THE
MOTION PICTURE
GUIDE

THIS VOLUME IS DEDICATED TO
THE MEMORY OF
JOHN FORD

THE
MOTION PICTURE
GUIDE

A - B

1927-1983

Jay Robert Nash
Stanley Ralph Ross

CINEBOOKS, INC.
Chicago, 1985
Publishers of THE COMPLETE FILM RESOURCE CENTER

Publishers: Jay Robert Nash, Stanley Ralph Ross; **Editor-in-Chief:** Jay Robert Nash; **Executive Editor:** Stanley Ralph Ross; **Associate Publisher and Director of Development:** Kenneth H. Petchenik; **Senior Editor-in-Charge:** Jim McCormick; **Senior Editors:** David Tardy, Robert B. Connelly; **Production Editor:** William Leahy; **Associate Editors:** Oksana Lydia Dominguez, Jeffrey H. Wallenfeldt, Edie McCormick, Michaela Tuohy, Jeannette Hori, Tom Legge; **Contributing Editors:** James J. Mulay (Chief Contributing Editor), Daniel Curran, Michael Theobald, Arnie Bernstein, Phil Pantone, Brian Brock; **Assistant Editors:** Marla Dorfman, Kim O. Morgan, Susan Doll, Marla Antelis, Debra Schwieder, Susan Fisher, Donna Roth, Marla Kruglik, Kristina Marcy, Sarah von Fremd, Wendy Anderson; **Art Production and Book Design:** Cathy Anetsberger; **Research Staff:** Shelby Payne (Associate Editor and Chief Researcher), William C. Clogston, Tobi Elliott, Carol Pappas, Rosalyn Mathis, Millicent Mathis, Andrea Nash; **Business/Legal:** Judy Anetsberger.

Associate Publishers: Howard Grafman, Lynn Christian, James and Monica Vrettos, Antoinette Mailliard, Brent H. Nettle, Michael Callie, Constance Shea, Barbara Browne Cramer, Alan Watts, Dr. Sir James R. Marks and Shirley R. Marks.

Editorial and Sales Offices: CINEBOOKS, 6135 N. Sheridan Road, Chicago, Illinois 60660.

Library of Congress Catalog Card Number: 85-071145
ISBN: 0-933997-00-0 THE MOTION PICTURE GUIDE (10 Vols.)
        0-933997-01-9 THE MOTION PICTURE GUIDE, Vol. I (A–B)

Printed in the United States
First Edition
This volume contains 2,805 entries.

2 3 4 5 6 7 8 9 10

Foreword

THE MOTION PICTURE GUIDE, the most important film encyclopedia *ever* written (all newly generated copy), compiled and published, inaugurates CINEBOOKS' continuing COMPLETE FILM RESOURCE CENTER. The present 12-volume encyclopedia, offering more than 50,000 entries of English-speaking (and notable foreign) films released theatrically and on video cassette, A through Z is, we can justifiably and proudly claim, *the only definitive and all-encompassing film encyclopedia in the world.* (NOTE: Major entries appear A-Z in volumes I-IX, with 1984 and a Miscellaneous Talkie List appearing in Volume IX, both A-Z, plus more than 3,000 major silent film entries appearing in Vol. X with a Miscellaneous A-Z Silent Film compilation appearing in Vol. X.)

For the general reader—one even mildly interested in motion pictures—THE MOTION PICTURE GUIDE (MPG) offers endless hours of browsing through lively synopses and fascinating anecdotal information on each and every favorite film, as well as thousands of little-known and lesser-known films, classics, and curiosities, heretofore ignored. THE GUIDE is a colorful history of motion pictures since the beginning, a reference work that will see constant day-to-day use.

For the student, teacher, historian, researcher, and serious amateur buff, THE MOTION PICTURE GUIDE will prove invaluable, offering hard data information in all vital areas: complete casts and roles played, running time, release dates, production and releasing companies, country of origin, color or black-and-white processes, creative and technical credits. For industry personnel, plot construction, production techniques (and hazards), financial successes or failures, as well as the public reactions, genres and themes for each film, should, we trust, prove enlightening and helpful in the planning and producing of future films.

For libraries and other archival institutions, of course, THE MOTION PICTURE GUIDE is indispensable as *the definitive reference work to motion pictures.* Which is to say: Finally, someone has done it!

This landmark work has been 25 years in the making—50 years of the joint research and source collections of the authors are totalled—with tens of thousands of sources consulted, collected and analyzed, including reviews, essays, biographies, autobiographies, all other compilations, bibliographies, correspondence, interviews conducted by the authors with film personalities, producers, directors, and creative technicians over the past quarter century, the harvest of two lifetimes spent chronicling the field of motion pictures (with a third lifetime concerned with the silent film era: Volume IX, compiled and written by Robert B. Connelly). And your authors have seen the films.

The result is an incomparable reference work containing the sum total of English-speaking (and notable foreign) films, as well as more than 35,000 in-depth entries on films of the silent period, plus an appendix-compendium of an additional 10,000 silent films. (We have included some apparently silent films in the talkie entries, such as SILENT MOVIE—where one word is actually uttered, "non"—THE THIEF, and some other experimental films such as the Italian production STORY WITHOUT WORDS, basically because these movies were made deep into the sound/talkie era and are generic to it.) The two index volumes (Vol. XI and XII) contain an alphabetical listing of more than 300,000 names, cross-referenced to their films, as they appear in the five A-Z compilations in Volumes I through X. Also included in the index volumes are all winners and nominees of the Academy Awards, the British Academy Awards, the New York Film Critics Circle Awards, and the film festival awards from Berlin, Cannes, and Venice. In addition, a special indices offers a compilation of all film series and background for each.

Nor have we forgotten the burgeoning VCR/cassette market. All films available on cassette at presstime have been identified in the last line of each entry, indicated by the notation "Cas." Those who rent video cassettes know that the cassettes rarely explain content; to these people THE MOTION PICTURE GUIDE will prove indispensable, giving as it does complete synopses of films on cassette. And for those parents in a quandary as to what they wish their young children to watch on pay TV or cassettes, we have provided a Parental Recommendation (under PR at the end of each entry), along with the MPAA rating—though we rate *all* films, whereas MPAA does not.

As a further service to user/readers, CINEBOOKS will offer weekly in-depth cassette availability reports through its CINE SEARCH division (which will also provide in-depth reports on all historical and contemporary film data for industry personnel and other subscribers). In addition to its initial 12 volumes of THE MOTION PICTURE GUIDE, CINEBOOKS will offer volumes covering all areas of the film field, including in-progress and definitive volumes detailing foreign films (a 16-volume country-by-country film encyclopedia), albeit several thousand notable foreign films are included in MPG. In preparation also is a 12-volume biographical encyclopedia of *all* film personnel—in front of and behind the cameras.

There are many existing compilations of motion pictures; that is, sets of old reviews from a single perspective and limited by scant time-of-release information and without the benefit of historical insight or in-depth research into individual productions and careers. These sets are also, regrettably, printed from near-unreadably reproduced reviews, haphazardly compiled and without a clear cross-reference system so that the general reader, the student, the historian, the teacher, the researcher, or the simply curious has only clumsy access, if that, to individual films. When the information is located, it is usually brief and often inaccurate.

Then there are the so-called genre compilations (westerns, sci-fi, horror, etc.), which offer selective film entries without any thought of being comprehensive (even though that claim is often made), glossing over inadequate, poorly researched and limited entries with more graphics than copy. By any standard these are not film encyclopedias, merely expensive pictorial volumes propped up with copy and masquerading as resource material when, in fact, they offer no real or all-inclusive value. At best, such volumes—and the review compilations mentioned earlier—offer only approximately 40 percent of the data available in MPG.

The mass-market and trade compilations that offer thumbnail sketches of selected films (the largest of which has 10,000 fewer entries than MPG) are of no use to the truly interested reader or dedicated scholar, since much of their information is both inaccurate and far too brief to be of value.

By way of contrast to the brevity of mass market guides are the essay collections that offer profoundly confusing and esoteric entries, selective rather than all-encompassing (one expensive set offers fewer than 1,500 entries in its 10 volumes; another covers only two decades, one in the silent years, the other of the 1960s, including X-rated films and amateur productions that might more charitably be classified as home movies). The latter offers no evaluative ratings or parental recommendations and lacks a point of historical reference, as well as being utterly useless as a reference tool for the history of film.

Not to be found in the MPG are X-rated films or unrated films of a similar nature since we do not consider such productions of filmic interest to the general reader or the serious researcher. Other categories such as documentaries (including entertainment documentaries like THAT'S ENTERTAINMENT), made-for-TV films, shorts, serials, and newsreels will not be found in the present ten volumes. CINEBOOKS will issue separate volumes in these categories in the near future, each as definitive and all-encompassing as the present ten-volume encyclopedia. CINEBOOKS will also publish a definitive annual beginning in 1986, covering all films, awards and pertinent events of each previous year.

THE MOTION PICTURE GUIDE (more than 15 million words) has come into being out of necessity. About 100 million Americans watch a movie each day, millions of VCR units and many millions more video cassettes are sold or rented, cable and pay-TV stressing motion pictures have expanded into enormous, deeply responsive markets, as has media coverage of this explosive field, and more movies, motion picture products, and firms have been born to meet the public demand. Foremost is the demand for information, from hard data to necessary critical evaluation, and this CINEBOOKS and its allied divisions will supply.

We trust that these volumes will meet the information needs of all readers, along with providing endless hours of entertainment, for here, truly, is the great cornucopia of movie information. We take great satisfaction in its accomplishment, but, more importantly, in our ability to offer, A through Z, THE MOTION PICTURE GUIDE to you, the viewer-reader.

Jay Robert Nash and Stanley Ralph Ross

HOW TO USE INFORMATION IN THIS GUIDE

ALPHABETICAL ORDER

All entries have been arranged alphabetically throughout this and all subsequent volumes. In establishing alphabetical order, all articles (A, An, The) appear after the main title (AFFAIR TO REMEMBER, AN). In the case of foreign films the article precedes the main title (LES MISERABLES appears in the letter L) which makes, we feel, for easier access and uniformity. Contractions are grouped together and these will be followed by non-apostrophized words of the same letters. B.F.'s DAUGHTER is at the beginning of the letter B, not under BF.

TITLES

It is important to know what title you are seeking; use the *complete* title of the film. The film ADVENTURES OF ROBIN HOOD, THE, cannot be found under merely ROBIN HOOD. Many films are known under different titles and we have taken great pains to cross-reference these titles. (AKA, also known as) as well as alternate titles used in Great Britain (GB). In addition to the cross-reference title only entries, AKAs and alternate titles in Great Britain can be found in the title line for each entry. An alphabetically arranged comprehensive list of title changes appears in the Index volume (Vol. X).

RATINGS

We have rated each and every film at critical levels that include acting, directing, script, and technical achievement (or the sad lack of it). We have a *five-star* rating, unlike all other rating systems, to signify a film superbly made on every level, in short, a masterpiece. At the lowest end of the scale is *zero* and we mean it. The ratings are as follows: *zero* (not worth a glance), *(poor), **(fair), ***(good), ****(excellent), *****(masterpiece, and these are few and far between). Half-marks mean almost there but not quite.

YEAR OF RELEASE

We have used in all applicable instances the year of United States release. This sometimes means that a film released abroad may have a different date elsewhere than in these volumes but this is generally the date released in foreign countries, not in the U.S.

FOREIGN COUNTRY PRODUCTION

When possible, we have listed abbreviated names of the foreign countries originating the production of a film. This information will be found within the parenthesis containing the year of release. If no country is listed in this space, it is a U.S. production.

RUNNING TIME

A hotly debated category, we have opted to list the running time a film ran at the time of its initial U.S. release but we will usually mention in the text if the film was drastically cut and give the reasons why. We have attempted to be as accurate as possible by consulting the most reliable sources.

PRODUCING AND DISTRIBUTING COMPANIES

The producing and/or distributing company of every film is listed in abbreviated entries next to the running time in the title line (see abbreviations; for all those firms not abbreviated, the entire firm's name will be present).

COLOR OR BLACK-AND-WHITE

The use of color or black-and-white availability appears as c or bw following the producing/releasing company entry.

CASTS

Whenever possible, we give *the complete cast and the roles played* for each film and this is the case in 95% of all entries, the only encyclopedia to ever offer such comprehensive information in covering the entire field. The names of actors and actresses are in Roman lettering, the names of the roles each played in Italic inside parentheses.

SYNOPSIS

The in-depth synopsis for each entry (when such applies) offers the plot of each film, critical evaluation, anecdotal information on the production and its personnel, awards won when applicable and additional information dealing with the production's impact upon the public, its success or failure at the box office, its social significance, if any. Acting methods, technical innovations, script originality are detailed. We also cite other productions involving an entry's personnel for critical comparisons and to establish the style or genre of expertise of directors, writers, actors and technical people.

REMAKES AND SEQUELS

Information regarding films that have sequels, sequels themselves or direct remakes of films can be found at the very end of each synopsis.

DUBBING AND SUBTITLES

We will generally point out in the synopsis when a foreign film is dubbed in English, mostly when the dubbing is poor. When voices are dubbed, particularly when singers render vocals on songs mimed by stars, we generally point out these facts either in the cast/role listing or inside the synopsis. If a film is in a foreign language and subtitled, we signify the fact in a parenthetical statement at the end of each entry (In Italian, English subtitles).

CREDITS

The credits for the creative and technical personnel of a film are extensive and they include: p (producer, often executive producer); d (director); w (screenwriter, followed by adaptation, if any, and creator of original story, if any, and other sources such as authors for plays, articles, short stories, novels and non-fiction books); ph (cinematographer, followed by camera system and color process when applicable, i.e., Panavision, Technicolor); m (composer of musical score); ed (film editor); md (music director); art d (art director); set d (set decoration); cos (costumes); spec eff (special effects); ch (choreography); m/l (music and lyrics); stunts, makeup, and other credits when merited. When someone receives two or more credits in a single film the credits may be combined (p&d, John Ford) or the last name repeated in subsequent credits shared with another (d, John Ford; w, Ford, Dudley Nichols).

GENRES/SUBJECT

Each film is categorized for easy identification as to genre and/or subject and themes at the left-hand bottom of each entry. (Western, Prison Drama, Spy Drama, Romance, Musical, Comedy, War, Horror, Science-Fiction, Adventure, Biography, Historical Drama, Children's Film, Animated Feature, etc.) More specific subject and theme breakdowns will be found in the Index (Vol. X).

PR AND MPAA RATINGS

The Parental Recommendation provides parents having no knowledge of the style and content of each film with a guide; if a film has excessive violence, sex, strong language, it is so indicated. Otherwise, films specifically designed for young children are also indicated. The Parental Recommendation (**PR**) is to be found at the right-hand bottom of each entry, followed, when applicable, by the **MPAA** rating. The PR ratings are as follows: **AAA** (must for children); **AA** (good for children); **A** (acceptable for children); **C** (cautionary, some objectionable scenes); **O** (completely objectionable for children).

KEY TO ABBREVIATIONS

Foreign Countries:

Arg.	Argentina
Aus.	Australia
Aust.	Austria
Bel.	Belgium
Braz.	Brazil
Brit.	Great Britain (GB when used for alternate title)
Can.	Canada
Chi.	China
Czech.	Czechoslovakia
Den.	Denmark
E. Ger.	East Germany
Fin.	Finland
Fr.	France
Ger.	Germany (includes W. Germany)
Gr.	Greece
Hung.	Hungary
Ital.	Italy
Jap.	Japan
Mex.	Mexico
Neth.	Netherlands
Phil.	Philippines
Pol.	Poland
Rum.	Rumania
S.K.	South Korea
Span.	Spain
Swed.	Sweden

Key to Abbreviations (continued)

Switz.	Switzerland
Thai.	Thailand
USSR	Union of Soviet Socialist Republics
Yugo.	Yugoslavia

Production Companies, Studios and Distributors (U.S. and British)

AA	ALLIED ARTISTS
ABF	Associated British Films
AE	Avco Embassy
AEX	Associated Exhibitors
AH	Anglo-Hollandia
AIP	American International Pictures
AM	American
ANCH	Anchor Film Distributors
ANE	American National Enterprises
AP	Associated Producers
AP&D	Associated Producers & Distributors
ARC	Associated Releasing Corp.
Argosy	Argosy Productions
Arrow	Arrow Films
ART	Artcraft
Astra	Astra Films
AY	Aywon
BA	British Actors
B&C	British and Colonial Kinematograph Co.
BAN	Banner Films
BI	British Instructional
BIFD	B.I.F.D. Films
BIP	British International Pictures
BJP	Buck Jones Productions
BL	British Lion
Blackpool	Blackpool Productions
BLUE	Bluebird
BN	British National
BNF	British and Foreign Film
Boulting	Boulting Brothers (Brit.)
BP	British Photoplay Production
BPP	B.P. Productions
BRIT	Britannia Films
BRO	Broadwest
Bryanston	Bryantston Films (Brit.)
BS	Blue Streak
BUS	Bushey (Brit.)
BUT	Butchers Film Service
BV	Buena Vista (Walt Disney)
CAP	Capital Films
CC	Christie Comedy
CD	Continental Distributing
CHAD	Chadwick Pictures Corporation
CHES	Chesterfield
Cineguild	Cineguild
CL	Clarendon
CLIN	Clinton
COL	COLUMBIA
Colony	Colony Pictures
COM	Commonwealth
COMM	Commodore Pictures
COS	Cosmopolitan (Hearst)
DE	Dependable Exchange
DGP	Dorothy Gish Productions
Disney	Walt Disney Productions
DIST	Distinctive
DM	DeMille Productions
DOUB	Doubleday
EAL	Ealing Studios (Brit.)
ECF	East Coast Films
ECL	Eclectic
ED	Eldorado
EF	Eagle Films
EFF & EFF	E.F.F. & E.F.F. Comedy
EFI	English Films Inc.
EIFC	Export and Import Film Corp.
EL	Eagle-Lion
EM	Embassy Pictures Corp.

EMI	EMI Productions
EP	Enterprise Pictures
EPC	Equity Pictures Corp.
EQ	Equitable
EXCEL	Excellent
FA	Fine Arts
FC	Film Classics
FD	First Division
FN	First National
FOX	20TH CENTURY FOX (and Fox Productions)
FP	Famous Players (and Famous Players Lasky)
FRP	Frontroom Productions
Gainsborough	Gainsborough Productions
GAU	Gaumont (Brit.)
GEN	General
GFD	General Films Distributors
Goldwyn	Samuel Goldwyn Productions
GN	Grand National
GOTH	Gotham
Grafton	Grafton Films (Brit.)
H	Harma
HAE	Harma Associated Distributors
Hammer	Hammer Films (Brit.)
HD	Hagen and Double
HM	Hi Mark
HR	Hal Roach
IA	International Artists
ID	Ideal
IF	Independent Film Distributors (Brit.)
Imperator	Imperator Films (Brit.)
IP	Independent Pictures Corp.
IN	Invincible Films
INSP	Inspirational Pictures (Richard Barthelmess)
IV	Ivan Film
Javelin	Javelin Film Productions (Brit.)
JUR	Jury
KC	Kinema Club
KCB	Kay C. Booking
Knightsbridge	Knightsbridge Productions (Brit.)
Korda	Alexander Korda Productions (Brit.)
Ladd	Ladd Company Productions
LAS	Lasky Productions (Jesse L. Lasky)
LFP	London Films
LIP	London Independent Producers
Lorimar	Lorimar Productions
LUM	Lumis
Majestic	Majestic Films
Mascot	Mascot Films
Mayflowers	Mayflowers Productions (Brit.)
Metro	Metro
MFC	Mission Film Corporation
MG	Metro-Goldwyn
MGM	METRO-GOLDWYN-MAYER
MON	Monogram
MOR	Morante
MS	Mack Sennett
MUT	Mutual
N	National
NG	National General
NGP	National General Pictures (Alexander Korda, Brit.)
NW	New World
Orion	Orion Productions
Ortus	Ortus Productions (Brit.)
PAR	PARAMOUNT
Pascal	Gabriel Pascal Productions (Brit.)
PDC	Producers Distributors Corp.

Key to Abbreviations (continued)

PEER	Peerless
PWN	Peninsula Studios
PFC	Pacific Film Company
PG	Playgoers
PI	Pacific International
PIO	Pioneer Film Corp.
PM	Pall Mall
PP	Pro Patria
PRC	Producers Releasing Corporation
PRE	Preferred
QDC	Quality Distributing Corp.
RAY	Rayart
RAD	Radio Pictures
RANK	J. Arthur Rank (Brit.)
RBP	Rex Beach Pictures
REA	Real Art
REG	Regional Films
REN	Renown
REP	Republic
RF	Regal Films
RFD	R.F.D. Productions (Brit.)
RKO	RKO RADIO PICTURES
Rogell	Rogell
Romulus	Romulus Films (Brit.)
Royal	Royal
SB	Samuel Bronston
SCHUL	B.P. Schulberg Productions
SEL	Select
SELZ	Selznick International (David O. Selznick)
SF	Selznick Films
SL	Sol Lesser
SONO	Sonofilms
SP	Seven Pines Productions (Brit.)
SRP	St. Regis Pictures
STER	Sterling
STOLL	Stoll
SUN	Sunset
SYN	Syndicate Releasing Co.
SZ	Sam Zimbalist
TC	Two Cities (Brit.)
T/C	Trem-Carr
THI	Thomas H. Ince
TIF	Tiffany
TRA	Transatlantic Pictures
TRU	Truart
TS	Tiffany/Stahl
UA	UNITED ARTISTS
UNIV	UNIVERSAL (AND UNIVERSAL INTERNATIONAL)
Venture	Venture Distributors
VIT	Vitagraph
WAL	Waldorf
WB	WARNER BROTHERS (AND WARNER BROTHERS-SEVEN ARTS)
WEST	Westminster
WF	Woodfall Productions (Brit.)
WI	Wisteria
WORLD	World
WSHP	William S. Hart Productions
ZUKOR	Adolph Zukor Productions

Foreign

ABSF	AB Svensk Film Industries (Swed.)
Action	Action Films (Fr.)
ADP	Agnes Delahaie Productions (Fr.)
Agata	Agata Films (Span.)
Alter	Alter Films (Fr.)
Arch	Archway Film Distributors
Argos	Argos Films (Fr.)
Argui	Argui Films (Fr.)
Ariane	Les Films Ariane (Fr.)
Athos	Athos Films (Fr.)
Belga	Belga Films (Bel.)

Beta	Beta Films (Ger.)
CA	Cine-Alliance (Fr.)
Caddy	Caddy Films (Fr.)
CCFC	Compagnie Commerciale Francais Einematographique (Fr.)
CDD	Cino Del Duca (Ital.)
CEN	Les Films de Centaur (Fr.)
CFD	Czecheslovak Film Productions
CHAM	Champion (Ital.)
Cinegay	Cinegay Films (Ital.)
Cines	Cines Films (Ital.)
Cineriz	Cinerez Films (Ital.)
Citel	Citel Films (Switz.)
Como	Como Films (Fr.)
CON	Concordia (Fr.)
Corona	Corona Films (Fr.)
D	Documento Films (Ital.)
DD	Dino De Laurentiis (Ital.)
Dear	Dear Films (Ital.)
DIF	Discina International Films (Fr.)
DPR	Films du Palais-Royal (Fr.)
EX	Excelsa Films (Ital.)
FDP	Films du Pantheon (Fr.)
Fono	Fono Roma (Ital.)
FS	Filmsonor Productions (Fr.)
Gala	Fala Films (Ital.)
Galatea	Galatea Productions (Ital.)
Gamma	Gamma Films (Fr.)
Gemma	Gemma Cinematografica (Ital.)
GFD	General Film Distributors, Ltd. (Can.)
GP	General Productions (Fr.)
Gray	(Gray Films (Fr.)
IFD	Intercontinental Film Distributors
Janus	Janus Films (Ger.)
JMR	Macques Mage Releasing (Fr.)
LF	Les Louvre Films (Fr.)
LFM	Les Films Moliere (Fr.)
Lux	Lux Productions (Ital.)
Melville	Melville Productions (Fr.)
Midega	Midega Films (Span.)
NEF	N.E.F. La Nouvelle Edition Francaise (Fr.)
NFD	N.F.D. Productions (Ger.)
ONCIC	Office National pour le Commerce et L'Industrie Cinematographique (Fr.)
Ortus	Ortus Films (Can.)
PAC	Production Artistique Cinematographique (Fr.)
Pagnol	Marcel Pagnol Productions (Fr.)
Parc	Parc Films (Fr.)
Paris	Paris Films (Fr.)
Pathe	Pathe Films (Fr.)
PECF	Productions et Editions Cinematographique Francais (Fr.)
PF	Parafrench Releasing Co. (Fr.)
PIC	Produzione International Cinematografica (Ital.)
Ponti	Carlo Ponti Productions (Ital.)
RAC	Realisation d'Art Cinematographique (Fr.)
Regina	Regina Films (Fr.)
Renn	Renn Productions (Fr.)
SDFS	Societe des Films Sonores Tobis (Fr.)
SEDIF	Societe d'Exploitation ed de Distribution de Films (Fr.)
SFP	Societe Francais de Production (Fr.)
Sigma	Sigma Productions (Fr.)
SNE	Societe Nouvelle des Establishments (Fr.)
Titanus	Titanus Productions (Ital.)
TRC	Transcontinental Films (Fr.)
UDIF	U.D.I.F. Productions (Fr.)
UFA	Deutsche Universum-Film AG (Ger.)
UGC	Union Generale Cinematographique (Fr.)
Union	Union Films (Ger.)
Vera	Vera Productions (Fr.)

A (NOTE: 1984 releases appear in Volume IX)

A NOUS LA LIBERTE***** (1931, Fr.) 104m SDFS bw

Henri Marchand *(Emile)*, Raymond Cordy *(Louis)*, Rolla France *(Jeanne)*, Paul Olivier *(Paul Imaque)*, Jacques Shelly *(Paul)*, Andre Michaud *(Foreman)*, Germaine Aussey *(Maud)*, Alexandre d'Arcy *(Gigolo)*, William Burke *(Old Convict)*, Vincent Hyspa *(Old Orator)*, Leon Lorin *(Deaf Old Man)*.

Classic satire on the dehumanization of industrial workers which preceded Chaplin's MODERN TIMES by five years. This quick-paced and amusing experiment has Cordy escaping prison to become a phonograph company tycoon. Marchand, a fellow inmate, later flees prison to work in his friend's factory where he meets and falls in love with fellow factory worker, France, overcoming the objections of her protective uncle, Olivier, with Marchand's help. Gangsters attempt to blackmail Cordy, exposing him to police as an escaped felon. Cordy witnesses the opening of his new factory where dozens of high-hatted social lions scramble greedily for banknotes left behind by the gangsters. Seeing police looking for him, the tycoon flees with his friend Marchand who has given up France to another worker she truly loves. Marchand and Cordy take to the open road, bumming their way to freedom. This Rene Clair masterpiece came into being when the director was traveling through an industrial suburb of Paris and spotted "a few wildflowers growing against a background of smoking factory chimneys. The contrast triggered something off in me and the idea crystalized." Emile, the tramp, was undoubtedly inspired by Chaplin and Louis is almost wholly drawn from the life of Charles Pathe, the French phonograph and film industry magnate. (In French, English subtitles.)

d&w, Rene Clair; ph, Georges Perinal; m, Georges Auric; ed, Clair, Rene Le Hanff; set d, Lazare Meerson.

Satire **Cas.** **(PR:A MPAA:NR)**

AARON LOVES ANGELA** (1975) 99m COL c

Kevin Hooks *(Aaron)*, Irene Cara *(Angela)*, Moses Gunn *(Ike)*, Robert Hooks *(Beau)*, Ernestine Jackson *(Cleo)*, Leon Pinkney *(Willie)*, Wanda Velez, Lou Quinones, Charles McGregor, Norman Evans, Alex Stevens, William Graeff Jr., Frank Aldrich, Jose Feliciano, Walt Frazier.

Sensitive romance story between a black youth and a Puerto Rican girl struggling to make their feelings known to each other is hampered by brutal ghetto types—dopesters, pimps, prostitutes in all their blatant glory—except for an awkward Mr. Cool type, uproariously played by Leon Pinkney.

p, Robert J. Anderson; d, Gordon Parks, Jr; w, Gerald Sanford; ph, Richard Kratina; m, Jose Feliciano; ed, William E. Anderson; stunts, Alex Stevens.

Romance **Cas.** **(PR:O MPAA:R)**

AARON SLICK FROM PUNKIN CRICK**
(1952) 95m PAR c (GB: MARSHMALLOW MOON)

Alan Young *(Aaron Slick)*, Dinah Shore *(Josie)*, Robert Merrill *(Bill Merridew)*, Adele Jergens *(Gladys)*, Minerva Urecal *(Mrs. Peabody)*, Martha Stewart *(Soubrette)*, Fritz Feld *(Headwaiter)*, Veda Ann Borg *(Girl in Red)*, Chick Chandler *(Pitchman)*.

A dull, uninspired musical, the plot has bashful Young courting Shore, his farm neighbor. The romance is uprooted when city folks Merrill and Jergens buy out Shore's farm for $20,000, believing it to contain oil deposits. Shore departs for the bright lights, which prompts Young to pursue her, wooing her back to the farm, while outwitting the slickers. A few humorous scenes bring alive the ancient (1919) play, particularly a purse-stealing involving Borg. Metropolitan Opera star Merrill is wasted in this lame songfest which offers such tunes as "I'd Like to Baby You," "Still Water," "Marshmallow Moon," and "Why Should I Believe in Love?"

p, William Perlberg, George Seaton; d&w, Claude Binyon (based on the play by Walter Benjamin Hare); ph, Charles B. Lang, Jr. (Technicolor); ed, Archie Marshek; md, Robert Emmett Dolan; m/l Jay Livingston, Ray Evans.

Musical **(PR:AA MPAA:NR)**

ABANDON SHIP!***
(1957, Brit.) 100m COL bw (GB: SEVEN WAVES AWAY)

Tyrone Power *(Alec Holmes)*, Mai Zetterling *(Julie)*, Lloyd Nolan *(Frank Kelly)*, Stephen Boyd *(Will McKinley)*, Moira Lister *(Edith Middleton)*, James Hayter *("Cookie" Morrow)*, Marie Lohr *(Mrs. Knudsen)*, Moultrie Kelsall *(Daniel Cane)*, Noel Willman *(Aubrey Clark)*, Victor Maddern *(Willie Hawkins)*, Gordon Jackson *(John Merritt)*, Clive Morton *(Gen. Barrington)*, Laurence Naismith *(Capt. Darrow)*, John Stratton *("Sparks" Clary)*, Eddie Byrne *(Michael Faroni)*, David Langton *(John Hayden)*, Ferdy Mayne *(Solly Daniels)*, Ralph Michael *(George Kilgore)*, Jill Melford *(Mrs. Kilgore)*, Clare Austin *(Mrs. Ruth Spencer)*, Derek Sidney *(Marie Pasquale)*, Danny Green *(Big Joe Woolsek)*, Austin Trevor *(Edward Wilton)*, Colin Broadley *(Mickey Stokes)*, Meurig Wyn-Jones *(Peter Kilgore)*, Orlando Martins *(Sam Holly)*, John Gray *(Aussie Smith)*, Finlay Currie *(Seaman)*.

Gripping sea adventure where survivors from a sunken luxury liner crowd a small boat commanded by Power whose initial aim is to save all. Many of those crammed into the boat or clinging to it in the water are sick or dying. It soon becomes apparent to the mortally injured Nolan, one of the ship's officers, that Power must exercise a survival-of-the-fittest rule. To prove his point, Nolan shockingly hurls himself into the sea, shouting to Power before he slips beneath the waves that he must get rid of the infirm or all will die. Knowing the food and water on board will not provide for all and, against the protests of his lover, Zetterling, and fellow officer and friend Boyd, Power weeds out the weak to save the strong. A telling portrait of survivors in crisis who first favor Power's actions, then later condemn him when a rescue ship appears on the horizon. Not for the squeamish.

p, John R. Sloan; d&w, Richard Sale; ph, Wilkie Cooper; m, Sir Arthur Bliss; ed, Ray Poulton; prod d, Wilfred Shingleton; art d, Ray Simm.

Adventure **(PR:C-O MPAA:NR)**

ABANDONED*** (1949) 78m UNIV bw (AKA: ABANDONED WOMAN)

Dennis O'Keefe *(Mark Sitko)*, Gale Storm *(Paula Considine)*, Jeff Chandler *(Chief McRae)*, Meg Randall *(Dottie Jensen)*, Raymond Burr *(Kerric)*, Marjorie Rambeau *(Mrs. Donner)*, Jeanette Nolan *(Maj. Ross)*, Mike Mazurki *(Hoppe)*, Will Kuluva *(DeCola)*, David Clarke *(Harry)*, William Page *(Scoop)*, Sid Tomack *(Humes)*, Perc Launders *(Dowd)*, Steve Darrell *(Brenn)*, Clifton Young *(Eddie)*, Ruth Sanderson *(Mrs. Spence)*.

Starkly photographed in semi-documentary style by William Daniels, this thinly budgeted film packs plenty of action and provides startlingly snappy dialog from first to last. Storm appears in a damp, grim Los Angeles looking for her missing sister, enlisting the aid of newsman O'Keefe, who discovers the vanished girl in the morgue, listed as an "unidentified suicide." Believing the girl has been murdered, O'Keefe launches a harrowing investigation. He turns up a baby-stealing ring fronted by calculating Rambeau and abetted by sleazy private detective Burr, who gives a marvelous performance as does the gang's chief goon, Mike Mazurki. O'Keefe survives shootouts and slugfests as he learns that the missing sister was killed when she tried to reclaim her illegitimate baby; moreover, Storm is almost murdered for her involvement and passed off as another suicide, but O'Keefe saves her life at the last moment. A fast-paced *film noir* gem.

p, Jerry Bresler; d, Joseph Newman; w, Irwin Gielgud (based on newspaper articles exposing a Los Angeles baby-stealing ring); ph, William Daniels; m, Walter Scharf; ed, Edward Curtiss; art d, Bernard Herzbrun, Robert Boyle; set d, Russell A. Gausman, Ruby R. Levitt; cos, Yvonne Wood.

Crime **(PR:C MPAA:NR)**

ABBOTT AND COSTELLO GO TO MARS* (1953) 77m UNIV bw

Bud Abbott *(Lester)*, Lou Costello *(Orville)*, Robert Paige *(Dr. Wilson)*, Mari Blanchard *(Allura)*, Martha Hyer *(Janie)*, Horace McMahon *(Mugsy)*, Jack Kruschen *(Harry)*, Jean Willes *(Captain)*, Joe Kirk *(Dr. Orvilla)*, Jack Tesler *(Dr. Holtz)*, Harold Goodwin *(Dr. Coleman)*, Anita Ekberg *(Venusian Woman)*, Hal Forrest *(Dr. Nedring)*, James Flavin, Russ Conway *(Policemen in Bank)*, Sid Saylor *(Man at Fountain)*, Paul Newlan *(Traffic Cop)*, Jackie Loughery *(Miss U.S.A.)*, Billy Newell *(Drunk)*, Grace Lenard *(French Girl)*, Tim Graham *(Cashier)*, Ken Christy *(Police Officer)*, Harry Lang *(French Waiter)*, Milt Bronson *(Announcer)*, Robert Forrest *(Observer)*, Dudley Dickerson *(Porter)*, Rex Lease *(Police Sergeant)*, Frank Marlowe *(Bartender)*, Bobby Barber *(Man)*, Miss Universe Contestants *(Venusian Handmaidens)*.

Shoddy production with plastic-thin futuristic sets in which B&L launch a spaceship by accident, one intended for Mars, landing first in New Orleans during Mardi Gras, then on Venus which is peopled only by gorgeous women who have banished all males from the planet. The sight gags and pratfalls are unimaginative and often dull, the boys' delivery merely expeditious. A good character actor, McMahon, is thrown away in the role of a bank robber who, along with sidekick Kruschen, forces B&L to blast off from New Orleans in a crazy escape attempt, going to Venus, then returning with B&L to NYC where the rocket slashes past the Statue of Liberty, the Empire State Building and other sites before landing in the arms of the law. Only the kiddies and super B&L fans will enjoy this mindless mess. (See ABBOTT & COSTELLO series, Index.)

p, Howard Christie; d, Charles Lamont; w, D. D. Beauchamp, John Grant (based on a story by Christie, Beauchamp); ph, Clifford Stine; ed, Russell Schoengarth; md, Joseph Gershenson.

Comedy **(PR:A MPAA:NR)**

ABBOTT AND COSTELLO IN HOLLYWOOD*** (1945) 84m MGM bw

Bud Abbott *(Buzz Kurtis)*, Lou Costello *(Abercrombie)*, Frances Rafferty *(Claire Warren)*, Robert Stanton *(Jeff Parker)*, Jean Porter *(Ruthie)*, Warner Anderson *(Norman Royce)*, Mike Mazurki *(Klondike Pete)*, Carleton G. Young *(Gregory Lemaise)*, Donald MacBride *(Dennis Kavanaugh)*, Arthur Space *(Director)*, Katharine Booth *(Louise)*, Edgar Dearing, Robert Emmett O'Connor *(Studio Cops)*, Marion Martin *(Miss Millbane)*, Bill Phillips *(Kavanaugh's Assistant)*, Marie Blake *(Secretary)*, Harry Tyler *(Taxi Driver)*, Skeets Noyes *(Assistant Director)*, Dick Alexander *(Prop Man)*, Dick Winslow *(Orchestra Leader)*, Jane Hale *(Cigarette Girl)*, Frank Scannell *(Waiter)*, Chester Clute *(Mr. Burvis)*, Lucille Ball, Butch Jenkins, Dean Stockwell, Preston Foster, Robert Z. Leonard, The Lyttle Sisters.

Above average B&L vehicle has the boys wheeling and dealing in filmdom as inept agents attempting to get a young singer, Stanton, the lead part in a musical, which leads to romps through studio sets, disruption of on-going productions, and a wild roller coaster ride finale. Costello's brief insomnia attack is a priceless bit of mirth, as is the boys' "earplug" routine (where Costello is wearing plugs and Abbott slaps him about for not listening), a bit that was later included in THAT'S ENTERTAINMENT, PART TWO. Some Hollywood personalities are thrown in for flavor and not a few laughs. B&L end this movie spoof as big-time agents in posh offices, as incompetent as when they began. The film, however, did not provide substantial BO returns for MGM to continue its option to make a B&L film each year. (See ABBOTT & COSTELLO series, Index.)

p, Martin A. Gosch; d, S. Sylvan Simon; w, Nat Perrin, Lou Breslow; ph, Charles Schoenbaum; ed, Ben Lewis; ch, Charles Walters; m/l Ralph Blane, Hugh Martin.

Comedy **Cas.** **(PR:AAA MPAA:NR)**

ABBOTT AND COSTELLO IN THE FOREIGN LEGION**
(1950) 79m UNIV bw

Bud Abbott *(Jonesy)*, Lou Costello *(Lou Hotchkiss)*, Patricia Medina *(Nicole)*, Walter Slezak *(Axmann)*, Douglas Dumbrille *(Hamud El Khalid)*, Leon Belasco *(Hassam)*, Marc Lawrence *(Frankie)*, Tor Johnson *(Abou Ben)*, Wee Willie Davis *(Abdullah)*, Fred Nurney *(Commandant)*, Sam Menacker *(Bertram)*, Henry Corden *(Ibrim)*, Paul Fierro *(Ibn)*, Jack Raymond *(Ali Ami)*, Dan Seymour *(Josef)*, Guy Beach *(Saleem)*, Alberto Morin *(Lieutnant)*, David Gorcey *(Newsboy)*, Charmienne Harker *(Arab Girl)*, Jack Shutta, Ernesto Morelli, Chuck Hamilton *(Thugs)*,

Ted Hecht *(Proprietor)*, Buddy Roosevelt *(Orderly)*, Mahmud Shaikhaly *(Referee)*, Bobby Barker *(Man)*.

Low-budget B&L effort with many bits taken from LOST IN A HAREM. The boys are wrestling promoters who find themselves in Algeria looking for one of their missing wrestlers and get involved in an espionage web woven by Medina, a sexy French undercover agent. They are then boondoggled into joining the Foreign Legion by slippery Slezak, a sadistic French army sergeant who caricatures Sgt. Markov in BEAU GESTE. The pair bumbles into exposing Slezak's traitorous collusions with evil sheik Dumbrille but offer little new humor other than a manic jeep drive through the sheik's camp. Uplifting is Lou's momentary wandering in the desert where he envisions absurd mirages, one being a NYC newsboy hawking papers. When Lou asks why he is in the middle of nowhere, the boy replies: "Can I help it if they gave me a bad corner?" For enthusiasts and little ones. (See ABBOTT & COSTELLO series, Index.)

p, Robert Arthur; d, Charles Lamont; w, John Grant, Martin Ragaway, Leonard Stern (based on a story by D. D. Beauchamp); ph, George Robinson; ed, Edward Curtiss.

Comedy **(PR:A MPAA:NR)**

ABBOTT AND COSTELLO IN THE NAVY (SEE: IN THE NAVY, 1941)

ABBOTT AND COSTELLO LOST IN ALASKA (SEE: LOST IN ALASKA, 1952)

ABBOTT AND COSTELLO MEET CAPTAIN KIDD** (1952) 70m WB c

Bud Abbott *(Rocky Stonebridge)*, Lou Costello *(Oliver "Puddin' Head" Johnson)*, Charles Laughton *(Captain Kidd)*, Hillary Brooke *(Captain Bonney)*, Fran Warren *(Lady Jane)*, Bill Shirley *(Bruce Martingale)*, Leif Erickson *(Morgan)*, Sid Saylor, Rex Lease, Frank Yaconelli *(Pirates)*, Bobby Barber *(Man)*.

Disappointing B&L programmer has the boys stranded on pirate-infested Tortuga Island, serving as waiters in an inn where they are given a love letter by Warren to be delivered to Shirley. They accidentally switch the letter for Captain Kidd's treasure map and are abducted by Laughton and female counterpart pirate Brooke and taken to Skull Island to seek Kidd's treasure. The voyage to the island and the romping about once there is tedious, with half-hearted routines from exhausted vaudeville material, not helped by a half dozen instantly forgettable tunes. Why Laughton launched himself into such lowbrow comedy still puzzles critics. He accepted the role without reading the script and, once on the set, was thoroughly befuddled by B&L's ad-libbing and their usual failure to provide the proper cues. (See ABBOTT & COSTELLO series, Index.)

p, Alex Gottlieb; d, Charles Lamont; w, Howard Dimsdale, John Grant; ph, Stanley Cortez; m, Raoul Kraushaar; ed, Edward Mann; m/l, Bob Rusell, Lester Lee.

Comedy **Cas.** **(PR:A MPAA:NR)**

ABBOTT AND COSTELLO MEET DR. JEKYLL AND MR. HYDE* 1/2 (1954) 76m UNIV bw

Bud Abbott *(Slim)*, Lou Costello *(Tubby)*, Boris Karloff *(Dr. Henry Jekyll)*, Craig Stevens *(Bruce Adams)*, Helen Westcott *(Vicky Edwards)*, Reginald Denny *(Inspector)*, John Dierkes *(Batley)*, Patti McKay, Lucille Lamarr *(Dancers)*, Henry Corden *(Javanese Actor)*, Marjorie Bennett *(Militant Woman)*, Carmen de Lavallade *(Javanese)*, Arthur Gould-Porter *(Bartender)*, Herbert Deans *(Victim)*, Judith Brian *(Woman on Bike)*, Clyde Cook, John Rogers *(Drunks)*, Gil Perkins *(Man on Bike)*, Hilda Plowright *(Nursemaid)*, Keith Hitchcock *(Jailer)*, Harry Cording *(Rough Character)*, Donald Kerr *(Chimney Sweep)*, Clive Morgan, Tony Marshe, Michael Hadlow *(Bobbies)*.

As two American cops sent to London to study crowd control, B&L are jailed after being in a riot prompted by equal rights leader Westcott. The boys, Westcott, and Stevens, playing a newsman in love with Westcott, are bailed out by Karloff who intends to murder Stevens over jealousy of Westcott. Karloff has been busy transforming animals into weird creatures (a cat that moos like a cow, a rabbit that barks like a dog), and murdering fellow doctors who have made fun of his theories, by injecting his special serum into himself for the lethal Mr. Hyde transformation (it is claimed that stuntman Edwin Parker played the monster in the more athletic scenes). B&L are hired by Karloff as bodyguards after Lou captures him as Hyde and puts him behind bars where, unseen, he changes back to Jekyll and is released. As B&L guard Karloff, their employer attempts to murder them and, in the ensuing chase, Lou is jabbed with a syringe containing Jekyll's formula and turns into a snarling monster, biting several bobbies who also turn into hairy-faced Hydes. The finale is a slapstick chase of monsters chasing monsters with more grunts than laughs provided. (See ABBOTT & COSTELLO series, Index.)

p, Howard Christie; d, Charles Lamont; w, Lee Loeb, John Grant (based on the novel *Dr. Jekyll and Mr. Hyde* by Robert Louis Stevenson); ph, George Robinson; md, Joseph Gershenson; ed, Russell Schoengarth; art d, Bernard Herzbrun, Eric Orbom;
set d, Russell A. Gausman; cos, Rosemary Odell; spec eff, David S. Horsley; makeup, Bud Westmore.

Comedy **Cas.** **(PR:A MPAA:NR)**

ABBOTT AND COSTELLO MEET FRANKENSTEIN****
(1948) 83m UNIV bw (GB: ABBOTT AND COSTELLO MEET THE GHOSTS)

Bud Abbott *(Chick Young)*, Lou Costello *(Wilbur Grey)*, Lon Chaney, Jr. *(Lawrence Talbot/The Wolf Man)*, Bela Lugosi *(Dracula)*, Glenn Strange *(The Monster)*, Lenore Aubert *(Sandra Mornay)*, Jane Randolph *(Joan Raymond)*, Frank Ferguson *(McDougal)*, Charles Bradstreet *(Dr. Stevens)*, Howard Negley *(Harris)*, Vincent Price *(Voice of The Invisible Man)*, Clarence Straight *(Man in Armor)*, Helen Spring *(Woman)*, Harry Brown *(Photographer)*, Joe Kirk, George Barton, Carl Sklover, Joe Walls *(Men)*, Paul Stader *(Sergeant)*, Bobby Barber *(Waiter)*.

Hilarious spoof where Universal threw all their monsters against B&L who play railway porters unwittingly delivering the "undead" bodies of The Monster and Dracula to a wax museum where they are revived with the help of Aubert who has pretended to be in love with Lou but is secretly Dracula's evil assistant intent on implanting Lou's brain inside The Monster's skull because he has become too intelligent and is therefore difficult to control by Dracula! Chaney, as Talbot/The Wolf Man, attempts to warn the boys against Dracula and The Monster. All the while Lugosi, as Dracula, flits about as a zany blood-starved bat who, naturally, lusts for Lou's veins. This was a big-budget film for B&L, almost $800,000, and it is superbly mounted and directed with impressive sets, properly mooded photography and a chilling score. The horror creatures, Chaney/Wolf Man, Lugosi/Dracula, Strange/The Monster (his third time in the role, having enacted it in HOUSE OF DRACULA and HOUSE OF FRANKENSTEIN), play for straight horror while B&L's comedic bits bounce off them like jai alai balls. Lugosi, who received $15,000 for his role in this film, spent off-camera time in pie-throwing contests with B&L, Chaney, and Strange, the latter tripping over a cable and breaking an ankle which caused Chaney to fill in as The Monster for one scene before Strange returned to finish the film in a cast. Costello at first did not want to make this film, reading the script and stating that it was not funny. It proved to be one of the funniest films B&L ever made, prompting later monster confrontation films with the zany duo. Chris Mueller, who created the scaly body for the CREATURE FROM THE BLACK LAGOON, fashioned the latex headpiece for Strange's monster. The film was an enormous box-office success largely due to the priceless lines that dot the dialog. Talbot to Lou: "I know you think I'm crazy, but in a half an hour the moon will rise and I'll turn into a wolf!" Lou to Talbot: "You and 20 million other guys." (See ABBOTT & COSTELLO series, Index.)

p, Robert Arthur; d, Charles T. Barton; w, Robert Lees, Frederic I. Rinaldo, John Grant (based on the novel *Frankenstein* by Mary Shelley); ph, Charles Van Enger; m, Frank Skinner; ed, Frank Gross; spec eff, David S. Horsley; makeup, Bud Westmore.

Comedy **Cas.** **(PR:A MPAA:NR)**

ABBOTT AND COSTELLO MEET THE INVISIBLE MAN 1/2** (1951) 82m UNIV bw

Bud Abbott *(Bud Alexander)*, Lou Costello *(Lou Francis)*, Nancy Guild *(Helen Gray)*, Adele Jergens *(Boots Marsden)*, Sheldon Leonard *(Morgan)*, William Frawley *(Det. Roberts)*, Gavin Muir *(Dr. Philip Gray)*, Arthur Franz *(Tommy Nelson)*, Sam Balter *(Radio Announcer)*, Sid Saylor *(Waiter)*, Billy Wayne *(Rooney)*, Bobby Barber *(Sneaky)*, John Day *(Rocky Hanlon)*, Edward Gargan *(Milt)*, Paul Maxey *(Dr. Turner)*, Herbert Vigran *(Stillwell)*, Frankie Van *(Referee)*, Carl Sklover *(Lou's Handler)*, George J. Lewis *(Torpedo)*, Ralph Dunn *(Motorcycle Cop)*, Harold Goodwin *(Bartender)*, Perc Launders *(Cop)*, Edith Sheets *(Nurse)*, Milt Bronson *(Ring Announcer)*, Richard Bartell *(Bald-headed Man)*, Charles Perry *(Rocky's Handler)*.

The boys graduate a fly-by-night detective school and immediately take on a murder case, that of Franz, a boxer accused of killing his manager, who hires them to prove him innocent. They visit Muir who shows them the formula which can turn a person invisible. (In homage there is a photo of Claude Rains, the original INVISIBLE MAN, on the wall.) When police arrive to arrest Franz, he injects himself with the serum and vanishes. Franz later explains to B&L that a mobster, Leonard, killed his manager when he, Franz, refused to throw a fight. The trio scheme to have Lou pretend to be a prizefighter and entrap Leonard in a similar fix so police will arrest him. Lou then takes on Day in a championship fight that has the invisible man throwing the punches and carrying a groggy Costello about the ring in the most hilarious part of the film, before Leonard and gang are rounded up. All in all, a pleasant film with consistent laughs. (See ABBOTT & COSTELLO series, Index.)

p, Howard Christie; d, Charles Lamont; w, Robert Lees, Frederic I. Rinaldo, John Grant (based on H. G. Wells' *Invisible Man*); ph, George Robinson; m, Joseph Gershenson; ed, Virgil Vogel.

Comedy **(PR:A MPAA:NR)**

ABBOTT AND COSTELLO MEET THE KEYSTONE KOPS** (1955) 79m UNIV bw

Bud Abbott *(Harry Pierce)*, Lou Costello *(Willie Piper)*, Fred Clark *(Joseph Gorman/Sergei Trumanoff)*, Lynn Bari *(Leota Van Cleef)*, Mack Sennett *(Himself)*, Maxie Rosenbloom *(Hinds)*, Frank Wilcox *(Snavely)*, Harold Goodwin *(Cameraman)*, Roscoe Ates *(Wagon Driver)*, Paul Dubov *(Jason)*, Henry Kulky *(Brakeman)*, Jack Daly *(Burglar)*, William Haade *(Hobo)*, Joe Devlin *(Policeman)*, Joe Besser *(Hunter)*, Harry Tyler *(Piano Player)*, Houseley Stevenson *(Pilot)*, Byron Keith *(Cop)*, Marjorie Bennett *(Fat Woman)*, Murray Leonard *(Studio Cop)*, Donald Kerr *(Projectionist)*, Charles Dorety *(Watermelon Peddler)*, Carole Costello *(Theater Cashier)*, Forrest Burns, Heinie Conklin, Don House *(Cops)*, Hank Mann.

Contrived period comedy where the boys buy the Edison Movie Studio in 1912 from con man Clark. After they discover they've been bilked, they follow the swindler to Hollywood where they become stunt men and finally discover Clark using the pseudonym Sergei Trumanoff and directing action films. B&L trap Clark as he is making off with the studio payroll and chase him to the airport, a marvelous chase worthy of any in the Sennett era; the preceding footage, unfortunately, does not live up to this highlight. Tired routines, blinded sight gags and a poor script add up to an average B&L programmer. (See ABBOTT & COSTELLO series, Index.)

p, Howard Christie; d, Charles Lamont; w, John Grant; ph, Reggie Lanning; m, Joseph Gershenson; ed, Edward Curtiss.

Comedy **(PR:A MPAA:NR)**

ABBOTT AND COSTELLO MEET THE KILLER, BORIS KARLOFF** (1949) 94m UNIV bw

Bud Abbott *(Casey Edwards)*, Lou Costello *(Freddie Phillips)*, Boris Karloff *(Swami Talpur)*, Lenore Aubert *(Angela Gordon)*, Gar Moore *(Jeff Wilson)*, Donna Martell *(Betty Crandall)*, Alan Mowbray *(Melton)*, James Flavin *(Inspector Wellman)*, Roland Winters *(T. Hanley Brooks)*, Nicholas Joy *(Amos Strickland)*, Mikel Conrad *(Sergeant Stone)*, Morgan Farley *(Gregory Milford)*, Percy Helton *(Abernathy)*, Victoria Horne *(Mrs. Hargreave)*, Claire Du Brey *(Mrs. Grimsby)*, Vincent Renno *(Mike Relia)*, Harry Hayden *(Lawrence Crandall)*, Murray Alper *(Joe)*, Patricia Hall *(Manicurist)*, Marjorie Bennett *(Maid)*, Harry Brown *(Medical Examiner)*, Beatrice Gray *(Woman)*, Frankie Van *(Bozzo)*, Billy Snyder, Eddie Coke *(Reporters)*, Jack Chefe *(Barber)*, Arthur Hecht *(Photographer)*, Ed Randolph *(Bootblack)*, Phil Shepard *(Bellboy)*.

When several murders occur at the Lost Caverns Hotel, bellhop Lou is suspected, especially after his pal, house detective Bud, tries to help him but casts more suspicion upon him. Karloff, who plays a mystic, attempts to hypnotize Lou and compel him to sign a bogus confession, but Lou's natural stupidity prevents success, one of the best scenes in this less than laugh-filled film. Police Inspector Wellman uses the bewildered bellhop to bait the real killer who is apprehended through Lou's stumbling moves. Karloff is not the killer, as the title suggests, but merely a red herring.

p, Robert Arthur; d, Charles T. Barton; w, Hugh Wedlock, Jr., Howard Snyder, John Grant; ph, Charles Van Enger; m, Milton Schwarzwald; ed, Edward Curtiss; spec eff, David S. Horsley; makeup, Bud Westmore.

Comedy **(PR:A MPAA:NR)**

ABBOTT AND COSTELLO MEET THE MUMMY** (1955) 79m UNIV bw

Bud Abbott *(Peter)*, Lou Costello *(Freddie)*, Marie Windsor *(Mme. Rontru)*, Michael Ansara *(Charlie)*, Dan Seymour *(Josef)*, Kurt Katch *(Dr. Gustav Zoomer)*, Richard Karlan *(Hetsut)*, Richard Deacon *(Semu)*, Mel Welles *(Iben)*, George Khoury *(Habid)*, Edwin Parker *(Kharis, The Mummy)*, Jan Arvan *(Waiter)*, Michael Vallon *(Dr. Azzui)*, Kem Dibbs, Mitchell Kowal, Ken Alton *(Policemen)*, Lee Sharon *(Blonde Girl)*, Hank Mann *(Native)*, Donald Kerr *(Newspaperman)*, Peggy King, Mazzone-Abbott Dancers, The Chandra-Kaly and Hi Dancers.

About to accompany Dr. Zoomer (Katch) to America from Egypt where they have been stranded, B&L find the archeologist murdered by cultists; a medallion falls into their hands and leads them to an ancient crypt where the mummy waits to terrorize them. The medallion is slipped into a hamburger which Lou eats and there is a great deal of fussing over his insides to locate the treasure, none of which is funny. A lame chuckle or two is all this cheaply produced film provides, the last made by B&L for Universal. Costello appears thin and wan in the film, Abbott heavier than his erstwhile partner. Costello had been suffering from rheumatic fever at the time.

p, Howard Christie; d, Charles Lamont; w, John Grant (based on a story by Lee Loeb); ph, George Robinson; m, Joseph Gershenson; ed, Russell Schoengarth.

Comedy **(PR:A MPAA:NR)**

ABBY** (1974) 89m AIP c

William Marshall *(Bishop Garnet Williams)*, Carol Speed *(Abby Williams)*, Terry Carter *(Rev. Emmett Williams)*, Austin Stoker *(Cass Potter)*, Juanita Moore *(Mama Potter)*, Charles Kissinger *(Dr. Hennings)*, Elliott Moffitt *(Russell)*, Nathan Cook *(Taft Hassan)*, Bob Holt *(voice of The Demon)*, Nancy Lee Owens *(Mrs. Wiggins)*.

Black exploitation film of THE EXORCIST variety has Marshall liberating a demon which soon houses itself within Speed who changes from nice girl to lascivious slattern venting hellish spleen upon one and all, bringing about the death of church organist Owens. An unimaginative script, erratic cross-cutting to replace expected special effects and a sophomoric approach to an already unbelievable subject renders this pic a loser.

p, William Girdler, Mike Henry, Gordon C. Layne; d, William Girdler; w, G. Cornell Layne; ph, William Asman; m, Robert O. Ragland; ed, Corky Ehlers, Henry Asman.

Horror **(PR:O MPAA:R)**

ABDICATION, THE** (1974, Brit.) 103 m WB c

Peter Finch *(Cardinal Azzolino)*, Liv Ullman *(Queen Christina)*, Cyril Cusack *(Oxenstierna)*, Graham Crowden *(Cardinal Barberini)*, Michael Dunn *(The Dwarf)*, Kathleen Byron *(Queen Mother)*, Lewis Fiander *(Father Dominic)*, Harold Goldblatt *(Pinamonti)*, Tony Steedman *(Carranza)*, Noel Trevarthen *(Ginetti)*, Richard Cornish *(Charles)*, James Faulkner *(Magnus)*, Ania Marson *(Ebba)*, Franz Drago *(Birgito)*, Suzanne Huddart *(Young Christina)*, Paul Rogers *(Altieri)*, Debbie Nicholson *(Young Ebba)*, Edward Underdown *(Christina's Father)*.

An utterly tedious, turgid historical drama set in 1654 where Ullman, in that vexing style of stammering gesture and frenetic word groping, ponders the problems of becoming a Catholic and losing her throne after traveling to Rome where she becomes enamored of a cardinal played woodenly by Finch. The viewer is not drawn in sympathy to her royal dilemma nor offered even a momentary respite from the film's arcane dialog. A boring waste of time—this film serves as a torpid example of how history comes to be thought of as dull and uninspiring. (Michael Dunn, a talented actor, died during this production and his replacement in the dwarf's role is noticeably different in manner and size.) One would be better entertained and informed by seeing Garbo's magnificent QUEEN CHRISTINA.

p, James Cresson, Robert Fryer; d, Anthony Harvey; w, Ruth Solff (based on her play); ph, Geoffrey Unsworth; m, Nino Rota; ed, John Bloom; art d, Alan Tomkins; cos, Farani, Peter J. Hall.

Historical Drama **(PR:C-O MPAA:PG)**

ABDUCTION* (1975) 100m Venture/Blackpool c

Judith Marie Bergan *(Patricia)*, David Pendleton *(Dory)*, Gregory Rozakis *(Frank)*, Leif Erickson *(Prescott)*, Dorothy Malone *(Mrs. Prescott)*, Lawrence Tierney *(FBI Agent)*, Presley Caton *(Angie)*, Catherine Lacy *(Carol)*, Andrew Rohrer *(Michael)*, Andrew Bloch *(Jake)*, Pat Hernon *(Newscaster)*, Dan Daniel *(Newscaster)*, John Bartholomew Tucker *(Newscaster)*, David Carroll *(Cop)*.

Awful kidnapping pic where Bergan is abducted by black radicals led by Pendleton, raped, attacked by lesbians and held for a strange ransom—the victim's father is ordered to dynamite a lavish high rise he has constructed for the opulent. The capitalist parent, Erickson, does exactly that in this low-budget production which was originally intended as a hardcore flic but softened to an unbearable "R." A doppelganger to the Patricia Hearst saga, the film was coincidentally based upon a Harrison James novel, published a year before Ms. Hearst was so ceremoniously snatched. Not worth a gander.

p, Kent E. Carroll; d, Joseph Zito; w, Carroll (based on the book *Black Abductor* by Harrison James); ph, Joao Fernandez; m, Ron Frangipane, Robbie Farrow; ed, James Macreading.

Crime **Cas.** **(PR:O MPAA:R)**

ABDUCTORS, THE** (1957) 80m FOX bw

Victor McLaglen, George Macready, Fay Spain, Carl Thayer, Gavin Muir, John Morley, Carlyle Mitchell, George Cisar, Pat Lawless, James Logan, Jason Johnson.

Recently released from prison, McLaglen attempts to free a fellow convict on the promise of a $100,000 payment, but after he and Macready kidnap the warden's daughter, Spain, the plot fails. Next the felonious pair attempt to snatch the body of Abraham Lincoln and hold it for ransom but confederate Muir drunkenly babbles their plans and Secret Service agents arrest the gang. Though this film is based upon a real incident, it fails to hold interest. The director is Victor McLaglen's son.

p, Ray Wander; d, Andrew V. McLaglen; w, Ray Wander; ph, Joseph La Shelle; m, Paul Glass.

Crime **(PR:A MPAA:NR)**

ABDUL THE DAMNED*1/2 (1935, Brit.) 111m BIP/CAP bw

Fritz Kortner *(Abdul Hamid II/Kislar)*, Nils Asther *(Kadar Pash)*, Adrienne Ames *(Therese Alder)*, John Stuart *(Talak Pash)*, Walter Rilla *(Hassan Bey)* Charles Carson *(Halmi Pasha)*, Patric Knowles *(Omar)*, Eric Portman *(Conspirator)*, Clifford Heatherley *(Doctor)*, Annie Esmond *(Lady)*, Arthur Hardy *(Ambassador)*, Robert Naylor, Warren Jenkins.

Overlong costumer depicts 1900 Turkey ruled by a paranoid potentate, Kortner, who ruthlessly destroys everyone he believes to be conspiring against him. Asther, as chief of police, blindly obeys his sultan's Nero-like orders but is pronounced guilty of plotting against his lord and is given a death decree, rescinded when Adrienne, a visiting Viennese actress who has fallen in love with Asther, agrees to join Kortner's harem. A stodgy historical opus.

d, Karl Grune; w, Ashley Dukes, Warren Strode, Roger Burford (based on a story by Robert Neumann); ph, Otto Kanturek; m, Hanns Eisler; art d, Clarence Elder, John Mead.

Drama **(PR:C MPAA:NR)**

ABDULLAH'S HAREM*1/2
(1956, Brit./Egypt.) 105m Sono c (GB: ABDULLA THE GREAT)

Gregory Ratoff *(Abdulla)*, Kay Kendall *(Ronnie)*, Sydney Chaplin *(Ahmed)*, Alex D'Arcy *(Marco)*, Marina Berti *(Aziza)*, Marti Stevens, Mary Costes.

A poor satire on Egypt's King Farouk enacted extravagantly by Ratoff who lusts after English model Kendall and, when she appears to fall in love with Chaplin, the king's chief advisor, Ratoff kidnaps her, unsuccessfully wooing her with the wealth of the Nile. During this palace frolic the people revolt, overthrowing the despot who ends his hours watching bellydancers as his kingdom collapses.

p&d, Gregory Ratoff; w, Boris Ingster, George Saint George (based on a story by Ismet Regeila); ph, Lee Garmes (Technicolor); m, Georges Auric; ed, Maurice Rootes.

Satire **Cas.** **(PR:O MPAA:NR)**

ABE LINCOLN IN ILLINOIS***
(1940) 110m RKO bw (GB: SPIRIT OF THE PEOPLE)

Raymond Massey *(Abraham Lincoln)*, Gene Lockhart *(Stephen Douglas)*, Ruth Gordon *(Mary Todd Lincoln)*, Mary Howard *(Ann Rutledge)*, Dorothy Tree *(Elizabeth Edwards)*, Harvey Stephens *(Ninian Edwards)*, Minor Watson *(Joshua Speed)*, Alan Baxter *(Billy Herndon)*, Howard da Silva *(Jack Armstrong)*, Maurice Murphy *(John McNeil)*, Clem Bevans *(Ben Battling)*, Herbert Rudley *(Seth Gale)*, Roger Imhof *(Mr. Crimmin)*, Edmund Elton *(Mr. Rutledge)*, George Rosener *(Dr. Chandler)*, Trevor Bardette *(John Hanks)*, Elisabeth Risdon *(Sarah Lincoln)*, Napoleon Simpson *(Gobey)*, Aldrich Bowker *(Judge Bowling Green)*, Louis Jean Heydt *(Mentor Graham)*, Harian Briggs *(Denton Offut)*, Andy Clyde *(Stage Driver)*, Leona Roberts *(Mrs. Rutledge)*, Florence Roberts *(Mrs. Bowling Green)*, Fay Helm *(Mrs. Seth Gale)*, Syd Saylor *(John Johnston)*, Charles Middleton *(Tom Lincoln)*, Alec Craig *(Trem Cogdall)*.

The popularity of Robert E. Sherwood's play prompted RKO to purchase and produce this episodic, somewhat static film even knowing that John Ford's much vaunted YOUNG MR. LINCOLN was in production at the time. Massey headed an impressive cast but he and the film covered too much ground to hold the viewer's attention, from Lincoln's early days as a young woodsman to his election to the Presidency in 1860, more a record of the Great Emancipator than a dramatic exposition of his life, including Lincoln's first love, his marriage, his early law practice, his debates with the feisty Douglas, played as a convincing bulldog by Lockhart. Hortatory speeches replace dialog and Massey is repeatedly seen not as a flesh-and-blood character but as a talking marble statue. Though critically successful, the public veered away from this Olympian Lincoln and the studio took a $750,000 loss.

p, Max Gordon; d, John Cromwell; w, Robert E. Sherwood (based on his play); ph, James Wong Howe; m, Roy Webb.

Drama **Cas.** **(PR:AA MPAA:NR)**

ABIE'S IRISH ROSE** (1928) 80m PAR bw

Jean Hersholt *(Solomon Levy)*, Charles Rogers *(Abie Levy)*, Nancy Carroll *(Rosemary Murphy)*, J. Farrell MacDonald *(Patrick Murphy)*, Bernard Gorcey *(Isaac Cohen)*, Ida Kramer *(Mrs. Isaac Cohen)*, Nick Cogley *(Father Whalen)*, Camillus Pretal *(Rabbi Jacob Samuels)*, Rosa Rosanova *(Sarah)*.

Initially produced as a silent film, the old theatrical chestnut was roasted over again by Paramount, ably directed by Victor Fleming, but made as an overlong gag with jokes that did not come off. To bolster its investment the studio cut down the film from its original 129 minutes to 80 minutes, added some vocal songs and snippets of dialog to zip up the lagging story of Abie's rise from the slums of New York, his fighting in France during WW I, and his love story with the beautiful Irish lass charmingly played by Nancy Carroll, a romance that leads to clashing families and sentimental fate. The critics universally panned the film but most were careful not to upset ethnic feelings. When *Variety's* "Rush" tore the tired story to pieces, the editors felt the need to tack the following comment on at the end of the review: "*Rush*, Al Greason, is of the Protestant faith.—Ed."

d, Victor Fleming; w, Julian Johnson, Herman Mankiewicz (based on the play by Anne Nichols); ph, Harold Rosson.

Comedy (PR:A MPAA:NR)

ABIE'S IRISH ROSE* (1946) 96m Crosby/UA bw

Joanne Dru (*Rosemary*), Richard Norris (*Abie*), Michael Chekhov (*Solomon Levy*), J. M. Kerrigan (*Patrick Murphy*), George E. Stone (*Isaac Cohen*), Vera Gordon (*Mrs. Cohen*), Emory Parnell (*Father Whalen*), Art Baker (*Rabbi Samuels*), Bruce Merritt (*Rev. Mr. Stevens*), Eric Blore (*Hotel Manager*), Harry Hays Morgan (*Hotel Clerk*).

The Nichols play which opened in 1922 and played for five years to the bewilderment of critics was back on the screen again (the first being the part-talkie in 1928) and this time really collapsed once and for all, audiences thoroughly rejecting the low-brow racial insults traded by the Jewish and Irish families feuding over the romance of their son and daughter. The coarse vaudevillian humor that bolstered such a tasteless show of slurs and slaps had faded with the roaring 1920s and so too did this film, thankfully.

p&d, Edward Sutherland; w, Anne Nichols (based on her play); ph, William Mellor; m, John Scott Trotter; art d, William Flanner.

Comedy (PR:C MPAA:NR)

ABILENE TOWN* (1946) 91m UA bw

Randolph Scott (*Dan Mitchell*), Ann Dvorak (*Rita*), Edgar Buchanan (*Bravo Trimble*), Rhonda Fleming (*Sherry Balder*), Lloyd Bridges (*Henry Dreiser*), Helen Boice (*Big Annie*), Howard Freeman (*Ed Balder*), Richard Hale (*Charlie Fair*), Jack Lambert (*Jet Younger*), Dick Curtis (*Ryker*), Eddie Waller (*Hannaberry*), Hank Patterson (*Doug Neil*), Earl Schenck (*Hazelhurst*).

Fast-paced actioner has Randolph Scott again donning the thumb-worn marshal's badge to clean up an end-of-the-trail cow town overrun with callous cattle barons and grim gunslingers, not dissimilar to the tales spun in VIRGINIA CITY and DODGE CITY. Scott is a Wyatt Earp-type lawman who slugs and shoots it out with the likes of Jack Lambert while Buchanan, the local sheriff, follows his own stereotype into drunken stupors. The good woman is played demurely by Rhonda Fleming while the wicked lady of the saloons is Ann Dvorak who shakes a mean leg and sings such ditties as "Every Time I Give My Heart," "All You Gotta Do," and "I Love It Out Here in the West." The customary ending is double-crossed when Scott goes off with the gambling hall cutie, forsaking sweet thing Fleming, a finish not so surprising when realizing that this better-than-average oater is based on a novel by Ernest Haycox who wrote STAGECOACH, another excellent western where the hero returns to the fallen angel.

p, Jules Levy; d, Edwin L. Marin; w, Harold Shumate (based on the novel *Trail Town* by Ernest Haycox); ph, Archie J. Stout; Otho Lovering, Richard Heermance; ch, Sammy Lee; m/l Fred Spielman, Kermit Goell.

Western Cas. (PR:A MPAA:NR)

ABILENE TRAIL ** (1951) 64m MON bw

Whip Wilson (*Kansas Kid*), Andy Clyde (*Sagebrush*), Tommy Farrell (*Ed Dawson*), Steve Clark (*Old Man Dawson*), Noel Neill (*Mary Dawson*), Dennis Moore (*Brandon*), Marshall Reed (*Slavens*), Lee Roberts (*Red*), Milburn Morante (*Chuck*), Ted Adams (*Sheriff*), Lyle Talbot (*Doctor*), Stanley Price (*Sheriff Warner*), Bill Kennedy (*Colter*).

Whip and his clowning companion Clyde are suspected of horse stealing but manage to clear themselves and catch the real culprits while working at the Dawson ranch where our all-in-black hero successfully woos the shy Miss Neill and manages a trail drive which culminates in the clearing of his good name. Some good outdoor footage and fight scenes.

p, Vincent M. Fennelly; d, Lewis Collins; w, Harry Fraser; ph, Gilbert Warrenton; md, Edward Kay; ed, Richard Heermance.

Western (PR:A MPAA:NR)

ABOMINABLE DR. PHIBES, THE* (1971, Brit.) 93m AIP c

Vincent Price (*Dr. Anton Phibes*), Joseph Cotten (*Dr. Vesalius*), Hugh Griffith (*Rabbi*), Terry-Thomas (*Dr. Longstreet*), Virginia North (*Vulnavia*), Audrey Woods (*Goldsmith*), Susan Travers (*Nurse Allan*), Alex Scott (*Dr. Hargreaves*), Peter Gilmore (*Dr. Kitaj*), Edward Burnham (*Dr. Dunwoody*), Peter Jeffrey (*Inspector Trout*), Maurice Kaufman (*Dr. Whitcombe*), Norman Jones (*Sgt. Schenley*), Derek Godfrey (*Crow*), John Cater (*Waverly*), Barbara Keogh (*Mrs. Frawley*), Sean Bury (*Lem Vesalius*), Walter Horsbrugh (*Ross*), Caroline Munro (*Mrs. Victoria Phibes*), David Hutcheson (*Dr. Hedgepath*), Dallas Adams, Alan Zipson (*Police Officials*).

A lunatic horror film about a lunatic doctor intent on murdering the physicians who butchered his departed wife while operating on her (Caroline Munro, seen in photos). Price has never been hammier than in this, his 100th film, so campy in fact that one wonders how he made it this far while mercilessly parodying himself. As the auto-injured Phibes, Price reconstructs his mutilated face and destroyed voice, able to speak only after plugging a cord extended from his neck into a phonograph! He devilishly devises gruesome ends for a bevy of quacks that are patterned after the plagues brought down on Ramses in ancient Egypt, from killer locusts to blood-sucking bats, chief surgeon Cotten being the main object of his maniacal plotting. The sets are awful, the plot ludicrous and dialog inane—what more could a horror freak desire? (Sequel: DR. PHIBES RISES AGAIN.)

p, Louis M. Heyward, Ronald S. Dunas; d, Robert Fuest; w, James Whiton, William Goldstein; ph, Norman Warwick; m, Basil Kirchin; ed, Tristam Cones; art d, Bernard Reeves; set d, Brian Eatwell; cos, Elsa Fennell.

Horror Cas. (PR:O MPAA:PG)

ABOMINABLE SNOWMAN OF THE HIMALAYAS, THE* (1957, Brit.) 83m Hammer/Clarion/FOX bw (AKA: ABOMINABLE SNOWMAN)

Forrest Tucker (*Tom Friend*), Peter Cushing (*Dr. John Rollason*), Maureen Connell (*Helen Rollason*), Richard Wattis (*Peter Fox*), Robert Brown (*Ed Shelley*), Michael Brill (*Andrew McNee*), Arnold Marie (*Lhama*), Anthony Chin (*Major Domo*), Wolfe Morris (*Kusang*).

Low-budget film (claimed to have been shot in the Pyrenees) with a lot of swirling snow as adventurer Tucker and botanist Cushing follow up the legendary reports of giant creatures, Yetis, living in the high Himalayas. They discover enormous footprints and are attacked by shaggy creatures that are never quite seen, due to chancy costuming no doubt. Further bogging down this tent-confining production is the interminable philosophical gobbledygook by so-called savants of the high mountains. More laugh able than frightening.

p, Aubrey Baring; d, Val Guest; w, Nigel Kneale; ph, Arthur Grant; m, Humphrey Searle; ed, Bill Lenny.

Fantasy Cas. (PR:A MPAA:NR)

ABOUT FACE* (1942) 43m Roach/UA bw

William Tracy (*Sgt. Doubleday*), Joe Sawyer (*Sgt. Ames*), Jean Porter (*Sally*), Marjorie Lord (*Betty Marlow*), Margaret Dumont (*Mrs. Culpepper*), Veda Ann Borg (*Daisy*), Joe Cunningham (*Col. Gunning*), Harold Goodwin (*Capt. Caldwell*), Frank Faylen (*Jerry*), Dick Wessel (*Charley*), Charles Lane (*Garage Manager*).

A silly, ineptly made film has army sergeants Tracy and Sawyer bumbling into trouble. Sawyer, playing his usual dumb-tough type, leads mild-mannered Tracy into a saloon brawl, gate-crashing a high society affair and an unexciting car crash scene. Not for anyone over age three.

p, Hal Roach, Fred Guiol; d, Kurt Neumann; w, Eugene Conrad, Edward E. Seabrook; ph, Paul Ivano; ed, Bert Jordan.

Comedy (PR:A MPAA:NR)

ABOUT FACE* (1952) 93m WB c

Gordon MacRae (*Tony Williams*), Eddie Bracken (*Boff Roberts*), Dick Wesson (*Dave Crouse*), Virginia Gibson (*Betty Long*), Phyllis Kirk (*Alice Wheatley*), Aileen Stanley, Jr. (*Lorna Carter*), Joel Grey (*Bender*), Larry Keating (*Col. Long.*), Cliff Ferre (*Lt. Jones*), John Baer (*Hal Carlton*).

A mediocre musical remake of BROTHER RAT with anemic direction and an equally bloodless script has MacRae, Bracken and Wesson as the cadets struggling through their final grades at Southern Military Institute, attempting to out-think an arrogant professor, Cliff Ferre, and, in Bracken's case, keep a secret wife under wraps. MacRae renders inadequate musical numbers with superior voice and talent but there's little to work with, the best being the ballad "There's No Other Girl For Me" and a big production number with Wesson and Gibson, "Spring Has Sprung." Bracken, who is always good for laughs as the whining buffoon, carries on hysterically when hearing that his hidden spouse is about to spring an offspring. Other tunes include "Tar Heels," "Reveille," "If Someone Had Told Me," "I'm Nobody" (delivered with gusto by Grey playing an oppressed underclassman), "S.M.I. March," "They Haven't Lost A Father Yet," and "Wooden Indian." All in all a pleasant but plodding programmer typifying Jack Warner's credo of making and remaking the WB properties that have done well in the past.

p, William Jacobs; d, Roy Del Ruth; w, Peter Milne (based on the play *Brother Rat* by John Monks, Jr., Fred F. Finklehoffe); ph, Bert Glennon; m/l, Charles Tobias, Peter De Rose; ed, Thomas Reilly; ch, LeRoy Prinz

Musical (PR:A MPAA:NR)

ABOUT MRS. LESLIE* (1954) 104m PAR bw

Shirley Booth (*Mrs. Vivien Leslie*), Robert Ryan (*George Leslie*), Marjie Millar (*Nadine Roland*), Alex Nicol (*Lan McKay*), Sammy White (*Harry Willey*), James Bell (*Mr. Poole*), Virginia Brissac (*Mrs. Poole*), Eileen Janssen (*Pixie*), Philip Ober (*Mort Finley*), Ellen Corby (*Mrs. Croffman*), Isaac Jones (*Jim*), Maidie Norman (*Camilla*), Henry Morgan (*Fred Blue*), Gale Page (*Marion King*), Laura Elliott (*Felice*), Ray Teal (*Barney*), Nana Bryant (*Mrs. McKay*), Pierre Watkin (*Lewis*), Ian Wolfe (*Mr. Pope*), Amanda Blake (*Gilly*), Percy Helton (*Hackley*), Ric Roman (*Ric*), Mabel Albertson (*Mrs. Sims*), Edith Evanson (*Mrs. Fine*), Joan Shawlee, Anne McCrea (*Girls at Night Club*), Benny Rubin (*TV Director*).

In her second film, after having scored a smash in COME BACK LITTLE SHEBA, Shirley Booth is ill-served in the role of a Beverly Hills rooming house landlady who looks back upon her romance with Ryan. Flashbacks show her wooed away from her NYC nightclub singing post by Ryan who takes her on a six-week vacation to the West Coast. She stays on as his mistress, though assuming the Leslie name. Booth knows little about Ryan's life and, after his death, learns that he was a tycoon airplane manufacturer. Revolving around this sudsy weeper are other minor stories, those of Mrs. Leslie's roomers, Nicol and Millar who fall in love on her premises, Janssen as an annoying teenager, and the salesman Morgan. The dialog is briefly bright but most of the film bogs down in murky melodrama with Ryan mismatched as the married-too-young lover. One handkerchief only.

p, Hal B. Wallis; d, Daniel Mann; w, Ketti Frings, Hal Kanter (based on the novel by Vina Delmar); ph, Ernest Laszlo; m, Victor Young; ed, Warren Low.

Romance (PR:A MPAA:NR)

ABOVE AND BEYOND* (1953) 122m MGM bw

Robert Taylor (*Col. Paul Tibbets*), Eleanor Parker (*Lucy Tibbets*), James Whitmore (*Maj. Uanna*), Larry Keating (*Maj. Gen. Vernon C. Brent*), Larry Gates (*Capt. Parsons*), Marilyn Erskine (*Marge Bratton*), Stephen Dunne (*Maj. Harry Bratton*), Robert Burton (*Gen. Samuel E. Roberts*), Hayden Rorke (*Dr. Ramsey*), Larry Dobkin (*Dr. Van Dyke*), Jack Raine (*Dr. Fiske*), Jonathan Cott (*Dutch Van Krik*), Jeff Richards (*Thomas Ferebee*), Dick Simmons (*Bob Lewis*), John McKee (*Wyatt Duzenbury*), Patrick Conway (*Radio Operator*), Christie Olson (*Paul Tibbets, Jr.*), William Lester (*Driver*), Barbara Ruick (*Mary Malone*), Jim Backus (*Gen. Curtis E. LeMay*), G. Pat Collins (*Maj. Gen. Creston*), Harlan Warde (*Chaplain Downey*), Crane Whittey (*Gen. Corlone*), Don Gibson (*Dexter*), John W. Baer (*Captain*), John Close (*Co-Pilot*), Lee MacGregor (*Gen. Robert's Aide*), Ewing Mitchell (*Gen. Wolfe*), Dorothy Kennedy (*Nurse*), (*Gen. Irvine*), Sam McKim (*Captain*), Robert Forrest (*M.P. Officer*), Dabbs Greer (*Haddock*), John Hedloe (*Lt. Malone*), Frank Gerslte (*Sgt. Wilson*), John Pickard (*Miller*), Gregory Walcott (*Burns*), Roger McGee (*Johnson*), Roger Fuller.

The dropping of atom bombs on Japan to end WW II was first dealt with by MGM in THE BEGINNING OR THE END but the studio had long wanted to deal with the intimate details of that earthquaking event, chiefly the story of the man who piloted the *Enola Gay* to her destiny over Hiroshima, Paul Tibbets. Robert Taylor forcefully enacts the role in this somewhat overlong production as the steely-nerved air force officer in charge of the operation, one which puts the top secret before personal feelings and lives; officers who make the slightest slip are instantly removed from their posts. The film jockeys between the carefully planned and absorbing preparations to drop the delicate bomb (details that sometimes become tedious) and a fairly mushy love affair between Taylor and Parker, his wife. Since he cannot reveal a tidbit of information to her and his manner becomes curt, the relationship is strained to the breaking point where Parker leaves him. Their scenes together are overacted, implausible and very sticky but then the pair, in their first film together (two more were to follow, VALLEY OF THE KINGS and MANY RIVERS TO CROSS) were torching offscreen in a love affair that would last until Taylor married a second time in 1954 to Ursula Thiess, and their personal involvement inescapably oozed onto celluloid. Whitmore gives a jocular performance as Tibbetts' aide. The most chilling aspect of the film is the final bomb run over Japan, an unforgettable filmic and historical record. Once the deed has been done, Taylor and Parker, the latter finally seeing her husband as a hero not an ogre, reunite in an even stronger marriage. Taylor was so enthusiastic about the film that he volunteered to become the first MGM star to go on TV to promote it, showing clips; up to that time the studio had utterly boycotted TV, refusing to allow its personnel before the television cameras, originally content to promote the pic with such cornball slogans as "The Love Story Behind the Billion Dollar Secret," a reflection of parts of the script written by Norman Panama and Melvin Frank, MGM scribes whose backgrounds were rooted in musical romances. The film's real value stems from the third scenarist, Beirne Lay, Jr., author of TWELVE O'CLOCK HIGH, and an air force veteran, who is largely responsible for the military segments.

p&d, Melvin Frank, Norman Panama; w, Beirne Lay, Jr., Frank Panama; ph, Ray June; m, Hugo Friedhofer; ed, Cotton Warburton; art d, Cedric Gibbons, Malcolm Brown; set d, Edwin B. Willis, Ralph Hurst; spec eff, A. Arnold Gillespie, Warren Newcombe.

War **(PR:A MPAA:NR)**

ABOVE SUSPICION*** (1943) 90m MGM bw

Joan Crawford *(Frances Myles)*, Fred MacMurray *(Richard Myles)*, Conrad Veidt *(Hassert Seidel)*, Basil Rathbone *(Sig von Aschenhausen)*, Reginald Owen *(Dr. Mespelbrunn)*, Richard Ainley *(Peter Galt)*, Cecil Cunningham *(Countess)*, Ann Shoemaker *(Aunt Ellen)*, Sara Haden *(Aunt Hattie)*, Felix Bressart *(Mr. A. Werner)*, Bruce Lester *(Thornley)*, Johanna Hofer *(Frau Kleist)*, Lotta Palfi *(Ottilie)*, Alex Papana *(Man in Paris)*, Rex Williams *(Gestapo Leader)*, Hans von Morhart *(Schmidt)*, William Yetter *(Hauptman)*, Steve Geray *(Anton)*, William "Wee Willie" Davis *(Hans)*, Lisa Golm *(Frau Schultz)*, Ludwig Stossel *(Herr Schultz)*, Ivan Simpson, Arthur Shields *(Porters)*, Henry Glynn *(Chauffeur)*, Eily Malyon *(Manageress)*, Matthew Boulton *(Constable)*, Marcelle Corday *(Maid)*, Frank Lackteen *(Arab Vendor)*, Charles de Ravenne *(Chasseur)*, Andre Charlot *(Cafe Manager)*, Frank Arnold *(Poet)*, George Davis *(Proprietor)*, Jack Chefe *(Coatroom Attendant)*, Felix Basch *(Guide)*, Edit Angold *(German Woman)*, Lisl Valetti *(Nazi Girl)*, Paul Weigel *(Elderly Man)*, Otto Reichow *(Gestapo Voice)*, Frank Reicher *(Col. Gerold)*, Peter Seal, Nicholas Vehr *(Col. Gerold's Aides)*, Henry Victor *(German Officer)*, Egon Brecher *(Gestapo Official)*, Walter O. Stahl *(Policeman)*.

This first-rate spy drama has newlyweds Crawford and MacMurray honeymooning in 1939 Germany but secretly acting as British agents to obtain details of a new Nazi weapon, a magnetic mine. There are clues and menacing creatures galore, from a torn page of a Liszt concerto to cryptic chessmen, from Rathbone, a sinister Gestapo chieftain tracking the pair, to Veidt, an underground leader aiding them. The couple travel from Paris to Salzburg while under constant threat but are foiled by Rathbone who imprisons Crawford in a remote Bavarian castle; she is saved by MacMurray and British agents before divulging her secrets and the pair, after a harrowing chase to the border, finally escape with lives and top secret information intact—a hectic, suspenseful thriller deftly directed by Thorpe. Crawford is excellent as the endangered but courageous wife, Rathbone exceptionally hateful as her evil pursuer, and MacMurray a lighthearted delight in the face of danger; at film's end, when he and Crawford cross safely over the Italian border, he doffs a jaunty Alpine hat and blithely utters: "How about some spaghetti?" This was Crawford's last film for MGM, after 17 years with the studio, Louis B. Mayer bluntly telling her it was time for her to "move on" and make way for the likes of Lana Turner. It was also Veidt's last film; the superb character actor, who had, in the 1930s, actually been imprisoned by the Nazis and who played Nazi commanders so convincingly as in CASABLANCA, died of a fatal heart attack shortly after completing this film.

p, Victor Saville, Leon Gordon; d, Richard Thorpe; w, Keith Winter, Melville Baker, Patricia Coleman (based on the novel by Helen MacInnes); ph, Robert Planck; m, Bronislau Kaper; ed, George Hively; art d, Randall Duell; cos, Irene, Gile Steele.

Spy Drama **(PR:A MPAA:NR)**

ABOVE THE CLOUDS** (1933) 68m COL bw (GB: WINGED DEVILS)

Robert Armstrong *(Scoop Adams)*, Richard Cromwell *(Dick Robinson)*, Dorothy Wilson *(Connie)*, Edmund Breese *(Crusty)*, Morgan Wallace *(Chandler)*, Dorothy Revier *(Dolly)*, Bessie Barriscale *(Mother)*, Geneva Mitchell *(Mabel)*, Luis Alberni *(Speakeasy Owner)*, Sherry Hall *(Doyle)*.

Early day cameraman story has Armstrong undoing himself with heavy drink and wild escapades while his apprentice, Cromwell, is left with his mistakes, taking the blame for superimposed photos, lost lenses and general foul-ups. Though Cromwell is fired from his job, he gets the girl, Wilson, and saves the day by recording the destruction of a dirigible. Excellent newsreel footage showing early-day naval maneuvers and aerial shots enhance a rather lame story and sophomoric dialog.

d, Roy William Neill; w, Albert De Mond (based on a story by George B. Seitz); ph, John Stumar; ed, John Rawlins.

Adventure **(PR:A MPAA:NR)**

ABOVE US THE WAVES*** (1956, Brit.) 92m RANK/REP bw

John Mills *(Cdr. Frazer)*, John Gregson *(Lt. Alec Duffy)*, Donald Sinden *(Lt. Tom Corbett)*, James Robertson Justice *(Adm. Ryder)*, Michael Medwin *(Smart)*, James Kenney *(Abercrombie)*, O. E. Hasse *(Captain of the "Tirpitz")*, William Russell *(Ramsey)*, Thomas Heathcote *(Hutchins)*, Lee Patterson *(Cox)*, Theodore Bikel *(German Officer)*, Lyndon Brook *(X2 Diver Navigator)*, William Russell *(Ramsey)*, Harry Towb *(McCleery)*, Anthony Newley *(X2 Engineer)*, Anthony Wager *(George)*, William Franklyn *(X2 No. 1)*, Leslie Weston *(Winley)*, Guido Lorraine *(Officer Interpretor)*.

A claustrophobic but chilling account of the British midget submarines that attempted to sink the giant German pocket battleship "Tirpitz" by planting underwater explosives on her hull in a foggy Norwegian fjord where the ship was riding at hidden anchorage. Mills and others are taken through their rigorous training for the near-suicidal mission with typical British resolve and resignation and are then abruptly sent forth. Two of the baby subs fail and their crews are picked up by affable German seamen; the third manages to plant an explosive that rocks the hulking warship but causes fatal damage to the sub. We do not see the "Tirpitz" founder but it is a fact that British subs did immobilize her for the duration of WW II in a daring September 1943 strike.

p, William MacQuitty; d, Ralph Thomas; w, Robin Estridge (based on a story by C. E. T. Warren, James Benson); ph, Ernest Steward; m, Arthur Benjamin; ed, Gerald Thomas.

War **(PR:A MPAA:NR)**

ABRAHAM LINCOLN* 1/2** (1930) 97m Griffith/UA bw

Walter Huston *(Abraham Lincoln)*, Una Merkel *(Ann Rutledge)*, Kay Hammond *(Mary Todd Lincoln)*, E. Alyn Warren *(Stephen Douglas)*, Hobart Bosworth *(Gen. Robert E. Lee)*, Fred Warren *(Gen. U. S. Grant)*, Henry B. Walthall *(Col. Marshall)*, Frank Campeau *(Gen. Sheridan)*, Francis Ford *(Sheridan's Aide)*, W. L. Thorne *(Tom Lincoln)*, Lucille La Verne *(Midwife)*, Helen Freeman *(Nancy Hanks Lincoln)*, Ian Keith *(John Wilkes Booth)*, Oscar Apfel *(Stanton)*, Otto Hoffman *(Offut)*, Edgar Deering *(Armstrong)*, Russell Simpson *(Lincoln's Employer)*, Helen Ware *(Mrs. Edwards)*, Charles Crockett *(Sheriff)*, Jason Robards, Sr. *(Herndon)*, Gordon Thorpe *(Tad Lincoln)*, James Bradbury, Sr. *(Gen. Scott)*, Cameron Prudhomme *(John Hay)*, Jimmy Eagles *(Young Soldier)*, Hank Bell, Carl Stockdale, George McQuarrie, Ralph Lewis, Robert Brower.

No greater film director or film pioneer existed than David Wark Griffith, whose silent classics INTOLERANCE, BIRTH OF A NATION and BROKEN BLOSSOMS, to name a few, had placed him at the pinnacle of his profession. Yet his transition from silent to talking pictures had been difficult and his prestige had dipped in the late 1920s. Griffith's ambitions for ABRAHAM LINCOLN were as keen as those he exhibited for his earlier masterpieces; the public and critics alike expected much of him, more than what he delivered in this film which has Walter Huston enacting an episodic version of Lincoln, from country bumpkin to early-day lawyer to the President marked for an assassin's bullet. Much of the film is stirring, particularly the Civil War battle scenesa marvelous sequence of cross-cutting and quick truck shots shows Sheridan's frantic ride down the Shenandoah Valley—and here the director was in his metier. But his utter reverence for his subject makes Lincoln appear somewhat stilted, as if posing dramatically for individual scenes, for posterity, to satisfy the image embedded in the public mind. Huston comes across early in the film as flesh and blood but later retreats into the mold of a marble statue, iron postures passing for pensiveness. The assassination scene is, ironically, less effective than the version Griffith rendered in BIRTH OF A NATION. The lead of that 1915 masterpiece, Henry B. Walthal, appears again, but this time as an aide to General Lee. The episodic nature of the film, as Griffith himself later realized, made the picture appear disjointed and often aimless. The great director left the production in ill health almost the minute after shooting the last scene. He later stated that the film was for him "a nightmare of the mind and nerves." The scenes between Hammond and Huston, when Lincoln meets the nervy Mary Todd, are genuinely comedic but less convincing are those between Huston and Merkel as the doomed Ann Rutledge. Griffith cannot be blamed for the incohesive story line; he wanted to concentrate on Lincoln's early love story as originally depicted in Benet's script, but mogul Joseph Schenck, who had taken over United Artists, backed him into an episodic approach and, upon completion of the film, ordered John Considine, Jr. to prevent Griffith from making any changes. Yet brilliant flashes of direction permeate the entire film which make it distinctively a product of the great master.

d, D. W. Griffith; w, Stephen Vincent Benet; ph, Karl Struss; m, Hugo Reisenfeld; ed, John Considine Jr.; set d, William Cameron Menzies.

Drama **Cas.** **(PR:AAA MPAA:NR)**

ABROAD WITH TWO YANKS** (1944) 80m UA bw

William Bendix *(Biff Koraski)*, Helen Walker *(Joyce Stuart)*, Dennis O'Keefe *(Jeff Reardon)*, John Loder *(Cyril North)*, George Cleveland *(Roderick Stuart)*, Janet Lambert *(Alice)*, James Flavin *(Sergeant Wiggins)*, Arthur Hunnicutt *(Arkie)*, Willard Jillson *(Handsome)*, Herbert Evans *(Michael)*, William Forrest *(Colonel Hart)*, John Abbott *(Salesman)*.

Zany slapstick, often mindless, is the thrust of this army comedy where two soldiers, Bendix and O'Keefe, clown together and compete over the attentions of curvaceous Helen Walker while stationed in Australia. So-so gags and predictable situations are elevated when O'Keefe steals Walker from the poetry-spewing Bendix by pretending he's schizophrenic and dangerous unless she complies with his every wish. A chase sequence develops between O'Keefe and Bendix, both having escaped the guard-house dressed as females, which proceeds disruptively through a charity ball. All in all, a low-brow redoing of the legendary Quirt and Flagg saga.

p, Edward Small; d. Allan Dwan; w, Charles Rogers, Wilkie Mahoney, Ted Sills; ph, Charles Lawton; m, Lud Gluskin; ed, Richard Heermance.

Comedy **(PR:A MPAA:NR)**

ABSENCE OF MALICE 1/2** (1981) 116m COL c

Paul Newman *(Gallagher)*, Sally Field *(Megan)*, Bob Balaban *(Rosen)*, Melinda Dillon *(Teresa)*, Luther Adler *(Malderone)*, Barry Primus *(Waddell)*, Josef Sommer *(McAdam)*, John Harkins *(Davidek)*, Don Hood *(Quinn)*, Wilford Brimley *(Wells)*, Arnie Ross *(Eddie Frost)*, Anna Marie Napoles *(Nickie)*, Shelley Spurlock *(Sarah Wylie)*, Joe Petrullo, Shawn McAllister *(Mobsters)*, Rooney Kerwin *(Walker)*, Oswaldo Calvo *(John)*, Clardy Malugen *(Donna)*, Sharon Anderson *(Secretary)*,

Jody Wilson *(Ragged Lady)*, Ilse Earl *(Nun)*, Alfredo Alvarez Colderon *(Rodriguez)*, Pat Sullivan *(Meersma)*, Bill Hindman *(Priest)*, Timothy Hawkins, John Archie, Ricardo Marquez *(FBI Agents)*, Kathy Suergiu, Jeff Gillen, Diane Zolten *(Reporters)*, Ted Bartsch *(Beverage Manager)*, Sugar Ray Mann *(Copy Boy)*, Richard O'Feldman *(Driver)*, Chuck Lupo *(Dock Boy)*, John DiSanti *(Longshoreman)*, Laurie V. Logan *(McAdam's Assistant)*, Patricia Matsdorff *(Susan)*, Gary Van Auken *(Marshall)*, Jack McDermott, Mark Harris, Bobbie-Ellyne Kosstrin, Lynn Parraga, Lee Sandman, Barry Hober *(News Staff)*.

An awkward attempt to profile the damage certain types of investigative reporters can bring about through unscrupulous ambition in getting their so-called exposes into print chiefly for a byline and professional recognition, a film that seemingly intends to counter ALL THE PRESIDENT'S MEN. Newman is the son of a dead mobster who runs a legitimate business in Miami with no connection to the crime syndicate other than a still-active uncle (Adler), yet a federal investigator (Balaban) believes Newman knows the intimate details about the disappearance of a labor leader and makes sure that reporter Field reads his confidential file on Newman which involves him in the disappearance. Field then implicates Newman in a story about the missing man, yet Newman provides an alibi covering the time of the disappearance; he was in Atlanta with a female friend, Dillon, arranging an abortion for her, one made necessary through an affair with another man. Field interviews Dillon and then callously prints the details of the abortion, causing Dillon to commit suicide. Newman takes his revenge by setting up a phony conspiracy which Field exposes, thus making herself and her paper subject to libel charges. A federal sachem, Brimley, arrives on the scene like some down-home *deus ex machina* (he is a blacksmith who entered the acting field as Jack Lemmon's aide in THE CHINA SYNDROME) to sort out the mess, put Field in her place and oust Balaban, the latter giving an annoying performance as a despicable bureaucrat. The film is confusing, too long and does not define its characters. Moreover, the acting, from Newman on down, is perfunctory and disappointing in a story that promises and does not deliver.

p&d, Sydney Pollack; w, Kurt Luedtke; ph, Owen Roizman; m, Dave Grusin; ed, Sheldon Kahn; prod d, Terence Marsh; cos, Bernie Pollack.

Drama **Cas.** **(PR:O MPAA:PG)**

ABSENT-MINDED PROFESSOR, THE*** (1961) 97m Disney/BV bw

Fred MacMurray *(Prof. Ned Brainard)*, Nancy Olson *(Betsy (Carlisle)*, Keenan Wynn *(Alonzo Hawk)*, Tommy Kirk *(Bill Hawk)*, Leon Ames *(Rufus Daggett)*, Elliott Reid *(Shelby Ashton)*, Edward Andrews *(Defense Secretary)*, Wally Brown *(Coach Elkins)*, Forrest Lewis *(Officer Kelly)*, James Westerfield *(Officer Hanson)*, Ed Wynn *(Fire Chief)*, David Lewis *(Gen. Singer)*, Belle Montrose *(Mrs. Chatsworth)*, Alan Carney *(Referee)*, Gage Clarke *(Rev. Bosworth)*, Alan Hewitt *(Gen. Hotchkiss)*, Jack Mullaney *(Captain)*, Raymond Bailey *(Adm. Olmstead)*, Wendell Holmes *(Gen. Poynter)*, Don Ross *(Lenny)*, Charlie Briggs *(Sig)*, Wally Boag *(TV Newsman)*.

Screwball comedy has quirkish MacMurray inventing flying rubber which he dubs "flubber," a substance, once added to rubber, which allows objects to leap into the air and even fly. This fantastic material is dabbed onto the soles of five of his school's stubby basketball players, allowing them to leap many feet into the air and thereby outscore their towering opposition in a crucial game and earn the necessary grants to keep the school afloat. Moreover, the professor injects his serum into his car which allows it to fly through the heavens while sinister Keenan Wynn tries to steal the formula and Nancy Olson tries to wed the scatterbrained Professor Brainard. The special effects will delight young and old. (Sequel: SON OF FLUBBER, 1964)

p, Walt Disney; d, Robert Stevenson; w, Bill Walsh (based on a story by Samuel W. Taylor); ph, Edward Colman; m, George Bruns; ed, Cotton Warburton; art d, Carroll Clark; spec eff, Peter Ellenshaw, Eustace Lycett, Robert A. Mattey.

Comedy/Fantasy **Cas.** **(PR:AAA MPAA:NR)**

ABSOLUTE QUIET*** (1936) 70m MGM bw

Lionel Atwill *(G. A. Axton)*, Irene Hervey *(Laura Tait)*, Raymond Walburn *(Governor Pruden)*, Stuart Erwin *(Chubby Rudd)*, Ann Loring *(Zelda Tadema)*, Louis Hayward *(Gregory Bengard)*, Wallace Ford *(Jack)*, Bernadene Hayes *(Judy)*, Harvey Stephens *(Barney Tait)*, Robert Gleckler *(Jasper Cowdray)*, J. Carroll Naish *(Kedro)*, Matt Moore *(Pilot)*, Robert Livingston *(Co-Pilot)*.

Offbeat melodrama has wealthy Atwill being robbed at his luxurious ranch by Wallace Ford and henchmen just as a plane carrying a cast of strange characters is forced to land in the desolate area. Walburn, as a blubbering corrupt governor fleeing his misdeeds, provides many laughs and the heroics are furnished by Louis Hayward, failed actor who takes on the robbers and shoots them down while Erwin, in the role of a jaded reporter, records the slaughter. Atwill is at the core of events, viciously manipulating his uninvited guests until he drops dead of a heart attack before his devoted secretary, Hervey. A bizarre treat with unexpected twists under the fast tempo of Seitz.

p, John W. Considine Jr.; d, George Seitz; w, Harry Clark (based on a story by George F. Worts); ph, Lester White; m, Franz Waxman; ed, Conrad A. Nervig.

Crime **(PR:C MPAA:NR)**

ABSOLUTION* (1981, Brit.) 95m EP c

Richard Burton *(Fr. Goddard)*, Dominic Guard *(Benjie)*, Dai Bradley *(Arthur)*, Billy Connolly *(Blakey)*, Andrew Kier *(Headmaster)*, Willoughby Gray *(Brig. Gen.* Walsh), Preston Lockwood *(Fr. Hibbert)*, Brook Williams *(Fr. Clarence)*, James Ottaway *(Fr. Matthews)*, John Plowman *(Fr. Piers)*, Robin Soans *(Fr. Henryson)*, Sharon Duce *(Louella)*, Trevor Martin *(Gladstone)*, Brian Glober, Dan Meaden *(Policemen)*.

Burton is a severe priest in a Catholic boarding school for boys. Students Guard and Bradley conspire to drive him insane with wild admissions in the confessional. An utterly depressing, pointless film which serves an an exercise in sadism and hatred, poorly written, aimlessly directed and photographed, it appears, with lenses kept in coal bins. The film might never have been released had it not included Burton, undoubtedly a quickie for the high-living actor.

p, Danny O'Donovan, Elliott Kastner; d, Anthony Page; w, Anthony Shaffer; ph, John Coquillon; m, Stanley Myers; ed, John Victor Smith; prod d, Natasha Kroll.

Drama **(PR:O MPAA:NR)**

ABUSED CONFIDENCE 1/2** (1938, Fr. ABUS DE CONFIANCE) 88m UDIF/COL bw

Danielle Darrieux *(Lydia)*, Charles Vanel *(Jacques Ferney)*, Valentine Tessier*(Helene Ferney)*, Therese Dorny *(Landlady)*, Jean Worms *(Judge)*, Pierre Mingand (Pierre), Gilbert Gil *(Paul)*, Yvette Lebon *(Alice)*, Svetlana Pitoeff *(Renee)*, Nicole de Rouves *(Waif)*.

An intriguing tale of a young woman going through law school; her grandmother dies and causes her to seek employment but she is met with lascivious proposals from several would-be employers. Darrieux then passes herself off as the daughter of a dead actress who had been the mistress of a now-famous writer, going to the author with this tale. Though married, he takes her in and finances her education. His wife, Tessier, discovers the lie but keeps silent, and sees the girl graduate and take up the law, defending a young girl who has committed the very kind of fraud of which she is guilty. In an impassioned conclusion, Darrieux addresses the jury and convinces members to free her client. A good psychological drama. (In French; English subtitles)

d, Henry Decoin; w, Decoin, Jean Boyer (based on a story by Pierre Wolff); ph, L. H. Burel; m, Georges Van Parys.

Drama **(PR:C-O MPAA:NR)**

ACAPULCO GOLD zero (1978) 105m Riddle c

Marjoe Gortner, Robert Lansing, John Harkins, Ed Nelson, Lawrence Casey, Randi Oakes, Phil Hoover.

Awful escapades on Kauai Island in Hawaii as Gortner, in an obnoxious performance, involves himself in a drug smuggling operation. Not worth blinking a single eye in its direction.

p, Allan F. Bodoh, Bruce Cohn; d, Burt Brinckerhoff; w, Don Enright, O'Brian Tomalin.

Crime **(PR:O MPAA:PG)**

ACCATTONE!** (1961, Ital.) 120m Arco/CD bw

Franco Citti *(Vittorio Accattone)*, Franca Pasut *(Stella)*, Silvana Corsini *(Maddalena)*, Paolo Guidi *(Ascenza)*, Adriana Asti *(Amore)*, Renato Capogna *(Renato)*, Roberto Scaringella *(Cartagine)*, Mario Cipriani *(Balilla)*, Piero Morgia *(Pio)*, Umberto Bevilacqua *(Salvatore)*, Elsa Morante *(Prisoner)*, Danilo Alleva *(Iaio)*, Polidor *(Becchino)*.

An unimpassioned, near-documentary film about a procurer and his street girls, a sleazy portrait without a laugh or a tear, directed by Pier Paolo Pasolini, whose GOSPEL ACCORDING TO SAINT MATTHEW and co-authorship of THE NIGHTS OF CABIRIA won him critical applause. Pasolini, who employs all non-professional actors in the film, studies his creations as if under a microscope, concentrating on Citti, a wastrel hating work but falling in love with a clean girl (Pasut) and attempting to take on a job which he quits in one day, returning to find his girls with other patrons. Citti turns to robbery and is killed. A raw look at a vulgar, disgusting street life peopled by apprehensive strangers.

p, Alfredo Bini; d&w, Pier Paolo Pasolini; ph, Tonino delli Colli; m, J. S. Bach, adapted by Carlo Rustichelli; ed, Nino Baragli.

Crime **(PR:O MPAA:NR)**

ACCENT ON LOVE* 1/2 (1941) 61m FOX bw

George Montgomery, Osa Massen, J. Carrol Naish, Cobina Wright Jr., Minerva Urecal, Stanley Clements, Thurston Hall, Irving Bacon, Oscar O'Shea, Leonard Carey, John T. Murray.

Grade B programmer glimmering Capra-antics has Montgomery quitting a cushy position with his father-in-law, Hall, and working as a WPA ditch digger; he falls in love with Massen, an immigrant, and sides with the impoverished dwellers of crumbling tenements, influencing Hall to aid the poor while divorcing his wife, Wright, to marry Massen. A helpless, hopeless mushy mishmash.

p, Walter Morosco, Ralph Dietrich; d, Ray McCarey; w, John Larkin (based on a story by Dalton Trumbo); ph, Charles Clarke; m, Emil Newman.

Romance **(PR:A MPAA:NR)**

ACCENT ON YOUTH 1/2** (1935) 77m PAR bw

Sylvia Sidney *(Linda Brown)*, Herbert Marshall *(Steven Gaye)*, Phillip Reed *(Dickie* Reynolds), Astrid Allwyn *(Genevieve Lang)*, Holmes Herbert *(Frank Galloway)*, Catherine Doucet *(Eleanor Darling)*, Ernest Cossart *(Flogdell)*, Donald Meek *(Orville)*, Dick Foran *(Butch)*, Lon Chaney Jr. *(Chuck)*, Samuel S. Hinds *(Benham)*, Florence Roberts *(Mrs. Benham)*, Laura Treadwell *(Mrs. Galloway)*, Elsie Clark *(Janet)*, Albert Taylor *(Cashier)*.

A solid love story where secretary Sidney falls hopelessly in love with an older man, Marshall, a playwright who employs her but avoids her affection. Marshall is superlative as the sensitive employer, overshadowing Sidney's sometimes histrionic performance. Reed is convincing as the athletic college boy and Cossart, as the stuffy butler, provides ample laughs. (Remade as BUT NOT FOR ME and MR. MUSIC.)

p, Douglas MacLean; d, Wesley Ruggles; w, Herbert Fields, Claude Binyon (based on the play by Samson Raphaelson); ph, Leon Shamroy; ed, Otho Lovering.

Romance **(PR:A MPAA:NR)**

ACCEPTABLE LEVELS 1/2** (1983, Brit.) 103m FP c

Kay Adshead *(Sue)*, Andy Rashleigh *(Simon)*, Patrick Higgins *(Tony McAteer)*, Tracey Lynch *(Roisin McAteer)*, Sally McCaffery *(Kathleen McAteer)*, George Shane *(Frank McAteer)*, Paul Jesson *(Major Green)*, Frances Barber *(Jill)*, Ina McElhinney *(Andy)*, Derek Halligan *(Ricky)*, Doyne Byrd *(Lawrence)*, Michael Gormley *(Father Docherty)*.

Study of a British TV crew interviewing a Belfast family in the war-strewn Catholic district focuses upon the death of a child hit by a stray plastic bullet fired by a British soldier. Adshead, as the chief reporter, becomes politically involved in the incident but her producer, Rashleigh, is apprehensive and, once back in London, makes sure that the most indicting footage is destroyed. Taut moments of a tough story are undermined by incoherent accents and tedious opening segments of a story seeming to have no destination. The film appears to be a production by committee, dragging along until everyone has put in their "bit." It is nevertheless a good, if unintentional, profile of self-indulgent, affluent British media reps who appear to be slumming among their stories and dining on expensive cuisine while mouthing meaningless empathy for the subjects of their lenses and microphones.

d, John Davies; w, Gordon Hann, Ellin Hare, Alastair Herron, Robert Smith, Kate McManus, Davies; ph, Robert Smith; m, Nick Garvey; ed, Hare; art d, Herron, McManus, Smith.

Drama **(PR:C MPAA:NR)**

ACCIDENT** (1967, Brit.) 105m LIP c

Dirk Bogarde *(Stephen)*, Stanley Baker *(Charley)*, Jacqueline Sassard *(Anna)*, Delphine Seyrig *(Francesca)*, Alexander Knox *(Provost)*, Michael York *(William)*, Vivien Merchant *(Rosalind)*, Harold Pinter *(Bell)*, Ann Firbank *(Laura)*, Brian Phelan *(Police Sergant)*, Freddie Jones *(Frantic Man)*, Nicholas Mosley *(Hedges)*, Terence Rigby *(Plainclothes Policeman)*, Jill Johnson *(Secretary)*, Jane Hillary *(Receptionist)*, Maxwell Findlater *(Ted)*, Carole Caplin *(Clarissa)*.

Morose story about the seduction of a university student after she undergoes a car crash which kills her boy friend; both Baker and Bogarde take advantage of the girl. Bogarde, an introspective professor reflecting upon the dead boy, a former student, tells the story leading up to the accident in a tedious, often boring series of flashbacks, more an exercise of self-indulgence than self-examination.

p, Joseph Losey, Norman Priggen; d, Losey; w, Harold Pinter (based on the novel by Nicholas Mosley); ph, Gerry Fisher (Eastmancolor); m, Johnny Dankworth; ed, Reginald Beck; art d, Carmen Dillon; cos, Beatrice Dawson.

Drama **Cas.** **(PR:O MPAA:NR)**

ACCIDENTAL DEATH** (1963, Brit.) 57m AA bw

John Carson *(Paul Lanson)*, Jacqueline Ellis *(Henriette)*, Derrick Sherwin *(Alan)*, Richard Vernon *(John Paxton)*, Joan Lodge *(Brenda)*, Gerald Case *(Inspector)*, Jacqueline Lacey *(Milly)*.

Mediocre Edgar Wallace story follows a plotting killer bent on murdering Ellis' patron in vengeance for misdeeds during WWII. The novel idea of permitting the viewer to see every move of the killer wears thin after the first half hour so that suspense is lacking.

p, Jack Greenwood; d, Geoffrey Nethercott; w, Arthur LaBern (based on the story "Jack O' Judgement" by Edgar Wallace).

Crime **(PR:C MPAA:NR)**

ACCIDENTS WILL HAPPEN** ½ (1938) 62m WB bw

Ronald Reagan *(Eric Gregg)*, Gloria Blondell *(Patricia Carmody)*, Dick Purcell *(Jim Faber)*, Sheila Bromley *(Nora Gregg)*, Addison Richards *(Blair Thurston)*, Hugh O'Connell *(John Oldham)*, Janet Shaw *(Mary Tarlton)*, Elliott Sullivan *(Burley Thorne)*, Anderson Lawlor *(Dawson)*, Spec O'Donnell *(Specs)*, Kenneth Harlan *(Nudnick)*, Don Barclay *(Dorsey)*, Earl Dwire *(Dr. Faris)*, Max Hoffman, Jr. *(Doc)*, John Butler *(Cosgrove)*, Edwin Stanley *(Judge)*, Allan Cavan *(Captain)*, Fern Barry *(Girl)*, Clinton Rosemond *(Black Man)*, Willard Parker *(Attendant)*, Al Herman *(Monty)*, Betty Farrington *(Sadie)*, Stuart Holmes *(Len)*, Frank Shannon *(Man on Crutches)*, Max Wagner *(Eddie)*, Jack Wise, John Harron, Myrtle Vandergrift, Cliff Saum *(Cops)*, Jeffrey Sayre *(Electric Company Man)*, Milton Kibbee *(Lineman)*, Wilfred Lucas *(Bailiff)*, Ralph Dunn *(Court Clerk)*, Richard Kipling *(Attorney)*, William Worthington *(Irate Car Owner)*, Loretta Rush *(Miss Mason)*, Pat O'Malley *(Conductor)*, Jimmy Fox, Betty Mack, Ralph Peters *(Passengers)*, Bernard Suss *(Mr. Philbert)*.

Insurance claims adjuster Reagan is married to a materialistic wife, Bromley, who involves in him phony claims causing him to lose his job. He joins forces with an attractive cigar store girl, Blondell (sister of actress Joan Blondell), and the twosome tirelessly track down the culprits of an insurance fraud ring, including Reagan's wayward wife, setting them up for police in a scam of their own. Reagan is vindicated and begins life all over again with Blondell at his side. A better than average B movie.

p, Bryan Foy; d, William Clemens; w, George Bricker, Anthony Coldeway (based on a story by Bricker); ph, William O'Connell; ed, Thomas Pratt.

Crime **(PR:A MPAA:NR)**

ACCOMPLICE* ½ (1946) 66m PRC bw

Richard Arlen *(Simon Lash)*, Veda Ann Borg *(Joyce Bonniwell)*, Tom Dugan *(Eddie Slocum)*, Michael Branden *(Sheriff Rucker)*, Marjorie Manners *(Evelyn Price)*, Earle Hodgins *(Jeff Bailey)*, Francis Ford *(Pete Connors)*, Edward Earle *(Jim Bonniwell)*, Herbert Rawlinson *(Vincent Springer)*, Sherry Hall *(Castleman)*.

Private eye Arlen, a bookish gumshoe, is called upon to find a missing husband, one married to the detective's old flame but, after several murders are committed, Arlen discovers that the ex-girl friend and her hubby have planned the vanishing act to shroud a bank swindle. Tepid whodunit with only a few exciting moments.

p, John K. Teaford; d, Walter Colmes; w, Irving Elman, Frank Gruber (based on Gruber's novel *Simon Lash, Private Detective*); ph, Jockey Feindel; m, Alexander Laszlo; ed, Robert Jahns.

Crime **(PR:A MPAA:NR)**

ACCORDING TO MRS. HOYLE* ½ (1951) 60m MON bw

Spring Byington *(Mrs. Hoyle)*, Anthony Caruso *(Morganti)*, Brett King *(Slattery)*, Tanis Chandler *(Angela Brown)*, Stephen Chase *(Judge Guthrie)*, Tristram Coffin *(Pat Dennison)*, James Flavin *(Prosecuting Attorney)*, Paul Bryar *(Willie)*, Charles Williams *(Charlie)*, Harry Lauter *(Gordon Warren)*, Michael Whalen *(Rev. Haverford)*, Leander de Cordova *(Minister)*, Wilbur Mack *(Hotel Clerk)*, Frank Jaquet *(Watchman)*, Marcelle Imhof *(Court Clerk)*, Baron James Lichter *(Bailiff)*, Ted Stanhope *(Clerk of Court)*, Joey Ray *(Policeman in Hospital)*, Rory Mallison, Don Harvey *(Detectives)*, Robert Karnes.

Lightweight programmer has Byington as a retired schoolteacher put upon by a group of ostensibly reformed gangsters, led by Caruso, who buy her rooming house and begin to summarily evict tenants. They are persuaded to allow the boarders to stay by Byington who mellows the thugs, except for Karnes who commits a robbery, forcing King to go with him, then hiding the loot in the boarding house before he is killed and King wounded. Byington stands trial and is acquitted, learning in court that her long-gone husband has died in prison and that King is her natural son: A mild tearjerker.

p, Barney Girard; d, Jean Yarbrough; w, W. Scott Darling, Girard (based on a novella by Jean Z. Owen): ph, Harry Neumann; ed, Roy V. Livingston.

Crime **(PR:A MPAA:NR)**

ACCOUNT RENDERED** (1957, Brit.) 59m RFD bw

Griffith Jones *(Robert Ainsworth)*, Ursula Howells *(Lucille Ainsworth)*, Honor Blackman *(Sarah Hayward)*, Ewen Solon *(Inspector Marshall)*, Robert Raikes *(Sergeant Berry)*, John Van Eyssen *(Clive Franklin)*, Philip Gilbert *(John Langford)*, Carl Bernard *(Gilbert Morgan)*

Limpid crime melodrama has Jones suspected of murdering Howells and setting forth to prove his innocence which, through some vague twists and turns, he does. The best thing about the film is the acting of curvacious Blackman as she aids the accused husband.

p, John Temple-Smith, Francis Edge; d, Peter Graham Scott; w, Barbara S. Harper (based on the novel by Pamela Barrington).

Crime **(PR:A MPAA:NR)**

ACCURSED, THE** (1958, Brit.), 88m Fantur/NR bw (GB:THE TRAITORS)

Donald Wolfit *(Col. Price)*, Robert Bray *(Maj. Shane)*, Jane Griffiths *(Vicki Toller)*, Anton Diffring *(Joseph Brezzini)*, Oscar Quitak *(Thomas Rilke)*, John Van Eyssen *(Lt. Grant)*, Rupert Davies *(Clinton)*, Carl Jaffe, Frederick Schiller, Colin Croft, Christopher Lee, Karel Stepanek.

When a group of former British underground agents have a reunion after the war, several of their members attempt to discover the killer of their comrades, one of their own number, as Wolfit realizes who has been a deep mole Nazi for years. An offbeat espionage whodunit with some nervy moments.

p, E. J. Fancey; d&w, Michael McCarthy; ph, Bert Mason; m, Jackie Brown; ed, Monica Kimick; art d, Herbert Smith; cos, Rene Coke.

Spy Drama **(PR:A MPAA:NR)**

ACCUSED** ½ (1936, Brit.) 83m Criterion/UA bw

Douglas Fairbanks, Jr. *(Tony Seymour)*, Dolores Del Rio *(Gaby Seymour)*, Florence Desmond *(Yvette Delange)*, Basil Sydney *(Eugene Roget)*, Athole Stewart *(President of Court)*, Cecil Humphreys *(Prosecuting Counsel)*, Esme Percy *(Morel)*, Edward Rigby *(Alphonse)*, George Moore Marriott *(Dubec)*, Cyril Raymond *(Guy Henry)*, Googie Withers *(Ninette)*, Roland Culver *(Henry Capelle)*

Married Apache dancers Fairbanks and Del Rio are booked into a Paris musical revue where the star of the show, sultry Desmond, makes a strong play for Fairbanks. He tells the vamp he is in love with his wife, but is seen leaving her dressing room by Del Rio. The wife next confronts the bitchy vixen—Desmond's performance is superbly hateful—and departs in a rage. The star is later found murdered with a knife used in the married couple's act and belonging to Del Rio. She is placed on trial for murder but the heavy circumstantial evidence is overturned in clever script bits and she is freed to rejoin her devoted spouse. An above-average whodunit with Fairbanks shining and Del Rio glimmering as one of the most beautiful women ever to adorn the screen.

p, Marcel Hellman; d, Thorton Freeland; w, Zoe Akins, George Barraud; ph, Victor Arminese; md, Percival Mackey; ch, Philip Buchal.

Crime **(PR:A MPAA:NR)**

ACCUSED (SEE: MARK OF THE HAWK,1957)

ACCUSED, THE*** (1949) 101m PAR bw (AKA: STRANGE DECEPTION)

Loretta Young *(Wilma Tuttle)*, Robert Cummings *(Warren Ford)*, Wendell Corey *(Lt. Ted Dorgan)*, Sam Jaffe *(Dr. Romley)*, Douglas Dick *(Bill Perry)*, Suzanne Dalbert *(Susan Duval)*, George Spaulding *(Dean Rhodes)*, Sara Allgood *(Mrs. Conner)*, Mickey Knox *(Jack Hunter)*, Frances Pierlot *(Dr. Vinson)*, Ann Doran *(Miss Rice)*, Bill Mauch *(Harry Brice)*, Carole Mathews *(Waitress)*.

Slippery psychology student Dick entices his teacher, Young, to a remote beach area where he attempts to seduce her, first kissing her then making lustier advances which Young resists. In her panic, the psychology professor grabs a steel bar, striking and killing Dick. She then drags the body to the water's edge and draws water into his lungs by administering artificial respiration in reverse while his head is beneath the water. Police discovering the body later determine Dick's death as one of accidental drowning. The distraught Young has hitchhiked home and taken an overdose of sleeping pills but is rushed to a hospital and saved. Corey conducts a routine police investigation which encompasses Young who also meets Cummings, Dick's guardian and attorney. Both men are enamored of Young but Corey puts enough evidence together, with the help of Dr. Romley, to have her indicted for Dick's murder. Cummings defends her brilliantly, proving justifiable homicide; Young's only guilt was hiding the crime which the jury sympathetically attributes to her unhinged frame of mind. She is acquitted and smilingly leaves court on Cummings' arm. Much of this *film noir* tale is shown in chilling flashbacks as Young hallucinates her way toward the realization of her deed. Corey is excellent as the hard-nosed sleuth and Sam Jaffe is an unimpassioned scientist whose careless attitude about human emotions evokes a deep shudder.

p, Hal B. Wallis; d, William Dieterle; w, Ketti Frings (based on the novel *Be Still, My Love* by June Truesdell); ph, Milton Krasner; m, Victor Young; ed, Warren Low; art d, Hans Dreier, Earl Hedrick; set d, Sam Comer, Grace Gregory; cos, Edith Head; spec eff, Gordon Jennings.

Crime **(PR:C MPAA:NR)**

ACCUSED OF MURDER** ½ (1956) 74m REP c

David Brian *(Lt. Roy Hargis)*, Vera Ralston *(Ilona Vance)*, Sidney Blackmer *(Hobart)*, Virginia Grey *(Sandra)*, Warren Stevens *(Stan)*, Lee Van Cleef *(Sgt. Lackey)*, Barry Kelley *(Capt. Smedley)*, Richard Karlan *(Chad Bayliss)*, Frank Puglia *(Caesar* Cipriano), Elisha Cook Jr. *(Whitey Pollock)*, Ian Mac Donald *(Trumble)*, Claire Carleton *(Marge)*, Greta Thyssen *(Myra Bayliss)*, Hank Worden *(Les Fuller)*, *Wally Cassell (Doorman)*, Robert Shayne *(Surgeon)*, Simon Scott *(Day Office Cop)*, John Damler *(Night Office Cop)*, Gil Rankin *(Fingerprint Policeman)*, Joseph Corey, Leon Tyler *(Jitterbugging Sailors)*, Harry Lewis *(Bartender)*, David Bair *(Parking Attendant)*, Bill Henry *(Walt)*, Bob Carney *(Waiter)*, Victor Sen Yung *(Houseboy)*.

Ralston is a nightclub singer suspected of murdering crooked lawyer Blackmer, although investigating detective Brian believes her innocent. His sidekick Van Cleef believes the opposite. Another red herring, Stevens, enacting the role of a gangster who had actually been assigned to murder Blackmer, is arrested but proves himself innocent. A woefully weak finish has Ralston confessing that Blackmer shot himself while she sat with him in his car. The reason? She refused to entertain his passions. A poor product of top crime writer W. R. Burnett, loaded with cliches and predictable turns. Ralston sings "You're In Love," an instantly disposable ballad.

p&d, Joseph Kane; w, Bob Williams, W. R. Burnett (based on Burnett's novel *Vanity Row)*; ph, Bud Thackery (Trucolor); m, R. Dale Butts; ed, Richard L. Ven Enger; art d, Frank Arrigo; m/l, Herb Newman, Buddy Brogman.

Crime (PR:A MPAA:NR)

ACCUSED—STAND UP**

(1930, Fr.) 105m PATHE bw (ACCUSEELEVEZ VOUS)

Gaby Morlay *(Gaby Delange)*, Simone Delve *(Yvette Dells)*, Nicole Rozay *(Nanette)*, Andre Roanne *(Andre Robert)*, Jean Dax *(Stage Manager)*, Andre Dubose *(Presiding Judge)*, Camille Bert *(Counsel for Defense)*, George Poulais *(Attorney General)*, Mihalesco *(The Janitor)*, Berthier *(The Cashier)*, Gaston Mauger *(The Manager)*, Andre Nicole *(The Doctor)*, Charles Vanel *(The Heavy)*.

Music hall star who attempts to seduce the male partner of one of the acts is found murdered, stabbed to death by the female partner's knife, one used in her act. Put on trial with circumstantial evidence weighing heavily against her, the dancer is saved when Bert hands Mihalesco the murder knife, then fires a shot that causes the theater janitor to throw the blade at him in a reflex action and in the same manner in which the victim was killed, thereby exposing himself as the killer; the dancer is freed and rejoins her partner in a happy ending. This story was later employed in the 1936 British film, ACCUSED, but the knife-throwing scene in court is a direct lift from THE TRIAL OF MARY DUGAN. An extremely theatrical film where silent histrionics were carried into a talkie production.

d, Maurice Tourneur; w, Mary Murillo (based on the novel by Jean Jose Frappa).

Crime (PR:A MPAA:NR)

ACCUSING FINGER, THE** ½ (1936) 61m PAR bw

Marsha Hunt *(Claire Patterson)*, Robert Cummings *(Jimmy Ellis)*, Paul Kelly *(Douglas Goodwin)*, Kent Taylor *(Jerry Welch)*, Harry Carey *(Senator Nash)*, Bernadene Hayes *(Muriel Goodwin)*, Sam Flint *(District Attorney)*, De Witt Jennings *(Warden)*, Ralf Harolde *(Spud)*, Fred Kohler *(Johnson)*, Hilda Vaughn *(Maid)*.

Cummings, a youthful defendant, is sent to the electric chair by a hardhitting district attorney, Kelly, one who prides himself on a 100% conviction rate. When his wife Hayes, is murdered, Kelly gets a dose of his own medicine and is convicted and sent to the death house, yet the circumstantial evidence against him is eventually shredded by a dogged investigator, Taylor. Most of the film is a polemic against capital punishment, an early-day morality effort diffused by a desultory plot line involving too many confusing subplots.

p. A. M. Botsford; d, James Hogan; w, Madeleine Ruthven, Brian Marlow, John Bright, Robert Trasker; ph, Henry Sharp; ed, Chandler House; md, Boris Morros.

Crime (PR:A MPAA:NR)

ACE, THE (SEE: GREAT SANTINI, THE, 1979)

ACE ELI AND RODGER OF THE SKIES** (1973) 92m FOX c

Cliff Robertson *(Eli)*, Eric Shea *(Rodger)*, Pamela Franklin *(Shelby)*, Rosemary Murphy *(Hannah)*, Bernadette Peters *(Allison)*, Alice Ghostley *(Sister Lite)*, Kelly Jean Peters *(Rachel)*, Don Keefer *(Mr. Parsons)*, Patricia Smith *(Wilma)*, Royal Dano *(Jake)*, Robert Hamm *(Dumb Dickie)*, Herb Gatlin *(Frank Savage)*, Arthur Malet *(Brother Watson)*, Ariane Munker *(Betty Jo)*, Hope Summers *(Laura)*, Jim Boles *(Abraham)*, Lew Brown *(Harrison)*, Brent Hurst *(Jeffrey)*, Rodger Peck *(Leroy)*, Jan Simms *(Mrs.* Parsons), Dixie Lee *(Mrs. Harrison)*, Claudia Bryar *(Ann)*, Felicity Van Runkle *(Linette)*, Pat O'Connor *(Brother Foster)*, Bill Quinn *(Mortician)*, Hubert Brotten *(Sheriff)*, Jerry Ayres *(Gambler)*, Penny Petropulos *(Bride)*, John O'Connell *(Groom)*, Gary L. Clothier *(Charlie)*.

Period piece has Robertson as an ex-WW I air ace who returns to the tranquility of the early 1920s but puts excitement back into his life by barnstorming through Kansas with his 11-year-old son, Shea, pitching woo and being wonderful to a bevy of adoring country females swooning at the very sight of his skullcap. Aerial photography is awesome but the script and acting are so shallow that Fox executives were embarrassed enough to give fake credits to the slots of producer, director and screenwriter.

p, Boris Wilson [Robert Fryer]; d, Bill Sampson [John Erman]; w, Chips Rosen [Claudia Salte] (based on a story by Steven Spielberg); ph, David M. Walsh; m, Jerry Goldsmith; ed, Louis Lombardo, Robert Belcher; art d, Jack Martin Smith, Joel Schiller; cos Theodora Van Runkle.

Adventure (PR:A MPAA:PG)

ACE HIGH** (1969, Ital.) 123m PAR c

Eli Wallach *(Cacopoulos)*, Terence Hill *(Cat Stevens)*, Bud Spencer *(Hutch)*, Brock Peters *(Thomas)*, Kevin McCarthy *(Drake)*, Steffen Zacharias *(Harold)*, Livio Lorenzon *(Paco Rosa)*, Tiffany Hoyveld *(Thomas' Wife)*, Remo Capitani *(Cangaceiro)*.

Beautifully photographed in Almeria, Spain, this spaghetti western apes Sergio Leone's profitable productions, its director Giuseppe Colizzi undecided whether to take his role model seriously or satirize the campy genre. Wallach plays a sinister fool who kills a bank robber and inadvertently collects a reward desired by bounty hunters Hill, doing a poor imitation of Clint Eastwood, and his hulking sidekick, Spencer. The terrible twosome then begin chasing Wallach who, in turn, is chasing three men who have sent him to prison for fifteen years for, naturally, reward money. Wallach is saved from a hanging by his pursuers Hill and Spencer only to vanish once more, seen again as he undoes his third victim, McCarthy, a gambler. A monstrous shoot-out then ensues between his pursuers and a host of hard cases, all being blown away with pistols that roar like cannons, accompanied by a cacophonous score that is ear-shattering. (Dubbed except for Wallach, McCarthy and Peters)

p, Finanziaria S. Marsco; d, Guiseppe Colizzi; w, Raifaele Mattela; ph, Marcello Masciocchi; m, Carlo Rustichelli; ed, Marcello Malvestitit; art d, Gastone Carsetti.

Western (PR:O MPAA:NR)

ACE IN THE HOLE (SEE: BIG CARNIVAL, THE, 1951)

ACE OF ACES*** (1933) 76m RKO bw

Richard Dix *(Lt. Rex Thorne)*, Elizabeth Allan *(Nancy Adams)*, Ralph Bellamy *(Major Blake)*, Theodore Newton *(Lt. Foster Kelly)*, Bill Cagney *(Lt. Meeker)*, Clarence Stroud *(Lt. Carroll Winstead)*, Joe Sauers, Frank Conroy, Bill Cagney, Howard Wilson, Helmuth Gorin, Art Jarrett, Anderson Lawlor, Frank Melton, Claude Gillingwater, Jr., Carl Eric Hanson, George Lollier.

Sculptor Dix resists enlistment at the outbreak of WW I, his decision based on scruples but his fiancee, Allan, interprets his actions as cowardice and tells him so. Dix promptly joins a flying corps, goes to France, and becomes one of the most ruthless killers in the sky, bringing down countless German planes. Allan, who has been serving behind the lines as a nurse, meets him in Paris in a brief rendezvous and is shocked by Dix's callous attitude. He returns to the fight a completely disillusioned man, resigned to death in the skies over France. The photography is crisp and brilliantly equal to that of HELL'S ANGELS and THE DAWN PATROL, vivid recreations of dogfights, spinouts and wild crashes, while massive armies, ignorant of the clean aviator's death, watch and wait from below.

p, Sam Jaffe; d, J. Walter Ruben; w, John Monk Saunders, H. W. Hanemann (based on Saunders' story "Bird of Prey"); ph, Henry Cronjager; ed, George Hively; md, Max Steiner.

War (PR:C MPAA:NR)

ACE OF ACES** (1982, Fr./Ger.) 100m Cerito/GAU c (L'AS DES AS)

Jean Paul Belmondo *(Joe Cavalier)*, Marie-Frances Pisier *(Journalist)*, Rachid Ferrache *(Karl)*, Frank Hoffmann *(Von Beckman)*, Gunther Meisner *(Hitler/His Sister)*.

Belmondo is a WW I ace shown in a docu-style prolog shooting down several German planes before appearing in 1936 Berlin where he is managing the French boxing team at the Olympiad. He becomes involved with some Jewish refugees and attempts to smuggle them out of the country but somehow leads the group right into Hitler's Bavarian mountain retreat where the Jews conceal themselves as band members fiddling for Hitler's party guests, a tasteless, utterly unfunny segment sure to arouse the sensitivities of anyone who can remember newsreels and photographs of Jewish musicians forced to play accompaniment to those being herded into gas chambers. The thoughtless script is not overcome by sharp photography and shrewd direction.

p, Alain Poire; d, Gerard Oury; w, Daniele Thompson, Oury; ph, Xavor Schwarzenberger; m, Vladimir Cosma, art d, Rolf Zehetbauer.

Drama (PR:O MPAA:NR)

ACE OF SPADES, THE** (1935, Brit.) 66m RA bw

Michael Hogan *(Nick Trent)*, Dorothy Boyd *(Nita)*, Richard Cooper *(Tony)*, Jane Carr *(Cleo Despard)*, Michael Shepley *(George Despard)*, Geraldine Fitzgerald *(Evelyn)*, Sebastian Shaw *(Trent)*, Felix Aylmer *(Lord Yardleigh)*, Bobbie Comber *(Andrews)*.

Smooth detective yarn where Trent learns how a girl consumed by jealousy has blackmailed her sister's fiance to bring about the death of a political foe.

p, Julius Hagen; d, George Pearson; w, Gerard Fairlie (based on the novel by John Crawford Fraser); ph, Ernest Palmer.

Crime (PR:A MPAA:NR)

ACES AND EIGHTS** (1936) 62m Colony/SYN bw

Tim McCoy *(Wild Bill Hickok)*, Jimmy Aubrey *(Lucky)*, Luana Walters *(Juanita)*, Wheeler Oakman *(Ace Morgan)*, Earl Hodgins *(Marshal)*, Frank Glennon *(Harden)*, Rex Lease *(Jose Hernendez)*, Joe Girard *(Don Hernendez)*, George Stevens *(Capt. Felipe)*, John Merton *(Gambler)*.

The title of this film is taken from the card hand gripped by Hickok in Deadwood when he was shot in the back by a cross-eyed drunk named Jack McCall on August 2, 1876, but that is all that is factual in this mythical saga of Hickok, one where McCoy does not even wear a six-gun and draws against no one, merely iron-grips his foes to the local hoosegow while managing to reform a ne'er-do-well son, save a ranch and clean up a gambling hall. All of it would be utter witless nonsense if it were not for the fact that it is the great Tim McCoy doing it.

p, Sig Neufeld, Leslie Simmonds; d, Sam Newfield; w, Arthur Durlan; ed, Joseph O'Donnell.

Western Cas. (PR:A MPAA:NR)

ACES HIGH*** (1977, Brit.) 114m Cine Artists/EMI c

Malcolm McDowell *(Gresham)*, Christopher Plummer *(Sinclair)*, Simon Ward *(Crawford)*, Peter Firth *(Croft)*, John Gielgud *(Headmaster)*, Trevor Howard *(Lt.-Col. Silkin)*, Richard Johnson *(Col. Lyle)*, Ray Milland *(Brig. Whale)* David Wood *(Thompson)*, David Daker *(Bennett)*, Elliott Cooper *(Wade)*, Pascale Christophe *(Croft's Girlfriend)*, Jeanne Patou *(Chanteuse)*.

The story of 76 Squadron, a crack group of WW I airmen led by McDowell who is astonishingly brave and deeply frightened but charges himself on whiskey to inspire his men. Plummer brings a sentimental understanding to the frayed nerves and apprehen sions of youngsters Firth and Ward, but the entire film is a grand *deja vu*, recounting the countless cliches of former war films, and deservedly so since it's based upon R. C. Sheriff's classic 1929 play, "Journey's End," although the play dealt with British infantry dying in the trenches of France. Milland, Howard and Johnson are excellent as the uncaring British brass ordering men to death while sipping vintage wine and wolfing down rich French entrees in a distant chateau. Much attention is given to young Firth who loses his virginity to sultry Christopher and then loses his life in a head-on collision with a German adversary. The aerial combat scenes are superb and worth the watching for enthusiasts.

p, S. Benjamin Fisz; d, Jack Gold; w, Howard Barker (based on R. C. Sherriff's play "Journey's End"); ph, Gerry Fisher, Peter Allwork; m, Richard Hartley; ed, Anne Coates; set d, Syd. Caine; spec eff, Derek Meddings.

War **(PR:C MPAA:PG)**

ACES WILD* (1937) 63m COM bw

Harry Carey *(Cheyenne Harry)*, Gertrude Messinger *(Martha)*, Snowflake *(Himself)*, Phil Dunham *(Anson)*, Ed Cassidy *(Blacksmith)*, Chuck Morrison *(Heck)*, Ted Lorch *(Kelton)*, William McCall *(Sheriff)*, Roger Williams *(Slim)*, Sonny *(Himself)*.

Primitive western with "the sun's in your eyes for the last time" dialog has Carey battling villianous outlaw Ted Lorch and his gang over stolen loot hidden in a secret mine shaft and, of course, winning the West once again. For Carey fans only.

p, William Berke; d, Harry Fraser; w, Monroe Talbot; ph, Robert Cline; ed, Arthur A. Brooks.

Western **(PR:A MPAA:NR)**

ACQUITTED* (1929) 62m COL bw

Lloyd Hughes *(Dr. Bradford)*, Margaret Livingston *(Marian)*, Sam Hardy *(Egan)*, Charles West *(McManus)*, Charles Wilson *(Nelson)*, George Rigas *(Tony)*, *Otto Hoffman (Smith)*.

Crotchety early talkie has gangster framing his moll, Livingston, for a murder he himself committed and, upon her release eight years later she manages to get the truth from her former lover who turns himself in to the police but not before warbling the song "What'll I Do?" Absolute idiocy.

p, Harry Cohn; d, Frank Strayer; w, Keene Thompson, James Seymour; ph, Ted Tetzlaff; ed, David Berg; art d, Harrison Wiley.

Crime **(PR:C MPAA:NR)**

ACROSS 110TH STREET** (1972) 102m UA c

Anthony Quinn *(Capt. Frank Mattelli)*, Yaphet Kotto *(Det. Lt. Pope)*, Anthony Franciosa *(Nick D'Salvio)*, Paul Benjamin *(Jim Harris)*, Ed Bernard *(Joe Logart)*, Richard Ward *(Doc Johnson)*, Norma Donaldson *(Gloria Roberts)*, Antonio Fargas *(Henry Jackson)*, Gilbert Lewis *(Shevvy)*, Marlene Warfield *(Mrs. Jackson)*, Tim O'Connor *(Lt. Hartnett)*, Nat Polen *(Lt. Reilly)*, Charles McGregor *(Chink)*, Frank Mascetta *(Don Gennaro)*, Joe Attles *(Mr. Jessup)*, Betty Haynes *(Mrs. Jessup)*.

Brutal, sadistic black exploitation movie has three black hoods robbing a fortune from a Mafia-controlled Harlem numbers bank and being tracked down by crooked cop Quinn who walks a thin line between his duties as a policeman and his obligations to the Mafia as a cop on the take. It is a race to see who gets the thieves first, the Mafia hoods or Quinn and his black partner, Kotto. Everyone loses here in a final bloodbath where Quinn is slain, along with Paul Benjamin, leader of the black gang, shot to pieces by Mafia henchmen just as Quinn corners Benjamin, and has him convinced to turn over the loot. Quinn was executive producer of this critically lambasted film of many murders, torture and castration.

p, Ralph Serpe, Fouad Said; d, Barry Shear; w, Luther Davis (based on the novel by Wally Ferris); ph, Jack Priestley; m, J. J. Johnson; ed, Bryan Brandt; art d, Perry Watkins.

Crime **Cas.** **(PR:O MPAA:R)**

ACROSS THE BADLANDS** (1950) 55m COL bw

Charles Starrett *(Steve Ransom/Durango Kid)*, Smiley Burnette *(Smiley Burnette)*, Helen Mowery *(Eileen Carson)*, Stanley Andres *(Sheriff Crocker)*, Bob Wilke *(Duke Jackson/Keeno Jackson)*, Dick Elliott *(Rufus Downey)*, Hugh Prosser *(Jeff Carson)*, Robert W. Cavendish *(Bart)*, Charles Evans *(Gregory Banion)*, Paul Campbell *(Pete)*, Harmonica Bill *(Harmonica Bill)*.

Starrett becomes a deputy sheriff and helps track down a gang which has been waylaying surveyors, preventing them from entering a secret canyon hideout, doing most of his sleuthing as the legendary Durango Kid in a disjointed, erratically constructed film that also has Burnette performing his cornball comedy with chubby cheer. Not one of Starrett's better efforts. (See DURANGO KID series, Index.)

p, Colbert Clark; d, Fred F. Sears, w, Barry Shipman; ph, Fayte Browne; ed, Paul Borofsky.

Western **(PR:A MPAA:NR)**

ACROSS THE BRIDGE*** (1957, Brit.) 103m RANK/IPF bw

Rod Steiger *(Carl Schaffner)*, David Knight *(Johnny)*, Marla Landi *(Mary)*, Noel Willman *(Chief of Police)*, Bernard Lee *(Det.-Inspector Hadden)*, Bill Nagy *(Paul Scarff)*, Eric Pohlmann *(Police Sgt.)* Alan Gifford *(Cooper)*, Ingeborg Wells *(Mrs. Scarff)*, Faith Brook *(Kay)*, Marianne Deeming *(Anna)*, Stanley Maxted *(Milton)*, Mark Baker, Jack Lester, Jon Farrell, Betty Cooper, Don Gilliland, John Gale, Richard Dunn, Philip Rose, Dan Jackson.

Powerful Graham Greene story of an international financier who has absconded with a fortune. Played masterfully by Steiger, he learns that authorities are after him in Europe while on a New York visit. In startling and crafty moves, Steiger evades the authorities in his flight southwest to Mexico, managing always to keep one step ahead of his pursuers. The great character actor embraces his role with sinister relish, particularly during a train trip where he chances upon Nagy who gets drunk and brags about his success, showing the wanted man his Mexican passport. In desperation Steiger murders the man, throws his body from the moving train and assumes his identity, that of Paul Scarff. But when he arrives in Mexico he learns that the dead man is traveling with a dog which he reluctantly removes from the baggage car. In Greene's grim twist of irony, Scarff is a wanted man and Steiger must endure the plight of his role model. Finally trapped in a seedy little Mexican town ruled by a corrupt police captain (Willman in a riveting performance), Steiger is undone by his own masquerade; Willman believes him to be Scarff, also a thief who stole a fortune, and holds him incommunicado in order to obtain a large slice of the loot. None of Steiger's considerable persuasiveness will convince the greedy cop that he is an impostor. A true Mexican stand-off ensues, both men pitting their superior attitudes against each other; Steiger, who affects a High German accent, finally crumbles and is released to live like a ragged vagrant, his only friend being the dog of the man he murdered, an animal he grows to love, so much so that in his final break for freedom, he chooses the dog over his own safety. An excellent psychological study with surprises most of the way. (Filmed in Spain.)

p, John Stafford; d, Ken Annakin; w, Guy Elmes, Denis Freeman (based on the novel by Graham Greene); ph, Reginald Wyer; m, James Bernard; ed, Alfred Roome.

Crime **(PR:C MPAA:NR)**

ACROSS THE GREAT DIVIDE*** (1976) 89m PI c

Robert Logan *(Zachariah)*, Heather Rattray *(Holly)*, Mark Hall *(Jason)*, George Flower *(Indian Chief)*.

Two determined orphans en route to Oregon travel the West and become hardier pioneers than their adult counterparts. Beautifully photographed on location, the film is delightfully devoid of excessive violence and the crude language many filmmakers feel obligated to include in reinforcing their "realistic" perspectives.

p, Arthur R. Dubs, d&w, Stewart Rafill; m, Gene Kauer, Douglas Lackey.

Western **Cas.** **(PR:AAA MPAA:G)**

ACROSS THE PACIFIC*1/2** (1942) 97m WB/FN bw

Humphrey Bogart *(Richard Lomas Leland)*, Mary Astor *(Alberta Marlow)*, Sydney Greenstreet *(Dr. Lorenz)*, Charles Halton *(A. V. Smith)*, Victor Sen Yung *(Joe Totsuiko)*, Roland Got *(Sugi)*, Lee Tung Foo *(Sam Wing On)*, Frank Wilcox *(Captain Morrison)*, Paul Stanton *(Colonel Hart)*, Lester Matthews *(Canadian Major)*, John Hamilton *(Court-martial President)*, Tom Stevenson *(Tall Thin Man)*, Roland Drew *(Captain Harknee)*, Monte Blue *(Dan Morton)*, Chester Gan *(Captain Higoto)*, Richard Loo *(First Officer Miyuma)*, Keye Luke *(Steamship Office Clerk)*, Kam Tong *(T. Oki)*, Spencer Chan *(Chief Engineer Mitsudo)*, Anthony Caruso *(Cab Driver)*, Philip Ahn *(Informer Inside Theater)*, Rudy Robles *(Filipino Assassin)*, Bill Hopper *(Orderly)*, Frank Mayo *(Trial Judge Advocate)* Garland Smith, Dick French, Charles Drake, Will Morgan *(Officers)*, Roland Drew *(Capt. Harkness)*, Jack Mower *(Major)*, Eddie Dew *(Man)*, Frank Faylen *(Barker)*, Ruth Ford *(Secretary)*, Eddie Lee *(Chinese Clerk)*, Dick Botiller *(Waiter)*, Beal Wong *(Usher)*, James Leong *(Nura)*, Paul Fung *(Japanese Radio Operator)*, Gordon De Main *(Dock Official)*.

With the success of THE MALTESE FALCON under his belt, young director John Huston took on this first-rate espionage adventure, using three principal pals from his previous film, Bogart, Astor and Greenstreet. A man still against the odds, Bogie is cashiered from the American Army, court-martialed for selling military secrets; to reinforce his disgrace he is publicly humiliated in the local officers' club where a fellow officer tears his captain's bars from his shoulder, ripping away part of his uniform. Going to Halifax, Bogart attempts to enlist in the Canadian Army but his unsavory reputation has preceded him; he is rejected and his status of pariah is entrenched. He intends to offer his services to Chiang Kai-Shek and boards a Japanese ship, the *Genoa Maru,* bound for the Pacific via the Panama Canal. On board Bogart meets a colorful lot—Astor, a high-style fashion designer going to the Canal Zone to visit her father; Greenstreet, a mysterious sociologist returning to his professorial post in Manila, a man who praises the Japanese to excess; T. Oki, a silent Japanese passenger who is replaced by another assuming his identity when the ship docks in New York. Here the viewer is allowed to see that Bogie is not the callous creature willing to sell his services to the highest bidder, but that his traitorous posture is only a cover for his true role of undercover agent; he has been planted on board to establish a liaison with Japanese agent Greenstreet and discover what he can about Astor. He takes money from the conniving doctor to reveal secret military operations at Panama where he had once been stationed, learning also that Astor is merely an innocent pawn of the Japanese who have been holding her father hostage while using his plantation as a staging area to blow up the priceless Canal. Bogie takes a terrible beating, as he did in THE MALTESE FALCON, and again at Greenstreet's sadistic orders. Yet he overcomes all odds, destroys the Japanese, saves the Canal, and gets the girl, a wonderfully impossible ending which brazenly spoofs the spy genre. Greenstreet is at his insidious best as are a host of Oriental actors—Luke, Loo, Tong, Ahn—the standard hateful crew who persecuted Americans from one war film to the next. (Many of these actors playing the roles of animalistic Japanese antagonists were Chinese or Filipinos; Loo was a Hawaiian who became so notorious that he feared walking American streets during WW II lest he be recognized and attacked, which happened on occasion.) Huston later told the story that he entered the service shortly before finishing the film and that he found it amusing to leave his friend Bogart in an impossible situation, preventing a logical conclusion. He had Bogie tied firmly to a chair with a half dozen Japanese guards pointing guns at him, then walked off the set to report to Washington where he would embark upon making startling documentaries such as THE BATTLE FOR SAN PIETRO. Journeyman director Vincent Sherman was brought into the production to wrap it up by a vexed Jack Warner. "It was up to Vince to figure a way to get Bogie out of that house," remarked Huston in *Open Book,* his autobiography. "His impossible solution was to have one of the Japanese soldiers in the room go berserk, Bogie escaped in the confusion with the comment: 'I'm not so easily trapped, you know!'" Actually Sherman had Monte Blue, playing Astor's dipsomaniac father, drunkenly attack the soldiers, creating a diversion so that Bogart could free himself and triumph. But Huston's tale made a good story and so too did this clever and amusing film.

p, Jerry Wald, Jack Saper; d, John Huston (final scenes by Vincent Sherman, uncredited); w, Richard Macaulay (based on the *Saturday Evening Post* serial "Aloha Means Goodbye" by Robert Carson); ph, Arthur Edeson; m, Adolph

Deutsch; ed, Frank Magee; art d, Robert Haas, Hugh Reticker; cos, Milo Anderson; spec eff, Byron Haskin, Willard Van Enger.

Spy Drama **(PR:A MPAA:NR)**

ACROSS THE PLAINS* 1/2 (1939) 54m MON bw

Jack Randall *(Cherokee)*, Frank Yaconelli *(Lopez)*, Joyce Bryant *(Mary)*, Hal Price *(Buckskin)*, Dennis Moore *(Kansas Kid)*, Glenn Strange *(Jeff)*, Robert Card *(Buff)*, Bud Osborn *(Lex)*, Dean Spencer *(Rip)*, Wylie Grant *(Rawhide)*, Rusty *(Rusty)*.

Fast action but poor plot has Randall and Moore, raised separately, after their parents are murdered by white renegades. The killers raise Moore, telling him that Indians have committed the deed; Indians find Randall and raise him. The brothers meet and tangle, with Randall avenging his dead parents by wiping out the outlaw band with his Indian friends and sidekick Yaconelli.

d, Spencer Bennett; w, Robert Emmett; ph, Bert Longenecker; ed, Robert Golden.

Western **(PR:A MPAA:NR)**

ACROSS THE RIO GRANDE** (1949) 56m MON bw

Jimmy Wakely *(Jimmy)*, Dub Taylor *(Cannonball)*, Reno Browne *(Sally Blaine)*, Riley Hill *(Steven Blaine)*, Dennis Moore *(Carson)*, Kenne Duncan *(Bardet)*, Ted Adams *(Sloan)*, Myron Healey *(Kane)*, Bud Osborne *(Stage Driver)*, Polly Burgin *(Cantina Singer)* Bob Curtis *(Lewis)*, Carol Henry *(Gill)*, Boyd Stockman *(Ed)*, William Bailey *(Sheriff)*, Bill Potter, Bob Woodward, Bud Osborne.

Wakely and his idiot friend Cannonball aid Hill in capturing the killers of his father, a band of thieves who have been smuggling silver across the Mexican border. Plenty of six-gun action and well-staged fistfights where tight gloves never slip and ten-gallon hats never topple.

p, Louis Gray; d, Oliver Drake; w, Ronald Davidson; ph, Henry Neumann; ed, John C. Fuller, md, Edward Kay.

Western **(PR:A MPAA:NR)**

ACROSS THE RIVER* (1965) 85m Sharf c

Lou Gilbert *(Obadiah)*, Kay Doubleday *(Monica)*, Samuel J. McCurry *(Superintendent)*, Archie Smith *(Bum)*, Lou Polan *(Store Owner)*, Robert F. Simon *(Policeman)*, Slavko Novytsky *(Sanitation Officer)*.

One of those improvisational films so popular in the 1960s where no statement was a statement, no story was an unspoken saga and no characterization meant the universal man doing whatever the universal man does. In this case, Gilbert is a hobo with a goat living in a shack next to New York's East River. He spends his hours peddling rags he has scrounged to niggardly dealers, then rescues a young girl from an attacker, taking her in and later, to provide the predictable unhappy ending of such turgid tales, steals a coat for her and drops into big city tragedy. None of it will move the viewer to any passion except to ask why such a meandering travelog could be considered feature material. All of it is the vanity of Stefan Sharff.

p,d&w, Stefan Sharff; ph, Tom Margraviti; m, Charles Gorss.

Drama **(PR:C MPAA:NR)**

ACROSS THE SIERRAS** (1941) 57m COL bw

Bill Elliott *(Wild Bill Hickok)*, Richard Fiske *(Larry)*, Luana Walters *(Alice)*, Dub Taylor *(Cannonball)*, Dick Curtis *(Mitch)*, Milt Kibbee *(Sheriff)*, LeRoy Mason *(Stanley)*, Ruth Robinson, John Dilson, Ralph Peters, Tex Cooper, Eddie Laughton, Carl Knowles, Tom London, Edmund Cobb, Jim Pierce, Art Mix.

Elliott is hunted, along with a storekeeper, by Curtis who has spent six years behind bars because of their testimony. Wild Bill, after knocking about several baddies and putting up with the zany antics of Dub Taylor, guns down his antagonist but Luana Walters, the girl he almost marries, will not abide a gunslinger so Elliott is compelled to ride off alone into the sunset once more. Walters, a talented one-time Paramount contract player, should have had a better fate than roughing such hayburners. Mostly for Elliott fans and the kids. (See WILD BILL HICKOK series, Index.)

d, D. Ross Lederman; w, Paul Franklin; ph, George Meehan; ed, James Sweeney.

Western **Cas.** **(PR:A MPAA:NR)**

ACROSS THE WIDE MISSOURI*** (1951) 78m MGM c

Clark Gable *(Flint Mitchell)*, Riccardo Montalban *(Ironshirt)*, John Hodiak *(Brecan)*, Adolphe Menjou *(Pierre)*, Maria Elena Marques *(Kamiah)*, J. Carroll Naish *(Looking Glass)*, Jack Holt *(Bear Ghost)*, Alan Napier *(Capt. Humberstone Lyon)*, George Chandler *(Gowie)*, Richard Anderson *(Dick)*, Henri Letondal *(Lucien Chennault)*, Douglas Fowley *(Tin Cup Owens)*, Ben Watson *(Markhead)*, Russell Simpson *(Hoback)*, Frankie Darro *(Cadet)*.

A florid pioneer epic, this film offers Gable as a blunt, tough, almost calculating trapper who marries Marques (an accomplished Mexican film star) because she is the daughter of a powerful Blackfoot chief, Holt, thinking the white man-hating tribe will allow him into their precious territory to trap the ample beaver, such pelts then being priceless. Surviving Indian attacks, Marques leads Gable and company a circuitous but safe route to the land of her people where she gives birth to a child. By then Gable no longer treats her as a pawn but is in love with her, devoted as his rugged character will permit (becoming what was then known as a "squaw man"). He and his trappers build a fort and make an alliance with the Indians but another warring Indian tribe attacks and kills Marques; Gable survives with the child. He thinks first to abandon the infant but turns back to spend his days with his offspring and Indian friends in the high mountains. Colorful performances from Menjou as a bottle-loving, carefree French trapper and Naish, an offbeat Indian chief. The photography is breathtaking, shot in the Rockies, but the use of a narrator (Howard Keel) to describe the episodic events and windy Indian monologs that must be translated, detract from a solid historical production.

p, Robert Sisk; d, William Wellman; w, Talbot Jennings (based on a story by Jennings and Frank Cavett and a book by Bernard DeVoto); ph, William Mellor; m, David Racksin; ed, John Dunn; art d, Cedric Gibbons, James Basevi.

Adventure **(PR:A MPAA:NR)**

ACT OF LOVE 1/2** (1953) 108m Litvak/UA bw

Kirk Douglas *(Robert Teller)*, Dany Robin *(Lisa)*, Barbara Laage *(Nina)*, Robert Strauss *(Blackwood)*, Gabrielle Dorzia *(Adele)*, Gregoire Aslan *(Commissaire)*, Marthe Mercadier *(Young Woman)*, Fernand Ledoux *(Fernand)*, Serge Reggiani *(Claude)*, Brigitte Bardot *(Mimi)*, Gilbert Geniat *(Mme. Henderson)*, George Mathews *(Henderson)*, Leslie Dwyer *(English Sergeant)*, Richard Benedict *(Pete)*.

In flashback while lounging on the Riviera, Douglas thinks back to the liberation of Paris in 1944 and his meeting a lonely girl, Robin; she is destitute and without papers. Douglas helps her, pretending to be married to her. Police list her as a prostitute when she fails to offer identification. Douglas desperately tries to marry the girl but his hard-headed CO, Mathews, refuses permission, patronizingly explaining that Euro- pean girls are all alike, deceitful and manipulating, wanting only to escape the poverty of war-torn Europe and migrate to America by using GIs through loveless marriages to obtain U.S. citizenship. Robin, stigmatized and ostracized, goes to the Seine River where she ends her life. Anatole Litvak's production is heavy-handed, morose and often depressing in that peculiar Germanic type of filmmaking born at UFA studios where all was shadow and much was murk. Yet it is a stylistic production that somehow truly captures that melancholy time when the world wound down from war while survivors faced only ruins as a future. Litvak arbitrarily changed the locale of the popular Alfred Hayes novel from Rome to Paris and was unhappy about the finished film, remarking "that it didn't work out as well as I thought it would."

p&d, Anatole Litvak; w, Irwin Shaw (based on the novel *The Girl on the Via Flaminia* by Alfred Hayes); ph, Armand Thirard; m, Michel Emer, Joe Hajos; ed, William Hornbeck.

Drama **(PR:C MPAA:NR)**

ACT OF MURDER, AN* 1/2**
(1948) 91m UNIV bw (AKA: LIVE TODAY FOR TOMORROW)

Fredric March *(Judge Calvin Cooke)*, Edmond O'Brien *(David Douglas)*, Florence Eldridge *(Catherine Cooke)*, Geraldine Brooks *(Ellie Cooke)*, Stanley Ridges *(Dr. Walter Morrison)*, John McIntire *(Judge Ogden)*, Frederic Tozere *(Judge Dayton)*, Will Wright *(Judge Jim Wilder)*, Virginia Brissac *(Mrs. Russell)*, Francis McDonald *(Mr. Russell)*, Mary Servoss *(Julia)*, Don Beddoe *(Pearson)*, Clarence Muse *(Mr. Pope)*, Ray Teal, Paul E. Burns, Taylor Holmes, Barry Kroeger.

A by-the-book judge, March, learns that his wife has an incurable disease. When Eldridge, March's real-life spouse, begins to endure incredible pain, he decides that she would be better off dead and he drives off a cliff with his wife at his side. She is killed and March survives, turning himself in to authorities and confessing to murder, demanding punishment for the crime of euthanasia. O'Brien, as his lawyer, brilliantly defends his client, arguing for the justification of March's act. Moreover, it is proved that Eldridge had taken a fatal dose of poison before taking her fatal ride with her husband and was already dead when hurtling over the cliff. March is freed but he is a changed man, no longer the unbending arbiter of another's fate but someone who has learned to judge as he was judged. Both March and Eldridge turn in superb performances, as does O'Brien, in portraying a sensitive subject.

p, Jerry Bresler; d, Michael Gordon; w, Michael Blankfort, Robert Thoeren (based on the novel *The Mills of God* by Ernst Lothar); ph, Hal Mohr; m, Daniele Amfitheatrof; ed, Ralph Dawson.

Drama **(PR:C MPAA:NR)**

ACT OF MURDER** (1965, Brit.) 62m Anglo-Amal./WB bw

John Carson *(Tim Ford)*, Anthony Bate *(Ralph Longman)*, Justine Lord *(Ann Longman)*, Duncan Lewis *(Will Peterson)*, Richard Burrell *(John Quick)*, Dandy Nichols *(Maud Peterson)*, Sheena Marshe *(Pauline)*, Norman Scace *(Watson)*, Robin Wentworth *(Constable)*, John Moore *(Publican)*, Michael Brennan *(Police Sergeant)*, Kenneth Laud *(Charlie)*, Marianne Stone *(Bobbie)*.

An actor attempts to win back his former mistress by putting stress on her husband—poisoning the family dog, farm animals at their country place, simulating a robbery attempt, then a real robbery of priceless antiques. The wife flees to London and the arms of her one-time lover while the husband stalks the antagonist, kills him, then commits suicide. An oddball whodunit with most of the clues apparent early on.

p, Jack Greenwood; d, Alan Bridges; w, Lewis Davidson; ph, James Wilson; m, Bernard Ebbing; ed, Derek Holding.

Crime **(PR:C MPAA:NR)**

ACT OF THE HEART* (1970, Can.) 103m Quest/UNIV c

Genevieve Bujold *(Martha Hayes)*, Donald Sutherland *(Father Michael Ferrier)*, Monique Leyrac *(Johane Foss)*, Bill Mitchell *(Russell Foss)*, Suzanne Langlois *(Housekeeper)*, Sharon Acker *(Adele)*, Ratch Wallace *(Diedrich)*, Jean Duceppe *(Parks Commissioner)*, Gilles Vigneault *(Coach Ti-Jo)*, Eric House *(Choirmaster)*.

Heavy-handed religious melodrama with Bujold as an innocent country girl raised in strict ways of the Bible who visits the city of Montreal to become the guardian of a precocious child who dies after being injured in a hockey game. She turns in trauma to a local priest, Sutherland, of whom she has long been enamored, blurting her love for him inside the confessional. Sutherland surprisingly responds in kind and leaves the priesthood to be with her. Once a choirsinger, Bujold turns to roadhouse performances to support the couple—Sutherland is a complete failure in the outer world—and her disillusionment is complete; her religious zealousness compels her to misinterpret Sutherland's philosophy by committing suicide upon a lonely hilltop. Sutherland had urged: "To consecrate something to Christ you must first rescue it for him, and in rescuing it, you must destroy it." This high-sounding claptrap prompts Bujold to cover her body with gasoline and immolate herself, sort of a Western form of suttee. A bleak, misleading film from Paul Almond whose ISABEL, another introspective potboiler, had pop critics swooning at one time. For extremely tolerant psychiatrists only.

p,d&w, Paul Almond; ph, Jean Boffety, m, Harry Freedman; ed, James Mitchell, art, d, Anne Pritcherd.

Drama **(PR:O MPAA:GP)**

ACT OF VENGEANCE* (1974) 90m AIP c

JoAnn Harris *(Linda)*, Peter Brown *(Jack)*, Jennifer Lee *(Nancy)*, Lisa Moore *(Karen)*, Connie Strickland *(Teresa)*, Patric Estrin *(Angie)*, Ross Elliot *(Sergeant Long)*, Steve Kanaly *(Tom)*, Tony Young *(Bud)*, Lada Edmund, Jr., *(Tiny)*, John Pickard *(Dr. Schetman)*, Ninette Bravo *(Joyce)*, Joan McCall *(Gloria)*, Stanley Adams *(Bernie/"Foulmouth")*.

Brutal, sadistic film graphically portrays a ski-mask-wearing rapist, Brown, attacking five different women, all of these victims later banding together to form a "Rape Squad," learning karate and other tricks to combat their attacker whom they seek out and an assortment of other hapless males who make extraordinary advances. A lamedog excuse to parade a most distasteful exploitation of sexual abuse, a film that does nothing to offer concrete measures in ameliorating a very real, day-to-day problem. Only those with untreated perversions will be fascinated.

p, Buzz Feitshans; d, Robert Kelljan; w, Betty Conklin, H. R. Christian; ph, Brick Marquard; m, Bill Marx; ed, Carl Kress.

Crime **(PR:O MPAA:R)**

ACT OF VIOLENCE*** (1949) 82m MGM bw

Van Heflin *(Frank R. Enley)*, Robert Ryan *(Joe Parkson)*, Janet Leigh *(Edith Enley)*, Mary Astor *(Pat)*, Phyllis Thaxter *(Ann)*, Berry Kroeger *(Johnny)*, Taylor Holmes *(Gavery)*, Harry Antrim *(Fred)*, Connie Gilchrist *(Martha)*, Will Wright *(Pop)*.

Grim, exciting *film noir* pic where Ryan, a crippled war veteran, seeks out Heflin to vent revenge for the latter's betrayal of fellow prisoners during WW II. When Heflin, a successful contractor, learns that he is being hunted he panics and his dormant feelings of guilt explode to the surface, coupled to fear created by Ryan's promise to kill him. In a masterful performance Heflin confesses to Leigh that he turned informer in a prison camp believing that the escape plan of his men was doomed to failure and that he would save their lives by blurting their plans; instead they were slaughtered, all except Ryan who was crippled for life and vowed vengeance. Ryan plays the psychological game of threatening phone calls, notes, messages to Leigh, so that Heflin believes he can protect his wife only by fleeing into the bowels of the city where social dregs offer no comfort, no escape. A sympathetic street tart is convincingly portrayed by Astor. Kroeger, a stone killer, hears of Heflin's plight and agrees to murder Ryan for a price. As Ryan closes in for the kill, Thaxter, his girl friend, pleads with him to give up his vendetta; he pauses, a sure target for Kroeger but, at the last minute, Heflin vindicates himself by sacrificing himself to save his pursuer. A hard-hitting melodrama with all-around tough performances.

p, William H. Wright; d. Fred Zinnemann; w, Robert L. Richards; ph, Robert Surtees; m, Bronislau Kaper; ed, Conrad A. Nervig; art d, Cedric Gibbons, Hans Peters; set d, Edwin B. Willis, Henry W. Grace; cos, Helen Rose.

Crime **(PR:C MPAA:NR)**

ACT ONE 1/2** (1964) 110m WB bw

George Hamilton *(Moss Hart)*, Jason Robards, Jr. *(George S. Kaufman)*, Jack Klugman *(Joe Hyman)*, Sam Levene *(Richard Maxwell)*, Ruth Ford *(Beatrice Kaufman)*, Eli Wallach *(Warren Stone)*, Joseph Leon *(Max Siegel)*, George Segal *(Lester Sweyd)*, Martin Wolfson *(Mr. Hart)*, Sam Groom *(David Starr)*, Sammy Smith *(Sam S. Harris)*, Louise Larabee *(Clara Baum)*, David Doyle *(Oliver Fisher)*, Jonathan Lippe *(Teddy Manson)*, Bert Convy *(Archie Leach)*, Sylvie Straus *(Mrs. Hart)*, Arno Selco *(Bernie Hart)*, Lulu B. King *(The Maid)*, Allen Leaf *(Harry the Waiter)*.

Film chronicles the development of Moss Hart from failed heavy dramatist to a shining star of comedic theater, but only when Kaufman, brilliantly acted by Robards, appears on the screen does the pic soar. Here the dialog sparkles with bon mots and metaphors and becomes thoroughly amusing. In prolog, we are compelled to suffer through Hart's early tribulations with an unpromising career and a shaky romance, scenes dipped into the kitchen sink for sudsy cliches, although the film is a faithful adaptation from the book, perhaps too faithful and too meticulous in that it bogs down with Hart's doubts and speculations along a literary level that is often arcane. Klugman is his usual phlegmatic self, but the biggest disappointment is Bert Convy enacting the role of a young Cary Grant (real name Archibald Leach), sans personality and appeal, a walk-through role that could have been matched by any pedestrian actor. All in all a good biopic with unique qualities for the literati.

p,d&w, Dore Schary (based on the book by Moss Hart); ph, Arthur J. Ornitz; m, Skitch Henderson; ed, Mort Fallick.

Biography **(PR:A MPAA:NR)**

ACTION FOR SLANDER 1/2** (1937, Brit.) 83m LFP/UA bw

Clive Brook *(Major George Daviot)*, Ann Todd *(Ann Daviot)*, Margaretta Scott *(Josie Bradford)*, Arthur Margetson *(Captain Bradford)*, Ronald Squire *(Charles Cinderford)*, Athole Stewart *(Lord Pontefract)*, Percy Marmont *(William Cowbit)*, Frank Cellier *(Sir Bernard Roper)*, Morton Selten *(Judge Trotter)*, Gus McNaughton *(Tandy)*, Francis L. Sullivan *(Sir Quinton Jessops)* Anthony Holles *(Grant)*, Enid Stamp-Taylor *(Jenny)*, Kate Cutler *(Dowager)*, Felix Aylmer *(Sir Eustace Cunningham)*, Lawrence Hanray *(Clerk of the Court)*, Albert Whelan *(Butler)*, Googie Withers *(Mary)*, Allan Jeayes *(Colonel)*.

All-star British cast performs regally in a talkative story concerning an officer accused of card cheating, an accusation that causes Brook to be completely ostracized by his peer group, club members and closest friends. He believes the only way to re-establish his good name is to bring legal action against his accuser, ergo the fascinating trial for slander that ensues and occupies most of the film. (In England the laws concerning slander and libel are such that individuals have greater recourse to protective action than in the U.S.) Many of the fine actors of the cast are wasted in walk-on roles—Squire, Selten, Stewart have little more than bits but the richness of the ensemble makes this film all the more appealing.

p, Victor Saville; d, Tim Whelan; w, Miles Malleson (based on the novel by Mary Borden); ph, Harry Stradling; m, Muir Mathieson; ed, Hugh Stewart; art d, Vincent Korda, Frederick Pusey.

Drama **(PR:A MPAA:NR)**

ACTION IN ARABIA** (1944) 75m RKO bw

George Sanders *(Gordon)*, Virginia Bruce *(Yvonne)*, Lenore Aubert *(Mouniran)*, Gene Lockhart *(Danesco)*, Robert Armstrong *(Reed)*, H. B. Warner *(Rashid)*, Alan Napier *(Latimer)*, Andre Charlot *(Leroux)*, Marcel Dalio *(Chakka)*, Robert Anderson *(Chalmers)*, Jamiel Hasson *(Kareem)*, John Hamilton *(Hamilton)*, Rafael Storm *(Hotel Clerk)*, Mike Ansara *(Hamid)*.

An American newspaper correspondent, Sanders, sniffs out intrigue in Damascus where, in a 1941 setting, Free French and German spies abound, all attempting to enlist the Arab tribes on their sides. After meeting mysterious Bruce, Sanders falls in love with her, then suspects her of being a Nazi agent before learning she is working with the French underground. Both follow German agents to a desert castle where they are meeting with wayward Arab sheiks who intend to bring their tribesmen to the Axis side for heavy pay. Sanders, with the help of the local constabulary, rounds up the Nazis and sheiks, ending up with Bruce on his arm. Much of the excellent desert footage for this pic was culled from many reels shot by Merian C. Cooper and E. B. Schoedsack, creators of KING KONG who had gone to Damascus and environs years earlier with the intention of shooting an epic for RKO that never materialized; the film was pulled off the shelf and cleverly incorporated into this production where Sanders shines as his highly polished self, excercising wry wit and bouncy banter.

p, Maurice Geraghty; d, Leonide Moguy; w, Philip MacDonald, Herbert Biberman; ph, Roy Hunt; ed, Robert Swink; spec eff, Vernon L. Walker.

Spy Drama **(PR:A MPAA:NR)**

ACTION IN THE NORTH ATLANTIC**** (1943) 126m WB/FN bw

Humphrey Bogart *(Joe Rossi)*, Raymond Massey *(Capt. Steve Jarvis)*, Alan Hale *(Boats O'Hara)*, Julie Bishop *(Pearl)*, Ruth Gordon *(Mrs. Jarvis)*, Sam Levene *(Chips Abrams)*, Dane Clark *(Johnny Pulaski)*, Peter Whitney *(Whitey Lara)*, Dick Hogan *(Cadet Robert Parker)*, Minor Watson *(Rear Adm. Hartridge)*, J. M. Kerrigan *(Caviar Jinks)*, Kane Richmond *(Ens. Wright)*, William von Brincken *(Ger. Sub Capt.)*, Chick Chandler *(Goldberg)*, George Offerman, Jr. *(Cecil)*, Don Douglas *(Lt. Commander)*, Ray Montgomery *(Aherne)*, Art Foster *(Pete Larson)*, Glenn Strange *(Tex Mathews)*, Creighton Hale *(Sparks)*, Elliott Sullivan *(Hennessy)*, Alec Craig *(McGonigle)*, Ludwig Stossel *(Capt. Ziemer)*, Dick Wessel *(Cherub)*, Frank Puglia *(Capt. Carpolis)*, Iris Adrian *(Jenny O'Hara)*, Irving Bacon *(Bartender)*, James Flavin *(Lieutenant Commander)*.

Excellent study of merchant marine crew during WW II and its murderous run to Murmansk, Russia, with vital war goods, the only chain of supply the free world then had with its Soviet ally. Bogart is a loyal, brave and rugged first mate to idealistic captain Massey, and they prove their mettle when their tanker is torpedoed and they and part of the crew barely survive a brutal ordeal at sea for eleven days on a raft. Rescued and returned to the U.S., the survivors are portrayed with sensitive and telling mini-plots, the captain utterly fatigued, grateful for clean sheets, his wife at his bedside, Bogart in a bar where he meets singer Bishop and later marries her. When Massey comes to collect his mate he finds him with Bishop, thinking her a girl of the streets and subtly attempts to buy her off until he discovers the pair have been married, an amusing yet touching scene. Massey and Bogart are given a spanking new Liberty Ship with most of their old crew members joined by a sharp Navy gun crew. They join a massive convoy en route to Murmansk but are repeatedly hounded by U-boats which take a pathetic toll of the mostly helpless tankers and freighters, despite the protection of Allied warships. The deadly anticipation of being torpedoed or bombed from the air permeates the crew of Massey's ship, eloquently expressed by Dane Clark whose fear is overcome by hatred for the Nazis who had imprisoned and murdered his relatives. Bogart and company battle through the Nazi attacks, managing to sink a surfaced sub by faking a ship fire and ramming it, then shooting down several German bombers as they approach Murmansk. When they finally dock, cheered on by other ships in port, Massey stirringly remarks that they are amidst "every flag in the world." A powerful document of a class of men given little due for their heroic role during WW II, one that lives up to its title—there is action aplenty. At the premiere of this film in New York, more than a dozen merchant mariners and several hundred U.S. sailors presented Jack Warner with the Merchant Marine Victory Flag.

p, Jerry Wald; d, Lloyd Bacon; w, John Howard Lawson (based on the novel by Guy Gilpatric); ph, Ted McCord; m, Adolph Deutsch; ed, Thomas Pratt, George Amy; art d, Ted Smith; set, d, Clarence I. Steensen; cos, Milo Anderson; makeup, Perc Westmore; spec eff, Jack Cosgrove, Edwin B. DuPar.

War **(PR:A MPAA:NR)**

ACTION OF THE TIGER** (1957) 91m MGM c

Van Johnson *(Carson)*, Martine Carol *(Tracy)*, Herbert Lom *(Trifon)*, Gustavo Rojo *(Henri)*, Tony Dawson *(Security Officer)*, Anna Gerber *(Mara)*, Yvonne Warren *(Katina)*, Helen Haye *(The Countess)*, Sean Connery *(Mike)*, Pepe Nieto *(Kol Stendho)*, Norman Macowan *(Trifon's Father)*, Helen Goss *(Farmer's Wife)*, Richard Williams *(Adbyll)*.

Ravishing Carol hires Johnson and his yacht in Athens to smuggle her into Albania where he is to locate her blind father, a prisoner of the Communist regime. With the help of Albanian bandits led by Herbert Lom in a characteristically powerful, moody role, Johnson and Carol succeed in rescuing the imprisoned man. Johnson flails his fists in every direction, from knocking out a half dozen plug-uglies in a cafe, to bruising a bunch of hardy security police, implausible but providing ample action. (Produced in Spain.)

p, Kenneth Harper; d, Terence Young; w, Robert Carson (based on the novel by James Wellard); ph, Edmund Dickinson; m, Humphrey Searle; ed, Frank Clarke.

Adventure **(PR:A MPAA:NR)**

ACTION STATIONS*

(1959, Brit.) 50m Aqua Films/New Realm bw (AKA: HI-JACK)

Paul Carpenter *(Bob Reynolds)*, Mary Martin *(Anna Braun)*, Joe Robinson *(Pete Archer)*, Ronald Leigh-Hunt *(Kleivar)*, Jack Taylor, Jacques Labreque.

The engraver in a counterfeiting operation tries to quit the gang when gang members kill a man. He and his daughter go to Spain, but his former associates track them down and kidnap the girl. Two friends of the hunted man, smugglers Carpenter and Robinson, rescue the girl while the bad guys meet their demise driving off a cliff. Marginally entertaining thriller. The Mary Martin of the cast is *not* the one who was beloved of U.S. musical comedy audiences during the 1940s and 1950s.

p E. J. Fancey; d,w&ph, Cecil H. Williamson.

Crime **(PR:A-C MPAA:NR)**

ACTORS AND SIN ** 1/2** (1952) 85m UA bw

ACTOR'S BLOOD: Edward G. Robinson *(Maurice Tilayou)*, Marsha Hunt *(Marcia Tilayou)*, Dan O'Herlihy *(Alfred O'Shea)*, Alice Key *(Tommy)*, Rudolph Anders *(Otto Lachsley)*, Rick Roman *(Clyde Veering)*, Peter Brocco *(Mr. Herbert)*, Elizabeth Root *(Mrs. Herbert)*, Joe Mell *(George Murry)*, Irene Martin *(Mrs. Murry)*, Herb Bernard *(Emile)*, Bob Carson *(Thomas Hayne)*; WOMAN OF SIN: Eddie Albert *(Orlando Higgens)*, Alan Reed *(J. B. Cobb)*, Tracey Roberts *(Miss Flannigan)*, Paul Guilfoyle *(Mr. Blue)*, Doug Evans *(Mr. Devlin)*, Jody Gilbert *(Mrs. Egelhofer)*, George Baxter *(Mr.* Brown), George Keymas *(Producer)*, Toni Carroll *(Movie Star)*, John Crawford *(Movie Hero)*, Kathleen Mulqueen *(Miss Wright)*, Alan Mendez *(Moriarity)*, Sam Rosen *(Joseph Danello)*, Jenny Hecht *(Daisy Marcher)*.

A two-part film, the first half being ACTOR'S BLOOD which presents Robinson as an esteemed Shakespearean actor who fiercely guides and protects the career of his actress-daughter, Hunt. A temperamental prima donna of great talent and even greater vanity, she loses her friends, husband and career through savage tantrums and then, gloomily staring at her wrecked career, takes poison for a suicidal curtain. Her father believes she has been driven to her death by ruthless co-actors and producers and he fakes her death as one of murder, later inviting detectives to a party of notables, telling them that one is the killer. The lights go out momentarily and, once on again, police find Robinson dying from a stab wound. With his dying gasp he blames someone in the perplexed crowd but police soon realize that he has murdered himself to cast suspicion on all and vindicate his daughter. The guests, in a bizarre scene, applaud the old actor's last performance. WOMAN OF SIN is much less muddled and more light-hearted, a typical Hechtian roasting of Hollywood and its conniving functionaries. Albert, a worldly agent too good for any client, reads a screenplay entitled *Woman of Sin* and laughingly rejects it as nonsense. But once a studio mogul mentions his interest in the script, Albert drops his suave manner like a bar bell and races pell-mell after the author whom he discovers to be a little girl of nine, Jenny Hecht (Ben's daughter). In a frenetic and masterful bit of acting, Albert doubles and then triples the price of the script while doggedly keeping the obnoxious little author under wraps and promising the moon to actors and technicians alike right down to the movie's premiere at Grauman's Chinese Theater in Hollywood. This is a side-splitting segment, especially when Albert is busy outwitting the pompous mogul flagrantly played by Alan Reed. Jenny Hecht is about the most annoying little girl to ever invade filmdom, perfectly cast by her father.

p,d&w, Ben Hecht; ph, Lee Garmes; m, George Antheil; ed, Otto Ludwig; set d, Howard Bristol.

Drama/Comedy **(PR:C MPAA:NR)**

ACTOR'S REVENGE, AN * 1/2** (1963, Jap.) 113m c (AKA: REVENGE OF YUKI-NO-JO, THE)

Kazuo Hasegawa, Fujiko Yamamoto, Ayako Wakao, Ganjiro Nakamura.

Strange tale of Kabuki actor—actually a female impersonator—popular in the 19th century, who encounters a wealthy businessman who had destroyed his family while on tour and who takes his revenge in not-too-subtle ways which result in a number of deaths. Sort of an Oriental COUNT OF MONTE CRISTO. Thoroughly unrewarding and utterly confusing.

d, Kon Ichikawa; w, Daisuke Ito, Natto Wada, Teinosuke Kinugasa; ph, Setsuo Kobayashi; m, Yasushi Akutagawa.

Drama **(PR:O MPAA:NR)**

ACTRESS, THE ** 1/2** (1953) 89m MGM bw

Spencer Tracy *(Clinton Jones)*, Jean Simmons *(Ruth Gordon Jones)*, Teresa Wright *(Annie Jones)*, Anthony Perkins *(Fred Whitmarsh)*, Ian Wolfe *(Mr. Bagley)*, Kay Williams *(Hazel Dawn)*, Mary Wickes *(Emma Glavey)*, Norma Jean Nilsson *(Anna)*, Dawn Bender *(Katherine)*.

A plodding, sometimes sensitive film about an aspiring actress, Simmons, whose father Tracy is a poor working man. He and his wife, Wright, are apprehensive about such a chancy career and try to convince their daughter to pursue another career, better yet, settle down with a dour suitor, Perkins. Simmons persists, even though she is turned down by Boston's leading theatrical impresario. Tracy taps his backbone and thrusts his child into the world, sending her to New York to find a role, giving her his only valuable, an expensive seaman's spyglass. A touching story which bogs down inside too much argumentative dialog. Tracy walks tolerantly through his role, Wright is the rock-ribbed mother and Simmons is often grating as the stage-struck daughter.

p, Lawrence Weingarten; d, George Cukor; w, Ruth Gordon (based on her play "Years Ago"); ph, Harold Rosson; md, Bronislau Kaper; ed, George Boemler; art d, Cedric Gibbons, Arthur Lonergan; set d, Edwin B. Willis, Emile Kuri; cos, Walter Plunkett; spec eff, Warren Newcombe.

Drama **(PR:A MPAA:NR)**

ADA** (1961) 109m MGM c

Susan Hayward *(Ada)*, Dean Martin *(Bo Gillis)*, Wilfrid Hyde-White *(Sylvester Marin)*, Ralph Meeker *(Colonel Yancey)*, Martin Balsam *(Steve Jackson)*, Frank Maxwell *(Ronnie Hallerton)*, Connie Sawyer *(Alice Sweet)*, Ford Rainey *(Speaker)*, Charles Watts *(Al Winslow)*, Larry Gates *(Joe Adams)*, Robert S. Simon *(Natfield)*, William Zuckert *(Harry Davers)*, *Mary Treen (Clubwoman)*.

Here is an improbable tale, one that takes the noble prostitute myth to Olympian heights, and, defying all belief, has dynamic Hayward, a professional whore who has reformed, marry a newly-elected state governor, happy-go-lucky Martin. Balsam, his press agent, and Hyde-White, his mentor and chief advisor, are enemies of Ada early on, cautioning Martin that her background might hurt his chances with the electorate (to say the least). Being a man of principle, he ignores them and goes on to govern with her at his side. Then, like some medieval drama, the film slices into various intrigues against Martin, all spawned by the power hungry Hyde-White who forces the lieutenant governor to resign then, when Martin refuses to follow his dictates, arranges for his official car to have a near-fatal accident in which Martin is almost killed. Hayward takes over the reins of government, unleashing a series of reform bills which her husband had set in motion. Hyde-White and crooked police chief Meeker try to block her actions by publicizing a tape recording containing the ecstatic outpourings of one of Hayward's former assignations. Before the state capitol crashes in on her, Martin recovers and stands by her through the cruel publicity, defeating their detractors. The viewer is hard put to accept such fairy tales and one wonders which state of the union would accept such an impossible couple to rule its destiny, yet tolerate such expensive shenanigans. For the sleepless, the mindless and those who have never cast their vote for anyone.

p, Lawrence Weingarten; d, Daniel Mann; w, Arthur Sheekman, William Driskill (based on the novel *Ada Dallas* by Wirt Williams); ph, Joseph Ruttenberg; m, Bronislau Kaper; ed, Ralph E. Winters; art d, George W. Davis, Edward Carfagno; cos, Helen Rose; m/l, "May the Lord Bless You Real Good," Warren Roberts, Wally Fowler (sung by Martin).

Drama **(PR:C MPAA:NR)**

ADALEN 31*** (1969, Swed.) 115m ABSF c (AKA: ADALEN RIOTS)

Peter Schildt *(Kjell)*, Kerstin Tidelius *(Mother)*, Roland Hedlund *(Father)*, Stefan Feierbach *(Ake)*, Marie De Goer *(Anna)*, Anita Bjork *(Wife)*, Olof Bergstrom *(Boss)*, Jonas Bergstrom *(Nisse)*, Olle Bjorling *(Strike-breaker)*, Pierre Lindstedt *(Foreman)*.

Creator of ELVIRA MADIGAN, Bo Widerberg, presents an historically poetic 1931 Sweden suddenly torn apart by labor unrest and a national strike that crippled the country and led to the nation's conversion to social democracy. Story concentrates on a young worker whose family is near destitution during the strike and his love for the boss's daughter, a union dissolved when her father brings in scabs to work the factory. In a scene reminiscent of the slaughter on the Odessa Steps in POTEMKIN, government troops close in on a peaceful striker's march and open fire, creating a bloodbath that ends the strike but also ends capitalism as it was then known in Sweden. A powerful documentary-style film with many rewarding moments.

d&w, Bo Widerberg; ph, Jorgen Perrson.

Drama **(PR:C MPAA:NR)**

ADAM AND EVE zero (1958, Mex.) 76m Constelacion

Carlos Baena *(Adam)*, Christiane Martel *(Eve)*.

Ridiculous film consisting of two actors and narrated in English; neither actor speaks as they flit about a misty Eden, enacting the biblical tale of their stay in Paradise and subsequent fall from grace. A sexploitation film, really, using a religious tale as a guise for grunts, gasps and low moans (which will no doubt be echoed by any viewer). Dreadful. (Filmed in Mexico, exact location unknown).

p&d, Albert Gout.

Fantasy **(PR:O MPAA:NR)**

ADAM AND EVELYNE**

(1950, Brit.) 82m Rank/TC bw (AKA: ADAM AND EVALYN)

Stewart Granger *(Adam Black)*, Jean Simmons *(Evelyne Wallace)*, Edwin Styles *(Bill Murray)*, Raymond Young *(Roddy Black)*, Helen Cherry *(Moira)*, Beatrice Varley *(Mrs. Parker)*, Joan Swinstead *(Molly)*, Wilfrid Hyde-White *(Colonel Bradley)*, Fred Johnson *(Chris Kirby)*, Peter Reynolds *(David)*, Geoffrey Denton *(Inspector)*, Brenda Hogan *(Christine)*, Irene Handl *(Manageress)*, John Forrest *(Tony)*.

Sophisticated melodrama solidly teams Granger as a gambler and Simmons as a homeless girl who thinks he is her father. Granger convinces her otherwise, telling her that she is the daughter of one of his dead friends and takes her in, clothing her in the finest gowns, presenting her with lavish surroundings and lying to her, saying he is a successful broker. His envious brother, Young, takes Simmons to Granger's swank gambling den just as police arrive, a raid the treacherous brother has arranged. Instead of leaving him, Simmons clings to Granger in his hour of need, the brother's hateful scheme failing to break up the loving couple.

p&d, Harold French; w, Noel Langley; ph, Guy Green; m, Mischa Spoliansky; ed, John D. Guthridge.

Romance **(PR:A MPAA:NR)**

ADAM AT 6 A.M.* (1970) 100m Solar/NGP c

Michael Douglas *(Adam Gaines)*, Lee Purcell *(Jerri Jo Hopper)*, Joe Don Baker *(Harvey Gavin)*, Charles Aidman *(Mr. Hooper)*, Marge Redmond *(Cleo)*, Louise Latham *(Mrs. Hopper)*, Grayson Hall *(Inez Treadley)*, Carolyn Conwell *(Mavis)*, Dana Elcar *(Van)*, Meg Foster *(Joyce)*, Richard Derr *(Roger Gaines)*, Anne Gwynne *(Mrs. Gaines)*, Ned Wertheimer *(Dr. Peters)*, Ed Call *(Orville)*, David Sullivan *(Leroy)*, Butch Youngblood *(Elwood)*, Bud Trone *(Ray)*, Jim Lantz *(Strawboss)*, Pat Randall *(Pearlie)*, Jo Ella Defenbaugh *(Marylist)*, Sharon Marshall *(Rosalie)*.

A too-young Douglas in the role of a semantics professor flees the urban life when a relative dies in rural Missouri; Douglas transplants himself for reasons of pure living and uncomplicated lifestyles. He learns that all people have problems and are problems to each other even in the sticks where they are sometimes weirder than any kook hitchhiking in southern California. A weak script, forgettable dialog, thin story, and the kind of shoddy direction for which TV production is infamous, knock unconscious a story already on its knees. Only rugged Joe Don Baker, foreman of a work crew, is convincing. This is the first Solar Production film owned by Steve McQueen in which McQueen did not star, the reasons being obvious. Moreover, the MPAA rating of GP is wholly misleading in that vulgar language, bare breasts and prophylactics used as comedy props repeatedly dot the production.

p, Rick Rosenberg, Robert Christiansen; d, Robert Scheerer; w, Stephen and Elinor Karpf; ph, Charles Rosher; m, Dave Grusin; ed, Jack McSweeney.

Drama **(PR:O MPAA:GP)**

ADAM HAD FOUR SONS* (1941) 108m COL bw**

Ingrid Bergman *(Emilie Gallatin)*, Warner Baxter *(Adam Stoddard)*, Susan Hayward *(Hester)*, Fay Wray *(Molly)*, OLDER BOYS: Richard Denning *(Jack)*, Johnny Downs *(David)*, Robert Shaw *(Chris)*, Charles Lind *(Phillip)*; YOUNGER BOYS: Billy Ray *(Jack)*, Steven Muller *(David)*, Wallace Chadweel *(Chris)*, Bobby Walberg *(Phillip)*; Helen Westley *(Cousin Phillipa)*, June Lockhart *(Vance)*, Pietro Sosso *(Otto)*, Gilbert Emery *(Dr. Lane)*, Renie Riano *(Photographer)*, Clarence Muse *(Sam)*.

In her second U.S. film (following her smash U.S. debut, INTERMEZZO), Bergman plays a long-suffering, sympathetic and misunderstood housekeeper for an American businessman, Baxter, whose wife, Wray, has just died. She lovingly raises his four young sons but leaves for Europe when Baxter's financial plight deepens, seeking other employment at his request. Some years later, when Baxter is again on his feet, he asks Bergman to return. She finds the sons almost grown and delighted to have her back, one of them, Downs, taking a new bride, Hayward, who is a scheming, vicious- streaked young lady who insists upon running the large household. In one of her better performances, Hayward degrades Bergman, cons Baxter into believing she is a sweet young thing, and cheats on Downs by attempting to seduce another brother, Denning, who will have nothing to do with her. The internecine warfare between Bergman and Hayward culminates in an out-and-out brawl and Baxter unwittingly sides with Hayward who showers crocodile tears on his shoulder (with a telling close-up as she displays a wicked smile over his shoulder while he comforts her). Hayward's malicious personality, however, is revealed to a visiting aunt, Westley, who suffers a relapse and Hayward is exposed as an uncontrollable vixen. Baxter finally admits his love for Bergman as the film ends. An excellent character study of a family in transition and growth (from the panic of 1907 to WW I), long a pet project of producer Robert Sherwood (no relation to the playwright) who purchased the rights to the Charles Bonner novel and held on to them until Columbia allowed him to venture into his first production. Ratoff's direction of this rather black-and-white tale is clear and crisp and standout performances are rendered by the heroic Bergman and the cuckolding Hayward, who begged Ratoff for the part of spoiler after having played nothing but sweet young things.

p, Robert Sherwood; d, Gregory Ratoff; w, William Hurlbutt, Michael Blankfort (based on the novel *Legacy* by Charles Bonner); ph, Peverell Marley; ed, Francis D. Lyon; art, d, Rudolph Sternad.

Drama Cas. (PR:A MPAA:NR)

ADAM'S RIB*1/2 (1949) 101m MGM bw**

Spencer Tracy *(Adam Bonner)*, Katharine Hepburn *(Amanda Bonner)*, Judy Holliday *(Doris Attinger)*, Tom Ewell *(Warren Attinger)*, David Wayne *(Kip Lurie)*, Jean Hagen *(Beryl Caighn)*, Hope Emerson *(Olympia La Pere)*, Eve March *(Grace)*, Clarence Kolb *(Judge Reiser)*, Emerson Treacy *(Jules Frikke)*, Polly Moran *(Mrs. McGrath)*, Will Wright *(Judge Marcasson)*, Elizabeth Flournoy *(Dr. Margaret Brodeigh)*, Janna Da Loos *(Mary, the Maid)*, Marvin Kaplan *(Court Stenographer)*, John Maxwell Sholes *(Court Clerk)*, David Clarke *(Roy)*, Gracille La Vinder *(Police Matron)*, William Self *(Benjamin Klausner)*, Paula Raymond *(Emerald)*, Tommy Noonan *(Reporter)*, Ray Walker *(Photographer)*, Sid Dubin *(Amanda's Assistant)*, Joe Bernard *(Mr. Bonner)*, Madge Blake *(Mrs. Bonner)*, Marjorie Wood *(Mrs. Marcasson)*, Lester Luther *(Judge Poynter)*, De Forrest Lawrence, John Fell *(Adam's Assistants)*, Roger David *(Hurlock)*, Anna Q. Nilsson *(Mrs. Poynter)*, Rex Evans *(Fat Man)*, Louis Mason *(Elevator Operator)*, Charles Bastin *(Asst. District Attorney)*, *(Witness)*, E. Bradley Coleman *(Subway Rider)*, Glenn Gallagher, Gil Patric, Harry Cody *(Criminal Attorneys)*, George Magrill, Bert Davidson *(Subway Guards)*.

Delightful comedy riddled with sophisticated laughs where Tracy, a tough, unbending D.A., is pitted against his beautiful lawyer-wife, Hepburn, in an attempted murder case that unleashes a battle of the sexes, almost wrecking Tracy's happy marriage. Judy Holliday, in her first of many scatter-brained roles (this part led to her getting the "dumb blonde broad" role in the Broadway and later film smash, BORN YESTERDAY), attempts to shoot another woman trysting with her slippery husband, Ewell (a hilarious performance), and is placed on trial, defended by Hepburn who is out to prove that the "unwritten law" applies to females as well as males, a charming equal rights advocate who soon tangles with her conservative husband whose life is further complicated when David Wayne begins to move blatantly in on Hepburn. Throughout the hijinks trial the marriage between Tracy and Hepburn begins to disintegrate as their courtroom resentments surface at home (in one amusing scene Tracy is giving Hepburn a rubdown and, while both lapse into acrimonious comments about their professional conduct, delivers a healthy whack to her bare behind—unseen by camera—which causes her to explode). Hepburn wins acquittal for Holliday through her rights issues but admits, as does a petulant Tracy, that there are basic differences between the sexes; *"Vive le difference!"* Tracy exclaims. A thoroughly witty, sharply directed fun film from Cukor and a spritely script from Gordon and Kanin, later nominated for an Oscar. One song, "Farewell Amanda," is lightweight fare from Cole Porter.

p, Lawrence Weingarten; d, George Cukor; w, Ruth Gordon, Garson Kanin; ph, George J. Folsey; m, Miklos Rozza; ed, George Boemler; art, d, Cedric Gibbons, William Ferrari; set d, Edwin B. Willis, Henry Grace; cos, Walter Plunkett; spec eff, A. Arnold Gillespie.

Comedy Cas. (PR:A MPAA:NR)

ADAM'S WOMAN1/2**

(1972, Austral.) 116m Edelman/WB c (AKA: RETURN OF THE BOOMERANG)

Beau Bridges *(Adam)*, Jane Merrow *(Bess)*, James Booth *(Dyson)*, Andrew Keir *(O'Shea)*, Tracy Reed *(Duchess)*, Peter O'Shaughnessy *(Barrett)* John Mills *(Sir Philip)*, John Warwick *(Croydon)*, Harry Lawrence *(Muir)*, Katy Wild *(Millie)*, Mark McManus *(Nobby)*, Harold Hopkins *(Cosh)*, Doreen Warburton *(Fat Anne)*, Clarissa Kaye *(Matron)*, Peter Collingwood *(Chaplain)*

It is the 1840s, Australia, when most of the country was a giant penal colony to which hardened felons and wrongly convicted citizens were sent by mean-spirited British magistrates. Bridges is one of the latter, an American sailor found guilty of a crime he did not commit in Liverpool and transported to the wild country beyond Sydney where he, along with other prisoners, is whipped, starved and maltreated at every turn. He escapes with Booth but is recaptured, Booth murdering a soldier and again escaping, a crime for which Bridges is wrongly convicted. He appeals to the governor, Mills, a kindly, sympathetic soul bent on reforming the brutal system, and is given the chance to marry a female prisoner and begin developing five acres of bushy outback land. Bridges weds Merrow (a top-flight actress who appeared in THE LION IN WINTER) and the two begin a settlement which flourishes, other married prisoners joining them. The settlement is destroyed by Booth, who has been living in the outback with a band of cutthroats, when he and his men set fire to the community. Mills summarily pardons Bridges and Merrow, allowing them to rebuild as free citizens while Booth gets his come uppance. A well-wrought story with exceptional photography that sometimes drags.

p, Louis F. Edelman; d, Phillip Leacock; w, Richard Fielder (based on a story by Lowell Barrington); ph, Wilmer C. Butler; m, Bob Young; ed, Anthony Buckley.

Adventure (PR:C MPAA:NR)

ADDING MACHINE, THE* (1969) 102m RF c**

Phyllis Diller *(Mrs. Zero)*, Milo O'Shea *(Zero)*, Billie Whitelaw *(Daisy)*, Sydney Chaplin *(Lt. Charles)*, Julian Glover *(Shrdlu)*, Raymond Huntley *(Smithers)*, Phil Brown *(Don)*, Libby Morris *(Ethel)*, Hugh McDermott *(Harry)*, Paddie O'Neil *(Mabel)*, Carol Cleveland *(Judy)*, Bruce Boa *(Detective)*, John Brandon *(First Cell Jailer)*, Kenny Damon *(Joe)*, Hal Galili *(Second Cell Jailer)*, Tony Caunter *(Third Cell Jailer)*, Bill Hutchinson *(Judy's Lover)*, Helen Elliott *(Second Apartment Girl)*, C. Denier Warren *(Jury Foreman)*, Tommy Duggan *(Judee)*, John Bloomfield, Helena Stevens, Alan Surtees, Christine Pryor, Cal McCord, Shirley Cooklin, Anthony Harwood *(Apartment Tenants)*, Bill Nagy *(Lawyer)*, Nicholas Stuart *(District Attorney)*, Gordon Sterne, Mike Reed *(Yard Guards)*, Lola Lloyd *(Coffee Girl)*, George Margo *(Gateman)*, Janet Brown *(Fat Woman)*, Janie Baron *(Thin Woman)*, John Cook *(Husband)*, George Roderick *(Hot Dog Vendor)*.

Well-acted film based on the 1923 Elmer Rice play has accomplished Irish actor O'Shea as the frustrated, wife-weary office employee who slaves for retirement only to be fired, replaced by an adding machine. He, in turn, murders his boss and is placed on trial, giving a marvelously moving performance from the witness stand; he is convicted and executed, glad to be rid of his shrewish wife, Diller, whose tongue-lashings and bitchy posturing make her a classic character of hate. Instead of going to Hades, O'Shea is transported to a heavenly area which is peopled by other compulsive killers all waiting to be reassigned to a new life in another being. The heavenly atmosphere is convincing and Chaplin, portraying O'Shea's otherworld guardian and guide to a new life, provides a brilliant bit of acting. The latter portion of the film dealing with the hereafter is imaginatively mounted, presented in almost surrealistic settings.

p,d&w, Jerome Epstein; ph, Walter Lassally; m, Mike Leander, Lambert Williamson; ed, Gerry Hambling; art, d, Jack Shampan; set d, Mike Pittel; cos, Gabriell Falk.

Drama (PR:C MPAA:NR)

ADDRESS UNKNOWN (1944) 80m COL bw**

Paul Lukas *(Martin Schulz)*, Carl Esmond *(Baron von Friesche)*, Peter Van Eyck *(Heinrich Schulz)*, Mady Christians *(Elsa)*, Morris Carnovsky *(Max Eisenstein)*, K. T. Stevens *(Griselle)*, Emory Parnell *(Postman)*, Mary Young *(Mrs. Delaney)*, Frank Faylen *(Jimmie Blake)*, Charles Halton *(Pip-Squeak)*, Erwin Kaiser *(Stage Director)*, Frank Reicher *(Professor Schmidt)*, Dale Cornell *(Carl)*, Peter Newmeyer *(Wilhelm)*, Larry Joe Olsen *(Youngest)*, Gary Gray *(Hugo)*.

Ponderous, poorly-constructed script shows Lukas as a German-American returning to Germany during the early Nazi era, one who becomes quickly indoctrinated in Hitler's racist philosophies to the point where he abandons his Jewish partner's daughter to her fate. The daughter, an actress engaged to Lukas' son, answers the Nazis' racial slurs from the stage and must flee for her life while Lukas himself falls prey to the Gestapo. The story is confusingly told through a series of letters exchanged between Lukas and his business partner, a device that makes the whole process tedious, if not boring. Director Menzies does what he can with a weak story and nevertheless turns out a sharply photographed production.

d, William Cameron Menzies; w, Herbert Dalmas (based on a story by Kressman Taylor); ph, Rudolph Mate; m, Ernst Toch; ed, Al Clark; md, M. W. Stoloff.

War (PR:A MPAA:NR)

ADELE HASN'T HAD HER SUPPER YET zero

(1978, Czech.) 100m CFP c (AKA: DINNER FOR ADELE, NICK CARTER IN PRAGUE)

Michal Docolomansky *(Nick Carter)*, Rudolf Hrusinsky *(Josef Ledvina)*, Milos Kopecky *(Baron Kratzman)*, Ladislav Pesek *(Professor Bocek)*, Nada Konvalinkova *(Kvetusa)*, Martin Ruzck *(Police Inspector Kauntiz)*, Vaclav Lohnisky *(Hotel Servant)*, Olga Schoberove *(Irma Gizela)*, Kveta Fialova *(Countess Thun)*.

Amateurish effort to satirize the detective heroics of Nick Carter, circa 1900, where director Oldrick Lipsky (who had a mild success with his animated feature LEMONADE JOE) uses myriad antiques and gadgets to enhance the invention-obsessed gumshoe but the whole thing, from the so-called nemesis of Carter, a slurping man-eating plant, Adele, to the detective's flight in a colorful balloon is neither funny nor interesting. It is merely one gimmick piled upon another, crudely introduced without being integral to the story. Docolomansky is a clownish Carter flitting about Prague looking for Adele in what he thinks are clever disguises, but are really gaudy costumes that make him stand out in any crowd. A cult film; certain buffs attempt to see art where there is none in this ridiculous, vacuous film.

d, Oldrich Lipsky; w, Jiri Brdecka; ph, Jaroslav Kuccra; m, Lubos Fiser; set, d, Vladimir Labsky, Milan Nejedly; spec eff, Jan Svankmaier.

Satire (PR:C MPAA:NR)

ADIEU PHILLIPINE* (1962, Fr./Ital.) 111m UNITEC/ALPHA bw

Yveline Cery *(Liliane)*, Stefania Sabatini *(Juliette)*, Jean-Claude Aimimi *(Michel)*, Vittorio Caprioli *(Pachala)*, Davide Tonelli *(Horatio)*.

So-called "New Wave" film dotes on the closeness of three 18-year-olds, two girls and a boy, and their growth together. A young worker meets the two girls, trying to romance both. They, in turn, devise foils for him but one ultimately becomes his true love. The simple story is the crux of this once very arty type of filmmaking, too simple (or simple-minded) to even provide a modicum of interest in a basic plotline, and overindulgence in the technical—no entertainment, no real action, no beginning, no middle, no end, just gentle, young, dull folks.

d&w, Jacques Rozier; ph, Rene Mathelin; ed, Marc Pavaux.

Drama (PR:C MPAA:NR)

ADIOS AMIGO** (1975) 87m Atlas c

Fred Williamson (Ben), Richard Pryor (Sam), Thalmus Rasulala (Noah), James Brown, Robert Phillips, Mike Henry, Suhaila Farhat, Victoria Jee, Lynne Jackson, Heidi Dobbs, Liz Treadwell, Joy Lober

Tame episodic excursion into what passes for comedic crimes committed by Richard Pryor, bumbling scams that never work and ultimately never pay, a backfiring real estate con, an abortive stagecoach robbery, an inept jailbreak. The entire production was dreamed up as black family entertainment by Fred Williamson who produced, wrote, directed and starred opposite Pryor. Though the film has no vulgar language or excessive violence it also has no story line, character development or interesting scenes other than a few witty ad-lib lines mumbled by Pryor who involves Williamson in his street swindles, laughs off his mistakes and runs off with the farewell, "Adios, amigo." Few will want to say hello to this one.

p,d&w, Fred Williamson; ph, Tony Palmieri; m, Luici de Jesus; ed, Gene and Eva Ruggiero.

Comedy (PR:C MPAA:PG)

ADIOS GRINGO*½ (1967, Ital./Fr./Span.) 98m Trans-Lux c

Guilano Gemma (Brent Landers), Evelyn Stewart (Lucy Tillson), Roberto Camardiel (Dr. Barfield), Jesus Puente (Tex Slaughter), Max Dean (Avery Ranchester), Peter Cross (Clayton Ranchester), Grant Laramy (Stan Clevenger), Jean Martin (Murphy), Monique Saint Clare (Maude Clevenger).

Incomprehensible spaghetti western with dubbed English where bandits and lawmen are indistinguishable in a woefully confusing film.

p, Bruno Tuchetto; d, George Finlay [Giorgio Stegani]; w, Jose Luis Jerez, Michele Villerot, Stegani; ph, Francisco Sempere; m, Benedetto Ghiglia; art d, Roman Calatayud; cos, Ed Michelson.

Western (PR:A MPAA:NR)

ADIOS SABATA** (1971, Ital./Span.) 106m Grimaldi/UA c

Yul Brynner (Sabata), Dean Reed (Ballantine), Pedro Sanchez (Escudo), Gerard Herter (Skimmel), Sal Borgese (September), Franco Fantasia (Ocano), Joseph Persaud (Gitano), Gianni Rizzo (Folgen), Salvatore Billa (Manuel), Massimo Carocci (Juan), Antonio Gradoli (Major).

Fast action, numerous gun battles and scores of bodies toppling from galloping horses don't bring this south-of-the-border oater beyond the average. Grimaldi's formula is the same as with his previous SABATA, only Brynner subs for Lee Van Cleef, a soldier of fortune dressed in the traditional black, who is joined by an American sharper and a Mexican bandit and his henchmen to filch a gold shipment from the short-termed Emperor Maximillian to finance Juarez' revolution. (Sequel: THE RETURN OF SABATA.)

p, Alberto Grimaldi; d, Frank Kramer [Gianfranco Paolini]; w, Renato Izzo, Paolini; ph, Sandro Mancori; m, Bruno Nicolai.

Western (PR:A MPAA:GP)

ADMIRABLE CRICHTON, THE**½
(1957, Brit.) 93m COL c (AKA: PARADISE LAGOON)

Kenneth More (Crichton), Diane Cilento (Tweeny), Cecil Parker (Lord Loam), Sally Ann Howes (Lady Mary), Martita Hunt (Lady Brocklehurst), Jack Watling (Treherne), Peter Graves (Brocklehurst), Gerald Harper (Ernest), Mercy Haystead (Catherine), Miranda Connell (Agatha), Miles Malleson (Vicar), Eddie Byrne (Captain), Joan Young (Mrs. Perkins), Brenda Hogan (Fisher), Peter Welch (Rolleston), Toke Townley (Lovegrove), Roland Cupram (Thomas).

Often filmed James M. Barrie classic (produced on Broadway in 1902, filmed as silent, MALE AND FEMALE), offers popular British star More in the role of the indefatigable butler who supervises the lives of his aristocratic employers marooned on a tropical island. Here the eldest of three daughters, Howes, falls in love with the newly appointed "governor" of the island which dashes the hopes of the family maid, Cilento. (Cecil Parker, whose yacht has been wrecked and family tossed to fortune, is marvelous as the helpless lord.) When the family is finally rescued by a passing ship, More resumes his Uriah Heep role and, rather than embarrass his employer by marrying above his station, nobly departs with the joyous maid. The film was shot in Bermuda with lush color; crisp direction brightens an otherwise staid tale.

p, Ian Dalrymple; d, Lewis Gilbert; w, Vernon Harris (based on the play by James M. Barrie); ph, Wilkie Cooper; m, Douglas Gamley; ed, Peter Hunt; cos, Bernard Nevill.

Drama/Adventure (PR:A MPAA:NR)

ADMIRAL NAKHIMOV** (1948, USSR) 95m Mosfilm bw

Alexi Dikki (Admiral Nakhimov), Vsevolod Pudovkin (Prince Menshikov), Eugene Samoilov (Lt. Buronou), Vladimir Vladislavsky (Capt. Laurov), N. Chapligin (Kornilov), V. Kovrigin (Baranovsky), L. Kniazev (Koshka), A. Khokhlov (Napoleon III) R. Simonov (Osman-Pasha), P. Galdeburov (Lord Raglan).

A difficult film to follow in that it has all-Russian dialog with a smattering of French with English subtitles. Director Pudovkin, who also appears as a foppish prince in a few scenes, offers a sweeping, sometimes magnificent view of one of Russia's traditional heroes, Nakhimov, who routed the Turkish fleet and armies during the Crimean conflict of 1853. The battle scenes, the naval combat done in miniature, are often breath-taking. Too much political rhetoric is spent indicting the British and French for forcing Russia into a defensive war and Pudovkin lingers languidly with his cameras for closeups that annoyingly expose hairy faces and rolling eyeballs, but Dikki is excellent as the forceful, decisive Nakhimov who overrides Czarist strategy to overcome the enemy, personally leading a wild bayonet charge in Sebastopol where he is killed by a British bullet. Of course the Soviet political message was worked into the film to dilute its historic accuracy. (In Russian; English subtitles.)

d, Vsevolod Pudovkin; w, I. Loukovsky; ph, A. Golovnia, T. Lobova.

War (PR:C MPAA:NR)

ADMIRAL WAS A LADY, THE** (1950) 87m UA bw

Edmond O'Brien (Jimmie Stevens), Wanda Hendrix (Jean Madison), Rudy Vallee (Mr. Pettigrew), Johnny Sands (Eddie), Steve Brodie (Mike), Richard Erdman (Ollie), Hillary Brooke (Mrs. Pettigrew), Richard Lane (The Fight Promoter), Garry Owen (The Private Eye), Fred Essler (The Store-Keeper).

O'Brien and three out-of-work vet buddies all chase Hendrix after she walks into their social club looking for a lost boyfriend who is being chased for wrongdoing by Rudy Vallee, a jukebox tycoon. Hendrix, a pert and funny WAVE, is disgusted by the fact that O'Brien, Sands, Erdman and Brodie have vowed never to work again; she shuns their clumsy advances which makes for some laughable scenes. To win her heart O'Brien climbs into a boxing ring to face a professional fighter in order to win a $100 purse to help out his lady love, a funny scene where he just barely manages to avoid being pulverized. It's apparent from the beginning that O'Brien will wind up with Hendrix but the chase is worth the watching.

p, Albert S. Rogell, Jack M. Warner; d, Rogell; w, Sidney Salkow, John O'Dea; ph, Stanley Cortez, Edward J. Kay; ed, William Ziegler; m/l, "Once Over Lightly," "Everything That's Wonderful," Al Stewart, Earl Rose.

Comedy **Cas.** (PR:A MPAA:NR)

ADMIRALS ALL** (1935, Brit.) 75m Stafford/RKO bw

Wynne Gibson (Gloria Gunn), Gordon Harker (Petty Officer Dingle), Anthony Bushell (Flag Lt. Steve Langham), George Curzon (Ping Hi), Joan White (Prudence Stallybrass), Henry Hewitt (Flag Captain Knox), Percy Walsh (Admiral Sir Westerham), Wilfrid Hyde-White (Mr. Stallybrass), Gwynneth Lloyd (Jean Stallybrass), Ben Weldon (Adolph Klotz).

Temperamental film star Gibson is pursued by Harker, a low-ranking Navy officer, their paths crossed meanly by a rigidly ridiculous and sometimes funny admiral, Walsh. This boy-chases-girl-and-gets-her plot has so many isolated scenes that are irrelevant to the vague story that one wonders if, after 20 minutes, one is watching the same movie.

p, John Stafford; d, Victor Hanbury; (based on the play by Ian Hay and Stephen King-Hall).

Comedy (PR:A MPAA:NR)

ADMIRAL'S SECRET, THE* (1934, Brit.) 71m Real Art/RKO bw

Edmund Gwenn (Adm. Pitzporter), James Raglan (Frank Bruce), Hope Davy (Pamela Pitzporter), Aubrey Mather (Capt. Brooke), Edgar Driver (Sam Hawkins), Abraham Sofaer (Don Pablo Y Gonzales), Dorothy Black (Donna Teresa), Andrea Malandrinos (Guido d'Elvira), D. J. Williams (Questa), Agnes Imlay.

Low-budget programmer is less than amusing as retired admiral Gwenn absconds with some jewels and is chased about by stumbling Spanish cutthroats.

p, Julius Hagen; d, Guy Newall; w, H. Fowler Mear (based on a play by Cyril Campion, Edward Dignon).

Comedy (PR:A MPAA:NR)

ADOLESCENT, THE** (1978, Fr./W.Ger.) 90m Carthago/PF c

Laetitia Chauveau (Marie), Simone Signoret (Mamie), Edith Clever (Eva), Jacques Weber (Jean), Francis Huster (Alexandre), Roger Blin (Romain).

A 12-year-old girl, Chauveau, leaves her Paris home and estranged parents just before the outbreak of WW II to spend a summer holiday in a remote village with her grandmother, Signoret, who plays a subtle soothsayer. The girl develops a heartthrob for a young Jewish doctor and begins to recognize mature feelings in herself, before returning to Paris to see her parents reunited. A somewhat doting, laboring film, directed by actress Jeanne Moreau, who presents more pastoral scenes than story.

p, Philippe Dussart; d&w, Jeanne Moreau; w, Henriette Jelinek; ph, Pierre Gautard; m, Philippe Sarde; ed, Albert Jurgenson.

Drama (PR:C MPAA:NR)

ADOLESCENTS, THE** (1967, Can.) 80m Pathe bw

"Fiametta: Micaela Esdra (Fiametta), Esmeralda Ruspoli (Livia); "Genevieve": Genevieve Bujold (Genevieve), Louise Marleau (Louise), Bernard Arcand (Bernard); "Marie-France and Veronica: Veronique Duval (Veronica), Nadine Ballot (Daniele), Marc Kalinoski (Marc), Michael Aracheguesne (Michel).

An episodic trilogy, this film suffers from lack of story and character development. In the first segment we see a little spoiled girl wandering about a lavish Florentine villa longing for a dead father, a morose portrait that brings to an end her mother's love affair with a young suitor. Next we have two girl friends attending a carnival and meeting a young man who favors one over a kiss which alienates the friendship of the other. In the final segment, two 16-year-olds experience their first sexual awareness in the streets of Paris. There is little with which to identify here for either adults or teenagers, except cliches passing for sensitivity.

"Fiametta": d&w, Gian Vittorio Baldi; "Genevieve": d, Michel Brault; w, Alex Pelletier; "Marie-France Veronica": d&w, Jean Rouch. SEQUENCE).

Drama (PR:C MPAA:NR)

ADOLF HITLER—MY PART IN HIS DOWNFALL*
(1973, Brit.) 102m Norcon/UA c

Spike Milligan, Jim Dale, Billy Maynard, Arthur Lowe, Windsor Davies, Tony Selby, Pat Coombs, Geoffrey Hughes.

Silly slapstick in the British vein, sort of a takeoff on M*A*S*H which shows Milligan as a WW II recruit in the various stages of his training. Appeal will be limited to those who enjoy delayed pratfalls.

d, Norman Cohen; w, John Bryne; ph, Terry Maher; m, Wilfred Burns.

Comedy **(PR:A MPAA:NR)**

ADOPTION, THE* (1978, Fr.) 93m LFM c

Geraldine Chaplin *(Wife)*, Jacques Perrin *(Husband)*, Patrick Norbert *(Etienne)*.

Following a fire in their barn, a childless couple find a teenager suffering an epileptic seizure in their country home. They take him in, oblivious to the certainty that he has set the fire, encouraging him to paint and seek medical attention which they finance. Moreover, the common-law adoption leads to the youth making love to the wife, impregnating her and then, when she is about to give birth, murdering her and her over-tolerant husband. A disastrous film offering nothing more than the experience of brutality endured by ultra-liberals bent on their own destruction and wallowing in blind, stupid beliefs that understanding will always be repaid in kind, a production reinforcing Mencken's jaundiced view that "It is a sin to think evil of others but it is seldom a mistake."

p, Arthur Cohn; d, Marc Grunebaum; w, Bernard Stora, Peter Krall, Magdeleine Dailloux, Grunebaum; ph, Luciano Tovoli; m, Michel Portal; ed, Kenout Peltier.

Drama **(PR:O MPAA:NR)**

ADORABLE ½** (1933) 87m FOX bw

Janet Gaynor *(The Girl)*, Henry Garat *(The Young Man)*, C. Aubrey Smith, *(The Prime Minister)*, Herbert Mundin *(The Detective)*, Blanche Frederici *(The Countess)*, Hans von Twardowski *(The Prince)*.

Princess Gaynor (posing as a manicurist) is attracted to a lowly lieutenant, Garat, whom she elevates through the ranks to general, then prince, making him a peer and eligible for marriage in the mythical kingdom of Hipsburgy-Legstadt. This light operetta is pure escapism and pleasing to the ear, with such songs as "My First Love to Last," "My Heart's Desire," "It's All For the Best," "I Loved You Wednesday," and the title song, "Adorable," all by Werner Richard Heymann. This was a lavish Fox production with a huge cast and tons of extras, a remake of the German (UFA) production of IHRE HOHEIT BEFIEHLT (HER MAJESTY COMMANDS), but entirely rewritten as a Gaynor vehicle.

d, William Dieterle; w, George Marion, Jr., Jane Storm (based on a story by Paul Frank and Billy Wilder); ph, John Seitz; m, Werner Richard Heymann; ed, Irene Morra, R.W. Bischoff; m/l Marion and Richard Whiting; ch, Sammy Lee.

Musical/Operetta **(PR:A MPAA:NR)**

ADORABLE CREATURES* ½ (1956, Fr.) 108m CVC/CD bw

Daniel Gelin *(Andre)*, Antonella Lualdl *(Catherine)*, Danielle Darrieux *(Christians)*, Martine Carol *(Minouche)*, Edwige Feuillere *(Denise)*, Renee Faure *(Alice)*, Marilyn Bufferd *(Evelyn)*, Daniel Lecourtois *(Jacques)*, Louis Selgner *(M. Dubreuil)*, Marie Glory *(Catherine's Mother)*, Georges Chamarat *(Catherine's Father)*, Jean-Marc Tennberg *(Pianist)*.

French sex farce goes far out of its way to present a host of shapely female bodies in various stages of undress. After Gelin tells his wife she's the only woman he has ever loved, several flashbacks reveal his myriad affairs. His conquests include Martine Carol as a materialistic money-grubber; Darrieux, a married woman cheating on her husband (who does a near-raw striptease); Feuillere, a sex-starved widow enticing lovers under the guise of a Maecenas, and more. Too much to be believable as anything other than a rather tawdry burlesque.

p, Jacques Roitfeld; d, Christian-Jaque; w, Charles Spaak, Jacques Companeez, Christian-Jaque; ph, Christian Matras; m, de Van Parys; ed, Jacques Desagneaux.

Satire/Comedy **(PR:O MPAA:NR)**

ADORABLE JULIA** (1964, Fr./Aust.) 97m Films-Etoile/JMR bw

Lili Palmer *(Julia)*, Charles Boyer *(Michel)*, Jean Sorel *(Tom)*, Jeanne Valerie *(Aive)*.

A famous but aging actress, Palmer, has a fling with a young lover but realizes it will be her last when she finally appreciates her tolerant, kind husband, Boyer. Sorel is the stoic lover and is about as appealing as a waste can. Corny around all the edges.

p, Wisner Mundus; d, Alfred Wiedemann; w, Marc-Gilbert Sauvajon, Guy Bolton, Pascal Jardin (based on the play by Somerset Maugham); ph, Werner Krien; ed, A. Wilhelm.

Comedy **(PR:C MPAA:NR)**

ADORABLE LIAR* ½

(1962, Fr.) 110m Elefilm/RIVERS bw (ADORABLE MENTEUSE)

Marina Vlady *(Juliette)*, Macha Meryl *(Sophie)*, Jean-Marc Bory *(Martin)*, Michel Vitold *(Tartuffe)*, Claude Nicot *(Sebastian)*, Jean-Francois Calve *(Brevant)*.

Capricious young woman flaunts her ability to lie, especially to lovers, believing that the more flamboyant the fabrication the more feminine her inner character will become, an absurd notion that disgusts her 40-year-old neighbor, a man she finally sets out to trap and does. A lighthearted but woefully lightweight production that will hold interest for only the first twenty-five minutes.

p, Fernand Rivers; d, Michel Deville; w, Nina Companeez, Deville; ph, Claude Lecomte; ed, Companeez.

Comedy **(PR:C MPAA:NR)**

ADRIFT* ½ (1971, Czech.), 108m MPO c

Rade Markovic *(Yanos)*, Milena Dravic *(Zuzka)*, Paula Pritchett *(Anada)*, Josef Kroner *(Stutterer)*, Vlado Muller *(Helmsman)*, Gustav Valach *(Balthazar)*, Ivan Darvas *(Kristof)*, Jaroslav Marvan *(Father-in-law)*, Janko Boldis *(Peter)*, Dezso Kiraly *(Doctor)*.

A moody slice of rustic life where a rigidly moral fisherman, Markovic, saves a naked girl from drowning and later suppresses his sexual attraction for her. This leads to raging jealousy whenever another man pays the slightest attention to her, and, after neglecting his wife's illness, guilt for the woman's death. The girl, Pritchett, is wholly oblivious to her rescuer's passion and goes about exuding as much life as a burnt-out coal. She falls into the river again and drowns, this time the fisherman watching her sink out of sight without making a move to help her. An undecided ending to a dismal story, one that should have been better from Kadar, the director of THE ANGEL LEVINE.

p, Julius Potocsny; d, Jan Kadar; w, Imre Gyongyossy, Elmar Klos, Kadar (based on the novel *Something Is Adrift in the Water* by Lajos Zilahy); ph, Vladimir Novotny; m, Zdenek Liska; ed, Josef Valusiak, Mihaly Morrell.

Drama **(PR:O MPAA:NR)**

ADULTERESS, THE**

(1959, Fr.) 105m Times Film Corp. bw (AKA: THERESE RAQUIN)

Simone Signoret *(Therese)*, Raf Vallone *(Laurent)*, Jacques Duby *(Camille)*, Roland Lesaffre *(The Sailor)*, Sylvie *(Mme. Raquin)*.

Housewife Signoret tires of her spineless husband and trysts with a brutal truckdriver, the two later conspiring to murder the spouse on a train. Vallone, as the truckdriver, kills the hapless husband, and the murder is witnessed by Lesaffre. He tries to blackmail the murderous pair and is killed for his pains. A poor, bleak portrait of a sordid, uninteresting affair that does a disservice to a powerful Zola novel.

d, Marcel Carne; w, Charles Spaak, Carne (based on the novel *Therese Raquin* by Emile Zola).

Crime **Cas.** **(PR:O MPAA:NR)**

ADULTEROUS AFFAIR zero

(1966, Can.) 84m Independent Film Artists/Executive Films-Manson bw (AKA: ROOM FOR A STRANGER; THE LOVE BLACKMAILER)

Jean Christopher *(Barbara)*, Bruce Gray *(Russ Taren)*, Sean Sullivan *(Frank)*, Faith Gardiner *(Lola)*, Brian James *(Stephen)*, Linda Gillespie *(Receptionist)*, Gillian Taylor *(Tina)*, Jean Cavall *(Telephone Man)*, Tony Pacioni *(Client)*.

Rancid potboiler starring Gray as a seedy blackmailer who photographs married woman Christopher having an affair while vacationing in Niagara Falls. Gray confronts Christopher with the pictures and tells her that he will show them to her husband unless she has sex with him. Luckily Gray is soon murdered by one of his other victims, putting an end to the nonsense.

p, Jack Ennis; d&w, Ted Leversuch (based on a story by Margot Stevens); ph, Stanley Lipinski; ed&md, John Bath; art d, Peter Douett; makeup, Peggy Stevens.

Drama **(PR:A MPAA:NR)**

ADVANCE TO THE REAR ½**

(1964) 97m MGM bw (GB: COMPANY OF COWARDS?)

Glenn Ford *(Capt Jared Heath)*, Stella Stevens *(Martha Lou)*, Melvyn Douglas *(Col. Claude Brackenby)*, Jim Backus *(Gen. Willoughby)*, Joan Blondell *(Jenny)*, Andrew Prine *(Pvt. Owen Selous)*, Jesse Pearson *(Cpl. Silas Geary)*, Alan Hale *(Sgt. Beauregard Davis)*, James Griffith *(Hugo Zattig)*, Whit Bissell *(Capt Queeg)*, Michael Pate *(Thin Elk)*, Yvonne Craig *(Ora)*, Chuck Roberson *(Monk)*, Bill Troy *(Fulton)*, Frank Mitchell *(Belmont)*, J. Lewis Smith *(Slasher O'Toole)*, Preston Foster *(Gen. Bateman)*, Harlan Warde *(Maj. Hayward)*, Allen Pinson *(Pvt. Long)*, Sugar Geise *(Mamie)*, Linda Jones *(Junie)*, Britta Ekman *(Greta)*, Paul Langton *(Maj. Forsythe)*, Charles Horvath *(Jones)*, Mary LeBow *(Mary)*, Joe Brooks *(Bannerman)*, Richard Adams *(Courier)*, Eddie Quillan *(Smitty)*, Paul Smith, Barnaby Hale *(Lieutenants)*, Harvey Stephens *(Gen. Dunlap)*, Robert Carson *(Col. Holbert)*, Janos Phohaska *(Flag Pole Sitter)*, Clegg Hoyt, John Day *(Loafers)*, Towyna Thomas *(Law and Order League)*, Sailor Vincent *(Deckhand)*, Bob Anderson *(Steamer Captain)*, Gregg Palmer *(Gambler)*, Kathryn Hart, Ann Blake *(League Ladies)*, Peter Ford *(Townsman)*, Ken Wales *(Lieutenant Aide)*.

Very funny film about a company of Union Army misfits during the Civil War with Douglas as the hard-headed, by-the-book commanding officer and Ford as his frustrated second-in-command. The bumbling men go through impossible antics, including an attack against Confederate troops without guns (they wind up hurling rocks at their foes). Stevens plays a sexy shady lady working for madam Blondell but she is really a Southern spy. Veteran western director Marshall does a quick-paced job on a sprightly script.

p, Ted Richmond; d, George Marshall; w, Samuel A. Peeples, William Bowers (based on the novel *The Company of Cowards* by Jack Schaefer); ph, Milton Krasner (Panavision); m, Randy Sparks; ed, Archie Marshek; art d, George W. Davis, Eddie Imazu; set d, Henry Grace, Budd S. Friend.

Comedy **(PR:A MPAA:NR)**

ADVENTURE*** (1945) 130m MGM bw

Clark Gable *(Harry Patterson)*, Greer Garson *(Emily Sears)*, Joan Blondell *(Helen Melohn)*, Thomas Mitchell *(Mudgin)*, Tom Tully *(Gus)*, John Qualen *(Model T)*, Richard Haydn *(Limo)*, Lina Romay *(Maria)*, Philip Merivale *("Old" Ramon Estado)*, Harry Davenport *(Dr. Ashlon)*, Tito Renaldo *("Young" Ramon Estado)*, Pedro de Cordoba *(Felipe)*, Chef Joseph Milani *(Rudolfo)*, Martin Garralaga *(Nick)*, Dorothy Granger *(Cashier)*, Elizabeth Russell, Barbara Billingsley, Rebel Randall, Sue Moore *(Dames)*, Esther Howard *(Blister)*, Florence Auer *(Landlady)*, Eddie Hart *(Milkman)*, Lee Phelps *(Bartender)*, Morris Ankrum *(Mr. Ludlow)*, Martha Wentworth *(Woman)*, Byron Foulger *(Rico)*, Audrey Totter *(Littleton)* Rex Ingram *(Black Preacher)*, Kay Medford *(Red)*, Stanley Andrews *(Officer)*, Bess Flowers *(Modiste)*, Tom Kingston *(Chip Man)*, Sayre Dearing *(Roulette Man)*, Claire McDowell.

This was Gable's first film after being mustered out of the Air Force following WW II (where he flew many missions over Germany and was decorated for heroism), and MGM ballyhooed its greatest star with an enourmous publicity campaign, headed with the slogan: "Gable's back and Garson's got him!" It wasn't the old boyish Gable of pranks or young anger but a seasoned man who had lived deeply his recent service years; it showed on his face and in his mannerisms but his role was tailor-made, that of a roughneck seaman who had been around the world and had the traditional girl in every port, but never a girl like Garson, a reserved, beautiful librarian whom he meets in a San Francisco library when trying to look up a history of the human soul for his friend and shipmate, Mitchell, superbly playing a superstitious Irishman who believes his soul "went up Powell Street," fleeing his body after a knife fight. The boisterous, freewheeling Gable sweeps Garson off her feet, as they used to say, in a dizzy courtship but then leaves her to sail away on another freighter. He returns to find her pregnant and gone to the old farm homestead to await the birth of their child; her friend Blondell gives him a ranting piece of her mind in the best scene of her small part. Gable does the right thing and settles down with Garson in a ramshackle house which he proceeds to renovate, but there is resentment on his part for being landlocked, a sullen attitude that does not change until the birth of the child. Here is one of the most moving portraits in any Gable film, the old country doctor, Davenport, struggling to bring a weak baby to life, an infant finally clutched desperately by father Gable who passionately talks him into breathing, into filling his lungs with that first sweet breath, a speech happily heard by an exhausted Garson in the next room that tells her that her wandering husband is home to stay, a little celluloid miracle worth the entire film. Critics at the time of the film's release universally and wrongly panned this light-hearted production, most likely expecting the old Gable of BOOM TOWN and TEST PILOT and disappointed at the middleaged man before them, playing opposite a sophisticated Garson instead of a steamy Lamarr or Turner (Garson enacted her role to perfection), but then what do critics know about everyday people, the birthing of babies, and the wellsprings of the human heart?

p, Sam Zimbalist; d, Victor Fleming; w, Frederick Hazlitt Brennan, Vincent Lawrence (based on the novel by Clyde Brion Davis); ph, Joseph Ruttenberg; m, Herbert Stothart; ed, Frank Sullivan; art d, Cedric Gibbons, Urie McCleary; set d, Edwin B. Willis; spec eff, Warren Newcombe.

Adventure/Drama **(PR:A MPAA:NR)**

ADVENTURE FOR TWO***

(1945, Brit.) 115m Two Cities/GFD bw (GB: DEMI-PARADISE, THE)

Laurence Olivier *(Ivan Dimitrevitch Kouzenetsoff)*, Penelope Dudley Ward *(Ann Tisdall)*, Marjorie Fielding *(Mrs. Tisdall)*, Margaret Rutherford *(Rowena Ventnor)*, Felix Aylmer *(Mr. Runalow)*, George Thorpe *(Herbert Tisdall)*, Leslie Henson *(Himself)*, Guy Middleton *(Richard Christie)*, Michael Shepley *(Mr. Walford)*, Edie Martin *(Miss Winnifred Tisdall, Aunt Winnie)*, Muriel Aked *(Mrs. Tisdall-Stanton)*, Jack Watling *(Tom Sellars)*, Joyce Grenfell *(Mrs. Pawson)*, Everley Gregg *(Mrs. Flannel)*, Aubrey Mallalieu *(Toomes, the Butler)*, Brian Nissen *(George Tisdall)*, John Schofield *(Ernie)*, David Kerr *(Mr. Jordan)*, Miles Malleson *(Box Office Manager)*, Marian Spencer *(Mrs. Teddy Beckett)*, Josephine Middleton *(Mrs. Tremlow)*, Margaret Withers *(Mrs. Elliston)*, Beatrice Harrison *(Beatrice Harrison)*, Wilfrid Hyde-White *(Waiter)*, Inge Perten *(Russian Doctor)*, Mavis Clair *(Barmaid)*, Alexis Chesnakoff *(Russian Delegate)*, Charles Paton *(Mr. Bishop)*, John Laurie, John Boxer *(British Sailors)*, George Street, Ben Williams *(Hecklers)*.

Olivier reaches down into his actor's bag of tricks and clutches another fascinating character, a Russian scientist who has invented an amazing propeller for ice breakers, a foreigner in a strange 1939 England, surrounded by customs, habits and people who prove all too perplexing to his Eastern European mind, a marvelous and wholly committed characterization that allows the viewer to see the reserved English through immigrant eyes. His landlady is hostile, those on the street are cold and guarded against him. When Olivier returns again in 1941, with his country and England united as allies against Nazi Germany, it is a completely different portrait, a people exuding warmth and friendship in the common cause. This strenuous role masterfully presented by one of the world's greatest actors was the first to really bring him into the ranks of that stellar group known later as superstars.

p&w, Anatole de Grunwald; d, Anthony Asquith; ph, Bernard Knowles; m, Nicholas Brodszky; ed, Jack Harris, Renee Woods; art d, Paul Sheriff, Carmen Dillon.

Drama **(PR:A MPAA:NR)**

ADVENTURE IN BALTIMORE½**

(1949) 89m RKO bw (GB: BACHELOR BAIT)

Robert Young *(Dr. Sheldon)*, Shirley Temple *(Dinah Sheldon)*, John Agar *(Tom Wade)*, Albert Sharpe *(Mr. Fletcher)*, Josephine Hutchinson *(Mrs. Sheldon)*, Charles Kemper *(Mr. Steuben)*, Johnny Sands *(Gene Sheldon)*, John Miljan *(Mr. Eckert)*, Norma Varden *(H. H. Hamilton)*, Carol Brannan *(Bernice Eckert)*, Charles Smith *(Fred Beehouse)*, Josephine Whittell *(Mrs. Eckert)*, Patti Brady *(Sis Sheldon)*, Gregory Marshall *(Mark Sheldon)*, Patsy Creighton *(Sally Wilson)*.

Packed with charm and warm family appeal, this film has Young as a youthful minister whose daughter, Temple, undergoes the painful and delightful (depending upon your perspective) transition from teenager to young woman: in a splendid waltz contest scene where she dances with her proud father, in another scene where Young chastises her for spreading rumors, and in a speech she delivers to stoic parishioners, one prepared by suitor Agar (her real life husband), wherein she shockingly, for that day, changes it into a women's rights diatribe. A consistently pleasing film.

p, Richard H. Berger; d, Richard Wallace; w, Lionel Houser (based on a story by Lesser Samuels, Christopher Isherwood); ph, Robert de Grasse; m, Frederick Hollander; ed, Robert Swink.

Comedy **(PR:AAA MPAA:NR)**

ADVENTURE IN BLACKMAIL**

(1943, Brit.) 70m Brit. Mercury/MGM bw (GB: BREACH OF PROMISE)

Clive Brook *(Peter Conroy)*, Judy Campbell *(Pamela Lawrence)*, C. V. France *(Morgan)*, Marguerite Allan *(Pamela Rose)*, Percy Walsh *(Saxon Rose)*, Dennis Arundell *(Philip)*, George Merritt *(The Professor)*, David Horne *(Sir Hamar)*, Charles Victor *(Sir William)*, Aubrey Mallalieu *(Judge)*, Tony Bazell *(Rex)*.

Playwright Brook is sued for breach of promise by Campbell but during the trial the accused, more out of compassion for the pleading young lady than a sense of guilt, shortcuts the verdict by agreeing to marry her. Following the nuptials, the pair go at it with bitter resentment for each other but they soften in one little truce after another until love becomes deep-rooted. Production values are on the shabby side but Brook's suave performance lifts the film above condemnation.

p, Richard Norton, Michael Brooke; d, Harold Huth, Roland Pertwee; w, Pertwee (based on a story by Emeric Pressburger); ph, Jack Cox; ed, Sidney Cole.

Romance **(PR:A MPAA:NR)**

ADVENTURE IN DIAMONDS½** (1940) 72m PAR bw

George Brent *(Capt. Stephen Bennett)*, Isa Miranda *(Felice Barclay)*, John Loder *(Michael Barclay)*, Nigel Bruce *(Col. J. W. Lansfield)*, Elizabeth Patterson *(Nellie)*, Matthew Boulton *(Lloyd)*, Rex Evans *(Jimmy)*, Cecil Kellaway *(Emerson)*, Walter Kingsford *(Wakefield)*, Ernest Truex *(Toutasche)*, Ralpi Forbes *(Mr. Perrins)*, Nikolayeva *(Mrs. Perrins)*, E. E. Clive *(Mr. Macpherson)*, Vera Lewis *(Mrs. Macpherson)*, Edward Gargan *(Lou)*, Charles Irwin *(Nelson)*, David Clyde *(Bartender)*, Rex Downing *(Buttons)*, Guy Bellis, Norman Ainsley *(Immigration Officers)*, Hi Roberts *(Bellhop)*, Major Sam Harris *(Bill)*, Roger Gray *(Sergeant at Airport)*, Wilfred Roberts *(Man)*, Carleton Young *(Sailor)*, Ambrose Barker *(Customs Official)*.

Loder and Miranda (her second American production following HOTEL IMPERIAL) arrive in South Africa to smuggle out a cache of diamonds but Brent, a government agent, plays a subtle game after falling in love with Miranda, pretending to help her obtain the gems, finally revealing his identity and enlisting her aid in rounding up the masterminds of the scheme. The pace is a bit slow and the script pockmarked with cliches but it's still an enjoyable cat-and-mouse film.

p, A. M. Botsford; d, George Fitzmaurice; w, Leonard Lee, Franz Schulz (based on a story by Frank O'Connor); ph, Charles Land, Jr.; ed, LeRoy Stone.

Crime **(PR:A MPAA:NR)**

ADVENTURE IN MANHATTAN½**

(1936) 73m COL bw (GB: MANHATTAN MADNESS)

Jean Arthur *(Clarie Peyton)*, Joel McCrea *(George Melville)*, Reginald Owen *(Blackton Gregory)*, Thomas Mitchell *(Phil Bane)*, Herman Bing *(Tim)*, Victor Killian *(Mark Gibbs)*, John Gallaudet *(McGuire)*, Emmet Vogan *(Lorimer)*, George Cooper *(Duncan)*, Robert Warwick *(Phillip)*.

Art connoisseur and criminologist McCrea is hired to track down art thieves, assisted by perky Arthur and goaded by Mitchell, the roaring newspaper editor who has employed him. The first 20 minutes zip along but the film then bogs down into some arcane dialog about art and jewel treasures, only to pick up for a slam-bang finale where the mastermind poses as a theatrical impresario who stages a war drama replete with loud explosions to divert attention from his band of thieves who are cracking safes in a bank adjacent to the theater. Lively *film noir*.

d, Edward Ludwig; w, Sidney Buchman, Harry Sauber, Jack Kirkland (based on the novel *Purple and Fine Linen* by May Dington); ph, Henry Freulich; ed, Otto Meyer.

Crime **(PR:A MPAA:NR)**

ADVENTURE IN ODESSA** (1954, USSR) 76m Kiev Film/ARTKINO c

Misha Mokrinsky *(Gleb)*, Mikhall Kuznetsov *(Belov)*, Anatoli Shimanyuk *(Vasya)*, Volodya Luschik *(Vadim)*, E. Samoilov *(Gleb's Father)*, Volodva Sudin *(Kolya)*, Natasha Morel *(Nina)*, I. Peltser *(Old Fisherman)*, A. Antomov *(Farm Chairman)*.

What begins as an interesting and sometimes provocative children's movie, where a group of Russian youngsters and their professor find a partially sunken gunboat and begin rebuilding it, is converted to film propaganda when the boat project is taken over by government directors who regiment the children's efforts to military precision, typically eliminating individual ambitions for the collective goal. (If the indoctrinating commissars could have kept their grubby hands off apparently good scripts, the Russian film archives would presently contain the exceptional instead of the politically predictable).

d, Lev Atamanov; w, Georgi Grebner (based on a story by Sergei Akasakov).

Adventure **(PR:C MPAA:NR)**

ADVENTURE IN SAHARA** (1938) 60m COL bw

Paul Kelly *(Jim Wilson)*, C. Henry Gordon *(Captain Savatt)*, Lorna Gray *(Carla Preston)*, Robert Fiske *(Lieutenant Dumond)*, Marc Lawrence *(Poule)*, Dick Curtis *(Karnoldl)*, Stanley Brown *(Rene Malrequx)*, Alan Bridge *(Corporal Dronov)*, Raphael Bennett *(Ladoux)*, Charles Moore *(Gungadin)*, Dwight Frye *(Gravet)*, Stanley Andrews *(Colonel Rancreux)*.

Gordon, in his usual typecast role of cruel overlord, here commands a detachment of Foreign Legionnaires with such brutality that he is sent at gunpoint by his men into the desert with a few loyal soldiers and scant supplies to fend for himself or perish (not unlike the legendary Capt. Bligh of MUTINY ON THE BOUNTY), but he vows to reach civilization and return for vengeance, which he does. When he and his men arrive at the desert outpost it is besieged by killer Arabs (the desert dwellers of the 1930s and 1940s films never seem to do anything other than attack isolated outposts and innocent caravans). Gordon and his men are mercifully allowed into the little fort to help beat back the attackers and Kelly and company are later decorated for bravery, then court-martialed for mutiny. Gordon is ultimately labeled a tyrant by Fiske, his aide, and properly punished. A routine, low-budget programmer with some exciting moments.

d, D. Ross Lederman; w, Maxwell Shane (based on a story by Samuel Fuller); ph, Frank Planer; ed, Otto Meyer; md, M. W. Stoloff.

Adventure **(PR:A MPAA:NR)**

ADVENTURE IN THE HOPFIELDS½**

(1954, Brit.) 60m Vandyke-Children's Film Foundation/ABF bw

Mandy Miller *(Jenny Quin)*, Mona Washbourne *(Mrs. McBain)*, Hilda Fenemore *(Mrs. Quin)*, Russell Waters *(Mr. Quin)*, Melvyn Hayes *(Reilly)*, Harold Lang *(Sam Hines)*, Wallas Eaton *(Postman)*, Leon Garcia, Molly Osborne, Jane Asher, Edward Judd.

After she breaks her mother's prized porcelain dog, Miller takes a job picking hops to pay for a replacement. She earns enough to buy a new one, but it is stolen by some other children. She chases the thieves to an old mill, where they capture her and tie her up. Lightning strikes the decrepit structure and sets it afire, but the hooligans return to rescue the young heroine just in time. Above-average children's film, with believable characters and story.

p, Roger Proudlock; d, John Guillermin; w, John Cresswell (based on the novel *The Hop Dog* by Nora Lavin and Molly Thorp); ph, Kenneth Talbot.

Children **(PR:AA MPAA:NR)**

ADVENTURE IN WASHINGTON** (1941) 82m COL bw

Herbert Marshall *(Senator John Coleridge)*, Virginia Bruce *(Jane Scott)*, Gene Reynolds *(Marty Driscoll)*, Samuel S. Hinds *(Senator Henry Owen)*, Ralph Morgan *(Senator Cummings)*, Vaughan Glaser *(Bundy)*, Charles Smith *(Collins)*, Dickie

Jones *(Abbott)*, Pierre Watkin *(Frank Conroy)*, J. M. Kerrigan *(Jim O'Brien)*, Tommy Bond *(Peewee Haynes)*, Billy Dawson *(Chubby Wells)*, Charles Lind *(Lenny Root)*, Mary Currier *(Miss Nolan)*.

A contrived plot with Marshall as a overindulgent senator and Bruce as his contrary girl friend, a radio personality running gossip over the airways, focuses upon the Senate pages and one little bounder who is selling government secrets to manipulating stockbrokers who, in turn, clean up in the billions. Marshall takes it upon himself to reform the wayward page, Reynolds. This is achieved when senators oversee a mock trial by the other pages who exonerate Reynolds for treasonable activities, as far-fetched a film as desperate Columbia scribes could manufacture. In reality, the page would be bounced onto the street, if not into prison. A thankless role for the expert Marshall, as were those enacted by Morgan, Hinds and Glaser, the latter being the too saintly major domo of the pages.

p, Charles R. Rogers; d, Alfred E. Green; w, Lewis R. Foster, Arthur Caesar; ph, Henry Sharp; ed, James Sweeney.

Drama **(PR:C MPAA:NR)**

ADVENTURE ISLAND*½ (1947) 66m PAR c

Rory Calhoun *(Mr. Herrick)*, Rhonda Fleming *(Faith Wishart)*, Paul Kelly *(Capt. Lochlin)*, John Abbott *(Mr. Hulsh)*, Alan Napier *(Mr. Atwater)*.

Filmed in Cinecolor with eye-catching tropical scenes, the story is a remake of EBB TIDE where three beachcombers, Kelly, Calhoun and Abbott, sign on board a small ship en route to Australia, its cargo, they later discover, being champagne which is really water. The ship anchors at a remote island for supplies and here the adventurers, along with fetching Fleming, encounter a lunatic, Napier, who rules the natives as a god-like figure, a murderous tyrant who kills Kelly and Abbott before being driven into a snake pit by Calhoun who sails off with Fleming. Low budget and poor script add up to a few captivating scenes, but mostly a dull trek through the foliage.

p, William Pine, William Thomas; d, Peter Stewart; w, Maxwell Shane (based on *Ebb Tide* by Robert Louis Stevenson); ph, Jack Greenhalgh (Cinecolor); m, Darrell Calker; ed, Howard Smith.

Adventure **(PR:A MPAA:NR)**

ADVENTURE LIMITED* (1934, Brit.) 69m B&D/PAR bw

Harry Milton *(Kim Berkeley)*, Pearl Argyle *(Anita Lorenzo)*, Sebastian Shaw *(Bruce Blandford)*, Sam Wilkinson *(Reginald Purdie)*, Clifford Heatherley *(Sir Matthew Muller)*, Hugh E. Wright *(Don Lorenzo/Montagu Phelps)*, Lawrence Hanray *(Simon Ledbury)*, Cecil Humphreys *(Gen Baroda)*.

Unfunny South American political farce where Wright is used to rescue his look-alike, a deposed president who has been imprisoned and awaits execution. Here the old-fashioned British music hall slapstick is in full force and will leave no one but the mindless laughing.

d, George King; w, George Dewhurst (based on the play "Trust Berkeley" by Cyril Campion).

Comedy **(PR:A MPAA:NR)**

ADVENTURE OF SALVATOR ROSA, AN½**
(1940, Ital.) 97m Stella/ESPERIA

Gino Cervi *(Salvator Rosa/Formica)*, Luisa Ferida *(Lucrezia)*, Rina Morelli *(Isabella of Torniano)*, Osvaldo Valenti *(Count of Lamberto)*, Ugo Cesari *(Giovanni)*, Umberto Sacripante *(A Peasant)*, Paolo Stoppa *(Another Peasant)*, Carlo Duse *(The Captain)*, Enzo Billotti *(Viceroy)*.

Rollicking action-packed Robin Hood of Italy story, taking place in the 17th century after the abortive Neapolitan Revolution. Cervi is the mighty Rosa, and also Formica, who leads a peasant revolt for water rights, while breaking up an ill-fated marriage between the Duchess Isabella and the dowery-lusting Count of Lamberto, Valenti, who gives a scary performance as a man consumed by greed. Cervi's portrayal mixes hero and buffoon, lover and fighter in an entertaining production.

d, Alessandro Blasetti; w, Ugo Scotti Berni, Guiseppe Zucca; ph, Berni; m, Alessandro Biasetti.

Adventure **(PR:A MPAA:NR)**

ADVENTURES OF SHERLOCK HOLMES' SMARTER BROTHER, THE****
(1975, Brit.) 91m FOX c

Gene Wilder *(Sigerson Holmes)*, Madeline Kahn *(Jenny)*, Marty Feldman *(Orville Sacker)*, Dom DeLuise *(Gambetti)*, Leo McKern *(Moriarty)*, Roy Kinnear *(Moriarty's Aide)*, John Le Mesurier *(Lord Redcliff)*, Douglas Wilmer *(Sherlock Holmes)*, Thorley Walters *(Dr. Watson)*, George Silver *(Bruner)*, Susan Field *(Queen Victoria)*.

Hilarious spoof of all the Holmes film adventures by director/writer Wilder who also stars as the utterly berserk younger brother of the great sleuth, consumed by jealousy over his brother's fame, detective acumen and mere presence in the same country. The obsessively quirkish Wilder must outdo his brother in everything, from fencing to inventions, from detecting the smallest clue to unraveling the most fiendish plot, in this case tracking down some vital state secrets that are missing and are about to fall into the clutching hands of, naturally, the evil Professor Moriarity, devilishly and deftly played by Leo McKern. Aiding the outlandishly courageous Wilder is wild-eyed Marty Feldman, a Scotland yard detective with photographic *hearing* and a mystery woman thrown in for witty non sequiturs, Kahn, in all her voluptuous pomp and puff. We tumble along with Wilder from one harrowing adventure to another as he draws ever nearer to the urgent papers, almost undone by a mad opera star, DeLuise, a total hedonist whose on-stage braying and prancing guarantees theatrical disaster. Wilder doggedly manages his job as a wholly side-splitting maniac only to be exposed as a decoy set up by his omnipotent brother (Wilmer) who has only pretended to be out of the country and has been operating behind the scenes with the venerable Watson (Walters), saving Wilder repeatedly from death and/or destruction. Both Holmes brothers triumph and so does this film, a portrait of delightful mayhem. (See SHERLOCK HOLMES series, Index.)

p, Richard A. Roth; d&w Gene Wilder; ph, Gerry Fisher; m, John Morris; ed, Jim Clark; ch, Alan Johnson; cos, Ruth Myers.

Comedy **Cas.** **(PR:AA MPAA:NR)**

ADVENTURERS, THE½**

(1951, Brit.) 86m Mayflower/RANK bw (AKA: GREAT ADVENTURE, THE; FORTUNE IN DIAMONDS)

Jack Hawkins *(Pieter Brandt)*, Peter Hammond *(Hendrik van Thaal)*, Dennis Price *(Clive Hunter)*, Gregoire Aslan *(Dominic)*, Charles Paton *(Barman)*, Siobhan McKenna *(Anne Hunter)*, Bernard Lee *(O'Connell)*, Ronald Adam *(Van Thaal)*, Martin Boddey *(Chief Engineer)*, Phillip Ray, Walter Harsburgh *(Men in Restaurant)*, Cyril Chamberlain *(Waiter)*.

Boer commando Hawkins, following the South African War in 1902, comes across a dead man whose pouch is brimming with diamonds. Thinking the war still on and that he might be taken captive and the gems confiscated, Hawkins buries the treasure and stumbles back to civilization where he learns peace has come. He enlists the aid of a disgruntled bartender, Aslan, another young Boer, Hammond, and a cashiered British officer, Price, who finances the expedition to the outback to retrieve the buried diamonds. En route, the greedy bunch fall out and attack each other, Hawkins murdering the haughty Englishman. The obsessed Hawkins then chases Hammond through a deserted gold mine where a cave-in finishes the killer, a handy retribution a la nature. Hawkins is powerful as the rugged Boer, Price is convincing as the aristocratic British victim and Hammond annoying as the apprentice Boer. McKenna's part as Hawkins' wife is a throw-away role. It is apparent that this production takes much from THE TREASURE OF THE SIERRA MADRE and from Von Stroheim's silent classic GREED but it is nevertheless an often gripping film.

d, David MacDonald; w, Robert Westerby; ph, Oswald Morris; m, Cedric Thorpe Davie; ed, V. Sagovsky.

Adventure **(PR:C MPAA:NR)**

ADVENTURERS, THE zero (1970) 171m PAR c

Bekim Fehmiu *(Dax Xenos)*, Charles Aznavour *(Marcel Campion)*, Alan Badel *(Rojo)*, Candice Bergen *(Sue Ann Daley)*, Ernest Borgnine *(Fat Cat)*, Leigh Taylor-Young *(Amparo)*, Fernando Rey *(Jaime Xenos)*, Thommy Berggren *(Sergei Nikovitch)*, Olivia de Havilland *(Deborah Hadley)*, John Ireland *(Mr. Hadley)*, Delia Boccardo *(Caroline de Coyne)*, Sydney Tafler *(Col. Gutierrez)*, Rossano Brazzi *(Baron de Coyne)*, Anna Moffo *(Dania Leonardi)*, Christian Roberts *(Robert)*, Yorgo Voyagis *(El Lobo)*, Jorge Martinez de Hoyos *(El Condor)*, Angela Scoular *(Denisonde)*, Yolanda Donlan *(Mrs. Erickson)*, Milena Vukotic *(April)*, Ferdy Mayne *(Sergei's Father)*, Jaclyn Smith *(Belinda)*, Katherine Balfour *(Roberto's Mother)*, Roberta Donatelli *(Ampara as a Child)*, Peter Graves *(Trustee Banker)*, John Frederick *(Mr. Erickson)*, Allan Cuthbertson *(Hugh)*, Zenia Merton *(Dax's Sister)*, Roberta Haynes *(Dax's Mother)*, Lois Maxwell *(Woman at Fashion Show)*, Loris Loddi *(Dax as a Child)*, Venessa Lee *(Trustee Banker's Wife)*, Michael Balfour *(Detective)*, Katia Christina *(Natalia)*, Katiushka Lanvin *(Marita)*, Nadia Scarpitia *(Giulia)*, Helen Ronee *(Lexie)*, Linda Towne *(Michelle)*, Joal Carlo *(Jose)*, Gisela Kopel *(Maid)*, David Canon *(Hadley's Secretary)*, Jose Luis Ospira *(Roberto)*, Manuelo Serrano *(Sergeant)*, Rey Vasquez *(Manuelo)*, Juan Esterlich *(Radio Announcer)*, Kiki Gonclaves *(General)*, Anthony Hickox *(Robert as a Child)*, Carl Ecklund *(Sergei as a Child)*, Christine Delit *(Brunette Girl Friend)*, Randi Lind *(Blonde Girl Friend)*, Marcus Beck *(Philippe)*.

Trash unto trash best describes this overblown, overlong, thoroughly disgusting major epic that wallows in human depravity for its own sake. Adapted from Harold Robbins' best-selling novel, a so-called *roman a clef* that describes every corrupt person who counts in South America, the film wanders after the life and times of Fehmiu, a Yugoslavian actor with no ability at all, not even the modest tool of clear speech—most times his conversation is unintelligible, garbled and swallowed, as if he were ashamed of the words the miserable script demands he utter. Here we have the story of a South American playboy who destroys everything and everybody in his path, a rapist and revolutionary, all because—and the rationale is jammed down the viewer's throat—he suffered trauma as a child, an experience that somehow is supposed to ameliorate his filthy transgressions against his fellow men. The trauma is produced during a revolution when Fehmiu witnesses the murder of his mother by bandits, his father, Rey, joining revolutionaries and, once the revolutionary leader triumphs, going to Italy with his father, a newly-appointed ambassador. In Italy Fehnmiu grows to sleazy manhood, wooing wealthy de Havilland for her money after his father is murdered by dictator Badel, his one-time friend. Naturally, the lover deserts the gullible matron once he has her money and he later marries Bergen, another wealthy girl who can't say no. Her child with Fehmiu is later killed in an accident and she turns her back on heterosexual activities, avidly pursuing lesbian love. Meanwhile, her errant husband is stirring up revolutionaries against his father's traitorous friend and trysting with any attractive female with money and/or power, which seems to be every good-looking woman in the mythical country of Corteguay; all find the swarthy Fehmiu irresistable and will sacrifice anything for him, including families, friends, home, country and self-respect. The hero ultimately avenges his father's murder by killing the dictator but is also killed by another emerging political fanatic. Blood, gore, raw and unattractive sex permeate this seemingly unending saga of the seamy side of South America which is just the way mogul Joseph E. Levine imagined it. Director Lewis Gilbert, who brought ALFIE to life, is a man without a movie, judging from his cameras and story, drowning in a mammoth budget that guarantees a completely tasteless and witless film, a digrace to the industry. (This is the film that Malcolm McDowell should have been forced to see repeatedly in A CLOCKWORK ORANGE, instead of the WW II concentration camp newsreels—it would have sent him around the bend a lot sooner.)

p&d, Lewis Gilbert; w, Michael Hastings, Gilbert (based on the novel by Harold Robbins); ph, Claude Renoir (DeLuxe Color); m, Antonio Carlos Jobim; ed, Anne V. Coates; prod d, Tony Masters,; art d, John Hoesli, Aureio Crugnola, Jack Maxted, Harry Pottle; set d, Vernon Dixon, Franco Fumagalli; cos, Ronald Paterson; spec eff, Cliff Richardson.

Adventure **(PR:O MPAA:R)**

ADVENTURES AT RUGBY (SEE: TOM BROWN'S SCHOOL DAYS, 1940)

ADVENTURE'S END*½ (1937) 68m UNIV bw

John Wayne *(Duke Slade)*, Diana Gibson *(Janet Drew)*, Moroni Olsen *(Rand Husk)*, Montagu Love *(Capt. Abner Drew)*, Maurice Black *(Blackie)*, Paul White *(Kalo)*, Cameron Hall *(Slivers)*, Patrick J. Kelly *(Matt)*, George Cleveland *(Tom)*, Oscar W. Sundholm *(Chips)*, James T. Mack *(Hooten)*, Glenn Strange *(Barzek)*, Wally Howe *(Kierce)*, Jimmie Lucas *(Flench)*, Ben Carter *(Stantial)*, Britt Wood *(Hardy)*.

Cheaply made seafaring tale offers a youthful Wayne on board a whaler as an ordinary sailor, although he is a professional pearl diver. Inside a poor script and unbelievable dialog, Duke manages to mumble a few passionate words to the captain's daughter, Gibson, whose father (Love) marries her to Wayne so that he will not have to give her hand to his brutish mate, Olson. Wayne almost single-handedly puts down a mutiny led by Olson, a task apparently more agreeable to him than being wedded. Children's fare only.

p, Trem Carr; d, Arthur Lubin; w, Ben G. Kohn, Scott Darling, Sid Sutherland (based on a story by Ben Ames Williams); ph, Gus Peterson, John Fulton; ed, Charles Craft.

Adventure **(PR:A MPAA:NR)**

ADVENTURES IN IRAQ*½ (1943) 64m WB bw

John Loder *(George Torrence)*, Ruth Ford *(Tess Torrence)*, Warren Douglas *(Doug Everett)*, Paul Cavanagh *(Sheik Ahmid Bel Nor)*, Barry Bernard *(Devins)*, Peggy Carson *(Timah)*, Bill Crago *(Captain Bill Carson)*, Martin Garralaga *(High Priest)*, Bill Edwards *(Radio Operator)*, Dick Botiller *(Patroling Guard)*, Eugene Borden *(Native Officer)*, Manuel Lopez *(Priest)*.

Routine actioner opens with Douglas flying a small plane through a storm over the desert, forced to land with his passengers, Loder and Ford, and struggle to a nearby encampment where a local sheik, Cavanagh, seizes them and holds them hostage, attempting to force the British Army to release three of his brothers who are about to be shot as Nazi spies. Before the captives meet a similar fate, a U.S. plane packed with rescuers lands nearby and saves the hero and his lady. Nothing saves this low-budget, shallow remake of THE GREEN GODDESS.

p, William Jacobs; d, D. Ross Lederman; w, George Bilson, Robert E. Kent (based on William Archer's play, "The Green Goddess"); ph, James Van Trees; ed, Clarence Kolster.

Adventure **(PR:A MPAA:NR)**

ADVENTURES IN SILVERADO**

(1948) 75m COL bw (AKA: ABOVE ALL LAWS)

William Bishop *(Driver)*, Forrest Tucker *("The Monk")*, Gloria Henry, Edgar Buchanan, Irving Bacon, Fred Sears.

Offbeat oater has stagecoach driver Bishop capturing a notorious hooded bandit known only as "The Monk," in a well-paced, often taut production ably handled by director Phil Karlson. This movie was supposedly based upon a real event recorded by Robert Louis Stevenson.

p, Ted Richmond, Robert Cohn; d, Phil Karlson; w, Kenneth Gamet, Tom Kilpatrick, Joe Pagano (based on *Silverado Squatters* by Robert Louis Stevenson); ph, Henry Freulich; ed, Henry Batista.

Western **(PR:A MPAA:NR)**

ADVENTURES OF A ROOKIE** (1943) 64m RKO bw

Wally Brown *(Jerry Miles)*, Alan Carney *(Mike Strager)*, Richard Martin *(Bob Prescott)*, Erford Gage *(Sgt. Burke)*, Margaret Landry *(Peggy Linden)*, Patti Brill *(Patsy)*, Rita Corday *(Ruth)*, Robert Anderson *(Sgt. Wilson)*, John Hamilton *(Colonel)*, Ruth Lee *(Mrs. Linden)*, Lorraine Krueger *(Eve)*, Ercelle Woods *(Margaret)*, Toddy Peterson *(Betty)*, Byron Foulger *(Mr. Linden)*.

Fairly dumb portrait of three young men drafted from various walks of life. Brown from a nightclub floor where he is performing, Carney, a hulking slug, from a shipping room, and Martin from the rich surroundings of his family mansionand their hijinks at training camp. Most of the jokes are puerile and the sight gags and pratfalls not worth a button on Chester Conklin's vest. RKO thought to pair Brown and Carney in a comedic B series but this first effort failed so miserably that executives abandoned the idea.

p, Bert Gilroy; d, Leslie Goodwins; w, Edward James (based on a story by William Bowers, M. Coates Webster); ph, Jack McKenzie; ed, Harry Marker.

Comedy **(PR:A MPAA:NR)**

ADVENTURES OF A YOUNG MAN***

(1962) 145m FOX c (AKA: HEMINGWAY'S ADVENTURES OF A YOUNG MAN)

Richard Beymer *(Nick Adams)*, Diane Baker *(Carolyn)*, Corinne Calvet *(Contessa)*, Fred Clark *(Mr. Turner)*, Dan Dailey *(Billy Campbell)*, James Dunn *(Telegrapher)*, Juano Hernandez *(Bugs)*, Arthur Kennedy *(Dr. Adams)*, Ricardo Montalban *(Major Padula)*, Susan Strasberg *(Rosanna)*, Jessica Tandy *(Mrs. Adams)*, Eli Wallach *(John)*, Edward Binns *(Brakeman)*, Whit Bissell *(Ludstrum)*, Philip Bourneuf *(Montecito)*, Paul Newman *(Ad Francis)*, Tullio Carminati *(Sig Griffi)*, Marc Cavell *(Eddy Bolton)*, Charles Fredericks *(Mayor)*, Simon Oakland *(Joe Bolton)*, Michael J. Pollard *(George)*, Pat Hogan *(Billy Tabeshaw)*.

The early short stories of Ernest Hemingway, representing some of his finest writing, centered upon his own youth, translated into the character of Nick Adams. Many of these ebullient vignettes were put together to form this often stirring, exciting film with Beymer as the wide-eyed, curious youth who begins his escapades in rural Michigan, hitting the open road to New York and some vague awaiting fame. The richness of the script is abetted by the arresting characters surrounding Beymer, making him look much better than his often wooden portrayal permits—Dailey as a drunken advance man for a cooch show for whom Beymer briefly works; promoter Clark; Montalban as an understanding Italian officer commanding Beymer in France during WW I; Wallach, one of the hospital orderlies who takes him under his wing when he becomes an ambulance corps officer; Hernandez, a kindly trainer; and the man he sticks to, the alcoholic, punch-drunk fighter, Newman, who can hardly be recognized under masterful gargoyle makeup (by Ben Nye), a shattering cameo performance where Newman took small billing just to enact the impossible role of Ad Francis whom Hemingway featured in "The Battler." Beymer meets the has-been pug on the open road and is warmly invited by Newman to join him and Hernandez at their campsite, sharing their meager food. The awe-struck Beymer thinks of the decrepit fighter as a hero. After a nap, Newman awakens with a murderous look, forgetting Beymer is a guest, accusing him of stealing his food, looking upon him as a strange interloper. Before he can attack the befuddled youth, Hernandez knocks out his fighter from behind with a skillet lid to protect the youth from harm. This sequence is worth the whole film, which later falls off in pace and almost comes to a standstill when Beymer, wounded in Europe, falls in love with an ill-starred nurse, Strasberg, whose performance exudes nothing more than a million-mile stare and a consistent monotone delivery which further infects Beymer's own lackluster performance, much to the discredit of director Ritt. The screenplay by Hotchner is slick, a good copy in dialog of the clipped Hemingway style, but then he had the master's original work from which to cull his scenes. The Waxman score is uplifting and moving and kudos go to cameraman Garmes for his crisp photography, proving him to be one of the sharpest lensmen in the business.

p, Jerry Wald; d, Martin Ritt; w, A. E. Hotchner (based on stories by Ernest Hemingway); ph, Lee Garmes (CinemaScope, DeLuxe Color); m, Franz Waxman; ed, Hugh S. Fowler; art d, John Martin Smith, Paul Groesse; set d, Walter M. Scott, Robert Priestley; cos, Don Feld.

Adventure/Drama **(PR:A MPAA:NR)**

ADVENTURES OF ARSENE LUPIN½**

(1956, Fr./Ital.) 103m Chavane/SNE/Gaumont c

Robert Lamoureux, O. E. Hasse, Lisolotte Pulver, Henri Rolland.

Slick thief commits several amazing jewel robberies in 1912 Germany with Lamoureux as the famous miscreant Lupin who seems justified in robbing the Kaiser's coffers.

p, Robert Sussfeld; d, Jacques Becker; w, Albert Simonin, Becker (based on stories by Maurice Leblanc); ph, Edmond Sechan; art d, Rino Mondellini.

Crime **(PR:A MPAA:NR)**

ADVENTURES OF BARRY McKENZIE*

(1972, Austral.) 117m LONGFORD c

Barry Crocker *(Barry McKenzie)*, Barry Humphries *(Edna Everage/Hoot/Barry Humphries)*, Paul Bertram *(Curly)*, Dennis Price *(Mr. Gort)*, Avice Landon *(Mrs. Gort)*, Peter Cook *(Dominic)*, Mary Anne Severne *(Lesley)*, Dick Bentley *(Detective)*, Spike Milligan *(Landlord)*, Jonathan Hardy *(Groove Courtenay)*, Julie Covington *(Blanche)*, Jenny Tomasin *(Sarah Gort)*, Chris Malcolm *(Sean)*, Judith Furze *(Claude)*, Maria O'Brien *(Caroline Thighs)*, John Joyce *(Maurie Miller)*, Margo Lloyd *(Mrs. McKenzie)*.

Thought to be chic when first released, this Australian import follows a brash young stand-up comic strip character on a visit to England and the zanies he encounters during his solo nightclub stands. Price, as Mr. Gort, a shell-shocked war victim, runs about dressed as a small boy with a stick, asking to be whipped for being disobedient. This kind of humor might edify bush country yokels used to hardscrabble violence but such cruel roles are about as humorous as a person being run over by a truck. There are a few laughs but these will mostly come from the throats of sophomores.

p, Phillip Adams; d, Bruce Beresford; w, Beresford, Barry Humphries (based on the comic strip "The Wonderful World of Barry McKenzie" by Humphries, Nicholas Garland); ph, Don McAlpine (Eastmancolor); m, Peter Best; ed, John Scott; cos, June Hamilton.

Comedy **(PR:C-O MPAA:NR)**

ADVENTURES OF BULLWHIP GRIFFIN, THE***

(1967) 110m Disney/BV c

Roddy McDowall *(Bullwhip Griffin)*, Suzanne Pleshette *(Arabella Flagg)*, Karl Malden *(Judge Higgins)*, Harry Guardino *(Sam Trimble)*, Bryan Russell *(Jack Flagg)*, Richard Haydn *(Quentin Bartlett)*, Liam Redmond *(Capt. Swain)*, Hermione Baddeley *(Irene Chesney)*, Cecil Kellaway *(Mr. Pemberton)*, Joby Baker *(Bandido Leader)*, Mike Mazurki *(Mountain Ox)*, Alan Carney *(Joe Turner)*, Parley Baer *(Chief Executioner)*, Arthur Hunnicutt *(Referee)*, Dub Taylor *(Timekeeper)*, Pedro Gonzalez-Gonzalez *(Bandido)*, Burt Mustin, Gil Lamb, John Qualen, Dave Willock.

Happy Disney effort for all the family shows McDowall, as a prim and proper butler in love with Pleshette to the point where he embarked on an ocean trip from Boston to California, with Pleshette at his side, to find Russell, her young brother, who has run away to the Gold Rush to seek his fortune. Once in the Golden State the Easterners are confronted with marvelous villains such as Malden, Guardino and Mazurki. (Baker, as a broadly played Mexican bandit, is particularly humorous.) To make ends meet Pleshette becomes a dancehall girl, singing for her supper, rescued from brutes by McDowall who performs with Mazurki an acrobatic, well-choreographed fist fight. The brother is finally found and the happy clan end together in an above-average entertaining film.

p, Walt Disney, Bill Anderson; d, James Neilson; w, Lowell S. Hawley (based on "By the Great Horn Spoon" by Sid Fleischman); ph, Edward Colman; m, George Bruns; cos, Bill Thomas; ch, Alex Plasschaert; m/l, Bruns, Mel Leven, Robert B. and Richard M. Sherman.

Adventure/Comedy **(PR:AAA MPAA:NR)**

ADVENTURES OF CAPTAIN FABIAN** (1951) 100m REP bw

Errol Flynn *(Capt. Fabian)*, Micheline Presle *(Lea Marriotte)*, Vincent Price *(George Brissac)*, Agnes Moorehead *(Jezebel)*, Victor Francen *(Henri Brissac)*, Jim Gerald *(Constable Gilpin)*, Helena Manson *(Mme. Pierrott)*, Howard Vernon *(Emil)*, Roger Blin *(Phillipe)*, Valentine Camax *(Housekeeper)*, Georges Flateau *(Judge Brissac)*, Zanie Campan *(Cynthia Winthrop)*, Reggie Nalder *(Constant)*, Charles Fawcett *(Defense Attorney)*, Aubrey Bower *(Mate)*.

Sea captain Flynn falls for Presle, a servant girl with ambitions in early-day New Orleans; she uses him to advance herself into rich households and manages an introduction to Price, a spineless dandy who marries her and, at her goading, kills his uncle for riches, a murder with which Flynn is charged. He escapes imprisonment, making it back to his ship, Presle at his side. As mobs close in on the hero and his crew at dosckside, a cache of ammunition explodes and kills the vixen Presle whose dead body is carried away by Flynn amidst debris and flames. One of Flynn's poorer efforts and done near the end of his career, the second production in cooperation with William Marshall and Flynn, another financial disaster for the great swashbuckler.

p&d, William Marshall; w, Flynn (and, uncredited, Charles Gross, based on the novel, *Fabulous Ann Madlock* by Robert Shannon); ph, Marcel Grignon; m, Rene Cloerec; ed, Henri Taverna; set d, Eugene Lourie, Max Douy; cos, Arlington Valles.

Adventure Cas. (PR:A MPAA:NR)

ADVENTURES OF CASANOVA** (1948) 83m EL bw

Arturo De Cordova *(Casanova)*, Lucille Bremer *(Lady Bianca)*, Turhan Bey *(Lorenzo)*, John Sutton *(Count de Brissac)*, George Tobias *(Jacopo)*, Noreen Nash *(Zanetta)*, Lloyd Corrigan *(D'Albernasi)*, Fritz Lieber *(D'Anneci)*.

Routine action programmer offers a rather hammy De Cordova playing a Robin Hood role in 1793 Sicily, battling the oppressive Austrian occupiers and wooing a host of love-starved ladies; he is sometimes exceptional in the partisan attacks and wields a mean blade in well-choreographed swordfights. John Sutton is at his oily tongued best as an insidious envoy of the Austrian monarch and Bremer is a convincing femme lead. Highlight of the film is a 10-minute swordfight between De Cordova and Sutton with the latter ultimately pierced through the middle. Bey and Tobias as the great lover's sidekicks are intriguing, the former for his exotic mannerisms, the latter for his funny bumbling and mouthing an accent that would be acceptable only in contemporary Brooklyn.

p, Leonard S. Picker (Bryan Foy); d, Roberto Galvadon; w, Crane Wilbur, Walter Bullock, Karen de Wolf; ph, John Greenhaigh; m, Hugo Friedhofer; ed, Louis H. Sachin.

Adventure/Romance (PR:A MPAA:NR)

ADVENTURES OF DON COYOTE** (1947) 65m Comet/UA c

Richard Martin *(Don Coyote)*, Frances Rafferty *(Maggie)*, Marc Cramer *(Dave)*, Val Carlo *(Sancho)*, Benny Bartlett *(Ted)*, Frank Fenton *(Big Foot)*, Byron Foulger *(Felton)*, Edwin Parker *(Joe)*, Pierce Lyden *(Jeff)*, Frank McCarroll *(Steve)*.

Martin and Carlo are Mexicano ranch hands who beat off a gang of evil gringos attempting to take over Rafferty's ranch so they can sell the valuable railroad rights. Plenty of action but Martin collapses as a romantic swain, pitching woo at attractive Rafferty as one might fork bales of hay.

p, Buddy Rogers, Ralph Cohn; d, Reginald Leborg; w, Bob Williams, Harold Tarshis; ph, Fred Jackman (Cinecolor); ed, Lynn Harrison.

Western (PR:A MPAA:NR)

ADVENTURES OF DON JUAN**** (1949) 110m WB c (GB: NEW ADVENTURES OF DON JUAN, THE)

Errol Flynn *(Don Juan)*, Viveca Lindfors *(Queen Margaret)*, Robert Douglas *(Duke de Lorca)*, Alan Hale *(Leporello)*, Romney Brent *(King Phillip III)*, Ann Rutherford *(Donna Elena)*, Robert Warwick *(Count De Polan)*, Jerry Austin *(Don Sebastian)*, Douglas Kennedy *(Don Rodrigo)*, Jeanne Shepherd *(Donna Carlotta)*, Mary Stuart *(Catherine)*, Helen Westcott *(Lady Diana)*, Fortunio Bonanova *(Don Serafino)*, Aubrey Mather *(Lord Chalmers)*, Una O'Connor *(Duenna)*, Raymond Burr *(Captain Alvarez)*, Tim Huntley *(Catherine's Husband)*, David Leonard *(Innkeeper)*, Leon Belasco *(Don De Cordoba)*.

Here is the essential Flynn, swashbuckler, lover, witty and wise, as well as capricious and not a little world-weary as the notorious lover and swordsman. The film opens with the dashing Lothario embracing a British noblewoman on her balcony, Flynn's light- hearted advances interrupted by the lady's enraged spouse who forces a duel upon the backpedaling lover of life. He reluctantly wounds the nobleman and is sent back to Spain in disgrace to be chastised by Lindfors, his queen who secretly loves him. She orders him to take over the royal fencing academy and stay out of trouble; Flynn obediently fends off the flighty advances of a bevy of luscious ladies, most of whom are married and sit in the gallery to watch him instruct his charges in the ways of swordsmanship, swooning at his every glance. Court intrigues envelop him when he learns that the scheming Duke de Lorca (Robert Douglas in a particularly well-acted role of evil conniving) is attempting to depose the monarchs and become dictator of Spain. Flynn, his ever-loyal aide Hale, and his idealistic pupils, take on the palace guards after Flynn unearths the necessary evidence to expose Douglas. In a magnificently choreographed duel inside the resplendent Madrid palace of his queen, Flynn battles the evil Douglas to death. Before leaving Spain once again, Flynn meets privately with Lindfors who blurts her love for him, begging him to take her with him on his adventures; she will gladly relinquish a crown for his embrace. There is too much nobility in Flynn/Don Juan to permit such a sacrifice; he tells her that she must remain queen to serve the needs of her people. We see the cavalier riding off with faithful Hale, stopped by a coach in which a beautiful woman sits, asking for directions (Nora Eddington, Flynn's second wife). The coach goes on, the woman batting her come-hither eyes, and Flynn hesitates. Hale cautions him against another immediate fling and Flynn replies in a great line of self-revelation: "There is a little Don Juan in every man and since I am Don Juan there is more of it in me." They laugh and ride in the direction of the fast-disappearing coach. This superbly mounted production was a long time in the making, scheduled by Jack Warner in spring 1945 and to be directed by Raoul Walsh. (Warner, the ever-alert entrepreneur, knew well what such a film would mean to a public that had become fascinated with Flynn's offscreen hedonism, his many wives, sexual reputation, even phony rape charges that ballooned his bedroom prowess and made the slogan "In like Flynn" a national cliche.) The film was not begun until fall 1947 and even then many doubted that it would ever see completion. Flynn's drinking and carousing had become excessive and production was stopped several times while he went on his Homeric toots. The toll of his self-indulgent flings began to show on his face and figure but that handsome wolf face still retained enough boyish charm and the body enough energy to complete what was the swashbuckler's last great film, one which Flynn played almost as a self-caricature, amused at the decline of the incredible hero he had become to millions of world-wide fans, a hero summarized in the fading Don Juan, a mythical, invincible character who could never be dislodged from legend. Though this film enjoyed great success in Europe, its American box office did not balance staggering production expenses. Warner thereafter cut Flynn's pictures to bone-marrow budgets and provided shabby scripts that quickly closed down one of the most spectacular careers in Hollywood. It is fitting that DON JUAN was Flynn's final swashbuckling curtain in that he had always wanted to play the role, one which his friend and mentor John Barrymore had done in the silent era. And, like Barrymore, Flynn followed that Sweet Prince's course of dedicated degeneration into an early good night, to the very last a lover, a hero, a courageous and unforgettable ghost.

p, Jerry Wald; d, Vincent Sherman; w, George Oppenheimer, Harry Kurnitz (based on a story by Herbert Dalmas); ph, Elwood Bredell (Technicolor); m, Max Steiner; ed, Alan Crosland, Jr.

Adventure (PR:A MPAA:NR)

ADVENTURES OF FRONTIER FREMONT, THE*** (1976) 106m Sun Classics c

Dan Haggerty *(Frontier Fremont)*, Denver Pyle *(Old Mountainan)*.

Haggerty, a St. Louis tinsmith, tires of the city life and heads for the mountains where he is happy communing with nature and the animals of the high mountains, almost a ringer remake of THE LIFE AND TIMES OF GRIZZLY ADAMS. Enjoyable family fare with spectacular photography.

p, Charles Selier, Jr.; d, Richard Friedenberg; w, David O'Malley; ph, George Stapleford (Techniscope color).

Adventure Cas. (PR:AAA MPAA:G)

ADVENTURES OF GALLANT BESS 1/2** (1948) 71m EL c

Cameron Mitchell *(Ted Daniels)*, Audrey Long *(Penny Gray)*, Fuzzy Knight *(Woody)*, James Millican *(Bud Millerick)*, John Harmon *(Blake)*, Ed Gargan *(Deputy)*, Harry V. Cheshire *(Doctor Gray)*, Cliff Clark *(Sheriff)*, Evelyn Eaton *(Billie)*, Herself *(Bess)*.

Mitchell is a wandering stunt rodeo rider whose beautifully trained horse Bess performs amazing tricks and becomes a heroine in her own right. The gypsy life for man and horse ends when Mitchell meets Long and love blossoms on the range. Superb outdoor photography matches a heart-warming story which will especially touch children.

d, Lew Landers; w, Matthew Rapf; ph, William Bradford (Cinecolor); ed, Harry Komer.

Western (PR:AAA MPAA:NR)

ADVENTURES OF GERARD, THE** (1970, Brit.) 91m Nigel Films/UA c

Peter McEnery *(Col. Etienne Gerard)*, Claudia Cardinale *(Countess Teresa)*, Eli Wallach *(Napoleon Bonaparte)*, Jack Hawkins *(Millefleurs)*, Mark Burns *(Col. Russell)*, Norman Rossington *(Sgt. Papilette)*, John Neville *(Duke of Wellington)*, Paolo Stoppa *(Count of Morales)*, Ivan Desny *(Gen. Lasalle)*.

A swaggering boisterous Hussar officer, McEnery, meets torrid Cardinale, an enticing noblewoman, falling in love with her during Napoleon's 1808 peninsula campaign in Spain. Cardinale is a spy for the British and enlists McEnery in her intrigues against oppressor Napoleon, played with manic fury by Wallach who chews up the scenery. A full-blown handsome production eschewing budget and sometimes comprehension, but presenting a sweeping historical perspective with extras aplenty (The Spanish army, always for hire, it seems, to the highest-bidding movie mogul). The court intrigues tend to the turgid and the love scenes between Cardinale and McEnery do not rise above the stereotype, but oh, those ignorant, clashing armies!

p, Henry Lester, Gene Gutowski; d, Jerzy Skolimowski; w, H. A. L. Craig, Lester, Gutowski, Skolimowski (based on stories by Arthur Conan Doyle); ph, Witold Sobocinski (DeLuxe color, Panavision); m, Riz Ortolani.

Adventure (PR:A MPAA:NR)

ADVENTURES OF HAJJI BABA** (1954) 92 m Wanger FOX c

John Derek *(Hajji Baba)*, Elaine Stewart *(Fawzia)*, Thomas Gomez *(Osman Aga)*, Amanda Blake *(Banah)* Paul Picerni *(Nur-El-Din)*, Rosemarie Bowe *(Ayesha)*, Donald Randolph *(Caliph)*, Melinda Markey *(Touareg)*, Peter Mamakos *(Executioner)*, Kurt Katch *(Caoush)*, Robert Bice *(Musa)*, Carl Milletaire *(Captain)*.

Thin grade-B take-off on Arabian Nights adventures is pregnant with swirling harem cuties, wide-edged blades and stilted dialog. Derek plays the impoverished Persian barber, Hajji Baba, who aspires to win the milky hand of princess Stewart, and does so through clever moves, also managing to best Picerni, an evil-minded, power-hungry prince who lusts after Stewart and all the land of Persia. When this film was first released audiences much less sophisticated than today perceived the production as an inept mess and laughed where no guffaws were scheduled in the script, particularly when scores of fetching harem ladies broke their necks to seduce the frenetic, too-intense Derek. The unintentional comedy is below par on all levels, almost pandering its sex sans sense.

p, Walter Wanger; d, Don Weis; w, Richard Collins; ph, Harold Lipstein (DeLuxe Color, CinemaScope); m, Dmitri Tiomkin; ed, William Austin; m/l, "Hajji Baba," Tiomkin, Ned Washington (sung by Nat "King" Cole).

Adventure (PR:C MPAA:NR)

ADVENTURES OF HAL 5, THE* (1958, Brit.) 59m Bushey/CFF bw

Peter Godsell *(Charles)*, William Russell *(Vicar)*, John Glyn Jones *(Mr. Goorlie)*, Janina Faye *(Moira)*, John Charlesworth *(Ralph)*, Edwin Richfield *(Cooper)*, David Morrell *(Dicey)*.

Sophomoric production involves the attempted theft of a family car by an unscrupulous garage owner. Done on such a childish level that even children might find it beneath them.

p, Gilbert Church; d&w,Don Sharp (based on the novel, *Hal 5 and the Haywards* by Henry Donald); ph, Jo Jago.

Children's Adventure (PR:A MPAA:NR)

ADVENTURES OF HUCKLEBERRY FINN, 1939

(SEE: HUCKLEBERRY FINN, 1939)

ADVENTURES OF HUCKLEBERRY FINN, THE** ½** (1960) 107m MGM c

Tony Randall *(The King)*, Eddie Hodges *(Huckleberry Finn)*, Archie Moore *(Jim)*, Patty McCormack *(Joanna)*, Neville Brand *(Pap)*, Mickey Shaughnessy *(The Duke)*, Judy Canova *(Sheriff's Wife)*, Andy Devine *(Mr. Carmody)*, Sherry Jackson *(Mary* Jane), Buster Keaton *(Lion Tamer)*, Finlay Currie *(Captain Sellers)*, Josephine Hutchinson *(Widow Douglas)*, Parley Baer *(Grangerford Man)*, John Carradine *(Slave* Catcher), Royal Dano *(Sheriff)*, Dolores Hawkins *(River Boat Singer)*, Sterling Holloway *(Barber)*, Dean Stanton *(Slave Catcher)*.

A spritely account of Mark Twain's all-American outdoors boy is also a bit on the cutesy side. Hodges as Huck goes through his episodic experiences along the Mississippi more like a picnic outing than the wild adventure Twain originally envisioned and the harrowing aspects of the story—Huck's escaping the wrath of a drunken father and other life-threatening events—have been eliminated for a tamer view, although Hodges' trip down the river on the raft with heavyweight slugger Archie Moore as Jim, the runaway black, is excellent, along with the exchanges of dialog between them. Randall as "The King" is a shining moment of devilish amusement and some real jeopardy as he cat-and-mouses Huck; his schizoid performance, beyond the splendor of the outdoors photography, is the best thing in this handsomely mounted production. Hodges was undoubtedly picked for his boyish looks but he lacks the inner spark that Jackie Coogan and Mickey Rooney gave to the role in previous productions (see HUCKLEBERRY FINN, 1931; HUCKLEBERRY FINN, 1938). Perhaps no one will ever fullfill the Twain image of Huckhalf boy, half man pushing his nose into any available adventure with delightful curiosity, innocence and courage. Hodges has the innocence and the decency of Huck but he strikes one as weak and artificial which Huck never was—he was the essence of unwitting bravery and boyish confidence. Hodges exhibits apprehension and vulnerability; his attitude demands that he be rescued from the smallest of perils, a posture unlike the great youth of the great river escapades.

p, Samuel Goldwyn, Jr.; d, Michael Curtiz; w, James Lee (based on the novel by Mark Twain); ph, Ted McCord (CinemaScope, MetroColor); m, Jerome Moross; ed, Frederic Steinkamp; art d, George W. Davis, McClure Capp; spec eff, A. Arnold Gillespie.

Adventure Cas. (PR:AAA MPAA:NR)

ADVENTURES OF ICHABOD AND MR. TOAD****** (1949) 68m Disney/RKO c

Voices of: Bing Crosby, Basil Rathbone, Eric Blore, Pat O'Malley, John Floyardt, Colin Campbell, Campbell Grant, Claude Allister, The Rhythmaires.

This feature-length cartoon, split into two sequences, is one of Disney's finest efforts, with his animators paying attention to every animated detail (a Disney hallmark, one that lifts his studio's product far above the flat animation of anything available today). The first sequence deals with that wonderful aristocratic Mr. Toad of Kenneth Grahame's British classic, *The Wind in the Willows,* a haughty amphibian too good for his fellow creatures, such as Mr. Pig and the stuff-shirted Mr. Rat, a leisure-class creature obsessed with planes and autos. A car, in fact, driven at impossible speeds by Mr. Toad and sold to him by a gang of thieving weasels, turns out to be stolen and the croaking hero must defend himself in court, this scene being masterful, subtly funny and instructional. The second segment deals with the *non compos mentis* Ichabod Crane from Washington Irving's "The Legend of Sleepy Hollow," delightfully narrated by Crosby who does all the voices and croons some eerie tunes with The Rhythmaires, climaxing in a genuinely scary scene where the Headless Horseman is in hot pursuit of Ichabod and his equally terrified horse, a pell-mell race through forests and glens that, for pure imaginative animation has gone unequalled. Superb family entertainment.

p, Walt Disney; d, Jack Kinney, Clyde Geronimi, James Algar; w, Erdman Penner, Winston Hibler, Joe Rinaldi, Ted Sears, Homer Brightman, Harry Reeves (based on the stories "The Legend of Sleepy Hollow" by Washington Irving and "The Wind in the Willows," by Kenneth Grahame); md, Oliver Wallace; m/l Don Raye, Gene De Paul.

Cartoon Feature (PR:AAA MPAA:NR)

ADVENTURES OF JACK LONDON (SEE: JACK LONDON, 1943)

ADVENTURES OF JANE, THE ½** (1949, Brit.) 55m New World/Keystone bw

Chrisabel Leighton-Porter *(Jane)*, Stanelli *(Hotelier)*, Michael Hogarth *(Tom Hawke)*, Wally Patch *(Customs Officer)*, Ian Colin *(Capt. Cleaver)*, Sonya O'Shea *(Ruby)*, Peter Butterworth *(Drunk)*, Sebastian Cabot *(Traveler)*.

Offbeat film played for laughs has a fake sea captain smuggling gems, exposed when he attempts to slip diamonds into an actress' bracelet. Not much funny here in a low-budget production.

p, Edward G. Whiting; d, Whiting, Alf Goulding; w, Whiting, Goulding, Con West (based on the comic strip character "Jane"); ph, Jack Rose.

Comedy (PR:A MPAA:NR)

ADVENTURES OF JANE ARDEN** (1939) 53m WB bw

Rosella Towne *(Jane Arden)*, William Gargan *(Ed Towers)*, James Stephenson *(Dr. Vanders)*, Benny Rubin *(Marvin Piermont)*, Dennie Moore *(Teenie Moore)*, Peggy Shannon *(Lola Martin)*, Edgar Edwards *(Bill Clifton)*, Pierre Watkin *(Albert Thayer)*, Maria Wrixon *(Martha Blanton)*, John Ridgely *(Reporter)*, Joe Devlin *(Thug)*, Raymond Bailey *(Thug)*, George Renevant *(Frenchman)*, Eddie Conrad *(Italian)*.

The comic strip heroine-sleuth comes to life in this rather tepid tale of gem smugglers who use beautiful women as covers for their operations, murdering them when they discover the ruse. The murders bring clue-sniffing Jane (Towne) into action as an investigative reporter directed by her blustery editor, Gargan. Ancillary characters, Moore as the lovelorn columnist and her boy friend Rubin, provide more interest than the lead roles, or at least they provide more humor. James Stephenson, as the mastermind of the smugglers, gives a standout portrayal in evil but this grade B whodunit still proves only a mildly provocative first-time directorial effort by former editor Morse.

p, Mark Hellinger; d, Terry Morse; w, Lawrence Kimble, Vincent Sherman, Charles Curran (based on comic strip characters created by Monte Barrett and Russell E. Ross); ph, L. W. O'Connell; ed, Harold McLernon.

Crime (PR:A MPAA:NR)

ADVENTURES OF KITTY O'DAY ½** (1944) 63m MON bw

Jean Parker *(Kitty)*, Peter Cookson *(Johnny)*, Tim Ryan *(Clancy)*, Ralph Sanford *(Mike)*, Bill Ruhl *(Tracey)*, Shelton Brooks *(Jeff)*, Bill Forrest *(Sauter)*, Lorna Grey *(Gloria)*, Hugh Prosser *(Nick)*, Dick Elliott *(Bascom)*, Byron Foulger *(Roberts)*, Jan Wiley *(Carla)*.

Above-average Monogram whodunit presents perky Jean Parker in one of the better O'Day productions, part of a successful B series, that has the snoopy telephone operator overhearing another plot which leads to three murders, which, naturally, Parker feels obligated to investigate on her own, getting herself and boy friend Cookson into scalding water with the cops. She solves the homicides and nabs the jewel thieves behind the killings while the bumbling police stand by in expected awe.

p, Lindsley Parsons; d, William Beaudine; w, Tim Ryan, George Callahan, Victor Hammond (based on a story by Victor Hammond); ph, Mack Stengler; ed, Richard Pike.

Crime (PR:A MPAA:NR)

ADVENTURES OF MARCO POLO, THE*** (1938) 100m Goldwyn/UA bw

Gary Cooper *(Marco Polo)*, Sigrid Gurie *(Princess Kukuchin)*, Basil Rathbone *(Ahmed)*, Ernest Truex *(Binguccio)*, George Barbier *(Kublai Khan)*, Binnie Barnes *(Nazama)*, Alan Hale *(Kaidu)*, H. B. Warner *(Chen Tsu)*, Robert Grieg *(Chamberlain)*, Ferdinand Gottschalk *(Persian Ambassador)* Henry Kolker *(Nicolo Polo)*, Hale Hamilton *(Maffeo Polo)*, Lotus Liu *(Visahka)*, Stanley Fields *(Bayan)*, Harold Huber *(Toctai)*, Eugene Hoo *(Chen Tsu's Son)*, Lana Turner *(Maid)*, Ward Bond *(Mongol* Guard), Helen Quan *(Chen Tsu's Daughter)*, Diane Toy *(Kaidu Entertainer)*, Granville Bates, Reginald Barlow, Theodore von Eltz *(Venetian Businessmen)*, Jason Robards, Sr. *(Messenger)*, Harry Kerua *(Kaidu Guard)*, Greta Granstedt *(Kaidu Maid)*, Soo Yong *(Chen Tsu's Wife)*, Mrs. Ng *(Chen Tsu's Mother)*, James Leong *(Tartar Warrior)*, Dick Alexander *(Ahmed's Aide)*, Harry Cording, Dick Rich, Joe Woody, Leo Fielding, Gloria Youngblood, Diana Moncardo, Mia Schioka, Dora Young.

The most lavish of four major films based on the exploits of the 13th-century Venetian traveler, Marco Polo, Goldwyn's version has Cooper and his whining, cringing aide, Truex, more pathetic than humorous, survive sandstorms, shipwrecks and avalanches en route to the Orient. As the first white man into China (or the first to record a visit), Cooper is a witty but wary Polo immersed in the court intrigues of Kublai Khan, expansively played by Barbier, and falls in love with Gurie, a princess coveted by the evil Rathbone, as he covets the Khan's enormous kingdom, murdering those in his climb to power, torturing others (in a special chamber where he amuses himself with wrist-breaking devices of his own invention). Rathbone schemes a way to have Cooper temporarily banished to the outlands controlled by Hale, the fun-loving bandit Kaidu, whom Cooper convinces to invade Pekin, to rescue the Khan from a Rathbone takeover and win amnesty and glory and heavy rewards. The attack against the walled city is breath-taking; thousands of extras were used, along with hundreds of horses in a thrilling cavalry charge. Rathbone's defending warriors send down a shower of arrows from the walls which are blown up by a new invention Cooper has discovered—gunpowder. He saves the day by freeing the Khan, conquering the city with Kaidu, dueling Rathbone to death, and having Gurie in his arms for what Hollywood then called a wow finish. This old-fashioned adventure yarn did not initially recoup its $2 million investment, a whopping sum for those days. Moreover, the film was hurt by what Goldwyn touted as his newest asset, Sigrid Gurie, whom he promoted as a "Norwegian Garbo," and "The Siren of the Fjords." Sleuths rooted out her real past, revealing that she was no foreign mystery woman of film, but had been born Sigrid Gurie Haukelid on May 11, 1911, in Brooklyn, N.Y., dead center in the middle of Flatbush. Her career took a prompt nosedive, taking this film with it. (Gurie's decline was rapid; she ended her career ten years later in 1948, after a series of uneventful roles for such poverty row firms as PRC.)

p, Samuel Goldwyn; d, Archie Mayo; w, Robert E. Sherwood (based on a story by N. A. Pogson); ph, Rudolph Mate; m, Hugo Friedhofer; md, Alfred Newman; ed, Fred Allen; art d, Richard Day; set d, Julia Heron; cos, Omar Kiam; spec eff, James Basevi.

Adventure (PR:A MPAA:NR)

ADVENTURES OF MARK TWAIN, THE****** (1944) 130m WB bw

Fredric March *(Samuel Clemens)*, Alexis Smith *(Olivia Langdon)*, Donald Crisp *(J. B. Pond)*, Alan Hale *(Steve Gillis)*, C. Aubrey Smith *(Oxford Chancellor)*, John Carradine *(Bret Harte)*, William Henry *(Charles Langdon)*, Robert Barrat *(Horace E.* Bixby), Walter Hampden *(Jervis Langdon)*, Joyce Reynolds *(Clara Clemens)*, Whitford Kane *(Joe Goodwin)*, Percy Kilbride *(Billings)*, Nana Bryant *(Mrs. Langdon)*, Dickie Jones *(Sam Clemens at age 15)*, Kay Johnson *(Jane Clemens)*, Jackie Brown *(Sam Clemens at age 12)*, Eugene Holland *(Huck Finn)*, Michael Miller *(Tom Sawyer)*, Joseph Crehan *(Promoter)*, Cliff Saum *(Prospector)*, Harry Tyler *(Assistant Editor)*, Roland Drew *(Editor)*, Douglas Wood *(William Dean Howells)*, Willie Best *(George)*, Burr Caruth *(Oliver W. Holmes)*, Harry Hilliard *(John G. Whittier)*, Brandon Hurst *(Ralph W. Emerson)*, Davison Clark *(Henry W. Longfellow)*, Monte Blue *(Captain)*, Paul Newlan *(Boss Deck Hand)*, Ernest Whitman *(Stoker)*, Emmett Smith *(Repeater)*, Pat O'Malley *(Captain's Mate)*, Chester Conklin *(Judge)*, George Lessey *(Henry H. Rogers)*, Dorothy Vaughan *(Kate Leary)*, Gloria Ann Crawford *(Susie as a child)*, Lynne Baggett *(Susie)*, Carol Joyce Coombs *(Clara as a child)*, Charlene Salerno *(Jean as a child)*, Joyce Tucker *(Jean)*, Charles Waldron *(Dr. Quintard)*, Paul Scardon *(Rudyard Kipling)*.

Here is a rich biography and a great profile rendered of the colorful Mark Twain, a masterpiece of incisive acting by March as the young adventurer who left Hannibal, Missouri, to learn the tricky ways of the mighty Mississippi as a navigator. (In one scene, when March is attempting to steer a riverboat through the fog-bound waters he hears a black deckhand, after throwing out a weight from the bow to determine the depth of water ahead, shout back: "Mark the twain (twine—the rope tied about the weight) . . . (feet)." And here is born the *nom de plume* of one of America's finest writers and humorists, Samuel Clemens/Mark Twain.) Sharp, witty dialog sparks along the story line as March moves from the Mississippi to the West as a newspaper editor, then on to the California Gold Rush with sidekick Alan Hale, meeting scribe Bret Harte, played well by John Carradine, and participating in the famous frog-jumping contest which later turned into one of Twain's finest and funniest stories. The love story between Twain and Olivia Langdon is beautifully played by March and Smith, understated and sensitive. The episodic film takes March from young manhood to old age, the in-between dramatically full of stirring events, winning his wife against the wishes of her parents, his growing stature as a writer, his dedication to U. S. Grant and the publication of his memoirs, even though it brings bankruptcy and the necessity to pay off his bills by lecturing himself to fatigue around the world. All of this March achieves with quiet nobility, projecting the forceful and courageous inner image that was truly the soul of the immortal Twain. Enhancing the production immeasurably was Sol Polito's crisp photography and the resonant and stirring score by Max Steiner.

p, Jesse L. Lasky; d, Irving Rapper; w, Alan LeMay, Harry Chandlee (based on an adaptation by LeMay and Harold M. Sherman of biographical material owned by the Mark Twain Co.); ph, Sol Polito, Laurence Butler, Edward Linden, Don Siegel, James Leicester; m, Max Steiner; ed, Ralph Dawson.

Adventure/Drama   **(PR:AAA   MPAA:NR)**

ADVENTURES OF MARTIN EDEN, THE*½   (1942) 87m COL bw
Glenn Ford (*Martin Eden*), Clarie Trevor (*"Connie" Dawson*), Evelyn Keyes (*Ruth Morley*), Stuart Erwin (*Joe Dawson*), Dickie Moore (*Johnny*), Ian MacDonald (*"Butch" Ragan*), Frank Conroy (*Carl Brissenden*), Rafaela Ottiano (*Marie Sylva*), Pierre Watkin (*Mr. Morley*), Regina Wallace (*Mrs. Morley*), Robert J. McDonald (*Judge*).

Stirring, sometimes upsetting Jack London tale of a sailor, Ford, serving on board a hellship, enduring brutal treatment and finally escaping the nightmare that was the fate of early-day seamen. He then vigorously campaigns for the publication of his memoirs and to free his fellow seaman, Erwin, wrongly imprisoned for mutiny. Ford triumphs, exposes the brutal captain and conditions and brings about Erwin's release, ending up not with wealthy socialite Keyes but Trevor, a girl from the gashouse district. A powerful indictment of a cruel merchant marine system with strong acting and solid production.

p, B. P. Shulberg; d, Sidney Salkow; w, W. L. River (based on a story by Jack London); ph, Franz F. Planer; ed, Al Clark.

Adventure   **(PR:A   MPAA:NR)**

ADVENTURES OF MICHAEL STROGOFF
                                    (SEE: SOLDIER AND THE LADY, 1937)

**ADVENTURES OF PC 49, THE **   (1949, Brit.) 67m Hammer bw
Hugh Latimer (*Archibald Berkeley-Willoughby*), John Penrose (*Barney*), Annette Simmonds (*Carrots*), Pat Nye (*Ma Benson*), Patricia Cutts (*Joan*), Arthur Brander (*Insp. Wilson*), Eric Phillips (*Sgt. Wright*), Martin Benson (*Skinny*).

Truck thieves are apprehended by an undercover British cop in a low-budget production that is tame on action and thin on acting ability.

p, Anthony Hinds; d, Godfrey Grayson; w, Alan Stranks, Vernon Harris (based on the British radio series by Stranks); ph, Cedric Williams.

Crime   **(PR:A   MPAA:NR)**

ADVENTURES OF QUENTIN DURWARD, THE
                                    (SEE: QUENTIN DURWARD, 1955)

ADVENTURES OF PICASSO, THE*   (1980, Swed.) 92m ABSF c
Gosta Ekman (*Picasso*), Hans Alfredson (*Picasso's Father*), Margaretha Krook (*Picasso's Mother*), Bernard Cribbins (*Gertrude Stein*), Wilfrid Brambell (*Alice B. Toklas*), Per Oscarsson (*Apollinaire*), Lennart Nyman (*Rousseau*), Lena Nyman (*Sirkkat*), Birgitta Anderson (*Ingrid Svensson Guggenheim*).

Sporadically funny but often tiring film that chronicles the life of Picasso, a painter with a sense of humor deeper than this episodic production. Ekman is a Swedish caricature of the great painter performing pratfalls and uttering vulgarities that give an oafish image rather than the bemused, incisive character that was Picasso. The forced portrait of a senile Dr. Albert Schweitzer mindlessly operating on a helpless Picasso is abysmal and in the poorest taste; such idiotic scenes seem to pass for satire in Sweden.

d, Tage Danielsson; w, Hans Alfredson, Danielsson, Gosta Ekman; ph, Tony Forsberg, Roland Sterner; m, Gunnar Svensson; ed, Jan Persson.

Comedy   **(PR:O   MPAA:NR)**

ADVENTURES OF RABBI JACOB, THE**
(AKA: THE MAD ADVENTURES OF RABBI JACOB) (1973, Fr.) 100m SNC c
Louis De Funes (*Victor*), Suzy Delair (*Germaine*), Marcel Dalio (*Rabbi Jacob*), Henry Guybert (*Salomon*), Claude Giraud (*Slimane*), Claude Pieplu (*Andreani*), Janet Brandt (*Tzipe*), Denise Provence (*Esther*), Renzo Montagni (*Fares*).

De Funes is a French Archie Bunker whose racism demands that Arabs, Jews, blacks and those other than his own race and nationality are all right in their place, which is not next to him. A comic with a penchant for burlesque—magnifying facial expressions, exaggerating physical reactions—he gets mixed up with an Arab coup d'etat, accidentally frees a kidnap victim and gets involved in a fantastic chase, all on the way to his daughter's wedding. Most of the mayhem is contrived but some genuine hilarity is found in scenes such as his falling with his pursuers into a vat of glutinous substance in a gum factory. Most of the humor is low-brow and suspiciously concocted to reinforce, it seems, instead of indict the racial slurs.

d, Gerard Oury; w, Oury, Daniel Thompson; ph, Henri Decae (Eastmancolor) ed, Albert Jurgenson.

Comedy   **(PR:C   MPAA:NR)**

ADVENTURES OF ROBIN HOOD, THE***   (1938) 102m WB/FN c
Errol Flynn (*Sir Robin of Locksley/Robin Hood*), Olivia de Havilland (*Maid Marian*), Basil Rathbone (*Sir Guy of Gisbourne*), Claude Rains (*Prince John*), Patric Knowles (*Will Scarlet*), Eugene Pallette (*Friar Tuck*), Alan Hale (*Little John*), Melville Cooper (*High Sheriff of Nottingham*), Ian Hunter (*King Richard the Lion-Hearted*), Una O'Connor (*Bess*), Herbert Mundin (*Much the Miller's Son*), Montagu Love (*Bishop of Black Canons*), Leonard Willey (*Sir Essex*), Robert Noble (*Sir Ralf*), Kenneth Hunter (*Sir Mortimer*), Robert Warwick (*Sir Geoffrey*), Colin Kenny (*Sir Baldwin*), Lester Matthews (*Sir Ivor*), Harry Cording (*Dickon Malbete*), Howard Hill (*Captain of Archers*), Ivan Simpson (*Tavern Proprietor*), Charles McNaughton (*Crippen*), Lionel Belmore (*Humilty Prin*), Janet Shaw (*Humilty's Daughter*), Crawford Kent (*Sir Norbert*), Austin Fairman (*Sir Nigel*), Leonard Mudie (*Town Crier*), Holmes Herbert (*Referee*).

No part was better suited to Errol Flynn than that of Robin Hood; from green woodsman's cap to brown hunting boots, the role belonged to him and he to it. Warners surrounded him with a sumptuous, lavish production and the finest supporting cast available to make what is undoubtedly the greatest adventure film ever produced, a feast for the eyes, a tonic for the heart and for the human spirit and undying belief in a legendary hero. All are matchless in their roles: Olivia de Havilland is the perfect Maid Marian, sweet, innocent, fair-minded even with Saxons, the sworn enemies of her Norman heritage. Rathbone is at his ruthless and cultured best as Sir Guy, and Rains is the insidious, scheming John incarnate. Hale as Little John is boisterous and devoted to Robin whom he beats in a hilarious duel with quarterstaffs. Pallette is a jovial but lethal Friar Tuck; Knowles a light-hearted Will Scarlett, Robin's first follower; O'Connor, Marian's maid, scatterbrained, loyal to death; Cooper, the cowardly sheriff full of bombast; and Hunter, resplendently noble as King Richard. The roles are umbilically tied to these players and forever etched in the public's mind. The story is tight, if not historically definitive, beginning with the capture of Hunter in Austria where he is held for ransom and the self-appointment of John as Regent of England in his absence. Against the false monarch, his nobles and the might of the ruling Norman class, a single Saxon knight, Flynn, defies the crown, swears his allegiance to Hunter and vows to raise the ransom his brother will not pay, stealing from the Norman caravans so foolish as to traverse Sherwood Forest, the impenetrable hideout of Robin and his merry men. One caravan with de Havilland is waylaid and she becomes Flynn's reluctant guest, first hating him and branding him an outlaw, then softening when seeing his kindness to the poor and the lame, then loving him for his humanity and indomitable spirit. By the time she is sent back to her Norman castle she is his ally. Rains and Rathbone connive a ruse to trap their quarry, establishing an archery contest which Flynn attends, beating all comers and winning a golden arrow from the hand of de Havilland. He is captured but de Havilland arranges for his escape. Her loyalty to the bandit is uncovered and John tells her he will condemn her to death after crowning himself in a matter of days. Flynn and his men are about to set upon another band of travelers but discover that it is Hunter and some of his crusaders who have returned to England incognito. They join with Robin and his men, disguised as monks, in the coronation of the usurper, disrupting the ceremonies with a battle royal in which Flynn duels the infamous Rathbone to death. Hunter banishes a petulant Rains and grants amnesty to the ban dits of Sherwood, restoring Flynn's title and lands and giving him the hand of de Havil land in marriage, the latter a royal command. With a boyish grin, Flynn takes his most precious prize in his arms and begins to leave the great hall of Nottingham Castle, replying: "May I obey all your commands with equal pleasure, sire." The lavish sets, Korngold's rich score, the cameras of Sol Polito and Tony Gaudio (the Warner Brothers workhorses of photography) which bathed the entire production in astounding color, and Curtiz's robust, quick-cutting direction made for a master-piece. The cost was enormous for 1938, more than $2 million, every dime put behind Warner's athletic star, the 28-year-old Flynn, but, oddly enough, the film was almost made with James Cagney as Robin Hood, Jack Warner's choice when he and producer Hal Wallis began putting the production together in 1935, but Cagney walked off the lot in a contract dispute and the project was shelved for two years. Flynn's overnight success with CAPTAIN BLOOD in 1935 established him as a great swashbuckler and the natural lead for ROBIN HOOD. Warner put a team of writers on the script, which draws most of its source material from Sir Walter Scott's *Ivanhoe*, as well as the 1890 light opera "Robin Hood" by De Koven-Smith (the latter being the only reference which depicted Robin and Sir Guy pitted against each other over the affection of Marian). Initially, director William Keighley took a crew to Chico, California, 100 miles north of Sacramento and filmed the lush vegetation inside Bidwell Park which later became Sherwood Forest. Jack Warner viewed Keighley's rushes and decided that more *elan vital* was needed and brought in his top action director, Curtiz, who directed all the interiors with great gusto, as well as additional outdoor scenes around Lake Sherwood, west of the San Fernando Valley. Rathbone studied particularly hard for his role of the evil Sir Guy, spending many hours with fencing instructor Fred Cavens, but Flynn ignored most of this tutored swordsmanship, relying upon his natural grace and exceptional athletic ability to convince viewers he was the better blade handler (he took great pride in doing most of his own stunts, including perilous leaps, falls, and the scaling of walls against Warner's dictates). The result was that the production was genuine from the first minute to the last and has remained one of the most popular films of all time.

p, Hal B. Wallis, Henry Blanke; d, Michael Curtiz, William Keighley; w, Norman Reilly Raine, Seton I. Miller (based on ancient Robin Hood legends); ph, Sol Polito, Tony Gaudio (Technicolor); m, Eric Wolfgang Korngold; ed, Ralph Dawson; art d, Carl Jules Weyl; cos, Milo Anderson; archery super, Howard Hill; fencing master, Fred Cavens.

Adventure   **Cas**   **(PR:AAA   MPAA:NR)**

ADVENTURES OF ROBINSON CRUSOE, THE*½   (1954) 90m UA c
Dan O'Herlihy (*Robinson Crusoe*), Jaime Fernandez (*Friday*), Felipe De Alba (*Capt. Oberzo*), Chel Lopez (*Bos'n*), Jose Chavez, Emilio Garibay (*Leaders of the Mutiny*).

The Defoe classic is well served by O'Herlihy as the shipwrecked and marooned British seaman on an isolated island where he fends for himself, taking refuge in a cave and living as did his ancient human predecessors. When cannibals visit his side of the island, the regressing caveman views them from afar, terrified. Then he realizes they are about to murder and eat one of their own and he frightens them off, saving the victim whom he calls Friday (Fernandez) since that happens to be the day of the tribesman's deliverance. At first he treats Hernandez as a slave, fearing he will murder him in his sleep. Then O'Herlihy softens and teaches his protege the ways of civilization. Not for ten more years (twenty-eight in all) does the marooned man see another vessel. Finally a privateer anchors nearby and takes a grateful O'Herlihy back to civilization. A superbly directed film by Bunuel which makes the viewer feel every inch of O'Herlihy's rugged survival, beautifully photographed in Mexico.

p, Oscar Dancigers, Henry Ehrlich; d, Luis Bunuel; w, Philip Roll, Bunuel (based on the novel *The Life and Strange Adventures of Robinson Crusoe* by Daniel Defoe); ph, Alex Philips (Pathecolor); m, Anthony Collins; ed, Carlos Savage, Alberto Valenzuela; set d, Edward Fitzgerald.

Adventure (PR:AA MPAA:NR)

ADVENTURES OF RUSTY** (1945) 69m COL bw

Ted Donaldson (*Danny Mitchell*), Margaret Lindsay (*Ann*), Conrad Nagel (*Hugh Mitchell*), Gloria Holden (*Louise Hover*), Robert Williams (*Will Nelson*), Addison Richards (*Psychiatrist*), Arno Frey (*Tausig*), Eddie Parker (*Ehrlich*), Bobby Larson (*Henry*), Douglas Madore (*Billy*), Gary Gray (*Herbie*), Ruth Warren (*Mrs. Nelson*), Ace (*Himself*).

Pleasant programmer has Donaldson adjusting to a new stepmother and adopting and getting a new pet, a vicious German Shepherd, one-time police dog gone wrong. There are some funny bits but most of the film drags along until the dog springs into action.

p, Rudolph C. Flothow; d, Paul Burnford; w, Aubrey Wisberg (based on a story by Al Martin); ph, L. W. O'Connell; ed, Reg Browne.

Children (PR:A MPAA:NR)

ADVENTURES OF SADIE, THE**
(1955, Brit.) 87m Renown/Fox c (GB: OUR GIRL FRIDAY)

Joan Collins (*Sadie Patch*), George Cole (*Jimmy Carroll*), Kenneth More (*Pat Plunkett*), Robertson Hare (*Professor Gibble*), Hermione Gingold (*Spinster*), Walter Fitzgerald (*Captain*), Hattie Jacques (*Mrs. Patch*), Felix Felton (*Mr. Patch*), Lionel Murton (*Barman*).

Collins and three men—Cole, More, Hare—are the only survivors of a shipwreck, stranded on a desert island. Cole, a jaded newsman, and Hare, a blue-nosed academic, are forever chasing the scantily clad Collins about, but More, an Irish stoker, ignores her until they are rescued. She is in love with the stoker and marries him on board ship but before they can reach civilization their ship goes down and they are marooned once again, but this time they are happy in their isolation.

p, George Minter; d, Noel Langley; w, Langley (based on the novel *The Cautious Amorist* by Norman Lindsay); ph, Wilkie Cooper (Eastmancolor); m, Ronald Binge; md, Muir Mathieson.

Comedy (PR:A MPAA:NR)

ADVENTURES OF SCARAMOUCHE, THE**
(1964, Fr./Span./Ital.) 98m Capitole Films c

Gerald Barray (*Scaramouche*), Michele Giradon (*Colette*), Gianna Maria Canale (*Suzanne*), Alberto de Mendoza (*M. de la Tour*), Jose Bruquera (*Marquis de Souchil*), Gonzalo Canas (*Pierrot*), Yvette Lebon (*Mme. de Pompignan*).

Poor remake of an oft-filmed classic has Barray prancing about Paris stealing the hearts of lofty Giradon and sultry Canale while attempting to win back through cunning and swordplay his birthright from Mendoza who plays a convincing villain. The colorful Sabatini story was first made as a silent with Ramon Novarro and Lewis Stone and then as a lavish talkie production, SCARAMOUCHE, in 1952 with Stewart Granger and Mel Ferrer, the latter remaining the best of the lot to date.

d, Antonio Isasi Isasmendi; w, Arthur Rigel, Colin Mann, Isasmendi (based on a story by Guido Malatesta from the novel by Rafael Sabatini); ph, Alejandro Ulloa.

Adventure (PR:C MPAA:NR)

ADVENTURES OF SHERLOCK HOLMES, THE****
(1939) 85m FOX bw (GB: SHERLOCK HOLMES)

Basil Rathbone (*Sherlock Holmes*), Nigel Bruce (*Dr. Watson*), Ida Lupino (*Ann Brandon*), Alan Marshal (*Jerrold Hunter*), Terry Kilburn (*Billy*), George Zucco (*Prof. Moriarty*), Henry Stephenson (*Sir Ronald Ramsgate*), E. E. Clive (*Inspector Bristol*), Arthur Hohl (*Bassick*), May Beatty (*Mrs. Jameson*), Peter Willes (*Lloyd Brandon*), Mary Gordon (*Mrs. Hudson*), Holmes Herbert (*Justice*), George Regas (*Mateo*), Mary Forbes (*Lady Conynham*), Frank Dawson (*Dawes*), William Austin (*Stranger*), Anthony Kemble Cooper (*Tony*), Leonard Mudie (*Barrows*), Ivan Simpson (*Gates*).

A taut script, sharp and witty dialog and attention to production detail make this one of the finest crime adventures ever made, a superb effort of the Rathbone-Bruce team who were to prove so successful in the subsequent series about the great sleuth. Rathbone is the quintessential Holmes, almost a physical doppelganger of the famous sketches by Sidney Paget that accompanied the original Doyle stories in *Strand Magazine*, long, lean, hawk-nosed, wearing his deerstalker's cap and Inverness coat, while Bruce matched him in the public's imagination as *the* Dr. Watson, bumbling, dogged and ever loyal, though Bruce in subsequent series played the role for more laughs than expected. Fox was the first to produce a film on Holmes with the Victorian setting in which he was born and the just-right fog-bound atmosphere, ancient buildings and hansom cabs double the pleasurable tension as Holmes is hot on the trail of the evil Professor Moriarty, aptly portrayed by Zucco (the role model for Moriarty in Doyle's works was the American mastermind thief Adam Worth). Zucco begins his devilish plot to steal the crown jewels by sidetracking Holmes with two foul murders, one involving Lupino, the only romantic element of the film, and, for a moment, Rathbone is caught off guard, investigating the murders rather than Zucco's real goal. At the last minute, the great detective realizes that Zucco is inside the Tower of London to steal the crown jewels and he commandeers a horse-drawn cab, racing it madly to the Tower where he confronts the genius thief who had vowed to Rathbone to "bring off right under your nose the most incredible crime of the century and you'll never suspect it until it's too late." The two fight to the death at the top of the Tower of London, with

Zucco taking the long fall (his character somehow always surviving to vex Rathbone again and again). All of Holmes' fascinating quirks and preoccupations were worked into Rathbone's character—his violin playing, his scientific experiments; the rooms he shared with Bruce at Baker Street were authentically recreated, marvelously cluttered with books and artifacts of crime. The movie was a success but Fox double-billed it with films offering weightier stars and it was instantly slotted as a second feature, one with a first-rate budget. Inexplicably, Fox executives came to think of the production in those terms and failed to continue the series which Universal later took over with less ambitious expense. Yet Rathbone was *the* Sherlock Holmes and more than happy with the role, once commenting: "Ever since I was a boy and first got acquainted with the great detective I wanted to be like him." Although many tried, no other actor duplicated the role, which, for Rathbone, was . . . elementary. (See SHERLOCK HOLMES series, Index.)

p, Darryl F. Zanuck, Gene Markey; d, Alfred Werker; w, Edwin Blum, William Drake (based on a play by William Gillette and works of Arthur Conan Doyle); ph, Leon Shamroy; md, Cyril J. Mockridge; ed, Robert Bischoff.

Crime Cas (PR:A MPAA:NR)

ADVENTURES OF TARTU*** (1943, Brit.) 103m MGM bw (AKA: TARTU)

Robert Donat (*Capt. Terence Stevenson*), Valerie Hobson (*Maruschka*), Walter Rills (*Insp. Otto Vogel*), Glynis Johns (*Paula Palacek*), Phyllis Morris (*Anna Palacek*), Martin Miller (*Dr. Novothy*), Anthony Eustrel (*Officer*), Percy Walsh (*Dr. Willendorf*), Frederic Richter (*Nestor*), John Penrose (*Lt. Krantz*), Mabel Terry Lewis (*Mrs. Stevenson*).

Donat is a British officer posing as a Rumanian ex-diplomat to penetrate a Nazi-controlled poison gas factory in Czechoslovakia; some harrowing intrigues with Gestapo agents and partisans make for exciting if sometimes confusing exploits, but Donat's performance is top-notch as Tartu.

p, Irving Asher; d, Harold S. Bucquet; w, Howard Emmet Rogers, John Lee Mahin, Miles Malleson (based on a story by John C. Higgins); ph, John J. Cox; m, Hubert Bath.

War/Spy Drama Cas (PR:A MPAA:NR)

ADVENTURES OF THE WILDERNESS FAMILY, THE***
(1975) 94m Pacific Intern. c

Robert F. Logan (*Skip*), Susan Damante Shaw (*Pat*), Hollye Holmes (*Jenny*), Ham Larsen (*Toby*).

Made in Utah, this back-to-nature film shows Logan as a construction worker fed up with city life and taking his family to the high mountains where his asthmatic daughter, Holmes, can breath clean fresh air. They build a log cabin and fend off attacks by ferocious bears while making friends with the tamer speciesraccoons, wild dogs, coyotesa paean of praise for the simpler life and a production that has universal family appeal.

p, Arthur R. Dubbs; d&w, Stewart Raffil; m, Gene Kauer, Douglas Lackey.

Adventure Cas (PR:AAA MPAA:G)

ADVENTURES OF TOM SAWYER, THE***1/2 (1938) 93m SELZ c

Tommy Kelly (*Tom Sawyer*), Jackie Moran (*Huckleberry Finn*), Ann Gillis (*Becky Thatcher*), May Robson (*Aunt Polly*), Walter Brennan (*Muff Potter*), Victor Jory (*Injun Joe*), David Holt (*Sid Sawyer*), Victor Kilian (*Sheriff*), Nana Bryant (*Mrs. Thatcher*), Olin Howland (*Schoolmaster*), Donald Meek (*Superintendent*), Charles Richman (*Judge Thatcher*), Margaret Hamilton (*Mrs. Harper*), Marcia Mae Jones (*Mary Sawyer*), Mickey Rentschler (*Joe Harper*), Cora Sue Collins (*Amy Lawrence*), Philip Hurlie (*Jim*).

Mark Twain's immortal Sawyer came to life in this excellent production with Kelly portraying a brave, adventure-seeking boy caught between the lifestyles of his very proper home overlorded by a tough but loving Robson as Aunt Polly and the wild roaming and trouble-seeking of his friend, Huckleberry Finn, ably portrayed by Moran. The great Sawyer adventures are faithfully recreated—the conning of the two boys into whitewashing his aunt's fence, a wild ride down the Mississippi on a raft, the witnessing of Injun Joe's crimes and the pursuit of Kelly and a terrified Ann Gillis into the giant cave by a truly frightening villain, Jory, who was never more at his menacing best than in this movie. After Tom kicks the killer from a precipice, he returns to save the town drunk, Brennan (wonderful as always) from being convicted of a murder committed by Injun Joe. The irascible boys even witness their own funeral ceremony before informing the grieving townsfolk that they are still alive. Selznick was his usual picky self in supervising this beloved classic story, conducting talent hunts through orphanages to fill the roles of Tom and Huck, but settled on professional actor Moran and finally unearthed a freckle-faced Brooklyn boy, Kelly, to play the role of Tom. He was slow to learn acting methods but he made a genuine Sawyer. (Kelly quit the movies after a few more films and later became a teacher.) Selznick's penchant for perfection resulted in the original director, H. C. Potter, walking off the set and being replaced by Taurog, which proved to be a happy accident in that Taurog's direction brought more to the production in terms of action and pace, and no little humor.

p, David O. Selznick, William H. Wright; d, Norman Taurog; w, John V. A. Weaver (based on the novel by Mark Twain); ph, James Wong Howe, Wilfrid Cline (Technicolor); m, Max Steiner; ed, Margaret Clancy; md, Lou Forbes.

Adventure/Children Cas (PR:AAA MPAA:NR)

ADVENTURESS, THE****
(1946, Brit.) 111m Individual/GFD bw (GB: I SEE A DARK STRANGER)

Deborah Kerr (*Bridie Quilty*), Trevor Howard (*Lt. David Bayne*), Raymond Huntley (*Miller*), Michael Howard (*Hawkins*), Norman Shelley (*Man in Straw Hat*), Liam Redford (*Timothy*), Brefni O'Rorke (*Michael O'Callaghan*), James Harcourt (*Grandfather*), W. G. O'Gorman (*Danny Quilty*), George Woodbridge (*Steve*), Garry Marsh (*Capt. Goodhusband*), Olga Lindo (*Mrs. Edwards*), Tom Macauley (*Lt. Spanswick*), David Ward (*Oscar Pryce*), Kathleen Harrison (*Waitress*), Harry Hutchinson (*Chief Mourner*), Harry Webster (*Uncle Joe*), Eddie Golden (*Terence Delaney*), Marie Ault (*Mrs. O'Mara*), Humphrey Heathcote (*Sgt. Harris*), John Salew (*Man in Bookshop*), David Tomlinson (*Intelligence Officer*), Kenneth Buckley (*R.T.O.*), Torin Thatcher (*Policeman*), Everley Gregg, Kathleen Boutall (*Women on*

Train), Pat Leonard (*Receptionist*), Katie Johnson (*Old Lady*), Gerald Case (*Col. Dennington*).

Kerr, making her fifth feature at age 24, appears as a high-spirited Irish lass who has been weaned on her grandfather's tales of British cruelty to the Irish; she leaves her small village of Ballygarry, spouting anti-British venom to a stranger, Huntley, on board a train to Dublin where the I.R.A. rejects her. But Huntley, a Nazi agent, uses her as a pawn, telling her that he represents another branch of the movement, involving her with the rescue of one "of the lads" imprisoned in a British prison; the prisoner is in reality another Nazi spy. Howard, as a British intelligence agent, gets on her trail, meets and falls in love with her, staying a step behind through one perilous adventure after another, to both protect her and uncover the Nazi spy ring. This is a highly suspenseful atmospheric film in the Hitchcockian tradition, mostly due to a superb script by Launder and Gilliat who authored THE LADY VANISHES. The acting, particularly by Kerr (who won the 1947 NY Film Critics Award for this role and her appearance in BLACK NARCISSUS), Howard and Huntley are superb in a high-production value film that has too long gone unsung.

p, Sidney Gilliat; d, Frank Launder; w, Gilliat, Launder, Wolfgang Wilhelm; ph, Wilkie Cooper; m, William Alwyn; ed, Thelma Myers.

Spy Drama   **(PR:A MPAA:NR)**

ADVENTUROUS BLONDE****1/2**   (1937) 60m WB bw

Glenda Farrell (*Torchy Blane*), Barton MacLane (*Steve McBride*), Anne Nagel (*Grace Brown*), Tom Kennedy (*Gahagan*), George E. Stone (*Pete*), Natalie Moorhead (*Theresa Gray*), William Hopper (*Matt*), Anderson Lawlor (*Hugo Brand*), Charley Foy (*Dud*), Bobby Watson (*Mugsy*), Charles Wilson (*Mortimer Gray*), Virginia Brissac (*Mrs. Hammond*), Leland Hodgson (*Harvey Hammond*), Raymond Hatton (*Maxie*), Frank Shannon (*Capt. McTavish*), James Conlon (*Dr. Bolger*), Granville Owen (*Dr. Nolly*), Walter Young (*Lawyer*), George Guhl (*Sergeant*), Al Herman (*Herman*).

Third in Warner's Torchy Blane series, Farrell plays the peppery female reporter about to marry MacLane when a police call interrupts the wedding. The call results in the death of an actor who had put in a prophetic fake homicide alarm to promote his career. Farrell is on the hunt for the killers, aggravating the cops, assisting her fiance, and, after some quick-paced adventures, nabs the culprits. Her marriage, naturally, is postponed until the next film. A good action-filled programmer. (See TORCHY BLANE series, Index.)

p, Bryan Foy; d, Frank McDonald; w, Robertson White, David Diamond; ph, Arthur Todd; ed, Frank Magee.

Crime   **(PR:A MPAA:NR)**

ADVERSARY, THE****1/2** (1973, Ind.) 100m Priya Films bw (PRATLDWANDI)

Dhritiman Chatterjee (*Siddhartha*), Krishnanbose (*Sutapa*), Jaysree Roy (*Keya*), Devraj Roy (*Tunu*).

A story of India's day-to-day struggle narrowed to a youth who must quit medical school because of his father's death and his efforts to find work and a place in a fluid, ambiguous society, one he does not resist, except in one instance when he and a large crowd are kept waiting by irritating bureaucrats. An often powerful story from Satyajit Ray, winner of the Grand Prix at Venice for THE COWARD.

d&w, Satyajit Ray (based on a story by Sunil Ganguly); ph, Soumendu Ray, Purmendu Base; m, S. Ray; ed, Dulal Dutta.

Drama   **(PR:A MPAA:NR)**

ADVICE TO THE LOVELORN***   (1933) 60m FOX/UA bw

Lee Tracy (*Toby Prentiss*), Sally Blane (*Louise Boley*), Sterling Holloway (*Benny*), Jean Adair (*Mrs. Prentiss*), Paul Harvey (*Gaskell*), Matt Briggs (*Richards*), Charles Levinson (*Circulation Manager*), C. Henry Gordon (*Kranz*), Isabel Jewell (*Rose*), Ruth Fallows (*Miss Howell*), May Boley (*Miss Lonelyhearts*).

Exceptional newspaper yarn, based on the minor masterpiece novel by Nathanael West, has Tracy as the wayward newsman demoted to writing the lonelyhearts column and becoming heavily involved with the problems of his readers. The novel's indictment of the corrupt newspaper publisher, so powerfully depicted in LONELYHEARTS, 1958, is dropped in favor of Tracy's pursuing crooked druggists victimizing customers. The overall production lifts this programmer out of grade B status and is a perfect example of Hollywood's first tempered stirrings in dealing with social problems (other than Warner Brothers, which made a crusade of it, via its gangster vehicles).

p, William Goetz, Raymond Griffith; d, Alfred Werker; w, Leonard Praskins (based on the novel *Miss Lonelyhearts* by Nathanael West); ph, James Van Trees, Sr.; ed, Alan McNeil; md, Alfred Newman.

Drama   **(PR:A MPAA:NR)**

ADVISE AND CONSENT****   (1962) 140m COL c

Henry Fonda (*Robert Leffingwell*), Charles Laughton (*Sen. Seabright "Seb" Cooley*), Don Murray (*Sen. Brigham Anderson*), Walter Pidgeon (*Sen. Bob Munson*), Peter Lawford (*Sen. Lafe Smith*), Gene Tierney (*Dolly Harrison*), Franchot Tone (*The President*), Lew Ayres (*Vice-President*), Burgess Meredith (*Herbert Gelman*), Eddie Hodges (*Johnny Leffingwell*), Paul Ford (*Sen. Stanley Dante*), George Grizzard (*Sen. Van Ackerman*), Inga Swenson (*Ellen Anderson*), Paul McGrath (*Hardiman Fletcher*), Will Geer (*Senate Minority Leader*), Betty White (*Sen. Bessie Adams*), Malcolm Atterbury (*Sen. Tom August*), Edward Andrews (*Sen. Knox*), J. Edward McKinley (*Sen. Hanson*), William Quinn (*Sen. Hendershot*), Tiki Santos (*Sen. Kanaho*), Raoul DeLeon (*Sen. Velez*), Tom Helmore (*British Ambassador*), Hilary Eaves (*Lady Maudulayne*), Chet Stratton (*Rev. Birch*), John Granger (*Ray Shaff*), Rene Paul (*French Ambassador*), Janet Jane Carty (*Pidge Anderson*).

Incisive study of American high politics, often as brutal as those who move through such shady wheelings and dealings, this film is a monument to how the American political system works for and against itself, sometimes hanging by the thread of one man's decision. Based on Allen Drury's best-selling novel, the integrity of this production is maintained from first to last with outstanding performances from the leads to a great collection of character actors. Fonda has been appointed to the omnipotent position of Secretary of State and the film revolves around confirmation

of that appointment by the U.S. Senate. Pidgeon and his cohorts are trying to push the appointment through, past such ancient pelicans as Laughton, a marvelous personification of a crusty old Dixiecrat who is more patriotic than political. Murray, a freshman senator whose vote in support of the nomination is vital, will not commit to his party leader, Pidgeon. This leads Grizzard, a ruthless, power-hungry colleague followed about by a ton of toadies, to attempt to blackmail Murray into siding with his voting block. He digs up Murray's former homosexual activities, an isolated incident really, from the ancient past and threatens to expose him unless he votes "the right way." The threat reaches Murray's wife and the young senator's marriage flounders; in resignation, Murray commits suicide. Moreover, Pidgeon's foes bring forward a strange, sweaty little man, Meredith, to testify that Fonda had once belonged to a Communist cell in their college days at the University of Chicago. One by one, Pidgeon's allies desert the nomination. Lawford, an apparently unscrupulous pawn and playboy senator indifferent to his duties, is enraged at Murray's blackmail and death and votes against Fonda but, in the end, the Senate is deadlocked, the final decision made by Ayres, who learns at the last moment that the President had died. Though this is his own party's nomination, he votes against it, saying: "I prefer to name my own Secretary of State." Laughton and democracy triumph over corrupt politics as the new President assumes office. Though the film sensationalizes Washington politics, its perspective is well-aimed and technically the film is as precise and careful as could be wanted, a more realistic if less human portrait of the Senate than portrayed in Capra's MR. SMITH GOES TO WASHINGTON. Both films proved to be unpopular with their role models who refused to comment on them.

p & d, Otto Preminger; w, Wendell Mayes (based on the novel by Allen Drury); ph, Sam Leavitt (Technicolor, Panavision): m, Jerry Fielding; ed, Louis Loeffler; art d, Lyle Wheeler; set d, Eli Benneche; cos, Hope Bryce.

Drama   **(PR:C MPAA:NR)**

AERIAL GUNNER****1/2**   (1943) 78m PAR

Chester Morris (*Foxy Pattis*), Richard Arlen (*Ben Davis*), Lita Ward (*Peggy Lunt*), Jimmy Lydon (*Sandy Lunt*), Dick Purcell (*Gadget Blaine*), Keith Richards (*Sgt. Jones*), Billy Benedict (*Private Laswell*), Ralph Sanford (*Barclay*).

A fast-paced, above-average programmer dealing with pre-combat air force training which Arlen narrates in flashback while recuperating in an Army hospital. He tells of his recruitment and training, his meeting with Morris, an antagonist from prewar days who turns out to be his training sergeant, and their mutual attempt to win the hand of Lita Ward, whose brother Lydon (playing a wimp, as usual) develops a fear of flying and crashes his plane during exercises. The squadron then departs for the South Pacific where Morris and Arlen land on an island and are trapped by occupying Japanese troops as they hurriedly attempt to repair their plane. Heroically, Morris stays behind, fighting off the enemy until Arlen can take off and fly to freedom. Tough portrayals and two-fisted action make this an excellent propaganda film of WWII, the story line not dissimilar to Arlen's smash silent movie WINGS.

p&d, William H. Pine; w, Maxwell Shane; ph, Fred Jackman, Jr.; ed, William Ziegler.

War   **(PR:A MPAA:NR)**

AFFAIR AT AKITSU**   (1980, Jap.) 113m Shochiku c

Mariko Okada (*Shinko*), Hiroyuki Nagato (*Shusaku Kawamoto*) with Sumiko Hidaka, Taiji Tonoyama, Masako Nakamura, Jinkichi Uno, Eijiro Tono, Fukuko Sayo, Teruo Yoshida.

Sickly student Nagato, emaciated and starving from the ravages of WWII, interrupts his wanderings at the village of Akitsu to be nursed back to health by a beautiful young girl, Okado. When they hear Japan has lost the war, both enter into a suicide pact (the then ideal—dying for the glory of the Emperor, sharing his shame, so to speak, as the disgraced warlord), but their fumblings and gropings toward death are futile and they decide to live and build a new life together. Most of the black humor dealing with the prolonged suicide attempts will be lost on Western viewers who regard such traditions as socially repugnant and criminal.

p, Masao Shirai; d, Yoshishige Yoshida; w, Yoshida (based on a story by Shinji Fujiwara); ph, Toichiro Narushima; m, Hikaru Hayashi; art d, Tatsuo Hamada; cos, Mariko Okada.

Drama   **(PR:O MPAA:NR)**

AFFAIR BLUM, THE**   (1949, Ger.) 109m Deutsche Film/AG bw

Kurt Erhardt (*Karl-Heinz Gabler*), Gisela Trowe (*Christine Burman*), Paul Bildt (*Judge Konrad*), Gerhard Blenert (*Schwerdtfeger*), Claus Becker (*Dr. Jacob Blum*), Renee Stobrawa (*Sabine*), Helmut Rudolph (*Wilschinski*), Arno Paulsen (*Wilhelm Platzer*), Karin Evans (*Lucie*), Maly Delschaft (*Anna*), Hans Christian Blech (*Bonte*).

A murder is committed by Erhardt, but Becker, a Jewish businessman remotely connected to the victim, is pinpointed as the murderer by anti-Semitic police officials, who build a web of circumstantial evidence around him aided by the real killer who provides alibis and explanations according to police instructions to protect himself and convict Becker. Bienert and Bildt give devastating performances as the biased detectives and Erhardt is both stupid and crafty as the killer. Becker is further hampered from obtaining justice by a pre-Hitler bureaucracy that blamed all Jews for Germany's post-WW I woes. Becker is saved at the last moment by one conscientious policeman who uncovers enough real evidence against Erhardt. This revealing and frightening movie is based upon a real incident occurring in 1926. (In German; English subtitles.)

d, Erich Engel; w, R. A. Stemmle; ph, Friedl Behn Grund, Karl Plintzer; m, Herbert Trantow.

Crime   **(PR:C MPAA:NR)**

AFFAIR IN HAVANA*   (1957) 71m AA bw

John Cassavetes (*Nick*), Raymond Burr (*Mallabee*), Sara Shane (*Lorna*), Lilia Lazo (*Fina*), Sergio Pena (*Valdes*), Celia Cruz (*Fiesta Singer*), Jose Antonio Rivero (*Rivero*), Miguel Angel Blanco (*Police Captain*).

Cassavetes seduces the wife of a crippled plantation owner, Burr, and is about to run off with the wanton woman (Shane) when Burr tells his greedy spouse that he only has ninety days to live and when he dies $20 million will be hers. Cassavetes gets the heave-ho and the wife settles back in the nest to await her fortune. Tiring of the wait, she pushes the wheelchair-bound Burr into his swimming pool and inherits the fortune ahead of schedule. Cassavetes learns the truth from a servant who is murdered by Shane (and she is killed in turn by the servant's wife). The lover returns to a Havana bar and his job at a piano which is where this sordid, dull adventure began. The most interesting aspects of this potboiler are the scenes, music and showgirls of pre-Castro Havana. All else is a disaster.

p, Richard Goldstone; d, Laslo Benedek; w, Burton Lane, Maurice Zimm (based on a story by Janet Green); ph, Alan Stensvold; ed, Stefan Arnsten.

Crime **(PR:O MPAA:NR)**

AFFAIR IN MONTE CARLO** (1953, Brit.) 90m ABPC/AA c (GB: 24 HOURS OF A WOMAN'S LIFE)

Merle Oberon *(Lindon Venning)*, Richard Todd *(The Boy)*, Leo Genn *(Robert Sterling)*, Stephen Murray *(Father Benoit)*, Peter Reynolds *(Peter)*, Joan Dowling *(Mrs. Barry)*, June Clyde *(Mrs. Roche)*, Peter Illing *(M. Blanc)*, Jacques Brunius *(Francois)*, Isabel Dean *(Miss Johnson)*, Peter Jones *(Bill)*, Yvonne Furneaux *(Henriette)*, Mara Lane *(Alice Brown)*, Robert Ayres *(Frank Brown)*.

Through the narration of a writer, the viewer sees a wealthy worldly woman, Oberon, attempt to reform a compulsive gambler, offering her love and fortune to prevent his habit from destroying him, an effort that fails miserably as does this poor sudser, although the background of the romantic Riviera and its fabulous casino provides some exotic interest.

p, Ivan Foxwell; d, Victor Saville; w, Warren Chetham Strode (based on Stefan Zweig's novel, *24 Hours In A Woman's Life*).

Romance **(PR:A MPAA:NR)**

AFFAIR IN RENO** (1957) 75m REP bw

John Lund *(Bill Carter)*, Doris Singleton *(Nora Ballard)*, John Archer *(Tony Lamarr)*, Angela Greene *(Gloria Del Monte)*, Alan Hale *(Deke)*, Harry Bartell *(Conrad Hertz)*, Howard McNear *(James T. James)*, Richard Deacon *(H. L. Denham)*, Thurston Hall *(J.B. Del Monte)*, Billy Vincent *(Pete)*.

An uninspiring little story of a PR man hired by a millionaire to go to Reno to prevent his daughter from marrying an opportunistic gambler. Should the gambler refuse to quit the relationship, the PR man, Lund, has $100,000 in cash from his tycoon employer to use in buying off the bounder. Most of this tiring tale is spent with Lund and Singleton, a lady gumshoe, fending off thieves after the cash. Archer is good as the slick gambler and so is Greene as the spoiled brat no sane father would keep single.

p, Sidney Picker; d, R. G. Springsteen; w, John K. Butler (based on a story by Gerald Drayson Adams); ph, Jack Marta; m, R. Dale Butts; ed, Tony Martinelli.

Crime **(PR:A MPAA:NR)**

AFFAIR IN TRINIDAD** (1952) 98m COL bw

Rita Hayworth *(Chris Emery)*, Glenn Ford *(Steve Emery)*, Alexander Scourby *(Max* Fabian), Valerie Bettis *(Veronica)*, Torin Thatcher *(Inspector Smythe)*, Howard Wendell *(Anderson)*, Karel Stepanek *(Walters)*, George Voskovec *(Dr. Franz Huebling)*, Steven Geray *(Wittol)*, Walter Kohler *(Peter Bronec)*, Juanita Moore *(Dominique)*, Gregg Martell *(Olaf)*, Mort Mills *(Martin)*, Robert Boon *(Pilot)*, Ralph Moody *(Coroner)*, Ross Elliott *(Neal Emery)*, Franz Roehn *(Refugee)*, Don Kohler *(Mr. Peters)*, Kathleen O'Malley *(Stewardess)*, Fred Baker *(Airport Clerk)*, Don Blackman *(Bobby)*, Ivan Browning, Roy Glenn, Joel Fluellen *(Fishermen)*.

An overdone spy melodrama which takes most of its inspiration from GILDA, this production served as Hayworth's return to the screen after a four-year absence (following her marriage to Prince Aly Khan she had announced she would never again appear in a film but the marriage collapsed and she was back with Harry Cohn of Columbia). Hayworth is a singer-dancer in a Trinidad dive owned by her husband who is murdered by international thief and spy Scourby. Police inspector Thatcher asks Hayworth to play up to Scourby and snoop into his affairs. At the same time Ford shows up to find out who killed Rita's husband, his brother, and gets into a lot of trouble, a thankless bumbling role for a strong actor. Scourby is finally exposed and his ring nabbed with Hayward winding up in Ford's arms. Highlights of the film show Rita doing sexy, hip-grinding dances to the tunes of "Trinidad Lady" and "I've Been Kissed Before." (Jo Ann Greer's voice was dubbed for Hayworth's in the vocals.) Valerie Bettis, who did the choreography for the two Hayworth numbers, and a famous name along Broadway, also appeared in the film as a drunken, empty-headed woman who exclaims after one of Hayworth's gyrations: "Gee, I wish I could dance like that." This, of course, was a great inside joke among the personnel of a production which was almost never made, thanks to the temperamental star. Hayworth had the script rewritten several times then rejected the final draft, walking off the set and stating she would not return until a complete revision was made. Cohn exploded, suspending her and preparing an expensive lawsuit against her, vowing to collect enormous damages from her. After looking over the lawyers' workups, Rita decided to bend to King Cohn's demands and returned to the studio to do the film which most critics agreed was trite in plot and, as far as the dances went, "vulgar and grotesque." Oddly, the film seems better today than when first released but that may be due to the Hayworth-Ford mystique and nostalgia for what we forget was corny in its day.

p&d, Vincent Sherman; w, Oscar Saul, James Gunn (based on a story by Virginia Van Upp, Berne Giler); ph, Joseph Walker; m, George Duning; ed, Viola Lawrence; art d, Walter Holscher; set d, William Kiernan; cos, Jean Lewis; m/l, Lester Lee, Bob Russell.

Spy Drama **(PR:C MPAA:NR)**

AFFAIR LAFONT, THE* 1/2 (1939, Fr.) 100m Transatlantic/CIPRA bw

Corinne Luchaire *(Claire)*, Annie Ducaux *(Catharine)*, Raymond Rouleau *(Michel Lafont)*, Roger Duchesne *(Robert)*, Pauline Carton *(Pauline)*, Jacques Copeau *(The Judge)*, Marguerite Angel *(Marguerite)*, Armand Bernard *(Secretary)*, Claude Dauphin *(Gerard)*, Leon Belleres *(Father)*, Dalio *(Money-Lender)*.

Lurid French melodrama has moments of superb acting inside an impossible plot. Ducaux's marriage is faltering because she cannot give her husband a child but her younger sister (Luchaire), after an affair with a ne'er-do-well, gives her child to Ducaux. She passes it off as her own to her husband, who has been on an African expedition. He accepts the child but Luchaire's lover begins blackmailing Ducaux, threatening to reveal the true parentage. The sister is also moved by parental urgings and demands Ducaux return the baby. When Ducaux refuses, Luchaire goes to the husband but before she can blurt her secret, Ducaux shoots her to death. Ducaux is excellent as the tortured wife but the plot is hopelessly unbelievable. (In French; English subtitles.)

d, Leonard Moguy; w, Hana Wilhelm, Gina Kaus (based on the novel by Kaus); ph, Ted Pahle; m, Wal-Berg.

Drama **(PR:O MPAA:NR)**

AFFAIR OF SUSAN* (1935) 62m UNIV bw

ZaSu Pitts *(Susan Todd)*, Hugh O'Connell *(Dudley Stone)*, Walter Catlett *(Gilbert)*, Thomas Dugan *(Jeff Barnes)*, Inez Courtney *(Mrs. Barnes)*, James Burke *(Hogan)*, Mae Busch *(Mrs. Hogan)*, Irene Franklin *(Mrs. Perkins)*, *Dorothy Granger, William Pawley, Buster Phelps, Monte Montague.*

Slipshod slapstick story of two wallflowers who spend a day at Coney Island, meeting an assortment of dopey men and using up their time on whirlwind rides, with Pitts carrying most of the forced comedy. Well photographed, some good action and an above-average score by Waxman can't save this one.

p, David Diamond; d, Kurt Neumann; w, Clarence Marks, H. M. Walker, Andrew Bennison (based on a story by Mann Page); ph, Norbert Brodine; m, Franz Waxman; ed, Phil Cahn.

Comedy **(PR:A MPAA:NR)**

AFFAIR OF THE SKIN, AN* (1964) 102m Zenith bw

Viveca Lindfors *(Victoria)*, Kevin McCarthy *(Allen McCleod)*, Lee Grant *(Katherine McCleod)*, Herbert Berghof *(Max)*, Diana Sands *(Janice)*, Nancy Malone *(Claire)*.

Ostentatious and contrived, this production is a mishmash of sexual rationales for one promiscuous affair after another, Lindfors as a fading model with a young lover she knows to be her last, McCarthy and Grant as unhappily wed neurotics, all spilling their mundane and morose tales to Sands. Only the photography landscaping New York is worth watching in this pretentious and artificial film which was once touted as a sophisticated view of sex.

p, Helen Levitt, Ben Maddow; d&w, Maddow.

Drama **(PR:O MPAA:NR)**

AFFAIR TO REMEMBER, AN*** (1957) 115m FOX c

Cary Grant *(Nickie Ferrante)*, Deborah Kerr *(Terry McKay)*, Richard Denning *(Kenneth)*, Neva Patterson *(Lois)*, Cathleen Nesbitt *(Grandmother)*, Robert Q. Lewis *(Announcer)*, Charles Watts *(Hathaway)*, Fortunio Bonanova *(Courbet)*, Matt Moore *(Father McGrath)*, Louis Mercier *(Mario)*, Geraldine Wall *(Miss Webb)*, Nora Marlowe *(Gladys)*, Sarah Selby *(Miss Lane)*, Genevieve Aumont *(Gabriello)*, Jesslyn Fax *(Landlady)*, Alberto Morin *(Bartender)*.

This grand soaper finds Grant traveling to New York aboard a luxury liner, and meeting Kerr. They draw close to one another but both have someone waiting for them and they agree that if they still feel the same way about each other in six months, they will meet again at the top of the Empire State Building. When the ship docks, Grant goes to Patterson and Kerr to Denning. Grant keeps the rendezvous six months later, but Kerr does not appear; she is run over by a car and permanently crippled en route to the meeting. Grant tries to forget all about her, but has a chance meeting with her some time later. Believing she would be a burden to him, Kerr discourages Grant's attempts to rekindle their affair. When he learns she is permanently disabled, he vows to stay at her side forever. This film is one of the most effective tearjerkers ever made and is brought to a sophisticated level by two consummate actors. (A remake of LOVE AFFAIR with Charles Boyer and Irene Dunne.)

p, Jerry Wald; d, Leo McCarey; w, Delmer Daves, McCarey (based on a story by McCarey, Mildred Cram); ph, Milton Krasner (CinemaScope, DeLuxe Color); m, Hugo Friedhofer; ed, James B. Clark; md, Lionel Newman; art d, Lyle R. Wheeler, Jack Martin Smith; set d, Walter M. Scott, Paul S. Fox; m/l, Harry Warren, Harold Adamson, McCarey (sung by Vic Damone).

Romance **(PR:A MPAA:NR)**

AFFAIR WITH A STRANGER** (1953) 89m RKO bw

Jean Simmons *(Carolyn Parker)*, Victor Mature *(Bill Blakely)*, Mary Jo Tarola *(Dolly Murray)*, Monica Lewis *(Janet Boothe)*, Jane Darwell *(Ma Stanton)*, Dabbs Greer *(Happy Murray)*, Wally Vernon *(Joe)*, Nicholas Joy *(George Craig)*, Olive Carey *(Cynthia Craig)*, Victoria Horne *(Mrs. Wallace)*, Lillian Bronson *(Miss Crutcher)*, George Cleveland *(Pop)*, Bill Chapin *(The Older Timmy)*.

An item in a gossip column sets off a chain reaction among friends of a writer and his wife who are reportedly breaking up. Told in flashbacks, we see the story of their meeting, the struggling playwright, the beauteous model and the birth of their child who dies on the opening night of his first play. Simmons adopts another child and Mature feels she no longer cares about his career; he begins playing around with sexy Lewis, the star of his new show, a tame affair that makes it into the gossip column, thus having the film come full circle. Simmons, however, is understanding and takes back her straying husband. A mediocre dose of suds and tears.

p, Robert Sparks; d, Roy Rowland; w, Richard Flournoy; ph, Harold J. Wild; ed, George Amy; m/l, "Kiss and Run," Sam Coslow (sung by Lewis).

Romance **(PR:A MPAA:NR)**

AFFAIRS IN VERSAILLES (SEE: ROYAL AFFAIRS IN VERSAILLES, 1957)

AFFAIRS OF A GENTLEMAN** (1934) 70m UNIV bw

Paul Lukas *(Gresham)*, Leila Hyams *(Gladys Durland)*, Patricia Ellis *(Jean Sinclair)*, Phillip Reed *(Carter Vaughn)*, Onslow Stevens *(Lyn Durland)*, Dorothy Burgess *(Nan* Fitzgerald), Lillian Bond *(Carlotta)*, Joyce Compton *(Foxey)*, Murray Kinnell *(Fletcher)*, Dorothy Libaire *(Gail Melville)*, Richard Carle *(Bindar)*, Wilfred Hari

(Sato), Sara Haden *(Gresham's Secretary)*, Charles Wilson *(Inspector)*, Gregory Gaye *(Bela)*.

Sensational fiction author Lukas is found dead at his desk, a letter from him stating that no one is to blame for his demise but police feel differently and begin investigating his ex-flames, all of whom Lukas jocularly scandalized in his books. Flashbacks show a party arranged by his publisher, Carle, which takes place the night before and one which is attended by the ex-girlfriends. In flashbacks, we see Lukas entertain several women that night before going to his study where he tells his valet, Kinnell, he intends to commit suicide—the world is too much with him—and the valet, it is revealed in the last scenes, suggests that Lukas leave a note so no one will be blamed for his death. He writes the note, then fires a shot into the floor which brings the valet on the run. Finding his employer still alive, he shoots him over an old grievance, thinking his tracks covered, but he does not reckon with that extra bullet in the floor which leads to his arrest. An above-average programmer which was certainly based upon the unsolved murder of film director William Desmond Taylor in 1922.

d, Edward L. Marin; w, Cyril Hume, Peter Ruric, Milton Krims (based on a play by Edith and Edward Ellis); ph, John Mescall.

Crime (PR:A MPAA:NR)

AFFAIRS OF A MODEL** (1952, Swed.) 82m Union Film bw

Alf Kjellin *(Erik Lunde)*, Maj-Britt Nilsson *(Dora Svensson)*, Marianne Lofgren *(Vera)*, Olaf Winnerstrand *(The Count)*, Stig Jarrel *(Consul-General)*, Oscar Winge *(Gregerson)*, Carl-Gunnar Wingard *(Bylund)*, Georg Funkquist *(Rune)*, Anna-Lisa Baude *(Fru Ohlsson)*, Sven Bergvali *(The General)*.

Nilsson is an unemployed artist's model who falls in love with a young sculptor, Kjellin. He, in turn, can think of her only as the perfect model without flesh-and-blood attraction. Both embark on a hectic crusade to convince the Swedish Parliament to sponsor a national monument to be sculpted by Kjellin. Not much story here and the film is further hampered by too-rapidly shown subtitles. (In Swedish; English subtitles.)

d, Gustaf Molander; w, Rune Lindstrom; ph, Aka Dahlquist; m, E. Eckert-Lundin.

Drama (PR:O MPAA:NR)

AFFAIRS OF A ROGUE, THE**

(1949, Brit.) 95m Two Cities/COL bw (GB:THE FIRST GENTLEMAN)

Jean Pierre Aumont *(Prince Leopold)*, Joan Hopkins *(Charlotte)*, Cecil Parker *(Regent)*, Ronald Squire *(Mr. Brougham)*, Athene Seyler *(Miss Knight)*, Anthony Hawtrey *(Sir Richard Croft)*, Gerald Heinz *(Dr. Stockmar)*, Margaretta Scott *(Lady Hartford)*, Jack Livesey *(Edward)*, Hugh Griffith *(Bishop of Salisbury)*, Joan Young *(Mrs. Griffiths)*, Betty Huntley-Wright *(Princess Elizabeth)*.

Ponderously directed film of British royalty in the early 19th century which traces the reign of the Prince Regent following the Napoleonic wars where Parker spends much time trying to marry off his unruly daughter, Hopkins, to a number of acceptable nobles, but to no avail in that she selects an impoverished German prince to wed. Aumont, as Leopold, is kind, devoted and very princely. His marriage to Hopkins (consuming the last half of the film) is joyous until the birth of their child when the baby and mother die during the delivery. A poorly mounted costume drama with a complicated script that moves at snail's pace.

p, Joseph Friedman; d, Alberto Cavalcanti; w, Nicholas Phipps, Reginald Long (based on a play by Norman Ginsbury); ph, Jack Hildyard; m, Lennox Berkeley; ed, Margery Saunders.

Drama (PR:A MPAA:NR)

AFFAIRS OF ADELAIDE**

(1949, U.S./Brit) 91m FOX bw (AKA: FORBIDDEN STREET GB: BRITANNIA MEWS)

Maureen O'Hara *(Adelaide Culver)*, June Allen *(Adelaide as a Child)*, Dana Andrews *(Gilbert Lauderdale/Henry Lambert)*, Dame Sybil Thorndike *(Mrs. Mounsey)*, Anthony Tancred *(Treff Culver)*, Anthony Lamb *(Treff as a Child)*, Wilfrid Hyde-White *(Mr. Culver)*, Fay Compton *(Mrs. Culver)*, Anne Butchart *(Alice Hambro)*, Suzanne Gibbs *(Alice as a Child)*, Diane Hart *(The Blazer)*, Heather Latham *(Blazer as a Child)*, Herbert Walton *(The Old Un)*, A. E. Matthews *(Mr. Bly)*, Mary Martlew *(Milly Lauderdale)*, Gwen Whitby *(Miss Bryant)*, Scott Harold *(Benson)*, Neil North *(Jimmy Hambro)*.

Morose story in murky Britannia Mews (a back alley where the down-and-out struggle to survive) relates how wealthy O'Hara falls in love with an alcoholic artist, marries him, and watches hopelessly as he dies in the poverty-stricken area in which she compels herself to live (art for art's sake), incurring the wrath of her disowning family. O'Hara remarries, this time to a failed lawyer who aids her in running a puppet theater for the street urchins, both husbands being played by the talented Andrews (the identical physical resemblance is offset a bit by makeup and personality changes, but is nevertheless a bit confusing). O'Hara's family finally comes around for the traditional happy ending.

p, William Perlberg; d, Jean Negulesco; w, Ring Lardner, Jr. (based on the novel *Britannia Mews* by Margery Sharp); ph, George Perinal, Denys Coop; m, Malcolm Arnold; ed, Richard Best.

Drama (PR:C MPAA:NR)

AFFAIRS OF ANNABEL*** (1938) 73m RKO bw

Jack Oakie *(Morgan)*, Lucille Ball *(Annabel)*, Ruth Donnelly *(Josephine)*, Bradley Page *(Webb)*, Fritz Feld *(Vladimir)*, Thurston Hall *(Major)*, Elisabeth Risdon *(Mrs. Fletcher)*, Granville Bates *(Mr. Fletcher)*, James Burke *(Muldoon)*, Lee Van Atta *(Robert Fletcher)*, Anthony Warde *(Bailey)* Edward Marr *(Martin)*, Leona Roberts *(Mrs. Hurley)*.

Zany press agent, to hype his scatterbrained client's flagging movie career, dreams up a dozen screwball stunts to get her publicity; creating one trouble spot after another for Ball, including a stint in a female reformatory. The last stunt backfires when Ball is kidnapped by real gangsters and forced to be party to a crime. In the end she is vindicated and Hollywood does pay attention to her at last, with Oakie taking the bows for her notoriety. He and Ball are both very funny, as is Thurston Hall as an escaped lunatic playing a mogul, Fritz Feld as a megalomaniac foreign director too good to direct any Hollywood script, and Ruth Donnelly, the wise secretary who constantly gets Oakie and his clients out of trouble. This is a fast-paced film with plenty of laughs.

p, Lou Lusty; d, Ben Stoloff; w, Bert Granet, Paul Yawitz (based on a story by Charles Hoffman); ph, Russell Metty; md, Roy Webb.

Comedy Cas. (PR:A MPAA:NR)

AFFAIRS OF CAPPY RICKS* (1937) 57m REP bw

Walter Brennan *(Cappy Ricks)*, Mary Brian *(Frankie Ricks)*, Lyle Talbot *(Bill Peck)*, Frank Shields *(Waldo Bottomley, Jr.)*, Frank Melton *(Matt Peasely)*, Georgia Caine *(Mrs. Peasely)*, Phyllis Barry *(Ellen)*, William B. Davidson *(Mr. Bottomley, Sr.)* Frank Shannon *(Captain Braddock)*, Howard Brooks *(Revere)*, Anthony Pawley *(Sailor)*, Sherry Hall *(Rankin)*, Don Rowan *(Riley)*, Will Stanton *(Steward)*.

Old salt Brennan spends most of his time trying to show his two daughters the real values in life, especially Brian who has thrown over a good man for a cad. Brennan takes the girls and their beaus on what appears to be a pleasure cruise but his boat is lost in a storm and the party must fend for itself on a deserted island where the girls learn that their choice in future husbands is faulty. They are finally picked up and returned to their true loves. A slow and banal production, far inferior to another Cappy Ricks production, THE GO-GETTER.

d, Ralph Staub; w, Lester Cole (based on a story by Peter B. Kyne); ph, Ernest Miller; ed, William Morgan.

Comedy (PR:A MPAA:NR)

AFFAIRS OF CELLINI, THE*** (1934) 90m FOX/UA bw

Constance Bennett *(Duchess of Florence)*, Fredric March *(Benvenuto Cellini)*, Frank Morgan *(Alessandro, Duke of Florence)*, Fay Wray *(Angela)*, Vince Barnett *(Ascanio)*, Jessie Ralph *(Beatrice)*, Louis Calhern *(Ottaviano)*, Jay Eaton *(Polverino)*, Paul Harvey *(Emissary)*, John Rutherford *(Captain of Guards)*.

A well-made bedroom farce has the versatile March as the hell-raising, womanizing rake and rascal, Benvenuto Cellini, a talented artist who would rather dabble with other men's wives than pursue a literary/artistic career. He begins by paying attention to his model, Wray, then diverting most of his energy to wooing gorgeous Bennett, whose bumbling, sputtering husband, Morgan (in one of many fine performances) blithely ignores the cuckolding and chases after model Wray. Meanwhile, Cellini's enemies—and there are scores of them—headed by Louis Calhern, fight a number of duels and he barely manages to escape death in some uninviting torture chambers. Director La Cava, who was to direct many of the great W. C. Fields films, produced a tongue-in-cheek movie where March parodies the part to perfection but most of his scenes with Morgan were stolen outright by the great character actor, no mean feat. A delightful, light-hearted film.

d, Gregory La Cava; w, Bess Meredyth (based on the play "The Firebrand," by Edwin Justus Mayer): ph, Charles Rosher; ed, Barbara McLean.

Comedy (PR:C MPAA:NR)

AFFAIRS OF DOBIE GILLIS, THE** (1953) 72m MGM bw

Debbie Reynolds *(Pansy Hammer)*, Bobby Van *(Dobie Gillis)*, Barbara Ruick *(Lorna Ellingboe)* Bob Fosse *(Charlie Trask)*, Hanley Stafford *(Mr. Hammer)*, Lurene Tuttle *(Mrs. Hammer)*, Hans Conried *(Prof. Amos Pomfritt)*, Charles Lane *(Prof. Obispo)*, Archer Mac Donald *(Harry Dorcas)*, Kathleen Freeman *(Happy Stella)*, Almira Sessions *(Aunt Naomi)*.

Tame, youth-oriented film shows Reynolds, Van, Ruick and Fosse as they enter their freshman year of college. The love blossoming, the escape from studies (much to the chagrin of stuffy teachers Conried and Lane), the stupid situations adolescents create and the inadvertent blowing up of the chemistry lab, are the highlights of this rather draggy production which is momentarily brightened by such songs as "I'm Through with Love," by Van, "All I Do Is Dream of You," by Reynolds and Van as they paddle a canoe, and two song and dance numbers with Reynolds, Van, Ruick and Fosse, "You Can't Do Wrong Doing Right," and "Those Endearing Young Charms." But mostly this one droops as low as a janitor's baggy pants with a script and scenes that are bald and humorless.

p, Arthur M. Loew, Jr.; d, Don Weis; w, Max Shulman; ph, William Mellor; ed, Conrad A. Nervig; md, Jeff Alexander; ch, Alex Romero.

Comedy/Musical (PR:A MPAA:NR)

AFFAIRS OF DR. HOLL**

(1954, Ger.) 101m Joseph Brenner Assoc. (AKA: ANGELIKA)

Maria Schell *(Angelika)*, Dieter Barsche *(Dr. Holl)*, Heidemarie Hatheyer *(Helga)*, Carl Wery *(Alberti)*, Otto Gebuhr *(Prof. Amriss)*, Franz Schafheitlin *(Prof. Godenbergh)*, Gerd Brudern *(Corvus)*, Lina Carstens *(Frau V. Bergmann)*, Claire Reigbert *(Housekeeper)*, Adrian Hoven *(Tonio)*, Marianne Koch *(Anna)*, Gustav Waldau *(Priest)*.

Slow-moving melodrama in which an incurably sick rich girl falls in love with her handsome, but boring, doctor. He marries her out of pity, but later realizes his love for her while discovering the miraculous cure for her "disease." Coming from a rather ho-hum era in German cinema, the film is memorable only for the beguiling presence of Maria Schell.

d, Friedrich A. Mainz; w, Thea Von Harbou; ph, Franz Weihmayr; m, Mark Lothar.

Drama (PR:A MPAA:NR)

AFFAIRS OF GERALDINE** (1946) 68m REP bw

Jane Withers *(Geraldine Cooper)*, James Lydon *(Willy Briggs)*, Raymond Walburn *(Amos Hartwell)*, Donald Meek *(Casper Millhouse)*, Charles Quigley *(J. Edmund Roberts)*, Grant Withers *(Henry Cooper)*, William Haade *(Wayne Cooper)*, Michael Branden *(Charlie March)*, Johnny Sands *(Danny)*, David Holt *(Percy McBride)*, Tanis Chandler *(Liza Jane)*, Harry V. Cheshire *(Judge Fricke)*, Josephine Whittell *(Belle Walker)*, Donia Russey *(Mrs. Hutchinson)*, Edith M. Griffith *(Mrs. Eddington)*, George Carleton *(Lawyer Darnell)*.

Withers suddenly inherits a fortune but her mother's dying request that her brothers find a good husband for her has Grant Withers and Haade dredging up all manner of goofs and clowns to come courting. Jane will have nothing to do with them or her long-standing boy friend, sappy Lydon, so she runs off to the big city where sharper Walburn, running a lovelorn clinic, sets her up under the bogus title of Madama L'Amour and sends her to side slick Quigley who almost wins her hand before Lydon and her brothers expose the suitor as a three-time bigamist. Lydon marries Withers at the end, reminding us one and all that beggars can't be choosers, even if they're rich!

p, Armand Schaefer, d, George Blair; w, John K. Butler (based on a story by Lee Loeb and Arthur Strawn); ph, John Alton; m, Morton Scott; ed, Tony Martinelli.

Comedy **(PR:A MPAA:NR)**

AFFAIRS OF JIMMY VALENTINE (SEE: UNFORGOTTEN CRIME, 1942)

AFFAIRS OF JULIE, THE* (1958, Ger.) 90m Trebitsch/BAKROS INTER. c

Lilo Pulver *(Juliane Thomas)*, Paul Hubschmid *(Dr. Jean Berner)*, Bernhard Wicki *(Paul Frank)*, Wolfgang Lukschy *(Juergen Kolbe)*, Rudolf Platte *(Edgar Stephan)*, Werner Finck *(Dr. Julius Weyer)*, Maria Sebalt *(Grace)*, Roland Kaiser *(Pips)*, Sonja Ziemann *(Sonja Ziemann)*, Max Schmeling.

Heavy-handed tale of Pulver batting large eyes at any man who'll pay attention to her, particularly playboy Hugschmid, whom she chases around St. Moritz, Switzerland (where the scenic shots help to compensate for the endlessly dull talk), Berlin and Hamburg, finally settling for down-to-earth Wicki, who has sought her hand through constant rebuffs. Little glamour and less story makes for a tedious hour and a half.

d, Helmut Kautner; w, Heinz Pauck, Kautner; ph, (Eastmancolor).

Comedy/Romance **(PR:C MPAA:NR)**

AFFAIRS OF MARTHA, THE ** 1/2**

(1942) 66m MGM bw (GB: ONCE UPON A THURSDAY)

Marsha Hunt *(Martha Lindstrom)*, Richard Carlson *(Jeff Sommerfield)*, Marjorie Main *(Mrs. McKissick)*, Virginia Weidler *(Miranda Sommerfield)*, Spring Byington *(Mrs. Sophie Sommerfield)*, Allyn Joslyn *(Joel Archer)*, Barry Nelson *(Danny OBrien)*, Frances Drake *(Sylvia Norwood)*, Melville Cooper *(Dr. Clarence Sommerfield)*, Ernest Truex *(Llewellyn Castle)*, Cecil Cunningham *(Mrs. Castle)*, William B. Davidson *(Homer Jacell)*, Inez Cooper *(Mrs. Jacell)*, Aubrey Mather *(Justin Peacock)*, Sara Haden *(Mrs. Peacock)*, Grady Sutton *(Junio Peacock)*, Margaret Hamilton *(Guinevere)*, Jody Gilbert *(Hadwig)*.

Excellent cast in a better than average B film offering an amusing plot wherein a household servant with an eye for scandal (or the imagination to create more than exists) writes a sensational book about her employers and ignites the gossips of the neighborhood, not to mention having a best-seller. Very funny in spots and humorous throughout.

p, Irving Starr; d, Jules Dassin; w, Isobel Lennart, Lee Gold; ph, Charles Lawton; m, Bronislau Kaper; ed, Ralph Winters; art d, Cedric Gibbons.

Comedy **(PR:A MPAA:NR)**

AFFAIRS OF MAUPASSANT***

(1938, Aust.) 86m Panta/GALLIC FILMS bw

Lili Darvas *(Marie Bashkirtseff)*, Han Jaray *(Guy de Maupassant)*, Szoke Szkall [S. Z. "Cuddles" Sakall] *(Dr. Walitzky)*, Attila Horbiger *(Bassleux)*, Anna Kallina *(Marie's Mother)*, Frida Richard *(Fortune Teller)*.

Well-done love story has painter Darvas being rescued by Jaray, who plays the mysterious writer de Maupassant, while a Paris mob of thugs swirls about her. He takes her home and then later to a fancy dress ball where she sees her teacher, Horbiger, who is jealous of her attentions from the writer whom he hates. Later she overhears Szkall tell the teacher that his recent examination of the frail Darvas reveals that she has an incurable ailment and that her death is imminent. Darvas returns home, collapses and takes to her bed to await the end. Jaray sees her before she dies, vowing his love. Director Koster maintains a brisk pace in this breezy film, his last before departing for Hollywood (one step away from the Nazis), as was the case of the great character actor Sakall. This film was lavish by any Austrian standards in that it commanded a $300,000 budget wherein most averaged $75,000 tops; it shows in sets of the moody Parisian street scenes and grand houses. (In German; English subtitles.)

d, Henry Koster; w, Felix Joachimson (based on the diary of Marie Bashkirtseff); ph, Willy Goldberger; m, Paul Abraham.

Romance **(PR:A MPAA:NR)**

AFFAIRS OF MESSALINA, THE zero (1954, Ital.) 120m COL

Memo Benassi, Maria Felix, Georges Marchal, Jean Chevrier, Jean Tissier, Michel Vitold, Giuseppe Varni, Germaine Kerjean, Delia Scala, Erno Crisa, Camillo Pilotto, Carla Ninchi, Ave Ninchi, Cesare Barbetti, Gino Saltamerenda.

How Italian director Gallone could take the tempestuous, torrid story of court intriguer Messalina, whose Roman Emperor husband Claudius was the essence of cruelty (second only to his nephew Caligula), and make of it a boring, drooping film without an ounce of merit can only be attributable to either improper diet or addled brains. Take your pick.

p,d&w, Carmine Gallone (based on an adaptation by Albert Valentin, Nino Novarese); m, Renzo Rossellini.

Adventure/Historical Drama **(PR:O PAA:NR)**

AFFAIRS OF SUSAN*** (1945) 110m PAR bw

Joan Fontaine *(Susan Darell)* George Brent *(Roger Berton)*, Dennis OKeefe *(Bill Anthony)*, Don DeFore *(Mike Ward)*, Rita Johnson *(Mona Kent)*, Walter Abel *(Richard Aiken)*, Byron Barr *(Chick)*, Mary Field *(Nancy)*, Frances Pierlot *(Uncle Jimmy)*, Lewis Russell *(Mr. Cusp)*, Vera Marshe *(Brooklyn Girl)*, Frank Faylen *(Brooklyn Boy)*, James Millican *(Major)*, Robert Sully *(Lieutenant)*, John Whitney *(1st Captain)*, Jerry James *(2nd Captain)*, Crane Whitney *(Colonel)*.

Fontaine is slick and funny as she plays four separate personalities in one girl, all of them remembered in flashback by different beaus. Abel proposes to her and is accepted. He then gives a party to celebrate and meets three men who have known and loved his wife-to-be—George Brent, a movie producer who married and divorced Fontaine; novelist Dennis OKeefe, who thought of her as an intellectual; and lumber tycoon DeFore, who met her after her divorce from Brent and endured endless nightclubbing with her, believing her to be a wonderful companion but a disgraceful liar. The three later embellish their stories of Fontaine at a bachelor dinner given by her fiance, Abel, and most the film is told in flashbacks, an effective and twisty technique which allows Fontaine a tour de force in ranging postures and attitudes, all of them delightfully funny.

p, Hal Wallis; d, William A. Seiter; w, Monroe Gorog, Richard Flournoy (based on a story by Thomas Monroe and Gorog); ph, David Abel; ed, Edna Warren.

Comedy **(PR:A MPAA:NR)**

AFFECTIONATELY YOURS ** 1/2** (1941) 87m WB bw

Merle Oberon *(Sue Marberry)*, Dennis Morgan *(Richard Ricky' Mayberry)*, Rita Hayworth *(Irene Malcolm)*, Ralph Bellamy *(Owen Wright)*, George Tobias *(Pasha)*, James Gleason *(Chester Phillips)*, Hattie McDaniel *(Cynthia)*, Jerome Cowan *(Cullen)*, Butterfly McQueen *(Butterfly)*, Renie Riano *(Mrs. Snell)*, Frank Wilcox *(Tom)*, Grace Stafford *(Miss Anderson)*, Carmen Morales *(Anita)*, Murray Alper *(Blair)*, William Haade *(Matthes)*, Pat Flaherty *(Harmon)*, James Flavin *(Tomassetti)*, DeWolfe Hopper, Craig Stevens, Frank Faylen, Garrett Craig, Keith Douglas, Ed Brian, Fred Graham, Nat Carr, Ann Edmonds, Billy Wayne, Alexis Smith, Henry Blair, Edward Gargan, Faye Emerson, Charles Drake, Charles Marsh.

Oberon wearies of hubby Morgan and his globe-trotting for a newspaper syndicate; she flies to Reno and gets an uncontested divorce, immediately submerging herself in a whirlwind courtship with ultragentleman Bellamy. (When was he anything but?) Morgan hears the news of his wife's disaffection when finishing a Russian assignment and flies back to the states, attempting every crazy stunt imaginable to win her back, while Hayworth, who outshines the stiffly British Oberon in every scene, goes after Morgan. Many funny scenes are not enough to pull this one up to the level of top screwball comedy mostly due to beautiful Oberon's inability to play her scenes expansively and handle banter, let alone take a pratfall which the script called for; it was embarrassing, not funny, to see a lady of such dignity attempt a Judy Canova fall. This was a hand-picked Jack Warner comedy and it shows. Warner wanted to be a standup comic all his life; the role of movie mogul was a second ambition, he later claimed in retirement, but what would one expect from a man who once attended a dinner in his honor, given by Mme. Chiang-Kai-Shek, and was called upon to give a speech before a long table of dignified Chinese-Americans. He slapped his forehead in mock shock, exclaiming: "You know, looking down this table reminds me me that I forgot to send out my laundry!" Not a single Oriental face cracked a smile. Fortunately, AFFECTIONATELY YOURS produced some smiles, even on the faces of McDaniel and McQueen, their first pairing since GONE WITH THE WIND. If you look closely, you'll see in this Lloyd Bacon farce novice actors who later became stars—Emerson as a nurse, Smith as a bridesmaid, Stevens as a guard.

p, Hal B. Wallis, Mark Hellinger; d, Lloyd Bacon; w, Edward Kaufman (based on a story by Fanya Foss and Aleen Leslie): ph, Tony Gaudio; m, Heinz Roemheld; ed, Owen Marks; md, Leo F. Forbstein; art d, Anton Grot; ch, Matty King.

Comedy **(PR:A MPAA:NR)**

AFRAID TO TALK** (1932) 74m UNIV bw

Eric Linden *(Ed Martin)*, Sidney Fox *(Peggy Martin)*, Tully Marshall *(Anderson)*, Louis Calhern *(Wade)*, Berton Churchill *(Manning)*, Edward Arnold *(Jig Skela)*, George Meeker *(Lennie)*, Mayo Methot *(Marge)*, Ian MacLaren *(Chief)*, Matt McHugh *(Joe Skela)*, Frank Sheridan *(Commissioner)*, Gustav von Seyffertitz *(Berger)*, Reginald Barlow *(Judge MacMurray)*, Edward Martindel *(Jamison)*, Robert Warwick *(Jake)*, Tom Jackson *(Benchley)*, Joyce Compton *(Alice)*, King Baggot.

Bellhop Linden witnesses a gangster assassination and is quickly gobbled up into the arms of a corrupt administration, politicians from the mayor down taking enormous bribes from gang bosses and nightclubbing with them, all the while deciding Linden's fate. He is finally charged with the killing and almost railroaded for a crime he did not commit. The locale of the city is obviously Chicago since there is a reference to the stockyards. All old hat crime situations with rub-outs, knock-offs, one-way rides, and dialog curled out of the side of the mouth, but its archaic feel of the Dillinger era is fascinating.

d, Edward L. Cahn; w, Tom Reed (based on the play "Merry Go Round" by Albert Maltz and George Sklar); ph, Karl Freund.

Crime **(PR:C MPAA:NR)**

AFRICA SCREAMS*** (1949) 79m UA bw

Bud Abbott *(Buzz Johnson)*, Lou Costello *(Stanley Livingston)*, Hillary Brooke *(Diana Emerson)*, Max Baer *(Boots)*, Buddy Baer *(Grappler)*, Clyde Beatty *(Clyde Beatty)*, Frank Buck *(Frank Buck)*, Shemp Howard *(Gunner)*, Joe Besser *(Harry)*.

A top-flight and generally unheralded B&L comedy opens with the boys working in the book department of a large store, Brooke coming to their counter and asking for an out-of-print tome entitled *Dark Africa*. To impress this well-dressed, attractive lady, Abbott tells her that his pal Costello was a personal friend of the author and accompa- nied him on many trips into jungles as a big game hunter. Brooke offers Costello a great sum of money if he will make a map for her expedition. The boys go to her mansion late that night and Costello draws a bogus map, but instead of collecting a reward they are abducted, taken to Africa and ordered to point out the way to a certain tribe; Brooke and her henchmen, the Baer brothers, are looking for some hidden diamonds. Stumbling along, the expedition meets with harrowing adventures and strange creatures, even famous lion tamers Beatty and Buck, as well as providing a ton of laughs as they are bounced about by giant apes, swirl down a jungle river (the studio tank where sideman Shemp Howard actually got seasick), and do some funny bits in gorilla costumes. The crooks are finally dispatched but Abbott has a breakdown (exhaustion from conning his pal), and returns to the U.S.; Costello stays on, finds the diamonds and, when back in America, buys the department store where he once worked, hiring Abbott as an elevator operator. The typical B&L off-set hijinks went on during this production, pie and seltzer water fights and an offscreen highlight that, had it been lensed, would have made this film one of the great curiosities of all time. The heavyweight prizefighting Baer brothers, playing Brooke's henchmen in the film, were visited on the set by Jack Dempsey and Gene Tunney, and the four of them staged an impromptu, one-round donnybrook, with Costello as the referee. There were no knockdowns or "long counts" but just the sight of these four legends battling each other (some actual blows were struck) would have sent fight fans into ecstasy. (See ABBOTT & COSTELLO series, Index.)

p, Edward Nassour; d, Charles Barton; w, Earl Baldwin; ph, Charles Van Enger; ed, Frank Gross; spec eff, Carl Lee.

Comedy **Cas.** **(PR:AA MPAA:NR)**

AFRICA—TEXAS STYLE!*** (1967 U.S./Brit.) 110m Vantors/PAR c

Hugh O'Brian *(Jim Sinclair)*, John Mills *(Wing Commander Howard Hayes)*, Nigel Green *(Karl Bekker)*, Tom Nardini *(John Henry)*, Adrienne Corri *(Fay Carter)*, Ronald Howard *(Hugo Copp)*, Charles Malinda *(Sampson)*, Honey Wamala *(Mr. Oyondi)*, Charles Hayes *(Veterinary)*, Stephen Kikumu *(Peter)*, Ali Twaha *(Turk)*, Mohammed Abdullah *(Witch Doctor)*, Hayley Mills *(Girl)*.

Fast-paced direction and action-filled scenes (as advertised) make this production first-rate, along with exceptional acting by John Mills who imports Texas cowboys O'Brian and Nardini to round up the thousands of wild animals that are being systematically killed into extinction, herding them onto a vast ranch reserve. The good guys are opposed by ruthless Green who presents obstacles to the humanitarian plan but is overcome in the end. In addition to that veteran character actor's superb portrait in villainy, Corri is attractive as the feminine lead and Howard is excellent as the concerned naturalist advising Mills. (Served as pilot for the TV series "Cowboy in Africa.")

p, Ivan Tors, Andrew Marton; d, Marton; w, Andy White; ph, Paul Beeson (Eastmancolor); m, Malcolm Arnold; ed, Henry Richardson.

Adventure **Cas.** **(PR:AA MPAA:NR)**

AFRICAN, THE** (1983, Fr.) 101m Renn/AMLF c (L'AFRICAIN)

Catherine Deneuve *(Charlotte)*, Philippe Noiret *(Victor)*, Jean-Francois Balmer *(Planchet)*, Joseph Momo *(Bako)*, Vivian Reed *(Josephine)*, Jacques Francois *(Patterson)*, Jean Benguigui *(Poulakis)*.

While scouting a resort site in Central Africa, travel executive Deneuve runs into her old flame Noiret who is the majo domo, storeowner and pilot for a one-man airline in the village she selects. Ancient animosities flare, then the two draw closer to each other, their affair interrupted by a gang of vicious ivory poachers who abduct Deneuve. Noiret goes after them in a well-filmed chase sequence, mows down the bad guys and frees his blonde paramour. Stereotypes abound—jungle pursuits, the cutting of a rope bridge to which Noiret desperately clings, a lot of hysterical pigmies running amuck.

p, Claude Berri; d, Philippe de Broca; w, Gerard Brach, de Broca; ph, Jean Penzer; m, Georges Delerue, Henri Lanoe; art d, Francois de Lamoth; cos, Sylvie Gautrelet; stunts, Daniel Verite.

Adventure/Romance **(PR:C MPAA:NR)**

AFRICAN FURY (SEE: CRY THE BELOVED COUNTRY, 1951)

AFRICAN MANHUNT zero (1955) 70m REP

Myron Healey *(Bob Kirby)*, Karen Booth *(Ann Davis)*, John Kellogg *(Sgt. Jed Drover)*, Ross Elliott *(Rene Carvell)*, Ray Bennett *(Dr. Clark)*, James Edwards *(Native Guide)*.

Crudely done studio setting, a few plants and jungle trees having seen better productions, go to make up the shoddy atmosphere in this safari film where Davis and two male friends escort a wanted criminal to the coast from central Africa, standing in awe every few minutes to watch grainy library footage of wild animals attacking each other. Not worth the trek.

p, Jerry Thomas; d, Seymour Friedman; w, Arthur Hoerl.

Adventure **(PR:A MPAA:NR)**

AFRICAN QUEEN, THE***** (1951, U.S./Brit.) 105m Horizon-Romulus/US c

Humphrey Bogart *(Charlie Allnut)*, Katharine Hepburn *(Rose Sayer)*, Robert Morley *(Rev. Samuel Sayer)*, Peter Bull *(Captain of "Louisa")*, *Theodore Bikel (1st Officer)*, Walter Gotell *(2nd Officer)*, Gerald Onn *(Petty Officer)*, Peter Swanick *(1st Officer at Shona)*, Richard Marner *(2nd Officer at Shona)*.

Here is a film that has everything—adventure, humor, spectacular photography, superb acting and exciting motion—oh, what motion. ("Great movies must move," said Louis B. Mayer.) This is the story of roustabout Bogart running a little tramp steamer with supplies to small villages in East Africa at the onset of WW I. He comes to a village which is overlorded by stuffy British missionary Morley (so British he can hardly speak, a marvelous performance of an out-of-place proper Edwardian), and his spinster sister, Hepburn, who is utterly devoted to her brother and his black flock; she tends the sick, plays the organ at church services and acts as if the savage wilds were nothing more than an extension of peaceful green England, rigidly adhering to teatime and parlor decorum. Bogart thinks the couple a bit batty but plays out forced niceties in an early hilarious scene where he sips tea out of a dainty cup with grimy hands while his stomach growls with hunger pangs and embarrassment twitches across that marvelously lined face. After dumping his supplies, Bogart leaves in his battered steamboat, "The African Queen," returning to find that German troops have invaded the village, torched its buildings, herded off the men as slave laborers and killed a protesting Morley (the scene of his violent demise is both traumatic and heart-rending through the reaction of a helpless Hepburn). Bogart offers to take the distraught woman back to civilization on the "Queen" and both start off downriver, Bogart swilling from an ample supply of gin and resentful at Hepburn's chidings and directives. He becomes amorous but she rebuffs his clumsy advances as they steam through the jungle. In a drunken burst of anger Bogart shouts: "You crazy psalm-singing skinny old maid!" Hepburn's hurt feelings show and he later apologizes, in the middle of which she proposes they sail down the Ulanga-Bora, Africa's most dangerous interconnecting rivers, to where the huge German warship "Louisa" commands a large Central Africa lake and use the explosives on board the "Queen" to blow the Germans sky-high. He thinks she has lost her mind, warning her of the incredible hazards en route, vicious rapids and falls, man-eating and poisonous water creatures, the towering fort at Shona where sharpshooting guards command every inch of the river. She is adamant and accuses him of cowardice. He rises to this bait and angrily agrees to the harebrained plan. Thus begins the wild and wonderful river adventure where the pair in the old, bobbing, steam-belching tub overcome every obstacle only to lose their way in the reedy channels at river's end. Famished and ill, they lie down to die at the bottom of the boat, lovers now. The wind finally pushes the "Queen" out onto the lake where they revive and see the enemy ship. Bogart fashions some makeshift torpedoes and inserts these through holes in the bow of the "Queen"; they make a night attack against the "Louisa" but a raging storm overturns the boat and both are picked up by the German warship at dawn, sentenced to be hanged on the yardarm as British spies, Peter Bull playing a particularly obnoxious German sea captain. Their touching last request, that they be married before the execution, is granted. With the ropes around their necks, Hepburn and Bogart exchange vows smilingly. All appears lost but the valiant "Queen" surfaces upside down, the torpedoes angled upward in the path of the "Louisa" which it strikes and sinks. As the warship goes down, Bogart and Hepburn joyously begin swimming toward a friendly shore, blissful as man-and-wife and accomplished saboteurs. The marvelous script, packed with sprightly dialog—unforgettable exchanges and comments by Bogart and Hepburn—was written as a straight drama by James Agee but director Huston and his stars played it with punchy tongue-in-cheek satire that filled the screen with hilarious humanity, a Hollywood film of the first order with one of the happiest endings on celluloid. An elaborate on-location production, early scenes were shot near Penthierville on the Lulaba River, then Huston moved the entire cast and the "Queen" 1,500 miles to where the Albert and Victoria Nile meet on a large lake in Uganda, which brought great hardships to the crew and actors. Everyone got deathly sick, including Lauren Bacall, traveling with husband Bogart, except Bogart and Huston who consistently downed large quantities of booze. "No insect's gonna bite me," remarked the laconic Bogie, "unless he wants to wind up a drunk!" Thus immunized, Huston and Bogart played constant pranks on the proper Hepburn who was first outraged at their behavior, once finding them up all night drinking, storming from her tent and shouting: "What's the meaning of this? We have to work tomorrow! You should all be in bed . . . and you should be ashamed of yourselves!" They weren't ashamed and enjoyed Hepburn's indignant attitude which was identical to the role she was playing. "She thought we were rascals, scamps, rogues," Huston later recalled in fond memory of the "Queen's" arduous location shooting. "We did everything we could to support this belief. We pretended to get roaring drunk. We even wrote dirty words in soap on her mirror. But eventually she saw through our antics and learned to trust us as friends." That trust showed in one of the most remarkable performances of Hepburn's illustrious career, and was responded to in kind by the great Bogie who deservedly won an Academy Award for portraying the kind-hearted drifter risking all for the woman he loves.

p, S. P. Eagle [Sam Spiegel]; d, John Huston; w, James Agee, Huston (based on the novel by C. S. Forester); ph, Jack Cardiff (Technicolor); m, Alan Gray; ed, Ralph Kemplen.

Adventure/Romance **Cas.** **(PR:AA MPAA:NR)**

AFRICAN TREASURE*

(1952) 70m MON bw (AKA: BOMBA AND THE AFRICAN TREASURE)

Johnny Sheffield *(Bomba)*, Laurette Luez *(Lita)*, Leonard Mudie *(Andy Barnes)*, Arthur Space *(Greg)*, Lane Bradford *(Hardy)*, Martin Garralaga *(Pedro)*, Lyle Talbot *(Gilroy)*, Robert Whitfield *(Eli)*, James Adamson *(Tolu)*, Jack Williams *(Drummer)*, Wesley Bly *(Timid Native)*, Sugar Foot Anderson *(Native Slave)*, Woodrow Wilson Strode *(Native Mail Boy)*.

Another attempt by Monogram to create a rousing African adventure, this one detailing the capture of two diamond smugglers by plucky jungle lad Sheffield, Saturday matinee stuff filled with the usual stock footage of frightening lions, elephants, and wildebeests. (See BOMBA, THE JUNGLE BOY series, Index.)

p, Walter Mirisch; d, Ford Beebe; w, Beebe; ph, Harry Neumann, md, Raoul Kraushaar; ed, Bruce Schoengarth; art d, Martin Obzina; set d, Robert Priestley.

Adventure **(PR:A MPAA:NR)**

AFTER MIDNIGHT WITH BOSTON BLACKIE** (1943) 64m COL bw

Chester Morris *(Boston Blackie)*, George E. Stone *(The Runt)*, Richard Lane *(Inspector Farraday)*, Cy Kendall *(Joe Herschel)*, George McKay *(Marty Beck)*, Al Hill *(Sammy Walsh)*, Walter Sande *(Sergeant Matthews)*, Ann Savage *(Betty Barnaby)*, Jan Buckingham *(Dixie Rose Blossom)*, Lloyd Corrigan *(Arthur Manleder)*, Walter Baldwin *(Diamond Ed Barnaby)*, Dick Elliott *(Justice Potts)*, Don Barclay, John Harmon.

Granite-jawed Morris as Blackie meets old flame Savage who tells him that her father, Baldwin, has just been released from prison and that he has hidden a sack of diamonds from an earlier robbery in a safe deposit box. She wants him to go straight and return the gems, asking Blackie to expedite matters; before the gumshoe can obtain the diamonds, he is arrested for Baldwin's murder. He escapes and discovers that Savage has been kidnapped by Kendall and his mob, holding her until she pinpoints the jewels. Blackie confronts the mob in Kendall's nightclub, shooting it out with several members and rounding up the mob while saving Savage. And, yes, our hero does return the jewels to their rightful owners. (SEE: Boston Blackie series.)

p, Sam White; d, Lew Landers; w, Howard J. Green (based on the book by Jack Boyle); ph, L. W. O'Connell; m, M.W. Stoloff; ed, Richard Fantl; art d, Lionel Banks.

Crime **(PR:A MPAA:NR)**

AFTER OFFICE HOURS* 1/2 (1932, Brit.) 78m BIP bw

Frank Lawton *(Hec)*, Heather Angel *(Pat)*, Viola Lyel *(Miss Janus)*, Garry Marsh *(Brewer)*, Eileen Peel *(Miss Bufton)*, Frank Royde *(Mr. Walker)*, Katie Johnson *(Miss Wilesden)*, Nadine March *(Miss Hooper)*.

Old maid secretary Lyel works behind the scenes to help love-smitten Lawton win the hand of Angel, a rather empty-headed secretary who will apparently fall in love with any man looking twice in her direction, oblivious to her own beauty and charm. Often tedious, consistently dull British programmer.

d, Thomas Bentley; w, Frank Launder, Bentley (based on the play "London Wall" by John Van Druten); ph, M.E. Palmer.

Romance (PR:A MPAA:NR)

AFTER OFFICE HOURS** (1935) 73m MGM bw

Constance Bennett (*Sharon Norwood*), Clark Gable (*Jim Branch*), Stuart Erwin (*Hank Parr*), Billie Burke (*Mrs. Norwood*), Harvey Stephens (*Tommy Bannister*), Katherine Alexander (*Mrs. Patterson*), Hale Hamilton (*Mr. Patterson*), Henry Travers (*Cap*), Henry Armetta (*Italian*), Charles Richman (*Jordan*), Herbert Bunston (*Barlow*).

Managing editor Gable fires Bennett from her newspaper job but later sees her being escorted by playboy Stephens. Gable believes that millionaire Hamilton is about to divorce his wife, Alexander, because she has been seeing Stephens on the sly, so he rehires Bennett to snoop on her boyfriend. Bennett, however, gets wise to Gable's using her and she throws herself at the playboy, going home with him after a party. Alexander follows them from the party and, while Bennett is in an upstairs bedroom, she enters Stephens' mansion and begins a row with him. He shoots her, then hides the body. He then takes Bennett home and—busy night for him—returns home, retrieves the body and takes it to Hamilton's home. Naturally, Hamilton is arrested for his wife's murder but Gable has been following Stephens' movements and confronts him, compelling him to give a full confession which runs in the next edition. Gable and Bennett scoop the world and wind up in each other's arms, talking about marriage and a two-day honeymoon, such are the demands of a working press. A pleasant but mindless film.

p, Bernard H. Hyman; d, Robert Z. Leonard; w, Herman J. Mankiewicz (based on a story by Laurence Stallings and Dale Van Every); ph, Charles Rosher; ed, Tom Held.

Crime (PR:A MPAA:NR)

AFTER THE BALL** (1932, Brit.) 70m GAU bw

Esther Ralston (*Elissa Strange*), Basil Rathbone (*Jack Harrowby*), Marie Burke (*Lavita*), Jean Adrienne (*Victorine*), George Curzon (*Peter Strange*), Clifford Heatherley (*Albuera*).

Sophisticated remake of the German bedroom farce OPERA BALL has Rathbone getting his promiscuous (and prominent) nose into an affair with a diplomat's wife. Or could it have been the maid? Lush and pretty with a handsome cast, the film has a definite, albeit simple charm.

p, Michael Balcon; d, Milton Rosmer; w, J. O. C. Orton; m, Otto Stransky; ph, Percy Strong; m/l, Stransky, Clifford Grey.

Comedy (PR:C MPAA:NR)

AFTER THE BALL**1/2 (1957, Brit.) 89m Romulus/IFD c

Pat Kirkwood (*Vesta Tilley*), Laurence Harvey (*Walter de Frece*), Jerry Stovin (*Frank Tanhill*), Jerry Verno (*Harry Ball*), Clive Morton (*Henry de Frece*), Marjorie Rhodes (*Bessie*), Leonard Sachs (*Richard Warner*), Ballard Berkeley (*Andrews*), Margaret Sawyer (*Tilly as a Child*), David Hurst (*Perelli*), George Margo (*Tony Pastor*), Rita Stevens (*Carmelita*), June Clyde (*Lottie Gilson*), Tom Gill (*Manager*), Peter Carlisle (*Oscar Hammerstein*), Charles Victor (*Stagehand*), Mark Baker (*George M. Cohan*), Terry Cooke (*Dan Leno, Jr.*).

Anemic biofilm of vaudeville entertainer Tilley, covering the years 1868-1920, and showing her act (once too often) as a male impersonator (which may or may not have inspired VICTOR/VICTORIA). Kirkwood does what she can with a poorly written script, putting zest into many old-time music hall numbers but she and Harvey, as her devoted manager-husband, shuffle through an agonizingly slow production toward paychecks. Director Bennett and writers Gregg and Blackmore did a great disservice to a famous British entertainer with their inept plodding.

p, Peter Rogers; d, Compton Bennett; w, Hubert Gregg, Peter Blackmore (based on Lady de Frece's memoirs, *Recollections of Vesta Tilley*); ph, Jack Asher; m, Muir Matheson; ed, Peter Boita.

Musical (PR:A MPAA:NR)

AFTER THE DANCE** (1935) 60m COL bw

Nancy Carroll (*Anne Taylor*), George Murphy (*Jerry Davis*), Thelma Todd (*Mabel Kane*), Jack La Rue (*Mitch*), Arthur Hohl (*Louis*), Wyrley Birch (*Warden*), Victor Kilian (*Kennedy*), George McKay (*Danny*), Thurston Hall, Robert Middlemass, Harry Barris, Virginia Sale.

Innocent of the crime for which he was convicted, Murphy escapes from prison and is taken in by hoofer Carroll; they begin a dance team that clicks but at the height of their success, Carroll's jealous former partner, LaRue, calls in the cops. Murphy is convinced by police to return to prison and serve out another two years while Carroll promises to wait for him, rejecting LaRue. It's all very trite and the ending too neat, but Murphy's dancing with Carroll is worth the watching.

d, Leo Bulgakov; w, Harold Shumate, Bruce Manning (based on a story by Harrison Jacobs); ph, Joseph August; ed, Otto Meyer; ch, Albertina Rasch; m/l, Harry Akst.

Musical (PR:A MPAA:NR)

AFTER THE FOG* (1930) 68m Beacon/Affiliated Exchanges Inc. bw

Mary Philbin, Russell Simpson, Edmund Jones, Carmelita Geraghty, Margaret Seddon, Allan Simpson, Joseph Bennett.

A lighthouse keeper's daughter, in love with a society chap, is confronted by her angry father wishing to speak with her about marrying above her station. Dad does his talking with an axe and Philbin answers with a pistol. Very poor, old-fashioned tale relies too heavily on dialogue and extreme situations. Philbin's presence is a curiosity.

d, Leander DeCordova; w, George Terwilliger, A. M. Statter; ph, Charles Boyle.

Drama (PR:C MPAA:NR)

AFTER THE FOX** (1966, U.S./Brit./Ital.) 102m UA c

Peter Sellers (*Aldo Vanucci*), Victor Mature (*Tony Powell*), Britt Ekland (*Gina Romantica*), Martin Balsam (*Harry*), Akim Tamiroff (*Okra*), Paolo Stoppa (*Polio*), Tino Buazzeli (*Siepi*), Mac Ronay (*Carlo*), Lidia Brazzi (*Mama Vanucci*), Lando

Buzzanca (*Police Chief*), Maria Grazia Buccella (*Bikini Girl*), Maurice Denham (*Chief of Interpol*), Tiberio Murgia, Francesco De Leone (*Detectives*), Carlo Croccolo (*Cafe Owner*), Nino Musco (*Mayor*), Pier Luigi Pizzi (*Doctor*), Lino Mattera (*Singer*), Daniele Vargas (*Prosecuting Counsel*), Franco Sportelli (*Judge*).

A visual delight, thanks to Director De Sica, this Sellers vehicle is loaded with belly laughs, guffaws and a stream of chuckles in a Simon script that is uneven but mostly up. As the flamboyant, inept Fox, a so-called master thief (he's been in prison seven of the last nine years), Sellers breaks jail because, as he explains patiently to an inmate, his sister, Ekland (Mrs. Sellers), a movie starlet, must be curbed of rapidly developing bad habits, and, as a second thought, he wants to arrange for the passage to Rome of $3 million in gold bullion stolen in Cairo. After his escape, Sellers pops up almost frame by frame in a host of easily indentifiable disguises—a prison doctor, a tourist cameraman, an Italian cop, and a zany New Wave film director where the great comedian gets to spoof *auteur* and avant-garde in a merciless portrayal. Part of that particular parody has Victor Mature making a movie inside the movie, an aging star trussed up with corsets and insisting he wear the threadbare trench coat and brimworn hat from his 1940s films, his trademarks so to speak. Mature is simply great in mocking his former *film noir* roles and beautifully interplays with Sellers. Also spoofed are the Italians themselves, their casual ways, indifference to authority, their passion for the carnal, all of the Italian actors zestily parodying the stereotypes of themselves and their country. Of precious memory are the scenes in the desert where De Sica himself is attempting to direct a movie during a violent sandstorm and having his equipment stolen by Sellers and Tamiroff. A bright bit of fluff with succulent linguine on the side.

p, John Bryan; d, Vittorio De Sica; w, Neil Simon, Cesare Zavattini; ph, Leonida Barboni (Technicolor); m, Burt Bacharach; ed, Russell Lloyd; art d, Mario Garbuglia; cos, Piero Tosi.

Comedy Cas. (PR:A MPAA:NR)

AFTER THE THIN MAN***1/2 (1936) 107m MGM bw

William Powell (*Nick Charles*), Myrna Loy (*Nora Charles*), James Stewart (*David Graham*), Joseph Calleia (*Dancer*), Elissa Landi (*Selma Landis*), Jessie Ralph (*Aunt Katherine Forrest*), Alan Marshal (*Robert Landis*), Sam Levene (*Lt. Abrams*), Teddy Hart (*Floyd Casper*), Dorothy McNulty [Penny Singleton] (*Polly Byrnes*), William Law (*Lum Kee*), Dorothy Vaughn (*Charlotte*), Maude Turner Gordon (*Helen*), William Burress (*General*), Thomas Pogue (*William*), George Zucco (*Dr. Adolph Kammer*), Tom Ricketts (*Henry the Butler*), Paul Fix (*Phil Byrnes*), Joe Caits (*Joe*), Edith Kingdom (*Hattie*), John Kelly (*Harold*), Joe Phillips (*Willie*), John T. Murray (*Jerry*), Zeffie Tilbury (*Lucy*), Clarence Kolb (*Lucius*), Jack Norton, Ed Dearing, Mary Gordon, Heinie Conklin, Ben Hall, Vince Barnett, Guy Usher, Harvey Parry, Richard Loo, Murray Alper, Billy Benedict, Sue Moore, Ernest Alexander, Charles Trowbridge, Constantine Romanoff, Bobby Watson, Harry Tyler.

Breezy and humorous sequel to THE THIN MAN, Powell and Loy are up to their ears in three quick murders after Landi, Powell's knock-out cousin, asks Powell/Nick to find her vanished husband, even though he's been unfaithfully having a tryst with a nightclub singer, McNulty (later Penny Singleton of Blondie fame), and is also blackmailing big shot Calleia. Powell learns that Stewart, at his naive and disarming best, has paid the husband to disappear because he still has a yen for McNulty, a former girl friend. All of this hazardous investigation proves to be the only stimulation inside the luxury-enjoying lives of Powell and Loy (she's rich and he drinks out of boredom except when on a case and of course she wants him on a case to curb the booze). The missing husband, Marshall, is killed, then Hart and an unseen janitor before Powell rounds up the usual suspects and plucks Stewart (one of the few roles where he was the bad guy) as the killer who went berserk out of jealousy for McNulty, killing the husband and witnesses to that killing. The script is tight, the direction swift and arresting and the cast is tops, MGM surrounding its two quipping stars with the best character actors on the lot. Hammett's style of snappy banter and cynical world views is kept intact by Goodrich and Hackett, making this *film noir* production all the more delectable. (See THIN MAN series, Index.)

p, Hunt Stromberg; d, W. S. Van Dyke; w, Frances Goodrich, Albert Hackett (based on a story by Dashiell Hammett); ph, Oliver T. Marsh; m, Herbert Stothart; ed, Robert J. Kern; art d, Cedric Gibbons; m/l, Arthur Freed, Nacio Herb Brown, Bob Wright, Walter Donaldson, Chet Forrest.

Crime (PR:A MPAA:NR)

AFTER TOMORROW** (1932) 70m FOX bw

Charles Farrell (*Peter Piper*), Marian Nixon (*Sidney Taylor*), Minna Gombell (*Elsie Taylor*), William Collier, Sr. (*Willie Taylor*), Josephine Hull (*Mrs. Piper*), William Pawley (*Malcolm Jarvis*), Greta Granstedt (*Betty*), Ferdinand Munier (*Mr. Beardsley*), Nora Lane (*Florence Blandy*).

Early talkie suffers from growing pains of the sound era; at the beginning, filmdom thought the only way to be effective was to present endless chatter but by the time this film was released the public was weary of the dull plays imported from Broadway and, preferably, England (because the diction was considered crisp and clear, no viewer could misunderstand the words). Here is one that deals with the hardships of a young man and woman who struggle to work and save so they can be married—a significant ploy for the Depression-tossed U.S. at the time—and are mostly separated while they slave to earn their pennies. At one reunion—after three years!—Nixon sees Farrell look "funny" at a passing woman and immediately suggests they go to a cabin for a weekend, mentioning the unheard-of word—"sex"—but he declines, saying it is better to wait until they are legally married (this concession aimed at the then strict censorship board, the Hays Office). They later have an innocent "sex talk" which was then sensational but is now, perhaps regrettably, amusing. This is a weary, sad story offering no relief to the viewer.

d, Frank Borzage; w, Sonya Levien (based on a play by John Golden, Hugh Stange); ph, James Wong Howe; ed, Margaret Clancy.

Drama/Romance (PR:A MPAA:NR)

AFTER TONIGHT***1/2 (1933) 70m RKO bw

Constance Bennett (*Carla*), Gilbert Roland (*Rudi*), Edward Ellis (*Col. Lieber*), Sam Godfrey (*Franz*), Lucien Percival (*Erlich*), Mischa Auer (*Adjutant Lehar*), Ben

Hendricks, Jr. *(Probert)*, Leonid Snegoff *(Pvt. Muller)*, Evelyn Carter Carrington *(Frau Stengel)*, John Wray *(Mitika)*.

Bennett is a Russian spy and Roland an Austrian captain, and they just happen to fall in love right smack dab in the middle of WW I. A complete lack of suspense or intrigue does not help the insipid love affair, which ends in a train depot where it began.

p, Merian C. Cooper; d, George Archainbaud; w, Jane Murfin, Albert Shelby LeVino, Worthington Miner (based on a story by Murfin); ph, Charles Rosher; ed, William Hamilton; md, Max Steiner.

Romance (PR:A MPAA:NR)

AFTER YOU, COMRADE** (1967, S. Afr.) 84m Continental c

Jamie Uys *(Igor Strogoff)*, Bob Courtney *(Granger J. Wellborne)*, Reinet Maasdorf *(Tanya Orloff)*, Angus Neill *(Johnny Edwards)*, Joe Stewardson *(Ed Sloane)*, Arthur Swemmer *(Anzonia)*, Frank Gregory *(Italian Mayor)*, Mimmi Poli *(Italian Butcher)*, Marjorie Gordon *(Hostel Matron)*, Emil Mofal *(Television Announcer)*, Sann De Lange *(Yugoslavian Mother)*, Wilhelm Esterhuizen *(Austrian Farmer)*, Victor Ivanoff *(Chief Russian Delegate)*, Keith Stanners-Bloxam *(Chief American Delegate)*, Ricky Arden *(Second Russian Delegate)*, George Bertolis *(Greek Sergeant)*, Bill Brewer *(Conference President)*.

A nice, funny political allegory in which the Russian and American delegates at a world committee meeting decide to resolve their differences via a walking race from Athens to Paris. Uys, virtually a one-man film crew, is a socially aware filmmaker, and although a bit sloppy, an interesting and promising humorist.

p,d&w, Jamie Uys; ph, Manie Botha; m, Sam Sklair.

Comedy (PR:A MPAA:NR)

AGAINST A CROOKED SKY** (1975) 89m Doty/Dayton c

Richard Boone *(Russian)*, Stewart Petersen *(Sam Sutter)*, Geoffrey Land *(Temkai)*, Jewel Blanch *(Charlotte Sutter)*, Gordon Hanson *(Shumeki)*, Henry Wilcoxon *(Cut Tongue)*.

A variation of John Ford's THE SEARCHERS in which crusty old trapper Boone and young, determined Petersen set out to find Blanch, Petersen's attractive sister who has been captured, of course, by evil, mindless Indians. It is a shame to see an actor like Boone, who can be very powerful when given the chance, stuck in a mediocre western that does not explore the genre's immense and varied complexities.

p, Lyman D. Dayton; d, Earl Bellamy; w, Douglas C. Stewart, Eleanor Lamb; ph, Joe Jackman (DeLuxe Color); m, Lex De Azevedo; ed, Marsh Hendry; art d, Carl Anderson; m/l, title song, Mac David.

Western Cas. (PR:C MPAA:G)

AGAINST ALL FLAGS** 1/2 (1952) 83m UNIV c

Errol Flynn *(Brian Hawke)*, Maureen O'Hara *(Spitfire Stevens)*, Anthony Quinn *(Roc Brasiliano)*, Alice Kelley *(Princess Patma)*, Mildred Natwick *(Molvina MacGregor)*, Robert Warwick *(Capt. Kidd)*, Harry Cording *(Gow)*, John Alderson *(Harris)*, Phil Tully *(Jones)*, Lester Matthews *(Sir Cloudsley)*, Tudor Owen *(Williams)*, Maurice Marsac *(Capt. Moisson)*, James Craven *(Capt. Hornsby)*, James Fairfax *(Barber)*, Bill Radovich *(Hassan)*, Michael Ross *(Swaine)*, Paul Newland *(Crop-Ear)*, Lewis Russell *(Oxford)*, Arthur Gould-Porter *(Lord Portland)*, Olaf Hytten *(King William)*.

Film opens in 1700 with Flynn being whipped before shipmates, a British officer being cashiered for desertion in the face of the enemy; that night he escapes the frigate with two companions and swims to the shore of Madagascar. The flogging has been a ruse; his real mission is to appear to be a renegade so that he can infiltrate the pirate stronghold. Dragged before a pirate tribunal, he is challenged by Quinn who wants him put to death, but O'Hara, a fierce female buccaneer, votes against this. (Her role is based on Anne Bonny, a real lady pirate.) Flynn becomes the navigator for Quinn's ship and gets involved in a bloody raid against a ship of the emperor of India with a number of harem girls taken prisoner. Flynn learns that one of them is the emperor's daughter and he conceals her, incurring the wrath of O'Hara, who is smitten with him and jealous. When the girl, Kelley, is sold on the block, Flynn tries to buy her but O'Hara bids higher, taking her home with her. Flynn manages to spike the pirate fort's cannons but is trapped by Quinn before he can escape and is tied with his aides to stakes at the water's edge, to be eaten alive by enormous crabs. O'Hara has ordered this gruesome end. She next appears to stab Flynn, but really cuts his bonds. Both sneak aboard Quinn's flagship where the princess is being held captive. In a wild hand-to-hand combat with rapier and pikestaff, Flynn kills Quinn and saves the princess. He then opens fire on the fort which signals the British fleet to enter the harbor. The swashbuckler is restored to his rank and is given custody of the beautiful O'Hara, promising with a smile to reform her. They set sail together, standing on the bridge of a fine ship, heading, of course, into a spendid sunset. This production, an exceptionally fast-actioner under the whiphand of director George Sherman, was delayed for five months while Flynn recovered from a broken ankle, the result of attempting a difficult stunt in the last week of shooting; Flynn, though aging, still insisted upon doing his own stunts. One he did not perform was accomplished by an uncredited double who, high on the yardarm, jabs his rapier through a sail and, while holding the hilt, slides down the sail as his blade slits it, a stunt first performed by Douglas Fairbanks, Sr. in THE BLACK PIRATE (1922). AGAINST ALL FLAGS was remade in 1967 as THE KING'S PIRATE with Doug McClure playing Flynn's role and Guy Stockwell that of Quinn's, a less ambitious production and one that almost descended to slapstick to glean laughs.

p, Howard Christie; d, George Sherman; w, Aeneas MacKenzie, Joseph Hoffman (based on a story by MacKenzie); ph, Russell Metty (Technicolor); m, Hans J. Salter; ed, Frank Gross; art d, Bernard Herzbrun, Alexander Golitzen: set d, Russell A. Gausman, Oliver Emert; cos, Edward Stevenson.

Adventure (PR:A MPAA:NR)

AGAINST THE LAW** (1934) 61m COL bw (GB: URGENT CALL)

Johnny Mack Brown *(Steve Wayne)*, Sally Blane *(Martha Gray)*, Arthur Hohl *(Kelly)*, George Meeker *(Bert Andrews)*, James Bush, Bradley Page, Ward Bond, Hooper Atchley, Al Hill, Joseph Crehan.

Fairly familiar plot has ambulance driver Brown trying to stop his intern buddy from falling in with the mob. Typical gangster action picture from the thirties that, for the time, was typically well done.

d, Lambert Hillyer; w, Harold Shumate; ph, Al Seigler; ed Otto Meyer.

Crime (PR:C MPAA:NR)

AGAINST THE TIDE* (1937, Brit.) 67m FOX bw

Robert Cockran *(Jim Leigh)*, Cathleen Nesbitt *(Margaret Leigh)*, Linden Travers *(Mary Poole)*, Jimmy Mageean *(Tom Jenkins)*, Herbert Cameron *(William Poole)*, Neil Carlton *(Bert Poole)*, Dorothy Vernon *(Mrs. Brewer)*.

Family turmoil erupts when a fisherman brings a fetching young thing home to his widowed mother who cannot abide another woman in the house and seethes jealousy toward the intended fiancee. Tepid as boiled beef.

p, Victor M. Greene; d, Alex Bryce; w, Greene; ph, Ronald Neame.

Drama (PR:A MPAA:NR)

AGAINST THE WIND** 1/2 (1948, Brit.) 96m Ealing/GFD bw

Robert Beatty *(Father Phillip)*, Jack Warner *(Max Cronk)*, Simone Signoret *(Michele)*, Gordon Jackson *(Johnny Duncan)*, Paul Dupuis *(Jacques Picquart)*, Gisele Preville *(Julie)*, John Slater *(Emile Meyer)*, Peter Illing *(Andrew)*, James Robertson Justice *(Ackerman)*, Sybilla Binder *(Malou)*, Helen Hanson *(Marie Berlot)*, Eugene Deckers *(Marcel van Hecke)*, Andre Morell *(Abbot)*, Gilbert Davis *(Commandant)*, Andrew Blackett *(Frankie)*, Arthur Lawrence *(Verreker)*, Leo de Pokorny *(Balthazar)*, Rory MacDermot *(Carey)*, Kenneth Hyde *(Captain Parker)*.

Polyglot group of volunteers is trained as British saboteurs in 1943 London and then parachuted into Belgium to blow up an office containing important Nazi records, as well as rescue Illing whom the Germans are pumping for vital infomation. The first forty minutes deal with the training period in semi-documentary style, a la 13 RUE MADELEINE, with Justice as the sabotage chief, sturdy, stoical and believable. Signoret, in her British film debut, has joined the force to forget a lost love and becomes involved with Jackson—their scenes together are understated and touching—while a host of character actors solidly play out the roles of other patriots—Beatty as a priest; Preville, who loves Beatty and whose neck is broken when landing in Belgium; Dupuis as a secret Nazi agent; Slater, who has disguised a famous face through plastic surgery in order to act as an anonymous saboteur. There was no length to which the British would not go in defeating their arch-enemy! The group accomplishes its mission but a heavy toll is paid in this well-mounted production.

p, Sidney Cole; d, Charles Crichton; w, T. E. B. Clarke, Michael Pertwee; ph, Lionel Banes, Paul Beeson; m, Leslie Bridgewater; ed, Alan Osbigton.

Spy Drama (PR:A MPAA:NR)

AGATHA* (1979, Brit.) 98m Sweetwal/WB c

Dustin Hoffman *(Wally Stanton)*, Vanessa Redgrave *(Agatha Christie)*, Timothy Dalton *(Archie Christie)*, Helen Morse *(Evelyn)*, Celia Gregory *(Nancy Neele)*, Tony Britton *(William Collins)*, Timothy West *(Kenward)*, Alan Badel *(Lord Brackenbury)*, Paul Brooke *(John Foster)*, Carolyn Pickles *(Charlotte Fisher)*, Robert Longden *(Pettelson)*, Donald Nithsdale *(Uncle Jones)*, Yvonne Gilan *(Mrs. Braithwaite)*, David Hargreaves *(Sgt. Jarvis)* Sandra Voe *(Therapist)*, Barry Hart *(Superintendent MacDonald)*, Tim Seely *(Capt. Rankin)*, Jill Summers *(Nancy's Aunt)*.

Agatha Christie, one of the world's most popular writers of detective fiction, utterly disappeared in 1926. She was later discovered at Hydro Harrowgate, a spa in Yorkshire, England. More than 15,000 persons searched high and low for the novelist who allegedly ran away after her husband Archibald told her he was leaving her for his secretary. Upon her return, Christie stated that she remembered nothing, had had a case of amnesia, such was the shock of her matrimonial break. That is the only story known. The film AGATHA is nothing more than writer Tynan's imagination, a shoddy creation of guessed-at events at best and, at worst, a travesty against the facts and Christie herself. The acting by Redgrave as Agatha is simply awful, even repulsive, as she flits furtively from scene to scene like a nervous pop-eyed hen, drawing attention to herself, hardly the moves of one traveling incognito. Moreover, the great talent of Hoffman is thoroughly wasted as an American reporter searching for Christie, finding her, and then, instead of writing the scoop, falling in love with her for a brief tryst and departing nobly to save her embarrassment when she "regains" her identity. The scenes between Hoffman and Redgrave are unfortunately laughable; he being diminutive and Redgrave, a big-boned woman, towering above him like some haggard Amazon. The idea here is that Agatha is intending to commit suicide in the therapy room by attaching electrodes (used for stimulation) to herself and turning up the juice, making it appear that her husband's secretary, also staying at the health resort, had murdered her, thus taking her revenge against hubby and lover. Hoffman uncovers her plan and stops her, telling her that her literary career comes first; she agrees. The dialog is stilted, corny, and absolutely pedestrian; Apted's direction crawls across a room like a bloated beetle. There is no suspense, no tension, and not even one good scene in this preposterous and ostentatious mess.

p, Jarvis Astaire, Garvik Losey; d, Michael Apted; w, Kathleen Tynan, Arthur Hopcraft (based on a story by Kathleen Tynan); ph, Vittorio Storaro; m, Johnny Mandel; ed, Jim Clark; art d, Simon Holland.

Romance Cas. (PR:C MPAA:PG))

AGATHA CHRISTIE'S ENDLESS NIGHT (SEE: ENDLESS NIGHT, 1971)

AGE FOR LOVE, THE* (1931) 81m Hughes/UA bw

Billie Dove *(Jean Hurd)*, Charles Starrett *(Dudley Crome)*, Lois Wilson *(Sylvia Pearson)*, Edward Everett Horton *(Horace Keats)*, Mary Duncan *(Nina Donnet)*, Adrian Morris *(Jeff Aldrich)*, Betty Ross Clarke *(Dot Aldrich)*, Vivian Oakland, Andre Beranger.

Confused, almost plotless film dealing with husbands and wives, female independence and having children, devotion and true love, and the institution of marriage. This is interesting subject matter for 1931, but without a coherent story or accessible characters, the ideas never bear fruit.

p, Howard Hughes; d, Frank Lloyd; w, Lloyd, Ernest Pascal, Robert E. Sherwood.

Drama   **(PR:A MPAA:NR)**

AGE OF CONSENT**   (1932) 100m RKO bw

Dorothy Wilson (*Betty*), Richard Cromwell (*Michael*), Eric Linden (*Duke*), Arline Judge (*Dora*), John Halliday (*David*), Aileen Pringle (*Barbara*), Reginald Barlow (*Swale*).

Underage girl and her collegiate boy friend must decide between their love and his pursuit of the old sheepskin. Well-intentioned, smart-looking picture that tries, as best as a film could in the thirties, to deal with post-adolescent sexuality.

d, Gregory La Cava; w, Sarah Y. Mason, Francis Cockrell (based on the stage play "Cross Roads" by Martin Flavin); ph, J. Roy Hunt; ed, Jack Kitchin.

Romance   **(PR:C MPAA:NR)**

AGE OF CONSENT**   (1969, Austral.) 98m Nautilus/COL c

James Mason (*Bradley Morahan*), Helen Mirren (*Cora*), Jack MacGowran (*Nat Kelly*), Neva Carr-Glyn (*Ma Ryan*), Antonia Katsaros (*Isabel Marley*), Michael Boddy (*Hendricks*), Harold Hopkins (*Ted Farrell*) Slim Da Grey (*Cooley*), Max Moldrun (*TV reporter*), Frank Thring (*Godfrey*), Dora Hing (*Receptionist*), Clarissa Kaye (*Meg*), Judy McGrath (*Grace*), Lenore Katon (*Edna*), Diane Strachan (*Susie*), Roberta Grant (*Ivy*), Prince Nial (*Jaspar*), Geoff Cartwright (*Newsboy*).

Disillusioned painter Mason chucks the superficial glamour of New York and returns to an island on the Great Barrier Reef where a weird assortment of characters come into his life—rich spinster Katsaros, a drunken harridan, Carr-Glyn, and her sexpot granddaughter Mirren. When Mason eyes Mirren swimming underwater he asks her to become his model and she willingly does, to earn money for hairdressing school. Enter MacGowran, an old pal of Mason's who ingratiates himself to Katsaros, then steals money from her, Mason's boat, and skips the island. Thievery is the order of the day, as Carr-Glyn steals the money her granddaughter has earned. Mirren chases her to a cliff where they struggle, with grandma taking the plunge to her death. Police investigate but accurately pronounce the old lady's demise as accidental, and MacGowran is captured and jailed by the police. Mason and Mirren sigh relief at avoiding arrest and retire to a cozy cottage. This was Mason's first Australian film in almost a decade, one that he later regretted. The film proved mostly boring and without charm despite his considerable effort in the role of the sensitive artist. MacGowran was the only other real actor in the crowd, an excellent heavy enacting one of his last screen roles. Some bedroom scenes are obnoxious if not offensive and this film barely squeaked past an "X" rating in Australia, getting an "R."

p, James Mason, Michael Powell; d, Powell; w, Peter Yeldham (based on the novel by Norman Lindsay); ph, Hannes Staudinger; m, Peter Sculthorpe; ed, Anthony Buckley; art d, Dennis Gentle.

Drama   **(PR:O MPAA:NR)**

AGE OF ILLUSIONS**   (1967, Hung.) 97m Mafilm/BRANDON bw

Andras Balint (*Janos*), Ilona Beres (*Eva*), Judit Halasz (*Habgab*), Kati Solyom (*Annie Klinger*), Bela Asztalos (*Laci*), Tamas Eross (*Matyl*), Laszlo Muranyi (*Gergely*), Cecilia Eszterggalyos (*Ballerina*), Miklos Gabor (*Chief Engineer*).

Young electrical engineer Balint takes one girl after another, refusing to commit emotional involvement, blaming it on his callous youth (so what else is new?). He falls in love with a newscaster, a beautiful TV personality, and finally locates her, only to find she is as lonely as he is, and just about as callous. Not much here but director Szabo turns in an acceptable if not stirring first film.

d&w, Istvan Szabo.

Romance   **(PR:O MPAA:NR)**

AGE OF INDISCRETION**   (1935) 77m MGM

Paul Lukas (*Robert Lenhart*), Madge Evans (*Maxine Bennett*), Helen Vinson (*Eve Lenhart*), May Robson (*Emma Shaw*), David Jack Holt (*Bill Lenhart*), Ralph Forbes (*Felix Shaw*), Catharine Doucet (*Jean Oliver*), Beryl Mercer (*Mrs. Williams*), Minor Watson (*Mr. Adams*).

An early divorce/child custody battle film that features Lukas and Vinson neglecting their child (Holt) while they selfishly pursue their own lives. Likeable enough, but not very interesting or unique in any way.

p, Philip Goldstone; d, Edward Ludwig; w, Leon Gordon, Otis Garrett (based on a story by Lenore Coffee); ph, Ernest Haller; ed, Hugh Winn.

Drama   **(PR:C MPAA:NR)**

AGE OF INFIDELITY**
(1958, Span.) 86m Janus/PATHE bw (AKA; DEATH OF A CYCLIST)

Lucia Bose (*Maria Jose*), Alberto Closas (*Juan*), Otello Toso (*Miguel*), Carlos Casaravilla (*Rafa*), Bruna Corra (*Matilde*), Julia Delgado Caro (*Dona Maria*).

Two illicit lovers, a professor and a tycoon's adulterous wife, are off on an interlude when they run over a bicyclist and leave him to die rather than reveal their identities to police. Their consciences are stricken as well as their wallets when a blackmailer threatens to expose the affair to the husband. They wriggle out of one danger after another, finally meeting violent ends, a directorial justification for their deed of manslaughter. A morose, choppy film without proper dissolves to signal an end to various scenes, plus poor English subtitles makes this one a chore. (In Spanish; English subtitles.)

d&w, Juan A. Bardem (based on a story by Luis F. de Igoa).

Drama/Crime   **(PR:O MPAA:NR)**

AGE OF INNOCENCE**   (1934) 71m RKO

Irene Dunne (*Countess Ellen Olenska*), John Boles (*Newland Archer*), Lionel Atwill (*Julius Beaufort*), Laura Hope Crews (*Mrs. Welland*), Helen Westley (*Granny Mingott*), Julie Haydon (*May Welland*), Herbert Yost (*Mr. Welland*), Theresa Maxwell-Conover (*Mrs. Archer*), Edith Van Cleve (*Janey Archer*), Leonard Carey (*Butler*).

Ambitious young attorney makes the mistake of falling for an intriguing soon-to-be-divorced Dunne, jeopardizing his engagement to the dull, but socially acceptable

Haydon. The lovely and charming Miss Dunne heads a very good cast in a sadly humdrum scandal picture.

d, Philip Moeller; w, Sarah Y. Mason, Victor Heerman (based on the novel by Edith Wharton); ph, James Van Trees; ed, George Hively.

Drama   **(PR:C MPAA:NR)**

AGE OF INNOCENCE* 1/2   (1977, Can.) 101m Judson/Willoughby c

David Warner, Honor Blackman, Cec Linder, Trudy Young, Tim Henry, Robert Hawkins, Lois Maxwell.

Canadian professor incites local veterans and families following WW II with his hortatory pacifist views. Such is the resentment of such radical behavior that riots and death threats ensue. Not much other than a political polemic with little acting above the sophomoric level and no entertainment value whatsoever.

d, Alan Bridges; w, Ratch Wallace; ph, Brian West; m, Lucio Agostini.

Drama   **(PR:A MPAA:NR)**

AGE OF THE MEDICI, THE*   (1979, Ital.) 252m Audio/BRANDON c

Marcello de Falco, Virginio Gazzolo.

An incredibly boring Rosselini vehicle in which he profiles twenty years of Florentine brilliance in the arts, the heart of the Renaissance, through the mercantile careers of Cosimo de Medici and Leon Alberti, two wealthy sponsors of art and artists. More than four hours are consumed to show what is no more than a parade of art gallery masterpieces. An excessively indulgent and pompous film.

d, Roberto Rosselini; w, Rosselini, Luciano Scaffa, Marcella Mariani; ph, Mario Montuori; m, Manuel De Sica; ed, Jolanda Benvenuti.

Biography   **(PR:C MPAA:NR)**

AGENCY*   (1981, Can.) 94m Farley c

Robert Mitchum (*Ted*), Lee Majors (*Philip*), Valerie Perrine (*Brenda*), Saul Rubinek (*Sam*), Alexandra Stewart (*Mimi*), Hayward Morse (*Tony*), Anthony Parr (*Charlie*), Michael Kirby (*Peters*), Gary Reinke (*Jones*), George Touliatos (*Sgt. Eckersly*), Jonathan Welsh (*Det. Ross*), Hugh Webster (*Inmate*), Franz Russell (*George*), Marylin Gardner (*Jill*), Malcolm Nelthorpe (*Cy*), Eric Donkin (*Henry*), Donald Davis (*Alexander*).

An involved, often confusing film which deals with an ad agency that plans a sneaky political campaign wherein voters are unwittingly swayed through subliminal messages hidden inside TV ads (a practice that was actually in effect some years ago and was stopped through legislation). A walk-through for Mitchum.

p, Robert Lantos, Stephen J. Roth; d, George Kaczender; w, Noel Hynd (based on the
novel by Paul Gottlieb); ph, Miklos Lente; m, Lewis Furey; ed, Kirk Jones; art d, Alicia Grunsky; cos, Olga Dimitrov.

Drama   **Cas.**   **(PR:O MPAA:R)**

AGENT 8 3/4**
(1965, Brit.) 98m RANK-RFD/Continental c (GB:HOT ENOUGH FOR JUNE)

Dirk Bogarde (*Nicholas Whistler*), Sylvia Koscina (*Vlasta Simenova*), Robert Morley (*Col. Cunliffe*), Leo McKern (*Simenova*), Roger Delgado (*Josef*), John le Mesurier (*Roger Allsop*), Richard Pasco (*Plakov*), Eric Pohlmann (*Galushka*), Richard Vernon (*Roddinghead*), Amanda Grinling (*Secretary*), Noel Harrison (*Johnnie*), Derek Nimmo (*Fred*), George Pravda (*Pavelko*), Frank Finlay (*Janitor*), Norman Bird (*Clerk*).

An unemployed writer, Bogarde, is sent to Prague on what he thinks is a goodwill visit by British minister Morley but then discovers that he is on an espionage mission for the intelligence service. A tame comedy of errors which does not come off as an intended spy spoof.

p, Betty E. Box; d, Ralph Thomas; w, Lukas Heller (based on the novel by Lionel Davidson).

Spy Comedy   **(PR:C MPAA:NR)**

AGENT FOR H.A.R.M.**   (1966) 84m UNIV c

Mark Richman (*Adam Chance*), Wendell Corey (*Jim Graff*), Carl Esmond (*Prof. Janos Steffanic*), Barbara Bouchet (*Ava Vestok*), Martin Kosleck (*Malko*), Rafael Campos (*Luis*), Alizia Gur (*Mid-Eastern Contact*), Donna Michelle (*Marian*), Robert Quarry (*Borg*), Robert Donner (*Morgue Attendant*), Steve Stevens (*Billy*), Horst Ebersberg (*Helgar*), Marc Snegoff (*Conrad*), Chris Anders (*Schloss*), Ray Dannis (*Manson*), Ronald Von (*Police Lieutenant*), Robert Christopher (*Police Officer*).

Another weak attempt to spoof the Bond films, as well as take advantage of their immense popularity, this production has Corey in a Washington office as an intelligence chief mapping every move for agent Richman whose job it is to protect a scientist from being abducted by Russian agents, moving one step ahead of the would-be kidnappers up and down the California coastline which makes for some scenic marvels but little story. Bouchet as the dangerous blonde is a showpiece and evil; little Kosleck, who made a career of playing evil little Nazis in WW II films, is the only offbeat interest here, and that says as much as possible about this lame-dog spoof.

p, Joseph F. Robertson; d, Gerd Oswald; w, Blair Robertson; ph, James Crab; m, Gene Kauer, Douglas Lackey.

Spy Comedy/Satire   **(PR:C MPAA:NR)**

AGGIE APPLEBY, MAKER OF MEN*
(1933) 73m RKO bw (GB: CUPID IN THE ROUGH)

Charles Farrell (*Adoniram Schlump*), Wynne Gibson (*Aggie Appleby*), William Gargan (*Red Branahan*), ZaSu Pitts (*Sybby*), Betty Furness (*Evangeline*), Blanche Friderici (*Aunt Katharine*).

Dim-witted Gibson turns a wimpy society boy into a tough guy and a roughneck into a sissy. Who does she really love? It appears to be Gargan but we are left with an unclear ending.

p, Pandro S. Berman; d, Mark Sandrich; w, Humphrey Pearson, Edward Kaufman (based on the play by Joseph O. Kesserling); ph, J. Roy Hunt; ed, Basil Wrangell; md, Max Steiner.

Comedy **(PR:A MPAA:NR)**

AGITATOR, THE* (1949) 95m Four Continents Films bw

William Hartnell *(Peter Pettinger)*, Mary Morris *(Lettie Shackleton)*, John Laurie *(Tom Tetley)*, Moore Marriott *(Ben Duckett)*, J. H. Roberts *(Mr. Ambler)*, George Carney *(Bill Shackleton)*, Frederick Leister *(Mark Overend)*, Joss Ambler *(Charles Sheridan)*, Elliott Mason *(Mrs. Pettinger)*, Cathleen Nesbitt *(Mrs. Montrose)*, Joyce Heron *(Helen Montrose)*, Edward Rigby *(Charlie Branfield)*, Phillip Godfrey *(Bert Roberts)*, Moira Lister *(Joan Shackleton)*, Beatrice Varley *(Mrs. Shackleton)*, Cyril Smith *(Dunham)*, Howard Douglas *(Taylor)*, Lloyd Pearson *(Derek Cunlyffe)*, Edgar Driver *(Smith)*, Bransby Williams *(Salvation Army Leader)*.

Well-meaning, idealistic young socialist Hartnell must face capitalistic reality's ugly eye when he inherits a factory. Uninteresting direction fails to breathe any life into this attempt at meaningful social comment.

p, Louis H. Jackson; d, John Harlow; w, Edward Dryhurst (based on W. Riley's novel, *Peter Pettinger*); ph, Arthur Grant; ed, Douglas Meyers.

Drama **(PR:A MPAA:NR)**

AGONY AND THE ECSTASY, THE*** (1965) 136m FOX c

Charlton Heston *(Michelangelo)*, Rex Harrison *(Pope Julius II)*, Diane Cilento *(Contessina de Medici)*, Harry Andrews *(Bramante)*, Alberto Lupo *(Duke of Urbino)*, Adolfo Celi *(Giovanni de Medici)*, Vanantino Venantini *(Paris de Grassis)*, John Stacy *(Sangallo)*, Fausto Tozzi *(Foreman)*, Maxine Audley *(Woman)*, Tomas Milian *(Raphael)*, Richard Pearson *(Cardinal)*.

Heston delivers a powerful, understated interpretation of one of the world's greatest artists, Michelangelo, albeit his persona exudes more agony (anger is a better word) than ecstacy as Pontiff Harrison commands him to paint the ceiling of the Sistine Chapel, which was completely recreated for this production, the largest indoor set in the world up to that time. Opening has Heston as the artistic rage of the Renaissance, the Medicis, the most powerful family in Europe, showering him with fat commissions for his sculpting in Florence. He is summoned by Harrison, playing a shrewd and demanding Pope Julius II, then head of church and state, and ordered to "decorate" the ceiling of the Sistine Chapel, a return to fresco painting at which Heston bridles. He undertakes the Herculean task, encouraged by an old flame, Cilento, married to another, but devoted to the artist, nurturing him with food and paying his rent because Harrison is a stingy Pontiff and ignores commissions due his artist. The work begins as a standard fresco, disgusting the perfectionist artist who runs away to work in a rock quarry, the Pontiff's troops later sent to find him. While working upon a mountaintop, Heston sees a vision of what he is to do in a magnificent cloud formation and returns to the chapel where he continues to work on a towering scaffold, lying on his back, the paint dripping onto his face, into his eyes until he is almost blinded and falls from the scaffold, severely injuring himself, then resuming his incredible task while still ill. He is constantly harrassed by the impatient Harrison who shouts up to him: "When will you make an end?" "When it's finished," is Heston's truculent reply—years of this, and the length of this painful chore is somehow too truly translated into the overlong film; the viewer begins praying that Heston will finish painting his interpretation of Genesis, and quickly! Some stirring moments include Heston's seeking out role models for his painting in local inns, hurriedly sketching the lined and dissipated faces of drunks, thieves and lepers, a source that would have horrified the Papacy had it known, and the completion of the God touching life into his man creation—is awesome. (The sixty-some technicians working on the recreation of the chapel ceiling duplicated the masterpiece in eye-popping color, the completely scaled set in the de Laurentiis Rome studio costing many millions.) The study in genius almost overcomes the tedium of the production but not quite. Fox executives thought the film would provide enormous box office returns for the studio's $12 million investment and were shocked to see only one third that amount return in domestic grosses.

p&d, Carol Reed; w, Philip Dunne (based on the novel by Irving Stone), ph, Leon Shamroy (DeLuxe Color); m, Alex North; ed, Samuel E. Beetley; art d, Jack Martin Smith; cos, Vittorio Nino Novarese; spec eff, L. B. Abbott, Emil Kosa, Jr.

Drama/Biography **Cas** **(PR:A MPAA:NR)**

AGOSTINO** (1962, Ital.) 90m Dino DeLaurentiis/Baltea bw

Paolo Colombo *(Agostino)* Ingrid Thulin *(His Mother)*, John Saxon *(Renzo)*.

A boy, Colombo, runs away from his widowed mother when she begins to devote herself to a new paramour. Falling in with a rough gang, the boy learns about life in some very harsh ways. An intelligent yet unemotional attempt to analyze the sadness and loneliness of a young boy's life. The striking Thulin is excellent as the mother and Colombo is very natural and appealing as the outcast boy.

d, Mauro Bolognini; w, Geoffredo Parise (based on a story by Alberto Moravia); ph, Aldo Tonti; m, Carlo Rustichelli; ed, Nino Baragli.

Drama **(PR:C MPAA:NR)**

AGUIRRE, THE WRATH OF GOD*** (1977, W. Ger.) 90m New Yorker c

Klaus Kinski *(Don Lope de Aguirre)*, Ruy Guerra *(Don Pedro de Ursua)*, Del Negro *(Brother Gaspar de Carvajal)*, Helena Rojo *(Inez)*, Cecilia Rivera *(Flores)*, Peter Berling *(Don Fernando de Guzman)*, Danny Ades *(Perucho)*.

Spanish conquistadores in Peru, under orders from Pizarro, explore a jungle river that hopefully will lead to the mythical city of gold, El Dorado. Kinski, a forceful second-in-command, violently takes control of the mission after a few members of the party are mysteriously killed by Indians. The descent into the jungle continues. More men are picked off by the silent, unseen natives. Kinski, obsessed with his new power and the vision of El Dorado, orders the former leader of the expedition hanged. The hellish journey begins again, and slowly but surely, everyone in the party is murdered, except Kinski, whose dream will not be destroyed by the death around him. On a spinning, uncontrollable raft in the middle of the river, the mad Kinski is joined by hundreds of tiny monkeys who fly out from the jungle to join this crazed man on his trip to nowhere. AGUIRRE is probably the best, or at least the most accessible, film of West German director Werner Herzog, who, along with a few others, revitalized German cinema in the 1970s. Herzog, the most poetic and spiritual of these filmmakers, put his heart and soul into AGUIRRE, one of the largest-budgeted independent films in history. It is a disturbing, haunting film that deals with obsession, power, death, and above all, man's inability to control his own destiny. One report has it that Herzog once pulled a gun on Kinski during the shooting of AGUIRRE, threatening that if Kinski quit the film, Herzog would kill him. Some sources say that it was Kinski who pulled the gun on Herzog, telling the director that he was pushing everyone too hard. The truth here does not matter. What does matter is the obvious determination in both actor and director to go beyond what is required, and to try to achieve something magical.

p,d&w, Werner Herzog; ph, Thomas Mauch (Eastmancolor); m, Popol Vuh; ed, Beate Mainka-Jellinghaus.

Drama **(PR:O MPAA:NR)**

A-HAUNTING WE WILL GO 1/2** (1942) 69m FOX bw

Stan Laurel *(Himself)*, Oliver Hardy *(Himself)*, Harry A. Jansen *(Dante the Magician)*, Sheila Ryan *(Margo)*, John Shelton *(Tommy White)*, Don Costello *(Doc Lake)*, Elisha Cook, Jr. *(Frank Lucas)*, Edward Gargan *(Foster)*, Addison Richards *(Malcolm Kilgore)*, George Lynn (Darby Mason), James Bush *(Joe Morgan)*, Lou Lubin *(Dixie Beeler)*, Robert Emmett Keane *(Phillips)*, Richard Lane *(Parker)*, Willie Best *(Waiter)*.

Laurel and Hardy unknowingly transport a live, wanted gangster over state lines in a coffin that they believe carries a corpse. Their various misadventures include a bit of playing around with Dante the Magician. Late Stan and Ollie vehicle that is a some- what sad reflection on their past uproarious work. (See LAUREL AND HARDY series, Index.)

p, Sol M. Wurtzel; d, Alfred Werker; w, Lou Breslow (based on a story by Breslow, Stanley Rauh); ph, Glen MacWilliams; m, Emil Newman; ed, Alfred Day; art d, Lewis Creber, Richard Day; set d, Thomas Little.

Comedy **(PR:AA MPAA:NR)**

AH, WILDERNESS!**** (1935) 101m MGM bw

Wallace Beery *(Sid Davis)*, Lionel Barrymore *(Nat Miller)*, Aline MacMahon *(Lily Davis)*, Eric Linden *(Richard Miller)*, Cecilia Parker *(Muriel McComber)*, Spring Byington *(Essie Miller)*, Mickey Rooney *(Tommy Miller)*, Charles Grapewin *(Mr. McComber)*, Frank Albertson *(Arthur Miller)*, Edward Nugent *(Wint Selby)* Bonita Granville *(Mildred Miller)*, Helen Flint *(Belle)*, Helen Freeman *(Miss Hawley)*.

Eugene ONeill's only comedy, written in five weeks, is a dream wish of the greatest American dramatist, the sweet unaffected boyhood he never had culminating in one long summer in which adolescence struggles into manhood, dragging with it idealistic poetry, innocence and gullible youth. Linden plays the young man with sincerity and some charming stupidity, as mother Byington busies herself with his problems, mischie- vous Rooney and snotty Granville vex him, as little brother and sister, father Barrymore nervously avoids instructing him in the ways of the world and boisterous, boozy uncle Beery teaches him the ways of the flesh. (Only certain fans with offbeat senses of humor can fully appreciate the always irreverent Beery, a classic case of nonconformity in a child-adult; to know him is to love him in any role even though the blue bloods and hoity-toity of the 1930s disavowed him for this roaring role.) Linden, who was 25 playing 18, is daffy in love with Parker but her father disapproves of the boy and, in frustration, he gets drunk for the first time (at uncle Beery's delighted urging) and slobbers over a tolerant woman of the streets, well played by Flint. (This very story element finds its way later into O'Neill's masterpiece, "Long Day's Journey Into Night.") Beery, the catalyst to misbehavior, does not escape unscathed; he is marvelously upbraided by tough old aunt, MacMahon, in a precious dinner table scene, besting him in banter and proving more than a match for his sneaky ways (and scene-stealing techniques). But all comes right for Linden. To the credit of talented director Brown the commencement exercises of his high school class are unforgettable, from the heroically struggling glee club singing, to one funny recitation after another, to the valedictory by Linden, wiseguy, wonderful youth personified. In the end, stoical Barrymore breaks down and has a moving heart-to-heart talk with his son, one that brings them closer than ever before, a fine, true moment of understanding between estranged generations. Remade as SUMMER HOLIDAY in 1948, a warm musical in which Rooney appears in the same vehicle but as the young man coming of age instead of the little terror lurking down the hall.

p, Hunt Stromberg; d, Clarence Brown; w, Albert Hackett, Frances Goodrich (based on the play by Eugene O'Neill); ph, Clyde De Vinna; m, Herbert Stothart; ed, Frank E. Hull; art d, Cedric Gibbons, William Horning.

Comedy **(PR:AAA MPAA:NR)**

AIDA** (1954, Ital.) 95m Oscar/EF c

Sophia Loren *(Aida, sung by Renata Tebaldi)*, Lois Maxwell *(Amneris, sung by Ebe Stignanai)*, Luciano Della Marra *(Radames, sung by Giuseppe Campora)*, Afro Poli *(Amonsaro, sung by Gino Bechi)*, Antonio Cassinelli *(Ramfis, sung by Giulio Neri)*, Enrico Formichi *(The Pharaoh, sung by Enrico Formichi)*.

Verdi's classic Egyptian love triangle has voluptuous Loren as a captured princess used as a personal slave by Maxwell, both loving Marra, captain of the king's guard. When he rebuffs the king's daughter, opting for Loren, both he and Loren are entombed alive while vowing their love for each other. The singing is superb but the cast is wholly inept, particularly Loren as the ill-starred Ethiopian princess who mouths her vocals as if gulping water, but this second lead role of her career brought her to the attention of DeMille and Carlo Ponti, the latter quickly putting her under contract and later marrying her. Filmed in an Italian studio during winter on a low budget, the heat was often turned off to save money which caused steam clouds to emit from the mouths of the actors. Hair driers were aimed at the faces of the actors to evaporate the steam. For dedicated opera fans only.

p, Ferruccio De Martino, Federico Teti; d, Clemente Fracassi; w, G. Castilli, A. Gobbi, Y. Salvucci (based on the opera by Giuseppe Verdi); ph, Piero Portalupi; md, Renzo Rossellin; ch, Margherita Wallman; set d, Flavio Mogherini.

Opera **(PR:A MPAA:NR)**

AIMEZ-VOUS BRAHMS (SEE: GOODBYE, AGAIN, 1961)

AIN'T MISBEHAVIN'**½ (1955) 81m UNIV c

Rory Calhoun *(Kenneth Post)*, Piper Laurie *(Sarah Hatfield)*, Jack Carson *(Hal North)*, Mamie Van Doren *(Jackie)*, Reginald Gardiner *(Piermont Rogers)*, Barbara Britton *(Pat)*, Dani Crayne *(Millie)*, Carl Post *(Andre Banet)*, Roger Etienne *(Corbini)*, Harris Brown *(Randall)*, Isabel Randolph *(Mrs. Moffit)*, George Givot *(Native Boatman)*, Peter Mamakos *(Andy)*.

Frothy musical with likeable cast shows chorus girl Laurie snaring millionaire businessman Calhoun but, to adapt to what she thinks is a more proper personality for high society, she begins changing her ways, from down-to-earth to snooty and snobbish which turns off Calhoun. Before she loses her mate Laurie comes to her senses and reverts to her normal self. Many sprightly tunes lift average story line from the mediocre; Laurie singing the title song, "The Dixie Mambo," "I Love That Rickey, Tickey, Tickey," all production numbers with a lot of hip-swinging from Laurie, Van Doren and Dani Crayne, and "A Little Love Can Go A Long Way."

p, Samuel Marx; d, Edward Buzzell; w, Philip Rapp, Devery Freeman, Buzzell (based on the story "Third Girl From the Right" by Robert Carson); ph, Wilfrid M. Cline (Technicolor); md, Joseph Gershenson; ch, Kenny Williams, Lee Scott; m/l, Paul Francis Webster, Sammy Fain, Charles Henderson, Sonny Burke, Sammy Cahn, Johnnie Scott.

Musical **(PR:A MPAA:NR)**

AIR CADET** (1951) 93m UNIV bw

Stephen McNally *(Major Jack Page)*, Gail Russell *(Janet Page)*, Alex Nicol *(Joe Czanoczek)*, Richard Long *(Russ Coulter)*, Charles Drake *(Captain Sullivan)*, Robert Arthur *(Walt Carver)*, Rock Hudson *(Upper Classman)*, Peggie Castle *(Pat)*, James Best *(Jerry Connell)*, Parley Baer *(Major Jim Evans)*.

Tough WW II veteran McNally teaches the usual mixed bag of young pilots the rigors of flying jet fighters. His mourning over comrades lost in the Big One wreaks havoc on his marriage, but his devotion to the hearty new recruits never falters. Some exciting air sequences shot by Clyde Da Vinna are the true highlights in this routine drama.

p, Aaron Rosenberg; d, Joseph Pevney; w, Robert L. Richards (based on a story by Robert Soderberg, Richards); ph, Cliff Stine, air ph, Clyde Da Vinna; ed, Russell Schoengarth; m, Joseph Gershenson; art d, Bernard Herzbrun, Edward Hou.

Drama **(PR:A MPAA:NR)**

AIR CIRCUS, THE** (1928) 86m FOX bw

Louise Dresser *(Mrs. Blake)*, David Rollins *(Buddy Blake)*, Arthur Lake *(Speed Doolittle)*, Sue Carol *(Sue Manning)*, Charles Delaney *(Charles Manning)*, Heinie Conklin *(Jerry McSwiggin)*, Earl Robinson *(Lt. Blake)*.

Two young aviators become determined flyers thanks to the help of a female pilot. Early Howard Hawks directorial effort that's fairly entertaining. According to reliable resources, prints of this film do not exist.

d, Howard Hawks, Lew Seiler; w, Seton I. Miller, Norman Z. McLeod, Hugh Herbert, William Kernell (based on a story by Graham Baker, Andrew Bennison); ph, Dan Clark; ed, Ralph Dixon.

Adventure/Drama **(PR:A MPAA:NR)**

AIR DEVILS* (1938) 70m UNIV bw

Larry Blake *(Horseshoe)*, Dick Purcell *(Slats)*, Beryl Wallace *(Marcia Bradford)*, Mamo Clark *(Lolano)*, Charles Brokaw *(Mordant)*, Minerva Urecal *(Miss Price)*, Forbes Murray *(Capt. Hawthorne)*, Paul Sutton *(Holo)*, LeRoy Mason *(Walker)*, Al Kikume *(Don Kahano)*, Michael Visaroff *(President)*, Billy Wayne *(Sgt. Jennings)*.

South Seas flying buddies, Blake and Purcell, vie for the affection of Wallace, but her heart belongs to another. A lot of double-crossing, fisticuffs, and dirty tricks in this inane quickie.

p, Trem Carr; d, John Rawlins; w, Harold Buckley, George Waggner (based on a story by Buckley); ph, Harry Neumann; ed, Charles Craft.

Drama **(PR:A MPAA:NR)**

AIR EAGLES* (1932) 72 m Big Productions bw

Lloyd Hughes, Norman Kerry, Shirley Grey, Matty Kemp, Otis Harlan, Berton Churchill, Katherine Ward.

Former WW I rivals, now carnival barnstormers, fight for the attention of Grey. The rotten German Kerry plans a payroll heist involving the kid brother of Hughes and, after the latter discovers the plot, the two aces battle to a simultaneous death. Since Grey has been in love with the kid brother all along, it's tough luck, guys.

p, W. Ray Johnson; d, Paul Whitman; ph, James Brown, Jr., Charles Marshall; w, Hampton Del Ruth.

Drama **(PR:C MPAA:NR)**

AIR FORCE**** (1943) 124m WB bw

John Ridgely *(Capt. Mike Quincannon)*, Gig Young *(Lt. Bill Williams)*, Arthur Kennedy *(Lt. Tommy McMartin)*, Charles Drake *(Lt. Munchauser)*, Harry Carey *(Sgt. Robby 01/2White)*, George Tobias *(Cpl. Weinberg)*, Ward Wood *(Cpl. Peterson)*, Ray Montgomery *(Pvt. Chester)*, John Garfield *(Sgt. Joe Winocki)*, James Brown *(Lt. Tex Rader)*, Stanley Ridges *(Maj. Mallory)*, Willard Robertson *(Col.)*, Moroni Olsen *(Col. Blake)*, Edward Brophy *(Sgt. J. J. Callahan)* Richard Lane *(Maj. W. G. Roberts)*, Faye Emerson *(Susan McMartin)*, Bill Crago *(Lt. Moran)*, Addison Richards *(Maj. Daniels)*, James Flavin *(Maj. A. M. Bagley)* Ann Doran *(Mary Quincannon)*, Dorothy Peterson *(Mrs. Chester)*, James Millican *(Marine with Dog)*, William Forrest *(Jack Harper)*, Murray Alper *(Corporal of Demolition Squad)*, George Neise *(Hickam Field Officer)*, Tom Neal *(Marine)*, Henry Blair *(Quincannon's Son)*, Warren Douglas *(Control Officer)*, Ruth Ford *(Nurse)*, William Hopper *(Sergeant)*, Walter Sande *(Joe)*, Leah Baird, Sol Gorss, George Offerman, Jr., James Bush, Theodore von Eltz, Rand Brooks, Lynne Baggett, Ross Ford.

This Howard Hawks war classic with tempered propaganda is a thrilling salute to the Air Force told through the exploits of one Boeing B-17, the "Mary Ann" by name, an inspiring, gripping tale with excellent performances all around. Film opens with the crews of nine Flying Fortresses taking off for points unknown, wives and mothers sending off their loved ones. Ridgely, the pilot, thinks it is a routine mission but when airborne he opens up his orders which direct him to fly to Hawaii. Just before the flight lands, Pearl Harbor is attacked by the Japanese (this is based on a real incident), hundreds of enemy planes destroying the fleet and the major airstrip, Hickam Field, forcing the unarmed fortresses to scatter to neighboring island landing strips. The "Mary Ann" lands on a remote island and is attacked by Japanese-Hawaiians but it manages to make emergency repairs and take off again, landing at a battered Hickam Field. There Kennedy learns that his sister, Emerson, has been wounded in the sneak attack while on a date with Brown. Kennedy and Young upbraid Brown but later learn that Emerson was wounded because of her own irresponsibility and that Brown had been a hero, shooting down four enemy planes before being shot down himself. The bomber is refueled and takes off for the grueling 7,000-mile trip to the Phillippines where fortresses are desperately needed, taking along pursuit pilot Brown. At Wake Island, 2300 miles from Hawaii (Drake, as a nervous apprentice navigator struggles to pinpoint the location), the plane stops to refuel, the crew witnessing a valiant Marine detachment which has been fighting off enormous Japanese forces. Before taking off members of the doomed Marine battalion convince Tobias to smuggle their mascot, a dog, on board the fortress. Once in the Philippines, the fortress undergoes several hazardous missions but is crippled on landing, Ridgely mortally wounded. His death-bed scene is prosaic as his crew stands about him and he hallucinates a take-off, giving instructions to which his mates respond, a moving understated scene that symbolizes the team spirit of the crew. Japanese troops move ever closer to the airfield where the crew members desperately attempt to repair the fortress which has been ordered burned so it will not fall into Japanese hands. Just before the plane is burned, Young and Brown, who replaces the dead Ridgely, get the fortress off the ground while its gunners mow down swarming Japanese troops. The plane heads for Australia as the Philippines fall but spot an enemy carrier force en route and radio American bombers based in Australia which fly to the attack in a rousing finale where the Japanese fleet is sent to the bottom. Garfield's role is that of a washed-out pilot turned gunner. He at first intends to get out of the service but after witnessing the carnage wrought by the Japanese he changes his mind and becomes a dedicated gunner. Carey is terrific as the tough old crew chief whose aviator son, he learns when landing in the Philippines, has been killed in the first attack while taking off. "He didn't even get into the air," says Carey when his son's handkerchief-bound effects are placed into his hands. Nichols' screenplay is powerful, with dialog that is both meaningful and believable. Hawks' direction is masterful in economy and pace; his handling of battle scenes, particularly when the plane is attacked by scores of Japanese Zeroes over Bataan, is harrowing and frighteningly realistic; the viewer is there, inside the plane as the gunners fight off the enemy planes. Also realistic was the plane itself. The Air Force gave Hawks the use of a real fortress (later lost in the Pacific), but interiors were shot inside a $40,000 model. Hawks was a veteran of the Air Corps of WW I so his own experience and love for the service shows in every scene. The film was shot outside Tampa, Florida.

p, Hal B. Wallis; d, Howard Hawks; w, Dudley Nichols; ph, James Wong Howe, aerial ph, Elmer Syer; m, Franz Waxman; ed, George Amy; md, Leo F. Forbstein; art d, John Huglies; spec eff, Roy Davidson, Rex Wimpy, H. F. Koenekamp.

War **(PR:A MPAA:NR)**

AIR HAWKS**½ (1935) 68m COL bw

Ralph Bellamy *(Barry)*, Wiley Post *(Wiley Post)*, Douglas Dumbrille *(Arnold)*, Tala Birell *(Letty Lynn)*, Robert Allen *(Lewis)*, Billie Seward *(Mona)*, Victor Kilian *(Tiny)*, Robert Middlemass *(Drewen)*, Geneva Mitchell *(Gertie)*, Wyrley Birch *(Holden)*, Edward Van Sloan *(Shulter)*, Bill Irving *(Leon)*, C. Franklin Parker *(Burbank)*, Peggy Terry *(Blondie)*, Al Hill *(Pete)*.

Two firms battle for airmail contracts which results in some exciting flying sequences, much of the footage from Post's actual transcontinental flights. An improbable sideline story involves the development and use of a deadly infra-red ray by one firm to knock down the opposition's planes. Above average aviation film.

d, Albert Rogell; w, Griffin Jay, Grace Neville; ph, Harry Freulich; ed, Richard Cahoon.

Adventure **(PR:A MPAA:NR)**

AIR HOSTESS* (1933) 67m COL bw

Evalyn Knapp *(Kitty King)*, James Murray *(Ted Hunter)*, Arthur Pierson *(Dick Miller)*, Jane Darwell *(Ma Kearns)*, J. M. Kerrigan *(Pa Kearns)*, Thelma Todd *(Sylvia Carleton)*, Mike Donlin *(Mike)*, Dutch Hendrian *(Spike)*.

Sit back and enjoy the non-stop thrills in the always exciting life of air hostess Knapp in mysterious and beautiful Albuquerque. Terribly boring, poorly acted picture that fails to get off the ground.

d, Al Rogell; w, Keene Thompson, Milton Raison (based on a story by Grace Perkins); ph, Joseph Walker.

Drama **(PR:A MPAA:NR)**

AIR HOSTESS** (1949) 60m COL bw

Gloria Henry *(Ruth Jackson)*, Ross Ford *(Dennis Hogan)*, Audrey Ford *(Lorraine Carter)*, Marjorie Lord *(Jennifer White)*, William Wright *(Fred MacCoy)*, Ann Doran *(Virginia Barton)*, Olive Deering *(Helen Field)*, Leatrice Joy *(Celia Hansen)*, Barbara Billingsley *(Madeline Moore)*, Harry Tyler *(Jeff Farrell)*, Jessie Arnold *(Mrs. Peabody)*, Irene Tedrow *(Miss Hamilton)*, Grady Sutton *(Ned Jenkins)*.

Thankfully not a remake of 1933's AIR HOSTESS, the film focuses on three stewardesses, one following in her sister's high heels, another seeking a wealthy husband, and the third becoming a hostess of the skies simply because her dead husband loved to fly. Likeable cast accentuates the satisfactory story.

p, Wallace MacDonald; d, Lew Landers; w, Robert Libott, Frank Burt (based on a story by Louise Rousseau); ph, Allen Siegler; ed, James Sweeney.

Drama **(PR:A MPAA:NR)**

AIR MAIL*** (1932) 83m UNIV bw

Pat O'Brien *(Duke Talbot)*, Ralph Bellamy *(Mike Miller)*, Gloria Stuart *(Ruth Barnes)*, Lillian Bond *(Irene Wilkins)*, Russell Hopton *(Dizzy Wilkins)*, Slim Summerville *(Slim McCune)*, Frank Albertson *(Tommy Bogan)*, Leslie Fenton *(Tony*

Dressler), David Landau *(Pop)*, Tom Corrigan *(Sleepy Collins)*, William Daly *(Tex Lane)*, Hans Furberg *(Heinie Kramer)*, Beth Milton *(Plane Attendant)*, Edmund Burns *(Radio Announcer)*, Jim Thorpe *(Indian)*, Lew Kelly *(Drunkard)*, Francis Ford, James Donlan, Louise MacIntosh, Frank Beals, Katherine Perry *(Passenger Plane Pilots)*, Jack Pennick, Alene Carroll.

Daredevil, reckless pilot O'Brien is hired by Bellamy when two of Bellamy's airmail pilots quit. O'Brien runs off with Bond, another pilot's wife, and Bellamy takes the most dangerous mission, crashing into a mountain. A penitent O'Brien lands on the mountain, damaging the plane, but he rescues his employer, then takes off but the damaged plane fails. O'Brien compels Bellamy to parachute, then crash-lands the plane. Critically injured, all the vain O'Brien can say while being rushed to the hospital is, "How do I look?" The film is almost identical in plot and character profiles to ONLY ANGELS HAVE WINGS (both written by Frank W. "Spig" Wead).

p, Carl Laemmle, Jr.; d, John Ford; w, Dale Van Every, Frank W. Wead (based on a story by Wead); ph, Karl Freund; ed, Harry W. Lieb; spec eff, John P. Fulton; aerial stunts, Paul Mantz.

Adventure **(PR:A MPAA:NR)**

AIR PATROL* (1962) 70m FOX bw

Willard Parker *(Lt. Vern Taylor)*, Merry Anders *(Mona Whitney)*, Robert Dix *(Sgt. Bob Castle)*, John Holland *(Arthur Murcott)*, Russ Bender *(Sgt. Lou Kurnitz)*, Douglas Dumbrille *(Millard Nolan)*, George Eldredge *(Howie Franklin)*, Ivan Bonar *(Oliver Dunning)*, Jack Younger, Glen Marshall, Ray Dannis, Stacey Winters, LaRue Farlow, Lee Patterson.

Detectives capture helicopter-flying art thieves by using a chopper of their own. No-name cast occupies space in this mundane chase picture.

p, Maury Dexter; d, Dexter; w, Henry Cross; ph, John M. Nicholaus, Jr. (CinemaScope); m, Albert Glasser; ed, Jodie Coplan; md, Glasser; set d, Harry Reif.

Adventure **Cas.** **(PR:C MPAA:NR)**

AIR POLICE* (1931) 60m Sono-Art World bw

Kenneth Harlan, Charles Delaney, Josephine Dunn, Richard Cramer, Arthur Thahasso, Tom London, George Chesebro.

Fearless air cop Harlan avenges the death of his partner by showing some nasty smugglers that airborne crime doesn't pay. Dull flight sequences help ruin this low-budget adventure.

d, Stuart Paton; w, Bennett Cohn (based on a story by Arthur Hoerl); ph, William Nobles; ed, Cohn.

Adventure **Cas.** **(PR:A MPAA:NR)**

AIR RAID WARDENS 1/2** (1943) 67m MGM bw

Stan Laurel *(Himself)*, Oliver Hardy *(Himself)*, Edgar Kennedy *(Joe Bledsoe)*, Jacqueline White *(Peggy Parker)*, Stephen McNally *(Dan Madison)*, Russell Hicks *(Major Scanlon)*, Nella Walker *(Millicent Norton)*, Howard Freeman *(J. P. Norton)*, Donald Meek *(Eustace Middling)*, Henry O'Neill *(Rittenhaus)*, Paul Stanton *(Captain Biddle)*, Robert Emmett O'Connor *(Charlie Beaugart)*, Lee Phelps, Martin Cichy *(Moving Men)*, Bert Moorhouse *(Warden)*, Don Costello *(Heydrich)*, William Tannen *(Joseph)*, Milton Kibbee *(Lem)*, Phil Van Zandt *(Herman)*, Frederic Worlock *(Otto)*, Betty Jaynes *(Waitress)*, Jack Gardner *(Johnson)*, Howard Mitchell *(Huxton Officer)*, Forrest Taylor, Edward Hearn *(Night Watchmen)*, Charles Coleman *(Butler)*, Rose Hobart *(Bank Secretary)*, Nolan Leary *(Gas Station Attendant)*.

L&H are miserable failures in every business they attempt, from selling fertilizer to running a pet shop. They close up shop and try to enlist, doing their bit for the war effort but all the services decline their assistance. The boys become air raid wardens but are constantly being pressured to resign by Freeman and his snooty wife Walker; during a practice air raid, the boys apply first aid to imaginary wounds on leading citizens whom they have strapped to boards in order to make them more cooperative, this being one of some hilarious scenes. Kennedy is uncooperative when L&H visit his home, refusing to observe the blackout by turning off his lights. The boys jump him in a patriotic donnybrook that leaves them all unconscious, having knocked each other senseless with beer bottles. When found, they are dismissed from the service for drunkenness. They redeem themselves later when they overhear a plot by Meek and O'Neill to sabotage the local magnesium plant and then round up the would-be saboteurs in a wild melee of slapstick action. Not one of L&H's better efforts but it does have its moments. (See LAUREL AND HARDY series, Index.)

p, B.F. Zeidman; d, Edward Sedgwick; w, Martin Rackin, Jack Jevne, Charles Rogers, Harry Crane; ph, Walter Lundin; m, Nathaniel Shilkret; ed, Irvine Warburton; art d, Cedric Gibbons; set d, Edwin B. Willis, Alfred Spencer.

Comedy **(PR:AAA MPAA:NR)**

AIR STRIKE* (1955) 63m Lippert bw

Richard Denning *(Cdr. Blair)*, Gloria Jean *(Marg Huggins)*, Don Haggerty *(Lt. Richard Huggins)*, Bill Hudson *(Lt. John Smith)*, Alan Wells *(Anthony Perini)*, John Kirby *(David Loring)*, William Hallop *(Lt. Cdr. Swanson)*, James Courtney *(Ens. James Delaney)*, Stanley Clements *(G. H. Alexander)*.

Navy squadron leader Denning whips up the boring young pilots of the U.S. carrier *Essex* for a terribly unexciting jet fighter attack. Not a single interesting or thrilling moment in the entire film.

p,d&w, Cy Roth; ph, Alan Stensvold; m, Andre Brummer; ed, George McGuire.

Drama/Adventure **(PR:A MPAA:NR)**

AIRBORNE** (1962) 78m Diamond bw

Bobby Diamond, Robert Christian, Mikel Angel, Bill Hale, Carolyn Byrd, Barbara Markham.

Farm boy Diamond shows the city boys at Fort Bragg's paratrooper training school the benefits of a good country upbringin'. Not much more than a positive look at the actual "Fighting 82nd," the movie is highlighted by some charming characterizations and well-shot parachuting footage.

p, Art Diamond; d, James Landis; w, Landis, ph, Larry Raimond.

Drama **(PR:A MPAA:NR)**

AIRPLANE! 1/2** (1980) 88m PAR c

Robert Hays *(Ted Striker)*, Julie Hagerty *(Elaine)*, Kareem Abdul-Jabbar *(Murdock)*, Lloyd Bridges *(McCroskey)*, Peter Graves *(Captain Oveur)*, Leslie Nielsen *(Dr. Rumack)*, Lorna Patterson *(Randy)*, Robert Stack *(Kramer)*, Stephen Stucker *(Johnny)*, Barbara Billingsley *(Jive Lady)*, Joyce Bulifant *(Mrs. Davis)*, James Hong *(Japanese General)*, Maureen McGovern *(Nun)*, Ethel Merman *(Lt. Hurwitz)*, Kenneth Tobey *(Air Controller Neubauer)*, Jimmie Walker *(Windshield Wiper Man)*, Howard Jarvis *(Man in Taxi)*.

Strictly slapstick revived from vaudeville, with triple-takes and broad burlesques of many an airplane pic, particularly THE CROWDED SKY and ZERO HOUR. A young pilot is forced to take over a pilotless jet liner after Graves and crew members grow ill eating the blueplate specials with a zany Nielsen encouraging Hays to fly the craft and even zanier ground officers Bridges and Stack giving him impossible instructions while the passengers grow ill, daffy, berserk, sex-crazed, maniacal, hysterical and utterly impossible. The onslaught of sight gags is overwhelming so that even the most dour viewer is reduced to laughing as the mass lunacy infects the funnybone. The only person who is not funny is limp-wristed Stucker who mocks the whole business with retarded gestures. A sort of Olson-and-Johnson of the air show which will leave most viewers with the same question at movie's end: "Why was I laughing?"

p, Jon Davison; d&w, Jim Abrahams, David and Jerry Zucker; ph, Joseph Biroc (Metrocolor); m, Elmer Bernstein; ed, Patrick Kennedy; set d, Anne D. McCulley; cos, Rosanna Norton; spec eff, Bruce Logan; ch, Tom Mahoney.

Comedy **Cas.** **(PR:C MPAA:PG)**

AIRPLANE II: THE SEQUEL** (1982) 85m PAR c

Robert Hays *(Ted Striker)*, Julie Hagerty *(Elaine)*, Lloyd Bridges *(McCroskey)*, Peter Graves *(Capt. Oveur)*, William Shatner *(Murdock)*, Chad Everett *(Simon)*, Stephen Stucker *(Jacobs)*, Oliver Robins *(Jimmie)*, Sonny Bono *(Bomber)*, Raymond Burr *(Judge)*, Chuck Connors *(Sarge)*, John Dehner *(Commissioner)*, Rip Torn *(Kruger)*, Kent McCord *(Unger)*, James A. Watson, Jr. *(Dunn)*, John Vernon *(Dr. Stone)*, Laurene London *(Testa)*, Wendy Phillips *(Mary)*, Jack Jones *(Singer)*, Art Fleming *(Himself)*, Frank Ashmore, Richard Jaeckel, John Hancock *(Controllers)*, Al White *(Witness)*, Lee Bryant *(Mrs. Hammen)*, John Larch *(Prosecuting Attorney)*, Oliver Robins *(Jimmy)*, Louis Giambalvo *(Witness)*, Leon Askin *(Anchorman)*, Sandahl Bergman *(Officer)*, James Noble *(Father of Flanagan)*, Lee Patterson *(Captain)*, Louise Sorel *(Stella)*.

An even more outrageous sequel to AIRPLANE! with sight gags and low-brow humor even lower and more disgusting than its predecessor (if that's possible), but here the novelty has worn off, worn thin, worn down, and worn out. Half of unemployed Hollywood joins the other half in this spoof of not a jet liner but a space shuttle about to crash. Most of the personalities flash by with little or nothing to do and less to say. Again Stephen Stucker appears as a humorless kibitzer but his role is no more or less worthless than the other cameos, really bits, in this sophomoric spoof.

p, Howard Koch; d&w, Ken Finkleman; ph, Joseph Biroc (Metrocolor); m, Elmer Bernstein; ed, Dennis Virkler.

Comedy **Cas.** **(PR:C MPAA:PG)**

AIRPORT** (1970) 137M UNIV c

Burt Lancaster *(Mel Bakersfeld)*, Dean Martin *(Vernon Demerest)*, Jean Seberg *(Tanya Livingston)*, Jacqueline Bisset *(Gwen Meighen)*, George Kennedy *(Patroni)*, Helen Hayes *(Ada Quonsett)*, Van Heflin *(D. O. Guerrero)*, Maureen Stapleton *(Inez Guerrero)*, Barry Nelson *(Lt. Anson Harris)*, Dana Wynter *(Cindy)*, Lloyd Nolan *(Harry Standish)*, Barbara Hale *(Sara)*, Gary Collins *(Cy Jordon)* John Findlater *(Peter Coakley)*, Jessie Royce Landis *(Mrs. Harriet DuBarry Mossman)*, Larry Gates *(Commissioner Ackerman)*, Peter Turgeon *(Marcus Rathbone)*, Whit Bissell *(Mr. Davidson)*, Virginia Grey *(Mrs. Schultz)*, Eileen Wesson *(Judy)*, Paul Picerni *(Dr. Compagno)*, Robert Patten *(Capt. Benson)*, Clark Howat *(Bert Weatherby)*, Lew Brown *(Reynolds)*, Llana Dowding *(Roberta Bakersfeld)*, Lisa Garritson *(Libby Bakersfeld)*, Patty Poulsen *(Joan)*, Jim Nolan *(Father Lonigan)*, Malila Saint Duval *(Maria)*, Ena Hartman *(Ruth)*, Jodean Russo *(Marie Patroni)*, Albert Reed *(Lt. Ordway)*, Sharon Harvey *(Sally)*, Dick Winslow *(Mrs. Schultz)*, Nancy Ann Nelson *(Bunnie)*, Mary Jackson *(Sister Felice)*, Janis Hansen *(Sister Katherine Grace)*, Lou Wagner *(Schuyler Schultz)*, Chuck Daniel *(Parks)*, Shelly Novack *(Rollings)*, Charles Brewer *(Diller)*.

Bizarre reshaping of GRAND HOTEL in the sky with disaster the key point and apprehension as the main story. A fanatic, Heflin, takes out a large insurance policy, then blows himself out of an in-flight jet which limps along for more than two hours looking for a place to land while a score of passengers' lives are capsulized (with her tiny part as a stowaway, Helen Hayes still managed to take an Academy Award for best supporting actress, proving her matchless talent can conquer any mediocre script). Then we have the frantic ground people sweating over microphones and runway equipment desperately attempting to move a stalled plane on the only runway available, all this during a blizzard while ground crew chief Kennedy huffs and puffs heroically. This film cost more than $10 million and Universal chiefs held their breath but they need not have worried—the production soared beyond a $45 million gross and spawned three sequels, one worse than the next.

p, Ross Hunter; d, George Seaton (additional sequences, Henry Hathaway); w, Seaton (based on the novel by Arthur Hailey); ph, Ernest Laszlo (Todd-AO, Technicolor); m, Alfred Newman; ed, Stuart Gilmore; art d, Preston Ames, Alexander Golitzen; cos, Edith Head.

Disaster **Cas.** **(PR:A MPAA:G)**

AIRPORT 1975** (1974) 107m UNIV c

Charlton Heston *(Alan Murdock)*, Karen Black *(Chief Stewardess Nancy Pryor)*, George Kennedy *(Joseph Patroni)*, Efrem Zimbalist Jr. *(Pilot Stacy)*, Susan Clark *(Mrs. Patroni)*, Helen Reddy *(Sister Ruth)*, Gloria Swanson *(Herself)*, Linda Blair *(Janice Abbott)*, Nancy Olson *(Abbott's Mother)*, Dana Andrews *(Small Plane Pilot)*,

Roy Thinnes *(Co-Pilot)*, Sid Caesar *(Talkative Passenger)*, Myrna Loy *(Mrs. Devaney)*, Ed Nelson *(Rescue Pilot)*, Larry Storch *(TV Newsman)*, Martha Scott *(Sister Beatrice)*, Norman Fell, Jerry Stiller, Conrad Janis *(Drinkers)*, Beverly Garland *(Mrs. Freeman)*, Augusta Summerland *(Swanson's Secretary)*, Guy Stockwell *(Col. Moss)*, Erik Estrada *(Navigator Julio)*, Ken Sanson *(Steward)*, Brian Morrison *(Junior Patroni)*, Christopher Norris, Irene Tsu *(Stewardesses)*.

Businessman Andrews has a heart attack while flying his small plane which smashes into a jumbo 747, killing the flight crew and leaving a gaping hole in the cockpit; the pilot's seat is quickly filled by courageous cross-eyed stewardess, Black, who flies the plane over hill and dale while the passengers recall their wicked ways and have apoplectic attacks on the side. Heston tries to give the hysterical Black instructions on flying the big crate and then thinks it best that he lower himself into the hole of the in-flight plane via helicopter (another pilot attempts it and gets splattered). He is successful and brings the ship to a perilous landing, the runway readied by gruff grounds chief Kennedy who has not stopped huffing and puffing from the original AIRPORT. This film is even more mindless than its predecessor with a whole new cast of miscasts, including Swanson who spends most of her moments making up that great silent film face. Loy is wasted as a drunk oblivious to her possible fate, and Reddy, a nun, plucking a guitar and blithely singing as the plane is about to crash, completes the absurdity of the film. The most astounding bit about the production was that a real 747 was employed (at $52,000 a day), no miniature, and that stunt man Joe Canutt actually spent an hour dangling out of the helicopter following the jet at 8,000 feet over the magnificent Rocky Mountains while shooting the transfer scene. Heston practiced flying a 747 at the American Airlines simulator in Dallas and then really flew the monster for an hour and a half. Universal's tally sheets were black on this one, $3 million investment for a $25 million-plus return, thus assuring the world of yet another sequel.

p, William Frye; d, Jack Smight; w, Don Ingalls; ph, Philip Lathrop; m, John Cacavas; ed, J. Terry Williams; art d, George C. Webb; cos, Edith Head.

Disaster **(PR:C MPAA:PG)**

AIRPORT '77** (1977) 113m UNIV c

Jack Lemmon *(Don Gallagher)*, Lee Grant *(Karen Wallace)*, Brenda Vaccaro *(Eve Clayton)*, Joseph Cotten *(Nicholas St. Downs II)*, Olivia de Havilland *(Emily Livingston)*, Darren McGavin *(Buchek)*, Christopher Lee *(Martin Wallace)*, Robert Foxworth *(Chambers)*, Robert Hooks *(Eddie)*, George Kennedy *(Patroni)* James Stewart *(Stevens)*, Monte Markham *(Banker)*, Kathleen Quinlan *(Julie)*, Gil Gerard *(Frank Powers)*, James Booth *(Ralph Crawford)*, Monica Lewis *(Anne)*, Maidie Norman *(Dorothy)*, Pamela Bellwood *(Lisa)*, Arlene Golonka *(Mrs. Stern)*, Tom Sullivan *(Steve)*, M. Emmet Walsh *(Dr. Williams)*, Michael Richardson *(Walker)*, Michael Pataki *(Wilson)*, George Furth *(Lucas)*, Richard Vanture *(Cdr. Guay)*.

Here we go again—it's time for a 747 to meet disaster once more with a host of colorful characters to worry about as they go down—and this time they go down 50 feet into the ocean. Billionaire James Stewart is transporting his vast and priceless art collection to Florida from Washington, DC. when thieves try to skyjack the plane, forcing pilot Lemmon to fly at water's edge to avoid radar detection. The plane sails through fog and strikes an oil derrick, sinking beneath the waves to rest on an underwater shelf, balancing on the edge of a fathomless trench. The thieves are killed but it becomes a race to save those on board in the water-tight compartments while they slowly use up their air supply. The usual panic grips the transparent stereotypes who pass for passengers—Christopher Lee as a famous oceanographer, Grant as his boozy wife, de Havilland as a wealthy art collector, Cotten, her one-time lover, and plane designer McGavin who admits he has a fear of flying (and drowning no doubt). Kennedy again puffs and huffs as Patroni, but from a massive rescue ship that manages to refloat the plane long enough to enable survivors to swim to safety; this proved tough on some—Vaccaro caught pneumonia while thrashing through the 2,000 gallons of water dumped onto the fast-sinking plane in the studio tank. Again Universal cleaned up with a gross of more than $16 million which put in order even another sequel, AIRPORT '79.

p, William Frye; d, Jerry Jameson; w, David Spector, Michael Scheff; ph, Philip Lathrop (Panavision, Technicolor); m, John Cacavas; ed, J. Terry Williams, Robert Watts; set d, Mickey S. Michaels; cos, Edith Head, Burton Miller, John Anderson, Sheila Mason; spec eff, Albert Whitlock; stunts, Stan Barrett.

Disaster **(PR:C MPAA:PG)**

AIRPORT '79 (SEE: CONCORDE, THE—AIRPORT '79, 1979)

AL CAPONE**** (1959) 105m AA bw

Rod Steiger *(Al Capone)*, Fay Spain *(Maureen)*, James Gregory *(Schaefer)*, Martin Balsam *(Kelly)*, Nehemiah Persoff *(Johnny Torrio)*, Murvyn Vye *(Bugs Moran)*, Joe De Santis *(Jim Colosimo)*, Lewis Charles *(Hymie Weiss)*, Robert Gist *(O'Banion)*, Sandy Kenyon *(Bones Corelli)*, Raymond Bailey *(Mr. Brancato)*, Al Ruscio *(Tony Genaro)*, Louis Quinn *(Joe Lorenzo)*, Ron Soble *(Scalisi)*, Steve Gravesi *(Anselmo)*, Ben Ari *(Ben Hoffman)*, Peter Dane *(Pete Flannery)*.

Excellent biofilm of one of the world's most ruthless men, an exacting and powerful performance by Steiger as the remorseless power-hungry Capone, with apt supporting roles by Gregory as the honest cop (his model taken from Captain John Stege of the Chicago PD), and Balsam as the corrupt slippery news reporter (based upon Jake Lingle of the *Tribune* who was murdered by Capone gunman Leo Vincent Brothers in 1931 for going over to Moran), Vye as blase gangster Bugs Moran. This is one of the most faithful *film noir* productions on record, detailing the actual meteoric rise of Capone, under the tutelage of Torrio, darkly played by Persoff, until he was boss supreme at age 25, making $50 million a year gross from bootleg hootch. We see Steiger appear in 1919 Chicago, becoming a bouncer for Big Jim Colosimo, an opera-loving old-time crime czar perfectly enacted by De Santis, arranging for the murder of Big Jim at Torrio's orders because the old man would not traffic in illegal booze (actually Capone himself killed Big Jim personally while disguised as a truck driver delivering pasta to Colosimo's Cafe in 1920). We witness the incredible gang wars between Capone-Torrio and the North Side Irish gang headed by O'Banion, Weiss, and Moran culminating in the St. Valentine's Day Massacre and an epilog that shows Capone going mad in Alcatraz as paresis of the brain eats him alive (as a result of untreated syphilis). It is far and away Steiger's greatest screen performance, enhanced at every savage turn by Wilson's quick-paced direction and Ballard's marvelously crisp camerawork.

p, John H. Burrows, Leonard J. Ackerman; d, Richard Wilson; w, Marvin Wald, Henry Greenberg; ph, Lucian Ballard; m, David Raksin; ed, Walter Hannemann; art d, Hilyard Brown.

Crime **(PR:C-O MPAA:NR)**

AL JENNINGS OF OKLAHOMA** (1951) 77m COL c

Dan Duryea *(Al Jennings)*, Gale Storm *(Margo St. Claire)*, Dick Foran *(Frank Jennings)*, Gloria Henry *(Alice Calhoun)*, Guinn "Big Boy" Williams *(Lon Tuttle)*, Raymond Greenleaf *(Judge Jennings)*, Stanley Andrews *(Marshal Slattery)*, John Ridgely *(Dan Hanes)*, James Millican *(Ed Jennings)*, Harry Shannon *(Fred Salter)*, Helen Brown *(Mrs. Salter)*, Robert Bice *(Pete Kinkaid)*, George J. Lewis *(Sammy Page)*, Jimmie Dodd *(Buck Botkin)*, Edwin Parker *(Doc Wrightmire)*, James Griffith *(Slim Harris)*, William "Bill" Phillips *(Bill Mertz)*, John Dehner *(Tom Marsden)*, Charles Meredith *(Judge Evans)*, William Norton Bailey *(Robert Kyle)*, Louis Jean Heydt *(John Jennings)*, Harry Cording *(Mike Bridges)*, Theresa Harris *(Terese)*.

Duryea and Foran, as the Jennings Brothers, begin their life of crime after vicious union troops ransack their Oklahoma home. They attempt to reform, even going to New Orleans, where Duryea meets lovely Storm and plans to marry, settling down into his law practice, but a vindictive detective exposes him and he's off with brother Foran again robbing trains and stages and banks until captured and imprisoned for five years, then released because of trial errors to become a successful lawyer, Storm at his side. Jennings sold Allied Artists his memoirs and acted as advisor on this potboiler which bears little or no resemblance to the truth. Jennings was the worst bandit in the Southwest and his robberies never netted much beyond a few dollars. So inept was he that during his first train holdup he raced alongside the moving locomotive, firing his pistol rapidly to signal the holdup; the engineer thought him just another cowboy having fun, pulled the whistle a few times and raced ahead of him. It was Jennings who *positively* identified J. Frank Dalton as the living Jesse James but he failed to inform the world how this ancient imposter grew a new finger when Jesse's had been blown off during the Civil War. The old fraud was successful in one robbery—this film.

p, Rudolph C. Flothow; d, Ray Nazarro; w, George Bricker; ph, W. Howard Greene (Technicolor); ed, Richard Fantl.

Western **(PR:A MPAA:NR)**

ALADDIN AND HIS LAMP** (1952) 67m MON c

Patricia Medina *(Jasmine)*, John Sands *(Aladdin)*, Richard Erdman *(Mirza)*, John Dehner *(Bokra)*, Billy House *(Kafan)*, Ned Young *(Hassan)*, Noreen Nash *(Passion Flower)*, Rick Vallin *(Captain of Guard)*, Charles Horvath *(Genie)*, Sujata *(Dancing Slave Girl)*, Arabella *(Maid-in-Waiting)*.

Lowly pickpocket Sands must thwart the evil prince in his attempt to woo the lovely daughter of the Caliph. Luckily, there's this lamp, see, and when you rub it . . . Lush color photography accentuates an already entertaining, but not very literal, adaptation of the Arabian Nights tale.

p, Walter Wanger; d, Lew Landers; w, Howard Dimsdale, Millard Kaufman; ph, Gilbert Warrenton (Cinecolor); m, Marlin Skiles; ed, Jack Ogilvie.

Fantasy/Adventure **Cas.** **(PR:AA MPAA:NR)**

ALAKAZAM THE GREAT! 1/2** (1961, Jap.) 84m Toei/AM-INT c

Frankie Avalon *(Alakazam)*, Dodie Stevens *(De De)*, Jonathan Winters *(Sir Quigley Broken Bottom)*, Arnold Stang *(Lulipopo)*, Sterling Holloway *(Narrator)*.

Very well done Japanese animated feature (English-dubbed) in which an arrogant monkey is forced to go on a journey where he learns about gluttony, greed, love, humility, *life*. Japanese animation has always had a unique graphic style and this highlights it extremely well. Winters' voice as Sir Quigley is outstanding.

English version: p, Lou Rusoff; w, Rusoff, Osamu Tezuka, Lee Kresel; ph, Seigo Otsuka, Komel Ishikawa, Kenji Sugiyama; ed, Salvatore Billitteri; m, Les Baxter; md, Al Simms.

Animated Feature **(PR:AAA MPAA:NR)**

ALAMBRISTA!*** (1977) 110m Filmhaus c

Domingo Ambriz *(Roberto)*, Trinidad Silva *(Joe)*, Linda Gillin *(Sharon)*, Paul Berrones *(Berto)*, George Smith *(Cook)*, Dennis Harris *(Sharon's Brother)*, Edward Olmos, Julius Harris *(Drunks)*, Mark Herder *(Cop)*, J. D. Hurt *(Preacher)*, Ned Beatty *(Anglo Coyote)*, Salvador Martinez *(Mexican Coyote)*, Felix Jose Alvarez *(Junkyard Cook)*, Lily Alvarez *(Pregnant Woman)*.

Innocent, wide-eyed youth Ambriz decides his future lies across the Mexican border in the U.S. and he slips over to undergo incredible exploitation as an illegal alien, slaving for peon wages to support his starving family. This film will not be popular with the law-and-order set but as a study in social persecution it's a powerful document.

p, Michael Hausman, Irwin W. Young; d,w&ph, Robert M. Young (DuArt Color); m, Michael Martin; ed, Ed Beyer; art d, Lily Kilvert.

Drama **(PR:C MPAA:NR)**

ALAMO, THE**** (1960) 192m Batjac/UA c

John Wayne *(Col. David Crockett)*, Richard Widmark *(Col. James Bowie)*, Laurence Harvey *(Col. William Travis)*, Frankie Avalon *(Smitty)*, Patrick Wayne *(Capt. James Butler Bonham)*, Linda Cristal *(Flaca)*, Joan O'Brien *(Mrs. Dickinson)*, Chill Wills *(Beekeeper)*, Joseph Calleia *(Juan Sequin)*, Ken Curtis *(Capt. Almeron Dickinson)*, Carlos Arruza *(Lt. Reyes)*, Jester Hairston *(Jethro)*, Veda Ann Borg *(Blind Nell)*, John Dierkes *(Jocko Robertson)*, Denver Pyle *(Gambler)*, Aissa Wayne *(Angelina Dickinson)*, Hank Worden *(Parson)*, Bill Henry *(Dr. Sutherland)*, Bill Daniel *(Col. Neill)*, Wesley Lau *(Emil)*, Chuck Roberson *(A Tennessean)*, Guinn "Big Boy" Williams *(Lt. Finn)*, Olive Carey *(Mrs. Dennison)*, Ruben Padilla *(Gen. Santa Anna)*, Richard Boone *(Gen. Sam Houston)*.

Excellent recreation of the defense of the Alamo in 1836 Texas where 187 Americans and Texicans stood against the onslaught of Santa Anna's armies (more than 7,000 men) for 13 days, equalling the heroic stands at Thermopylae, Rorke's Drift and Bataan. The movie deals with how those men came to be inside the mission converted to a tiny fort in the dusty village of San Antonio, particularly Travis, played archly by Harvey, Bowie, enacted angrily by Widmark and Crockett, expansively played by John Wayne, coonskin cap and all. (Boone, in two small but telling scenes, is excellent as Sam Houston.) Wayne, whose Batjac Productions spent more than $15 million mounting this superb epic (shot in 91 days) produced, starred and directed (with an uncredited assist from his good friend John Ford, especially the crushing battle scenes at the incredible finale). He presented an old-fashioned patriotic movie at a time when such deep sentiments were disavowed and many a film critic not worth his stars and stripes condemned the film with such unjust terms such as "yesteryear theatricalism." One idiotic reviewer stated that Harvey "seems awfully young for commander of the garrison." Had he bothered to check, as did those doing spendid research for this film, he would have learned that William Barrett Travis died on the battlements of the fort he commanded at age 25. True, Wayne and friends do wax eloquently and sometimes a bit overlong about the joys and fruits of freedom and the kind of sacrifice it takes to maintain freedom but that is exactly the kind of talk that went on down there at the Alamo more than 140 years ago. Moreover, Grant's sparkling screenplay crackles with wit and humor, making those of that long-ago period appear real and the overall production is doggedly faithful to the historical facts. THE ALAMO is entertaining and awesome, with beautiful camera work by Clothier and a stirring score that haunts the memory by Trojan movie composer Tiomkin. Much time is spent developing the rivalry between Harvey/Travis and Widmark/Bowie, both attempting to take command of the fort. This, too, is based upon actual fact, as is the moving scene where Harvey draws a line in the dirt and asks every man who is willing to defend the Alamo, knowing it means doom, to cross it. Of course Wayne/Crockett, with a colonel's rank that matched Travis and Bowie, crosses it with alacrity with his Tennesseans, followed by the rest. This film is an inspiring history lesson, it is high drama well played and it should be seen by everyone seeking the meaning of liberty, and the reason why men give up their lives for an ideal and for their fellow man, all somehow crystallized by Wayne before meeting his death as the immortal Davy Crockett, the words rolling from that leather-lined face: "Republic . . . I like the sound of the word."

p&d, John Wayne; w, James Edward Grant; ph, William H. Clothier (Todd-AO, Technicolor); m, Dmitri Tiomkin; ed. Stuart Gilmore; art d, Alfred Ybarra; spec eff, Lee Zavitz; technical supervision, Frank Beetson, Jack Pennick; m/l, Paul Francis Webster.

War **Cas.** **(PR:AA MPAA:NR)**

ALASKA* (1944) 76m MON bw

Kent Taylor, John Carradine, Margaret Lindsay, Dean Jagger, Nils Asther, Iris Adrian, George Cleveland, Lee White, Jack Norton, Glenn Strange, Dewey Robinson, Dick Scott, John Maxwell.

Low-budget saga has Taylor looking for both gold and thieves during the Gold Rush, while romancing a seemingly disinterested Lindsay. Jagger, Carradine and other stal wart character actors are wasted in this throw-away story.

p, Lindsay Parsons; d, George Archainbaud; w, George Wallace Sayre, Harrison Orkow, Malcolm Stuart Boylan (based on Jack London's story "Flush of Gold"); ph, Archie Stout, Mack Stengler; ed, Richard Currier; md, Edward Kay.

Adventure **(PR:A MPAA:NR)**

ALASKA HIGHWAY* (1943) 66m PAR bw

Richard Arlen *(Woody Ormsby)*, Jean Parker *(Ann Coswell)*, Ralph Sanford *(Frosty Gimble)*, Joe Sawyer *(Roughhouse)*, Bill Henry *(Steve Ormsby)*, John Wegman *(Sgt.* Swithers), Harry Shannon *(Pop Ormsby)*, Edward Earle *(Blair Caswell)*, Keith Richards *(Hank Lincoln)*, Eddie Quillan *(Pompadour Jones)*.

Two brothers blazing a trail through the frozen wilderness for the Army Corps of Engineers fall for the same girl. Typical romance stuff set against the harsh Alaskan tundra.

p, Bill Pine, Bill Thomas; d, Frank McDonald; w, Maxwell Shane, Lewis R. Foster; ph, Fred Jackman, Jr.; ed, William Ziegler.

Drama **(PR:A MPAA:NR)**

ALASKA PASSAGE* (1959) 71m Associated Producers Inc./FOX bw

Bill Williams *(Al)*, Nick Dennis *(Pete)*, Nora Hayden *(Tina)*, Leslie Bradley *(Mason)*, Lyn Thomas *(Janet)*, Jess Kirkpatrick *(Barney)*, Fred Sherman *(Radabaugh)*, Raymond Hatton *(Hank)*, Tommy Cook *(Hubie)*, Jorie Wyler *(Claudette)*, Greg Martell *(McCormick)*, Court Shepart *(MacKilliop)*, Ralph Sanford *(Anderson)*.

Uninteresting adventures of truckers transporting goods over some of the iciest roads imagineable. Low-budget production contains one rather exciting chase scene.

p, Bernard Glasser; d, Edward Bernds; w, Bernds; ph, William Whitney (Regal Scope); m, Alex Alexander; ed, Richard C. Meyer.

Adventure/Drama **(PR:A MPAA:NR)**

ALASKA PATROL** (1949) 61m Burwood/Film Classics bw

Richard Travis *(Tom Norman/Battick)*, Helen Westcott *(Mary Lynn)*, Jim Griffith *(Operative Dale)*, Emory Parnell *(Capt. Roburt)*, Dick Fraser *(Operative Farrell)*, Ralf Harolde *(Steele)*, Selmer Jackson *(Capt. Wright)*, Gene Ross *(Ehrlich)*, William Tannen *(Dajek)*, Pierre Watkin *(Mr. Sigmund)*, Otto Reichow *(Balser)*, Paul Bryar *(Cmdr. Braddock)*, William Haade *(Anorus)*, Jason Robards *(Dr. Loring)*.

Naval intelligence officer Travis poses as an enemy agent in order to break up a spy ring holing up in chilly Alaska. Reasonably well-made spy picture done with a documentary-like style.

p, James Burkett; d, Jack Bernhard; w, Arthur Hoerl; ph, Marcel LePicard; ed, Charles Craft.

Spy/Drama **(PR:A MPAA:NR)**

ALASKA SEAS*½ (1954) 78m PAR bw

Robert Ryan *(Matt Kelly)*, Jan Sterling *(Nicky)*, Brian Keith *(Jim Kimmerly)*, Gene Barry *(Verne Williams)*, Richard Shannon *(Tom Erickson)*, Ralph Dumke *(Jackson)*, Ross Bagdasarian *(Joe)*, Fay Roope *(Walt Davis)*, Timothy Carey *(Wycoff)*, Peter Coe *(Grego)*, Jim Hayward *(Jailer)*, Aaron Spelling *(Knifer)*, William Fawcett *(Silversmith)*, Earl Holliman *(Indian Boy)*, Richard Kipling *(Croupier)*, Eugene Roth *(Dan)*, Abel Fernandez *(Reichie)*.

Ruthless, unlikable Ryan tries to monopolize salmon fishing in his area, strong-arming everyone out of the business, including best friend Keith. Good cast is wasted in cliched, tedious story. Remake of SPAWN OF THE NORTH.

p, Mel Epstein; d, Jerry Hopper; w, Geoffrey Homes, Walter Doniger (based on a story by Barrett Willoughby); ph, William C. Mellor; md, Irvin Talbot; ed, Archie Marshek.

Adventure/Drama **(PR:A MPAA:NR)**

ALBERT, R.N.** (1953, Brit.) 88m Eros bw (AKA: BREAK TO FREEDOM)

Anthony Steel *(Lt. Geoffrey Ainsworth)*, Jack Warner *(Capt. Maddox)*, Robert Beatty *(Lt. Jim Reid)*, William Sylvester *(Lt. "Texas" Norton)*, Michael Balfour *(Lt. Henry Adams)*, Guy Middleton *(Capt. Barton)*, Paul Carpenter *(Lt. Erickson)*, Moultrie Kelsall *(Cdr. Dawson)*, Eddie Byrne *(Cdr. Brennan)*, Geoffrey Hibbert *(Lt. Craig)*, Peter Jones *(Lt. Browne)*, Frederick Valk *(Camp Kommandant)*, Anton Diffring *(Hauptmann Schultz)*, Frederick Schiller *(Hermann)*, Walter Gotell *(Feldwebel)*, Peter Swanwick *(Obergefreiter)*.

Typical British prison camp escape film with tough but classy officers utilizing a papier mache dummy to trick their German captors. Anton Diffring stands out among the quite good cast as a totally evil Nazi.

d, Lewis Gilbert; w, Vernon Harris, Guy Morgan (based on play by Morgan and Edward Sammis); ph, Jack Asher; m, Malcolm Arnold; ed, Charles Hesse.

War Drama **(PR:A MPAA:NR)**

ALBUQUERQUE** (1948) 89m PAR bw (AKA: SILVER CITY)

Randolph Scott *(Cole Armin)*, Barbara Britton *(Letty Tyler)*, George "Gabby" Hayes *(Juke)*, Lon Chaney *(Steve Murkill)*, Russell Hayden *(Ted Wallace)*, Catherine Craig *(Celia Wallace)*, George Cleveland *(John Armin)*, Karolyn Grives *(Myrtle Walton)*, Bernard J. Nedell *(Sheriff Linton)*, Russell Simpson *(Huggins)*, Jody Gilbert *(Pearl)*, Dan White *(Jackson)*, Irving Bacon *(Dave Walton)*, John Halloran *(Matt Wayne)*, Walter Baldwin *(Judge)*.

Scott rides into town and aids a small stagecoach line that is being threatened by the local power-hungry tyrant who happens to be Scott's uncle. Lackluster direction holds back an otherwise pleasant western.

p, William Pine, William Thomas; d, Ray Enright; w, Gene Lewis, Clarence Upson Young (based on the novel by Luke Short); ph, Fred Jackman, Jr.; m, Darrell Calker; ed, Howard Smith.

Western **(PR:A MPAA:NR)**

ALCATRAZ ISLAND*½ (1937) 64m Cosmopolitan/WB bw

Ann Sheridan *(Flo Allen)*, Mary Maguire *(Ann Brady)*, Dick Purcell *(Harp Santell)*, Addison Richards *(Fred MacClane)*, George E. Stone *(Tough Tony Burke)*, Doris Lloyd *(Miss Marquand)*, Charles Trowbridge *(Warden Jackson)*, Veda Ann Borg *(The Red Head)*, Edward Keane *(Crandall)*, Ed Stanley *(U.S. Attorney)*, John Litel *(Gat Brady)*, Gordon Oliver *(George Drake)*.

Soft-hearted gangster begins to appreciate love and freedom after a stay on the "Rock." Aside from the unique appeal of the story's location, there's not much worth watching here.

d, William McGann; w, Crane Wilbur (based on Wilbur's story "Alcatraz"); ph, L. W. O'Connell; ed, Frank Dewar.

Crime **(PR:A MPAA:NR)**

ALERT IN THE SOUTH**
(1954, Fr.) 115m Neptune-Fonorama/Sirius c (ALERTE AU SUD)

Erich von Stroheim *(Conrad)*, Jean-Claude Pascal *(Jean)*, Giana Maria Canale *(Natalie)*, Peter Van Eyck *(Howard)*, Lia Amanda *(Michele)*, Jean Murat *(Colonel)*.

Moroccan intrigue focuses upon Pascal whose friend is murdered; he seeks vengeance, first with French thugs, pretending to be a cashiered officer, then with a gang of thieves headed by a German gambler, falling in love with the gambler's protege, Canale, then winding up in a remote desert fort commanded by a berserk German general who refuses to believe WW II is over. Pascal is finally rescued from this madness, taking his beefy ballerina with him, for which any viewer will be thankful.

d&w Jean Devalvre (based on the novel by Pierre Nord); ph, Lucien Joulin; ed, Louis Devalvre.

Adventure **(PR:A MPAA:NR)**

ALEX AND THE GYPSY*½ (1976) 99m FOX c

Jack Lemmon *(Alexander Main)*, Genevieve Bujold *(Maritza)*, James Woods *(Crainpool)*, Gino Ardito *(The Golfer)*, Robert Emhardt *(Judge)*, Joseph X. Flaherty *(Morgan)*, Todd Martin *(Roy Blake)*, Victor Pinhiero *(Sanders)*.

Cynical bailbondsman Lemmon takes custody of past lover Bujold after she is charged with assaulting her present repulsive boyfriend. Romance begins to ooze into their lonely, depressing lives, but it is never fully realized. A complete lack of empathy for the characters involved destroys a potentially quirky love story. A poor role choice in Lemmon's career.

p, Richard Shepherd; d, John Korty; w, Lawrence B. Marcus (based on the novella *The Bailbondsman* by Stanley Elkins); ph, Bill Butler (DeLuxe Color); m, Henry Mancini; ed, Don Cambern; prod d, Bill Malley.

Drama **(PR:C MPAA:R)**

ALEX IN WONDERLAND** (1970) 110m MGM c

Donald Sutherland *(Alex)*, Ellen Burstyn *(Beth)*, Meg Mazursky *(Amy)*, Glenna Sergent *(Nancy)*, Viola Spolin *(Mother)*, Andre Phillipe *(Andre)*, Michael Lerner *(Leo)*, Joan Delaney *(Jane)*, Neil Burstyn *(Norman)*, Leon Frederick *(Lewis)*, Carol O'Leary *(Marlene)*, Paul Mazursky *(Hal Stern)*, Moss Mabry *(Mr. Wayne)*, Federico Fellini, Jeanne Moreau *(Themselves)*.

Autobiographical look at modern Hollywood centering on a young director's desperate need to follow up his debut smash with another hit. Some self-righteous jabs at hip, money-hungry producers hit the comedy target, as do the cameos by Moreau and Fellini, but the film never really finds its niche. Ellen Burstyn, as usual, is marvelous as Sutherland's wife.

p, Larry Tucker; d, Paul Mazursky; w, Mazursky, Tucker; ph, Laszlo Kovacs; m, Tom O'Horgan; ed, Stuart H. Pappe; prod d, Pato Guzman; set d, Audrey Blasdel.

Comedy   **(PR:C   MPAA:R)**

ALEXANDER GRAHAM BELL
(SEE: STORY OF ALEXANDER GRAHAM BELL, THE, 1939)

ALEXANDER HAMILTON**1/2   (1931) 70m WB bw

George Arliss (Alexander Hamilton), Doris Kenyon (Mrs. Hamilton), Dudley Digges (Sen. Timothy Roberts), Alan Mowbray (George Washington), Ralf Harolde (Mr. Reynolds), June Collyer (Mrs. Reynolds), Montagu Love (Chief Justice Jay), Lionel Belmore (Gen. Philip Schuyler), Morgan Wallace (James Monroe), Gwendolin Logan (Martha Washington), John T. Murray (Count Talleyrand), Charles Evans (Whalen), John Larkin (Zesial), Evelyn Hall (Mrs. Bingham), Russell Simpson (First ex-Soldier), James Durkin (Second ex-Soldier).

Antique film still suffers from transitional shudders from silent to talkie in uneven sound recordings as the very hammy Arliss, once considered to be a theatrical giant, slips and slides about as Hamilton, the financier of early America's coffers, while conducting a behind-the-scenes affair as a small boy might sneak into the pantry for cookies. Very stagy and mostly ineffective.

d, John G. Adolfi; w, Julian Josephson, Maude Howell (based on the play by George Arliss and Mary Hamlin); ph, James Van Trees.

Biography   **(PR:A   MPAA:NR)**

ALEXANDER NEVSKY****   (1939) 87m Mosfilm/AMKINO bw

Nikolai Cherkassov (Prince Alexander Yaroslavich Nevsky), N. P. Okhlopkov (Vassily Buslai), A. L. Abrikossov (Gavrilo Olexich), D. N. Orlov (Ignat. Master Armourer), V. K. Novikov (Pavsha, Governor of Pskov), N. N. Arski (Domash, Nobleman of Novgorod), V. O. Massalitinova (Amefa Timofeyevna, Mother of Buslai), V. S. Ivasbeva (Olga, a Novgorod Girl), A. S. Danilova (Vassilissa), V. L. Ersbov (Master of the Teutonic Order), S. K. Blinnikov (Tverdillo, Traitorous Mayor of Pskov), I. I. Lagutin (Anani, a Monk), L. A. Fenin (The Bishop), N. A. Rogozbin (The Black-robed Monk).

Eisenstein classic of 13th-century Russia offers a lavish panorama of ancient warfare with masses of troops that stretch to the horizon in horrific battle garb and enough action to satiate the most adventurous viewer. The story concerns the invasion of Russia by the Tartars from one side and the Teutonic Knights of Germany from the other. Eisenstein shows a decaying land where invaders plunder at will, the morale of the populace at low ebb and its leaders fearful and indecisive. Finally, the moody and volatile Prince Nevsky, memorably played by Cherkassov, is summoned to lead his people in their death struggle against the oppressors. A valiant and intelligent noble, Cherkassov begins building an army, a campaign that takes up half the film, then fights an incredible and decisive battle at Lake Peipus in 1242 where his strategy proves successful. The battle scenes are overwhelming—thousands and thousands of men (Eisenstein had use of the Russian army at will) fill the screen—the Teutonic Knights in their flowing crusaders' costumes, their heads topped with helmets fashioned in the forms of gargoyles, ogres, and fierce animals (purposely designed to frighten the enemy), and the Russian army of peasants and nobles, all hacking with sword, mace, spear, pike, and axe, until the armor-burdened Germans are driven into the lake by the thousands to drown. Eisenstein's attention to detail is meticulous down to every piece of equipment and weapon, every horse blanket and homemade shoe used in that long-ago era, and the mounting of his monument to Russia's ancient hero is no less than superb. (It is therefore all the more curious to see this great director showing old Novgorod with elegant temples and mosques of white stucco when, in the 13th century, it was nothing more than a crude community of wooden huts and rutted dirt streets.) The dialog is in Russian with English subtitles that flash by so fast that to concentrate upon them is to lose the film's visual momentum. This is Russian filmmaking at its best and most demonstrative, but Eisenstein's battle scenes were undoubtedly inspired by Griffith's silent classic, BIRTH OF A NATION (the director many times over acknowledged his debt to Griffith). (In Russian; English subtitles.)

d, Sergei Eisenstein, D. I. Vassillev; w, Eisenstein, Peter Pavlenko; m, Sergei Prokofiev; ph, Edward Tisse; subtitles, Julian Leigh.

War   **Cas.**   **(PR:C   MPAA:NR)**

ALEXANDER THE GREAT***   (1956) 143m UA c

Richard Burton (Alexander the Great), Fredric March (Philip of Macedonia), Claire Bloom (Barsine), Danielle Darrieux (Olympias), Harry Andrews (Darius), Stanley Baker (Attalus), Niall MacGinnis (Parmenio), Peter Cushing (Memnon), Michael Hordern (Demosthenes), Barry Jones (Aristotle), Marisa De Leza (Eurydice), Gustavo Rojo (Cleitus), Ruben Rojo (Philotas), William Squire (Aeschines), Helmut Dantine (Nectanebus), Friedrich Ledebur (Antipater), Peter Wyngarde (Pausanias), Virgilio Texeira (Ptolemy), Teresa Del Rio (Roxane), Julio Pena (Arsites), Jose Nieto (Spithridates), Carlos Baena (Nearchus), Larry Taylor (Perdiccas), Jose Marco (Harpalus), Ricardo Valle (Hephaestion), Carmen Carulla (Stateira), Jesus Luque (Aristander), Ramsey Ames (Drunken Woman), Mario De Barros (Messenger), Ellen Rossen (Apites), Carlos Acevedo (Orchas).

Engrossing spectacle wherein director Rossen undertakes to show the conquest of the world by Alexander of Greece in the fourth century, B.C. In early scenes, the consummate actor, March, is King Philip of Macedonia, a powerful ruler who appears both ruthless and slightly mad. He is plotted against by his unfaithful wife, Darrieux, and nobles, and disliked by his son Alexander (Burton), and his friends. March loves his son but distrusts his teachers, including Jones as Aristotle, feeling he is learning loftier thoughts than should be harbored by princely mountain warriors. They battle over philosophy and March's flagrant mistreatment of Darrieux, but the insidious mother-wife has her revenge by arranging for March's assassination so that her son Burton will become king. One of March's most memorable scenes occurs after he wins a bloody battle, then orders the prisoners executed. Burton attempts to intervene, calling his father a barbarian when he refuses to spare the lives of his

defeated foes. Drunk, standing on a mountain precipice that overlooks the battle carnage, March does a wild dance of death while bitterly mocking his son's words in sing-song: "Philip the Barbarian, Philip the Barbarian!" Following his father's murder, Burton turns on his mother, then unites his father's followers and conquers Greece, then cuts the Gordian knot and enters vast Persia to destroy the armies of Darius, then on and on, conquering one country after another, including the enormous tracts of India, all of the then known world, motivated by the belief that spreading the Greek way of life and philosophy will enlighten all people. Burton is at his stormy, growling best in portraying the warrior who died at 32 of an illness, leaving his empire to the "strongest" of his lieutenants, who immediately begin battling for spoils. Bloom, as Burton's faithful wife, provides the love interest but is seen only briefly, with Rossen concentrating upon the innumerable battles which are displayed brilliantly (the film being shot in Spain and Italy). Other sequences where Burton and his followers philosophize about fate and their roles in destiny are overlong and sometimes outright boring. Krasker's lensing is rich and clear, encompassing every detail down to the last spear-tosser.

p,d&w, Robert Rossen; ph, Robert Krasker (CinemaScope, Technicolor); m, Mario Nascimbene; ed, Ralph Kempler; set d, Andre Andrejew; cos, David Ffolkes; spec eff, Cliff Richardson.

Biography/War   **(PR:A   MPAA:NR)**

ALEXANDER'S RAGTIME BAND***1/2   (1938) 105m FOX bw

Tyrone Power (Roger Grant), Alice Faye (Stella Kirby), Don Ameche (Charlie Dwyer), Ethel Merman (Jerry Allen), Jack Haley (Davey Lane), Jean Hersholt (Prof. Heinrich), Helen Westley (Aunt Sophie), John Carradine (Taxi Driver), Paul Hurst (Bill), Wally Vernon (Himself), Ruth Terry (Ruby), Douglas Fowley (Snapper), Eddie Collins (Cpl. Collins), Joseph Crehan (Stage Manager), Robert Gleckler (Eddie), Dixie Dunbar (Specialty), Joe King (Charles Dillingham), Charles Coleman (Head Waiter), Stanley Andrews (Colonel), Charles Williams (Agent), Jane Jones, Otto Fries, Mel Kalish (Trio), Grady Sutton (Babe), Selmer Jackson (Manager Radio Station), Tyler Brooks (Assistant Stage Manager), Donald Douglas (Singer), James Flavin, Jack Pennick (Sergeants), Harold Goodwin (M.P.), Edward Keane (Major), Ralph Dunn (Captain), Charles Tannen (Secretary), Robert Lowery (Reporter), Eleanor Wesselhoeft (Martha), Kings Men Quartet, Cully Richards, Arthur Rankin, Cecil Weston, Kay Griffith, Sam Ash, Pop Byron, Edwin Stanley, Lynne Barkley.

Energetic and handsomely mounted musical has Power and Ameche battling over the affections of Faye in a chronological span that stretches from 1915 to 1938, with 28 Irving Berlin compositions filling the production. Fox's three most popular stars had just finished making IN OLD CHICAGO when they were rushed into this film which had been long in preparation. Power, an aristocratic Knob Hill product, takes up ragtime, discarding his musical education in the classical field, much to the chagrin of his professor (Hersholt) and his aunt (Westley). He puts together a band and is booked into a Barbary Coast dive, finding the music for "Alexander's Ragtime Band" on the bar, left there by a tempestuous young singer, Faye. Power uses the music to make his band, naming his group after the title song, then taking on Faye as his vocalist. Struggling young composer Ameche is smitten with Faye and brings producer Dillingham to listen to Power and Faye. He turns down the band but offers Faye a starring role in a Broadway production; Faye is urged by Ameche to take the job and Power becomes angry. After a confrontation, Faye goes off on her own and becomes an overnight success while Power and his band play on in the tank towns. When WW I breaks out, Power enlists and is put in charge of an army band, performing on Broadway where Faye, who really loves him, sits in the audience, waiting to see him. Before she can reach him, Power and his band march out of the theater going directly to their embarking troop ships. Faye and Ameche later marry, she becoming the toast of New York, he becoming a celebrated composer. Faye sees Power upon his return from France and knows she loves only him. She and Ameche agree to divorce but Power remains ignorant of their separation, beginning a new band with a powerful vocalist, Merman, and they become the nightclub and theatrical rage. As Power's star rises, Faye's descends until she is reduced to singing in cheap honky-tonks. Hearing of Power's debut at Carnegie Hall, she watches lovingly from the wings. He sees her, pulls her on-stage and she sings their hit number, the title song, ending in his arms to begin a new life. Hokey, corny, and predictable as this film is, it's still one of the most enjoyable movies ever made and for the very reasons that caused many a critic to sneer: its prosaic style, down-to-earth portrayals, petty jealousies and hates make for great Americana. The was two years in preparation and cost Fox more than $2 million. Its period sets were unique and fashioned to the times perfectly. One featured a half dozen 1500-pound cut glass chandeliers imported from Czechoslovakia, such were the perfectionist demands of producer Zanuck. There were no lags in King's snappy direction. There simply was no time for boredom since a new production fills almost every scene, 26 old and never-to-be-forgotton Berlin numbers and two new ditties—"My Walking Stick" and "Now It Can Be Told." Berlin himself said, "I'd rather have Alice Faye introduce my songs than any other singer I know" when asked to comment on the film that served as the greatest showcase for his memorable music.

p, Darryl F. Zanuck; d, Henry King; w, Kathryn Scola, Lamar Trotti; ph, Peverell Marley; ed, Barbara McLean; md, Alfred Newman; art d, Bernard Herzbrun, Boris Leven; set d, Thomas Little; ch, Seymour Felix; cos, Gwen Wakeling; m/l, Irving Berlin.

Musical   **(PR:AAA   MPAA:NR)**

ALF 'N' FAMILY**1/2
(1968, Brit.) 100m Associated London-BL/Sherpix c (GB: TILL DEATH DO US PART)

Warren Mitchell (Alf Garnett), Dandy Nichols (Else Garnett), Anthony Booth (Mike), Una Stubbs (Rita Garnett), Liam Redmond (Mike's Father), Bill Maynard (Bert), Brian Blessed (Sergeant), Sam Kydd (Fred), Frank Thornton (Valuation Officer), Cleo Sylvestre (Girl at Wedding Party), Ann Lancaster, Michael Robbins, Bob Grant, Jack Jordan, Edward Evans, Madge Brindley, Pat Coombes, Shelagh Fraser, Bill Ward, Leslei Noyes, Brenda Kempner.

Theatrical version of the popular British TV series, which was the inspiration for the long-running "All In The Family" on U.S. television. Basically plotless, the film follows the lives of a cockney family beginning during WW II. Mitchell, the model for "Archie Bunker," plays the rascist, foul-mouthed, opinionated head of the house, constantly spouting his pearls of wisdom regarding politics, society, and religion. The film covers his marriage to Nichols; the birth of his daughter, Stubbs; her marriage to hippie-type Booth; and the family's eventual move from a London slum to the suburbs. Ray Davies of the British rock band "The Kinks" provides the title song. Worth a look, especially for "All In The Family" fans.

p, Beryl Vertue, Jon Pennington; d, Norman Cohen; w, Johnny Speight (based on the TV series by Speight); ph, Harry Waxman (Eastmancolor); m, Wilfred Burns; ed, Anthony Lenny; prod d, Terry Knight; m/l, title song, Ray Davies.

Comedy **(PR:C MPAA:NR)**

ALFIE*** (1966, Brit.) 114m Lewis Gilbert Prod./Sheldrake/PAR c

Michael Caine *(Alfie)*, Shelley Winters *(Ruby)*, Millicent Martin *(Siddie)*, Julia Foster *(Gilda)*, Jane Asher *(Annie)*, Shirley Anne Field *(Carla)*, Vivien Merchant *(Lily)*, Eleanor Bron *(The Doctor)*, Denholm Elliott *(Abortionist)*, Alfie Bass *(Harry)*, Graham Stark *(Humphrey)*, Murray Melvin *(Nat)*, Sydney Tafler *(Frank)*.

A breezy, colorful, sad odyssey, where Caine as Alfie goes through life without a backbone, a decision, a future, apparently loving every second of an existence that is decidedly amoral (a more modern word for the judgmental term "immoral" but meaning the same thing). Caine plays the role of a sexual bum, hoboing his way through the bedrooms of equally promiscuous women, less offensive and certainly more affirmative than their uncertain paramour. First Alfie meets Foster whom he impregnates and cares for but cannot bring himself to marry. He goes on to tersely tryst with Field, a dedicated hedonist, Asher, an egotist, Winters, a wealthy user of male whores, and Merchant, a married woman who is looking for passion but finds pregnancy and abortion, both arranged by Alfie. Only at the end does this wardrobe wanderer express any kind of remorse for the women he has made unhappy and the pointless life he leads but by then most viewers hate him too much to care. A well-made film with measured, convincing portrayals, particularly by the reserved Caine as the cockney swain, but the characters, by-products of the 1960s, are basically unappealing on all counts. One remembers the song and the line: "What's it all about, Alfie?" And one answers: The cluck will never know.

p&d, Lewis Gilbert; w, Bill Naughton (based on his play); ph, Otto Heller (Technicolor); m, Sonny Rollins; ed, Thelma Connell.

Drama **(PR:O MPAA:NR)**

ALFIE DARLING* (1975, Brit.) 102m Signal Films/EMI c

Alan Price *(Alfie)*, Jill Townsend *(Abby)*, Paul Copley *(Bakey)*, Joan Collins *(Fay)*, Sheila White *(Norma)*, Annie Ross *(Claire)*, Hannah Gordon *(Dora)*, Roger Lumont *(Pierre)*, Rula Lenska *(Louise)*, Minah Bird *(Gloria)*, Derek Smith *(Harold)*, Vicki Michelle *(Bird)*, Brian Wilde *(Doctor)*, Robin Parkinson *(Parker)*, Rosaline Elliott *(Secretary)*, Jenny Hanley *(Receptionist)*, Timothy Peters, Ben Aris, Hugh Walters *(Ad Men)*, Sally Bulloch *(Clerk)*, Brian Anthony *(Airport Official)*, Sean Roantree *(Fitter)*, Constantin de Goguel *(Police Inspector)*, Graham Ashley *(Customs Official)*, Patsy Densitt *(Penny)*, Mark Scoones *(Boy)*, Terence Taplin *(Photographer)*, Ian Woodward *(Male Model)*, Marianne Broom, *(Female Model)*.

More sexual adventures from Naughton's tirelessly tiring character Alfie, this time Price, instead of Michael Caine, doing the dishonors as a roving truck driver who has a lady waiting for him at every stop. When he meets the beauteous Townsend, who is almost as much a heel as he is, the similarity leads to mutual respect, then avowed love and plans for marriage. In a flagrantly contrived ending, the nuptials are called off when she dies in a plane crash, leaving a saddened Alfie to go slinking to other seductions. Everything about this film is cheap—the story, direction, camerawork and especially the acting.

p, Dugald Rankin; d&w, Ken Hughes (based on the novel by Bill Naughton); ph, Ousama Rawi (Technicolor); m, Alan Price; ed, John Trumper; set d, Denise Exshaw.

Drama **(PR:O MPAA:NR)**

ALFRED THE GREAT** (1969, Brit.) 122m MGM c

David Hemmings *(Alfred)*, Michael York *(Guthrum)*, Prunella Ransome *(Aelhswith)*, Colin Blakely *(Asher)*, Julian Glover *(Athelstan)*, Ian McKellan *(Roger)*, Alan Dobie *(Ethelred)*, Peter Vaughan *(Buhrud)*, Julian Chagrin *(Ivar)*, Barry Jackson *(Wulfstan)*, Vivien Merchant *(Freda)*, Christopher Timothy *(Cedric)*, John Rees *(Cuthbert)*, Andrew Bradford *(Edwin)*, Michael Billington *(Offa)*, Ralph Nossek *(Bishop)*.

Hemmings, reluctant leader of the Brits, protects England from bloodthirsty Danes who have kidnapped his wife. Tedious historical drama highlighted by a few well-choreographed battle scenes. The cast is outstanding, but has little to do.

p, Bernard Smith, James R. Webb; d, Clive Donner; w, James R. Webb, Ken Taylor (based on a story by Webb); ph, Alex Thomson (Metrocolor); m, Raymond Leppard; ed, Fergus McDonnell; prod d, Michael Stringer; art d, Ernest Archer; spec eff, Robert A. MacDonald; cos, Jocelyn Rickards.

Historical Drama **(PR:C MPAA:NR)**

ALFREDO, ALFREDO* (1973, Ital.) 97m RPA-Rizzoli Films-Francoriz/PAR c

Dustin Hoffman *(Alfredo)*, Stefania Sandrelli *(Mariarosa)*, Carla Gravina *(Carolina)*, Clara Colosimo *(Carolina's Mother)*, Daniele Patella *(Carolina's Father)*, Danika La Loggia *(Mariarosa's Mother)*, Saro Urzi *(Mariarosa's Father)*, Luigi Baghetti *(Alfredo's Father)*, Duilio Del Prete *(Oreste)*.

Badly dubbed sexpotboiler, including Hoffman's voice, about a meek bank clerk who goes daffy for voluptuous Sandrelli, marries her and is then horror-struck to find that she bores him every waking moment. He impregnates her and, while she awaits the child, Hoffman goes off with Gravina, a more attractive companion, but he cannot divorce because of Italy's stringent laws. His lawyers battle for his new love and, with a help from changing laws, he is granted the divorce and marries Gravina. A stumbling, mumbling mess of a film which does much to confirm the notion that actors have no sense of career direction.

d, Pietro Germi; w, Leo Benvenuti, Piero De Bernardi, Tullio Pinelli, Pietro Germi; ph, Aiace Parolin (Technicolor); m, Carlo Rustichelli; ed, Sergio Montanari; set d, Carlo Egidi.

Comedy **(PR:O MPAA:R)**

ALF'S BABY* (1953, Brit.) 75m Adelphi/ACT bw

Jerry Desmonde *(Alf Donkin)*, Pauline Stroud *(Pamela Weston)*, Olive Sloane *(Mrs. Matthews)*, Peter Hammond *(Tim Barton)*, Sandra Dorne *(Enid)*, Roy Purcell *(Sgt. Bob Mackett)*, C. Denier Warren *(Cedric Donkin)*, Mark Daly *(Will Donkin)*, Roddy Hughes *(Mr. Prendergast)*.

Inane comedy has Desmonde and two of his brothers adopting a girl who later falls in love with a thief. The brothers must come to the rescue.

p, John Harlow; d, Maclean Rogers; w, A. P. Dearsley (based on the play "It Won't Be a Stylish Marriage" by Dearsley); ph, Ted Lloyd.

Comedy **(PR:A MPAA:NR)**

ALF'S BUTTON*½ (1930, Brit.) 96m Gaumont bw/color sequences

Tubby Edlin *(Alf Higgins)*, Alf Goddard *(Bill Grant)*, Nora Swinburne *(Lady Isobel Fitzpeter)*, Polly Ward *(Liz)*, Humberston Wright *(Eustace)*.

Early British comedic reworking of the Aladdin's lamp story has WW I soldier Edlin finding a button made from the aforementioned torch. Pleasant but forgettable laugher notable for its fantasy sequences done in the early pastel Pathe color process.

p, L'Estrange Fawcett; d, W. P. Kellino; w, Fawcett (based on the play by W. A. Darlington); ph, Percy Strong.

Fantasy/Comedy **(PR:AA MPAA:NR)**

ALF'S BUTTON AFLOAT*½ (1938, Brit.) Gainsborough/GFD bw

Bud Flanagan *(Alf Higgins)*, Chesney Allen *(Ches)*, Jimmy Nervo *(Cecil)*, Teddy Knox *(Teddy)*, Charlie Naughton *(Charlie)*, Jimmy Gold *(Jimmy)*, Alastair Sim *(Eustace)*, Wally Patch *(Sgt. Hawkins)*, Peter Gawthorne *(Capt. Driscol)*, Glennis Lorimer *(Frankie Driscol)*, James Carney *(Lt. Hardy)*, Agnes Laughlin *(Lady Driscol)*, Bruce Winston *(Mustapha)*.

Another adventure of the Marine's button fashioned from the magic lamp of Aladdin which allows Alf to obtain impossible wishes which turn his fate comedic. This film will only be appreciated by the elderly remembering British music hall spoofs, more low-brow slapstick than high adventure. Memorable among the cast is Sim.

p, Edward Black; d, Marcel Varnel; w, Marriott Edgar, Val Guest, Ralph Smart (based on W. A. Darlington's play "Alf's Button"); ph, Arthur Crabtree; md, Louis Levy.

Fantasy/Comedy **(PR:A MPAA:NR)**

ALF'S CARPET* (1929, Brit.) 65m BIP bw

Pat *(Bill)*, Patachon *(Alf)*, Janice Adair *(Joan)*, Gerald Rawlinson *(Jimmy Donaldson)*, Gladys Hamer *(Lizzie Fletcher)*, Philip Hewland *(Djinn)*, Edward O'Neill *(Father)*, Frank Perfitt *(Caliph)*.

Nonsensical early talkie has a London bus driver discover a magic carpet which he uses to save a friend from the clutches of an evil sheik, thus winning the hand of the friend's daughter. No magic at all.

d, W. P. Kellino; w, Val Valentine, Arthur Leclerq, Blanche Metcalfe (based on the novel by W.A. Darlington); ph, Theodor Sparkuhl.

Fantasy/Comedy **(PR:A MPAA:NR)**

ALGIERS***** (1938) 95m UA bw

Charles Boyer *(Pepe Le Moko)*, Sigrid Gurie *(Ines)*, Hedy Lamarr *(Gaby)*, Joseph Calleia *(Slimane)*, Gene Lockhart *(Regis)*, Johnny Downs *(Pierrot)*, Alan Hale *(Grandpere)*, Mme. Nina Koshetz *(Tania)*, Joan Woodbury *(Aicha)*, Claudia Dell *(Marie)*, Robert Greig *(Giroux)*, Stanley Fields *(Carlos)*, Charles D. Brown *(Max)*, Ben Hall *(Gil)*, Armand Kalis *(Sergeant)*, Leonid Kinsky *(L'Arbi)*, Walter Kingsford *(Louvain)*, Paul Harvey *(Janvier)*, Bert Roach *(Bertier)*, Luana Walters *(Waitress)*.

Down and along the shadowy, labyrinthine alleyways of the Casbah, a notorious bastion in French Algiers that harbored all manner of criminals, the viewer is introduced to a remarkable thief and lover, Pepe Le Moko, wonderfully enacted by Charles Boyer, already a reigning sex symbol of the screen. Boyer has fled Paris to escape pursuing police; he is wanted for stealing jewels and takes refuge in the Casbah, a quarter actually controlled by the French underworld in which no detective dare make an arrest. Calleia is the crafty, insidious French detective who meets with Boyer regularly but plays a waiting game, watching for the moment the wanted man will step from the Casbah and into the arms of his officers. Boyer grows restless, longing for the grand life of Paris, resenting the mooning woman devoted to him (Gurie) until a dazzling Parisian beauty, Lamarr (in her American film debut), walks into his life as a tourist slumming among dangerous criminals. Even though she is engaged, Lamarr invents excuses to slip back into the Casbah to meet Boyer. Both of them are now madly in love but Lamarr, thinking Pepe has been killed, leaves for Paris, booking passage on a liner. Boyer dashes to dockside, buying a ticket and rushing on board. Calleia is right behind him, arresting him and taking him off the ship. Suddenly Boyer sees Lamarr and begins to run to her. Calleia thinking he is attempting to escape, shoots and kills him. The tragic Lamarr sails away alone to France. The understated love scenes between Boyer and Lamarr are moving and forcefully passionate, and the entire film drips with authenticity, as well as superb character enactments from Calleia, and Gene Lockhart as the sleazy informer willing to sell Boyer out for a pittance. Cromwell's direction is crisp, even though he reshot this movie almost scene for scene from the earlier French version, PEPE LE MOKO, directed by Julien Duvivier and starring Jean Gabin, Line Noro, and Mireille Balin. Producer Walter Wanger saw the original and just had to have it for American production. He first tried to sign up Dolores Del Rio for the role of the sultry Gaby, but they never got to the contract stage. Then Sylvia Sidney turned down the role, preferring to commit to a Broadway play (she could never abide filmmaking, albeit she was a marvelous actress on screen.) Wanger accidentally met Lamarr, who was under contract to MGM and waiting for her first American role, and convinced Louis B. Mayer to loan her out for ALGIERS, which made her an international star shortly after the film's release. It is perhaps her best remembered part, one she never quite equalled, irrespective of the number of vamps she so energetically played. The film was remade in 1948 as THE CASBAH with Tony Martin as Pepe, Yvonne De Carlo as Ines, Peter Lorre as the detective Slimane and Marta Toren as Gaby; only Lorre approached the caliber of acting found in ALGIERS.

p, Walter Wanger; d, John Cromwell; w, John Howard Lawson, James M. Cain (based on the novel *Pepe Le Moko* by Roger D'Ashelbe); ph, James Wong Howe; m, Vincent Scotto, Muhammed Ygner Buchen; ed, Otho Lovering, William Reynolds; art d, Alexander Toluboff; cos, Omar Kiam, Irene.

Drama/Crime **Cas.** **(PR:C MPAA:NR)**

ALI BABA* (1954, Fr.) 95m Film Cyclope/Cinedia c

Fernandel, Samia Gamal, Dieter Borsche, Henri Vilbert, Delmont.

Slave ventures out to pick up his master's new wife, falls in love with her himself, joins a band of thieves to obtain money, and wins the hand of the lovely Gamal. French comic Fernandel tries to carry this sorry version of the ancient tale, but succeeds in picking up only a few scattered laughs.

d, Jacques Becker; w, Becker, Marc Maurette, Cesare Zavattini; ph, Robert Le Fehvre; m, Paul Misraki; ed, Marguerite Renoir.

Comedy/Adventure **(PR:A MPAA:NR)**

ALI BABA AND THE FORTY THIEVES*½** (1944) 87m UNIV c

Maria Montez *(Amara)*, Jon Hall *(Ali Baba)*, Turhan Bey *(Jamiel)*, Andy Devine *(Abdullah)*, Kurt Katch *(Hulagu Khan)*, Frank Puglia *(Cassim)*, Fortunio Bonanova *(Baba)*, Moroni Olsen *(Caliph)*, Ramsey Ames *(Nalu)*, Chris-Pin Martin *(Fat Thief)*, Scotty Beckett *(Ali as a Child)*, Yvette Duguay *(Amara as a Girl)*, Noel Cravat *(Mongol Captain)*, Jimmy Conlin *(Little Thief)*, Harry Cording *(Mahmoud)*.

A lush and lavish Arabian Nights fantasy yarn that put the Jon Hall-Maria Montez love team on the map, this tempestuous tale shows Mongol monster Katch, with the aid of traitor Puglia, murdering the Caliph of Bagdad (Olsen), and taking over his vast domain. The Caliph's son Beckett runs away to the hills with the royal seal and comes upon a band of noble brigands led by Bonanova and roly-poly, laugh-a-minute Devine. He watches from hiding as the leader cries out before a solid wall of rock: "Open Sesame!" ("Open sez me!") The rock magically parts to allow the forty thieves to gallop inside their cavernous hiding place. Beckett beckons the rock to open for him, entering to find fabulous riches, gems, and gold stolen by the band. Members discover him and are about to slit his throat when kindly Bonanova and Devine take a liking to the feisty boy, dubbing him "Ali Baba," the adopted son of the leader. He grows up to be Hall, fearless leader of the thieves (all of whom wear the identical robes of white and red), inheriting Bonanova's mantle, the only resistance leader still opposing the ruthless Katch who has gutted the country. Hall waylays a caravan carrying Puglia's beautiful daughter, Montez, but she has acted as a decoy for the Khan and Hall is captured. Devine escapes to alert the band and lead them into Bagdad, plucking their leader from the chopping block in the main square just before his head is to be severed at Katch's orders. Montez is later abducted and taken to the cave but Hall returns her to Bagdad when he cannot bring himself to take her life in vengeance for her father's betrayal; he loves her. He is later informed that Montez also loves him but is about to be forced to marry the repugnant Katch. Hall and his band ride to the rescue, entering the Khan's palace, it appears, while hidden in large oil jars, ostensibly a gift to the wicked ruler. Katch, suspecting a ruse, has forty sabre-wielding dancers entertain his visitors, the dance ending in a frightful scene where each dancer plunges his sword into a jar; the thieves, of course, are not inside, but emerge elsewhere to battle the palace guards and open the gates to let the townsfolk in. The Khan's troops are defeated and Katch done in at the hands of a righteous Hall who scoops up the sultry and willing Montez at film's heroic and happy end. There is much in the script that is reminiscent of THE ADVENTURES OF ROBIN HOOD but set in the Middle East of ancient times. Some have likened this film to a western set in Arabia of old but the film holds its own as a fast-action film with wonders and miracles aplenty to excite any child and amuse any adult, and is so rich in color, eye-filling pastels, that every rock is golden, every sword is silver, every piece of silk a sliver of the rainbow. Universal's only reason for remaking the film in 1965 as THE SWORD OF ALI BABA was to use half the footage from the original, such was its splendor.

p, Paul Malvern; d, Arthur Lubin; w, Edmund L. Hartmann; ph, George Robinson, W. Howard Green; m, Edward Ward; ed, Russell Schoengarth; art d, John B. Goodman, Richard H. Riedel; set d, R. A. Gausman, Ira S. Webb; spec eff, John P. Fulton.

Adventure/Fantasy **(PR:AAA MPAA:NR)**

ALI BABA GOES TO TOWN½** (1937) 80m FOX bw

Eddie Cantor *(Ali Baba)*, Tony Martin *(Yusuf)*, Roland Young *(Sultan)*, June Lang *(Princess Miriam)*, Louise Hovick *(Sultana)*, John Carradine *(Ishak)*, Virginia Field *(Dinah)*, Alan Dinehart *(Boland)*, Douglas Dumbrille *(Prince Musah)*, Raymond Scott Quintet *(Themselves)*, Peters Sisters, Jeni Le Gon *(Specialties)*, Maurice Cass *(Omar, The Rug Maker)*, Warren Hymer, Stanley Fields *(Tramps)*, Paul Hurst *(Captain)*, Sam Hayes *(Radio Announcer)*, Douglas Wood *(Selim)*, Sidney Fields *(Assistant Director)*, Ferdinand Gottschalk *(Chief Councilor)*, Charles Lane *(Doctor)*, Pearl Twins *(Specialty)*.

A variation of A CONNECTICUT YANKEE IN KING ARTHUR'S COURT, stars funnyman Cantor as a bum who goes to work as a Hollywood extra, taking sleeping pills while on the set of an Arabian Nights epic. He dreams he is back in ancient Bagdad where the sultan makes him his chief minister. In a spoof of FDR's New Deal, Cantor abolishes the army, levies heavy taxation on the indignant, angry rich, and sets in motion massive works projects to put people back into jobs, a tailor-made message for the Depression-torn 1930s. He is almost done in by his enemies but discovers a flying carpet and uses this to frighten opponents into submission before waking from his dream of empire. An amusing, well-done farce with many tuneful ditties sprucing up the sometimes inane script, including "Swing is Here to Stay," "Twilight in Turkey," and "Laugh Your Troubles Away" (Mack Gordon, Harry Revel, Raymond Scott).

p, Darryl F. Zanuck; d, David Butler; w, Harry Tugend, Jack Yellen (based on a story by Gene Towne, Gene Fowler, Graham Baker); ph, Ernest Palmer; ed, Irene Morra; art d, Bernard Herzbrun; set d, Thomas Little; cos, Gwen Wakeley.

Musical **(PR:AAA MPAA:NR)**

ALIAS A GENTLEMAN** (1948) 74m MGM bw

Wallace Beery *(Jim Breedin)*, Tom Drake *(Johnny Lorgen)*, Dorothy Patrick *(Elaine Carter)*, Gladys George *(Madge Parkson)*, Leon Ames *(Matt Enley)*, Warner Anderson *(Capt. Charlie Lopen)*, John Qualen *(No End)*, Sheldon Leonard *(Harry Bealer)*, Trevor Bardette *(Jig Johnson)*, Jeff Corey *(Zu)*, Marc Krah *(Spats Edwards)*, William Forrest *(Carruthers)*.

Oil is found on simple-minded, corn-bred Beery's farm and his old pals from the lock-up try to muscle in by convincing Beery that Patrick is his long-lost daughter, then kidnaping her. Fairly entertaining but dumb comedy designed as a vehicle for Beery.

p, Nat Perrin; d, Harry Beaumont; w, William R. Lipman (based on a story by Peter Rurie); ph, Ray June; ed, Ben Lewis.

Comedy **(PR:A MPAA:NR)**

ALIAS BIG SHOT½** (1962, Argen.) 90m Rio Negro Prod. bw

Walter Vidarie *(Toribio)*, Tonia Carrero *(Wife)*, Lautaro Murua *(Boss)*, Alberto Argibay *(Friend)*, Nora Palmer *(Girl)*.

Taut crime drama where Vidarie dreams of a singing career but supports himself through stealing and smuggling; well-fashioned profile of the rise of a petty hoodlum through the slums and poverty that shaped him. (In Spanish, with English subtitles)

d, Lautaro Murua; w, Bernardo Kordon, Agusto Roa; ph, Oscar Melly; ed, Sauto Benavente.

Crime **(PR:C MPAA:NR)**

ALIAS BILLY THE KID*½ (1946) 56m REP bw

Sunset Carson *(Himself)*, Peggy Stewart *(Ann Marshall)*, Tom London *(Dakota)*, Roy Barcroft *(Matt Conroy)*, Tex Terry *(Buckskin)*, Tom Chatterton *(Ed Pearson)*, Russ Whiteman *(Peewee)*, Pierce Lyden *(Sam)*, Stanley Price *(Frank Pearson)*, James Linn *(Jack)*, Edward Cassidy *(Sheriff)*.

One of Carson's lesser efforts has him battling a gang led by villain posing as the notorious outlaw Billy; even the action is unaccountably tame, including the love interest with Stewart.

p, Bennett Cohen; d, Thomas Carr; w, Betty Burbridge, Earle Snell (based on a story by Norman Sheldon); ph, Bud Thackery; ed, Charles Craft.

Western **(PR:AA MPAA:NR)**

ALIAS BOSTON BLACKIE** (1942) 67m COL bw

Chester Morris *(Boston Blackie)*, Adele Mara *(Eve Sanders)*, Richard Lane *(Inspector Farraday)*, George E. Stone *(The Runt)*, Lloyd Corrigan *(Arthur Manleder)*, Walter Sande *(Det. Mathews)*, Larry Parks *(Joe Trilby)*, George McKay *(Roggi McKay)*, Cy Kendall *(Jumbo Madigan)*, Paul Fix *(Steve Caveroni)*, Ben Taggart *(Warden)*, Lloyd Bridges *(Bus Driver)*, Ernie Adams *(Doorman)*, Edmund Cobb *(Police Sergeant)*, Sidney Miller *(Bellhop)*, Bud Geary *(Cop)*, Duke York *(Johnson)*.

Blackie attends a Christmas show in prison, amused by the performances of some of the more talented inmates, including Parks whose magic act is a cover for a prison break (a similar technique was used for a crashout in Bogart's THE BIG SHOT). Parks escapes, Blackie on his tail. Parks is determined to track down and kill the double who is really responsible for the crime that imprisoned him. Blackie not only recaptures Parks but apprehends the doppelganger, which leads to the release of the innocent man. (See BOSTON BLACKIE series, Index.)

d, Lew Landers; w, Paul Yawitz; ph, Phil Tannura; ed, Richard Fantl.

Crime **(PR:A MPAA:NR)**

ALIAS BULLDOG DRUMMOND**

(1935, Brit.) 62m Gaumont bw (GB: BULLDOG JACK)

Fay Wray *(Ann Manders)*, Jack Hulbert *(Jack Pennington)*, Claude Hulbert *(Algy Longworth)*, Ralph Richardson *(Morelle)*, Paul Graetz *(Salvini)*, Gibb McLaughlin *(Denny)*, Atholl Fleming *(Bulldog Drummond)*, Henry Longhurst *(Melvor)*, Cyril Smith *(Duke)*.

Hulbert doubles for Drummond (Fleming) who is sick in the hospital and takes on a tough case, apprehending a gang of vicious jewel thieves. He actually lays siege to their lair, shooting it out with the entire mob, capturing all except the leader, a maniac played superbly by Richardson. In a thriller finale, Richardson locks himself in the motorman's cab of a subway train on which Hulbert and Wray are riding and drives it at full throttle toward destruction, a hectic finish that provides enough tension to make up for earlier lagging scenes. (See BULLDOG DRUMMOND series, Index.)

p, Michael Balcon; d, Walter Forde; w, H. C. McNeile, Gerard Fairlie, J. O. C. Orton, Sidney Gilliat; ph, M. Greenbaum; ed, Otto Ludwig.

Crime **(PR:A MPAA:NR)**

ALIAS FRENCH GERTIE*½ (1930) 66m RKO bw

Bebe Daniels *(Marie)*, Ben Lyon *(Jimmy)*, Robert Emmett O'Connor *(Kelcey)*, John Ince *(Mr. Matson)*, Daisy Belmore *(Mrs. Matson)*, Betty Pierce *(Nellie)*.

Cute gangster couple Daniels and Lyon find true happiness despite shootings, the police, prison, etc. You won't know whether to laugh or fall asleep during this uneven 1930s crime picture.

d, George Archainbaud; w, Bayard Veiller (based on Veiller's "The Chatterbox"); ph, J. Roy Hunt.

Crime **(PR:A MPAA:NR)**

ALIAS JESSE JAMES½** (1959) 92m Hope Enterprises/UA c

Bob Hope *(Milford Farnsworth)*, Rhonda Fleming *(The Duchess)*, Wendell Corey *(Jesse James)*, Jim Davis *(Frank James)*, Gloria Talbott *(Indian Maiden)*, Will Wright *(Titus Queasley)*, Mary Young *(Ma James)*, Sid Melton *(Fight Fan)*, George E. Stone *(Gibson Girl Fan)*, James Burke *(Charlie)*, Joe Vitale *(Sam Hiawatha)*. Guest Stars *(unbilled)*: Hugh O'Brian *(Wyatt Earp)*, Ward Bond *(Maj. Seth Adams)*, James

Arness *(Matt Dillon)*, Roy Rogers *(Himself)*, Fess Parker *(Davy Crockett)*, Gail Davis *(Annie Oakley)*, James Garner *(Bret Maverick)*, Gene Autry *(Himself)*, Jay Silverheels *(Tonto)*, Bing Crosby *(Himself)*, Gary Cooper *(Himself)*.

Eastern insurance man Hope takes out a policy on Corey, not knowing that he is the famous outlaw. Going west to protect his client, Hope is set up as Jesse James so that Corey can collect on his own insurance by simply waiting for Hope to get shot. Fairly amusing send-up of wild west cliches highlighted by the surprise appearance of some famous Hollywood gunslingers who come to the star's rescue.

p, Jack Hope; d, Norman McLeod; w, William Bowers, Daniel D. Beauchamp (based on a story by Robert St. Aubrey, Bert Lawrence); ph, Lionel Lindon (DeLuxe Color); ed, Marvin Coil, Jack Bachom; md, Joseph J. Lilley; art d, Hal Pereira, Roland Anderson; set d, Sam Comer, Bertram Granger; cos, Edith Head.

Comedy (PR:A MPAA:NR)

ALIAS JIMMY VALENTINE* 1/2 (1928) 75m MGM bw

William Haines *(Jimmy Valentine)*, Karl Dane *(Swede)*, Lionel Barrymore *(Doyle)*, Leila Hyams *(Rose)*, Tully Marshall *(Avery)*, Howard Hickman *(Mr. Lane)*, Billy Butts *(Bobby)*, Evelyn Mills *(Little Sister)*.

Insignificant crime drama, played for laughs, about the notorious, good-willed safe-cracker. Notable only for the fact that this was the first MGM talkie made in commercial desperation to counter the flood of WB talking releases. Even MGM big shots Mayer, Schenck and Thalberg reluctantly agreed to make this film, thinking talkies still a novelty that *might* fade. (A remake of the 1920 silent film.)

d, Jack Conway; w, Sarah Y. Mason, A. P. Younger, Joe Farnham; ph, Merritt B. Gerstad; ed, Sam S. Zimbalist; set d, Cedric Gibbons; cos, David Cox.

Crime (PR:A MPAA:NR)

ALIAS JOHN LAW* (1935) 59m Supreme bw

Bob Steele, Roberta Gale, Earl Dwire, Buck Connors, Jack Rockwell, Steve Clark, Horace Murphy.

Poor programmer has Steele riding circles around himself while scooping up rustlers. A lot of gunplay but the action is so confused that the viewer will have a hard time determining whether it's the good or bad guys toppling from the saddle.

p, A. W. Hackel; d, Robert N. Bradbury; w, Forbes Parkhill.

Western (PR:A MPAA:NR)

ALIAS JOHN PRESTON* 1/2 (1956, Brit) 66m Danziger/BL bw

Betta St. John *(Sally Sandford)*, Alexander Knox *(Dr. Walton)*, Christopher Lee *(John Preston)*, Sandra Dorne *(Maria)*, Patrick Holt *(Stranger)*, Betty Anne Davies *(Mrs. Sandford)*, John Longden *(Mr. Sandford)*, Bill Fraser *(Joe Newton)*, John Stuart *(Dr. Underwood)*.

Lee rises in the social structure of a small town, not realizing his real personality which slowly comes to the surface through a series of dreams. A poorly developed psychological drama where Knox proves to the schizoid Lee that his nightmares of murder are very real indeed.

p, Edward J. and Harry Lee Danziger, Sid Stone; d, David Macdonald; w, Paul Tabori; ph, Jack Smith.

Crime (PR:A MPAA:NR)

ALIAS MARY DOW** (1935) 65m UNIV bw

Sally Eilers *(Sally Gates)*, Raymond Milland *(Peter Marshall)*, Henry O'Neill *(Henry Dow)*, Katherine Alexander *(Evelyn Dow)*, Chick Chandler *(Jimmy Kane)*, Baby Jane *(Mary Dow)*, Addison Richards *(Martin)*, Lola Lane *(Minna)*, Clarence Muse *(Rufe)*.

Husband of a dying woman asks a cheap cafe waitress to pose as their long-lost daughter before his beloved wife slips unhappily away. Standard soap-opera stuff highlighted by a charming characterization by Milland as Eilers' love interest.

d, Kurt Neumann; w, Forrest Halsey, William A. Johnston; (based on a story by Gladys Unger, Rose Franken, Arthur Caesar); ph, Joseph Valentine; ed, Phil Cohn.

Drama (PR:A MPAA:NR)

ALIAS MARY SMITH* (1932) 61m Like/Mayfair bw

John Darrow, Gwen Lee, Raymond Hatton, Henry B. Walthall, Blanche Mehaffey, Myrtle Stedman, Edmund Breese, Alec B. Francis, Matthew Betz, Jack Grey, Ben Hall, Harry Strang.

Reporters help solve a murder by investigating the removal and eventual rediscovery of a key set of fingerprints. Humdrum mystery lacks any elements of suspense, humor, or intrigue.

d, E. Mason Hopper; w, (based on a story by Edward T. Lowe); ph, Jules Cronjager; ed, Byron Robinson.

Mystery (PR:A MPAA:NR)

ALIAS NICK BEAL*** (1949) 92m PAR bw (GB: THE CONTACT MAN)

Ray Milland *(Nick Beal)*, Audrey Totter *(Donna Allen)*, Thomas Mitchell *(Joseph Foster)*, Geraldine Wall *(Martha Foster)*, George Macready *(Rev. Thomas Gaylord)*, Henry O'Neill *(Judge Ben Hobbs)*, Daryll Hickman *(Larry Price)*, Fred Clark *(Frankie Faulkner)*, Nestor Paiva *(Carl, Bartender)* King Donovan *(Peter Wolfe)*, Arlene Jenkins *(Aileen)*, Douglas Spencer *(Henry Cuthbert)*, Charles Evans *(Paul Norton)*, Maxine Gates *(Josie)*, Erno Verbes *(Mr. Cox)*, Steve Pendleton *(Det. Hill)*, Stuart Holmes, Phil Van Zandt, Tom Dugan, Joe Whitehead, Charles Flickinger, Donya Dean, John Shay, James Davies, Pepito Perez.

Mitchell is a crusading judge who aspires to the governorship and, in an off moment, remarks that he'd sell his soul to the devil if he could win the post, ironically so that he could do good for mankind. Milland, as Nick Beal, another guise of the Devil, appears to aid Mitchell at every turn on his political rise, using as his surrogate the conniving Totter. But when Milland comes to collect that elusive soul, both Mitchell and Totter outwit him with the help of Protestant minister Macready, the judge's close friend. Milland is excellent as old Beelzebub in modern dress for this contemporary "Faust" morality play, never overstating his evil presence, bathed eerily in shadows, hovering just over there in the dark, stepping forth to demonstrate his fire and brimstone with a lighted match, a little trail of smoke that passes for fog, and Mitchell is both a convincing law-minded judge and a frightened soul. Lindon's lighting is a minor masterwork of grays and softly defined shadows and Waxman's score is murky and full of foreboding. Farrow's direction fully utilizes the well-written script and the strange set designs to effect an otherworld feeling.

p, Endre Bohem; John Farrow; w, Jonathan Latimer (based on a story by Mindret Lord); ph, Lionel Lindon; m, Franz Waxman; ed, Edna Warren; art d, Hans Dreier, Franz Bachelin; set d, Sam Comer, Ross Dowd; cos, Mary Kay Dodson.

Drama (PR:A MPAA:NR)

ALIAS THE BAD MAN* 1/2 (1931) 62m Tiffany bw

Ken Maynard, Virginia Browne Faire, Charles King, Lee McKee, Robert Homans, Frank Mayo, Ethan Allen, Irving Bacon, Jack Rockwell.

Average Maynard western has heroic Ken battling the typically cruel cattle rustlers who murdered Faire's pappy. Go get 'em, Ken!

p, Phil Goldstone, d, Phil Rosen; w, Earle Snell (based on a story by Ford Beebe); ph, Arthur Reed; ed, Martin G. Cohn.

Western Cas. (PR:A MPAA:NR)

ALIAS THE CHAMP* (1949) 60m REP bw

Robert Rockwell *(Lt. Ron Peterson)*, Barbara Fuller *(Colette)*, Audrey Long *(Lorraine)*, Jim Nolan *(Al Merlo)*, John Harmon *(Chuck Lyons)*, Sammy Menacker *(Sam)*, Joseph Crehan *(Tim Murphy)*, John Hamilton *(Police Comm. Bronson)*, Stephen Chase *(D.A. Gould)*, Frank Scannell *(Bert Tracy)*, Frank Yaconelli *(Head Waiter)*, Emmett Vogan *(Doc Morgan)*, John Wald *(Telecaster)*, Gorgeous George, Mike Ruby, Jim Lennon, Bomber Kulkovich [Henry Kulky], Billy Varga, Bobby Manogoff, George Temple, Super Swedish Angel, Jack "Sockeye" McDonald.

Racketeers try to muscle in on the professional wrestling game. Gorgeous George is set up for a murder rap when he won't do business with the bad guys. It's the old "crime invades the ring" theme with boxing gloves being replaced by the fanciful outfits, odd hairdos, and larger-than-life characters of television wrestling shows. Nothing worth paying attention to here unless you're a never-say-die Gorgeous George fan.

p, Stephen Auer; d, George Blair; w, Albert DeMond; ph, John MacBurnie; ed, Harold Minter; m/l, Ned Washington, Al Newman, Richard Cherwin.

Crime Drama (PR:A MPAA:NR)

ALIAS THE DEACON** (1940) 74m UNIV bw

Bob Burns *(Deke Caswell)*, Mischa Auer *(Andre)*, Peggy Moran *(Phyllis)*, Dennis O'Keefe *(Johnny Sloan)*, Edward Brophy *(Stuffy)*, Thurston Hall *(Jim Cunningham)*, Spencer Charters *(The Sheriff)*, Jack Carson *(Sullivan)*, Guinn "Big Boy" Williams *(Bull Gambatz)*, Virginia Brissac *(Elsie Clark)*, Bennie Bartlett *(Willie Clark)*, Mira McKinney *(Mrs. Gregory)*, Janet Shaw *(Mildred Gregory)*.

Offbeat humorous story, a remake of Universal's 1927 silent version, has Burns discovered in the back of a truck which is also hauling hitchhiker Peggy Moran. Both are dumped in a small town where Burns' sanctimonious manner convinces one and all he is a wandering church deacon when all the while he is a card sharp who takes the local yokels in the back rooms. His brief romancing of Moran, the girl, is weak but one poker game in particular is extremely well done. Most of the funny stuff is slapstick performed hit-and-miss by town barber Auer and Williams, a punch-drunk fighter who's always hearing bells.

p, Ben Pivar; d, Christy Cabanne; w, Nat Perrin, Charles Grayson (based on the play by John H. Hymer and LeRoy Clemens); ph, Stanley Cortez; ed, Milton Carruth.

Comedy (PR:A MPAA:NR)

ALIAS THE DOCTOR* 1/2 (1932) 69m First National bw

Richard Barthelmess *(Karl Muller)*, Marian Marsh *(Lotti Brenner)*, Lucille La Verne *(Mother Brenner)*, Norman Foster *(Stephan Brenner)*, Adrienne Dore *(Anna)*, Oscar Apfel *(Keller)*, John St. Polis *(Dr. Niergardt)*, Wallis Clark *(Kleinschmidt)*, Claire Dodd *(Mrs. Beverly)*, George Rosener *(Von Bergman)*, Boris Karloff *(Autopsy Surgeon)*, Reginald Barlow *(Professor)*, Arnold Lucy *(The Deacon)*, Harold Waldridge *(Willie)*, Robert Farfan *(Franz)*.

Austrian doctor Barthelmess takes the blame for a friend's illegal operation and goes to prison. Urged by his stepmother, he returns to surgery after his release from jail. After his sordid past is discovered by the authorities, he performs one more operation (saving his stepmother's life) and runs off to a little farm to marry his half-sister Marsh. Unappealing melodrama with the cast's American accents sounding curiously out of place in the Teutonic surroundings. A note to Karloff fans: Boris appears in a small role as an autopsy surgeon (Dr. Frankenstein?) but was replaced in some prints by Nigel De Brulier when the British censor regarded some scenes as a bit gruesome and Karloff was unavailable for the re-shooting.

d, Lloyd Bacon; w, Houston Branch, Charles Kenyon (based on the story by Imre Foeldes); ph, Barney McGill; ed, William Holmes; art d, Anton Grot.

Drama (PR:A MPAA:NR)

ALIBI** (1929) 90m UA bw

Chester Morris *(No. 1065/Chick Williams)*, Harry Stubbs *(Buck Bachman)*, Mae Busch *(Daisy Thomas)*, Eleanor Griffith *(Joan Manning)*, Irma Harrison *(Toots)*, Regis Toomey *(Danny McGann)*, Al Hill *(Brown)*, James Bradbury, Jr. *(Blake)*, Elmer Ballard *(Soft Malone)*, Kiernan Cripps *(Trask)*, Purnell B. Pratt *(Pete Manning)*, Pat O'Malley *(Tommy Glennon)*, DeWitt Jennings *(O'Brien)*, Edward Jennings *(Geo. Stanislaus David)*, Virginia Flohri, Edward Jardon *(Singers in Theater)*.

Police don't sleep until ruthless killer Morris is apprehended. Gritty, exciting low-budget crime melodrama from Roland West, who was one of very few independent producer/directors in Hollywood during the late 1920s early 1930s.

p, Roland West; d, West; w, West, C. Gardner Sullivan (based on the play "Nightstick" by John Wray, J. C. Nugent, and Elaine Sterne Carrington); ph, Ray

June; m, Hugo Riesenfeld; ed, Hal Kern; art d, William Cameron Menzies; ch, Fanchon.

Crime **(PR:C MPAA:NR)**

ALIBI* (1931, Brit.) 70m Twickenham/Woolf and Freedman bw

Austin Trevor *(Hercule Poirot)*, Franklyn Dyall, Mercia Swinburne, J. H. Roberts, Elizabeth Allan, John Deverell, Mary Jerrold, Ronald Ward, Harvey Braban, Clare Greet, Diana Beaumont, Earle Grey.

Unsuccessful attempt to capture the suspense of the popular British stage play based on an Agatha Christie story in which the killer of a doctor is tracked down. The London stage version featured Charles Laughton; this film, unfortunately, does not.

p, Julius Hagen; d, Leslie S. Hiscott; w, H. Fowler Mear (based on the play by Michael Morton and Agatha Christie, from the novel *The Murder of Roger Ackroyd* by Christie); ph, Sydney Blythe.

Crime/Mystery **(PR:A MPAA:NR)**

ALIBI, THE** (1939, Fr.) 82m B-N Films/COL bw

Erich von Stroheim *(Prof. Winckler)*, Louis Jouvet *(Inspector Calas)*, Albert Prejean *(Laurent)*, Jany Holt *(Helene)*, Phillippe Richard *(Gordon)*, Margo Lico *(Dany)*, Florence Marly *(The Blonde)*, Fun-Sen *(The Professor's Assistant)*, Maurice Baquet *(Gerard)*, Roger Blin *(Kretz)*.

Cunning nightclub mind-reader von Stroheim spots an old enemy one evening and mercilessly kills him. Seeking the perfect alibi, he bribes the club hostess, Holt, into saying that they had spent the night together. Thinking he is in the clear, von Stroheim has yet to deal with the perceptive and determined Parisian police inspector, masterfully played by Jouvet, who is assigned to the case. Von Stroheim, having virtually given up on Hollywood at the time, uses his powerful presence well in this taut, multinational thriller. (In French; English subtitles.)

d, Pierre Chenal; w, Marcel Achard, J. Companeez, R. Juttke; m, Georges Auric, Jacques Dallin; English subtitles, Clement Douenias.

Crime/Mystery **(PR:C MPAA:NR)**

ALIBI, THE 1/2** (1943, Brit.) 66m REP bw

Margaret Lockwood *(Helene Andoine)*, Hugh Sinclair *(Insp. Calas)*, James Mason *(Andre Laurent)*, Raymond Lovell *(Prof. Winkler)*, Enid Stamp-Taylor *(Dany)*, Hartley Power *(Gordon)*, Jane Carr *(Delia)*, Rodney Ackland, Edana Romney *(Winkler's Assistants)*, Elisabeth Welch *(Singer)*, Olga Lindo *(Mlle. Loureau)*, Muriel George *(Mme. Bretonnet)*, George Merritt *(Bourdille)*, Judy Gray *(Josette)*, Philip Leaver *(Dodo)*, Derek Blomfield *(Gerard)*, Clarie Wear's Embassy Orchestra.

Uninteresting remake of 1939's THE ALIBI which starred Erich von Stroheim. As in that film, a nightclub psychic kills a man and uses the bar hostess to obtain his alibi. Mason gives a suave performance, but that's about the only worthwhile contribution.

p, Josef Somlo; d, Brian Desmond Hurst; w, R. Carter, R. Juttke, J. Companeez (based on a story by Marcel Achard); ph, W. McLeod; ed, Alan Jaggs.

Crime/Mystery **(PR:C MPAA:NR)**

ALIBI FOR MURDER* (1936) 61m COL bw

William Gargan *(Perry Travis)*, Marguerite Churchill *(Lois Allen)*, Gene Morgan *(Brainy)*, John Gallaudet *(Billy Howard)*, Romaine Callender *(E. J. Easton)*, Egon Brecher *(Sir Conrad Stava)*, Drue Leyton *(Mrs. Foster)*, Wade Boteler *(Conroy)*, Dwight Frye *(McBride)*, Raymond Lawrence *(Harkness)*.

Radio newsman Gargan begins to play sleuth when a top scientist he is sent to interview is murdered. Easily dismissible mystery picture.

d, D. Ross Lederman; w, Tom Van Dycke; ph, George Meehan; ed, William A. Lyon.

Crime/Mystery **(PR:A MPAA:NR)**

ALIBI IKE** (1935) 73m WB bw

Joe E. Brown *(Frank X. Farrell)*, Olivia de Havilland *(Dolly)*, Roscoe Karns *(Cary)*, William Frawley *(Cap)*, Joseph King *(Owner)*, Ruth Donnelly *(Bess)*, Paul Harvey *(Crawford)*, Eddie Shubert *(Jack Mack)*, G. Pat Collins *(Lieutenant)*, Spencer Charters *(Minister)*, Gene Morgan *(Smitty)*, Jack Norton *(Reporter)*, George Riley *(Ball Player)*, Cliff Saum *(Kelly)*, Joseph Crehan *(Conductor)*, Jed Prouty *(Jewelry Merchant)*, Jack Cheatham *(Operator)*, Eddy Chandler, Bruce Mitchell *(Detectives)*, Fred "Snowflake" Toones *(Elevator Operator)*, Gordon "Bill" Elliott, Milton Kibbee *(Fans)*, Selmer Jackson *(Announcer)*, Frank Sully *(Player)*.

Screwball comedy pits Brown against the world and professional baseball as an unorthodox, eccentric pitcher who possesses a marvelous bag of tricks and oddball pitches which generally see him win. When things go wrong, particularly his miserable batting, he always has a zany excuse, ergo the sobriquet, Alibi Ike. In between his field antics, Brown manages to meet de Havilland, the sister of the wife of the team's owner. He proposes, but is rejected after he makes a foolish remark. As the big game approaches, Brown is kidnaped by gamblers who have bet heavily on the opposition, knowing they'll win if the star pitcher is not on the mound. He escapes and, after a wild chase, returns to the playing field just in time to save the game and win de Havilland. A routine Brown vehicle but one popular with his numerous fans. Brown made about two films a year though the 1930s for Warner Bros., all proving to be consistent money-makers, but few of them ever rose above the pedestrian level. This was de Havilland's first appearance on screen, followed quickly by THE IRISH IN US and A MIDSUMMER NIGHT'S DREAM. She was upset at being thrust into this modest-budget film as a debut, complaining to Jack Warner that such fare was a waste of her talent. Warner, in typically gruff manner, informed her that she was on contract and the public had to see her often enough for her name to be established as a star; the 18-year-old actress nodded bravely and went on with her chores, but never again was she compelled to appear in any WB programmers.

p, Edward Chodorov; d, Ray Enright; w, William Wister (based on a story by Ring Lardner); ph, Arthur Todd; md, Leo F. Forbstein; ed, Thomas Pratt; art d, Esdras Hartley.

Comedy **(PR:AA MPAA:NR)**

ALIBI INN* (1935, Brit.) 53m MGM bw

Molly Lamont *(Mary Talbot)*, Frederick Bradshaw *(Jack Lawton)*, Ben Welden *(Saunders)*, Gladys Jennings *(Anne)*, Olive Sloane *(Queenie)*, Brian Buchel *(Masters)*, Wilfrid Hyde-White *(Husband)*.

Inexpensive little production shows how an inventor is wrongly convicted for a crime he has not committed; Bradshaw breaks out of prison and finds the jewel thieves who have murdered a night watchman, vindicating himself.

p&d, Walter Tennyson; w, Sydney and Muriel Box.

Crime **(PR:A MPAA:NR)**

ALICE ADAMS*** (1935) 99m RKO bw

Katharine Hepburn *(Alice Adams)*, Fred MacMurray *(Arthur Russell)*, Fred Stone *(Mr. Adams)*, Evelyn Venable *(Mildred Palmer)*, Frank Albertson *(Walter Adams)*, Ann Shoemaker *(Mrs. Adams)*, Charles Grapewin *(Mr. Lamb)*, Grady Sutton *(Frank Dowling)*, Hedda Hopper *(Mrs. Palmer)*, Jonathan Hale *(Mr. Palmer)*, Janet McLeod *(Henrietta Lamb)*, Virginia Howell *(Mrs. Dowling)*, Zeffie Tilbury *(Mrs. Dresser)*, Ella McKenzie *(Ella Dowling)*, Hattie McDaniel *(Malena)*.

She lives only a block or so from the wrong side of the tracks. Her friends all come from wealthy families and she pretends that she and her family actually enjoy the status of her peer group, a pretense that grows into a dangerous conviction. She is Alice Adams, Booth Tarkington's social-climbing but likable heroine, and she was never better played than by Hepburn who brought a fiery temperament, clutching coyness and bold aggressiveness as well as down-home sensitivity to the part which won for her a second Academy Award nomination, after MORNING GLORY in 1933. Alice is naive and frustrated in her desire to escape her middle-class, small-town environment. Her family of hopeless clods drags her down to grim reality at every turn, as does her clerk-typist job, yet she has hope of escape through her rich friends who are really nothing more than sophisticated snobs, shallow where she is full, purposeless in the face of her ambition to succeed. They merely tolerate her as a source of amusement, frivolously inviting her to an exclusive party where she meets several men, including Grady Sutton, a limp-wristed son of wealth; others who look down on her; and the man of her dreams, rich, handsome and gracious MacMurray, who plays his part with unexpected sensitivity. He is attracted to her and also conned into believing that her family is well-to-do. Hepburn builds them up even more, inflating their importance and then risking all by inviting her hero to dinner at her home. In preparation for this momentous occasion, her mother, Shoemaker, becomes infected with Alice's vibrant aspira- tions and insists that her husband, Stone, quit his job at a glue factory and go into business for himself, marketing a glue process which he has invented. But the night of the big dinner party is a disaster. MacMurray sits quietly through an ordeal of fierce posturing and ostentatious behavior by Alice's family as they "put on the dog" in trying to impress him with their social place which, of course, is all transparent. One of the funniest bits is when the family's part-time cook, Hattie McDaniel, a woman of questionable morals, chews gum incessantly and makes suggestive remarks while sloppily serving the family, offering up a meal that MacMurray realizes no self-respecting stomach would accept. He backs away gracefully and one is left to believe that Tarkington's ending in the novel, as it was in the 1923 silent version with Florence Vidor, would be maintained, that Alice and her oafish family would be deserted by Prince Charming, especially after MacMurray hears that Alice's brother, Albertson, has stolen from his employer. But this forlorn fate, movie execs concluded, would not do for the public of the 1930s with its own forlorn fate crushing it in the Great Depression. Prince Charming does return to Alice, vowing his love for her. Her father is backed by a millionaire in his new glue process and her brother is forgiven for his transgression. And, because of this finale, the film was a smash success, as important for Hepburn as it was for 30-year-old director George Stevens, this being his first major film.

p, Pandro S. Berman; d, George Stevens; w, Dorothy Yost, Mortimer Offner (based on the novel by Booth Tarkington); ph, Robert De Grasse; m, Max Steiner; ed, Jane Loring; art d, Van Nest Polglase; cos, Walter Plunkett.

Comedy/Drama **Cas.** **(PR:A MPAA:NR)**

ALICE DOESN'T LIVE HERE ANYMORE 1/2** (1975) 112m WB c

Ellen Burstyn *(Alice Hyatt)*, Kris Kristofferson *(David)*, Billy Green Bush *(Donald Hyatt)*, Diane Ladd *(Flo)*, Lelia Goldoni *(Neighbor Bea)*, Harvey Keitel *(Ben Everhart)*, Lane Bradbury *(Ben's Wife)*, Vic Tayback *(Mel)*, Jodie Foster *(Audrey)*, Valerie Curtin *(Vera)*, Murray Moston *(Bar Owner Jacobs)*, Harry Northrup *(Bartender)*, Alfred Lutter *(Tommy Hyatt)*, Mia Bendixsen *(Young Alice)*.

Widow Burstyn and her young son are on the road, en route to Monterey and a singing career, although Burstyn's goal is distant and her ambition a thin one, a fact she recognizes, but does not quite accept. Following the death of her husband, the slovenly housewife drives off toward escapism but only finds misery after taking up with brutal, egomaniacal Keitel (whose psychopathic performances are now traditional, branding him as one of the most repugnant screen characters in the history of film, his own unimaginative stereotype). Director Scorsese sinks into the usual mire of foul-mouthed dialog, a distasteful trademark that feebly and mistakenly attempts to prove that all people speak from the gutter. After being mercilessly abused by Keitel, Burstyn moves on through other mediocre adventures until meeting small rancher Kristofferson who treats her and her son with dignity and respect, offering them that happy home they are seeking. A moving film but one that dwells on the more depressing aspects of life in the holy name of Scorsese's so-called art. Kristofferson is a weak hero; his one-dimensional talent of the big stare and the unfaltering monotone is as convincing and uplifting as a recording from telephone infomation. This film is unique in that it shifts the perspective to a heroine after decades of male-dominated films, even though the elements of that perspective are mostly vile and uninviting.

p, David Susskind, Audrey Maas; d, Martin Scorsese; w, Robert Getchell; ph, Kent L. Wakeford (Technicolor); m, Richard LaSalle; ed, Marcia Lucas; prod d, Toby Carr Rafelson.

Drama **Cas.** **(PR:O MPAA:PG)**

ALICE IN THE CITIES*** (1974, W. Ger.) 110m Bauer bw

Rudiger Vogler *(Phillip)*, Yella Rottlander *(Alice)*, Elisabeth Kreuzer *(Lisa)*, Edda

Kochi (Edda), Didi Petrikat *(The Girl)*, Ernest Bohm *(The Agent)*, Sam Presti *(The Car Salesman)*, Lois Moran *(Girl at Ticket Counter)*, Hans Hirschmuller, Sybille Baier, Mirko.

Reporter Vogler is given temporary custody of a little girl, Rottlander, after a chance meeting with the girl's mother in America. Together, the two wander around Germany searching for Rottlander's grandmother. Director Wenders, the most American- influenced of the new German filmmakers (he loves the films of Nicholas Ray and rock and roll), is an artist not interested in fast-paced plots or happy-go-lucky characters. What he does care about are simple people, the bonds they make with each other, and the types of environment they choose to live in and those they choose to avoid. In ALICE IN THE CITIES, Wenders is much more intrigued by the visual contrast between neon/metal America and the quiet German countryside. The factors that make up the friendship between Rottlander and the brooding Vogler are much more important than the "will they find her relatives?" plot. This approach may not appeal to many filmgoers who like their stories fast and simple, but ALICE weaves a pleasant spell on those willing to sit back and patiently observe.

p, Peter Genee; d, Wim Wenders; w, Wenders, Veith der Furstenberg; ph, Robby Muller, Martin Schafer; ed, Peter Przygodda, Barbara von Weitershausen.

Drama (PR:A MPAA:NR)

ALICE IN WONDERLAND*** (1933) 90m PAR bw

Charlotte Henry *(Alice)*, Richard Arlen *(Cheshire Cat)*, Roscoe Ates *(Fish)*, William Austin *(Gryphon)*, Gary Cooper *(White Knight)*, Jack Duffy *(Leg of Mutton)*, Leon Errol *(Uncle Gilbert)*, Louise Fazenda *(White Queen)*, W. C. Fields *(Humpty Dumpty)*, Alec B. Francis *(King of Hearts)*, Skeets Gallagher *(White Rabbit)*, Cary Grant *(Mock Turtle)*, Lillian Harmer *(Cook)*, Raymond Hatton *(Mouse)*, Sterling Holloway *(Frog)*, Edward Everett Horton *(Mad Hatter)*, Roscoe Karns *(Tweedledee)*, Baby LeRoy *(Joker)*, Lucien Littlefield *(Father William's Son)*, Mae Marsh *(Sheep)*, Polly Moran *(Dodo Bird)*, Jack Oakie *(Tweedledum)*, Edna May Oliver *(Red Queen)*, George Ovey *(Plum Pudding)*, May Robson *(Queen of Hearts)*, Charlie Ruggles *(March Hare)*, Jackie Searle *(Dormouse)*, Alison Skipworth *(Duchess)*, Ned Sparks *(Caterpillar)*.

An all-star cast, in fact anyone who was anybody on Paramount's lot in 1933 made up the incredible characters in this surrealistic version of Lewis Carroll's nonsensical and often frightening fantasy. Alice is quietly reading in her garden when she notices a rabbit diving into a hole; she inspects the opening which suddenly enlarges so that she falls into it, down and down, landing in a luxuriant garden. Again she spots the rabbit, who runs off, claiming he's late. She and runs after him only to stop to eat toadstools and grow enormous. After eating again, she grows tiny, so small that she almost drowns in the tears she shed when she was gigantic. Strange creatures who are not what they appear surround her. She saves a baby from harm only to wind up holding a squirming pig. She attends the Mad Hatter's tea party, realizing that all there are insane, and flees, only to find herself in a courtroom where an even crazier Queen of Hearts threatens to cut off her head unless she testifies to please her royal highness. The Queen's vicious guards rush her and are on the verge of destroying her when Alice calls it quits, angrily shouting: "Why, you're nothing more than a pack of cards!" With this abrupt realization, Alice, well played by Charlotte Henry, awakens from what must be one of the most fearful nightmares on record. Most of the superstars in this fascinating but offbeat production are thoroughly unrecognizable, buried under pounds of makeup or smothered in cumbersome costumes—Grant as the Mock Turtle, Cooper as the White Knight could have been extras for all the costuming that buried their identities. Oakie as Tweedledum is identifiable, as are Fields as Humpty-Dumpty, Horton as the Mad Hatter, Holloway as the frog, and Oliver as the Queen, but this is due to their distinctive voices. The film is a technical marvel for 1933 with its lavish sets, costuming and makeup but beyond that the film suffers from a lack of identity, except for Henry. (Oddly, Ida Lupino was first scheduled to play the part of Alice, brought by Paramount from England for that very purpose, but studio heads changed their minds after testing Brooklyn-born Henry for the role.)

p, Louis D. Lighton; d, Norman McLeod; w, Joseph L. Mankiewicz, William Cameron Menzies (from the novels *Alice's Adventures in Wonderland* and *Alice Through the Looking Glass* by Lewis Carroll); ph, Henry Sharp, Bert Glennon; m, Dmitri Tiomkin; ed, Edward Hoagland; art d, Robert Odell; spec eff, Gordon Jennings, Farciot Edouart; masks and cos, Wally Westmore, Newt Jones.

Fantasy Cas. (PR:AAA MPAA:NR)

ALICE IN WONDERLAND*** (1951) 74m Disney/RKO c

Kathryn Beaumont *(Alice)*, Ed Wynn *(Mad Hatter)*, Richard Haydn *(Caterpillar)*, Sterling Holloway *(Cheshire Cat)*, Jerry Colonna *(March Hare)*, Verna Felton *(Queen of Hearts)*, Pat O'Malley *(Walrus-Carpenter-Dee & Dum)*, Bill Thompson *(White Rabbit and Dodo)*, Heather Angel *(Alice's Sister)*, Joseph Kearns *(Doorknob)*, Larry Grey *(Bill)*, Queenie Leonard *(Bird in the Tree)*, Dink Trout *(King of Hearts)*, Doris Lloyd *(The Rose)*, James Macdonald *(Dormouse)*, The Mellomen *(Card Players)*.

Disney's beautifully animated version of Alice (one of six: Nonparell Feature Film Co., 1915; another silent in 1922; Paramount, 1933; Bunin, 1951; Horne Productions, 1972) remains the most popular today in that it was aimed at the children's market, with Disney eliminating the intellectual aspects of Carroll's story and playing it as a straight crazy dream/nightmare. (Walt was never above frightening the pants off anyone.) The depth of photographic field and the startling color, as well as the detail of animation and distinctive voices, particularly of Wynn as the Mad Hatter, Holloway as the Cheshire Cat, Colonna as the March Hare and Felton's Queen of Hearts, are memorable. A delight for children and the young at heart.

p, Walt Disney; d, Clyde Geronimi, Hamilton Luske, Wilfred Jaxon; anim d, Milt Kahl, Ward Kimball, Frank Thomas, Eric Larson, John Lounsberry, Ollie Johnston, Wolfgang Reitherman, Marc Davis, Les Clark, Norm Ferguson; w, Winston Hibler, Bill Peet, Joe Rinaldi, Bill Cottrell, Joe Grant, Del Connell, Ted Sears, Erdman Penner, Milt Banta, Dick Kelsey, Dick Huemer, Tom Oreb, John Walbridge (based on the stories of Lewis Carroll); anim, Hal King, Judge Whitaker, Hal Ambro, Bill Justice, Phil Duncan, Bob Carlson, Don Lusk, Cliff Nordberg, Harvey Toombs, Fred Moore, Marvin Woodward, Charles Nichols, Hugh Fraser; effects anim, Josh Meador, Dan MacManus, George Rowley, Blaine Gibson; m, Oliver Wallace; m/l, Bob Hilliard, Sammy Fain, Gene DePaul, Mack David, Jerry Livingston, Al Hoffman.

Fantasy Cas. (PR:AAA MPAA:NR)

ALICE IN WONDERLAND 1/2** (1951, Fr.) 83m Bunin/Souvaine c

Stephen Murray *(Lewis Carroll)*, Pamela Brown *(Queen Victoria)*, Carol Marsh *(Alice)*, Felix Aylmer *(Dr. Liddel)*, Ernest Milton *(Vice Chancellor)*, David Read *(The Prince Consort)*, Raymond Bussieres *(The Tailor)*, Elizabeth Henson *(Lorena)*, Joan Dale *(Edith)*, VOICES OF CHARACTERS: Stephen Murray *(Knave of Hearts)*, Pamela Brown *(Queen of Hearts)*, Felix Aylmer *(Cheshire Cat)*, Ernest Milton *(White Rabbit)*, David Read *(King of Hearts)*, Raymond Bussieres *(Mad Hatter)*.

An intellectual approach to the Lewis Carroll classic aims for satire and an adult view which is almost as impossible as the full-tilt juvenile approach taken by Disney because the stories lie somehwere in between. Here live action and puppets tell the oft-told tale of Alice following the rabbit down the hole and into assorted fantasies, grim and delightful. American Bunin was invited to produce this lofty film bhy the French government which fiananced it and, ironically, the very equipment used for stop-motion animation and color was that formerly used by Nazi propagandists when occupying Paris during WW II and later captured by the French.

p, Lou Bunin; d, Dallas Bower; w, Henry Myers, Albert Lewin, Edward Eliscu (based on stories by Lewis Carroll).

Fantasy/Children (PR:A MPAA:NR)

ALICE, OR THE LAST ESCAPADE 1/2** (1977, Fr.) 93m Filmel-PHPG c

Sylvia Kristel *(Alice)*, Charles Vanel *(Vergennes)*, Jean Carmet *(Colas)*, Andre Dussollier *(Man)*, Fernand Ledoux *(Doctor)*, Thomas Chabrol *(Boy)*, Bernard Russelet *(Husband)*.

Haunting nightmare-like tale of a pretty young wife who leaves her overbearing husband, drives off, and stops at an old house when her windshield cracks. She spends the night in the house after being tended to by an old man who seems to expect her, and prepares to drive off in a newly fixed car. Finding no way out, she is told to "accept" her situation by a young man and she realizes that she is in limbo. After she walks down a dark cellar, the woman's body is seen hanging out of her demolished car. She has finally met Death. College philosophy course idea is given a lush photographic treatment by the Hitchcock-influenced Frenchman Chabrol.

d, Claude Chabrol; w, Chabrol; ph, Jean Rabier; ed, Monique Fardoulis; m, Pierre Jansen.

Drama/Fantasy (PR:C MPAA:NR)

ALICE, SWEET ALICE**

(1978) 108m AA c (AKA: COMMUNION, HOLY TERROR)

Paula Sheppard *(Alice)*, Brooke Shields *(Karen)*, Linda Miller *(Catherine)*, Jane Lowry *(Aunt Annie)*, Alphonso DeNoble *(Alphonso)*, Rudolph Willrich *(Father Tom)*, Mildred Clinton *(Mrs. Tredoni)*, Niles McMaster *(Dom Spages)*, Michael Hardstark *(Detective)*, Gary Allen *(Uncle)*, Tom Signorelli *(Brenner)*, Louisa Horton *(Psychiatrist)*, Antonino Rocco *(Funeral Attendant)*, Lillian Roth *(Pathologist)*.

Low-budget thriller about a teenage girl who is thought to be a killer. Not much here except exploitation and a bit too much gore, though the suspense is maintained through a weak story, mostly due to the director, Sole, an imitator of Polanski.

p, Richard K. Rosenberg; d, Alfred Sole; w, Rosemary Rityo, Sole; ph, John Friberg, Chuck Hall (Technicolor); m, Stephen Lawrence; ed, Edward Salier.

Crime Cas. (PR:O MPAA:R)

ALICE'S ADVENTURES IN WONDERLAND*

(1972, Brit.) 96m Horne/ANE

Fiona Fullerton *(Alice)*, Michael Crawford *(White Rabbit)*, Ralph Richardson *(Caterpillar)*, Flora Robson *(Queen of Hearts)*, Peter Sellers *(March Hare)*, Robert Helpmann *(Mad Hatter)*, Dudley Moore *(Dormouse)*, Michael Jayston *(Dodgson)*, Spike Milligan *(Gryphon)*.

This slowly paced version of the often-filmed Lewis Carroll classic is the worst of the lot, even more ponderous and groping than Paramount's cumbersome 1933 effort. A great deal of top talent—Richardson, Sellers, Robson, Moore—is completely wasted in this limp, lame, and unenthusiastic production. Strictly for the youngsters, and even they might yawn it up.

p, Derek Horne; d&w, William Sterling (based on stories by Lewis Carroll); ph, Geoffrey Unsworth (Eastmancolor); m, John Barry; set d, Michael Stringer; art d, Norman Dorme.

Fantasy Cas. (PR:A MPAA:G)

ALICE'S RESTAURANT** (1969) 111m UA c

Arlo Guthrie *(Arlo)*, Pat Quinn *(Alice)*, James Broderick *(Ray)*, Michael McClanathan *(Shelly)*, Geoff Outlaw *(Roger)*, Tina Chen *(Mari-chan)*, Kathleen Dabney *(Karin)*, William Obanhein *(Officer Obie)*, Seth Allan *(Evangelist)*, Monroe Arnold *(Bluegrass)*, Joseph Boley *(Woody)*, Pete Seeger *(Himself)*, Vinnette Carroll *(Lady Clerk)*, Sylvia Davis *(Marjorie)*, Simm Landres *(Jacob)*, Eulalie Noble *(Ruth)*, Louis Beachner *(Dean)*, Mac Intryre Dixon *(lst Deconsecration Minister)*, Rev. Dr. Pierce Middleton *(2nd Deconsecration Minister)*, Donald Marye *(Funeral Director)*, Shelley Plimpton *(Reenie)*, M. Emmet Walsh *(Group W Sergeant)*, Lee Hays *(Himself)*,Ronald Weyland *(1st Cop)*, Eleanor Wilson *(Landlady)*, Simon Deckard *(Medic)*, Thomas De Wolfe *(Waiter)*, Judge James Hannon *(Himself)*, Graham Jarvis *(Music Teacher)*, John Quill *(2nd Cop)*, Frank Simpson *(Sergeant)*.

A jittery, disjointed drop-out film extolling the virtues of the on-the-bum, noncommittal, nonconformist life limply enacted by Guthrie and company, a cult film of the late 1960s, popular with hippie types. Most of it is in bad taste and based upon Guthrie's arrest as a litterbug (he dumped some food and was arrested for littering, writing a song about this heroic exploit which later kept him from being drafted to fight in Viet Nam, a little ditty that undoubtedly did not endear Arlo to anyone serving in that war). One poignant scene does occur, Arlo visiting his dying father Woody, the great folk singer, but this fillip hardly ameliorates a travesty of tedium, pranks, and *non compos mentis* musings passing for a movie.

p, Hillard Elkins, Joe Manduke; d, Arthur Penn; w, Venable Herndon, Penn (based on Arlo Guthrie's "The Alice's Restaurant Massacre" record) ph, Michael Nebbia (DeLuxe Color); m, Guthrie; ed, Dede Allen.

Drama **Cas.** **(PR:O MPAA:R)**

ALIEN*** (1979) 124m Brandywine-Shusett/FOX c

Tom Skerritt *(Dallas)*, Sigourney Weaver *(Ripley)*, Veronica Cartwright *(Lambert)*, Harry Dean Stanton *(Brett)*, John Hurt *(Kane)*, Ian Holm *(Ash)*, Yaphet Kotto *(Parker)*.

A murderous life form terrorizes the crew of an outer-space mineral tanker. Owing quite a bit to Howard Hawks' THE THING, ALIEN is a very suspenseful film, more in the horror genre than in science fiction. Containing some very grisly, but inventive, special effects sequences (the chest-burster has become a bloody classic), the film is one of few that succeeds in creating a believable futuristic world. In terms of design, ALIEN is a visual feast that is indebted heavily to the work of surrealist H. R. Giger and French comic book artist Moebius. Aside from its striking style and suspenseful narrative, the picture is sadly lacking in characterization and emotion.

p, Gordon Carroll, David Giler, Walter Hill; d, Ridley Scott; w, Dan O'Bannon (based on a story by O'Bannon, Ronald Shusett); ph, Derek Vanlint; m, Jerry Goldsmith; ed, Jerry Rawlings, Peter Weatherley; prod d, Michael Seymour; set d, Ian Whittaker; cos, John Mollo; Alien design, H. R. Giger, Roger Dicken; spec eff, Carlo Rambaldi, Bernard Lodge.

Horror/Science Fiction **Cas.** **(PR:O MPAA:R)**

ALIEN CONTAMINATION zero (1982, Ital.) 90m Cannon c

Ian McCulloch, Louise Marleau, Marino Mase, Siegfried Rauch, Gisela Hahn.

Awful ALIEN rip-off has McCulloch fighting alien eggs that squirt goo which causes people to explode. The eggs are controlled by a laughable one-eyed Martian blob who is intent on conquering Earth. Bad special effects and inane dialog make this cheap exploitation product more laughable than chilling.

p, Claudio Mancini; d, Lewis Coates [Luigi Cozzi]; w, Cozzi.

Science Fiction Drama **(PR:O MPAA:R)**

ALIEN THUNDER**
(1975, US/Can.) 90m Onyx-Al/Cinerama c (AKA: DAN CANDY'S LAW)

Donald Sutherland, Chief Dan George, Kevin McCarthy, Jean Duceppe, George Tootoosis, Francine Racette.

Mountie Sutherland sets out across 1890s Saskatchewan wilderness to capture Chief Dan George, accused of stealing a cow and possibly murdering another Mountie Another variation of *Les Miserables* that has Sutherland spending more than a year tracking down the cunning Indian. Exquisitely photographed with a fine cast, the film is still a bit slow and not very compelling.

p, Marie Josee Raymond; d, Claude Fournier; w, George Malko; ph, Fournier.

Adventure **(PR:C MPAA:PG)**

ALIMONY* (1949) 71m Equity/EA bw

Martha Vickers *(Kitty Travers)*, John Beal *(Dan Barker)*, Hillary Brooke *(Linda Waring)*, Laurie Linde *(Helen Drake)*, Douglas Dumbrille *(Burt Crail)*, James Guilfoyle *(Paul Klinger)*, Marie Blake *(Mrs. Nesbitt)*, Leonid Kinskey *(Joe Wood)*, Ralph Graves *(George Griswold/Curtis P. Carter)*, William Ruhl, Fred Richards, Harry Lauter.

Heartless woman, hell-bent on destroying good relationships, marrying wealthy men, getting divorced, and pocketing huge alimony payments, is finally discovered by the long arm of the law. Laughable.

p, Constantin J. David; d, Alfred Zeisler; w, Laurence Lipton, George Bricker, Sherman L. Lowe (based on a story by Lowe, Royal K. Cole); ph, Gilbert Warrenton; ed, Joseph Gluck; m/l, L. Wolfe Gilbert, Alexander Laszlo, Fred Frederick.

Drama **(PR:C MPAA:NR)**

ALIMONY MADNESS zero (1933) 63m Golden Arrow/Mayfair

Helen Chandler *(Joan Armstrong)*, Leon Waycoff *(John Thurman)*, Edward Earle *(Joel Mason)*, Charlotte Merriam *(Eloise Thurman)*, Blanche Frederici *(Mrs. Van)*, Albert Vaughn *(Mary)*.

Hopelessly insipid melodrama concerning the trial of a woman accused of killing her husband's first wife.

p, Fanchon Royer; d, B. Reeves Eason; w, John Thomas Neville; ph, Ernest Miller; ed, Jeanne Spencer.

Drama **(PR:C MPAA:NR)**

ALIVE AND KICKING*** (1962, Brit.) 95m Pathe/Seven Arts bw

Sybil Thorndike *(Dora)*, Kathleeen Harrison *(Rosie)*, Estelle Winwood *(Mabel)*, Stanley Holloway *(MacDonagh)*, Liam Redmond *(Old Man)*, Marjorie Rhodes *(Old Woman)*, Richard Harris *(Lover)*, Olive McFarland *(Lover)*, John Salew *(Solicitor)*, Eric Pohlmann *(Captain)*, Colin Gordon *(Birdwatcher)*, Joyce Carey *(Matron)*, Anita Sharp Bolster *(Postmistress)*, Paul Farrell *(Postman)*, Patrick McAlinney *(Policeman)*, Raymond Manthorpe *(Little Boy)*.

Thorndike, Harrison and Winwood leave their tranquil Old Folks' Home surroundings when they discover that they are to be separated. Eluding the police, army, navy, and air force in a manner that would make the cast of any British POW camp movie proud, the three spunky old ladies hop on a speedboat and get picked up by the crew of a Soviet fishing vessel. Neatly avoiding going to Mother Russia with the sailors, the ladies are dropped off on a remote Irish isle where they meet an eccentric American millionaire, pose as his nieces, and bring economic prosperity to the island village by setting up a knitting operation. A delightfully zany British comedy that gets addedspark from the three main actresses and the ever-precocious Holloway, who plays the millionaire.

p, Victor Skutzeky; d, Cyril Frankel; w, Denis Cannan, ph, Gilbert Taylor; m, Philip Green; ed, Bernard Gribble.

Comedy **(PR:AA MPAA:NR)**

ALIVE ON SATURDAY* 1/2 (1957, Brit.) 58m C&G Films/ABP

Guy Middleton *(George Pilbeam)*, Patricia Owens *(Sally Parker)*, Geoffrey Goodhart *(Joseph H. Parker)*, John Witty *(Slade)*, Jessica Cairns *(Maisie)*, John Salew *(Melito)*, Charles Lloyd Pack *(Gorman)*, Wallas Easton *(Garton)*.

Forced effort has a tycoon from America hoodwinked into believing a hobo is really a prince of a Balkan country; he begins financing the bum's revolution, only to realize his mistake millions of dollars later. Unfunny programmer offers little beyond this thin plot.

p, Geoffrey Goodhart, Brandon Fleming; d, Alfred Travers; w, Fleming.

Comedy **(PR:A MPAA:NR)**

ALL ABOUT EVE***** (1950) 138m FOX bw

Bette Davis *(Margo)*, Anne Baxter *(Eve)*, George Sanders *(Addison De Witt)*, Celeste Holm *(Karen)* Gary Merrill *(Bill Simpson)*, Hugh Marlowe *(Lloyd Richards)*, Thelma Ritter *(Birdie)*, Marilyn Monroe *(Miss Casswell)*, Gregory Ratoff *(Max Fabian)*, Barbara Bates *(Phoebe)*, Walter Hampden *(Aged Actor)*, Randy Stuart *(Girl)*, Craig Hill *(Leading Man)*, Leland Harris *(Doorman)*, Barbara White *(Autograph Seeker)*, Eddie Fisher *(Stage Manager)*, William Pullen *(Clerk)*, Claude Stroud *(Pianist)*, Eugene Borden *(Frenchman)*, Helen Mowery *(Reporter)*, Steven Geray *(Captain of Waiters)*.

Baxter is Eve Harrington, a sweet young thing aspiring to a theatrical part. At least she appears sweet and naive when she approaches star Davis like an awe-struck fan, flattering the older actress and ingratiating herself to her. In a passionate response to Baxter's hard-luck story, Davis makes her her secretary and she later appears at a party in New York with a sterling array of the theatrical world— Sanders, acerbic theater critic; his "protege," Monroe, a vacuous sexy blonde; pompous producer Ratoff; director Merrill, who is also Davis' fiance; Marlowe, a famous playwright and his wife Holm. Baxter plays up to Sanders, Merrill, and Marlowe as a wide-eyed innocent novice actress who would be ever so grateful for any kind of part—even a walk-on. Davis is first amused by her secretary's posturing but then her experience tells her that the young lady is a bit manipulative; she responds to Baxter's cunning ways by getting unpleasantly plastered, telling off one and all. Holm, after being charmed by Baxter, gets her a try-out in her husband's play as Davis' understudy and when she gets the job, Davis explodes, now fully realizing, as did her maid Ritter from the start, that Baxter is a conniving and vicious climber, masking her ruthless ambition beneath loads of charm and, when Davis tries to expose her, feigning deep injury at the hands of the woman she ostensibly worships. All of this subtle competition, obvious only to Davis, drives the star to maddening outbursts, tantrums according to Merrill and Marlowe, who interpret Davis' actions and biting attacks as that of a prima donna completely out of control. The play goes on but Holm, still believing Baxter is being wrongfully characterized by Davis, arranges a "break" for the scheming understudy by taking Davis away to a country place for a few days, then making sure that her car will run out of gas so she cannot catch the train back to New York in time for her performance. Baxter goes on in her place and is magnificent, winning plaudits from Sanders, whom she has played up to like some slobbering sycophant. Now that she has her foothold before the stagelights, Baxter attempts to steal Merrill's affections from Davis but is turned down, a rejection witnessed by the insidious Sanders. Then Baxter urges Marlowe to give her the lead in his next play, using blackmail, saying to Holm that she will reveal how she arranged to have her play Davis' role unless the part is given to her, instead of Davis. Holm, after the shock of recognizing Baxter as a career-crazy vixen who will stop at nothing, is saved from losing face and her friendship with Davis when the great actress decides to retire and marry Merrill (Davis' real husband at the time of this movie). Baxter gets the part and goes on to instant stardom. She wins the coveted Sarah Siddons Award, and, flush with triumph, she brags in her dressing room to Sanders that she intends to stay on top by forcing a divorce between Holm and Marlowe, then marrying Marlowe and having him write plays exclusively for her. Sanders proves he is as ruthless as she is, and for that reason, he explains, they belong together. He has kept a close chronicle of Baxter's deceits, betrayals, and dirty tricks. He tells her that unless she becomes his wife, he will reveal all and utterly destroy her career. Trapped, Baxter agrees to become his woman. Ironic justice appears in the form of another sweet young thing, Bates, whom Baxter later finds in her dressing room, admiring herself in a mirror. She tells Baxter that she wants to be just like her, that she will do anything to be near the great actress, Baxter. Succumbing to the girl's oozing flattery, Baxter takes her on as an aide, just as Davis had done. Sanders comes to Baxter's door to present her with the Sarah Siddons statuette but finds Bates, who takes it from him to give to Baxter, their exchange of glances promising future trysts. Bates stands before the dressing mirror holding the award, assuming Baxter's mantle and image. She is to repeat the same moves, go down the same road, toward a terrible fate aimed at the destruction of Baxter's career and her own at the hands of another scheming would-be star, and another, and another. This film is brilliantly written with witty, biting and satiric lines, directed so tightly that there is not an inch of room for boredom or disbelief. It is a scathing indictment of the New York theatrical world, presented much the same way Billy Wilder exposed the movie world in SUNSET BOULEVARD, both films produced the same year. The acting is outstanding, Davis and Baxter performing at their best, Davis as the consummate stage actress betrayed by her own kindness, condescending as it may be, and Baxter as the thoroughly shallow creature who will fake her own talent to the top and stay there until her lack of substance is ultimately exposed. Director Mankiewicz uses his camera as an audience, framing each shot as a stage setting which would be ineffective for anything other than this theatrical saga. Equally impressive are Thelma Ritter as the savvy maid who has seen it all happen before, Sanders, as the despicable caustic critic, Marlowe, as the egotistical playwright, and Merrill, as the sensitive director. Even Monroe, never greatly endowed with in-depth acting ability, is superbly type-cast as Sanders describes her: "A graduate of the dramatic school of Copacabana." A sparkling masterpiece. The Broadway musical "Applause" is based on this film.

p, Darryl F. Zanuck; d, Joseph L. Mankiewicz; w, Mankiewicz (based on the story "The Wisdom of Eve" by Mary Orr); ph, Milton Krasner; m, Alfred Newman; ed, Barbara McLean; art d, Lyle Wheeler, George W. Davis; cos, Edith Head.

Drama **Cas.** **(PR:A MPAA:NR)**

ALL-AMERICAN, THE** (1932) 73m UNIV bw(GB: SPORT OF A NATION)

Richard Arlen *(Garry King)*, Andy Devine *(Andy Moran)*, Gloria Stuart *(Ellen Steffens)*, James Gleason *(Chick Knipe)*, John Darrow *(Bob King)*, Preston Foster *(Steve Kelly)*, Merna Kennedy *(Gloria Neuchard)*, Harold Waldrige *(Willie Walsh)*, Huntley Gordon *(Harcourt)*, Earl McCarthy *(Ted Brown)*, Ethel Clayton *(Mrs. Brown), June Clyde (Betty Poe)*, Walter Brennan, Margaret Lindsay, Jack LaRue, James Flavin, Florence Roberts.

Big-headed college football star quits school to make it rich quick selling bonds, but loses his money and stature pretty fast thanks to cheap women and gambling. Before his brother falls victim to the same pattern, the star returns to the hard-hitting field hoping to make the kid wise up. Devine's comedic presence adds a little spice to this pleasant story.

d, Russell Mack; w, Frank Weed, Ferdinand Reyney (based on story by Richard Schayer, Dale Van Every); ph, George Robinson.

Drama **(PR:A MPAA:NR)**

ALL-AMERICAN, THE** (1953) 82m UNIV bw (GB: THE WINNING WAY)

Tony Curtis *(Nick Bonelli)*, Lori Nelson *(Sharon Wallace)*, Richard Long *(Howard Carter)*, Mamie Van Doren *(Susie Ward)*, Gregg Palmer *(Cameron)*, Paul Cavanagh *(Prof. Banning)*, Herman Hickman *(Jumbo)*, Barney Phillips *(Clipper Colton)*, Jimmy Hunt *(Whizzer)*, Stuart Whitman *(Zip Parker)*, Douglas Kennedy *(Tate Hardy)*, Donald Randolph *(David Carter)*, Frank Gifford *(Stan Pomeroy)*, Tom Harmon *(Tom Harmon)*, Jim Sears *(Dartmore Quarterback)*, Elmer Willhoite *(Kenton)*, Don Moomaw *(Jones)*, Fortune Gordein *(Gronski)*, George Bozanic *(McManus)*.

All-American quarterback Curtis quits school after his parents are killed in a bus accident. After a brief period of mourning and moping, he attends a rich, snobby school, and eventually starts to tear up their football field. After avoiding jeers from the snotty rich boys on the team and the temptation of Van Doren's off-limit bar, Curtis becomes a gridiron champ with the help of understanding girl friend Nelson. Not a direct remake of 1932's film of the same title, but pretty much the same amount of entertainment value. Curtis does a good job and it's nice to see some actual football stars and coaches on the screen.

p, Aaron Rosenberg; d, Jesse Hibbs; w, D. D. Beauchamp, Robert Yale Libett (based on a story by Leonard Freeman); ph, Maury Gertsman; ed, Edward Curtiss.

Drama **(PR:A MPAA:NR)**

ALL-AMERICAN BOY, THE * (1973) 118m WB c

Jon Voight *(Vic Bealer)*, Carol Androsky *(Rodine)*, Anne Archer *(Drenna Valentine)*, Gene Borkan *(Rockoff)*, Ron Burns *(Larkin)*, Rosalind Cash *(Poppy)*, Jeanne Cooper *(Nola Bealer)*, Peggy Cowles *(Bett Van Daumee)*, Leigh French *(Lovette)*, Ned Glass *(Arty)*, Bob Hastings *(Ariel Van Daumee)*, Kathy Mahoney *(Shereen Bealer)*, Art Metrano *(Jay David Swooze)*, Jaye P. Morgan *(Magda)*, Harry Northup *(Parker)*, Nancie Phillips *(Connie Swooze)*, Jeff Thompson *(High Valentine)*.

Pathetic film about a "never-was" boxer (Voight) who hangs around a small town populated by similar losers. Too bad nobody told director Eastman about the difference between heroic tragedy and irritating, manipulated pathos. THE ALL-AMERICAN BOY sat on the producer's shelf for a few years before its release and it should have remained there, happily collecting dust.

p, Joseph T. Naar, Saul J. Krugman; d&, Charles Eastman; ph, Philip Lathrop; ed, Christopher Holmes; art d, Carey O'Dell.

Drama **(PR:0 MPAA:R)**

ALL-AMERICAN CHUMP* (1936) 63m MGM bw

Stuart Erwin *(Elmer)*, Robert Armstrong *(Hogan)*, Betty Furness *(Kitty)*, Edmund Gwenn *(Jeffrey Crane)*, Harvey Stephens *(Crawford)*, Edward Brophy *(Murphy)*, E. E. Clive *(Brantley)*, Dewey Robinson *(Al)*, Eddie Shubert *(Butch)*, Spencer Charters *(Abiah Smith)*.

Easygoing country boy Erwin turns out to be a mathematical genius and is exploited by a couple of big-city gangsters. You want laughs? You're not going to find them here.

p, Lucien Hubbard, Michael Fessler; d, Edwin L. Marin; w, Lawrence Kimble; ph, Charles Clarke; m, Dr. William Axt.; ed, Frank G. Hull.

Comedy **(PR:A MPAA:NR)**

ALL-AMERICAN CO-ED*1/2 (1941) 48m Roach/UA bw

Frances Langford *(Virginia)*, Johnny Downs *(Bob Sheppard)*, Marjorie Woodworth *(Bunny)*, Noah Beery, Jr. *(Slinky)*, Esther Dale *(Matilda)*, Harry Langdon *(Hap Holden)*, Alan Hale, Jr. *(Tiny)*, Kent Rogers *(Henry)*, Allan Lane, Joe Brown, Jr., Carlyle Blackwell, Jr. *(Seniors)*, Irving Mitchell *(Doctor)*, Lillian Randolph *(Washwoman)*.

After a neighboring all-girl school insults them, the members of a Quinceton college fraternity decide to enter Downs in the girls' beauty contest. Donning his best dress, Downs goes off and does what a man has to do. Freud would have had a field day with this slapstick Hal Roach quickie.

p, Hal Roach [Le Roy Prinz]; d, Prinz; w, Cortland Fitzsimmons, Kenneth Higgins; ph, Robert Pittack; ed, Bert Jordan; m/l, Walter G. Samuels, Charles Newman, Lloyd B. Norlin.

Comedy **(PR:A MPAA:NR)**

ALL-AMERICAN SWEETHEART* (1937) 62m COL bw

Patricia Farr *(Connie Adams)*, Scott Colton *(Lance Corbett)*, Gene Morgan *(Coach Dolan)*, Jimmy Eagles *("Squirt" Adams)*, Arthur Loft *(Cap Collender)*, Joe Twerp *(Giblets Offenbach)*, Ruth Hilliard *(Amy Goss)*, Donald Briggs *(Johnny Ames)*, Louis DaPron *(Andy Carter)*, Allen Brook *(Joe Collins)*, Frank C. Wilson *(Alfred)*.

Racketeers get their feet wet when they try to manipulate the local college rowing team. Is there anything thirties movie gangsters didn't try to control?

d, Lambert Hillyer; w, Grace Neville, Fred Niblo, Jr., Michael L. Simmons (based on a story by Robert E. Kent); ph, Benjamin Kline; ed, James Sweeney.

Crime **(PR:A MPAA:NR)**

ALL-AROUND REDUCED PERSONALITY—OUTTAKES, THE**

(1978, Ger.) 98m Basis-Film Verlich/Zweites Deutsches Fernsehen bw

Helke Sander *(Edda Chiemnyjewski)*, Joachim Baumann, Frank Burckner, Eva Gagel, Ulrich Gressieker, Beate Kopp, Andrea Nabakowski, Helga Storck, Gesine Strempel, Ronny Tanner, Abisag Tuellmann, Ulla Ziermann, Gisela Zies.

An independent woman photographer tries to cope with economic hardship in a dehumanizing Berlin. An emotionally cold feminist film that points the finger not only at the male-dominated business world, but at the submissive people who allow themselves to be manipulated. Excellent photography reflecting Sander's inner feeling adds to the sad isolation created by the narrative.

d, Helke Sander; w, Sander; ph, Katia Forbert; ed, Ursula Hoef.

Drama **(PR:A MPAA:NR)**

ALL ASHORE** (1953) 80m COL color

Mickey Rooney *(Francis "Moby" Dickerson)*, Dick Haymes *(Joe Carter)*, Peggy Ryan *(Gay Night)*, Ray McDonald *(Skip Edwards)*, Barbara Bates *(Jane Stanton)*, Jody Lawrence *(Nancy Flynn)*, Fay Roope *(Commodore Stanton)*, Jean Willes *(Rose)*, Rica Owen *(Dotty)*, Patricia Walker *(Susie)*, Edwin Parker *(Sheriff Billings)*, Dick Crockett *(Guard)*, Frank Kreig *(Arthur Barnaby)*, Ben Welden *(Bartender)*, Gloria Pall *(Lucretia)*, Joan Shawlee *(Hedy)*.

Poor man's ON THE TOWN has sailors Rooney, Haymes, and McDonald posing as entertainers on Catalina so they can earn some spending money while they're on shore leave. Mediocre songs do nothing to help the routine story, although Rooney does a nifty bit of clowning.

p, Jonie Taps; d, Richard Quine; w, Blake Edwards, Quine (based on a story by Edwards and Robert Wells); ph, Charles Lawton, Jr.; md, Morris Stoloff; m/l, Wells, Fred Karger, Lee Scott.

Musical Comedy **(PR:AA MPAA:NR)**

ALL AT SEA*1/2 (1935, Brit.) 60m FOX bw

Tyrell Davis *(Joe Finch)*, Googie Withers *(Daphne Tomkins)*, James Carew *(Julius Mablethorpe)*, Cecily Byrne *(Mary Maggs)*, Rex Harrison *(Aubrey Bellingham)*, Dorothy Vernon *(Mrs. Humphrey)*, James Harcourt *(Mr. Humphrey)*, Colin Lesslie *(Tony Lambert)*.

A meek-mannered clerk quits his job after receiving a small inheritance and lavishes it upon himself on a sea cruise during which he pretends to be a successful author, attracting glamorous females but getting himself in hot water. Tepid programmer.

d&w, Anthony Kimmins (based on the play by Ian Hay); ph, Roy Kellino.

Comedy **(PR:A MPAA:NR)**

ALL AT SEA*1/2 (1939, Brit.) 75m British Lion bw

Sandy Powell *(Sandy Skipton)*, Kay Walsh *(Diana)*, John Warwick *(Brown)*, Gus McNaughton *(Nobby)*, George Merritt *(Bull)*, Leslie Perrins *(Williams)*, Franklin Dyall *(Dr. Stolk)*, Robert Rendel *(Sir Herbert)*, Aubrey Mallalieu *(Prof. Myles)*

Idiotic story concerning a factory worker who is sent on an errand but instead of delivering a message inadvertently enlists in the Navy. When stumbling upon spies, he saves an explosives formula. A weak effort to make fun of the then-growing war tensions between England and Germany.

p&d, D. Herbert Smith; w, Gerald Elliott, Reginald Long; ph, Hone Glendinning.

Comedy **(PR:A MPAA:NR)**

ALL AT SEA*** (1958, Brit.) 87M MGM bw (GB: BARNACLE BILL)

Alec Guinness *(Captain Ambrose)*, Irene Browne *(Mrs. Barrington)*, Percy Herbert *(Tommy)*, Harold Goodwin *(Duckworth)*, Maurice Denham *(Crowley)*, Victor Maddern *(Figg)*, George Rose *(Bullen)*, Jackie Collins *(June)*, Junia Crawford *(Evie)*, Lloyd Lamble *(Superintendent Browning)*, Charles Cullum *(Major Kent)*, Joan Hickson *(Mrs. Kent)*, Alexander Harris *(Adrian)*, Warren Mitchell *(Artie White)*, Miles Malleson *(Erudite Angler)*, Sam Kydd *(Frogman)*, Frederick Piper *(Harry)*, Harry Locke *(Peters)*, Richard Wattis *(Registrar of Shipping)*, Eric Pohlmann *(Liberamanian Consul)*, Newton Blick *(Bank Manager)*, Donald Pleasence *(Teller)*, Alec Guinness *(Ambrose's Six Ancestors)*.

Often hilarious film about the scion of a seafaring family trailing back to the stone age, Guinness, who has one problem—he gets deathly ill when the waters are the slightest bit choppy. To solve his dilemma, Guinness opens up a seafarer's hotel and amusement pier, basking in glory that was never his as well as making money. In flashbacks, we see Guinness in the multiple roles of his ancestors: a Stone Age seaman who is berserk by any standard, an inept lieutenant to Admiral Drake, and a wacky naval officer during WW I. Here the great impersonator is in his element, but as the modern weakling he is less inspiring, until turning about bravely when the local citizens, jealous of his newfound prosperity, attempt to destroy his pier. He rallies his sailing buddies and puts up a valiant slapstick battle, saving the old homestead.

p, Michael Balcon; d, Charles Frend; w, T. E. B. Clark; ph, Douglas Slocombe; m, John Addison; ed, Jack Harris.

Comedy **(PR:A MPAA:NR)**

ALL AT SEA*1/2 (1970, Brit.) 60m Anvil/CFF c

Gary Smith *(Steve)*, Steven Mallett *(Ian)*, Stephen Childs *(Douglas)*, Norman Bird *(Mr. Danvers)*, Sara Nicholls *(Vicky)*, Lee Chamberlain *(Jim)*, Ali Soussi *(Hello)*, Peter Copley *(Mr. Gordon)*, Joan Sterndale-Bennett *(Miss Fisby)*, Simon Lack *(Mr. Parker)*

Anemic youngster story about a group of schoolchildren who take a cruise to Portugal and North Africa and, after seeing a thief stealing a rare painting in Tangier, set out to capture him. Short on adventure and long on tedium.

p, Hugh Stewart; d, Ken Fairbairn; w, Patrica Latham.

Children **(PR:A MPAA:NR)**

ALL BY MYSELF** (1943) 63m UNIV bw

Rosemary Lane *(Val Stevenson)*, Evelyn Ankers *(Jean Wells)*, Patric Knowles *(Dr. Bill Perry)*, Neil Hamilton *(Mark Turner)*, Grant Mitchell *(J. D. Gibbons)*, Louise

Beavers (*Willie*), Sarah Edwards (*Woman*), Loumell Morgan Trio, Tip, Tap, and Toe.

Ad man Knowles forgets all about his attractive partner, Ankers, when he falls for torch singer Lane. Aside from a fine job from Ankers, nothing in this routine musical can elevate its below-par status.

p, Bernard W. Burton; d, Felix Feist; w, Hugh Wedlock, Jr., Howard Snyder (based on a story by Dorothy Bennett, Linde Hannah); ph, Paul Ivano; ed, Charley Maynard.

Musical   **(PR:A MPAA:NR)**

ALL CREATURES GREAT AND SMALL***   (1975, Brit.) 92m EMI bw

Simon Ward, Anthony Hopkins, Lisa Harrow, Brian Sirner, Freddie Jones, T. P. McKenna, Brenda Bruce, John Collin, Daphne Oxenford, Christine Buckley, Jane Collins.

Warm-hearted story of a country vet and his practice in rural England which deals with the day-to-day feeding and care of animals and the children who love them. Excellent family entertainment. (Sequel: IT SHOULDN'T HAPPEN TO A VET)

p, David Susskind, Duane Bogie; d, Claude Whatham; w, Hugh Whitemore (based on the book by James Herriot); ph, Peter Suschitzky; m, Wilfred Josephs.

Children   **Cas.**   **(PR:AAA MPAA:NR)**

ALL FALL DOWN**1/2   (1962) 111m MGM bw

Eva Marie Saint (*Echo OBrien*), Warren Beatty (*Berry-Berry Willart*), Karl Malden (*Ralph Willart*), Angela Lansbury (*Annabel Willart*), Brandon de Wilde (*Clinton Willart*), Constance Ford (*Mrs. Mandel*), Barbara Baxley (*Schoolteacher*), Evans Evans (*Hedy*), Jennifer Howard (*Myra*), Madame Spivy (*Bouncer*), Albert Paulsen (*Capt. Ramirez*), Henry Kulky (*Sailor*), Colette Jackson (*Dorothy*), Paul Bryar (*Manager of Sweet Shop*).

Hard-hitting performances by de Wilde and Beatty as two brothers with polarized personalities highlight a generally depressing film. DeWilde idolizes Beatty, refusing to see him for the callous, indifferent and ruthless fellow he is. Malden and Lansbury are superb as the tolerant mother and father who take in Saint. When Beatty returns home he quickly seduces the woman, makes her pregnant, then deserts her, causing Saint to commit suicide. DeWilde, who has loved the woman from afar, finally realizes the true character of his brother and sets out to kill him. When confronting Beatty, however, he loses heart as Beatty sobs like a helpless child. He leaves him, forever free of the spell, finally matured into manhood. The film overreaches itself in making its point and much of it is sordid and dismal for its own sake but the acting is both compelling and memorable. Playwright Inge, author of this film, ironically chose to end his life as did Saint in the film.

p, John Houseman; d, John Frankenheimer; w, William Inge (based on the novel by James Leo Herlihy); ph, Lionel Lindon; m, Alex North; ed, Fredric Steinkamp; art d, George W. Davis, Preston Ames; set d, Henry Grace, George R. Nelson; cos, Dorothy Jeakins.

Drama   **(PR:) MPAA:NR)**

ALL FOR MARY**   (1956, Brit.) 79m RANK c

Nigel Patrick (*Clive Morton*), Kathleen Harrison (*Nannie Cartwright*), David Tomlinson (*Humpy Miller*), Jill Day (*Mary*), David Hurst (*M. Victor*), Leo McKern (*Gaston Nikopopoulos*), Nicholas Phipps (*General*), Joan Young (*Mrs. Hackenfleuger*), Lionel Jeffries (*Maitre d'Hotel*), Paul Hardtmuth (*Porter*), Fabia Drake (*Opulent Lady*), Tommy Farr (*Bruiser*), Charles Lloyd Pack (*Doctor*), Robin Brown (*American Boy*), Dorothy Gordon (*W.R.A.C. Orderly*).

Two British tourists and a rich, obnoxious Greek vie for the affections of Day while all are on holiday in Switzerland. Tired old formula given the standard British treatment, resulting in an enjoyable, but far from classic comedy.

p, J. Arthur Rank; d, Wendy Toye; w, Peter Blackmore, Paul Soskin (based on the play by Harold Brock, Kay Bannerman); ph, Reginald Wyer; m, Robert Farnon; ed, Frederick Wilson.

Comedy   **(PR:A MPAA:NR)**

ALL HANDS ON DECK*   (1961) 98m FOX c

Pat Boone (*Lt. Donald*), Buddy Hackett (*Garfield*), Dennis O'Keefe (*Lt. Comdr. O'Gara*), Barbara Eden (*Sally Hobson*), Warren Berlinger (*Ensign Rush*), Gale Gordon (*Comdr. Bintle*), David Brandon (*Lt. Kutley*), Joe E. Ross (*Bos'n*), Bartlett Robinson (*Lt. Comdr. Anthony*), Paul von Schreiber (*Mulvaney*), Ann B. Davis (*Nobby*), Jody McCrea (*Lt. J. G. Schuyler*), Pat McCaffrie (*Gruber*).

Hopelessly silly shipboard comedy involving wholesome Boone, shapely Eden, crazy Hackett, a turkey, a pelican, and a cross-bred egg. It's all against navy regulations, but it's all forgotten in the end. Forget the movie, period.

p, Oscar Brodney; d, Norman Taurog; w, Jay Sommers (based on a novel by Donald R. Morris); ph, Leo Tover; m, Cyril J. Mockridge; ed, Frederick Y. Smith; art d, Jack Martin Smith, Walter M. Simonds.

Comedy   **(PR:A MPAA:NR)**

ALL I DESIRE**1/2   (1953) 79m UNIV bw

Barbara Stanwyck (*Naomi Murdoch*), Richard Carlson (*Henry Murdoch*), Lyle Bettger (*Dutch Heinemann*), Marcia Henderson (*Joyce Murdoch*), Lori Nelson (*Lily Murdoch*), Maureen O'Sullivan (*Sara Harper*), Richard Long (*Russ Underwood*), Billy Gray (*Ted Murdoch*), Lotte Stein (*Lena Engstrom*), Dayton Lummis (*Col. Underwood*), Fred Nurney (*Peterson*), Guy Williams, Charles Hand.

Actress Stanwyck, divorced from her family, returns to her home town to see her daughter in a school play. Although her lifestyle is much different than the complacent townspeople's, she stays in an attempt to rebuild her family. Director Sirk, a talented social commentator via his soap-opera-like films, was apparently displeased with the happy ending insisted upon by producer Hunter, but Stanwyck's powerful perform ance of a strong woman and the director's dissection of small-town values make this a still-compelling drama, typical of Sirk's excellent work.

p, Ross Hunter; d, Douglas Sirk; w, James Gunn, Robert Blees, Gina Kaus,(based on the novel *Stopover* by Carol Brink); ph, Carl Guthrie; ed, Milton Carruth; m, Joseph Gershenson; art d, Bernard Herzbrun, Alexander Golitzen; set d, Russell A. Gausman, Julia Heron; cos, Rosemary Odell; ch, Kenny Williams.

Drama   **(PR:A MPAA:NR)**

ALL IN**   (1936, Brit.) 71m Gainsborough/GAU bw

Ralph Lynn (*Archie Slott*), Gina Malo (*Kay Slott*), Jack Barty (*Tingaling Tom*), Claude Dampier (*Toop*), Sydney Fairbrother (*Genesta Slott*), Garry Marsh (*Lilleywhite*), Robert Nainby (*Eustace Slott*), O. B. Clarence (*Hemingway*), Gibb McLaughlin (*Rev. Cuppleditch*), Glennis Lorimer (*Kitty*), Fewlass Llewellyn (*Dean of Plinge*), W. Graham Brown, Joan Kemp-Walsh, Bryan Powley, Edwin Durer.

Decent comedy stars Lynn as a man who inherits a stable of race horses. His aunt, a fervent foe of gambling, wants him to turn the building into a home for working girls. A pair of con men show up and soon Lynn not only owns the horses, but a failing wrestling arena as well. Fast-moving and quite enjoyable.

p, Michael Balcon; d, Marcel Varnel; w, Leslie Arliss, Val Guest (based on the play "Tattenham Corner" by Bernard Merivale and Brandon Fleming); ph, Jack Cox.

Comedy   **(PR:A MPAA:NR)**

ALL IN A NIGHT'S WORK**1/2   (1961) 94m PAR c

Dean Martin (*Tony Ryder*), Shirley MacLaine (*Katie Robbins*), Charlie Ruggles (*Dr. Warren Kingsley, Sr.*), Cliff Robertson (*Warren Kingsley, Jr.*), Norma Crane (*Marge Coombs*), Gale Gordon (*Oliver Dunning*), Jerome Cowan (*Sam Weaver*), Jack Weston (*Lasker*), Ian Wolfe (*O'Hara*), Mabel Albertson (*Mrs. Kingsley, Sr.*), Mary Treen (*Miss Schuster*), Rex Evans (*Carter*), Roy Gordon (*Albright*), Charles Evans (*Col. Ryder*), Ralph Dumke (*Baker*), John Hudson (*Harry Lane*), Gertrude Astor (*Customer*), Rosemary Bawe (*Tony's Friend*).

Flaky MacLaine is suspected to be the mysterious woman who spent the night with a rich publishing kingpin, leaving the old geezer dead with a smile on his face. Fearing a scandal and a tremendous blackmail scheme, Martin, heir to the publishing business tries to seduce her and lets her know that he's aware of her sinister "plans." MacLaine, innocent nut that she is, is offended by his accusations and runs off. Martin, realizing that he's made a mistake and is really in love, follows. Enjoyable business-world comedy that uses MacLaine's dizzy charm well. Martin wanders through the film as if he can't wait for the director to yell, "Cut!"

p, Hal B. Wallis; d, Joseph Anthony; w, Edmund Beloin, Maurice Richlin, Sidney Sheldon (based on a story by Margit Veszi and a play by Owen Elford); ph, Joseph LaShelle; m, Andre Previn; ed, Howard Smith; art d, Hal Pereira, Walter Tyler.

Comedy   **Cas.**   **(PR:C MPAA:NR)**

ALL MEN ARE ENEMIES*   (1934) 78m Rocket/FOX bw

Hugh Williams (*Tony*), Helen Twelvetrees (*Katha*), Mona Barrie (*Margaret*), Herbert Mundin (*Noggins*), Henry Stephenson (*Scrope*), Walter Byron (*Walter Ripton*), Una O'Connor (*Annie*), Matt Moore (*Allerton*), Halliwell Hobbes (*Clarendon*), Rafaela Ottiano (*Filomena*), Mathilde Comont (*Mamina*).

No, it's not a radical feminist lesbian propaganda film from the 60s, it's a terrible 30s melodrama telling the story of lovers separated by the war reuniting despite the problems created by their present involvements. This picture was to make male lead Hugh Williams a big star, which it didn't.

d, George Fitzmaurice; w, Samuel Hoffenstein, Lenore Coffee (based on the novel by Richard Aldington); ph, John Seitz; m, Louis DeFrancesco; ed, Harold Schuster.

Drama   **(PR:A MPAA:NR)**

ALL MINE TO GIVE**

                        (1957) 103m UNIV c (GB: THE DAY THEY GAVE BABIES AWAY)

Glynis Johns (*Mamie*), Cameron Mitchell (*Robert*), Rex Thompson (*Robbie*), Patty McCormack (*Annabella*), Ernest Truex (*Dr. Delbert*), Hope Emerson (*Mrs. Pugmire*), Alan Hale (*Tom Cullen*), Sylvia Field (*Lelia Delbert*), Royal Dano (*Howard Tyler*), Reta Shaw (*Mrs. Runyon*), Stephen Wooton (*Jimmie*), Butch Bernard (*Kirk*), Yolanda White (*Elizabeth*), Rita Johnson (*Katie Tyler*), Ellen Corby (*Mrs. Raiden*), Rosalyn Boulter (*Mrs. Stephens*), Francis DeSales (*Mr. Stephens*), Jon Provost (*Bobbie*).

You'll have to keep wringing out your handkerchief during this heartwarming tale of an oldest child's efforts to find his baby siblings homes on Christmas Day after the death of his widowed mom. An intelligent, talented cast saves what could have been a hopelessly schmaltzy tearjerker.

p, Sam Wiesenthal; d, Allen Reisner; w, Dale and Katherine Eunson (based on the *Cosmopolitan* magazine story, "The Day They Gave Babies Away" by Katherine Eunson); ph, William Skall; m, Max Steiner; ed, Alan Crosland, Jr.

Drama   **Cas.**   **(PR:AA MPAA:NR)**

ALL MY SONS****   (1948) 93m UNIV bw

Edward G. Robinson (*Joe Keller*), Burt Lancaster (*Chris Keller*), Mady Christians (*Kate Keller*), Louisa Horton (*Ann Deever*), Howard Duff (*George Deever*), Frank Conroy (*Herbert Deever*), Lloyd Gough (*Jim Bayliss*), Arlene Francis (*Sue Bayliss*), Henry Morgan (*Frank Lubey*), Elisabeth Fraser (*Lydia Lubey*), Walter Soderling (*Charles*), Therese Lyon (*Minnie*), Charles Meredith (*Ellsworth*), William Johnstone (*Attorney*), Herbert Vigran (*Wertheimer*), Harry Harvey (*Judge*), Pat Flaherty (*Bartender*), George Sorel (*Headwaiter*), Helen Brown (*Mrs. Hamilton*), Herbert Haywood (*McGraw*), Joseph Kerr (*Norton*), Jerry Hausner (*Halliday*), Frank Kreig (*Foreman*), William Ruhl (*Ed*), Al Murphy (*Tom*), Walter Boon (*Jorgenson*), Richard La Marr (*Workman*), Victor Zimmerman, George Slocum (*Attendants*).

Arthur Miller's powerful drama tells the story of Robinson, a small-town manufacturer enjoying prosperity following WW II, and that of his doting wife, Christians, and devoted son, Lancaster. Into this apparently tranquil scene steps Horton, who had once been engaged to Robinson's other son Larry, killed in action during the war, even though his mother, Christians, will not accept that grim fact, insisting that her son is only missing, that one day he will come home to her. When Horton begins to fall in love with Lancaster, Christians forbids such a relationship, saying that it is a betrayal of Larry, that Horton should wait for her son to return so that they can be married. Moreover, Horton's brother (Duff) violently opposes marriage between his sister and Lancaster, saying that Robinson's entire family is "blood-stained" because of Robinson's corrupt practices during the war when he manufactured vital military parts. Lancaster begins to investigate, going to see Robinson's partner who is serving time in prison for purposely shipping defective parts to the front, parts that caused plane crashes killing 21 men. The partner, Conroy, tells Lancaster that he is innocent, that Robinson was the one who ordered the parts shipped and escaped prosecution through a legal technicality. Lancaster later confronts Robinson who admits his culpability, losing his son's affection. Then Lancaster shows his father a letter Horton has given to him, one written to her by Larry before his death, which states how Larry intended to go on a suicide mission to make up for his father's criminal and unpatriotic act. The shock of being exposed leads the volatile Robinson to commit suicide. Lancaster and Horton, in love with each other, leave to build a new life in another town where the stigma of Robinson's deed will not follow them. Robinson provides a gripping performance, one of his best, showing the human frailty of his character in all its naked fury and shame, a role matched only by Lancaster's tense, taut presence as an embittered war veteran. Their scenes together are full of sparks and compassion.

p, Chester Erskine; d, Irving Reis; w, Erskine (based on the play by Arthur Miller); ph, Russell Metty; m, Leith Stevens; ed, Ralph Dawson; art d, Bernard Herzbrun, Hilyard Brown; set d, Russell A. Gausman, Al Fields.

Drama **(PR:C MPAA:NR)**

ALL NEAT IN BLACK STOCKINGS** 1/2** (1969, Brit.) 106m NG/Warner-Pathe c

Victor Henry *(Ginger)*, Susan George *(Jill)*, Jack Shepherd *(Dwyer)*, Clare Kelly *(Mother)*, Anna Cropper *(Sis)*, Harry Towb *(Issur)*, Vanessa Forsyth *(Carole)*, Terence de Marney *(Gunge)*, Jasmina Hamzavi *(Babette)*, Nita Lorraine *(Jocasta)*.

Cynical story of a young cad (Henry) who finally settles down with the "right" girl, even though his good-for-nothing mate had impregnated the girl while both were drunk at a party. Resenting the newborn child, his wife, and his basic existence, Henry's eyes start to wander towards new women. British working-class locale and characters add to the realism in this look at a serious flaw in society, but the film is too cold and bleak for its own good.

p, Leon Clore; d, Christopher Morahan; w, Jane Gaskell, Hugh Whitemore (based on the novel by Gaskell); ph, Larry Pizer; m, Robert Cornford; ed, Misha Norland; art d, David Brockhurst.

Drama **(PR:C MPAA:NR)**

ALL NIGHT LONG** 1/2** (1961, Brit.) 95m RANK

Patrick McGoohan *(Johnny Cousin)*, Marti Stevens *(Delia Lane)*, Betsy Blair *(Emily)*, Keith Michel *(Cass Michaels)*, Paul Harris *(Aurelius Rex)*, Richard Attenborough *(Rod Hamilton)*, Bernard Beaden *(Berger)*, Maria Velasco *(Benny)*, Harry Towb *(Phales)*, Dave Brubeck, Johnny Dankworth, Charles Mingus, Tubby Hayes, Keith Christie, Ray Dempsey, Allen Gantley, Bert Courtley, Barry Morgan, Kenny Napper, Colin Purbrook, Johnny Scott, Geoffrey Holder *(Themselves)*.

Jazz group reworking of Shakespeare's "Othello" with drummer McGoohan (in the Iago role) trying to destroy the marriage of bandleader Harris and his wife Stevens, in hopes of becoming the bandleader himself. An admirable attempt to give the typical jazz picture a dramatic structure; the most memorable parts of the film are undoubtedly the brief appearances by greats Dave Brubeck and Charles Mingus.

p, Bob Roberts; d, Michael Relph, Basil Dearden; w, Nel King, Peter Achilles; ph, Ted Scaife; ed, John Guthridge.

Drama **(PR:C MPAA:NR)**

ALL NIGHT LONG** 1/2** (1981) 88m UNIV c

Gene Hackman *(George Dupler)*, Barbra Streisand *(Cheryl Gibbons)*, Diane Ladd *(Helen Dupler)*, Dennis Quaid *(Freddie Dupler)*, Kevin Dobson *(Bobby Gibbons)*, William Daniels *(Richard H. Copleston)*, Hamilton Camp *(Buggams)*, Terry Kiser *(Ultra-Sav Day Manager)*, Charles Siebert *(Nevins)*, Vernee Watson *(Emily)*, Raleigh Bond *(Ultra-Sav Doctor)*, Annie Girardot *(French Teacher)*, Mitzi Hoag *(Nurse)*.

Drugstore manager Hackman rebels against suburbia, his wife, his son, being middle-aged, small-business, and just about anything else he can think of while having an affair with San Fernando Valley housewife Streisand. Although this frantic Southern California comedy never reaches the level of absurdity it should have, Hackman, aided by some fine writing by Richter, turns in an appealing, complex performance as George Dupler, an average guy who has simply had enough. Hackman, one of America's finest actors, has the uncanny ability to turn in an understated but intriguing portrayal in just about any film he is in. It's too bad that this obscure coupling with Streisand didn't reach the heights (or audience) it could have.

p, Leonard Goldberg, Jerry Weintraub; d, Jean-Claude Tramont; w, W. D. Richter; ph, Philip Lathrop; m, Ira Newborn, Richard Hazard; ed, Marion Rothman; prod d, Peter Jamison; set d, Linda Spheeris; cos, Albert Wolsky.

Comedy **Cas.** **(PR:C MPAA:R)**

ALL NUDITY SHALL BE PUNISHED** 1/2** (1974, Brazil) 102m Faria c

Paulo Porto *(Father)*, Darlene Gloria *(Severine)*, Paulo Sacks *(Son)*, Paulo Cesar *(Brother)*, Isabel Ribeiro *(Aunt)*, Hugo Carvana *(Bolivian)*.

Satirical look at a wealthy, proud family whose grief over their matriarch's death and strict morals are completely forgotten when a beautiful prostitute enters their lives. Pleasant, sexy comedy from one of a new group of Brazilian filmmakers determined to tear away at South American social and political values.

p, Paulo Porto; d, Arnaldo Jabor; w, Jabor (based on a play by Nelson Rodrigues); ph, Lauro Escorel; ed, Rafael Justo Valverde.

Comedy **(PR:O MPAA:NR)**

ALL OF ME** 1/2** (1934) 70m PAR bw

Fredric March *(Don Ellis)*, Miriam Hopkins *(Lydia Darrow)*, George Raft *(Honey Rogers)*, Helen Mack *(Eve Haron)*, Nella Walker *(Mrs. Darrow)*, William Collier, Jr. *(Jerry Helman)*, Gilbert Emery *(Dean)*, Blanche Frederici *(Miss Haskell)*, Kitty Kelly *(Lorraine)*, Guy Usher *(District Attorney)*, John Marston *(Nat Davis)*, Edgar Kennedy *(Guard)*.

Strange March vehicle which he shares in a strong sub-plot with Raft, a film going in two different directions at the same time. March is an engineering teacher wanting to escape a crowded campus for a special project near Boulder Dam. His wealthy student-mistress, Hopkins, is reluctant to rough it in the wilds with him. While they talk it over they meet a couple in a nightclub, Raft, a thief, and his girl, Mack. Raft tells his girl friend Mack that March and Hopkins are only "a couple of lugs learnin' about life," and explains to his upper-class companions the meaning of a low-born life. He steals Hopkins' purse, not for his own ends, but to help his pregnant girl friend. He later breaks jail to be with her in her hour of need, a break arranged for by a compassionate Hopkins. Raft kills a cop in his escape and takes Hopkins and Mack to a hotel room which the police besiege. As Hopkins cowers in a corner during a wild shootout, Raft and Mack vow their eternal love and that they will never again be separated. They step to the window and together make a death dive to the street far below. Hopkins has learned the meaning of true love and devotion, returning to March and going West with him into a new life. The improbable ending was highly criticized when first released, as was the first part of the film which is mostly blathering talk and the almost complete disappearance of March in the second half which is given over to Raft's melodramatics and a wow finish.

p, Louis Lighton; d, James Flood; w, Sidney Buchman, Thomas Mitchell (based on the play "Chrysalis" by Rose Porter); ph, Victor Milner; ed, Otho Lovering; m/l, Ralph Rainger, Leo Robin.

Drama **(PR:C MPAA:NR)**

ALL OVER TOWN* 1/2** (1937) 63m REP bw

Ole Olsen *(Olsen)*, Chic Johnson *(Johnson)*, Mary Howard *(Joan Eldridge)*, Harry Stockwell *(Don Fletcher)*, Franklin Pangborn *(Costumer)*, James Finlayson *(MacDougal)*, Eddie Kane *(Bailey)*, Stanley Fields *(Slug)*, D'Arcy Corrigan *(Davenport)*, Lew Kelly *(Martin)*, John Sheehan *(McKee)*, Earle Hodgins *(Barker)*, Gertrude Astor *(Mamie)*, Blanche Payson *(Mrs. Wilson)*, Otto Hoffman *(Phillips)*, Fred Kelsey *(Inspector Murphy)*.

Tired, worthless vaudevillian comedy with forgotten comics Olsen and Johnson trying to save a theatrical boarding house from the bank. Look hard and fast for Alan Ladd in a barely noticeable part.

p, Leonard Fields; d, James Horne; w, Jack Townley, Jerome Chodorov (based on a story by Richard English); ph, Ernest Miller.

Comedy **Cas.** **(PR:A MPAA:NR)**

ALL OVER THE TOWN** 1/2** (1949, Brit.) 88m RANK/GFD

Norman Wooland *(Nat Hearn)*, Sarah Churchill *(Sally Thorpe)*, Cyril Cusack *(Gerald Vane)*, Ronald Adam *(Sam Vane)*, Bryan Forbes *(Trumble)*, James Hayter *(Baines)*, Fabia Drake *(Miss Gelding)*, John Salew *(Sleek)*, Edward Rigby *(Grimmett)*, Patric Doonan *(Burton)*, Eleanor Summerfield *(Beryl Hopper)*, Trevor Jones *(Tenor)*, Sandra Dorne *(Marlene)*, Frederick Leister *(Wainer)*.

Ex-soldier Wooland returns to his home town and takes over the small newspaper, annoying the local businessmen who had been controlling the paper's content. Good- spirited British village comedy promising nothing more than a pleasant story.

p, Ian Dalrymple; d, Derek Twist; w, Twist, Michael Gordon (based on a play by R. F. Delderfield); ph, C. Pennington-Richards, Nigel C. Huke.

Comedy **(PR:AA MPAA:NR)**

ALL QUIET ON THE WESTERN FRONT******* (1930) 140m UNI bw

Louis Wolheim *(Katczinsky)*, Lew Ayres *(Paul Baumer)*, John Wray *(Himmelstoss)*, George "Slim" Summerville, *(Tjaden)*, Russell Gleason *(Muller)*, William Bakewell *(Albert)*, Scott Kolk *(Leer)*, Walter Browne Rogers *(Behm)*, Ben Alexander *(Kemmerick)*, Owen Davis, Jr. *(Peter)*, Harold Goodwin *(Detering)*, Pat Collins *(Lieut. Berlenck)*, Richard Alexander *(Westhus)*, Arnold Lucy *(Professor Kantorek)*, Heinie Conklin *(Hammacher)*, Edmund Breese *(Herr Mayer)*, Bodil Rosing *(Wachter)*, Bill Irving *(Ginger)*, Marion Clayton *(Miss Baumer)*, Beryl Mercer *(Mrs. Baumer)*, Edwin Maxwell *(Mr. Baumer)*, Yola d'Avril *(Suzanne)*, Renee Damonde, Poupee Andriot *(French Girls)*, Bertha Mann *(Sister Libertine)*, Joan Marsh *(Poster Girl)*, Fred Zinnemann *(Man)*.

Here is one of the great anti-war films ever made, a trenchant indictment of war, as well as the most graphic war film of its day, equalled perhaps by only one or two films since its time. Ironically, the film's greatest impact was in the U.S., despite the fact that it presented the German side of WW I, or profiled the front-line troops, young boys who were led to slaughter on the Western Front. The story centers on Ayres, an energetic, sensitive youth who is recruited, along with his entire class, by a war-mongering professor (Lucy) advocating "glory for the Fatherland." He and his friends enlist, are trained by Wray, kindly postmaster turned brutal corporal, and sent to the front lines to taste battle, blood, and death. Ayres comes under the protective wing of old veteran Wolheim, one of the ugliest and most wonderful character actors ever to grace the screen with an enormous talent. Wolheim teaches his young charges when to drop to the ground during a bombardment, how to "hug Mother earth," how not to bury one's head too deep to avoid concussion, how to get through wire and slither like a snake through no man's land, while all the while foraging but mostly stealing food; the German army is already on its last legs and its supplies are dwindling, its troops starving. One by one, Ayres' boyhood friends are killed, blown up under a barrage, machine-gunned to death in useless charges. Older soldiers such as Slim Summerville, who provides momentary comic relief inside the awful chaos, become as grim as their day-to-day survival. Summerville remarks: "Me and the Kaiser; we are both fighting, with the only difference the Kaiser isn't here." Wolheim is more acid in his views, telling Ayres in a moment of dugout respite: "At the next war, let all the Kaisers, Presidents, Generals, and diplomats go into a big field and fight it out first amongst themselves. That will satisfy us and keep us at home." Ayres does go home himself, after miraculously recovering from a near-fatal wound. He lies to his sick mother, Mercer, telling her that it "isn't so bad" at the front, that he has all the food he wants and is kept warm and mostly safe. When she cautions him about loose women he tells her not to worry (he's already experienced his first affair with some French girls who have traded their favors for a loaf of bread and a roll of sausage). Returning to his school he hears his teacher giving the same jingoistic speech to a new group of even younger boys and is asked to tell the youths about the glories of the war. "We fight; we try not to be killed," he begins lamely, then blurts in anger at the man who sent him and his friends to early deaths: "You still think it's beautiful to die for your country. The first bombardment taught us better! When it comes to dying for your country, it's better not to die at all!" He is hissed and booed from the classroom, branded a traitor. By then it means little to Ayres, a young man grown old within a year of battle. He is now filled with the memory of war, awful nightmares such as the moment when he dove into a shell crater and stabbed a French soldier, watching him slowly die through the night, covering his mouth to prevent him from crying out in pain so that passing enemy troops would not find him, then begging him not to die, trying to prevent him from bleeding to death. When the soldier does die, Ayres takes his papers, promising the corpse that he will take care of his family. (The silent comedian Raymond Griffith begged for this cameo part of the dying French Soldier and got it, giving an incredible performance without uttering a word.) Ayres returns to the front, not using up his leave; he is more at home in battle now, resigned to his fate. Most of his old company has been decimated, replaced by green troops, more "cannon fodder." But he does find Wolheim still alive, foraging to feed the youngsters. Just as they meet, a passing enemy plane drops a bomb, wounding Wolheim. Ayres begins carrying him to a first-aid tent but another bomb splinter kills him and Ayres discovers his best friend is dead by the time he reaches the medics. Ayres is back in the trenches alone on a seemingly peaceful day. He sees a butterfly land just beyond the trench—as a youth he had collected the species—and he begins to reach for it, just as an enemy sniper focuses in on him. He reaches further and a shot rings out. His hand twitches, then goes limp; the youth is dead. As a grim epilog we see black hills covered with endless crosses and superimposed on this Ayres and his classmates marching away, turning to look hauntingly at the viewer, accusingly if you will, a generation staring back from an early grave dug by politicians and saber-rattling generals. The impact of this film is devastating, emotionally draining, and so riveting and realistic that it should be forever etched in the mind of any viewer. Milestone's magnificent direction is clipped and economical, not a shot is wasted, from the period of training to the awesome war scenes, both French and German troops charging across no-man's-land into bone-ripping bombardment and machine-gun fire that cuts down hundreds (one quick scene shows a human hand, sliced from its corpse, still clutching a piece of barbed wire). Universal spared no expense in its production, converting more than twenty acres of a large California ranch into battlefields occupied by more than 2,000 ex-servicemen as extras. The world had never seen anything like this film, hard warfare the way it is, brutal gunfire, merciless death on all sides, grim, dirty, relentless. THE BIG PARADE, the only film of the silent era attempting to chronicle WW I, offered some harrowing moments but its happy ending was fantasy. Here were the true horrors of war in all their monstrous forms, fashioned in a film that is unforgettable, yet, after its initial release, some foreign countries refused to run it. Poland inexplicably banned it as being pro-German. In Germany, the Nazis went crazy with anger over the film, labeling it anti-German. Joseph Goebbels, later propaganda minister, denounced the film in rabid speeches. He personally led pickets in front of the few theaters daring to show the film, labeling it pacifistic. He ordered storm troopers in Berlin to riot inside theaters showing the film. These thugs threw rocks through the screens and let loose snakes and rats among the panicking audiences. The Censor Board later banned the movie, stating that it sought to "damn the reputation of Germany." Producer Carl Laemmle, Jr. (son of Universal's founder), fought back, calling press conferences and stating that the film, which had cost Universal $1,250,000 (then a staggering amount), was designed to establish good will toward Germany and its people, not to condemn either, that its anti-war theme would help to curb future wars. *Variety* agreed wholeheartedly, urging the League of Nations to support it, stating that that titular body "could make no better investment than to buy the master print, reproduce it in every language for every nation to be shown every year until the word 'War' shall have been taken out of the dictionaries." Other Americans hated the film and said so; Maj. Frank Pease, who headed the Hollywood Technical Directors Institute, labeled the film brazen "propaganda," adding that it was created to "undermine belief in the Army and in authority." Pease even tried to have the film banned in the U.S., with little success. The Nazis had greater success in punishing the great author of this book, Erich Maria Remarque, who had fought on the Western Front and had been wounded five times. He was hounded by Nazi goons until leaving the country and shortly thereafter his bank accounts were confiscated and all his books burned in public. Remarque immigrated to the U.S. where he continued to write his stirring novels, profiling the Nazi menace in such books as *The Road Back, Three Comrades, The Black Obelisk* and *The Arch of Triumph.* Universal was sensitive to all manner of reaction regarding this triumphant film. ZaSu Pitts, noted chiefly for her comedic roles, appeared in the original print as Ayres' mother, but when the film was previewed, audiences, to Laemmle's horror, began laughing at her most dramatic scenes with Ayres. She had recently appeared in a popular comedy so the viewers were primed for laughter. The film was pulled and all of Pitts' scenes were reshot with Beryl Mercer replacing her, yet the European prints had already been sent abroad so Pitts remained as Ayres' mother in its first foreign run. The film's star, 20-year-old Ayres, proved to be as sensational off screen as the film itself. A mild-mannered youth who was discovered playing in the band at the posh Coconut Grove nightclub in downtown Los Angeles, he was hired as a bit player and shot to fame by playing opposite Greta Garbo in THE KISS in 1929, followed by ALL QUIET ON THE WESTERN FRONT (selected for this film by dialog director George Cukor). He proved as pacifistic as the hero he played (the film reportedly formed his rigid non-violent convictions). After appearing in the popular Dr. Kildare series he shocked America at the beginning of WW II by stating that he was a conscientious objector and fell into mass disfavor. Yet he was redeemed in the public eye when it was made known that he served bravely throughout the war as a medic who risked his life repeatedly under fire to save wounded soldiers. The film received an Academy Award as Best Picture and Milestone, who was best known up to that time as the Oscar-winning director of the 1927 silent war comedy, TWO ARABIAN NIGHTS (for which he became the first and last director to win in the category of comedy-directing), took home an Oscar for ALL QUIET ON THE WESTERN FRONT. The extravagant three-hour TV remake in 1979, costing $6 million and featuring Richard Thomas in the Ayres role, had nowhere the impact or quality of the original film, an exercise in utter futility. Nothing can match the 1930 production of ALL QUIET ON THE WESTERN FRONT. It is truly one of a kind. Sequel: THE ROAD BACK.

p, Carl Laemmle, Jr.; d, Lewis Milestone; w, Del Andrews, Maxwell Anderson, George Abbott, (and, uncredited, Milestone) (based on the novel by Erich Maria Remarque); ph, Arthur Edeson (and, uncredited, Karl Freund); m, David Broekman; ed, Edgar Adams, Milton Carruth; art d, Charles D. Hall, William R. Schmidt; spec eff, Frank H. Booth.

War **Cas.** **(PR:C MPAA:NR)**

ALL RIGHT, MY FRIEND***1/2** (1983, Japan) 119m Kitty/Toho c

Peter Fonda (*Gonzy Traumerai*), Jinpachi Nezu (*Doctor*), Reona Hirota (*Mimimi*), Hiroyuki Watanabe (*Hachi*), Yoshiyuki Noo (*Monika*), Kumi Aoichi (*Reiko*).

Borrowing from E. T., SUPERMAN, DR. NO, and a host of other American movies, director Murakami tells the not-too-serious tale of super-human alien Fonda who arrives in Japan and the three good-natured souls who try to keep him hidden from the evil business organization called the Doors, who wish to clone Fonda and build a master race. Sound pretty dumb and schlocky? Well, you're right.

p, Hidenori Taga; d&w Ryu Murakami; ph, Kozo Okazaki; ed, Sachiko Yamaji; md, Kazuhiko Katch; art d, Osamu Yamaguchi.

Science Fiction **(PR:A MPAA:NR)**

ALL SCREWED UP****1/2** (1976, Ital.) 105m New Line Cinema c

(AKA: ALL IN PLACE; NOTHING IN ORDER)

Luigi Diberti (*Gigi*), Lina Polito (*Mariuccia*), Nino Bignamini (*Carletto*), Sara Rapisarda (*Adelina*), Guiliana Calandra (*Biki*), Isa Danieli (*Isotta*), Eros Pagni (*Bagonghi*).

Half comedy, half drama detailing the lives of some rural folks who move to the city where they find adjustment next to impossible. Director Wertmuller typically indulges herself with overlong and pointless scenes shot for aesthetic gratification but some brilliance does shine through. (In Italian; English subtitles.)

p, Romano Cardarelli; d&w, Lina Wertmuller; ph, Guiseppe Rotunno; m, Piero Piccioni; ed, Franco Fraticelli; set d&cos, Enrico Job.

Drama/Comedy **Cas.** **(PR:O MPAA:NR)**

ALL THAT GLITTERS***1/2** (1936, Brit.) 72m GS Enterprises bw

Jack Hobbs (*Jack Tolley*), Moira Lynd (*Angela Burrows*), Aubrey Mallalieu (*Flint*), Kay Walsh (*Eve Payne-Coade*), Annie Esmond (*Mrs. Payne-Coade*), Fred Duprez (*Mortimer*), John Robinson (*Taylor*), Dick Francis (*Derek Montague*).

Silly production has the past owner of a gold mine outwitting swindlers attempting to mulct his claim from him. Not much of a story and little humor adds up to a yawner.

p, A. George Smith; d, Maclean Rogers; w, Denison Clift; ph, Geoffrey Faithfull.

Comedy **(PR:A MPAA:NR)**

ALL THAT HEAVEN ALLOWS**** (1955) 89m UNIV c

Jane Wyman (*Cary Scott*), Rock Hudson (*Ron Kirby*), Agnes Moorehead (*Sara Warren*), Conrad Nagel (*Harvey*), Virginia Grey (*Alida Anderson*), Gloria Talbot (*Kay Scott*), William Reynolds (*Ned Scott*), Jacqueline De Witt (*Mona Flash*), Charles Drake (*Mick Anderson*), Leigh Snowden (*Jo-Ann*), Donald Curtis (*Howard Hoffer*), Alex Gerry (*George Warren*).

Small-town widow Wyman falls in love with gardener/outdoorsman Hudson, who is 15 years her junior. Succumbing to the pressure of her family and social peers, she stops seeing the equally loving Hudson and settles into a lonely little niche. Finally rebelling against her boring, conformist surroundings, she goes to Hudson's farm and, after a melodramatic near-miss, the two finally end up in each other's arms. One of the greatest neglected talents of American film (particularly the 1950s), Douglas Sirk used the typical melodrama as a structure for his analysis of existing social values, the power of love, and the need for human expression. ALL THAT HEAVEN ALLOWS is one of his finest works, a lushly stylized and photographed commentary on the emotional numbness of suburban life, a lifestyle that condemns those who show spirit and vitality. Wyman and Hudson, typical Sirk heroes, transcend the cold world around them to build a new life through love. Sirk was not an idealist, his criticism of people is too strong for one, but his films convey a sense of hope, a sense, interestingly, that was dropped by German director Rainer Werner Fassbinder in his social melodramas that are heavily influenced by Sirk.

p, Ross Hunter; d, Douglas Sirk; w, Peggy Fenwick (based on a story by Edna Lee, Harry Lee); ph, Russell Metty (Technicolor); m, Frank Skinner, Joseph Gershenson; ed, Frank Gross, Fred Baratta; art d, Alexander Golitzen, Eric Orbom; set d, Russell A. Gausman, Julia Heron; cos, Bill Thomas.

Drama **(PR:A MPAA:NR)**

ALL THAT JAZZ****1/2** (1979) 123m COL/FOX c

Roy Scheider (*Joe Gideon*), Jessica Lange (*Angelique*), Ann Reinking (*Kate Jagger*), Leland Palmer (*Audrey Paris*), Cliff Gorman (*David Newman*), Ben Vereen (*O'Connor Flood*), Erzebet Foldi (*Michelle*), Michael Tolan (*Dr. Ballinger*), Max Wright (*Joshua Benn*), William La Messena (*Jonesy Hecht*), Chris Chase (*Leslie Perry*), Deborah Geffner (*Victoria*), Kathryn Doby (*Kathryn*), Anthony Holland (*Paul Dann*), Robert Hitt (*Ted Christopher*), David Margulies (*Larry Goldie*), Sue Paul (*Stacy*), Keith Gordon (*Young Joe*), Frankie Man (*Comic*), Alan Heim (*Eddie*), John Lithgow (*Lucas Sergeant*).

Scheider, as Bob Fosse's alter ego, is a hell-bent-for-leather choreographer maniacally driving his dancers and himself while preparing a musical and at the same time editing a movie, so exhausting a chore that he suffers a fatal heart attack and hallucinates wild choreographic numbers before the end (not unlike the visions of Jose Ferrer in his last moments as Lautrec in MOULIN ROUGE where the dancers of the Folies Bergere come prancing by his deathbed.) The dancing is the acrobatic frenzied sort which Fosse fans adore but the story is a paean of self-praise that is more than embarrassing, in fact it's blatantly self-serving. The photography is superb, especially of the dance sequences, but it would have been better to get a more solid story before the cameras. This semi-autobiographical opus grossed $20 million.

p, Robert Alan Arthur; d, Bob Fosse; w, Arthur, Fosse; ph, Giuseppe Rotunno (Technicolor); m, Ralph Burns; ed, Alan Heim; set d, Philip Rosenberg; cos, Albert Wolsky; ch, Fosse.

Musical/Drama Cas. (PR:O MPAA:R)

ALL THAT MONEY CAN BUY
(SEE: DEVIL AND DANIEL WEBSTER, THE, 1941)

ALL THE BROTHERS WERE VALIANT* 1/2** (1953) 94m MGM c

Robert Taylor *(Joel Shore)*, Stewart Granger *(Mark Shore)*, Ann Blyth *(Priscilla Holt)*, Betta St. John *(Native Girl)*, Keenan Wynn *(Silva)*, James Whitmore *(Fetcher)*, Kurt Kasznar *(Quint)*, Lewis Stone *(Capt. Holt)*, Robert Burton *(Asa Worthen)*, Peter Whitney *(James Finch)*, John Lupton *(Dick Morrell)*, Jonathan Cott *(Carter)*, Mitchell Lewis *(Cook)*, James Bell *(Aaron Burnham)*, Leo Gordon *(Peter How)*, Michael Pate *(Varde)*, Clancy Cooper *(Smith)*, Frank deKova *(Stevenson)*, Henry Rowland *(Jones)*.

Taylor and Granger are brothers in a family that traditionally makes its trade in whaling but Granger, filled with wanderlust, goes off to seek exotic adventures, landing on an island where, with the help of native St. John, he finds a cache of priceless black pearls. Meanwhile, back in New England, down-to-earth Taylor woos and wins Blyth, who was once engaged to Granger. Married, the couple set off on whaling business but Taylor believes his brother may still be alive and steers a searching course across the Pacific. He locates Granger who has escaped the island after natives, angry over his theft of their sacred pearls, have killed St. John and narrowly missed taking Granger's life. Once Granger is on board the family ship he begins to make advances to Blyth and foment unrest among the crew members, telling them to forget harpooning whales and turn the ship about and make sail for the island to retrieve the black pearls he has dropped in shallow water. Lust for riches inflames the crew to mutiny against skipper Taylor who appears to be a coward, refusing to attack his brother, and losing Blyth's respect. He is locked in irons as Granger takes over the crew and is about to win Blyth's favor. Then Taylor escapes with the help of some loyal hands and a five-by-five brawl ensues on board, with Taylor's side losing. Just as Taylor is about to be killed, Granger's sibling instincts come to the fore and he steps in front of his brother to receive a mortal wound. At the sight of their leader dying the mutinous crew members lay down their weapons and Blyth flies to her husband's arms. Taylor is able to write in his log that his brother died valiantly, not a traitor, as the ship sails peacefully for home. Bathed in beautiful color photography, this film is a fast-paced yarn that makes up for its implausible script with action aplenty and rich production values. Taylor did not like the story nor working with Granger, whom he thought too stuffy, but their scenes together were strong and convincing. This was the last film made by MGM's venerable character actor Lewis Stone, best known as Judge Hardy in the popular Andy Hardy series; two weeks after completing this film, Stone, dressed in bathrobe, pajamas, and slippers, age 74, raced from his home in the middle of the night to chase teenagers vandalizing his property and died on the sidewalk of a heart attack. (First filmed by MGM in 1923, remade as a silent in 1928 as ACROSS TO SINGAPORE with Joan Crawford and Ramon Novarro and Ernest Torrence as the saintly and devilish brothers.)

p, Pandro S. Berman; d, Richard Thorpe; w, Harry Brown (based on the novel by Ben Ames Williams); ph, George Folsey (Technicolor); m, Miklos Rozsa; ed, Ferris Webster; spec eff, A. Arnold Gillespie, Warren Newcombe.

Adventure (PR:A MPAA:NR)

ALL THE FINE YOUNG CANNIBALS* 1/2 (1960) 112m MGM c

Robert Wagner *(Chad Bixby)*, Natalie Wood *(Salome Davis)*, Susan Kohner *(Catherine McDowall)*, George Hamilton *(Tony McDowall)*, Pearl Bailey *(Ruby Jones)*, Jack Mullaney *(Putney Tinker)*, Onslow Stevens *(Joshua Davis)*, Anne Seymour *(Mrs. Bixby)*, Virginia Gregg *(Ada Davis)*, Mabel Albertson *(Mrs. McDowall)*, Louise Beavers *(Rose)*, Addison Richards *(Mr. McDowall)*.

Ah, the idle rich! With nothing to do but fool around with each other's husbands and wives, you would think they could be happy, but alas, no. In this complete waste of film stock, unhappy but incredibly wealthy couples Wagner/Kohner and Wood/Hamilton must deal with a little tot that Wagner and Wood happened to create before they married their present spouses. No, the title has nothing to do with their decision.

p, Pandro S. Berman; d, Michael Anderson; w, Robert Thom (based on the "The Bixby Girls" by Rosamond Marshall); ph, William H. Daniels (CinemaScope, Metrocolor); m, Jeff Alexander; ed, John McSweeney, Jr.; art d, George W. Davis.

Drama (PR:C MPAA:NR)

ALL THE KING'S HORSES* 1/2 (1935) 86m PAR bw

Carl Brisson *(King Rudolph/Carl Rocco)*, Mary Ellis *(Elaine, the Queen)*, Edward Everett Horton *(Peppi)*, Katherine DeMille *(Mimi)*, Eugene Pallette *(Con Conley)*, Arnold Korff *(Baron Kraemer)*, Marina Schubert *(Steffi)*, Stanley Andrews *(Count Batthy)*.

Poor musical about a Hollywood actor visiting a small country; he is the king's look-alike and the trouble he starts with the beautiful queen culminates in this absurd operetta lifted from *The Prisoner of Zenda*. All the king's horses and all the king's men couldn't put Humpty Dumpty back together again and they'd have even more trouble with this rotten egg.

p, William LeBaron; d, Frank Tuttle; w, Tuttle, Frederick Stefani (based on the play by Frederick, Herendeen, Edward Horan from the operetta by Laurence Clark, Max Glersberg); ph, Henry Sharp; m, Sam Coslow; ch, LeRoy Prinz.

Musical Comedy (PR:A MPAA:None)

ALL THE KING'S MEN*** 1/2** (1949) 109m COL bw

Broderick Crawford *(Willie Stark)*, Joanne Dru *(Anne Stanton)*, John Ireland *(Jack Burden)*, John Derek *(Tom Stark)*, Mercedes McCambridge *(Sadie Burke)*, Shepperd Strudwick *(Adam Stanton)*, Ralph Dumke *(Tiny Duffy)*, Anne Seymour *(Lucy Stark)*, Katharine Warren *(Mrs. Burden)*, Raymond Greenleaf *(Judge Stanton)*, Walter Burke *(Sugar Boy)*, Will Wright *(Dolph Pillsbury)*, Grandon Rhodes *(Floyd McEvoy)*, H. C. Miller *(Pa Stark)*, Richard Hale *(Hale)*, William Bruce *(Commissioner)*, A. C. Tillman *(Sheriff)*, Houseley Stevenson *(Madison)*, Truett Myers *(Minister)*, Phil Tully *(Football Coach)*, Helene Stanley *(Helene Hale)*, Judd Holdren *(Politician)*, Paul Ford *(Man)*, Ted French *(Dance Caller)*.

Willie Stark (Crawford) is a creature from the backwaters of a southern state illiterate, well-intentioned, groping for identity. He is seen as the viewer sees him,—through the scrutinizing eyes of Ireland, a newsman who first meets Crawford when he is fumbling about as a political hopeful, his local campaign dying because of his ineffective delivery and obscure identity. He warns of a poorly constructed school building among many of his accusations against the state machine but goes unheard and loses his race, buried by a political organization having the power and wealth to control the election. Dogged, Crawford begins to study law while his wife, Seymour, and adopted son, Derek, suffer but support him. Then the school building Crawford had cited as dangerous collapses, killing scores of youngsters. The people in his community become enraged, remembering Crawford's warning, and the ground swell of support for his candidacy begins. Again Crawford goes on the stump, this time backed by insidious machine politicians who intend to use him but make sure he loses by insisting that he deliver statistically boring speeches which diminish rather than increase his following. Ireland and a political aide, McCambridge, take him aside and show him exactly how he is being manipulated. Crawford explodes and at the very next rally tosses away the speech prepared for him and launches into a down-home address, labeling himself a sucker and a hick, "just like all you hicks." His fiery outburst ignites the people, who identify with him, loving his blazing oratory which has been born out of anger. He loses again but in the next election, once more backed by the machine, Crawford is a wiser candidate, using the same backwoods appeal but playing both ends against the middle by wheeling and dealing with the very forces he appears to attack in public. He wins this time by a landslide, becoming governor of the state. Crawford builds new highways, hospitals, bridges, and schools, appearing to improve his state vastly, but the underpinnings of his administration are rotten with corruption, bribes, payoffs, and intimidation (Crawford maintains a private army of police and armed thugs who make sure no one publicly objects to his fascist methods). Crawford's mania for power increases until he insists a respectable girl, Dru, become his mistress, and ruins the career of her uncle, an upstanding judge who dies prematurely under the pressure of Crawford's underhanded tactics. In retaliation for dumping his sister and his uncle's death, Strudwick, a sensitive doctor, decides to rid the state of the demagogue and shoots Crawford in the foyer of the Capitol Building, being killed himself in a hail of bullets fired by bodyguards. This grimly realistic film, long a pet project of producer-director-writer Robert Rossen served as a break-out film for Crawford who had previously been confined to B films. In it, he let loose a fierce and awesome character whose cunning, brutality, and ambition forever locked in the public imagination, a tour de force never again equalled by the actor and one which deservedly won him an Academy Award. The character of Willie Stark as profiled in the novel by Robert Penn Warren was most certainly inspired by Louisiana bigwig Huey Pierce Long, the notorious "Kingfish" who ruled the state as governor and later senator with an iron hand, soaking the wealthy and building public works projects during the depression more to enhance his own status than to benefit his constituents. And it was Long's own demagoguery, so accurately profiled in this film, that brought about his own assassination in 1935 by Dr. Carl Austin Weiss, a 29-year-old Baton Rouge physician whose sister may or may not have been raped by Long. Rossen's film exemplifies with compelling scenes the life it chronicled, one of raw power. McCam bridge as the equally callous and conniving political aide almost matched Crawford's animal dynamism, also winning an Oscar for her tough performance. Rossen shot the film in Stockton, California, a working-class town, enlisting the aid of hundreds of citizens as extras and bit players, and these folk helped to give that added edge of authenticity to the production. A hallmark political film. (McCambridge's debut.)

p,d&w, Robert Rossen (based on the novel by Robert Penn Warren); ph, Burnett Guffey; m, Louis Gruenberg; ed, Al Clark.

Drama (PR:C MPAA:NR)

. . . ALL THE MARBLES 1/2**
(1981) 112m MGM/UA c (GB: CALIFORNIA DOLLS, THE)

Peter Falk *(Harry)*, Vicki Frederick *(Iris)*, Laurence Landon *(Molly)*, Burt Young *(Eddie)*, Tracy Reed *(Diane)*, Ursaline Bryant-King *(June)*, John Hancock *(Big John)*, Claudette Nevins *(Solly)*, Richard Jaeckel *(Referee)*.

Veteran action director Aldrich fails to bring this curious mixture of mildly sexual comedy and sports drama to life. Falk, as the manager of a tag-team women's wrestling pair body-slamming their way to the top, has a comfortable, humorous rapport with Frederick and Landon (who play his wrestlers), but the natural-flowing comedy is lost when the film takes on a cliche come-from-behind seriousness. The two female newcomers are both pretty and talented, but the movie itself is a bit disappointing.

p, William Aldrich; d, Robert Aldrich; w, Mel Frohman; ph, Joseph Biroc (Metrocolor); m, Frank De Vol; ed, Irving C. Rosenblum, Richard Lane; prod d, Carl Anderson; art d, Beala Neel; cos, Bob Mackie.

Comedy Cas. (PR:C MPAA:R)

ALL THE OTHER GIRLS DO! 1/2**
(1967, Ital.) 90m Harlequin International/Noonan Warfield c

Rosemarie Dexter *(Giovenella)*, Jacques Perrin *(Gabrielie)*, Folco Lulli *(His Father)*, Magali Noel *(Giovenella's Sister)*, Gina Rovere *(Giovenella's Mother)*, Bice Valori *(Giovenella's Father)*, Luisa Dalla Noce *(Mistress)*.

Small-time story about a boy and girl who shyly attempt a first affair, urged on by a hedonist father, Lulli, whose expansive vulgarity is the absurd highlight of this otherwise tame sex farce.

p, Saggitario Tirso; d, Silvio Amadio; w, Amadio, Carlo Romano.

Romance (PR:C MPAA:NR)

ALL THE PRESIDENT'S MEN*½** (1976) 138mm WB c

Dustin Hoffman *(Carl Bernstein)*, Robert Redford *(Bob Woodward)*, Jack Warden *(Harry Rosenfeld)*, Martin Balsam *(Howard Simons)*, Hal Holbrook *(Deep Throat)*, Jason Robards *(Ben Bradlee)*, Jane Alexander *(Bookkeeper)*, Meredith Baxter *(Debbie Sloan)*, Ned Beatty *(Dardis)*, Stephen Collins *(Hugh Sloan, Jr.)*, Penny Fuller *(Sally Aiken)*, John McMartin *(Foreign Editor)*, Robert Walden *(Donald Segretti)*, Frank Wills *(Frank Wills)*, F. Murray Abraham *(1st Arresting Officer)*, David Arkin *(Bachinski)*, Henry Calvert *(Barker)*, Dominic Chianese *(Martinez)*, Bryan E. Clark *(Arguing Attorney)*, Nicholas Coster *(Markham)*, Lindsay Ann Crouse *(Kay Eddy)*, Valerie Curtin *(Miss Milland)*, Cara Duff-MacCormick *(Tammy Ulrich)*, Gene Dynarski *(Clerk)*, Nate Esformes *(Gonzales)*, Ron Hale *(Sturgis)*, Richard Herd *(McCord)*, Polly Holliday *(Secretary)*, Kames Karen *(Lawyer)*, Paul Lambert *(Editor)*, Frank Latimore *(Judge)*, Gene Lindsey *(Baldwin)*, Anthony Mannino *(Officer)*, Allyn Ann McLerie *(Carolyn)*, James Murtaugh *(Clerk)*, John O'Leary *(Attorney)*, Jess Osuna *(FBI Man)*, Neva Patterson *(Angry Woman)*, George Pentecost *(George)*, Penny Peyser *(Sharon)*, Joshua Shelly *(Al)*, Sloane Shelton *(Sister)*, Lelan Smith *(Officer)*, Jaye Stewart *(Librarian)*, Ralph Williams *(Ray)*, George Wyner *(Attorney)*.

Unlike most politically oriented films, this production was a landmark achievement in relating just how Woodward and Bernstein came upon the greatest newspaper scoop of the last decade, the Watergate scandal and the ruination of Nixon's administration. Hoffman as Bernstein is his usual jittery, quirkish self, relentlessly probing for informa- tion in the ongoing investigation he launched with Woodward (Redford). Like most great stories, it begins routinely with the reporters covering a lackluster burglary. But their discovery that two of the break-in artists have the phone numbers of Howard Hunt, a White House aide and CIA consultant, leads them to dig deeper, contacting other aides and cabinet members and receiving so many contradictory stories that they delve even deeper, until the scandal begins to take shape, most of their heavy leads provided by a mysterious political bigshot who calls them anonymously and meets with them in a Washington, D.C., parking area to guide them toward their eventual sensational revelations—the man the reporters dubbed "Deep Throat" by virtue of his rasping voice (or so they said). Redford seems to amble too easily through his part, annoyed at his partner's slovenly habits but working toward the same end with equal fervor. Jason Robards is excellent as Ben Bradlee, their tough-and-rough, hard-to-bluff boss at the Washington *Post*, played more as an editor out of THE FRONT PAGE than the usually cautious executive of today's media, one who overlooks his reporters' minor errors and supports them through their ferreting, and one who protectively watches over them, particularly when they receive death threats. The long and exciting investigation by the aristocratic WASP (Woodward/Redford) and the street savvy Jew (Bernstein/Hoffman) is both compelling and rewarding as, scene for scene, the viewer discovers what they discover, shock for shock, as the whole ugly mess finds its way into one edition after another, until Nixon resigns. A first-rate production employing aerial shots, tracking, and cut-away techniques that help the film to increase its tempo. The gratuitous vulgar language employed mars an already good script, the street language completely unnecessary to either character portrayal or the story itself, obviously included at the insistence of some nitwit movie executive eager to sensationalize an already sensational story.

p, Walter Coblenz; d, Alan J. Pakula; w, William Goldman (based on the book by Carl Bernstein, Bob Woodward); ph, Gordon Willis (Panavision, Technicolor); m, David Shire; ed, Robert L. Wolfe; prod d, George Jenkins; set d, George Gaines.

Drama Cas. (PR:C MPAA:PG)

ALL THE RIGHT MOVES½** (1983) 91m FOX c

Tom Cruise *(Stef)*, Craig T. Nelson *(Nickerson)*, Lea Thompson *(Lisa)*, Charles Cioffi *(Pop)*, Paul Carafotes *(Salvucci)*, Christopher Penn *(Brian)*, Sandy Faison *(Suzie)*, Paige Price *(Tracy)*, James A. Baffico *(Bosko)*, Donald A. Yanessa *(Coach)*, Walter Briggs *(Rifleman)*, Leon Robinson *(Shadow)*.

High school football star Cruise dreams of getting out of his mundane steel-town home via an athletic scholarship. An understanding girl friend and father help Cruise deal with his overbearing coach, well-played by Craig T. Nelson. A well-executed, competently acted film that becomes much too cliche-ridden and melodramatic as it progresses. Cruise is good, but displays less charisma and charm than in the entertaining RISKY BUSINESS. This was veteran cinematographer Michael Chapman's directorial debut, and he did a fair job, but the real eye-catcher among the cast and crew is Lea Thompson, who impressively plays Cruise's girl friend.

p, Stephen Deutsch; d, Michael Chapman; w, Michael Kane; ph, Jan DeBont; m, David Campbell; ed, David Garfield; art d, Mary Ann Biddle; set d, Ernie Bishop; cos, Deborah Hopper, Joseph Roveto.

Drama Cas. (PR:C MPAA:R)

ALL THE RIGHT NOISES½** (1973, Brit.) 92m FOX c

Tom Bell *(Len)*, Olivia Hussey *(Val)*, Judy Carne *(Joy)*, John Standing *(Bernie)*, Edward Higgins *(Ted)*, Chloe Franks *(Jenny Lewin)*, Gareth Wright *(Ian)*, Gordon Griffith *(Terry)*, Robert Keegan *(Mr. Lewin)*, Lesley-Ann Down *(Laura)*, Yootha Joyce *(Mrs. Byrd)*, Paul Whitsun-Jones *(Performer)*, Nicolette Roeg *(Performer)*.

Late entry in the "Angry Young Man" school of British filmmaking has happily married electrician Bell finding himself in the midst of an affair with an aspiring 15-year-old actress (Hussey). After a pregnancy scare, Hussey and Bell part amicably as the latter decides to go back to his wife. A well-told, very well-acted tale that lacks the punch of earlier films in the genre like THIS SPORTING LIFE.

p, Max Raab; d&w, Gerry O'Hara (based on his novel); ph, Gerry Fisher; m, Melanie; ed, Antony Gibbs; art d, Terry Pritchard.

Drama (PR:O MPAA:PG)

ALL THE WAY, BOYS*½ (1973, Ital.) 105m AE c

Terence Hill *(Plata)*, Bud Spencer *(Salud)*, Cyril Cusack *(Mad Man)*, Michel Antoine *(Caveira)*, Rene Kolldehoff *(Mr. Ears)*.

Sophomoric slapstick deals with a hopeless, hapless air freight line wobbling over the Andes and its inept, inane crew and owners. Shabby production values and witless story add up to a large waste of time.

p, Italo Zingarelli; d&w, Giuseppe Colizzi; ph, Marcel Masciocchi (DeLuxe Color); m, Guido and Maurizio De Angelis.

Comedy Cas. (PR:C MPAA:G)

ALL THE WAY HOME*½** (1963) 107m PAR bw

Jean Simmons *(Mary)*, Robert Preston *(Jay)*, Pat Hingle *(Ralph)*, Aline MacMahon *(Aunt Hannah)*, Thomas Chalmers *(Joel)*, John Cullum *(Andrew)*, Ronnie Claire Edwards *(Sally)*, Michael Kearney *(Rufus)*, John Henry Faulk *(Walter Starr)*, Lylah Tiffany *(Great-Great-Granmaw)*, Mary Perry *(Grand-Aunt Sadie)*, Georgia Simmons *(Jessie)*, Edwin Wolfe *(John Henry)*, Ferdie Hoffman *(Father Jackson)*.

Poignant small-town Americana tale, based on James Agee's Pulitzer Prize-winning autobiographical novel, has Preston as a happy-go-lucky father and Simmons as a sturdy but compassionate mother to Kearney, their son. It is through his eyes that the story is told, a simple but heart-tugging one where Preston dies and the family members adjust to the great hole in their lives. Kearney made his first film appearance here and his innocence and fresh-faced personality fit his role perfectly. Hingle, as the dour, heavy-drinking mortician brother who handles the funeral, is appropriately mean-spirited and easy to dislike. Excellent sets lend authenticity to the era of 1915 Knoxville, Tenn. (Agee's birthplace), portrayed as the hometown of this admirable family. Producer Susskind allegedly cut a full hour of this film before its release.

p, David Susskind; d, Alex Segal; w, Philip Reisman, Jr. (based on the play by Tad Mosel, and the novel *A Death in the Family* by James Agee); ph, Boris Kaufman; m, Bernard Green; ed, Carl Lerner.

Drama (PR:A MPAA:NR)

ALL THE WAY UP½** (1970, Brit.) 97m Granada/Anglo Amalgamated c

Warren Mitchell *(Fred Midway)*, Pat Heywood *(Hilda Midway)*, Elaine Taylor *(Eileen* Midway), Kenneth Cranham *(Tom Midway)*, Vanessa Howard *(Avril Hadfield)*, Richard Briers *(Nigel Hadfield)*, Adrienne Posta *(Daphne Dunmore)*, Bill Fraser *(Arnold Makepiece)*, Terence Alexander *(Bob Chickman)*, Maggie McGrath *(Mrs. Chickman)*, Clifford Parrish *(Mr. Hadfield)*, Lally Bowers *(Mrs. Hadfield)*, Janet Monta *(Stripper)*.

Not very intelligent but determined insurance salesman Mitchell vows to bring his family up the social ladder. Entertaining British comedy that lacks the sophistication and wit of its predecessors.

p, Philip Mackie; d, James MacTaggart; w, Mackie (based on David Turner's play, "Semi-Detached"); ph, Dick Bush (Technicolor); m, Howard Blake; ed, Roy Watts; prod d, Ivan King; cos, Sandra Moss.

Comedy (PR:A MPAA:NR)

ALL THE YOUNG MEN½** (1960) 86m Jaguar/COL bw

Alan Ladd *(Kincaid)*, Sidney Poitier *(Towler)*, James Darren *(Cotton)*, Glenn Corbett *(Wade)*, Mort Sahl *(Crane)*, Ana St. Clair *(Maya)*, Paul Richards *(Bracken)*, Dick Davalos *(Casey)*, Lee Kinsolving *(Dean)*, Joe Gallison *(Jackson)*, Paul Baxley *(Lazitech)*, Charles Quinlivan *(Lieutenant)*, Michael Davis *(Cho)*, Marlo Alcalde *(Hunter)*, Maria Tsien *(Korean Woman)*, Ingemar Johansson *(Torgil)*.

A marine platoon of 45 men is ordered to hold a mountain pass near Wosan early in the Korean War when Chinese Communists were swarming all over MacArthur's tiny army. Quinlivan is mortally wounded and hands over his command to Poitier, a novice sergeant, which angers most of the men since Ladd is the most experienced in the platoon; although he has lost his stripes, he is the man expected to lead. Poitier tries to enlist Ladd's help but he is rebuffed; Ladd feels that he is a "black man with an axe to grind." Dissension and uncertainty permeate the defenders until a massive attack is made on their position and a faltering Poitier gives way to Ladd's authority. The marines under Ladd's command stop the attack with only a few survivors, Ladd being terribly wounded when a Chinese tank which he blows up runs over his leg, requiring amputation. Battle has, however, unified the men, Ladd and Poitier becoming close friends, so much so that when Ladd later requires a transfusion he accepts the blood of Poitier with gratitude. This was a journeyman film for Ladd and a thankless role for Poitier who is the real star, yet the simple story of men fighting and dying together against impossible odds is compelling and has powerful moments.

p,d&w, Hall Bartlett; ph, Daniel Fapp; m, George Duning; ed, Al Clark; art d, Carl Anderson

War (PR:A MPAA:NR)

ALL THESE WOMEN½**

(1964, Swed.) 80m Janus c (AKA: NOW ABOUT ALL THESE WOMEN)

Jarl Kulle *(Cornelius)*, Georg Funkquist *(Tristan)*, Allan Edwall *(Jillker)*, Eva Dahlbeck *(Adelaide)*, Karin Kavli *(Madame Tussaud)*, Harriet Andersson *(Isolde)*, Gertrud Fridh *(Traviata)*, Bibi Andersson *(Humian)*, Barbro Hjort af Ornas *(Beatrice)*, Mona Malm *(Cecilia)*.

Weak satire about a womanizing musician who uses his cello-playing as a modern troubadour to woo his paramours while attempting to get a writer to pen his life story by constantly playing the writer's musical opus. Not too funny and not the least bit entertaining, a rare Bergman bomb.

p&d, Ingmar Bergman; w, Erland Josephson, Bergman; ph, Sven Nykvist (Eastmancolor); cos, Mago.

Drama/Satire (PR:O MPAA:NR)

ALL THINGS BRIGHT AND BEAUTIFUL*½**

(1979, Brit.) 94m Susskind/WORLD c (GB: IT SHOULDN'T HAPPEN TO A VET)

John Alderson *(James)*, Colin Blakely *(Siegfried)*, Lisa Harrow *(Helen)*, Bill Maynard *(Hinchcliffe)*, Paul Shelly *(Richard)*, Richard Pearson *(Granville)*, Rosemary Martin *(Mrs. Dalby)*, Raymond Francis *(Col. Bosworth)*, John Barrett *(Crump)*, Philip Stone *(Jack)*, Clifford Kershaw *(Kendall)*, Kevin Moreton *(William)*, Liz Smith *(Mrs. Dodds)*, Leslie Sarony *(Kirby)*, Gwen Nelson *(Mrs. Kirby)*, Juliet Cooke *(Jean)*, Stacy Davies *(Harry)*, Christine Hargreaves *(Mrs. Butterworth)*, May Warden *(Mrs. Tompkins)*, Richard Griffiths *(Sam)*, Ian Hastings *(Jackson)*.

Compassionate veterinarian takes care of animals and children alike in a small British community during the Depression. A thoroughly uplifting non-violent film all the family can enjoy with only one message: life is more fascinating than depressing sociological studies passing for drama. (Sequel: ALL CREATURES GREAT AND SMALL)

p, Margaret Matheson; d, Eric Till; w, Alan Plater (based on the books by James Herriot); ph, Arthur Ibbetson; m, Laurie Johnson; ed, Thom Noble; prod d, Geoffrey Drake.

Children **(PR:AAA MPAA:G)**

ALL THIS AND HEAVEN TOO* 1/2** (1940) 140m WB bw

Bette Davis *(Henriette Deluzy Desportes)*, Charles Boyer *(Duke De Praslin)*, Jeffrey Lynn *(Reverend Henry Field)*, Barbara O'Neil *(Duchesse De Praslin)*, Virginia Weidler *(Louise)*, Walter Hampden *(Pasquier)*, Harry Davenport *(Pierre)*, Fritz Leiber *(Albe)*, Helen Westley *(Mme. Le Maire)*, Sibyl Harris *(Mlle. Maillard)*, Janet Beecher *(Miss Haines)*, Montagu Love *(Marechal Sebastiani)*, George Coulouris *(Charpentier)*, Henry Daniell *(Broussels)*, Ian Keith *(Delangle)*, June Lockhart *(Isabelle)*, Ann Todd *(Berthe)*, Richard Nichols *(Raynald)*, Madge Terry *(Madame Gauthier)*, Christian Rub *(Loti)*, Frank Reicher *(Police Official)*, Victor Kilian *(Gendarme)*, Edward Fielding *(Dr. Louis)*, Egon Brecher *(Doctor)*, Ann Gillis *(Emily Schuyler)*, Mary Anderson *(Rebecca Jay)*, Peggy Stewart *(Helen Lexington)*, Creighton Hale *(Officer)*, Mary Forbes, Georgia Caine, Natalie Moorhead *(Ladies)*, Claire Du Brey, Virginia Brissac, Brenda Fowler *(Nuns)*, Mrs. Gardner Crane *(Madame Gauthier)*.

Based upon the Rachel Lyman Field novel (as popular as *Gone With the Wind* in its day), this sprawling 19th-century soap opera possesses amazing production values and a high caliber of acting surprising for its genre. Based upon a scandalous relationship between a French nobleman, the Duke De Praslin, and the governess of his children and the even greater notoriety of the murder of his wife over the governess' affections, WB threw the full weight of its production geniuses to achieve a marvelous tearjerker which gave full vent to the deep acting talents of Davis. As Henriette Deluzy Desportes, Davis is hired by Boyer (as the Duke De Praslin) which instantly incurs the wrath of the sultry Duchess, Barbara O'Neil, a Corsican beauty who is insanely jealous of her debonair husband. Davis quickly endears herself to the children but O'Neil resents her strengthening position, going to the local priest, Leiber, to seek advice and complain. He tells her bluntly to spend more time with her children, counsel she ignores. After Davis nurses one of her children back to health from a near-fatal bout with diphtheria, O'Neil angrily leaves for Corsica to visit her parents. When she hears groundless rumors that Davis and Boyer are having an affair, she returns home, furious, demanding Davis be dismissed, but she promises the governess a sterling letter of introduction to her next position, a promise she does not keep. Davis, almost destitute after moving from the De Praslin home, is suddenly arrested for the murder of O'Neil; the Duke is charged with killing his wife and Davis is charged with being his accomplice. Moreover, the strong friendship Boyer has with King Louis Philippe, and the resultant public opinion about his suspected crime, compels the monarch to abdicate. To save his king further embarrassment and Davis the agony of standing trial for a crime she has not committed—he has truly loved her all along but has displayed only the manner of a kindly employer—Boyer takes poison. Davis is rushed to his deathbed where he nobly clears her of any involvement in his wife's murder, assuming full responsibility. Davis, to avoid further notoriety, emigrates to the U.S. to teach in an exclusive girls' school, a position arranged for her by Rev. Henry Field (Lynn), her one and only friend. Here she faces the silent accusations of her class until she candidly tells the students the entire story, a touching scene that ends with the girls supporting her. Davis masterfully plays her role with restraint, careful never to cross over the line into histrionics, which a lesser actress handling such a fragile character might have done. Litvak's direction is taut and properly moody despite the great length of the film.

p, Hal B. Wallis, David Lewis; d, Anatole Litvak; w, Casey Robinson (based on the novel by Rachel Lyman Field); ph, Ernest Haller; m, Max Steiner; ed, Warren Low; md, Leo F. Forbstein; art d, Carl Jules Weyl; cos, Orry-Kelly.

Drama/Romance **(PR:A MPAA:NR)**

ALL THROUGH THE NIGHT** 1/2** (1942) 107m WB bw

Humphrey Bogart *(Gloves Donahue)*, Conrad Veidt *(Hall Ebbing)*, Kaaren Verne *(Leda Hamilton)*, Jane Darwell *(Ma Donahue)*, Frank McHugh *(Barney)*, Peter Lorre *(Pepi)*, Judith Anderson *(Madame)*, William Demarest *(Sunshine)*, Jackie Gleason *(Starchie)*, Phil Silvers *(Waiter)*, Wallace Ford *(Spats Hunter)*, Barton MacLane *(Marty Callahan)*, Edward Brophy *(Joe Denning)*, Martin Kosleck *(Steindorff)*, Jean Ames *(Annabelle)*, Ludwig Stossel *(Mr. Miller)*, Irene Seidner *(Mrs. Miller)*, James Burke *(Forbes)*, Ben Welden *(Smitty)*, Hans Schumm *(Anton)*, Charles Cane *(Spence)*, Frank Sully *(Sage)*, Sam McDaniel *(Deacon)*.

Extremely funny spoof of spy dramas, as well as a thrilling, dizzy-paced crime tale, this Bogart vehicle proves to be one of most enjoyable of his WB productions. Bogie is a top-drawer gambler, Gloves Donahue, respected high and low along Broadway (not unlike Arnold Rothstein), who goes to his favorite restaurant where waiter Silvers goes into a panic because he does not have Bogart's favorite cheesecake on hand, desperately explaining that Miller's Bakery made no delivery that day. Bogie and sidekicks Demarest and McHugh (both at their wise-guy best) are later called by Ma Donahue (Darwell) to check up on baker Miller (Stossel) who has vanished. They find him murdered in the basement of the bakery and launch an investigation, tracking down a young woman, Verne, whom Ma has seen visiting Miller's shop. She is a singer at the Duchess nightclub which Bogart visits, encountering MacLane who is his gambling rival, and assorted henchmen, including Brophy, who owns the club with MacLane. Bogie waves away their threats to throw him out and sits down to listen to Verne sing "All Through the Night," the title song, eyeing her piano accompanist, Lorre, who later responds nervously to Bogart's questions about Miller. Going to visit the singer backstage, Bogart finds Brophy shot in the throat in a back hall; he cannot speak but communicates with his hand, thrusting up five fingers before dying. Bogart explains to Demarest and McHugh the meaning of Brophy's signal—"Five, don't you get it? Fivers! Fifth columnists!" With that he and his pals follow the fleeing Lorre to a waterfront warehouse. As they search about, they are jumped, knocked unconscious and tied up. Bogart comes to as Verne is freeing him and he investigates the upper floors where he and Demarest find secret rooms containing short-wave radios and other spy apparatus, along with a Nazi flag and a portrait of Hitler adorning the wall. Further checking finds them entering an adjoining building that houses the Continental Art Galleries owned and operated by Veidt, the spymaster. Bogart buys an antique at an auction (in a bidding scene that no doubt inspired the one with Cary Grant in NORTH BY NORTHWEST 15 years later). He then tries to grill Veidt and his sinister-looking aide, Anderson, later learning that Verne is being forced to work for the Nazi underground organization; her father, in a German concentration camp, will be killed unless she does what Veidt commands. Bogart finds Veidt's secret book and, grabbing Verne, makes his escape, followed by a gang of Nazi goons. The book reveals that Verne's father has already been murdered in Germany; further, Bogart learns from Verne that Lorre murdered the baker because he refused to cooperate with Veidt and gang, and an important meeting of the Nazis is about to take place wherein plans will be finalized for the blowing up of half of New York harbor. Bogart and friends, aided by MacLane and his rough pals, invade Veidt's lair and pulverize the fascists until police arrive to take in the spies. Veidt, however, escapes after shooting Lorre who refuses to take the fall for him. The master spy takes off in a motorboat loaded with explosives, intending to blow up a U.S. warship riding at anchor in the harbor. Bogart manages to leap into the boat just as it speeds from dockside, battling with Veidt. Steering the boat away from its course, Bogart dives overboard while Veidt is carried into a wharf and is killed by the explosion. The warship is saved, the Nazis are neatly rounded up and gambler Bogart, with Verne on his arm, becomes a hero. The film, with its many climaxes, holds its suspense throughout with Lorre more sinister than his role in M, from which some of the plot—the idea of the underworld hunting down one of its own—is lightly scooped. Olivia de Havilland and George Raft were originally intended to play the Bogart-Verne roles but both had production commitments, Raft in MANPOWER, de Havilland in HOLD BACK THE DAWN.

p, Hal B. Wallis; d, Vincent Sherman; w, Leonard Spigelgass, Edwin Gilbert (based on a story by Spigelglass and Leonard Ross); ph, Sid Hickox; m, Adolph Deutsch; ed, Rudi Fehr; art d, Max Parker; m/l, "All Through the Night," Johnny Mercer, Arthur Schwartz; "Cherie, I Love You So," Lillian Goodman.

Spy Drama **(PR:A MPAA:NR)**

ALL WOMAN zero

(1967) 83m Franklin-Three Stories High/Joseph Brenner bw (AKA: SCHIZO; ALL GIRL)

Robert Alda *(Wally)*, Rebecca Sand *(Kitty)*, William Redfield *(Tod)*, Midge Ware *(Martha)*, Patricia Alison *(Virginia)*, Lonney Lewis *(Marty)*, Daniel Negrin *("Him")*, Kathy Sands *(Little Girl)*, Phil Bruns *(Drunk)*, Beverly Lawrence *(Birdie)*.

Alda is a young composer who becomes involved with the personal affairs of three women who move into an adjoining apartment. Sand is a widow plagued by dreams of her dead husband. Ware is a dancer who falls in love with her partner. She learns he has had a homosexual affair and realizes her love for him is more maternal than romantic. Alison believes she has found her long-lost father, but when the man posing as her father attempts to rape her, she must be rescued by her boy friend. A nasty exploitation picture, produced in 1958 but not released until 1967 with the addition of several sex scenes.

p&d, Frank Warren.

Drama **(PR:O MPAA:NR)**

ALL WOMEN HAVE SECRETS* 1/2 (1939) 59m PAR bw

Jeanne Cagney *(Kay)*, Joseph Allen *(John)*, Virginia Dale *(Jennifer)*, Peter Hayes *(Slats)*, Betty Moran *(Susie)*, John Arledge *(Joe)*, Lawrence Grossmith *(Professor Hewitt)*, Una O'Connor *(Mary)*, George Meeker *(Doc)*.

Married college couples appear to have more trouble than their single counterparts. Dull B picture treading over the same husband-and-wife turmoil material.

p, Edward T. Lowe; d, Kurt Neuman; w, Dale Eunson, Agnes Christine Johnson; ph, Theodor Sparkuhl; ed, Arthur Schmidt; m/l, Ned Washington, Victor Young.

Drama **(PR:A MPAA:NR)**

ALLEGHENY UPRISING 1/2** (1939) 81m RKO bw (GB:THE FIRST REBEL)

John Wayne *(Jim Smith)*, Claire Trevor *(Janie)*, George Sanders *(Capt. Swanson)*, Brian Donlevy *(Callendar)*, Wilfrid Lawson *(MacDouglas)*, Robert Barrat *(Duncan)*, John F. Hamilton *(Professor)*, Moroni Olsen *(Calhoon)*, Eddie Quillan *(Anderson)*, Chill Wills, *(McCammon)*, Ian Wolfe *(Poole)*, Wallis Clark *(McGlashan)*, Monte Montague *(Morris)*, Olaf Hytten *(General Gage)*.

Pre-Revolutionary War frontiersman Wayne stops bad guy Donlevy from selling booze and guns to the local Indians, while defying Sanders, a British captain turned tyrant. Pleasant post-STAGECOACH team-up of Wayne and Trevor, but not very memorable. (In an effort to mollify English viewers, RKO execs ordered some of the more anti-British dialog softened.)

p, P. J. Wolfson; d, William A. Seiter; w, Wolfson; ph, Nicholas Musuraca; ed, George Crone.

Action **Cas.** **(PR:A MPAA:NR)**

ALLEGRO NON TROPPO* 1/2** (1977, Ital.) 85m Specialty bw/c

Maurisio Nichetti, Nestor Garay, Maurizio Micheli, Maria Luisa Giovanninni.

A high-spirited, energetic animated feature that expands on FANTASIA's idea of using classical music pieces as a basis for cartoon movement. Director Bozzetto's style is frantic in pace and occasionally violent, but his use of color and line is dazzling. Each segment of the film is rich and funny, but the evolution of life from the last few drops of a Coca-Cola bottle set to Ravel's "Bolero" is a true showstopper.

d, Bruno Bozzetto; w, Bozzetto, Guido Manuli, Maurizio Nichetti; anim., Bozzetto, Giuseppe Lagana, Walter Cavazzuti; Giovanni Ferrari, Giancarlo Cereda, Giorgio Valentini, Guido Manuli, Paolo Abicocco, Giorgio Forlani (Technicolor); ed, Giancarlo Rossi; m, Debussy, Dvorak, Ravel, Sibelius, Vivaldi, Stravinsky.

Animated **Cas.** **(PR:A MPAA:NR)**

ALLERGIC TO LOVE**½   (1943) 64m UNIV bw

Martha O'Driscoll (Pat), Noah Beery, Jr. (Kip), David Bruce (Roger), Franklin Pangborn (Ives), Fuzzy Knight (Charlie), Maxie Rosenbloom (Max), Henry Armetta (Louie), Marek Windheim (Dr. Kardos), Paul Stanton (Mr. Bradley), Olive Blakeney (Mrs. Bradley), Grady Sutton (Cuthbert), William Davidson (Mr. Henderson), John Hamilton (Dr. McLaughlin), George Chandler (Joe), Olin Howlin (Sam Walker), Lotte Stein (Mrs. Beamish), Edna Holland (Miss Peabody), Dudley Dickerson (Whitney), Antonio Triana and Montes, Chinita Guadalajara Trio.

Mildly amusing farce begins with O'Driscoll and Beery as newlyweds, sailing to South America on their honeymoon. She breaks out with acute hay fever, replete with uncontrollable sneezing. Bruce, vying for the lady's hand, is a doctor who happens to be on board and sneakily decides that the only way the couple can live happily ever after is to divorce; Beery causes the hay fever, says Bruce. This ridiculous premise is carried to the shores of South America where Beery gets wise and cold-cocks the scheming physician. Only a few bright moments in this trekking programmer.

p, Warren Wilson; d, Edward Lilly, w, Wilson (based on a story by Jack Townley, John Larkin); ph, George Robinson; ed, Philip Cahn.

Comedy   **(PR:A MPAA:NR)**

ALLIGATOR***½   (1980) 94m Group 1 c

Robert Forster (David Madison), Robin Riker (Marisa), Michael Gazzo (Police Chief), Perry Lang (Kelly), Jack Carter (Mayor), Henry Silva (Col. Brock), Bart Braverman (Reporter), Dean Jagger (Tycoon), Sue Lyon, Angel Tompkins. (News Reporters).

Title creature, after being flushed down a toilet as a baby, grows to monstrous proportions over a 12-year period by feasting on the discarded bodies of animals chock full of illegal growth hormones with which a chemical company has been experimenting. After a while, the big guy gets hungry and wreaks reptilian havoc on Los Angeles, even getting some sort of revenge by slurping down the chemical plant's owner, Jagger. Cop Forster and scientist Riker team up to destroy the gator and start up a romance as well. Sure this sounds stupid, and it is, but it's quite a bit of fun, too. Screenwriter Sayles, whose own work as a director has been critically acclaimed, and director Teague have loaded ALLIGATOR with visual puns, film-buff jokes, and a few frightening moments as well. Forster is very likable as the problem-ridden cop and Riker, an attractive but tough redhead, is wonderfully charismatic as the herpetologist whose Mom and Dad threw that little thing down the toilet years ago. All in all, a fine example of what a sense of humor can do with a low budget and an old idea.

p, Brandon Chase; d, Lewis Teague; w, John Sayles; ph, Joseph Mangine (DeLuxe Color).

Horror   **Cas.**   **(PR:O MPAA:R)**

ALLIGATOR NAMED DAISY, AN***½   (1957, Brit.) 88m RANK c

Donald Sinden (Peter Weston), Diana Dors (Vanessa Colebrook), Jean Carson (Moira), James Robertson Justice (Sir James), Stanley Holloway (General), Roland Culver (Col. Weston), Margaret Rutherford (Prudence Croquet), Avice Landone (Mrs. Weston), Stephen Boyd (Albert), Richard Wattis (Hoskins), Henry Kendall (Valet), Michael Shepley (Judge), Charles Victor (Sergeant), Ernest Thesiger (Notcher), Wilfrid Lawson (Irishman), George Moon (Al).

Pleasant, average fellow Sinden returns home from vacation to find that he has become the owner of a pet alligator. The film's plot concerns itself with Sinden having to choose between his heiress fiancee and a cute little Irish girl that he recently met, but the richness of the film comes through its charming characters' reactions to Daisy. A very funny film with an excellent supporting cast.

p, Raymond Stross; d, J. Lee Thompson; w, Jack Davies; ph, Reginald Wyer (VistaVision, Technicolor); ed, John D. Guthridge; ch, Alfred Rodrigues; m/l, Sam Coslow.

Comedy   **(PR:A MPAA:NR)**

ALLIGATOR PEOPLE, THE**½   (1959) 73m FOX bw

Beverly Garland (Jane Marvin), George Macready (Dr. Mark Sinclair), Richard Crane (Paul Webster), Lon Chaney, Jr. (Mannon), Frieda Inescort (Mrs. Henry Hawthorne), Vince Townsend, Jr. (Toby), Ruby Goodwin (Lou Ann), Boyd Stockman (Paula Double), John Merrick (Nurse No. 1), Lee Warren (Nurse No. 2), Bruce Bennett (Dr. Erik Lorimer), Doug Kennedy (Dr. Wayne McGregor), Bill Bradley (Patient No. 6), Dudley Dickerson (Porter), Hal K. Dawson (Conductor).

Doctor experimenting in the Louisiana bayou country discovers a serum derived from the title reptile that allows humans to regenerate lost limbs. Too bad it has this peculiar side effect that eventually changes the serum receiver into a 'gator. Rather interesting horror film with an unusual premise. Garland and Chaney turn in a couple of above-par performances.

p, Jack Leewood; d, Roy Del Ruth; w, Orville H. Hampton (based on a story by Hampton and Charles O'Neal); ph, Karl Struss; m, Irving Gertz; ed, Harry Gerstad; art d, Lyle R. Wheeler, John Mansbridge.

Horror   **(PR:C MPAA:NR)**

ALLOTMENT WIVES, INC.*½   (1945) 80m MON bw (AKA:WOMAN IN THE CASE)

Kay Francis (Sheila), Paul Kelly (Major Pete Martin), Otto Kruger (Whitney Colton), Gertrude Michael (Gladys Smith), Teala Loring (Connie), Bernard Nedell (Spike Malone), Matty Fain (Louie Moranto), Anthony Warde (Agnew), Jonathan Hale (General Gilbert), Selmer Jackson (Deacon Sam), Evelynn Eaton (Ann Farley).

Government agent Kelly foils a group of heartless (and stupid) women who marry servicemen for those huge sums of money they earn. An unbelievable, laughable mess.

p, Jeffrey Bernerd, Kay Francis; d, William Nigh; w, Harvey H. Gates, Sidney Sutherland (based on a story by Sutherland); ph, Harry Neumann; ed, William Austin; art d, Dave Milton.

Drama   **(PR:A MPAA:NR)**

ALLURING GOAL, THE*½   (1930, Ger.) Tober-Tonfilm/Emelka bw

Richard Tauber, Maria Elsner, Oscar Sima, Lucie Englisch.

Unlike an American, who would have told the story of a baseball player or dance hall girl, German director Reichmann spins the saga of an opera singer's climb to the top of the classical ladder. Knowing the weight of some of those tenors, let's hope the rungs can hold them. Weak direction and poor use of music hamper this prettily packaged film.

d, Max Reichmann.

Drama   **(PR:A MPAA:NR)**

ALMOST A BRIDE   (SEE: KISS FOR CORLISS, A, 1949)

ALMOST A DIVORCE*½   (1931, Brit.) 75m British and Dominions/W&F bw

Nelson Keys (Richard Leighton), Sydney Howard (Mackintosh), Marjorie Binner (Angela Leighton), Eva Moore (Aunt Isobel), Kay Hammond (Maisie), Kenneth Kove (Detective).

Drunken Howard almost ruins the marriage of best pal Keys. Poor comic outing that fails to reach any type of fun pace.

p, Herbert Wilcox; d, Arthur Varney Serrao, Jack Raymond; w, Brock Williams (based on a story by Serrao); ph, Henry Harris.

Comedy   **(PR:A MPAA:NR)**

ALMOST A GENTLEMAN*½   (1938, Brit.) 78m BUT bw

Billy Bennett (Bill Barker), Kathleen Harrison (Mrs. Barker), Gibb McLaughlin (Bartholomew Quist), Marcelle Rogez (Mimi), Mervyn Johns (Percival Clicker), Basil Langton (Andrew Sinker), Harry Terry (Jim), Dorothy Vernon (Mrs. Garrett).

Ridiculous forced comedy where a group of unsophisticated people easily believe that a grubby night watchman is really a glue manufacturer of enormous wealth. Only for the mindless.

p, Sidney Morgan; d, Oswald Mitchell; w, Morgan, Mitchell; ph, Geoffrey Faithfull.

ALMOST A GENTLEMAN zero

(1939, Brit.) 64m RKO bw (GB: MAGNIFICENT OUTCAST)

James Ellison (Dan Preston), Helen Wood (Shirley Haddon), Robert Kent (Robert Mabrey), June Clayworth (Marian Mabrey), Robert Warwick (Major Mabrey), Leonard Penn (Arthur), John Wray (Crack Williams), Brandon Tynan (Jason Troop), Earl Hodgins (Ira Willis), Harlan Briggs (Doc Rollins), Ace, the Wonder Dog.

Ace, the Wonder Dog, is accused of murder! Terrible kiddie matinee fare with a premise not even a mewling infant would swallow.

p, Cliff Reid; d, Leslie Goodwins; w, David Silverstein, Jo Pagano (based on a story by Harold Shumate); ph, J. Roy Hunt; ed, Desmond Marquette.

Children   **(PR:A MPAA:NR)**

ALMOST A HONEYMOON*½   (1930, Brit.) 100m BIP/Elstree

Clifford Mollison (Basil Dibley), Donald Calthrop (The Butler), Dorothy "Dodo" Watts (Rosalie Quilter), Lamont Dickson (Cuthbert de Gray), C. M. Hallard (Sir James Jephson).

Awfully stupid British comedy that has vagabond Mollison accidentally sleeping with old maid Watts. Dreadfully boring.

d, Monty Banks; w, Banks, Walter Mycroft (based on the play by Walter Ellis); ph, Jack Cox.

Comedy   **(PR:A MPAA:NR)**

ALMOST A HONEYMOON*½   (1938, Brit.) 80m Welwyn/Pathe bw

Tommy Trinder (Peter Dibley), Linden Travers (Patricia Quilter), Edmond Breon (Aubrey Lovitt), Frederick Burtwell (Charles), Vivienne Bennett (Rita Brent), Arthur Hambling (Adolphus), Aubrey Mallalieu (Clutterbuck), Betty Jardine (Lavinia Pepper), Ian Fleming (Sir James Hooper), Wally Patch (Bailiff).

Poor remake of a poor 1930 programmer, but this time the accidental bedroom arrangements are made by a rich gent who gives the keys to an attractive girl but forgets she is occupying his bed when he returns to sleep it off.

p, Warwick Ward; d, Norman Lee; w, Kenneth Horne, Ralph Neale (based on the play by Walter Ellis); ph, Bryan Langley.

Comedy   **(PR:A MPAA:NR)**

ALMOST ANGELS**½   (1962) 93m BV c

Peter Weck (Max Heller), Vincent Winter (Toni Fiala), Sean Scully (Peter Schaefer), Hans Holt (Director Eisinger), Fritz Echardt (Father Fiala), Bruni Lobel (Frau Fiala),Hermann Furthmosek (Choirmaster), Hans Christian (Choirmaster), Walter Regelsberger (Choirmaster), the Vienna Boys Choir.

One lad's adventures in the Vienna Boys Choir. Mediocre Disney fare with a bare-bones structure used mainly as a basis for plenty of singing, featuring the music of Brahms, Schubert and Strauss.

d, Steven Previn; w, Vernon Harris (based on an idea by R. A. Stemmle); ph, Kurt Grigoleit (Technicolor).

Children   **(PR:AAA MPAA:NR)**

ALMOST HUMAN zero   (1974,Ital.) Dania/Jos. Brenner c

Tomas Milian (Julio Sacchi), Henry Silva (Inspector Walter Grandi), Anita Strindberg (Iona Tucci), Raymond Lovelock (Carmine), Laura Belli (Mary Lou), Guido Alberti (Mary Lou's Father).

Violent creep Milian kidnaps wealthy Belli and goes on a killing spree until the ransom is paid. Tough cop Silva goes beyond the law and takes care of Milian in his own way, getting sent to prison for his vigilante tactics. Horrible, bloody rip-off of DIRTY HARRY and DEATH WISH that was originally marketed to U.S. audiences as a sci-fi/horror film.

p, Luciano Martino; d, Umberto Lenzi; ph, (Eastmancolor); m, Ennio Morricone; ed, Eugenio Alabiso.

Horror   **(PR:O MPAA:R)**

ALMOST MARRIED**½   (1932) 50m FOX bw

Violet Heming (*Anita*), Ralph Bellamy (*Denee Maxwell*), Alexander Kirkland (*Capristi*), Alan Dinehart (*Inspector Slante*), Eva Dennison (*Lady Laverling*), Grace Hampton (*Aunt Mathilda*), Herbert Bunston (*Lord Laverling*), Maria Alba (*Mariette*), Herbert Mundin (*Butler*), Mary Gordon (*Cook*).

Nice guy Bellamy marries Heming in order to save her from imprisonment in Russia, but later finds she's already married to crazy Kirkland who has this strange habit of strangling women. When Kirkland escapes from an asylum, the horror begins. Muddled suspense film aided by Kirkland's eccentric, compelling performance and first-time director Menzies' clear visual style.

d, William Cameron Menzies, Marcel Varnel; w, Wallace Smith, Guy Bolton (based on the novel *Devil's Triangle* by Andrew Soutar); ph, John Mescall; ed, Harold Schuster.

Horror/Suspense   **(PR:C MPAA:NR)**

ALMOST MARRIED**½   (1942) 65m UNIV bw

Jane Frazee (*Gloria Dobson*), Robert Paige (*James Manning III*), Eugene Pallette (*Dr. Dobson*), Elizabeth Patterson (*Aunt Matilda*), Charles Coleman (*Michael*), Maude Eburne (*Mrs. Clayton*), Will Lee (*Hurley*), Olin Howland (*Bright*), Mary Forbes, Ray Walker, Lionel Pape, Herbert Haywood.

To escape an unpromising engagement Paige runs after singer Frazee who agrees to a mock marriage to help him disentangle himself, but the couple fall in love after the ceremony. Frazee winds up with a stellar nightclub career *and* a wealthy husband. Not bad for her, but the viewer is terribly short-changed by this blah story.

p, Ken Goldsmith; d, Charles Lamont; w, Hugh Wedlock, Jr., Howard Snyder (based on a story by Theodore Reeves); ph, Jerome Ash; ed, Edward Curtiss.

Romance   **(PR:A MPAA:NR)**

ALMOST PERFECT AFFAIR, AN*½   (1979) 93m PAR c

Keith Carradine (*Hal*), Monica Vitti (*Maria*), Raf Vallone (*Freddie*), Christian De Sica (*Carlo*), Dick Anthony Williams (*Jackson*), Henri Garcin (*Lt. Montand*), Anna Maria Horsford (*Amy Zon*).

Ambitious young director Carradine, determined to get his "personal" film into the Cannes festival, gets some assistance from producer's wife Vitti. Being in France, the two, naturally, decide to have an affair. Uneven, unfunny film from hit-and-miss director Michael Ritchie.

p, Terry Carr; d, Michael Ritchie; w, Walter Bernstein, Don Petersen; (based on a story by Michael Ritchie, Don Petersen); ph, Henri Decae (DeLuxe Color); ed, Richard Harris; m, Georges Delerue; art d, Willy Holt; cos, Tanine Autre.

Romance/Comedy   Cas.   **(PR:C MPAA:PG)**

ALMOST SUMMER*½   (1978) 88m Motown/UNIV c

Bruno Kirby (*Bobby DeVito*), Lee Purcell (*Christine Alexander*), John Friedrich (*Darryl Fitzgerald*), Didi Conn (*Donna DeVito*), Thomas Carter (*Dean Hampton*), Tim Matheson (*Kevin Hawkins*), Petronia Paley (*Nicole Henderson*), David Wilson (*Duane Jackson*), Sherry Hursey (*Lori Öttinger*), Harvey Lewis (*Stanley Lustgarten*).

Teen romance abounds during a high school election. Cute cast is worth watching in this sometimes boring campaign between sophomoric politicians.

p, Rob Cohen; d, Martin Davidson; w, Judith Berg, Sandra Berg, Davidson, Marc Reid Rubel; ph, Stevan Larner (Technicolor); m, Charles Lloyd, Ron Altbach; ed, Lynzee Klingman; art d, William M. Hiney.

Romance   **(PR:A MPAA:PG)**

ALMOST TRANSPARENT BLUE**½ (1980, Jap.) 103m Kitty Film/TOHO c

Kunihiko Mitamura (*Ryu*), Mari Nakayama (*Lilly*), Haruhiko Saito (*Yoshiyama*), Keiko Wakasa (*Kei*), Togo Igawa (*Okinawa*), Narumi Tokura (*Reiko*), Yuri Takase (*Moko*), Goro Masaki (*Kazuo*).

Insightful film of alienated Japanese youth of the 1960s (the social upheaval was not confined to the U.S.) where a disillusioned young man, Mitamura, meets and falls in love with an older woman, Nakayama, advancing slowly toward a sexual relationship which is oft-times pitiful, such as their lovemaking outside a rainswept U.S. Air Force base while high on mescaline. Decidedly repugnant scenes mar a beautifully directed and photographed film, even though the rampant sex in the novel by director Murakami was toned down for Japan's normally reserved film audiences.

p, Hidenori Taga, Kei Ijisato; d&w, Ryu Murakami (based on his novel); ph, Shuya Schigawa; m, Masaru Hoshi; ed, Hatoko Yamaji; art d, Hiroshi Wada.

Romance/Drama   **(PR:O MPAA:NR)**

ALOHA zero   (1931) 85m TIF bw

Ben Lyon, Raquel Torres, Robert Edeson, Alan Hale, Thelma Todd, Marian Douglas, Otis Harlan, T. Roy Barnes, Robert Ellis, Donald Reed, Al St. John, Dickie Moore, Marcia Harris.

Utter nonsense about an island girl who marries a white man and cannot adjust to the life of a different society. She returns to her native land and throws herself into a volcano.

d, Al Rogell; w, Leslie Mason, W. Totman.

Drama   **(PR:A MPAA:NR)**

ALOHA, BOBBY AND ROSE**½   (1975) 88m CineArtists/COL c

Paul LeMat (*Bobby*), Dianne Hull (*Rose*), Tim McIntire (*Buford*), Leigh French (*Donna Sue*), Noble Willingham (*Uncle Charlie*), Martine Bartlett (*Rose's Mother*), Robert Carradine (*Moxey*).

Updated rip-off of BONNIE AND CLYDE has auto mechanic LeMat and car wash worker Huil becoming mixed up in a robbery and finding themselves on the run. LeMat, an interesting actor, is lost in this mediocre bit of Americana.

p, Fouad Said; d, Floyd Mutrux; w, Mutrux; ph, William A. Fraker (Metrocolor); ed, Danford B. Greene.

Drama   Cas.   **(PR:C MPAA:PG)**

ALOMA OF THE SOUTH SEAS***½   (1941) 76m PAR c

Dorothy Lamour (*Aloma*), Jon Hall (*Tanoa*), Lynne Overman (*Corky*), Philip Reed (*Revo*), Katherine deMille (*Kari*), Fritz Leiber (*High Priest*), Dona Drake (*Nea*), Esther Dale (*Tarusa*), John Barclay (*Ilkali*), Norma Jean Nelson (*Aloma as a Child*), Evelyn Del Rio (*Nea as a Child*), Scotty Beckett (*Tanoa as a Child*), Billy Roy (*Revo as a Child*), Noble Johnson (*Moukali*), Ella Neal, Dena Coaker, Emily LaRue, Patsy Mace, Dorothy Short, Paula Terry, Carmella Cansino, Esther Estrella (*Aloma's Handmaidens*), John Bagni (*Native*), Nina Campana (*Toots*), Charlene Wyatt, Janet Dempsey (*Girls*).

Top-drawer South Seas romance has a Tahitian chief selecting a bride for his young son who is then sent off for a Harvard education. Upon his return aboard Overman's ship—the captain acting as mentor to Hall and protector to Lamour—the youth, now grown into Hall, is determined not to marry someone promised to him 15 years earlier. Hall meets Lamour, not knowing she is his intended, and both fall deeply in love. The match is almost interrupted by a jealous native girl, DeMille, and even more vengeance-seeking sub-chieftain Reed, the latter trying to kill Hall several times so he can have Lamour. Hall manages to escape Reed's wrath in the middle of a volcanic eruption that almost destroys the entire island, standing at film's end with Lamour atop a rocky crag, looking out to sea at a fading sun of rich red. (This is a remake of a 1926 silent version starring Gilda Gray and directed by Maurice Tourneur, based on a play by John B. Hymer and Leroy Clemens.) The color of this production is lavish, the songs and dances authentic and well choreographed and the miniatures of the eruption represent the best in special effects. Though the story is somewhat lightweight and borrows a bit from THE HURRICANE in which Hall and Lamour doubled as a love team for the first dynamic time, director Santell keeps the film moving at a brisk trot through exotic settings. The color quality and lighting allow the eyes to feast.(The color process used in this film, known as IB Technicolor, produced the richest colors ever impregnated on film, laboriously and expensively made by superimposing three strips of tinted film which were then treated with vegetable coloring, a process that, unlike the emulsion process employed after WW II, guaranteed the color lasting almost forever, whereas in the later process the color simply wears out. Oddly, the Hollywood moguls, after WW II, felt that the IB Technicolor process was simply too expensive and time-consuming and sold all of the studio equipment for this process to China, which has continued to use it, providing incredibly rich color for its films; when U.S. and other production companies now wish to use this process they must go to China and pay a premium price, far in excess of what it would have cost had the equipment been retained—another massive *faux pas* on the part of less than visionary Louis B. Mayer and company.)

p, B. G. De Sylva; d, Alfred Santell; w, Frank Butler, Seena Owen, Lillian Hayward (based on a story by Owen and Curt Siodmak, from the Hymer-Clemens play); ph, Karl Struss (Technicolor); ed, Arthur Schmidt; spec eff, Gordon Jennings; m/l Frank Loesser, Frederick Hollander.

Adventure/Romance   **(PR:A MPAA:NR)**

ALONE AGAINST ROME*½   (1963, Ital.) 100m Medallion bw

Rossana Podesta, Jeffries Lang, Philippe Leroy

Almost incomprehensible costumer has an invading army under a renegade Italian warrior attempt to destory Rome and punish Podesta for loving another. Utter Latin drivel.

p, Marco Vicario; d, Herbert Wise (based on the novel *The Gladiator* by Gasted Green).

Adventure   **(PR:C MPAA:NR)**

ALONE IN THE DARK**½   (1982) 92m New Line Cinema c

Jack Palance (*Frank Hawkes*), Donald Pleasence (*Dr. Leo Bain*), Martin Landau (*Bryon "Preacher" Sutcliff*), Dwight Schultz (*Dan Potter*), Erland Van Lidth (*Ronald "Fatty" Elster*), Deborah Hedwall (*Nell Potter*), Lee Taylor-Allen (*Tonie Potter*), Phillip Clark (*Tom Smith/Skaggs*).

Four killers escape from an asylum during a blackout and terrorize the home of a disliked doctor. Seeing familiar Hollywood faces as the murderers instead of the usual mindless hulks is what highlights this slash 'em up horror film. Pleasence's humorous portrayal of the asylum operator is a nice counterweight to the grisly death scenes.

p, Robert Shaye; d, Jack Sholder; w, Sholder; ph, Joseph Mangine; m, Renato Serio; ed, Arline Garson; art d, Peter Monroe.

Horror   Cas.   **(PR:O MPAA:R)**

ALONE IN THE STREETS**½   (1956, Ital.) 81m Carroll Pictures bw

Carlo Tamberlani (*Police Commissioner*), Brunella Bovo (*Peppino's Step-Sister*), Marco Vicario (*Her Fiance*), Tecla Scrano (*Step-Mother*), Peppino, Stellina and other children in Naples (*Themselves*).

Sometimes charming little drama about Neapolitan waifs and how they survive poverty and starvation, in this case it's Peppino, who sells lottery tickets to support his mother and 3-year-old Stellina, the darling little girl who follows him everywhere. The children were taken directly from the streets of Castellammare near Naples for this film by director Siano. They are not left destitute in the film, adopted, so to speak, by Tamberlani, the kindly police magistrate. How the children survived beyond this film production is unknown.

p, Edoardo Capolino; d&w, Silvio Siano; m, Franco Longelia.

Drama/Children   **(PR:C MPAA:NR)**

ALONE ON THE PACIFIC***½ (1964, Jap.) 104m Ishihara International c
(AKA: MY ENEMY THE SEA)

Yuiro Ishihara (*The Youth*), Kinuyo Tanaka (*His Mother*), Masayuki Mori (*His Father*), Ruriko Asoka (*His Sister*), Hajime Hana (*His Friend*).

This film is a fine testimony to the human spirit, a well-crafted film, one where Ishihara fulfills his boyhood dream of crossing the ocean. He paddles his little craft past the coast guard in Osaka Bay and is immediately hurled into deep waters by a raging blue-black typhoon that bids fair to send him to his ancestors. He survives the storm, and flashbacks of the youth's life show his stern father and understanding mother, a loving sister and devoted friend, all of whom he tells of his desire to sail to America. Throughout the impossible voyage, through more storms, doldrums, days and days without food or water, the plucky, determined youth courageously sails onward to complete his dream, often babbling to his tiny boat, The Mermaid (in scenes recalled from THE OLD MAN AND THE SEA.) Nothing can tempt him from his goal, including the help offered from a passing ship and a circling plane. At one point he spots a floating newspaper which shows a picture of a dog and this tearfully reminds him of his pet at home. One harrowing adventure follows another until the youth, near collapse and resignation to failure, looks up to see the Golden Gate Bridge. His little boat sails into San Francisco Bay triumphant. Excellent film fare, sharply directed and well acted.

p, Akira Nakai; d, Kon Ichikawa; w, Natto Wada (based on a logbook by Kenichi Horie); ph, Yoshihiro Yamazaki; m, Yasushi Akatagaw, Tohru Takemitsu.

Adventure/Children (PR:AAA MPAA:NR)

ALONG CAME JONES***1/2

(1945) 90m Cinema Artists/International Pictures/RKO

Gary Cooper (Melody Jones), Loretta Young (Cherry de Longpre), William Demarest (George Fury), Dan Duryea (Monte Jarrad), Frank Sully (Cherry's Brother), Russell Simpson (Pop de Longpre), Arthur Loft (Sheriff), Willard Robertson (Luke Packard), Don Costello (Gledhill), Ray Teal (Kriendler), Walter Sande (Ira Waggoner), Lane Chandler (Boone), Frank Cordell (Coach Guard), Lou Davis, Ed Randolph, Tommy Coates (Coach Passengers), Tony Roux (Old Mexican), Erville Alderson (Bartender), Paul Sutton (Man at Bar), Herbert Heywood, Frank Hagney, Ralph Littlefield, Ernie Adams (Townsmen), Lane Watson (Town Character), Paul E. Burns (Small Man), Chris-Pin Martin (Store Proprietor), Jack Baxley (Rancher on Street), Doug Morrow (Rifleman), Ralph Dunn (Cotton), Geoffrey Ingham, John Merton, Tom Herbert (Card Players), Charles Morton (Fat Card Player), Lee Phelps (Deputy), Billy Engle (Wagon Driver), Bob Kortman, Frank McCarroll, Hank Bell, Chalky Williams (Posse).

In his first role as producer, Cooper turns out a savory spoof of all westerns, particularly a satire on the type of strong, silent hero he himself had established. As an inept, gunshy saddle bum, Jones/Cooper rides into town with his carping sidekick, Demarest, only to be mistaken for bad man Duryea. He wins the respect of the townfolk, admiration he has sought all his life, even though it is on the dark side. But the charade collapses when Cooper proves he cannot hit the side of a barn with any carefully aimed bullet and he is almost sent to boot hill when Duryea finally shows up to challenge him. Our hero is saved by a sharpshooting damsel, Young, whom he has been unsuccessfully wooing. When she learns he is not a baddie she takes quick action, disposes of Duryea with a well-directed (and well-deserved) bullet, and Cooper winds up in her arms. A witty, thoroughly entertaining film with snappy scenes directed by Heisler, who had edited Cooper's films as early as 1934 (beginning with King Vidor's THE WEDDING NIGHT).

p, Gary Cooper; d, Stuart Heisler; w, Nunnally Johnson (based on a story by Alan Le May); ph, Milton Krasner; m, Arthur Lange, Hugo Friedhofer, Charles Maxwell; ed, Thomas Neff; prod d, Wiard B. Ihnen; set d, Julia Heron; cos, Walter Plunkett.

Western Cas. (PR:A MPAA:NR)

ALONG CAME LOVE*1/2

(1937) 65m PAR bw

Irene Hervey (Emmy Grant), Charles Starrett (John Patrick O'Ryan), Doris Kenyon (Mrs. Gould), H. B. Warner (Dr. Martin), Irene Franklin (Mrs. Grant), Bernadene Hayes (Sarah Jewett), Ferdinand Gottschalk (Mr. Vincent), Charles Judels (Joe).

Shopgirl Hervey and young pediatrician Starrett fall for each other during the scandal ous arrest of Hervey's mother at a burlesque house. A light-hearted comedy with nothing to offend, but with nothing to recommend, either.

p, Richard A. Rowland; d, Bert Lytell; w, Austin Strong, Arthur Caesar; ph, Ira Morgan; md, Boris Morros.

Comedy (PR:A MPAA:NR)

ALONG CAME SALLY*1/2

(1934, Brit.) 70m Gainsborough/GAU bw (GB: AUNT SALLY)

Cicely Courtneidge (Mademoiselle Zaza/Sally Bird), Sam Hardy (Michael "King" Kelly), Phyllis Clare (Queenie), Billy Milton (Billy), Hartley Power ("Gloves" Clark), Ben Weldon (Casion), Enrico Naldi (Little Joe), Ann Hope (Joan), Ivor McLaren (Madison), Rex Evans (Percy), Tubby Cipen (Tubby).

Ambitious nightclub singer Courtneidge assumes the identity of a French star and fools a gang of New York racketeers, saving the club at which she works from their slimy clutches. Miss Courtneidge is not the most compelling or entertaining screen star and this, of course, does not help this terribly slow British production.

p, Michael Balcon; d, Tim Whelan; w, Whelan, Guy Bolton, Austin Medford, A. R. Rawlinson; ph, Charles Van Enger; m, Harry Woods; ch, Edward Royce.

Musical Comedy (PR:A MPAA:NR)

ALONG CAME YOUTH*1/2

(1931) 74m PAR bw

Charles Rogers (Larry Brooks), Frances Dee (Elinor Farrington), Stuart Erwin (Ambrose), William Austin (Eustace), Evelyn Hall (Lady Prunella), Leo White (Senor Cortes), Mathilde Comont (Senora Cortes), Betty Boyd (Sue Long), Arthur Hoyt (Adkins), Sybil Grove (Maid), Herbert Sherwood (Doorman), Charles West (Chauffeur).

Pretty rich girl Dee mistakes sandwich boy Rogers for the wealthy suitor her aunt has been foisting upon her. Uninspiring romantic comedy.

d, Lloyd Corrigan, Norman Z. McLeod; w, George Marion, Jr., (based on a story by Maurice Bedel); ph, Henry Gerrard.

Comedy (PR:A MPAA:NR)

ALONG THE GREAT DIVIDE**1/2

(1951) 88m WB bw

Kirk Douglas (Len Merrick), Virginia Mayo (Ann Keith), John Agar (Billy Shear), Walter Brennan (Pop Keith), Ray Teal (Lou Gray), Hugh Sanders (Frank Newcombe), Morris Ankrum (Ed Roden), James Anderson (Dan Roden), Charles Meredith (The Judge).

Guilt-ridden marshal Douglas (he believes he is responsible for his father's death) saves Brennan from a lynch mob and the pair set out across the desert to the nearest town in hopes of a fair trial. Brennan is found guilty, but before the sentence can be carried out, Douglas pins the murder on mob leader Anderson. After neatly disposing of the actual murderer with his six-gun, Douglas and Mayo (Brennan's dutiful daughter) ride off into the sunset. Douglas' first western is aided by veteran action director Walsh's storytelling capabilities and Sid Hickox's excellent photography, but the picture as a whole is too reminiscent of past tales of the West and relatively unexciting. Song: "Down in the Valley."

p, Anthony Veiller; d, Raoul Walsh; w, Walter Doniger, Lewis Meltzer; ph, Sid Hickox; m, David Buttolph; ed, Thomas Reilly.

Western (PR:C MPAA:NR)

ALONG THE NAVAJO TRAIL**1/2

(1945) 66m REP bw

Roy Rogers (Roy Rogers), George "Gabby" Hayes (Gabby Whittaker), Dale Evans (Lorry Alastair), Douglas Fowley (J. Richard Bentley), Nestor Paiva (Janza), Sam Flint (Breck Alastair), Emmett Vogan (Roger Jerrold), Roy Barcroft (Rusty Channing), David Cota (Lani), Edward Cassidy (Sheriff Clem Wagner), Bob Nolan and the Sons of the Pioneers.

With the aid of a band of gypsies, Rogers helps break up a cattle syndicate pressuring local ranchers. As usual for Roy, a pleasant outing featuring equal shares of gunfights and songs. He sings the title tune and "How Are You Doing in the Heart Department?" and the Sons of the Pioneers sing "Cool Water." (See ROY ROGERS series, Index.)

p, Edward J. White; d, Frank McDonald; w, Gerald Geraghty (based on a novel by William C. MacDonald); ph, William Bradford; ed, Tony Martinelli; m/l, Larry Markes, Dick Charles, Eddie De Lange, Charles Newman, Arthur Altman, Bob Nolan, Gordon Forster, Jack Elliott.

Western (PR:A MPAA:NR)

ALONG THE OREGON TRAIL*1/2

(1947) 64m REP bw

Monte Hale, (Himself), Adrian Booth (Sally Dunn), Max Terhune (Himself), Clayton Moore (Gregg Thurston), Roy Barcroft (Jake Stoner), LeRoy Mason (John Fremont), Will Wright (Jim Bridger), Wade Crosby (Tom).

Trail guide Hale leads a group exploring the Oregon trail into uncharted territory, uncovering land-greedy Moore who is manipulating local indians in order to scare off pioneers. Average Republic western interesting for the presence of Moore a few years before he became famous as TV's Lone Ranger.

p, Melville Tucker; d, R. G. Springsteen; w, Earle Snell; ph, Alfred S. Keller; ed, Arthur Roberts.

Western (PR:A MPAA:NR)

ALONG THE RIO GRANDE*1/2

(1941) 65m RKO bw

Tim Holt (Jeff), Ray Whitley (Smokey), Betty Jane Rhodes (Mary), Emmett Lynn (Whopper), Robert Fiske (Doc Randall), Hal Taliaferro (Sheriff), Carl Stockdale (Turner), Slim Whitaker (Pete), Monte Montague (Kirby), Ruth Clifford (Paula), Harry Humphrey (Pop).

Standard Tim Holt western, this one focusing on the capture of a border rustler/thief. Holt and friends join the outlaw band to nab Fiske when he crosses the Mexican border into the U.S. Fast action but little story.

p, Bert Gilroy; d Edward Killy; w, Arthur V. Jones, Morton Grant (based on a story by Stuart Anthony); ph, Frank Redman; ed, Frederic Knudson; m/l, Fred Rose, Ray Whitley.

Western (PR:A MPAA:NR)

ALPHA BETA**1/2

(1973, Brit.) 67m Memorial/Unset c

Albert Finney (Man), Rachel Roberts (Woman).

Essentially a filmed stage play detailing the disintegration of a British middle-class marriage. It's not cinematic in the least, but Finney's and Roberts' performances are amazingly powerful, and make the picture worth watching.

p, Timothy Burrill; d, Anthony Page; w, E. A. Whitehead (based on his play); ph, Charles Stewart (Technicolor); ed, Tom Priestly.

Drama (PR:C MPAA:NR)

ALPHABET MURDERS, THE*1/2

(1966) 90m MGM bw (GB: THE ABC MURDERS)

Tony Randall (Hercule Poirot), Anita Ekberg (Amanda Beatrice Cross), Robert Morley (Hastings), Maurice Denham (Japp), Guy Rolfe (Duncan Doncaster), Sheila Allen (Lady Diane), Margaret Rutherford (Miss Marple), James Villiers (Franklin), Julian Glover (Don Fortune), Grazina Frame (Betty Barnard), Clive Morton ("X"), Cyril Luckham (Sir Carmichael Clarke), Richard Wattis (Wolf), David Lodge (Sergeant), Patrick Newell (Cracknell), Austin Trevor (Judson), Alison Seebohn (Miss Sparks).

Ridiculous detective Randall stops a sadistic killer from working his way through an alphabetical victim list. Agatha Christie and her legendary detective, Poirot, get a not-at-all serious treatment in this unbelievably unfunny comic mystery.

p, Lawrence P. Bachmann; d, Frank Tashlin; w, David Pursall, Jack Seddon (based on the Agatha Christie novel The ABC Murders); ph, Desmond Dickinson; m, Ron Goodwin; ed, John Victor Smith.

Comedy/Mystery (PR:A MPAA:NR)

ALPHAVILLE, A STRANGE CASE OF LEMMY CAUTION***1/2

(1965, Fr.) 98m Athos/PATHE bw

Eddie Constantine (Lemmy Caution), Anna Karina (Natasha Von Braun), Akim Tamiroff (Henri Dickson), Laszlo Szabo (Doctor), Howard Vernon (Prof. Von

Braun), Michel Delahaye *(Von Braun's Assistant)*, Jean-Andre Fieschi *(Prof. Heckel)*, Jean-Louis Comolli *(Prof. Jeckell)*.

Intergalactic special agent Constantine travels to the mysterious Alphaville to investigate the disappearance of Tamiroff, a member of Constantine's agency. Discovering that Vernon rules the ultra-conformist Alphaville with the aid of his computer, Alpha 60, Constantine destroys both man and machine, saving those who dare to be different. Perhaps the most non-conformist director in film history, Godard uses the secret agent/sci-fi structure as a mere springboard to bounce off his ideas on an unquestioning, uncaring society, particularly that of his native Paris, whose modern motels and office buildings are used as the structures of Alphaville. Intellectually stimulating while still entertaining, ALPHAVILLE is one of Godard's more accessible films.

p, Andre Michelin; d, Jean-Luc Godard; w, Godard; ph, Raoul Coutard; m, Paul Misraki; ed, Agnes Guillemot.

Science Fiction Cas. (PR:A MPAA:NR)

ALRAUNE 1/2** (1952, Ger.) 90m STYRIA bw

Hildegard Neff *(Alraune)*, Erich von Stroheim *(Ten Brinken)*, Karlheinz Boehm *(Frank Braun)*, Harry Meyen *(Count Geroldingen)*, Harry Helm *(Dr. Mohn)*, Denise Vernanc *(Governess)*, Julia Koschka *(Princess Wolkonska)*

Oddball sci-fi horror film has madman scientist von Stroheim inseminating a prostitute with the seed of a ruthless murderer, the child maturing to Neff, whose beauty attracts young men by the score and whose evil ways send them to their doom through murder and suicide. Neff, whose wooden appearance and monotone deliv ery make her seem nothing more than a glassy-looking mannequin, finally falls in love with a boyish Boehm but just as they are about to consummate their relationship she is shot dead by an insanely jealous von Stroheim, her scientific foster father, exposing his deep-seated incestuous desires. The last eerie moments of this murky film—shot in so much shadow that eyestrain is inevitable—are filled with von Stroheim's Teutonic, immobile face, unflinchingly staring up at the hangman's noose toward which he climbs ever so slowly up the gallows steps while inky fog enfolds him. Though this film takes itself seriously, the comic aspects are inescapable and one laughs where gasps should be.

d, Arthur Maria Rabenalt; w, Fritz Rotter (based on the novel by H. H. Ewers); ph, Freidl Behn-Grund; m, Werner Heymann.

Horror/Science Fiction (PR:O MPAA:NR)

ALSINO AND THE CONDOR 1/2** (1983, Nicaragua) 89m Libra Cinema 5 c

Dean Stockwell *(Frank)*, Alan Esquivel *(Alsino)*, Carmen Bunster *(Alsino's Grandmother)*, Alejandro Parodi *(The Major)*, Delia Casanova *(Rosario)*, Marta Lorena Perez *(Lucia)*, Reinaldo Miravalle *(Don Nazario, the Birdman)*, Marcelo Gaete *(Lucia's Grandfather)*, Jan Kees De Roy *(Dutch Adviser)*.

A devastating view of Nicaragua torn to pieces by war, its people in poverty and starvation, all seen through the eyes of a wonderful little actor, Esquivel, whose only desire is to escape the havoc and misery, daydreaming his life away so that he imagines himself an exotic bird flying above the jungles and rotting cities, breathing the clean air of the high mountains, finding peace. Though thin on story, the production level is high, with arresting photography. This was the first film produced in Nicaragua following the Sandinista revolution. (In Spanish; English subtitles.)

p, Herman Littin; d, Miguel Littin; w, M. Littin, Isidora Aguirre, Tomas Perez Turrent; ph, Jorge Herrera, Pablo Martinez; m, Leo Brower; ed, Meriam Talavera; art d, Elly Menz.

Drama (PR:C MPAA:NR)

ALTERED STATES 1/2** (1980) 102m WB c

William Hurt *(Eddie Jessup)*, Blair Brown *(Emily Jessup)*, Bob Balaban *(Arthur Rosenberg)*, Charles Haid *(Mason Parrish)*, Thaao Penghlis *(Eccheverria)*, Miguel Godreau *(Primal Man)*, Dori Brenner *(Sylvia Rosenberg)*, Peter Brandon *(Hobart)*, Charles White Eagle *(The Brujo)*, Drew Barrymore *(Margaret Jessup)*, Megan Jeffers *(Grace Jessup)*.

Obsessive scientist Hurt, disregarding his wife, family, and friends, attempts to find the truth about his inner self and man's relationship to the universe, almost becoming a misshapen monster in the process. Essentially, a big-budget, modern-day version of a 1960s acid-trip movie in which South American mushrooms and isolation tanks bring hallucinations to life. Flamboyant and talented but terribly self-indulgent director Russell takes a confusing Chayefsky story, puts it in a pretty package, but fails to bring any sense to the silly affair. A feast for special effects lovers and drugged philosophy majors only.

p, Howard Gottfried; d, Ken Russell; w, Sidney Aaron [Paddy Chayefsky] (based on the novel Chayefsky); ph, Jordan Croneweth (Technicolor); m, John Corigliano; ed, Eric Jenkins; spec eff, Bran Ferren; makeup, Dick Smith.

Science Fiction/Drama Cas. (PR:O MPAA:R)

ALVAREZ KELLY 1/2** (1966) 110m COL c

William Holden *(Alvarez Kelly)*, Richard Widmark *(Col. Tom Rossiter)*, Janice Rule *(Liz Pickering)*, Patrick O'Neal *(Maj. Albert Stedman)*, Victoria Shaw *(Charity Warwick)*, Roger C. Carmel *(Capt. Angus Ferguson)*, Richard Rust *(Sergeant Hatcher)*, Arthur Franz *(Captain Towers)*, Donald Barry *(Lt. Farrow)*, Duke Hobbie *(John Beaurider)*, Harry Carey, Jr. *(Cpl. Peterson)*, Howard Caine *(McIntyre)*, Mauritz Hugo *(Ely Harrison)*, G. B. Atwater *(Gen. Kautz)*, Robert Morgan *(Capt. Williams)*, Paul Lukather *(Capt. Webster)*, Stephanie Hill *(Mary Ann)*, Indus Arthur *(Melinda)*, Clint Ritchie *(Union Lieutenant)*.

Holden is an avaricious cattleman of Irish-Mexican ancestry in this less than even, often offbeat, western Civil War drama. At first he makes a deal to sell 5,000 head of prime cattle to Union officer O'Neal, but en route to the delivery station he is waylaid by Widmark and a band of tough Confederate troopers, ordered to teach Widmark's unskilled drovers how to handle a large herd of cattle so Holden's cows can be driven into Confederate territory. The journey is fraught with action, from attacking Indians to running gunfights with Union troops, all after the prize beef. The film lags toward the end but a climactic stampede overwhelms the viewer. Widmark is particularly menacing in this film, a ruthless cutthroat who will perform any abusive act to advance the Lost Cause, even shooting off one of Holden's fingers to signify that he means business when they first meet, an encounter arranged for by Shaw, who feigns the gentle southern belle until she can contact Widmark to abduct her house guest Holden. Rule plays a sexy loose woman (not unlike her contemporary role of married slattern in THE CHASE); she belongs to Widmark and when he learns that Holden has dallied with her his temper blazes to white heat and he promises to kill the cowboy when the drive is finished. Holden's performance is not in keeping with his usual intensive effort, due, no doubt, to a 26-week absence from any filmmaking. Critics noted his almost withdrawn attitude, particularly with Widmark, who fiercely steals one scene after another.

p, Sol C. Siegel; d, Edward Dmytryk; w, Franklin Coen, Elliott Arnold (based on a story by Coen); ph, Joseph MacDonald (Panavision, Eastmancolor); m, John Green; ed, Harold F. Kress; m/l, title song, Johnny Mercer (sung by the Brothers Four).

Western/War Cas. (PR:A MPAA:NR)

ALVIN PURPLE 1/2** (1974, Aus.) 97m Hexagon/Roadshow c

Graeme Blundell *(Alvin Purple)*, George Whaley *(Dr. McBurney)*, Penne Hackforth-Jones *(Dr. Liz Sort)*, Elli Maclure *(Tina)*, Noel Ferrier *(Judge)*, Jill Foster *(Mrs. Horwood)*.

Simple Aussie Blundell tries to face up to the fact that women find him irresistible. Clever, adult comedy from Down Under featuring a talented group of fresh faces.

p&d, Tim Burstall; w, Alan Hopgood; ph, John Seale, M, Brian Cadd.

Comedy Cas. (PR:C MPAA:R)

ALVIN RIDES AGAIN 1/2** (1974, Aus.) 89m Hexagon/Roadshow c

Graeme Blundell *(Alvin Purple "Balls" McGee)*, Alan Finney *(Spike Dooley)*, Brionny Behets *(Nymphomaniacal Taxi Passenger)*, Abigail *(Mae)*, Frank Thring *("Fingers")*, Chantal Contouri *(Boobs LaTouche)*, Frank Wilson *(House Detective)*, Jeff Ashby *(Loopy Schneider)*, Jon Finlayson *(Magician)*, Noel Ferrier *("The Hatchet")*.

Sequel to the successful ALVIN PURPLE has sexually magnetic Blundell getting mixed up with a look-alike American gangster. Not as clever and a bit more vulgar than its predecessor, the film still has a certain charm, thanks to its star.

p, Tim Burstall; d, David Bilcock, Robin Copping; w, Burstall, Alan Hopgood, Alan Finney; ph, Copping; m, Brian Cadd; ed, Edward McQueen-Mason; art d, Bill Hutchinson.

Comedy Cas. (PR:O MPAA:NR)

ALWAYS A BRIDE* 1/2 (1940) 58m FN/WB bw

Rosemary Lane *(Alice Bond)*, George Reeves *(Michael Stevens)*, John Eldredge *(Marshall Winkler)*, Virginia Brissac *(Lucy Bond)*, Francis Pierlot *(Pete Bond)*, Oscar O'Shea *(Dan Jarvis)*, Ferris Taylor *(Mayor Loomis)*, Joseph King *(Franklyn)*, Phyllis Ruth *(Mary Ann Coleridge)*, Lucia Carroll *(Receptionist)*, Jack Mower *(Martin)*, Tom Wilson *(Charlie)*.

Confused Lane dumps her boring fiance Eldredge and runs off with lazy but happy Reeves. Weak, uninteresting attempt at comedy, with nothing to separate it from a thousand others just like it.

d, Noel M. Smith; w, Robert E. Kent (based on the play by Barry Conners); ph, Charles Schoenbaum; ed, Frank Magee.

Comedy (PR:A MPAA:NR)

ALWAYS A BRIDE 1/2** (1954, Brit.) 83m GFD bw

Peggy Cummins *(Clare Hemsley)*, Terence Morgan *(Terence Winch)*, Ronald Squire *(Victor Hemsley)*, James Hayter *(Dutton)*, Marie Lohr *(Dowager)*, Geoffrey Sumner *(Teddy)*, Charles Goldner *(Manager)*, David Hurst *(Beckstein)*, Jacques Brunius *(Inspector)*, Jill Day *(Singer)*, Sebastian Cabot *(Taxi Driver)*, Jacques Brown *(Manager)*, Dino Galvani *(Magistrate)*.

British treasury investigator falls for the daughter of a con man planning a big scam in Monte Carlo. Delightful English comedy with Cummins turning in a charming portrayal.

p, Robert Garrett; d, Ralph Smart; w, Smart, Peter Jones; ph, C. Pennington-Richards; m, Benjamin Frankel; ed, Alfred Roome.

Comedy (PR:A MPAA:NR)

ALWAYS A BRIDESMAID* 1/2 (1943) 61m UNIV bw

The Andrews Sisters *(Themselves)*, Patric Knowles *(Tony Warren)*, Grace McDonald *(Linda Marlowe)*, Billy Gilbert *(Nick)*, Charles Butterworth *(Col. Winchester)*, Edith Barrett *(Mrs. Cavanaugh)*, O'Neill Nolan *(Rigsy)*, Annie Rooney *(Annie)*, Addison Richards *(Martin Boland)*, Charles Cane *(Police Lieutenant)*, Philip Van Zandt *(Waiter)*, The Jivin' Jacks and Jills.

Illegal manufacturer uses a lonely hearts club as a front during wartime. McDonald, the local asst. D.A., works in conjunction with the jiving Andrews Sisters to trap the crook in a plot which is only an excuse to parade some entertaining song and dance numbers.

d, Eric C. Kenton; w, Mel Ronson (based on a story by Oscar Brodney); ph, Louis Da Pron.

Musical (PR:A MPAA:NR)

ALWAYS ANOTHER DAWN* (1948, Aus.) 65m EM/UNIV bw

Charles Tingwell, Guy Doleman, Queenie Ashton, Betty McDowell, Douglas Herald, Charles Zoll, Max Gibb.

Not-too-thrilling exploits of the Australian navy during WW II are depicted in this average war picture. Too many flag-waving speeches get in the way of a story centered around the battle of the Coral Sea.

p, Tom McCreadie; d, McCreadie; w, Zelma Roberts; ph, George Malcolm.

War (PR:A MPAA:NR)

ALWAYS GOODBYE* (1931) 62m FOX bw

Elissa Landi *(Lila)*, Lewis Stone *(Graham)*, Paul Cavanagh *(Carlson)*, John Garrick *(Cyril)*, Frederick Kerr *(Sir George Boomer)*, Herbert Bunston *(Merson)*, Lumsden Hare *(Blake)*.

Landi, who's been continually jilted by males in the past, finally meets "Mr. Right," diamond dealer Stone. Further complicating her life are suave crook Cavanagh and Garrick, who pursues her because he believes her to be an heiress, particularly when she is sporting Stone's gems. Sort of an early-day GOODBYE GIRL without the humor.

d, William Cameron Menzies, Kenneth MacKenna; w, Kate McLaurin; ed, Harold Schuster.

Drama (PR:A MPAA:NR)

ALWAYS GOODBYE**   (1938) 75m FOX bw

Barbara Stanwyck (*Margot Weston*), Herbert Marshall (*Jim Howard*), Ian Hunter (*Phillip Marshall*), Cesar Romero (*Count Giovanni Corini*), Lynn Bari (*Jessica Reid*), Binnie Barnes (*Harriet Martin*), John Russell (*Roddy*), Mary Forbes (*Martha Marshall*), Albert Conti (*Benoit*), Marcelle Corday (*Nurse*), Franklin Pangborn (*Bicycle Salesman*), George Davis, Ben Welden (*Taxi Drivers*).

With the aid of kindly doctor Marshall, Stanwyck gives up her illegitimate child for adoption. Years later, the now-grown and wealthy boy receives assistance from a strange woman (Stanwyck) who exposes his fiancee as an unscrupulous vixen out for his money. A passable vehicle for Stanwyck, one of the finest actresses of the 1930-1950 era.

p, Raymond Griffith; d, Sidney Lanfield; w, Kathryn Scola, Edith Skouras (based on a story by Gilbert Emery, Douglas Doty); ph, Robert Planck; ed, Robert Simpson; md, Louis Silvers; art d, Bernard Herzbrun, Hans Peters; set d, Thomas Little; cos, Royer.

Drama (PR:A MPAA:NR)

ALWAYS IN MY HEART**   (1942) 93m WB bw

Kay Francis (*Marjorie Scott*), Walter Huston (*MacKenzie Scott*), Gloria Warren (*Victoria Scott*), Patty Hale (*Booley*), Frankie Thomas (*Martin Scott*), Una O'Connor (*Angie*), Sidney Blackmer (*Philip Ames*), Armida (*Lolita*), Frank Puglia (*Joe Borrelli*), Russell Arms (*Red*), Anthony Caruso (*Frank*), Elvira Curci (*Rosita*), John Hamilton (*Warden*), Harry Lewis (*Steve*), Herbert Gunn (*Dick*), Borrah Minevitch and His Rascals.

Gifted musician Huston, convicted of a crime he didn't commit, is released from prison after years of separation from his family. He finally finds them in a small coastal town and is delighted to learn that his singing daughter has carried on the family tradition.

p, Walter MacEwen, William Jacobs; d, Joe Graham; w, Adele Comandini (based on a play by Dorothy Bennett, Irving White); ph, Sid Hickox; m, Heinze Reinhold; ed, Thomas Pratt.

Drama (PR:AA MPAA:NR)

ALWAYS IN TROUBLE**   (1938) 69m FOX bw

Jane Withers (*Jerry Darlington*), Jean Rogers (*Virginia Darlington*), Arthur Treacher (*Rogers*), Robert Kellard (*Pete Graham*), Eddie Collins (*Uncle Ed Darlington*), Andrew Tombes (*J. C. Darlington*), Nana Bryant (*Mrs. Darlington*), Joan Woodbury (*Pearl Mussendorfer*), Joseph Sawyer (*Buster Mussendorfer*), Charles Lane (*Donald Gower*), Pat Flaherty (*Gideon Stubbs*).

Withers' pop strikes it rich in the oil fields and mom prods the family into joining the ranks of the social elite, much to the chagrin of father and the kids. After a yachting jaunt goes sour and a run-in with a zany bunch of smugglers led by the delightful Treacher, Withers, mom, and dad return to their humble existence, chucking the trappings of the idle rich.

p, John Stone; d, Joseph Santley; w, Karen De Wolf, Robert Chapin (based on a story by Albert Treynor and Jeff Moffit); ph, Lucien Andriot; m, Samuel Kaylin; ed, Nick De Maggio.

Comedy (PR:AA MPAA:NR)

ALWAYS LEAVE THEM LAUGHING**   (1949) 115m WB bw

Milton Berle (*Kip Cooper*), Virginia Mayo (*Nancy Egan*), Ruth Roman (*Fay Washburn*), Bert Lahr (*Eddie Egan*), Alan Hale (*Mr. Washburn*), Grace Hayes (*Mrs. Washburn*), Jerome Cowan (*Elliot Montgomery*), Lloyd Gough (*Monte Wilson*), Ransom Sherman (*Richards*), Iris Adrian (*Julie Adams*), Wally Vernon (*Comic*), Cecil Stewart and His Royal Rogues, O'Donnell and Blair, Max Showalter, The Moroccans.

Small-time comic Berle, realizing that his career is going nowhere fast, takes a chance on using his own material and becomes a success. Depending on whether you're a fan of Uncle Milty or not, this jump from TV to the big screen will either be a laugh riot or a dud, but the manic slapstick will win the kids over.

p, Jerry Wald; d, Roy Del Ruth; w, Melville Shavelson, Jack Rose (based on a story by Max Schulman and Richard Mealand); ph, Ernest Haller; ed, Clarence Kolster; ch, LeRoy Prinz; m/l, Sammy Cahn.

Comedy (PR:A MPAA:NR)

ALWAYS TOGETHER**½   (1947) 78m FN/WB bw

Robert Hutton (*Donn Masters*), Joyce Reynolds (*Jane Barker*), Cecil Kellaway (*Jonathan Turner*), Ernest Truex (*Mr. Bull*), Don McGuire (*McIntyre*), Ransom Sherman (*Judge*), Douglas Kennedy (*Doberman*).

Movie fanatic Reynolds is left a million dollars by dying millionaire Kellaway. When her aspiring writer husband finds out about the gift, he turns into a jerk and demands alimony when Reynolds seeks a divorce. Another log of confusion is tossed on the fire when Kellaway recovers and wants his money back. Quirky, somewhat enjoyable comedy best remembered for the guest appearances of Humphrey Bogart, Errol Flynn, Dennis Morgan, Janis Paige, Eleanor Parker, and Alexis Smith as inhabitants of the cinematic fantasy world within Reynolds' mind.

p, Alex Gottlieb; d, Frederick de Cordova; w, Phoebe and Henry Ephron, I. A. L. Diamond; ph, Carl Guthrie; m, Werner Heymann; ed, Folmar Blangsted; art d, Leo K. Kuter; set d, Jack McConaghy; cos, Travilla; spec eff, William McGann, Edwin B. DuPar; makeup, Perc Westmore.

Comedy (PR:A MPAA:NR)

ALWAYS VICTORIOUS**   (1960, Ital.) 75m Bamberger/UFA c

Vittorio De Sica (*Capt. Ernesto di Rossi*), Folco Lulli (*Sciacciabratta*), Heinz Reincke (*Hans Richter*), Ingnar Zelsberg (*Anna*), Helene Remy (*Irma*), Lionella Carell (*Mrs. Sciacciabratta*), Piero Lulli (*Franco*), Marco Gugliemi (*Alberto*), Aldo Pedinotti (*Carlo*).

Lightweight farce offers De Sica as a skipper of a fruit and vegetable boat plying its commerce between Leghorn and Genoa during WW II. Trouble arises due to a crew of inexperienced landlubbers, able seamen already serving on more important vessels. Folco Lulli is amusing as the surly second-in-command, looking out for his absent-minded captain, who sees intrigue and destruction over every wave. It is apparent that Italy's top director took on such pedestrian chores to glean enough capital to finance his considerably more artistic efforts. (In Italian, English subtitles.)

p, Peter Bamberger; d, Wolfgang Staudte; w, Emillio Concini, Duccio Tessari.

Satire/Comedy (PR:A MPAA:NR)

AM I GUILTY?**   (1940) 71m Supreme bw

Ralph Cooper (*Dr. James Dunbar*), Sybil Lewis (*Joan Freeman*), Sam McDaniel (*John D. Jones*), Lawrence Criner (*"Trigger" Bennett*), Marcella Moreland (*Marcella*), Arthur T. Ray (*Dr. Freeman*), Reginald Fenderson (*Slick*), Monte Hawley (*Tracy*), "Tia Juana" Matthew Jones (*Monk*), "Pigmeat" Markham (*Proprietor*), Jesse Brooks (*Dr. Fairchild*), Napoleon Simpson (*John Parks*), Clarence Brooks (*Lt. Harris*), Cleo Desmond (*Mrs. Thompson*), Ida Coffin (*Mrs. Smith*), Lillian Randolph (*Mrs. Jones*), Vernon McCallan (*Judge*), Eddie Thompson (*Lawyer*), Mae Turner (*Dunbar's Mother*), Alfred Grant (*Intern*), Gurnsey Morrow (*Pete*).

Early attempt at meaningful black social drama has a young black doctor trying to decide between personal success (treating rich gangsters) or helping others by starting a clinic for the poor. Ambitious for its time, the film still falls victim to stereotyping and cliche situations.

p, A. W. Hackell; d, Samuel Neufeld; w, Sherman Lowe (based on a story by George Sayre and Earl Snell); ph, Robert Cline.

Drama (PR:A MPAA:NR)

AMANTI   (SEE: PLACE FOR LOVERS, A, 1969, Ital./Fr.)

AMARCORD***   (1974, Ital.) 127m F.C.-PECF/WB-NW c

Magali Noel (*Gradisca*), Bruno Zanin (*Titta*), Pupella Maggio (*Titta's Mother*), Armando Brancia (*Titta's Father*), Giuseppe Ianigro (*Titta's Grandfather*), Nando Orfei (*Pataca*), Ciccio Ingrassia (*Uncle Teo*), Luigi Rossi (*Lawyer*), Gennaro Ombra (*Bisein*), Josiane Tanzilli (*Volpina*), Antonietta Beluzzi (*Tobacconist*), Gianfilipo Carcano (*Don Baravelli*), Ferruccio Brembilla (*Fascist Leader*), Dina Adorni (*Math Teacher*), Marcello di Falco (*The Prince*), Aristide Caporale (*Giudizio*), Alvaro Vitali (*Naso*), Bruno Scagnetti (*Ovo*), Bruno Lenzi (*Gigliozzi*), Fernando Vona (*Candela*), Donatella Gambini (*Aldina*), Franca Magno (*Zeus*), Marco Misul (*Philosophy Teacher*), Mario Silvestri (*Italian Teacher*), Fides Stagni (*Art Teacher*), Mario Liberati (*"Ronald Coleman," Theater Owner*), Domenenico Pertica (*Blindman*).

It seems that as Fellini's style developed into a pictorial of the bizarre fragments of his imagination, his ability to weave a structure adding continuity to his visuals diminished. Such is the case with AMARCORD, a collection of memories about a seaside village (very similar to Fellini's boyhood town of Rimini) in the 1930s. Incidents are viewed from the perspective of Zanin, playing an impressionable youth, and it is through his eyes that Fellini takes a penetrating look at family life, religion, education, and politics. Among the characters are Zanin's constantly battling mother and father, and a priest who listens to confession only to spark his own deviant imagination. Though Italy is under control of the Fascists, the regime's oppressiveness remains an obscurity to the naive villagers, who worship an immense, daunting banner of the face of Il Duce. At the film's end, Zanin's mother dies, marking the youth's passage into manhood and the time for him to leave the security and the memories of the village behind. Though there is hardly a character in AMARCORD who is unscathed by Fellini's biting wit, the director still shows a great amount of love for these people. Unique personality traits, those things that reveal weaknesses and, thus, humanness, are valued by Fellini for the color and variety they add to the world. AMARCORD won the Academy Award for Best Foreign Film in 1974.

p, Franco Cristaldi; d, Federico Fellini; w, Fellini, Tonino Guerra; ph, Giuseppe Rotunno; m, Nino Rota; ed, Ruggiero Mastroianni; art d & cos, Danilo Donati.

Drama/Fantasy Cas. (PR:O MPAA:R)

AMATEUR, THE**   (1982) 111m FOX c

John Savage (*Heller*), Christopher Plummer (*Lakos*), Marthe Keller (*Elisabeth*), Arthur Hill (*Brewer*), Ed Lauter (*Anderson*), Nicholas Campbell (*Scraeger*), Jan Rubes (*Kaplan*), Graham Jarvis (*Porter*), Chapelle Jaffe (*Gretchen*), Jan Triska (*Rodzenko*), Miguel Fernandes (*Botaro*), Lynne Griffin (*Sara*), John Marley (*Molton*), Jacques Godin (*Argus*), George Coe (*Rutledge*), Vladimir Valenta (*Ludvik*).

After the murder of his girl friend by terrorists, CIA computer technician Savage blackmails his bosses into training him as a professional killer. Sneaking behind the Iron Curtain, Savage sets out to destroy the terrorist gang. A good cast and a great premise for an espionage/revenge film is ruined by implausibility and confusion.

p, Joel B. Michaels, Garth H. Drabinsky; d, Charles Jarrott; w, Robert Littell, Diana Maddox (based on Littell's novel); ph, John Coquillon (Technicolor); m, Ken Wannberg; ed, Richard Halsey; art d, Richard Wilcox.

Spy Drama Cas. (PR:C MPAA:R)

AMATEUR CROOK zero   (1937) 62m Royal

Herman Brix Bruce Bennett (*Jimmy Baxter*), Joan Barclay (*Betsy*), Monte Blue (*Crone*), Jack Mulhall (*Jaffin*), Vivian Oakland (*Mrs. Flint*), Jimmy Aubrey (*Armand*), Fuzzy Knight (*Jape*).

Poor production involves Barclay attempting to recover stolen jewels from her father's safe with Brix, later Bruce Bennett, helping her to nab the baddies. Nothing of value.

p, Sam Katzman; d, Katzman; ph, Bill Hyer.

Crime **(PR:A MPAA:NR)**

AMATEUR DADDY* (1932) 7lm FOX bw

Warner Baxter *(Jim Gladden)*, Marian Nixon *(Sally Smith)*, Rita LaRoy *(Lottie Pelgram)*, Lucille Powers *(Olive Smith)*, William Pawley *(2nd Fred Smith)*, David Landau *(Sam Pelgram)*, Clarence Wilson *(Bill Hansen)*, Frankie Darro *(Pete Smith)*, Joan Breslaw *(Nancy Smith)*, Gail Kornfeld *(Lily Smith)*, Joe Hachey *(Sam Pelgram, Jr.)*, Edwin Stanley *(1st Fred Smith)*.

Good-natured Baxter vows to take care of a dying buddy's family despite the ridicule of the family's cold-hearted neighbors. Admirable attempt to capture some real human emotion in a tense situation is spoiled with some typical easy answers at the conclusion. Excellent photography by James Wong Howe.

d, John Blystone; w, Doris Malloy, Frank Dolan (based on the novel *Scotch Valley* by Mildred Cram); ph, James Wong Howe; ed, Louis Loeffler.

Drama **(PR:A MPAA:NR)**

AMATEUR GENTLEMAN*** (1936, Brit.) 93m Criterion/UA bw

Douglas Fairbanks Jr.*(Barnabas Barty)*, Elissa Landi *(Lady Cleone)*, Gordon Harker *(Natty Bell)*, Basil Sydney *(Chichester)*, Hugh Williams *(Ronald)*, Irene Browne *(Lady Huntstanton)*, Athole Stewart *(Marquess of Camberhurst)*, Coral Browne *(Pauline d'Arville)*, Margaret Lockwood *(Georgina Huntstanton)*, Frank Pettingell *(John Barty)*, Esme Percy *(Townsend)*, Gilbert Davis *(Prince Regent)*.

Good actioner with Fairbanks at his dashing best, posing as a foppish gent while attempting to clear his father's name of a crime he did not commit. Finally cornering the true thief and murderer, Sydney, Fairbanks takes him on in the ring and pounds him senseless before turning him over to the police. Some spectacular scenes, particularly ballroom sequences, give this production a lavish impression, albeit the male dancers are a little more light on their feet than direction might call for. Landi, a stunning beauty and solid actress, is unfortunately given little to do in this intriguing yarn.

p, Marcel Hellman; d, Thornton Freeland; w, Clemence Dane, Edward Knoblock (based on the novel by Jeffrey Farnol); ph, Gunther Krampf; ed, Conrad von Molo; ch, Quentin Todd.

Adventure **(PR:A MPAA:NR)**

AMAZING ADVENTURE, THE (SEE: ROMANCE AND RICHES, 1937, Brit.)

AMAZING COLOSSAL MAN, THE** (1957) 81m AIP bw

Glenn Langan *(Lt.-Col. Glenn Manning)*, Cathy Downs *(Carol Forrest)*, William Hudson *(Dr. Paul Lindstrom)*, James Seay *(Col. Hallock)*, Larry Thor *(Dr. Eric Coulter)*, Russ Bender *(Richard Kingman)*, Lynn Osborn *(Sgt. Taylor)*, Diana Darrin *(Typist)*, William Hughes *(Control Officer)*, Hank Patterson *(Henry)*, Scott Peters *(Sgt. Lee Carter)*, Myron Cook *(Capt. Thomas)*, Jack Kosslyn, Jean Moorehead, Frank Jenks, Bill Cassady, Edmund Cobb, Paul Hahn, June Jocelyn, Stanley Lachman.

Army colonel Langan is exposed to massive amounts of radiation after an atomic experiment backfires. Unexpectedly, he is not killed, but his body chemistry is altered, causing him to grow at the rate of ten feet per day. When reaching the height of seventy feet, the radioactivity seems to affect Langan's brain too, and he begins to wreak havoc on nearby Las Vegas. Not simply looking for a jumbo-sized poker game, the colossal man is finally killed in a rather exciting conclusion at Boulder Dam. One of the first atomic mutation horror films of the fifties, and one of the most absurdly entertaining. The scenes detailing Langan's growth and his attack on Vegas are quite memorable.

p, Bert I. Gordon; d, Gordon; w, Mark Hanna, Gordon; ph, Joseph Biroc; m, Albert Glasser; ed, Ronald Sinclair; spec eff, Gordon.

Science Fiction **(PR:A MPAA:NR)**

AMAZING DOBERMANS, THE* 1/2 (1976) 96m Golden c

Fred Astaire *(Daniel Hughes)*, James Franciscus *(Lucky Vincent)*, Barbara Eden *(Justine Pirot)*, Jack Carter *(Solly Kramer)*, Billy Barty *(Clown)*, Parley Baer *(Circus Owner)*.

Undercover agent Franciscus enlists the aid of Astaire's trained pooches in nabbing small-time hood Carter. Rather sad to see Astaire wasting his time in this mediocre kids' film.

p, David Chudnow; d, Byron Chudnow; w, Michael Kraike, William Goldstein, Richard Chapman (based on a story by Kraike, Goldstein); ph, Jack Adams (CFI Color); m, Alan Silvestri; ed, James Potter.

Children **Cas.** **(PR:AAA MPAA:G)**

AMAZING DR. CLITTERHOUSE, THE*** (1938) 87m WB bw

Edward G. Robinson *(Dr. Clitterhouse)*, Claire Trevor *(Jo Keller)*, Humphrey Bogart *(Rocks Valentine)*, Gale Page *(Nurse Randolph)*, Donald Crisp *(Inspector Lane)*, Allen Jenkins *(Okay)*, Thurston Hall *(Grant)*, John Litel *(Prosecuting Attorney)*, Henry ONeill *(Judge)*, Maxie Rosenbloom *(Butch)*, Curt Bois *(Rabbit)*, Bert Hanlon *(Pal)*, Ward Bond *(Tug)*, Vladmir Sokoloff *(Popus)*, Billy Wayne *(Candy)*, Robert Homans *(Lt. Johnson)*, William Worthington, Larry Steers, Ed Mortimer *(Guests)*, William Haade *(Watchman)*, Thomas Jackson *(Connors)*, Edward Gargan *(Sergeant)*, Ray Dawe, Bob Reeves *(Policemen)*, Winifred Harris *(Mrs. Ganswoort)*, Eric Stanley *(Dr. Ames)*, Loia Cheaney *(Nurse Donor)*, Wade Boteler *(Captain MacLevy)*, Libby Taylor *(Mrs. Jefferson)*, Edgar Dearing *(Patrolman)*, Sidney Bracy *(Chemist)*, Irving Bacon *(Jury Foreman)*, Vera Lewis *(Woman Juror)*, Bruce Mitchell *(Bailiff)*, Ronald Reagan *(Announcer's Voice)*.

Robinson is a book-writing criminologist (Dr. Clitterhouse) fascinated with hoodlums and thieves, so eager to test the physiological reactions of criminals at the time of their crimes—do they sweat, does the heart beat faster, when does panic set in?—that he actually commits several jewel robberies, then contacts an infamous fence who turns out to be Trevor. She, in turn, introduces Robinson to a gang of super crooks headed by Bogart (with the unmistakably professional name of "Rocks Valentine"), and he masterminds several jobs for them. Bogart becomes jealous of Robinson's natural leadership abilities; he appears to be taking over the gang out of sheer brain power. Bogie locks Robinson in a cold-storage vault during a fur heist. Rosenbloom, Trevor's right hand man, rescues Robinson who decides it is time to depart the criminal world. He returns to his practice but Bogart trails him and threatens to expose him as a thief unless he goes on masterminding robberies for him. Pretending to accept the proposition, Robinson pours Bogart a drink, slipping poison into it. He then records Bogie's every twitch, with the help of his ever-faithful nurse, Page, until the gangster dies. Next he turns himself in and while Trevor, Page, and Crisp, a visiting Scotland Yard inspector startled by the whole fantastic story, watch dumbfounded in court, Robinson pleads guilty to murdering Bogart by reason of insanity. Once on the witness stand he adamantly states that he was sane when he poisoned the crook; he did it to advance the cause of psychological science, don't you see? The jury does see what they think is a crazy man. Only an insane person would plead insanity then claim soundness of mind. With this their only rationale, jury members vote to free Robinson who goes off chatting with nurse Page on one arm and fence Trevor on the other. The mere impossibility of this plot, taken from a drama originally starring Cedric Hardwicke in England and on Broadway, coupled to Robinson's bemused and farcically constructed character, makes this an entertaining satire on the entire gangster cycle so energetically produced by the Brothers Warner, a delightful film the viewer will take seriously until realizing that both legs are not only being pulled but yanked hard, especially by Wexley and Huston who wrote the sharp, bantering dialog and script and Litvak, whose moody directorial genius caricaturizes the filmic nightmares that earlier lurked inside Germany's UFA studios.

p, Anatole Litvak, Robert Lord; d, Litvak; w, John Wesley, John Huston (based on the play by Barre Lyndon); ph, Tony Gaudio; m, Max Steiner; ed, Warren Low; art d, Carl Jules Weyl; cos, Milo Anderson.

Crime **(PR:C MPAA:NR)**

AMAZING GRACE* (1974) 97m UA c

Moms Mabley *(Grace)*, Slappy White *(Forthwith Wilson)*, Moses Gunn *(Welton J. Walters)*, Rosalind Cash *(Creola Waters)*, Stepin Fetchit *(Cousin Lincoln)*, Butterfly McQueen *(Clarine)*, Jim Karen *(Annenberg)*, George Miles *(Strokes)*, Gary Bolling *(William)*, Dolph Sweet *(Mayor Scott)*

Terrible throwback to the racist "yassuh boss" black films of the 1930s has crusty old Mabley shaping up mayoral candidate Gunn. Aging actors recreating tired old roles apparently never heard of the civil rights movement.

p, Matt Robinson, d, Stan Lathan; w, Robinson; ph, Ed Brown, Sr., Sol Negrin (DeLuxe Color); m, Coleridge Taylor Perkinson; ed, Paul L. Evans; art d, Robert Wightman; set d, Richard Nelson.

Comedy **(PR:A MPAA:G)**

AMAZING MR. BEECHAM, THE*

(1949, Brit.) Two Cities/GFD bw (AKA: THE CHILTERN HUNDREDS)

Cecil Parker *(Benjamin Beecham)*, A. E. Matthews *(Lord Lister)*, David Tomlinson *(Lord Tony Pym)*, Lana Morris *(Bessie Sykes)*, Helen Backlin *(June Farrell)*, Marjorie Fielding *(Lady Molly)*, Tom Macaulay *(Jack Cleghorn)*, Joyce Carey *(Lady Caroline)*, Charles Cullum *(Colonel)*, Anthony Steel *(Adjutant)*.

British hijinks has a rebellious butler campaign against the snobbish son of his employer for a political post, with all the caste-system jokes thrown in to confuse anyone not living in England. Barely manages a good laugh.

p, George H. Brown; d, John Paddy Carstairs; w, William Douglas Home, Patrick Kirwan (based on the play by Home); ph, Jack Hildyard.

Comedy **(PR:A MPAA:NR)**

AMAZING MR. BLUNDEN, THE** (1973, Brit.) 99m HEMISPHERE c

Laurence Naismith, James Villiers, Diana Dors, David Lodge, Lynne Frederick, Dorothy Alison, Rosalyn Lander, Marc Granger.

Extremely confused story about a ghost who employs a widow with two young children to take over his abandoned country mansion where the children meet two ghost children and through them solve an ancient mystery. Too scary for children and too befuddling for the average viewer to sort out. Most of the responsibility for this disjointed film rests with director Jeffries, whose cuts are confusing; the point of view meanders, as do the camera and script.

d&w, Lionel Jeffries (based on the story "The Ghosts" by Antonio Barker); ph, Gerry Fisher; m, Elmer Bernstein.

Mystery **(PR:C MPAA:NR)**

AMAZING MR. FORREST, THE* (1943, Brit.) 71m PRC bw

Edward Everett Horton *(Treadwell)*, Otto Kruger *(Mike Chadwick)*, Jack Buchanan *(John Forrest)*, Jack LaRue *(Alberni)*, Georgia Withers *(Alice Forrest)*, Syd Walker *(Younce)*, David Burns *(Beretti)*, Walter Rilla *(Prince Homouska)*, Charles Carson *(Charles Cartwright)*, Leslie Perrins *(Harper)*, Ronald Shiner *(Spider Ferris)*.

Supposed comedy about the breakup of a group of jewel thieves falls with a dull thud. Horton, as always, is delightful, despite the material.

p, Walter C. Mycroft, Jack Buchanan; d, Thornton Freeland; w, Ralph Spence; ph, Claude Friese-Greene; ed, E. B. Jarvis.

Comedy **(PR:A MPAA:NR)**

AMAZING MR. WILLIAMS 1/2** (1939) 80m COL bw

Melvyn Douglas *(Kenny Williams)*, Joan Blondell *(Maxine Carroll)*, Clarence Kolb *(McGovern)*, Ruth Donnelly *(Effie)*, Edward Brophy *(Moseby)*, Donald MacBride *(Bixler)*, Don Beddoe *(Deever)*, Jonathan Hale *(Mayor)*, John Wray *(Stanley)*.

Slick, intelligent flatfoot Douglas gets into hot water with his superiors when he aids fugitive Wray, whom he believes to be innocent. Blondell is cute and sexy as Douglas' gal who wishes he'd pay as much attention to her as he does on seeing justice done. Funny, well-paced police picture that gets its spark from its romantic side angle.

p, Everett Riskin; d, Alexander Hall; w, Dwight Taylor, Sy Bartlett (based on a story by Bartlett); ph, Arthur Todd; m, Morris W. Stoloff; ed, Viola Lawrence; art d, Lionel Banks.

Police Drama **(PR:A MPAA:NR)**

AMAZING MR. X, THE (SEE: SPIRITUALIST, THE, 1948)

AMAZING MRS. HOLLIDAY*** (1943) 97m UNIV bw

Deanna Durbin *(Ruth)*, Edmond O'Brien *(Tom)*, Barry Fitzgerald *(Timothy)*, Arthur Treacher *(Henderson)*, Harry Davenport *(Commodore)*, Grant Mitchell *(Edgar)*, Frieda Inescourt *(Karen)*, Elisabeth Risdon *(Louise)*, Jonathan Hale *(Ferguson)*, Esther Dale *(Lucy)*, Gus Schilling *(Jeff)*, J. Frank Hamilton *(Dr. Kirke)*, Christopher Severn, Yvonne Severn, Vido Rich, Mila Rich, Teddy Infuhr, Linda Bieber, Diane Dubois, Bill Ward, and the Chinese Baby *(The Children)*.

A rather Cinderella-like adventure with Durbin trying to get a group of orphan children out of South China and to safety in America. Fitzgerald poses Durbin as the wife of his former boss (a steamship magnate lost at sea) and manages to establish the kids in the huge family mansion. She confesses her fraud to the magnate's grandson, O'Brien, who protects her and the children. All turns out well in the end when the magnate shows up alive after all and takes the kids under his wing. Pleasant outing highlighted by two songs sung by Durbin in Chinese.

p&d, Bruce Manning; w, Frank Ryan, John Jacoby (based on a story by Boris Ingster, Leo Townsend); ph; Woody Bredell; m, Frank Skinner, H. J. Salter; ed, Ted Kent; md, Charles Previn.

Musical Adventure (PR:AAA MPAA:NR)

AMAZING MONSIEUR FABRE, THE ½** (1952, Fr.) 78m Futter bw

Pierre Fresnay *(Jean Henri Fabre)*, Elina La Bourdette *(Countesse de Latour)*, Andre Randall *(John Stuart Mill)*, Georges Tabet *(Director of Avignon)*, Oliver Hussenot *(Dean of Avignon)* Espanita Cortez *(Empress Eugenie)*, Paul Boniface *(Victor Duruy)*, Jacques Emmanuel *(Charles Delegrave)*, Albert Culloz *(Jules Fabre)*, France Descaut *(Antonio Fabre)*, Catherine Culloz *(Claire Fabre)*, J. P. Maurin *(Prince Imperial)*, Elizabeth Hardy *(Marle Fabre)*, Pierre Bertin *(Napoleon III)*.

Tame biography of the great French entomologist Fabre shows how his fascination for the insect world made of him a recluse, truculently refusing to even tutor the son of Napoleon III because such work would detract from his obsessive studies. The telling of this man's sedentary life is both uninspiring and tedious, but the incredible views of the insect world are fascinating, showing black and red ants warring, the defeated black ants committing suicide rather than becoming slaves, two male scorpions battling to the death to possess a female who kills the winner after mating with him, the worlds of spiders, centipedes, and flies, all presented in microscopic wonder.

p, Walter Futter; d, Henri Diamand-Berger; w, Jack Kirkland (based on his story).

Biography (PR:A MPAA:NR)

AMAZING QUEST OF ERNEST BLISS, THE (SEE: ROMANCE AND RICHES, 1936)

AMAZING TRANSPARENT MAN, THE zero (1960) 58m AIP

Marguerite Chapman *(Laura)*, Douglas Kennedy *(Joey Faust)*, James Griffith *(Krenner)*, Ivan Triesault *(Dr. Ulof)*, Red Morgan *(Julian)*, Carmel Daniel *(Maria)*, Edward Erwin *(Drake)*, Jonathan Ledford *(Smith)*, Norman Smith, Patrick Cranshaw *(Security Guards)*, Kevin Kelly *(Woman)*, Dennis Adams, Stacy Morgan *(State Policemen)*.

Awful production which director Ulmer shot at a Texas state fair to employ amateur futuristic sets then on display. The nothing story has mad scientist Triesault making crook Kennedy invisible so he can steal radioactive materials the cuckoo doctor requires to continue his bizarre experiments. Kennedy instead opts to use his transparent form in an abortive bank robbery. The most pleasing thing about this hodgepodge of a story is the alluring Chapman, who plays Kennedy's sultry moll.

p, Lester D. Guthrie; d, Edgar G. Ulmer; w, Jack Lewis; ph, Meredith Nicholson; m, Darrell Calker; ed, Jack Ruggiero; prod d, Ernest Fegte; set d, Louise Caldwell; spec eff, Roger George.

Science Fiction/Crime Cas. (PR:C MPAA:NR)

AMAZON QUEST* (1949) 75m FC bw

Tom Neal *(Tom)*, Carole Matthews *(Teresa)*, Carole Donne *(Anna)*, Joe Crehan *(DeRuyter)*, Ralph Graves *(Anna's Attorney)*, Don Zelaya *(Lobato)*.

Routine jungle actioner replete with tropical safaris, savages, tom-toms, and wildlife. Most of the location footage was lifted from a German film, GREEN HELL. Plot concerns the efforts of Neal to clear his father's name after scandalmongers claim the old man had run off with a Brazilian jungle siren. In reality Neal's father (an unbilled actor from the German film) has been on a mission to find rubber plant seeds for a Far East development. Not much here to recommend.

p, Max Alexander; d, S. K. Seeley; w, Al Martin (based on a story by Irwin Gielgud); ph, Guy Rowe; ed, Norman Cerf.

Adventure (PR:A MPAA:NR)

AMBASSADOR BILL** (1931) 68m FOX bw

Will Rogers *(Bill Harper)*, Marguerite Churchill *(The Queen)*, Greta Nissen *(Countess Ilka)*, Tad Alexander *(King Paul)*, Raymond Milland *(Lothar)*, Gustav von Seyffertitz *(Prince de Polikoff)*, Arnold Korff *(The General)*, Ferdinand Munier *(Senator Pillsbury)*, Edwin Maxwell *(Monte)*, Ernest Wood *(Northfield Slater)*, Tom Ricketts *(Littleton)*, Theodore Lodi *(French Ambassador)*, Herbert Bunston *(British Ambassador)*, Russ Powell *(Drunk)*, Ben Turpin *(The Butcher)*.

Hokum about an Oklahoma cattleman, Rogers, who is appointed American ambassador to a country whose king has been exiled amid spasmodic revolutions by its inhabitants. Rogers saves the day with his rustic observations and home spun philosophy. For Will Rogers fans only.

d, Sam Taylor; w, Guy Bolton (based on the story "Ambassador from the United States" by Vincent Sheean); ph, John Mescall; ed, Harold Schuster; art d, Duncan Cramer.

Comedy (PR:A MPAA:NR)

AMBASSADOR'S DAUGHTER, THE** (1956) 102m UA c

Olivia de Havilland *(Joan)*, John Forsythe *(Danny)*, Myrna Loy *(Mrs. Cartwright)*, Adolphe Menjou *(Sen. Cartwright)*, Tommy Noonan *(Al)*, Francis Lederer *(Prince Nicholas Obelski)*, Edward Arnold *(Ambassador Fiske)*, Minor Watson *(Gen. Harvey)*.

Daughter of the American ambassador to France comes to the aid of American soldiers when grumpy senator Menjou thinks about closing off Paris to the good-time-loving servicemen. Mistaking her for a Dior model, sergeant Forsythe falls for the lovely de Havilland, unaware of her position. De Havilland, pushing forty, is amazingly attractive and easily carries off what would have been thought of as a younger actress' role, but her distinct charm still can't save the hopelessly lightweight material. Menjou and Loy, in almost thankless roles, nearly steal the film in a pair of delightfully witty performances.

p,d&w, Norman Krasna; ph, Michael Kelber (CinemaScope, Technicolor); ed, Roger Dwyre; art d, Leon Barsacqu; md, Jacques Metchen; cos, Christian Dior.

Comedy (PR:A MPAA:NR)

AMBUSH* (1939) 60m PAR bw

Gladys Swarthout *(Jane Hartman)* Lloyd Nolan *(Tony Andrews)*, William Henry *(Charlie Hartman)*, William Frawley *(Inspector Weber)*, Ernest Truex *(Mr. Gibbs)*, Broderick Crawford *(Randall)*, Rufe Davis *(Sheriff)*, Raymond Hatton *(Hardware Store Owner)*, Hartley Tufts *(Sidney)*, Antonio Moreno *(Capt. Gonzales)*, Harry Fleischman *(Capt. Bosen)*, Clem Bevans *(Pop Stebbins)*, Billy Lee *(Boy in Restaurant)*, Polly Moran *(Cora)*, Wade Boteler *(Bank Guard)*.

Fairly exciting robbery picture spiced up with deft touches of humor from its principals and a truly intense extended getaway sequence, a getaway spoiled by the spineless sister of one of the crooks who panics after she has helped to engineer the bank robbery.

d, Kurt Neumann; w, Laura and S. J. Perelman (based on a story by Robert Ray); ph, William Meller; ed, Stuart Gilmore.

Crime (PR:A MPAA:NR)

AMBUSH** (1950) 89m MGM bw

Robert Taylor *(Ward Kinsman)*, John Hodiak *(Capt. Ben Lorrison)*, Arlene Dahl *(Ann Duverall)*, Don Taylor *(Lt. Linus Delaney)*, Jean Hagen *(Martha Conovan)*, Bruce Cowling *(Tom Conovan)*, Leon Ames *(Maj. Beverly)*, John McIntire *(Frank Holly)*, Pat Moriarity *(Sgt. Mack)*, Charles Stevens *(Diablito)*, Chief Thundercloud *(Tana)*, Ray Teal *(Capt. J.R. Wolverson)*, Robin Short *(Lt. Storrow)*, Richard Bailey *(Lt. Tremaine)*.

Indian scout Taylor tracks down Dahl's sister in Apache country in this tough, but easygoing western. Miss Dahl's costumes in this picture caused quite a stir among American males. Needless to say, they didn't exactly accentuate her *acting* talent.

p, Armand Deutsch; d, Sam Wood; w, Marguerite Roberts (based on a story by Luke Short); ph, Harold Lipstein; ed, Ben Lewis.

Western (PR:A MPAA:NR)

AMBUSH AT CIMARRON PASS** (1958) 73m FOX bw

Scott Brady *(Sgt. Matt Blake)*, Margia Dean *(Theresa)*, Baynes Barron *(Corbin)*, William Vaughan *(Henry)*, Ken Mayer *(Corp. Schwitzer)*, John Manier *(Pvt. Zach)*, Keith Richards *(Pvt. Lasky)*, Clint Eastwood *(Keith Williams)*, John Merrick *(Pvt. Nathan)*, Frank Gerstle *(Sam Prescott)*, Dirk London *(Johnny Willows)*, Irving Bacon *(Stanfield)*, Desmond Slattery *(Cobb)*.

Cavalry sergeant Brady, transporting a prisoner across Apache country, runs into a group of rebels roaming around aimlessly after the Civil War. At first there is antagonism, but then the parties unite under an Indian attack. Although Eastwood dismissed AMBUSH as one of the worst westerns ever made, it is mildly entertaining and provided the future superstar with his first major feature film role.

p, Herbert E. Mendelson; d, Jodie Copeland; w, Richard G. Taylor, John K. Butler; ph, John M. Nickolaus; m, Paul Sawtell, Bert Shefter; ed, Carl L. Peirson.

Western (PR:A MPAA:NR)

AMBUSH AT TOMAHAWK GAP** (1953) 73m COL c

John Hodiak *(McCord)*, John Derek *(Kid)*, David Brian *(Egan)*, Marie Elena Marques *(Indian Girl)*, Ray Teal *(Doc)*, John Qualen *(Jonas P. Travis)*, Otto Hulett *(Stranton)*, Percy Helton *(Marlowe)*, Trevor Bardette *(Sheriff)*, John Doucette *(Bartender)*.

Surprisingly violent western with Derek, Hodiak, Brian, and Teal just out of prison and looking for their buried loot. Trouble starts when the partners can't find their money, and things only get worse when the Apaches ride into town in search of scalps.

p, Wallace McDonald; d, Fred F. Sears; w, David Lang; ph, Henry Fruelich (Techni color); m, Ross Dimaggio; ed, Aaron Stell.

Western (PR:C MPAA:NR)

AMBUSH BAY*** (1966) 107m UA c

Hugh O'Brian *(First Sgt. Steve Corey)*, Mickey Rooney *(Sgt. Ernest Wartell)*, James Mitchum *(Pvt. James Grenier)*, Pete Masterson *(Sgt. William Maccone)*, Harry Lauter *(Cpl. Alvin Ross)*, Greg Amsterdam *(Cpl. Stanley Parrish)*, Jim Anuao *(Pvt. Henry Reynolds)*, Tony Smith *(Pvt. George George)*, Clem Stadler *(Capt. Alonzo Davis)*, Amado Abello *(Amado)*, Juris Sulit *(Midori)*, Max Quismundo *(Max)*, Bruno Punzalan *(Ramon)*, Tisa Chang *(Miyazaki)*, Buff Fernandez *(Lt. Tokuzo)*, Joaquin Farjado *(Capt. Kayamatsu)*, Limbo Lagdameo *(Man)*, Nonong Arceo *(Soldier)*.

Competent WW II pic follows a group of Marines led by O'Brian as they make their way through a Japanese-held island in the Philippines. The mission requires making contact with a Japanese-American girl who holds important information vital to the success of General MacArthur's planned invasion. The Marines have only 96 hours to complete their mission and return. Exciting war picture helped by lush jungle locations and decent cast.

p, Hal Klein; d, Ron Winston; w, Marve Feinburg, Ib Melchoir; ph, Emmanuel Rojas (DeLuxe Color); m, Richard La Salle; ed, John Schreyer.

War (PR:C MPAA:NR)

AMBUSH IN LEOPARD STREET**   (1962, Brit.) 60m Luckwell bw

James Kenney (*Johnny*), Michael Brennan (*Harry*), Bruce Seton (*Nimmo*), Norman Rodway (*Kegs*), Jean Harvey (*Jean*), Pauline Delany (*Cath*), Marie Conmee (*Myra*).

An aging thief comes out of retirement to plan a last big job, the ambushing of a heavily guarded diamond shipment, enlisting the aid of old pros and novices whose nervousness and inexperience adds up to a miserable failure.

p, Bill Luckwell, Jack MacGregor; d, J. Henry Piperno; w, Bernard Spicer, Ahmed Faroughy (based on the story by Spicer).

Crime   **(PR:C MPAA:NR)**

AMBUSH TRAIL*   (1946) 60m PRC bw

Bob Steele (*Curley Thompson*), Syd Saylor (*Sam Hawkins*), I. Stanford Jolley (*Hatch Bolton*), Lorraine Miller (*Alice Rhodes*), Charles King (*Al Craig*), Bob Carson (*Ed Blane*), Budd Buster (*Jim Ugley*), Kermit Maynard (*Walter Gordon*), Frank Ellis (*Frank Gwen*), Edward Cassidy (*Marshall Dowes*).

Obscure oater concerning Steele's attempts to stop the bad guys from ruining the local ranchers. Stranger-in-town Steele dispenses justice while Saylor-the-sidekick goes for laughs.

p, Arthur Alexander; d, Harry Fraser; w, Elmer Clifton; ph, Jack Greenhalgh; ed, Roy Livingston; md, Lee Zahler.

Western   **Cas.**   **(PR:A MPAA:NR)**

AMBUSH VALLEY*   (1936) 57m Reliable bw

Bob Custer, Victoria Vinton, Eddie Phillips, Wally Wales, Hal Taliaferro, Vane Calvert, Ed Cassidy, Denver Dixon, Oscar Gahan, Roger Williams.

Thieves and rustlers gang up on Custer, who battles for Vinton's favor and corrals the bad guys in a poor actioner.

p, William Steiner; d, Raymond Samuels [B. B. Ray]; w, Bennett Cohen.

Western   **(PR:A MPAA:NR)**

AMBUSHERS, THE**   (1967) 101m COL c

Dean Martin (*Matt Helm*), Senta Berger (*Francesca*), Janice Rule (*Sheila*), James Gregory (*MacDonald*), Albert Salmi (*Ortega*), Kurt Kasznar (*Quintana*), Beverly Adams (*Lovey*), David Mauro (*Nassim*), Roy Jenson (*Karl*), John Brascia (*Rocco*), Linda Foster (*Linda*).

Tedious Matt Helm pic in which Martin must rescue kidnapped Rule from the evil clutches of Salmi. Pedestrian script and direction, too little emphasis on gadgetry, and a lackluster performance from Martin weaken the potential for a good time. Third in the Helm series.

p, Irwin Allen; d, Henry Levin; w, Herbert Baker (based on the book by Donald Hamilton); ph, Burnett Guffey, Edward Coleman (Technicolor); m, Hugo Montenegro; ed, Harold F. Kress; art d, Joe Wright.

Spy Drama   **(PR:A MPAA:NR)**

AMELIE OR THE TIME TO LOVE**½   (1961, Fr.) 105m Port Royal/Indusfilm bw

Marie-Jose Nat (*Amelie*), Jean Sorel (*Alain*), Sophie Daumier (*Emmannuelle*), Clotilde Joano (*Fany*), Jean Babilee (*Pierre*), Louise De Vilmorin (*Loyse*)

Sad girl Nat, grieving over the departure of her cousin Sorel with a vampish actress, dies before Sorel comes back to her to confess his love. Alone now, he sets out for the isolated life of a sailor. Familiar melodramatic plot is given a caring, atmospheric treatment by emotionally aware director Drach.

d, Michel Drach; w, Drach (based on a novel by Michele Angot); ph, Jean Tournier; ed, Genevieve Winding.

Drama   **(PR:A MPAA:NR)**

AMERICA, AMERICA**

                (1963) 177m WB bw (GB: THE ANATOLIAN SMILE)

Stathis Giallelis (*Stavros Topouzoglou*), Frank Wolff (*Vartan Damadian*), Harry Davis (*Isaac Topouzoglou*), Elena Karam (*Vasso Topouzoglou*), Estelle Hemsley (*Grandmother*), Gregory Rozakis (*Hohanness Gardashian*), Lou Antonio (*Abdul*), Salem Ludwig (*Odysseus Topouzoglou*), John Marley (*Garabet*), Joanna Frank (*Vartuhi*), Paul Mann (*Aleko Sinnikoglou*), Linda Marsh (*Thomna Sinnikoglou*), Robert H. Harris (*Aratoon Kebabian*), Katharine Balfour (*Sophia Kebabian*).

Story of a young Greek immigrant's struggle in the United States and the harsh realities he faces. A nicely told, occasionally highly emotional story, but the main purpose of the film seems to be to exist as a reason for the filmmaker to pat himself on the back. The stunning black-and-white photography is by Haskell Wexler.

p,d&w, Elia Kazan (based on his book); ph, Haskell Wexler; m, Manos Hadjidakis; ed, Dede Allen.

Drama   **(PR:A MPAA:NR)**

AMERICAN DREAM, AN*

                (1966) 103m WB c (GB: SEE YOU IN HELL, DARLING)

Stuart Whitman (*Stephen Rojack*), Janet Leigh (*Cherry McMahon*), Eleanor Parker (*Deborah Kelly Rojack*), Barry Sullivan (*Roberts*), Lloyd Nolan (*Barney Kelly*), Murray Hamilton (*Arthur Kabot*), J. D. Cannon (*Sgt. Leznicki*), Susan Denberg (*Ruta*), Les Crane (*Nicky*), Warren Stevens (*Johnny Dell*), Joe DeSantis (*Eddie Ganucci*), Stacy Harris (*O'Brien*), Paul Mantee (*Shago Martin*), Harold Gould (*Ganucci's Lawyer*), George Takei (*Ord Long*), Kelly Jean Peters (*Freya*).

TV talk show host Whitman, in a frenzied fight with his bitch of a wife Parker, pushes her out of their penthouse apartment. Trying to palm it off as a suicide, Whitman is betrayed by his old flame Leigh. A strong beginning intensified by Parker's powerful portrayal of the wife is a false, untrustworthy pointer to the quality of the rest of this cynical, unsympathetic look at 1960s society.

p, William Conrad; d, Robert Gist; w, Mann Rubin (based on the novel by Norman Mailer); ph, Sam Leavitt (Technicolor); m, Johnny Mandel; ed, George Rohrs; m/l, Mandel, Paul Francis Webster.

Drama   **(PR:O MPAA:NR)**

AMERICAN EMPIRE***   (1942) 82m UA bw (GB: MY SON ALONE)

Richard Dix (*Dan Taylor*), Leo Carrillo (*Dominique Beauchard*), Preston Foster (*Paxton Bryce*), Frances Gifford (*Abby Taylor*), Robert H. Barrat (*Crowder*), Jack La Rue (*Pierre*), Guinn "Big Boy" Williams (*Sailaway*), Cliff Edwards (*Runty*), Merrill Guy Rodin (*Paxton Bryce, Jr.*), Chris-Pin Martin (*Augustin*), Richard Webb (*Crane*), William Farnum (*Louisiana Judge*), Etta McDaniel (*Wida May*), Hal Taliaferro (*Malone*).

Following the Civil War three men, Dix, Foster and Carrillo, the latter incongruously playing a French Creole, establish a vast cattle ranch in Texas. Carillo is caught selling off part of the herd and is sent on his way but he keeps raiding the cattle, making a fortune from his rustling, then enticing Foster into his schemes until hero Dix stands alone against them, his only ally being Gifford, his sister and Foster's wife. In a final swoop, Carillo and Foster try to move all of Dix's cattle but Foster's son is killed in the stampede. The renegade comes to his senses and helps Dix beat off Carillo and company. Superior action film with high production values, excellent photography and a good script where the dialog rings true and without cliche.

p, Harry Sherman; d, William McGann; w, J. Robert Bren, Gladys Atwater, Ben Grauman Kohn; ph, Russell Harlan; m, Gerard Carbonarn; ed, Carrol Lewis.

Western   **Cas.**   **(PR:A MPAA:NR)**

AMERICAN FRIEND, THE***

(1977, Ger.) 127m Road Movies Filmproduktion/Filmverlag-Der Autoren-Les Films Moli/New Yorker c

Dennis Hopper (*Ripley*), Bruno Ganz (*Jonathan Zimmermann*), Lisa Kreuzer (*Marianne Zimmermann*), Gerard Blain (*Raoul Minot*), Nicholas Ray (*Derwatt*), Samuel Fuller (*The American*), Peter Lilienthal (*Marcangelo*), Daniel Schmid (*Ingraham*), Jean Eustache (*Friendly Man*), Rudolf Schundler (*Gantner*), Sandy Whitelaw (*Doctor in Paris*), Lou Castel (*Rodolphe*).

Ganz, a humble and quiet picture framer living in Hamburg, thinks that he may be dying from a blood disease. Hopper, a cowbody wheeler-dealer who flits around Europe, finds out about Ganz's illness and sets him up as a pawn for gangster Blain. Blain, convincing Ganz that as long as he is going to die, he should make some quick money for his wife and child, offers him the well-paying job of a mafia assassin. At first Ganz refuses, then goes ahead with the deal and kills the targeted man in the Paris metro. Hopper and Ganz slowly become friends, with their alliance solidifying in a somewhat botched second assassination where Hopper comes to Ganz's aid. In a frenzied final confrontation with American gangsters who've captured Blain, Hopper and Ganz and his wife escape to the beach where they prepare to destroy all evidence of their connection to the mafia. Surprisingly, Ganz abandons his friend on the beach and drives off with his wife. As Hopper, irritated and mumbling, wanders across the sand, Ganz quietly dies at the wheel of his car.

d, Wim Wenders; w, Wenders (based on the novel *Ripley's Game* by Patricia Highsmith); ph, Robby Muller; m, Jurgen Knieper; ed, Peter Przygodda; art d, Sickerts.

Drama   **Cas.**   **(PR:) MPAA:NR)**

AMERICAN GIGOLO zero   (1980) 117m PAR c

Richard Gere (*Julian*), Lauren Hutton (*Michelle*), Hector Elizondo (*Sunday*), Nina Van Pallandt (*Anne*), Bill Duke (*Leon Jaimes*), Brian Davies (*Charles Stratton*), K. Callan (*Lisa Williams*), Tom Stewart (*Mr. Rheiman*), Patti Carr (*Judy Rheiman*), David Cryer (*Lt. Curtis*), Carole Cook (*Mrs. Dobrun*), Carol Bruce (*Mrs. Sloan*), Frances Bergen (*Mrs. Laudner*), Macdonald Carey (*Hollywood Actor*), William Dozier (*Michelle's Lawyer*), Peter Turgeon (*Julian's Lawyer*), Robert Wightman (*Floyd Wicker*), Richard Derr (*Mr. Williams*), Jessica Potter (*Jill*).

Male prostitute Gere, who specializes in delighting Beverly Hills matrons, is set up as the scapegoat in a kinky sex murder. Will his lover Hutton, a politician's wife, risk scandal and provide Gere with an alibi? Only the producers of this sleazy vile movie would care. Director Schrader overloads his film with synthetic style—in the music, the photography, the costumes, the look of the actors—but neglects to create a character or a situation in which any average human being would really take interest. Gere, who can be used as an actor and not just a male model, is as about as appealing here as a frustrated dog that gets a five-hundred-dollar-a-shot stud fee. This is a perverse film devoted to perversity and with no redeeming qualities whatsoever, typical of Schrader's apparently sadistic intent to pillory his audience with every kind of degenerate act he can manufacture. Garbage.

p, Jerry Bruckheimer; d&w, Paul Schrader; ph, John Bailey (Metrocolor); m, Giorgio Moroder; ed, Richard Halsey; art d, Ed Richardson; set d, Mark Fabus.

Drama   **Cas.**   **(PR:O MPAA:R)**

AMERICAN GRAFFITI****   (1973) 110m UNIV c

Richard Dreyfuss (*Curt*), Ronny Howard (*Steve*), Paul LeMat (*John*), Charlie Martin Smith (*Terry*), Cindy Williams (*Laurie*), Candy Clark (*Debbie*), Mackenzie Phillips (*Carol*), Wolfman Jack (*Himself*), Harrison Ford (*Falfa*), Bo Hopkins (*Joe*), Manuel Padilla, Jr. (*Carlos*), Beau Gentry (*Ants*), Kathy Quinlan (*Peg*), Tim Crowley (*Eddie*), Terry McGovern (*Mr. Wolfe*), Jan Wilson (*Girl*), Caprice Schmidt (*Announcer*), Jana Bellan (*Budda*), Joe Spano (*Vic*), Chris Pray (*Al*), Susan Richardson (*Judy*), Donna Wehr (*2nd Carhop*), Jim Bohan (*Policeman Holstein*), Ron Vincent (*Jeff Pazzuto*), Fred Ross (*Ferber*), Jody Carlson (*Girl in Studebaker*), Cam Whitman (*Balloon Girl*), John Bracci (*Gas Station Attendant*), Debbie Celiz (*Wendy*), Lynn Marie Stewart (*Bobbie*), Ed Greenberg (*Kip Pullman*), Suzanne Somers (*Blonde in T-Bird*), Gordon Analla (*Bozo*), Lisa Herman (*Girl in Dodge*), Debralee Scott (*Falfa's Girl*), Charles Dorsett (*Man at Accident*), Stephen Knox (*Kid at Accident*), Bob Pasaak (*Dale*), Joseph Miksak (*Man*), George Meyer (*Bum*), William Niven (*Clerk*), James Cranna (*Thief*), Del Close (*Manin Alley*), Charlie Murphy (*Old Man*), Jan Dunn (*Old Woman*), Johnny Weissmuller, Jr (*Badass I*), Scott Beach (*Mr. Gordon*), Al Nalbandian (*Hank*), Herby and the Heartbeats, Flash Cadillac and the Continental Kids.

Hallmark film of the 1970s, GRAFFITI's action and great cast of characters are seen in the time span of one night in 1962, a night of cruising through the streets of a small California town, in touching and telling vignettes. Howard, the clean-cut All-American boy, is about to leave for college the next day; Dreyfuss, the class intellectual, has doubts about his future and that of the world; Williams, playing Howard's girl friend and Dreyfuss' sister, is upset, almost depressed, at Howard's impending departure. Smith, the bumpkin of the class, is a hopeless case; his only ambition is to be a "cool dude" and he lickspittles after older boys who possess fast cars and have sexy girls at their sides. Older boy LeMat is an antique car devotee who thinks he is a "cool dude," but who is really nothing more than a hot-rodder. After the school dance everyone goes cruising. LeMat picks up 13-year-old Phillips, thinking she is much older until she climbs into his 1932 Ford Deuce Coupe, then becoming embarrassed as she chatters his ears off. Howard and Williams, driving about in his 1958 Impala, talk about their tomorrows; he is full of desires for the future, she tearfully believing her life is over at 17. Everyone meets at Mel's Drive-In where exchanges of the groping teenagers seem to reveal their entire personalities in microcosm. LeMat, who is thought by the group to be the great dragster of the town, takes great pride in driving to a junkyard to point out cars to Phillips that have been destroyed in drag races, their drivers killed. He later meets Ford who is driving a 1955 Chevy and is challenged to a duel. The entire group gathers to watch the race on remote Paradise Road where Ford's car crashes from a blowout (he is not killed). Smith, the hopeless bumbler of the group, feels he has lived his ultimate moments. An older, attractive girl, Candy Clark, has deigned to cruise with him and he has witnessed a near fatal crash which only his peer group has been entitled to see. (The drag race is not unlike that shown in REBEL WITHOUT A CAUSE and this film owes much to that Nicholas Ray masterpiece; in fact GRAFFITI duplicates much from that film, replacing the sinister with the sweet). The next morning situations are reversed. Howard has succumbed to Williams' blandishments. He decides not to go on to college but stay with his girl friend. The undecided Dreyfuss suddenly refuses to "stay 17 forever," and goes off to a university. In a tacked-on epilog somber significance is gratuitously added to this plotless, aimless film as the viewer is informed that Howard later became an insurance agent, Dreyfuss a writer, LeMat a fatality in a drunk-driving accident, and Smith a victim of the Viet Nam war. These post-adolescent facts only attempt to unify a disjointed story but the appeal of this film is in its fragmentary scenes as the nervous camera, as explosive as acne, jumps frantically from character to character to present a powerful collage of American youth on the brink of maturity. Poignant, often priceless in its dialog and mannerisms, GRAFFITI has the innocence of a Saturday afternoon matinee yet it is as unsure and inexperienced as its characters, a happy accident that nostalgically captures one balmy night in America. At its San Francisco premiere, although enthusiastically received, Universal bigwigs sniggered at the film's murky lighting and told producer Coppola and director Lucas that they might not release the film, that it was an "unfinished product." The agitated Coppola immediately offered to buy the property and release it himself. The executives, to Universal's financial credit, refused; the film would gross more than $55 million. This proved an incredible feat on the ledger books in that GRAFFITI was produced for only $750,000, shot in northern California in only 25 days. It also made stars of a host of young actors Ford, Howard, LeMat, Dreyfuss, Hopkins, Quinlan, Clark, Williams, Somers. Director Lucas later admitted that the film was largely autobiographical, based upon his own teenage hot-rodding in Modesto, California. The enormous success of this film and its gigantic financial rewards allowed Lucas to finance the greatest grossing film of all time—STAR WARS. The success also spawned numerous imitations, and inspired the TV show, "Happy Days," with Howard as the star.

p, Francis Ford Coppola, Gary Kurtz; d, George Lucas; w, Lucas, Gloria Katz, Willard Huyck; ph, Ron Everslage, Jan D'Alquen (Technicolor); ed, Verna Fields, Marcia Lucas; art d, Dennis Clark; set d, Douglas Freeman; cos, Aggie Guerard Rodgers.

Comedy **Cas.** **(PR:C MPAA:PG)**

AMERICAN GUERRILLA IN THE PHILIPPINES, AN***

(1950) 105m, FOX c (GB: I SHALL RETURN)

Tyrone Power *(Ensign Chuck Palmer)*, Micheline Presle *(Jeanne Martinez)*, Tom Ewell *(Jim Mitchell)*, Bob Patten *(Lovejoy)*, Tommy Cook *(Miguel)*, Juan Torena *(Juan Martinez)*, Jack Elam *(The Speaker)*, Robert Barrat *(Gen. Douglas MacArthur)*, Carleton Young *(Col. Phillips)*, Maria Del Val *(Senora Martinez)*, Eddie Infante *(Col. Dimalanta)*, Orlando Martin *(Col. Benson)*, Miguel Anzures *(Native Traitor)*, Chris de Varga, Eduardo Rivera *(Japanese Officers)*, Arling Gonzales, Fred Gonzales *(Radio Operators)*, Sabu Camacho *(Bo)*, Rosa del Rosario, Kathy Ruby, Erlinda Cortez *(Partisans)*.

Based on the actual exploits of Navy Lt. I. D. Richardson in the Philippines, Power and fellow seamen refuse to surrender to the Japanese after the fall of Bataan in 1942 and attempt to hack their way through the jungle to Leyte, expecting to find a small boat that will take them to Australia to continue the fight. Along the way they pick up the attractive wife of a friendly planter, Presle, taking her with them. The group commandeers a small craft but a storm sinks it eight miles out at sea and the survivors must swim to shore where Filipino partisans pick them up, hiding them in the jungle. In the many months to follow Power, Ewell and others evade the Japanese patrol hunting them, then meet with resistance leaders, taking a message to MacArthur's representative in Mindanao on the promise that passage to Australia will be arranged for them. Instead Power and his group are ordered back to Leyte where he establishes a radio network, prints money and newspapers for the government of Free Leyte and begins manufacturing arms for the guerrillas. Power and Presle fall in love but make no plans until she hears that her husband, Torena, has been killed by the Japanese. But the lovers have little time to dally since MacArthur's promised invasion of Leyte is now in full swing. Power and his group make radio contact with American troops, directing them to key positions but the Japanese intercept these messages and pinpoint the location of the guerrillas. They close in, trapping the group in an abandoned church, killing most of Power's men before American troops appear to destroy the enemy. Power personally greets MacArthur and is commended for his brave and extraordinary work. (Robert Barrat, playing the great American general, had earlier appeared in the same role for John Ford's classic WW II drama, THEY WERE EXPENDABLE.) Power's performance is energetic, intense and reliably heroic. Ewell as his griping, sardonic aide, brings realism to a surrealistic situation. French actress Presle, whom Fox was attempting to build to star status, is a tempting souffle but with little acting range. The great director Fritz Lang shrugged off the impossible story, explaining to Peter Bogdanovich that he took on the film because "I have to eat." Though critics pummeled the film at the time, it appears now as a top-notch action production with great pace and gusto, having the necessary elements of tension and drive, with an excellent score and lush photography.

p, Lamar Trotti; d, Fritz Lang; w, Trotti (based on the novel by Ira Wolfert); ph, Harry Jackson (Technicolor); m, Cyril J. Mockridge; ed, Robert Simpson; art d, Lyle Wheeler, J. Russell Spencer; set d, Thomas Little, Stuart Reiss; cos, Travilla, Charles LeMaire; spec eff, Fred Sersen.

War **(PR:A MPAA:NR)**

AMERICAN HOT WAX*** (1978) 91m PAR c

Tim McIntire *(Alan Freed)*, Fran Drescher *(Sheryl)*, Jay Leno *(Mookie)*, Laraine Newman *(Teenage Louise)*, Carl Earl Weaver, Al Chalk, Sam Harkness, Arnold McCuller *(The Chesterfields)*, Jeff Altman *(Lennie Richfield)*, Moosie Drier *(Artie Moress)*, John Lehne *(District Attorney)*, Kenny Vane *(Prof. La Plano)*, Chuck Berry, Jerry Lee Lewis, Screamin' Jay Hawkins *(Themselves)*.

Loads of fun in this unassuming celebration of the early days of rock n' roll. Plot concerns the efforts of Alan Freed (a 1950s disk jockey credited with popularizing the term "rock and roll") to gain acceptance for this new form of popular music despite the efforts of local police to quell it. McIntire protrays Freed in a particularly energetic performance. The music dominates the movie with especially enjoyable guest appearances by Chuck Berry, Jerry Lee Lewis, and Screamin' Jay Hawkins. The film manages to recreate the excitement of the rock movies of the 1950s.

p, Art Linson; d, Floyd Mutrux; w, John Kaye; ph, William A. Fraker (Metrocolor); ed, Melvin Shapiro, Ronald J. Fagan; art d, Elayne Barbara Ceder.

Musical **Cas.** **(PR:A MPAA:PG)**

AMERICAN IN PARIS, AN***** (1951) 113m MGM c

Gene Kelly *(Jerry Mulligan)*, Leslie Caron *(Lise Bouvier)*, Oscar Levant *(Adam Cook)*, Georges Guetary *(Henri Baurel)*, Nina Foch *(Milo Roberts)*, Eugene Borden *(George Mattieu)*, Martha Bamattre *(Mathilde Mattieu)*, Mary Jones *(Old Lady Dancer)*, Ann Codee *(Therese)*, George Davis *(Francois)*, Hayden Rorke *(Tommy Baldwin)*, Paul Maxey *(John McDowd)*, Dick Wessel *(Ben Macrow)*.

No one could argue the authentic look of this marvelous musical; even the French Government, highly critical of any film profiling its beloved Paris, agreed that the entire production was genuine down to the last cobblestone. Yet only a few of the opening scenes were live shots of Paris, the rest of the film being photographed on MGM's creative back lot where a Parisian neighborhood was reproduced with meticulous care by Edwin P. Willis and Keogh Gleason. The simple story is pure Hollywood but it works as a tonic on the heart. Kelly, who created the spellbinding choreography for the entire production, is a young GI who has stayed on in Paris to paint. Though he is unsuccessful he is happy living and working in his cramped one-room Montmartre garret. His one friend, Levant, is a piano player in a nearby cafe, a sarcastic and morose individual who offers nothing but discouragement to Kelly (Levant in character and as he was). Guetary, a successful revue singer, is another friend who does encourage the young painter while informing him that he is going to marry a wonderful girl, an 18-year-old dancer Guetary has rescued from the Nazis during the war. Kelly, meanwhile, is discovered by rich widow Foch; she buys his paintings and encourages her rich friends to do the same, a worldly sharp-talking woman who expects Kelly to be her bought man. Kelly, innocently enjoying his new-found success, goes to a nightclub where he meets and falls in love with a young girl, Caron. She fends him off but later agrees to a date, then tells him that she is engaged to Guetary. They are both in love but do the noble thing and decide not to meet again. Foch next makes demands upon Kelly and he refuses to play the gigolo, even if it means losing a Maecenas. All looks bleak as Oscar Levant at midnight but Guetary is also noble; realizing Caron is in love with his friend, he gives her up. The lovers fly into each other's arms and life is sweet again. Based upon Gershwin's work, this musical has a freshness and charm unlike many musicals that overreach and fabricate. The music and dance numbers blend perfectly with the story. Kelly and Levant team up for song and dance on "Tra-La-La," then harmonize By Strauss. Kelly, in one of the most delightful sequences, dances with street children who jump and leap with him in his typical acrobatic efforts. Guetary's tenor belts out a wonderful tune, "I'll Build a Stairway to Paradise," in a top-hatted review number and he harmonizes with Kelly on "S'Wonderful" where they are oddly singing about the same girl, each not knowing the other is in love with Caron. The highlight of the film is the fantasy ballet fantasized by Kelly, a terrific 17-minute sequence not equalled in musicals before or after this film, one that cost MGM $450,000 to mount, and one that brought "culture" of a higher sort to a public that loved it. This sequence was done after the film was finished, with art director Preston Ames, who was an art student in Paris in the late 1920s, painting magnificent 40-foot high backdrops around a Place de la Concorde set all in the style of French artist Raoul Dufy. (The elderly, wheelchair-bound Dufy was shown the sequence by Kelly at a special screening and wept when he saw it, then asked to see it again.) Everything about this film was superb, from Minnelli's direction to the Gershwin tunes, rendered with lush orchestration. In all, twenty-two numbers, all Gershwin greats, were included in the production, plus the third movement from the "Concerto in F" which was first produced in 1929 for Ziegfeld's "Show Girl." Revived were "Embraceable You," "Nice Work If You Can Get It," and a new tune, "Our Love Is Here to Stay." Kelly's dance numbers are spectacular and unforgettable, reflecting a genius choreographer and a dancer of grace, *joie de vivre*, style and a unique talent equalled only by Fred Astaire. This landmark film forever identified MGM as *the* maker of musicals. In addition to the seven Oscars this film deservedly won, Kelly was given a special Academy Award "in appreciation of his versatility as an actor, singer, director and dancer, and especially for his brilliant achievements in the art of choreography on film." Right on all counts, including Kelly's sharp eye for talent for it was he who spotted Leslie Caron in the Ballets des Champs Elysees, and made an overnight star of this marvelous dancer.

p, Arthur Freed; d, Vincente Minnelli; w, Alan Jay Lerner; ph, Alfred Gilks, ballet ph, John Alton (Technicolor); md, John Green, Saul Chaplin; ed, Adrienne Fazan; art d, Cedric Gibbons, Preston Ames; set d, Edwin B. Willis, Keogh Gleason; spec eff, Warren Newcombe; m/l, George and Ira Gershwin.

Musical Cas. (PR:AAA MPAA:NR)

AMERICAN LOVE* 1/2

(1932, Fr.) 85m Braunberger Richebe bw (FR: AMOUR A L'AMERICAINE)

Spinelly, Andre Luguet, Pauline Carton, Suzette Mais, Romain Bouquet, Carette.

Lackluster farce has Spinelly playing a jilted American millionairess who chases her French lover through France in an effort to capture him. A case of mistaken identity occurs when she is convinced that a young newlywed is, in fact, her lover. She spends the rest of the movie trying to win him back despite his bride's protestations. Unbeliev able premise hurts the film, as well as an unappealing performance by Spinelly.

d, Claude Heymann; w, Mouezy-Eon and Spitzer; m, Misraki and Ray Ventura.

Comedy (PR:A MPAA:NR)

AMERICAN MADNESS**** (1932) 75m COL bw

Walter Huston *(Dickson)*, Pat O'Brien *(Matt)*, Kay Johnson *(Mrs. Dickson)*, Constance Cummings *(Helen)*, Gavin Gordon *(Cluett)*, Robert Ellis *(Dude Finlay)*, Jeanne Sorel *(Cluett's Secretary)*, Walter Walker *(Schultz)*, Berton Churchill *(O'Brien)*, Arthur Hoyt *(Ives)*, Edward Martindel *(Ames)*, Edwin Maxwell *(Clark)*, Robert Emmett O'Connor *(Inspector)*, Anderson Lawler *(Charlie)*.

Like many an excellent Capra film to follow, central theme here is the idealistic individual against the cruelty of the faceless crowd. Huston is a bank president who has been making loans to depositors without sufficient collateral (much the same way Fredric March does as a benevolent banker in THE BEST YEARS OF OUR LIVES). He explains to a suspicious and narrow-minded board of directors that such loans are necessary for the growth of the country and can be made on the basis of character. (This film was made at the onset of FDR's New Deal and advanced much of Roosevelt's philosophy.) The board of directors disagrees and puts him on warning. He is also on warning from his wife, Johnson, whom he has neglected, giving all his attention to his bank. He even forgets their wedding anniversary and she responds angrily by going on the town with sleazy Gordon, an unscrupulous bank cashier who later arranges a robbery which causes a run on the bank. Ex-convict O'Brien, another cashier devoted to Huston, and employee Cummings, do all they can to stem the run on the banka truly memorable scene of utter panic—by calling small business men indebted to Huston to make more deposits to prevent the bank's collapse. (Capra uses this device most effectively in IT'S A WONDERFUL LIFE when small depositors come to Jimmy Stewart's rescue.) Meeting again before his board of directors at the height of the panic a near-exhausted Huston staunchly maintains his policy, insisting that he will put his own fortune behind the bank to stem the tide. The directors know, however, this will be insufficient but they are moved to see the small business people rally to Huston's support and they finally commit their own capital which barely saves the institution. Huston's marriage is not saved, however, since he believes his wife to be unfaithful once discovering how she has dallied with Gordon, an Iago who does get his comeuppance. He demands of her complete trust as his investors have demanded of him. Both have failed him, really, only a few remaining to support him through his great crisis. Like the single set interiors of GRAND HOTEL, Capra filmed AMERICAN MADNESS totally within an enormous bank set, all the action taking place inside board rooms and vaults and behind tellers' cages, moving his camera with fluid truck and dolly shots, boom shots, and quick cuts that keep up the already established frenetic pace. To further create this sense of urgency, Capra cut out all dissolves (a device used to indicate the passing of time) and used only quick cuts; he overlapped speeches and then had his actors hurry through their actions and dialog. He called it "kicking up the pace." AMERICAN MADNESS reassured the public that Hooverism and all the conservative horrors that had created the Great Depression was gone, that a new breed of creative banker was at the helm, one like the magnificent Huston who states in the movie: "Unemployed money leads to unemployed men. . . . The answer is bank money, fuel to start industry's wheels turning again. Hoarding money in vaults makes as much sense as pouring oil back into oil wells!" Capra had struck a blow against the hoarders, the nay-sayers and the do-nothings and he had made a superlative film, even dreaming that it might win some sort of Academy Award. It didn't. When Capra mentioned the possibility of this film being nominated, Harry Cohn, the crass head of Columbia, snorted: "Forget it. You ain't got a Chinaman's chance. They only vote for that arty junk!"

d, Frank Capra; w, Robert Riskin; ph, Joseph Walker; ed, Maurice Wright.

Drama (PR:A MPAA:NR)

AMERICAN POP* (1981) 97m COL c

VOICES: Ron Thompson *(Tony/Pete)*, Marya Small *(Frankie)*, Jerry Holland *(Louie)*, Lisa Jane Persky *(Bella)*, Jeffrey Lippa *(Zalmie)*, Roz Kelly *(Eva Tanguay)*, Frank DeKova *(Crisco)*, Richard Singer *(Benny)*, Elsa Raven *(Hannele)*, Ben Frommer *(Palumbo)*, Amy Levitt *(Nancy)*, Leonard Stone *(Leo)*, Eric Taslitz *(Little Pete)*, Gene Borkan *(Izzy)*, Richard Moll *(Poet)*, Beatrice Colen *(Prostitute)*.

This animated feature, poorly detailed, attempts to chronicle popular American music from the turn of the century to Rock with no clear point of view or focus upon character development. A Ralph Bakshi self-indulgent effort to justify Rock and its weird sisters by trying to say that all earlier music led up to its domination of adolescent ears, which, of course, is nonsense. Low production value, an artless script and an unschooled, poorly researched view of history add up to a waste of time for any viewer.

p, Martin Ransohoff; d, Ralph Bakshi; w, Ronni Kern; ph, R&B Efx (Metrocolor); m, Lee Holdridge; ed, David Ramirez.

History/Animation (PR:O MPAA:R)

AMERICAN PRISONER, THE**

(1929 Brit.) 70m British International/Elstree bw

Carl Brisson *(Lt. Stark)*, Madeleine Carroll *(Grace Malherb)*, Cecil Barry *(Peter Norcutt)*, Carl Harbord *(Lt. Burnham)*, A. Bromley Davenport *(Squire Malherb)*, Nancy Price *(Lovey Lee)*, Reginald Fox *(Capt. Mainwaring)*, Charles Ashton *(Carberry)*, Harry Terry *(Bosun Knapps)*, John Valentine *(Cdr. Miller)*, Robert English *(Col. Governor)*, Edmond Dignon *(Leverett)*.

Uneven performances mar this early talking costume drama set during a European conflict in 1815. The father of a young girl, Carroll, is forced to push his daughter into a marriage with the villainous Barry, who holds a debt over the family's head. Enter escaped American prisoner Brisson, who has been wounded by the French in his run for freedom. Carroll nurses the dashing soldier back to health and they run off together when the war ends. Carroll does a decent job, but Barry and Brisson look as if they have trouble taking this melodramatic material seriously.

d, Thomas Bentley; w, Eliot Stannard, Garnett Weston (based on the novel by Eden Phillpotts); ph, Rene Guissatt.

Drama (PR:A MPAA:NR)

AMERICAN ROMANCE, AN*** (1944) 151m MGM c

Brian Donlevy *(Steve Dangos)*, Ann Richards *(Anna)*, Walter Abel *(Howard Clinton)*, John Qualen *(Anton Dubechek)*, Horace McNally *(Teddy Dangos)*.

Good performance by Donlevy as a poor Czech immigrant who rises to become a powerful industrialist. Director Vidor spent two years and $3 million bringing this uniquely American success story to the screen. We follow the immigrant from Ellis Island, through his difficult period while working in Minnesota's iron ore mines, until he reaches the top of the industry as an auto manufacturer. His troubles don't end there. There are unions to contend with and strikes to settle. We leave him in his old age, overseeing a new airplane development business. Virtuoso performance by Donlevy from young immigrant to old industrialist keeps this overlong saga moving. Richards is good as the woman he marries after meeting her in the mining town of his youth.

p&d, King Vidor; w, Herbert Dalmas, William Ludwig (based on a story by Vidor); ph, Harold Rosson (Technicolor); m, Louis Gruenberg; ed, Conrad A. Nervig.

Drama (PR:A MPAA:NR)

AMERICAN SOLDIER, THE***

(1970 Ger.) 80m Anti-teater bw (GER: DER AMERIKANISCHE SOLDAT)

Karl Scheid *(Ricky)*, Elga Sorbas *(Rosa)*, Jan George *(Jan)*, Hark Bohm *(Doc)*, Eva Ingeborg Scholz *(Ricky's Mother)*, Kurt Raab *(Ricky's Brother)*, Marius Aicher *(Cop)*, Gustl Datz *(Police Chief)*, Marquand Bohm *(Private Detective)*, Rainer Werner Fassbinder *(Franz)*, Katrin Schaale *(Magdalena Fuller)*, Ulli Lommel *(Gypsy)*, Irm Hermann *(Whore)*, Ingrid Caven *(Songstress)*, Margareta von Trotta *(Maid)*.

The third part of Fassbinder's gangster trilogy. Said to have been shot in ten days, SOLDIER is the story of an American Viet Nam vet of German descent who returns to his native Munich as a hired killer. Three policemen have retained his services to eliminate a number of "undesirables" they have a quarrel with. Through a series of events the mercenary ends up killing the girl friend of one of the corrupt cops. A gunfight ensues between the soldier, who is aided by his friend Franz (played by Fassbinder), and the cops. Though not for all tastes, Fassbinder's films are cynical examinations of traditional Hollywood styles. His films have stong elements of parody and the freshness of his vision will be among the most lasting influences of the New German Cinema. AMERICAN SOLDIER is one of Fassbinder's earliest films (he made more than 40 before he died tragically in 1983 at the age of 37), is not as strong or as developed as his later masterpieces, but it is well worth seeing.

d&w, Rainer Werner Fassbinder; ph, Dietrich Lohmann; m, Peer Raben; ed, Thea Eymasz; prod d, Kurt Raab.

Crime (PR:C MPAA:NR)

AMERICAN SUCCESS COMPANY, THE*** (1980) 94m COL c

Jeff Bridges *(Harry)*, Belinda Bauer *(Sarah)*, Ned Beatty *(Mr. Elliot)*, Steven Keats *(Rick Duprez)*, Bianca Jagger *(Corinne)*, John Glover *(Ernst)*, Mascha Gonska *(Greta)*, Michel Durrell *(Herman)*, Eva-Maria Meineke *(Mrs. Heinemann)*, Gunter Meisner *(Maitre D)*, David Brooks *(Gunter)*, Marie Bardishewski *(Landlady)*, Sebastian Baur, Peter Brensing, Judy Brown, Michael Burger, Andrew Burleigh, Claudia Butenuth, Peter Capell, Loyd Catlett, Peter Chelsom, Conrad Dechert, Eunice Dechert, Erland Erlandson, Stephen Frances, Josef Frolich, Claudia Golling, Wolfgang Klein, Ann Kligge, Regina Mardeck, Michaela May, Shelagh McLeod, Elisabeth Neumann-Viertel, Osman Ragheb, William Richert, Ute Willing.

Critics either love director William Richert's bizzare black comedies, or they hate them. In his previous film, WINTER KILLS, he took on the Kennedy family myth and the craziness of American power brokers. In THE AMERICAN SUCCESS COMPANY, Bridges stars (as he did in WINTER KILLS) as the nice-guy son of credit card tycoon Beatty. It seems that the kid can't do anything right and is constantly being reminded of that fact by his dad and his oversexed wife Bauer. To prove he can be a success, Bridges becomes a gangsterish tough guy and gets what he wants by pushing people around. He even hires an experienced prostitute, Jagger, to teach him how to be a supreme lover. This change of attitude works, and Bridges is on his way to being a powerful man. Though not as thematically complex or fascinating as WINTER KILLS, this film has a wonderful sense of style. Richert's films always look good. Fabulous sets, good casts, and inventive cinematography are all characteristics of these odd examinations of the American power structure.

p, Daniel H. Blatt, Edgar J. Scherick; d, William Richert; w, Richert, Larry Cohen (based on a story by Cohen); ph, Anthony Richmond; m, Maurice Jarre; ed, Ralph E. Winters; art d, Werner Achmann; cos, Robert DeMora, Helga Pinnow; ch, Cecilia Gruessing.

Comedy/Drama (PR:C MPAA:PG)

AMERICAN TRAGEDY, AN*** (1931) 96m PAR bw

Phillips Holmes *(Clyde Griffiths)*, Sylvia Sidney *(Roberta Alden)*, Frances Dee *(Sondra Finchley)*, Irving Pichel *(Orville Mason)*, Frederick Burton *(Samuel Griffiths)*, Claire McDowell *(Mrs. Samuel Griffiths)*, Wallace Middleton *(Gilbert Griffiths)*, Vivian Winston *(Myra Griffiths)*, Emmett Corrigan *(Belknap)*, Lucille La Verne *(Mrs. Asa Griffiths)*, Charles B. Middleton *(Jephson)*, Albert Hart *(Titus Alden)*, Fanny Midgely *(Mrs. Alden)*, Arline Judge *(Bella Griffiths)*, Evelyn Pierce *(Bertine Cranson)*, Arnold Korff *(Judge)*, Elizabeth Forrester *(Jill Trumbell)*, Imboden Parrish

(Earl Newcomb). Russell Powell *(Coroner Fred Heit)*, Richard Kramer *(Deputy Sheriff Kraut)*.

The Theodore Dreiser novel was brought to the screen by Paramount at a costly figure and it is a straightforward telling of the story: Holmes, a young and ambitious office worker distantly related to wealth seeks to enter high society. He is given a functionary position in a plant and, as a fringe relative, occasionally invited to the home of a wealthy relative whose beautiful daughter, Dee, takes a liking to him. But before Holmes can win her heart, her prestige and become moneyed, he dallies with factory worker Sidney, almost compelling her to have a tryst with him or face unemployment. Director von Sternberg shows one scene where Holmes receives a note from Sidney in response to his demands. He goes into an alcove where only the camera can see him read the note and the smug smile of triumph upon his face. When the girl becomes pregnant, Holmes takes Sidney to a small resort and suggests they go boating. On the lake at night while she pleads for marriage to protect her good name, an argument erupts and the boat is overturned. Sidney drowns while Holmes swims ashore. He tries to cover up the death but is discovered and put on trial. Fully one-third of the film is taken up with his murder trial where he is abandoned by his rich patrons, except for Dee who loves him. Holmes is found guilty of purposely drowning Sidney and sent to the electric chair. This film was remade by George Stevens in 1951 as A PLACE IN THE SUN but the two films differ greatly. Von Sternberg, as consummate a director as Stevens, opted to tell the tale as Dreiser had written it, emphasizing the youth's scheming, manipulative nature, his quietly ruthless ambition to better himself at any price, and his outright guilt of murdering a woman he had victimized. Dreiser had spent weeks attending the sensational 1906 trial of Chester Gillette who was found guilty of drowning his sweetheart, Grace "Billie" Brown, so he could marry a socially prominent girl; before going to the electric chair the vainglorious Gillette, a handsome youth, sold his autograph to female thrill-seekers so he could afford catered meals in his death cell. The author, who took ten years to write the novel, fully based his story on this callous youth, and von Sternberg emulates Dreiser's conviction that the youth was entirely guilty, unlike Stevens who leaves a nagging doubt in the remake. In his mannered way, von Sternberg shows in devastating takes the rotting inner character of Holmes as he plans the seduction of Sidney and later her murder, feigning innocence at the end. He also places the emphasis of sympathy where it belongs, on the victimized girl. Stevens would later portray the victim, Shelley Winters, as a relentlessly hounding nag, a thoroughly repugnant character who almost deserved to be drowned for interrupting the torrid affair between Elizabeth Taylor and Montgomery Clift. Although von Sternberg dwells too long on some scenes to make his point, his version has powerful impact and takes on an almost surrealistic air. The great Russian director Sergei Eisenstein was first contracted by Adolph Zukor, head of Paramount, to write and direct this film, but when he turned in his manuscript the studio executive panicked. He had written a proletarian view, altering much of the novel's viewpoint, intending to film the story as one where the youth was victimized by a society of capitalistic tyrants, a society that compelled the youth to murder to obtain the good life. Zukor turned down the anti-American script and hired von Sternberg to redo everything, complaining to the director that his studio had already spent a half million dollars developing a script that was going nowhere. As von Sternberg later told Andrew Sarris: "I . . . went to work writing my own script. I eliminated the sociological elements which, in my opinion, were far from being responsible for the dramatic accident with which Dreiser had concerned himself." Yet Dreiser did a complete turn-about. Upon the release of the von Sternberg film, he sued Paramount for a fortune, stating that he liked the Eisenstein script better. He lost the case. The von Sternberg film remains a source of debate to this day but it is highly provocative and visually rewarding, with Sidney giving a powerful, standout performance. The photography of Lee Garmes is detailed and arresting in almost every scene.

d, Josef von Sternberg; w, Samuel Hoffenstein (based on the novel by Theodore Dreiser); ph, Lee Garmes; art d & set d, Hans Dreier.

Drama **(PR:C MPAA:NR)**

AMERICAN WEREWOLF IN LONDON, AN 1/2** (1981) 97m UNIV c

David Naughton *(David Kessler)*, Jenny Agutter *(Alex Price)*, Griffin Dunne *(Jack Goodman)*, John Woodvine *(Dr. Hirsch)*, Brian Glover *(Chess Player)*, David Schofield *(Dart Player)*, Lila Kaye *(Barmaid)*, Paul Kember *(Sgt. McManus)*, Don McKillop *(Inspector Villiers)*, Frank Oz *(Mr. Collins)*, Anne Marie Davies *(Nurse Gallagher)*, Paula Jacobs *(Mrs. Kessler)*, Gordon Sterne *(Mr. Kessler)*, Mark Fisher *(Max)*, Michele Brisigotti *(Rachel)*.

Often funny, sometimes frightening spoof of monster movies has Naughton and Dunne hiking on the moors when they are attacked by a wolf. Dunne is horribly torn to shreds and Naughton is bitten while killing the beast. Once in a London hospital he meets and falls in love with a nurse, Agutter, who attends his wounds. She takes him into her home where he begins to have lycanthropic seizures, turning into a werewolf and then stalking the residents of London, tearing them limb from limb. He awakens naked inside of a zoo cage containing wild wolves, to make his precarious way back to Agutter's apartment. The seizures finally consume Naughton while he sits in a theater talking to the ghost of his dead partner. Once more a werewolf, Naughton kills all in the audience and then attacks an army of bobbies in the streets. He retreats down an alley and is held at bay. Agutter arrives and tries to communicate with the beast but he leaps for her. At that moment he is shot to death. Although this film begins with a great deal of humor, the excessive gore and bloodletting utterly destroy the good build-up. Coupled to this violence for its own sake is a stream of gutter language that further alienates the hero from mainstream audiences. In the end the best thing about this offbeat production is the amazing special effects achieved in showing Naughton's transformation from man to hideous werewolf. After that, it's just another cliche-ridden horror tale.

p, George Folsey, Jr.; d&w, John Landis; ph, Robert Paynter (Technicolor); m, Elmer Bernstein; ed, Malcolm Campbell; art d, Leslie Dilley; cos, Deborah Nadoolman; makeup, Rick Baker.

Comedy/Horror **Cas.** **(PR:O MPAA:R)**

AMERICAN WIFE, AN**

(1965, Ital.) 115m Sancro Films/SADI c (UNA MOGLIE AMERICANA)

Ugo Tognazzi *(Ricardo)*, Rhonda Fleming *(Oil Heiress)*, Graziella Granata *(Hostess)*, Juliet Prowse *(Wife)*, Marina Vlady *(Carole)*, Ruth Laney *(Girl)*, Carlo Mazzone *(Carlo)*, Louisette Rousseau *(Call Girl)*.

Misdirected spoof on emancipated, rich American widows and how they are sought by an opportunistic Italian teacher. Tognazzi is hired away from his academic pursuits in Italy to travel to the U.S. as an interpreter for a businessman. Once in the states he quickly learns from fellow countrymen how easy it is to marry a grass widow and become a citizen, enjoying the country bountiful. First he experiences sexual encounters in Miami Beach, then Texas millionairess Fleming toys with him for kicks, as does Prowse, until the scheme seems exhaustingly impossible. Blatant sex, pot smoking, infidelity, usury, and a host of other unsavory images are thrown up as a universal portrait of U.S. morality under the guise of humor; the film falls flat due to a cliched European perspective of the U.S. A few laughs, a lot of long looks at curvaceous Fleming and Prowse, and bad dubbing make for an inadequate import.

d, Gian Luigi Polidoro; w, Rodolfo Sonego, Rafael Azoona, Ennio Flaiano, Polidoro; ph, Benito Frattari, Marcello Gatti, Enzo Sarafin (Technicolor); ed, Eraldo Da Roma.

Comedy **(PR:O MPAA:NR)**

AMERICANA*** (1981) 91m Carradine/Sherwood c

David Carradine *(Soldier)*, Barbara Hershey *(Girl)*, Michael Greene *(Garage Man)*.

Haunting film about Carradine, a Viet Nam vet, who drifts into a small Kansas town and becomes obsessed with fixing a broken down merry-go-round that was once the pride of the community. The townsfolk distrust the stranger and resist his efforts to revive their lives. Beautiful allegorical treatment of America's attitude toward its Viet Nam veterans and the slow healing process needed after the war. A labor of love for Carradine who co-produced and directed. A great example of creative, low-budget filmmaking.

p, David Carradine, Skip Sherwood; d, David Carradine; w, Richard Carr; ph, Michael Stringer; m, Craig Hundley, David Carradine; ed, David Kern.

Drama **Cas.** **(PR:C MPAA:PG)**

AMERICANIZATION OF EMILY, THE** (1964) 115m MGM bw

James Garner *(Lt. Cmdr. Charles Madison)*, Julie Andrews *(Emily Barham)*, Melvyn Douglas *(Admiral William Jessup)*, James Coburn *(Lt. Cmdr. "Bus" Cummings)*, Joyce Grenfell *(Mrs. Barham)*, Edward Binns *(Admiral Thomas Healy)*, Liz Fraser *(Sheila)*, Keenan Wynn *(Old Sailor)*, William Windom *(Capt. Harry Spaulding)*, John Crawford *(Chief Petty Officer Paul Adams)*, Douglas Henderson *(Capt. Marvin Ellender)*, Edmond Ryan *(Admiral Hoyle)*, Steve Franken *(Young Sailor)*, Paul Newlan *(Gen. William Hallerton)*, Gary Cockrell *(Lt. Victor Wade)*, Alan Sues *(Enright)*, Bill Fraser *(Port Commander)*, Lou Byrne *(Nurse Captain)*, Alan Howard *(Port Ensign)*, Linda Marlow *(Pat)*, Janine Gray, Judy Carne, Kathy Kersh.

Garner is a thorough coward, a Navy officer hiding in a London office while his fellow servicemen are being killed in European raids. He has plenty of time to kill and money to spend and he selects prudish Andrews as the woman he spoils with his affluence and luxury. A widow—she has also lost her father and brother in the war—Andrews resists Garner's advances, telling him, "I fall in love too easily. I shatter too easily." Yet she succumbs to the good life and falls in love again. Garner, however, receives a ridiculous assignment with his roommate, free-and-easy Coburn, who spends every spare moment in bed with a gaggle of whores. Garner and Coburn are to land on Omaha Beach before any invasion troops and record the first death of a Navy man. Once on the assignment Garner realizes that either he or Coburn is slated for this less than envious honor. The premise of this film is preposterous and the leads merely saunter through their unattractive roles from a contrived script that bends over backward to profile in cheap, lunatic terms the architects of the D-Day Invasion for the sake of forced humor. A large let-down of a concept that could have been meaningful and touching.

p, Martin Ransohoff; d, Arthur Hiller; w, Paddy Chayefsky (based on the novel by William Bradford Huie); ph, Philip Lathrop; m, Johnny Mandel; ed, Tom McAdoo; cos, Bill Thomas.

Comedy/Drama **(PR:C MPAA:NR)**

AMERICANO, THE** (1955) 85m RKO c

Glenn Ford *(Sam Dent)*, Frank Lovejoy *(Bento Hermanny)*, Cesar Romero *(Manoel)*, Ursula Thiess *(Marianna Figuerido)*, Abbe Lane *(Teresa)*, Rudolfo Hoyos Jr. *(Cristino)*, Salvador Baguez *(Capt. Gonzales)*, Tom Powers *(Jim Rogers)*, Dan White *(Barney Dent)*, Frank Marlowe *(Captain of Ship)*, George Navarro *(Tuba)*, Nyra Monsour *(Tuba's Sister)*.

Good cast and unusual location (Brazil) save this otherwise average oater that involves a range war between an evil cattle baron and the farmers who attempt to settle on the grazing land. Ford, an American confused by these south-of-the-border activities, teams up with Robin Hood-type bandit Romero to defeat villain Lovejoy.

p, Robert Stillman; d, William Castle; w, Guy Trosper (based on a story by Leslie T. White); ph, William Snyder; m, Roy Webb; ed, Harry Marker.

Western **Cas.** **(PR:A MPAA:NR)**

AMERICATHON* (1979) 85m Lorimar/UA c

Peter Riegert *(Eric)*, Harvey Korman *(Monty)*, Fred Willard *(Vanderhoff)*, Zane Buzby *(Mouling)*, Nancy Morgan *(Lucy)*, John Ritter *(Chet)*, Richard Schaal *(Jerry)*, Elvis Costello *(Earl)*, Chief Dan George *(Sam)*, Tommy LaSorda *(Announcer)*, Jay Leno *(Larry)*, Peter Marshall *(Himself)*, Meat Loaf *(Oklahoma Roy)*, Howard Hesseman *(Kip)*, Geno Andrews *(Chris)*, Robert Beer *(David Eisenhower)*, Terry McGovern *(Danny)*, Nellie Bellflower *(VP Advertising)*, Jimmy Weldon *(VP Research)*, David Opatoshu, Allan Arbus *(Hebrabs)*.

Shoddy comedy with a potentially funny premise. It is 1998. Chet Roosevelt (great-grandson of Franklin) is President. The U.S. Government runs out of money. The President is forced to hold an international telethon to raise enough money to bail out the most powerful nation in the free world. Sounds like it could be funny? It isn't.

The film is ruined by a lousy cast, episodic subplots involving a White House aide, Willard, who conspires with an Arab/Jewish terrorist organization (The Herabs. Hebrew/Arabs. Get it? Ha. Ha.) to overthrow the ailing government, and a production company that was more interested in selling soundtrack albums than making a decent comedy. (The casting of rock stars Costello and Meat Loaf was supposed to sell records. It didn't.) The whole thing was a misguided attempt by some Hollywood executives to pander to a mindless teenage audience. As it turned out, the teenage audience wasn't all that mindless. They stayed away in droves and the movie bombed.

p, Joe Roth; d, Neil Israel; w, Israel, Michael Mislove, Monica Johnson (based on a play by Philip Proctor and Peter Bergman); ph, Gerald Hirschfeld; m, Earl Brown Jr., David Pomeranz; Elvis Costello, Alan Parsons, Reggie Knighton, Jim Steinman; ed, John C. Howard; cos, Daniel Paredes; ch, Jamie Rogers.

Comedy Cas. (PR:C MPAA:PG)

AMIN—THE RISE AND FALL zero (1982, Kenya) 101m International Films/Continental c

Joseph Olita *(Idi Amin)*, Geoffrey Keen *(British Commissioner)*, Denis Hills *(Himself)*, Leonard Trolley *(Bob Astles)*, Andre Maranne *(French Ambassador)*, Diane Mercer *(His Wife)*, Tony Sibbald *(Canadian Commissioner)*, Thomas Baptiste *(Dr. Oloya)*, Louis Mahoney *(Freedom Fighter)*, Ka Vundia *(Malyamungu)*, Sophie Kind *(French Ambassador's Daughter)*, Marlene Dogherty *(Mrs. Dora Bloch)*.

Sick violent chronicle of Uganda tyrant Idi Amin offers nothing more than a string of atrocities—hacked-up bodies, bullet-ridden bodies, blown-up bodies—tied to Amin's savage regime. An awful waste of good film.

p&d, Sharad Patel; ph, Harvey Harrison; ed, Keith Palmer.

Drama Cas. (PR:O MPAA:R)

AMITYVILLE HORROR, THE** (1979) 126m AM-INT c

James Brolin *(George Lutz)*, Margot Kidder *(Kathleen Lutz)*, Rod Steiger *(Fr. Delaney)*, Don Stroud *(Fr. Bolen)*, Natasha Ryan *(Amy)*, K. C. Martell *(Greg)*, Meeno Peluce *(Matt)*, Michael Sacks *(Jeff)*, Helen Shaver *(Carolyn)*, Val Avery *(Sgt. Gionfriddo)*, Amy Wright *(Jackie)*, Murray Hamilton *(Fr. Ryan)*, John Larch *(Fr. Nuncio)*, Irene Dailey *(Aunt Helena)*.

Amazingly successful horror film from the amazingly successful book about the unlucky Lutz family that is terrorized by their new home's past demons. Swarms of flies appear out of nowhere, pipes ooze slime, and Rod Steiger chews up the scenery as the priest determined to rid the house of its evil. Effective but stupid fright film. The real estate game isn't what it used to be.

p, Ronald Saland, Elliot Geisinger; d, Stuart Rosenberg; w, Sandor Stern (based on the book by Jay Anson); ph, Fred J. Koenekamp; m, Lalo Schifrin; ed, Robert Brown; art d, Jim Swados; visual eff d, William Cruse; spec eff, Delwyn Rheaume.

Horror Cas. (PR:O MPAA:R)

AMITYVILLE 3-D* (1983) 105m Dino DeLaurentiis/Orion c

Tony Roberts *(John Baxter)*, Tess Harper *(Nancy Baxter)*, Robert Joy *(Elliot West)*, Candy Clark *(Melanie)* John Beal *(Harold Caswell)*, Leona Dana *(Emma Caswell)*, John Harkins *(Clifford Sanders)*, Lori Loughlin *(Susan Baxter)*, Meg Ryan *(Lisa)*.

Cynical, determined reporter Roberts ignores just about everybody's warnings when he decides to investigate a supposedly haunted house. Explosive ending and a few good 3-D effects can't help this stinker. The third dimension they should have tried to create is believability.

p, Stephen F. Kesten; d, Richard Fleischer; w, William Wales; ph, Fred Schuler (DeLuxe Color); m, Howard Blake; ed, Frank J. Urioste; art d, Giorgio Postiglione; set d, Justin Scoppa; spec eff, Michael Wood.

Horror Cas. (PR:O MPAA:PG)

AMITYVILLE II: THE POSSESSION* (1982) 104m Dino DeLaurentiis/Orion c

Burt Young *(Anthony Montelli)*, Rutanya Alda *(Deloris Montelli)*, James Olson *(Fr. Adamski)*, Jack Magner *(Sonny Montelli)*, Diane Franklin *(Patricia Montelli)*, Andrew Prine *(Fr. Tom)*, Leonardo Cimino *(Chancellor)*, Brent Katz *(Mark Montelli)*, Erica Katz *(Jan Montelli)*, Moses Gunn *(Detective Turner)*.

Troubled teenage son of a simple, middle-class family is possessed by some form of evil lurking in his home's basement. The kid finally goes over the deep end and hacks apart his entire family. Vague themes of incest and family abuse give the final grisly scenes a nasty, disturbing quality in an otherwise laughable film. Actually a sequel to 1979's AMITYVILLE HORROR, AMITYVILLE II tries to create an explanation for the future terrors that will befall the Lutz family, but fails miserably as a competent piece of entertainment.

p, Ira N. Smith, Stephen R. Greenwald; d, Damiano Damiani; w, Tommy Lee Wallace (based on a book by Hans Holzer); ph, Franco Digiacomo (DeLuxe Color), m, Lalo Schifrin; ed, Sam O'Steen; prod d, Pierluigi Basile; art d, Ray Recht; set d, George Dititta, Jr.; spec eff makeup, John Caglione, Jr.; spec eff, Glen Robinson.

Horror Cas. (PR:O MPAA:R)

AMONG HUMAN WOLVES** (1940, Brit.) 61m Film Alliance/Anglo-American bw (GB: SECRET JOURNEY)

Basil Radford *(John Richardson)*, Silvie St. Claire *(Helen Richardson)*, Thorley Walters *(Von Raugwitz)*, Peter Gawthorne *(General Von Raugwitz)*, Tom Helmore *(Capt. Benolt)*, Joseph Ambler *(Col. Blondin)*, George Hayes *(Inspector Walter)*, Kiwi *(Himself)*.

Poorly made wartime espionage film from the British involving the theft of a secret cartridge from Paris by a German spy. The spy dashes back to the Fatherland with agents from the Allied forces right on his tail. Not only are they to get the cartridge back, but they are to gather important military data for intelligence purposes. They are aided by an English girl who seduces the son of a German general who is involved in some top-secret Axis operations. Typical spy film hurt by almost total incompetence in the technical areas.

p, John Corfield; d, John Baxter; w, Michael Hogan (based on the story "Lone Wolves" by Charles Robert Dumas); ph, James Wilson.

Spy Drama (PR:A MPAA:NR)

AMONG THE LIVING*** (1941) 67m PAR bw

Albert Dekker *(John Raden/Paul Raden)*, Susan Hayward *(Millie Pickens)*, Harry Carey *(Dr. Ben Saunders)*, Frances Farmer *(Elaine Raden)*, Gordon Jones *(Bill Oakley)*, Jean Phillips *(Peggy Nolan)*, Maude Eburne *(Mrs. Pickens)*, Frank M. Thomas *(Sheriff)*, Harlan Briggs *(Judge)*, Archie Twitchell *(Tom Reilly)*, Ernest Whitman *(Pompey)*, Dorothy Sebastian *(Woman in Cafe)*, William Stack *(Minister)*.

Homicidal maniac returns to his home town and begins a killing spree, disrupting the life of his twin brother. Dekker does very well with a dual role in this moody, unusual B-picture, but the real interest in this film is generated by the presence of Hayward and Farmer, the two female stars. AMONG THE LIVING was a tremendous boost to the just-beginning career of Hayward, her lively, engaging performance catching the eye of more than one producer at the time. Sadly, this is one of the later films of the gifted Farmer, her tragic bout with alcohol and mental illness coming soon after this picture. The brilliant photography by Theodor Sparkuhl is a very early example of the *film noir* chiaroscuro style.

p, Sol C. Siegel; d, Stuart Heisler; w, Lester Cole, Garrett Fort (based on a story by Brian Marlowe, Cole); ph, Theodor Sparkuhl; m, Gerard Carbonara; ed, Everett Douglas.

Drama (PR:C MPAA:NR)

AMONG THE MISSING* (1934) 62m COL bw

Henrietta Crosman, Richard Cromwell, Billie Seward, Arthur Hohl, Ivan Simpson, Ben Taggart, Wade Boteler, Harry C. Bradley, Claire DuBrey, Douglas Cosgrove, Paul Hurst.

Laughably implausible story of an old woman who is fed up with her family, so she leaves them and becomes a cook in the home of a respectable dealer of antiques who also happens to be the local jewel thief. There she meets one of the young gang members and his girl friend. She takes an immediate liking to the couple and wants to help the kids go straight. The young thief decides it is time to retire, but he must go on one last job. The old lady follows him and just when he is about to be caught, she takes the jewels from him and is captured by the police. She refuses to talk but the kid confesses, gets a suspended sentence, marries his girl, and the old lady goes back to her family.

d, Al Rogell; w, Fred Niblo Jr., Herbert Asbury (based on a story by Florence Wagner); ph, Joseph August; ed, John Rawlins.

Crime (PR:A MPAA:NR)

AMONG VULTURES* (1964, Ger./Ital./Fr./Yugo.) 102m Rialto Film/Atlantis (UNTER GEIERN) Film/S.N.C./Jadran Film c

Stewart Granger *(Shurehand)*, Pierre Brice *(Winnetou)*, Elke Sommer, Gotz George, Walter Barnes, Renato Baldini.

Third in a series of German westerns based on German author Karl May's novels involving the characters of "Shurehand" and "Winnetou the Warrior". Granger (replacing Lex Barker in the series) who plays Shurehand and Brice (a French actor) who plays Winnetou team up to rescue Sommer from outlaw George who is out to get her and her money. Granger introduces an element of parody to his role for the first time in the series.

p, Preben Philipsen; d, Alfred Vohrer; w, Eberhard Kleindorff, Johanna Sibelius (based on the book by Karl May); ph, Karl Lob.

Western (PR:A MPAA:NR)

AMOROUS ADVENTURES OF MOLL FLANDERS, THE½** (1965) PAR c

Kim Novak *(Moll Flanders)*, Claire Ufland *(Young Moll)*, Richard Johnson *(Jemmy)*, Angela Lansbury *(Lady Blystone)*, Vittorio De Sica *(The Count)*, Leo McKern *(Squint)*, George Sanders *(The Banker)*, Lilli Palmer *(Dutchy)*, Peter Butterworth *(Grunt)*, Dandy Nichols *(Orphanage Supt.)*, Noel Howlett *(Bishop)*, Cecil Parker *(Major)*, Barbara Couper *(The Major's Wife)*, Daniel Massey *(Elder Brother)*, Darren Nesbitt *(Younger Brother)*, Ingrid Hafner *(Elder Sister)*, June Watts *(Younger Sister)*, Judith Furse *(Miss Glowber)*, Anthony Dawson *(Officer of Dragoons)*, Roger Livesey *(Drunken Person)* Jess Conrad *(lst Mohock)*, Noel Harrison *(2nd Mohock)*, Alex Scott *(3rd* Mohock), Alexis Kahner *(4th Mohock)*, Mary Merrall *(A Lady)*, Richard Wattis *(Jeweler)*, Terence Lodge *(Draper)*, Reginald Beckwith *(Doctor)*, Lionel Long *(Singer in Prison)*, David Lodge *(Ship's Captain)*, David Hutcheson *(A Nobleman)*, Hugh Griffith *(Prison Governor)*, Michael Trubshawe *(Lord Mayor of London)*, Richard Goolden *(The Ordinary)*, Leonard Sachs *(Prison Doctor)*, Basil Dignam *(Lawyer)*, Michael Brennan *(The Turnkey)*, Liam Redmond *(Convict Ship Captain)*, Neville Jason *(Convict Ship Officer)*.

Bawdy comedy starring Novak as the title character in this female version of TOM JONES. She plays a poor 18th-century lass who wants to become a woman of substance. While attempting to achieve this, she goes through a series of affairs and marriages that take up most of the movie. Unfortunately, she falls in love with a lowly highwayman who rents a giant ship to fool her into thinking he is wealthy. The plan doesn't work and she marries a rich banker, Sanders, who soon dies of a heart attack, leaving her with a vast fortune. She is then free to marry her dashing robber and live as a lady of wealth. The film tries to recreate the same sense of farce and craziness that made TOM JONES such a success, but ultimately fails for being too derivative. Novak tries hard, but she just can't handle what the material demands.

p, Marcel Hellman, d, Terence Young, w, Denis Cannan, Roland Kibbee (based on the works of Daniel Defoe); ph, Ted Moore (Panavision, Technicolor); m, John Addison; ed, Frederick Wilson; art d, Syd Cain; cos, Elizabeth Haffenden, Joan Bridge; ch, Pauline Grant.

Comedy/Farce (PR:C MPAA:NR)

AMOROUS MR. PRAWN, THE**
(1964, Brit.) 89m BLC bw (AKA: THE PLAYGIRL AND THE WAR MINISTER)

Joan Greenwood *(Lady Fitzadam)*, Cecil Parker *(Gen. Fitzadam)*, Ian Carmichael *(Cpl. Sidney Green)*, Robert Beatty *(Larry Hoffman)*, Dennis Price *(Prawn)*, Liz Fraser *(Suzie Tidmarsh)*, Reg Lye *(Uncle Joe)*, Bridget Armstrong *(Biddy O'Hara)*, Derek Nimmo *(Willie Maltravers)*, Harry Locke *(Albert Huggins)*, Robert Nichols *(Sam Goulansky)*, Roddy McMillan *(Mac)*, Godfrey James *(Sergeant at Exchange)*, Finlay Currie *(Lochaye)*, Patrick Jordan *(Sergeant of Guard), Gerald Sim, Geoffrey Bayldon (Operators), Eric Woodburn (Landlord), John Dunbar, Jack Stewart (Men in Bar), Sandra Dorne (Dusty Babs), Eric Francis (Postman), Michael Ripper (Angus), Drew Russell (Airman), Michael Hunt (RAF Sergeant), Ronald Brittain (Parade Sergeant Major).*

Parker is a retiring army general who is in need of some cash to purchase his retirement cottage. While he's gone on maneuvers, his faithful wife, Greenwood, comes up with the perfect solution to their financial dilemma. She decides to convert her husband's military headquarters in Scotland into a hotel for tourists. She enlists the aid of the general's loyal army staff to fill in as chefs, maids, bellhops, and chauffeurs. The scheme turns out to be a bigger success than she anticipated. Things look grim when Parker returns unexpectedly, but he thinks it's a good idea and he'd like to get revenge on the war office anyway. Trouble arises when the minister of the state of war shows up to rent a room. He decides to remain silent when he discovers the misuse of government property, because the young blonde he is caught in bed with is not his wife. It's a broad comedy with especially funny sequences showing the staff trying to camouflage the hotel when unexpected military personnel arrive.

p, Leslie Gilliat; d, Anthony Kimmins; w, Kimmins, Nicholas Phipps (based on the play by Kimmins); ph, Wilkie Cooper; m, John Barry; ed, Thelma Connell; art d, Albert Witherick; cos, Hardy Aimes; makeup, George Partleton.

Comedy (PR:A MPAA:NR)

AMOS 'N' ANDY* 1/2
(1930) 70m Radio bw (AKA: CHECK AND DOUBLE CHECK)

Freeman F. Gosden *(Amos)*, Charles V. Correll *(Andy)*, Sue Carol *(Jean Blair)*, Charles Morton *(Richard Williams)*, Ralf Harolde *(Ralph Crawford)*, Edward Martindel *(John Blair)*, Irene Rich *(Mrs. Blair)*, Rita La Roy *(Elinor Crawford)*, Russell Powell *(Kingfish)*, Robert E. Homans *(Nathan)*, Pat Conway *(Cop)*.

Weak comedy from the popular radio comedians Gosden and Correll. All the radio characters make appearances including the Kingfish, Powell, and the Mystic Knights. While the white men who play Amos N' Andy could get away with imitating the voices of black men on the radio, watching them perform in black-face is a bit much to take. The music is played by Duke Ellington's Orchestra.

d, Melville Brown; w, J. Walter Ruben; ph, William Marshall; m/l, Bert Kalmar, Harry Ruby.

Comedy (PR:A MPAA:NR)

AMOUR, AMOUR* (1937, Fr.) 85m GFFA bw

Le Gallo, Colette Broldo, Henri Marchand, Sylvio de Pedrelli Delaitre, Paul Menant, Jaques Tarride, Polaire.

Story of a dim jeweler who would be robbed constantly if not for a faithful employee who keeps him out of trouble. Most of the film looks like an excuse to show off Paris' best stores, restaurants, and tourist spots.

p, Leon Poirier, d, Robert Bilbal, w, Pierre Batcheff (based on the novel by Paul Maret); m. A. Demurger.

Comedy (PR:A MPAA:NR)

AMPHIBIOUS MAN, THE** (1961, USSR) 100m Sovexport/Lenfilm c

K. Korieniev *(Sea Devil)*, M. Virzinskaya *(Alicia)*.

Fable-like tale of a scientist who has turned his only son into an amphibious man who lurks in the waters of a small fishing village. The fishermen have named the creature the "Sea Devil". One day the Sea Devil saves the daughter of one of the fisherman from a shark and falls in love. The girl is promised to another and the Sea Devil comes ashore in search of his beloved. Interesting underwater sequences.

d, Y. Kasancki; w, A. Blajaev, Y. Kasancki (based on a book by Blajaev); m, Tirentev.

Adventure (PA:AA MPAA:NR)

AMPHYTRYON** (1937, Ger.) 88m Globe/UFA bw

Henri Garat *(Amphitryon/Jupiter)*, Armond Bernard *(Sosias/Mercury)*, Jeanne Boitel *(Alcmene)*, Odette Florelle *(Myrismis)*, Marguerite Moreno *(Juno)*.

German musical spectacular based on Greek mythology, starring French performers. Lavish production surrounds the story of Alcmene, Boitel, who longs for the return of her husband Amphytrion (Garat) from war. The god Jupiter (also played by Garat) notices the lovely mortal woman and descends to Earth in human form to seduce her. Alcmene succumbs to the disguised god's charms, but she is saved because Jupiter drinks too much and passes out before they can consummate the affair. Jupiter's wife, Juno, comes to Earth and drags her husband back to Olympus. A slightly cumbersome film, but good for mythology buffs.

p, Guenther Stapenhorst; d, Reinhold Schuenzel; w, Schuenzel, Albert Valentin, Serge Veher; m/l, Francois Doelle, Veher.

Musical (PR:A MPAA:NR)

AMSTERDAM AFFAIR, THE 1/2**
(1968 Brit.) 91m London Independent Producers/Trio Films Group c

William Marlowe *(Martin Ray)*, Catherine Von Schell *(Sophie Ray)*, Wolfgang Kieling *(Van Der Valk)*, Pamela Ann Davy *(Elsa de Charmoy)*, Josef Dubin-Behrman *(Eric de Charmoy)*, Lo Van Hensbergen *(Magistrate)*, Guido de Moor *(Piet Ulbricht)*.

British murder mystery concerning a young writer, Marlowe, who is accussed of killing his ex-mistress, whom he hated. Enter the detective, Kieling, who is not fully convinced of the writer's guilt. Due to pressure from his superiors, the detective is forced to wrap up the case quickly, but he and the writer's wife, Von Schell, continue the investigation after hours. Eventually one of the dead woman's lovers appears to be the actual murderer and the writer's wife allows herself to be used as bait to catch him. Typical mystery/thriller stuff made special by Kieling's performance as the tough-guy detective.

p, William Gell, Howard Barnes; d, Gerry O'Hara; w, Edmund Ward (based on novel *Love in Amsterdam* by Nicolas Freeling); ph, Gerry Fisher (Eastmancolor); m, Johnny Scott; ed, Barry Peters.

Mystery/Thriller (PR:C MPAA:NR)

AMSTERDAM KILL, THE** (1978, Hong Kong) 89m Golden Harvest/COL c

Robert Mitchum *(Quinlan)*, Bradford Dillman *(Odums)*, Richard Egan *(Ridgeway)*, Leslie Nielsen *(Knight)*, Keye Luke *(Chung Wei)*, George Cheung *(Jimmy Wong)*, Chan Sing *(Assassin)*.

Routine international crime drama with a tedious pace begins with several important figures around the world being killed and Dillman, head of the U.S. Drug Enforce ment Agency in Hong Kong, calling in middle-aged has-been lawman Mitchum to track down the source leaking information which has led to the deaths of the agency's contacts. Mitchum leaves his poverty-row flat in London, flying to Hong Kong where he laconically encounters a host of almost fatal attacks by parties unknown, his visit to the British Crown Colony offering a perfect excuse for some gorgeous photography of the exotic port. Several bodies later, Mitchum unearths a single lead, the word "Juliana," which leads him to Amsterdam. Here, among the colorful flower beds, he learns that a single person is attempting to take over the world drug traffic; he outlives a long and near-boring gun battle (if that's possible), and discovers the high-ranking traitor leaking the information, a political sachem who commits suicide before the authorities can close in. This film is disappointingly inactive for a story line that promises a lot of snap. Moreover, Mitchum underplays his role as the old world-weary crime fighter with such *sotto voce that he appears at times to be sleepwalking.*

p, Andre Morgan; d, Robert Clouse; w, Clouse, Gregory Tiefer; ph, Alan Hume (Panavision, Technicolor); m, Hal Schaefer; ed, Allan Holzman, Gina Brown; art d, John Blezard, K.S. Chen; spec eff, Gene Grigg.

Crime Cas. (PR:O MPAA:R)

AMY 1/2** (1981) 100m BV c

Jenny Agutter *(Amy Medford)*, Barry Newman *(Dr. Ben Corcoran)*, Kathleen Nolan *(Helen Gibbs)*, Chris Robinson *(Elliot Medford)*, Lou Fant *(Lyle Ferguson)*, Margaret O'Brien *(Hazel Johnson)*, Nanette Fabray *(Malvina)*, Otto Rechenberg *(Henry Watkins)*, Lance LeGault *(Edgar Wamback)*, Lucille Benson *(Rose)*, Jonathan Daly *(Clyde)*, Lonny Chapman *(Virgil)*, Brian Frishman *(Melvin)*, Jane Daly *(Molly)*, Dawn Jeffory *(Caroline)*, Francis Bay *(Mrs. Lindey)*, Peggy McCay *(Mrs. Grimes)*, Len Wayland *(Grimes)*, Virginia Vincent *(Edna)*, Norman Burton *(Caruthers)*, David Hollander *(Just George)*, Bumper *(Wesley)*, Alban Branton *(Eugene)*, Ronnie Scribner *(Walter)*.

Agutter plays the title character who leaves her rich husband to teach at a special school for the deaf and blind in this Disney picture set at the turn of the century. Once she arrives at the school, she meets and befriends one of the doctors, Newman, and the two of them set out to teach the handicapped children how to play football. The film climaxes with a big football game between the deaf and blind kids and the "normal" children of the area. Though the script doesn't realistically deal with the male mentality of the early 1900s, which would have made Agutter's achievements more difficult, the film is admirable and a good bet for children.

p, Jerome Courtland; d, Vincent McEveety; w, Noreen Stone; ph, Leonard J. South (Technicolor); m, Robert F. Brunner; ed, Gregg McLaughlin; art d, John B. Mansbridge, Mark W. Mansbridge; cos, Jack Sandeen.

Drama Cas. (PR:AAA MPAA:G)

ANASTASIA**** (1956) 105m FOX c

Ingrid Bergman *(Anastasia)*, Yul Brynner *(Bounine)*, Helen Hayes *(Empress)*, Akim Tamiroff *(Chernov)*, Martita Hunt *(Baroness von Livenbaum)*, Felix Aylmer *(Russian Chamberlain)*, Sacha Pitoeff *(Petrovin)*, Ivan Desny *(Prince Paul)*, Natalie Schafer *(Lissenskaia)*, Gregoire Gromoff *(Stepan)*, Karel Stepanek *(Vlados)*, Ina de la Haye *(Marusia)*, Hy Hazell *(Maxime)*, Katherine Kath *(Blonde Lady)*, Olga Valery *(Countess Baranova)*, Tamara Shayne *(Xenia)*, Peter Sallis *(Grischa)*, Polycarpe Pavloff *(Schischkin)*.

Impostor or grand duchess of Russia, daughter of the last Czar? There was no doubt in the mind of any viewer after watching Bergman's sublime performance that she was the presumably lost and unhappy Romanoff princess. This was the actress' comeback after a long absence from American screens and she played her part with such intense feeling that it won over audiences across the land, as well as a well-earned Academy Award. She is found in Paris in 1928, destitute, suicidal, contemplating the inky waters of the Seine by expatriate White Russian General Brynner who instantly sees in her a likeness to Anastasia, the youngest daughter of Czar Nicholas of Russia, who was said to have somehow survived the slaughter of the Romanoff family at Ekaterinberg in 1918 at the hands of a Bolshevik execution squad. A schemer aware that millions of rubles had been deposited by the Czar in foreign banks years earlier and that Anastasia, if alive, would be heir to this fortune, Brynner immediately sets in motion a grand hoax. Once he himself believes that Bergman can physically pass for Anastasia, he and other Russian exiles begin to groom the bewildered, withdrawn woman in the ways of royalty, compelling her to put to memory a mass of details concerning the Romanoff family, its heritage, myriad relatives, living and dead, habits, customs, an avalanche of minutiae that overwhelms Bergman who has no idea who she is. Near collapse, attempting to run away, she is caught by Brynner who is suddenly gentle with her, unexpectedly understanding. He tells her that if she does run away she gives up any hope of ever being anything worthwhile, especially of learning her own identity. The temptatyon prompts her to go on with the charade. She is introduced to Aylmer, one-time Russian minister to the Czar, who dismisses her out of hand as an impostor. Bergman, surprising herself, rebukes the nobleman for speaking to a grand duchess in such a manner, projecting a royal bearing that instantly convinces the elderly statesman that he is indeed in the presence of his sovereign's daughter. The display even astounds the cynical Brynner who begins to think that Bergman is more than a nobody, that she just might be the princess. One great test remains. She must confront the Dowager Empress, Helen Hayes, who plays her royal role as if born for it (as with most of the parts ever played by this indefatigable peerless actress). Hayes at first refuses to see Bergman; she has had her heart wrenched time and again by impostors claiming to be one or another of her four departed granddaughters, particularly the youngest, Anastasia. Royal members who have met Bergman, Hunt and Desny, are convinced she is authentic and persuade Hayes to finally give her an audience. The meeting between Bergman and Hayes is worth the entire movie, a taut, suspenseful, utterly captivating encounter where Bergman attempts to convince her grandmother that she is Anastasia and Hayes, rebuffing the idea, countering every bit of proof with a challenge, explaining how she could have learned such information outside the royal family. Bergman is defeated, crushed. She is about to leave, go into the oblivion of the nameless when she begins to cough excitedly. Hayes stares at her, asking her if she is ill. "I always cough when I'm nervous," replies Bergman, then calling Hayes by a pet name. Hayes is startled into belief, explaining that only Anastasia would know the name she has used and that her granddaughter displayed a nervous cough when excited. She embraces Bergman as Anastasia, pronouncing her the missing Romanoff but asking that if she is an impostor not to tell her because her heart cannot stand another letdown. All of the exiled Russian royalty in Copenhagen accept Bergman as Anastasia, now that she is endorsed by the Dowager Empress. She is received at a courtly ball and publicly acknowledged. Desny, as Prince Paul, has fallen in love with her and plans to marry Bergman. Yet she cannot wed the handsome suitor, she tells Hayes; she's in love with the adventurer Brynner. Hayes tells her that having a throne or crown is worthless without love and encourages Bergman to follow the dictates of her heart. She does, giving up all, and leaving with Brynner. Bergman's performance is nothing less than majestic; here she ranges from a mentally disturbed itinerant to a regal woman born to the purple, a gradual transformation that is a wonder to behold. Bergman's role turned American audiences away from the conviction that she was an "immoral" woman; almost eight years earlier, after a stellar film career which had made her a premier actress of American films, Bergman had had an illegitimate child with Italian director Roberto Rossellini while married to another man and was ostracized by her employers and fans. ANASTASIA changed all that. The illustrious Bergman was back, greater than ever, and the public would never again let her go.

p, Buddy Adler; d, Anatole Litvak; w, Arthur Laurents (based on the play by Marcelle Maurette, adapted by Guy Bolton); ph, Jack Hildyard (CinemaScope, DeLuxe Color); m, Alfred Newman; ed, Bert Bates; art d, Andrei Andrejew, Bill Andrews; set d, Andrew Low; cos, Rene Hubert.

Drama **(PR:A MPAA:NR)**

ANATAHAN* (1953, Jap.) 90m Dalwa bw (AKA: SAGA OF ANATAHAN)

A. Negishi *(The Queen Bee)*, T. Sugunuma *(Her Husband)*, K. Sawamura, S. Nakayama, J. Fujikawa, H. Kondoh, S. Mivashita *(The Five Drones)*, K. Onoe, T. Bandoh *(The Two Skippers)*, R. Kineya *(Samisen Player)*, D. Tamura, T. Kitagawa *(The Homesick Ones)*, T. Suzmk *(The Patriot)*.

Pretentious film that famed director Joseph von Sternberg made in Japan. Self-consciously arty, the plot chronicles the tale of a woman marooned on a small island that is inhabited by thirty lecherous men. The metaphorical meaning of the material is put forth by calling the woman "The Queen Bee" and the men "drones." Poor performances, laughable material, and a bizarre cultural combination (native German von Sternberg spending a record-breaking amount of money to produce a Japanese film), almost push this effort into farce. A miserable failure.

p, K. Takimura; d&ph, Joseph von Sternberg (based on a book by Michiro Maruyama); m, A. Ifukube; ed, M. Miyata.

Drama **(PR:C MPAA:NR)**

ANATOMIST, THE*½ (1961, Brit.) 73m BIP bw

Alistair Sim, George Cole, Jill Bennet, Michael Ripper, Margaret Gordon.

Fumbling slapstick attempts to make fun of bodysnatching capers which are about as funny as a cemetery, night or day. The only redeeming aspect of this dismal grinder are the few moments when Sim is given something to do.

d, Leonard William (based on the play by James Bridie).

Comedy/Horror **(PR:C MPAA:NR)**

ANATOMY OF A MARRIAGE (MY DAYS WITH JEAN-MARC AND MY NIGHTS WITH FRANCOISE)½** (1964 Fr.) 97m Janus bw

Marie-Jose Nat *(Francoise)*, Jacques Charrier *(Jean-Marc)*, Michel Subor *(Roger)*, Giani Esposito *(Ettore)*, Macha Meril *(Nicole)*, George Riviere *(Phillipe)*, Michele Giradon *(Patricia)*, Jacqueline Porel *(Line)*, Yves Vincent *(Granjouan)*, Yvan Chiffre *(Christian)*, Anne Caprille *(Mme. Monnier)*, Corinne Armand *(Christina)*, Michel Tureau *(Milou)*, Marie-Claude Breton *(Minouche)*.

Strange attempt to tell two versions of the same story by making two short films and showing them one after the other. The subject is the dissolution of a marriage. One film shows us the woman's recollections of the events surrounding the separation. To her, her husband was unambitious, lazy, and insecure. She tried to help him make more of himself but her efforts proved fruitless. She is forced to become the breadwinner, has an affair, and becomes a successful career woman. She leaves him thinking it was his jealousy that ruined the marriage. The other film (which was shown in a different theatre located nearby when first screened in N.Y.C.) shows us the husband's version of the same events, which of course, are quite different. He thinks that it was his wife's infidelity that ruined the marriage. He was happy with his career and recalls that he was forced to end his work in the small town they lived in due to his wife's immoral behavior. He claims that she became successful because she slept her way to the top. When both films are over, we are left to make up our own minds as to where the truth lies. While the attempt at creating a unique movie-going experience is admirable, the film ultimately fails due to the necessary gap between viewing the two films. If, through editing, the stories were juxtaposed, incident for incident, wife's version and husband's version immediately, the effect might have been more powerful. The other problem with the film is the characters themselves. These are venal, petty people and there is no reason we should care about either of them. An interesting failure.

p&d, Andre Cayette; w, Cayette, Louis Sapin, Maurice Auberge; ph, Roger Felloux; m, Louniguy.

Drama **(PR:O MPAA:NR)**

ANATOMY OF A MURDER**** (1959) 160m COL bw

James Stewart (Paul Biegler), Lee Remick (Laura Manion), Ben Gazzara (Lt. Frederick Manion), Arthur O'Connell *(Parnell McCarthy)*, Eve Arden *(Maida)*, Kathryn Grant *(Mary Pilant)*, Joseph N. Welch *(Judge Weaver)*, Brooks West *(Mitch Lodwick)*, George C. Scott *(Claude Dancer)*, Murray Hamilton *(Alphonse Paquette)*, Orson Bean *(Dr. Smith)*, Alexander Campbell *(Dr. Harcourt)*, Joseph Kearns *(Mr. Burke)*, Russ Brown *(Mr. Lemon)*, Howard McNear *(Dr. Dompierre)*, Ned Wever *(Dr. Raschid)*, Jimmy Conlin *(Madigan)*, Ken Lynch *(Sgt. Durgo)*, Don Russ *(Duane Miller)*, Lloyd Le Vasseur *(Court Clerk)*, Royal Beal *(Sheriff Battisfore)*, John Qualen *(Sulo)*, James Waters *(An Army Sergeant)*, Duke Ellington *(Pie-Eye)*, Irving Kupcinet *(Distinguished Gentleman)*.

A slick, terse *film noir* production that concentrates its action in a courtroom where a host of colorful bizarre personalities cavort in a sensational murder trial. Gazzara is an Army lieutenant accused of murdering a bartender who reportedly beat up and raped his wife, Remick. He is defended by one-time prosecutor Stewart who first refuses the case then takes it on as a challenge. His opponent, sophisticated big-town prosecutor Scott, maintains that Gazzara's motive was not a noble defense of his wife but that Remick, who has a reputation of being free-and-easy with her favors, really carried on a love affair with the murdered bartender, that Gazzara put the bruises on her face when beating the truth from her and that he then willfully killed his victim in a jealous rage. Stewart's researcher, drunken O'Connell, digs up an old case where a husband had killed another man attacking his wife, pleaded not guilty as acting under "an irresistible impulse, and had been acquitted. Stewart uses the same plea and seals his case by putting the murdered man's stepdaughter, Grant, on the witness stand where she portrays the victim as having been a ravisher of young women. As conclusive proof she offers a pair of panties torn from Remick during the rape and since missing; she has found them in her own laundry room, proving that the murdered man hid them there, and, concludes the jury, also proving that Gazzara had killed to defend his wife's honor. Stewart wins his case but not his fee; when he and O'Connell drive to Gazzara's mobile home to collect they find a note from their former client reading that he and Remick had an "irresistible impulse" to leave without paying their legal fees. The complex roles are handled with great skill, particularly by Gazzara as the callous, haughty accused, Remick as his sexpot wife, and Stewart and Scott whose courtroom bantering and cleverness is a joy to behold, with Stewart's "gee-whiz" persona eventually overcoming the super-confident Scott. Joseph Welch, a noted Boston attorney turned actor, is particularly impressive as the trial judge. Audiences of the day, however, were shocked to hear all-American Stewart openly talking of contraceptives, sex, and rape. Once controversial, the film is now merely good drama with the deft stamp of Preminger on every scene.

p&d, Otto Preminger; w, Wendell Mayes; ph, Sam Leavitt; m, Duke Ellington; ed, Louis R. Loeffler; set d, Howard Bristol.

Crime Drama **(PR:C MPAA:NR)**

ANATOMY OF A PSYCHO* (1961) 75m Unitel bw

Ronnie Burns *(Mickey)*, *Pamela Lincoln (Pat)*, Darrell Howe *(Chet)*, Russ Bender *(Frank)*, Don Devlin *(Moe)*, Robert W. Stabler *(Prosecuting Attorney)*, Pat McMahon *(Arthur)*, Judy Howard *(Sandy)*, Frank Kiliman *(Bobbie)*, Mike Grainger *(Lt. Mac)*, John B. Lee *(District Attorney)*, Charles J. Simon *(Judge)*.

Mass-murder plan enacted by the brother of a man sent to the gas chamber; the killer plans to destroy every person connected to his brother's conviction. A low-budget, inanely scripted film with no viewer interest whatsoever.

p&d, Brooke L. Peters; w, Jane Mann, Larry Lee.

Crime **(PR:C MPAA:NR)**

ANATOMY OF A SYNDICATE (SEE: BIG OPERATOR, THE, 1959)

ANATOMY OF LOVE* (1959, Ital.) 92m Kassier/Lux bw

Vittorio De Sica, Sophia Loren, Toto, Michel Simon, Lea Padovani, Sylvie, Elisa Cegani, Marcello Mastroianni.

Dull assemblage of five short Italian melodramatic vignettes. The first story stars Mastroianni and Padovani as destitute parents who are forced to abandon their baby which they can't afford to feed. The second episode has De Sica and Cegani as former aristocrats who have fallen on hard times. They have a bittersweet reunion on the set of a movie they have been cast as extras in. The third part tells the story of a priest trying to talk a young woman out of committing suicide. The fourth vignette stars De Sica again as a happy cab driver with a zest for life. The final episode stars Loren as a woman who is being pursued by a love-crazed man with a camera. None of the five episodes is particularly good, which makes it hard to sit through all five.

d, S. Blasetti; continuity, Suso Cecchi D'Amico and Alessandro Blasseti.

Drama **(PR:C MPAA:NR)**

ANCHORS AWEIGH**** (1945) 143m MGM c

Frank Sinatra *(Clarence Doolittle)*, Gene Kelly *(Joseph Brady)*, Kathryn Grayson *(Susan Abbott)*, Jose Iturbi *(Himself)*, Dean Stockwell *(Donald Martin)*, Carlos Ramirez *(Carlos)*, Henry O'Neill *(Adm. Hammond)*, Leon Ames *(Commander)*, Rags Ragland *(Police Sergeant)*, Edgar Kennedy *(Police Captain)*, Pamela Britton *(Girl from Brooklyn)*, Henry Armetta *(Hamburger Man)*, Billy Gilbert *(Cafe Manager)*, Sharon McManus *(Little Girl Beggar)*, James Burke *(Studio Cop)*, James Flavin *(Radio Cop)*, Chester Clute *(Iturbi's Assistant)*, Grady Sutton *(Bertram Kramer)*, Peggy Maley *(Lana Turner Double)*, Sondra Rodgers *(Iturbi Secretary)*, Gary Owen, Steve Brodie *(Soldiers)*, Charles Coleman *(Butler)*, Milton Parsons *(Bearded Man)*, Renie Riano *(Waitress)*, Alex Callam *(Commander)*, Harry Barris, John James, Wally Cassell, Douglas Cowan, Henry Daniels, Jr., Hanna, William "Bill" Phillips, Tom Trout *(Sailors)*, Esther Michelson *(Hamburger Woman)*, William

Forrest *(Movie Director)*, Ray Teal *(Asst. Movie Director)*, Milton Kibbee *(Bartender)*.

Top-notch 1940s musical has two sailors, Sinatra and Kelly, on shore leave in Hollywood where conniver Kelly tells innocent Sinatra he will fix him up with glamour queens. Instead Kelly runs into bit movie player Grayson who aspires to become a leading singer. Kelly cavalierly promises to get her an audition with Iturbi but his scheme backfires and he tries to foist Sinatra onto Grayson. The shy Sinatra, however, has fallen in love with a girl from Brooklyn, Britton. Grayson, who eventually performs for Iturbi and receives a contract, ends up in the arms of Kelly who realizes that he loves her. The somewhat thin pilot is magnificently overcome by Kelly's spectacular dancing, particularly with an animated mouse, cartoon character, Jerry of Tom and Jerry fame; it was this film that established Kelly as a superstar. Sinatra crooned such pleasant ditties as "The Charm of You," "We Hate to Leave," and "I Fall in Love Too Easily" by Jule Styne and Sammy Cahn. Grayson exercises her famous vibrato with such songs as "Jalousie" and "All of a Sudden My Heart Sings."

p, Joe Pasternak; d, George Sidney; w, Isobel Lennart (based on a story by Natalie Marcin); ph, Robert Planck, Charles Boyle (Technicolor); m, George Stoll; ed, Adrienne Fazan; art d, Cedric Gibbons, Randall Duell; set d, Edwin B. Wills, Richard Pefferle; cos, Irene, Kay Dean; ch, Gene Kelly; m/l, Jule Styne, Sammy Cahn.

Musical **(PR:AAA MPAA:NR)**

AND BABY MAKES THREE** (1949) 83m COL bw

Robert Young *(Vernon Walsh)*, Barbara Hale *(Jacqueline Walsh)*, Robert Hutton *(Herbert Fletcher)*, Janis Carter *(Wanda York)*, Billie Burke *(Mrs. Fletcher)*, Nicholas Joy *(Mr. Fletcher)*, Lloyd Corrigan *(Dr. William Parnell)*, Howland Chamberlin *(Otto Stacy)*, Melville Cooper *(Gibson)*, Louise Currie *(Miss Quigley)*, Grandon Rhodes *(Phelps Burbridge)*, Katherine Warren *(Miss Ellis)*, Wilton Graff *(Root)*, Joe Sawyer, James Cardwell *(Police Officers)*.

Screwball comedy involving a recently divorced couple, Young and Hale, who discover that they are about to have a baby. Deciding against a rebound marriage to the stuffy Hutton, Hale wants Young back and tries to steal him away from glamour blonde Carter by distracting him with the unusual cravings associated with pregnancy. Typical comedy of the period.

p, Robert Lord; d, Henry Levin; w, Lou Breslow, Joseph Hoffman; ph, Burnett Guffey; ed, Viola Lawrence.

Comedy **(PR:A MPAA:NR)**

AND GOD CREATED WOMAN**

(1957, C.U. Fr.) 95m Iena-UCIL-Cocinor/Kingsley International c (AKA: AND WOMAN . . . WAS CREATED)

Brigitte Bardot *(Juliette)*, Curt Jurgens *(Eric)*, Jean-Louis Trintignant *(Michel)*, Christian Marquand *(Antoine)*, Georges Poujouly *(Christian)*, Jean Tissier *(M. Vigier-Lefranc)*, Jeanne Marken *(Mme. Morin)*, Marie Glory *(Mme. Tardieu)*, Isabelle Corey *(Lucienne)*, Jean Lefebvre *(Rene)*, Philippe Grenier *(Perri)*, Jacqueline Ventura *(Mme. Vigier-Lefrance)*, *Jany Mourey (Bonne Femme)*, Jacques Giron *(Roger)*, Paul Faivre *(Mons. Morin)*, Leopoldo Frances *(Dancer)*, Toscano *(Rene)*.

Sex kitten Bardot was never lovelier than in this most sensational and popular of her many erotic films. Here she plays the 18-year-old wife of Trintignant, only to be close to his brother, Marquand, whom she attempts to seduce, while also flirting with millionaire Jurgens. The entire film is a showcase for Bardot's sexy wardrobe (or the lack of it), from short-shorts to next-to-nothing bikinis. Bardot's assignations are brought to a quick end when Trintignant bounces her around a bit, insisting she behave herself and become a full-time wife; she happily succumbs to his forceful ways, exemplifying the old lyric "He beats me, too/What can I do?/He's my man!" Though this film began in the U.S. art houses, the peepshowers poured in to see the blonde sexpot from France, producing a reported $4 million gross. The film made an overnight success of Bardot but she never again matched this success.

p, Raoul J. Levy; d, Roger Vadim; w, Vadim, Levy; ph, Armand Thirard (CinemaScope, Eastmancolor); m, Paul Misrake; ed, Victoria Mercanton; art d, Jean Andre.

Drama **Cas.** **(PR:O MPAA:NR)**

AND HOPE TO DIE*** (1972 Fr./U.S.) 140m FOX c

Robert Ryan *(Charley)*, Aldo Ray *(Mattone)*, Tisa Farrow *(Pepper)*, Jean-Louis Trintignant *(Tony)*, Lea Massari *(Sugar)*, Jean Gaven *(Rizzio)*, Nadine Nabokov *(Majorette)*, Andre Lawrence *(Gypsy)*, Daniel Breton *(Paul)*

A moody, somewhat arty gangster film with an outstanding cast. Trintignant stars as a Frenchman trying to escape his past. He goes to Canada, where he becomes an unwitting participant in a mob hit. The gangsters take him in and make him one of the group. The aging leader of the gang, Ryan, has planned a big robbery, but the heist goes foul and results in the deaths of most of the gang members. The film has some interesting editing, including intercuts of the gang planning the robbery with scenes of French children playing games. The counterpoint of the images is disturbing and haunting.

p, Serge Siberman; d, Rene Clement; w, Sebastien Japrisot; ph, Edmond Wilson (Eastmancolor); m, Francis Lai; ed, Roger Dwyre.

Crime **(PR:C MPAA:PG)**

. . . AND JUSTICE FOR ALL** (1979) 120m COL c

Al Pacino *(Arthur Kirkland)*, Jack Warden *(Judge Rayford)*, John Forsythe *(Judge Fleming)*, Lee Strasberg *(Grandpa Sam)*, Jeffrey Tambor *(Jay Porter)*, Christine Lahti *(Gail Packer)*, Sam Levene *(Arnie)*, Robert Christian *(Ralph Agee)*, Thomas Waites *(Jeff McCullaugh)*, Larry Bryggman *(Warren Fresnell)*, Craig T. Nelson *(Frank Bowers)*, Dominic Chianese *(Carl Travers)*, Victor Arnold *(Leo Fauci)*, Vincent Beck *(Officer Leary)*, Michael Gorrin *(Elderly Man)*, Baxter Harris *(Larry)*, Joe Morton *(Prison Doctor)*, Alan North *(Deputy Sheriff)*, Tom Quinn *(Desk Clerk Kiley)*, Beverly Sanders *(Sherry)*, Connie Sawyer *(Gitel)*, Charles Siebert *(Assistant District Attorney Keene)*, Robert Symonds *(Judge Burns)*, Keith Andes *(Marvin Bates)*, Stephen Blackmore *(Robert Wenke)*, Vasili Bogazianos *(Avillar)*, Jack Hollander *(Prison Warden)*.

Contrived escapades of a young and idealistic lawyer, Pacino, who sees his clients abused and wrongly punished by a judicial system gone haywire. A transvestite client who cannot tolerate prison hangs himself, another young man is sent to prison for a series of abuses that stem from a broken tail-light on his car (he is eventually shot to death while attempting to break prison despite Pacino's whining pleas to surrender). The lawyer's only friend is a wacko judge, Warden, who restores order in his court by firing his automatic into the ceiling, spends his lunch hours perched on a high window ledge of the courthouse, and entertains himself by flying about crazily in a helicopter, crashing one and almost killing himself and Pacino, his terrified passenger. Pacino is subsequently asked to defend Forsythe, a venal, self-righteous judge he hates and who hates him. Forsythe is accused of sadistically raping and beating a young woman. He selects Pacino to defend him because he believes the altruistic lawyer will do his utmost to save a person he dislikes out of pure principle (which is about as realistic and reasonable as staring into the sun to improve one's vision). Pacino undertakes to undo the judge, gathering overwhelming evidence against him. Then, in what is supposed to be the dramatic climax, he attacks his client in court with such venomous zeal that he is literally dragged from the courtroom screaming: "I'm gonna get him!" No character development, ridiculous situations and a miserably written script attempting to indict corrupt legal and judicial systems add up to a tiresome and pointless film where Pacino is wasted as a witness to a parade of lunatics. The pity is that a truly important film could have been made to demonstrate the condescending and selfish caste system which the legal field has sadly become. Instead we get this cartoon which comfortably profiles only those lawyers and jurists too bizarre to be realistically accepted as representative of a mistrusted profession.

p, Norman Jewison, Patrick Palmer; d, Jewison; w, Valerie Curtin, Barry Levinson; ph, Victor J. Kemper (Metrocolor); m, Dave Grusin; ed, John F. Burnett; art d, Peter Samish; set d, Richard MacDonald; cos, Ruth Myers.

Drama **Cas.** **(PR:O MPAA:R)**

AND MILLIONS WILL DIE* (1973) 104m COL c

Richard Basehart, Susan Strasberg, Leslie Nielsen, Peter Sumner, Tony Wager.

Idiotic tale has Basehart and other scientists searching for a time bomb containing deadly nerve gas which is buried somewhere beneath the streets of Hong Kong. The only attraction here is the lush on-location photography of the British Crown Colony.

d, Leslie Martinson.

Crime **(PR:C MPAA:NR)**

AND NOW FOR SOMETHING COMPLETELY DIFFERENT**

(1972, Brit.) 89m COL

Graham Chapman, John Cleese, Eric Idle, Terry Jones, Michael Palin, Terry Gilliam, Carol Cleveland, Connie Booth.

Some of the best of the BBC TV's "Monty Python's Flying Circus" blackout sketches reshot for the big screen. Although the cast is brilliant and the material generally funny, the whole thing suffers the transition from a 30-minute TV show to a full-length feature. The gang from Python did much better with their follow-up film MONTY PYTHON AND THE HOLY GRAIL. Recommended for "Python" fans.

p, Victor Lownes; d, Ian MacNaughton; w, Graham Chapman, John Cleese, Terry Gilliam, Eric Idle, Terry Jones, Michael Palin; ph, David Muir; ed, Thom Noble; art d, Colin Grimes; animations, Terry Gilliam.

Comedy **Cas.** **(PR.O MPAA:PG)**

AND NOW MIGUEL** (1966) 95m UNIV c

Pat Cardi *(Miguel)*, Michael Ansara *(Blas)*, Guy Stockwell *(Perez)*, Clu Gulager *(Johnny)*, Joe De Santis *(Padre de Chavez)*, Pilar Del Rey *(Tomasita)*, Peter Robbins *(Pedro)*, Buck Taylor *(Gabriel)*, Edmund Hashim *(Eli)*, Emma Tyson *(Faustina)*, Richard J. Brehm *(Bonafacio)*, Heil F. Waters *(Wool Buyer)*, James Hall *(Ranger)*, J. Scott Carroll *(Shearer)*, Father Ralph W. Pairon *(Priest)*, Sister Katrina *(Sister)*.

Simple tale of a young boy's desire to some day shepherd the flocks of sheep that his family has owned for many generations. Action takes place in New Mexico and suffers somewhat from the lengthy scenes of outdoor dinners and sheep shearing. Cardi is sufficiently wholesome to retain interest.

p, Robert B. Radnitz; d, James B. Clark; w, Ted Sherdeman, Jane Klove (based on the novel by Joseph Krumgold); ph, Clifford Stine (Technicolor); m, Philip Lambro; ed, Hugh S. Fowler.

Drama **(PR:AA MPAA:NR)**

AND NOW MY LOVE*** (1975, Fr.) 121m AE c

Marthe Keller *(Sarah/Her Mother/Her Grandmother)*, Andre Dussollier *(Simon)*, Charles Denner *(Sarah's Father/Operator/Sarah's Grandfather)*, Carla Gravina *(Sarah's Italian Girl Friend)*, Charles Gerard *(Simon's Friend)*, Gilbert Becaud *(Himself)*, Alain Basnier *(Understudy)*, Daniel Boulanger *(14-18-Year-Old Hero)*, Elie Choraqui *(Amorous Union Man)*, Nathalie Courval *(Wife of the Lawyer)*, Andre Falcon *(Lawyer)*, Angelo Infanti *(A Stud)*, Annie Kerani *(A Woman of Simon)*, Sam Lethrone *(Restaurant Owner)*, Judith Magre *(Wife of the Operator)*, Gerard Sire *(Director of L'Usine)*, Gabriele Tinti *(Six-day Husband)*, Venantino Venantini *(Very Italian Italian Man)*, Harry Walter *(Lover Among Many)*, Yvan Tanguy *(General's Aide)*.

An episodic view of three generations of Parisians. French director Lelouch views a relationship of two young lovers as parallel to their parents and grandparents. Star Keller plays a total of three roles covering three generations. In her most contemporary role, as Sarah, she falls in love with pop-singer Becaud when she is a teenager. At the same time her future lover, Dussollier, is jailed for stealing Becaud's records from a record store. As they mature, both change. She goes from spoiled bourgeoisie brat to a socially conscious adult, he from an ex-con to actor in movies, starting with porno films, leading into more commercial cinema, and eventually becoming a recognized filmmaker. Through a juggling of chronologies, the film interjects a variety of ideologies, social observations, and a love of the filmmaking process itself. Not for all tastes.

d, Claude Lelouch; w, Lelouch, Pierre Uytterhoeven; ph, Jean Collomb (Technicolor); m, Francis Lai; ed, George Klotz; art d, Francois De Lamothe.

Romance/Drama **(PR:C MPAA:PG)**

AND NOW THE SCREAMING STARTS** (1973, Brit.) 87m Amicus/Cinerama c

Peter Cushing *(Dr. Pope)*, Herbert Lom *(Henry Fengriffen)*, Patrick Magee *(Dr. Whittle)*, Ian Ogilvy *(Charles Fengriffen)*, Stephanie Beacham *(Catherine Fengriffen)*, Guy Rolfe *(Maitland)*, Geoffrey Crutchley *(Silas)*, Rosalle Crutchley *(Mrs. Luke)*, Janet Key *(Bridget)*, Gillian Lind *(Aunt Edith)*, Sally Harrison *(Sarah)*, Lloyd Labie *(Sir John Westcliffe)*, Norman Mitchell *(Constable)*, Frank Forsyth *(Servant)*.

Gothic horror involving a curse on a young woman, Beacham, who lives with her husband, Ogilvy, in a large mansion. The spooky goings-on are interrupted by the arrival of Cushing who has come to investigate. The group is terrorized by a disembodied hand and an ax-wielding psycho. Lom plays the ancestor that caused the curse in the first place. Stunning art direction for a low-budget film.

p, Milton Subotsky, Max J. Rosenberg; d, Roy Ward Baker; w, Roger Marshall; ph, Denys Coop; ed, Peter Tanner; art d, Tony Curtis.

Horror **Cas.** **(PR:O MPAA:PG)**

AND NOW TOMORROW 1/2** (1944) 86m PAR bw

Loretta Young *(Emily Blair)*, Alan Ladd *(Dr. Merek Vance)*, Susan Hayward *(Janice Blair)*, Barry Sullivan *(Jeff Stoddard)*, Beulah Bondi *(Aunt Em)*, Cecil Kellaway *(Dr. Weeks)*, Helen Mack *(Angeletta Gallo)*, Anthony Caruso *(Peter Gallo)*, Grant Mitchell *(Uncle Wallace)*, Jonathan Hale *(Dr. Sloane)*, George Carlton *(Meeker)*, Connie Leon *(Hester)*.

Medical melodrama starring Ladd as a doctor who grew up on the wrong side of the tracks, returning to his home town to practice medicine. He meets Young, the daughter of the most powerful man in town, who has contracted meningitis and gone deaf. Though Ladd has always resented the rich family, he just happens to have developed a new serum to cure her deafness. As the movie progresses, the doctor and patient go from active antagonism to genuine respect (and perhaps love?) for each other. A subplot involving Young's sister, Hayward, who falls in love with her sibling's fiancee, Sullivan (who has lost interest in Young because of her ailment), makes it easier for the cured Young to join Ladd in Pittsburgh and start a new life. Maudlin material is helped by a competent cast of professionals. Mystery writer Raymond Chandler co-wrote the screenplay.

p, Fred Kohlmar; d, Irving Pichel; w, Frank Parton, Raymond Chandler (based on the novel by Rachel Field); ph, Daniel Fapp, Farciot Edouart; m, Victor Young; ed, Duncan Mansfield.

Drama **(PR:A MPAA:NR)**

AND ONE WAS BEAUTIFUL* 1/2 (1940) 68m MGM bw

Robert Cummings *(Ridley Crane)*, Laraine Day *(Kate Lattimer)*, Jean Muir *(Helen Lattimer)*, Billie Burke *(Mrs. Lattimer)*, Ann Morriss *(Gertrude Hunter)*, Esther Dale *(Margaret)*, Charles Waldron *(Stephen Harridge)*, Frank Milan *(George Olcott)*, Rand Brooks *(Joe Havens)*, Paul Stanton *(Arthur Prince)*, Ruth Tobey *(Zillah Torrington)*.

Uninteresting Cinderella story of two sisters, Day and Muir, who are in love with the same man. One of the sisters, Muir, is a carefree glamour girl who sets out to conquer Cummings. The other sister, Day, is sweet and unassuming, and it is she Cummings falls for. Things change when Cummings is sent to prison for a hit-and-run charge, which Muir committed. Being too much of a gentleman the honorable, but foolish, Cummings takes the fall. Muir keeps her mouth shut and lets the dummy go to prison. Day finds out the truth and works for Cummings' release. The authorities soon let him free and the couple wed. Predictable and overly talky, the film holds little interest.

p, Frederick Stephani; d, Robert Sinclair; w, Harry Clark (based on a story by Alice Duer Miller); ph, Ray June; ed, Conrad A. Nervig.

Drama **(PR:A MPAA:NR)**

AND QUIET FLOWS THE DON 1/2** (1960 USSR) 107m UA bw

Ellina Bystritskaya *(Aksinya)*, Pyotr Glebov *(Grigory)*, Zinaida Kirienko *(Natalya)*, Danilo Ilchenko *(Pantelei Melekhox)*, Nikolai Smirnov *(Pytor)*, Lyudmila Khityayeva *(Darya)*, Natalya Arkangelskaya *(Dunyashka)*, Alexander Blagovestov *(Stepan Lekathov)*, Igor Dmitriev *(Yevgeni Listnitsky)*, William Shatunovsky *(Shtockman)*.

Made in Russia in 1957, this film was part of the US-Soviet cultural exchange program that took place in the early 1960s. AND QUIET FLOWS THE DON is the first of three films dealing with the life of the fiery Cossack Grigory (Glebov). We follow the Cossack through his early disagreements with his father (including a loveless, arranged marriage), battles in WW I, and an affair with another Cossack's wife. Though the material is fairly standard, the scenery is exotic and beautiful and it is nice to see locations inside Russia that Hollywood hasn't been able to utilize.

d&w, Sergei Gerasimov (based on the novel by Mikhail Sholokhov); m, Yuri Levitin.

Drama **(PR:A MPAA:NR)**

AND SO THEY WERE MARRIED*** (1936) 72m COL bw

Melvyn Douglas *(Stephen Blake)*, Mary Astor *(Edith Farnham)*, Edith Fellows *(Brenda Farnham)*, Jackie Moran *(Tommy Blake)*, Donald Meek *(Hotel Manager)*, Dorothy Stickney *(Miss Peabody)*, Romaine Callender *(Ralph P. Shirley)*, Douglas Scott *(Horace)*, Margaret Armstrong *(Horace's Butler)*, George McKay *(Janitor)*, Wade Boteler *(Police Captain)*, Charles Irwin *(Tom Phillips, a Drunk)*, Gene Morgan, William Irving *(Drunks)*, Ernie Alexander, Dennis O'Keefe *(Drunks in Car)*, Charles Arnt, Joseph Caits *(Captains of Waiters)*, Phyllis Godfrey *(Ellen)*, Olaf Hytten *(Secretary)*, Jay Eaton *(James)*, Hooper Atchley *(Fred Cutler)*, Beatrice Curtis, Beatrice Blinn *(Guests)*, Gennaro Curci *(Greek)*, Alan Bridge *(Motor Cop)*, Jessie Perry *(Maid)*, Margaret Morgan *(Stout Woman)*, Adolf Faylauer *(Bald-Headed Man)*, Kernan Cripps *(Turnkey)*, Anne Schaefer *(House keeper)*, Gus Reed *(Assistant Captain of Waiters)*.

Pleasing comedy starring Douglas and Astor as single parents who meet while at a winter resort and fall in love. Problems arise when the couple's children take an immediate dislike to each other and try their hardest to keep their parents from marrying. The kids' scheme works and Douglas and Astor call things quits, but now the two little pests have found a camaraderie together and decide they have made a mistake. The two previously devilish kids now turn Cupid and try to patch things up between their parents. Good comedy helped by outstanding performances from the principals.

p, B. P. Schulberg; d, Elliot Nugent; w, Doris Anderson, Joseph Anthony, A. Laurie Brazee (based on a story by Sarah Addington); ph, Henry Freulich; m, Howard Jackson; ed, Gene Milford.

Comedy **(PR:AA MPAA:NR)**

AND SO THEY WERE MARRIED

(SEE: JOHNNY DOESN'T LIVE HERE ANYMORE, 1944)

AND SO TO BED* 1/2 (1965, Ger.) 112m Medallion/Stadthalle bw

Hildegard Neff *(Call Girl)*, Thomas Fritsch *(Scholar)*, Alexandra Stewart *(Professor's Wife)*, Martin Held *(Professor)*, Daliah Lavi *(Secretary)*, Peter Van Eyck *(Boss)*, Nadia Tiller *(Boss's Wife)*, Peter Parten *(Student)*, Daniele Gaubert *(French Girl)*, Angelo Santi *(Bellhop)*, Lilli Palmer *(Actress)*, Paul Hubschmid *(Diplomat)*.

German sexy comedy with Fritsch as a young man who starts a sexual chain reaction with a call girl, Neff, who teaches him the finer points of lovemaking. The young student then takes this knowledge into an affair with his Professor's wife. The professor retaliates by sleeping with his secretary, the secretary then sleeps with. . . etc. Until, at the end, a diplomat picks up the call girl and film comes full circle. Lamebrain idea is not done well at all. There is a strange appearance by Palmer toward the end of the movie.

d, Alfred Weidermann.

Comedy **(PR:O MPAA:NR)**

AND SOON THE DARKNESS* (1970, Brit.) 100m Warner-Pathe/EMI c

Pamela Franklin *(Jane)*, Michele Dotrice *(Cathy)*, Sandor Eles *(Paul)*, John Nettleton *(Gendarme)*, Clare Kelly *(Schoolmistress)*, Hanna-Maria Pravda *(Mme. Lassal)*, John Franklin *(Old Man)*, Claude Bertrand *(Lassal)*, Jean Carmet *(Renier)*.

Suspense-thriller about two British nurses, Franklin and Dotrice, being menaced by a crazed sex-murderer while on a cycling vacation in France. Contrived mystery complete with red herrings, suspicious noises, mistaken identities, and a village of French peasants no one can trust. Dumb.

p, Albert Fennel, Brian Clemens; d, Robert Fuest; w, Brian Clemens, Terry Nation; ph, Ian Wilson (Technicolor); m, Laurie Johnson; ed, Ann Chegwidden.

Crime **(PR:O MPAA:PG)**

AND SUDDEN DEATH* (1936) 60m PAR bw

Randolph Scott *(Lt. James Knox)*, Frances Drake *(Betty Winslow)*, Tom Brown *(Jackie Winslow)*, Billy Lee *(Bobby Sanborn)*, Fuzzy Knight *(Steve Bartlett)*, Terry Walker *(Bangs)*, Porter Hall *(District Attorney)*, Charles Quigley *(Mike Andrews)*, John Hyams *(J. R. Winslow)*, Joseph Sawyer *(Sgt. Sanborn)*, Oscar Apfel *(Defense Counsel)*, Don Rowan *(Sgt. Maloney)*, Jimmy Conlin *(Mr. Tweets)*, Maidel Turner *(Dodie Sloan)*, Charles Arnt *(Archie Sloan)*, Wilma Francis *(Nurse)*, Herbert Evans *(Meggs)*.

Preachy drama about a young woman, Drake, who takes the rap for her brother on a hit-and-run charge. Film waffles between being a stern warning to traffic violators and a somewhat daft romance movie with Drake falling in love with traffic officer Scott. The brother, Brown, eventually confesses on his death bed, and Drake and Scott live happily ever after. Pretty tedious.

p, A. M. Botsford; d, Charles Barton; w, Joseph Moncure March (based on a story by Theodore Reeves, Madeleine Ruthven, and an essay by J. C. Furness); ph, Alfred Gilks.

Drama **(PR:A MPAA:NR)**

AND SUDDENLY IT'S MURDER! 1/2** (1964, Ital.) 90m Royal bw

Alberto Sordi *(The Commendatore)*, Vittorio Gassman *(Remo)*, Sylvana Mangano *(Marini)*, Dorian Gray *(The Commendatore's Wife)*, Nino Manfredi *(Quirino)*, Franca Valeri *(Giovanna)*, Bernard Blier *(Police Superintendent)*, Georges Rivere *(Playboy)*.

Typical breakneck Italian stretch-the-situation-until-it-snaps comedy involving three Italian couples who are thrown together in Monte Carlo while on holiday. The couples become the main suspects in a murder case when a corpse is found in one of their suitcases. They all scramble to find suitable alibis, with embarassing results. The material itself is implausible and tiresome, but the performers are fine and make this outing enjoyable.

p, Dino de Laurentiis; d, Mario Camerini; w, Rodolfo Sonego, Giorgio Artorio, Stefano Strucchi, Luciano Vincenzoni.

Comedy **(PR:C MPAA:NR)**

AND THE ANGELS SING*** (1944) 95m PAR bw

Dorothy Lamour *(Nancy Angel)*, Fred MacMurray *(Happy Morgan)*, Betty Hutton *(Bobby Angel)*, Diana Lynn *(Josie Angel)*, Mimi Chandler *(Patti Angel)*, Raymond Walburn *(Pop Angel)*, Eddie Foy, Jr. *(Fuzzy Johnson)*, Frank Albertson *(Oliver)*, Mikhail Rasumny *(Schultz)*, Frank Faylen *(Holman)*, George McKay *(House Man)*, Harry Barris *(Saxy)*, Donald Kerr *(Mickey)*, Pere Launders *(Miller)*, Tom Kennedy *(Potatoes)*, Erville Alderson *(Mr. Littlefield)*, Edgar Dearing *(Man)*, Tim Ryan *(Stage Door Man)*, Jimmy Conlin *(Messenger)*, Leon Belasco *(Waiter at "Polonaise Cafe")*, Douglas Fowley *(N.Y. Cafe Manager)*, Siegfried Arno *(Mr. Green)*, William Davidson *(Theatrical Agent)*, Otto Reichow *(Polish Groom)*, Hillary Brooke *(Polish Bride)*, Julie Gibson *(Cigarette Girl)*, Arthur Loft *(Stage Manager)*, Matt McHugh *(Doorman at "33 Club")*, Libby Taylor *(Attendant in Powder Room)*, Drake Thornton *(Page Boy)*, Buster Phelps *(Spud)*, Jack Norton *(Drunk)*, Buddy Gorman *(Messenger)*, Roland Dupree *(Boy)*, Louise La Planche *(Ticket Taker)*.

Zany comedy-musical offers four struggling singing sisters led by Lamour and the always frenetic Hutton who does a scat number with such energy that she appears manic, a jiggling, wiggling flailing body and a pair of lungs that would deafen a crowd in the Roman Colosseum. Lamour and MacMurray, he being a sax player and protector of the female vocal group, are in love. Hutton is in love with MacMurray but he does not reciprocate which makes for the old love triangle plus hot sparks from sibling rivalry. MacMurray spends a great deal of time running between Lamour and Hutton, so careful not to offend either that he becomes a nervous wreck. The Angel Sisters act is destitute at one point so MacMurray and sidekick Eddie Foy, Jr., get jobs as singing waiters in a Polish restaurant; both do a knockout, funny number dressed in exaggerated Tyrolean costumes, slapping the blazes out of themselves. Lamour sings "It Could Happen to You," and the sister act does "Hello, Mary, How Does Your Garden Grow?" a nifty war propaganda tune built around a Victory Garden motif. Oddly, no one renders the song from which the title of this film is taken. Though a bit on the goofy side, this well-produced pic offers up many a laugh and pleasing song.

p, E. D. Leshin; d, Claude Binyon; w, Melvin Frank, Norman Panama; ph, Karl Struss; ed, Edna Warren; md, Victor Young; art d, Hans Dreier, Hal Pereira; m/l, Johnny Burke, Jimmy Van Heusen.

Comedy/Musical   **(PR:A   MPAA:NR)**

AND THE SAME TO YOU*   (1960, Brit.) 70m Monarch bw

Brian Rix (Dickie Dreadnought), Leo Franklyn (Rev. Sydney Mullett), William Hartnell (Wally Burton), Vera Day (Cynthia), Tommy Cooper (Horace), Dick Bentley (George Nibbs), Tony Wright (Percy Gibbons), Renee Houston (Mildred), John Robinson (Pomphret), Sidney James (Sammy Gatt), Miles Malleson (Bishop), Ronald Adam (Trout), Shirley Ann Field (Iris), Terry Scott (PC).

Weak programmer stabs at humor when a clergyman's nephew decides to become a boxer but outwardly maintains a religious appearance with his crude manager pretending to be a church official. More knuckles than chuckles.

p, William Gell; d, George Pollock; w, John Paddy Carstairs, John Junkin (based on the play by A. P. Dearsley).

Comedy   **(PR:A   MPAA:NR)**

AND THE SHIP SAILS ON***

(1983, Ital./Fr.) 132m RAI/VIDES c (E LA NAVE VA)

Freddie Jones (Orlando), Barbara Jefford (Ildebranda Cuffari), Victor Poletti (Fuciletto), Peter Cellier (Sir Reginald), Elisa Marinardi (Teresa Valegnani), Norma West (Sir Reginald's Wife), Paolo Paolini (Orchestra Conductor), Sarah Jane Varley (Dorothy), Fiorenzo Serra (Grand Duke of Harzock), Pina Bausch (Princess Lheremia), Pasquale Zito (Count of Bassano), Linda Polan (Ines Ione), Phillip Locke (Prime Minister), Jonathan Cecil (Ricotin), Maurice Barrier (Ziloev), Fred Williams (Lepori), Janet Suzman (Edmea Tetua).

Wacky Fellini movie involving a shipload of eccentric show-biz types who set sail in 1914 to a small island to scatter the ashes of a great soprano who recently died. While the first-class cabins contain businessmen, opera colleagues, comedians, dukes, counts, and princesses, the steerage contains a whole flock of Serbo-Croation freedom fighters on the run from the assassination of Archduke Ferdinand. An Austro-Hungarian battleship arrives and demands that the freedom fighters be turned over to them or the cannons will fire. Shot entirely on the sound stage at Cinecitta studios. Typical craziness from Fellini.

p, Franco Cristaldi; d, Federico Fellini; w, Fellini, Tonino Guerra; ph, Giuseppe Rotunno; m, Gianfranco Plenixio; ed, Ruggero Mastroianni, art d, Dante Ferreti.

Comedy   **Cas.**   **(PR:A   MPAA:NR)**

AND THE WILD, WILD WOMEN*¹/₂   (1961, Ital.) 85m Rima Films bw

Anna Magnani (Aggie), Giulietta Masina (Lina), Christina Gaioni (Marietta), Miriam Bru (Vittorina), Renato Salvatori (Piero).

Disjointed film about a group of female prisoners and their internecine wars does little to enhance the career of the great Magnani. Poor dubbing makes this uninspired drama even worse.

p, Guiseppe Amato; d, Renato Castellani; w, Suso Cecchi D'Amico (based on the novel by Isa Mari); m, Roman Vlad.

Drama   **(PR:C-O   MPAA:NR)**

AND THEN THERE WERE NONE****

(1945) 97m FOX bw (GB:TEN LITTLE NIGGERS)

Barry Fitzgerald (Judge Quincannon), Walter Huston (Dr. Armstrong), Louis Hayward (Philip Lombard), Roland Young (Blore), June Duprez (Vera Claythorne), Sir C. Aubrey Smith (Gen. Mandrake), Judith Anderson (Emily Brent), Mischa Auer (Prince Starloff), Richard Haydn (Rogers), Queenie Leonard (Mrs. Rogers), Harry Thurston (Fisherman).

Classic Agatha Christie whodunit takes place on a desolate island off the English coast to which ten strangers travel, all invited to spend an evening in the sprawling, eerie mansion. Among the colorful characters are Huston, a sinister doctor; Smith, a dictatorial militarist; and Auer, a zany impostor claiming royal blood. All of the guests, who find their host Fitzgerald murdered, have something to hide, evil acts in their pasts. In collective terror, it dawns on the guests that they have been marooned on the island for only one purpose: All are to be murdered in retribution for their transgressions. And like the nursery rhyme, they forfeit their lives in one horrible murder after another, all the while trying to figure out who the murderer is. The romantic interest is sustained by the dashing Hayward and the exquisitely beautiful Duprez (her lisp imperceptible). Only three survive the man-made nightmare, one committing suicide at the surprising conclusion, which we won't reveal. French director Clair took his time with this production, his cameras playing cat-and-mouse with each victim, the perfect pace for the story as it was originally conceived by Christie and tightly adapted by that superb screenwriter Nichols. (Remade in 1965 and 1974 as TEN LITTLE INDIANS, both films inferior to the original.)

p, Harry M. Popkin; d, Rene Clair; w, Dudley Nichols (based on the story "Ten Little Niggers" by Agatha Christie); ph, Lucien Andriot; ed, Harvey Manger.

Mystery   **Cas.**   **(PR:A   MPAA:NR)**

AND THEN THERE WERE NONE 1965 (SEE: TEN LITTLE INDIANS,1965)

AND THEN THERE WERE NONE

1974 (SEE: TEN LITTLE INDIANS, 1974)

AND THERE CAME A MAN**   (1968, Ital.) 90m Brandon Films c

Rod Steiger (Intermediary), Adolfo Celi (Msgr. Radini Tedeschi), Rita Bertocchi (Pontiff's Mother), Pietro Gelmi (Pontiff's Father), Antonio Bertocchi (Uncle Xavier).

A less than desired film about the saintly Pope John XXIII, played by Steiger in a half-theatrical, half-documentary production that cuts from actual color footage of the Pontiff to dramatic vignettes enacted by Steiger, chronicling this great man's rise from peasant surroundings to leader of the Catholic Church, Steiger reading passages from John's diary in voice-over during the showing of the clips. The story suffers through this erratic technique and viewer attention is tugged in two directions. Steiger's masterful talent does come to the surface in one powerful and poignant scene where he goes to confession, heard by an alcoholic and weepingly repentant priest. Only Steiger speaks English while the other voices are dubbed from the Italian, so poorly that they sound as if they are speaking through hollow tin cans.

p, Harry Saltzman; d, Ermanno Olmi; w, Vincenzo Labella, Olmi.

Religious Drama/Documentary   **(PR:AAA   MPAA:NR)**

AND WOMEN SHALL WEEP*¹/₂   (1960, Brit.) 65m Ethio Films/RFD bw

Ruth Dunning (Mrs. Lumsden), Max Butterfield (Terry Lumsden), Gillian Vaughan (Brenda Wilkes), Richard O'Sullivan (Godfrey Lumsden), Claire Gordon (Sadie MacDougall), David Gregory (Desmond Peel), David Rose (Woody Forrest), Leon Garcia (Ossie Green).

A turgid tearjerker on the film noir fringe where an impoverished widow with two sons is forced to reveal one as the murderer of a pawnbroker. Aside from the mother's agonizing decision, there is little story value here.

p, Norman Williams; d, John Lemont; w, Lemont, Leigh Vance.

Crime   **(PR:C   MPAA:NR)**

ANDERSON TAPES, THE**¹/₂   (1971) 98m COL c

Sean Connery (Anderson), Dyan Cannon (Ingrid), Martin Balsam (Haskins), Ralph Meeker (Delaney), Alan King (Angelo), Christopher Walken (The Kid), Val Avery (Parelli), Dick Williams (Spencer), Garrett Morris (Everson), Stan Gottlieb (Pop), Paul Benjamin (Jimmy), Anthony Holland (Psychologist), Richard B. Schull (Werner), Conrad Bain (Dr. Rubicoff), Margaret Hamilton (Miss Kaler), Judith Lowry (Mrs. Hathaway), Max Showalter (Bingham), Janet Ward (Mrs. Bingham), Scott Jacoby (Jerry Bingham), Norman Rose (Longene), Meg Miles (Mrs. Longene), John Call (O'Leary), Ralph Stanley (D'Medico), John Braden (Vanessi), Paula Trueman (Nurse), Michael Miller (1st Agent), Michael Prince (Johnson), Frank Macetta (Papa Angelo), Jack Doroshow (Eric), Michael Clary (Eric's Friend), Hildy Brooks (Receptionist), Robert Dagny (Doctor), Bradford English (TV Watcher), Reid Cruckshanks (Judge), Tom Signorelli (Sync Man), Carmine Caridi, George Patelis, William Da Prato (Detectives), Michael Fairman (Sgt. Claire), Sam Coppola (Private Detective).

Tough ex-convict Connery, an habitual criminal, is looking for a big score immediately upon leaving prison, going to the syndicate to seek funds to back a massive robbery; he intends to steal the "guts" out of a posh East Side New York apartment building (not unlike the famous Dakota Building, residence of superstars and the fabulously wealthy—where John Lennon of the Beatles once lived). Rounding up a gang of top-flight thieves, Connery proceeds to plan and carry out his caper unaware that he is being taped at every turn for reasons other than this impending crime, in fact various agencies have been taping Connery since his release from prison to establish his links with organized crime. Though lawmen from all areas record Connery's every move, as he is entering the posh apartment complex with his men, breaking into each apartment that is unoccupied—he has determined in advance what tenants are present and those who are not—and the systematic looting of each place. Those listening in on the myriad tape devices, so many as to give the horrific impression that the whole world is bugged, do nothing but listen; local police are accidentally tipped off and they close in, gunning down Connery and company. This film is a curious filmic precursor to the Watergate break-in, employing the same devices and techniques as later used by Nixon's bizarre henchmen.

p, Robert M. Weitman; d, Sidney Lumet; w, Frank R. Pierson (based on the novel by Lawrence Sanders); ph, Arthur Ornitz (Technicolor); m, Quincy Jones; ed, Joanne Burke; art d, Philip Rosenberg.

Crime   **Cas.**   **(PR:C-O   MPAA:GP)**

ANDREI ROUBLOV***   (1973, USSR) 185m Mosfilm c/bw

Anatoll Solonitzine (Andrei Roublov), Ivan Lapikov (Kirill), Nikolai Grinko (Daniel), Nikolai Sergueiev (Theophane), Irma Raouch (Simpleton), Nikolai Bourliaiev (Boriska), Youn Nasarov (Grand Duke).

Meticulously constructed film duplicates the 15th-century world of icon painter Roublov who is tempest tossed between participating in the social upheavals of his era or standing back to merely record its triumphs and failures. Roublov, for the sake of history (as well as the interminable Russian propaganda that distorts historical facts for its own political ends), takes part in a peasant uprising against nobles, forced to kill a man in protecting a woman, this act being so repugnant to him that he renounces his art. He does take up his painting once again, producing innumerable and startling icons. It is at this point that the black-and-white sequences end and radiant color bursts forth on the screen to deeply focus upon the artist's wonderful work. This segment alone, so breathtaking in its lavish color and settings, is worth the whole film.

d, Andrei Tarkovsky; w, Andrei Mikhalkov-Kontchalovsky, Tarkovsky; ph, Vadim Youssov; m, Vlatcheslav Ovtchinnikov; ed, N. Beliava, L. Lararev.

Drama/History   **(PR:A   MPAA:NR)**

ANDREW'S RAIDERS   (SEE: GREAT LOCOMOTIVE CHASE, THE, 1956)

ANDROCLES AND THE LION**   (1952) 98m RKO bw

Jean Simmons (Lavinia), Alan Young (Androcles), Victor Mature (Captain), Robert Newton (Ferrovius), Maurice Evans (Caesar), Elsa Lanchester (Megaera), Reginald

Gardiner *(Lentulus)*, Gene Lockhart *(Menagerie Keeper)*, Alan Mowbray *(Editor)*, Noel Willman *(Spintho)*, John Hoyt *(Cato)*, Jim Backus *(Centurion)*, Lowell Gilmore *(Metelius)*.

Animal lover Young removes a thorn from title beast and later meets the same animal in a Roman arena where captured Christians are the day's entree. Secondary storyline is about ill-fated love between Simmons and Mature. Loose adaptation of G. B. Shaw's play that makes a pleasant enough studio picture.

p, Gabriel Pascal; d, Chester Erskine; w, Erskine, Ken Englund (based on the play by George Bernard Shaw); ph, Harry Stradling; m, Frederick Hollander; ed, Roland Cross.

Comedy **Cas.** **(PR:A MPAA:NR)**

ANDROID*** (1982) 80m New World c

Klaus Kinski *(Dr. Daniel)*, Brie Howard *(Maggie)*, Norbert Weisser *(Keller)*, Crofton Hardester *(Mendes)*, Kendra Kirchner *(Cassandra)*, Don Opper *(Max. 404)*.

Charming low-budget sci-fi film in which fanatical scientist Kinski, obsessed with constructing the perfect android, must deal with escaped convicts invading his private space station laboratory. Kinski's helper, Opper, a simple robot, falls in love with a pretty female convict and becomes jealous of Kirchner, who will render the Max series obsolete. Opper's portrayal of Max is delightful and interesting, as is the entire movie. ANDROID is a perfect example of what talent and originality can do with a small budget.

p, Mary Ann Fisher; d, Aaron Lipstadt; w, James Reigle, Don Opper (based on an idea by Will Reigle); ph, Tim Suhrstedt (DeLuxe Color); m, Don Preston; ed, Andy Horvitch; art d, K. C. Schelbel, Wayne Springfield.

Science Fiction **Cas.** **(PR:O MPAA:R)**

ANDROMEDA STRAIN, THE 1/2** (1971) 127m UNIV c

Arthur Hill *(Dr. Stone)*, David Wayne *(Dr. Dutton)*, James Olson *(Dr. Hall)*, Kate Reid *(Dr. Leavitt)*, Paula Kelly *(Nurse)*, George Mitchell *(Old Man)*, Ramon Bieri *(Major)*.

Research satellite carrying an alien virus crashes into a small Arizona town, the bug killing all of the inhabitants except a baby and an old wino. Top scientists from across the country are rounded up in order to identify and control the potentially plague-like germ. Intriguing, suspenseful story is somewhat hampered by a dull cast. The last sequence will have you on the edge of your seat.

p&d, Robert Wise; w, Nelson Gidding (based on the novel by Michael Crichton); ph, Richard H. Kline (Panavision, Technicolor); m, Gil Melle; ed, Stuart Gilmore, John W. Holmes; prod d, Boris Leven; art d, William Tuntke; set d, Ruby Levitt.

Science Fiction **Cas.** **(PR:A MPAA:G)**

ANDY 1/2** (1965) 86m Deran/UNIV bw

Norman Alden *(Andy)*, Tamara Daykarhonova *(Mrs. Cliadakis)*, Zvee Scooler *(Mr. Cliadakis)*, Ann Wedgeworth *(Margie)*, Murvyn Vye *(Bartender)*, Al Nessor *(Sommerville)*, Warren Finnerty *(Simovich)*.

Realistic, caring film about the everyday life of a mentally retarded man. Emotional and touching without sentimentalizing, the story is aided by a gifted cast of unknowns.

p,d&w, Richard C. Sarafian; ph, Ernesto Capparos; ed, Aram Avakian.

Drama **(PR:A MPAA:NR)**

ANDY HARDY COMES HOME** (1958) 80m MGM bw

Mickey Rooney *(Andy Hardy)*, Patricia Breslin *(Jane Hardy)*, Fay Holden *(Mother Hardy)*, Cecilia Parker *(Marian)*, Sara Haden *(Aunt Milly)*, Joey Forman *(Bezzy Anderson)*, Jerry Colonna *(Doc)*, Vaughn Taylor *(Thomas Chandler)*, Frank Ferguson *(Mayor Benson)*, William Leslie *(Jack Bailey)*, Tom Duggan *(Councilman Warren)*, Jeanne Baird *(Sally Anderson)*, Gina Gillespie *(Cricket)*, Jimmy Bates *(Chuck)*, Teddy Rooney *(Andy, Jr.)*, Johnny Weissmuller, Jr. *(Jimmy)*, Pat Cawley *(Betty Wilson)*.

Rooney, now a west coast lawyer working for an aviation firm, returns to his home town of Carvel with family in tow in order to explore the possibilities of setting up a new aircraft factory. He runs into trouble with a greedy landowner who tries to manipulate the townspeople against Rooney, but the simple folk soon sway back in support of him. After a 12-year absence from the Hardy series, Rooney returned to the stock MGM vehicle with this film. An entertaining and good-natured picture, as were the previous tales of Andy's teen years. (See ANDY HARDY series, Index.)

p, Red Doff; d, Howard W. Koch; w, Edward Everett Hutshing, Robert Morris Donley (based on characters created by Aurania Rouveral); m/l, Mickey Rooney, Harold Spina.

Comedy **(PR:AAA MPAA:NR)**

ANDY HARDY GETS SPRING FEVER*** (1939) 88m MGM bw

Lewis Stone *(Judge Hardy)*, Mickey Rooney *(Andy Hardy)*, Cecilia Parker *(Marian Hardy)*, Ann Rutherford *(Polly Benedict)*, Fay Holden *(Mrs. Hardy)*, Sara Haden *(Aunt Milly)*, Helen Gilbert *(Rose Meredith)*, Terry Kilburn *(Stickin' Plaster)*, George Breakston *(Beezy)*, Sidney Miller *(Sidney)*, Charles Peck *(Tommy)*, Stanley Andrews *(James Willet)*, Byron Foulger *(Mark Hansen)*, Robert Kent *(Lt. Charles Copley)*, Maurice Costello *(Member of Audience)*.

Attractive dramatics teacher Gilbert becomes the center of innocent Rooney's busy world. He is at first infatuated with her, then blurts his love and asks for her hand in marriage. When hearing that she is engaged to another he goes into a tailspin, seemingly never to recover, but Judge Hardy (Stone) and the rest of Rooney's family help to heal his injured heart, including girl friend Rutherford. A pleasing and humorous outing, this seventh in a delightful series and the first directed by veteran moviemaker Van Dyke. (See ANDY HARDY series, Index.)

d, W. S. Van Dyke II; w, Kay Van Riper; ph, Lester White; ed, Ben Lewis.

Comedy **(PR:AAA MPAA:NR)**

ANDY HARDY MEETS DEBUTANTE 1/2** (1940) 89m MGM bw

Lewis Stone *(Judge Hardy)*, Mickey Rooney *(Andy Hardy)*, Fay Holden *(Mrs. Hardy)*, Cecelia Parker *(Marian Hardy)*, Judy Garland *(Betsy Booth)*, Sara Haden *(Aunt Milly)*, Ann Rutherford *(Polly Benedict)*, Tom Neal *(Aldrich Brown)*, Diana Lewis *(Daphne Fowler)*, George Breakston *(Beezy)*, Cy Kendall *(Mr. Carrillo)*, George Lessey *(Underwood)*, Addison Richards *(Mr. Benedict)*.

While Stone is in New York taking care of some legal matters, Rooney decides to try to meet glamor girl Lewis with the aid of his chum Garland. Naturally, they're the two who fall for each other. Above-average Hardy picture highlighted, of course, by Garland's presence. (See ANDY HARDY series, Index.)

d, George B. Seitz; w, Annalee Whitmore, Thomas Seller; ph, Sidney Wagner, Charles Lawton; ed, Harold F. Kress.

Comedy **(PR:AAA MPAA:NR)**

ANDY HARDY'S BLONDE TROUBLE*** (1944) 107m MGM bw

Lewis Stone *(Judge Hardy)*, Mickey Rooney *(Andy Hardy)*, Fay Holden *(Mrs. Hardy)*, Sara Haden *(Aunt Milly)*, Bonita Granville *(Kay Wilson)*, Jean Porter *(Katy Henderson)*, Keye Luke *(Dr. Lee)*, Herbert Marshall *(Dr. M.J. Standish)*, Lee Wilde *(Lee Walker)*, Lyn Wilde *(Lyn Walker)*, Marta Linden *(Mrs. Townsend)*, Jackie Moran *(Spud)*, Tommy Dix *(Mark)*.

Rooney goes to his dad's alma mater but almost instantly gets into trouble by paying too much attention to several girls, including the Wilde twins who make life so miserable for him that he plans to leave college in disgrace. The venerable Stone arrives unexpectedly and sets his son straight. Granville and the Wilde twins are precocious and cute, doing some smart song-and-dance numbers, including "You'd Be So Easy to Love." Marshall as the school's dean is the essence of polished culture, the perfectly understanding counterpart to slapdash Rooney. (See ANDY HARDY series, Index.)

d, George B. Seitz; w, Harry Ruskin, William Ludwig, Agnes Christine Johnson; ph, Lester White; m, David Snell; ed, George White; art d, Cedric Gibbons.

Comedy **(PR:AAA MPAA:NR)**

ANDY HARDY'S DOUBLE LIFE 1/2** (1942) 91m MGM bw

Lewis Stone *(Judge Hardy)*, Mickey Rooney *(Andy Hardy)*, Fay Holden *(Mrs. Hardy)*, Cecilia Parker *(Marian Hardy)*, Ann Rutherford *(Polly Benedict)*, Sara Haden *(Aunt Milly)*, Esther Williams *(Sheila Brooks)*, William Lundigan *(Jeff Willis)*, Susan Peters *(Wainwright College Girl)*, Robert Pittard *(Botsy)*, Arthur Space *(Stedman's Attorney)*, Howard Hickman *(Lincoln's Attorney)*, Frank Coghlan, Jr. *(Red)*, Mantan Moreland *(Prentiss)*, Bobby Blake *(Tooky)*.

Rooney gets himself into a sticky situation when the two girls he has proposed to both decide to accept. There are some hilarious scenes where frantic Rooney tries to sell his old jalopy in order to make the next payment on it. Rather witty Andy Hardy tale with Williams making an impressive early film appearance. (See ANDY HARDY series, Index.)

d, George B. Seitz; w, Agnes Christine Johnson; ph, John Mescal; m, Daniele Amifitheatrof; ed, Gene Ruggiero; art d, Cedric Gibbons.

Comedy **(PR:AAA MPAA:NR)**

ANDY HARDY'S PRIVATE SECRETARY** (1941) 101m MGM bw

Lewis Stone *(Judge Hardy)*, Mickey Rooney *(Andy Hardy)*, Fay Holden *(Mrs. Hardy)*, Ian Hunter *(Steven Land)*, Ann Rutherford *(Polly Benedict)*, Kathryn Grayson *(Kathryn Land)*, Todd Karns *(Harry Land)*, John Dilson *(Mr. Davis)*, Addison Richards *(George Benedict)*, George Breakston *(Beezy)*, Margaret Early *(Clarabelle Lee)*, Gene Reynolds *(Jimmy MacMahon)*, Donald Douglas *(Mr. Harper)*.

After failing his final high school exam before heading off to college, Rooney is given a second chance by an understanding faculty. Rather routine episode, although Grayson, in an early part, is quite watchable as Rooney's part-time secretary. (See ANDY HARDY series, Index.)

d, George B. Seitz; w, Jane Murfin, Harry Ruskin, ph, Lester White; ed, Elmo Vernon.

Comedy **(PR:AAA MPAA:NR)**

ANGEL 1/2** (1937) 98m PAR bw

Marlene Dietrich *(Maria Barker)*, Herbert Marshall *(Sir Frederick Barker)*, Melvyn Douglas *(Anthony Halton)*, Edward Everett Horton *(Graham)*, Ernest Cossart *(Walton)*, Laura Hope Crews *(Grand Duchess Anna Dmitrievna)*, Herbert Mundin *(Greenwood)*, Ivan Lebedeff *(Prince Vladimir Gregorovitch)*, Dennie Moore *(Emma)*, Lionel Pape *(Lord Davington)*, Phyllis Coghlan *(Maid at Barker Home)*, Leonard Carey, Gerald Hamer, James Finlayson *(Footmen)*, Eric Wilton *(English Chauffeur)*, Michael S. Visaroff *(Russian Butler)*, Olaf Hytten *(Photographer)*, Gwendolen Logan *(Woman with Maria)*, George Davis, Arthur Hurni *(Taxi Drivers)*, Joseph Romantini *(Headwaiter)*, Duci Kerekjarto *(Prima Violinist)*, Suzanne Kaaren *(Girl who Gambles)*, Louise Carter *(Flower Woman)*, Major Sam Harris *(Extra at Club)*, Gino Corrado *(Assistant Hotel Manager)*, Herbert Evans *(Lord's Butler)*.

"The Lubitsch Touch" barely fondles this sophisticated melodrama which profiles Dietrich as the bored wife of a British nobleman, Marshall, who has neglected if not ignored her for quite some time. She angrily goes off to Paris without informing her husband to see an old friend, Crews, an expatriate Russian duchess running a posh bordello. Here Douglas, an American visiting Paris, meets Dietrich and plies her with attention to which she happily responds, agreeing to have dinner with him. The two then make the rounds of Paris sites and monuments, but when Dietrich thinks Douglas is getting serious, she disappears, returning to England and Marshall, who has hardly noticed her absence. When the couple go to the races, Dietrich spots Douglas in the crowd and flees. Douglas, however, recognizes Marshall as an old WW I comrade and he is invited to dinner. Finally Douglas comes face-to-face with his "angel," realizing at dinner that she is married. The undercurrent of this scene is powerful but neither Dietrich nor Douglas betray their feelings. When Dietrich again vanishes from home, Marshall follows her and sees her meeting secretly with Douglas. He realizes his error in taking his beautiful wife for granted; Marshall asks Dietrich to return home with him but it looks as if she will depart with Douglas. At the last minute she goes to Marshall and sails to England. Not one of Dietrich's better outings, due no doubt to a stilted script that is too often saved by Lubitsch's adroit direction, Hollander's moving score and Dreier's majestic sets but the story line is still too hard to swallow despite all the gloss, like a dumpling turned to stone. At the end of this film the great Lubitsch marked his 25th anniversary as a director; Dietrich had an enormous cake delivered to the set decorated with the words "Congratulations, Ernst . . . Marlene." She personally cut a piece and fed it to Lubitsch while he was still smoking one of his famous long cigars. That probably went down better than the rushes of this near miss.

p&d, Ernst Lubitsch; w, Samson Raphaelson, Guy Bolton, Russell Medcraft (based on a play by Melchior Lengyel); ph, Charles Lang; m, Frederick Hollander; ed, William Shea; md, Boris Morros; art d, Hans Dreier, Robert Usher; spec eff, Farciot Edouart; m/l, "Angel," Hollander, Leo Robin.

Drama   (PR:C MPAA:NR)

ANGEL*   (1982, Irish) 90m Motion Picture Co. c

Stephen Rea (Danny), Alan Devlin (Bill), Veronica Quilligan (Annie), Peter Caffrey (Ray), Honor Heffernan (Deirdre) Ray McAnally (Bloom).

A powerful Irish feature film about a saxophone player who witnesses the murder of his manager and a deaf-and-dumb girl who was an innocent witness to the crime. The musician becomes obsessed with finding the killers and getting revenge. In the process, he, too, becomes a murderer. Great performance by Rea as the sax player. First-time director Jordan does a magnificent job. Strong stuff.

p, Barry Blackmore; d&w, Neil Jordan; ph, Chris Menges; m, Paddy Meegan; ed, Pat Duffner; art d, John Lucas.

Crime/Drama   (PR:C MPAA:NR)

ANGEL AND SINNER*   (1947, Fr.) 84m AFE bw (BOULE DE SUIF)

Micheline Presle (Boule de Suif), Louis Salou (Lt. Eyrick), Palau (Carre-Lamadon), Roger Carel (Le Major Falsborg), Marcel Simon (Le Comte), Alfred Adam (Cornudet), Jean Brochard (Loiseau), Michel Saline (Otto Grossling), Denis DInes (Le Cure), Bertha Bovy, Suzet Mais.

Variety of French citizens from different social groups flee Nazi-occupied Paris. They are halted by a ruthless Prussian officer who forces Presle to submit to his desires, threatening that he'll kill the other members of the party if she does not. When another German tries the same thing a few moments later, Presle, recalling that she received no support from her countrymen, goes against their recommendations, and this time kills the brute. Cynical moral tale that is well acted, and exquisitely photographed.

p, Louis Wips; d, Christian-Jacque; w, Henri Jeanson, Louis d'Helo (based on the stories "Boule de Suif" and "Mam'zelle Fifi" by Guy de Maupassant); ph, Christian Matras; art d, Leon Barsacq, Clavel.

Drama   (PR:C MPAA:NR)

ANGEL AND THE BADMAN*1/2   (1947) 100m REP bw

John Wayne (Quirt Evans), Gail Russell (Prudence Worth), Harry Carey (Wistful McClintock), Bruce Cabot (Laredo Stevens), Irene Rich (Mrs. Worth), Lee Dixon (Randy McCall), Stephen Grant (Johnny Worth), Tom Powers (Dr. Mangrum), Paul Hurst (Carson), Olin Howlin (Bradley), John Halloran (Thomas Worth), John Barton (Lila), Craig Woods (Ward Withers), Marshall Reed (Nelson), Hank Worden (Townsman), Pat Flaherty (Baker Brother).

First film produced by and starring John Wayne in this story of an outlaw trying to change his life. Wayne, wounded, collapses on the doorstep of a Mormon family. While they nurse him back to health, he begins to fall in love with the daughter, Russell. Gradually the gunslinger begins to realize that his outlaw days are numbered and he begins to change his ways, even though he is obsessed with killing the murderer, Cabot, of his foster-father. Though the Mormons have had a great influence on him, Wayne sets out to get his revenge. Russell follows and gets Wayne to turn over his gun to her before he can kill Cabot. Cabot is taken care of by the local Sheriff, Carey, who guns him down before he can kill a defenseless Wayne. Wayne and Russell ride off to start a new life together. Great performances from a top-notch cast make this gentle western well worth seeing. Though the film didn't do well at the box office at the time, it stands up better today than most of Wayne's other, more action-packed westerns.

p, John Wayne; d&w, James Edward Grant; ph, A.J. Stout; m, Richard Hageman; ed, Harry Keller; md, Cy Fever; art d, Ernest Fegte; m/l, Kim Gannon, Walter Kent.

Western   Cas.   (PR:A MPAA:NR)

ANGEL, ANGEL, DOWN WE GO zero
                        (1969) 93m AIP c (AKA: CULT OF THE DAMNED)

Jennifer Jones (Astrid), Jordan Christopher (Bogart), Roddy McDowall (Santoro), Holly Near (Tara Nicole), Lou Rawls (Joe), Charles Aidman (Willy Steele), Davey Davison (Anna Livia), Marty Brill (Maitre d'), Hiroko Watanabe (Masseuse), Carol Costello, Danielle Aubry, Sandrine Gobet, Joan Calhoun, Rudy Battaglia, George Ostos, Ron Allen, Romo Vincent.

Confusion reigns in this sick film about Hollywood decadence. Christopher stars as a leader of a vile rock and roll band (among whose members are McDowall and Rawls) who invade the lives of a rich family. The leader of the band seduces the 18-year-old Near and her mother, Jones. Later, Jones is taken on a one-way skydiving jump fitted with a faulty parachute, and her husband is found hung from the diving board of the family swimming pool. All of the performers look like they don't know what is going on and the lousy rock songs sung by Christopher don't help. This film, which bears a disturbing similarity to the events that took place at the Polanski/Tate home, was produced some time before the Manson cult murders took place, but was released about the same time the newspaper headlines were filled with descriptions of the horrible event.

p, Jerome F. Katzman; d&w, Robert Thom; ph, Jack Warren (Movielab Color); m, Fred Karger; ed, Eve Newman; art d, Gabriel Scognamillo; ch, Wilda Taylor; m/l, Barry Mann, Cynthia Weil.

Crime   (PR:O MPAA:R)

ANGEL BABY*   (1961) 97m Allied Artists bw

George Hamilton (Paul Strand), Mercedes McCambridge (Sarah Strand), Salome Jens (Angel Baby), Joan Blondell (Mollie Hays), Henry Jones (Ben Hays), Burt

Reynolds (Hoke Adams), Roger Clark (Sam Wilcox), Dudley Remus (Otis Finch), Victoria Adams (Ma Brooks), Harry Swoger (Big Cripple), Barbara Biggart (Farm Girl), Davy Biladeau (Little Boy).

Mute girl Jens, after having her speech restored by faith healer Hamilton, becomes a healer herself. After being exploited by unscrupulous Reynolds and labeled a fake, Jens heals a lame child and her faith is restored. Melodramatic southern gothic aided by good performances from both veterans and newcomers, and fine photography from Wexler.

p, Thomas F. Woods; d, Paul Wendkos; w, Orin Borsten, Paul Mason, Samuel Roeca (based on the novel Jenny Angel by Elsie Oaks Barber); ph, Haskell Wexler, Jack Marta; m, Wayne Shanklin; ed, Betty J. Lane; art d, Val Tamelin; set d, Sid Clifford.

Drama   (PR:C MPAA:NR)

ANGEL COMES TO BROOKLYN, AN*   (1945) 70m REP bw

Kaye Dowd (Karen James), Robert Duke (David Randall), David Street (Paul Blake), Barbara Perry (Barbara), Charles Kemper (Phineas Aloysius Higby), Marguerite D'Alvarez (Madam Della), Bob Scheerer (Bob), Alice Tyrrell (Susie), June Carroll (Kay), Rodney Bell (Oscar), Betzi Beaton (Tiny), Jay Presson (Johnson), Joe Cappo (Joe), Sherle North (Roxie), Billie Haywood (Theresa), Cliff Allen (Cliff), C. Montague Shaw (Sir Henry Bushnell), Eula Morgan (Olga Ashley), Harry Rose (Michael O'Day), Frank Scannell (Brian Hepplestone), Mike Ricigliano (Man in Hat), Jack McClendon (Shadow Dancer), Jimmy Conlin (Cornelius Terwilliger), Ralph Dunn (Sgt. O'Rourke).

Guardian angel Kemper comes down to earth to help a bunch of kids put on a Broadway show. He induces a producer to put up the money but his unorthodox methods cause the head angel in charge of actors on high to be vexed no end. Kemper provides some laughs but, beyond the amusing idea, the film is a letdown.

p, Leonard Sillman; d, Leslie Goodwins; w, Stanley Paley, June Carroll (based on a story by Carroll, Lee Wainer); ph, Jack Marta; ed, Tony Martinelli, m/l, Sanford Green, Carroll.

Musical Comedy   (PR:AA MPAA:None)

ANGEL FACE*   (1953) 91m RKO bw

Robert Mitchum (Frank), Jean Simmons (Diane), Mona Freeman (Mary), Herbert Marshall (Mr. Tremayne), Leon Ames (Fred Barrett), Barbara O'Neil (Mrs. Tremayne), Kenneth Tobey (Bill), Raymond Greenleaf (Arthur Vance), Griff Barnett (The Judge), Robert Gist (Miller), Morgan Farley (Juror), Jim Backus (District Attorney Judson), Bess Flowers (Barrett's Secretary), Alex Gerry (Lewis, Frank's Attorney), Gertrude Astor (Matron).

A beautiful but mentally unbalanced girl, Simmons, plans to kill her rich stepmother. Her first attempt fails when Mitchum, an ambulance driver, rushes to the scene and revives O'Neil. Simmons likes his looks and thinks to make good use of the strapping Mitchum, hiring him as the family chauffeur. Next Simmons fixes the family car so that O'Neil goes over a cliff to her death, taking with her Simmons' father, Marshall, whom Simmons truly loves; she had not meant for him to die. Simmons and Mitchum are both charged with murder and are defended by a shrewd lawyer, Ames, who insists they get married to draw sympathy from the jury. They are freed but Mitchum realizes that his new wife is a killer to the bone, and decides to leave her. As they are driving to the bus station, Simmons stalls the car, puts it in reverse, and both roar over a cliff to their deaths. Many of the twists and turns of this outrageous melodrama are indebted to THE POSTMAN ALWAYS RINGS TWICE, particularly the courtroom machinations of Ames, who played a similar role in POSTMAN. Here, however, we have a Satanic female intent on murder instead of two lovers bumbling into homicide. For all of its unbelievability, ANGEL FACE is consistently suspenseful under Preminger's sure direction. In short, you're never sure what that crazy woman will do next.

p&d, Otto Preminger; w, Frank Nugent, Oscar Millard (based on a story by Chester Erskine); ph, Harry Stradling; m, Dmitri Tiomkin; ed, Frederic Knudtson; art d, Albert S. D'Agostino, Carroll Clark; set d, Darrell Silvera, Jack Mills; cos, Michael Woulfe.

Crime   (PR:C MPAA:NR)

ANGEL FROM TEXAS, AN*   (1940) 69m WB bw

Eddie Albert (Peter Coleman), Wayne Morris (Mr. McClure), Rosemary Lane (Lydia Weston), Jane Wyman (Marge Allen), Ronald Reagan (Mr. Allen), Ruth Terry (Valerie Blayne), John Litel (Quigley), Hobart Cavanaugh (Mr. Robelink), Ann Shoemaker (Mrs. Coleman), Tom Kennedy (Chopper).

Texas yahoo Albert invests his mother's life savings into a shaky theater production hoping that his girl friend Lane will become a star. Humdrum farce that tried to recapture the success of BROTHER RAT but failed. Interesting now only for the presence of Reagan and Wyman.

p, Robert Fellows; d, Ray Enright; w, Fred Niblo, Jr., Bertram Millhauser (based on the play "The Butter and Egg Man," by George S. Kaufman); ph, Arthur L. Todd; ed, Clarence Kolster.

Comedy   (PR:A MPAA:NR)

ANGEL IN EXILE*   (1948) 90m REP bw

John Carroll (Charlie Dakin), Adele Mara (Raquel Chavez), Thomas Gomez (Dr. Esteban Chavez), Barton MacLane (Max Giorgio), Alfonso Bedoya (Ysidro Alvarez), Grant Withers (Sheriff), Paul Fix (Carl Spitz), Art Smith (Ernie Coons), Tom Powers (Warden), Ian Wolfe (Health Officer), Howland Chamberlin (J. H. Higgins), Elsa Lorraine Zepeda (Carmencita), Mary Currier (Nurse).

Ex-con Carroll uses a Mexican mine as a cover in his plan to filter out gold hidden away from a past robbery. Carroll has a change of heart when the local villagers look at his success with the mine as a message from God. Prolific and talented director Dwan does a nice job with this simple uplifting tale.

d, Allan Dwan, Phillip Ford; w, Charles Larson; ph, Reggie Lanning; m, Nathan Scott; ed, Arthur Roberts.

Drama   (PR:A MPAA:NR)

ANGEL IN MY POCKET** (1969) 105m UNIV c

Andy Griffith *(Sam)*, Jerry Van Dyke *(Bubba)*, Kay Medford *(Racine)*, Lee Meriwether *(Mary Elizabeth)*, Henry Jones *(Will Sinclair)*, Edgar Buchanan *(Axel Gresham)*, Gary Collins *(Art Shields)*, Parker Fennelly *(Calvin)*, Jack Dodson *(Norman Gresham)*, Elena Verdugo *(Lila Sinclair)*, Margaret Hamilton *(Rhoda)*, Ruth McDevitt *(Nadine)*, Richard Van Fleet *(Harry Toback)*, Bob Hastings *(Ted Palish)*, Jim Boles *(Corby Gresham)*, Leonard Stone *(Paul Gresham)*, Steve Franken *(Zimmerman)*, Larry D. Mann *(Bishop Morenschild)*, Al Checco *(Byron)*, Margaret Ann Peterson *(Mrs. Toback)*, Peggy Mondo *(Charlotte)*, Beverly Powers *(Charlene De Gaulle)*, Joy Harmon *(Miss Holland)*, Benny Rubin *(Dad Schrader)*, Herbie Faye *(Mr. Welch)*, George Tapps *(Ace Black)*, Eddie Quillan *(Rev. Beckwith)*, Michael Barrier *(Mr. Grant)*, Buddy Foster *(Sammy)*, Todd Starke *(Dink)*, Amber Smale *(Rachel)*, Susan Seaforth *(Mrs. Grant)*, Athena Lorde *(Mrs. Corby Gresham)*, Grace Albertson *(Mrs. Will Sinclair)*, Robert Lieb *(Cyrus Sinclair)*, Claudia Bryar *(Mrs. Axel Gresham)*, Tani Phelps *(Mrs. Palish)*, Monty Margetts *(Mrs. Chase)*, Eve Bruce *(Miss USA)*, Lynn Fields *(Miss France)*, Gloria Mills *(Miss Soviet Union)*, Chela Bacigalupo *(Miss South America)*, Anne Besant *(Miss England)*, Linda Carol *(Miss Egypt)*, Bonnie Sue Schwartz *(Majorette)*, Jesslyn Fax *(Mrs. Styles)*, Stuart Nisbet *(Sheriff)*, Ellen Corby *(Older Woman)*, Kathryn Minner *(Mrs. Williams)*, Mary Gregory *(Secretary)*, Rufe Davis *(Older Man)*.

Griffith is a parson who helps settle a small-town political rivalry by helping elect newcomer Collins and getting rid of old-timer Buchanan and Jones. Light-hearted cornpone comedy was a return to feature films for Griffith after his great success on television.

p, Edward J. Montague; d, Alan Rafkin; w, Jim Fritzell, Everett Greenbaum; ph, William Margulies (Techniscope, Technicolor); m, Lyn Murray; ed, Sam E. Waxman; m/l, Jerry Keller, Dave Blume.

Comedy **(PR:AA MPAA:G)**

ANGEL LEVINE, THE** (1970) 105m UA c

Zero Mostel *(Morris Mishkin)*, Harry Belafonte *(Alexander Levine/the angel)*, Ida Kaminska *(Fanny Mishkin)*, Milo O'Shea *(Dr. Arnold Berger)*, Gloria Foster *(Sally)*, Barbara Ann Teer *(Welfare Lady)*, Eli Wallach *(Storeclerk)*, Anne Jackson *(Customer)*.

Sentimental tale of an old Jewish man, Mostel, who has lost his faith in God and himself after a series of personal and business losses. Enter a black angel from heaven, Belafonte, who has to earn his wings by convincing the depressed Mostel that his life does have meaning. The whole thing is a rip-off of Frank Capra's classic, IT'S A WONDERFUL LIFE, and suffers an originality problem because of it, but Mostel and Belafonte are appealing and the supporting cast is fine.

p, Chriz Schultz; d, Jan Kadar; w, Bill Gunn, Ronald Ribman (based on a story by Bernard Malamud); ph, Richard Kratine (DeLuxe Color); m, William Eaton; ed, Carl Lerner; art d, George Jenkins; set d, Ben Rutter; cos, Dom Rodriguez.

Drama **(PR:A MPAA:GP)**

ANGEL OF VIOLENCE, 1981 (SEE: MS. 45, 1981)

ANGEL ON MY SHOULDER*** ½** (1946) 95m UA bw

Paul Muni *(Eddie Kagle)*, Anne Baxter *(Barbara Foster)*, Claude Rains *(Nick)*, Onslow Stevens *(Dr. Higgins)*, George Cleveland *(Albert)*, Hardie Albright *(Smiley)*, James Flavin *(Bellamy)*, Erskine Sanford *(Minister)*, Marion Martin *(Mrs. Bentley)*, Jonathan Hale *(Chairman)*, Murray Alper *(Jim)*, Joan Blair *(Brazen Girl)*, Fritz Leiber *(Scientist)*, Kurt Katch *(Warden)*, Sarah Padden *(Agatha)*, Addison Richards *(Big Harry)*, Ben Welden *(Shaggsy)*, George Meeker *(Mr. Bentley)*, Lee Shumway *(Bailiff)*, Russ Whiteman *(Interne)*, James Dundee, Mike Lally, Saul Gores, Duke Taylor *(Gangsters)*, Edward Keane *(Prison Yard Captain)*, Chester Clute *(Kramer)*.

A witty, caustic and exciting film, this is a reverse from the script Segall wrote for HERE COMES MR. JORDAN, but here it is not heavenly messengers trading off bodies for a misappropriated soul. The action is coming the other way, from the fiery depths where the flamboyant Rains, as a calculating and often funny Devil, makes a deal with lost soul Muni, a former gangster killed by a henchman, Albright. He will help Muni take his revenge on Albright if the gangster will occupy the body of a saintly judge who has prevented too many souls from slipping into Hell. No sooner does Muni occupy the judge's body than his traitorous henchman conveniently falls from a high ledge and is killed. Rains has kept his part of the bargain but Muni evades his responsibility to old Beelzebub. First he has difficulty in adjusting to his new surroundings, the judge's mansion and servants, and particularly his fiance, Baxter. His crude manners, speech habits, and decidedly homicidal attitude alarm the judge's friends but it is thought that he is suffering from a breakdown due to his workload, so he is humored and pampered, which makes Muni all the more irritable. Some hilarious scenes are produced by this marvelous actor as he slowly makes the transition from gutter thug to polished jurist. After listening to a sermon he realizes that Rains can never reclaim him as long as he does no evil and he becomes an even more dedicated reformer than the soul he has replaced, which sends Rains into fits of rage. He also falls in love with Baxter but realizes that he has no right to her affection as a spiritual impostor. In the end Muni believes the judge has the right to live out his life, entitled to the happiness he has earned. The gangster-turned-do-gooder makes a pact with Rains. He will return to Hades but as a trustee with wide-ranging privileges. Rains sneers refusal but Muni tells him that his prestige will collapse if it be known in Hell that the boss almost lost a soul through ineptitude. Bitterly agreeing to the deal, Rains and Muni descend on a street-level garbage elevator, Rains carping: "This is sheer blackmail!" Muni gives him a wink, replying: "You ought to know, Nick, you ought to know." Muni, whose film career was slipping a bit, had high hopes for ANGEL ON MY SHOULDER but was dissatisfied with Mayo's direction, demanding perfection in every scene from a man who was used to producing fast-paced commercial films. The two argued over almost every line which made the entire company uneasy. Tragically, a grip fell to his death from a scaffold during the end-of-production party. The film is nevertheless marvelous entertainment, with a great actor giving his usual riveting performance. Rains, who played an angel in HERE COMES MR. JORDAN, is superbly sinister as the man from below.

p, Charles R. Rogers; d, Archie Mayo; w, Harry Segall, Roland Kibbee (based on a story by Segall); ph, James Van Trees; m, Dmitri Tiomkin; ed, Asa Clark; art d, Bernard Herzbrun; spec eff, Harry Redmond, Jr.

Fantasy/Comedy **Cas.** **(PR:A MPAA:NR)**

ANGEL ON THE AMAZON** (1948) 86m REP bw (GB: DRUMS ALONG THE AMAZON)

George Brent *(Jim Warburton)*, Vera Ralston *(Christine Ridgeway)*, Brian Aherne *(Anthony Ridgeway)*, Constance Bennett *(Dr. Karen Lawrence)*, Fortunio Bonanova *(Sebastian Ortega)*, Alfonso Bedoya *(Paulo)*, Gus Schilling *(Dean Hartley)*, Richard Crane *(Johnny McMahon)*, Walter Reed *(Jerry Adams)*, Ross Elliott *(Frank Lane)*, Konstantin Shayne *(Dr. Jungmeyer)*, Charles LaTorre *(Waiter)*, Elizabeth Dunne *(Housekeeper)*, Alberto Morin *(Radio Operator)*, Dick Jones *(George)*, Alfredo DeSa *(Brazilian Reporter)*, Tony Martinez *(Bellhop)*, Gerardo Sei Groves *(Native)*, John Trebach *(Waiter)*, Manuel Paris *(Night Desk Clerk)*.

Routine jungle actioner starring Ralston as a woman who lives in the rain forest to soothe her distraught mind after the death of her daughter. It seems that Miss Ralston has stopped aging due to shock, and on one of her hunting excursions she meets up with a party of explorers led by Brent, whose plane has crashed. She rescues the group and Brent begins to fall in love with this jungle beauty until her age begins to catch up with her and her hair greys and face wrinkles. Oh well, there's always Constance Bennett.

p&d, John H. Auer; w, Lawrence Kimble (based on a story by Earl Felton); ph, Reggie Lanning; m, Nathan Scott; ed, Richard L. Van Enger; md, Morton Scott; art d, James Sullivan; set d, John McCarthy Jr., George Milo; spec eff, Howard and Theodore Lydecker.

Adventure **(PR:A MPAA:NR)**

ANGEL PASSED OVER BROOKLYN, AN
(SEE: MAN WHO WAGGED HIS TAIL, THE, 1961, Span./Ital.)

ANGEL STREET (SEE: GASLIGHT, 1940)

ANGEL UNCHAINED* (1970) 86m AIP c

Don Stroud *(Angel)*, Luke Askew *(Tremaine)*, Larry Bishop *(Pilot)*, Tyne Daly *(Merilee)*, Aldo Ray *(Sheriff)*, Neil Moran *(Magician)*, Jean Marie *(Jackie)*, Bill McKinney *(Shotgun)*, Jordan Rhodes *(Tom)*, Peter Laurence *(Dave)*, Pedro Regas *(Injun)*, Linda Smith *(Wendy)*.

Motorcycle gang leader Stroud enlists the aid of some commune hippies in fighting against the closed-minded but violent inhabitants of a small town. Typical early seventies biker exploitation movie with a few fair action scenes.

p, Hal Klein, Lee Madden; d, Madden; w, Jeffrey Alladin Fiskin (based on a story by Madden); ph, Irving Lippman; m, Randy Sparks; ed, Fred Feitshans, Jr.

Drama **(PR:C MPAA:GP)**

ANGEL WHO PAWNED HER HARP, THE** (1956, Brit.) 76m BL bw

Felix Aylmer *(Joshua Webman)*, Diane Cilento *(The Angel)*, Jerry Desmonde *(Parker)*, Robert Eddison *(The Voice)*, Joe Linnane *(Ned Sullivan)*, Sheila Sweet *(Jenny Lane)*, Phillip Guard *(Len Burrows)*, Genitha Halsey *(Mrs. Burrows)*, Edward Evans *(Sgt. Lane)*, Elaine Wodson *(Mrs. Lane)*, Alfie Bass *(Lennox)*.

Curious angel Cilento, feeling the need to observe mortal behavior, visits earth and befriends pawnshop owner Aylmer. Well-made, charming British picture with the standard serious/comedic blend of 1950s English film

p, Sidney Cole; d, Alan Bromly; w, Charles Terrot, Cole (based on the novel by Terrot); ph, Arthur Grant; m, Anthony Hopkins; ed, John Merritt.

Fantasy/Comedy **(PR:A MPAA:NR)**

ANGEL WITH THE TRUMPET, THE** (1950, Brit.) 98m London Films/BL

Eileen Herlie *(Henrietta Stein)*, Basil Sydney *(Francis Alt)*, Norman Wooland *(Prince Rudolf)*, Maria Schell *(Anna Linden)*, Olga Edwards *(Monica Alt)*, John Justin *(Paul Alt)*, Andrew Cruikshank *(Otto Alt)*, Oskar Werner *(Herman Alt)*, Anthony Bushell *(Baron Hugo Traun)*, Wilfrid Hyde-White *(Simmerl)*, Campbell Cotts *(Gen. Paskiewicz)*. Dorothy Batley *(Pauline Drauffer)*.

Sad, sad tale of a woman who marries the man her family wishes her to wed, and not Wooland, the man she truly loves. Years after her lover's suicide, Herlie joins him before the Gestapo can get to her because of her Jewish ancestry. Depressing film that heavily emphasizes interpretation of character.

p, Karl Hartl; d, Anthony Bushell; w, Hartl, Franz Tassie; ph, Robert Krasker; m, Willy Schmidt-Geniner; ed, Reginald Beck.

Drama **(PR:C MPAA:NR)**

ANGEL WORE RED, THE** (1960) 99m MGM bw

Ava Gardner *(Soledad)*, Dirk Bogarde *(Arturo Carrera)*, Joseph Cotten *(Hawthorne)*, Vittorio De Sica *(Gen. Clave)*, Aldo Fabrizi *(Canon Rota)*, Arnoldo Foa *(Insurgent Major)*, Finlay Currie *(The Bishop)*, Rossano Rory *(Mercedes)*, Enrico Maria Salerno *(Capt. Botargas)*, Robert Bright *(Father Idlefonso)*, Franco Castellani *(Jose)*, Bob Cunningham *(Mac)*, Gustavo De Nardo *(Major Garcia)*, Nino Castelnuevo *(Capt. Trinidad)*, Aldo Pini *(Chaplain)*.

Good performances can't save this insipid tale of a priest and a prostitute, Bogarde and Gardner, who are thrown together in the midst of the Spanish Civil War. Bogarde has had a lapse of faith and turned in his collar to help the Falangist rebels. On the way he meets and falls for good-hearted, patriotic hooker, Gardner. Soon they are captured by the Loyalists, who want a religious statue, for morale reasons, that only Bogarde knows the whereabouts of. During his confinement, the priest decides to pick up his faith and go back to the Lord. Gardner accepts the news and dies heroically for the rebel cause. Lack of a clear political position (the Falangists and the Loyalists both appear to be villains at times) in writer/director Nunnally Johnson's material cloud the drama between the characters.

p, Goffredo Lombardo; d&w, Nunnally Johnson; ph, Giuseppe Rotunno; m, Propislau Kaper; ed, Louis Loeffler; art d, Piero Filippone; cos, Maurizio Chiara.

War/Romance **(PR:A MPAA:NR)**

ANGELA**

(1955, Ital.) 81m FOX bw

Dennis O'Keefe (Steve Catlett), Mara Lane (Angela Towne), Rossano Brazzi (Nino), Arnoldo Foa (Cpt. Ambrosi), Galeazzo Benti (Gustavo Venturi), Enzo Fiermonte (Sgt. Collins), Nino Crisman (Bertolati), Giovanni Fostini (Tony), Francesco Tensi (Dr. Robini), Maria Teresa Paliani (Girl of Beauty Shop), Gorella Gori (Nurse), Aldo Pini (Doorkeeper).

O'Keefe directs and stars in this sordid tale of an American ex-GI who stays in Rome after the war. He becomes involved with a beautiful woman, Lane, who has killed her boss, which causes both of them to run as fugitives from the law and the woman's husband. O'Keefe kills the hubby in self defense, and then realizes that this lady is trouble and lets the cops take her away. Surviving the war must have been easy compared to this.

p, Steven Pallos; d, Dennis O'Keefe; w, Jonathan Rix [Dennis O'Keefe], Edoardo Anton (based on a story by Steven Carruthers); ph, Leonida Barboni; m, Mario Nascimbene; ed, Giancarlo Cappelli.

Drama   (PR:A MPAA:NR)

ANGELA zero

(1977, Can.) 100m Montreal Travel Co. c

Sophia Loren (Angela), Steve Railsback (Jean), John Vernon (Ben), John Huston (Hogan), Yvon Dufour, Michelle Rossignol, Ian Lapointe, Luce Guilboult, Andre Cousineau.

A very beefy Loren delivers a baby, then abandons her tricks as a prostitute and becomes a waitress in Montreal to support the child. Her man, Vernon, returns from the Korean War, immediately tosses her to the floor, and they have sex (in the space of about 15 seconds). He hears the baby crying and immediately suspects that it is the child of another, though Loren insists that she had written him about the child, that it is his. Disbelieving, Vernon goes back to working for underworld boss Huston, telling him that he cannot concentrate on any capers while the child is present in his house. Huston has the boy kidnapped as a favor and Vernon goes off on a stick-up but is turned in by Loren who knows he is behind the abduction. Vernon is captured, vowing revenge against Loren, and is shipped off to prison. It is twenty plus years later, 1976, and Loren is now the owner of a posh restaurant, falling in love with a youth, Railsback, who delivers meat to her kitchen. He is none other than her own grown-up child, set up in his job by the evil Huston. The youth's carnal cravings for Loren culminate just as she hears that Vernon has been released from prison and is gunning for her. Railsback jumps Loren, throws her to the floor (like father, like son), rips away her blouse, buries his head in her bosom, just as Vernon bursts into the room to inform Loren that she is having sex with her own son, then shoots both of them before being killed by Railsback. With her dying gasp Loren looks up lovingly at Railsback, touches his face maternally and cries: "My baby!" A dreadful film from beginning to end, one where the principals move about like puppets muttering inane dialog from a script that could have been written by an illiterate monkey. Huston is wasted. Loren is phlegmatic and appears overweight, no more attractive than a fishmonger's wife gone to seed. Vernon is his usual obnoxious self, overacting every scene, and Railsback is instantly forgettable as the unwittingly incestuous son. The entire film is done in low-key lighting, so low key as to strain the eyes with its murky scenes. This production was obviously one of those Canadian deals where Canada fronted the financing on the usual condition that most of the talent employed be Canadian, sort of vanity filmmaking where Hollywood stars avail themselves of quick big bucks in return for the use of their names to front a host of mediocre and unemployed Canadian actors and technicians. The result here is an insult to viewers who expect a professional film production. The only benefit such a film might serve is to be foisted upon the Canadian Parliament in a special viewing so its members can see how government funds are squandered.

p, Julian Melzack, Claude Heroux; d, Boris Sagal; w, Charles Israel; ph, Marc Champion; m, Henry Mancini; ed, Yves Langlois, art d, Keith Pepper; set d, Ronald Fauteux; spec eff, John Thomas.

Drama/Crime   Cas.   (PR:O MPAA:NR)

ANGELE**

(1934 Fr.) 130m Pagnol bw

Orane Demazis (Angele), Fernandel (Saturnin), Henri Puopon (Clarius), Delmont (Amedee), Andrez (Louis), Mme. Toinon (Mother), Jean Servais (Albin).

Overlong French film starring Demazis as a young peasant girl who is seduced by a pimp from the big city. The procurer takes the girl from the farm and puts her to work on the streets. Soon she has an illegitimate child and her father sends one of his helpers to go fetch his wayward daughter. The angry father takes both his daughter and her baby and locks them in the cellar. Demazis' old sweetheart finds out that she's being held prisoner and helps her get away to the mountains when a flood hits the cellar. Guilty that she has left her father, the couple return to the farm to face the music. Dad softens and gives his consent for them to marry. Strictly for fans of French melodrama.

p&d, Marcel Pagnol (based on a novel by Jean Glono).

Drama   (PR:C MPAA:NR)

ANGELIKA

(SEE: AFFAIRS OF DR. HOLL, 1954)

ANGELINA**

(1948, Ital.) 90m Lux-Ors/President bw

Anna Magnani (Angelina), Nando Bruno (Pasquale), Ave Ninchi (Carmeja), Agnese Dubbini (Cesira), Ernesto Almirante (Luigi), Armando Migliari (Callisto Carrone), Vittorio Mittini (Roberto), Maria Donati (Mrs. Carrone), Maria Grazia Franci (Annetta), Franco Zefferelli (Filippo Carrone), Gianni Glori (Libero).

Feisty mama Magnani fights for better living conditions in her neighborhood. Fair neo-realist drama highlighted by a few fine performances.

p, Paolo Frasca; d, Luigi Zampa; w, Zampa, Suso Cecchi D'Amico, Piero Tellini, Anna Magnani; ph, Paoli Craveri.

Drama   (PR:C MPAA:NR)

ANGELO**

(1951, Ital.) 97m Scalera bw

Renato Baldini (Matteo Belfiore), Umberto Spadaro (Don Gennaro), Iole Fierro (Catari), Little Angelo (Angelo).

Absorbing tale about an ex-convict who returns home to find that his wife has had a child by a black GI during the war. Emotional Italian film dealing with compassion and the ability to forgive.

d&w, Francesco de Robertis; ph, Carlo Bellero.

Drama   (PR:C MPAA:NR)

ANGELO IN THE CROWD**

(1952, Ital.) 90m Continental bw

Angelo Maggio (Angelo), Umberto Spadaro (La Spada), Isa Pola (Countess Melitta), Dante Maggio (Emma), Luisella Beghi (Sister Luisa), Lia Murano (Ninuccia), Aldo Capacci (Pietro), Nino Milano (Bruno), Maria Parisi (Sora Rosa), Ugo de Pascale (Goldstein), Desiderio Nobile (Blumfield), Silvio Bagolini (Cav. Bartolozzi), Oscar Andriani (Comm. Petroni), Anna Silena (Sister Beatrice), Edoardo Toniono (Geo. Flores), Giovanna Galletti (Giocatrice), Lora Silvani (Cameriera).

A sequel to 1951's ANGELO, this film follows the title lad as he escapes from a Catholic orphanage and wanders around the city streets. Creative use of naturalistic photography enhances the boy's story.

p, Mario Borghi; d, Leonardo DeMitri; w, Alessi Paternostro; ph, Carlo Bellero; m, Gino Filippini; ed, Titti D'Alvino, Mario Mengoli.

Drama   (PR:A MPAA:NR)

ANGELO MY LOVE**

(1983) 115m Cinecom International c

Angelo Evans (Himself), Michael Evans (Himself), Ruthie Evans (Herself), Tony Evans (Himself), Debbie Evans (Herself), Steve "Patalay" Tsigonoff (Himself), Millie Tsigonoff (Herself), Frankie Williams (Himself), George Nicholas (Himself), Katherina Ribraka (Patricia), Timothy Phillips (School Teacher), Lachlan Youngs (Student Reporter), Jennifer Youngs (Student Reader), Louis Garcia (Hispanic Student), Margaret Millan Gonzalez (Old Woman), Cathy Kitchen (Country Singer), Jan Kitchen (Mother), Debbie Ristick (Peaches), William Duvall, John Duvall (Opera Singers), Nick Costello, Diana Costello (Godparents), Johnny Ristick, Yelka Ristick (Bride's Parents), John Williams (Greek Dancer).

Offbeat drama that mixes semi-documentary style and approach in chronicling the exploits of New York gypsies, particularly the provocative Angelo Evans, who is an expert hustler and sometimes amusing clown. A pet project of actor Robert Duvall, who directed, will find few viewers able to sustain interest in an overlong look at a community alien and sarcastically hostile to mainstream America.

d&w, Robert Duvall; ph, Joseph Friedman; ed, Stephen Mack.

Drama   Cas.   (PR:O MPAA:NR)

ANGELS ALLEY*½

(1948) 66m MON bw

Leo Gorcey (Slip), Huntz Hall (Sach), Gabriel Dell (Ricky), Billy Benedict (Whitey), David Gorcey (Chuck), Frankie Darro (Jimmy), Nestor Paiva (Tony Lucarno), Rosemary LaPlanche (Daisy Harris), Geneva Gray (Josie O'Neill), Bennie Bartlett ("Jag" Harmon), John Eldredge (Willis), Nelson Leigh (Father O'Hanlon), Tommie Menzies (Boomer), Mary Gordon (Mrs. Mahoney), Dick Paxton (Jockey Burns), Buddy Gorman (Andy Miller), Robert Emmett Keane (Attorney Felix Crowe).

Typical Bowery Boys outing has the gang breaking up a car thief outfit. (See BOWERY BOYS series, Index.)

p, Jan Grippo; d, William Beaudine; w, Edmond Seward, Tim Ryan, Gerald Schnitzer; ph, Marcel Le Picard; m, Edward J. Kay; ed, William Austin; art d, Dave Milton.

Comedy   (PR:A MPAA:NR)

ANGELS BRIGADE*

(1980) 87m Arista c

Sylvia Anderson, Lieu Chinh, Jacqulin Cole, Liza Greer, Robin Greer, Susan Kiger, Noela Velasco, Jack Palance, Peter Lawford, Jim Backus, Neville Brand, Pat Buttram, Arthur Godfrey, Alan Hale.

Dull actioner has a group of female avengers equipping a van with armor and weapons so that they can drive about destroying drug dealers. Idiotic vigilantism.

p&d, Greydon Clark; w, Alvin Fast, Clark; ph, Dean Cundy; m, Gerald Lee.

Crime   (PR:O MPAA:R)

ANGELS DIE HARD*

(1970) 87m New World c

Tom Baker (Blair), William Smith (Gentleman Tim), R. G. Armstrong (Mel Potter), Alan De Witt (Undertaker), Connie Nelson (Nancy Davis), Carl Steppling (Sheriff Davis), Frank Leo (Deputy Martin), Gary Littlejohn (Piston), Rita Murray (Naomi), Mikel Angel (Dirty Davis), William Bonner (Houston), Michael Donovan O'Donnell (Monk), Leslie Otis (Tommy), Dianne Turley (Patsy), Beach Dickerson (Shank), Michael Stringer (Seed), Richard Compton (Restaurant Owner), Bambi Allen (Owner's Wife).

Another biker film, this one with Baker and Smith as the leaders of a gang seeking revenge on a town where one of their number was murdered. Despite the efforts of the Sheriff's daughter, Nelson, to quell the violence, all hell breaks loose and it's bikers vs. townsfolk in a bloody battle. As it turns out, the Sheriff himself committed the original murder, and the cyclists get their revenge.

p, Charles Beach Dickerson; d&w, Richard Compton; ph, Arch Archambault (Movielab Color); m, Richard Hieronymous; ed, Tony de Zarraga.

Crime   Cas.   (PR:O MPAA:R)

ANGELS FROM HELL*

(1968) 86m AIP c

Tom Stern (Mike), Arlene Martel (Ginger), Ted Markland (Smiley), Stephen Oliver (Speed), Paul Bertoya (Nutty Norman), James Murphy (Tiny Tim), Jack Starrett (Capt. Bingham), Jay York, Pepper Martin, Bob Harris, Saundra Gayle, Suzy Walters, Luana Talltree, Susan Holloway, Judith Garwood, Susanne Sidney, Steve Rogers.

Executive producer Joe Solomon's follow-up to the highly successful biker film HELL'S ANGELS ON WHEELS, this time starring Stern as a returned Vietnam vet who builds the ultimate outlaw biker gang as a protest against the Establishment that sent him off to war. The 500 bikers invade a town whose sheriff had killed one of their members (Sound familiar? See ANGELS DIE HARD). The usual bloodbath ensues. Interesting thematic ideas (Vietnam vet disillusioned with America) are clouded by the vast amounts of sex and violence associated with the biker genre.

p, Kurt Neumann; d, Bruce Kessler; w, Jerome Wish; ph, Herman Knox (Perfect Color); m, Stu Phillips; ed, William Martin.

Crime **(PR:O MPAA:NR)**

ANGELS HARD AS THEY COME* (1971) 90m New World c

Scott Glenn *(Long John)*, Charles Dierkop *(General)*, Gilda Texter *(Astrid)*, James Iglehart *(Monk)*, Gary Littlejohn *(Axe)*, Gary Busey *(Henry)*, Janet Wood *(Vicki)*, Don Carerra *(Juicer)*, Brendan Kelly *(Brain)*, Larry Tucker *(Lucifer)*, Cheri Latimer *(Cheri)*, Marc Seaton *(Louie)*, John Taylor *(Crab)*, Dennis Art *(Rings)*, Niva Davis *(Clean Sheila)*, Hal Marshall *(Dr. Jagger)*, Steve Slauson *(Magic)*.

Early film produced and co-written by Jonathan Demme who went on to direct MELVIN AND HOWARD and SWING SHIFT. Another outlaw biker film, this time involving hippies. Nothing special about the material, but look for some soon-to-be-stars in the cast, including Glenn who played Alan Shepard in THE RIGHT STUFF, and Busey, who starred in THE BUDDY HOLLY STORY. The music is performed by the group Carp.

p, Jonathan Demme; d, Joe Viola; w, Demme, Viola; ph, Steve Katz (Metrocolor); m, Richard Hieronymous; ed, Joe Ravetz; art d, Jack Fisk.

Crime **Cas.** **(PR:O MPAA:R)**

ANGEL'S HOLIDAY** (1937) 74m FOX bw

Jane Withers *(Angel)*, Robert Kent *(Nick)*, Joan Davis *(Strivers)*, Sally Blane *(Pauline Kaye)*, Harold Huber *(Bob Regan)*, Frank Jenks *(Butch)*, Ray Walker *(Crandall)*, John Qualen *(Waldo)*, Lon Chaney Jr. *(Louie)*, Al Lydell *(Gramp)*, Russell Hopton *(Gus)*, Paul Hurst *(Sgt. Murphy)*, John Kelly *(Maxie)*, George Taylor *(Eddie)*, Cy Kendall *(Chief of Police)*, Charlie Arnt *(Everett)*, Virginia Sale *(Hatchet-Faced Woman)*, Emmett Vogan *(Radio Officer)*, Irving Bacon *(Fingerprint Expert)*, Tom London *(Truck Driver)*, Frank Moran *(Tough Man)*, James Flavin *(Detective)*, Harrison Greene *(Fat Man)*.

Child star Withers, niece of the town's newspaper editor, comes to the rescue of a famous movie star, Blane, who has returned to her home town to promote her latest movie. A group of gangsters kidnaps the movie queen and holds her for ransom. Withers, with the aid of newspaper reporter Kent, takes on the racketeers and frees the starlet. Typical tough little kid movie.

p, John Stone; d, James Tinling; w, Frank Fenton, Lynn Root; ph, Daniel B. Clark; ed, Nick DeMaggio; md, Samuel Kaylin; m/l, Harold Bill, Bill Telaak.

Drama **(PR:A MPAA:NR)**

ANGELS IN DISGUISE*½ (1949) 63m MON bw

Leo Gorcey *(Slip)*, Huntz Hall *(Sach)*, Billy Benedict *(Whitey)*, David Gorcey *(Chuck)*, Benny Bartlett *(Butch)*, Gabriel Dell *(Gabe Moreno)*, Bernard Gorcey *(Louie Dumbrowsky)*, Mickey Knox *(Angles)*, Edward Ryan *(Carver)*, Richard Benedict *(Miami)*, Joseph Turkel *(Johnny Mutton)*, Ray Walker *(Jim Cobb)*, William Forrest *(Roger T. Harrison)*, Pepe Hern *(Bertie Spangler)*, Marie Blake *(Millie)*, Roy Gordon *(Johnson/Foreman)*, Jane Adams *(Nurse)*, Don Harvey *(Hodges)*, Tristram Coffin *(Bookkeeper)*.

Poor outing of the cheaply produced Bowery Boys series (so inexpensively produced that backlighting was mostly ignored so that the shadows of the actors were visible as they moved in front of the camera lights.) Here Gorcey, Hall, and company set out as do-gooders but their generosity backfires into problems which take too long to solve. Replete with Gorcey's malapropisms and Hall's ultra-dumb antics. (See BOWERY BOYS series, Index.)

p, Jan Grippo; d, Jean Yarbrough; w, Charles B. Marion, Gerald Schnitzer, Bert Lawrence; ph, Marcel Le Picard; ed, William Austin; md, Edward Kay; art d, Dave Milton.

Comedy **(PR:A MPAA:NR)**

ANGELS IN THE OUTFIELD*½**

(1951) 99m MGM c (GB: ANGELS AND THE PIRATES)

Paul Douglas *(Guffy McGovern)*, Janet Leigh *(Jennifer Paige)*, Keenan Wynn *(Fred Bayles)*, Donna Corcoran *(Bridget White)*, Lewis Stone *(Arnold P. Hapgood)*, Spring Byington *(Sister Edwitha)*, Bruce Bennett *(Saul Hellman)*, Marvin Kaplan *(Timothy Durney)*, Ellen Corby *(Sister Veronica)*, Jeff Richards *(Dave Rothberg)*, John Gallaudet *(Reynolds)*, King Donovan *(McGee)*, Don Haggerty *(Rube Robinson)*, Paul Salata *(Tony Minelli)*, Fred Graham *("Chunk")*, John McKee *(Bill Baxter)*, Patrick J. Molyneaux *(Patrick J. Finley)*.

Silly, but fun, baseball film starring Douglas as the gruff manager of a ball club firmly entrenched in the basement, that suddenly finds itself climbing to first place for no apparent reason. Enter lady reporter Leigh who prints a newspaper story about a little orphan girl who swears she's seen angels standing among Douglas' ballplayers, trying to help them win. Soon after, Douglas is hit in the head by a line drive and admits to the press that indeed, angels have been helping the team. The baseball commissioner, Stone, thinks he's gone nuts and starts an investigation into the manager's sanity. It doesn't matter because the team goes on to win the pennant. Great performances by all make this a little gem of a film. Dwight Eisenhower, interviewed during his Presidency, named this his favorite movie.

p&d, Clarence Brown; w, Dorothy Kingsley, George Wells (based on a story by Richard Conlin); ph, Paul C. Vogel; m, Daniel Amfitheatrof; ed, Robert J. Kern.

Comedy **(PR:AAA MPAA:NR)**

ANGELS OF DARKNESS* (1956, Ital.) 90m Excelsior/Supra bw

Linda Darnell *(Lola Baldi)*, Valentina Cortesa *(Vally)*, Lea Padovani *(Franca)*, Giulietta Masina *(Rosita)*, Anthony Quinn *(Francesco Caserto)*, Lilla Brignone *(Tamara)*, Roberto Risso *(Bruno)*, Maria Pia Casilio *(The Young Girl)*, Carlo Dapporto *(Vittorio)*.

Three impoverished prostitutes, Darnell, Cortesa and Padovani, are thrown out of their only home, a bordello slated for destruction. Darnell returns home to live with her mother but townsfolk knowing her profession shun her and she leaves to live a nomadic existence. Cortesa is lucky enough to find Quinn who proposes but on their wedding day her past is revealed and she runs off to be killed by a speeding auto. Padovani is the only one who finds peace with her small child. Badly dubbed, the film is a terrible tearjerker, insipid and boring for the most part, and for the other part just boring. This disaster did work a small miracle, however, for Anthony Quinn, whose career had been sliding downhill fast. He befriended Masina and through her met her husband, director Federico Fellini; she also got him the role opposite her in LA STRADA that made Quinn an overnight international sensation, no longer the slick villain, the crazy Indian or the suave gangster but a grimy slob with a cruel streak and a hidden conscience that sometimes surfaced to save his repugnant character, a type Quinn would exploit in one subsequent film after another. This miserable film was not even complete when Fellini began shooting LA STRADA.

p&d, Giuseppe Amato; w, Giuseppe Mangione, Cesare Zavattini, Gigliola Falluto, Bruno Paolinelli, Amato (based on the novel *New Life* by Paolinelli); ph, Anchise Brizzi; m, Renzo Rossellini; ed, Gabriele Varriale; art d, Virgilio Marchi.

Drama **(PR:O MPAA:NR)**

ANGELS OF THE STREETS**

(1950, Fr.) 80m Synops-Robert Paul/MGM bw (LES ANGE DU PECHE)

Renee Faure *(Anne-Marie)*, Jany Holt *(Therese)*, Sylvie *(The Prioresss)*, Mila Parely *(Madeleine)*, Marie-Helene Daste *(Mother St. John)*, Yolande Laffon *(Madame Lamaury)*, Paula Dehelly *(Mother Dominique)*, Sylvia Monfort *(Agnes)*, Gilberte Terbois *(Sister Marie-Joseph)*, Louis Seigner *(Prison Warden)*.

Filmed in 1943 by famed director Bresson, ANGELS OF THE STREETS concerns a nun, Faure, who becomes obsessed with saving the soul of a woman convict. The ambitious nun pushes so hard for the convict's salvation that her superiors begin to get angry. The convict herself senses that the nun isn't helping her to save her soul, but to further her own religious career. (In French; English subtitles.)

p, Roland Tual; d, Robert Bresson; w, Jean Giraudoux, Bresson, R. L. Bruckberger; ph, Philippe Agostini; m, Jean Jacques Grunewald; ed, Yvonne Martin; art d, Rene Renoux.

Drama **(PR:C MPAA:NR)**

ANGELS ONE FIVE** (1954, Brit.) 97m A-B Pathe/Templar bw

Jack Hawkins *("Tiger" Small)*, Michael Denison *(Peter Moon)*, Dulcie Gray *(Nadine Clinton)*, John Gregson *("Septic" Baird)*, Cyril Raymond *(Barry Clinton)*, Veronica Hurst *(Betty Carfax)*, Harold Goodwin *(Wailes)*, Norman Pierce *(Bonzo)*, Geoffrey Keen *(CSM)*, Harry Locke *(Lookout)*, Philip Stainton *(PC)*, Vida Hope *(WAAF)*, Amy Veness *(Aunt Tabitha)*, Ronald Adam *(Controller)*.

British WW II air battle movie which never gets in the air. Instead of seeing exciting dogfights in the skies, we stay down on the ground and see the battles through the eyes and ears of those in the operational control room. Plotted maps, flashing lights, and big boards generate the excitement in this war film. Despite good performances by Hawkins and Denison, it's kind of like watching a telephone switchboard operator. Interesting, but not thrilling.

p, John Gossage, Derek Twist; d, George More O'Ferrall; w, Derek Twist (based on a story by Pelham Groom); ph, Christopher Challis; m, John Woodridge; ed, Daniel Birt.

War **(PR:A MPAA:NR)**

ANGELS OVER BROADWAY**** (1940) 78m COL bw

Douglas Fairbanks, Jr. *(Bill O'Brien)*, Rita Hayworth *(Nina Barona)*, Thomas Mitchell *(Gene Gibbons)*, John Qualen *(Charles Engle)*, George Watts *(Hopper)*, Ralph Theodore *(Dutch Enright)*, Eddie Foster *(Louie Artino)*, Jack Roper *(Eddie Burns)*, Constance Worth *(Sylvia Marbe)*, Richard Bon *(Sylvia's Escort)*, Frank Conlan *(Joe)*, Walter Baldwin *(Rennick)*, Jack Carr *(Tony)*, Al Seymour *(Jack)*, Jimmy Conlin *(Proprietor)*, Ethelreda Leopold *(Cigarette Girl)*, Edward Earle *(Headwaiter)*, Catherine Courtney *(Miss Karpin)*, Al Rhein, Jerry Jerome, Roger Gray, Harry Strang *(Gamblers)*, Bill Lally *(Doorman)*, Tommy Dixon *(Checkroom Boy)*, Fred Sweeney *(Hugo)*, Carmen D'Antonio *(Specialty Dancer)*, Carlton Griffin *(Waiter)*, Stanley Brown *(Master of Ceremonies)*, Patricia Maier *(Girl)*, Lee Phelps *(Police Lieutenant)*, Henry Antrim *(Court Clerk)*, Blanche Payson *(Large Woman)*, Caroline Frasher *(Streetwalker)*, Billy Wayne *(Taxi Driver)*, Walter Sande *(Lunch Wagon Waiter)*, Art Howard *(Night Court Judge)*, Ben Hecht.

One of the most unheralded fine films ever to come out of Hollywood, this was an all-Ben Hecht production, a marvelous and exciting film that annoyed the critics of the day for not pandering to the mindless and humorless. Four characters and a host of supporting players make a single Broadway night come to life with zip and wit. Mitchell, as a glossy-tongued, alcoholic playwright, saves Qualen, who is about to commit suicide after embezzling several thousand dollars. "Dismiss your hearse," Mitchell urges him. "Live, little man, and suffer!" The zany playwright has a scheme that is sure fire, he believes, taking big-time cardsharps in a battle royal, using Qualen's stolen loot to build a fortune. It's quite simple. Since most gamblers play out their winning streak, the trick is to get into a big-time game, then pull out with the winnings long before you're expected to throw in the chips. Enter slick Fairbanks (associate producer of this film), who shills for a top-drawer poker game, and his devoted but equally sharp girl friend Hayworth. Fairbanks spots Qualen as an easy mark and intends to suck him into the game and take him for everything. Nothing, of course, goes according to anyone's plans as Hecht's clever script twists and turns its way to a startling and pleasant conclusion. The performances are captivating, particularly by Mitchell and Fairbanks, and the dialog sparkles with Hecht's poetic irony: "This town's a giant dice game—come on seven!" Because the film featured Rita Hayworth, who had been hand-picked for stardom by Columbia's boss Harry Cohn, Hecht was surprisingly given free reign on this production and went unhampered by interfering producers and studio bureaucrats to create an unpredictable Broadway saga on the screen, one with perilous pace and panache.

p&w, Ben Hecht; d, Hecht, Lee Garmes; ph, Garmes; m, George Antheil; ed, Gene Havlick; md, Morris Stoloff; art d, Lionel Banks; cos, Ray Howell.

Drama **(PR:A MPAA:NR)**

ANGELS WASH THEIR FACES½** (1939) 86m WB bw

Ann Sheridan *(Joy Ryan)*, Ronald Reagan *(Pat Remson)*, Billy Halop *(Billy Shafter)*, Bonita Granville *(Peggy Finnigan)*, Frankie Thomas *(Gabe Ryan)*, Bobby Jordan *(Bernie)*, Bernard Punsley *(Sleepy Arkelian)*, Leo Gorcey *(Lee Finegan)*, Huntz Hall *(Huntz)*, Gabriel Dell *(Luigi)*, Henry O'Neill *(Mr. Remson Sr.)*, Eduardo Ciannelli

(Martino), Berton Churchill *(Mayor Dooley)*, Minor Watson *(Maloney)*, Margaret Hamilton *(Miss Hannaberry)*, Jackie Searle *(Alfred Goonplatz)*, Bernard Nedell *(Kroner)*, Cy Kendall *(Hynos)*, Dick Rich *(Shuffle)*, Grady Sutton *(Gildersleeve)*, Aldrich Bowker *(Turnkey)*, Marjorie Main *(Mrs. Arkelian)*, Robert Strange *(Simpkins)*, Egon Brecher *(Mr. Smith)*, Sibyl Harris *(Mrs. Smith)*, Frank Coughlin Jr. *(Boy)*, Claude Wisberg *(Al)*, Nat Carr, Garry Owen *(Drivers)*, Jack Wagner *(Marsh)*, Harry Strang *(Assistant Turnkey)*, John Ridgely, John Harron, Max Hoffman Jr. *(Reporters)*, Jack Clifford, Tom Wilson, Eddy Chandler *(Cops)*.

Ronald Reagan and the Dead End Kids star in this mediocre sequel to the James Cagney classic ANGELS WITH DIRTY FACES. The lame story concerns Thomas, one of the gang, who gets framed as an arsonist. The Dead End Kids set out to clear their pal's name with the help of District Attorney O'Neil and his son Reagan. Reagan, by the way, happens to be in love with the accused's sister, Sheridan, so he had to work extra hard on the case to get his potential brother-in-law out of the slammer. The gang eventually gathers enough evidence to clear Thomas and Reagan nabs the real firebugs. Most of the modern-day entertainment value in the picture comes from watching the future President of the United States deal with the likes of Hall and Gorcey. (See BOWERY BOYS series, Index.)

d, Ray Enright; w, Michael Fessier, Niven Busch, Robert Buckner (based on an idea by Jonathan Finn); ph, Arthur L. Todd; ed, James Gibbon; md, Leo F. Forbstein.

Drama **(PR:A MPAA:NR)**

ANGELS WITH BROKEN WINGS** (1941) 72m REP bw

Binnie Barnes *(Sybil Barton)*, Gilbert Roland *(Don Pablo Vincente)*, Mary Lee *(Mary Wilson)*, Billy Gilbert *(Billy Wilson)*, Jane Frazee *(Jane Lord)*, Edward Norris *(Steve Wilson)*, Katharine Alexander *(Charlotte Lord)*, Leo Gorcey *(Punchy)*, Lois Ranson *(Lois Wilson)*, Leni Lynn *(Leni Lord)*, Marilyn Hare *(Marilyn Lord)*, Sidney Blackmer *(Guy Barton)*, Tom Kennedy *(Gus)*.

Dull romantic comedy starring Alexander and Blackmer as a couple who try to marry despite the efforts of Alexander's children to block their path to the altar. The kids try to distract their mother with the dashing Norris, who is an Argentine cattle baron. After a dozen hokey incidents, the kids decide that the marriage would be okay after all and they clear the way for the wedding. Can't anybody control their kids in these movies?

p, Albert J. Cohen; d, Bernard Vorhaus; w, George Carleton Brown, Bradford Ropes (based on an idea by Brown); ph, Ernest Miller; ed, Murray Seldeen; m/l, Jule Styne, Eddie Cherkose.

Comedy **(PR:A MPAA:NR)**

ANGELS WITH DIRTY FACES***** (1938) 97m WB bw

James Cagney *(Rocky Sullivan)*, Pat O'Brien *(Jerry Connelly)*, Humphrey Bogart *(James Frazier)*, Ann Sheridan *(Laury Ferguson)*, George Bancroft *(Mac Keefer)*, Billy Halop *(Soapy)*, Bobby Jordan *(Swing)*, Leo Gorcey *(Bim)*, Bernard Punsley *(Hunky)*, Gabriel Dell *(Patsy)*, Huntz Hall *(Crab)*, Frankie Burke *(Rocky as a Boy)*, William Tracy *(Jerry as a Boy)*, Marilyn Knowlden *(Laury as a Girl)*, Joe Downing *(Steve)*, Adrian Morris *(Blackie)*, Oscar O'Shea *(Guard Kennedy)*, Edward Pawley *(Guard Edwards)*, William Pawley *(Bugs the Gunman)*, Charles Sullivan, Theodore Rand *(Gunmen)*, John Hamilton *(Police Captain)*, Earl Dwire *(Priest)*, The St. Brendan's Church Choir *(Themselves)*, William Worthington *(Warden)*, James Farley *(Railroad Yard Watchman)*, Pat O'Malley, Jack C. Smith *(Railroad Guards)*, Roger McGee, Vince Lombardi, Sonny Bupp, A. W. Sweatt *(Boys)*, Chuck Stubb *(Red)*, Eddie Syracuse *(Maggione Boy)*, George Sorel *(Headwaiter)*, Robert Homans *(Policeman)*, Harris Berger *(Basketball Captain)*, Lottie Williams *(Woman)*, Harry Hayden *(Pharmacist)*, Dick Rich, Stevan Darrell, Joe A. Devlin *(Gangsters)*, Donald Kerr, Jack Goodrich, Al Lloyd, Jeffrey Sayre, Charles Marsh, Alexander Lockwood, Earl Gunn, Carlyle Moore *(Reporters)*, Lee Phelps, Jack Mower *(Detectives)*, Belle Mitchell *(Mrs. Maggione)*, William Edmunds *(Italian Storekeeper)*, Charles Wilson *(Buckley the Police Chief)*, Vera Lewis *(Soapy's Mother)*, Eddie Brian *(Newsboy)*, Billy McClain *(Janitor)*, Claude Wisberg *(Hanger-On)*, Frank Hagney, Dick Wessel, John Harron *(Sharpies)*, Wilbur Mack *(Croupier)*, Frank Coghlan, Jr., David Durand *(Boys in Poolroom)*, Mary Gordon *(Mrs. Patrick McGee)*, George Offerman, Jr. *(Older Boy in Poolroom)*, Joe Cunningham *(Managing Editor)*, James Spottswood *(Record Editor)*, John Dilson *(Chronicle Editor)*, Charles Trowbridge *(Norton J. White)*, Tommy Jackson *(Press City Editor)*, Ralph Sanford, Galan Galt *(Policemen at Call-Box)*, Emory Parnell, Wilfred Lucas, Elliott Sullivan *(Police Officers)*, William Crowell *(Whimpering Convict)*, Lane Chandler, Ben Hendricks *(Guards)*, Sidney Bracey, George Taylor, Oscar G. Hendrian, Dan Wolheim, Brian Burke *(Convicts)*, John Marston *(Well Dressed Man)*, Poppy Wilde *(Girl at Gaming Table)*.

One of the most stirring, colorful and thoroughly memorable gangster films ever made, so distinctive that this film, more than any other, symbolized Cagney as the tough guy with a sentimental weakness for women, kids, and most of all the undying friendship with a priest, an alter-ego haunting him from boyhood to the electric chair. Cagney is Rocky Sullivan, a gangster with so many unforgettable mannerisms that imitators pick this role to emulate. We see Cagney as a youth, the boyish Rocky portrayed by doppelganger Frankie Burke, and William Tracy as a youthful O'Brien, growing up in New York's lower East Side, a melting pot for the unschooled immigrant class who struggle to survive in poverty and crime. Burke and Tracy rob a boxcar of pens but yard police chase them, catching Burke because he cannot run as fast as Tracy who clambers over a fence to make good his escape. The code of silence is in effect even with these youngsters of the streets as Burke refuses to identify his friend; he goes to reformatory and graduates to prison after committing one crime after another. Tracy takes the road less traveled, reforming after seeing Burke's fate and going into the ministry. Years pass and we now see Cagney as the adult Rocky, just released from prison. He rents a room in his old neighborhood from Sheridan, whom he used to pick on when they were children. Next he looks up his friend, O'Brien, Father Jerry, who is the caretaker of a broken-down parish and the shepherd of a rough bunch of boys, the Dead End Kids. Then he pays a call on his lawyer, Bogart, who has been keeping $100,000 for him, and meets rackets boss Bancroft. Both promise to cut Cagney in on their lucrative operations, including a one-third ownership of the swanky El Toro Club. When they think he is out of sight, both plot to have Cagney murdered, but he kidnaps Bogart and keeps him in an old hide-out used by the Dead End Kids as a meeting place. Bancroft attempts to have Cagney murdered but a gang member is shot to death in his place, riddled as he stands inside a telephone booth (the same way real-life gangster Vincent "Mad Dog" Coll was shot to death in New York in 1932). Bancroft finally pays off Cagney who keeps Bogart's extortion ledgers, to assure himself of receiving one-third of all the gang's racket money. He sends some of this money to O'Brien so he can build a new gymnasium for his boys but the priest returns the cash, knowing it's dirty money. O'Brien launches a radio and newspaper campaign against Cagney, Bancroft, and Bogart with Cagney's tolerant blessing. Sheridan by this time has become Cagney's girl. One touching scene has them standing in front of the window of Cagney's tenement room looking out to the Manhattan skyline. "See those white lights up there," he tells her. "That's where you belong." She falls in love with him, knowing their love affair is doomed. They go to the El Toro Club where Cagney leaves Sheridan playing roulette, entering Bancroft's office to overhear the boss and Bogart planning to kill his priest friend O'Brien. Bancroft draws his revolver but Cagney is faster, shooting him down and then blasting Bogart as he attempts to escape. (Bogart's cringing, whining hand-quivering appeal for life before the lethal Cagney is almost a duplicate of his cowardly death at Cagney's hands in THE ROARING TWENTIES.) The shootings bring the police, dozens of them, swarming about a warehouse into which Cagney retreats. He trades bullet for bullet with the cops, running from floor to floor, window to window. Machinegun fire blazes everywhere; real bullets were used in this scene (as they had been in 1931's PUBLIC ENEMY when Cagney was almost gunned down). Remembering the close call he had seven years earlier when an expert machinegunner shot up the corner of a building and almost hit the actor, Cagney balked. During the warehouse gun battle, the actor asked director Curtiz to superimpose the actual fire, but the feisty Hungarian refused, insisting on authenticity. Cagney told the director that he would not be in front of the window when the expert fired. He wasn't and his decision saved his life, a hail of live bullets blowing through a window pane where Curtiz wanted Cagney to place his head. During the gun battle, O'Brien and Sheridan break through police lines and plead with the captain to allow O'Brien to go in and bring out his pal Cagney. He enters the tear gas-filled warehouse and persuades his friend to surrender. Once outside Cagney attempts to make a break but is captured. A cop holds up his two guns and says "empty." Cagney gives him a sinister grin and spits: "So's your thick head, copper!" He is quickly tried and sentenced to the electric chair. O'Brien visits him in the death house, asking him to go to the chair as a coward so that the Dead End Kids will no longer admire him. "You're asking me for the only thing I got," he snarls. "I won't do it." But he does go to the chair begging for life until the current cuts him off in midscream, one of the most chilling moments in the history of the film. In a poignant final scene O'Brien goes to the Dead End Kids who ask him if the newspapers are correct, that their hero Cagney died like "a yellow rat." "It's true," he tells them, "now let's go say a prayer for a boy who couldn't run as fast as I could." Some of the most humorous scenes in this film occur between Cagney and the roughneck kids, when he first finds them in his old hideout and buys them food and corrupts them with money, but later supports O'Brien in trying to make them play a civilized game of basketball without fouling opposing team members. The Dead Enders had been playing havoc on the set throughout the film up to this point; they had cornered Bogart, shouting at him: "So you think you're tough, huh!" The boys jumped him and tore his pants away, running off with them. Then they tried to bully Cagney, especially Leo Gorcey who kept ad-libbing his scenes during the basketball game, destroying the other actors' concentration and cues. During a break Cagney slapped Gorcey hard on the forehead with a stiff-arm, startling him, then poked him in the chest. In his autobiography Cagney is quoted as firmly telling Gorcey: "Now listen—we've got work to do and there'll be no more of this goddamn nonsense. We're going to do it the way we're told to do it. Understand?" Gorcey nodded meekly. "You're not dealing with Bogart," one of the other kids told Gorcey. The boys behaved after that, realizing that Bogart seemed tough but Cagney really was tough. The marvelous character played by Cagney had a curious role model. All the exaggerated mannerisms he employed—the uncomfortable twisting of the neck when he enters the church to see O'Brien, as if his tie is too tight, the lifting of his shoulders, the wincing, biting of the lower lip so that the upper teeth show—all came from a New York pimp Cagney had observed in his youth, a man who stood on a corner all day long going into weird gyrations, pitching, shouting out: "Whaddya hear, whaddya say?" (A line used constantly by Cagney in the film.) "I did those gestures maybe six times in the pictures," he also states in his autobiography, "and the impressionists have been doing me doing him ever since." Cagney received an Academy Award nomination for his characterization of Rocky Sullivan but he would wait four more years before getting an Oscar for YANKEE DOODLE DANDY. The theme of two boyhood friends going down different paths, one to respectability, the other to crime, was a popular one in the 1930s, used in other films such as DEAD END and MANHATTAN MELODRAMA. (See BOWERY BOYS series, Index.)

p, Sam Bischoff; d, Michael Curtiz; w, John Wexley, Warren Duff (based on a story by Rowland Brown); ph, Sol Polito; m, Max Steiner; ed, Owen Marks; art d, Robert Haas.

Crime **Cas.** **(PR:C MPAA:NR)**

ANGI VERA*** (1980, Hung.) 96m New Yorker c

Veronika Papp *(Vera Angi)*, Erzsi Paszior *(Anna Trajan)*, Eva Szabo *(Maria Muskat)*, Tamas Dunai *(Istvan Andre)*, Laszlo Halasz *(Comrade Sas)*, Laszlo Horvath *(Josef Neubauer)*.

Well produced political drama profiling Papp as a young girl attempting to succeed in the dictatorial Stalinist regime of 1948 with powerful scenes that expose the Commu- nist repression of the country, an amazing document in that it indicts the very system which funded this film. (In Hungarian; English subtitles.)

d&w, Pal Gabor (based on the novel by Endre Veszi); ph, Lajos Koltai; m, Gyorgy Selmeczi; ed, Eva Karmento; art d, Andras Gyorky; cos, Eva Zs.

Drama **(PR:C MPAA:NR)**

ANGRY BREED, THE* (1969) 89m Commonwealth United c

Jan Sterling *(Gloria Patton)*, James MacArthur *(Deek Stacey)*, William Windom *(Vance Patton)*, Jan Murray *(Mori Thompson)*, Murray McLeod *(Johnny Taylor)*,

Lori Martin *(Diane Patton)*, Melody Patterson *(April Wilde)*, Karen Malouf *(Jade)*, Suzi Kaye *(Ginny Morris)*.

Incredibly incoherent story of a returned Viet Nam vet, McLeod, who hangs around Hollywood trying to sell a screenplay. While living on Malibu beach, he rescues the daughter of big-shot movie producer Windom from the dirty deeds of a band of bikers. Windom thanks the vet for saving his daughter, but tells him to stay away from her, and that his script is lousy. Now the going gets really weird. The bikers return, and their leader, MacArthur, happens to be an actor who is interested in playing the lead in our hero's script. Then somebody breaks out the LSD, rock music, and bizarre costumes, and the film goes into an extended hallucinatory party scene. In addition, look for Jan Murray (Jan Murray?!) as a homosexual talent scout.

p&d, David Commons.

Drama **(PR:O MPAA:NR)**

ANGRY HILLS, THE** (1959, Brit) 105m MGM bw

Robert Mitchum *(Michael Morrison)*, Elisabeth Mueller *(Lisa)*, Stanley Baker *(Konrad Heisler)*, Gia Scala *(Eleftheria)*, Theodore Bikel *(Tassos)*, Sebastian Cabot *(Chesney)*, Peter Illing *(Leonidas)*, Leslie Phillips *(Ray Taylor)*, Donald Wolfit *(Dr. Stergiou)*, Marius Goring *(Comdr. Oberg)*, Jackie Lane *(Maria)*, Kieron Moore *(Andreas)*, George Pastell *(Papa Panos)*, Patrick Jordan *(Bluey)*, Marita Constaniou *(Kleopatra)*, Stanley Van Beers *(Tavern Proprietor)*, Alec Mango *(Papa Philibos)*.

Somewhat confusing war picture set during the Nazi occupation of the Balkans. Mitchum stars as a cynical American newspaper reporter who agrees to deliver the names of the Greek resistance fighters to British intelligence in London for a fee of $20,000. The Nazis and their confederates find out and chase Mitchum across Greece for the information. Not even Robert Aldrich's usually tight direction could save this wobbly script.

p, Raymond Stross; d, Robert Aldrich; w, A. I. Bezzerides (based on the novel by Leon Uris); ph, Stephan Dade (CinemaScope); m, Richard Bennet; ed, Peter Tanner.

War/Espionage **(PR:A MPAA:NR)**

ANGRY ISLAND** 1/2 (1960, Jap.) 90m Bentley c (KAJIKKO)

Kazuo Suzuki *(Tetsu Nakaya)*, Shigeo Tezuka *(Teizo Terada)*, Teruo Shibata *(Mitsuo Ito)*, Yasuo Tsuchiya *(Kotaro)*, Shigeaki Goto *(Taichi)*, Yukio Akiyama *(Susumu)*, Kiyoshi Komiyama *(Tadasi)*, Sankichi Ishihara *(Kazuo)*, Gen Sato *(Naoji)*, Terumi Futagi *(Kinuko)*, Mosao Oda *(Yoshikawa)*, Saburo Ukida *(Izo)*.

Beautifully photographed tale based on a true incident in the Sea of Japan in 1931, when it was discovered that young boys were being taken from Japanese reformatories and sold as slaves to fishermen, who made them row their boats. The boys were treated cruelly by the fishermen, who starved and beat them. Produced by Masafumi Soga who also produced Akira Kurosawa's classic RASHOMON.

p, Masafumi Soga; d, Seiji Nisamatau; w, Yoko Mizuki (based on her story "The Rowers"); ph, Selichi Kizuka (Eastmancolor); m, Yasushi Akatagawa.

Drama **(PR:A MPAA:NR)**

ANGRY MAN, THE** (1979 Fr./Can.) 105m UA c (L'HOMME EN COLERE)

Lino Ventura *(Romain)*, Angie Dickinson *(Karen)*, Laurent Malet *(Julien)*, Hollis McLaren *(Nancy)*, Donald Pleasence *(Pumpelmayer)*, Chris Wiggins *(MacKenzie)*.

Pedestrian story of a French widower, Ventura, who travels to Canada to identify the body of his son, who was gunned down in a shootout with police. It turns out the dead boy is not his son, so the father vows to go into the Canadian underworld and bring back his boy. The two have had a strained relationship ever since the death of the boy's mother in a forest fire. The boy had always blamed his father for her death and finally fled to Canada. Ventura enlists the aid of an ex-con waitress, Dickinson, to help him in his search. Not only are Ventura and Dickinson looking for the boy, but the Under- world is also after him because the kid plans to flee to California with some of the mob's money. Finally all forces clash at the US/Canada border. Lackluster script helped by nice locations and good performances.

p, Alexandre Mnouchkine; d, Claude Pinoteau; w, Jean-Claude Carriere, Pinoteau, Charles Israel; ph, Jean Boffety (Eastmancolor); m, Claude Bolling; ed, Marie-Josee Yoyotte; art d, Earl Preston.

Crime/Drama **(PR:C MPAA:NR)**

ANGRY RED PLANET, THE* (1959) 83m AIP c

Gerald Mohr *(O'Banion)*, Nora Hayden *(Iris Ryan)*, Les Tremayne *(Prof. Gettell)*, Jack Kruschen *(Sgt. Jacobs)*, Paul Hahn *(Gen. Treegar)*, J. Edward McKinley *(Prof. Weiner)*, Tom Daly *(Dr. Gordon)*, Edward Innes *(Gen. Prescott)*.

Dumb, uninteresting science-fiction film with the planet Mars being the target for space explorers. The group lands on the "angry red planet," battles some unfriendly Martian plants, gets back in their ship, and returns to Earth. Filmed with a gimmick called "Cinemagic," which basically made everything look like a negative with pinkish tonality. Amazing.

p, Sid Pink, Norman Maurer; d, Ib Melchior; w, Melchior, Pink (based on a story by Pink); ph, Stanley Cortez (Eastmancolor); m, Paul Dunlap; ed, Ivan J. Hoffman.

Science Fiction **(PR:A MPAA:NR)**

ANGRY SILENCE, THE** 1/2 (1960, Brit.) 95m Beaver/BL bw

Richard Attenborough *(Tom Curtis)*, Pier Angeli *(Anna Curtis)*, Michael Craig *(Joe Wallace)*, Bernard Lee *(Bert Connolly)*, Alfred Burke *(Travers)*, Geoffrey Keen *(Davis)*, Laurence Naismith *(Martindale)*, Russell Napier *(Sid Thompson)*, Penelope Horner *(Pat)*, Brian Bedford *(Eddie Barrett)*, Brian Murray *(Gladys)*, Norman Bird *(Roberts)*, Beckett Bould *(Billy Armstrong)*, Oliver Reed *(Mick)*, Edna Petrie *(Harpy)*, Lloyd Pearson *(Howarth)*, Norman Shelley *(Seagrave)*, Daniel Farson *(Himself)*, Alan Whicker *(Himself)*.

Moody industry drama has Attenborough (who headed this production company) selected by insidious union organizer Burke to lead the revolt in his factory. In a confused, groping performance, Attenborough attempts to organize fellow workers, bringing about a wildcat strike and misery to his co-laborers for which he is vilified, then beaten up and ostracized while his wife, Angeli, and family suffer. Attenborough's intense performance does not clarify this film's murky motivation. It's hard to tell from the script and direction if Attenborough is trying to indict unions or capitalism, perhaps a little of both, the message being somewhere right of man's intolerance of man's ignorance.

p, Richard Attenborough, Bryan Forbes; d, Guy Green; w, Forbes (based on a story by Michael Craig, Richard Gregson); ph, Arthur Ibbetson; m, Malcolm Arnold; ed, Anthony Harvey.

Drama **(PR:C MPAA:NR)**

ANIMAL CRACKERS*** (1930) 97m PAR bw

Groucho Marx *(Capt. Jeffrey Spaulding)*, Harpo Marx *(The Professor)*, Chico Marx *(Signor Emanuel Raveld)*, Zeppo Marx *(Horatio Jamison)*, Lillian Roth *(Arabella Rittenhouse)*, Margaret Dumont *(Mrs. Rittenhouse)*, Louis Sorin *(Roscoe Chandler)*, Hal Thompson *(John Parker)*, Margaret Irving *(Mrs. Whitehead)*, Kathryn Reece *(Grace Carpenter)*, Richard Greig *(Hives)*, Edward Metcalf *(Hennessey)*.

Zany comedy featuring the zaniest film comics ever opens with a party in Dumont's posh mansion where a priceless oil painting is unveiled. The rest of the story—if you can call it that—deals with the painting's theft and recovery. Even though the script was written tightly, the movie appears to be one big ad-lib in the style of COCONUTS, the first smash film by the Marx boys. Groucho's wise-guy delivery is fast-paced as usual, but even he is repelled at times by his own kitsch and forced bon mots, turning at one point to the camera to grimace and half-apologize, saying: "Well, *all* the jokes can't be good! You've got to expect that once in a while." (He does sing the memorable "Hooray For Captain Spaulding.") Harpo is in usual delightful and daffy character, handing his leg to his brothers, blowing bubbles that turn to smoke, letting loose a shower of silverware from his endless coat pockets (all gags repeated from COCONUTS). Chico is again the antagonist and hurler of straight lines who gets a few licks in on brother Groucho and then has his ear pulled so hard for it that he is tossed on a table top. Not as amusing as HORSEFEATHERS or DUCK SOUP, this film nevertheless breaks more than a few funny bones on a reckless story dominated by the human cyclones who made the vehicle a stage hit before bringing it to the screen. (As a play, ANIMAL CRACKERS ran for three years around the country before Paramount signed up its maniacal stars.) Groucho's periodic trips to the camera to carp about the story and his brothers' antics is an inside parody of the techniques then being used in Eugene O'Neill's dramatic hit "Strange Interlude." There are many more inside jokes employed, so inside that the brothers never suggest their meanings to the viewer, who should be grateful. (See MARX BROTHERS series, Index.)

d, Victor Heerman; w, Morris Ryskind (based on the musical play by Ryskind and George S. Kaufman); ph, George Foley; m/l, Bert Kalmar, Harry Ruby.

Comedy **Cas.** **(PR:AAA MPAA:NR)**

ANIMAL FARM** (1955, Brit.) 75m RKO c

Voice of all animals, Maurice Denham; Narrator, Gordon Heath.

George Orwell's classic novel animated by the British. Story concerns a barnyard revolution led by a pig, Napoleon, who perverts the cause and becomes just as bad as the regime they overthrew. The animation is okay, but the allegorical nature of the subject matter is better served in print.

p&d, John Halas, Joy Batchelor; w, Halas, Batchelor, Lothar Wolff, Borden Mace, Philip Stapp, (based on the fable by George Orwell) ph, S. J. Griffiths (Technicolor); m, Matyas Seiber.

Animation/Fable **Cas.** **(PR:A MPAA:NR)**

ANIMAL HOUSE (SEE: NATIONAL LAMPOON'S ANIMAL HOUSE, 1978)

ANIMAL KINGDOM, THE***
(1932) 90m RKO bw (GB: THE WOMAN IN HIS HOUSE)

Ann Harding *(Daisy Sage)*, Leslie Howard *(Tom Collier)*, Myrna Loy *(Cecilia Henry)*, Neil Hamilton *(Owen)*, William Gargan *(Regan)*, Henry Stephenson *(Rufus Collier)*, Ilka Chase *(Grace)*, Leni Stengel *(Franc)*, Donald Dillaway *(Joe)*.

Well-acted romantic vehicle for Howard which will appeal to the more intellectual and sophisticated. He is a rich publisher who leaves his artist-mistress Harding to marry socially active Loy, only to discover that the security of married life does not exist, that his wife is a Lorelei who is encouraging an affair with another man, Hamilton. In fact Loy acts more like a free-wheeling mistress than a wife and Harding is more loyal and loving like a wife than a mistress. The age-old love triangle is freshly presented with Howard's emotions being tugged by both women. His colorful butler, Gargan, doesn't help matters; he's an ex-fighter who makes himself at home with guests, pouring himself drinks and oafishly acting as if on the same peer level, a wonderful supporting part played to the hilt by this veteran character actor. Howard finally sees the errors of his ways, the shallowness of Loy and the completeness of Harding. Putting on his hat, he tells Loy: "I'm going back to my wife," meaning his mistress, and departs. This was a faithful adaptation of the very successful stage play by Philip Barry, produced by David O. Selznick, always a stickler for authenticity and maintaining the integrity of the original story as he was later to prove with inexhaustible fury with GONE WITH THE WIND. At first Selznick did not want Loy playing Howard's wife (although he later said he insisted that she play the part at the start). His first choice was the cool blonde, Karen Morley, who had played the trampy mistress to Osgood Perkins in SCARFACE, but after he saw Loy's screen test for the part (she was then not considered star material), Selznick was convinced that she would be the perfect wifely vixen. Of course, this marvelous actress vindicated Selznick's final decision by giving a masterful performance of the scheming flirt, but it was Howard who carried the film with his usual sensitive portrayal of the gentleman most men wished to be.

p, David O. Selznick; d, Edward H. Griffith; w, Horace Jackson (based on the play by Philip Barry); ph, George Folsey; ed, Daniel Mandell.

Drama **(PR:A MPAA:NR)**

ANIMALS, THE* 1/2 (1971) 86m Levitt-Pickman/XYZ c

Henry Silva *(Chatto)*, Keenan Wynn *(Pudge Elliot)*, Michele Carey *(Alice McAndrew)*, John Anderson *(Sheriff Allan Pierce)*, Joseph Turkel *(Peyote)*, Pepper

Martin (Jamie), Bobby Hall (Cat Norman), Peter Hellmann (Karl), William Bryant (Sheriff Martin Lord), Peggy Stewart (Mrs. Emily Perkins).

Somewhat vile western starring Carey as a schoolteacher who is pulled off a stagecoach and gang-raped by Wynn and his outlaw gang. A helpful Apache, Silva, nurses the woman back to health and then teaches her how to shoot. The pair then go out in search of the rapists, whereupon Carey promptly castrates Wynn and goes insane. A confused Sheriff kills Silva by mistake, thinking he was the guilty party. Bloody revenge tale is weakened by a lame central performance by Carey. Silva is a standout as the Apache. A similar film released the same year, HANNIE CAULDER, with Raquel Welch, handles the same material with a little more sensitivity.

p, Richard Bakalyan; d, Ron Joy; w, Hy Mizrahi; ph, Keith Smith (Techniscope, Technicolor); m/l, Rupert Holmes, Danny Jordan.

Western   (PR:O   MPAA:R)

ANITA GARIBALDI**

(1954, Ital.) 78m A.P.G.F. Prod./I.F.E. bw (CAMICIE ROSSE)

Anna Magnani (Anita Garibaldi), Raf Vallone (Giuseppe Garibaldi), Alain Cuny (Bueno), Jacques Sernas (Gentile), Carlo Ninchi (Ciceruacchio), Gino Leurini (Andrea), Serge Reggiani (Lantini), Michel Auclair (A Volunteer).

Labored war film honoring Italy's fiery military adventurer Garibaldi which, through smoke and lackluster clash of arms, recounts the soldier's Risorgimento campaigns, showing Vallone stoic on horseback and his wife, Magnani, on a bigger horse, urging and ordering their men in and out of battle. A tiresome film with no character development whatsoever; even the battle scenes are confusing and poorly organized. The story line is one of simple conquest with the blatant adage about a stronger woman behind a strong man. Not that strong in that Magnani, a fine actress wasted in a thankless role, succumbs during a battle in her husband's arms while mouthing a ridiculous patriotic monolog.

d, Goffredo Alessandrini, Francesco Rosi; w, E. Biagi, R. Renzi, S. Bolchi.

War   (PR:C   MPAA:NR)

ANN CARVER'S PROFESSION*

(1933) 71m COL bw

Fay Wray (Ann Carver), Gene Raymond (Bill Graham), Claire Dodd (Carole Rodgers), Arthur Pierson (Ken), Claude Gillingwater (Judge Bingham), Frank Albertson (Jim Thompson), Frank Conroy (Baker), Jessie Ralph, Robert Barrat, Edward Keane, Diana Bori.

Overwrought independent woman tale featuring Wray (fresh from her battle with KING KONG) as a female super-lawyer. She handles civil, corporate, and criminal law equally well. She intimidates experienced judges with her impressive knowledge of legalese. Her poor husband, a fumbling architect, feels completely impotent compared to his wife. He quits his nowhere job and becomes a nightclub singer. At his newfound place of employment, he gets involved with a shady lady who drinks herself to death and he is accused of her murder. Guess who defends the poor sot. That's right, his wife the super-lawyer! The final, melodramatic summation of the case to the jury by Wray got unintentional laughs in 1933.

d, Eddie Buzzell; w, Robert Riskin; ph, Teddy Tetzlaff; ed, Maurice Wright.

Drama   (PR:A   MPAA:NR)

ANN VICKERS*1/2

(1933) 73m RKO bw

Irene Dunne (Ann Vickers), Walter Huston (Barney Dolphin), Conrad Nagel (Lindsay), Bruce Cabot (Resnick), Edna May Oliver (Malvina Wormsor), Sam Hardy (Russell Spaulding), Mitchell Lewis (Capt. Waldo), Helen Eby-Rock (Kitty Cignac), Gertrude Michael (Mona Dolphin), J. Carroll Naish (Dr. Sorell), Sarah Padden (Lil), Reginald Barlow (Chaplain), Rafaella Ottiano (Feldermus), Irving Bacon (Waiter), Edwin Maxwell (Defense Attorney), Jane Darwell (Mrs. Gates), Arthur Hoyt (Mr. Penny).

Empty adaptation of Sinclair Lewis' novel starring Dunne as a social worker striving to improve conditions in the nation's prisons and other civil liberties challenges. The producers made a big mistake when they tried to cram Lewis' novel into a 75-minute running time, and build a romance between Huston and Dunne.

d, John Cromwell; w, Jane Murfin (based on Sinclair Lewis' novel); ph, David Abel, Edward Cronjager; ed, George Nicholls, Jr.; md, Max Steiner.

Drama   **Cas.**   (PR:A   MPAA:NR)

ANNA**1/2

(1951, Ital.) 110m Ponti-DeLaurentiis/I.F.E. bw

Silvana Mangano (Anna), Gaby Morlay (Mother Superior), Raf Vallone (Andrea), Jacques Dumesnil (Professor Ferri), Vittorio Gassman (Vittorio), Patrizia Mangano (Luisa), Natascia Mangano (Lucia), Dina Romano (Sister Virginia), Rosita Pisano (Sister Carmela), Bianca Doria (A Mother), Rocco D'Assunta (A Father), Lilla Rocco (A Nurse), Dina Perbellini (A Patient), Emilio Petacci (The Colonel), Tina Lattanzi (Mother of Andrea), Mariemma Bardi (A Nurse), Piero Lulli (Dr. Manzi).

Sizzling Mangano, whose voluptuous body filled American screens in BITTER RICE to the edification of males everywhere here plays a novitiate nun working in a hospital. Her past catches up with her when her former lover, Vallone, is wheeled in, and shot by Gassman, another of her lovers, both having once fought for her favors. While tending the gentle Vallone, Mangano relives in flashback her experiences with both men, first Gassman, a brutish, carnal truckdriver with an insatiable sex drive who meets her while she is performing sexy, snaky dances in a smoky bistro and goes on to mistreat her as much or more than he did in BITTER RICE, then Vallone, the good man with the gentle touch. Through a series of sordid adventures, the viewer is finally brought back to the present and Mangano's spiritual resolve to become a full-fledged nun. (With her background it's hard to imagine a great many choices.) Solid acting by Gassman and Vallone and a steaming performance by Mangano (perhaps the most sensuous woman ever to grace Italian cinema) make for some spellbinding moments, even though dubbed.

p, Carlo Ponti, Dino De Laurentiis; d, Alberto Lattuada, Giuseppe Berto, Dino Risi; w, Ivo Perilli, Franco Brusati, Rodolfo Sonego; ph, Otello Marelli; m, Nino Rota; ed, Gabriele Varriale.

Drama   (PR:C-O   MPAA:NR)

ANNA**1/2

(1981,Fr./Hung.) 90m GAU c (UNE MERE, UNE FILLE)

Marie-Jose Nat (Anna), Jan Novicki (Janos), Marie Lebee (Marie), Teri Tordai (Madam Aubier), Dunai Tamas (M. Aubier), Lazlo Galffy (Anna's Son).

More melodrama from Hungarian director Marta Meszaros (THE HERITAGE 1980). Nat plays a Hungarian clothes designer who sees a young French tourist and becomes convinced that it is her long-lost daughter. She pursues the young woman and even arranges a meeting with her family, who are visiting Hungary on holiday. The girl's French mother balks at answering Nat's prying personal questions and the family goes back to France. Nat follows and learns that the daughter is ill and has been hospitalized. The girl needs a kidney transplant and her French mother admits that indeed, the child was adopted. Since her adopted mother's kidneys won't match, Nat volunteers one of her own to save her daughter's life. Good direction helps the otherwise overly dramatic situation. Two entirely silent scenes are standouts.

p, Evelyn July; d, Marta Meszaros; w, Meszaros, Gyula Hernadi; ph, Tamas Andor (Eastmancolor); ed, Agnes Hranitsky; art d, Eva Martin; m, Zsolt Dome.

Drama   (PR:A   MPAA:NR)

ANNA AND THE KING OF SIAM****

(1946) 128m FOX bw

Irene Dunne (Anna), Rex Harrison (The King), Linda Darnell (Tuptin), Lee J. Cobb (Kralahome), Gale Sondergaard (Lady Thiang), Mikhail Rasumny (Alak), Dennis Hoey (Sir Edward), Tito Renaldo (Prince, as a Man), Richard Lyon (Louis Owens), William Edmunds (Monshee), John Abbott (Phya Phrom), Leonard Strong (Interpreter), Mickey Roth (Prince as a Boy), Connie Leon (Beebe), Diane von den Ecker (Princess Fa-Ying), Si-Lan Chen (Dance Director), Marjorie Eaton (Miss MacFarlane), Helena Grant (Mrs. Cartwright), Stanley Mann (Mr. Cartwright), Addison Richards (Capt. Orton), Neyle Morrow (Phra Palat), Julian Rivero (Government Clerk), Chet Voravan (Siamese Guard), Dorothy Chung, Jean Wong (Amazon Guards).

Entertaining tale of an English tutor who travels to Siam in 1862 with her young son, hired to educate the harem and 67 children of the rather savage king, who covets Western culture but insists upon maintaining Siam's customs and some particularly barbaric traditions. The story is drawn from the real life of 33-year-old Mrs. Anna Leonowens, who actually traveled to Siam, and is brilliantly played by Dunne who is repelled by Harrison, the king (in his first American film), and his inexplicable Eastern ways. She also meets and befriends the king's first wife, Sondergaard, long relegated to the back rooms of the imperial palace, and pretty Darnell, a young addition to the harem who falls in love with another and is tragically executed by the king for being unfaithful, a kingly edict that sours Dunne on Harrison whom she has grown to like. All of the players are excellent in their roles, including supporting actor Cobb, as the king's chief minister. Well lighted and lensed, director Cromwell keeps the story frisky and less sentimental than the musical remake, THE KING AND I. Dunne is the perfect British governess-tutor and Harrison is simply majestic as the king who gropes toward sensitivity and Western reason, battling his authoritarian instincts all the way. Richly costumed and boasting lavish sets, it's a wonder this production was not done in color.

p, Louis D. Lighton; d, John Cromwell; w, Talbot Jennings, Sally Benson (based on the book by Margaret Landon); ph, Arthur Miller; m, Bernard Wheeler, William Darling; set d, Thomas Little, Frank E. Hughes; spec eff, Fred Sersen.

Drama   (PR:A   MPAA:NR)

ANNA CHRISTIE***1/2

(1930) 86m MGM bw

Greta Garbo (Anna Christie), Charles Bickford (Matt Burke), George F. Marion (Chris Christopherson), Marie Dressler (Marthy Owen), James T. Mack (Johnny the Harp), Lee Phelps (Larry).

Stagey, somewhat preciously presented O'Neill classic with primitive sound techniques are all overcome by magnificent performances from Garbo, Dressler and Bickford. The great silent sphinx of the movies first talked in this film (advertised with enormous letters "GARBO TALKS!") as she plays the deserted offspring of a sailor father who leaves her with a mean-streaked farm family before she goes off to walk the streets as a common prostitute. Giving up the profession, Garbo finds her father, Marion, living on a barge as broken down as his mistress, Dressler. She moves in with them and during a storm she and her father save another sailor, Bickford, from drowning. Bickford falls in love with her and proposes. She startles him and her father in emotional revenge for past wrongs done to her by angrily blurting out her background as a whore. Sickened, Bickford abandons her but finds that he can't live without her, realizing that he, too, has committed errors. He returns, again asking her to marry him. She agrees to marry the forceful Irishman for a slightly glimmering closeout. The public fascination with the mysterious Garbo heightened this film's popularity, holding captive critics and viewers alike from her first opening lines in a bar when ordering a waiter in husky tones to gimme a whiskey, ginger ale on the side—and don't be stingy, baby!" Dressler, as the ancient prostitute commiserating with Garbo throughout the film, mugs fiercely for the camera but in one scene when the tipsy harridan pours out her heart to Garbo she is awesome in her touching pathos and rich humanity. Much of the film's creakiness is due to the crude and cumbersome sound equipment used when Hollywood was lumbering from the silent era into the age of the talkies. This equipment hampered Clarence Brown's direction in that he was restrained from using cameras freely, having to settle for set shots where the players were compelled to walk into the framed scene. In some instances the cameras were actually bolted to the floor of the sound stage to prevent movement and unnecessary noise. Brown, a superb silent film director who had studied from 1915 to 1920 under Maurice Tourneur, was known for pictorial excellence and sensitivity in handling romance films. Once at MGM Brown became famous as one of the few directors who could manage the temperamental Garbo, directing her in two distinguished movies, FLESH AND THE DEVIL and A WOMAN OF AFFAIRS. He would go on to shepherd her most important talkies beyond ANNA CHRISTIE, including ROMANCE, INSPIRATION, ANNA KARENINA, and CONQUEST. Brown's experience with talkies was limited before he took on ANNA CHRISTIE, having directed the all-talkie NAVY BLUES and WONDER OF WOMEN, a part-talkie. Garbo's acting in ANNA CHRISTIE sometimes appears as exaggerated as the desperate sound techniques where dialog seems to click on and off as if some unsure craftsman were flicking a switch. She clutches the breast a bit too frantically and flails arms too frenetically, gestures undoubtedly held over from the silent days when fierce posturing was the norm, but her haunting, lovely face, her almost baritone voice, resolute timing, and interaction with fellow players makes this a stellar performance. The great actress was dissatisfied with her role but gave endless kudos to Dressler. She remade the film in German with Jacques Feyder who had directed THE KISS, her last silent movie, and she later stated that she preferred this version. (The O'Neill drama was first filmed in 1923 with Blanche Sweet and William Russell.)

d, Clarence Brown; w, Frances Marion (based on the play by Eugene O'Neill); ph, William Daniels; ed, Hugh Wynn; art d, Cedric Gibbons; cos, Adrian.

Drama **Cas.** **(PR:C MPAA:NR)**

ANNA CROSS, THE** (1954, USSR) 85m Artinko/Gorky c

Anna Larlonova *(Anna)*, A. Sashin-Nikolsky *(Pytor Leontievich, her father)*, Mikhail Zharov *(Modest Alexseyvich)*, A. Vertinsky *(Prince)*, N. Belevtzeva *(Princess)*, I. Murzayeva *(Mavra Grigorievna)*.

Unusual approach to the usual Bolshevik propaganda typical of Russian cinema. This film features the decadent pre-revolutionary Russian upper-class in their full glory, with large opulent dress balls as opposed to the normal Soviet hard-working-peasants-vs.-the-Cossacks films that they usually cranked out to glorify the revolution. Story concerns a beautiful young debutante who is forced to marry an old government official for the family's financial security. Eventually she dumps the old creep for a young lover. Soon after, as she struts down the streets with her young stud, her brother and father are evicted from their home (presumably by the bitter old government official) and wander the snow-covered streets begging the girl to go back to her husband.

d&w, I. Annensky (based on a story by Anton Chekhov); ph, G. Reisgoff (Sovcolor); m. L. Schwartz.

Drama **(PR:A MPAA:NR)**

ANNA KARENINA**** (1935) 85m MGM bw

Greta Garbo *(Anna Karenina)*, Fredric March *(Vronsky)*, Freddie Bartholomew *(Sergei)*, Maureen O'Sullivan *(Kitty)*, May Robson *(Countess Vronsky)*, Basil Rathbone *(Karenin)*, Reginald Owen *(Stiva)*, Reginald Denny *(Yashvin)*, Phoebe Foster *(Dolly)*, Gyles Isham *(Levin)*, Buster Phelps *(Grisha)*, Ella Ethridge *(Anna's Maid)*, Joan Marsh *(Lili)*, Sidney Bracey *(Valet)*, Cora Sue Collins *(Tania)*, Joe E. Tozer *(Butler)*, Guy D'Ennery *(Tutor)*, Harry Allen *(Cord)*, Mary Forbes *(Princess Sorokino)*, Ethel Griffies *(Mme. Karatasoff)*, Harry Beresford *(Matve)*.

A remake of the silent movie LOVE with John Gilbert, this splendid, moody Garbo vehicle tells the tragic Tolstoy tale with great sensitivity under Brown's direction. Garbo as the immortal Anna of 19th-century Russia, is the pampered wife of Rathbone, a rich government leader. When hearing that her brother, Owen, is womanizing and ruining his marriage she travels to his side, pleading reform. She meets and falls in love with March, a dashing officer, whom she continues to see after returning home. Asking Rathbone for a divorce, she is told that if she makes such an unheard-of move, she will be deprived of her son. Abandoning her family, the love-consumed woman runs off with March. He resigns his commission and they at first live happily together. But he grows restless, longing for his carefree army days, and the star-crossed lovers finally argue and separate. Garbo rushes to the train station when learning that March is leaving for another post. Here she see him saying goodbye to another woman and realizes that all that mattered in her life is no more. Dramatically she resigns herself to fate and steps in the path of an oncoming train. Director Brown played the entire story to his beloved actress, bathing Garbo in soft lighting that seems to caress her classic features. No longer adorned in the extravagant costumes attending her silent films (which one wag described as "a theatrical dressmaker's advertisement"), her gowns are luxurious but subdued in keeping with her understated acting style. Garbo is a sad woman here; only in her scenes with the electric March does she bubble with carefree happiness, registering that unique throaty laughter curled around a thick Swedish accent. She is unforgettable as the love-hungry Anna, whose desires are crushed by selfish and unfeeling men. Producer Selznick mounted a meticulous, almost rigidly faithful adaptation with sumptuous and authentic sets and scenes, although he had great difficulty in getting March to make the film. The 37-year-old actor was fed up with costume epics and had just made a costumer, WE LIVE AGAIN (remade from RESURRECTION). He told Selznick that he wanted modern roles and would only do ANNA KARENINA if ordered to by his bosses. He was so ordered and did it with consummate skill. At first Selznick tried to talk Garbo out of doing the Russian classic, asking her to consider doing another film, DARK VICTORY, later done by Bette Davis at Warner Brothers. George Cukor was also Selznick's first choice as director but Garbo opted for her favorite, Clarence Brown (and William Daniels who was known as "Garbo's camerman"; both Brown and Daniels, in deference to the sensitive actress, always insisted that all of the actress' scenes be shot on closed sets with only vital crew members present). What Garbo wanted she got. Here it was another masterful film

p, David O. Selznick; d, Clarence Brown; w, Clemence Dane, Salka Viertel, S. N. Behrman (based on the novel by Count Leo Tolstoy); ph, William Daniels; m, Herbert Stothart; ed, Robert J. Kearn; ch, Marguerite Wallmann, Chester Hale.

Drama **Cas.** **(PR:A MPAA:NR)**

ANNA KARENINA*** (1948, Brit.) 139m LFP-Korda/BL

Vivien Leigh *(Anna Karenina)*, Ralph Richardson *(Alexei Karenin)*, Kieron Moore *(Count Vronsky)*, Sally Ann Howes *(Kitty Scherbatsky)*, Niall MacGinnis *(Levin)*, Martita Hunt *(Princess Betty Tversky)*, Marie Lohr *(Princess Scherbatsky)*, Michael Gough *(Nicholai)*, Hugh Dempster *(Stefan Oblonsky)*, Mary Kerridge *(Dolly Oblonsky)*, Heather Thatcher *(Countess Lydia Ivanova)*, Helen Haye *(Countess Vronsky)*, Austin Trevor *(Col. Vronsky)*, Ruby Miller *(Countess Meskov)*, John Longden *(General Serpuhousky)*, Leslie Bradley *(Korsunsky)*, Michael Medwin *(Doctor)*, Jeremy Spenser *(Giuseppe)*, Gino Cervi *(Enrico)*, Frank Tickle *(Prince Scherbatsky)*, Mary Martlew *(Princess Nathalia)*, Ann South *(Princess Sorokina)*, Guy Verney *(Prince Makhotin)*, Beckett Bould *(Matvey)*, Judith Nelmes *(Miss Hull)*, Valentina Murch *(Annushka)*, Theresa Giehse *(Marietta)*, John Salew *(Lawyer)*, Patrick Skipwith *(Sergei)*.

This remake of the Garbo classic has different values and approaches that enhance Vivien Leigh's magnetic performance of the ill-starred Anna who leaves stuffy bureaucrat of a husband, Richardson, for an adventurous army officer, Moore, only to be discarded and sent to suicide in front of an onrushing train when husband, child and lover are lost to her. Unlike the 1935 version, the psychological elements of this tragedy are underscored and registered with powerful impact through Leigh who is more victim than Garbo was catalyst, her raw emotions distorting and finally destroying a once-orderly, though predictably dull, life. Leigh is positively riveting and Richardson as the priggish, pompous government official is properly vengeful and vexing. Only Moore, as the self-centered lover, is a letdown, rendering a rather wooden performance. Korda's production is spectacular with a great supporting cast, countless extras, and authentic 19th-century sets that are mouth-openers. Duvivier's direction is moody, quick-paced, and sometimes frightening, with angles and cuts that sequentially distort the image of a woman slipping deeper and deeper into her own destruction.

p, Alexander Korda; d, Julien Duvivier; w, Jean Anouilh, Guy Morgan, Duvivier (based on the novel by Count Leo Tolstoy); ph, Henri Alekana, Robert Walker; m, Constant Lambert; ed, Russell Lloyd; prod d, Andre Andrejew; cos, Cecil Beaton; spec eff, W. Percy Day.

Drama **(PR:A MPAA:NR)**

ANNA LUCASTA** (1949) 86m COL bw

Paulette Goddard *(Anna Lucasta)*, William Bishop *(Rudolf Strobel)*, Oscar Homolka *(Joe Lucasta)*, John Ireland *(Danny Johnson)*, Broderick Crawford *(Frank)*, Will Geer *(Noah)*, Gale Page *(Katie)*, Mary Wickes *(Stella)*, Whit Bissell *(Stanley)*, Lisa Golm *(Theresa)*, James Brown *(Buster)*, Dennie Moore *(Blanche)*, Anthony Caruso *(Eddie)*.

All-white movie version of a successful stage play that featured an all-black cast. Story concerns Goddard, a young streetwalker, who is tossed out of the house by her lecherous father Homolka. When the family sees a chance to marry her off for some big money, they drag her back and wed her to a southern farmer. Goddard falls in love with her arranged spouse and blocks her family's attempt at grabbing his dough. Pretty risque material for the time.

p, Philip Yordan; d, Irving Rapper; w, Yordan, Arthur Laurents (based on the play by Yordan); ph, Sol Polito; ed, Charles Nelson.

Drama **(PR:C MPAA:NR)**

ANNA LUCASTA½** (1958) 97m UA bw

Eartha Kitt *(Anna Lucasta)*, Sammy Davis Jr. *(Danny Johnson)*, Frederick O'Neal *(Frank)*, Henry Scott *(Rudolph Slocum)*, Rex Ingram *(Joe Lucasta)*, Georgia Burke *(Theresa)*, James Edwards *(Eddie)*, Rosetta Lenoire *(Stella)*, Isabelle Cooley *(Katie)*, Alvin Childress *(Noah)*, Claire Leyba *(Blanche)*, John Proctor *(Stanley)*, Charles Swain *(Lester)*, Issac Jones *(Cop)*, Wally Earl *(Secretary)*.

Remake of the 1949 version, this time with an all-black cast. Standout performances by Ingram as the father and Davis as the boy friend give this one a slight edge over the original. Yordan again adapted his play for the screen.

p, Sidney Harmon; d, Arnold Laven; w, Philip Yordan (based on his play); ph, Lucien Ballard; m, Elmer Bernstein; ed, Richard C. Meyer.

Drama **(PR:C MPAA:NR)**

ANNA OF BROOKLYN** (1958, Ital.) 106m Circeo Cinema/RKO bw

Gina Lollobrigida, Dale Robertson, Vittorio De Sica, Peppino de Felippo, Amedeo Nazzari, Gabriella Palotta.

Wealthy widow Lollobrigida returns to her native Italy from Brooklyn to seek out an appropriate husband, dallying with various prospects in a small village. Not much story and less dramatic appeal in a listless script and direction that focuses almost solely upon Gina's physical attributes.

d, Reginald Denham, Carlo Lasticati; w, Ettore Margadonna, Dino Risi; ph, Giuseppe Rotunno; m, Alessandro Cicognini, Vittorio De Sica.

Romance **(PR:C MPAA:NR)**

ANNA OF RHODES** (1950, Gr.) 78m Gloria Films bw

Katy Panos *(Anna Roditi)*, Lambros Constantaras *(Aris)*, Yannis Prineas *(Panaghis Roditis)*, Nicos Matheos *(Yannis)*, Lelos Jacovides *(Pantelis)*, Persa Vlahos *(Hariclea)*, Dimos Starenlos *(Giovani Rejilli)*, Aliki Alpha *(Aliki)*.

Slow-moving tale of a young Greek soldier who pretends to be a fascist during the Italian occupation of the Isle of Rhodes. We follow the soldier and his girl friend as they try to drive the fascists off the island. One of the first films produced in Greece after the war.

d, Michael Gazlades, John Flippou; w, G. Assimakopoulos, V. Spyropoulos, P. Papaloukas; m, Nick Giakovief, Jack Jacovides.

War **(PR:A MPAA:NR)**

ANNABEL TAKES A TOUR** (1938) 66m RKO bw

Jack Oakie *(Lanny Morgan)*, Lucille Ball *(Annabel)*, Ruth Donnelly *(Josephine)*, Bradley Page *(Webb)*, Ralph Forbes *(Viscount)*, Frances Mercer *(Natalie)*, Donald McBride *(Thompson)*, Alice White *(Marcella)*, Pepito *(Poochy)*, Chester Clute *(Pitcairn)*, Jean Rouverol *(Laura)*, Clare Verdera *(Viscountess)*, Edward Gargan *(Longshoreman)*, Lee Phelps *(Delivery Man)*, Major Sam Harris, Robert Warwick *(Race Track Officials)*, Milton Kibbee.

Second in the series of Annabel comedies starring Ball as a goofy actress who gets herself in all sorts of jams. This picture has her on a promotional tour for her latest film. On the road, she gets involved with a harebrained publicity stunt that has her and a famous song writer romantically linked. The stunt works until Ball actually falls in love with the writer and wants to quit the movie biz to marry him. Unfortunately for her, he's not interested, and besides, he's already married. Standard screwball outing.

p, Lou Lusty; d, Lew Landers; w, Bert Granet, Olive Cooper (based on a story by

Joe Bigelow and characters created by Charles Hoffman); ph, Russell Metty, ed, Harry Marker.

Comedy   Cas.   (PR:A MPAA:NR)

ANNABELLE'S AFFAIRS★★   (1931) 76m FOX bw

Victor McLaglen (*John Rawson*), Jeanette MacDonald (*Annabelle Leigh*), Roland Young (*Ronald Wimbleton*), Sam Hardy (*James Ludgate*), William Collier, Sr. (*Wickham*), Ruth Warren (*Lottie*), Joyce Compton (*Mabel*), Sally Blane (*Dora*), George Andre Beranger (*Archer*), Walter Walker (*Gosling*), Ernest Wood (*McFadden*), Jed Prouty (*Bolson*), Hank Mann (*Summers*), Wilbur Mack (*Assistant Hotel Manager*), Louise Beavers (*Ruby*).

Light comedy starring MacDonald as a newlywed whose husband gives her stock in a lucrative mining enterprise and tells her not to part with it. Hours later, the husband she barely knows leaves on a business trip. MacDonald accidentally loses the stock covering a bad loan she made with her husband's millionaire rival. With the knowledge that her husband is returning soon, MacDonald poses as a cook and gets herself a job in the millionaire's home in hopes that she can get her hands on the stock. Usual screwball situation helped by a good cast.

d, Alfred Werker; w, Leon Gordon (based on the play "Good Gracious Annabelle" by Clare Kummer); ph, Charles Clarke; ed, Margaret Clancy; cos, Dolly Tree.

Comedy   (PR:A MPAA:NR)

ANNAPOLIS FAREWELL★★   (1935) 75m PAR bw (GB: GENTLEMEN OF THE NAVY)

Sir Guy Standing (*Cdr. Fitzhugh*), Rosalind Keith (*Madeline Deming*), Tom Brown (*Morton "Click" Haley*), Richard Cromwell (*Boyce Avery*), John Howard (*Duncan Haley*), Benny Baker (*Zimmer*), Louise Beavers (*Miranda*), Minor Watson (*Commodore Briggs*), Samuel S. Hinds (*Dr. Bryant*), Ben Alexander (*Adams*), William Collier Sr. (*Rumboat Charlie*), Wheeler Oakman (*Cdr. Lawson*).

Average Naval Academy picture complete with a group of plebes being hazed by the upper-classmen and the one tough punk, Brown, who needs to be taught a lesson. Standing plays an old naval retiree who lives by the college to be near the service which is so dear to his heart. At his last hurrah Standing dresses up in his old uniform and boards the ship that he once commanded which is about to be used for target practice by the Navy.

p, Louis D. Lighton; d, Alexander Hall; w, Dale Van Every, Frank Craven, Grover Jones, Williams Slavens McNutt (based on a story by Stephen M. Avery); ph, Ted Tetzlaff; ed, Doane Harrison.

Drama   (PR:A MPAA:NR)

ANNAPOLIS SALUTE★ (1937) 65m RKO bw (GB: SALUTE TO ROMANCE)

James Ellison (*Bill Marton*), Marsha Hunt (*Julia Clemmens*), Harry Carey (*Chief Martin*), Van Heflin (*Clarke Parker*), Ann Hovey (*Bunny Oliver*), Arthur Lake (*Tex Clemmens*).

Typical tale of young cadets going from boys to men. The highlight of this one is a lengthy boat race. Dull script is helped by a decent cast of character actors.

d, Christy Cabanne; w, John Twist (based on a story by Cabanne); ph, Russell Metty; ed, Ted Cheesman.

Drama   (PR:A MPAA:NR)

ANNAPOLIS STORY, AN★★   (1955) 81m AA c (GB: BLUE AND THE GOLD, THE)

John Derek (*Tony*), Diana Lynn (*Peggy*), Kevin McCarthy (*Jim*), Alvy Moore (*Willie*), Pat Conway (*Dooley*), L. Q. Jones (*Watson*), John Kirby (*Macklin*), Don Haggerty (*Prentiss*), Barbara Brown (*Mrs. Scott*), Betty Lou Gerson (*Mrs. Lord*), Fran Bennett (*Connie*), Robert Osterloh (*Austin*), John Doucette (*Boxing Coach*), Don Kennedy (*McClaren*), Tom Harmon (*Announcer*).

Story of two brothers, Derek and McCarthy, who go through Annapolis together. Their relationship is strained when they both fall in love with Lynn. Their bitterness continues after graduation and into the Korean War. In the end brotherhood wins when Derek saves McCarthy after he is shot down into the ocean off Korea. Decent direction by Siegel and a good supporting cast save this otherwise cliche outing.

p, Walter Mirisch; d, Don Siegel; w, Dan Ullman, Geoffrey Homes (based on a story by Dan Ullman); ph, Sam Leavitt (Technicolor); ed, William Austin; m, Marlin Skiles; m/l, Joseph W. Crosley, Skiles.

War   (PR:A MPAA:NR)

ANNE-MARIE★   (1936, Fr.) 85m AureaFilms bw

Annabella (*Anne-Marie*), Pierre Richard-Willm (*The Inventor*), Jean Murat (*The Thinker*), Abel Jacquin (*The Detective*), Pierre Labry (*The Peasant*), Paul Azais (*The Boxer*), Christian Gerard (*The Lover*).

French potboiler starring Annabella as a young daredevilish gal who is in love with a bizarre inventor. She also knows five dashing young pilots who teach her how to fly planes. The pilots don't like the inventor because he's not as adventurous as they are. One day Annabella jumps in a plane and attempts to make a record-breaking flight, only to be lost in a storm. The pilots and the inventor put aside their differences and join together to rescue her. Overlong and pointless film that could have been done as a chapter to THE PERILS OF PAULINE.

p, P. J. de Venloo; d, Raymond Bernard; w, Antoine de Saint-Exupery; ph, Kruger and Fossard.

Adventure   (PR:A MPAA:NR)

ANNE OF GREEN GABLES★★   (1934) 80m RKO bw

Anne Shirley (*Anne Shirley*), Tom Brown (*Gilbert Blythe*), O. P. Heggie (*Matthew Cuthbert*), Helen Westley (*Marilla Cuthbert*), Sara Haden (*Mrs. Barry*), Murray Kinnell (*Mr. Phillips*), Gertrude Messinger (*Diana*), June Preston (*Mrs. Blewett's Daughter*), Charley Grapewin (*Dr. Tatum*), Hilda Vaughn (*Mrs. Blewett*).

Shirley stars in this homespun tearjerker as we follow her from a pigtailed orphan to young womanhood. Good performances and beautiful Canadian locations help this adaptation of L. M. Montgomery's heart-tugging novel.

d, George Nicholls, Jr.; w, Sam Mintz (based on the novel by L. M. Montgomery); ph, Lucien Andriot; m, Max Steiner; ed, Arthur Schmidt; md, Steiner.

Drama   Cas.   (PR:A MPAA:NR)

ANNE OF THE INDIES★★   (1951) 81m FOX c

Jean Peters (*Anne*), Louis Jourdan (*Capt. Pierre Francois La Rochelle*), Debra Paget (*Molly*), Herbert Marshall (*Dr. Jameson*), Thomas Gomez (*Blackbeard*), James Robertson Justice (*Red Dougal*), Francis Pierlot (*Herkimer*), Sean McClory (*Hackett*), Holmes Herbert (*English Sea Captain*), Byron Nelson (*Bear Handler*), Douglas Bennett (*Bear Wrestler*), Mario Siletti (*Auctioneer*), Bob Stephenson (*Tavern Host*), Carleton Young (*Pirate Mate*), Lynn Davies (*Carib Woman*), Lester Matthews (*Wherry*), Olaf Hytten (*Cdr. Harris*), William Walker (*Servant*), Sheldon Jett (*Innkeeper*), Gene Ramey (*Singer*), Harry Carter (*Pirate*).

Unusual swashbuckler with Peters as a female pirate captain. Plot concerns the efforts of French naval officer Jourdan to get his wife and ship back from the British. The British, wanting to end Peters' piracy, blackmail him into leading the lady pirate into their clutches. Peters escapes and gets revenge on Jourdan by kidnaping his wife. She later softens and helps the couple escape before a big sea battle with Blackbeard. A bit silly, but it moves along at a rapid pace.

p, George Jessel; d, Jacques Tourneur; w, Phillip Dunne, Arthur Caesar (based on a story by Herbert Ravenel Sass); ph, Harry Erickson (Technicolor); m, Franz Waxman; ed, Robert Fritch.

Adventure   (PR:A MPAA:NR)

ANNE OF THE THOUSAND DAYS★★★★   (1969, Brit.) 145m UNIV c

Richard Burton (*King Henry VIII*), Genevieve Bujold (*Anne Boleyn*), Irene Papas (*Queen Katherine*), Anthony Quayle (*Wolsey*), John Colicos (*Cromwell*), Michael Hordern (*Thomas Boleyn*), Katharine Blake (*Elizabeth Boleyn*), Peter Jeffrey (*Norfolk*), Joseph O'Conor (*Fisher*), William Squire (*Thomas More*), Valerie Gearon (*Mary Boleyn*), Vernon Dobtcheff (*Mendoza*), Gary Bond (*Smeaton*), Terence Wilton (*Lord Percy*), Denis Quilley (*Weston*), Esmond Knight (*Kingston*), T. P. McKenna (*Norris*), Michael Johnson (*George Boleyn*), Marne Maitland (*Campeggio*), Nora Swinburne (*Lady Kingston*), June Ellis (*Bess*), Cyril Luckham (*Prior Houghton*), Brook Williams (*Brereton*), Lesley Paterson (*Jane Seymour*), Kynaston Reeves (*Willoughby*), Amanda Jane Smythe (*Baby Elizabeth*), Nicola Pagett (*Princess Mary*).

Superbly acted costumer tells the story of Henry VIII, Burton, who, in 1526, discards his wife Katherine of Aragon, Papas, lusting after a pretty young thing named Anne Boleyn, Bujold. But she is as crafty and ruthless as her sovereign. Though Burton orders Bujold to court as a lady-in-waiting, she resists his incessant advances, stating that any child born to them must be decreed legitimate, which puts off the satyr-like king. For six years Bujold plays her cat-and-mouse game, as Burton orders royal ladies in and out of his bed with the alacrity of a pinball flipper. Burton roars in this role, snarling, sneering, and often giving out with that famous Welsh whine, at times attempting to pluck sympathy out of a wholly unsympathetic character, yet his flourish and flamboyance are certainly in character, as is his subtle manipulation of statesmen and churchmen. Quayle, as Cardinal Wolsey, attempts a modicum of dignity but collapses into senility when he fails to have Bujold's marriage to another annulled. Colicos, playing the evil Iago, Cromwell, solves the king's dilemma by simply breaking with the Vatican, naming Burton head of the Church of England and dispensing with any religious controls. Burton seizes the wealth of the Catholic Church in England, weds Bujold after a quick divorce is arranged, and proceeds to the nuptial bed. The match produces a daughter, Elizabeth (Smythe as a baby, Blake as an adolescent.) When a son is later born dead, Burton seizes upon this hapless event as an excuse to abandon his worried queen and woo the attractive Jane Seymour (Paterson) whom he decides to marry. But what to do with Bujold? Colicos, who enacts his part as if born for it, frames the Queen with a trumped-up adultery charge, at Burton's enthusiastic request, and she is condemned, going to the block after a short reign of a thousand days, no doubt regretting her words: "Power is exciting as love, I discover." Burton does not witness her execution but rides off unperturbed to see Paterson while the teenage heir to the throne, Blake, chillingly poses before a mirror, pretending to be Queen of England. Based on the 1948 Maxwell Anderson play, there is a touch of soap opera here—which might explain the film's then-substantial gross of $7 million—but its lavish sets and brilliant photography, its cunning performance by Burton, the epitome of the royal fox and oaf, depending upon his merciless whims, and Bujold's arresting talent (the French-Canadian actress had scored well in ISABEL a year earlier), made for a grand, bawdy, and often enlightening historical film. Producer Wallis had done well with just such a vehicle in 1964, when audiences were awed by Jean Anouilh's BECKET and he had had good luck with another Anderson play, "Elizabeth the Queen," which he converted to the screen as THE PRIVATE LIVES OF ELIZABETH AND ESSEX with Bette Davis and Errol Flynn. A pattern of success fast emerged after this film with others dealing with the chuckling tyrant Henry, notably A MAN FOR ALL SEASONS. A year earlier Peter O'Toole and Katharine Hepburn stunned audiences with a similar historical drama, THE LION IN WINTER. Oddly, Charles Laughton's Henry the VIII is almost comical and benign compared with Burton's amoral, insidious king while Robert Shaw's Henry in A MAN FOR ALL SEASONS is downright savage. All of the interpretations are probably correct in attempting to capture this enigmatic sovereign. Burton, who received an Oscar nomination for his powerful role (losing out to John Wayne for TRUE GRIT), enjoyed his character enormously, as did his wife, Elizabeth Taylor, who entertained herself by stepping onto the set to play a masked courtesan attending a costume ball; to make it complete, 11-year-old Kate Burton played a servant girl and 12-year-old Liza Todd Burton was a street urchin.

p, Hal B. Wallis; d, Charles Jarrott; w, Bridget Boland, John Hale (based on the play by Maxwell Anderson, adapted by Richard Sokolove); ph, Arthur Ibbetson (Panavision, Technicolor); m, Georges Delerue; ed, Richard Marden; prod d, Maurice Carter; art d, Lionel Couch; set d, Peter Howitt; cos, Margaret Furse; ch, Mary Skeaping.

Drama   Cas.   (PR:C-O MPAA:M)

ANNE OF WINDY POPLARS*½ (1940) 85m RKO bw

Anne Shirley *(Anne Shirley)*, James Ellison *(Tony Pringle)*, Henry Travers *(Matey)*, Patric Knowles *(Gilbert Blythe)*, Slim Summerville *(Jabez Monkman)*, Elizabeth Patterson *(Rebecca)*, Louise Campbell *(Katherine Pringle)*, Joan Carroll *(Betty Grayson)*, Katherine Alexander *(Ernestine Pringle)*, Minnie Dupree *(Kate)*, Alma Kruger *(Mrs. Stephen Pringle)*, Marcie Mae Jones *(Jen Pringle)*, Ethel Griffles *(Hester Pringle)*, Clara Blandick *(Mrs. Morton Pringle)*, Gilbert Emery *(Stephen Pringle)*, Wright Kramer *(Morton Pringle)*, Jackie Moran *(Boy)*.

Dull and uninspired tale of an ambitious young teacher, Shirley, who arrives in a small town to assume the vice-principal position of the school. She soon runs afoul of the ruling family of the town and becomes the scapegoat of a local feud. Education eventually triumphs. A near-sequel to ANNE OF GREEN GABLES.

p, Cliff Reid; d, Jack Hively; w, Michael Kanin, Jerry Cady (based on the novel by L. M. Montgomery); ph, Frank Redman; ed, George Hively.

Drama **(PR:A MPAA:NR)**

ANNE ONE HUNDRED** (1933, Brit.) 66m B&D/PAR bw

Betty Stockfield *(Anne Briston)*, Gyles Isham *(Nixon)*, Dennis Wyndham *(March)*, Evelyn Roberts *(Burton Fraim)*, Allan Jeayes *(Penvale)*, Eric Hales *(Masters)*, Quinton McPherson *(Mole)*.

A girl being vexed by another vying for her boy friend's attentions suddenly gets the upper hand by inheriting a soap company; her generosity with new-found wealth wins the hearts of all. A sudsy tale with a few bubbles.

d, Henry Edwards; w, Sewell Collins (based on Collins' play "Anne 100," and the novel *Rescuing Anne* by Edgar Franklin).

Drama **(PR:A MPAA:NR)**

ANNIE*** (1982) 130m COL c

Albert Finney *(Daddy Warbucks)*, Carol Burnett *(Miss Hannigan)*, Bernadette Peters *(Lily)*, Ann Reinking *(Grace Farrell)*, Tim Curry *(Rooster)*, Aileen Quinn *(Annie)*, Geoffrey Holder *(Punjab)*, Roger Minami *(Asp)*, Toni Ann Gisondi *(Molly)*, Rosanne Sorrentino *(Pepper)*, Lara Berk *(Tessie)*, April Lerman *(Kate)*, Lucie Stewart *(Duffy)*, Robin Ignico *(July)*, Edward Herrmann *(FDR)*, Lois DeBanzie *(Eleanor Roosevelt)*, Peter Marshall *(Bert Healy)*, Loni Ackerman, Murphy Cross, Nancy Sinclair *(Boylan Sisters)*, I. M. Hobson *(Drake)*, Lu Leonard *(Mrs. Pugh)*, Mavis Ray *(Mrs. Greer)*, Pam Blair *(Annette)*, Colleen Zenk *(Celette)*, Victor Griffin *(Saunders)*, Jerome Collamore *(Frick)*, Jon Richards *(Frack)*, Wayne Cilento *(Photographer)*, Ken Swofford *(Weasel)*, Larry Hankin *(Pound Man)*, Irving Metzman *(Bundles)*, Angela Martin *(Mrs. McKracky)*, Kurtis Epper Sanders *(Spike)*.

Delightful musical based on the comic strip character "Little Orphan Annie" features many a memorable song and pleasant dance numbers to which the versatile Finney, as Daddy Warbucks, the leggy-spritely Reinking, and Quinn, an adorable near-perfect Annie, tap, shuffle, waltz, glide, and leap for all their hearts. A great supporting cast includes Burnett spoofing the heartless Hannigan role of overseer to a phalanx of orphan girls and Holder as Punjab the magician servant of Warbucks who finds no feat impossible for his mysterious talents. A slim story has Annie escaping from Burnett's orphanage, being returned, then selected as a child to spend a short time with billionaire Warbucks who grows to love her, showing her the lights of Broadway, introducing her to FDR (Herrman who overplays the great man to caricature), and almost loses her when Burnett and her brother, Curry, and his girl friend, Peters (indifferent efforts at best by both) come up with a scheme to claim the reward offered by Warbucks if Quinn's real parents can be found. Failing, they abduct the child, she escapes, and a wild chase ensues, until the villains are brought to embarrassing justice and Quinn is restored to the loving arms of Finney and Reinking. Finney is excellent as the right-wing Warbucks, rubbing his bald pate and succumbing to the precocious wiles of Quinn. Reinking is fetching and dances well, albeit the choreography here is less energetic than her frenetic acrobatics in ALL THAT JAZZ. Burnett is somewhat of a disappointment as the orphanage overseer, going through the same mugging and predictable double-takes she wore out viewers with on TV. Yet the musical contains the unforgettable song "Tomorrow" which receives several renditions and is worth the whole film. The production itself is rich, too rich for the coffers of Columbia, it later proved, costing between $42 and $52 million, with an impossible goal of $150 million to break even, putting this film into the exorbitant realm of such financial disasters as HEAVEN'S GATE, INCHON and COTTON CLUB. Producer Ray Stark strutted so with pride that he crowed: "This is the film I want on my tombstone!" *Time* Magazine reviewed the film, directed by 74-year-old Huston in his first attempt at a musical, by replying to Stark with the devastating words: "Funeral services may be held starting this week at a theater near you." The expenses spiraled from the first when Columbia paid a record $9.5 million for the rights to the long-running stage hit. A single street set cost more than $1 million. But the production proved the old Hollywood adage about unrealistic executives possessed with wildcatter's fever: "If there's no oil, dig deeper."

p, Ray Stark; d, John Huston; w, Carol Sobieski (based on the stage production book by Thomas Meehan, Charles Strouse, Martin Charnin and the comic strip "Little Orphan Annie"); ph, Richard Moore (Panavision, Metrocolor, Dolby Stereo); ed, Michael A. Stevenson; prod d, Dale Hennesy; art d, Robert Guerra, Diane Wager; cos, Theoni V. Aldredge; ch, Arlene Phillips; m/l, Charles Strouse, Martin Charnin.

Musical **Cas.** **(PR:AAA MPAA:PG)**

ANNIE GET YOUR GUN*½** (1950) 107m MGM c

Betty Hutton *(Annie Oakley)*, Howard Keel *(Frank Butler)*, Louis Calhern *(Buffalo Bill)*, J. Carrol Naish *(Chief Sitting Bull)*, Edward Arnold *(Pawnee Bill)*, Keenan Wynn *(Charlie Davenport)*, Benay Venuta *(Dolly Tate)*, Clinton Sundberg *(Foster Wilson)*, James H. Harrison *(Mac)*, Bradley Mora *(Little Jake)*, Susan Odin *(Jessie)*, Diane Dick *(Nellie)*, Chief Yowlachie *(Little Horse)*, Eleanor Brown *(Minnie)*, Evelyn Beresford *(Queen Victoria)*, Andre Charlot *(President Loubet of France)*, John Mylong *(Kaiser Wilhelm II)*, Nino Pipitone *(King Victor Emanuel of Italy)*.

Sprightly song-fest film that surprisingly captivated audiences wanting musicals in that there is little dancing throughout but the tunes became instant standards and the large sets, armies of extras, and Wild West motif offset the missing choreography. In a glove-fitting role, Hutton blasts her way on and off screen as the sharp-shooting Annie Oakley Mozie (1860-1926), a homely girl from the Ozarks who becomes queen of Buffalo Bill's renowned Wild West Show, pitting her talents against marksman Keel whom she loves and loses because of her ability to best him, winning him in the end by following Sitting Bull's (Naish) advice when facing off head to head in a final shootout with her idol: "You miss, you win." Keel is excellent as the smug star of the show, Naish, the versatile character actor, top-notch as a shrewd Sitting Bull, Calhern superb as a noble but slippery Buffalo Bill, Arnold solid as his show biz rival, and Wynn his usual truculent self. Standout numbers include "Doin' What Comes Natur'lly" sung by Hutton and siblings, "My Defenses Are Down" boomed by Keel, "I'm An Indian Too" with Hutton and a horde of leaping, lunging redskins, and the fantastic finale number with hordes of cowboys and indians, "There's No Business Like Show Business." MGM execs struggled to find the perfect Annie Oakley, first considering Judy Canova, Betty Garrett and Doris Day, then opted for Judy Garland who was reportedly fired because of her incessant temper tantrums. Hutton was finally brought in to save the day which she did with unbridled enthusiam, giving one of the greatest performances of her life. Even the choice of director was muddled by MGM moguls. First Busby Berkeley was nominated, then Charles Walters, but George Sidney got the assignment and created a bedazzling, memorable film. (Musical remake of ANNIE OAKLEY.)

p, Arthur Freed; d, George Sidney; w, Sidney Sheldon (based on the musical play, m/l, Irving Berlin, book, Herbert and Dorothy Fields); ph, Charles Rosher (Technicolor); md, Adolph Deutsch; ed, James E. Newman; art d, Cedric Gibbons, Paul Groesse; ch, Robert Alton.

Musical/Western **(PR:AAA MPAA:NR)**

ANNIE HALL**** (1977) 93m UA c

Woody Allen *(Alvy Singer)*, Diane Keaton *(Annie Hall)*, Tony Roberts *(Rob)*, Carol Kane *(Allison)*, Paul Simon *(Tony Lacey)*, Colleen Dewhurst *(Mom Hall)*, Janet Margolin *(Robin)*, Shelley Duvall *(Pam)*, Christopher Walken *(Duane Hall)*, Donald Symington *(Dad Hall)*, Helen Ludlam *(Grammy Hall)*, Mordecai Lawner *(Alvy's Dad)*, Joan Newman *(Alvy's Mom)*, Jonathan Munk *(Alvy at 9)*, Ruth Volner *(Alvy's Aunt)*, Martin Rosenblatt *(Alvy's Uncle)*, Hy Ansel *(Joey Nichols)*, Rashel Novikoff *(Aunt Tessie)*, Marshall McLuhan, Dick Cavett *(Themselves)*, Russell Horton *(Man in Theater Line)*, Christine Jones *(Dorrie)*, May Boylan *(Miss Reed)*, Wendy Girard *(Janet)*, John Doumanian *(Coke Fiend)*, Bob Maroff, Rick Petrucelli *(Men Outside Theater)*, Chris Gampel *(Doctor)*, Dan Ruskin *(Comedian at Rally)*, John Glover *(Actor Boy Friend)*, Bernie Styles *(Comic's Agent)*, Johnny Haymer *(Comic)*, Ved Bandbu *(Maharishi)*, Lauri Bird *(Tony Lacey's Girl Friend)*, Jeff Goldblum, William Callaway, Jim McKrell, Roger Newman, Alan Landers, Jean Sarah Frost *(Lacey's Party Guests)*, Vince O'Brien *(Hotel Doctor)*, Humphrey Davis *(Alvy's Psychiatrist)*, Veronica Radburn *(Annie's Psychiatrist)*, Robin Mary Paris *(Actress in Rehearsal)*, Charles Levin *(Actor in Rehearsal)*, Michael Karm *(Rehearsal Director)*, Petronia Johnson, Shaun Casey *(Tony's Dates at Nightclub)*, Lou Picetti, Loretta Tupper, James Burge, Shelley Hack, Albert Ottenheimer, Paula Trueman *(Street Strangers)*, Beverly D'Angelo *(Actress in Rob's TV Show)*, David Wier, Keith Dentice, Susan Mellinger, Hamit Perezic, James Balter, Eric Gould, Amy Levitan *(Alvy's Classmates)*, Gary Allen, Frank Vobs, Margaretta Warwick *(Schoolteachers)*, Gary Muledeer *(Man at Health Food Restaurant)*, Sigourney Weaver *(Alvy's Date Outside Theater)*, Walter Bernstein *(Annie's Date Outside Theater)*.

Very funny spoof on modern-day sexual arrangements with Allen playing a neurotic, insecure, indecisive comedy writer (which is how he really began his career in early TV), meeting and falling madly in love with midwestern hick Keaton, who aspires to become a singer. They fumble about in the early stages of their relationship like two teenagers groping toward sex and self-identity, mouthing one cliche after another, only twisted in the Allen style to the wry, the incisive and the sublimely ridiculous. Allen meets with Keaton's family, Dewhurst and Symington, a mother and father who all but ignore the nincompoopish-looking city slicker. Despite this disapproval, they move in together but Allen becomes so insecure about their affair that he pounces on Keaton's every move, interpreting these acts as rejection and disaffection. When Keaton finally sings a solo—"Seems Like Old Times"—in a Manhattan club, she is spotted by record tycoon Simon who asks her to move to Hollywood to work (and live) with him; star-struck, she accepts, leaving Woody in the lurch. The story is so simple it embraces the moronic but that is part of its charm, along with Allen's flashbacks to childhood (with Munk doing a side-splitting characterization of a young Woody), and constant asides to the camera similar to STRANGE INTERLUDE, a device that sometimes has to carry the laughs. (Oddly, Allen is not a bit funny when removing his glasses, only tired looking.) In the flashbacks, Allen himself moves about freely as a grown man, unseen by others, commenting on various scenes, a technique borrowed freely from Bergman's WILD STRAWBERRIES. And always there are the priceless Allen lines. He observes that Keaton habitually smokes a joint before their every love act, then says to her: "Why don't you take sodium pentothal? Then you could sleep through the whole thing!" Close to an autobiography, Allen made sure there was no advance publicity on ANNIE HALL; in fact, the entire story, one long ad-lib, really, was kept a tight secret until its premiere, which made the entire production fresh and startling, again pointing out in extravagant terms and scenes the follies and foibles of man, and in particular, a hopeless nerd whose mannered idiocies always make the viewer feel superior, a tried and true method to assure popularity. (The film originally grossed almost $19 million.) Annoying is the glib Tony Roberts, Allen's perennial sidekick, whose hip and silky ways, thoroughly amoral outlook, and a lifestyle picked up in the main aisle of Nieman-Marcus is funny for the moment and later repugnant, which may or may not have been Allen's intention. Superior though the film certainly is, lovable in a snotty sort of way, there remains at every subsequent viewing a hole that grows larger where a life should have been instead of a throwaway line. The film won Academy Awards for best picture, best director, and best screenplay.

p, Charles H. Joffe; d, Woody Allen; w, Allen, Marshall Brickman; ph, Gordon Willis; ed, Ralph Rosenblum, Wendy Greene Bricmont; art d, Mel Bourne; set d, Robert Drumheller, Justin Scoppa, Jr., Barbara Kreiger; cos, Ruth Morley, George Newman, Marilyn Putnam, Ralph Lauren, Nancy McArdle.

Comedy **Cas.** **(PR:C-O MPAA:PG)**

ANNIE LAURIE** (1936, Brit.) 82m Mondover-BUT bw

Will Fyffe *(Wiill Laurie)*, Polly Ward *(Annie Laurie)*, Bruce Seton *(Jamie Turner)*, Vivienne Chatteron *(Maggie Laurie)*, Romilly Lunge *(John Anderson)*, Percy Walsh *(Alec Laury)*, Frederick Culley *(Robert Anderson)*, Evelyn Barnard *(Elspeth McAlpine)*, Quinton McPherson *(Small)*.

The adopted daughter of a lowly merchant loses her job but is determined to salvage a life and uses her natural abilities as a dancer to become a star in musical reviews. Ward is a delightfully good hoofer, bringing this programmer above par.

p, Walter Tennyson, Wilfred Noy; d, Tennyson; w, Frank Miller; ph, Jack Parker.

Comedy (PR:A MPAA:NR)

ANNIE, LEAVE THE ROOM* ½** (1935, Brit.) 76m Twickenham/UNIV bw

Eva Moore *(Mrs. Morley)*, Morton Selten *(Lord Spendlove)*, Jane Carr *(Adrienne Ditmar)*, Davina Craig *(Annie)*, Richard Cooper *(Hon. Algernon Lacey)*, Jane Welsh *(Lady Mary)*, Ben Welden *(Raisins)*, Arthur Finn *(Al Gates)*, Edward Underdown *(John Brandon)*, Alfred Wellesley.

Selten is an impoverished peer reliant on his mother-in-law for his finances. A film crew offers him a large sum of money for use of his manor house and he accepts, flirting with the film's starlet during shooting. Selten does a screen test with his maid, and she gets a contract while he finds his mother-in-law is on the film company's board of directors. Sporadically amusing.

p, Julius Hagen, d, Leslie Hiscott; w, Michael Barringer (based on the play "Spendlove Hall" by Norman Cannon); ph, William Luff.

Comedy (PR:A MPAA:NR)

ANNIE OAKLEY*** (1935) 79m RKO bw

Barbara Stanwyck *(Annie Oakley)*, Preston Foster *(Toby Walker)*, Melvyn Douglas *(Jeff Hogarth)*, Moroni Olsen *(Buffalo Bill)*, Pert Kelton *(Vera Delmar)*, Andy Clyde *(MacIvor)*, Chief Thundercloud *(Sitting Bull)*, Margaret Armstrong *(Mrs. Oakley)*, Delmar Watson *(Wesley Oakley)*, Philo McCullough *(Officer)*, Eddie Dunn, Ernie S. Adams *(Wranglers)*, Harry Bowen *(Father)*, Theodore Lorch *(Announcer)*, Sammy McKim *(Boy at Shooting Gallery)*.

Lively historical fare presents Stanwyck as the rugged Ozark sharpshooter, particularly fine in the opening scenes when she is discovered as an awkward, backwoods character, thoroughly uncultured and untutored in the sophisticated ways of civilization. She joins Buffalo Bill's Wild West Show and becomes its star marksman, vying for attention with male sharpshooter Foster whom she loves. The show's manager, Douglas, is hopelessly in love with Annie but he doesn't stand a chance as Stanwyck goes tenaciously after Foster and wins him with the help of a bumbling Chief Thundercloud as Sitting Bull, her mentor. Thundercloud provides many a laugh in his attempt to cope with the white man's ways, particularly folding beds and gaslight. The film is elaborately produced with scores of indians and cowboys making up Cody's legendary show, although the facts are bent a bit for dramatic effect. Stevens' direction is fast-paced and innovative. This was Stanwyck's first western film, a genre she would return to periodically with great success. (Remade as the musical ANNIE GET YOUR GUN.)

p, Cliff Reid; d, George Stevens; w, Joel Sayre, John Twist (based on a story by Joseph A. Fields, Ewart Adamson); ph, J. Roy Hunt; ed, Jack Hively; md, Alberto Columbo; art d, Van Nest Polglase, Perry Ferguson.

Western Cas. (PR:AAA MPAA:NR)

ANNIVERSARY, THE*** (1968, Brit.) 95m FOX/HAMMER (British) c

Bette Davis *(Mrs. Taggart)*, Sheila Hancock *(Karen Taggart)*, Jack Hedley *(Terry Taggart)*, James Cossins *(Henry Taggart)*, Christian Roberts *(Tom Taggart)*, Elaine Taylor *(Shirley Blair)*, Timothy Bateson *(Mr. Bird)*, Arnold Diamond *(Headwaiter)*.

Disturbing black comedy with Davis (wearing an eye patch) as the world's most possessive mom. Plot concerns the yearly gathering of her three sons to celebrate her wedding anniversary to their deceased father whom she hated. One son, Cossins, is a transvestite, which mother approves of, another, Roberts, spites her by bringing home his pregnant girl friend, and the third, Hedley, who managed to marry, announces he's leaving the country. Mom tries to control these developments by telling Hedley that his children have been killed in a car wreck, putting her glass eye under the pillow of Roberts' girl friend, and encouraging Cossins to steal women's undergarments off the neighbor's clothesline. Davis is great, but the film suffers from the staginess of the play on which it was based.

p, Jimmy Sangster; d, Roy Ward Baker; w, Sangster (based on the play by Bill MacIlwraith); ph, Henry Waxman (Technicolor); m, Philip Martell; ed, Peter Wetherley.

Comedy (PR:O MPAA:NR)

ANONYMOUS VENETIAN, THE zero (1971) 91m AA c

Tony Musante *(Enrico)*, Florinda Bolkan *(Valeria)*, Toti Cal Monte *(House Owner)*, Alessandro Grinfan *(Factory Manager)*, Brizio Montinaro *(Waiter)*, Giuseppe Bella *(South Technician)*.

Torporous talky tearjerker about a man dying of a brain tumor (Musante) who meets with his estranged wife, Bolkan, to discuss what went wrong in their relationship while strolling about Venice. Insipid dialog, inert direction and even the canals seem dismal. Not worth a glance.

p, Turi Vasile; d, Enrico Maria Salerno; w, Salerno, Guiseppe Berto; ph, Marcello Gatti (Eastmancolor); m, Stelvio Cipriani.

Drama (PR:C MPAA:GP)

ANOTHER CHANCE (SEE: TWILIGHT WOMEN, 1952)

ANOTHER DAWN** (1937) 73m WB bw

Kay Francis *(Julia Ashton)*, Errol Flynn *(Captain Denny Roark)*, Ian Hunter *(Colonel John Wister)*, Frieda Inescort *(Grace Roark)*, Herbert Mundin *(Wilkins)*, Billy Bevan *(Hawkins)*, Kenneth Hunter *(Sir Charles Benton)*, G. P. Huntley Jr. *(Lord Alden)*, Clyde Cook *(Sgt. Murphy)*, Richard Powell *(Henderson)*, Charles Irwin *(Kelly)*, David Clyde *(Campbell)*, Spencer Teakle *(Fromby)*, Ben Welden *(Victor Romkoff)*, Mary Forbes *(Mrs. Benton)*, Eily Malyon *(Mrs. Farnold)*, Reginald Sheffield *(Wireless Operator)*, Charles Austin *(Yeoman)*, Tyrone Brereton *(Soldier)*, Yorke Sherwood *(Station Master)*, Will Stanton *(John's Caddy)*, Neal Kennedy *(Julia's Caddy)*, J. R. Tozer *(Butler)*, Martin Garralaga *(Ali, the Servant)*, Major Sam Harris *(Guest)*, Leonard Mudie *(Doctor)*, Jack Richardson *(Lang)*, Stefan Moritz *(Arab Horseman)*, Clare Vedera *(Innkeeper)*.

Tepid love triangle set in the Sahara stars 28-year-old Flynn as the dashing young officer who falls for his commander's wife, Francis, because she reminds him of his great love who was killed in WW I. Pretty dull goings on until a rather lame battle scene between the British and the Arabs ensues during a sandstorm. Highlight is the magnificent musical score by Korngold which is better than the film for which it was written.

p, Hal B. Wallis; d, William Dieterle; w, Laird Doyle; ph, Tony Gaudio; m, Erich Wolfgang Korngold; ed, Ralph Dawson; md, Hugo Friedhofer, Milan Roder; art d, Robert Hass; cos, Orry-Kelly;

Romance (PR:A MPAA:NR)

ANOTHER FACE** ½** (1935) 72m RKO bw

Wallace Ford *(Joe Haynes)*, Brian Donlevy *(Dawson Dutra)*, Phyllis Brooks *(Sheila)*, Erik Rhodes *(Asst. Director)*, Molly Lamont *(Mary)*, Alan Hale *(Kellar)*, Addison Randall *(Tex)*, Paul Stanton *(Director)*, Edward Burns *(Cameraman)*, Charles Wilson *(Capt. Spellman)*, Hattie McDaniel *(Maid)*, Sy Jenks *(Janitor)*, Oscar Apfel *(Doctor)*, Inez Courtney *(Mamie)*, Emma Dunn *(Sheila's Mother)*, Ethel Wales *(Aunt Hattie)*, Frank Mills *(Muggsie)*.

Offbeat gangster-comedy starring Donlevy as an ugly crook who has his face changed by a plastic surgeon. He is so pleased with the results that he decides to go to Hollywood and become a movie actor. While in Hollywood he is identified by the one person who remembers him from the old days. Humorous scenes of former tough guy hamming it up on the set are good for laughs.

p, Cliff Reid; d, Christy Cabanne; w, Ray Mayer, Thomas Dugan, Garrett Graham, John Twist; ph, Jack MacKenzie; ed, George Hively; md, Roy Webb.

Comedy (PR:A MPAA:NR)

ANOTHER LANGUAGE*** ½** (1933) 75m MGM bw

Helen Hayes *(Stella Hallam)*, Robert Montgomery *(Victor Hallam)*, Louise Closser Hale *(Mom Hallam)*, John Beal *(Jerry Hallam)*, Henry Travers *(Pop Hallam)*, Margaret Hamilton *(Helen Hallam)*, Willard Robertson *(Harry Hallam)*, Irene Cattell *(Grace Hallam)*, Minor K. Watson *(Paul Hallam)*, Hal Dawson *(Walter Hallam)*, Maidel Turner *(Etta Hallam)*, William Farnum *(Sculpting Instructor)*, Sherry Hall *(Purser)*.

Montgomery brings home his new bride, Hayes, to the ancestral hearth only to be met by a domineering, selfish mother, Hale, in one of the best roles of her career. Hubby's family is all snob, the essence of small town Babbitry, a pervasive attitude that all but wrecks the infant marriage. Hayes is splendid as the victimized wife struggling for identity and love while Montgomery attempts first to mollify mama then does the stalwart thing to save his wife from social oblivion. A faithful adaptation of the Franken play.

p, Walter Wanger; d, Edward H. Griffith; w, Herman J. Mankiewicz, Gertrude Purcell, Donald Ogden Stewart (based on the play by Rose Franken); ph, Ray June; ed, Hugh Wynn.

Romance (PR:A MPAA:NR)

ANOTHER MAN, ANOTHER CHANCE***

(1977 Fr/US) 132m UA c (FR: UN AUTRE HOMME, UNE AUTRE CHANCE)

James Caan *(David Williams)*, Genevieve Bujold *(Jeanne Leroy)*, Francis Huster *(Francis Leroy)*, Jennifer Warren *(Mary)*, Susan Tyrrell *(Debbie/Alice)*, Rossie Harris *(Simon)*, Linda Lee Lyons *(Sarah)*, Diana Douglas *(Mary's Mother)*, Fred Stuthman *(Mary's Father)*, Bernard Behrens *(Springfield)*, Oliver Clark *(Evans)*, William Bartman *(Telegrapher)*, Burton Gilliam *(Sheriff Murphy)*, Richard Farnsworth *(Stagecoach Driver)*, Walter Barnes *(Foster)*, Walter Scott *(Bill)*.

Another romance from French director Claude Lelouch. Bujold plays a young French woman who flees Paris for America in 1870 with her boy friend to escape the Franco-Prussian War. The couple make their way out West, get married, have a baby, and set up a photography studio. One day her husband is killed by the angry father of a hanged man whom he had photographed. Her story is paralleled with the life of American veterinarian Caan, who also lives in the West. His wife is raped and killed one evening when he is in town playing pool. Caan and Bujold finally meet and fall in love, though Caan is obsessed with finding the killers of his wife. A slightly long, but fascinating film that spans quite a few settings and genres.

p, Alexandre Mnouchkine, Georges Dancigers; d&w, Claude Lelouch; ph, Jacques Lefrancois, Stanley Cortez (Eastmancolor); m, Francis Lai; ed, Georges Klotz, Fabien Tordjmann; art d, Robert Clatworthy.

Romance (PR:C-O MPAA:PG)

ANOTHER MAN'S POISON*** (1952, Brit.) 90m Eros/UA bw

Bette Davis *(Janet Frobisher)*, Gary Merrill *(George Bates)*, Emlyn Williams *("Dr." Henderson)*, Anthony Steel *(Larry Stevens)*, Barbara Murray *(Chris Dale)*, Reginald Beckwith *(Mr. Bigley)*, Edna Morris *(Mrs. Bunting)*.

Bravura performance by Davis who almost does a caricature of herself as she smokes her way through a dozen cartons of cigarettes, neurotically brushes her hair and snaps her fingers to punctuate meaningful lines in a melodramatic crime story that has more twists and turns than California's Route 1. She is a mystery writer in love with Steel, winning him away from her secretary, Murray, to whom he is engaged. Just when things look good, Davis' husband, a convict, escapes prison and, when he seeks out her remote home on the Yorkshire moors as a refuge, they battle and he is killed. Another convict who has escaped with the dead man, Merrill (Davis' off-screen husband at the time), arrives and learns Davis has killed his partner. He tells her that he and her husband have just robbed a bank, agreeing to dump her husband's body in a lake close by if she passes him off as her husband until the search for him dies down. Davis introduces Merrill as her long-departed husband, just returned from Malaya, she says, to a suspicious Williams, the vet who has been treating her horse. Merrill brutally convinces Davis to shield him by murdering her horse. She then plots to kill him, sending him on a useless errand in a jeep with faulty brakes. The jeep crashes over an embankment, sinking into the lake, joining the husband's body. But Merrill survives, returning to tell an hysterical Davis that authorities are sure to drag the lake now to recover the jeep and possible occupants and will next find the body. Frantic, Davis gives Merrill poisoned brandy. His body is found by Williams and Davis tells the vet that Merrill murdered her husband and was impersonating the victim. Williams says he suspected as much all along and that the police are on the way, that he has informed them she was in peril. Davis collapses in relief—her impossible schemes have succeeded. To revive her, Williams gives her some of the poisoned brandy. Coming around she realizes that her own insidious plotting has assured her own death. Davis laughs maniacally, then dies. Justice triumphs through irony and blunder in one of the most ridiculous plots ever concocted for film, yet it is all miraculously saved by Davis' histrionic, scenery-gnawing performance. She is a wild woman whose own devices are more intricate and shifty than any mystery she could ever write. Merely watching this great star use every acting trick in the book to bring about believability is a treat.

p, Douglas Fairbanks, Jr., Daniel M. Angel; d, Irving Rapper; w, Val Guest (based on the play "Deadlock" by Leslie Sands); ph, Robert Krasker; m, Paul Sawtell; ed, Gordon Hales; art d, Cedric Dawe.

Crime **(PR:C MPAA:NR)**

ANOTHER PART OF THE FOREST*** (1948) 106m bw

Fredric March *(Marcus Hubbard)*, Ann Blyth *(Regina Hubbard)*, Edmond O'Brien *(Ben Hubbard)*, Florence Eldridge *(Lavinia Hubbard)*, Dan Duryea *(Oscar Hubbard)*, John Dall *(John Bagtry)*, Dona Drake *(Laurette)*, Betsy Blair *(Birdie Bagtry)*, Fritz Leiber *(Colonel Isham)*, Whit Bissell *(Jugger)*, Don Beddoe *(Penniman)*, Wilton Graff *(Sam Taylor)*, Virginia Farmer *(Clara Bagtry)*, Libby Taylor *(Cora)*, Smoki Whitfield *(Jake)*.

March is a marvelous creature for power in this Hellman play which backs into THE LITTLE FOXES by presenting the Hubbard family 20 years earlier. The tyrannical cruelty displayed by March is a wonder to watch as he lords it over his southern neighbors by flaunting his wealth. He ruthlessly profited from the misery of Confederate troops during the Civil War and now has nothing but contempt for the genteel folk of the Lost Cause. He degrades his sons, O'Brien and Duryea, the latter giving another fascinating performance as the whining, spineless coward Oscar. Only money and power appeal to the savage patriarch but O'Brien, the eldest son who is banished by March for standing up to him, unearths the skeletal secret in the Hubbard cupboard, that his father was directly responsible for the deaths of many Confederate troops. Just as ruthless as his father, O'Brien threatens to reveal this awful tale unless the family fortune is turned over to him. March relents and falls from power, proving to be utterly hollow. All his children turn on him, but wife Eldridge, the only decent member of this hideous clan, stands by March, telling her vicious offspring she wishes never to see them again. This utterly depressing film is salvaged through intense performances that rivet the viewer, along with the literate, acerbic script.

p, Jerry Bresler; d, Michael Gordon; w, Vladimir Pozner (based on the play by Lillian Hellman); ph, Hal Mohr; m, Daniele Amfitheatrof; ed, Milton Carruth.

Drama **(PR:C MPAA:NR)**

ANOTHER SHORE* (1948, Brit.) 91m GFD/Ealing bw

Robert Beatty *(Gulliver)*, Moira Lister *(Jennifer)*, Stanley Holloway *(Alastair)*, Michael Medwin *(Yellow)*, Sheila Manahan *(Nora)*, Fred O'Donovan *(Coghlan)*, Desmond Keane *(Parkes)*, Maureen Delaney *(Mrs. Gleason)*, Dermot Kelly *(Boxer)*, Michael Golden *(Broderick)*, Michael O'Mahoney *(Fleming)*, W.A. Kelly *(Roger)*, Wilfred Brambell *(Moore)*.

Dull British yarn about a young man, Beatty, who wants to set sail for a South Sea island and live there. Since he is broke and cannot find anyone to foot the bill, he hangs around the city's most dangerous street corners waiting to rescue a rich person who will be grateful enough to send him to his paradise. Then along comes a stunning blonde who distracts him from his Tahitian daydreams.

p, Michael Balcon; d, Charles Crichton; w, Walter Meade (based on the novel by Kenneth Reddin); ph, Douglas Slocombe; m, Georges Auric; ed, Bernard Gribble.

Comedy **(PR:A MPAA:NR)**

ANOTHER SKY* (1960, Brit.) 83m Harrison bw

Victoria Grayson *(Rose Graham)*, Catherine Lacey *(Selena Prouse)*, Lee Montague *(Michael)*, Ahmed Ben Mahomed *(Ahmed)*, Tayeb *(Tayeb)*, Alan Forbes *(Bancroft)*.

Tedious middle eastern romance starring Grayson as a lonely British girl who falls in love with a Moroccan musician with whom she has nothing in common (including language). Soon after they consummate the relationship, the musician disappears into the desert. The girl spends the rest of the film searching for him until she runs out of energy, money, and hope.

p, Aymer Maxwell; d&w, Gavin Lambert.

Romance **(PR:A MPAA:NR)**

ANOTHER THIN MAN*** (1939) 101m MGM bw

William Powell *(Nick Charles)*, Myrna Loy *(Nora Charles)*, Virginia Grey *(Lois MacFay)*, Otto Kruger *(Assistant District Attorney Van Slack)*, C. Aubrey Smith *(Colonel MacKay)*, Ruth Hussey *(Dorothy Waters/Linda Mills)*, Nat Pendleton *(Lt. Guild)*, Patric Knowles *(Dudley Horn)*, Tom Neal *(Freddie Coleman)*, Phyllis Gordon *(Mrs. Bellam)*, Sheldon Leonard *(Phil Church)*, Don Costello *(Diamond Back Vogel)*, Harry Bellaver *(Creeps Binder)*, William A. Poulsen *(Nicky Charles, Jr.)*, Muriel Hutchinson *(Smitty)*, Abner Biberman *(Dum Dum)*, Marjorie Main *(Mrs. Dolley)*, Asta *(Himself)*, Ralph Dunn *(Expressman)*, Horace MacMahon *(Chauffeur)*, Doodles Weaver *(Gatekeeper)*, George Guhl, Paul Newlan, Joe Devlin *(Bodyguards)*, Paul E. Burns *(Ticket Agent)*, Milton Parsons *(Coroner)*, Milton Kibbee, Dick Elliott, Thomas Jackson, Edward Gargan *(Detectives)*, William Tannen *(State Trooper)*, Joe Downing, Matty Fain *(Hoods)*, Martin Garralaga *(Informant)*, Alphonse Martel, Alberto Morin *(Waiters)*, Nestor Paiva *(Headwaiter)*, Frank Sully, John Kelly, Murray Alper *(Fathers)*, Shemp Howard *(Wacky)*, Edward Hearn *(Detective)*, Alex D'Arcy *(Gigolo)*.

Sub-standard outing for the Powell-Loy duo in the legendary roles of Nick and Nora Charles from the pen of master detective writer Hammett. They arrive in New York to spend some of Loy's considerable fortune when they are asked by Smith to come to his Long Island estate; he is fearful that someone is trying to kill him, he tells them, and asks if Powell will look into some puzzling actions by his relatives and friends. The couple, with their baby son (William Anthony Poulsen, a part later assumed by Dean Stockwell as the Charles boy grew older) and nurse, encamp at Smith's rambling estate where the colonel is murdered as prophesied. As Powell consumes innumerable drinks, with Loy hiding the keys to the liquor cabinet in order to keep him on track, two more people are killed. All the while countless wild characters, from show biz types to sentimental gangsters, flit in an out of scenes so fast it's hard to keep the suspects in order without a scorecard. But the jocular, half-tipsy Powell does his usual round-up at film's end to identify Grey as the killer of the colonel, murder committed for inheritance. More mystery than comedy dominates this sometimes draggy production where the script is less inspired than previous THIN MAN efforts. The atmosphere and sets, along with stellar performances by the principals, can't offset a weak story. This was Powell's first film after a two-year absence from the screen due to illness. (Ses THIN MAN series, Index.)

p, Hunt Stromberg, W. S. Van Dyke; w, Frances Goodrich, Albert Hackett (based on a story by Dashiell Hammett); ph, Oliver T. Marsh, William Daniels; m, Edward Ward; ed, Frederick Y. Smith; art d, Cedric Gibbons.

Crime **(PR:A MPAA:NR)**

ANOTHER TIME, ANOTHER PLACE** (1958) 95m PAR bw

Lana Turner *(Sara Scott)*, Barry Sullivan *(Carter Reynolds)*, Glynis Johns *(Kay Trevor)*, Sean Connery *(Mark Trevor)*, Terrence Longdon *(Alan Thompson)*, Sidney James *(Jake Klein)*, Martin Stephens *(Brian Trevor)*, Doris Hare *(Mrs. Bunker)*, Julian Somers *(Hotel Manager)*, John Le Mesurier *(Dr. Aldridge)*, Cameron Hall *(Alfy)*, Jane Welsh *(Jonesy)*, Robin Bailey *(Captain Barnes)*, Bill Fraser *(R. E. Sergeant)*.

Melodramatic weeper shot in England featuring Turner as an American correspondent in London who has a fling with British correspondent Connery (in one of his first roles.) Just before Connery boards a plane to cover a story, he tells the shocked Turner that he is married and has a child. Connery's plane crashes and he is killed. Turner has a nervous breakdown and checks herself into a hospital. Upon her release, still obsessed with Connery, she finds his home and goes to meet his wife and child. This tear-jerker was released four months ahead of schedule to capitalize on Turner's notoriety during the Johnny Stompanato murder trial.

p, Joseph Kaufman, Lewis Allen; d, Lewis Allen; w, Stanley Mann (based on the novel by Lenore Coffee); ph, Jack Hildyard; m, Douglas Gamley; ed, Geoffrey Foot; md, Muir Mathieson; art d, Tom Monahan; cos, Laura Nightingale.

Drama **(PR:A MPAA:NR)**

ANOTHER TIME, ANOTHER PLACE 1/2**
(1983, Brit.) 101m Umbrella/Rediffusion c

Phyllis Logan *(Janie)*, Giovanni Mauriello *(Luigi)*, Gian Luca Favilla *(Umberto)*, Claudio Rosini *(Paolo)*, Paul Young *(Dougal)*, Gregor Fisher *(Beel)*, Tom Watson *(Finlay)*, Jennifer Piercey *(Kirsty)*, Denise Coffey *(Meg)*, Yvonne Gilan *(Jess)*.

Low-budget feature from the British concerning the cultural differences between a community of Scotsmen and a trio of Italians trapped together during WW II. One of the Italians, Mauriello, becomes fascinated with a young Scottish housewife, Logan. Logan, too, finds the Italian appealing and warms to his loving personality and zest for life which contrasts sharply with the cold, hard life she leads with her husband. Shot on super 16mm and blown up to 35mm.

p, Simon Perry; d&w, Michael Radford (based on the novel by Jessie Kesson); ph, Roger Deakins; m, John McLeod; ed, Tom Priestly; art d, Hayden Pearce.

Drama **Cas.** **(PR:C MPAA:NR)**

ANTHONY ADVERSE*** (1936) 139m WB bw

Fredric March *(Anthony Adverse)*, Olivia de Havilland *(Angela Guessippi)*, Edmund Gwenn *(John Bonnyfeather)*, Claude Rains *(Don Luis)*, Anita Louise *(Maria)*, Louis Hayward *(Denis Moore)*, Gale Sondergaard *(Faith Paleologus)*, Steffi Duna *(Neleta)*, Billy Mauch *(Anthony as a Child)*, Donald Woods *(Vincent Nolte)*, Akim Tamiroff *(Carlo Cibo)*, Ralph Morgan *(Debrulle)*, Henry O'Neill *(Father Zavier)*, Pedro De Cordoba *(Brother Francois)*, George E. Stone *(Sancho)*, Luis Alberni *(Tony Guessippi)*, Fritz Leiber *(Ouvard)*, Joseph Crehan *(Capt. Elisha Jorham)*, Rafaela Ottiano *(Signora Buvino)*, Rollo Lloyd *(Napoleon Bonaparte)*, Leonard Mudie *(De Bourrienne)*, Marilyn Knowlden *(Florence as a Child)*, Mathilde Comont *(Cook Guessippi)*, Eily Malyon *(Mother Superior)*, J. Carroll Naish *(Maj. Doumet)*, Scotty Beckett *(Anthony's Son)*, Paul Sotoff *(Ferdinando)*, Frank Reicher *(Coach Driver)*, Clara Blandick *(Mrs. Jorham)*, Addison Richards *(Capt. Matanaza)*, William Ricciardi *(Coachman)*, Grace Stafford *(Lucia)*, Boris Nicholai *(Courier)*.

Overlong but spectacular film true to the immensely popular novel by Hervey Allen in its adaptation has 39-year-old March playing Adverse, the illegitimate son of Hayward, an army officer and Louise, who is married to Rains, a Spanish don. Hayward is killed in a duel by Rains and the boy is left at a convent, his early childhood tended by O'Neill, a kindly priest. At age ten the boy is adopted by Gwenn, a wealthy Scottish tradesman in Leghorn where he is apprenticed, befriending the daughter of the family cook, Howard. Both children are then seen in young adulthood as March and de Havilland, deeply in love and planning to marry, she having a lovely voice and an ambition for the opera (de Havilland's singing was dubbed by Diana Gaylen). When her father obtains a considerable amount of money de Havilland moves from Leghorn but March, traveling for his stepfather on business, later finds her singing in an opera chorus. They marry (in the novel they have an affair) but de Havilland takes a job elsewhere, leaving a note about her destination, a missive that is blown away, the wind taking with it March's happiness. He prospers as he takes over Gwenn's interests, traveling around the world, by now embittered, a hard drinker. Just when March appears to sink into degeneracy, he again finds de Havilland on a trip to Paris from the West Indies where he has spent many years. She is now the toast of France, a famous opera star who is also mistress to Napoleon Bonaparte (Lloyd). Also, he finds that Rains and Gwenn's one-time assistant, Sondergaard, have conspired to cheat him out of the business left to him by the dying Gwenn who has truly loved his adopted son. He outwits the connivers and learns that Gwenn was really his grandfather. March attempts to revive his life with de Havilland but they both know that it is impossible, that the omnipotent Bonaparte's shadow blankets their future. As a supreme gift of love de Havilland gives March their child (his existence unknown to March until this time); the boy, Scotty Beckett, and his father sail for America and a new life. This massive tearjerker, an elaborate historical soaper, really, is saved by brilliant performances from March and the 20-year-old de Havilland. Rains is superbly wicked as the evil Don Luis, the kind of part in which he reveled. Gale Sondergaard matched him here in malevolence. Gwenn is Rains' perfect counterpart, a man so understanding and kind as to be saintly. Novelist Allen, after his book was translated into 20 languages, was at first concerned that Warner Bros. would ruin the story, but director LeRoy and writer Gibney slashed the rambling saga and still retained the basic concepts. Korngold's score is majestic and melancholic, befitting the romantic tragedy of the starcrossed lovers. Natale Carossio capably directed the opera sequences.

p, Henry Blanke; d, Mervyn LeRoy; w, Sheridan Gibney (based on the novel by Hervey Allen); ph, Tony Gaudio; m, Erich Wolfgang Korngold; ed, Ralph Dawson; md, Leo F. Forbstein; art d, Anton Grot; cos, Milo Anderson; technical ad, Dwight Franklin.

Historical Romance   **(PR:A MPAA:NR)**

ANTHONY OF PADUA zero   (1952, Ital.) 78m Oro/TRANS GLOBAL bw

Aldo Fiorelli (Antonio), Aldo Fabrizi (Ezzelino Da Romano), Alberto Pomerani (Fernando), Silvana Pampanini (Anita).

Awful attempt to profile the Franciscan monk of feudal times, somehow attached to a flashback by a WW I veteran, which is no more than an excuse to exhibit insane battles where scores of knights are slaughtered and sadistic punishments meted out to dissenters, while the bounteous Pampanini parades in the near-altogether for no purpose other than explicit exposure. The script is nonsensical, witless and an insult to any moron.

d, Pietro Francisci; w, Raul DeSarro, Florenzo Florentini, Giorgio Grazlosi, Francisci.

Historical Drama   **(PR:O MPAA:NR)**

ANTI-CLOCK zero   (1980) 107m International Film Exchange

Sebastian Saville (Joseph Sapha/Prof. Zanov), Suzan Cameron (Sapha's Mother), Liz Saville (Sapha's Sister), Louise Temple (Madame Aranovitch).

Awful, pretentious, overlong nuclear comedy about a man's journey to a higher consciousness. Once free of everyday worries, our hero, Saville, becomes acutely aware of the harmony between his atoms and those of the rest of the universe. Saville spends most of the film making ridiculously pretentious statements such as, "The present is terrifying because it is irrevocable." This would have been a rotten short film, but as a feature it is an unbearable intellectual ego trip for directors Arden and Bond. Arden goes so far as to sing a few songs she wrote for the soundtrack. Most of the song lyrics are along the same philosophical lines as, "If a tree falls, and no one is there to hear it, does it make a sound?" Deep. This is the kind of film that gives art-houses and film schools a bad name.

p, Jack Bond; d, Jane Arden, Bond; w&m, Arden.

Drama   **(PR:C-O MPAA:NR)**

ANTIGONE*   (1962 Gr.) 93m Norma bw

Irene Papas, Manos Katrakis, Maro Kontou, Nikos Kazis, Ilia Livikou.

Lavish Greek production given to Sophocles' tragedy set in Thebes. Story concerns Antigone (Papas) who defies the King after her two brothers are killed in a fight to determine which of them will be next in line for the throne. Antigone is sentenced to death and buried alive in a cave. Impeccable treatment of the classic Greek tale with an outstanding performance by Papas.

d&w, George Tzavellas; ph, Dinos Katsourdis; m, Arghyris Kounadis.

Drama   **(PR:A MPAA:NR)**

ANTOINE ET ANTOINETTE*   (1947 Fr.) 98m Gaumont bw

Roger Pigaut (Antoine), Claire Mattei (Antoinette), Noel Roquevert (Roland), Annette Poivre (Juliette), Jacques Meyran (Barbelot), Emile Dtain (Father-in-law), Paulette Jan (Huguette), Gaston Modot (Official), G. Oury (Customer), Francois Joux (Bridegroom), Pierre Trabaud (Riton), Huguette Saget (Bride).

Appealing French comedy starring Pagaut and Mattei as a young married couple. He works as a bookbinder, she as a salesgirl. Plot revolves around a desperate search for a lost lottery ticket.

d, Jacques Becker; w, Francoise Giroux, Becker, Maurice Griffe; ph, Pierre Montazel; m, Jean-Jacques Grunewald; ed, Marguerite Renoir; art d, Robert-Jules Garnier.

Comedy   **(PR:A MPAA:NR)**

ANTONIO DAS MORTES*   (1970, Braz.) 100m Grove c

Mauricio do Valle (Antonio das Mortes), Odete Lara (Laura), Othon Bastos (Teacher), Hugo Carvana (Police Chief), Jofre Soares (Colonel), Rosa Maria Penna (Saint), and the people of Milagres.

Powerful political film has mercenary do Valle tracking down insurgents, killing all in a band, dispatching the leader in hand-to-hand combat in a wild bullet-ridden finale, only to discover that his real sympathies are with the rebels. Brazil's lush vegetation, mountains, and plains are beautifully photographed in this polemic which seems to lionize the likes of Che Guevara while indicting the cruel and impersonal landlords of a South American dictatorship.

p, Claude-Antoine; d&w Glauber Rocha; ph, Alfonso Beato (Eastmancolor); m, Marlos Nobre.

War   **(PR:C-O MPAA:NR)**

ANTONY AND CLEOPATRA*   (1973, Brit.) 160m Rank c

Charlton Heston (Antony), Hildegard Neil (Cleopatra), Eric Porter (Enobarbus), John Castle (Octavius Caesar), Fernando Rey (Lepidus), Juan Luis Galiardo (Alexas), Carmen Sevilla (Octavia), Freddie Jones (Pompey), Peter Arno (Menas),

Luis Barboo (Varrius), Fernando Bilbao (Menecrates), Warren Clarke (Scarus), Roger Delgado (Soothsayer), Julian Glover (Proculeius), Sancho Gracia (Canidius), Garrick Hagan (Eros), John Hallam (Thidias), Sergio Krumbel (2nd Messenger), Jane Lapotaire (Charmian), Jose Manuel Martin (Guard), Joe Melia (1st Messenger), Manolo Otero (Sentry), Monica Peterson (Iras), Emiliano Redondo (Mardian), Aldo Sambrel (Ventidius), Felipe Solano (Soldier), Doug Wilmer (Agrippa).

Shakespearean drama starring Heston as a tense and obdurate Antony, suffers from too much historical hodgepodge. In fact, the film is so underproduced (for $1,600,000) that it relies solely on the importance of Heston's beautifully concentrated scenes. Neil is adequate as the Egyptian vamp but in no way compares with Vivien Leigh in CAESAR AND CLEOPATRA or even the trampy vixen enacted by Elizabeth Taylor in CLEOPATRA. Totally fascinating is Porter, Heston's unctuous aide who deserts him in the face of Octavius' armies. The script is commendably faithful to the Immortal Bard but in that sense almost stagey. This film saw no U.S. release after completion.

p, Peter Snell; d&w, Charlton Heston (based on the play by William Shakespeare); ph, Rafael Pacheco (Todd-AO, Technicolor); m, John Scott, Augusto Alegero; ed, Eric Boyd-Perkins; prod d, Maurice Pelling; art d, Jose Alguero, Jose Ma Alarcon.

Drama   **Cas.**   **(PR:A MPAA:NR)**

ANTS IN HIS PANTS*   (1940, Aus.) 71m British Empire Films bw

Will Mahoney (Barney O'Hara), Shirley Ann Richards (Eve Cameron), Jean Hatton (Pat), Evie Hayes (Kitty Katkin), Alec Kellaway ("Killer"), John Fleeting (John Wynyard), Sidney Wheeler (Worthington Howard), Ronald Whelan (Max), Guy Hastings (Colonel Cameron), Harry Adby (Sharkey), Lou Vernon (Signor Rudolpho), Harold Meade (Sir James Hall), Bob Geraghty (Pressman).

Australian musical drama starring Mahoney as a partner in a sideshow carnival who enters himself in a boxing match to raise money to save sweet little girl Hatton's voice. He wins the bout and has enough cash to send the kid abroad to the throat specialists.

d&w, William Freshman; ph, George Heath; m/l, Will Mahoney, Bob Geraghty.

Musical/Drama   **(PR:AA MPAA:NR)**

ANY GUN CAN PLAY**   (1968, Ital./Span.) 103m Golden Eagle/RAF Vado, L'Ammazzo, e Torno c

Edd Byrnes (Clayton), Gilbert Roland (Monetero), George Hilton (The Stranger), Kareen O'Hara (Wapa), Pedro Sanchez (Paiondo), Gerard Herter (Backman).

Spaghetti western unusual for the appearance of Byrnes ("77 Sunset Strip") and veteran American actor Roland. Interesting opening sequence in which three strangers ride into town, dead ringers for Clint Eastwood, Lee Van Cleef, and Hugh O'Brian, where they run into a man, Hilton, with three coffins who guns them down. It's a joke meant to declare that this spaghetti gunslinger, Hilton, is going to bury the stars of the old Italian westerns. Not a chance. Stick to Leone's films.

d. Enzo G. Castellari; ph, (Eastmancolor).

Western   **(PR:C MPAA:NR)**

ANY MAN'S WIFE*   (1936) 67m Republic bw

Wynne Gibson (Grace Minturn), Warren Hull (Dr. Douglas Bruce), Jackie Moran (Michael O'Halloran), Charlene Wyatt (Lily O'Halloran), Sidney Blackmer (Jim Minturn), Hope Manning (Leslie), G. P. Huntley Jr. (Ted Frost), Robert Greig (Butler), Helen Lowell (Hettie), Vera Gordon (Mrs. Levinsky).

Sappy story concerning Gibson's efforts to save her marriage by taking in two street waifs, Moran and his sister Wyatt. The little sister needs an expensive operation to cure her paralysis and Gibson arranges it thinking it would look good to the judge during the divorce proceedings. Genuine love develops between the children and Gibson and she wins back her husband to boot. Hokum tear-jerker.

d, Karl Brown; w, Adele Buffington (based on the novel Michael O'Halloran by Gene Stratton-Porter); ph, Jack Marta; m, Alberto Columbo.

Drama   **(PR:A MPAA:NR)**

ANY NUMBER CAN PLAY¹⁄₂**   (1949) 102m MGM bw

Clark Gable (Charley Enley Kyng), Alexis Smith (Lon Kyng), Wendell Corey (Robbin Elcott), Audrey Totter (Alice Elcott), Frank Morgan (Jim Kurstyn), Mary Astor (Ada), Lewis Stone (Ben Gavery Snelerr), Barry Sullivan (Tycoon), Marjorie Rambeau (Sarah Calbern), Edgar Buchanan (Ed), Leon Ames (Dr. Palmer), Mickey Knox (Pete Senta), Richard Robert (Lew "Angle" Debretti), William Conrad (Frank Sistina), Darryl Hickman (Paul Enley Kyng), Caleb Peterson (Sleigh), Dorothy Comingore (Mrs. Purcell), Art Baker (Mr. Reardon).

Gable is a big-shot gambler running an honest casino, a noble dice-roller who, in the words of one of his employees "is a nut for human dignity." Ethical and decent (not your average crap-shooter), Gable is innocently if not logically perplexed at the disdain shown for his chosen career by his estranged wife, Smith, and disaffected son, Hickman. One evening finds him staking venerable MGM character actor Stone, a down-and-out gambler, to $500 which he promptly loses at Gable's tables and then tries to commit suicide but is prevented from blowing away his gray head by Gable. Meanwhile Gable's spineless brother-in-law, Corey, has been blackmailed into allowing two crooks to shoot loaded dice at the casino. At the same time Gable hears that his son is in jail, charged with starting a fight. He bails his son out but the youth refuses to leave with him, going with his mother who later takes the boy to Gable's gambling den to witness an above-the-board operation, particularly a showdown between Gable and wealthy Frank Morgan who has been winning all night. Morgan taunts Gable, saying that he intends to get even after years of losing, and asks if there is any limit. Gable stakes his entire fortune in a head-to-head roll of the dice and wins. When the two crooked dice shooters, Robert and Conrad—both marvelous villains—attempt to rob the casino Gable disarms them and sends them on their way. Such bravado persuades Hickman that his father is a courageous and noble soul and he comes around to showing some affection, as does the icy Alexis Smith. With a typical beau geste, Gable realizes that he can have his family back but without his casino. He stakes his club and plays his employees for the premises in a game he knows he will lose, then departs with his family to build a new career. Stilted and unrealistic, this Gable vehicle is arresting for LeRoy's terse, professional direction and the star's commanding performance, although Corey gives an anemic effort and Smith's is bloodless. More interesting are Gable's colorful patrons, Morgan, Stone, Mary Astor, and Marjorie Rambeau, along with his staff members Sullivan, Buchanan, Knox, and Peterson.

p, Arthur Freed; d, Mervyn LeRoy; w, Richard Brooks (based on the novel by Edward Harris Heath); ph, Harold Rosson; m, Lennie Hayton; ed, Ralph E. Winters; art d, Cedric Gibbons, Urie McCleary.

Drama (PR:A MPAA:NR)

ANY NUMBER CAN WIN*** (1963 Fr.) 110m MGM bw

Jean Gabin (Charles), Alain Delon (Francis), Viviane Romance (Ginette), Maurice Biraud (Louis), Carla Marlier (Brigitte), Jose De Vilallonga (Grimp), Germaine Montero (Francis' Mother), Jean Carmet (Barman), Dora Doll (Countess), Henri Virlojeux (Marie), Rita Cadillac (Lilliane), Anne Marie Coffinet (Marcelle), Jimmy Davis (Sam), Dominique Davray (Leone), The Ben Tyber Ballet Troupe.

Terrific caper movie featuring Gabin as an ex-con who returns from prison determined to pull off one last, big robbery. He recruits his cellmate Delon and together they plan to rob the casino at Cannes. Good pacing, taut direction, gorgeous scenery, and excellent performances make this film noir production quite entertaining.

p, Jacques Bar; d, Henri Verneuil; w, Albert Simonin, Michel Audiard, Verneuil (based on the novel by John Trinian); m, Michel Magne.

Crime (PR:A MPAA:NR)

ANY WEDNESDAY** (1966) 109m WB c (GB: BACHELOR GIRL APARTMENT)

Jane Fonda (Ellen Gordon), Jason Robards (John Cleves), Dean Jones (Cass Henderson), Rosemary Murphy (Dorothy Cleves), Ann Prentiss (Miss Linsley), Jack Fletcher (Felix), Kelly Jean Peters (Girl in Museum), King Moody (Milkman), Monty Margetts (Nurse).

Robards is good as a likable once-a-week philanderer in this sex comedy based on the stage play by Muriel Resnik. Fonda plays his mindless Wednesday date and Jones is the man who wrecks Robards' weekly habit. Murphy recreates her Broadway role as Robards' long-suffering wife. Luckily the film takes advantage of real N.Y.C. exteriors and avoids the staginess of most adaptations.

p, Julius J. Epstein; d, Robert Ellis Miller; w, Julius J. Epstein (based on the play by Muriel Resnik); ph, Harold Lipstein (Technicolor); m, George Duning; ed, Stefan Arnstein; cos, Dorothy Jeakins.

Comedy (PR:C-O MPAA:NR)

ANY WHICH WAY YOU CAN**1/2 (1980) 116m WB c

Clint Eastwood (Philo Beddoe), Sondra Locke (Lynne Halsey-Taylor), Geoffrey Lewis (Orville), William Smith (Jack Wilson), Harry Guardino (James Beekman), Ruth Gordon (Ma), Michael Cavanaugh (Patrick Scarfe), Barry Corbin (Fat Zack), Roy Jenson (Moody), Bill McKinney (Dallas), William O'Connell (Elmo), John Quade (Cholla), Al Ruscio (Tony Rapoli Sr.), Dan Vadis (Frank), Camila Ashland (Hattie), Dan Barrows (Baggage Man), Michael Brockman (Moustache Officer), Julie Brown (Candy), Glen Campbell (Himself), Dick Christie (Jackson Officer), Rebecca Clemons (Buxon Bess), Anne Ramsey (Loretta Quince), Logan Ramsey (Luther Quince), Jim Stafford (Long John), Lynn Hallowell (Honey Bun).

Sequel to Eastwood's phenomenally successful good ol' boy comedy, EVERY WHICH WAY BUT LOOSE, has Philo (Eastwood) retiring from brawling for dollars and settling down with his country-western singer girl friend, Locke, his zany landlady, Gordon, and his friend the orangutan, Clyde. This rest and relaxation is not to be. The mob offers Eastwood big bucks to participate in one last fight. He must take on his old nemesis, Smith, in a King-of-the-Streetfighters brawl. Eastwood can't resist the challenge, and besides, the gangsters have kidnaped his girl just to make sure the fight goes on. The lengthy fight takes place in every bar across the town of Jackson Hole, Wyoming. A much gentler follow-up to the original film, ANY WHICH WAY YOU CAN takes the time to humanize the characters, and shows them as passionate human beings instead of the fighting machines they were in the first film. Some very funny moments highlighted by a parallel seduction scene showing Eastwood/Locke in one motel room, and Clyde trying to put a few holds on a female orangutan next door. Locke is the biggest disappointment, a thoroughly inanimate actress with a tiresome deadpan delivery, unappealing, unattractive, and mostly inexcusable as a performer. Silly, but fun.

p, Fritz Manes; d, Buddy Van Horn; w, Stanford Sherman (based on characters created by Jeremy Joe Kronsberg); ph, David Worth (DeLuxe Color); ed, Ferris Webster, Ron Spang; md, Snuff Garrett; art d, William J. Creber; set d, Ernie Bishop; cos, Glenn Wright.

Comedy/Action Cas. (PR:C MPAA:PG)

ANYBODY'S BLONDE* (1931) 60m Action Pictures bw

Dorothy Revier (Janet), Reed Howes (Dan O'Hara), Lloyd Whitlock (Steve Crane), Edna Murphy (Myrtle), Nita Martin (Ginger), Gene Morgan (Stew), Henry Walthall (Editor), Arthur Housman (O'Hara's Manager), Pat O'Malley (Reporter), Richard Cramer (Riley).

Crummy murder mystery with Revier as lonely hearts columnist whose boxer brother is murdered. She gets a job at the local nightclub as a dancer to find the killer. This stuff was cliche in 1931.

p, Ralph M. Like; d, Frank Strayer; w, Betty Burridge; ph, Jules Cronjager.

Mystery/Drama (PR:A MPAA:NR)

ANYBODY'S WAR zero (1930) 90m PAR

Charles Mack (Amos Crow), George Moran (Willie), Joan Peers (Mary Jane Robinson), Neil Hamilton (Ted Reinhart), Walter Weems (Sgt. Skipp), Betty Farrington (Camilla), Walter McGrail (Capt. Davis).

Awful comedy with two white guys in blackface playing inept dogcatchers who get drafted into the army. Most of the action takes place in boot camp where the stupid draftees shoot craps until they get shipped out. Fine if you like racist, ignorant comedy.

d, Richard Wallace; w, Lloyd Corrigan, Hector Turnbull (based on "The Two Black Crows in the A.E.F."); ph, Alan Siegler.

Comedy (PR:A MPAA:NR)

ANYBODY'S WOMAN** (1930) 80m PAR bw

Ruth Chatterton (Pansy Gray), Clive Brook (Neil Dunlap), Paul Lukas (Gustav Saxon), Huntly Gordon (Grant Crosby), Virginia Hammond (Katherine Malcolm), Tom Patricola (Eddie Calcio), Juliette Compton (Ellen), Cecil Cunningham (Dot), Charles Gerrard (Walter Harvey), Harvey Clark (Mr. Tanner), Sidney Bracey (The Butler), Gertrude Sutton (The Maid).

Comedy romance with Brook as a lawyer whose rich society wife dumps him to marry someone even richer. This drives poor Brook to drink, and while he's stewed, he meets a chorus girl, Chatterton, who wants to be a lady. When he sobers up the next morning he is stunned to find out he has married the girl. He wants to get rid of her, but can't bear to kick her out because she is so devoted to him. Though his family is horrified, and his friends can't believe it, he decides to make a go of it. Brooks falls in love with Chatterton and the two make a new life together.

d, Dorothy Arzner; w, Zoe Akins, Doris Anderson (based on a story by Gouverneur Morris); ph, Charles Lang; ed, Jane Loring.

Comedy/Romance (PR:A MPAA:NR)

ANYONE CAN PLAY** (1968, Ital.) 110m Documento/PAR c (LE DOLCI SIGNORE)

Ursula Andress (Norma), Virna Lisi (Luisa), Marisa Mell (Paola), Claudine Auger (Esmeralda), Brett Halsey (Carlo), Jean Pierre Cassel (Aldo), Frank Wolff (Cesare), Marco Guglielmi (Berto), Mario Adorf (Traffic Cop).

Overlong, confusing Italian sex farce dealing with the infidelities of four bourgeois couples. Andress is the victim of a psychopathic obsession that can only be held in check by rampant adultery, Lisi cannot resist any man, Mell is driven to sudden strip-teases, and Auger is visiting the three of them to get away from an inevitable fling with a friend of the family. The Italians have produced better.

p, Gianni Hecht Lucari; d, Fausto Saraceni; w, Ettore Scola, Ruggero Maccari; ph, Ennio Guarnieri; m, Armando Trovajoli; ed, Gianna Baragli.

Comedy/Satire (PR:O MPAA:NR)

ANYONE FOR VENICE? (SEE: THE HONEYPOT, 1967)

ANYTHING CAN HAPPEN** (1952) 107m PAR bw

Jose Ferrer (Giorgi), Kim Hunter (Helen Watson), Kurt Kasznar (Nuri Bey), Eugenie Leontovich (Anna Godiedze), Oscar Karlweiss (Uncle Besso), Oscar Beregi (Uncle John), Mikhail Rasumny (Tariel Godiedze), Nick Dennis (Chancho), Gloria Marlowe (Luba Godiedze), Otto Waldis (Sandro), Alex Danaroff (Pavli), Natasha Lytess (Madame Greshkin).

Pleasant comedy based on a true story about a lovable group of Russian immigrants headed by Ferrer who come to make a new life in America. Ferrer is fine as he struggles with the English language, courts the equally lovable Hunter, and eventually becomes the owner of a California orange grove.

p, William Perlberg; d, George Seaton; w, Seaton, George Oppenheimer (based on the book by George and Helen Papashvily); ph, Daniel L. Fapp; m, Victor Young; ed, Alma Macrorie.

Comedy (PR:A MPAA:NR)

ANYTHING FOR A SONG* (1947, Ital.) 76m Superfilm bw

Ferruccio Tagliavini (Mario Gualducci), Carlo Romani (Bodoloni), Luisa Rossi (Anna), Tino Scotti (Parcotti), Aldo Silvani (Cavencelli), Carlo Campanini (Giulio), Vera Carmi (Elena), Luigi Cimara (Conte), Virgilio Riento (Gualducci).

Farfetched musical comedy starring Tagliavini as the son of an eggplant processor who wants to abandon the family business and become a singer. His departure is delayed while he raises enough money to cure a blind girl. Anything is better than this. (In Italian; English subtitles.)

p, S. A. Grandi; d, Carlo Bugiani; w, Mario Mattoli; ph, Charles Suln; m, Cilea, Donizetti, Cardillo.

Musical Comedy (PR:A MPAA:NR)

ANYTHING FOR A THRILL* (1937) 59m Maurice Conn bw

Frankie Darro (Dan Mallory), Kane Richmond (Cliff Mallory), June Johnson (Jean Roberts), Ann Evers (Betty Kelley), Johnstone White (The Earl), Horace Murphy (Mr. Kelley), Eddie Hearn (Collins), Frank Marlow (Joe).

Unbelievably vapid tale of a brother-and-sister team who want to become newsreel photographers. The pair save a professional cameraman's career by getting footage of a camera-shy heiress. The heiress is so taken with the kids that she turns around and buys the newsreel firm. The plucky camerakids then foil a plot by crooks who want to steal a few million from their benefactor. Yes, and it all happens in the space of 59 minutes.

p, Martin G. Cohen; d, Les Goodwins; w, Joseph O'Donnell, Stanley Lowenstein (based on a story by Peter B. Kyne); ph, Jack Greenhalgh; ed, Richard G. Wray.

Drama (PR:A MPAA:NR)

ANYTHING FOR LOVE (SEE: 11 HARROWHOUSE, 1974)

ANYTHING GOES*** (1936) 92m PAR bw (AKA: TOPS IS THE LIMIT)

Bing Crosby (Billy Crocker), Ethel Merman (Reno Sweeney), Charlie Ruggles (Rev. Dr. Moon/Moonface Martin), Ida Lupino (Hope Harcourt), Grace Bradley (Bonnie Le Tour), Arthur Treacher (Sir Evelyn Oakleigh), Robert McWade (Elisha J. Whitney), Richard Carle (Bishop Dobson), Margaret Dumont (Mrs. Wentworth), Jerry Tucker (Junior), Edward Gargan, Harry Wilson, Matt McHugh, Bud Fine (Pug Uglies), Billy Dooley (Ship's Photographer), Matt Moore (Ship's Captain), Rolfe Sedan (Bearded Man).

Cole Porter's 1934 stage smash is brought to the screen with Crosby as the altruistic pursuer of Lupino. He thinks she is being kidnaped and, to save her, follows her and her abductors aboard an ocean liner, pretending to be Ruggles' henchman, only to discover that she is a runaway heiress (much like Claudette Colbert in IT

HAPPENED ONE NIGHT filmed two years earlier by Columbia). Crosby's attentions to Lupino are happily returned but he is constantly in hiding from his boss who coincidentally happens to be on the ship. Then Lupino learns that Crosby is a gangster and refuses to see him. He explains that it's only an impersonation after the ship docks in England and they embrace in the back seat of a cab. The story is decidedly weak but the music is terrific and the dialog offbeat and funny. Victor Moore was originally selected as the gag gangster eventually played by Ruggles, saying the role would miscast him, as it did the too-gentle Ruggles. Merman, as the nightclub singer, a Texas Guinan-type hostess, belts out the memorable "I Get a Kick Out of You." Crosby delightfully croons the title song, "You're the Top," and "There'll Always Be a Lady Fair." Additonal Porter songs include "All Through the Night," and "Blow, Gabriel Blow." Others are "Am I Awake?," "My Heart and I," "Hopelessly in Love," and "Shanghai-De-Ho," (Frederick Hollander, Leo Robin); "Moonburn" (Hoagy Carmichael, Edward Heyman); and "Sailor Beware" (Richard Whiting, Robin), rendered by Crosby and ship's crew members in a particularly rousing production number. Teenaged Lupino is excellent as the spoiled heiress but the film drags a bit under Milestone's deliberate direction, a director more suited to serious drama.

p, Benjamin Glazer; d, Lewis Milestone; w, Howard Lindsay, Russel Crouse, Guy Bolton, P.G. Wodehouse (based on the musical by Cole Porter); ph, Karl Struss; ed, Eda Warren; art d, Hans Dreier, Ernst Fegte; set d, A. E. Freudeman.

Musical **(PR:A MPAA:NR)**

ANYTHING GOES½** (1956) 106m PAR c

Bing Crosby *(Bill Benson)*, Donald O'Connor *(Ted Adams)*, Jeanmaire *(Gaby Duval)*, Mitzi Gaynor *(Patsy Blair)*, Phil Harris *(Steve Blair)*, Kurt Kasznar *(Victor Lawrence)*, Richard Erdman *(Ed Brent)*, Walter Sande *(Alex Todd)*, Archer MacDonald *(Otto)*, Argentina Brunetti *(Suzanne)*, Alma Macrorie *(French Baroness)*, Dorothy Newmann *(German Woman)*, James Griffith *(Paul Holiday)*.

Crosby, an aging stage crooner, and O'Connor, an up-and-coming TV singer, join forces to produce a musical, searching for a female lead. On board a ship bound for Europe they discover Mitzi Gaynor and Jeanmaire, not only signing them to contracts but winning their hearts. A routine story, weaker than its original (which was silly enough) is bolstered by Cole Porter's wonderful music, and energetic dancing from O'Connor and the female leads, Jeanmaire, as an accomplished ballerina, and Gaynor, whose movements are best described as refined burlesque. Songs include "I Get A Kick Out of You," "You're the Top," "All Through the Night," "You Can Bounce Right back," and "It's De-Lovely." This was Crosby's first reunion on film with O'Connor since SING YOU SINNERS, made in 1938, and it was Crosby's last film under his Paramount contract.

p, Robert Emmett Dolan; d, Robert Lewis; w, Sidney Sheldon (based on the play by P. G. Wodehouse, Guy Bolton, music by Cole Porter revised by Russell Crouse, Howard Lindsay); ph, John F. Warren (VistaVision, Technicolor); ed, Frank Bracht; ch, Nick Castle; m/l, James Van Heusen, Sammy Cahn.

Musical **(PR:A MPAA:NR)**

ANYTHING MIGHT HAPPEN** (1935, Brit.) 66m Real Art bw

John Garrick *(Nicholson/Raybourn)*, Judy Kelly *(Kit Dundas)*, Martin Walker *(Kenneth Waring)*, Aubrey Mather *(Seymour)*, D. J. Williams *(Brown)*, Albert Whelan *(Strickland)*.

A reformed gangster suddenly gets into trouble, accused of crimes he has not committed; he tracks down the real culprit who is his exact double. Not much of a story and weak acting add up to a mediocre production.

p, Julius Hagen; d, George A. Cooper; w, H. Fowler Mear (based on the novel by Lady Evelyn Balfour); ph, Ernest Palmer.

Crime **(PR:A MPAA:NR)**

ANYTHING TO DECLARE?*½ (1939, Brit.) 76m Rembrandt/Butcher bw

Claude Hulbert *(Claude Fishlock)*, Reginald Purdell *(Pete Nutter)*, Barbara Greene *(Rosemary Edghill)*, Davy Burnaby *(Lord Fishlock)*, Frederick Burtwell *(Col. Edghill)*, Jack Melford *(Capt. Torrent)*, Arthur Hambling *(Sgt.-Maj. Hornett)*, Edward Lexy *(Sgt. Butterworth)*, Edmond Breon *(Colonel)*, Ralph Truman *(Zanner)*, Dorothy Seacombe *(Mrs. Hornett)*.

Lightheaded spoof about an inventor who creates a new mechanism for tanks which is stolen by spies whom he captures, rescuing his vital plans. Dumb programmer with little action and not too many laughs.

p, Jerome Jackson; d, Roy William Neill; w, Austin Melford, Reginald Purdell; ph, Geoffrey Faithfull.

Comedy **(PR:A MPAA:NR)**

ANZIO** (1968, Ital.) 117m COL c (GB: THE BATTLE FOR ANZIO)

Robert Mitchum *(Dick Ennis)*, Peter Falk *(Cpl. Rabinoff)*, Robert Ryan *(Gen. Carson)*, Earl Holliman *(Sgt. Stimler)*, Mark Damon *(Richardson)*, Arthur Kennedy *(Gen. Lesly)*, Reni Santoni *(Movie)*, Joseph Walsh *(Doyle)*, Thomas Hunter *(Andy)*, Giancarlo Giannini *(Cellini)*, Anthony Steel *(Gen. Marsh)*, Patrick Magee *(Gen. Starkey)*, Arthur Franz *(Gen. Howard)*, Tonio Selwart *(Gen. Von Mackensen)*, Elsa Albani *(Emilia)*, Wayde Preston *(Col. Hendricks)*, Venantino Venantini *(Capt. Burns)*, Annabella Andreoli *(Anna)*, Wolfgang Preiss *(Marshal Kesselring)*, Stefanella Giovannini *(Diana)*, Marcella Valeri *(Assunta)*, Enzo Turco *(Pepe)*, Wolf Hillinger *(Hans)*.

Disappointing war film dramatizing the bloody battle in Italy. Mitchum plays the cynical reporter who turns up everywhere. Awful Jack Jones theme song sets the tone for the rest of this misguided effort. Most of the cast is picked off by a German sniper on the retreat to the Allied beachhead. A good cast wasted.

p, Dino DeLaurentiis; d, Edward Dmytryk; w, Harry A. L. Craig (based on the book by Wynford Vaughan-Thomas); ph, Giuseppe Rotunno; m, Riz Ortolani; ed, Alberto Gallitti, Peter Taylor; art d, Luigi Scaccianoce; m/l, Ortolani, Jerome "Doc" Pomus.

War **(PR:A MPAA:NR)**

APACHE*** (1954) 91m Hecht-Lancaster/UA c

Burt Lancaster *(Massai)*, Jean Peters *(Nalinle)*, John McIntire *(Al Sieber)*, Charles Buchinsky (Charles Bronson) *(Hondo)*, John Dehner *(Weddle)*, Paul Guilfoyle *(Santos)*, Ian MacDonald *(Glagg)*, Walter Sande *(Lt. Col Beck)*, Morris Ankrum *(Dawson)*, Monte Blue *(Geronimo)*.

A tough, brutal western where the acrobatic Lancaster, one of Geronimo's sub-chiefs, refuses to surrender, conducting a one-man war against the cavalry, battling with knife, arrow, and gun. Swarms of troopers attempt to kill him, though they are led by white scout McIntire who is sympathetic to the Indians' plight. In fact, the perspective here is a novel one for the day, strictly from the hunted man's point of view, depicting Indians as human beings. Peters is a sensuous mate to Lancaster, supporting his struggle, while her father, Guilfoyle, sells out the renegade. Charles Bronson, using his real name, Buchinsky, appears as an Apache soldier, giving his usual leaden performance. One-time matinee idol Blue is a less-than-effective Geronimo, who was a real terror. UA compelled Lancaster to change the ending of this film; he wanted his hero to be shot to death by troopers after he had made peace and settled down to farm the land. Instead, he is exonerated, despite slaying a dozen men, because he has conducted a legitimate war and is therefore entitled to the provisions of peace settlements accorded warring nations, if that makes any sense.

p, Harold Hecht; d, Robert Aldrich; w, James R. Webb (based on the novel *Bronco Apache* by Paul I. Wellman); ph, Ernest Laszlo (Technicolor); m, David Raksin; ed, Alan Crosland, Jr.; art d, Nicolai Remisoff; set d, Joseph Kish.

Western **Cas.** **(PR:A MPAA:NR)**

APACHE AMBUSH** (1955) 68m COL bw

Bill Williams *(James Kingston)*, Richard Jaeckel *(Lee Parker)*, Alex Montoya *(Joaquin Jironza)*, Movita *(Rosita)*, Adele August *(Ann)*, Tex Ritter *(Trager)*, Ray "Crash" Corrigan *(Mark Calvin)*, Ray Teal *(Sgt. O'Roarke)*, Don C. Harvey *(Major McGuire)*, James Flavin *(Col. Marshall)*, George Chandler *(Chandler)*, Forrest Lewis *(Silas Parker)*, George Keymas *(Tweedy)*, Victor Millan *(Manoel)*, Harry Lauter *(Bailey)*, Bill Hale *(Bob Jennings)*, Robert Foulk *(Red Jennings)*.

Interesting western finds Abraham Lincoln in the aftermath of the Civil War sending a mixed group of Union and Confederate soldiers on a mission to drive a herd of cattle from Texas to the northern states. On the way the group finds a shipment of repeating rifles that is about to be sold to the Apaches, the Mexicans, and/or Confederate renegades intent on capturing Texas. A giant battle between the Apaches and the Mexicans ensues.

p, Wallace MacDonald; d, Fred F. Sears; w, David Lang; ph, Fred Jackman Jr.; m, Mischa Bakaleinikoff; ed, Jerome Thoms.

Western **(PR:A MPAA:NR)**

APACHE CHIEF* (1949) 59m Lippert bw

Alan Curtis *(Young Eagle)*, Tom Neal *(Lt. Brown)*, Carol Thurston *(Watona)*, Russell Hayden *(Black Wolf)*, Fuzzy Knight *(Nevada Smith)*, Trevor Bardette *(Big Crow)*, Francis McDonald *(Mohaska)*, Ted Hecht *(Pani)*, Allan Wells *(Lame Bull)*, Roy Gordon *(Col. Martin)*, Billy Wilkerson *(Grey Cloud)*, Roderic Redwing *(Tewa)*, Dale Blanchard *(Indian Boy)*, Hazel Nilsen *(White Faun)*, Charles Soldani *(Councillor)*.

Boring tale of two rival indian tribes. One, led by Curtis, believes that white men and red men can live in peace while the other, led by Hayden, murders and pillages. When the white soldiers have had enough of this they hire Curtis to capture the renegade redskin. A hand-to-hand struggle between the two chiefs follows and justice triumphs. Might have been interesting if real Indians played the Apaches.

p, Leonard S. Picker; d, Frank MacDonald; w, George D. Green (based on a story by Green, Picker); ph, Benjamin Kline; ed, Stanley Frazen.

Western **(PR:A MPAA:NR)**

APACHE COUNTRY* (1952) 62m COL bw

Gene Autry *(Himself)*, Pat Buttram *(Himself)*, Carolina Cotton *(Carolina Cotton)*, Harry Lauter *(Dave Kilrain)*, Mary Scott *(Laura Rayburn)*, Sydney Mason *(Walter Rayburn)*, Francis X. Bushman *(Cdr. Latham)*, Greg Barton *(Luke Thorn)*, Tom London *(Patches)*, Byron Foulger *(Bartlett)*, Frank Matts *(Steve)*, Mickey Simpson *(Tom Ringo)*.

Bad Autry oater where the star looks bored and tired with the series. Typical white-man-keeps-indians-drunk-so-they-do-his-bidding plot, with Autry sent in by the government to put an end to it. Autry sings "Melt Your Cold Cold Heart." (See GENE AUTRY series, Index.)

p, Armand Schaefer; d, George Archainbaud; w, Norman S. Hall; ph, William Bradford; m, Paul Mertz; ed, James Sweeney.

Western **(PR:A MPAA:NR)**

APACHE DRUMS*** (1951) 74m UNIV c

Stephen McNally *(Sam Leeds)*, Coleen Gray *(Sally)*, Willard Parker *(Joe Madden)*, Arthur Shields *(Rev. Griffin)*, James Griffith *(Lt. Glidden)*, Armando Silvestre *(Pedro-Peter)*, Georgia Backus *(Mrs. Keon)*, Clarence Muse *(Jehu)*, Ruthelma Stevens *(Betty Careless)*, James Best *(Bert Keon)*, Chinto Gusman *(Chache)*, Ray Bennett *(Mr. Keon)*.

Moody western produced by Lewton who was better known for horror films such as I WALKED WITH A ZOMBIE and CAT PEOPLE. Plot involves the efforts of a group of settlers who defend the town of Spanish Boot from a lengthy indian attack. Standout battle sequence with the citizens holed up in the town church shows off Lewton's penchant for areas of light and dark. Worth a look.

p, Val Lewton; d, Hugo Fregonese; w, David Chandler (based on *Stand at Spanish Boot* by Harry Brown); ph, Charles P. Boyle (Technicolor); m, Hans J. Salter; ed, Milton Carruth.

Western **(PR:A MPAA:NR)**

APACHE GOLD**

(1965, Ger.) 91m COL c (AKA: WINNETOU THE WARRIOR, WINNETOU)

Lex Barker *(Old Shatterhand)*, Mario Adorf *(Santer)*, Pierre Brice *(Winnetou)*, Marie Versini *(Nscho-tschi)*, *Ralf Wolter (Sam Hawkins)*, Walter Barnes *(Bill Jones)*, Mavid

Popovic *(Intschu-tschuna)*, Dunja Rajter *(Belle)*, Chris Howland *(British Journalist)*, Husein Cokic, Demeter Bitenc, Niksa Stefanini, Branko Spoljar, Vlado Krstulovic, Ilija Ivezic, Teddy Stotsek, Tomoslav Erak, Hrvoje Evob, Antun Nalis, Vladimir Bosnjak, Ana Kranjcec.

Barker is a railway detective known as Old Shatterhand and Brice is his fierce but noble Indian foe, Winnetou, in an action-jammed western with offbeat images reflecting how German filmmakers see the indomitable Apaches, here being victimized by a ruthless railroad magnate intent on carving up Indian territory for the right-of-way of his iron horse. The second in a series based upon Winnetou, a character created by European pulp writer Karl May, whose writings, irrespective of their historical inaccuracies, were at one time the most popular in Europe. (His perspective is more in keeping with James Fenimore Cooper's Indian sagas centered along America's North-east coast than realistic focus upon the savage Southwest.)

p, Horst Wendlandt; d, Harald Reinl; w, H. G. Petersson (based on the novel *Winnetou* by Karl May; ph, Ernst W. Kalinke (CinemaScope, Eastmancolor); m, Martin Bottcher.

Western **(PR:A MPAA:NR)**

APACHE KID, THE* (1941) 56m REP bw

Don "Red" Barry *(Pete Dawson)*, Lynn Merrick *(Barbara Taylor)*, Leroy Mason *(Nick Barter)*, Robert Fiske *(Joe Walker)*, John Elliott *(Judge Taylor)*, Forbes Murray *(Commissioner)*, Monte Montague *(Sheriff)*, Al St. John *(Dangle)*, Fred Toones *(Snowflake)*.

Dull "Robin Hood" story starring a surly Barry as an outraged cowboy who holds up a stagecoach to pay off a group of roadworkers who are being shafted by the town boss. Republic released better westerns.

p&d, George Sherman; w, Eliot Gibbons, Richard Murphy; ph, Harry Neumann; m, Cy Feuer; ed, Les Orlebeck.

Western **(PR:A MPAA:NR)**

APACHE RIFLES** (1964) 90m Admiral/FOX c

Audie Murphy *(Jeff Stanton)*, Michael Dante *(Red Hawk)*, Linda Lawson *(Dawn Gillis)*, L. Q. Jones *(Mike Greer)*, Ken Lynch *(Hodges)*, Joseph A. Vitale *(Victorio)*, Robert Brubaker *(Sgt. Cobb)*.

Change-of-rascist-attitude western starring Murphy who commands an army outpost in Arizona. Murphy can't stand Indians until he falls in love with a half-breed missionary, Lawson. His change of heart is frustrated by the intolerant gold-seeking white miners who start a war with the Apaches. Refreshing for its portrayal of Indians as a sympathetic group.

p, Grant Whytock; d, William H. Witney; w, Charles B. Smith; ph, Arch R. Dalzell (DeLuxe Color); ed, Whytock.

Western **(PR:A MPAA:NR)**

APACHE ROSE* (1947) 75m REP c

Roy Rogers *(Roy Rogers)*, Dale Evans *(Billie Colby)*, Olin Howlin *(Alkali Elkins)*, George Meeker *(Reed Calhoun)*, John Laurenz *(Pete)*, Russ Vincent *(Carlos Vega)*, Minerva Urecal *(Felicia)*, LeRoy Mason *(Hilliard)*, Donna DeMario *(Rosa Vega)*, Terry Frost *(Sheriff Jim Mason)*, Conchita Lemus *(Dancer)*, Tex Terry *(Likens)*, Bob Nolan and The Sons of the Pioneers, Trigger.

Roy Rogers' first color western features the singing cowboy as an oil wildcatter trying to obtain the rights to an old Spanish land grant. Gamblers headquartered on a ship offshore conspire to get the land first. Evans plays a kind of Tugboat Annie of the West. Dale sprightly sings "There's Nothin' Like Coffee in the Morning," and Roy croons the title song, "Ride, Vaquero," and is particularly good on "Wishing Well." The Sons of the Pioneers do a fine rendition of "Jose." (See ROY ROGERS series, Index.)

p, Edward J. White; d, William Witney; w, Gerald Geraghty; ph, Jack Marta (Trucolor); m, Jack Elliott, Tim Spencer, Glenn Spencer; ed, Les Orlebeck.

Western **Cas.** **(PR:A MPAA:NR)**

APACHE TERRITORY** (1958) 72m Rorvic/COL c

Rory Calhoun *(Logan Cates)*, Barbara Bates *(Jennifer Fair)*, John Dehner *(Grant Kimbrough)*, Carolyn Craig *(Junie Hatchett)*, Thomas Pittman *(Lonnie Foreman)*, Leo Gordon *(Zimmerman)*, Myron Healey *(Webb)*, Francis De Sales *(Sgt. Sheehan)*, Frank De Kova *(Lugo)*, Reg Parton *(Conley)*, Bob Woodward *(Graves)*, Fred Krone *(Styles)*.

Calhoun stars as a drifter who finds himself helping a group of back-biting settlers under Indian attack. Most of the ungrateful pilgrims run to their deaths in spite of the cowboy's efforts to save them. Calhoun eventually defeats the redskins and rides off into the sunset with Bates. Based on a Louis L'Amour novel, and co-produced by Calhoun.

p, Rory Calhoun, Victor M. Orsatti; d, Ray Nazarro; w, Charles R. Marion, George W. George (based on Frank Moss' adaptation of the Louis L'Amour novel); ph, Irving Lippman (Eastmancolor); ed, Al Clark.

Western **(PR:A MPAA:NR)**

APACHE TRAIL** (1942) 66m MGM bw

Lloyd Nolan *(Trigger Bill)*, Donna Reed *(Rosalia Martinez)*, William Lundigan *(Tom Folliard)*, Ann Ayars *(Constance Selden)*, Connie Gilchrist *(Senora Martinez)*, Chill Wills *('Pike' Skelton)*, Miles Mander *(James V. Thorne)*, Gloria Holden *(Mrs. James V. Thorne)*, Ray Teal *(Ed Cotton)*, Grant Withers *(Lestrade)*, Fuzzy Knight *(Juke)*, Trevor Bardette *(Amber)*, Tito Renaldo *(Cochee)*, Frank M. Thomas *(Maj. Lowden)*, George Watts *(Judge Keeley)*.

Nolan and Lundigan play brothers defending themselves against an Apache uprising caused by the theft of a peace pipe. Good B western with a decent cast of character actors. Later remade as APACHE WAR SMOKE which isn't bad either.

p, Samuel Marx; d, Richard Thorpe; w, Maurice Geraghty (based on a story by Ernest Haycox); ph, Sidney Wagner; m, Sol Kaplan; ed, Frank Sullivan

Western **(PR:A MPAA:NR)**

APACHE UPRISING** (1966) 90m PAR c

Rory Calhoun *(Jim Walker)*, Corinne Calvet *(Janice MacKenzie)*, John Russell *(Vance Buckner)*, Lon Chaney *(Charlie Russell)*, Gene Evans *(Jess Cooney)*, Richard Arlen *(Capt. Gannon)*, Robert H. Harris *(Hoyt Taylor)*, Arthur Hunnicut *(Bill Gibson)*, DeForest Kelley *(Toby Jack Saunders)*, George Chandler *(Jace Asher)*, Jean Parker *(Mrs. Hawkes)*, Johnny Mack Brown *(Sheriff Ben Hall)*, Donald Barry *(Henry Belden)*, Abel Fernandez *(Young Apache)*, Robert Carricart *(Chico Lopez)*, Paul Daniel *(Old Antone)*.

In the middle of hostile Apache country, crooked stagecoach businessman Harris and cunning thief Russell are thwarted in their plans to rob a relay station of its gold by Calhoun and his honest pals. Kelley, famous to many as Dr. McCoy on TV's "Star Trek," hams it up as a wicked, paranoid gunfighter in this routine western.

p, A. C. Lyles; d, R. G. Springsteen; w, Harry Sanford, Max Lamb (based on the novel *Way Station* by Sanford, Max Steeber); ph, W. Wallace Kelley (Technicolor); m, Jimmie Haskell; ed, John Schreyer.

Western **(PR:A MPAA:NR)**

APACHE WAR SMOKE** (1952) 67m MGM bw

Gilbert Roland *(Peso)*, Glenda Farrell *(Fanny Webson)*, Robert Horton *(Tom Herrera)*, Barbara Ruick *(Nancy Dekker)*, Gene Lockhart *(Cyril R. Snowden)*, Henry Morgan *(Ed Cotten)*, Patricia Tiernan *(Lorraine Sayburn)*, Hank Worden *(Amber)*, Myron Healey *(Pike Curtis)*, Emmett Lynn *(Les)*, Argentina Brunetti *(Madre)*, Bobby Blake *(Luis)*, Douglas Dumbrille *(Maj. Dekker)*,

Roland, a legendary bandito, holes up at forgotten bastard son Horton's way station, hiding from crazed Apaches who have accused him of killing some braves. Although he has no love for his long-lost father, Horton refuses to give the possibly innocent Roland to the angry indians in return for the safety of the others at the station. Some tension builds up among members of the threatened group but it dissipates quickly, the makers of the film never exploring the material that deeply and never reaching the necessary level of suspense.

p, Hayes Goetz; d, Harold Kress; w, Jerry Davis (based on a story by Ernest Haycox); ph, John Alton; ed, Newell P. Kimlin.

Western **(PR:A MPAA:NR)**

APACHE WARRIOR½** (1957) 73m FOX

Keith Larsen *(Apache Kid)*, Jim Davis *(Ben)*, Rodolfo Acosta *(Marteen)*, John Miljan *(Nantan)*, Eddie Little, Michael Carr *(Apaches)*, George Keymas *(Chato)*, Lane Bradford *(Sgt. Gaunt)*, Eugenia Paul *(Liwana)*, Damian O'Flynn *(Major)*, Dehl Berti *(Chikisin)*, Nick Thompson *(Horse Trader)*, Ray Kellogg, Allan Nixon, Karl Davis *(Bounty Men)*, David Carlisle *(Cavalry Leader)*.

Apache scout Larsen, aiding good friend Davis and others in the U.S. Cavalry in the tracking down of renegade Indians after Geronimo's defeat, is himself hunted when he kills the man who murdered his brother. When he finally captures Larsen, Davis lets his Apache friend go, realizing that he was obeying a personal code and not the white man's law. Supposedly based on the notorious outlaw, The Apache Kid, this above-average western is notable for its fair portrayal of Indians exemplified in the friendship that grows between Larsen and Davis.

p, Plato Skouras; d, Elmo Williams; w, Carroll Young, Kurt Neumann, Eric Norden (based on a story by Neumann, Young); ph, John M. Nickolaus, Jr. (Regalscope); m, Paul Dunlap; ed, Jodie Copelan.

Western **(PR:A MPAA:NR)**

APACHE WOMAN** (1955) 82m Golden State/ARC c

Lloyd Bridges *(Rex Moffet)*, Joan Taylor *(Anne Libeau)*, Lance Fuller *(Armand)*, Morgan Jones *(Macey)*, Paul Birch *(Sheriff)*, Jonathan Haze *(Tom Chandler)*, Paul Dubov *(Ben)*, Lou Place *(Carrom)*, Gene Marlowe *(White Star)*, Dick Miller *(Tall Tree)*, Chester Conklin *(Mooney)*, Jean Howell *(Mrs. Chandler)*.

Government agent Bridges arrives in a small Arizona town and sets out to investigate a series of murderous robberies supposedly committed by a wild group of Apaches who refuse to exist peacefully on the reservation. While constantly calming the white townspeople's call for retaliation against *any* Indians, Bridges discovers that the crimes are the brainchild of demented, college-educated half-breed Fuller and his motley white gang. Taylor aids Bridges in his capture of the thieves, even though Fuller is her brother. The second western by Hollywood legend Corman is noteworthy for its anti-racist theme and untraditional style, but it still remains an average western.

p, Roger Corman; d, Corman; w, Lou Rusoff; ph, Floyd Crosby (Pathe Color); m, Ronald Stein; ed, Ronald Sinclair.

Western **(PR:A MPAA:NR)**

APARAJITO***

(1959, India) 105m Epic/Aurora bw (GB: THE UNVANQUISHED)

Pinaki Sen Gupta *(Apu, as a boy)*, Smaran Ghosal *(Apu, as an adolescent)*, Karuna Banerji *(Mother)*, Kanu Banerji *(Father)*, Ramani Sen Gupta *(Old Uncle)*, Charu Ghosh *(Nanda Babu)*, Subodh Ganguly *(Headmaster)*, Kali Charan Ray *(Press Proprietor)*, Santi Gupta *(Landlord's Wife)*, K. S. Pandey *(Pandey)*, Sudipta Ray *(Nirupama)*, Ajay Mitra *(Anil)*.

A young boy and his newly widowed mother struggle for existence in a small Indian town. Resisting a life in the priesthood, the boy persuades his mother to send him to school. Having done well in his studies over the years, the boy, now a young adult, wins a scholarship to the university in Calcutta. Engulfed in city life and very demanding school work, Ghosal forgets about his mother. Finally returning for a visit after his exams, Ghosal discovers that his mother has died and that she never wanted to inform him of her illness for fear that it would disrupt his academic goals. Somewhat shaken and saddened, Ghosal returns to Calcutta. APARAJITO is the second chapter in THE APU TRILOGY, perhaps the finest and certainly the most famous group of films from India. Director Ray, a painter and commercial artist, devoted his time, money, and passion to a personal project that many considered impossible, the cinematic adaptation of the popular Bengali novel, *Pather Panchali*. Although very slow-moving, the films are considered to be among the finest of the 1950s, winning numerous awards and gaining praise for the amazing sitar music of composer/performer Ravi Shankar. APARAJITO, being the "middle" of the story of Apu, lacks the power of the first and third films (PATHER PANCHALI and THE WORLD OF APU) but it nonethe less is an excellent look at Indian society and the average people who inhabit this still-mysterious part of the world.

p,d&w, Satyajit Ray (based on the novel *Pather Panchali* by Bibhutibhusan Bandapaddhay); ph, Subroto Mitra; m, Ravi Shankar; ed, Dulala Dutta; art d, B. Chandragupta.

Drama   **Cas.**   **(PR:A   MPAA:NR)**

APARTMENT, THE***   (1960) 125m UA bw

Jack Lemmon (*C. C. Baxter*), Shirley MacLaine (*Fran Kubelik*), Fred MacMurray (*J. D. Sheldrake*), Ray Walston (*Mr. Dobisch*), David Lewis (*Mr. Kirkeby*), Jack Kruschen (*Dr. Dreyfuss*), Joan Shawlee (*Sylvia*), Edie Adams (*Miss Olsen*), Hope Holiday (*Margie MacDougall*), Johnny Seven (*Karl Matuschka*), Naomi Stevens (*Mrs. Dreyfuss*), Frances Weintraub Lax (*Mrs. Lieberman*), Joyce Jameson (*The Blonde*), Willard Waterman (*Mr.Vanderhof*), David White (*Mr. Eichelberger*), Benny Burt (*Bartender*), Hal Smith (*Santa Claus*), Dorothy Abbott (*Office Worker*)

In his climb up the corporate ladder of success, office worker Lemmon finds the rungs almost as slippery as his own weaseling, ingratiating personality. The insurance clerk, to please his middle-management bosses, loans out his apartment so they can conveniently carry on their sordid extramarital affairs without the bother of hotels and prying bellboys. The superiors promise to put in a good word with the big boss, MacMurray, in obtaining him a promotion. Suddenly the conniving device works like a charm. Lemmon is given a sprawling office, a secretary, and a key to the executive washroom in a surprise promotion. MacMurray confers with the new corporate leader and informs Lemmon that he alone brought about this good fortune after learning that the key to his apartment was available. He, too, is carrying on an affair and requests use of the valued apartment, to which Lemmon agrees with lickspittle speed. Now that he has "arrived," Lemmon doffs a bowler hat, slings a walking cane on his arm, and goes after the girl he adores, MacLaine, a rather simple-minded but cute elevator operator in his office building. He is crushed to learn that she is the one having the affair with the much-married MacMurray. The grim irony of the situation deepens when MacMurray tells MacLaine that he cannot marry her, even though he has been stringing her along with this promise. She takes an overdose in Lemmon's apartment after her lover leaves but the plotting occupant finds her in the nick of time, revives her and blurts out his love for her. He tenderly nurses MacLaine while she recuperates, preparing meals in unique fashion, such as straining spaghetti through the threads of his tennis racket. Returning to work, Lemmon realizes the shallow amorality he and his colleagues have been practicing. When MacMurray again asks for his apartment key, Lemmon refuses, telling off the boss and quitting. He returns to the apartment where MacLaine joins him after learning that he has given up his career for her. It's almost all Lemmon's film, as director Wilder promised it would be after the two made SOME LIKE IT HOT. His scenes with MacLaine are priceless, the interacting properly forced, groping, then genuinely warm and affectionate as they fall in love. This was the first film in which the pert, pixieish MacLaine emerged with a display of real talent. They are the only likable people in a really shoddy story where Wilder purposely spotlighted the new morality of the sixties, a popular adultery that undoubtedly led to the rise of certain social diseases that threaten our present existence, seeing these warped customs as more comic than tragic, spoofing the new moderns while, at the finish, upholding the old moral traditions. MacMurray is a great standout heel, at one point blandly stating that he has lied to MacLaine all along and never had any intention of leaving his wife for her, later commenting wryly: "When you've been married to a woman 12 years you just don't sit down to a breakfast table and say 'Pass the sugar. I want a divorce.' It's not that easy." MacMurray's mail was overwhelmingly against this portrayal, an avalanche of missives insisting that he play only "nice guys" henceforth. It stunned the actor so that he never again took on a role where his moral character could be criticized, comfortably staying in the Disney camp. MacLaine's forlorn, neurotic, almost empty- headed cutie would have been as tawdry and repugnant as a cheap hooker had she not underplayed the role, guided, of course, by the iron-handed Billy Wilder. Lemmon was given free rein by the director, who compared Lemmon with Chaplin and thought he could do no evil. He didn't, masterfully working every scene in and out of a wheedling creature whose marvelous conscience finally boils to the top and steams through his ears. In keeping with his habit, Wilder shot the film right up to its finish without knowing the ending, handing his stars wet mimeographed script pages about twenty minutes before the final scenes. Quick readers, Lemmon and MacLaine then wrapped the film in one take. In describing this unforgettable and yet unsavory story, Lemmon later remarked: "Billy Wilder grew a rose in a garbage pail." Just as Wilder's SUNSET BOULEVARD destroyed the ancient images of sacrosanct Hollywood, THE APARTMENT is the iconoclast's raspberries to American businessmen who had coupled immorality to success. Both Lemmon and MacLaine were nominated for Oscars but were passed over, although Wilder received the statuette for Best Director, Diamond for Best Screenplay, and the film won Best Picture. MacLaine later got a strange nod of recognition from an unexpected source for her portrayal of the elfin floozy. In the book *Don't Fall Off the Mountain* she recalled meeting an interpreter for Nikita Khrushchev who was then addressing the United Nations in New York. The Russian envoy told the actress: "The Premier sends his regards, wishes to be remembered to you, and says he's just seen your new picture, THE APARTMENT, and you've improved." (This film was later converted into the smash Broadway play "Promises, Promises.")

p&d, Billy Wilder; w, Wilder, I. A. L. Diamond; ph, Joseph LaShelle (Panavision); m, Adolph Deutsch; ed, Daniel Mandell; art d, Alexander Trauner; set d, Edward G. Boyle.

Comedy/Drama   **Cas.**   **(PR:C-O   MPAA:NR)**

APARTMENT FOR PEGGY***   (1948) 96m FOX c

Jeanne Crain (*Peggy*), William Holden (*Jason*), Edmund Gwenn (*Professor Henry Barnes*), Gene Lockhart (*Professor Edward Bell*), Griff Barnett (*Dr. Conway*), Randy Stuart (*Dorothy*), Marion Marshall (*Ruth*), Pati Behrs (*Jeanne*), Henri Letondal (*Prof. Roland Pavin*), Houseley Stevenson (*Prof. T. J. Beck*), Helen Ford (*Della*), Almira Sessions (*Mrs. Landon*), Charles Lane (*Prof. Collins*), Ronald Burns

(*Delivery Boy*), Gene Nelson (*Jerry*), Bob Patten, William Sheehan, Joan Wrae, Geraldine Jordon, Kaye Lake (*Students*), Mae Marsh (*Woman*), Ann Staunton, Theresa Lyon (*Nurses*), Betty Lynn (*Wife*), Hal K. Dawson, Robert Williams, Charles Tannen, Frank Scannell (*Salesmen*)

A heartwarming film concerning the adjustment of WW II vet Holden and his young wife, Crain, and their search for values and roots in the turbulent, avaricious boom years of the late 1940s. Seaton's subtle direction depicts the young couple's everyday struggles to deal with trailer life, laundromats, and store bargains. All the while Holden attempts to get through college on the G.I. bill and find a decent place for his wife to live. Crain finds an old college professor, Gwenn, living alone in a large house depressed, thinking of suicide; he has come to believe that his life is over, that the ideals and noble purposes of the past have been forgotten. She convinces him to rent his attic to her and hubby and both turn the place into a cozy apartment. Their positive, optimistic views and natural ebullience revitalize Gwenn who decides to fill his remaining years with constructive work. A superior film, thanks to Seaton's deft direction and script which testifies to the magnificence of the human heart, one that also indicts the slimy postwar profiteers who made life miserable for American youth but could not suppress its indefatigable spirit. A significant role for Holden in that it brought him high praise from critics, establishing him as a solid lead. Gwenn, who had just triumphed in the classic MIRACLE ON 34TH STREET, which Seaton had also directed, was never more touching or memorable.

p, William Perlberg; d&w, George Seaton (based on a story by Faith Baldwin); ph, Harry Jackson (Technicolor); m, David Raksin; ed, Robert Simpson; md, Lionel Newman; art d, Lyle Wheeler, Richard Irvine; set d, Thomas Little, Walter M. Scott.

Drama   **(PR:A   MPAA:NR)**

APE, THE*   (1940) 63m MON bw

Boris Karloff (*Dr. Bernard Adrian*), Maris Wrixon (*Frances Clifford*), Gertrude Hoffman (*Mrs. Clifford*), Henry Hall (*Sheriff Jeff Holliday*), Gene O'Donnell (*Danny Foster*), Dorothy Vaughan (*Jane*), Jack Kennedy (*Tomlin*), Jessie Arnold (*Mrs. Brill*).

Crazed doctor Karloff, obsessed with finding a cure for paralysis after his crippled daughter's death, is convinced that the secret cure can be found in the spinal fluid of human beings. Killing an escaped circus ape, Karloff dons the animal's hide, murders innocent townspeople, drains their precious spinal fluid, and returns to his lab. The serum does indeed cure his surrogate-daughter patient Clifford, but the formula dies with Karloff when he is shot and killed by the police while dressed as the rampaging ape. Not some of Karloff's best work at all, THE APE never finds the right groove, veering between odd thriller and ridiculous mad scientist tale.

p, Scott R. Dunlap; d, William Nigh; w, Curt Siodmak, Richard Carroll (based on a play by Adam Hull Shirk); ph, Harry Neumann; m, Edward Kay; ed, Russell Schoengarth, art d, E. R. Hickson.

Horror   **Cas.**   **(PR:C   MPAA:NR)**

APE MAN, THE*   (1943) 64m MON bw (GB: LOCK YOUR DOORS)

Bela Lugosi (*Dr. Brewster*), Wallace Ford (*Jeff Carter*), Louise Currie (*Billie Mason*), Minerva Urecal (*Agatha Brewster*), Henry Hall (*Dr. Randall*), Ralph Littlefield (*Zippe*), J. Farrell MacDonald (*Captain*), George Kirby (*Butler*), Wheeler Oakman (*Brady*), Emil Van Horn (*The Ape*).

Jeckyll-ish doctor Lugosi gains simian characteristics after consuming a secret potion. With an actual gorilla as an accomplice, Lugosi drains the spinal fluid from murdered victims and uses it as the catalytic ingredient in changing back to his "normal" self. Gutsy reporters Ford and Currie, investigating the recent killings, are nearly taken off the story permanently by Lugosi and his ape, but are saved in the nick of time by the police. Unintentionally funny Lugosi outing reminiscent, at times, of Monogram's 1940 Karloff vehicle, THE APE. Monogram never used the talent of Karloff and Lugosi well. The stars' best work can be seen in their classics for Universal.

p, Sam Katzman, Jack Dietz; d, William Beaudine; w, Barney Sarecky; ph, Mack Stengler; ed, Carl Pierson.

Horror   **Cas.**   **(PR:C   MPAA:NR)**

APE WOMAN, THE**   (1964, Ital.) 100m CC CHAM-Interfilm/EM

Ugo Tognazzi (*Antonio Focaccia*), Annie Girardot (*Maria*), Achille Majeroni, Elvira Paoloni, Ugo Rossi, Filippo Pompa Marcelli, Ermeldinda De Felice.

Good-for-nothing Tognazzi accidentally comes across Girardot, a beautiful woman whose body is covered with fur, and convinces her to let him set her up as a sideshow attraction. Considering her pitiful yet fascinating, Tognazzi marries "The Ape Woman," giving him the legal right to star her in an obscure strip-tease act. Girardot becomes pregnant and things look hopeful for the little family, but she and the child die during a painful birth. Feeling pressure from his debtors, Tognazzi remorsefully mummifies the two bodies and continues his side-show attraction. The unusual, distasteful subject matter is given a strong, emotional treatment by its director and talented cast, but the obscure, curious tone of the film falters throughout, never finding a comfortable niche. The film is based on the true story of Julia Pastrana, a 19th-century Mexican woman who was covered with hair. She died in childbirth (allegedly of a broken heart when she saw her still-born fur-covered offspring). Her manager-husband had both bodies embalmed and exhibited them in Europe. Over the years the corpses were passed from showman-to-showman until they vanished sometime between the World Wars. The French version of this film ends with the birth of a normal baby, and all Girardot's hair falling out, leaving her happy and normal.

p, Carlo Ponti; d, Marco Ferreri; w, Ferreri, Rafael Azcona; ph, Aldo Tonti; m, Teo Usuelli; ed, Mario Serandrei; cos. Piero Tosi.

Drama   **(PR:C   MPAA:NR)**

APOCALYPSE NOW*1/2   (1979) 139m UA c

Marlon Brando (*Col. Kurtz*), Robert Duvall (*Lt. Col. Kilgore*), Martin Sheen (*Capt. Willard*), Frederic Forrest (*Chef*), Albert Hall (*Chief*), Sam Bottoms (*Lance*), Larry Fishburne (*Clean*), Dennis Hopper (*Photo Journalist*), G. D. Spradlin (*General*), Harrison Ford (*Colonel*), Scott Glenn (*Civilian*), Bill Graham (*Agent*), Cyndi Wood,

Colleen Camp, Linda Carpenter (Playmates), Jack Thibeau, Damien Leake, Glenn Walken, Jerry Ross.

This brilliant, bizarre and confusing film brought producer-director Coppola great kudos; he was hailed as the creator of the greatest war (or anti-war) film ever made, yet subsequent viewings show considerable flaws and wide gaps in the story line that are merely filled in with Brando's incomprehensibility. Sheen, a captain high on war and suffering from battle fatigue, is ordered to take a four-man crew up the Mekong River into Cambodia where he is to exterminate Brando, a berserk American colonel who has set up a ruthless dictatorship on an island. As the gunboat proceeds upriver, Sheen and his men, whom he regards as "rock and rollers with one foot in their graves," come under fire which jangles the nerves of the executioner, haunting him with memories of previous battles. They stop at an American helicopter base where Sheen accompanies Duvall, a wacko colonel who "loves the smell of napalm in the morning," on a raid against a Vietcong stronghold. The copters fly in blaring Wagner's "Ride of the Valkyries" which, according to Duvall, "scares hell out of the slopes," and then proceed to bomb and strafe everyone in sight. The gunboat continues upriver to a USO site where thousands of GIs are near frantic at the sight of Playboy Playmates bumping and grinding sexily on stage; several soldiers become so aroused they rush the stage and the talentless girls must be taken away to prevent gang rape. Sheen resumes his journey with the boat being attacked from shore; some crew members are killed but he finally reaches Brando's island stronghold. Signs of his dictatorship among the mountain tribesmen are every-where—severed heads of dissenters impaled on poles, corpses hanging from trees. American stragglers greet Sheen, fanatical followers of Brando, notably Hopper, a neurotic photographer. The executioner is granted an audience with Brando, who resides in the damp darkness of a cave, meditating on life and death, telling Sheen that "moral terror" is necessary for the preservation of civilization. Despite his inner admiration for Brando—it is never made clear why diehard soldier Sheen should feel this way—the execution is carried out and Sheen escapes with Bottoms as the natives close in on the retreating gunboat. Coppola, as usual, was expansive and almost as self-indulgent in this production as was his temperamental star, Brando, beginning with a $12 million budget and going over $31 million before his 238-day shooting schedule ended, his costs so excessive that he had to sink his own money into the production. The film was also held up as Sheen recovered from a heart attack. The movie originally was a financial disaster, grossing little more than $5 million above budget, but Coppola did produce an awesome movie which depicts the ultra-insanity of the Vietnam War. Everything here is perverted, from those commanding troops to the sleazy entertainment given American soldiers (instead of Bob Hope and wisecracks there are talentless floozies; instead of resolute and somber militarists there is madness, schizophrenia, paranoia and murder by order). The photography and production values are faultless as Coppola reproduced the flavor of the Vietnam-Cambodian jungle—its suffocating foliage, its lurking dangers—in the Philippines. But the introspective passages slow down the slim story, first exemplified by Sheen, then in the rambling, incohesive monologs mumbled by Brando which echo chillingly in his cave (reportedly inspired by Joseph Conrad's arcane Heart of Darkness) but one never clearly understands the madman's point of view, which might be the point, yet such obfuscating tirades could have been encapsulated for the sake of the viewer suffering through selfishly produced surrealistic scenes. Here again was a message no one understood, but accepted in the name of muddled art. The juxtaposition of Coppola's swift and paralyzing action and the leaden weight of Brando's boring monologs did not justify the fizzling finale. We are given the tremendous build-up of Technicolor battle only to be offered an end in the shadows of a cave with a madman whose philosophy and rhetoric are about as interesting as those of a drugged-out guru contemplating his navel at the top of Big Sur. The point, of course, is that war is pointless and horrible and inhuman, and in those regards APOCALYPSE NOW succeeds with devastating accuracy. Yet it lacks anything and everything really human—love, humor (outside the display of madness), reason, understanding, and people to whom the normal viewer can relate. There is no real feeling here for the Vietnam struggle where hundreds of thousands of Americans fought and more than 50,000 died, a universal attitude that is found in THE DEER HUNTER and even THE GREEN BERETS. Coppola's intense interpretation of that war is technically impressive and shocking, but it is woefully short on humanity.

p&d, Francis Ford Coppola; w, John Milius, Coppola; ph, Vittorio Storaro (Technivision, Technicolor); m, Carmine Coppola, Francis Ford Coppola; ed, Richard Marks; prod d, Dean Tavoularis; art d, Angelo Graham; set d, George R. Nelson; cos, Charles E. James; narr, Michael Herr.

War   Cas.   (PR:O   MPAA:R)

APOLLO GOES ON HOLIDAY**   (1968, Ger./Swed.) 90m
A. Th. Damaskinos & V. Michaelides A.E./T.V.S. of Stockholm c

Thomas Fritsch (Prince), Helena Nathaneal (Guide), Athenodoros Proussalis (Bus Driver), Georges Bartis (Photographer), Ulla Bergryd, Ulf Brunnberd, Caroline Christensen (Tourists), Eftihia Partheniadou (Woman Hitchhiker).

Young prince Fritsch, spying beautiful tour guide Nathaneal from his helicopter while touring Greece, escapes from his overbearing entourage and joins the girl's tour group posing as a humble visitor. The two fall in love, but Fritsch, knowing that he has duties and responsibilities to his country, leaves her, never revealing his true identity. Greek/Swedish reworking of ROMAN HOLIDAY is a pleasure for romantics, but it lacks the personality and charm of the Audrey Hepburn vehicle.

p, A. Th. Damaskinos, V. Michaelides; d, Georges Skalenakis; w, Yannis Tziotis, V. Scnitzeff; ph, Tony Forsberg; m, Yannis Marcopoulos; ch, Yannis Emirzas.

Romance   (PR:A   MPAA:NR)

APOLOGY FOR MURDER*   (1945) 67m PRC bw
Ann Savage (Toni Kirkland), Hugh Beaumont (Kenny Blake), Charles D. Brown (Ward McGee), Russell Hicks (Kirkland), Pierre Watkin (Craig Jordan), Bud Buster (Caretaker), Norman Willis (Allen Webb), Eva Novak (Maid), Archie Hall (Paul), Elizabeth Valentine (Rancher's Wife), Henry Hall (Warden), Wheaton Chambers (Minister), George Sherwood (Lt. Edwards).

Reporter Beaumont, sapped of his morals by his lover Savage, agrees to assist in the killing of her husband. Echoes of James M. Cain ring throughout the plot of this forgettable little mystery.

p, Sigmund Neufeld; d, Sam Newfield; w, Fred Minton; ph, Jack Greenhalgh; ed, Holbrook N. Todd; md, Leo Erdody.

Crime   (PR:A   MPAA:NR)

APPALOOSA, THE** (1966) 98m UNIV c (GB: SOUTHWEST TO SONORA)
Marlon Brando (Matt Fletcher), Anjanette Comer (Trini), John Saxon (Chuy Medina), Emilio Fernandez (Lazaro), Alex Montoya (Squint Eye), Miriam Colon (Ana), Rafael Campos (Paco), Frank Silvera (Ramos), Larry D. Mann (Priest), Argentina Brunetti (Yaqui Woman).

Near the Mexican border loner Brando, a hoary buffalo hunter whose wife has been murdered by Indians, enters a church to promise God that he will begin a new sinless life, breeding beautiful Appaloosa horses (similar in markings but bigger than pintos). While thus occupied, Comer steals his horse from the front of the church to escape her sadistic boy friend, Saxon, a bandit chief. She is returned to Saxon who later offers Brando money for the animal but is refused. The bandit and his men then waylay Brando in the desolate wilds, taking his horse and humiliating him by dragging him rope-tied through a rocky stream. He recovers from his terrible wounds, goes to Saxon's Mexican hideout and loses a wrestling match wherein he is stung by a scorpion and left to die. Brando cuts out the poison with broken glass and, with Comer's help, again revives and again goes to the bandit's camp where he shoots several henchmen and leaves with Comer who hates Saxon, she says, ever since she was sold to him as a child. Saxon and cronies pursue the pair, trapping them in the mountains. Brando, realizing he loves the girl more than his horse, lets the Appaloosa go. Saxon shoots at the horse, his hiding place revealed, and Brando kills him. He and Comer than mount the prize animal and ride away to begin anew. Director Furie's stylistic method of dwelling on certain scenes, a penchant for exasperating close-ups so large as to blot out the screen and confuse the vision, worked effectively in his IPCRESS FILE but here his shots of teeth, horses' eyes, guns, Brando's jowls and Comer's brow are merely specious, distracting, and as amateurish as a TV director shooting into the sun for reflection or allowing water on the camera lens to remind the viewer that technicians are present. Moreover, this film is a blatant exploitation of Brando's recently completed ONE-EYED JACKS, with a story and location that are almost identical. Furie, to be fair, also had difficulty with Brando, a truculent actor who insisted that his interpretation of his character take precedence over Furie's (what else is new?). This was the great actor's second excursion into the western genre and the more he immersed himself into the Old West, the more bizarre his characters became, until he sank into the bubble-bathed idiocy of THE MISSOURI BREAKS.

p, Alan Miller; d, Sidney J. Furie; w, James Bridges, Roland Kibbee (based on the novel by Robert MacLeod). ph, Russell Metty (Techniscope, Technicolor): m, Frank Skinner; ed, Ted J. Kent; art d, Alexander Golitzen, Alfred Sweeney; cos, Rosemary Odell, Helen Colvig.

Western   (PR:C   MPAA:NR)

APPASSIONATA**½   (1946, Swed.) 93m Lux/Saga bw
Viveca Lindfors (Marla), Georg Rydeberg (Dahlhoff), Alf Kjellin (Erik), Georg Funquist (Hellenius).

An established concert pianist and a determined young musician vie for the affections of the lovely Lindfors. Familiar story is enhanced by the presence of Miss Lindfors (in one of her last Swedish films before going to Hollywood) and by the off-screen piano playing of W. Witkowsky, one of the finest Polish pianists.

d&w, Olaf Molander.

Drama   (PR:A   MPAA:NR)

APPLAUSE***   (1929) 80m PAR bw
Helen Morgan (Kitty Darling), Joan Peers (April Darling), Fuller Mellish, Jr. (Hitch Nelson), Jack Cameron (Joe King), Henry Wadsworth (Tony), Dorothy Cumming (Mother Superior).

Morgan, the rage of Broadway musicals and nightclubs during the 1920s, is a fading burlesque singing star—she is shown to age on the stage as her born-in-a-trunk daughter grows up in a convent. The pathetic Morgan, who debuted on the screen with this tearjerker and who was to die of cirrhosis of the liver in 1941 at age 41, is being two-timed by a slippery boy friend, not unlike the real men in the torch singer's life. Moreover, she attempts to save her grown-up child from the clutches of fakes and ne'er-do-wells, losing her daughter's love in the melancholy end. Poignant though dated, this early talkie is rich in old burlesque backstage atmosphere and has many innovative techniques introduced by Mamoulian in his directorial debut. Then there is Morgan's singing, which is captivating and distinctive, a plaintive voice of the cabaret society that was only a memory when this film was made at Paramount's Astoria, Long Island (N.Y.) studio.

p, Monta Bell; d, Rouben Mamoulian; w, Garrett Fort (based on the novel by Beth Brown); ph, George Folsey; ed, John Bassler.

Drama   (PR:A   MPAA:NR)

APPLE, THE*   (1980 U.S./Ger.) 90m N.F. Geria III/Cannon c
Catherine Mary Stuart (Bibi), George Gilmour (Alphie), Grace Kennedy (Pandi), Allan Love (Dandi), Joss Ackland (Topps), Vladek Sheybal (Boogalow), Ray Shell (Snake), Miriam Margolyes (Landlady), Leslie Meadows (Ashley), Derek Deadman (Bulldog), Gunter Notthoff (Fatdog), Michael Logan (James), Clem Davies (Clark), George S. Clinton (Joe), Coby Recht (Jean-Louis), Francesca Poston (Vampire), Iris Recht (Domini).

Vaguely Faustian futuristic musical that has devilish record producer Sheybal seducing innocent folk-singing couple Stuart and Gilmour into his group of high-tech emotionless stars. Tempted by the inhabitants of Sheybal's sinful colony where sex and drugs are in great supply, Stuart and Gilmour finally reject the cold lifestyles of their new world and join a group of radicals. Handsomely packaged musical, shot in Berlin, that lacks the strong songs and/or performers that are necessary to carry off this type of pop allegory.

p, Menahem Golan, Yoram Globus; d&w, Golan; ph, David Gurfinkle (Panavision); m, Coby and Iris Recht; ed, Alain Jakubowicz; prod d, Jurgen Kiebach; cos, Ingrid Zore; ch, Nigel Lythgoe.

Musical/Science Fiction (PR:C-O MPAA:PG)

APPLE DUMPLING GANG, THE** (1975) 100m BV c

Bill Bixby (Russell Donavan), Susan Clark (Magnolia Dusty Clydesdale), Don Knotts (Theodore Ogilvie), Tim Conway (Amos), David Wayne (Col. T. T. Clydesdale), Slim Pickens (Frank Stillwell), Harry Morgan (Homer McCoy), John McGiver (Leonard Sharpe), Don Knight (John Wintle), Clay O'Brien (Bobby Bradley), Brad Savage (Clovis Bradley), Stacy Manning (Celia Bradley), Dennis Fimple (Rudy Hooks), Pepe Callahan (Clemons), Iris Adrian (Poker Polly), Fran Ryan (Mrs. Stockley), Bing Russell (Herm Dally), James E. Brodhead (The Mouthpiece), Jim Boles (Easy Archie), Olan Soule (Rube Cluck), Tom Waters (Rowdy Joe Dover), Dawn Little Sky (Big Foot), Richard Lee-Sung (Oh So), Arthur Wong (No S'o), Dick Winslow (Slippery Kid), Bill Dunbar (Fast Eddie), Wally Berns (Cheating Charley).

Handsome gambler Bixby finds himself stuck with three orphaned children in the Old West. Agreeing to a "friendly" marriage with tough female coach driver Clark, the couple escorts the children to their dead father's abandoned gold mine where, as luck would have it, they find a huge lump of the valuable stuff. Into the pleasant picture come two outlaw gangs, one consisting of the bumbling Conway and Knotts, and the other headed by the vicious Pickens. After defeating both in a very Disney-like fashion, the makeshift family settles down to farm life with Clark and Bixby deciding to make their relationship a bit more than platonic. A rather pleasant period comedy that made quite a sum of money for the studio in its economically weak post-Walt period. A delightful cast of character actors helps the childish story, with Conway and Knotts beginning what would become a somewhat famous, but very simple-minded, film comedy duo.

p, Bill Anderson; d, Norman Tokar; w, Don Tait (based on a book by Jack M. Bickham); ph, Frank Phillips (Technicolor); m, Buddy Baker; ed, Ray deLeuw; art d, John B. Mansbridge, Walter Tyler.

Western Comedy Cas. (PR:AAA MPAA:G)

APPLE DUMPLING GANG RIDES AGAIN, THE*1/2 (1979) 88m BV c

Tim Conway (Amos), Don Knotts (Theodore), Tim Matheson (Private Jeff Reid), Kenneth Mars (Marshall), Elyssa Davalos (Millie), Jack Elam (Big Mac), Robert Pine (Lt. Ravencroft), Harry Morgan (Major Gaskill), Ruth Buzzi (Tough Kate), Audrey Totter (Martha), Richard X. Slattery (Sgt. Slaughter), John Crawford (Sheriff), Cliff Osmond (Wes Hardin), Ted Gehring (Frank Starrett), Morgan Paull (Corporal No. I), Robert Totten, James Almanzar, Shug Fisher, Rex Holman, Roger Mobley, Ralph Manza, Stu Gilliam, A. J. Bakunas, Dave Class, Louie Elias, Jimmy Van Patten, Jay Ripley, Nick Ramus, George Chandler, Bryan O'Byrne, Jack Perkins, John Wheeler, Art Evans, Ed McReady, Ted Jordan, Pete Renaday, Bobby Rolofson, Tom Jackman, Joe Baker, Allan Studley, Mike Masters, John Arndt, Bill Erickson, Vince Deadrick, Gary McLarty, Bill Hart, Mickey Gilbert, Wally Brooks, Stacie Elias, Mike Elias.

Stupid slapstick Western comedy in which jerky, clumsy outlaws Knotts and Conway get mixed up in Matheson's investigation of dastardly Pine's attempt to disrupt the goings-on at Morgan's fort. If the APPLE DUMPLING predecessor to this film is to be taken as a reference point, the sequel lacks the warmth and good-natured spirit of its ancestor. Knotts and Conway's constant pratfalls and frightened, anxious looks may be a riot for the kids, but anyone over the age of six will find them just plain dumb.

p, Ron Miller, Tom Leetch; d, Vincent McEveety; w, Don Tait, (based on characters created by Jack M. Bickham); ph, Frank Phillips (Technicolor); ed, Gordon D. Brenner; art d, Norman Rockett, John B. Mansbridge, Frank T. Smith.

Western Comedy Cas. (PR:AA MPAA:G)

APPOINTMENT, THE* (1969) 100m Marpol/MGM c

Omar Sharif (Federico Fendi), Anouk Aimee (Carla), Lotte Lenya (Emma Valadier), Fausto Tozzi (Renzo), Ennio Balbo (Ugo Perino), Didi Perego (Nany).

Passionate lawyer Sharif steals Aimee away from her fiance (who happens to be Sharif's partner) and marries her, but begins to doubt his love when he suspects her of being a secret high-priced prostitute. Just as Sharif is about to come to terms with his jealousy, Aimee kills herself, a victim of her husband's obsessive accusations. Uninspired, emotionally void tragic love story that never reveals the substructure beneath its characters' surface emotions.

d, Sidney Lumet; w, James Salter (based on a story by Antonio Leonviola); ph, Carlo di Palma (Metrocolor); m, John Barry; ed, Thelma Connell; prod d, Piero Gherardi.

Drama (PR:O MPAA:R)

APPOINTMENT FOR LOVE*** (1941) 88m UNIV bw

Charles Boyer (Andre Casall), Margaret Sullavan (Jane Alexander), Rita Johnson (Nancy Benson), Eugene Pallette (George Hastings), Ruth Terry (Edith Meredith), Reginald Denny (Michael Dailey), Cecil Kellaway (OLeary), J. M. Kerrigan (Timothy), Roman Bohnen (Dr. Gunther), Gus Schilling (Gus), Virginia Brissac (Nora), Mary Gordon (Martha).

Top-drawer, sophisticated comedy has suave playwright Boyer marrying dedicated doctor Sullavan who tells him that his numerous past affairs mean nothing to her clinical mind, that she harbors not a drop of jealousy, which certainly proves otherwise. The couple's honeymoon is interrupted with an emergency hospital call, a sign of things to come. Sullavan insists that each of them have separate apartments in the same building in accordance with their working schedules and that they meet only once a day, at 7 a.m., a situation which makes for some very funny episodes that are loaded with double-entendres, culminating when the pair inadvertently enter each other's apartments out of schedule for a surprising wow finish. Excellent acting, production values and skillfull direction add up to a delightful film.

p, Bruce Manning; d, William A. Seiter; w, Manning, Felix Jackson (based on a story by Ladislaus Bus-Fekete; ph, Joseph Valentine; m, Frank Skinner; ed, Ted Kent.

Comedy-Romance (PR:A MPAA:NR)

APPOINTMENT FOR MURDER* (1954, Ital.) 91m Lux Film/Ital. Film Export

Umberto Spadaro (Det. Pietrangeli), Della Scala (Silvia), Andrea J. Bosic (Aldo Manni), Marco Vicario (Giorgio Morelli), Natale Cirino (Palermo), Dorian Grey (Vandina).

Incredibly slow-moving Italian murder mystery that has veteran actor Spadaro questioning Bosic in the killing of his wife, finally breaking him down into a doubtful confession. Too many writers overkilled this script. (In Italian; English subtitles.)

d, Paccio Bandini; w, Sandro Continenza, Ennio de Concini, Mario Monicelli, Stefano Vanzina, Bandini; ph, Renato del Frate, Ugo Nudi; m, Gine Marinuzzi, Jr.; art d, Alberto Boccianti.

Mystery (PR:C MPAA:NR)

APPOINTMENT IN BERLIN** (1943) 77m COL bw

George Sanders (Keith Wilson), Marguerite Chapman (Ilse Preissing), Onslow Stevens (Rudloph Preissing), Gale Sondergaard (Gretta van Leyden), Alan Napier (Col. Patterson), H. P. Sanders (Sir Douglas Wilson), Don Douglas (Bill Banning), Jack Lee (Babe Forrester), Alec Craig (Smitty), Leonard Mudie (MacPhail), Frederic Worlock (Von Ritter), Steven Geray (Henri Bader), Wolfgang Zilzer (Cripple).

Ex-RAF officer Sanders, feigning disillusionment with his country, flees to Berlin to become an anti-British radio propagandist for the Nazis, but in reality is sending back secret information via a word/phrase code while he is on the air. When he is found out by the Germans, he enlists the aid of pretty German girl Chapman and another British agent, Sondergaard, in plotting his escape. Both women are killed, as is Sanders when the Nazi plane he is flying back to England is destroyed. A rather pessimistic wartime picture whose clever plot and cast make it a bit more intelligent than the standard film of its type.

p, Samuel Bischoff; d, Alfred E. Green; w, Horace McCoy, Michael Hogan (based on a story by B. F. Fineman); ph, Franz F. Planer; ed, Al Clark, Reg Browne.

War (PR:A MPAA:NR)

APPOINTMENT IN HONDURAS** (1953) 79m RKO c

Glenn Ford (Steve Corbett), Ann Sheridan (Sylvia Sheppard), Zachary Scott (Harry Shepherd), Rodolfo Acosta (Reyes), Jack Elam (Castro), Ric Roman (Jiminez), Rico Alaniz (Bermudez), Paul Zaramba (Luis), Stanley Andrews (Capt. McTaggart).

Adventurer Ford is hired by outside interests to trek through the Honduran jungle to deliver money to an ousted presidente, hoping the cash will help the jefe get reinstated. Taking feuding Americano couple Sheridan and Scott as hostages, Ford avoids escaped convicts, revolutionaries, snakes, ants, piranhas, wasps, and alligators in his dogged attempt to complete the transaction. Luckily, Scott is killed, and Ford gets the girl, too. Attempt at rousing jungle adventure is made interesting by director Tourneur's visualization of the environment and a surprisingly gutsy performance by Ford.

p, Benedict Bogeaus; d, Jacques Tourneur; w, Karen de Wolfe; ph, Joseph Biroc (Scenic-Scope, Technicolor); m, Louis Forbes; ed, James Leicester.

Adventure Cas. (PR:A MPAA:NR)

APPOINTMENT IN LONDON** (1953, Brit.) 96m Mayflower/BL bw

Dirk Bogarde (Cdr. Tim Mason), Ian Hunter (Capt. Logan), Dinah Sheridan (Eve Canyon), Bill Kerr (Lieut. Bill Brown), Bryan Forbes (Pilot Officer Greene), William Sylvester (Mac), Charles Victor (Dobbie), Anne Leon (Pamela Greene), Walter Fitzgerald (Dr. Mulvaney), Anthony Shaw (Smithy), Carl Jaffe (General).

Hot-shot flyer Bogarde, determined to make 90 bombing runs on Germany before he is given desk duty, is grounded after his 89th by his unsympathetic higher-ups. When a fellow flyer is injured, Bogarde, going against orders, takes his place and makes an heroic 90th run. Although it could easily court-martial him, the upper echelon decides to decorate Bogarde instead. Occasionally exciting air battles liven up this tale of WW II heroism and determination.

p, Maxwell Setoon, Aubrey Baring; d, Philip Leacock; w, John Wooldridge, Robert Westerby; ph, Stephen Dade; m, Wooldridge; ed, V. Sagovsky.

War (PR:A MPAA:NR)

APPOINTMENT WITH A SHADOW*1/2 (1958) 73m UNIV bw

George Nader (Paul Baxter), Joanna Moore (Penny), Brian Keith (Lt. Spencer), Virginia Field (Florence Knapp), Frank de Kova (Dutch Hayden), Stephen Chase (Sam Crewe).

World-weary reporter Nader is the only witness to the slaying of a man the public suspects to be a gangland boss. When Nader discovers that the murdered man was an impostor set up by the actual mobster, he tries to spread the truth, but is doubted because of his reputation as a drunk. Far-fetched city melodrama that makes the mistake of trying to combine tough social issues (alcoholism) with a gutsy crime story.

p, Howie Horwitz; d, Richard Carlson; w, Alec Coppel, Norman Jolley (based on a story by Hugh Pentecost); ph, William E. Snyder; m, Joseph Gershenson; ed, George Gittens.

Crime (PR:A MPAA:NR)

APPOINTMENT WITH CRIME**1/2 (1945, Brit.) 91m BN/Anglo-Amer. bw

William Hartnell (Leo Martin), Raymond Lovell (Loman), Robert Beatty (Inspector Rogers), Herbert Lom (Gregory Lang), Joyce Howard (Carol Dane), Alan Wheatley (Noel Penn), Cyril Smith (Sergeant Weeks), Elsie Wagstaffe (Mrs. Wilkins), Ian Fleming (Prison Governor), Wally Patch (Joe Fisher), Ian McLean (Det. Mason), Harry Lane (Big Mike), Ken Warrington (Winckle), Frederick Morant (Harry Millerton).

Released from prison, Hartnell plans an elaborate scheme to rob the former partners who double-crossed him. Excellently done caper film filled with detailed, inventive characterizations, especially Lom's.

p, Louis H. Jackson; d, John Harlow; w, Harlow (based on a story by Michael Leighton); ph, James Wilson, Gerald Moss.

Crime (PR:A MPAA:NR)

APPOINTMENT WITH DANGER*   (1951) 90m PAR bw

Alan Ladd *(Al Goddard)*, Phyllis Calvert *(Sister Augustine)*, Paul Stewart *(Earl Boettiger)*, Jan Sterling *(Dodie)*, Jack Webb *(Joe Regas)*, Stacy Harris *(Paul Ferrar)*, Henry Morgan *(George Soderquist)*, David Wolfe *(David Goodman)*, Dan Riss *(Maury Ahearn)*, Harry Antrim *(Taylor, Postmaster)*, Geraldine Wall *(Mother Ambrose)*, George J. Lewis *(Leo Cronin)*, Paul Lees *(Gene Gunner)*.

Tough Ladd film where he is a detective for the little known Postal Inspection Service investigating the murder of a fellow inspector. He convinces a nun, the only witness, Calvert, to identify the killer, Morgan. Instead of arresting the man, Ladd works his way into a gang of ruthless thieves who murdered his partner when he learned of their intentions to steal a mail shipment containing huge amounts of money. Ladd passes himself off as a corrupt postal worker aiding them for a piece of the action, a suspenseful and often terrifying position where hazard is present at every turn as the ever-suspicious gang members probe his background, particularly Webb, who rightly believes he is an agent. Webb, unlike his latter-day Sergeant Friday role, is a stone psychopath here, one who even frightens gang leader Stewart into blurting: "Somewhere in your blood there's a crazy bug. Get a cure or you'll get us all killed." Ladd himself is as tough as any of the gang members. The film presents great *film noir* dialog. He is accused of not knowing what love is, and immediately spits back: "Sure I do—it's something that goes on between a man and a .45 that won't jam!" Ladd must overcome Webb's suspicion and attempts to befriend him by playing a squash match with the psycho. The scene is one of the most suspenseful in crime films, one where both men use the missile as a deadly weapon, attempting to literally drive it through each other. The film also contains perhaps the most brutal murder in the history of *film noir*, one where Webb must kill his closest friend on mob orders. Morgan is known to have been identified by the nun and is told to leave town. When he dallies, Webb murders him, beating him to death with the bronzed shoes of Morgan's long-lost baby boys, the only humanizing mementos the thief possesses. Webb then becomes obsessed with killing the nun who identified his dead partner, even after the robbery takes place. Ladd stops him and the rest of the gang in a powerful conclusion that produces relentless gunfire and several cadavers, all of them bad guys. Ladd is superlative as the determined agent, Stewart is silky and deadly as the gang leader and Sterling, as the gun moll who tries unsuccessfully to seduce the hero, does a bang-up job. But it is Webb as the maniacal killer who freezes the viewer's blood to the bone.

p, Robert Fellows; d, Lewis Allen; w, Richard Breen, Warren Duff; ph, John Seitz; m, Victor Young; ed, LeRoy Stone.

Crime   **(PR:C   MPAA:NR)**

APPOINTMENT WITH MURDER* 1/2   (1948) 67m Falcon/FC bw

John Calvert *(Falcon)*, Catherine Craig *(Lorraine)*, Jack Reitzen *(Norton)*, Lyle Talbot *(Fred Muller)*, Robert Conte *(Count Dalo)*, Fred Brocco *(Donatti)*, Ben Welden *(Minecci)*, Carlos Schipa *(Farella)*, Ann Demitri *(Italian Woman)*, Pat Lane *(Customs Officer)*, Eric Wilton *(Butler)*, Robert Nadell, Michael Mark *(Baggage Clerks)*, Carole Donne *(Miss Connors)*, Gene Carrick, Frank Richards *(Thugs)*, Carl Sklover *(Guard)*, Jay Griffith *(Detective)*, Jack Chefe *(Hotel Clerk)*.

Private investigator Calvert tracks down some stolen classic paintings, following suspected thief Reitzen in Los Angeles and then in Italy. Typical entry in the low-budget, unambitious Falcon detective series. (See FALCON series, Index.)

p&d, Jack Bernhard; w, Don Martin (based on a story by Joel Malone, Harold Swanton); ph, Walter Strange; m, Karl Hajos; ed, Asa Boyd Clark.

Mystery   **(PR:A   MPAA:NR)**

APPOINTMENT WITH VENUS   (SEE: ISLAND RESCUE, 1952)

APPRENTICESHIP OF DUDDY KRAVITZ, THE*

(1974, Can.) 120m International Cinemedia Centre/Astral Films of Canada/PAR c

Richard Dreyfuss *(Duddy)*, Micheline Lanctot *(Yvette)*, Jack Warden *(Max)*, Randy Quaid *(Virgil)*, Joseph Wiseman *(Uncle Benjy)*, Denholm Elliott *(Friar)*, Henry Ramer *(Dingleman)*, Joe Silver *(Farber)*, Zvee Scooler *(Grandfather)*, Robert Goodier *(Calder)*, Allan Rosenthal *(Lennie)*, Barry Baldaro *(Paddy)*, Allan Migicovsky *(Irwin)*, Barry Pascal *(Bernie Farber)*, Susan Friedman *(Linda)*, Jacques Durette *(Bodyguard)*, Jonathan Robinson *(Rabbi)*, Edward Resmini *(Bernie Alt-man)*, Vincent Cole *(Moe)*, Henry Gamer *(Lawyer)*, Lou Levitt *(Rubin)*, Sonny Oppenheim *(Cohen)*, Lionel Schwartz *(Arnie)*, Mickey Eichen *(Cuckoo)*, Robert Desroches *(Laplante)*, Judith Gault *(Tarty Woman)*, Norman Taviss *(Grandfather Farber)*, Capt. L. Lussier, The Cadets of the St. Basile-le-Grand Cadet Corps 2831.

Dreyfuss, a zealous Jewish boy determined to become rich in the world, loses all personal contact with women, friends, and family in his desperate business transactions. A strong, often very funny film that points out the potential emotional loss in the pressure to succeed put on the young by families. Not anti-Semitic, the film means to point out the corruption of youth and power of greed in all young people, not the Jews alone, although the film did receive many negative reactions from Jewish groups, as did the book it is based on. Dreyfuss, who later went on to become one of the better-known faces of the 1970s, turns in an early great performance, making Duddy simultaneously loathsome, funny, and vulnerable. British actor Elliott masterfully portrays the washed-up British director Dreyfuss hires to make Bar Mitzvah movies for his relatives. In the most hilarious scene in the film, Dreyfuss' relatives are stunned to see that "artsy" filmmaker Elliott has juxtaposed Bar Mitzvah scenes with footage detailing African tribal dances celebrating the circumcision rights of the young warriors. Although there are quite a few holes in the script and Dreyfuss may be a bit unappealing to many, THE APPRENTICESHIP OF DUDDY KRAVITZ is a sad, funny, memorable film.

p, John Kemeny; d, Ted Kotcheff; w, Mordecai Richler (based on Richler's novel, adaptation by Lionel Chetwynd); ph, Brian West (Panavision, Bellevue-Pathe Color); m, Stanley Meyers; ed, Thom Noble; prod d, Anne Pritchard.

Drama   **Cas.**   **(PR:A   MPAA:PG)**

APRES L'AMOUR*   (1948, Fr.) 95m Films Osso bw

Pierre Blanchar *(Francois Mezaule)*, Simone Renant *(Nicole Mezaule)*, Giselle Pascal *(Germaine)*, Fernand Fabre *(Fournier)*, Gabrielle Fontan *(Catou)*, Germaine Ledoyen *(Sister)*.

Well-crafted Tourneur domestic drama portrays a Nobel Prize-winning author at the turn of the century tolerating a wife who flagrantly cheats on him with a drunken newspaperman; Blanchar himself has cheated on Renant with Pascal, a mistress now dead. When Renant discovers that her husband has another child, being tended by Ledoyen, she takes the child home with her to care for as one of her own. Ironically, the child is one of her own in that Blanchar has, years earlier, switched the child born to his mistress and that born of his marriage. An intriguing, well-acted and sharply directed film; the masterful Tourneur was able to shoot this movie for $83,000, much less than the budget he was allowed, this in a day when French directors insisted upon massive budgets to make even the most pedestrian films.

p, Emile Nathan; d, Maurice Tourneur; w, Jean Bernard Luc (based on the play by Pierre Wolff and Henry Duvernois); ph, A. Trirard; m, Marc Lanjean.

Drama   **(PR:O   MPAA:NR)**

APRIL BLOSSOMS**

(1937, Brit.) 80m Alliance/MGM bw (AKA: APRIL ROMANCE)

Richard Tauber *(Schubert)*, Jane Baxter *(Vicki)*, Carl Esmond *(Rudi)*, Athene Seyler *(Archduchess)*, Paul Graetz *(Wimpassinger)*, Charles Carson *(Lafont)*, Marguerite Allan *(Baroness)*, Edward Chapman *(Meyerhoffer)*, Lester Matthews *(Schwindt)*, Gibb McLaughlin *(Bauernfeld)*, Ivan Samson *(Hutten Bremmer)*, Cecil Ramage *(Vogl)*, Spencer Trevor *(Colonel)*, Frederick Lloyd *(The Police Captain)*, Hugh Dempster *(Will)*, Bertha Belmore *(Madame)*.

In 1820's Vienna, Baxter falls in love with one of the Archduchess' dragoons, Esmond. The two wish to marry, but royal decree forbids a dragoon to wed a commoner. Baxter enlists the aid of composer Tauber, an old flame, in convincing the Archduchess to let the young couple wed. Her majesty, having once been in love with her old music master, is swayed by the convincing Tauber and allows the marriage. Slow-moving tale of Viennese society lacks the hearty singing or style and grace needed to carry off a musical period piece.

p, Walter C. Mycroft; d, Paul L. Stein; w, John Drinkwater, Roger Burford, Paul Perez, G. H. Clutsam (based on a story by Franz Schulz); ph, Otto Kanturek, Bryan Langley; set d, Clarence Elder, David Rawnsley.

Musical/Romance   **(PR:A   MPAA:NR)**

APRIL FOOLS, THE* 1/2   (1969) 95m Jalem/NG c

Jack Lemmon *(Howard Brubaker)*, Catherine Deneuve *(Catherine Gunther)*, Peter Lawford *(Ted Gunther)*, Harvey Korman *(Benson)*, Sally Kellerman *(Phyllis Brubaker)*, Melinda Dillon *(Leslie Hopkins)*, Kenneth Mars *(Don Hopkins)*, Janice Carroll *(Mimsy Shrader)*, Jack Weston *(Potter Shrader)*, David Doyle *(Walters)*, Gary Dubin *(Stanley Brubaker)*, Susan Barrett *(Party Singer)*, Dee Gardner *(Secretary)*, Tom Ahearne *(Doorman)*.

Unhappily married to ultimate suburban shrew Kellerman, Lemmon falls in love with the equally unhappy Deneuve at his corporate boss's cocktail party. The romance between the two builds and oddly intensifies when he realizes that Deneuve is boss Lawford's wife. When Deneuve suggests that they both leave their sad lives behind and fly off together to her home, Paris, Lemmon agrees and says farewell to the suburban executive wasteland. An optimistic romance that got lost in the 1960's shuffle, THE APRIL FOOLS displays a beautiful relationship between Lemmon (in a fine performance), and the hauntingly gorgeous Deneuve, an excellent actress who just happens to have one of the most striking faces in film. Although it lacks the intensity and sophistication that could have made it a classic, the film still has a definite charm and appeal.

p, Gordon Carroll; d, Stuart Rosenberg; w, Hal Dresner; ph, Michel Hugo (Technicolor); m, Marvin Hamlisch; ed, Bob Wyman; prod d, Richard Sylbert; art d, Robert Luthardt; set d, William Kiernan; m/l, title song, Burt Bacharach, Hal David (sung by Dionne Warwick).

Romantic Drama   **(PR:C   MPAA:M)**

APRIL IN PARIS**   (1953) 101m WB c

Doris Day *(Dynamite Jackson)*, Ray Bolger *(S. Winthrop Putnam)*, Claude Dauphin *(Philippe Fouquet)*, Eve Miller *(Marcia)*, George Givot *(Francois)*, Paul Harvey *(Secretary Sherman)*, Herbert Farjeon *(Joshua Stevens)*, Wilson Millar *(Sinclair Wilson)*, Raymond Largay *(Joseph Welmar)*, John Alvin *(Tracy)*, Jack Lomas *(Cab Driver)*.

When the U.S. State Department mistakenly sends chorus girl Day an invitation to the arts festival in Paris, they decide to stick with the offer when Miss Day makes a public case out of the affair. On board the ship to France, Day falls for timid soul Bolger even though he is bethrothed to Miller. The musical numbers really sprout up in Paris, as does the romance between Bolger and Day. When he learns that his shipboard marriage to Miller was a fluke, Bolger scurries off to Day for a final number. Heavily laden with forgettable tunes and uninspired hoofing, the film is made colorful by the delightful Day and Bolger as well as the Technicolor photography.

p, William Jacobs; d, David Butler; w, Jack Rose, Melville Shavelson; ph, Wilfred M. Cline (Technicolor); ed, Irene Morra; ch, LeRoy Prinz; m/l, E. Y. Harburg, Sammy Cahn, Vernon Duke.

Musical Comedy   **(PR:A   MPAA:NR)**

APRIL LOVE**   (1957) 99m FOX c

Pat Boone *(Nick Conover)*, Shirley Jones *(Liz Templeton)*, Dolores Michaels *(Fran)*, Arthur O'Connell *(Jed)*, Matt Crowley *(Dan Templeton)*, Jeanette Nolan *(Henrietta)*, Brad Jackson *(Al Turner)*.

City boy Boone moves to a Kentucky town, bringing with him nothing more than his minor theft record. Once there, Boone falls for homespun Jones, and a certain horse on one of the racing farms as well. Getting over his initial dislike of country living, Boone wins the heart of Jones and quite a few horse races as a sulky driver, too. This remake of HOME IN INDIANA, essentially a showcase for the talents of the squeaky-clean Boone, is a pleasant enough teen romance where the often neglected charm and vocal capabilities of Miss Jones get some good exposure.

p, David Weisbart; d, Henry Levin; w, Winston Miller (based on a novel by George Agnew Chamberlain); ph, Wilfrid Cline (CinemaScope, DeLuxe Color); ed, William

B. Murphy; md, Alfred Newman, Cyril J. Mockridge; m/l, Paul Francis Webster, Sammy Fain.

Romantic Musical (PR:AA MPAA:NR)

APRIL 1, 2000* (1953, Aust.) 90m Wien-Film bw

Hilde Krahl *(World Security Council President)*, Josef Meinrad *(Prime Minister)*, Kall Ehmann *(Cabinet Chief)*, Elisabeth Stemberger *(Secretary)*, Judith Holzmeister *(Senora Equsquiza)*, Curd Juergens [Curt Jurgens] *(Capitano Herakles)*, Peter Gerhard *(Hieronymus Gallup)*, Guido Wieland *(Alessandro Vitalini)*, Heinz Moog *(Hajji Halef Omar)*, Ulrich Bettac *(Moderato Robinson)*, Robert Michal *(Wei Yao Chee)*, Waltraut Haas *(Mitzi)*, Harry Fuss *(Franz)*, Hans Moser *(Composer)*, Paul Hoerbiger *(Augustin)*.

In the year 2000, the people of Austria decide that it's about time they were a free and independent nation. Obviously made during the post-war years, the film is more of an historical look at the happy Austrian people than a futuristic comedy dealing with the fictitious World Security Council and its handling of a possible revolution.

d, Wolfgang Liebeneiner; w, Rudolf Brunngraber, Ernst Marboe; ph, Fritz Arno Wagner, Karl Lob, Sepp Ketterer; m, Josef Fiedler; set d, Otto Niedermoser.

Comedy (PR:A MPAA:NR)

APRIL ROMANCE (SEE: APRIL BLOSSOMS, 1937)

APRIL SHOWERS** 1/2** (1948) 93m WB bw

Jack Carson *(Joe Tyme)*, Ann Sothern *(June Tyme)*, Robert Alda *(Billy Shay)*, S. Z. Sakall *(Mr. Curly)*, Robert Ellis *(Buster)*, Richard Rober *(Al Wilson)*, Joseph Crehan *(Mr. Barnes)*, Ray Walker *(Mr. Barclay)*, John Gallaudet *(Mr. Gordon)*, Phillip van Zandt *(Mr. Swift)*, Billy Curtis *(Vanderhouten)*.

Turn-of-the-century vaudevillians Carson and Sothern have modest success as hoofers until their talented child, Ellis, joins the family on stage as a great little dancer; the trio bring down the house and their West Coast success leads to a chance at Big Time Broadway but just as their act is to score at the Palace, members of the Gerry Society movement have police close them down for allowing a child under 16 to perform on stage. (This was an era in which the Gerry Society was a real bugbear, dictating lifestyles to entertainers with children.) Carson, whose ego is now rabid—he considers his recent success all due to his own talent—reacts to this setback as a personal affront to his genius. He takes to drink, verbally abuses his wife and child, and sinks into backwater oblivion as they return to the more liberal West Coast to continue performing without him, being managed by Alda, who has eyes for the shapely Sothern. Carson sobers up, takes the pledge, and reclaims his family after a terrific screen fight with sleazy Alda, beating the pulp out of the double-dealing agent-manager (a scene which should vicariously edify most performers, writers, and other talent tied to ten-percenters.) Carson rejoins his family on stage for a happy and touching ending. The acting here, like the production values (the scenes are meticulously in period), is above average and the music is pleasant. Songs include: the title tune, "Put on Your Old Gray Bonnet," "Cuddle Up a Little Closer," "Carolina in the Morning," "Every Little Movement Has a Meaning All Its Own," "Mr. Lovejoy and Mr. Gay," along with new tunes, "The World's Most Beautiful Girl" by Kim Gannon and Ted Fetter, and "Little Trouper" by Gannon and Walter Kent.

p, William Jacobs; d, James V. Kern; w, Peter Milne (based on the story "Barbary Host" by Joe Laurie, Jr.); ph, Carl Guthrie; m, Ray Heindorf; ed, Thomas Reilly.

Musical (PR:A MPAA:NR)

ARABELLA** (1969, U.S./Ital.) 88m UNIV c

Virna Lisi *(Arabella Danesi)*, James Fox *(Giorgio)*, Margaret Rutherford *(Princess Maria)*, Terry-Thomas *(The Hotel Manager, The General, The Duke)*, Antonio Casagrande *(Filberto)*, Giancarlo Giannini *(Saverio)*.

Rutherford, an aging aristocrat heavily indebted to her country's tax department, receives aid from her devoted granddaughter Lisi in obtaining a large sum of money in a very short time. Entertaining European comedy that used Lisi's personal and physical charm to great advantage. In the film's funniest scenes, Lisi tries to seduce the wallets out of a General, a Duke, and a hotel manager, all played by the delightfully hammy Terry-Thomas.

p, Maleno Malenotti; d, Mauro Bolognini; w, Adriano Barocco; ph, Ennio Guarnieri (Technicolor); m, Ennio Morricone; ed, Eraldo Da Roma; art d, Alberto Boccianti.

Comedy (PR:A MPAA:M)

ARABESQUE*** (1966) 107m UNIV c

Gregory Peck *(David Pollock)*, Sophia Loren *(Yasmin Azir)*, Alan Badel *(Beshraavi)*, Kieron Moore *(Yussef Kassim)*, Carl Duering *(Hassan Jena)*, John Merivale *(Sloane)*, Duncan Lamont *(Webster)*, George Coulouris *(Ragheeb)*, Ernest Clark *(Beauchamp)*, Harold Kasket *(Mohammed Lufti)*, Gordon Griffin *(Fanshaw)*.

Solid espionage caper has Peck as an American professor at Oxford; he is approached by a Mid-East political leader, Duering, and asked to spy on a politically ambitious oil tycoon, Badel, who is attempting to take over his country. Peck, a code expert, is then asked to come to the home of Badel where he is given an involved cipher which he is to solve, but before he finishes his work he meets stunning Sophia Loren. She is Badel's mistress and warns him that as soon as he finishes deciphering the coded message he will be terminated. They both escape the building, Peck actually abducting Loren at scissors-point. Their escapades really begin, replete with wild chases, killings, and horrible assassinations, all of which Peck and Loren survive, finishing in each other's arms. Donen repeated CHARADE in the making of this film, rightly assuming that that film's success deserved another almost identical in plot, which ARABESQUE certainly is. Loren was draped in gowns by Dior and was equally fetching in a small bath towel prior to her showering with Peck, he being fully clothed and hiding in her shower. (Dior's bill and other wardrobe expenses for the Italian sexpot exceeded $100,000; this included more than fifty pairs of shoes which Donen excused by having her lover, Badel, consumed with a shoe fetish!)

p&d, Stanley Donen; w, Julian Mitchell, Stanley Price, Pierre Martin (based on the novel *The Cipher* by Gordon Cotler); ph, Christopher Challis (Technicolor); m, Henry Mancini; ed, Frederick Wilson; art d, Reece Pemberton.

Spy Drama (PR:C MPAA:NR)

ARABIAN ADVENTURE* 1/2 (1979, Brit.) 98m EMI/Orion-WB c

Christopher Lee *(Alquazar)*, Milo O'Shea *(Khasim)*, Oliver Tobias *(Prince Hasan)*, Emma Samms *(Princess Zuleira)*, Puneet Sira *(Majeed)*, John Wyman *(Bahloul)*, John Ratzenberger *(Achmed)*, Shane Rimmer *(Abu)*, Hal Galili *(Asaf)*, Peter Cushing *(Wazir Al Wuzara)*, Capucine *(Vahishta)*, Mickey Rooney *(Daad El Shur)*, Elizabeth Welch *(Beggarwoman)*, Suzanne Danielle *(Eastern Dancer)*, Athar Malik *(Mahmoud)*, Jacob Witkin *(Omar, the Goldsmith)*, Milton Reid *(Genie)*.

STAR WARS meets the Arabian Nights in this special-effects extravanganza that pits heroic prince Tobias against evil sorcerer Lee. Cushing, Rooney, O'Shea, and Capucine, all enjoying their brief playtime in a flashy costume, help Tobias in his desperate attempt to defeat Lee and save his beloved Samms from the sorcerer's clutches, but it is engaging street waif Sira who gives Tobias a mystical rose, the key to destroying Lee. Someone somewhere must have laid down a law saying that a film for children has to be flashy and stupid, and ARABIAN ADVENTURE is not a law-breaker.

p, John Dark; d, Kevin Connor; w, Brian Hayles; ph, Alan Hume; m, Ken Thorne; ed, Barry Peters; prod d, Elliot Scott; art d, Jack Maxsted; spec eff, George Gibbs.

Fantasy/Adventure (PR:AA MPAA:G)

ARABIAN NIGHTS*** (1942) 86m UNIV c

Sabu *(Ali Ben Ali)*, Jon Hall *(Haroun al Raschid)*, Maria Montez *(Sherazad)*, Leif Erikson *(Kamar)*, Billy Gilbert *(Ahmad)*, Edgar Barrier *(Hadan)*, Richard Lane *(Corporal)*, Turhan Bey *(Captain)*, John Qualen *(Aladdin)*, Shemp Howard *(Sinbad)*, "Wee Willie" Davis *(Valda)*, Thomas Gomez *(Hakim the Slave Trader)*, Jeni Le Gon *(Dresser to Sherazad)*, Robert Greig *(Eunuch-Story Teller)*, Charles Coleman *(Eunuch)*, Adia Kuznetzoff *(Slaver)*, Emory Parnell *(Harem Sentry)*, Harry Cording *(Blacksmith)*, Robin Raymond *(Slave Girl)*, Carmen D'Antonio, Virginia Engels, Nedra Sanders, Mary Moore, Veronika Pataky, Jean Trent, Frances Gladwin, Rosemarie Dempsey, Patsy Mace, Pat Starling, June Ealey *(Harem Girls)*, Andre Charlot, Frank Lackteen, Anthony Blair, Robert Barron, Art Miles, Murdock MacQuarrie *(Bidders)*, Elyse Knox *(Duenna)*, Burna Acquanetta *(Ishya)*, Ernest Whitman *(Nubian Slave)*, Eva Puig *(Old Woman)*, Ken Christy *(Provost Marshal)*, Johnnie Berkes *(Blind Beggar)*, Cordell Hickman, Paul Clayton *(Black Boys)*, Phyllis Forbes, Peggy Satterlee, Helen Pender, Eloise Hardt *(Virgins)*, Alaine Brandes *(Street Slave Girl)*, Jamiel Hasson, Crane Whitley, Charles Alvarado *(Officers)*, Duke York *(Archer)*, Mickey Simpson *(Hangman)*, Amador Gutierrez, Ben Ayassa Wadrassi, Edward Marmolejo, Daniel Barone *(Tumblers)*.

Producer Wanger played fast and loose with the 1880s stories penned by British explorer Sir Richard Burton but his version of the ARABIAN NIGHTS is nevertheless action-filled and so rich in color as to dazzle any skeptic's eye. Hall, the legal heir to the throne of the Caliph, is attacked and almost murdered by his evil brother, Erickson, who seizes the throne. A sultry dancing girl, Montez, find the wounded Hall and nurses him back to health. They fall in love and Hall sets off on a series of adventures accompanied by Sabu, his trusted almost slavish friend, Qualen, an aging Aladdin in search of his mislaid lamp, and idiotic Shemp Howard, a bragging shiftless Sinbad in his declining years, all aboard the vessel of Billy Gilbert, he of the famous sneeze. The dialog is stilted and mawkish but the action is almost non-stop and Montez is beauty personified in her scanty, shimmering silks. In the end, Hall overturns the rule of his wicked brother and mounts the throne, taking with him the exotic Montez and bestowing favors upon his loyal friends and subjects. It's all adolescent adventure but great fun and the production is lavish in all areas, particularly the costumes, sets, and wonderful lush color, achieved with glass shots and painted backdrops.

p, Walter Wanger; d, John Rawlins; w, Michael Hogan, True Boardman; ph, Milton Krasner; m, Frank Skinner; ed, Philip Cahn; md, Charles Previn; prod d, Jack Otterman, Alexander Golitzen; set d, R. A. Gausman, Ira S. Webb; cos, Vera West.

Fantasy/Adventure (PR:AAA MPAA:NR)

ARABIAN NIGHTS 1/2**

(1980, Ital./Fr.) 155m PEA (Rome)/Les Productions Artistes Associes (Paris)/UA c

Ninetto Davoli, Franco Merli, Ines Pellegrini, Luigina Rocchi, Francesco Paolo Governale, Zeudi Biasolo, Franco Citti, Tessa Bouche, Margareth Clementi, Alberto Argentino.

An Arabian prince, searching for his lost love, a slave girl, listens to a variety of odd, sexually explicit stories during his journey, before finding and marrying a slave girl. Pasolini, one of the strangest and most self-indulgent men ever to sit behind a movie camera, saw ARABIAN NIGHTS as the final chapter in his odd, erotic classic trilogy, the film's predecessors being DECAMERON and THE CANTERBURY TALES. The final result is a disjointed collection of realistic, sensual tales set in such exotic places as Yemen, Eritrea, Persia, and Nepal. Pasolini, a practicing realist with a surrealist's sensibilities, is a filmmaker whose works either offend, bore, or fascinate. ARABIAN NIGHTS is rather disappointing, its unstructured narrative alienating, its eroticism confusing, and its players a bit stiff. For fans of the director's work only.

p, Alberto Grimaldi; d&w, Pier Paolo Pasolini; ph, Giuseppe Ruzzolini (Technicolor); m, Ennio Morricone; ed, Enzo Ocone, Nino Baragli, Tatiana Casini; art d, Dante Ferretti.

Fantasy (PR:O MPAA:NR)

ARCH OF TRIUMPH*** (1948) 120m Enterprise/UA bw

Ingrid Bergman *(Joan Madou)*, Charles Boyer *(Dr. Ravic)*, Charles Laughton *(Haake)*, Louis Calhern *(Morosow)*, Ruth Warrick *(Kate Hergstroem)*, Roman Bohnen *(Dr. Veber)*, Stephen Bekassy *(Alex)*, Ruth Nelson *(Madame Fessler)*, Curt Bois *(Tattooed Waiter)*, J. Edward Bromberg *(Hotel Manager)*, Michael Romanoff *(Alidze)*, Art Smith *(Inspector)*, John Laurenz *(Col. Gomez)*, Leon Lenoir *(Captain Spanish)*, Franco Corsaro *(Novarro)*, Nino Pipitoni *(Gen. Aide)*, Vladimir Rasbevsky *(Nugent)*, Alvin Hammer *(Milan Porter)*, Jay Gilpin *(Refugee Boy)*, Ilia Khmara *(Russian Singer)*, Andre Marsauden *(Roulette Croupier)*, Hazel Brooks *(Sybil)*, Byron Foulger *(Policeman)*, William Conrad *(Official)*, Peter Virgo *(Polansky)*.

Boyer is a refugee physician without passport, operating illegally in Paris under an assumed name. He spots a drifter, Bergman, as she is about to throw herself into the Seine. She explains that her lover has committed suicide and she is at wit's end. He returns with her to her room, arranging for her to avoid prying questions from police and coroner, finds a room for her and a job singing at his favorite club, the Scheherazade, a gathering place for White Russian emigres and the social elite of Paris; his best friend, Calhern, a one-time colonel in the Czar's Imperial Guard, is the club's doorman. Bergman falls in love with Boyer but he is afraid to return that love, knowing that at any moment he might be picked up and deported. The two share calvados, meet in their lonely rooms and draw closer together in a world where the German war machine is about to attack France. There is the air of doom and foreboding everywhere. Bergman learns that Boyer was in Spain during the Civil War, serving the Loyalist cause. When she asks what he did in Spain, Boyer blurts: "Cut off legs." They vacation briefly on the Riviera, meeting socialite friends, but Boyer's own kindness is his undoing. Once back in Paris he stops to help an injured workman in the street and an officious French plainsclothesman, Conrad, insists upon seeing his papers. Boyer is deported, calling his only friend Calhern, instructing him to tell Bergman nothing. By the time he returns he finds that she has quit her job and is now the mistress of Bekassy, a rich, possessive playboy. He meets with her in her lavish new apartment but refuses to go on seeing her while she is with another man. Boyer has other things on his mind; he has spotted Laughton, a brutal SS leader visiting Paris, the same Nazi thug who has murdered his wife. Ingratiating himself to Laughton who does not recognize a former victim of his tortures, Boyer takes the Nazi for a drive through the Bois where he kills him. To accomplish this mission he has staked out his victim, waiting for days in a hotel room for a phone call, totally ignoring Bergman who wants to return to him but thinks he is seeing another woman. By the time Boyer disposes of Laughton, Calhern tells him Bergman has been shot by her jealous lover. He rushes to her side to ease her pain in her dying moments. The next day war is declared between France and Germany and Boyer leaves his hotel with Calhern to be processed by police, knowing he will again be deported. The two friends promise to meet when the war is over. In undertaking the widely popular novel by Erich Maria Remarque, veteran director Milestone (who had directed another Remarque story, ALL QUIET ON THE WESTERN FRONT, with great success), had to deal with a large, complicated story and capture the forlorn and dismal mood of its protagonists, and the oppressive suspense of a country waiting to be attacked by its neighbor. All of this Milestone managed but the story, overlong in itself, bogged down his direction which has great moments. The acting by all is superior, Boyer being the ideal lost person, Ravic, matched in melancholy by Bergman. Calhern enacts one of his best roles as the jaunty, jocular Russian philosopher but Laughton's Nazi is a caricature and his accent is positively atrocious. The film is much better than the estimates rendered by critics of the day, with high production values and unforgettable scenes that can only be attributed to master director Milestone. The unfavorable criticism, however, coupled to the public's desire to forget the recently finished war, contributed to the film's box office failure. The newly created Enterprise Studios invested more than $5 million in this sprawling tale, earning back only a third of that amount, causing the company to be stillborn.

p, David Lewis; d, Lewis Milestone; w, Harry Brown, Milestone (based on the novel by Erich Maria Remarque); ph, Russell Metty; m, Louis Gruenberg; ed, Mario Castegnaro.

Drama **Cas.** **(PR:C MPAA:NR)**

ARCTIC FLIGHT*½ (1952) 78m MON bw

Wayne Morris *(Mike)*, Lola Albright *(Martha)*, Alan Hale, Jr. *(Wetherby)*, Carol Thurston *(Saranna)*, Phil Tead *(Squid)*, Tom Richards *(Karluck)*, Anthony Garson *(Miksook)*, Kenneth McDonald *(Father Francois)*, Paul Bryar *(Hogan)*, Dale Van Sickle *(Dorgan)*.

Arctic pilot Morris, taking a group of passengers up to Alaska, suspects that business man hunter Hale is really a Communist spy. After convincing the others of his suspicions, Morris chases Hale across the frozen tundra, the latter trying to make it to the Russian-occupied Big Diomede. The two men fight, Hale escapes, but is shot by Russian soldiers when he cannot show them the proper identification papers, having lost them in the scuffle with Morris. The pilot returns to the small Alaskan town from which he started the chase and into the arms of Albright, the newly assigned school teacher. Typical 50's anti-Communist drivel with fair, uninspired performances from Morris and Hale.

p, Lindsley Parsons; d, Lew Landers; w, George Bricker, Robert Hill (based on the story, "Shadow of the Curtain," by Ewing Scott); ph, Jack Russell; ed, Leonard Herman.

Adventure **(PR:A MPAA:NR)**

ARCTIC FURY* (1949) 61m RKO bw

Del Cambre*(Dr. Thomas Barlow)*, Eve Miller *(Mrs. Barlow)*, Gloria Petroff *(Emily Barlow)*, Don Riss *(Narrator)*, Merrill McCormick *(Trapper)*, Fred Smith *(Uncle Jim)*.

Dull telling of the real-life adventure of a doctor, played by Cambre, who, on a gallant mission to a disease-ridden Arctic village, was lost in a plane crash in the frozen North. Courageously fighting his way back across the tundra, Cambre runs into various forms of arctic wildlife before being rescued. Mannequin-like performances by the leads don't help this wretched treatment of a good, inspiring story.

p, Boris Petroff; d, Norman Dawn, Fred R. Feitshans; w, Charles F. Royal (based on a story by Dawn); ph, Dawn, Jacob Hull, Edward Kull, William C. Thompson; ed, Feitshans.

Adventure **(PR:AA MPAA:NR)**

ARCTIC MANHUNT* (1949) 69m UNIV bw

Mikel Conrad *(Mike Jarvis)*, Carol Thurston *(Narana)*, Wally Cassell *(Tooyuk)*, Helen Brown *(Lois Jarvis)*, Harry Harvey *(Carter)* Russ Conway *(Landers)*, Paul E. Burns *(Hotel Clerk)*, Quianna *(Eskimo Girl)* Chet Huntley *(Narrator)*.

Ex-con Conrad, ditching insurance investigators, flees to Alaska in an effort to spread out some cash stolen long ago. Posing as a missionary to avoid suspicion, he falls in love with an Eskimo girl, but must leave her when the investigators come calling. Alone in the wilderness, Conrad dies an icy death. Typical "Crime Doesn't Pay" drama that's supposed to be interesting because of its setting.

p, Leonard Goldstein; d, Ewing Scott; w, Oscar Brodney, Joel Malone (based on Scott's story, "Narana of the North"); ph, Irving Glassberg; m, Milton Schwarzwald; ed, Otto Ludwig.

Crime **(PR:A MPAA:NR)**

ARE HUSBANDS NECESSARY?½** (1942) 79m PAR bw

Ray Milland *(George Cugat)*, Betty Field *(Mary Elizabeth Cugat)*, Patricia Morison *(Myra Ponsonby)*, Eugene Pallette *(Bunker)*, Charles Dingle *(Duncan Atterbury)*, Leif Erickson *(Bill Stone)*, Elisabeth Risdon *(Mrs. Westwood)*, Richard Haydn *(Chuck)*, Kathleen Lockhart *(Laura Atterbury)*, Phillip Terry *(Cory Cartwright)*, Cecil Kellaway *(Dr. Buell)*, Anne Revere *(Anna)*, Charles Lane *(Mr. Brooks)*, Charlotte Wynters *(Mrs. Finley)*, Clinton Rosemond *(Enos)*, Olive Blakeney *(Miss Bumstead)*, Cecil Cunningham *(Miss Jenkins)*.

Effervescent and spontaneous comedy about a conservative banker, Milland, and his spendthrift wife Field who live beyond their means, she charging everything in sight and running up ghastly bills which Milland tries to pay. Their financial situations only start off the laughs, then Field decides to adopt a child, a move Milland tries to block. This leads to battling and some wild scenes until Milland is confronted with the child who immediately softens his heart. Fast-paced and generally funny throughout.

p, Fred Kohlmar; d, Norman Taurog; w, Tess Schlesinger, Frank Davis (based on the novel *Mr. and Mrs. Cugat* by Isabel Scott Rorick); ph, Charles Lang; ed, LeRoy Stone.

Comedy **(PR:A MPAA:NR)**

ARE THESE OUR CHILDREN?* (1931) 75m RKO bw

Eric Linden *(Eddie Brand)*, Rochelle Hudson *(Mary)*, Arline Judge *(Florence Carnes)*, Ben Alexander *(Nick Crosby)*, Robert Quirk *(Bennie Gray)*, Roberta Gale *(Giggles)*, Mary Kornman *(Dumbell)*, William Orlamond *(Heine Krantz)*, Beryl Mercer *(Grandmother Morton)*, Billy Butts *(Bobby Brand)*, Jimmy Wang *(Sam Kong)*, Robert McKenzie *(Taxi Driver)*, Earl Pingee *(Charlie)*, Russell Powell *(Sam)*, Harry Shutan *(Defense Attorney)*, Ralf Harolde *(Prosecutor)*.

Well-intentioned high-school student Linden eventually becomes a lousy juvenile delinquent after hanging around with the wrong crowd at jazz clubs swigging booze. Trying to impress his playboy pals and hussy girl friends one night, Linden tells them he can get free booze from a friend of the family who owns a small food store. When the old geezer refuses Linden, the lad shoots him. On his way to the electric chair, the depressed youth, now realizing the error of his ways, apologizes to his family and walks the last few steps proud, but sad. Horribly hokey and ridiculous picture that was supposed to point out the way youth can be easily swayed into a seedy life.

d&w, Wesley Ruggles; w, Howard Estabrook; ph, Leo Tover.

Crime/Drama **(PR:A MPAA:NR)**

ARE THESE OUR PARENTS?* (1944) 73m MON bw

Helen Vinson *(Myra Salisbury)*, Lyle Talbot *(George Kent)*, Ivan Lebedeff *(Alexis)*, Noel Neill *(Terry Salisbury)*, Richard Byron *(Hal Bailey)*, Addison Richards *(Clint Davis)*, Emma Dunn *(Ma Henderson)*, Ian Wolfe *(Pa Henderson)*, Robin Raymond *(Mona Larson)*, Anthony Warde *(Sam Bailey)*, Jean Carlin *(Meg)*, Claire McDowell *(Miss Winfield)*, Emmett Vogan *(Commissioner)*, Edgar Norton *(Butler)*.

Teenage society girl runs away from her exclusive boarding house and hangs out with a boy from the wrong side of the tracks. Feeling unloved and uncared for by her parents, the girl, and the boy, begin to delve into various forms of mischief. When the two are accused of a murder, the investigating officer blames their juvenile delinquency on their unattentive parents. Ridiculous switch on the typical teen delinquent movie that attempts to point out that the source of the crime is in the criminal's upbringing. Early social liberalism falls dreadfully flat.

p, Jeffrey Bernerd; d, William Nigh; w, Michel Jacoby (based on a story by Hilary Lynn); ph, Harry Neumann; ed, Johnny Link.

Teen Drama **(PR:A MPAA:NR)**

ARE WE CIVILIZED?* (1934) 70m Raspin bw

William Farnum *(Paul Franklin, Sr.)* Anita Louise *(Norma Bockner)*, Frank McGlynn *(Abraham Lincoln, Felix Bockner)*, Leroy Mason *(Paul Franklin, Jr.)* Oscar Apfel *(Dr. Leonard Gear)*, Stuart Holmes *(Col. Salter)*, Alin Cavin *(Moses)*, Conrad Siderman *(Buddha)*, Sidney T. Pink *(Confucius)*, Harry Burkhart *(Caesar)*, Charles Requa *(Christ)*, J. C. Fowler *(Mohammed)*, Bert Lindley *(Christopher Columbus)*, Aaron Edwards *(George Washington)*, William Humphries *(Napoleon)*.

Farnum gnaws on the scenery as an idealistic news chief in a fictitious European country who tries to convince the nation's fascist leader that peace is the best answer. "Newsreel" footage of Christ, Mohammed, Buddha, and Confucius is shown while Farnum make his over-excited plea for the good side of human nature. Sappy attempt to reveal what could have happened in Nazi Germany if the filmmakers had only been given the chance; could be used today for a quick chuckle at any United Nations meeting.

p, Edwin Carewe; d, Carewe; w, Harold Sherman.

Drama **(PR:A MPAA:NR)**

ARE YOU A MASON?*½ (1934, Brit.) 70m Real Art/UNIV bw

Sonnie Hale *(Frank Perry)*, Robertson Hare *(Amos Bloodgood)*, Davy Burnsby *(John Halton)*, Gwyneth Lloyd *(Eva)*, Bertha Belmore *(Mrs. Bloodgood)*, Joyce Kirby *(Lulu)*, Lewis Shaw *(George Fisher)*, Michael Shepley *(Ernest Morrison)*, Davina Craig *(Annie)*, May Agate *(Mrs. Halton)*.

Having posed as a Mason in order to be able to go out at night, Hare runs into trouble when his daughter and son-in-law, whom he believes to be an actual Mason, come for a visit. The humor is supposed to erupt when Hale, the son-in-law, actually another fake Mason, and Hare try to impress each other with their knowledge of Masonic order, neither of them knowing what in God's name they're doing. Simple-minded British comedy that contains a fair share of laughs.

p, Julius Hagen; d, Henry Edwards; w, H. Fowler Mear (based on a play by Leo Ditrichstein, Emanuel Lederer).

Comedy **(PR:A MPAA:NR)**

ARE YOU LISTENING?*
(1932) 73m MGM bw

William Haines (Bill Grimes), Madge Evans (Laura), Anita Page (Sally), Karen Morley (Alice), Neil Hamilton (Clayton), Wallace Ford (Larry), Jean Hersholt (George Wagner), Joan Marsh (Honey), John Miljan (Russell), Murray Kinnell (Carson), Ethel Griffies (Mrs. Peters).

Radio writer Haines is tricked into a pseudo-confession in the accidental killing of his wife on a radio phone-in show. Sloppy melodrama was one of the first to use the radio business as a setting for passionate crime.

d, Harry Beaumont; w, Dwight Taylor (based on a story by J. P. McEvoy); ph, Harold Rosson; ed, Frank Sullivan.

Drama (PR:A MPAA:NR)

ARE YOU THERE? zero
(1930) 60m FOX bw

Beatrice Lillie (Shirley Travis), John Garrick (Geoffrey), Olga Baclanova (Countess Helenka), George Grossmith (Duke of St. Pancras), Jillian Sand (Barbara Blythe), Roger Davis (Barber), Gustav von Seyffertitz, Nicholas Soussanin (Barbers), Richard Alexander, Henry Victor (International Crooks), Lloyd Hamilton (Hostler).

Unbelievably dumb musical featuring Lillie as an aristocratic girl who happily breaks into song at the fox hunt, the ball, the appearance of thieves, etc.

d, Hamilton MacFadden; w, Harlan Thompson; ph, Joseph Valentine; ed, Al De Gaetano; md, Arthur Kay; art d, Stephen Goosson, Duncan Cramer; ch, Edward Dolly; cos, Sophie Wachner; m/l, Grace Henry, Morris Hamilton.

Musical Comedy (PR:AA MPAA:NR)

ARE YOU WITH IT?** 1/2
(1948) 89m UNIV bw

Donald O'Connor (Milton Haskins), Olga San Juan (Vivian Reilly), Martha Stewart (Bunny La Fleur), Lew Parker (Goldie McGoldrick), Walter Catlett (Jason Carter), Pat Dane (Sally), Ransom Sherman (Mr. Bixby), Louis Da Pron (Bartender), Noel Neill (Terry), Julie Gibson (Ann), George O'Hanlon (Buster), Eddie Parks (Herman Bogel), Raymond Largay (Mr. Mapleton), Jody Gilbert (Mrs. Henkle), Howard Negley (Ed McNaughton), Charles Bedell (Barker).

Mathematics whiz O'Connor decides to apply his genius at carnival games and winds up saving Parker's carnival from a pair of swindlers. O'Connor's witty portrayal and outstanding dancing make this otherwise trite musical a pleasure.

p, Robert Arthur; d, Jack Hively; w, Oscar Brodney (based on a musical comedy by Sam Perrin, George Balzer); ph, Maury Gertsman; m, Walter Scharf; ed, Russell Schoengerth; ch, Louis Da Pron; m/l, Sidney Miller, Inez James.

Musical Comedy (PR:AA MPAA:NR)

ARENA**
(1953) 83m MGM c

Gig Young (Bob Danvers), Jean Hagen (Meg Hutchins), Polly Bergen (Ruth Danvers), Henry Morgan (Lew Hutchins), Barbara Lawrence (Sylvia Morgan), Robert Horton (Jackie Roach), Lee Aaker (Teddy Hutchins), Lee Van Cleef (Smitty), Marilee Phelps (Smitty's Wife), Jim Hayward (Cal Jamison), George Wallace (Buster Cole), Stuart Randall (Eddie Elstead).

Egotistic rodeo star Young takes up with tramp Hagen when loving wife Bergen leaves him, unable to stand his vanity. During a big rodeo in Tucson, Young makes up with Bergen after his life is saved by Morgan who sacrifices himself to a rampaging Brahma bull. Hopelessly melodramatic reworking of Nicholas Ray's THE LUSTY MEN complete with cardboard performances from everyone except Van Cleef. Originally released in 3-D.

p, Arthur M. Loew, Jr.; d, Richard Fleischer; w, Harold Jack Bloom (based on a story by Arthur Loew, Jr.); ph, Paul C. Vogel (Anscocolor); ed, Cotton Warburton.

Western/Drama (PR:A MPAA:NR)

ARENA, THE zero
(1973) 83m New World c

Pam Grier (Mamawi), Margaret Markov (Bodicia), Lucretia Love (Deidre), Paul Muller, Daniel Vargas, Marie Louise, Mary Count, Sara Bay, Vic Karis, Sid Larence, Anthony Vernon, Dick Palmer, Anna Melita, Christopher Oakes, Peter Cester, Jho Jhenkins, Ivan Gasper, Piertro Torrisi, Salvatore Baccaro.

Cheap Roger Corman sexploitation film where Grier, Markov and other Amazons perform as gladiators in ancient Rome. While the script has a bevy of awful actors mouth platitudes about women's rights, they flaunt their flesh in scanty combat garb like second-rate burlesque queens and carve up each other in bloodbaths. Anyone not seeing through Corman's slippery ploy has no business watching films. Those who do have no business watching this one.

p, Mark Damon; d, Steve Carver; w, John and Joyce Corrington; ph, Aristide Massaccesi; m, Francesco De Masi; ed, Joe Dante, Jann Carver.

Historical Drama (PR:O MPAA:R)

AREN'T MEN BEASTS?**
(1937, Brit.) 73m ABPC/Wardour bw

Robertson Hare (Herbert Holly), Alfred Drayton (Thomas Potter), Billy Milton (Roger Holly), June Clyde (Marie), Ruth Maitland (Selina Potter), Ellen Pollock (The Vamp), Frank Royde (A Policeman), Victor Stanley (Harry Harper), Charles Mortimer (Detective), Frederick Morant (George Deck), Anne Boyd (Louise Baker), Judy Kelly (Yvette Bingham), Kathleen Harrison (Annie).

Hare's son, about to be married to Clyde, is accused of being a philanderer by French tramp Pollock at the altar. Hare then sets out to prove his son's innocence, which includes posing as the boy's aunt. Quite funny British comedy made palatable by Hare's delightful presence.

p, Walter C. Mycroft; d, Graham Cutts; w, Marjorie Deans, William Freshman (based on the stage play by Vernon Sylvaine); ph, Roy Kellino.

Comedy (PR:A MPAA:NR)

ARENT WE ALL?**
(1932, Brit.) 67m PAR bw

Gertrude Lawrence (Margot), Hugh Wakefield (Lord Grenham), Owen Nares (Willie), Harold Huth (Von Elsen), Marie Lohr (Lady Frinton), Rita Page (Cabaret Dancer), Renee Gadd (Kitty Lake), Aubrey Mather (Vicar), Emily Fitzroy (Angela).

Lawrence, timid girl about to be married to playboy Nares, is discovered to have had a minor indiscretion in the past. Before hypocrite Nares can make any accusations, fair-minded Wakefield, the boy's father, invites the old lover to the wedding. Stiff-upper-lip comedy that falters quite a bit in narrative structure, is made very watchable by the mesmerizing Lawrence.

p, Walter Morosco; d, Harry Lachman; w, Basil Mason, Gilbert Wakefield (based on the play by Frederick Lonsdale); ph, Rudolph Mate.

Comedy (PR:A MPAA:NR)

ARENT WE WONDERFUL?** 1/2
(1959, Ger.) 120m Constantin/Filmaufbrau bw

Johanna von Koczian (Kirsten), Hansjorg Felmy (Hans Boeckel), Wera Frydtberg (Wera), Robert Graf (Bruno Tiches), Elizabeth Flickenschildt (Frau Meisegeler), Ingrid van Bergen (Evelyne), Jurgen Goslar (Schally), Tatjana Sais (Frau Haflingen), Liesl Karlstadt (Frau Roselieb), Michl Lang (Herr Roslieb), Wolfgang Neuss (Erklarer/Narrator), Wolfgang Muller (Hugo/Narrator).

When the Nazis begin to take control of Germany, Graf quickly joins the party to boost his feelings of superiority and toughness. Felmy, on the other hand, although not a radical, loses his job because he refuses to join the Nazis. After the war, Felmy, a newspaper editor, exposes now-industrial kingpin Graf as a former ruthless war criminal. Graf kills himself before he can be brought up on charges. Despite its serious, self-analytical subject matter, this German film is really very funny. Looking at the problems the German people faced during the war years with a tongue-in-cheek approach, director Hoffmann does not lessen the emotional impact, he just makes it easy to take and understand.

p&d, Kurt Hoffmann; w, Heinz Pauck, Gunther Neumann (based on a novel by Hugo Hartung); ph, Richard Angst; m, Franz Grothe.

Comedy (PR:A MPAA:NR)

ARGENTINE NIGHTS* 1/2
(1940) 72m UNIV bw

The Ritz Brothers (Al, Harry, Jimmy), The Andrews Sisters (Maxine, Patty, La Verne), Constance Moore (Bonnie Brooks), George Reeves (Eduardo), Peggy Moran (Peggy), Anne Nagel (Linda), Kathryn Adams (Carol), Ferike Boros (Mama Viejos), Paul Porcasi (Papa Viejos).

The Ritz Brothers, the comedy portion of a revue traveling in Argentina, enlist the aid of new revue members, The Andrews Sisters, in winning back a small South American hotel from a pair of con men. Average vehicle for the Ritz's slapstick antics noteworthy as the first film appearance of WW II sweethearts, Maxine, Patty, and La Verne. (See RITZ BROTHERS series, Index.)

p, Ken Goldsmith; d, Albert S. Rogell; w, Arthur T. Horman, Ray Golden, Sid Kuller (based on a story by J. Robert Bren, Gladys Atwater); ph, Elwood Bredell; ed, Frank Gross; m/l, Sammy Cahn, Saul Chaplin, Sid Kuller, Ray Golden, Hal Borne, Don Raye, Hughie Prince, Vic Schoen.

Musical Comedy (PR:AA MPAA:NR)

ARGYLE CASE, THE**
(1929) 85m WB bw

Thomas Meighan (Alexander Kayton), H. B. Warner (Hurley), Lila Lee (Mary Morgan), John Darrow (Bruce Argyle), ZaSu Pitts (Mrs. Wyatt), Bert Roach (Joe), Wilbur Mack (Sam), James Quinn (Skidd), Gladys Brockwell (Mrs. Martin), Douglas Gerrard (Finley), Alona Marlowe (Kitty), Lew Harvey (Man).

The murder of the head of the house of Argyle leads to some hammy sleuthing by Meighan. While through the sets scurry secret service agents, and killers lurk behind false walls and escape through wooden panels—the kind of hokey thriller techniques that died with the silents. The acting by Warner and Lila Lee is noteworthy and, as a period piece, the film is worth watching.

d, Howard Bretherton; w, Harvey Thew (based on the play by Harriet Ford, Harvey J. O'Higgins, William J. Burns); ph, J. G. Van Trees; ed, Thomas Pratt.

Mystery/Crime (PR:A MPAA:NR)

ARGYLE SECRETS, THE* 1/2
(1948) 63m Eronel/FC bw

William Gargan (Harry), Marjorie Lord (Maria), Ralph Byrd (Lt. Samson), Jack Reitzen (Panama), John Banner (Mr. Winter), Barbara Billingsley (Miss Court), Alex Fraser (Joe McBrod), Peter Brocco (Scanlon), George Anderson (Pierce), Mickey Simpson (Gil), Alvin Hammer (Pinky), Carole Donne (Nurse), Mary Tarcal (Mrs. Rubin), Robert Kellard (Melvyn), Kenneth Greenwald (Irving), Herbert Rawlinson (Dr. Van Selbin).

Reporter Gargan tracks down some papers that will show that some leading Americans collaborated with the Nazis during the war. After discovering a trail of bodies and nearly becoming a corpse himself, Gargan exposes the traitors. Often exciting low-budget thriller.

p, Alan H. Posner, Sam X. Abarbanel; d, Cyril Endfield; w, Endfield (based on "The Argyle Album" as presented on "Suspense" radio program); ph, Mack Stengler; ed, Greg Tallas.

Mystery Cas. (PR:A MPAA:NR)

ARIANE**
(1931, Ger.) 78m Vereinigte Starfilm/Nerofilm bw (AKA: THE LOVES OF ARIANE)

Elisabeth Bergner (Ariane), Rudolf Forster (Konstantin), Annemarie Steinsieck (Tante Warwara), Hertha Guthmar (Olga), Theodor Loos (The Teacher), N. Wassiljeff (The Student), Alfred Gerasch (The Doctor).

Young, innocent Bergner falls madly in love with older, wiser Forster. At first the simple businessman regards the affair as a thing to be quickly ended, but then realizes his deep love for the girl. Early German talkie that would have been easily dismissed as a simple love story if not for the amazing performance of now-forgotten Bergner.

d, Paul Czinner, w, Czinner, Carl Mayer (based on the novel by Claude Anet); ph, Adolf Schlasy, Adolf Jansen.

Drama (PR:A MPAA:NR)

ARIANE, RUSSIAN MAID* (1932, Fr.) 85m Natan bw

Gaby Morlay *(Ariane)*, Rachel Devirys *(Aunt Warwara)*, Maria Fromet *(Olga)*, Victor Francen *(Constantin)*, Jean Sax *(The Professor)*, Durthal *(Dr. Kundert)*.

Director Czinner's second try at filming Claude Anet's novel about a young innocent who falls in love with an older man is incredibly inferior to his German version made a year earlier with the haunting Elisabeth Bergner as Ariane.

d&w, Paul Czinner (based on the novel by Claude Anet).

Drama (PR:A MPAA:NR)

ARISE, MY LOVE*** (1940) 100m PAR bw

Claudette Colbert *(Augusta Nash)*, Ray Milland *(Tom Martin)*, Dennis O'Keefe *(Shep)*, Walter Abel *(Phillips)*, Dick Purcell *(Pink)*, George Zucco *(Prison Governor)*, Frank Puglia *(Father Jacinto)*, Esther Dale *(Susie)*, Paul Leyssac *(Bresson)*, Ann Codee *(Mme. Bresson)*, Stanley Logan *(Col. Tubbs-Brown)*, Lionel Pape *(Lord Kettlebrock)*, Aubrey Mather *(Achille)*, Cliff Nazarro *(Botzelberg)*, Michael Mark *(Botzelberg's Asst.)*, Jesus Topete *(Guard)*, Nestor Paiva *(Uniformed Clerk)*, Fred Malatesta *(Mechanic)*, Juan Duval *(Spanish Driver)*, Paul Bryar *(Desk Clerk)*, George Davis *(Porter)*, Alan Davis *(Cameraman)*, Jean Del Val *(Conductor)*, Jon Easton *(Waiter at Cafe Magenta)*, Eugene Borden, Jean De Briac *(Waiters at Maxim's)*, Sarah Edwards, Fern Emmett *(Spinsters)*, Jacques Vanaire, Olaf Hytten, Louis Mercier, Guy Repp *(Employees)*, Paul Everton *(Husband)*, Mrs. Wilfrid North *(Wife)*, Maurice Maurice, Marcel de la Brosse, Francois Richier *(French Newsboys)*, Douglas Kennedy *(College Boy)*, Charles de Ravenne *(Bellboy)*, Charles Bastin *(Elevator Boy)*, Nadia Petrova *(Girl at Maxim's)*, Major Fred Farrell *(Cab Driver)*, Reginald Sheffield *(Steward)*, Tempe Pigott *(Woman in Irish Pub)*, Rafael Storm, Alphonse Martell *(French Correspondents)*, Hans Fuerberg *(German Sentry)*, Sherry Hall *(American Correspondent)*, Leyland Hodgson *(English Correspondent)*.

Tough reporter Colbert, stationed in France, becomes sick and tired of writing about fashion and decides to do a hard-hitting war story. She travels to Spain to investigate the whereabouts of noted rebel Milland and ends up freeing him from Zucco's jail by posing as his wife. They steal a plane and escape back to France, where their exploits become page one news. Colbert is given a Berlin assignment by her editors for her daring reporting, and she gladly accepts, partly to escape the amorous advances of her "husband" Milland. She takes a train to Berlin, but runs into Milland in one of the cars. The two realize their love for each other and decide to spend a few days (and nights) at a secluded French inn. At that moment, the Nazis invade Poland, and "ace" reporter Colbert misses the story completely. When their ship back to the states is torpedoed, Colbert and Milland escape without injury, but the event makes them realize that the work they could do in the war is far more important (for the moment) than their new-found love. Milland joins the RAF and Colbert returns to the typewriter. Highly enjoyable, fast-paced wartime adventure/comedy with a delightful chemistry very evident between Colbert and Milland. The script by Brackett and Wilder is a treasure chest of humorous innuendo and hard, but sweet, characterizations. All in all, a lovely wartime romantic comedy.

p, Arthur Hornblow, Jr.; d, Mitchell Leisen; w, Charles Brackett, Billy Wilder (based on Jacques Thery's adaptation of a story by Benjamin Glaser, John S. Toldy); ph, Charles Lang; m, Victor Young; ed, Doane Harrison; art d, Hans Dreier, Robert Usher.

Romantic Comedy (PR:A MPAA:NR)

ARISTOCATS, THE*** (1970) 78m BV c

Voice Talents: Maurice Chevalier *(Title Song)*, Scatman Crothers *(Scat Cat)*, Paul Winchell *(Chinese Cat)*, Lord Tim Hudson *(English Cat)*, Vito Scotti *(Italian Cat)*, Thurl Ravenscroft *(Russian Cat)*, Dean Clark *(Berlioz)*, Liz English *(Marie)*, Gary Dubin *(Toulouse)*, Nancy Kulp *(Frou Frou)*, Pat Buttram *(Napoleon)*, George Lindsay *(Lafayette)*, Monica Evans *(Abigail)*, Carole Shelley *(Amelia)*, Charles Lane *(Lawyer)*, Hermione Baddeley *(Madame)*, Roddy Maude-Roxby *(Butler)*, Bill Thompson *(Uncle Waldo)*, Phil Harris *(O'Malley)*, Eva Gabor *(Duchess)*, Sterling Holloway *(Roquefort)*.

The last of the high-quality Disney cartoon features. Disney himself had participated in its conception in 1963 and the film took four years to produce at a cost of $4 million. The final product is an enjoyable mix of fine animation (although nowhere near the quality of the earlier Disney animated features), catchy songs, and outstanding voice characterizations. The story concerns an eccentric, wealthy Frenchwoman who leaves her fortune to her cat Duchess (Gabor) and her three kittens. The woman's butler is next in line for the fortune if anything should happen to the cats. The butler finds out and is determined to get rid of the animals. He drugs the felines and dumps them in the countryside with the hope that they won't find their way home. The cats meet up with a tough alley cat (Harris) who helps them regain their fortune. On the way they meet a wide variety of animals and they even stop to listen to the Scat Cat (Crothers) and his jazz band. Maurice Chevalier came out of retirement to sing the film's theme song.

p, Wolfgang Reitherman, Winston Hibler; d, Reitherman; w, Larry Clemmons, Vance Gerry, Ken Anderson, Frank Thomas, Eric Cleworth, Julius Svendsen, Ralph Wright, Tom Rowe, Tom McGowan; ph, (Technicolor); m, George Bruns; ed, Tom Acosta; md, Walter Sheets; anim d, Milton Kahl, Oliver M. Johnston, Jr., Franklin Thomas, John Lounsberry; prod d, Ken Anderson; char anim, Hal King, Eric Larson, Eric Cleworth, Julius Svendsen, Fred Hellmich, Walt Stanchfield, Dave Michener; background anim, Al Dempster, Bill Layne, Ralph Hulett; layout, Don Griffith, Basil Davidovich, Sylvia Roemer; anim effects, Dan MacManus, Dick Lucas; m/l, Richard M. Sherman, Robert B. Sherman, Terry Gilkyson, Floyd Huddleston, Al Rinker.

Animated Adventure (PR:AAA MPAA:G)

ARIZONA (SEE: MEN ARE LIKE THAT, 1931)

ARIZONA*** (1940) 125m COL bw

Jean Arthur *(Phoebe Titus)*, William Holden *(Peter Muncie)*, Warren William *(Jefferson Carteret)*, Porter Hall *(Lazarus Ward)*, Paul Harvey *(Solomon Warner)*, George Chandler *(Haley)*, Byron Foulger *(Pete Kitchen)*, Regis Toomey *(Grant Oury)*, Paul Lopez *(Estevan Ochoa)*, Colin Tapley *(Bert Massey)*, Uvaldo Varela *(Hilario Gallego)*, Edgar Buchanan *(Judge Bogardus)*, Earl Crawford *(Joe Briggs)*, Griff Barnett *(Sam Hughes)*, Ludwig Hardt *(Meyer)*, Patrick Moriarty *(Terry)*, Frank Darien *(Joe)*, Syd Saylor *(Timmins)*, Wade Crosby *(Longstreet)*, Frank Hill *(Mono)*, Nina Campana *(Teresa)*, Addison Richards *(Captain Hunter)*.

Epic western originally intended for Gary Cooper became Holden's first horse opera which is built mostly around Arthur as Tucson's first female citizen, a hellcat who bests bad men at every turn as they struggle to turn the 1860 town of mud huts into a city. Holden appears as a wanderer heading for California, catching Arthur's eye and winning her heart so that she abandons her breeches for dresses, but she can't turn him from his wanderlust. He departs and she throws herself into the task of establishing a freight line which William and Hall attempt to destroy with raids and warring Apaches inflamed by the villains. Just when the Indians are about to burn out Arthur's entire line, Holden appears with the cavalry to save the day. In a spectacular finish he turns a wild herd of stampeding cattle into the center of the onrushing Apache horde to send them flying and win tomboy Arthur. The film suffers from overlong scenes, albeit the photography is superb, reflecting meticulous period sets and majestic scenery; much of this film was later used by Columbia as stock footage for its low-budget programmers, one way execs thought to recoup the studio's then-hefty budget of $2 million. Director Ruggles, who triumphed with CIMARRON in 1931, employed hundreds of Tuscon natives as extras and was a stickler for historic accuracy, a penchant that sometimes slows down the pace and zigzags the story line. The film is nevertheless an enjoyable big western with plenty of action.

p&d, Wesley Ruggles; w, Claude Binyon (based on a story by Clarence Budington Kelland); ph, Joseph Walker, Harry Hollenberger, Fayte Brown; m, Victor Young; ed, Otto Meyer, William Lyon; md, M.W. Stoloff.

Western (PR:A MPAA:NR)

ARIZONA BADMAN* (1935) 58m Kent bw

Reb Russell, Lois January, Edmund Cobb, Tommy Bupp, Ben Corbett.

Rock-bottom budget provides for a nonsensical oater where Russell attempts to round up a vicious gang single-handedly, but gets beaten to a pulp before overcoming the bad guys.

p, Willis Kent; d, S. Roy Luby.

Western Cas. (PR:A MPAA:NR)

ARIZONA BOUND** (1941) 58m MON bw

Buck Jones, Tim McCoy, Raymond Hatton, Luana Walters, Dennis Moore, Kathryn Sheldon, Tris Coffin, Horace Murphy.

First in the series of "Rough Rider" oaters starring Jones, Hatton, and McCoy. Plot concerns the efforts of Jones to clean up Mesa City and send the villainous Moore out of town. Jones enlists the aid of McCoy, a gun-slinging reverend, and Hatton, a simple cowhand, to help him regain control of the heroine's (Walters), stagecoach franchise and do battle with Moore's army of hoods. (See ROUGH RIDER series, Index.)

p, Scott R. Dunlap; d, Spencer Bennet; w, Jess Bowers; ph, Harry Neumann; m, Edward Kay; ed, Carl Pierson.

Western Cas. (PR:A MPAA:NR)

ARIZONA BUSHWHACKERS** (1968) 87m PAR c

Howard Keel *(Lee Travis)*, Yvonne De Carlo *(Jill Wyler)*, John Ireland *(Dan Shelby)*, Marilyn Maxwell *(Molly)*, Scott Brady *(Tom Rile)*, Brian Donlevy *(Major Smith)*, Barton MacLane *(Sheriff Grover)*, James Craig *(Ike Clanton)*, Roy Rogers, Jr. *(Roy)*, Reg Parton *(Curly)*, Montie Montana *(Stage Driver)*, Eric Cody *(Bushwhacker)*.

Keel plays a Confederate prisoner-of-war who takes advantage of Abe Lincoln's offer for volunteers to enlist in the Union army and patrol the Western territories. He is sent to an Arizona town where he must teach a crooked sheriff and evil saloonkeeper a lesson. Average effort made somewhat interesting by the presence of old western-movie veterans Ireland, Brady, Donlevy, and MacLane.

p, A. C. Lyles; d, Lesley Selander; w, Steve Fisher (based on a story by Fisher, Andrew Craddock); ph, Lester Shorr (Technicolor); m, Jimmie Haskell; ed, John F. Schreyer; art d, Hal Pereira, Al Roelofe.

Western (PR:A MPAA:NR)

ARIZONA COLT*

(1965, Ital./Fr./Span.) 104m Leone-Orphee-Arturo Gonzales c (AKA: MAN FROM NOWHERE)

Giuliano Gemma *(Arizona Colt)*, Fernando Sancho *(Gordon Watch)*, Corinne Marchand *(Jane)*, Roberto Camardiel *(Whisky)*, Rosalba Neri *(Dolores)*, Giovanni Pazzafini *(Kay)*, Pietro Tordi *(Priest)*, Andrea Bosic *(Pedro)*, Gerard Lartigau *(John)*, Mirko Ellis *(Sheriff)*, Gianni Solaro, Otto Rock, Renato Chiantoni, Valentino Macchi, Tom Felleghi, Emma Baron.

Uninspired spaghetti outing featuring Gemma as an ungrateful outlaw who refuses to join Sancho's gang after they bust him out of the hoosegow. Instead he helps defend the tiny town of Blackstone against Sancho's marauders. Nothing special.

p, Elio Scardamagali; d, Michele Lupo; w, Ernesto Gastaldi; ph, Guglielmo Maniori.

Western (PR:C MPAA:NR)

ARIZONA COWBOY, THE** (1950) 67m REP bw

Rex Allen *(Rex Allen)*, Teala Loring *(Laramie Carson)*, Gordon Jones *(I. Q. Barton)*, Minerva Urecal *(Cactus Kate Millican)*, James Cardwell *(Hugh Davenport)*, Roy Barcroft *(Slade)*, Stanley Andrews *(Jim Davenport)*, Harry V. Cheshire *(David Carson)*, Edmund Cobb *(Sheriff Fuller)*, Joseph Crehan *(Col. Jefferson)*, Steve Darrell *(Sheriff Mason)*, Douglas Evans *(Radio Announcer)*, John Elliott *(Ace Allen)*, Chris-Pin Martin *(Pedro Morales)*, Frank Reicher *(Maj. Sheridan)*, George H. Lloyd *(Fogarty)*, Lane Bradford *(Applegate)*.

The first in a series of 31 westerns featuring the singing cowboy Rex Allen. Routine plot has Allen crooning away as he tries to prove his father innocent of a theft. Lackluster cast and direction make it hard to understand how the series lasted so long.

p, Franklin Adreon; d, R. G. Springsteen; w, Bradford Ropes; ph, William Bradford; m, Stanley Wilson; ed, Harry Keller.

Western   **Cas.**   **(PR:A MPAA:NR)**

ARIZONA CYCLONE*   (1934) 51m Imperial bw

Wally Wales [Hal Taliaferro], Franklyn Farnum, Karla Cowan.

Rustlers and thieves gang up against battling Wally who wins through in an awful oater that looks as if it were filmed in a coal bin.

p, William Pizor; d, Robert Emmett Tansey; w, Tansey.

Western   **(PR:A MPAA:NR)**

ARIZONA CYCLONE**   (1941) 59m UNIV bw

Johnny Mack Brown (Tom), Fuzzy Knight (Muleshoe), Nell O'Day (Claire), Kathryn Adams (Elsie), Herbert Rawlinson (Randolph), Dick Curtis (Quirt), Robert Strange (Draper), Glenn Strange (Jessup).

Yet another Johnny Mack Brown oater, and this one's not half bad. The plot concerns the efforts of an unscrupulous banker who is out to get in on Brown's wagon freight business by means fair or foul. The usual romance and singing take place, but the direction in the action scenes is exceptionally well done.

p, Will Cowan; d, Joseph H. Lewis; w, Sherman Lowe; ph, Charles Van Enger; ed, Paul Landres.

Western   **Cas.**   **(PR:A MPAA:NR)**

ARIZONA DAYS* **1/2**   (1937) 57m GN bw

Tex Ritter (Tex), Ethelind Terry (Jean), Syd Saylor (Hopper), William Faversham (McGill), Eleanor Stewart (Marge), Forrest Taylor (Price), Snub Pollard (Cook), Glenn Strange (Pete), Horace Murphy (Sheriff), Earl Dwire (Workman), Budd Buster (Higginbotham), Salty Holmes (Salty), William Desmond (Stranger).

Another singing cowboy oater featuring Tex Ritter. In this one Ritter joins a traveling medicine show which gives him ample opportunity to warble a half-dozen tunes while he romances Stewart and foils villain Taylor's plans.

p, Edward Finney; d, John English; w, Sherman Lowe (based on a story Lindsley Parsons); ph, Gus Peterson.

Western   **Cas.**   **(PR:A MPAA:NR)**

ARIZONA FRONTIER* **1/2**   (1940) 55m MON bw

Tex Ritter (Tex Whitedeer), Evelyn Finley (Honey Lane), Slim Andrews (Slim), Jim Thorpe (Gray Cloud), Tristram Coffin (Lt. James), Frank LaRue (Farley), Gene Alsace (Bisbee), Dick Cramer (Graham), Jim Pierce (Kansas), Chick Hannon, Sherry Tansey (Outlaws), Hal Price (Joe Lane), Art Wilcox and his Arizona Rangers, Whiteflash, the Horse.

Ritter is a government agent who is sent west to investigate some Indian raids on a railway outfit. His clues lead not to the reservation but to a nearby army battalion headed by Coffin. Ritter's attempted ambush failed and he's captured, but with the help of Thorpe, he's able to escape and round up the outlaws. Songs include "Wastin' Time" and "Red River Valley."

p, Edward Finney; d, Al Herman; w, Robert Emmett Tansey; ph, Marcel LePicard; ed, Robert Golden; md, Frank Sanucci; m/l, Sanucci, Slim Andrews.

Western   **(PR:A MPAA:NR)**

ARIZONA GANGBUSTERS*   (1940) 57m PRC bw

Tim McCoy (Tim), Pauline Hadden (Sue Lambert), Forrest Taylor (Lambert), Lou Fulton (Lanky), Arno Frey (Schmidt), Julian Rivero (Gringo), Jack Rutherford (Thorpe), Otto Reichow (Haas), Lita Cortez (Lola), Kenny Duncan (Dan Kirk), Elizabeth LaMal (Mrs. Kirk), Ben Corbett, Frank Ellis, Carl Mathews, Curley Dresden.

Poor outing for the venerable McCoy (a real-life cowboy) who must undo the machinations of a corrupt town administration before facing down the baddies.

p, Sigmund Neufeld; d, Peter Stewart [Sam Newfield]; w, Joseph O'Donnell; ph, Jack Greenhalgh; ed, Holbrook N. Todd; md, Lew Porter.

Western   **(PR:A MPAA:NR)**

ARIZONA GUNFIGHTER*   (1937) 58m REP bw

Bob Steele (Colt Ferron), Jean Carmen (Beth Lorimer), Ted Adams (Wolf Whitson), Ernie Adams (Grizzly Barr), Lew Meehan (Snake Bralt), Steve Clark (Sheriff), John Merton (Farley), Karl Hackett (Durkin), A.C. Henderson (Governor Gray).

Steele stars in another of his series of low-budget westerns. Steele, perhaps the worst actor of the B oater cowboys, is forced to show emotions in this one, which was a big mistake on director Newfield's part. Steele handles anger, sadness, love, and joy with the same stoic grimace. Apparently, Steele noticed this himself because it was the last film he made with producer Hackel.

p, A. W. Hackel; d, Sam Newfield; w, George Plympton (based on a story by Harry F. Olmsted); ph, Robert Cline; ed, Roy Claire.

Western   **Cas.**   **(PR:A MPAA:NR)**

ARIZONA KID, THE* **1/2**   (1930) 88m FOX bw

Warner Baxter (The Arizona Kid), Mona Maris (Lorita), Carol Lombard (Virginia Hoyt), Mrs. Jiminez (Pulga), Theodore Von Eltz (Nick Hoyt), Arthur Stone (Snakebite Pete), Walter P. Lewis (Sheriff Andrews), Jack Herrick (The Hoboken Hooker), Wilfred Lucas (His Manager), Hank Mann (Bartender Bill), De Sacia Mooers (Molly), Larry McGrath (Homer Snook), Jim Gibson (Stage Driver).

A sequel to the first Cisco Kid talkie, IN OLD ARIZONA (1929), starring Baxter who is this time billed as "The Arizona Kid." While the first film was a critical and popular success (it won Academy Award nominations for best picture and best director), the sequel is a lackluster attempt to recapture the previous magic. Plot concerns Baxter who is hiding from the law in Rockville, Arizona. The former bandit lives off the proceeds from his private gold mine, but the sheriff suspects the miner of robbing a stagecoach. Meanwhile, Baxter has thrown dance-hall girl Maris over for a treacherous vamp, Lombard. When Baxter realizes that Lombard and her equally

villainous husband, Eltz, are trying to steal his gold, he dispatches the evil pair and rides off with Maris.

d, Alfred Santell; w, Ralph Block; ph, Glen MacWilliams; ed, Paul Weatherwax; set d, Joseph Wright; cos, Sophie Wachner.

Western   **(PR:A MPAA:NR)**

ARIZONA KID, THE**   (1939) 61m REP bw

Roy Rogers (Roy), George "Gabby" Hayes (Gabby), Sally March (Laura), Stuart Hamblen (McBride), Dorothy Sebastian (Bess Warren), Earl Dwire (Dr. Radford), David Kerwin (Dave), Peter Fargo (Sheldon), Fred Burns (Melton).

Better than usual Rogers outing set during the turmoil of the Civil War. Action takes place in Missouri soon after the state vows its loyalty to the Union. Angry Confederates ignore the oath and form outlaw bands of guerrillas who terrorize the area. Rogers is a Union captain who must order the execution of his close friend Kerwin for participating in the marauding. Unusually complex and emotional plot-line make this singing cowboy film worth a look.

p&d, Joseph Kane; w, Luci Ward, Gerald Geraghty (based on a story by Ward); ph, William Nobles; ed, Lester Orlebeck; md, Cy Feuer.

Western   **Cas.**   **(PR:A MPAA:NR)**

ARIZONA LEGION**   (1939) 58m RKO bw

George O'Brien (Boone Yeager), Laraine Johnson (Letty Meade), Carlyle Moore, Jr. (Lt. Ives), Chill Wills (Whopper Hatch), Edward Le Saint (Judge Meade), Harry Cording (Whiskey Joe), Tom Chatterton (Commissioner Teagle), William Royle (Dutton), Glenn Strange (Kirby), Monty Montague (Dawson), Joe Rickson (Dakota), Robert Burns (Tucson Jones).

Decent B western starring the popular cowboy actor O'Brien as the commander of a group of federal agents known as the Legionnaires out to bust a group of crooks who have taken over a small town. O'Brien joins the bandits in an effort to uncover the leader of the crime cult. Wills is good as O'Brien's story-telling sidekick.

p, Bert Gilroy; d, David Howard; w, Oliver Drake (based on a story by Bernard McConville); ph, Harry Wild; ed, Frederic Knudtson; md, Roy Webb.

Western   **(PR:A MPAA:NR)**

ARIZONA MAHONEY*   (1936) 58m PAR bw

Joe Cook (Mahoney), Robert Cummings (Randall), June Martel (Sue Bixby), Larry Crabbe (Talbott), Marjorie Gateson (Safrony), John Miljan (Lloyd), Dave Chasen (Flit), Irving Bacon (Smoky), Richard Carle (Sheriff), Billy Lee (Kid), Fred Kohler, Sr. (Blair).

Misguided attempt to combine a circus comedy and a serious western into some sort of coherent entertainment. This confused film stars Cook as a circus performer whose act is being shot out of a cannon, and his piano-playing partner, Cummings, as they try to end the reign of terror by rustlers Kohler and Miljan. The situations are stretched out of shape to find excuses for having the paths of the circus performers and the rustlers cross.

p, A. M. Botsford; d, James Hogan; w, Robert Yost, Stuart Anthony (based on a Zane Grey novel); ph, George Clemens; ed, James Smith; art d, Hans Dreier, Robert Odell.

Western   **(PR:A MPAA:NR)**

ARIZONA MANHUNT* **1/2**   (1951) 60m REP bw

Michael Chapin (Red), Eilene Janssen (Judy), James Bell (Sheriff White), Lucille Barkley (Clara Drummond), Roy Barcroft (Pete Willard), Hazel Shaw (Jane Rowan), John Baer (Deputy Jim Brown), Harry Harvey (Dr. Sawyer), Stuart Randall (Scar), Ted Cooper (Charlie).

Republic was getting desperate to breathe new life into their westerns by the 1950s and the last attempt they made starred two children as "The Rough-Ridin' Kids" in a short series of horse operas. The plot of this one details the efforts of the kids, Chapin and Janssen, to set the daughter of an outlaw on the straight and narrow. Not only are they successful with this conversion, but they capture a whole band of outlaws to boot. (See ROUGH-RIDIN' KIDS series, Index.)

p, Rudy Ralston; d, Fred C. Brannon; w, William Lively; ph, John MacBurnie; ed, Irving M. Schoenberg.

Western   **(PR:A MPAA:NR)**

ARIZONA MISSION   (SEE: GUN THE MAN DOWN, 1956)

ARIZONA NIGHTS*   (1934) 62m Reliable bw

Jack Perrin, Ben Corbett, Charles French, Al Ferguson.

Confused horser has Perrin chasing outlaws who seem to outwit him at every turn until he miraculously captures the entire gang. Dumbbell script.

p&d, Bernard B. Ray; w, Bennett Cohn.

Western   **(PR:A MPAA:NR)**

ARIZONA RAIDERS, THE**   (1936) 57m PAR bw

Larry Crabbe (Laramie Nelson), Raymond Hatton (Tracks Williams), Marsha Hunt (Harriet Lindsay), Jane Rhodes (Lenta Lindsay), Johnny Downs (Lone Alonzo Mulhall), Grant Withers (Monroe Adams), Don Rowan (Luke Arledge), Arthur Aylesworth (Andy Winthrop), Richard Carle (Boswell Abernathy), Herbert Haywood (Sheriff), Petra Silva (Tiny).

Comedy is emphasized in this western featuring FLASH GORDON star Larry "Buster" Crabbe as a happy-go-lucky outlaw who saves himself from being hanged and picks up two partners, Hatton, a horse thief and bigamist, and a lovesick kid, Downs. The trio gallop into a variety of farcical situations.

p, A. M. Botsford; d, James Hogan; w, Robert Yost, John Krafft (based on the novel Riders of the Spanish Peaks by Zane Grey); ph, Leo Tover; ed, Chandler House.

Western   **Cas.**   **(PR:A MPAA:NR)**

ARIZONA RAIDERS** **1/2**   (1965) 88m COL c

Audie Murphy (Clint), Michael Dante (Brady), Ben Cooper (Willie Martin), Buster Crabbe (Capt. Andrews), Gloria Talbott (Martina), Ray Stricklyn (Danny Bonner),

George Keymas *(Montana)*, Fred Krone *(Matt Edwards)*, Willard Willingham *(Eddie)*, Red Morgan *(Tex)*, Fred Graham *(Quantrill)*.

Historical inaccuracies fly like a desert sandstorm in this Murphy western detailing the saga of Quantrill's Raiders immediately after the Civil War. Murphy and Cooper join Quantrill's guerrillas as he is driven out of the South and into Arizona territory. The pair is captured by Union officer Crabbe who sentences them to 20 years of hard labor. Soon after, Crabbe is appointed chief of the newly formed Arizona Raiders and he offers the ex-Confederate rebels full amnesty if they join him and help end Quantrill's bloody run through the territory. The effect of the film is marred somewhat by the misrepresentation of the facts; Quantrill was never anywhere near Arizona in his life, and the "Arizona Raiders" weren't actually formed until 1902. But then if all westerns had to follow the history books, 90 percent of them would never have been made.

p, Grant Whytock; d, William Witney; w, Alex Gottlieb, Mary and Willard Willingham (based on a story by Frank Gruber, Richard Schayer); ph, Jacques Marquette (Techniscope, Technicolor); m, Richard LaSalle; ed, Grant Whytock; art d, Paul Sylos, Jr.

Western **Cas.** **(PR:A MPAA:NR)**

ARIZONA RANGER, THE 1/2** (1948) 64m RKO bw

Tim Holt *(Bob Wade)*, Jack Holt *(Rawhide)*, Nan Leslie *(Laura Butler)*, Richard Martin *(Chito Rafferty)*, Steve Brodie *(Quirt)*, Paul Hurst *(Ben Riddle)*, Jim Nolan *(Nimino)*, Robert Bray *(Jasper)*, Richard Benedict *(Gil)*, William Phipps *(Mae)*, Harry Harvey *(Peyton)*.

Tim Holt and his father Jack team up playing father and son in this western from RKO. Young Holt returns home from war after being discharged from Roosevelt's Rough Riders and refuses to join the family ranching business much to the Dad's dismay. The pair become estranged when Holt, Jr. sets out on his own, haunted by the memories of the war and unable to settle down. In his travels, he comes across wife-abuser Brodie, whom he sets straight. Brodie's wife falls in love with her savior and Holt slowly comes out of his war-induced shell. Eventually Holt is reunited with his father and goes back to the ranch. Interesting material about the healing process that ex-soldiers go through after a war must have seemed very relevant to the feelings of returning WW II vets at the time of this film's release.

p, Herman Schlom; d, John Rawlins; w, Norman Houston; ph, J. Roy Hunt; m, Paul Sawtell; ed, Desmond Marquette.

Western **Cas.** **(PR:A MPAA:NR)**

ARIZONA ROUNDUP* (1942) 56m MON bw

Tom Keene, Hope Blackwood, Frank Yaconelli, Hal Price, Edward Cassidy, Jack Ingram, Steve Clark, Nick Moro, Tex Palmer, Rocky Camron.

Idiotic oater where Keene and sidekicks take on an army of baddies while taming a rough town where to say hello is to get a punch in the face.

p&d, Robert Emmett Tansey; w, Tansey, Frances Kavanaugh.

Western **(PR:A MPAA:NR)**

ARIZONA STAGECOACH* 1/2 (1942) 58m MON bw

Ray Corrigan, John King, Max Terhune, Nell O'Day, Slim Whitaker, Steve Clark, Kermit Maynard, Charles King, Carl Mathews, Jack Ingram, Frank Ellis, Dick Cramer.

Fair horser has the trio of friends, led by Corrigan, ride into trouble, backstep from the badmen, then take them on head-to-head after some cruel murders. Terhune provides the scant laughs.

p, George W. Weeks; d, S. Roy Luby; w, Arthur Hoerl.

Western **Cas.** **(PR:A MPAA:NR)**

ARIZONA TERRITORY* 1/2 (1950) 56m MON bw

Whip Wilson *(Jeff)*, Andy Clyde *(Luke)*, Nancy Saunders *(Doris)*, Dennis Moore *(Lance)*, John Merton *(Kilborn)*, Carl Mathews *(Steve)*, Carol Henry *(Joe)*, Bud Osborne *(Stableman)*, Frank Austin *(Assayer)*.

Standard horse opera starring the flashy "Whip" Wilson. Unfortunately, Whip" wasn't all that handy with a whip and, therefore, we only see him use one four times through the course of the film, albeit ineffectually. Routine plot concerns Wilson and U.S. Marshal Clyde's efforts to end the activities of a West/East counterfeiting ring.

p, Vincent M. Fennelly; d, Wallace W. Fox; w, Adele Buffington; ph, Harry Neumann; ed, Richard Heermance.

Western **(PR:A MPAA:NR)**

ARIZONA TERROR* (1931) 65m Tiffany bw

Francis Natteford, Ken Maynard, Lina Basquette, Hooper Atchley, Michael Visaroff.

Dull and unnecessarily long Maynard outing as a cowboy who goes after a murdering ring of thieves who have shot his partner. Maynard is framed for the shooting of a cattleman by the hoods he's after and he spends the rest of the film trying to get himself out of this jam.

d, Phil Rosen; w, John Francis Natteford.

Western **Cas.** **(PR:A MPAA:NR)**

ARIZONA TERRORS** (1942) 56m REP bw

Don "Red" Barry *(Jim Bradley)*, Lynn Merrick *(Lila Adams)*, Al St. John *(Hardtack)*, Reed Hadley *(Halliday, Don Pedro)*, John Maxwell *(Larry Madden)*, Frank Brownlee *(Henry Adams)*, Rex Lease *(Briggs)*, Lee Shumway *(Sheriff Wilcox)*, Tom London *(Wade)*.

Pretty good, action-packed oater starring Barry, who tries to save a group of landowners from being kicked off their property by the villainous Hadley. Barry even bumps into President McKinley when he lands on top of the Presidential train to avoid being captured by the baddies.

p&d, George Sherman; w, Doris Schroeder, Taylor Caven; ph, Ernest Miller.

Western **(PR:A MPAA:NR)**

ARIZONA TO BROADWAY 1/2** (1933) 66m FOX bw

James Dunn *(Smiley Wells)*, Joan Bennett *(Lynn Martin)*, Herbert Mundin *(Kingfish Miller)*, Sammy Cohen *(Morris Blitz)*, Theodore Von Eltz *(Wayne)*, Merna Kennedy *(Flo)*, Earle Foxe *(Sandburg)*, J. Carrol Naish *(Tommy)*, Max Wagner *(Pete)*, Walter Catlett *(Ned Flynn)*, Jerry Lester *(Jimmy Dante)*.

Next to FOG OVER FRISCO, this film may be the fastest in pace ever put on celluloid, so clipped and startling in cuts that the technique might have been the unintentional work of an overworked editor, Loeffler. The feel and atmosphere of the crime-ridden year of 1933 is very much in curious evidence as Dunn, a leader of a confidence gang, entices small-town girl Bennett to try her luck in the big city. She does, changing from sweet thing to hard street dame giving Dunn what he dishes out. A great assortment of colorful characters wisecrack and cavort through scene after spastic scene, running over dialog (as Capra intentionally used to speed up action in AMERICAN MADNESS), accelerating actions and skipping any logical transitions in their rush to Broadway where cops chase burlesque-attending gangsters and con men stand on every corner looking for prey, with suckers aplenty falling into their insidious traps. A hectic, almost dizzying film that holds attention to the last neurotic minute. (Remade as JITTERBUGS.)

d, James Tinling; w, William Conselman, Henry Johnson; ed, Louis Loeffler.

Crime/Romance **(PR:A MPAA:NR)**

ARIZONA TRAIL** (1943) 57m UNIV bw

Tex Ritter *(Johnnie)*, Fuzzy Knight *(Kansas)*, Dennis Moore *(Wayne Trent)*, Janet Shaw *(Martha Brooks)*, Jack Ingram *(Ace Vincent)*, Erville Alderson *(Dan Trent)*, Joseph Greene *(Doc Wallace)*, Glenn Strange *(Matt Baker)*, Dan White *(Sheriff)*, Art Fowler *(Curley)*, Johnny Bond and his Red River Valley Boys.

Not another Johnny Mack Brown western, but it was supposed to be. Brown was slated for the lead, but he left Universal for Monogram and Ritter, who was originally set in a supporting role, was given the lead. Decent stoty line concerns Ritter and Moore's efforts to rescue their father's land from an unscrupulous sod baron.

p, Oliver Drake; d, Vernon Keays; w, William Lively; ph, William Sickner; ed, Alvin Todd.

Western **(PR:A MPAA:NR)**

ARIZONA TRAILS* (1935) 56m Superior bw

Bill Patton, Edna Aslin, Ed Carey, Denver Dixon.

Inferior horse opera with Patton accused of crimes he did not commit and having to clear himself while punching his way through a phalanx of heavies.

p, Victor Adamson [Denver Dixon]; d, Alan James; w, Tom Camden.

Western **(PR:A MPAA:NR)**

ARIZONA WHIRLWIND* (1944) 59m MON bw

Ken Maynard, Hoot Gibson, Bob Steele *(Themselves)*, Ian Keith *(Polini)*, Myrna Dell *(Ruth Hampton)*, Don Stewart *(Donny Davis)*, Charles King *(Duke Rollins)*, Karl Hackett *(Steve Lynch)*, George Chesebro *(Ace)*, Dan White *(Jim Lockwood)*, Charles Murray Jr. *(Ted Hodges)*, Frank Ellis *(Lefty)*.

The last film Maynard made with the "Trail Blazers" because of his increasing irritation with the rock-bottom budgets of these crude oaters. Plot concerns the usual three, Maynard, Gibson and Steele, as they foil a diamond smuggling ring run by King and Hackett. (See TRAIL BLAZERS series, Index.)

p&d, Robert Tansey; w, Frances Kavanaugh; ph, Edward Kull; ed, John C. Fuller.

Western **Cas.** **(PR:A MPAA:NR)**

ARIZONA WILDCAT** (1938) 69m FOX bw

Jane Withers *(Mary Jane Patterson)*, Leo Carrillo *(Manuel Hernandez)*, Pauline Moore *(Caroline Reed)*, William Henry *(Donald Clark)*, Henry Wilcoxon *(Richard Baldwin)*, Douglas Fowley *(Rufe Calloway)*, Etienne Girardot *(Judge White)*, Harry Woods *(Ross Harper)*, Rosita Harlan *(Margarita)*.

Light-hearted western featuring spunky child star Withers that takes place in the Arizona territory of 1870. Withers pulls all her usual mischief in an attempt to clear her foster-father's (Carrillo) name when he is accused of robbing the gold shipment from the local stagecoach line. Carrillo, a former bandit, reunites his old gang and goes after the corrupt sheriff who tried to frame him.

p, John Stone; d, Herbert I. Leeds; w, Barry Trivers, Jerry Cady (based on a story by Frances Hyland, Albert Ray); ph, Lucien Andriot; ed, Fred Allen.

Western/Comedy **(PR:AA MPAA:NR)**

ARIZONIAN, THE** (1935) 75m RKO bw

Richard Dix *(Clay Tallant)*, Margot Grahame *(Kitty Rivers)*, Preston Foster *(Tex Randolph)*, Louis Calhern *(Jake Mannen)*, James Bush *(Orin Tallant)*, Ray Mayer *(McClosky)*, Joseph Sauers *(Pompey)*, Francis Ford *(Comstock)*.

Dix is marshal of Silver City who takes on Calhern and his motley band of outlaws. The odds are impossible so reformed bandit Foster gives Dix a helping hand to subdue the bad guys while beautiful Grahame wins the lantern-jawed lawman's heart. The action is well-paced and believable under veteran director Vidor's hand and Nichols' script is tight and sensitive (he would write the classic STAGECOACH six years later). Above average film remade as THE MARSHAL OF MESA CITY with George O'Brien in 1939.

p, Cliff Reid; d, Charles Vidor; w, Dudley Nichols; ph, Harold Wenstrom; ed, Jack Hively; md, Roy Webb.

Western **(PR:A MPAA:NR)**

ARKANSAS JUDGE* 1/2 (1941) 71m REP bw

Leon Weaver *(Abner)*, Frank Weaver *(Cicero)*, June Weaver *(Elviry)*, Roy Rogers *(Tom Martel)*, Spring Byington *(Mary Shoemaker)*, Pauline Moore *(Margaret)*, Frank M. Thomas *(August Huston)*, Veda Ann Borg *(Hettie Huston)*, Eily Malyon *(Widow Smithers)*, Loretta Weaver *(Violey)*, Minerva Urecal *(Miranda Wolfson)*, Beatrice Maude *(Mrs. Neill)*, Harrison Greene *(Mr. Neill)*, Barry Macollum *(Mr. Melvany)*, George Rosener *(Mr. Beaudry)*, Monte Blue *(Mr. Johnson)*, Frank Darien *(Henry Marden)*, Russell Hicks *(John Root)*, Edwin Stanley *(Judge Carruthers)*.

Rustic drama starring the ever-popular Weaver family who usually deal in home-spun comedies. This one takes place in the sleepy town of Peaceful Valley where nothing ever happens. One day $50 is stolen from a widow's cracker barrel and the community flies into an uproar. An innocent scrubwoman is almost run out of town on a rail, but Judge Abner (Weaver) settles things down with his usual homey finesse. June Weaver, who plays the Judge's wife, sings a few down-home tunes to give the audience a breather from the intense drama.

p, Armand Schaefer; d, Frank McDonald; w, Dorrell and Stuart McGowan (based on an adaptation by Ian Hunter, Ring Lardner, Jr., Gertrude Purcell of Irving Stone's novel); ph, Ernest Miller; ed, Ernest Nims; md, Cy Feuer.

Drama   **(PR:A MPAA:NR)**

ARKANSAS TRAVELER, THE* 1/2   (1938) 83m PAR bw

Bob Burns (*The Traveler*), Fay Bainter (*Martha Allen*), John Beal (*Johnnie Daniels*), Jean Parker (*Judy Allen*), Lyle Talbot (*Matt Collins*), Irvin S. Cobb (*Constable*), Dickie Moore (*Benny Allen*), Porter Hall (*Mayor Daniels*).

Bucolic melodrama starring Burns as a vagabond who blows into a quiet town just in time to save the local newspaper, which is run by the widow and young daughter of an old friend, from the unscrupulous designs of a corrupt politician. Burns gives a Will Rogers-like performance, especially when dispensing rustic witticisms and sage advice.

p, George M. Arthur; d, Alfred Santell; w, Viola Brothers Shore, George Sessions Perry (based on a story by Jack Cunningham); ph, Leo Tover; ed, Paul Weatherwax; md, Boris Morros.

Drama   **(PR:A MPAA:NR)**

ARM OF THE LAW*   (1932) 62m Trojan/MON bw

Rex Bell, Marceline Day, Lina Basquette, Bryant Washburn, Robert Emmett O'Connor, Robert Frazer, Dorothy Revier, Dorothy Christy, Donald Keith, Larry Bathin, Gilbert Clayton, Wallace McDonald, William V. Mong, Snowflake.

Sluggish murder mystery involving a female nightclub performer whose reputation with the men leads to a divorce from her husband. She turns up dead and the ex-wife of one of her lovers, and the dancer's business lawyer become the main suspects. Things look grim for the pair until a feisty newspaper reporter uncovers who the real killer is.

d, Louis King, w, Leon Lee (based on *The Butterfly Mystery* by Arthur Hoerl).

Mystery   **(PR:A MPAA:NR)**

ARMCHAIR DETECTIVE, THE* 1/2   (1952, Brit.) 60m Meridian bw

Ernest Dudley (*Himself*), Hartley Power (*Nicco*), Sally Newton (*Penny*), Derek Elphinstone (*Insp. Carter*), Iris Russell (*Jane*), David Oxley (*Terry*), Lionel Gross (*Sergeant*).

Murky murder mystery has radio singer wrongly accused of killing her boss and her co-worker setting out to prove her innocence. Nothing for which the BBC would take credit.

p, Donald Ginsberg, Derek Elphinstone; d, Brendan J. Stafford; w, Ernest Dudley, Elphinstone (based on the British radio series by Dudley); ph, Gordon Lang.

Crime/Mystery   **(PR:A MPAA:NR)**

ARMED AND DANGEROUS* 1/2
                (1977, USSR) 123m (WOORUZHYON I OCHEN OPASEN)

Donatas Banionis, Ludmila Senchina, Vsevolod Abdulov, Sergei Martinson, Leonid Bronevoy, Lev Durov.

Highly unusual western from the Soviet Union starring Banionis, Abdulov, and Soviet pop star Senchina as a miner, a journalist, and a cabaret singer. Together they try to save the stakes of gold miners from villain Martinson and his boys when oil is struck on the real estate. Meticulous attention to authenticity and western flavor still can't hide the fact that it was produced by Europeans.

p&d, Vladimir Vainstok; w, Vladimir Vladimirov, Pavel Finn; ph, Konstantin Ryzhov.

Western   **(PR:A MPAA:NR)**

ARMORED ATTACK   (SEE: NORTH STAR, THE, 1943)

ARMORED CAR* 1/2   (1937) 64m UNIV bw

Robert Wilcox (*Larry Wills*), Judith Barrett (*Ella*), Irving Pichel (*Walinsky*), Cesar Romero (*Petack*), Inez Courtney (*Blind Date*), Tom Kennedy (*Tiny*), David Oliver (*Bubbles*), William Lundigan (*Hutchins*), Harry Davenport (*Pop Logan*), Joe King (*Sheridan*), Richard Tucker (*Hale*), Rollo Lloyd (*Organist*), John Kelly (*Frenchy*), Stanley Blystone (*Lt. Shores*), Paul Fix (*Slim*).

Wilcox plays a private detective who gets a job as an armored car guard knowing he'll be fired. Wilcox is a clever man because he is able to join the robbery gang he's been looking to bust by pretending to seek revenge on the armored car company. The gang takes the detective in, thinking he'll provide them with the inside scoop on how to crack the bank. Routine actioner hurt by lackluster direction and a no-name cast.

p, E. M. Asher; d, Lewis R. Foster; w, Foster, Robert N. Lee (based on a story by William Pierce); ph, Stanley Cortez; ed, Frank Gross.

Crime   **(PR:A MPAA:NR)**

ARMORED CAR ROBBERY**   (1950) 67m RKO bw

Charles McGraw (*Cordell*), Adele Jergens (*Yvonne*), William Talman (*Purvus*), Douglas Fowley (*Benny*), Steve Brodie (*Mapes*), Don McGuire (*Ryan*), Don Haggerty (*Cuyler*), James Flavin (*Phillips*), Gene Evans (*Foster*).

Surprisingly good caper film starring McGraw as a cop out to get revenge on a gang that killed his buddy during an armored car holdup. The gang is led by Talman, who masterminds a meticulously planned scheme to rob an armored car at its last cash pick-up of the day. McGraw and his crime fighters shoot it out with the crooks, but Talman and his gang manage to escape. The film then turns into a cat-and-mouse game between the cops and robbers. All of the crooks are slowly picked off with the

exception of Talman, who nearly gets away in a chartered plane. Taut and exciting direction with good performances by a relatively unknown cast.

p, Herman Schlom; d, Richard Fleischer; w, Earl Felton, Gerald Drayson Adams (based on a story by Robert Angus, Robert Leeds); ph, Guy Roe; ed, Desmond Marquette.

Crime   **(PR:A MPAA:NR)**

ARMORED COMMAND* 1/2   (1961) 98m AA bw

Howard Keel (*Col. Devlin*), Tina Louise (*Alexandra Bastegar*), Warner Anderson (*Lt. Col. Wilson*), Earl Holliman (*Sgt. Mike*), Carleton Young (*Capt. Macklin*), Burt Reynolds (*Skee*), James Dobson (*Arab*), Marty Ingels (*Pinhead*), Clem Harvey (*Tex*), Maurice Marsac (*Jean Robert*), Thomas A. Ryan (*The Major*), Peter Capell (*Little General*), Charles Nolte (*Capt. Swain*).

Uneven war/spy drama that takes place during the 7th U.S. Army's push in the Vosges Mountains. Louise plays a Nazi Mata Hari who is sent by the Germans to infiltrate and report on any plans by the U.S. She is planted near the tank corps where kind-hearted Holliman finds her and brings her to headquarters. Soon all the G.I.s are climbing over each other for her attentions. Reynolds, the obnoxious loudmouth of the corps, wins her favors which sparks a lengthy fight between he and Holliman. Luckily, the colonel, Keel, sees the fight and breaks it up in time for all the G.I.s to get involved in a tank battle with the Panzers. Louise is gunned down by Holliman after being caught sniping at Americans from her bedroom window, and the U.S. beats the Nazis. Pretty good action with competent performances by all the principals, though the pace does get slowed a bit by the melodrama.

p&w, Ron W. Alcorn; d, Byron Haskin; ph, Ernest Haller; m, Bert Grund; ed, Walter Hannemann; art d, Hans Berthel.

War/Spy Drama   **(PR:C MPAA:NR)**

ARMS AND THE GIRL   (SEE: RED SALUTE, 1935)

ARMS AND THE MAN**   (1932, Brit.) 85m Wardour/BIP bw

Barry Jones (*Capt. Bluntschli*), Anne Grey (*Raina Petkoff*), Maurice Colbourne (*Sergius Seranoff*), Angela Baddeley (*Louka*), Frederick Lloyd (*Maj. Paul Petkoff*), Wallace Evenett (*Niccola*), Margaret Scudamore (*Catherine Petkoff*), Charles Morton (*Plechanoff*).

In the late 1800s, a Bulgarian soldier deserts and hides out in a young woman's apartment. George Bernard Shaw's acerbic play is followed too closely in this turgid production where Jones, Grey and others render ordinarily snappy dialog lifeless and dull.

d&w, Cecil Lewis (based on the play by George Bernard Shaw); ph, J. J. Cox, James Wilson.

Comedy   **(PR:A MPAA:NR)**

ARMS AND THE MAN**   (1962, Ger.) 96m Casino Films c

O. W. Fischer (*Bluntschli*), Liselotte Pulver (*Raina*), Ellen Schwiers (*Louka*), Jan Hendriks (*Sergius*), Ljuba Welitsch (*Katharina*), Kurt Kasznar (*Petkoff*), Manfred Inger (*Nicola*).

Shaw's satiric, anti-militaristic play receives a fairly good presentation as Fischer, the cowardly soldier, hides in Pulver's bedroom, while her fiance, Hendriks, blindly attacks the Serbian army on behalf of Bulgaria. The witty dialog and acid-like attacks on rabid nationalism are evident and the production is much superior to the 1932 British version. Pulver is convincing as the girl who first hates the deserter than falls in love with him after listening to his logical arguments against war.

p, H. R. Sokal, P. Goldbaum; d, Franz Peter Wirth; w, Johanna Sibellus, Eberhard Keindorff (based on the play by George Bernard Shaw); ph, (Agfacolor):m, Franz Grothe.

Comedy   **(PR:A MPAA:NR)**

ARMY BOUND*   (1952) 60m MON bw

Stanley Clements (*Frank Cermak*), Karen Sharpe (*Jane Harris*), Steve Brodie (*Matt Hall*), John Fontaine (*Lieut. Peters*), Harry Hayden (*Mr. Harris*), Lela Bliss (*Mrs. Harris*), Gil Stratton (*Burt*), Danny Welton (*Steve*), Mona Knox (*Gladys*), Jean Dean (*Hortense*), Louis Tomei (*Herb Turner*), Joey Ray (*George*).

Notable only because it was Monogram's last programmer before the company changed its name to Allied Artists and concentrated on lengthier, bigger-budget films. Plot concerns a midget-car driver who gets drafted only to find that his commanding officer is a former racer with whom he's earlier competed. Usual nonsense involving the romancing of a girl; the kid patches things up with C.O. by saving his life during a fire in the arsenal.

p, Ben Schwalb, d, Paul Landres; w, Al Martin; ph, Harry Neumann; m, Marlin Skiles; ed, Bruce Schoengarth.

Action   **(PR:A MPAA:NR)**

ARMY GAME, THE**   (1963, Fr.) 87m bw Les Films du Carrosse/SEDIF (TIRE AU FLANC; AKA: THE SAD SACK)

Christian de Tiliere (*Jean Lerat*), Ricet-Barrier (*Joseph*), Jacques Balutin (*Corporal*), Serge Davri (*Colonel*), Annie Lefebure (*Annie*), Germaine Risse (*The Aunt*), Francois Truffaut, Bernadette Lafont.

Zany and contrived fantasy epitomizing the so-called "New Wave" French films of the late 1950s and early 1960s which was nothing more than a return to nihilistic Dadaism which, in its 1920s heyday, was another word for practical jokes. Based on an ancient vaudeville farce, the film deals with a group of French Army trainees going through their rigors as the actors and director de Givray spoof the military and everything else in sight. Not much of a story and a lot of sophomoric nonsense such as de Tiliere imagining himself performing a ballet with a ravishing dancer over the obstacle course. The forced humor is blatant and appears in the English subtitles; at one point a skywriter smokes up the sky with the words "Le Cahier du Cinema," which is translated as "Read Variety." Director de Givray even has his mentor Francois Truffaut make a cameo appearance and takes delight in a bumbling safe-cracking scene that spoofs RIFIFI. Not really funny, most of this puerile "inside joke" film would have served better as a brief skit on French TV.

p, Francois Truffaut; d, Claude de Givray; w, de Givray, Truffaut, Andre Mouezy-Eon (based on the play "Tire Au Flanc"); ph, Raoul Coutard; m, Ricet-Barrier, J. M. Defaye; ed, Claudine Bouche.

Comedy/Satire **(PR:C-O MPAA:NR)**

ARMY GIRL** (1938) 90m REP bw

Madge Evans *(Julie Armstrong)*, Preston Foster *(Dike Conger)*, James Gleason *(Hennessy)*, H. B. Warner *(Col. Armstrong)*, Ruth Donnelly *(Leila Kennet)*, Neil Hamilton *(Capt. Schuyler)*, Heather Angel *(Mrs. Bradley)*, Billy Gilbert *(Cantina Pete)*, Ralph Morgan *(Maj. Kennet)*, Barbara Pepper *(Riki)*, Ralph Byrd *(Capt. Marvin)*, Guinn "Big Boy" Williams *(Harry Ross)*, Robert Warwick *(Brig. Gen. Matthews)*, Allen Vincent *(Capt. Bradley)*, Pepito *(Pedro)*, Paul Stanton *(Maj. Thorndike)*, Dewey Robinson *(Bartender)*.

Saga of the growing pains the U.S. Army experienced when going from horses to tanks. Evans, daughter of Army post commander Warner, falls for tank specialist Foster. Foster proves that tanks can do more than cavalry by setting up a race between his vehicle and a horse on a prearranged course. In the end, Evans gets Foster and the Army gets tanks.

p, Sol C. Siegel; d, George Nicholls, Jr., B. Reeves Easton; w, Barry Trivers, Samuel Ornitz (based on an idea by Charles L. Clifford); ph, Ernest Miller, Harry Wild; m, Alberto Columbo; ed, William Morgan.

Military/Romance **(PR:A MPAA:NR)**

ARMY SURGEON* (1942) 63m RKO bw

James Ellison *(Capt. James Mason)*, Jane Wyatt *(Beth Ainsley)*, Kent Taylor *(Lt. Philip Harvey)*, Walter Reed *(Bill Drake)*, James Burke *(Brooklyn)*, Jack Briggs *(Major Wishart)*, Cyril Ring *(Major Peterson)*, Eddie Dew *(Ship Orderly)*, Ann Codee *(Flower Woman)*, Russell Wade *(Soldier)*, Richard Martin *(Soldier)*.

Monotonous WW I trench romance starring Wyatt as a lady doctor who lies and tells the Army she's just a nurse so she will be sent to the front where the action is. She falls in love with an army surgeon among the blood and bullets, but things get sticky when her old beau shows up wounded after flying in a few dogfights. Dull and uninspired, only highlighted by some old newsreel footage of WW I battle scenes.

p, Bert Gilroy; d, A. Edward Sutherland; w, Barry Trivers, Emmet Lavery (based on a story by John Twist); ph, Russell Metty; m, Roy Webb; ed, Samuel E. Beetley; md, C. Bakaleinikoff.

War **(PR:A MPAA:NR)**

ARMY WIVES* (1944) 68m MON bw

Elyse Knox *(Jerry)*, Marjorie Rambeau *(Mrs. Shannahan)*, Rick Vallin *(Barney)*, Dorothea Kent *(Louise)*, Murray Alper *(Mike)*, Hardie Albright *(Verne)*, Kenneth Brown *(Pat Shannahan)*, Billy Lenhart *(Billy Shannahan)*, Eddie Dunn *(Sgt. Shannahan)*, Jimmy Conlin *(Stan)*, Ralph Langford *(Burke)*, Dorothy Christy *(Mrs. Lowry)*, Phil Warren *(Benson)*, Ralph Lewis *(Kirby)*.

Uninteresting little drama chronicling the efforts of a young couple trying to get married while he's in the army. The usual troubles with travel, living quarters, rationing, and dealing with the ever-present military bureaucracy are detailed, much to the boredom of the audience.

p, Lindsley Parsons; d, Phil Rosen; w, R. Harrison Orkow (based on an idea by Joel Levy, Jr.); ph, Mack Stengler; ed, William Austin.

Military/Romance **(PR:A MPAA:NR)**

ARNELO AFFAIR, THE*** (1947) 86m MGM bw

John Hodiak *(Tony Arnelo)*, George Murphy *(Ted Parkson)*, Frances Gifford *(Anne Parkson)*, Dean Stockwell *(Ricky Parkson)*, Eve Arden *(Vivian Delwyn)*, Warner Anderson *(Sam Leonard)*, Lowell Gilmore *(Avery Border)*, Michael Brandon *(Roger Alison)*, Ruth Brady *(Dorothy Alison)*, Ruby Dandridge *(Maybelle)*, Joan Woodbury *(Claire Lorrison)*.

Arch Oboler's second film (following BEWITCHED) is half *film noir*, half psychological mystery, certainly not a whodunit in that we know early in the film that the culprit is none other than Hodiak, a slick, evil-minded Chicago nightclub owner with whom Gifford falls in love. Her husband is rich lawyer Murphy, an affable type who is so aboveboard that he finds it impossible to believe that his wife would two-time him. The thoroughly corrupt Hodiak turns in a stellar performance as an emotional sadist reveling in the hypnotic hold he has over Gifford, twisting her love for him in any direction whim dictates, murdering a former paramour who gets in the way of his new conquest and almost driving Gifford to suicide before he is undone. The dialog is cleverly written and well delivered, so fast at times that one believes that it is accompa nied by more action than really exists on the screen. Murphy is perfect as the trusting cuckolded husband and Gifford, one of the reigning queens of B films in the 1940s, turns in a superlative performance as the transfixed female. Oboler's terse direction and Salerno's moody photography create a suspenseful and compelling film.

p, Jerry Bresler; d&w, Arch Oboler (based on a story by Jane Burr); ph, Charles Salerno; m, George Rassman; ed, Harry Kemer.

Crime/Romance **(PR:A MPAA:NR)**

ARNOLD* (1973) 94m Cinerama c

Stella Stevens *(Karen)*, Roddy McDowall *(Robert)*, Elsa Lanchester *(Hester)*, Shani Wallis *(Jocelyn)*, Farley Granger *(Evan Lyons)*, Victor Buono *(Minister)*, John McGiver *(Governor)*, Bernard Fox *(Constable Hooks)*, Patric Knowles *(Douglas Whitehead)*, Jamie Farr *(Dybbi)*, Norman Stuart *(Arnold)*, Ben Wright *(Jonesy)*, Wanda Bailey *(Flo)*, Steven Marlo, Leslie Thompson *(Dart Players)*.

Dull-witted comedy thriller starring Stevens as the mistress of a deceased nobleman who marries the stiff posthumously to inherit his fortune. While the dead man lies in state, a series of killings occur. The victims are: playboy brother McDowall, flaky sister Lanchester, lawyers Granger and Knowles, handyman Farr, and widow Wallis. The whole thing comes off like a cheap made-for-TV movie of the week.

p, Andrew J. Fenady; d, Georg Fenady; w, Jameson Brewer, John Fenton Murray; ph, William Jurgenson (DeLuxe Color); m, George Duning; ed, Melvin Shapiro; art d, Monty Elliot; cos, Oscar Rodrigues, Vou Le Giokaris; m/l, title song, Andrew J. Fenady (sung by Shani Wallis).

Comedy/Thriller Cas. **(PR:C MPAA:PG)**

AROUND THE TOWN* (1938, Brit.) 68m BL bw

Vic Oliver *(Ollie)*, Irene Ware *(Norma Wyngold)*, Finlay Currie *(Sam Wyngold)*, Jimmy Kennedy *(Michael Carr)*, Tin Pan Alley Trio, Leslie Carew, 3 Hillbillies, Rhythm Sisters, Terry's Juveniles, 2 Charladies, Al & Bib Garvet, Pat McCormack, Maurice Winnick and his Band.

As an excuse to parade some pretty hackneyed music hall revues, a weak story has a talent agent acting as a tourist guide to a wealthy American producer and his daughter, shuttling them from one show to another. The singing and dancing are as anemic and forgettable as the story line.

p&d, Herbert Smith; w, Fenn Sherie; Ingram d'Abbes; ph, George Stretton.

Musical **(PR:A MPAA:NR)**

AROUND THE WORLD½** (1943) 90m RKO bw

Kay Kyser *(Kay)*, Mischa Auer *(Mischa)*, Joan Davis *(Joan)*, Marcy McGuire *(Marcy)*, Wally Brown *(Pilot)*, Alan Carney *(Joe Gimpus)*, Georgia Carroll *(Georgia)*, Harry Babbitt *(Harry)*, Ish Kabibble *(Ish)*, Sully Mason *(Sully)*, Julie Conway *(Julie)*, Diane Pendleton *(Diane)*, Kay Kyser's Band *(Themselves)*, Jack and Max *(Specialty)*, Al Norman *(Specialty)*, Lucienne and Ashour *(Specialty)*, Little Fred's Football Dogs *(Specialty)*, Jadine Wong and Li Sun *(Specialty)*, Robert Armstrong *(General)*, Joan Barclay *(Barclay)*, Margie Stewart *(Marjorie)*, Barbara Hale *(Barbara)*, Rosemary La Planche *(Rosemary)*, Barbara Coleman *(Coleman)*, Shirley O'Hara *(Shirley)*, Sherry Hall *(Clipper Steward)*, Joan Valerie *(Countess Olga)*, Frank Puglia *(Native Dealer)*, Peter Chong *(Mr. Wong)*, Duncan Renaldo *(Dragoman)*, Chester Conklin *(Waiter)*, Selmer Jackson *(Consul)*, Louise Currie *(WAC)*, James Westerfield *(Bashful Marine)*, Philip Ahn *(Foo)*.

Pleasant musical featuring Kyser and his band as they travel throughout the world spreading entertainment. Stops along the way include Australia, India, Chungking, Cairo, and North Africa. While the comedy is a bit labored, the musical numbers are good. These include: "Doodle-Ee-Doo," "He's Got a Secret Weapon," "Candelight and Wine," "Great News in the Making," "They Chopped Down the Old Apple Tree," "A Moke from Shamokin" all by Harold Adamson and Jimmy McHugh.

p&d, Allan Dwan; w, Ralph Spence; ph, Russell Metty; ed, Theron Warth; md, C. Bakaleinikoff; art d, Albert S. D'Agostino, Hal Herman; set d, Darrell Silvera; ch, Nick Castle; m/l, Jimmy McHugh, Harold Adamson.

Musical **(PR:A MPAA:NR)**

AROUND THE WORLD IN 80 DAYS**** (1956) 175m Michael Todd/UA c

David Niven *(Phileas Fogg)*, Cantinflas *(Passepartout)*, Shirley MacLaine *(Princess Aouda)*, Robert Newton *(Inspector Fix)*, Charles Boyer *(Monsieur Casse)*, Joe E. Brown *(Station Master)*, Martine Carol *(Tourist)*, John Carradine *(Colonel Proctor Stamp)*, Charles Coburn *(Clerk)*, Ronald Colman *(Railway Official)*, Melville Cooper *(Steward)*, Noel Coward *(Hesketh-Baggott)*, Finlay Currie *(Whist Partner)*, Reginald Denny *(Police Chief)*, Andy Devine *(First Mate)*, Marlene Dietrich *(Hostess)*, Luis Miguel Dominguin *(Bullfighter)*, Fernandel *(Coachman)*, Hermione Gingold *(Sportin' Lady)*, Jose Greco *(Dancer)*, Sir John Gielgud *(Foster)*, Sir Cedric Hardwicke *(Sir Francis Gromarty)*, Trevor Howard *(Falletin)*, Glynis Johns *(Companion)*, Buster Keaton *(Conductor)*, Evelyn Keyes *(Flirt)*, Beatrice Lillie *(Revivalist)*, Peter Lorre *(Steward)*, Edmund Lowe *(Engineer)*, Victor McLaglen *(Helmsman)*, Colonel Tim McCoy *(Commander)*, Mike Mazurki *(Character)*, John Mills *(Cabby)*, Alan Mowbray *(Consul)*, Robert Morley *(Ralph)*, Edward R. Murrow *(Narrator)*, Jack Oakie *(Captain of "S. S. Henrietta")*, George Raft *(Bouncer at Barbary Coast Saloon)*, Gilbert Roland *(Achmed Abdullah)*, Cesar Romero *(Henchman)*, Frank Sinatra *(Saloon Pianist)*, Red Skelton *(Drunk)*, Ronald Squire, A. E. Mathews, Basil Sydney *(Club Members)*, Ava Gardner *(Spectator)*, Harcourt Williams *(Hinshaw)*.

Niven is the punctual Phileas Fogg of the famous Jules Verne novel who makes a bet with his fellow club members in London that he can encircle the globe within eighty days, this in 1872 when travel went at snail's pace. To win the 20,000 pounds, Niven is accompanied by the great Mexican mimic Cantinflas (real name Mario Moreno), who plays his bumbling valet in a grandiose fashion reminiscent of Chaplin (his bullfight scene is priceless). En route Niven picks up Shirley MacLaine, a misplaced princess, and is doggedly pursued by a London detective, Newton, who believes the globe-trotter has somehow robbed the Bank of England. Around these leads producer Todd wrapped an army of stars, persuading, cajoling, and coaxing 46 famous personalities to appear in bit parts. In fact, they all but bury the leads in their endless appearances which made for widespread box-office appeal in that audiences loved playing the identifying game. (This was the film that began the trend of stars appearing in cameo roles.) Not to say that the great stars don't come through; all their parts are played with consummate skill, small as they are (living up to the theatrical credo that "there are no small parts, only small actors"). Niven's race is in itself a thrilling adventure, offering expansive use of colorful vignettes. First he sails for the Continent from England only to find a train tunnel blocked. He rents a balloon and sails over the Pyrenees to Spain (where Cantinflas performs hilariously in the ring), then by steamer to Marseilles and then a boat to India where Niven and his servant save a beautiful princess, MacLaine, from being burned alive on her dead husband's funeral pyre (a quaint Indian custom known as suttee wherein the widowed woman sacrifices her life to honor her deceased spouse and, no doubt, to help decrease the country's always burgeoning population). They travel onward by train but they run out of track; Colman, a polite railway official, tells them they must proceed by other means because the railroad is incomplete. They rent an elephant and make their way to an Indian port, then sail for Hong Kong, then Japan, then across the wide Pacific to San Francisco where Dietrich entertains them as a Barbary Coast dance hall girl, singing to the piano music banged out by Frank Sinatra. (A marvelous cutaway shows Red Skelton, a drunken saloon customer, wildly stuffing his pockets with free lunch food before tough bouncer Raft runs him out of the place by the seat of his pants.) Next the trio cross the great mountains and plains, first by train which breaks down after a wild Indian attack, then by a weird contraption which passes for a sailboat but which runs on the railway tracks. Time is running out so when Niven cannot book passage for England he rents a small steamer owned by Oakie but this runs out of fuel in mid-Atlantic. At Niven's orders the ship is stripped to its hull and engine to feed its roaring boilers but, alas, he arrives in England minutes too late. He has lost the great wager but he has fallen in love with MacLaine and proposes. She happily accepts and Cantinflas is sent out to make arrangements for the wedding. In so doing he learns that they have arrived not late but a day early, having crossed the International Dateline. Niven races to his club and, just as the clock is nearing the last minute, claims his bet. The film was a resounding success due to its dazzling cast, a lively script from the renowned humorist, S.J. Perelman (John Farrow and James Poe also worked on the screenplay), and Anderson's solid direction, a surprise from a relatively unknown director. Great credit should be given to film editor Gene Ruggiero who, with Paul Weatherwax, was handed seemingly countless reels of film by Todd who begged them to put it together in some reasonable order. "I told him to go away for two weeks and leave us alone," Ruggiero later stated, "and then we cut the monster down to something that made sense." The outtakes alone for this production would easily make up two more films if they could be found. The showing of the film was also aided by the Todd-AO widescreen process, used for the second time (the first being for OKLAHOMA!). The film has grossed over $25 million since 1956 and these were non-inflated dollars. But Todd himself put the production together for a song. He offered Colman, for instance, either a token check or a Cadillac for his bit part. Colman took the car. When later asked if he had worked one afternoon for the car, the distinguished actor snorted: "No, for a lifetime." Actually, Noel Coward was the most difficult to recruit but Todd worked on him relentlessly until he agreed to appear in his first American film in 20 years. (Said Coward: "Todd bullied me over an inferior lunch and I gave in.") Edward R. Murrow was brought in to do a prolog and Todd counted him among his "50 stars," although there are 46, including Peter Lorre, doing a sort of Mr. Moto reprise as a Japanese ship steward. "I didn't have to sell anybody after we got rolling," Todd later commented. "My problem was keeping stars *out*." The part of the cavalry colonel who rides to the rescue with his troops against attacking Indians was coveted by John Wayne but Todd gave the role to Tim McCoy who was an actual colonel and had been a professional cowboy. The great showman spared no detail in mounting his production, using almost 70,000 people in thirteen countries which gave seventy make-up artists headaches. More than 100 natural settings and 140 special sets were constructed for the shooting, with 2,000-plus camera set-ups, the most ever used. Everything about this big, beautiful movie smacks of authenticity, of excitement, and of massive showmanship not seen since Barnum. It proved to be a great bonanza for Todd and, more important, a cornucopia of entertainment for audiences around the world.

p, Michael Todd; d, Michael Anderson; w, S. J. Perelman (uncredited, John Farrow, James Poe) (based on the novel by Jules Verne); ph, Lionel Lindon (Todd-AO, Eastmancolor); m, Victor Young; ed, Gene Ruggiero, Paul Weatherwax; art d, James W. Sullivan, Ken Adams; set d, Ross Dowd; cos, Miles White; ch, Paul Godkin; spec eff, Lee Zavitz.

Adventure Cas. (PR:AAA MPAA:NR)

AROUND THE WORLD UNDER THE SEA** (1966) 110m MGM c

Lloyd Bridges *(Dr. Doug Standish)*, Shirley Eaton *(Dr. Maggie Handford)*, Brian Kelly *(Dr. Craig Mosby)*, David McCallum *(Dr. Phil Volker)*, Keenan Wynn *(Hank Stahl)*, Marshall Thompson *(Dr. Orin Hillyard)*, Gary Merrill *(Dr. August Boren)*, Ron Hayes *(Brinkman)*, George Shibata *(Prof. Hamuru)*, Frank Logan *(Capt. of Diligence)*, Don Wells *(Sonar Man)*, Donald Linton *(Vice President)*, George DeVries *(Lt. of Coast Guard)*, Tony Gulliver *(Officer)*, Joey Carter *(Technician)*, Celeste Yarnall *(Secretary)*, Paul Gray *(Pilot)*.

Great underwater photography somewhat buoys this silly aquatic adventure brought to you by the makers of the successful TV program "Sea Hunt." Bridges is again at the helm as the leader of an expedition in a deep sea submarine to investigate underwater volcanic eruptions. Along the way the sub is almost sucked into a volcano and eaten by a sea monster. Good supporting cast makes a stab at maintaining the credibility.

p&d, Andrew Marton; w, Arthur Weiss, Art Arthur; ph, Clifford Poland (Technicolor); underwater ph, Lamar Boren; m, Harry Sukman; ed, Warren Adams; diving sequences, Ricou Browning.

Adventure Cas. (PR:A MPAA:NR)

AROUSERS, THE*

(1973) 84m New World c (AKA: SWEET KILL; A KISS FROM EDDIE)

Tab Hunter, Cherie Latimer, Linda Leider, Isabel Jewell, Nadyne Turney, Roberta Collins, Brandy Herred, Angel Fox, Katie McKeown, John Aprea, Josh Green, Rory Guy, Sandy Kenyon.

Low-budget horror show has Hunter as a psychopath living in Venice, California, seeking out women to love, finding he cannot feel affection, then murdering his bed partners, not unlike the sick protagonist of LOOKING FOR MR. GOODBAR. The film indulges in gore which lessens what could have been a fair chiller, but then nothing could have helped Hunter's monotone, stale delivery.

p, Tamara Asseyev; d&w, Curtis Hanson; ph, Daniel Lacombre, Floyd Crosby, Edmund Anderson (Metrocolor); m, Charles Bernstein; ed, Gretel Erlich.

Horror Cas. (PR:O MPAA:R)

ARRANGEMENT, THE* (1969) 125m WB c

Kirk Douglas *(Eddie & Evangelos)*, Faye Dunaway *(Gwen)*, Deborah Kerr *(Florence Anderson)*, Richard Boone *(Sam Anderson)*, Hume Cronyn *(Arthur)*, Michael Higgins *(Michael)*, John Randolph Jones *(Charles)*, Carol Rossen *(Gloria)*, Anne Hegira *(Thomna)*, William Hansen *(Dr. Weeks)*, Charles Drake *(Finnegan)*, Harold Gould *(Dr. Liebman)*, E. J. Andre *(Uncle Joe)*, Michael Murphy *(Father Draddy)*, Philip Bourneuf *(Judge Morris)*, Dianne Hull *(Ellen)*.

Great cast totally ruined by Kazan's overwrought direction in this adaptation of his own best-selling novel. Douglas plays an incredibly successful advertising executive with a beautiful wife, Kerr, and a lovely mistress, Dunaway. He is filled with self-loathing and sees life as a series of compromises and arrangements. One day he decides to end it all by driving his sports car into a truck. He survives the crash physically after a long convalescence, but is still disturbed mentally. While in the hospital, his mistress has left him for another man, and his father, Boone, is terminally ill and bedridden in a hospital waiting to die. Douglas flies to New York and snatches his father from the hospital and takes him to the family home on Long Island. He then tracks down Dunaway and talks her into living with him in the family mansion. Kerr has finally had enough of this and gets lawyer Cronyn to have her father-in-law readmitted to the hospital, and has Douglas and his floozy kicked out. Douglas goes completely nuts and sets the joint on fire. Dunaway runs back to her lover with Douglas hot on her trail. He confronts her at her apartment where he is shot by Dunaway's angry boy friend. He survives the wound; Kerr and Dunaway put aside their differences and together they bring him back from his mental abyss. The film ends with a freeze frame of Douglas at his father's grave in a totally ambiguous finish. Overlong and basically lightweight, the picture never develops Douglas' character into a man the audience should care about. Kazan's heavy-handed direction, which includes frustratingly inept flashbacks and fantasy scenes, cloud any kind of real perceptions he may have had regarding his main character. A real shame.

p,d&w, Elia Kazan (based on his novel); ph, Robert Surtees (Technicolor); m, David Amram; ed, Stefan Arnstein; art d, Malcolm C. Bert.

Drama Cas. (PR:O MPAA:R)

ARREST BULLDOG DRUMMOND** (1939, Brit.) 60m PAR w

John Howard *(Capt. Hugh C. Drummond)*, Heather Angel *(Phyllis Clavering)*, H. B. Warner *(Col. Nielson)*, Reginald Denny *(Algy Longworth)*, E. E. Clive *(Tenny)*, Jean Fenwick *(Lady Beryl Ledyard)*, Zeffie Tilbury *(Aunt Meg)*, George Zucco *(Rolf Alferson)*, Leonard Mudie *(Robin Gannett)*, Evan Thomas *(Smith)*, Clyde Cook *(Constable Sacker)*, David Clyde *(Constable McThane)*, George Rigas *(Soongh)*, Neil Fitzgerald *(Sir Malcolm McLeonard)*, Claude Allister *(Sir Basil Leghorne)*, John Sutton *(Inspector Tredennis)*, Ferdinand Munier *(Old Maj. Trumleigh)*, John Rogers *(Guggins)*, Frank Baker *(Cop)*, John Davidson *(Gumba)*.

Only fair outing for the sleuth as solidly played by Howard. Just as he is preparing to marry Angel, Howard accidentally discovers the body of an inventor who has created a futuristic atomic detonating machine which can set off explosives a half-mile away. Howard is accused of the killing but trails the real culprits to a strange island, his fiancee and friends in tow. Here he confronts the villains and rounds up the gang before they can set off a British ammunition depot. Has some entertaining moments from a fine cast. (See BULLDOG DRUMMOND Series, Index.)

p, Stuart Walker; d, James Hogan; w, Stuart Palmer (based on the novel by H. C. McNelle); ph, Ted Tetzlaff; ed, Stewart Gilmore.

Crime/Mystery (PR:A MPAA:NR)

ARRIVEDERCI, BABY!* (1966, Brit.) 100m PAR c

Tony Curtis *(Nick Johnson)*, Rosanna Schiaffino *(Francesca)*, Lionel Jeffries *(Parker)*, Zsa Zsa Gabor *(Gigi)*, Nancy Kwan *(Baby)*, Fenella Fielding *(Fenella)*, Anna Quayle *(Aunt Miriam)*, Warren Mitchell *(Conte de Rienzi*/Maximilian), Mischa Auer *(Romeo)*, Noel Purcell *(Capt. O'Flannery)*, Alan Gifford *(American Brasshat)*, Joseph Furst *(German Brasshat)*, Monti De Lyle *(Butler)*, Bernard Spear *(French Inspector)*, Eileen Way *(Italian Dressmaker)*, Bruno Barnabe *(Head Waiter)*, Gabor Baraker *(Gypsy Baron)*, Tony Baron *(Ruby's Boy Friend)*, Eunice Black *(Matron)*, John Brandon, Windsor Davis *(Radio Engineers)*, Franco DeRosa *(Romano)*, Iole Marinelli, Miki Iveria *(Maids)*, Henri Vidon *(Priest)*, Raymond Young *(Photographer)*.

Lousy murder-sex comedy starring Curtis as a modern-day Bluebeard who kills off his various wives for their money. Humor is based on graphic portrayals of drownings, electrocutions, and other means of murder. Curtis finally meets his match with his last mate who is planning to kill *him*. The whole affair leaves a bad taste in one's mouth.

p,d&w, Ken Hughes (based on a story by Hughes, Ronald Harwood, suggested by "The Careful Man" by Richard Deming); ph, Denys Coop (Panavision, Technicolor); m, Dennis Farnum; ed, John Shirley; cos, Elizabeth Haffenden.

Comedy (PR:C-O MPAA:NR)

ARROW IN THE DUST** (1954) 79m AA c

Sterling Hayden *(Bart Laish)*, Coleen Gray *(Christella)*, Keith Larsen *(Lt. King)*, Tom Tully *(Crowshaw)*, Jimmy Wakely *(Carqueville)*, Tudor Owen *(Tillotson)*, Lee Van Cleef *(Crew Boss)*, John Pickard *(Lybarger)*, Carleton Young *(Pepperis)*.

Hayden stars as an army deserter who is forced to assume leadership of a wagon train that has been under constant Indian attack. Among the members of the caravan is an unscrupulous white, Owen, who has a wagonload of repeating rifles that the savages want to get their hands on. Once Hayden puts two and two together he destroys the rifles and the Indians leave. The cavalry arrives and escorts the wagon train into Laramie where Hayden is arrested for desertion and given a light sentence. Everything turns out fine in the end because the girl he met on the wagon train, Gray, will be waiting for him when he gets out. Lackadaisical direction by Selander spoils the good performances.

p, Hayes Goetz; d, Lesley Selander; w, Don Martin (based on the novel by L. L. Foreman); ph, Ellis W. Carter (Technicolor); m, Marlin Skiles; ed, William Austin, m/l, Jimmy Wakely.

Western (PR:A MPAA:NR)

ARROWHEAD** 1/2** (1953) 105m PAR c

Charlton Heston *(Ed Bannon)*, Jack Palance *(Toriano)*, Katy Jurado *(Nita)*, Brian Keith *(Capt. North)*, Mary Sinclair *(Lela Wilson)*, Milburn Stone *(Sandy MacKinnon)*, Richard Shannon *(Lt. Kirk)*, Lewis Martin *(Col. Weybright)*, Frank de Kova *(Chief Chattez)*, Robert Wilke *(Sgt. Stone)*, Peter Coe *(Spanish)*, Kyle James *(Jerry August)*, John M. Pickard *(John Gunther)*, Pat Hogan *(Jim Eagle)*.

Heston is an Indian-hating cavalry scout (his role based on the life of Al Sieber) who particularly loathes Apaches, stating to one and all that he knows them, having been raised by them. The story centers upon the return of de Kova's tribe to the reservation and Toriano's (Palance) return to his tribe from an eastern prison where he has been held as an incorrigible but has learned the white man's ways. Heston brands him a renegade when he returns but is ignored and then fired from his post when he persists in telling the military that Palance will lead the tribe to war. James and Hogan are named scouts for the cavalry but Hogan betrays the troop as they rendezvous with Palance for a peace meeting. Heston arrives to help the troopers counterattack and finally, in a hand-to-hand battle kills Palance, which brings about peace. Though the tale is often far-fetched, it is nevertheless based on fact and Heston's performance is fascinating in its offbeat appeal of a truculent rebel. Keith is a strong second lead as Heston's officer friend. Katy Jurado plays a treacherous, backstabbing halfbreed mistress to Heston with such conviction that she appears to enjoy the viperous role. Love interest is nil with Mary Sinclair as Heston's white woman, a part she enacts with the zeal of an ostrich.

p, Nat Holt; d&w, Charles Marquis Warren (based on the novel by W. R. Burnett); ph, Ray Rennahan (Technicolor); m, Paul Sawtell; ed, Frank Bracht.

Western **(PR:C MPAA:NR)**

ARROWSMITH**** (1931) 108m Goldwyn/UA bw

Ronald Colman *(Dr. Martin Arrowsmith)*, Helen Hayes *(Leora)*, A. C. Anson *(Prof. Gottlieb)*, Richard Bennett *(Sondelius)*, Claude King *(Dr. Tubbs)*, Beulah Bondi *(Mrs. Tozer)*, Myrna Loy *(Joyce Lanyon)*, Russell Hopton *(Terry Wickett)*, De Witt Jennings *(Mr. Tozer)*, John Qualen *(Henry Novak)*, Adele Watson *(Mrs. Novak)*, Lumsden Hare *(Sir Robert Fairland)*, Bert Roach *(Bert Tozer)*, Charlotte Henry *(Young Girl)*, Clarence Brooks *(Oliver Marchand)*, Walter Downing *(City Clerk)*, David Landau, James Marcus, Alec B. Francis, Sidney McGrey, Florence Britton, Bobby Watson.

Idealistic doctor Colman is obsessed with finding a cure for bubonic plague and dedicates his life to pure research in the West Indies. His devoted and self-sacrificing wife, Hayes, dies of the very disease Colman attempts to eradicate; in a powerful and poignant scene he must witness the death of the woman who has given her life to his ambition. Compounding his guilt is the memory of Loy, who plays the sleek other woman with sensuous allure. Colman first flirts with Loy but ultimately rejects her. He must also choose between his coveted research and practicing medicine when the plague breaks out among the natives. Using up his priceless germ cultures, he ruins his scientific work by using this to inoculate plague victims and stopping the epidemic. Colman, until the making of A TALE OF TWO CITIES, thought ARROWSMITH his best film (completed the same year as THE UNHOLY GARDEN, universally considered to be the distinguished actor's worst film). Although Ford took some liberties with the popular Sinclair Lewis novel, such as "opening up" the film with broad shots of cattle being inoculated, his direction and Howard's script faithfully tell the tale. Ford's smooth direction incisively tells Colman's altruistic story while profiling the image of the medical profession as god-like in the public mind. Lewis viewed the film and pronounced it a fine interpretation, stating that he realized Howard had to necessarily boil down many of his complex and interwoven themes for clarity's sake. Ford, always a feisty character, could not stand interference from producer Goldwyn. When the producer appeared on the set, Ford yelled: "Cut!" Then he walked off without a word until Goldwyn returned to his office or the golf course. At one point the equally stubborn producer lingered for hours on the set and Ford packed his rods into a car and went off for a week's fishing. The budget-minded Goldwyn thereafter steered clear of Ford's set until the film was completed. ARROWSMITH was immensely popular with audiences and was listed as one of the year's best films by the New York *Times*; it was nominated as Best Picture but lost out to GRAND HOTEL. The strange alchemy between Colman and Hayes is beguiling, he being the British sophisticate with a wry sense of humor and lofty speech, she the homespun American woman whose values are like the roots of an oak tree. Yet the pairing works with unforgettable magic.

p, Samuel Goldwyn; d, John Ford; w, Sidney Howard (based on the novel by Sinclair Lewis); ph, Ray June; m, Alfred Newman; ed, Hugh Bennett; set d, Richard Day.

Drama **(PR:A MPAA:NR)**

ARSENAL STADIUM MYSTERY, THE* (1939, Brit.) 84m G&S Films/GDF

Leslie Banks *(Inspector Slade)*, Greta Gynt *(Gwen Lee)*, Ian Maclean *(Sgt. Clinton)*, Esmond Knight *(Raille)*, Liane Linden *(Inga)*, Brian Worth *(Philip Morring)*, Anthony Bushell *(Jack Dyce)*, Richard Norris *(Setchley)*, Wyndham Goldie *(Kindilett)*, Dennis Wyndham *(Commissionaire)*, Maire O'Neill *(Mrs. Kirwan)*.

The intrigue, tepid as it is presented, involves the poisoning of a star footballer, Bushell, during a championship match, and the ensuing investigation to find the killer.

p, Josef Somio, Richard Norton; d, Thorold Dickinson; w, Dickinson, Donald Bull (based on the novel by Leonard Gribble); ph, Desmond Dickinson.

Crime **(PR:A MPAA:NR)**

ARSENE LUPIN*** (1932) 64m MGM bw

John Barrymore *(Duke of Charmerace)*, Lionel Barrymore *(Guerchard)*, Karen Morley *(Sonia)*, John Miljan *(Prefect of Police)*, Tully Marshall *(Gourney-Martin)*, Henry Armetta *(Sheriff's Man)*, George Davis *(Sheriff's Man)*, John Davidson *(Butler)*, James Mack *(Laurent)*, Mary Jane Irving *(Marie)*.

The first time the Great Profile and his scene-stealing brother Lionel appear together on film is a treat. John is the infamous super-burglar Lupin and Lionel his determined detective pursuer. A great deal of theorizing between the two about crime and criminals subordinates action but provides for some marvelous interaction as each attempts to get the upper hand and the center of each frame of film. John suavely plays the crook, understating his lines and letting Lionel throw all the roundhouse punches, counterboxing with deft deliveries, seeming to almost throw away his best lines. Moreover, the viewer never sees John in the act of thieving which adds even more mystique to his character. Sexy Karen Morley provides the love interest for John, whose last caper is as bold as his character, the theft of the Mona Lisa from the Louvre (somewhat in the manner of Vincenzo Peruggia who actually stole the painting in 1911). But in this super caper John is foiled by detective Lionel who proves to be his intellectual match. Yet the cop admires his crafty opponent, and, while they are en route to the police station, Lionel hypothesizes that a wily criminal just might slip from the cab as it moves over the bridge, dive into the water, and swim away. This is the action John promptly takes while brother Lionel fires a few perfunctory shots in his direction, purposely aiming high, then later reports shooting his adversary, saying he has drowned. The teaming of the Barrymores was no accident. Mogul Louis B. Mayer adored Lionel, thinking him the greatest living actor, and Thalberg considered John as America's top thespian. They waited until John's contract expired at Warner Bros., and, a minute later, hired the Great Profile at $150,000 a film, hurrying the brothers into ARSENE LUPIN. A sheer delight, this Barrymore vehicle where the great acting brothers perform for each other as well as the viewer.

d, Jack Conway; w, Carey Wilson, Bayard Veiller, Lenore Coffee (based on the play by Maurice LeBlanc and Francis de Croisset); ph, Oliver T. Marsh; ed, Hugh Wynn.

Crime **(PR:A MPAA:NR)**

ARSENE LUPIN RETURNS 1/2** (1938) 81m MGM bw

Melvyn Douglas *(Arsene Lupin/Rene Farrand)*, Virginia Bruce *(Lorraine DeGrissac)*, Warren William *(Steve Emerson)*, John Halliday *(Count De Grissac)*, Nat Pendleton *(Joe Doyle)*, Monty Woolley *(George Bouchet)*, George Zucco *(Martell)*, E. E. Clive *(Alf)*, Rollo Lloyd *(Duval)*, Vladimir Sokoloff *(Ivan Pavloff)*, Tully Marshall *(Monelli)*, Leonard Penn, Harry Tyler, Chester Clute *(Reporters)*, Jonathan Hale *(Chief of D.C.I.)*, Lillian Rich *(Telephone Operator)*, Harvey Clark *(Assistant Manager)*, Jack Norton *(Hotel Manager)*, Robert Emmett Keane *(Watkins)*, Pierre Watkin *(Mr. Carter)*, Joseph King *(Inspector Hennessey)*, Del Henderson *(Plainclothesman)*, George Davis *(Guard at Dock)*, Frank Dawson *(Franz)*, Stanley Fields *(Groom)*, Mitchell Lewis, William Norton Bailey, Chris Frank *(Detectives)*, Robert Middlemass *(Sergeant)*, Perry Ivins *(Fingerprint Man)*, Egon Brecher *(Vasseur)*, Ian Wolfe *(A. LeMarchand)*, Ruth Hart *(Phone Girl)*, Otto Fries *(Truck Driver)*, Priscilla Lawson *(Switchboard* Operator), Jacques Vanaire, Robert O'Connor *(Gendarmes)*, Sid D'Albrook *(Detective Alois)*, William H. Royle *(Burly Detective)*, George Douglas, Jean Perry *(Gendarmes)*, Frank Leigh *(English Eddie)*.

A less than enthusiastic sequel to the Barrymore original talkie, the action drags for the first third of the film while the plot is slowly unraveled, one where William, a fired FBI agent operating a security agency, escorts a fabulous jewel from New York to Europe via steamer. Douglas, as Lupin, makes a late entrance to plot the theft of the $250,000 gem. Bruce, a fetching passenger, is slowly wooed by Douglas and later is revealed to be one of his confederates involved in the laborious scheme which culminates in a rather absurd cops-and-robbers chase, spoiling the meticulous story line. Douglas is a believable Lupin but is at times too much the gentleman for his notorious character. The up-and-down pace is unnerving and little suspense holds the viewer since it is obvious what everyone's after. Yet Douglas' pleasing performance lifts the film above the routine.

p, John W. Considine; d, George Fitzmaurice; w, James Kevin McGuinness, Howard Emmett Rogers, George Harmon Coxe; ph, George Folsey; m, Franz Waxman; ed, Ben Lewis; art d, Cedric Gibbons.

Crime Drama **(PR:A MPAA:NR)**

ARSENIC AND OLD LACE**** (1944) 118m WB bw

Cary Grant *(Mortimer Brewster)*, Raymond Massey *(Jonathan Brewster)*, Priscilla Lane *(Elaine Harper)*, Josephine Hull *(Abby Brewster)*, Jean Adair *(Martha Brewster)*, Jack Carson *(O'Hara)*, Edward Everett Horton *(Mr. Witherspoon)*, Peter Lorre *(Dr. Einstein)*, James Gleason *(Lt. Rooney)*, John Alexander *("Teddy Roosevelt" Brewster)*, Grant Mitchell *(Rev. Harper)*, Edward McNamara *(Brophy)*, Garry Owen *(Taxi Driver)*, John Ridgely *(Saunders)*, Vaughan Glaser *(Judge Cullman)*, Chester Clute *(Dr. Gilchrist)*, Charles Lane *(Reporter)*, Edward McWade *(Gibbs)*, Leo White *(Man in Phone Booth)*, Spencer Charters *(Marriage License Clerk)*, Hank Mann *(Photographer)*, Lee Phelps *(Umpire)*.

Riotously funny film adaptation of the smash Broadway comedy (which ran for almost four years), coddled and coaxed into hilarious existence by master director Capra and wonderfully enacted by Grant and his two zany aunts Hull and Adair, playing the lovable Brewster sisters who are the pillars of Brooklyn society, except for their secret pen chant of poisoning old male callers with their homemade elderberry wine, to put them out of their misery. The gruesome fact that they have been practicing this mercy killing for years is not discovered by their doting nephew Grant until he unearths a body in the window seat just before his nuptials with Lane. He has already been putting up with a madly eccentric uncle, Alexander, who thinks he is Teddy Roosevelt and is forever charging wildly up the stairs to his bedroom. Grant is at his wits' end when he discovers more bodies buried in the basement (their graves dug happily by Alexander, who believe he is tunneling out the Panama Canal.) Though directed into slapstick, Grant provides a spellbinding performance of a man uncertain as to whether or not to turn in his sweet old lady aunts to the police. To complicate matters, another Brewster brother, Massey, a much-wanted murderer with horrible scars on his face (with the stitches still intact!) arrives to hide out with the aunts. He is accompanied by Lorre, a maniacal little doctor who put the scars on Massey's horrid face in an abortive facelifting. They both terrorize the aunts and Grant, who gets dizzy running back and forth between his aunt's home and Lane's, the girl next door who is at first perplexed, then angry at Grant for inexplicably stalling their wedding; he has been postponing the ceremony in the belief that he might be as insane as his aunts and uncles. After many zany machinations, the police arrive, arrest fugitive Massey who, along with his sisters, is sent to an asylum, their commitment papers signed by an all-too-willing Lorre wanting to escape the lunatic clutches of Massey. Before they are happily trundled off to the loony bin, the sweet little old aunts inform Grant that he's not really their nephew but the son of their cook. He is free to marry his lady love Lane and goes off to the church. Most of the play's great laugh lines are kept intact. In one instance Jack Carson, as a cop, is told by a superior to go into the basement with Massey and check out the thought-to-be-ridiculous statement that bodies are buried down there. "Do I Have to?" Carson replies in dumbbell pose, "I mean, look at this guy, Sarge (referring to Massey) . . . He looks like Boris Karloff!" (Karloff had played the role on stage.) One line, the punch ending of the play, was cut by the then censorship board, one where Grant learns he is free of hereditary insanity, yelling elatedly to his fiance: "Elaine! Did you hear? Do you understand? I'm a bastard!" The film was Capra's pet from beginning to end. He saw the play in New York and rushed backstage to buy the property only to be told that Warner Brothers (his studio was

Columbia) had optioned the film rights. He immediately went to the WB studio and had Jack Warner's own people prepare a modest budget, $400,000 for a hectic four-week shooting schedule and then presented the figures to the boss. Jack Warner was delighted at getting the popular property for so little (although Grant, then at the zenith of his career as Hollywood's top farcical actor, demanded and got $100,000 for his role.) Capra used only one interior set, that of the spooky old house belonging to the aunts and an exterior set of the house next to an ancient cemetery and part of Lane's house next door. The lighting was low-keyed, from dusk to night, in keeping with the eerie atmosphere. Capra came in on schedule as was his professional wont and produced a romping rip-snorting black comedy that remains a classic to this day.

p&d, Frank Capra; w, Julius J. and Philip G. Epstein (based on the play by Joseph Kesselring); ph, Sol Polito; m, Max Steiner; ed, Daniel Mandell; art d, Max Parker; spec eff, Byron Haskin, Robert Burks.

Comedy **Cas.** **(PR:A MPAA:NR)**

ARSON FOR HIRE* (1959) 67m AA bw

Steve Brodie *(John)*, Lyn Thomas *(Keely)*, Frank Scannell *(Pop)*, Antony Carbone *(Foxy)*, John Merrick *(Clete)*, Jason Johnson *(Yarbo)*, Robert Riordan *(Boswell)*, Wendy Wilde *(Marily)*, Walter Reed *(Hollister)*, Lari Lane *(Cindy)*, Reed Howes *(Barney)*, Lyn Osborn *(Jim)*, Frank Richards *(Dink)*, Ben Frommer *(Hot Dog Vendor)*, Lester Dorr *(Dispatcher)*, Florence Useem *(Nurse)*, Tom Hubbard *(Ben)*.

Crummy actioner involving a nasty fireman, Hubbard, who heads an arson ring that burns down big buildings and then blackmails the owners to split the insurance money. Fire Inspector Brodie gets to the bottom of things. Pretty dull when the stock footage of horrendous fires isn't on screen. This was originally the B picture on a double-bill with the equally monotonous British giant-monster-on-the-loose pic THE GIANT BEHEMOTH.

p, William F. Broidy; d, Thor Brooks; w, Tom Hubbard; ph, William Margulies; ed, Herbert R. Hoffman.

Action/Crime **(PR:A MPAA:NR)**

ARSON GANG BUSTERS*½ (1938) 65m REP bw (AKA: ARSON RACKET SQUAD)

Robert Livingston *(O'Connell)*, Rosalind Keith *(Joan)*, Jackie Moran *(Jimmy)*, Warren Hymer *(Tom)*, Jack LaRue *(Morgan)*, Clay Clement *(Hamilton)*, Selmer Jackson *(Commissioner)*, Emory Parnell *(Riley)*, Walter Sande *(Oscar)*, Jack Rice *(Bradbury)*, Lloyd Whitlock *(Martin)*.

Livingston stars as an intrepid firefighter who gets off the hook and ladder and into a trench coat to investigate a group of shady insurance underwriters who have been burning down half the town to make some big bucks. Livingston was better known for the series of westerns he did for the studio.

d, Joe Kane; w, Alex Gottlieb, Norman Burnstine; ph, Ernest Miller; ed, Edward Mann.

Crime **(PR:A MPAA:NR)**

ARSON, INC.** (1949) 64m Screen Guild bw

Robert Lowery *(Joe Martin)*, Anne Gwynne *(Jane)*, Marcia Mae Jones *(Bella)*, Douglas Fowley *(Fender)*, Edward Brophy *(Pete)*, Byron Foulger *(Peyson)*, Gaylord Pendleton *(Murph)*, Maude Eburne *(Grandma)*, Lelah Tyler *(Mrs. Peyson)*, William Forrest *(Firechief)*, John Maxwell *(Detective)*, Richard David *(Junior Peyson)*, Emmett Vogan *(Night Watchman)*.

Lowery stars as a young fireman who is transferred to the arson squad to go under cover and stop a gang of thieves who set fires to cover their tracks. Not bad for a film that was shot in seven days at a cost of $60,000.

p, William Stephens; d, William Berke; w, Arthur Caesar, Maurice Tombragel; ph, Carl Berger; ed, Edward Mann.

Crime **(PR:A MPAA:NR)**

ARSON SQUAD*½ (1945) 66m PRC bw

Frank Albertson *(Tom Mitchell)*, Robert Armstrong *(Capt. Joe Dugan)*, Grace Gillern *(Judy Mason)*, Byron Foulger *(Amos Baxter)*, Chester Clute *(Samuel Purdy)*, Arthur Loft *(Cyrus Clevenger)*, Jerry Jerome *(Mike Crandall)*, Stewart Garner *(Bill Roberts)*, Edward Cassidy *(Chief O'Neil)*.

Yet another tale chronicling the trials and tribulations of a big-city fire department as they deal with an insidious rash of arson. Armstrong is the chief of the arson squad, and Albertson is the insurance investigator and together they uncover a ring of hoods making quick cash burning down local warehouses.

p, Arthur Alexander; d, Lew Landers; w, Arthur St. Clair; ph, Ben Kline; ed, Holbrook Todd; md, Lee Zahler.

Crime **(PR:A MPAA:NR)**

ART OF LOVE, THE½** (1965) 99m UNIV c

James Garner *(Casey)*, Dick Van Dyke *(Paul)*, Elke Sommer *(Nikki)*, Angie Dickinson *(Laurie)*, Ethel Merman *(Mme. Coco)*, Carl Reiner *(Rodin)*, Pierre Olaf *(Carnot)*, Miiko Taka *(Chou Chou)*, Roger C. Carmel *(Zorgus)*, Irving Jacobsen *(Fromkis)*, Jay Novello *(Janitor)*, Naomi Stevens *(Mrs. Fromkis)*, Renzo Cesana *(Pepe)*, Leon Belasco *(Prince)*, Louis Mercier *(Judge)*, Maurice Marsac *(Prosecutor)*, Fifi D'Orsay *(Fanny)*, Marcel Hillaire *(Executioner)*, Dawn Willere *(Couchette)*, Nancy Martin *(Margo)*, Victoria Carroll *(Yvette)*, Sharon Shore *(Betti)*, Astrid De Brea *(Cerise)*.

Overloaded comedy, written by Carl Reiner, about an American artist living in Paris, Van Dyke, and his roommate, a struggling author, Garner. Van Dyke decides to give up painting and go back to his rich girl friend in the states who has been paying the pair's bills. Garner panics and tries a variety of methods to keep the painter in Paris, including a fake suicide which backfires, appearing to be real. When the painter returns he has to go underground because Garner discovers that a dead painter's work sells for much more dough than a living painter's. The authorities begin to think that Garner murdered Van Dyke to get rich and his roommate must reappear at the last minute to save his buddy's neck. Good cast handles the material well but the film is so bloated with lunacy that it is hard to keep up with.

p, Ross Hunter; d, Norman Jewison; w, Carl Reiner (based on a story by Richard Alan Simmons, William Sackheim); ph, Russell Metty (Technicolor); m, Cy Coleman; ed, Milton Carruth.

Comedy **(PR:A MPAA:NR)**

ARTHUR*½ (1931, Fr.) 90m Osso bw (LE CULTE DE BEAUTE)

Boucot *(Arthur Michoux)*, Edith Mero *(Mado, His Wife)*, Lily Zevaco *(Antoine, His Cousin)*, Robert Dartres *(Roger Beautromel)*, Berval *(Hubert Fondragon)*.

French musical comedy about a beauty parlor owner who ignores the daily temptations of the ladies because he loves his wife. That is, until he finds out his wife has taken up with his best friend. The beautician then decides to make a play for his best friend's wife. Typical French sex farce adapted from a successful stage show.

p, Adolphe Osso; d, Leonce Perret (based on the Paris stage play); m, Ed Flamert.

Musical Comedy **(PR:C MPAA:NR)**

ARTHUR*½** (1981) 117m Orion/WB c

Dudley Moore *(Arthur Bach)*, Liza Minnelli *(Linda Marolla)*, John Gielgud *(Hobson)*, Geraldine Fitzgerald *(Martha Bach)*, Jill Eikenberry *(Susan Johnson)*, Stephen Elliott *(Burt Johnson)*, Ted Ross *(Bitterman)*, Barney Martin *(Ralph Marolla)*, Thomas Barbour *(Stanford Bach)*, Anne DeSalvo *(Gloria)*, Marjorie Barnes *(Hooker)*, Dillon Evans *(Oak Room Maitre D')*, Maurice Copeland *(Uncle Peter)*, Justine Johnston *(Aunt Pearl)*, Paul Vincent *(Oak Room Waiter)*, Mary Alan Hokanson *(Secretary)*, Paul Gleason *(Executive)*, Phyllis Somerville *(Saleslady)*, Irving Metzman *(Security Guard)*, Joe Doolan, John Doolan, Melissa Ballan *(Kids in Street)*, Florence Tarlow *(Mrs. Nesbitt)*, Lou Jacobi *(Plant Store Owner)*, Gordon Press *(Prize Man)*, Marcella Lowry *(Harriet)*, Jerome Collamore *(Johnson Butler)*, Mark Fleischmann *(Waiter)*, Helen Hanft *(Perry's Wife)*, John Bentley *(Perry)*, Raymond Serra *(Racetrack Owner)*, Peter Evans *(Preston)*, Dominic Guastaferro *(Party Guest)*, Phil Oxnam *(Orderly)*, Richard Hamilton *(Bill)*, George Riddle *(Bartender)*, Lawrence Tierney *(Man in Coffee Shop)*, Bobo Lewis *(Lady in Coffee Shop)*, B. Constance Barry, Kurt Schlesinger *(Wedding Guests)*.

In a successful return to 1930s-style screwball comedy, Moore reprises his triumph in 10 as a dissolute playboy who would rather be drunk day and night than face the reality of his wealth and lofty social position. When thinking about the WASP witch to whom he is betrothed, Eikenberry, Moore literally dives into a bottle. Though a bit unconvincing as the poor little rich boy in middle age looked after by kindly valet Gielgud, who is closer to him than his own father, Moore is brilliant and often hilarious after meeting working girl Minnelli; he is intrigued by her commonplace manners, outspoken ways, and even her occasional shoplifting. After deciding that he wants Minnelli, Moore tries to brush off his fiancee, telling Eikenberry over a drunken dinner that he doesn't love her and that she would be better off without him. She nods like a rich robot at his every insult, holds his hand lovingly with a stupid stare, and promises they will be happy. He can't shake her. Also, his father and grandmother threaten to cut him off from his $750 million inheritance if he continues to see low-class Minnelli. He visits Minnelli to tell her that he can't marry her but must go through with his family's plans; she more or less tells him to drop dead and he almost does by drinking himself into a stupor, before picking up Minnelli on the way to marry Eikenberry, announcing to the shocked socialites gathered in church that he loves another and that the wedding is off. He is attacked viciously by would-be father-in-law Elliott until tough old Fitzgerald steps up to protect her grandson. She insists, however, that she'll leave him penniless unless he marries on a proper level. Showing more grit than in his entire lifetime, Moore refuses, saying he'll get a job to support Minnelli. The thought of actual labor so frightens Fitzgerald that she relents, welcoming Moore and Minnelli to her family and fortune. Moore is often wonderful if not predictable in his role of the spoiled scion of wealth, Minnelli is terrific as the candid lady of the masses, and Gielgud's loyal and sarcastic servant proves him to be one of the world's most adaptable actors. The highly polished production is well-paced and imaginatively directed, yet there is a disturbing aspect to the film; it is hard to imagine today's more informed public idolizing Moore's position of luxury as it would have in Depression-torn 1931, then as a desperate form of escape from dooming poverty. He is amusing but unrealistic; he is entertaining, but as a predictable anachronism. Today he comes across not as a zany, to-hell-with-it man of means, but as a very talented actor playing at being filthy rich.

p, Robert Greenhut; d&w, Steve Gordon; ph, Fred Schuler (Technicolor); m, Burt Bacharach; ed, Susan E. Morse; prod d, Stephen Hendrickson; cos, Jane Greenwood.

Comedy **Cas.** **(PR:C MPAA:PG)**

ARTHUR TAKES OVER** (1948) 63m FOX bw

Lois Collier *(Margaret Bixby)*, Richard Crane *(James Clark)*, Skip Homeier *(Arthur Bixby)*, Ann E. Todd *(Valerie Jeanne Bradford)*, Jerome Cowan *(George Bradford)*, Barbara Brown *(Fiora Bixby)*, William Bakewell *(Lawrence White)*, Howard Freeman *(Bert Bixby)*, Joan Blair *(Mrs. Bradford)*, Almira Sessions *(Mrs. Barnafogle)*, Jeanne Gail *(Betty Lou)*.

Feeble comedy starring Collier, who keeps her marriage to sailor Crane a secret until she can muster up enough courage to tell her mother, Brown, the news. Brown had already arranged for her daughter to marry the local rich man. Things get hectic when Collier's younger brother Homeier hatches a plan to take the heat off Sis and announces that he is engaged, thinking it will distract their mother from the problem at hand.

p, Sol M. Wurtzel; d, Malcolm St. Clair; w, Mauri Grashin; ph, Benjamin Kline; ed, Roy Livingston.

Comedy **(PR:A MPAA:NR)**

ARTISTS AND MODELS*½** (1937) 95m PAR bw

Jack Benny *(Mac Brewster)*, Ida Lupino *(Paula)*, Richard Arlen *(Alan Townsend)*, Gail Patrick *(Cynthia)*, Ben Blue *(Jupiter Pluvius)*, Judy Canova *(Toots)*, Cecil Cunningham *(Stella)*, Donald Meek *(Dr. Zimmer)*, Hedda Hopper *(Mrs. Townsend)*, Sandra Storme *(Model)*, Madelon Grey *(Marjorie)*, Alan Birmingham *(Craig Sheldon)* Kathryn Kay *(Lois)*, Jerry Bergen *(Bartender)*, Mary Shepherd, Gloria Wheeden *(Water Waltzers)*, Del Henderson *(Lord)*, Virginia Brissac *(Seam-*

stress), Henry and Harry C. Johnson *(Jugglers)*, Jack Stary *(Cycling Star)*, Harvey Poirier *(Sharpshooter)*, David Newell *(Romeo)*, Jane Weir *(Miss Gordon)*, Edward Earle *(Flunky)*, Howard Hickman *(Mr. Currie)*, Pat Moran *(Tumbler)*, Martha Raye, Andre Kostelanetz and Orchestra, Russell Patterson's Personettos, Louis Armstrong and Orchestra, Judy, Anne, and Zeke Canova, The Yacht Club Boys, Connie Boswell *(Specialties)*, Peter Arno, McClelland Barclay, Arthur William Brown, Rube Goldberg, John LaGatta, Russell Patterson *(Artists)*

A solidly entertaining musical, this film presents the irrepressible Benny as the lead for the first time. He is the head of an advertising agency with Arlen as his almost only client and, given his wild antics and crazy notions, it's hard to understand why Arlen stays with him. His show biz oriented staff spends every waking second coming up with wow musical numbers to sell Arlen's products, which is a nifty way of presenting one great act after another without the bother of an overpowering story (no musical worth its song-and-dance ever overworked a plot.) Benny is also given the task of crowning a queen of the Artists and Models Ball. One of his staff members, Lupino, goes after the crown to be awarded at the ball sponsored by Arlen, but is snubbed because she is a professional model and not from the upper crust. She grows even more determined and travels to Miami to compete, going up against blueblood Patrick, who is dabbling in modeling. Meanwhile Benny provides hilarious laughs when he is mistaken by underwear salesmen as a model and, in another riotous scene, when becoming involved with Meek, a bashful doctor. Before Lupino wins her way with Arlen and queenship, a number of delightful performers go into their acts: Ben Blue and Judy Canova do an eccentric dance number, Andre Kostelanetz and his band play "Whispers in the Dark" (by Leo Robin and Frederick Hollander), Connie Boswell belts out some tunes, as do the Yacht Club Boys (the Adler, Kern, Kelly and Mann Combo). The culmination of this quick-paced songfest is the Artists and Models Ball, which takes place at the Miami nightclub where most of the film's action is centered. The tunes presented include: "Pop Goes the Bubble," "Stop, You're Breaking My Heart," (Ted Koehler, Burton Lane); "I Have Eyes" (Ralph Rainer, Leo Robin); "Public Melody Number One" (Koehler, Harold Arlen) (a massive production number a la Busby Berkeley which was choreographed by Vincente Minnelli, who left Hollywood after this film, thinking his first try a failure); and "Mr. Esquire," (Koehler, Victor Young) (a number performed by the Personettes, a fanciful puppet act). The entertainment never stops in this one. Just when one show stopper ends, Martha Raye goes into a zany routine or the great Louis Armstrong blasts out a solo. A class act all the way.

p, Lewis Gensler; d, Raoul Walsh; w, Walter DeLeon, Francis Martin (based on a story by Sig Herzig and Gene Thackery); ph, Victor Milner; m, Victor Young; ed,Ellsworth Hoagland; ch, LeRoy Prinz, Vincente Minnelli.

Musical **(PR:AAA MPAA:NR)**

ARTISTS AND MODELS**1/2 (1955) 108m PAR c

Dean Martin *(Rick Todd)*, Jerry Lewis *(Eugene Fullstack)*, Shirley MacLaine *(Bessie Sparrowbush)*, Dorothy Malone *(Abigail Parker)*, Eddie Mayehoff *(Mr. Murdock)*, Eva Gabor *(Sonia)*, Anita Ekberg *(Anita)*, George Winslow *(Richard Stilton)*, Jack Elam *(Ivan)*, Herbert Rudley *(Chief Samuels)*, Richard Shannon *(Agent Rogers)*, Richard Webb *(Agent Peters)*, Alan Lee *(Otto)*, Kathleen Freeman *(Mrs. Muldoon)*, Art Baker *(Himself)*, Emory Parnell *(Kelly)*, Carleton Young *(Col. Drury)*, Nick Castle *(Specialty Dancer)*.

Idiotic Lewis has nightmares and talks in his sleep; Martin, a struggling roommate artist writes down the babble and uses this gobbledygook in selling a successful cartoon strip. Many of Lewis' inane mutterings, however, smack of spies and espionage. The CIA, as well as enemy agents, begins to investigate the innocuous pair. Neighboring girls Malone and MacLaine, the latter a struggling model, patiently await proposals from the nomadic pair who dally with fleshpots Gabor and, especially, the Amazonian lady bountiful, Ekberg, before winding up with the down-to-earth ladies in their rooming house. The finish at the Artists and Models Ball is less than spectacular but the film does offer the memorable "Inamorata," sung by Martin and later used in a dance number pertly performed by MacLaine. Other tunes include "Lucky Song," "You Look So Familiar," and a particularly appealing tune, "Why You Pretend," done by Martin and Lewis in their dingy room as a tuneful commentary on their lack of food. On the whole a pleasant vehicle for the mercurial team that later blew through the top of the tube because of temperament. Eddie Mayehoff, as the mugging, boisterous publisher of gory comic books is actually funnier than Lewis. (It is hard to imagine now exactly what in Lewis' frenetic, almost spastic mannerisms momentarily caught the public's fancy; he is still revered in France as a great comic, but that may be the subtle French way of sneering at American comedy.)

p, Hal B. Wallis; d, Frank Tashlin; w, Tashlin, Hal Kanter, Herbert Baker (based on a play by Michael Davidson and Norman Lessing); ph, Daniel L. Fapp (VistaVision, Technicolor); m, Walter Scharf; ed, Warren Low; cos, Edith Head; ch, Charles O'Curran; m/l, Harry Warren, Jack Brooks.

Musical **(PR:A MPAA:NR)**

ARTISTS AND MODELS ABROAD**1/2 (1938) 90m PAR bw (GB: STRANDED IN PARIS)

Jack Benny *(Buck Boswell)*, Joan Bennett *(Patricia Harper)*, Mary Boland *(Mrs. Isabel Channing)*, Charley Grapewin *(James Harper)*, Joyce Compton *(Chickie)*, The Yacht Club Boys *(Themselves)*, Fritz Feld *(Dubois)*, G. P. Huntley *(Elliot Winthrop)*, Monty Woolley *(Gantvoort)*, Adrienne d'Ambricourt *(Mme. Brissard)*, Andre Cheron *(Brissard)*, Jules Raucourt *(Chaumont)*, Phyllis Kennedy *(Marie)*, Mary Parker *(Punkins)*, Sheila Darcy *(Becky)*, Yvonne Duval *(Red)*, Gwen Kenyon *(Miss America)*, Joyce Mathews *(Jersey)*, Dolores Casey *(Dodie)*, Marie De Forest *(Kansas)*, Alex Melesh *(Count Vassily Vossilovitch)*, Georges Renevant, Nicholas Soussanin *(Prefects of Police)*, Francisco Maran *(Assistant to Prefect)*, Chester Clute *(Simpson)*, Louis Mercier *(Simpson)*, Louis Van den Ecker *(Cabby)*, Charles de Ravenne *(Porter)*, Joseph Romantini *(Grocery Boy)*, Robert du Couedic, Eddie Davis, Alphonse Martel, Ray de Ravenne, Arthur Dulac *(Waiters)*, Armand Kaliz *(Headwaiter)*, George Kerebel, Saverio Rinaldo *(Busboys)*, Gennaro Curci *(Proprietor)*, Jean Perry, Constant Franke *(Gendarmes)*, Paul Cremonesi, Robert Graves *(Chefs)*, Eugene Beday *(Watchman)*, George Davis *(Leader of Guards)*, Paco Moreno, Jacques Vanaire, Eugene Borden, Fred Cavens, Manuel Paris *(Guards)* Jean De Briac, Fred Malatesta *(Treasury Officials)*, David Mir *(Attendant)*, Georges de Gombert *(Reporter)*, Ferdinand Schumann-Heink *(German Reporter)*, Ken Gibson *(American Reporter)*, Joseph de Beauvolers, Martial de Serrand *(Exposition Guards)*, Paul Bryar *(Hotel Clerk)*, Peter Camlin *(Assistant Manager)*, Andre Marsaudon, Roque Guinart *(Plainclothesmen)*, Ed Agresti *(Doorman)*, William Emile *(Secretary)*, Cliff Nazarro *(Guide)*, Albert d'Arno, Harry Lamont, Maurice Brierre, Tony Merlo *(Kitchen Helpers)*, Linda Yale *(Tailor-Made Model)*, Donald Boucher *(Page Boy)*, George Calliga *(Keyboard Operator)*, Marie Burton, Paula de Cardo, Carol Parker, Helaine Moler, Evelyn Keyes, Laurie Lane, Nora Gale, Maria Doray *(Girls)*, Ethel Clayton *(Woman)*.

The sequel to the original Benny musical farce fell far short of its producers' hopes and audience expectation. The droll comedian is stranded in Paris and puts together a super fashion show which is all song-and-dance. Benny also welcomes Coburn and daughter Bennett, thinking they are penniless, but he is a Texas oil tycoon who eventually saves the troupe when disaster looms. Geared as a vehicle for the broadly popular Benny, much of the snap and spontaneity of the original is missing, replaced by elaborate sets that minimize the music. Only four undistinguished tunes permeate an otherwise pedestrian production: "You're Broke, You Dope," by the Yacht Club Boys, "What Have You Got That Gets Me," "Do the Buckaroo," and the vocal ensemble number expected to become popular but didn't, "You're Lovely, Madame" (all by Ralph Rainer and Leo Robin). The result is a big but empty musical without a great deal of music, a production that later prompted its sarcastic star to mutter: "It was lousy." Well, it sure couldn't claim to be a stepcousin to AN AMERICAN IN PARIS.

p, Arthur Hornblow, Jr.; d, Mitchell Leisen; w, Howard Lindsay, Russell Crouse, Ken England (based on a story by Lindsay, Crouse from an idea by J. P. McEvoy); ph, Ted Tetzlaff; ed, Doane Harrison; md, Boris Morros; art d, Hans Dreier, Ernst Fegte; cos, Edith Head; spec eff, Farciot Edouart.

Musical **(PR:A MPAA:NR)**

ARTURO'S ISLAND*1/2 (1963, Ital.) 93m MGM bw

Reginald Kernan *(Wilhelm)*, Key Meersman *(Nunziata)*, Vanni De Maigret *(Arturo)*, Luigi Giuliani *(Tonino Stella)*, Gabriella Giorgielli *(Teresa)*.

Offbeat, truly depressing film about a young boy left alone in a huge house on a remote island and his resultant fantasies and terrors.

p, Carlo Ponti; d, Damiano Damiani; w, Damiani, Ugo Liberatore, Enrico Ribulzi, Cesare Zavattini (based on the novel by Elsa Morante).

Adventure **(PR:C MPAA:NR)**

AS GOOD AS MARRIED** (1937) 73m UNIV bw

John Boles *(Alexander Drew)*, Doris Nolan *(Sylvia Parker)*, Walter Pidgeon *(Fraser James)*, Tala Birell *(Princess Cherry Bouladoff)*, Alan Mowbray *(Wally)*, Katherine Alexander *(Alma)*, Esther Ralston *(Miss Danforth)*, Ernest Cossart *(Quinn)*, Mary Phillips *(Laura)*, Dorothea Kent *(Poochie)*, David Oliver *(Ernie)*, Harry Davenport *(Jessup)*, Billy Schaefer *(Page)*, Elsa Christiansen *(Jean Stafford)*, Walter Byron *(Man)*.

Tepid comedy featuring Nolan as a loyal young secretary who marries her boss to keep him out of trouble with the ladies, and to avoid his financial ruin. None of the spark that should accompany this marriage of circumstances is dealt with, therefore making the whole thing somewhat pointless.

d, Eddie Buzzell; w, F. Hugh Herbert, Lynn Starling (based on an idea by Norman Krasna); ph, Merritt Gerstad; ed, Philip Cahn; md, Charles Previn.

Comedy **(PR:A MPAA:NR)**

AS HUSBANDS GO**1/2 (1934) 65m FOX bw

Warner Baxter *(Charles Lingard)*, Helen Vinson *(Lucille Lingard)*, Warner Oland *(Hippolitus)*, Catherine Doucet *(Emmie Sykes)*, Eleanor Lynn *(Peggy Sykes)*, Frank O'Conner *(Jake Canon)*, Jay Ward *(Wilbur)*, G. P. Huntley Jr. *(Ronald)*.

Okay adaptation of a popular stage play starring Vinson as a married American woman visiting Paris and almost succumbing to the British charms of Huntley. Upon her return to the States she is shocked to find that her English almost-lover has turned up stateside and has become fishing buddies with her unsuspecting husband Baxter. Good dialog and idyllic Iowa countryside locations make this a pleasant little comedy, which looks far enough removed from the stage to be entertaining visually. Upon release, 15 minutes of the footage was cut out, leaving the narrative somewhat choppy.

p, Jesse Lasky; d, Hamilton McFadden; w, Sonya Levien, Sam Behrman (based on the stage play by Rachel Crothers); ph, Hal Mohr.

Comedy **(PR:A MPAA:NR)**

AS LONG AS THEYRE HAPPY*** (1957, Brit.) 95m GFD/RANK c

Jack Buchanan *(John Bentley)*, Janette Scott *(Gwen)*, Jean Carson *(Pat)*, Brenda de Banzie *(Stella)*, Jerry Wayne *(Bobby Denver)*, Diana Dors *(Pearl)*, Hugh McDermott *(Barnaby)*, David Hurst *(Dr. Schneider)*, Athene Seyler *(Mrs. Arbuthnot)*, Joan Sims *(Linda)*, Nigel Green *(Peter)*, Dora Bryan *(Mavis)*, Gilbert Harding *(Gilbert Harding)*, Joan Hickson *(Barmaid)*, Susan Lyall Grant *(Ist Bobbysoxer)*, Jean Aubrey *(2nd Bobbysoxer)*, Peter Illing *(French Sergeant)*, Edie Martin *(Woman)*, Arnold Bell *(Ship's Purser)*, Pauline Winter *(Miss Prendergast)*, Hattie Jacques *(Party Girl)*.

Buchanan plays a stuffy British stockbroker whose home is thrown into chaos when a popular American singer comes to visit. His two daughters, one a bobbysoxer, the other a Parisian existentialist, are mad about the singer and go into a frenzy that drives their father crazy. Mom, de Banzie, thinks it's all harmless and sees it as a good opportunity to rib her fuddy-duddy husband. Adapted from a hit stage play.

p, Raymond Stross; d, J. Lee Thompson; w, Alan Melville (based on the play by Vernon Sylvaine); ph, Gilbert Taylor (Eastmancolor); m, Stanley Black; ed, John Guthridge; ch, Paddy Stone, Irving Davies, m/l, Sam Coslow.

Comedy **(PR:A MPAA:NR)**

AS LONG AS YOU'RE NEAR ME** (1956, Ger.) 94m N.D.F./W.B. c (SOLANGE DU DA BIST)

Maria Schell, O. W. Fischer, Brigitte Horney, Hardy Kruger, Mathias Wieman, Paul Bildt.

An actress of limited talent but working regularly as a bit player has her career almost destroyed by a vainglorious film director who insists upon making her a great star. This mediocre production seems to be inspired by the scenes between Orson Welles and Dorothy Comingore in CITIZEN KANE, where the great man insists his talentless mistress become a great opera diva, but the similarity drastically ends there. Schell is often interesting but sinks into too much sputtering bathos. Poorly dubbed English over the incongruous German.

d, Harald Braun; w, Jochen Huth (English dialog, Bert Reisfeld); ph, Helmuth Ashley; m, Werner Eisbrenner; ed, Claus Boro.

Drama **(PR:A MPAA:NR)**

AS THE DEVIL COMMANDS* (1933) 70m COL bw

Alan Dinehart, Mae Clarke, Neil Hamilton, Charles Sellon, Charles Coleman, John Sheehan.

Turgid melodrama/mystery concerning an evil lawyer who frames the aide of a dying, rich invalid on a murder rap. The invalid pleads for a fatal injection to end his suffering, but the aide will not do it. The lawyer gets the old man to sign his fortune over to the aide and then gives him the fatal injection, making it appear that the aide killed the invalid for his money. The aide gets life in prison instead of the death penality, which is what the lawyer wanted, so the evil attorney frees the aide by faking a suicide note from the deceased. Then the lawyer makes the mistake of trying to kill the only witness to all this, but only wounds him. The witness talks, the lawyer gets prison, and the aide gets the fortune and the girl. Unbelievably complicated and ridiculous.

d, Roy William Neill, Keane Thompson; w, Dam Nelson (based on a story by Jo Swerling); ph, Glen Rominger.

Mystery **(PR:A MPAA:NR)**

AS THE EARTH TURNS** (1934) 73m WB bw

Jean Muir *(Jen)*, Donald Woods *(Stan)*, Emily Lowry *(School Teacher)*, William Janney *(Ollie)*, David Landau *(Mark Shaw)*, Dorothy Peterson *(Mil Shaw)*, Dorothy Appleby *(Doris)*, Arthur Hohl *(George Shaw)*.

Farm drama set in Maine detailing the hardships and joys of three farming families. One family is hardworking and frugal, another is headed by a lazy, venal man, and the third is made up of Polish immigrants led by their amibitious son who is determined to make good in America. Muir plays the simple farmer's daughter who falls in love with the Polish boy and helps him make a success of his farm.

d, Alfred E. Green; w, Ernest Pascal (based on the book by Gladys Hasty Carroll); ph, Byron Haskin.

Drama **(PR:A MPAA:NR)**

AS THE SEA RAGES* (1960 Ger.) 76m COL bw

Maria Schell *(Mana)*, Cliff Robertson *(Clements)*, Cameron Mitchell *(Psarathanas)*.

Boring fishing drama set in the Adriatic starring Robertson as an heroic seaman who helps overthrow the tyrannical rule of Mitchell, who controls the fishing community with an iron hand. Schell is the local girl who falls in love with stranger Robertson and is left to mourn his passing when he sacrifices his life as a gesture of peace. Shot by Germans, dubbed into English, the film doesn't have much to recommend it, except beautiful scenery of the Adriatic Sea.

p, Carl Szokoll; d, Horst Haechler; w, Jeffery Dell, Jo Eisinger (based on the screenplay by Walter Ulbrich and the novel *Raubfischer in Hellas* by Werner Helwig); ph, Kurt Hasse; m, Frederich Meyer; ed, Arndt Heyne; art d, Otto Pischinger, Harta Hareiter, Tihomir Piletic.

Drama **(PR:A MPAA:NR)**

AS YOU DESIRE ME*** (1932) 71m MGM bw

Greta Garbo *(Zara)*, Melvyn Douglas *(Count Bruno Varelli)*, Erich von Stroheim *(Carl Salter)*, Owen Moore *(Tony)*, Hedda Hopper *(Madame Mantari)*, Rafaela Ottiano *(Lena)*, Warburton Gamble *(Baron)*, Albert Conti *(Captain)*, William Ricciardi *(Pietro)*, Roland Varno *(Albert)*.

A bizarre, always fascinating film with two of the world's most intriguing characters—Garbo and von Stroheim—who square off in histrionic battle. Based on the Luigi Pirandello play, the film offers Garbo as a *demi-mondaine* who has seen greater days she cannot remember. Her amnesia stems from a violent incident occuring in WW I. At the time she was an Italian countess whose palace was overrun by invading Austrian troops. She is raped by drunken soldiers (similar to the horrific experience undergone by Sophia Loren in TWO WOMEN) and the resultant trauma causes her mind to go blank. She wanders off into the Balkan backwaters only to emerge as a singer in a cheap nightclub. She wears a blonde wig and is adorned in a tight-fitting black cat suit, an outlandish sartorial vamp image undoubtedly designed to spoof the much-discussed garb of Marlene Dietrich who was busy shocking audiences of the era with strangely mannish or next-to-nothing costumes. Garbo's paramour is a cruel-streaked novelist, von Stroheim, a calculating possessive character who makes love to Garbo by whipping her head backwards, holding her in an iron grip, and crushing her lips in the manner of a tank smashing a hedgerow. She responds to him mechanically, accepting her gutter life as if born to it. All this changes when Moore comes into the club and recognizes her; he had painted her wedding portrait years earlier and reminds her of a past she cannot remember. He convinces her to return to her husband, Douglas, who still mourns her disappearance. She leaves the incensed von Stroheim and moves into a world of posh nobility while her husband worshipfully reintroduces her to blueblood society where she is snubbed. Garbo's life is further complicated when the vengeance-seeking lover, von Stroheim, appears with another woman, insisting that she is really the lost countess and that Garbo is nothing but a scheming impostor. Von Stroheim's claimant is revealed to be a phony and the novelist is sent packing. Garbo remains with her adoring Douglas but she is uncertain at the end whether or not she is indeed his true wife. The film was not a resounding success; audiences of the day were not used to such subtle moralities and problems. (Two decades later audiences responded well to a similar story, ANASTASIA.) The viewer then wanted stories with clearly established heroes and villains; justice had to triumph with a club in its hands. Moreover, the production was rushed on short notice since Garbo's MGM contract was to end 40 days after she had completed GRAND HOTEL earlier that year, and the studio wanted to make the most of its superstar. Though given a lavish production, Garbo resented the studio's greedy race to milk her name into one more film. The ever generous star asked that the man studio bosses had humilated years earlier, von Stroheim, appear in the film. When Mayer and Thalberg objected, she insisted and they bowed to her wishes. Von Stroheim's career was at low ebb; he had not directed a film in years and acted in only mediocre productions up to that time. This would be the most distinguished part he would play until making LA GRANDE ILLUSION five years later, but even during the making of AS YOU DESIRE ME the once-great director-actor suffered doubts and fears of failure that left him bedridden. Before these nervous attacks he would phone Garbo at home, telling her that he could not appear on the set in the morning, that he was near collapse. She would then call production chief Thalberg and tell him that *she* was "indisposed" and could not appear for the next day's shooting, thus heroically protecting her colleague. This Garbo did time and again until von Stroheim's scenes were completed, the kind of marvelous gesture that proved there was a great human being inside a great actress. Almost immediately after the film ended, Garbo went aboard the Swedish liner "Gripsholm" incognito, having already announced that she would never again appear before the cameras. AS YOU DESIRE ME, her 20th film, would be her last, she said. But there would be seven more, among them outstanding triumphs such as QUEEN CHRISTINA, ANNA KARENINA, CAMILLE, and NINOTCHKA, thankfully.

d, George Fitzmaurice; w, Gene Markey (based on the play by Luigi Pirandello); ph, William Daniels; ed, George Hively.

Drama **(PR:A MPAA:NR)**

AS YOU LIKE IT*** (1936, Brit.) 96m FOX bw

Elisabeth Bergner *(Rosalind)*, Laurence Olivier *(Orlando)*, Sophie Stewart *(Celia)*, Henry Ainley *(Exiled Duke)*, Leon Quartermaine *(Jacques)*, Mackenzie Ward *(Touchstone)*, Richard Ainley *(Sylvius)*, Felix Aylmer *(Duke Frederick)*, Aubrey Mather *(Corin)*, Austin Trevor *(le Beau)*, J. Fisher White *(Adam)*, John Laurie *(Oliver)*, Dorice Fordred *(Audrey)*, Stuart Robertson *(Amiens)*, Peter Bull *(William)*, Joan White *(Phebe)*.

One of the first adaptations of Shakespeare in the talking movies. Shot in England over a period of eight months, AS YOU LIKE IT is a good, but not outstanding, presentation. Bergner is the daughter of exiled Duke Ainley. She falls in love with Olivier, who is the son of one of her father's courtiers. Olivier is very proper and reserved and in order for Bergner to get his attention and gain his favor, she diguises herself as a boy and follows him. Eventually Olivier becomes fond of the boy and Bergner becomes jealous of herself. Soon all truth is revealed and Bergner resumes her proper identity and the pair marry.

p, Joseph M. Schenck; d, Paul Czinner; w, J. M. Barrie, Robert Cullen (based on the play by William Shakespeare); ph, Hal Rosson, Jack Cardiff; md, William Walton; set d, Lazare Meerson; cos, John Armstrong; ch, Ninelle De Valois.

Drama **Cas.** **(PR:A MPAA:NR)**

AS YOU WERE* (1951) 68m Lippert bw

Joe Sawyer, William Tracy, Russell Hicks, John Ridgeley, Sondra Rogers, Joan Vohs, Margie Liszt, Rolland Morris, Ed Dearing, Roger McGee, Chris Drake, Maris Wrixon, John Parrish, Ruth Lee.

Zero production values and a dumbbell script about two warring sergeants at training camp adds up to total waste of time.

p, Hal Roach, Jr.; d, Fred L. Guiol; w, Edward R. Seabrook.

Comedy **(PR:A MPAA:NR)**

AS YOUNG AS WE ARE* 1/2 (1958) 75m PAR bw

Robert Harland *(Hank Moore)*, Pippa Scott *(Kim Hutchins)*, Majel Barrett *(Joyce Goodwin)*, Ty Hungerford *(Roy Nielson)*, Barry Atwater *(Mr. Peterson)*, Carla Hoffman *(Nina)*, Ellen Corby *(Mettie McPherson)*, Harold Dyrenforth *(Mr. Evans)*, Ross Elliott *(Bob)*, Linda Watkins *(Mrs. Hutchins)*, Beverly Long *(Marge)*, Mack Williams *(Dr. Hutchins)*.

Inspired drama starring Scott as a youthful-looking schoolteacher who accepts a job teaching in a desert community. A week before school starts she meets local lad Harland who falls in love with her. She likes the boy and they spend the week together. When school begins both are shocked to learn that he is one of her students. Harland refuses to break off the relationship, but Scott gets him to return to his old girl friend Hoffman. Nice production and good performances help the somewhat silly material.

p, William Alland; d, Bernard Girard; w, Meyer Dolinsky (based on a story by Dolinsky, Alland); ph, Haskell Boggs; ed, Everett Douglas.

Drama **(PR:C NPAA:NR)**

AS YOUNG AS YOU FEEL*** (1951) 77m FOX bw

Monty Woolley *(John Hodges)*, Thelma Ritter *(Della Hodges)*, David Wayne *(Joe)*, Jean Peters *(Alice Hodges)*, Constance Bennett *(Lucille McKinley)*, Marilyn Monroe *(Harriet)*, Allyn Joslyn *(George Hodges)*, Albert Dekker *(Louis McKinley)*, Clinton Sundberg *(Frank Erickson)*, Minor Watson *(Cleveland)*, Ludwig Stossel *(Conductor)*, Renie Riano *(Harpist)*, Wally Brown *(Gallagher)*, Rusty Tamblyn *(Willie)*, Roger Moore *(Saltonstall)*.

Good comedy starring Woolley as a 65-year-old worker who is forcibly retired from his job at the Acme Printing Co. because of his age. Outraged by his ouster he decides to get back at boss Dekker by impersonating the president of the conglomerate that owns the printing company. Posing as the head honcho, he forces Dekker to remove the forced retirement policy of the company. Woolley then gets nationwide press coverage from an eloquent speech he makes on the dignity of man that creates a national fervor of approval. The company realizes that he's a fake, but can't proceed against him legally because of the negative public opinion they would endure, so they are forced to give him his old job back. Look for Marilyn Monroe in an early performance as Dekker's secretary.

p, Lamar Trotti; d, Harmon Jones; w, Lamar Trotti (based on a story by Paddy Chayefsky); ph, Joe MacDonald; m, Cyril Mockridge; ed, Robert Simpson; md, Lionel Newman.

Comedy **(PR:A MPAA:NR)**

ASCENDANCY** (1983, Brit.) 92m British Film Institute c

Julie Covington *(Connie)*, Ian Charleson *(Ryder)*, John Phillips *(Wintour)*, Susan Engel *(Nurse)*, Phillip Locke *(Dr. Strickland)*, Kieran Montague *(Dr. Kelso)*.

First feature film from British documentary filmmaker Edward Bennett, an initial cinematic response to the problems between England and Ireland. Set just after WW I, the story deals with a young girl from a wealthy family who protests the horrors of Belfast with crippling effects on her body. The girl loses the use of her right arm soon after her brother is killed on the battlefield. This is followed by her becoming mute when the growing tension between the Catholics and the Protestants explodes. However, there is an inherent problem in creating a successful exploration of the deep emotional aspects of the Irish problem using this kind of metaphor. The silence of the girl is an interesting symbol, but it alienates an audience from the character it is supposed to identify with. The audience must provide the motivations and emotions of the main character because she cannot respond verbally. The director, therefore, is forced to provide purely visual images that comment on the material.

p, Penny Clark, Ian Elsey; d, Edward Bennett; w, Bennett, Nigel Gearing; ph, Clive Tickner; m, Ronnie Leahy; ed, Charles Rees, George Akers; art d, Jamie Leonard.

Drama **(PR:C MPAA:NR)**

ASCENT TO HEAVEN (SEE: MEXICAN BUS RIDE, 1951)

ASH WEDNESDAY* (1973) 99m PAR c

Elisabeth Taylor *(Barbara Sawyer)*, Henry Fonda *(Mark Sawyer)*, Helmut Berger *(Erich)*, Keith Baxter *(David)*, Maurice Teynac *(Dr. Lambert)*, Margaret Blye *(Kate Sawyer)*, Monique Van Vooren *(German Woman)*, Heening Schlueter *(Bridge Player)*, Dino Mele *(Mario)*, Kathy Van Lypps *(Mandy)*, Dina Sassoli *(Nurse Ilsa)*, Carlo Puri *(Paolo)*, Andrea Esterhazy *(Comte D'Arnoud)*, Jill Pratt *(Simone)*, Irina Wassilchikoff *(Silvana Del Campo)*, Muki Windisch-Graetz *(Viet Hartung)*, Nadia Stancioff *(Helga)*, Rodolfo Lodi *(Prince Von Essen)*, Raymond Vignale *(Gregory De Rive)*, Jose De Vega *(Tony Gutierrez)*, Samantha Starr *(Samantha)*, Elena Tricoli *(Elena)*, Maria Grazia Marescalchi *(Saleslady)*, Sandra Johnson *(Sandy)*.

Taylor stars as a 55-year-old woman whose looks have gone during her lengthy, unhappy marriage to rich lawyer Fonda. In a last-ditch attempt to save her marriage, she flies to Italy to get complete plastic surgery to rejuvenate her face, breasts, buttocks and hands. After some fairly disturbing and gory scenes of the operations, Taylor emerges looking twenty years younger. While she awaits the arrival of Fonda, a sleazy playboy, Berger, seduces her. She uses the creep for one evening to prove to herself that she is still attractive, and then reveals her new look to her husband. Fonda is impressed with the results, but announces that he has fallen in love with a younger woman and he is seeking a divorce. The couple split amicably, but sadly, each going to begin a new life. Another in the long string of mediocre films that Taylor lent her talent to in the last 15 years. Fonda appears only in the last half-hour.

p, Dominick Dunne; d, Larry Peerce; w, Jean-Claude Tramont; ph, Ennio Guarnieri (Technicolor); m, Maurice Jarre; ed, Marion Rothman; art d, Philip Abramson.

Drama **(PR:C MPAA:R)**

ASHANTI** 1/2** (1979) 117m COL c

Michael Caine *(Dr. David Linderby)*, Peter Ustinov *(Suleiman)*, Beverly Johnson *(Anansa Linderby)*, Kabir Bedi *(Malik)*, Omar Sharif *(The Prince)*, Rex Harrison *(Brian Walker)*, William Holden *(Jim Sandell)*, Zia Mohyeddin *(Djamel)*, Winston Ntshona *(Ansok)*, Tariq Yunus *(Faid)*, Tyrone Jackson *(Dongaro)*, Jean-Luc Bideau *(Marcel)*, Johnny Sekka *(Capt. Bradford)*.

A superb cast and a promising story full of exciting elements can't save what becomes a turgid chase movie that drags the viewer endlessly through Middle East sand dunes. Caine's beautiful black wife, Johnson, is kidnaped by Ustinov, a loathsome slave trader who intends to make a fortune on her sale. Director Fleischer dwells painfully on the brutalities visited upon the slaves, particularly the females, as Ustinov's henchmen whip, kick, punch, and herd them from oasis to oasis, heading for purchase points. Following at a less than hectic pace is Caine, aided at times by Harrison, an adventurer, Holden, a helicopter pilot, and Bedi, a fierce nomad who has an old score to settle with Ustinov and does so with blade-wielding accuracy. Too much camera lingers on Johnson as her slender body is more and more revealed as her flimsy dress is worn to tatters during the trek, a focal point bordering on voyeurism, until she is finally delivered to a royal sheik, Sharif, whose yacht is about to sail. Sharif is not only bored stiff but whimsically decides to risk his neck by buying the wife of a World Health Office doctor (she herself is a physician), but in the end the filthy rich bounder is foiled by Caine, who arrives in the traditional nick of time to pluck his winsome bride from the lustful clutches of the kidnapers. An expensive movie, shot on startling locations, the story does not come off because of lame direction and a script that meanders in and out of senseless dialog. The considerable acting talent of the cast is wasted and only the excellent lensing by Tonti sustains attention.

p, George-Alain Vuille; d, Richard Fleischer; w, Stephen Geller (based on the novel *Ebano* by Alberto Vasques-Figueroa); ph, Aldo Tonti (Panavision); m, Michael Melvoin; prod d, Aurelio Crugnola; art d, Kuli Sander.

Adventure/Drama **(PR:O MPAA:R)**

ASHES AND DIAMONDS*** (1961, Pol.) 105m Janus bw (POPIOL I DIAMENT)

Zbigniew Cybulski *(Maciek)*, Eva Krzyzewska *(Christine)*, Adam Pawlikowski *(Andrzej)*, Waclaw Zastrzezynski *(Szczuka)*, Bogumil Kobiela *(Drewnowski)*, Jan Ciecierski *(Porter)*, Stznilaw Milski *(Pienionzek)*, Arthur Mlodnicki *(Kotowicz)*, Halina Kwiatkoska *(Mrs. Staniewicz)*, Ignancy Machowski *(Waga)*, Zbigniew Skowronski *(Slomka)*, Barbara Krafft *(Stefka)*, Alexander Sewruk *(Swiencki)*.

Vivid film by Polish director Andrzej Wajda chronicling the events of the day the Germans surrendered in WW II. We follow a young Polish resistance fighter who is determined to find and assassinate the new Polish Communist leader. The film has a mood of cynicism, nostalgia, and melancholy to it that is haunting. It is full of brilliant visuals showing Poland among the ruins, with its new oppressors rising to power, all detailed in crisp black-and-white photography. A very powerful film. Winner of the 1959 Venice Film Festival, British Film Critics' Guild Award, and the Vancouver Film Festival 1960. (In Polish; English subtitles.)

d, Andrzej Wajda; w, Wajda, Jerzy Andrzejewski (based on the novel by Andrzejewski); m, Aroclaw Radio Quintet; ph, Jerzy Wojcik; ed, Halina Nawrocka; art d, Roman Mann.

War/Drama **(PR:C MPAA:NR)**

ASK A POLICEMAN** (1939, Brit.) 83m MGM bw

Will Hay *(Sgt. Dudfoot)*, Graham Moffatt *(Albert)*, Moore Marriott *(Harbottle)*, Glennis Lorimer *(Emily)*, Peter Gawthorne *(Chief Constable)*, Charles Oliver *(Squire)*, Herbert Lomas *(Coastguard)*, Pat Aherne *(Motorist)*.

Farcical comedy about a village police station where no crime has occurred in over ten years. The cops are bored stiff so they decide to entrap someone by planting a keg of brandy on the beach and arresting whoever grabs it as a smuggler. As it turns out, a second keg shows up and the bumbling cops actually uncover a real smuggler in their midst.

p, Edward Black; d, Marcel Varnel; w, Marriot Edgar, Val Guest (based on a story by Sidney Gilliat); ph, Derick Williams.

Comedy **(PR:A MPAA:NR)**

ASK ANY GIRL*** (1959) 98m MGM c

David Niven *(Miles Doughton)*, Shirley MacLaine *(Meg Wheeler)*, Gig Young *(Evan Doughton)*, Rod Taylor *(Ross Taford)*, Jim Backus *(Mr. Maxwell)*, Claire Kelly *(Lisa)* Elisabeth Fraser *(Jeannie Boyden)*, Dody Heath *(Terri Richards)*, Read Morgan *(Bert)*, Carmen Phillips *(Refined Young Lady)*, Helen Wallace *(Hotel Manager)*, Myrna Hansen, Kasey Rogers, Carrol Byron, Norma French, Kathy Reed *(Girls)*, Mae Clarke *(Woman on Train)*.

MacLaine stars as a small-town girl who comes to Manhattan in search of a husband in this charming sex comedy. After bouncing in and out of several jobs because she wouldn't knuckle under to the amorous advances of her respective bosses, MacLaine finally settles down to work for brothers Niven and Young as a secretary and researcher for their motivational agency. She sets her marital sights on Young and enlists the aid of older brother Niven. Things turn around and it's Niven that she falls for. Good cast of supporting players, and a standout performance by MacLaine make this one well worth sitting through.

p, Joe Pasternak; d, Charles Walters; w, George Wells (based on the novel by Winifred Wolfe); ph, Robert Bronner (CinemaScope, Metrocolor); m, Jeff Alexander; ed, John McSweeney Jr.; cos, Helen Rose.

Comedy **(PR:A MPAA:NR)**

ASK BECCLES* (1933, Brit.) 68m B&D/PAR bw

Garry Marsh *(Eustace Beccles)*, Mary Newland *(Marion Holforth)*, Abraham Sofaer *(Baki)*, Allan Jeayes *(Matthew Blaise)*, John Turnbull *(Inspector Daniels)*, Evan Thomas *(Sir Frederick Boyne)*, Eileen Munro *(Mrs. Rivers)*, Fewlass Llewellyn *(Sir James Holforth)*.

Business consultant steals a priceless gem but pangs of conscience cause him to return the diamond when an innocent man is arrested in his place. A droll comedic attempt that struggles for laughs as well as telling a muddled story.

d, Redd Davis; w, Cyril Campion (based on the play by Campion, Edward Dignon).

Comedy **(PR:A MPAA:NR)**

ASKING FOR TROUBLE* 1/2 (1942, Brit.) 81m BN bw

Max Miller *(Dick Smith)*, Carol Lynne *(Jane Smythe)*, Mark Lester *(Gen. Smythe)*, Wilfrid Hyde-White *(Pettifer)*, Billy Percy *(George)*, Eleanor Hallam *(Margarita)*, Aubrey Mallalieu *(Gen. Fortescue)*, Kenneth Kove *(Capt. Fortescue)*, Chick Elliott *(Mandy Lou)*, Raymond Glendenning *(Commentator)*.

Stupid story about a low-life bookie trying to save the daughter of a stuffy general from the clutches of a big-game hunter by pretending to be an even-bigger-game hunter, with music hall numbers thrown into a bottomless script. The only thing big about this Miller opus is its failure.

p, Wallace Orton; d, Oswald Mitchell; w, Mitchell, Con West.

Comedy **(PR:A MPAA:NR)**

ASPHALT JUNGLE, THE***** (1950) 112m MGM bw

Sterling Hayden *(Dix Handley)*, Louis Calhern *(Alonzo D. Emmerich)*, Jean Hagen *(Doll Conovan)*, James Whitmore *(Gus Ninissi)*, Sam Jaffe *(Doc Erwin Riedenschneider)*, John McIntire *(Police Commissioner Hardy)*, Marc Lawrence *(Cobby)*, Barry Kelley *(Lt. Ditrich)*, Anthony Caruso *(Louis Ciavelli)*, Teresa Celli *(Maria Ciavelli)*, Marilyn Monroe *(Angela Phinlay)*, William Davis *(Timmons)*, Dorothy Tree *(May Emmerich)*, Brad Dexter *(Bob Brannon)*, John Maxwell *(Dr. Swanson)*, James Seay *(Janocek)*, Thomas Browne Henry *(James X. Connery)*, Don Haggerty *(Andrews)*, Helene Stanley *(Jeannie)*, Henry Rowland *(Franz Schurz)*, Raymond Roe *(Tallboy)*.

One of the greatest crime classics ever filmed, the Huston production deals with a single caper, the robbery of a swanky jewelry firm, elaborately schemed by master criminal Jaffe, who is financially backed by corrupt lawyer Calhern. In cross-cutting, we see Jaffe, an unrepentant, habitual criminal of intellectual bent, released from prison, going to a big city to immediately seek financing for a robbery he has meticulously planned behind bars. Also shown is Hayden, in one of the finest performances of his see-saw career, a lumbering, no-nonsense hooligan down on his luck and looking for some sort of score that will get him back to his native Kentucky; his ambition is to buy back his father's horse farm, a desire lost on dumb but good-natured Hagen, the mistreated mistress who adores him. Jaffe, after meeting with crooked lawyer Calhern, recruits Hayden through his friend and fence, Whitmore, a cat-loving hunchback who runs a diner and is tough as nails. Caruso, a professional box man, is next enlisted to blow the safe under Jaffe's direction while Lawrence, never more sleazy than in this role, a nervous bookie, doles out cash for the operation at Calhern's behest. (Hayden notices him perspiring as he counts out bills and asks him about it; Lawrence blurts: "I always sweat when I handle money.") The robbery is accomplished but a watchman interrupts the trio as they are leaving and Caruso is mortally wounded. He is taken home by getaway driver Whitmore and dies surrounded by his large, wailing Italian family. Other odd circumstances contribute to the undoing of the thieves. A corrupt cop, Kelley, who has been extorting money from Lawrence, beats the story of the robbery out of him; he names lawyer Calhern, Whitmore and the others. Before police arrive, Jaffe and Hayden go to Calhern with the millions in stolen gems to collect their money. The lawyer, with Dexter, a private detective fronting muscle for him, tries to double-cross them, but Hayden kills Dexter as he is shot. He gives Jaffe the jewels, takes some cash, and tells the mastermind to flee, a last criminal *beau geste*. After they depart, police arrive at Calhern's hideaway. He is with dumb blonde mistress Monroe and, when confronted with Lawrence's accusations, Calhern goes into another room, ostensibly to write a letter explaining matters to his bedridden wife, then blows out his brains. Quickly now, the police dragnet, led by McIntyre, closes in. Whitmore is arrested and thrown into a cell next to Lawrence, trying to kill him for informing by reaching through the bars. Jaffe, who has hired a cabbie to drive him to Cleveland, stops in a cafe and dallies too long to watch a sexy teenager jitterbug, giving her nickels for the juke box. Police arrest him as he steps from the cafe. "How long have you been out here?" he inquires of a cop. A couple of minutes, he is told. "About as long as it takes to play a phonograph record," Jaffe muses, seeing how he has been foiled by his own perversion. The last of the gang is Hayden, who makes his break for freedom by driving furiously toward Kentucky with Hagen at his side; she persuades him to stop at a doctor's (Maxwell) home in a small town. He is patched up but hears the doctor calling police from another room to report a gunshot wound. He flees and by dawn he is still at the wheel of the car shown racing through the Kentucky hills. Hayden is dying, delirious, babbling about his lost youth. At the same moment McIntyre is holding a press conference, telling reporters that only one of the gang remains at large, "a hardened killer, a hooligan, a man without human feeling or human mercy." Hayden is almost dead at the wheel of the car, stating "If Pa just hangs on to that black colt everything's going to be all right." He stops the car, staggers through a gate and into a field, where he collapses. Beautiful race horses come to him as Hagen races for help. The horses surround the stricken gangster as he dies inside his own pathetic past. Huston directed this superb production with lightning speed, developing his characters incisively but not at the expense of the quickly unraveling plot, one that comes apart at the seams like the plans of the criminals. Jaffe had not appeared in films for some time, having been on the stage, and his role once more made him one of Hollywood's most sought-after character actors. Hayden's career had been drowning in mediocre roles and this film brought him back to superstar status. Calhern, Whitmore, Caruso and Lawrence are nothing short of excellent in their shadowy roles. Monroe, a chorus girl with no future whatever, was plucked from obscurity by Huston who, more than anyone at the time, was responsible for setting off her career with the role of the naive, voluptuous mistress. Rosson's moody photography and Rozsa's moving score further enhance this *film noir* masterpiece.

p, Arthur Hornblow, Jr.; d, John Huston; w, Ben Maddow, Huston (based on the novel by W. R. Burnett); ph, Harold Rosson; m, Miklos Rozsa; ed, George Boemler; art d, Cedric Gibbons, Randall Duell; set d, Edwin B. Willis, Jack D. Moore.

Crime (PR:C MPAA:NR)

ASPHYX, THE** (1972, Brit.) 93m Paragon c (AKA: SPIRIT OF THE DEAD)

Robert Stephens (*Hugo*), Robert Powell (*Giles*), Jane Lapotaire (*Christina*), Alex Scott (*President*), Ralph Arliss (*Clive*), Fiona Walker (*Anna*), Terry Scully (*Pauper*), John Lawrence (*Mason*), Davis Gray (*Vicar*), Tony Caunter (*Warden*), Paul Bacon (*lst Member*).

Lackluster gothic horror concerning the efforts of British aristocrat Stephens, whose hobbies are metaphysics and photography, to capture the soul when it leaves the body. The Greeks called this phenomenon "the asphyx." Stephens succeeds in his experiments, but the asphyx turns out to be an uncontrollable demon. More a mood piece than an out-and-out horror, the film's most notable achievement is the excellent cinematography by Freddie Young, who also shot LAWRENCE OF ARABIA.

p, John Brittany; d, Peter Newbrook; w, Brian Comfort; ph, Freddie Young (Todd-AO 35).

Horror Cas. (PR:C MPAA:PG)

ASSASSIN, THE* (1953, Brit.) 95m UA bw

Richard Todd *(Edward Mercer)*, Eva Bartok *(Adriana)*, John Gregson *(Renzo Occello)*, George Coulouris *(Spadoni)*, Margot Grahame *(Rosa Melitus)*, Walter Rilla *(Count Boria)*, John Bailey *(Lt. Longo)*, Sidney James *(Bernardo)*, Michael Balfour *(Moretto)*, Martin Boddey *(Gufo)*, Sydney Tafler *(Boldesca)*, Miles Malleson *(Crespi)*, Eric Pohlmann *(Gostini)*.

Tedious and confusing mystery set in Venice. Story concerns the search of Todd, a government agent, for a former WW II hero who has become an assassin. Chase scenes over the rooftops of Venice and a music score composed by Nino Rota are the highlights of this otherwise dull actioner.

p, Betty E. Box; d, Ralph Thomas; w, Victor Canning (based on his novel *Venetian Bird)* m, Nino Rota.

Crime (PR:A MPAA:NR)

ASSASSIN, THE*

(1965, Ital./Fr.) 105m Titanu-Vides-SGC bw (AKA: THE LADY KILLER OF ROME)

Marcello Mastroianni *(Nello Poletti)*, Salvo Randone *(Commissioner Palumbo)*, Andrea Checci *(Morello*, Micheline Presle *(Adalgisa de Matteis)*, Cristina Gajoni *(Antonella)*, Mac Ronay *(Suicide Victim)*, Max Cartier *(Adalgisa's Friend)*, Giovanna Gagliardo *(Rosa)*, Enrico Maria Salerno, Bruno Scipioni, Franco Ressel, Toni Ucci, Paolo Panelli, Corrado Zingaro.

Mastrioianni, a well-to-do, unscrupulous businessman, is accused of murder and placed under arrest. His repugnant past is revealed but he is found innocent and released, having undergone a complete personality change for the better.

p, Franco Cristaldi; d, Elio Petri; w, Petri, Tonino Guerra, Pasquale Festa Campanile, Massimo Franciosa; ph, Carlo Di Palma; m, Piero Piccioni; ed, Ruggero Mastroianni; art d, Renzo Vespignani; set d, Carlo Egidi.

Crime (PR:O MPAA:NR)

ASSASSIN* (1973, Brit.) 83m Permini c

Ian Hendry, Edward Judd, Frank Windsor, Ray Brooks, John Hart Dyke.

Cold war spy melodrama has Hendry on a mission from MI5 to assassinate a secret agent working in the British Air Ministry. A weak effort that makes no pretense about plot or acting ability.

d, Peter Crane; w, Michael Sloan; ph, Brian Johnson; m, Zack Lawrence.

Spy Drama (PR:C MPAA:NR)

ASSASSIN FOR HIRE** (1951, Brit.) 67m Merton Park bw

Sydney Tafler *(Antonio Riccardi)*, Ronald Howard *(Inspector Carson)*, John Hewer *(Guiseppi Riccardi)*, Kathryn Blake *(Maria Riccardi)*, Gerald Case *(Sgt. Scott)*, Ian Wallace *(Charlie)*, Martin Benson *(Catesby)*, Ewen Solon *(Fred)*.

Slick professional murderer is arrested for a killing he did not perform; he is ironically convicted and punished in a weird triumph of justice. Interesting twist and above-average performances from Howard and Tafler.

p, Julian Wintle; d, Michael McCarthy; w, Rex Rientis.

Crime (PR:C MPAA:NR)

ASSASSINATION BUREAU, THE*** (1969, Brit.) 106m PAR c

Oliver Reed *(Ivan Dragomiloff)*, Diana Rigg *(Sonya Winter)*, Telly Savalas *(Lord Bostwick)*, Curt Jurgens *(Gen. von Pinck)*, Philippe Noiret *(Lucoville)*, Warren Mitchell *(Weiss)*, Beryl Reid *(Madame Otero)*, Clive Revill *(Cesare Sado)*, Kenneth Griffith *(Popescu)*, Vernon Dobtcheff *(Muntzov)*, Annabella Incontrera *(Elenora)*, Jess Conrad *(Angelo)*, George Couloris *(Swiss Peasant)*, Ralph Michael *(Editor)*, Katherine Kath *(Mme. Lucoville)*, Eugene Deckers *(Desk Clerk)*, Olaf Pooley *(Swiss Cashier)*, George Murcell *(Pilot)*, Michael Wolf *(Officer)*, Gordon Sterne *(Corporal)*, Peter Bowles, William Kendall *(Clients at Mme. Otero's)*, Jeremy Lloyd *(English Officer)*, Roger Delgado, Maurice Browning, Clive Gazes, Gerik Schjelderup *(Bureau Members)*, Milton Reid, Frank Thornton.

Fun farce based on a Jack London story detailing the activities of a group of international assassins who knock off whomever they think needs killing. Intrepid female reporter Rigg noses into the group and pays their leader, Reed, a large sum of money to have his own assassins assassinate him. Reed accepts the challenge, seeing it as a good opportunity to rejuvenate his organization. He has his assassins try to eliminate him, while he, in turn, will try to terminate them. A wacky cat-and-mouse game between the group and their leader takes them racing across Europe, climaxing in a Zeppelin. Great cast who play the whole thing with tongue in cheek.

p, Michael Relph; d, Basil Dearden; w, Relph (based on "The Assassination Bureau Limited" by Jack London, Robert Fish); ph, Geoffrey Unsworth (Technicolor); m, Ron Grainer; ed, Teddy Darvas; art d, Relph; cos, Beatrice Dawson.

Comedy (PR:O MPAA:M)

ASSASSINATION OF TROTSKY, THE**

(1972 Fr./Ital.) 105m Cinerama c Richard Burton *(Leon Trotsky)*, Alain Delon *(Frank Jacson)*, Romy Schneider *(Gita)*, Valentina Cortese *(Natasha Trotsky)*, Enrico Maria Salerno *(Salazar)*, Luigi Vannucchi *(Ruiz)*, Duilio Del Prete *(Felipe)*, Jean Desailly *(Alfred Rosmer)*, Simone Valere *(Marguerite Rosmer)*, Carlos Miranda *(Sheldon Harte)*, Peter Chatel *(Otto)*, Mike Forest *(Jim)*, Marco Lucantoni *(Seva)*, Claudio Brook *(Roberto)*, Hunt Powers *(Lou)*, Gianni Lofredo *(Sam)*, Pierangelo Civera *(Pedro)*.

By no means a good film, but not as bad as some might think. Burton (in an admittedly questionable piece of casting) plays the aging revolutionary Trotsky in his waning years while in exile in Mexico. Delon is the mysterious assassin who eventually slams an ice axe into the brain of Trotsky. The assassination scene is accurate in reflecting the events that took place in Trotsky's office that day. Needless to say, the film is somewhat muddled, but there are small moments that give some insight into the tragedy of the last days of the exiled revolutionary's life. An interesting failure.

p, Josef Shaftel; d, Joseph Losey; w, Nicholas Mosley; ph, Pasquel De Santis (Eastmancolor); m, Egisto Macchi; ed, Reggie Beck; art d, Arrigo Equini.

Historical Drama (PR:O MPAA:R)

ASSAULT* 1/2 (1971, Brit.) 90m Rank c (AKA: IN THE DEVIL'S GARDEN)

Suzy Kendall *(Julie West)*, Frank Finlay *(Det. Chief Supt. Velyan)*, Freddie Jones *(Reporter)*, James Laurenson *(Greg Lomax)*, Lesley-Anne Down *(Tessa Hurst)*, Tony Beckley *(Leslie Sanford)*, Anthony Ainley *(Mr. Bartell)*, Dilys Hamlett *(Mrs. Sanford)*, James Cosmo *(Det. Sgt. Beale)*, Patrick Jordan *(Sgt. Milton)*, Alan Cuthbertson *(Coroner)*, Anabel Littledale *(Susan Miller)*, Tom Chatto *(Police Doctor)*, Kit Taylor *(Doctor)*, Jan Butlin *(Day Receptionist)*, William Hoyland *(Chemist in Hospital)*, John Swindells *(Desk Sergeant)*, Jill Cary *(Night Receptionist)*, David Essex *(Man in Chemist Shop)*, Valerie Shute *(Girl in Chemist Shop)*, John Stone *(Fire Chief)*, Siobhan Quinlan *(Jenny Greenaway)*, Marianne Stone *(Matron)*, Janet Lynn *(Girl in Library)*.

Kendall stars as an art teacher at a school plagued by murders of their young, female students. She is determined to get to the bottom of the mystery by offering herself up as a decoy so the police can catch the killer. Among the suspects are the local newspaper reporter, the sleazy husband of the school principal, and a young doctor. Average thriller.

p, Peter Rogers; d, Sidney Hayers; w, John Kruse (based on the novel *The Ravine* by Kendal Young); ph, Ken Hodges (Panavision); m, Eric Rogers; ed, Tony Palk; art d, Lionel Couch; set d, Peter James Howitt; cos, Courtenay Elliot.

Crime Cas. (PR:O MPAA:NR)

ASSAULT OF THE REBEL GIRLS (SEE: CUBAN REBEL GIRLS, 1959)

ASSAULT ON A QUEEN** (1966) 106m PAR c

Frank Sinatra *(Mark Brittain)*, Virna Lisi *(Rosa Lucchesi)*, Tony Franciosa *(Vic Rossiter)*, Richard Conte *(Tony Moreno)*, Alf Kjellin *(Eric Lauffnauer)*, Errol John *(Linc Langley)*, Murray Matheson *(Captain)*, Reginald Denny *(Master-at-Arms)*, John Warburton *(Bank Manager)*, Lester Matthews *(Doctor)*, Val Avery *(Trench)*, Laurence Conroy *(Junior Officer)*, Gilcrist Stuart, Ronald Long, Leslie Bradley, Arthur E. Gould-Porter *(Officers)*.

Complex caper film about an attempted robbery of the Queen Mary. Sinatra stars as an American who is hired by a rich Italian, Lisi, and her German partner Kjellin to help renovate a sunken German U-boat and use it to threaten to sink the luxury liner if the thieves are not allowed to board and plunder the ship. A series of mistakes by the gang leads to the German about to torpedo the ocean liner, but he is stopped by Sinatra who escapes with Lisi in a dinghy and they drift toward South America. The producers tried to generate the same magic that made Sinatra's OCEAN'S 11 so popular. They didn't succeed but the results aren't too bad.

p, William Goetz; d, Jack Donohue; w, Rod Serling (based on the novel by Jack Finney); ph, William H. Daniels (Panavision, Technicolor); m, Duke Ellington; ed, Archie Marshek; cos, Edith Head.

Crime/Adventure (PR:A MPAA:NR)

ASSAULT ON AGATHON* (1976, Brit./Gr.) 96m Nine Network c

Nico Minardos *(Cabot Cain)*, Nina Van Pallandt *(Maria Christopherous)*, John Woodvine *(Inspector Matt Fenrek)*, Marianne Faithful *(Helen Rochefort)*, Kostas Baladimas *(Vito Glabianco)*, George Moussou *(Agathon)*, Dimitri Aronis *(Claus Cernik)*, Takis Kavouras *(Inspector Krnj)*, Tina Spathi *(Katrina)*, Walter Hessig *(Captain Tsamados)*.

Confusing espionage film set in Greece dealing with the re-emergence of the long-believed-dead guerilla leader Agathon, who plans a new revolution. Interpol agent Woodvine is sent to stop the insidous movement. Dozens of killings and explosions can't hide the fact that the narrative is choppy and confusing. Strange supporting roles from Van Pallandt and Faithful who used to be the close friends of Mick Jagger and Keith Richards, members of the rock band The Rolling Stones.

p, Nico Minardos; d, Laslo Benedek; w, Alan Caillou (based on his novel); ph, George Arvanitis, Aris Stavrou; m, Ken Thorne.

Spy Drama Cas. (PR:O MPAA:NR)

ASSAULT ON PRECINCT 13*** (1976) 91m Turtle Releasing Co. c

Austin Stoker *(Bishop)*, Darwin Joston *(Wilson)*, Laurie Zimmer *(Leigh)*, Martin West *(Lawson)*, Tony Burton *(Wells)*, Charles Cyphers *(Starker)*, Nancy Loomis *(Julie)*, Peter Bruni *(Ice Cream Man)*, John J. Fox *(Warden)*, Kim Richards *(Kathy)*, Henry Brandon.

Early film in the career of HALLOWEEN director John Carpenter that many consider to be his best film to date. It is a low-budget, taut, well-directed update of the Howard Hawks classic western RIO BRAVO, set in modern-day Los Angeles. The story concerns a lengthy siege by a multi-racial street gang on a soon-to-be-closed police station. The gang has murdered a young girl and her father has run to the station for help. The man is in a state of shock and cannot speak to the one cop, Stoker, and two secretaries, Zimmer and Loomis, who are waiting for the moving vans to take what's left of the station's file cabinets. Unexpectedly, two death-row prisoners arrive and are put in holding cells until the prison authorities can find a place to put them, due to the overcrowding of the state prison. As night falls, the street gang attacks in full force, peppering the station with bullets shot from silencers. The gang cuts the electricity and phone lines and the station is left alone in the center of the neighborhood, helpless. The inmates demand to be let loose so they can defend themselves, and they prove to be honorable men. Loomis is killed and Zimmer turns out to be just as tough as any woman in a Howard Hawks film. The shadowy photography, great editing, snappy dialog, and a moody synthesizer score by Carpenter himself, make this one of the most successful homages to the Hawks brand of filmmaking, and a very impressive film in its own right.

p, J. S. Kaplan; d&w, John Carpenter; ph, Douglas Knapp (Metrocolor); m, Carpenter; ed, John T. Chance; art d, Tommy Wallace; cos, Louise Kyes.

Action Cas. (PR:O MPAA:R)

ASSIGNED TO DANGER*½ (1948) 63m EL bw

Gene Raymond *(Dan Sullivan)*, Noreen Nash *(Bonnie)*, Robert Bice *(Frankie Mantell)*, Martin Kosleck *(Joe Gomez)*, Gene Evans *(Joey)*, Ralf Harolde *(Matty Farmer)*, Jack Overman *(Biggie Kritz)*, Mary Meade *(Evie)*.

Average gangster pic starring Raymond as an insurance investigator who is forced to pose as a doctor while investigating a huge payroll robbery. Gang leader Bice is wounded in the hold-up and when the mobsters see Raymond poking around the hideout, they drag him in and make him fix up the boss. The mobster's wife, Nash, is attracted to the stranger, causing tension at the hideout before the gangsters are rounded up.

p, Eugene Ling; d, Oscar [Budd] Boetticher; w, Ling (based on a story by Robert E. Kent); ph, Lewis W. O'Connell; ed, W. Donn Hayes.

Crime (PR:A MPAA:NR)

ASSIGNMENT IN BRITTANY** (1943) 94m MGM bw

[Jean] Pierre Aumont *(Capt. Metard)*, Susan Peters *(Anne Pinot)*, Richard Whorf *(Kerenor)*, Margaret Wycherly *(Mme. Corlay)*, Signe Hasso *(Elise)*, Reginald Owen *(Col. Trane)*, John Emery *(Capt. Deichgraber)*, George Coulouris *(Capt. Holz)*, Sarah Padden *(Albertine)*, Miles Mander *(Col. Fournier)*, George Brest *(Henri)*, Darryl Hickman *(Etienne)*.

Complicated WW II espionage yarn about a plan by the French underground to plant Nazi leader look-alike Aumont among the Huns to get vital information regarding a secret U-boat base off the coast of Brittany. Usual WW II film, with touches of Nazi terror and the French humming "The Marseillaise" at the climax. This movie represented the first U.S. starring exposure for Aumont (who temporarily dropped the "Jean" from his hyphenated front handle) and Hasso, although both were well known in their home countries (France and Sweden, respectively).

p, J. Walter Ruben; d, Jack Conway; w, Anthony Veiller, William H. Wright, Howard Emmett Rogers (based on the novel by Helen MacInnes); ph, Charles Rosher; m, Lennie Hayton; ed, Frank Sullivan.

Spy Drama (PR:A MPAA:NR)

ASSIGNMENT K* (1968, Brit.) 96m COL c

Stephen Boyd *(Philip Scott)*, Camilla Sparv *(Toni Peters)*, Leo McKern *(Smith)*, Robert Hoffmann *(Paul Spiegler)*, Michael Redgrave *(Harris)*, Jan Werich *(Dr. Spiegler)*, Jeremy Kemp *(Hall)*, Jane Merrow *(Martine)*, Vivi Bach *(Erika Herschel)*, David Healy *(David)*, Geoffrey Bayldon *(Boffin)*, Carl Mohner *(Inspector)*, Werner Peters *(Kramer)*, Ursula Howells *(Estelle)*, Friedrich von Ledebur *(Proprietor)*, Dieter Geissler *(Kurt)*, John Alderton *(George)*, Basil Dignam *(Howlett)*, Joachim Hansen *(Heinrich Herschel)*, Marthe Harell *(Mrs. Peters)*, Trudi Hochfilzer *(Ski Instructress)*, Friedrich von Thun *(Rolfe)*, Catherina von Schell *(Maggi)*, Herbert Fuchs *(Bavarian Tourist)*, Peter Capell *(Chalet Landlord)*, Heinz Leo Fischer *(Joseph)*, Karl Otto Alberty *(Detective)*, Helmut Schneider *(Stranger)*, Andrea Allen *(Mini Skirt)*, Rosemarie Reede *(English Nurse)*, Mia Nardi *(German Nurse)*, Jenny White *(Air Hostess)*, Olga Linden *(Nightclub Blonde)*, Alistair Hunter *(Doorman)*, Gert Weidenhof *(Porter)*, Alexander Allerson *(Salesman)*.

Uninspired espionage picture starring Boyd posing as a toy manufacturer who is actually a British agent whose cover is blown. He also makes the disturbing discovery that his girl friend is in the employ of the Germans. Overlong and boring, the film is padded with seemingly endless footage of skiing.

p, Ben Arbeid, Maurice Foster; d, Val Guest; w, Guest, Bill Strutton, Foster (based on the novel *Department K* by Hartley Howard); ph, Ken Hodges (Technicolor); m, Basil Kirchin; ed, Jack Slade; art d, John Biezard; cos, Yvonne Blake.

Spy Drama (PR:A MPAA:NR)

ASSIGNMENT: KILL CASTRO (SEE: CUBA CROSSING, 1980)

ASSIGNMENT OUTER SPACE zero
(1961, Ital.) 79m Ultra-Titanus/AIP bw (AKA: SPACE MEN)

Rik von Nutter *(Ray Peterson)*, Gabriella Farinon *(Lucy)*, Archie Savage *(Al)*, Dave Montresor *(George)*, Alan Dijon *(The Commander)*, Jack Wallace *(Narrator, English Version)*.

A computer goes haywire and causes a huge spacecraft to veer uncontrollably off course, crashing for earth; another craft is sent to intercept the crippled ship and remedy its mechanical problems but the rescue crew, while avoiding perils in space, takes up the whole film battling over sexy Farinon's favors. Not worth a glance.

p, Hugo Grimaldi; d, Antonio Margheriti; w, Vassily Petrov; ph, Marcello Masciocchi; m, J. K. Broady; md, Gordon Zahler; spec eff, Caesar Peace.

Scince Fiction (PR:C MPAA:NR)

ASSIGNMENT—PARIS*** (1952) 84m COL bw

Dana Andrews *(Jimmy Race)*, Marta Toren *(Jeanne Moray)*, George Sanders *(Nick Strang)*, Audrey Totter *(Sandy Tate)*, Sandro Giglio *(Grischa)*, Donald Randolph *(Anton Borvitch)*, Herbert Berghof *(Andreas Ordy)*, Ben Astar *(Vajos)*, Willis Bouchey *(Biddle)*, Earl Lee *(Dad Pelham)*, Maurice Doner *(Victor)*, Leon Askin *(Franz)*, Paul Hoffman *(Kedor)*, Jay Adler *(Henry)*, Peter Votrian *(Jan)*, Georgianna Wulff *(Gogo)*, Don Gibson *(Male Phone Operator)*, Joe Forte *(Barker)*, Mari Blanchard *(Wanda Marlowe)*, Don Kohler *(Bert)*, Hanne Axman *(Secretary)*, Paul Javor *(Laslo Boros)*.

Hard-hitting espionage thriller has Andrews as a reporter assigned to Budapest office of the New York *Herald Tribune* by editor Sanders to help fellow reporter Toren support a story that government plotters are trying to make a deal with Tito to overthrow a Communist dictatorship. Andrews finds that an American businessman has been arrested as a spy and has died in prison but not before leaving a photo showing Tito conferring with the plotters. Andrews manages to smuggle the photo back to Paris before being arrested and beaten into admitting that he is a spy. Through the intervention of another man wanted by the Communists, Andrews finds freedom and returns to love, Toren, and a happy editor Sanders. Tension and suspense are held throughout the film by attention to details, the surveillance of Red spies and censors and a dozen close calls with death, ably directed by Parrish. There is an eerie feeling to this film in that much of what is profiled came into very real existence four years later with the outbreak of the abortive Hungarian Revolution.

p, Samuel Marx, Jerry Bresler; d, Robert Parrish; w, William Bowers (based on the story "Trial by Terror" by Pauline and Paul Gallico); ph, Burnett Guffey, Ray Cory; m, George Duning, ed, Charles Nelson.

Spy Drama (PR:A MPAA:NR)

ASSIGNMENT REDHEAD (SEE: MILLION DOLLAR MANHUNT,1956)

ASSIGNMENT TERROR zero
(1970, Ger./Span./Ital.) 86m Prades c (EL HOMBRE QUE VINO DEL UMMO; AKA: DRACULA VS. FRANKENSTEIN)

Michael Rennie, Paul Naschy, Karin Dor, Craig Hill, Patty Shepard.

Abysmal horror show as Rennie, an alien from another world, finds werewolf Naschy in dire straits and nurses him back to health, along with Dracula, the Mummy and the Frankenstein monster in order to take over planet earth. Moronic script, inept direction and adolescent acting, along with crude dubbing, adds up to an insult to any intelligent viewer.

p, Jaime Prades; d, Tulio Demicheli, Hugo Fregonese; w, Jacinto Molina.

Horror/Science Fiction (PR:C-O MPAA:NR)

ASSIGNMENT TO KILL* (1968) 98m WB-Seven Arts c

Patrick O'Neal *(Richard Cutting)*, Joan Hackett *(Dominique)*, John Gielgud *(Curt Valayan)*, Herbert Lom *(Matt Wilson)*, Eric Portman *(Notary)*, Peter Van Eyck *(Walter Green)*, Oscar Homolka *(Inspector Ruff)*, Leon Greene *(Big Man)*, Kent Smith *(Eversley)*, Philip Ober *(Bohlen)*. Fifi D'Orsay *(Mrs. Hennie)*, Eva Soreny *(Landlady)*, Cynthia Baxter *(Felice Valayan)*.

Good cast can't save this tedious private eye film set in Switzerland. O'Neal is an insurance investigator who is hired to find out why so many of shipping tycoon

Gielgud's ships are sinking mysteriously. Lom plays Gielgud's evil employee who is up to no good. Too much dialog and not enough action fail to hold interest.

d&w, Sheldon Reynolds; ph, Harold Lipstein, Enzo Barboni (Panavision, Technicolor); m, William Lava; ed, George Rohrs; art d, John Beckman.

Crime **(PR:C MPAA:M)**

ASSISTANT, THE**
(1982, Czech.) 93m Ceskoslovensky/Slovak c (POMOCNIK)

Gabor Kanz *(Valent Lancaric)*, Elo Romancik *(Riecan)*, Ildika Pesci *(Mrs. Riecan)*, Marta Sladeckova *(Eva)*, Milan Kis *(Filadelfi)*, Ivan Mistrik *(Dobrik)*, Jozef Ropog *(Torok)*, Hana Talpova *(Vilma)*, Julius Satinsky *(Dr. Lielik)*, Roman Mecznarowski *(Blascak)*.

Another metaphorical slam at the capitalist system from the Eastern European cinema. This one is better than most. Kanz stars as a butcher's assistant whose sexual appetite is used as a metaphor for capitalist acquisition. The helper promptly beds his boss's overweight, materialistic wife and his young, hot-to-trot daughter. The butcher, of course, is above all the nonsense. He is a hard-working, frugal man who shuns the results of his wife's get-rich-quick schemes. The end of the film is somewhat anti-climactic with the noble butcher leaving his business and family to pursue more pure life goals. Decent performances by the principal players make this glorification of socialism a little easier to take.

d, Zoro Zahon; w, Zahon, Ondrej Sulaj (based on a novel by Ladislav Ballek); ph, Jozef Simoncic; m, Svetozar Stur; ed, Maximilian Remen.

Drama **(PR:C MPAA:NR)**

ASSOCIATE, THE*** (1982, Fr./Ger.) 94m EB-COL c (FR: L'ASSOCIE)

Michel Serrault *(Julien Pardot)*, Claudine Auger *(Agnes)*, Catherine Alric *(Alice)*, Judith Magre *(Mme. Brezol)*, Mathieu Carriere *(Louis)*, Bernard Haller *(Hellzer)*.

Very funny comedy starring Serrault as a 50-year-old nebbish who never made it big in business due to his blah personality. To get around this problem he invents a fictitious business partner from England named "Mr. Davis." With the help of Mr. Davis, Serrault's financial counseling firm skyrockets to success. The elusive Mr. Davis lends an air of mystery to the company that investors find appealing. The more money the company makes, the harder it is for Serrault to keep up the charade. He finds that answering phone calls with a British accent is not enough. There are customers who demand personal meetings with his partner, women who bring in new-born babies claiming they have been fathered by Mr. Davis, and female groupies who speculate on the fictitious businessman's sexual prowess. Finally Serrault has had enough of his charming, albeit invisible partner, and decides to kill him off. He fakes a kidnap note and purchases a skeleton from a medical supply company, making it appear that Davis has been murdered. The trick works too well and the police arrest Serrault for the murder of his imaginary partner. The finale is as funny as the rest of the film. Good cast headed by Serrault who was a big hit in LA CAGE AUX FOLLES.

d, Rene Gainville; w, Gainville, Jean-Claude Carriere (based on the novel *My Partner, Mr. Davis* by Jenaro Prieto); ph, Etienne Szabo (Fujicolor); m, Mort Shuman; ed, Raymonde Guyot; art d, Sidney Bettex.

Comedy **(PR:A MPAA:NR)**

ASTERO* (1960, Gr.) 80m Finos Films c

Aliki Vouyouklaki *(Astero)*, Titos Vandis *(Mitros)*, Athanassia Moustaka *(Assimina)*, Dimitrios Papmichail *(Thimios)*, Georgia Vassiliadou *(Stamatina)*, Stefanos Stratigos *(Thanos)*, Koula Lemvessi *(Maroula)*.

Boring Greek village drama concerning a young couple whose courtship is ended by the boy's father who has arranged for him to marry another. The girl's father has also arranged a marriage to a wealthy family, but she flees into the mountains in protest. After some hysterics, there is a happy ending.

d, Dino Dimopoulos; w, Alekos Sakellarios (based on a story by Paul Nirvanas); m, T. Morakis.

Drama **(PR:A MPAA:NR)**

ASTONISHED HEART, THE*** (1950, Brit.) 92m RANK/UNIV bw

Noel Coward *(Christian Faber)*, Celia Johnson *(Barbara Faber)*, Margaret Leighton *(Leonora Vail)*, Joyce Carey *(Susan Birch)*, Graham Payn *(Tim Verney)*, Amy Veness *(Alice Smith)*, Ralph Michael *(Philip Lucas)*, Michael Hordern *(Ernest)*, Patricia Glyn *(Helen)*, Everley Gregg *(Miss Harper)*.

Coward, a suave British psychiatrist, is first personally interested in a patient, Leighton, a stunning blonde with wily ways, then intrigued, then helplessly in love, abandoning his 10-year marriage to Johnson who, as an almost unbelievably understanding wife, encourages her husband to have his fling with the siren to get her out of his system. Instead, Coward becomes a jealous, possessive lover who loses his head and finally plunges to his death when Leighton grows bored with him and finally dismisses his love. Though a somber and sometimes depressing film, the majestic performances of its leading players make it compelling, almost as obsessive in the watching as Coward is in his quick self-destruction.

p, Sidney Box; d, Terence Fisher, Anthony Darnborough; w, Noel Coward (based on his play); ph, Jack Asher; m, Coward; ed, V. Sagovsky.

Drama/Romance **(PR:C MPAA:NR)**

ASTOUNDING SHE-MONSTER, THE zero
(1958) 60m AIP bw (GB:MYSTERIOUS INVADER)

Robert Clarke *(Dick Cutler)*, Kenne Duncan *(Nat Burdell)*, Marilyn Harvey *(Margaret Chaffee)*, Jeanne Tatum *(Esther Malone)*, Shirley Kilpatrick *(Monster)*, Ewing Brown *(Brad Conley)*.

Idiotic story about an alien, Kilpatrick, who lands in a remote area and kills some hoodlums by her mere touch, inadvertently freeing Clarke and Harvey who are being held for ransom. Kilpatrick is killed when an acid bomb created by Clarke eats through her space suit. Cheaply made and written for three-year-olds, this is another amateurish effort to ensnare the insatiable sci-fi viewers who would be better off staring at an empty fish tank and imagining their own other-world creations.

p&d, Ronnie Ashcroft; w, Frank Hall; ph, William C. Thomas; m, Guenther Kauer; cos, Maureen.

Science Fiction **(PR:C MPAA:NR)**

ASTRO-ZOMBIES, THE zero (1969) 90m Geneni c

Wendell Corey *(Holman)*, John Carradine *(Dr. DeMarco)*, Tom Pace *(Eric Porter)*, Joan Patrick *(Janine Norwalk)*, Rafael Campos *(Juan)*, Tura Satana *(Satanna)*, William Bagdad *(Franchot)*, Joseph Hoover *(Chuck Edwards)*, Vincent Barbi *(Tiros)*, Victor Izay *(Dr. Petrovich)*, Wally Moon *(Mike Webber)*, John Hopkins *(Thompson)*, Egon Sirany *(Foreign Agent)*, Lynette Lantz *(Ginger)*, Vic Lance *(Chauffeur)*, Janis Saul *(Lynn)*, Rod Wilmoth *(Astro-Zombie)*.

Just Awful. One of the all-time worst sci-fi pictures. Carradine stars as a mad scientist who makes zombies in his cellar. The "why" of all this is never fully explained, but the zombies go around ripping out people's vital organs. Enter FBI agent Corey (who died soon after filming) who stands around making official pronouncements regarding the investigation of this hideous activity. Throw in some Chinese communists and foreign agents from Mexico led by soft-core porn director Russ Meyer favorite Satana, and you've got one really bad movie. Wayne Rogers of TV's "M*A*S*H" fame co-produced and co-wrote this rancid celluloid mess.

p&d, Ted V. Mikels; w, Mikels, Wayne Rogers; ph, Robert Maxwell (Eastmancolor); m, Nico Karaski; ed, Art Names; art d, Wally Moon.

Science Fiction **Cas.** **(PR:C MPAA:NR)**

ASYLUM***
(1972, Brit.) 88m Amicus/Cinerama c (AKA: HOUSE OF CRAZIES)

Peter Cushing *(Smith)*, Britt Ekland *(Lucy)*, Herbert Lom *(Byron)*, Patrick Magee *(Dr. Rutherford)*, Barry Morse *(Bruno)*, Barbara Parkins *(Bonnie)*, Robert Powell *(Dr. Martin)*, Charlotte Rampling *(Barbara)*, Sylvia Syms *(Ruth)*, Richard Todd *(Walter)*, James Villiers *(George)*, Geoffrey Bayldon *(Max)*, Ann Firbank *(Anna)*, John Franklyn-Robbins *(Stebbins)*, Megs Jenkins *(Miss Higgins)*.

Creepy British horror told in four separate stories written by Robert Bloch. In the first episode, Todd dismembers his wife and wraps the pieces in paper which he then places in the freezer. Soon the parts come to life and crawl around seeking revenge. The second story stars Cushing as a grieving father who brings some special cloth to tailor Morse for a suit that will bring his dead son back to life. The third part is a tale of schizophrenia featuring Ekland as the evil half of Rampling. The final chapter has Lom as an insane inventor who makes tiny robot dolls that murder at his command. Great cast of horror veterans, well written script, and a deft execution.

p, Max J. Rosenberg, Milton Subotsky; d, Roy Ward Baker; w, Robert Bloch; ph, Denys Coop (Technicolor); ed, Peter Tanner; art d, Tony Curtis.

Horror **Cas.** **(PR:O MPAA:PG)**

AT DAWN WE DIE*
(1943, Brit.) 85m Smith/REP bw (GB: TOMORROW WE DIE)

John Clements *(Jean Batiste)*, Godfrey Tearle *(The Mayor)*, Hugh Sinclair *(Maj. von Kleist)*, Greta Gynt *(Marie DuSchen)*, Judy Kelly *(Germaine)*, Yvonne Arnaud *(Mme. Labouche)*, Karel Stepanek *(Seitz)*, Bransby Williams *(Matthieu)*, F. R. Wendhausen *(Commandant)*, Allan Jeayes *(Pogo)*, Gabrielle Brune *(Frissette)*, David Keir *(Jacquier)*.

Contrived espionage melodrama where Clements is unconvincing as a British agent in occupied France, thinking Gynt is a traitor but realizing she is a patriot at film's end. Typical propaganda stuff with wooden acting by Tearle and other first-rate talent interpreting Nazis as hellbent buffoons, not the insidious crafty and evil creatures they truly were.

p, S.W. Smith; d, George King; w, Anatole de Grunwald (based on a story by Dorothy Hope); ph, Otto Heller.

Spy Drama **(PR:A MPAA:NR)**

AT GUNPOINT1/2** (1955) 80m AA c (GB: GUNPOINT)

Fred MacMurray *(Jack Wright)*, Dorothy Malone *(Martha Wright)*, Walter Brennan *(Doc Lacy)*, Tommy Rettig *(Billy)*, Skip Homeier *(Bob Dennis)*, John Qualen *(Livingstone)*, Harry Shannon *(Marshal MacKay)*, Whit Bissell *(Clark)*, Irving Bacon *(Ferguson)*, Jack Lambert *(Kirk)*, Frank Ferguson *(Henderson)*, James Anderson *(Barlow)*, John Pickard *(Alvin)*, Charles Morton *(Bartender)*, Anabel Shaw *(Mrs. Clark)*, Rick Vallin *(Moore)*, Stephen Wootton *(Joey Clark)*, Kim Charney *(Eddie Ferguson)*, Mimi Gibson *(Cynthia Clark)*, James Lilburn *(Wally)*, James Griffith *(The Stranger)*, Harry Lauter *(Federal Marshal)*, Byron Foulger *(Larry, the Teller)*, Keith Richards, Lyle Latell *(Men in Saloon)*, Bill Forman *(Bank Customer)*, Leighton Noble *(Bob, the New Teller)*, Barbara Woodell *(Mrs. Canfield)*, Gertrude Astor *(Woman)*, Charles Courtney *(Horseman)*, Harry Strang *(Postmaster)*.

Some vicious gunmen ride into the small town of Plainview but storekeeper MacMurray foils their bank robbery by getting off a lucky shot that kills the ringleader, a shot that the peace-loving shop owner fires by accident. The townsfolk hail him a hero but their enthusiasm turns sour when gunmen Homeier, Lambert, Pickard, and others return to seek vengeance. Then a reign of terror ensues while the outlaws bide their time, knowing the circuit-riding marshal will not visit the town for days. The town turns against MacMurray and wife Malone, except for staunch friend Brennan, a local doctor. MacMurray's general store is boycotted and he is even asked to leave town so the baddies won't cause trouble. He refuses, going into a showdown against the outlaws; his bravery, even though he knows he will be killed, and the exhortations of Brennan, bring the citizens around so that all do their bit to destroy the menacing killers. MacMurray turns in a fine performance as does Malone, Rettig, their son, and old reliable Brennan, in a film that has a little from a lot of films, such as BAD DAY AT BLACK ROCK, BROKEN ARROW, and most certainly HIGH NOON, the most imitated western of them all. But the movie still stands on its own, thanks to MacMurray's riveting role.

p, Vincent M. Fennelly; d, Alfred Werker; w, Daniel B. Ullman; ph, Ellsworth Fredricks (Technicolor); m, Carmen Dragon; ed, Edna Warren.

Western **Cas.** **(PR:A MPAA:NR)**

AT LONG LAST LOVE** (1975) 118m FOX c

Burt Reynolds *(Michael Oliver Pritchard III)*, Cybill Shepherd *(Brooke Carter)*, Madeline Kahn *(Kitty O'Kelly)*, Duilio Del Prete *(Johnny Spanish)*, Eileen Brennan *(Elizabeth)*, John Hillerman *(Rodney James)*, Mildred Natwick *(Mabel Pritchard)*, Quinn Redeker *(Phillip)*, J. Edward McKinley *(Billings)*, John Stephenson *(Abbott)*, Peter Dane *(Williams)*, William Paterson *(Murray)*, Lester Dorr *(Doorman)*, Liam Dunn *(Harry)*, Elvin Moon *(Elevator Boy)*, M. Emmet Walsh *(Harold)*, Burton Gilliam *(Man at Racetrack)*, Albert Lantieri *(Bookmaker)*, Len Lookabaugh *(Workman)*.

Famed critic-turned-director Peter Bogdanovich's infamous attempt at recreating the lush musicals of the 1930s. The studio provided all that money could buy, creating fabulous art-deco sets, hiring the best technicians in Hollywood and filling the film with more than a dozen Cole Porter classics. Bogdanovich's fatal flaw was in his casting. The critics jumped all over poor Cybill Shepherd for her performance (which probably had more to do with her relationship with Bogdanovich than her acting.) Yes, she was miscast, but she handles the material as well as she can and, after all, who can compete with Ginger Rogers? An even more questionable piece of casting is that of Reynolds as the lead. The man may have a charming smile and a goofy, likable manner, but he's no Fred Astaire and he just can't sing. The plot, such as it is, is just an excuse to show off the fancy sets that accompany the story and four idle rich folk who break out into song and dance at the drop of a hat. The film does have many successful qualities to it and Bogdanovich did make the film *appear* to be a 1930s Hollywood musical. The fault of the film may not be the director's alone, but shared with the mentality of the movie business that no longer supports or nurtures the kind of performing talent that would have made AT LONG LAST LOVE a total success.

p,d&w, Peter Bogdanovich; ph, Laszlo Kovacs (DeLuxe Color); ed, Douglas Robertson; md, Artie Butler; art d, John Lloyd; set d, Jerry Wonderlich; cos, Bobbie Mannix; ch, Albert Lantieri, Rita Abrams; m/l, Cole Porter.

Musical (PR:A MPAA:G)

AT SWORD'S POINT** ½** (1951) 81m RKO c (GB: SONS OF THE MUSKETEERS)

Cornel Wilde *(D'Artagnan)*, Maureen O'Hara *(Claire)*, Robert Douglas *(Lavalle)*, Gladys Cooper *(Queen)*, June Clayworth *(Claudine)*, Dan O'Herlihy *(Aramis)*, Alan Hale Jr. *(Porthos)*, Blanche Yurka *(Mme. Michon)*, Nancy Gates *(Princess Henriette)*, Edmund Breon *(Queen's Chamberlain)*, Peter Miles *(Louis)*, George Petrie *(Chalais)*, Moroni Olsen *(Old Porthos)*, Boyd Davis *(Dr. Fernand)*, Holmes Herbert *(Mallard)*, Lucien Littlefield *(Corporal Gautier)*, Claude Dunkin *(Pierre)*.

Entertaining costume drama set in medieval France detailing the problems of Queen Cooper who is helpless against the sinister Duke Douglas who plans to marry Princess Gates and remove her younger brother from the path to the throne by having him killed. Helpless, that is, until the children of the original four musketeers arrive and foil the nefarious plot. The highlight is O'Hara as a female swordsman who is just as skilled and deadly as her male counterparts. Good fun.

p, Sid Rogell; d, Lewis Allen; w, Walter Ferris, Joseph Hoffman (based on a story by Aubrey Wisberg, Jack Pollexfen); ph, Ray Rennahan (Technicolor); m, Roy Webb; ed, Samuel E. Beetley, Robert Golden.

Adventure Cas. (PR:A MPAA:NR)

AT THE CIRCUS*** (1939) 86m MGM bw

Groucho Marx *(Attorney Loophole)*, Chico Marx *(Antonio)*, Harpo Marx *(Punchy)*, Kenny Baker *(Jeff Wilson)*, Florence Rice *(Julie Randall)*, Eve Arden *(Peerless Pauline)*, Margaret Dumont *(Mrs. Dukesbury)*, Nat Pendleton *(Goliath)*, Fritz Feld *(Jardinet)*, James Burke *(John Carter)*, Jerry Marenghi *(Little Professor Atom)*, Barnett Parker *(Whitcomb)*.

Slippery lawyer Groucho and two idiotic circus employees, Chico and Harpo, attempt to save a bankrupt circus through their impossible schemes. Baker, who is in debt $10,000, must find a way to pay off his creditors or lose his circus. Groucho saves the day by selling the circus for one day at a mammoth social gathering in Dumont's opulent mansion but before this big production number finale the unpredictable brothers go through their antics, Harpo playing a funny game of checkers with a seal as his adviser, Chico performing a pianolog in a circus wagon, Groucho walking on a ceiling with sarcastic Eve Arden. At one point, Arden takes Groucho's money and stuffs it into her bra; Groucho sends a barb in the direction of the then censor's office by remarking to the camera: "There must be some way of getting that money back without getting in trouble with the Hays office." A wild finish has the frantic trio doing impossible gyrations on the flying rings while attempting to avoid an escaped gorilla. Songs abound, with Baker and Rice dueting on "Two Blind Loves" which became a minor hit, "Step Up and Take a Bow," by Harold Arlen, "Blue Moon" by Rogers and Hart which Harpo renders on his harp, backed up with a band of black children, and the most arresting tune sung by Groucho in that marvelous off-key voice, "Lydia, The Tattooed Lady," by Arlen and E. Y. Harburg. This film really marks the decline of the Marx Brothers into Hollywood production numbers and relinquishing of their distinctive set pieces (such as the crammed stateroom sequence in A NIGHT AT THE OPERA or the spoofs of literary classics in HORSEFEATHERS) as they slipped from original satire to studio burlesque. The film is nevertheless a Marx must. (See MARX BROTHERS series, Index.)

p, Mervyn Leroy; d, Edward Buzzell; w, Irving Brecher; ph, Leonard M. Smith; m, Franz Waxman; ed, William H. Terhune; ch, Bobby Connolly.

Comedy/Musical Cas. (PR:AAA MPAA:NR)

AT THE EARTH'S CORE* (1976, Brit.) 89m AIP c

Doug McClure *(David Innes)*, Peter Cushing *(Dr. Abner Perry)*, Caroline Munro *(Dia)*, Cy Grant *(Ra)*, Godfrey James *(Ghak)*, Sean Lynch *(Hooja)*, Keith Barron *(Dowsett)*, Helen Gill *(Maisie)*, Anthony Verner *(Gadsby)*, Robert Gillespie *(Photographer)*, Michael Crane *(Jubal)*, Bobby Parr *(Sagoth Chief)*, Andee Cromarty *(Slave Girl)*.

Incredibly inept and silly adaptation of Edgar Rice Burroughs' adventure yarn. McClure is a lackluster hero who joins scientist Cushing in his machine that burrows its way into the earth until reaching the society of Pellucidar, inhabited with hokey flying creatures. The special effects look like they've been done in somebody's basement, and the monsters appear to have been rented from the corner costume shop, yet the film's graphic violence makes it unacceptable for even the younger viewers. Two other equally feeble films were part of this series of Burroughs' adaptations entitled THE LAND THAT TIME FORGOT and THE PEOPLE THAT TIME FORGOT.

p, John Dark; d, Kevin Connor; w, Milton Subotsky (based on the novel by Edgar Rice Burroughs); ph, Alan Hume (Movielab Color); m, Mike Vicars; ed, John Ireland, Barry Peters; art d, Bert Davey; set d, Michael White.

Adventure Cas. (PR:C MPAA:PG)

AT THE RIDGE** (1931) 56m TIF bw

Bob Steele *(Jim Sullivan)*, Al "Fuzzy" St. John *(Timbers)*, Al Jennings *(Mike Logan)*, Caryl Lincoln *(Pola Valdez)*, Noah Hendricks *(Alabam)*.

An offbeat oater where Steele and sidekick St. John must drive a herd of horses across a state line before rustlers can overtake them. The rustlers are led by Jennings, a real-life bad man who turned to acting when he reformed. Here, oddly enough, Jennings is an undercover marshal riding with the bad guys to obtain information on their evil doings.

p, Trem Carr; d, John P. McCarthy; w, Bob Quigley (based on a story by James Rhodes); ph, Harry Neumann; ed, Frank Balsam.

Western (PR:A MPAA:NR)

AT THE STROKE OF NINE** (1957, Brit.) 72m Tower/GN bw

Patricia Dainton *(Sally Bryant)*, Stephen Murray *(Stephen Garrett)*, Patrick Barr *(Frank)*, Dermot Walsh *(MacDonnell)*, Clifford Evans *(Insp. Hudgell)*, Leonard White *(Thompson)*, Reg Green *(Toby)*, Frank Atkinson *(Porter)*.

Psycho drama has an insane concert pianist abducting a female reporter, announcing that he will murder her in five days unless his bizarre demands are met. The frantic search for the loonie by police offers some interesting scenes with fair suspense.

p, Jon Pennington, Harry Booth, Michael Deeley; d, Lance Comfort; w, Pennington, Booth, Deeley; ph, Gerald Gibbs.

Crime (PR:A MPAA:NR)

AT WAR WITH THE ARMY** ½** (1950) 92m PAR bw

Dean Martin *(Sgt. Puccinelli)*, Jerry Lewis *(Pfc, Korwin)*, Mike Kellin *(Sgt. McVey)*, Jimmie Dundee *(Eddie)*, Dick Stabile *(Pokey)*, Tommy Farrell *(Cpl. Clark)*, Frank Hyers *(Cpl. Shaughnessy)*, Dan Dayton *(Sgt. Miller)*, William Mendrek *(Capt. Caldwell)*, Kenneth Forbes *(Lt. Davenport)*, Paul Livermore *(Pvt. Edwards)*, Ty Perry *(Lt. Terray)*, Jean Ruth *(Millie)*, Angela Greene *(Mrs. Calwell)*, Polly Bergen *(Helen)*, Douglas Evans *(Colonel)*, Steve Roberts *(Doctor)*, Al Negbo *(Orderly)*, Dewey Robinson *(Bartender)*.

The third Martin and Lewis comedy, this one has the boys taking on the military in the tradition of the other great comedy teams, Laurel and Hardy, and Abbott and Costello. Lewis steals the show as a bumbling private who can't seem to do anything right, and Martin is the cool first sergeant who sings most of the songs and sets up most of the gags for Lewis. The highlight of this picture is the pair imitating Bing Crosby and Barry Fitzgerald in a musical parody of GOING MY WAY.

p, Fred F. Finklehoffe; d, Hal Walker; w, Finklehoffe (based on the play by James B. Allardice); ph, Stuart Thompson; m/l, Mack David, Jerry Livingston.

Comedy Cas. (PR:A MPAA:NR)

ATHENA** ½** (1954) 95m MGM c

Jane Powell *(Athena)*, Debbie Reynolds *(Minerva)*, Virginia Gibson *(Niobe)*, Nancy Kilgas *(Aphrodite)*, Dolores Starr *(Calliope)*, Jane Fischer *(Medea)*, Cecile Rogers *(Ceres)*, Edmund Purdom *(Adam Calhorn Shaw)*, Vic Damone *(Johnny Nyle)*, Louis Calhern *(Grandpa Mulvain)*, Evelyn Varden *(Grandma Salome Mulvain)*, Linda Christian *(Beth Hallson)*, Ray Collins *(Mr. Tremaine)*, Carl Benton Reid *(Mr. Griswalde)*, Howard Wendell *(Mr. Grenville)*, Henry Nakamura *(Roy)*, Steve Reeves *(Ed Perkins)*, Kathleen Freeman *(Miss Seely)*, Richard Sabre *(Bill Nichols)*.

Offbeat musical takes us down the path less traveled to view a health-faddist family of seven musically gifted daughters named after constellations and governed by eccentric grandparents, particularly Varden who communes with the faraway galaxies. Powell works hard to infatuate stuffy Bostonian lawyer Purdom and Reynolds entrances crooner Damone as they slog through a boggy script and routine direction by Thorpe. Powell and Reynolds render separate versions of "Love Can Change the Stars," Powell delivers "Chacun Le Sait," and Damone, in a big, pompous production number, sings "Venezia." He does much better with "The Girl Next Door" and, with Reynolds, "Imagine." Other songs include "I Never Felt Better" and Vocalize" (all by Hugh Martin and Ralph Blane). Calhern is exceptional as the muscle-building grandfather and Christian is a sultry counter-character to Powell's often-embarrassing sweet young thing.

p, Joe Pasternak; d, Richard Thorpe; w, William Ludwig, Leonard Spigelgass; ph, Robert Planck (Eastmancolor); ed, Gene Ruggiero; md, George Stoll; ch, Valerie Bettis.

Musical (PR:A MPAA:NR)

ATLANTIC** (1929, Brit.) 87m Elstree bw

Franklin Dyall *(John Rool)*, Madeleine Carroll *(Monica)*, John Stuart *(Lawrence)*, Ellaline Terriss *(Alice Rool)*, Monty Banks *(Dandy)*, Donald Calthrop *(Pointer)*, John Longden *(Lanchester)*, Arthur Hardy *(Maj. Boldy)*, Helen Haye *(Clara Tate-Hughes)*, D.A. Clarke-Smith *(Freddie Tate-Hughes)*, Joan Barry *(Betty Tate-Hughes)*, Francis Lister *(Padre)*, Sydney Lynn *(Capt. Collins)*, Syd Crossley *(Wireless Operator)*, Dino Galvani *(Steward)*, Danny Green *(Passenger)*.

Very early talkie concerning the final voyage of a trans-Atlantic ocean liner that bears an amazing resemblance to the "Titanic." Based on an unsuccessful stage play that ran in England, there is not much of a plot, but the film devotes itself to detailing the horror of the events that took place that fateful evening in the North Atlantic. The picture concentrates on the tragedy of families and friends being split up among the chaos, nervous crew members who try to keep the passengers calm, and the mechanics of trying to save lives on a sinking ocean liner. The footage from this film is powerful and has been used in other films dealing with the same subject matter. There was also a German-language version of ATLANTIC shot at the same time on the same sets using a cast of actors from Germany. It became the first "all-talking" picture released in that country.

p&d, E. A. Dupont; w, Victor Kendall (based on the play "The Berg" by Ernest Raymond); ph, Charles Rosher.

Drama **(PR:A MPAA:NR)**

ATLANTIC ADVENTURE*½ (1935) 68m COL bw

Nancy Carroll *(Helen)*, Lloyd Nolan *(Dan)*, Harry Langdon *(Snapper)*, Arthur Hohl *(Frank)*, Robert Middlemass *(Van Dieman)*, John Wray *(Mitts)*, E. E. Clive *(McIntosh)*, Dwight Frye *(Spike)*, Nana Bryant *(Mrs. Van Dieman)*.

The usual intrepid reporter nonsense starring Nolan as a newspaperman who gets canned because he left the scene of a story early to take his waiting fiancee, Carroll, to dinner. Nolan gets a tip that the murderer of the District Attorney is skipping town on the next ocean liner, so, in an attempt to vindicate himself, he grabs his loyal photographer Langdon and his fiancee and they board the ship. Nolan is such a great reporter that not only does he capture the killer, but a gang of jewel thieves as well.

d, Albert Rogell; w, John T. Neville, Nat Dorfman (based on a story by Diana Bourbon); ph, John Stumar; ed, Ted Kent.

Crime **(PR:A MPAA:NR)**

ATLANTIC CITY*½ (1944) 86m REP bw

Constance Moore *(Marilyn Whitaker)*, Brad Taylor *(Brad)*, Charley Grapewin *(Jake Taylor)*, Jerry Colonna *(Professor)*, Robert B. Castaine *(Carter Graham)*, Adele Mara *(Bar Maid)*, Pierre Watkin *(Senator)*, Harry Tyler *(Sherman)*, Stanley Andrews *(Rogers)*, Donald Kerr *(Oaks)*, Charlie Williams *(Man on the Street)*, Daisy Mothershed *(The Maid)*, Jack Kenny & Al Shean *(Gallagher & Shean)*, Gus Van, Charles Marsh *(Van & Schenck)*, Paul Whiteman and His Orchestra, Louis Armstrong and His Orchestra, Buck & Bubbles, Dorothy Dandridge, Belle Baker, Joe Frisco.

Below average musical starring Taylor as an overly ambitious young man who builds an entertainment empire on the Boardwalk. While he amasses his own theater, nightclub, amusement park, and department store, he alienates his friends. He learns his lesson when tragedy strikes and the pier burns down, forcing him to realize that his friends are more valuable than mere money. Musical entertainment provided by Paul Whiteman, Louis Armstrong, and Dorthy Dandridge, comedy by Gallagher & Shean, Van & Schenck, and Buck & Bubbles. All have been better elsewhere.

p, Albert J. Cohen; d, Ray McCarey; w, Doris Gilbert, Frank Gill Jr., George Carleton Brown (based on a story by Arthur Caesar); ph, John Alton; m, Walter Scharf, Albert Newman, Joseph Dubin; ed, Richard L. Van Enger; ch, Seymour Felix.

Musical **(PR:A MPAA:NR)**

ATLANTIC CITY****

(1981, U.S./Can.) 104m PAR c (AKA: ATLANTIC CITY, U.S.A.)

Burt Lancaster *(Lou)*, Susan Sarandon *(Sally)*, Kate Reid *(Grace)*, Michel Piccoli *(Joseph)*, Hollis McLaren *(Chrissie)*, Robert Joy *(Dave)*, Al Waxman *(Alfie)*, Robert Goulet *(Singer)*, Moses Znaimer *(Felix)*, Angus MacInnes *(Vinnie)*, Sean Sullivan *(Buddy)*, Wally Shawn *(Waiter)*, Harvey Atkin *(Bus Driver)*, Norma Dell'Agnese *(Jeanne)*, Louis Del Grande *(Mr. Shapiro)*, John McCurry *(Fred)*, Eleanor Beecroft *(Mrs. Reese)*, Cec Linder *(President of Hospital)*, Sean McCaan *(Detective)*, Vincent Glorioso *(Young Doctor)*, Adele Chatfield-Taylor *(Florist)*, Tony Angelo *(Poker Player)*, Sis Clark *(Toll Booth Operator)*, Gennaro Consalvo *(Casino Guard)*, Lawrence McGuire *(Pit Boss)*, Connie Collins *(Connie Bishop)*, John Allmond *(Police Commissioner)*, John Burns *(Anchorman)*, Ann Burns, Marie Burns, Jean Burns *(Singers in Casino)*.

Lancaster, in a smashing performance, is an aging fringe criminal who hangs around Atlantic City doing odd jobs and taking care of a broken-down gun moll, Reid, with money, sometimes servicing her sexually; he had been a gopher for her deceased husband, a real gangster during the heyday of the Boardwalk. The small-timer lives inside a past not his own, identifying with yesteryear's notorious gangsters, bragging that he was once a friend of Benjamin "Bugsy" Siegel. Sarandon, who works in an oyster bar and who is going to school to learn how to become a professional croupier, has a room next to Lancaster's and he watches her bathe at night, washing herself down with lemons to destroy the stink of fish. Sarandon's ambitious husband, Joy, appears with a cache of drugs he has stolen from the mob. He makes friends with Lancaster then uses him as an "errand boy" to sell the drugs. Syndicate hoods unearth Joy and brutally murder him before he can collect the money from Lancaster. Later, Joy's killers locate Sarandon and threaten to kill her unless she turns over the narcotics stolen by her husband, but Lancaster comes to the rescue and kills both thugs with a gun he has been carrying around for decades, surprising himself. He laughs hysterically at the shooting, "I killed them, I killed them both—did you see it?" His imagined background and braggadocio have come to be reality. Lancaster flees with Sarandon but, after a brief tryst in a motel room, she leaves with most of the cash he has accumulated through the drug sales. He sends her on her way to France to learn the gambling business, living up to his projected noble image, admitting to her that he never really knew Siegel or any other big-time gangster, that he has been a small-timer all his life, a liar, an impostor. Lancaster then returns to nurture Reid. French director Malle, creator of the dubious PRETTY BABY, presents a tightly shot film with little wasted footage but his nostalgia for America's seamy side of history is often far-fetched, with a foreign perspective that distorts rather than clarifies. The script by Guare is taut; its dialog sparkles with originality and is far superior to TAKING OFF, which he wrote for Milos Forman. Aside from Lancaster's absolutely engrossing performance, the film leaves a sad impression of emptiness, similar to the vacant lots in Atlantic City left by the destroyed hotels of yesterday, and Lancaster somehow represents the new plastic casinos risen in their place, shining expensive towers without personal history, without grandeur, without real tinsel.

p, Denis Heroux; d, Louis Malle; w, John Guare; ph, Richard Ciupka; m, Michel LeGrand; ed, Suzanne Baron; prod d, Anne Pritchard; cos, Francois Barbeau; m/l, "Atlantic City, My Old Friend" Paul Anka.

Crime/Drama **Cas.** **(PR:C-O MPAA:R)**

ATLANTIC CONVOY** (1942) 66m COL bw

Bruce Bennett *(Capt. Morgan)*, Virginia Field *(Lida Adams)*, John Beal *(Carl Hansen)*, Clifford Severn *(Sandy Brown)*, Larry Parks *(Gregory)*, Stanley Brown *(Eddie)*, Lloyd Bridges *(Bert)*, Victor Kilian *(Otto)*, Hans Schumm *(Cdr. von Smith)*, Erik Rolf *(Gunther)*, Eddie Laughton *(Radio Operator)*.

Action-packed war drama featuring Beal as a weather operator working with the U.S. air patrol off the coast of Iceland. Our hero is suspected of being a Nazi spy by his superiors because of his uncanny ability to predict when the next Allied ship will be sunk by a German U-Boat. To prove his innocence, Beal volunteers to ride with a pilot to rescue some British children and their nanny who have been stranded at sea. When the pilot is wounded, Beal is forced to land the plane without landing gear, saving the children. This event really throws suspicion on Beal because no one knew he could fly a plane and his superiors assume he was keeping it a secret that soon would be revealed in an insidious Nazi plot. As it turns out, one of the children Beal rescues is actually a Nazi cabin boy who is to make contact with a fishing boat/spy ship to provide them with the necessary information to sink more Allied ships. Beal discovers this and becomes a hero when he prevents the disaster and helps sink the spy vessel.

p, Collbert Clark; d, Lew Landers; w, Robert Lee Johnson; ph, Henry Freulich; m, M.W. Stoloff; ed, James Sweeney.

War **(PR:A MPAA:NR)**

ATLANTIC FERRY* (1941, Brit.) 108m WB bw (GB: SONS OF THE SEA)

Michael Redgrave *(Charles MacIver)*, Valerie Hobson *(Mary Ann Morison)*, Griffith Jones *(David MacIver)*, Hartley Power *(Samuel Cunard)*, Margaretta Scott *(Susan Donaldson)*, Bessie Love *(Begonia Baggot)*, Milton Rosmer *(George Burns)*, Frederick Leister *(Morison)*, Edmund Willard *(Robert Napier)*, Henry Oscar *(Eagles)*, Charles Victor *(Grogan)*, Frank Tickle *(Donaldson)*, David Keir *(Stubbs)*, Felix Aylmer *(Bank President)*.

Big budget, big cast, big bore of a British epic chronicling the efforts of two brothers, Redgrave and Jones, to build the first steamship to sail the Atlantic. Set in 1837, the costumes and sets look nice, but the story is tedious and cliche-ridden, with the two brothers struggling to build their dream.

d. Walter Forde; w, Gordon Wellesley, Edward Dryhurst, Emeric Pressburger (based on a story by Derek MacIver, Wynne MacIver); ph, Basil Emmott.

Drama **(PR:A MPAA:NR)**

ATLANTIC FLIGHT* (1937) 59m MON bw

Dick Merrill *(Dick Bennett)*, Jack Lamble *(Carter)*, Paula Stone *(Gail)*, Weldon Heyburn *(Bill)*, Ivan Lebedeff *(Baron)*, Milburn Stone *(Pokey)*

Pretty rotten airplane picture starring actual flyer Merrill who had flown to London and back in 48 hours. Monogram grabbed the pilot and signed him up to do a movie. The result is an embarrassing effort by all concerned. Plot details the efforts of rival plane owners, Merrill and a phoney baron, Lebedeff, to prove whose craft is better in a national air race. The baron crashes and is injured, and the heroic Merrill jumps into his plane and flies to London and back in 48 hours with a newly discovered serum that saves his rival's life. Merrill looks extremely uncomfortable when he isn't in the cockpit.

p, William Berke; d, William Nigh; w, Scott Darling, Erna Lazarus; ph, Paul Ivano.

Drama **(PR:A MPAA:NR)**

ATLANTIS, THE LOST CONTINENT*½ (1961) 91m MGM c

Anthony Hall *(Demetrios)*, Joyce Taylor *(Antillia)*, John Dall *(Zaren)*, Bill Smith *(Captain of the Guard)*, Edward Platt *(Azor)*, Frank DeKova *(Sonoy)*, Berry Kroeger *(Surgeon)*, Edgar Stehli *(King Kronas)*, Wolfe Barzell *(Petros)*, Jay Novello *(Xandros)*, Buck Maffei *(Andres)*.

Uninspired George Pal effort starring Hall as a Greek sailor who saves Princess Taylor and is seduced into going to Atlantis where he is suddenly enslaved by the evil Dall. The villain has been transforming slaves into animal-men a la Dr. Moreau and he also has harnessed atomic power to annihilate his opposition. Once Hall gets fed up with this nonsense he organizes the slaves, overthrows the evil ruler and sinks Atlantis into the ocean. Pal's THE TIME MACHINE (1960) is much better.

p&d, George Pal; w, Daniel Mainwaring (based on a play by Sir Gerald Hargreaves); ph, Harold E. Wellman (Metrocolor); m, Russell Garcia; ed, Ben Lewis; art d, George W. Davis, William Ferrari; spec eff, A. Arnold Gillespie, Lee Le Blanc, Robert Hoag.

Adventure/Fantasy **(PR:A MPAA:NR)**

ATLAS* (1960) 84m Filmgroup c

Michael Forrest *(Atlas)*, Frank Wolff *(Praximedes)*, Barboura Morris *(Candia)*, Walter Maslow *(Garnis)*, Christos Exarchos *(Indros)*, Andreas Philippides *(Talectos)*, Theodore Dimitriou *(Gallus)*, Miranda Kounelaki *(Ariana)*, Sascha Dario *(Ballerina)*.

Cheaply produced mini-epic with a dozen extras in cardboard costumes masked as massive armies; even producer Corman subbed as a sword-wielding soldier to make up for a lack of cast. Made in Greece, the pitifully weak story has Olympic champion Forrest battling Wolff over the earthy favors of Morris; the dialog is strictly street corner Brooklyn and the film is a bottom-of-the-barrel imitation of HERCULES—a film that wasn't that good to begin with. not good either.

p&d, Roger Corman; w, Charles Griffith; ph, Basil Maros; m, Ronald Stein; ed, Michael Luciano; cos, Barbara Comeau.

Adventure/Fantasy **(PR:C-O MPAA:NR)**

ATLAS AGAINST THE CYCLOPS*

(1963, Ital.) 100m Medallion c (MACISTE NELLA TERRA DEI CICLOPI)

Mitchell Gordon (Maciste), Chelo Alonso (Capys), Vira Silenti (Penelope), Paul Wynter (Mumba), Dante Di Paolo (Ifito), Aldo Bufi-Landi (Sirone), Germano Longo (Agisandro), Giotto Tempestini (Aronio), Massimo Righi (Efros), Flavio (Penelope's Son), Aldo Padinotti (Cyclops).

Awful Italian epic has muscleman Gordon staggering around as Atlas, killing a one-eyed giant to rescue a baby while battling a sinister queen bent on his destruction.

p, Ermanno Donati, Luigi Carpentieri; d, Antonio Leonuiola; w, O. Biancoli, Gino Mangini (based on a story by Biancolli); ph, Riccardo Pallottini (Eastmancolor); m, Carlo Innocenzi; ed, Mario Serandrei; art d, Alberto Boccianti; cos, Giuliano Papi.

Adventure/Fantasy   **(PR:A MPAA:NR)**

ATLAS AGAINST THE CZAR zero

(1964, Ital.) 90m Medallion c (AKA: MACISTE AGAINST THE CZAR; SAMSON VERSUS THE GIANT KING)

Kirk Morris, Gloria Milland.

Moronic muscleman film has Olympic hero destroying hordes of soldiers (maybe ten or twelve) for the conquest and love of Milland. Not worth the flexing of an eyelash.

d, Amerigo Anton.

Adventure/Fantasy   **(PR:A MPAA:NR)**

ATOLL K   (SEE: UTOPIA, 1950)

ATOM AGE VAMPIRE*   (1961, Ital.) 87m Topaz Films bw

Alberto Lupo (Prof. Levyn), Susanne Loret (Jeannete), Sergio Fantoni (Pierre), Roberto Berta (Sacha), Franca Paridi Strahl (Monique).

Bizarre B film offers up Lupo as a berserk professor who falls in love with torch singer Loret. When she is horribly disfigured in a car accident he remedies her marred face by injecting her with serum from the glands of the dead, causing her to turn into a vampire. Lupo himself regularly transforms himself, inexplicably, into a reptilian monster, supposedly from his exposure to Hiroshima bomb victims he has been treating. Fantoni and friends finally seek out the awful pair and destroy them. About as scary as a little boy shaking a thunder sheet. Producer Bava's reputation as Italy's most renowned creator of sci-fi and horror films was built upon this picture and such tepid productions as TERRORE NELLO SPACIO and DIABOLIK.

p, Mario Bava; d, Anton Guilio Majano, Richard McNamara; w, Majano, Piero Monviso, Gino de Sanctis, Alberto Befilacqua, John Hart; ph, Aldo Giordano; m, Armando Trovajoli; art d, Walter Martigli, Giuseppe Ranieri; spec eff, Ugo Amadoro.

Horror/Science Fiction   **Cas.**   **(PR:C MPAA:NR)**

ATOMIC BRAIN, THE*

(1964) 72m Emerson Films bw (AKA: MONSTROSITY)

Frank Gerstle (Doctor), Erika Peters (Nina), Judy Bamber (Bee), Marjorie Eaton (Hazel), Frank Fowler (Victor), Margie Fisco (Zombie).

Eaton is a wealthy but aging widow, seeking eternal youth. She employs Gerstle, a mad doctor, to put her brain into the body of a young woman—any young, beautiful woman will do—and he operates on three abducted females, two of whom become zombies killing off townsfolk. The third victim is his own pet project; he insert's a cat's brain into the woman and she turns into a carnivorous feline. A soggy, sorry sight.

p, Jack Pollexfen, Dean Dillman, Jr.; d, Joseph V. Mascelli; w, Vi Russell, Sue Dwiggens, Dillman.

Horror/Science Fiction   **(PR:O MPAA:NR)**

ATOMIC CITY, THE*

(1952) 84m PAR bw

Gene Barry (Dr. Addison), Lydia Clarke (Martha Addison), Michael Moore (Russ Farley), Nancy Gates (Ellen), Lee Aaker (Tommy Addison), Milburn Stone (Harold Mann), Bert Freed (Emil Jablons), Frank Cady (Weinberg), Houseley Stevenson, Jr. (Gregson), Leonard Strong (Clark), Harry Hausner (Pattiz), John Damler (Peter Rassett), George M. Lynn (Robert Kalnick), Olan Soule (Mr. Fenton), Anthony Warde (Arnie Molter).

Taut crime drama with Los Alamos as the backdrop features Barry as a nuclear physicist whose son is kidnaped by terrorists who want the bomb-making formula as ransom. The gang hides in Los Angeles where Barry and the FBI are hot on the trail. The gang then runs back to Los Alamos and hides in the mountains. The kid escapes and has to find his own way down the mesa.

p, Joseph Sistrom; d, Jerry Hopper, w, Sydney Boehm; ph, Charles B. Lang, Jr.; m, Leith Stevens; ed, Archie Marshek.

Crime   **(PR:A MPAA:NR)**

ATOMIC KID, THE*   (1954) 86m REP bw

Mickey Rooney (Blix Waterberry), Robert Strauss (Stan Cooper), Elaine Davis (Audrey Nelson), Bill Goodwin (Dr. Rodell), Whit Bissell (Dr. Pangborn), Joey Forman (M.P. in Hospital), Hal March (Ray), Peter Leeds (Bill), Fay Roope (General Lawler), Stanley Adams (Wildcat Hooper), Robert E. Keane (Mr. Reynolds).

A none-too-funny nuclear comedy starring Rooney as a prospector looking for uranium when he is caught in the center of an atomic blast. He survives because of a peanut butter sandwich he was eating at the time. (Nothing like spreading more nuclear disinformation.) It seems the atomic energy has given him the power to do all sorts of comical things like winning at Las Vegas slot machines without touching them. Pretty stupid stuff attributable to Blake Edwards who wrote the original story.

p, Maurice Duke; d, Leslie H. Martinson; w, Benedict Freedman, John Fenton Murray (based on a story by Blake Edwards); ph, John L. Russell, Jr.; m, Van Alexander.

Comedy   **(PR:A MPAA:NR)**

ATOMIC MAN, THE*   (1955, Brit.) 93m AA bw (GB: TIMESLIP)

Gene Nelson (Mike Delaney), Faith Domergue (Jill Friday), Joseph Tomelty (Insp. Cleary), Donald Gray (Maitland), Vic Perry (Vasquo), Peter Arne (Stephen

Maitland), Launce Maraschal (Editor), Charles Hawtrey (Scruffy), Martin Wyldeck (Dr. Preston), Carl Jaffe (Dr. Marks), Barry Mackay (Insp. Hammond).

Nelson and Domergue, atomic scientists, find a fellow worker alive after having believed him dead, discovering that his brain thinks seven seconds ahead of actual time and he is capable of predicting the momentary future. Crooks abduct the scientist to use him for a robbery scheme but they are foiled by Nelson. Dumb movie with an interesting premise.

p, Alex Snowden; d, Ken Hughes; w, Charles Eric Maine, Hughes.

Science Fiction   **(PR:A MPAA:NR)**

ATOMIC SUBMARINE, THE*   (1960) 72m AA bw

Arthur Franz (Reef), Dick Foran (Wendover), Brett Halsey (Carl), Tom Conway (Sir Ian Hunt), Paul Dubov (Dave), Bob Steele (Griff), Victor Varconi (Kent), Joi Lansing (Julie), Selmer Jackson (Admiral), Jack Mulhall (Murdock), Jean Moorhead (Helen), Richard Tyler (Carney), Sid Melton (Chester), Ken Becker (Powell).

Futuristic tale of an atomic sub sailing to the North polar cap to investigate disappearances of freight and passenger submarines in the area. A cyclops space monster with myriad tentacles living in an underwater saucer and bent on conquering the world is what the five crew members find. In a good special-effects battle the invader is destroyed. The internecine battles of crew members do little to enhance the basic story which is also muddied by overuse of news clips of atomic subs (one of which is shown passing the same iceberg several times). One script error has atomic scientists referring to the magnetic and geographical North poles as one and the same. A nevertheless entertaining sci-fi thriller.

p, Alex Gordon; d, Spencer G. Bennet; w, Orville H. Hampton; ph, Gilbert Warrenton; m, Alexander Laszlo, Neil Brunnenkant; ed, William Austin; art d, Don Ament, Dan Heller; set d, Harry Reif; spec eff, Jack Rabin, Irving Block, Louis DeWitt.

Science Fiction   **(PR:A MPAA:NR)**

ATRAGON ½**

(1965, Jap.) 90m AIP/Totto c (KAITEI GUNKAN, ATORAGON, ATARAGON; AKA: THE FLYING SUPERSUB)

Tadao Takashima (Commercial Photographer), Yoko Fujiyama (Capt. Shinguchi's Daughter), Yu Fujiki (Capt. Shinguchi), Kenji Sawara, Akemi Kita, Tetsuko Kobayashi, Akihiko Hirata, Hiroshi Koizumi, Jun Tazaki, Ken Uehara.

Better then average Japanese sci-fi film dealing with the evil undersea society of Mu which has been sucking all the energy out of the center of the Earth and causing quakes on the surface to destroy the non-aquatic people. As usual, the world's only hope is with a batty ex-submarine commander whose supership "Atragon" can stop the terror. Atragon is able to sail on the land, sea, and air, but the skipper isn't interested in saving the Earth until his daughter is kidnaped by the Mu. Great special effects keep this one afloat.

p, Yuko Tanaka; d, Inoshiro Honda; w, Shinichi Sekizawa; ph, Hajime Koizumi (Anamorphic, Pathe Color); m, Akira Ifukube; spec eff, Eiji Tsuburaya.

Science Fiction   **(PR:A MPAA:NR)**

ATTACK!*

(1956) 107m UA bw

Jack Palance (Lt. Costa), Eddie Albert (Capt. Cooney), Lee Marvin (Col. Bartlett), Robert Strauss (Pvt. Bernstein), Richard Jaeckel (Pvt. Snowden), Buddy Ebsen (Sgt. Tolliver), William Smithers (Lt. Woodruff), Jon Shepodd (Cpl. Jackson), Jimmy Goodwin (Pvt. Ricks), Steven Geray (Short German), Peter Van Eyck (Tall German), Louis Mercier (Old Frenchman), Strother Martin (Sgt. Ingersol).

No sensibilities are spared in this brutal portrait of infantry warfare, featuring a powerful performance by Palance. In 1944 Belgium, Albert, a stone coward, orders one of his platoons forward into a position where they are surrounded and slowly destroyed as its leader, Palance, begs via radio for help. Albert, however, is afraid to commit his reserve troops, let alone go near the battle he has created. Palance's men, Ebsen, Strauss, Jaeckel, and others are particularly effective as mud-slogging GIs dealing with their own problems as well as the predicament Albert has brought about. One-by-one they die, until only Palance is able to make it back to headquarters, where he intends to kill Albert but is himself killed. Marvin, Albert's superior, ruthlessly overlooks the coward's unpardonable conduct, believing he will be politically useful after the war. A devastating profile of real war done with expert craftsmanship.

p&d, Robert Aldrich; w, James Poe (based on the play "The Fragile Fox" byNorman Brooks); ph, Joseph Biroc; m, Frank DeVol; ed, Michael Luciano.

War   **(PR:O MPAA:NR)**

ATTACK AND RETREAT   (SEE: ITALIANO BRAVA GENTE, 1965)

ATTACK OF THE CRAB MONSTERS* ½   (1957) 62m AA bw

Richard Garland (Dale Drewer), Pamela Duncan (Martha Hunter), Russell Johnson (Hank Chapman), Leslie Bradley (Dr. Karl Weigand), Mel Welles (Jules Deveroux), Richard Cutting (Dr. James Carson), Beech Dickerson (Ron Fellows), Tony Miller (Jack Somers), Ed Nelson (Ens. Quinlan).

Another Roger Corman low-budget wham-bam quickie sci-fi film with silly looking monsters and fairly laughable dialog. This one concerns an expedition to a Pacific island to study the effects of atomic radiation, and to find out what happened to the last group of scientists which disappeared. What they find is two giant crabs who have eaten the last group of explorers, absorbed their knowledge, and imitated their human voices to entrap more victims. Good premise and some scary moments make this inane fun.

p&d, Roger Corman; w, Charles Griffith; ph, Floyd Crosby; m, Ronald Stein; ed, Charles Gross.

Science Fiction   **Cas.**   **(PR:A MPAA:NR)**

ATTACK OF THE 50 FOOT WOMAN*   (1958) 65m AA bw

Allison Hayes (Nancy Archer), William Hudson (Harry Archer), Yvette Vickers (Honey Parker), Roy Gordon (Dr. Cushing), George Douglas (Sheriff Dubbitt), Ken Terrell (Jessup Stout), Otto Waldis (Dr. Von Loeb), Eileen Stevens (Nurse), Mike Ross (Tony), Frank Chase (Charlie).

Really bad sci-fi film starring Hayes as a woman who grows into a giant overnight. She goes on the rampage after she learns that her sleazy husband has been shacking up with some floozy. The 50 foot woman finally finds her hubby in a fancy mansion, busts up the place, and squeezes her little gigolo to death. The local law enforcement officer then blows the big gal away with a riot gun. Worth seeing for laughs.

p, Bernard Woolner; d, Nathan Hertz; w, Mark Hanna; ph, Jacques R. Marquette; m, Ronald Stein; ed, Edward Mann.

Science Fiction **Cas.** **(PR:A MPAA:PR)**

ATTACK OF THE GIANT LEECHES zero

(1959) 62m AIP bw (AKA: THE GIANT LEECHES)

Ken Clark (*Steve Benton*), Michael Emmet (*Cal Moulton*), Yvette Vickers (*Liz Walker*), Bruno Ve Sota (*Dave Walker*), Gene Roth (*Sheriff*), Jan Shepard (*Nan Greyson*), Tyler McVey (*Doc Greyson*).

Dippy scare film where leeches in a swamp thrive on human flesh (extras wearing suction cup-like diver's suits which, when stretched over their air tanks, make them look like hunchbacks. A low-life bunch of swamp dwellers includes Ve Sota, a bar owner who catches his wife making love to another and forces both into the swamp to be eaten. Murkily filmed, the acting is almost as ridiculous as the story, if that's possible.

p, Gene Corman; d, Bernard Kowalski; w, Leo Gordon.

Horror **(PR:C-O MPAA:NR)**

ATTACK OF THE KILLER TOMATOES* (1978) 87m NAI/Four Square c

David Miller (*Mason Dixon*), George Wilson (*Jim Richardson*), Sharon Taylor (*Lois Fairchild*), Jack Riley (*Agriculture Official*), Rock Peace (*Wilbur Finletter*), Eric Christmas (*Senator Polk*), Al Sklar (*Ted Swan*), Ernie Meyers (*President*), Jerry Anderson (*Major Milis*), Ron Shapiro (*Newspaper Editor*).

There is an unwritten law in the movie business that states you cannot make a cult film intentionally. A cult film's appeal must come from the total sincerity of the filmmakers who felt, at the time of shooting, that the film in production was going to be a serious effort that would be a proud addition to whatever genre it was being made in. Then, when the audience laughs the film out of the first-run houses and into the midnight show circuit, it becomes a cult classic. This is not the case with ATTACK OF THE KILLER TOMATOES. This film was designed to appeal to cult audiences with a cynical eye at bad acting, ridiculous special effects, and hysterical dialog. Unfortunately the results are none too funny. The film tries too hard at being ridiculous, and though the idea of savage vegetables rolling around the city splattering innocent bystanders sounds funny, actually sitting through nearly 90 minutes of it is enough to make anyone long for ATTACK OF THE 50 FOOT WOMAN. There are some genuinely funny moments and the song parodies are good, but overall it is a failed effort.

p, Steve Peace, John De Bello; d, De Bello; w, Costa Dillon, Peace, De Bello; ph, John K. Culley; m, Gordon Goodwin, Paul Sundfur.

Comedy **Cas.** **(PR:C MPAA:PG)**

ATTACK OF THE MAYAN MUMMY zero

(1963, U.S./Mex.) 77m Medallion

Nina Knight, Richard Webb, John Burton, Steve Conte, Bruno Ve Sota.

Woman is mesmerized by a greedy scientist into becoming her former self in ancient Egypt so the scientist can obtain the loot of the Nile. Much of the footage is gleaned from the Mexican-made AZTEC MUMMY, and even that was not worth watching once.

p&d, Jerry Warren; w, Gilberto Solares, Alfredo Salazar.

Horror **(PR:C MPAA:NR)**

ATTACK OF THE MUSHROOM PEOPLE*

(1964, Jap.) 70m Daiei/AIP bw (AKA: MATANGO, UNGUS OF TERROR, CURSE OF THE MUSHROOM PEOPLE)

Akira Kubo, Kenji Sahara, Yoshio Tsuchiya, Hiroshi Koizumi, Mike Yashiro, Kumi Mizuno.

A lunatic in a padded cell tells the tale of a boatload of vacationers being stranded on a mysterious, fog-shrouded island where they begin eating toadstools, then turn into giant toadstools themselves as the fungus takes over. The only two humans remaining normal are two lovers but the woman craves the toadstools so much she weakens and eats one, joining the staggering vegetables who used to be her friends. Only the youth escapes to the mainland and an insane asylum to recount the weird experience. Of course, no one believes him until mushroom-like growths begin to appear on his face. It's too much for any intelligent mind to accept, but this film remains a cult movie to the sci-fi/fantasy aficionados.

p, Tomoyuki Tanaka; d, Inoshiro Honda; w, Takeshi Kimura; ph, Hajime Koizumi; spec eff, Eiji Tsuburaya.

Science Fiction/Fantasy **(PR:A MPAA:NR)**

ATTACK OF THE PUPPET PEOPLE* ¹/₂ (1958) 78m AIP bw

John Agar (*Bob Westley*), John Hoyt (*Mr. Franz*), June Kenny (*Solly Reynolds*), Michael Mark (*Emil*), Jack Kosslyn (*Sgt. Peterson*), Marlene Willis (*Laura*), Ken Miller (*Stan*), Laurie Mitchell (*Georgia*), Scott Peters (*Mac*), Susan Gordon (*Agnes*), June Jocelyn (*Brownie Leader*), Jean Moorhead (*Janet*), Hank Patterson (*Doorman*), Hal Bogart (*Mailman*), Troy Patterson (*Elevator Operator*), Bill Giorgio (*Janitor*), George Diestel (*Switchboard (Operator)*), Jaime Forster (*Ernie*), Mark Lowell (*Salesman*).

Bizarre horror/sci-fi from special-effects master Bert I. Gordon stars Hoyt as a lonely dollmaker who has developed a way to shrink people. He miniaturizes anyone unlucky enough to step into his shop and he keeps them around to amuse him when he is bored. Most of the victims are teenagers who don't really mind their shrunken state because they don't have to go to school anymore and they can spend all their time dancing to rock 'n' roll records for the goofy dollmaker. Along comes troublemaker Agar who does not like being small and fights to regain his stature. Good miniature work and clever camera angles pull off the special effects, but the story is pretty silly and good only for laughs.

p&d, Bert I. Gordon; w, George Worthing Yates (based on a story by Gordon); ph, Ernest Laszlo; m, Albert Glasser; ed, Ronald Sinclair.

Science Fiction **(PR:A MPAA:NR)**

ATTACK OF THE ROBOTS*

(1967, Fr./Span.) 85m AIP bw (CARTES SUR TABLE)

Eddie Constantine (*Lemmy Caution*), Sophie Hardy, Fernando Rey.

Constantine is an invulnerable Interpol agent who outwits a power-hungry scientist, Rey, bent on killing off the world's heads of state and replacing them with killer robots. The producers undoubtedly skipped their homework; Interpol is strictly a collector of international crime data and has no working agents. But then they also skipped making a film with any sense.

d, Jesse Franco; w, Jean-Claude Carriere.

Science Fiction **Cas.** **(PR:C MPAA:NR)**

ATTACK ON THE IRON COAST* (1968, U.S./Brit.) 90m UA c

Lloyd Bridges (*Maj. James Wilson*), Andrew Keir (*Capt. Owen Franklin*), Sue Lloyd (*Sue Wilson*), Mark Eden (*Lt. Cdr. Donald Kimberley*), Maurice Denham (*Sir Frederick Grafton*), Glyn Owen (*Lt. Forrester*), Howard Pays (*Lt. Graham*), George Mikell (*Capt. Strasser*), Simon Prebble (*Lt. Smythe*), Keith Buckley (*1st Commando*), Bill Henderson (*2nd Commando*), Gavin Breck (*3rd Commando*), Walter Gotell (*Van Horst*), Michael Wolf (*Lt. Kramer*), John Welsh (*Cansley*), Joan Crane (*Wren Officer*), Ernest Clark (*A.V.M. Woodbridge*), Richard Shaw (*German Infantry Sergeant*) Victor Beaumont (*German Battery Commander*), John Albineri (*German Gunnery Sergeant*), John Kelland (*Flag Lieutenant*), Mark Ward (*Timmy Wilson*), Dick Haydon (*Pringle*), John Golightly (*Helmsman*), Murray Evans (*Bosun's Mate*), Robin Hawdon (*Radar Man*), Sean Barrett (*Radio Man*).

Bridges stars as a commando leader who leads his group of brave soldiers on a suicide mission to knock out a German naval stronghold on the French coast in this average WW II thriller. Competent, if uninspired, war picture shot in England.

p, John C. Champion; d, Paul Wendkos; w, Herman Hoffman (based on a story by Champion); ph, Paul Beeson (DeLuxe Color); m, Gerard Schurmann; ed, Ernie Hosler; art d, Bill Andrews.

War **(PR:A MPAA:NR)**

ATTEMPT TO KILL* (1966, Brit.) 57m Merton Park/AA bw

Derek Farr (*Inspector Minter*), Tony Wright (*Gerry Hamilton*), Richard Pearson (*Frank Weyman*), Freda Jackson (*Mrs. Weyman*), Patricia Mort (*Elisabeth Gray*), J. G. Devlin (*Elliott*), Clifford Earl (*Sgt. Bennett*), Denis Holmes (*Fraser*).

Scotland Yard carries on a massive hunt for conmen who plan to murder an important businessman, an investigation which bogs down into theory too often but revives for some harrowing moments.

p, Jack Greenwood; d, Royston Morley; w, Richard Harris (based on the novel *The Lone House Mystery* by Edgar Wallace); ph, Bert Mason; ed, Edward Jarvis.

Mystery **(PR:A MPAA:NR)**

ATTENTION, THE KIDS ARE WATCHING* (1978, Fr.) 100m Adel/UA c

Alain Delon (*Man*), Francoise Brion (*Secretary*), Richard Constantini (*Dimitri*), Sophie Renoir (*Marlene*), Thierry Torchet (*Boule*), Tiphaine Leroux (*Laetitia*), Henri Vilbert (*Gardener*), Marco Perrin (*Policeman*).

Spoiled group of French children, under a maid's care at their parents' villa, spend most of their time lazing in front of a television set, mesmerized by exceedingly violent films. One day, at their secluded beach, the mischievous kids push the sleeping maid out to sea in a rubber raft. She becomes hysterical when she wakes up and falls into the deep water. The children make an attempt to save her, but she drowns. Seeing this not as a tragedy, but an opportunity for wild independence, the children fail to report the "accident" and have a festive time at the villa. Delon, a stranger, mysteriously arrives and tells the little group that he has witnessed their "prank." After terrorizing them with insinuations of premeditated murder and possible retribution, Delon is seduced by an older girl while her brother obtains one of their father's prized guns. As he tries to escape amid gunfire, Delon is killed by an exploding television set. The children dispose of the body, and, when their parents return from vacation, insist that the maid ran away and left them alone. The understanding parents pat them on their heads and the little angels go back to their normal existence. Unusual commentary on television violence and its effect on children was a pet project of star Delon's, but he made the mistake of casting himself in a role that calls for a more disturbing presence. Owing to William Golding's *Lord of the Flies* for its ideas of child brutality, the film manages to convey the twisted reasoning of its young protagonists almost too well.

d, Serge Leroy; w, Christopher Frank, Leroy, (based on a book by Laird Koenig and Peter Dixon); ph, Claude Renoir (Eastmancolor); ed, Fernand Cespi.

Drama **(PR:C MPAA:NR)**

ATTIC, THE* (1979) 97m Atlantic c

Carrie Snodgress (*Louise*), Ray Milland (*Wendell*), Ruth Cox (*Emily*), Angel (*Dickey*), Rosemary Murphy (*Mrs. Perkins*), Francis Bay (*Librarian*), Marjorie Eaton (*Mrs. Fowler*), Fern Barry (*Mrs. Mooney*), Michael Rhodes (*Sailor*), Patrick Brennan (*David*), Mark Andrews (*Gardener*), Dick Welsbacher (*Bureau of Missing Persons*), Phil Speary (*Travel*).

Snodgress is a stay-at-home spinster who has devoted her entire life to her invalid father, Milland, a cruel tyrant who dominates her mind and prevents her from contact with the outside world, particularly any meetings with men. She finally rebels in horrible retribution. A fair psychological thriller that could have been better.

p, Raymond M. Dryden, Phillip Randall; d, George Edwards; w, Tony Crechales, Edwards; ph, Gary Graver (CFI Color); m, Hod David Schudson; ed, Derek Parsons; art d, Tom Rasmussen; set d, Tana Cunningham-Curtis.

Suspense Drama **Cas.** **(PR:C-O MPAA:NR)**

ATTILA*

(1958, Ital.) 87m Lux c

Anthony Quinn (*Attila*), Sophia Loren (*Honoria*), Henri Vidal (*Ezio*), Irene Papas (*Grune*), Colette Regis (*Galla Placida*), Ettore Manni (*Bleda*), Christian Marquand (*Hun Leader*), Claude Laydu (*Valentiniano*), Eduardo Ciannelli (*Onegesio*),

Georges Brehat, Guido Celano, Carlo Hinterman *(Roman Consuls)*, Mario Feliciani, Piero Pastore, Aldo Pini, Marco Gugliemi *(Hun Chieftains)*.

Ludicrous costume epic has Quinn murderering his keen-minded brother, ordering the treacherous Roman Loren put to death, and lopping off thousands of Roman soldiers' heads on his successful trek to Rome. Before Quinn can pillage the great city, the Pope makes a quick call to God and orders up a tempestuous storm that sends the rampaging Hun and his fur-clad followers back to their homeland. Quinn sleepwalks through this silly piece of "history" occasionally spouting brilliant lines of dialog like, "Today Rome, tomorrow the world!"

p, Carlo Ponti, Dino De Laurentiis; d, Pietro Francisci; w, Ennio DeConcini, Primo Zeglio; ph, Aldo Tonti (Technicolor); Karl Struss; m, Enzo Masetti; ed, Leo Catozzo; spec eff, Ivor Beddoes, Stephen Grimes; ch, Gusa Geert.

Historical Drama (PR:C MPAA:NR)

ATTORNEY FOR THE DEFENSE* (1932) 70m COL bw

Edmund Lowe *(Burton)*, Evelyn Brent *(Val Lorraine)*, Constance Cummings *(Ruth Barry)*, Donald Dilloway *(Paul Wallace)*, Dorothy Peterson *(Mrs. Wallace)*, Bradley Page *(Nick Quinn)*, Nat Pendleton *(Mugg)*, Dwight Frye *(Wallace)*, Douglas Haig *(Paul as a Boy)*, Wallace Clark *(Crowell)*, Clarence Muse *(Jeff)*.

Lowe, a clever lawyer more interested in his own reputation than justice, secures a conviction for innocent man Frye through his manipulation of circumstantial evidence. This event begins to haunt Lowe and he gets the chance to make good in clearing Dilloway, Frye's son, years later during his murder trial. Wishy-washy analysis of lawyers that lacks the gutsy digging into the justice system that would have made it unique.

d, Irving Cummings; w, Jo Swerling (based on a story by J. K. McGuinness); ph, Ted Tetzlaff; ed, Gene Havelick.

Drama (PR:A MPAA:NR)

AU HASARD, BALTHAZAR*****
(1970, Fr.) 95m New Line Cinema c (AKA: BALTHAZAR)

Anne Wiazemsky *(Marie)*, Francois Lafarge *(Gerard)*, Philippe Asselin *(Marie's Father)*, Nathalie Joyaut *(Marie's Mother)*, Walter Green *(Jacques)*, Jean-Claude Guilbert *(Arnold)*, Pierre Klossowski *(Merchant)*, Francois Sullerot *(Baker)*, M. C. Fremont *(Baker's Wife)*, Jean Remignard *(Notary)*.

A poignant, beautiful and ugly film full of sensitivity and brutality, this is a powerful portrait of humanity seen through the life of a donkey who is first the loving plaything of small children in rural France, then a working beast of burden named by a sullen child. As the girl grows up, the donkey's fortunes worsen with the young woman's. She is gang-raped and dies; her sadistic lover, a leader of a motorcycle gang, in turn, tortures the donkey by setting its tail on fire. The donkey's life intersects with many of its owners, a brutal farmer who beats the animal but is finished off in grim irony. The donkey has a respite in becoming a momentary circus star, then again a beast tilling the soil, ending its days with a simple-minded but loving old man who considers the animal a saint. A great film made with uncompromising honesty and devastating reality, which, according to Jean-Luc Godard, "is really the world in an hour and a-half." Music includes Franz Schubert's "Piano Sonata No. 20."

p, Mag Bodard; d&w, Robert Bresson; ph, Ghislain Cloquet; m, Jean Wiener; ed, Raymond Lamy; art d, Pierre Charbonnier.

Drama (PR:C-O MPAA:NR)

AUDREY ROSE** (1977) 112m UA c

Marsha Mason *(Janice Templeton)*, Anthony Hopkins *(Elliot Hoover)*, John Beck *(Bill Templeton)*, Susan Swift *(Ivy Templeton)*, Norman Lloyd *(Dr. Lipscomb)*, John Hillerman *(Scott Velie)*, Robert Walden *(Brice Mack)*, Philip Sterling *(Judge Langley)*, Ivy Mones *(Mary Lou Sides)*, Stephen Pearlman *(Russ Rothman)*, Aly Wassil *(Maharishi Gupta Pradesh)*, Mary Jackson *(Mother Veronica)*, Richard Lawson, David Wilson *(Policemen)*, Tony Brande *(Detective Fallon)*, Elizabeth Farley *(Carole* Rothman), Ruth Manning *(Customer in Store)*, Stanley Brock *(Cashier in Store)*, David Fresco *(Dominick)*, Pat Corley *(Dr. Webster)*, Eunice Christopher *(Mrs. Carbone)*, Karen Anders *(Maria)*.

The happy lives of couple Mason and Beck are disrupted when stranger Hopkins appears claiming that their daughter Swift contains the reincarnated spirit of his dead little girl. They dismiss his strange tale, then begin to notice that their daughter *has* been acting a little odd lately. Subtle, uninteresting tale of the supernatural that features strong performances from Mason and Hopkins, but has none of the frightening touches of a previous Wise horror tale, THE HAUNTING. Another disappointment in the ups-and-downs career of the director.

p, Joe Wizan, Frank De Felitta; d, Robert Wise; w, De Felitta (based on his novel); ph, Victor J. Kemper (DeLuxe Color); m, Michael Small; ed, Carl Kress; prod d, Harry Horner; set d, Jerry Wunderlich; cos, Dorothy Jeakins, Sheldon Levine, Shirlee Strahm.

Horror Cas. (PR:C MPAA:PG)

AUGUST WEEK-END* (1936, Brit.) 70m Chesterfield bw

Valerie Hobson *(Claire Barry)*, G. J. Huntley, Jr. *(Kim Sherwood)*, Paul Harvey *(George Washburne)*, Betty Compson *(Ethel Ames)*, Claire McDowell *(Alma Washburne)*, Frank Melton *(Ronnie)*, Dorothea Kent *(Midge Washburne)*, Maynard Holmes *(Dave Maxwell)*, Edgar Norton *(Grimsby)*, Gigi Parrish *(Elinor)*, Howard Hickman *(Spencer)*, Paul Irving *(Steinfeld)*, Pat West *(Taxi Driver)*.

Bored with his lush, wealthy surroundings and family, an entrepreneur relaxes and enjoys life a bit too much, becoming mixed up in an income tax scandal. When he realizes that he truly loves his wife and children, everything seems to work out. Easygoing aristocratic comedy with an uninspired cast typical of the period.

p, George R. Batcheller; d, Charles Lamont; w, Paul Perez (based on a magazine story by Faith Baldwin); ph, M. A. Anderson.

Comedy (PR:A MPAA:NR)

AUGUSTINE OF HIPPO**
(1973, Ital.) 120m Entertainment Marketing c (AGOSTINO DI IPPONA)

Dary Berkani, Virgilio Gazzolo, Bruco Cataneo, Leonardo Fioravanti, Dannunzio Papini, Bepy, Mannejuolo, Livio Galassi, Fablo Carriba.

Historical look at the Bishop of Hippo, a North African prelate, and his life and times during the decline of the Roman Empire, another chronicle from Rossellini in a many-part series that is more self-indulgent than dramatically revealing.

p, Francesco Orefici; d, Roberto Rossellini; w, Rossellini, Marcella Mariani, Luciano Scaffa, Carlo Cremona; m, Mario Nascimbene; ed, Iolanda Benvenuti.

Historical drama (PR:A MPAA:NR)

AULD LANG SYNE* 1/2 (1929, Brit.) 75m Welsh-Pearson-Elder/FP bw

Harry Lauder *(Sandy McTavish)*, Pat Aherne *(Angus McTavish)*, Dodo Watts *(Marie McTavish)*, Dorothy Boyd, Hugh E. Wright.

A silent with six songs added, the film stars Lauder as a dour Scotsman in London to visit his son and daughter, Aherne and Watts. He believes Aherne is a student and Watts is a nurse, but, in reality, he's a boxer and she's a dancer. A fair film and a good example of of the transition from silent to sound.

p&d, George Pearson; w, Pearson, Hugh E. Wright, Patrick L. Mannock; ph, Bernard Knowles.

Comedy (PR:A MPAA:NR)

AULD LANG SYNE* 1/2 (1937, Brit.) 72m Fitzpatrick/MGM bw

Andrew Cruickshank *(Robert Burns)*, Christine Adrian *(Jean Armour)*, Richard Ross *(Gavin Hamilton)*, Marian Spencer *(Clarinda)*, Malcolm Graham *(Gilbert Burns)*, Doris Palette *(Highland Mary)*, Jenny Laird *(Alison Begbie)*.

Romantic but turgid account of the great Scottish poet set in the late eighteenth century. Although some of the bard's greatest sonnets are given nodding treatment, his literary life is merely the topping to his tepid love affairs. Not much to recite.

p&d, James A. Fitzpatrick; w, W. K. Williamson; ph, Hone Glendinning.

Drama (PR:A MPAA:NR)

AUNT CLARA 1/2** (1954, Brit.) 84m Lesslie-LFP/BL bw

Ronald Shiner *(Henry Martin)*, Margaret Rutherford *(Clara Hilton)*, A. E. Matthews *(Simon Hilton)*, Fay Compton *(Gladys Smith)*, Nigel Stock *(Charles Willis)*, Jill Bennett *(Julie)*, Reginald Beckwith *(Alfie Pearce)*, Raymond Huntley *(Rev. Maurice Hilton)*, Eddie Byrne *(Fosdick)*, Sidney James *(Honest Sid)*, Diana Beaumont *(Dorrie)*, Garry Marsh *(Arthur Cole)*, Gillian Lind *(Doris Hilton)*, Ronald Ward *(Cyril Mason)*.

Rutherford is a saintly old lady whose crusty uncle dies and leaves her five racing greyhounds, a broken-down pub, and a successful brothel. When confronted with her property the old lady becomes near apoplectic but shrewdly finds a way to convert the tainted dowry to her pious purposes. A charming film dotted with cameos by noted British comics.

p&d, Anthony Kimmins; w, Kenneth Horne, Roy Miller (based on the novel by Noel Streatfield); ph, C. Pennington-Richards; m, Benjamin Frankel.

Comedy (PR:A MPAA:NR)

AUNT FROM CHICAGO 1/2** (1960, Gr.) 90m Finos bw

Georgia Vassiliadou *(Aunt Calliopi)*, Orestis Makris *(General Charilaos)*, Margarita Papageorgiou *(Maria)*, Tzeni Karezi *(Helen)*, Celly Navropoulou *(Katina)*, Niki Papadatou *(Angela)*, Dimitrios Papamichail *(Kostas)*, Stefanos Stratigos *(Yakis)*, Theodore Dimitriou *(Cardis)*.

Militaristic retired general Makris, afraid that his strictly-raised daughters may never find husbands, sends for his matchmaking sister in Chicago. Upon arrival in Athens, Vassiliadou introduces the girls to booze, rock'n'roll, and, most important, prospective suitors. Delightful Greek comedy highlighted by Vassiliadou, a beefy, toothy, overexuberant woman who brings an Americanized spark of life into the sedate family.

d&w, Alekos Sakelarios; m, Takis Morakis.

Comedy (PR:C MPAA:NR)

AUNTIE MAME** 1/2** (1958) 143m WB c

Rosalind Russell *(Mame Dennis)*, Forrest Tucker *(Beauregard Burnside)*, Coral Browne *(Vera Charles)*, Fred Clark *(Mr. Babcock)*, Roger Smith *(Patrick Dennis)*, Patric Knowles *(Lindsay Woolsey)*, Peggy Cass *(Agnes Gooch)*, Jan Handzlik *(Patrick Dennis as a Child)*, Joanna Barnes *(Gloria Upson)*, Pippa Scott *(Pegeen Ryan)*, Lee Patrick *(Mrs. Upson)*, Willard Waterman *(Mr. Upson)*, Robin Hughes *(Brian O'Bannion)*, Connie Gilchrist *(Norah Muldoon)*, Yuki Shimoda *(Ito)*, Brook Byron *(Sally Cato)*, Carol Veazie *(Mrs. Burnside)*, Henry Brandon *(Acacius Page)*.

A showcase for the spectacular talents of Russell, who made the play a Broadway hit. She is the eccentric and colorful aunt who adopts an orphan boy, exposing him to all manner of extravagant and bizarre characters in the 1920s and 1930s. Tucker is perfect as the blustering North Carolina millionaire who marries Mame, then leaves her a filthy rich widow when he falls from a Matterhorn crag. Peggy Cass, the common-as-dirt secretary Mame encourages to "live a little," is hilarious and non-plused when realizing she is an unwed mother, and Clark is perfectly sneaky as the scheming banker desperate to get the boy out of the flamboyant woman's hands. Browne steals many a scene from Russell as her carping, dispsomaniac lady friend who somehow epitomizes the Lost Generation. There are stagy lapses, however, where the bon mots go on too long and wordy scenes that could have been chopped down. All in all, a solid, amusing vehicle for a captivating actress.

d, Morton Da Costa; w, Betty Comden, Adolph Green (based on the novel *Mame* by Patrick Dennis and the play by Jerome Lawrence, Robert E. Lee); ph, Harry Stradling, Sr. (Technirama, Technicolor); m, Bronislau Kaper; ed, William Ziegler; md, Ray Heindorf; art d, Malcolm Bert; set d, George James Hopkins; cos, Orry-Kelly.

Comedy Cas. (PR:A MPAA:NR)

AUSTERLITZ** $^{1}/_{2}$

(1960, Fr./Ital./Yugo.) 170m CFPI-Lyre-Galatea-Dubrava/LUX c (AKA: THE BATTLE OF AUSTERLITZ)

Rossano Brazzi *(Lucien Bonaparte)*, Claudia Cardinale *(Pauline)*, Martine Carol *(Josephine)*, Maria Ferrero *(Elise)*, Ettore Manni *(Murat)*, Jean Marais *(Carnot)*, Georges Marchal *(Lannes)*, Jack Palance *(Weirother)*, Vittorio De Sica *(Pope)*, Michel Simon *(Grognard)*, Orson Welles *(Robert Fulton)*, Pierre Mondy *(Napoleon Bonaparte)*.

Ambitious effort by silent film great Gance (whose NAPOLEON ranks among the finest of that era); the muddled script, however, bends over backward to make more of the cameos from stars than necessary and thereby distorts the story line leading to the titanic battle between Napoleon and the overwhelming armies of European allies. It never takes off and even the battle scenes are disjointed and meaningless as the 70-year-old Gance beats the drum too loudly for France's former days of glory and almost approaches militaristic propaganda for a benign dictator. The $4 million price tag for this empty opus was staggering at the time, almost sending its producers into bankruptcy.

p, Alexander Salkind; d&w, Abel Gance; ph, Henri Alekan (Dyaliscope, Eastmancolor); ed, Leonide Azar, Yvonne Martin.

Historical Drama **Cas.** **(PR:A MPAA:NR)**

AUTHOR! AUTHOR!** (1982) 110m FOX c

Al Pacino *(Travalian)*, Dyan Cannon *(Alice Detroit)*, Tuesday Weld *(Gloria)*, Alan King *(Kreplich)*, Bob Dishy *(Finestein)*, Bob Elliott *(Patrick Dicker)*, Ray Goulding *(Jackie Dicker)*, Eric Gurry *(Igor)*, Elva Leff *(Bonnie)*, B. J. Barie *(Spike)*, Ari Meyers *(Debbie)*, Benjamin H. Carlin *(Geraldo)*, Ken Sylk *(Roger Slessinger)*, James Tolkan *(Lt. Glass)*, Tony Munafo *(Officer Kapinsky)*, Reuben Singer *(Oliver Cromwell)*, Cosmo F. Allegretti *(Fippsy Fippininni)*, Kevin McClarnon *(Ted Brawn)*, Lori Tan Chinn *(Mrs. Woo)*, Richard Belzer *(Seth Shapiro)*, Andre Gregory *(J. J.)*, Judy Graubart *(Miss Knoph)*, Jaime Tirelli *(Taxi Driver)*, Frederic Kimball *(Larry Kotzwinkle)*.

Pacino is a successful playwright whose work is constantly interrupted by his neurotic wife and pestering but lovable children, some by Weld and some from Weld's previous three marriages. Just as Pacino anxiously nears completion of his first play in two years, Weld decides to seek her own "identity" and departs to live with another man. Pacino is left in the lurch, having to manage the children as well as rehearsals and his new leading lady, Cannon, with whom he begins a tenuous affair. Cannon is completely unsuited for the role, having no stage presence whatsoever, acting like some street-corner girl who happens to be a reigning queen of legitimate theater. Weld is just annoying, a sociopath really, and why Pacino still wants her is a question for that character's analyst. Pacino as a sensitive, introspective playwright is unbelievable and often embarrassingly ridiculous; his posture is more apt to a truck-driver expressing himself with a crowbar. Only the children with their bright and precocious behavior and inquisitive dialog save this shabby memoir from being a total loss.

p, Irwin Winkler; d, Arthur Hiller; w, Israel Horovitz; ph, Victor J. Kemper (TVC Lab Color); m, Dave Grusin; ed, William Reynolds; prod d, Gene Rudolf; set d, Alan Hicks; cos, Gloria Gresham.

Comedy **Cas.** **(PR:A MPAA:PG)**

AUTUMN CROCUS* (1934, Brit.) 70m Dean/Auten bw

Ivor Novello *(Andreas Steiner)*, Fay Compton *(Jenny Gray)*, Jack Hawkins *(Alaric)*, Diana Beaumont *(Audrey)*, Muriel Aked *(Miss Mayne)*, Esme Church *(Edith)*, Frederick Ranalow *(Feldmann)*, Mignon O'Doherty *(Frau Feldmann)*, George Zucco *(Rev. Mayne)*.

Schoolteacher Compton, visiting the Austrian Alps, falls in love with innkeeper Novello, then sadly learns that he is a married father. Weepy romance that makes the mistake of assuming that the tragic plot situation will be enough to evoke emotional interest. Novello and Compton do absolutely nothing to inject life into their characters.

p, Basil Dean; d, Dean (based on a play by C. L. Anthony); ph, Robert Martin.

Romance **(PR:A MPAA:NR)**

AUTUMN LEAVES*** (1956) 107m COL bw

Joan Crawford *(Milly)*, Cliff Robertson *(Burt Hanson)*, Vera Miles *(Virginia)*, Lorne Greene *(Mr. Hanson)*, Ruth Donnelly *(Liz)*, Shepperd Strudwick *(Dr. Couzzens)*, Selmer Jackson *(Mr. Wetherby)*, Maxine Cooper *(Nurse Evans)*, Marjorie Bennett *(Waitress)*, Frank Gerstle *(Mr. Ramsey)*, Leonard Mudie *(Colonel Hillyer)*, Maurice Manson *(Dr. Masterson)*, Bob Hopkins *(Desk Clerk)*, Frank Arnold *(Butcher)*, Ralph Volkie *(Doorman)*, Robert Sherman *(Paul's Voice)*, Abdullah Abbas *(Mexican Vendor)*, Mary Benoit, Paul Bradley, Bess Flowers.

Crawford, a lonely spinster in her early forties, leaves her New England home after her father's death and travels to California. With men assuming that the still-attractive woman must be married, Crawford continues her lonely life until she meets shy, kind Robertson at a restaurant. Although he is only in his twenties and naive about women, Robertson falls in love with Crawford and begs her to marry him. She refuses, citing the difference in their ages as too great a barrier. Alone and withdrawn, Crawford returns to her home only to have Robertson appear a few weeks later, still proposing marriage. Unable to resist his urgent, passionate request, Crawford agrees to the ceremony. After a pleasant honeymoon, Crawford's understanding of Robertson's life is turned upside down by the appearance of Miles, who claims to be the first wife of Robertson, wanting to talk to him about some legal matters. When Crawford confronts Robertson with this information, he starts to display mentally unstable, occasionally violent characteristics. When Robertson discovers that his weird, tyrannical father had been sleeping with Miles during his marriage to her, Robertson goes berserk, almost killing Crawford when he returns home. Crawford sadly commits Robertson to an institution and, after he is cured, the two get back together, Crawford overcoming her hesitancy to live with the previously deranged man. Released a year after the nihilist *film noir* classic KISS ME DEADLY, the film recaptured the twisted qualities of the human mind in this intense "soap opera" about loneliness, despair, and mental illness. The building up of a pleasant romantic tale and then plunging into a whirlwind of schizophrenic violence has the same effect as seeing a hammer shatter a shiny piece of glass. Almost like a nightmare going on in Crawford's mind, the film's visual style gets more and more distorted and the lighting very harsh as Robertson's schizophrenia builds. Crawford is wonderful and the rest of the cast, particularly Robertson, do an outstanding job. Crawford and Aldrich would again work together on another odd tale, WHATEVER HAPPENED TO BABY JANE?

p, William Goetz; d, Robert Aldrich; w, Jack Jevne, Lewis Meltzer, Robert Blees; ph, Charles Lang; m, Hans Salter; ed, Michael Luciano; md, Morris Stoloff; m/l, Joseph Kosma, Jacques Prevert, Johnny Mercer (sung by Nat "King" Cole.

Drama **(PR:C MPAA:NR)**

AUTUMN MARATHON**

(1982, USSR) 90m Mosfilm-Lenfilm-Goskino/International Film Exchange c

Oleg Basilashvili *(Andrei)*, Natalia Gundareva *(Nina)*, Marina Neyelova *(Alla)*, Yevgeny Leonov *(Vasily)*.

Cute Soviet comedy about a compulsively late English translator who can't seem to find enough time for his wife, mistress, publisher, students, *and* an old friend who needs to be bailed out of jail. Simple, enjoyable satire on everyday Soviet life from fairly prolific director Danelia.

d, Georgi Danelia; w, Aleksandr Volodin; ph, Sergei Vronsky.

Comedy **(PR:A MPAA:NR)**

AUTUMN SONATA zero (1978, Swed.) 97m ITC/NEW WORLD c

Ingrid Bergman *(Charlotte)*, Liv Ullmann *(Eva)*, Lena Nyman *(Helena)*, Halvar Bjork *(Viktor)*, Georg Lokkeberg *(Leonardo)*, Knut Wigert *(Professor)*, Eva Von Hanno *(Nurse)*, Erland Josephson *(Josef)*, Linn Ullmann *(Eva as a Child)*, Arne Bang-Hansen *(Uncle Otto)*, Gunnar Bjornstrand *(Paul)*.

An insipidly ultra-boring emotional exercise by much-vaunted director Bergman whose overuse of extreme close-ups of Ingrid and Liv are meaningless in that both actresses are taxed to exhausting every twitch and tic known to womankind. The story, anemic as it is, deals with Bergman's visit to her two daughters, one being Nyman, a hopeless bedridden woman dying of an unknown disease who can only moan through the film unsympathetically. She is the favorite. The rock-strong Ullmann, the other daughter, who is less favored by her mother, finally confronts Bergman in head-to-head anger and frustration at being taken for granted. Ullmann's performance is absolutely terrible; she is either mumbling her way through incoherent monologs or groping around like some uncontrollable spastic in her torrent of abuse aimed at mother Bergman, who makes a resolute but condescending effort in a role that cannot be anything other than that of a functional waste can into which Ullmann "artistically" heaves up her lines. This badly dubbed monstrosity is obviously a cruel inside joke by Ingmar Bergman in parody of female sensitivity.

p, Lew Grade, Martin Starger; d&w, Ingmar Bergman; ph, Sven Nykvist (Eastmancolor); ed, Sylvia Ingmarsdotter; prod d, Anna Asp; cos, Inger Pehrsson.

Drama **Cas.** **(PR:O MPAA:PG)**

AVALANCHE* $^{1}/_{2}$ (1946) 68m PRC bw

Bruce Cabot *(Steve Batchellor)*, Roscoe Karns *(Red Kelly)*, Helen Mowery *(Ann Watson)*, Veda Ann Borg *(Claire Jeremy)*, Regina Wallace *(Mrs. Carlton Morris)*, John Good *(Sven Worden)*, Philip Van Zandt *(Malone)*, Eddie Parks *(Mr. Carlton Morris)*, Wilton Graff *(Austin Jeremy)*, Harry Hays Morgan *(Duncan)*, Eddie Ryan *(Jean)*, Eddy Waller *(Sam)*, Syd Saylor *(Bartender)*, Joe, the Raven.

Cabot and Karns, a pair of unlikely T-Men in search of a tax evader hiding millions, end their search in a mountain lodge (in the tradition but not the elegance of GRAND HOTEL.) Here they sift through a goodly batch of suspects while several mysterious murders occur and stock footage of Idaho ski resorts abounds. The miserable script gives nothing to Cabot's lifeless love affair with Mowery. Karns fails to provide any humor before the pair find the killer and the money. The funniest character in the film is a trained raven walking up and down the lodge bar picking up empty glasses in its beak. There is an avalanche, but only in stock footage.

p, Pat Di Cicco; d, Irving Allen; w, Andrew Holt; ph, Jack Greenhalgh; m, Lucien Moraweck, Rene Garriguenc; ed, Louis Sackin; md, Lud Gluskin.

Mystery **(PR:A MPAA:NR)**

AVALANCHE* (1978) 91m New World c

Rock Hudson *(David Shelby)*, Mia Farrow *(Caroline Brace)*, Robert Forster *(Nick Thorne)*, Jeanette Nolan *(Florence Shelby)*, Rick Moses *(Bruce Scott)*, Steve Franken *(Henry McDade)*, Barry Primus *(Mark Elliott)*, Cathey Paine *(Tina Elliott)*, Peggy Browne *(Annette Rivers)*, Pat Egan *(Cathy Jordan)*, Joby Baker *(TV Director)*, Cindy Luedke *(Susan Maxwell)*, John Cathey *(Ed the Pilot)*, Angelo Lamonea *(Bruce's Coach)*.

Bed-hopping ski lodge owner Hudson, ex-wife Farrow, and the usual variety of character types become trapped when a monstrous avalanche envelops the inn with a blanket of snow and ice. They're eventually rescued and Hudson realizes that he should have listened to the locals and built in a different spot. Stupid entry in one of the worst genres ever created, the disaster film. Hudson and Farrow give their characters the same amount of excitement one would expect to see from a slug crawling up a wet rock.

p, Roger Corman; d, Corey Allen; w, Claude Pola, Allen (based on a story by Frances Doel; ph, Pierre-William Glenn (Metrocolor); m, William Kraft; ed, Stuart Schoolnick, Larry Bock; art d, Phillip Thomas; prod d, Sharon Compton; spec eff, Lewis Teague.

Disaster **Cas.** **(PR:O MPAA:PG)**

AVALANCHE EXPRESS* $^{1}/_{2}$ (1979) 88m Lorimar/FOX c

Robert Shaw *(Marenkov)*, Lee Marvin *(Wargrave)*, Linda Evans *(Elsa Lang)*, Maximillian Schell *(Bunin)*, Mike Connors *(Haller)*, Joe Namath *(Leroy)*, Horst Bucholz *(Scholten)*, David Hess *(Geiger)*, Arthur Brauss *(Neckermann)*, Kristine Nel *(Helga Mann)*, Sylva Langover *(Olga)*.

CIA agent Marvin uses defector Shaw as bait to lure Soviet agent and biological warfare genius Schell aboard their train traveling through Europe. Hoping to eliminate the dangerous Schell, Marvin's plans are interrupted by a thundering river of snow. Top-notch tough guys Marvin and Shaw do the best they can in this poorly handled espionage tale. Shaw, an often neglected and underrated talent, died before the film's soundtrack was completed.

p&d, Mark Robson; w, Abraham Polonsky, (based on the novel by Colin Forbes); ph, Jack Cardiff (Panavision); m, Allyn Ferguson; ed, Garth Craven; prod d, Fred Tuch; cos, Mickey Shirard; spec eff, John Dykstra.

Spy Drama **(PR:C MPAA:PG)**

AVANTI!** (1972) 144m Phalanx-Jalem/UA c

Jack Lemmon *(Wendell Armbruster)*, Juliet Mills *(Pamela Piggott)*, Clive Revill *(Carlo Carlucci)*, Edward Andrews *(J. J. Blodgett)*, Gianfranco Barra *(Bruno)*, Franco Angrisano *(Arnold Trotta)*, Pippo Franco *(Mattarazzo)*, Franco Acampora *(Armando Trotta)*, Giselda Castrini *(Anna)*, Raffaele Mottola *(Passport Officer)*, Lino Coletta *(Cipriani)*, Harry Ray *(Dr. Fleischmann)*, Guidarino Guidi *(Maitre d')*, Giacomo Rizzo *(Barman)*, Antonino Faa'Di Bruno *(Concierge)*, Yanti Sommer, Janet Agren *(Nurses)*, Aldo Rendine *(Rossi)*, Maria Rosa Sclauzero, Melu Valente *(Hostesses)*.

Corporate executive Lemmon travels to Italy to claim his father's body, the old man having been killed in an automobile accident while on vacation. Upon arrival, Lemmon discovers that dad died with the English mistress he had been sneaking off to a little Italian island with for the last ten years. Lemmon then meets Mills, the chubby but cute daughter of his father's mistress, and the two end up recreating their respective parents' affair. Becoming frustrated under a mountain of bureaucratic red-tape, Lemmon and Mills decide to bury the deceased couple on the island paradise that they had held so dear in the past. Fun, often lively (although too long) Billy Wilder comedy that sits somewhere in the middle of the list of the director's work. Lemmon does a good job, but Mills is a chunky treasure, as is Revill, who plays a wacky hotel owner who is constantly trying to fix things. The comedy unexpectedly does not arise out of the reincarnated affair, but out of the endless bureaucracy surrounding the couple. The contemporary references to Henry Kissinger, Billy Graham, and Julie and David Eisenhower fall dreadfully flat, but the majority of the comedy is on target.

p&d, Billy Wilder; w, Wilder, I. A. L. Diamond (based on a play by Samuel Taylor); ph, Luigi Kuveiller (DeLuxe Color); Carlo Rustichelli; ed, Ralph E. Winters; art d, Ferdinando Scarfiotti.

Comedy **(PR:C MPAA:R)**

AVENGER, THE* (1931) 62m COL bw

Buck Jones, Dorothy Revier, Edward Peil, Sr., Otto Hoffman, Sidney Bracey, Edward Hearn, Walter Percival, Paul Fix, Frank Ellis, Al Taylor, Slim Whitaker, Silver, the Horse.

It seems that the studio made Jones don a sombrero and a black mustache to capitalize on the popularity of Mexican western heroes at the time and the result is this ridiculous oater about a mysterious Mexican rider who's determined to avenge his brother's death.

p, Sol Lesser; d, Roy William Neill; w, George Morgan (based on a story by Jack Townley); ph, Charles Van Enger; ed, Ray Snyder.

Western **(PR:A MPAA:NR)**

AVENGER, THE* (1933) 64m MON bw

Ralph Forbes *(Norman Craig)*, Adrienne Ames *(Ruth Knowles)*, Arthur Vinton *(James Gordon)*, Claude Gillingwater *(Witt)*, Charlotte Merriam *(Sally)*, J. Carroll Naish *(Hanley)*, Berton Churchill *(Forster)*, Thomas Jackson *(McCall)*.

Once freed from prison, former D.A. Forbes makes it clear that he'd like to get back at the men who framed him. When five men disappear, apparently murdered, Forbes becomes the likely suspect. Then former girl friend Ames proves that the men are alive, hidden away somewhere; she exposes their plan to get rid of Forbes by making him appear to be their murderer. Confusing, manipulative revenge drama that never makes its point clear.

d, Edwin L. Marin; w, Brown Holmes, Tristram Tupper (based on a novel by John Goodwin); ph, Sid Hickox.

Mystery **(PR:A MPAA:NR)**

AVENGER, THE*

(1964, Fr./Ital.) 108m Medclion c (AKA: THE LAST GLORY OF TROY)

Steve Reeves *(Aeneas)*, Giacomo Rossi Stuart *(Eurialo)*, Carla Marlier *(Lavinia)*, Gianni Garko *(Turno)*, Liana Orfei *(Camilla)*, Mario Ferrari *(Latino)*, Enzo Fiermonte *(Acate)*, Nerio Bernardi *(Drance)*, Luciano Benetti *(Sergeste)*, Lula Selli *(Amata)*, Roberto Bettoni *(Pallante)*, Maurice Poli *(Mezensio)*, Benito Stefanelli *(Niso)*, Pietro Capanna *(Bisia)*.

Absurd muscleman film set in ancient times where Reeves is Aeneas battling Etruscans for the honor of Troy. The most exciting scene is a stampede of angry bulls which are no doubt looking for the producer of this dubbed mess.

p, Albert Band, Giorgio Venturini; d, Giorgio Rivalta; w, Ugo Liberatore.

Fantasy **(PR:C MPAA:NR)**

AVENGER, THE* (1966, Ital.) 92m BRC Produzione Film/Estela Films c

Franco Nero, Cole Kitosch, Jose Suarez, Elisa Montes, Livio Lorenzon, Jose Guardiola.

Unremarkable Italian western has determined Nero gunning down the man who killed his father, only to discover that the fellow happened to be his half-brother's dad. Nero's lackadaisical performance adds to the tiresome quality of this guilt/revenge loser.

p, Manolo Baolognini; d, Ferdinando Baldi; w, Baldi, Franco Rossette; ph, Enzo Barboni.

Western **(PR:C MPAA:NR)**

AVENGERS, THE***

(1942, Brit.) 87m PAR bw (GB: THE DAY WILL DAWN)

Ralph Richardson *(Lockwood)*, Deborah Kerr *(Kari Alstead)*, Hugh Williams *(Colin Metcalfe)*, Griffith Manes *(Inspector Gunter)*, Francis L. Sullivan *(Wettau)*, Roland Culver *(Naval Attache)*, Niall McGinnis *(Olaf)*, Finlay Currie *(Alstead)*, Bernard Miles *(McAllister)*, Patricia Medina *(Ingrid)*, Elizabeth Mann *(Gerda)*, Henry Oscar *(Editor)*, John Warwick *(Milligan)*, David Horne *(Evans)*, Henry Hewitt *(News Editor)*, Ann Farrer *(Evans' Secretary)*.

Solid WW II action film with Williams as a foreign correspondent who organizes a Norwegian village, falling in love with native girl Kerr. They help to pinpoint a Nazi U-boat base for the RAF and later lead British commandos to German strongholds which are overwhelmed. Richardson appears only in the first half of this film as mentor to the raid (during the dark days of the war a full-scale invasion of Nazi-occupied Europe was no more than a remote plan).

p, Paul Soskin; d, Harold French; w, Terence Rattigan, Anatole de Grunwald, Patrick Kirwan (based on a story by Frank Owen); ph, Cyril Knowles; ed, Michael C. Chorlton.

War **(PR:A MPAA:NR)**

AVENGERS, THE* (1950) 90m REP bw

John Carroll *(Don Careless/Francisco Suarez)*, Adele Mara *(Maria Moreno)*, Mona Maris *(Yvonne)*, Roberto Airaldi *(Col. Luis Corral)*, Jorge Villoldo *(Don Rafael Moreno)*, Vincente Padula *(El Mocho/Hernandez)*, Vivian Ray *(Carmencita)*, Cecile Lezard *(Pamela)*, Juan Olaguivel *(Sancho)*, Eduardo Gardere, Angel M. Gordordo Palacios *(Fencing Doubles)*, Fernando Lamas *(Andre LeBlanc)*.

Carroll, a mysterious adventurer, wanders into a small Spanish settlement in South America, falls in love with Mara, and stops her from falling under the romantic spell of the man plotting to overthrow her governor father. Argentina-based Republic cheapie that doesn't take its swords and thumping hearts very seriously. Lamas makes his screen debut with a small role that would catch MGM's eye, paving the road to Latin Lover-dom and Esther Williams' swimming pool.

p, John H. Auer; d, Auer; w, Lawrence Kimble, Aeneas MacKenzie (based on Rex Beach's novel *Don Careless*); ph, Pablo Tabernero; m, Nathan Scott; ed, Marvin J. Coil.

Adventure **(PR:A MPAA:NR)**

AVENGING HAND, THE** (1936, Brit.) 64m Stafford bw

Noah Beery *(Lee Barwell)*, Kathleen Kelly *(Gwen Taylor)*, Louis Borell *(Pierre Charrell)*, James Harcourt *(Sam Hupp)*, Charles Oliver *(Toni Visetti)*, Reginald Long *(Charles Mason)*, Ben Welden *(Slug Clarke)*, Tarver Penna *(Conrad Colter)*, Penelope Parkes *(Elizabeth)*, Billie de la Volta *(Muriel)*, Bela Mila *(Mrs. Penworthy)*.

There is lot of creeping about, darting shadows and dark-hatted menaces who flit through this programmer where a group of hotel guests all turn out to be thieves searching for a cache of stolen loot. Has some interesting moments but is leaden with stilted dialog.

p, John Stafford; d, Victor Hanbury; w, Akos Talnay, Reginald Long.

Mystery **(PR:A MPAA:NR)**

AVENGING RIDER, THE* (1943) 56m RKO bw

Tim Holt *(Brit)*, Cliff "Ukulele Ike" Edwards *(Ike)*, Ann Summers *(Jean)*, Davison Clarke *(Grayson)*, Norman Willis *(Red)*, Karl Hackett *(Sheriff Allen)*, Earl Hodgins *(Deputy)*, Edward Cassidy *(Sheriff Lewis)*, Kenneth Duncan *(Blackie)*, Bud McTaggart *(Baxter)*, Bud Osborne *(Wade)*, Bob Kortman *(Harris)*.

Fearless Holt and happy-go-lucky Edwards are jailed when they are assumed to be part of an outlaw gang that murdered a local gold mine owner, who just happened to be an old friend of the cowpoke duo. They break out, unearth the identities of the *real* killers, are tossed back in the hoosegow, and have to escape once again before actually nabbing the guilty parties. Average Holt western that's given a small amount of whimsy from the silly Edwards.

p, Bert Gilroy; d, Sam Nelson; w, Harry O. Hoyt, Morton Grant; ph, J. Roy Hunt; ed, John Lockert.

Western **(PR:A MPAA:NR)**

AVENGING WATERS* (1936) 57m COL bw

Ken Maynard, Beth Marion, Ward Bond, Wally Wales Hal Taliaferro), Edmund Cobb, Zella Russell, John Elliott, Glenn Strange.

Routine oater has Maynard taming a town, winning the girl, and herding an army of bad men into jail without too much effort, action, script, direction, or personal zeal.

p, Larry Darmour; d, Spencer G. Bennet; w, Nate Gatzert; ed, Dwight Campbell.

Western **(PR:A MPAA:NR)**

AVIATOR, THE* (1929) 73m WB bw

Edward Everett Horton *(Robert Street)*, Patsy Ruth Miller *(Grace Douglas)*, Johnny Arthur *(Hobart)*, Lee Moran *(Brown)*, Edward Martindel *(Gordon)*, Armand Kaliz *(Major Gaillard)*, Kewpie Morgan *(Sam Robinson)*, Phillips Smalley *(John Douglas)*, William Bailey *(Brooks)*.

Timid writer Horton poses as the author of a book on aviation to help out a publisher friend and ends up in a daring flying contest, hoping to win the love of flyboy-obsessed Miller. Virtually a line-for-line remake of THE HOTTENTOT, which also starred Horton, that had the prim and proper hero posing as a top horseman and not a pilot. Occasionally funny vehicle for the humorous Horton.

d, Roy Del Ruth; w, Arthur Caesar, Robert Lord, DeLeon Anthony (based on a play by James Montgomery); ph, Chick McGill; ed, William Holmes.

Comedy **(PR:A MPAA:NR)**

AVIATOR'S WIFE, THE** (1981, Fr.) 104m New Yorker c

Philippe Marlaud *(Francois)*, Marie Riviere *(Anne)*, Anne-Laure Meury *(Lucie)*, Mathieu Carriere *(Christian)*, Philippe Caroit *(Friend)*, Carolie Clement *(Colleague)*, Lisa Heredia *(Girl Friend)*, Haydee Caillot *(Blonde)*, Mary Stephen, Neil Chan *(Tourists)*, Rosette *(Concierge)*, Fabrice Luchini *(Mercillat)*.

Lightweight lovers' story with Marlaud and Riviere having an affair but carrying on with others all the while. Has some charming moments but the dialog is a bit soggy and a lot of scenes are included only to make the director of MAUD, CLAIRE, and CHLOE look good. But then such sexual free-for-all stories don't require much substance. (In French; English subtitles.)

p, Margaret Menegoz; d&w, Eric Rohmer; ph, Bernard Lutic, Romain Windig; ed, Cecile Decugis.

Romance (PR:O MPAA:NR)

AWAKENING, THE* (1938, Brit.) 64m Cosmopolitan bw

Eric Elliott *(Dr. Christian Adrian)*, Eve Gray, Rex Walker.

Tame love triangle between an older doctor, his young protege, and the woman they both covet. Slow moving and sluggish even in the clinches.

d, Alfonse Frenguelli; w, Nigel Byass.

Romance (PR:A MPAA:NR)

AWAKENING, THE** (1958, Ital.) 97m Rizzoli-Pallavacini bw

Anna Magnani *(Sister Letizia)*, Eleonora Rossi Drago *(Assunta)*, Antonio Cifariello *(Peppino)*, Piero Boccia *(Salvatore)*, Luisa Rossi *(Salvatore's Aunt)*.

Street waif Cifariello, abandoned by his uncaring mother and her sleazy lover, is taken in by kindly nun Magnani. When her love for the little boy becomes so great that she actually contemplates leaving the Church in order to be a full-time mother, her dilemma is sadly resolved when the boy's real mother returns for her son. Magnani gives a passionate, sad, and emotionally charged performance as a lonely nun who sees her true calling in the soul of the sweet and kind Cifariello. Although the story line owes quite a bit to THE BELLS OF ST. MARY'S and the heartstring-tugging can get a bit much, the film retains a definite power thanks to the dynamic Magnani.

d, Mario Camerini; w, Cesare Zavattini, Camerini (based on their story "Suor Letizia"); m, A. F. Lavagnino.

Drama (PR:AA MPAA:NR)

AWAKENING, THE* 1/2 (1980) 102m Orion/WB c

Charlton Heston *(Matthew Corbeck)*, Susannah York *(Jane Turner)*, Jill Townsend *(Anne Corbeck)*, Stephanie Zimbalist *(Margaret Corbeck)*, Patrick Drury *(Paul Whittier)*, Bruce Myers *(Dr. Khalid)*, Nadim Sawalha *(Dr. El Sadek)*, Ian McDiarmid *(Dr. Richter)*, Ahmed Osman *(Yussef)*, Miriam Margolyes *(Kadira)*, Michael Mellinger *(Hamid)*, Leonard Maguire *(John)*, Ishia Bennison *(Nurse)*, Madhav Sharma *(Doctor)*, Chris Fairbanks *(Porter)*, Michael Halphie, Roger Kemp *(Doctors)*.

Archeologist Heston, obsessed with the legend of an Egyptian princess, Kara, travels to the Middle East to uncover her tomb. Disregarding the curse associated with the legend of Kara killing her father after a forced incestuous affair, Heston pillages the burial site, in the name of science, of course, and brings the loot back to a museum in his home town of London, unaware of the fact that his daughter was born at the moment he broke the seal on Kara's tomb. A quick eighteen years fly by and Heston's daughter, Zimbalist, becomes possessed by the long-dormant spirit of Kara. Bodies start to pile up and Heston starts to piece together the bizarre happenings. Adapted from an obscure Bram Stoker novel, this return to the Egyptian mummy type of horror film is quite a joke, mainly because of Heston's ridiculous impersonation of a British scientist. Zimbalist, however, gives her character a rather eerie quality and, combined with the incestuous theme, suggests that the film could have been a rather disturbing horror story.

p, Robert Solo, Andrew Scheinman, Martin Shafer; d, Mike Newell; w, Allan Scott, Chris Bryant, Clive Exton (based on the novel, *The Jewel of Seven Stars,* by Bram Stoker); ph, Jack Cardiff (Technicolor); m, Claude Bolling; ed, Terry Rawlings; prod d, Michael Stringer; art d, Lionel Couch; cos, Phyllis Dalton.

Horror Cas. (PR:O MPAA:R)

AWAKENING OF JIM BURKE* 1/2 (1935) 70m COL bw

Jack Holt *(Jim Burke)*, Florence Rice *(Tess Hardie)*, Kathleen Burke *(Laura)*, Jimmie Butler *(Jimmie Burke)*, Robert Middlemass *(Bill Duke)*, Wyrley Birch *(Lem Hardie)*, Ralph M. Remley *(Blink)*.

Holt, an outdoorsy, tough construction foreman, becomes fed up with his violin-playing sissy son and decides to turn the boy into a he-man with some good, hard work. Holt takes Butler's precious fiddle away and forces the kid to develop callouses while sweet Rice and trampy Burke vie for Holt's affections. The family clash is resolved when the now-manly Butler saves his father's life in a construction accident. Holt settles down with Rice, and Butler returns to music knowing he could knock out any guy who calls him a sissy in the future. Aside from the anti-aesthetic theme being pounded out in a very muscle-headed manner, the film contains a rather simple, likable father and son camaraderie.

d, Lambert Hillyer; w, Michael Simmons; ph, Benjamin Kline; ed, John Rawlins.

Drama (PR:A MPAA:NR)

AWAY ALL BOATS** (1956) 114m UNIV c

Jeff Chandler *(Capt. Jeb Hawks)*, George Nader *(Lt. Dave MacDougall)*, Julie Adams *(Nadine MacDougall)*, Lex Barker *(Cdr. Quigley)*, Keith Andes *(Dr. Bell)*, Richard Boone *(Lt. Fraser)*, William Reynolds *(Ens. Kruger)*, Charles McGraw *(Lt. Mike O'Bannion)*, Jock Mahoney *(Alvick)*, John McIntire *(Old Man)*, Frank Faylen *(Chief "Pappy" Moran)*, Grant Williams *(Lt. Sherwood)*, Floyd Simmons *(Lt. Robinson)*, Don Keefer *(Ens. Twitchell)*, Sam Gilman *(Lt. Randall)*.

Hardened Navy captain Chandler trains a bunch of green sailors in the South Pacific during WW II. To keep his men from fighting among themselves, Chandler sets himself up as an elitist snob who cares little for anyone, thus allowing the seamen to vent their anger at him. Former Merchant Marine Nader picks up on Chandler's game and eventually gets the rest of the men to understand Chandler's situation and respect their captain. Under a kamikaze attack and other threats from the wily Japanese, the entire crew pulls together in the great tradition of the U.S. Navy. Pretty much a wide-screen, colorful advertisement for the seafaring branch of the armed forces, the film's inter-crew melodramatics get a bit heavy-handed, detracting from the thrilling intensity of a few of the battle scenes.

p, Howard Christie; d, Joseph Pevney; w, Ted Sherdeman (based on the novel *Away All Boats* by Kenneth M. Dodson); ph, William Daniels (VistaVision, Technicolor); m, Frank Skinner; ed. Ted J. Kent.

War (PR:A MPAA:NR)

AWFUL DR. ORLOFF, THE zero

(1964, Span/Fr.) 90m Hispamer/Sigma III Corp bw (GRITOS EN LA NOCHE; L'HORRIBLE DR. ORLOFF; AKA: CRIES IN THE NIGHT)

Howard Vernon *(Dr. Orloff)*, Conrado Sanmartin *(Detective)*, Ricardo Valle *(Monster)*, Maria Silva, Venancio Muro, Perla Cristal, Mara Laso, Felix Dafauce, Faustino Cornejo, Diana Lorys.

Vernon is Orloff, a crackpot scientist who attempts to correct his daughter's mutilated face by grafting the skin of murdered women to that of his offspring, while giving her transfusions of blood drained from his victims. His aide, Valle, a lascivious hunchback, is shown slavishly probing the bodies of the dead females and horrid scenes explicitly depict the skinning of the bodies by Vernon. Valle is really the physician's brother, we later learn, who is actually dead, murdered by Vernon after the doctor found him in bed with his wife, but transformed into a cretinous robot to do Vernon's bidding. Lorys, a fearless ballerina, finally destroys the pair. This film spawned a number of similar disgusting films which drew the sado-masochist fans by the droves. A half-hearted attempt is made here and in subsequent subculture films like this to posture a surrealistic approach with zany zooming and erratic cutaways to further heighten the psychopathic nature of the characters. Sensationalism at its most distasteful.

p, Serge Newman, Leo Lax; d&w, Jesus Franco; ph, Godofredo Pacheco.

Horror (PR:O MPAA:NR)

AWFUL TRUTH, THE 1/2** (1929) 68m Pathe bw

Ina Claire *(Lucy Warriner)*, Henry Daniell *(Norman Warriner)*, Theodore von Eltz *(Edgar Trent)*, Paul Harvey *(Dan Leeson)*, Blanche Frederici *(Mrs. Leeson)*, Judith Vosselli *(Josephine Trent)*, John Roche *(Jimmy Kempster)*.

The first talkie version of Arthur Richman's 1922 stage hit, which was filmed as a silent in 1925. It's the familiar tale of a couple who plan to divorce but soon realize they need each other after all. Passable entertainment, though nowhere near as well-done as the 1937 version.

p, Maurice Revnes; d, Marshall Neilan; w, Arthur Richman, Horace Jackson, Rollo Lloyd (based on the play by Richman); ph, David Abel; ed, Jackson, Frank E. Hull.

Comedy (PR:A MPAA:NR)

AWFUL TRUTH, THE***** (1937) 90m COL bw

Irene Dunne *(Lucy Warriner)*, Cary Grant *(Jerry Warriner)*, Ralph Bellamy *(Daniel Leeson)*, Alexander D'Arcy *(Armand Duvalle)*, Cecil Cunningham *(Aunt Patsy)*, Molly Lamont *(Barbara Vance)*, Esther Dale *(Mrs. Leeson)*, Joyce Compton *(Dixie Belle Lee/Toots Binswanger)*, Robert Allen *(Frank Randall)*, Robert Warwick *(Mr. Vance)*, Mary Forbes *(Mrs. Vance)*, Claud Allister *(Lord Fabian)*, Zita Moulton *(Lady Fabian)*, Scott Colton *(Mr. Barnsley)*, Wyn Cahoon *(Mrs. Barnsley)*, Paul Stanton *(Judge)*, Mitchell Harris *(Jerry's Attorney)*, Alan Bridge, Edgar Dearing *(Motor Cops)*, Leonard Carey *(Butler)*, Miki Morita *(Japanese Servant)*, Frank Wilson *(M.C.)*, Vernon Dent *(Police Sergeant)*, George C. Pearce *(Caretaker)*, Bobby Watson *(Hotel Clerk)*, Byron Foulger *(Secretary)*, Kathryn Curry *(Celeste)*, Edward Peil, Sr. *(Bailiff)*, Bess Flowers *(Viola Heath)*, John Tyrrell *(Hank)*, Edward Mortimer *(Lucy's Attorney)*.

Superb lighthearted production which became the epitome of the screwball comedies of the 1930s. Grant tells wife Dunne that he is going on a short Florida vacation but spends his time playing poker with the boys, then establishes his alibi by burning himself brown under a sunlamp as a convincer. When he returns home he finds his wife absent and then she appears with D'Arcy, a dashing voice teacher. Both assume infidelity on each other's part and, after a rousing round of accusations, decide to accept a 90-day interlocutory divorce, their main courtroom battle settling over the custody of Mr. Smith, their pet dog (Asta of the THIN MAN series). Not only does Dunne continues to see D'Arcy, but she befriends Texas oil baron Bellamy while Grant looks up an old flame, Compton, a sexy nightclub singer. Both go their separate ways but are emotionally drawn back to each other under one pretext after another. Grant, exercising his visiting rights to see his dog, drops in on Dunne who has hidden D'Arcy in her bedroom. Then Bellamy's stuffy parents, potential in-laws, arrive and Dunne absentmindedly sends Grant into the same bedroom where he discovers the sheepish voice coach and promptly pummels him. The commotion creates another crazy confrontation between the pair. When Grant meets and begins to fall for socialite Lamont, Dunne invades a party at her mansion, pretending to be drunk and carrying on wildly until Grant escorts her home, but she convinces him to drive her to their mountain retreat where they play a cat-and-mouse game, finally succumbing to the deep love they have for each other and making up. Director McCarey exercised a great deal of his own whim and humor in making this classic comedy which had been a 1922 stage hit, filmed as a silent in 1925 with Agnes Ayres and Warner Baxter, then in 1929 with Henry Daniell and Ina Claire. He took the basic premise of the play but improvised greatly, adding witty, sophisticated dialog and bits of hilarious business. He encouraged the actors to try anything they thought funny. In six weeks the film was in the can, a wonderfully inventive, dizzy-paced film that has since become a classic where the laughs never stop coming. It was such a success that Grant and Dunne were teamed again in MY FAVORITE WIFE, another splendid comedy and a touching tearjerker, PENNY SERENADE. THE AWFUL TRUTH won an Oscar nomination and was the first of McCarey's long string of comedies and great melodramas. (The film was remade in 1953 as LET'S DO IT AGAIN with Jane Wyman and Ray Milland, but did not come near this version.)

p&d, Leo McCarey; w, Vina Delmar (based on the play by Arthur Richman); ph, Joseph Walker; ed, Al Clark; md, Morris Stoloff; art d, Stephen Gooson, Lionel

Banks; set d, Babs Johnstone; cos, Kalloch; m/l, "My Dreams Have Gone With the Wind," Ben Oakland, Milton Drake.

Comedy   **(PR:A   MPAA:NR)**

AZAIS*   (1931, Fr.) 105m Halk bw

Max Dearly *(Le Baron Wurtz)*, Simone Rouviere *(Suzette Wurtz)*, Pierre Stephen *(Felix Borneret)*, Jeanne St. Bonnet *(Comtesse Romani)*, Gaston Dupray *(Luquin)*, Henriette Delannoy *(La Baronne Wurtz)*, Pizani *(Stromboli)*.

Optimistic private tutor lives the philosophyof, "If something bad happens, something good must be happening somewhere else, so why not be there?" Intellectually slanted French aristocracy farce in which comic Dearly chomps every piece of scenery he can get his teeth around.

p, Jacques Halk; d, Rene Hervil (based on the play by Georges Berr and Rene Verneuil).

Comedy   **(PR:A   MPAA:NR)**

AZTEC MUMMY, THE zero
(1957, Mex.) 65m Cinematografica Calderon bw (EL ROBOTHUMANO; LA MOMIA AZTECA CONTRA EL ROBOT HUMANO; AKA: THE AZTEC MUMMY VS THE HUMAN ROBOT)

Ramon Gay, Rosita Arenas, Luis Aceves Castaneda, Arturo Martinez, Jesus Murcielago Velazquez, Salvador Lozano, Crox Alvarado, Guillermo Hernandez, Alejandro Cruz.

Part of a Mexican horror series, all directed by Rafael Lopez Portillo, the monster is a long-haired mummy called Popoca, which, in this cheap potboiler, guards a cache of sacred jewels which are coveted by Castaneda, a sinister doctor. He constructs his own monster from metal and human flesh, a top-heavy robot that appears as if it will fall over from the flick of an index finger. The mummy, of course, destroys this ridiculous adversary, and survives as a sort of monster hero. Two more of these insults, LA MOMIA AZTECA and LA MADICION DE LA MOMIA AZTECA, were added to the screen.

p, Guillermo Calderon; d, Rafael Lopez Portillo; w, Calderon, Alfredo Salazar; ph, Enrique Wallace.

Horror   **Cas.**   **(PR:O   MPAA:R)**

AZURE EXPRESS**   (1938, Hung.) 68m Standard bw

Antal Pager *(Thomas Rak)*, Klari Tolnay *(Tery)*, Lajos Basthy *(Denes Banath)*, Zita Szeleczky *(Erna)*, Ferenc Vendrey *(Uncle)*.

Pager, a clumsy, shy schoolmaster, finds suicidal girl Tolnay wandering the streets the night before his wedding. He takes her back to his apartment, feeds her, gives her a place to sleep, and nearly misses the ceremony the next day. At the train station, on his way to a honeymoon in Venice, Pager is separated from his new bride when he steps off the train to buy a ticket for the wandering Tolnay. Pager's wife, Szeleczky, fearful that her parents in Venice will think that she is fibbing about having landed a husband, asks a fellow traveler to pose as Pager. Pager himself and Tolnay find *their* way to Venice and are assumed to be husband and wife. After the actual wedding couple is reunited, Tolnay and Basthy (the temporary husband) decide they should get married, too. Delightful comedy from a country whose films get little exposure in other parts of the globe.

d, Bela Bologh; w, Laszlo Pacsery (based on the play "Budapest-Wien" by Szanto and Szecsen); m, Carlo de Fries.

Comedy   **(PR:A   MPAA:NR)**

B

B. F.'S DAUGHTER**   (1948) 107m MGM bw (GB: POLLY FULTON)

Barbara Stanwyck (*Polly Fulton*), Van Heflin (*Thomas W. Brett*), Richard Hart (*Robert S. Tasmin*), Charles Coburn (*B. F. Fulton*), Keenan Wynn (*Martin Delwyn Ainsley*), Margaret Lindsay (*Apples Sandler*), Spring Byington (*Gladys Fulton*), Marshall Thompson (*Sailor*), Barbara Laage (*Eugenia Taris*), Thomas E. Breen (*Major Riley*), Fred Nurney (*Olaf*), Edwin Cooper (*General Waldron*), Tom Fadden (*Mr. Holmquist*), Davison Clark (*Doorman*), Anne O'Neal (*Receptionist*), Hal K. Dawson (*Frederick X. Gibson*), Laura Treadwell (*Emily Lovelace*), Bill Harbach (*Co-Pilot*), David Newell (*Captain*), Mary Jo Ellis, Lisa Kirby, Josette Deegan (*Girls*), Florence Wix, Major Sam Harris (*Wedding Guests*), Pierre Watkin (*Joe Stewart*), Mickey Martin, Gene Coogan, Jack Stenlino, Joe Recht (*Soldiers*).

Beyond the simple structure of its boy-meets-girl theme, this film, the first Stanwyck made for MGM in twelve years, explores the rampantly popular socialism that swept the U.S. in the early 1930s, a massive reaction to a crushing economic depression. Heflin, in an excruciating performance of self-examination and go-to-Hell idealism, is the ultra-liberal college professor down on capitalism. He meets and falls in love with Stanwyck who is entranced with his mind; she throws over stuffy lawyer Hart and weds the intellectual. Yet everything Heflin attempts, from lectures to writing, ends in failure until Stanwyck uses her father's wealth and power to further his career. He had married her not knowing tycoon Coburn was her father, a fact he resents upon learning it. When he finds that his future has been guaranteed by a man epitomizing the rich industrialists, Heflin's love for Stanwyck turns to loathing. (Coburn is brilliant as the benevolent father—Maecenas B. F. Fulton). Only when the self-contained, independent Stanwyck later admits that she needs Heflin—by then the terrible 1930s have melted into the war-torn 1940s and he is in uniform—does the self-styled, too-righteous intellectual forgive her for a happy ending. The script is gutsy, terse, and to the point, especially when Stanwyck and Heflin pit one lifestyle against another. Keenan Wynn is a standout in a role he always plays to perfection, a sleazy opportunist, in this case a radio commentator who builds his career by slashing Fulton and friends to pieces; he lives to regret his empty iconoclasm. Director Leonard's guiding hand is firmly in control throughout and he wastes no time in boiling down and telling the difficult Marquand story. There are several "Messages" in B. F.'s DAUGHTER, and this time Louis B. Mayer did not use Western Union but his very own studio to send them.

p, Edwin H. Knopf; d, Robert Z. Leonard; w, Luther Davis (based on the novel by John P. Marquand); ph, Joseph Ruttenberg; m, Bronislau Kaper; ed, George White; md, Charles Previn; art d, Cedric Gibbons, Daniel B. Cathcart; set d, Edwin B. Willis, Jack D. Moore; cos, Irene; spec eff, Warren Newcombe.

Drama   (PR:A MPAA:NR)

B.S. I LOVE YOU*¹/₂   (1971) 99m FOX/Motion Pictures International c

Peter Kastner (*Paul Bongard*), JoAnna Cameron (*Marilyn Michele*), Louise Sorel (*Ruth*), Gary Burghoff (*Ted*), Richard B. Shull (*Harris*), Joanna Barnes (*Jane Ink*), John Gerstad (*Paul's Father*), Mary Lou Mellace (*Car Rental Girl*), Jeanne Sorel (*Paul's Mother*), Joe Kottler (*Cab Driver*), Tom Ruisinger (*Travel Agent*), Frank Orsatti (*Manuel*), Barry Woloski (*Hippie*).

Monotonous rip-off of THE GRADUATE starring Kastner as a young bed-hopping TV commercial producer who has an affair with the boss, Barnes, and her 18-year-old daughter, Cameron. He finally gives the madness up and goes back to his girl friend in Connecticut. Another independently made Canadian film apparently designed to be a tax shelter for its investors.

p, Arthur M. Broidy; d&w, Steven Hillard Stern; ph, David Dans (DeLuxe Color); m, Jimmy Dale, Mark Shekter; art d, Ernst Fegte; ed, Melvin Shapiro; m/l, Mark Shekter.

Comedy   (PR:O MPAA:R)

BABBITT**   (1934) 75m FN/WB bw

Aline MacMahon (*Myra Babbitt*), Guy Kibbee (*George F. Babbitt*), Claire Dodd (*Tanis Judique*), Maxine Doyle (*Verona Babbitt*), Glen Boles (*Ted Babbitt*), Minna Gombell (*Mrs. Reisling*), Alan Hale (*Charlie McKelvey*), Berton Churchill (*Judge Thompson*), Russell Hicks (*Commissioner Gurnee*), Nan Gray (*Eunice Littlefield*), Arthur Aylesworth (*Zeke*), Harry Tyler (*Martin Gunch*), Mary Treen (*Miss McGoun*).

Sluggish adaptation of Sinclair Lewis' classic novel (first filmed as a silent in 1924) with a standout performance by Kibbee as the title character. Story of life in a small midwestern town not helped by lackadaisical direction and an overlong opening sequence where we follow Kibbee around the house to establish atmosphere.

p, Sam Bischoff; d, William Keighley; w, Mary McCall, Jr. (based on an adaptation by Tom Reed, Niven Busch of the novel by Sinclair Lewis); ph, Arthur Todd; m, Leo F. Forbstein; ed, Jack Killifer; art d, John Hughes.

Drama   (PR:A MPAA:NR)

BABE RUTH STORY, THE*   (1948) 106m MON/AA bw

William Bendix (*Babe Ruth*), Claire Trevor (*Claire Hodgson*), Charles Bickford (*Brother Mathias*), Sam Levene (*Phil Conrad*), William Frawley (*Jack Dunn*), Gertrude Niesen (*Nightclub Singer*), Fred Lightner (*Miller Huggins*), Stanley Clements (*Western Union Boy*), Bobby Ellis (*Babe Ruth as a Boy*), Lloyd Gough (*Baston*), Matt Briggs (*Col. Ruppert*), Paul Cavanagh (*Dr. Menzies*), Pat Flaherty (*Bill Corrigan*), Tony Taylor (*The Kid*), Richard Lane (*Coach*), Mark Koenig (*Himself*), Harry Wismer, Mel Allen (*Sports Announcers*), H. V. Kaltenborn (*News Announcer*), Knox Manning (*Narrator*).

The greatest baseball player ever (although you'd get odds on it anywhere the present favorite reigns) is ably, if not excessively, enacted by that wonderful lantern-jawed character actor Bendix who brings bravado and color to every frame of film. His lady love Trevor follows him loyally through one tight spot after another, rooting louder than any bleacher fan as Ruth's second wife (his first is not mentioned) and equally sympathetic is Levene as Bendix's Boswell, albeit real sports announcers Allen and Wismer pitch in to help chronicle the explosive career of the Sultan of Swat. Ruth is taken as a boy (Ellis) from his father's Baltimore saloon to an orphanage where kindly Bickford helps to squeeze delinquency from his oversized frame and sends him on to the sandlot where baseball becomes his first nature. Then the adult Bendix takes over, first as a speed-demon hurler for the Boston Red Sox and then as the most powerful batsman in the world, playing for the New York Yankees, managed by Miller Huggins (Lightner in an exceptional portrayal) who takes care of the Bambino as one would a wild and wonderful child. Bendix works hard in what is perhaps the finest role of his long career; he studied films of Ruth endlessly until he was able to perfectly imitate his stance, his walk, his unique mannerisms and facial expressions. He became so good at being Ruth that it is difficult to tell where the Bendix action shots leave off and the newsreel clips of the real Ruth begin. Further, he imbues the character with the same heart and warmth for which the Babe was famous. And, yes, he does call his shot by pointing to center field and smacking a home run to that very spot, all for that little boy in the hospital, or was it two boys, or a million?

p, Joe Kaufman; d, Roy Del Ruth; w, Bob Considine, George Callahan (based on the book by Considine); ph, Phillip Tannura; m, Edward Ward; ed, Richard Heermance; tech. ad, Pat Flaherty.

Sport Drama   (PR:AAA MPAA:NR)

BABES IN ARMS*¹/₂**   (1939) 93m MGM bw

Mickey Rooney (*Mickey Moran*), Judy Garland (*Patsy Barton*), Charles Winninger (*Joe Moran*), Guy Kibbee (*Judge Black*), June Preisser (*Rosalie Essex*), Grace Hayes (*Florrie Moran*), Betty Jaynes (*Molly Moran*), Douglas McPhail (*Don Brice*), Rand Brooks (*Jeff Steele*), Leni Lynn (*Doby Martini*), John Sheffield (*Bobs*), Henry Hull (*Maddox*), Barnett Parker (*William*), Ann Shoemaker (*Mrs. Barton*), Margaret Hamilton (*Martha Steele*), Joseph Crehan (*Mr. Essex*), George McKay (*Brice*), Henry Roquemore (*Shaw*), Lelah Taylor (*Mrs. Brice*), Lon McCallister (*Boy*).

This is the first Garland/Rooney film directed by Busby Berkeley and set the tone for the next trio of films to come. Based (just barely) on the Rodgers and Hart play of the same name, Winninger and Hayes are old vaudevillians who begin a touring show utilizing many of their senior pals. Their children want to go along but the old folks refuse, so the kids start their own show. Rooney, pushed on by Garland, writes the show that he will star in as well as direct (a portent of the way Rooney was to become in later years). Mick lives in a state school for underprivileged kids and they've been given a month out of stir to prove what they can do or it's off to a trade high school as Margaret Hamilton (MGM's resident witch) demands. They don't have enough money for the show, then June Preisser, as an ex-child-star, agrees to lay out the cash if *she* can have the lead. Garland is thunderstruck but understands the realities of show business and backs off to become the understudy. June, who is desperate to make a comeback as a teenager, never makes it to opening night and Judy goes on in her place. A few complications ensue (a sudden downturn of the weather) but all ends happily as Mickey is invited to bring his show to Broadway by Henry Hull, a famous New York producer and pal of Winninger's. Garland and Berkeley didn't get along from the start and she struggled mightily to get her energy level up to Rooney's. Later biographies claim that she was already on handfuls of diet and pep pills. (Second leads McPhail and Jaynes were married when the picture was made and divorced in 1941. He was discharged from the US Army in Spring 1944 for emotional problems and committed suicide in December, 1944.)

p, Arthur Freed; d, Busby Berkeley; w, Jack McGowan, Kay Van Riper (based on the musical play by Richard Rodgers and Lorenz Hart); ph, Ray June; ed, Frank Sullivan; art d, Cedric Gibbons, Merrill Pye; cos, Dolly Tree; m/l, Richard Rodgers, Lorenz Hart, Arthur Freed, Gus Arnheim, Abe Lyman, E. Y. Harburg, Harold Arlen, Freed, Nacio Herb Brown.

Musical   Cas.   (PR:AAA MPAA:NR)

BABES IN BAGDAD*¹/₂   (1952) 79m UA c

Paulette Goddard (*Kyra*), Gypsy Rose Lee (*Zohara*), Richard Ney (*Ezar*), John Boles (*Hassan*), Thomas Gallagher (*Sharkhan*), Sebastian Cabot (*Sinbad*), Macdonald Parke (*Caliph*), Natalie Benesh (*Zelika*), Hugh Dempster (*Omar*), Peter Bathurst (*Officer*).

Silly attempt at satire as the ladies of the harem go on strike and the Arabian Knights get annoyed at the lack of action. So do we. Paulette Goddard (by this time divorced from Chaplin and remarried to Erich Maria Remarque) was 41 when she made this and already over the hill. Gypsy Rose Lee (as the joke goes, we hardly recognized her with her clothes on) displays a neat turn for repartee but hardly has enough to do. Richard Ney, who must have held some sort of record by playing his real-life wife's (Greer Garson) son in MRS. MINIVER, is boring. He wisely got out of the business, became a stock-and-bonds type and made a fortune. It's Lysistrata sideways.

p, Edward J. and Harry Lee Danziger; d, Edgar G. Ulmer; w, Felix Feist, Joe Anson; ph, Jack Cox; m, J. Leoz; ed, Edith Lenny.

Satire/Comedy   (PR:A MPAA:NR)

BABES IN TOYLAND***
(1934) 77m MGM bw (AKA: MARCH OF THE WOODEN SOLDIERS)

Stan Laurel *(Stanley Dum)*, Oliver Hardy *(Oliver Dee)*, Charlotte Henry *(Bo-Peep)*, Felix Knight *(Tom-Tom)*, Henry Kleinbach [Brandon] *(Barnaby)*, Florence Roberts *(Widow Peep)*, Ferdinand Munier *(Santa Claus)*, William Burress *(Toymaker)*, Virginia Karns *(Mother Goose)*, Johnny Downs *(Little Boy Blue)*, Jean Darling *(Curly Locks)*, Frank Austin *(Justice of the Peace)*, Gus Leonard *(Candle Snuffer)*, Alice Dahl *(Little Miss Muffett)*, Peter Gordon *(Cat and the Fiddle)*, Sumner Getchell *(Tom Thumb)*, Kewpie Morgan *(Old King Cole)*, John George *(Barnaby's Minion)*, Billy Bletcher *(Chief of Police)*, Alice Cook *(Mother Hubbard)*, Alice Moore *(Queen of Hearts)*.

A terrific vehicle for the classic comedy style of Laurel and Hardy. As Stanley Dum and Oliver Dee, they become the unsung heroes of Toyland when they save the Widow Peep's daughter, Bo, from marrying the evil Barnaby; save the widow's abode (a multi-level shoe); save Tom-Tom from his exile to Bogeyland; and ultimately rid Toyland of the evil Barnaby forever. In a priceless prediction of things to come, Santa's chief toymaker admonishes his moronic but lovable helpmates Stan and Ollie: "I told you to make 600 hundred wooden soldiers one foot high and you made 100 soldiers six feet high!") There is nothing too spectacular about this picture, but it's one where you root for the good guys and boo the villains. Henry as Bo Peep and Knight as Tom Tom are a "cutesy" duo, so sweet you could stir them into your coffee. Kleinbach is a perfect villain. The other characters are portrayed well, and are believable as Mother Goose creations. It's an enjoyable family movie although any six-year-old can figure out early on that they will all live happily ever after. The "March of The Toys" is five minutes of raucous action that ends the film on a high note: E flat above C. (See LAUREL & HARDY series, Index.)

p, Hal Roach; d, Gus Meins, Charles Rogers; w, Nick Grinde, Frank Butler (based on the musical comedy by Victor Herbert); ph, Art Lloyd, Francis Corby; ed, William Terhune, Bert Jordan; md, Harry Jackson; m/l, Victor Herbert, Glen MacDonough); Ann Ronell, Frank Churchill.

Musical Fantasy (PR:AAA MPAA:NR)

BABES IN TOYLAND** (1961) 106m BV c

Ray Bolger *(Barnaby)*, Tommy Sands *(Tom Piper)*, Annette Funicello *(Mary Contrary)*, Ed Wynn *(Toymaker)*, Tommy Kirk *(Grumio)*, Kevin Corcoran *(Boy Blue)*, Henry Calvin *(Gonzorgo)*, Gene Sheldon *(Roderigo)*, Mary McCarty *(Mother Goose)*, Ann Jillian *(Bo Peep)*, Brian Corcoran *(Willie Winkie)*, Marilee and Melanie Arnold *(Twins)*, Jerry Glenn *(Simple Simon)*, John Perri *(Jack-be-Nimble)*, David Pinson *(Bobby Shaftoe)*, Bryan Russell *(The Little Boy)*, James Martin *(Jack)*, Liana Dowding *(Jill)*.

Remake of the original 1934 Laurel and Hardy film; were it not for Stan and Ollie, the original might have been a misfire, so you can well imagine that this version is not as good as that one. Sheldon mimes Laurel and Calvin essays Hardy but it's to no avail. No question that a lot of money was spent on this holiday release but most of it was wasted due to the miscasting of Bolger as the villain and the dullness of Sands and Funicello as the young lovers. Any Victor Herbert score is singable and this one, with Oscar-nominated George Bruns doing the adaptation, is better than most. Yet the picture seems to have no center, no heart. It's half-fantasy, half-reality and is a triumph of special effects over material. A generally disappointing film with only Bolger and Wynn to recommend it. The finale of the attack of the toy soldiers is colorful and exciting but there is a lot of waiting around to get to that.

p, Walt Disney; d, Jack Donohue; w, Joe Rinaldi, Ward Kimball, Lowell S. Hawley (based on the operetta by Victor Herbert, Glen MacDonough; m/l, Herbert, Mel Leven); ph, Edward Colman (Technicolor); ed, Robert Stafford; cos, Bill Thomas; ch, Tommy Mahoney.

Musical Fantasy Cas. (PR:AAA MPAA:NR)

BABES ON BROADWAY*** 1/2** (1941) 121m MGM bw

Mickey Rooney *(Tommy Williams)*, Judy Garland *(Penny Morris)*, Fay Bainter *(Miss Jones)*, Virginia Weidler *(Barbara Jo)*, Ray McDonald *(Ray Lambert)*, Richard Quine *(Morton Hammond)*, Donald Meek *(Mr. Stone)*, Alexander Woollcott *(Himself)*, Luis Alberni *(Nick)*, James Gleason *(Thornton Reed)*, Emma Dunn *(Mrs. Williams)*, Frederick Burton *(Prof. Morris)*, Cliff Clark *(Inspector Moriarty)*, William A. Post, Jr. *(Announcer)*, Carl Stockdale *(Man)*, Dick Baron *(Butch)*, Will Lee *(Waiter)*, Donna Reed *(Secretary)*, Joe Yule *(Mason, Aide to Reed)*, Anne Rooney, Dorothy Morris, Maxine Flores *(Pit Astor Girls)*, Stop, Look and Listen Trio.

Mickey Rooney is truly skin stretched over enthusiasm in this nonstop musical comedy. He runs away from the pack (and it's not that Garland and the rest don't do a good job, it's just that Mickey is at his best) in this backstage youth musical about a bunch of youngsters struggling to get their opportunity to shine on Broadway. BABES ON BROADWAY is the sequel to BABES IN ARMS, and outdoes it! Mickey dances, sings, mimes a score of excellent impressions as he leads the way for the continuous entertainment. Berkeley does his usual inventive job in directing. (Busby was not a dancer; he was a director who knew how to stage and where to put the camera, but he left the dance work to assistants.) Look for Rooney's father, Joe Yule, as Mason. A highlight for theatrical fans is the scene where Rooney and Garland walk into the Duchess Theater and relive magical moments from the theater's past: scenes from Mansfield's "Cyrano," Harry Lauder singing a Scot ditty, Fay Templeton, complete with bustle, Blanche Ring doing "Rings On My Fingers," and a show-stopping Carmen Miranda impression by Rooney, accurate down to the platform shoes and fruit-covered hat.

p, Arthur Freed; d, Busby Berkeley; w, Fred Finklehoffe, Elaine Ryan (based on a story by Burton Lane); ph, Lester White; ed, Frederick Y. Smith; md, Georgie Stoll; cos, Kalloch; m/l, E. Y. Harburg, Burton Lane, Ralph Freed, Roger Edens, Harold J. Rome.

Musical (PR:AAA MPAA:NR)

BABES ON SWING STREET* (1944) 69m UNIV bw

Ann Blyth *(Carol Curtis)*, Peggy Ryan *(Trudy Costello)*, Andy Devine *(Joe Costello)*, Leon Errol *(Malcolm Curtis)*, Anne Gwynne *(Frances Carlyle)*, Kirby Grant *(Dick Lorimer)*, June Preisser *(Fern Wallace)*, Alma Kruger *(Martha Curtis)*, Billy Dunn *(Billy Harper)*, Sidney Miller *(Corny Panatowsky)*, Marion Hutton, The Freddie Slack Orchestra, The Rubenettes.

Another "Hey gang, let's put on a show!" musical starring Ryan as the president of a group of Settlement House intellects who decide to stage a singing and dancing extravaganza in order to raise enough cash to send ten of their number to music school. Many obstacles must be overcome to get the show on the road including talking Blyth's crusty aunt, Kruger, into letting them perform in the large hall she owns. Nothing special.

p, Bernard W. Burton; d, Edward Lilley; w, Howard Dinsdale, Eugene Conrad (based on an idea, Brenda Weisberg); ph, Jerome Ash; m, Sam Freed Jr.; ed, Fred R. Feitshans, Jr.; ch, Louis DePron; m/l Sidney Miller, Inez James.

Musical (PR:A MPAA:NR)

BABETTE GOES TO WAR**
(1960, Fr.) 106m COL c (BABETTE S'EN VA-T-EN)

Brigitte Bardot *(Babette)*, Jacques Charrier *(Gerard)*, Hannes Messemer *(Von Arenberg)*, Yves Vincent *(Capt. Darcy)*, Ronald Howard *(Fitzpatrick)*, Francis Blanche *(Schulz)*, Rene Havard *(Louis)*, Pierre Bertin *(Duke)*.

Bardot stars as an innocent French refugee who is used by British Intelligence and sent from Blighty to Paris as live bait. Her job is to use her feminine wiles to kidnap a Nazi general and convince other Germans that he is, in fact, a British agent. If this is accomplished, the invasion of England can be averted. Well, we all know that England was not invaded so it is safe to say that Bardot did what was necessary to keep the Hun away. Bardot is succulent as Babette but even her attributes cannot save this from being a mild comedy at best. It's slow-moving and silly in spots and can't hold a candle to many WW II comedies that came out around the same time.

p, Raoul J. Levy; d, Christian Jaque; w, Jean Ferry (based on a story by Levy and Gerard Oury); ph, Armand Thirard (CinemaScope, Eastmancolor); m, Gilbert Becaud; ed, Jacques Desagneaux.

Satire/Comedy (PR:C MPAA:NR)

BABIES FOR SALE** (1940) 65m COL bw

Rochelle Hudson *(Ruth Williams)*, Glenn Ford *(Steve Burton)*, Miles Mander *(Dr. Rankin)*, Joseph Stefani *(Dr. Gaines)*, Georgia Caine *(Miss Talbot)*, Isabel Jewell *(Edith Drake)*, Eva Hyde *(Gerda Honaker)*, Selmer Jackson *(Mr. Kingsley)*, Mary Currier *(Mrs. Kingsley)*, Edwin Stanley *(Mr. Edwards)*, Douglas Wood *(Dr. Aleshire)*, John Qualen *(Mr. Anderson)*, Helen Brown *(Mrs. Anderson)*.

Early expose on the illegal adoption business with Ford as the angry newspaper reporter crusading to stop the baby trade. Sleazy doctor Mander entices vulnerable mothers to his maternity home where he delivers the kids and talks the women into signing away the rights to their infants. Film is hurt by the lengthy scenes of footprinting babies (an important detail that later hangs the villainous Doc) and the miscasting of Mander as the doctor.

d, Charles Barton; w, Robert D. Andrews (based on a story by Robert Chapin, Joseph Carole); ph, Benjamin Kline; ed, Charles Nelson.

Drama (PR:C MPAA:NR)

BABY, THE zero (1973) 102m Scotia International c

Anjanette Comer, Ruth Roman, Mariana Hill, Suzan Zenor, David Manzy.

Sloppy thriller has Roman as a drunk psycho whose husband has run off years earlier, leaving her with an infant son; to express her hatred for men she keeps her so-called "baby" (an older teenager nearing manhood) in diapers, gurgling incoherently in his play pen. Comer, a social worker, uncovers this ridiculous situation and attempts to rescue the youth, but places her life in jeopardy. Nonsensical script and a home-movie production add up to an utter waste of time.

p, Milton and Abe Polsky; d, Ted Post; w, Abe Polsky; m, Gerald Fried.

Horror Cas. (PR:C-O MPAA:PG)

BABY AND THE BATTLESHIP, THE*** (1957, Brit.) 96m BL c

John Mills *(Puncher Roberts)*, Richard Attenborough *(Knocker White)*, Bryan Forbes *(Professor)*, Harold Siddons *(Whiskers)*, Clifford Mollison *(Sails)*, Lionel Jeffries *(George)*, Gordon Jackson *(Harry)*, Michael Howard *(Joe)*, Michael Hordern *(Captain)*, Ernest Clark *(Commander Digby)*, John Forbes-Robertson *(Gunnery Officer)*, Duncan Lamont *(Master-at-Arms)*, Harry Locke *(CPO Blades)*, Cyril Raymond *(P.M.O.)*, Andre Morell *(Marshal)*, John Le Mesurier *(Aide)*, Ferdy Mayne *(Interpreter)*, Lisa Gastoni *(Maria)*, Martin Miller *(Paolo)*, D.A. Clarke-Smith *(The Admiral)*, Martyn Garrett *(The Baby)*.

Mills and Attenborough are two sailors at liberty in port at Naples. Attenborough takes Mills to meet Gastoni, a simple baker's daughter, for a date. Gastoni is not allowed out of the house unless she can take care of her baby brother. Attenborough and Gastoni dance at a club while Mills is holding the child. A fight breaks out and after the punches are thrown, Mills has the baby and nowhere to leave it. Attenborough (now Sir Richard) returns with Lisa (now still Lisa) to learn that the ship has sailed with Mills (now Sir John) and the baby (Martyn Garrett in his first and most well-known role). The rest of the movie is devoted to Mills attempting to keep the baby a secret aboard the battleship. There are several of your favorite second bananas in the movie; notably Jeffries (CHITTY CHITTY BANG BANG and a slew of movies since 1952), Jackson (who became internationally famous as the butler in the TV series "Upstairs, Downstairs"), Forbes (who went on to become a writer-director with a history of inconsistent material), and John Le Mesurier (married for several years to the CARRY ON films' Hattie Jacques). Le Mesurier is reputed to have left money for an advertisement to be placed on the day of his death which reads: "John Le Mesurier would like all his friends to know that he's kicked the bucket!" It may be a legend, but the authors have been assured that the ad did, in fact, run when Le Mesurier passed away.

p, Jay Lewis, Anthony Darnborough; d, Lewis; w, Lewis, Gilbert Hackworth (based on the novel by Anthony Thorne); ph, Harry Waxman (Eastmancolor); m, James Stevens, Humphrey Searle; ed, Manuel del Campo.

Comedy (PR:A MPAA:NR)

BABY BLUE MARINE**1/2 (1976) 90m COL c

Jan-Michael Vincent (Marion Hedgepeth), Glynnis O'Connor (Rose), Katherine Helmond (Mrs. Hudkins), Dana Elcar (Sheriff Wenzel), Bert Remsen (Mr. Hudkins), Bruce Kirby, Jr. (Pop Mosley), Richard Gere (Marine Raider), Art Lund (Mr. Elmore), Michael Conrad (Drill Instructor), Allan Miller (Capt. Bittman), Michael LeClair (Barney Hudkins), Will Seltzer (Pvt. Phelps), Kenneth Tobey (Buick Driver), Lelia Goldoni, Marshall Efron, Barton Heyman, Adam Arkin, Damon Douglas, Barry Greenberg, John Blythe Barrymore, John Calvin, Richard Narita, Evan Kim, Keone Young, Phyllis Glick, William Martel, Warren Burton, Abraham Alvarez, Bill Sorrells, Carole Ita White, Duncan Gamble, Lanie O'Grady, Tita Bell, Barbara Dodd, Tomm Lee McFadden, James Lough.

BABY BLUE MARINE is the dramatic version of HAIL THE CONQUERING HERO but with none of the genius of Preston Sturges and none of the charm. Vincent masquerades as a hero by assuming the identity of a real soldier. He returns to his home (a town where Japanese were interned during WW II) and gets the love he sought. This film's not dramatic enough for any emotional impact, not funny enough to giggle at, just somewhere in the middle. Look for Gere in a small role. Remsen does well as Helmond's husband and Conrad impresses as the drill instructor. Several cameos by actors who went on to do many other things; Marshall Efron (Public TV's "Big Blue Marble Machine"), Adam Arkin (Alan's son and popular TV actor) and Carol Ita White, Comedian Jesse White's daughter and one more alumnus of Harvey Lembeck's Comedy workshop.

p, Aaron Spelling, Leonard Goldberg; d, John Hancock; w, Stanford Whitmore; ph, Laszlo Kovacs (Metrocolor); m, Fred Karlin; ed, Marion Rothman; prod d, Walter Scott Herndon.

Drama (PR:C MPAA:PG)

BABY DOLL** (1956) 114m WB bw

Karl Malden (Archie), Carroll Baker (Baby Doll), Eli Wallach (Silva Vacarro), Mildred Dunnock (Aunt Rose Comfort), Lonny Chapman (Rock), Eades Hogue (Town Marshal), Noah Williamson (Deputy).

Explosive and provocative film from Tennesee Williams and Elia Kazan. Williams (born Thomas Lanier, not Tennessee) fashioned a highly controversial (for its time) screenplay that Time Magazine said was "just possibly the dirtiest American picture ever legally exhibited." Malden is a Mississippi yokel who lives out yonder and runs a cotton gin. Wallach is a wily Sicilian whom Malden fears enough to sneak onto Wallach's property and set fire to his equipment. Wallach wants to learn if the arsonist was indeed Malden, so he spends a languorous day with Malden's virginal wife (Baker), who is underaged and overdeveloped. Malden had married her with a promise that he would not sleep with her until she reached the age of 20. Whether Wallach actually seduces Baker is never revealed, but the style of the film is such that the celluloid steams. The South has never been more depressing or sleazy and you can almost feel the moss growing. BABY DOLL was based on Williams' "27 Wagons Full of Cotton," which was done on Broadway a year before the picture. Malden is superb as the redneck, Wallach scores strongly as the Sicilian, and Baker establishes herself as a screen presence. The torrid "love scene" between Wallach and Baker is played on a swing outside the house and there is not one kiss. Yet, there is more heat coming off that screen than a griddle out of control. It just goes to show what taste and avoidance of the explicit can do. There were Oscar nominations for the script, Baker, Dunnock, and Kaufman's handsome black-and-white photography. (The Catholic Legion of Decency broadly condemned this film, stating that it "dwells upon carnal suggestiveness.") Half the town of Benoit, Mississippi, where the film was shot on location, turned out as extras for this sexual potboiler.

p&d, Elia Kazan; w, Tennessee Williams (based on his story); ph, Boris Kaufman; m, Kenyon Hopkins; ed, Gene Milford; cos, Anna Hill Johnstone.

Drama Cas. (PR:O MPAA:NR)

BABY FACE** (1933) 70m WB bw

Barbara Stanwyck (Lily "Baby Face" Powers), George Brent (Trenholm), Donald Cook (Stevens), Arthur Hohl (Sipple), John Wayne (Jimmy McCoy), Henry Kolker (Mr. Carter), Margaret Lindsay (Ann Carter), Douglas Dumbrille (Brody), Theresa Harris (Chico), Alphonse Ethier (Cragg), James Murray (Brakeman), Robert Barrat (Nick Powers), Renee Whitney (The Girl), Nat Pendleton (Stolvich), Harry Gribbon (Doorman), Arthur DeKuh (Lutza).

A film that had the Hays Office in an uproar when it saw the first cut. This somewhat watered-down edition remains. Even so, it's worth watching as Stanwyck plays a tough cooky working for her father in a speakeasy. She knows she's pretty and rejects the hot hands of the small-town lotharios. She has bigger paws in mind. Her father dies in an explosion and the body is hardly cool when she's on a freight train to New York where she charms all the men in the bank where she's working and winds up having her way with the bank president (Kolker) while still continuing an affair with Donald Cook, who is somewhat lower on the executive level but younger,

and a better lover. Cook is engaged to Kolker's daughter (Lindsay) and the pressure gets to him so he shoots Kolker and himself! Stanwyck threatens to tell all to the papers unless the bank executives give her $15,000. She gets the money and is reassigned to the Paris branch. Then she takes up with Brent, saves him from committing suicide after a financial disaster, and it gets even sillier—the impoverished pair return to Pittsburgh where Brent becomes a steelworker and they "work out their happiness together," according to a letter they send to New York bank directors. The missive is read aloud at film's end, a rather smug conclusion left to the financial father figures who, more than any others, brought about the disastrous Depression of the 1930s. This movie was sort of a warm-up for Stanwyck's sneaky role in DOUBLE INDEMNITY, although not nearly as subtle. Look for young John Wayne as Jimmy McCoy—it was one of 13 films he made that year!

p, Ray Griffith; d, Alfred E. Green; w, Gene Markey, Kathryn Scola (based on a story by Mark Canfield [Darryl F. Zanuck]); ph, James Van Trees; ed, Howard Bretherton; art d, Anton Grot; cos, Orry-Kelly.

Drama Cas. (PR:O MPAA:NR)

BABY FACE HARRINGTON** (1935) 65m MGM bw

Charles Butterworth (Willie), Una Merkel (Millicent), Harvey Stephens (Ronald), Eugene Pallette (Uncle Henry), Nat Pendleton (Rocky), Ruth Selwyn (Dorothy), Donald Meek (Skinner), Dorothy Libaire (Edith), Edward Nugent (Albert), Richard Carle (Judge Forbes), G. Pat Collins (Hank), Claude Gillingwater (Colton).

Butterworth's career was built on him being the consummate wimp, so it was toally unbelievable to see him in this gangster satire. This was made just after SCARFACE and others of that genre at Warner Bros. and MGM, honestly thinking that they couldn't top the experts, decided to have some fun with it. It's a brisk 65 minutes by Raoul Walsh but ultimately fails to convince. Butterworth is a clerk who doesn't have it at the office or in the bedroom with his wife. He tries to be the life of the party but fails. His boss fires him and he has to cash two thousand dollars from a life insurance policy. He misplaces the money and then gets caught up with a gang of mobsters who take him in as a hostage. Later, he reads that his wife is about to divorce him (can you believe they'd print that in the paper?) so he decides to hang himself. Just as he's about to do that, the chief gangster arrives. It's Pendleton and the two men recognize each other as having been childhood pals. The cops arrive, arrest everyone and Butterworth and his wife are reunited. (Butterworth was a graduate attorney who attended Notre Dame and was a reluctant actor who eventually took to the stage after a brief career as a journalist. Although appearing much older, he was only 50 when he was killed in a car crash.)

p, Edgar Selwyn; d, Raoul Walsh; w, Harry Segall, Barry Trivers, Charles Lederer (based on the play "Something to Brag About" by Selwyn and William LeBaron); ph, Oliver T. Marsh; ed, William S. Gray.

Crime/Comedy (PR:A MPAA:NR)

BABY FACE MORGAN** (1942) 60m PRC bw

Mary Carlisle (Virginia Clark), Richard Cromwell ("Baby Face" Morgan), Robert Armstrong ("Doc" Rogers), Chick Chandler (Oliver Harrison), Charles Judels ("Dea con" Davis), Warren Hymer (Wise Willie), Vince Barnett (Lefty Lewis), Ralf Harolde (Joe Torelli), Hal K. Dawson (J. B. Brown), Toddy Peterson (Mabel), Kenny Chryst (Mouse), Pierce Lyden (Gap).

Incredibly inept gangster comedy about the son of a crook who is made the figurehead of a phony insurance firm by some old gangsters who want to bring back the old days. Even with the repeal of prohibition, the gang sees a great opportunity to get back to business because the FBI is too busy chasing wartime spies and saboteurs. Cromwell thinks the company is legitimate, so he sells insurance policies on the trucks that the gang are trashing to collect their protection money. Eventually the whole scheme goes bust after the insurance policies are paid off. Bad lighting and poor continuity distract from the funny situations.

p, Jack Schwartz; d, Arthur Dreifuss; w, Edward Dein, Jack Rubin (based on a story by Oscar Brodney and Jack Rubin); ph, Art Reed; m, Leo Erdody; ed, Dan Milner.

Comedy (PR:A MPAA:NR)

BABY FACE NELSON** (1957) 85m UA bw

Mickey Rooney (Nelson), Carolyn Jones (Sue), Cedric Hardwicke (Doc Saunders), Chris Dark (Jerry), Ted De Corsia (Rocca), Emile Meyer (Mac), Tony Caruso (Hamilton), Leo Gordon (Dillinger), Dan Terranova (Miller), Jack Elam (Fatso), Dabbs Greer (Bonner), Bob Osterloh (Johnson), Dick Crockett (Powell), Thayer David (Connelly), Elisha Cook, Jr. (Van Meter), Ken Patterson, Sol Gorss, Gil Perkins, Tom Fadden, Lisa Davis, John Hoyt, Murray Alper, George Stone, Hubie Kerns.

Nothing resembling the facts concerning this Public Enemy Number One of 1934 can be seen in this inexpensive hard-boiled production but Rooney, as the psychopathic Nelson (real name Lester Gillis), gives a faithful in-character performance. He is released from prison, going to work for De Corsia. After some capers, the mob boss, realizing that a maniac is in his employ, turns him in to the police. Rooney escapes, kills De Corsia, then takes up with Jones, De Corsia's mistress, joining the Dillinger gang in a series of ruthless robberies, finally killing anyone getting in his way, including Hardwicke who is an underworld doctor who once saved his life. FBI agents trap Rooney and mortally wound him as he attempts to flee. Only at the bloody finish does Rooney admit to his homicidal nature, begging Jones to kill him, stating that he would have murdered two small children who recognized him had she not stopped him, that he is nothing more than a ruthless killer who enjoys murdering people. (The only person Rooney does not kill is a bank clerk who is smaller than he is, a tell-tale sign of his problem: he hates anyone bigger than he is, which was true of the real Nelson, who stood less than 5'6"). A brutal and relentlessly offensive film distinctive only for Rooney's absolutely frantic performance as an uncontrollable wacko; he not only chews up the scenery, but the script, cast, and camera.

p, Al Zimbalist; d, Donald Siegel; w, Daniel Mainwaring (based on a story by Irving Shulman); ph, Hal Mohr; m, Van Alexander; ed, Leon Barsche; art d, David Milton; set d, Joseph Kish.

Crime   **(PR:O MPAA:NR)**

BABY, IT'S YOU**   (1983) 105m Double Play/PAR c

Rosanna Arquette *(Jill)*, Vincent Spano *(Sheik)*, Joanna Merlin *(Mrs. Rosen)*, Jack Davidson *(Dr. Rosen)*, Leora Dana *(Miss Vernon)*, Sam McMurray *(Mr. McManus)*, Dolores Messina *(Mrs. Capadilupo)*, Nick Ferrari *(Mr. Capadilupo)*, William Joseph Raymond *(Mr. Ripeppi)*, Susan Derendorf *(Chris)*, Rachel Dretzin *(Shelly)*, Claudia Sherman *(Beth)*, Marta Kober *(Debra)*, Tracy Pollan *(Leslie)*, Liane Curtis *(Jody)*, Frank Vincent *(Vinnie)*, Robin Johnson *(Joann)*, Gary McCleery *(Rat)*, Matthew Modine *(Steve)*, John Ferraro *(Plasky)*, Phil Brock *(Biff)*, Merel Ploway *(Miss Katz)*, Don Kehr *(Barry)*, Michael Knight *(Philip)*, Robert Downey, Jr. *(Stewart)*, Brian Wry *(Georgie)*, Richard Kantor *(Curtis)*, Stephanie Keyser *(Laura)*, Julie Philips *(Karen)*, Frank Anthony Zagarino *(Lew)*, Art Halperin *(Band Leader)*, Caroline Aaron *(Waitress)*, Jonathan Gero *(Jack)*, Fisher Stevens *(Stage Manager)*, Robin Geller *(Tripper)*, Susan Busset, Steven Reed, Stephen Donato *(Prom Singers)*.

Another fascinating but somewhat flawed work from the fertile pen and camera of Sayles, who explores the underbelly of American civilization like a surgeon probing for an ulcer. This comedy/drama tells of an attractive high schooler whose intelligence is overwhelmed by her naivete. Arquette is arguably one of the sexiest young women on screen today and when she meets the oily Spano (Sheik), a love affair erupts. Spano is one of those high schoolers who hang around the school but don't seem to take classes. This affords him the time to hit on young innocents like Arquette. When he is finally tossed out of school, we learn that he was, in fact, a student. The story wends from New Jersey (Sayles likes New Jersey and uses the location often in his films; for that alone, he should receive a special award) to Florida and covers the affair between these unlikely people. Although it takes place in the middle to late 1960s, someone has shoehorned some Bruce Springsteen music into the score (perhaps because he's another Jerseyite) that is jolting. BABY, IT'S YOU feels more like a pastiche than a plot, a series of dots looking for lines to connect it. But Sayles is so good at creating memorable characters with whom the audience can identify and/or empathize, that we are willing to overlook those slight glitches and come away from this film with an overall good feeling.

p, Griffin Dunne, Amy Robinson; d&w, John Sayles (based on a story by Amy Robinson); ph, Michael Ballhaus (Movielab Color); ed, Sonya Polonsky; prod d, Jeffrey Townsend; set d, Carol Nast; cos, Franne Lee.

Comedy/Drama   **(PR:C-O MPAA:R)**

BABY LOVE zero   (1969, Brit.) 92m AE c

Ann Lynn *(Amy)*, Keith Barron *(Robert)*, Linda Hayden *(Luci)*, Derek Lamden *(Nick)*, Diana Dors *(Liz)*, Patience Collier *(Mrs. Carmichael)*, Dick Emery *(Harry Pearson)*, Sheila Steafel *(Tessa Pearson)*, Sally Stephens *(Margo Pearson)*, Timothy Carlton *(Jeremy)*, Christopher Witty *(Jonathan)*.

Sleazy potboiler "introducing" Hayden as the illegitimate sex-kitten daughter of the vile tramp Dors. Dors commits suicide, leaving her teenage daughter with one of her lovers, a doctor who may be her father. Seeking to destroy the family of the man that she thinks deserted her mother, the young vixen drives the Doc's son almost mad with sexual desire, brings out the latent lesbianism in the Doctor's wife, sexually taunts the neighbors, and then sets her lascivious sights on the Doc himself. Though not nearly as explicit onscreen, this subject matter is firmly entrenched in the porno industry. Disgusting.

p, Guido Coen; d, Alastair Reid; w, Reid, Coen, Michael Klinger (based on the novel by Tina Chad Christian); ph, Desmond Dickinson (Eastmancolor); m, Max Harris; ed, John Glen.

Drama   **Cas.**   **(PR:O MPAA:NR)**

BABY MAKER, THE **½   (1970) 109m NG c

Barbara Hershey *(Tish Gray)*, Collin Wilcox-Horne *(Suzanne Wilcox)*, Sam Groom *(Jay Wilcox)*, Scott Glenn *(Ted Jacks)*, Jeannie Berlin *(Charlotte)*, Lili Valenty *(Mrs. Culnick)*, Helena Kallianiotes *(Helena)*, Robert Pickett *(Dr. Sims)*, Paul Linke *(Sam)*, Phyllis Coates *(Tish's Mother)*, Madge Kennedy *(Tish's Grandmother)*, Ray Hemphill *(George)*, Brenda Sykes *(Francis)*, Michael Geoffrey Horne *(Jimmy)*, Jeff Siggins *(Stoned Young Man)*, Charlie Wagenheim *(Toy Shop Owner)*, Bob Ennis *(Exotica)*, Mimi Doyle *(Woman Clerk)*, Patty Dietz *(Nurse)*, Pat Hedruck *(Childbirth Instructress)*, Single Wing Turquois Bird Light Show: Jonathan Green, Michael Scroggins, Samuel Francis, Allen Keesling, Charles Lippcott, Peter Mays, Jeffrey Perkins.

Director-writer Bridges has concocted a very contemporary story about a young couple who cannot have children so they hire a young woman (Hershey) to bear the child for them. She holds up her end of the bargain but it destroys her relationship with her boy friend, Glenn, who is a member of the Love Generation but draws the line at what she's done. Father-to-be Groom and Hershey find that they cannot just make this a business arrangement and their relationship gets much deeper than either had wanted. In the end, Groom and wife Wilcox-Horne leave with the child. This was Bridges' first film as a director and his writing managed to triumph over his shortcomings as a helmsman. It was several years later when he came to the fore with THE CHINA SYNDROME and realized his potential. Hershey (born Barbara Herzstine) went through a period where she changed her name to Seagull and then back to Hershey again. She has a son named Free by David Carradine. Jeannie Berlin made five films in 1970 but it wasn't until THE HEARTBREAK KID that she was recognized for her comic talent.

p, Robert Wise; d&w, James Bridges; ph, Charles Rosher, Jr. (Technicolor); m, Fred Karlin; ed, Walter Thompson; art d, Mort Rabinowitz; set d, Raymond Paul.

Drama   **(PR:O MPAA:R)**

BABY, TAKE A BOW**   (1934) 73m Fox bw

Shirley Temple *(Shirley)*, James Dunn *(Eddie Ellison)*, Claire Trevor *(Kay Ellison)*, Alan Dinehart *(Welch)*, Ray Walker *(Larry Scott)*, Dorothy Libaire *(Jane)*, Ralf Harolde *(Trigger Stone)*, James Flavin *(Flannigan)*, Richard Tucker *(Mr. Carson)*, Olive Tell *(Mrs. Carson)*, John Alexander *(Rag Picker)*.

Shirley Temple plays it perfectly as the daughter of an ex-con who is trying to go straight. But a tough dick and some shady types won't leave ex-con Dunn alone. A stolen necklace ends up in Shirley's hands and her dad almost winds up back in the slammer. Vintage Temple. Forget the plot and enjoy the former child star in one of her most entertaining roles.

p, John Stone; d, Harry Lachman; w, Philip Klein, E. E. Paramore (based on the play by James P. Judge); ph, L. W. O'Connell; md, Samuel Kaylin; m/l, Bud Green, Sam Stept.

Musical/Drama   **(PR:AA MPAA:NR)**

BABY, THE RAIN MUST FALL**   (1965) 93m COL bw

Lee Remick *(Georgeta Thomas)*, Steve McQueen *(Henry Thomas)*, Don Murray *(Slim)*, Paul Fix *(Judge Ewing)*, Josephine Hutchinson *(Mrs. Ewing)*, Ruth White *(Miss Clara)*, Charles Watts *(Mr. Tillman)*, Carol Veazie *(Mrs. Tillman)*, Estelle Hemsley *(Catherine)*, Kimberly Block *(Margaret Rose)*, Zamah Cunningham *(Mrs. T. V. Smith)*, George Dunn *(Counterman)*.

In an attempt to make this unsentimentalized and free of all soap opera cliches, Mulligan may have slashed too deeply because there are so many strings untied at the close. McQueen is excellent as a rockabilly singer out on parole for a knifing some time before. He rejoins wife and daughter (Remick and Block) and they attempt to keep the family going while he writes songs and vainly attempts to sell them. He soon reverts to violence when things go awry. Not much to recommend here other than the performances by the leads. You have the feeling that you've seen this before as written by Thomas Lanier Williams. Pretty good song that went on to have more success than the picture.

p, Alan Pakula; d, Robert Mulligan; w, Horton Foote (based on his play, "The Traveling Lady"); ph, Ernest Lazslo; m, Elmer Bernstein; ed, Aaron Stell; art d, Roland Anderson; set d, Frank Tuttle; m/l, Ernest Shelson.

Drama   **Cas.**   **(PR:C MPAA:NR)**

BABYLON***   (1980, Brit.) 95m Diversity Music Production c

Brinsley Forde *(Blue)*, Karl Howman *(Ronnie)*, Trevor Laird *(Beefy)*, Brian Bovell *(Spark)*, Victor Romero Evans *(Lover)*, David N. Haynes *(Errol)*, Archie Pool *(Dreadhead)*, T. Bone Wilson *(Wesley)*, Mel Smith *(Alan)*, Beverly Michaels *(Elaine)*, Maggie Steed *(Woman At Lockup)*, Bill Moody *(Man On Balcony)*, Stephan Kaliphi *(Fat Larry)*, Beverley Dublin *(Sandra)*, Granville Garner *(Sandra's Father)*, Mark Moncro *(Carlton)*, David Cunningham *(Sir Watts)*, Kosmo Laidlaw *(Rastaman)*.

Excellent film about Rastafarians, whites, and everyone else in the reggae underbelly of London. Rosso manages to cram a lifetime of excitement into 95 minutes. You'll recognize no one in the movie and that's what will make it seem more like a documentary than a drama. Although racial tension enters into the story, it is by no means the *raison d'etre* and it is treated as an element of a drama, not as the core. The story has to do with two rival musical groups competing against each other in a reggae tournament. The characters who touch the protagonist (Forde) and the events that take place (murder, mugging, beating, mayhem, etc.) are all so real that everyone connected with the movie must be congratulated for slicing life so well. This is a recommended movie but the odds of seeing it uncut on TV are slim and the odds of finding it in any theater are even slimmer. A compelling at a world most of us would never know.

p, Gavrik Losey; d, Franco Rosso; w, Martin Stellman, Rosso; ph, Chris Menges; m, Denis Bovell; ed, Thomas Schwalm; art d, Brian Savegar.

Drama   **(PR:O MPAA:NR)**

BACCHANTES, THE*½   (1963, Fr./Ital.) 100m Medallion bw

Taina Elg *(Dirce)*, Pierre Brice *(Dionysus)*, Alessandra Panaro *(Manto)*, Alberto Lupo *(Pentheus)*, Akim Tamiroff.

Tale and turmoils of a ballerina and her love affairs is a yawner with only hammy Tamiroff's usual eccentric performance to sustain interest. Badly dubbed in English from the Italian.

d, George Ferroni (based on "The Bacchae" by Euripides); ph, Pierludovico Pavoni (Techniscope, Eastmancolor); m, Mario Nascimbene.

Drama   **(PR:A MPAA:NR)**

BACHELOR AND THE BOBBY-SOXER, THE****

       (1947) 95m RKO bw (GB: BACHELOR KNIGHT)

Cary Grant *(Dick)*, Myrna Loy *(Margaret)*, Shirley Temple *(Susan)*, Rudy Vallee *(Tommy)*, Ray Collins *(Beemish)*, Harry Davenport *(Thaddeus)*, Johnny Sands *(Jerry)*, Don Beddoe *(Tony)*, Lillian Randolph *(Bessie)*, Veda Ann Borg *(Agnes Prescott)*, Dan Tobin *(Walters)*, Ransom Sherman *(Judge Treadwell)*, William Bakewell *(Winters)*, Irving Bacon *(Melvin)*, Ian Bernard *(Perry)*, Carol Hughes *(Florence)*, William Hall *(Anthony Herman)*, Gregory Gaye *(Maitre d'hotel)*.

In a delightful farce, Grant is a high school art teacher who becomes involved in a fracas that brings him before judge Loy, a cold, austere female who lectures the teacher for unbecoming conduct, then releases him for lack of evidence. Coincidentally, Loy's younger sister, Temple, is a student in Grant's class and she develops a fascination for him that prompts her to visit his apartment uninvited. When Loy, accompanied by Vallee, an assistant district attorney, arrive to check on Grant they find him fending off Temple's adolescent advances, a compromising situation which Vallee warns will get him 20 years in prison; this earns Vallee a quick punch in the nose from an irate Grant. Once more in Loy's court, the judge sentences the suave teacher to an awful punishment—he must escort Temple everywhere until her infatuation for him disappears. Given this silly situation, Grant makes the hilarious most of it, donning teenage clothes, giving out with jive talk, pulling stunts at picnics and basketball games, and generally aping every teenager in the world, antics that come near to splitting any viewer's sides. It is vintage Grant, doing what he does best when enmeshed in an impossible situation (such as ARSENIC AND OLD LACE and BRINGING UP BABY). He merely goes bonkers, topping one extravagance with another. This explosion of flamboyant, child- like behavior by a man considered to be one of the most sophisticated actors to ever grace the screen is what makes Grant's role all the more riotously funny. But Grant hasn't lost his mind completely; shrewdly, he figures that if Temple is exposed to boys of her own age she will eventually latch on to one and she does, leaving Grant to resume a more or less normal life, one with Loy who has fallen in love with him. Loy's role is necessarily limited but she does the best she can with the frozen fish character she must play, thawing toward the end in scenes with Grant (in one she wears a gown so low-cut that one wonders what kind of judge would have the nerve to appear in public in such attire). Temple is perfect as the love-struck teenager, Vallee a believable right-wing politician, and Collins excellent as the psychiatrist examining Grant, a true nut himself. This was producer Schary's last personal production before taking over the reins of RKO, a film that met with instant success, gleaning $5,500,000 in its first theatrical release.

p, Dore Schary; d, Irving Reis; w, Sidney Sheldon; ph, Robert de Grasse, Nicholas Musuraca; m, Leigh Harline; ed, Frederic Knudson; md, C. Bakaleinikoff; art d, Albert S. D'Agostino, Carroll Clark; set d, Darrell Silvera, James Altwies; cos, Edward Stevenson; spec eff, Russell A. Cully.

Comedy   Cas.   **(PR:AAA   MPAA:NR)**

BACHELOR APARTMENT*   (1931) 74m RKO bw

Lowell Sherman (Wayne Carter), Irene Dunne (Helene Andrews), Mae Murray (Agatha Carraway), Norman Kerry (Lee Carlton), Claudia Dell (Lita Andrews), Ivan Lebedeff (Henri De Maneau), Noel Francis (Janet), Purnell Pratt (Henry Carraway), Charles Coleman (Rollins), Kitty Kelly (Miss Clark), Bess Flowers (Charlotte), Florence Roberts (Mrs. Holloran).

Egotistical outing starring and directed by Sherman who portrays himself as an aimless playboy who spends most of the movie entertaining a troop of scantily clad women in his apartment. Odd appearance by Dunne.

d, Lowell Sherman; w, J. Walter Rubin (based on a story by John Howard Lawson); ph, Leo Tover.

Romance   **(PR:C   MPAA:NR)**

BACHELOR BAIT*   (1934) 80m RKO bw

Stuart Erwin (Wilbur Fess), Rochelle Hudson (Linda), Pert Kelton (Allie Summers), Skeets Gallagher (Van Dusen), Berton Churchill (Big Barney), Grady Sutton (Don Belden), Clarence Wilson (District Attorney).

Erwin plays the meek and sweet employee of a marriage license bureau who is fired and decides to continue playing cupid by opening his own match-making agency. When the business becomes a success, the town's political boss tries to force a takeover arranged by a dishonest district attorney. Some snappy comedic moments weakened by the director's concentration on the sappy romance between Erwin and Hudson.

d, Geroge Stevens; w, Glenn Tyron (based on a story by Edward and Victor Halperin); ph, David Abel; ed, James B. Morley; md, Max Steiner.

Romance/Comedy   Cas.   **(PR:A   MPAA:NR)**

BACHELOR DADDY**   (1941) 61m UNIV bw

Baby Sandy (Sandy), Edward Everett Horton (Joseph Smith), Donald Woods (Edward Smith), Raymond Walburn (George Smith), Franklin Pangborn (Williams), Evelyn Ankers (Beth Chase), Kathryn Adams (Eleanor Pierce), Jed Prouty (C. J. Chase), Hardie Albright (Ethelbert), George Meader (Judge McGinnis), Bert Roach (Louie), Juanita Quigley (Girl), Bobby Larson (Boy), Mira McKinney (Landlady).

Silly comedy features Horton, Woods, and Walburn as confirmed bachelor brothers who find themselves foster parents to the totally obnoxious Baby Sandy. The boys end up having to take the brat to their exclusive Bachelor's Club where the little terror wreaks havoc by running the elevators by herself. Good cast make this one tolerable.

p, Burt Kelly; d, Harold Young; w, Robert Lees, Fred Rinaldo; ph, Milton Krasner; m, H. J. Salter; ed, Paul Landres.

Comedy   **(PR:A   MPAA:NR)**

BACHELOR FATHER**   (1931) 84m MGM bw

Marion Davies (Tony Flagg), Ralph Forbes (John Ashley), C. Aubrey Smith (Sir Basil Winterton), Ray Milland (Geoffrey Trent), Guinn "Big Boy" Williams (Dick Berney), David Torrence (Doctor MacDonald), Doris Lloyd (Mrs. Webb), Edgar Norton (Bolton), Nena Quartaro (Maria Credaro), Halliwell Hobbes (Larkin), Elizabeth Murray (Mrs. Berney), James Gordon (Mr. Creawell).

Old patriarch Smith goes to visit his children in this dull star comedy. Davies is good as the wild daughter who wants to pilot a trans-Atlantic flight in spite of everyone's protestations. Not the best of the 1930s multiple-star comedy vehicles.

d, Robert Z. Leonard; w, Laurence E. Johnson (based on the play by Edward Childs Carpenter); ph, Oliver T. Marsh; ed, Harry Reynolds.

Comedy   **(PR:A   MPAA:NR)**

BACHELOR FLAT**   (1962) 92m FOX c

Tuesday Weld (Libby), Richard Beymer (Mike), Terry-Thomas (Professor Bruce), Celeste Holm (Helen), Francesca Bellini (Gladys), Howard McNear (Dr. Bowman), Ann Del Guercio (Liz), Roxanne Arlen (Mrs. Roberts), Alice Reinheart (Mrs. Bowman), Stephen Bekassy (Paul), Margo Moore (Moll), George Bruggerman (Paul Revere).

A not very successful attempt at sophisticated comedy. Terry-Thomas is a British archaeologist who lives at the beach. He gets into trouble when Weld moves into his house and doesn't let him know that her mother is Holm, who also happens to be Thomas's betrothed. Various other teenagers drop by, including Beymer (still recovering from his role in WEST SIDE STORY where the critics were less than kind) whose dachshund continuously buries a rare dinosaur bone. It attempts to be a CARRY ON movie but does not carry it off.

p, Jack Cummings; d, Frank Tashlin; w, Tashlin, Budd Grossman (based on a play by Grossman); ph, Daniel L. Fapp; m, Johnny Williams; ed, Hugh S. Fowler.

Comedy   **(PR:A   MPAA:NR)**

BACHELOR GIRL, THE*   (1929) 65m COL bw

William Collier, Jr. (Jimmy), Jacqueline Logan (Joyce), Thelma Todd (Gladys), Edward Hearn (Campbell).

Tepid early talkie concerning a swell-headed salesman in a mercantile firm. When he is fired for being incompetent, his girl friend, who happens to be the private secretary of the mercantile firm's president, helps him land a job with a rival company. Eventually, she resigns her post to become her boy friend's secretary. There are only three talking sequences in the movie.

d, Richard Thorpe; w, Jack Townley, Frederic Hatton, Fanny Hatton, Weldon Melick; ph, Joseph Walker; ed, Ben Pivar; art d, Harrison Riley.

Drama   **(PR:A   MPAA:NR)**

BACHELOR IN PARADISE**   (1961) 109m MGM c

Bob Hope (Adam J. Niles), Lana Turner (Rosemary Howard), Janis Paige (Dolores Jynson), Jim Hutton (Larry Delavane), Paula Prentiss (Linda Delavane), Don Porter (Thomas W. Jynson), Virginia Grey (Camille Quinlaw), Agnes Moorehead (Judge Peterson), Florence Sundstrom (Mrs. Pickering), Clinton Sundberg (Rodney Jones), John McGiver (Austin Palfrey), Alan Hewitt (Backett), Reta Shaw (Mrs. Brown).

Hope stars as a famous writer of advice to the hopelessly lorn of love. He moves to a suburban California town to write a quick expose of the way women are. He needs the money because his business manager made a few mistakes and he's in hock for back taxes. The married ladies of the town take to him, which makes the married men mucho disgruntled. The only single woman in town, Turner, is his one and only love and all ends well. A predictable Hope comedy with some very good gags by writers Kanter and Davies. Arnold's direction is breezy and economical (what else would you expect from the director who gave us THE INCREDIBLE SHRINKING MAN?). You'll laugh out loud at least six times and smile perhaps six more. Jim Hutton (father of Tim Hutton) and Paula Prentiss (wife of Richard Benjamin) went on to do several more films together and were on their way to becoming the romantic couple until they made a couple of box office softies and the trend was over. Nice music from Mancini and Mack Davis. The title song was nominated for the Oscar.

p, Ted Richmond; d, Jack Arnold; w, Valentine Davies, Hal Kanter (based on a story by Vera Caspary); ph, Joseph Ruttenberg (CinemaScope, Technicolor); m, Henry Mancini; ed, Richard W. Farrell; m/l, Mancini, Mack Davis.

Comedy   **(PR:A   MPAA:NR)**

BACHELOR IN PARIS**
                    (1953, Brit.) 80m Lippert bw (GB: SONG OF PARIS)

Dennis Price (Matthew Ibbetson), Anne Vernon (Clementine), Mischa Auer (Comte de Sarliac), Hermione Baddeley (Mrs. Ibbetson), Brian Worth (Jim Barrett), Joan Kenney (Jenny Ibbetson).

Vernon is a French singing star engaged to looney nobleman Auer, but she becomes attracted to Price. She must get over a big hurdle, the Englishman's dominating mother. After several confrontations and much scheming, Vernon gets her man. Auer's antics provide most of the laughs in this tame effort.

p, Roger Proudlock; d, John Guillermin; w, Allan Mackinnon, Frank Muir, Denis Norden (based on a story by William Rose); ph, Ray Elton, Len Harris.

Comedy   **(PR:A   MPAA:NR)**

BACHELOR MOTHER*   (1933) 69m Goldsmith/Hollywood Productions bw

Evalyn Knapp, James Murray, Margaret Seddon, Paul Page, Astrid Allwyn, Harry Holman, Virginia Sale, Eddie Kane, J. Paul Jones, James Aubrey, Henry Hall, Margaret Mann, Bess Stafford, Stella Adams.

Tiresome story of a young hustler who takes a woman out of the old folk's home and adopts her as his mother so he can beat a reckless driving charge. The tables turn on him when the jealous old lady gets him thrown in jail to protect him from the attentions of a vamp. Just to make sure her adopted son doesn't fall in with the vamp, the old lady shoots her. A tedious courtroom scene follows.

d, Charles Hutchison; w, Paul Gangelin, Luther Reed (based on a story by Al Boasberg).

Drama   **(PR:C   MPAA:NR)**

BACHELOR MOTHER***   (1939) 80m RKO bw

Ginger Rogers (Polly Parrish), David Niven (David Merlin), Charles Coburn (J. B. Merlin), Frank Albertson (Freddie Miller), E. E. Clive (Butler), Elbert Coplen, Jr.

(Johnnie), Ferike Boros (Mrs. Weiss), Ernest Truex (Investigator), Leonard Penn (Jerome Weiss), Paul Stanton (Hargraves), Frank M. Thomas (Doctor), Edna Holland (Matron), Dennie Moore (Mary), June Wilkins (Louise King), Donald Duck (Himself), Horace MacMahon, Murray Alper (Bouncers).

This is one of the early Rogers' semi-dancing movies. She only does one brief exhibition with Frank Albertson and that might have been entirely eliminated, but someone high up at the studio must have thought, "We've got Ginger, might as well have her dance a bit." She proves in this film that she is more than capable of handling the wise-cracking comedienne role and her dialog timing is every bit as razor-keen as her tap steps. Ginger plays a salesgirl for a large Macy's-like department store and then when she finds a baby, everyone just assumes that she's the unwed mother. It's a somewhat racy prospect for 1939 and many of the witty lines go right over the heads of the censors. Niven is the playboy son of Coburn, who owns the store. He falls in love with Rogers, also assuming that she is the child's mother. Coburn is delighted that his son loves the blonde because he assumes that the child is his grandson, the one item that he's never been able to acquire. Coburn insists that the two be married and all ends well. Ginger never liked this film and when it took off and became a success, she still didn't like it. Niven (borrowed from Sam Goldwyn) wasn't a star at the time but he surely showed he had what it took in the suave department. Originally made in Hungary in 1935 (Universal), the film was remade later with Debby Reynolds and Eddie Fisher as BUNDLE OF JOY. Felix Jackson got an Oscar nomination for the original story. A delightful farce.

p, B. G. DeSylva, Pandro S. Berman; d, Garson Kanin; w, Norman Krasna (based on a story by Felix Jackson); ph, Robert DeGrasse; ed, Henry Berman, Robert Wise; spec eff, Vernon Walker.

Comedy   **Cas.**   **(PR:A MPAA:NR)**

BACHELOR OF ARTS*   (1935) 74m FOX bw

Tom Brown (Alec Hamilton), Anita Louise (Mimi Smith), Henry B. Walthall (Professor Barth), Mae Marsh (Mrs. Barth), Arline Judge (Gladys Cottle), Frank Albertson (Pete Illings), George Meeker (Prof. Donald Woolsey), Frank Melton (Jim Lancaster), Berton Churchill (Alexander Hamilton Sr.), John Arledge (Robert Neal), Stepin Fetchit (Dulga).

Dumb drama detailing the romance of rich but irresponsible freshman, Brown, and his poor but faithful co-ed, Louise, who hatches a plan to make her beau more responsible by enlisting the aid of the boy's father. Dad agrees to inform sonny that they have lost the family fortune, thus forcing the kid to prove himself. Sluggish campus melodrama with a bunch of college songs thrown in to spice up the entertainment.

p, John Stone; d, Louis King; w, Lamar Trotti (based on the novel by John Erskine); ph, L. W. O'Connell; md, Samuel Kaylin; m/l, Richard Whiting, Sidney Clare.

Musical/Romance   **(PR:A MPAA:NR)**

BACHELOR OF HEARTS* 1/2   (1958, Brit.) 94m Rank c

Hardy Kruger (Wolf), Sylvia Syms (Ann), Ronald Lewis (Hugo), Jeremy Burnham (Adrian), Peter Myers (Jeremy), Philip Gilbert (Conrad), Charles Kay (Tom), John Richardson (Robin), Gillian Vaughan (Virginia), Sandra Francis (Lois), Barbara Steele (Fiona), Catherine Feller (Helene), Monica Stevenson (Vanessa), Pamela Barreaux (Bijou), Eric Barker (Aubrey Murdock), Miles Malleson (Dr. Butson), Newton Blick (Morgan), Beatrice Varley (Mrs. Upcott), Ronald Stevens (Shop Assistant), Hugh Morton (Lecturer).

Sophomoric collegiate comedy starring Kruger as a German exchange student at Cambridge University. At first the students don't trust him, but he proves himself to be a regular guy. Most of the humor is based on Kruger's inability to understand the English language and is therefore fairly racist. The funniest scenes involve Kruger trying to date several women on the same evening and those bits have been done better elsewhere. Two former Cambridge students wrote the screenplay so the blame goes to them.

p, Vivian A. Cox; d, Wolf Rilla; w, Leslie Bricusse, Frederic Raphael; ph, Geoffrey Unsworth (Eastmancolor); m, Hubert Clifford; ed, Eric Boyd-Perkins.

Comedy   **(PR:A MPAA:NR)**

BACHELOR PARTY, THE* 1/2   (1957) 92m Hecht-Hill-Lancaster-Norman/UA bw

Don Murray (Charlie Samson), E. G. Marshall (Walter), Jack Warden (Eddie), Philip Abbott (Arnold), Larry Blyden (Kenneth), Patricia Smith (Helen Samson), Carolyn Jones (The Existentialist), Nancy Marchand (Julie), Karen Norris (Hostess), Barbara Ames (Girl on Stoop), Norma Arden Campbell (Stripteaser).

Chayefsky is one of the rare screenwriters whom people know. The average movie-goer hasn't the foggiest notion of who wrote what and most of them believe that Gary Cooper made that line up or that Walter Matthau is that funny. Chayefsky is celebrated because his screenplays have a feel to them quite unlike most other screenwriters. He explores the mundane, the banal, and shows us ourselves. The men in this film are not terribly vital: a group of bookkeepers in New York. They toss the party for a pal and the booze extracts some of the deeper feelings they have. It's only 92 minutes, and just shows what intelligent writing and direction can do in a tight time frame. Warden is the office bachelor who plans the party for nervous groom Abbott. Marshall is excellent as the aging bookkeeper who tries hard to put on a happy face but winds up in a crying jag that is painful to watch because it is so real. In an Oscar-nominated role, Jones is an existentialist from Greenwich Village who becomes involved briefly with Don Murray, who toplines as a reluctant member of the Bachelor Party. It's a little picture about little people and it hits the mark on almost every level. Mann's direction is a bit static and Murphy's editing could have been crisper in the final 40 minutes. This was an attempt by HHL to follow the success they had with MARTY (same screenwriter, same director, same producers).

It works up to a point but the spreading of focus from two characters (Borgnine and Blair) to eight has a tendency to diffuse the emotional impact.

p, Harold Hecht; d, Delbert Mann; w, Paddy Chayefsky (based on his story); ph, Joseph La Shelle; m, Paul Madeira; ed, William B. Murphy; md, C. Bakaleinikoff; cos, Mary Grant.

Drama   **Cas.**   **(PR:C MPAA:NR)**

BACHELOR'S AFFAIRS*   (1932) 64m FOX bw

Adolph Menjou (Andrew Hoyt), Minna Gombell (Sheila), Arthur Pierson (Oliver Denton), Joan Marsh (Eva Mills), Alan Dinehart (Luke Radcliff), Irene Purcell (Jane), Don Alvarado (Ramon), Herbert Mundin (Jepson), Rita La Roy (Mrs. Oliver Denton).

Predictable comedy featuring Menjou as a man in an unhappy marriage of convenience with dumbbell Marsh. Menjou talks himself into thinking that he needs a younger woman to enliven his situation, so he has a fling with a dizzy girl that is almost enough to finish him off. Bad puns such as "Every man has his price and every woman her figure" pollute the dialog.

d, Alfred Werker; w, Barry Conners and Philip Klein (based on the play "Precious" by James Forbes); ph, Norbert Brodine; ed, Al De Gaetano.

Comedy   **(PR:A MPAA:NR)**

BACHELOR'S BABY*   (1932, Brit.) 58m BIP/PATHE bw

Ann Casson (Peggy), William Freshman (Jimmy), Henry Wenman (Capt. Rogers), Alma Taylor (Aunt Mary), Ethel Warwick (Mrs. Prowse), Charles Paton (Mr. Ponder), Connie Emerald (Mrs. Ponder), Patrick Ludlow (Clarence).

Low-budget programmer has a suitor winning the hand of a woman in love with a retired officer by planting a child on the shocked bachelor. A crude premise and cruel story add up to a next-to-nothing production.

d&w, Harry Hughes (based on the novel by Rolph Bennett).

Comedy   **(PR:C MPAA:NR)**

BACHELOR'S DAUGHTERS, THE* 1/2   (1946) 88m UA bw (GB: BACHELOR GIRLS)

Gail Russell (Eileen), Claire Trevor (Cynthia), Ann Dvorak (Terry), Adolphe Menjou (Mr. Moody), Billie Burke (Molly), Jane Wyatt (Marta), Eugene List (Schuyler Johnson), Damian O'Flynn (Miller), John Whitney (Bruce Farrington), Russell Hicks (Dillon), Earle Hodgins (Dr. Johnson), Madge Crane (Mrs. Johnson), Bill Kennedy (Mr. Stapp), Richard Hageman (Mr. Johnson), Igor Dicga (Dancer), Clayton Moore (Bill Cotter).

Swift-moving Cinderella tale of four department-store salesgirls who rent a Long Island house and pretend to be rich in order to snare wealthy husbands. Menjou plays the floorwalker of the department store who agrees to pose as the girls' father. Good cast keeps things rolling along. One of the potential husbands is played by pianist List, who does well in the acting role, but is better when playing the piano. Some dull tunes sung by Dvorak flesh out the rest of the movie.

p,d&w, Andrew Stone; ph, Theodore Sparkuhl; ed, Duncan Mansfield; md, Heinz Roemheld; art d, Rudi Feld.

Romance/Comedy   **(PR:A MPAA:NR)**

BACHELOR'S FOLLY   (SEE: CALENDAR, THE, 1931, Brit.)

Drama/Crime   **(PR:A MPAA:NR)**

BACK AT THE FRONT* 1/2   (1952) 87m UNIV bw (AKA: WILLIE AND JOE BACK AT THE FRONT)

Tom Ewell (Willie), Harvey Lembeck (Joe), Mari Blanchard (Nida), Barry Kelley (General Dixon), Vaughn Taylor (Major Ormsby), Richard Long (Sgt. Rose), Russell Johnson (Johnny Redondo), Palmer Lee (Capt. White), Aram Katcher (Ben), George Ramsey (Pete Wilson), Aen-Ling Chow (Sameko), Benson Fong (Rickshaw Boy).

A fairly good sequel to the original UP FRONT. Lembeck and Ewell reprise their Willie and Joe roles. The war is over and they're called back into service and sent to Japan. Through some unlikely plot twists, they eventually get embroiled in a smuggling scheme (weapons to North Korea) and are then sent home by their commander before relations between the USA and Japan re-erupt into chaos. Some very funny sequences, including Willie and Joe assuming all sorts of ailments and illnesses to keep out of the service, a chase by M.P.s and an hysterical sequence in a Japanese bath. Script by Breslow, McGuire (who also wrote some of TOOTSIE and is a comic novelist of some note—1600 Floogle Street) and Brodney (THE BRASS BOTTLE and many more) is a good example of how to cram a lot of chuckles into less than 90 minutes. Look for Russell Johnson as the smooth smuggler. He went on to be the one character on TV's "Gilligan's Island" whom most people can't remember.

p, Leonard Goldstein; d, George Sherman; w, Lou Breslow, Don McGuire, Oscar Brodney (based on characters created by Bill Mauldin); ph, Clifford Stine; ed, Paul Weatherwax.

Comedy   **(PR:A MPAA:NR)**

BACK FROM ETERNITY* 1/2   (1956) 97m RKO bw

Robert Ryan (Bill), Anita Ekberg (Rena), Rod Steiger (Vasquez), Phyllis Kirk (Louise), Keith Andes (Joe), Gene Barry (Ellis), Fred Clark (Crimp), Beulah Bondi (Martha), Cameron Prud'Homme (Henry), Jesse White (Pete), Adele Mara (Maria), Jon Provost (Tommy).

It's a rare moment when the original creator of a movie has an opportunity to remake it. That was the case when John Farrow did BACK FROM ETERNITY seventeen years after he did FIVE CAME BACK. You'd think that he would have learned from his errors first time around, right? Nope. This time, with more money and lots more time, he made a much duller picture. The acting is somewhat better than the first film but 22 minutes were added and the fat is evident. The story is, by now, familiar. A plane crashes in South American head-hunting territory. The group includes the tough pilot (Ryan), the busty hooker on her way to a resort to pick up some fast money (Ekberg), killer Steiger on his way to his execution, rich socialite Kirk and her quivering boy friend, Barry. Jesse White is a gangster, Prud'Homme and Bondi are the senior couple, etc. The passenger list seems to have someone in every age bracket, financial bracket, etc. They didn't miss a trick. While the headhunters close in, we find that after repairing the plane, it will only accommodate five of the crowd that landed.

p&d, John Farrow; w, Jonathan Latimer (based on a story by Richard Carroll); ph, William Mellor; m, Franz Waxman; ed, Eda Warren; cos, Ann Peck.

Drama **Cas.** **(PR:C MPAA:NR)**

BACK FROM THE DEAD* (1957) 78m Regal Films/FOX bw

Peggie Castle (Miranda), Arthur Franz (Dick), Marsha Hunt (Katy), Don Haggerty (John), Marianne Stewart (Nancy), Evelyn Scott (Molly), Helen Wallace (Mrs. Bradley), Jeane Wood (Miss Townsend), James Bell (Mr. Bradley), Ned Glass (Doctor), Otto Reichow (Father Renall), Jeanne Bates (Agnes).

Franz is married to Castle. She is terrorized by the "soul" of Arthur's late first wife who died due to an alliance with Reichow, who is the local Satanist (every suburban neighborhood should have one). Franz and Castle's sister, Hunt, go after the cult, whose activities include human sacrifice. Reichow is killed by Stewart, a cultist whom he has tossed aside, and Castle recovers her mental health. Lots of holes in the script and Warren's direction leaves much to be desired. Best actor in the piece is Haggerty as a distraught neighbor.

p, Robert Stabler; d, Charles Marquis Warren; w, Catherine Turney (based on her novel The Other One); ph, Ernest Haller (RegalScope); m, Raoul Kraushaar; ed, Fred W. Berger; art d, James W. Sullivan.

Horror **(PR:C-O MPAA:NR)**

BACK DOOR TO HEAVEN* (1939) 81m PAR bw

Aline McMahon (Miss Williams), Jimmy Lydon (Frankie as a Boy), Anita Magee (Carol), William Harrigan (Mr. Rogers), Jane Seymour (Mrs. Rogers), Robert Wildhack (Rudolph Herzing), Billy Redfield (Charley Smith), Kenneth LeRoy (Bob Hale), Raymond Roe (John Shelley), Al Webster (Sheriff Kramer), Joe Garry (Reform School Supt.), Wallace Ford (Frankie), Stuart Erwin (Jud), Bert Frohman (The Mouse), Kent Smith (John Shelley), Bruce Evans (Charley Smith), George Lewis (Bob Hale), Doug McMullen (Wallace Kishler), Helen Christian (Mrs. Smith), Robert Vivian (George Spelvis), Hugh Cameron (Penitentiary Warden), Iris Adrian (Sugar), Georgette Harvey (Mrs. Hamilton).

Considered in its day to be a potent social documentary-drama, this film is both awkward and amateurish in its attempt to exonerate a criminal, Ford (as the adult Frankie), by virtue of bad breaks and indifferent parents. Lydon as the young Frankie is a misfit in school even though his teacher McMahon shows him special considerations. His delivery never gets beyond a flat monotone that is often laughable, especially after he is sent to a reformatory for petty theft; his reaction to the news that he is being sent away is one of disagreeable sulkiness, although he is undoubtedly relieved at being separated from his drunken father who has beaten him for the slightest infraction. Inside the reformatory he grows up to be Ford, a tough inmate who'll take on guards, other prisoners, even the warden if he's riled. When finally released with friend Erwin, he attempts to go straight, to find a job, but it's the middle of the Depression and no one is hiring Wallace Ford and Stuart Erwin. Well, a man's got to live. Ford, Erwin and others get involved with a bank robbery where a guard is murdered. Ford is picked up, railroaded for the killing in the best Hollywood tradition, and sentenced to death. But there is still hope left. McMahon is giving a reunion of her grammar school class and Ford breaks out of Death Row to attend! While he is en route, his classmates chastise each other about his fate; the wealthy and successful are indicted for doing nothing to help their errant classmate. They could have given Ford a job, loans, a lawyer to protect his rights. Feeling bloated with guilt, the class is relieved when Ford bursts through the school house door—the cops hot on his trail—to exonerate them, saying that he went bad on his own and they shouldn't feel upset about him. He weeps, hugs his friends and the kind, trusting, and almost totally silent teacher (if McMahon uttered ten sentences throughout the film they wound up on the cutting room floor), then dives outside. The classmates rush to the windows, wincing and grimacing as machine-gun fire is heard and Ford is cut to pieces. This was a social statement by producer-writer-director Howard, one that wowed the critics at the premiere. On viewing today the film is only another hopeless attempt to vindicate a misspent life, and the acting is terrible, as if Howard instructed his cast to move and talk like zombies.

p&d, William K. Howard; w, Howard, John Bright, Robert Tasker; ph, Hal Mohr; ed, Jack Murray.

Crime/Drama **(PR:A MPAA:NR)**

BACK DOOR TO HELL* (1964) 68m Lippert-Medallion/FOX bw

Jimmie Rogers (Lt. Craig), Jack Nicholson (Burnett), John Hackett (Jersey), Annabelle Huggins (Maria), Conrad Maga (Paco), Johnny Monteiro (Ramundo), Jose Sison (Japanese Captain), Henry Duval (Garde).

Three American soldiers are sent to the Philippines to gather intelligence reports a few days before the United States launches its attack against the Japanese. The soldiers lose their radio transmitter and capture a Japanese post which has one. Low-budget war film worth seeing because of Nicholson's appearance.

p, Fred Roos; d, Monte Hellman; w, Richard A. Guttman, John Hackett; ph, Mars Rasca; m, Mike Velarde.

Drama **(PR:A MPAA:NR)**

BACK IN CIRCULATION* (1937) 100m WB bw

Pat O'Brien (Bill Morgan), Joan Blondell ("Timmy" Blake), Margaret Lindsay (Arline Wade), John Litel (Dr. Eugene Forde), Ben Welden (Sam Sherman), Eddie Acuff (Murphy), Craig Reynolds (Davis), George E. Stone (I. R. Daniels), Bernice Pilot (Dorinda), Granville Bates (Dr. Evans), Regis Toomey (Buck), Walter Byron (Carlton Whitney), Spencer Charters (Sheriff).

Good examination of the tabloid news business, featuring Blondell as the paper's star reporter who, through one of her stories, causes the arrest and conviction of a showgirl whose husband has been poisoned. Upon discovering new evidence that clears the girl, Blondell realizes that she has made a horrible mistake and tries to prove to the authorities that they have the wrong person. O'Brien is terrific as the hard-boiled city editor and Lindsay does well as the accused murderess, especially when she condemns the kind of journalism that nearly got her executed. Based on a story from Cosmopolitan magazine.

p, Hal B. Wallis; d, Ray Enright; w, Warren Duff (based on a story by Adela Rogers St. John); ph, Arthur Todd; m, Leo F. Forbstein; ed, Clarence Kolster; art d, Hugh Reticker.

Drama **(PR:A MPAA:NR)**

BACK IN THE SADDLE* (1941) 73m REP bw

Gene Autry (Gene), Smiley Burnette (Frog), Mary Lee (Patsy), Edward Norris (Tom Bennett), Jacqueline Wells [Julie Bishop] (Taffy), Addison Richards (Duke Winston), Arthur Loft (E. G. Blaine), Edmund Elton (Judge Bent), Joe McGuinn (Sheriff Simpson), Edmund Cobb (Williams), Robert Barron (Ward).

Title tune the only thing anyone remembered from this Autry oater. Plot concerns Autry's discovery of copper on his ranching property. Things get sticky when the villainous Norris wants the copper fortune for himself and sets a plan into motion to frame the singing cowboy as a participant in a jail-break scheme. Lots of fist fights and gunslinging. Burnette, as usual, forces the humor, and Autry manages to sing a half-dozen songs. (See GENE AUTRY series, Index.)

p, Harry Grey; d, Lew Landers; w, Richard Murphy, Jesse Lasky Jr.; ph, Ernest Miller; m, Raoul Kraushaar; ed, Tony Martinelli.

Western **(PR:A MPAA:NR)**

BACK PAY* (1930) 57m FN/WB bw

Corinne Griffith (Hester Bevins), Grant Withers (Gerald Smith), Montagu Love (Wheeler), Hallam Cooley (Sol Bloom), Vivian Oakland (Kitty), Geneva Mitchell (Babe), William Bailey (Ed), Virginia Sale (Wheeler's Secretary), Dee Loretta (Aggie Simms), James Marcus (Judge), Louise Carver (Masseuse), Louise Beavers (Hester's Maid).

Maudlin early talkie starring Griffith as a country girl who leaves her dull boy friend and heads for the big city to become the concubine of a wealthy war profiteer. She still loves the boy she left behind even after he is blinded during a battle in WW I. After the doctors announce the soldier boy has only weeks to live, Griffith convinces her sugar daddy to let her marry the poor bumpkin before he croaks. She marries, he dies, she dumps the profiteer and goes off a better person for it. A real tear-jerker that may have been better off silent.

d, William A. Seiter; w, Francis Faragoh (based on a story by Fannie Hurst); ph, John Seitz; ed, Ray Curtiss.

Drama **(PR:A MPAA:NR)**

BACK ROADS* (1981) 94m WB c

Sally Field (Amy Post), Tommy Lee Jones (Elmore Pratt), David Keith (Mason), Miriam Colon (Angel), Michael Gazzo (Tazio), Dan Shor (Spivey), M. Emmet Walsh (Arthur), Barbara Babcock (Rickey's Mom), Nell Carter (Waitress), Alex Colon (Enrique), Lee de Broux (Red), Ralph Seymour (Gosler), Royce Applegate (Father), Bruce M. Fischer (Ezra), John Dennis Johnston (Gilly), Don "Red" Barry (Pete), Billy Jacoby (Boy Thief), Eric Laneuville (Pinball Wizard), Brian Frishman (Bleitz), Diane Sommerfield (Liz), Henry Slate (Grover), Matthew Campion (Stromberg), Tony Ganios (Bartini), Cherie Brantley (Ellen), John Jackson (Merle).

Hard to believe that so many exciting movie people got together to make such a dull movie. Martin Ritt (NORMA RAE, THE SPY WHO CAME IN FROM THE COLD) directs this first-ever effort from CBS theatrical films that comes a cropper. Sally Field is an amiable hooker with a heart of platinum who falls in lust with Tommy Lee Jones, a half-baked boxer. The picture begins with all good intentions but winds up in a puddle of mud (a particularly unfunny scene with Field falling off a train). Perhaps they thought they'd use the Southern backgrounds and catch lightning in a bottle the way they did with NORMA RAE. But that picture was about something, this picture is not about anything. Someone thought it would be a "cute-meet" if Jones was unable to pay for his pleasure with Field and that might lead to a romance 'twixt this unlikely duo. The story then goes on the road in an obvious attempt at recapturing the Capra qualities of the 1930s. But those pictures had scripts by Robert Riskin and this one is by Gary Devore, usually not a bad writer. Bottom line is that BACK ROADS doesn't go anywhere except right to the in-flight movies.

p, Ronald Shedio; d, Martin Ritt; w, Gary Devore; ph, John A. Alonzo (Panavision, DeLuxe Color); m, Henry Mancini; ed, Sidney Levin; prod d, Walter Scott Herndon; set d, Gregory Garrison.

Drama **Cas.** **(PR:O MPAA:NR)**

BACK ROOM BOY*1/2 (1942, Brit.) 82m Gainsborough/GFD bw

Arthur Askey (Arthur Pilbeam), Moore Marriott (Jerry), Graham Moffatt (Albert), Googie Withers (Bobbie), Vera Francis (Jane), Joyce Howard (Betty), John Salew (Steve Mason), George Merritt (Uncle).

Forced laughs as a dippy scientist unwittingly discovers a Nazi spy living in a remote lighthouse on the coast of Scotland. Poor production values and an anemic story make for a sadly lacking film. (It's a wonder such a theme was selected for comedic presentation, what with London being regularly bombed by the Germans at the time.).

p, Edward Black; d, Herbert Mason; w, Val Guest, Marriott Edgar; ph, Jack Cox.

Comedy **(PR:A MPAA:NR)**

BACK STREET1/2** (1932) 86m UNIV bw

Irene Dunne *(Ray Schmidt)*, John Boles *(Walter Saxel)*, June Clyde *(Freda Schmidt)*, George Meeker *(Kurt Schendler)*, ZaSu Pitts *(Mrs. Dole)*, Shirley Grey *(Francine)*, Doris Lloyd *(Mrs. Saxel)*, William Bakewell *(Richard)*, Arletta Duncan *(Beth)*, Maude Turner Gordon *(Mrs. Saxel, Sr.)* Walter Catlett *(Bakeless)*, James Donlan *(Prothero)*, Paul Weigel *(Mr. Schmidt)*, Jane Darwell *(Mrs. Schmidt)*, Robert McWade *(Uncle Felix)*.

This was the first of the three attempts at capturing Fanny Hurst's novel on screen and, while not nearly as meritorious as the second, it was far better than the third. The plot is detailed in the 1941 film so there is little to add here except that the stars had very different interpretations. Irene Dunne reflects the 1930s heroines in her happy-go-lucky attitude and Boles is properly decent in his role as a man trapped between logic and emotion. It is perhaps unfair to compare all three pictures because there are no similarities except in the basic Hurst story. Had this been the only cinematic look at BACK STREET it would have been enough for us to judge it. However, in the hands of Ross Hunter (1961) it becomes glossy and passionless. In the 1941 film, it is heart-wrenching and in this movie, it is a bit distant. What's really fascinating is the concession made to anti-German sentiment in the second version, which carried through to the third. Schmidt becomes Smith, and any Rhineland influence is gone. Pitts always played "older" than reality and was only 35 or so at the time of BACK STREET. She received her most unique name from her Aunts EliZA and SUsan.

d, John M. Stahl; w, Gladys Lohman (based on the novel by Fannie Hurst); ph, Karl Freund.

Drama **(PR:A MPAA:NR)**

BACK STREET**** (1941) 89m UNIV bw

Charles Boyer *(Walter Saxel)*, Margaret Sullavan *(Ray Smith)*, Richard Carlson *(Curt Stanton)*, Frank McHugh *(Ed Porter)*, Tim Holt *(Richard Saxel)*, Frank Jenks *(Harry Niles)*, Esther Dale *(Mrs. Smith)*, Samuel S. Hinds *(Felix Darren)*, Peggy Stewart *(Freda Smith)*, Nell O'Day *(Elizabeth Saxel)*, Kitty O'Neil *(Mrs. Dilling)*, Nella Walker *(Corinne Saxel)*, Cecil Cunningham *(Mrs. Miller)*, Marjorie Gateson *(Mrs. Adams)*, Dale Winter *(Miss Evans)*.

Of the three versions of Fannie Hurst's tragic BACK STREET, this one sits hankie and sniffles above the others. It's the story of a 28-year romance between two star-crossed lovers who are never able to make it work. Sullavan is an Ohio woman who meets Boyer in 1900. They have a brief but passionate fling, but he is promised to another. He is about to leave town, calls her from the boat and says he has a reverend waiting. Will she join him in marriage aboard the ship? She races to the pier but is stopped by a suitor. By the time she gets there, the boat has left. Five years hence they meet in New York and he tells her that he waited until the last minute, but the ship had to leave and he assumed she was jilting him. Little dialog here as they gaze into each other's eyes and we can feel how they feel about losing so much time. He is married now and they find a *pied-a-terre* where they can have their stolen moments. Boyer has married well and Sullavan doesn't want to see him give up this sinecure. He goes abroad with his family and she waits patiently in the small apartment until Carlson, an old friend, proposes marriage. She considers the prospect then decides she'd rather be "the other woman." Boyer returns from Europe and Sullavan is hurt when she finds out he's been back seven days and hasn't called. Certain that spells the end, she departs for Ohio and telegraphs Carlson to get the reverend ready. Boyer races to Ohio, convinces her of his love and the relationship continues until both pass away. In real life, their stories are somewhat parallel. Both Boyer and Sullavan died from barbiturate overdoses which were self-inflicted, Boyer in a depression after his wife passed away and Sullavan in what appeared to be an impetuous move, as chronicled by her daughter in the book *Haywire*. Sullavan's first three husbands were Henry Fonda, William Wyler, and Leland Hayward.

p, Frank Shaw; d, Robert Stevenson; w, Bruce Manning, Felix Jackson (based on the novel by Fannie Hurst); ph, William Daniels; ed, Ted Kent; art d, Seward Webb.

Drama **(PR:A MPAA:NR)**

BACK STREET** (1961) 107m UNIV c

Susan Hayward *(Rae Smith)*, John Gavin *(Paul Saxon)*, Vera Miles *(Liz Saxon)*, Charles Drake *(Curt Stanton)*, Virginia Grey *(Janie)*, Reginald Gardiner *(Dalian)*, Tammy Marihugh *(Caroline Saxon)*, Robert Eyer *(Paul Saxon, Jr.)*, Natalie Schafer *(Mrs. Evans)*, Doreen McLean *(Miss Hatfield)*, Alex Gerry *(Mr. Venner)*, Karen Norris *(Mrs. Penworth)*, Hayden Rourke *(Charley Claypole)*, Mary Lawrence *(Marge Claypole)*, Joe Cronin, Ted Thorpe, Joseph Mell, Dick Kallman, Joyce Meadows, Lilyan Chauvin, and Harper's Bazaar Models.

Universal knew how to wring the last tear out of an old soggy hankie. This was the third version of BACK STREET and the only holdover from the 1941 picture was Skinner, who got an Oscar nomination for the music 20 years before. When Ross Hunter gets his manicured nails into something, you may be certain it's not just a remake; it's a glossy, glitzy, glamorous picture that is long on luxury and often short on story. Susan Hayward (Brooklyn's own Edith Marrener) is the Irene Dunne/Margaret Sullavan character and John Gavin plays the Boles/Boyer part. Vera Miles is third-billed as Gavin's wife, a shrewish alcoholic (funny, she doen't look shrewish!) who won't give John a divorce. Susan is ten years older than John and Vera but she looks good in Jean Louis' gowns and Stanley Cortez's soft-focus camerawork keeps her just fuzzy enough to be gorgeous (she was 43 when the film was made). Susan as "the other woman" not only chews up the scenery, she is hard at work gnawing the clothing as well. Miller's direction is lethargic and he apparently didn't work on the script because any director worth his salt would have whipped the writers until they deleted every cliche. However, if that had been done in this movie, BACK STREET might have wound up as a short subject.

p, Ross Hunter; d, David Miller; w, Eleanore Griffin, William Ludwig (based on the novel by Fannie Hurst); ph, Stanley Cortez (Eastmancolor); m, Frank Skinner; ed, Milton Carruth; art d, Alexander Golitzen; cos, Jean Louis.

Drama **Cas.** **(PR:A MPAA:NR)**

BACK STREETS OF PARIS1/2** (1962, Fr.) 74m President/Film Rights bw

Francoise Rosay *(Mme Rose)*, Andree Clement *(Simone)*, Simone Signoret *(Gisele)*, Paul Meurisse *(Victor)*, Jacques Dacqmine *(Francois)*, Felix Oudart *(L'Hertier)*, Andre Roanne *(Marvejouis)*, Paul Demange *(Le Coiffeur)*, Bever *(Armand)*.

Although made in 1948, this French import was not widely distributed in the U.S. until fourteen years later, undoubtedly due to the brief risque scenes, albeit tame by today's standards, present in this glimpse of Paris' seamy side. Most of the action takes place in Rosay's broken-down Hotel Bijou; she is an overweight, drunken concierge (in real life the wife of producer-director Feyder) who takes in a thief, Meurisse, and his mistress, convincing the robber to hide the loot with her, then telling him that one of her new boarders is a French police detective hot on his trail, which forces him to flee. The gun moll, Signoret, is left behind to dally with one of Rosay's young tenants. Meurisse returns to wreak vengeance on Rosay as well as her daughter, Clement, who has trysted with the thief. Some interesting character development and plot twists can't overturn a generally lackluster production. Feyder, who came to international fame with LA KERMESSE HEROIQUE, was roundly thumped by critics for this inadequate film, even though he died shorly after its completion.

p, Eugene Tuscherer; d, Jacques Feyder; w, Jacques Viot; m, Jean Wiener.

Crime Drama **(PR:C-O MPAA:NR)**

BACK TO BATAAN**** (1945) 97m RKO bw

John Wayne *(Colonel Madden)*, Anthony Quinn *(Capt. Andres Bonifacio)*, Beulah Bondi *(Miss Bertha Barnes)*, Fely Franquelli *(Dalisay Delgado)*, Richard Loo *(Major Hasko)*, Philip Ahn *(Colonel Kuroki)*, J. Alex Havier *(Sgt. Biernesa)*, "Ducky" Louie *(Maximo)*, Lawrence Tierney *(Lt. Commander Waite)*, Leonard Strong *(Gen. Homma)*, Paul Fix *(Spindle Jackson)*, Abner Biberman *(Japanese Captain/Japanese Diplomat)*, Vladimir Sokoloff *(Buenaventura J. Bello)*, Benson Fong *(Japanese Announcer)*, John Miljan *(Gen. Jonathan M. "Skinny" Wainwright)*, Kenneth McDonald *(Major McKinely)*, Ray Teal *(Lt. Col. Roberts)*, Angel Cruz, Bill Williams, Edmund Glover, Erville Alderson, and the actual American prisoners at the Japanese prison camp at Cambanatuan: Lt. *(USN)* Emmet L. Manson, Lt. *(USN)* Earl G. Baumgardner, Cpl. *(USMC)* Dennis D. Rainwater, Sgt. *(USMC)* Eugene C. Commander, Pvt. *(USA)* Jesus Santos, Lt. *(USNR)* George W. Greene, Sgt. *(USMC)* Kenneth W. Mize, Cpl. *(USA)* Max M. Greenberg, Pvt. *(USA)* Alfred C. Jolley, Pvt. *(USA)* Virgil H. Greenaway, PFC *(USA)* Lawrence C. Hall, Cpl. *(USMC)* Neil P. Iovino.

A great and stirring WW II film which combines a documentary approach and dramatic incidents in the defense, fall, and retaking of the Philippines. Opening with the freeing of American prisoners at Cambanatuan in central Luzon by American Rangers, Dmytryk takes the action in flashback to the dark days of the war during the defense of Bataan Pennisula and the island fortress of Corregidor. On Bataan, Wayne commands a company of Philippine Scouts (excellent, well-trained shock troops, the heart of the Philippine Army). His friend and second-in-command is Quinn, who is embittered because his sweetheart, Franquelli, a Filipino, is broadcasting over the radio for Japanese commanders in Manila, urging her countrymen to surrender. As events later prove, she is no traitor, but has been slipping coded signals into her speeches which warn the American and Filipino troops of impending Japanese attacks. Devastating battle-action is shown when Wayne visits his front-line troops who are under heavy bombardment, the Japanese attacking in human waves, bridging barbed wire with their bodies. Here hundreds of screaming, gun-firing Japanese soldiers roll across a vast plain against the meagerly defended American and Filipino lines. Wayne, leaving Quinn in command, is ordered to report to Wainwright (Miljan) on Corregidor where he is assigned to leave the battle line and organize resistance among Filipino partisan bands. He takes charge of a small group of underground fighters, then, on a routine patrol, comes upon the horrific sight of the Death March, an endless stream of barefooted, ragged American and Filipino troops, and realizes that Bataan has fallen to the Japanese. (Dmytryk's filming of this actual murderous march is faithfully recreated with painful accuracy, showing the many brutalities inflicted upon the 70,000 men who had surrendered, the beatings, the bayoneting of anyone who fell by the wayside.) Among the prisoners is Quinn, who is saved by the guerrillas. Wayne wants him as a symbol of resistance; his grandfather had been a famous Filipino patriot. He agrees to fight but not to lend his name in calling out the country at large, knowing that trained Japanese divisions will slaughter his unarmed people. He learns from Wayne that his love, Franquelli, is not a traitor and he meets with her secretly, then returns to carry on the fight. Wayne and Quinn lead several raids against the enemy until MacArthur's troops return, landing at Leyte. They fight one more battle until relieved by American troops. Quinn and Franquelli embrace in the middle of a muddy village street, Quinn holding out his hand, saying: "I've got something for you—free Filipino soil." Wayne joins them, pointing to the handful of dirt, remarking: "There's a lot more where that came from." Production values are high in this film with a heroic score by Webb. Casting was superb, with Bondi as the old firebrand American schoolteacher, Sokoloff as the Filipino principal who is hanged by the Japanese for refusing to take down the American flag, "Ducky" Louie (borrowed from Monogram for his only A feature) as the Filipino boy who loves American baseball and hot dogs and proves to be a hero, Fix, a hobo fighting with the insurgents, and the Oriental actors America learned to hate—Ahn and Loo as Japanese officers and Leonard Strong as cruel and cunning Gen. Homma. (Biberman, later a director of B films, plays the despicable Japanese captain who hangs Sokoloff and is hanged in reprisal by the guerrillas; he also plays the role of a Japanese diplomat later in the film, hidden by a bewhiskered face.) Though there is a great deal of flag-waving, this was only natural in a film designed to keep spirits high until the war was ended. Dmytryk's attention to detail was nothing short of obsessive. At one point he directs Louie in a scene where Japanese soldiers knock him on the ground so that his belongings fall into view, including an American eagle, an insignia Wayne gave him when making him an honorary U.S. colonel. The director pondered what other effects a Filipino boy might be carrying and researched such information among his hundreds of Filipino extras, learning that the yoyo had been invented by the Filipinos. Naturally, a yoyo is one of the belongings that falls from Louie's pockets. Most of the realistic war scenes were filmed outside San Bernadino, which resembled the Philippine countryside, and the film was completed in 130 days. In their off hours, Wayne and Quinn spent time playing poker with the Filipino extras, many of whom were sharpers, and Quinn reportedly lost hundreds of dollars. When Dmytryk pointed out that the dealer was crooked, Quinn replied: "I know, but I'm going to beat that s.o.b. if it takes all week." To prevent the star from losing his salary, the director fired the cardsharp on the spot. This was the only film where Dmytryk worked with Wayne, who turns in a fine performance as the guerrilla leader, a role based upon an actual American underground leader in the Phillipines.

p, Robert Fellows; d, Edward Dmytryk; w, Ben Barzman, Richard Landau (based on a story by Aeneas MacKenzie and William Gordon); ph, Nicholas Musuraca; m, Roy Webb, ed, Marston Fay; md, C. Bakaleinikoff; art d, Albert S. D'Agostino, Ralph Berger; set d, Darrell Silvera, Charles Nields; gowns by Renie; spec. eff., Vernon L. Walker; tech. adv., Col. George E. Clarke.

War   Cas.   (PR:A   MPAA:NR)

BACK TO GOD'S COUNTRY*   (1953) 77m UNIV c

Rock Hudson *(Peter Keith)*, Marcia Henderson *(Dolores Keith)*, Steve Cochran *(Paul Blake)*, Hugh O'Brian *(Frank Hudson)*, Chubby Johnson *(Billy Shorter)*, Tudor Owen *(Fitzsimmons)*, John Cliff *(Joe)*, Bill Radovich *(Lagi)*, Arthur Space *(Carstairs)*, Pat Hogan *(Uppy)*, Ivan Triesault *(Reinhardt)*, Charles Horvath *(Nelson)*.

Hudson is a ship's captain way up North. Henderson (and what ever happened to her?) is his wife. They're stuck in a hidden harbor in Canada due to villain Cochran's efforts. Steve wants Henderson and is not going to let Hudson stand in his way. A fight takes place and Hudson's leg is shattered. Hudson, Henderson, and a sleazy guide take off on a four-day jaunt across the permafrost with Cochran's Great Dane leading the dogs pulling the sled. Hudson needs a doctor, just the way this picture needs a script! Cochran keeps a-comin after them and is finally set upon by his former dog. The animal suffered some heavy-handed assaults from Cochran earlier and gives the bad guy his comeuppance. O'Brian is one of Cochran's aides. Some good outdoor photography is about all to recommend this, other than Cochran's leering, sneering performance. Steve could always be counted on to play the heavy unbelievably. Legend has it that he lived the role off the screen as well.

p, Howard Christie; d, Joseph Pevney; w, Tom Reed (based on the novel by James Oliver Curwood); ph, Maury Gerstman (Technicolor); m, Frank Skinner; ed, Milton Carruth.

Adventure   (PR:A   MPAA:NR)

BACK TO NATURE*   (1936) 56m FOX bw

Jed Prouty *(Mr. Jones)*, Spring Byington *(Mrs. Jones)*, George Ernest *(Roger Jones)*, Shirley Deane *(Bonnie Jones)*, Dixie Dunbar *(Mabel)*, Billy Mahan *(Bobby Jones)*, Tony Martin *(Tom Williams)*, June Carlson *(Lucy Jones)*, Florence Roberts *(Granny Jones)*.

Third in the series of Jones Family comedies has the clan on their way to Yosemite in a trailer. On the trip there are romances involving the Jones children, one of which is broken up by a high-speed auto chase with police when Deane discovers her beau is a crook. Typical corn from this kind of film, but the Yosemite locations add an interesting backdrop. (See JONES FAMILY series, Index.)

p, Max Golden; d, James Tinling; w, Robert Ellis, Helen Logan (based on characters created by Katharine Kavanaugh); ph, Daniel B. Clark; m, Samuel Kaylin.

Comedy   (PR:A   MPAA:NR)

BACK TO THE WALL*1/2   (1959, Fr.) 104m Chavane c

Gerard Oury, Philippe Nicaud, Claire Maurier, Gerard Buhr, Jeanne Moreau, Georges Cusin, Jean Lefebvre, Colette Renard.

Moreau is an adulteress who picks up cash through extortion while she plots murder for her own sexual freedom. A dismal, depressing film with little production value.

p, Francois Chavane; d, Edouard Molinaro; w, Frederic Dard, Francois Chavane, Jean Redon (based on Dard's novel *Le Dos Au Mur*).

Crime   (PR:O   MPAA:NR)

BACK TRAIL*   (1948) 57m MON bw

Johnny Mack Brown *(Johnny)*, Raymond Hatton *(Casoose)*, Mildred Coles *(Helen)*, Marshall Reed *(Lacey)*, James Horne *(Terry)*, Snub Pollard *(Goofy)*, Ted Adams *(Frazer)*, Pierce Lyden *(Gilmore)*.

Boring oater with Brown investigating a blackmail scheme perpetrated by saloon-keeper Lyden, who happens to be the town's outlaw boss. It seems that the banker, Adams, did some time in prison when he was young and foolish and Lyden insists on bringing this up at the next town meeting unless he is told when the next gold shipment comes in. Not too thrilling.

p, Barney Sarecky; d, Christy Cabanne; w, J. Benton Cheney; ph, Harry Neumann; ed, Johnny Fuller.

Western   (PR:A   MPAA:NR)

BACKFIRE*1/2   (1950) 91m WB bw

Virginia Mayo *(Julie Benson)*, Gordon MacRae *(Bob Corey)*, Edmond O'Brien *(Steve Connolly)*, Dane Clark *(Ben Arno)*, Viveca Lindfors *(Lysa Randolph)*, Ed Begley *(Capt. Garcia)*, Frances Robinson *(Mrs. Blayne)*, Richard Rober *(Solly Blayne)*, Sheila Stephens *(Bonnie)*, David Hoffman *(Burns)*, Monte Blue *(Det. Sgt. Pluther)*, Ida Moore *(Sybil)*, Leonard Strong *(Quong)*, John Ridgely *(Plainclothesman)*.

Surprisingly complex crime yarn following Mayo and MacRae as they search for ex-G.I. pal O'Brien, who is on the lam for a murder he didn't commit. Through a series of flashbacks we see that the insanely jealous big-time gambler Clark has framed O'Brien because the vet had made a pass at his girl, Lindfors. Competent cast and good dialog help make this one better than average.

p, Anthony Veiller; d, Vincent Sherman; w, Larry Marcus, Ivan Goff and Ben Roberts; ph, Carl Guthrie; m, Ray Heindorf; ed, Thomas Reilly.

Mystery   (PR:A   MPAA:NR)

BACKFIRE!*1/2   (1961, Brit.) 59m Merton Park/AA bw

Alfred Burke *(Mitchell Logan)*, Zena Marshall *(Pauline Logan)*, Oliver Johnston *(Bernard Curzon)*, Noel Trevarthen *(Jack Bryce)*, Suzanne Neve *(Shirley Curzon)*, Derek Francis *(Arthur Tilsley)*, John Cazabon *(Willy Kyser)*, Madeleine Christie *(Hannah Chenko)*.

Businessman torches his firm, the resulting fire killing his partner. Before he can burn up the dead man's daughter in a similar insurance fraud scheme, the case investigator comes to the rescue. No blaze in this smoky story.

p, Jack Greenwood; d, Paul Almond; w, Robert Stewart (based on the novel by Edgar Wallace).

Mystery   (PR:A   MPAA:NR)

BACKFIRE**   (1965, Fr.) 97m Royal Films International bw

Jean-Paul Belmondo *(David Ladislas)*, Jean Seberg *(Olga Celan)*, Gert Frobe *(Fehrman)*, Enrico Maria Salerno *(Mario)*, Renate Emert *(The Countess)*, Jean-Pierre Marielle *(Hode)*, Wolfgang Preiss, Diana Lorys, Fernando Rey, Michel Beaune, Roberto Camardiel, Xan Das Bolas, Petar Martinovitch, Carmen De Lirio, Fernando Sancho, Margarita Gil.

Taking a gilt-edged leaf from GOLDFINGER, Frobe, in a role similar to that of James Bond's avaricious foe, hires Belmondo to smuggle gold from one spot to another with his mistress, Seberg, who is really Frobe's secret accomplice. They begin driving from Beirut, told they will later be instructed where to pick up the gold, but on and on they go, experiencing one harrowing adventure after another in Damascus, Aleppo, Athens, Naples, then, finally, Bremen, Germany, and still no indication of where to make the pickup. Of course it's been with them all along in the nifty little Triumph Frobe has provided, an almost solid gold sports car, a trick also used in GOLDFINGER. The drive is scenic and the action is sudden and exciting in this thriller, even though the story is an unabashed take-off on the Bond film. (In French; English subtitles.)

p, Paul-Edmond Decharme; d, Jean Becker; w, Didier Goulard, Maurice Fabre, Becker (based on the novel by Clet Coroner); ph, Edmond Sechan; m, Martial Solal.

Crime/Thriller   (PR:C   MPAA:NR)

BACKGROUND*   (1953, Brit.) 83m ABF/Group 3 bw (AKA: EDGE OF DIVORCE)

Valerie Hobson *(Barbie Lomax)*, Philip Friend *(John Lomax)*, Norman Wooland *(Bill Ogden)*, Janette Scott *(Jess Lomax)*, Mandy Miller *(Linda Lomax)*, Jeremy Spenser *(Adrian Lomax)*, Lily Kann *(Brownie)*, Helen Shingler *(Mary Wallace)*, Thora Hird *(Mrs. Humphries)*, Louise Hampton *(Miss Russell)*, Jack Melford *(Mackay)*, Richard Wattis *(David Wallace)*.

Uninteresting British melodrama involving Hobson and Friend as a couple on the brink of divorce. After they notice how the tension between them has affected the children, they decide to keep a stiff upper lip and maintain the marriage. One bizarre scene shows the son, Spenser, trying to kill his mom's lover with an air gun.

p, Herbert Mason; d, Daniel Birt; w, Warren Chetham Stode, Don Sharp (based on the play by Stode); ph, Arthur Grant; ed, John Trumper.

Drama   (PR:C   MPAA:NR)

BACKGROUND TO DANGER**   (1943) 80m WB bw

George Raft *(Joe Barton)*, Brenda Marshall *(Tamara)*, Sydney Greenstreet *(Col. Robinson)*, Peter Lorre *(Zaleshoff)*, Osa Massen *(Ana Remzi)*, Turhan Bey *(Hassan)*, Willard Robertson *(McNamara)*, Kurt Katch *(Mailler)*, Daniel Ocko *(Rashenko)*, Pedro de Cordoba *(Old Turk)*, Frank Puglia *(Syrian Vendor)*, Steve Geray *(Raeder)*, Curt Furberg *(Von Popen)*, Frank Reicher *(Rudick)*, Jean De Briac, George Renavent, Paul Porcasi, Demetris Emanuel, Michael Mark, Kurt Krueger, Ray Miller, William Netter, Otto Reichow, Charles Irwin, Antonio Samaniego, Irene Seidner, Lisa Golm, Manart Kippen, William Edmunds, William Vaughn, Nestor Paiva, Charles La Torre, Lou Marcelle, Dave Kashner.

American agent Raft, pretending to be a machinery salesman, travels to Turkey via train where he meets sophisticated Massen who thrusts secret documents on him before she is murdered in an Ankara hotel room adjoining his. The envelope she has entrusted to him contains oddly marked maps; just after she hides them, agents burst into Raft's room and take him at gunpoint to see Nazi master spy Greenstreet who demands the maps which show where German troops will invade Turkey, just after that neutral government has been alienated from its unofficial ally, Russia, through another series of plots. When Raft refuses to turn over anything, he is mercilessly beaten but before Nazi goons kill him he is rescued by Lorre and his sister Marshall, who tell him they are Russian agents, also seeking the maps. But Raft no longer has them; they have been stolen by Greenstreet's agents. The American invades the fat spy's lavish estate where he finds Lorre and Marshall held prisoner. Raft manages to free himself and Marshall from the Nazi clutches with the help of Lorre, who sacrifices himself so they can escape at the last minute. A curve-slicing car chase ensues with Raft racing after Greenstreet, catching him, compelling him to destroy the secret plans, then sending him on his way back to Berlin where all know he will be imprisoned, perhaps executed, for his failure. The fat man goes off, wincing at his fate and Raft, with Marshall on his arm, "cements Russian-American relations" by heading for Cairo. The film is quick-paced and properly moody in lensing, having all the ambiance of an Eric Ambler thriller, this being his second spy book to be converted to the screen (albeit the first, JOURNEY INTO FEAR, is a far superior production). The story is confusing at times, and bogs down in the middle, where it's difficult to tell who is spying for what country, but the presence of the volatile Lorre and the sneaky Greenstreet, the most perfect pair of rascally spies, overshadows the occasional lassitudes. Raft is very good as the American agent, though he at times seems colorless, but then he has to contend with fascinating scene stealers Greenstreet and Lorre. Ironically, this film was made as a follow-up to Warner Bros.' immensely popular CASABLANCA: Raft had originally turned down the role Bogart played in that classic and when he tried to duplicate Bogie's character, he and BACKGROUND TO DANGER fell short of the success of its predecessor.

p, Jerry Wald; d, Raoul Walsh; w, W. R. Burnett (based on the novel *Uncommon Danger* by Eric Ambler); ph, Tony Gaudio; m, Frederick Hollander; ed, Jack Killifer; md, Leo F. Forbstein; art d, Hugh Reticker; set d, Casey Roberts; spec eff, Warren Lynch, Willard Van Enger.

Spy Drama   **(PR:A MPAA:NR)**

BACKLASH*   (1947) 66m FOX bw

Jean Rogers (*Catherine Morland*), Richard Travis (*Richard Conroy*), Larry Blake (*Lt. Jerry McMullen*), John Eldridge (*John Morland*), Leonard Strong (*The Stranger*), Robert Shayne (*James O'Neil*), Louise Currie (*Marian Gordon*), Douglas Fowley (*Red Bailey*), Sara Berner (*Dorothy*), Richard Benedict (*Det. Sgt. Tom Carey*), Wynne Larke (*Pat McMullen*), Susan Klimist (*Maureen*).

Perplexing murder mystery about an attorney, Eldridge, who picks up a murderous hitchhiker. The good Samaritan becomes the suspect in a murder case himself when an estrangement from his wife and some bad business dealings cast suspicion on him. Two detectives, Blake and Travis, sift through the clues and interrogate all the suspects as they slowly weave their way into a series of flashbacks which become unnecessarily slow and complicated. Strange structure ruins an otherwise interesting narrative.

p, Sol M. Wurtzel; d, Eugene Forde; w, Irving Elman; ph, Benjamin Kline; m, Darrell Calker; ed, William F. Claxton.

Mystery   **(PR:A MPAA:NR)**

BACKLASH*   (1956) 83m UNIV c

Richard Widmark (*Jim Slater*), Donna Reed (*Karyl Orton*), William Campbell (*Johnny Cool*), John McIntire (*Jim Bonniwell*), Barton MacLane (*George Lake*), Edward Platt (*Sheriff Marson*), Harry Morgan (*Tony Welker*), Bob Wilke (*Jeff Welker*), Reg Parton (*Tom Welker*), Robert Foulk (*Sheriff Olson*), Phil Chambers (*Dobbs*), Gregg Barton (*Sleepy*), Fred Graham (*Ned McCloud*), Frank Chase (*Cassidy*).

John Sturges, who directed some of the best outdoors epics ever (BAD DAY AT BLACK ROCK, THE GREAT ESCAPE, GUNFIGHT AT THE O.K. CORRAL, THE MAGNIFICENT SEVEN) should have looked more closely at the script Aaron Rosenberg, former USC football star and producer of many interesting films (TONY ROME, WINCHESTER 73, THE GREAT MAN, THE GLENN MILLER STORY), missed when he put this one together for Universal. Widmark is a gunman searching for his father, McIntire, who sold out five of his pals to attacking Indians, then escaped with a trove of $60,000 in gold with which he built a career as a rustler. Reed is the widow of one of the dead men. She and Widmark join forces to get to the truth and they wind up together. McIntire is excellent as the villain. Morgan, Wilke and Parton are quite unlikely as three brothers. They are so different in size, shape, and facial characteristics that it's hard to believe someone actually cast them. Morgan, whose real name is Henry, changed it to Harry shortly after THE OX-BOW INCIDENT because he didn't want to be confused with Henry Morgan, the radio comedian, who starred in SO THIS IS NEW YORK. Henry Morgan ran into trouble with an ex-wife and exiled himself from New York, dropping in occasionally to do TV game shows. Harry Morgan has gone on to do many TV series ("Pete and Gladys," "Dragnet," "M*A*S*H," among others) and hasn't stopped working since.

p, Aaron Rosenberg; d, John Sturges; w, Borden Chase (based on the novel by Frank Gruber); ph, Irving Glassberg (Technicolor); m, Herman Stein; ed, Sherman Todd; cos, Rosemary Odell.

Western   **(PR:A MPAA:NR)**

BACKSTAGE*   (1937, Brit.) 65m GAU bw

Anna Neagle (*Marjorie Kaye*), Arthur Tracy (*Bob Grant*), Jane Winton (*Ray Madison*), Ellis Jeffreys (*Lady Madeleine*), Muriel George (*Mrs. Kaye*), Alexander Field (*Alf Sparkes*), Antony Holles (*Impresario*), William Freshman (*Joe*), Helena Pickard (*Pixie*), Queenie Leonard (*Queenie*), Ralph Reader (*Ralph*).

Street singer is discovered by British chorus girl. The American singer gets an opportunity to pinch hit for the ailing vocal star of the show and becomes an overnight success. Will success spoil Arthur Tracy? Well, almost. Routine yarn with some nice musical numbers.

p&d, Herbert Wilcox; w, Laura Whetter; ph, F. A. Young; m/l, Harry Woods.

Musical   **(PR:A MPAA:NR)**

BACKTRACK*   (1969) 95m UNIV c

Neville Brand (*Reese*), James Drury (*Ramrod*), Doug McClure (*Trampas*), Peter Brown (*Chad*), William Smith (*Riley*), Philip Carey (*Capt. Parmalee*), Fernando Lamas (*Capt. Estrada*), Rhonda Fleming (*Carmelita*), Ida Lupino (*Madame Dolores*), Royal Dano (*Faraway*), Gary Clark (*Steve*), Randy Boone (*Randy*).

This picture was originally made for TV as a "Virginian" episode that introduced the characters from another Universal series, "Laredo." However, it was released as a feature. Chase, a first-rate western writer (RED RIVER, LONE STAR, MONTANA) did the script for this saga of McClure being sent to Mexico by Drury (in a very small role) to get a bull. During the trip he gets involved with the Texas Rangers and helps them as they find a train that has been robbed with everyone aboard having been murdered, except for a tiny baby. The picture takes off from there with action every few minutes, encounters with perfidious villains (Lamas is terrific as a Mexican captain who can't be trusted any farther than you can throw a taco), attractive women (Fleming is the tough owner of a saloon), and Lupino gloriously overplaying as a south-of-the- border widow with a passion for Brand (who was the fourth most decorated soldier in WW II). Other good performances by Dano and Smith, perhaps the slimmest and the most muscular character men in the business, in that order.

p, David J. O'Connell; d, Earl Bellamy; w, Borden Chase; ph, Richard H. Kline, John Russell, Andrew Jackson; m, Jack Marshall; ed, Michael R. McAdam, art d, George Patrick, Howard E. Johnson.

Western   **(PR:A MPAA:G)**

BAD AND THE BEAUTIFUL, THE***   (1952) 116m MGM bw

Lana Turner (*Georgia Lorrison*), Kirk Douglas (*Jonathan Shields*), Walter Pidgeon (*Harry Pebbel*), Dick Powell (*James Lee Bartlow*), Barry Sullivan (*Fred Amiel*), Gloria Grahame (*Rosemary Bartlow*), Gilbert Roland (*Victor "Gaucho" Ribera*), Leo G. Carroll (*Henry Whitfield*), Vanessa Brown (*Kay Amiel*), Paul Stewart (*Syd Murphy*), Sammy White (*Gus*), Elaine Stewart (*Lila*), Ivan Triesault (*Von Ellstein*), Kathleen Freeman (*Miss March*), Jonathan Cott (*Assistant Director*), Marietta Canty (*Ida*), Lucille Knoch (*Blonde*), Steve Forrest (*Leading Man*), Perry Sheehan (*Secretary*), Francis X. Bushman (*Eulogist*), Robert Burton (*McDill*), George Lewis (*Actor in Screen Test*), William "Bill" Phillips (*Assistant Director*), Madge Blake (*Mrs. Rosser*), Stanley Andrews (*Sheriff*), Dorothy Patrick (*Arlene*), Karen Verne (*Rosa*), Peggy King (*Singer*), Ben Astar (*Joe*), Bess Flowers (*Joe's Friend at Party*), Dee Turnell (*Linda*), Louis Calhern (*Voice on the Recording*), Harold Miller, Alyce May, Frank Scannell, Dabbs Greer, William Tannen, Sara Spencer, Barbara Thatcher, Sharon Saunders, Erwin Selwyn, Norman Salina, Kathy Qualen.

The quintessential movie on the movies, this film is graced with performances that approach and/or capture perfection from all the leads. Three separate stories revolve around Douglas, a complex, creative and charming producer whose cunning charac- ter and ruthless ways allow him to climb to the top of the Hollywood heap. The film opens with three Hollywood greats, Turner, Powell, and Sullivan, visiting the deserted studios of Douglas for a nocturnal meeting with his production chief Pidgeon. They are asked to star, write, and direct Douglas' next movie, a blockbuster that will get his studio out of hock. Douglas will be making a conference call from Europe any moment to tell them about it, Pidgeon says. The three, who all hate Douglas, are about to walk out, but Pidgeon persuades them to remain until they hear the studio boss out. While waiting for the transatlantic call each remembers in flashback the devastating personal experiences with the wildly ambitious Douglas. Sullivan opens with a burial scene. In a rainswept graveyard, Douglas attends his father's funeral; the dead man's awful reputation causes one of the spectators, Sullivan, to pass critical remarks about him which Douglas overhears. He later refuses to pay Sullivan, a fledgling director, the professional mourner's fee he doles out to the crowd. The director visits Douglas later at the deserted Hollywood mansion once occupied by his father to apologize. They become friends and go to work for B-film producer Pidgeon, one of the few friends of Douglas' father. Douglas produces and Sullivan directs a clunker called *The Cat Men* which, through innovative techniques, becomes a smash hit. The pair go on to make several successful B movies until Douglas wangles a major film out of Pidgeon, but on the proviso that he produce it with a major director, Triesault; he promptly deserts friend Sullivan who later becomes a top director on his own. A firmly entrenched big shot who now heads Pidgeon's poverty-row-studio-turned-giant, Douglas notices in a screen test a blonde extra, Turner, the alcoholic, loose-living daughter of a dead silent-screen star. He reforms her, grooms her for stardom, and makes her a top actress. Turner falls in love with Douglas but, after her first big hit, unexpectedly visits his mansion to find him with another woman, vampy Stewart. Douglas goes into a rage, rejecting her. Hysterical, Turner drives madly away, almost killing herself when her car goes out of control. In the last segment, Douglas convinces author Powell to adapt his popular novel for the screen, moving him and southern belle wife, Grahame, to Hollywood. To prevent her from interfering with Powell and the script he so desperately wants, Douglas has leading man Gilbert seduce Grahame, taking her on a tete-a-tete plane trip. The small plane crashes in the mountains, killing Gilbert and Grahame. Douglas becomes Powell's pillar of support while getting him to finish the script, but then later slips, remarking how he had warned Gilbert not to take the plane with Powell's wife, an affair he earlier denied knowing about. Powell knocks Douglas down and goes off to become a top screenwriter. At film's end Douglas calls Pidgeon's office from Europe to talk to the three persons he has wounded most in life, asking them all to join him on one last magnificent production. They sneer, laugh, and begin to walk out, but are drawn magnetically to the voice describing the wonderful project, each going to the phone, snaring the receiver, listening, fascinated, ready. This film has kept buffs guessing as to the real-life identities of the leading players. Some believe that Douglas' role model was Val Lewton, the extravagant, driving producer of mini-horror films of the 1940s that have become cult classics. Since Lewton made CAT PEOPLE and Douglas produces THE CAT MEN in the film, the identifications are established. But the character is really based upon mogul David O. Selznick, whose father Lewis J. Selznick was an early Hollywood mogul battling giants Adolph Zukor (PAR) and Louis B. Mayer (MGM) into bankruptcy. The parallels between the Douglas character and Selznick are unmistakable, particularly his beginnings as a B film producer (Selznick worked in this capacity at MGM), his grooming of star Jennifer Jones who later became Selznick's wife, and his making of a colossal Civil War film which, of course, was Selznick's production of GONE WITH THE WIND. Although Selznick was never as ruthless as the Douglas character, he was certainly as involved with every aspect of production as is Douglas, making decisions from expensive sets to sequins on the gowns of extras. Selznick's fortune was literally made on the back of Louis B. Mayer. It was Mayer who was chiefly instrumental in destroying the career of Selznick's father and his hatred for the elder Selznick lingered long. After giving the young David a job in his studio's B-film division, mostly out of guilt, Mayer learned that his daughter Irene was seeing the fledgling producer. "Keep away from that schnook," Mayer told his daughter. "He'll be a bum just like his old man!" (As quoted from *The Moguls* by Norman Zierold.) The Pidgeon part of Harry Pebbel is most certainly based upon the cost-conscious B-production chief at MGM, Harry Rapf, for whom Selznick first went to work. Pidgeon's oft-stated remark: "Give me pictures that end with a kiss and black ink on the books" is straight out of Rapf's penny-pinching philosophy. Schnee's sharp script, which acutely profiles every type of Hollywood character, from the grubbing agent to the mighty mogul, prototypes Turner's role with easy identification, that of Diana Barrymore, the tragedy-struck daughter of the Great Profile, John Barrymore. More "inside" ploys were used in the production; Turner's own makeup man and hairdresser, Del Armstrong and Helen Young, appear in the film in their real-life roles, as does Alyce My, Turner's regular stand-in. Cost-conscious MGM used many sets from its previous productions for this film, showing them in their naked construction, such as the sweeping staircase used earlier in Turner's MERRY WIDOW. The Powell role, an excellent understated profile, is best identified with the writer F. Scott Fitzgerald, whose romance of Hollywood turned sour and who was also married to a Southern belle (Zelda Sayre Fitzgerald, who died not in a plane crash but in a raging fire consuming an insane asylum where she was being treated). For Douglas, the role of mogul Jonathan Shields was a tour de force seldom equalled by this captivating actor. Turner, also, gives one of her finest performances, particularly in the absolutely riveting scene where her car goes out of control, a masterpiece of lensing by Surtees and direction by Minnelli, his finest film. Driving wildly from her lover's mansion, Turner begins sobbing as the camera closes in on her anguished face. She becomes hysterical, screaming, shrieking out her pain as she lets loose the wheel, her ermine-wrapped body quivering, the car going out of control, turning dizzily while horns honk and lights from other cars shoot like lightning bolts through the car's windows. For this Minnelli had a special machine built which spun the car while the camera remained steady, zooming in and out to capture the frenetic scene which builds to a crescendo, suddenly halted when Turner, in a final lunge for life, jams her foot down on the brake. It is truly one of the great cinematic highlights in the history of film, capturing despair, fear and futility in an unforgettable scene that will wrench the heart and etch the mind of any viewer. Raksin's stirring, moody score is superb. The sets by Willis and Gleason, especially in the roomy, dust-laden Loring and Shields mansions, the movie lots, sets and studio offices, totally reflect the Hollywood that is no more but which is now forever preserved in this always fascinating classic.

p, John Houseman; d, Vincente Minnelli: w, Charles Schnee (based on a story by George Bradshaw); ph, Robert Surtees; m, David Raksin; ed, Conrad A. Nervig; art d, Cedric Gibbons, Edward Carfagno; set d, Edwin B. Willis, Keogh Gleason; cos, Helen Rose; spec eff, A. Arnold Gillespie, Warren Newcombe; makeup, William Tuttle.

Drama **(PR:C MPAA:NR)**

BAD BASCOMB 1/2** (1946) 111m MGM bw

Wallace Beery *(Zeb Bascomb)*, Margaret O'Brien *(Emmy)*, Marjorie Main *(Abbey Hanks)*, J. Carrol Naish *(Bart Yancy)*, Frances Rafferty *(Dora)*, Marshall Thompson *(Jimmy Holden)*, Russell Simpson *(Elijah Walker)*, Warner Anderson *(Luther Mason)*, Donald Curtis *(John Fulton)*, Connie Gilchrist *(Annie Freemont)*, Sara Haden *(Tillie Lovejoy)*, Renio Riano *(Lucy Lovejoy)*, Jane Green *(Hanna)*, Henry O'Neill *(Gov. Winton)*, Frank Darien *(Elder McCabe)*, Joseph Crehan *(Gov. Ames)*, Clyde Fillmore *(Gov. Clark)*, Arthur Space *(Sheriff)*, Eddie Acuff *(Corporal)*, Stanley Andrews *(Col. Cartright)*.

A bankrobber, Beery, and his partner, Naish, hide out among a group of Mormon settlers on their way to Utah. On the trail Beery develops a fatherly affection for a little orphan girl, O'Brien, who makes him realize the errors of his ways. The Mormons look up to the robber and he becomes their involuntary leader during an indian attack. Through Naish would like to grab the Mormon's gold and ride off, he too respects the group and gives up any thought of thievery. Typically corny "good bad man" story helped by good performances from Beery, O'Brien and Naish.

p, Orville O. Dull; d, S. Sylvan Simon; w, William Lipman, Grant Carrett (based on a story by D. A. Loxley); ph, Charles Schoenbaum; ed, Ben Lewis.

Western **(PR:AA MPAA:NR)**

BAD BLONDE* 1/2 (1953, Brit.) 80m Lippert bw

Barbara Payton *(Lorna Vecchi)*, Frederick Valk *(Guiseppe Vecchi)*, John Slater *(Charlie)*, Sidney James *(Sharkey)*, Tony Wright *(Johnny Flanagan)*, Marie Burke *(Mrs. Vecchi)*, Selma Vaz Dias *(Mrs. Corelli)*, Enzo Coticchia *(Corelli)*, George Woodbridge *(Inspector)*, Bettina Dickson *(Barmaid)*, John Brooking *(Parnes)*.

Barbara Payton, who starred in the newpapers as often as she did in movies, headlines this weak melodrama made in England. Payton is the knockout spouse of Valk, a heavyweight prizefight manager. Valk handles Wright, who turns the lady on. She tells the young palooka that she's pregnant and that they have to get rid of her husband. They do this by drowning him. His mother suspects the worst and confronts Payton, who admits that she is not expecting. Wright can't take the pressure and confesses. Payton, living up to the title of the film, kills him with poison. Picture smacks of truth, though, with a bit of the 1927 Snyder-Gray case and few others as background. Handled by a different production team and cast with different stars, this might have made some noise.

p, Anthony Hinds; d, Reginald LeBorg; w, Guy Elmes, Richard Landau (based on the novel by Max Catto); ph, Walter Harvey; m, Ivor Slaney; ed, James Needs.

Drama **(PR:C MPAA:NR)**

BAD BOY* (1935) 56m FOX bw

James Dunn *(Eddie Nolan)*, Dorothy Wilson *(Sally Larkin)*, Louise Fazenda *(Mrs. Harris)*, Victor Kilian *(Sid)*, John Wray *(Fred Larkin)*, Luis Alberni *(Tony)*, Beulah Bondi *(Mrs. Larkin)*, Allen Vincent *(Bob Carey)*.

Dull-witted comedy concerning Dunn as an aimless pool shark trying to become respectable so that he can marry his girl, Wilson. He makes the mistake of hustling a businessman on his lunch hour, who turns out to be the girl's father. All ends well when the kids helps out with the arrest of a couple of gangsters. Some forgettable songs are thrown in for good measure.

p, Edward Butcher; d, John Blystone; w, Alan Rivkin (based on a story by Vina Delmar); ph, Bert Glennon; md, Arthur Lange; m/l, Lew Pollack, Paul Webber.

Musical/Comedy **(PR:A MPAA:NR)**

BAD BOY* 1/2 (1938, Brit.) 69m Radius bw (AKA: BRANDED)

John Warwick *(Nick Bryan)*, John Longden *(Inspector Thompson)*, Kathleen Kelly *(Ann Travers)*, Gabrielle Brune *(Ena Bryan)*, Brian Buchel *(Tony Santell)*, Richard Norris *(Joe Morgan)*, Edie Martin *(Mrs. Bryan)*, Ernest Sefton *(Sam Barnes)*.

Ex-convict trying to reform rescues his sister from the clutches of his old crime boss. Routine histrionics with a pat story and dull dialog.

p, Vaughan N. Dean; d&w, Lawrence Huntington (based on a story by R. Astley Richards); ph, Stanley Grant.

Crime Drama **(PR:A MPAA:NR)**

BAD BOY* (1939) 56m Atlas/Gateway bw (GB: PERILOUS JOURNEY)

Johnny Downs *(John Fraser)*, Rosalind Keith *(Madelin Kirby)*, Helen MacKellar *(Mrs. Fraser)*, Spencer Williams Jr. *(Terry)*, James Robbins *(Steve Carson)*, Holmes Herbert *(Mr. McNeil)*, Dick Cramer *(George)*, Harry Lang *(Vanetti)*.

Absurd crime drama stars Downs as a hard-working architect who becomes a gangster chief because of his wild night-life activities and penchant for the ponies. Robbins plays the crooked co-worker who ensnares Downs into a life of crime by preying on his weaknesses. Doltish premise and lack of decent stars make this pretty hard to sit through.

d, Herbert Meyer; w, Richard C. Kahn; ph, Jack Greenhalgh; ed, Ray Luby.

Crime **(PR:A MPAA:NR)**

BAD BOY* 1/2 (1949) 85m AA/MON bw

Lloyd Nolan *(Marshall Brown)*, Jane Wyatt *(Mrs. Marshall Brown)*, Audie Murphy *(Danny Lester)*, James Gleason *(The Chief)*, Stanley Clements *(Bitsy)*, Martha Vickers *(Lila Strawn)*, Rhys Williams *(Arnold Strawn)*, James Lydon *(Ted Hendry)*, Dickie Moore *(Charlie)*, Selena Royle *(Judge Prentiss)*, Tommy Cook *(Floyd)*, William Lester *(Joe Shields)*, Walter Sande *(Texas Oil Man)*, Stephen Chase *(Sheriff Wells)*, Charles Trowbridge *(Dr. Fletcher)*, Francis Pierlot *(Mr. Pardee)*, Florence Auer *(Mrs. Meechan)*, George Beban *(Bell Captain)*, BIll Walker *(Ollie)*, Barbara Woodell *(Mrs. Strawn)*.

Earnest attempt at depicting the work done by the Boy's Club ranch at Copperas Cove, Texas. The story is simple: a bad boy (Murphy in his first major role, four years after having been *the* hero of WW II) gets some heavy time after an armed robbery. They turn him over to the guys at Copperas Cove, figuring they might be able to rehabilitate him. It doesn't work, so they do further research and learn that his antisocial behavior is mainly due to a mistaken belief that he was responsible for the death of his mother, and Murphy is saved. Not a bad film, though a bit thick on the moralizing. Nolan and Wyatt, as the folks who run the farm, do a fine job and Clements almost steals the movie with his winning comedic ways. Moore, who went on to write a book about his youth in the movies that ruffled a lot of feathers, and Lydon (HENRY ALDRICH, LIFE WITH FATHER, many more) are excellent as other juvenile delinquents. Cook, on the other hand, is his customary dull self. Gleason as The Chief is perfect.

p, Paul Short; d, Kurt Neumann; w, Robert Hardy Andrews (based on a story by Andrews, Short); ph, Karl Struss; m, Paul Sawtell; ed, William Austin.

Crime Drama **(PR:A MPAA:NR)**

BAD BOYS***   (1983) 123m EMI/UNIV-Associated Film Distributors c

Sean Penn (Mick), Reni Santoni (Pramon Herrera), Esai Morales (Paco), Jim Moody (Gene Daniels), Eric Gurry (Horowitz), Clancy Brown (Viking), Ally Sheedy (J. C. Walenski), Robert Lee Rush (Tweety), John Zenda (Wagner).

Production credits are sometimes longer than the film, but not in the case of this 123-minute opus that may go too long for its own good. This is THE BLACK-BOARD JUNGLE of the 1980s in that it's just as searing and gut-wrenching as the breakthrough picture was in the 1950s. Penn stars as an angry young juvenile delinquent who, after a series of incidents and crimes, is thrown into the slammer where his mates are the scum of the earth. Writer Dilello and director Rosenthal have collaborated for excellent results. Penn soon becomes top dog in this kennel, but his reign is short-lived when an old enemy rapes Penn's girl friend on the outside and is sent to the same prison. The battle commences. BAD BOYS is disturbing, sometimes annoying, often painful, and never boring. The makers have taken a difficult subject, infused it with interesting people, some wit and a lot of careful thought. As in any film that attempts to make a broad statement, BAD BOYS has occasional forays that lead nowhere but, on balance, it's a fair work that takes the subject seriously without taking itself pedantically.

p, Robert Solo; d, Richard Rosenthal; w, Richard Dilello; ph, Bruce Surtees, Donald Thorin (Technicolor); m, Bill Conti; ed, Antony Gibbs; prod d, J. Michael Riva.

Drama   **Cas.**   **(PR:O MPAA:R)**

BAD CHARLESTON CHARLIE zero   (1973) 91m International Cinema c

Ross Hagen (Charlie Jocobs), Kelly Thordsen (Thad), Hoke Howell (Claude), Dal Jenkins (Ku Klux Klan Leader), Carmen Zapata (Lottie), Mel Berger (Fat Police Chief), John Carradine (Reporter), Ken Lynch (Sheriff Koontz), John Dalk (Promoter), Tony Lorea (Criminal).

Rancid period-piece gangster comedy with a cast of no-names. Hagen and Thordsen are two bumbling coal miners who turn into equally inept big-time gangsters. Carradine is the only recognizable face in the picture and it is said to have been his 401st movie. He should have quit at 400. Incompetent director Nagy made a living in still photography before this mistake.

p, Ross Hagen; d, Ivan Nagy; w, Hagen, Nagy, Stan Kamber; ph, Michael Neyman (Eastmancolor); m, Luchi DeJesus; ed, Walter Thompson, Richard Garritt; art d, Raymond Markam.

Comedy   **(PR:A MPAA:PG)**

BAD COMPANY*   (1931) 65m Pathe/RKO bw

Helen Twelvetrees (Helen), Ricardo Cortez (Goldie Gorio), John Garrick (Steve), Paul Hurst(Butler), Frank Conroy (Markham King), Frank McHugh (Doc), Edgar Kennedy (Buff), Kenneth Thompson (Barnes), Emma Dunn (Emma), William V. Mong (Henry), Wade Boteler (Monk), Al Iteman (Pearson), Harry Carey, Sr. (McBaine), Robert Keith (Professor).

Moll, mobsters, and a mundane tale of racketeering in the 1930s. The audience is expected to believe that girl has no idea she is mixed up with a bunch of bad guys. Pure hokum.

p, Charles R. Rogers; d, Tay Garnett; w, Garnett, Thomas Buckingham (based on a story by Jack Lait); ph, Arthur Miller; ed, Claude Berkeley; md, Arthur Lange.

Crime Drama   **(PR:A MPAA:NR)**

BAD COMPANY*   (1972) 93m PAR c

Jeff Bridges (Jake Rumsey), Barry Brown (Drew Dixon), Jim Davis (Marshal), David Huddleston (Big Joe), John Savage (Loney), Jerry Houser (Arthur Simms), Damon Cofer (Jim Bob Logan), Joshua Hill Lewis (Boog Bookin), Charles Tyner (Farmer), Geoffrey Lewis, Raymond Guth, Edward Lauter (Big Joe's Gang), Jean Allison, Ned Wertimer (Dixon's Parents), Ted Gehring (Zeb), Claudia Bryar (Mrs. Clum), John Boyd (Prisoner), Monika Henried (Min), Todd Martin (Sergeant).

Draft-dodging is evidently an old American custom, according to thjis screenplay by Benton and Newman. BAD COMPANY is a comedy-drama about the Civil War equivalent of the Viet Nam protesters. Instead of going north to Canada, these young men wend their ways west. Bridges, Brown, Houser, Cofer, Savage, and Lewis are a bunch of young easterners who drift out beyond the Mississippi and encounter several adventures. A segmented movie, BAD COMPANY manages to sustain interest by deft direction and an intelligent screenplay. The movie shows the down side of the Old West, deprivation, the cold, the murders, and very little of the dime-novel glamor that young men read about in their gaslit Manhattan rooms. It's a mixture of comedy and drama and when it's funny, it's terrific. Ed Lauter and Geoffrey Lewis stepped out and made names for themselves after this movie but Huddleston got involved in TV and starred and produced one of the worst television shows ever made, a turkey on NBC about a Mayor called "Hizzoner."

p, Stanley R. Jaffe; d, Robert Benton; w, David Newman, Benton; ph, Gordon Willis (Technicolor); m, Harvey Schmidt; ed, Ralph Rosenblum; art d, Robert Gundlach; set d, Audrey Blaisdel.

Drama   **(PR:A MPAA:NR)**

BAD DAY AT BLACK ROCK***   (1955) 81m MGM c

Spencer Tracy (John J. MacReedy), Robert Ryan (Reno Smith), Anne Francis (Liz Wirth), Dean Jagger (Tim Horn), Walter Brennan (Doc Velie), John Ericson (Pete Wirth),Ernest Borgnine (Coley Trimble), Lee Marvin (Hector David), Russell Collins (Mr. Hastings), Walter Sande (Sam).

A powerful, lightning-paced film where Tracy, in another tour de force, arrives at a broken-down little town straddling the Santa Fe tracks, shocking the dozen or so grubby inhabitants who have not seen the Super Chief stop in four years. The one-armed stranger goes to the local hotel where he asks the whereabouts of a Japanese farmer. As soon as Tracy utters the name of "Komoko" hotel owner Ericson

freezes, telling him there are no vacancies. Tracy sees a number of room keys and helps himself, but is ousted from his room by local lout Marvin, one of the thugs working for town boss and landowner Ryan. Meekly, Tracy moves to another room, then continues asking where he might find the Japanese farmer. (The Japanese were still not popular in the U.S., particularly in this time setting of late 1945, just after the end of WW II.) Jagger, the alcoholic town sheriff and Ryan appointee, tells Tracy nothing, but he learns the whereabouts of Komoko's farm from local doctor Brennan and rents a jeep from Francis, going to the site and finding an unmarked grave. By the time he returns to town, he realizes that he will never leave Black Rock alive; his death has been decreed by Ryan. In one harrowing scene, Tracy is driven off the road by Borgnine who repeatedly rams his car into the jeep. Beer gut Borgnine next provokes a fight in a local beanery. Tracy, sitting on a stool and about to eat a bowl of chili, is approached by the bully boy who tells him he's sitting on his stool. Tracy moves. Next Borgnine spices up Tracy's chili by dumping an entire bottle of catsup into it. Tracy pushes the bowl away, still refusing to fight. Then Borgnine calls him a coward and the one-armed man explodes in an incredible display of judo, first cutting off Borgnine's breath with a neck chop,and, when the lumbering thug charges him, Tracy flips him one-armed through the diner's screen door. Borgnine staggers to his feet and lunges once more, this time twisted up and around until he thuds to the floor, a physical wreck. The judo display leaves Marvin and the others awestruck, but Tracy is still marked for death. He cannot call state police since the phones are closed to him, as is the telegraph. Ryan confronts him, asking him what he wants in the town. A psychopath, Ryan raves about outsiders coming to Black Rock looking for "the old West, the wild West, the undeveloped West . . . why don't they leave us alone?" Tracy quips: "Leave you alone to do what?" Ryan, learning that Tracy lost his arm in the war ("That's tough"), tells how he tried to enlist right after Pearl Harbor but that he was rejected as 4-F. He also reveals his psychopathic hatred for all Japanese, including dirt-farmer Komoko. Tracy learns later that, in a drunken fit of super-patriotism, Ryan, Borgnine, Marvin, and others tried to scare off the farmer, then killed him and secretly buried his body. Before Tracy can be murdered, he is helped by Brennan and Ericson to subdue Marvin, then drives to a secluded spot with Francis to face down Ryan. Francis, who has set up Tracy, stalls the jeep, then runs toward her lover Ryan who kills her for "knowing too much." Ryan begins firing at the jeep and the seemingly helpless Tracy, who slips to the ground, fills an empty bottle with gas, stuffs his tie into the neck and lights it, a Molotov cocktail which he hurls at Ryan, who catches fire and collapses in agony. Before leaving town, Tracy explains to Brennan that he has come to Black Rock to give a medal to Komoko; the farmer's dead son was a war hero and was responsible for saving Tracy's life. Brennan asks that the medal be left with the town. Tracy agrees, then leaves on the Super Chief. Tracy is at his subdued, confident best, Ryan perfectly oozes xenophobia, Borgnine and Marvin are their most hateful. Sturges' direction is superbly timed and Kaufman's literate script was so memorable that many of its lines quickly passed into public use.

p, Dore Schary; d, John Sturges; w, Millard Kaufman (based on a story by Howard Breslin); ph, William C. Mellor (CinemaScope, Eastmancolor); m, Andre Previn; ed, Newell P. Kimlin; art d, Cedric Gibbons, Malcolm Brown; set d, Edwin B. Willis, Fred MacLean.

Crime Drama   **(PR:A MPAA:NR)**

BAD FOR EACH OTHER*   (1954) 83m COl bw

Charlton Heston (Dr. Tom Owen), Lizabeth Scott (Helen Curtis), Dianne Foster (Joan Lasher), Mildred Dunnock (Mrs. Mary Owen), Arthur Franz (Dr. Jim Crowley), Ray Collins (Dan Reasonover), Marjorie Rambeau (Mrs. Roger Nelson), Lester Matthews (Dr. Homer Gleeson), Rhys Williams (Doc Scobee), Lydia Clarke (Rita Thornburg), Cris Alcaide (Pete Olzoneski), Robert Keys (Joe Marzano), Frank Tully (Tippy Kashdo), Ann Robinson (Lucille Grettett), Dorothy Green (Ada Nicoletti).

BAD FOR EACH OTHER may be harmful to your health. A real bore fashioned from Horace McCoy's story "Scalpel," it tells of Heston (who has never been stiffer or more self-righteous) having to choose between a career as a society doctor or doing what he was trained to do: helping people. He opts for money and the wiles of Lizabeth Scott. (It is rumored that the "E" which Scott no longer has in her name was sold, early in her career, to comedian Joe E. Lewis who did not have a middle initial of his own.) Late in the movie, Heston renounces his love of Mammon and decides to aid the miners who have been trapped in the usual cave-in. It should go without saying that there's another altruistic nurse hanging around who will help Heston through the bends of giving up his lucrative practice and becoming a doctor of the people again. Some excellent character actors are totally wasted in this film, notably Williams, Collins and the always-believable Dunnock.

p, William Fadiman; d, Irving Rapper; w, Irving Wallace, Horace McCoy (based on the novel by McCoy); ph, Franz Planer; m, Mischa Bakaleinikoff; ed, Al Clark.

Drama   **(PR:A MPAA:NR)**

BAD GIRL*   (1931) 90m FOX bw

Sally Eilers (Dorothy Haley), James Dunn (Eddie Collins), Minna Gombell (Edna Driggs), William Pawley (Jim Haley), Frank Darien (Lathrop).

Adaptation of a play tells the story of a young woman, Eilers, who meets a young man, Dunn, on a Coney Island boat, goes home with him, and is indiscreet enough to conceive a child out of wedlock. The couple marry one step ahead of the obstetrician. Dunn must give up his life-long dream of owning his own radio store to provide for his new bride and child. He even goes so far as to enter himself in a boxing match to win $40 to pay the doctor bills. Pretty sappy stuff.

d, Frank Borzage; w, Edwin Burke (based on the novel and the play by Vina Delmar); ph, Chester Lyons; ed, Margaret Clancy.

Melodrama   **(PR:C MPAA:NR)**

BAD GIRL, 1959 (SEE: TEENAGE BAD GIRL, 1959, Brit.)

BAD GUY* 1/2 (1937) 64m MGM bw

Bruce Cabot (*Lucky Walden*), Virginia Grey (*Kitty*), Edward Norris (*Steve Carroll*), Jean Chatburn (*Betty*), Cliff Edwards (*Hi-Line*), Charley Grapewin (*Dan Grey*), Warren Hymer (*Shorty*), John Hamilton (*Warden*), Clay Clement (*Bronson*).

Story of two brothers, Cabot and Norris, who work at a power plant. Cabot is the misguided sibling who is sent to prison for murdering a local gambler. He convinces Dunn to help him break out of the hoosegow by applying high-voltage electricity to the prison's iron bars. The plan fails when Cabot is forced into contact with the juice and is fried to a crisp. Somewhat silly tale is bogged down by lengthy sequences showing the two brothers dealing with all manner of electrical problems on the job.

d, Edward Cahn; w, Earl Felton (based on the story "High Voltage" by J. Robert Bren, Kathleen Shepard, Hal Long); ph, Lester White; m, Edward Ward; ed, Ben Lewis.

Drama (PR:A MPAA:NR)

BAD LANDS** 1/2 (1939) 70m RKO bw

Robert Barrat (*Sheriff*), Noah Beery Jr. (*Chile Lyman*), Guinn "Big Boy" Williams (*Billy Sweet*), Douglas Walton (*Mulford*), Andy Clyde (*Cliff*), Addison Richards (*Rayburn*), Robert Coote (*Eaton*), Paul Hurst (*Curley Tom*), Francis Ford (*Garth*), Francis McDonald (*Manuel Lopez*).

Saga of an uneasy posse, led by Barrat, which goes into the Arizona desert in hot pursuit of a group of marauding Indians. The men become trapped in the middle of nowhere and begin to succumb, one-by-one, to the blistering heat and Indian sniper attacks. Unusually nasty role for Beery and a good supporting cast make this one better than average. (A thin remake of THE LOST PATROL.)

p, Robert Sisk; d, Lew Landers; w, Clarence Upson Young; ph, Frank Redman; ed, George Hively.

Western (PR:A MPAA:NR)

BAD LITTLE ANGEL** (1939) 72m MGM bw

Virginia Weidler (*Patsy*), Gene Reynolds (*Tommy Wilks*), Guy Kibbee (*Luther Marvin*), Ian Hunter (*Jim Creighton*), Elizabeth Patterson (*Mrs. Perkins*), Reginald Owen (*Edwards, Valet*), Henry Hull (*Red Wilks*), Lois Wilson (*Ellen Creighton*), Mitchell Lewis, Esther Dale, Cora Sue Collins, Ann Todd.

Average waif-on-the-run-from-the-orphanage tale starring Weidler as the ragamuffin whose faith in the Bible sees her through the rough spots. While on the lam she meets up with shoe-shine boy Reynolds, who befriends her and introduces her to Hunter, the local newspaper editor, who takes her home to the wife. Kibbee is good as the town's skinflint and Hull is interesting as the shoe-shine boy's alcoholic father.

d, William Thiele; w, Dorothy Yost (based on a story by Margaret Turnbull); ph, John Seitz; m, Edward Ward; ed, Frank Sullivan.

Drama (PR:AA MPAA:NR)

BAD LORD BYRON, THE** (1949, Brit.) 83m Triton/GFD bw

Dennis Price (*Lord Byron*), Mai Zetterling (*Teresa Guiccioli*), Joan Greenwood (*Lady Caroline Lamb*), Linden Travers (*Augusta Leigh*), Sonia Holm (*Arabella Millbank*), Raymond Lovell (*John Hobhouse*), Leslie Dwyer (*Fletcher*), Denis O'Dea (*Prosecution*), Nora Swinburne (*Lady Jersey*), Ernest Thesiger (*Count Guiccioli*), Irene Browne (*Lady Melbourne*), Barry Jones (*Col. Stanhope*), Henry Oscar (*Count Gamba*), Archie Duncan (*John Murray*), Liam Gaffney (*Tom Moore*), John Salew (*Samuel Rogers*), Wilfrid Hyde-White (*Mr. Hopton*), Betty Lynne (*Signora Segati*), Zena Marshall (*Italian*).

Lord Byron is dying in Greece and dreams of a court of inquiry being held to determine whether or not he is entitled to go to Heaven. One flashback after another, showing various parts of his life, all with an appalling sameness about them, makes this picture seem much longer than it is. A lavish production marred by an ill-conceived screenplay credited to five writers—so the adage about too many cooks also applies in movies. How such an exciting life could be transformed into such a static and dull exercise is almost beyond human ken. Yet the production values and the earnest acting by the ensemble (Zetterling and Greenwood were never more delicious) merits attention.

p, Sidney Box [Aubrey Baring]; d, David MacDonald; w, Terence Young, Anthony Thorne, Peter Quennell, Lawrence Kitchen, Paul Holt; ph, Stephen Dade, David Harcourt; m, Cedric Thorpe Davie; ed, James Needs.

Biography (PR:A MPAA:NR)

BAD MAN, THE* 1/2 (1930) 80m FN/WB bw

Walter Huston (*Pancho Lopez*), Dorothy Revier (*Ruth Pell*), James Rennie (*Gilbert Jones*), O. P. Heggie (*Henry Taylor*), Sidney Blackmer (*Morgan Pell*), Marion Byron (*Angela Hardy*), Guinn "Big Boy" Williams (*Red Giddings*), Arthur Stone (*Pedro*), Erville Alderson (*Hardy*), Harry Semels (*Jose*).

Huston is the only reason to sit through this western as he plays the swaggering, gleam-toothed Mexican bandit Lopez eventually shot to pieces by Texas Rangers. Remade from a silent film, the script suffers from the melodramatic plotting that characterized the worst films of that era. Inexplicable attraction to this material was demonstrated by a remake in 1937 as WEST OF SHANGHAI and again in 1941. Director Badger worked on the classic silent IT (1927).

d, Clarence Badger; w, Howard Estabrook (based on the play by Porter Emerson Browne); ph, John Seitz; ed, Frank Ware.

Western (PR:A MPAA:NR)

BAD MAN, THE** 1/2 (1941) 70m MGM bw (GB:TWO-GUN CUPID)

Wallace Beery (*Pancho Lopez*), Lionel Barrymore (*Uncle Henry Jones*), Laraine Day (*Lucia Pell*), Ronald Reagan (*Gil Jones*), Henry Travers (*Mr. Hardy*), Chris-Pin Martin (*Pedro*), Tom Conway (*Morgan Pell*), Chill Wills (*Red Giddings*), Nydia Westman (*Angela Hardy*), Charles Stevens (*Venustiano*).

Yet another version of the Pancho Lopez story, this one with Beery as the lovable Mexican bandit. It's a real contest between Beery and Barrymore (who plays Reagan's wheelchair-ridden grandfather) to see who can growl, bluster, and generally chew up the scenery more. Plot concerns the troubles of Reagan and Barrymore who are about to lose the ranch because they can't pay the mortgage. Into their lives ride Beery and his bandits. Reagan had saved the outlaw's life earlier and now the grateful thief pays back the favor by taking care of the mortgage and reuniting Ronnie with his sweetheart. Not a great film by any stretch of the imagination, but it's fun to watch Beery and Barrymore stealing scenes from the future President.

p, J. Walter Ruben; d, Richard Thorpe; w, Wells Root (based on the play by Porter Emerson Browne); ph, Clyde De Vinna; ed, Conrad Nervig.

Western (PR:A MPAA:NR)

BAD MAN FROM RED BUTTE* 1/2 (1940) 58m UNIV bw

Johnny Mack Brown (*Gil Brady/Buck Halliday*), Bob Baker (*Gabriel Hornsby*), Fuzzy Knight (*Spud Jenkins*), Anne Gwynne (*Tibby Mason*), Lloyd Ingraham (*Turner*), Lafe McKee (*Dan Todhunter*), Bill Cody Jr. (*Skip Todhunter*).

Yes, another Johnny Mack Brown oater by the usual director, Taylor, with the usual cast, Brown, Knight, and Baker, shot on the usual locations. This one has Brown playing a dual role as a cowboy with an evil twin brother. The evil twin is wanted for murder and of course the posse is after the wrong brother. Romantic interest is provided by Gwynne who plays, you guessed it, a schoolteacher.

d, Ray Taylor; w, Sam Robbins; ph, William Sickner; ed, Paul Landres; m/l, Everett Carter, Milton Rosen.

Western (PR:A MPAA:NR)

BAD MAN OF BRIMSTONE*** (1938) 89m MGM bw

Wallace Beery("*Trigger*" *Bill*), Virginia Bruce (*Loretta Douglas*), Dennis O'Keefe (*Jeffrey Burton*), Joseph Calleia (*Ben*), Lewis Stone (*Mr. Jack Douglas*), Guy Kibbee ("*Eight Ball*" *Harrison*), Bruce Cabot ("*Blackjack*" *McCreedy*), Cliff Edwards (*Buzz McCreedy*), Guinn "Big Boy" Williams (*Vulch McCreedy*), Arthur Hohl (*Doc Laramie*), Noah Beery (*Ambrose Crocker*), John Qualen (*Loco*), Charley Grapewin (*Barney Lane*), Robert Barrat (*Hank Summers*).

Beery is a good-hearted outlaw who discovers his long-lost son, O'Keefe, has taken up prize-fighting. This development disturbs Pop who directs the kid's attention to law school and, in the process, becomes a changed man. But old habits die hard and with the appearance of the villainous Cabot, Beery is forced to strap on his pistols and go for one last showdown. Beery finally finds his niche with this material and doesn't overdo the hamminess that characterized many of his earlier western bandit performances. Good script, interesting performances by a top-flight cast, and an exciting climax make this one worth sitting through. Note: Film was originally released with a sepia tone tint but most prints that exist today will be black & white.

p, Harry Rapf; d, J. Walter Reuben; w, Cyril Hume, Richard Mailbaum (based on a story by Rueben, Maurice Rapf); ph, Clyde De Vinna; ed, Frank Sullivan.

Western (PR:A MPAA:NR)

BAD MAN OF DEADWOOD* (1941) 61m REP bw

Roy Rogers (*Bill Brady*), George "Gabby" Hayes (*Prof. Blackstone*), Carol Adams (*Linda*), Henry Brandon (*Carver*), Herbert Rawlinson (*Judge Gary*), Sally Payne (*Sally Blackstone*), Hal Taliaferro (*Ripper*), Jay Novello (*Monte*), Horace Murphy (*Seth Belden*), Monte Blue (*Sheriff*), Ralf Harolde (*Jake Marvel*), Jack Kirk (*Clem*).

Another in the never-ending series of Roy Rogers westerns. This one has Rogers helping a town regain control of its destiny by kicking out a group of crooked businessmen who have taken over all of Deadwood, eliminating the competition. Rogers once again proves he can keep the West safe for free enterprise and bad cowboy songs. (See ROY ROGERS series, Index.)

p&d, Joseph Kane; w, James R. Webb; ph, William Nobles; m, Cy Feuer; ed, Charles Craft.

Western **Cas.** (PR:A MPAA:NR)

BAD MAN'S RIVER* (1972, Span.) 90m Scotia International c

Lee Van Cleef (*King*), James Mason (*Montero*), Gina Lollobrigida (*Alicia*), Simon Andreu (*Angel*), Diana Lorys (*Dolores*), John Garko (*Pace*), Aldo Sanbrell (*Canales*), Jess Hahn (*Odie*), Daniel Martin (*False Montero*), Luis Rivera (*Orozco*), Lone Ferk (*Conchita*), Eduardo Fajardo (*Duarte*), Sergio Fantoni (*Fierro*), Per Barclay (*Reverend*).

Van Cleef stars as an outlaw embroiled in a hopelessly complicated scheme by Lollobrigida and Mason who con the Mexican government out of $1 million. The film becomes bogged down as the Mexican army, a band of revolutionaries, and even Billy The Kid, all try to get their hands on the dough. Stupid western that emulates what was bad about the worst spaghetti product from Italy. A real low point in Mason's career.

p, Bernard Gordon; d, Gene Martin; w, Martin, Philip Yordan; ph, Alexander Ulloa (Eastmancolor); m, Waldo de los Rios; ed, Antonio Ramirez de Loayra; art d, Julio Molino.

Western **Cas.** (PR:A MPAA:PG)

BAD MEN OF MISSOURI** 1/2 (1941) 75m FN/WB bw

Dennis Morgan (*Cole Younger*), Jane Wyman (*Mary Hathaway*), Wayne Morris (*Bob Younger*), Arthur Kennedy (*Jim Younger*), Victor Jory (*William Merrick*), Alan

Baxter (Jesse James), Walter Catlett (Mr. Pettibone), Howard da Silva (Greg Bilson), Faye Emerson (Martha Adams), Russell Simpson (Hank Younger), Virginia Brissac (Mrs. Hathaway), Erville Alderson (Mr. Adams), Hugh Sothern (Fred Robinson), Sam McDaniel (Wash), Dorothy Vaughan (Mrs. Dalton), William Gould (Sheriff Brennan), Robert Winkler (Willie Younger), Ann Todd (Amy Younger), Roscoe Ates (Lafe).

Solid story dealing with the notorious Younger brothers, albeit the facts are highly distorted. Morgan, Kennedy, and Morris take up the outlaw trail after northern carpet- baggers pillage their lands and cruelly kill friends and family. By accident, they meet Baxter, a weird Jesse James, who is robbing a train Baxter and gang intend to rob. (The James and Younger brothers were united from their beginnings as members of Quantrill's guerrillas during the Civil War and were even distantly related; they rode together until the Youngers were captured after the disastrous raid against a Northfield, Minnesota bank in 1878, the James boys escaping.) The film begins with Civil War battle scenes culled from D. W. Griffith's silent classic, THE BIRTH OF A NATION. More accurate profiles of these notorious bandits are found in JESSE JAMES; THE GREAT NORTHFIELD, MINNESOTA RAID; and THE LONG RIDERS. Director Enright moves this version along speedily.

p, Harlan Thompson; d, Ray Enright; w, Charles Grayson (based on a story by Robert E. Kent); ph, Arthur L. Todd; ed, Clarence Kolster.

Western   **(PR:A MPAA:NR)**

BAD MEN OF THE BORDER* 1/2   (1945) 56m UNIV bw

Kirby Grant, Fuzzy Knight, Armida, John Eldredge, Francis McDonald, Barbara Sears, Edmund Cobb, Pierce Lyden, Gene Stutenroth [Gene Roth], Glenn Strange.

Kirby pretends to be a bandit, working his way into an outlaw band passing counterfeit bills. He rounds up the baddies and bogus bills, and fetching Armida to boot. Routine oater.

p&d, Wallace Fox; w, Adele Buffington; ph, Maury Gertsman; ed, Philip Cahn; art d, Abraham Grossman, John B. Goodman; set d, Russell A. Gausman, Ralph Sylos.

Western   **(PR:A MPAA:NR)**

BAD MEN OF THE HILLS*
            (1942) 58m COL bw (GB: WRONGLY ACCUSED)

Charles Starrett (Steve Carlton), Russell Hayden (Lucky Shelton), Cliff Edwards (Harmony Haines), Luana Walters (Laurie Bishop), Alan Bridge (Sheriff Arnold), Guy Usher (Doctor Mitchell), Joel Friedkin (Judge Malotte), Norma Jean Wooters (Buckshot), John Shay (Marshal Upjohn), Dick Botiller (Brant).

Another oater featuring Starrett as a U.S. marshal assigned to stop a murderous sheriff from ransacking the local ranchers. The usual fist fights, shootouts, and singing fill the bill.

p, Jack Fier; d, William Berke; w, Luci Ward; ph, Benjamin Kline; ed, Richard Fantl.

Western   **(PR:A MPAA:NONE)**

BAD MEN OF THUNDER GAP*
            (1943) 57m PRC bw (AKA: THUNDERGAP OUTLAWS)

Dave "Tex" O'Brien, Jim Newill, Guy Wilkerson, Janet Shaw, Jack Ingram, Michael Vallon, Charles King, Lucille Vance, Tom London, I. Stanford Jolley, Bud Osborne, Jimmy Aubrey, Cal Strumm's Rhythm Rangers.

Dull horser has O'Brien framed for a crime he didn't commit and his considerable struggle to locate the culprit and clear his name. This was another outing in PRC's Texas Ranger series. Of curious note is O'Brien's method of shooting his six-gun, similar to that of a small boy swatting pesky flies.

p, Alfred Stern, Arthur Alexander; d, Al Herman; w, Elmer Clifton; ph, Robert Cline; ed, Charles Henkel, Jr.; md, Lee Zahler.

Western   **(PR:A MPAA:NR)**

BAD MEN OF TOMBSTONE* 1/2   (1949) 74m MON/AA bw

Barry Sullivan (Tom), Marjorie Reynolds (Julie), Broderick Crawford (Morgan), Fortunio Bonanova (Mingo), Guinn "Big Boy" Williams (Red), John Kellogg (Curly), Mary Newton (Ma Brown), Louis Jean Heydt (Mr. Stover), Virginia Carroll (Mrs. Stover), Dick Wessel (Bartender), Claire Carleton (Nellie), Olin Howlin (Proprietor), Robert H. Barrat (Sheriff), Dennis Hoey (Mr. Smith), Dick Foote (Jerry).

An early offbeat western where the bad guys, Sullivan and Crawford, are stone gunslingers without compassion or a single sincere thought of reform, characters loosely based on the McLoury-Clanton gang of Tombstone. The real brutality and senseless killing of the Old West is summarized by Sullivan, a gun-happy murderer who shoots a gambler to death because he cheated him out of a horse months earlier. Reynolds is his equally callous lady friend who merely suggests reforming as a whim, and Crawford is apt as the thick-headed, brutish gang leader who dies in the middle of the street with his minions, trying to take as many helpless souls with him to Boot Hill as possible.

p, Frank Maurice, Hyman King; d, Kurt Neumann; w, Philip Yordan, Arthur Strawn (based on the novel The Last of Badmen by Jay Monaghan); ph, Russell Harlan; ed, Richard Heermance; m/l, "Girl on the Flying Trapeze," by Neumann, Clarence Marks.

Western   **(PR:C MPAA:NR)**

BAD NEWS BEARS, THE** 1/2   (1976) 102m PAR c

Walter Matthau (Coach Buttermaker); Tatum O'Neal (Manda Whurlizer), Vic Morrow (Roy Turner), Joyce Van Patten (Cleveland), Ben Piazza (Councilman Whitewood), Jackie Earle Haley (Kelly Leak), Alfred W. Lutter (Ogilvie), Brandon Cruz (Joey Turner), Shari Summers (Mrs. Turner), Joe Brooks (Umpire), Maurice Marks (Announcer), Quinn Smith (Lupus), Gary Lee Cavagnaro (Engelberg), Erin

Blunt (Ahmad), David Stambaugh (Toby Whitewood), Jaime Escobedo, George Gonzales (Agilar Boys), David Pollock, Chris Barnes, Scott Firestone, Brett Marx (Other Boys).

Charming and funny film that bridges the gap between children and adults. Rated PG for the language, that should not deter most from seeing this gentle and warm poke-in-the-ribs at the Little League system. Ritchie, who often goes overboard (PRIME CUT, SEMI-TOUGH) was held in check on this and fashioned a lovely picture about a rag-tag team that manages to overcome all odds and get second place. Right there is the key to the intelligence of the Bill Lancaster (Burt's son) script. Most writers would have had the title team win the championship, but that, in truth, is a lot of hooey, so Lancaster opted for the truth: a respectful second. Matthau is wonderful as the one-time minor leaguer who manages the team. O'Neal is his girl pitcher. Lots of preaching in this movie, but you'll never notice it for a second. Points are made with such deftness that the only memory you'll carry away is of having watched a terrifically emotional and hilarious movie. Fielding joins with Georges Bizet for the musical background and the effect is electric as "Carmen" underscores the game sequences. Baseball is a tough game to show in a movie. This is one of the best examples of how to do it right. Morrow scores as the rival coach and Van Patten (sister of Dick, wife of Dennis Dugan) is superior as a league official. Then again, she's good in just about everything she does.

p, Stanley R. Jaffe; d, Michael Ritchie; w, Bill Lancaster; ph, John A. Alonzo (Movielab Color); m, Jerry Fielding; ed, Richard A. Harris; prod d, Polly Platt; set d, Cheryal Kearney.

Comedy   **Cas.**   **(PR:C MPAA:PG)**

BAD NEWS BEARS GO TO JAPAN, THE* 1/2   (1978) 91m PAR c

Tony Curtis (Marvin Lazar), Jackie Earle Haley (Kelly Leak), Tomisaburo Wakayama (Coach Shimizu), Hatsune Ishihara (Arika), George Wyner (Network Director), Lonny Chapman (Louis the Gambler), Matthew Douglas Anton (E. R. W. Tillyard, III), Erin Blunt (Ahmad Rahim), George Gonzales (Miguel Agilar), Brett Marx (Jimmy Feldman), David Pollock (Rudy Stein), David Stambaugh (Toby Whitewood), Jeffrey Louis Starr (Mike Engleberg), Scoody Thornton (Mustapha Rahim).

Despite a script by the originator, Bill Lancaster, and producing chores handled by THE BAD NEWS BEARS director, Michael Ritchie, this one falls apart almost before it gets to first base. Haley and several of the players have returned but the bloom is off the rose on this third film in the BEARS cycle. It's somewhat more energetic than the previous year's BREAKING TRAINING and the Japanese locations are a plus but so much silliness has been substituted for the solid situations and characterizations of the first film that it's hard to believe the same people had anything to do with both pictures. Script overlooks the kids most of the time in favor of the relationship between Curtis (the coach) and Wakayama (the Japanese coach). Plot has to do with the Bears coming to the land of the Rising Sun to play the Japanese all-stars. Ordinary twists—Curtis is a martinet, despised by the kids (except for Scoody Thornton) who finally manages to understand what he's doing wrong and is reformed just before the final call of "Play Ball." Whereas BAD NEWS BEARS was a home run, the next two pictures were ignominious called-out-on-strikes.

p, Michael Ritchie; d, John Berry; w, Bill Lancaster; ph, Jean Polito, Kozo Okazaki (Movielab Color); m, Paul Chihara; ed, Richard A. Harris; prod d, Walter Scott Herndon.

Comedy   **Cas.**   **(PR:C MPAA:PG)**

BAD NEWS BEARS IN BREAKING TRAINING, THE* (1977) 99m PAR c

William Devane (Mike Leak), Clifton James (Sy Orlansky), Jackie Earle Haley (Kelly Leak), Jimmy Baio (Carmen Ronzonni), Chris Barnes (Tanner Boyle), Erin Blunt (Ahmad Abdul Rahim), Jaime Escobedo, George Gonzales (Agilar Boys), Alfred Lutter (Ogilvie), Brett Marx (Jimmy Feldman), David Pollock (Rudi Stein), Quinn Smith (Timmy Lupus), David Stambaugh (Toby Whitewood), Jeffrey Louis Starr (Mike Engleberg), Fred Stuthman (Caretaker), Dolph Sweet (Coach Manning), Lane Smith (Officer Mackie), Pat Corley (Coach Morrie Slater).

Some of the kids return for this pale sequel to THE BAD NEWS BEARS but the adults have moved on to greener ballfields and this picture suffers from their loss. Michael Pressman is no Michael Ritchie and Brickman's script (based on the characters created by Bill Lancaster) is weak. The Bears go to Houston where Haley recruits his dad, Devane, to coach the kids in an Astrodome playoff game. Whereas a lot of the language was azure in the original, this time it's cerulean blue and sounds smarmy rather than cute. Stanley Jaffe produced the original but Leonard Goldberg, an old TV hand, came aboard to handle this sequel. His TV expertise is immediate. If we were watching this at home, we'd have shut it off.

p, Leonard Goldberg; d, Michael Pressman; w, Paul Brickman (based on characters created by Bill Lancaster); ph, Fred J. Koenekamp (Movielab Color); m, Craig Safan; ed, John W. Wheeler; art d, Steve Berger; set d, Fred R. Price; cos, Jack Martell; m/l, Safan, Norman Gimbel.

Comedy   **Cas.**   **(PR:C MPAA:PG)**

BAD ONE, THE*   (1930) 70m UA bw

Dolores Del Rio (Lita), Edmund Lowe (Jerry Flanagan), Don Alvarado (The Spaniard), Blanche Frederici (Madame Durand), Adrienne D'Ambricourt (Madame Pompier), Ullrich Haupt (Pierre Ferrande), Mitchell Lewis (Borloff), Ralph Lewis (Blochet), Charles McNaughton (Petey), Yola D'Avril (Gida), John Sainpolis (Judge), Henry Kolker (Prosecutor), George Fawcett (Warden), Victor Potel (Sailor), Harry Stubbs (Sailor), Tom Dugan (Sailor), Boris Karloff (Guard).

This melodrama gets so heavy that, at times, one thinks it may be a straight-faced comedy. Del Rio dances for a living in a sailor's hang-out in Marseilles. It appears to be a tavern but closer inspection marks it as a brothel. She meets Lowe and agrees to marry him. An old beau arrives and Lowe gets jealous; there's a fight and the result is a death, a trial, and a sentence for Lowe to an unreasonable facsimile of Devil's Island. Since the only females allowed on the island are the wives of the guards, Del Rio agrees to marry the most brutal guard there . . . just to be near her amour. Soon enough, there's a prison riot. Lowe proves his courage, gets a pardon and he and Dolores plan to return to his native Brooklyn. Some strange editing in this one. They established that this is an island, a distance from any other landfall and suddenly, near the end, there is a bridge to the mainland that is blown up. Karloff plays a small role as a guard. He was, at the time, 43 years old and a year away from international stardom as the Frankenstein monster.

p, Joseph M. Schenck, John W. Considine, Jr.; d, George Fitzmaurice; w, Carey Wilson, Howard Emmet Rogers (based on a story by John Farrow); ph, Karl Struss; m, Hugo Riesenfeld; ed, Donn Hayes; art d, William Cameron Menzies, Paul French; cos, Alice O'Neill.

Drama (PR:C MPAA:NR)

BAD SEED, THE* (1956) 127m WB bw

Nancy Kelly (Christine), Patty McCormack (Rhoda), Henry Jones (LeRoy), Eileen Heckart (Mrs. Daigle), Evelyn Varden (Monica), William Hopper (Kenneth), Paul Fix (Bravo), Jesse White (Emory), Gage Clarke (Tasker), Joan Croydon (Miss Fern), Frank Cady (Mr. Daigle).

THE BAD SEED is an erratic but compelling film that lingers long after the fade-out. Patty McCormack is memorable as the eight-year-old liar, cheat and murderess whose mother is convinced that she is a bad seed. Mother, of course, is right, but no one believes her. LeRoy deftly maneuvers what could have been a stagy and talky script (based on the stage hit by Maxwell Anderson) and keeps the action going. McCormack has murdered a schoolmate because the other boy received a medal for penmanship. Then we learn of the death of an old woman. Then Jones, the janitor, is burned. (One of the most macabre scenes in this bizarre film shows Jones deviling McCormack with thoughts of retribution, telling her that there are two types of electric chairs awaiting bad children: "They have a blue one for little boys and a pink one for little girls.") Nancy Kelly attempts suicide but fails and Patty is finally. . . . but no, if you haven't seen the picture, we'd rather not reveal the ending. At the end of the film LeRoy has the cast take a bow, the way they do on the stage, and that takes away some of the acrid taste. The Broadway play had the terror child getting away with murder in the end, a finish the Johnston Office (then the official censor, Eric Johnston succeeding Will Hays) would not tolerate; it demanded and got a "just" finale. Heckart is wonderful as the alcoholic mother of the dead schoolmate and was one of three actresses (Kelly, McCormack) to get Oscar nominations. Harold Rosson also received a nomination. Look for White (the lonely Maytag Man) as Emory.

p&d, Mervyn LeRoy; w, John Lee Mahin (based on the play by Maxwell Anderson and the novel by William March); ph, Hal Rosson; m, Alex North; ed, Warren Low; cos, Moss Mabry.

Horror/Drama (PR:C MPAA:NR)

BAD SISTER*1/2 (1931) 68m UNIV bw

Conrad Nagel (Dick Lindley), Sidney Fox (Marianne), Bette Davis (Laura), ZaSu Pitts (Minnie), Slim Summerville (Sam), Charles Winninger (Mr. Madison), Emma Dunn (Mrs. Madison), Humphrey Bogart (Corliss), Bert Roach (Wade Trumbull), David Durand (Hedrick Madison).

A knock-out cast in a drag-out movie. Sidney Fox is a rich deb, daughter of small-town businessman Winninger. She is bored by the local gentry and falls under the oily spell of Bogart, a conman who has come to town to bilk and fleece the local yokels. Fox is convinced by Bogart to forge Daddy's name on a letter of endorsement. He shows this letter to the town's merchants, collects a bundle, and slips out, after convincing Fox to elope with him. But Bogart shows his true colors and deserts her in a seedy hotel. Meanwhile, Fox's sister, Davis, has been quietly in love for years with Nagel, a handsome physician who courted Fox to no avail. Davis and Nagel fall in love and when Fox returns from being used by the foul Bogie, she accepts the proposal of Roach, a wealthy young man-about-town who is all sincerity. This film was made when Bogart was 32, five years before he was to be propelled to the top as Duke Mantee in THE PETRIFIED FOREST. This was the film debut for both Davis and Fox, who died in 1942 at the age of 32.

p, Carl Laemmle, Jr.; d, Hobart Henley; w, Raymond L. Schrock, Tom Reed, Edwin Knopf (based on the novel The Flirt by Booth Tarkington); ph, Karl Freund; ed, Ted J. Kent.

Drama (PR:A MPAA:NR)

BAD SISTER* (1947, Brit.) 97m RANK bw (GB: THE WHITE UNICORN)

Margaret Lockwood (Lucy), Dennis Price (Richard Glover), Ian Hunter (Philip Templar), Joan Greenwood (Lottie Smith), Guy Middleton (Fobey), Catherine Lacey (Miss Carter), Mabel Constanduros (Nurse), Paul Dupuis (Paul), Eileen Peel (Joan), Toots Lockwood (Norey), Lily Kann (Shura), Valentine Dyall (Storton), Joan Rees (Alice Waters), Stewart Rome (Charles Madden).

The lives of two unhappy women, loaded with flashbacks and lots of schmaltz. Greenwood winds up in an institution for delinquents after attempting to kill herself and her baby. A kindly matron befriends her. The two women talk endlessly about their messed-up love lives. A sorry showing.

p, Harold Huth; d, Bernard Knowles; w, Flora Sandstrom (based on her novel, The Milkwhite Unicorn); ph, Reginald H. Wyer.

Drama (PR:A MPAA:NR)

BADGE OF HONOR* (1934) 62m Mayfair bw

Buster Crabbe (Bob Gordon), Ruth Hall (Helen Brewster), Ralph Lewis (Brewster),Betty Blythe (Mrs. Van Alstyne), John Trent (Larkin).

Crabbe stars in this action-filled drama as an out-of-town society boy who poses as a newspaper reporter. During the course of this film Crabbe gets involved in everything from car chases to barroom brawling. The only thing he doesn't do is swim, which one can assume is supposed to be a refreshing change of pace for Crabbe, who got to show off his underwater prowess in just about every role he was assigned.

d, Spencer Gordon Bennet; w, George Morgan (based on a story by Robert Emmett); ed, Fred Bain.

Drama (PR:A MPAA:NR)

BADGE OF MARSHAL BRENNAN, THE* (1957) 74m AA bw

Jim Davis (Stranger), Arleen Whelan (Murdock), Lee Van Cleef (Shad Donaphin), Louis Jean Heydt (Col. Donaphin), Carl Smith (Sheriff), Marty Robbins (Felipe), Harry Lauter (Dr. Steve Hale), Douglas Fowley (Marshal), Lawrence Dobkin (Chickamon).

Second-rate western obviously made for people who have never seen a first-rate western. Davis takes the badge of dying lawman Fowley. Davis is a criminal racing away from a fleeing posse. The badge has some sort of mystical effect on him, and he takes on Van Cleef and Heidt, who are the kingpins of a town. They run the cattle in and out of this burg and are in the midst of trying to pawn some sick steers off on unsuspecting buyers. Davis assumes the identity of the dead lawman and battles the bad guys to a conclusion. Not a bad story but terribly handled by the production team. It gets one star for the appearances of Davis (who went on to international fame on TV's "Dallas"); Van Cleef (who became a major star in spaghetti westerns, then came back to the U.S. and enjoyed a brief TV series); and Douglas Fowley (who was brilliant as the mad director in SINGING IN THE RAIN).

p&d, Albert C. Gannaway; w, Thomas G. Hubbard; ph, Charles Straumer; m, Rame Indriss; ed, Asa Clark; m/l,"Man on the Run," Hal Levy, Gannaway (sung by Harve Presnell.)

Western (PR:A MPAA:NR)

BADGE 373* (1973) 116m PAR c

Robert Duvall (Eddie Ryan), Verna Bloom (Maureen), Henry Darrow (Sweet William), Eddie Egan (Scanlon), Felipe Luciano (Ruben), Tina Cristiani (Mrs. Caputo), Marina Durell (Rita Garcia), Chico Martinez (Frankie Diaz), Jose Duval (Ferrer), Louis Cosentino (Gigi Caputo), Luis Avalos (Chico), Nubia Olivero (Mrs. Diaz), Sam Schact (Asst. D.A.), Edward F. Carey (Commissioner), John Marriott (Superintendent), Pete Hamill (Reporter), Joel Veiga (Manuel), Mark Tendler (Bouncer), Robert Weil (Hans), Rose Ann Scarmardella, Larry Applebaum, John McCurry, Bob Farley, Tracy Walter, John Scanlon, Jimmy Archer, Ric Mancini, Mike O'Dowd, Robert Miano, Pompie Pomposello, Hector Troy.

They tried to do a sequel to THE FRENCH CONNECTION and failed with BADGE 373. Was it because they had different actors, different screenwriters, different directors and the movies were made by different studios? Could be. Both FRENCH CONNECTION movies were made at Fox with Hackman. The first one took four Oscars. BADGE 373 takes the cake for boredom. Duvall is an angry cop, not unlike the Kirk Douglas role in DETECTIVE STORY, except that Duvall is a bigot, foul-mouthed, pot-bellied, raiding illegally, double-crossing friend and foe alike. His character is supposedly patterned after the real-life Eddie Egan (who plays Scanlon). Egan also is billed as tech advisor so you know he gave them his input. Duvall is a sociopath who hates Puerto Ricans and in New York, that can limit your acquaintances. The biggest surprise is real-life Puerto Rican activist Felipe Luciano (as Ruben) who comes across with the only conviction shown on the screen. Verna Bloom does her hapless role in the only way she knows how; with intelligence. Screenwriter Pete Hamill plays a reporter named Pete and is believable as a reporter. Unfortunately, he was not as believable as a screenwriter. Howard Koch (Sr.) directed for maximum yawns.

p&d, Howard W. Koch; w, Pete Hamill; ph, Arthur J. Ornitz (Technicolor); m, J. J. Jackson; ed, John Woodcock; art d, Philip Rosenberg.

Crime (PR:O MPAA:R)

BADGER'S GREEN*1/2 (1934, Brit.) 68m British & Dominions/Brit. PAR bw

Valerie Hobson (Molly Butler), Bruce Lister (Dickie Wetherby), Frank Moore (Dr. Wetherby), David Horne (Maj. Forrester), Sebastian Smith (Mr. Twigg), John Turnbull (Thomas Butler), Wally Patch (Mr. Rogers), Elsie Irving (Mrs. Wetherby).

A business scheme backfires when villagers rebel against commercial buildings being put up on a cricket field. Weak script does a disservice to a good cast, providing laugh lines that have no punch.

d, Adrian Brunel; w, R. J. Davis, Villet Powell (based on the play by R. C. Sherriff).

Comedy (PR:A MPAA:NR)

BADGER'S GREEN** (1949, Brit.) 62m GFD bw

Barbara Murray (Jane Morton), Brian Nissen (Dickie Wetherby), Garry Marsh (Maj. Forrester), Kynaston Reeves (Dr. Wetherby), Laurence Naismith (Mr. Butler), Mary Merrall (Mrs. Wetherby), Jack McNaughton (Mr. Twigg), Sam Rogers (Norman Pierce).

Remake of the 1934 film, this time with better production values, but not much can help the forced situations and contrived humor where the villagers are up in arms over a business scheme to convert a cricket field to a commercial complex.

p, John Croydon; d, John Irwin; w, William Fairchild (based on the play by R. C. Sheriff); ph, Walter Harvey.

Comedy (PR:A MPAA:NR)

BADLANDERS, THE*   (1958) 85m MGM c

Alan Ladd (*Peter Van Hock*), Ernest Borgnine (*John McBain*), Katy Jurado (*Anita*), Claire Kelly (*Ada Winton*), Kent Smith (*Cyril Lounsberry*), Nehemiah Persoff (*Vincente*), Robert Emhardt (*Sample*), Anthony Caruso (*Comanche*), Adam Williams (*Leslie*), Ford Rainey (*Warden*), John Day (*Lee*).

THE BADLANDERS is an adult western remake of THE ASPHALT JUNGLE. Ladd replaces Sam Jaffe as the brains behind the plot and Borgnine plays the Sterling Hayden hood role. The plot is basically the same, with Ladd finishing out a sentence at Yuma prison. He feels he's been cheated out of his stake in a mine by Smith, the mine's owner, who had him sent up on false charges. Ladd enlists Borgnine, another of Smith's victims. Smith hates his wife and is fooling around with Kelly. They plan to take off for the continent. Meanwhile, she falls for Ladd, who arrives at the hotel where Smith keeps her. Borgnine tumbles for Jurado, a hooker with a heart of guess what? She falls head over heels for Borgnine (they did in real life as well) and they vow to make it work. Persoff, an old pal of Ladd's, joins them and the three men enter Smith's gold mine, set dynamite and blow up a section to reveal a thick vein of the real stuff. Smith has euchred them, though, and arrives with Williams, a crooked cop. Smith is hoist on his own petard when Borgnine attacks him and he and Ladd and Persoff cut out. Borgnine stays with Jurado and Ladd leaves with Kelly. The film was not a hit, although Ladd gave his finest western performance (other than SHANE) and Borgnine had his best role since MARTY. Watch the movie and see if you can recognize it as the same plot of the W. R. Burnett novel that inspired the John Huston film made just eight years earlier.

p, Aaron Rosenberg; d, Delmer Daves; w, Richard Collins (based on the novel *The Asphalt Jungle* by W. R. Burnett); ph, John Seitz (CinemaScope, Metrocolor); ed, William H. Webb, James Balotto.

Western   **(PR:A MPAA:NR)**

BADLANDS*   (1974) 95m WB c

Martin Sheen (*Kit*), Sissy Spacek (*Holly*), Warren Oates (*Father*), Ramon Bieri (*Cato*), Alan Vint (*Deputy*), Gary Littlejohn (*Sheriff*), John Carter (*Rich Man*), Bryan Montgomery (*Boy*), Gail Threlkeld (*Girl*), Charles Fitzpatrick (*Clerk*), Howard Ragsdale (*Boss*), John Womack, Jr. (*Trooper on plane*), Dona Baldwin (*Maid*), Ben Bravo (*Gas Station Attendant*), Terrence Malick (*Salesman*).

Stark, brutal reenactment of the Charles Starkweather-Carol Fugate murder spree through Nebraska and surrounding states in 1958, with Sheen playing the killer garbageman lashing out against a society that ignores his existence and Spacek as his misguided teenage consort. Sheen is forceful and properly weird as the mass murderer, killing Oates, Spacek's disapproving father, when he forbids his daughter to date him, then a host of others. (Starkweather and Fugate, although she later denied killing anyone, were responsible for the deaths of ten innocent people.) The locale in the movie is changed to South Dakota but almost all the characteristics of the real culprits are intact, the strutting Sheen pretending to be James Dean in REBEL WITHOUT A CAUSE, the mindless Spacek as the teenage toady. Basically, these two social rejects act out of boredom, practicing moronic humor and lethal anger on all who look sideways at them or don't look at them at all. Starkweather really summed up his own nitwit personality, and that played by Sheen, when he stated: "The more I looked at people the more I hated them, because I knowed they wasn't any place for me with the kind of people I knowed." The script brings no new insight to these basically uninteresting people and the direction is that of an amateur dabbling in documentaries. A cult film; those who truly hate films as a medium designed to inspire and enlighten love this one. It has all the fascination of prying into a cavity with a bent hairpin.

p,d&w, Terrence Malick; ph, Brian Probyn, Tak Fujimoto, Steve Larner (Consolidated Color); m, George Tipton; ed, Robert Estrin; art d, Jack Fisk.

Crime   **Cas.**   **(PR:O MPAA:PG)**

BADLANDS OF DAKOTA¹/₂   (1941) 74m UNIV bw

Robert Stack (*Jim Holliday*), Ann Rutherford (*Anne Grayson*), Richard Dix (*Wild Bill Hickok*), Frances Farmer (*Jane*), Broderick Crawford (*Bob Holliday*), Hugh Herbert (*Rocky*), Andy Devine (*Spearfish*), Lon Chaney Jr. (*Jack McCall*), Fuzzy Knight (*Hurricane Harry*), Addison Richards (*General Custer*), Bradley Page (*Chapman*), Samuel S. Hinds (*Uncle Wilbur*), Dwight Latham, Walter Carlson, Guy Bonham (*The Jesters*).

Great programmer with an incredibly good cast in this western detailing the gold rush in the Black Hills of Dakota. Stack, a sheriff, and Crawford, an outlaw, play brothers whose paths cross the likes of Wild Bill Hickok (Dix), Calamity Jane (Farmer), and General Custer (Richards). Farmer is a standout as the rough and tumble Jane who is in love with bad-guy Crawford. Climax occurs when Farmer is forced to halt the robbery of the town's bank by shooting her lover dead. Worth a look.

p, George Waggner; d, Alfred E. Green; w, Gerald Geraghty (based on a story by Harold Shumate); ph, Stanley Cortez; m, H. J. Salter.

Western   **(PR:A MPAA:NR)**

BADLANDS OF MONTANA   (1957) 75m FOX bw

Rex Reason (*Steve*), Margia Dean (*Emily*), Beverly Garland (*Susan*), Keith Larsen (*Rick*), Emile Meyer (*Hammer*), Russ Bender (*George*), Robert Cunningham (*Paul*), Ralph Peters (*Sammy*), Lee Tung Foo (*Ling*), Stanley Farrar (*Rayburn*), Rankin Mansfield (*Travis*), William Phipps (*Walt*), John Pickard (*Vince*), Paul Newlan (*Marshal*), John Lomma (*Bank Teller*), Jack Kruschen (*Cavalry Sergeant*), Elena DaVinci (*1st Girl*), George Taylor (*Bank Teller*), William Forester (*Bank Manager*), Larry Blake (*1st Outlaw*), Ralph Sanford (*Marshal Sloan*), William Tanner (*2nd Outlaw*), Roydon Clark (*Posseman*), Helen Jay (*2nd Girl*).

Much better than average oater finds Reason being run out of the town he wants to lead as mayor. He is tricked into a gunfight and manages to kill his opponent. Forced to earn a living outside the law, he takes up with a gang, becomes a criminal, and is eventually wounded and captured. He is brought back to his town by some friends where he recovers and is eventually elected sheriff. Proving again that it takes a thief to catch a thief, it takes an outlaw to stop an outlaw, and Reason faces his old gang when they attack the town. Meyer is the leader of the bad gang and Garland is his nubile daughter. Reason convinces Garland to leave the gang and come over the line onto the side of the law. Good technical credits, even good music. Reason is convincing and Garland never looked prettier.

p,d&w, Daniel B. Ullman; ph, Frederick Gately (RegalScope); m, Irving Gertz; ed, Neil Brunenkant; m/l, "The Man with the Gallant Gun" Gertz, Hal Levy (sung by Bob Grabeau).

Western   **(PR:A MPAA:NR)**

BADMAN'S COUNTRY¹/₂   (1958) 85m Peerless/WB bw

George Montgomery (*Pat Garrett*), Neville Brand (*Butch Cassidy*), Buster Crabbe (*Wyatt Earp*), Karin Booth (*Lorna*), Gregory Wolcott (*Bat Masterson*), Malcolm Atterbury (*Buffalo Bill Cody*), Russell Johnson (*Sundance*), Richard Devon (*Harvey Logan*), Morris Ankrum (*Mayor Coleman*), Dan Riss (*Marshall McAfee*).

Brand leads a bushel-basket-full of the sleaziest outlaws. They are lurking outside Abilene and waiting for a trainload of gold to come chugging through. Montgomery would like to gull the outlaws into Abilene where they can be ambushed and more easily dealt with. The locals are against it, even though the outlaws dominate the town. They are finally convinced, the battle takes place and all ends well. Film is notable in that it uses the characters of Earp, Garrett, Masterson and Cody—any one of whom would be enough to carry the story. But the producers, not adhering to the architectural doctrine that "less is more" opted for "more is more" and gave us this plot. Hampton writes a good, tight screenplay and this is a better-than-average western with lots of excitement, suspense and action. This picture was made in the days when everyone hoped they could get a hit title song (HIGH NOON) so The Mellowmen sing producer Kent's original ditty! (A piece of music that should be in everyone's collection of western title songs.)

p, Robert E. Kent; d, Fred F. Sears; w, Orville H. Hampton; ph, Benjamin H. Kline; m, Irving Gertz; ed, Grant Whytock; m/l, title song, Kent, (sung by The Mellowmen).

Western   **(PR:A MPAA:NR)**

BADMAN'S GOLD*¹/₂   (1951) 56m UA bw

Johnny Carpenter (*Johnny*), Alyn Lockwood (*Bess Benson*), Troy Tarrell (*Bob Benson*), Kenne Duncan (*Rance*), Verne Teters (*Sheriff*), Jack Daly (*Professor*), Daisy (*Daisy*), Emmett Lynn (*Miner*).

B-western featuring Carpenter as the lean, tough marshal who is sent to help a local lawman (Teters) find out who's looting the stagecoaches. Carpenter enlists the aid of Lockwood and Tarrell who help him defeat the baddies. Daisy the dog may have been the same pup used in the BLONDIE series, although it was produced by Columbia from 1938 through 1950. Since BADMAN'S GOLD was made after the last BLONDIE feature, it's safe to say that the dog made a conscious career choice and was not on loan-out from Harry Cohn (who was always reluctant to do that). This picture was obviously shot for very little money and some of the exteriors are noticeably interiors. Not very good, but fans of Daisy will love it.

p&d, Robert Tansey; w, Robert Emmett, Alyn Lockwood.

Western   **(PR:A MPAA:NR)**

BADMAN'S TERRITORY   (1946) 97m RKO bw

Randolph Scott (*Mark Rowley*), Ann Richards (*Henryette Alcott*), George "Gabby" Hayes (*Coyote*), Ray Collins (*Col. Farewell*), James Warren (*John Rowley*), Morgan Conway (*Bill Hampton*), Virginia Sale (*Meg*), John Halloran (*Hank McGee*), Andrew Tombes (*Doc Grant*), Richard Hale (*Ben Wade*), Harry Holman (*Hodge*), Chief Thundercloud (*Chief Tahlequah*), Lawrence Tierney (*Jesse James*), Tom Tyler (*Frank James*), Steve Brodie (*Bob Dalton*), Phil Warren (*Grat Dalton*), William Moss (*Bill Dalton*), Nestor Paiva (*Sam Bass*), Isabel Jewell (*Belle Starr*), Emory Parnell (*Bitter Creek*), John Hamilton (*Commissioner*), Robert E. Homans (*Trial Judge*).

Scott stars as a Texas sheriff who must enter a kind of no-man's land of Oklahoma in search of his younger brother. His quest takes him into a mass hideout of outlaw gangs including the Daltons, the James Boys, Sam Bass, and Belle Starr. RKO pulled out all the stops and stretched historical accuracy to the breaking point by placing every famous outlaw bunch in the same picture. Sequel in 1949, RETURN OF THE BAD MEN.

p, Nat Holt; d, Tim Whelan; w, Jack Natteford, Luci Ward, Clarence Upson Young, Bess Taffel; ph, Robert De Grasse; m, Roy Webb; ed, Philip Martin Jr.

Western   **(PR:A MPAA:NR)**

BAGDAD   (1949) 82m UNIV c

Maureen O'Hara (*Princess Marjan*), Paul Christian (*Hassan*), Vincent Price (*Pasha Al Nadim*), John Sutton (*Raizul*), Jeff Corey (*Mohammad Jad*), Frank Puglia (*Saleel*), David Wolfe (*Mahmud*), Fritz Leiber (*Emir*), Otto Waldis (*Marengo*), Leon Belasco (*Beggar*), Ann Pearce (*Tirza*).

A typical Arabian Nights story with gorgeous Maureen O'Hara as the daughter of a sheik. She returns from England to find her daddy done in, his followers gone, and the money missing. Christian, leader of a group called The Black Riders, is blamed for the dastardly deed but since he's a handsome devil and you just know he's the male lead, there's no way he can be the true villain. You're right, of course, if you suspect Price as the rotter who lurks behind the action. Christian, who is also known as Paul Hubschmid in Europe, did not impress in his American debut, but he did go on to do some good work in FUNERAL IN BERLIN, SKULLDUGGERY and others. Good technical credits and a slightly confused script from Andrews pull at each other. It's almost, but not quite, a spoof of the genre. Maureen sings three songs written by Frank Skinner and Jack Brooks and does a nice job (the title song, "Love is Strange," and "Song of the Desert"). Miss O'Hara's brother, Charles Fitzsimons, is a well-known TV producer who acted briefly, playing the role of McCloskey, the man who defeats Spencer Tracy in the mayor's race in THE LAST HURRAH.

p, Robert Arthur; d, Charles Lamont; w, Robert H. Andrews; ph, Russell Metty (Technicolor); ed, Russell Schoengarth.

Adventure (PR:A MPAA:NR)

BAHAMA PASSAGE* (1941) 62m PAR c

Madeline Carroll (Carol), Sterling Hayden (Adrian), Flora Robson (Mrs. Ainsworth), Leo G. Carroll (Delbridge), Mary Anderson (Mary), Cecil Kellaway (Capt. Jack Risingwell), Leigh Whipper (Morales), Dorothy Dandridge (Thalia), Jani LeGon (Maid), Fred Kohler, Jr. (Purser).

Poor drama featuring Hayden as a lonely young islander who falls in love with Madeline Carroll, the daughter of the man—the other Carroll, Leo G.—hired to manage the business end of the salt mine that is the mainstay of the atoll's economy. While the love-sick couple chase each other on the beach, Carroll's old man has to deal with a native workers' revolt. Nice color photography of the island is the only excuse for this yawner.

p&d, Edward H. Griffith; w, Virginia Van Upp (based on the novel Dido Cay by Nelson Hayes); ph, Leo Tover; ed, Eda Warren.

Romance (PR:A MPAA:NR)

BAILOUT AT 43,000* (1957) 78m UA bw

John Payne (Maj. Paul Peterson), Karen Steele (Carol Peterson), Paul Kelly (Col. Hughes), Richard Eyer (Kit Peterson), Constance Ford (Frances Nolan), Eddie Firestone (Capt. Mike Cavallero), Adam Kennedy (Lt. Simmons), Gregory Gay (Reinach), Steven Ritch (Maj. Goldman), Richard Crane (Capt. Nolan).

Writer Monash has done what many might have considered impossible; he took several interesting characters, a background of test piloting, and he made it all come out dull. Monash, who later went on to produce TV's of "Peyton Place" betrays his leanings to soap opera with a tiring story about Payne and the development of a special ejection seat for fighter planes. Payne is called back to the service, much to his chagrin. When two other pilots are out of the running (one dies with a broken neck, the other has an emergency operation) Payne must show his mettle. He does. This is as routine a film as one can find, and gets a star for the performances. BAILOUT AT 43,000 was Paul Kelly's final film. It was also the last film made under the Pine-Thomas aegis. Tough to go out on such a low note, especially after having done more than 80 movies, many of them notably entertaining.

p, William Thomas, Howard B. Pine; d, Francis D. Lyon; w, Paul Monash; m, Albert Glasser; ed, George Gittens; cos, Alvena Tomin.

Adventure (PR:A MPAA:NR)

BAIT*1/2 (1950, Brit.) 73m Advance/Adelphi bw

Diana Napier (Eleanor Panton), John Bentley (Ducane), John Oxford (Bromley), Patricia Owens (Anne Hastings), Kenneth Hyde (Jim Prentiss), Sheila Robins (Nina Revere), Willoughby Goddard (John Hartley).

In a vicious love reprisal, Napier, who heads a gang of thugs, frames Bentley for the murder of her brother. Dumb premise and script make for a tedious production which is not worth more than a nod or two.

d, Frank Richardson; w, Mary Bendetta, Francis Miller (based on the play by Richardson); ph, Ernest Palmer.

Crime (PR:A MPAA:NR)

BAIT** (1954) 79m COL bw

Cleo Moore (Peggy), John Agar (Ray), Hugo Haas (Marko), Emmett Lynn (Foley), Bruno VeSota (Webb), Jan Englund (Waitress), George Keymas (Chuck), Prolog by Sir Cedric Hardwicke.

Hugo Haas always made interesting films. This one is a meld between THE POSTMAN ALWAYS RINGS TWICE and THE TREASURE OF THE SIERRA MADRE. Haas and Agar find a lost gold mine that Haas has been looking for. Haas has promised Agar half the action. Then the old reprobate decides to get rid of Agar and uses Moore, his wife, as the bait (hence the title). Haas specialized in really low-budget pictures with high concepts. Lots of the action takes place in a small cabin, not unlike Chaplin's in THE GOLD RUSH. This is about as sexy as theatrical films got in 1954. Haas attempts to catch Moore and Agar en flagrante delicto so he can kill the younger man and call it justifiable. The plan backfires and Haas (who always looked like Walter Slezak's brother—not Walter Slezak, but his brother) is vanquished. There is something intensely brooding about many of Haas' films, and this one is no exception. Given higher budgets and better scripts, he might have been a second-rate Hitchcock.

p&d, Hugo Haas; w, Samuel W. Taylor; ph, Edward P. Fitzgerald; m, Vaclav Divina; ed, Robert S. Eisen; m/l, Martin Schwab.

Drama (PR:C MPAA:NR)

BAKER'S HAWK*** (1976) 96m Doty-Dayton c

Clint Walker (Dan Baker), Burl Ives (Mr. McGraw), Diane Baker (Jenny Baker), Lee H. Montgomery (Billy Baker), Alan Young (Mr. Carson), Taylor Lacher (Sweeney), Bruce M. Fischer (Blacksmith), Cam Clarke (Morrie), Phil Hoover (Sled), Danny Bonaduce (Robertson), Brian Williams (Jeremy), Burt Mustin (General), Martin Eric (Wattle).

What a pleasant relief to see a good western again. After HEAVEN'S GATE and THE MISSOURI BREAKS, here comes BAKER'S HAWK. Hoodlum vigilantes are trying to get Ives out of the neighborhood. He is a recluse who would just like to be left alone. Montgomery becomes the old coot's pal, then enlists Walker, his father, in helping to foil the villains. It's a throwback to earlier days in westerns when men were men and women were women and the old values and ethics and morals were easily recognizable. This was long before westerns became psychological and boring. A well-photographed film with lots of natural footage, good animal stock and a sincerity that can be felt in every frame. The score by Lex De Azevedo is just right as are all other technical credits. Kudos to Doty-Dayton for proving that a good western can be made for a price, without sacrificing taste.

p&d, Lyman D. Dayton; w, Dan Greer, Hal Harrison, Jr. (based on the novel by Jack Bickham); ph, Bernie Abramson (DeLuxe Color); m, Lex De Azevedo; ed, Parkie Singh; prod d, Bill Kenney; set d, Tony Montenaro, Sig Tinglof; cos, Tom Dawson.

Western (PR:A MPAA:G)

BAKER'S WIFE, THE**** (1940, Fr.) 130m La Societe des Films Marcel Pagnol bw (LA FEMME DU BOULANGER)

Raimu (The Baker), Ginette Leclerc (The Baker's Wife), Charles Moulin (The Shepherd), Robert Vattier (The Priest), Robert Bassac (The School Teacher), Charpin (The Marquis), Maximiliene.

David Merrick attempted to capture the joy of THE BAKER'S WIFE in a stage presentation in 1976, two years after Marcel Pagnol passed away. The show, which starred Topol (Tevya in the film version of FIDDLER ON THE ROOF) and Patti Lupone (star of the stage version of "Evita") closed on the road, despite the tuneful score by Stephen Schwartz. In Pagnol's lighter-than-air screen version, he tells the story of Provence baker Raimu, who is readying his first loaves of bread in his new town. Fernand Chapin, the Marquis, arrives and introduces his shepherd, Charles Moulin, who will call on the baker regularly from now on for the marquis' bread. Moulin is immediately attracted to Ginette LeClerc, the Baker's Wife of the title. She is much younger than her spouse and terribly unhappy. This combination draws her to Moulin and they make plans to run away together. On Sunday, without his wife to wake him, Raimu oversleeps and the bread is burnt. Despite eyewitness reports, the baker will not hear of his wife's infidelity and he convinces himself that she has gone off to visit her mother. Even the priest makes a veiled reference to the case at Mass but Raimu doesn't listen and gets drunk at the local bar. The villagers wonder when he'll get back to baking their bread and they are shocked to learn that he has no intention of resuming his baking chores until his wife returns. The Marquis leads them all on a military foray and LeClerc is eventually found on a small island with Moulin by the priest, Vattier, who has been riding on the shoulders of Bassac as they march through the swamps to get to the cuckolding couple. When Moulin sees the priest, his guilt overcomes him and he flees. Ginette is stunned by his behavior and returns to the town and her husband. Raimu is thrilled to have her back and says nary a word about her affair. Instead, he scolds the cat (an oblique reference to his wife) for staying out late. Leclerc answers for the cat and assures Raimu that the pussy will never leave home again. A wonderful closing for a charming picture. (In French; English subtitles.)

p, Hakim Brothers; d&w, Marcel Pagnol (based on Jean Giono's novel Jean Le Bleu); ph, R. Lendruz, N. Daries; m, Vincent Scotto; ed, Suzanne de Troeye.

Comedy (PR:C MPAA:NR)

BAL TABARIN* (1952) 84m REP bw

Muriel Lawrence (Judy Allen), William Ching (Don Barlow), Claire Carleton (Stella Simmons), Steve Brodie (Joe Goheen), Steven Geray (Inspector Manet), Carl Milletaire (Little Augie), Jan Rubini (Violinist), Tom Powers (Eddie Mendies), Gregory Gay (Dufar), Adrienne d'Ambricourt (Madam Ramquet), Herbert Deans (Inspector Llewelyn), French Can-Can Dancers.

Musical action as we follow the adventures of Lawrence as she hides out in Paris from the crooks who murdered her boss, who was a jewel fence. Most of the action revolves around the title nightclub which gives Lawrence a chance to belt out a few tunes while waiting for mobster Brodie to come after the jewel cache she is carrying. Luckily, the French Police arrive in time to prevent disaster.

p, Herbert J. Yates; d, Philip Ford; w, Houston Branch; ph, Reggie Lanning, Michael Kelber; m, R. Dale Butts; ed, Tony Martinelli; m/l, Jack Elliot, Tom Mack.

Musical/Drama (PR:A MPAA:NR)01144

BALALAIKA**1/2 (1939) 102m MGM bw

Nelson Eddy (Peter), Ilona Massey (Lydia), Charles Ruggles (Nicki), Frank Morgan (Danchenoff), Lionel Atwill (Marakov), C. Aubrey Smith (Gen. Karagin), Joyce Compton (Masha), Dalies Frantz (Dimitri), Walter Woolf King (Sibirski), Phillip Terry (Lieut. Smirnoff), Frederick Worlock (Ramensky), Abner Biberman (Leo), Arthur W. Cernitz (Capt. Pavloff), Roland Varno (Lt. Nikitin), George Tobias (Slaski), Paul Sutton (Anton), Willy Costello (Capt. Testoff), Paul Irving (Prince Morodin), Mildred Shay (Jeanette Sibirsky), Alma Kruger (Mrs. Danchenoff), Zeffie Tilbury (Princess).

Eddy (who looks naked without Jeanette MacDonald) is a Russian prince who masquerades as a member of the proletariat in order to get close to Massey, a singer at a local cafe. Eddy arranges for Massey to have her debut at the Imperial Opera but on that very night, Eddy's father is shot by Red assassins and one of them is Massey's father. The story swings from pre-revolutionary Russia to pre-WW II Paris. Massey goes to Siberia with other members of her family, but they are freed when the Revolution hits. Eddy flees to Paris and becomes a celebrity singer while working in a boite owned by a one-time Russian nobleman (Ruggles). It's a lavish picture filled with music and Eddy's rendition of "Stille Nacht" ("Silent Night") is memorable and one of his best moments on screen. Massey was expected to become the next Garbo . She was attractive, personable and had a fine figure. It just didn't happen, though, and was soon doing second-rate horror films that were far beneath her abilities. But in BALALAIKA, she was young, had stars in her eyes, and the world was hers...for a while.

p, Lawrence Weingarten; d, Reinhold Schunzel; w, Leon Gordon, Charles Bennett, Jacques Deval (based on the operetta by Eric Maschwitz, George Ponford and Bernard Gruen); ph, Joseph Ruttenberg, Karl Freund; m, Herbert Stothart; ed, George Boemler; m/l, Stothart, Gus Kahn, Bob Wright, Chet Forrest.

Musical   **(PR:A MPAA:NR)**

BALCONY, THE*   (1963) 84m City Film Corp./Continental bw

Shelley Winters (Madam Irma), Peter Falk (Police Chief), Lee Grant (Carmen), Ruby Dee (Thief), Peter Brocco (Judge), Jeff Corey (Bishop), Joyce Jameson (Penitent), Arnette Jens (Horse), Leonard Nimoy (Roger), Kent Smith (General).

A low-budget adaptation of Genet's play that is an improvement on the stage piece. Gone is much of the blue language that seemed to be there to shock and nothing else. Maddow's screenplay takes the best of the play and makes it better. This literary work preceded "Fantasy Island" by several years but there are many similarities. The "Balcony" is a brothel where you can have your fantasies realized. It's administered by Winters (slimmer, prettier than Ricardo Montalban) and her occasional lover, Police Chief Falk (taller, funnier than Herve Villechaize). It's an adult fantasy about this fabulous whorehouse where you can even pay with your credit card. The plot is loose but the attention to details is marvelous. A worthwhile film despite what you may have heard from bluenoses and rednecks who didn't understand it. Also interesting because of the early appearances of Nimoy (Spock in STAR TREK), Joyce Jameson (now a well-known astrologer syndicated in hundreds of newspapers), Lee Grant (now also a director), and Jeff Corey, (for years Hollywood's favorite acting coach).

p, Joseph Strick, Ben Maddow; d, Strick; w, Maddow (based on the play by Jean Genet; translated by Bernard Frecthman); ph, George Folsey; m, Igor Stravinsky; ed, Chester W. Schaeffer.

Drama/Fantasy   **(PR:O MPAA:NR)**

BALL AT SAVOY*   (1936, Brit.) 69m Stafford/Radio bw

Conrad Nagel (John Egan), Marta Labarr (Anita), Lu Anne Meredith (Mary), Fred Conyngham (George), Aubrey Mather (Herbert), Fred Duprez (Mason), Bela Mila (Terese), Dino Galvani (Manager), Monte de Lisle (Stranger), Esther Kiss (Suzanne), Tony de Lungo (Maitre d'Hotel), Broun Barnaby (Train Conductor).

Dim musical starring Nagel as a baron who poses as a waiter to meet the girl of his dreams, Labarr, who is an opera singer. The plot thickens when the baron/waiter is accused of being a jewel thief. Remake of a German film and set in Cannes.

p, John Stafford; d, Victor Hanbury; w, Akos Tolney, Reginald Long (based on the book by Alfred Grunwald and Fritz Lohner-Beda); ph, James Wilson; m, Paul Abraham.

Musical   **(PR:A MPAA:NR)**

BALL AT THE CASTLE*

(1939, Ital.) 95m Industria Cinematographiche Italiane bw (BALLO AL CASTELLO)

Alida Valli (Greta Larsen), Antonio Centa (Tenente Paola Karinsky), Carlo Lombardi (Il Principe Giorgio), Sandra Ravel (Rita Valenti), Giuseppe Pierozzi (Ballet Master Petrovich), Carrado De Cenzo (Il Principe Nicola), Vasco Creti (Sebastiano Larsen), Guido Notario (Director Of The Theatre), Ermino d O'Olivio (Substitute Ballet Master).

Creaky Cinderella tale of a young ballerina, Valli, who is unknowingly picked up and brought to her dance class by the Crown Prince. The class thinks she has become the Prince's girl and Valli becomes upset when she learns that her promotion to premier ballerina wasn't based on her talent, but on her instructor's fears of offending the Prince. For ballet aficionados only.

d, Massimilino Nuefeld; w, Carlo Della Posta, Oreste Biancoli; ph, Valcav Vich; m, Fragna; ch, Mara Dousse.

Romance   **(PR:A MPAA:NR)**

BALL OF FIRE*   (1941) 111m Goldwyn/RKO bw

Gary Cooper (Prof. Bertram Potts), Barbara Stanwyck (Sugarpuss O'Shea), Oscar Homolka (Prof. Gurkakoff), Henry Travers (Prof. Jerome), S. Z. "Cuddles" Sakall (Prof. Magenbruch); Tully Marshall (Prof. Robinson), Leonid Kinsky (Prof. Quintana), Richard Haydn (Prof. Oddly), Aubrey Mather (Prof. Peagram), Allen Jenkins (Garbage Man), Dana Andrews (Joe Lilac), Dan Duryea (Duke Pastrami), Ralph Peters (Asthma Anderson), Kathleen Howard (Miss Bragg), Mary Field (Miss Totten), Charles Lane (Larson), Charles Arnt (McNeary), Elisha Cook, Jr. (Cook), Alan Rhein (Horseface), Eddie Foster (Pinstripe), Will Lee (Benny, "the Creep"), Aldrich Bowker (Justice of the Peace), Addison Richards (District Attorney), Kenneth Howell, Tommy Ryan, Pat West, Ed Mundy, June Horne, Geraldine Fissette, Ethelreda Leopold, George Barton, Walter Shumway, Doria Caron, Merrilee Lannon, Catherine Henderson, Helen Seamon, Jack Perry, Mildred Morris, Gerald Pierce, Francis Sayles, Lorraine Miller, Chet De Vito, Pat Flaherty, George Sherwood, Lee Phelps, Ken Christy, Del Lawrence, Eddy Chandler, Dick Rush, Johnnie Morris, Edward Clark, Gene Krupa and His Orchestra.

Despite the presence of a fine cast of farceurs, a director who knows what he's doing, and screenwriters who've been there before with great success, BALL OF FIRE just misses being the wacko comedy it should have been. Perhaps everyone was trying too hard to live up to their reputations and they should have just relaxed and had more fun. This feels a bit labored. Cooper is a stodgy linguist researching slang for a new encyclopedia. In order to get closer to it, he recruits Stanwyck, a

stripper who knows exactly what color the cat's pajamas should be and why it's 23, not 24 or 22 Skiddoo. Cooper lives in a huge house with seven other profs and she moves in with them to avoid the long arm of the law. The old guys get to like her, go to see her perform (they are truly fish out of water) and enjoy her presence in their otherwise dusty lives. She's engaged to gangster Andrews (horribly miscast) and is supposed to tie the knot soon but she falls for Cooper and decides to try it with him instead. There's a veritable corps de comedy in the character actors here. One look at the cast list will convince anyone that scene-stealing would have been the byword if not under the firm Hawks hand. It's 15 minutes too long to be a comedy classic, but the Wilder/Brackett dialog should be memorized by any fledgling playwright. (Remade as A SONG IS BORN.)

p, Samuel Goldwyn; d, Howard Hawks; w, Charles Brackett, Billy Wilder (based on the story "From A to Z" by Thomas Monroe, Wilder); ph, Gregg Toland; m, Alfred Newman; ed, Daniel Manell; art d, Perry Ferguson; set d, Julie Heron; m/l, "Drum Boogie," Gene Krupa.

Comedy   **Cas.**   **(PR:A MPAA:NR)**

BALLAD IN BLUE   (SEE: BLUES FOR LOVERS, 1966, Brit.)

BALLAD OF A GUNFIGHTER* ½   (1964) 84m Bill Ward/Parade bw

Marty Robbins (Himself), Joyce Reed (Secora), Bob Barron (McCord), Nestor Paiva (Padre), Michael Davis (Miguelito), Charlie Aldrich (Amigo), Laurette Luez (Felina).

The near-legendary country singer Marty Robbins' only starring role in a movie based on his million-selling record, "El Paso." Robbins and his bandit buddy have a falling out over a pretty cowgirl. An independent production and a low-budget curiosity.

p,d&w, Bill Ward; ph, Brydon Baker; ed, Jack Cornall, Bill Keith; set d, Raymond G. Boltz; cos, Muriel Pool.

Western   **(PR:A MPAA:NR)**

BALLAD OF A SOLDIER**   (1960, USSR) 89m Mosfilm/Kingsley bw

Vladimir Ivashov (Alyosha), Shanna Prokhorenko (Shura), Antonina Maximova (Alyosha's Mother), Nikolai Kruchkov (General), Evgeni Urbanski (Invalid).

Moving, often heart-tearing profile of a beardless boy soldier who, in order to win a few days leave, performs an incredibly heroic act at the front during WW II. The story deals with Ivashov's adventures en route to his mother, first encountering and helping a legless soldier, Urbanski. Next he delivers a bar of soap to the wife of a comrade at the front only to find in shame that she is living with another man. Allowed to travel in a boxcar to his native city, the soldier is suddenly joined by a young, pretty girl hitching a ride and they form an innocent, touching, but brief, friendship. Most of Ivashov's time is used up on others, but he does manage to see his mother before hurrying back to fight the Nazis. Although many scenes and twists smack of ALL QUIET ON THE WESTERN FRONT, much of the film is sheer poetry as director Chukhrai plays his cameras quickly on the principal actors with a vast wartime panorama always moving in the background. Deft touches enrich the film, such as the girl's (Prokhorenko) beautiful hair blowing in the breeze, almost waving goodbye when she makes her farewell, a baby blowing bubbles while sitting on the stairs leading from the apartment where the youth has nervously delivered the soap to the cheating wife. This is Soviet filmmaking at its finest, even though there is the unmistakable tinge of propaganda. A winner of Golden Gate and Cannes Festival Awards. (In Russian; English subtitles.)

d, Grigori Chukhrai; w, Valentin Yoshow, Chukhrai; m, Michael Siv.

War Drama   **Cas.**   **(PR:A MPAA:NR)**

BALLAD OF A HUSSAR**   (1963, USSR) 94m Mosfilm/Artkino c

Larissa Golubkina (Shura), Yuri Yakoviev (Rzhevsky), Igor Ilyinsky (Kutuzov), Tatyana Shmyga (Masha).

If you like Russian films, opera, and melodramas about the Napoleonic invasion, you may like this movie. Mother Russia actually takes some heavy spoofing in this well-made musical that is sort of the Soviet version of some of the MGM musicals of the 1940s and 1950s. The plot is something Friml might have rejected as being too silly; and he would have been right. Golubkina is due to marry an ass. She sets out to prick his pomposity. In accomplishing this, she becomes an authentic hero and doesn't reveal that she is not a he until near the end of the movie. You can just picture Kathryn Grayson and Edmond Purdom in the leads, with "Cuddles" Sakall and Phil Silvers doing the comic relief. One of the very rare pictures with a sense of humor to come out of the Soviet Union. It was many years between this and MOSCOW DOES NOT BELIEVE IN TEARS (1980).

d, Eldar Ryazanov; w, A. Gladkov; ph, Leonid Kralnekov; m, Tikhon Khrennikov.

Musical   **(PR:A MPAA:NR)**

BALLAD OF CABLE HOGUE, THE* ½   (1970) 121m WB c

Jason Robards (Cable Hogue), Stella Stevens (Hildy), David Warner (Joshua), Strother Martin (Bowen), Slim Pickens (Ben), L. Q. Jones (Taggart), Peter Whitney (Cushing), R. G. Armstrong (Quittner), Gene Evans (Clete), William Mims (Jensen), Kathleen Freeman (Mrs. Jensen), Susan O'Connell (Claudia), Vaughn Taylor (Powell), Max Evans (Webb), James Anderson (Preacher), Felix Nelson (William).

Peckinpah demonstrated a sense of humor in THE BALLAD OF CABLE HOGUE which had not been seen since his early TV days when he ran one of the best and most overlooked cowboy shows ever, "The Westerner" with Brian Keith. Robards is a prospector abandoned in the desert and left to die by Martin and Jones. (They worked together again that same year in THE BROTHERHOOD OF SATAN.) Instead of dying, he finds water in a previously arid spot, opens a rest stop for thirsty travelers, and prospers. Stevens is a hot number determined to sleep her way to riches and, after a brief fling with Robards, she decides to move on to greener sheets, fleeing to San Francisco. Warner pops in and out as a preacher who can't decide if he should save souls or live a life of dedicated hedonism. Hedonism wins. If you're expecting blood and guts and slow-motion death, forget it. Peckinpah decided to make a different movie here and different it was indeed. Not a hit at the box office (the title was terrible), it will remain as one of his finest. It's funny, touching, and never crosses into mawkish sentimentality. It is at its best when chronicling what was happening when the Old West was passing and creeping mercantilism was advancing across the face of western society. Second only to his classic RIDE THE HIGH COUNTRY in 1962.

p, Phil Feldman, Sam Peckinpah, William Faralla; d, Peckinpah; w, John Crawford, Edmund Penney; ph, Lucien Ballard (Technicolor); m, Jerry Goldsmith; ed, Frank Santillo, Lou Lombardo; art d, Leroy Coleman; cos, Robert Fletcher; m/l, Richard Gillis, Goldsmith.

Western (PR:C MPAA:R)

BALLAD OF COSSACK GLOOTA**

(1938, USSR) 83m Soyuzdetfilm/Amkino

Vitla Seleznev (Mousie), K. Nassonov (Commissar), N. Sokolov (Grandfather), Lenia Shekhman (Zhigan), Kostia Tirtov (Sashko), N. Russinova (Mother), A. Grechhany (Goloven), N. Starostin (Ataman Kozolup), N. Gorlow (Ataman Levka), A. Zhutyev (Vassily), Y. Martsinchik (Polish Officer).

Well done Russian youth film about two boys, Shekhman and Tirtov, whose village has been overrun by Polish mercenaries. The boys fight the cold and hunger as they make their way to the Russian Army to get help for their people. A little heavy on the Red propaganda at times, but not too bad. (In Russian; English subtitles.)

d, Igor Savchenko; w, A. Galdar; ph, Y. Fogelman; m, S. Potolski.

Drama (PR:A MPAA:NR)

BALLAD OF GREGORIO CORTEZ, THE*** (1983) 104m EM c

Edward James Olmos (Cortez), Tom Bower (Boone Choate), Bruce McGill (Bill Blakely), James Gammon (Sheriff Fly), Alan Vint (Sheriff Trimmell), Tim Scott (Sheriff Morris), Pepe Serna (Romaldo Cortez), Brion James (Capt. Rogers), Barry Corbin (Abernethy), Rosana DeSoto (Carolot Munoz).

An Independent production originated at Robert Redford's Sundance Institute in Utah and was a cult film practically before the film was dry. The picture, like ODE TO BILLY JOE, TAKE THIS JOB AND SHOVE IT and ALICE'S RESTAURANT, is based on a song that was written about an actual event. Cortez was a San Antonio cowhand in 1901 who was arrested in a case of mistaken identity. Because no one could properly translate into Spanish for him, Cortez fought back and accidentally slew a sheriff in what today would be deemed self-defense. Director Robert Young (not to be confused with film and television actor) then takes us on an 11-day manhunt with Olmos, as Cortez, hightails it for Mexico. He is pursued by the legendary Texas Rangers (who once sent a lone Ranger in to quell a huge prison riot; when the warden said "One man? They only sent one man?," the Ranger shrugged and answered, "Wal, y'only got one riot!") as well as a small army of others who can't catch the mercurial Olmos. The press made him a hero and, after escaping several traps, he turned himself in when he learned that his family had been arrested and were being held prisoners. It uses the flashback technique of several people seeing the same event and offering varying accounts of what happened. The remainder of the film is the trial and the near-lynching of the protagonist. Since the original courthouse and jail still exist, they were used to lend an air of absolute reality to the film. This could have been an overblown paean to peons, but the taste evinced by the creators is apparent everywhere, so we see a slice of what life must have been like at the turn of the century. This story falls into that genre that Faulkner spoke of: "An appealing person struggles against insurmountable odds in search of a worthwhile goal." That same rule of thumb can be applied to everything from ROCKY to NORTH BY NORTHWEST. For fledgling screenwriters, it's a phrase to live by. Olmos would go on to achieve small-screen fame as the stoical Lt. Castillo on "Miami Vice."

p, Michael Hausman; d, Robert M. Young; w, Victor Villasenor (based on the novel *With His Pistol in His Hands* by Americo Paredes); ph, Ray Villalobos, Young (DuArt Color); m, W. Michael Lewis, Edward James Olmos; ed, Richard Soto; art d, Stuart Wurtzel.

Western **Cas.** (PR:C-O MPAA:PG)

BALLAD OF JOSIE**1/2 (1968) 102m UNIV c

Doris Day (Josie Minick), Peter Graves (Jason Meredith), George Kennedy (Arch Ogden), Andy Devine (Judge Tatum), William Talman (Charlie Lord), David Hartman (Fonse Pruitt), Guy Raymond (Doc), Audrey Christie (Annabelle Pettijohn), Karen Jensen (Deborah Wilkes), Elisabeth Fraser (Widow Renfrew), Linda Meiklejohn (Jenny), Shirley O'Hara (Elizabeth), Timothy Scott (Klugg), Don Stroud (Bratsch), Paul Fix (Alpheus Minick), Harry Carey (Mooney), John Fiedler (Simpson), Robert Lowery (Whit Minick), Teddy Quinn (Luther Minick).

Harmless Doris Day western/comedy with Day as a frontier feminist who accidentally kills her drunkard husband with a pool cue. Needing to support herself and her son, she opens her own sheep farm, much to the dismay of the locals. Enter Kennedy as the rancher who wants to run her out of business and Graves as her hero. Good fun for Day fans.

p, Norman MacDonnell; d, Andrew V. McLaglen; w, Harold Swanton; ph, Milton Krasner; m, Frank DeVol; ed, Otho S. Lovering, Fred A. Chulak; art d, Alexander Golitzen, Addison Hehr; m/l, Floyd Huddleston, Don Costa, Jack Lloyd, Gene de Paul.

Western/Comedy (PR:A MPAA:NR)

BALLAD OF NARAYAMA** (1961, Jap.) 98m Shochiku c

Kinuyo Tanaka (Orin), Teiji Takahashi (Tatsuhei), Yuko Mochizuki (Tama-yan), Danko Ichikawa (Kesakichi), Keiko Ogasawara (Mutsu-yan), Seiji Miyaguchi (Mata-yan), Yunosuke Ito (Mata-yan's son), Ken Mitsuda (Teru-Yan).

One of those so-called "sensitive" Japanese films so popular in the early 1960s which took a primitive custom of ancient Nippon and tried to explain and ameliorate its barbaric nature. Director Kinoshita shows how, in long centuries past, it was the tradition to herd the sickly aged onto the barren wastes of Mount Narayama where the elements would soon put them out of their misery and beyond the painful responsibility of their struggling and starving offspring. One old woman in her seventies accepts her fate but stoically lingers, surviving on sheer will power. Another elderly victim rebels at being sent to his death on the mountain by his brutal son who kills him and is, in turn, killed. The production is high in value and the photography stunning.

p, Ryuzo Ohtani; d&w, Keisuke Kinoshita (based on the novel by Shichiro Fukazawa); ph, Hiroyuki Kusuda (Grandscope, Fujicolor); m, R. Kineya, M. Nozawa; ed, Yoshi Sugihara; art d, Kisuka Ito.

Historical Drama (PR:C MPAA:NR)

BALLERINA** (1950, Fr.) 90m Memnon/Lux bw

Violette Verday (Nicole), Gabrielle Dorziot (Aunt), Henri Guisol (Jeweler), Romney Brent (Director), Nicolas Orloff (Loulou), Jean Mercure (Dancer).

Lyrical French ballet movie about a young dancer who daydreams about the men in her life. One is a petty thief, one a jeweler, one a middle-aged producer, and one a young dancer. Of course these fantasies include dancing, which is photographed nicely. Another film for ballet fans.

d&w, Ludwig Burger; ph, Robert Le Febre; ed, Jacques Poitrenaud.

Fantasy/Romance (PR:A MPAA:NR)

BALLOON GOES UP, THE* (1942, Brit.) 58m New Realm bw

Ethel Revnell (Ethel), Gracie West (Gracie), Donald Peers (Sgt. Jim), Ronald Shiner (Sgt. Shiner), Elsie Wagstaffe (Welfare Officer), Mrs. Masemore Morris (Lady Hurst), Gordon McLeod (Doctor).

Daffy tuner has entertainers impersonating military officers at a barrage-balloon site in order to nab Nazi spies. Ridiculous excuse to parade corny music hall numbers.

p, E. J. Fancey; d, Redd Davis; w, Val Valentine; ph, Stephen Dade.

Musical (PR:A MPAA:NR)

BALTHAZAR (SEE: AU HASARD BALTHAZAR, 1970)

BALTIC DEPUTY*1/2 (1937, USSR) 107m Lenfilm/Amkino bw

Nikolai Cherkassov (Prof. Polezhayev), Marta Domasheva (His Wife), Boris Livanov (Bocharov), Otto Zhakov (Vorobiev), Alexander Melnikov (Kuprianov).

Russian propaganda as Cherkassov plays a young botanist who is so thrilled with the Revolution that he goes out to the peasants to spread the word and aid the farmers with his scientific knowledge of planting and raising crops. The only thing that upsets him is his fellow scientists' distrust of the Bolsheviks. But it doesn't matter because the Red peasants, soldiers, and sailors respect his efforts to improve the country. The flag waving gets a bit hard to take. (In Russian; English subtitles.)

d, Alexander Zarkhl and Joseph Heifetz; w, David Dell, Zarkhl, Heifetz, and Leonid Rakhmanov (based on a story by Rakhmanov); ph, Hoissaye Kaplan.

Drama (PR:A MPAA:NR)

BALTIMORE BULLET, THE**1/2 (1980) 103m AE c

James Coburn (Nick Casey), Omar Sharif (The Deacon), Bruce Boxleitner (Billie Joe Robbins), Ronee Blakley (Carolina Red), Jack O'Halloran (Max), Calvin Lockhart (Snow White), Michael Learner (Paulie), Paul Barselou (Cosmo), Cissie Cameron (Sugar), Jeff Temkin (Sportscaster), Willie Mosconi (Sportscaster), Shep Sanders (Robin), Jon Ian Jacobs (Baron), Ed Bakey (Skinny), Robert Hughes (Ricco), Rocknee Tarkington (Gunner), Shay Duffin (Al), Thomas Castranova (Ernie), Eric Laneuville (Purvis), William M. Vint (Frankie), Lou Butera, Irving Crane, Richie Florence, Allan Hopkins, Peter Margo, Ray Martin, Jim Mataya, Steve Mizerak, Jim Rempe, Michael Sigel.

THE BALTIMORE BULLET is a combination of THE HUSTLER and ROCKY and about 20 other pictures, but that's okay because it's sort of fun. John Brascia (producer, co-writer) is a former ballroom dancer (team of Brascia and Tybee) who decided to make a movie about his second love: pool. Coburn takes Boxleitner under his wing and, when they meet in the ultimate match, Coburn says, "I taught you everything you know, kid. But I didn't teach you everything I know." Many real pool champs people the film. Sharif is the bad guy with O'Halloran, the behemoth, as a frightening henchman. Blakley improves on her NASHVILLE work and shows that she has an acting career if she really wants one. Major problem is that Coburn appears to have just a little too much class to be the frazzled pool hustler. His lingo is more billiards than pool. Some misanthropy and cheap anti-women jokes in the script might cause militants to hiss. Women's libbers take note: This film is not for thee. Keep an eye out for Steve Mizerak (the pool player in the beer commercials) and Irving Crane, one of the deans of the game.

p, John F. Brascia; d, Robert Ellis Miller; w, Brascia, Robert Vincent O'Neil; ph, James A. Crabe (Eastmancolor); m, Johnny Mandel; ed, Jerry Brady; prod d, Herman Blumenthal; art d, Adrian Gorton; cos, Patricia Ann Norris.

Drama **Cas** (PR:C MPAA:PG)

BAMBI**** (1942) 70m Disney/RKO c

Featuring the voices of Bobby Stewart (Bambi), Peter Behn (Thumper), Stan Alexander (Flower), Cammie King (Phylline), Donnie Dunagan, Hardie Albright, John Sutherland, Tim Davis, Sam Edwards, Sterling Holloway, Ann Gillis.

BAMBI might well have been called THUMPER because it is the little rabbit that steals the picture away from the deer. We watch Bambi mature from youth through co-leader of the herd, with his father. It could be the story of any youngster facing trials and tribulations, except that this youngster is an animal. He loses his mother to a hunter's bullet (there wasn't a dry eye in the house during that scene), he fights for his doe, Phylline, and must kill his rival for her cold nose. He then saves her from a horde of mad dogs. The culminating scene of a forest fire ranks among the animated highlights in the history of the technique. Thumper provides all the comedy as he teaches Bambi how to make it in the forest. The funniest scene is the rabbit attempting to show Bambi how to slide across the ice. To see Disney's animation so many many years ago and to see what now passes for TV animation is to realize that the art has gone backward. There is virtually no mention of humans in the movie and the only word Bambi fears is "Man" because that word symbolizes the attack on the tranquility of the sylvan forest. This is definitely a film for the entire family, but small children become wrapped up in the story and may, in fact, identify with Bambi to the point where bad dreams might occur. This is not a psychological interpretation, just the result of having seen the film at an impressionable age and never quite recovering. Songs include "Let's Sing A Gay Little Spring Song," "Love Is A Song," "Little April Shower," "The Thumper Song," and "Twitterpated," (Frank Churchill, Larry Morey).

p, Walt Disney, David D. Hand; w, Perce Pearce, Larry Morey (based on the story by Felix Salten); m, Frank Churchill, Edward Plumb (conducted by Alexander Steinert); seq. dir., James Algar, Bill Roberts, Norman Wright, Paul Satterfield, Sam Armstrong, Graham Heid; animators, Milton Kahl, Eric Larson, Franklin Thomas, Oliver M. Johnston, Jr.

Feature-Length Cartoon (PR:AAA MPAA:NR)

BAMBOLE!**
(1965, Ital.) 111m Royal Films/COL bw (AKA: FOUR KINDS OF LOVE; THE DOLLS)

THE TELEPHONE CALL: Virna Lisi (Luisa), Nino Manfredi (Giorgio), Alicia Bradet (Armenia), TREATISE ON EUGENICS: Elke Sommer (Ulla), Maurizio Arena (Massimo), Piero Focaccia (Valerio), THE SOUP: Monica Vitti (Giovanna), Orazio Orlando, John Karlsen, Roberto De Simone, MONSIGNOR CUPID: Gina Lollobrigida (Beatrice), Jean Sorel (Vincenzo), Akim Tamiroff (Monsignor Arcudi).

Tepid inspection of everyday Italian life told in a quartet of uninteresting stories supposedly based on Boccaccio's Decameron tales. It's really an excuse to parade a bevy of Italian sexpots—Lisi, Vitti, Lollobrigida, and the tantalizing Teuton, Sommer, but they somehow, in this shabby production, manage to look unappealing.

p, Gianni Hecht Lucari; d, Dino Risi, Luigi Comencini, Franco Rossi, Mauro Bolognini (based on Giovanni Boccaccio's Tales of the Decameron).

Drama (PR:C MPAA:NR)

BAMBOO BLONDE, THE**1/2 (1946) 68m RKO bw

Frances Langford (Louise Anderson), Ralph Edwards (Eddie Clark), Russell Wade (Patrick Ransom, Jr.), Iris Adrian (Montana), Richard Martin (Jim Wilson), Jane Greer (Eileen Sawyer), Glenn Vernon (Shorty Parker), Paul Harvey (Patrick Ransom, Sr.), Regina Wallace (Mrs. Ransom), Jean Brooks (Marsha), Tom Noonan (Art Department), Dorothy Vaughan (Mom).

A silly but pleasing war romance film that is truly a whirlwind production. Langford is singing in a two-bit Manhattan nightclub owned by Edwards where she meets B-29 pilot Wade. After a one-night romantic interlude, Wade goes off to the Pacific; on Saipan his pranksterish crew paints Langford's picture on the nose of its plane which becomes the scourge of the Pacific, sinking Japanese battleships and downing a host of Zeros. The fame of the plane and its name, THE BAMBOO BLONDE, inspires huckster Edwards to promote his club, singer, and a line of products under that name to a fortune. Wade returns, spurns his fiancee, Greer, and winds up in the arms of the honey-voiced Langford. The script and story are put together with cheap glue; even though Langford's voice is wonderful, the only memorable song she warbles is "Dreaming Out Loud." One of the most absurd production numbers is a brief slapdash chorus-crushing thing called "Moonlight Over the Islands," which helped to set Langford's career adrift.

p, Herman Schlom [Sid Rogell]; d, Anthony Mann; w, Olive Cooper, Lawrence Kimble (based on a story by Wayne Whittaker); ph, Frank Redman; ed, Les Millbrook; ch, Charles O'Curran; m/l, Mort Greene, Lou Pollack.

War Romance (PR:A MPAA:NR)

BAMBOO PRISON, THE** (1955) 79m COL bw

Robert Francis (Sgt. Bill Rand), Dianne Foster (Tanya Clayton), Brian Keith (Cpl. Brady), Jerome Courtland (Arkansas), E. G. Marshall (Fr. Francis Dolan), Earle Hyman (Doc Jackson), Jack Kelly (Slade), Richard Loo (Hsai Tung), Keye Luke (Li Ching), Murray Matheson (Clayton), King Donovan (Pop), Dick Jones (Jackie), Pepe Hern (Ramirez), Leo Gordon (Pike), Weaver Levy (Meatball), George Keymas (Metaxas), Denis Martin (Cockney).

THE BAMBOO PRISON is the Korean version of STALAG 17, down to the traitor in their midst, the apparent villain, some hijinks, etc. While nowhere as good as the former, there is much of merit in this film. It has many interesting plot twists and the theme of Americans turning to Communism under the brainwashing techniques of the North Koreans was, and still is, a fascinating topic. Keye Luke (Number One Son in many CHARLIE CHAN movies) makes a fine interrogator, as does Richard Loo. Leo Gordon does well as Pike and E.G. Marshall plays a phony priest so well that you want to confess everything to him. (When once asked what his initials stand for, Marshall said, "Everybody's Guess.")

p, Bryan Foy; d, Lewis Seiler; w, Edwin Blum, Jack DeWitt (based on a story by DeWitt); ph, Burnett Guffey; m. Mischa Bakaleinikoff; ed, Henry Batista.

War (PR:A MPAA:NR)

BAMBOO SAUCER, THE* (1968) 100m World Entertainment/NTA c

Dan Duryea (Hank Peters), John Ericson (Fred Norwood), Lois Nettleton (Anna Karachev), Bob Hastings (Garson), Vincent Beck (Zagorsky), Bernard Fox (Ephram), Robert Dane (Miller), Rico Cattani (Dubovsky), James Hong (Sam Archibald), Bartlett Robinson (Rhodes), Nick Katurich (Gadyakoff), Bill Mims (Vetry), Nan Leslie (Dorothy Vetry), Andy Romano (Blanchard).

Just plain awful sci-fi/anti-Cold War film starring Duryea (in his last role) as the head of an American expedition to find a hidden UFO in Red China. While hiking through the mountains the explorers meet a Soviet team who have the same idea. Both groups band together because of the intense fear of being discovered by the Chinese. Three of the group end up being taken for a ride on the space ship which zooms all the way to Saturn before being brought back as a gesture of universal brotherhood. Blech.

p, Jerry Fairbanks; d&w, Frank Telford (based on a story by Rip Von Ronkel and John Fulton); ph, Hal Mohr (DeLuxe Color); ed, Richard Harris; m, Edward Paul; art d, Theodore Holsopple; spec eff, Fulton, Glen Robinson.

Science Fiction/Adventure **Cas.** (PR:A MPAA:NR)

BANANA MONSTER, THE (SEE: SCHLOCK, 1971)

BANANA PEEL**1/2 (1965, Fr.) 97m Pathe bw (PEAU DE BANANE)

Jeanne Moreau (Cathy), Jean-Paul Belmondo (Michel), Claude Brasseur (Charlie), Gert Frobe (Lachard), Jean-Pierre Marielle (Reynaldo), Alain Cuny (Montemps).

Gang of con artists, led by Belmondo and Moreau, slowly weave a web to trap greedy millionaire Frobe. Director Marcel Ophuls (son of the great Max Ophuls) presents a breezy, often witty film that confuses the actors as much as the viewer, an intentional ploy designed to show mass avarice taking over the gang so that everyone is stealing from everyone else. It becomes impossible to tell the crooks from the straights, but it's still fun. (In French; English subtitles.)

p, Paul-Edmonde DeCharme; d, Marcel Ophuls; w, Claude Sautet, Daniel Boulanger, Ophuls; ph, Jean Rabler; m, Ward Swingle.

Comedy (PR:C MPAA:NR)

BANANA RIDGE*1/2 (1941, Brit.) 87m ABPC/Pathe bw

Robertson Hare (Willoughby Pink), Alfred Drayton (Mr. Pound), Isabel Jeans (Sue Long), Nova Pilbeam (Cora Pound), Adela Dixon (Mrs. Pound), Patrick Kinsella (Jones), Valentine Dunn (Mrs. Pink), Stewart Rome (Sir Ramsey Flight), John Stuart (Staples).

Ancient plot revived when an old lover suddenly appears to shock a wealthy man by presenting him with a bastard son she insists is his. The claim is false but the scheming lady parlays the offspring for plenty in a farce that never delivers the laughs.

p&d, Walter C. Mycroft; w, Mycroft, Lesley Storm, Ben Travers (based on the play by Travers); ph, Claude Friese-Greene.

Comedy (PR:A MPAA:NR)

BANANAS*** (1971) 82m UA c

Woody Allen (Fielding Mellish), Louise Lasser (Nancy), Carlos Montalban (Gen. Vargas), Natividad Abascal (Yolanda), Jacob Morales (Esposito), Miguel Suarez (Luis), David Ortiz (Sanchez), Rene Enriquez (Diaz), Jack Axelrod (Arroyo), Howard Cosell (Himself), Roger Grimsby (Himself), Don Dunphy (Himself), Charlotte Rae (Mrs. Mellish), Stanley Ackerman (Dr. Mellish), Dan Frazer (Priest), Martha Greenhouse (Dr. Feigen), Conrad Bain (Semple), Tigre Perez (Perez), Baron DeBeer (Ambassador), Arthur Hughes (Judge), John Braden (Prosecutor), Dorthi Fox (J. Edgar Hoover), Dagne Crane (Sharon), Axel Anderson, Ted Chapman, Ed Barth, Nicholas Saunders, Eulogio Peraza, Norman Evans, Robert O'Connel, Robert Dudley, Marilyn Hengst, Ed Crowley, Beeson Carroll, Allen Garfield, Princess Fatosh, Dick Callinan.

As Woody Allen's career flourished, he combined his writing and performing talents with his directorial eye and has now been assured a bust in the Comedy Hall of Fame. Before helming ANNIE HALL and MANHATTAN, he did a number of what might be called "Allen In The Rough"—pictures that were often hysterical and also embarrassing. Many of the gags were unrelated shticks that he'd culled from his own nightclub routines and stuck into the movies because he'd heard "live" laughter as response and knew they would work on screen. In BANANAS, Woody is his usual neurotic New Yorker. This time he's trying to make it with Lasser (one-time Allen wife), a political activist. She'll have nothing to do with him (Allen used to complain that was the case in real life) as she is totally immersed in the revolution taking place in a Caribbean country named San Marcos. As fate would have it (and in a manner that defies synopsizing) Woody winds up president of San Marcos in a false red beard and with all the attendant woes. He returns to the USA, is unmasked as a fraud, is tried for subversion and winds up getting married to Lasser with narration by Howard Cosell as the couple consummates their union for ABC's "Wide World of Sports." There are many side-splitting scenes in BANANAS and just as many gags that gag. It's a shame the movie wasn't made after Woody's directorial enlightenment.

p, Charles H. Joffe, Jack Grossberg; d, Woody Allen; w, Allen, Mickey Rose; ph, Andrew M. Costikyan (DeLuxe Color); m, Marvin Hamlisch; ed, Ron Kalish; prod d, Ed Wittstein; cos, Gene Coffin; m/l, "Quiero La Noche," Hamlisch (sung by

Yomo Toro Trio), "'Cause I Believe in Loving," Hamlisch, Howard Liebling (sung by Jake Holmes).

Comedy   **Cas.**   **(PR:C MPAA:NR)**

BAND OF ANGELS****

(1957) 125m WB c

Clark Gable (*Hamish Bond*), Yvonne De Carlo (*Amantha Starr*), Sidney Poitier (*Rau-Ru*), Efrem Zimbalist, Jr. (*Ethan Sears*), Rex Reason (*Seth Parton*), Patric Knowles (*Charles de Marigny*), Torin Thatcher (*Capt. Canavan*), Andrea King (*Miss Idell*), Ray Teal (*Mr. Calloway*), Russ Evans (*Jimmee*), Carolle Drake (*Michele*), Raymond Bailey (*Stuart*), Tommie Moore (*Dollie*), William Forrest (*Aaron Starr*), Noreen Corcoran (*Young Manty Starr*), Jack Williams (*Runaway Slave*), Zelda Cleaver (*Sukie*), Juanita Moore (*Budge*), Joe Narcisse (*Shad*), Marshall Bradford (*Gen. Butler*), Charles Heard (*Helper*), Roy Barcroft (*Gillespie, the Overseer*), Curtis Hamilton (*Jacob, the Coachman*), Riza Royce (*Mrs. Hopewell*), Jim Hayward (*Sheriff*), Larry Blake (*Town Crier*), Guy Wilkerson (*Minister*), Bob Steele, Mayo Loizeau, June-Ellen Anthony, Carla Merry, Dan White, Jean G. Harvey, Alfred Meissner, William Fawcett, Ewing Mitchell, Morgan Shaan, Paul McGuire, Martin Smith, Ann Doran, Milas Clark, Jr., Walter Smith, Charles Horvath, William Schallert, Carl Harbaugh, Anthony Ghazlo, Ann Staunton, Robyn Faire.

De Carlo's father dies, leaving her without a dime and forcing her to leave an exclusive girls' school. She then learns that she has Negro blood in her veins and is taken to New Orleans to be sold on the block. Before any mean-minded plantation owner can covet this beauty, Gable, a powerful and mysterious landowner, buys De Carlo and ensconces her inside his lavish mansion; after some resistance she becomes his mistress, growing to love this kindly savior. Comes the Civil War, the Yankees close in on the South, capturing New Orleans and recruiting ex-slaves to the colors, including Poitier, Gable's right-hand overseer whom he calls "My Claw" (sort of a soft profile of the legendary black leader Bras Coupe) and who deserts his master to join the Union Army, hating Gable's kindness and loathing part-black sister De Carlo for becoming his mistress. Risking execution by disobeying Yankee orders, Gable burns his crops and retreats to one of his remote plantations where Poitier hunts him down but in the end lets him go, realizing that Gable has raised him as a son. Gable is joined by De Carlo and they sail away with old salt Thatcher, who had once been in the slave trade with Gable. This is the terrible secret Gable reveals earlier to De Carlo in a wildly moving scene while sitting drunk in his New Orleans patio, a raging summer storm crashing overhead. Everyone in the film gives a top performance, even sultry De Carlo, who always had a penchant for overacting. Gable almost does a reprise of his magnificent Rhett Butler role in GONE WITH THE WIND. Reason, as De Carlo's one-time suitor and later a Bible-belching Union officer, is effective as a lustful religious nut. His friend, Zimbalist, is a bit unbelievable as the soft-spoken Union officer who aids De Carlo after Reason rejects her when he learns she is part black. Poitier does not have a likable role but does what he can with a surly, graceless character. Thatcher is great as the rollicking sea captain and Knowles is properly hateful as the smug, bigoted and pompous plantation owner who lusts after De Carlo. Walsh's direction is at its fleetest in a fine adaptation of the Robert Penn Warren novel. Steiner's score thunders and hums and calls plaintively, while the lensing by Ballard shows the Old South in all its glories and gluttonies.

d, Raoul Walsh; w, John Twist, Ivan Goff, Ben Roberts (based on the novel by Robert Penn Warren); ph, Lucien Ballard (Warner Color); m, Max Steiner; ed, Folmar Blangsted; art d, Franz Bachelin; cos, Marjorie Best.

Historical Drama/Adventure   **(PR:A MPAA:NR)**

BAND OF ASSASSINS**

(1970, Jap.) 122m Mifune/Toho c (SHINSENGUMI)

Toshiro Mifune, Isami Kondo, Keiju Kobayashi, Kinya Kitaoli, Rentaro Mikuni.

Late nineteenth-century Japan setting provides a colorful backdrop to a violent saga of the Shinsen, a secret military organization that supported through execution and terror a weak, oft-degenerate aristocracy. There's a whole lot of grunting going on, along with beheadings, murders, and intrigues so intricate as to make any Sumo wrestler lose weight. The brisk pace and inexplicable cutaways make up for a script that is senseless to any Westerner.

d, Tadashi Sawashima; w, Kenro Matsuura; ph, Kozuo Yamdada; m, Masau Sato.

Historical Drama   **(PR:C MPAA:NR)**

BAND OF OUTSIDERS**

(1966, Fr.) 95m Anouchka-Orsay/Royal bw (AKA: BANDE A PART, THE OUTSIDERS)

Anna Karina (*Odile*), Claude Brasseur (*Arthur*), Sami Frey (*Franz*), Louisa Colpeyn (*Mme. Victoria*), Daniele Girard (*English Teacher*), Ernest Menzer (*Arthur's Uncle*), Chantal Darget (*Arthur's Aunt*), Michele Seghers (*Pupil*), Claude Makovski (*Pupil*), Georges Staquet (*Legionnaire*), Michel Delahaye (*Doorman at School*).

A group of dreamy young people fantasize and then enact a robbery which subsequently involves them in a murder, a dream gone to bloody nightmare. This is an interesting if not thoroughly depressing film where Godard plays upon the winter grayness of Paris suburbs, this dismal background permeating the characters, almost forcing them into a fatalistic move, students outside authority, mingling with gangsters, prostitutes, pimps, the worst dregs of the great city. Though family members are represented, these young people have already severed their emotional relations with relatives. Although there are moments of levity, such as Karina, Brasseur, and Frey doing an impromptu chorus-line dance in a cheap cafe, they have abandoned the real joys of youth, opting for the naive philosophy that doom and gloom is chic, an attitude that brings their cloistered views into bloody collision with their own safety and mortality. Godard's certain art is present in every scene but the film's depressing climate and predictable story prevent it, for the most part, from rising above the mediocre.

p, Philippe Dussart; d&w, Jean-Luc Godard (based on the novel *Fool's Gold/Pigeon Vole* by Dolores Hitchens); ph, Raoul Coutard; m, Michel Legrand; ed, Agnes Guillemot, Francoise Collin.

Crime Drama   **(PR:C-O MPAA:NR)**

BAND OF THIEVES**

(1962, Brit.) 69m Filmvale/RFD bw

Acker Bilk (*Himself*), Jimmy Thompson (*Hon. Derek Delaney*), Jennifer Jayne (*Anne*), Geoffrey Sumner (*Governor*), Maudie Edwards (*Duchess of Hartlepoole*), Chairman Innes (*Mrs. Van Der Ness*), Arthur Mullard (*Getaway*), Michael Peake (*Warder*), Colin Smith (*Flash*), Norrie Paramor, Peter Haigh, Carol Denne.

Strange combination of crime and musical theme where ex-cons take their jazz band on tour, using it as a cover for robberies by its members. Not a good jam session.

p, Lance Comfort, Bill Chalmers, Harold Shampan; d, Peter Bezencenet; w, Lyn Fairhust.

Musical   **(PR:A MPAA:NR)**

BAND PLAYS ON, THE*

(1934) 87m MGM bw

Robert Young (*Tony*), Stuart Erwin (*Stuffy*), Leo Carrillo (*Angelo*), Betty Furness (*Kitty*), Ted Healy (*Joe*), Preston Foster (*Howdy*), Russell Hardie (*Mike*), William Tannen (*Rosy*), Robert Livingston (*Bob Stone*), Norman Phillips, Jr. (*Stuffy as a Child*), David Durand (*Tony as a Child*), Sidney Miller (*Rosy as a Child*), Beaudine Anderson (*Mike as a Child*), Betty Jean Graham (*Kitty as a Child*).

Monotonous tale of four street punks who are brought before a kindly judge for stealing a Ford. The Judge sends the kids to a football camp where the coach, Foster, teaches them the meaning of teamwork, loyalty, and honor. Bad job of matching newsreel footage of football crowds with the staged shots proves distracting.

d, Russell Mack; w, Bernard Schubert, Ralph Spence, Harvey Gates (based on the stories, "Blackfield" by Byron Morgan, J. Robert Bren and "The Gravy Game" by Harry Stuhldreher, W. Thorton Martin); ph, Leonard Smith; ed, William Levanway.

Drama   **(PR:A MPAA:NR)**

BAND WAGGON**

(1940, Brit.) 85m Gainsborough/GFD bw

Arthur Askey (*Big-Hearted Arthur*), Jack Hylton (*Himself*), Richard Murdoch (*Stinker*), Pat Kirkwood (*Pat*), Moore Marriott (*Jasper*), Peter Gawthorne (*Claude Pilkington*), Wally Patch (*Commissionaire*), Donald Calthrop (*Hobday*), Jack Hylton's Band, Freddy Schweitzer, Bruce Trent, Sherman Fisher Girls, Michael Standing, C. H. Middleton, Jasmine Bligh, Jonah Barrington.

Fair entertainment from apprentice comics who take over a haunted castle and convert it to a TV station, belting out tunes on one hand, and nabbing Nazi spies with the other. Another example of stretching a nonsense situation to the ridiculous in order to present music hall numbers, but it's a pleasing absurdity.

p, Edward Black; d, Marcel Varnel; w, Marriott Edgar, Val Guest (based on the radio series by Harry S. Pepper, Gordon Crier, Vernon Harris); ph, Henry Harris.

Musical   **(PR:A MPAA:NR)**

BAND WAGON, THE****

(1953) 111m MGM c

Fred Astaire (*Tony Hunter*), Cyd Charisse (*Gaby Berard*), Oscar Levant (*Lester Marton*), Nanette Fabray (*Lily Marton*), Jack Buchanan (*Jeffrey Cordova*), James Mitchell (*Paul Byrd*), Robert Gist (*Hal Benton*), Thurston Hall (*Col. Tripp*), Ava Gardner (*The Movie Star*), LeRoy Daniels (*Shoeshine Boy*), Jack Tesler (*Ivan*), Dee Turnell, Elynne Ray, Peggy Murray, Judy Landon (*Girls in Troupe*), Jimmie Thompson, Bert May (*Boys in Troupe*), John Lupton (*Jack, the Promoter*), Owen McGivney (*Prop Man*), Sam Hearn (*Agent*), Herb Vigran, Emory Parnell (*Men on Train*), Ernest Anderson (*Porter*), Frank Scannon, Stu Wilson, Roy Engel (*Reporters*), Al Hill (*Shooting Gallery Operator*), Paul Bradley (*Dancer in Park/Waiter*), Bobby Watson (*Bobby, the Dresser*), Lotte Stein (*Chambermaid*), Smoki Whitfield (*Chauffeur*), Dick Alexander, Al Ferguson (*Stagehands*), Betty Farrington (*Fitter*), Bess Flowers (*Lady on Train*).

The story is strictly from Cornsville and the actors all know it, so THE BAND WAGON is a satire of itself. The plot should tell all: aging Hollywood dancer (Astaire) comes to Broadway because his movies aren't doing business. Fabray and Levant (playing Comden and Green, authors of the screenplay) are a couple of New York playwrights who conceive a musical for their pal, Astaire. Buchanan is the theatrical wizard who takes what is essentially a simple story and makes a Faustian allegory out of it. Buchanan says, "The Faust legend always works" and how right he is, because, only a few years later, DAMN YANKEES was a stage and screen smash. Charisse is a ballerina pressed into stage service. She and Astaire do not hit it off (she thinks he's old and decrepit; he was 54 at the time) and he's afraid she's too tall for him. The play is a flop but we never get to see what it's about as the story concentrates on backstage machinations. After a disastrous opening night, all the warring factions decide to toss aside differences and work for the benefit of the show (would that were true in real life). It is, of course, a hit. Some of the highlight musical numbers are: "A Shine On Your Shoes"—done in a 42nd Street penny arcade; "Dancing In The Dark"—a memorable dance duet between Cyd and Fred; and, of course, the legendary "Triplets" by Fred, Nan, and Jack. Dietz and Schwartz never did get the recognition for their superb songwriting skills. Smith designed the musical numbers and Kidd did the choreography. If the only musical a person ever saw was THE BAND WAGON, that would be enough to establish the genre. Note: Listen closely to the lyrics of "That's Entertainment"—still as witty and sophisticated today as they were then.

p, Arthur Freed; d, Vincente Minnelli; w, Betty Comden, Adolph Green; ph, Harry Jackson (Technicolor); md, Adolph Deutsch; ed, Albert Akst; ch, Michael Kidd, Oliver Smith; m/l, Howard Dietz, Arthur Schwartz.

Musical   **Cas.**   **(PR:A MPAA:NR)**

BANDE A PART   (SEE: BAND OF OUTSIDERS, 1964)

BANDIDO**   (1956) 92m UA c

Robert Mitchum *(Wilson)*, Ursula Thiess *(Lisa)*, Gilbert Roland *(Escobar)*, Zachary Scott *(Kennedy)*, Rudolfo Acosta *(Sebastian)*, Henry Brandon *(Gunther)*, Douglas Fowley *(McGee)*, Jose I. Torvay *(Gonzalez)*, Victor Junco *(Lorenzo)*, Alfonso Sanchez Tello *(G. Brucero)*, Arturo Manrique *(Adolfo)*, Margarito Luna *(Santos)*, Miguel Inclan *(Priest)*, with Jose A. Espinosa, Jose Munoz, Manuel Sanchez Navarro, Antonio Sandoval, Alberto Pedret.

Mitchum stars as an American mercenary looking for action in Mexico during the Revolution. He is hired by bandit leader Roland to intercept an arms shipment being delivered to the government troops by Scott. Mitchum not only discovers the guns, but the charms of Scott's wife, Thiess. The film falls into a series of gun battles and double-crosses until the guns wind up with Roland and Mitchum rides off with Thiess. Standard adventure with Mitchum playing his part tongue-in-cheek.

p, Robert L. Jacks; d, Richard Fleischer; w, Earl Felton; ph, Ernest Laszlo (DeLuxe Color); m, Max Steiner; ed, Robert Golden; art d, John Martin Smith.

Western/Adventure   **(PR:A   MPAA:NR)**

BANDIDOS*   (1967, Ital.) 94m Epic Film/Hespeira Films c

Enrico Maria Salerno, Terry Jenkins, Venatino Venatini, Maria Martin, Marco Guglielmi, Chris Huerta.

Salerno (who dubbed Clint Eastwood in the Italian version of A FISTFUL OF DOLLARS) plays a sharpshooter who is viciously beaten up by an outlaw. The beating ends his days as a sharpshooter, but does nothing to dull his desire for revenge. Very stringy spaghetti western.

p, Solly V. Bianco; d, Max Dillmann; w, Romano Migliorini, Giambattista Mussetto, Juan Cobos; ph, Emilio Foriscot.

Western   **(PR:A   MPAA:NR)**

BANDIT, THE**   (1949, Ital.) 77m Lux/Times bw

Anna Magnani *(Lydia)*, Amadeo Nazzari *(Ernesto)*, Carla Del Poggio *(Maria)*, Carlo Campanini *(Carlo)*, Mino Doro *(Mirko)*, Folco Lulli *(Andrea)*, Eliana Banducci *(Rosetta)*.

Minor Italian neo-realist film starring Nazzari as a disillusioned soldier who becomes a crime chieftain to survive in postwar Italy. Only his love for his companion's small daughter keeps him in touch with the feelings he had before the war. Magnani is good as Nazzari's girl friend. (In Italian; English subtitles.)

d, Alberto Lattuada; w, O. Diancoli, M. Caudani, E. M. Margadonna; ph, Aldo Tonti.

Drama   **(PR:A   MPAA:NR)**

BANDIT KING OF TEXAS**   (1949) 60m REP bw

Allan "Rocky" Lane *(Himself)*, Black Jack *(His Stallion)*, Eddy Waller *(Nugget Clark)*, Helene Stanley *(Cynthia Turner)*, Jim Nolan *(Dan McCabe)*, Harry Lauter *(Tremm Turner)*, Robert Bice *(Gus)*, John Hamilton *(Marshal John Turner)*, Lane Bradford *(Cal Barker)*, George H. Lloyd *(Dobson)*, Steve Clark *(Tom Samson)*, I. Stanford Jolley *(Willets)*, Danni Nolan *(Emily Baldwin)*, Richard Emory *(Jim Baldwin)*.

Rocky is suspected of being involved with the villains who are selling nonexistent land to unwary frontier settlers. Once the people learn that the land is invisible, the villain Nolan kills the poor folks and steals their money. Rocky enlists the aid of Waller (who is particularly good as the town's jeweler) and Lauter (the marshal's son). A heap of riding, shooting, punching, kicking varmints and everything a devoted western fan might enjoy. This is better than most westerns of the period, mainly due to Cooper's intelligent screenplay and Brannon's no-nonsense direction.

p, Gordon Kay; d, Fred Brannon; w, Olive Cooper; ph, John MacBurnie; m, Stanley Wilson; ed, Irving M. Schoenberg.

Western   **(PR:A   MPAA:NR)**

BANDIT OF SHERWOOD FOREST, THE**   (1946) 85m COL c

Cornel Wilde *(Robert of Nottingham)*, Anita Louise *(Lady Catherine Maitland)*, Jill Esmond *(The Queen Mother)*, Edgar Buchanan *(Friar Tuck)*, Henry Daniell *(The Regent)*, George Macready *(Fitz-Herbert)*, Russell Hicks *(Robin Hood)*, John Abbott *(Will Scarlett)*, Lloyd Corrigan *(Sheriff of Nottingham)*, Eva Moore *(Mother Meg)*, Ray Teal *(Little John)*, Leslie Denison *(Allan-A-Dale)*, Ian Wolfe *(Lord Mortimer)*, Maurice R. Tauzin *(The King)*, Mauritz Hugo, Philip Van Zandt, Robert Williams, Harry Cording, Ralph Dunn, Dick Curtis *(Men-at-Arms)*, Nelson Leigh, George Eldredge, Robert Scott *(Robin Hood's Men)*, Ferdinand Munier *(Inn-keeper)*, Dan Stowell, Lane Chandler *(Outlaws)*, Ted Allan *(Captain of the Watch)*, Gene Stutenroth *(Jailer)*, Jimmy Lloyd *(Crossbowman)*, Holmes Herbert *(Baron)*.

The son of Robin Hood, Wilde, returns to Sherwood Forest to save England's young King and the Magna Carta from the evilness of the wayward regent Daniell. Nice color photography, decent sets, and a good cast of character actors help the average story line.

p, Leonard S. Picker, Clifford Sanforth; d, George Sherman, Henry Levin; w, Wilfred H. Pettitt, Melvin Levy (based on the novel *The Son Of Robin Hood* by Paul A. Castleton); ph, Tony Gaudio, William Snyder, George Meehan Jr. (Technicolor); m, Hugo Friedhofer; ed, Richard Fantl; md, Morris Stoloff; art d, Stephan Goosson, Rudolph Sternad; set d, Frank Kramer.

Adventure   **(PR:AA   MPAA:NR)**

BANDIT OF ZHOBE, THE*   (1959) 80m COL c

Victor Mature *(Kasin Khan)*, Anne Aubrey *(Zenda)*, Anthony Newley *(Stokes)*, Norman Wooland *(Maj. Crowley)*, Dermot Walsh *(Capt. Sounders)*, Walter Gotell *(Azhad Khan)*, Sean Kelly *(Lt. Wylie)*, Paul Stassino *(Hatti)*, Laurence Taylor *(Ahmed)*, Dennis Shaw *(Hussu)*, Murray Kash *(Zecco)*, Maya Koumani *(Tamara)*.

THE BANDIT OF ZHOBE is an American western in every sense of the word. It has the jut-jawed hero (Mature), the sweet young thing (Aubrey) and the dumb comic relief that embarrasses viewers (Newley). Yes, it's a true western except that it all takes place in Inja (never India). The story by Richard (who is still, in the middle 1980's, working for Broccoli, doing James Bond screenplays) has Mature as an Indian leader whose family as been wiped out by the British. Truth is, it wasn't the British at all but a rival group of Indians wearing British red coats. By the time the picture is over, the misunderstanding is rectified and everyone shakes hands. Mature (who got his big break on Broadway in "Lady In The Dark" as the handsome Hollywood hunk) is a bit long in the tooth and thick in the waist to play roles with this much derring-do. Newley, who began as The Artful Dodger in the original OLIVER TWIST, does his usual mugging act and is tiresome. It's all chase and melodrama with little care for characterizations.

p, Irving Allen, Albert Broccoli; d&w, John Gilling (based on a story by Richard Maibaum); ph, Ted Moore, Cyril Knowles (CinemaScope, Eastmancolor); m, Kenneth V. Jones; ed, Bert Rule; md, Muir Mathieson; cos, Elsa Fennell; m/l, Jones, Len Praverman; makeup, Colin Garde.

Western   **(PR:A   MPAA:NR)**

BANDIT QUEEN*   (1950) 69m Lippert bw

Barbara Britton *(Lola)*, Willard Parker *(Dan Hinsdale)*, Phillip Reed *(Joaquin Murietta)*, Barton MacLane *(Jim Harden)*, Martin Garralaga *(Fr. Antonio)*, Victor Kilian *(Jose Montalve)*, Thurston Hall *(Governor)*, Angie *(Nino)*, Anna Demetrio *(Maria)*, Paul Marion *(Manuel)*, Pepe Hern *(Raphael)*, Lalo Rios *(Juan)*, Cecile Weston *(Zara Montalve)*, John Merton *(Hank)*, Carl Pitti *(McWilliams)*, Hugh Hooker *(Dawson)*, Jack Ingram *(Barton)*, Mike Conrad *(Capt. Gray)*, Jack Perrin *(Mr. Grayson)*, Minna Phillips *(Mrs. Grayson)*, Margia Dean *(Carol Grayson)*, Felipe Turich *(Ortiz)*, Joe Dominguez *(Morales)*, Trina Varela *(Mrs. Morales)*, Nancy Laurents *(Ann)*, Roy Butler *(Guard)*, Elias Gomboa *(Waiter)*, Chuck Roberson *Deputy)*.

Barbara Britton is the daughter of some original Californians (read "Mexicans") who comes home from a trip to see her mother and father murdered. These original Californians had the land under which lots of gold was situated. Barbara decides to become the female equivalent of Zorro and takes her revenge against MacLane (who did some sort of dirty work in almost every picture he made) and Parker. Reed essays the role of fabled Murietta who rode the range at that time. The idea of a feminine Zorro or Robin Hood is a good one but the treatment misses.

p&d, William Berke; w Victor West, Budd Lesser (based on a story by West); ph, Ernest W. Miller; ed, Carl Pierson.

Western   **(PR:A   MPAA:NR)**

BANDIT RANGER*   (1942) 58m RKO bw

Tim Holt, Cliff "Ukulele Ike" Edwards, Joan Barclay, Kenneth Harlan, LeRoy Mason, Glenn Strange, Jack Rockwell, Bob Kortman, Dennis Moore, Frank Ellis, Jack Rockwell, Bud Geary, Russell Wade, Ernie Adams, Lloyd Ingraham, Tom London.

Tim wages a one-man saddle war against marauding cattle thieves, subduing the baddies and saving Barclay, the lady in peril. Routine sage grinder, one of six Holt oaters rushed into dusty existence by RKO between May and July 1942, before its rising B star, Holt, was drafted into the service. Songs include: "Move Along" and "Musical Jack" by Ray Whitley and Fred Rose.

p, Bert Gilroy; d, Lesley Selander; w, Bennett R. Cohen, Morton Grant (based on a story by Cohen); ed, Les Millbrook; md, Paul Sawtell.

Western   **(PR:A   MPAA:NR)**

BANDIT TRAIL, THE* 1/2   (1941) 59m RKO bw

Tim Holt *(Steve)*, Ray Whitley *(Smokey)*, Janet Waldo *(Ellen Grant)*, Lee "Lasses" White *(Whopper)*, Morris Ankrum *(Red)*, Roy Barcroft *(Joel Nesbitt)*, J. Merrill Holmes *(Sheriff Saunders)*, Eddy Waller *(Tom Haggerty)*, Glenn Strange *(Idaho)*, Frank Ellis *(Al)*, Joseph Eggenton *(Andrew Grant)*, Guy Usher *(Mayor)*, Jack Clifford *(Kurt Halliday)*, Bud Osborne *(Tint)*.

After a chiseling banker claps an unfair mortgage on his father's ranch, Holt joins a gang and robs the bank. Remorse gets the better of him and he repays the money. Then, to win Waldo's heart, he becomes the marshal of the town of Remington, cleaning up the bad guys, including his former outlaw pals. The working title of this average horser wound up as the title of the lead song, "Outlaw Trail," by Ray Whitley and Fred Rose.

p, Bert Gilroy; d, Edward Killy; w, Norton S. Parker (based on a story by Arthur T. Horman); ph, Harry Wild; ed, Frederic Knudtson.

Western   **(PR:A   MPAA:NR)**

BANDITS OF CORSICA, THE**

(1953) 81m Global/UA bw (GB: RETURN OF THE CORSICAN BROTHERS)

Richard Greene *(Mario/Carlos)*, Paula Raymond *(Christina)*, Raymond Burr *(Jonatto)*, Dona Drake *(Zelda)*, Raymond Greenleaf *(Paoli)*, Lee Van Cleef *(Nerva)*, Frank Puglia *(Riggio)*, Nestor Paiva *(Lorenzo)*, Peter Mamakos *(Diegas)*, Paul Cavanagh *(Dianza)*, Peter Brocco *(Angelo)*, George Lewis *(Arturo)*, Clayton Moore *(Ricardo)*, Virginia Brissac *(Maria)*, Francis J. McDonald *(Grisha)*, Michael Ansara *(Blacksmith)*, William Forrest *(Marquis)*, John Pickard *(Coachman)*.

If you liked THE CORSICAN BROTHERS (Douglas Fairbanks, 1941), you probably won't like this sequel. Richard Greene is pleasant and all that, but he's no

Doug. Mario Franchi leads a faction who wishes to unseat Burr and bring home rule to the people of Corsica. His twin brother Carlos (from whom he was separated at birth) is a Gypsy and the two of them get together to overthrow Burr. So far it's very much like the original in which the two brothers combined to overthrow Akim Tamiroff. The switch comes when we learn that Carlos has fallen in love with Mario's wife, Raymond, and intends to do his brother in, thus taking over the Franchi fortune and the Franchi female. There is a battle between the siblings and . . . well, can you guess who comes out on top? For a hint, when was the last time you saw a Gypsy hero? Ansara, who never stopped working in the 1950s, has a small role as the blacksmith, as does Moore, playing Ricardo. The best things about the film are Schayer's screenplay, Nazzaro's direction, and Burr's villainy. Despite his size in recent years, Burr remains an overlooked heavy who should have fared better at the critics' hands.

d, Ray Nazzaro; w, Richard Schayer (based on a story by Frank Burt); ph, George E. Diskant; m, Irving Gertz; ed, Grant Whytock.

Adventure   **(PR:A MPAA:NR)**

BANDITS OF DARK CANYON*   (1947) 59m REP bw

Allan "Rocky" Lane *(Himself)*, Bob Steele *(Ed Archer)*, Eddy Waller *(Nugget)*, Roy Barcroft *(Jeff Conley)*, John Hamilton *(Ben Shaw)*, Linda Johnson *(Joan Shaw)*, Gregory Marshall *(Billy Archer)*, Francis Ford *(Horse Trader)*, Eddie Acuff *(Faraday)*, LeRoy Mason *(Guard)*, Jack Norman *(Sheriff)*.

Lane stars as a Texas Ranger who helps an escaped convict, Steele, clear his name on a phony murder charge. It turns out that the "victim" is alive and working with the innocent con's best friend to swipe his fortune.

p, Gordon Kay; d, Philip Ford; w, Bob Williams; ph, John MacBurnie; ed, Les Orlebeck.

Western   **(PR:A MPAA:NR)**

BANDITS OF EL DORADO*   (1951) 54m COL bw (GB: TRICKED)

Charles Starrett *(Steve Carson)*, Smiley Burnette *(Himself)*, George J. Lewis *(Jose Vargas)*, Fred Sears *(Capt. Henley)*, John Dehner *(Charles Bruton)*, Clayton Moore *(Morgan)*, Jack O'Mahoney *(Starling)*, John Doucette *(Tucker)*, Max Wagner *(Paul)*, Henry Kulky *(Spade)*, Mustard and Gravy.

Western whose only interest is seeing Moore (The Lone Ranger) without the mask, and Dehner as a young man. A short film, it manages to pack lots of story into the time frame, but no real emotional involvement. There are no featured women and the loss is evident. Who gets excited about a movie where everyone is a baritone? Starrett is a Texas Ranger masquerading as The Durango Kid, an outlaw. He goes to Mexico in search of a criminal underground's ringleader and gets his man. Burnette plays himself and offers whatever humor can be found. A few funny songs are also included. Keep an eye out for a young Kulky as well as Jock Mahoney (who later became one of the many Tarzans) using the name of Jack O'Mahoney. (See DURANGO KID series, Index.)

p, Colbert Clark; d, Ray Nazarro; w, Barry Shipman; ph, Fayte Browne; m, Rossi DiMaggio; ed, Paul Borofsky.

Western   **(PR:A MPAA:NR)**

BANDITS OF ORGOSOLO***   (1964, Ital.) 98m Pathe-Contemporary bw (BANDITI A ORGOSOLO)

Michele Cossu *(Michele)*, Peppeddu Cuccu *(Peppeddu)*, Vittorina Pisano *(Mintonia)*.

Vittorio De Seta (not to be confused with Vittorio De Sica) may eventually be confused with the other Vittorio if he keeps up this kind of work. It's one of those classic Italian stories about a Sardinian shepherd who cannot escape his fate. He is unfairly accused of murder and robbery and chased all over the countryside. He becomes a mountain bandit but we realize from the start that he is the true victim of circumstances. BANDITS OF ORGOSOLO looks and feels more like a documentary than a staged piece. The actors are unrecognizable and they work with a deliberate pace that is seldom seen in contemporary films. If made in the 1940s, the film would have established De Seta as a genius. But, like Miniver Cheevy, he was born too late and you, reading this acknowledgement of the movie, may be the last person to recall the picture. Tsk, tsk.

p&d, Vittorio De Seta; w, De Seta, Vera Gherarducci; ph, De Seta; m, Valentino Bucci; ed, Jolanda Benvenuti; set d, Vera Gherarducci; cos, Marilu Carteny.

Adventure   **(PR:A MPAA:NR)**

BANDITS OF THE BADLANDS*1/2   (1945) 55m REP bw

Sunset Carson, Peggy Stewart, Monte Hale, Forrest Taylor, Si Jenks, John Merton, Wade Crosby, Jack Ingram, Alan Ward, Fred Graham.

Mediocre Carson oater has the hero overwhelming a horde of thieves and saving Stewart's honor and ranch. A yawner, even for the horses.

p, Bennett R. Cohen; d, Thomas Carr; w, Doris Schroeder; ph, Bud Thackery; ed, Arthur Roberts; md, Richard Cherwin; art d, James Sullivan.

Western   **(PR:A MPAA:NR)**

BANDITS OF THE WEST*   (1953) 54m REP

Allan "Rocky" Lane *(Himself)*, Eddy Waller *(Nugget Clark)*, Cathy Downs *(Joanne Collier)*, Roy Barcroft *(Bud Galloway)*, Trevor Bardette *(Jeff Chadwick)*, Ray Montgomery *(Steve Edrington)*, Byron Foulger *(Eric Strikler)*, Harry Harvey *(Judge Wolters)*, Robert Bice *(Dutch Clyburn)*.

Another Lane western, this one dealing with the efforts of local ranchers to halt the installation of the first natural gas system in Texas. In the old days it used to be farmers that the ranchers got upset about.

d, Harry Keller; w, Gerald Geraghty; ph, Bud Thackery; ed, Tony Martinelli.

Western   **(PR:A MPAA:NR)**

BANDITS ON THE WIND**   (1962, Jap.) 113m Toho c

Yosuke Natsuki *(Taro)*, Izumi Yukimora *(Kayo)*, Makato Sato *(Gale)*, Akiko Wakabayashi *(Yuri)*.

Blood, guts, sex, and power are the themes of this 15th-century Samurai drama from Toho. A group of bandits takes refuge in a small village and is mistaken for a once-prosperous family who lived in the town years ago. The bandits continue the charade and help the failing citizenry get off their duffs and back into the mainstream. The villagers adore these strangers and take them into their hearts. But it's for naught as the really bad guys come in and slaughter the reformed bandits. Sounds like a typical gang war in East Los Angeles. Well-photographed, good music, somewhat slow at 110 minutes, but a good example of the genre.

p, Tomoyuki Tanaka; d, Hiroshi Inagaki; w, Masato Ide; ph, Kazuo Yamada (Tohoscope); m, Kan Ishii.

Historical Drama   **(PR:A MPAA:NR)**

BANDOLERO!*1/2   (1968) 107m FOX c

James Stewart *(Mace Bishop)*, Dean Martin *(Dee Bishop)*, Raquel Welch *(Maria)*, George Kennedy *(Sheriff Johnson)*, Andrew Prine *(Roscoe Bookbinder)*, Will Geer *(Pop Chaney)*, Clint Richie *(Babe)*, Denver Pyle *(Muncie Carter)*, Tom Heaton *(Joe Chaney)*, Rudy Diaz *(Angel)*, Sean McClory *(Bobbie)*, Harry Carey *(Cort Hyjack)*, Donald Barry *(Jack Hawkins)*, Guy Raymond *(Ossie Grimes)*, Perry Lopez *(Frisco)*, Jock Mahoney *(Stoner)*, Dub Taylor *(Attendant)*, Big John Hamilton *(Bank Clerk)*, Bob Adler *(Ross Harper)*, John Mitchum, *(Bath House Customer)*, Joseph Patrick Cranshaw *(Bank Clerk)*, Roy Barcroft *(Bartender)*.

Badmen Stewart and Martin have their hands full dodging the law after they and fellow gang members break out of jail. They've also taken a reluctant Welch along as hostage. Pursuing the gang are Kennedy and his posse. Despite a great cast and a top-notch director, the movie is a rather dull western.

p, Robert J. Jacks; d, Andrew V. McLaglen; w, James Lee Barrett (based on a story by Stanley L. Hough); ph, William H. Clothier (Panavision, DeLuxe Color); m, Jerry Goldsmith; ed, Folmar Blangsted; art d, Jack Martin Smith, Alfred Sweeney, Jr.

Western   **(PR:A MPAA:NR)**

BANG BANG KID, THE*1/2
(1968, U.S./Span./Ital.) 90m Westside-L.M. Film-Domino/Ajay c (AKA: BANG BANG)

Guy Madison *(Bear Bullock)*, Sandra Milo *(Gwenda Skaggel)*, Tom Bosley *(Merriweather Newberry)*, Riccardo Garrone *(Killer Kissock)*, Joe Caffarel *(Mayor Skaggel)*, Dianik *(Betsy Skaggel)*, Giustino Durano *(Hotchkiss)*.

Ridiculous Spanish western with Madison as a sort of feudal lord of a mining town. (He has even gone so far as to import a castle from Europe in which to live.) The citizens finally become fed up with taking orders from this loony, so they try to hire a new sheriff. Their efforts become frustrated because Madison's men gun down all the applicants. Suddenly Bosley rides into town with his metal robot "The Bang Bang Kid." The Kid can defend the town and not be killed. That is, of course, if Bosley can get the machine working properly. Much of the comedy (and the movie) is taken up by Bosley's tinkering with the robot like a surgeon. Once the metal machine is running, it's only a matter of time until Madison is sent packing. The film is funny in a silly manner, but constant fantasy sequences of Madison seeing the whole town as if it were in the Middle Ages become distracting.

p, Sidney Pink; d, Stanley Prager; w, Howard Berk; ph, Antonio Macasoli (Movielab Color); m, Nico Tedenco.

Western   **(PR:A MPAA:NR)**

BANG, BANG, YOU'RE DEAD*1/2
(1966) 92m AIP c (GB: OUR MAN IN MARRAKESH; AKA: MARRAKESH)

Tony Randall *(Andrew Jessel)*, Senta Berger *(Kyra Stanovy)*, Terry-Thomas *(El Caid)*, Herbert Lom *(Mr. Casimir)*, Wilfrid Hyde-White *(Arthur Fairbrother)*, Gregoire Aslan *(Achmed)*, John Le Mesurier *(George Lillywhite)*, Klaus Kinski *(Jonquil)*, Margaret Lee *(Samia Voss)*, Emil Stemmler *(Hotel Clerk)*, Helen Sanguineti *(Madame Bouseny)*, Sanchez Francisco *(Martinez)*, William Sanguineti *(Police Chief)*, Hassan Essakali *(Motorcycle Policeman)*, Keith Peacock *(Philippe)*, Burt Kwouk *(Export Manager)*.

Not much to recommend in this film which features Randall and Berger as a tourist and a secret agent involved with gangsters in an exotic Moroccan locale. This is not to be confused with BANG! YOU'RE DEAD, the 1954 British suspenser. The jokes don't work, the photography is awful, the actors seem to look as though they wish they were all in Marbella. Some of the best second bananas on the stalk are in this film and Klaus Kinski, Terry-Thomas and Herbert Lom are the only elements that save this from no film at all.

p, Harry Alan Towers; d, Don Sharp; w, Peter Yeldam; ph, John Von Kotze (Technicolor); m. Malcolm Lockyer; ed, Teddy Darvas.

Spy Comedy   **(PR:A MPAA:NR)**

BANG THE DRUM SLOWLY***   (1973) 96m PAR c

Robert De Niro *(Bruce Pearson)*, Michael Moriarty *(Henry Wiggen)*, Vincent Gardenia *(Dutch Schnell)*, Phil Foster *(Joe Jaros)*, Ann Wedgeworth *(Katie)*, Patrick McVey *(Pearson's Father)*, Heather MacRae *(Holly Wiggen)*, Selma Diamond *(Tootsie)*, Barbara Babcock, Maurice Rosenfield *(Team Owners)*, Tom Ligon *(Piney Woods)*, Andy Jarrell *(Ugly Jones)*, Marshall Efron *(Bradley Lord)*, Barton Heyman *(Red Traphagen)*, Donny Burks *(Perry)*, Hector Elias *(Diego)*, Tom Signorelli *(Goose Williams)*, Jim Donahue *(Canada Smith)*, Nicolas Surovy *(Aleck Olson)*,

Danny Aiello *(Horse)*, Hector Troy *(George)*, Tony Major *(Jonah)*, Alan Manaon *(Dr. Loftus)*, Ernesto Gonzales *(Dr. Chambers)*, Jack Hollander, Lou Girolami *(Tegwar Players)*, Arnold Kapnick *(Detective)*, Jean David *(Dutch's Wife)*, Bea Blau *(Joe's Wife)*, Herb Henry *(Keith Crane)*, Dorothy Nuebert *(Bruce's Mother)*, Pierrino Mascarino *(Sid Goldman)*, Kaydette Grant *(Gem)*, Dell Bethel *(Third Base Coach)*, Forrest Wynn *(Bat Boy)*, Vince Camuto, Jeff Sartorius, Willie Lemmey, Doug Major.

A well-done but unremittingly depressing story about a baseball catcher, De Niro, who is dying of Hodgkin's disease. Moriarty, the team's star pitcher, becomes dedicated to De Niro when he learns of his fatal illness. This is sort of the baseball version of "Brian's Song," the TV movie that swept all the awards the year it was presented. One of De Niro's earliest roles, and it is poles apart from the enigmatic loners he would later specialize in. Here is a quintessential bumpkin, a man who would (and does) wear a "Smiley Face" t-shirt under a sports jacket. He is very effective as the doomed ballplayer, as is Moriarty as the sympathetic Henry Wiggen, the central character in a number of baseball novels authored by Mark Harris. More than an illness story, this is a baseball story and Harris and Hancock have done one of the best baseball movies ever. The dugout scenes smack of reality and one can almost smell the socks in the dressing room. Gardenia received an Academy Award nomina- tion for supporting work and there might have been more awards for the movie had it not been such a dull item at the box office. The producer plays the part of one of the team's owners and when he talks about money, you can really believe him. Foster, who was the Dodgers' biggest booster until they betrayed Brooklyn and moved west, is excellent as a coach.

p, Maurice and Lois Rosenfield; d, John Hancock; w, Mark Harris (based on the novel by Harris); ph, Richard Shore (Movielab Color); m, Stephen Lawrence; ed, Richard Marks; prod d, Robert Gundlach.

Sports Drama **Cas.** **(PR:A MPAA:NR)**

BANG! YOU'RE DEAD**½ (1954, Brit.) 88m Wellington/BL bw (AKA: GAME OF DANGER)

Jack Warner *(Bonsell)*, Derek Farr *(Detective Grey)*, Veronica Hurst *(Hilda)*, Michael Medwin *(Bob Carter)*, Gordon Harker *(Mr. Hare)*, Anthony Richmond *(Cliff Bonsell)*, Sean Barrett *(Willy)*, Beatrice Varley *(Mrs. Maxted)*, Philip Saville *(Ben Jones)*, John Warwick *(Sgt. Gurney)*, Toke Townley *(Jimmy Knuckle)*.

Mystery in which blame for a shooting goes to the wrong man. In reality, a young boy has committed the killing accidentally by playing with a gun he thought was a toy pistol. Interesting parallel story line shows detectives gathering clues leading to the boy, and the stark terror growing within the nine-year-old as the truth comes closer. Good performance by Richmond as the boy.

p&d, Lance Comfort; w, Guy Elmes, Ernest Borneman; ph, Brandar J. Stafford; m, Eric Spear; ed, Francis Bieber.

Mystery/Suspense **(PR:C MPAA:NR)**

BANISHED** (1978, Jap.) 109m Toho c (HANARE GOZE ORIN; AKA: MELODY IN GRAY)

Shima Iwashita *(Orin)*, Yoshio Harada *(Big Man)*, Tomoko Naraoka *(Teruyo)*, Taiji Teneyama *(Mountain Man)*, Toru Abe *(Besho)* Jun Hamamura *(Saito)*.

A compelling movie about a blind woman who is sensuous and sultry but who cannot exercise her passions due to her condition. Exquisitely photographed and intelligently directed, it details the ups and downs of the woman who has been trained by the Goze, a group of blind Geishas. As long as she remains chaste, she can be secure with the Goze; once her virginity is gone, she is banished. The film gets very sad and eventually depressing. Yet, as in so many Japanese films, it never dwells on depression, nor does it mawkishly aim for sentimentality. Instead, it presents what it considers the truth and moves on to the next sequence. It is difficult to compare this kind of film to American or even European pictures, mainly because the rules seem to change once we cross the Pacific. The same story in another setting might not have worked.

p, Kiyoshi Iwashita, Seikichi Iizumi; d, Mashahero Shinoda; w, Keiji Hasebe, Shinoda (based on the novel by Tsutomu Minagami); ph, Kazuo Miyagawa; m, Toru Takemitsu; art d, Kiyoshi Awazu.

Drama **(PR:C MPAA:NR)**

BANJO* (1947) 67m RKO

Sharyn Moffett *(Pat)*, Jacqueline White *(Elizabeth)*, Walter Reed *(Dr. Bob)*, Una O'Connor *(Harriet)*, Herbert Evans *(Jeffries)*, Louise Beavers *(Lindy)*, Ernest Whitman *(Jasper)*, Lanny Ross *(Ned)*, Theron Jackson *(Exodus)*, Howard McNeely *(Genesis)* and Banjo as himself.

Cliche-ridden orphan tale starring Moffett as a ragamuffin who loses her father under the hooves of a spooked horse on their Georgia plantation. The girl and her faithful pooch "Banjo" are sent off to live with her grouchy aunt in Boston. The aunt takes an immediate dislike to the dog and sends it back to Georgia. Moffett runs off after her hound the first chance she gets. The aunt, seeing the child's love for the dog, feels guilty and reunites them.

p, Lillie Hayward; d, Richard O. Fleischer; w, Hayward; ph, George E. Diskant; m, Alexander Laszlo; ed, Les Millbrook.

Drama **(PR:AA MPAA:NR)**

BANJO ON MY KNEE*** (1936) 95m FOX bw

Barbara Stanwyck *(Pearl)*, Joel McCrea *(Ernie Holley)*, Helen Westley *(Grandma)*, Buddy Ebsen *(Puddy)*, Walter Brennan *(Newt Holley)*, Walter Catlett *(Warfield Scott)*, Anthony Martin *(Chick Bean)*, Minna Gombell *(Ruby)*, George Humbert *(Jules)*, Spencer Charters *(Tope)*, Cecil Weston *(Hattie)*, Louis Mason *(Eph)*, Hilda Vaughn *(Gertha)*, Victor Kilian *(Slade)*, Katherine DeMille *(Leota Long)*, Teresa Harris *(Blues Singer)*, Eddy Waller *(Truck Driver)*, Salty Holmes *(Jug Blower)*, Davison Clark *(Police Sergeant)*, The Hall Johnson Choir.

A happy tale of a young couple, McCrea and Stanwyck, who get married, but before they can get things going, McCrea has a battle with Kilian (the villain) and thinks that he's killed him so he takes it on the lam up the Mississippi. Kilian lives and further complications arise when Stanwyck runs off to New Orleans with Catlett, a skirt-chasing lowlife photographer. That doesn't work out and she gets a job washing dishes in a local restaurant. This becomes the focal point for much of the film as Brennan (Joel's daddy) arrives to do a one-man-band routine. Stanwyck sings a duet with Martin (who was using the name Anthony Martin in those days) and brings down the house. Culmination occurs when DeMille tries to wreck a boat that Stanwyck, McRea, and Brennan are riding on. There's lots to like in this film; Stanwyck sings and dances better than you might think, but a close look at her bio reveals that she got her start hoofing and chirping in the Ziegfeld Follies and other stage reviews. Ebsen again acquits himself as a fine singer/dancer with absolutely no foreshadowing of the huge TV success that was to come in his white-haired years. Some nice songs, lovely photography of the river and good fun all around. Songs include "Where the Lazy River Goes By," (Stanwyck on vocal); "With A Banjo On My Knee," "There's Something in the Air," (Harold Adamson, Jimmy McHugh); and the venerable "St. Louis Blues" (W. C. Handy).

p, Nunnally Johnson; d, John Cromwell; w, Johnson (based on the novel by Harry Hamilton); ph, Ernest Palmer; ed, Hans Fritch; md, Arthur Lange; art d, Hans Peters; set d, Thomas Little; cos, Gwen Wakeling.

Musical **(PR:A MPAA:NR)**

BANK ALARM* (1937) 64m Condor/GN bw

Conrad Nagel *(Alan O'Connor)*, Eleanor Hunt *(Bobbie Reynolds)*, Vince Barnett *(Bulb)*, Frank Milan *(Turner)*, Wilma Francis *(Kay)*, William Thorne *(Inspector Macy)*, Wheeler Oakman *(Karlotti)*, Charles Delaney *(Duke)*, Phil Dunham *(Curtis)*, Sid D'Albrook *(Grimes)*, Pat Gleason *(Barney)*, Wilson Benge *(Overman)*, Henry Roquemore *(Sheriff)*.

Standard crime drama starring Nagel as a G-man in hot pursuit of a band of bank robbers. While following the trail of blood, bills, and empty banks Nagel manages to get himself into several car chases, gunfights, and some romance with Hunt. He then lets the gangsters kidnap her so that he can rescue her in the end. A western with trenchcoats and cars.

p, George A. Hirliman; d, Louis Gasnier; w, David S. Levy, J. Griffin Jay; ph, Mack Stengler; m, Abe Meyer; ed, Dan Milner.

Crime **(PR:A MPAA:NR)**

BANK DICK, THE**** (1940) 69m UNIV bw GB: BANK DETECTIVE, THE)

W. C. Fields *(Egbert Souse)*, Cora Witherspoon *(Agatha Souse)*, Una Merkel *(Myrtle* Souse), Evelyn Del Rio *(Elsie Mae Adele Brunch Souse)*, Jessie Ralph *(Mrs. Hermisillo Brunch)*, Franklin Pangborn *(J. Pinkerton Snoopington)*, Shemp Howard *(Joe Guelpe)*, Richard Purcell *(Mackley Q. Greene)*, Grady Sutton *(Og Oggilby)*, Russell Hicks *(J. Frothingham Waterbury)*, Pierre Watkin *(Mr. Skinner)*, Al Hill *(Repulsive Rogan)*, George Moran *(Loudmouth McNasty)*, Bill Wolfe *(Otis)*, Jack Norton *(A. Pismo Clam)*, Pat West *(Assistant Director)*, Reed Hadley *(Francois)*, Heather Wilde *(Miss Plupp)*, Harlan Briggs *(Doctor Stall)*, Bill Alston *(Mr. Cheek)*, Jan Duggan *(Woman in Bank)*, Kay Sutton *(Young Woman on Bench)*, Fay Adler *(Bank President's Secretary)*, Bobby Larson *(Boy in Bank)*, Russel Cole *(Bank Clerk)*, Pat O'Malley *(Cop)*, Billy Mitchell *(Black Bank Customer)*, Eddie Dunn *(James, the Chauffeur)*, Emmett Vogan *(Hotel Desk Clerk)*, Margaret Seddon *(Old Lady in Car)*, Eddie Acuff *(Reporter)*, Mary Field *(Woman)*.

Classic Fields vehicle of manic mirth. The great comedian is an unemployed, much-henpecked (what else) family man not too eagerly seeking work when he accidentally captures a bank robber and is rewarded with a guard job inside the bank. (In a hilarious bit, snooty bank president Watkin congratulates Fields for his daring exploit by saying: "Allow me to extend to you a hearty handshake," and then disdainfully touches Fields' outstreched hand with the tips of his fingers.) When not busy bothering customers (apprehending a customer's son brandishing a toy gun inside the bank), Fields is running between his horrid family and The Black Pussy Cat Cafe where proprietor Howard spends most of his time pouring Fields, his only customer, a series of stiff ones. His bumbling brings about a risky investment, made by nitwit bank clerk Sutton, Fields' future son-in-law, where bank funds are funneled to a conman selling phony stock. Bank examiner Pangborn next arrives to check the books. Fields goes through rollicking gyrations and schemes to keep the official snoop away from the telltale ledgers, including having Howard give Pangborn a Mickey Finn; he indicates this ploy by repeatedly asking Howard, "Has my friend Michael Finn, MICHAEL FINN, been in?" while winking and thumbing in Pangborn's direction until Howard gets the blatant hint. Fields takes the sick-to-death Pangborn to a hotel where he is diagnosed by a fake physician as deathly ill, and is told that he must stay in bed for several days, enough time for Fields and Sutton to try to replace the money. The obstinate Pangborn struggles back to his responsibilities and, just before he discovers the missing money, a bank robber appears and robs the till once more, taking Fields along as a hostage. After a wild ride, Fields manages to apprehend the crook and gain a huge reward. We also see him as a film director being carried about like some marvelous maharaja, basking in glory. In the end, however, he steps from a mansion where his obnoxious family now treats him as royalty, spots the scurrying Howard, and then chases wildly after him toward the inevitable destination, The Black Pussy Cat Cafe and its elixirs. Fields, who wrote the script under one of his standard impossible pseudonyms, set the story in the town of Lompoc, a ridiculous-sounding name that appealed to him, as did most phonetically offbeat names (albeit there is a town called Lompoc in California which Fields certainly knew). His own character is named Souse, which he pronounces Sou-say; the rest of the world calls him "souse," as in drunk. Fields' personal drinking problem at the time was reaching heroic and debilitating proportions; he had developed a kidney ailment that made work often painful. THE BANK DICK would be his last major film; five more would follow in which he would have relatively minor roles. He would die on Christmas Day, 1946, at age 67. Close friend Thomas Mitchell visited him a few days before this great clown passed on. Mitchell found a Bible at Fields' bedside. The self-avowed agnostic appeared flustered at his friend's discovery. "Bill, of all people," Mitchell said, "what are *you* doing with a Bible?" Replied W. C. with squinting eyes and a corner-of-the-lip delivery: "Looking for loopholes."

d, Edward Cline; w, Mahatma Kane Jeeves [Fields]; ph, Milton Krasner; ed, Arthur Hilton; art d, Jack Otterson.

Comedy   **Cas.**   **(PR:A MPAA:NR)**

BANK HOLIDAY*
     (1938, Brit.) 86m Gainsborough/GFD bw (AKA: THREE ON A WEEKEND)

John Lodge (*Stephen Howard*), Margaret Lockwood (*Catherine*), Hugh Williams (*Geoffrey*), Rene Ray (*Doreen*), Merle Tottenham (*Milly*), Linden Travers (*Ann Howard*), Wally Patch (*Arthur*), Kathleen Harrison (*May*), Garry Marsh (*Manager*), Jeanne Stuart (*Miss Mayfair*), Wilfred Lawson (*Police Sergeant*), Felix Aylmer (*Surgeon*), Alf Goddard, Michael Rennie, Arthur West Payne, David Anthony, Angela Glynne.

Forgettable heart-tugger about a nurse, Lockwood, whose patient dies while giving childbirth on the day she (the nurse) is about to leave on a vacation with her lover. The memory of the dead woman's grieving husband haunts the nurse on her holiday and she has a miserable time. She returns to London just in time to save the distraught husband from committing suicide. At the close, there is every reason to believe that the nurse and the widower will find happiness together.

p, Edward Black; d, Carol Reed; w, Rodney Ackland, Roger Burford (original story by Hans Wilhelm and Ackland); ph, Arthur Crabtree.

Drama   **(PR:C MPAA:NR)**

BANK MESSENGER MYSTERY, THE*   (1936, Brit.) 56m Hammer bw

George Mozart (*George Brown*), Francesca Bahrle (*Miss Brown*), Paul Neville (*Harper*), Marilyn Love, Frank Tickle, Kenneth Kove.

Angered over being fired, a bank cashier enlists the aid of professional thieves to rob his own bank. Unexciting caper story with lame script and direction.

p, Will Hammer; d&w, Lawrence Huntington.

Crime   **(PR:A MPAA:NR)**

BANK RAIDERS, THE*1/2   (1958, Brit.) 60m Film Workshop/RFD bw

Peter Reynolds (*Terry*), Sandra Dorne (*Della*), Sydney Tafler (*Shelton*), Lloyd Lamble (*Inspector Mason*), Rose Hill (*Mrs. Marling*), Arthur Mullard (*Linders*), Tim Ellison, Ann King, Dennis Taylor, Robert Bruce, Jeanne Kent, Roberta Wooley.

Small-time chiseler is taken in by a big-time gang who plan a bank robbery and, to silence a witness, kidnap a girl employee who is saved by the chiseler. Not much of a caper or film.

p, Geoffrey Goodhart; d, Maxwell Munden; w, Brandon Fleming; ph, Henry Hall.

Crime   **(PR:A MPAA:NR)**

BANK SHOT*   (1974) 83m UA c

George C. Scott (*Walter Ballantine*), Joanna Cassidy (*El*), Sorrell Booke (*Al G. Karp*), G. Wood (*Chief FBI Agent*), Clifton James (*Frank "Bulldog" Steiger*), Robert Balaban (*Victor Karp*), Bibi Osterwald (*Mums*), Frank McRae (*Herman X*), Don Calfa (*Stosh Gornik*), Harvey Evans (*Irving*), Hank Stohl (*Johnson*), Liam Dunn (*Painter*), Jack Riley (*Jackson*), Pat Zurica (*Man in Privy*), Harvey J. Goldenberg, Jamie Reidy (*Policemen*).

What a disappointment is this far-fetched and silly TV-like movie from what would appear to be a fine creative group. We say "TV" because that's precisely what it looks like from start to finish, with the only difference being the presence of Scott. Donald Westlake's weak novel is overdone to a turn by Mayes'adaptation and Champion's direction. He was an odd choice as he'd only done one film, MY SIX LOVES, and that was 11 years earlier. Scott stars as a bank robber, in the largest sense of the word. Using house-moving equipment, Scott and his cohorts rob a bank by dragging it away with them. The remainder of the film is a chase that never quite pays off. With Robert Reed, in the lead you might have seen this on any given Friday night on the American Broadcasting Co. One of the few standouts is Riley in a small role as Jackson. Riley has since appeared in many films, notably ATTACK OF THE KILLER TOMATOES and TO BE OR NOT TO BE.

p, Hal Landers, Bobby Roberts; d, Gower Champion; w, Wendell Mayes (based on the novel by Donald Westlake); ph, Harry Stradling, Jr. (DeLuxe Color); m, John Morris; ed, David Bretherton; art d, Albert Brenner; set d, George Gaines.

Crime/Comedy   **(PR:A MPAA:NR)**

BANNERLINE*   (1951) 87m MGM bw

Keefe Brasselle (*Mike Perrivale*), Sally Forrest (*Richie Loomis*), Lionel Barrymore (*Hugo Trimble*), Lewis Stone (*Josh*), J. Carrol Naish (*Frankie Scarbine*), Larry Keating (*Stambaugh*), Spring Byington (*Mrs. Loomis*), Warner Anderson (*Roy*), Elisabeth Risdon (*Mrs. Margaret Trimble*), Michael Ansara (*Floyd*), John Morgan (*Al*).

An interesting premise is what highlights this Metro release. Brasselle is a young reporter who comes up with the idea of publishing a bogus front page detailing all the civic reforms that Barrymore, a dying professor, has espoused in the town. Then Brasselle enlists Lewis Stone, who runs the paper's morgue, to help him and they manage to get the phony front page tacked onto the regular newspaper. Brasselle is hoping the townspeople will take notice and rise up against Naish, who is the local

heavyweight gangster. Like most Americans, the townspeople are too busy with their own problems and let the whole thing slide. Naish, however, is incensed. His hoodlums beat the banjo eyes out of Brasselle (who also played Eddie Cantor, you might recall) and the authorities finally do take notice. Naish is defeated, Brasselle takes up with Forrest and it all wraps up well. Schnee writes some sharp dialog and the Raphaelson story eschews the usual cliches. Weis' direction is slow (as it was in most of his career) but the material is worthy.

p, Henry Berman; d, Don Weis; w, Charles Schnee (based on a story by Samson Raphaelson); ph, Harold Lipstein; m, Rudolph G. Kopp; ed, Frederick Y. Smith.

Drama   **(PR:A MPAA:NR)**

BANNING*   (1967) 102m UNIV c

Robert Wagner (*Banning*), Anjanette Comer (*Carol*), Jill St. John (*Angela*), Guy Stockwell (*Linus*), James Farentino (*Chris*), Susan Clark (*Cynthia*), Howard St. John (*J. Pallister Young*), Mike Kellin (*Kalielle*), Gene Hackman (*Tommy Del Gaddo*), Sean Garrison (*Tyson*), Logan Ramsey (*Doc*), Edmon Ryan (*Stuart Warren*), Oliver McGowan (*Sen. Brady*), Lucille Meredith (*Maggi Andrews*), Bill Cort (*Tony*).

Messy soap opera concerning bored rich folks at the country club. Wagner is featured as the lead stud and assistant golf pro whom all the women are hot for. Farentino plays the sneaky ex-caddie who wants Wagner's job and will do anything to get it. St. John is the sex-bomb who wants to bed Wagner, and the whole thing is as boring as it sounds. Watch for Hackman in an early role. Good score by Quincy Jones.

p, Dick Berg; d, Ron Winston; w, James Lee (based on a story by Hamilton Maule); ph, Loyal Griggs (Technicolor); m, Quincy Jones; ed, J. Terry Williams.

Drama   **(PR:C MPAA:NR)**

BANZAI*   (1983, Fr.) 100m Renn/AMLF c

Michel Coluche (*Michel Bernardin*), Valerie Mairesse (*Isabelle Morizet*), Francois Perrot (*Boss*), Eva Darlan (*Carole*), Marthe Villalonga (*Mme. Bernardin*), Jean-Marie Proslier (*A Businessman*), Didier Kaminka (*Paul*).

Claude Berri, who directed some of the more interesting French comedies of the 1960s and 1970s (PAPA'S CINEMA, LE SEX SHOP, MAZEL TOV OU LE MARRIAGE, etc.) produced this hodge-podge and allowed another Claude (Zidi) to direct it. Perhaps they should have traded hats. This one doesn't work. It's an ornate piece of fluff about a nerd (Coluche) who works for the Parisian version of Travelers Aid and gets into all sorts of scrapes attempting to help tourists in distress. The picture jets from Tunisia to New York to Hong Kong and never settles in to let us like it. In Africa, Coluche misguidedly frees an anti-government official which leads to a rebellion. In New York, he is taken to be a drug smuggler (the man couldn't smuggle Alka-Seltzer, much less cocaine) and in Hong Kong, he winds up embroiled with the underworld. Where are the frothy French comedies of yesteryear? These people have been watching too many Jerry Lewis pictures and have forgotten the lovely tradition their predecessors established. It looks as though a lot of money was spent on it to little avail. They should have realized that special effects and whiz-bang gags are no substitute for character comedy and honest reactions. Fernandel...where are you now that we need you?

p, Claude Berri; d, Claude Zidi; w, Zidi, Didier Kaminka, Michel Fabre; ph, Jean-Jacques Tarbe; m, Vladimir Cosma; ed, Nicole Saulnier; art d, Pay Ling Wang, Claude Guilhem; spec eff, Derek Meddings, Paul Wilson.

Comedy   **(PR:C-O MPAA:NR)**

BAR L RANCH*   (1930) 60m Big Four bw

Buffalo Bill Jr. (*Bob Tyler*), Wally Wales [Hal Taliaferro] (*Frank Kellogg*), Yakima Canutt (*Steve*), Betty Baker (*Gene Polk*), Ben Corbett (*Barney McCool*), Fern Emmett, Robert Walker.

Obscure early western talkie about cattle rustling. Slapstick fist-fights, repetitious horseback chases, and no major stars make this one pretty hard to take.

p, F. E. Douglas; d, Harry Webb; w, Carl Krusada (based on a story by Bennett R. Cohen); ph, William Nobles; ed, Fred Bain.

Western   **(PR:A MPAA:NR)**

BAR SINISTER, THE*1/2   (1955) 88m MGM c (GB: IT'S A DOG'S LIFE)

Jeff Richards (*Patch McGill*), Jarma Lewis (*Mabel Maycroft*), Edmund Gwenn (*Jeremiah Nolan*), Dean Jagger (*Mr. Wyndham*), Willard Sage (*Tom Tattle*), Sally Fraser (*Dorothy Wyndham*), Richard Anderson (*George Oakley*), J. M. Kerrigan (*Paddy Corbin*).

Bizarre turn-of-the-century film featuring a bull terrier, Wildfire, as a hound who rises from the mean streets of the Bowery to live in luxury with the rich Jagger. Richards finds the pooch and decides to make a buck off him by holding dog fights in the local saloon. Wildfire loves his manager, but when Richards dumps him, the dog finds himself taken in by the kindly Gwenn who is a household employee of the wealthy, but crusty, Jagger. Wildfire works his magic on the dog-hating Jagger and the whole thing has a happy ending.

p, Henry Berman; d, Hermann Hoffman; w, John Michael Hayes (based on a story by Richard Harding Davis); ph, Paul C. Vogel (CinemaScope, Eastmancolor); m, Elmer Bernstein; ed, John Dunning.

Drama   **(PR:A MPAA:NR)**

BAR 20*   (1943) 54m UA bw

William Boyd (*Hopalong Cassidy*), Andy Clyde (*California*), George Reeves (*Lin Bradley*), Dustin Farnum (*Marie Stevens*), Victor Jory (*Mark Jackson*), Douglas Fowley (*Slash*), Betty Blythe (*Mrs. Stevens*), Bob Mitchum (*Richard Adams*), Francis McDonald (*One Eye*), Earle Hodgins (*Tom*).

Usual Hopalong fare, this time with Boyd, Reeves, and Clyde after stagecoach robbers who had the audacity to steal Hoppy's cattle-buying money. Robert Mitchum, who did quite a few Hopalong Cassidy films, plays a good guy for the first time in the series. (See HOPALONG CASSIDY series, Index.)

p, Harry Sherman; d, Lesley Selander; w, Morton Grant, Norman Houston, Michael Wilson; ph, Russell Harlan; ed, Carroll Lewis; art d, Ralph Berger.

Western (PR:A MPAA:NR)

BAR 20 JUSTICE* (1938) 70m PAR bw

William Boyd *(Hopalong Cassidy)*, George Hayes *(Windy Halliday)*, Russell Hayden *(Lucky Jenkins)*, Paul Sutton *(Slade)*, Gwen Gaze *(Ann Dennis)*, Pat O'Brien *(Frazier)*, Joseph DeStefani *(Perkins)*, William Dunkin *(Buck Peters)*, Walter Long *(Pierce)*, H. Bruce Mitchell *(Ross)*, John Beach *(Dennis)*.

Hoppy goes after some outlaw miners who have been stealing ore from heroine Gaze's mine. In order to catch the villains in the act, Boyd must spend much of the movie crawling around in dark mine shafts, making it kind of hard to enjoy the wide expanse of western scenery one could usually rely on when things got this dull. (See HOPALONG CASSIDY series, Index.)

p, Harry Sherman; d, Lesley Selander; w, Arnold Belgard, Harrison Jacobs (based on a story by Clarence E. Mulford); ph, Russell Harlan; ed, Robert Warwick; art d, Lewis J. Rachmil.

Western Cas. (PR:A MPAA:NR)

BAR 20 RIDES AGAIN* (1936) 65m PAR bw

William Boyd *(Hopalong Cassidy)*, Jimmy Ellison *(Johnny Nelson)*, Jean Rouverol *(Margaret Arnold)*, George Hayes *(Windy)*, Frank McGlynn Jr. *(Red Conners)*, Harry Worth *(Nevada)*, Paul Fix *(Gila)*, Ethel Wales *(Clarissa Peters)*, J. P. McGowen *(Buck Peters)*, Joe Rickson *(Herb Layton)*, Al St. John *(Cinco)*, John Merton *(Carp)*, Frank Layton *(Elbows)*, Chill Wills and his Avalon Boys *(Themselves)*.

Hopalong oater pits the Bar 20 boys against cattle-rustler Worth who dreams of building a Napoleonic empire in the West. Only notable because this was the film that riders-to-the-rescue sequence) that became so routine in the following films of the series. (See HOPALONG CASSIDY series, Index.)

p, Harry Sherman; d, Howard Bretherton; w, Doris Schroeder, Gerald Geraghty (based on a story by Clarence Mulford); ph, Archie Stout; ed, Edward Schroeder.

Western (PR:A MPAA:NR)

BAR Z BAD MEN* (1937) 57m REP bw

Johnny Mack Brown, Lois January, Ernie Adams, Jack Rockwell, Tom London, Dick Curtis, Milburn Morante, Horace Murphy, Tex Palmer, Budd Buster, Frank Ball, George Morrell, Horace B. Carpenter, Art Dillard, Oscar Gahan.

Dull western has smiling Johnny gun down several rustlers and stop a stampede before winning the winsome January. Even the cattle seem tired.

p, A.W. Hackel; d, Sam Newfield; w, George Plympton (based on a story by James P. Olson).

Western Cas. (PR:A MPAA:NR)

BARABBAS*** (1962, Ital.) 144m COL c

Anthony Quinn *(Barabbas)*, Silvana Mangano *(Rachel)*, Arthur Kennedy *(Pontius Pilate)*, Katy Jurado *(Sara)*, Harry Andrews *(Peter)*, Vittorio Gassman *(Sahak)*, Jack Palance *(Torvald)*, Ernest Borgnine *(Lucius)*, Norman Wooland *(Rufio)*, Valentina Cortese *(Julia)*, Michael Gwynn *(Lazarus)*, Douglas Fowley *(Vasasio)*, Robert Hall *(Gladiator Captain)*, Lawrence Payne *(Disciple)*, Arnold Foa *(Joseph of Arimathea)*, Roy Mangano *(Christ)*, Ivan Triesault *(Emperor)*, Joe Robinson *(Gladiator)*, Guido Celano *(Scorpio)*, Spartaco Nale *(Overseer)*, Enrico Glori *(Important Gentleman)*, Carlo Giustini, Frederich Ledebur, Gianni De Benedetto *(Officers)*, Rina Braido *(Tavern Reveler)*, Tullio Tomadoni *(Blind Man)*, Maria Zanoli *(Beggar Woman)*.

Quinn is the murderer and thief pardoned in place of Christ. He wrings every emotion out as he is trapped in a mine collapse, stoned, fights a gladiator, and escapes death by cross, arrow, and lions. It's technically good but terribly long and Fry's screenplay seems to have been written under the influence of too much capuccino. Lots of spectacular sequences including the burning of Rome (always popular in these kinds of epics), the arena, sweating in the sulphur mines, etc. Director Fleischer earns his money in this one. Sort of an all-star-cast, which means not quite as big a roster of names as Irwin Allen usually offers. Silvana Mangano (wife of the producer) is Gassman's former girl friend who has turned to Christ. Gassman is Quinn's cellmate and does a fine job. Palance is the mean gladiator who enjoys hurting and killing people. He is most believable. Lots of violence in this movie as is usual in stories taken from that most violent of all books, the Bible. Kennedy plays Pontius Pilate with just the right note of smarminess, and Jurado and Borgnine (who liked to work together at the time because they were married) also turn in good jobs. Odd that the role of Christ gets billing near the bottom of the cast line. He's played by Roy Mangano, brother to the female lead and brother-in-law of the producer. Nepotism is here to stay. All right . . . we all know who died on the cross and now we know the name of the man who was saved, but can you tell us the name of the man who died next to Jesus? Think hard now. If you saw THE HOODLUM PRIEST (1961) starring Don Murray, you'll remember that he was named for that other man . . . Dismas. See? Movies *do* teach us things!

p, Dino De Laurentiis; d, Richard Fleischer; w, Christopher Fry (based on the novel by Par Lagerkvist); ph, Aldo Tonti (Technicolor, Technirama); m, Mario Nascimbene; ed, Raymond Poulton; cos, Maria DeMatteis.

Historical/Drama Cas. (PR:C MPAA:NR)

BARBADOS QUEST (SEE: MURDER ON APPROVAL, 1956, Brit.)

BARBARELLA*

(1968, Fr./Ital.) 98m PAR c (AKA: BARBARELLA, QUEEN OF THE GALAXY)

Jane Fonda *(Barbarella)*, John Phillip Law *(Pygar)*, Anita Pallenberg *(Black Queen)*, Milo O'Shea *(Concierge)*, David Hemmings *(Dildano)*, Marcel Marceau *(Prof. Ping)*, Ugo Tognazzi *(Mark Hand)*, Claude Dauphin *(President of Earth)*.

Silly sexploitation sci-fi film concerns the space adventures of Fonda in the cartoon-strip title role, directed tediously by Vadim, whose only aim was to produce another sex kitten, but this time in outer space. Beneath the credits, Fonda does a slow strip out of her space suit while floating in a 40th-century capsule heading for the planet Lythion. Upon landing she befriends counterrevolutionary Hemmings with whom she has sex by taking pills and touching fingers. She meets blind angel Law who becomes her hero, although he himself is subjected to rape by Pallenberg, the Black Queen. A host of other weird creatures assail and jeopardize the pair as they make their way through labyrinthine worlds within this world, ostensibly to lift the spirits of Law so that he will be able to fly once again. This he does, Fonda riding his back, as they escape the machinations of Pallenberg and her hideous minions. All of this nonsense, filmed at De Laurentiis' Rome studios, adds up to softcore striptease but played straight so that it doesn't even approach camp. The special effects are as thin as cellophane; the unimaginative sets, although massive, smokescreen an overall cheapness of production. The entire film is nothing more than an excuse to parade Fonda's flesh in a comic-strip vehicle that edifies only the most moronic. Even the flesh is boring.

p, Dino De Laurentiis; d, Roger Vadim; w, Terry Southern, Brian Degas, Claude Brule, Jean-Claude Forest, Clement Biddle Wood, Tudor Gates, Vittorio Bonicelli, Vadim (based on the book by Forest); ph, Claude Renoir (Panavision, Technicolor): m, Bob Crewe, Charles Fox; ed, Victoria Mercanton; art d, Enrico Fea.

Science Fiction Cas. (PR:O MPAA:NR)

BARBARIAN, THE** (1933) 82m MGM bw (GB: A NIGHT IN CAIRO)

Ramon Novarro *(Jamil)*, Myrna Loy *(Diana)*, Reginald Denny *(Gerald)*, Louise Closser Hale *(Powers)*, C. Aubrey Smith *(Cecil)*, Edward Arnold *(Achmed)*, Blanche Frederici *(Mrs. Hume)*, Marcelle Corday *(Marthe)*, Hedda Hopper *(American Tourist)*, Leni Stengel *(German Tourist)*.

Loy stars as an American tourist in Egypt, and Novarro is the Egyptian guide trying to woo her in this 1933 retread of Edgar Selwyn's racy (for the 1920s) stage play "The Arab." The guide eventually reveals that he's a prince and, after many light-hearted desert chases, draggings, and protestations, Loy finally succumbs to Novarro's charms. Remarkable only for the absolutely beautiful photography of Loy, including a rather risque (for a Depression-era MGM film) nude bathing scene.

d, Sam Wood; w, Anita Loos, Elmer Harris (based on a story by Edgar Selwyn); ph, Harold Rosson; m, Herbert Stothart; ed, Tom Held.

Romance (PR:C MPAA:NR)

BARBARIAN AND THE GEISHA, THE** (1958) 105m FOX c

John Wayne *(Townsend Harris)*, Eiko Ando *(Okichi)*, Sam Jaffe *(Henry Heusken)*, So Yamamura *(Tamura)*, Norman Thomson *(Ship Captain)*, James Robbins *(Lt. Fisher)*, Morita *(Prime Minister)*, Kodaya Ichikawa *(Daimyo)*, Hiroshi Yamoto *(Shogun)*, Tokujiro Iketaniuchi *(Harusha)*, Fuji Kasai *(Lord Hotta)*, Takeshi Kumagai *(Chamberlain)*.

Truth may be stranger than fiction, but as the screenplay for THE BARBARIAN AND THE GEISHA demonstrated, it can also be duller. President Franklin Pierce sends US Consul Townsend Harris (John Wayne) to Japan to negotiate a series of treaties, both diplomatic and commercial. The Japanese have no interest in talking to the man and he is rudely treated. He is told to leave, but refuses and moves into a rat-infested house with three Chinese servants and Jaffe, his interpreter. The governor, Yamamura, introduces Ando into the Harris residence as a servant, but she is really there to spy on the Americans. She soon learns that Wayne is a good man and she falls in love with him. The rest of the movie is fanciful conjecture in many places, with hara-kiri, a broken love affair, a successful end to the mission, etc. The movie is more like a history lesson than an entertainment. Not that history isn't exciting, it's just written and shot in a passionless fashion, most unusual from the director who gave us THE MALTESE FALCON among other great films.

p, Eugene Frenke; d, John Huston; w, Charles Grayson (based on the story by Ellis St. Joseph); ph, Charles G. Clarke (CinemaScope, DeLuxe Color); m, Hugo Friedhofer; ed, Stuart Gilmore; art d, Lyle R. Wheeler, Jack Martin Smith.

Biography/Historical Drama (PR:A MPAA:NR)

BARBAROSA*** (1982) 90m UNIV c

Willie Nelson *(Barbarosa)*, Gary Busey *(Karl)*, Isela Vega *(Josephina)*, Gilbert Roland *(Don Braulio)*, Danny De La Paz *(Eduardo)*, Alma Martinez *(Juanita)*, George Voskovec *(Herman)*, Sharon Compton *(Hilda)*, Howland Chamberlin *(Emil)*, Harry Caesar *(Sims)*, Wolf Muser *(Floyd)*, Kai Wulff *(Otto)*, Roberto Contreras *(Cantina Owner)*, Luis Contreras *(Angel)*, Itasco Wilson *(Mattie)*, Robert Paul English *(Horse Trader)*, Bruce Smith *(Photographer)*, Sonia DeLeon *(Old Whore)*, Joanelle Romero *(Young Whore)*, Michael O'Rourke *(Brother)*, Berkley H. Garrett *(Bartender)*, Allison Wittliff *(Emily)*.

Country singer Nelson is an amiable outlaw who befriends Busey while roaming the Texas border country. Nelson is constantly trying to avoid assassination attempts by his wife's relatives because of a family feud. Busey is also on the run from another family feud. A beautifully filmed, nicely philosophic western. Busey and Nelson make a nice team, and the performances are all good.

p, Paul N. Lazarus III, William D. Wittliff; d, Fred Schepisi; w, William D. Wittliff; ph, Ian Baker (Panavision, Todd AO); m, Bruce Smeaton; ed, Don Zimmerman, David Ramirez.

Western Cas. (PR:C MPAA:PG)

BARBARY COAST***   (1935) 91m Goldwyn/UA bw

Miriam Hopkins (Mary Rutledge), Edward G. Robinson (Louis Chamalis), Joel McCrea (James Carmichael), Walter Brennan (Old Atrocity), Frank Craven (Col. Marcus Aurelius Cobb), Brian Donlevy (Knuckles), Clyde Cook (Oakie), Harry Carey (Slocum), Matt McHugh (Broncho), Otto Hoffman (Peebles), Rollo Lloyd (Wigham), J.M. Kerrigan (Judge Harper), Donald Meek (McTavish), Roger Gray (Sandy Ferguson), Wong Chung (Ah Wing), Russ Powell (Sheriff), Fredrik Vogeding (Ship's Captain), Dave Wengren (1st Mate), Anders Van Haden (Mc-Cready, 2nd Mate), Jules Cowles (Pilot), Cyril Thornton (Steward), Clarence Wertz (Drunk), Harry Semels (Lookout), Bert Sprotte, Claude Payton, Frank Benson, Bob Stevenson (Passengers), David Niven (Sailor Thrown Out of Saloon), Constantine Romanoff (Bouncer), Victor Potel (Wilkins), Patricia Farley (Dance Hall Girl), Hank Mann, Doc Wilson (Waiters), Harry Holman (Mayor), Ethel Wales (Mayor's Wife), Herman Bing (Fish Peddler), Kit Guard (Kibitzer), Jim Thorpe (Indian), Tom London (Ringsider).

A gaudy, tumultuous story, jammed with director Hawks' special action, this film rollicks with all the zest of 1850 San Francisco. Hopkins is a genteel lady from the East who finds her intended dead when arriving in the roughhouse city (at the time S.F. was a great, brawling seaport, the major American city on the Pacific; L.A. was only an adobe village to the south). Newspaper publisher Craven offers to take Hopkins in, but she refuses and is soon swept into the waterfront life of Robinson, crime czar of the city, becoming a plumed shill for his notoriously crooked roulette wheel, freely admitting that she is mercenary, only out for the percentage of gold she fleeces from gullible miners under her spell. Robinson is his typically snarling, wonderfully offensive self. He demands and gets Hopkins' affections but is snubbed by the town's upper crust. In one scene, while standing outside his sprawling saloon palace, the Bella Donna (writers Hecht and MacArthur thought it funny to name the place after a deadly drug), Robinson waves to an official passing by with his wife in a carriage. They ignore him and Robinson explodes, telling Hopkins: "I'll fix him and that horse-face he calls his wife!" On a trip to the gold fields, Hopkins meets and falls in love with young miner. On a visit to the Bella Donna, he loses all his money and takes a job as a dishwasher. Later, he and Hopkins attempt to flee the city, with Robinson in pursuit. The seemingly star-crossed lovers attempt to board a ship about to sail but Robinson stops them, shooting and wounding McCrea. Hopkins, at her tearful, whining best, then begs Robinson to spare the young man, promising that if he does, she will stay with him and cherish his cruel affection. Realizing that she is truly in love with McCrea and rejecting her terms, Robinson blusters off, letting the pair escape, walking into the waiting arms of vigilantes who intend to hang him for the destruction of Craven's newspaper, which had tried to expose his shady operations. This was a vintage Hecht-MacArthur script, full of wisecracks, sexual innuendoes and enough twists and turns to obscure the basic love triangle. The writers, who churned out the script in about a week (MacArthur swimming around in a pool while Hecht sat nearby at a typewriter, the two of them shouting out their competitive lines), of course concentrated on the evil character of Robinson, who embodies the soul of corruption. McCrea and Hopkins are simpy by comparison, but the story rolls along like a roller coaster, crowded, noisy, full of teeming life.

p, Samuel Goldwyn; d, Howard Hawks; w, Ben Hecht, Charles MacArthur; ph, Ray June; md, Alfred Newman; ed, Edward Curtis.

Adventure   (PR:A MPAA:NR)

BARBARY COAST GENT**   (1944) 87m MGM bw

Wallace Beery (Honest Plush Brannon), Binnie Barnes (Lil Damish), John Carradine (Duke Cleat), Bruce Kellogg (Bradford Bellamy III), Frances Rafferty (Portia Adair), Chill Wills (Sheriff Hightower), Noah Beery Sr. (Pete Hannibal), Henry O'Neill (Colonel Watrous), Ray Collins (Johnny Adair), Morris Ankrum (Alec Veeder), Donald Meek (Bradford Bellamy I), Addison Richards (Wade Gamelin), Harry Hayden (Elias Porter), Paul E. Burns (Tim Shea), Paul Hurst (Jake Compton), Victor Kilian (Curry Slake), Cliff Clark (Jack Coda), Louise Beavers (Bedelia).

Set in the 1880s, Beery stars as a conman who is run out of San Francisco's Barbary Coast and heads for Nevada's gold rush where he is welcomed as a big financier. He discovers an actual gold mine and is forced to sell shares to the locals. When ex-partners Carradine and Ankrum show up to grab his payroll, Beery becomes a Robin Hood thief, stealing to save the local mine. Once caught, he becomes the first prisoner in the jail he helped to build.

p, Orville O. Dull; d, Roy Del Ruth; w, William R. Lipman, Grant Garrett, Harry Ruskin; ph, Charles Salerno, Jr.; ed, Adrienne Fazan.

Western   (PR:A MPAA:NR)

BARBARY PIRATE*   (1949) 64m COL bw

Donald Woods (Maj. Tom Blake), Trudy Marshall (Anne Ridgeway), Lenore Aubert (Zoltah), Stefan Schnabel (Yusof, Bey of Tripoli), Ross Ford (Sam Ridgeway), John Dehner (Murad Reis), Matthew Boulton (Tobias Sharpe), Nelson Leigh (Rindeff), Joe Mantell (Dexter Freeman), Frank Reicher (Cathcart), Holmes Herbert (Thomas Jefferson), Frank Jaquet (Capt. Crawford), William Fawcett (Ezra Fielding), Russell Hicks (Commodore Preble).

Cheapie by Sam Katzman about pirates marauding around Tripoli. Woods is an Army officer sent to Tripoli to uncover who it is in Washington that is tipping off the pirates as to what's being shipped where. Lots of sabers, and rapiers, some decolletage, a whole bunch of stock shots, and a generally fast-moving story. BARBARY PIRATE is the kind of movie that played third on a Saturday triple bill in the 1940s and 1950s. Mantell went on to achieve cult fame as Borgnine's best friend in MARTY, receiving an Oscar nomination.

p, Sam Katzman; d, Lew Landers; w, Robert Libott, Frank Burt; ph, Ira H. Morgan; ed, James Sweeney.

Adventure   (PR:A MPAA:NR)

BARBED WIRE**   (1952) 61m COL bw

Gene Autry (Himself), Pat Buttram (Buckeye Buttram), Anne James (Cay Kendall), William Fawcett (Uncle John Copeland), Leonard Penn (Steve Ruttledge), Michael Vallon (August Gormley), Terry Frost (Perry), Clayton Moore (Bailey), Edwin Parker (Ed Parker), Sandy Sanders (Hendley).

Gentleman Gene is a cattle buyer who finds out that a battle between cattle ranchers and homesteaders is threatening to cut off his supply of heifers. The folks who own the land aren't allowing the cattle people to go across it with their herds, and the steers have been rerouted hundreds of miles out of the way. Penn, as a wealthy landowner, and his cohorts have made claims on thousands of acres and are hoping to put a railroad across the valuable territory. They fence off enormous sections of land with barbed wire and the cattlemen can't drive their animals north. Gene discovers the plot and with the help of Buttram, Government agent and pal, and Anne James, a crusading newspaper editor, defeats the bad 'uns. Now, if that's not enough for a tight 61 minutes, Gene also has time to serenade all his fans with "Mexicali Rose" and "Old Buckaroo." (See GENE AUTRY series, Index.)

p, Armand Schaefer; d, George Archainbaud; w, Gerald Geraghty; ph, William Bradford; m, Mischa Bakaleinikoff; ed, James Sweeney.

Western   (PR:A MPAA:NR)

BARBER OF SEVILLE, THE*   (1947, Ital.) 110m Tespi/Excelsior bw

Ferruccio Tagliavini (Count Almaviva), Tito Gobbi (Figaro), Nelly Corradi (Rosina), Vito de Tarranto (Don Bartolo), Italo Tajo (Don Basilio), Natalia Nicolini (Berta), Nino Mazziotti (Fiorello).

Great costumes and fabulous sets can't save a dull opera that's photographed like a stage play. Aggravating commentator interrupts before every act to explain what's going to happen, which just slows the film down more. Tagliavini was a highly-touted tenor at the time.

p, Marie and Ugo Trombetti; d, Mario Gosta; w, Deems Taylor (based on the opera by Giacomo Rossini); ph, Massimo Terano; art d, Libero Petrassi; cos, Giorgio Foeldes.

Opera   (PR:A MPAA:NR)

BARBER OF SEVILLE*   (1949, Fr.) 98m Spalier bw

Lucienne Jourfier (Rosine), Renee Gilly (Marceline), Louis Musy (Bartholo), Roger Bourdin (Basile), Roger Bussonet (Figaro), Raymond Amade (Almaviva).

The French made the same mistakes the Italians did two years earlier. This one's worse because the singers weren't that great.

p, Claude Dolbert; d, Jean Loubignac; md, Louis Musy; m/l, Giacomo Rossini, Castil-Blaise.

Opera   (PR:A MPAA:NR)

BARBER OF SEVILLE, THE***   (1973, Ger./Fr.) 141m United/Beta c

Teresa Berganza (Rosina), Stefania Malagu (Berta), Hermann Prey (Figaro), Luigi Alva (Count Almaviva), Enzo Dara (Bartolo), Paolo Montarsolo (Basilio), Renato Cesari (Fiorello), Hans Kraemmer (Ambrogio), Luigi Roni (Officer), Karl Schaidler (Notary).

It took 30 years but somebody finally thought to move the camera around and photograph this opera like it was a movie and not a stage play. Great sets and costumes, good sound recording, and creative visuals make this the best of the batch of BARBER OF SEVILLE films. It was about time. Let's hope it ends here. The music was performed by the orchestra and chorus of La Scala, Milan.

d&ph, Ernst Wild; m, Giacomo Rossini; md, Claudio Abbado; art d, Jean Pierre Ponelle.

Opera   (PR:A MPAA:NR)

BARBER OF STAMFORD HILL, THE*1/2   (1963, Brit.) 64m BL bw

Megs Jenkins (Mrs. Werner), John Bennett (Mr. Figg), Maxwell Shaw (Dober), John Graham (Mr. Luster), Trevor Peacock (Willy), David Franks (Lennie), Judi Bloom (Marilyn), Dilys Hamlett (Mother), Eric Thompson (1st Customer), Wensley Pithey (Mr. O), Barry Keegan (2nd Customer), Matthew Peters (Boy).

Suprisingly short (for 1963) film features Bennett as a lonely Jewish barber whose social life consists of playing chess on Friday night with his dim-witted friend Shaw. One day the barber decides to propose to a widow with two children, but she scares him off and he goes back to playing chess on Friday nights. Very good cast, but pathetic subject matter makes this tedious.

p, Ben Arbeid; d, Casper Wrede; w, Ronald Harwood; ph, Arthur Lavis; m, George Hall; ed, Thelma Connell.

Drama   (PR:A MPAA:NR)

BARBERINA*1/2

(1932, Ger.) 78m Zelnik bw (BARBERINA, DIE TAENZERIN VON SANS SOUCI)

Otto Gebuehr (Frederick II), Lil Dagover (Barberina), Rosa Valetti (Her mother), Hans Stuewe (Baron Cocceji), Hans Junkermann (Baron Poellnitz), Hans Brausaewetter (Moeller), Margot Walter (Eve), Iris Arlan (Demoiselle Brigelli), Paul Otto (Cagliostro).

Melodramatic telling of the Frederick the Great story starring Gebuehr as the lonely conqueror who falls in love with an Italian dancer. Things go well between the two for awhile, but the dancer takes off with a younger man and Frederick stares out the castle windows looking pathetic. Who cares if you hold half the known world if your castle is empty?

p&d, Friedrich Zelnik; w, Herren Carlson and Behrend; ph, Friedl Behn-Grun; m, Marc Roland.

Historical Drama   (PR:A MPAA:NR)

BARCAROLE*½ (1935, Ger.) 83m UFA bw

Lida Baarova *(Giacinta)*, Gustav Froehlich *(Colloredo)*, Willy Birgel *(Zubaran)*, Elsa Wagner *(Elvira)*, Will Dohm *(Motta)*, Hubert von Meyerinck *(Lopuchin)*, Hilde Huldebrand *(Ludovisca)*, Emilia Unda *(Wirtin)*.

Dumb drama about a gambler who bets his life he can seduce the wife of a fellow club member. He succeeds, but also falls in love with the woman and pretends he failed in order to preserve her honor. The husband shoots the gambler dead, and as his dying request, he tells a trusted friend not to let the woman find out about the bet. It all takes place in the space of one evening.

d, Gerhard Lamprecht; w, Gerhard Menzel (based on "The Tales of Hoffman" by Offenbach); m, Hans-Otto Borgmann.

Drama **(PR:A MPAA:NR)**

BARE KNUCKLES zero (1978) 90m Intercontinental Releasing Corp. c

Robert Viharo *(Zachary Kane)*, Sherry Jackson *(Jennifer Randall)*, Michael Heit *(Richard Devlin)*, Gloria Hendry *(Barbara Darrow)*, John Daniels *(Black)*.

Heit is a cut-up as he plays a knife-wielding maniac slashing his way into your heart. He specializes in slicing women who bleed on cue. Bounty hunter Viharo is hot on the trail—with all that blood, Heit is hard to miss. Mostly fight scenes with little or no time for any character development. The kind of film you see on obscure cable channels or, perhaps, on non-scheduled airlines.

p,d&w, Don Edmonds; ph, Dean Cundey (Metrocolor); m, Vic Caesar; ed, Robert Freeman; prod d, Michael Riva; stunts, Jim Winburn.

Adventure **(PR:O MPAA:R)**

BAREFOOT BATTALION, THE** (1954, Gr.) 89m Leon Brandt bw

Maria Costi *(Alexandra)*, Nicos Fermas *(Black Marketeer)*, Vassilios Frangadakis *(Andrea)*, Antonios Voulgaris *(Niko)*, Stavros Krozos *(Dimitri in 1943)*, Apostolis Bekiaros *(Dimitri in 1953)*, Christos Solouroglou *(Joe)*, Ketty Gyni *(Martha)*, Evangelos Yiotopoulos *(Jacob)*, George Axiotis *(Thanos)*, Kostas Rigas *(Professor)*, Nicholas Zaharias *(Stavros)*.

Based on a true occurrence, THE BAREFOOT BATTALION was, in fact, a real group of young people who fought in the Greek Resistance during WW II. The kids stole from the Nazis in order to finance their exploits and to help the poor. It's a tribute to the pluckiness of the teens and tots who made up Greece's youth during those dark days. The actual exploits were many, including helping a downed US airman to safety in Egypt. The technical aspects are so dismal that any interest in the film will be dulled. If you can look past the foggy quality of the film, you cannot fail to be touched by the story. Just two of the children depicted are professional actors, and you are defied to tell which ones they are. Director/editor Tallas has extracted heart-rending per- formances from one and all.

p, Peter Boudoures; d, Gregg Tallas; w, Nico Katsiotes (based on a story by Katsiotes and Tallas); m, Mikis Theodorakis; ed, Tallas.

War **(PR:A MPAA:NR)**

BAREFOOT BOY** (1938) 60m MON bw

Jackie Moran *(Billy Whittaker)*, Marcia Mae Jones *(Pige Blaine)*, Claire Windsor *(Valerie Hale)*, Ralph Morgan *(John Hale)*, Charles D. Brown *(Calvin Whittaker)*, Helen MacKeller *(Martha Whittaker)*, Bradley Metcalf *(Kenneth Hale)*, Frank Puglia *(Hank)*, Matty Fain *(Blake)*, Marilyn Knowlden *(Julia Blaine)*, Henry Roquemore *(Ben Blaine)*, Roger Grey *(Pop)*, Earle Hodgins *(Sheriff)*, Johnnie Morris *(Jeff Blaine)*.

Decent juvenile fare starring Morgan as the wholesome youngster who puts spoiled newcomer Metcalf through some grief before he is assimilated into the neighborhood. Boyhood pranks take up most of the action until the boys unite to clear Metcalf's dad when he's falsely arrested for robbery.

p, E. B. Derr; d, Karl Brown; w, John T. Neville; ph, Gilbert Warrenton; ed, Finn Ulback.

Drama **(PR:A MPAA:NR)**

BAREFOOT CONTESSA, THE*½** (1954) 128m UA c

Humphrey Bogart *(Harry Dawes)*, Ava Gardner *(Maria Vargas)*, Edmond O'Brien *(Oscar Muldoon)*, Marius Goring *(Alberto Bravano)*, Valentina Cortesa *(Eleanora Torlato-Favrini)*, Rossano Brazzi *(Vincenzo Torlato-Favrini)*, Elizabeth Sellars *(Jerry)*, Warren Stevens *(Kirk Edwards)*, Franco Interlenghi *(Pedro)*, Mari Aldon *(Myrna)*, Bessie Love *(Mrs. Eubanks)*, Diana Decker *(Drunken Blonde)*, Bill Fraser *(J. Montague Brown)*, Alberto Rabagliati *(Night Club Proprietor)*, Enzo Staiola *(Busboy)*, Maria Zanoli *(Maria's Mother)*, Renato Chiantoni *(Maria's Father)*, John Parrish *(Mr. Black)*, Jim Gerald *(Mr. Blue)*, Riccardo Rioli *(Gypsy Dancer)*, Tonio Selwart *(The Pretender)*, Margaret Anderson *(The Pretender's Wife)*, Gertrude Flynn *(Lulu McGee)*, John Horne *(Hector Eubanks)*, Robert Christopher *(Eddie Blake)*, Anna Maria Paduan *(Chambermaid)*, Carlo Dale *(Chauffeur)*.

THE BAREFOOT CONTESSA is one of those movies that one remembers as better than it actually was. O'Brien won an Oscar for his role and Joe Mankiewicz was nominated as writer, but that's about it. A very complex story finds Gardner dancing in a Madrid nightclub. Stevens has hired Bogart, a faded director, to write and direct a movie about a glamorous woman. Gardner likes Bogart and hates Stevens but agrees to make the movie. She is an instant star. Stevens, in a thinly disguised portrayal of Howard Hughes, throws a party for fellow millionaire Marius Goring. Bogart and Elizabeth Sellars, his girl friend/script girl, arrive. Goring has eyes for Gardner, invites her to join him on his yacht. Stevens forbids it and she defies him. O'Brien, the toadying press agent, goes to work for Goring. There is no way that Goring is going to get Gardner, but since people assume that he is sleeping with her, that's enough to soothe Goring's insecurities. At a local casino, Gardner takes some of Goring's cash and tosses it out the window to her latest lover. Goring begins to lose and accuses Gardner of bringing him ill fortune. Goring berates Gardner in public until he is stopped by Brazzi, a count, who whacks Goring and takes Gardner out of the casino. They fall in love and Bogart gives the bride away at the wedding. Some time later, Gardner tells Bogart that her beloved husband is impotent, the result of a wound sustained during the war. Gardner loves her husband so much that she wants to make him a father. Bogart suggests that might be a bad idea. Brazzi is a very proud man and might not enjoy the thought of his wife getting pregnant by someone else. Gardner leaves Bogart's hotel room and he looks out the window to see Brazzi's car following Gardner's auto. Bogart gets into his car, races to the fabulous house they occupy but he is too late. Two shots are heard from the servant's quarters. Brazzi walks out carrying his dead wife. They call the police and the film ends where it began, at the cemetery. THE BAREFOOT CONTESSA is marked by Mankiewicz's sharp wit, sometimes too much wit. When there is one character cracking wise, fine. When you have two, okay. But when almost everyone sounds as though they were sitting around the writer's table at the MGM commissary, suddenly credibility goes out the window. Often it seems as though the screenwriter is writing for his friends, rather than for the broad, popular audience that makes a movie a hit.

p,d&w, Joseph L. Mankiewicz; ph, Jack Cardiff (Technicolor); m, Mario Nascimbene; ed, William Hornbeck; art d, Arrigo Equini; cos, Fontana.

Drama **Cas.** **(PR:A MPAA:NR)**

BAREFOOT EXECUTIVE, THE*** (1971) 96m BV c

Kurt Russell *(Steven Post)*, Joe Flynn *(Francis X. Wilbanks)*, Harry Morgan *(E. J. Crampton)*, Wally Cox *(Mertons)*, Heather North *(Jennifer Scott)*, Alan Hewitt *(Farnsworth)*, Hayden Rourke *(Clifford)*, Raffles *(Himself)*, John Ritter *(Roger)*, Jack Bender *(Tom)*, Tom Anfinsen *(Dr. Schmidt)*, George N. Neise *(Network Executive)* Ed Reimers *(Announcer)*, Morgan Farley *(Advertising Executive)*, Glenn Dixon *(Sponsor)*, Robert Shayne *(Sponsor)*, Tris Coffin *(Sponsor)*, J. B. Douglas *(Network Executive)*, Ed Prentiss *(Justice Department)*, Fabian Dean *(Jackhammer Man)*, Iris Adrian *(Woman Shopper)*, Jack Smith *(Clatworthy)*, Eve Brent, Sandra Gould, James Flavin, Pete Renoudet, Judson Pratt, Vince Howard, Hal Baylor, Bill Daily, Dave Wilcox, Anthony Teague, Edward Faulkner.

A very funny satire about the TV business that may have more truth to it than one would believe. Action takes place at UBC, a TV network that's always last in the ratings. One of the pages has a girl friend who owns a pet chimp that has an unerring eye and ear for picking hit TV shows. Russell uses the simian to great advantage, gets Flynn fired (the former program director) and becomes the *wunderkind* of TV. Once the secret is out, everyone wants the brilliant chimp and complications ensue. Lots of serious laughter here from a basically funny situation cooked up by Garrett and Kahn (who were married at the time) and Billett and a good-natured screenplay by McEveety. Fred Silverman, who really was the network genius at all three nets before his deserved fall from grace, loved apes and used to attempt programming shows with them constantly. They never worked. One wonders if he had an ape that picked the shows? Look for a very young John Ritter already showing his stuff as Roger. Flynn and Morgan (as the network president) offer solid support as usual.

p, Bill Anderson; d, Robert Butler; w, Joseph L. McEveety (based on a story by Lila Garrett, Bernie Kahn, Stewart C. Billett); ph, Charles F. Wheeler (Technicolor); m, Robert F. Brunner; ed, Robert Stafford; art d, John B. Mansbridge, Ed Graves; cos, Chuck Keehne, Emily Sundby; m/l, Brunner, Bruce Belland.

Comedy **(PR:AAA MPAA:G)**

BAREFOOT IN THE PARK*** (1967) 104m PAR c

Robert Redford *(Paul Bratter)*, Jane Fonda *(Corie Bratter)*, Charles Boyer *(Victor Velasco)*, Mildred Natwick *(Mrs. Ethel Banks)*, Herbert Edelman *(Telephone Man)*, James Stone *(Delivery Man)*, Ted Hartley *(Frank)*, Mabel Albertson *(Aunt Harriet)*, Fritz Feld *(Restaurant Proprietor)*.

Laughs galore in this first screenplay by Simon, based on his Broadway success. Simon has made it a point to write about his life and this light, very funny and often charming screenplay must be drawn from his own experiences. Saks, who had been an actor for so many years (A THOUSAND CLOWNS), makes a smashing impression in his first directorial stint. Redford and Fonda live five flights up in Greenwich Village. Fonda thinks it's lovely and he, ever the conservative attorney, hates it. To worsen matters, Boyer lives above them and has to go through their apartment to get to his. Boyer's reputation is that of a ladies' man with a touch of madness. Fonda adores the old reprobate and fixes him up with her mother, stodgy Mildred Natwick. A blind date in an Albanian restaurant follows. Redford and Natwick are ill from the food, drink, and the five-story climb to the apartment. (The long climb is a running joke and used to its best advantage by Edelman, reprising his role from the Broadway show as the telephone repairman. Edelman went on to greater success in several films and TV.) Natwick spends the night in Boyer's apartment after she takes a fall on the ice. Meanwhile, Fonda and Redford are battling about his inability to let himself go—like the night he refused to go barefoot in Central Park. He explains that it was 17 degrees and raining, but Fonda won't hear of it and demands a divorce. Natwick prevails on Jane to give Bob another chance and film comes to conclusion with Redford wacked out of his skull and barefoot in the park. Redford was on Broadway, as was Natwick, but Fonda nosed out Elizabeth Ashley for the femme lead. Most people don't recall that Redford was a fine light comedian before he began to do movies with messages. He never liked dressing up in suit and tie and spent most of his time in cowboy gear on the set. He could have been the next Cary Grant.

p, Hal Wallis; d, Gene Saks; w, Neil Simon (based on his play); ph, Joseph LaShelle (Technicolor); m, Neal Hefti; ed, William H. Lyon; cos, Edith Head; m/l, title song, Hefti, Johnny Mercer.

Comedy **Cas.** **(PR:A MPAA:NR)**

BAREFOOT MAILMAN, THE*¹/₂   (1951) 81m COL c

Robert Cummings *(Sylvanus Hurley)*, Terry Moore *(Adie Titus)*, Jerome Courtland *(Steven Pierton)*, John Russell *(Theron)*, Will Geer *(Dan Paget)*, Arthur Shields *(Ben Titus)*, Trevor Bardette *(Oat McCarty)*, Arthur Space *(Piggott)*, Frank Ferguson *(Doc Bethune)*, Percy Helton *(Dewey Durgan)*, Ellen Corby *(Miss Della)*, Renie Riano *(Miss Emily)*, Robert Lynn *(Farrell)*, Mary Field *(Mrs. Thomas)*.

A strange film with a cast that one might think would bid for comedy, but no. It takes place in Florida a hundred years ago when the mail was delivered on foot. Courtland, who went on to become a director and producer (PETE'S DRAGON for Disney), is the barefoot mailman of the title and Cummings is a conman escaping from the long arm of the New York law. Moore dresses up as a little girl so she won't be molested by anyone on the trail. (How times have changed!) The trio team up and make the walk from Palm Beach to Miami. Along the way, they are attacked by a group of beachcombers and Moore (who was only 22 at the time) is kidnaped. Eventually, Cummings saves her. In the last third of the movie, Cummings reverts to his conman ways and attempts to bilk a group of settlers of their savings. He sees the folly of his ways soon enough and changes, just in time, as it were, because the settlers deal harshly with Russell's beachcombers and would have done the same with SOB (Sweet Old Bob). It was many years later that Geer and Corby teamed up again for a television series that delighted America for many years, "The Waltons." There are some interesting underwater sequences as well as a few exciting shots of alligators but, by and large, this picture is not nearly as good as it should have been.

p, Robert Cohn; d, Earl McEvoy; w, James Gunn, Francis Swan (based on the novel by Theodore Pratt); ph, Ellis W. Carter (Supercinecolor); m, George Duning; ed, Aaron Stell.

Adventure   (PR:A   MPAA:NR)

BAREFOOT SAVAGE   (SEE: SENSUALITA, 1954, Ital.)

BARGAIN, THE*   (1931) 68m FN/WB bw

Lewis Stone *(Maitland White)*, Evalyn Knapp *(Vorencia)*, Charles Butterworth *(Geoffrey)*, Doris Kenyon *(Nancy)*, John Darrow *(Roderick White)*; Oscar Apfel *(G. T. Warren)*, Una Merkel *(Etta)*.

Tedious adaptation of the 1923 play, "You and I," which was the tale of a rich father who had forsaken an art career in his youth to go into the economically safer area of business. He has spent his life regretting that decision and now moves to make sure his son won't make the same mistake. Director Minton also performed the same chore on the play.

d, Robert Minton; w, Robert Presnell (based on Philip Barry's play "You and I").

Drama   (PR:A   MPAA:NR)

BARGEE, THE**   (1964, Brit.) 106m ABF/Warne-Pathe c

Harry H. Corbett *(Hemel)*, Hugh Griffith *(Joe)*, Eric Sykes *(The Mariner)*, Ronnie Barker *(Ronnie)*, Julia Foster *(Christine)*, Miriam Karlin *(Nellie)*, Eric Barker *(Foreman)*, Derek Nimmo *(Dr. Scott)*, Norman Bird *(Waterways Supervisor)*, Richard Briers *(Tomkins)*, Brian Wilde *(Policeman)*, George A. Cooper *(Office Official)*, Grazina Frame *(Girl in Office)*, Jo Rowbottom *(Cynthia)*, Edwin Apps *(Barman)*, Godfrey Winn *(Announcer)*.

Banal British life-on-the-canals comedy heavily influenced by the creators of the BBC TV series "Steptoe and Son." (The Americans borrowed the concept and turned it into the hit show "Sanford and Son.") The film is directed by Wood, who staged the TV show, and the movie stars one of its leads, Corbett, who played Steptoe, Jr. Plot concerns freedom-loving Corbett, a confirmed bachelor, who has a reputation with the ladies. While he runs his barge up and down the British waterways, he is lured into marriage by the daughter of a lock-keeper whom he has put in a family way. Pretty oafish premise for a full-length comedy.

p, W. A. Whittaker; d, Duncan Wood; w, Ray Galton, Alan Simpson; ph, Harry Waxman (Technicolor); m, Frank Cordell; ed, Richard Best.

Comedy   (PR:C   MPAA:NR)

BARKER, THE*   (1928) 86m FN/WB bw

Milton Sills *(Nifty Miller)*, Dorothy Mackaill *(Lou)*, Betty Compson *(Carrie)*, Douglas Fairbanks Jr. *(Chris Miller)*, Sylvia Ashton *(Ma Benson)*, George Cooper *(Hap Spissel)*, S. S. Simon *(Col. Gowdy)*.

Very early talkie in which young Fairbanks is attracted to the carnival life despite the protestations of his father who wants to send him to law school. Most of the film is silent, with the sound sequences running three, nine, 11, and 15 minutes respectively.

p, Al Rockett; d, George Fitzmaurice; w, Benjamin Glazer, Herman Mankiewicz, Joe Jackson (based on the play by Kenyon Nicholson); ph, Lee Garmes; m, Louis Silvers; ed, Stuart Heisler; cos, Max Ree.

Drama   (PR:A   MPAA:NR)

BARKLEYS OF BROADWAY, THE***   (1949) 109m MGM c

Fred Astaire *(John Barkley)*, Ginger Rogers *(Dinah Barkley)*, Oscar Levant *(Ezra Miller)*, Billie Burke *(Mrs. Belney)*, Gale Robbins *(Shirlene May)*, Jacques Francois *(Jacques Barredout)*, George Zucco *(The Judge)*, Clinton Sundberg *(Bert Felsher)*, Inez Cooper *(Pamela Driscoll)*, Carol Brewster *(Gloria Amboy)*, Wilson Wood *(Larry)*, Jean Andren *(First Woman)*, Laura Treadwell *(Second Woman)*, Margaret Bert *(Mary)*, Hans Conreid *(Ladislaus Ladi)*, Frank Ferguson *(Mr. Perkins)*, Dee Turnell *(Blonde)*.

A handsome but somewhat empty production with a plot as thin as Twiggy. Fred and Ginger (in a role originally conceived for Judy Garland—who had to bow out due to "illness") are The Barkleys, a highly successful musical team. Ginger longs

to spread her wings on the dramatic stage and leaves Fred. After a middle section that is singularly unmemorable, they get back together for the finale. This is not one of their best efforts, despite sharp work by Levant, Burke, and almost all other supporters. Fabray recently said that her time with Astaire in THE BAND WAGON was one of the worst experiences she's ever had. Astaire is reputed to be aloof, cold and distant (all three mean the same and all three have been used to describe him). Yet, in this film, as in most of the movies he made, Fred managed to get the job done. Someone said that Fred and Ginger were a perfect team because they complemented each other in that he gave her Class and she gave him Sex. In THE BARKLEYS OF BROADWAY the weakest part is the score. Warrren and Ira Gershwin didn't give them much to work with. Highligts include "My One And Only Highland Fling," George and Ira Gershwin's "They Can't Take That Away From Me," and Levant's rendering of "The Sabre Dance."

p, Arthur Freed; d, Charles Walters; w, Betty Comden, Adolph Green; ph, Harry Stradling (Technicolor); m, Lenny Hayton; ed, Albert Akst; art d, Cedric Gibbons, Edward Carfagno; ch, Hermes Pan; anim, Irving G. Reis; cos, Irene; m/l, Harry Warren, Ira Gershwin.

Musical   (PR:A   MPAA:NR)

BARN OF THE NAKED DEAD zero

(1976) 86m Twin World c (AKA: TERROR CIRCUS)

Andrew Prine, Manuella Theiss, Sherry Alberoni, Gyl Roland, Al Cormier, Jennifer Ashley.

Awful bloodbath film where a lunatic busies himself by torturing abducted females while his father, transformed into a sub-human creature by radiation, slaughters citizens in remote Nevada areas. Low budget garbage.

p&d, Gerald Cormier; w, Roman Valenti, Ralph Harolde.

Horror   (PR:.O MPAA:NR)

BARNACLE BILL**   (1935, Brit.) 90m City/BUT bw

Archie Pitt *(Bill Harris)*, Joan Gardner *(Jill Harris)*, Gus McNaughton *(Jack Baron)*, Jean Adrienne *(Mary Bailey)*, Sybil Jason *(Jill as a Child)*, Denis O'Neil *(Shorty)*, O. B. Clarence *(Uncle George)*, Henrietta Watson *(Aunt Julia)*, Minnie Rayner *(Mrs. Bailey)*, Iris Darbyshire *(Florrie)*, Tully Comber *(Harry Fordyce)*, Arthur Neal *(Frank Atkinson)*, Frank Titterton, Donna le Bourdais.

Long-widowed seaman sacrifices his career and comfort for his only daughter's happiness. Decent production marred by saccharine script and melodramatic tear-jerking.

p, Basil Humphreys; d, Harry Hughes; w, Aveling Ginever (based on a story by Archie Pitt).

Drama   (PR:A   MPAA:NR)

BARNACLE BILL**   (1941) 90m MGM bw

Wallace Beery *(Bill Johansen)*, Marjorie Main *(Marge Cavendish)*, Leo Carrillo *(Pico Rodriguez)*, Virginia Weidler *(Virginia Johansen)*, Donald Meek *(Pop Cavendish)*, Barton MacLane *(John Kelly)*, Connie Gilchrist *(Mamie)*, Sara Haden *(Aunt Letty)*, William Edmunds *(Joe Petillo)*, Don Terry *(Dixon)*, Alec Craig *(MacDonald)*, Monte Montague *(Dolan)*, Irving Bacon *(Deckhand)*, Harry Fleischman *(Detective)*, Francis Pierlot *(Minister)*, Harry Semels *(Tony)*, George Guhl *(Harry)*, Charles Lane *(Auctioneer)*, Art Miles *(Driver)*, Marie Genardi *(Mrs. Petillo)*, William Forrest *(Naval Officer)*, James Millican *(Sailor)*, Milton Kibbee, Frank Yaconelli *(Fishermen)*.

Beery plays the scrappy owner of a small fishing boat who, through the influence of his girl friend, Main, and daughter, Weidler, gets wrapped up with big-time fish-contractor MacLane. With a loan from Main, Beery buys a large schooner to be used as a refrigeration vessel for MacLane's operation. Beery is not happy with his work and dreams of sneaking off to the South Seas in his new boat. A hurricane stops him and he decides to stick it out and marry the loyal and supportive Main. Pleasant outing for Beery fans.

p, Milton Bren; d, Richard Thorpe; w, Jack Jevne, Hugo Butler (based on a story by Jevne); ph, Clyde De Vinna; ed, Frank E. Hull.

Drama   (PR:A   MPAA:NR)

BARNACLE BILL, 1958   (SEE: ALL AT SEA, 1958, Brit.)

BARNUM WAS RIGHT*   (1929) 55m UNIV bw

Glenn Tryon *(Freddie Farell)*, Merna Kennedy *(Miriam Locke)*, Otis Harlan *(Samuel Locke)*, Basil Radford *(Standish)*, Clarence Burton *(Martin)*, Lew Kelly *(Harrison)*, Isabelle Keith *(Phoebe O'Dare)*, Gertrude Sutton *(Sarah)*.

Title refers to P.T. Barnum's remark, "There's a sucker born every minute." In this adaptation of the play Tryon is the poor boy who has to wait to marry his sweetheart until he can raise some serious money. Meanwhile, the girl's father wants her to marry the local English multi-millionaire.

d, Del Lord; w, Hutchinson Ford (based on the play by Philip Bartholomae and John Meehan); ph, Jerome Ash; w, Arthur Ripley, Ewart Adamson (based on a story by Hutchinson Boyd and a play by Philip Bartholomae, John Meehan).

Drama   (PR:A   MPAA:NR)

BARNYARD FOLLIES*¹/₂   (1940) 68m REP bw

Mary Lee *(Bubbles Martin)*, Rufe Davis *(Bucksaw Beechwood)*, June Storey *(Louise Dale)*, Jed Prouty *(Sam)*, Victor Kilian *(Hiram Crabtree)*, Joan Woodbury *(Dolly)*, Carl "Alfalfa" Switzer *(Alfalfa)*, Robert Homans *(The Fire Inspector)*, Dorothy Harrison *(Queen of Dairyland)*, Harry "Pappy" Cheshire *(Pappy)*, Mary Jane De Zurik, Carolyn De Zurik *(Cackle Sisters)*, Jim Jeffries *(Announcer)*, The Kidoodlers *(Themselves)*, Ralph Bowman *(Jeff)*, Isabel Randolph *(Mrs. Uppington)*.

Rustic musical comedy concerning a group of youngsters who try to save their 4-H club. Some grouchy townsfolk try to block the club financially, but the clever kids decide to put on a show to raise the $5,000 bucks needed to keep America safe for agriculture. Songs include "Big Boy Blues," "Barnyard Holiday," "Lollipop Lane" (Fred Lane, Johnny Marvin); "Mama Don't Allow It" (Charles Davenport); "Poppin' the Corn" (Sol Meyer, Jule Styne).

p, Armand Schaefer; d, Frank MacDonald; w, Dorell and Stuart McGowen (based on a story by Robert T. Shannon); ph, Ernest Miller; ed, Charles Craft; md, Cy Feuer; ch, Josephine Earl.

Musical   **(PR:A MPAA:NR)**

BAROCCO*¹/₂   (1976, Fr.) 102m Films La Boetie c

Isabelle Adjani (Laure), Gerard Depardieu (Samson), Marie-France Pisier (Nelly), Jean-Claude Brialy (Walt), Julien Guiomar (Gauthier), Helene Surgere (Antoinette), Claude Brasseur (Jules).

Pretentious film made by a former film critic. Depardieu plays two parts, neither of them very well. Adjani seems to use only two expressions in the film, a smile or a whine. Marie-France Pisier is your standard whore with a heart of gold and Brialy is wasted. Techine must have had something in mind when he wrote the script with Goldin. Perhaps there is an homage to the German films of the 1930s or the *film noir* movies in the US. Whatever it is, we missed it and all that comes across is a flabby love story set against a confusing crime background.

p, Andre Genoves, Alain Sarde; d, Andre Techine; w, Techine, Marilyn Goldin; ph, Bruno Nuytten (Eastmancolor); m, Philippe Sarde; ed, Claude Merlin.

Drama   **(PR:O MPAA:NR)**

BARON BLOOD*¹/₂   (1972, Ital.) 90m AIP c

Joseph Cotten (Becker/The Baron), Elke Sommer (Eva), Massimo Girotti (Uncle Karl), Antonio Cantafora (Peter Kleist), Alan Collins (Fritz), Nicoletta Elmi (Gretchen), Rada Rassimov (Occult Lady), Dieter Tressier (Castle Owner), Humi Raho (Inspector).

Cult director Bava offers this story of a haunted castle that is being renovated by a hotel conglomerate. The workers wake up the ghost of the sadistic Baron, Cotten, who goes on a rampage of torture and mayhem. Sommer runs through the castle looking scared and screaming at the top of her Teutonic voice. Cotten looks as if he wished he were someplace else (and he is).

p, Alfred Leone; d, Mario Bava; w, Vincent Forte, William A. Bairn; ph, Emilio Varriano (Technicolor); m, Les Baxter; ed, Carlo Reali; art d, Enzo Bulgarelli.

Horror   **(PR:C MPAA:PG)**

BARON MUNCHAUSEN*

                  (1962, Czech.) 81m Ceskoslovensky Film c (AKA: BARON PRASIL)

Milos Kopecky, Rudolf Jelinek, Jana Brejchova.

Whimsical sci-fi film has an astronaut picking up the notorious liar Munchausen on the moon and returning him to earth for some silly escapades. Not much exciting happens but the live action played before painted backdrops is interesting.

d&w, Karel Zeman (based on the novel by Gottfried Burger); ph, Jiri Tarantile; m, Zdenek Liska.

Science Fiction/Fantasy   **(PR:A MPAA:NR)**

BARON OF ARIZONA, THE***   (1950) 96m Lippert bw

Vincent Price (James Addison Reavis), Ellen Drew (Sofia Peralta-Reavis), Vladimir Sokoloff (Pepito), Reed Hadley (Griff), Robert Barrat (Judge Adams), Robin Short (Lansing), Barbara Woodell (Carry Lansing), Tina Rome (Rita), Margia Dean (Marquesa), Edward Keane (Surveyor Miller), Gene Roth (Father Guardian), Karen Kester (Sofia as a Child), Joseph Green (Gunther), Fred Kohler, Jr. (Demming), Tristram Coffin (McCleary), Angelo Rosito (Angie), I. Stanford Jolley (Secretary of Interior), Terry Frost (Morelle), Zachary Yaconelli (Greco), Adolfo Ornelas (Martinez), Wheaton Chambers (Brother Gregory), Robert O'Neil (Brother Paul), Stephen Harrison (Surveyor's Assistant).

Ambitious western for budget-bound Lippert is based upon a real conman and artful forger, James Addison Reavis. Price, in one of his best roles, spends years forging ancient land grants that give the rights to almost all of the land in Arizona to the near-extinct Peralta family, of blueblood Mexican lineage. He then marries Drew, last of the line. Next, as husband of the endowed lady, he lays claim to the entire state, briefly taking over Arizona as his personal fiefdom, proclaiming himself a baron. Not for money does Price covet such vast lands, but for regal power which goes to his head and is finally his undoing. A powerful and colorful film, second to be directed by the gifted Fuller, which shows a large slice of pioneer life in early America.

p, Carl K. Hittleman; d&w, Samuel Fuller; ph, James Wong Howe; m, Paul Dunlap; ed, Arthur Hilton.

Western   **(PR:A MPAA:NR)**

BARONESS AND THE BUTLER, THE**   (1938) 75m FOX bw

William Powell (Johann Porok), Annabella (Baroness Katrina), Helen Westley (Countess Sandor), Henry Stephenson (Count Albert Sandor), Joseph Schildkraut (Baron Georg Marissey), J. Edward Bromberg (Zorda), Nigel Bruce (Major Andros), Lynn Bari (Klari), Maurice Call (Announcer), Ivan Simpson (Count Domo), Alphonse Ethier (President), Claire DuBrey (Secretary), Wilfred Lucas, Sidney Bracy, Frank Baker (Members of Parliament), Eleanor Wesselhoeft (Housekeeper), George Davis (Radio Technician), Margaret Irving (Countess Olga).

Making her American film debut, Annabella is woefully miscast as the Baroness, due to several problems: her English was not yet ready to be heard by human ears and her comedic talents still needed refining. She is the married daughter of the Hungarian Prime Minister (Stephenson), and her husband (Schildkraut) doesn't know how to handle this spitfire. Powell is the butler in the castle and eventually becomes leader of the opposition party. In that capacity, he makes an impassioned

speech on behalf of old-age pensions, relief programs, and the reduction of armaments, a speech that could have been made this morning in Congress. The butler returns as a full-fledged politician and announces his love for the baroness. It's all a lot of nonsense and bears no resemblance to reality or even to good farce (THE MOUSE THAT ROARED, etc.) in a royal household. Powell is dapper and debonair and Lang peoples the screen with all the best second bananas because he knew he'd need them to make this thing fly. It didn't. (Annabella, born Suzette Charpentier, began her career with a small role in Gance's NAPOLEON and was married to Tyrone Power in the 1940s before returning to her native France and retirement.)

p, Raymond Griffith; d, Walter Lang; w, Sam Hellman, Lamar Trotti, Kathryn Scola (based on the play by Ladislaus Bus-Fekete); ph, Arthur Miller; ed, Barbara MacLean; md, Louis Silvers; art d, Bernard Herzbrun, Hans Peters; set d, Thomas Little.

Comedy   **(PR:A MPAA:NR)**

BARQUERO***   (1970) 108m UA c

Lee Van Cleef (Travis), Warren Oates (Remy), Forrest Tucker (Mountain Phil), Kerwin Mathews (Marquette), Mariette Hartley (Anna), Marie Gomez (Nola), Armando Silvestre (Sawyer), John Davis Chandler (Fair), Craig Littler (Pitney), Ed Bakey (Happy), Richard Lapp (Poe), Harry Lauter (Steele), Brad Weston (Driver), Thad Williams (Gibson), Armand Alzamora (Lopez), Frank Babich (Roland), Terry Leonard (Hawk), Bennie Dobbins (Encow), Rita Conde (Layeta).

Van Cleef plays an honorable ferry operator and Tucker portrays a grizzled mountain man who defend a budding border settlement from the absolutely evil Oates and his gang. Oates is terrific as the psychopathic outlaw who destroys everything in his path. The film becomes a battle of wits between Oates and Van Cleef as each decides how to get rid of the other. Bloody oater owes much to the spaghetti westerns of Leone. Not bad if you can take the intensity.

p, Hal Klein; d, Gordon Douglas; w, George Schenck and William Marks; ph, Jerry Finnerman (DeLuxe Color); m, Dominic Frontiere; cos, Ray Phelps.

Western   **(PR:O MPAA:PG)**

BARRACUDA*   (1978) 98m REP c (AKA: THE LUCIFER PROJECT)

Wayne David Crawford, Jason Evers, Roberta Leighton, William Kerwin, Bert Freed, Cliff Emmich.

Dull attempt to horrify through an environmental disaster where chemicals cause tame fish to turn carnivorous and drive swimmers insane. Junk production methods and amateur script offer no excitement whatsoever.

p&w, Wayne Crawford, Harry Kerwin; d, Kerwin; m, Klaus Schultze.

Horror   **(PR:C MPAA:NR)**

BARRANCO*   (1932, Fr.) 102m Halk bw

Tramel (Florestan Fertiolis/Old Carabe), Rosine Derean (Aline del' Estranglebleu), Rene Donnio (Overlook), Gaston Jaquet (Stanton Muir).

Dumb film starring French comedian Tramel as a hobo who inherits a Mexican silver mine. Usual poor-guy-gets-rich goings on.

d, Andre Berthomieu.

Comedy   **(PR:A MPAA:NR)**

BARRETTS OF WIMPOLE STREET, THE****

                          (1934) 110m MGM bw (AKA: FORBIDDEN ALLIANCE)

Fredric March (Robert Browning), Norma Shearer (Elizabeth Barrett), Charles Laughton (Edward Moulton Barrett), Maureen O'Sullivan (Henrietta Barrett), Katherine Alexander (Arabel Barrett), Una O'Connor (Wilson), Ian Wolfe (Harry Bevan), Marion Clayton (Bella Hedley), Ralph Forbes (Capt. Surtees Cook), Vernon Downing (Octavius Barrett), Neville Clark (Charles Barrett), Matthew Smith (George Barrett), Robert Carleton (Alfred Barrett), Alan Conrad (Henry Barrett), Peter Hobbes (Septimus Barrett), Ferdinand Munier (Dr. Chambers), Leo Carroll (Dr. Ford-Waterlow), Margaret Seddon (Woman), George Kirby (Coachman), Winter Hall (Clergyman), Lowden Adams (Butler), Robert Bolder (Old Man), Flush (Elizabeth's Dog).

This movie got two Academy nominations, Best Picture and Best Actress (Shearer). The count was woefully short because this was, in fact, one of the premier films of 1934, if not the entire decade. Shearer as Elizabeth Barrett and March as Robert Browning find happiness in each other's arms. Shearer is an invalid who is all but held captive by her dictatorial and overly protective father, played exquisitely by Laughton. She's confined to her room with nothing but her dog and her love for poetry. March appears on the scene and is watched carefully by Laughton, who seems to have more than paternal feelings for his daughter. She eventually leaves with March and her recovery is astonishing; all she needed was the love of a good man. It sounds more simplistic than it plays because there are several layers of psychological drama beneath the surface and each performance is a gem of restraint (except for Laughton) under Franklin's guidance. There are those who prefer the 1957 version (also directed by Franklin) because all of the actors were British and the sets seemed more authentic. We felt this was the definitive film, though it was short of the 1931 play that made Katherine Cornell a household word.

p, Irving Thalberg; d, Sidney Franklin; w, Ernest Vajda, Claudine West, Donald Ogden Stewart (based on the play by Rudolph Besier); ph, William Daniels; ed, Margaret Booth; art d, Cedric Gibbons; cos, Adrian.

Drama/Biography   **(PR:A MPAA:NR)**

BARRETTS OF WIMPOLE STREET, THE****   (1957) 105m MGM c

Jennifer Jones (Elizabeth), John Gielgud (Barrett), Bill Travers (Robtert Browning), Virginia McKenna (Henrietta), Susan Stephen (Bella), Vernon Gray (Capt. Surtees

Cook), Jean Anderson *(Wilson)*, Maxine Audley *(Arabel)*, Leslie Phillips *(Harry Bevan)*, Laurence Naismith *(Dr. Chambers)*, Moultrie Kelsall *(Dr. Ford-Waterlow)*, Michael Brill *(George)*, Kenneth Fortescue *(Octavius)*, Nicholas Hawtrey *(Henry)*, Richard Thorpe *(Alfred)*, Keith Baxter *(Charles)*, Brian Smith *(Septimus)*.

A very rare remake of a very famous story that was first done as a play in 1931, then as a movie in 1934, then again as a movie in 1957. The rarity is caused by the fact that the same director, Franklin, helmed both versions. Jones is the frail poetess-daughter of Gielgud. (She is hardly frail, though, and looks as robust as any pink-cheeked and gorgeous woman can be, although she was in her late thirties when the film was produced.) Her father has an almost incestuous adoration for her and keeps her under wraps, confining her to his London house. She is understandably lonely and depressed as her only compatriots are her volumes, her servants, her horde of brothers (all wonderfully played by bright young men of the period) and her dog. Travers, a rich-in-love-and-warmth poet, meets and sweeps her off the couch. Suddenly, the almost-expired young woman blooms like a morning glory at dawn. Gielgud, in a masterpiece of understated terror, is insidious as he attempts to smash the Jones-Travers relationship before it attains fruition. Jones finally leaves her father's house and marries Travers. Gielgud, in a parting fit of anger, wants to have Jones' beloved dog destroyed as repayment for her perfidy. He is disappointed to learn that she anticipated that move and took the animal with her. Gielgud's eyes narrow; she's out of his clutches forever, but he still has several other children he can manipulate. THE BARRETTS OF WIMPOLE STREET is a subtle movie, perhaps too much so for the period. It's the kind of film you have to watch, without interruption. The sets, the colors, the costumes, are all perfection. A high- gloss, high-quality movie in every way.

p, Sam Zimbalist; d, Sidney Franklin; w, John Dighton (based on the play by Rudolph Besier); ph, F.A. Young (Metrocolor); m, Bronislau Kaper; ed, Frank Clark; art d, Alfred Junge; cos, Elizabeth Haffenden; m/l, Herbert Stothart.

Drama/Biography **(PR:A MPAA:NR)**

BARRICADE** (1939) 71m FOX bw

Alice Faye *(Emmy Jordan)*, Warner Baxter *(Hank Topping)*, Charles Winninger *(Samuel J. Cady)*, Arthur Treacher *(Upton Ward)*, Keye Luke *(Ling)*, Willie Fung *(Yen)*, Doris Lloyd *(Mrs. Ward)*, Eily Malyon *(Mrs. Little)*, Joan Carroll *(Winifred)*, Leonid Snegoff *(Boris, Russian Consul)*, Philip Ahn *(Col. Wai Kang)*, Jonathan Hale *(Asst. Sec. of State)*, Moroni Olsen *(Managing Editor)*, Harry Hayden *(Telegraph Manager)*.

Faye is a nightclub singer running away from a murder charge and posing as a Russian emigre on a train going to Shanghai. She meets Baxter, a newspaperman who drinks the way newspapermen are supposed to drink, heavily and noisily. Bandits attack the area ahead and the train detours. Alice seeks safety in the American Consulate and Warner soon follows. Winninger runs the consulate in his customary believable man- ner, but that's about all that's believable in this rag-tag film that's been edited so deeply it's hard to even wonder what they had in mind when they began shooting. The rest of the picture has to do with the rescue of American missionaries, bandits, shootings, chases, sieges, the President of the United States personally calling Baxter back and Faye planning to marry Baxter after she clears herself of a real murder charge (not alleged, as so often happens in melodrama; Alice *did* kill the guy). The sidebar stories about BARRICADE are more interesting than the film. For example, it was never really finished, and editor Dennis took a handful of disparate scenes (as we know, movies are not shot in sequence, except on rare occasions) and put them together to attempt to make a story. Faye's hair styles change in the middle of a sequence sometimes; Schildkraut and Bromberg, two of the best character men of the period, were in the movie but totally edited out of the final print. Treacher has fewer than five lines of dialog and received fourth billing, so we know he had lots more to do in the original script. Two years prior, cinematographer Freund won an Oscar for his work on THE GOOD EARTH and he continued his sharp China eye here.

p, Darryl F. Zanuck; d, Gregory Ratoff; w, Granville Walker; ph, Karl Freund; m, David Buttolph; ed, Jack Dennis; art d, Bernard Herzbrun, Haldane Douglas; set d, Thomas Little; cos, Royer.

Adventure **(PR:A MPAA:NR)**

BARRICADE* 1/2 (1950) 75m WB c

Dane Clark *(Bob Peters)*, Raymond Massey *(Boss Kruger)*, Ruth Roman *(Judith Burns)*, Robert Douglas *(Aubry Milburn)*, Morgan Farley *(The Judge)*, Walter Coy *(Benson)*, George Stern *(Tippy)*, Robert Griffin *(Kirby)*, Frank Marlowe *(Brandy)*, Tony Martinez *(Peso)*.

Massey is the villain of the piece. He portrays a mean gold mine owner who uses criminals on the run to dig for ore. Clark and Roman are both fugitives and arrive at this chain-gang-like compound. Robert Douglas is a lawyer whose brother used to own the mine and whom Massey eliminates in order to secure it. Don't think too hard about how this one winds up. Massey, who made a living for years playing trustworthy humanitarians, is a good enough actor to make us believe that he's a rat. Clark does his customary fine job and Roman is darkly attractive. A passable film, but not worth late-night watching. (Loose remake of THE SEA WOLF.)

p, Saul Elkins; d, Peter Godfrey; w, William Sackheim; ph, Carl Guthrie; ed, Clarence Kolster.

Western **(PR:A MPAA:NR)**

BARRIER, THE* (1937) 90m PAR bw

Leo Carrillo *(Poleon Doret)*, Jean Parker *(Necia)*, James Ellison *(Lt. Burrell)*, Robert Barrat *(John Gale)*, Otto Kruger *(Stark)*, Andy Clyde *(No Creek Lee)*, Addison Richards *(Runnion)*, Sara Haden *(Alluna)*, J. M. Kerrigan *(Sgt. Thomas)*, Sally Martin *(Molly)*, Fernando Alvarado *(Johnny)*, Alan Davis *(Sgt. Tobin)*.

Gorgeous scenery cannot save this ho-hum melodrama. Barrat kidnaps the young daughter of the woman he once loved and raises her to think she is a half-breed Indian. The child grows and becomes frustrated because she thinks she may never marry the man of her dreams, Ellison, because the army would never let a lieutenant wed an Indian.

p, Harry Sherman; d, Lesley Selander; w, Bernard Schubert, Harrison Jacobs, Mordaunt Sharp (based on a story by Rex Beach); ph, George Barnes; m, Maurice Lawrence; md, Boris Morros; m/l, Jack Stern, Harry Tobias.

Western **(PR:A MPAA:NR)**

BARRIER** (1966, Pol.) 83m Film Polski bw

Jan Nowicki *(He)*, Joanna Szczerbic *(She)*, Tadeusz Lomnicki *(Doctor)*, Zygmunt Malonowicz *(Eddy)*, Andrej Herder *(Manius)*.

An episodic film where Nowicki travels through Poland to encounter poverty, bureau- cratic waste, laziness on the part of proletarian workers, and a few inspired people whose lives are caught up in their crafts and arts. More of a travelog than a dramatic film, albeit a love affair is briefly offered.

d&w, Jerzy Skolimowski; ph, Jan Laskowski; m, Krzysztof Komeda; ed, H. Prugar; art d, Roman Wolyniec, Z. Straszewski.

Drama **(PR:A MPAA:NR)**

BARRY LYNDON*** (1975, Brit.) 184m Hawk-Peregrine/WB c

Ryan O'Neal *(Barry Lyndon)*, Marisa Berenson *(Lady Lyndon)*, Patrick Magee *(The Chevalier)*, Hardy Kruger *(Capt. Potzdorf)*, Steven Berkoff *(Lord Ludd)*, Gay Hamilton *(Nora)*, Leonard Rossiter *(Capt. Quin)*, Godfrey Quigley *(Capt. Grogan)*, Arthur O'Sullivan *(Highwayman)*, Diana Koerner *(German Girl)*, Marie Kean *(Barry's Mother)*, Frank Middlemass *(Sir Charles Lyndon)*, Murray Melvin *(Reverend Runt)*, Philip Stone *(Graham)*, Leon Vitali *(Lord Bullingdon)*, Dominic Savage *(Lord Bullingdon as Child)*, David Morley *(Brian Lyndon)*, Andre Morell *(Lord Wendover)*, Michael Hordern *(Narrator)*, John Bindon, Roger Booth, Billy Boyle, Jonathan Cecil, Peter Cellier, Geoffrey Chater, Anthony Dawes, Patrick Dawson, Bernard Hepton, Anthony Herrick, Barry Jackson, Wolf Kahler, Patrick Laffan, Hans Meyer, Ferdy Mayne, David George Sewell, Anthony Sharp, John Sharp, Roy Spencer, John Sullivan, Harry Towb.

At a little more than three hours in length, BARRY LYNDON is terribly fat. And yet it is such a visual delight that we are tempted to forgive its excesses. Tempted, but not compelled. Every shot is framed beautifully; all the details are exquisite, costumes are stylish, and the overall feeling is as though we were there. So what went wrong? Certainly not O'Neal who gave one of his best performances as the 18th-century Pal Joey who climbs over everyone on his way up the ladder. Not any of the actors, from Berenson to the narration of Hordern. Was it the script? Perhaps. Kubrick was too respectful of the book and didn't want to leave anything out so he left everything in. It is not the sort of movie that one can watch with one eye. So much happens and so many scenes are packed with subtleties that we must pay attention to BARRY LYNDON. In today's TV world, where 30-second commercials often have as many as 20 shots, we may have become too enamored of speed to be able to sit back and enjoy as languorous as film as this one from Kubrick. It's a movie mural, and how many of us can walk up to a mural in a museum and look at it for any length of time? In this case, it was 184 minutes. Nevertheless, it's worthwhile and, in the future, cinema students and revival theaters will play this film. Chances are it will never recover the cost, at least not until the next century. Still, you should see it. There were no motion picture cameras around in his time, but if there had been and if a movie were made then of his life, it couldn't have been more authentic than BARRY LYNDON.

p, d&w, Stanley Kubrick (based on the novel by William Makepeace Thackeray); ph, John Alcott (Metrocolor); m, Leonard Rosenman; ed, Tony Lawson; prod d, Ken Adam; art d, Roy Walker; set d, Vernon Dixon.

Historical Drama **Cas.** **(PR:C-O MPAA:PG)**

BARRY MC KENZIE HOLDS HIS OWN* 1/2
(1975, Aus.) 120m Roadshow Release c

Barry Crocker *(Barry McKenzie/Ken McKenzie)*, Barry Humphries *(Edna Everage/Sen. Douglas Manton/Dr. Meyer de Lamphrey/Buck-toothed Englishman)*, Donald Pleasence *(Eric, Count Plasma)*, Dick Bentley *(Col. Lucas)*, Ed Devereaux *(Sir Alec Ferguson)*, Tommy Trinder *(Arthur McKenzie)*, Roy Kinnear *(Bishop of Paris)*, John Le Mesurier *(English Emigrant)*, Beatrice Aston *(Cherylene McKenzie)*, Katya Wyeth *(Germaine)*, Marcelle Jordine *(Rhonda Cutforth-Jones)*.

Boorish, boozy, sexy, silly, inane, vulgar, crude and, in the end, a funny sequel to THE ADVENTURES OF BARRY MC KENZIE. Filled with many, many Australian expressions that will mean absolutely nothing to anyone who hasn't spent time in a billabong or under a wallaroo. Crocker and Humphries, in many roles, headline this fun tribute to an Australian abroad, based on the adult comic strip which appeared in the British journal, *Private Eye.* Nothing and no one is safe from the eye of Beresford who directed and co-wrote the script with Humphries. Forget the plot, the sight gags are hysterical, like Crocker (as Reverend Ken McKenzie) making a crucifix out of beer cans and holding it up in front of Pleasence (as Count Plasma, the foppish vampire) who promptly disintegrates into a skeleton. The film includes many British supporting players—Trinder, Le Mesurier, Kinnear, et al. They should put out a listener's guide to the Aussie expressions. How in the world is anyone going to know that "Brewer's Droop" means the inability to gain and/or sustain sexual potency? Worth seeing if you take someone from Melbourne or Adelaide or Sydney with you to act as an interpreter.

p&d, Bruce Beresford; w, Barry Humphries, Beresford; ph, Don McAlpine; m, Peter Best; ed, William Anderson; prod d, John Stoddart.

Adventure **Cas.** **(PR:C MPAA:NR)**

BARS OF HATE*   (1936) 57m Times Release bw

Regis Toomey (*District Attorney*), Sheila Terry (*The Girl*), Snub Pollard (*Pickpocket*), Molly O'Day, Robert Warwick, Fuzzy Knight, Gordon Griffith, Arthur Loft, Jack Cowell, John Elliot.

Poor programmer has Terry trying to save her brother, who has been framed, from the electric chair. She gets help from Pollard, an underworld type, and Toomey, a sympathetic D.A. The dialog sounds like the babble of children imitating adults and the criminal heavies are ridiculous, mouthing British accents and dressed to kill. Most of the film presents car, train, and plane chase footage culled from unknown serials. The direction is draggy and the camerawork seems to be handled by someone with the permanent shakes.

d, Al Herman; w, Al Martin (based on a story by Peter B. Kyne); ph, Billy Hyer; ed, Dan Milner.

Crime   (PR:A MPAA:NR)

BARTLEBY*1/2   (1970, Brit.) 78m Pantheon/BL c

Paul Scofield (*The Accountant*), John McEnery (*Bartleby*), Thorley Walters (*The Colleague*), Colin Jeavons (*Tucker*), Raymond Mason (*Landlord*), Charles Kinross (*Tenant*), Neville Barber (*First Client*), Robin Asquith (*Office Boy*), Hope Jackman (*Tealady*), John Watson (*Doctor*), Christine Dingle (*Patient*), Rosalind Elliot (*Secretary*), Tony Parkin (*Clerk*).

A very literary story (from a Herman Melville tale) about a young man who is out of touch with his surroundings and eventually withdraws into the ultimate cocoon. McEnery is Bartleby, a clerk who refuses to adjust to the society around him. He gets a job with Scofield, an accountant, but won't do what is required of him. McEnery has a code of behavior from which he will not deviate, nor will he explain it. Exasperated, Scofield finds he must eventually must fire the young man. Fine...except that Bartleby will not accept the sacking and comes in every day nevertheless. Bartleby is eventually taken to a hospital where it is learned that he is suffering from a cornucopia of ailments. Scofield is, at first, glad to be rid of the boy, but then finds himself intrigued by McEnery's actions. He goes to the hospital and finds the lad dead. And that's that. It's brooding, slow and annoying at times, but the vision of McEnery as Bartleby is not easily forgotten. Scofield, who works far too little in films, gives a supremely intelligent portrayal of a man caught between logic and emotion. He's done fewer than ten movies and we all suffer from that absence.

p&w, Anthony Friedman, Rodney Carr-Smith; d, Friedman (based on a story by Herman Melville); ph, Ian Wilson (Eastmancolor); m, Roger Webb; ed, John C. Smith; art d, Simon Holland.

Drama   (PR:A MPAA:NR)

BARTON MYSTERY, THE*   (1932, Brit.) 76m British & Dominions/PAR bw

Ursula Jeans (*Ethel Standish*), Ellis Jeffreys (*Lady Marshall*), Lyn Harding (*Beverly*), Ion Swinley (*Richard Standish*), Wendy Barrie (*Phyllis Grey*), Joyce Bland (*Helen Barton*), Tom Helmore (*Harry Maitland*), O.B. Clarence (*Sir Everard Marshall*), Franklyn Bellamy (*Gerald Barton*), Wilfred Noy (*Griffiths*).

A man accused of murder is cleared when a woman confesses. She is cleared when a fake medium admits that she killed the victim, a blackmailer, in self-defense. Routine mystery first made as a silent in 1920.

p, Herbert Wilcox; d, Henry Edwards; w, (based on a play by Walter Hackett).

Crime   (PR:A MPAA:NR)

BASHFUL BACHELOR, THE*1/2   (1942) 78m RKO bw

Chester Lauck (*Lum*), Norris Goff (*Abner*), ZaSu Pitts (*Geraldine*), Grady Sutton (*Cedric*), Oscar O'Shea (*Squire Skimp*), Louise Currie (*Marjorie*), Constance Purdy (*Widder Abernathy*), Irving Bacon (*Sheriff*), Earle Hodgins (*Joe*), Benny Rubin (*Pitch Man*).

Rural comedy starring Lauck and Goff as Lum and Abner. Abner trades a delivery car for a race horse, but all turns out the nag wins a big race.

p, Jack William Votion; d, Malcolm St. Clair; w, Chandler Sprague (based on a story by Charles Lauck and Norris Goff); ph, Paul Ivano; ed, Duncan Mansfield; md, Lud Gluskin.

Comedy   (PR:A MPAA:NR)

BASHFUL ELEPHANT, THE*1/2   (1962, Aust.) 82m AA bw

Molly Mack (*Tristy*), Helmut Schmidt (*Kurt*), Buddy Baer (*Tavern Owner*), Fritz Weiss (*Father Francis*), Arnulf Schroeder (*Police Inspector*), Hans Schumm (*Fritz*), Hans Posenbacher (*Constable*), Gernot Duda (*Policeman*), Jeffrey (*Dog*), Valle (*Elephant*).

Most of this movie has to do with the elephant trainer's romance and should have been edited out. However, that would have left very little film on the reel. This is supposedly a moppet movie with Molly Mack as a sweet, innocent homeless child looking for foster parents in Austria. It has to do with crossing the Iron Curtain, a helpful dog, and an elephant. The title is totally misleading as it makes one think of Disney, Dumbo, etc. This elephant is hardly bashful and the overlay of the secondary story takes it out of the realm of FKO (For Kiddies Only) and makes it far more adult. Former boxer Buddy Baer (Brother of Max Baer and Uncle to Max Baer, Jr., of "The Beverly Hillbillies" TV show) is about the only face you'll recognize—unless, of course, you are really up on your Austrian screen actors.

p,d&w, Dorrell and Stuart E. McGowan; ph, George Tyson, Hans Nikel; m/l, Ronald Stein (sung by Raffaela).

Children   (PR:A MPAA:NR)

BASKET CASE*   (1982) 90m Analysis Releasing c

Kevin Van Hentenryck (*Duane Bradley*), Terri Susan Smith (*Sharon*), Beverly Bonner (*Casey*), Lloyd Pace (*Dr. Harold Needleman*), Diana Browne (*Dr. Judith Kutter*), Robert Vogel (*Hotel Manager*), Bill Freeman (*Dr. Julian Lifflander*), Joe Clarke (*Brian "Mickey" O'Donovan*), Dorothy Strongin (*Josephine*), Ruth Neuman (*Aunt*), Richard Pierce (*Mr. Bradley*), Kerry Ruff (*Detective*).

Van Hentenryck walks Times Square and carries a basket inside which is something that sucks up burgers. It's not a friendly little monster, it's a Siamese twin mutant ready to wreak revenge on the physicians who separated him from his brother. Story goes through various peregrinations in and around the sleaziest area of New York and is ultimately an idiotic put-on.

p, Edgar Ievins; d&w, Frank Henenlotter; ph, Bruce Torbet; m, Gus Russo; ed, Henenlotter; spec eff, Kevin Haney, John Caglione.

Horror   Cas.   (PR:O MPAA:NR)

BASKETBALL FIX, THE*   (1951) 65m Realart bw

John Ireland (*Pete Ferreday*), Marshall Thompson (*Johnny Long*), Vanessa Brown (*Pat Judd*), William Bishop (*Mike Taft*), Hazel Brooks (*Lily Courtney*), John Sands (*Jed Black*), Bobby Hyatt (*Mickey Long*), Walter Sande (*Nat Becker*), Ted Pierson (*Lt. Garrett*), Johnny Phillips (*Reporter*), Lester Sharp (*Jewelry Salesman*).

Ireland is a sportswriter who narrates this tale of basketball scandal. Up-and-coming cager Thompson finds himself up to his neck in gambling debts and tries to shave a few points off the big game so bad guy Bishop will ease up. Unfortunately, the gaming commission notices and his career is over. Gambling doesn't pay.

p, Edward Leven; d, Felix Feist; w, Peter R. Brooke, Charles K. Peck, Jr.; ph, Stanley Cortez; m, Raoul Kraushaar; ed, Francis D. Lyon.

Drama   (PR:A MPAA:NR)

BAT, THE**   (1959) 80m AA bw

Vincent Price (*Dr. Malcolm Wells*), Agnes Moorehead (*Cornelia Van Gorder*), Gavin Gordon (*Lt. Anderson*), John Sutton (*Warner*), Lenita Lane (*Lizzie Allen*), Elaine Edwards (*Dale Dailey*), Darla Hood (*Judy Hollender*), John Bryant (*Mark Fleming*), Harvey Stephens (*Carter Fleming*), Mike Steele (*Jack Bailey*), Riza Royce (*Mrs. Patterson*), Robt. B. Williams (*Detective*).

Mary Roberts Rinehart and Agatha Christie were cut from the same cloth: musty velvet. Both loved the old-dark-house story, replete with weird characters, creaking doors, etc. THE BAT is a murderer who likes his murder in a jugular vein. He rips throats when he isn't searching for one million dollars worth of securities stashed in the house. It will not harm your viewing one whit to disclose that Vincent Price is the murderer. His leers and ogles and grimaces soon indicate his true character. Moorehead is Miss Rinehart, a mystery writer with a penchant for overreacting. The rest of the cast is good but not great. The movie betrays its stage origins by being too talky and far too insulated.

p, C.J. Tevlin; d&w, Crane Wilbur (based on the novel and play by Mary Roberts Rinehart and Avery Hopwood); ph, Joseph Biroc; m, Louis Forbes; ed, William Austin; art d, David Milton.

Mystery   (PR:C MPAA:NR)

BAT PEOPLE, THE**   (1974) 95m AIP c (AKA: IT LIVES BY NIGHT)

Stewart Moss (*Dr. John Beck*), Marianne McAndrew (*Cathy*), Michael Pataki (*Sergeant.*), Paul Carr (*Dr. Kipling*), Arthur Space (*Tramp*), Robert Berk (*Motel Owner*), Pat Delaney (*Ms. Jax*), George Paulsin (*Youth in car*), Bonnie Van Dyke (*Girl in Car*), Jeni Kulik (*Nurse Attacked*), Laurie Brooks Jefferson (*Nurse*).

Moss is a biologist who is bitten by a bat while exploring a desert cave; he is changed into a blood-lusting batman creature which does not inspire his new bride nor enliven his honeymoon. Good special effects but a lame script and only mediocre acting.

p, Lou Shaw; d, Jerry Jameson; w, Shaw; ph, Matthew Leonetti (DeLuxe Color); m, Artie Kane; ed, Tom Stevens.

Horror   (PR:C MPAA:PG)

BAT WHISPERS, THE*   (1930) 82m UA bw

Chance Ward (*Police Lieutenant*), Richard Tucker (*Mr. Bell*), Wilson Benge (*The Butler*), Dewitt Jennings (*Police Captain*), Sidney D'Albrook (*Police Sergeant*), S.E. Jennings (*Man in Black Mask*), Grayce Hampton (*Cornelia Van Gorder*), Maude Eburne (*Lizzie Allen*), Ben Bard (*The Unknown*), Spencer Charters (*The Caretaker*), Una Merkel (*Dale Van Gorder*), Charles Dow Clark (*Detective Jones*), Hugh Huntley (*Richard Fleming*), William Bakewell (*Brook*), Gustav Von Seyffertitz (*Dr. Venrees*), Chester Morris (*Detective Anderson*).

THE BAT WHISPERS was apparently the first movie to use the now-hoary device of appealing to the audience at the end of film to keep mum about the ending. Morris unravels the mystery of The Bat's identity (it's based on the play by Mary Roberts Rinehart and Avery Hopwood). To reveal a plot such as this would be to do a disservice to a potential viewer so merely be aware that nothing is what it seems. Tucker (Bell) is not well-remembered, despite having appeared in hundreds of films and having begun his career at the dawn of the film's creation with the Edison Company in 1913. Morris is but one of many "brother acts" in show business; his brother, Adrian, played a carpetbagger in GONE WITH THE WIND. Director West also directed the 1926 silent version of this classic mystery; the sets are top-notch, presenting the proper eerie atmosphere.

p, d&w, Roland West (based on the novel and play by Mary Roberts Rinehart and Avery Hopwood); ph, Robert H. Planck; ed, James Smith.

Mystery/Comedy   (PR:A MPAA:NR)

BATAAN**   (1943) 113m MGM bw

Robert Taylor (*Sgt. Bill Dane*), George Murphy (*Lt. Steve Bentley*), Thomas Mitchell (*Cpl. Jake Feingold*), Lloyd Nolan (*Cpl. Barney Todd/Danny Burns*), Lee Bowman (*Capt. Lassiter*), Robert Walker (*Leonard Purckett*), Desi Arnaz (*Felix*

Ramirez), Barry Nelson (*F. X. Matowski*), Phillip Terry (*Gilbert Hardy*), Roque Espiritu (*Cpl. Juan Katigbak*), Kenneth Spencer (*Wesley Epps*), J. Alex Havier (*Yankee Salazar*), Tom Dugan (*Sam Malloy*), Donald Curtis (*Lieutenant*), Lynne Carver, Mary McLeod, Dorothy Morris (*Nurses*), Bud Geary (*Infantry Officer*), Ernie Alexander (*Wounded Soldier*), Phil Schumacher (*Machine Gunner*).

Tough, uncompromising war story of a group of determined American and Filipino soldiers fighting on Bataan, knowing they must delay the hordes of advancing Japanese troops and that they will be doomed in their attempt. Based on the heroic defense of the Philippines in early 1942, this film examines soldiers from all points of America, as well as Filipinos fighting for their own soil, with a rugged and inspiring performance from Taylor as the grim but kind-hearted sergeant commanding the small group in a rear-guard action, protecting MacArthur's ragged army as it limped away down the narrow peninsula where it would make its stand for three harrowing months. Bowman, originally commanding the group, is killed early and Taylor takes over with an approving nod from Murphy, a pilot trying to repair his crippled plane. Mitchell and Nolan are old troopers; Nolan is using a phony name because he is wanted for stabbing another soldier in a brawl. Taylor knows this but overlooks the impersonation, realizing that Nolan will give his life for the cause. Robert Walker, in his screen debut, is a youthful, naive, all-American boy, gum-chewing his optimistic views and refusing to the last to believe that none will get out alive. One by one, the all male cast is picked off (not unlike the forlorn members of THE LOST PATROL) until only a handful is left to fend off a wild attack by countless Japanese crawling toward their positions while adorned with shrubbery. Murphy finally gets his plane repaired but is mortally wounded while taking off and crashes suicidally into a dismantled bridge the Japanese are frantically trying to repair, destroying the massive structure. The hand-to-hand combat is startling and as brutal as real warfare, men fighting to the death with guns, bayonets, knives and hands. Next to WAKE ISLAND, this was the first A film presented to female audiences which showed the realism of modern war, the kind of experiences their sons, brothers, fathers and husbands were truly undergoing, and it proved a mass shocker, but one that gave audiences nationwide a devastating portrait of the enemy, resolved in the last-ditch stand of one-time matinee idol Taylor. No longer was Taylor to be remembered as the rather foppish youth clutching a dying Garbo in CAMILLE. He was the hard-as-nails sergeant of BATAAN who, with all his men dead and buried, their helmets slanted upon upturned rifles at the heads of graves, digs his own grave, climbs inside, and waits with machine guns at the ready while the insidious enemy crawls forward beneath a layer of fog, inching snakelike toward him. He sees them, hundreds of them, and shouts as he blazes away: "C'mon, suckers, come and get me—what are you waiting for? Didn't think we were here, did you, you dirty, rotten rats! We're still here—we'll always be here!" And the camera closes in to be filled with his gunsmoke rather than see his end at the hands of the enemy. Tay Garnett's direction is appropriately action-filled and the lulls are properly taken up with establishing each man's identity. Taylor, later described by Garnett as "one of the world's great gentlemen," gave an inspired performance. This was his last film for MGM before he became a fighter pilot for the U.S. Navy. (He was an accomplished aviator before enlisting. His wife at the time, Barbara Stanwyck, visited the BATAAN set and boasted about her hubby's flying abilities to Garnett: "Bob can do anything a bird can do, except balance himself on a barbed wire fence.") When Garnett heard that BATAAN was to be filmed, he went to MGM boss Louis B. Mayer and practically begged for the directorial assignment. Mayer hesitated. Garnett said he would take a cut in pay to do it. Mayer agreed.

p, Irving Starr; d, Tay Garnett; w, Robert D. Andrews (based partly on the 1934 film THE LOST PATROL); ph, Sidney Wagner; m, Bronislau Kaper; ed, George White; art d, Cedric Gibbons; spec eff, Arnold Gillespie, Warren Newcombe.

War   **(PR:C MPAA:NR)**

BATHING BEAUTY**1/2   (1944) 101m MGM c

Red Skelton (*Steve Elliott*), Esther Williams (*Caroline Brooks*), Basil Rathbone (*George Adams*), Bill Goodwin (*Willis Evans*), Ethel Smith (*Organist*), Jean Porter (*Jean Allenwood*), Carlos Ramirez (*Carlos*), Donald Meek (*Chester Klazenfrantz*), Nana Bryant, Ann Codee, Francis Pierlot, Margaret Dumont, Janis Paige, Jacqueline Daly, Harry James and His Orchestra with Helen Forrest, Xavier Cugat and His Band with Lina Romay.

Star-studded swimming musical featuring Skelton as a goofy songwriter who is in love with college aquaette Williams. Incredible water dance numbers with Cugat and James kicking out the tunes. Skelton breaks up the dancing with some of his patented comedy bits. The escapist plot, thin as plastic, involves a songwriter enrolling at a women's school to be near his wife who is the swimming instructor. Great music includes such tunes as "I Cried for You," sung by Helen Forrest (Arthur Freed, Gus Arnheim, Abe Lyman), "Bim, Bam, Boom," by Cugat's orchestra, Lina Romay on vocal (J. Camacho, Noro Morales), "Tico-Tico," by organist Ethel Smith (Zequinha Abreu), "Hora Staccato," belted by James (Grigoras Dinicu, Jascha Heifetz), "I'll Take the High Note," "Trumpet Blues," "Magic is the Moonlight" ("Te Quiero Dijiste"), "By the Waters of Minnetonka," and "Loch Lomond."

p, Jack Cummings; d, George Sidney; w, Dorothy Kingsley, Allen Boretz, Frank Waldman, Joseph Schrank (based on a story by Kenneth Earl, M. M. Musselman; ph, Harry Stradling (Technicolor); m, Johnny Green; ed, Blanche Sewell.

Musical   **(PR:A MPAA:NR)**

BATMAN**1/2   (1966) 105m FOX c

Adam West (*Batman/Bruce Wayne*), Burt Ward (*Robin/Dick Grayson*), Lee Meriwether (*Catwoman/Kitka*), Cesar Romero (*The Joker*), Burgess Meredith (*The Penguin*), Frank Gorshin (*The Riddler*), Alan Napier (*Alfred*), Neil Hamilton (*Commissioner Gordon*), Stafford Repp (*Chief O'Hara*), Madge Blake (*Aunt Harriet Cooper*), Reginald Denny (*Commodore Schmidlapp*), Milton Frome (*Vice Admiral*

Fangschliester), Gil Perkins (*Bluebeard*), Dick Crockett (*Morgan*), George Sawaya (*Quetch*).

Big-screen version of the popular television series. The producers let out all the stops on this one by having every one of the dynamic duo's favorite villains team up to take over the world. Batman himself goes whole hog and drags out all the "bat" hardware; the batcycles, the batboat, the batplane, etc. Shot in the same campy style that characterized the TV show, the whole cast looks like it is having a great time chewing up the scenery. Meredith as the Penguin and Gorshin as the Riddler are the villainous standouts.

p, William Dozier; d, Leslie H. Martinson; w, Lorenzo Semple, Jr. (based on characters created by Bob Kane); ph, Howard Schwartz (DeLuxe Color); m, Nelson Riddle; ed, Harry Gerstad; m/l, theme, Neal Hefti.

Action   **(PR:AA MPAA:NR)**

BATTLE, THE**1/2
(1934, Fr.) 85m GAU bw (AKA: THUNDER IN THE EAST, HARA-KIRI)

Charles Boyer (*Marquis Yorisaka*), John Loder (*Fergan*), Merle Oberon (*Marquise Yorisaka*), Betty Stockfield (*Betty Hockley*), V. Inkijinoff (*Hirata*), Miles Mander (*Feize*), Henri Fabert (*The Admiral*).

Strong cast in a story about a Japanese naval officer (Boyer) who forces his wife to mimic Occidental life. Boyer is so ambitious that he manipulates and forces his delicate wife, Oberon, into an extramarital situation with Loder, the British naval attache who is serving aboard Boyer's vessel as an observer. There are Japanese naval maneuvers taking place and Boyer wants to learn what Loder thinks of them. He uses his wife as a pawn in the intelligence game. In order to get to read Loder's report on the maneuvers, Boyer arranges the liaison between his wife and John. In the end, Loder dies in an explosion and Boyer commits hara-kiri due to having betrayed his wife whom he truly loved more than he loved his country. This is a unique setting for a well-done film, the likes of which have never been seen before or since—that a military man would sacrifice his wife on the altar of gaining naval knowledge was a strong pill for many in the audience to take and this was not the success that had been expected. Loder (born John Lowe in 1898) made many films in his lengthy career and is particularly remembered for his work in NOW VOYAGER.

p, Leon Garganoff; d, Nicolas Farkas; w, Bernard Zimmer, Robert Stevenson, Farkas (based on the novel *La Bataille* by Claude Farrere); ph, Roger Hubert; m, Andre Gailhard; ed, Choudens.

War/Romance   **(PR:A MPAA:NR)**

BATTLE AT APACHE PASS, THE**   (1952) 85m UNIV c

John Lund (*Maj. Jim Colton*), Jeff Chandler (*Cochise*), Beverly Tyler (*Mary Kearny*), Bruce Cowling (*Neil Baylor*), Susan Cabot (*Nono*), John Hudson (*Lt. George Bascom*), Jimmy Best (*Cpl. Hassett*), Regis Toomey (*Dr. Carter*), Richard Egan (*Sgt. Bernard*), Hugh O'Brian (*Lt. Harley*), Palmer Lee (*Joe Bent*), William Reynolds (*Lem Bent*), Jay Silverheels (*Geronimo*), Tommy Cook (*Little Elk*), Jack Elam (*Mescal Jack*), Richard Garland (*Culver*), Jack Ingraham (*Johnny Ward*), John Baer (*Pvt. Bolin*), Paul Smith (*Ross*).

Chandler plays Apache chief Cochise (he had played him before in BROKEN ARROW), who is out to stop renegade chief Geronimo (Silverheels) from going on the warpath. He enlists the aid of cavalry officer Lund and together they discover that an overly ambitious Indian Affairs representative has stirred up all the trouble by giving Geronimo delusions of grandeur. Not the greatest western ever made, but interesting for its portrayal of Indians as rational human beings able to cooperate with the white man.

p, Leonard Goldstein; d, George Sherman; w, Gerald Drayson Adams; ph, Charles Boyle (Technicolor); m, Hans J. Salter; ed, Ted J. Kent.

Western   **(PR:A MPAA:NR)**

BATTLE AT BLOODY BEACH*1/2
(1961) 83m FOX bw (GB: BATTLE ON THE BEACH)

Audie Murphy (*Craig Benson*), Gary Crosby (*Marty Sackler*), Dolores Michaels (*Ruth Benson*), Alejandro Rey (*Julio Fontana*), Marjorie Stapp (*Caroline Pelham*), Barry Atwater (*Pelham*), E. J. Andre (*Dr. Van Bart*), Dale Ishimoto (*Blanco*), Lillian Bronson (*Delia Ellis*), Miriam Colon (*Nahni*), Pilar Seurat (*Camota*), William Mims (*McKeever*), Ivan Dixon (*Tiger Blair*), Kevin Brodie (*Timmy Thompson*), Sara Anderson (*Mrs. Thompson*), Lloyd Kino (*Japanese Lieutenant*).

Audie Murphy was *the* hero of WW II and no sooner did he get mustered out than the movie industry snatched him up and he began fighting the war all over again on film, except that this time the bullets weren't real. In BATTLE AT BLOODY BEACH, Audie is a civilian working with Filipino guerrillas during WW II. He is desperately trying to find his wife, Michaels, from whom he was separated while on their honeymoon in Manila. A triangle has formed because Dolores, thinking that Audie was killed by the Japanese, has fallen for Rey, one of the leaders of the resistance. Audie and his pal, Gary Crosby, fight the Japanese, eventually locate Dolores, and she and Audie are brought back together when Rey gallantly strolls away to allow the married couple to continue their lives (not unlike what Rick did for the Lazlos in CASABLANCA). Story, production, and half the script was done by veteran Richard Maibaum who became the chief writer for the James Bond films in later years.

p, Richard Maibaum; d, Herbert Coleman; w, Maibaum, Willard Willingham (based on a story by Maibaum); ph, Kenneth Peach (CinemaScope); m, Henry Vars; ed, Jodie Copelan.

War   **(PR:A MPAA:NR)**

BATTLE BENEATH THE EARTH*   (1968, Brit.) 91M MGM c

Kerwin Matthews (*Cdr. Shaw*), Viviane Ventura (*Tila Yung*), Robert Ayres (*Adm. Hillebrand*), Peter Arne (*Dr. Arnold Kramer*), Martin Benson (*Gen. Chan Lu*), Earl

Cameron (Hawkins), Peter Elliott (Kengh Lee), Al Mulock (Sgt. Mulberry), Michael McStay (Train Commander), Edward Bishop (Lt. Cmdr. Vance Cassidy), Bill Nagy (Col. Talbot Wilson), Sarah Brackett (Meg Webson), Paula Li Shiu (Dr. Amn), David Spenser (Maj. Chai), Carl Jaffe (Dr. Galissi), Norma West (Susan Kramer), Larry Cross (Broadcaster), Bessie Love (Matron), Bee Duffell (Matron's Friend), Bill Hutchinson (Lanchek), Martin Terry (Mine Foreman), Frank Lieberman, Roy Pattison (Police), Chela Matthison (Nurse).

Red scare film has the Chinese burrowing a complex series of tunnels beneath the earth where they plan to plant atomic warheads under every major population center. Luckily the good ol' U.S. Navy discovers the plot and stops the godless heathens in their tracks.

p, Charles Vetter, Charles Reynolds; d, Montgomery Tully, w, Lance Z. Hargreaves; ph, Kenneth Talbot (Technicolor); art d, Jim Morahan; m, Ken Jones; ed, Sidney Stone.

Science Fiction　　　　　　**Cas.**　　　　　　**(PR:A MPAA:NR)**

BATTLE BEYOND THE STARS**　　　　　　(1980) 104m New World c

Richard Thomas (Shad), Robert Vaughn (Gelt), Darlanne Fluegel (Sador), George Peppard (Cowboy), Sybil Danning (St. Exmin), Sam Jaffe (Dr. Hephaestus), Morgan Woodward (Cayman), Steve Davis (Quopeg), Earl Boen, John McGowans (Nestor No. 1 and No. 2), Larry Meyers, Laura Cody (Kelvin), Lynn Carlin (Nell), Jeff Corey (Zed), Julia Duffy (Mol), Eric Morris (Feh), Marta Kristen (Lux), Doug Carleson (Pok), Ron Ross (Dab), Terrance McNally (Gar), Don Thompson (Cush), Daniel Carlin (Pez), Ansley Carlin (Wok), Whitney Rydbeck, Dallas Clarke, Dan Vincent, Rick Davidson, Ron Henschel, Brian Coventry, Kerry Frank.

Pleasant sci-fi picture that owes its life to several other movies, including THE MAGNIFICENT SEVEN which, in turn, owes its life to THE SEVEN SAMURAI. Ambitiously expensive by New World's standards, plot is about a peacenick planet attacked by a bunch of bad guys. They have to get someone to do their dirty work, so they hire Peppard. Danning (who has been seen to greater advantage in some cheesecake layouts) is the female mercenary who gets hot when she is at war. Saxon is the chief rat and Thomas is Mr. Nice Guy. Sayles' screenplay never takes itself to heart, so the badinage is relaxed and often funny, instead of the terse and often boring words in so many sci-films. Woodward is wasted, but Jaffe does a cute turn as an arms merchant. Look for Whitney Rydbeck in a tiny role. He played the gay robot in SLEEPER and is one of America's best mimes. (Loose remake of THE SEVEN SAMURAI.)

p, Ed Carlin; d, Jimmy T. Murakami; w, John Sayles (based on a story by Sayles and Ann Dyer); ph, Daniel Lacambre; m, James Horner; ed, Allan Holtzman, Bob Kizer; art d, Jim Cameron, Charles Breen; set d, John Zabrucky; cos, Durinda Rice Wood; spec eff, C. Comisky, Ken Jones; miniatures, Mary Schallock.

Science Fiction　　　　　　**Cas.**　　　　　　**(PR:C MPAA:NR)**

BATTLE BEYOND THE SUN zero　　　　　　(1963) 75m Film Group/AIP c

Edd Perry, Arla Powell, Andy Stewart, Bruce Hunter

Inane intergalactic space war film with opposing monsters shaped like the male and female sex organs. This is a typical Roger Corman garbage film, taken out of a Russian wastecan called NIEBO ZOWIET, a USSR product that originally showed America as a capitalistic power out to destroy all other systems and the Communist countries out to defend the rights of man (there's a switch!). Corman bought the film, hired Francis Ford Coppola to reshape it into a futuristic movie and the result was two ambiguous hemispheric powers battling to the death in space. Cretinous at best.

p, Thomas Colchart; d, Alexander Kozyr, Colchart; w, Nicholas Colbert, Edwin Palmer.

Science Fiction　　　　　　　　　　**(PR:O MPAA:NR)**

BATTLE CIRCUS**　　　　　　(1953) 89m MGM bw

Humphrey Bogart (Maj. Jeb Webbe), June Allyson (Lt. Ruth McCara), Keenan Wynn (Sgt. Orvil Statt), Robert Keith (Lt. Col. Hillary Whalters), William Campbell (Capt. John Rustford), Perry Sheehan (Lt. Lawrence), Patricia Tiernan (Lt. Rose Ashland), Adele Longmire (Lt. Jane Franklin), Jonathan Cott (Adjutant), Ann Morrison (Lt. Edith Edwards), Helen Winston (Lt. Graciano), Sarah Selby (Capt. Dobbs), Danny Chang (Korean Child), Philip Ahn (Korean Prisoner), Steve Forrest (Sergeant), Jeff Richards (Lieutenant), Dick Simmons (Capt. Norson).

This movie was the forerunner to M*A*S*H in that it was about a Mobile Army Surgical Corps in the Korean War. Allyson is a self-sacrificing nurse who comes to Korea to serve at Bogart's hospital, just a few miles behind the lines. He's attracted to her and the incongruous romance begins in between his attempts at getting her to stop doing dumb things and taking needless chances. Because the hospital is mobile, it just picks up and moves often, depending on how far the enemy has come forward or gone backward. Wynn, a former circus type, knows how to pull up stakes so he takes care of moving the equipment and providing what little humor there is. Bogart is a hard drinker and tries to avoid any real entanglement with Allyson but they eventually get together after their path of love has run its bumpy course. Bogart was totally out of place in this role and acted like it. The only way you knew it wasn't just a little potboiler for second features is by the presence of some heavyweight actors on the screen. Look hard for Steve Forrest in one of his earliest roles. Singularly undistinguished except for Bogart's presence.

p, Pandro S. Berman; d&w, Richard Brooks (based on a story by Allen Rivkin and Laura Kerr); ph, John Alton; m, Lennie Hayton; ed, George Boemler.

War　　　　　　　　　　　　　**(PR:A MPAA:NR)**

BATTLE CRY**1/2　　　　　　(1955) 147m WB c

Van Heflin (Maj. Huxley), Aldo Ray (Andy), Mona Freeman (Kathy), Nancy Olson (Pat), James Whitmore (Sgt. Mac), Raymond Massey (Gen. Snipes), Tab Hunter (Danny), Dorothy Malone (Elaine), Anne Francis (Rae), William Campbell (Ski), John Lupton (Marion), Justus E. McQueen (L. Q. Jones), Perry Lopez (Joe Gomez), Fess Parker (Speedy), Jonas Applegarth (Lighttower), Tommy Cook (Ziltch), Felix Noriego (Crazy Horse), Susan Morrow (Susan), Carleton Young (Maj. Wellman), Rhys Williams (Enoch Rogers), Allyn McLerie (Waitress), Gregory Walcott (Sgt. Beller), Frank Ferguson (Mr. Walker), Sarah Selby (Mrs. Forrester), Willis Bouchey (Mr. Forrester), Glen Denning (Sea Bags), Chick Chandler (Chaplain), James Whitmore (Narrator), Fred Hanson, Jack Downs, Lee Allen, Victor Millan.

Huge, sprawling movie based on a Leon Uris novel. It's an essentially disappointing movie because it focuses more on sexual relationships (Ray and Olson; Hunter and Freeman; and Malone, Lupton and Francis) than it does on the story, which takes a group of soldiers in a communications battalion through their training on Saipan, then to New Zealand where they jump off to glory, or death. Heflin is believable as the tough major who combines gentleness with the necessary discipline to mold his youthful charges into fighting machines. In the love department, Ray comes across like a new sex symbol and his story (with Nancy Olson) is the most realized. All the small roles are by first-rate actors (with the exception of Cook) and the music by Steiner was good enough to garner an Oscar nomination. Raoul Walsh, who spent much of his career doing action films (OBJECTIVE BURMA, WHITE HEAT, WHAT PRICE GLORY?) is hampered by the Uris script. This is not unique in that some novelists cannot bear to cut one word of their work so they just put it into screenplay form and their contracts forbid any slashes. Thus, we get overblown, fat films. One other sidelight . . . a young actor named Justus E. McQueen had a small part in this movie. He played the role of a character named L. Q. Jones and he liked that name so much that he took it for his own. Justus McQueen was no more and L. Q. Jones became a successful actor and sometime producer (THE BROTHERHOOD OF SATAN, THE WILD BUNCH, THE HUNTING PARTY, MOTHER, JUGS AND SPEED).

p, Raoul Walsh; w, Leon W. Uris (based on his novel); ph, Sid Hickox (CinemaScope, Warnercolor); m, Max Steiner; ed, William Zeigler.

War　　　　　　**Cas.**　　　　　　**(PR:A MPAA:NR)**

BATTLE FLAME**1/2　　　　　　(1959) 78m AA

Scott Petrie (1st Lt. Frank Davis), Elaine Edwards (Mary), Robert Blake (Cpl. Pacheco), Wayne Heffley (Teach), Gordon Jones (Sgt. McKelvey), Ken Miller (Orlando), Arthur Walsh (Nawlins), Richard Harrison (2nd Lt. Wechsler), Gary Kent (Gilchrist), Peggy Moffitt (Nurse Fisher), Jean Robbins (Nurse Claycomb), Richard Crane (Dr. Stoddard).

A quintet of United States nurses is captured by North Korean Forces and Brady is the Marine who leads the desperate mission to rescue them. In doing so, he falls in love with Edwards. Ordinary war-type film with lots of stock footage and lots of boring dialog. At least one-quarter of the film (or so it feels) is wasted on sitting around and bitching about being in the service. Robert Blake, somewhere between his youth and his rediscovery in IN COLD BLOOD, is hardly noticed as the grown-up version of the Mexican child he played in THE TREASURE OF THE SIERRA MADRE. Look for Walsh, one-time nightclub comedian who had a brief acting career, and was best known for his role as Junior, Spencer Tracy's son, in THE LAST HURRAH.

p, Lester A. Samson; d, R. G. Springsteen; w, Elwood Ullman (based on a story by Samson, Ullman); ph, Carl Guthrie; m, Marlin Skiles; ed, William Austin.

War　　　　　　　　　　　　　**(PR:A MPAA:NR)**

BATTLE FOR MUSIC***　　　　　　(1943, Brit.) 87m Strand/Anglo-American bw

Hay Petrie, Mavis Clarke, Joss Ambler, Charles Carson, Dennis Wyndham, Ben Williams, Anthony Holles, Jack Hylton, J. B. Priestley.

Semi-documentary account of the London Philharmonic Orchestra's struggles during WW II. German bombings destroy the orchestra's hall and instruments, but famed author Priestley, playing himself, stages a benefit concert that provides needed funds. The music is superb and this unusual film is well worth seeing.

p&d, Donald Taylor; w, St. John L. Clowes.

Docu-drama　　　　　　　　　　**(PR:A MPAA:NR)**

BATTLE FOR THE PLANET OF THE APES**　　　　　　(1973) 86m FOX c

Roddy McDowall (Caesar), Claude Akins (Aldo), John Huston (Lawgiver), Natalie Trundy (Lisa), Severn Darden (Kolp), Lew Ayres (Mandemus), Paul Williams (Virgil), Austin Stoker (MacDonald), Noah Keen (Teacher), Richard Eastham (Mutant Captain), France Nuyen (Alma), Paul Stevens (Mendez), Heather Lowe (Doctor), Bobby Porter (Cornelius), Michael Sterns (Jake), Cal Wilson (Soldier), Pat Cardi (Young Chimp), John Landis (Jake's Friend), Andy Knight (Mutant On Motorcycle).

Last and weakest of the APES series has McDowall once again playing Caesar, the uneasy leader of the apes, as he struggles to build a decent simian society. Trouble arrives in the form of Akins who plays the gorilla general who wants to turn the place into a monkey boot-camp. Look for John Huston as an orangutan. (See PLANET OF THE APES series, Index.)

p, Arthur P. Jacobs; d, J. Lee Thompson; w, John William Corrington, Joyce Hooper Corrington (based on a story by Paul Dehn and characters created by Pierre Boulle); ph, Richard H. Kline (Panavision, DeLuxe Color); m, Leonard Rosenman; ed, Alan L. Jaggs, John C. Horger.

Science Fiction　　　　　　**Cas.**　　　　　　**(PR:A MPAA:G)**

BATTLE HELL**
(1956, Brit.) 99m Herbert Wilcox bw (GB: YANGTSE INCIDENTS)

Richard Todd *(Lt. Cdr. Kerans)*, William Hartnell *(Leading Seaman Frank)*, Akim Tamiroff *(Col. Peng)*, Keye Luke *(Capt. Kuo Tai)*, Donald Houston *(Lt. Weston)*, Robert Urquhart *(Flight Lt. Fearnley)*, Sophie Stewart *(Nurse Dunlap)*, James Kenney *(Lt. Hett)*, Richard Leech *(Lt. Strain)*, Michael Brill *(Lt. Berger)*, Barry Foster *(McCarthy)*, Thomas Heathcote *(Mr. Monaghan)*, Sam Kidd *(Walker)*, Ewen Solon *(Williams)*, Brian Smith *(Martin)*, John Charlesworth *(Roberts)*, Kenneth Cope *(Mr. McNamara)*, Alfred Burke *(Petty Officer)*, Keith Rawlings *(Crocker)*, Ian Bannen *(Bannister)*, Basil Dignam *(British Ambassador)*.

The true-life story of a British ship, the H.M.S. Amethyst, and its crew, which became stranded on the Communist-dominated-Yangtze River in 1949. After a rousing battle scene, the movie focuses on the battered survivors. A well-made film from an Eric Ambler script.

p, Herbert Wilcox; d, Michael Anderson; w, Eric Ambler (based on the book *Escape of the Amethyst* by Laurence Earl); ph, Gordon Dines.

War **Cas.** **(PR:A MPAA:NR)**

BATTLE HYMN** (1957) 108m UNIV c

Rock Hudson *(Dean Hess)*, Anna Kashfi *(En Soon Yang)*, Dan Duryea *(Sgt. Herman)*, Don DeFore *(Capt. Skidmore)*, Martha Hyer *(Mary Hess)*, Jock Mahoney *(Maj. Moore)*, Alan Hale *(Mess Sergeant)*, James Edwards *(Lt. Maples)*, Carl Benton Reid *(Deacon Edwards)*, Richard Loo *(Gen. Kim)*, Philip Ahn *(Old Man)*, Bartlett Robinson *(Gen. Timberidge)*, Simon Scott *(Lt. Hollis)*, Teru Shimada *(Korean Official)*, Carleton Young *(Maj. Harrison)*, Art Millan *(Capt. Reardon)*, William Hudson *(Navy Lieutenant)*, Paul Sorenson *(Sentry)*, Children of the Orphan's Home in Korea.

True story of Dean Hess (Hudson) a WW II pilot who became a minister, then went to Korea during that conflict and established a home for orphan children. Rock Hudson does a fine job as the selfless Hess in this factual saga that is so incredible it often seems like the stuff that scripts are made of. But Hess functioned as tech advisor and we are assured it's all true. Hyer does well as Mrs. Hess and Duryea shows that he can play light as well as heavy in an unaccustomed role as comic relief. Although it would appear at the start that Hess is suffering from a guilt complex due to a bombing raid he made during WW II, one comes away with the feeling that Hess is a good man, that he would have done what he did anyhow. Music by Oscar-winning Frank Skinner is in keeping with his soap-opera expertise. Since it is a true-life story, there is no professional script structure to the movie; i.e., beginning, middle and end. There is a lot of middle.

p, Ross Hunter; d, Douglas Sirk; w, Charles Grayson, Vincent B. Evans (based on the life of Col. Dean Hess); ph, Russell Metty (CinemaScope, Technicolor); m, Frank Skinner; ed, Russell Schoengarth; art d, Alexander Golitzen, Emrich Nicholson; set d, Russell A. Gausman, Oliver Emert; cos, Bill Thomas.

War **(PR:A MPAA:NR)**

BATTLE IN OUTER SPACE*
(1960) 90m COL c (USCHI DAI SENSO; AKA: THE WORLD OF SPACE)

Ryo Ikebe, Kyoko Anzai, Koreya Senda, Yoshio Tsuchiya, Kisaya Ito, Kozo Nomura, Minoru Takada, Fuyuki Murakami, Leonard Stanford, Harold Conway, George Wyman, Elise Richter, Leonard Walsh, Malcolm Pearce.

A simplistic science-fiction film with a familiar plot: Aliens from another planet come to take us over. The earth retaliates in a totally implausible fashion and we are once again saved. Lots of errors in plot, dubbing, special effects and some terrible looping, yet, for all its goofiness, the picture does have some good moments and is filled with action, rather than violence, so kids will probably enjoy the picture more than adults. Some fine miniature scenes and good color lensing.

p, Yuko Tanaka; d, Inoshiro Honda; w, Shinichi Sekizawa (based on a story by Jotaro Okami); ph, Hajime Koizumi (Tohoscope, Eastmancolor); m, Akira Ifukube; ed, Kazuji Taira; art d, Teruaki Ando; spec eff, Eiji Tsuburaya.

Science Fiction **(PR:A MPAA:NR)**

BATTLE OF ALGIERS, THE*** (1967, Ital./Alger.) 120m Magna/Rizzoli bw

Yacef Saadi *(Kader)*, Jean Martin *(Colonel)*, Brahim Haggiag *(Ali La Pointe)*, Tommaso Neri *(Captain)*, Samia Kerbash *(One of the Girls)*; Fawzia el Kader *(Halima)*, Michele Kerbash *(Fathia)*, Mohamed Ben Kassen *(Petit Omar)*.

THE BATTLE OF ALGIERS secured Oscar nominations as Best Foreign Film, as well as nominations for Solinas as screenwriter and Pontecorvo as director. All of them were well-deserved, but the movie lost out to CLOSELY WATCHED TRAINS. THE BATTLE OF ALGIERS proudly announces at the start of the picture that not one foot of the film is newsreel or documentary. Watching the movie, it's hard to believe, because it it is so powerful and so true-to-life that it could have come off the seven o'clock news. The movie engendered chaos wherever it was shown as it is almost a primer for guerrilla warfare and patently communistic in every sense. Putting aside the propaganda and the Marxist/Maoist beliefs of its creators, THE BATTLE OF ALGIERS stands on its own as a searing, memorable movie. FLN assassinates French police! Police secure Casbah! FLN terrorism continues, French vigilantes retaliate! French bomb innocent Arabs! Arabs send three women to blow up crowd in French Quarter! Paratroopers arrive! A reign of torture begins! FLN asks for general strike! Paratroopers hunt down and kill FLN leaders but it all erupts again two years later and French rule is doomed. And that's what this picture is; a series of exclamation points made by Pontecorvo, a concerned" filmmaker, whose reputation for being unstinting kept him out of the movie business until 1970, when he teamed to make BURN, another concerned" picture that was as boring as this was exciting. There are no stars, nothing chic, no phony melodramatics. THE BATTLE OF ALGIERS should not be missed.

p, Antonio Musu, Yacef Saadi; d, Gino Pontecorvo; w, Pontecorvo, Franco Solinas; ph, Marcello Gatti; m, Pontecorvo, Ennio Morricone; ed, Mario Serandrei, Mario Morra.

War **(PR:C MPAA:NR)**

BATTLE OF AUSTERLITZ (SEE: AUSTERLITZ, 1960)

BATTLE OF BLOOD ISLAND* (1960) 64m Filmgroup bw

Richard Devon *(Moe)*, Ron Kennedy *(Ken)*.

Smarmy socially relevant war pic with two antagonistic G.I.s trapped together on a Japanese island about to be blown to atoms. The soldiers, one Jewish, one Christian, spend most of the film scowling and yelling at each other until they have to pull together to save themselves. This material has been handled better elsewhere.

d&w, Joel Rapp; ph, Jacques Marquette; ed, Carlo Lodato.

War **(PR:A MPAA:NR)**

BATTLE OF BRITAIN, THE**** (1969, Brit.) 133m Spitfire Prod./UA c

Harry Andrews *(Senior Civil Servant)*, Michael Caine *(Sqd. Ldr. Canfield)*, Trevor Howard *(Air Vice Marshal Keith Park)*, Curt Jurgens *(Baron von Richter)*, Ian McShane *(Sgt. Pilot Andy)*, Kenneth More *(Group Capt. Baker)*, Laurence Olivier *(Air Chief Marshal Sir Hugh Dowding)*, Nigel Patrick *(Group Capt. Hope)*, Christopher Plummer *(Sq. Ldr. Harvey)*, Michael Redgrave *(Air Vice Marshal Evill)*, Ralph Richardson *(British Minister in Switzerland)*, Robert Shaw *(Sq. Ldr. Skipper)*, Patrick Wymark *(Air* Vice Marshal Trafford Leigh-Mallory), Susannah York *(Section Officer Maggie Harvey)*, Michael Bates *(Warrant Officer Warrick)*, Isla Blair *(Andy's wife)*, John Baskcomb *(Farmer)*, Tom Chatto *(Willoughby's Asst. Controller)*, James Cosmo *(Jamie)*, Robert Flemyng *(Wing Commander Willoughby)*, Barry Foster *(Sq. Ldr. Edwards)*, Edward Fox *(Pilot Officer Archie)*, W. G. Foxley *(Sq. Ldr. Evans)*, David Griffin *(Sgt. Pilot Chris)*, Jack Gwillim *(Sr. Air Staff Officer)*, Myles Hoyle *(Peter)*, Duncan Lamont *(Flt. Sgt.* Arthur), Sarah Lawson *(Skipper's Wife)*, Mark Mahez *(Pasco)*, Andre Maranne *(French N.C.O.)*, Anthony Nichols *(A Minister)*, Nicholas Pennell *(Simon)*, Andrzey Scibor *(Ox)*, Jean Wladon *(Jean-Jacques)*, Wilfried van Aacken *(Gen. Osterkamp)*, Karl Otto Alberty *(Chief of Staff Luftwaffe)*, Alexander Allerson *(Maj. Brandt)*, Dietrich Frauboes *(Feldmarschall Milch)*, Alf Jungermann *(Brandt's Navigator)*, Peter Hager *(Feldmarschall Kesselring)*, Wolf Harnish *(Gen. Fink)*, Reinhard Horras *(Bruno)*, Helmut Kircher *(Boehm)*, Paul Newhaus *(Maj. Foehn)*, Malte Petzel *(Beppo Schmid)*, Manfred Reddemann *(Maj. Falke)*, Hein Reiss *(Reichmarschall Goering)*, Rulf Stiefel *(Hitler)*.

A great, stirring saga of England's defense of its homeland with a staggering starstudded cast; its overlong docudrama style is compensated by excellent portrayals, irrespective of the limited roles. Caine, Plummer and More have the meatier parts with love interest provided by York, Plummer's WAAF wife, hating the war and craving affection. Olivier is at his documentary best as Sir Hugh Dowding whose crafty tactics with his limited fighter command induced the Luftwaffe to make fatal errors that led to its destruction. Shaw is superb as an exhausted but relentlessly tough fighter commander ordering his men again and again into the air. Not only is this a proper paean of praise for the noble RAF in its "Finest Hour" but nodding recognition is given to the Czech and Polish flyers who fought alongside their British comrades. Except for Jurgens, the German actors are mere caricatures of the Nazi high command (Stiefel is ludicrous as a berserk Hitler who, with a red beard, could pass for a German Yosemite Sam). The aerial photography of the German bombing and the dogfights between the British and German fighters are spectacular and fascinating and it was the high production value of these segments which cost the producers the bulk of their $12 million investment (they lost a reported $10 million!). Praise also goes to Sir William Walton for his "Battle of the Air" theme, heroic and memorable. Ironically, Adolf Galland, one of the sharpest German aces to vex the British during WW II, was used as a technical adviser on the film.

p, Harry Saltzman, S. Benjamin Fisz; d, Guy Hamilton; w, James Kennaway, Fisz, Wilfred Greatorex; ph, Freddie Young, Bob Huke (Panavision, Technicolor); m, Sir William Walton, Ron Goodwin (conducted by Malcolm Arnold); prod d, Sydney Streeter; art d, Maurice Carter, Bert Davey, Jack Maxsted, William Hutchinson, Gil Parrondo; spec eff, Cliff Richardson; Glen Robinson; aerial dir, David Bracknell; ed, Bert Bates; Brit. tech. adv, Capt. Hamish Mahaddie, Capt. Tome Gleave, Wg.-Cdr. Robert Wright, Wg.-Cdr. Robert Standord-Tuck, Squadron Ldr. Ginger Lacey, Squadron Ldr. B. Drobinski, Wg. Cdr. Claire Legge; Ger. adv., Adolf Galland, Hans Brustellin, Franz Frodl.

War **Cas.** **(PR:A MPAA:G)**

BATTLE OF BROADWAY** (1938) 84m FOX bw

Victor McLaglen *(Big Ben Wheeler)*, Brian Donlevy *(Chesty Webb)*, Louise Hovick [Gypsy Rose Lee] *(Linda Lee)*, Raymond Walburn *(Homer C. Bundy)*, Lynn Bari *(Marjorie Clark)*, Jane Darwell *(Mrs. Rogers)*, Robert Kellard *(Jack Bundy)*, Sammy Cohen *(Turkey)*, Esther Muir *(Opal Updyke)*, Eddie Holden *(Svenson)*, Hattie McDaniel *(Agatha)*, Paul Irving *(Prof. Halligan)*, Frank Morgan *(Pinky McCann)*, Andrew Tombes *(Judge Hutchins)*.

Silly tale of two buddies, McLaglen and Donlevy, who go to New York City to break up an affair between their boss's son and a showgirl. While in the Big Apple, the two become embroiled in some Broadway hi-jinks and they both fall for the same nightclub singer. Suddenly, the boss himself shows up and steals the singer from both of them. Script is on the dim side, but McLaglen and Donlevy make a good team.

p, Sol M. Wurtzel; d, George Marshall; w, Lou Breslow, John Patrick (based on a story by Norman Houston); ph, Barney McGill; ed, Jack Murray; md, Louis Silvers; m/l, Sidney Claire, Harry Akst.

Comedy **(PR:A MPAA:NR)**

BATTLE OF GALLIPOLI**

(1931, Brit.) 75m British Instructional/Capitol bw (GB: TELL ENGLAND)

Carl Harbord (Edgar Doe), Tony Bruce (Rupert Ray), Dennis Hoey (The Padre), C. M. Hallard (The Colonel), Frederick Lloyd (Capt. Hardy), Gerald Rawlinson (Lieut. Doon), Fay Compton (Mrs. Doe), Hubert Harben (Mr. Ray).

Harbord and Bruce play two young soldiers who are enthusiastic for warfare until they experience the horror firsthand. Remade as a much better film by Australian director Peter Weir in 1980 as GALLIPOLI.

p, H. Bruce Woolfe; d, Anthony Asquith, Geoffrey Barnes; w, Asquith (based on the novel by Ernest Raymond); ph, Jack Parker, Stanley Rogers, James Rodwell; ed, Mary Field; art d, Arthur Woods.

War   **(PR:A MPAA:NR)**

BATTLE OF GREED*   (1934) 59m Crescent bw

Tom Keane, Gwynne Shipman, James Bush, Jimmy Butler, Budd Buster, Lloyd Ingraham, Bob Callahan, Henry Rocquemore, Ray Bennett, Robert Fiske, Carl Stockdale.

Typical oater starring Keane who runs into Mark Twain, Bush, running the newspaper in the Virginia mining town where the film's action takes place.

p, E. B. Derr; d, Howard Higgins; w, John T. Neville; ph, Paul Ivano; ed, Donald Barrett.

Western   **(PR:A MPAA:NR)**

BATTLE OF LOVE'S RETURN, THE*   (1971) 82m Standard Films c

Lloyd Kaufman (Abacrombie), Lynn Lowry (Dream Girl), Andy Kay (The Loafer), Stanley Kaufman (Mr. Crumb), Ida Goodcuff (Elderly Woman), Jim Crispi (Bridge Foreman), Bernard Brown (Det. Glass), Roderick Ghyka (Dr. Finger), Bonnie Sacks (Army Sergeant), Robert S. Walker (Preacher).

This messy, low-budget, independent comedy that somehow found a distributor was shot on 16mm and deals with a young man's problems coping with life in the big city. Director-writer Kaufman also stars as the inept young man who can't seem to do anything right. After seeing this, the autobiographical elements of the material become crystal clear.

p, Lloyd Kaufman, Frank Vitale; d,w&ed, Kaufman; ph, Vitale; m, Kaufman, Andre Golino.

Comedy   **(PR:A MPAA:G)**

BATTLE OF PARIS, THE*   (1929) 80m PAR bw

Gertrude Lawrence (Georgie), Charles Ruggles (Zizi), Walter Petrie (Tony), Gladys DuBois (Suzanne), Arthur Treacher (Harry), Joe King (Jack).

A musical comedy version of WW I which is not very musical nor very funny. Lawrence is a singer working with Ruggles, a pickpocket, and she falls in love with American artist Petrie (after Ruggles picks his pocket) and then becomes his model. Songs include: "Here Comes The Bandwagon," and "They All Fall In Love" (Cole Porter), "Housekeeping For You," and "What Makes My Baby Blue" (Howard Dietz, Jay Gorney). Reviewers took more shots at this primitive talkie when it opened than were probably fired during the war. All the dialog is with songs written by Cole Porter.

d, Robert Florey; w, Gene Markey; m, Cole Porter; ph, George Folsey.

Musical   **(PR:A MPAA:NR)**

BATTLE OF ROGUE RIVER* 1/2   (1954) 70m COL c

George Montgomery (Maj. Frank Archer), Richard Denning (Stacey Wyatt), Martha Hyer (Brett McClain), John Crawford (Capt. Richard Hillman), Emory Parnell (Sgt. McClain), Michael Granger (Chief Mike), Freeman Morse (Pvt. Reed), Bill Bryant (Corporal), Charles Evans (Matt Parish), Lee Roberts (Lt. Keith Ryan), Frank Sully (Kohler), Steve Ritch (1st Brave), Bill Hale (Henry), Wes Hudman (Roy), Jimmy Lloyd (Hamley), Willis Bouchey (Maj. Wallich).

Another of Katzman's cheapies; this time it's Cowboys and Indians rather than Bowery Boys and Cops. Montgomery is a no-nonsense martinet in the cavalry. His job is to bring some sort of tranquility to the area around Rogue River. Denning is the heavy; he leads a group of villains who try to keep the Injuns in a state of war paint so all of the rich Oregon mineral lands can be grabbed off by a horde of Northwestern-type carpetbaggers. There are no surprises in the ably directed film (by Castle, who went on to become a major force in low-budget horror movies) and it will please all but the discriminating.

p, Sam Katzman; d, William Castle; w, Douglas Heyes; ph, Henry Freulich (Technicolor); ed, Charles Nelson.

Western   **(PR:A MPAA:NR)**

BATTLE OF THE AMAZONS*   (1973, Ital./Span.) 92m Riccardo Billi c

Lincoln Tate (Zeno), Lucretia Love (Eraglia), Robert Vidmark (Llio), Solvi Stubing (Sinade), Paola Tedesco (Valeria), Mirta Miller (Melanippe), Benito Stefanelli (Erno), Genia Woods (Antiope).

Amazon queen and her female warriors strut their stuff in ancient Asia Minor. The neighborhood bullies decide to take over a nearby village, but the martial arts-trained farmers rake them over. A giant flop.

p, Riccardo Billi; d, Al Bradley; w, Mario Amendola, Bruno Corbucci (based on a story by Fernando Izcaino Cases); m, Franco Micalizzi.

Historical Adventure   **(PR:A MPAA:NR)**

BATTLE OF THE BULGE*** 1/2   (1965) 167m Cinerama/WB c

Henry Fonda (Lt. Col. Kiley), Robert Shaw (Col. Hessler), Robert Ryan (Gen. Grey), Dana Andrews (Col. Pritchard), George Montgomery (Sgt. Duquesne), Ty

Hardin (Schumacher), Pier Angeli (Louise), Barbara Werle (Elena), Charles Bronson (Wolenski), Werner Peters (Col. Kohler), Hans Christian Blech (Conrad), James MacArthur (Lt. Weaver), Telly Savalas (Guffy), Karl Otto Alberty (Von Diepel), William Conrad (Narrator), Steve Rowland, Donald Pickering.

When director Ken Annakin is good (TRIO, parts of THE LONGEST DAY) he is very good, but when he is bad, which is more often than he's good, he's terrible. But that's not the case in BATTLE OF THE BULGE which has to rank as his best picture ever. At 167 minutes, it's a fat picture with not enough plot to satisfy the time. Robert Shaw is a master tactician in the German tank corps. His counterparts on the other side of the Bastogne are Fonda, Ryan, and Andrews in standard wartime characterizations. Fonda keeps after his superiors by telling them that he expects an attack from the other side. They won't hear of it. Fonda is vindicated and the rest of the film is an inch-by-inch view of the battle. The movie is very inaccurate and any veteran of the real battle laughs at the idea of the climax taking place on a butte with squadrons of tanks facing each other down in a mechanized HIGH NOON. Bill Conrad's narration is totally out of keeping with the rest of the movie. This is a foot-slogging, dirty account of war with little of the John Wayne heroics. In that alone, it merits your attention.

p, Milton Sperling, Philip Yordan; d, Ken Annakin; w, Yordan, Sperling, John Melson; ph, Jack Hildyard (Panavision, Technicolor); m, Benjamin Frankel; ed, Derek Parsons; cos, Laure De Zarate.

War   **Cas.**   **(PR:A MPAA:NR)**

BATTLE OF THE CORAL SEA**   (1959) 80m COL bw

Cliff Robertson (Lt. Comm. Jeff Conway), Gia Scala (Karen Philips), Teru Shimada (Cdr. Mori), Patricia Cutts (Lt. Peg Whitcomb), Rian Garrick (Al Schechter), Gene Blakely (Lt. Len Ross), L.Q. Jones (Yeoman Halliday), Robin Hughes (Maj. Jammy Harris), Tom Laughlin (Ens. Franklin), Eiji Yamashiro (Oshikawa), James T. Goto (Capt. Yamazaki), K. L. Smith (CPO Connors), Carlyle Mitchell (Adm. McCabe), Larry Thor (Army Major), Patrick Westwood (Simes).

Undistinguished war film about the battle that turned the tide in the Pacific Theater in WW II. Kandel (whose father is Aben Kandel, also a screenwriter) turned out the story and co-wrote the screenplay with Ullman and it is appalling that they missed the whole point of the fracas. The film concentrates on a submarine that recons the area before the battle. After that's done, they begin to return to port, are captured, and tossed into a Japanese prison where they are aided by Scala, as a Eurasian, who helps three officers flee the island on a torpedo boat. This done, the men arrive safely home and inform their commanders about what's happening. Robertson is downright boring under Wendkos' equally languorous direction. Does the man ever smile? Best actors in the bunch are the Japanese; when a person watches a WW II film and begins rooting for the Japanese, you know something has gone wrong in the conception. There's just not enough battle in BATTLE OF THE CORAL SEA.

p, Charles H. Schneer; d, Paul Wendkos; w, Daniel Ullman, Stephen Kandel (based on a story by Kandel); ph, Wilfrid Cline; m, Ernest Gold; ed, Chester W. Schaeffer.

War   **(PR:A MPAA:NR)**

BATTLE OF THE NERETVA***

(1971, Yugo./Ital./Ger.) 175m Jadran Film-Bosna Film-Commonwealth-United-Eichberg/AIP c

Yul Brynner (Viado), Hardy Kruger (German Captain), Franco Nero (Italian Captain), Sylva Koscina (Sister), Orson Welles (Senator), Curt Jurgens (German General), Anthony Dawson (Italian General), Milena Dravic (Girl), Sergei Bondarchuk (Artillery Man), Liubisa Samardzic (Novak), Bata Zivonolovic (Partisan Captain), Boris Dvornik (Partisan), Oleg Vidov (Nicola).

A $12 million war epic with a strong international cast. The story focuses on the Yugoslav partisans who in 1943 gallantly battled German and Italian troops. The good guys won this one and the movie is also a winner for anyone who enjoys a decent war movie.

p, Veljko Bulajic; w, Stevo Bulajic, Ratko Durovic, Ugo Pirro, Bulajic; ph, Tomislav Winter (Technicolor); m, Vladimir Raiteric-Kraus; ed, Vojislav Bjenjas.

War   **Cas.**   **(PR:A MPAA:NR)**

BATTLE OF THE RAILS** 1/2

(1949, Fr.) 87m Clement/Mayer-Burstyn bw (LA BATAILLE DU RAIL)

Clarieux (Railroad Worker), Daurand (Railroad Worker), Deagneaux (Chief Operator), Tony Laurent (Carmargue), Leray (Station Master), Redon (Engineer), Pauleon (Railroad Worker), Rauzena (Yard Worker), Lozach (Railroad Worker), Salina (Railroad Worker), Woll (Railroad Worker), Charles Boyer (Narrator).

Boyer narrates a patriotic docudrama about French railway workers who sabotaged the movement of freight and passenger trains in France during its WW II occupation by the Nazis, most of the actors taken from actual positions they occupied in the French railway system. Clement's direction is so realistic as to give the impression that we are watching startling newsreel footage. It is easy to see this historic film inspired most of the plot for John Frankenheimer's THE TRAIN.

p&d, Rene Clement; w, Colette Audry; ph, Henri Alekan; m, Yves Baudrier.

War   **(PR:A MPAA:NR)**

BATTLE OF THE RIVER PLATE, THE, SEE

(SEE: PURSUIT OF THE GRAF SPEE, 1957)

BATTLE OF THE SEXES, THE***

(1960, Brit.) 88m Bryantston/Continental bw

Peter Sellers (Mr. Martin), Robert Morley (Robert MacPherson), Constance Cummings (Angela Barrows), Ernest Thesiger (Old MacPherson), Jameson Clark (Andrew Darling), Moultrie Kelsall (Graham), Alex MacKenzie (Robertson), Roddy McMillan (Macleod), Donald Pleasence (Irwin Hoffman), James Gibson (Night Watchman), Abe Barker (Mr. Meekie), Noel Howlett (Mr. White), Gordon Phillott

(*Mr. Munson*), Macdonald Parke (*C. J.*), Patricia Hayes (*Jeannie MacDougall*), Eric Woodburn (*Wine Shop Owner*), Donald Bissett (*Tobacconist*), Althea Orr (*American Wife*), Sydney Keith (*American Husband*), Sam Wanamaker (*Narrator*).

Thinly adapted from a Thurber short story and transplanted from America to Edinburgh, the film is nevertheless a witty and humorous rendition where so-called efficiency expert Sellers, a meek, and retiring sort, tries to save textile manufacturer Morley from the brash takeover by shrewd American Cummings. His plan is simple, merely dispose of the lady, and thus we enter the battle of male vs female. In Sellers' words: "No need to use violence; many a battle has been won without striking a blow." The subtle machinations and plot twists are adroitly presented by director Crichton who masterminded THE LAVENDER HILL MOB. A very funny film with the laughs on the sophisticated side, albeit the proper doses of slapstick enliven the action.

p&w, Monja Danischewsky; d, Charles Crichton (based on the short story "The Catbird Seat" by James Thurber); ph, Freddie Francis; m, Stanley Black.

Comedy   **Cas.**   **(PR:A MPAA:NR)**

BATTLE OF THE V1   (SEE: MISSILES FROM HELL, 1958)

BATTLE OF THE VILLA FIORITA, THE*
(1965, Brit.) 111m WB c (AKA: AFFAIR AT THE VILLA FIORITA)

Maureen O'Hara (*Moira*), Rossano Brazzi (*Lorenzo*), Richard Todd (*Darrell*), Phyllis Calvert (*Margot*), Martin Stephens (*Michael*), Elizabeth Dear (*Debby*), Olivia Hussey (*Donna*), Maxine Audley (*Charmian*), Ursula Jeans (*Lady Anthea*), Ettore Manni (*Father Rossi*), Richard Wattis (*Travel Agent*), Finlay Currie (*M.C.*), Clelia Matania (*Celestina*), Rosi Di Pietro (*Giuletta*).

Excellent production and stunning photography can't overcome a lachrymose soap-opera story where luscious O'Hara falls for Italian composer Brazzi and plans to leave her husband, Todd. Her children intervene and save a marriage that is no less boring than the tepid affair.

p,d&w, Delmer Daves (based on the novel by Rumer Godden); ph, Oswald Morris (Panavision, Technicolor); m, M. Spoliansky; ed, Bert Bates; art d, Carmen Dillon.

Romance   **(PR:A MPAA:NR)**

BATTLE OF THE WORLDS*
(1961, Ital.) 84m Ultra/Sicilia Cinematografica c (IL PIANETA DEGLI UOMINI SPENTI; GUERRE PLANETARI; AKA: PLANET OF THE LIFELESS MEN)

Claude Rains (*Prof. Benson*), Bill Carter (*Fred Steel*), Umberto Orsini (*Bob Cole*), Maya Brent (*Eva*), Jacqueline Derval (*Cathy*), Carol Denell (*Mrs. Collins*), Renzo Palmer (*Gen. Varrick*), Carlo D'Angelo, Maria Mustari, Guiliano Gemma.

Far-fetched space yarn is saved somewhat by Rains' controlled performance (he was 72 at the time, only finding work in Italy). A meteorite appears to be on a collision course with Earth but Rains, a top scientist, tells his associates not to fear; the crash will not take place. It doesn't. Instead the meteorite launches spaceships which begin firing on Earth. Rains learns that the orb has been sent from a dead planet where the computers still do all the thinking. Fascinated, he contacts the main computer to learn its deep wisdom, but he is killed by Earth's militarists before learning the secrets of space (when will we ever learn?). Impressive sets and sharp direction by Margheriti offset a docile cast and contrived dialog, suffering further from poor English dubbing.

p, Thomas Sagone; d, Anthony Dawson [Antonio Margheriti]; ph, Raffaello Masciocchi; w, Vassily Petrov; ed, George Serallon.

Science Fiction   **(PR:A MPAA:NR)**

BATTLE STATIONS*
(1956) 81m COL bw

John Lund (*Fr. Joe McIntyre*), William Bendix (*Buck Fitzpatrick*), Keefe Brasselle (*Chris Jordan*), Richard Boone (*The Captain*), William Leslie (*Ens. Pete Kelly*), John Craven (*Cdr. James Matthews*), James Lydon (*Squawk Hewitt*), Claude Akins (*Marty Brennan*), George O'Hanlon (*Patrick Mosher*), Eddie Foy, III (*Tom Short*), Jack Diamond (*William Halsey*), Chris G. Randall (*Archie Golder*), Robert Forrest (*John Moody*), Dick Cathcart (*Eddie*), Gordon Howard (*Lt. Hanson*), James Lilburn (*Williams*), Frank Connor, Eric Bond (*Bosuns*).

Everything you wanted to know about routine life on an aircraft carrier during WW II with some battle footage thrown in to discourage total boredom. Richard Boone and William Bendix do their best to keep this film from sinking.

p, Bryan Foy; d, Lewis Seiler; w, Crane Wilbur (based on a story by Charles S. Gould); ph, Burnett Guffey; m, Mischa Bakaleinikoff; ed, Jerome Thoms.

War   **(PR:A MPAA:NR)**

BATTLE STRIPE   (SEE: MEN, THE, 1950)

BATTLE TAXI*
(1955) 82m UA bw

Sterling Hayden (*Capt. Russ Edwards*), Arthur Franz (*Lt. Pete Stacy*), Marshall Thompson (*2nd Lt. Tim Vernon*), Leo Needham (*S/Sgt. Slats Klein*), Jay Barney (*Lt. Col. Stoneham*), John Goddard (*Wounded G.I.*), Robert Sherman (*Lt. Joe Kirk*), Joel Marston (*Lt. Marty Staple*), John Dennis (*M/Sgt. Joe Murdock*), Dale Hutchinson (*Blue Boy Three-Gene*), Andy Andrews (*Lazy Joker Two*), Vance Skarsted (*Lt. Smiley Jackson*), Michael Colgan (*Medic Capt. Larsen*), Capt. Vincent McGovern (*Co-Pilot Harry*).

Sterling Hayden stars as leader of a Korean War air rescue group. His major task appears to be convincing his pilots that they should listen to the maxin that "there are old pilots and there are bold pilots but there are no old, bold pilots." Although the picture was made with the cooperation of the Department of Defense, perhaps this worked as a hindrance in that the filmmakers may have been censored by the government. Consequently, all that's seen is several rescues with very little story in between.

p, Ivan Tors, Art Arthur; d, Herbert L. Strock; w, Malvin Wald (based on a story by Wald and Arthur); ph, Lothrop B. Worth; m, Herman Sukman; ed, Jodie Copelan.

War   **(PR:A MPAA:NR)**

BATTLE ZONE*
(1952) 81m AA bw

John Hodiak (*Danny*), Linda Christian (*Jeanne*), Stephen McNally (*Mitch*), Martin Milner (*Andy*), Dave Willock (*Smitty*), Jack Larson (*O'Doole*), Richard Emory (*Lt. Orlin*), Philip Ahn (*Korean*), Carleton Young (*Colonel*), John Fontaine (*Lt. Pilot*), Todd Karnes (*Officer*), Gil Stratton, Jr. (*Runner*).

The story of Marine combat photographers during the Korean War. Hodiak and McNally not only get involved in some action-packed heroics behind North Korean lines, but both are also vying for the love of the same girl—a Red Cross nurse (Christian). Solid acting and a good mix of combat footage and studio-staged warfare.

p. Walter Wanger; d, Lesley Selander; w, Steve Fisher; ph, Ernest Miller; m, Marlin Skiles; ed, Jack Ogilvie.

War   **(PR:A MPAA:NR)**

BATTLEAXE, THE*
(1962, Brit.) 66m Danziger bw

Jill Ireland (*Audrey Page*), Francis Matthews (*Tony Evers*), Joan Haythorne (*Mrs. Page*), Michael Beint (*Dodson*), Olaf Pooley, Richard Caldicott, Juliette Manet.

Weak comedic effort where Matthews files a lawsuit against Ireland for breach of promise, pummeling the law in court to prove that Haythorne, the possessive, domineering mother, is responsible. The mother-in-law (or future mother-in-law) role takes an awful beating in this cliche-ridden farce.

p, John Ingram; d, Godfrey Grayson; w, M. M. Mc Cormack.

Comedy   **(PR:A MPAA:NR)**

BATTLEGROUND***
(1949) 118m MGM bw

Van Johnson (*Holley*), John Hodiak (*Jarvess*), Ricardo Montalban (*Roderigues*), George Murphy (*Pop Stazak*), Marshall Thompson (*Jim Layton*), Jerome Courtland (*Abner Spudler*), Don Taylor (*Standiferd*), Bruce Cowling (*Wolowicz*), James Whitmore (*Kinnie*), Douglas Fowley (*Kipp Kippton*), Leon Ames (*The Chaplain*), Guy Anderson (*Hansan*), Thomas E. Breen (*Doc*), Denise Darcel (*Denise*), Richard Jaeckel (*Bettis*), Scotty Beckett (*William J. Hooper*), Brett King (*Lt. Teiss*), Ian MacDonald (*Gen. McAuliffe*), and the original "Screaming Eagles" of the 101st Airborne Division.

Excellent story of an American squad of foot soldiers trapped by the Germans in 1944 Bastogne, shown in basic survival terms and presenting a great cross-section of citizen soldiers. Although many of MGM's one-time matinee idols appear, none appropriately reaches beyond the common men they are playing. Johnson is the wise-cracking, girl-chasing GI "inconvenienced" by the war; Hodiak the conscientious small-time newspaperman turned soldier. At one point, when food is running out in besieged Bastogne, Johnson and Hodiak see an elderly woman picking through a garbage can. "I don't see that," Johnson says in disgust, turning away. "Well, I see it," retorts Hodiak. "I'll always see it and I never want anyone to forget it!" Whitmore is terrific as the tobacco-chomping, frozen-foot sergeant, as tough as a whole Panzer division. Montalban was never better than as the Mexican-American from southern California who delights in seeing snow for the first time, frolicking in the flakes as would a child. Others fall into believable stereotypes—Thompson as the bashful replacement; Courtland as the hillbilly who can't sleep with his boots on, a situation which leads to his demise; smart-aleck Fowley who entertains his compatriots by constantly clicking his poorly fitted false teeth (GI issue); the rich boy, Taylor, a role later played to the hilt in STALAG 17; Ames as the chaplain; Jaeckel and Beckett as boy soldiers maturing quickly under fire. And there is a fine little cameo performance by MacDonald as the American general who is asked to surrender by the Germans and prosaically replies: "Nuts!" Darcel is one of the few females with any kind of role and she busies herself as a French lady cutting bread so wildly that she almost cleaves a mammary, much to the alarm of Johnson. Although the action is on the down side, director Wellman expertly gives attention to the human side of war. (Scriptwriter Pirosh knew his story line since he served at Bastogne.) BATTLEGROUND was a special project of Dore Schary's, who brought it from RKO to MGM where he had been named production chief (it was his first production credit at MGM). MGM mogul Louis B. Mayer had told Irving Thalberg, his wonder boy in charge of production during the 1920s and 1930s, that the WW I silent epic THE BIG PARADE would never go over in 1925; Mayer repeated his mistake by saying no to Schary's BATTLEGROUND, insisting that the public was not ready to relive WW II. He was again wrong; millions flocked to see the film, particularly veterans who identified with the many types of soldiers therein represented. Made over his strenuous objections, BATTLEGROUND proved to be the source of the rift between Mayer and Schary that would eventually lead to Mayer's ouster.

p, Dore Schary; d, William Wellman; w, Robert Pirosh; ph, Paul C. Vogel; m, Lennie Hayton; ed, John Dunning; spec eff, Peter Balbursch.

War   **(PR:A MPAA:NR)**

BATTLES OF CHIEF PONTIAC*
(1952) 71m REA bw

Lex Barker (*Kent McIntire*), Helen Westcott (*Winifred Lancester*), Lon Chaney, Jr. (*Chief Pontiac*), Berry Kroeger (*Col. Von Weber*), Roy Roberts (*Major Gladwin*), Larry Chance (*Hawkbill*), Katherine Warren (*Chia*), Ramsey Hill (*Gen. Amherst*), Guy Teague (*Von Weber's Aide*), James Fairfax (*Sentry*), Abner George (*Doctor*).

The British and Indians go at it after a peace deal worked out by Ranger lieutenant Lex Barker falls apart due to brutality on the white man's side. A real hatchet job on historical fact. Chaney, of WOLF MAN fame, and Barker, who later played TARZAN, are the film's only saving grace.

p, Jack Broder; d, Felix Feist; w, Jack De Witt; ph, Charles Van Enger; m, Elmer Bernstein; ed, Philip Cahn.

Western   **(PR:A MPAA:NR)**

BATTLESTAR GALACTICA*   (1979) 120m UNIV c

Richard Hatch *(Capt. Apollo)*, Dirk Benedict *(Lt. Starbuck)*, Lorne Greene *(Cdr. Adama)*, Ray Milland *(Uri)*, Lew Ayres *(Adar)*, Jane Seymour *(Serina)*, Wilfrid Hyde-White *(Anton)*, John Colicos *(Count Baltar)*, Laurette Spang *(Cassiopea)*, John Fink *(Dr. Page)*, Terry Carter *(Col. Tighe)*, Herb Jefferson, Jr. *(Lt. Boomer)*, Maren Jensen *(Athena)*, Tony Swartz *(Lt. Jolly)*, Noah Hathaway *(Boxey)* Ed Begley, Jr. *(Ens. Greenbean)*, Rick Springfield *(Lt. Zac)*, Randi Oakes *(Young Woman)*, Norman Stuart *(Statesman)*, David Greenan *(Bridge Officer)*, Sarah Rush *(Woman on Duty)*, David Matthau *(Operative)*, Chip Johnson, Geoffrey Binney *(Warriors)*, Paul Coufos *(Pilot)*, Bruce Wright *(Deck Hand)*.

Futuristic Earthmen travel the universe in search of a legendary planet called Earth. This movie is a re-edited version of the television series, with the addition of Sensurround. Just as bad as the failed series. Lorne Greene should never have sold The Ponderosa. (This giant, empty shell of a movie was released theatrically in Canada and Europe.)

p, Leslie Stevens; d, Richard A. Colla; w, Glen A. Larson; ph, Ben Colman (Sensurround, Technicolor); m, Stu Phillips; ed, Robert L. Kimble, Leon Ortiz-Gill, Larry Strong; art d, John E. Chilberg, II; spec eff, Apogee, Inc.

Science Fiction   **Cas.**   **(PR:A MPAA:NR)**

BATTLETRUCK** ½
                   (1982) 91m New World c (AKA: WARLORDS OF THE 21ST CENTURY)

Michael Beck *(Hunter)*, Annie McEnroe *(Carlie)*, James Wainwright *(Straker)*, John Ratzenberger *(Rusty)*, Randolph Powell *(Judd)*, Bruno Lawrence *(Willie)*, Diana Rowan *(Charlene)*, John Bach *(Bone)*.

As in MAD MAX, civilization, as we know it, is over. There is no fuel to be found. An outlaw army, led by Wainwright, does have this huge truck and somehow they manage to have enough gasoline. Wainwright has James Bond-villain dreams but his daughter, McEnroe, will have none of it. She departs, takes up with Beck, and moves into a tranquil community run by Ratzenberger. Wainwright is not thrilled about his only daughter taking up with these peaceniks, so he decides to wreak revenge. The outcome, good triumphs over evil, is predictable from the opening credits. Good actors, lots of action, not as speed-crazed as either of Mel Gibson's Australian films. This was made in New Zealand on a small budget and looks a lot better than most of the similar chase films done in the U.S.

p, Lloyd Phillips, Rob Whitehouse; d, Harley Cokliss; w, Irving Austin, Cokliss, John Beech; ph, Chris Menges (Colorfilm); m, Kevin Peek; ed, Michael Harton; prod d, Gary Hansen; art d, Ron Highfield; spec eff, Jonnie Burke.

Science Fiction   **(PR:C MPAA:PG)**

BATTLING BELLHOP, THE   (SEE: KID GALAHAD, 1937)

BATTLING BUCKAROO*
                   (1932) 61m Kent bw (GB: HIS LAST ADVENTURE)

Lane Chandler, Doris Hill, Yakima Canutt, Ted Adams, Lafe McKee, Olin Francis, Bart Carre.

Absurd, badly produced oater with Chandler chasing rustlers and thieves to impress and win the love of Hill. Not worth the effort.

p, Willis Kent; d, Armand Schaefer; w, Oliver Drake.

Western   **(PR:A MPAA:NR)**

BATTLING MARSHAL*   (1950) 55m Astor bw

Sunset Carson, Pat Starling, Forrest Matthews, Lee Roberts, Al Terry, Richard Bartell, Dale Carson.

Carson makes a mistake as a lawman and takes the rest of the film to get even with the baddies. Not one of Sunset's better outings.

p, Walt Mattox; d, Oliver Drake; w, Rose Kreves.

Western   **Cas.**   **(PR:A MPAA:NR)**

BAWDY ADVENTURES OF TOM JONES, THE** ½
                                                                 (1976, Brit.) 94m UNIV c

Nicky Henson *(Tom Jones)*, Trevor Howard *(Squire Western)*, Terry Thomas *(Mr. Square)*, Arthur Lowe *(Dr. Thwackum)*, Georgia Brown *(Jenny Jones/Mrs. Waters)*, Joan Collins *(Black Bess)*, William Mervyn *(Squire Alworthy)*, Murray Melvin *(Blifil)*, Madeline Smith *(Sophia)*, Geraldine McEwan *(Lady Bellaston)*, Jeremy Lloyd *(Lord Fellamar)*, Janie Greenspun *(Daisy)*, Michael Bates *(Madman)*, Hilda Fenemore *(Mrs. Belcher)*, Patricia MacPherson *(Molly Seagram)*, Isabel Dean *(Bridget)*, James Hayter *(Briggs)*, Frank Thornton *(Whitlow)*, Gladys Henson *(Mrs. Wilkins)*, Joan Cooper *(Nellie)*, Maxine Casson *(Prudence)*, Judy Buxton *(Lizzie)*, Arthur Howard *(Old Vicar)*, John Forrest *(Captain Blifil)*, Arnold Diamond *(Noisy Reveller)*, Griffith Davies *(Tilehurst)*.

This is not a sequel, nor is it a remake. Instead, it's a musical version of TOM JONES that had its birth in Las Vegas, Nevada. Back in the late 1960s, MacPherson and Holden thought it might be fun to add some bare skin, cut down the sets and musicalize the Fielding classic. It worked on the small Vegas stage, not so well on the screen. Still, it is a bit of fun and the music doesn't detract from the rollicking speed of the story. Look for a brief bit by Joan Collins as the highwaywoman, one of the rare films around in which she doesn't bare her boobs. Terry-Thomas, Howard, Melvin and Lloyd (who also wrote the screenplay) are delicious as they get right into the spirit and overplay all the way. Although not up to the merits of the original TOM JONES, this film is much better than you might think but not as good as you might

hope. Lots of leers, ogles, antics, slamming doors, laughs, wenches and just about everything else you'd expect from a movie with such a title.

p, Robert Sadloff; d, Cliff Owen; w, Jeremy Lloyd (based on the musical "Tom Jones" by Don MacPherson, adapted from the novel *Tom Jones* by Henry Fielding); ph, Douglas Slocombe (Technicolor); m, Ron Grainer; ed, Bill Blunden; cos, Beatrice Dawson; art d, Jack Shampan; m/l, Paul Holden, Claude Hitchcock, Gordon K. McCallum.

Musical   **(PR:O MPAA:R)**

BAXTER**   (1973, Brit.) 105m NG c

Patricia Neal *(Dr. Clemm)*, Jean-Pierre Cassel *(Roger Tunnell)*, Britt Ekland *(Chris Bentley)*, Lynn Carlin *(Mrs. Baxter)*, Scott Jacoby *(Rober Baxter)*, Sally Thomsett *(Nemo)*, Paul Eddington *(Mr. Rawling)*, Paul Maxwell *(Mr. Baxter)*, Ian Thomson *(Dr. Walsh)*, Ronald Leigh-Hunt *(Mr. Fishie)*, Frances Bennett *(Mrs. Newman)*, George Tovey *(George)*.

Story is centered about a youth with a speech defect who endures the emotional stress of his parents' crumbling marriage. A weepy, unhappy film where the miseries are relentless, saved only in the scenes where Neal appears as an heroic speech therapist.

p, Arthur Lewis; d, Lionel Jeffries; w, Reginald Rose; ph, Geoffrey Unsworth; m, Michael J. Lewis; ed, Teddy Darvas; art d, Anthony Pratt.

Drama   **(PR:C MPAA:PG)**

BAY OF ANGELS** ½   (1964, Fr.) 85m Pathe bw (LA BAIE DES ANGES)

Jeanne Moreau *(Jackie)*, Claude Mann *(Jean)*, Paul Guers *(Caron)*, Henri Nassiet *(Jean's Father)*.

An intense look into the minds of gamblers with Moreau as a married woman who leaves husband and child to play at Nice. Mann is a boring young man who has had a streak of luck at the casino tables when he meets Moreau. She begins to win and thinks he may be her good luck charm. Soon enough she loses it all and stays with Mann as she has no place else to go. He is hurt when she admits that she only desires him because she thinks he can help her win at the tables. She walks away from him, then returns and film goes to conclusion without drawing one; we don't know if she will stay with the young man and quit gambling or go back to risking everything on a turn of the wheel. The title of the film is most unfortunate because it gives no indication of the stark theme. Moreau is good as the disenchanted woman who only finds excitement when risking everything. Mann is less effective as the young man. Contributing well is Nassiet as Mann's father. They have a sharp argument in the first third of the film that sets the tone for Mann's behavior.

d&w, Jacques Demy; ph, Jean Rabier; m, Michel Legrand; ed, Anne-Marie Cotret; art d, Bernard Evein.

Drama   **(PR:C MPAA:NR)**

BAY OF SAINT MICHEL, THE**
                   (1963, Brit.) 73m RANK bw (AKA: PATTERN FOR PLUNDER)

Keenan Wynn *(Nick Rawlings)*, Mai Zetterling *(Helene Bretton)*, Ronald Howard *(Bill Webb)*, Rona Anderson *(Pru Lawson)*, Trader Faulkner *(Dave Newton)*, Edward Underdown *(Col. Harvey)*, Michael Peake *(Capt. Starkey)*, Rudolph Offenbach *(Father Laurent)*, Victor Beaumont *(Man in the "Boite d'Or")*, Paul Bogdan *(Gen. von Kreisling)*, Rita Webb *(Landlady)*, Murray Kash *(Boorish Man)*, Mike Jenkinson *(Drunken Sailr)*, Harvey Hall *(SS Officer)*, Sidney Gross *(Barman)*, Patrick Darren *(Stuart)*, Sally Aylward *(Barmaid)*, Michael Landeau *(French Officer)*.

Ex-commandos are rounded up by their former leader and return to Normandy to find a fabulous treasure hidden by a Nazi general. A lot of digging and no rewards in this mediocre production.

p&d, John Ainsworth; w, Christopher Davis; ph, Stephen Dade; m, Johnny Douglas; ed, Tristram Cones; md, Douglas; art d, Duncan Sutherland.

Adventure   **(PR:A MPAA:NR)**

BAYOU* ½   (1957) 83m UA bw

Peter Graves *(Martin)*, Lita Milan *(Marie)*, Douglas Fowley *(Herbert)*, Tim Carey *(Ulysses)*, Jonathan Haze *(Bos)*, Edwin Nelson *(Etienne)*, Eugene Sondfield *(Jean Titho)*, Evelyn Hendrickson *(Doucette)*, Milton Schneider *(Cousine)*, Michael R. Romano *(Felician)*.

Peter Graves plays an architect who is as unsure of himself as Gary Cooper was self-confident in THE FOUNTAINHEAD. Graves arrives in the bayou area to attempt to convince a New Orleans politician to okay plans for a new building. While in the mossy outback, Graves meets Milan, smouldering offspring of Doug Fowley who plays the role as though he were auditioning for "Hee Haw." Graves falls in love with the Cajun queen and stays on in the area, eventually involving himself with the business of the locals. This runs him afoul of Tim Carey who has leering eyes for Milan. A fight ensues and Graves bests Carey. The picture was made on location and most of the talent was imported to Louisiana. It didn't help. The movie never rises above being a pallid imitation of a second-rate Tennessee Williams' set of characters. Cult films fans will recognize Jonathan Haze (Bos) in a silent role. This was three years before he was to play the greatest role of his life: Seymour in the never-to-be-forgotten LITTLE SHOP OF HORRORS.

p, M. A. Riggs; d, Harold Daniels; w, Edward I. Fessler; ph, Ted and Vincent Salzis; m, Fessler; ed, Maury Wright.

Drama   **(PR:A MPAA:NR)**

BE MINE TONIGHT**   (1933, Brit.) 78m GAU bw

Jan Kiepura (Enrico Ferraro), Sonnie Hale (Koretsky), Magda Schneider (Mathilde), Edmund Gwenn (Mayor Pategy), Athene Seyler (Mrs. Pategy), Betty Chester (Nonstop Nora), Aubrey Mather (Belthasar).

A harassed opera star flees to a small town for peace and quiet. Picture is an English reproduction of a German-made musical. Noteworthy effort.

p, Herman Fellner, Josef Somio; d, Anatole Litvak; w, Irma Von Cube, A. Joseph; ph, Fritz Arno Wagner, Willie Goldberger.

Musical   **(PR:A MPAA:NR)**

BE MY GUEST* 1/2   (1965, Brit.) 82m Three Kings bw

David Hemmings (Dave), Stephen Marriot (Ricky), John Pike (Phil), Andrea Monet (Erica), Ivor Salter (Herbert), Anna King (Margaret), Avril Angers (Mrs. Pucil), Joyce Blair (Wanda), David Healy (Hilton Bass), Tony Wager (Artie), David Lander (Routledge), Robin Stewart (Matthews), Monica Evans (Dyllis), Douglas Ives (Stewart).

A London family purchases a seaside guest hotel. To attract guests, son of the family and a local pop group sponsor a talent contest. Some good British pop groups appear along with Jerry Lee Lewis.

p&d, Lance Comfort; w, Lyn Fairhurst; ph, Basil Emmott; m, Malcolm Lockyer; ed, Sid Stone.

Drama/Musical   **(PR:A MPAA:NR)**

BE YOURSELF**   (1930) 65m UA bw

Fannie Brice (Fannie Field), Robert Armstrong (Jerry Moore), Harry Green (Harry Field), Gertrude Astor (Lillian), G. Pat Collins (McCloskey), Budd Fine (Step), Marjorie "Babe" Kane (Lola), Rita Flynn (Jessica), Jimmy Tolson (Himself).

Music and comedy surround a thin plot about a down-and-out boxer trying to make it big. Some good laughs by Brice (married to Billy Rose) and a great burlesque by her of Dante's Inferno. She sings "Cookin' Breakfast for the One I Love" (Billy Rose, Henry Tobias), the best tune in the film. Other songs include "Kicking A Hole in The Sky", "Sasha, The Passion of the Pasha," (Rose, Ballard MacDonald, Jesse Greer), and "When A Woman Loves A Man" (Rose, Ralph Rainger).

d, Thornton Freeland; w, Freeland, Max Marcin (based on a story by Joseph Jackson); ph, Karl Struss, Robert H. Planck; ed, Robert J. Kern; set d, William Cameron Menzies, Park French; cos, Alice O'Neill; ch, Maurice L. Kusell.

Musical Comedy   **(PR:A MPAA:NR)**

BEACH BALL** 1/2   (1965) 83m PAR c

Edd Byrnes (Dick), Chris Noel (Susan), Robert Logan (Bango), Gail Gilmore (Deborah), Aron Kincaid (Jack), Mikki Jamison (Augusta), Don Edmonds (Bob), Brenda Benet (Samantha), Anna Lavelle (Polly), James Wellman (Mr. Wolf).

Bikinis, beaches, beach balls, and a plot that has something to do with three aspiring rock-and-rollers who are trying to pay for their instruments. Good, nonsensical 1960s rock and roll/surf movie. The Righteous Brothers make an appearance along with the Supremes, The Four Seasons, and other great groups.

p, Bart Patton, d, Lennie Weinrib; w, David Malcolm; ph, Alfred Taylor (Technicolor); m, Frank Wilson; ed, Karl Wald; m/l, Chester Pipkin, Frank Wilson, Al Capps, Eddie Holland, Brian Holland, Lamont Dozier.

Musical   **(PR:A MPAA:NR)**

BEACH BLANKET BINGO***   (1965) 100m AIP c

Frankie Avalon (Frankie), Annette Funicello (Dee Dee), Deborah Walley (Bonnie Graham), Harvey Lembeck (Eric Von Zipper), John Ashley (Steve Gordon), Jody McCrea (Bonehead), Donna Loren (Donna), Marta Kristen (Lorelei), Linda Evans (Sugar Kane), Timothy Carey (South Dakota Slim), Donna Michelle (Animal), Mike Nadler (Butch), Patti Chandler (Patti), Don Rickles (Big Drop), Paul Lynde (Bullets), Buster Keaton (Himself), Earl Wilson (Himself), Bobbi Shaw (Bobbi).

Annette keeps Frankie in tow after he falls for Linda Evans. Subplots about a mermaid who falls in love with a nitwit, a villainous "drunkard," and motorcycle gangs. The classic beach movie of the 1960s with Don Rickles and Buster Keaton adding their shtick to all the nonsense. Lots of great rock-and-roll.

p, James H. Nicholson, Samuel Z. Arkoff; d, William Asher; w, Sher and Leo Townsend; ph, Floyd Crosby (Panavision, Pathecolor); m, Les Baxter; ed, Fred Feitshans, Eve Newman; art d, Howard Campbell.

Musical Comedy   **(PR:A MPAA:NR)**

BEACH GIRLS**   (1982) 91m Crown International c

Debra Blee (Sarah), Val Kline (Ginger), Jeana Tomasina (Ducky), James Daughton (Scott), Adam Rourke (Uncle Carl), Dan Barrows, Herb Braha, Mary Jo Catlett, Fern Fitzgerald, Tessa Richarde, Judson Vaughn, George Kee Cheung, Channing Clarkson, Paul E. Richards, Bert Rosario, Jacqueline Jacobs.

BEACH GIRLS is better than you might expect. It is a 1980s version of the old Avalon/Funicello movies but, at that, is actually funnier than those early boobs-and-sand pictures were. Cute girls, fairly good music, outrageous puns, sight gags and a good-natured attitude take this out of the realm of soft-porn teenage junk and into the realm of teenage fun. You probably may not recognize anyone here except for Mary Jo Catlett who has since gone on to star in many commercials. Best thing about this R-rated teen fare is that nobody dies in a horrible fashion—which is what's been happening in so many teen films these days. There are no villains and there is no tension, just a lot of laughs and acres and acres of skin. Music is performed by Arsenal.

p, Marilyn J. Tenser, Michael D. Castle; d, Pat Townsend; w, Patrick Duncan, Phil Groves; ph, Michael Murphy (DeLuxe Color); m, Michael Lloyd; ed, George Bowers; art d, Kenneth Herzenroder; cos, Kristin Nelson.

Comedy   **Cas.**   **(PR:C-O MPAA:R)**

BEACH GIRLS AND THE MONSTER, THE*   (1965) 70m U.S. Films bw/c

Jon Hall (Otto Lindsey), Sue Casey (Vicki), Walker Edmiston (Mark), Arnold Lessing (Richard), Elaine DuPont (Jane Howard), Read Morgan (Sheriff), Clyde Alder (Deputy), Gloria Neil (Bunny), Tony Roberts (Brad), Dale Davis (Tom), Carolyn Williamson (Sue).

Oceanographer Jon Hall battles beach monster and flirtatious wife on the shores of Waikiki. Some good suspenseful moments, but overall a cheapie scare flick.

p, Edward Janis; d, Jon Hall; w, Joan Gardner; m, Frank Sinatra, Jr.; ph, Dale Davis (Technicolor).

Horror   **(PR:C MPAA:NR)**

BEACH HOUSE PARTY   (SEE: WILD ON THE BEACH, 1965)

BEACH PARTY**   (1963) 104m James A. Nicholson/AIP c

Bob Cummings (Professor Sutwell), Dorothy Malone (Marianne), Frankie Avalon (Frankie), Annette Funicello (Dolores), Harvey Lembeck (Eric Von Zipper), Jody McCrea (Deadhead), John Ashley (Ken), Morey Amsterdam (Cappy), Eva Six (Ava), Dick Dale and the Del-Tones (Musicians), David Landfield (Ed), Dolores Wells (Sue), Valora Noland (Rhonda), Bobby Payne (Tom), Duane Ament (Big Boy), Candy Johnson (Perpetual Motion Dancer), Roger Bacon (Tour Guide), Yvette Vickers, Sharon Garrett (Yogi Girls) with assorted surfers, beach girls, beach boys, motorcycle rats and motorcycle mice.

Sappy but painless picture that proved to be a bonanza for AIP. This was the first of several films in the genre that starred Frankie, Annette, and, later, Fabian. Cummings is an anthropologist studying teenage sex habits at Malibu. If this picture is any indication, there were no sex habits in those years. Malone is his secretary and is totally misused in the part. Nothing much happens except a lot of teenage jealousy, questions about going all the way, etc. Lembeck provides most of the humor in a sharp satire of Brando's "Wild One." To this day, producers are attempting to make surfing movies and recapture the box office business that the BEACH PARTY pictures enjoyed. Frankie was already married with children at the time but that fact was kept very quiet. Annette was dating and later married and divorced her agent, Jack Gilardi. John Ashley went on to become a successful low-budget maker of absurd horror films.

p, James H. Nicholson, Lou Rusoff; d, William Asher; w, Rusoff; ph, Kay Norton (Panavision, Pathecolor); m, Les Baxter; ed, Homer Powell; cos, Marge Corso.

Musical/Teen   **Cas.**   **(PR:A MPAA:NR)**

BEACH PARTY, ITALIAN STYLE   (SEE: EIGHTEEN IN THE SUN, 1964)

BEACH RED**   (1967) 105m UA c

Cornel Wilde (Capt. MacDonald), Rip Torn (Sgt. Honeywell), Dewey Stinger III (Mouse), Patrick Wolfe (Cliff), Burr De Benning (Egan), Jean Wallace (Julie MacDonald), Linda Albertano (Girl in Baltimore), Jan Garrison (Susie), Gene Blakely (Goldberg), Genki Koyama (Col. Sugiyama), Fred Galang (Lt. Domingo), Dale Ishimoto (Capt. Tanaka), Michael Parsons (Sgt. Lindstrom), Jaime Sanchez (Colombo), Norman Pale (Nikato), Michio Hazama (Capt. Konito), Masako Ohtsuki (Sugiyama's Wife).

Wilde produced, directed, and starred in this anti-war film which focuses on the efforts of an American unit to take a Japanese-held island in the Pacific during WW II. Solid acting, sincere war picture that suffers from slack pacing.

p&d, Cornel Wilde; w, Clint Johnston, Donald A. Peters, Jefferson Pascal (based on a novel Sunday Red Beach by Peter Bowman); ph, Cecil R. Cooney (DeLuxe Color); m, Col. Antonio Buenaventura; ed, Frank P. Keller.

War   **(PR:A MPAA:NR)**

THE BEACHCOMBER***

(1938, Brit.) 86m Mayflower(Pommer-Laughton) PAR bw (AKA: VESSEL OF WRATH)

Charles Laughton (Ginger Ted), Elsa Lanchester (Martha Jones), Tyrone Guthrie (Dr. Jones), Robert Newton (Controleur), Dolly Mollinger (Lia), Rosita Garcia (Kati), J. Solomon (Sgt. Henrik), Fred Groves (Dutch Sea Captain), Elliot Makeham (Native Head Clerk), Mah Foo (Ho), Ley On (Ah King), D.J. Ward (Albert), S. Alley (Mechanic).

Originally released as VESSEL OF WRATH, this movie was excised considerably before it was allowed to be shown in the USA. Laughton is a drunken beachcomber in the Dutch Islands who is taken in hand by Guthrie, a self-righteous minister, and his sister, Lanchester. In the end, Laughton marries Lanchester (as he did in real life) and returns to England where he opens a bar. If that sounds vaguely like the plot of THE AFRICAN QUEEN you're right. Guthrie is much like Morley and Lanchester is quite the same as Hepburn. Laughton, of course, was far too fey to play anything but what he appeared to be. Newton growls well as the local authority. (Early in their married life, Charles and Elsa lived in a Soho house that once belonged to Karl Marx, who is buried in England; it was around that time that she learned he was homosexual, but it didn't seem to matter much in their marriage as they were more great friends than great lovers. They were married 33 years until his death in 1962.)

p&d, Erich Pommer; w, B. Van Thal (based on an adaptation by Bartlett Cormack of a novel by W. Somerset Maugham); ph, Jules Kruger, Gus Drisse; m, Richard Addinsell; ed, Robert Hamer.

Drama   **Cas.**   **(PR:A MPAA:NR)**

THE BEACHCOMBER**½   (1955, Brit.) 90m MacQuitty Prod/UA c

Glynis Johns (Martha), Robert Newton (Ted), Donald Sinden (Ewart Gray), Paul Rogers (Owen), Donald Pleasence (Tromp), Walter Crisham (Vederala), Michael Hordern (Headman), Auric Lorand (Alfred), Tony Quinn (Ship's Captain), Ah Chong Choy (Wang), Ronald Lewis (Headman's son), Jean Rollins (Amao), Lizabeth Rollins (Girl at Maputiti), Michael Mellinger (Medical Orderly).

Maugham loved to write about the South Seas—Sadie Thompson of RAIN, THE MOON AND SIXPENCE and others. In THE BEACHCOMBER, he spins the tale of Newton, a drunk—lolling about in between attacks of the d.t.'s. The only other white residents of this tropical island are a minister and his sister (Rogers and Johns). This film was done in 1938 with Laughton as the wastrel but this version is slightly better as the secondary roles (Sinden as a government official, Pleasence as a clerk, Hordern as the tribal chief) are more defined. When cholera erupts, Newton straightens out his act and he and Glynis go to work to stem the epidemic. Four years before, another film about a drunk and a missionary's sister was made. It took place in Africa, but the similarities are nevertheless evident. That film was THE AFRICAN QUEEN. Newton died shortly after this film was released and has yet to be replaced.

p, William MacQuitty; d, Muriel Box; w, Sydney Box (based on a story by W. Somerset Maugham) ph, Reginald Wyer (Technicolor); m, Francis Chagrin; ed, Jean Barker; cos, Dorothy Sinclair.

Drama   (PR:A   MPAA:NR)

BEACHHEAD***   (1954) 89m UA c

Tony Curtis (Burke), Frank Lovejoy (Sgt. Fletcher), Mary Murphy (Nina), Eduard Franz (Bouchard), Skip Homeier (Reynolds), John Doucette (Major Scott), Alan Wells (Biggerman), Sunshine Akira Fukunaga (Japanese Sailor), Dan Aoki (Sniper), Steam-boat Mokuahi (Malanesian).

Taut war drama has a platoon of Marines trying to rescue a plantation owner-spy (Franz) and a vital message from a Japanese-held island. All are killed as they try to escape, except Lovejoy, Curtis, and Murphy, Franz's daughter. The jungle rot and creatures almost come off the screen in this extremely realistic film, tightly directed by Heisler. Koch's production (he was one of the witty writers on CASABLANCA) is fulsome and rich with unique dialog from writer Simmons, albeit some of the scenes are a bit too fearsome. At one point Curtis stares at Murphy who has been urging him to leave her behind because she has been slowed with a twisted ankle. "The Japs," Curtis hisses, "do you think I can leave you to them?" The thought causes Murphy's eyes to almost pop from her pretty skull as she desperately embraces her lover-rescuer. Shot in the lush jungles of Hawaii, the production is rich in color, but the special effects, particularly the miniature battle between Japanese and American gunboats, look like they might have been shot in a large bathtub. Nevertheless a gripping, fraught-with-danger film.

p, Howard W. Koch; d, Stuart Heisler; w, Richard Alan Simmons (based on the novel I've Got Mine by Richard G. Hubler); ph, Gordon Avil (Technicolor); m, Emil Newman, Arthur Lange; ed, John F. Schreyer.

War   (PR:C   MPAA:NR)

BEADS OF ONE ROSARY, THE**   (1982, Pol.) 116m Zespol/Cinegate c

Augustyn Halotta, Marta Straszna, Fransiszek Pieczka, Ewa Wisniewska, Jan Gogdol, Stanislow Zaczk, Jerzy Rzepka, Ryszard Jasny, Wladyslaw Gulch, Rosa Richert, Antoni Wolny, Maksymilian Baron.

Retired old miner refuses to be relocated to a cheesebox apartment in a high-rise, resisting all manner of encouragement and intimidation by friends, relatives, and authorities. Pleasant comedy by non-professional actors.

d&w, Kazimierz Kutz; ph, Wieslaw Zdort; m, Wojciech Kilar; ed, Josef Bartczak, Miroslawa Filipiak; art d, Andrej Plocki, Miroslawa Krelik, S. Burzynski.

Comedy/Drama   (PR:A   MPAA:NR)

BEAR, THE**   (1963, Fr.) 85m Cinedis/EM c (L'OURS)

Renato Raschel (Medard), Francis Blanche (Chappius), Gaucha (The Bear), Daniel Lecourtois (Director), Cora Camoin, Gaby Basset, Yvette Etievant, Marcel Loche.

THE BEAR is a French version of "Mr. Ed" or "Francis the Talking Mule." Gaucha is a bear who lives in a zoo. When Raschel discovers the bear can talk, no one will believe him. He arranges a nuit d'amor with a polar bear for Gaucha. Raschel's boss at the zoo is a sadistic type (Blanche) and gets his comeuppance when the bear reports the man's conversation. This should have been a terrific kiddie flick but it wasn't because the makers didn't know the difference between wit and drama and, so they gave us very little of either. They seemed to have their eye on a sequel before they finished the original.

d, Edmond Sechan; w, Roger Mauge, Sechan (based on a story by Mauge); ph, Andre Villard (Eastmancolor), m, Jean Prodromides; ed, Jacqueline Thiedot; art d, Rene Renoux.

Fantasy   (PR:AA   MPAA:NR)

BEAR ISLAND*½   (1980, Brit.-Can.) 118m Taft Int./COL c

Donald Sutherland (Frank Lansing), Vanessa Redgrave (Hedi Lindquist), Richard Widmark (Otto Gerran), Christopher Lee (Lechinski), Barbara Parkins (Judith Ruben), Lloyd Bridges (Smithy), Lawrence Dane (Paul Hartman), Patricia Collins (Inge Van Zipper), Michael Reynolds (Heyter), Nicholas Cortland (Jungbeck), August Schellenberg (Marine Technician), Candace O'Connor (Lab Assistant), Joseph Golland (Meteorological Assistant), Bruce Greenwood (Technician), Hagen Beggs (Larsen), Michael Collins (Ship's Captain), Terry Kelly (Radio Operator), Terry Waterhouse (Helicopter Pilot).

A terribly expensive and incomprehensible Canadian/British film sporting a plot that cannot be explained and the most ludicrous Norwegian (Vanessa Redgrave) and

German (Richard Widmark) accents ever attempted. It has something or other to do with a United Nations expedition on an obscure North Atlantic Island. They find some old Nazi submarines filled with, of course, gold bullion. Shot in Canada and partially in Alaska, this picture lost almost every penny of its $12 million budget. When not spouting politics, Redgrave took time off to play the dullest character she's ever attempted. A few good action scenes but most of the picture is as frozen as the tundra it was shot upon. A good cast is absolutely wasted on an ill-conceived picture, a blurry script, and dull direction.

p, Peter Snell; d, Don Sharp; w, Sharp, David Butler, Murray Smith (based on the novel by Alistair MacLean); ph, Alan Hume; ed, Tony Lower.

Adventure   Cas.   (PR:C   MPAA:PG)

BEARS AND I, THE**   (1974) 89m BV c

Patrick Wayne (Bob Leslie), Chief Dan George (Chief A-Tas-Ka-Nay), Andrew Duggan (Commissioner Gaines), Michael Ansara (Oliver Red Fern), Robert Pine (John McCarten), Val DeVargas (Sam Eagle Speaker), Hal Baylor (Foreman).

Disney film about a Vietnam vet who adopts three motherless bear cubs and also gets involved with an Indian tribe fighting to get its land rights back. Beautiful Canadian Rockies photography adds to a tender story.

p, Winston Hibler; d, Bernard McEveety; w, John Whedon (based on the novel by Robert Franklin Leslie); ph, Ted D. Landon (Technicolor); m, Buddy Baker; ed, Gregg McLaughlin; art d, John B. Mansbridge.

Drama   (PR:C   MPAA:G)

BEAST, THE**   (1975, Fr.) 102m (Anatole Dauman) c

Serpa Lane (Romilda), Lisbeth Hummel (Lucy), Elizabeth Kaza (Virginia), Pierre Benedetti (Mathrurin), Guy Trejan (Pierre), Dalio (Duc), Armontel (Priest).

This is the Polish version of BEAUTY AND THE BEAST. And we're not attempting to be funny by that remark. This is a dream-like story that takes place half in reality and half in the minds of the actors. The woman eventually kills the beast with her lovemaking but the story is so convoluted, what with Rolls-Royces and a Catholic Cardinal and a priest who likes to kiss his two choir boys and . . . hey, it's worth seeing if you're into religious eroticism.

w&d, Walerian Borowczyk; ph, Bernard Daillencourt, Marcel Grignon (Eastmancolor); ed, Borowczyk, art d, Alain Guille.

Fantasy   Cas.   (PR:O   MPAA:NR)

BEAST FROM THE HAUNTED CAVE*½   (1960) 65m Filmgroup bw

Michael Forest (Gill), Sheila Carol (Gypsy), Frank Wolff (Alex), Richard Sinatra (Marty), Wally Campo (Byron).

Gold bullion thieves hole up in an isolated cabin and find more than they bargained for as they are attacked by a monster of cobwebs. Good acting and nice photography of Black Hills in South Dakota help this one.

p, Gene Corman; d, Monte Hellman; w, Charles Griffith; ph, Andy Costikyan, Anthony Carras.

Horror   (PR:C   MPAA:NR)

BEAST FROM 20,000 FATHOMS, THE**   (1953) 80m WB bw

Paul Christian (Tom Nesbitt), Paula Raymond (Lee Hunter), Cecil Kellaway (Prof. Elson), Kenneth Tobey (Col. Evans), Donald Woods (Capt. Jackson), Jack Pennick (Jacob), Lee Van Cleef (Cpl. Stone), Steve Brodie (Sgt. Loomis), Ross Elliott (George Ritchie), Ray Hyke (Sgt. Willistead), Mary Hill (Nesbitt's Secy.), Michael Fox (Doctor), Alvin Greenman (1st Radar Man), Frank Ferguson (Dr. Morton), King Donovan (Dr. Ingersoll).

Not a bad monster film, featuring the usual atomic explosion that causes all the trouble. This time, it's responsible for releasing a long-frozen monster in the Arctic. When Christian tells what's happened, no one believes him and they think it's Arctic Fever (sort of like the boy who cried "Monster!"). The monster makes it way down the northeastern coast of the U.S., arriving in New York City where it cuts a swath across Gotham not unlike Godzilla did a while later. Then it's back into the Atlantic and eventual reappearance at Coney Island where it gets involved in the roller coaster area and is finally shot by a radioactive isotope. Lots of good monster sequences overshadow any acting in the movie. The scenes at Coney Island are very good, but if the beast were to surface these days in that neighborhood, he'd be frightened to walk the streets. Excellent Ray Harryhausen special effects.

p, Hal Chester, Jack Dietz, Bernard W. Burton; d, Eugene Lourie; w, Lou Morheim, Fred Freiberger (based on a story by Ray Bradbury); ph, Jack Russell; m, David Buttolph; ed, Bernard W. Burton.

Horror   (PR:C   MPAA:NR)

BEAST IN THE CELLAR, THE*½   (1971, Brit.) 87m Tigon/Cannon c

Beryl Reid (Ellie Ballantyne), Flora Robson (Joyce Ballantyne), Tessa Wyatt (Joanna Sutherland), John Hamill (Cpl. Alan Marlow), T. P. McKenna (Superintendent Paddick), David Dodimead (Dr. Spencer), Christopher Chittell (Baker), Peter Craze (Roy), John Kelland (Sgt. Young), Vernon Dobtcheff (Sir Bernard Newsmith), Dafydd Harvard (Stephen Ballantyne).

Robson and Reid are spinster sisters who brick up a mad brother, Harvard, in their cellar, trying to suppress a family secret that soon gets out of hand to terrorize the neighborhood. Too talky and overdrawn to be properly frightening.

p, Graham Harris, d&w, James Kelly; ph, Harry Waxman; m, Tony Macauley.

Horror   Cas.   (PR:C   MPAA:NR)

BEAST MUST DIE, THE*   (1974, Brit.) 93m Cinerama c

Calvin Lockhart (Tom Newcliffe), Peter Cushing (Dr. Christopher Lundgren), Charles Gray (Bennington), Anton Diffring (Pavel), Marlene Clark (Caroline Newcliffe), Ciaran Madden (Davina Gilmore), Tom Chadbon (Paul Foote), Michael

Gambon (Jan Jamokowksi), Sam Mansaray (Butler), Andrew Lodge (Pilot), Carl Bohun (First Hunter), Eric Carte (Second Hunter).

A black millionaire who owns an English estate invites an odd assortment of guests to his manor. The millionaire believes one of his guests is a werewolf and he wants to hunt him. Not very hair-raising.

p, Max J. Rosenberg, Milton Subotsky; d, Paul Annett; w, Michael Winder; p, Jack Hildyard (Technicolor); m, Douglas Gamley; ed, Peter Tanner; art d, John Stoll.

Horror　　　　　　　　　**Cas.**　　　　　　　**(PR:A MPAA:PG)**

BEAST OF BABYLON AGAINST THE SON OF HERCULES
(SEE: HERO OF BABYLON, 1963)

BEAST OF BUDAPEST, THE*1/2　　　　(1958) 72m Barlene/AA bw

Gerald Milton (Zagon), John Hoyt (Prof. Tolnai), Greta Thyssen (Christi), Michael Mills (Charles Tolnai), Violet Rensing (Marissa), John Mylong (Gen. Foldessy), Joseph Turkel (Martin), Booth Colman (Lt. Stefko), Svea Grunfeld (Teresa), John Banner (Dr. Kovach), Charles Brill (Josef), Kurt Katch (Geza), Robert Blake (Karolyi), Tommy Ivo (Moricz), Colette Jackson (Elizabeth).

Although the title might make one think this was a middle-European horror story, it is, in fact, a slow recreation of the Hungarian Revolution of 1956. A Hungarian militarist (Mylong) has a daughter (Rensing) who is as ardent a Communist as can be uncovered. She loves Mills, who comes from a liberal family headed by his professor-father, Hoyt. They are kept apart by their politics. "The Beast" in the title is Milton and he portrays the real man who kept an iron hand on the Hungarians. In 72 minutes, director Mayo attempts to synthesize the entire revolution, tell a couple of love stories, indicate the duplicity of the Hungarian Secret Police, and outline the drama between a boy and his father as they argue about what's best for their country. We all know what happened when the Russkies swept in and tanked the town. Hungary has not been out of the Communist grip since. One of the major flaws of this film is that the stock shots are so good and so real that everything on either side of them seems contrived. Joe Turkel (Martin) only seems to come to life under the hand of Kubrick (PATHS OF GLORY, THE SHINING) and is misused here.

p, Archie Mayo; d, Harmon C. Jones; w, John McGreevey (based on a story by Louis Stevens); ph, Carl Guthrie; m, Marlin Skiles; ed, George White.

Drama/War　　　　　　　　　　　　　**(PR:C MPAA:NR)**

BEAST OF BLOOD*1/2
(1970, U.S./Phil.) 90m Sceptre/Hemisphere c (AKA: RETURN TO THE HOR-
RORS OF BLOOD ISLAND)

John Ashley (Bill), Celeste Yarnell (Myra), Alfonso Carvajal (Ramu), Lisa Belmonte (Laida), Bruno Punzalan (Razak), Eddie Garcie (Dr. Lorca), Angel Buenaventura, Beverly Miller, Johnny Long.

Ridiculous monster movie has Ashley visiting the terrible island where a monster with green blood terrorizes the natives. She meets Yarnell, a reporter after a good story (and this isn't it). Garcie is a latter-day Dr. Frankenstein, trying to graft a head on the monster from local, murdered contributors in an attempt to correct the monster's evil thinking. Yarnell is kidnaped by the mad doctor but is saved at the last moment by Ashley and natives who kill the monster after he has murdered Garcie. A sequel to MAD DOCTOR OF BLOOD ISLAND, this film is poorly produced and is about as scary as Boris Karloff out of makeup.

p,d&w, Eddie Romero (based on a story by Beverly Miller); ph, Justo Paulino; m, Tito Arevalo; ed, Ben Barcelon; art d, Ben Otico; set d, Bobby Bautista; spec eff, Teofilo Hilario.

Horror　　　　　　　　　　　　　　**(PR:C-O MPAA:GP)**

BEAST OF HOLLOW MOUNTAIN, THE**　　　　(1956) 81m UA c

Guy Madison (Jimmy Ryan), Patricia Medina (Sarita), Eduardo Noriega (Enrique Rios), Carlos Rivas (Felipe Sanchez), Mario Navarro (Panchito), Pascual Garcia Pena (Pancho), Julio Villareal (Don Pedro), Lupe Carriles (Margarita), Manuel Arvide (Martinez), Jose Chavez (Manuel), Margarito Luna (Jose), Roberto Contreras (Carlos), Lobo Negro (Jorge), Jorge Trevino (Shopkeeper), Armando Gutierrez (Employee).

This is a most unusual film in that it provides the viewers with a completely new genre, a science-fiction Western. Now, sometimes disparate ingredients, no matter how much you like them, just don't mix. You might enjoy sour cream and you might just love licorice, but the two of them together are a yeeccchhh. THE BEAST OF HOLLOW MOUNTAIN is not a yecchhh but it isn't an "Oh Boy!" either. Madison (born Robert Moseley) is a rancher and happily partnered with Rivas on a spread near Hollow Mountain. For years, there have been tales of the swamp that surrounds the mountain, but nobody paid much mind. They should have. Filmed in Mexico, this film used some interesting special effects and a new animation process known as Regiscope. The story wasn't much; Noriega is the heavy, Medina is the heroine, a couple of fights, some pale love scenes, etc. What piques the interest is the techniques and the combination of the two styles. Since then, of course, there have been numerous combinations: disaster-comedies, horror-comedies, western-terror, and so on. With a better script and more money spent on production, this might have been a much-remembered movie.

p, William and Edward Nassour; d, Edward Nassour; w, Robert Hill, Jack DeWitt (based on a story by Willis O'Brien); ph, Jorge Stahl, Jr. (DeLuxe Color); m, Raoul La Vista; ed, Holbrook Todd, Maury Wright.

Science Fiction/Western　　　　　　**(PR:A MPAA:NR)**

BEAST OF MOROCCO　　　　(SEE: HAND OF NIGHT, THE, 1967)

BEAST OF THE CITY, THE***
(1932) 74m COS/MGM bw (AKA: CITY SENTINEL)

Walter Huston (Jim Fitzpatrick), Jean Harlow (Daisy), Wallace Ford (Edward Fitzpatrick), Jean Hersholt (Sam Belmonte), Dorothy Peterson (Mary Fitzpatrick), Tully Marshall (Michaels), John Miljan (District Attorney), Emmett Corrigan (Chief of Police), Warner Richmond (Tom), Sandy Roth (Mac), J. Carroll Naish (Cholo), Edward Coppo (Fingerprint Expert), George Chandler (Reporter), Nat Pendleton (Abe Gorman), Arthur Hoyt (Witness), Julie Haydon (Blonde), Clarence Wilson (Coroner), Charles Sullivan (Cop in Hall), Morgan Wallace (Police Captain), Mickey Rooney (Mickey Fitzpatrick).

Hard-hitting crime melodrama where Huston takes on a city's (probably Chicago) corrupt administration, police department and the countless gangs shooting up the citizenry. Huston, as obsessed with righteousness as Clint Eastwood is four decades later in DIRTY HARRY, investigates a killing and then arrests politically connected crime boss Hersholt and three others. The men are soon released and Huston is reassigned to the boondocks for his transgression. Now the gangsters run amuck, openly shooting anyone who opposes them. Huston prevents a bank robbery and becomes the city's hero, the public demanding that he head the police department. He is reluctantly appointed to the position of police chief and immediately launches a massive clean-up, bending the law to corral gangsters, crooked politicians, and cops alike. In a gruesome finale, the good cops line up a vicious gang of hoodlums and machine-gun them to death, sort of a reversal of the St. Valentine's Day Massacre. (The audiences of the day cheered wildly in theaters at the sight of this mass extermination!) In a thick sub-plot, sexy Harlow, in her first MGM film after her contract had been sold by Howard Hughes to Mayer for $60,000, is Hersholt's gun moll. Ford, Huston's weak-willed brother, who expects quick promotion now that his sibling heads the force, is assigned to watch Harlow but falls in love with her and then takes payoffs from Hersholt's minions. He redeems himself by going with Huston and 12 other officers in the final gunfight that sees everyone shot to pieces, including Ford and Harlow. MGM's head of production Thalberg wanted to compete with the successful gangster vehicles produced by Warner Bros. in the early 1930s and hired W.R. Burnett of LITTLE CAESAR fame to write the story. Burnett called on memories of Chicago mob activities and culled some plot lines from his western novel St. Johnson, then turned it over to scriptwriter Mahin. The finished film caused the MGM moguls, used to frothy musicals, to go into shock. The brutality of the film was certainly not in keeping with Mayer's "family films" program and he decreed that this classic film noir product be sent through the B-film circuit, only to play second to "major" films. Newspaper mogul William Randolph Hearst, who owned Cosmopolitan, was incensed that his film was so mismanaged.

d, Charles Brabin; w, John Lee Mahin (based on a story by W. R. Burnett); ph, Norbert Brodine; ed, Anne Bauchens.

Crime　　　　　　　　　　　　　**(PR:C-O MPAA:NR)**

BEAST OF THE DEAD　　　　(SEE: BEAST OF BLOOD, 1970)

BEAST OF YUCCA FLATS, THE*1/2　　　　(1961) 60m Crown bw

Douglas Mellor, Larry Aten, Barbara Francis, Bing Stafford, Linda Bielima, Tor Johnson, John Morrison, Tony Cardoza, Bob Labansat, Jim Oliphant.

A well-known intellectual and scientist is pursued by Commie rats and winds up in an Atomic Testing area. The insidious radiation he encounters turns him into a monster. Honest attempt at making a brief protest picture but the producers didn't have enough money to accord this any sort of production value. As is the case of many low-budget films, a narration is used rather than much sound-on-film because it is easier and much cheaper to do it that way.

p, Anthony Cardoza, Roland Morin, d&w, Coleman Francis; ph, John Cagle; m, Irwin Nafshun, Al Remington; ed, Francis.

Science Fiction/Horror　　　　　　**(PR:C MPAA:NR)**

BEAST WITH A MILLION EYES, THE zero　　　　(1956) 78m AM bw

Paul Birch (Allan Kelly), Lorna Thayer (Carol Kelly), Dona Cole (Sandy Kelly), Dick Sargent (Larry), Leonard Tarver (Him), Chester Conklin (Old Man Webber).

The Kellys live in the desert and all is well until an alien lands in a space ship. This creature plans to dominate earthlings by mind-projection. Birds go after humans (did Hitchcock see this movie?) and normally tranquil animals turn vicious. Finally, by dint of love between them, the Kellys manage to vanquish the being and the spacecraft flies off, although we never see whether the alien went with it. The big question in this cheap, cheap movie is what was Chester Conklin doing in the film? Chester was one of Chaplin's favorites and appeared in MODERN TIMES and THE GREAT DICTATOR, as well as hundreds of shorts for Sennett. His first well-known role was in GREED and he was quite a cut-up in HAIL THE CONQUERING HERO. So again we ask, what was he doing in this turkey? Would that he were around to answer.

p&d, David Karmansky, w, Tom Filer, ph, Everett Baker, m, John Bickford, ed, Jack Killeser.

Science Fiction　　　　　　**Cas.**　　　　**(PR:A MPAA:NR)**

BEAST WITH FIVE FINGERS, THE***　　　　(1946) 88m WB/FN bw

Robert Alda (Bruce Conrad), Andrea King (Julie Holden), Peter Lorre (Hilary Cummins), Victor Francen (Francis Ingram), J. Carrol Naish (Ouidio Castanio), Charles Dingle (Raymond Arlington), John Alvin (Donald Arlington), David Hoffman (Duprex), Patricia White (Clara), Barbara Brown (Mrs. Miller), William Edmunds (Antonio), Belle Mitchell (Giovanna), Pedro DeCordoba (Horatio), Ray Walker (Miller).

A taut, genuinely scary psychodrama which gave vent to Lorre's weird mannerisms and produced some marvelous special effects created by director Florey. An invalided, retired concert pianist living in a rural Italian villa dies mysteriously, leaving his considerable wealth to his private nurse in a newly drafted will. When the will is contested by the pianist's associates, the villa and its occupants are suddenly terrorized by an unknown creature which turns out to be the disembodied hand of the pianist which has been severed by Lorre, the rich man's personal secretary. Lorre is sorely vexed at being cut out of the will and cut off from the villa which contains a tremendous library on astrology, of which he is an obsessive student. Accompanied by a chilling score and startling sound effects, the hand stalks the hallucinating Lorre from behind books, across rooms, out of boxes. No matter what Lorre does to stop it—nailing it to a desk, throwing it into a fire—he cannot escape its final vengeance. Florey, who had originally been drafted by Universal to direct FRAKENSTEIN in 1931 (taken off that project to create MURDERS IN THE RUE MORGUE, 1932), wanted large expressionistic sets for THE BEAST WITH FIVE FINGERS, along with absolute control. He got nothing of the kind, but still managed to provide a good little thriller. The closeups of the disembodied and menacing hand were taken of Florey's very own five fingers. To accomplish shots showing the hand playing the piano, pianist Erwin Nyrigegyhazi was covered in black with only his hand shown moving across the keyboard. This was Warner Brothers' sole contribution to the horror genre in the 1940s and one of the best of that period.

p, William Jacobs; d, Robert Florey; w, Curt Siodmak (based on a story by William Fryer Harvey); ph, Wesley Anderson; m, Max Steiner; ed, Frank Magee; art d, Stanley Fleischer.

Horror **(PR:C MPAA:NR)**

BEAST WITHIN, THE* (1982) 90m MGM/UA c

Ronny Cox *(Eli MacCleary)*, Bibi Besch *(Caroline MacCleary)*, Paul Clemens *(Michael MacCleary)*, Dan Gordon *(Judge Curwin)*, R. G. Armstrong *(Doc)*, Kitty Moffat *(Amanda)*, L. Q. Jones *(Sheriff)*, Ramsay King *(Edwin)*, John Dennis Johnston *(Horace)*, Ron Soble *(Tom)*, Luke Askew *(Dexter)*, Meshach Taylor *(Deputy)*.

Besch and Cox are on their honeymoon in Mississippi (which may have been their first mistake). She is raped by someone or something with hairy legs (could have been almost anyone on the Ol' Miss football team). Time flies and we are now 17 years later. Besch's son is not the kind of kid you'd like to introduce to your daughter. Matter of fact, he's weird and not feeling too well. Mom and Dad take him back to Mississippi to see if there's any connection between what's bothering him and that hairy thing we met in reel one. Clemens, as the son, needs no makeup to show us the pain of being half-monster, half-teenager (which may be redundant) in the early sequences. Made on location in Raymond, Mississippi, this is an obvious attempt by producer Bernhard to recapture the success he once had with THE OMEN. It didn't work. THE OMEN had tension followed by gore. All this has is gore.

p, Harvey Bernhard, Gabriel Katzka; d, Phillipe Mora, w, Tom Holland (based on a novel by Edward Levy); ph, Jack L. Richards (DeLuxe Color); m, Les Baxter; ed, Robert Brown, Bert Livitt; prod d, David M. Haber; makeup eff, Thomas R. Burman.

Horror **Cas.** **(PR:O MPAA:R)**

BEASTMASTER, THE*1/2 (1982) 118m MGM/UA c

Marc Singer *(Dar)*, Tanya Roberts *(Kiri)*, Rip Torn *(Maax)*, John Amos *(Seth)*, Josh Milrad *(Tal)*, Rod Loomis *(Zed)*, Ten Hammer*(Young Dar's father)*, Ralph Strait *(Sacco)*, Billy Jacoby *(Young Dar)*.

A quickie attempt at cashing in on the early 1980s spate of sci-fi and fantasy films. This one features Rip Torn (his real first name is Elmore) as the heavy, Roberts (who went on to become SHEENA), Amos and Singer as THE BEASTMASTER. Singer, who was particularly good as Christian in the version of "Cyrano" for PBS, is wasted in this confused story of a boy whose mother was a cow. This somehow gives him the ability to make animals do his bidding. Not much action, no excitement, no business, no interest.

p, Paul Pepperman, Sylvio Tabet; d, Don Coscarelli, w, Coscarelli, Pepperman; ph, John Alcott (CFI color); m, Lee Holdridge; ed, Ray Watts; prod d, Conrad E. Angone; cos, Betty Pecha Madden.

Fantasy **Cas.** **(PR:C MPAA:PG)**

BEASTS OF BERLIN*1/2
(1939) 87m PDC bw (AKA: HITLERBEAST OF BERLIN)

Roland Drew *(Hans)*, Steffi Duna *(Elsa)*, Greta Granstedt *(Anna)*, Alan Ladd *(Karl)*, Lucien Prival *(Sachs)*, Vernon Dent *(Lustig)*, John Ellis *(Schulz)*, George Rosener *(Wunderlich)*, Bodil Rosing *(Frau Kohler)*, Hans von Twardowski *(Albert)*, Willie Kaufman *(Herr Kohler)*, Hans Joby *(Lippert)*, Frederick Giermann *(Pommer)*, Clem Wilenchick *(Klee)*, Henry von Zynda *(Erlich)*, John Voight *(Kleswig)*, Hans Schumm *(Schaefer)*, John Peters *(Kruger)*, Hans von Morehart *(Braun)*, Walter Stahl *(Col. Hess)*, Josef Forte *(Berkley)*, Francisco Moran *(Jouvet)*, Fred Mellinger *(Ratig)*, Dick Welles *(Buchman)*, A. Palasthy, Walter Thiele, Paul Panzer, Fred Vogeding, Abe Dinovitch, Bob Stevenson, Anna Lisa.

BEASTS OF BERLIN was made before the USA entered the war and while people like Joe Kennedy and Charles Lindbergh were still trying to patch things up with the Hitler regime. Therefore, the film was banned for a while and was released only after serious cuts were made in the content. Because of those edits, the movie only touches the surface about Hitler and life inside The Third Reich. The slim plot has to do with the dissemination of anti-government propaganda and the underground plots of a few good Germans. The last two-thirds of the picture depicts the cruelty of the concentration camps and is followed by the hero escaping to Switzerland. Amazing that the picture came out at all as Charlie Chaplin had a terrible time convincing people he was telling the truth in THE GREAT DICTATOR. The Father Coughlins of America and the various rightist groups backed the little Austrian almost until the middle of 1941. The movie made a big splash when it came out due to the inhumanity shown. Little did the world know that it was not even close to the brutal truth. For its good intentions, this movie should get four stars. Unfortunately, their intentions were better than their release print and we can only judge the final result. The only "name" performer was Ladd.

p&d, Sherman Scott; (based on Shephard Traube's story "Goose Step"); ph, Jack Greenhalgh; m, Dave Chudnow; ed, Robert Crandall, Holbrook Todd.

Drama **(PR:C MPAA:NR)**

BEASTS OF MARSEILLES, THE**
(1959, Brit.) Dial/RFD bw (GB: SEVEN THUNDERS)

Stephen Boyd *(Dave)*, James Robertson Justice *(Dr. Martout)*, Kathleen Harrison *(Mme. Abou)*, Tony Wright *(Jim)*, Anna Gaylor *(Lise)*, Eugene Deckers *(Emile Blanchard)*, Rosalie Crutchley *(Therese Blanchard)*, Katherine Kath *(Mme. Parfait)*, James Kenney *(Eric Triebel)*, Anton Diffring *(Col. Trautman)*, Martin Miller *(Schlip)*, George Coulouris *(Bourdin)*, Carl Duering *(Major Grautner)*, Edric Connor *(Abou)*.

Prisoners of war escape and are aided by Justice, ostensibly a kind-hearted physician, but, as the POWs later prove, really a merciless mass poisoner who has been murdering those wanted by the Nazis and stealing their goods. A loosely drawn portrait of real-life French mass killer Marcel Petiot which offers a thin script and unimpressive production techniques.

p, Daniel M. Angel; d, Hugo Fregonese; w, John Baines (based on the novel by Rupert Croft-Cooke); m, Anthony Hopkins; ph, Wilkie Cooper.

Horror/War **(PR:C MPAA:NR)**

BEAT GENERATION, THE*(1959) 95m MGM bw (AKA: THIS REBEL AGE)

Steve Cochran *(Dave Culloran)*, Mamie Van Doren *(Georgia Altera)*, Ray Danton *(Stan Hess)*, Fay Spain *(Francee Culloran)*, Louis Armstrong *(Himself)*, Maggie Hayes *(Joyce Freenfield)*, Jackie Coogan *(Jake Baron)*, Jim Mitchum *(Art Jester)*, Cathy Crosby *(The Singer)*, Ray Anthony *(Harry Altera)*, Dick Contino *(Singing Beatnik)*, Irish McCalla *(Marie Baron)*, Vampira *(Poetess)*, Billy Daniels *(Dr. Elcott)*, Maxie Rosenbloom *(Wrestling Beatnik)*, Charles Chaplin Jr. *(Lover Boy)*.

THE BEAT GENERATION is little more than a title that some executive thought would get the patrons away from the TV sets and into the theatre. Cochran is a cop chasing Danton, a rapist of married women. There is little difference between hero and heavy because Cochran is a rat when he deals with the victims. Danton eventually rapes Cochran's wife, Fay Spain, and when she learns she's pregnant, she doesn't know by whom! Eventually, Cochran gets Danton and sees, through him, the folly of his own misanthropic attitude. Small parts are cast well. Slapsie Maxie Rosenbloom, former light-heavyweight champ, is funny as a dumb wrestler.

p, Albert Zugsmith; d, Charles Haas, w, Richard Matheson, Louis Meltzer; Walter H. Castle (CinemaScope); ed, Ben Lewis; cos, Kitty Mager; ch, Hamil Petrof; m/l, Louis Armstrong, Albert Glasser, Walter Kent, Tom Walston, Meltzer.

Crime Drama **(PR:C MPAA:NR)**

"BEAT" GIRL (SEE: WILD FOR KICKS, 1962, Brit.)

BEAT THE BAND* (1947) 67m RKO bw

Frances Langford *(Ann)*, Ralph Edwards *(Eddie)*, Phillip Terry *(Damon)*, June Clayworth *(Willow)*, Mabel Paige *(Mrs. Peters)*, Andrew Tombes *(Professor)*, Donald MacBride *(Duff)*, Mira McKinney *(Mrs. Rogers)*, Harry Harvey *(Mr. Rogers)*, Grady Sutton *(Harold)*.

Country girl arrives in a big city to take operatic lessons and falls into the hands of a bandleader who is after her money. The legendary Gene Krupa band belts out some hot numbers in this one, and they are worth the price of admission. Songs include: "I'm In Love," "Kissin' Well," "I've Got My Fingers Crossed," "Beat the Band" (Mort Greene, Leigh Harline).

p, Michel Kraike; d, John H. Auer; w, Lawrence Kibble (based on a play by George Abbott); ph, Frank Redman; ed, Samuel E. Beetley.

Musical/Comedy **(PR:A MPAA:NR)**

BEAT THE DEVIL**** (1953) 100m Romulus-Santana/UA bw

Humphrey Bogart *(Billy Dannreuther)*, Gina Lollobrigida *(Maria Dannreuther)*, Jennifer Jones *(Gwendolyn Chelm)*, Robert Morley *(Peterson)*, Peter Lorre *(O'Hara)*, Edward Underdown *(Harry Chelm)*, Ivor Barnard *(Maj. Ross)*, Marco Tulli *(Ravello)*, Marion Perroni *(Purser)*, Alex Pochet *(Hotel Manager)*, Aldo Silviani *(Charles)*, Guilio Donnini, Saro Urzi, Juan De Landa, Manuel Serano, Mimo Peli.

A screwball, wacky comedy-drama that is played as straight as MACBETH and is therefore funnier than any movie in the past few years. Five desperate and disparate men (Bogart, Lorre, Morley, Barnard and Tulli) are out to garner control over land in East Africa which they believe contains a rich uranium ore lode. Their scuzzy steamer is in port in Italy. Bogart is married to Gina (an odd choice for the role but she proves to be more than adept at the straight-faced comedy) and the other four are their "business associates." Bogart and Gina meet another couple, Jones and Underdown. She's in a blonde wig and off-the-wall, he's a prig-and-a-half at first glance but he is, in reality, a phony peer. Jones rattles on about her hubby's uranium holdings, all lies. The "associates" think they are being gulled by Bogart when it appears that Bogie is after Jones and Gina is hot for Underdown. The boat leaves for Africa, then blows up and seven survivors make it to shore and are taken in by a hostile group of Arabs. Their lives are saved when Bogart manages to charm the evil Arab police chief by promising the man an opportunity to meet his idol, Rita Hayworth. Underdown is supposed to have drowned and this causes Jones, a pathological liar, to tell the truth. The four villains are taken in by the Italian police, then Jones gets a telegram from her still-alive husband and is delighted to learn that Underdown made it to Africa and acquired the uranium-rich land the others yearned for. If all the aforementioned sounds like a hodge-podge, you're right. But it is such wonderful nonsense that there isn't a moment when the picture doesn't take a left turn when you expect it to turn right. A cult film that was *not* a success the first time around, BEAT THE DEVIL is a parody of THE MALTESE FALCON, THE

TREASURE OF THE SIERRA MADRE and KEY LARGO; all Huston films. A sheer delight.

d, John Huston; w, Huston, Truman Capote (based on the novel by James Helvick); ph, Oswald Morris; m, Franco Mannino; ed, Ralph Kemplin; art d, Wilfred Shingleton; md, Lambert Williamson.

Comedy/Drama   **(PR:A MPAA:NR)**

BEATNIKS, THE*   (1960) 78m Barjul bw

Tony Travis, Peter Breck, Karen Kadler, Joyce Terry, Charles Delaney.

A rip-off of THE BEAT GENERATION (which was terrible to begin with), this movie claims to reveal the dark secrets of the high-living beatniks (a so-called generation that was no more than a handful of drugged-out, failed poets and half-baked novelists with no conception of literature, life or themselves). The story is banal at best. Travis is heard singing along with a juke box tune by an agent who promises to make him a big-time star, but these fanciful ambitions are destroyed when his buddy, Breck, a certifiable lunatic, commits murder. A waste of time as was the whole moronic Beat Movement.

p, Ron Miller; d, Paul Frees; w, Arthur Julian, Frees.

Drama   **(PR:O MPAA:NR)**

BEAU BANDIT*   (1930) 71m RKO bw

Rod La Rocque (Montero), Mitchell Lewis (Coloso), Doris Kenyon (Helen), Charles B. Middleton (Perkins), George Duryea [Tom Keene] (Howard), Walter Long (Bobcat), Jim Donlan (Buck).

Wealthy cowboy suitor hires a notorious bandit to rub out his rival for the girl he loves. Bandit decides to go to work for the girl instead. Not a bad choice in an otherwise bad movie.

p, William LeBaron; d, Lambert Hillyer; w, Wallace Smith; ph, Jack MacKenzie; ed, Archie F. Marshek; art d, Max Ree.

Western   **(PR:A MPAA:NR)**

BEAU BRUMMELL*   (1954) 111m MGM c

Stewart Granger (Beau Brummell), Elizabeth Taylor (Lady Patricia), Peter Ustinov (Prince of Wales), Robert Morley (King George III), James Donald (Lord Edwin Mercer), James Hayter (Mortimer), Rosemary Harris (Mrs. Fitzherbert), Paul Rogers (William Pitt), Noel Willman (Lord Byron), Peter Dyneley (Midget), Charles Carson (Sir Geoffrey Baker), Ernest Clark (Doctor Warren), Peter Bull (Mr. Fox), Mark Dignam (Mr. Burke), Desmond Roberts (Colonel), David Horne (Thurlow), Ralph Truman (Sir Ralph Sidley), Elwyn Brook-Jones (Mr. Tupp), George De Warfaz (Doctor Dubois), Henry Oscar (Dr. Willis), Harold Kasket (Mayor).

Lavish remake of the 1924 silent starring John Barrymore, this one has Granger in the role of the audacious rags-to-riches dandy who becomes the chief adviser to the Prince of Wales, played to the pleasure-seeking hilt by Ustinov. Granger rises from poverty and, using borrowed money, gambling winnings, and the help of powerful friends met at private London casinos, meets Ustinov and quickly ingratiates himself to the future king (George IV). He also enamors blue-blood Taylor, who falls in love with him. When he finally confronts Ustinov with some truthful if indiscreet statements, Granger is banished. His pride will not let him seek help from his friends nor Taylor, and he dies in poverty in France, but not before king Ustinov visits him on his deathbed. Taylor's acting, despite her ravishing beauty, is an embarrassment, but the film is redeemed by Granger's sharply timed panache and bravado. The cinematography, sets, and costuming for this period chronicle of George Bryan Brummel are outstanding. Shot on location in England's lush countryside, many of the interior shots were taken inside a perfectly intact 15th-century mansion, Ockwell Manor, located near Windsor Castle.

p, Sam Zimbalist; d, Curtis Bernhardt; w, Karl Tunberg (based on the play by Clyde Fitch); ph, Oswald Morris (Eastmancolor); m, Richard Addinsell; ed, Frank Clarke; art d, Alfred Junge; cos, Elizabeth Haffenden.

Historical Drama   **(PR:A MPAA:NR)**

BEAU GESTE***   (1939) 114m PAR bw

Gary Cooper (Beau Geste), Ray Milland (John Geste), Robert Preston (Digby Geste), Brian Donlevy (Sgt. Markoff), Susan Hayward (Isobel Rivers), J. Carrol Naish (Rasinoff), Albert Dekker (Schwartz), Broderick Crawford (Hank Miller), Charles Barton (Buddy McMonigal), James Stephenson (Maj. Henri de Beaujolais), Heather Thatcher (Lady Patricia Brandon), G. P. Huntley, Jr. (Augustus Brandon), James Burke (Lt. Dufour), Henry Brandon (Renouf), Arthur Aylesworth (Renault), Harry Woods (Renoir), Harold Huber (Voisin), Stanley Andrews (Maris), Donald O'Connor (Beau as a Child), Billy Cook (John as a Child), Martin Spellman (Digby as a Child), David Holt (Augustus as a Child), Ann Gillis (Isobel as a Child), Harvey Stephens (Lt. Martin), Barry Macollum (Krenke), Ronnie Rondell (Bugler), Frank Dawson (Burdon, the Butler), George Chandler (Cordier), Duke Green (Glock), Thomas Jackson (Colonel in Recruiting Office), Jerome Storm (Sergeant Major), Joseph Whitehead (Sergeant), Harry Worth, Nestor Paiva (Corporals), George Regas, Francis McDonald (Arab Scouts), Carl Voss, Joe Bernard, Robert Perry, Larry Lawson, Henry Sylvester, Joseph William Cody (Legionnaires), Joe Colling (Trumpeter O. Leo), Gladys Jeans (Girl in Port Said Cafe).

Superb adventure tale loaded with drama, action and mystery as Cooper embodies the title role with quiet magnificence. The film opens with a relief column of Legionnaires crossing the desert dunes to Fort Zinderneuf, which greets the newcomers with eerie silence. Commander Stephenson fires a signal shot and is answered by a bullet that kicks up the sand in front of the column. A bugler is sent to investigate and finds all inside the fort dead, noticing a dead Legionnaire and a sergeant also dead on the parapet, the sergeant's hand containing a confession that he has stolen a fabulous gem called "The Blue Water." When the column enters the

fort, the bodies of these two men have disappeared. Next the troops hear shots outside the fort and pursue what they think are tribal invaders. The fort suddenly erupts into flames, setting off the arsenal which destroys Zinderneuf. In a 15-year flashback we see three boys, the Geste brothers, Beau enacted by an ebullient O'Connor, all playing inside a great English mansion, then at a pond where they undergo the ceremony of giving one of their "deceased" toy sailors a "Viking Funeral," sending the sailor off with a toy dog at its feet on a little paper boat into the pond after setting it on fire; it burns and sinks. The boys are cared for by kindly Thatcher, an impoverished blueblood who is so desperate to give the orphaned brothers a good home (along with another child, Gillis), that she secretly sells the treasured family jewel, "The Blue Water," to raise the necessary funds. O'Connor witnesses the transaction from hiding and watches Thatcher replace the gem with a fake. Years later, with the boys grown into Cooper, Milland, and Preston, and the little girl bloomed into Hayward, the lord of the manor, Huntley, appears seeking the great sapphire. To prevent Thatcher from having to admit her secret transaction, Cooper steals the phony gem, leaves a note for his brothers admitting the theft, and joins the Foreign Legion. Preston and Milland follow, meeting Cooper at a training post where informer and thief Naish (in one of his most repugnant roles) learns that the brothers possess a great jewel. He tells the crafty Donlevy, playing the sadistic Sgt. Markov, who arranges for the brothers to be separated, taking Milland and Cooper with him and a company of troopers to relieve desolate Fort Zinderneuf, and sending Preston, now a bugler, to another post, Fort Tokotu. At Zinderneuf, the youthful lieutenant in charge dies of illness and the maniacal Donlevy takes over, creating a hellish nightmare for his troops who plan a mutiny which is suppressed by Donlevy. Since Cooper and Milland had refused to take part in the overthrow, Donlevy spares them punishment but brutally orders them to execute the mutineers. They refuse and he is about to shoot them when a desert tribe attacks the fort. The Legionnaires rush to the battlements and die at their posts. To make it appear that his men are still alive, Donlevy braces their bodies to the wall with rifles affixed with bayonets, sending his least favorite troopers to the tower as lookouts where they will be exposed and meet certain death (including his insidious informant Naish). With almost all the men dead, Donlevy shoots Cooper, then frantically searches his body for the jewel but is stopped by Milland who threatens him. Donlevy is about to kill Milland but Cooper comes to life and trips him up while Milland drives a bayonet into the tryant's chest. Cooper dies in Milland's arms, giving him the two notes he has written, one to be placed in Donlevy's hand, the other to be given to Thatcher in England. Milland sees the relief column arrive and fires a warning shot. Remembering the boyhood promises he and his brothers made to each other—that they would give each other noble "Viking Funerals"—Milland puts Cooper's body in the barracks with Donlevy's corpse nearby, remarking "there is a dog at your feet," then sets the fort on fire and slips over a wall to wait behind a remote sand dune. The bugler sent by the relief column to investigate is Preston, who also joins his brother Milland. As they make their way back to England, Preston dies heroically at the hands of tribesmen. Milland returns to the ancestral manor and the girl he loves, Hayward. Thatcher reads Cooper's note, tearfully realizing his chivalric sacrifice, saying, "Beau Geste—no one was better named!" Cooper's great performance is backed up solidly by Milland and Preston while Hayward has only a few brief appearances as the love interest and doesn't get a chance to act. Donlevy almost steals every scene he's in with a squinty-eyed, snarling performance that will scare the blazes out of any viewer, while Naish's hyena-like caricature of Rasinoff is unforgettable. Great support comes from veteran heavies Dekker, Woods, and Huber, enacting the mutinous Legionnaires. Crawford and Barton are laugh reliefs as sidekicks to the Gestes. The French Foreign Legion, founded in 1831 as a shock troop unit to quell colonial uprisings, especially in French North Africa, was open to all nationalities; enlistees were asked no questions, a policy that drew to its ranks a host of colorful and mysterious individuals escaping from the law in other lands, fleeing family problems (as was the case with Beau Geste), or those merely seeking harrowing adventure. P. C. Wren, the author of this captivating story, was in the latter group, an Oxford University graduate who sailed on four-masters, labored in mines, and had been a cavalryman in the British Army before joining the Legion. He served and was wounded while in the Indian Army during WW I; mustered out as an invalided major, Wren spent his time penning the Geste saga which became a world-wide best-seller when published and was made into a great silent movie by Paramount in 1926 with Ronald Coleman as Beau, Ralph Forbes as John and Neil Hamilton as Digby. When Wellman was brought in to remake the silent version he was instructed to follow the original almost to the letter which he did, even using the same locale, the spreading desert dunes of Yuma, Arizona, where a new Fort Zinderneuf was completely rebuilt. Paramount executives thought it would be impressive to run the first reel of the silent version before showing the 1939 remake to reviewers in a formal screening, to show what sound could do to improve a classic. It was a scheme that almost blew up in their faces; one reviewer liked the silent version better and said so, but most agreed that the Wellman remake was superior and it is, also standing head and shoulders in direction, acting and production values above the third version made in 1966. The 1939 BEAU GESTE deservedly earned Oscar nominations for Donlevy and Hans Dreier and Robert Odell for Art Direction. This was Cooper's last film under his Paramount contract, after which he became a free agent, making THE REAL GLORY and the unforgettable THE WESTERNER for Samuel Goldwyn. He was only three years away from his first Academy-Award-winning role in the stirring SERGEANT YORK.

p&d, William A. Wellman; w, Robert Carson (based on the novel by Percival Christopher Wren); ph, Theodor Sparkuhl, Archie Stout; m, Alfred Neeman; ed, Thomas Scott; art d, Hans Dreier, Robert Odell; tech ad, Louis Van Der Ecker.

Adventure   **(PR:A MPAA:NR)**

BEAU GESTE*   (1966) 105m UNIV c

Guy Stockwell (Beau), Doug McClure (John), Leslie Nielsen (DeRuse), Telly Savalas (Dagineau), David Mauro (Boldini), Robert Wolders (Fouchet), Leo

Gordon (*Kraus*), Michael Constantine (*Rostov*), Malachi Throne (*Kerjacki*), Joe De Santis (*Beaujolais*), X Brands (*Vallejo*), Michael Carr (*Sergeant*), George Keymas (*Platoon Sgt.*), Patrick Whyte (*Surgeon*), Ted Jacques (*Captain*), Jeff Nelson, David Gross, Hal Hooper, Chuck Wood, Duane Grey, Vic Lundin (*Legionnaires*), Ava Zamora (*Dancer*).

You may well ask, why remake BEAU GESTE when it was so good the first two times around? Well, Universal had the rights and some hot TV actors and thought they could sneak it past an unsuspecting public, so they did. Wonder of wonders, this third version was not nearly as dismal as you might think. Further, it was not anywhere as disgusting as the comedy version by Marty Feldman, THE LAST REMAKE OF BEAU GESTE (1977). In Ronald Colman's version (1926) and the more popular Gary Cooper edition in 1939, there were three Geste brothers. This time there are only two and they are Americans. Stockwell and McClure are in the Foreign Legion, with Stockwell having taken responsibilitiy for a crime he didn't commit. Once there, they incur the wrath of the sadistic Savalas (nowhere near as memorable as Brian Donlevy or even Noah Beery in the 1926 film). Heyes wrote and directed with a strong hand and didn't make the mistake of thinking he could helm a better picture than Wellman's 1939 movie, so he went about doing a *different* picture. Emphases were changed and a great deal of care was taken in secondary casting. Gordon, Constantine and Throne are excellent and Wolders, whom everyone thought would be a star, does well as a daydreaming Frenchman. (Wolders married Merle Oberon and lived the life we all dream of.) Good entertainment from start to finish.

p, Walter Seltzer; d&w, Douglas Heyes (based on the novel by Percival Christopher Wren); ph, Bud Thackery (Technicolor); m, Hans J. Salter; ed, Russell F. Schoengarth; art d, Alexander Golitzen.

Adventure   **(PR:A   MPAA:NR)**

BEAU IDEAL*¹/₂   (1931) 82m RKO bw

Frank McCormack (*Carl Neyer*), Ralph Forbes (*John Geste*), Lester Vail (*Otis Madison*), Otto Matieson (*Jacob Levine*), Don Alvarado (*Ramon Gonzales*), Bernard Siegel (*Ivan Radinoff*), Irene Rich (*Lady Brandon*), Myrtle Stedman (*Mrs. Frank Madison*), Loretta Young (*Isobel Brandon*), John M. St. Polls (*Judge Advocate*), Joseph de Stefani (*Prosecuting Attorney*), Paul McAllister (*Sergeant Frederic*), Hale Hamilton (*Major Labaudy*), George Rigas (*The Emir*), Leni Stengel (*Zuleika*).

Ralph Forbes, who played a leading role in the 1926 silent BEAU GESTE, returns in the same role in this sequel. This is the second sequel after the silent sequel BEAU SABRE based on the original 1926 silent movie, and is the first of the three to use sound. Desert battles, light romance, but don't go charging out to get a copy of the print. The film lost $350,000 and is considered one of the poorest RKO productions of the 1930s.

d, Herbert Brenon; w, Elizabeth Meehan; ph, J. Roy Hunt.

Adventure   **(PR:A   MPAA:NR)**

BEAU JAMES**¹/₂   (1957) 105m PAR c

Bob Hope (*Jimmy Walker*), Vera Miles (*Betty Compton*), Paul Douglas (*Chris Nolan*), Alexis Smith (*Allie Walker*), Darren McGavin (*Charley Hand*), Joe Mantell (*Bernie Williams*), Horace McMahon (*Prosecutor*), Richard Shannon (*Dick Jackson*), Willis Bouchey (*Arthur Julian*), Sid Melton (*Sid Nash*), George Jessel (*Himself*), Walter Catlett (*Al Smith*).

A real let-down, considering the story material available from the most colorful mayor New York City ever had, the singing, dancing, and quipping James J. Walker. Hope is shown rising from political obscurity with the mighty arm of Tammany pushing him upward (in the form of bulky Douglas) until he becomes Mayor of Gotham, a job he never takes seriously, allowing corrupt minions and a police force on the take to loot the city coffers and collect bribes in the millions. Most of the dull plot is consumed with Walker's love affair with dancer Betty Compton who went on, after dumping Walker, to an unspectacular film career, angrily played by a furrow-browed, carping Miles, battling for her man with estranged wife Smith, who seems to be walking about in a stupor. Although the production values are high and the glittering aura of the Roaring Twenties comes through loud and clear, Hope cannot deal with the dramatics, and merely wisecracks his way through a role he caricaturizes and at times almost reduces to burlesque. He does deliver Walker's own famous line about three things a man must do in life, "be born, die, and testify," relating to his testimony before the famous Seabury investigators who brought down the corrupt Walker regime. Well, Jimmy did make sure that New Yorkers never paid more than a nickel for a subway ride. The price is a lot higher to watch this one.

p, Jack Rose; d, Melville Shavelson; w, Rose, Shavelson (based on the biography of Walker by Gene Fowler); ph, John F. Warren (VistaVision, Technicolor); m, Joseph J. Lilley; ed, Floyd Knudtson; ch, Jack Baker.

Biography   **(PR:A   MPAA:NR)**

BEAU PERE*   (1981, Fr.) 120m New Line c

Patrick Dewaere (*Remi*), Ariel Besse (*Marion*), Maurice Ronet (*Charly*), Nicole Garcia (*Martine*), Nathalie Baye (*Charlotte*), Maurice Risch (*Nicolas*), Genevieve (*Simone*), Macha Meril (*Birthday Hostess*), Pierre Lerumeur (*Pediatrician*), Yves Gasc (*Landlord*), Rose Thierry (*Landlord's Wife*), Henri-Jacques Huet (*Restaurant Manager*), Michel Berto (*Professor*), Catherine Alcover (*Emergency Doctor*).

Distasteful, overlong film where the widowed Dewaere is lusted after and finally seduced by his 14-year-old daughter, Besse, presenting the offensive cliche of the embryonic nymph of insatiable appetite. Poor production standards and a miserable script pretentiously affecting sensitivity to excuse its real offering makes this one a sham.

p, Alain Sarde; d&w, Bertrand Blier; ph, Sacha Vierny; m, Philippe Sarde; ed, Claudine Merlin; art d, Theobald Meurisse; cos, Michele Cerf.

Drama   **Cas.**   **(PR:O   MPAA:NR)**

BEAUTIFUL ADVENTURE*   (1932, Ger.) 87m UFA bw

Alfred Abel (*Graf d'Eguzon*), Ida Wuest (*Graefin d'Eguzon*), Wolf Albach-Retty (*Andre d'Eguzon*), Kaethe Haack (*Jeantine*), Kaethe von-Nagy (*Helene de Trevillac*), Adele Sandrock (*Frau de Trevillac*), Otto Wallburg (*Valentin le Barroyer*), Hilde Hildebrand (*Frau de Serignan*), Julius Falkenstein (*Herr Chartrain*), Gertrid Wolle (*Frau Chartrain*), Kurt Vespermann (*Herr Desmigneres*), Blandine Ebinger (*Frau Desmigneres*), Julius E. Herrmann (*Herr Dubois*), Ferdinand Hart (*Herr Durand*), Lydia Pollman (*Jeanne*).

Light yarn about a young girl who balks at an arranged marriage to a fat man. Instead, she takes off with her young lover. Remake of a popular German film based on a French stage play. Poorly received here.

p, Guenther Stapenhorst; d, Reinhold Schuenzel; w, Schuenzel, Emerich Pressburger (based on play by Etienne Rey and Robert de Flers); ph, Fritz Arno Wagner, Robert Baberske.

Romance   **(PR:A   MPAA:NR)**

BEAUTIFUL BLONDE FROM BASHFUL BEND, THE *   (1949) 76m FOX c

Betty Grable (*Freddie*), Cesar Romero (*Blackie Jobero*), Rudy Vallee (*Charles Hingleman*), Olga San Juan (*Conchita*), Sterling Holloway (*Basserman Boy*), Hugh Herbert (*Doctor*), El Brendel (*Mr. Jorgenson*), Porter Hall (*Judge O'Toole*), Pati Behrs (*Roulette*), Margaret Hamilton (*Mrs. O'Toole*), Danny Jackson (*Basserman Boy*), Emory Parnell (*Mr. Hingleman*), Alan Bridge (*Sheriff*), Chris-Pin Martin (*Joe*), J. Farrell McDonald (*Sheriff Sweetzer*), Richard Hale (*Mr. Basserman*), Georgia Caine (*Mrs. Hingleman*), Esther Howard (*Mrs. Smidlap*), Harry Hayden (*Conductor*), Chester Conklin (*Messenger Boy*), Mary Monica McDonald (*Freddie, Age 6*), Torben Meyer (*Dr. Schultz*), Dewey Robinson (*Bartender*), Richard Kean (*Dr. Smidlap*), Harry Tyler (*Station Agent*), Dudley Dickerson (*Pullman Porter*), Russell Simpson (*Grandpa*).

Even a fair-to-middling Sturges production is better than most comedies by other writer/directors, and in THE BEAUTIFUL BLONDE FROM BASHFUL BEND, Preston attempts to meld a western to a Feydeau farce. He misfires a bit but when he hits, cheeks hurt from laughing. Grable (in a take-off on Annie Oakley) is a markswoman whose boy friend, Romero, has been catting around. She takes a shot at him and hits a judge (Hall) in error. A warrant goes out for her arrest and she flees to another town where she takes a job as a schoolmarm and convinces everyone that she is the sweet, virginal type (quite a bit different from the hell-raiser in the first reel). Vallee is the town's richest citizen, mostly because he owns a gold mine, so Betty goes after him and he falls in love with her. Just when all seems to be going swell for Betty, there's a gun battle, a kidnaping, and a host of other complications that lead to a trial. Betty's in court, winds up grabbing a gun, and sending another bullet in the direction of the judge's rear end. The movie actually plays better than it sounds. It's burlesque, with none of the subtleties of UNFAITHFULLY YOURS or the Capra-like hope of SULLIVAN'S TRAVELS, but it does get funny in places and Betty's charms are shown to their full advantage. This was Sturges' last movie in the U.S. Some years later he wrote and directed a dreadful potboiler in France, THE DIARY OF MAJOR THOMPSON.

p,d&w, Preston Sturges (based on a story by Earl Felton); ph, Harry Jackson (Technicolor); m, Cyril Mockridge; ed, Robert Fritch.

Comedy   **(PR:A   MPAA:NR)**

BEAUTIFUL BUT BROKE*¹/₂   (1944) 74m COL bw

Joan Davis (*Dottie*), John Hubbard (*Bill Drake*), Jane Frazee (*Sally Richards*), Judy Clark (*Sue Ford*), Bob Haymes (*Jack Foster*), Danny Mummert (*Rollo*), Byron Foulger (*Maxwell McKay*), George McKay (*Station Master*), Ferris Taylor (*Mayor*), Isabel Withers (*Mrs. Grayson*), John Eldredge (*Waldo Main*), Grace Hayle (*Birdie Benson*), John Dilson (*Putnam*), Joe King (*Mr. Martin*), Emmett Vogan (*Hotel Manager*).

Airwaves comic Joan Davis turns to the medium of the motion picture in this musical comedy about a lady booking agent who has her troubles with an all-female band. Tunes include: "Pistol Packin' Mama" (Al Dexter), "Just Another Blues" (Jimmy Paul, Dick Charles, Larry Marks), "Shoo-Shoo Baby" (Phil Moore), "Mama, I Want to Make Rhythm" (Walter Kent, Richard Byron, Richard Jerome), "Mr. Jive Has Gone To War" (L. Wolfe Gilbert, Ben Oakland), "Take the Door to the Left" (James Cavanaugh, Walter G. Samuels), and "We're Keeping It Private" (Mort Greene, Walter Donaldson).

p, Irving Briskin; d, Charles Barton; w, Monte Brice; ph, L. W. O'Connell; md, M. W. Stoloff; ed, Richard Fantl; art d, Lionel Banks.

Musical Comedy   **(PR:A   MPAA:NR)**

BEAUTIFUL BUT DEADLY   (SEE: DON IS DEAD, THE, 1973)

BEAUTIFUL CHEAT, THE*¹/₂   (1946) 59m UNIV bw

Bonita Granville (*Alice*), Noah Beery, Jr. (*Prof. Haven*), Margaret Irving (*Olympia*), Irene Ryan (*Miss Kent*), Carol Hughes (*Dolly*), Tom Dillon (*Cassidy*), Lester Matthews (*Harley*), Edward Fielding (*Dr. Pennypacker*), Tommy Bond (*Jimmy*), Milburn Stone (*Lucius Haven*), Edward Gargan (*Blue Moon Manager*), Margaret Irving (*Olympia Haven*), Sarah Selby (*Athena Haven*), Eddy Chandler, Lee Phelps (*Cops*).

Sociologist undertakes study of juvenile deliquents for publisher and becomes paternally involved with an attractive young secretary at a reform school. Bright little comedy with pleasant music.

p&d, Charles Barton; w, Ben Markson; ph, Woody Bredell; ed, Ray Snyder.

Comedy   (PR:A MPAA:NR)

BEAUTIFUL PRISONER, THE*

(1983, Fr.) 88m Argos Films c (LA BELLE CAPTIVE)

Daniel Mesguich (*Walter*), Cyrielle (*Sara*), Gabrielle Lazure (*Marie-Ange*), Daniel Emilfork (*Inspector Francis*), Roland Dubillard (*Van de Reeves*), Francois Chaumette (*Dr. Morgentodt*).

Alain Robbe-Grillet, who wrote the script for LAST YEAR AT MARIENBAD as well as the screenplays and direction of L'IMMORTELLE and TRANS-EUROPE EXPRESS, is responsible for this allegorical melange filled with symbolism, dream-sequences and fantasy and . . . are you asleep yet? With music by Shubert and Duke Ellington (can you imagine those two jamming together?), Robbe-Grillet takes us into Walter's (Daniel Mesguich) mind for a roller-coaster ride. He and his wife Sara (Cyrielle) move into a new abode and he promptly falls in love with a mysterious young woman who vanishes, then reappears. He subsequently learns that she died seven years ago. This is told to him by her father, a physician who is not satisfied with making sick people well; he want to make dead people communicate. (Why can't we let the dead sleep in peace instead of continuously attempting to contact them and find out what's beyond the pale?) Anyhow, it's a little of this and a little of that and I'm sure the intellectuals will go for our throats and say "You didn't understand the underlying truth, the images, the ultimate and deep meaning of the movie." They're right. We didn't. And you may not either.

p, Bernard Bouix; d, Alain Robbe-Grillet; w, Robbe-Grillet, Framl Verpillat; ph, Henri Alekan; ed, Bob Wade; prod d, Aime Deude; cos, Piet Bolscher.

Fantasy   (PR:C MPAA:NR)

BEAUTIFUL STRANGER**

(1954, Brit.) 89m BL bw (AKA: TWIST OF FATE)

Ginger Rogers (*Johnny Victor*), Stanley Baker (*Louis Galt*), Herbert Lom (*Emil Landosh*), Jacques Bergerac (*Pierre Clement*), Margaret Rawlings (*Marie Galt*), Eddie Byrne (*Luigi*), Ferdy Mayne (*Chief of Police*).

Rogers is a poor showgirl living in the fabulous villa owned by Baker, her wealthy lover. He promises that his divorce will be final soon and they can wed and live gaudily ever after. She then learns that he has no intention of shedding the first Mrs. Baker. What she doesn't know, however, is that the source of his income comes from forging British gold coins. She meets Bergerac, a struggling French artist; they fall in love and the rest is a few complications followed by smooth sailing. (Ginger and Jacques were married at the time although it's hard to realize how they made it work for the five years it did.) Jacques is almost totally unintelligible and could truly use printed English titles at the bottom of the screen when he speaks English! Twenty years later, Lom was doing the same comic role in the PINK PANTHER films. Rogers was 43 when this was made, a bit long in the tooth to play a starving showgirl. She was also 16 years older than Baker, who was supposed to be her protector. One oddity about the film is that the song was written by Jose Ferrer and Ketti Frings, who wrote the screenplay for such films as ABOUT MRS. LESLIE and COME BACK, LITTLE SHEBA.

p, Maxwell Seton, John R. Sloan; d, David Miller; w, Robert Westerby, Carl Nystrom (based on a story by Rip Van Ronkel, Miller); ph, Ted Scaife; m, Malcolm Arnold; ed, Alan Osbiston; m/l "Love Is A Beautiful Stranger," Jose Ferrer, Ketti Frings.

Crime Drama   (PR:C MPAA:NR)

BEAUTIFUL SWINDLERS, THE**

(1967, Fr./Ital./Jap./Neth.) 90mUlysse Productions/Ellis bw (AKA: WORLD'S GREATEST SWINDLES)

AMSTERDAM: Nicole Karen, Jan Teulings; PARIS: Jean-Pierre Cassel, Catherine Deneuve, Francis Blanche, Sacha Briquet, Jean-Louis Maury. TOKYO: Nie Hama, Ken Mitsuda. NAPLES: Gabriella Giorgelli, Beppe Mannaiuolo, Guido Guiseppone.

Four episodes with tepid stories that are supposed to profile the various kinds of cons who prey on the innocent. In Amsterdam, the best of the lot, directed by Polanski, a young woman convinces a doddering old man to buy her an expensive necklace, promising to return sexual favors. Once she has the necklace she runs away and trades it for a parrot, giving the necklace to an old salt who has no idea how expensive it is. In Paris a sucker buys the Eiffel Tower (a play on the machinations of Victor "The Count" Lustig, who actually sold the Tower *twice* to scrap metal dealers) but is arrested when he attempts to charge visitors a toll. In Naples, prostitutes, to avoid being sent out of the city, marry old men in retirement villages at the urging of their pimp, who believes this will give his girls immunity. The scheme backfires when all the elderly men refuse to let their wives work at night. In the most gruesome of this dubious quartet, a Japanese barmaid in Tokyo serves her elderly escort noodles and then gleefully watches him choke to death on them, later trying to pawn his false teeth which she believes to be platinum; they are worthless and she is arrested for murder. (In native languages; English subtitles.)

p, Pierre Roustang; English titles, Herman G. Weinberg; AMSTERDAM: d, Roman Polanski; w, Polanski, Gerard Brach; ph, Jerzy Lipman; m, Krysztof Komeda; ed, Rita von Royen; PARIS: d, Claude Chabrol; ph, Jean Rabier; m, Pierre Jansen; ed, Jacques Gaillard; NAPLES: d, Ugo Gregoretti; ph, Tonino Delli Colli; m, Piero Umiliani; TOKYO: d, Hiromichi Horikawa; ph, Asakazu Nakai; m, Keitaro Miho.

Drama/Comedy   (PR:O MPAA:NR)

BEAUTY AND THE BANDIT*

(1946) 77m MON bw

Gilbert Roland, Martin Garralaga, Frank Yaconelli, Ramsay Ames, Vida Aldana, George J. Lewis, William Gould, Dimas Sotello, Felipe Turch, Glenn Strange, Alex Montoya.

A poor outing for one of Monogram's Cisco Kid series, this one has Roland as the Mexican Robin Hood saving the deed to the old homestead and earning the love of the ranch lass and owner. The action is tame and the story and dialog instantly forgettable.

p, Scott R. Dunlap; d, William Nigh; w, Charles Belden.

Western   (PR:A MPAA:NR)

BEAUTY AND THE BARGE*½

(1937, Brit.) 71m Twickenham/Wardour bw

Gordon Harker (*Capt. Barley*), Judy Gunn (*Ethel Smedley*), Jack Hawkins (*Lt. Seton Boyne*), George Carney (*Tom Codd*), Margaret Rutherford (*Mrs. Baldwin*), Ronald Shiner (*Augustus*), Michael Shepley (*Herbert Manners*), Margaret Yarde (*Mrs. Porton*), Sebastian Smith (*Maj. Smedley*), Margaret Scudamore (*Mrs. Smedley*), Anne Wemys (*Lucy Dallas*).

The daughter of a British Army major runs away and is taken in by a bargeman who adopts her. She is won back into her father's camp by one of his officers who pretends to be a sailor on the barge and with whom she falls in love. Contrived piece of piffle.

p, Julius Hagen; d, Henry Edwards; w, H. Fowler Mear (based on the play by W. W. Jacobs); ph, Sydney Blythe, William Luff.

Comedy   (PR:A MPAA:NR)

BEAUTY AND THE BEAST*****

(1947, Fr.) 90m Discina International/Lopert Films bw (LA BELLE ET LAETE)

Jean Marais (*Avenant/The Beast/The Prince*), Josette Day (*Beauty*), Marcel Andre (*The Merchant*), Mila Parely (*Adelaide*), Nane Germon (*Felice*), Michel Auclair (*Ludovic*).

Cocteau's fantasy, a visual masterpiece so overwhelming that it is often difficult to follow the simple tale. The merchant father (Andre) is adored by his daughter Beauty (Day) who slaves for him and her sisters. When the father accidentally comes upon a deserted castle and picks a rose, he is confronted by a hideous beast (Marais) adorned in the finery of a prince. The Beast informs the merchant that he must die for violating his rose garden, but he allows the terrified man to return home to bid his family farewell. When the merchant explains his terrible fate to Day she volunteers to take his place and fearlessly goes to the mysterious castle. Instead of slaying her, Marais falls hopelessly in love with her, proposing to her nightly, only to be refused. She is in love with a handsome prince (also Marais). Day is allowed to return home to visit her dying father and while there she realizes that she loves the Beast; as a measure of trust he has given her the key to his treasure room and tells her that if she does not return to him at the required hour he will perish of grief. Day's wicked sisters steal the key to the treasure room, giving it to Day's betrothed who, full of greed, races off to the castle. She is late returning to the Beast, delayed while looking for the key. When she does return she finds the Beast dying of grief. Her prince breaks into the treasure room where a statue of Diana comes to life and sends an arrow into him. He dies and turns into the hideous Beast, while the Beast turns into the handsome prince, united in a heavenly atmosphere with Day. The whole surrealistic experience marvels the senses with camerawork that has seldom been equalled. The sets are both awesome and fascinating, the decor of the castle patterned after illustrations by Gustave Dore. Many of the castle's exteriors were shot at the Chateau de Raray outside Senlis, Cocteau taking visual advantage of the estate's strange animal statuary which dots the landscape, and the exquisite Rochecorbon manor house in Ille-et-Vilaine. The brilliant poet suffered through a production hampered by limited funds, accidents, and even his own severe illness where the company had to shut down until he was released from the hospital. Cocteau wrote an extraordinary account about his first film (*Beauty and the Beast, Diary of a Film*) where he admits to urging composer Auric to provide a score that broke all the rules: "At my request, Georges Auric has not kept (the musical score) to the rhythm of the film but cut across it so that when film and music come together it seems as though by the grace of God." He drove his cinematographer to do the impossible: "People have decided once and for all that fuzziness (soft or out-of-focus shots) is poetic. No, since in my eyes poetry is precision, numbers. I'm pushing Alekan in precisely the opposite direction from what fools think is poetic." Art director Berard took Cocteau's astounding ideas and transformed them into wonderful sets, amazing costumes and the Beast's marvelous mask, one that made him almost attractive instead of ugly. BEAUTY AND THE BEAST is a memorable and enduring film, from the first frame to the last.

p, Andre Paulve; d&w, Jean Cocteau (based on the fairy tale by Mme. Leprince de Beaumont); ph, Henri Alekan; m, Georges Auric; ed, Claude Iberia; art d, Christian Berard; makeup, Hagop Arakelian; tech adv, Rene Clement; English titles, Irving Drutman.

Fantasy   **Cas.**   (PR:A MPAA:NR)

BEAUTY AND THE BEAST zero

(1963) 79m UA c

Joyce Taylor (*Lady Althea*), Mark Damon (*Duke Eduardo*), Eduard Franz (*Baron Orsini*), Michael Pate (*Prince Bruno*), Merry Anders (*Princess Sybil*), Dayton Lummis (*Count Roderick*), Walter Burke (*Grimaldi*), Charles Waggenheim, Tom Cound, Herman Rudin, Alexander Lockwood, Meg Wyllie.

Damon is the Beast and Taylor is Beauty in this terrible rip-off of the Cocteau classic, a film that should have stayed in the can or never have been filmed at all. The makeup looks wholly unlike Cocteau's creation, more like that of a chimp in search of a tall tree. Dreadful.

p, Robert E. Kent; d, Edward L. Cahn; w, George Bruce, Orville H. Hampton (based on the fairy tale by Mme. Leprince de Beaumont); ph, Gilbert Warrenton (Technicolor); ed, Robert Carlisle; art d, Franz Bachelin; makeup, Jack P. Pierce.

Fantasy   (PR:C MPAA:NR)

BEAUTY AND THE BOSS*
(1932) 75m WB bw

Marian Marsh (*Susie Sachs*), Warren William (*Baron Von Ullrich*), Charles Butterworth (*Ludwig*), Frederick Kerr (*The Count*), Mary Doran (*Polly*), Lillian Bond (*Girl at Bar*), Polly Walters (*Ludwig's Girl*), Robert Greig (*Chappel*), Yola D'Avril (*Girl in Bath Tub*), Barbara Leonard (*Girl With Dog*).

Young girl lands a job in a Viennese bank as a stenographer and entertains ambitions to marry her wealthy employer. The boss, however, likes to play around so stenog's road to success is a difficult one. Another B movie version of Cinderella.

d, Roy Del Ruth; w, Joseph Jackson (based on the play, "The Church Mouse" by Paul Frank and Ladislaus Fodor); ph, Barney McGill; art d, Anton Grot.

Comedy/Drama (PR:A MPAA:NR)

BEAUTY AND THE DEVIL**1/2
(1952, Fr./Ital.) 8lm Universalie-Enie/Franco-London bw

Michel Simon (*Prof. Faust, Mephisto*), Gerard Philipe (*Henri, Young Faust*), Nicole Besnard (*Marguerite*), Simone Valere (*The Princess*), Carlo Ninchi (*The Prince*), Tullio Carminati (*Diplomat*), Raymond Cordy (*Servant*), Gaston Modot (*Gypsy*), Paolo Stoppa (*Official*).

Solid Faust story where Simon does double duty as the frustrated alchemist and the visitor from Hades who describes himself as a "second-rate devil," one who tempts the wisdom-seeking Faust with a promise of universal knowledge in exchange for his soul. In this version, the scientist does not make the bargain and is only tempted with eternal youth, mistresses, and the power sent on his way. Good production, with Simon in an outstanding performance and good support from Philipe as the young Faust, and Besnard as a startling Marguerite.

p, Salvo D'Angelo; d, Rene Clair; w, Clair, Armand Salacrou; ph, Michel Kelber; m, Roman Vlad; ed, James Cuenet; art d, Leon Barsacq.

Drama (PR:A MPAA:NR)

BEAUTY FOR SALE*1/2
(1933) 85m MGM bw (GB:BEAUTY)

Madge Evans (*Letty*), Alice Brady (*Mrs. Sherwood*), Otto Kruger (*Sherwood*), Una Merkel (*Carol*), May Robson (*Mrs. Merrick*), Phillips Holmes (*Burt Barton*), Eddie Nugent (*Bill*), Hedda Hopper (*Madam Sonia*), Florine McKinney (*Jane*), Isobel Jewell (*Hortense*), Louise Carter (*Mrs. Lawson*), John Roche (*Robert Abbott*), Charles Grapewin (*Gordon*).

A humorous look at some single women who work in a beauty shop and dream about Mr. Right. One of these beauties lucks out and meets the tall, handsome, and wealthy stranger she has been dreaming about while giving shampoos. Some good comedic bits add life to this run-of-the-mill movie.

d, Richard Boleslawski; w, Zelda Sears, Eve Greene (based on the novel *Beauty* by Faith Baldwin); ph, James Wong Howe; ed, Blanche Sewell.

Comedy (PR:A MPAA:NR)

BEAUTY FOR THE ASKING*
(1939) 68m RKO bw

Lucille Ball (*Jean Russell*), Patric Knowles (*Denny Williams*), Donald Woods (*Jeffrey Martin*), Frieda Inescourt (*Flora Barton*), Inez Courtney (*Gwen Morrison*), Leona Maricle (*Eva Harrington*), Frances Mercer (*Patricia Wharton*), Whitney Bourne (*Peggy Ponsby*), Ann Evers (*Lois Peabody*), George Andre Beranger (*Cyril*).

A cosmetic business in New York City is the backdrop for this light story about unrequited love and a marriage for money. A slow-moving yarn with Lucy playing a serious role.

p, B. P. Fineman; d, Glenn Tryon; w, Doris Anderson, Paul Jerrico; ph, Frank Redman; ed, George Crone.

Drama (PR:A MPAA:NR)

BEAUTY JUNGLE, THE**
(1966, Brit.) 114m RANK c (AKA:CONTEST GIRL)

Ian Hendry (*Don Mackenzie*), Janette Scott (*Shirley*), Ronald Fraser (*Walter*), Edmund Purdom (*Carrick*), Jean Claudio (*Armand*), Kay Walsh (*Mrs. Freeman*), Norman Bird (*Freeman*), Juanina Faye (*Elaine*), Tommy Trinder (*Charlie Dorton*), David Weston (*Harry*), Francis Matthews (*Taylor*), Jerry Desmonde (*Organizer*), Peter Ashmore (*Lucius*), Jacqueline Jones (*Jean Watson*), Alizia Gur (*Miss Peru*), Jackie White (*Barbara*), Leila Williams (*Second Chaperone*), Raymond Young (*Globe Organizer*), Marianne Stone (*Typist*), Sylvia Steel (*Janet*), Eve Arden (*Angela*), Jacqueline Wallis (*Julie*), Margaret Nolan (*Caroline*), Nicki Peters (*Cora*).

A pretty stenographer, Scott, climbs the ranks in various beauty queen competitions and makes it to the top—but encounters lots of pitfalls and disillusionment. A penetrating look at "the beauty contest jungle." Good camerawork and score, although much is for the sake of parading flesh.

p&d, Val Guest; w, Robert Muller, Guest; ph, Arthur Grant (Eastmancolor); m, Laurie Johnson; ed, Bill Lenny.

Drama (PR:C MPAA:NR)

BEAUTY ON PARADE*1/2
(1950) 66m COL bw

Robert Hutton (*Gil McRoberts*), Ruth Warrick (*Marian Medford*), Lola Albright (*Kay Woodstock*), John Ridgely (*Jeffrey Woodstock*), Hillary Brooke (*Gloria Barton*), Wally Vernon (*Sam Short*), Jimmy Lloyd (*Johnny Fennell*), Donna Gibson (*Mona Booker*), Frank Sully (*Murph*), Robert C. Hasha (*Walker*).

BEAUTY ON PARADE is a precursor to Michael Ritchie's SMILE in that it, too, follows the inner workings of a beauty pageant. Warrick is the ex-beauty queen who left a chic life to take up the role of housewife. She has champed at the bit ever since and when her gorgeous daughter, Albright, qualifies for the Miss USA contest, Warrick becomes the ultimate stage mother' and pushes her daughter to the brink. In doing so, Warrick just about ruins her marriage and her daughter's romance with

Hutton, a newspaperman. By feature's end, Warrick has realized the folly of her ways and returned to her doting husband, Ridgely. Hutton takes off with Albright, who relinquishes her queenly seat in favor of her adoration for Hutton. Lots of bare skin, bathing suits, innocent fun. Good idea ruined by dull screenplay.

p, Wallace MacDonald; d, Lew Landers; w, Arthur Orloff, George Bricker (story by Orloff); ph, Vincent Farrar; m, Mischa Bakaleinikoff; ed, Aaron Stell.

Drama (PR:A MPAA:NR)

BEAUTY PARLOR*
(1932) 66m Chesterfield bw

Barbara Kent (*Sally*), Joyce Compton (*Joan*), John Harron (*Jeffery Colt*), Dorothy Revier (*Stella*), Albert Gran (*Burke*), Wheeler Oakman (*Fremont*), Mischa Auer (*Herman Bauer*), Betty Mack (*Lou*).

The lives of two manicurists, Kent and Compton, and several customers of a hotel barber shop are interwoven. The movie is an attempt by an independent film company to capitalize on this popular genre film, but nothing can improve the looks of this one.

p, George R. Batcheller; d, Richard Thorpe; w, Harry Sauber (based on a story by Marion Orth); ph, M. A. Anderson.

Drama (PR:A MPAA:NR)

BEBO'S GIRL**1/2
(1964, Ital.) 110m Lux-Ultra-Vides bw

Claudia Cardinale (*Mara*), George Chakiris (*Bebo*), Marc Michel (*Stefano*), Dany Paris (*Liliana*), Emilo Esposito (*Mara's Father*), Monique Vita (*Ines*), Mario Lupi (*Lidori*), Pier Luigi Catocci (*Priest Ciolfi*), Carla Calo (*Mara's Mother*), Ugo Chitti (*Arnaldo*), Bruno Scipioni (*Mauro*).

A country girl falls in love with a partisan she scarcely knows. The partisan has killed a man during the war and is in jail for the crime. Claudia Cardinale, in one of her finest roles, turns her back on a good life for this mysterious lover. Both picture and characters grow on you.

p, Franco Cristaldi; d, Luigi Comencini; w, Comencini, Marcello Fondato (based on a novel by Carlo Cassola); ph, Gianni di Venanzo; m, Carlo Rustichelli.

Drama (PR:A MPAA:NR)

BECAUSE I LOVED YOU*
(1930, Ger.) 97m UFA/American bw (DICH HAB ICH GELIEBT)

Mady Christians (*Inge Lund*), Walter Jankulm (*Otto Radney*), Hans Bluwe (*Dr. Hubert Baumgart*), Marion Conradi (*Marlechen*), Carl Platen (*Oberregusseur Kecgber*), Sophie Pagay (*Frau Werner*), Trude Berliner (*Edith Karin*), Fritz Alberti (*Justizrat Korner*), Hans Mierendorff (*Direktor Sommer*), Jaro Furth (*Sanitatsrat Brink*), Hans Sternberg (*Der Theaterdirektor*), Hermann Picha (*Der Inspizient*), Andre Pilot (*Der Conferencier*).

First German-language film released in the U.S. Story deals with an actress who leaves the stage to get married, has a brief affair before her marriage, and ends up losing her child.

p, Aafa Robis; d, Rudolf Walther-Fein; w, Walter Reisch; ph, Fugsland and Holzki; m/l, Ed May, Bruno Balz.

Drama (PR:C MPAA:NR)

BECAUSE OF EVE*1/2
(1948) 67m International Pictures bw

Joseph Crehan (*Dr. West*), Wanda McKay (*Sally Stevens*), John Parker (*Bob Stephens*), Robert Leaver (*Nicholas Wilde*).

Film ostensibly made to combat juvenile delinquency. It touches on everything from venereal disease to illegitimate children. Prospective husband and wife discuss with family doctor these sensitive topics. Interesting to see horrified attitudes of the times towards these problems.

p, William Daniels; d, Howard Bretherton; w, Larry Allen, Walter A. Lawrence; ph, Arthur Martineli, Elmer Moss; ed, Dede Allen.

Drama (PR:C-O MPAA:NR)

BECAUSE OF HIM**1/2
(1946) 100m UNIV bw

Deanna Durbin (*Kim Walker*), Franchot Tone (*Paul Taylor*), Charles Laughton (*Sheridan*), Helen Broderick (*Nora*), Stanley Ridges (*Charlie Gilbert*), Donald Meek (*Martin*), Charles Halton (*Mr. Dunlap*), Regina Wallace (*Head Nurse*), Douglas Wood (*Samuel Hargood*), Lynn Whitney (*Martha Manners*).

Laughton lends a soupcon of class to this otherwise ordinary film about a down-on-her-luck actress who finagles her way into a big-time stage presentation on Broadway. Playwright Tone is not pleased with Deanna's presence in the play and takes his name off the billing. (In reality, the playwright has final approval of the cast and this could not happen today, according to the rules of the Dramatist's Guild.) She scores with crowds and critics alike, and it winds up for the best with Deanna in Tone's arms. Laughton takes the acting kudos with a performance that would go well with eggs in the morning. Since he is playing exactly that, an overplaying emoter, we can resist any criticism on his going over the top. And it isn't that he gets all the great lines, it's merely that he's the most with what he has. Deanna is in good voice as always and, if she weren't against such a consummate actor in Laughton, she might have fared better. Keep an eye out for Helen Broderick as Nora and then marvel over the fact that she is Broderick Crawford's mother! Not much of a resemblance except in the acting genes.

p, Felix Jackson; d, Richard Wallace; w, Edmund Beloin (based on a story by Beloin, Sig Herzig); ph, Hal Mohr; m, Miklos Rozsa: ed, Ted Kent.

Musical (PR:A MPAA:NR)

BECAUSE OF YOU*1/2
(1952) 95m UNIV bw

Loretta Young (*Christine Carroll*), Jeff Chandler (*Steve Kimberly*), Alex Nicol (*Mike Monroe*), Frances Dee (*Susan Arnold*), Alexander Scourby (*Dr. Breen*), Lynne

Roberts *(Rosemary Balder)*, Mae Clarke *(Peachie)*, Gayle Reed *(Kim)*, Billy Wayne *(George)*, Frances Karath *(Judy)*.

A soap opera that never rinses out. Young, who looks the same today as she did in 1952 and 1932, is an ex-convict on parole. She marries and does not tell anyone of her sordid past. When her former pals involve her in another crime, albeit innocently, her husband divorces her. Young and Chandler make a fine romantic duo but some of the scenes are so laden with tears that they almost become ludicrous. Good production values and proper music by Oscar-winning Frank Skinner (who used to specialize in soaps and did two of the three versions of BACK STREET).

p, Albert J. Cohen; d, Joseph Pevney; w, Ketti Frings (based on a story by Thelma Robinson); ph, Russell Metty; m, Frank Skinner; ed, Virgil Vogel.

Romance   **(PR:A   MPAA:NR)**

BECAUSE THEY'RE YOUNG**   (1960) 97m COL bw

Dick Clark *(Neil)*, Michael Callan *(Griff)*, Tuesday Weld *(Anne)*, Victoria Shaw *(Joan)*, Roberta Shore *(Ricky)*, Warren Berlinger *(Buddy)*, Doug McClure *(Jim)*, Linda Watkins *(Frances McCalla)*, Chris Robinson *(Patcher)*, Rudy Bond *(Chris)*, Wendell Holmes *(Mr. Donlan)*, Philip Coolidge *(Mr. Rimer)*, Bart Patton *(Kramer)*, Stephen Talbot *(Eric)*, Kathryn Card *(Mrs. Wellenberg)*, Paul Genge *(Pekarek)*, Susan Odin *(Plump Girl)*, Frances Karath *(Girl Friend)*, James Darren, Duane Eddy and The Rebels.

Dick Clark proves himself a competent actor as he stars in this routine melodrama about life in a big-city high school. Clark is the new teacher in town and sort of a well-scrubbed Glenn Ford (THE BLACKBOARD JUNGLE) except that Ford had to contend with the tough likes of Sidney Poitier, Vic Morrow, and Jamie Farr and Clark must put up with McClure, Callan, and Berlinger. Clark, a do-gooder, involves himself in the lives of a few students and trouble begins. Columbia had some fine young actors in their stable at the time and all were used to good advantage in this film. Callan, the former dancer from "West Side Story," acquits himself well, as does another erstwhile Broadwayite, Berlinger. Gunn's scripting almost defeats the self-conscious direction by Wendkos, who went on to carve himself out an undistinguished career in TV films.

p, Jerry Bresler; d, Paul Wendkos; w, James Gunn (based on *Harrison High* by John Farris); ph, Wilfrid Cline; m, Johnny Williams; ed, Chester A. Schaeffer; m/l, Don Costa, Aaron Schroeder, Wally Gold, Duane Eddy, Lee Hazelwood, Hal Mann, Bernie Lowe.

Drama   **(PR:C   MPAA:NR)**

BECAUSE YOU'RE MINE*¹/₂   (1952) 103m MGM c

Mario Lanza *(Renaldo Rossano)*, Doretta Morrow *(Bridget Batterson)*, James Whitmore *(Sgt. Batterson)*, Dean Miller *(Ben Jones)*, Paula Corday *(Francesca Landers)*, Jeff Donnell *(Patty Ware)*, Spring Byington *(Mrs. Montville)*, Curtis Cooksey *(Gen. Montville)*, Don Porter *(Capt. Loring)*, Eduard Franz *(Albert Parkson Foster)*, Bobby Van *(Artie Pilcer)*, Ralph Reed *(Horsey)*, Celia Lovsky *(Mrs. Rossano)*, Alexan der Steinert *(Maestro Paradori)*.

Sammy Cahn and Nicholas Brodzsky garnered an Oscar nomination for the title song that Lanza warbles, but that's about it for this clunky, trite musical featuring the Golden Throat. In a forerunner of what actually did happen to a different kind of singer, Elvis Presley, Lanza is an opera singer at army training camp. He is pampered because of his image. He falls for Whitmore's sister, Morrow (a chirper in her own right) and a fight ensues. A few funny scenes, the best of which is a duet between Whitmore, as a classically oriented non-com, and Lanza. Lots and lots of singing, perhaps too much, where there might have been more story. But Lanza's fans only cared about his terrific tenor voice. If you like Mario, then you'll go mad for all the opera as well as the pop songs. A few good lines and some fine music but it's nowhere near THE GREAT CARUSO for excitement. Bobby Van does a neat tap dance that has absolutely nothing to do with the movie.

p, Joe Pasternak; d, Alexander Hall; w, Karl Tunberg, Leonard Spigelgass (based on a story by Ruth Brooks Flippen, Sy Gomberg); ph, Joseph Ruttenberg (Technicolor); m, Johnny Green; ed, Albert Akst; m/l, Sammy Cahn, Nicholas Brodzsky, Paul Francis Webster, Irving Aaronson, John Lehmann, Raymond Sinatra.

Musical Comedy   **(PR:AA   MPAA:NR)**

BECKET****   (1964, Brit.) 148m PAR c

Richard Burton *(Thomas Becket)*, Peter O'Toole *(King Henry II)*, Donald Wolfit *(Bishop Folliot)*, Sir John Gielgud *(King Louis VII)*, Martita Hunt *(Queen Matilda)*, Pamela Brown *(Queen Eleanor)*, Sian Phillips *(Gwendolyn)*, Paolo Stoppa *(Pope Alexander III)*, Gino Cervi *(Cardinal Zambelli)*, David Weston *(Brother John)*, Felix Aylmer *(Archbishop of Canterbury)*, Veronique Vendell *(Pretty French Girl)*, Gerald Lawson *(English Peasant)*, Jennifer Hilary *(His Daughter)*, Riggs O'Hara *(Prince Henry)*, John Phillips *(Bishop of Winchester)*, Frank Pettingell *(Bishop of York)*, Hamilton Dyce *(Bishop of Chichester)*, Linda Marlowe *(Farmer's Daughter)*, Patrick Newall *(William of Corbeil)*, Geoffrey Bayldon *(Brother Philip)*, Graham Stark *(Pope's Secretary)*, Victor Spinetti *(French Tailor)*, Magda Knopke *(Girl on Balcony)*, Niall MacGinnis, Percy Herbert, Christopher Rhodes, Peter Jeffrey *(Henry II's Barons)*.

BECKET won but a single Oscar (screenplay from another medium by Anhalt) and was nominated for seven others. It should have won at least four of those. It's too fat and not nearly as action-packed as it could have been. An improvement over the stage-bound Anouilh play, BECKET tells the story of two great friends, Burton as Becket and O'Toole as Henry II, whose relationship almost borders on homosexuality, despite both being great wenchers. Burton is O'Toole's chancellor until consecrated Archbishop of Canterbury, almost in jest, by O'Toole. Becket takes the

job seriously and defends the church from royal onslaughts. The two men drift further apart as Burton goes deeper into his ecclesiastical role and the king realizes that he must be killed after the two men meet for an attempted reconciliation in a wonderful scene on horseback at a British beach. Ostensibly a story regarding the separation of church and state, Anouilh and Anhalt followed history closely and added their own undercur- rent of sexual tension between the men although this is so subtle that it was lost on many viewers. All technical credits are excellent and so is every actor. Many wonderful touches abound, including the scene where forks are introduced into the court. Wallis, whose career spanned six decades (everything from LITTLE CAESAR, CASABLANCA, and GUNFIGHT AT THE O.K. CORRAL to various Elvis Presley films) established himself in the Pantheon of Producers with BECKET.

p, Hal B. Wallis; d, Peter Glenville; w, Edward Anhalt (based on the play by Jean Anouilh); ph, Geoffrey Unsworth (Technicolor); m, Laurence Rosenthal; ed, Anne Coates; prod d, John Bryan; art d, Maurice Carter; cos, Margaret Furse.

Historical Drama   **Cas.**   **(PR:C   MPAA:NR)**

BECKY SHARP**   (1935) 83m Pioneer Prod./RKO c

Miriam Hopkins *(Becky Sharp)*, Frances Dee *(Amelia Sedley)*, Cedric Hardwicke *(Marquis of Steyne)*, Billie Burke *(Lady Bareacres)*, Alison Skipworth *(Miss Crawley)*, Nigel Bruce *(Joseph Sedley)*, Alan Mowbray *(Rawdon Crawley)*, Colin Tapley *(William Dobbin)*, G.P. Huntley, Jr. *(George Osborne)*, William Stack *(Pitt Crawley)*, George Hassell *(Sir Pitt Crawley)*, William Faversham *(Duke of Wellington)*, Charles Richman *(General Tufto)*, Doris Lloyd *(Duchess of Richmond)*, Leonard Mudie *(Tarquin)*, Bunny Beatty *(Lady Blanche)*, Charles Coleman *(Bowles)*, May Beatty *(Briggs)*, Finis Barton *(Miss Floyers)*, Olaf Hytten, Pauline Caron, James "Hambone" Robinson, Elspeth Dudgeon, Tempe Pigott, Ottola Nesmith, Will Geer.

BECKY SHARP is a landmark film in that it provided us with the very first all-color (Technicolor) picture although there had been many other color films before, most notably Universal's KING OF JAZZ in 1930. Audiences oohed and ahhhed at the technique but came to sleep through the movie. This was as much a milestone as THE JAZZ SINGER or "Fred Ott's Sneeze" because it offered the closest color to real life but the joy ended there. A loose adaptation of Thackeray's *Vanity Fair*, BECKY SHARP falls flat on almost every level, mostly because of a dull screenplay filled with caricatures rather than characterizations. Trouble plagued this picture from the moment Jock Whitney and Cornelius Vanderbilt Whitney decided to invest their own money in it. Director Lowell Sherman died and Mamoulian tossed out all of Sherman's footage and started from scratch. The story, for what it's worth, concerns the ultimate golddigger, an anti-heroine who makes it from the lowest Gorkian depths to the side of a throne. Beautiful to watch but boring from the fade-in, BECKY SHARP was the third version of VANITY FAIR to be filmed. Mabel Ballin starred in a 1923 release and Myrna Loy tried it in 1932. Critics were certain that this new process would doom black and white films forever, just as sound had tolled the knell for silent films.

p, Kenneth MacGowan; d, Rouben Mamoulian; w, Francis Edward Faragoh (based on a play by Langdon Mitchell and *Vanity Fair*; by William Makepeace Thackeray) ph, Ray Rennehan (Technicolor); m, Roy Webb; ed, Archie Marshek; prod d, Robert Edmond Jones; ch, Russell Lewis.

Drama   **Cas.**   **(PR:C   MPAA:NR)**

BED AND BOARD**   (1971, Fr.) 95m Les Films du Carrosse-Valoria/Fida/COL c

Jean-Pierre Leaud *(Antoine)*, Claude Jade *(Christine)*, Hiroko Berghauer *(Kyolo)*, Barbara Laage *(Executive Secretary)*, Daniel Ceccaldi *(Mons. Darbon)*, Claire Duhamel *(Mme. Darbon)*, Pierre Fabre *(The Sneerer)*, Claude Vega *(Strangler)*, Bill Kearns *(American Customer)*, Daniel Boulanger *(Tenor)*, Silvana Blasi *(Tenor's Wife)*, Daniele Gerard *(Servant)*, Jacques Jouanneau *(Bistro Landlord)*, Marie Irakane *(Housekeeper)*, Serge Rousseau *(Unknown Person)*, Pierre Maguelon *(Customer in Bistro)*, Annick Asty *(Mother of Young Violinist)*, Rispal *(Pensioner)*, Christian De Tiliere *(String-puller)*, Ada Lonati *(Hotel Owner)*.

Part of the continuing story profiling the life of a fun-loving Frenchman, Antoine, played hungrily by Leaud. Leaud falls in love and marries Jade, has a child, then experiments with adultery by having an uninteresting affair with Berghauer before the close-out. Director Truffaut's dwelling upon scenes thought to be tender is really a matter of self-indulgence. There simply isn't enough story to tell and most of the plot and characters remain inert. (Loose sequel: LOVE ON THE RUN.)

p&d, Francois Truffaut; w, Truffaut, Claude De Givray, Bernard Revon; ph, Nestor Almendros; art d, Jean Mandaroux.

Drama   **(PR:C   MPAA:NR)**

BED AND BREAKFAST*   (1930, Brit.) 80m GAU bw

Jane Baxter *(Audrey Corteline)*, Richard Cooper *(Toby Entwhistle)*, Sari Maritza *(Anne Entwhistle)*, Alf Goddard *(Alf Dunning)*, David Hawthorne *(Bernard Corteline)*, Cyril McLaglen *(Bill)*, Ruth Maitland *(Mimosa Dunning)*, Muriel Aked *(Mrs. Boase)*, Frederick Volpe *(Cannon Boase)*, Mike Johnson *(Henry)*, Matthew Boulton *(Sergeant)*

Married couple has a quarrel: the husband decides to teach his wife a lesson, and wife decides to do the same. So it's switch partners for a while. Subplot involves burglars, police, and more mixed-up happenings. A silly farce.

p, L'Estrange Fawcett; d, Walter Forde; w, H. Fowler Mear (based on the play by Frederick Whitney).

Comedy   **(PR:A   MPAA:NR)**

BED AND BREAKFAST* (1936, Brit.) 58m Coronel bw

Barry Lupino (*Bert Fink*), Mabel Poulton (*The Maid*), Frank Miller (*Charles Blake*), Daphne Courtney (*Margaret Reynolds*), Florence LeRoy (*Landlady*).

A doddering old thespian comes to the aid of those younger than he, helping a typist, an author, and a composer to solve seemingly impossible problems. Not as charming and perky as it could have been.

p&d, Walter West; w, Frank Miller.

Drama **(PR:A MPAA:NR)**

BED OF ROSES*1/2 (1933) 70m RKO bw

Constance Bennett (*Lorry Evans*), Joel McCrea (*Mike*), John Halliday (*Paige*), Pert Kelton (*Minnie*), Samuel Hinds (*Father Doran*).

Two women graduate from reform school and decide to snare a couple of men on a steamer rollin' down the Mississippi towards New Orleans. A sort of neat tongue-in-cheek kind of movie with former Ziegfeld comedienne Pert Kelton getting the best lines.

p, Merian C. Cooper; d, Gregory LaCava; w, Wanda Tuchock, Eugene Thackrey; ph, Charles Rosher; ed, Basil Wrangel; md, Max Steiner; art d, Van Nest Polglase, Charles Kirk.

Drama **(PR:A MPAA:NR)**

BED SITTING ROOM, THE***1/2 (1969, Brit.) 80m UA c

Rita Tushingham (*Penelope*), Ralph Richardson (*Lord Fortnum*), Peter Cook (*Inspector*), Dudley Moore (*Sergeant*), Spike Milligan (*Mate*), Michael Hordern (*Blues Martin*), Roy Kinnear (*Plastic Man*), Richard Warwick (*Allan*), Arthur Lowe (*Father*), Mona Washbourne (*Mother*), Ronald Fraser (*Field Marshall Sgt.*), Dandy Nichols (*Ethyl Shroake*), Frank Thornton (*BBC Man*), Henry Woolf (*Electricity Man*), Ron Brody (*Dwarf*), Gordon Rollings (*Patient*).

A very weird picture that stemmed from a famous weird place, the mind of Spike Milligan, once of the Goon Show (wtih Sellers, Secombe and Michael Bentine). It's an offbeat, effective look at London after the bombs have been dropped. Very episodic segments of several survivors (most of whom are famous faces on British TV) as they make their ways around the ruins of a once-great city. It's obscure in many ways and the producers didn't seem to mind that people walked out saying "What was that?" Bizarre but wildly imaginative, the actors all seemed to be having an hysterical time of it as Lowe (Father) turns into a parrot, Washbourne becomes a chest of drawers, Tushingham announces that she's 17 months pregnant and Richardson metamorphoses into a bed sitting room! It's, at best, not the funniest situation imaginable, and yet the players and the creators manage to keep the humor flying thick and fast. Cook and Moore are side-splitting as government bureaucrats and Feldman is seen briefly as a Communist.

p&d, Richard Lester; w, John Antrobus, Charles Wood (based on a play by Antrobus and Spike Milligan); ph, David Watkin; m, Ken Home; ed, John Victor Smith.

Comedy Fantasy **(PR:C MPAA:NR)**

BEDAZZLED***1/2 (1967, Brit.) 104m FOX c

Peter Cook (*George Spiggot*), Dudley Moore (*Stanley Moon*), Eleanor Bron (*Margaret*), Raquel Welch (*Lillian Lust*),Alba (*Vanity*), Robert Russell (*Anger*), Barry Humphries (*Envy*), Parnell McGarry (*Gluttony*), Danielle Noel (*Avarice*), Howard Goorney (*Sloth*), Michael Bates (*Inspector Clarke*), Bernard Spear (*Irving Moses*), Robin Hawdon (*Randolph*), Michael Trubshawe (*Lord Dowdy*), Evelyn Moore (*Mrs. Wisby*), Charles Lloyd Pack (*Vicar*), Lockwood West (*St. Peter*), Betty Cooper (*Sister Phoebe*).

No one and nothing is safe from Cook and Moore's barbed screenplay of BEDAZZLED. They take shots at nuns, priests, the upper classes of England, Lyndon Baines Johnson, Julie Andrews, the Prime Minister and, eventually, God. This is the kind of movie that religious people expect to go up in a puff of smoke. It's a devilish plot with Moore as a short short order cook in love with Bron, a waitress with sex exuding from every pore. Cook is the Devil ("Faust *always* works!" said Jack Buchanan in THE BAND WAGON, and he was right) who grants him several wishes. Naturally, all of them go awry (or there would be no comedy) and Moore winds up in a nun's habit as one of the Order of Leaping Berelians, which consists of several sisters who do their penance on trampolines. Cook and Moore are brilliant in their abilities to move from character to character with just a change of voice (not unlike Peter Sellers in that all of his best portrayals began with the vocal inflections) and the movie never flags. Where it does fall down is in the taste department as they never seem to let Hell enough alone. Nevertheless, it's much funnier than what you'll see in the 1980s, albeit just a trifle dated. Raquel Welch is at her sexiest as Lust but Ms. Bron is the standout female as the recalcitrant waitress. Bron appeared with the Monty Python group on stage in London and is best recalled for her wonderful work as Bill Daniels' wife in TWO FOR THE ROAD done the year earlier (1966), also directed by Donen.

p&d, Stanley Donen; w, Peter Cook, Dudley Moore (based on a story by Cook); ph, Austin Dempster (Panavision, DeLuxe Color); m, Moore; ed, Richard Marden.

Comedy Fantasy **Cas.** **(PR:C MPAA:NR)**

BEDELIA** (1946, Brit.) 90m GFD bw

Margaret Lockwood (*Bedelia*), Ian Hunter (*Charlie Carrington*), Barry K. Barnes (*Ben Chaney*), Anne Crawford (*Ellen*), Beatrice Varley (*Mary*), Louise Hampton (*Hannah*), Jill Esmond (*Nurse Harris*), Julien Mitchell (*Dr. McAbee*), Kynaston Reeves (*Mr. Bennett*), Olga Lindo (*Mrs. Bennett*), John Salew (*Alec Johnstone*), Claudie Bailey (*Captain McKelvey*).

Greedy woman poisons three husbands for their money. She is about to do away with number four, when an investigator assigned to the case steps in. Margaret Lockwood appears in one of her best villainous roles, played this time with subtlety.

p, Isadore Goldsmith; d, Lance Comfort; w, Herbert Victor, Vera Caspary (based on her novel); ph, Frederick A. Young, Harold Julius.

Drama **(PR:A MPAA:NR)**

BEDEVILLED** (1955) 85m MGM c

Anne Baxter (*Monica Johnson*), Steve Forrest (*Gregory Fitzgerald*), Victor Francen (*Father Du Rocher*), Simone Renant (*Francesca*), Maurice Teynac (*Trevelle*), Robert Christopher (*Tony Lugacetti*), Ina de la Hye (*Mama Lugacetti*), Joseph Tomelty (*Father Cunningham*), Oliver Hussenot (*Remy Hotel Manager*), Jean Ozenne (*Priest in Seminary*), Jacques Hilling (*Taxi Driver*), Raymond Bussieres (*Concierge*).

Forrest is on his way to the Seminary when he meets and falls for Baxter, a nightclub singer with a shady past. But since Forrest is about to take the final priestly vows, his concern for Baxter is humanitarian rather than sexual. Anne is a bad girl, having killed her married lover. So what we have here is the spectre of temptation over the young priest. Will the pleasures of the flesh outstrip the vows? It all takes place in France, and the Parisian backgrounds help make the film more interesting than it really is. In the end, Forrest opts for the cloth and Baxter, in a rare moment of self-sacrifice, walks out to face the waiting guns of the killers who've been chasing her down for the aforementioned murder. It's a quasi-religioso tale that never fully comes to grips with itself. There are hints of Sadie Thompson and the Reverend as well as overtones of Mary Magdalene. You won't recognize anyone but Anne and Steve.

p, Henry Berman; d, Mitchell Leisen; w, Jo Eisenger; ph, F. A. Young (Eastmancolor); m, William Alwyn; ed, Frank Clarke; md, Muir Matheson; m/l, Paul Durand, Richard Driscoll.

Crime Drama **(PR:C MPAA:NR)**

BEDFORD INCIDENT, THE***1/2 (1965, Brit.) 102m COL bw

Richard Widmark (*Capt. Eric Finlander, USN*), Sidney Poitier (*Ben Munceford*), James MacArthur (*Ens. Ralston*), Martin Balsam (*Lt. Cmdr. Chester Potter*), Wally Cox (*Sonarman, 2nd Class*), Eric Portman (*Cmdr. Wolfgang Schrepke*), Michael Kane (*Cmdr. Allison*), Phil Brown (*Chief Pharmacist Mate McKinley*), Gary Cockrell (*Lt. Bascombe*), Warren Stanhope (*Pharmacist's Mate Strauss*), Donald Sutherland (*Pharmacist's Mate Nerny*), Colin Maitland (*Seaman Jones*), Edward Bishop (*Lt. Hacker*), George Roubicek (*Lt. Burger*).

Widmark is the captain of a newly launched destroyer. His mission is to root out hostile subs in the North Atlantic. Along for the ride (in a role that never once refers to his color) is Poitier, a newspaperman documenting the ship's travels. MacArthur is a young ensign who is ridden mercilessly by Widmark. Contact with a Russian sub is made and the hunt begins with Widmark stalking relentlessly until an atomic weapon is accidentally fired by MacArthur. Taut, suspenseful, but not neglectful of the lighter side (Cox as the Sonar operator who collapses of exhaustion), THE BEDFORD INCIDENT marked Harris' first directorial assignment after a host of memorable producing chores (THE KILLING, PATHS OF GLORY, LOLITA) and he does well in sustaining the tension of Poe's Cold War script. Widmark co-produced, but never let that get in the way of his totally believable portrait of a man obsessed with his work and his devotion to his country. In a small role, Sutherland makes no impression at all.

p&d, James B. Harris; w, James Poe (based on the novel by Mark Rascovich); ph, Gil Taylor; m, Gerard Schurmann; ed, John Jympson.

Adventure **Cas.** **(PR:C MPAA:NR)**

BEDKNOBS AND BROOMSTICKS***1/2 (1971) 117m BV c

Angela Lansbury (*Eglantine Price*), David Tomlinson (*Emelius Browne*), Roddy McDowall (*Mr. Jelk*), Sam Jaffe (*Bookman*), John Ericson (*Col. Heller*), Bruce Forsyth (*Swinburne*), Reginald Owen (*Gen. Teagler*), Tessie O'Shea (*Mrs. Hobday*), Arthur E. Gould-Porter (*Capt. Greer*), Ben Wrigley (*Street Sweeper*), Rick Traeger, Manfred Lating (*German Sergeants*), John Orchard (*Vendor*), Roy Smart (*Paul*), Cindy O'Callaghan (*Carrie*), Ian Weighall (*Charlie*), Robert Holt (*Voice of Codfish*), Lennie Weinrib (*Voice of Secretary Bird and Lion*).

Billed as the successor to MARY POPPINS, BEDKNOBS AND BROOMSTICKS is filled with unique special effects that still have audiences oohing and ahhhing. Lansbury owns a seaside house in England and has three children foisted on her during WW II. At first, the cockney trio isn't thrilled about being relocated. Then they learn that Lnasbury is studying witchcraft by mail and has a host of mischief planned for the Nazis if they ever land in Jolly Olde. With a bedstead as their magic carpet, Lnasbury takes the kids on a wonderful ride into several fantastic worlds. Animation is neatly mixed with live action and all performances are good, but the film flattens out quickly because there is no real driving force behind the story (other than the threat of the German invasion). The Sherman Brothers, who are among the best film composers around (MARY POPPINS, THE HAPPIEST MILLIONAIRE, THE SLIPPER AND THE ROSE and more), did not come up with any memorable tunes for this one, although they did get an Oscar nomination for "The Age Of Not Believing." An Oscar was awarded to for the special visual effects. Nominations also went for Art and Costumes. Irwin Kostal was also nominated for Music Adaptation but lost to John Williams for FIDDLER ON THE ROOF.

p, Bill Walsh; d, Robert Stevenson; w, Walsh, Don DaGradi (based on the book by Mary Norton); ph, Frank Phillips (Technicolor); ed, Cotton Warburton; art d, Peter Ellenshaw, John Mansbridge; cos, Bill Thomas; anim d, Ward Kimball; spec eff, Danny Lee, Eustace Lycett, Alan Maley; m/l, Richard M. and Robert B. Sherman.

Fantasy **Cas.** **(PR:AAA MPAA:G)**

BEDLAM*** (1946) 78m RKO bw

Boris Karloff (*Master Sims*), Anna Lee (*Neil Rowen*), Billy House (*Lord Mortimer*), Glen Vernon (*The Gilded Boy*), Jason Robards (*Oliver Todd*), Joan Newton (*Dorothea*), Richard Fraser (*Hannay*), Ian Wolfe (*Sidney Long*), Leland Hodgson (*John Wilkes*), Elizabeth Russell (*Mistress Simms*).

The great Karloff plays the sadistic head of an English asylum where inmates are tortured and otherwise mistreated. When an actress, Lee, tries to change conditions, she ends up as an inmate. Historically accurate, this is more than just another horror movie. Bedlam was the nickname for Mary's of Bethlehem Hospital for the Insane, which operated in 1773.

p, Val Lewton; d, Mark Robson; w, Robson, Carlos Keith; ph, Nicholas Musuraca; m, Roy Webb; ed, Lyle Boyer; art d, Albert S. D'Agostino, Walter Keller; set d, Darrell Silvera, John Sturtevant; spec eff, Vernon L. Walker.

Horror   **Cas.**   **(PR:C MPAA:NR)**

BEDSIDE* (1934) 63m FN/WB bw

Warren William (*Louis*), Jean Muir (*Caroline*), Allen Jenkins (*Sparks*), David Landau (*Smith*), Kathryn Sergava (*Maritza*), Donald Meek (*Dr. Wiley*).

An expelled medical student takes up a practice without a license. When his girl friend nurse is struck by an auto and an operation is necessary to save her life, he admits his lack of credentials and then proceeds to save her. Hopeless bedside manner.

p, Sam Bischoff; d, Robert Florey, w, Manuel Seff, Harvey Thew, Rian James (based on a story by Lillian Hayward, James Whanton); ph, Sid Hickok.

Drama   **(PR:A MPAA:NR)**

BEDSIDE MANNER** (1945) 79m UA bw

John Carroll (*Morgan Hale*), Ruth Hussey (*Hedy Fredericks*), Charles Ruggles (*Doc Fredericks*), Ann Rutherford (*Lola*), Claudia Drake (*Tanya*), Renee Godfrey (*Stella*), Esther Dale (*Gravitt*), Grant Mitchell (*Mr. Pope*), Joel McGinnis (*Tommy Smith*), John James (*Dick Smith*), Frank Jenks (*Harry Smith*), Bert Roach (*George*), Vera Marsh (*Mary*), Sid Saylor (*Elmer Jones*), Earl Hodgins (*Mr. Perkins*), Mary Currier (*Mrs. Livingston*), Constance Purdy (*Mrs. Moriarity*), Mrs. Gardner Crane (*Mrs. Pringle*), Joe Devlin (*Head Waiter*), Dimitrios Alexis (*Waiter*), Don Brody (*Good-Looking Stranger*).

An overworked doctor, Ruggles, in a war-boom town wants his doctor niece, Hussey, to stay around and help him, but she's en route to Chicago. Ruggles talks an airplane test pilot (Carroll) his daughter likes into staging a fake accident so she'll stick around. Dumb plot but a pretty decent comedy.

p&d, Andrew Stone; w, Frederick Jackson, Malcolm Stuart Boylan (based on a story by Robert Carson); ph, James Van Trees, John Mescall; ed, James Smith.

Comedy   **(PR:A MPAA:NR)**

BEDTIME FOR BONZO**1/2 (1951) 83m UNIV bw

Ronald Reagan (*Prof. Peter Boyd*), Diana Lynn (*Jane*), Walter Slezak (*Prof. Hans Neumann*), Lucille Barkley (*Valerie Tillinghast*), Jesse White (*Babcock*), Herbert Heyes (*Dean Tillinghast*), Herbert Vigran (*Lt. Daggett*), Harry Tyler (*Knicksy*), Ed Clark (*Fosdick*), Ed Gargan (*Policeman*), Joel Friedkin (*Mr. DeWitt*), Brad Browne (*Chief of Police*), Elizabeth Flournoy (*Miss Swithen*), Howard Banks (*Policeman*), Perc Landers (*Fireman*), Brad Johnson (*Student*), Bill Mauch (*Student*), Ann Tyrrell.

DeCordova, for years the "Tonight Show" producer, began life as a director and does a creditable job on this nonsensical comedy. Reagan, one-time sports reporter and sportscaster turned actor, is a psychology prof at Sheridan College. He's engaged to Barkley, the dean's daughter, but her father (Heyes) is against the marriage because Reagan's father was a criminal and Heyes fears that Reagan may have inherited some of the genes. Reagan thinks that environment counts more than heridity in determining personality and, to prove it, steals Bonzo, the college's sulking chimp, and decides to raise it himself and show how love and proper surroundings can overcome anything. He hires Lynn as a nanny. Lynn and Reagan bring up Bonzo in an atmosphere of kindness rather than chaos. Lots of complications follow, including a robbery by Bonzo, the threat to sell him to Yale for research, police accusing Reagan of the theft, etc. It ends with Reagan, Lynn, and Bonzo driving off on their honeymoon. BEDTIME FOR BONZO is better than the title would lead you to believe. Lynn is lovely, Bonzo (who died tragically with his four stand-ins in a trailer fire) is hysterical and Slezak, as another professor, is very good. Reagan was an adept *farceur* who didn't mind being upstaged by an animal, something many other actors have avoided. (Sequel: BONZO GOES TO COLLEGE.)

p, Michel Kraike; d, Frederick DeCordova; w, Val Burton, Lou Breslow (based on a story by Raphael David Blau, Ted Berkman); ph, Carl Guthrie; m, Frank Skinner; ed, Ted J. Kent.

Comedy   **Cas.**   **(PR:AA MPAA:NR)**

BEDTIME STORY, A** (1933) 87m PAR bw

Maurice Chevalier (*Rene*), Helen Twelvetrees (*Sally*), Edward Everett Horton (*Victor*), Adrienne Ames (*Paulette*), Earle Fox (*Max*), Betty Lorraine (*Suzanne*), Gertrude Michael (*Louise*), Ernest Wood (*Robert*), Reginald Mason (*General*), Henry Kolker (*Agent de Police*), George MacQuarrie (*Henry Joudain*), Paul Panzer (*Concierge*).

Being a star and then retiring before one is four years of age is usually reserved for animal actors. Not so in the case of Ronald Leroy Overacker, also known as Baby Leroy. Here was a child who began his career before he was six months old (and before there were laws about how long a child could be on the set), had a fabulous run in such films as IT'S A GIFT, TILLIE AND GUS, THE OLD-FASHIONED WAY

and was already over the hill before he may have been properly toilet-trained. Chevalier, as a wealthy Vicomte, comes back to Paris after hunting game for about a year. Michael, his fiancee, has an appointment she cannot cancel so, with a night to kill, the debonair Maurice arranges three dates with three old amours, one every couple of hours with Ray, Ames and Lorraine, each more sensuous than the next. In the middle of his carefully planned evening, he finds a baby abandoned in his limo, left there by poor parents. Maurice is fascinated by the child. (This also happened in real life; Leroy's folks were separated and Chevalier offered to adopt Leroy.) He hires Twelvetrees as a nanny for Mons. Baby. Maurice cleans up his life and begins to live for the child, arranging his life around the boy's welfare. When he takes the baby to a party at his fiancee's house, she is mortified and tosses the engagement ring back at him, thinking that this might cause him to realize that she is more important than this mysterious child. But *au contraire*, Maurice is thrilled to be rid of Gertrude, gives the ring to Helen, and the two of them presumably spend the rest of their lives together with the scene-stealing Leroy. It's cute, faintly amusing, and worth seeing if only for Leroy.

p, Ernest Cohen; d, Norman Taurog; w, Waldemar Young, Nunnally Johnson, Benjamin Glazer (based on Roy Horniman's novel *Bellamy The Magnificent*); ph, Charles Lang; ed, Otho Lovering; m/l, Ralph Rainger, Leo Robin.

Musical Comedy   **(PR:AA MPAA:NR)**

BEDTIME STORY* (1938, Brit.) 71m Admiral/GN bw

Jack Livesey (*Sir John Shale*), Lesley Wareing (*Judy*), Eliot Makeham (*Uncle Toby*), Dorothy Dewhurst (*Lady Blundell*), Margery Morris (*Isabel*), Michael Bazalgette (*Prince*), Jonathan Field (*Butler*).

Wareing is an orphan living with her aunt. She runs away and pretends to be an American heiress in order to get passage on a ship for New York. When the scheme fails, she travels to the farm of her uncle. There, she falls in love with the ex-fiance of her cousin and finds happiness. Weak and forgettable drama.

p, Victor M. Greene; d&w, Donovan Pedelty (based on a play by Walter Ellis); ph, Ernest Palmer.

Drama   **(PR:A MPAA:NR)**

BEDTIME STORY*** (1942) 83m COL bw

Fredric March (*Lucius Drake*), Loretta Young (*Jane Drake*), Robert Benchley (*Eddie Turner*), Allyn Joslyn (*William Dudley*), Eve Arden (*Virginia Cole*), Helen Westley (*Emma Harper*), Joyce Compton (*Beulah*), Tim Ryan (*Mac*), Olaf Hytten (*Alfred*), Dorothy Adams (*Betsy*), Clarence Kolb (*Collins*), Andrew Tombes (*Pierce*).

Under no circumstances can you confuse this with the abysmal Niven/Brando film of the same name made a generation later. This is cinema-sophistication at its best. March is a playwright married to actress Young for seven years. They are both at the top of their profession. He'd like her to star in his next show, but she wants to retire to their Connecticut hideaway. This disagreement causes a divorce and her subsequent marriage to Joslyn, a stuffy banker. Fred never relents and wins Loretta back, just in time for her to star in the show that he wanted her to do in the first place. If that sounds trivial, be aware that it's the school and period of Gable and Grant comedies, and even though it does not jump off the screen, this ranks as one of the better romantic comedies. If this movie were made today, the director would be hailed as a comedy genius, given his own building at the studio and allowed millions in failures before the executives got wise to him. In 1942, it was just another picture directed by Hall (LITTLE MISS MARKER, HERE COMES MISTER JORDAN and loads more). Arden and Benchley in their accustomed roles as second bananas are worth the price of admission.

p, B. P. Schulberg; d, Alexander Hall; w, Richard Flournoy (based on a story by Horace Jackson and Grant Garrett); ph, Joseph Walker; ed, Viola Lawrence.

Comedy   **(PR:A MPAA:NR)**

BEDTIME STORY*1/2 (1964) 99m UNIV c

Marlon Brando (*Freddy*), David Niven (*Lawrence*), Shirley Jones (*Janet*), Dody Goodman (*Fanny Eubank*), Aram Stephan (*Andre*), Parley Baer (*Col. Williams*), Marie Windsor (*Mrs. Sutton*), Rebecca Sand (*Miss Trumble*), Frances Robinson (*Miss Harrington*), Henry Slate (*Sattler*), Norman Alden (*Dubin*), Susanne Cramer (*Anna*), Cynthia Lynn (*Frieda*), Ilse Taurins (*Hilda*), Francine York (*Gina*).

A disappointing attempt at comedy, considering the names of the creators and the adroitness of the stars. Maybe it's that certain people just should not be given jobs outside their ken. One wouldn't cast Niven in a Clint Eastwood role so why cast Brando in a Niven role? This is supposedly a light comedy by Shapiro (PILLOW TALK, OPERATION PETTICOAT) and Henning (Creator of "The Beverly Hillbillies"), but the souffle falls flat due to Brando's heavy performance. Brando and Niven are two conmen in Europe. After we see their various ploys, the two men meet, team up, and are rendered asunder when both fall for Jones, who is, they are told, a "soap queen." Thinking that she may be a Lever Brothers sister or either Miss Procter or Gamble, they both turn their attentions to her. The truth is that she is the winner of a beauty contest. Lots of silliness, a contest for Shirley's affections, Brando posing as a cripple (always lots of laughs) and more and more. Lighthearted but heavy-handed, this picture would have driven the women's liberation groups mad because all of the distaffers are portrayed in a less-than-intelligent fashion. Good work by all the second bananas and a nice score by Salter.

p, Stanley Shapiro; d, Ralph Levy; w, Shapiro, Paul Henning; ph, Clifford Stine (Eastmancolor); m, Hans J. Salter; ed, Milton Carruth; art d, Alexander Golitzen, Robert Clatworthy.

Comedy   **(PR:C MPAA:NR)**

BEEN DOWN SO LONG IT LOOKS LIKE UP TO ME* (1977) 90m PAR c

Barry Primus (*Gnossos*), Linda DeCoff (*Kristin*), David Downing (*Heff*), Susan Tyrell (*Jack*), Philip Shafer (*Calvin*), Bruce Davison (*Fitzgore*), Zack Norman (*Mojo*), Raul Julia (*Juan*).

Various vignettes that view society through the eyes of the so-called Beat Generation. A truckload of cliches, hip jargon, and nothing much to recommend this film.

p, Robert Rosenthal; d, Jeffrey Young; w, Robert Schlitt (based on the novel by Richard Farina); ph, Urs Furrer (Movielab Color); m, Gary Sherman; ed, Nicholas Meyers, Bruce Witkin; art d, William Molyneux; m/l, Gene Pistilli.

Drama (PR:A MPAA:NR)

BEES, THE* (1978) 83m New World c

John Saxon (John Norman), Angel Tompkins (Sandra Miller), John Carradine (Dr. Sigmund Humel), Claudio Brook (Dr. Miller). Alicia Encinias (Alicia).

To call this a B movie would be to deliver a cliched joke! This is, in fact, a C movie. One of several movies about the Hymenoptera (KILLER BEES with Gloria Swanson, THE SWARM, Irwin Allen's disaster of Disaster Film), THE BEES has a few twists and turns, mainly the idea that the Bees have a collective intelligence that is rankled by what is happening to the ecology of the earth. A silly film and even Angel Tompkins doesn't look as pretty as she is. Tompkins is yet another graduate of the Harvey Lembeck comedy workshop in Hollywood but she gets no opportunity to use her comic abilities in this inane film.

p,d&w, Alfredo Zacharias; ph, Leon Sanchez (CFI Color); m, Richard Gillis; ed, Mort Tubor, Sandy Nervig; spec eff, Jack Rabin.

Disaster Cas. (PR:C MPAA:PG)

BEES IN PARADISE** (1944, Brit.) 75m Gainsborough bw

Arthur Askey (Arthur Tucker), Anne Shelton (Rouana), Peter Graves (Peter Lovell), Max Bacon (Max Holer), Jean Kent (Jani), Ronald Shiner (Ronald Wild), Antoinette Cellier (Queen), Joy Shelton (Almura), Beatrice Varley (Moagga).

A silly notion gone crazy—four flyers stranded on a South Atlantic island are treated like princes by the all-female population and gleefully respond until they learn that after their honeymoons they must, by law, commit suicide. Not only that but we get music, too, which is about as frothy as the premise.

p, Edward Black; d, Val Guest; w, Guest, Marriott Edgar; ph, Phil Grindrod.

Musical/Comedy (PR:A MPAA:NR)

BEFORE DAWN** ¹/₂ (1933) 60m RKO bw

Stuart Erwin (Dwight Wilson), Dorothy Wilson (Patricia Merrick), Warner Oland (Dr. Cornelius), Dudley Digges (Horace Merrick), Gertrude W. Hoffman (Mattie), Oscar Apfel (O'Hara), Frank Reicher (Joe Valerie), Jane Darwell (Mrs. Marble).

A mysterious mansion, three murders, $1 million in a dead gangster's buried loot and a patient in a Vienna hospital all contribute to this mystery. Detective Erwin searching for fake mystics arrives on the scene and saves pretty girl Wilson from disappearing. Fun movie with Warner Oland playing it like Charlie Chan. Very fast-paced whodunnit thanks to Pichel's taut direction.

d, Irving Pichel; w, Garrett Fort, Marian Dix, Ralph Block (based on a story by Edgar Wallace); ph, Lucien Andriot; ed, William Hamilton; md, Max Steiner.

Mystery (PR:A MPAA:NR)

BEFORE HIM ALL ROME TREMBLED* ¹/₂

(1947, Ital.) 110m Excelsa/Superfilm bw

Anna Magnani (Ada), Gino Sinimberghi (Franco), Edda Albertini (Lena), Steffen Bude-Wab (Franz), Carlo Duse (Police Officer), Joop Von Hulzen (Webb), Guido Natari (Doctor), Tino Scotti (Mechanic), Guglielmo Sinaz (Stagehand), Guiseppe Varni (Stagehand).

Singers with Rome's Royal Opera hide a wounded English agent, Von Hulzen, during World War II. This story of the Italian underground parallels somewhat the opera "Tosca," of which there is a performance during the film. Interesting movie which music lovers will especially enjoy. (In Italian; English subtitles).

d, Carmine Gallone; ph, Anchise Brizzi; m, Giacomo Puccini; md, Luigi Ricci; English titles, Armando V. Macatuso.

War/Opera (PR:A MPAA:NR)

BEFORE I HANG** (1940) 62m COL bw

Boris Karloff (Dr. John Garth), Evelyn Keyes (Martha Garth), Bruce Bennett (Dr. Paul Ames), Edward Van Sloan (Dr. Ralph Howard), Ben Taggart (Warden Thompson), Pedro de Cordoba (Victor Sondini), Wright Kramer (George Wharton), Barton Yarborough (Stephen Barclay), Don Beddoe (Captain McGraw), Robert Fiske (District Attorney), Kenneth MacDonald (Anson), Frank Richards (Otto Kron).

In his search for a cure for death, elderly scientist Boris Karloff kills an aged pauper and is sentenced to death. In prison, with the help of the prison doctor, he continues his experiments and, by injecting himself with the blood of a hanged convict, reverses his old age. There is only one problem in that the serum turns him on to killing. Believe it or not, Karloff's serious approach to the role has you convinced.

p, Wallace MacDonald; d, Nick Grinde; w, Robert D. Andrews; ph, Benjamin Kline; md, Morris W. Stoloff; ed, Charles Nelson; art d, Lionel Banks.

Horror Cas. (PR:A MPAA:NR)

BEFORE I WAKE (SEE: SHADOW OF FEAR, 1956, Brit.)

BEFORE MIDNIGHT* (1934) 63m COL bw

Ralph Bellamy (Trent), June Collyer (Janet), Claude Gillingwater (Fry), Betty Blythe (Mavis).

Murder at a minute before midnight in an old house. On the scene is a detective, Bellamy, who knows about the crime but fails to prevent it. So who did it? Run-of-the-mill mystery with some confusing flashbacks.

d, Lambert Hillyer; w, Robert Quigley; ph, John Stumar; ed, Otto Meyer.

Mystery (PR:A MPAA:NR)

BEFORE MORNING* (1933) 56m Stage and Screen/Greenblatt bw

Leo Carrillo (Dr. Gruelle), Lora Baxter (Elsie Manning), Taylor Holmes (Leo Bergman), Blaine Cordner (Horace Barker), Louise Prussing (Mrs. Nichols), Russell Hicks (James Nichols), Louis Jean Heydt (Neil Kennedy), Jules Epailly (Ben Ayoub), Constance Bertrand (Diane), Terry Carroll (Doris).

A man is poisoned and his wife and mistress are both confronted by a blackmailer. It turns out, however, that the blackmailer is really a police inspector who has adopted this ruse to determine who killed the victim. Film is more deadly than poison.

p, Louis Weiss; d, Arthur Hoerl; ph, Walter Strenge; ed, Joe Silverstein.

Mystery (PR:A MPAA:NR)

BEFORE THE REVOLUTION* ¹/₂ (1965, Ital.) 115m Cineriz/IRIDE bw

Adriana Asti (Gina), Francesco Barilli (Boy), Alain Midgette (Agostino), Morando Morandini (Teacher), Domenico Alpi (Fabrizio's Father).

When the poor friend of an upper-class boy commits suicide, the wealthy lad, Barilli, begins to question his own life and outlook. There is a tendency for too much talk, but otherwise a film with considerable appeal.

d&w, Bernardo Bertolucci; ph, Aldo Scavarda; m, Gino Paoli, Ennio Morricone; ed, Roberto Perpignani.

Drama (PR:C MPAA:NR)

BEFORE WINTER COMES** (1969, Brit.) 107 COL c

David Niven (Major Giles Burnside), Topol (Janovic), Anna Karina (Maria Holz), John Hurt (Lieutenant Francis Pilkington), Anthony Quayle (Brigadier-General Bewley), Ori Levy (Captain Kamenev), John Collin (Sergeant Woody), Karel Stepanek (Count Derassy), Guy Deghy (Kovacs), Mark Malicz (Komenski), Gertan Klauber (Russian Major), Anna-Maria Pravda (Beata), George Innes (Bill), Tony Selby (Ted), Christopher Sandford (Johnny), Jerry Tarrant, John Savident (British Corporals), Britt Bern (Marta), Gisela Fritsch (Anna), Harry Kalenberg (Policeman), Karin Schroeder (Pregnant Girl), Peter Mathes (Malik).

They tried so hard to give us a message in BEFORE WINTER COMES that they forgot they were making a movie. It's 1945 in Austria and Niven is in charge of displaced persons. Topol, in a part not unlike the Tevya he played some years later, is a multilingual interpreter who helps Niven with the various tongues he must listen to. Topol turns out to be a Russian deserter and not the Slav he claims to be. When the time comes for him to be turned over to the Russians, Hurt (in a very early screen role—his third after WILD AND WILLING and A MAN FOR ALL SEASONS) tries to prevent Niven from giving Topol back to the Commies. Big holes in the story and motivations, so big that one might think a reel might have been removed. Karina is luminous as always but doesn't have much to do. Topol (born Chaim Topol) later became a producer but never did achieve the international fame that was expected after his smashing job in BEFORE WINTER COMES.

p, Robert Emmett Ginna; d, J. Lee Thompson; w, Andrew Sinclair (based on the story "The Interpreter" by Frederick L. Keefe); ph, Gilbert Taylor (Technicolor); m, Ron Grainer; ed, Willy Kemplen; art d, John Blezard.

Drama (PR:C MPAA:NR)

BEG, BORROW OR STEAL* (1937) 70m MGM bw

Frank Morgan (Ingraham Steward), Florence Rice (Joyce Steward), John Beal (Bill Cherau), Janet Beecher (Mrs. Agatha Steward), Herman Bing (Von Giersdorff), Erik Rhodes (LeFevre), George Givot (Izmanov), E. E. Clive (Lord Braemer), Tom Rutherfurd (Horace Miller), Cora Witherspoon (Mrs. Miller), Reginald Denny (Clifton Summitt), Vladimir Sokoloff (Sascha), Harlan Briggs (Mr. Miller).

An American expatriate in Paris lives the life of a con man but gets caught up in his own lies when he invites his separated wife and daughter to come abroad. Worthless piece of entertainment, despite consummate actor Morgan's considerable effort.

p, Frederick Stephani; d, William Thiele; w, Leonard Lee, Harry Ruskin, Marion Parsonnet; ph, William Daniels; ed, Conrad A. Nervig; md, William Axt.

Drama (PR:A MPAA:NR)

BEGGAR STUDENT, THE* (1931, Brit.) 66m Amalgamated Films bw

Shirley Dale (Tania), Lance Fairfax (Carl Romaine), Jerry Verno (Jan Janski), Frederick Lloyd (Col. Ollendorff), Mark Daly (Sergeant) Jill Hands (Broni), Margaret Halstan (Countess Novalska), Ashley Cooper (Nicki).

Weak rendition of the German opera with low production values and hardly any script at all, let alone character development and plot. The sound on this early talkie is abysmal.

p, John Harvel; d, Harvel, Victor Hanbury; w, John Stafford, Hans Zerlett (based on the operetta "Der Bettelstudent" by Carl Milloecker and R. Gene).

Opera (PR:A MPAA:NR)

BEGGAR STUDENT, THE* (1958, Ger.) 97m Sam Baker Associates c

Gerhard Riedmann (Symon Rymanowisz), Waltraut Haas (Countess Laura), Elma Karlowa (Countess Bronislawa), Ellen Kessler (Katya), Alice Kessler (Mira), Dick Price (Count Kaminsky), Fita Benkhoff (Countess Palmatica), Gunther Philipp (Jan Janicki), Gustav Knuth (Col. Ollendorf), Rudolf Vogel (Enterich), Karl Lieffen (Major Wangenheim), Jost Siethoff (Lt. Schwintz).

Remake of an 18th-century period piece based on an operetta in which boy meets girl, they overcome adversity and live happily ever after. Pretty tunes, attractive ladies but otherwise a stale movie, as bad as the original.

d, Werner Jacobs; w, Fritz Boetiger (based on the operetta "Der Bettelstudent" by Carl Milloecker, R. Gene); ph, Ernst W. Kalinke, Heinz Schnackerz (Eastmancolor).

Opera **(PR:A MPAA:NR)**

BEGGARS IN ERMINE** (1934) 70m MON bw

Lionel Atwill *(John Dawson)*, H. B. Walthall *(Marchant)*, Betty Furness *(Joyce)*, Jameson Thomas *(James Marley)*, James Bush *(Lee Marley)*, Astrid Allwyn *(Vivian)*, George Hayes *(Joe Wilson)*, Stephen Gross *(Scott Taggart)*.

Bizarre Atwill role as a cripple who organizes beggars throughout the world into a financial force on the marketplace. Background of steel mill life also interesting. Worth seeing because of Atwill's performance and appearance by young Betty Furness.

d, Phil Rosen; w, Tristram Tupper (based on a novel by Esther Lynd Daly); ph, Gilbert Warrenton.

Drama **Cas.** **(PR:A MPAA:NR)**

BEGGARS OF LIFE**** (1928) 80m PAR bw

Wallace Beery *(Oklahoma Red)*, Louise Brooks *(Nancy)*, Richard Arlen *(Jim)*, Edgar Blue Washington *(Mose)*, H.A. Morgan *(Skinny)*, Andy Clark *(Skelly)*, Mike Donlin *(Bill)*, Roscoe Karns *(Hopper)*, Robert Perry *(Arkansas Snake)*, Johnnie Morris *(Rubin)*, George Kotsonaros *(Baldy)*, Jacques Chapin *(Ukle)*, Robert Brower *(Blind Sims)*, Frank Brownlee *(Farmer)*.

An impressive early part-talkie, BEGGARS OF LIFE expresses a brilliant naturalism in its portrayal of Depression era hoboes. Arlen is a hungry, unkempt wanderer drawn into a country house in hopes of a hot meal. Peeking through the dusty screen door he sees an older man sitting motionless at a dinner table. Upon closer inspection, he finds the man a victim of a gunshot wound to the head. Demure Brooks enters and explains she killed the man, her adopted guardian, when he tried to rape her. Dressed in boy's clothes, she leaves with Arlen in hopes of hopping a freight train to safety. They settle down in a hobo camp led by Perry. When Perry's rival Beery arrives, a power struggle ensues, Beery takes over the camp, and expresses his desire for Brooks. Evading a trio of detectives who are after Brooks, the hoboes board a train which heads into the mountains. Beery holds "court," sentencing Arlen to be thrown off the train and granting himself exclusive rights to Brooks, touching off a brawl among the hoboes. The detectives have boarded the train and are close to capturing Brooks when Beery pulls a pin separating the car from the rest of the train. The runaway car plummets downhill before coming safely to a stop. Brooks and Arlen, with Washington and an injured friend, take refuge in a nearby cabin. Returning with a car and feminine attire for Brooks, Beery attempts to convince her to leave with him. He eventually recognizes the deep love Brooks and Arlen have for each other and allows them to escape in his car. In the meantime the injured hobo has died and Beery dresses the corpse in Brooks' discarded "boy" clothes and props it up on a lumber car. The detectives arrive and Beery sets the car on fire, then attracts the attention of the detectives who gun him down. Beery's ploy works, as the detectives believe Brooks has also perished in the gun battle and fire. Many miles away, Brooks and Arlen head for safety. While a silent version of the film does exist, the sound version of BEGGARS OF LIFE made significant in-roads in recording techniques. According to David O. Selznick, it was Wellman who first used a microphone on a boom, despite the insistence of sound engineers that mikes had to be stationery. Selznick recalled a confrontation between Wellman and the sound engineer: "Wellman, who had a quick temper, got very angry, took the microphone himself, hung it on a boom, gave orders to record—and moved it." Brooks never again equalled the success she achieved in BEGGARS OF LIFE (her German films for G.W. Pabst—PANDORA'S BOX, DIARY OF A LOST GIRL—are legendary however), mainly because she had no desire to become a Hollywood starlet. Wellman later cast her in PUBLIC ENEMY (1931), but when she chose to take a trip to New York instead, the part went to Jean Harlow.

d, William Wellman; w, Benjamin Glazer, Jim Tully (based on a story by Tully); ph, Henry Gerrard; ed, Alyson Shaffer.

Drama **(PR:A-C MPAA:NR)**

BEGGAR'S OPERA, THE*** (1953) 94m Imperadio/WB c

Laurence Olivier *(Capt. MacHeath)*, Stanley Holloway *(Lockit)*, George Devine *(Peachum)*, Mary Clare *(Mrs. Peachum)*, Athene Seyler *(Mrs. Trapes)*, Dorothy Tutin *(Polly Peachum)*, Daphne Anderson *(Lucy Lockit)*, Hugh Griffith *(The Beggar)*, Margot Grahame *(The Actress)*, Dennis Cannan *(The Footman)*, George Rose *(lst Turnkey)*, Yvonne Furneaux *(Jenny Diver)*, Cyril Conway, Edward Pryor, Felix Felton, Oliver Hunter, Sandra Dorne, Eileen Harvey, Edith Coats, Kenneth Williams, Tamba Alleney, John Kidd, Joycelyn James, John Baker.

THE BEGGAR'S OPERA is an attempt at recreating the original play by John Gay on film. It was also done as THE THREEPENNY OPERA with a score by Bertolt Brecht and Kurt Weill. The music in this version is by Sir Arthur Bliss with lyrics by Christopher Fry (THE LADY'S NOT FOR BURNING) as well as some additional dialog for the Cannan screenplay. Olivier stars as MacHeath ("Just a jacknife has MacHeath, babe, and he keeps it out of sight") with Holloway as Lockit, Griffith as the Beggar and the wonderful Seyler (she gave one of the funniest performances in *any* comedy in MAKE MINE MINK and for years specialized in classical stage work) as Mrs. Trapes. It's on two levels, in that Olivier does a play within a play as a criminal prisoner in Newgate who creates an opera based on his own life. It's very complex and may have been better done in MAN OF LA MANCHA. An ambitious project that never quite comes off. Olivier and Holloway did their own singing, but the others were dubbed. Olivier has a pleasant but airy baritone voice and did well to stay out of musicals. The attempt was bold and so was the failure at the box office but, for film enthusiasts, it remains an interesting curiosity.

p, Laurence Olivier, Herbert Wilcox; d, Peter Brook; w, Dennis Cannan, Christopher Fry (based on John Gay's comic opera); ph, Guy Green (Technicolor); m, Sir Arthur Bliss; ed, Reginald Beck.

Opera/Drama **(PR:C MPAA:NR)**

BEGINNING OF THE END* ½ (1957) 73m AB-PT Pictures Corp./REP bw

Peggy Castle *(Audrey)*, Peter Graves *(Ed)*, Morris Ankrum *(Gen. Hanson)*, Richard Benedict *(Cpl. Mathias)*, James Seay *(Capt. Barton)*, Thomas B. Henry *(Col. Sturgeon)*, Than Wyenn *(Frank)*, John Close *(Maj. Everett)*, Don C. Harvey *(1st Patrolman)*, Larry J. Blake *(2nd Patrolman)*, Steve Warren *(1st Soldier)*, Frank Connor *(2nd Soldier)*, Don Eltner *(3rd Soldier)*, Frank Chase *(4th Soldier)*, Pierre Watkin *(Taggert)*, Frank Wilcox *(Gen. Short)*.

Bert Gordon went on from this turkey to make some bigger and worse movies such as EMPIRE OF THE ANTS, FOOD OF THE GODS, THE AMAZING COLOSSAL MAN, CYCLOPS and several others. You've seen this plot a thousand times, but here it is . . . Several people die near a government testing station. Radioactive material has caused fruits and vegetables to grow to enormous proportions. Now . . . you have your choice of which insect gets a dose of the radioactive stuff in order to become huge. In FOOD OF THE GODS, it was wasps and worms and chickens and rats that became Cadillac-sized. In EMPIRE OF THE ANTS it was, of course, those knuckleheaded picnic pests. In this movie, it's grasshoppers! In an American version of the typical Japanese Godzilla film, the grasshoppers attack Chicago, tear up the Loop and are finally killed when it is learned that they cannot stand the waters of Lake Michigan. A ludicrous, cliche-filled movie. Graves (James Arness' brother) and Benedict, who went on to be a very successful TV director, do good work, as does that old war horse, Watkin, who began his career in 1935 and should have known better than to take a job in a movie as flawed as BEGINNING OF THE END.

p&d, Bert I. Gordon; w, Fred Freiberger, Lester Corn.

Science Fiction **(PR:C MPAA:NR)**

BEGINNING OR THE END, THE*** (1947) 110m MGM bw

Brian Donlevy *(Maj-Gen. Leslie R. Groves)*, Robert Walker *(Col. Jeff Nixon)*, Tom Drake *(Matt Cochran)*, Beverly Tyler *(Ann Cochran)*, Audrey Totter *(Jean O'Leary)*, Hume Cronyn *(Dr. J. Robert Oppenheimer)*, Hurd Hatfield *(Dr. John Wyatt)*, Joseph Calleia *(Dr. Enrico Fermi)*, Godfrey Tearle *(President Roosevelt)*, Victor Francen *(Dr. Marre)*, Richard Haydn *(Dr. Chisholm)*, Jonathan Hale *(Dr. Vannevar Bush)*, John Litel *(K. T. Keller)*, Henry O'Neill *(Gen. Thomas F. Farrell)*, Warner Anderson *(Capt. Parsons, USN)*, Barry Nelson *(Col. Paul Tibbets, Jr.)*, Art Baker *(President Truman)*, Ludwig Stossel *(Dr. Albert Einstein)*, John Hamilton *(Dr. Harold C. Urey)*.

The story of the development of the Atomic Bomb. There is also a love plot interwoven throughout the film and other subplots. Very realistic performances, masterful scripting and production. MGM head Mayer heard that Paramount intended to film a similar story so he rushed this one into production, determined to have the A-Bomb exclusively for his studio, buying the story from Hal Wallis for a hefty but unspecified amount.

p, Samuel Marx; d, Norman Taurog; w, Frank Wead; ph, Ray June, Warren Newcombe; m, Daniele Amfitheatrof; ed, George Hoemier.

Drama **(PR:A MPAA:NR)**

BEGUILED, THE** (1971) 105m UNIV c

Clint Eastwood *(John McBurney)*, Geraldine Page *(Martha)*, Elizabeth Hartman *(Edwina)*, Jo Ann Harris *(Carol)*, Darleen Carr *(Doris)*, Mae Mercer *(Hallie)*, Pamelyn Ferdin *(Amy)*, Melody Thomas *(Abigail)*, Peggy Drier *(Lizzie)*, Pattie Mattick *(Kanie)*.

Many critics adored this picture, just as many didn't. Count us in the latter. Clint is a wounded Union soldier convalescing at a southern girls' school. They attempt a black comedy but it never gets more than dark gray as the schoolgirls get curious and then sensuous about their lame visitor. It's funny when it shouldn't be, sentimental to a fault and has one of the goriest scenes ever shot with Page amputating Clint's leg. He claims she's doing this because he wouldn't bless her with his favors. Clint kills one of the girls' turtles. Well! That gets their dander up and they retaliate by feeding him poisoned mushrooms until he dies. Universal executives were livid when they heard that Siegel and Eastwood planned to have the lead character killed. They claimed that audiences would reject the notion of the hero's demise at the hands of a bunch of . . . women! It was a smash in Europe but failed to ignite any excitement in the U.S. Although it's rare when it happens, in this case the studio chiefs were right. Actually, they were wrong for making the movie in the first place. Eastwood fans want to see him as a winner (DIRTY HARRY, etc.), not as a meek or mild loser (BRONCO BILLY, PAINT YOUR WAGON). THE BEGUILED was made well with excellent technical credits but casting Clint in this role is as mistaken as putting Dom De Luise in a comedy (another grave error made by several producers in the seventies and eighties).

p&d, Don Siegel; w, John B. Sherry, Grimes Grice (based on the novel by Thomas Cullinan); ph, Bruce Surtees (Technicolor); m, Lalo Schifrin; ed, Carl Pingitore; cos, Helen Colvig; makeup, Bud Westmore.

Comedy **Cas.** **(PR:O MPAA:R)**

BEHAVE YOURSELF ½** (1951) 81m RKO bw

Farley Granger *(Bill Denny)*, Shelley Winters *(Kate Denny)*, Margalo Gilmore *(Mrs. Carter)*, William Demarest *(O'Ryan)*, Francis L. Sullivan *(Fat Fred)*, Lon Chaney, Jr. *(Pinky)*, Sheldon Leonard *(Bert)*, Marvin Kaplan *(Max)*, Henry Corden *(Numi)*, Glenn Anders *(Stam)*, Allen Jenkins *(Detective)*, Elisha Cook, Jr. *(Jonas)*, Hans Conreid *(Gillie)*.

Hit-and-miss comedy with odd casting of Winters and Granger as a young married couple. Archie, the dog, follows Granger home. Winters thinks the dog is an anniversary gift but it is, in reality, a specially trained animal that bad guys Leonard and Kaplan have lost. They advertise for the dog's return. Granger answers and uncovers a murder. Then it happens again. Soon, the screen is littered with corpses. It tries a bit too hard to have ARSENIC AND OLD LACE overtones with some sharp secondary casting: Leonard, who went on to become one of the most successful TV producers in America; Kaplan, who doesn't seem to have aged since he began his career on one of TV's earliest sitcoms, "Meet Millie" with Elena Verdugo; Demarest, another TV star in "My Three Sons"; Corden, who starred in "The Monkees" as the rock group's landlord; Conreid, whose career goes well back into radio when he was "My Friend Irma's" neighbor, Prof. Kropotkin; and, of course, everyone's favorite punk . . . Elisha Cook, Jr., who made a career out of sniveling. For the character roles alone, BEHAVE YOURSELF is worth seeing. The story was co-authored by Tarloff, who later went on to share an Oscar for the screenplay for FATHER GOOSE.

p, Jerry Wald, Norman Krasna, Stanley Rubin; d, George Beck; w, Beck (based on a story by Beck, Frank Tarloff); ph, James Wong Howe; m, Leigh Harline; ed, Paul Weatherwax; m/l, Lew Spence, Buddy Ebsen.

Comedy   **(PR:C MPAA:NR)**

BEHEMOTH, THE SEA MONSTER*

(1959, Brit.) 72m Eros bw (AKA: THE GIANT BEHEMOTH)

Gene Evans (*Steve Karnes*), Andre Morell (*Professor James Bickford*), Leigh Madison (*Jeanie*), Henry Vidon (*Tom*), John Turner (*John*), Jack McGowran (*Dr. Sampson*), Maurice Kaufmann (*Submarine Officer*), Leonard Sachs (*Scientist*).

Scientists track down radioactive sea monster off the coast of Britain. An A-Bomb, of course, sets free a dinosaur which immediately heads for London to chew up its great historical landmarks (they never bother the slums). Evans finally does the monster in by shooting a torpedo filled with radium into its bulk. But before it goesjust one more landmark, please—it crushes London Bridge with its death-rattling tail. Low budget torpedoed this effort.

p, David Diamond; d, Douglas Hickox, Eugene Lourie; w, Lourie; ph, Desmond Davies; m, Ted Astley; ed, Lee Doig.

Science Fiction   **(PR:A MPAA:NR)**

BEHIND CITY LIGHTS**

(1945) 68m REP bw

Lynne Roberts (*Jean Lowell*), Peter Cookson (*Lance Marlow*), Jerome Cowan (*Perry Borden*), Esther Dale (*Sarah Lowell*), William Terry (*Ben Coleman*), Victor Kilian (*Daniel Lowell*), Moroni Olsen (*Curtis Holbrook*), William Forrest (*Detective Peterson*), Emmett Vogan (*Jones*), Joseph J. Greene (*Gab Culson*), Frank Scannell (*Charles Matthews*), Tom London (*Andrew Coleman*), George Cagleton (*Doctor Blodgett*), Bud Geary (*Fred Haskins*).

Country girl Roberts walks out of wedding for city life and hooks up with two city slickers who turn out to be jewel thieves. After some narrow brushes with the law, Roberts returns to her farm boy fiance. Some laughs, sentiment and thrills.

p, Joseph Bercholz; d, John English; w, Richard Weil; ph, William Bradford; m, Richard Cherwin; m/l, Jule Styne.

Musical   **(PR:A MPAA:NR)**

BEHIND CLOSED SHUTTERS**

(1952, Ital.) 90m Lux bw

Massimo Girotti (*Roberto*), Eleonora Rossi (*Sandra*), Giulietta Masina (*Pippo*), Liliana Gerace (*Lucia*), Andriana Sivieri (*Iris*), Ottavio Senoret (*Signorino*), Caserina Gheraldi (*Gianna*), Antonio Nicotra (*Barale*), Renato Baldini (*Primavera*), Sidney Gordon (*Inspector*), Gilarda Sapienza (*The Religious Girl*).

A girl's search for her missing sister leads her through the sordid world of the Genovese waterfront. Filmed in semi-documentary fashion to give a realistic slice-of-life film.

p, Luigi Rovere; d, Luigi Comencini; w, Missimo Mida, Gianni Puccini, Franco Solinas, Sergio Solima; ph, Antonio Belviso; m, Carlo Rusticheli; ed, Rolando Benedetti.

Drama   **(PR:O MPAA:NR)**

BEHIND GREEN LIGHTS**

(1935) 68m Mascot bw

Norman Foster (*Dave Britten*), Judith Allen (*Mary Kennedy*), Sidney Blackmer (*Raymond Cortell*), Purnell Pratt (*Jim Kennedy*), Theodore Von Eltz (*J. C. Owen*), Edward Gargan (*Moran*), Kenneth Thomson (*Conrad*), Ford Sterling (*Max Schultz*), Jane Meredith (*Mrs. Gorham*), John Davidson (*Peasley*), Hooper Atchley (*District Attorney*).

Movie takes a good slap at shyster lawyers with a story treated from a cop's point of view and shows how such lawyers are able to keep crooks and gunmen out of jail. Foster is a little too tame and trusting for his role of hardboiled detective nabbing one public enemy after another. Good expose for this.

p, Nat Levine; d, Christy Cabanne; w, James Gruen, Colbert Clark (based on a book of the same name by Capt. Cornelius W. Willemse); ph, Ernie Miller, Jack Marta.

Crime Drama   **(PR:A MPAA:NR)**

BEHIND GREEN LIGHTS**

(1946) 64m FOX bw

Carole Landis (*Janet Bradley*), William Gargan (*Sam Carson*), Richard Crane (*Johnny Williams*), Mary Anderson (*Nora Bard*), John Ireland (*Detective Engelhofer*), Charles Russell (*Arthur Templeton*), Roy Roberts (*Max Calvert*), Mabel Paige (*Flossie*), Stanley Prager (*Ruzinsky*), Charles Tannen (*Ames*), Fred Sherman (*Zachary*), Don Beddoe (*Dr. Yager*), Bernard Nedell (*Bard*), Tom Moore (*Metcalfe*), Harry Seymour (*Kaypee*), Jimmy Cross (*King*), Charles Arnt (*Wintergreen*).

A policeman, Gargan, is torn between his devotion to duty and the opportunity to do something dishonest for political gain. Most of the action takes place around the press room of a police station. Gargan's life is further complicated when he falls for Landis who is suspected of a political murder. A fair whodunit that doesn't leave you guessing.

p, Robert Bassler; d, Otto Brower; w, W. Scott Darling, Charles G. Booth; ph, Joe MacDonald; m, Emil Newman; ed, Stanley Rabjohn.

Crime Drama   **(PR:A MPAA:NR)**

BEHIND JURY DOORS*

(1933) 67m Mayfair bw

Helen Chandler, William Collier, Jr., Blanche Frederici, Franklin Parker.

A young reporter becomes interested in the case of a physician convicted of murder and helps to prove his innocence. Stop the presses on this one.

p, Franchon Royer; d, Breezy Eason; w, John Thomas Neville (based on a story by Frank E. Fenton); ph, Earl N. Crain; ed, Jeanne Spencer.

Crime Drama   **(PR:A MPAA:NR)**

BEHIND LOCKED DOORS**

(1948) 61m EL bw

Lucille Bremer (*Kathy Lawrence*), Richard Carlson (*Ross Stewart*), Doug Fowley (*Larson*), Tom Browne Henry (*Dr. Clifford Porter*), Herbert Heyes (*Judge Drake*), Ralf Harolde (*Fred Hopps*), Gwen Donovan (*Madge Bennett*), Morgan Farley (*Topper*), Trevor Bardette (*Mr. Purvis*), Dickie Moore (*Jim*).

Newsman, Carlson, has himself committed to an insane asylum where he believes a political crook is hiding from the law. There is a $10,000 reward for the crook's arrest. While in the asylum, Carlson is suspected of faking a mental condition and, as the tension mounts, he almost undergoes a real nervous breakdown before solving the case. Some frightening moments when one of the resident lunatics gets loose and wreaks havoc. Nice little suspense drama.

p, Eugene Ling; d, Oscar "Budd" Boetticher, Jr.; w, Malvin Wald, Ling (based on a a story by Wald); ph, Guy Roe; m, Irving Friedman; ed, Norman Colbert; art d, Edward L. Ilou; set d, Armor Marlowe, Alexander Orenbach; cos, Frances Ehren; spec eff, George J. Teague.

Mystery   **(PR:A MPAA:NR)**

BEHIND LOCKED DOORS zero

(1976, S. Africa) 80m Box Office International c

Eve Reeves, Joyce Denner, Daniel Garth, Ivan Hager, Irene Lawrence.

Sleazy sexual version of the Frankenstein story where Garth appears to help Reeves and Denner when they run out of gas on a desolate road, takes them to his lair and begins his tortuous transformations. Not worth a whimsical blink.

p&d, Charles Romine; w, Romine, Stanley H. Brasloff.

Horror   **(PR:O MPAA:R)**

BEHIND OFFICE DOORS**

(1931) 82m RKO bw

Mary Astor (*Mary Linden*), Robert Ames (*James Duneen*), Ricardo Cortez (*Bonnie Wales*), Kitty Kelly (*Delores Kogan*), Edna Murphy (*Daisy Presby*), Catherine Dale Owen (*Ellen Robison*), Charles Sellon (*Ritter*), William Morris (*Robinson*).

A movie aimed at women which shows who really can wield power in an office organizational setup. Astor is the guiding secretarial light behind executive Ames who takes her for granted until Cortez makes his play and she almost falls. At the last second Ames proposes, for a fast turnabout.

d, Melville Brown; w, Carey Wilson (based on a story by Alan Brener Schultz).

Drama   **(PR:A MPAA:NR)**

BEHIND PRISON GATES**

(1939) 63m COL bw

Brian Donlevy (*Red Murray*), Jacqueline Wells [Julie Bishop] (*Sheila Murphy*), Joseph Crehan (*Warden O'Neil*), Paul Fix (*Petey Ryan*), George Lloyd (*Marty Conroy*), Dick Curtis (*Capt. Simmons*), Richard Fisk (*Lyman*).

Donlevy, in a fine performance, is a secret operative who goes to prison to uncover where a pair of bank robbers and cop killers have hidden the stolen money. Harrowing moments occur when Donlevy's identity is almost discovered. Good prison movie.

d, Charles Barton; w, Arthur T. Horman, Leslie T. White; ph, Allen G. Siegler; ed, Richard Fantl.

Crime Drama   **(PR:A MPAA:NR)**

BEHIND PRISON WALLS**

(1943) 64m PRC bw (GB: YOUTH TAKES A HAND)

Alan Baxter (*Jonathan MacGlennon*), Gertrude Michael (*Elinor Cantwell*), Tully Marshall (*James J. MacGlennon*), Edwin Maxwell (*Percy Webb*), Jacqueline Dalya (*Mimi*), Matt Willis (*Frank Lucacelli*), Richard Kipling (*Frederick Driscoll*), Olga Sabin (*Yette Kropatchek*), Isabelle Withers (*Whitey O'Neill*), Lane Chandler (*Reagan*), Paul Everton (*Warden*), George Guhl (*Doc*), Regina Wallace (*Mrs. Cantwell*).

Honest son, Baxter, gets steel tycoon dad, Marshall, sent to prison and winds up there himself. While in jail, son tries to convert pop from capitalist to moderate socialist. Good father-son comedy. This was veteran Marshall's last film; he died shortly after the movie's completion, having made his film debut in 1914.

p, Arthur Ripley; d, Steve Sekely; w, Van Norcross (based on a story by W.A. Ulman, Jr.); ph, Marcel Le Picard; ed, Holbrook N. Todd; md, David Chudnow.

Comedy   **(PR:A MPAA:NR)**

BEHIND STONE WALLS*

(1932) 58m Action Pictures bw

Robert Elliott, Priscilla Dean, Eddie Nugent, Ann Christy, Robert Ellis, George Chesebro.

Cheating wife shoots lover, but her stepson shoulders the blame to protect father from learning the truth. Stonewall this one.

d, Frank Strayer; w, George B. Seitz; ph, Jules Cronjager; ed, Byron Robinson.

Drama (PR:A MPAA:NR)

BEHIND THAT CURTAIN*** (1929) 91m FOX bw

Warner Baxter (*John Beetham*), Lois Moran (*Eve Mannering*), Gilbert Emery (*Sir Frederic Bruce*), Claude King (*Sir George Mannering*), Philip Strange (*Eric Durand*), Boris Karloff (*Sudanese Servant*), Jamiel Hassen (*Habib Hanna*), Peter Gawthorne (*Scotland Yard Inspector*), John Rogers (*Alf Pornick*), Montague Shaw (*Hilary Galt*), Finch Smiles (*Galt's Clerk*), Mercedes De Valasco (*Neinah*), E. L. Parks (*Charlie Chan*).

A crackerjack melodrama that has a few interesting sidelights to it. This movie introduced Karloff to sound (in a role so small that it didn't have a character name) and, in a small cameo, we see the detective who would last longer than just about any other on the screen, Charlie Chan, in his third screen appearance. In this version, the redoubtable Chan is a lieutenant with Scotland Yard and is played by Parks, one of the many Occidentals who did the role. King hires Shaw to pry into the background of Strange who wants to marry Moran, a rich young woman and King's niece. Shaw is quickly murdered and King then learns that Strange has married Moran and they've gone off to India. Baxter, an old pal who has long harbored the warmies for Lois, sees that she is not happy with Strange; the man is a cheat, liar, drunk, etc. She'd love to dump the cad and go back home. They leave together on a chartered plane. The picture winds up in San Francisco, where Baxter is giving a lecture when Strange comes in and starts shooting, but is quickly dispatched by Parks. This is a fast-moving mystery with more twists than San Francisco's Lombard Street. It may get a bit confusing at times but worth staying with as the conclusion is worthwhile. Gilbert Emery (born Gilbert Emery Bensley Pottle) never achieved the success expected of him and was relegated to stereotype roles.

p, William Fox; d, Irving Cummings; w, Sonya Levien, Clarke Silvernail (based on the novel by Earl Derr Biggers); ph, Conrad Wells, Dave Ragin, Vincent Farrar; ed, Alfred De Gaetano.

Mystery (PR:C MPAA:NR)

BEHIND THE DOOR (SEE: MAN WITH NINE LIVES, THE, 1940)

BEHIND THE EIGHT BALL**½
(1942) 59m Universal bw (GB: OFF THE BEATEN TRACK)

Al Ritz, Jimmy Ritz, Harry Ritz (*The Three Jolly Jesters*), Carol Bruce (*Joan Barry*), Dick Foran (*Bill Edwards*), Grace McDonald (*Babs*), Johnny Downs (*Danny*), William Demarest (*Police Chief McKenzie*), Richard Davies (*Clay Martin*), William Ruhl (*Officer Flynn*), Kernan Cripps (*Officer Doyle*), Lew Kelly (*Hank, the Stagehand*), Ray Kellogg (*Dunham Vocalist*), Russell Hicks (*Harry B. Kemp*), Jack Arnold (*Vinton Haworth*), Bobby Leonard, Johnnie Berkes, Claire Whitney, Ruth Lee, Duke York.

The Ritz Brothers get involved in auditioning for a play, murder, and mayhem. Nice dumb Ritz Brothers movie with broad comedy, burlesque and good 1940s band music. Songs include "Bravest of the Brave,' "You Don't Know What Love Is," "Keep 'Em Laughing," "Atlas," "Mr. Five By Five," "Wasn't It Wonderful?" "Riverboat Jamboree," "Golden Wedding Day," "Don't You Think We Ought To Dance?" (Don Raye, Gene De Paul), "When My Baby Smiles At Me" (Andrew B. Sterling, Harry von Tilzer). (See RITZ BROTHERS series, Index.)

p, Howard Benedict; d, Edward F. Cline; w, Stanley Roberts, Mel Ronson; ph, George Robinson; md, Charles Previn; ed, Maurice Wright.

Musical/Comedy (PR:A MPAA:NR)

BEHIND THE EVIDENCE* (1935) 70m COL bw

Norman Foster (*Tony Sheridan*), Donald Cook (*Ward Cameron*), Sheila Mannors (*Ruth Allen*), Geneva Mitchell (*Rita Sinclair*), Samuel Hinds (*J. T. Allen*), Frank Darien (*Herbert*), Pat O'Malley (*Lt. James*), Gordon De Main (*Capt. Graham*), Edward Keane (*Hackett*).

An ex-millionaire playboy, Foster, becomes a newspaper reporter and solves a series of holdups. Foster spends most of his time battling his old grump editor. The news on this movie is not very good.

d, Lambert Hillyer; w, Harold Shumate; ph, Henry Freulich; ed, Richard Cahoon.

Drama (PR:A MPAA:NR)

BEHIND THE HEADLINES** (1937) 58m RKO bw

Lee Tracy (*Eddie Haines*), Diana Gibson (*Mary Bradley*), Donald Meek (*Potter*), Paul Guilfoyle (*Art Martin*), Philip Huston (*Bennett*), Frank M. Thomas (*Naylor*), Tom Kennedy (*Tiny*), Doodles Weaver (*Duggan*).

Newspaper reporter Tracy competes with a lady reporter, Gibson, on the trail of bank robbers. The race for a scoop becomes so fierce that the fragile relationship between Tracy and Gibson almost snaps but is patched together when the smart-talking Tracy rescues his girl from gangsters. Fast-paced direction and above average dialog on a programmer with plenty of bantering humor.

p, Cliff Reid; d, Richard Rosson; w, J. Robert Bren, Edmund I. Hartman (from a story by Thomas Ahearn); ph, Russell Metty; ed, Harry Marker.

Drama (PR:A MPAA:NR)

BEHIND THE HEADLINES*½ (1956, Brit.) 67m Kenilworth/RFD bw

Paul Carpenter (*Paul Banner*), Hazel Court (*Maxine*), Adrienne Corri (*Pam Barnes*), Alfie Bass (*Sammy*), Ewen Solon (*Supt. Faro*), Harry Fowler (*Alfie*), Trevor Reid (*Mr. Bunting*), Olive Gregg (*Mrs. Bunting*).

A blackmailing showgirl is murdered and reporters sniff out the killer of the blonde schemer. Weak script and stiff direction offer little suspense in this routine yarn.

p, Guido Coen; d, Charles Saunders; w, Allan Mackinnon (based on the novel by Robert Chapman); ph, Geoffrey Faithfull.

Crime/Mystery (PR:A MPAA:NR)

BEHIND THE HIGH WALL*½ (1956) 85m UNIV bw

Tom Tully (*Frank Carmichael*), Sylvia Sidney (*Hilda Carmichael*), Betty Lynn (*Anne MacGregor*), John Gavin (*Johnny Hutchins*), Don Beddoe (*Todd MacGregor*), John Larch (*William Kiley*), Barney Phillips (*Tom Reynolds*), Ed Kemmer (*Charlie Rains*), John Beradino (*Carl Burkhardt*), Rayford Barnes (*George Miller*), Herbert C. Lytton (*Prof. Reese*), Nicky Blair (*Roy Burkhardt*), David Garcia (*Morgan*), William Forrest (*Corby*), Frances Osborne (*Mrs. Loomis*), Peter Leeds, Jim Hyland (*Detectives*), Bing Russell, Dale Van Sickel, George Barrows, Ray Darmour (*Guards*).

Screenplay by Bloom, another writer born and raised in Coney Island, fails to grip the emotions as Tully stars as a prison warden with Sidney as his crippled wife. Story is that Tully is kidnaped by convicts. Gavin (Ambassador to Mexico in the Reagan administration) is forced to go along. The truck in which they're riding is wrecked and villains are killed with only Gavin and Tully surviving. One hundred thousand bucks is stolen by Tully who lets Gavin be sentenced for getting involved in a prison break in which an officer is killed. Gavin is remanded to the death house and escapes. The cops catch him and his life is saved when Tully confesses that Gavin had nothing to do with the break and was inadvertently dragged into it. Look for Beradino (former baseball player) and Peter Leeds, Jack Benny's favorite TV foil. (Remake of THE BIG GUY, 1939.)

p, Stanley Rubin; d, Abner Biberman; w, Harold Jack Bloom (based on a story by Wallace Sullivan and Richard K. Polimer); ph, Maury Gertsman; m, Ted J. Gershenson; ed, Ted J. Kent; cos, Bill Thomas.

Crime/Drama (PR:C MPAA:NR)

BEHIND THE IRON CURTAIN (SEE: IRON CURTAIN, THE, 1948)

BEHIND THE IRON MASK*½
(1977) Sascha Wien/COL c (AKA: THE FIFTH MUSKETEER)

Beau Bridges (*King Louis*), Sylvia Kristel (*Marie-Therese*), Ursula Andress (*Mme. de la Valliere*), Cornel Wilde (*D'Artagnan*), Ian McShane (*Fourquet*), Lloyd Bridges (*Aramis*), Alan Hale, Jr. (*Porthos*), Helmut Dantine (*Ambassador*), Olivia De Havilland (*Queen Anne*), Jose Ferrer (*Athos*), Rex Harrison (*Colbert*).

Evil twin takes over the throne by imprisoning legitimate monarch and making him wear an iron mask. Top-notch cast salvages this one.

p, Ted Richmond; d, Ken Annakin, w, David Ambrose (based on novel, *The Man in the Iron Mask*, by Alexandre Dumas and a screenplay by George Bruce); ph, Jack Cardiff (Eastmancolor); m, Riz Ortolani; art d, Theo Harisch; ed, Malcolm Cooke; cos, Tony Pueco.

Adventure (PR:C MPAA:PG)

BEHIND THE MAKEUP** (1930) 65m PAR bw

Hal Skelly (*Hap Brown*), William Powell (*Gardoni*), Fay Wray (*Marie*), Kay Francis (*Kitty Parker*), E. H. Calvert (*Dawson*), Paul Lukas (*Boris*), Agostino Borgato (*Chef*), Jacques Vanaire (*Valet*), Jean De Briac (*Sculptor*), Torben Meyer (*Waiter*), Bob Perry (*Bartender*).

They were already doing backstage dramas and the sound era had only just begun. Powell is the heavy in this seamy tale of former circus clowns. Skelly is a successful small-time performer working in New Orleans. He saves Powell's life when the latter is literally starving to death. Powell is from a famous family of European clowns and Skelly proposes they do a two-act. Powell is above the slapstick kind of thing and wants to perform only high-class (read "unfunny") material. They try it and it bombs. Powell leaves and Skelly later finds him doing the very same act that Skelly wanted to do in the first place. Powell apologizes, loses his new partner, and he and Skelly take up where they left off, with Skelly getting smaller billing. Powell eventually steals Skelly's girl friend and marries her, then instantly begins to cheat. He also loses all the team's money on gambling. When Kay Francis, the second girl, tosses Powell aside, he does a Davy Jones and walks into the water until he floats. One can only presume that Skelly and Fay Wray, the former g.f. and now Powell's widow, will get back together. Now that's a heck of a lot of story for 65 minutes. Worthwhile viewing, if only to see Powell in the unaccustomed role of a backstabbing, cheating, lying thief.

d, Robert Milton; w, George Manker Watters, Howard Estabrook (based on a story by Mildred Cram); ph, Charles Lang; ed, Doris Drought; m/l, Leo Robin, Sam Coslow, Newell Chase.

Drama (PR:C MPAA:NR)

BEHIND THE MASK** (1932) 68m COL bw

Jack Holt (*Hart*), Constance Cummings (*Julie*), Boris Karloff (*Henderson*), Claude King (*Arnold*), Bertha Mann (*Edwards*), Edward Van Sloan (*Steiner*), Willard Robertson (*Hawkes*).

A mad doctor, Van Sloan, is the head of a drug syndicate. When he knocks off people who know too much, he doesn't fill the caskets with their bodies, but with dope. Karloff, in his first role following FRANKENSTEIN, is merely another thug helping Secret Service agent Holt, a disappointment for his legion of fans. Despite the serial-like plot of storm-raging nights, eerie graveyards and a laboratory crackling with strange electrical instruments, the film packs a lot of campy interest. Van Sloan, the kindly, moralistic character of DRACULA and FRANKENSTEIN, here turns lunatic, savoring the vivisection of his victims.

p, Harry Cohn; d, John Francis Dillon; w, Jo Swerling (based on his story "In the Secret Service"); ph, Ted Tetzlaff; ed, Otis Garrett.

Crime/Drama **(PR:C MPAA:NR)**

BEHIND THE MASK* (1946) 67m MON bw

Kane Richmond *(Lamont Cranston)*, Barbara Read *(Margo Lane)*, George Chandler *(Shrevie)*, Joseph Crehan *(Cardona)*, Pierre Watkin *(Weston)*, Dorothea Kent *(Jennie)*, Joyce Compton *(Lulu)*, Marjorie Hoshelle *(Mac Bishop)*, June Clyde *(Edith Merrill)*, Robert Shayne *(Brad Thomas)*, Lou Crosby *(Marty Greane)*, Edward Gargan *(Dixon)*, Bill Christy *(Copy Boy)*, James Cardwell *(Jeff Mann)*, Nancy Brinkman *(Susan)*, Dewey Robinson *(Head Waiter)*, Marie Harmon *(Girl)*, Ruth Cherrington *(Dowager)*, James Nataro *(Reporter)*.

"The Shadow" must prove himself innocent of the murder of a newspaper columnist. He breaks up a bookie ring and blackmail operation along the way. The contrived comedy situations introduced into the plot destroy the mood.

p, Joe Kaufman; d, Phil Karlson; w, George Callahan (based on "The Shadow" radio character); ph, William A. Sickner; ed, Ace Herman.

Crime Drama **(PR:A MPAA:NR)**

BEHIND THE MASK 1/2** (1958, Brit.) 99m GW Films c

Michael Redgrave *(Sir Arthur Benson Gray)*, Tony Britton *(Philip Selwood)*, Carl Mohner *(Dr. Carl Romek)*, Niall MacGinnis *(Neil Isherwood)*, Vanessa Redgrave *(Pamela Gray)*, Ian Bannen *(Alan Crabtree)*, Brenda Bruce *(Elizabeth Fallon)*, Lionel Jeffries *(Walter Froy)*, Miles Malleson *(Sir Oswald Pettiford)*, John Welsh *(Col. Langley)*, Ann Firbank *(Mrs. Judson)*, Jack Hedley *(Dr. Galbraith)*, Hugh Miller *(Examiner)*, Mary Skinner *(Theatre Sister)*, Margaret Tyzack *(Night Sister)*, John Gale *(Mr. John Greenwood)*.

A strange title that makes one think of Zorro, not a hospital drama. The producers must have thought we'd understand that the mask they refer to is a surgical one, not a mask to hide one's identity. Lots of plots, sub-plots and counter-plots in this Dope Opera which is not to be confused with the Boris Karloff 1932 feature of the same name. Redgrave and MacGinnis are the two senior surgeons who run the country hospital. They are diametrically opposed as to how it should function. This gives birth to several complications and the medical highlight of the film: a heart operation shown on a closed-circuit TV screen. This film introduced Vanessa Redgrave to the movie industry and she showed immediate promise. Good casting in the smaller roles and Miles Malleson is excellent as the chairman of the hospital's board. (Malleson was a playwright, screenwriter and actor whose personal life was filled with sexual intrigue, quite unlike the potty roles he played such as the celibate Dr. Chasuble in THE IMPORTANCE OF BEING EARNEST.)

p, Sergei Nolbandov, Josef Somlo; d, Brian Desmond Hurst; w, John Hunter (based on the novel *The Pack* by John Rowan Wilson); ph, Robert Krasker (Eastmancolor); m, Geoffrey Wright; ed, Alan Morrison.

Drama **(PR:C MPAA:NR)**

BEHIND THE MIKE* 1/2 (1937) 68m UNIV bw

William Gargan *(George Hayes)*, Judith Barrett *(Jane Arledge)*, Don Wilson *(Tiny Martin)*, Sterling Holloway *(Tommy Astor)*, William Davidson *(Cyrus Wittles)*, Gerald Oliver Smith *(Robert Ainesley)*, Charles Brokaw *(Harry Fox)*, Spencer Charters *(Pete Jones)*, Grady Sutton *(Curly Conway)*, Harlan Briggs *(Sheriff)*, Roy Atwell *(Vale)*, Jerry Mandy *(First Violinist)*.

Don Wilson, Jack Benny's radio announcer, shows a flair for acting in this comedy about the world of radio. Gargan and Barrett are rival radio producers battling for programs and sponsorship, adversarial positions that almost wreck their love life. Gargan has a self-destructive habit of telling off sponsors, but he is saved from his own folly by pal Wilson, jovial and with a voice that radiates comfort and care. Gags don't hold up, but Wilson does.

p, Lou Brock; d, Sidney Salkow; w, Barry Trivers; ph, Elwood Bredell; ed, Phil Cahn.

Comedy **(PR:A MPAA:NR)**

BEHIND THE NEWS* (1941) 75m REP bw

Lloyd Nolan *(Stuart Woodrow)*, Doris Davenport *(Barbara Shaw)*, Frank Albertson *(Jeff Flavin)*, Robert Armstrong *(Vic Archer)*, Paul Harvey *(Hardin S. Kelly)*, Charles Halton *(Neil Saunders)*, Eddie Conrad *(Enrico)*, Harry Tyler *(Monroe)*, Dick Elliott *(Foster)*, Archie Twitchell *(Reporter)*, Veda Ann Borg *(Bessie)*, Milton Parsons *(Eddie)*.

Journalism school scholarship winner befriends a boozy former news ace and gets the pro to straighten up his act. The two of them go on to upset a crime scheme. Nothing worthwhile in this cheapie.

p, Robert North; d, Joseph Santley; w, Isabel Dawn, Boyce De Gaw; ph, Jack Marta; md, Cy Feuer; ed, Ernest Nims.

Drama **(PR:A MPAA:NR)**

BEHIND THE RISING SUN*** (1943) 88m RKO bw

Margo *(Tama)*, Tom Neal *(Taro)*, J. Carrol Naish *(Publisher)*, Robert Ryan *(Lefty)*, Gloria Holden *(Sara)*, Don Douglas *(O'Hara)*, George Givot *(Boris)*, Adeline Reynolds *(Grandmother)*, Leonard Strong *(Tama's Father)*, Iris Wong *(Woman Secretary)*, Wolfgang Zilzer *(Max)*, Shirley Lew *(Servant)*, Benson Fong *(Japanese Officer)*, Lee Tung Foo *(Dinner Guest)*, Mike Mazurki *(Japanese Wrestler)*, William Yip *(Japanese Officer)*, H. T. Tsiang *(Policeman)*, Luke Chan *(Officer)*, Bruce Wong *(First Agent)*, Leon Lontoc *(Japanese Guard)*, Mei Lee Foo *(Geisha Girl)*, Allan Jung *(Capt. Matsuda)*, Abner Biberman *(Inspector)*, Connie Leon *(Tama's Mother)*, Nancy Gates *(Sister)*, Fred Essler *(Takahashi)*, Philip Ahn *(Japanese Officer)*, Daisy Lee *(Takahashi's Servant)*, Richard Loo *(Japanese Officer)*, Barbara Jean Wong *(Girl Given Dope)*, Beal Wong *(Japanese Major)*, Charles Lung *(Broker)*, Robert Katcher *(Prof. Namachi)*.

A slam-bang, flag-waving, anti-Japanese movie that was released at the nadir of the war and served to rally moviegoers behind the War Bond effort that went on in every theater. Lavery and Dmytryk (who teamed earlier on a highly successful RKO film called HITLER'S CHILDREN) tell the story of a Japanese publisher, Naish, forcing his son, Neal, to join the Japanese Army against his will. Lots of atrocities to show the Japanese as inhuman. Highlight action sequence is a battle between American boxer Ryan and Japanese ju-jitsu expert Mazurki. Looking at the picture today it seems simple. But taken at the time it was made, BEHIND THE RISING SUN stirred a lot of hearts and served to unite the states. Somewhat ludicrous is the casting of Margo, Mazurki, Neal and Naish as Asians but that's the way it was back then. The audiences cheered when Naish committed hara-kiri.

d, Edward Dmytryk; w, Emmett Lavery, Sr. (based on the book by James R. Young); ph, Russell Metty; m, Roy Webb; ed, Joseph Noriega; spec eff, Vernon L. Walker.

War **Cas.** **(PR:C MPAA:NR)**

BEHIND YOUR BACK** (1937, Brit.) 70m Crusade/PAR bw

Jack Livesey*(Archie Bentley)*, Dinah Sheridan *(Kitty Hugon)*, Elizabeth Astell *(Gwen Bingham)*, Stella Bonheur *(Lady Millicent Coombe)*, Desmond Marshall *(Leslie Woodford)*, Rani Waller *(Mary Woodford)*, Kenneth Buckley *(Albert Clifford)*, Toni Edgar Bruce *(Clara Bradley)*, Raymond Lovell *(Adam Adams)*, Jimmy Mageean *(Man from the Stalls)*.

An improbable but interesting story has a wise playwright solve the many problems of her leading actors before the opening night of her play. Fairly good script and direction bring this one above the mediocre.

p, Victor M. Greene; d&w, Donovan Pedelty (based on the play by Charles Landstone); ph, Stanley Grant.

Drama **(PR:A MPAA:NR)**

BEHOLD A PALE HORSE* 1/2** (1964) 118m COL bw

Gregory Peck *(Manuel Artiguez)*, Anthony Quinn *(Captain Vinolas)*, Omar Sharif *(Father Francisco)*, Mildred Dunnock *(Pilar)*, Raymond Pellegrin *(Carlos)*, Paolo Stoppa *(Pedro)*, Daniela Rocca *(Rosanna)*, Christian Marquand *(Lt. Zaganar)*, Marietto Angeletti *(Paco Degas)*, Perette Pradier *(Maria)*, Zia Mohyeddin *(Luis)*, Rosalie Crutchley *(Teresa)*, Mollie Urquhart, Jean-Paul Molinot, Laurence Badie, Martin Benson, Jean-Claude Berck, Claude Berri, Claude Confortes, Michel Lonsdale, Alain Saury, Jose-Luis Vilallonga, Elisabeth Wiener.

The Spanish Civil War ended many years earlier but Peck is still fighting it, not unlike those Japanese who were found on obscure islands so many years after the end of WW II. Peck, miscast as a Spaniard, leads forays from France and Spain and continues an almost one-man effort for a while after the war. Twenty years later, Peck is told that his mother, Dunnock, is dying in Spain. He doesn't realize that it's a trap set by Quinn, the vicious Spanish police chief who has been after Peck for years. Dunnock, knowing that her son has been set up, pleads with Sharif, her priest, to tell Peck what's happening. Sharif feels that he is a human being before he is a Spaniard, so he tells Peck the truth while on a trip to Lourdes. Despite this, Peck goes to visit his mother at the hospital. He kills the man who set him up (Pellegrin) and is then killed by Quinn's men. Quinn will wonder forever why Peck came back. Lots of preachy moralizing and allegory in this art film that never had the great commercial success expected. Peck is very good, Quinn is superb, and everyone involved with this subtle and yet powerful movie should take a bow.

p&d, Fred Zinnemann; w, J. P. Miller (from the novel *Killing A Mouse On Sunday* by Emeric Pressburger); ph, Jean Badal; m, Maurice Jarre; ed, Walter Thompson; art d, Auguste Capelier.

War/Drama **Cas.** **(PR:C MPAA:NR)**

BEHOLD MY WIFE* (1935) 79m PAR bw

Sylvia Sidney *(Tonita Stormcloud)*, Gene Raymond *(Michael Carter)*, Julie Compton *(Diana Carter-Curson)*, Laura Hope Crews *(Mrs. Carter)*, H. B. Warner *(Mr. Carter)*, Monroe Owsley *(Bob Prentice)*, Kenneth Thomson *(Jim Curson)*, Ann Sheridan *(Mary White)*, Dean Jagger *(Pete)*, Charlotte Granville *(Mrs. Sykes)*, Eric Blore *(Benson)*, Charles B. Middleton *(Juan Stormcloud)*, Ralph Remley *(Jenkins)*, Cecil Weston *(Gibson)*, Dewey Robinson *(Bryan)*, Edward Gargan *(Connoly)*, Olin Howland *(Mattingly)*, Greg Whitespear *(Medicine Man)*, Jim Thorpe *(Indian Chief)*, Otto Hoffman *(Minister)*, Nella Walker *(Mrs. Copperwaithe)*, Gwenllian Gill *(Miss Copperwaithe)*, Charles Wilson *(Police Captain)*, Fuzzy Knight *(Photographer)*.

Raymond, son of a wealthy family, decides to teach his folks a lesson after they won't let him marry a pretty stenographerhe goes West and brings back his new wife, Sidney, the daughter of an Indian chief. In this offbeat movie, racial hate is explored on a prosaic level and is confused when Compton shoots her extramarital lover and Sidney is blamed for it. Raymond goes to the police and confesses the killing, but detectives put them in a room together, turn on a hidden microphone, and hear that both are innocent; they are released to resume their marriage. Strong cast and a good perform- ance by Ann Sheridan can't help this one.

p, B. P. Schulberg; d, Mitchell Leisen; w, Vincent Lawrence, Grover Jones (based on the novel *Translation of a Savage,* by Sir Gilbert Parker); ph, Leon Shamroy.

Drama **(PR:C MPAA:NR)**

BEING, THE* 1/2 (1983) 79m BFV c

Martin Landau *(Garson Jones)*, Jose Ferrer *(Mayor)*, Ruth Buzzi *(Mayor's Wife)*, Dorothy Malone *(Marge)*, Rexx Coltrane *(Mortimer)*, Marianne Gordon Rogers *(Laurie)*, Kent Perkins *(Dudley)*.

Made in 1980 under the name EASTER SUNDAY (the horror movie producers were running out of dates for their titles after HALLOWEEN and FRIDAY THE THIRTEENTH,etc.), this inept film had its creators decide to change the name of the picture rather than incur the wrath of those churchgoers who feel that Easter Sunday is sacred. This is a mystery-horror film but the biggest mystery is how they ever managed to convince two Oscar winners (Malone for WRITTEN ON THE WIND and Ferrer for his memorable CYRANO DE BERGERAC) to appear in this cinematic Valium. The plot, for what it's worth, goes something like this: People in a small Idaho town are disappearing and nobody knows how or where. Coltrane wants to find out why but Ferrer, as the mayor, stands in his way because this is a big potato town and that's their main income, so why jeopardize it for the sake of a few vanishing citizens? (Does this sort of sound like the plot of JAWS?) Someone suggests it might be the nuclear (yawn) dump outside of town but Landau says, "Nah. The place is as safe as your mother's arms." Hah! The more fool he. Well, the story finally gets around to being The Creature From The Nuclear Dump.

p, William Osco; d&w, Jackie Kong; ph, Robert Ebinger; m, Don Preston; ed, David Newhouse; art d, Alexia Corwin.

Horror   **Cas.**   **(PR:C MPAA:R)**

BEING THERE*** (1979) 130m Lorimar/UA c

Peter Sellers (Chance), Shirley MacLaine (Eve Rand), Melvyn Douglas (Benjamin Rand), Jack Warden (President Bobby), Richard Dysart (Dr. Robert Allenby), Richard Basehart (Vladmir Skrapinov), Ruth Attaway (Louise), Dave Clenon (Thomas Franklin), Fran Brill (Sally Hayes), Denise DuBarry (Johanna Franklin), Oteil Burbridge (Lolo), Ravenell Keller III (Abbaz), Brian Corrigan (Policeman), Alfredine Brown (Old Woman), Donald Jacob (David), Ernest M. McClure (Jeffery), Kenneth Patterson (Butler), Richard Venture (Wilson), Arthur Grundy (Arthur), W.C. "Mutt" Burton (Lewis), Henry B. Dawkins (Billings), Georgine Hall (Mrs. Aubrey), Nell Leaman (Constance), Villa Mae Barkley (Teresa), Alice Hirson (First Lady), James Noble (Kaufman), Sandy Ward (Sen. Slipshod), Danna Hansen (Mrs. Slipshod), Mitch Kreindel (Dennis Watson), Katherine De Hetre (Kinney), Sam Weisman (Colson), Elya Baskin (Karpatov), Thann Wyenn (Ambassador Gaufridi).

Perfection. Never have two hours and ten minutes gone by so quickly. Sellers is an innocent illiterate who has lived in a house with an old man ever since he can remember. The old man dies and Sellers must leave the cocoon. He has never been in the real world and only knows of it through watching television, his one and all-consuming passion. On the streets, he is hit by a limousine owned by MacLaine who is married to a kingmaker, a man behind all the President's men (Douglas). Sellers' honesty is charming and his prosaic answers seduce Douglas and MacLaine and eventually the President (Warden in a sensational performance). Sellers becomes a national celebrity by appearing on his favorite medium, television. His answers to complex questions are beautiful. We, the audience, realize that he is talking about gardening (he had been a gardener at his former residence) but the audience in the film finds all sorts of hidden meanings to his simple words. His truthfulness attracts the policy makers in the political party and by the film's end they are seriously considering Sellers as a presidential nominee. That, in a nutshell, is the story, yet the details would take many nutshells to cover. Sellers hadn't been this good since his early British comedies. MacLaine is sincere and funny as the sex-starved wife. Douglas is such a presence on screen that it's difficult to look at anyone else in a scene if Douglas is there. The movie was made in Los Angeles, Washington, D.C. and at The Biltmore, Vanderbilt's incredible North Carolina mansion. As in the case of ONE FLEW OVER THE CUCKOO'S NEST, BEING THERE took many years to get done. It was worth the wait. Though ostensibly labeled a comedy, BEING THERE goes way beyond comedy, beyond satire, and out into a world of its own.

p, Andrew Braunsberg; d, Hal Ashby; w, Jerzy Kosinski (based on his novel); ph, Caleb Deschanel (Technicolor); m, John Mandel; ed, Don Zimmerman; art d, James Schoppe; set d, Robert Benton; makeup, Charles Schram, Frank Westmore.

Comedy   **Cas.**   **(PR:C MPAA:PG)**

BELA LUGOSI MEETS A BROOKLYN GORILLA*
(1952) 74m REA bw (AKA: BOYS FROM BROOKLYN, THE)

Bela Lugosi (Dr. Zabor), Duke Mitchell (Duke Mitchell), Sammy Petrillo (Sammy Petrillo), Charlita (Nona), Muriel Landers (Salome), Al Kikume (Chief Rakos), Mickey Simpson (Chula), Milton Newberger (Bongo), Martin Garralaga (Pepe Borde), Ramona, the Chimp (Himself).

Mad scientist Lugosi comes across two zanies in a tropical jungle and tries to get rid of them because of jealousy over a pretty girl. He turns one of the two into a gorilla. Lugosi is at his usual scary best, but the movie is at its worst with Mitchell and Petrillo doing awful imitations of Martin and Lewis.

p, Jack Broder; d, William Beaudine; w, Tim Ryan, "Ukie" Sherin, Edmond G. Seward; ph, Charles Van Enger; ed, Phil Cahn.

Horror/Comedy   **Cas.**   **(PR:A MPAA:NR)**

BELIEVE IN ME* (1971) 86m MGM c

Michael Sarrazin (Remy), Jacqueline Bisset (Pamela), Jon Cypher (Alan), Allen Garfield (Stutter), Kurt Dodenhoff (Matthew), Marcia Jean Kurtz (ER Nurse), Kevin Conway (Clancy), Roger Robinson (Angel), Antonio Fargas (Boy), Milt Kamen (Attending Physician), Susan Doukas (Ward Nurse), Suzannah Norstrand (Sylvia), Ultra Violet (ER Patient), Dr. William Abruzzi (Lecturer), Matthew Anton (David Kieser), Elizabeth Brown (Saleslady), Tony Capodilupo (Max Trencher), Tom Foral (Michael), Katherine Helmond (Saleslady), Tom Lacy (Store Mgr.) Barbara Thurston (Margaret), Larry Weber (Dr. Markham), Jan Saint (Morgue Attendant).

Director Hagmann had an altogether too brief career in TV and films (THE STRAWBERRY STATEMENT) before returning to the world of commercials where he made an international name doing such campaigns as the Chaplin series for IBM. His firm hand is evident in BELIEVE IN ME, the hard-hitting story of a young intern,

Sarrazin, who is hooked and who entices his lover, Bisset, to join him in the pleasures of drugs. He's high on speed most of the time. She joins him, almost inadvertently, and their lives begin a downward spiral. Painful to watch at times, it made no concession to commercialism and consequently suffered at the box office. Excellent work all around from the creative team and from the supporting cast, particularly Garfield and Cypher, as Bisset's physician-brother who tries to get them off amphetamines. (Cypher later enjoyed great stage success as Peron in Broadway's "Evita.")

p, Robert Chartoff, Irwin Winkler; d, Stuart Hagmann; w, Israel Horovitz; ph, Dick Kratins, Richard C. Brooks (Metrocolor); m, Fred Karlin; ed, John C. Howard; art d, Robert Gundlach.

Drama   **(PR:O MPAA:R)**

BELL' ANTONIO (1962, Ital.) 101m Hakim/EM bw

Marcello Mastroianni (Antonio Magnano), Claudia Cardinale (Barbara Puglisi), Pierre Brasseur (Alfio Magnano), Rina Morelli (Mrs. Magnano), Tomas Milian (Eduardo).

Up-and-down drama concerns Mastroianni and wife Cardinale, a beautiful young woman married to a man for about a year before discovering that he's impotent. Mastroianni has the reputation of being a worldly womanizer and his boastful father Brasseur brags at the drop of a noodle about the sexual prowess of his father, himself, and his Lothario son. It's a frustrating and embarrassing situation which is stupidly handled in a script that resolves the problem not through psychological treatment but by Cardinale's wealthy father who, with the help of a Catholic bishop, has the marriage annulled, and his daughter sent off into another marriage as one would mate a farm animal, all of this in spite of the fact that Cardinale loves Mastroianni. Even more puzzling is how this handsome devil stands by mutely and lets the woman of his life be taken from him. A good story with sharp direction goes to pot quickly and we are left with limp linguine, no sauce.

p, Raphael Hakim; d, Mauro Bolognini; w, Pier Paolo Pasolini, Gino Vissentini (based on the novel by Vitaliano Brancati); ph, Armando Nannuzzi; m, Piero Piccioni; ed, Nino Baragli; md, Piccioni; art d, Carlo Egidi, Piero Tosi.

Drama   **(PR:C-O MPAA:NR)**

BELL, BOOK AND CANDLE* (1958) 106m COL C

James Stewart (Sheperd Henderson), Kim Novak (Gillian Holroyd), Jack Lemmon (Nicky Holroyd), Ernie Kovacs (Sidney Redlitch), Hermione Gingold (Mrs. De Pass), Elsa Lanchester (Queenie), Janice Rule (Merle Kittridge), Phillipe Clay (French Singer), Bek Nelson (Secretary), Howard McNear (Andy White), The Brothers Candoli (Musicians), Wolfe Barzell (Proprietor), Joe Barry (Exterminator), Gail Bonney (Merle's Maid), Monty Ash (Herb Store Owner).

Delightful spoof on witchcraft where publisher Stewart falls beneath the love spell put on him by beautiful witch Novak on Christmas Eve after he walks into her art store. Stewart postpones his wedding to Rule and slavishly follows Novak about. She, being a witch, is incapable of love but enjoys taking a man away from her stuck-up friend Rule. Lemmon, Novak's mischievous warlock brother, complicates matters by co-authoring a book on magic with drunken Kovacs, one that Stewart intends to publish (while under a spell), and it is through their revelations that Stewart discovers he has been hexed into affection. He is steered by Lemmon and Kovacs to another powerful witch, Gingold, who concocts a vile potion to counteract Novak's spell. One of the funniest scenes shows Stewart having to drink this odious witch's brew. The spell is broken and Stewart confidently returns to Novak to snap his fingers in her face. Novak suddenly loses her powers and even her "familiar," a cat named Pyewacket, will not respond to her, going to Lanchester, her aunt, another practicing witch. Stewart, through the magical machinations of Lanchester, finds himself in a curio shop run by Novak; she has completely changed her ways and is out of the art and witch business. Stewart sees her crying, and she herself realizes that she is shedding real tears, a sign that she is no longer a witch and that she is actually in love with Stewart. Stewart is genuinely in love with her and all ends well. Except that Lemmon and his magic-loving friends continue to kill the motors of running cars and put out the street lights of San Francisco. Good score, witty dialog and shrewd direction make this a top comedy with cast members at their very best.

p, Julian Blaustein; d, Richard Quine; w, Daniel Taradash (based on the play by John Van Druten); ph, James Wong Howe (Technicolor); m, George Duning; ed, Charles Nelson; art d, Cary Odell; set d, Louis Diage.

Comedy   **Cas.**   **(PR:A MPAA:NR)**

BELL-BOTTOM GEORGE*1/2 (1943, Brit.) 97m COL bw

George Formby (George), Anne Firth (Pat), Reginald Purdell (Birdie Edwards), Peter Murray Hill (Shapley), Charles Farrell (Jim Benson), Eliot Makeham (Johnson), Manning Whiley (Church), Hugh Dempster (White), Dennis Wyndham (Black), Jane Welsh (Rita), Peter Gawthorne (Adm. Coltham).

Rejected for service, Formby loses the love of his girl. He next impersonates a sailor and apprehends some spies to become a local hero and win back the girl. An overlong launching for an unseaworthy production.

p, Ben Henry; d, Marcel Varnel; w, Peter Fraser, Edward Dryhurst (based on a story by Richard Fisher and Peter Cresswell); ph, Roy Fogwell.

Comedy   **(PR:A MPAA:NR)**

BELL FOR ADANO, A*1/2** (1945) 104m FOX bw

Gene Tierney (Tina), John Hodiak (Maj. Joppolo), William Bendix (Sgt. Borth), Glenn Langan (Lt. Livingstone), Richard Conte (Nicolo), Stanley Prager (Sgt. Trampani), Henry Morgan (Capt. Purvis), Montague Banks (Guiseppe), Reed Hadley (Cdr. Robertson), Roy Roberts (Col. Middleton), Hugo Haas (Fr. Pensovecchio), Marcel Dalio *(Zito)*, Fortunio Bonanova *(Gargano)*, Henry Armetta *(Errante)*, Roman Bohnen *(Erba)*, Luis Alberni *(Cacopardo)*, Eduardo Ciannelli *(Mayor Nasta)*, William Edmunds *(Tomasino)*, Yvonne Vautrot *(Francisca)*, John Russell *(Capt. Anderson)*, Anna Demetrio *(Rosa)*, James Rennie *(Lt. Col. Sartorius)*, Charles La Torre *(Mercurio Salvatore)*, Charles Judels *(Alfronti)*, Frank Jaquet *(Basile)*, Gino Corrado *(Zapulla)*, Peter Cusanelli *(Craxi)*, Minor Watson *(Gen. McKay)*, Grady Sutton *(Edward)*, Joseph Milani *(Capello)*, Edward Hyans *(M.P.)*.

Hodiak is a tough Army major who is given the job of reestablishing a small Italian town's civil administration just after the war. Adano is war-ravaged, its citizens starving and in rags. Hodiak must feed the people as well as instill in them trust of the Americans. He stops the lynching of the former Fascist mayor but deals harshly with others who have backed Mussolini. His life is further complicated when he falls in love with a local girl, stunning Tierney. Strong support comes from Bendix, who gives a superbly understated performance of the kind-hearted major's orderly, and Conte, one of the returning POW Italian soldiers. As a gesture of understanding and affection for the people in his charge, Hodiak goes to long lengths to retrieve the huge church bell which symbolizes the town's spirit and which has been stolen. It is replaced in the tower and tolls upon Hodiak's departure, one which is attended by the grateful citizens. A well-done adaptation of Hersey's powerful novel.

p, Louis D. Lighton, Lamar Trotti; d, Henry King; w, Trotti, Norman Reilly Raine (based on the novel by John Hersey); ph, Joseph La Shelle; m, Alfred Newman; ed, Barbara McLean.

War/Drama (PR:A MPAA:NR)

BELL JAR, THE*½ (1979) 117m Peerce-Goldston/AE c

Marilyn Hassett *(Esther)*, Julie Harris *(Mrs. Greenwood)*, Anne Jackson *(Dr. Nolan)*, Barbara Barrie *(Jay Cee)*, Robert Klein *(Lenny)*, Donna Mitchell *(Jean)*, Mary Louise Weller *(Doreen)*, Scott McKay *(Mr. Gilling)*, Jameson Parker *(Buddy)*, Thaao Penghlis *(Marco)*, Carol Monferdini *(Hilda)*, Debbie McLeod *(Betsy)*, Meg Mundy *(Bea Ramsey)*, Elizabeth Hubbard *(Vikki St. John)*, Karen Howard *(Toni LaBouchere)*, Margaret Hall *(Jane McLode)*, Mary Ann Johnson, Roxanne Hart, David Faulkner, Dan Hamilton, Nicholas Guest, Alana Davis, Leslie Goldstein, Shelley Rogers, Beth McDonald, Brenda Currin, Ruth Antonofsky, Christine Estabrook, Ruth Van Poons, Gil Rogers, Carolyn Hurlburt, Allan Eisennman, Dan Hamilton.

Sylvia Plath committed suicide at 30. THE BELL JAR is her story and should have been dramatic. Though adhering closely to the book, the script never examines the reasons Plath had her mental problems and the nervous breakdown that eventually preceded her death. The drama is lost and the story meanders under Peerce's direction. Peerce, son of opera singer Jan Peerce, was either courting or married to Hassett when this picture was made and the nepotism is evident. Other than GOODBYE, COLUMBUS, Peerce's work has been very serious, serious to the point of tedium (A SEPARATE PEACE, ASH WEDNESDAY among others). A good cast otherwise; performances by Jackson, Barrie, and Weller (so good in NATIONAL LAMPOON'S ANIMAL HOUSE) are outstanding, and Harris as the suicide's mother is, as usual, on the money. The plot is simply that Hassett gets increasingly depressed when her father dies and eventually takes her own life. It begins as a downer and goes down from there.

p, Michael Todd, Jr., Jerrold Brandt, Jr. (Robert Goldston); d, Larry Peerce; w, Marjorie Kellogg (based on the novel by Sylvia Plath); ph, Gerald Hirschfield; m, Gerald Fried; ed, Marvin Wallowitz; cos, Donald Brooks.

Autobiography/Drama Cas. (PR:O MPAA:R)

BELLA DONNA*½ (1934, Brit.) 91m Twickenham/GAU bw

Conrad Veidt *(Mahmoud Baroudi)*, Mary Ellis *(Mona Chepstow)*, Cedric Hardwicke *(Dr. Isaacson)*, Jeanne Stuart *(Lady Harwich)*, "Eve" *(Native Dancer)*, John Stuart *(Nigel Armine)*, Rodney Millington *(Ibrahim)*, Michael Shepley *(Dr. Hartley)*.

Complicated plot about a woman poisoner with a great Veidt role as a diabolical Egyptian. Veidt is positively Satanic as he pummels and pushes his victims, mostly women, about and, strangely enough, they appear to like it. Hardwicke is his usual majestic self but Ellis, as the American heroine, seems to be in a stupor, as if someone cruelly shoved her before the cameras and demanded she act for the first time. The sets and decor are impressive but the direction slows it all down to a painful crawl.

d, Robert Milton; w, Vera Allinson, H. Fowler Mear (based on a novel by Robert Hichens and a play by James Bernard Fagan); ph, Sydney Blythe.

Drama (PR:A MPAA:NR)

BELLA DONNA* (1983, Ger.) 105m WDR/SFB etc. c

Fritz Praetorius *(Fritz)*, Krystana Janda *(Lena)*, Erland Josephson *(Max)*, Kurt Raab, Angela Gockel, Brigitte Horney.

This is a co-production between Joachim von Vietinghoff and Westdeutscher Rundfunk (WDR) and Sender Freies Berlin (SFB) and Joachim von Mengershausen and Hans Kwiet. Judging from this picture, I don't think any of them will become household names. One of the thinnest books in the world is alleged to be "One Thousand Years Of German Humor" and BELLA DONNA lends credability to that contention. It's an unremitting downer about a depressing saxophonist pining for a band singer with whom he works on a boat that cruises around a lake in Berlin. His regular girl friend is dying of cancer (always a million laughs) and he mopes around trying to figure out who he is. Janda sings well and does a few nice songs. Josephson came over from Sweden to help out on this turkey but he should have stayed in Stockholm. The picture rambles like a senator's speech and doesn't really go anywhere; sort of like a boat cruising around a lake in Berlin. Now, if they would have *sunk* the ship. . .

d&w, Peter Keglevic; ph, Edward Klosinski; m, Astor Piazolla; ed, Sigrum Jaeger.

Drama (PR:C MPAA:NR)

BELLAMY TRIAL, THE** (1929) 95m MGM bw

Leatrice Joy *(Sue Ives)*, Betty Bronson *(Girl Reporter)*, Edward Nugent *(Boy Reporter)*, George Barraud *(Pat Ives)*, Margaret Livingston *(Mimi Bellamy)*, Kenneth Thomson *(Stephen Bellamy)*, Margaret Seddon *(Mother Ives)*, Charles B. Middleton *(District Attorney)*, Charles Hill Mailes *(Defense Attorney)*, William Tooker *(Judge Carver)*.

Two defendants are on trial for a murder they did not commit. Story is based on a love triangle, with a gruesome scene for a 1929 movie. A plaster cast of the dead woman's bust is displayed in court with an open knife wound into which the prosecution repeatedly jabs a knife. Middleton, the D.A. doing the thrusting, was an accomplished vaudevillian with the kind of crispy diction film producers sought desperately to overcome the shaky sound techniques. A great deal of dialog, but only toward the end of the picture, inserted after the fact to accommodate burgeoning public interest in the talkies. It is well done, though, and coupled with the capable acting, story line, and direction, make this and interesting film.

d, Monta Bell; w, Joe Farnham (based on a novel by Frances Noyes Hart); ph, Arthur Miller; ed, Frank Sullivan; set d, Cedric Gibbons; cos, Gilbert Clark.

Mystery (PR:C MPAA:NR)

BELLBOY, THE** (1960) 72m PAR bw

Jerry Lewis *(Stanley)*, Alex Gerry *(Manager)*, Bob Clayton *(Bell Captain)*, Sonnie Sands, Eddie Shaeffer, Herkie Styles, David Landfield *(Bellboys)*, Bill Richmond *(Man in Black as Stan Laurel)*, Larry Best *(Apple Man)*, Jimmy and Tilly Gerard *(Fighting Couple)*, Duke Art, Jr., Eddie Barton, Howard Brooks, Paul Gerson, H. S. Gump, B. S. Pully, Maxie Rosenblum, Benny Ross, Joe E. Ross, Mike Zetz, Milton Berle, Cary Middlecoff, The Novelites, Joe Levitch.

The film is very short, occasionally funny, and virtually plotless. It also serves to make one wonder what the French see in Jerry Lewis. Perhaps they think he is the successor to Charlot (Chaplin) or Hulot (Tati), but this is Lowblow with Lewis as the Bellboy at the Fontainebleau hotel in a series of almost unrelated sight gags. Richmond had been Lewis' drummer, then became his screenwriter in later years. At best, this is a kiddie movie with enough laughs if you're not too discriminating. Lewis may have thought this character would be his Little Tramp or M. Hulot. There's little dialog in the film and none from the Bellboy, so the film did do well in foreign markets where word-play jokes don't make it.

p,d&w, Jerry Lewis; ph, Haskell Boggs; m, Walter Scharf; ed, Stanley Johnson; art d, Hal Pereira, Henry Bumstead; ch, Nick Castle.

Comedy Cas. (PR:AA MPAA:NR)

BELLE DE JOUR*½** (1968, Fr.) 100m Paris Film Prod/AA c

Catherine Deneuve *(Se'verine Se'rizy)*, Jean Sorel *(Pierre Serizy)*, Michel Piccoli *(Henri Husson)*, Genevieve Page *(Mme. Anais)*, Pierre Clementi *(Marcel)*, Francisco Rabal *(Hippolyte)*, Francois Fabian *(Charlotte)*, Maria Latour *(Mathilde)*, Georges Marchal *(The Duke)*, Macha Meril *(Renee Fevret)*, Muni *(Pallas)*, Iska Khan *(Asiatic Client)*, D. de Roseville *(Coachman)*, Michel Charrel *(Footman)*, Brigitte Parmentier *(Severine as Child)*, Francis Blanche *(M. Adolphe)*, Francois Maistre *(The Teacher)*, Bernard Fresson *(Pock-Marked Man)*, Dominique Dandrieux *(Catherine)*, Marc Eyraud, Bernard Musson, Adelaide Blasquez.

A surrealistic voyage into the mind of a woman who is married to a handsome surgeon who dotes on her but whose odd quirks lead her to a life of afternoon prostitution in order to awaken some deep-seated need. Fantasy and reality are blended seamlessly and we are never certain if what we see is the actuality or another of her erotic daydreams. Deneuve is elegantly decadent as the bored housewife who learns that a bordello exists nearby. She is told this by Piccoli, a friend of Sorel, her adoring husband. She is turned on as Piccoli tells her of the enslavement of the women at the brothel. Deneuve shows up at the maison and offers her services from two until five every afternoon (hence the name BELLE DE JOUR). After one bad incident, she settles in and has several affairs and even more daydreams. Clementi, sort of a 1960s BORSALINO, takes a liking to her. Piccoli eventually arrives at the whorehouse and Deneuve spots him and promptly quits, lest he tell her husband. Clementi finds out her real situation and threatens blackmail. Clementi shoots Sorel, causing him to be paralyzed and mute. The police dispatch Clementi and the finale has *two* endings, and we are never certain if we are seeing the truth, a lie, or a dream? It's almost, but not quite, pornography. And it's almost, but not quite, a great movie. Bunuel tries so hard to pose questions that he forgets we have come to the cinema for entertainment and/or enlightenment, rather than to have the director play cinematic tricks on us. But Bunuel enjoyed his little joke and did it again up to and including THE DISCREET CHARM OF THE BOURGEOISIE.

p, Robert and Raymond Hakim, Luis Bunuel; d, Bunuel; w, Bunuel, Jean-Claude Carriere (based on the novel by Joseph Kessel); ph, Sacha Vierny (Eastmancolor); ed, Walter Spohr; art d, Robert Clavel.

Drama (PR:O MPAA:NR)

BELLE LE GRAND*½ (1951) 90m REP bw

Vera Ralston *(Belle Le Grand)*, John Carroll *(John Kilton)*, Muriel Lawrence *(Nan Henshaw)*, William Ching *(Bill Shanks)*, Hope Emerson *(Emma McGee)*, Grant Withers *(Shannon)*, Stephen Chase *(Montgomery Crane)*, John Qualen *(Corky McGee)*, Henry Morgan *(Abel Stone)*, Charles Cane *(Cal)*, Thurston Hall *(Parkington)*, Marietta Canty *(Daisy)*, Glen Vernon *(Bellboy)*.

In case you were wondering why Vera Ralston worked so much when she really didn't have that much talent, be advised that she only worked for Republic Pictures for many years and the man who owned Republic was the man she slept with . . . Herbert Yates, her husband. In this western musical, Vera displays her usual stuff as a lady gambler in early San Francisco. She and John Carroll join forces. Carroll is a silver miner whom Chase attempts to ruin. It's a fairly standard plot and seems to serve only as a vehicle for Vera and the songs by Lawrence. It's a confused and often silly film but the Young score makes it somewhat worthwhile.

p, Herbert J. Yates; d, Allan Dwan; w, D.D. Beauchamp (based on the story by by Peter B. Kyne); ph, Reggie Lanning; m, Victor Young; ed, Harry Keller; art d, James Sullivan; cos, Adele Palmer.

Western   **(PR:A   MPAA:NR)**

BELLE OF NEW YORK, THE**   (1952) 82m MGM c

Fred Astaire (*Charlie Hill*), Vera-Ellen (*Angela Bonfils*), Marjorie Main (*Mrs. Phineas Hill*), Keenan Wynn (*Max Ferris*), Alice Pearce (*Elsie Wilkins*), Clinton Sundberg (*Gilfred Spivak*), Gale Robbins (*Dixie McCoy*), Lisa Ferraday (*Frenchie*), Henry Slate (*Clancy*), Carol Brewster, Meredith Leeds, Lyn Wilde (*Frenchie's Girls*), Buddy Roosevelt (*Cab Driver*), Roger Davis (*Judkins*), Dick Wessel, Percy Helton, Tom Dugan (*Bowery Bums*).

Fred Astaire is usually only as good as his material. In the case of THE BELLE OF NEW YORK, that means only so-so. Fred is a bachelor playboy during the Gay Nineties. He falls over toupee for Vera-Ellen, who is a Bowery social worker type (not unlike Sarah Brown in GUYS AND DOLLS). Fred goes so far as to get a real job in order to impress Vera-Ellen who is as pure as any heroine can be. And that's the plot. Into this, they cram several songs to fill out the rather brief time of the movie. Lots of good secondary support from Main, Helton, Wynn, Pearce, and Sundberg. The role of Clancy is played by Henry Slate, one of the Slate Brothers trio who opened a Hollywood nightclub in the 1950s that was the place to go for several years and gave birth to the career of Don Rickles, who used to insult different celebrities every night, but saved his most seething invective for the owners. The movie could have used some of Rickles' humor. Songs include: "Oops," "Bachelor's Dinner Song," "When I'm Out With the Belle of New York," "I Wanna Be A Dancin' Man" (Johnny Mercer, Harry Warren), and "Let A Little Love Come In" (Roger Edens).

p, Arthur Freed; d, Charles Walters; w, Robert O'Brien, Irving Elinson (based on an adaptation by Chester Erskine of a play by Hugh Morton); ph, Robert Planck (Technicolor); ed, Albert Akst; md, Adolph Deutsch; art d, Cedric Gibbons, Jack Martin Smith; cos, Helen Rose, Gile Steele; ch, Robert Alton.

Musical   **(PR:A   MPAA:NR)**

BELLE OF OLD MEXICO*   (1950) 70m REP c

Estelita Rodriguez (*Rosita*), Robert Rockwell (*Kip Armitage III*), Dorothy Patrick (*Deborah*), Thurston Hall (*Horatio Huntington*), Florence Bates (*Nellie Chatfield*), Dave Willock (*Tommy Mayberry*), Gordon Jones (*Tex Barnet*), Fritz Feld (*Dr. Quincy*), Anne O'Neal (*Mrs. Abercrombie*), Nacho Galindo (*Pico*), Joe Venuti (*Himself*), Edward Gargan (*Sam*), Carlos Molina and Orchestra.

A semi-musical about Rockwell, a college president, going South-of-the-Border to adopt the kid sister of a pal from WW II. Sis turns out to be a curvy full-grown lady (Rodriguez) and the stuffy college types bitch about the adoption. It also doesn't please Rockwell's snooty fiance, Patrick. If you've already guessed that Patrick gets dumped and Rockwell and Rodriguez wind up doing the Mexican Hat Dance together, you're way ahead of the producers of this picture. Shot in Trucolor, Republic's process, it's just the right kind of movie to see after eating a tamale.

p, Edward J. White; d, R.G. Springsteen; w, Bradford Ropes and Francis Swann; ph, Jack Marta (Trucolor); m, Stanley Wilson; ed, Harold Minter; m/l, Walter Kent, Walton Farrar.

Musical   **(PR:A   MPAA:NR)**

BELLE OF THE NINETIES½   (1934) 73m PAR bw

Mae West (*Ruby Carter*), Roger Pryor (*Tiger Kid*), John Mack Brown (*Brooks Claybourne*), John Miljan (*Ace Lamont*), Katherine DeMille (*Molly Brant*), James Conlan (*Kirby*), Stuart Holmes (*Dirk*), Harry Woods (*Slade*), Edward Gargan (*Stogie*), Libby Taylor (*Jasmine*), Warren Hymer (*St. Louis Fighter*), Benny Baker (*Blackie*), Morrie Cohan (*Butch*), Tyler Brooke (*Comedian*), Sam McDaniel (*Brother Eben*), Tom Herbert (*Gilbert*), Frederick Burton (*Col. Claybourne*), Augusta Anderson (*Mrs. Claybourne*), Sam Flint (*Fire Chief*), Wade Boteler (*Editor*), George Walsh (*Leading Man*), Eddie Borden (*Comedian*), Fuzzy Knight (*Comedian*), Kay Deslys (*Beef Trust Chorus Girl*), Frank Rice (*Best Man*), Gene Austin (*Crooner*), Walter Walker, Mike Mazurki, Edward Hearn, James Pierce.

BELLE OF THE NINETIES is not one of West's best but it's still better than most other comedies of the period. West was heavily censored by the powers-that-were and the result is a somewhat choppy musical comedy that missed on a few burners but hit the spot everywhere else. West is a nightclub performer and Pryor is a boxer. They fall into each other's arms without falling into each other's hands and West exhibits early women's liberation tendencies by making her own way in a man's world. The funny lines come one after another. West says, "It's better to be looked over than overlooked" and, when asked (by Miljan): "You were born in Saint Louis. What part?" West replies, "Why all of me." Miljan says: "I must have your golden hair, fascinating eyes, alluring smile, lovely arms and your form divine . . ." to which West answers: "Wait a minute! Is this a proposal, or are you taking an inventory?" The bluenoses cut most of West's sexual innuendoes but enough remain for us to get the idea. Lots of music, too, with Duke Ellington and his orchestra and West singing several tunes including "My Old Flame" and a few black spirituals for the Bible Belters. West wasn't used to Leo McCarey's style of directing and there was a bit of a problem between the two. In the end, one can see the seams and the differences in the way these two comedic talents looked at things. It was shortly after this that Johnny Mack Brown became a star.

p, William LeBaron; d, Leo McCarey; w, Mae West; ph, Karl Struss; ed, Leroy Stone; art d, Hans Dreier, Bernard Herzbrun; cos, Travis Banton; m/l, Arthur Johnston, Sam Coslow.

Comedy   **(PR:C   MPAA:NR)**

BELLE OF THE YUKON* ½   (1944) 83m RKO c

Randolph Scott (*Honest John Calhoun*), Gypsy Rose Lee (*Belle Devalle*), Dinah Shore (*Lettie Candless*), Charles Winninger (*Pop Candless*), Bob Burns (*Sam Slade*), Florence Bates (*Viola*), Guinn "Big Boy" Williams (*Marshall Maitland*), William Marshall (*Steve*), Robert Armstrong (*George*), Victor Kilian (*The Professor*), Edward Fielding (*C. V. Atterbury*), Wanda McKay (*Cherie Atterbury*), Charles Soldani (*Fire Chief*).

Randolph Scott is a reformed confidence man fleeing north from the law. He now operates a successful dance hall-gambling establishment and thwarts Armstrong, the bad guy who wants to turn it crooked. Lee and Shore help boost this musical out of the mediocre. Songs include "Like Someone in Love," "Sleigh Ride in July," sung by Shore; "Belle Of The Yukon," "Every Girl Is Different" (Johnny Burke, Jimmy Van Heusen); "I Can't Tell Why I Love You But I Do, Do, Do" (Will Cobb, Gus Edwards).

p&d, William A. Seiter; w, James Edward Grant (based on a story by Houston Branch); ph, Ray Rennahan (Technicolor); m, Arthur Lange; ed, Ernest Nims; ch, Don Loper.

Musical   **(PR:A   MPAA:NR)**

BELLE STARR*   (1941) 87m FOX c

Randolph Scott (*Sam Starr*), Gene Tierney (*Belle Starr*), Dana Andrews (*Major Thomas Crall*), John Sheppard [Sheppard Strudwick] (*Ed Shirley*), Elizabeth Patterson (*Sarah*), Chill Wills (*Blue Duck*), Louise Beavers (*Mammy Lou*), Olin Howland (*Jasper Tench*), Paul Burns (*Sergeant*), Joseph Sawyer (*John Cole*), Joseph Downing (*Jim Cole*), Howard Hickman (*Col. Thornton*), Charles Trowbridge (*Col. Bright*), James Flavin (*Sergeant*), Charles Middleton (*Carpetbagger*).

This movie and the facts of history have nothing in common, yet Tierney makes such a beautiful, if mythical, Belle in radiant color that it is impossible to take your eyes from her. In this romanticized version, Belle takes up with Confederate guerrilla leader Scott after her mansion is burned. Together they continue to fight for "The Lost Cause," long after Lee's surrender, battling Yankees, banks, railroads, and sheriffs until Tierney, loved by the Yankee captain (Andrews) pursuing her and Scott, is killed as she rides to warn her husband of an ambush. Wills gives good support as Scott's chief aide. Ironically, he is named Blue Duck, which was the name of Belle's second husband in real life after Sam Starr was shot to death. In reality, Belle was a common horse thief and prostitute who once dressed up in a velvet gown and adorned her body with pistols while sitting atop a horse she had stolen for an early photo. She had the face of an aged crone, one that would stop a freight train, but Fox transformed this mean-minded hatchet-faced bushwhacker into the lovely Tierney and the uninformed world reveled in the spectacle. Since GONE WITH THE WIND had been released only two years earlier, Tierney was instructed to affect a Southern drawl a la Scarlett O'Hara and she even has a mammy, Beavers, similar to Hattie McDaniel. Belle never lived in a glorious mansion as does Tierney; she was a Missouri low-life who slept with any outlaw who would have her, including the notorious Cole Younger with whom she had a child, Pearl. She married Sam Starr in 1880, 15 years after the Civil War; neither of them ever fought for the South, only their own mercenary selves, ending in the dust of lonely Oklahoma roads. In addition to the absolutely marvelous photography of this film, Newman's score is bold and haunting, one of his best.

p, Kenneth Macgowan; d, Irving Cummings; w, Lamar Trotti (based on a story by Niven Busch, Cameron Rogers); ph, Ernest Palmer, Ray Rennahan (Technicolor); m, Alfred Newman; ed, Robert Simpson.

Western   **(PR:A   MPAA:NR)**

BELLE STARR'S DAUGHTER*   (1947) 86m Alson/FOX bw

George Montgomery (*Tom Jackson*), Rod Cameron (*Bob "Bittercreek" Yauntis*), Ruth Roman (*Rose of Cimarron*), Wallace Ford (*Bailey*), Charles Kemper (*Gaffer*), William Phipps (*Yuma*), Edith King (*Mrs. Allen*), Jack Lambert (*Brone*), Freddy Libby (*Slim*), Isabel Jewell (*Belle Starr*), Larry Johns (*Jed Purdy*), Kenneth MacDonald (*Jim Davis*).

Ruth Roman believes that marshal Montgomery killed her famous outlaw mother. Actually, some of her own men did the deed. A routine sequel to the 1941 production of BELLE STARR.

p, Edward L. Alperson; d, Lesley Selander, w, W. R. Burnett; ph, William Sickner; m, Dr. Edward Kilenyi; ed, Jason Bernie.

Western   **(PR:A   MPAA:NR)**

BELLES OF ST. CLEMENTS, THE**   (1936, Brit.) 68m British & Dominions/PAR bw

Evelyn Foster (*Eve Chester*), Meriel Forbes (*Natalie de Mailliere*), Basil Langton (*Billy Grant*), Isobel Scaife (*Maisie Carstairs*), Enid Lindsey (*Miss Nelson*), Sonia Somers (*Miss Grant*), Tosca von Bissing, Don Tidbury, Arthur Metcalfe, Frederick Bradshaw.

Refusing to accept an arranged marriage, a schoolgirl runs away only to be picked up by a suspected car thief and become involved with his problems. Tepid soap opera that gets worse from the first ten minutes.

p, Anthony Havelock-Allan; d, Ivar Campbell; w, Terence Rattigan (based on a story by Ivar and Sheila Campbell).

Drama   **(PR:A   MPAA:NR)**

BELLES OF ST. TRINIAN'S, THE*** (1954, Brit.) 91m London Films/BL

Alastair Sim *(Millicent and Clarence Fritton)*, Joyce Grenfell *(Sgt. Ruby Gates)*, George Cole *(Flash Harry)*, Vivienne Martin *(Arabella)*, Eric Pohlmann *(Sultan of Makyad)*, Lorna Henderson *(Princess Fatima)*, Hermione Baddeley *(Miss Drownder)*, Betty Ann Davies *(Miss Waters)*, Rene Houston *(Miss Brimmer)*, Beryl Reid *(Miss Dawn)*, Balbina *(Mlle. de St. Emilion)*, Jane Henderson *(Miss Holland)*, Diana Day *(Jackie)*, Lloyd Lamble *(Supt. Kemp-Bird)*, Jill Braidwood *(Florrie)*, Annabelle Covey *(Maudie)*, Pauline Drewitt *(Celia)*, Jean Langston *(Rosie)*, Guy Middleton *(Eric Rowbotham Smith)*, Richard Wattis *(Manton Bassett)*.

Very funny comedy based on Ronald Searles's cartoons of a monstrous girls' school known as St. Trinian's. Plot has to do with the horsenaping of a famous steed being foiled by some of the Trinian's girls. Sim is delicious as the headmistress as well as her ne'er-do-well brother. Cole (so good in the KITE segment of the Maugham film QUARTET) is a tough who is the salesman who peddles the gin the girls make in their lab. Grenfell gets a lot of laughs as the police spy. This one was a winner, but the ensuing sequels (BLUE MURDER AT ST. TRINIAN'S, THE PURE HELL OF ST. TRINIAN'S, THE GREAT ST. TRINIAN'S TRAIN ROBBERY) were drivel.

p, Frank Launder, Sidney Gilliat; d, Launder; w, Launder, Gilliat and Val Valentine; ph, Stanley Pavey; m, Malcolm Arnold; ed, Thelma Connell.

Comedy **Cas.** **(PR:AA MPAA:NR)**

BELLES ON THEIR TOES** 1/2** (1952) 88m FOX c

Jeanne Crain *(Ann Gilbreth)*, Myrna Loy *(Mrs. Gilbreth)*, Debra Paget *(Martha)*, Jeffrey Hunter *(Dr. Bob Grayson)*, Edward Arnold *(Sam Harper)*, Hoagy Carmichael *(Tom Bracken)*, Barbara Bates *(Ernestine)*, Robert Arthur *(Frank Gilbreth)*, Verna Felton *(Cousin Lenora)*, Roddy McCaskill *(Bob Gilbreth)*, Carol Nugent *(Lily Gilbreth)*, Tina Thompson *(Jane Gilbreth)*, Teddy Driver *(Jack Gilbreth)*, Tommy Ivo *(William Gilbreth)*, Jimmy Hunt *(Fred Gilbreth)*, Anthony Sydes *(Don Gilbreth)*, Martin Milner *(Al Lynch)*, Clay Randolph *(Martin Dykes)*, June Hedin *(Jane, Age 22)*, Robert Easton *(Franklyn Dykes)*, Cecil Weston *(Emily)*, Syd Saylor *(Cab Driver)*.

BELLES ON THEIR TOES is the sequel to CHEAPER BY THE DOZEN and has everything the first picture had, with one notable exception: Clifton Webb. This may be one of the first women's liberation-themed films as it details the story of Loy carrying on with the business after Webb's death. With the 12 kids to help and hinder her, Loy continues in the industrial engineering field and encounters serious prejudice against women. Arnold, as a wealthy industrialist, lets Loy work for him, training young engineers. She does a bang-up job and makes enough money for the children's educations. It's not easy to have 12 stories going simultaneously so the authors opt for one major sub-plot; Hunter as a medical man falls for eldest daughter Crain and they eventually marry. Loy is particularly good as an emerging woman who gets righteously indignant when called for and yet never loses the femininity that makes her so attractive. Whereas so many movie widows float helplessly until the next man swims through the sea to rescue them, Loy's character meets adversity face-to-face and triumphs, proving that a woman is the equal of a man in any field—except mothering; in that she has a large edge.

p, Samuel G. Engel; d, Henry Levin; w, Phoebe and Henry Ephron (based on a book by Frank B. Gilbreth, Jr., Ernestine Gilbreth Carey.); ph, Arthur E. Arling (Technicolor); m, Cyril Mockridge; ed, Robert Fritch; md, Lionel Newman.

Comedy **(PR:AAA MPAA:NR)**

BELLISSIMA*** (1952, Ital.) 130m Bellisima/CEL-INCOM bw

Anna Magnani *(Maddalena Cecconi)*, Walter Chiari *(Alberto Annovazzi)*, Tina Apicella *(Maria Cecconi)*, Gastone Renzelli *(Spartaco Cecconi)*, Arturo Bragaglia *(Photographer)*, Alessandro Blasetti *(Himself)*, Tecla Scarano *(Elocution Teacher)*, Linda Sina *(Mimmetta), Vittorio Glori, Iris, Geo Taparelli, Mario Chiari.*

An important movie for any stage or screen mother to see as it quite accurately depicts what goes on in the industry. Magnani is superb as the Italian version of Rose (GYPSY), a Roman Momma who tries to get her daughter a movie job. The child gets a screen test and she and Magnani furtively watch as the screen test is seen by various employees of the film studio. The child (Apicella) is terrible and the comments are devastating to mother and daughter alike. Magnani walks into the room and berates them for their meanness. Later, the studio gets in touch with Magnani and says they do have another role for Apicella, but Magnani turns it down and opts to return to her husband. The picture is long, sometimes funny, sometimes brutal, always interesting, and still affecting. It has been released in three different lenghts; 95, 100 and 130 minutes. The shorter versions are easier to watch, though they lack the character development of the long version. Magnani, who starred in such landmark films as THE ROSE TATTOO, OPEN CITY, and THE MIRACLE, has never been better than she is in BELLISSIMA.

d, Luchino Visconti; w, Suso Cecchi D'Amico, Francisco Rosi (based on a story by Cesare Zavattini); ph, Piero Portalupe; m, Franco Mannino; ed, Mario Serandel.

Drama **(PR:C MPAA:NR)**

BELLMAN, THE** 1/2** (1947, Fr.) 95m Moulin D'Or/Mage bw (SORTILEGES)

Lucien Coedel *(The Bellman)*, Fernand Ledoux *(Fabret)*, Renee Faure *(Catherine)*, Madeleine Robinson *(Marthe)*, Roger Pigaut *(Pierre)*, Georges Tourrell *(Commandant of Gendarmes)*, Sinoel *(The Old Woman)*, Pierre Labry *(The Village Outsider)*.

The bellman's job is to sound a bell high in the French Alps to keep travelers from becoming lost. Instead, Coedel murders lost travelers. Excellent French horror movie, although you wouldn't know that from the title.

d, Christian Jaques; w, Jacques Prevert (based on the novel, *Horseman of Riouclare*, by Claude Boncompain); ph, Louis Page.

Horror **(PR:C MPAA:NR)**

BELLS, THE** (1931, Brit.) 75m BSFP/PDC bw

Donald Calthrop *(Mathias)*, Jane Welsh *(Annette)*, Edward Sinclair *(Sgt. Christian* Nash), O. B. Clarence *(Watchman)*, Wilfred Shine *(Philosopher)*, Ralph Truman *(Blacksmith)*.

A racist burgomeister in Alsace murders a Jew but his conscience will not allow him to maintain his silence. After some agonizing self-examination, he confesses. This was one of the many films banned by Propaganda Minister Josef Goebbels when the Nazis took over Germany in 1933. A remake of the 1926 silent starring Lionel Barrymore, with Boris Karloff.

p, Isidore Schlesinger, Sergei Nolbandov; d, Oscar M. Werndorff, Harcourt Templeman; w, C. H. Dand (based on the play by Erckmann and Chatrian); ph, Gunther Krampf.

Crime Drama **(PR:C MPAA:NR)**

BELLS zero

(1981, Can.) 79m Co-Co/New World c (AKA: MURDER BY PHONE, THE CALLING)

Richard Chamberlain *(Nat)*, John Houseman *(Stanley)*, Robin Gammell *(Noah)*, Sara Botsford *(Ridley)*, Barry Morse *(Waites), Gary Reineke (Lt. Meara)*.

Terrible attempt to make a thriller out of an impossible device, one used by an indiscriminate killer who kills his random victims over the phone. This nonsense was whipped up by writers Shryack and Butler who insulted even the mindless with THE CAR and embraced the ridiculous in THE GAUNTLET. Chamberlain and Houseman, who play detective in tracking down the killer, should have known better than to have appeared in such drivel.

p, Robert Cooper, Brian Walker; d, Michael Anderson; w, Dennis Shryack, Michael Butler, John Kent Harrison; ph, Reginald Morris.

Horror **Cas.** **(PR:O MPAA:NR)**

BELLS ARE RINGING*** 1/2** (1960) 126m MGM c

Judy Holliday *(Ella Peterson)*, Dean Martin *(Jeffrey Moss)*, Fred Clark *(Larry Hastings)*, Eddie Foy, Jr. *(J. Otto Prantz)*, Jean Stapleton *(Sue)*, Ruth Storey *(Gwynne)*, Dort Clark *(Inspector Barnes)*, Frank Gorshin *(Blake Barton)*, Ralph Roberts *(Francis)*, Valerie Allen *(Olga)*, Bernie West *(Dr. Joe Kitchell)*, Steven Peck *(1st Gangster)*, Gerry Mulligan *(Ella's Blind Date)*, Nancy Walters.

Neat adaptation of the stage play with Holliday reprising her Broadway success. Judy runs an answering service and gets passionately involved in the lives of her customers. Martin is miscast as the love interest, although he is more lively than usual. West is hysterical as the dentist who wants to be a songwriter. West later became a millionaire TV writer-producer with Norman Lear's company and later with his own series, "Three's Company." Mulligan, who plays Judy's blind date, was married to Miss Holliday at the time of her death. He went on to marry and divorce Sandy Dennis. Jazz fans will recognize him as the dean of the baritone sax. Stapleton, in one of her earliest appearances, scores as Sue, as does Gorshin in the role of a beatnik who wants to be a serious actor. The two big songs were "Just In Time" and "The Party's Over." This might have been better with a different male lead and more attention paid to dancing and less to talking. The dialog seemed much better in the stage version, although that's probably not true. It's just that films require a different kind of rhythm to the words, and many playwrights have never mastered cinema and vice versa. Holliday was a marvelous talent who died in her early forties. This film, BORN YESTERDAY (Oscar winner),and THE SOLID GOLD CADILLAC were her best roles.

p, Arthur Freed; d, Vincente Minnelli; w, Betty Comden, Adolph Green (based on the musical play by Comden, Green and Jule Styne); ph, Milton Krasner (CinemaScope Eastmancolor); m, Styne; ed, Adrienne Fazan; art d, George W. Davis, Preston Ames; cos, Walter Plunkett; ch, Charles O'Curran; m/l, Styne, Comden, Green.

Musical Comedy **Cas.** **(PR:AA MPAA:NR)**

BELLS GO DOWN, THE** 1/2** (1943, Brit.) 90m EAL/UA bw

Tommy Trinder *(Tommy Turk)*, James Mason *(Ted Robbins)*, Philip Friend *(Bob)*, Mervyn Johns *(Sam)*, Billy Hartnell *(Bookes)*, Finlay Currie *(Dist. Officer MacFarlane)*, Philippa Hiatt *(Nan)*, Meriel Forbes *(Susie)*, Beatrice Varley *(Ma Turk)*, Norman Pierce *(Pa Robbins)*, Muriel George *(Ma Robbins)*, Julien Vedey *(Lou Freeman)*, Richard George *(P.C. O'Brien)*, Victor Weske *(Peters)*, Leslie Harcourt *(Alfie Parrot)*, Lesley Brook *(June)*, Frederick Culley *(Vicar)*, Stanley Lothbury *(Verger)*, Johnnie Schofield *(Milkman)*.

The plot of THE BELLS GO DOWN will sound like a bummer because it details war, death, sadness, and all the factors that go into a B-movie tear-jerker. But that's not the case as MacDougall and Black (author of the original novel) have devised a funny and heart-warming script using the above elements. Friend and Hiatt are a young twosome about to be wed in East London. They decide to hold off due to the outbreak of war. Phil joins the AFS (Auxiliary Fire Service) and serves under Currie and Mason, who run the unit. Despite animosities between the professional firefighters and the amateurs, they unite as one every time "Air Nazi" schedules a flight over London. Friend and Hiatt eventually get married and their home is burned down while he is busily saving a warehouse across the road. Trinder, a greyhound bettor, and Johns, a petty thief, also volunteer and are part of the coterie of interesting characters. Trinder dies while attempting vainly to save Currie, and Friend and Hiatt name their new child after him, in honor of his valor. Johns has been avoiding a cop all through the movie and now finds he must save the self-same bobby from drowning. What must be recalled is that what was happening on screen in this movie was also happening in real life outside! Ealing filmed this in between air raids. Screenwriter MacDougall may be better remembered for scripting THE

FOREMAN WENT TO FRANCE, THE MAN IN THE WHITE SUIT, and THE MOUSE THAT ROARED.

p, Michael Balcon; d, Basil Dearden; w, Roger MacDougall (based on the novel by Stephen Black), ph, Ernest Palmer; m, Roy Douglas; ed, Mary Habberfield; art d, Michael Relph.

Comedy/War (PR:A MPAA:NR)

BELLS OF CAPISTRANO*¹/₂ (1942) 78m REP bw

Gene Autry (Gene), Smiley Burnette (Frog Millhouse), Virginia Grey (Jennifer Benton), Lucien Littlefield (Pa McCracken), Morgan Conway (Shag Johnson), Claire DuBrey (Ma McCracken), Charles Cane (Tex), Joe Strauch, Jr. (Tadpole Millhouse), Maria Shelton (Jackie Laval), Tristram Coffin (Jed Johnson), Jay Novello (Jenkins), Al Bridge (Jake), Eddie Acuff (Sign Poster), Champion, the Horse.

"The Singing Cowboy's" last film before he went into the army for the next four years. In this one, he sides with a young woman who owns a rodeo show and is facing some unscrupulous competition. Standard Autry western with lots of good action. Songs include "Don't Bite The Hand That's Feeding You," "At Sundown," and "Forgive Me." (See GENE AUTRY series, Index.)

p, Harry Grey; d, William Morgan; w, Lawrence Kimple; ph, Reggie Lanning; ed. Edward Mann; md, Morton Scott; m/l, Jimmie Morgan, Thomas Holer, Milton Ager, Jack Yellen, Fred Stryker, Jerry Charleston, Sol Meyer, Walter Donaldson.

Western (PA:A MPAA:NR)

BELLS OF CORONADO** (1950) 67m REP c

Roy Rogers (Himself), Trigger, the Smartest Horse in the Movies, Dale Evans (Pam Reynolds), Pat Brady (Sparrow Biffle), Grant Withers (Craig Bennett), Leo Cleary (Dr. Frank Harding), Clifton Young (Ross), Robert Bice (Jim), Stuart Randall (Sheriff), John Hamilton (Linden), Edmond Cobb (Rafferty), Eddie Lee (Shanghai), Rex Lease (Foreman), Lane Bradford (Jenks), Foy Willing and the Riders of the Purple Sage.

Roy Rogers (born Leonard Slye in Cincinnati, 1912) and Dale Evans (born Frances Octavia Evans in 1912) team up with Trigger (now stuffed and standing at the Rogers' hotel in Apple Valley, California) in this tightly edited, fast-moving modern story about uranium robbers who are selling the ore to a foreign power. Roy is an insurance investigator trying to get to the bottom of the mine owner's death and the disappearance of the ore. He eventually learns that the chief thief is Cleary, playing the kind of doctor that Kildare would love: avuncular and kindly. The gang attempts to get the ore aboard a plane and escape, but is foiled by Roy in the finale. Somehow, in just 67 minutes, the plot is unfolded, love happens between Roy and Dale, Brady gets a chance to do some of his funny stuff and Roy finds time to sing the title song and "Save A Smile For A Rainy Day." Dale does "Got No Time For The Blues" with the Riders Of The Purple Sage. Trigger doesn't sing a note but he can do just about everything else. (See ROY ROGERS series, Index.)

p, Edward J. White; d, William Witney; w, Sloan Nibley; ph, John Mac Burnie (Trucolor); ed, Tony Martinelli; m/l, Sid Robin, Foy Willing, Aaron Gonzales.

Western Cas. (PR:AA MPAA:NR)

BELLS OF ROSARITA*** (1945) 68m REP bw

Roy Rogers (Himself), George "Gabby" Hayes (Baggy Whittaker), Dale Evans (Sue Farnum), Adele Mara (Patty Phillips), Grant Withers (William Ripley), Janet Martin (Rosarita), Addison Richards (Slim Phillips), Roy Barcroft (Maxwell), Sons of the Pioneers (Themselves), Wild Bill Elliott, Allan "Rocky" Lane, Don "Red" Barry, Robert Livingston, Sunset Carson.

The daughter of an ex-circus man is about to be ripped off by her dead dad's former partner. Enter Roy, Trigger, Gabby, and a host of other western heroes to the rescue. A classic! Great action, songs by Roy and Dale, and a menagerie of bad guys. (See ROY ROGERS series, Index.)

p, Edward J. White; d, Frank McDonald; w, Jack Townley; ph, Ernest Miller; md, Morton Scott; ed, Arthur Roberts.

Western Cas. (PR:AAA MPAA:NR)

BELLS OF ST. MARY'S, THE**** (1945) 126m Rainbow/RKO bw

Bing Crosby (Father Chuck O'Malley), Ingrid Bergman (Sister Benedict), Henry Travers (Mr. Bogardus), Ruth Donnelly (Sister Michael), Joan Carroll (Patsy), Martha Sleeper (Patsy's Mother), William Gargan (Joe Gallagher), Rhys Williams (Dr. McKay), Dickie Tyler (Eddie), Una O'Connor (Mrs. Breen), Bobby Frasco (Tommy), Matt McHugh (Clerk), Edna Wonacott (Delphine), Jimmy Crane (Luther), Minerva Urecal (Landlady), Cora Shannon (Old Lady), Gwen Crawford, Aina Constant, Eva Novak (The Sisters).

Touchingly sentimental, but strong at all the broken places, this is the sequel to the great GOING MY WAY and does exactly what film writer James Agee said it could not do, "repeat the unrepeatable." Crosby, a trouble-shooting priest, is sent to financially ailing St. Mary's where he takes over the parish and runs smack into charming, clever, spiritually uplifting Bergman, a Mother Superior who rules her students with a gentle but decisive hand. She is too rigid for Crosby and he too permissive for her; their verbal fencing is a joy to behold, especially when Bergman and Crosby clash over how the students are to be instructed. He is rather cavalier and would rather croon than preach. Yet he is effective, bringing together separated parents Gargan and Sleeper, to the delight of their daughter, Carroll. And the old groaner knew just how to tug the heart with "Adeste Fidelis," "O, Sanctissima," the title song and, with a children's choir, and, alone, with the lyrical "In the Land of Beginning Again," and the sprightly "Aren't You Glad You're You." Bergman owns every scene she's in, deservedly so, especially when dealing with a failing student and teaching a youngster how to box (by reading from a book by Gene Tunney) so

he can stand up to a tough kid. And it is Bergman, not Crosby, who charms the local skinflint landowner Travers into not only turning over his property to St. Mary's but erecting a spectacular new school and gym for the students. Her scenes with Crosby are indeed special and she delivers an unforgettable line, smiling at him and saying: "Did anyone ever tell you that you have a dishonest face, for a priest, I mean?" Then there is the departure of Bergman after she learns she has TB and must go away for a cure. This supreme actress manages such pathos with quiet dignity that will wrench anyone's heart. McCarey's direction is magnificent, Barnes' camera excellent, Nichols' script sparkling, and Dolan's score inspiring. McCarey, Crosby, and Bergman had all won Oscars the year earlier (Bergman and McCarey for GASLIGHT and Crosby for GOING MY WAY). At the time Crosby was the most popular film star in America. There was no way RKO could miss. It didn't. THE BELLS OF ST. MARY'S was the top box-office hit of 1945, earning a staggering $3,715,000. William Flannery's impressive set of St. Mary's cathedral, much in need of repairs, was used the next year in Val Lewton's production of BEDLAM, a truly frightening horror film starring Boris Karloff.

p&d, Leo McCarey; w, Dudley Nichols (based on a story by McCarey); ph, George Barnes; m, Robert Emmett Dolan; ed, Harry Marker; art d, William Flannery; set d, Darrell Silver; cos, Edith Head.

Drama Cas. (PR:AAA MPAA:NR)

BELLS OF SAN ANGELO*** (1947) 71m REP c

Roy Rogers (Himself), Dale Evans (Lee Madison), Andy Devine (Cookie), John McGuire (Rex Gridley), Olaf Hytten (Mr. Lionel Bates), David Sharpe (Gus Ulrich), Fritz Leiber (The Padre), Hank Patterson (The Old Timer), Fred S. Toones (The Cook), Eddie Acuff (Bus Driver), Sons of the Pioneers (Themselves).

This time it's Dale Evans, playing an authoress who writes western novels, who outwits the bad guys. When Roy and Dale find themselves in a tight spot, it's a chapter from her current book that bails them out of the mess. The first of the "violent" Rogers films in which people who got punched suffered bloody noses. This was the first Rogers film in which Devine appeared. Roy sings "A Cowboy's Dream of Heaven," and Dale warbles "I Love the West." The right stuff. (See ROY ROGERS series, Index.)

p, Edward J. White; d, William Witney; w, Sloan Nibley; ph, Jack Marta; ed, Lee Orlebeck; m/l, Jack Elliot, Tim Spencer.

Western (PR:A MPAA:NR)

BELLS OF SAN FERNANDO* (1947) 74m Screen Guild bw

Donald Woods (Michael), Gloria Warren (Maria), Shirley O'Hara (Nita), Byron Foulger (Garcia), Paul Newlan (Gueyon), Anthony Warde (Mendoza), Monte Blue (Governor), Claire DuBrey (Manta), David Leonard (Padre), Gordon Clark (Enrico), Gilbert Galvan (Perdido), Felipe Turich (Mule Driver).

An Irish seaman, Woods, wanders into a valley in early California during Spanish rule and confronts a cruel overseer. Warren, the love interest, sings "Land of Make Believe." Movie doesn't ring any bells.

p, James S. Burkett; d, Terry Morse; w, Jack Dewitt, Renault Duncan; ph, Robert Pattack; ed, George McGuire.

Drama (PR:A MPAA:NR)

BELOVED** (1934) 80m UNIV bw

John Boles (Carl Hausmann), Gloria Stuart (Lucy Hausmann), Albert Conti (Baron Von Hausmann), Dorothy Peterson (Baroness Von Hausmann), Morgan Farley (Eric), Ruth Hall (Patricia), Anderson Lawler (Rountree), Richard Carle (Judge Belden), Lucille Gleason (The Duchess), Mae Busch (Marie), Lucille La Verne (Mrs. Briggs), James Flavin (Wilcox), Bessie Barriscale (Mrs. Watkins), Montague Shaw (Talbot), Neysa Nourse (Laurette), Peggy Terry (Alice), Mickey Rooney, Edmund Breese, Louise Carter, Oscar Apfel, Fred Kelsey, Holmes Herbert, Mary Gordon.

The plot follows the life of a man from age ten in Vienna in 1840 to past the age of 90 in New York City in 1933. Boles fights in the Austrian revolution of 1848, battles for the Union in the Civil War and winds up giving violin lessons in New York. His son is a family disgrace until he dies heroically in the Spanish-American War. The grandson, Farley, becomes a brilliant violinist and is responsible for arranging to have Boles' symphony, the work of a lifetime, performed before his death. Too much material crammed into too short a time frame. Look for a tiny Mickey Rooney in a tiny early role.

p, Bennie F. Zeidman, Carl Laemmle, Jr.; d, Victor Schertzinger; w, Paul Gangelin, George O'Neil (based on a story by Gangelin); ph, Merritt Gerstad; m, Victor Schertzinger, Howard Jackson; md, Sam Wineland.

Drama (PR:A MPAA:NR)

BELOVED BACHELOR, THE** (1931) 72m PAR bw

Paul Lukas (Michael Morda), Dorothy Jordan (Mitzi Stressman), Betty Van Allen (Mitzi Stressman, Age 6), Charlie Ruggles (Jerry Wells), Vivienne Osborne (Elinor Hunter), Leni Stengel (Julie Stressman), John Breeden (Jimmy Martin), Harold Minjir (Winthrop Cole), Marjorie Gateson (Hortense Cole), Alma Chester (Martha), Guy Oliver (John Adams).

Love story involving a man who loses his lover and then falls in love with his adopted daughter. They feign indifference, but finally face their emotions. Film is an acting vehicle designed for Paul Lukas, and was successful at the box office.

d, Lloyd Corrigan; w, Raymond Griffith, Agnes Brand Leahy, Sidney Buchman (based on a play by Edward H. Peple); ph, Charles Rosher.

Drama (PR:A MPAA:NR)

BELOVED BRAT**   (1938) 78m WB bw (GB: A DANGEROUS AGE)

Bonita Granville (*Roberta*), Dolores Costello (*Helen Cosgrove*), Donald Crisp (*Mr. Morgan*), Donald Briggs (*Williams*), Natalie Moorhead (*Mrs. Morgan*), Lucille Gleason (*Miss Brewster*), Emmett Vogan (*Jenkins*), Lola Cheaney (*Mrs. Jenkins*), Mary Doyle (*Miss Mitchell*), Ellen Lowe (*Anna*), Paul Everton (*Judge Harris*), Bernice Pilot (*Mrs. White*), Priscilla Lyon (*Sylvia*), Doris Brenn (*Jackie*), Patsy Mitchell (*Betty Mae*), Stymie Beard (*Pinkie*), Meredith White (*Arabella*), Carmencita Johnson (*Estella*).

Costello, one-time leading lady of the silents, is the patient mother, doubling as a teacher, who handles young Granville, an obnoxious, impossible teenager creating problems for her indulgent family. Crisp is the equally understanding father. Soggy script and an unappealing production offers little.

p, Bryan Foy; d, Arthur Lubin; w, Lawrence Kimble (based on a story, "Too Much of Everything" by Jean Negulesco); ph, George Barnes; ed, Fred Richards.

Drama   **(PR:A MPAA:NR)**

BELOVED ENEMY***   (1936) 90m Goldwyn/UA bw

Merle Oberon (*Helen Drummond*), Brian Aherne (*Dennis Riordan*), Karen Morley (*Cathleen*), Theodore Von Eltz (*O'Brian*), Jerome Cowan (*O'Rourke*), David Niven (*Gerald Preston*), John Burton (*Hall*), Leyland Hodgson (*Hawkins*), David Torrence (*Alroyd*), Henry Stephenson (*Lord Athleigh*), Donald Crisp (*Burke*), Ra Hould (*Jerry*), Wyndham Standing (*Thornton*), Robert Strange (*Perrins*), Lionel Pape (*Crump*), Granville Bates (*Ryan*), P. J. Kelly (*Rooney*), Leo McCabe (*Connor*), Pat O'Malley (*Callahan*), Jack Mulhall (*Casey*), Claude King (*Col. Loder*), Donald Barry.

Just as THE INFORMER could be remade today without losing any of its power and immediacy, such is the case with BELOVED ENEMY, a drama about "the Troubles" in Ireland. Where the picture goes astray is that the screenwriters solve the problems, all through the love of a British woman (Oberon) for her Irish swain (Aherne). At the end of the exciting and believable Goldwyn movie, there is the one segment which we cannot believe. But before that, the screen is charged with fiery passion, good chase sequences, fine melodrama and touching dialog as the two lovers talk about the stupidity of killing in the name of political gain. Strong performances from everyone involved. It supposedly takes place during the revolution of 1921 but it might have happened the day before yesterday. Worth watching.

p, Samuel Goldwyn; d, H. C. Potter; w, John Balderston, Rose Franken, William Brown Meloney, David Hart (from a story by Balderston); ph, Gregg Toland; m, Alfred Newman; ed, Sherman Todd.

Drama   **(PR:C MPAA:NR)**

BELOVED IMPOSTER*   (1936, Brit.) 86m Stafford/RKO bw

Rene Ray (*Mary*), Fred Conyngham (*George*), Germaine Aussey (*La Lumiere*), Penelope Parkes (*Connie*), Edwin Ellis (*Herbert*), Charles Oliver (*Pierre*), Fred Groves (*Jack Harding*), Bela Mila (*Mona*), Tony de Lungo (*Gavani*), Lawrence Hanray (*Arthur*), Leslie "Hutch" Hutchinson, Quinton McPherson, Sidney Culver, Phil Thomas, Bombardier Billy Wells, Gwen Farrar, Caligary Brothers.

Offbeat musical concerns a vain waiter—would-be show business star—who believes he has murdered a beautiful singer, a girl who has rejected his advances. A directionless film.

p, John Stafford; d, Victor Hanbury; w, Connery Chappell (based on the novel *Dancing Boy* by Ethel Mannin).

Musical   **(PR:A MPAA:NR)**

BELOVED INFIDEL***   (1959) 123m FOX c

Gregory Peck (*F. Scott Fitzgerald*), Deborah Kerr (*Sheilah Graham*), Eddie Albert (*Carter*), Philip Ober (*John Wheeler*), Herbert Rudley (*Stan Harris*), John Sutton (*Lord Donegall*), Karin Booth (*Janet Pierce*), Ken Scott (*Robinson*), Buck Class (*Dion*), A. Cameron Grant (*Johnson*), Cindy Ames (*Miss Bull*).

Top production and stars give this one all they're worth but it could have been better. The film deals with the brief love affair between Graham and Fitzgerald in his last year of life while attempting to write screenplays in Hollywood to support his wife in an asylum and his daughter in a private school, as well as redeem a failing literary career. He meets an ambitious English writer, Graham, whom he takes under his wing. Peck is miscast (he is dark-haired and towers well over six feet, where Fitzgerald was 5'7" and fair-haired) and he plays the role nobly, even when drunk, which is most of the time, having to be taken care of by the beautiful Kerr (who is also miscast in that she is a mature woman here where Graham was only a slip of a girl-lady aspiring to be a gossip columnist). The story is more Graham's than Fitzgerald's, and she is portrayed as his rescuer, a dubious role we must accept on faith. She is at first charmed by Peck, then, becoming his mistress, plagued by his drinking and insults. When he discovers she is not the blueblood she claims to be, he cruelly degrades her; he also interferes in her career much more than one would believe. And the whole story comes down to Peck's sudden death at an early age while with his paramour. (Fitzgerald died in Graham's company while reading a Princeton alumni magazine, chewing on a Hershey bar, and sipping a Coke. He had a massive heart attack, brought on, no doubt, by years of guzzling cheap gin, but he was sober at the time.) Albert plays a sort of Robert Benchley role and gives it as much credit as he can, Benchley (and Dorothy Parker, the only one to go to Fitzgerald's funeral) being the writer's friend. It's a sad, almost wasted film which dwells not on Fitzgerald's courage and magnificent talent, but on his failure and Graham's triumph, an image not in keeping with today's perspective of that tragic giant.

p, Jerry Wald; d, Henry King; w, Sy Bartlett (based on the book by Sheilah Graham and Gerold Frank), ph, Leon Shamroy (CinemaScope, De Luxe Color); m, Franz Waxman; ed, William Reynolds; m/l, title song, Paul Francis Webster, Waxman.

Biography   **(PR:A MPAA:NR)**

BELOVED VAGABOND, THE*½   (1936, Brit.) 68m Toeplitz/COL bw

Maurice Chevalier (*Paragot*), Betty Stockfield (*Joanna*), Margaret Lockwood (*Blanquette*), Desmond Tester (*Asticot*), Austin Trevor (*Count Verneuil*), Peter Haddon (*Maj. Waters*), Charles Carson (*Charles Rushworth*), Kathleen Nesbitt (*Mme. Boin*), Barbara Gott (*Concierge*), D. J. Williams (*Undertaker*), C. Denier Warren (*Railway Clerk*).

This was the third time around for THE BELOVED VAGABOND story and, hopefully, the last. While they shot this one in English, they were doing the same thing in French, so it had the distinction of being dull in two languages. Chevalier loves his boss' daughter, but when she decides to marry someone else, he quits his architectural job and goes back to France (which is one of the reasons Chevalier agreed to make the film after being off-screen for three years). Chevalier is traveling with Tester when they meet a gypsy woman (Lockwood) and begin a strolling minstrel trio act with her. After a while, Chevalier realizes that Lockwood loves him but before this can get any stickier, he tells her that he must get Desmond back to England for the school year at the end of summer. Back in Blighty, Chevalier learns that Joanna (Stockfeld) didn't get married and she'd like to take matters up with him again. It doesn't take Chevalier long to realize that she's a money-hungry, venal woman with whom he could never be happy. So, with that, he returns to France to find Lockwood and tell her he loves her. A few songs, some snappy patter but, by and large, a weak effort.

p, Ludovico Toeplitz; d, Kurt [Curtis] Bernhardt; w, Hugh Mills, Walter Creighton, Arthur Wimperis (based on the novel *The Beloved Vagabond* by William J. Locke); ph, Franz Planer; md, Leslie Bridgewater.

Drama/Musical   **(PR:A MPAA:NR)**

BELOW THE BELT**½   (1980) 91m Aberdeen-RLF-Tom-Mi/ATLANTIC c

Regina Baff (*Rosa Rubinsky*), Mildred Burke (*Herself*), John C. Becher (*Promoter*), Annie McGreevey (*The Beautiful Boomerang*), Jane O'Brien (*Terrible Tommy*), Sierra Pecheur (*Verne Vavoom*), Gregory Rozakis (*Peddler*), Frazer Smith (*Terry*), Shirley Stoler (*Trish*), Dolph Sweet (*LeRoi*), K.C. Townsend (*Thalia*), Paul Brennan (*Stepfather*), Titi Paris (*Hilda*), Billie Mahoney (*Jean*), James Gammon (*Luke*), Ric Mancini (*Tio*), Ray Scott, Voices of the Firesign Theater.

An engaging but artless look at the world of female wrestling. ALL THE MARBLES came out just a while later and was too slick in treatment for the subject matter. Just as ROLLER DERBY, the Dayton, Ohio, docudrama effectively captured that milieu, so, too, does this film wrap up "wrassling." Baff masquerades as "The Mexican Spitfire" on the cornpone circuit. She is trained by the dean of lady wrestlers, Burke, playing herself. Eventually, she meets the royal scuzz of wrestling, O'Brien. Even though this was released in 1980, it was made six years before and has a plot not unlike ROCKY (1976). Fowler is an excellent director with an eye for documentary that gives us the feeling we are seeing real people in real situations. The lack of slickness is what sets this picture apart and what ultimately sinks it. We are used to seeing movies with top-level technical credits and this one doesn't have that. What it does have, though, is heart.

p&d, Robert Fowler; w, Fowler, Sherry Sonnett (based on the novel *To Smithereens* by Rosalyn Drexler); ph, Alan Metzger (TVC color); m, Jerry Fielding; ed, Stephen Zaillion; m/l, Fielding, David McKechnie.

Comedy   **Cas.**   **(PR:C MPAA:R)**

BELOW THE BORDER**   (1942) 57m MON bw

Buck Jones (*Buck Roberts*), Tim McCoy (*Tim McCall*), Raymond Hatton (*Sandy*), Linda Brent (*Rosita*), Eva Puig (*Aunt Maria*), Charles King (*Slade*), Dennis Moore (*Joe*), Bud Osborne (*Scully*), Ted Mapes (*Max*), Silver (*Himself*).

Buck and his friends clean up a gang that has been rustling cattle and doing other nasty things. Old-time cowboy actors do a bang-'em-up job. (See ROUGH RIDERS series, Index.)

p, Scott R. Dunlop; d, Howard P. Bretherton; w, Jess Bowers; ph, Harry Neumann; ed, Carl Pierson.

Western   **Cas.**   **(PR:A MPAA:NR)**

BELOW THE DEADLINE*½   (1936) 69m GN bw

Cecilia Parker (*Molly Fitzgerald*), Russell Hopton (*Terry Mulvancy*), Theodor Von Eltz (*Flash Ackroyd*), Thomas Jackson (*Pearson*), Warner Richmond (*Diamond Dutch*), John St. Polis (*Abrams*), Robert Frazer (*Palmer*), Charles Delaney (*Artie Nolan*), Kathryn Sheldon (*Aunt Mary*), Robert E. Homans (*Capt. Symonds*).

Cop Hopton is framed in a jewel heist. In escaping police, he gets involved in a train wreck, gets a new face, and returns to New York to prove his innocence. Lethargically paced, yet sometimes engrossing.

p, George R. Batcheller; d, Charles Lamont; w, Ewart Adamson; ph, M. A. Anderson.

Crime Drama   **(PR:A MPAA:NR)**

BELOW THE DEADLINE**   (1946) 65m MON bw

Warren Douglas (*Joe Hilton*), Ramsay Ames (*Lynn Turner*), Jan Wiley (*Vivian*), Paul Maxey (*Arthur Brennan*), Philip Van Zandt (*Oney Kessel*), John Harmon (*Pinky*), Bruce Edwards (*Sam Austin*), George Meeker (*Jeffrey Hilton*), Clancy Cooper (*Nichols*), Cay Forrester (*Blonde*), Alan Bridge (*Turner*), George Eldredge (*Vail*), William Ruhl (*Welsh*).

Douglas is an embittered WW II veteran who takes over his brother's gambling operations when Meeker is killed. Despite pleas from friends and lady love, Douglas will not reform but is blatantly out to get all he can, and is almost killed by rival gangsters when a reform administration takes over. Fast-action film is above average for a Monogram programmer.

p, Lindsley Parsons; d, William Beaudine; w, Harvey Gates, Forrest Judd; ph, Harry Neumann; ed, Ace Herman.

Crime Drama **(PR:A MPAA:NR)**

BELOW THE SEA*** (1933) 78m COL bw

Ralph Bellamy *(Steve McCreary)*, Fay Wray *(Diane Templeton)*, Fredrik Vogeding *(Karl Schlemmer)*, Esther Howard *(Lily)*, Trevor Bland *(Waldridge)*, William J. Kelly *(Dr. Chapman)*, Paul Page *(Jackson)*.

Deep-sea adventure has soldier of fortune Vogeding on a quest for $3 million in bullion still on a sunken German U boat. Bellamy scowls through high action as a strong and courageous scuba diver enchanted by ingenue Wray. Kelly's acting flows well as head of the scientific expediton. Bellamy's fight with an octopus makes this film unforgettable.

d, Albert Rogell; w, Jo Swerling; ph, Joseph Walker; ed, Jack Dennis.

Adventure **(PR:A MPAA:NR)**

BELSTONE FOX, THE*** (1976, Brit.) 103m RANK/FOX c

Eric Porter *(Asher)*, Rachel Roberts *(Cathie)*, Jeremy Kemp *(Kendrick)*, Bill Travers *(Tod)*, Dennis Waterman *(Stephen)*, Heather Wright *(Jenny)*.

A hunting hound and baby fox settle into a happy friendly relationship which remains until man pits them against each other in a horse-and-hound hunt. Porter is solid as the huntsman who brings the baby fox to be nurtured by the hound. Hats off to the trainers and technical experts who let the animals steal the show.

p, Julian Wintle; d, James Hill; ph, John Wilcox, James Allen (Todd-AO, Eastmancolor); m, Laurie Johnson; ed, Peter Tanner; art d, Hazel Peizer.

Drama **Cas.** **(PR:AAA MPAA:G)**

BEN 1/2** (1972) 95m Cinerama c

Lee Harcourt Montgomery *(Danny Garrison)*, Joseph Campanella *(Cliff Kirtland)*, Arthur O'Connell *(Bill Hatfield)*, Rosemary Murphy *(Beth Garrison)*, Meredith Baxter *(Eve Garrison)*, Kaz Garas *(Joe Greer)*, Paul Carr *(Kelly)*, Richard Van Fleet *(Reade)*, Kenneth Tobey *(Engineer)*, James Luisi *(Ed)*, Lee Paul *(Careu)*, Norman Alden *(Policeman)*, Scott Garrett *(Henry Gary)*, Arlen Stuart *(Mrs. Gray)*, Richard Drasin *(George)*.

When a young boy, Montgomery, befriends an educated and influential rodent named Ben, they organize an army of varmints which terrorize the city's populace. Impeccable performances crest this exciting crisis movie. Better stand on a chair for this one. Michael Jackson sings "Ben's Song."

p, Mort Briskin; d, Phil Karlson; w, Gilbert A. Ralston (based on characters created by Stephen Gilbert); ph, Russell Metty (DeLuxe Color); m, Walter Scharf; ed, Henry Gerstad; art d, Rolland M. Brooks; cos, Ray Harp, Mina Mittleman.

Horror **(PR:A MPAA:PG)**

BEN HUR***** (1959) 212m MGM c

Charlton Heston *(Judah Ben-Hur)*, Jack Hawkins *(Quintus Arrius)*, Stephen Boyd *(Messala)*, Haya Harareet *(Esther)*, Hugh Griffith *(Sheik Ilderim)*, Martha Scott *(Miriam)*, Sam Jaffe *(Simonides)*, Cathy O'Donnell *(Tirzah)*, Finlay Currie *(Balthasar)*, Frank Thring *(Pontius Pilate)*, Terence Longden *(Drusus)*, Andre Morell *(Sextus)*, Marina Berti *(Flavia)*, George Relph *(Tiberius)*, Adi Berber *(Malluch)*, Stella Vitelleschi *(Amrah)*, Jose Greci *(Mary)*, Laurence Payne *(Joseph)*, John Horsley *(Spintho)*, Richard Coleman *(Metellus)*, Duncan Lamont *(Marius)*, Ralph Truman *(Aide to Tiberius)*, Richard Hale *(Gaspar)*, Reginald Lal Singh *(Melchoir)*, David Davies *(Quaestor)*, Dervis Ward *(Jailer)*, Claude Heater *(The Christ)*, Mino Doro *(Gratus)*, Robert Brown *(Chief of Rowers)*, John Glenn *(Rower No. 42)*, Maxwell Shaw *(Rower* No. 43), Emile Carrer *(Rower No. 28)*, Tutte Lemkow *(Leper)*, Howard Lang *(Hortator)*, Ferdy Mayne *(Captain of Rescue Ship)*, John Le Mesurier *(Doctor)*, Stevenson Lang *(Blind man)*, Aldo Mozele *(Barca)*, Thomas O'Leary *(Starter at Race)*, Noel Sheldon *(Centurion)*, Hector Ross *(Officer)*, Bill Kuehl *(Soldier)*, Aldo Silvani *(Man in Nazareth)*, Diego Pozzetto *(Villager)*, Dino Fazio *(Marcello)*, Michael Cosmo *(Raimondo)*, Aldo Pial *(Cavalry Officer)*, Remington Olmstead *(Decurian)*, Victor De La Fosse *(Galley Officer)*, Enzo Fiermonte *(Galley Officer)*, Hugh Billingsley *(Mario)*, Tiberio Mitri *(Roman at Bath)*, Pietro Tordi *(Pilate's Servant)*, Jerry Brown *(The Corinthian)*, Otello Capanna *(The Byzantine)*, Luigi Marra *(Syrian)*, Cliff Lyons *(Lubian)*, Edward J. Auregul *(Athenian)*, Joe Yrigoyan *(Egyptian)*, Alfredo Danesi *(Armenian)*, Raimondo Van Riel *(Old Man)*, Mike Dugan *(Seaman)*, Joe Canutt *(Sportsman)*.

One of the great movie spectacles, BEN-HUR is a tour de force for Heston, as was THE TEN COMMANDMENTS. In remaking the silent classic (1927, with Ramon Novarro and Francis X. Bushman), quality-conscious director Wyler presented a modern interpretation of the novel by General Lew Wallace, published in 1880. Heston, a wealthy patrician prince once friendly with Romans occupying his country of Judea, turns against them in revolt after witnessing their many transgressions, particularly indicting the Emperor Tiberius (Relph) who has the Romans convinced they belong to a master race, not unlike the crazy credo preached by Hitler centuries later. Boyhood friend Messala (Boyd), now a Roman Tribune, visits Heston to ask for the names of those leading the revolt. Heston refuses to identify the leaders, calling them patriots. Boyd leaves furious, now Heston's sworn enemy. Days later, the new Roman governor enters the city, his parade watched from a rooftop by Heston and his sister Tirzah (O'Donnell). She accidentally brushes against a loose roof tile which falls to the street, frightening the governor's skittish horse, throwing him into a wall and injuring him. Boyd uses this incident to take his vengeance, arresting Heston and his entire family, cruelly explaining: "I wanted your help. Now you have given it to me. By making this example of you, I discourage treason. By condemning, without hesitation, an old friend, I shall be feared." The entire family is sent into slavery, Heston and dozens of others taken to Tyrus. En route, in a small town named Nazareth, Heston collapses from lack of water which has been specifically denied to him. He begs God for help and suddenly a carpenter's son, Jesus, gives him water. A Roman guard rushes forward but when facing the Nazarene, whose whole presence seems adorned in blinding light, the soldier is dumbstruck and silently retreats. Heston is dragged on his way but not before gaining great strength at the sight of Jesus, who has saved his life. He becomes a galley slave on a boat commanded by Hawkins; Macedonian pirates attack the ship. A fierce battle ensues and the ship is boarded. Hawkins is knocked into the sea, his heavy armor quickly pulling him down. Heston, who has freed himself and several other slaves as the ship begins to sink, dives into the water and saves Hawkins' life, holding onto wreckage which floats away from the battle. Hawkins, in gratitude, sponsors Heston in Rome where he becomes a champion chariot racer in the great arena. Years pass and he becomes the adopted son of Hawkins, as well as a worldly citizen of the great city, but he is obsessed with finding his mother and sister and returns to Judea to visit Boyd, coming not as a slave but as the son of a Roman counsul. He asks that Boyd find his loved ones and the Roman agrees, realizing Heston now represents great power. At his home Heston meets Harareet, the daughter of a loyal family servant, with whom he later falls in love and marries. She tells him that his mother and sister are dead, a lie; the two have been living as lepers, a condition caused by many years in prison, and do not want Heston to know of their plight. When hearing that his loved ones are dead, Heston explodes and decides to meet Boyd in a chariot race, a match long promoted by rich sheik Griffith. The arch-enemies meet in the arena and begin their wild ride, Boyd destroying one chariot after another by cutting into their wheels with specially fixed blades on his own, whipping his opponents and crashing into them until their bodies and debris from their chariots lie strewn upon the sand while thousands roar approval. The race is finally down to Boyd and Heston and Boyd attempts the same maneuvers, almost destroying Heston's chariot, but Heston manages to lock the wheel of his chariot behind that of Boyd's, then rushes forward, pulling it off its axle. Boyd's chariot collapses; he is dragged forward by his racing horses, bruised, bleeding; he rolls, a bloody pulp, into the middle of the track where remaining chariots roar over him, while Heston goes on to win the great race. Taken to aneoom beneath the coliseum, Boyd lies dying. Heston comes to him and is greeted with hissing hatred as Boyd tells him that his mother and sister are not dead, that he is to "look for them in the Valley of the Lepers, if you can recognize them. The race is *not* over!" With this horrible news the arch-villain dies. Heston goes to the Valley of the Lepers, secretly following Harareet who has been taking food to O'Donnell and Scott for years. Heston rushes forward and despite his mother's wild protests, he embraces her and learns that his sister is dying. He takes them to Jerusalem to see a great healer but they find him condemned to death when they reach the city. Heston watches as Jesus struggles through a crowd, carrying the cross upon which he is to die. He recognizes Jesus as the one who saved his life and tries to give him water but is pushed away by soldiers, though Jesus sees him. The family leaves the city after Christ has been crucified; a thunderstorm breaks overhead and the rainwater covers O'Donnell and Scott. In shock they look at their flesh which is no longer covered with sores; they have been cured. Heston and his loved ones rejoice. The last scene shows an empty cross with a shepherd driving his flock before it. The majesty of this film is captured in almost every frame by Wyler, who tells the gigantic story in human, understated terms, albeit the great chariot race was directed by action expert Andrew Marton. Everything about BEN-HUR was enormous; more than 300 sets were employed, taken from 15,000 sketches, these sets covering more than 340 acres. The arena housing the chariot race consumed eighteen acres, the largest single set in film history. The five-story stands were packed with 8,000 extras and 40,000 tons of sand were taken from beaches to make the track. Scores of Yugoslavian horses were imported for the spectacular twenty-minute race which took three months to shoot. More than a thousand workers slaved for a year to build the colossal arena. Rome's Cinecitta Studios were gutted of more than a million props and here sculptors labored to make more than 200 pieces of giant statues. Also unique were the wide-screen cameras employed, 65 millimeters wide to achieve sharp deep focus. MGM lavished about $12,500,000 on this stupendous production, which brought them near bankruptcy, but the returns were staggering, a gross of $40 million. Veteran stunt man Yakima Canutt taught Boyd and Heston how to manage the cumbersome chariots for the great race which is probably the best action sequence of the film. Heston is simply splendid as the enlightened Ben-Hur and Boyd is the perfect sinister Messala, a role he never quite equalled. (He was scheduled to play opposite Elizabeth Taylor in CLEOPATRA but was replaced by Burton when contractual disputes arose; one might wonder what would have happened to a lot of personal lives if Burton, who was compelled to wear Boyd's costumes in the film, had not ridden so heroically into Liz's confused life.) More than 50,000 people were involved in making this epic which swept 12 Oscars, notably for Best Picture, to Wyler for direction, Heston for acting, and the shifty-eyed Griffith for supporting actor; also winning, deservedly so, was Surtees for cinematography and Rozsa for a great bravura score. Gillespie and MacDonald, who handled the special effects, also won and no wonder; the miniature sea battle appears startlingly real and life-size. The wide-screen, stereophonic sound of this marvelous epic only added to a production that epitomizes Hollywood's finest effort, a film the industry had been unconsciously aiming to produce for half a decade. Much credit should go to the tireless production mastermind Sam Zimbalist, who had produced QUO VADIS in Rome nine years earlier. The effort was superhuman and it killed him; Zimbalist died shortly before the film's completion and its triumph is a tribute to his memory. Though Tunberg receives lone credit for the script, a host of other writers contributed in one form or another, including such stellar literary lights as Maxwell Anderson, S.N. Behrman, Gore Vidal, and Christopher Fry. The effort was worthwhile in every sense, producing three-and-a-half hours of unforgettable greatness on film.

p, Sam Zimbalist; d, William Wyler; w, Karl Tunberg (based on the novel by Lew Wallace); ph, Robert L. Surtees (Camera 65, Panavision, Technicolor); m, Miklos Rozsa; ed, Ralph E. Winters, John Dunning; art d, William Horning, Edward Carfagno; cos, Elizabeth Haffenden; spec eff, Arnold Gillespie, Robert MacDonald; associate directors, Andrew Marton, Yakima Canutt, Mario Soldati.

Historical Drama   Cas.   (PR:A   MPAA:NR)

BEND OF THE RIVER**

(1952) 91m UNIV c (GB: WHERE THE RIVER BENDS)

James Stewart (Glyn McLyntock), Arthur Kennedy (Cole Garret), Julia Adams (Laura Baile), Rock Hudson (Trey Wilson), Lori Nelson (Marjie), Jay C. Flippen (Jeremy Baile), Stepin Fetchit (Adam), Henry Morgan (Shorty), Chubby Johnson (Cap'n Mello), Howard Petrie (Tom Hendricks), Frances Bavier (Mrs. Prentiss), Jack Lambert (Red) Royal Dano (Long Tom), Frank Chase (Wasco), Cliff Lyons (Willie), Frank Ferguson.

Kennedy is about to be lynched as a horse thief when Stewart, once a border raider from Missouri, saves his life. Stewart is now working as a guide for a group of farmers on their way to Oregon. A grateful Kennedy joins him and they lead the wagon train. They are attacked and repel a band of Shoshone Indians, then arrive in Portland. Flippen, the farmers' leader, gets local Petrie to take care of transportation for the group. The farmers go upriver and settle in for the long winter. When Petrie's promised supplies fail to get to the newly built village, Stewart and Flippen race into Portland to see what went wrong. In the short while since they've been gone, Portland has turned into a boom town due to a gold rush. Petrie can make a lot more money selling his supplies to newly rich miners so he refuses to make good on the deal with the farmers. Guns roar and Stewart and Flippen get the goods and race upriver on a boat. They arrive and Kennedy is a different man now. He is entrapped by the lure of easy money and wants to sell the supplies and cattle to miners, who are willing to pay inflated prices. Kennedy takes Flippen and his daughter, Adams, as hostages. A final battle has Stewart drowning Kennedy in the exciting penultimate scene. Flippen and Adams realize that Stewart is now a changed man so they welcome him as part of their community. Good performances, a slightly simple plot, fine action direction from Mann. Rock Hudson in one of his earliest roles and Frances Bavier before she joined Andy Griffith for their memorable TV series.

p, Aaron Rosenberg; d, Anthony Mann; w, Borden Chase (based on the novel Bend of the Snake by Bill Gulick); ph, Irving Glassberg (Technicolor); m, Hans J. Salter; ed, Russell Schoengarth; art d, Bernard Herzbrun, Nathan Juran; set Russell A. Gausman, Oliver Emert; cos, Rosemary Odell.

Western   (PR:C   MPAA:NR)

BENEATH THE PLANET OF THE APES**

(1970) 95m FOX c

Charlton Heston (Taylor), James Franciscus (Brent), Kim Hunter (Zira), Maurice Evans (Dr. Zaius), Linda Harrison (Nova), Paul Richards (Mendez), Victor Buono (Fat Man), James Gregory (Ursus), Jeff Corey (Caspay), Natalie Trundy (Albina), Thomas Gomez (Minister), David Watson (Cornelius), Don Pedro Colley (Negro), Tod Andres (Skipper), Gregory Sierra (Gorilla Sergeant), Lou Wagner (Lucius).

The adventure continues when Heston suddenly disappears in the ape civilization. Franciscus and Hunter begin searching for Heston and find the ape tribes inside the earth, led by nutsy Buono whose headquarters is inside the ruins of Grand Central Station, where a live A-Bomb is worshipped like a god until someone jiggles it and the planet goes poof. Many of the sets shown in ruins were left over from HELLO DOLLY. Roddy McDowall does not appear in this one, this time occupied with directing DEVIL'S WIDOW, but he did slip into the studio to make some recordings so that his voice comes out of one of the apes. The best of the four sequels following the successful PLANET OF THE APES. Interesting look at nuclear holocaust through Krasner's average camera technique. Rosenman's musical score easily inflates the drama. (See PLANET OF THE APES series, Index.)

p, Arthur P. Jacobs; d, Ted Post; w, Paul Dehn, Mort Abrahams; ph, Milton Krasner (Panavision, DeLuxe Color); m, Leonard Rosenman; ed, Marion Rothman; art d, Jack Martin Smith, William Creber; set d, Walter M. Scott, Sven Wickman.

Adventure   Cas.   (PR:AA   MPAA:NR)

BENEATH THE 12-MILE REEF**

(1953) 102m FOX c

Robert Wagner (Tony Petrakis), Terry Moore (Gwyneth Rhys), Gilbert Roland (Mike Petrakis), J. Carrol Naish (Soak), Richard Boone (Thomas Rhys), Angela Clarke (Mama), Peter Graves (Arnold), Jay Novello (Sinan), Jacques Aubuchon (Sofotes), Gloria Gordon (Penny), Harry Carey, Jr. (Griff), James Harakas (Card), Charles Wagenheim (Paul), Marc Krah (Fat George), Rush Williams (David Rhys), Jonathan Jackson, Guy Carleton, Frank Joyner, Jack Pappas, William Llewellyn Johnstone, Jack Burke.

This is sort of Romeo and Juliet under water. Wagner is the son of Greek diver Roland, Moore is the daughter of WASP diver Boone. They are all in the sponge gathering business and both families have been at each other for eons. Boone's group is from Key West and has its own designated (by them) area where they hunt sponges and hook the creatures from the shallow depths. The Greeks operate out of Tarpon Springs and go much deeper. A battle between clans ensues when Roland poaches in Boone territory. He's killed while diving at the l2-mile reef, so Wagner has to dive where his Dad died in order to become the leader of family. In doing so, he battles the requisite octopus, then has an underwater fight with Graves, beating then saving him. The problem with many underwater films is that, no matter how fast the people and fish swim, it always seems to be in slow motion. This picture is no exception. (Moore claims she was married to Howard Hughes during

this time. Watching the movie, one can definitely see her attraction. She was quite a looker in her day.)

p, Robert Bassler; d, Robert D. Webb; w, A.I. Bezzerides; ph, Edward Cronjager (CinemaScope, Technicolor); m, Bernard Herrmann; ed, William Reynolds; spec eff, Ray Kellogg; underwater ph, Till Gabbani.

Adventure   Cas.   (PR:A   MPAA:NR)

BENEATH WESTERN SKIES*

(1944) 56m REP bw

Bob Livingston (Johnny Revere), Smiley Burnette (Frog Milhouse), Effie Laird (Carrie Stokes), Frank Jacquet (Samuel Webster), Tom London (Earl Phillips), Charles Miller (Lem Toller), Joe Strauch Jr. (Tadpole), Leroy Mason (Bull Bricker), Kenne Duncan (Rod Barrow), Charles Dorety (Spike), Jack Kirk (Wainwright), Bud Geary (Hank).

An improbable tale, even for a grade B western: Livingston is rendered an amnesia victim after being hit on the head and is easily convinced by outlaws that he's one of them. He joins in several robberies until he is again struck on the head, reverts to normal good guy, and rounds up his deceivers.

p, Louis Gray; d, Spencer Bennet; w, Albert DeMond, Bob Williams (based on an original story by DeMond); ph, Ernest Miller; ed, Charles Craft.

Western   (PR:A   MPAA:NR)

BENGAL BRIGADE*

(1954) 86m UNIV c (GB: BENGAL RIFLES)

Rock Hudson (Jeff Claybourne), Arlene Dahl (Vivian Morrow), Ursula Theiss (Latah), Torin Thatcher (Col. Morrow), Arnold Moss (Rajah Karem Jee), Dan O'Herlihy (Capt. Ronald Blaine), Michael Ansara (Maj. Puran Singh), Harold Gordon (Hari Lal), Shep Menken (Bulbir), Leslie Denison (Capt. Ian McLeod), John Dodsworth (Capt. Guy Fritz-Morrell), Ramsay Hill (Maj. Jennings), Sujata and Asoka (Themselves).

Hudson stars as the leader of a troop of Sepoys in India. He leads them into action against orders, then resigns his commission when he is brought on the carpet. Moss is a villainous rajah bent on heaving the British out of the sub-continent. Hudson convinces Moss that he's a traitor and joins the villain. By fade-out, Hudson has saved his Sepoys, his girl friend (Dahl) and her father, Thatcher. Benedek is only as good as his material. He directed THE WILD ONE and DEATH OF A SALESMAN but he also directed this movie and THE KISSING BANDIT, which just goes to show that no director, no matter how skilled, can triumph over a lousy script. There are many directors, however, who can take a wonderful script and dull it up or punch it down. Gershenson's score is excellent and if this had been a first-rate movie, the music would have merited an Oscar nomination.

d, Ted Richmond; d, Laslo Benedek; w, Richard Alan Simmons, Seton I. Miller (based on a novel by Hall Hunter); ph, Maury Gertsman (Technicolor); m, Joseph Gershenson; ed, Frank Gross.

Adventure   (PR:A   MPAA:NR)

BENGAL TIGER**

(1936) 62m WB bw

Barton MacLane (Cliff Ballenger), June Travis (Laura), Warren Hull (Joe Larson), Paul Graetz (Carl Homan), Joseph Crehan (Hinsdale), Richard Purcell (Nick DeLargo), Carlyle Moore Jr. (Ambulance Driver).

Best friends in love with the same woman battle it out with the help of a tiger and a circus fire. One gets killed and the other gets the girl and tiger. Acceptable acting bolsters dramatic substance, but not enough. Hold onto your cats.

d, Louis King; w, Roy Chanslor and Earl Felton; ph, L. William O'Connell.

Drama   (PR:A   MPAA:NR)

BENGAZI**

(1955) 79m Panamint/RKO bw

Richard Conte (Gillmore), Victor McLaglen (Donovan), Richard Carlson (Levering), Mala Powers (Aileen), Richard Erdman (Selby), Hillary Brooke (Nora), Maury Hill (Peters), Jay Novello (Basim), Gonzales Gonzales (Kamal).

Fairly interesting adventure story that begins in Bengazi and winds up in the Sahara. Conte is a Yank with a history not unlike Ric Blaine's in CASABLANCA and McLaglen is a burly Irishman without a single scruple. They team up with Erdman in a search for the gold that Arab nomads have hidden in an old mosque for safekeeping during WW II. Carlson, a British official and Powers, McLaglen's daughter, also join in the search. The gold is found, but the natives are angered at the desecration of their house of worship. A battle between the Arabs and the mosque-robbers ends the film. This might have been a variation of von Stroheim's GREED as that is the motivating force behind all the action and there are many scenes in the desert. The similarity ends there. Look for Gonzalez Gonzalez as Kamal. GG got his start as a contestant on the old Groucho TV show and provided America with ten of the funniest minutes ever seen on television. He was then taken to the film community's heart and hasn't stopped working.

p, Sam Wiesenthal, Eugene Tevlin; d, John Brahm; w, Endre Bohem, Louis Vittes (story by Jeff Bailey); ph, Joseph Biroc; m, Roy Webb; ed, Robert Golden; cos, Michael Woulfe.

Crime Drama   (PR:A-C   MPAA:NR)

BENJAMIN*** ½

(1968, Fr.) 108m Parc-Marianne/PAR c (BENJAMIN OU LES MEMOIRES D'UN PUCEAU; AKA: THE DIARY OF AN INNOCENT BOY)

Michele Morgan (Countess de Valandry), Catherine Deneuve (Anne de Clecy), Pierre Clementi (Benjamin), Michel Piccoli (Count Phillipe), Francine Berge (Marion), Anna Gael (Celestine), Catherine Rouvel (Victorine), Jacques Dufilho (Camille), Odile Versois (Married Woman).

Comedy detailing the coming of age of 17-year-old Clementi, beginning with his introduction into the 18th-century country estate of his titled relatives. Deneuve is an orphan on a neighboring estate. Clementi trysts with her, who trysts with Piccoli, who trysts with Morgan, who, though insane about Piccoli, takes more than a passing interest in her nephew Clementi. A gracious, technically adept satire, redolent of THE RULES OF THE GAME (1950), LA DOLCE VITA (1961), and many other mannered sexual tragicomedies, from a director whose works are infrequently released abroad.

p, Mag Bodard; d, Michel Deville; w, Nina Companeez, Deville; ph, Ghislain Cloquet (Technicolor); cos, Rita Bayance.

Comedy **(PR:O MPAA:NR)**

BENJAMIN*** (1973, Ger.) 95m Willy Bogner/FOX c

Philip Sonntag, Helmut Trunz, Billy Kidd, Suzy Chaffee, Art Furrer, Herman Goelliner, the Bonne Ski Ballet.

Computer foul-up results in the selection of a humble accountant as the predicted winner of a major ski championship. The problem is, he's never been on skis before. Great cast of well-known skiers and brilliant photography performed on skis by Bogner and Trunz.

p&d, Willy Bogner; w, Bogner, Juergen Guett (based on a story by Bogner); ph, Bogner, Helmut Trunz (Eastmancolor); m, Gary Wright, Eberhard Schoerer; ed, Bettyna Lewertoff, Brigitte Hubner.

Comedy **(PR:AA MPAA:NR)**

BENJI***¹/2 (1974) 85m Mulberry Square c

Higgins (Benji), Patsy Garrett (Mary), Allen Fiuzat (Paul), Cynthia Smith (Cindy), Peter Breck (Dr. Chapman), Frances Bavier (Lady with Cat), Terry Carter (Officer Tuttle), Edgar Buchanan (Bill), Tom Lester (Riley), Christopher Connelly (Henry), Deborah Walley (Linda), Mark Slade (Mitch), Herb Vigran (Lt. Samuels), Larry Swartz (Floyd), J. D. Young (Second Policeman), Erwin Hearne (Mr. Harvey), Katie Hearne (Mrs. Harvey), Don Puckett (Plainclothesman), Ed DeLatte (Bob Fielding), Victor Raider Wexler (Payton), Charles Starkey (Custodian), Ben Vaughn (Man).

Unlike the pallid sequels, BENJI is a captivating and irresistible film. Benji, whose real name is Higgins, starred for several years on TV's "Petticoat Junction" (1963-1969) and took home many Patsy Awards for his abilities. If Higgins were a human, he might be accused of overacting but it wears well on a dog and this dog is an actor, not merely a mutt who licks and jumps. Higgins is a dog of questionable lineage who lives in a vacant house. He is adopted by a family. When that family's children (Smith and Fiuzat) are kidnaped and taken to the very same house Higgins used to occupy, the dog attempts to communicate this to various people but it's not easy. Eventually, someone listens to the dog, the kids are saved, and the movie ends happily. Much of the film is shot from the dog's-eye view and it works perfectly. The human acting is good, but not as good as the animal star. Still, it's great fun from the first "arf." Think of how smart dogs are . . . they can understand hundreds of words in *our* language and yet *we* can't understand one of *theirs*. It was old home week for Higgins and Edgar Buchanan who also worked on "Petticoat Junction." For the record, Higgins is one of the rare animals not trained by Weatherwax. *His* trainer is Frank Inn. (Sequel: FOR THE LOVE OF BENJI.)

p,d&w, Joe Camp; ph, Don Reddy; m, Euel Box; ed, Leon Smith; prod d, Harland Wright.

Comedy **Cas.** **(PR:AAA MPAA:G)**

BENNY GOODMAN STORY, THE**¹/2 (1956) 116m UNIV c

Steve Allen (Benny Goodman), Donna Reed (Alice Hammond), Berta Gersten (Mom Goodman), Herbert Anderson (John Hammond), Robert F. Simon (Pop Goodman), Sammy Davis Sr. (Fletcher Henderson), Dick Winslow (Gil Rodin), Barry Truex (Benny Goodman at 16), David Kasday (Benny Goodman at 10), Hy Averback (William Alexander), Wilton Graff (Mr. Hammond), Shep Menken (Harry Goodman), Harry James, Gene Krupa, Martha Tilton, Lionel Hampton, Ziggy Elman, Ben Pollack, Teddy Wilson, Edward "Kid" Ory.

Allen impresses mightily in his first acting job as the incomparable Benny Goodman. Anytime a musical biography is attempted, if the person is famous enough, it's dangerous to toy with the truth. In the case of THE GLENN MILLER STORY there was the added drama of his unexpected death. In this case, Goodman has the standard rags to riches history of so many musical personalities and, despite Davies' often inventive and intelligent script, truth can get tiresome. Davies also directs with as much aplomb as he can muster, but it's uphill in the dramatic scenes because the audience is waiting for the musical numbers that dot the screenplay. Every major musician whom Benny played with is represented and the film is jam-packed with music, with Goodman doing the clarinet playing for Allen. To the producers' credit they don't shy away from any of Goodman's humble beginnings and his Jewish Mama and Papa are well repped by Gersten and Simon. Goodman was one of the first bandleaders who integrated his musicians, but little is made of that. There were leaders well into the 1970s who kept their bands lily-white and refused to mix or match. Their music suffered for it. A rare appearance by Sammy Davis *Senior* in an acting role as the late Fletcher Henderson, as well as Hy Averback as Goldman's manager are highlights. Averback later became a respected film and TV director after beginning as a radio announcer (I LOVE YOU, ALICE B. TOKLAS).

p, Aaron Rosenberg; d&w, Valentine Davies; ph, William Daniels (Technicolor); m, Joseph Gershenson, Henry Mancini, Sol Yaged, Alan Harding, Harold Brown); ed, Russell Schoengarth; cos, Bill Thomas.

Musical Biography **(PR:AA MPAA:NR)**

BENSON MURDER CASE, THE** (1930) 69m PAR bw

William Powell (Philo Vance), Natalie Moorhead (Fanny Del Roy), Eugene Pallette (Sergeant Heath), Paul Lukas (Adolph Mohler), William Boyd (Harry Gray), E. H. Calvert (District Attorney Markham), May Beatty (Paula Banning), Mischa Auer

(Albert), Otto Yamaoka (Sam), Charles McMurphy (Burke), Dick Rush (Welch), Richard Tucker (Anthony Benson), Perry Ivins (Dealer).

Tucker, a notorious womanizer and wealthy stockbroker, is shot to death in his country estate and it's Powell/Vance into the breach. Powell has been a guest at the estate and he does the usual roundup of suspects before nailing the killer. This so-so film ranges far afield from the original Van Dine novel which was based upon the mysterious 1920 murder of card wizard and millionaire Joseph Elwell, a killing that has gone unsolved to this day.

d, Frank Tuttle; w, Bartlett Cormack (based on the novel by S. S. Van Dine); ph, A. J. Stout; ed, Doris Drought.

Mystery **(PR:A MPAA:NR)**

BENVENUTA** (1983, Fr.) 103m Nouvelle Imagerie-UGC-Europe 1-FR3-Opera/Artificial Eye c

Fanny Ardant (Benvenuta), Vittorio Gassman (Livio), Mathieu Carriere (Francois), Claire Wauthion (Inge), Francoise Fabian (Jeanne), Philipe Geluck (Father), Anne Chappuis (Mother).

Once again, the tale of a single woman in love with a very married man. But this one has a difference. It's told on two levels, in reality and in fantasy. It flashes forward and back in various time frames and concerns a screenwriter tracking down the author of a scandalous book so he can write a script from it. The female author insists that her book was purely imagination and bore no resemblance to her own life. She eventually admits that Benvenuta was a real person and tells the story. Cut from here to there as the two stories unfold. Gassman, as the man in the book, and Ardant, as the woman, are excellent in making us believe their passion, but the task of keeping both stories going eventually defeats the Flemish filmmaker Delvaux. Two parallel stories is not new, but anyone attempting it had better look at Lelouche's AND NOW MY LOVE before attempting it. In BENVENUTA they may have chewed off more than they could bite.

p, Jean-Claude Batz; d&w, Andre Delvaux (from novel La Confession Anonyme by Suzanne Lilar); ph, Charles Van Damme (Eastmancolor); m, Frederic Devreese; ed, Albert Jurgenson, Jean Goudier; art d, Claude Pignot.

Romance **(PR:C MPAA:NR)**

BEQUEST TO THE NATION (SEE: NELSON AFFAIR, THE, 1973, Brit.)

BERKELEY SQUARE*** (1933) 87m Lasky/FOX bw

Leslie Howard (Peter Standish), Heather Angel (Helen Pettigrew), Valerie Taylor (Kate Pettigrew), Irene Browne (Lady Ann Pettigrew), Beryl Mercer (Mrs. Barwick), Colin Keith-Johnston (Tom Pettigrew), Alan Mowbray (Maj. Clinton), Lionel Barrymore (Innkeeper), Juliette Compton (Duchess of Devonshire), Betty Lawford (Marjorie Frant), Ferdinand Gottschalk (Mr. Throstle), Samuel S. Hinds (The American Ambassador), Olaf Hytten (Sir Joshua Reynolds), David Torrence (Lord Stanley).

Posh production of a sophisticated Broadway play which ran for 50-carriage trade weeks. The film, with Howard beautifully managing his difficult role, is centered about a British mansion which manages to somehow transport modern-day Howard back into the 18th century and into the body of a foppish ancestor. Howard falls in love with a girl in a bygone age, saves her from assorted problems, and is then tragically torn back to the present where he meets her modern counterpart. It's a unique twist on Twain's A Connecticut Yankee in King Arthur's Court, and the first time such a time-lapse film was produced. Great style and Howard's haunting, lyrical presence lift this film far above the average. (Remade as THE HOUSE ON THE SQUARE and I'LL NEVER FORGET YOU.)

p, Jesse L. Lasky; d, Frank Lloyd; w, Sonya Levien, John L. Balderston (based on Balderston's play); ph, Ernest Palmer; ed, Harold Schuster; m, Louis de Francesco; set d, William Darling.

Fantasy/Romance **(PR:A MPAA:NR)**

BERLIN ALEXANDERPLATZ* (1933, Ger.) 90m Allianz/Capital bw

Heinrich George (Franz Bieberkopf), Bernhard Minetti (Reinhold), Margarete Schlegel (Mieze), Albert Florath (Pums), Paul Westermeier (Henschke).

Ex-con George, trying to go straight, gets his wife killed by gangsters when he won't cooperate by paying their requested amount. Shining performance by Schlegel saves movie from distasteul subtitling.

d, Phil Jutzl; w, Alfred Doeblin, Hans Wilhelm (based on the novel by Doeblin); ph, Erich Giese.

Drama **(PR:A MPAA:NR)**

BERLIN CORRESPONDENT**¹/2 (1942) 70m FOX bw

Virginia Gilmore (Karen Hauen), Dana Andrews (Bill Roberts), Mona Maris (Carla), Martin Kosleck (Capt. von Rau), Sig Rumann (Dr. Dietrich), Kurt Katch (Weiner), Erwin Kalser (Mr. Hauen), Torben Meyer (Manager), Williams Edmunds (Gruber), Hans Schumm (Gunther), Leonard Mudie (English Prisoner), Hans von Morhart (Actor), Curt Furberg (Doctor), Henry Rowland (Pilot), Christian Rub (Prisoner).

Good WW II action movie with plenty of harrowing moments, even on the far-fetched side, has Andrews as an enterprising foreign correspondent who acts more like an espionage agent. He smuggles out of Nazi Germany vital information on Axis plans just prior to Pearl Harbor in his seemingly innocuous news reports. Gilmore is a Nazi counter-intelligence agent who dallies with him in order to discover how he is operating, but becomes emotionally attached when learning that his chief source of information is her father. Father, daughter, and newsman escape to Switzerland at the last moment. Andrews is his usual convincing and dashing self, Gilmore an attractive bit of fluff, and that wonderful Rumann burlesques a pompous Nazi even more than in his role of camp sergeant in STALAG 17. Kosleck, who made a career of playing Dr. Goebbels in WW II films, appears as a Gestapo sadist. The fast-paced film owes much to MISTER V, a British production starring Leslie Howard.

p, Bryan Foy; d, Eugene Forde; w, Steve Fisher, Jack Andrews; ph, Virgil Miller; m, Emil Newman; ed, Fred Allen.

Spy Drama   (PR:A MPAA:NR)

BERLIN EXPRESS**½   (1948) 86m RKO bw

Merle Oberon (Lucienne), Robert Ryan (Robert Lindley), Charles Korvin (Perrot), Paul Lukas (Dr. Bernhardt), Robert Coote (Sterling), Reinhold Schunzel (Walther), Roman Toporow (Lt. Maxim), Peter Von Zerneck (Hans Schmidt), Otto Waldis (Kessler), Fritz Kortner (Franzen), Michael Harvey (Sgt. Barnes), Tom Keene (Major), Jim Nolan (Train Captain), Arthur Dulac (Steward), Ray Spiker, Bruce Cameron (Huskies), Charles McGraw (Col. Johns), Buddy Roosevelt (M.P.), David Clarke (Army Technician).

It's three years after Adolf and Eva died in the bunker and there are still Nazis roaming Germany trying their best to prevent reunification. Ryan, Coote, and Toporow are a trio of Yank, Brit and Russky officers who are assigned to root out these underground vermin and set the country back on the right track. Filmed in Frankfurt and Berlin, the bombed-out backgrounds lend a great deal of credibility to the movie. Lukas is excellent as the German leader who wants to unify the country. History proved them all wrong, though, as the country remains divided. Ryan always gave a wonderful performance and was one of just a few actors who respected the script. This may have been because Ryan's first love was playwriting and he did, in fact, win an award for that at Dartmouth. This was his follow-up to CROSSFIRE and established him as the star he was to be for the remainder of his life.

p, Bert Granet; d, Jacques Tourneur; w, Harold Medford (based on a story by Curt Siodmak); ph, Lucien Ballard; m, Frederick Hollander; ed, Sherman Todd; md, C. Bakaleinikoff; art d, Albert S. D'Agostino, Alfred Herman; set d, Darrell Silvera, William Stevens; cos, Orry-Kelly; ch, Charles O'Curran.

Drama   **Cas.**   (PR:C MPAA:NR)

BERMONDSEY KID, THE*½   (1933, Brit.) 75m FN/WB bw

Esmond Knight (Eddie Martin), Pat Paterson (Mary), Ellis Irving (Joe Dougherty), Ernest Sefton (Lou Rodman), Clifford McLaglen (Bates), Eve Gray (Toots), Syd Crossley (Porky), Winifred Oughton (Mrs. Bodge), Len Harvey (Himself).

A newsboy who is a top boxing contender is compelled to meet his best friend, who is ill, in the ring to battle for the championship. A worn-out tearjerker that collapses in the first round.

p, Irving Asher; d, Ralph Dawson; w, W. Scott Darling (based on a story by Bill Evans).

Drama   (PR:A MPAA:NR)

BERMUDA AFFAIR*   (1956, Brit.) 77m Bermuda/COL bw

Gary Merrill (Bob), Ron Randell (Chuck), Zena Marshall (Chris), Kim Hunter, Don Gibson, Robert Arden.

Korean War vets Merrill and Randell open an airline in Bermuda. Merrill has an affair with Randell's wife, but redeems himself by sacrificing his own life to save his partner. An affair to forget.

p, Coolidge Adams; d, Edward Sutherland; Robert J. Shaw; ph, Harry W. Smithy.

Drama   (PR:A MPAA:NR)

BERMUDA MYSTERY*   (1944) 65m FOX bw

Preston Foster (Steve Carromond), Ann Rutherford (Constance Martin), Charles Butterworth (Dr. Tilford), Helene Reynolds (Angela), Jean Howard (Mrs. Tilford), Richard Lane (Det. Donovan), Roland Drew (Mr. Best), John Eldredge (Mr. Brooks), Theodore von Eltz (Mr. Cooper), Pierre Watkin (Mr. Bond.)

Obvious whodunit takes unlikely detective Foster and naive Rutherford on an insurance merry-go-round of murders only to find the wife of one of the dead men is the culprit. Distinguishing feature is mediocrity.

p, William Girard; d, Benjamin Stoloff; w, W. Scott Darling (from a story by John Larkin); ph, Joseph La Shelle; m, Arthur Lange; ed, Norman Colbert; md, Emil Newman.

Mystery   (PR:A MPAA:NR)

BERNADETTE OF LOURDES**½   (1962, Fr.) 90m Janus bw

Daniele Ajoret, Nadine Alari, Robert Arnoux, Blanchette Brunoy, Jean Clarieux, Lise Delamare, Jean-Jacques Delbo, Francoise Engel, Michele Grellier, Bernard Lajarrige, Renaud Marie, Charles Moulins, Henri Nassiet, Francoise St. Laurent, Madeleine Sologne.

Uncomplicated story of the French peasant girl, Bernadette, who frequently visited a remote grotto where she beheld holy visions and was later given sainthood by the Vatican. Uplifting version of a stirring story which suffers from a powerful earlier production, SONG OF BERNADETTE, starring Jennifer Jones.

p, Georges de la Grandiere; d, Robert Darene; Gilbert Cesbron; m, Maurice Thiret.

Biography   (PR:A MPAA:NR)

BERNARDINE* ½   (1957) 94m FOX c

Pat Boone (Beau), Terry Moore (Jean), Janet Gaynor (Mrs. Wilson), Richard Sargent (Sanford Wilson), Dean Jagger (Fullerton Weldy), James Drury (Lt. Beaumont), Ronnie Burns (Griner), Walter Abel (Mr. Beaumont), Natalie Schafer (Mrs. Beaumont), Isabel Jewell (Ruby), Jack Costanzo and Orchestra (Themselves), Edit Angold (Hilda), Val Benedict (Friedelhauser), Ernestine Wade (Cleo), Russ Conway (Mr. Mason), Tom Pittman (Olson), Hooper Dunbar (Kinswood).

BERNARDINE is Fox's answer to the Presley films. Boone, who first achieved national recognition on Arthur Godfrey's TV show, is the white on white hero, one

of several young and definitely un-sleazy students, who create a mythical girl named Bernardine that they would all love to love. Moore is new in town. She's a telephone operator who meets the exact standards that the boys have laid down for their dream woman. Slim story has Sargent (later to star with Liz Montgomery in "Bewitched" when Dick York had to leave due to a bad back) falling in love with Moore, then having to cease seeing her while he studies for finals. Boone has his older brother, Drury (who became "The Virginian") take Terry out to keep her away from the clutching lounge lizards in the town. Drury and Moore fall in love, Sargent runs off to join the service, returns home 18 months later, sadder but wiser. BERNARDINE doesn't have much to recommend it. Boone says "gee" a lot and looks as though he's doing an imitation of himself. Janet Gaynor returned to the screen after a long absence in this film. One would have hoped she might have chosen a better vehicle. The original play is by Mary Chase, who wrote HARVEY and several others. This one also featured an invisible lead as Bernardine was just as invisible as the legendary six-foot rabbit. The similarity ends there.

p, Samuel G. Engel; d, Henry Levin; w, Theodore Reeves (based on a play by Mary Chase); ph, Paul Vogel (CinemaScope, DeLuxe Color); m, Lionel Newman; ed, David Bretherton; cos, Mary Wills, Charles LeMaire; m/l, Johnny Mercer, Nick Kenny, Charles Kenny, J. Fred Coots; ch, Bill Foster.

Musical   (PR:AA MPAA:NR)

BERSERK**   (1967) 98m COL c

Joan Crawford (Monica Rivers), Ty Hardin (Frank Hawkins), Diana Dors (Matilda), Michael Gough (Dorando), Judy Geeson (Angela Rivers),Robert Hardy (Supt. Brooks), Geoffrey Keen (Comm. Dalby), Sidney Tafler (Harrison Liston), George Claydon (Bruno), Ambrosine Philpotts (Miss Burrows), Ted Lune (Skeleton Man), Philip Madoc (Lazlo), Peter Burton (Gustavo), Golda Casimir (Bearded Lady), Milton Reid (Strong Man), Marianne Stone (Wanda), Miki Iveria (Gypsy Fortune Teller), Howard Goorney (Emil), Reginald Marsh (Sgt. Hutchins), The Billy Smart Circus.

First a high-wire walker falls from his quivering perch and it is learned that his wire has been cut. Crawford suggests to Gough that he play up the killing to promote business, a cold-hearted notion that fills her partner with disgust. He is later found murdered and everyone under the big top suspects Crawford and is terrified that she might strike at any moment. Hardin, a new high-wire artist, arrives and does a spectacular act over a bed of spikes, carrying on an affair with the older Crawford which is apparently more lethal. Geeson, Crawford's daughter, arrives after being thrown out of school and is put to work in the circus. Knife-thrower Burton is seen tampering with the wires on which Hardin walks and a short time later a knife is hurled into Hardin's back while he is doing his act, sending him to horrible death on the spikes below. The knife-thrower has been seen, however. It is Geeson, Crawford's daughter, who has gone crazy because her mother has neglected her (or, at least, that's an explanation given) and has been knocking off her mother's performers out of spite. Before the cuffs can be locked about her wrists, Geeson runs screaming into a raging storm and is struck by a fallen live wire and killed, but not before dying in her mother's arms, begging for love, understanding, sympathy and instant absolution, all of which the guilty parent immediately gushes. Neither pretty nor interesting, this film is another unnecessary stain upon the career of a great actress who sank into sleaze, not through need of money but through the same kind of vanity that sent Norma Desmond down the staircase to the cameras in SUNSET BOULEVARD.

p, Herman Cohen; d, Jim O'Connor; w, Aben Kandel, Cohen; ph, Desmond Dickinson (Technicolor); m, Patrick John Scott; ed, Raymond Poulton; art d, Maurice Felling; set d, Helen Thomas; cos, Jay Hutchinson Scott.

Crime/Mystery/Horror   (PR:O MPAA:NR)

BEST FOOT FORWARD***   (1943) MGM 93m c

Lucille Ball (Herself), William Gaxton (Jack O'Riley), Virginia Weidler (Helen Schlessenger), Tommy Dix (Elwood), Nancy Walker (Nancy), Gloria DeHaven (Minerva), Kenny Bowers (Dutch), June Allyson (Ethel), Jack Jordan (Hunk), Beverly Tyler (Miss Delaware Water Gap), Chill Wills (Chester Short), Henry O'Neill (Maj. Reeber), Sara Haden (Miss Talbert), Donald McBride (Capt. Bradd), Bobby Stebbins (Greenie), Darwood Kaye (Killer), Morris Ankrum (Col. Harkrider), Nana Bryant (Mrs. Dalyrimple), Harry James and His Music Makers.

Military prep school graduates put designs on Ball to make her their prom queen. Many lap slappers with Nancy Walker as the highlight. Colorful, elaborate production is cleverly tempoed by Buzzell. Songs include: "Ev'ry Time," "Three Men On A Date," "Wish I May," "Buckle Down Winsocki," "The Three B's," "Alive and Kicking" (Martin Blane), "Two O'Clock Jump" (Count Basie, Harry James, Benny Goodman), "The Flight Of The Bumble Bee" (Rimsky-Korsakov).

p, Arthur Freed; d, Edward Buzzell; w, Irving Brecher, Fred Finklehoffe; ph, Leonard Smith (Technicolor); ed, Blanche Sewell; md, Lennie Hayton.

Musical   (PR:A MPAA:NR)

BEST FRIENDS zero   (1975) 83m Crown International c

Richard Hatch (Jesse), Suzanne Benton (Kathy), Doug Chapin (Pat), Ann Noland (Jo Ella), Renee Paul, Ralph Montgomery, Roger Bear, John McKee, Bonnie Erkel, Julie.

Suzanne Benton (A BOY AND HIS DOG) is the best thing about this primitive movie. Chapin and Hatch are best friends who probably would be homosexuals if they weren't so busy being macho. A hodgepodge film with no apparent reason for being. Hatch is a member of the naturalistic school of acting and underplays so much that Chapin, who is not overdoing things, seems to be disgustingly gross by comparison. Benton, in the middle, does a neat job.

p&d, Noel Nosseck; w, Arnold Somkin; ph, Stephen M. Katz (Movielab Color); m, Rick Cunha; ed, Robert Gordon; art d, Jodie Tillen.

Drama (PR:O MPAA:NR)

BEST FRIENDS** (1982) 116m WB c

Burt Reynolds (*Richard Babson*), Goldie Hawn (*Paula McCullen*), Jessica Tandy (*Eleanor McCullen*), Barnard Hughes (*Tim McCullen*), Audra Lindley (*Ann Babson*), Keenan Wynn (*Tom Babson*), Ron Silver (*Larry Weisman*), Carol Locatell (*Nellie Ballou*), Richard Libertini (*Jorge Medina*), Peggy Walton-Walker (*Carol Brandon*), Noah Hathaway (*Lyle Ballou*), Mickey Martin (*Robbie Ballou*).

Reynolds keeps making deals, but he hasn't made a decent movie for some time. Levinson (director of DINER, THE NATURAL) and Curtin (together they wrote AND JUSTICE FOR ALL) wrote what is supposed to be their story, about two writers who collaborate on their work as well as their marriage. Nice try at a "relationship" film,but Jewison can't triumph over what appears to be a lack of enthusiasm on the screen. It's a gentle film with no end of neat touches. Silver is excellent as a phony Hollywood producer (was he getting his characterization from anyone connected with this film?). Tandy and Hughes, as Hawn's parents are marvelous as are Lindley and Wynn as Reynold's parents. Hawn shows admirable restraint and emerges as a person, not a caricature. The problem was that there was no actual story; it's a series of incidents that must have been very personal to the writers and the creative staff behind the picture but meant little or nothing to the great unwashed who plunk down their hard-earned money at the box office. So it just goes to prove that stars of such magnitude as Reynolds and Hawn or Gene Hackman and Lee Marvin (PRIME CUT, another Joe Wizan failure) cannot win an audience when they don't have a producer to select the project and the director who may be right for the project.

p, Norman Jewison, Patrick Palmer; d, Jewison; w, Valerie Curtin, Barry Levinson; ph, Jordan Cronenweth (Technicolor); m, Michel Legrand; ed, Don Zimmerman; art d, Joe Russo; cos, Betsy Cox.

Romance/Comedy Cas. (PR:A MPAA:PG)

BEST HOUSE IN LONDON, THE**½ (1969, Brit.) 97m MGM c

David Hemmings (*Benjamin Oakes*), Joanna Pettet (*Josephine Pacefoot*), George Sanders (*Sir Francis Leybourne*), Dany Robin (*Babette*), Warren Mitchell (*Count Pandolfo*), John Bird (*Home Secretary*), William Rushton (*Sylvester Wall*), Bill Fraser (*Inspector MacPherson*), Maurice Denham (*Editor of "Times"*), Wolfe Morris (*Chinese Trade Attache*), Martita Hunt (*Headmistress*), Arnold Diamond (*Charles Dickens*), Hugh Burden (*Lord Tennyson*), John DeMarco (*Oscar Wilde*), Jan Holden (*Lady Dilke*), Mike Lennox (*Algernon Charles Swinburne*), Arthur Howard (*Mr. Fortnum*), Clement Freud (*Mr. Mason*), Neal Arden (*Dr. Livingston*), Walter Brown (*Mr. Barrett*), Suzanne Hunt (*Miss Elizabeth Barrett*), Carol Friday (*Flora*), Marie Rogers (*Phoebe*), Tessie O'Shea (*Singer*), Avril Angers (*Flora's Mother*), Betty Marsden (*Felicity*).

The young blades of London are miffed when they learn that the World's Oldest Profession is about to be banned in their town. They appeal to Bird, the Home Secretary, and he suggests "The French System." Sanders is made the House's first proprietor and appoints Robin (his girl friend) as the designated Mistress. Sanders then leaves to visit his opium plantation and is killed by the Indian natives. His money goes to Pettet, his social-reformer niece who must now deal with all of the questionable behavior attached to running such a business. Hemmings is Sanders' son (he plays two roles, both overdone) who wants to get the money and the house. Lots of running around, silliness, a few laughs. This predated RAGTIME by many years but the technique of mixing real and fictional characters was valid even then. Fortnum and Mason, Watson and Holmes, Dickens, Wilde, Livingston, Tennyson, et al. are all used to maximum advantage. If you can overlook the movie's inconsistencies, it's a pleasant way to spend 97 minutes. This was Hunt's final film after a career that spanned five decades. Born in Argentina of British parents, her first film was SERVICE FOR LADIES in 1932.

p, Phillip Breen, Kurt Unger; d, Phillip Savile; w, Denis Norden; ph, Alex Thomson (Metrocolor); m, Mischa Spoliansky; cos, Yvonne Blake.

Comedy (PR:O MPAA:NR)

BEST LITTLE WHOREHOUSE IN TEXAS, THE* (1982) 114m UNIV c

Burt Reynolds (*Sheriff*), Dolly Parton (*Mona Strangely*), Dom DeLuise (*Melvin*), Charles Durning (*Governor*), Jim Nabors (*Deputy Fred*), Robert Mandan (*Senator Wingwood*), Lois Nettleton (*Dulcie Mae*), Theresa Merritt (*Jewel*), Noah Beery (*Edsel*), Raleigh Bond (*Mayor*), Barry Carbin (*C. J.*), Ken Magee (*Mansel*), Mary Jo Catlett (*Rita*), Mary Louise Wilson (*Modene*), Howard K. Smith (*Himself*), Paula Shaw (*Wulla Jean*), Lee Ritchie (*Governor's Aide*), Alice Drummond (*Governor's Secretary*), Karyn Harrison (*Chicken Girl*), Randy Bennett (*Privates Boy*).

The immensely talented Parton is in need of expert advice in chosing her roles, and there is no better indication than in this dud. THE BEST LITTLE WHOREHOUSE was a minor musical that had its beginnings on Westheimer Road in Houston, then on to Broadway where the title brought the people in. There's nary a song to hum in the whole score. At a cost of more than $25 million the film fails to titillate except for an outstanding performance by Durning that merited an Oscar nomination. It's big, noisy and synthetic as polyester. Reynolds is the sheriff of the town and he has to close down Dolly's whorehouse after DeLuise exposes the goings-on. DeLuise camps it to a point where he's no longer funny, just to be pitied. It seems that's about all he can do these days. He's become more androgynous than his wife, Carol, a brilliant comedienne in her own right. Durning is the governor who reluctantly orders the whorehouse shut. That this play was a hit on Broadway is astonishing. That it was a bust on the screen proves again that the rest of America may be more sophisticated than the Big Apple. Colin Higgins' direction is as lifeless as the script.

Dolly and Nettleton and the hard-working dancers under the watchful *eye of* choreographer Stevens make it acceptable, if nothing more.

p, Thomas Miller, Edward Milkis, Robert Boyett; d, Colin Higgins; w, Larry L. King, Peter Masterson, Higgins (based on the play); ph, William A. Fraker (Panavision, Technicolor); ed, Pembroke J. Herring, David Bretherton, Jack Hofstra, Nicholas Eliopoulous, Walter Hanneman; cos, Theodora Van Runkle; ch, Tony Stevens; m/l, Carol Hall, Dolly Parton, Pat Williams.

Musical Comedy Cas. (PR:O MPAA:NR)

BEST MAN, THE***½ (1964) 102m UA bw

Henry Fonda (*William Russell*), Cliff Robertson (*Joe Cantwell*), Edie Adams (*Mabel Cantwell*), Margaret Leighton(*Alice Russell*), Shelley Berman (*Sheldon Bascomb*), Lee Tracy (*Art Hockstader*), Ann Sothern (*Mrs. Gamadge*), Gene Raymond (*Dan Cantwell*), Kevin McCarthy (*Dick Jensen*), Mahalia Jackson (*Herself*), Howard K. Smith (*Himself*), John Henry Faulk (*T. T. Claypoole*), Richard Arlen (*Oscar Anderson*), Penny Singleton (*Mrs. Claypoole*), George Kirgo (*Speechwriter*), George Furth (*Tom*), Anne Newman (*Janet*), Mary Lawrence (*Mrs. Merwin*), H. E. West (*Senator Lazarus*), Michael MacDonald (*Zealot*), William R. Eberson (*Governor Merwin*), Natalie Masters (*Mrs. Anderson*), Blossom Rock (*Cleaning Woman*), Bill Stout (*Himself*), Tyler McVey (*Chairman*), Sherwood Keith (*Doctor*).

An excellent film about the backroom boys of politics. Released during the Presidential year of 1964, it was unsettling to many politicians as Vidal's knife went through their jugulars. Major problem was that soap started to creep into what might have been a memorable and provocative movie. Fonda and Robertson are battling for their party's nomination. Fonda, as you might well imagine, is the candidate of high ideals and Robertson is the sleazebag who will do anything to get elected. Fonda's wife (Leighton) has held off getting the divorce so he won't alienate the female voters. Tracy is the dying President who hasn't put his support behind either man on the eve of the convention. Robertson has a dossier on Fonda's emotional instability (in later years, this happened with Tom Eagleton) and will use it to get what he wants. Then we learn that Cliff had a rendezvous with another *man* some years ago! Fonda is hesitant to use that information, nice guy that he is. Tracy dies and Fonda announces to the convention that he is throwing his support behind yet another candidate, thereby rendering Robertson defenseless and out of the running. You could see Stevenson in Fonda, McCarthy or Nixon in Robertson, and a bit of Truman in Oscar-nominated Tracy, who died before making another film. Vidal's dialog is razor-sharp as is Wexler's photography.

p, Stuart Millar, Lawrence Turman; d, Franklin Schaffner; w, Gore Vidal (based on his play); ph, Haskell Wexler; m, Mort Lindsey; ed. Robert Swink; cos, Dorothy Jeakins.

Drama (PR:C MPAA:NR)

BEST MAN WINS, THE* (1935) 75m COL bw

Edmund Lowe (*Tobu*), Jack Holt (*Nick*), Bela Lugosi (*Dr. Boehm*), Florence Rice (*Ann*), Forrester Harvey (*Harry*).

Best-buddy champion scuba divers Hart and Lowe are at odds when Lowe gets involved with jewel thieves after losing an arm saving Hart's life. The reason? To get out of debt and back on his feet financially. Half the team drowns on the job.

d, Erle Kenton; w, Ben G. Kohn; ph, John Stumar; ed, Otto Meyer.

Adventure (PR:A MPAA:NR)

BEST MAN WINS** (1948) 73m COL bw

Edgar Buchanan (*Jim Smiley*), Anna Lee (*Nancy Smiley*), Robert Shayne (*Judge Carter*), Gary Gray (*Bob Smiley*), Hobart Cavanaugh (*Amos*), Stanley Andrews (*Sheriff Dingle*), George Lynn (*Mr. Crow*), Bill Sheffield (*Monty Carter*), Marietta Canty (*Hester*), Paul Burns (*Bartender*).

Young son supports wandering-gambler father Buchanan's efforts to win back his wife who divorced him while he was away and is about to marry another man. Smooth editing by Sweeney strengthens good points of the film.

p, Ted Richmond; d, John Sturges; w, Edward Husbach (based on Mark Twain's "The Celebrated Jumping Frog of Calaveras County"); ph, Vincent Farrar; ed, James Sweeney.

Drama (PR:AA MPAA:NR)

BEST OF ENEMIES* (1933) 72m FOX bw

Buddy Rogers (*Jimmie Hartman*), Marian Nixon (*Lena Schneider*), Frank Morgan (*William H. Hartman*), Joseph Cawthorn (*Gus Schneider*), Greta Nissen (*The Blonde*), William Lawrence (*August*), Arno Frey (*Emil*), Anders Van Haden (*Professor Herman*).

Conflict between Cawthorn and Morgan is tempered when the son and daughter of each of the arch-enemies meet and fall in love. Producer went through three directors, thereby diluting the film's impact.

d, Rian James; w, Sam Mintz; ph, L. W. O'Connell; ed, Margaret Clancy; set d, William Darling.

Comedy/Romance (PR:A MPAA:NR)

BEST OF ENEMIES, THE*** (1962) 104m COL bw

David Niven (*Maj. Richardson*), Michael Wilding (*Lt. Burke*), Harry Andrews (*Capt. Rootes*), Noel Harrison (*Lt. Hilary*), Ronald Fraser (*Cpl. Prefect*), Bernard Cribbins (*Pvt. Tanner*), Duncan MacRae (*Sgt. Trevethan*), Robert Desmond (*Pvt. Slinger*), Kenneth Fortescue (*Lt. Tomlinson*), Michael Trubshawe (*Col. Brownlow*), Alberto Sordi (*Capt. Blasi*), David Opatoshu (*Capt. Bernasconi*), Amedeo Nazzari (*Maj. Fornari*), Aldo Giuffre (*Sgt. Todini*), Pietro Marascalchi (*Cpl. Bortolini*), Tiberio Mitri (*Cpl. Moccia*), Bruno Cattaneo (*Pvt. Mattone*), Pippo Fazio (*Sgt. Spadoni*), Allesandro Ninchi (*Sub. Lt. Del Pra*).

Witty, incisive look at the futility of war without being preachy. Niven and Wilding crash in the desert of Ethopia in 1941 while on an observation flight. They are taken in by Sordi, who leads an Italian patrol. Sordi allows them to go free when they promise to let his patrol roam freely and take refuge in an old fort. Later, Niven is ordered to attack that fort, and does so with great annoyance as it means breaking his word. The two men capture each other and the rest of the film is a continuous barrage of jokes, witticisms and fun. Sordi spoke almost no English when this movie was made and had to learn his English by rote. You'd never know it. Cribbins is very funny as Tanner. He went on to score well in many British movies as well as in the role of Nathan Detroit in the National Theatre's version of "Guys and Dolls." Cribbins is one of those rare actors who can do an American accent and make you believe it. If you'll notice, there is not a single female in the movie; a tribute to the writer, Pulman, who wisely felt that the overlay of any distaff roles would destroy the delicacy of the story. Pulman achieved his greatest worldwide fame when he adapted Robert Graves' *I, Claudius* for TV.

p, Dino De Laurentiis; d, Guy Hamilton; w, Jack Pulman (based on the story by Luciano Vincenzoni, adaptation by Age Scarpelli, Subo Cecchi); ph, Giussepe Rotunno; m, Nino Rota; ed, Buri Bates; cos, Ezio Frigerio, Dario Cecchi.

War Comedy **(PR:A MPAA:NR)**

BEST OF EVERYTHING, THE** (1959) 122m FOX c

Hope Lange *(Caroline Bender)*, Stephen Boyd *(Mike)*, Suzy Parker *(Gregg)*, Martha Hyer *(Barbara)*, Diane Baker *(April)*, Brian Aherne *(Mr. Shalimar)*, Robert Evans *(Dexter Key)*, Brett Halsey *(Eddie)*, Donald Harron *(Sidney Carter)*, Sue Carson *(Mary Agnes)*, Linda Hutchings *(Jane)*, Lionel Kane *(Paul)*, Ted Otis *(Ronnie Wood)*, Louis Jourdan *(David Savage)*, Joan Crawford *(Amanda Farrow)*, David Hoffman *(Joe)*, Theodora Davitt *(Margo Stewart)*, Girls in typing pool: Alena Murray, Rachel Stephens, Julie Payne.

Overly complex and glossy soap opera with several stories going at once. Crawford (she of the wide shoulders) is a tough businesswoman editing a number of readables and having an affair with a married man we never see. There's a little of Ginger Rogers in LADY IN THE DARK as well as Helen Gurley Brown in SEX AND THE SINGLE GIRL here. Her frustrated sex life causes her to wreak havoc on her employees. A lot of smarminess and cheating is featured in this thin story. Hyer is having an affair with Harron, who is also married. Baker becomes pregnant by Evans who suggests she get rid of the baby with an illegal operation. (Evans went on to become the very successful producer of CHINATOWN, among others.) Parker is having it away with Jourdan who tosses her out to take up with Hansen. Have you had enough yet? Well, it goes on and on. Wald, the producer (who supposedly was the inspiration for Schulberg's *What Makes Sammy Run*) loved this kind of movie and did it once before with PEYTON PLACE. He and director Negulesco had greater success a few years before with JOHNNY BELINDA. The major problem with THE BEST OF EVERYTHING is that there is so much happening that there is no time for any development of characters and so everyone is a thumbnail sketch where an oil painting is needed. The song got an Oscar nomination for Newman and Cahn, who earlier won Oscars for "All The Way," "Call Me Irresponsible," "High Hopes," and "Three Coins In The Fountain."

p, Jerry Wald; d, Jean Negulesco; w, Edith Sommer, Mann Rubin (based on the novel by Rona Jaffe); ph, William C. Mellor (DeLuxe Color); m, Alfred Newman; ed, Robert Simpson; cos, Adele Palmer; m/l, Newman, Sammy Cahn.

Drama/Romance **(PR:C-O MPAA:NR)**

BEST OF THE BADMEN*** (1951) 83m RKO c

Robert Ryan *(Jeff Clanton)*, Claire Trevor *(Lily Fowler)*, Jack Buetel *(Bob Younger)*, Robert Preston *(Matthew Fowler)*, Walter Brennan *(Doc Butcher)*, Bruce Cabot *(Cole Younger)*, John Archer *(Curley Ringo)*, Lawrence Tierney *(Jesse James)*, Barton MacLane *(Joad)*, Tom Tyler *(Frank James)*, Bob Wilke *(Jim Younger)*, John Cliff *(John Younger)*, Lee MacGregor *(Lieutenant)*, Emmett Lynn *(Oscar)*, Carleton Young *(Wilson)*.

Another James-Younger saga where the lionized outlaws are persuaded, as members of Quantrill's guerrillas, to surrender, receive amnesty following the Civil War, and take up lawful pursuits. Ryan, Buetel, Cabot, Tierney, Tyler, and others accept. Preston, a backstabbing Union detective, has no intention of allowing the ex-Confederates to live in peace; all have huge rewards on their heads and he plans to kill them in ambush and collect. Ryan learns of the plans and tries to warn the Southern boys but Preston captures him and he is sentenced to hang. Trevor, Preston's estranged wife, helps Ryan to escape and he rejoins the outlaw band, which is presented as more law-abiding than their pursuers (which was certainly not the case in real life). They rob banks and trains in which Preston has an interest. Ryan finally faces Preston in a shootout, kills the villain, and is exonerated to live happily ever after with Trevor, while the outlaws continue their criminal careers. Ryan is powerful and rugged in his role, one that lifts this production out of the average oater class, and his support is tough, with witty remarks spurting from Cabot, Brennan, and others from a clever script that never bothers with the facts. Russell directs with professional smoothness. This was the first film of Buetel, Howard Hughes' protege and star of the inflated western, THE OUTLAW, since making that potboiler in 1941, a 10-year lapse which no one in Hollywood, including Buetel, ever explained.

p, Herman Schlom; d, William D. Russell; w, Robert Hardy Andrews, John Twist (based on a story by Andrews); ph, Edward Cronjager (Technicolor); m, Paul Sawtell; ed, Desmond Marquette.

Western **(PR:A MPAA:NR)**

BEST THINGS IN LIFE ARE FREE, THE* ½** (1956) 104m FOX c

Gordon MacRae *(B.G. "Buddy" De Sylva)*, Dan Dailey *(Ray Henderson)*, Ernest Borgnine *(Lew Brown)*, Sheree North *(Kitty)*, Tommy Noonan *(Carl)*, Murvyn Vye *(Manny)*, Phyllis Avery *(Maggie Henderson)*, Larry Keating *(Sheehan)*, Tony Galento *(Fingers)*, Norman Brooks *(Al Jolson)*, Jacques D'Amboise *(Specialty Dancer)*, Roxanne Arlen *(Perky Nicholas)*, Bryon Palmer *(Hollywood Star)*, Linda Brace, Patty Lou Hudson, Larry Kerr, Julie Van Zandt, Charles Victor, Eugene Borden, Harold Miller, Paul Glass.

Thoroughly charming biography of De Sylva, Brown, and Henderson, a trio of songwriters responsible for a score of hits. MacRae, Borgnine, and Dailey are excellent as the three cleffers. Not much of a story; just the usual saga of pals who get together and have some success until greed and ambition take over and threaten to split them, but, in the end, they reconcile and go on writing hummable tunes. There is hardly enough room for a story after hearing only a soupcon of their songs like "Birth Of The Blues" and "Black Bottom" (the film's two production sequences, ably choreographed by Rod Alexander), "Good News" done by Sheree North (in a role that allows her to act, for a change), "Button Up Your Overcoat," "It All Depends On You," "Keep Your Sunnyside Up," the title song and Norman Brooks doing a black-and-white impression of Al Jolson singing "Sonny Boy." Vye chimes in ably as a 1920s gunsel who wants to muscle in and Borgnine handles him in a lovely scene. "Tough" Tony Galento, former heavyweight boxer, proves he can act as well as he takes punches in the role of Fingers, a henchman of another hood who likes Borgnine and wants to protect him. Some good jokes from Bowers and Ephron (story by, would you believe, John O'Hara?) and breezy direction by Curtiz. All in all, a lovely way to spend 104 minutes with Oscar-nominated music by Newman.

p, Henry Ephron; d, Michael Curtiz; w, William Bowers, Phoebe Ephron (based on a story by John O'Hara); ph, Leon Shamroy (DeLuxe Color); m, Lionel Newman; ed. Dorothy Spencer; ch, Rod Alexander, Bill Foster.

Musical Biography **(PR:AA MPAA:NR)**

BEST WAY, THE** (1978, Fr.) 90m Specialty c

Patrick Dewaere *(Marc)*, Patrick Bouchitey *(Phillippe)*, Christine Pascal *(Chantel)*, Claude Pieplu *(Father)*.

Good portrayal of two counselors at a boys' summer camp with witty dialog and some funny incidents. This was the first film by writer-director Miller, protege of Truffaut and Godard.

p&d, Claude Miller; w, Luc Beraud, Miller; ph, Bruno Nytten (Eastmancolor); ed, Jean Bernard Bonis.

Drama **(PR:C MPAA;NR)**

BEST YEARS OF OUR LIVES, THE***** (1946) 172m Goldwyn/RKO

Myrna Loy *(Milly Stephenson)*, Fredric March *(Al Stephenson)*, Dana Andrews *(Fred Derry)*, Teresa Wright *(Peggy Stephenson)*, Virginia Mayo *(Marie Derry)*, Cathy O'Donnell *(Wilma Cameron)*, Hoagy Carmichael *(Butch Engle)*, Harold Russell *(Homer Parrish)*, Gladys George *(Hortense Derry)*, Roman Bohnen *(Pat Derry)*, Ray Collins *(Mr. Milton)*, Steve Cochran *(Cliff)*, Minna Gombell *(Mrs. Parrish)*, Walter Baldwin *(Mr. Parrish)*, Dorothy Adams *(Mrs. Cameron)*, Don Beddoe *(Mr. Cameron)*, Erskine Sanford *(Bullard)*, Marlene Aames *(Luella Parrish)*, Michael Hall *(Rob Stephenson)*, Charles Halton *(Prew)*, Ray Teal *(Mr. Mollett)*, Dean White *(Novak)*, Howland Chamberlin *(Thorpe)*, Victor Cutler *(Woody Merrill)*, Pat Flaherty *(Construction Foreman)*.

"I don't care if it doesn't make a nickel," Sam Goldwyn reportedly stated in a classic malapropism about this classic film, "I just want every man, woman, and child in America to see it." The colorful producer got the idea for the film after reading a *Life* Magazine article about returning veterans of WW II and their difficulties in adjusting to civilian life. He hired MacKinlay Kantor to write a script but instead the author wrote a novella in blank verse which was then converted by Robert E. Sherwood, Goldwyn's close friend, into one of the greatest screenplays ever written. There is no film like it, this masterpiece about returning American servicemen following WW II. Three servicemen in particular are shown returning to their home town: March, Andrews and Russell, full of the awful memories of war and doubts about their future in a country they find difficult to remember. After sharing space on board a bomber that flies them home, the three take a cab to their separate addresses, first sailor Russell to a bungalow where his startled parents greet him, apprehensive at the sight of his empty sleeves and the hooks that have replaced his hands. (Russell, the only non-professional actor in the cast, lost his hands as a paratrooper on D-Day.) In a family gathering, he embarrassingly spills a cold drink and flees to the confines of his uncle's (Carmichael) saloon. Middle-aged sergeant March steps into his expensive apartment (he had been a banker before going off to war) to startle his children, whom he motions to keep quiet. In the kitchen, his wife (Loy) suddenly stops her work, looks up with an intuitive expression, then steps into the long hall to see her husband standing at the end of it. The scene is electrifying as they silently, gratefully, go into each other's arms. March, unsteady that evening in talking to a family now changed, his daughter, Wright, grown into a young lady, his son, Hall, a young man in college, insists they all go out on the town. He, Loy, and Wright end up in Carmichael's lounge where they meet Russell and Andrews, the latter a heavily decorated Air Force captain. Andrews has found no one at home, his blonde, brassy wife (Mayo) is gone. He drinks heavily, then is taken home by Loy and Wright when he cannot get into his wife's apartment. Put to sleep in Wright's bedroom, he has nightmares of his bombing runs over Germany; Wright enters the bedroom and quiets him. In the morning, half remembering the party, he apologizes and returns to Mayo's apartment, but Wright is smitten with him. Mayo's only delight in having Andrews home is his service pay and his dashing uniform, which she insists he wear everywhere, but he wants nothing more to do with the service—the war is over and Andrews desperately wants to get a job and get on with his life. In many ways, he is the most tragic of the lot, since no doors are open to him, only the lowly soda-jerking and counter sales job he had in a large drugstore before the war. He takes it to survive. March goes back to his bank and begins making loans to servicemen without collateral. Bank President Collins subtly calls him on the carpet and, at a banquet that night March gets stiff. Before the stuffy bankers he rises and speaks a parable about how he was asked by a superior officer during the war to order his men to take a hill. But the officer had no collateral, March points out. "No collateral—no hill. So we didn't take the hill . . . and we lost the war." He has drawn the line of battle—he will continue to make loans to servicemen on faith. Russell's crisis is dealing with the girl next door he was to marry before the war, O'Donnell, whom he avoids. One evening she comes to him, pleading that they wed. He attempts to shock her into rejecting him, taking her to his bedroom where he asks that she perform the duties assumed by his father every night before he goes to sleep. He has her remove his robe, then the halter to which the mechanical hooks are attached. "Now I'm completely helpless," he tells her, explaining that he cannot ever open the bedroom door in case of an emergency. O'Donnell smiles, covers him, and kisses him goodnight. He lies there alone after she leaves, staring at the ceiling, tears streaming from his eyes. It doesn't matter at all to his girl that he is crippled for life. Andrews' marriage quickly goes downhill after he loses his job by punching a radical (Teal) for starting a brawl with Russell. Mayo begins running around with Cochran (the eternal cad), and Wright begins to see Andrews. March breaks up the relationship and Andrews decides to leave town. He packs his bags in the broken-down apartment occupied by his boozy father, Bohnen, and his stepmother, George, leaving for points unknown. After he leaves, in a bittersweet scene, his impoverished old father reads the military citations he has left behind, swelling with pride over the heroic exploits of his son. Andrews, after booking a flight leaving Boone City, wanders through a massive graveyard of WW II bomber and fighter planes, crawling into a dust-strewn bomber and going to the bombardier's position. The camera closes in on him, then to the front of the bomber as the score rumbles with bass notes that simulate the roar of engines; Wyler dollies his camera forward so that the motorless plane appears to be taking off. Then the camera appears to creep up from behind Andrews inside the plane as he sits transfixed, reliving the horrors of war, his head slowly lowering over a bombsight that is not there. The spell is broken by the voice of a construction foreman who orders him from the plane. Andrews, realizing that the planes are being converted into prefabricated housing (from shields to ploughs), asks for, and gets a job. He stays in Boone City and attends Russell's marriage to O'Donnell, where he again meets March, Loy, and Wright. After the ceremonies, Andrews goes to Wright, kisses her, and it is implicit that they will be together. "You know what'll it be, don't you, Peggy," he tells her. "It may take us years to get anywhere. We'll have no money, no decent place to live. We'll have to work—get kicked around." Through this Wright's smile fills the screen as they once more kiss and the film ends. Wyler masterfully directed this sensitive, loving film, detailing with a finite eye the adjustment of the servicemen to their families, an indifferent peacetime society, and, in Russell's case, the agonizing role of the permanently handicapped. Toland's deep-focus photography enhances every scene. Friedhofer's score is compelling and memorable, and every actor gives the performance of his or her career. Loy is the perfect wife, March, who received an Oscar as Best Actor, is a delight to behold as the compassionate father, husband, and banker. Andrews is utterly believable and sympathetic as the out-of-place hero, and Russell, who earned an Oscar for Supporting Player, gives a powerful, complex performance as the wonderful boy next door who exchanged his hands for a free world. There was much apprehension in the making of this film. Everyone told Goldwyn that it was too serious and would flop, according to Loy who was later quoted as saying: "But Sam had faith in it and in the long run he was right." Loy herself was apprehensive of director Wyler who had a reputation for demanding that stars undergo endless takes, but she found he was right and gave him one of her finest efforts. Warm, moving, poignant, and realistic to the point of touching upon the lives of all Americans in that more innocent and optimistic era, THE BEST YEARS OF OUR LIVES reflects the best Hollywood could do, or might ever do. Goldwyn was right. Every man, woman and child should see this film, from one generation to the next.

p, Samuel Goldwyn; d, William Wyler; w, Robert E. Sherwood (based on the blank verse novella *Glory for Me* by MacKinlay Kantor); ph, Gregg Toland; m, Hugo Friedhofer; ed, Daniel Mandell; art d, George Jenkins, Perry Ferguson; set d, Julia Heron; cos, Sharaff.

Drama   **Cas.**   **(PR:A MPAA:NR)**

BETRAYAL*½   (1932, Brit.) 65m Fogwell Films bw.

Stewart Rome *(John Armytage)*, Marjorie Hume *(Diana Armytage)*, Leslie Perrins *(Clive Wilson)*, Henry Hewitt *(Sir Robert Blackburn KC)*, J. Fisher White *(John Lawrence KC)*, Frank Atherley *(Judge)*, E. H. Williams *(Butler)*, Charles Childerstone *(Doctor)*.

Avaricious lady weds wealthy man but shows her growing affection for him when he shoots her former boy friend and comes to his rescue. Not much here beyond a tepid triangle.

d&w, Reginald Fogwell (based on the play "No Crime of Passion" by Hubert G. Griffith).

Crime   **(PR:A MPAA:NR)**

BETRAYAL**½   (1939, Fr.) 85m World bw (TARAN KOVA)

Annie Vernay *(Elizabeth Tarakanova)*, Suzy Prim *(Catherine II of Russia)*, Pierre-Richard Willm *(Count Orloff)*, Roger Karl *(Prince Radziwill)*, Abel Jacquin, Bergeron, Janine Merrey.

Empress Prim's romance dies when she sends favorite attendant Willm to take crown-aspiring Vernay a prisoner. Instead, Vernay enchants him and he tries to save her from being jailed. Ozep's potent direction keeps intrigue ahead of extravagance.

p, S. Nebenzahl; d, Fedor Ozep; w, Companeez and Jacoby (based on the novel

The Princess Tarakova by G. P. Danilevski); ph, Curt Courant; m, Ricardo Zandenat.

Drama   **(PR:A MPAA:NR)**

BETRAYAL, THE*   (1948) 183m Astor bw

Lou Vernon *(Ned Washington)*, Edward Fraction *(Nelson Boudreaux)*, Leroy Collins *(Martin Eden)*, Jessie Johnson *(Preble)*, William Byrd *(Jack Stewart)*, Myra Stanton *(Deborah)*, Frances De Young *(Mrs. Bowles)*, Arthur McCool *(Joe Bowles)*, Vernetties Moore *(Eunice)*, Barbara Lee *(Jessie)*.

Young black farmer Collins struggles with personal conflicts of racial intermarriage and economic hardships. Film is locked in by stilted and artificial dialog, creating a dull domestic drama without action.

p,d&w, Oscar Michbeaux; ph, N. Spoor.

Drama   **(PR:A MPAA:NR)**

BETRAYAL, THE*½   (1958, Brit.) 82m UA bw

Philip Friend, *(Michael McCall)*, Diana Decker *(Janet Hillyer)*, Philip Saville *(Bartel)*, Peter Bathurst *(Insp. Baring)*, Peter Burton *(Tony Adams)*, Ballard Berkeley *(Lawson)*, Harold Lang *(Clay)*.

Pilot blinded in WW II enlists the help of a model to track down snitch who turned him over to the Germans during the war.

p. Edward J. and Harry Lee Danzinger; d, Ernest Morris; w, Brian Clemens, Eldon Howard

Crime   **(PR:A MPAA:NR)**

BETRAYAL***½   (1983, Brit.) 95m FOX c

Jeremy Irons *(Jerry)* Patricia Hodge *(Emma)*, Ben Kingsley *(Robert)*.

Harold Pinter is sort of like sushi. You either won't go near it or you love it so much that you make a pig of yourself. In BETRAYAL, Pinter paints a portrait of a *menage a trois*. Sure, it's been done before, but Pinter borrows from the failed Sondheim-Furth musical MERRILY WE ROLL ALONG (which, in turn, was borrowed from a movie) to tell us the story backwards! He begins at the end and flashes back to the beginning, much in the manner of peeling an artichoke to get to the heart. Kingsley is a book publisher whose wife, Hodge, is having an affair with Irons, a literary agent. It begins after the affair is over, takes us through the emotional liaison and ends as they meet. Kingsley is an immensely talented actor whose Oscar for GHANDI was no fluke. He is the fulcrum which moves the story backward (or forward, as the case may be) and says more with fewer words than any ham essaying Hamlet. Director David Jones (not to be confused with the former Monkee) manages to fashion a brisk film, despite having to deal with Pinter's patented pauses. According to the dictates of the script, Hodge should have been the center of attraction but she fails to come across with the requisite sensuousness that might move these two disparate men. BETRAYAL begins long (first scene is nearly 30 minutes) and ends short, but is never confusing. Once you've swallowed the gimmick of the time warp, it's easy enough to keep up with the activities. Pinter can sometimes be infuriating and even more so when he refuses to explain anything to the press.

p, Sam Spiegel; d, David Jones; w, Harold Pinter (based on his play); ph, Mike Fash; m, Dominic Muldowney; ed, John Bloom; prod d, Eileen Diss; cos, Jane Robinson, Jean Muir.

Drama   **Cas.**   **(PR:O MPAA:R)**

BETRAYAL FROM THE EAST*   (1945) 82m RKO bw

Lee Tracy *(Eddie)*, Nancy Kelly *(Peggy)*, Richard Loo *(Tanni)*, Abner Biberman *(Yamato)*, Regis Toomey *(Scott)*, Philip Ahn *(Kato)*, Addison Richards *(Capt. Bates)*, Bruce Edwards *(Purdy)*, Hugh Hoo *(Araki)*, Sen Yung *(Omaya)*, Roland Varno *(Kurt)*, Louis Jean Heydt *(Marsden)*, Jason Robards, Sr. *(Hildebrand)*.

An ex-G.I., Tracy, thought to be a mercenary by Japanese agents, is contacted to steal military plans for the defense of the Panama Canal. He allows the Japanese to think he's going along with their plans with the help of a beautiful American counterspy, Kelly, and a great deal of imagination. He succeeds in putting one over on the enemy, but at the cost of his life and that of his lady. Drew Pearson narrates and wrote the epilog, giving an aura of validity to a fictional gung-ho story of love and honor.

d, William Berke; w, Kenneth Gamet, Aubrey Wisberg (based on the book by Alan Hynd); ph, Russell Metty; m, Roy Webb; ed, Duncan Mansfield; md, Constantin Bakaleinikoff; art d, Albert S. D'Agostino; set d, Darrell Silvera, William Stevens; spec eff, Vernon L. Walker.

War   **(PR:AA: MPAA: NR)**

BETRAYED*   (1954) 107m MGM c

Clark Gable *(Col. Pieter Deventer)*, Lana Turner *(Carla Van Oven)*, Victor Mature *(The Scarf)*, Louis Calhern *(Gen. Ten Eyck)*, O.E. Hasse *(Col. Helmut Dietrich)*, Wilfrid Hyde-White *(Gen. Charles Larraby)*, Ian Carmichael *(Capt. Jackie Lawson)*, Niall MacGinnis *(Blackie)*, Nora Swinburne *(The Scarf's Mother)*, Roland Culver *(Gen. Warsleigh)*, Leslie Weston *(Pop)*, Christopher Rhodes *(Chris)*, Lilly Kann *(Jan's Grandmother)*, Brian Smith *(Jan)*, Anton Diffring *(Capt. Von Stanger)*.

Flashy cloak-and-dagger drama with plenty of action and suspense. Turner, never sexier despite going from blonde to brunette for this actioner, is a woman of dubious background, accused of collaborating with the Nazis in Holland. She is recruited by intelligence chief Gable to redeem herself by returning to Holland to work for an underground operative known only as "The Scarf" (Mature), the very same dashing agent who has saved Gable's life earlier. After rigorous training when Gable falls for the sultry recruit, Turner is smuggled into Holland to ostensibly sing for her supper as a pub entertainer to whom the Nazis flock, all attempting to bed her. One steamy scene has a German officer running his hands up and down Turner's fleshy leg as she warbles a song (voice-over done by Diana Coupland). After hours, Lana busies herself with spy chores for Mature but soon learns that the best agents connected with this operation are being discovered and executed. Turner is thought to be up to her old tricks again and Gable sneaks into Holland to kill his protege. But he learns that it is Mature who is the villain and traitor. It turns out that Victor has a severe case of Momism, that his mother (Swinburne) was wrongly accused of being a Nazi collaborator and for this indignity he takes his revenge by betraying the Allies. Gable tricks him into a trap and kills him, then escapes with Turner and British troops retreating from the disastrous raid on Arnhem, a wildly abortive battle massively treated in A BRIDGE TOO FAR in 1977. Gable was to star opposite Ava Gardner in BETRAYED, but Turner was brought in at the last moment. "The King" of Hollywood was putting on weight and his career seemed to be in decline; this was the last film he made under his $500,000-a-year contract with MGM, but he would make better films and more money in his last six years of life as a freelancer. Moreover, MGM mogul Dore Schary let Gable go, thinking he was finished. Yet MOGAMBO, made before BETRAYED, with Gable, Grace Kelly, and Ava Gardner (who had replaced Turner) made so much money for MGM that Schary later wanted Gable back and could not get him. Gable seems tired throughout BETRAYED but his presence was still commanding. Gable and Turner had appeared in earlier vehicles where their love scenes steamed (HONKY TONK, SOMEWHERE I'LL FIND YOU), so much so in HONKY TONK that Gable's then wife, Carole Lombard, stormed onto the set and warned her husband to stay away from blonde bombshell Turner. But the fire was gone in BETRAYED; Gable was 54 and Turner 33 and when he kissed her, quipped one reviewer, "it was like a husband with a hangover." Mature gives a flamboyant performance full of romp, camp, and caricature. The lensing on location in Holland is splendid, as are all other production efforts, but the plot and dialog are somewhat stilted.

p&d, Gottfried Reinhardt; w, Ronald Millar, George Froeschel; ph, F. A. Young (Eastmancolor); m, Walter Goehr; ed, John Dunning, Raymond Poulton; art d, Alfred Junge; cos, Balmain; m/l, "Johnny Come Home" Goehr, Millar.

War **(PR:C MPAA:NR)**

BETRAYED WOMEN*½ (1955) 70m AA bw

Carole Mathews *(Kate)*, Beverly Michaels *(Honey)*, Peggy Knudsen *(Nora)*, Tom Drake *(Jeff)*, Sara Haden *(Darcy)*, John Dierkes *(Cletus)*, Esther Dale *(Mrs. Ballard)*, Paul Savage *(Baby Face)*, Darlene Fields *(Mrs. Mabry)*, John Damler *(Mabry)*, G. Pat Collins *(Hostage Guard)*, Burt Wenland *(1st Guard)*, Pete Kellett *(2nd Guard)*.

How can anyone resist a title like BETRAYED WOMEN? Unfortunately, that's the best part of this sadistic prison film. Michaels is a tough woman who has been remanded to jail. She and Mathews hate each other immediately but join forces in a prison break from this maximum-security facility. Drake, as the warden, is held as a hostage with the prison matron and another inmate, Knudsen, who is in love with the warden. While not as disgusting or obvious as Billy Fine's CONCRETE JUNGLE, a movie which goes over the same territory, it's difficult to believe that there is not one person with a sense of humor to be found.

p, William F. Broidy; d, Edward L. Cahn; w, Steve Fisher (based on a story by Paul L. Peil); ph, John Martin; m, Edward J. Kay; ed, Ace Herman, Chandler House; cos, Tommy Thompson.

Crime **(PR:C MPAA:NR)**

BETSY, THE* (1978) 120m AA c

Laurence Olivier *(Loren Hardeman, Sr.)*, Robert Duvall *(Loren Hardeman III)*, Katherine Ross *(Sally Hardeman)*, Tommy Lee Jones *(Angelo Perino)*, Jane Alexander *(Alicia Hardeman)*, Lesley-Anne Down *(Lady Bobby Ayres)*, Joseph Wiseman *(Jake Weinstein)*, Kathleen Beller *(Betsy Hardeman)*, Edward Herrmann *(Dan Weyman)*, Paul Rudd *(Loren Hardeman, Jr.)*, Roy Poole *(Duncan)*, Richard Venture *(Mark Sampson)*, Titos Vandis *(Angelo Luigi Perino)*, Clifford David *(Joe Warren)*, Inga Swenson *(Mrs. Craddock)*, Whitney Blake *(Elizabeth Hardeman)*, Carol Williard *(Roxanne)*, Read Morgan *(Donald)*, Charlie Fields *(Loren III as a Boy)*.

How can you go wrong with the four corners of the American Dream? Sex, power, money, and automobiles. Harold Robbins' book was wall-to-wall raunch and this picture goes the other way. Petrie, a classy director, puts a patina of taste on the film that it doesn't deserve. The Betsy, a car named after the company founder's daughter, is to be unveiled to the public. It's a gem of an auto, and therein lies the problem. With no built-in obsolescence, it can be an albatross—not unlike the indestructible fabric in THE MAN IN THE WHITE SUIT that threatened to put the textile workers out of business. Olivier is the patriarch, Duvall is his grandson (not unlike the Ford family, where Henry Sr.'s son Edsel died young and his grandson took over), Jane Alexander is Duvall's spouse and Ross is Olivier's lover as well as being his daughter-in-law (married to Rudd). Whereas the book was first-rate third-rate trash, this film is fourth-rate third-rate trash.

p, Harold Robbins, Robert Weston; d, Daniel Petrie; w, Walter Bernstein, William Bast (based on the novel by Robbins); ph, Mario Tosi (Technicolor); m, John Barry; ed, Rita Roland; prod d, Herman A. Blumenthal; cos, Dorothy Jeakins.

Drama **Cas.** **(PR:C MPAA:R)**

BETTER A WIDOW*

(1969, Ital.) 105m Ultra Films/UNIVL c (MEGLIO VEDOVA)

Virna Lisi *(Rosa)*, Peter McEnery *(Tom Proby)*, Gabriele Ferzetti *(Don Calogero)*, Jean Servais *(Baron Misceni)*, Agnes Spaak *(Prostitute)*, Nino Terzo *(Carmelo)*, Carla Calo *(Rosa's Governess)*, Salvatore Fucile *(Don Santo)*, Roy Bosier *(Orchestra Conductor)*, Bruno Lauzi *(Hotel Manager)*, Adriano Vitale *(Chauffeur-Killer)*.

Unfunny comedy concerned with the Italian criminal elements, from Mafia to Camorra, is utterly confusing and appeared as if it were shot without a script. Not worth the attention, even to see the voluptuous Lisi cavort about.

p, Turi Vasile; d, Duccio Tessari; w, Ennio De Concini, Tessari (based on a story by De Concini); ph, Ennio Guarnieri (Technicolor); m, Carlo Rustichelli; ed, Romano Trina, Mario Morra; cos, Adriana Berselli.

Drama **(PR:O MPAA:NR)**

BETTER LATE THAN NEVER** (1983) 87m WB c

David Niven *(Nick)*, Art Carney *(Charley)*, Maggie Smith *(Anderson)*, Kimberley Partridge *(Bridget)*, Catherine Hicks *(Sable)*, Lionel Jeffries *(Hargreaves)*, Melissa Prophet *(Marlene)*.

It's always a source of amazement when several talented people band together to make a movie that misses. Where do they go wrong? Script? Well, this one was written by Forbes (after other uncredited writers took a whack at it) whose scripting included screenplays for COCKLESHELL HEROES, THE CAPTAIN'S TABLE, ONLY TWO CAN PLAY, THE L-SHAPED ROOM, and directing by Forbes, THE SLIPPER AND THE ROSE, INTERNATIONAL VELVET, THE WRONG BOX, etc. So that can't be it. What about the producers? Haley Junior and Niven Junior both have extensive credits including THAT'S ENTERTAINMENT (Haley) and THAT'S DANCING. Surely the stars can't be faulted. David Niven, in one of his last appearances, managed to do what he could to lift the material, and Carney can always be counted on to deliver a solid performance. Hicks (who played Marilyn Monroe in the TV film) was perfect and Maggie Smith is always a delight. Okay, *you* try to figure it out. Here's the story: Bridget is the orphaned daughter of a very rich couple. Her grandmother (dead before the film begins) has left her a fortune and the news that either Niven or Carney is her true grandfather (She slept with both of them to produce her child and never was sure which one was the father). Bridget must choose between Niven, who is a down-and-out song-and-dance man working a Riviera nightclub (other than La Cage Aux Folles), and Carney, a failed New York photographer. The problem is that this film is as predictable as a rumbling stomach after a bowl of chili.

p, Jack Haley Jr., David Niven Jr.; d&w, Bryan Forbes; ph, Claude Lecomte, Gerry Fisher; m, Henry Mancini; ed, Phillip Shaw; prod d, Peter Mullins.

Comedy **Cas.** **(PR:C MPAA:PG)**

BETTY CO-ED* (1946) 68m COL bw

Jean Porter *(Joanne Leeds)*, Shirley Mills *(Gloria Campbell)*, William Mason *(Bill Brewster)*, Rosemary LaPlanche *(Glenda Warren)*, Kay Morley *(Louise Morgan)*, Jackie Moran *(Ted Harris)*, Edward Van Sloan *(A. J. A. Woodruff)*, George Meader *(Plimpton)*, Daisy Moran *(Joyce Lee)*, Ray Bennett *(Michael Leeds)*.

Carnival singer Porter gets herself accepted into a social-climbing sorority and reforms its snobbish attitudes. Script and directing do nothing but the obvious with the obvious. College campus wasted in Anderson's camera work. Believe it if you will, but it'll never happen.

p, Sam Katzman; d, Arthur Dreifuss; w, Dreifuss, George H. Plympton; ph, M. A. Anderson; ed, Henry Batista.

Drama **(PR:A MPAA:NR)**

BETWEEN FIGHTING MEN* (1932) KBS 62m World Wide bw

Ken Maynard, Ruth Hall, Josephine Dunn, Wallace MacDonald, Albert J. Smith, Walter Law, James Bradbury Jr., John Pratt.

Deep-seated hatred between sheepmen and cowmen brings this story to the surface. Hall, the orphaned daughter of a sheepherder, is adopted by the cow puncher who instigated the murder of her father. His son and adopted son both fall in love with the girl—one conveniently getting shot to eliminate future conflict. Dependable and predictable story doesn't take away from the fun.

p, Burt Kelly, Sam Bischoff, William Saal; d, Forrest Sheldon; w, Betty Burbridge and Forrest Sheldon.

Western **(PR:A MPAA:NR)**

BETWEEN HEAVEN AND HELL½** (1956) 94m FOX c

Robert Wagner *(Sam Gifford)*, Terry Moore *(Jenny)*, Broderick Crawford *(Waco)*, Buddy Ebsen *(Willie)*, Robert Keith *(Col. Gozzens)*, Brad Dexter *(Joe Johnson)*, Mark Damon *(Terry)*, Ken Clark *(Morgan)*, Harvey Lembeck *(Bernard Meleski)*, Skip Homeier *(Swanson)*, L. Q. Jones *(Kenny)*, Tod Andrews *(Ray Mosby)*, Biff Elliot *(Tom Thumb)*, Bart Burns *(Raker)*, Frank Gerstle *(Col. Miles)*, Carl Switzer *(Savage)*, Gregg Martell *(Sellers)*, Frank Gorshin *(Millard)*, Darlene Fields, Ilene Brown, Scotty Morrow, Pixie Parkhurst, Brad Morrow, Scatman Crothers.

Rich landowner Wagner, who has been raised with the usual southern prejudices and has mistreated his sharecroppers, enters the service shortly after Pearl Harbor. Most of the story dwells upon Wagner's southern background in the life of landed gentry before going with his all-southern national guard unit to the Pacific war where avuncular Keith is an understanding colonel. Wagner threatens another hometown bigot who is an officer and is transferred to a remote suicide hill comanded by psychopathic, loud-mouthed, illiterate Crawford, playing Willie Stark in the army. Crawford is protected from his own men, whom he mistreats so cruelly that they all want to kill him, by two young punks, Gorshin and Homeier (both seem to typecast themselves in such roles). Wagner befriends Ebsen, a sharecropper
him the errors of his social viewpoint in a great understated performan
Japanese close in on the hill, Wagner, in a spectacular running figh
Both are wounded but survive to be sent back to the states. Crawfo
are conveniently killed by the enemy to keep the military rolls
billed as an action-packed film, only the final scenes deliver e
Moore is functional in filling sweaters as Wagner's girl back ho
who was being groomed to replace Tyrone Power at Fo
together in BENEATH THE TWELVE-MILE REEF, prom
team. Wagner never became Power and the duo fizzled on

time that rugged Humphrey Bogart was asked what he thought of new young actors like Wagner. "He's the boy next door," snorted Bogie, "but who in the hell is gonna pay a buck to see the boy next door?")

p, David Weisbart; d, Richard Fleischer; w, Harry Brown (based on the novel by Francis Gwaltney); ph, Leo Tover (CinemaScope, DeLuxe Color); m, Hugo Friedhofer; ed, James B. Clark; cos, Mary Willis.

War Drama   **(PR:A MPAA:NR)**

BETWEEN MEN**   (1935) 60m Supreme bw

Johnny Mack Brown (*Johnny Wellington*), William Farnum (*Wellington Rand*), Beth Marion (*Gale Winters*), Earl Dwire (*Trent*), Lloyd Ingraham (*Sir George Thorn*).

Brown grows up under the care of titled gentleman Farnum when his father presumes he has been murdered. When the boy grows up, he goes to New Mexico for Marion, the grandaughter Farnum ostracized when he refused to approve her marriage. All's well that ends happily ever after.

p, A.W, Hackel; d&w, Robert N. Bradbury; ph, Bert Longnecker.

Western   **Cas.**   **(PR:A MPAA:NR)**

BETWEEN MIDNIGHT AND DAWN**   (1950) 89m COL bw

Mark Stevens (*Rocky Barnes*), Edmund O'Brien (*Dan Purvis*), Gale Storm (*Kate Mallory*), Donald Buka (*Ritchie Garris*), Gale Robbins (*Terry Romaine*), Anthony Ross (*Lt. Masterson*), Roland Winters (*Leo Cusick*), Tito Vuolo (*Romano*), Grazia Narciso (*Mrs. Romano*), Madge Blake (*Mrs. Mallory*), Lora Lee Michel (*Kathy*), Jack Del Rio (*Louis Franissi*), Philip Van Zandt (*Joe Quist*), Cliff Bailey (*Sgt. Bailey*), Tony Barr (*Harry Yost*), Peter Mamakos (*Cootie Adams*), Earl Breitbard (*Rod Peters*), Wheaton Chambers (*Building Super*), Frances Morris (*Super's Wife*).

Stevens and O'Brien are patrol-car pals who break up the activities of Buka, a notorious gangster. Buka, whose ears were also so close to his head that he looked like Louis Calhern's son, gets into a shoot-out with Stevens and O'Brien and is captured. He escapes jail and seeks out his captors, killing Stevens. He is trapped again when visiting his moll, Robbins. He uses a small child as a shield and almost gets away with it until O'Brien finishes him off. Storm is the sweetie that Stevens and O'Brien both like. With Mark out of the way, Ed can move in and does. Buka is excellent as the killer and Robbins sings well in her role as the nightclub tootsie. Roland Winters is quite good as a gangster and almost makes you forget how ordinary he was in the six CHARLIE CHAN features he made for Monogram.

p, Hunt Stromberg; d, Gordon Douglas; w, Eugene Ling (story by Gerald Drayson Adams, Leo Katcher); ph, George E. Diskant; m, George Duning; ed, Gene Havlick.

Crime   **(PR:C MPAA:NR)**

BETWEEN THE LINES***   (1977) 101m Midwest Film c

John Heard (*Harry*), Lindsay Crouse (*Abbie*), Jeff Goldblum (*Max*), Jill Eikenberry (*Lynn*), Bruno Kirby (*David*), Gwen Welles (*Laura*), Stephen Collins (*Michael*), Lewis J. Stadlen (*Stanley*), Michael J. Pollard (*Hawker*), Lane Smith (*Roy Walsh*), Marilu Henner (*Danielle*), Susan Haskins (*Sarah*), Ray Barry (*Herbert Fisk*), Douglas Kenney (*Doug Henkel*), Jon Korkes (*Frank*), Richard Cox (*Wheeler*), Joe Morton (*Ahmad*), Gary Springer (*Jason*), Charles Levin (*Paul*), Guy Bond (*Austin*).

Joan Micklin Silver's HESTER STREET was a little gem that successfully recreated the life of the Jewish immigrants at the turn of the century on New York's lower East Side. BETWEEN THE LINES again demonstrates that she is a director with excellent taste and the ability to wring every last penny out of a budget and put it up there on the screen. The story takes place at one of those alternative newspapers like the *Village Voice* or *The LA Weekly*. Nobody makes much money but the compensations are in a different realm. Heard is an investigative reporter and photographer. Crouse (named after playwrights Lindsay and Crouse—LIFE WITH FATHER, STATE OF THE UNION) and he have a go at it. There are several stories happening simultaneously in BETWEEN THE LINES; two of the more exciting characters are Goldblum (THE BIG CHILL) and Bruno Kirby as the odder balls around the publication. Bits are all good. Look for Michael J. Pollard in a teeny role as the hawker. Henner has a small part as Danielle and proves unmemorable. BETWEEN THE LINES was made for about one-third of what Burt Reynolds gets as his personal fee for a movie. This cost a mere $800,000 and the husband-wife Silver team managed to bring in a first-rate picture. Caution to the studios, though, about giving directors like this too much money. With small budgets, they must rely on talent and ingenuity. With large budgets, they produce THE BLUES BROTHERS.

p, Raphael D. Silver; d, Joan Micklin Silver; w, Fred Barron (based on a story by Barron, David M. Helpern, Jr.); ph, Kenneth Van Sickle (Panavision, TVC Color); m, Michael Kamen; ed, John Carter; cos, Patrizia Von Brandenstein.

Drama   **Cas.**   **(PR:C MPAA:R)**

BETWEEN TIME AND ETERNITY**1/2   (1960, Ger.) 98m New Terra/UNIV c

Lilli Palmer (*Nina Bohlen*), Willy Birgel (*Prof. Bohlen*), Ellen Schwiers (*Consuela*), Carlos Thompson (*Manuel*), Robert Lindner (*Erich V. Hausserman*), Peter Capell (*Police Inspector*).

... tear-jerker about a middle-aged woman, Palmer, doomed by an ... ess and desperately seeking pleasure in an abortive last fling.

... Rebenalt; w, Robert Thoeren; m, Bert Grund; ph, (PatheColor).

(PR:A MPAA:NR)

...VOMEN*   (1937) 84m MGM bw

... Meighan), Maureen O'Sullivan (*Claire Donahue*), Virginia ... eonard Penn (*Tony Woolcott*), Cliff Edwards (*Snoopy*), ... gle), Charley Grapewin (*Dr. Webster*), Helen Troy (*Sally*),

Grace Ford (*Nurse Howley*), June Clayworth (*Eleanor*), Edward Norris (*Dr. Barth*), Anthony Nace (*Tom Donahue*), Hugh Marlowe (*Priest*).

Erich von Stroheim wrote the soapy story for this sappy saga of Tone, an earnest surgeon, who is in love with petite O'Sullivan (Mia Farrow's mama). She loves him as well, but is trapped in a marriage with a layabout alky (Nace) and her nursely compassion knows no bounds, so she is not about to leave the lad. Tone meets Bruce, who is rich and suffering from appendicitis. They are soon wed (the way to a woman's heart is through her appendix?). Virginia doesn't appreciate the hours Tone keeps in his medical practice and lets him know in no uncertain terms. Nace goes to the hospital for emergency surgery, but Tone is out high-stepping with his wife so the man dies. With him out of the way, Tone dumps Bruce and returns to O'Sullivan for the predictable fade-out. Not one medical cliche is overlooked. Grapewin struggles with the material and loses. He is best be remembered as Uncle Henry in THE WIZARD OF OZ, Jeeter Lester in TOBACCO ROAD and Grandpa Joad in THE GRAPES OF WRATH.

d, George B. Seitz; w, Carey Wilson, Frederick Stephani, Marlon Parsonnet (based on a story by Erich von Stroheim); ph, John Seitz; m, Dr. William Axt; ed, W. Donn Hayes; spec eff, John Hoffman.

Drama   **(PR:C MPAA:NR)**

BETWEEN TWO WOMEN**   (1944) 83m MGM bw

Lionel Barrymore (*Dr. Leonard Gillespie*), Van Johnson (*Dr. Red Adams*), Marilyn Maxwell (*Ruth Edley*), Gloria DeHaven (*Edna*), Keenan Wynn (*Tobey*), Keye Luke (*Dr. Lee Wong How*), Alma Kruger (*Molly Byrd*), Tom Trout (*Eddie Harmon*), Walter Kingsford (*Dr. Edwin Carew*), Marie Blake (*Sally*), Nell Craig (*Nurse Parker*).

Dual theme has wealthy debutante Maxwell aiming to marry handsome doctor Johnson, and anorectic DeHaven as the psychiatric patient he cures. At the same time, hospital operator Blake requires surgery and our hero performs it and saves the girl. Slow pace from Goldbeck undermines story. DeHaven sings "I'm In the Mood for Love" with some skill. (See DR. GILLESPIE series, Index.)

p&d, Willis Goldbeck; w, Harry Ruskin; ph, Harold Rossom; m, David Snell; ed, Adrienne Fazan; art d, Cedric Gibbons, Edward Carfagno.

Drama   **(PR:A MPAA:NR)**

BETWEEN TWO WORLDS**1/2   (1944) 112m WB bw

John Garfield (*Tom Prior*), Paul Henreid (*Henry*), Sydney Greenstreet (*Thompson*), Eleanor Parker (*Ann*), Edmund Gwenn (*Scrubby*), George Tobias (*Pete Musick*), George Coulouris (*Lingley*), Faye Emerson (*Maxine*), Sara Allgood (*Mrs. Midget*), Dennis King (*Rev. William Duke*), Isobel Elsom (*Mrs. Cliveden-Banks*), Gilbert Emery (*Cliveden-Banks*), Lester Matthews (*Dispatcher*), Pat O'Moore (*Clerk*).

A remake of OUTWARD BOUND (1930, starring Leslie Howard), and based on a hit play, the film opens as Henreid and Parker, emigrant Austrians fleeing Nazi air raids, are inside a limousine heading for a transatlantic liner. A bomb explodes nearby, hurling them from the vehicle. Returning to their flat, the despondent couple decide to commit suicide and turn on the gas. Suddenly they find themselves aboard a ship which is fog-bound and without a specific destination. One by one, they identify those passengers in the limousine, all of whom have been killed by the bomb. They then realize that they are on board a ship of the dead, a vessel sailing between life and eternity. Garfield is a smart-cracking newsman who seems out of place and has little to do or say. As was his habit when having no meat to his role, he overacts in the scenes he is given. Before the death ship reaches its destination, Greenstreet comes aboard as the Examiner. He determines who goes to what place, presumably Heaven or Hell. In the case of the suicides, he first states that their terrible crime against themselves demands that they sail endlessly through the fog-bound waters of limbo. Henreid and Parker beg for another chance, and Greenstreet relents with compassion. The couple come to in their flat in time to turn off the gas and return to the world of the living. Director Blatt took a fragile fantasy and approached it with stark realism, a technique that does not work. Greenstreet is good in his role of divine judge and Gwenn, as the sole crew member serving the doomed passengers, is properly mysterious.

p, Mark Hellinger; d, Edward A. Blatt; w, Daniel Fuchs (based on the play by Sutton Vane); ph, Carl Guthrie; ed, Rudi Fehr.

Fantasy   **(PR:A MPAA:NR)**

BETWEEN US GIRLS*   (1942) 88m UNIV bw

Diana Barrymore (*Caroline Bishop*), Robert Cummings (*Jimmy Blake*), Kay Francis (*Christine Bishop*), John Boles (*Steven Forbes*), Andy Devine (*Mike Kilinsky*), Ethel Griffies (*Gallagher*), Walter Catlett (*Desk Sergeant*), Guinn "Big Boy" Williams (*Father of the Boys*), Scotty Beckett (*Leopold*), Andrew Tombes (*Doctor*), Peter Jamerson (*Harold*), Mary Treen (*Mary Belle*), Lillian Yarbo (*Phoebe*), Irving Bacon (*Soda Dispenser*).

Barrymore plays a 20-year-old actress caught up in a ridiculous array of situations designed to hide her mother's real age. Barrymore hasn't the ability to sustain a major role for the unimaginatively produced movie.

p&d, Henry Koster; w, Myles Connolly, True Boardman (based on the play "Le Fruit Vert" by Regis Gignoux and Jacques Thery); ph, Joe Valentine; md, Charles Previn; ed, Frank Gross; art d, Jack Otterson, Richard Riedel; cos, Vera West.

Drama   **(PR:C MPAA:NR)**

BEWARE*   (1946) 64m Astor bw

Louis Jordan (*Lucius Brokenshire Jordan*), Frank Wilson (*Professor Drury*), Emory Richardson (*Dean Hargraves*), Valerie Black (*Miss Anabelle Brown*), Milton Woods (*Benjamin Ware III*).

Singer Jordan saves college from financial demise then makes off with women's physical education teacher Black. Unimpressive production with camerawork from Malkames painful to the eyes. All-black cast makes this a pioneer for its time.

p, Savini-Berle-Adams; d, Bud Pollard; w, John E. Gordon; ph, Don Malkames; ed, Bud Pollard; m/l, Morry Lasco, Fleecy Moore, Dick Adams, Claude Demetrius, Bill Tennyson, Bob Hillard, Dick Miles, William Davis, Duke Groner, Charles Stewart, Herman Fairbanks, Dick Watson, Louis Jordan, Irene Higginbotham, Dan Fisher, Ervin Drake, Lucky Millender, Jerry Black.

Musical　　　　　　　　　　　　　　　　　　　**(PR:A　MPAA:NR)**

BEWARE, MY LOVELY*¹⁄₂　　　　　　(1952) 77m RKO bw

Ida Lupino (Mrs. Gordon), Robert Ryan (Howard), Taylor Holmes (Mr. Armstrong), Barbara Whiting (Ruth Williams), James Williams (Mr. Stevens), O. Z. Whitehead (Mr. Franks), Dee Pollock (Grocery Boy).

BEWARE, MY LOVELY is the kind of film they make for TV these days. Ryan is a mental defective who makes a hand-to-mouth living by doing odd jobs. He is seen escaping from a small town and we presume it's because he's committed a murder. Now he arrives at widow Lupino's doorstep, ingratiates himself, and goes to work. As the film continues, we see little hints of Ryan's problems. Lupino is a little slow to catch on and when she eventually realizes that this guy is a nut case, it's too late. He locks her up and we are then involved in a series of violent premises that never quite get violent. They attempted to make it suspenseful but director Horner is not Hitchcock, who might have made something out of this story. In the end, Ryan leaves, having forgotten why he was there, and Ida is saved. It's a small film with a fairly tight script and a good idea. The execution is not as good as the concept and it winds up as murky melodrama.

p, Collier Young; d, Harry Horner; w, Mel Dinelli (based on his story and play "The Man"); ph, George E. Diskant; m, Leith Stevens; ed, Paul Weatherwax.

Drama　　　　　　　　　　　　　　　　　　　**(PR:C　MPAA:NR)**

BEWARE OF BLONDIE**　　　　　　　(1950) 64m COL bw

Penny Singleton (Blondie), Arthur Lake (Dagwood), Larry Simms (Alexander), Marjorie Kent (Cookie), Adele Jergens (Toby Clifton), Dick Wessel (Mailman), Jack Rice (Ollie), Alyn Lockwood (Mary), Emory Parnell (Herb Woodley), Isabel Withers (Harriet Woodley), Danny Mummert (Alvin), Douglas Fowley (Adolph), William E. Green (Samuel P. Dutton).

Dagwood's boss, Mr. Dithers, misguidedly takes a vacation thinking that Dagwood Bumstead can look after the business. The more fool he. Jurgens is a vamp who can see that Dagwood is a naive suburbanite. She uses the old badger game and Dagwood is in big trouble until the redoubtable Blondie (Penny Singleton) rescues him. It's all good fun and innocent as a new-born babe. Plenty of laughs, a lot of silliness, much predictability, and a general feeling of fun. (See BLONDIE series, Index.)

p, Milton Feldman; d, Edward Bernds; w, Jack Henley (based on characters created by Chic Young); ph, Henry Freulich, Vincent Farrar; ed, Richard Fantl.

Comedy　　　　　　　　　　　　　　　　　　**(PR:AA　MPAA:NR)**

BEWARE OF CHILDREN*　　　　(1961, Brit.) 86m GHW/AIP bw (GB: NO KIDDING)

Leslie Phillips (David Robinson), Geraldine McEwan (Catherine Robinson), Julia Lockwood (Vanilla), Irene Handl (Mrs. Spicer), Noel Purcell (Tandy), Joan Hickson (Cook), June Jago (Matron), Cyril Raymond (Col. Matthews), Esma Cannon (District Nurse), Alan Gifford (Edgar Treadgold), Sydney Tafler (Mr. Rockbottom), Brian Oulton (Vicar), Eric Pohlmann (King), Patricia Jessel (Queen), Brian Rawlinson (Will), Michael Sarne (Henri), Joy Shelton (Mrs. Rockbottom), Marian Mather (Helen Treadgold).

Phillips and McEwan inherit considerable land and, do-gooders that they are, turn the estate into a children's camp which brings their lives to chaos when hordes of kids commit endless pranks that are not as funny as pratfalls. No trip in the country.

p, Peter Rogers; d, Gerald Thomas; w, Norman Hudis, Robin Estridge (based on the book by Verily Anderson); ph, Alan Hume; m, Bruce Montgomery; ed, John Shirley; cos, Joan Ellacott.

Comedy　　　　　　　　　　　　　　　　　　　**(PR:A　MPAA:NR)**

BEWARE OF LADIES**　　　　　　　(1937) 62m REP bw

Donald Cook (George Martin), Judith Allen (Betty White), George Meeker (Freddie White), Goodee Montgomery (Gertie), Russell Hopton (Randy Randall), William Newell (Sniff), Dwight Frye (Swanson).

Young newspaper reporter Allen falls for hopeful district attorney Cook, thereby securing his downfall when a compromising photo is obtained by her estranged husband. Production weakened when exciting points become giggly rather than dramatic.

p, Nat Levine; d, Irving Pichel; w, L. C. Dublin; ph, William Nobles; ed, Ernest Nims.

Drama　　　　　　　　　　　　　　　　　　　**(PR:A　MPAA:NR)**

BEWARE OF PITY***　　　　　　　(1946, Brit.) 105m TC bw

Lilli Palmer (Baroness Edith), Albert Lieven (Lt. Anton Marek), Cedric Hardwicke (Dr. Albert Condor), Gladys Cooper (Klara Condor), Linden Travers (Ilona Domansky), Ernest Thesiger (Baron Emil de Kekesfalva), Peter Cotes (Cusma), Freda Jackson (Gypsy).

Crippled baroness Palmer commits suicide after learning Lieven has denied their engagement to his army comrades. He has more sympathy than love for her. Commendable camera work from Williams with an expertly done screenplay by Lipscomb.

d, Maurice Elvey; w, W. P. Lipscomb (based on the novel by Stefan Zweig); ph, Derick Williams.

Romance　　　　　　　　　　　　　　　　　　**(PR:A　MPAA:NR)**

BEWARE SPOOKS**　　　　　　　　(1939) 65m COL bw

Joe E. Brown (Roy Gifford), Mary Carlisle (Betty Lou Winters), Clarence Kolb (Commissioner Lewis), Marc Lawrence (Slick Eastman), Don Beddoe (Nick Bruno), George J. Lewis (Danny Emmett).

After ineptly handling a cinch arrest, Brown finds sought-after criminals at Coney Island and traps them in a spookhouse. Above par camera work by Siegler highlights sagging spots and keeps the comedy interesting.

p, Robert Sparks; d, Edward Sedgwick; w, Richard Flournoy, Albert Duffy, Brian Marlow; ph, Allen G. Siegler; ed, James Sweeney; md, M. W. Stoloff.

Comedy　　　　　　　　　　　　　　　　　　　**(PR:A　MPAA:NR)**

BEWARE! THE BLOB*　　(1972) 88m Jack H. Harris c (AKA: SON OF BLOB)

Robert Walker, Gwynne Gilford, Richard Stahl, Richard Webb, Godfrey Cambridge, Carol Lynley, Shelley Berman, Burgess Meredith.

J. R. directs! "Dallas" star Larry Hagman handled the directorial chores on this mindless sequel to THE BLOB (1958). Small-town youth Walker exterminates a shapeless mass which inhales everything in its path, terrorizing his home turf. Sharp photography from Hamm is the saving grace in this overlong film. Hagman shows no flair for direction.

p, Anthony Harris; d, Larry Hagman; w, Jack Woods, Harris (based on a story by Richard Clair and Harris); ph, Al Hamm (DeLuxe Color); m, Mort Garson; ed, Tony de Zarraga.

Horror　　　　　　　　　　　　Cas.　　　　　　**(PR:A　MPAA:NR)**

BEWITCHED***　　　　　　　　　(1945) 65m MGM bw

Phyllis Thaxter (Joan Alris Ellis), Edmund Gwenn (Dr. Bergson), Henry H. Daniels, Jr. (Bob Arnold), Addison Richards (John Ellis), Francis Pierlot (Dr. George Wilton), Sharon McManus (Little Girl in Zoo), Gladys Blake (Glenda), Will Wright (Mr. Herkheimer), Horace [Stephen] McNally (Eric Russell), Oscar O'Shea (Capt. O'Malley), Minor Watson (Governor), Virginia Brissac (Governor's Wife), Audrey Totter's voice (Karen).

Intended as a low-budget B film, Arch Oboler's startling radio show "Alter Ego" was his first directorial chore, and he turned it into a classy chiller, retitled BEWITCHED. (Oboler had for years been transfixing radio audiences with his scary "Lights Out" show.) Thaxter is the schizophrenic killer, a woman with another deadly personality, who is examined and revealed by psychiatrist Gwenn who hypnotizes Thaxter on the eve of her execution. She has murdered her boyfriend. Under treatment, the crime is relived in flashback and an evil personality (voice wonderfully rendered by Totter) called Karen is chillingly shown to lurk inside the woman. Other flashbacks show how her devoted friend McNally saves her in court only to have the good personality erupt screaming, "I did kill him!" The struggle between the two personalities to dominate is absolutely fascinating as Thaxter gives the performance of her life. A terrific little chiller predating by a dozen years the multiple personality films THE THREE FACES OF EVE and LIZZIE. Kaper's eerie and arresting score is a cold hand at the back of the neck.

p, Jerry Bresler; d&w, Arch Oboler (based on Oboler's story, "Alter Ego"); ph, Charles Salerno, Jr.; m, Bronislau Kaper; ed, Harry Komer.

Suspense/Mystery　　　　　　　　　　　　　　**(PR:C　MPAA:NR)**

BEYOND A REASONABLE DOUBT**　　(1956) 80m RKO bw

Dana Andrews (Tom Garrett), Joan Fontaine (Susan Spencer), Sidney Blackmer (Austin Spencer), Philip Bourneuf (Thompson), Shepperd Strudwick (Wilson), Arthur Franz (Hale), Edward Binns (Lt. Kennedy), Robin Raymond (Terry), Barbara Nichols (Sally), William Leicester (Charlie Miller), Dan Seymour (Greco), Rusty Lane (Judge), Joyce Taylor (Joan), Carleton Young (Kirk), Trudy Wroe (Hat Check Girl), Joe Kirk (Clerk), Charles Evans (Governor), Wendell Niles (Announcer).

A second-rate plot distinguished by a first-rate cast. Andrews is a writer who witnesses an execution and then has a discussion with editor Blackmer, who suggests the two carry out a ruse to show the fallibility of circumstantial evidence. Blackmer encourages Andrews to confess to murder and go to trial, with Blackmer holding back evidence which will prove Andrews is innocent. Andrews goes along with the plan, and later confesses to an the unsolved murder of a girl. He is arrested and put on trial, but Blackmer is killed in a car accident before he can produce the evidence which will free Andrews. Andrews' conviction seems certain, until Blackmer's lawyer uncovers a letter from the dead man which details the ruse, and he uses it to clear Andrews. Later, however, in a conversation with Fontaine, Blackmer's daughter, the truth comes out—Andrews did actually murder the girl. BEYOND A REASONABLE DOUBT is a ludicrous story, very hard to swallow. Lang, who should have known better, must have directed this with his good eye closed.

p, Bert Friedlob; d, Fritz Lang; w, Douglas Morrow; ph, William Snyder; m, Herschel Burke Gilbert; ed, Gene Fowler, Jr.

Mystery　　　　　　　　　　　　　　　　　　　**(PR:C　MPAA:NR)**

BEYOND AND BACK*　　　　　　(1978) 93m Sunn Classic c

Brad Crandal (Narrator), Vern Adix (Plato), Linda Bishop (Army Nurse), Shelley Osterloh (Louisa May Alcott), Beverly Rowland (Mrs. Houdini), Janet Bylund (Nurse), Richard Cannaday (Physician), Maxilyn Capel (Dr. Stevens), Bill Carroll (Doctor), David Chandler (Nobleman), Hyde Clayton (Sam), Elaine Daniel (Janice), Lori Davis (Little Girl), Stewart Falcone (Dr. Meyers).

Sunn Classic has done it again. They've taken 93 minutes of yawn and made it into an audience grabber. This company should hire itself out as marketers for the rest of the industry because they do the most with the least. Witness IN SEARCH OF NOAH'S ARK and MYSTERIOUS MONSTERS, two of the worst and yet most successful (for their price) pictures ever. In BEYOND AND BACK, Sunn examines the phenomenon of death and rebirth, surely a subject any living person has thought of. They weigh a dead person's soul, they interview people who have died, "gone over," and come back and they generally assure us that there is life after death. The question is . . . is there sleep while watching this movie? And the answer is, again, a resounding "yes."

p, Charles Sellier, Jr.; d, James L. Conway; w, Stephen Lord (based in part on book by Ralph Wilkerson); ph, Henning Schellerup; m, Bob Summers; ed, James D. Wells; art d, Charles Bennett; spec eff, Doug Hubbard; stunt d, Alan Biss.

Docu-Drama   **Cas.**   **(PR:A MPAA:NR)**

BEYOND ATLANTIS zero   (1973, Phil.) 88m Dimension c

John Ashley, Patrick Wayne, Leigh Christian, George Nader, Lenore Stevens, Sidney Haig.

Ashley is up to his usual garbage film in the horror genre, a dirt-cheap production. Ashley, Haig, and Wayne attempt to steal pearls from natives on an uncharted island, but Nader, the demonic leader of a killer cult, stands in their way. Christian adds the spice as Nader's helpmate. Nitwit story.

p, Eddie Romero, John Ashley; d, Romero; w, Charles Johnson; ph, (Metrocolor).

Horror   **Cas.**   **(PR:O MPAA:NR)**

BEYOND EVIL* 1/2   (1980) 94m IFI/Scope III c

John Saxon (Larry), Lynda Day George (Barbara), Michael Dante (Del), Mario Milano (Albanos), Janice Lynde (Alma), David Opatoshu (Dr. Solomon), Anne Marisse (Leia), Zitto Kazaan (Esteban).

Janice Lynde has been dead a long time. She made a deal with (who else?) the Devil, so she was able to rise from the dead and knock off her hubby. Lynde is the driving force behind this otherwise listless film. Lynda Day George and John Saxon (two actors who deserve a lot better than this lame script) move into Alma's house. Alma does her best to get rid of them. End of story. Michael Dante plays the best friend of the two leads, a role once made famous by Ronald Reagan in several Warner Brothers movies.

p, David Baughn, Herb Freed; d, Freed; w, Paul Ross, Freed (based on a story by Baughn); ph, Ken Plotin (Metrocolor); ed, Rick Westover.

Horror   **Cas.**   **(PR:A MPAA:NR)**

BEYOND FEAR* 1/2   (1977, Fr.) 95m CINE III c (Au-dela Dela Peur)

Michel Bouquet (Claude), Michel Constantin (Guilloux), Marilu Tolo (Nicole), Paul Crauchet (Inspector), Michel Creton (Legoff).

This is the French version of THE DESPERATE HOURS, except it doesn't have Fredric March or Humphrey Bogart or anything else to merit much attention. Basic story is that Bouquet gets some gangster information inadvertently. The mobsters find out where he lives and take over his house. He is on the outside and they threaten his family unless he shows up. He promises he won't talk if they allow him to speak to his wife every 30 minutes. The wife's brother finds out about the situation and alerts the police. Some suspense, a couple of turns, but that's about it.

d&w, Yannik Andrei; ph, Pierre Petit (Eastmancolor); m, Alain Goraguer.

Crime Drama   **Cas.**   **(PR:C MPAA:NR)**

BEYOND GLORY** 1/2   (1948) 82m PAR bw

Alan Ladd (Rockwell "Rocky" Gilman), Donna Reed (Ann Daniels), George Macready (Maj. Gen. Bond), George Coulouris (Lew Proctor), Harold Vermilyea (Raymond Denmore, Sr.), Henry Travers (Pop Dewing), Luis Van Rooten (Dr. White), Tom Neal (Henry Daniels), Conrad Janis (Raymond Denmore, Jr.), Margaret Field [Maggie Mahoney] (Cora), Paul Lees (Miller), Dick Hogan (Cadet Sgt. Eddie Loughlin), Audie Murphy (Thomas), Geraldine Wall (Mrs. Daniels), Charles Evans (Mr. Julian), Russell Wade (Cadet), Vincent Donahue (John Craig), Steve Pendleton (Gen. Prescott), Harland Tucker (Col. Stoddard), Edward Ryan (Cadet).

Ladd blacked out during a key battle in Tunisia and is convinced that this lapse was responsible for the death of his commanding offier (Neal). After his discharge, the incident continues to haunt him so he visits the widow (Reed) and they fall in love. With her encouragement he enters West Point and is doing well in his studies when he gets involved with a board of enquiry and the old claim is dragged up by the attorney for a spoiled plebe (Janis). Ladd is a good deal older than the other cadets and under great pressure from several directions. He leaves the Point and a court martial is called for. With Reed and Travers behind him, he returns to the Academy and the trial continues. Finally, a young soldier who was there tells everyone in court that Ladd was innocent of any wrongdoing and had passed out due to an artillery bombardment when Neal was killed. When a relieved Ladd says, "Why didn't you say this before?" Loughlin (Hogan) replies, "You never asked me!" What an ignominious cop-out for what otherwise was an interesting movie. Janis went on to become a regular on many TV shows but his first loves are Dixieland music and his trombone. In the 1950s he ran a group called The TailGate Jazz Band, and in the 1980s he continues to play with The Beverly Hills Unlisted Jazz Band whenever he isn't working in a film or on television.

p, Robert Fellows; d, John Farrow; w, Jonathan Latimer, Charles Marquis Warren, William Wister Haines; ph, John Seitz; m, Victor Young; ed, Eda Warren.

Drama   **(PR:A MPAA:NR)**

BEYOND MOMBASA**   (1957) 90m COL bw

Cornel Wilde (Matt Campbell), Donna Reed (Ann Wilson), Leo Genn (Ralph Hoyt), Ron Randell (Elliott Hastings), Christopher Lee (Gil Rossi), Dan Jackson (Ketimi), Eddie Calvert (Trumpet Player), Bartholomew Sketch (Native Boss), Clive Morton (Irate Englishman), Macdonald Parke (Tourist), Virginia Bedard (Tourist's Wife), Julian Sherrier (Desk Clerk), Ed Johnson (Dacall Chief), Roy Purcell (George Campbell).

Wilde is somewhat more lively than his usual somnambulist self as a devil-may-care drifter who joins his brother in Africa to mine uranium in a deserted gold dig. Upon arrival, Wilde learns that his brother has been murdered by . . . The Leopard Men! Both of Wilde's brother's partners deny any knowledge of the mine. Wilde doesn't believe them (Lee and Randell), nor does he believe the theory that his brother was done in by this quasi-religious cult. Genn is the missionary who turns out to be the heavy, Reed is his niece. (Why is it that many of these B-movie heavies have nieces but never daughters?) It's a western plot set in East Africa and a far cry from Wilde's best picture, also set in Africa, THE NAKED PREY.

p, Tony Owen; d, George Marshall; w, Richard English, Gene Levitt (based on story "The Mark Of The Leopard" by James Eastwood); ph, Frederick A. Young; m, Humphrey Searle; ed, Ernest Walter.

Adventure   **(PR:A-C MPAA:NR)**

BEYOND REASONABLE DOUBT**   (1980, New Zeal.) 127m Endeavour c

David Hemmings (Inspector Hutton), John Hargreaves (Arthur Allen Thomas), Martyn Sanderson (Lem Demler), Tony Barry (Detective John Hughes), Grant Tilly (David Morris), Diana Rowan (Vivien Thomas), Ian Watkin (Kevin Ryan), Terence Cooper (Paul Temin), Marshall Napier (Constable Wyllie), John Bach (Detective Murray Jeffries), Bruce Allpress (Detective Stan Keith), Bruno Lawrence (Pat Vesey), Peter Hayden (Graham Hewson).

This film is not to be confused with BEYOND A REASONABLE DOUBT (1956, Fritz Lang). One of the most compelling murder crimes in the Down Underworld was the murder of Mr. and Mrs. Harvey Crewe. Eventually, a man named Arthur Thomas was tried and found guilty. He was later pardoned as David Yallop's book opened the case again, not unlike the situation between Jimmy Stewart and Richard Conte in CALL NORTHSIDE 777. What's more, both films are based on real cases and resulted in the innocent parties being released. The roles were cast with an eye toward the actors actually looking like the true protagonists in the story but that will mean little outside New Zealand or Australia. Actually, the film won't mean much either if the producers are expecting a certain amount of curiosity on the part of the public. BEYOND REASONABLE DOUBT does stand on its own merits, though, and Hemmings is chilling as the inspector who seems to have it in for the innocent scapegoat.

p, John Barnett; d, John Laing; w, David Yallop; ph, Alan Bollinger (Eastmancolor); m, Dave Fraser; ed, Michael Horton; art d, Kay Hawkins.

Docu-Drama   **Cas.**   **(PR:C MPAA:NR)**

BEYOND THE BLUE HORIZON**   (1942) 76m PAR c

Dorothy Lamour (Tama), Richard Denning (Jakra), Jack Haley (Squidge), Walter Abel (Thornton), Helen Gilbert (Carol), Patricia Morison (Sylvia), Frances Gifford (Charlotte), Elizabeth Patterson (Mrs. Daly), Abner Biberman (La'Oa), Ann Todd (Tama as a child), Edward Fielding (Judge Alvin Chase), Charles Stevens (Panao), Ann Doran (Margaret Chase), Charles Cane (Broderick), Frank Reicher (Sneath), Gerald Oliver Smith (Chadwick), Inez Palange (Native Nurse), Barbara Britton (Pamela).

A silly film that is saved by the good humor of the people in it and the obvious realization that none of them believe one word of the script. Denning is a lion tamer for a failing circus. Lamour is a jungle girl on her way to the states to pick up a fortune her parents left her when they died in her youth. Haley is the circus' tub-thumper and he tries to get Lamour to join up with the one-ring business to attempt to get more publicity. Lamour's relations don't believe she is who she claims she is and from there it just gets to be more of a botch. Lamour looks good in a sarong and there are a few cute moments with a chimp but that's about it. Britton plays a small role as Pamela. The year before, she made her screen test with star Denning and it was some time later when she starred with him in the TV series "Mr. and Mrs. North." She may be best remembered as "The Revlon Girl" on TV's "64 Thousand Dollar Question."

p, Monta Bell; d, Alfred Santell; w, Frank Butler (based on a story by E. Lloyd Sheldon, Jack DeWitt); ph, Charles Boyle; ed, Doane Harrison; art d, Hans Dreier, Earl Hedrick; m/l, Frank Loesser, Jule Styne, Mort Greene, Harry Revel.

Comedy Drama   **(PR:A MPAA:NR)**

BEYOND THE CITIES*   (1930, Brit.) 70m Piccadilly/PAR bw

Carlyle Blackwell (Jim Campbell), Edna Best (Mary Hayes), Alexander Field (Sam), Lawrence Hanray (Gregory Hayes), Helen Haye (Amy Hayes), Eric Maturin (Hector Braydon), Percy Parsons (Boss).

Cheated out of his life savings by a corrupt lawyer, Blackwell leaves England and emigrates to Canada. While he is trying to make a go of ranching, an airplane crashes nearby. Blackwell aids a young lady survivor who is suffering amnesia following the crash. He eventually learns she is the lawyer's daughter, but still saves her from marrying a conniving suitor. American stage and screen actor Blackwell, "the Clark Gable of the silents" with film credits dating back to 1909, emigrated to England after his popularity at home diminished with the advent of talkies. His acting career faded and he tried his hand at producing, directing, and writing, with modest success.

p&d, Carlyle Blackwell; w, Blackwell, Noel Shannon.

Drama   **(PR:A MPAA:NR)**

BEYOND THE CURTAIN* 1/2   (1960, Brit.) 88m RANK bw

Richard Greene (*Jim Kyle*), Eva Bartok (*Karin von Seefeldt*), Marius Goring (*Hans Koertner*), Lucie Mannheim (*Frau von Seefeldt*), Andree Melly (*Linda*), George Mikell (*Pieter*), John Welsh (*Turner*), Dennis Shaw (*Krumm*), Annette Karell (*Governor*), Gaylord Cavallaro (*Twining*), Leonard Sachs (*Waiter*).

Forced drama about how an airline stewardess held captive with her plane in East Germany. She is rescued by the pilot who loves her. Dour story with no action and witless script.

d, Compton Bennett; w, John Cresswell, Bennett (based on the novel *Thunder Above* by Charles F. Blair); ph, Eric Cross; m, Eric Pakeman.

Drama   **(PR:A   MPAA:NR)**

BEYOND THE DOOR zero   (1975, Ital./U.S.) 100m Film Ventures c

Juliet Mills (*Jessica*), Richard Johnson (*Dimitri*), David Colin, Jr. (*Robert*), Elizabeth Turner, Gabriele Lavia.

Unbelievably blatant copy of the Friedkin-Blatty THE EXORCIST, so much so that we are told Warner Bros. took legal action against the producers. Mills (John's daughter, Hayley's sister, and the Professor's Nanny) does the Burstyn role. She's the spouse of a record producer. She's pregnant with a demoniacal child, the result of a liaison 'twixt her and Johnson, who we suppose is the Devil. In this, they are also ripping off ROSEMARY'S BABY. They use all the tricks seen in THE EXORCIST and hardly bother to add anything new. There is nothing good to say about this movie other than it made a lot of money for its producers.

p, Ovidio Assonitis, Giorgio Rossi; d, Oliver Hellman; w, Richard Barrett; ph, (DeLuxe Color); m, Riz Ortolani; spec eff, Donn Davison, Wally Gentleman.

Horror   **Cas.**   **(PR:O   MPAA:R)**

BEYOND THE DOOR II zero

(1979, Ital.) 92m Film Ventures c (AKA: SHOCK)

Daria Nicolodi (*Dora*), John Steiner (*Bruno*), David Colin, Jr. (*Marco*), Ivan Rassimov (*Carlos*).

This sequel to BEYOND THE DOOR was the last work of monster movie mogul Mario Bava and like the original, deals with possession, using one member of the original cast, David Colin, Jr., as a young boy possessed by a supernatural power. His mother is married for the second time to a man with a mysterious past who is not what he appears to be. She suffers from amnesia and, not surprisingly, given her family situation, horrible dreams. This film has been touted as being much better than the original. It's not.

p, Juri Vasile; d&ph, Mario Bava; w, Lamberto Bava.

Horror   **Cas.**   **(PR:O   MPA:NR)**

BEYOND THE FOG zero

(1981, Brit.) 86m Independent-International c (AKA: TOWER OF EVIL, HORROR ON SNAPE ISLAND)

Bryant Haliday (*Brent*), Jill Haworth (*Rose*), Anna Palk (*Nora*), Jack Watson (*Hamp*), Mark Edwards (*Adam*), Derek Fowlds (*Dan*), John Hamill (*Gary*), Candace Glendenning (*Penny*), Dennis Price (*Bakewell*), George Coulouris (*Gurney*), Robin Askwith (*Des*), Serretta Wilson (*Mac*), Fredric Abbott (*Saul*), Mark McBride (*Michael*), William Lucas (*Det. Hawk*), Anthony Valentine (*Dr. Simpson*), Marianne Stone (*Nurse*).

Madman lives only to devise new ways in which to murder helpless people. A sleazy script, awful acting, and pure exploitation of the genre adds up to a large waste of time.

p, Richard Gordon; d&w, Jim O'Connolly (based on a story by George Baxt); ph, Desmond Dickinson (Eastmancolor); m, Ken Jones; ed, Henry Richardson; art d, Disley Jones.

Horror   **(PR:O   MPAA:R)**

BEYOND THE FOREST*   (1949) 95m WB bw

Bette Davis (*Rosa Moline*), Joseph Cotten (*Dr. Lewis Moline*), David Brian (*Neil Latimer*), Ruth Roman (*Carol*), Minor Watson (*Moose*), Dona Drake (*Jenny*), Regis Toomey (*Sorren*), Sara Selby (*Mildred*), Mary Servoss (*Mrs. Welch*), Frances Charles (*Miss Elliot*).

Ms. Davis never liked this slow, overdone melodrama and she was not alone. Critics massacred it with extreme prejudice across the country when it was released. This was the final film on Davis' Warner Bros.' contract, and a rotten way for such a great lady to exit. Davis plays a bitchy young woman in a small midwest town who is married to Cotten, a pleasant but dull physician. Davis has the hots for Brian, a wealthy manufacturer from Chicago. She leaves home and goes to Chicago to meet Brian, who rebuffs her, saying that he intends marrying a wealthy socialite. Defeated, Davis returns to the yawning life with Cotten. Brian changes his mind, dumps the lady, and tells Davis she must divorce her husband and marry him. This conversation is heard by Watson, caretaker at Brian's hunting lodge. Davis is now pregnant by Cotten and Watson says he'll tell Brian of her impending motherhood if she doesn't come across. Davis kills Watson and makes it looks accidental. Now she tells Cotten that she's leaving him for Brian. He refuses to allow her to go until after his child is born. She knows he can perform an abortion, but he steadfastly refuses so she jumps off an embankment. The miscarriage takes place but she develops peritonitis. Why her condition goes unchecked is never explained but, in a feverish state, she gets out of bed, staggers toward the train station to catch the express to Chicago. She never makes it, dies on the street in much the same way Cagney did in so many other Warner Bros. films. The comeuppance is achieved. Davis overplays this so much that she appears to be a female impersonator doing Bette Davis. She's a psychopathic slut with absolutely no redeeming virtues. How anyone could have approved this script for shooting is a mystery.

p, Henry Blanke; d, King Vidor; w, Lenore Coffee (based on the novel by Stuart Engstrand); ph, Robert Burks; m, Max Steiner; ed, Rudi Fehr; cos, Edith Head; makeup, Perc Westmore.

Romance/Drama   **(PR:C   MPAA:NR)**

BEYOND THE LAST FRONTIER**   (1943) 57m REP bw

Eddie Dew (*John Paul Revere*), Smiley Burnette (*Frog Milhouse*), Harry Woods (*Big Bill Hadley*), Bob Mitchum (*Trigger Dolan*), Kermit Maynard (*Clyde Barton*), Lorraine Miller (*Susan Cook*), Ernie Adams (*Kincaid*), Curley Dresden (*Ranger*), Wheaton Chambers (*Doc Jessup*).

Spies Dew and Burnette chase each other throughout this good guys vs. bad guys story centered around illegal trade. Production hides behind poor location lighting, but is still satisfactory. Mitchum in an early, small-billed part, is a good-bad guy who becomes a hero at the finish.

p, Louis Gray; d, Howard Bretherton; w, John K. Butler, Morton Grant; ph, Bud Thackery; m, Mort Glickman; ed, Charles Craft.

Western   **(PR:A   MPAA:NR)**

BEYOND THE LAW**   (1934) 58m COL bw

Tim McCoy (*Tim*), Shirley Grey (*Helen*), Addison Richards (*Morgan*), Lane Chandler, Dick Rush, Harry Bradley, Morton Laverre (*John Merton*).

When ex-con mechanic Richards is framed for murder and railroad robbery, his daughter lures railroad detective McCoy to prove her father's innocence. Nothing outstanding, but fun anyway.

d, D. Ross Lederman; w, Harold Shumate; ph, A. Siegler; ed, Otto Mayer.

Adventure   **(PR:A   MPAA:NR)**

BEYOND THE LAW* 1/2

(1967, Ital.) 85m Sanscrosiap/ROXY bw (Al Di La Della Legge)

Lee Van Cleef (*Bandit Turned Sheriff*), Gordon Mitchell (*Bat-cloaked Villain*), Antonio Sabato, Lionel Stander, Graziella Granata, Ann Smymer.

There are several very funny moments in this spaghetti western about a bad guy (Van Cleef) who turns good in order to get close to a payroll that he wants to steal. Mitchell is the villain Van Cleef shoots when he attempts to take a second payroll. Nobody takes anything seriously for one moment. This was made during the time when Lionel Stander was living outside the country, a victim of the continuing HUAC blacklisting. He was forced to leave the US (after attempting to work on stage and in unrelated fields), moved to Rome, and enjoyed immediate success in movies such as this.

p, Alfonso Sansone, Enrico Chroscicki; d, Giorgio Stegani; w, Warren Kiefer, Fernando DiLeo, Mino Roli, Stegani; ph, Enzo Serafin; ed, Jan Welt.

Western   **(PR:C   MPAA:NR)**

BEYOND THE LAW**   (1968) 110m Grove Press/Evergreen bw

Rip Torn (*Popcorn*), George Plimpton (*Mayor*), Norman Mailer (*Lt. Francis Xavier Pope*), Mickey Knox (*Mickey Berk*), Buzz Farbar (*Rocco Gibraltar*), Beverly Bentley (*Mary Pope*), Mary Lynn (*Ilse Fuchs*), Marcia Mason (*Marcia Stillwell*), John Maloon (*John Francis*), Mary Wilson Price (*Judy Grundy*), Peter Rosoff (*Subway Arrestee*), Noel Parmental (*Asst. District Attorney*), Edward Bonnetti (*Wife Killer*), Jack Richardson (*Jack Scott*), Michael McClure (*Grahr*), Harold Conrad (*Perry Fuchs*).

Mailer wrote the story, directed the actors, and played a part himself in this almost totally improvised movie about one night in a fictitious Manhattan precinct house. He's ripped off DETECTIVE STORY in the locale and even some of the ambience. The TV series "Barney Miller" may have been inspired by this movie. Mailer is the Irish captain who oversees the precinct zoo. Torn and playwright McClure are two Hell's Angels, Richardson is a gambler, and Beverly Bentley does well as Mailer's wife. But the outstanding surprise is Plimpton doing a parody of former mayor John V. Lindsay. Plimpton is so funny (and we're still not sure if this was deliberate or not) that one wonders why Alan Alda had to be hired to play Plimpton in PAPER TIGER. This was Mailer's second film, the first being WILD 90 which went directly into the john from the cutting room. BEYOND THE LAW is another thing entirely. Despite being improvised, it *feels* scripted and the actors act as though there was a method to their work, rather than The Method! Co-producer Farbar impresses as Rocco and should have followed a path as an actor.

p, Norman Mailer, Buzz Farbar; d, Mailer; w, improvised by actors (based on story by Mailer); ph, D. A. Pennebaker, Nicholas Proferes, Jan Welt; m, Frank Conroy; ed, Welt, Mailer, Lana Jokel.

Crime   **(PR:C   MPAA:NR)**

BEYOND THE LIMIT* 1/2

(1983) 102m PAR c (GB: HONORARY CONSUL, THE)

Michael Caine (*Charlie Fortnum*), Richard Gere (*Dr. Plarr*), Bob Hoskins (*Colonel Perez*), A. Martinez (*Aquino*), Geoffrey Palmer (*Ambassador*), Elpidia Carrillo (*Clara*), Joaquim De Almeida (*Leon*), Domingo Ambriz (*Diego*), Stephanie Cotsirilos (*Marta*).

Once again, a fine, natural talent, Caine, is wasted on a film that would be better served by cutting it up and making it into guitar picks. Based on Graham Greene's 1973 *The Honorary Consul*, Christopher Hampton's screenplay has managed to take us on a trip between tedium and apathy. The story is that Dr. Plarr (Gere) helps some revolutionaries kidnap the U.S. Ambassador. While doing this, he knocks up the British Consul's wife. But the terrorists kidnap the wrong guy, see? They get Caine (The Consul) instead. Then they tell one and all that they're going to execute the poor chump if the usual political prisoners aren't released from jail. Never mind it's the wrong man, they'll do it anyhow. The plot was done in a much better way in Tanaka's HIGH AND LOW (1963) because the moral dilemma in that film concerned a child. Caine's character is drunkenly similar to Finney's in UNDER THE VOLCANO but Caine manages to underplay whereas Finney chewed up not only the sets, he was gnawing on the landscape by the time the film ended. Gere, of course, takes his clothes off a few times so his fans can see he hasn't gained any weight. He hasn't gained any ability either because his accent is as British as Toshiro Mifune's. It's a political thriller that fails to thrill. The other acting jobs are good, especially Hoskins as a South American police chief who makes the decision to end the hostage problem. He should have done it earlier—103 minutes earlier.

p, Norma Heyman; d, John MacKenzie; w, Christopher Hampton (based on the novel *The Honorary Consul* by Graham Greene); ph, Phil Meheux (Rank Color); m, Stanley Myers, Richard Harvey; ed, Stuart Baird; m/l, theme, Paul McCartney.

Spy Drama   **Cas.**   **(PR:C   MPAA:R)**

BEYOND THE LIVING   (SEE: NURSE SHERRI, 1978)

BEYOND THE PECOS**   (1945) 58m UNIV bw

Rod Cameron, Eddie Dew, Fuzzy Knight, Jennifer Holt, Gene Stutenroth (Gene Roth), Jack Ingram, Henry Wills, Jack Rockwell, Robert Homans, Frank Jacquet, Jim Thorpe, Al Ferguson, Forrest Taylor, Dan White.

Cameron and Dew battle over Holt's affections and the rights to oil lands that border both their sprawling ranches. Some good action sequences overcome a stereotyped script.

p, Oliver Drake; d, Lambert Hillyer; w, Bennett Cohen (based on a story by Jay Karth); ed, Ray Snyder, md, Paul Sawtell.

Western   **(PR:A   MPAA:NR)**

BEYOND THE POSEIDON ADVENTURE*   (1979) 122m WB c

Michael Caine *(Mike Turner)*, Sally Field *(Celeste Whitman)*, Telly Savalas *(Capt. Stefan Svevo)*, Peter Boyle *(Frank Massetti)*, Jack Warden *(Harold Meredith)*, Shirley Knight *(Hannah Meredith)*, Shirley Jones *(Gina Rowe)*, Karl Malden *(Wilbur)*, Slim Pickens *(Tex)*, Veronica Hamel *(Suzanne)*, Angela Cartwright *(Theresa Mazzetti)*, Mark Harmon *(Larry Simpson)*, Paul Picerni *(Kurt)*, Patrick Culliton *(Doyle)*, Dean Ferrandini *(Castorp)*.

Caine has this remarkable ability to survive Allen's alleged creativity. He's managed to keep his career going despite this movie and THE SWARM and that, in itself, is a tribute to his immense personal charm. Not so for Allen, who has managed to become a schlockmeister of disaster and bad taste, the epitome of shoddy moviemaking. You can always tell an Allen film, even without looking at the credits. A name cast, a terrible event, and dialog that ranges from boring to embarrassing. Gallico's same premise as luxury liner gets hit by tidal wave (odd that it hasn't affected the cruise line business at all). Caine, Malden, and Field battle Savalas for salvage rights. Biff Bam, an explosion and they're all stuck inside the boat. The whole thing is soggy cardboard. (Sequel to THE POSEIDON ADVENTURE.)

p&d, Irwin Allen; w, Nelson Gidding (based on the novel by Paul Gallico); ph, Joseph Biroc (Panavision, Technicolor); m, Jerry Fielding; ed, Bill Brame; cos, Paul Zastupnevich.

Disaster   **(PR:A-C   MPAA:PG)**

BEYOND THE PURPLE HILLS* **1/2   (1950) 69m COL bw

Gene Autry *(Himself)*, Pat Buttram *(Mike Rawley)*, Jo Dennison *(Mollie Rayburn)*, Don Beddoe *(Amos Rayburn)*, James Millican *(Rocky Morgan)*, Don Reynolds *(Chip Beaumont)*, Hugh O'Brian *(Jack Beaumont)*, Roy Gordon *(Judge Beaumont)*, Harry Harvey *(Sheriff Whiteside)*, Gregg Barton *(Ross Pardee)*, Bob Wilke *(Jim Connors)*, Ralph Peters *(Tim)*, Frank Ellis *(Corey)*, John Cliff *(Dave Miller)*, Sandy Sanders *(Doghouse)*.

Gene is a small-town sheriff who reluctantly arrests O'Brian for the murder of O'Brian's father. Now Gene and we know that Hugh is innocent, so Autry goes off in search of the real killer. After a passel of fist fights, gunshots and a few songs tossed in for good measure, Gene gets to the bottom of things and learns that Millican is the henchman and Beddoe is the dastardly designer of the dirty deed. Buttram deals the comedy and Reynolds is a young trick rider who cavorts on Champion's back. Title song was co-written by former New York News columnist Nick Kenny. (See GENE AUTRY series, Index.)

p, Armand Schaefer; d, John English; w, Norman S. Hall; ph, William Bradford; ed, Richard Fantl; m/l, Charles and Nick Nenny.

Western   **(PR:A   MPAA:NR)**

BEYOND THE REEF zero   (1981) 91m UNIV c

Dayton Ka'ne *(Tikayo)*, Maren Jensen *(Diana)*, Kathleen Swan *(Milly)*, Keahi Farden *(Jeff)*, Oliverio Maciel Diaz *(Manidu)*, George Tapare *(Hawaiian)*, David Nakuna *(Mischima)*, Robert Atamu *(Maku)*, Bob Spiegel *(Turpin)*.

Dino De Laurentiis went to the south seas, built a hotel to house his crew and cast, then shot two movies. One was HURRICANE and the other wasn't. The one that wasn't was BEYOND THE REEF. It would be easy to poke fun at such an inept picture by calling it Beyond Belief, but we must have pity for the poor lass who produced the movie, Rafaella De Laurentiis. She has to live down the name of the man who gave us such classics as THE WHITE BUFFALO and WATERLOO. (Now come on, be fair! He also produced LA STRADA, BITTER RICE and THE BIBLE.) This is Boy Meets Shark time. Ka'ne and Jensen are an item. A tiger shark named Manidu (that's the shark's name, honest!) guards a heap of sacred black pearls from outsiders. Come too close and the shark eats you. (Unless, of course, you are a show business attorney, in which case the shark allows you to pass unhurt; it's called "professional courtesy.") The kids overlook the shark's penchant for flesh, establish a relationship with the beast, and save his life so he can go out and eat some more unsuspecting surfers. Picture sounds terrible but looks pretty good. If silent movies ever come back, BEYOND THE REEF may have a chance.

p, Raffaella DiLaurentiis; d, Frank C. Clark; w, Louis LaRusso II, Jim Carabatsos (based on Clement Richer's novel *Tikoyo And His Shark*); ph, Sam Martin (Technicolor); m, Francis Lai; ed, Ian Crafford, John Jympson; ch, Coco Ellacott.

Adventure   **(PR:C   MPAA:PG)**

BEYOND THE RIO GRANDE*   (1930) 50m Biltmore bw

Jack Perrin, Franklyn Farnum, Buffalo Bill, Jr., Pete Morrison, Edmund Cobb.

Weak, padded story makes determining a plot impossible. Careless production detracts further from this light-action western whose best asset is Noble's photography. Outside of a few poorly choreographed fist fights, the cowboys merely meander from town to town.

p, F. E. Douglas; d, Harry Webb; ph, William Noble.

Western   **(PR:A   MPAA:NR)**

BEYOND THE ROCKIES***   (1932) 55m David Selznick bw

Tom Keene, Rochelle Hudson, Marie Wells, Ernie Adams, Julian Rivero, Hank Bell, Tom London, William Welsh, Ted Adams.

Mischievous do-gooders Keene, Rivero, Adams, and Hudson foil cattle rustlers when they get the goods on boss woman Wells. Finely developed script directed by Allen moves the story swiftly and smoothly.

p, Harry Joe Brown; d, Fred Allen; w, John McCarthy; ph, Ted McCord, ed, William Clemmens; art d, R. E. Tyler.

Western   **(PR:A   MPAA:NR)**

BEYOND THE SACRAMENTO***   (1941) 58m COL bw (GB: POWER OF JUSTICE)

Bill Elliott *(Wild Bill Hickok)*, Evelyn Keyes *(Lynn Perry)*, Dub Taylor *(Cannonball)*, Frank LaRue *(Jeff Adams)*, Don Beddoe *(Warden McKay)*, Bradley Page *(Cord Crowley)*, Norman Willis *(Nelson)*.

Action fast and fighting often in this western which has Elliott saving a frontier town from swindlers Page and LaRue. Keyes is just okay as the plain-jane heroine. This movie rates for its chases and swindlers. (See WILD BILL HICKOK series, Index.)

p, Leon Barsha; d, Lambert Hillyer; w, Luci Ward; ph, George Meehan; ed, James Sweeney.

Western   **(PR:A   MPAA:NR)**

BEYOND THE TIME BARRIER*   (1960) 75m AIP bw

Robert Clarke *(Maj. William Allison)*, Darlene Tompkins *(Trirene)*, Arianne Arden *(Markova)*, Vladmir Sokoloff *(The Supreme)*, Stephen Bekassy *(Karl Kruse)*, John van Dreelen *(Dr. Bourman)*, Red Morgan *(The Captain)*, Ken Knox *(Col. Martin)*, Don Flournoy *(Mutant)*, Tom Ravick *(Mutant)*, Neil Fletcher *(Air Force Chief of Staff)*, Jack Herman *(Dr. Richman)*, William Shapard *(Gen. York)*, James Altgens *(Secretary Patterson)*, John Loughney *(Gen. LaMont)*, Russell Marker *(Col. Curtis)*.

A crude and somewhat childish science fiction film about what Earth will be like in the year 2024. We've gone underground to avoid all the nuclear fallout and the usual crew of despots, nubile wenches, and evil flunkies are the foils for Robert Clarke's protagonist. Clarke was also the producer and would have done better if he'd hired another actor. Pierce's screenplay is filled with mumbo-jumbo, five-syllable words, all serving to make the story that much more unbelievable instead of lending an air of credibility. Clarke is a test pilot who crosses into the next dimension when he hits a particular speed. This done, he has to save the future. Not a bad idea for a "Twilight Zone" episode, but not enough to sustain 75 minutes.

p, Robert Clarke; d, Edgar G. Ulmer; w, Arthur G. Pierce; ph, Meredith M. Nicholson; m, Darrell Calker; ed, Jack Ruggiero; cos, Jack Masters.

Science Fiction   **(PR:C   MPAA:NR)**

BEYOND THIS PLACE   (SEE: WEB OF EVIDENCE, 1959, Brit.)

BEYOND TOMORROW**   (1940) 81m Academy Productions/RKO bw

Harry Carey *(George Melton)*, C. Aubrey Smith *(Allan Chadwick)*, Charles Winninger *(Michael O'Brien)*, Alex Melesh *(Josef Butler)*, Maria Ouspenskaya *(Madame Tanya)*, Helen Vinson *(Arlene Terry)*, Rod LaRocque *(Phil Hubert)*, Richard Carlson *(James Houston)*, Jean Parker *(Jean Lawrence)*, J. Anthony Hughes *(Officer Johnson)*, Robert Homans *(Sergeant)*, Virginia McMullen *(Radio Station Secretary)*, James Bush *(Jace Taylor)*, William Bakewell *(David Chadwick)*.

Three wealthy bachelor friends, Carey, Smith, and Winninger, feeling lonely on Christmas Eve, conspire to attract guests for dinner at their home in New York City. Carlson, an unemployed former rodeo performer from Texas, and Parker end up as the dinner guests, and also end up falling in love with each other. The benevolent trio befriends the couple, and all is jolly until the three men are killed in an airplane crash. They return as spirits and are horrified to find that Carlson, who has proven to be a talented singer, is caught up in the show business world, ignoring Parker and falling prey to stage actress Vinson. Winninger has little success in getting Carlson and Parker back together, and then Vinson's jealous ex-husband shoots Carlson. He's about to die on an operating table, but Winninger appeals to The Almighty, and Carlson survives, presumably to live happily ever-after with Parker. Ridiculous premise without the charm of such fantasies as HERE COMES MR. JORDAN, HEAVEN CAN WAIT, and ANGEL ON MY SHOULDER; poorly written, hammily acted and it's only saving grace is White's superb lensing supervised by Garmes, one of the world's greatest cinematographers. Garmes put together the independent company for this production which went out of business after offering such contrived pieces; Garmes was much more successful in his collaborative productions with Ben Hecht, creating such minor classics as CRIME WITHOUT PASSION, but then he had the benefit of a master scriptwriter.

p, Lee Garmes; d, A. Edward Sutherland; w, Adele Comandini (based on a story by Mildred Cram and Comandini); ph, Lester White; ed, Otto Ludwig, spec eff, Ned

Mann, Jack Cosgrove, Howard Anderson; m/l, "Jeannie With The Light Brown Hair," "It's Raining Dreams" Harold Spina, Charles Newman.

Fantasy **Cas.** **(PR:A MPAA:NR)**

BEYOND VICTORY** (1931) 70m Pathe-RKO bw

Bill Boyd *(Bill)*, ZaSu Pitts *(Fritzie)*, Lew Cody *(Lew)*, Marion Shilling *(Ina)*, James Gleason *(Jim)*, Lissi Arna *(Katherine)*, Theodore Von Eltz *(Maj. Sparks)*, Mary Carr *(Mother)*, Russell Gleason *(Russell)*.

Four soldiers at the front ponder their choices to enlist and leave a loving woman alone back home. Two get killed to prove national prejudices are wrong. Comic relief from Gleason and Pitts gives fair production a few memorable scenes.

p, E. D. Derr; d, John Robertson; w, Horace Jackson, James Gleason; ed, Daniel Mandell; md, Francis Gromon.

Drama **(PR:C MPAA:NR)**

BHOWANI JUNCTION** (1956) 110m MGM c

Ava Gardner *(Victoria Jones)*, Stewart Granger *(Col. Rodney Savage)*, Bill Travers *(Patrick Taylor)*, Abraham Sofaer *(Surabhai)*, Francis Matthews *(Ranjit Kasel)*, Marne Maitland *(Govindaswami)*, Peter Illing *(Ghanshyam)*, Edward Chapman *(Thomas Jones)*, Freda Jackson *(The Sadani)*, Lionel Jeffries *(Lt. Graham McDaniel)*, Alan Tilvern *(Ted Dunphy)*.

Somewhat disappointing adaptation of John Masters' novel about a young half-breed woman (Gardner) who comes back to India to find her country bubbling over with anger on the eve of the English leaving for good. Granger, jut-jawed and handsome as ever (Stewart Granger, by the way, was born Jimmy Stewart but had to change his name for obvious reasons), is in charge of some troops at Bhowani Junction. His job is to keep leftists from sabotaging the trains. Gardner is apparently in love with Travers, also a half-caste. She kills an Englishman who's trying to assault her and is taken in by the Commie Chief, Illing. After a series of adventures (crowd riots, a train wreck, etc.), Gardner, who has been having some trouble trying to decide if she's an Indian or a European, concludes that it doesn't make a bit of difference and it all ends happily ever after. A simple-minded film about a very important period in world history. After seeing this film, we know little more about India than we did before seeing it. Director Cukor is out of his element with this movie.

p, Pandro S. Berman; d, George Cukor; w, Sonya Levien, Ivan Moffat (based on the novel by John Masters); ph, F. A. Young (Eastmancolor); m, Miklos Rozsa; ed, Frank Clark, George Boemler; cos, Elizabeth Haffenden.

Historical Drama **(PR:C MPAA:NR)**

BIBLE . . . IN THE BEGINNING, THE*** (1966) 174m FOX c

Michael Parks *(Adam)*, Ulla Bergryd *(Eve)*, Richard Harris *(Cain)*, John Huston *(Noah/Narrator)*, Stephen Boyd *(Nimrod)*, George C. Scott *(Abraham)*, Ava Gardner *(Sarah)*, Peter O'Toole *(The Three Angels)*, Zoe Sallis *(Hagar)*, Gabriele Ferzetti *(Lot)*, Eleonora Rossi Drago *(Lot's Wife)*, Franco Nero, Robert Rietty, Grazia Maria Spina, Claudie Lange, Adriana Ambesi, Alberto Lucantoni, Luciano Conversi, Pupella Maggio, Peter Heinze, Angelo Boschariol, Anna Maria Orso, Eric Leutzinger, Gabriella Pallotta, Rosanna De Rocco.

They should have called this "Genesis" as it really concerns only the first book of the Bible. It's hard to screw up the Greatest Story Ever Told but they come awfully close in this overblown epic. Nevertheless, it rates attention just for the sheer audacity of such an undertaking. It's Huston's film all the way, as he directs, co-stars (as Noah) and narrates this $18 million epic. In the 1980s it would have been triple that amount. All the usual biblical stories are seen: Eve and the serpent, Cain and Abel, Noah and the Flood, the tower of Babel, Abraham starting the Arab and the Jewish segments, etc. The movie did not do as well as the producers had hoped (what movie does?) and is still in the red. Huston used the screen the way Michelangelo used the Sistine Chapel ceiling. It's a series of magnificent set pieces, all very logically scripted by Fry and a host of other often uncredited writers but failing to make the emotional impact one might expect from material so powerful. Scott was a bit young to play the patriarch Abraham and Parks never convinced us he was Adam. Ulla Bergryd, who played Eve, seemed to have dropped from sight shortly thereafter and was not seen again.

p, Dino De Laurentiis; d, John Huston; w, Christopher Fry, Jonathan Griffin, Ivo Perilli, Vittorio Bonicelli; ph, Giuseppe Rotunno (DeLuxe Color); m, Toshiro Mayuzumi; cos, Maria De Matteis; ch, Katherine Dunham.

Drama **Cas.** **(PR:AA MPAA:NR)**

BICYCLE THIEF, THE*****

(1949, Ital.) 90m Mayer-Burstyn/De Sica bw (LADRI DI BICICLETTE)

Lamberto Maggiorani *(Antonio)*, Lianella Carell *(Maria)*, Enzo Staiola *(Bruno)*, Elena Altieri *(The Lady)*, Vittorio Antonucci *(The Thief)*, Gino Saltamerenda *(Bajocco)*, Fausto Guerzoni *(Amateur Actor)*.

THE BICYCLE THIEF is a landmark film on every level. It's honest, beautiful, and deceptively simple. Reviewers praised it unanimously when it was first released for its power, some even likening it to KING LEAR. Here is an Italian neo-realistic movie without sex or tricks, just sincerity. It's the story of ordinary, forgotten people, the kind of people who never have movies made about them. Maggiorani is reasonably happily married to Carell. He uses a bicycle to get back and forth to work. One day, his bike is stolen by Antonucci. Now, this bike is no mere two-wheeler; it symbolizes his ability to earn a living, feed his family, make a life for himself. So finding it takes on a Grail-like quest. Enzo Staiola is his son and the two of them begin a hegira around Rome in search of the elusive vehicle. It all takes place on a Sunday and the bike must be found by nightfall because Maggiorani needs it for Monday. Their trials and peregrinations take them to a brothel, to the used bike mart, to a religious mission serving free lunches and around the crowded streets of Rome. By using the bike as the focal point, De Sica exposes the indifference of the authorities, the church's uncaring attitude, the general inhumanity of the residents of a big city. In desperation, Maggiorani steals a bike himself, is caught and trounced while his son watches. The boy comes of age and the picture ends. These were all non-actors at the time the film was made and De Sica elicited haunting performances from them. Dialog is as spare as a talking picture can be and the black-and-white photography, deliberately rough in spots, serves to make an audience feel they are watching a documentary. It never goes over the top and all emotions are real, rather than manufactured. Perhaps an apocryphal story concerns De Sica searching for money and being offered the needed dough by an American producer, provided that Cary Grant play the lead. De Sica, of course, was true to his dream and declined the offer. Can you imagine Grant as the poor, downtrodden Antonio? It's like Fred Astaire as Ratso Rizzo! Oscar for Best Foreign Film awarded to Zavattini.

p&d, Vittorio De Sica; w, Cesare Zavattini (based on the novel by Luigi Bartolini); ph, Carlo Montuori; m, Allesandro Cigognini; ed, Eraldo Da Roma; art d, Antonio Traverso.

Drama **(PR:A-C MPAA:NR)**

BIDDY* (1983, Brit.) 86m Sands Film Prod. c

Celia Bannerman *(Biddy)*, Patricia Napier *(Mother)*, Sam Ghazoros, Luke Duckett, Miles Parsey, David Napier *(Tom)*, Kate Elphick, Sabine Goodwin, Emily Hone *(Mathilda)*, Sally Ashby *(Susan)*, John Dalby *(Mr. Tove)*, Amelda Brown *(The Wife)*.

We've all seen Nannies in British films. Sometimes they're mad, as in Jimmy Sangster's THE NANNY (Bette Davis), sometimes they're as befuddled as Miss Prism (Margaret Rutherford) in THE IMPORTANCE OF BEING EARNEST, and sometimes they just wither away and die as in BIDDY. It's a sure bet that very few people will see this film. Made for what looks like just a few shillings, BIDDY details the years between middle-age and "we're going to have to put her away." It all takes place in the 19 century and is a sincere effort to depict the way it was. It's obviously been made with great fondness but the technical attempts are woefully inadequate. "A" for effort but "Z" for execution.

p, Richard Goodwin; d&w, Christine Edzard; ph, Alec Mills, m, Michael Sanvoisin.

Drama **(PR:A MPAA:NR)**

BIG AND THE BAD, THE**

(1971, Ital./Fr./Span.) 84m Sancrosiap-Terzafilm-Roitfeld/Atlantida c

Bud Spencer, Jack Palance, Francisco Rabal, Renato Cestie, Dany Saval, Luciano Catenacci.

Slapstick spaghetti western has Spencer pursued by gunman Palance whose sister Spencer has seduced. Witty script is well paced by Lucidi, who uses humor charmingly. Saturday afternoon delight.

p, Alfonso Sasone, Enrico Chroscicki; d, Maurizio Lucidi; w, Rafael Azcona; ph, Aldo Tonti.

Western **(PR:C MPAA:NR)**

BIG BAD MAMA zero (1974) 87m New World c

Angie Dickinson *(Wilma McClatchie)*, William Shatner *(William J. Baxter)*, Tom Skerritt *(Fred Diller)*, Susan Sennett *(Billy Jean McClatchie)*, Robbie Lee *(Polly McClatchie)*, Noble Willingham *(Barney)*, Joan Prather *(Jane Kingston)*, Royal Dano *(Rev. Johnson)*, William O'Connell *(Preacher)*, Ralph James *(Sheriff)*. Dick Miller *(Bonny)*, Tom Signorelli *(Dobbs)*, John Wheeler *(Lawyer)*, Sally Kirkland *(Barney's Woman)*, Wally Berns *(Legionnaire)*, Shannon Christie *(Stripper)*, Michael Talbott *(Sheriff's Son)*, Rob Berger *(Charlie)*, Charles Pinney *(Kingston)*, Georgia Lee *(Mrs. Kingston)*, Jay Brooks *(Wesley)*, Paul Linke *(Bank Teller)*, Mickey Fox *(Hattie)*, William F. Engle *(Fred)*.

Dickinson, whose acting ability has always been confined to her shapely legs, appears as a sort of sexy Ma Barker, circa 1932, insisting that her daughters take up kidnaping, robbery, rum-running, lesbianism, prostitution, to name a few of the activities that fascinate her. This is a vintage Roger Corman production which means sleaze in its most disgusting and unimaginative form, as banal as a tawdry peep show in the divey part of town. Angie is seldom in her clothes as she and Shatner, way out of cast and looking confused, loot the country, kill cops and citizens, fornicate with each other, and Angie's sultry daughters (Lee and Sennett) before being gunned down in the most contrived manner, accepting death so that the kids can enjoy the fruits of their robberies. The cynical script sneers at its viewers with utter contempt, a favorite ploy of artless Hollywood hacks, and the production meanly poses as authentic by virtue of old cars and ancient wardrobe. A terrible rip-off of BONNIE AND CLYDE that offers nothing but misinformation and canned sex. The Great American Music Band supplies the music.

p, Roger Corman; d, Steve Carver; w, William Norton, Frances Doel; ph, Bruce Logan (Metrocolor); m, David Grisman; ed, Tina Hirsch; art d, Peter Jamison; cos, Jac McAnelley.

Crime Drama **Cas.** **(PR:O MPAA:R)**

BIG BEAT, THE** (1958) 82m UNIV c

William Reynolds *(John Randall)*, Andra Martin *(Nikki Collins)*, Gogi Grant *(Cindy Adams)*, Jeffery Stone *(Danny Phillips)*, Rose Marie *(May Gordon)*, Hans Conried *(Vladimir Skilsky)*, Bill Goodwin *(Joseph Randall)*, Howard Miller *(himself)*, Jack Straw *(Chick)*, Phil Harvey *(Director)*, Ingrid Goude *(Secretary)*, Steve Drexel *(Piano Player)*.

Reynolds gets the chance to spice up a recording company's catalog but neglects distributing the new platters. Comedy builds and everyone ends up happy. Smooth job from editor Curtis connects Glassberg's fresh camera style.

p&d, Will Cowan; w, David P. Harmon; ph, Irving Glassberg, m, Joseph Gershenson; ed, Edward Curtiss.

Comedy   **(PR:A MPAA:NR)**

BIG BIRD CAGE, THE zero   (1972) 88m New World c

Pam Grier (*Blossom*), Anitra Ford (*Terry*), Candice Roman (*Carla*), Teda Bracci (*Bull Jones*), Carol Speed (*Mickie*), Karen McKevic (*Karen*), Sid Haig (*Django*).

Women living out prison terms plan an escape which results in the massacre of all but two participants. Technical effort is only functional with lots of T & A to cover amateur script and performances. Nudity, sex, violence, raw language, comic relief as frequent as cheers at a football game.

p, Jane Schaffer; d&w, Jack Hill; ph, Philip Sacdalan (Metrocolor); m, William Castleman, William Loose; ed, James Mitchell, Jere Huggins; art d, Ben Otico.

Crime Drama   Cas.   **(PR:O MPAA:R)**

BIG BLOCKADE, THE* 1/2   (1942, Brit.) 73m Ealing bw

Leslie Banks (*Taylor*), Michael Redgrave (*Russian*), Will Hay (*Skipper*), John Mills (*Tom*), Frank Cellier (*Schneider*), Robert Morley (*Von Geiselbrecht*), Alfred Drayton (*Direktor*),Bernard Miles (*Mate*), Marius Goring (*Propaganda Officer*), Austin Trevor (*U-boat Captain*), Michael Rennie (*George*), Morland Graham (*Dock Official*), Albert Lieven (*Gunter*), John Stuart (*Naval Officer*), Joss Ambler (*Stoltenhoff*), Michael Wilding (*Captain*), David Evans (*David*), George Woodbridge (*Quisling*), Quentin Reynolds, Frank Owen, Hon. David Bowes-Lyon, Hugh Dalton.

Good cast making up the staffs of the Ministry of Economic Warfare, Navy, and the RAF to concentrate talents on a blockade of Germany during WW II. The production values of this grinder, however, are low with flat direction.

p, Alberto Cavalcanti; d, Charles Frend; w, Charles Frend, Angus Macphail; ph, Wilkie Cooper, Douglas Slocombe.

War   **(PR:A MPAA:NR)**

BIG BLUFF, THE*   (1933) 58m Tower bw (GB: WORTHY DECEIVERS)

Reginald Denny, Claudia Dell, Jed Prouty, Cyril Chadwick, Donald Keith, Leigh Smith.

Technical disaster has Denny hired to impersonate an English lord who gained his title by marrying a social climber. Our hero turns out to be authentic in this unwieldy comedy. Basically slow-moving technical effort with a good script idea melted into nothingness.

d&w, Reginald Denny; ph, Lee Zahler; m, Byron Robinson; ed, C. S. Franklin; art d, Jason S. Brown.

Drama   **(PR:A MPAA:NR)**

BIG BLUFF, THE* 1/2   (1955) 70m UA bw

John Bromfield (*Ricardo DeVilla*), Martha Vickers (*Valerie Bancroft*), Robert Hutton (*Dr. Peter Kirk*), Rosemarie Bowe (*Fritzie Darvel*), Eve Miller (*Marsha Jordan*), Max Palmer (*Fullmer*), Eddie Bee (*Don Darvel*), Robert Bice (*Dr. Harrison*), Pierre Watkin (*Winthrop*), Beal Wong (*Art Dealer*), Rusty Wescoatt (*Frank*), Mitchel Kowal (*Coroner*), Jack Daly (*M.C.*), Paul McGuire (*Butler*), George Conrad (*Bellboy*), Kay Garrett (*Walter*).

Vickers is a widow in delicate health. She has been told to move to Los Angeles for the climate. Slick and oily Bromfield marries her for her money. Miller is Vickers' faithful secretary. She correctly suspects Bromfield of being all mustache and no substance. With the help of good guy doctor Hutton, the gigolo is exposed. An attempt at *film noir* that winds up *gris.*

p&d, W. Lee Wilder; w, Fred Freiberger (based on a story by Mildred Lord); ph, Gordon Avil; m, Manuel Compinsky; ed, T. O. Morse.

Crime Drama   **(PR:C MPAA:NR)**

BIG BONANZA, THE**   (1944) 69m REP bw

Richard Arlen (*Jed Kilton*), Robert Livingston (*Sam Ballou*), Jane Frazee (*Chiquita McSweeney*), George "Gabby" Hayes (*Hap Selby*), Lynne Roberts (*Judy Parker*), Bobby Driscoll (*Spud Kilton*), J.M. Kerrigan (*Jasper Kincaid*), Russell Simpson (*Adam Parker*), Frank Reicher (*Dr. Ballou*), Cordell Hickman (*Abraham*), Howard Soo Hoo (*Jimmy*), Roy Barcroft (*Don Pendleton*), Fred Kohler, Jr. (*Roberts*), Monte Hale (*The Singer*).

Escaped U.S. Army officer Arlen returns home to find a life of crime growing around boyhood buddy Livingston who has been romantically linked with dance hall girl Frazee. Vivid performances are given by main characters in this fast-paced photo graphic delight.

p, Eddy White; d, George Archainbaud; w, Dorrell McGowan, Stuart McGowan, Paul Gangelin (based on a story by Robert Presnell, Leonard Praskins); ph, Reggie Lanning; ed, Tony Martinelli.

Drama   **(PR:C MPAA:NR)**

BIG BOODLE, THE**   (1957) 84m UA bw (GB: NIGHT IN HAVANA)

Errol Flynn (*Ned Sherwood*), Pedro Armendariz (*Col. Mastegui*), Rossana Rory (*Fina Ferrer*), Gia Scala (*Anita Ferrer*), Sandro Giglio (*Armando Ferrer*), Jacques Aubuchon (*Miguel Collada*), Carlos Rivas (*Carlos Rubin*), Charles Todd (*Griswold*), Guillermo Alvarez Guedes (*Casino Manager*), Carlos Mas (*Chuchu*), Rogelio Hernandez (*Salcito*), Velia Martinez (*Secretary*), Aurora Pita (*Sales Girl*).

A sad film for Flynn when the great swashbuckler was close to the end of his career, gone to flab and indifference. Flynn is a Havana casino croupier who inadvertently comes into the possession of plates for counterfeit pesos. Mysterious criminals stalk him to regain the plates. This results in an overlong chase through the streets of pre-Castro Havana, a seedy black-and-white travelog of dives, dens, casinos, and

mantraps, footage that is more interesting than the story itself. Flynn is beaten to a pulp but still emerges the hero.

p, Lewis F. Blumberg; d, Richard Wilson; w, Jo Eisinger (based on the novel by Robert Sylvester); ph, Lee Garmes; m, Raul Lavista; ed, Charles L. Kimball; prod d, Henry Spitz.

Crime Drama   **(PR:C MPAA:NR)**

BIG BOSS, THE***   (1941) 70m COL bw

Otto Kruger (*Jim Maloney*), Gloria Dickson (*Sue Peters*), John Litel (*Bob Dugan*), Don Beddoe (*Cliff Randall*), Robert Fiske (*George Fellows*), George Lessey (*Sen. Williams*), Joe Conti (*Tony*).

Orphaned brothers separated as children meet as adults when they are pitted against each other on opposite sides of the political fence. Beddoe delivers an expert perform ance as the illusionless reporter. Direction paces actors well, involving the audience in the characters' struggles.

p, Wallace MacDonald; d, Charles Barton; w, Howard J. Green; ph, Benjamin Kline; ed, Viola Lawrence.

Drama   **(PR:A MPAA:NR)**

BIG BOUNCE, THE zero   (1969) 102m WB-Seven Arts c

Ryan O'Neal (*Jack Ryan*), Leigh Taylor-Young (*Nancy Barker*), Van Heflin (*Sam Mirakian*), Lee Grant (*Motel Resident*), James Daly (*Ray Richie*), Robert Webber (*Bob Rogers*), Cindy Eilbacher (*Cheryl*), Noam Pitlik (*Sam Turner*), Victor Paul (*Comacho*), Kevin O'Neal (*Boy in Buggy*), Charles Cooper (*Senator*).

Rotten sexual soap opera filled with laughable dialog and gratuitous nudity. O'Neal, in his feature-film debut, plays a tough young cucumber picker on a massive farm owned by Daley. The macho field-hand becomes embroiled in a hot romance with the sleazy teenage mistress of the plantation owner. The sex kitten, Young, gets her kicks from making love on tombstones in the local cemetery and other bizarre activities. Veteran actor Heflin plays the local justice of the peace, who also runs the motel where Grant and her young daughter live. Grant, too, is in love with the cucumber picker, but he is not interested. For this rejection, and a variety of other reasons, she commits suicide. Finally, Young ends up committing a murder while out to get some kicks, and lies through her teeth to save herself. O'Neal has had enough, packs his bags, and leaves the farm, with Young giving him the raised finger salute, which is a fitting final image to this rancid piece of trash.

p, William Dozier; d, Alex March; w, Robert Dozier (based on a novel by Elmore Leonard); ph, Howard R. Schwartz (Technicolor); m, Michael Curb; ed, William Ziegler; art d, Serge Krizman.

Drama   **(PR:O MPAA:R)**

BIG BOY**   (1930) 68m WB bw

Al Jolson (*Gus*), Claudia Dell (*Annabel Bedford*), John Harron (*Joe*), Franklin Batie (*Jim*), Lew Harvey (*Doc Wilbur*), Eddie Phillips (*Coley Reed*), Lloyd Hughes (*Jack Bedford*), Louise Closser Hale (*Mrs. Bedford*).

A very strange film that is quite outdated. Jolson does most of the movie in blackface as a stable boy who is given the chance to ride "Big Boy" in the Kentucky Derby. Gamblers, bad guys, all the usual cliches abound. Jolson sings a number of songs including an inexplicable flashback to post-Civil War days for a leaden comedy sequence with Jolson leading a choir in a host of black spirituals. At the film's conclusion, Jolson comes out in white face, tells the audience that a Jolson movie should end with a song, and he does "Tomorrow's Another Day." Why is this done? After asking a few old-timers, they said that Jolson's blackface character must have been so convincing that Warner Bros. wanted to make sure the audience knew it was Jolie under that dark makeup. Jolson, Babe Ruth, and Bill Robinson (Bojangles) are all reputed to have attended the St. Mary's Industrial Home For Boys in Baltimore. How's that for an alumni association?

d, Alan Crosland; w, William K. Wells, Perry Vekroff (based on the stage play "Big Boy" by Harold Atteridge.)

Musical Comedy   **(PR:A MPAA:NR)**

BIG BRAIN, THE**   (1933) 71m RKO bw (GB: ENEMIES OF SOCIETY)

George E. Stone (*Max Werner*), Phillip Holmes (*Terry Van Sloan*), Fay Wray (*Cynthia Glennon*), Minna Gombell (*Margy*), Lillian Bond (*Dorothy Norton*), Reginald Owen (*Lord Darlington*), Berton Churchill (*Col. Higginbotham*), Reginald Mason (*Lord Latham*), Sam Hardy (*Slick Ryan*), Randall Stake (*Scoop*), Edgar Norton (*Butler*), Charles McNaughton (*Wallack*), Lucien Littlefield (*Justice of the Peace*).

Midget barber Stone makes it to easy street as a fake stock promoter only to be discovered by Wray, who turns him over to the cops. Holmes, the protagonist of AN AMERICAN TRAGEDY (1931), is wasted in this programmer. The story appears to be based upon Peter-to-Paul swindler Charles Ponzi, who gleaned millions from suckers before his simpleton scheme was exposed in 1920.

d, George Archainbaud; w, Sy Bartlett; ph, Arthur Edeson; ed, Rose Loewinger.

Comedy   **(PR:A MPAA:NR)**

BIG BRAWL, THE** 1/2   (1980) 95m WB c

Jackie Chan (*Jerry*), Jose Ferrer (*Dominici*), Kristine De Bell (*Nancy*), Mako (*Herbert*), Ron Max (*Leggetti*), David Sheiner (*Morgan*), Rosalind Chao (*Mae*), Lenny Montana (*John*), Pat Johnson (*Carl*), Mary Ellen O'Neill (*Dominici's Mother*), H. B. Haggerty (*Kiss*), Chao-Li Chi (*Kwan*), Joycelyne Lew (*Miss Wong*).

This is definitely one of the better martial arts pictures in that it has a wonderful sense of humor about itself. There are those who claim that martial arts and comedy don't mix. The audience that wants to see Bruce Lee and his clones has no other desire than to hear bones break and windpipes crunch. Not so, if we are to believe the box office results on this Jackie Chan-starrer. Chan is a good actor as well as being a good yeller. Oddly enough, picture is situated in Chicago in the late 1930s, so it looks like a color version of an old Warner Bros. movie. Ferrer hires Chan to fight in a Big Brawl, with the winner-taking-all. Plot doesn't matter in this one, but some fine characters do. O'Neill as a Ma Barker type, De Bell as Chan's sweet thing and Montana as a menacer, are all top-notch. Even if you hate this kind of film, you might enjoy this one.

p, Fred Weintraub, Terry Morse, Jr.; d&w, Robert Clouse (based on a story by Clouse, Weintraub); ph, Robert Jessup (Panavision, Technicolor); m, Lalo Schifrin; ed, George Greenville; art d, Joe Altadonna.

Martial Arts **Cas.** **(PR:C MPAA:R)**

BIG BROADCAST, THE** (1932) 80m PAR bw

Bing Crosby *(Bing Hornsby)*, Stu Erwin *(Leslie McWhinney)*, Leila Hyams *(Anita Rogers)*, Sharon Lynn *(Mona)*, George Burns *(George)*, Gracie Allen *(Gracie)*, George Barbier *(Clapsaddle)*, Ralph Robertson *(Announcer)*, Alex Melish *(Bird and Animal Man)*, Spec O'Donnell *(Office Boy)*, Anna Chandler *(Mrs. Cohen)*, Tom Carrigan *(Officer)*, Dewey Robinson *(Basso)*, Leonid Kinskey *(Ivan)*, Kirsten Flagsted *(Herself)*, James Craig *(Steward)*, Irving Bacon *(Prisoner)*, Edgar Norton *(Secretary to T. F. Bellows)*.

The real reason for making this film was to show the viewing public what many of their favorite radio stars looked like. It was a smash hit despite a slim story. Crosby, who was catapulted to stardom from his role in THE BIG BROADCAST, works at a radio station managed by Burns. The station is in big financial trouble and only a raft of appearances by several stars can save it. The well-known specialty acts included Cab Calloway, Kate Smith, The Vincent Lopez Orchestra, the Boswell Sisters, Arthur Tracy, and others. It was in this film that Crosby crooned what was to later become his theme song: "When The Blue of the Night Meets the Gold of the Day." Burns and Allen are very funny with George getting more and more frustrated by Gracie's dumb stenographer act. The movie lacked a driving story and seemed to be more a panoply of short sequences. It didn't make much difference to the public as the movie spawned several others in a highly successful series. Tracy was known as "The Street Singer" and enjoyed enormous popularity on radio but he never did register on film and eventually moved to England where he made a few pictures and was best remembered for his record, "Marta, Rambling Rose Of The Wildwood."

d, Frank Tuttle; w, George Marion, Jr. (based on the play "Wild Waves" by William Ford Manley); ph, George Folsey; m/l, Ralph Rainger and Leo Robin.

Musical Comedy **(PR:AA MPAA:NR)**

BIG BROADCAST OF 1936, THE 1/2** (1935) 97m PAR bw

Jack Oakie *(Spud)*, George Burns *(George)*, Gracie Allen *(Gracie)*, Fayard Nicholas *(Dash)*, Harold Nicholas *(Dot)*, Akim Tamiroff *(Boris)*, Lyda Roberti *(Countess Ysobel de Narglia)*, Wendy Barrie *(Sue)*, Henry Wadsworth *(Smiley)*, Samuel S. Hinds *(Captain)*, Benny Baker *(Herman)*, C. Henry Gordon *(Gordonio)*, Specialities by: Bing Crosby, Ethel Merman, Amos 'n' Andy, Ray Noble's band, Ina Ray Hutton's band, Mary Boland, Charlie Ruggles, Bill Robinson, Willie West and McGinty, Vienna Boys Choir, Sir Guy Standing, Gail Patrick, David Holt, Virginia Weidler.

It took three years to get to number two in the BIG BROADCAST series of films. Believe it or not, this broadcast featured *television* in 1936! Oakie manages a fly-by-night station and he doubles as the voice of "The Great Lover" (sort of a precursor to "The Continental" on 1950s TV). He is kidnaped by a man-crazy countess who is loaded with money. George and Gracie have the rights to a television device that her uncle invented (Burns and Allen fans will recall that Gracie always had an uncle who was doing *something* mad at all times) that can broadcast as well as receive, like a CB radio. The plot has 12 twists per minute, most of which are in there to give the specialty acts an opportunity to strut their stuff. The finale is right out of a Marx Brothers movie, with about as much logic to it. A very pleasant outing for all involved, with particular kudos to Willie West and McGinty for their house-breaking act that remains, to this day, a classic bit of vaudeville business. The Nicholas Brothers continued their career into the 1980s in Las Vegas and, when last seen, were still delighting audiences.

p, Benjamin Glazer; d, Norman Taurog; w, Walter DeLeon, Francis Martin, Ralph Spence; ph, Leo Tover; ch, LeRoy Prinz; m/l, Ralph Rainger, Richard Whiting, Leo Robin, Dorothy Parker, Mack Gordon, Harry Revel, Ray Noble.

Musical Comedy **(PR:AA MPAA:NR)**

BIG BROADCAST OF 1937, THE*** (1936) 100m PAR bw

Jack Benny *(Jack Carson)*, George Burns *(Mr. Platt)*, Gracie Allen *(Mrs. Platt)*, Bob Burns *(Bob Black)*, Benny Fields *(Himself)*, Frank Forest *(Frank Rossman)*, Ray Milland *(Bob Miller)*, Shirley Ross *(Gwen Holmes)*, Martha Raye *(Patsy)*, Benny Goodman and his orchestra, Leopold Stokowski and his symphony orchestra, Louis DaPron, Eleanore Whitney, Larry Adler, Virginia "Pigtails" Weidler, David Holt, Billy Lee.

Burns and Allen are back. This time they're joined by Benny and Bob Burns for comedy and a host of specialty acts, as usual. At 100 minutes, it felt a trifle long, but the comedy was quick and the music never seemed to stop. Benny runs a radio station and is in constant trouble with his sponsors. George and Gracie are the Platts, a couple who do the Platt Golf Ball program. Benny and Gracie are always running afoul of each other. Much of the action takes place in and around the radio station with a few well-chosen forays into various New York nightclubs of the era. Leon and Eddie's, Lindy's, the Paradise, the Onyx, and El Morocco are featured. Music all over the place with Goodman getting the best visual representation and Stokowski being given the best editing. The inclusion of Leopold Stokowski added a cachet to this third BIG BROADCAST that the first two didn't have. The producers must have felt strongly about the cultural aspect of classical movies as they added Kirsten Flagstad to the next film, with less integrated results. This is not quite a comedy and not quite a musical but, whatever it is, if you love Jack Benny, you'll love this film.

p, Lewis E. Gensler; d, Mitchell Leisen; w, Walter DeLeon, Francis Martin (based on a story by Barry Trivers, Arthur Kober, Erwin Gelsey); ph, Theodore Sparkuhl; ed, Stuart Heisler; m/l, Leo Robin, Ralph Rainger.

Musical Comedy **(PR:AA MPAA:NR)**

BIG BROADCAST OF 1938, THE*** (1937) 94m PAR bw

W. C. Fields *(T. Frothingill Bellows/S. B. Bellows)*, Martha Raye *(Martha Bellows)*, Dorothy Lamour *(Dorothy Wyndham)*, Shirley Ross *(Cleo Fielding)*, Russell Hicks *(Capt. Stafford)*, Dorothy Howe *(Joan Fielding)*, Lionel Pape *(Lord Droopy)*, Patricia Wilder *(Honey Chile)*, Rufe Davis *(Turnkey)*, Grace Bradley *(Grace Fielding)*, Lynne Overman *(Scoop McPhail)*, Bob Hope *(Buzz Fielding)*, Ben Blue *(Mike)*, Leif Erickson *(Bob Hayes)*.

Large departure from the first three BROADCAST pictures as Fields takes over from Burns and Allen in the comedy department. W. C. owns an ocean liner and pits it in a race against another ship at 100 per hour speeds! (The boats are supposedly able to convert electrical power from radio broadcasts and send that power to the propellers.) Most of the action takes place in the show room of the boat and this, too, is a rostrum for many old and new radio stars to do their acts. Fields is often hysterical as he takes time out to do his billiards and golf routines. Specialties by the Shep Fields orchestra, Tito Guizar, and a very bizarre outing by Kirsten Flagstad who sings "Die Walkure" for no apparent reason other than someone connected with the picture must have wanted to hear it. A young fellow from Broadway came aboard the movies in this film. He sang the song that became his trademark; "Thanks For The Memories" by Rainger and Robin. It was Leslie Townes Hope, better known as Bob, and the tune won an Oscar for best song that year.

p, Harlan Thompson; d, Mitchell Leisen; w, Walter DeLeon, Francis Martin, Ken Englund (adaptation by Howard Lindsay, Russel Crouse of a story by Frederick Hazlitt Brennan); ph, Harry Fischbeck; ed, Eda Warren, Chandler House; md, Boris Morros; art d, Hans Dreier, Ernst Fegte; cos, Edith Head; spec eff, Gordon Jennings; ch, LeRoy Prinz; anim, Leon Schlesinger; m/l Leo Robin, Ralph Rainger, Tito Guizar.

Musical Comedy **(PR:AA MPAA:NR)**

BIG BROWN EYES 1/2** (1936) 76m PAR bw

Cary Grant *(Danny Barr)*, Joan Bennett *(Eve Fallon)*, Walter Pidgeon *(Richard Morey)*, Lloyd Nolan *(Russ Cortig)*, Alan Baxter *(Cary Butler)*, Marjorie Gateson *(Mrs. Cole)*, Isabel Jewell *(Bessie Blair)*, Douglas Fowley *(Benny Bottle)*, Henry Kleinbach *(Don Butler)*, Ed Jones *(Chauffeur)*, Eddie Conrad *(Joe)*, Francis McDonald *(Malley)*, Charles Martin *(Red)*, Charlie Wilson *(Prosecuting Attorney)*, Joe Picorri *(Defense Attorney)*, Sam Flint *(Martin)*, Helen Brown *(Mother)*, Edwin Maxwell *(Editor)*, Doris Canfield *(Myrtle)*, Dolores Casey *(Cashier)*, Joseph Sawyer *(Jack Sully)*.

Bennett is a wisecracking manicurist in a hotel barbershop (was there ever a 1930s heroine who wasn't a wisecracker?) and meets anyone who is anyonea Damon Runyon cast of characters. She is in love with Grant, a city detective,who is enamored of her but somewhat wary of her glibness. Cary investigates a jewelry heist of rich Gateson and Joan is jealous of his attentions to her. She loses her manicuring job and, in a bit of convenience that only Hollywood could create, she immediately catches on as a reporter and goes out to investigate a child murder. Jewell is a witness who inadvertently informs Joan that Fowley may be involved. She writes a story to that effect and Fowley, who is in jail, fears gang reprisals for having "named" the killer (he didn't say a word but she abused the power of the press to intimate that) and so does,in fact, put the finger on Nolan. The subsequent trial is a travesty and Lloyd, who pays off everyone, is freed. Joan is fired and Cary quits the police force. Soon enough, a new story begins. It has something to do with jewel thieves and framing Nolan and a mess of other complications. Some truly dumb attempts at comedy in all the wrong places mar the overall effect of what might have been an enjoyable mystery. See if you can spot radio/TV star Jinx Falkenburg as a manicurist.

p, Walter Wanger; d, Raoul Walsh; w, Walsh, Bert Hanlon (based on a story by James Edward Grant); ph, George Clemens; ed, Robert Simpson; md, Boris Morros; art d, Alexan- der Toluboff, cos, Helen Taylor.

Mystery **(PR:A MPAA:NR)**

BIG BUS, THE** (1976) 88m PAR c

Joseph Bologna *(Dan Torrance)*, Stockard Channing *(Kitty Baxter)*, John Beck *(Shoulders O'Brien)*, Rene Auberjonois *(Father Kudos)*, Ned Beatty *(Shorty Scotty)*, Bob Dishy *(Dr. Kurtz)*, Jose Ferrer *(Ironman)*, Ruth Gordon *(Old Lady)*, Harold Gould *(Prof. Baxter)*, Larry Hagman *(Parking Lot Doctor)*, Sally Kellerman *(Sybil Crane)*, Richard Mulligan *(Claude Crane)*, Lynn Redgrave *(Camille Levy)*, Richard B. Shull *(Emery Bush)*, Stuart Margolin *(Alex)*, Howard Hesseman *(Scotty's Aide Jack)*, Mary Wilcox *(Mary Jane Beth Sue)*, Walter Brooke *(Mr. Ames)*, Vic Tayback *(Goldie)*, Murphy Dunne *(Tommy Joyce)*, Raymond Guth, Miriam Byrd-Nethery, Dennis Kort *(Farm Family)*, James Jeter *(Bus Bartender)*.

Spoof from the pens of two master spoofers (Freeman and Cohen) that doesn't get beyond the second bus stop. Freeman and Cohen wrote one of the funniest films ever in START THE REVOLUTION WITHOUT ME but come up short with this one. It must have read well in the script, but it just doesn't play. It's like AIRPLANE on the road. A huge behemoth of a nuclear-powered bus, driven by Bologna and designed by Channing and Gould, gets into all sorts of sight gags and that's it. It's almost like an Irwin Allen movie in that it has an all-star cast and a disaster. It's also almost as funny as an Irwin Allen movie, except that he thinks his pictures are serious. Solid actors all through, delivering cliche material with ho-hum direction by

Frawley (MUPPETS MOVIE). Hagman, Kellerman, Hesseman (completing the trio of people whose names end in "man") do some cute cameos and Vic Tayback is seen in one of his earlier screen jobs. Once again, a tremendous waste of money and time on a project so ill-conceived it might have come from the mind of Fred Silverman (who later did the same thing for TV except he called it "Supertrain"). The highlight of the film is Dunne's portrayal of the ultimate cocktail pianist.

p&w, Fred Freeman, Lawrence J. Cohen; d, James Frawley; ph, Harry Stradling, Jr. (Movielab Color); m, Joel Schiller; ed, Edward Warschika.

Comedy   Cas.   (PR:A MPAA:PG)

BIG BUSINESS*   (1930, Brit.) 76m Sheridan/FOX bw

Frances Day (Pamela Fenchurch), Barrie Oliver (Barrie), Virginia Vaughan (Kay), Anthony Ireland (Jimmy), Ben Welden (Fenchurch), Jimmy Godden (Oppenheimer), Billy Fry (Augustus).

Enterprising partners combine their talents and expertise to stage a cabaret, thereby saving a nightclub and the careers of an unfortunate group of musicians haplessly named Arthur Roseberry's Symphonic Syncopated Orchestra.

p&d, Oscar M. Sheridan; w, Oscar M. Sheridan, Hubert W. David

Musical   (PR:A MPAA:NR)

BIG BUSINESS*   (1934, Brit.) 53m WB/FN bw

Eve Gray (Sylvia Brent), Ernest Sefton (Mac), James Finlayson (PC), Hal Walters (Spike), Maude Zimbla (Nina).

Out-of-work double of unsuccessful businessman proves there is justice after all by pulling the firm out of the red for his pal.

p, Irving Asher; d, Cyril Gardner; w, Gardner, Claude Hulbert.

Comedy   (PR:A MPAA:NR)

BIG BUSINESS*   (1937) 61m Fox bw

Jed Prouty (John Jones), Shirley Deane (Bonnie Jones), Spring Byington (Mrs. John Jones), Russell Gleason (Herbert Thompson), Kenneth Howell (Jack Jones), Allan Lane (Ted Hewett), Florence Roberts (Granny Jones), Billy Mahan (Bobby Jones), Marjorie Weaver (Vicky), Frank Conroy (Leland Whitney), Wallis Clark (Mr. Rodney).

Pa Jones Prouty gets mixed up in an oil swindle when football star Lane leads him astray with deceitful flattery. Byington is self-possessive as Ma Jones while the direction is earmarked by a rush job. A bad gag. (See JONES FAMILY series, Index.)

d, Frank Strayer; w, Robert Ellis, Helen Logan; ph, Edward Snyder; ed, Al DeGaetano; md, Samuel Kaylin; art d, Chester Gore.

Drama   (PR:A MPAA:NR)

BIG BUSINESS GIRL*1/2   (1931) 72m WB/FN bw

Loretta Young (Claire McIntyre), Frank Albertson (John Saunders), Ricardo Cortez (Ralph Clayton), Joan Blondell (Pearl), Frank Darien (Luke Winters), Dorothy Christy (Mrs. Emery), Mickey Bennett (Joe), Bobby Gordon (Messenger Boy), Nancy Dover (Sarah Ellen), Virginia Sale (Sally Curtis), Oscar Apfel (Walter Morley).

Monotonous tale of a young married couple who have trouble maintaining their marriage due to work schedules. Albertson plays a jazz-band leader who must travel to Paris for a gig. Young is the wife he leaves behind. She decides to go to New York and get a job as an advertising copy writer. When the band leader returns from Paris he is shocked to find his wife and her boss smooching in their apartment. The boss swears he didn't know she was married, and then does everything he possibly can to spur a divorce between the two so he can move in on his employee. The tired humor and ridiculous shock device (the audience doesn't find out that the couple is actually married until the boss does) make this hard to sit through. The entirely forgettable jazz tunes don't help either.

d, William Seiler; w, Robert Lord (based on a story by Patricia Reilly, Harold N. Swanson); ph, Sol Polito; ed, Peter Frisch.

Drama   (PR:A MPAA:NR)

BIG CAGE, THE**   (1933) 71m UNIV bw

Clyde Beatty (Himself), Anita Page (Lillian Langley), Andy Devine (Scoops), Vince Barnett (Soupmeat), Raymond Hatton (Timothy O'Hara), Mickey Rooney (Jimmy), Reginald Barlow (John Whipple).

Nearly bankrupt circus owner Beatty sets out to recover from a bad season. Neuman's clever staging improves standard acting in this biography of Beatty's wild life. Great fight with the cats.

d, Kurt Neuman; w, Clyde Beatty, Edward Anthony.

Drama   (PR:A MPAA:NR)

BIG CAPER, THE*1/2   (1957) 84m UA bw

Rory Calhoun (Frank Harber), Mary Costa (Kay), James Gregory (Flood), Robert Harris (Zimmer), Roxanne Arlen (Doll), Corey Allen (Roy), Paul Picerni (Harry), Pat McVey (Sam Loxley), James Nolan (Waldo Harrington), Florenz Ames (Paulmeyer), Louise Arthur (Alice Loxley), Roscoe Ates (Keeler), Terry Kelman (Bennie), Melody Gate (Bitsy).

Rory and Costa pretend to be a young, sidewardly mobile couple who have come to this small town to make a life for themselves. In truth, they are part of a bank robbery gang led by Gregory. Costa is Gregory's girl and she and Calhoun are tossed together by Gregory's mastermind plot. That's his mistake. The two of them fall for each other and are reformed by the life they pretend to lead. Harris is excellent as a psycho pyromaniac whose job is to set fire to a warehouse and dynamite a school in order to divert attention from the robbery of the small-town bank. Allen plays a

muscular oaf with a brain like a pea. It's not unlike the sadist he did so well in REBEL WITHOUT A CAUSE. He has since become a TV director with excellent credits.

p, William Thomas, Howard Pine; d, Robert Stevens; w, Martin Berkeley (based on a novel by Lionel White); m, Albert Glasser; ed, George Gittens.

Crime Drama   (PR:C MPAA:NR)

BIG CARNIVAL, THE*1/2**
(1951) 111m PAR bw (AKA: ACE IN THE HOLE; THE HUMAN INTEREST STORY)

Kirk Douglas (Charles Tatum), Jan Sterling (Lorraine), Bob Arthur (Herbie Cook), Porter Hall (Jacob Q. Boot), Frank Cady (Mr. Federber), Richard Benedict (Leo Minosa), Ray Teal (Sheriff), Lewis Martin (McCardle), John Berks (Papa Minosa), Frances Dominguez (Mama Minosa), Gene Evans (Deputy Sheriff), Frank Jaquet (Smollett), Harry Harvey (Dr. Hilton), Bob Bumpas (Radio Announcer), Geraldine Hall (Mrs. Federber), Richard Gaines (Nagel), Paul D. Merrill, Stewart Kirk Clawson, Bob Kortman, Ralph Moody, Edith Evanson, William Fawcett, Frank Keith, Bill Sheehan, Basil Chester, Joe J. Merrill, Ken Christy, Bert Moorhouse, Martha Maryman, Larry Hogan, Lester Dorr, Iron Eyes Cody, Jack Roberts.

Unrelentingly cynical, this is a portrait of a boozy but ruthlessly ambitious newspaperman, Douglas, down on his luck and desperate to improve it at any cost, including the life of the man providing the big story. Benedict gets stuck in a mine shaft after part of it caves in on him. Remembering the sensational newspaper story of 1925 when Floyd Collins was trapped in a cave for days as rescuers attempted to free him, Douglas scurries to the mine shaft, digging his way to where Benedict is trapped, telling him help is on the way. He next convinces the digging crew not to shore up the shaft which will free the trapped man in a matter of hours, but to drill through solid rock from above to get to him, giving him days in which to build a big story. Next he telephones his old editor out East and tells him he's sitting on a scoop; he has locked up the story through Benedict's slattern wife, Sterling, who operates a greasy spoon in a nearby one-horse town, promising her money through syndication rights. The small New Mexico town begins to fill up with gawking sightseers, other newsmen angry at being denied any news sources, and hawkers of wares, from western garb to hot dogs and balloons, a circus atmosphere of the morbid and the ghoulish, not dissimilar to those drivers compelled by some strange inner quirk to slow down to gaze at accidents along the road. Douglas milks the story for all it's worth, sending out reams of copy about the trapped man, particularly daily interviews with him which only Douglas is allowed to conduct. He also carries on a torrid love affair with the wife while directing her public posture for the press. At one point Douglas insists that she go to church to pray for a husband she does not love and, in fact, was about to divorce before he got trapped looking for arrowheads. Sterling refuses, smirking: "I don't pray. Kneeling bags my nylons." There is no mercy in this film, which expands with more and more profiteers exploiting Benedict's situation. Religious fanatics move in, chanting "We're Coming, Leo," then singing out the words as if at a revival meeting. But before Douglas and the trampy wife can cash in, Benedict dies of pneumonia and the scheming couple get their comeuppance by not realizing a profit, as have others they've brought to the area, by the man's death. The film is well crafted by the brilliant writer-director Wilder, but it shows too blatantly his jaundiced view of the world, without the humor he lavished in THE APARTMENT or SOME LIKE IT HOT. True, Wilder's forte has always been to mirror human weakness, moral frailty, as in DOUBLE INDEMNITY, vanity or lust as in SUNSET BOULEVARD, but here he is merely a consummate artist presenting a technically admirable film without a sliver of compassion or a morsel of hope for the human race, leaving only a bitter vision. Douglas is superb as the rotten-to-the-core newsman and Sterling vamps it to the hilt, while Teal does his usual conniving bit as a corrupt sheriff and Hall is the typical squirmish small-town publisher. The only idealistic viewpoint is represented by young Arthur, the photographer working with Douglas, but his helplessness and final turn against his one-time hero Douglas is as weak-willed and inept as Wilder's powers of evil are overwhelming.

p&d, Billy Wilder; w, Wilder, Lesser Samuels, Walter Newman; ph, Charles B. Lang; m, Hugo Friedhofer; ed, Arthur Schmidt; art d, Hal Pereira, Earl Hedrick; set d, Sam Comer, Ray Moyer; makeup, Wally Westmore; m/l, "We're Coming, Leo" Ray Evans, Jay Livingston.

Drama   (PR:O MPAA:NR)

BIG CAT, THE*1/2   (1949) 75m EL c

Lon McCallister (Danny Turner), Peggy Ann Garner (Doris), Preston Foster (Tom Eggers), Forrest Tucker (Gil Hawks), Skip Homeier (Jim), Sara Haden (Mary), Irving Bacon (Matt Cooper), Gene Reynolds (Wid).

Phil Karlson, one of the better action directors around (PHENIX CITY STORY, WALKING TALL) doesn't get much to work with in this outdoors drama about the hunt for a cougar. One sensational fight sequence between Foster and Tucker (almost as good as the Wayne-MacLaglen bout in THE QUIET MAN and better than the fight in the first remake of THE SPOILERS) stands out but the rest of the picture leaves much to be desired. Homeier (who had dropped the name Skippy by this time) is wasted as is Reynolds, the child actor who went on to become the millionaire producer of "M*A*S*H" and other TV shows.

p, William Moss; d, Phil Karlson; w, Morton Grant, Dorothy Yost (based on a story by Grant); ph, W. Howard Greene (Technicolor); m, Paul Sawtell; ed, Harvey Manger; md, Irving Friedman; art d, Frank Durlauf; set d, Ben S. Bone.

Adventure   Cas.   (PR:C MPAA:NR)

BIG CATCH, THE*   (1968, Brit.) 55m IF bw

David Gallacher (Ewan Cameron), Ronald Sinclair (Lindsay Murray), Andrew Byatt (Anderson), Simon Orr (Ian), Murray Forbes (Graham), James Copeland (Mr. Cameron), Michael O'Halloran (Campbell Murray), Willie Joss (Willie John).

A group of Scottish children band together to save a little boy swept onto a reef by the tide. Script and director struggle for meager content.

p, Laurence Henson, Edward McConnell; d, Henson; w. Henson, Charles Gormley

Children **(PR:A MPAA:NR)**

BIG CHANCE, THE* (1933) 63m Eagle bw

John Darrow, Merna Kennedy, Natalie Moorhead, Mickey Rooney, Matthew Betz, Hank Mann, J. Carroll Naish, Eleanor True Boardman.

There's the corrupt gym groupies, life-educated father-type trainer, demure girl, rival who has been around the block a few times, and a cub who admires the boxer in this formula movie. Recording knocks out film.

d, Al Herman.

Drama **(PR:A MPAA:NR)**

BIG CHANCE, THE* (1957, Brit.) 61m RFD bw

Adrienne Corri *(Diana)*, William Russell *(Bill)*, Ian Colin *(Adam)*, Penelope Bartley *(Betty)*, Ferdy Mayne *(Alpherghis)*, John Rae *(Jarvis)*, Douglas Ives *(Stan Willett)*, Robert Raglan *(Inspector)*.

Unhappily married clerk, in love with a socialite, decides the enterprising way to whisk her away to Panama is to rob a travel agency. No racy item.

p, John Temple-Smith, Francis Edge; d&w, Peter Graham Scott (based on the novel by Pamela Barrington); ph, Walter J. Harvey.

Crime **(PR:A MPAA:NR)**

BIG CHASE, THE ** (1954) 84m Lippert bw

Glenn Langan, Adele Jergens, Lon Chaney, Jr., Jim Davis, Douglas Kennedy, Jay Lawrence, Phil Arnold, Jack Daly, Gil Perkins, Tom Walker, Jack Breed, Wheaton Chambers, Iris Menshell.

Langan, who astounded himself in THE AMAZING COLOSSAL MAN, is a new cop on the juvenile beat who refuses a promotion to a more dangerous position because his wife, Jergens, is afraid he'll be killed and her forthcoming baby be left fatherless. This ploy backfires when Langan becomes involved in a murder case and has to pursue payroll thief Chaney into Mexico via helicopter. Langan survives to see his child born and take the promotion. Not a bad action film despite the forced script, and tepid direction from the man who gave us CAT WOMEN OF THE MOON.

p, Robert L. Lippert, Jr.; d, Arthur Hilton; w, Fred Freiberger.

Crime Drama **(PR:A MPAA:NR)**

BIG CHIEF, THE 1/2** (1960, Fr.) 105m Continental bw (LE GRAND CHEF)

Fernandel *(Antione, "Black Eagle")*, Gino Cervi *(Paul, "Snake Eye")*, Papouf *(Erie, "Sly Fox")*, Jean-Jacques Delbo *(M. Jumelin)*, Noelle Norman *(Mme. Jumelin)*, Georges Chamarat *(Butler)*, Albert Michel, Dominique Davray *(Tenants)*, Mare Dekock *(Their Son)*, Florence Blot *(Governess)*, Maurice Nasil *(Detective)*, Germaine Michel *(Landlady)*, Bover *(Maurice Rivoire)*, Madeleine Barbulee *(Mme. Rivoire)*.

This is the Gallic version of William Sidney Porter's "The Ransom of Red Chief" which was done as part of O. HENRY'S FULL HOUSE in 1952. Both this and the earlier English-language picture have much to recommend them, but the Oscar Levant and Fred Allen piece was much shorter and thus takes the nod. If you haven't heard the story, it's simple: two would-be kidnapers steal a young man who comes from a wealthy family. In order to keep the boy happy while they await the ransom, both men dress as Indians—that being the lad's pleasure. But the kid is such a rotten child that the family refuses to pay ransom for him and eventually the kidnapers are forced to send the boy back with their own money in payment for the family accepting his return. It doesn't run more than a few pages and padding it out to 105 minutes was a mistake, despite Fernandel's superb clowning. O. Henry's stories all had *ideas* behind them. They also had beginnings, middles and ends, something seldom seen in many of the esoteric short stories published in the past several years. (In French; English subtitles.)

p, Ralph Baum; d, Henri Verneuil; w, Verneuil, Henri Troyat, Jean Manse (based on O. Henry's story "The Ransom Of Red Chief"); ph, Roger Huberts; m, Gerard Calvi; ed, Borys Lewin; Eng. titles, Herman G. Weinberg.

Children's Comedy **(PR:AA MPAA:NR)**

BIG CHILL, THE*** (1983) 103m COL c

Glenn Close *(Sarah)*, Tom Berenger *(Sam)*, William Hurt *(Nick)*, Jeff Goldblum *(Michael)*, Mary Kay Place *(Meg)*, Kevin Kline *(Harold)*, Meg Tilly *(Chloe)*, Don Galloway *(Richard)*, JoBeth Williams *(Karen)*, James Gillis *(Minister)*, Ken Place *(Peter)*.

THE BIG CHILL is the IBM of movies; it has absolutely everything, except heart. Kasdan, who comes out of a Detroit advertising agency, has done his first really original work here, after emulating the old Saturday morning serials in STAR WARS and RAIDERS where he also should have paid homage to the Batman TV series. BODY HEAT owed its birth to Raymond Chandler but in THE BIG CHILL, Kasdan (and co-writer Benedek) touch upon something that must have affected their lives; the death of a friend and the reunion of old pals at the funeral. We felt it was more contrivance than anything else and it might have made a better play. John Sayles handled the subject with more passion in THE RETURN OF THE SECAUCUS SEVEN, but he didn't have a major studio and major financing to help him, so he just had to be satisfied with content. All of the characters have a problem and the little touches are better than the grand plan in THE BIG CHILL. It's talk, talk, talk, which skirts issues instead of confronting them. Very good acting on everyone's part and Kasdan does not make the mistake that so many new directors make; an exercise in self-indulgence allowing the camera to be the star. To his credit, Kasdan is as unobtrusive a director as Lubitsch was. He stands aside and lets the actors act. One kept wishing for more fireworks, but THE BIG CHILL is as shallow as a soap dish in its conception. The people in the picture are the wild-eyed radicals of the 1960s who sold out in the 1970s and have not accepted their positions in the 1980s. Kasdan is capable of far better work and might eventually take his place with the top director/writers as soon as he goes a little deeper inside himself.

p, Michael Shamberg; d, Lawrence Kasdan; w, Kasdan, Barbara Benedek; ph, John Bailey (Metrocolor); ed, Carol Littleton; prod d, Ida Random; set d, George Gaines.

Drama **Cas.** **(PR:C MPAA:R)**

BIG CIRCUS, THE 1/2** (1959) 108m AA c

Victor Mature *(Hank Twirling)*, Red Buttons *(Randy Sherman)*, Rhonda Fleming *(Helen Harrison)*, Kathryn Grant *(Jeannie Weirling)*, Vincent Price *(Hans Hagenfeld)*, Gilbert Roland *(Aerialist)*, Peter Lorre *(Skeeter)*, David Nelson *(Tommy Gordon)*, Adele Mara *(Mama Colino)*, Howard McNear *(Mr. Lomax)*, Charles Watts *(Jonathan Nelson)*, Steve Allen *(Guest Star)*, and the world's greatest circus acts.

A rare film from Allen in that it doesn't have the huge star cast nor the single, great disaster. But Irwin was much younger when this film was made and hadn't perfected his cliches yet. It's a beautifully shot movie about a circus on the brink of failure. Mature is the boss, Price is his ringmaster, Lorre is a top clown. There's the usual fire, escaped beast, heavy financial woes, etc., all serving to put the circus into deeper trouble. Buttons is a cold banker who has been called upon to examine the workings of the circus before a loan can be granted. In the end, Red is called upon to be a clown and an aerialist. Fleming is a publicity woman and doesn't get too much to do in the film except look red-headed and attractive. Many famous circus acts are featured and almost steal the thunder from the cast. The Human Cannonball (Zacchini), Berg's Seals, Carr's Chimps, Dick Walker's lions, and so on. Roland is excellent as an aerialist who walks Niagara Falls on a wire in order to publicize the circus. Actual crossing was done by Gene Mendez. Nice song by Fain and Webster that wasn't the hit everyone expected. After THE GREATEST SHOW ON EARTH there were very few films that captured the spirit of a circus and did not flag under predictable stories. Happy to say, this is one of the Big Top films that has merit.

p, Irwin Allen; d, Joseph Newman; w, Allen, Charles Bennett, Irving Wallace (based on a story by Allen); ph, Winton Hoch (Technicolor); m, Paul Sawtell, Bert Shefter; ed, Adrienne Fazan; cos, Paul Zastupnevich; ch, Barbette; m/l, Sammy Fain, Paul Francis Webster.

Adventure **(PR:A MPAA:NR)**

BIG CITY 1/2** (1937) 80m MGM bw

Spencer Tracy *(Joe Benton)*, Luise Rainer *(Anna Benton)*, Charley Grapewin *(The Mayor)*, Janet Beecher *(Sophie Sloane)*, Eddie Quillan *(Mike Edwards)*, Victor Varconi *(Paul Roya)*, Oscar O'Shea *(John C. Andrews)*, Helen Troy *(Lola Johnson)*, William Demarest *(Beecher)*, John Arledge *(Buddy)*, Irving Bacon *(Jim Sloane)*, Guinn Williams *(Danny Devlin)*, Regis Toomey *(Fred Hawkins)*, Edgar Dearing *(Tom Reilly)*, Paul Harvey *(District Attorney Gilbert)*, Andrew J. Tombes *(Insp. Matthews)*, Clem Bevans *(Grandpa Sloane)*, Grace Ford *(Mary Reilly)*, Alice White *(Peggy Devlin)*, Jack Dempsey, James J. Jeffries, Jimmy McLarnin, Maxie Rosenbloom, Jim Thorpe, Frank Wykoff, Jackie Fields, Man Mountain Dean, Gus Sonnenberg, George Godfrey, Joe Rivers, Cotton Warburton, Bull Montana, Snowy Baker, Taski Hagio.

In this war-of-the-taxicabs film, unions and union organizers come off as distasteful, this in an era when the union was battling for its very existence. Tracy and his immigrant Russian wife Rainer are caught up in the turmoil; he is an independent driver refusing to join any organization, she his loyal supporter. The screen is filled with brawls and taxis smashing into each other like battering rams. When a taxi garage is bombed, Rainer is inexplicably blamed for the crime, involving the deaths of several drivers. The district attorney has no evidence but, despite Tracy's vociferous objections, manages to have her deported. Before her ship sails, in one of the most ludicrous scenes on record, the frantic husband bursts into Jack Dempsey's Broadway Restaurant where the mayor and other bigwigs are dining and pleads for his wife's return. Mayor Grapewin decides on the spot that Tracy has enough evidence to prove his wife innocent and, contrary to federal laws in force at the time, overrules higher authorities and stipulates Rainer can stay in America. Next comes the mad dash for the departing boat, Tracy, the mayor, and others racing for the pier in taxicabs, while opposing drivers try to wreck their cars. They reach the ship just in the nick of time, pluck Rainer from her cabin and put her in an ambulance where she delivers a baby (!) while Tracy battles the opposition union leader to a pulpy victory; he then goes off with his new family to enjoy the fruits of American freedom. Hokey and contrived, this Borzage saga would have been nothing more than mediocre fare had it not been for the considerable talents of Tracy and Rainer and the able direction of Borzage, who zipped up the pace and delivered all the action he could create in lieu of an intelligent script.

p, Norman Krasna; d, Frank Borzage; w, Dore Schary, Hugo Butler (based on a story by Krasna); ph, Joseph Ruttenberg; m, William Axt; ed, Frederick Y. Smith; art d, Cedric Gibbons.

Drama **(PR:A MPAA:NR)**

BIG CITY 1/2** (1948) 103m MGM bw

Margaret O'Brien *(Midge)*, Robert Preston *(Rev. Andrews)*, Danny Thomas *(Cantor Feldman)*, George Murphy *(Patrick O'Donnell)*, Karin Booth *(Florence Bartlett)*, Edward Arnold *(Judge Abercrombie)*, Butch Jenkins *(Lewis Keller)*, Betty Garrett *("Shoo-Shoo" Grady)*, Lotte Lehmann *("Mamma" Feldman)*, Connie Gilchrist *(Martha)*, Page Cavanaugh Trio.

Musical THREE GODFATHERS tale starring O'Brien as a lonely waif who is adopted by three young men of different faiths. Thomas is a Jewish cantor, Murphy is an Irish cop, and Preston is a Protestant minister. Everything goes well until

Murphy decides to get married and wants O'Brien to be part of his family. There is bad blood between the friends until kindly Judge Arnold and little tyke O'Brien work out a solution acceptable to all. Good production values, charming musical numbers, and standout performances by the principals keep this somewhat hokey material from being too maudlin.

p, Joe Pasternak; d, Norman Taurog; w, Whitfield Cook, Anne Morrison Chaplin, Aben Kandel (based on a story by Miklos Laszlo, adapted by Nanette Kutner); ph, Robert Surtees; m, George Stoll; ed, Gene Ruggiero; m/l, Irving Berlin, Fred Spieian, Janice Torre, Jimmy McHugh, Inez James, Sidney Miller, Walter Popp, Jerry Seelen.

Musical **(PR:AA MPAA:NR)**

BIG CITY, THE** (1963, India) 131m Bansal bw (MAHANAGAR)

Madhabi Mukherjee *(Aratee)*, Anil Chatterjee *(Subrata)*, Haren Chatterjee *(Father)*, Haradhan Banerjee *(Mukherjee)*, Vicky Redwood *(Edith Simmons)*, Jaya Bhaduri *(Sister)*.

Bank official in Calcutta insists that his wife work to make ends meet. When his bank fails, the wife must support the entire family, which leads to conflict. Interesting portrait of family life in India where a feminist is as rare as a quagga.

p, R.D. Bansal; d&w, Satyajit Ray (based on the novel by Narendra Nath Mitra); ph, Subrata Mitra; m, Ray; ed Dulal Dutta.

Drama **(PR:A MPAA:NR)**

BIG CITY BLUES*** (1932) 65m WB bw

Joan Blondell *(Vida)*, Eric Linden *(Bud Reeves)*, Inez Courtney *(Faun)*, Evalyn Knapp *(Jo-Jo)*, Guy Kibbee *(Hummel)*, Lyle Talbot *(Sully)*, Gloria Shea *(Agnes)*, Walter Catlett *(Gibbony)*, Jobyna Howland *(Serena)*, Humphrey Bogart *(Adkins)*, Josephine Dunn *(Jackie)*, Grant Mitchell *(Station Agent)*, Thomas Jackson *(Quelkin)*, Ned Sparks *(Stackhouse)*, Sheila Terry *(Lorna)*, Tom Dugan *(Red)*, Betty Gillette *(Mabel)*, Edward McWade *(Baggage Master)*, J. Carrol Naish *(Bootlegger)*, Voice of Dick Powell *(Radio Announcer)*, Clarence Muse *(Nightclub Singer)*, Dennis O'Keefe *(Dice Spectator)*, Herman Bing, Torben Meyer *(Waiters)*, Selmer Jackson *(Joe)*.

Linden is visting Manhattan from a small town in Indiana. He meets his cousin Catlett and ends up with unexpected troubles. Catlett throws a party at Linden's hotel room and a young girl is killed by a bottle someone throws. Everyone flees, including Linden, along with his new-found girl friend Blondell. Of course Linden is the leading suspect, but his name is cleared when the real killer is found hanging in a closet after committing suicide. Linden returns to Indiana, but makes enough money to come back and marry Blondell. Some good direction. The script contains gags that are stale but there's some nice use of dissolves and atmospheric shots. The innocent country boy swept up in the big city was a popular theme for Warner Bros. films at the time. Watch for Bogart in one of his first film appearances.

p, Mervyn LeRoy; w, Ward Morehouse, Lillie Hayward (based on the play by Morehouse); ph, James Van Trees; m, Ray Heindorf, Bernhard Kaun; ed, Ray Curtis; md, Leo F. Forbstein; art d, Anton Grot.

Drama **(PR:C MPAA:NR)**

BIG CLOCK, THE**** (1948) 95m PAR bw

Ray Milland *(George Stroud)*, Charles Laughton *(Earl Janoth)*, Maureen O'Sullivan *(Georgette Stroud)*, George Macready *(Steven Hagen)*, Rita Johnson *(Pauline York)*, Elsa Lanchester *(Louise Patterson)*, Harold Vermilyea *(Don Klausmeyer)*, Dan Tobin *(Ray Cordette)*, Henry Morgan *(Bill Womack)*, Richard Webb *(Nat Sperling)*, Tad Van Brunt *(Tony Watson)*, Elaine Riley *(Lily Gold)*, Luis Van Rooten *(Edwin Orlin)*, Lloyd Corrigan *(McKinley)*, Margaret Field *(Secretary)*, Philip Van Zandt *(Sidney Kislav)*, Henri Letondal *(Antique Dealer)*, Douglas Spencer *(Bert Finch)*, Frank Orth *(Burt, the Bartender)*, Bobby Watson *(Milton Spaulding)*, Frances Morris *(Grace Adams)*, B.G. Norman *(George, Jr.)*, Theresa Harris *(Daisy)*, James Burke *(Building Cop)*, Erno Verebes *(Bartender)*, Noel Neill *(Elevator Operator)*, Earle Hodgins *(Guide)*, Edna Holland *(Staff Member)*, Lane Chandler *(Doorman)*, Lester Dorr *(Cabby)*, Bert Moorehouse *(Editor)*, Bess Flowers *(Stylist in Conference Room)*, Napoleon Whiting *(Bootblack)*, Diane Stewart *(Girl)*, Eric Alden, Ralph Dunn, Harry Anderson *(Guards)*.

Top-notch *film noir* production fraught with suspense, twisting its unique plot and characters to a clever and frightening conclusion. Milland is the shrewd editor of *Crimeways Magazine* which is published by Laughton, a megalomaniacal media tycoon who lords it over his myriad employees in his own skyscraper, treating one and all as peons. A stickler for time (time is money), Laughton prides himself on the clock mechanism in the tower which controls the clocks throughout his building and is never off a second. Milland, who has been working for years like a dog to build *Crimeways* into Laughton's leading magazine, is finally taking a vacation with his long-suffering wife, O'Sullivan, but Laughton demands he perform some duties, so he misses his train to West Virginia. O'Sullivan leaves without him and he stays behind, depressed, hitting the sophisticated Manhattan bars where he meets Johnson who, unknown to Milland, happens to be Laughton's mistreated mistress. In an expansive and boozy moment, Milland buys a heavy piece of bric-a-brac for Johnson and then purchases a picture by eccentric saloon artist Lanchester. That night Johnson goes home with Milland who leaves just as Laughton arrives at Johnson's apartment. Laughton does not recognize Milland but the editor certainly sees his boss. The jealous publisher demands that Johnson tell him who she was out with and the two get into a raging argument. At one point Johnson calls Laughton every name she can think of and he retaliates by crushing her skull with Milland's present. He is seen leaving by Milland. Milland later departs, going to see his wife the next day. When the murder is discovered Laughton goes to his second-in-command, opportunistic, calculating Macready (was he ever anything else?), admitting his crime and begging him to help him cover it up. Macready knows that without Laughton his career is doomed so he calls Milland who is at a cabin with his wife, explaining the situation and that they know Johnson was with a man celebrating in bars before she was murdered. Clearly Laughton and Macready intend to pin the blame for the killing on the other man, in this case Milland. The editor realizes he must prevent himself from being framed so he agrees to return to NYC to head the *Crimeways* manhunt for the unknown man. Using his "clueboard" and the host of editorial investigators he has specially trained, Milland conducts a crazy search for himself, sending his people off on wild goose chases while he tries to establish his own innocence. Several witnesses who saw Milland with Johnson are rounded up and Milland busies himself by hiding from them in the office building, frantically trying to find the cab driver who had driven Laughton to Johnson's apartment, a man paid by Laughton to leave town. O'Sullivan returns and Milland fends off his own investigators. He is almost exposed several times. Then Lanchester is found and brought to the offices, promised a reward if she will draw a sketch of the man who was with Johnson and bought the painting on the murder night. She recognizes Milland but does not give him away. She sketches a picture of the killer then shows it to Laughton in a hilarious moment. Her work is so abstract that it could represent King Tut or the Empire State Building. By now Laughton and Macready are on to Milland, who is pinpointed by one of their witnesses. He takes refuge in the tower which houses the massive mechanism that runs the clocks. Morgan, Laughton's bodyguard, finds Milland and the two struggle, Milland knocking out Morgan and making his way to Laughton's office where he accuses him of the murder. Laughton immediately demands that Macready take the fall for him, that he will get him out of prison. When Macready refuses, Laughton shoots him and runs for an elevator. He forces the doors open and backs into the shaft, about to shoot Milland. Laughton falls the long way down the shaft screaming, much the same way, with an upward zoom of the camera, that Hitchcock showed his villain falling from the top of the Statue of Liberty in SABOTEUR. Milland is reunited with O'Sullivan for a happy if exhausted ending. Farrow's direction is superb as he keeps the story moving and introduces fast cuts from one threatening character to the next, aided greatly by Latimer's taut scripting which offers a great deal of black humor to relieve tension in this dark, edge-of-the seat classic.

p, Richard Maibaum; d, John Farrow; w, Jonathan Latimer (based on the novel by Kenneth Fearing); ph, John Seitz; m, Victor Young; ed, Gene Ruggiero; art d, Hans Dreier, Roland Anderson, Albert Nozaki; set d, Sam Comer, Ross Dowd; cos, Edith Head; spec eff, Gordon Jennings; m/l, title song, by Jay Livingston, Ray Evans.

Crime Drama **(PR:C MPAA:NR)**

BIG COMBO, THE** (1955) 86m Security-Theodora/AA bw

Cornel Wilde *(Diamond)*, Richard Conte *(Brown)*, Brian Donlevy *(McClure)*, Jean Wallace *(Susan)*, Robert Middleton *(Peterson)*, Lee Van Cleef *(Fante)*, Earl Holliman *(Mingo)*, Helen Walker *(Alicia)*, Jay Adler *(Sam Hill)*, John Hoyt *(Dreyer)*, Ted De Corsia *(Bettini)*, Helene Stanton *(Rita)*, Roy Gordon *(Audubon)*, Whit Bissell *(Doctor)*, Philip Van Zandt *(Mr. Jones)*, Steve Mitchell, Baynes Barron, Rita Gould, Tony Michaels, Bruce Sharpe, Michael Mark, Donna Drew.

THE BIG COMBO is a mean-spirited melodrama that was a preview of sadism to come in movies. Some stomach-wrenching scenes that offended eyes then (the censor had some whacks at it) and still manage to induce frowns. Wilde is an honest cop who is manhandled by Conte and his thugs, Donlevy, Holliman, and Van Cleef. Wilde also has a yen for cool blonde Wallace (Mrs. Wilde in real life, at that time) who is Conte's girl friend. Conte's wife, Walker, is not thrilled that he has another lady and eventually spills the beans on his operation, thus giving Wilde the necessary ammo for his investigation. This is an often confused script with lots of holes in the logic. The torture scenes are gratuitous and Wilde's performance is a cut below ordinary. Lewis's tough direction and the fine secondary performances by Adler, Hoyt, De Corsia (who was to score so well in Kubrick's THE KILLING), and Middleton save the film.

p, Sidney Harmon; d, Joseph Lewis; w, Phillip Yordan; ph, John Alton; m, David Raksin; ed, Robert Eisen; cos, Don Loper.

Crime **Cas.** **(PR:O MPAA:NR)**

BIG COUNTRY, THE* 1/2** (1958) 166m UA c

Gregory Peck *(James McKay)*, Jean Simmons *(Julie Maragon)*, Carroll Baker *(Patricia Terrill)*, Charlton Heston *(Steve Leech)*, Burl Ives *(Rufus Hannassey)*, Charles Bickford *(Maj. Henry Terrill)*, Alfonso Bedoya *(Ramon)*, Chuck Connors *(Buck* Hannassey), Chuck Hayward *(Rafe)*, Buff Brady *(Dude)*, Jim Burk *(Cracker)*, Dorothy Adams *(Hannassey Woman)*, Terrill Cowboys: Chuck Roberson, Bob Morgan, John McKee, Jay Slim Talbot.

Huge, sprawling western with just about everything; brilliant photography, superb music, an intelligent script, and excellent performances, including one from Heston that is one of the best of his wooden career. Wyler was so taken by Heston that he starred him in his next film BEN HUR and Heston walked away with an Oscar. THE BIG COUNTRY didn't do as well in the Academy Awards as many thought. Ives took the Oscar for Best Supporting Actor and Moross secured a nomination. Story is that Peck, an ex-captain on a ship, has come West to marry Baker and live on the ranch of her father (Bickford). He meets and instantly dislikes Heston, who is the foreman of the ranch. Bickford and Ives are feuding, and have been forever. The hatred even extends to Baker. Seeing this side of her, Peck and she move away from each other and he soon falls for Simmons, local schoolmarm, who owns the only water for miles around. Simmons has resisted being bought out by both sides and is eventually kidnaped by the Ives bunch. Peck trails them, meets and gains the respect of Ives, who then has a face-to-face confrontation with Bickford. The two old coots shoot and kill each other. Peck and Simmons move to her ranch, Heston and Baker take over the big spread. If you like westerns you'll love THE BIG COUNTRY. If you hate westerns, you'll still enjoy this picture because the story could have taken place in a board room, at sea, or anywhere else strong personalities clash. It's too long, true, and could easily lose 20 minutes. Sharper editing was needed and some more attention paid to a few of the supporting roles; Connors overdoes it as Ives' lout son, Rafe, who attempts to rape Jean.

p&d, William Wyler; w, James R. Webb, Sy Bartlett, Robert Wyler (based on an adaptation by Jessamyn West, R. Wyler of the novel by Donald Hamilton); ph, Franz F. Planer (Technirama, Technicolor); m, Jerome Moross; ed, Robert Belcher, John Faure; cos, Emile Santiago, Yvonne Wood.

Western **(PR:A MPAA:NR)**

BIG CUBE, THE** (1969) 91m WB c

Lana Turner *(Adriana Roman)*, George Chakiris *(Johnny Allen)*, Richard Egan *(Frederick Lansdale)*, Dan O'Herlihy *(Charles Winthrop)*, Karin Mossberg *(Lisa Winthrop)*, Pamela Rogers *(Bibi)*, Carlos East *(Lalo)*, Augusto Benedico *(Dr. Lorenz)*, Victor Junco *(Delacroix)*, Norma Herrera *(Stella)*, Pedro Galvan *(University Dean)*, Regina Thorne *(Queen Bee)*, The Finks *(Themselves)*.

Jealous stepdaughter Mossberg conspires with psychedelic drug dealer Chakiris to drive newlywed stepmother Turner mad because she is withholding the girl's inheritance. Mossberg is a hippie, attracted to medical student Chakiris who is selling LSD sugar cubes to beach bums, resulting in an OD death. Pop knows all this so he refuses to give his permission for her to marry the loser, who is really just after her money. When Dad dies, the pair give Turner acid in hopes of securing the family fortune, and nearly commit murder. Daughter Mossberg begins to see the light and turns to a friend of the family, Egan, for help in bringing Turner back to sanity. Cast-out Chakiris ends up on skid row with an overdose of his own medicine. Disconnected montage from director Davidson is annoying in a fair entertainment vehicle.

p, Lindsley Parsons; d, Tito Davidson; w, William Douglas Lansford (based on a story by Davidson and Edmundo Baez); ph, Gabriel Figueroa; m, Val Johns; ed, Carlos Savage, Jr.; spec eff, Charlatan Prods.

Drama **(PR:O MPAA:M)**

BIG DADDY* (1969) 68m Syzygy/United c (AKA: PARADISE ROAD)

Victor Buono *(A. Lincoln Beauregard)*, Joan Blondell, Chill Wills, Tisha Sterling, Reed Sherman, Billy Benedict, John Hale, Virginia Sale, Tanya Lemani, Ned Romero, Don McArt, Kelton Garwood, Wendy Wickstrom, Carol Schmidt, Rhonda Scott, Lennie Geer, Louis Hart, William Foster, Hank Worden, Arline Hunter.

Low-budget effort set in the Florida Everglades where Buono defends his moronic swamp girl lover from Sherman. Not surprisingly, the story line is weak and serves only as a frame for two subplots involving voodoo rites and man-eating alligators. Presented by M.A. Ripps, king of the Southern drive-in trash movies. Buono, Blondell, and Wills should erase this from their resumes.

p,d&w, Carl K. Hittleman; ph, Morrison B. Paul; m, Alan Hyams; ed, Carlo Lodato, Margaret Royce; art d, Rudi Feld; set d, Fred Price.

Adventure/Drama **(PR:O MPAA:NR)**

BIG DAY, THE** (1960, Brit.) 62m Independent Artists/Bryanston bw

Donald Pleasence *(Victor Partridge)*, Andree Melly *(Nina Wentworth)*, Colin Gordon *(George Baker)*, Harry H. Corbett *(Jackson)*, William Franklyn *(Selkirk)*, Susan Shaw *(Phyllis Selkirk)*, Molly Urquhart *(Mrs. Deeping)*, Betty Marsden *(Mabel Jackson)*.

A businessman is in job competition with his manager's brother-in-law and a crack salesman. His marriage is in trouble and he's got a mistress to further complicate things. Another cheaply made quickie.

p, Arthur Alcott; d, Peter Graham Scott; w, Bill MacIlwraith.

Drama **(PR:A MPAA:NR)**

BIG DEAL ON MADONNA STREET, THE*½** (1960) 91m Lux/United Motion Picture Organization

Vittorio Gassman *(Peppe)*, Renato Salvatori *(Mario)*, Rossana Rory *(Norma)*, Carla Gravina *(Nicoletta)*, Claudia Cardinale *(Carmelina)*, Carlo Pisacane *(Capannelle)*, Tiberio Murgia *(Ferribotte)*, Memmo Carotenuto *(Cosimo)*, Marcello Mastroianni *(Tiberio)*, Toto *(Dante)*.

Very funny spoof of RIFIFI has Gassman, a fine dramatic actor and superb clown when needed, leading a group of incompetent burglars attempting to loot a jewelry store on Madonna Street. Gassman works out an elaborate route into the store via the adjoining apartment, but he falls in love with the occupant and this causes innumerable delays. Mastroianni, another hard-pressed inept thief, cannot go to the burglary as planned because his wife is working and he must perform baby-sitting chores. Pisacarne cannot concentrate on the plan because he is constantly eating and the expert boxman Toto, who explains in detail how to blow a safe, vanishes competely at the time of break-in. The burglary is a disaster as the elaborate apparatus the crooks design shatters walls, smashes pipes, and unleashes a flood. They exhaust themselves in getting into the store when it is obvious that they could as easily have broken the front door lock. It's such a mess that the tool-dropping thieves give up and go home to look for honest employment. The entire procedure is hilarious, thanks to the fine acting, a consistently humorous script, and sharp direction. (Remade as CRACKERS.)

p, Franco Cristaldi; d, Mario Monicelli; w, Suso Cecchi D'Amico, Argo Scarpelli, Monicelli.

Comedy **(PR:A MPAA:NR)**

BIG DOLL HOUSE, THE* (1971) 93m New World c

Judy Brown *(Collier)*, Roberta Collins *(Alcott)*, Pam Grier *(Grear)*, Brooke Mills *(Harrad)*, Pat Woodell *(Bodine)*, Sid Haig *(Harry)*, Christiane Schmidtmer *(Miss Dietrich)*, Kathryn Loder *(Lucian)*, Jerry Franks *(Fred)*, Jack Davis *(Dr. Phillips)*, Gina Stuart *(Ferina)*, Letty Mirasol *(Leyte)*, Shirley De Las Alas *(Guard)*.

Female exploitation film has Brown, Grier, and others in a prison where guards and warden treat them as dirt, exercising a great deal of sadism while the prisoners scheme to escape. The script, direction, and acting offer no escape to the viewer in the kind of film that supposedly spoofs itself but in reality is just inept and amateurish.

p, Jane Schaffer; d, Jack Hill; w, Don Spencer; ph, Freddie Conde (DeLuxe Color); m, Hall Daniels; prod d, Ben Otico.

Crime **(PR:O MPAA:R)**

BIG EXECUTIVE** (1933) 70m PAR bw

Ricardo Cortez *(Victor Conway)*, Richard Bennett *(Commodore Richardson)*, Elizabeth Young *(Helena Grant)*, Sharon Lynn *(Miss Healy)*, Dorothy Peterson *(Mrs. Conway)*, Barton MacLane *(Harry the Guide)*, Charles Middleton *(Sheriff)*, Pop Kenton *(Coroner)*, Maude Eburne *(Coroner's Wife)*.

Success after failure after success, executive Cortez is driven into hock by competitor Bennett, the grandfather of his sweetheart Young. Overstated set design takes attention away from all but Bennett's good performance.

d, Erle C. Kenton; w, Laurence Stallings; ph, Harry Fischbeck.

Drama **(PR:A MPAA:NR)**

BIG FELLA** (1937, Brit.) 73m Lion-Beaconsfield bw

Paul Robeson *(Joe)*, Elizabeth Welch *(Miranda)*, Roy Emerton *(Spike)*, James Hayter *(Chuck)*, Lawrence Brown *(Corney)*, Eldon Grant *(Roy Oliphant)*, Marcelle Rogez *(Marietta)*, Eric Cowley *(Mr. Oliphant)*, Joyce Kennedy *(Mrs. Oliphant)*.

Robeson gets caught in blackmail when he finds a missing child and takes him to cafe singer Welch. The kid threatens to say he was kidnaped by them if he is returned to his folks. An offbeat, but fascinating tale much in debt to O. Henry's story, "The Ransom of Red Chief."

d, J. Elder Wills; w, Fenn Sherie, Ingram d'Abbes (based on the novel by Claude McKay); ph, Cyril Bristow; m, Eric Ansell, Hugh Williams, G.H. Clutsam.

Musical **(PR:A MPAA:NR)**

BIG FISHERMAN, THE** (1959) 180m BV c

Howard Keel *(Simon Peter)*, Susan Kohner *(Fara)*, John Saxon *(Voldi)*, Martha Hyer *(Herodias)*, Herbert Lom *(Herod Antipas)*, Ray Stricklyn *(Deran)*, Marian Seldes *(Arnon)*, Alexander Scourby *(David Ben-Zadok)*, Beulah Bondi *(Hannah)*, Jay Barney *(John the Baptist)*, Charlotte Fletcher *(Rennah)*, Mark Dana *(Zendi)*, Rhodes Reason *(Andrew)*, Henry Brandon *(Menicus)*, Brian Hutton *(John)*, Thomas Troupe *(James)*, Marianne Stewart *(Ione)*, Jonathan Harris *(Lysias)*, Phillip Pine *(Lucius)*, Leonard Mudie, James Griffith, Peter Adams, Jo Gilbert, Michael Mark, Joe Di Reda, Stuart Randall, Herbert Rudley, Francis McDonald, Don Turner.

Long, often-enraging and totally miscast, THE BIG FISHERMAN features a nonsinging Keel as Saint Peter. Most of the film actually concerns the love story between Saxon and Kohner. It's just so much biblical nonsense because such liberties are taken that any serious student of the life and surrounding events will take exception. Douglas wrote the novel but made the mistake of entrusting it to the wrong people. The movie is distinguished by the fact that it was made entirely in the San Fernando Valley (this was before the realtors took over and made it a million-plus population suburb of Los Angeles), has numerous technical mistakes: microphone boom shadows, kleig lights, Martha Hyer's vaccination mark. To make a love story the focal point of such a potentially dynamic saga of history's most memorable era was a bad decision. One of the rare bummers by Disney in those years.

p, Rowland V. Lee; d, Frank Borzage; w, Howard Estabrook, Lee (based on a novel by Lloyd C. Douglas); ph, Lee Garmes (Technicolor); m, Albert Hay Malotte; ed, Paul Weatherwax; cos, Renie.

Biblical Drama **(PR:A-C MPAA:NR)**

BIG FIX, THE*½ (1947) 82m PRC bw

James Brown *(Ken Williams)*, Sheila Ryan *(Lillian)*, Noreen Nash *(Ann Taylor)*, Regis Toomey *(Lieutenant Brenner)*, Tom Noonan *(Andy Rawlins)*, John Shelton *(Del Cassini)*, Charles McGraw *(Armiston)*, Charles Mitchell *(Harry)*, John Morgan *(Joe)*, Nana Bryant *(Mrs. Carter)*, Howard Negley *(Coach Ambrose)*.

Confused story about the fixing of college basketball games, with Brown being framed by Nash, Ryan's older sister. Nash is killed but not before admitting that she brought in the gangsters to corrupt the kids. The basketball team also comes to the rescue by thumping the gangsters for an absurd finale. Oddly, the premise for this film was enacted in reality across the nation four years later in the most notorious basketball fixing on record.

p, Ben Stoloff, Marvin D. Stahl; d, James Flood; w, George Bricker, Aubrey Wisberg (based on a story by Sonja Chernus and George Ross, adapted by Joe Malone); ph, Virgil Miller; m, Emil Cadkin; ed, Norman Colbert; md, Irving Friedman; art d, Perry Smith; set d, Armor Marlowe.

Sports Drama **(PR:A MPAA:NR)**

BIG FIX, THE½** (1978) 108m UNIV c

Richard Dreyfuss *(Moses Wine)*, Susan Anspach *(Lila)*, Bonnie Bedelia *(Suzanne)*, John Lithgow *(Sam Sebastian)*, Ofelia Medina *(Alora)*, Nicholas Coster *(Spitzler)*, F. Murray Abraham *(Eppis)*, Fritz Weaver *(Oscar Procari, Sr.)*, Jorge Cervera, Jr. *(Jorge)*, Michael Hershewe *(Jacob)*, Rita Karin *(Aunt Sonya)*, Ron Rifkin *(Randy)*, Larry Bishop *(Wilson)*, Andrew Block *(Michael Linker)*, Sidney Clute *(Mr. Johnson)*, John Cunningham *(Hawthorne)*, Frank Doubleday *(Jonah's Partner)*, Joyce Easton *(Woman in Mercedes)*, Martin Garner *(Bittleman)*, Danny Gellis *(Simon)*, William

Glover *(Commentator)*, Kathryn Grody *(Wendy Linker)*, Murray MacLeod *(Perry)*, Ray Martucci *(Policeman)*, Bob O'Connell *(Policeman)*, Lupe Ontiveros *(Maid)*.

Everyone loved THE BIG FIX except the public. Critics fell over each other describing the nuances and the portrayal of a sixties radical who had become a detective. Simon's novel read lots better than his screenplay which is a confused hodgepodge. Dreyfuss is a former Chicago Seven type who takes a case having to do with the sabotaging of a politician's campaign by smear tactics (not unlike the Nixon/Voorhies allegations of the Fifties). The trail goes from Bel Air to the barrios and is a generally interesting story with some satirical pokes at the people in and of The Big Orange. Susan Anspach is delicious as Dreyfuss's employer. This is one of Lithgow's *(Sam)* earliest roles, before he became everyone's favorite supporting actor. F. Murray Abraham, who later went on to be Salieri in AMADEUS does nice work as Eppis, which means something' in Yiddish. Abraham is really something. In dealing with people from that era, Kasdan does better with THE BIG CHILL. This was an attempt to meld a mystery against some morality. It doesn't quite make it but has enough sidebar material to keep you from falling asleep. Look for Joey Bishop's son, Larry, as Wilson and soap opera star Nicholas Coster as Spitzler. Simon wrote a far more interesting book about the Jewish cop, Moses Wine, and his super-leftist Aunt *(Karin)*, *Peking Duck,* and it had to do with a tour to mainland China. They should have filmed that one instead.

p, Carl Borack, Richard Dreyfuss; d, Jeremy Paul Kagan; w, Roger L. Simon (based on his novel); ph, Frank Stanley; m, Bill Conti; ed, Patrick Kennedy; prod d, Robert F. Boyle; cos, Edith Head; art d, Raymond Brandt; set d, Mary Ann Biddle.

Comedy   **(PR:C   MPAA:PG)**

BIG FOOT*   (1973) 83m Gemini-American/Ellman c

Chris Mitchum *(Rick)*, John Carradine *(Jasper B. Hawks)*, Joi Lansing *(Joi Landis)*, Lindsay Crosby *(Wheels)*, Ken Maynard *(Mr. Bennett)*, Joy Wilkerson *(Peggy)*, John Mitchum *(Elmer Briggs)*, Doodles Weaver *(Forest Ranger)*, Haji Lamme *(Haji)*, James Stellar *(Big Foot)*.

Up in the Northwest forest the missing link (if a skinny guy in a shabby gorilla suit can be considered as such) kidnaps women so he can hear the pitter patter of little Bigfeet. Carradine wants to catch him to create a side show. There's a fight between the creature and a bear, some motorcyle gang action, lots of bikini-clad girls, and ex-B western star Maynard in a supporting role. Pretty hokey stuff.

p, Anthony Cardoza; d, Robert F. Slatzer; w, Slatzer, James Gordon White; ph, Wilson S. Hong (DeLuxe Color); m, Richard A. Podolor; ed, Bud Hoffman, Hugo Grimaldi; art d, Norman Houle; spec eff, Harry Woolman; makeup, Louis Lane, John Elliott; m/l, title song, Podolor (sung by Don Jones).

Horror   **Cas.**   **(PR:O   MPAA:PG)**

BIG FRAME, THE*   (1953, Brit.) 66m RKO bw (GB: THE LAST HOURS)

Mark Stevens *(Paul Smith)*, Jean Kent *(Louise Parker)*, Garry Marsh *(Foster)*, John Bentley *(Clark Sutton)*, Dianne Foster *(Dianne Wrigley)*, Jack Lambert *(John Parker)*, Leslie Perrins *(Dr. Morrison)*, Brian Coleman *(Tom Wrigley)*, Duncan Lamont *(Bristow)*, Cyril Smith *(Roper)*, Thora Hird *(Maid)*.

Smugglers conspire to murder and double-cross one another. Standard technical efforts with lifeless acting make this a lower-case film. Obscure-course whodunit leaves viewers out in the cold.

p, Robert S. Baker and Monty Berman; d, David MacDonald; w, Steve Fisher, John Gilling; ph, Monty Berman; m, William Hill-Rowan; ed, Reginald Beck.

Drama   **(PR:A   MPAA:NR)**

BIG GAMBLE, THE*   (1931) 65m RKO-Pathe bw

Bill Boyd *(Alan Beckwith)*, Dorothy Sebastian *(Beverly)*, Warner Oland *(Mr. North)*, William Collier, Jr. *(Johnny)*, James Gleason *(Squint)*; ZaSu Pitts *(Nora)*, June MacCloy *(May)*, Geneva Mitchell *(Trixie)*, Ralph Ince *(Webb)*, Fred Walton *(Butler)*.

Penniless gambler Boyd decides to pay off his debts with insurance policy money brought by his death. Slow-moving quasi-comedy lacks follow-through everywhere.

d, Fred Niblo; w, Octavus Roy Cohen, Walter DeLeon, F. McGrew Willis; ph, Hal Mohr; ed, Joseph Kane; md, Arthur Lange.

Comedy   **(PR:A   MPAA:NR)**

BIG GAMBLE, THE**   (1961) 98m FOX c

Stephen Boyd *(Vic Brennan)*, Juliette Greco *(Marie Brennan)*, David Wayne *(Samuel Brennan)*, Dame Sybil Thorndyke *(Aunt Cathleen)*, Gregory Ratoff *(Daltenberg)*, Harold Goldblatt *(Father Frederick)*, Philip O'Flynn *(John Brennan)*, Maureen O'Dea *(Margaret Brennan)*, Mary Kean *(Cynthia)*, Alain Saury *(Naval Lieutenant)*, Fergal Stanley *(Davey)*, Fernand Ledoux *(High Official)*, J.G. Devlin *(Irish Truck Driver)*, Jacques Marin *(Hotel Manager)*, Jess Hahn *(1st Mate)*.

Boyd is an Irishman who departs for Africa with his French wife (Greco) and his wimpy cousin (Wayne). They plan to open a trucking business and make all sorts of money. They soon learn that Africa is no easy place to earn a living. In the course of the film they must drive a huge truck into the heart of the darkness; a truck like that is a very valuable commodity in that area and literally worth its weight in whatever precious metal can be found. It's a series of misadventures and soon becomes somewhat repetitious, despite the glorious photography and a nice comic relief by Wayne. Ratoff and Thorndyke are wasted as is Goldblatt, a veteran of the Abbey Players.

p, Darryl F. Zanuck, d, Richard Fleischer (African sequence d, Elmo William); w, Irwin Shaw; ph, William C. Mellor (Eastmancolor); m, Maurice Jarre; ed, Roger Dwyre; art d, Jean D'Eaubonne.

Adventure   **(PR:A   MPAA:NR)**

BIG GAME, THE**   (1936) 73m RKO bw

Phillip Houston *(Clark)*, James Gleason *(George)*, June Travis *(Margaret)*, Bruce Cabot *(Calhoun)*, Andy Devine *(Pop)*, C. Henry Gordon *(Brad Anthony)*, Guinn "Big Boy" Williams *(Pete)*, John Arledge *(Spike Adams)*, Frank M. Thomas *(Coach)*, Barbara Pepper *(Lois)*, Edward Nugent *(Drunk)*, Margaret Seddon *(Mrs. Jenkins)*, Billy Gilbert *(Fisher)*, John Harrington *(Dawson)*, Murray Kinnell *(Dean)*, Jay Berwanger *(U. of Chicago)*, William Shakespeare *(Notre Dame)*, Robert Wilson *(Southern Methodist)*, James Moscrip *(Stanford)*, Irwin Klein *(NYU)*, Gomer Jones *(Ohio State University)*, Robert "Bones" Hamilton *(Stanford)*, Frank Alustiza *(Stanford)*.

Gamblers influence college admissions requirements when they recruit uneducated coal miners to play on the school's football team. When the star player is kidnaped and a riot on the football field occurs the expertly photographed film gains momentum. Top-notch technical effort makes this a fair but flat movie.

p, Pandro S. Berman; d, George Nicholls, Jr.; w, Irwin Shaw (based on the story by Francis Wallace); ph, Harry Wild; ed, Frederic Knudtson.

Sports Drama   **(PR:A   MPAA:NR)**

BIG GAME, THE   (SEE: FLESH AND THE WOMAN, 1954, Fr./Ital.)

BIG GAME, THE*   (1972) 90m Comet c

Stephen Boyd, France Nuyen, Ray Milland, Cameron Mitchell, Brendon Boone, Michael Kirner, John Stacy, George Wang, John Van Dreelan.

Weak story about big-game hunters with big-star names and small-time interest. Shot in semi-documentary fashion, the only redeeming virtue of this confusing tale is the on-location camera work in South Africa, lensing that captures the rugged terrain like a pretty travelog.

p, Stanley Norman; d&w, Robert Day; ph, Mario Fioretti.

Adventure   **(PR:C   MPAA:NR)**

BIG GUNDOWN, THE**   (1968, Ital.) 84m COL c

Lee Van Cleef *(Jonathan Corbett)*, Tomas Milian *(Cuchilo)*, Luisa Rivelli *(Lizzie)*, Fernando Sancho *(Capt. Segura)*, Nieves Navarro *(Widow)*, Benito Stefanelli *(Jess)*, Walter Barnes *(Brokston)*, Maria Granada *(Rosita)*, Lanfranco Ceccarelli *(Jack)*, Robert Camardiel *(Jellicol)*, Nello Pazzafini *(Hondo)*, Spartaco Conversi *(Mitchell)*, Romano Puppo *(Rocky)*, Tom Felleghi *(Chet)*, Calisto Calisti *(Miller)*, Antonio Casas *(Dance)*, Jose Torres *(Nathan)*.

Sharp-shooting lawman Van Cleef trails murdering rapist Milian along the U.S. Mexican border. The famous bounty hunter gets the cocky young Mexican eventually, despite Milian's evasive maneuvers. All this and more since millionaire Barnes wants to contract Van Cleef to make possible the building of a railroad across Texas into Mexico. Mild excitement occurs in some fight scenes but generally the fast pace is set by Morricone's music, complemented by eye-catching photography from Carlini in this spaghetti western.

p, Alberto Grimaldi; d, Sergio Sollima; w, Sergio Donati & Solima (based on the story by Franco Solinas & Fernando Morand); ph, Carlo Carlini (Technicolor); m, Ennio Morricone; ed, Adriana Novelli; art d, Raphael Perri.

Western   **(PR:A   MPAA:NR)**

BIG GUNS   (SEE: NO WAY OUT, 1972, Ital.)

BIG GUSHER, THE* 1/2   (1951) 68m COL bw

Wayne Morris *(Kenny Blake)*, Preston Foster *(Hank Mason)*, Dorothy Patrick *(Betsy Abbott)*, Paul E. Burns *(Cappy Groves)*, Emmett Vogan *(Jim Tolman)*, Eddie Parker *(Bartender)*, Fred F. Sears *(Sheriff)*.

Two oilfield roughnecks, Foster and Morris, become independents with Burns, an old-timer who uses a divining rod to find the black gold. Patrick uses her wiles to attempt delaying the drilling as she's in the employ of heavy Vogan. Love triumphs when Dorothy falls for Preston and joins his alliance. Fairly standard yarn featuring everything you'd expect in an oilfield story; the fire, the iron pipes breaking loose and threatening the protagonists, lots of punches. It's sort of a budget version of BOOM TOWN.

p, Wallace MacDonald; d, Lew Landers; w, Daniel Ullman (from story by Harold Greene); ph, Wm. Whitley; ed, Aaron Stell.

Adventure   **(PR:A   MPAA:NR)**

BIG GUY, THE***   (1939) 78m UNIV bw

Victor McLaglen *(Warden Whitlock)*, Jackie Cooper *(Timmy Hutchins)*, Edward Brophy *(Dippy)*, Peggy Moran *(Joan Lawson)*, Ona Munson *(Mary Whitlock)*, Russell Hicks *(Lawson)*, Jonathan Hale *(Jack Lang)*, Edward Pawley *(Chuck Burkhart)*, George McKay *(Buzz Miller)*.

Fast-moving melodrama where McLaglen is a captain of the guards at a reformatory, elevated to the position of acting warden after apprehending escaped prisoners, including Cooper. He also obtains some gangster loot but instead of turning this in, he holds onto the stolen money for family security. Cooper is wrongly tried and convicted for a killing connected with the break and is sentenced to death. He tearfully accuses McLaglen of stealing the money from the gangsters engineering the break, explaining that he only wanted to be free to get money to further his education. At first it appears that McLaglen will let the innocent youth go to the chair. Then a berserk trusty and Cooper break out of Death Row and McLaglen stops them, receiving a fatal wound. Before he dies, he admits keeping the money and that Cooper is innocent. The film is told in compassionate terms with excellent technical values and heart-tugging performances from Cooper and McLaglen.

d, Arthur Lubin; w, Lester Cole (based on the story "No Power on Earth" by Wallace Sullivan, Richard K. Polimer).

Crime Drama   **(PR:A   MPAA:NR)**

BIG HAND FOR THE LITTLE LADY, A***
(1966) 95m WB c (GB: BIG DEAL AT DODGE CITY)

Henry Fonda *(Meredith)*, Joanne Woodward *(Mary)*, Jason Robards *(Henry Drummond)*, Charles Bickford *(Benson Tropp)*, Burgess Meredith *(Doc Scully)*, Kevin McCarthy *(Otto Habershaw)*, Robert Middleton *(Dennis Wilcox)*, Paul Ford *(Ballinger)*, John Qualen *(Jesse Buford)*, James Kenny *(Sam Rhine)*, Allen Collins *(Toby)*, Jim Boles *(Pete)*, Gerald Michenaud *(Jackie)*, Virginia Gregg *(Mrs. Drummond)*, Chester Conklin *(Old Man in Saloon)*, Mae Clarke *(Mrs. Craig)*, Ned Glass *(Owney Price)*, James Griffith *(Mr. Stribling)*, Noah Keen *(Sparrow)*, Milton Selzer *(Fleeson)*, Louise Glenn *(Celie Drummond)*, William Cort *(Arthur)*.

Great little comedy western with a surprise ending starring Fonda and Woodward as a farm couple who get involved in a big-stakes poker game while traveling to their new home in Texas. A compulsive gambler, Fonda puts up the family's life savings against experienced card-players like rancher Robards, lawyer McCarthy and the richest undertaker in the territory, Bickford. When he realizes he's about to lose all, the tension spurs a heart attack incapacitating him for the rest of the game. He begs the players to let his wife finish his hand and they reluctantly agree. She ends up with a very good hand and the local banker advances her $1,000 on the strength of it. Woodward wins big, wiping out all the big-time players, who accept their fate with aplomb. After the gamblers leave, Fonda suddenly recovers and it turns out that the farm couple are con artists who were in cahoots with the banker to take the rich card players for all the money they had. Outstanding cast, well-paced script, and deft execution make this an enjoyable 90 minutes.

p&d, Fielder Cook; w, Sidney Carroll (based on his teleplay, "Big Deal At Laredo"); ph, Lee Garmes (Technicolor); m, David Raksin; ed, George Rohrs.

Western/Comedy **(PR:A MPAA:NR)**

BIG HANGOVER,THE** (1950) 82m MGM bw

Van Johnson *(David Maldon)*, Elizabeth Taylor *(Mary Belney)*, Percy Waram *(John Belney)*, Fay Holden *(Martha Belney)*, Leon Ames *(Carl Bellcap)*, Edgar Buchanan *(Uncle Fred Mahoney)*, Selena Royle *(Kate Mahoney)*, Gene Lockhart *(Charles* Parkford), Rosemary DeCamp *(Claire Bellcap)*, Phillip Ahn *(Dr. Lee)*, Gordon Richards *(Williams)*, Matt Moore *(Mr. Rumlie)*, Pierre Watkin *(Samuel C. Lang)*, Russell Hicks *(Steve Hughes)*.

Norman Krasna, who won an Oscar for writing PRINCESS O'ROURKE, takes on producing and directing chores as well in this odd film about a man who gets dizzy at the mere sniff of any alcohol. Johnson is an attorney with a strange allergy to booze, the result of having been almost drowned by casks of brandy in the basement of a monastery. Waram is his boss and Liz Taylor is the daughter who helps him overcome the allergy. The secondary story has to do with Johnson deciding between being a rich man's attorney or taking up the cudgel for the poor and oppressed (Phillip Ahn, before he invested his money and became a noted Chinese restaurateur in California, despite being of Korean parentage). During this film Liz was being courted by Glenn Davis, famous footballer with West Point (he and Doc Blanchard were known as Mr. Inside and Mr. Outside), whom she eventually married. Good supporting cast includes Leon Ames (born Leon Wycoff), who had three TV series when he wasn't selling cars from his San Fernando Valley dealership.

p,d&w, Norman Krasna; ph, George Folsey; m, Adolph Deutsch; ed, Frederick Y. Smith.

Drama **(PR:A-C MPAA:NR)**

BIG HEART, THE 1965 (SEE: MIRACLE ON 34TH STREET, 1947)

BIG HEARTED HERBERT*** (1934) 60m WB bw

Aline McMahon *(Elizabeth Kainess)*, Guy Kibbee *(Big Hearted Herbert Kainess)*, Patricia Ellis *(Alice Kainess)*, Helen Lowell *(Martha)*, Phillip Reed *(Andrew Goodrich)*, Robert Barrat *(Jim Lawrence)*, Henry O'Neill *(Goodrich Sr.)*, Marjorie Gateson *(Amy Goodrich)*, Nella Walker *(Mrs. Goodrich)*, Trent Durkin *(Junior Kainess)*, Jay Ward *(Robert Kainess)*, Hale Hamilton *(Mr. Havens)*, Claudia Coleman *(Mrs. Havens)*.

Successful plumber turned bathroom equipment manufacturer has trouble spending money so brings plain folks home for a dinner which humbles the host. Competent all- around work offers more than a few belly laughs.

d, William Keighley; w, Lillie Hayward, Ben Markson (based on the play by Sophie Kerr, Anna Steese Richardson from a story by Kerr); ph, Arthur Todd.

Comedy **(PR:A MPAA:NR)**

BIG HEAT, THE**** (1953) 89m COL bw

Glenn Ford *(Dave Bannion)*, Gloria Grahame *(Debby Marsh)*, Jocelyn Brando *(Katie Bannion)*, Alexander Scourby *(Mike Lagana)*, Lee Marvin *(Vince Stone)*, Jeanette Nolan *(Bertha Duncan)*, Peter Whitney *(Tierney)*, Willis Bouchey *(Lt. Wilkes)*, Robert Burton *(Gus Burke)*, Adam Williams *(Larry Gordon)*, Howard Wendell *(Commissioner Higgins)*, Cris Alcaide *(George Rose)*, Michael Granger *(Hugo)*, Dorothy Green *(Lucy Chapman)*, Carolyn Jones *(Doris)*, Ric Roman *(Baldy)*, Dan Seymour *(Atkins)*, Edith Evanson *(Selma Parker)*, Joe Mell *(Dr. Kane)*, Sid Clute *(Bartender)*, Norma Randall *(Jill)*, Linda Bennett *(Joyce)*, Herbert Lytton *(Martin)*, Ezelle Poule *(Mrs. Tucker)*, Byron Kane *(Dr. Jones)*, Ted Stanhope *(Butler)*, Mike Ross *(Segal)*, Bill Murphy *(Reds)*, Phil Arnold *(Mike)*, Mike Mahoney *(Dixon)*, Pat Miller *(Intern)*, Paul Maxey *(Fuller)*, Charles Cane *(Hopkins)*, Kathryn Eames *(Marge)*, Al Eben *(Harry Shoenstein)*, Harry Lauter *(Hank O'Connell)*, Phil Chambers *(Hettrick)*, Robert Forrest *(Bill Rutherford)*, John Crawford *(Al)*, John Doucette *(Mark Reiner)*.

A tough and uncompromising crime drama, starkly photographed and without a continuous score, the absence of which underlines the hard-hitting dialog and the sound of smacking fists and thudding bullets, this Fritz Lang film is as brutal as his M was frightening. Ford is an uncorruptible cop who learns that another detective has killed himself. He investigates and is told by the widow, Nolan, that her husband was despondent over a fatal disease. Ford disbelieves the story but is ordered to investigate no further by his superiors. Ford meets a bar hostess, Green, who was the suicide's mistress; she tells him that the dead cop left a long suicide note which exposes widespread city corruption, behind which is mob boss Scourby and that widow Nolan is using the note to blackmail Scourby for a fortune. Green's corpse—she had obviously been tortured before being killed—is later found on a lonely stretch of road and Ford now believes her story. He goes to Scourby's mansion, arriving in the midst of a party, and confronts the mob boss who explodes and unleashes his bodyguard. Ford beats the goon half senseless, then departs, swearing he'll pin the Green death on him, and expose his rotten empire. Scourby orders Ford killed. A bomb is placed in his car but it kills Ford's wife, Brando, and now Ford really goes all out for Scourby's throat. His superiors tell him he's off the case, promising they'll find his wife's killer. He calls them liars and throws down his badge, thereafter operating alone. He meets with Grahame, mistress to Scourby's right-hand enforcer, Marvin, pumping her for information. Grahame pays the price for this meeting; Marvin later beats her up, then throws scalding coffee on her face, scarring her for life. (Hell hath no fury as a woman scorned, the man once said, but an even more horrible fate awaits Marvin at the hands of the woman he hath scarred.) Grahame immediately goes to Ford, who nurses her. In return for his kindness, Grahame tells him about three murders Scourby and Marvin have committed. She also realizes that Ford will not be able to nail Scourby legally until the suicide note is released, knowing that it will be mailed, as Nolan has told Scourby, if she is ever killed. Grahame goes to Nolan and shoots her. The letter is automatically mailed by a Nolan accomplice as Grahame returns to her loutish lover Marvin, telling him that she has destroyed the gang. Then his comeuppance as she hurls scalding coffee into his face. Raging, Marvin shoots her just as Ford arrives. The cop beats Marvin to a pulp before turning him over to friendly cops. He kneels to speak to the dying Grahame who hides her disfigured face in her mink coat, telling her about his wife. The mobsters are jailed and Ford goes back to his police work. This film, along with a spate of others, was spawned by the 1950 U.S. Senate crime investigations conducted via TV by Sen. Estes Kefauver, which pinpointed widespread corruption by organized crime throughout America. Fritz Lang's THE BIG HEAT, meaning the heat brought down by the policeman (not the scalding coffee, as one wag put it), is one of the best expose films dealing with the national crime cartel, including HOODLUM EMPIRE, Robert Wise's startling CAPTIVE CITY, and Phil Karlson's hard-hitting KANSAS CITY CONFIDENTIAL. Lang's ferocious gangster film is directed with immaculate care, showing not so much violence on film as showing the reaction to violence while examining the human side of its results, the victims, rather than the criminals. Ford gives one of his best performances as the dedicated and courageous cop, Scourby is properly ruthless and oily, Grahame the perfect beautiful tramp with a conscience, and Marvin is the loathsome creature of all our nightmares. Rich characterizations, a taut, telling script by Boehm, and sharp lensing in keeping with the theme by Charles Lang contribute to this *film noir* standout.

p, Robert Arthur; d, Fritz Lang; w, Sydney Boehm (based on the serial in the *Saturday Evening Post* by William P. McGivern); ph, Charles Lang; m, Daniele Amfitheatrof; md, Mischa Bakaleinikoff; ed, Charles Nelson; art d, Robert Peterson; set d, William Kiernan; cos, Jean Louis.

Crime Drama **Cas.** **(PR:C MPAA:NR)**

BIG HOUSE, THE*** ½** (1930) 84m MGM bw

Chester Morris *(John Morgan)*, Wallace Beery *(Butch Schmidt)*, Lewis Stone *(Warden James Adams)*, Robert Montgomery *(Kent Marlowe)*, Leila Hyams *(Ann Marlowe)*, George F. Marion *(Pop Riker)*, J. C. Nugent *(Mr. Marlowe)*, Karl Dane *(Olsen)*, De Witt Jennings *(Captain Wallace)*, Mathew Betz *(Gopher)*, Claire McDowell *(Mrs. Marlowe)*, Robert Emmet O'Connor *(Donlin)*, Tom Wilson *(Sandy, the Guard)*, Eddie Foyer *(Dopey)*, Roscoe Ates *(Putnam)*, Fletcher Norton *(Oliver)*, Adolph Seidel *(Prison Barber)*, Eddie Lambert, Michael Vavitch.

One of the most successful prison films ever produced, THE BIG HOUSE follows three inmates, Morris, Beery, and Montgomery, a forger, a killer, and a rather innocuous youth convicted of manslaughter. Morris escapes, going to Montgomery's sister, Hyams, for aid, falling in love with her before he is recaptured and returned to prison, vowing to go straight. Beery is the top bull con, settling fights and running the yard; he plans a big break to escape the sadistic guards and the endless stoolpigeons. But weak-willed Montgomery informs warden Stone of the impending escape attempt and when Beery and other inmates make their play, they are met by horrific gunfire. It's a battle royal where Montgomery is killed, as is Beery, cut to pieces by machine-gun fire. Morris finally restores order in the prison block, for which he is paroled so that he can join Hyams. Grimly realistic, often brutal, this was the granddaddy of all prison films, exposing the mean conditions, the paranoia, the vicious system that deepened criminal resolves among inmates. It spawned a host of other prison films, notably 20,000 YEARS IN SING SING and I AM A FUGITIVE FROM A CHAIN GANG. Hill's uncompromising direction captures all the ugliness and futility of prison life and Beery (in a role originally intended for Lon Chaney, Sr.) is the perfect goonish ringleader of the inmates, half clown, half menace, soft-hearted, soft-headed, but with a killer instinct that is iron-streaked. Morris performed one of his best roles as the intelligent member of the threesome while Montgomery, at the beginning of his film career, is uncharacteristically spineless, a wretched, despicable cringer wholly without character. Stone, as always,is the establishment stalwart wanting to improve conditions but helpless as a warden who can only kill those attempting to break out of his prison. The film was inspired by a particularly bloody riot in Auburn (N.Y.) prison a year earlier.

d, George Hill; w, Frances Marion, Joe Farnham, Martin Flavin; ph, Harold Wenstrom; ed, Blanche Sewell; art d, Cedric Gibbons.

Prison Drama **(PR:C MPAA:NR)**

BIG HOUSE, U.S.A.*** (1955) 82m UA bw

Broderick Crawford (Rollo Lamar), Ralph Meeker (Jerry Barker), Reed Hadley (James Madden), Randy Farr (Nurse Emily Evans), William Talman (Machinegun Mason), Lon Chaney, Jr. (Alamo Smith), Charles Bronson (Benny Kelly), Peter Votrian (Danny Lambert), Roy Roberts (Chief Ranger Erickson), Willis B. Bouchey (Robertson Lambert.)

This hard-hitting film begins when Meeker kidnaps a young boy and takes him deep into Colorado's Royal George Park, where the boy attempts to escape and is accidentally killed in a fall. Meeker still collects $200,000 ransom money, but he is captured after hiding the loot and sent to prison. Here he meets tough cons Crawford, Talman, Chaney, Bronson, and others who plan and execute a successful escape, taking Meeker back to the site of the kidnaping to collect his loot. Hadley and other G-men are joined by rangers and local police, who trap the gang in a to-the-death shoot-out which ends with the culprits dead or captured. A particularly brutal scene after the prison break has psychopath Crawford kill fellow con Bronson, then, to prevent his corpse from being identified, burns away his face and fingerprints with a blowtorch, a scene undoubtedly inspired by the use of such devices in Mark Hellinger's classic prison film, BRUTE FORCE. Good action and outdoor photography, coupled to frightening performances from Crawford, as a berserk con, and Meeker, as a calculating kidnaper, make for a tension-filled, first-rate production.

p, Aubrey Schenk; d, Howard W. Koch; w, John C. Higgins; ph, Gordon Avil; m, Paul Dunlap; ed, John F. Schreyer; cos, George A. Thompson.

Crime Drama (PR:O MPAA:NR)

BIG JACK*¹/₂ (1949) 85m MGM bw

Wallace Beery (Big Jack Horner), Richard Conte (Dr. Alexander Meade), Marjorie Main (Flapjack Kate), Edward Arnold (Mayor Mahoney), Vanessa Brown (Patricia Mahoney), Clinton Sundberg (C. Patronius Smith), Charles Dingle (Mathias Taylor), Clem Bevans (Saltlick Joe), Jack Lambert (Bud Valentine), Will Wright (Will Farnsworth), William "Bill" Phillips (Teddy), Syd Saylor (Pokey).

Wallace is at his beeriest in this ghoulish comedy about a man who steals bodies from graves in the name of medical research. Conte is about to be hanged for desecrating graves when he is saved by Beery and his outlaw gang because they need a physician to treat Wally's leg. That taken care of, Beery wants Conte to stay with the gang, but Richard escapes and sets himself up in a new place. Because of his experiments on corpses, Conte is able to perform surgery and save a woman's life. This was Beery's last movie and not a great way to ring down the curtain on a career that included such memorable movies as GRAND HOTEL, TREASURE ISLAND, AH, WILDERNESS, and his Oscar-winning performance in THE CHAMP.

p, Gottfried Reinhardt; d, Richard Thorpe; w, Gene Fowler, Marvin Borowsky, Otto Van Eyes (based on a story by Robert Thoeren); ph, Robert Surtees; m, Herbert Stothart; ed, George Boemler.

Western Comedy (PR:C MPAA:NR)

BIG JAKE** (1971) 109m National General c

John Wayne (Jacob McCandles), Richard Boone (John Fain), Maureen O'Hara (Martha McCandles), Patrick Wayne (James McCandles), Chris Mitchum (Michael McCandles), Bobby Vinton (Jeff McCandles), Bruce Cabot (Sam Sharpnose), Glenn Corbett (O'Brien), Harry Carey, Jr. (Pop Dawson), John Doucette (Buck Dugan), Jim Davis (Head of Lynching Party), John Agar (Bert Ryan), Gregg Palmer (John Goodfellow), Robert Warner (Will Fain), Jim Burke (Trooper), Dean Smith (Kid Duffy), John Ethan Wayne (Little Jake McCandles), Virginia Capers (Delilah), William Walker (Moses Brown), Jerry Gatlin (Stubby), Tom Hennesy (Saloon Brawler), Don Epperson (Saloon Bully), Everett Creach (Walt Devries), Jeff Wingfield (Billy Devries), Hank Worden (Hank).

Wayne brought in old friends, family, and associates to help him make BIG JAKE and the resulting film is a disappointment. Directed by George Sherman, who had worked with Wayne when he was just a rising star at Republic in the "Three Mesquiteers" series of the late 1930s, the film is marred somewhat by lackadaisical direction and gratuitous violence. Plot concerns the kidnaping of wealthy rancher Wayne's young grandson (played by Wayne's real-life son Ethan) by a vicious band of hoods led by Boone. Wayne sets out with his sons, Pat Wayne (also Duke's real-life offspring) and Mitchum to drop off the $1 million ransom demanded by the kidnapers. Cabot tags along as an old Indian scout and there is the usual horseplay between father and sons, with the Duke reminding everyone that though his age is creeping up on him, he's still someone to be reckoned with. The film ends with an unusually bloody finale for a Wayne film, where the bad guys get their just desserts. Wayne, Boone, and Cabot are very good. O'Hara looks like she's just doing Wayne a favor (none of the wonderful spark that made MCLINTOCK! such a success is evident here), and Pat Wayne and singer Vinton just don't have much screen presence. These weaknesses piled on a mediocre script add up to a very weak Wayne outing.

p, Michael Wayne; d, George Sherman; w, Harry Julian Fink, R. M. Fink; ph, William Clothier (Panavision, Technicolor); m, Elmer Bernstein; ed, Harry Gerstad; art d, Carl Anderson; set d, Raymond Moyer; spec eff, Howard Jensen.

Western (PR:O MPAA:GP)

BIG JIM McLAIN** (1952) 90m WB bw

John Wayne (Big Jim McLain), Nancy Olson (Nancy Vallon), James Arness (Mal Baxter), Alan Napier (Sturak), Veda Ann Borg (Madge), Gayne Whitman (Dr. Gelster), Hal Baylor (Poke), Robert Keys (Edwin White), Hans Conried (Robert Henried), John Hubbard (Lt. Cmdr. Clint Grey), Sara Padden (Mrs. Lexiter), Mme. Soo Yong (Mrs. Nomaka), and Dan Liu, Paul Hurst, Vernon McQueen.

Wayne and Arness go to Hawaii to investigate the inner workings of a terrorist group headquartered there. They are both special agents assigned to rooting out Commie rats. Wayne falls in love with Olson, who works for Whitman, a suspect psychiatrist. Wayne and Arness learn the name of the contact man for the terrorists, get into his house, speak to his landlady and get the names of several of the head honchos, a number of whom are highly placed people. After a wild-goose chase that fills up the middle of the film (bath house, religious institution, way-out sections of Oahu), Wayne tells a group of prominent people at a party that he knows who is involved in the organization and arrests are imminent. This isn't the truth but Wayne knows the rats will be smoked out by the ploy. And they are. Arness is captured and killed when Whitman gives him too much of a truth serum. Now Wayne is really annoyed! Arness was the only man in the movie that Wayne could look straight in the eye. He enlists the local police and they beat the terrorists in a smashing conclusion. Olson, by the way, was totally innocent so she and Wayne walk off into the Hawaiian sunset to listen to ukuleles forever. At one time, Wayne was considered for the role of Dillon on the TV series "Gunsmoke." He turned it down but recommended a young fella he'd worked with a short time before; Arness, brother of Peter Graves (born Aurness.) The rest was TV history. Alan Napier, tall and elegant Sturak in this film, achieved worldwide popularity as Alfred, the butler, in the "Batman" TV series.

p, Robert Fellows; d, Edward Ludwig; w, James Edward Grant, Richard English, Eric Taylor; ph, Archie Stout; m, Emil Newman; ed, Jack Murray.

Spy Drama (PR:C MPAA:NR)

BIG JOB, THE*** (1965, Brit.) 88m Warner-Pathe bw

Sidney James (George Brain), Sylvia Syms (Myrtle Robbins), Dick Emery (Fred "Booky" Binns), Joan Sims (Mildred Gamely), Lance Percival (Tim "Dipper" Day), Jim Dale (Harold); Edina Ronay (Sally Gamely), Deryck Guyler (Police Sergeant), Brian Rawlinson (First Workman), Reginald Beckwith (Registrar), David Horne (Judge).

Bank robbers James, Emery, and Percival return from a 15-year prison sentence to claim their reward only to find the prairie tree they hid it in is now in the front lawn of a police station. Technical efforts up to par with cast.

p, Peter Rogers; d, Gerald Thomas; w, Talbot Rothwell; ph, Alan Hune; ed, Rod Keys; m, Eric Rogers.

Comedy (PR:A MPAA:NR)

BIG KNIFE, THE**** (1955) 111m UA bw

Jack Palance (Charles Castle), Ida Lupino (Marion Castle), Shelley Winters (Dixie Evans), Wendell Corey (Smiley Coy), Jean Hagen (Connie Bliss), Rod Steiger (Stanley Hoff), Ilka Chase (Patty Benedict), Everett Sloane (Nat Danziger), Wesley Addy (Hank Teagle), Paul Langton (Buddy Bliss), Nick Dennis (Nick), Bill Walker (Russell), Mike Winkelman (Billy Castel), Mel Wells (Bearded Man), Robert Sherman (Bongo Player), Strother Martin (Stillman), Ralph Volke (Referee), Michael Fox (Announcer).

A cruel and even vicious film based on the Clifford Odets play, THE BIG KNIFE is a tour de force for Palance who is a superstar in tinseltown. Palance refuses to renew his contract with Hoff Studios, enraging mogul Stanley Hoff (Steiger), but pleasing his estranged wife Lupino who has asked the one-time stage star to extricate himself from Steiger's creative-financial stranglehold. But the decision to shun Steiger has caused Palance to drink heavily and retreat into the arms of mistress Hagen. Steiger arrives to first cajole, then beg, then blackmail Palance into signing a new contract. He offers more money, even withdraws an historic pen with which to sign the contract, a pen Steiger claims was used by MacArthur to sign the Japanese surrender document on board the U.S.S. Missouri in 1945. Palance laughs in his face. Then Steiger plays his trump card. Unless Palance reconsiders, he will expose the fact that it was he, not Hagen's husband, who was guilty of a hit-and-run accident where Hagen's husband took the blame (at the studio's request to save its star) and went to jail for manslaughter. Steiger leaves in a rage, telling Palance he must sign soon or face prison. Steiger's aide, oily Corey, a press agent who will perform any unsavory chore his boss demands, stays behind to hear Palance express his worries about Winters, a bit player who was with him in the car when the accident occured. Corey tells him not to worry; he'll fix things up with Winters. Palance begins to waver and Lupino has had enough. She leaves as he hits the bottle. Moreover, he soon learns that Corey has gotten Winters drunk and shoved her in front of a speeding car which killed her. In one last effort to cure himself of his Hollywood malady, Palance goes to Lupino, begging her to stay with him, that he'll somehow overcome Steiger and return to the clean life of stage actor and reconstruct their marriage. She takes her time considering, a pause he interprets as rejection. By the time she agrees to stay with him, Palance is dead in the bathtub, his wrists slashed. Director Aldrich's unflinching use of a candid, almost documentary style results in a devastating mirror image of Hollywood at its most ruthless. It is grim, without humorous respite, and one is left awe-struck at the total lack of compassion. The film is uncompromising, irrespective of the name-dropping of real personalities (Kazan, Wilder, Wyler, etc.) to authenticate the atmosphere. The script blares the philosophy that it is not only windy at the top but lethal. Lupino is a bit too motherly as a concerned wife, but Steiger is outstanding as the tyrannical mogul, even though his character rests on a stereotyped foundation. Just watching his histrionics is a treat, and seeing the bravura counterattack by Palance is even more edifying. This is a tough film, not for youngsters, and best for those able to endure the kind of emotional exhaustion produced by such films as LONG DAY'S JOURNEY INTO NIGHT and PATTERNS.

p&d, Robert Aldrich; w, James Poe (based on the play by Clifford Odets); ph, Ernest Laszlo; m, Frank DeVol; ed, Michael Luciano; art d, William Glasgow.

Drama (PR:O MPAA:NR)

BIG LAND, THE** (1957) 93m Jaguar/WB c (GB: STAMPEDE)

Alan Ladd (*Morgan*), Virginia Mayo (*Helen*), Edmond O'Brien (*Jagger*), Anthony Caruso (*Brog*), Julie Bishop (*Kate Johnson*), John Qualen (*Sven Johnson*), Don Castle (*Draper*), David Ladd (*David Johnson*), Jack Wrather, Jr. (*Olaf Johnson*), George J. Lewis (*Dawson*), James Anderson (*Cole*), Don Kelly (*Billy*), Charles Watts (*McCullough*).

Below-average western starring Ladd as an angry cattle-driver who is outraged at villain-buyer Caruso's price per head. Caruso happens to be the only buyer in the territory who has access to the railroad, and therefore he can undercut the price of cattle to $1.50 instead of the $10.00 a head the ranchers were expecting. Ladd meets up with a washed-up, alcoholic architect, O'Brien, after saving him from being lynched. They decide, with the help of Ladd's railroad developer friend Castle, to build their own town where the cattlemen can come to sell their cattle at reasonable prices and ship them by train. Excited by the challenge, O'Brien sobers up and draws up the plans for the new town. The grand opening of the cattle town is stopped by Caruso and his thugs, who shoot O'Brien and then destroy the settlement by causing a stampede. Ladd has finally been pushed too far. He puts aside his hatred for violence (the horror of the Civil War had taken its toll on him), straps on his guns, and goes out to settle things with the evil Caruso and his men. While the Ladd character is well drawn and interesting, the film rambles in the middle and takes much too long to get to the main conflict. O'Brien's performance is very good, but Caruso does no more with his villainous cattle buyer than scowl and leer. These fatal weaknesses just add another chapter in the long slide downward in Ladd's once-promising career.

p, George C. Bertholon; d, Gordon Douglas; w, David Dortort, Martin Rackin (based on an adaptation by Dortort of *Buffalo Grass* by Frank Gruber); ph, John Seitz (WarnerColor); m, David Buttolph; ed, Thomas Teily; m/l, "I Leaned on a Man" Wayne Shanklin, Leonard Rosenman.

Western **(PR:A MPAA:NR)**

BIG LEAGUER*½ (1953) 70m MGM bw

Edward G. Robinson (*John B. "Hans" Lobert*), Vera-Ellen (*Christy*), Jeff Richards (*Adam Polachuk*), Richard Jaeckel (*Bobby Bronson*), William Campbell (*Julie Davis*), Carl Hubbell (*Himself*), Paul Langton (*Brian McLennan*), Lalo Rios (*Chuy Agilar*), Bill Crandall (*Tippy Mitchell*), Frank Ferguson (*Wally Mitchell*), John McKee (*Dale Alexander*), Mario Siletti (*Mr. Polachuk*), Al Campanis (*Himself*), Bob Trocolor (*Himself*), Tony Ravish (*Himself*).

All the usual baseball corniness in this Bob Aldrich film that will have true fans asleep before the first inning is over. Curious casting of Robinson and Vera-Ellen as his niece. Edward G. is an aging former player who now runs the training camp for the New York Giants (of blessed memory) in Florida. His job is to whip a bunch of raw recruits into shape. Actually, the plot is not unlike AN OFFICER AND A GENTLE-MAN or THE D.I. in that all three are concerned with young men in a training camp with a tough leader barking at them. The customary stereotypes accrue: Jaeckel as the Robert Redford type in THE NATURAL, a baseball *wunderkind*; Rios as the Cuban; Crandall as the young man who secretly hates the game but is only in it to please his father, a former major-league star. This film has all the cliches that THE NATURAL omitted.

p, Matthew Rapf; d, Robert Aldrich; w, Herbert Baker (based on a story by John McNulty and Louis Morheim); ph, William Mellor; m, Alberto Colombo; ed, Ben Lewis.

Sports Drama **(PR:A MPAA:NR)**

BIG LIFT, THE*** (1950) 120m FOX bw

Montgomery Clift (*Danny MacCullough*), Paul Douglas (*Hank*), Cornell Borchers (*Frederica*), Bruni Lobel (*Gerda*), O. E. Hasse (*Stieber*), Danny Davenport (*Private*), and American military personnel stationed in Germany.

A semi-historical look at the airlift that kept Berlin functioning when the Russians decided to blockade the city. The movie was filmed entirely on location in West Berlin and around Templehof airport. Seaton had a Herculean job in making this subject palatable as this was only five years after the end of WW II and there were many Americans who could not have cared less about the plight of the Germans. Clift is a pilot and Douglas is the ground operations non-com who hates the Germans because of his war experiences. Seaton doesn't avoid the issue of bad memories: he goes right for it. Clift is in love with Borchers, who does a fine first-performance-in-films as the heroine who is ultimately revealed to be the villainess. Douglas and Clift are the only Hollywood "names" in the film. The other actors are all local Germans and contribute mightily to the reality of the movie, especially Hasse who was brilliant as the German commander in Litvak's DECISION BEFORE DAWN. It's a bit slow and gets a mite preachy, but that's easy to overlook as the movie was made very shortly after the Russian blockade and objectivity was hard to come by in those Cold War days. Clift pulled some star turns while the film was being made and was not beloved by either cast or crew. He became a scene stealer around this time and attempted it in the two-shots with Douglas. Once the redoubtable Douglas saw what was transpiring, he stepped on Clift's foot and Monty wisely backed off and became a good scout, at least around Douglas.

p, William Perlberg; d&w, George Seaton; ph, Charles G. Clark; m, Alfred Newman; ed, Robert Simpson; spec eff, Fred Sersen.

Drama **(PR:A-C MPAA:NR)**

BIG MONEY** (1930) 80m Pathe bw

Eddie Quillan (*Eddie*), James Gleason (*Tom*), Robert Armstrong (*Ace*), Miriam Seegar (*Joan McCall*), Margaret Livingston (*Mae*), Dorothy Christy (*Leila*), Morgan Wallace (*Durkin*), Robert Edeson (*Mr. McCall*).

Unlucky professional gambler and bank messenger Quillan gets caught up with card sharks and is nearly bankrupt. Just to keep it interesting, Armstrong comes in to save the day and gives a nice performance as the wise and trusted gambling counselor. Precise directing increases suspense.

d, Russell Mack; w, Walter De Leon, Mack (based on a story by De Leon); ph, John Mescall; ed, Joseph Kane; art d, Carroll Clark; cos, Gwen Wakeling.

Drama **(PR:A MPAA:NR)**

BIG MONEY, THE** (1962, Brit.) 86m RANK/Lopert c

Ian Carmichael (*Willie Frith*), Belinda Lee (*Gloria*), Kathleen Harrison (*Mrs. Frith*), Robert Helpmann (*The Reverend*), James Hayter (*Mr. Frith*), George Coulouris (*The Colonel*), Jill Ireland (*Doreen Frith*), Renee Houston (*Bobby*), Leslie Phillips (*Receptionist*), Harold Berens (*Bookmaker*).

A British comedy where the performers triumph over the thin material. Carmichael is the white sheep of a family of thieves. He finds it almost impossible to think larcenously until he comes upon a suitcase filled with banknotes. The money turns out to be counterfeit and Carmichael must now get rid of the bogus bills. Belinda Lee plays Carmichael's girl friend and she is the weakest link in the acting. Helpmann, as a clergyman/crook, is okay but should stick to roles as a dancer (THE RED SHOES, TALES OF HOFFMAN). Jill Ireland, a few years before she left husband David McCallum ("The Man from UNCLE") for Charles Buchinski (Charles Bronson), is cute and Leslie Phillips, who went on to a distinguished career as a CARRY ON person as well as a West End stage star, impresses as the receptionist. It's kinda like BREWSTER'S MILLIONS except the money is phony.

p, Joseph Yanni; d, John Paddy Carstairs; w, John Baines; ph, Jack Cardiff (Technicolor); m, Van Phillips; ed, Alfred Roome, Hugh Stewart.

Comedy **(PR:A MPAA:NR)**

BIG MOUTH, THE** (1967) 107m COL c

Jerry Lewis (*Gerald Clamson*), Harold J. Stone (*Thor*), Susan Day (*Suzie Cartwright*), Buddy Lester (*Studs*), Del Moore (*Mr. Hodges*), Paul Lambert (*Moxie*), Jeannine Riley (*Bambi Berman*), Leonard Stone (*Fong*), Charlie Callas (*Rex*), Frank DeVol (*Bogart*), Vern Rowe (*Gunner*), Dave Lipp (*Lizard*).

Eccentric fisherman Lewis catches a frogman who is searching for sunken treasure and the fun begins. The frogman hands Lewis a map, mumbling something about diamonds and their hiding place before a gang of thugs in a power boat show up to send him for the Deep Six. From then on it's one long and tiresome chase after Lewis to obtain the map, a take-off, really, on IT'S A MAD MAD MAD MAD WORLD filmed four years earlier. Lewis relies on his bugwit characterizations with pratfalls, screwball expressions and berserk mannerisms to glean laughs where none really deserve to exist.

p&d, Jerry Lewis; w, Lewis, Bill Richmond (based on a story by Richmond); ph, W. Wallace Kelley, Ernest Laszlo (PatheColor); m, Harry Betts; ed, Russel Wiles; prod d, Lyle Wheeler; set d, Frank Tuttle.

Comedy **(PR:AA MPAA:NR)**

BIG NEWS** (1929) 75m Pathe bw

Robert Armstrong (*Steve Banks*), Carole Lombard (*Margaret Banks*), Tom Kennedy (*Sgt. Ryan*), Warner Richmond (*Phelps*), Wade Boteler (*O'Neil*), Sam Hardy (*Joe Reno*), Louis Payne (*Hensel*), James Donlan (*Deke*), Cupid Ainsworth (*Vera Wilson*), Gertrude Sutton (*Helen*), Charles Sellon (*Addison*), Herbert Clark (*Pells*), George Hayes (*Reporter*), Lew Ayres (*Copy Boy*), Dick Cramer (*Hood*), Clarence H. Wilson (*Coroner*), Vernon Steele (*A Reporter*).

Early talkie newspaper drama featuring Armstrong as a tough reporter who is fired when he goes after gangster Hardy, who happens to be a big advertiser in the *Courier*. Armstrong continues investigating the crook on his own and comes up with solid evidence that proves Hardy guilty of murder. The city editor, Sellon, reinstates his ace reporter on the strength of the evidence, but Hardy overhears the conversation and when Armstrong leaves the mobster kills the editor, making it appear that the reporter did it. All turns out well in the end when it is discovered that the entire murder has been recorded on the editor's dictaphone. Sound is used to good advantage, showing off Armstrong's talent for spitting out rapid-fire dialog, the constantly clacking typewriters in the newspaper office, and the key element that saves the hero is a device that records sound.

d, Gregory LaCava; w, Walter DeLeon, Jack Jungmeyer (based on the play "For Two Cents" by George S. Brooks); ph, Arthur Miller; ed, Doane Harrison.

Drama **(PR:A MPAA:NR)**

BIG NIGHT, THE* (1951) 70m UA bw

John Barrymore, Jr. (*George La Main*), Preston Foster (*Andy LaMain*), Joan Lorring (*Marion Rostina*), Howard St. John (*Al Judge*), Dorothy Comingore (*Julie Rostina*), Philip Bourneuf (*Dr. Lloyd Cooper*), Howland Chamberlin (*Flanagan*), Emil Meyer (*Packingpaugh*), Myron Healey (*Kennealy*), Mauri Lynn (*Tery Angelus*).

Stanley Ellin is a helluva writer and Joseph Losey can be a superb director, but together they are dreadful in this mean-spirited film of revenge. Barrymore is a teenager who watches Foster, his father, get beaten by St. John. Barrymore goes after St. John in Losey's attempt at natural-lighting-to-make-it-look-like-foreign-movie-style. Barrymore eventually gets to St. John, a gunshot is fired, St.John goes down. Barrymore races home, cops come, Dad accepts the blame, tells officers that he did it. Then we learn that St. John is only the recipient of a "flesh wound" and all is forgiven. The only reason to see this movie is for the curious performance of Dorothy Comingore as Julie. Comingore, you may recall, was one of the pivotal characters in CITIZEN KANE and almost disappeared after that famous performance as Kane's second wife, the dreadful opera singer.

p, Philip A. Waxman; d, Joseph Losey; w, Stanley Ellin, Losey (based on the novel by Ellin); ph, Hal Mohr; m, Lyn Murray; ed, Edward Mann.

Teenage Drama (PR:C MPAA:NR)

BIG NIGHT, THE** (1960) 87m Maycliff/PAR bw

Randy Sparks (Frank), Venetia Stevenson (Ellie), Dick Foran (Ed), Jesse White (Wegg), Dick Contino (Carl Farrow), Frank Ferguson (Dave), Paul Langton (Spencer), House Peters, Jr. (Robert Shaw), Bob Padget (Tony), Marc Cavell (Jerry), Kay Kuter (Mailman), Anna Lee (Mrs. Turner).

Money stolen in a wild robbery falls into the hands of a couple who put it aside and are then sought out by the thieves. Taut little crime yarn for a low-budget production.

p, Vern Alves; d, Sidney Salkow; w, Rich Hardman; m, Richard Lasalle; cos, Bill Edwards, Bernice Pontrelli.

Crime Drama (PR:C MPAA:NR)

BIG NOISE, THE** (1936) 58m WB bw (GB: MODERN MADNESS)

Guy Kibbee (Julius Trent), Warren Hull (Ken Mitchell), Alma Lloyd (Betty Trent), Dick Foran (Don Andrews), Marie Wilson (Daley), Henry O'Neill (Charlie Caldwell), Olin Howland (Harrison), Virginia Brissac (Mrs. Trent), Andre Beranger (Rosewater), Edward McWade (Douglas), Robert Emmett Keane (Aldrich), William Davidson (Welford Andrews), Al Hill (Slug Batterson), Eddie Shubert (Machine Gun Nolan), William Pawley (Dutch Schmidt), George Lloyd (Morelli).

Kibbee is a retired millionaire who buys a dry-cleaning plant to keep busy but bristles when gangsters move in (as did Capone in Chicago when taking over the dry-cleaning businesses) to extort money. He rounds up some employees and, supported by wife Brissac, cleans up the mobs where the police have failed. Ridiculous premise with a few laughs provided by a talking parrot. Alma Lloyd is the daughter of director Frank Lloyd.

d, Frank Lloyd; w, Edward Hartman, George Bricker, William Jacobs; ph, L. William O'Connell; ed, Terry Morse.

Drama (PR:A MPAA:NR)

BIG NOISE, THE* (1936, Brit.) 65m FOX bw

Alastair Sim (Finny), Norah Howard (Mary Miller), Fred Duprez (Henry Hadley), Grizelda Hervey (Consuelo), C. Denier Warren (E. Pinkerton Gale), Viola Compton (Mrs. Dayton), Peter Popp (Jenkins), Howard Douglas (Gluckstein), Reginald Forsyth and his Band.

Moguls of an oil company conceive of a plan promoting a simple clerk into a position of authority in order to make him the scapegoat of their devious schemes.

p, John Findlay; d, Alex Bryce; w, Gerard Fairlie (based on a story by Gene Markey, Harry Ruskin); ph, Stanely Grant.

Comedy (PR:A MPAA:NR)

BIG NOISE, THE**1/2 (1944) 74m FOX bw

Stan Laurel (Himself), Oliver Hardy (Himself), Doris Merrick (Evelyn), Arthur Space (Hartley), Louis Arco (German Officer), Beal Wong (Japanese Officer), Veda Ann Borg (Mayme), Bobby Blake (Egbert), Frank Fenton (Charlton), Ken Christy (Speaker), Charles Wilson (Conductor), Jack Norton (Drunk), Francis Ford (Station Attendant), James Bush (Hartman), Phil Van Zandt (Dutchy), Esther Howard (Aunt Sophie), Harry Hayden (Butler), Selmer Jackson (Manning), Edgar Dearing (Motor Policeman), Robert Dudley (Grandpa).

By the time they made this, Laurel and Hardy had been working together for almost twenty years. In comparison to many other L&H pictures, it is woeful. But compared to what passes for comedy lately, it's hysterical! They made three more films after this one and none was particularly good or successful; this was about the last of it and, for that alone, it merits watching. Stan and Ollie are mail-order detectives hired to guard a new bomb at the inventor's house. The house is incredibly modern (what the futuristic set designers thought houses would be like in the 1980s) and understandably befuddles them. Criminals attempt to steal the explosive but are foiled by Stan and Ollie. Highlights include the boys finding themselves in a drone airplane that's being used for target practice. Some political overtones here (it was made during WW II) and a number of laughs, but not as many as we'd come to expect. This was producer Wurzel's last film after a 30-year career at Fox. Look for Bobby Blake (born Michael Gubitosi, later known as Robert Blake) as Egbert Hartley. Also . . . Laurel and Hardy aficionados will recall Edgar Dearing as the fuming motorcycle policeman in TWO TARS. He does it again here, 16 years later and still fuming. (See LAUREL & HARDY series, Index.)

p, Sol M. Wurtzel; d, Malcolm St. Clair; w, Scott Darling; ph, Joe MacDonald; m, Cyril J. Mockridge; ed, Norman Colbert; md, Emil Newman; art d, Lyle Wheeler, John Ewing; set d, Thomas Little, Al Orenbach; cos, Yvonne Wood; makeup, Guy Pearce; spec eff, Fred Sersen.

Comedy (PR:AA MPAA:NR)

BIG OPERATOR, THE**1/2
(1959) 90m MGM bw (AKA: ANATOMY OF A SYNDICATE)

Mickey Rooney (Little Joe Braun), Steve Cochran (Bill Gibson), Mamie Van Doren (Mary Gibson), Ray Danton (Oscar Wetzel), Mel Torme (Fred McAfee), Jim Backus (Cliff Heldon), Jackie Coogan (Edward Brannel), Ray Anthony (Slim Clayburn), Ben Gage (Bert Carr), Charles Chaplin Jr. (Bill Tragg), Billy Daniels (Tony Webson), Jay North (Timmy Gibson), Joey Forman (Raymond Baily), Ziva Rodann (Alice McAfee).

Rooney does his customary believable job as a Hoffa-like labor boss being skewered by a panel of Senators. He hides behind the Fifth Amendment but his tongue slips once when asked about one of his hoodlums and the rest of the picture is one shock

after another. Cochran plays a straight heroic type whose son is kidnaped by Rooney's goons when Cochran mounts an offense against Rooney's tyrannical rule of the union. Suspense is high and so is the violence: Torme, Cochran's best friend, is burned, a hood is tossed into a cement mixer. This film was made by the same group that did the dreadful THE BEAT GENERATION the same year. Zugsmith, Haas, Danton, Cochran, Coogan, Vampira Anthony, Daniels, Van Doren, and Charles Chaplin, Jr., were all involved in both movies. One was tripe and this one had some merit. So then . . . what's the difference? Obviously it was the script. Smith and Rivkin respected the Gallico story and provided cast and crew with a no-nonsense, tense story that never flags. When the film community begins to appreciate that it all begins with the word and that no star will triumph over bad material, movies will be a lot better off. (Remake of JOE SMITH, AMERICAN.)

p, Red Doff, Albert Zugsmith; d, Charles Haas; w, Robert Smith, Allen Rivkin (from story by Paul Gallico); ph, Walter H. Castle; m, Van Alexander; ed, Ben Lewis.

Crime Drama (PR:O MPAA:NR)

BIG PARTY, THE** (1930) 60m Fox bw

Sue Carol (Flo Jenkins), Dixie Lee (Kitty Collins), Walter Catlett (Mr. Goldfarb), Frank Albertson (Jack Hunter), Richard Keene (Eddie Perkins), Charles Judels (Dupuy), "Whispering" Jack Smith.

Married playboys Catlett and Judels are partners in a dress shop who can't shake their single habits regarding women. Production starts off fast and keeps the pace. The womanizing premise popular in the 1920s but fast fading as the Depression deepened is only a weak excuse to parade some good songs which include "Nobody Knows But Rose" (James Hanley, Joseph McCarthy), "Bluer Than Blue Over You," "Good For Nothing But Love" (William Kernell, Harlan Thompson), and "I'm Climbing Up A Rainbow" (Edward G. Nelson, Harry Pease).

p, William Fox; d, John Blystone; w, Harlan Thompson, J. Edwin Robbins.

Musical (PR:A MPAA:NR)

BIG PAYOFF, THE** (1933) 70m MAS bw

Lucien Littlefield, Ralph Ince, Barbara Kent, J. Farrell MacDonald, Glenn Tryon, Sally Blane, Victor Jory, Rinty the dog.

Police officers found in hard-to-believe situations tangle with gangsters. Fast-moving tightly directed job from poverty row Mascot.

d, Ford Beebe (based on Peter Kyne's story "Pride of the Legion".)

Crime Drama (PR:A MPAA:NR)

BIG POND, THE**1/2 (1930) 78m PAR bw

Maurice Chevalier (Pierre Mirande), Claudette Colbert (Barbara Billings), George Barbier (Mr. Billings), Marion Ballou (Mrs. Billings), Elaine Koch (Jennie), Nat Pendleton (Pat O'Day), Frank Lyon (Ronnie), Andree Corday (Toinette).

While they were making THE BIG POND at the Astoria studio in New York, they were also shooting the French version, LA GRANDE MER, and, believe it or not, the second one was better. Chevalier always felt more at home in his native tongue (who can blame him?) and the evidence is apparent in the former version. Maurice is a poor but honorable tour guide working in Venice who falls in love with heiress Claudette Colbert. Her father, Barbier, and her fiance, Lyon, would like to get rid of this guy but Claudette's mother, Ballou, shares her daughter's fascination with Chevalier. The men are convinced Maurice is a fortune hunter but he is given a job at old man Barbier's gum factory. He works so hard that he can barely function at her nightly soirees and this apparently bolsters her father's contention that he really cares little for her. Maurice continues work in the chewing gum factory until he accidentally drenches some gum with rum and races to the office where he convinces Barbier to manufacture the new discovery. Earlier in the film, Maurice had sung a love song to Claudette and now that he has to write the ads for the new product, he borrows from himself, changes the words, and uses the same melody for the rum-gum jingle. Are you still there? Claudette is miffed at the commercialization of "their song" and vows to run off and marry Lyons. Maurice wakes up in time to kidnap the willing Claudette and they take off on a combination business and honeymoon trip. Four songs, including Chevalier's favorite: "You Brought a New Kind of Love to Me." Pleasant enough but not one of Maurice's or Claudette's best.

d, Hobart Henley; w, Robert Presnell, Garrett Fort, Preston Sturges (based on a story by George Middleton, A. E. Thomas); ph, George Folsey; ed, Emma Hill; m/l, Al Lewis, Al Sherman, Lew Brown, B. G. DeSylva, Ray Henderson, Irving Kahal, Pierre Norman, Sammy Fain.

Musical/Romance (PR:A MPAA:NR)

BIG PUNCH, THE** (1948) 50m WB bw

Wayne Morris (Chris Thorgenson), Lois Maxwell (Karen Long), Gordon MacRae (Johnny Grant), Mary Stuart (Midge Parker), Eddie Dunn (Ed Hardy), Marc Logan (Milo Brown), Charles March (Sam Bancroft).

Minister turned boxer MacRae is accused of murdering a policeman but is acquitted when his innocence is proven by recently made small-town friends. Some of the story seems to be taken from Garfield's BODY AND SOUL, produced a year earlier.

p, Saul Elkins; d, Sherry Shourds; w, Bernard Girard (based on a story by George Carleton Brown); ph, Carl Guthrie; m, William Lava; ed, Frank Magee; md, Leo F. Forbstein; art d, Charles H. Clarke; set d, William Wallace.

Drama (PR:A MPAA:NR)

BIG RACE, THE** (1934) 62m Showmen's bw (GB: RAISING THE WIND)

Boots Mallory (Patricia), John Darrow (Bob Hamilton), Paul Hurst (Skipper), Frankie Darro (Jockey), Phillips Smalley (Hamilton, Sr.), Katherine Williams (Deborah), Georgia O'Dell (Mrs. Hemingway), James Flavin (Bill Figg), Skipper Zeliff (Ferguson), Oscar (Ezra), Richard Terry (Riley).

Darrow and Smalley are at odds as father-and-son horse trainers competing for the big handicap. Independently, they learn a trusted employee fixed a race by drugging one of the favorites. Well-performed comedy slowed down by cheapy production.

d, Fred Newmeyer; w, Hugh Cummings.

Drama **(PR:AA MPAA:NR)**

BIG RED*½ (1962) 89m BV c

Walter Pidgeon *(James Haggin)*, Gilles Payant *(Rene Dumont)*, Emile Genest *(Emile Fornet)*, Janette Bertrand *(Terese Fornet)*, George Bouvier *(Baggageman)*, Doris Lussier *(Farmer Mariot)*, Roland Bedard *(Conductor)*, Teddy Burns Goulet *(Engineer)*.

BIG RED is a big yawn. Typical "boy and his dog" story from Disney that has little to recommend it past some songs by the Sherman brothers. Pidgeon is a stiff businessman who is shown the advantages of family life by Payant and Champion Red Aye Scraps,the dog who plays Big Red. The picture is just too cute for its own good and the attempt at doing an understated kiddy film only results in being so understated that children will fall asleep rather than get involved.

p, Walt Disney, Winston Hibler; d, Norman Tokar; w, Louis Pelletier (based on a novel by Jim Kjelgaard); ph, Edward Colman (Technicolor); m, Oliver Williams; ed, Grant K. Smith; m/l, Robert and Richard Sherman.

Children **Cas.** **(PR:AA MPAA:NR)**

BIG RED ONE, THE*** (1980) 113m Lorimar/UA c

Lee Marvin *(Sergeant)*, Mark Hamill *(Griff)*, Robert Carradine *(Zab)*, Bobby DiCicco *(Vinci)*, Kelly Ward *(Johnson)*, Siegfried Rauch *(Schroeder)*, Stephane Audran *(Walloon)*, Serge Marquand *(Rensonnet)*, Charles Macaulay *(General/Captain)*, Alain Doutey *(Broban)*, Maurice Marsac *(Vichy Colonel)*, Colin Gilbert *(Dog Face POW)*, Joseph Clark *(Shep)*, Ken Campbell *(Lemchek)*, Doug Werner *(Switolski)*, Perry Lang *(Kaiser)*, Howard Delman *(Smitty)*, Marthe Villalonga *(Madame Marbaise)*, Giovanna Galetti *(Woman in Sicilian Village)*, Gregori Buimistre *(The Hun)*, Shimon Barr *(German Male Nurse)*, Matteo Zoffoli *(Sicilian Boy)*, Avrahan Ronai *(German Field Marshal)*, Galit Rotman *(Pregnant Frenchwoman)*.

The title is a mystery to those who don't know that it refers to the First Infantry Division. This picture had been rattling around Fuller's fertile brain for more than three decades and he finally got it down on celluloid but it came too late. It's a WW II story that takes place in Europe and Africa during the campaign of '42-45 and it attempts to tell the whole story of that era through the ten eyes of five foot-sloggers. Fuller's genius is evident when you realize that his budget was miniscule and he intercut many battle scenes to cover the fact that he really didn't have a lot of people to work with. It's a flag-waving movie (John Wayne was once slated to star in it back in the fifties) that celebrates the patriotism of the War. Trouble is that the era may have passed and what once might have been a smash hit became just another war movie. The point being that timing is so important. A lousy film that's released at the right time will do ten times the business of a good film that comes out at the wrong time. This was a good film that was released at the wrong time.

p, Gene Corman; d&w, Samuel Fuller; ph, Adam Greenberg (Metrocolor); m, Dana Koproff; ed, Morton Tubor.

War **Cas.** **(PR:C MPAA:PG)**

BIG SEARCH, THE (SEE: EAST OF KILIMANJARO, 1957)

BIG SCORE,THE* (1983) 85m Almi c

Fred Williamson *(Frank Hooks)*, John Saxon *(Davis)*, Richard Roundtree *(Gordon)*, Ed Lauter *(Parks)*, Nancy Wilson *(Angie Hooks)*, D'Urville Martin *(Easy)*, Michael Dante *(Jackson)*, Bruce Glover *(Koslo)*, Joe Spinell *(Mayfield)*, Frank Pesce *(J. C.)*, Tony King *(Jumbo)*, James Spinks *(Cheech)*, Karl Theodore *(Huge)*, Ron Dean *(Kowalski)*.

This one looks like DIRTY HARRY in blackface, but Williamson doesn't have the wherewithal to carry off the characterization. The locale is Chicago and the story is that of a cop who is dispatched from the force when a lot of money disappears and he's accused of it. This, of course, allows him to hunt the bad dudes on his own with none of the red tape that ties up policemen. Williamson, who also directed, has occasionally helmed some decent adventure pictures and he would probably be much better off if he stayed behind the camera rather than cavorting in front of it. Saxon and Roundtree, who began the whole genre in the late Ernest Tidyman's SHAFT series, play cops with their usual aplomb. Lauter, as the C-I-C (Cop In Charge) is on the money. Are you sick to death of drug bust pictures? If so, avoid this one. But if you like murder, mayhem, and excessive violence, you'll probably love THE BIG SCORE. Fernandes' photography is one of the film's few pluses.

p, Michael S. Landes, Albert Schwartz; d, Fred Williamson; w, Gail Morgan Hickman; ph, Joao Fernandes (TVC Color); m, Jay Chattawy; ed, Dan Loewenthal.

Crime Drama **Cas.** **(PR:C MPAA:R)**

BIG SHAKEDOWN, THE*½ (1934) 64m WB bw

Charles Farrell *(Jimmy Morrell)*, Bette Davis *(Norma Frank)*, Ricardo Cortez *(Barnes)*, Glenda Farrell *(Lil)*, Allen Jenkins *(Lefty)*, Henry O'Neill *(Sheffner)*, G. Pat Collins *(Gyp)*, Adrian Morris *(Trigger)*, Dewey Robinson *(Slim)*, John Wray *(Gardinella)*, Philip Faversham *(John)*, Earle Foxe *(Carey)*, Samuel S. Hinds *(Kohlsadt)*, Sidney Miller *(Jewish Boy)*, Elinor Jackson *(Woman)*, Charles B. Williams *(Timid Man)*, Robert Emmett O'Connor *(Regan, the Bartender)*, Ben Taggert *(Cop)*, Oscar Apfel *(Doctor)*, John Hyams *(Smith)*, Edward LeSaint *(Fillmore)*, Frank Layton *(Dr. Boutellier)*.

Overblown crime melodrama starring Farrell as an unassuming druggist who gets pulled into a phony medicine scheme engineered by former bootlegger Cortez. The druggist agrees to become involved in the plan because he falls for the mobster's claims that it would be beneficial to the poor, who can buy his medicine at lower prices. Farrell's motivations aren't entirely humanitarian; he also sees the scheme as a good way to make a few extra dollars so he can marry his sweetheart, Davis. Soon after the marriage, Davis announces she's in a family way and Farrell wants out of the illegal business. He is persuaded to stay with a blackjack and threats on his pregnant wife. Days later, Davis is rushed to the hospital in serious condition due to premature labor. She loses the baby and nearly her own life when some of the mobster's bogus medicine is administered unknowingly by her doctors. Farrell finally snaps, goes to the medicine factory, and shoots Cortez, who tumbles into a vat of acid. The material stretches believability at every plot turn, and the dispatching of the villain is almost too much to take without laughing.

p, Samuel Bischoff; d, John Francis Dillon; w, Niven Busch, Rian James (based on a story by Sam Engels); ph, Sid Hickox; ed, James Gibbon.

Crime **(PR:A MPAA:NR)**

BIG SHOT, THE* (1931) 65m RKO-Pathe bw (GB: THE OPTIMIST)

Eddie Quillan *(Ray)*, Maureen O'Sullivan *(Doris)*, Mary Nolan *(Fay Turner)*, Roscoe Ates *(Barber)*, Belle Bennett *(Mrs. Thompson)*, Arthur Stone *(Old Timer)*, Otis Harlan *(Dr. Peasley)*, Louis John Bartels *(Mr. Howell)*, Edward McQuade *(Uncle Ira)*, Frank Darien *(Postmaster)*.

Con men dupe Quillan into purchasing useless swamps which are later discovered to be priceless sulphur deposits which make him rich. O'Sullivan, whom Quillan has earlier saved after a car crash, races to tell him the good news before the con artists can buy back the real estate. This kind of rural comedy went out during the early 1930s, thankfully.

p, Charles Rogers; d, Ralph Murphy; w, Joseph Fields, Earl Baldwin; ph, Arthur Miller; ed, Charles Craft.

Comedy **(PR:A MPAA:NR)**

BIG SHOT, THE** (1937) 66m RKO bw

Guy Kibbee *(Mr. Simms)*, Cora Witherspoon *(Mrs. Simms)*, Dorothy Moore *(Peggy)*, Gordon Jones *(Chet)*, Russell Hicks *(Drake)*, Frank M. Thomas *(Murdock)*, Dudley Clements *(McQuade)*, George Irving *(Police Chief)*, Maxine Jennings *(Gloria)*, Barbara Pepper *(Mamie)*, Tom Kennedy *(Bugs)*. John Kelly *(Deuces)*, Eddie Gribbon *(Soapy)*, Al Hill *(Spots)*, Donald Kirke *(Johnny Cullen)*.

Kibbee, a village vet, inherits a fortune from a big-city uncle and moves to Gotham at his wife's (Witherspoon) insistence so that he can launch his daughter, Moore, into society. The money, however, comes with a vicious mob once bossed by the deceased uncle and Kibbee's troubles increase as he disposes of the gangsters. A nitwit story with little production value.

d, Edward Killy; w, Arthur T. Horman, Bert Granet (based on a story by Lawrence Pohle, Thomas Ahearn); ph, Nicholas Musuraca; ed, Jack Hively.

Comedy **(PR:A MPAA:NR)**

BIG SHOT, THE½** (1942) 82m WB bw

Humphrey Bogart *(Duke Berne)*, Irene Manning *(Lorna Fleming)*, Richard Travis *(George Anderson)*, Susan Peters *(Ruth Carter)*, Stanley Ridges *(Martin Fleming)*, Minor Watson *(Warden Booth)*, Chick Chandler *(Dancer)*, Joseph Downing *(Frenchy)*, Howard da Silva *(Sandor)*, Murray Alper *(Quinto)*, Roland Drew *(Faye)*, John Ridgely *(Tim)*, Joseph King *(Toohey)*, John Hamilton *(Judge)*, Virginia Brissac *(Mrs. Booth)*, William Edmunds *(Sarto)*, Virginia Sale *(Mrs. Miggs)*, Ken Christy *(Kat)*, Wallace Scott *(Rusty)*.

This one is almost a remake of a half-dozen other Bogie crime films, loosely plotted and lamely directed by Seiler but with a terrific finale chase patterned after Bogart's mountainous car race in HIGH SIERRA the year earlier. Bogart has just been released from prison. He is out of money, a gang, and a girl. Moreover he has lost his nerve. Downing and Drew, two hoodlums, run into Bogie, slap him around, then offer him a job on a caper. He needs money and agrees but doesn't show up at the break-in, persuaded not to go by Manning, an old flame married to criminal lawyer Ridges. Downing and Drew are caught but later escape, vowing vengeance on Bogie. He is later framed for the attempted burglary and sent to prison, escaping with Chandler during a prison show where Chandler does a wild blackface dummy dance (he is killed before going over the wall). A guard is killed by Bogie who is now wanted for murder. Picking up Manning, the couple flee to a north woods retreat but police follow and a wild chase along the snow-bound roadways ensues with motorcycle cops flying into snowbanks. One gets off a lucky shot that kills Manning. Bogie goes to her husband, believing rightly that Ridges has tipped the cops and is responsible for Irene's death. He confronts the criminal lawyer who panics, offering money, safety. Bogie says no and Ridges goes for his gun. Both men fire, Ridges being killed; Bogie is mortally wounded. Bogie calls the warden at the prison, telling him that another inmate, Travis, being held for the murder of the guard during his escape is innocent, that he not only shot the guard but has just murdered Ridges. He is picked up, taken to the prison hospital. Travis, the inmate Bogie has cleared, is at his deathbed to watch him go out. "Big shot," snorts Bogie about himself, taking a drag from a cigarette which drops to the floor. A male nurse grinds it out with an immaculate white shoe, which ends this drawn-out Bogie repeater. Bogart was then earning $114,000 a year from Warners, agreeing to make this kind of film or any other they wanted for the money, including the stellar CASABLANCA he made the same year.

p, Walter MacEwen; d, Lewis Seiler; w, Bertram Millhauser, Abem Finkel, Daniel Fuchs; ph, Sid Hickox; m, Adolph Deutsch; ed, Jack Killifer; art d, John Hughes; cos, Milo Anderson; makeup, Perc Westmore.

Crime Drama **(PR:A MPAA:NR)**

BIG SHOW, THE*** (1937) 70m REP bw (AKA: HOME IN OKLAHOMA)

Gene Autry *(Himself and Tom Ford)*, Smiley Burnette *(Frog)*, Kay Hughes *(Marion)*, Sally Payne *(Toodles)*, William Newell *(Wilson)*, Max Terhune *(Max)*, Charles Judels *(Swartz)*, Rex King *(Collins)*, Harry Worth *(Rico)*, Mary Russell *(Mary)*, Christine Maple *(Elizabeth)*, Champion.

Autry plays a dual role as himself and his own stuntman, the western star skipping out on an appearance at the Texas Centennial in Dallas (where on-location scenes were filmed) and the double taking over the role, which confuses two girls engaged to both men, as well as gangsters looking for the star and being pummeled by the stuntman. It's top-notch Autry fare with plenty of action and a lot more humor than is found in most of his oaters. Gene sings "Lady Known as Lulu" and "Mad about You." The hillbilly songs are backed up by the western swing of the Light Crust Doughboys and the Sons of the Pioneers. In the latter group was a young, handsome singer named Leonard Slye, later renamed Roy Rogers, who had a fist fight with Autry, when using the name Dick Weston, in another Autry horse opera, THE OLD CORRAL. (See GENE AUTRY series, Index.)

P, Nat Levine; d, Mark V. Wright; w, Dorrell and Stuart McGowan; ph, William Nobles, Edgar Lyons; ed, Robert Jahns; m/l, Sam H. Stept, Ned Washington, Ted Koehler.

Comedy/Western Cas. (PR:A MPAA:NR)

BIG SHOW, THE* 1/2 (1961) 113m FOX c

Esther Williams *(Hillary Allen)*, Cliff Robertson *(Josef Everard)*, Nehemiah Persoff *(Bruno Everard)*, Robert Vaughn *(Klaus Everard)*, Margia Dean*(Carlotta Martinez)*, David Nelson *(Eric Solden)*, Carol Christensen *(Garda Everard)*, Kurt Fecher *(Hans)*, Renata Mannhardt *(Teresa)*, Franco Andrei, Peter Capell, Stefan Schnabel, Carleton Young, Philo Hauser, Mariza Tomic, Gerd Vesperman.

Those interested in esoterica might recognize this film as sort of a remake of the western BROKEN LANCE which was, in turn, the sagebrush remake of HOUSE OF STRANGERS, Joe Mankiewicz's version of Jerome Weidman's novel. In this case, it's not a ranch or a bank but a circus. Persoff is the cruel father and, although only five years older then Cliff Robertson in real life, manages to convince in the role. Vaughan is the rotten son who wants to take over the business. The picture is told in flashback, for no apparent reason, and uses lots of circus footage to fill out the time. Good, solid acts are seen but the film is a bore, despite the presence of Esther Williams who does a fine job as a wealthy U.S. woman who falls in love with Robertson. It doesn't have the scope of THE GREATEST SHOW ON EARTH or the suspense of TRAPEZE and falls far short of being the circus epic the producers must have imagined.

p, Ted Sherdeman, James B. Clark; d, Clark; w, Sherdeman; ph, Otto Heller (CinemaScope, Technicolor); m, Paul Sawtell, Bert Shefter; ed, Benjamin Laird; cos, Teddy Turai-Rossi; art d, Ludwig Reiber.

Drama (PR:A MPAA:NR)

BIG SHOW-OFF, THE** (1945) 60m REP bw

Arthur Lake *(Sandy Elliott)*, Dale Evans *(June Mayfield)*, Lionel Stander *(Joe Bagley)*, George Meeker *(Wally Porter)*, Paul Hurst *(The Devil)*, Marjorie Manners *(Mitzi)*, Sammy Stein *(Boris the Burglar)*, Louis Adlon *(Muckenfuss)*, Dan Toby *(Announcer)*.

Honky-tonk pianist Lake puts the moves on Evans, then finds himself humbled in a wrestling match after he pretends to be a famous wrestler. Evans sings her own composition, "Only One You," while other songs include "Cleo from Rio," and "Hoops My Dear," by Dave Oppenheim and Roy Ingraham. This one never gets off the mat.

p, Sydney M. Williams; d, Howard Bretherton; w, Leslie Vadney, Richard Weil; ph, Jack Greenhalgh; md, David Chudnow; art d, Frank Dexter; set d, E. H. Reif.

Drama (PR:C MPAA:NR)

BIG SKY, THE* 1/2** (1952) 140m Winchester/RKO bw

Kirk Douglas *(Deakins)*, Dewey Martin *(Boone)*, Elizabeth Threatt *(Teal Eye)*, Arthur Hunnicutt *(Zeb)*, Buddy Baer *(Romaine)*, Steven Geray *(Jourdonnais)*, Hank Worden *(Poordevil)*, Jim Davis *(Streak)*, Henri Letondal *(Ladadie)*, Robert Hunter *(Chouquette)*, Booth Colman *(Pascal)*, Paul Frees *(MacMasters)*, Frank de Kova *(Moleface)*, Guy Wilkerson *(Longface)*, Don Beddoe *(Horse Trader)*, George Wallace, Max Wagner, Sam Ash, Barbara Hawks, Frank Lackteen, Jay Novello, William Self.

A stirring but overlong northwest frontier epic from Hawks which depicts the adventures of two young Kentuckians at the turn of the nineteenth century. Douglas and Martin search for Martin's uncle, Hunnicut, a noted trapper and frontiersman, finding him in a St. Louis jail (into which they are thrown for brawling). All are bailed out by riverboat captain and trader Geray who needs Hunnicut to guide his French company more than 1,000 miles distant into Blackfoot Indian territory where he intends to trade for expensive fur pelts. On board the large keelboat is a Blackfoot princess, Threatt, to whom Martin is attracted. In her silent response (he does not speak the language and their brief conversations must be interpreted by uncle Hunnicut) it is apparent that she loves him. A thieving renegade, Davis, and his band, allied with a large party of Crow Indians, attack the boat party, trying to eliminate the fur-trading competitors. They are beaten off and Douglas and Martin later kill Davis and his henchman. When the expedition finally reaches Blackfoot country, its members are hailed in friendship because they have returned princess Threatt safely. (It is never explained what the Indian lady was doing so far East in the first place.) Martin is reluctant to stay with the woman he loves but, at the last minute, he bids farewell to Douglas and friends and settles with the Blackfoot tribe. Douglas was the only star in this languid, leisurely Hawks film which is superbly written by Nichols who was chosen especially by the director to do the scripting. The scenery is magnificent, even in black and white, shot on location in the Grand Teton National Park. Tiomkin's score is lyrical and haunting, on occasions full of his typical stirring bombast (he had recently won two Oscars for score and song for HIGH NOON). The Russian-born composer also created the score for Hawks' epic western RED RIVER. Aside from the fascinating up-river struggle where the men must pull the boat by rope while hostile Indians lurk nearby, the most interesting character is that of the wizened Hunnicut as the old trapper; he manages to steal almost every scene.

p&d, Howard Hawks; w, Dudley Nichols (based on the novel by A. B. Guthrie); ph, Russell Harlan; m, Dmitri Tiomkin; ed, Christian Nyby; art d, Albert D'Agostino, Perry Ferguson.

Adventure (PR:A MPAA:NR)

BIG SLEEP, THE***** (1946) 118m WB bw

Humphrey Bogart *(Philip Marlowe)*, Lauren Bacall *(Vivian)*, John Ridgely *(Eddie Mars)*, Louis Jean Heydt *(Joe Brody)*, Elisha Cook, Jr. *(Jones)*, Regis Toomey *(Bernie Ohls)*, Sonia Darren *(Agnes)*, Bob Steele *(Canino)*, Martha Vickers *(Carmen)*, Tom Rafferty *(Carol Lundgren)*, Dorothy Malone *(Girl in Bookshop)*, Charles Waldron *(General Sternwood)*, Charles D. Brown *(Norris)*, Tom Fadden *(Sidney)*, Ben Welden *(Pete)*, Trevor Bardette *(Art Huck)*, James Flavin *(Cronjager)*, Joy Barlowe *(Cab Driver)*, Thomas Jackson *(Wilde)*, Peggy Knudsen *(Mona Mars)*, Theodore Von Eltz *(Geiger)*, Carole Douglas *(Librarian)*, Dan Wallace *(Owen Taylor)*, Tanis Chandler, Deannie Best *(Waitresses)*, Lorraine Miller *(Hat Check Girl)*, Shelby Payne *(Cigarette Girl)*, Forbes Murray, Joseph Crehan, Emmett Vogan.

One of the best Raymond Chandler yarns ever brought to the screen, THE BIG SLEEP comes magically alive through Hawks' careful direction and Bogart's persona which is twin to his character of Philip Marlowe. Bogie is summoned to the lavish mansion of wealthy Waldron, a dying man who survives by staying in his greenhouse. He asks Bogie to look after his young daughter, Vickers, and investigate why she is being blackmailed by a smut book dealer (Von Eltz), but his real aim is to have Bogart find his missing friend Shawn Regan. Bogie goes to Von Eltz's home and finds him shot to death with Vickers sitting idly nearby in a drugged state. He rushes her home where he strikes up a liaison with the other daughter, Bacall. He next finds Heydt, a small-time racketeer, has the photos with which Vickers has been blackmailed. Bogart obtains these, but Heydt is killed by an unknown gunman before he can reveal more. At every turn, Bogart hears about a big-shot gambler, Ridgely, who seems to be behind the six killings that occur, including that of Cook, whose girl friend, Darrin, has been using him in Heydt's blackmail scheme. At one point Bogie witnesses Cook's death, standing helpless in the next room, as he is sadistically poisoned to death by Steele, who plays the cold-blooded killer Canino, Ridgely's top gunsel. Bogart tracks down Steele at a farmhouse but is himself trapped, managing to escape with Bacall's help; she is there visiting Ridgely's wife, Knudson, the woman Shawn Regan was supposed to have run off with. Through a ruse, Bogart manages to kill Steele and both he and Bacall go to Geiger's house where Ridgely finally shows up, admitting that he has killed Von Eltz and Heydt and was responsible for several other deaths, but not Regan's. Regan was killed by Vickers when he rejected her advances. Ridgely's men are waiting outside, guns at the ready, but Bogart shoots the gang boss and then orders the wounded man out the door where he is mistaken for Bogart and killed. Bogie calls the police, having solved the mystery, promising that Vickers will be sent to an asylum, not to prison. He holds Bacall in his arms as they hear the approaching wail of police sirens. The unwieldy plot designed by Chandler kept Hawks busy trying to figure out the puzzle; at one point during the production Hawks could not determine who killed the Sternwood chauffeur, so he called the author. Chandler reportedly stated: "How should I know? You figure it out," and hung up. The director also had problems with the great novelist William Faulkner, one of those who worked on the marvelous script. Faulkner, the story goes, tolds Hawks that working at the Warner Brothers Studio cramped his writing style. He asked if he couldn't work on the script at home. Hawks agreed! After many days went by and he didn't hear from Faulkner, the director frantically called The Garden of Allah apartment complex where the writer was staying. He was informed that Faulkner had left town. Hawks finally found Faulkner in his hometown of Oxford, Mississippi. "What are you doing there, Bill?" he asked. "Well," replied the laconic Faulkner, "you said I could go home and write, didn't you?" Apocryphal or not, the story is in keeping with the colorful production, which boasts a sparklingly witty script, one of the best in the genre, with electric lines that crackle between Bacall and Bogart, especially when they first meet and Bogart takes the spoiled heiress down a few pegs. She complains about his manners and Bogart nods: "I don't like them either; I grieve over them on long winter evenings." She looks him over, saying, "And you're not very tall." "Next time I'll come on stilts," he retorts. It was on the set of THE BIG SLEEP that the Bogart and Bacall love-team image on and offscreen was cemented, although their first sizzling union on screen was in TO HAVE AND HAVE NOT. Chandler, miffed at not being able to write the screenplay to his own novel, was uncooperative but Hawks actually made more sense of the impossible story than what the novel conveyed, while retaining its chilling mystery, sudden violence, and sparkling characters, creating a *film noir* masterpiece.

p&d, Howard Hawks; w, William Faulkner, Jules Furthman, Leigh Brackett (based on the novel by Raymond Chandler); ph, Sidney Hickox; m, Max Steiner; md, Leo F. Forbstein; ed, Christian Nyby; art d, Carl Jules Weyl; set d, Fred MacLean; cos, Leah Rhodes; spec eff, E. Roy Davidson.

Mystery/Crime Drama Cas. (PR:C MPAA:NR)

BIG SLEEP, THE 1/2 (1978, Brit.) 99m UA c

Robert Mitchum *(Philip Marlowe)*, Sarah Miles *(Charlotte Sternwood)*, Richard Boone *(Lash Canino)*, Candy Clark *(Camilla Sternwood)*, Joan Collins *(Agnes Lozelle)*, Edward Fox *(Joe Brody)*, John Mills *(Inspector Carson)*, Jimmy Stewart

(Gen. Sternwood), Oliver Reed *(Eddie Mars)*, Harry Andrews *(Butler Norris)*, Colin Blakely *(Harry Jones)*, Richard Todd *(Barker)*, Diana Quick *(Mona Grant)*, James Donald *(Inspector Gregory)*, John Justin *(Arthur Geiger)*, Simon Turner *(Karl Lundgren)*, Martin Potter *(Owen Taylor)*, David Savile *(Rusty Regan)*, Dudley Sutton *(Lanny)*, Don Henderson *(Lou)*, Nik Forster *(Croupier)*, Joe Ritchie *(Taxi Driver)*, Patrick Durkin *(Reg)*, Derek Deadman *(Man in Bookstore)*.

THE BIG SLEEP is the right name for this cinematic quaalude. Raymond Chandler, who was more Los Angeles than smog, wrote about the city of the Angels in a unique way. To transfer the story to England (Kastner lives in England and Winner is British) is like putting a Mickey Spillane story in Peoria. Mitchum plays Bogart, Miles plays Bacall, Clark plays Martha Vickers, and so on. The 1946 version was a sprightly, sharp, funny screenplay by Jules Furthman, Leigh Brackett, and Faulkner, as in William, and never flagged for a second. This is nowhere on every level except cinematography. Some very good British and American actors are hamstrung by the turgid screenplay (Winner) and the ordinary direction (Winner, again). But what else can we expect from the director of THE SENTINEL and WON TON TON? Mitchum is hired by Stewart's daughters, Clark and Miles. Mills, Todd, and Fox are the British cops and Edward Fox is wasted in a small role. Joan Collins (before "Dynasty") has a medium-sized part as a bookstore employee. This picture proves the theory that it doesn't pay to remake a movie unless you can make it better. Mitchum did it once before in FAREWELL, MY LOVELY which was a somewhat better picture, despite having the same producer.

p, Elliot Kastner, Michael Winner; d&w, Winner; ph, Robert Paynter (DeLuxe Color); m, Jerry Fielding; ed, Freddie Wilson; prod d, Harry Pottle; art d, John Graysmark; cos, Rob Beck.

Mystery   **Cas.**   **(PR:C MPAA:R)**

BIG SOMBRERO, THE *½   (1949) 77m COL c

Gene Autry *(Himself)*, Elena Verdugo *(Estrellita Estrada)*, Stephen Dunne *(James Garland)*, George J. Lewis *(Juan Vazcaro)*, Vera Marshe *(Angie Burke)*, William Edmunds *(Luis Alvarado)*, Martin Garralaga *(Felipe Gonzales)*, Gene Stutenroth *(Ben McBride)*, Neyle Morrow *(Tico)*, Bob Cason *(Stacy)*, Pierce Lyden *(Farmer)*, Rian Valente *(Esteban)*, Antonio Filauri *(Pablo)*, and Champion, the Horse.

Gene Autry as Gene Autry, Elena Verdugo as a sexy senorita, and Dunne as the villain in this somewhat predictable story of a gigolo-type (Dunne) who wants to marry Elena in order to gain control of her rich rancho. Gene comes into the picture and, like Mighty Mouse, "saves the day." Plenty of punches, punch lines, gunplay, and melodies are offered. Gene manages five songs as well as a triple medley in betweeen bouts of derring-do. Autry parlayed a pleasant face and voice into millions and wound up as major stockholder of a huge broadcasting conglomerate as well as the California Angels baseball team. (See GENE AUTRY series, Index.)

p, Armand Schaefer; d, Frank McDonald; w, Olive Cooper; ph, William Bradford (Cinecolor); ed, Henry Batista.

Western Musical   **(PR:A MPAA:NR)**

BIG SPLASH, THE*   (1935, Brit.) 66m BL/MGM bw

Frank Pettingell *(Bodkin)*, Finlay Currie *(Hartley Bassett)*, Marguerite Allan *(Germaine)*, Drusilla Wills *(Mrs. Bodkin)*, Roy Royston *(Jack Trent)*, Ben Welden *(Crook)*, Percy Parsons *(Crook)*.

An engaged millionaire, either gunshy about marriage or else used to having everything done for him, hires a married man to take his place. Not a lot of laughs.

p, Herbert Smith; d, Leslie Hiscott; w, Michael Barringer.

Comedy   **(PR:A MPAA:NR)**

BIG STAMPEDE, THE**   (1932) 63m WB bw

John Wayne *(John Steele)*, Noah Beery *(Sam Crew)*, Mae Madison *(Ginger Malloy)*, Luis Alberni *(Sonora Joe)*, Berton Churchill *(Gov. Lew Wallace)*, Paul Hurst *(Arizona)*, Sherwood Bailey *(Pat Malloy)*, Lafe McKee, Frank Ellis, Hank Bell, Duke the Horse.

Beery draws down his eyebrows as the displeased cattle rustler who kills one sheriff only to find Wayne, the new sheriff, is good at crossing over the law and making friends with bandits. Remake of LAND BEYOND THE LAW from Ken Maynard's silent which Warners repeated wtih Dick Foran in 1936.

p, Leon Schlesinger; d, Tenny Wright; w, Kurt Kempler (based on a story by Marion Jackson); ph, Ted McCord; ed, Frank Ware.

Western   **(PR:A MPAA:NR)**

BIG STEAL, THE***   (1949) 71m RKO bw

Robert Mitchum *(Duke)*, Jane Greer *(Joan)*, William Bendix *(Blake)*, Patric Knowles *(Fiske)*, Ramon Navarro *(Col. Ortega)*, Don Alvarado *(Lt. Ruiz)*, John Qualen *(Seton)*, Pascual Garcia Pena *(Manuel)*.

Don Siegel, in one of his earliest efforts, helmed this chase movie about Mitchum and Greer chasing Knowles across Mexico (where it was filmed). Knowles has an Army payroll worth several hundred G's. Meanwhile, Bendix is after Mitchum. Lots of holes in the story but it doesn't matter as Siegel's sharp direction, Homes' and Adams' tight script, and Beetley's editing keep the action going with nary a flag. Mitchum is full of energy as a framed officer trying to get the real perpetrator of the deed. (In later years, he's become something of an actor of the somnambulistic school.) It's well-crafted surprise.

p, Jack J. Gross; d, Don Siegel; w, Geoffrey Homes, Gerald Drayson Adams (based on *The Road To Carmichael's* by Richard Wormser.); ph, Harry J. Wild; m, Leigh Harline; ed, Samuel E. Beetley.

Crime   **Cas.**   **(PR:C MPAA:NR)**

BIG STORE, THE**½   (1941) 84m MGM bw

Groucho Marx *(Wolf J. Flywheel)*, Chico Marx *(Ravelli)*, Harpo Marx *(Wacky)*, Tony Martin *(Tommy Rogers)*, Virginia Grey *(Joan Sutton)*, Margaret Dumont *(Martha Phelps)*, Douglass Dumbrille *(Mr. Grover)*, William Tannen *(Fred Sutton)*, Marion Martin *(Peggy Arden)*.

Five was a magic number for the Marx Brothers. This was their fifth and last film for MGM, and they also made five for Paramount. It wasn't their finest, nor was it their lowest, but even medium Marx is better than no Marx at all. Groucho is hired to guard the body of Tony Martin, owner of The Big Store, a department store whose manager is Douglas Dumbrille, a villain who would love to get rid of Tony. That's about the plot; the rest is Mack Sennett-type chases, a turn on the harp for Harpo, a little piano for Chico, some leering at Margaret Dumont by Groucho, and the movie is over. Just when you think they can't slap the stick any louder, they do it. Tony Martin sings "Tenement Symphony" —all about "The Cohens and The Kellys," and what it is doing in this movie is beyond us, but it's a nice number and Martin is a good singer. Married to Cyd Charisse for almost 40 years, Tony Martin (born Alvin Morris, his father and uncle were also in show business as musicians) was also married to Alice Faye. Writer Hal Fimberg also wrote IN LIKE FLINT years later and writer Sid Kuller continues to be one of Hollywood's best special material writers.

p, Louis K. Sidney; d, Charles Riesner; w, Sid Kuller, Hal Fimberg, Ray Golden (based on a story by Nat Perrin); ph, Charles Lawton; m, Georgie Stoll; ed, Conrad A. Nervig; ch, Arthur Appell; m/l, Hal Borne, Ben Oakland, Artie Shaw, Milton Drake, Kuller, Fimberg, Golden.

Comedy   **(PR:AA MPAA:NR)**

BIG STREET, THE**½   (1942) 88m RKO bw

Henry Fonda *(Little Pinks)*, Lucille Ball *(Gloria)*, Barton MacLane *(Case Ables)*, Eugene Pallette *(Nicely Nicely Johnson)*, Agnes Moorehead *(Violette)*, Sam Levene *(Horsethief)*, Ray Collins *(Professor B)*, Marion Martin *(Mrs. Venus)*, William Orr *(Decatur Reed)*, George Cleveland *(Col. Venus)*, Hans Conried *(Louie)*, Vera Gordon *(Mrs. Lefkowitz)*.

Lucy got her first major role as the arrogant moll of a small-time hood (MacLane). Fonda is a mild-mannered busboy who saves Lucy's dog from being run over. He's loved her, in a mild-mannered way, from afar and she decides to treat him nicely after his bravery. This endears her to him even more. MacLane slaps Lucy around and she is crippled and placed in a wheelchair but that hasn't changed her surly attitude. She wants to go to Florida and find a rich man. Fonda and she hitchhike to the Orange state, and much of that distance is with Henry pushing Lucy's wheelchair. Once in Florida, he rounds up a host of Broadwayites who are there for the winter and arranges a party for Lucy where everyone will come and pay homage to her. She has no idea that Fonda did all of this and is so moved by everyone at the party that she musters her last bit of strength, stands, and dances with Henry. The effort is too great and she dies in his arms, but she has gone out the way she wanted to go—at a party in her honor. This Damon Run-yarn is a charming, touching, and often funny little film that presaged GUYS AND DOLLS by several years, but you could see where the genre was going. Eugene Pallette is a fine "Nicely-Nicely" and two of Orson Welles' crowd register strongly in small bits, Agnes Moorehead as Violette (Pallette's moll) and Ray Collins as the betting king of Mindy's (in real life, Lindy's) restaurant.

p, Damon Runyon; d, Irving Reis; w, Leonard Spigelgass (based on the story "Little Pinks" by Runyon); ph, Russell Metty; m, Roy Webb; ed, William Hamilton; spec eff, Vernon L. Walker; m/l, Morte Greene, Harry Revel.

Comedy   **(PR:A MPAA:NR)**

THE BIG SWITCH *   (1970, Brit.) 80m Miracle/ScreenCom c (GB: STRIP POKER)

Sebastian Breaks *(John Carter)*, Virginia Wetherell *(Karen)*, Jack Allen *(Hornsby-Smith)*, Derek Aylward *(Karl Mendez)*, Erika Raffael *(Samantha)*, Douglas Blackwell *(Bruno Miglio)*, Julie Shaw *(Cathy)*, Jane Howard *(Jane)*, Roy Stone *(Al)*, Nicholas Hawtrey *(Gerry)*, Brian Weske *(Mike)*, Gilly Grant *(Sally)*, Desmond Cullum-Jones *(Chief Inspector)*, Derek Martin, Steve Emerson *(Heavies)*, Tracey Yorke, Lena Ellis *(Strippers)*.

Playboy Breaks picks up Raffael in a nightclub and takes her home for a night of passion. Stepping out briefly, he returns to find her murdered. Fearful of a scandal, he decides not to call the police, and becomes embroiled with a gang of blackmailers. Eventually, he finds his boss, Allen, is the leader of the gang and that Raffael (who faked her death) is in cahoots with him. After several chases and gun battles the crooks are captured and Breaks is cleared of any wrongdoing.

p,d&w, Pete Walker; ph, Brian Tufano (Eastmancolor); m, Harry South; ed, Peter Austen-Hunt, Nehema Milner.

Crime   **(PR:O MPAA:NR)**

BIG TIMBER*½   (1950) 73m MON bw

Roddy McDowall *(Jimmy)*, Jeff Donnell *(Sally)*, Lyn Thomas *(June)*, Gordon Jones *(Jocko)*, Tom Greenway *(Rocky)*, Robert Shayne *(Dixon)*, Ted Hecht *(Bert)*, Lyle Talbot *(lst Logger)*.

Short, fairly interesting story of a tree surgeon, McDowall, who comes to a logging camp somewhere in the Pacific Northwest. He tries very hard to be a good logger and falls for Jeff Donnell. Another logger, Jones, gives him a hard time and all ends well when Roddy shows his mettle by saving the foreman's life. There have been very few good stories about logging the great outdoors other than THE BIG TREES, SOMETIMES A GREAT NOTION, COME AND GET IT, and NEVER GIVE AN INCH. Perhaps they should stop making them? Lyle Talbot (whose real name is Hollywood) took a small role in this film but distinguished himself in many movies since. The same year this was made, Talbot had the distinction of appearing in one of the funniest films ever done, CHAMPAGNE FOR CAESAR. Talbot is one of those actors the public always recognizes but never remembers by name.

p, Lindsley Parsons; d, Jean Yarbrough; w, Warren Wilson; ph, William Sickner; m, Edward J. Kay; ed, Leonard Herman.

Outdoors Drama   **(PR:A-C   MPAA:NR)**

BIG TIME**   (1929) 85m FOX w

Lee Tracy (Eddie Burns), Mae Clarke (Lily Clark), Daphne Pollard (Sybil), Josephine Dunn (Gloris), Stepin Fetchit (Eli), John Ford (Himself).

Tracy is a Broadway dancer who marries actress Clark and together they become the toast of the town. When he gets involved with an underhanded aspiring actress, he ends up as a down-and-out Hollywood extra. Early talkie with some interesting backstage atmosphere.

d, Kenneth Hawks; w, Sidney Lanfield, William K. Wells (based on a story by Wallace Smith); ph, L. William O'Connell; ed, Al De Gaetano; cos, Sophie Wachner.

Drama   **(PR:A   MPAA:NR)**

BIG TIME OR BUST**   (1934) 61m Tower bw (GB: HEAVEN BOUND)

Regis Toomey, Gloria Shea, Edwin Maxwell, Walter Byron, Nat Carr, Charles Delaney, Hooper Atchley.

Irresponsible but great diver Toomey falls in love and marries assistant Shea. She is pursued by wealthy playboy Byron and gains her own fame overnight with his help. Shea constantly reminds him she loves her crowd-pleasing husband; Byron responds by not attempting to embrace her. High-fashion technical work can't turn around cornball story.

d, Sam Neufeld; w, G. W. Sayre (based on his story); ph, Harry Forbes.

Drama   **(PR:A   MPAA:NR)**

BIG TIP OFF, THE*½   (1955) 79m AA bw

Richard Conte (Johnny Denton), Constance Smith (Penny Conroy), Bruce Bennett (Bob Gilmore), Cathy Downs (Sister Joan), James Millican (Lt. East), Dick Benedict (First Hood), Sam Flint (Father Kearney), Mary Carroll (Sister Superior), Murray Alper (Hal Trenton), Lela Bliss (Mrs. Marshall), Harry Guardino (2nd Hood), G. Pat Collins, George Sanders, Frank Hanley, Virginia Carroll, Allen Wells, Pete Kellett, Tony Rock, Tony DiMario, Cecil Elliott, Robert Carraher.

THE BIG TIP OFF is so confusing that it might have made a better board game than it did a movie. Conte is a small-time newspaperman who won't disclose the source of his underworld info; a series of anonymous telephone tips. Bennett is a phony who runs telethons, then takes the lion's share of the money. Lots of flashbacks which only serve to confuse matters even further. Smith and Conte wind up together at the conclusion. Particularly muddling is the presence of Cathy Downs as a nun. There are several religious overtones here and no one seems to know why. Perhaps too much was edited out and we missed something.

p, William F. Broidy; d, Frank McDonald; w, Steve Fisher; ph, John Martin; m, Edward J. Kay; ed, Chandler House.

Crime Drama   **(PR:C   MPAA:NR)**

BIG TOWN**   (1932) 57m Invincible bw

Lester Vail, Frances Dade, John Lilern, Geoffrey Bryant, Edith Broder, Diane Bori, Alan Brooks, Bernard Randall, Thomas Holer, A. J. Herbert, Shannon Day, Herschel Mayall, Jason LaCurto, Walter Arnim, Gloria Grey and Edward Bower.

Newspaper editor breaks the big story when he discovers who is behind vice murders and why they were committed. The terminators do in only those who won't pay their protection money. Muffled production with good camera effort from Rogeili and Malkames.

d&w, Arthur Hoerl; ph, Bernard Rogan; ed, Jack Miner.

Drama   **(PR:C   MPAA:NR)**

BIG TOWN*   (1947) 59m PAR bw

Phillip Reed (Steve Wilson), Hillary Brooke (Lorelei Kilbourne), Robert Lowery (Pete Ryan), Byron Barr (Vance Crane), Veda Ann Borg (Vivian LeRoy), Nana Bryant (Mrs. Crane), Charles Arnt (Mr. Peabody).

Crusading editor Reed brings integrity to a major daily newspaper after being burned by yellow journalism. Unfortunately, the city room looks fake. Action takes off in the beginning but slows down to a crawl because of unnatural dialog, stilted direction and technical efforts.

p, William Pine, William C. Thomas; d, Thomas; w, Geoffrey Homes (based on the radio program "Big Town" by Homes and Maxwell Shane); ph, Fred Jackman; m, Darrell Calker; ed, Howard Smith; art d, F. Paul Sylos.

Drama   **(PR:AA   MPAA:NR)**

BIG TOWN AFTER DARK**

(1947) 70m PAR bw (AKA: UNDERWORLD AFTER DARK)

Phillip Reed (Steve Wilson), Hillary Brooke (Lorelei Kilbourne), Richard Travis (Chuck LaRue), Anne Gillis (Susan Peabody), Vince Barnett (Louie Snead), Joe Sawyer (Monk), Douglas Blackley (Jake Sebastian), Charles Arnt (Amos Peabody), Joe Alben Jr. (Wally Blake), William Haade (Marcus), Arthur Space (Fletcher), Dick Keese (Jimmy O'Brien), Sumner Getchell (Barry Cushman).

Out again helping shake down crime in the big city, crusading editor Reed exposes his publisher's kidnaping which is connected with mob-controlled poker clubs. Money man menaces niece Gillis and leads her uncle into blackmail. Reed is supported by sparky police reporter Brooke who helps justice prevail and sees the crooks get theirs.

p, William Pine, William C. Thomas; d, Thomas; w, Whitman Chambers (based on the radio program "Big Town"); ph, Ellis W. Carter; ed, Howard Smith; art d, F. Paul Sylos; set d, Glenn Thompson, Alfred Kegerris.

Crime Drama   **(PR:AA   MPAA:NR)**

BIG TOWN CZAR*   (1939) 61m UNIV bw

Barton MacLane (Phil Daley), Tom Brown (Danny Daley), Eve Arden (Susan Warren), Jack La Rue (Mike Luger), Frank Jenks (Sid Travis), Walter Woolf King (Paul Burgess), Oscar O'Shea (Pa Daley), Esther Dale (Ma Daley), Horace MacMahon (Punchy), Ed Sullivan (Himself).

In his attempt to lead organized illegal activity from the tenements, mob social climber MacLane finds himself charged with murder. It's a frame born out of clashes with a rival family, responsible for the dirty work. Then kid brother Brown drops out of college to follow in MacLane's footsteps and gets bumped off in the feud which brings on the final shootout.

p, Ken Goldsmith; d, Arthur Lubin; w, Edmund L. Hartmann (based on a story by Ed Sullivan); ph, Ellwood Bredell; ed, Phillip Cahn.

Drama   **(PR:C   MPAA:NR)**

BIG TOWN GIRL**½   (1937) 68m FOX bw

Claire Trevor (Fay Loring), Donald Woods (Mark Tracey), Alan Dinehart (Larry Edwards), Alan Baxter (James Mead), Murray Alper (Marty), Spencer Charters (Isaiah Wickenback), Maurice Cass (Mr. Huff).

Trevor sings her way to radio stardom masquerading as a French countess to evade her escaped-convict husband. This also protects her from an anxious newspaperhawk. Dependable entertainment from this first-class production.

p, Milton Feld; d, Frank R. Strayer; w, Lou Breslow, John Patrick, Robert Ellis, Helen Logan (based on stories by Darrell Ware, Frances Whiting Reid); ph, Lucien Andriot; md, Samuel Kaylin; m/l, Sidney Clare, Harry Akst.

Drama   **(PR:A   MPAA:NR)**

BIG TOWN SCANDAL**   (1948) 61m PAR bw

Phillip Reed (Steve Wilson), Hillary Brooke (Lorelei Kilbourne), Stanley Clements (Tommy Malone), Darryl Hickman (Skinny Peters), Carl "Alfalfa" Switzer (Frankie Sneed), Roland Dupree (Dummy).

Crusading editor Reed uncovers a professional gambling ring when he takes charge of paroled teenagers and provides them with a basketball court and recreation. Wise guy Clements promotes betting with the bad boys and gives them a place to hide stolen goods. His newly reformed buddies try getting Clements to give up a life of crime and one is killed in the effort. Okay production with standard performances.

p, William Pine, William C. Thomas; d, Thomas; w, Milton Raison (based on the radio program "Big Town"); ph, Ellis W. Carter; m, Darrell Calker; ed, Howard Smith; md, David Chudnow; art d, Charles H. Clarke; set d, Glenn Thompson, Alfred Keggeris.

Crime Drama   **(PR:AA   MPAA:NR)**

BIG TRAIL, THE***   (1930) 125m FOX bw-c

John Wayne (Breck Coleman), Marguerite Churchill (Ruth Cameron), El Brendel (Gussie), Tully Marshall (Zeke), Tyrone Power, Sr. (Red Flack), David Rollins (Dave Cameron), Frederick Burton (Pa Bascom), Charles Stevens (Lopez), Russ Powell (Windy Bill), Helen Parrish (Honey Girl), Louise Carver (Gussie's Mother-in-Law), William V. Mong (Wellmore), Dodo Newton (Abigail), Jack Peabody (Bill Gillis), Ward Bond (Sid Bascom), Marcia Harris (Mrs. Riggs), Marjorie Leet (Mary Riggs), Emalie Emerson (Salrey), Frank Rainboth (Ohio Man), Andy Shufford (Ohio Man's Son), Gertrude and Lucille Van Lent (Sisters), DeWitt Jennings (Boat Captain), Alphonse Ethier (Marshall).

Wayne was working as a property man, a kid just out of college, when director John Ford noticed him, promising him a substantial role in the future. When director Walsh was fielding about for the male lead in the film, Ford recommended Wayne, telling Walsh, who appeared in Griffith's THE BIRTH OF A NATION in 1915, and who would go on to become one of the best action directors in the business (OBJECTIVE BURMA, THEY DIED WITH THEIR BOOTS ON) that he "liked the looks of this new kid with a funny walk, like he owned the world." Walsh went to Wayne and explained that he was about to make a frontier epic and wanted him in the film. Wayne was dumfounded and thought he was going to get a bit part. When showing up for the first day's shooting, he was told that he had the lead in this early talkie. The tall youth almost keeled over. "But I don't even have any training in speaking lines," Wayne pleaded. "Speaking lines?" Walsh growled. "Forget that. Hell, all you gotta do is sit good on a horse and point!" The film deals with the first covered wagon train to cross the rugged Oregon Trail, beginning in St. Louis, going over the plains, up and over the high mountains with Wayne leading the impossible way and looking magnificent on horseback as he pointed and pointed. There is the traditional Indian attack, the pioneers beating off the redskins from their circle of wagons, a spectacular buffalo hunt, and a devastating scene where the entire cast was almost drowned when fording a river during a fierce rainstorm (Walsh always kept the cameras rolling). There is little plot other than the great trek West through the wilderness of Nebraska and Wyoming where the film was shot, with Wayne vying for Churchill's attentions with Tully Marshall and David Rollins. Walsh's direction is superb as he captures the thrilling outdoor action in this epic which cost Fox $2 million to produce, a fortune in those days. Further, the film was one of the first to be made in Grandeur, a 55mm wide-screen color process so impressive that the premiere audience jumped to its feet and cheered at the conclusion. Most viewers, however, only saw the film on the standard 35mm black-and-white screen, and this took away much of the impact. Moreover, the interior scenes were awkward, the sound freakish in that experimental sound era, and Wayne's amateur theatrics embarrassing, although most excused him as a newcomer. It didn't help matters when Fox producers insisted that Lumsden Hare, the studio voice coach, compel Wayne to make himself sound like an Englishman in buckskin so that each preciously recorded word could be understood. It all came out stilted, forced and unreal, unlike the outdoor scenes Walsh so expertly molded. Using different leading players, Fox released Spanish and German versions of this film and they also failed. Wayne next drifted into the oblivion of "poverty row" studios that would have him making sagebrush grinders for nine years until Ford once again came to the rescue by giving him the lead in his classic STAGECOACH.

d, Raoul Walsh; w, Jack Peabody, Marie Boyle, Florence Postal, (based on a story by Hal G. Evarts and Walsh); ph, Lucien Andriot, Arthur Edeson (Grandeur); m, Arthur Kay; ed, Jack Dennis; art d, Harold Miles, Fred Sersen.

Western (PR:A MPAA:NR)

BIG TREES, THE* (1952) 89m WB c

Kirk Douglas (John Fallon), Eve Miller (Alicia Chadwick), Patrice Wymore (Daisy Fisher), Edgar Buchanan (Yukon Burns), John Archer (Frenchy LeCroix), Alan Hale, Jr. (Tiny), Roy Roberts (Judge Crenshaw), Charles Meredith (Elder Bixby), Harry Cording (Cleve Gregg), Ellen Corby (Mrs. Blackburn).

THE BIG TREES is a remake of the 1938 VALLEY OF THE GIANTS and it suffers by comparison. Everybody who lives in and around Eureka, California, and who has the slightest interest in the lumber business is against the religious sect that resides in the redwoods. This includes Kirk Douglas who is a lumberjack extraordinaire. Kirk is just one of three rival factions that want the land the religious folks have settled. His greediness is eventually overcome by the love of Eve Miller, one of the religious people. This is a choppy and uneven picture with lousy dialog and worse performances. Douglas reputedly did this picture with no pay in order to get out of his contract with Jack Warner. This one spelled "Timber" at the box office.

p, Louis F. Edelman; d, Felix Feist; w, John Twist, James R. Webb (based on a story by Kenneth Earl); ph, Bert Glennon (Technicolor); m, Heinz Roemheld; ed, Clarence Kolster.

Outdoors Drama Cas. (PR:A-C MPAA:NR)

BIG WEDNESDAY* 1/2 (1978) 126m WB c

Jan-Michael Vincent (Matt), William Katt (Jack), Gary Busey (Leroy), Patti D'Arbanville (Sally), Lee Purcell (Peggy Gordon), Sam Melville (Bear), Robert Englund (Fly), Barbara Hale (Mrs. Barlow), Fran Ryan (Lucy), Reb Brown (Enforcer).

This picture may have cost more than every other surfing movie ever made all put together. It is also the most pretentious film of its kind in creation. Whereas Bruce Brown and MacGillvray and Freeman made surfumentaries with nothing more than fun intended, Milius, who always seems to have some allegorical intent underlying his work, infuses the movie with heavy-handed philosophy and all-around dumbness. It's a segmented film that shows the coming of age of pals through the medium of the beach. The best part of it is MacGillvray's photography. How Milius keeps working after THE WIND AND THE LION, DILLINGER and now this, is the miracle of Hollywood. It's the Peter Principle of Failing Upward. Busey and Katt are believable despite what Milius and co-writer Aaberg have given them to say.

p, Buzz Fetshans; d, John Milius; w, Milius, Dennis Aaberg; ph, Bruce Surtees (Panavision, Metrocolor); m, Basil Poledouris; ed, Robert L. Wolfe, Tim O'Meara; art d, Dean Mitzner.

Drama Cas. (PR:A-C MPAA:PG)

BIG WHEEL, THE* (1949) 92m UA bw

Mickey Rooney (Billy Coy), Thomas Mitchell (Red Stanley), Michael O'Shea (Vic Sullivan), Mary Hatcher (Louise Riley), Spring Byington (Mrs. Mary Coy), Lina Romay (Dolores Raymond), Steve Brodie (Happy), Allen Jenkins (George), Richard Lane (Reno Riley).

Mickey Rooney stars as a race car driver whose late father also tooled those speed wagons around the track. He becomes a hot-rodder and inadvertently causes the death of another driver. Soon, his reputation as a daredevil precedes him and no owner will give him a car to race. He hits the Eastern circuit and, after trying several different things, winds up in Gasoline Alley at the Indy track. Mary Hatcher sticks with him through thin and thinner and she is finally rewarded when Mickey comes to his senses after he comes in third at Indy, in a race he thought he had won. Hattie McDaniel sings a song for no apparent reason and Spring Byington and Thomas Mitchell are wasted as Mickey's mother and her beau. Mickey was 29 when this picture was made and that was his awkward age. He was too old to be the cute elf and too young to have those age lines that he owns now. Rooney remains one of America's gifts to the world of movies.

p, Harry M. Popkin, Samuel H. Steifel, Mort Briskin; d, Edward Ludwig; w, Robert Smith; ph, Ernest Laszlo; m, Nat Finston; ed, Walter Thompson.

Adventure (PR:A-C MPAA:NR)

BIGAMIST, THE* (1953) 79m Filmakers bw

Edmond O'Brien (Harry Graham), Joan Fontaine (Eve Graham), Ida Lupino (Phyllis Martin), Edmund Gwenn (Mr. Jordan), Jane Darwell (Mrs. Connelly), Kenneth Tobey (Tom Morgan), John Maxwell (Judge), Peggy Maley (Phone Operator), Mack Williams (Prosecuting Attorney), James Todd (Mr. Forbes), James Young (Executive), Lillian Fontaine (Miss Higgins), John Brown (Dr. Wallace), Matt Dennis (Himself), Jerry Housner (Roy), Kem Dibbs (Tanner Driver), Kenneth Drake (Court Clerk), Mac Kim (Boy on the Street), George Lee (Head Waiter).

Married traveling salesman O'Brien gets bored in Los Angeles and picks up lonely greasy-spoon cook Lupino, then marries her when she announces her pregnancy.

Number one wife Fontaine maintains their manufacturer's outlet in San Francisco. When they try to adopt a child, she discovers wife number two. There's a court battle which leaves the viewer annoyed with a vague ending. The judge promises to pass judgment the following week and that's all. Viewers are left speculating.

p, Collier Young; d, Ida Lupino; w, Young (based on a story by Larry Marcus, Lou Schor); ph, George Diskant; m, Leith Stevens; ed, Stanford Tischler; m/l, Matt Dennis, David Gillam.

Drama (PR:C MPAA:NR)

BIGGER THAN LIFE* (1956) 95m FOX c

James Mason (Ed Avery), Barbara Rush (Lou), Walter Matthau (Wally), Robert Simon (Dr. Norton), Christopher Olsen (Richie Avery), Roland Winters (Dr. Rurich), Rusty Lane (La Porte), Rachel Stephens (Nurse), Kipp Hamilton (Pat Wade), Betty Caulfield (Mrs. La Porte), Virginia Carroll (Mrs. Jones), Renny McEvoy (Mr. Jones), Bill Jones (Mr. Byron), Dee Aaker (Joe), Jerry Mather (Freddie), Portland Mason (Nancy), Natalie Masters, Richard Collier, Lewis Charles, William Schallert John Monoghan, Gus Schilling, Alex Frazer, Mary McAdoo, Gladys Richards, David Bedell, Ann Spencer, Nan Dolan, Mary Carver, Eugenia Paul.

A very unusual subject matter for everyone involved here. Mason, who also produced, is an American teacher (quite an incongruity) who becomes a willing pawn in a miracle drug experiment. The drug is cortisone and the film explores the assets and liabilities of the medicine. Mason becomes addicted to the stuff and it affects his mind, causing him to become egomaniacal and filled with incredibly manic plans. The addiction destroys his relationship with Rush, his wife, and Olsen, his son. Mason has a tough time with the role and considered his casting a boo-boo. Matthau registers strongly as Mason's pal and all secondary parts are done well under the sure hand of Nick Ray. Some basic errors were made in this film; the juxtapositioning of color and CinemaScope against such a black-and-white story was the first mistake. Mason's casting was another, and the general overall tone of pessimism didn't match the look. Yes, there's a happy ending, but, by that time, many of the people will be turned off, hopelessly depressed and in search of a warm pizza.

p, James Mason; d, Nicholas Ray; w, Cyril Hume, Richard Maibaum (based on an article by Berton Roueche); ph, Joe MacDonald (CinemaScope, DeLuxe Color); m, David Raksin; ed, Louis Loeffler; art d, Lyle Wheeler, Jack Martin Smith; cos, Mary Wills.

Drama (PR:C MPAA:NR)

BIGGEST BUNDLE OF THEM ALL, THE** (1968) 105m MGM c

Vittorio De Sica (Cesare Celli), Raquel Welch (Juliana), Robert Wagner (Harry), Godfrey Cambridge (Benny), Davey Kaye (Davey), Francesco Mule (Tozzi), Edward G. Robinson (Professor Samuels), Victor Spinetti (Captain Giglio), Yvonne Sanson (Teresa), Mickey Knox (Joe Ware), Femi Benussi (Uncle Carlo's Bride), Paola Borboni (Signora Rosa), Andrea Aureli (Carabiniere), Aldo Bufi Landi (Capitano del Signore), Carlo Croccolo (Franco), Roberto De Simone (Uncle Carlo), Piero Gerlini (Lt. Naldi), Ermelinda De Delice (Emma), Gianna Dauro (Signora Clara), Carlo Rizzo (Maitre d'Hotel), Nino Musco (Chef), Calisto Calisti (Inspector Bordoni).

Disappointing crime comedy about a nutty group of Americans: Wagner, Welch, Cambridge, Kaye, and Mule, who try to kidnap mobster De Sica while he attends the funeral in Naples of an old mob associate. The kidnapers are shocked to learn that not only can't the old hood raise the $50,000 ransom they demand, but that he is flat broke and being supported by his mistress. De Sica proposes that he include the kidnapers in on a big heist he's been planning, the theft of $5 million worth of platinum ingots when they're being shipped on. The inexperienced crooks agree and the robbery turns into a comedy of errors that finally ends with the loot falling out of the B-25 bomber the gang uses to make its getaway to Morocco. Good cast (including a cameo by Robinson, who blueprints the heist) can't rescue this spotty effort.

p, Josef Shaftel; d, Ken Annakin; w, Shaftel, Sy Salkowitz, Riccardo Aragno (based on a story by Shaftel); ph, Piero Portalupi (Panavision, Metrocolor); m, Riz Ortolani; ed, Ralph Sheldon; art, d, Arrigo Equini.

Comedy (PR:A MPAA:NR)

BIKINI BEACH** (1964) 100m AIP c

Frankie Avalon (Frankie & Potato Bug), Annette Funicello (Dee Dee), Martha Hyer (Vivien Clements), John Ashley (Johnny), Don Rickles (Big Drag), Harvey Lembeck (Eric Von Zipper), Keenan Wynn (Harvey Huntington Honeywagon), Jody McCrea (Deadhead), Candy Johnson (Candy), Danielle Aubrey (Lady Bug), Meredith MacRae (Animal), Delores Wells (Sniffles), Paul Smith (First Officer), James Westerfield (Second Officer), Donna Loren (Donna), Janos Prohaska (Clyde), Timothy Carey (South Dakota Slim), Val Warren (Teenage Werewolf), Little Stevie Wonder, The Pyramids & The Exciters Band.

In an embarrassing portrayal of a Beatle-like English singer named Potato Bug, Avalon endangers his chances with steady Funicello. Taxing his acting responsibilities, Avalon also has to perform his usual beach bum role. The sandy turf is threatened by wealthy publisher Wynn who wants to evict the surfers from the beach in favor of building a senior citizens' community. Romance ensues when teacher Hyer straightens him out. Technical effort is above the acting efforts, yeah, yeah, yeah.

p, James H. Nicholson, Samuel Z. Arkoff; d, William Asher; w, Asher, Leo Townsend, Robert Dillion; ph, Floyd Crosby (Pathecolor); m, Les Baxter, Al Simms; ed, Fred Feitshans; art d, Daniel Haller; m/l, Guy Hemric, Jerry Styner, Gary Usher, Roger Christian, Jack Merrill, Red Gilson.

Comedy Cas. (PR:A MPAA:NR)

BILL AND COO** (1947) 6lm REP c

Ken Murray, George Burton, Elizabeth Walters.

Heartwarming tale of a bird sanctuary where habitants are threatened by menace Jimmy the Crow. The blackbird is later bagged by lovebird Bill. Chirpendale is the model village home to several hundred birds. Spectacular scene has feathered friends tightrope walking as circus performers and executing aerial work with much skill. First- rate film has no human acting. Incredible achievement from Murray and Burton putting feathers in their caps.

p, Ken Murray; d, Dean Reisner; w, Royal Foster, Reisner (based on an idea from Murray's "Blackouts"); ph, Jack Marta (Trucolor); m, David Buttolph; ed, Harold Minter; md, Lionel Newman; m/l, Buttolph, Lionel Newman, Foster, B. G. DeSylva, Lew Brown, Ray Henderson.

Animal   Cas.   (PR:AAA MPAA:NR)

BILL CRACKS DOWN* (1937) 61m REP bw (GB: MEN OF STEEL)

Grant Withers (Tons Walker), Beatrice Roberts (Susan), Ranny Weeks (Bill Reardon), Judith Allen (Elaine Witworth), William Newell (Porkey), Pierre Watkin (William Reardon), Roger Williams (Steve), Georgia Caine (Mrs. Witworth), Greta Meyer (Hilda), Edgar Norton (Jarvis).

Unconvincing and careless story of a father who leaves his son the family business, which happens to be a steel mill, with certain restrictions. The heir is a playboy and unless he gains some experience working under a black superintendent, the kid will lose his inheritance to the veteran mill hand who can't even dictate a literate business letter. They have a year to work it out, after which the loyal employee will gain control of the company if dad's demands aren't met. During that time, the man pop left in charge of the plant steals the sheltered boy's girl and vice-versa. In the end, they resolve their bitter feelings toward each other. Poor cast and trite dialog drain this comedy of fun.

p, William Burke; d, William Nigh; w, Dorrell McGowan, Stuart McGowan (based on the story by Owen Francis, Morgan Cox); ph, William Nobles; ed, Edward Mann.

Comedy   (PR:A MPAA:NR)

BILL OF DIVORCEMENT, A**** (1932) 70m Selznick/RKO bw

John Barrymore (Hillary Fairfield), Billie Burke (Margaret Fairfield), Katharine Hepburn (Sydney Fairfield), David Manners (Kit Humphrey), Henry Stephenson (Doctor Alliot), Paul Cavanagh (Gray Meredith), Elizabeth Patterson (Aunt Hester), Gayle Evers (Bassett), Julie Haydon (Party Guest).

This was the second of three versions of the Clemence Dane play. The first was a British import in 1922 and RKO did it again with Adolph Menjou and Maureen O'Hara in 1940. But this version is the definitive one with Barrymore at the top of his profession and a radiant Hepburn in her debut performance. Barrymore is a man who has been living in a mental hospital for the past quarter of a century. He escapes on the day his wife, Burke, is divorcing him. Hepburn is in love with Manners and she is unaware to learn of the mental illness in her blood. This causes her to say farewell to her lover, as she is convinced she can never bear children with the stigma of insanity hanging over them. Barrymore, whose illness was triggered by a shellshock in WW I, is sane enough to step aside and let his wife remarry. His performance is superb as Cukor elicits a sensitive and caring man from beneath all the bravado. Hepburn, who was to work with Cukor again and again, was only twenty-four at the time. Her appearance was electric and sent critics reaching for new superlatives such as "absorbing," "neural stridency," "eugenic," "half Botticelli and half bobbed-hair bandit," and more. All true.

p, David O. Selznick; d, George Cukor; w, Howard Estabrook, Harry Wagstaff Gribble (based on the play by Clemence Dane); ph, Sid Hickox; m, Max Steiner; ed, Arthur Roberts; art d, Carroll Clark; cos, Josette De Lima; makeup, Mel Burns; tech d, Marion Balderstone; Piano concerto by W. Franke Harling.

Comedy/Drama   (PR:A-C MPAA:NR)

BILL OF DIVORCEMENT**1/2 (1940) 70m RKO bw (AKA: NEVER TO LOVE)

Maureen O'Hara (Sidney Fairfield), Adolphe Menjou (Hilary Fairfield), Fay Bainter (Margaret Fairfield), Herbert Marshall (Gray Meredith), Dame May Whitty (Hester Fairfield), Patric Knowles (John Storm), C. Aubrey Smith (Dr. Alliot), Ernest Cossart (Dr. Pumphrey), Kathryn Collier (Basset), Lauri Beatty (Susan).

Depressing, but engrossing remake of the classic Hepburn and Barrymore 1932 melodrama of the same name, this time with Menjou as the insane father and O'Hara (in one of her first roles) as the loyal daughter. Menjou escapes from the mental institution and shows up on his wife's doorstep on Christmas to find that she's divorced him and is ready to remarry. His sudden reappearance shocks everyone, including his daughter O'Hara, who is also engaged. When she learns that her father's insanity is hereditary, she refuses to marry on the chance she may bear children with the disease, and spends the rest of her days caring for her father.

p, Lee Marcus; d, John Farrow; w, Dalton Trumbo (based on the play by Clemence Dane); ph, Nicholas Musuraca; ed, Harry Marker.

Drama   (PR:C MPAA:NR)

BILLIE** (1965) 86m UA c

Patty Duke (Billy), Jim Backus (Howard Carol), Jane Greer (Agnes Carol), Warren Berlinger (Mike Benson), Billy DeWolfe (Mayor Davis), Charles Lane (Coach Jones), Dick Sargent (Matt Bullitt), Susan Seaforth (Jean Matthews), Ted Bessell (Bob Matthews), Richard Deacon (Principal Wilson), Bobby Diamond (Eddie Davis), Michael Fox (Ray Case), Clive Clerk (Ted Chekas), Harlan Warde (Dr. Hall), Jean MacRae (Nurse Webb), Allan Grant (Himself), Georgia Simmons (Mrs. Hosenwacker), Arline Anderson (Mrs. Clifton), Layte Bowden (Miss Channing),

Mathew M. Jordan (Reporter), Shirley J. Shawn (Mrs. Harper), Maria Lennard (Adele Colin), Brenna Howard (Mary Jensen), Craig W. Chudy (Starter).

Tomboy Duke plays a high school track star who sets an example for the less talented men's team. Fair technical effort with Duke projecting a few songs about her frustrations. Predictable situations with obvious resolutions leave film dangling.

p&d, Donald Weis; w, Ronald Alexander (based on his play "Time Out for Ginger"); ph, John Russell (Technicolor); m, Dominic Frontiere; ed, Adrienne Frazan; art d, Arthur Lonergan; ch, David Winters.

Drama   (PR:A MPAA:NR)

BILLION DOLLAR BRAIN* (1967, Brit.) 111m UA c

Michael Caine (Harry Palmer), Karl Malden (Leo Newbigin), Francoise Dorleac (Anya), Oscar Homolka (Col. Stok), Ed Begley (Gen. Midwinter), Guy Doleman (Col. Ross), Vladek Sheybal (Dr. Eiwort), Milo Sperber (Basil), Mark Elwes (Birkinshaw).

An awful adaptation of the Len Deighton book; laboriously slow, overly plotted, and almost without humor. Caine is again Harry Palmer and no longer working in Intelligence. He accepts an assignment to deliver some mysterious "eggs" to Helsinki where he meets Malden, a one-time CIA agent. Malden is involved with Begley, a nut-case who thinks the only good Communist is a dead Communist. Begley wants to defeat the Reds by attacking their satellite countries one by one with his own army. The story goes from Latvia to Texas; from London to the North Pole area; from the ridiculous to the inane. This abortion totally wastes all the actors and the great sadness is that it was Francoise Dorleac's last movie before her fatal car crash. Saltzman, Russell, and everyone else involved with the creation of the screen version should hang their heads. The actors are compelled to slog through a muddy, illconceived film.

p, Harry Saltzman; d, Ken Russell; w, John McGrath (based on the novel by Len Deighton); ph, David Harcourt; m, Richard Rodney Bennett; ed, Alan Osbiston.

Spy Drama   (PR:C MPAA:NR)

BILLION DOLLAR HOBO, THE* (1977) 96m International Picture Show c

Tim Conway (Vernon Praiseworthy), Will Geer (Choo Choo Trayne), Eric Weston (Steve), Sydney Lassick (Mitchell), John Myhers (Leonard Cox), Frank Sivero (Ernie), Sharon Weber (Jen), Victoria Carroll (Barbara Henderson), Sheela Tessler (Rita).

Tim Conway's license plate, in real life, used to be "13 WEEKS" because it referred to the length of time his TV series used to last. This movie probably didn't last 13 days in the theaters. Conway (whose real name is Tom; he had to change it when he joined the Screen Actors Guild so he wouldn't be confused with Tom Conway, the actor who played THE FALCON and who was George Sanders' brother) is a bumbler who learns that he is the only remaining relative of the fabulously wealthy Choo Choo Trayne (Geer, in his last performance), to give you an idea of the intelligence level. He has to duplicate the same hobohemian life that his aged relative did in order to glean the money. The rest of the story is as predictable as the sun rising in the East. Conway is getting to be more and more of a caricature of himself. The refreshing character he brought to TV on "McHale's Navy" has never matured and he seems to be doomed to doing the same thing again and again. A sad state for a man who had enormous potential. You can take a child to this, provided the child isn't too discerning. But over the age of six you'll find them nodding off.

p, Lang Elliott; d, Stuart E. McGowan; w, McGowan, Tim Conway, Roger Beatty; ph, Irv Goodnoff (DeLuxe Color); m, Michael Leonard.

Comedy   Cas.   (PR:A MPAA:G)

BILLION DOLLAR SCANDAL* (1932) 76m PAR bw

Robert Armstrong (Fingers Partos), Constance Cummings (Doris Masterson), Olga Baclanova (Anne), Frank Morgan (Masterson), James Gleason (Ratsy), Irving Pichel (Griswold), Warren Hymer (Kid McGurn), Frank Albertson (Babe), Berton Churchill (The Warden), Sidney Toler (Carter B. Moore).

Fight manager and professional masseur Armstrong sweet talks his way out of prison with friendly warden Churchill and becomes a wealthy oil baron's private gym instructor. By being observant, attentive, and a good listener, Armstrong picks up market tips which make him rich. The boss gives him a bum steer after discovering the ex-con's kid brother is messing around with his daughter. Pickpocket Gleason and punch-drunk fighter Hymer help Armstrong carry out his bets with able performances though bad script sinks their comedic efforts.

p, Charles Rogers; d, Harry Joe Brown; w, Willard Mack, Beatrice Banyard (based on a story by Gene Towne); ph, Charles Stumar.

Drama   (PR:A MPAA:NR)

BILL'S LEGACY*1/2 (1931, Brit.) 57m Twickenham/Ideal bw

Leslie Fuller (Bill Smithers), Mary Clare (Mrs. Smithers), Angela Joyce (Countess), Syd Courtenay (Count), Ethel Leslie (Bride), Ivan Crowe (Groom).

Idiotic tale about a paperhanger who manages to buy a race horse after inheriting a small amount of money and how he loses the little wad and the chance to step into the winner's circle. Low-brow grinder with stock racetrack footage carrying an almost non-existent story.

p, Julius Hagen; d, Harry J. Revier; w, Leslie Fuller and Syd Courtenay.

Comedy   (PR:A MPAA:NR)

BILLY BUDD**1/2 (1962) 123m UA bw

Robert Ryan (Master-at-Arms Claggart), Peter Ustinov (Capt. Edward Fairfax Vere), Melvyn Douglas (The Dansker), Terence Stamp (Billy Budd), John Neville (Lt. John Ratcliffe), Ronald Lewis (Jenkins), Lee Montague (Squeak), Paul Rogers (Lt.

Seymour), Niall MacGinnis *(Capt. Graveling)*, John Meillon *(Kincaid)*, Ray McAnally *(O'Daniel)*, Robert Brown *(Talbot)*.

The saddest words of tongue or pen . . . "what might have been." BILLY BUDD is a "what might have been" picture. The story was almost impossible to make into a movie because its more of an operatic plot, replete with good and evil allegorically depicted. Stamp stars as Billy, an ingenuous young man sadistically treated by Ryan, master-at-arms aboard a late-18th-century fighting ship of the British navy. Ustinov, who also produced, directed, and co-wrote the screenplay with Robert Rossen, is the captain of the ship, a man who stands in the middle and cannot make up his mind. There is no question that Ustinov is a prodigious and Protean talent, but he truly took on more than he could handle in all these categories. A good cast and crisp photography but soggy editing which could have easily lopped 20 minutes off the running time.

p&d, Peter Ustinov; w, Ustinov, Robert Rossen (based on the novel by Herman Melville); ph, Robert Krasker (CinemaScope); m, Anthony Hopkins; ed, Jack Harris; cos, Anthony Mendelson.

Drama/Adventure Cas. (PR:C MPAA:NR)

BILLY IN THE LOWLANDS* (1979) Theatre Co. of Boston/FIF INC c

Henry Tomaszewski *(Billy Shaughnessy)*, Paul Benedict *(Father)*, David Morton *(Joey)*, David Clennon *(Social Worker)*, Ernie Lowe *(Officer Duncan)*, Genevieve Reale *(Liz)*, Bronia Wheeler *(Mother)*, Robert Owczarek *(Uncle)*.

This is one of those movies made by a small independent group of people who apparently did it for love. It was done on half a shoestring and, unfortunately, shows it. Fairly standard story of the Bad Boy, the parental problems with the drunken father, and like that. The only person you may ever see come out of this picture is Tomaszewski, if he shortens his name. He's quite believable in the title role. Other than that, very little to recommend. (Loose sequel: THE DARK END OF THE STREET.)

p, Nick Egleson; d&w, Jan Egleson; ph, D'Arcy Marsh; m, The Nighthawks; ed, J. Egleson, Marsh.

Drama (PR:A-C MPAA:NR)

BILLY JACK* (1971) 112m WB c

Tom Laughlin *(Billy Jack)*, Delores Taylor *(Jean Roberts)*, Clark Howat *(Sheriff Cole)*, Bert Freed *(Posner)*, Julie Webb *(Barbara)*, Ken Tobey *(Deputy)*, Victor Izay *(Doctor)*, Debbie Schock *(Kit)*, Stan Rice *(Martin)*, Teresa Kelly *(Carol)*, Katy Moffatt *(Maria)*, Susan Foster *(Cindy)*, Paul Bruce *(Councilman)*, Lynn Baker *(Sarah)*, David Roya *(Bernard)*, Susan Sosa *(Sunshine)*, Gwen Smith *(Angela)*, John McClure *(Dinosaur)*, Cissie Colpitts *(Miss Eyelashes)*.

Unbelievably successful at the box-office, this cynical, hypocritical film has taken on cult status in recent years. BILLY JACK starred, was written, and directed by Laughlin, who encouraged the film (and his personal image) to be sold as the 1970s answer to Robin Hood, canonizing himself in the advertising. The material played upon all the best aspects of the socially conscious movements of the 1960s, and then perverted them by preaching that violence is indeed the solution to problems as long as it's for the right cause. The plot concerns Laughlin as a half-breed American Indian Vietnam vet, who is wandering throughout the Southwest. He comes across a racist community whose leader, Freed, and his son, Roya, constantly harass a progressive school for unwanted children of all races, which is run by Taylor (Mrs. Laughlin). If that isn't enough, Freed also runs a company that catches wild horses and sells the meat for dog dood. One day the children from the school venture into the downtown area to buy ice cream. The children are refused service, and a young pacifist Indian, Rice, is beaten by Roya, who is trying to impress his father. Laughlin arrrives and beats the daylights out of Roya using Hapkido, but then he, in turn, is pounced on by a group of good ol' boys who punch him out until the local sheriff, Howat, breaks things up. Seeking revenge, Roya rapes the schoolteacher, but Taylor does not tell Laughlin because she knows the martial arts expert will kill the rapist. Roya then seeks out and murders the Indian boy, Rice. Laughlin figures things out and goes after the rapist/killer. Roya manages to get one shot off, wounding Laughlin, who then beats the boy to death. On the way back to town, Laughlin is ambushed by a racist deputy, and he, too, is killed by our hero. Wanted by the police for two killings, Laughlin seeks sanctuary in a church. Reporters and cops find him and the schoolteacher convinces him to give up and stand trial. As he is led off to jail, the children rally around him in support and raise their fists in salute. Two sequels followed: THE TRIAL OF BILLY JACK (1974) and BILLY JACK GOES TO WASHINGTON (1977). Neither was as financially successful as the original, which gleaned a whopping $32 million at the box office.

p, Mary Rose Solti; d, T. C. Frank [Tom Laughlin]; w, Frank, Teresa Christina [Delores Taylor]; ph, Fred Koenekamp, John Stephens (Technicolor); m, Mundell Lowe; ed, Larry Heath, Marion Rothman.

Action/Drama Cas. (PR:O MPAA:GP)

BILLY JACK GOES TO WASHINGTON** (1977) 155m Taylor-Laughlin Dist. c

Tom Laughlin *(Billy Jack)*, Delores Taylor *(JeanRoberts)*, E.G. Marshall *(Sen. Joseph Paine)*, Teresa Laughlin *(Staff Worker)*, Sam Wanamaker *(Bailey)*, Lucie Arnaz *(Saunders McArthur)*, Dick Gautier *(Gov. Hubert Hopper)*, Pat O'Brien *(Vice President)*.

Long, arduous, and sometimes agitating rip-off of MR. SMITH GOES TO WASHINGTON. Except that, in this case, they actually give credit to the original screenwriter (Sidney Buchman, from a story by Lewis R. Foster) and the producer is, in fact, the son of the original director, Frank Capra. This is another remake that never should have happened. Laughlin is not Stewart (who starred in the original) or Buchman or Capra, Sr. He attempts to wear all of those hats and just misses on every account. Laughlin is a pretty fair actor, not a bad director, and a serviceable screenwriter. But when he attempts to do them all, something has to suffer. In this case, it's the movie. Laughlin is the naive senator who battles Marshall (in the Claude Rains role) and expatriate Sam Wanamaker (in the Edward Arnold part). It's talky, has violence, and virtually none of the humor of the original. Nor does it have the fun relationship between Stewart and Jean Arthur. The Arthur character is divided between Lucie Arnaz and Delores Taylor, Laughlin's wife, who does service as executive producer and co-author of the screenplay. If it wasn't made with such obvious sincerity, it would be a vanity production. But the Laughlins are sincere about what they do and one of these days they are going to do it right.

p, Frank Capra, Jr.; d, T. C. Frank [Tom Laughlin]; w, Frank, Teresa Christina [Delores Taylor]; ph, Jack Merta; m, Elmer Bernstein; art d, Hilyard Brown.

Drama (PR:C MPAA:NR)

BILLY LIAR*½** (1963, Brit.) 98m Vic Films/Warner-Pathe bw

Tom Courtenay *(Billy Fisher)*, Julie Christie *(Liz)*, Wilfred Pickles *(Geoffrey Fisher)*, Mona Washbourne *(Alice Fisher)*, Ethel Griffies *(Florence)*, Finlay Currie *(Duxbury)*, Rodney Bewes *(Arthur Crabtree)*, Helen Fraser *(Barbara)*, George Innes *(Eric Stamp)*, Leonard Rossiter *(Shadrack)*, Godfrey Winn *(Disc Jockey)*, Ernest Clark *(Prison Governor)*, Leslie Randall *(Danny Boone)*, Gwendolyn Watts *(Rita)*, Patrick Barr, Anna Wing, Elaine Stevens, George Ghent.

BILLY LIAR is a first-rate comedy-fantasy that featured Tom Courtenay in a role which Albert Finney had played in the stage version by Waterhouse and Hall. (Courtenay and Finney later worked together in THE DRESSER.) No one will argue the plot's derivation. It's the Anglo version of Thurber's SECRET LIFE OF WALTER MITTY, with Courtenay as the dreamer who works for a funeral director but, who retreats into a fantasy world. Billy is also a pathological liar who, like Oscar Wilde said, doesn't lie for gain, just for the sheer joy of lying. Billy is involved with three young women, two of whom share an engagement ring. Christie is terrific as a sweet young thing who is willing to overlook anything her charming Billy tosses at her. All secondary roles are sharply etched and wonderfully acted under the sure hand of John Schlesinger in his third feature. (The first two were TERMINUS and A KIND OF LOVING, two superb films that failed to garner any sort of audience. With this film, Schlesinger's reputation soared and he went on to make DARLING and get an Oscar nomination.) This story has had many incarnations. First the play, then this film, then a musical and TV series. Billy's life proves . . . if at first you're not believed, lie, lie again.

p, Joseph Janni; d, John Schlesinger; w, Keith Waterhouse, Willis Hall (based on their play); ph, Denys Coop; m, Richard Rodney Bennett; ed, Roger Cherrill.

Drama Cas. (PR:A-C MPAA:NR)

BILLY ROSE'S DIAMOND HORSESHOE

(SEE: DIAMOND HORSESHOE, 1945)

BILLY ROSE'S JUMBO (SEE: JUMBO, 1962)

BILLY THE KID** (1930) 95m MGM bw

John Mack Brown *(Billy)*, Wallace Beery *(Barrett)*, Kay Johnson *(Claire)*, Karl Dane *(Swenson)*, Wyndham Standing *(Tunston)*, Russell Simpson *(McSween)*, Blanche Frederici *(Mrs. McSween)*, Roscoe Ates *(Old Stuff)*, Warner P. Richmond *(Ballinger)*, James Marcus *(Donovan)*.

Very early wide-screen (70mm) western directed by Vidor and starring Brown as the Kid and Beery as Pat Garrett. Filled with historical inaccuracies (including an ending that sees Beery waving and smiling as he allows the Kid and his girl to escape, instead of gunning the Kid down like his real-life counterpart did), the film is notable for the participation of silent cowboy star William S. Hart, who served as a technical advisor on the shoot, and led the producers to the actual locations in New Mexico where the historical events took place. These touches of realism give the film a gritty, true-to-life look that was rare for westerns of that period. The plot concerns Beery's capture of Brown after a lengthy siege on his hideout. Brown is brought to trial, escapes, and is allowed to go free by Beery who can't bring himself to shoot the dynamic outlaw. The ending is total poppycock as far as the facts are concerned and two finales were shot, the British release getting the version where Beery guns down the Kid. A second telling of the legend, which was not much better, was shot in 1941 starring Robert Taylor as the Kid. Look to Sam Peckinpah's PAT GARRETT AND BILLY THE KID (1973) for the best version of this material.

d, King Vidor; w, Wanda Tuchock, Laurence Stallings, Charles MacArthur (based on *The Saga of Billy the Kid* by Walter Noble Burns); ph, Gordon Avil; ed, Hugh Wynn.

Western (PR:A MPAA:NR)

BILLY THE KID½** (1941) 94m MGM c

Robert Taylor *(Billy Bonney)*, Brian Donlevy *(Jim Sherwood)*, Ian Hunter *(Eric Keating)*, Mary Howard *(Edith Keating)*, Gene Lockhart *(Dan Hickey)*, Lon Chaney, Jr. *(Spike Hudson)*, Henry O'Neill *(Tim Ward)*, Guinn "Big Boy" Williams *(Ed Bronson)*, Cy Kendall *(Cass McAndrews, Sheriff)*, Ted Adams *(Buzz Cobb)*, Frank Conlan *(Judge Blake)*, Frank Puglia *(Pedro Gonzales)*, Mitchell Lewis *(Bart Hodges)*, Dick Curtis *(Kirby Claxton)*, Grant Withers *(Ed Shanahan)*, Joe Yule *(Milton)*, Earl Gunn *(Jessie Martin)*, Eddie Dunn *(Pat Shanahan)*, Carl Pitti *(Bat Smithers)*, Kermit Maynard *(Thad Decker)*, Ethel Griffies *(Mrs. Hanky)*, Chill Wills *(Tom Patterson)*, Olive Blakeney *(Mrs. Patterson)*.

Another horribly inaccurate version of the Billy the Kid story, this time starring Taylor in his first foray into the western genre. The plot has Taylor ride into a Southwest town and join up with Lockhart's gang of outlaws. Here he meets old boyhood friend Donlevy, who is now marshal of the territory. (This character is obviously patterned after Pat Garrett, but the script calls him Jim Sherwood for some unknown reason.) Taylor begins to change his shady ways when he is befriended by kindly landowner Hunter and Donlevy's fiancee, Howard. This is not to be because one of Lockhart's men murders Hunter and Taylor goes wild, gunning down all those responsible for the killing. Donlevy tries to convince the Kid to give up and stand trial, but Taylor refuses and lets the marshal kill him in a showdown. The performances are good and the color photography is excellent, but the film may as well have been about an entirely fictional outlaw because the story bears no resemblance to the actual last days of Billy the Kid.

p, Irving Asher; d, David Miller; w, Gene Fowler (based on a story by Howard Emmett Rogers, Bradbury Foote, suggested by book *The Saga of Billy the Kid* by Walter Noble Burns); ph, Leonard Smith, William V. Skall (Technicolor); m, David Snell; ed, Robert J. Kern.

Western   **(PR:A   MPAA:NR)**

BILLY THE KID IN SANTA FE*   (1941) 66m PRC bw

Bob Steele (*Billy the Kid*), Al St. John (*Fuzzy*), Rex Lease, Marin Sais, Dennis Moore, Karl Hackett, Steve Clark, Hal Price, Charles King, Frank Ellis, Dave O'Brien, Kenne Duncan, Curley Dresden.

An uninspired western programmer in which the Kid is on the run in Santa Fe after being wrongly accused of murder. Steele meets up with a cowhand whose brother was lynched by Steele's nemesis. Together, they hunt the outlaw down and deal him a full hand of justice. (See BILLY THE KID series, Index.)

p, Sigmund Neufeld; d, Sherman Scott [Sam Newfield]; w, Joseph O'Donnell; ed, Holbrook N. Todd; md, Johnny Lange, Lew Porter.

Western   **(PR:A   MPAA:NR)**

BILLY THE KID IN TEXAS*   (1940) 44mm PRC bw

Bob Steele (*Billy the Kid*), Terry Walker (*Mary*), Al St. John (*Fuzzy*), Carleton Young (*Gil*), Charles King (*Dave*), John Merton (*Flash*), Frank LaRue (*Jim*), Charles Whitaker (*Windy*).

Go-get-'em Steele does his best to put bandits (destroying a small western town) out of business while protecting resident cowpunchers from the rustlers. Implausible western has the kid rob a bank with a sheriff, who also has a bounty on his head. Acting not as good as usual for Steele with shameful technical efforts. (See BILLY THE KID series, Index.)

p, Sigmund Neufeld; d, Peter Stewart; w, Joseph O'Donnell; ph, Jack Greenhalgh; md, Lew Porter; ed, Holbrook N. Todd.

Western   **Cas.**   **(PR:A   MPAA:NR)**

BILLY THE KID RETURNS***   (1938) 51m REP bw

Roy Rogers (*Billy the Kid*), Smiley Burnette (*Frog*), Lynne Roberts (*Ellen*), Morgan Wallace (*Morganson*), Fred Kohler, Sr. (*Matson*), Wade Boteler (*Garrett*), Edwin Stanley (*Miller*), Horace Murphy (*Moore*), Joseph Crehan (*Conway*), Robert Emmett Keane (*Page*).

Likable singing cowboy Rogers puts the little bank robber behind a badge once again, restoring law and order to Lincoln County with the help of comedian Burnette. Big film made a name for Rogers. Fast action musical roundup with technical efforts strong and imaginative. Good novelty numbers from drummer salesman Burnette. Songs include "Born to the Saddle," "Trail Blazing," "When Sun Is Setting on the Prairie," "When I Camped Under the Stars," and "Dixie Instrument Song." (See BILLY THE KID series, Index.)

p, Charles E. Ford; d, Joseph Kane; w, Jack Natteford; ph, Ernest Miller; m/l, Eddie Cherkose, Smiley Burnette.

Western   **Cas.**   **(PR:A   MPAA:NR)**

BILLY THE KID TRAPPED**   (1942) 59m PRC bw

Buster Crabbe (*Billy the Kid*), Al St. John (*Fuzzy*), Bud McTaggart (*Jeff*), Anne Jeffreys (*Sally*), Glenn Strange (*Stanton*), Walter McGrail (*Judge McConnell*), Ted Adams (*Sheriff Masters*), Jack Ingram (*Harton*), Milton Kibbee (*Judge Clarke*), Eddie Phillips (*Dave*), Budd Buster (*Montana*), Jack Kinney, Jimmy Aubrey, Wally West, Bert Dillard, Kenne Duncan, George Chesebro, Carl Mathews, Dick Cramer, Ray Henderson, Curley Dresden, Augie Gomez, Horace B. Carpenter, Herman Hack, James Mason, Hank Bell, Oscar Gahan.

Bandit Crabbe and his comedic sidekick St. John are rescued from a hanging by outlaws wanting to use the Kid's name to carry out stick-ups and murders. Fast-paced gunfights and fist fights put the bad guys behind bars. Our heroes are later falsely accused of another crime. Horsemanship and photography balance swift direction. No assistance needed. (See BILLY THE KID series, Index.)

p, Sigmund Neufeld; d, Sherman Scott [Sam Newfield]; w, Oliver Drake; ph, Jack Greenhalgh; m, Johnny Lange, Lew Porter; ed, Holbrook N. Todd.

Western   **(PR:A   MPAA:NR)**

BILLY THE KID VS. DRACULA**   (1966) Circle/EM 73m c

Chuck Courtney (*Billy the Kid*), John Carradine (*Vampire Uncle*), Melinda Plowman (*Betty*), Walter Janovitz (*Franz Oster*), Harry Carey, Jr. (*Ben*), Roy Barcroft (*Marshal Griffin*), Olive Carey (*Dr. Henrietta Hull*), Hannie Landman (*Lila Oster*), Marjorie Bennett (*Mrs. Ann Bentley*), William Forrest (*James Underhill*), George Cisar (*Joe Blake*), Charlita (*Nana*), Virginia Christine (*Eva Oster*), Richard Reeves, Max Kleven, Jack Williams, William Challee.

Packed full of funny dialog, this film makes great bad weather fun. Vampire Carradine poses as the uncle of pretty golden-haired ranch owner Plowman. Conflicts arise when outlaw Courtney, her foreman, decides to marry and settle down with the sweet young thing.

p, Carroll Case; d, William Beaudine; w, Carl Hittleman (based on his story); ph, Lothrop Worth (Pathe Color); m, Raoul Kraushaar; ed, Roy Livingston; art d, Paul Sylos; set d, Harry Reif.

Western/Horror   **Cas.**   **(PR:A   MPAA:NR)**

BILLY THE KID WANTED**   (1941) 62m PRC bw

Buster Crabbe (*Billy the Kid*), Al St. John (*Fuzzy*), Dave O'Brien (*Jeff*), Glenn Strange (*Matt*), Charles King (*Saunders*), Slim Whitaker (*Sheriff*), Howard Masters (*Stan*), Choti Sherwood (*Jane*), Joe Newfield (*Child*), Budd Buster (*Storekeeper*), Frank Ellis (*Bart*), Curly Dresden, Wally West.

In an effort to save humble pioneer homesteaders from being swindled out of their land by racketeers, outlaw underdog Crabbe crosses over to the legal side of the law and foils the bad guys. Consistent comedy saves this otherwise ho-hum cowpuncher. (See BILLY THE KID series, Index.)

p, Sigmund Neufeld; d, Sherman Scott [Sam Newfield]; w, Fred Myton; ph, Jack Greenhalgh; ed, Holbrook N. Todd.

Western   **(PR:A   MPAA:NR)**

BILLY THE KID'S FIGHTING PALS*   (1941) 59m PRC bw

Bob Steele (*Billy*), Al St. John (*Fuzzy*), Phyllis Adair (*Ann*), Carleton Young, (*Jeff*), Charles King (*Badger*), Curley Dresden (*Burke*), Edward Peil, Sr. (*Hardy*), Hal Price (*Burroughs*), George Chesebro (*Sheriff*), Forrest Taylor (*Hanson*), Budd Buster (*Mason*), Julian Rivero (*Lopez*).

Ridiculous western starring Steele as the Kid and Young and St. John as his "fightin' pals" who come across a mortally wounded U.S. Marshal who was ambushed by the evil villain Piel and his gang who have taken over a small border town. The trio decide to fulfill the dying marshal's mission and kick the bums out. A bizarre subplot has Piel and his men digging a tunnel across the border into Mexico for smuggling purposes, but it's never made clear just what needs to be smuggled through the tunnel. For die-hard oater fans only. (See BILLY THE KID series, Index.)

p, Sigmund Neufeld; d, Sherman Scott [Sam Newfield]; w, George Plympton; ph, Jack Greenhalgh; ed, Holbrook N. Todd; md, Dave Chudnow.

Western   **(PR:A   MPAA:NR)**

BILLY THE KID'S RANGE WAR*   (1941) 60m PRC bw

Bob Steele (*Billy the Kid*), Joan Barclay (*Ellen*), Al St. John (*Fuzzy*), Carleton Young (*Jeff*), Rex Lease (*Buck*), Milton Kibbee (*Leonard*), Karl Hackett (*Williams*), Ted Adams (*Sheriff*), Julian Rivero (*Romero*), John Ince (*Hastings*), Alden Chase (*Dave*), Howard Master (*Jenkins*), Buddy Roosevelt (*Spike*), Ralph Peters (*Jailer*).

When outlaws try to frame Steele for murder, he finds crooked sheriff Adams is really behind it all. To add spice, a gang leader holds up the stage to get a government contract for his steamship line. Poor film technique does not thread killings as a possible frame since Steele is shown in other parts of the country when the crimes take place. Because viewers know from the start what's what, the device makes for a slow, flimsy oater. (See BILLY THE KID series, Index.)

p, Sigmund Neufeld; d, Peter Stewart [Sam Newfield]; w, William Lively; ph, Jack Greenhalgh; m, Lew Porter.

Western   **(PR:A   MPAA:NR)**

BILLY THE KID'S ROUNDUP**   (1941) 55m bw

Buster Crabbe (*Billy the Kid*), Al St. John (*Fuzzy*), Carleton Young (*Jeff*), Glenn Strange (*Vic*), Charles King (*Ed*), Slim Whitaker (*Sheriff*), John Webster (*Dan*).

Crooked deputy replaces honest sheriff he had murdered only to be avenged by the good guy's buddies. When the press tries to oppose the crooked sheriff in an election, the bad guys put the old publisher and his girl Friday out of business by wrecking the print shop. Comedian St. John lightens up the mood, but sharpie Crabbe makes the movie. (See BILLY THE KID series, Index.)

p, Sigmund Neufeld; d, Sherman Scot [Sam Newfield]t; w, Fred Myton; ph, Jack Greenhalgh.

Western   **(PR:A   MPAA:NR)**

BILLY TWO HATS**1/2

(1973, Brit.) 80m UA c (AKA: THE LADY AND THE OUTLAW)

Gregory Peck (*Deans*), Desi Arnaz, Jr. (*Billy*), Jack Warden (*Gifford*), Sian Barbara Allen (*Esther*), David Huddleston (*Copeland*), John Pearce (*Spencer*), Dawn Littlesky (*Squaw*), Vincent St. Cyr, Zev Berlinsky, Henry Medicine Hat, Antony Scott (*Indians*).

The first western shot in Israel (as opposed to cheap runaway productions in Spain or Italy) stars Peck as a grizzled old Scottish bandit who teams up with a young half-breed, Arnaz, to pull a robbery. Things go badly and the two accidentally kill a citizen and the haul only nets them $420. Arnaz is captured and Peck rescues him only to be severely wounded by a gunshot to his leg. Now the tables are turned and the older, more experienced outlaw must rely on the young bandit. While on the run they encounter the homestead of an old rancher and his young wife. Peck pays the rancher to take him in his wagon to the nearest doctor, which is four days' ride away. Left alone together, Arnaz and the rancher's wife form a carnal liaison and are caught by the racist sheriff, Warden, who has been on the outlaw's trail since his escape. At the same time, the rancher is killed and Peck mortally wounded by savage Indians on the trail. Routine western redeemed somewhat by Peck's performance.

p, Norman Jewison, Patrick Palmer; d, Ted Kotcheff; w, Alan Sharp; ph, Brian West; m, John Scott; art d, Tony Pratt; spec eff, Les Hillman.

Western   **(PR:O   MPAA:PG)**

BIMBO THE GREAT* (1961, Ger.) 92m WB c

Claus Holm *(Bimbo Tagore)*, Germaine Damar *(Lilo)*, Elma Karlowa *(Yvonne)*, Marina Orschel *(Marianne)*, Helmut Schmidt *(Kovacs)*, Paul Hartmann *(Williams)*, Lisa Gussack *(Monica)*, Loni Heuser *(Circus Agent)*.

Joseph E. Levine imported BIMBO THE GREAT from Germany and should have left it there. A very predictable circus story with all the usual plot points; a fire, several circus acts, a murder. Bimbo should have stayed in limbo. There is nothing turkey-like about the movie; it's an honest attempt handled somewhat saggingly. The actors do what they can with the tired script.

p, Alexander Gruter; d, Harold Phillip; w, Hans Raspotnik, Harold Phillip, Erich Kroehnke; ph, Willy Winterstein (Eastmancolor); m, Theo Mackeben, Klaus Orgermann; ch, John Scapar; m/l, Vic Mizzy, Mitchell Parish.

Drama (PR:A MPAA:NR)

BINGO BONGO1/2** (1983, Ital.) 108m Intercapital Films/COL c

Adriano Celentano *(Bingo Bongo)*, Carole Bouquet *(Laura)*.

BINGO BONGO is the Italian version of TARZAN, but played for laughs, which is, perhaps, the way the latest Tarzan *should* have been played. Celentano, an enormously popular actor and singer in Italy, essays the title role, a man who grew up with monkeys, is captured in the jungle, and hauled back to "civilization." (Just imagine him coming back to the treehouse and mopping his brow as he says "Phew! It's a *city* out there, Jane!") Laura, an attractive anthropologist, teaches him to talk, the correct way to eat pasta, and how to fall in love. He does just that but she doesn't think it's a good idea. How does she introduce her parents to her in-laws, a pair of orangutans? Lots of laughs, in a good, low-comedy way, almost a throwback to Mack Sennett in several scenes. Good, clean comedy that you can take any child to.

p, Mario and Vittorio Cecchi Gori; d, Pasquale Festa Campanile; w, Enrico Oldoini, Franco Ferrrini, Laura Toscano, Franco Marotta; ph, Aldo Contini (Technicolor); m, Pinucchio Pirazzoli.

Comedy (PR:AAA MPAA:NR)

BINGO LONG TRAVELING ALL-STARS AND MOTOR KINGS, THE1/2** (1976) 110m Motown-Pan Arts/UNIV c

Billy Dee Williams *(Bingo)*, James Earl Jones *(Leon)*, Richard Pryor *(Charlie Snow)*, Rico Dawson *(Willie Lee)*, Sam "Birmingham" Briston *(Louis)*, Jophery Brown *(Champ Chambers)*, Leon Wagner *(Fat Sam)*, Tony Burton *(Isaac)*, John McCurry *(Walter Murchman)*, Stan Shaw *(Esquire Joe Calloway)*, DeWayne Jessie *(Rainbow)*, Ted Ross *(Sallie Potter)*, Mabel King *(Bertha)*, Sam Laws *(Henry)*, Alvin Childress *(Horace)*, Ken Force *(Honey)*, Carl Gordon *(Mack)*, Anna Capri *(Prostitute)*, Joel Fluellen *(Mr. Holland)*, Sarina C. Grant *(Pearline)*.

If you love the grand old American sport of baseball, you'll enjoy this good-natured look at the old Negro Leagues, B.J.R. (Before Jackie Robinson). There is no accounting for taste and there is no way to understand why this Motown picture didn't turn many turnstiles. The script was a fine mix of humor and pathos and honest drama. The direction was brisk. The photography and production design were first-rate. What happened to make it a flop? Tired of being abused by the owners of all-black teams, Williams forms an independent team, and is joined by other black stars. Their former employers conspire to put the Bingo Long All-Stars out of business, but the team succeeds in barnstorming the country, playing amateur white teams and achieving some success. In the climactic final game, Williams' team is pitted against a team of all stars from the black league; if his team wins, it gets a spot in the league, but if it loses, the players have to return to the servitude of their former teams. Williams and Jones are very good in their roles as the star pitcher and catcher, and Pryor does a nice comic turn as the player who poses as a Cuban and then an Indian in an attempt to overcome Major League baseball's color barrier. Entertaining and well worth a look.

p, Rob Cohen; d, John Badham; w, Hal Barwood, Matthew Robbins; ph, Bill Butler (Panavision, Technicolor); m, William Goldstein; ed, David Rawlins; cos, Bernard Johnson.

Comedy Cas. (PR:A-C MPAA:PG)

BIOGRAPHY OF A BACHELOR GIRL1/2** (1935) 84m MGM bw

Ann Harding *(Marion)*, Robert Montgomery *(Kurt)*, Edward Everett Horton *(Nolan)*, Edward Arnold *(Feydak)*, Una Merkel *(Slade)*, Charles Richman *(Kinnicott)*, Greta Meyer *(Minnie)*, Willard Robertson *(Process Server)*, Donald Meek *(Mr. Irish)*.

Artist dynamo Harding, whose career was boosted by her first flame, a rising politician, meets up with editor Montgomery who disdains capitalist bureaucracy and all its components after he was left holding his father's hand when his dad was shot down in a labor war. Outstanding scene between Richman and Harding on metabolism, the subject of conversation. Good technical support, solid direction and excellent performances make this one above average.

p, Irving Thalberg; d, Edward H. Griffith; w, Anita Loos, Horace Jackson (based on the play "Biography" by S. N. Behrman); ph, James Wong Howe; m, Herbert Stothart; ed, William S. Gray; art d, Cedric Gibbons.

Comedy (PR:A MPAA:NR)

BIONIC BOY, THE*
(1977, Hong Kong/Phil.) 95m BAS Film Production/RJR Films c

Johnson Yap, Ron Rogers, Susan Beacher, Carole King, Clem Parsons, David McCoy, Steve Nicholson, Kerry Chandler, Debbie Rogers, Kathleen Scherini

An Interpol agent is killed by gangsters after he saves the life of a wealthy industrialist who stood in their way. When the rest of his family is killed in a car crash, the Interpol agent's badly injured son is fitted with heavy-duty artificial limbs. With the help of his father's friends at Interpol, he wipes out the gangsters, save for the boss who heads for sequel land. This was a cheap attempt to combine the popularity of martial arts films and the popular television show "The Six Million Dollar Man." Poorly made profiteer.

p, Bobby A. Suarez; d, Leody M. Diaz; w, Romeo N. Galang; ph, Arnold Alvaro.

Spy Drama (MPAA:NR)

BIQUEFARRE** (1983, Fr.) 90m Midas/Millia Films c

Henri Rouquier *(Henri)*, Maria Rouquier *(Maria)*, Roget Malet *(Raoul)*, Marius Benaben *(Lucien)*, Helene Benaben *(Hortense)*, Andre Benaben *(Marcel)*, Francine Benaben *(Martine)*, Marie-Helene Benaben *(Genevieve)*, Roch Rouquier *(Roch)*, Raymon Rouquier *(Raymond)*, Georgette Rouquier *(Jeanette)*.

This semi-documentary is the 35-years-later sequel to George Rouquier's FARREBIQUE and has been shown in tandem with the original in various theaters. Both FARREBIQUE and BIQUEFARRE have to do with a family of farmers. In the first film, the highlight was the coming of electricity to the theretofore unelectrified farm. In the sequel, the drama comes when one farmer sells his farm to another. You can't call it a documentary because the actors have been staged, and yet most of the actors are real people so this falls between two stools. If you liked Robert Flaherty, you might like this picture. Nothing much happens in BIQUEFARRE but it still holds interest because of its reality.

p, William Gilcher, Marie-Francois Mascaro, Bertrand van Effenterre; d, George Rouquier; ph, Andre Villard; m, Yves Gilbert; ed, Genevieve Louveau.

Docudrama (PR:A MPAA:NR)

BIRCH INTERVAL*** (1976) 103m GAMMA III c

Eddie Albert *(Pa Strawacher)*, Rip Torn *(Thomas)*, Ann Wedgeworth *(Marie)*, Susan McClung *(Jessie)*, Brian Part *(Samuel)*, Jann Stanley *(Esther)*, Bill Lucking *(Charlie)*, Margaret Leary *(Hattie)*, Anne Revere *(Mrs. Tanner)*, George Eveling *(Aaron Byler)*, Eunice Lehman *(Mrs. Byler)*, Doug Fishel, Jr. *(Josh)*, Patricia Elliott *(Martha)*, William Morgan, Jr. *(Andrew)*, Andrew Gates *(Mason)*, John Keffer *(Borsy)*, David Gates *(Pissy)*, Robin Strosnider *(Crazy Girl)*, Joanna Crawford *(Lady on Bus)*.

A sensitive and compelling film that nobody went to see. Perhaps it was the title, the fact that there were no big names on the marquee, whatever. McClung is a "city cousin" who comes to the Amish country to live with relatives Torn and Albert. Radnitz has made a career of doing intelligent, but seldom seen, movies. In the past, he's produced SOUNDER, ISLAND OF THE BLUE DOLPHINS, A DOG OF FLANDERS, and others and none has been terribly successful. Still, he manages to raise money and to make these movies for a small but appreciative audience. The look at the Amish life is fascinating and all performances are good, particularly that by Anne Revere. It's handsome, well-written and well-directed, and if you are one of the few people who saw it, you won't forget BIRCH INTERVAL.

p, Robert B. Radnitz; d, Delbert Mann; w, Joanna Crawford (based on her novel); ph, Ura B. Furrer (Movielab Color); m, Leonard Rosenman; ed, Robbe Roberts; prod d, Walter Scott Herndon; set d, Marvin March.

Drama (PR:A MPAA:PG)

BIRD OF PARADISE1/2** (1932) 80m RKO bw

Dolores Del Rio *(Luana)*, Joel McCrea *(Johnny Baker)*, John Halliday *(Mac)*, Richard "Skeets" Gallagher *(Chester)*, Creighton [Lon] Chaney, Jr. *(Thornton)*, Bert Roach *(Hector)*, Napoleon Pukui *(The King)*, Sofia Ortega *(Mahumahu)*, Agostino Borgator *(The Medicine Man)*.

A lavish South Seas romance with a thin story line but wonderful graphics is about all RKO could muster when filming Richard Walton Tully's ancient play for the first time. McCrea is a wealthy playboy on a pleasure cruise, his yacht accidentally driven onto a coral reef, which lands him on an exotic Polynesian island where he meets the devastatingly beautiful Del Rio, the reigning princess. They promptly fall in love, but are pulled in different directions by their own kind. McCrea's friends sneer at his aim to marry this foreign woman, describing the rigors of miscegenation, while the natives insist that Del Rio keep herself pure. Under their bizarre superstitions and rites, she must be held aloof, untouched, ready to appease the gods should they become disturbed. What this means becomes gruesomely obvious when the island volcano begins to erupt. It is Del Rio's job to propitiate the volcano god's angry lust as the "bride of Peli" by diving into Peli's lava-belching mouth. Against McCrea's imploring, Del Rio is helplessly drawn to her native tradition and ends her life to save her tribe. The production, shot on location in Hawaii, is lush with shots of coral reefs, sandy beaches, dense jungles, and towering mountains, permeated with half-naked natives performing tribal dances. Del Rio, Mexico's first international film star, displays a scantily clad, almost perfect body. Her limited acting talents and language difficulties were overcome in a role that requires the child-like performance of an innocent native whose sophistication is buried in a foreign character. There is a good and humorous play on Del Rio's language limitations when McCrea attempts to teach her English. The production, which cost a then-whopping $1 million, was initially hampered in Hawaii when the "kono wind" appeared and stripped the palm trees. Crew workers had to spend days on end nailing branches back onto the trees before shooting began. But you'd never know this from the beautiful black-and-white results which stunned audiences first seeing the film. (Cinematographer De Vinna had won an Oscar in 1928 for his work in WHITE SHADOWS IN THE SOUTH SEAS.) Unique was Max Steiner's score, rich and bombastic, the first score to run continuously throughout a film. RKO executives thought this might distract audiences but it proved to enhance a basically weak story. McCrea, of course, is the perfect all-American red-blooded boy, bedazzled with his South Seas lover, hand-picked by Vidor, who had accumulated a divergent number of credits up to that time: BILLY THE KID, THE CHAMP. the film was shot in record time, twenty-four days, since McCrea and Del Rio had other film commitments waiting, and some makeup scenes were reshot in the studio backlot. Vidor was unhappy with the script at the start, complaining to Selznick, who had just taken over production at RKO, that there was not too much to the story. The producer shrugged and replied in typical fashion: I don't care what story you use as long as we call it BIRD OF PARADISE and Del Rio jumps into a flaming volcano at the finish." Selznick got what he wanted, as usual. (Remade in 1951 by Fox in color with even less story.)

p, David O. Selznick; d, King Vidor; w, Wells Root, Leonard Praskins, Wanda Tuchok (based on the play by Richard Walton Tully); ph, Clyde De Vinna, Edward Cronjager, Lucien Andriot; m, Max Steiner; art d, Carroll Clark; ch, Busby Berkeley; song, Milia Rosa, Peter de Rose.

Romance/Adventure Cas. (PR:C MPAA:NR)

BIRD OF PARADISE* 1/2 (1951) 101m FOX c

Louis Jourdan *(Andre Laurence)*, Debra Paget *(Kalua)*, Jeff Chandler *(Tenga)*, Everett Sloane *(The Beachcomber)*, Maurice Schwartz *(The Kahuna)*, Jack Elam *(The Trader)*, Prince Lei Lani *(Chief)*, Otto Waldis *(Skipper)*, Alfred Zeisler *(Van Hook)*, Mary Ann Ventura *(Noanoa)*, David K. Bray *(Chanter)*, Sam Monsarrat *(Tenga's Friend)*, Violet Nathaniel *(Chiefess)*, Solomon Pa *(Chief's Man)*.

They cast movies strangely years ago. Chandler is a South Seas native and his sister, Paget, is a sort of a Fijian Princess. Schwartz is a medicine man, the ever-urbane Sloane is a beachcomber, and none of it makes any sense in this handsomely mounted remake of the 1932 Joel McCrea/Dolores Del Rio version of the same Richard Tully play. Daves wears too many hats as he attempts to make a silk purse out of this. The story is very basic; Jourdan accompanies Chandler to his island home, falls in love with Paget. They woo (against all native traditions) and their courting courts disaster and predictions of terrible things from the witch doctors. A local volcano erupts and Paget's answer is to assume responsibility for the whole thing and to throw herself into the volcano to appease it. Phew! Talk about guilt! Paget (born Debralee Griffin) does a good job but is about as believable as Schwartz is as a medicine man. (Maurice Schwartz was one of the greatest actors of the Yiddish stage and introduced the character of TEVYA in an early Yiddish-language film.)

p,d&w, Delmer Daves; (based on a play by Richard Walton Tully); ph, Winton C. Hoch (Technicolor); m, Daniele Amfitheatrof; ed, James B. Clark.

Romance/Adventure Cas. (PR:C MPAA:NR)

BIRD WATCH, THE* 1/2

(1983, Fr.) 90m Pamter's/FR3/GAU c (LA PALOMBIERE)

Jean-Claude Bourbault *(Paul)*, Christiane Millet *(Claire)*, Nadine Raynaud *(Sylvette)*, Georges Vaur *(Father)*, Daniel Jegou *(The Rival)*.

"La Palombiere" is the French word for the tree-top cabin where Bourbault and Millet hold their trysts. It's not as comfortable as a Holiday Inn or even a Ramada but when you live in the Dordogne region of France, you can't very well choose accommodations for a fling. Bourbault is a shlump who works for the city. Millet is a beautiful teacher who has come to this tiny burg for a three-month job. Bourbault declares his love, is rebuffed. He tries again, she says no. She finally has nothing better to do so they begin their affair but both know full well that this cannot last. The director/co-writer's first film was made in the obscure dialect of Occitan (HISTOIRE D'ADRIEN) and won an award at Cannes. This will win no awards but it does offer a peek into life in Southwest France. It's a fair film, nothing stupendous, nothing embarrassing. But these days, more must be offered to the public than what LA PALOMBIERE has to give.

p, Ariel Zeitun, Claude Gildas; d, Jean-Peirre Denis; w, Denis; ph, Denis Gheerbrant (Eastmancolor); m, Jean Musy; ed, Anne Baudry; art d, Pierre Salet; m/l, Laurence Matalon.

Romance (PR:C MPAA:NR)

BIRD WITH THE CRYSTAL PLUMAGE, THE****

(1970, Ital./Ger.) 98m Glazier/UM c (L'UCELLO DALLE PLUME DI CRISTALLO; AKA: THE PHANTOM OF TERROR)

Tony Musante *(Sam Dalmas)*, Suzy Kendall *(Julia)*, Eva Renzi *(Monica)*, Enrico Maria Salerno *(Morosini)*, Mario Adorf *(Berto)*, Renator Romano *(Dover)*, Umberto Rano *(Ranieri)*.

A heart-stopping Hitchcockian melodrama with excellent acting from all involved. Director Argento uses humor, much like Hitchcock, to counterpoint the suspense, but it doesn't ever make you feel that the master is being ripped off. Musante is a Yank scribe in Roma and, walking home one night, he sees Renzi being murdered in an art gallery. He can't make out the killer but the police decide to keep him covered as this is but one of several murders of lone women. Musante cooperates with the police, but also goes out on his own investigation which takes him into the underbelly of the Eternal City. Memorable characters abound and Storaro's camera work is sensational. There are several terrifying sequences, one after another, and none gratuitous. What makes this picture so good is that it is totally believable and does not wallow in excessive violence. With a different title and better marketing, this movie would have been a smash.

p, Salvatore Argento; d&w, Dario Argento; ph, Vittorio Storaro (Eastmancolor); m, Ennio Morricone.

Crime Adventure Cas. (PR:C MPAA:PG)

BIRDMAN OF ALCATRAZ**** (1962) 147m UA bw

Burt Lancaster *(Robert Stroud)*, Karl Malden *(Harvey Shoemaker)*, Thelma Ritter *(Elizabeth Stroud)*, Betty Field *(Stella Johnson)*, Neville Brand *(Bull Ransom)*, Edmond O'Brien *(Tom Gaddis)*, Hugh Marlowe *(Roy Comstock)*, Telly Savalas *(Feto Gomez)*, Crahan Denton *(Kramer)*, James Westerfield *(Jess Younger)*, Chris Robinson *(Young Convict)*.

Lancaster plays a tough, withdrawn convict, Robert Stroud, who is doing life for an Alaskan murder and is almost later executed when he murders a guard at Leavenworth (this killing, in real life, was never explained by Stroud, who knifed a guard in front of the entire prison population in the mess hall). Ritter is Stroud's over-protective mother, who goes to the White House and begs for her son's life. (In reality, Mrs. Stroud met with Mrs. Woodrow Wilson, then actually running things as her husband was ill in the last months of his administration. His death sentence was commuted to life, provided Stroud was never paroled). The uncompromising inmate's life is changed when a small bird flies into his cell, a sick bird which he manages to cure by putting together some homemade medicine. This leads to Stroud's obsession with birds and deep studies which made him into one of the world's most learned ornithologists, developing cures for ill birds, even the most exotic. Stroud was allowed to build a bird hospital of sorts at Leavenworth. A wall into another cell was opened so he could expand his crude laboratory. A kindly guard, played with compassion by Brand, provides Lancaster with implements and chemicals, encouraging him at every turn, but he receives not a whit of thanks from the truculent prisoner. His nemesis appears in the form of Malden, a new prison warden. When Lancaster does not give Malden the proper respect, his bird laboratory is limited by the warden. But by then Lancaster has written several booklets on his bird cures and these have made him famous. One of his devotees, Field, comes to him, offering to set up a joint partnership outside the walls. She'll market his bird remedies. Lancaster agrees and on her subsequent visits it becomes apparent that she is in love with the man, offering to marry him. Before Lancaster decides, his possessive mother Ritter intervenes and wrecks the plan; Lancaster then tells Ritter he never wants to see her again. After defying Malden repeatedly, Lancaster is sent to Alcatraz, the notorious "Rock" in San Francisco Bay, where the most incorrigible prisoners were sent (Capone, Doc Barker, Alvin Karpis). Here he continues his studies and work, but stern-faced Malden arrives to take over the institution. He curtails Lancaster's activities after finding a manuscript which the prisoner has written, one outlining prison abuses by administrators. Then, in 1946, a massive riot breaks out, one which Lancaster helps to quell, earning him back his privileges. He finally comes to terms with Malden and is removed to the federal country club at Springfield, Ill., where infirm prisoners were sent to die. Lancaster has a touching meeting with O'Brien, playing the part of author Gaddis, who brought Stroud's story to the world, as he comes ashore from Alcatraz. The film has great production value, a deliberate and often moving script, and taut direction from Frankenheimer, a black-and-white specialist. But it is Lancaster's bravura performance which holds this lengthy movie together, long after the mystique of his character would have faded at the hands of another. Oddly, Stroud was nothing like the tough, taciturn character Lancaster embodies. He was a sneaky, whining, cringing type whose raging homosexuality, more than anything else, caused him to be permanently confined in isolation.

p, Stuart Miller, Guy Trosper; d, John Frankenheimer; w, Trosper (based on the book by Thomas E. Gaddis); ph, Burnett Guffey; m, Elmer Bernstein; ed, Edward Mann.

Crime Drama Cas. (PR:C MPAA:NR)

BIRDS, THE*** (1963) 120m UNIV c

Rod Taylor *(Mitch Brenner)*, Tippi Hedren *(Melanie Daniels)*, Jessica Tandy *(Lydia Brenner)*, Suzanne Pleshette *(Annie Hayworth)*, Veronica Cartwright *(Cathy Brenner)*, Ethel Griffies *(Mrs. Bundy)*, Charles McGraw *(Sebastian Sholes)*, Ruth McDevitt *(Mrs. MacGruder)*, Joe Mantell *(Salesman)*, Doodles Weaver *(Fisherman)*, Richard Deacon *(Man in Elevator)*, Alfred Hitchcock *(Man in Front of Pet Shop with White Poodles)*.

An emotionally disturbing film, Hitchcock's THE BIRDS takes the simple approach that even the most innocuous of creatures, our feathered friends, can and will turn upon the two-legged creatures ground-bound beneath them. Without his usual MacGuffin (Hitchcock's term for the item or individual sought that causes all the suspense, uranium in NOTORIOUS, a missing diplomat in FOREIGN CORRESPONDENT), the master of mystery relies purely on the shock value of nature revenging itself inexplicably upon humans in THE BIRDS. There is a story, to be sure, a weak one penned by Evan Hunter (a third-rate crime writer out of his element) where Taylor deserts teacher Pleshette for cool blonde Hedren, and a mediocre profile of Tandy who is worried over becoming too possessive of her son. But the angst Hitchcock creates with the residents of remote Bodega Bay over the bird attacks—when and where will they strike next?—is the meat of the movie. The rear projection (a favorite Hitchcock technique) and special effects are uncustomarily predictable in this film but that is of no matter. The birds flock in, thousands of them, to the community, waiting, lurking, about to pounce and peck their victims to death. They are everywhere and the viewer's heart stops time and again, waiting for these normally loving creatures to turn killer. Taylor meets Hedren in a San Francisco pet shop where he treats her flippantly. Intrigued, the playgirl follows him to Bodega Bay, ostensibly to deliver a pet bird to a friend, but really to develop a relationship with Taylor. She is attacked by a seagull, receiving a slight head wound which causes her to stay overnight with teacher Pleshette. Strange things begin to happen at Bodega Bay. A children's outdoor party is attacked by flocks of birds. The winged creatures begin to gather in vast numbers on rooftops and phone wires. Tandy finds a farmhouse wrecked, the farmer dead, his body shredded, his eyes gouged out. Then children, including Taylor's young daughter, Cartwright, are attacked as they leave their school by swooping, diving, pecking birds, a scene considered to be the most vicious ever recorded by Hitchcock. (It was achieved by having the children run down a road, waving their arms, beating off attacking birds that were not there; special effects artist Ub Iwerks later added the birds, plus arranged for some close-ups where his specially trained crows landed on a few children.) The kids reach safety, Cartwright and a friend being saved by Hedren who drags them into her car. Down in the town the local folk cannot believe the story Hedren and Taylor later tell them in a local restaurant. A local ornithologist pooh-poohs the notion that the docile birds, billions of them, would ever turn against mankind. Then birds attack a gas station across the street, causing a man to drop a lighted match into gasoline spilled by an attendant attacked by birds. The place blows up, fire and smoke spiraling upward. Hedren is trapped outside in a phone booth, trying to call for help, birds diving suicidally into the booth, smashing against the glass which splinters but does not give way. It is a nightmare come to life in broad daylight. A terrific long shot shows Bodega Bay in the distance, a small, peaceful community in panic, the smoke from the raging gasoline fire towering upward as a sign of holocaust and doom. Taylor spirits Hedren away to his home. En route, Taylor finds Pleshette, his former girl friend, pecked to death in front of her home; she has died to protect some of her school children from the killer birds. That night Taylor frantically boards up the windows. The birds cover the house, pecking relentlessly away at the heavy wood, as they attempt to get inside and kill the humans. At one point Taylor must board up a kitchen door that looks as if it had been sprayed with shotgun pellets. Hedren, hearing noises upstairs, goes to an attic room, steps inside, and shines a flashlight on an army of waiting birds who, for two agonizing minutes, attack her, cutting her to pieces before Taylor can drag her from the room and close the door. (This scene alone took a week to film.) At dawn, the battered family, Taylor leading the way, almost creep outside, moving quietly through thousands of birds, to get into a car and slowly drive away for a finish that is less than satisfying. Much has been written and said of this film, one of Hitchcock's less-than-reliable biographers stating that the director secretly lusted after his new star, cool blonde Hedren, she of the long legs, high cheekbones and million-mile stare, whom he was grooming to replace Grace Kelly, albeit the former model's acting ability was no more than that of a walking zombie. It was also said that Hitchcock was voyeuristically raping Hedren via his attacking birds in the horrific attic room scene, which is stretching the wildest notion to the absurd. (Now that Hitch is dead the vultures feed on his artistic corpse much like the ferocious birds the director made infamous.) Technically, the film is a marvel, with more than 350 special-effects shots employed. In one scene, where the birds are spread about over hill and dale, coating the landscape, 30-some pieces of film were put together for the effect. Hitchcock, by the time of this film, was reaching further and further to appease his expectant audience. THE BIRDS made up in shock for what it lacked in mystery, and there was some basis in fact for the story since a small West Coast community had, years earlier, been attacked by flocks of birds for no apparent reason. The only excuse Hitchcock gave was an indirect one, where the academic restaurant customer explains that the birds might take revenge on man for destroying the planet's ecology. Whatever, the film remains Hitchcock's most outlandish, most fiendish, and one of his most memorable.

p&d, Alfred Hitchcock; w, Evan Hunter (based on the story by Daphne du Maurier); ph, Robert Burks (Technicolor); m, Bernard Herrmann; ed, George Tomasini; prod d, Norman Deming; set d, Robert Boyle, George Milo; cos, Edith Head; spec eff, Ub Iwerks; bird trainer, Ray Berwick.

Mystery/Suspense   **Cas.**   **(PR:C   MPAA:NR)**

BIRDS AND THE BEES, THE½   (1956) 94m PAR c

George Gobel (*George Hamilton*), Mitzi Gaynor (*Jean Harris*), David Niven (*Col. Harris*), Reginald Gardiner (*Gerald*), Fred Clark (*Mr. Hamilton*), Harry Bellaver (*Marty Kennedy*), Hans Conried (*Duc Jacques de Montaigne*), Margery Maude (*Mrs. Hamilton*), Clinton Sundberg (*Purser*), Milton Frome (*Assistant Butler*), Rex Evans (*Burrows*), King Donovan (*Writer*), Mary Treen (*Mrs. Burnside*), Charles Lane (*Jenkins*), Bartlett Robinson, Douglas Evans, Barry Bernard, Kathryn Card, Vera Burnett, John Benson, Matt Moore, Valerie Allen.

Lots of good, solid comic performances and a pleasant script where Ol' Lonesome George (who was a very hot TV star at the time) is a vegetarian. Trouble is that his dad, Clark, is a very important meat packer. Returning on a ship from a trip to The Dark Continent, George falls for Gaynor, who is part of a card-playing cadre of grifters. David Niven is Mitzi's dad and annoyed that she's fallen for this wimp. Bellaver (excellent in TV's "Naked City") tells George the truth about his loved one and George leaves Mitzi. Later, Mitzi gets an invite to the huge estate, reestablishes herself with George, they fall in love again after a number of twists and turns, most of them funny, and all ends well. A remake of the much superior THE LADY EVE.

p, Paul Jones; d, Norman Taurog; w, Sidney Sheldon, Preston Sturges (based on a story by Monckton Hoffe); ph, Daniel F. Fapp (Technicolor); m, Walter Scharf; ed, Archie Marshek; cos, Edith Head; ch, Nick Castle; m/l, Harry Warren, Mack David.

Comedy   **(PR:A   MPAA:NR)**

BIRDS COME TO DIE IN PERU**

(1968, Fr.) 95m UNIV c (LES OISEAUX VONT MOURIR AU PERU; AKA: BIRDS IN PERU)

Jean Seberg (*Adriana*), Maurice Ronet (*Rainier*), Pierre Brasseur (*Le Mari*), Danielle Darrieux (*Fernande*), Jean Pierre Kalfon (*Le Chauceur*), Michael Buades (*Alejo*), Pierre Koulak (*Bouncer*), Henry Czarniak (*Camionneur*).

Gary wrote and directed this movie starring his wife, Seberg, as a nymphomaniac. It begins with a bang as she is being pummeled by a group of Peruvians in Carnival gear on a beach. She next moves to a seashore whorehouse and sleeps with Darrieux, an old hooker. Soon enough she's in the arms of several others. Seberg, we now learn, is as nuts as she is nubile and the picture degenerates into a pyschosexual rambling with Gary raging unchecked. One can hardly say the name of Seberg without adding "poor" to it. Poor Jean Seberg was a star in her teens in Otto Preminger's SAINT JOAN, then on to the landmark BREATHLESS and several others where she began to achieve an honest sort of stardom. Marrying Gary changed her career and she eventually died in 1979 in questionable circumstances and under a political cloud due to her alleged relationships with some of America's rebels.

p, Jacques Natteau, d&w, Romain Gary (based on his short story); ph, Christian Matras (Eastmancolor); m, Kenton Coe.

Drama   **(PR:C   MPAA:NR)**

BIRDS DO IT*   (1966) 88m COL c

Soupy Sales (*Melvin Byrd*), Tab Hunter (*Lt. Porter*), Arthur O'Connell (*Prof. Wald*), Edward Andrews (*Gen. Smithburn*), Doris Dowling (*Congresswoman Clanger*), Beverly Adams (*Claudine Wald*), Louis Quinn (*Sgt. Skam*), Frank Nastasi (*Yellowcab Driver*), Burt Taylor (*Devlin*), Courtney Brown (*Arno*), Russell Saunders (*Clurg*), Julian Voloshin (*Prof. Nep*), Bob Bersell (*Doorman*), Warren Day (*Curtis*), Jay Lasky (*Willie*), Burt Leigh (*Radar Operator*).

Stupid comedy starring Sales as a special government janitor who is hired to keep the dust off of United States nuclear missiles. (Dust had previously ruined a $5 million missile project.) Enter counter-agent Hunter and his bumbling spies who try to sabotage Sales' clean-up efforts. The highlight of this dim venture has Sales flying around Florida on his own when he is exposed to negatively ionized particles which make him weightless.

p, Ivan Tors; d, Andrew Marton; w, Arnie Kogen, Art Arthur (based on a story by Leonard Kaufman); ph, Howard Winner (Pathe Color); m, Samuel Matiovsky; ed, Irwin Dumbrille.

Comedy   **(PR:A   MPAA:NR)**

BIRDS OF A FEATHER*   (1931, Brit.) 52m Baxter and Barter bw

Haddon Mason (*Michael*), Dorothy Bartlam (*Vera*), Edith Saville, Robert Horton, Gladys Dunham.

Truce between unconventional and conventional lifestyles. Individual striving for intellectual and artistic greatness curbs his personal goals to secure the love of a widowed artist's daughter. Not too romantic.

p, P. Macnamara; d, Ben R. Hart.

Romance   **(PR:AA   MPAA:NR)**

BIRDS OF A FEATHER**   (1935, Brit.) 65m UNIV bw

George Robey (*Henry Wortle*), Horace Hodges (*Lord Cheverton*), Eve Lister (*Lady Susan*), Jack Melford (*Rudolph*), Veronica Brady (*Mrs. Wortle*), Julian Royce (*Warrington*), Denier Warren (*Taylor*), Diana Beaumont (*May Wortle*), Ian Wilson (*Peter*), Fred Hearne (*Herbert*), Billy Percy (*Horace*), Sebastian Shaw (*Jack Wortle*), Charles Mortimer (*Sir Michael*), Eve Chipman (*Lady Rossiter*), Maud Locker (*Cook*).

Fun comedy-thriller has hidden treasure discovered when a poor but titled family rents their castle to the family of a millionaire sausage manufacturer. To mask their identities, the bluebloods pose as servants. Children of both fall in love after a series of amusing events.

p, John Barter; d, John Baxter; w, Con West, Gerald Elliott (based on the play "A Rift in the Loot" by George Foster); ph, Ernest Palmer.

Comedy   **(PR:A   MPAA:NR)**

BIRDS OF PREY   (SEE: PERFECT ALIBI, THE, 1930, Brit.)

BIRDS, THE BEES AND THE ITALIANS, THE**   (1967) 115m 7 Arts bw

Virna Lisi (*Milena Zulian*), Gastone Moschin (*Osvaldo Bisigato*), Nora Ricci (*Gilda Bisgato*), Alberto Lionello (*Toni Gasparini*), Olga Villi (*Ippolita Gasparini*), Franco Fabrizi (*Lino Bensetti*), Beba Loncar (*Noemi Castellan*), Gigi Ballista (*Giancinato Castellan*).

Mild comedy supported by suspenders throughout, begins with high-society married citizens at a wild party, then leads to a shy bookkeeping bank official who takes up with a shop girl, falls hopelessly in love, and leaves home to secure her passions. The last part reveals sexual perversions of prominent citizens who seduce an under-aged country girl.

p, Robert Haggiag, Pietro Germi; d, Germi; w, Age Scarpelli, Germi, Luciano Vincanzoni (based on a story by Scarpelli, Germi); ph, Aiace Parolin; m, Carlo Rustichelli.

Comedy   **(PR:O   MPAA:NR)**

BIRTH OF A BABY**   (1938) 72m Special Pictures bw

Eleanor King (*Mary Burgess*), Richard Gordon (*Dr. Wilson*), Ruth Matteson (*Julia Norton*), Josephine Dunn (*Mrs. Bromley*), William Post, Jr. (*John Burgess*), Frederica Going (*Mrs. Perry*), Helen Hawley (*Mrs. Burgess*), Kathleen Comegys (*Mrs. Wilson*), Robert Ober (*Mr. Case*), Edith Gresham (*Mrs. Case*), Walter Gilbert (*Mr. Perry*).

Informative filming of the process one couple goes through in preparation for the birth of their first child. They consult a reputable doctor early and often as the film follows them stage by stage to the delivery. Shocking highlight is viewing the actual birth, now commonplace in both television and film. Production is way ahead of its time, offering educational value and wisdom on a subject once confined to intimate discussion mainly among women, since men were not then allowed in the delivery room. This film was subjected to censorship when released for commercial play. Mainly a documentary film with an important message.

p, Jack Skirball; d, A. E. Christie; w, Burke Symon, Arthur Jarrett; ph, George Webber; ed, Sam Citron.

Docudrama   **(PR:C   MPAA:NR)**

BIRTH OF THE BLUES***   (1941) 80m PAR bw

Bing Crosby (*Jeff Labert*), Mary Martin (*Betty Lou Cobb*), Brian Donlevy (*Memphis*), Carolyn Lee (*Aunt Phoebe Cobb*), Eddie "Rochester" Anderson (*Louey*), Jack Teagarden (*Pepper*), J. Carrol Naish (*Blackie*), Cecil Kellaway (*Mr. Granet*), Warren Hymer (*Limpy*), Horace McMahon (*Wolf*).

Here's a jazz film that begins with Dixieland and ends with The Dorseys, Duke Ellington, Ted Lewis, George Gershwin, Paul Whiteman, and Louis Armstrong. It also has Bing Crosby singing several numbers, playing a romantic clarinetist, showing the others how to run a band, etc. Further, you've got Donlevy as sort of a white Satchmo and Mary Martin and Rochester and a host of terrific secondary players. Never mind the hoked-up plot of the gangsters (Naish) and a riot and a lot of other unbelievable filler. This picture crams loads of fun into 80 minutes and even though it attempts to tell the story of "how jazz came up the river from New Orleans" and doesn't quite make it, you'll smile from start to finish. Lots of comedy, almost wall-to-wall music, it makes you just want to go down to the levee (I said "to the levee!"). The music adaptation was good enough to warrant an Oscar nomination for Dolan.

p, B. G. DeSylva; d, Victor Schertzinger; w, Harry Tugend, Walter DeLeon (based on a story by Tugend); ph, William Mellor; m, Robert Emmett Dolan; ed, Paul Weatherwax; art d, Hans Dreier, Ernst Fegte; cos, Edith Head; m/l, Johnny Mercer, Gus Edwards, Dolan, Tugend, DeSylva, Lew Brown, Ray Henderson, Edward Madden, W.C. Handy.

Musical   **(PR:A MPAA:NR)**

BIRTHDAY PARTY, THE**   (1968, Brit.) 123m Continental c

Robert Shaw (*Stanley Weber*), Patrick McGee (*Shamus McCann*), Dandy Nichols (*Meg Bowles*), Sydney Tafler (*Nat Goldberg*), Moultrie Kelsall (*Petey Bowles*), Helen Fraser (*Lulu*).

Early film by the director of THE FRENCH CONNECTION (1971), William Friedkin, who sadly over-directed this adaptation of Harold Pinter's play. Shaw plays a pianist who was once involved in organized crime and has been hiding out at Nichols' boarding house for nearly a year. The action takes place at an uneasy birthday party thrown in the somewhat unstable Shaw's honor. Tafler and McGee, two hoods who have come after Shaw, show up and mentally torture him to the point of madness before they take him for a one-way ride. Pinter is always difficult to adapt to the screen and Friedkin does a nice job with the actors. The handling of Pinter's cryptic dialog is superb, but the director clouds and confuses the film with overly tricky camera placement and an annoying switch from color to black & white during a lengthy blind man's bluff game played at the party.

p, Max Rosenberg, Milton Subotsky; d, William Friedkin; w, Harold Pinter (based on his play); ph, Denys Coop (Technicolor); ed, Tony Gibbs; art d, Edward Marshall.

Drama   **(PR:C MPAA:G)**

BIRTHDAY PRESENT, THE**   (1957, Brit.) 100m BL bw

Tony Britton (*Simon Scott*), Sylvia Syms (*Jean Scott*), Jack Watling (*Bill Thompson*), Walter Fitzgerald (*Sir John Dell*), Geoffrey Keen (*Colonel Wilson*), Howard Marion Crawford (*George Bates*), John Welsh (*Chief Customs Officer*), Lockwood West (*Mr. Barraclough*), Harry Fowler (*Charlie*), Frederick Piper (*Careers Officer*), Cyril Luckham (*Magistrate*), Thorley Walters (*Photographer*), Ernest Clark (*Barrister*).

Britton plays a rising executive who gets thrown into prison when he tries smuggling an expensive watch through customs, having already traded for the gift intended to surprise his wife. All-around fine technical efforts add a sense of authenticity.

p, Jack Whittingham; d, Pat Jackson; w, Whittingham; ph, Ted Scaife; m, Clifton Parker; ed, Jocelyn Jackson.

Drama   **(PR:C MPAA:NR)**

BISCUIT EATER, THE**   (1940) 82m PAR bw

Billy Lee (*Lonnie McNeil*), Cordell Hickman (*Text*), Richard Lane (*Harve McNeil*), Lester Matthews (*Mr. Ames*), Helene Millard (*Mrs. McNeil*), Snowflake (*Sermon*), Promise, the dog.

Hickman is a Georgia backwoods boy who discovers a dog left behind to survive in the wilderness. The animal stakes out a territory and protects it, frightening the boy and his friends many times before they all become pals. Then Promise, the dog, wins top honors for them as a field tracking dog. Highly emotional production with location shots indicative of close attention to detail.

p, Jack Moss; d, Stuart Heisler; w, Stuart Anthony, Lillie Hayward (based on a story by James Street); ph, Leo Tover; ed. Everett Douglas.

Drama   **(PR:AA MPAA:NR)**

BISCUIT EATER, THE**½   (1972) 90m BV c

Earl Holliman (*Harve McNeil*), Lew Ayres (*Mr. Ames*), Godfrey Cambridge (*Willie Dorsey*), Patricia Crowley (*Mrs. McNeil*), Beah Richards (*Charity Tomlin*), Johnny Whitaker (*Lonnie McNeil*), George Spell (*Text Tomlin*), Clifton James (*Mr. Eben*).

Remake of the 1940 classic has a white boy and a black boy together as friends in the backwoods of Georgia. They discover a dog stalking his territory and make hesitant attempts to tame the wild animal. When everybody relaxes, the dog decides to get his pedigree by winning top honors in fence-jumping competition. Unfortunately, this movie, for all its charm, lacks the quality production of the original; but if you didn't see it, you'll enjoy this one.

p, Bill Anderson; d, Vincent McEveety; w, Lawrence Edward Watkin; m, Robert F. Brunner; ph, Richard A. Kelley (Technicolor); art d, John B. Mansbridge, Al Roelofs.

Drama   **(PR:AAA MPAA:G)**

BISHOP MISBEHAVES, THE**

(1933) 85m MGM bw (GB: BISHOP'S MISADVENTURES, THE)

Maureen O'Sullivan (*Hester*), Edmund Gwenn (*Bishop*), Lucille Watson (*Lady Emily*), Reginald Owen (*Guy Waller*), Dudley Digges (*Red*), Norman Foster (*Donald*), Lillian Bond (*Mrs. Waller*), Melville Cooper (*Collins*), Charles McNaughton (*French*), Etienne Girardot (*Brooke*).

The daughter of an inventor seeks out the man who has stolen one of Pop's inventions. When a bishop changes his career momentarily to a private detective, the patent papers are secured and all is well. Hysterical and above all well-timed

comedy with acting and production balanced. This was Edmund Gwenn's first Hollywood film. He would become one of the industry's finest character actors.

d, E. A. Dupont; w, Leon Gordon, George Auerbach (based on the play by Frederick Jackson); m, Edward Ward; ed, James Newcom.

Comedy/Mystery   **(PR:AA MPAA:NR)**

BISHOP MURDER CASE, THE***   (1930) 91m MGM bw

Basil Rathbone (*Philo Vance*), Leila Hyams (*Belle Dillard*), Roland Young (*Arnesson*), George Marion (*Adolph Drukker*), Alec B. Francis (*Prof. Bertrand Dillard*), Zelda Sears (*Mrs. Otto Drukker*), Bodil Rosing (*Grete Menzel*), Carroll Nye (*John E. Sprigg*), Charles Quartermaine (*John Pardee*), James Donlan (*Sgt. Ernest Heath*), Sidney Bracey (*Pyne*), Clarence Geldert (*District Attorney Markham*), Delmar Daves (*Raymond Sperling*), Nellie Bly Baker (*Beedle*).

Classic sleuth Rathbone snoops through thick and thin suspects to uncover the killer of a young man found on an archery range with an arrow through his heart. Three possible suspects are promptly killed and two others die of presumed heart attacks due to overexcitement. Tension builds around the remaining suspects, an elderly sly-mannered hunchback, a crazed fanatic, and a fellow in love with the niece of an elderly professor. Most of the action takes place in the old gent's house. Our hero reveals the truth by tying together the events a la Sherlock Holmes and Agatha Christie with a logical explanation, the ending less than surprising. Fine character work by performers adding that special touch of eccentric horror and mystery. Watch for the sudden change from a silent, tense sequence to a police car screaming down the street. (See PHILO VANCE series, Index.)

d, Nick Grinde, David Burton; w, Lenore J. Coffee (based on the story by S. S. Van Dine), ph, Roy Overbaugh; ed, William Le Vanway.

Mystery   **(PR:A MPAA:NR)**

BISHOP'S WIFE, THE***   (1947) 105m RKO bw

Cary Grant (*Dudley*), David Niven (*Henry Brougham*), Loretta Young (*Julia Brougham*), Monty Woolley (*Prof. Wutheridge*), James Gleason (*Sylvester*), Gladys Cooper (*Mrs. Hamilton*), Elsa Lanchester (*Matilda*), Sara Haden (*Mildred Cassaway*), Karolyn Grimes (*Debby Brougham*), Tito Vuolo (*Maggenti*), Regis Toomey (*Mr. Miller*), Sarah Edwards (*Mrs. Duffy*), Margaret McWade (*Miss Trumbull*).

Niven is an Episcopalian Bishop praying for money to build a new church. His marriage is apparently over and his faith is quivering when Grant arrives. He's an Angel who uses his powers so sparingly that he might have been from Welcome Wagon. Loretta Young, as Niven's wife, never learns Cary is from Up There as he helps her achieve some peace on earth. Niven keeps looking for money to erect his cathedral and can't find it. Cary manages to put Loretta and David back together and never once do we feel that he's been intrusive. Under Koster's direction, everyone seems to be having a good time, enjoying the script, and never mocking it. The picture does get a bit long and it does pale by comparison to the book but it was a welcome smile in 1947 and will provide the same today.

p, Samuel Goldwyn; d, Henry Koster; w, Robert E. Sherwood, Leonardo Bercovici (based on a novel by Robert Nathan); ph, Gregg Toland; m, Hugo Friedhofer: ed, Monica Collingwood; md, Emil Newman; art d, Charles Henderson; set d, Julie Heron; cos, Irene Sharaff.

Comedy-Fantasy   **Cas.**   **(PR:A MPAA:NR)**

BITE THE BULLET***   (1975) 131m COL c

Gene Hackman (*Sam Clayton*), Candice Bergen (*Miss Jones*), James Coburn (*Luke Matthews*), Ben Johnson (*Mister*), Ian Bannen (*Norfolk*), Jan-Michael Vincent (*Carbo*), Mario Arteaga (*Mexican*), Robert Donner (*Reporter*), Robert Hoy (*Lee Christie*), Paul Stewart, (*J. B. Parker*), Jean Willes (*Rosie*), John McLiam (*Gebhardt*), Dabney Coleman (*Jack Parker*), Jerry Gatlin (*Woodchopper*), Sally Kirkland (*Honey*), Walter Scott, Jr. (*Steve*).

Spendid period piece about an endurance horse race. The plot is not unlike THE GREAT RACE or THOSE MAGNIFICENT MEN IN THEIR FLYING MACHINES in that a disparate group is assembled, lots of secondary stories are opened, and the race begins. Very episodic rather than having a driving force behind it. Brooks writes and directs well but there are very few people who can do both on the same picture and it is the writing to the story that we haven't seen before. There is nothing to the story that we haven't seen before. The participants gather, we learn too little about them and their motivations for running this incredible race on horseback, the race begins, things happen. BITE THE BULLET looks good, the music by North was good enough to get an Oscar nomination, and it ranks head (if not shoulders) over many other westerns. It offers some excellent performances, crisp direction and overall professionalism of the entire cast and crew. What keeps it from being a great western (FORT APACHE, HIGH NOON) is that the audience is seldom involved in the lives of the riders other than in a peripheral sense. If you're watching a horse race and you don't have a bet down and don't much care about who wins . . . then a horse race is a mighty dull way to spend two minutes or 131 minutes.

p,d&w, Richard Brooks; ph, Harry Stradling, Jr. (Metrocolor); m, Alex North; ed, George Granville; art d, Robert Boyle; set d, Robert Signorelli.

Adventure   **Cas.**   **(PR:C MPAA:)**

BITER BIT, THE*   (1937, Brit.) 49m FOX bw (GB: CALLING ALL MA'S)

Billy Caryll (*Billy Smith*), Hilda Munday (*Hilda Smith*), Margaret Yarde (*Ma-in-law*), Anthony Shaw (*Arthur Parkins*), Julien Vedey (*Italian*), Charles Castella (*Barman*).

Age-old story of a wimpy husband cavorting about with other women to escape being harangued by his nagging wife.

p, Ivor McLaren; d, Redd Davis; w, Al Booth; ph, Ray Kellino.

Comedy   **(PR:A MPAA:NR)**

BITTER CREEK** (1954) 74m AA bw

Wild Bill Elliott *(Clay Tyndall)*, Carleton Young *(Quentin Allen)*, Beverly Garland *(Gail Bonner)*, Claude Akins *(Vance Morgan)*, Jim Hayward *(Dr. Prentiss)*, John Harmon *(A. Z. Platte)*, Veda Ann Borg *(Whitey)*, Dan Mummert *(Jerry Bonner)*, John Pickard *(Oak Mason)*, Forrest Taylor *(Harley Pruitt)*, Dabbs Greer *(Sheriff)*, Mike Ragan *(Joe Venango)*, Zon Murray *(2nd Rider)*, John Larch *(Gunman)*, Joe Devlin *(Pat Cleary)*, Earl Hodgins *(Charles Hammond)*, Florence Lake *(Mrs. Hammond)*, Jane Easton *(Oak's Girl)*.

This is one of the better Elliott westerns, and it's due, in great part, to a fine script by George Waggner, who went on to become a very respected film and TV director (THE WOLF MAN, many "Batman" episodes) and whose credit always read: George WaGGner. Bill arrives in Bitter Creek trying to find out who killed his brother. Nobody wants to help Elliott as it seems that Young, one of the wealthier people in those parts, may have been behind the murder. Bill investigates and Garland believes Young's story of total innocence. Later, she realizes the rancher is a liar and she winds up with Elliott after the denouement. This film has many of the best western second leads in it; Borg, who always played the hard-boiled blonde, Akins, and many more. The action never stops in the picture, except to make some telling dialog points. A fine example of how to make a good movie for short money.

p, Vincent Fennelly; d, Thomas Carr; w, George Waggner; ph, Ernest Miller; m, Raoul Kraushaar; ed, Sam Fields.

Western **(PR:A MPAA:NR)**

BITTER HARVEST** (1963, Brit.) 96m RANK c

Janet Munro *(Jeannie Jones)*, John Stride *(Bob Williams)*, Anne Cunningham *(Ella)*, Alan Badel *(Karl Denny)*, Vanda Godsell *(Mrs. Pitt)*, Norman Bird *(Mr. Pitt)*, Terence Alexander *(Andy)*, Richard Thorp *(Rex)*, Barbara Ferris *(Violet)*, William Lucas *(David Medwin)*, Daphne Anderson *(Nancy Medwin)*, Derek Francis *(Mr. Jones)*, Mary Merrall *(Aunt Louise)*, May Hallatt *(Aunt Sarah)*, Colin Gordon *(Charles)*, Thora Hird *(Mrs. Jessup)*, Allan Cuthbertson *(Mr. Eccles)*.

Small-town girl Munro gets swept off her hitch-hiking boots by a sleazebag and then gets the idea that London is to be her golden opportunity. She meets a bartender who falls for her but she just wants to use him, because that's what the city has taught her. She gets caught up in the social register then leaves the party forever with an overdose of sleeping pills to cure her disillusionment. A whimpering finish for a depressing film!

p, Albert Fennell; Leslie Parkyn; d, Peter Graham; w, Ted Willis (based on Patricia Hamilton's novel *The Secret Has a Thousand Skies*); ph, Ernest Steward; m, Laurie Johnson; ed, Russell Lloyd.

Drama **(PR:C MPAA:NR)**

BITTER RICE***

(1950, Ital.) 107m De Laurentiis/Lux bw (AKA: RISO AMARO)

Silvana Mangano *(Silvana)*, Doris Dowling *(Francesca)*, Vittorio Gassman *(Walter)*, Raf Vallone *(Marco)*, Checco Rissone *(Aristide)*, Nico Pepe *(Beppe)*, Adriana Sivieri *(Celeste)*, Lia Croelli *(Amelia)*, Maria Grazia Francia *(Gabriella)*, Ann Maestri *(Irene)*, Mariemma Bardi *(Gianna)*.

Fine, moody film that captures the bare survival atmosphere of Italy after WW II when the country lay in ruins and everyone scraped for a living. In this case it's the very well equipped Mangano who parades about in a bursting sweater, short-shorts and torn nylons as she works with hundreds of other women in the rice fields of the Po Valley. Mangano fairly smokes the screen with her sultry performance, revealing as much of her voluptuous body as censors of the time would permit, as well as an unexpected amount of real acting talent. (It was Mangano who paved the way for the invasion of the Italian sexpot actresses into U.S. theaters, long before Gina and Sophia burst, literally, upon the screen; also, like Sophia with Carlo Ponti, Mangano's career would be wholly shaped by her producer, De Laurentiis who, like Ponti, would marry his sexy protege.) The story concerns the young woman and two men, Vallone, a down-to-earth, responsible and respectable man who wants to marry her, and a rotten-to-the core thief on the run, Gassman. (The threesome would repeat essentially the same characters in ANNA.) Naturally, Mangano goes for Gassman who mistreats her, berates and rapes her, but not before she steals his money. Only Vallone has a redeeming character but little backbone; he stands by helplessly while Mangano and Gassman tryst, then destroy each other. Gassman is superb as a sneering, instantly dislikable villain. De Santis' direction is of the natural school, devoid of glamor, full of sweat and bodies, love on straw bunks, sex offered along the highway. Somehow it is not repugnant but real, as emotions are sliced from characters like one might cut an overrripe tomato. Tart or not, there's plenty of juice. (In Italian; English subtitles.)

p, Dino De Laurentiis; d, Giuseppe De Santis; w, De Santis, Carlo Lizzani, Gianni Puccini (based on a story by De Santis and Lizzani); ph, Otello Martelli; m, Goffredo Petrassi; English titles, Clare Catalano.

Drama **(PR:O MPAA:NR)**

BITTER SPRINGS** (1950, Aus.) 90m British Empire Films bw

Tommy Trinder *(Tommy)*, Chips Rafferty *(Wally King)*, Gordon Jackson *(Mac)*, Jean Blue *("Ma" King)*, Charles Tingwell *(John King)*, Nonnie Piper *(Emma King)*, Nicky Yardly *(Charlie)*, Michael Pate *(The Trooper)*, Henry Murdoch *(Black Jack)*.

Unnatural enemies Rafferty and a tribe of Aborigines conflict when Rafferty moves onto the tribe's hunting grounds. How they make peace is the enchantment of this must-see heartwarmer. Production effort is top notch.

p, Michael Balcon; d, Ralph Smart; w, W. P. Lipscomb, M. Danischewsky; ph, George Heath; ed, Bernard Gribble.

Drama **(PR:A MPAA:NR)**

BITTER SWEET** 1/2** (1933, Brit.) 76m British & Dominion bw

Anna Neagle *(Sari Linden)*, Fernand Graavey *(Carl Linden)*, Esme Percy *(Hugh Devon)*, Clifford Heatherly *(Herr Schlick)*, Ivy St. Helier *(Manon La Crevette)*, Miles Mander *(Captain Auguste Lutte)*, Pat Paterson *(Dolly)*, Hugh Williams *(Vincent)*.

Neagle finally woos Graavey into marriage only to find he is a compulsive gambler as well as a remarkable violinist. He works in a cafe, playing popular ballads, then spends his wages on gambling, an obsession that finally brings tragedy when he is murdered by other gamblers. Outstanding musical score, superb photography, and book and lyrics reflect the universal genius of Coward.

p&d, Herbert Wilcox; w, Noel Coward (operetta); ph, F. A. Young.

Operetta **(PR:A MPAA:NR)**

BITTER SWEET*** (1940) 92m MGM c

Jeanette MacDonald *(Sarah Millick)*, Nelson Eddy *(Carl Linden)*, George Sanders *(Baron Von Tranisch)*, Ian Hunter *(Lord Shayne)*, Felix Bressart *(Max)*, Edward Ashley *(Harry Daventry)*, Lynne Carver *(Dolly)*, Diana Lewis *(Jane)*, Curt Bois *(Ernst)*, Fay Holden *(Mrs. Millick)*, Sig Rumann *(Herr Schlick)*.

Filmed once before with Anna Neagle in 1933 from Noel Coward's 1929 operetta, BITTER SWEET should have been a much bigger hit than it was but the screenplay by Lesser Samuels did not enhance the original plot and score by Coward. It made money, though, and survives today as an interesting example of MacDonald and Eddy in their prime. Jeanette is a Victorian belle who scandalizes her family on the eve of her marriage to Edward Ashley by running off with Nelson, her singing teacher. They marry and go to live in Vienna. Poverty soon follows and they become street singers with Bois and Bressart. Nelson has written an operetta but can interest no producers so life gets more difficult until Jeanette captures the eyes of Hunter and Sanders, two gambling opponents. Hunter thinks her singing brings his good fortune but Sanders has only base desires for the comely soprano. Sanders hires Jeanette to sing at his cafe with husband Nelson at the keyboard. Sanders begins overturing Jeanette and this is reported to Nelson by Ashley and his new wife, Lewis. Nelson doesn't believe anyone could be such a cad but eventually sees it for himself at an audition of his operetta. He must duel for her honor and is no match for Sanders who rapiers him on the spot. Nelson dies in Jeanette's arms but the operetta is eventually produced through the auspices of impresario Charles Judels, a pal of Hunter's. Beautiful Coward songs ("I'll See You Again" "Zigeuner" and more) and exquisite photography almost triumph over some of the wooden acting. Sanders, as the cad, kills Eddy in the fastest duel in screen history.

p, Victor Saville; d, W. S. Van Dyke II; w, Lesser Samuels (based on the operetta by Noel Coward); ph, Oliver T. Marsh, Allen Davey (Technicolor); m, Coward; ed, Harold F. Kress; md, Herbert Stothart; ch, Ernst Matray; m/l, Coward, Gus Kahn.

Operetta **(PR:A MPAA:NR)**

BITTER TEA OF GENERAL YEN, THE*** (1933) 87m COL bw

Barbara Stanwyck *(Megan Davis)*, Nils Asther *(General Yen)*, Gavin Gordon *(Dr. Robert Strike)*, Lucien Littlefield *(Mr. Jackson)*, Toshia Mori *(Mah-Li)*, Richard Loo *(Captain Li)*, Clara Blandick *(Mrs. Jackson)*, Walter Connolly *(Jones)*, Moy Ming *(Dr. Lin)*, Robert Wayne *(Reverend Bostwick)*, Knute Erickson *(Dr. Hansen)*, Ella Hall *(Mrs. Hansen)*, Arthur Millette *(Mr. Pettis)*, Helen Jerome Eddy *(Miss Reed)*, Martha Mattox *(Miss Avery)*, Jessie Arnold *(Mrs. Blake)*, Emmett Corrigan *(Bishop Harkness)*, Miller Newman *(Dr. Mott)*, Arthur Johnson *(Dr. Shuler)*, Willie Fung *(Officer)*, Adda Gleason *(Mrs. Bowman)*, Daisy Robinson *(Mrs. Warden)*, Doris Llewellyn *(Mrs. Meigs)*, Nora Cecil, Lillian Leighton, Harriet Lorraine *(Missionaries)*, Milton Lee, Ray Young.

Stanwyck arrives in Shanghai to marry missionary Gordon, a wedding of convenience. When the couple move through a danger zone threatened by warring factions to rescue some Chinese orphans, they are suddenly in the middle of a shooting revolution. The crowds panic and Stanwyck is swept into the arms of troops under the command of Asther, an infamous warlord. She soon discovers that Asther has no intention of releasing her; he is fascinated with this white woman whom he slowly attempts to seduce. Asther is unlike any other Chinese warlord in history. His manners are courtly, he speaks fluent English, spouts poetry, and defers to the woman's comfort. At one point he tells her the story of an ancestor who tried once to catch the moon and fell into the Yellow River and drowned, a prophecy of his own star-crossed passion. Connolly is splendid as Asther's opportunistic American financial adviser. When all of Asther's aides desert him only Stanwyck and Connolly stay by his side as enemies close in for the kill. Grieving Asther more than such disloyalty is the fact that he cannot possess the one thing he desires most in life, Stanwyck. He takes his bitter tea, laced heavily with poison, and puts himself beyond misery. Stanwyck plays her victimized role with aplomb and shines most brightly in the dream sequences where she envisions Asther as her lover. The subject was taboo when Capra made this unusual film; miscegenation was a real bugbear then. It was unthinkable for a white woman to wind up in the arms of a Chinese, even a most sophisticated Oriental as Asther certainly represented. The film, despite its gentle, almost poetic approach, did not do well because of the racial issue. England and several other countries banned the film for its radical love theme and women were repelled by Asther, one-time silent screen idol who had played opposite the great Garbo. He was no longer the handsome, tall Lothario. Director Capra had stiff upper lids attached to his eyes and cut his eyelashes short to give him Oriental eyes (which caused severe strain, requiring Asther to have constant medical attention). Asther was now a leering "Yellow Peril" in hot pursuit of lily-white Stanwyck. Capra's film is full of *sturm und drang*. It teems with exotic life and customs and is fascinating in its meticulous detail of Oriental life, due to the perfectionism of its splendid director. In one scene, when Capra brought on more than a thousand extras to attack a train, stage-trained Connolly, playing the American adventurer, fell out of a boxcar and promptly broke his leg. He played the rest of the film on crutches, using these implements to help steal more scenes.

p, Walter Wanger; d, Frank Capra; w, Edward Paramore (based on the novel by Grace Zaring Stone); ph, Joseph Walker; m, W. Frank Harling; ed, Edward Curtis; cos, Edward Stevenson, Robert Kalloch.

Drama   (PR:C   MPAA:NR)

BITTER TEARS OF PETRA VON KANT, THE**¹/₂
(1972, Ger.) 124m Tango/New Yorker c (DIE BITTEREN TRAENEN DER PETRA VON KANT)

Margit Carstensen *(Petra von Kant)*, Irm Hermann *(Marlene)*, Hanna Schygulla *(Karin)*, Eva Mattes *(Gabriele)*, Katrin Schaake *(Sidonie)*, Gisela Fachelday *(Valerie)*.

Brilliant German director'Rainer Werner Fassbinder's thirteenth film in less than four years is a strange, but haunting melodrama concerning Carstensen, who divorces her husband when she realizes that she no longer loves him and that she is sexually attracted to her secretary, Schygulla. Fassbinder explores the lesbian relationship with sensitivity (he was homosexual) and finds that just as many of the games that exist in a heterosexual relationship (love/hate, freedom/slavery, overbearing jealousy) are present in a homosexual one. The film is shot in an unusually artificial visual style that is marked by lush, overly decorative sets and performed in an extremely melodramatic manner.

p,d&w, Rainer Werner Fassbinder; ph, Michael Ballhaus (Kodakcolor); m, Giuseppe Verdi, The Platters, Walker Brothers; ed, Thea Eymes; art d, Kurt Raab.

Melodrama   (PR:O   MPAA:NR)

BITTER VICTORY**¹/₂   (1958, Fr.) 97m COL bw (AMERE VICTOIRE)

Curt Jurgens *(Maj. Brand)*, Richard Burton *(Capt. Leith)*, Ruth Roman *(Mrs. Brand)*, Raymond Pellegrin *(Makron)*, Anthony Bushell *(Gen. Paterson)*, Alfred Burke *(Lt. Col. Callander)*, Christopher Lee *(Sgt. Barney)*, Sean Kelly *(Lt. Barton)*, Ramon De Larrocha *(Lt. Sanders)*, Nigel Green *(Pvt. Wilkins)*, Harry Landis *(Pvt. Berowining)*, Jo Davray *(Pvt. Spicer)*, Sumner Williams *(Pvt. Anderson)*, Ronan O'Casey *(Sgt. Dunnigan)*, Fred Matter *(Col. Lutze)*, Andrew Crawford, Raoul Delfosse.

Odd amalgam of a French film, starring a British, German, and American trio, directed by an American and written by three men from different countries. Perhaps that's what goes wrong with this flawed war story of two men in the African campaign during WW II. Burton knows that Jurgens is a coward, Jurgens knows that Burton has been diddling Roman, Curt's wife. Jurgens attempts to kill Burton a few times (scorpion bite, etc.) and finally succeeds. Jurgens comes home to earn a medal for his alleged valor but the rest of his life is a shambles as Roman sees him for what he is. Ray has the ability to make almost anything interesting and Burton can make the most turgid words seem fascinating. Rare story points in that Burton, who is the hero, is eventually killed and Jurgens remains alive. It's a basic mistake and an attempt to be ironic that fails. Audiences want to see their heroes win.

p, Paul Graetz, Robert Laffont; d, Nicholas Ray; w, Ray, Rene Hardy, Gavin Lambert (based on the novel by Hardy); ph, Michel Kilber; m, Maurice LeRoux; cos, Jean Zay.

War/Adventure   (PR:C   MPAA:NR)

BITTERSWEET LOVE**   (1976) 90m AE c

Lana Turner *(Claire)*, Robert Lansing *(Howard)*, Celeste Holm *(Marian)*, Robert Alda *(Ben)*, Scott Hylands *(Michael)*, Meredith Baxter Birney *(Patricia)*, Gail Strickland *(Roz)*, Raymond Masur *(Alex)*, Denise DeMirjian *(Nurse Morrison)*, John Friedrich *(Josh)*, Amanda Gavin *(Judy)*, Jerome Guardino *(Psychiatrist)*.

Although it's barely ninety minutes in length, this picture seems much much longer, a good idea that has been talked to death. Birney and Hylands meet, she gets pregnant, they are in love. Then they learn that they are half-brother and half-sister. What to do? Turner is Birney's mother and Lansing is Hyland's father. Thirty years ago they had a one-nighter and so Lansing is the father of both children. It takes a bit more than a half-hour to learn this and the rest of the picture becomes an endless debate of should we abort or not. No shock, no story.

p, Joseph Zappala, Gene Slott, Joel B. Michaels; d, David Miller; w, Adrian Morrall, D. A. Kellogg; ph, Stephen Katz (DeLuxe Color); m, Ken Wannberg; ed, Bill Butler; art d, Vince Cresciman.

Drama   **Cas.**   (PR:C   MPAA:R)

BIZARRE BIZARRE**   (1939, Fr.) 84m Lenauer bw (DROLE DE DRAMA)

Louis Jouvet *(Vicar of Bedford)*, Francoise Rosay *(Margaret Molyneux)*, Michel Simon *(Irwin Molyneux /Felix Chapel)*, Jean Louis Barrault *(William Kramps)*, Jean Pierre Aumont *(The Milkman)*, Nadine Vogel *(Eva)*, Alcover *(Detective)*, Guisol *(Reporter)*, Jeanne Lory *(Mrs. McPhearson)*, M. Duhamel *(Man in Mourning)*.

Amusing French farce starring Simon as the unassuming head of a bourgeois household who makes his living writing crime novels with ideas supplied by his daughter. One day his quiet existence is plunged into chaos when his cousin, a Vicar, arrives for the weekend unannounced. The writer's wife is thrown into a panic because her servants have walked out, so she assumes the cooking duties, but refuses to help entertain and hides from the cousin in the kitchen. Simon explains that his wife is out of town visiting friends, but the Vicar thinks things rather mysterious and spreads the word that the crime writer has murdered his wife. Soon Scotland Yard shows up to investigate, and the whole situation is straightened out. (In French, English subtitles.)

p, Corniglion Molinier; d, Marcel Carne; w, Jacques Prevert (based on a story by J. Storer-Clouston); ph, Roger Kahan.

Comedy   **Cas.**   (PR:A   MPAA:NR)

BLACK ABBOT, THE*   (1934, Brit.) 56m REA/RKO bw

John Stuart *(Frank Brooks)*, Judy Kelly *(Sylvia Hillcrest)*, Richard Cooper *(Lord Jerry Pilkdown)*, Ben Welden *(Charlie Marsh)*, Drusilla Wills *(Mary Hillcrest)*, Edgar Norfolk *(Brian Heslewood)*, Farren Soutar *(John Hillcrest)*, Cyril Smith *(Alf Higgins)*, John Turnbull *(Inspector Lockwood)*.

Money is the name of the game when a band of crooks decide to add ransom to their list of credits and hold a wealthy man hostage in his own home for the cash. Little tension and less story.

p, Julius Hagen; d, George A. Cooper; w, H. Fowler Mear (based on the novel by Phillip Godfrey *The Grange Mystery*).

Crime   (PR:A   MPAA:NR)

BLACK ACES**   (1937) 59m UNIV bw

Buck Jones *(Ted Ames)*, Charles King *(Less)*, Kay Linaker *(Sandy McKenzie)*, Fred Mackaye *(Len Stoddard)*, W. E. Laurence *(Boyd Loomis)*, Raymond Kortman *(Henry Kline)*.

Jones plays a wimpy cattleman who is teased by everyone until Linaker stands up to defend him. Sudden bravery brought on by fear of the gallows brings the cowpoke to his senses. Good directing and production by Jones.

p&d, Buck Jones; w, Frances Guihan; ph, Allen Thompson; ed, Bernard Loftus.

Western   (PR:A   MPAA:NR)

BLACK AND WHITE IN COLOR***
                    (1976, Fr.) 100m AA c (LA VICTOIRE EN CHANTANT)

Jean Carmet *(Sergeant Bosselet)*, Jacques Dufilho *(Paul Rechampot)*, Catherine Rouvel *(Marinette)*, Jacques Spiesser *(Hubert Fresnoy)*, Dora Doll *(Maryvonne)*, Maurice Barrier *(Caprice)*, Claude Legros *(Jacques Rechampot)*, Jacques Monnet *(Pere Simon)*, Peter Berling *(Pere Jean De La Croix)*, Marius Beugre Boignan *(Barthelemy)*, Baye Macoumba Diop *(Lamartine)*, Aboutbaker Toure *(Fidele)*, Dieter Schidor *(Kraft)*, Marc Zuber *(Major Anglais)*, Klaus Huebel *(Haussmann)*, Mamadou Coulibaly *(Oscar)*, Memel Atchori *(Assomption)*, Jean-Francoise Eyou N'Guessan *(Marius)*, Natou Koly *(Charlotte)*, Tanoh Kouao *(John)*.

First feature film by director Jean-Jacques Annaud is a satirical look at the warfare mentality set in West Central Africa at the start of WW I. The story involves a remote French trading post and a nearby German settlement that have co-existed peacefully for years until it is learned that the war has started. Suddenly, patriotic fervor sweeps both camps and a mini-war erupts between them. The French, led by Carmet, launch a disastrous attack on the Germans which fails miserably. The French army is then taken over by the formerly socialist geographer, Spiesser, who throws away his ideals and becomes an ardent militarist. The film won an Oscar for Best Foreign Film in 1976.

p, Arthur Cohn, Jacques Perrin, Giorgio Silagni; d, Jean-Jacques Annaud; w, Annaud, Georges Conchon; ph, Claude Agostini (Eastmancolor); m, Pierre Bachelet; ed, Francoise Bonnot; art d, Max Douy.

Satire   (PR:C   MPAA:PG)

BLACK ANGEL***   (1946) 80m UNIV bw

Dan Duryea *(Martin Blair)*, June Vincent *(Catherine)*, Peter Lorre *(Marko)*, Broderick Crawford *(Captain Flood)*, Wallace Ford *(Joe)*, Hobart Cavanaugh *(Jake)*, Constance Dowling *(Mavis Marlowe)*, Freddie Steele *(Lucky)*, Ben Bard *(Bartender)*, John Phillips *(Kirk Bennett)*.

Interesting *film noir* starring Vincent as a woman who tries to clear her estranged husband's name after he is convicted and sentenced to death for the murder of his nightclub singer lover. The only clue to the crime is a missing, heart-shaped brooch that had been stolen from the victim. Vincent suspects that the dead woman's husband, an alcoholic songwriter, Duryea, actually committed the murder, but she finds that his alibi is airtight. He was on a bender that night and he had a friend lock him in his room. Duryea decides to help Vincent, and together they get a job as a nightclub act (she singing, he playing piano) in sleazy Lorre's bar. Lorre had known the dead woman and is known to be heavily involved in the underworld, but police detective Crawford tells the pair that he cannot be the murderer because the cops had been tailing him that night. Meanwhile Duryea has fallen in love with Vincent and tells her so. She gently tells him that she is still in love with her husband and cannot become involved. This sends the crushed Duryea back to the bottle, and in an alcoholic haze he suddenly remembers that he did indeed kill his wife while he was drunk and blocked the incident from his mind. The songwriter turns himself in to free Vincent's husband, and is led off to jail resigned to his fate. Though somewhat melodramatic, the film has a dense visual style with terrific opening and closing camera movements that sweep across the action. The opening shot directly foreshadows the ending, wrapping the film in a circular pattern that reflects on the mystery itself. Stark shadows and gloomy lighting are typical of this genre and are used to full effect. The acting by all players is outstanding, and Duryea's re-living of the murder through an almost surrealistic haze is superb.

p, Tom Knight, Roy William Neill; d, Neill; w, Roy Chanslor (based on the novel by Cornell Woolrich); ph, Paul Ivano; m, Frank Skinner; ed, Saul A. Goodkind; m/l, Jack Brooks; art d, Jack Otterson, Martin Obzina; set d, Russell A. Gausman, E. R. Robinson; cos, Vera West.

Mystery   (PR:A   MPAA:NR)

BLACK ANGELS, THE zero   (1970) 89m Merrick International c

King John III *(Johnny Reb)*, Des Roberts *(Chainer)*, Linda Jackson *(Jackie)*, James Whitwirth *(Big Jim)*, James Young-El *(Jimmy)*, Clancy Syrko *(Lt. Harper)*, Beverly Gardner *(Wallflower)*, John Donavan *(Frenchy)*, Gene Stowell *(Fixer)*, Miller Pettit *(One-Eye)*, Frank Donato *(Clyde)*, The Choppers Gang *(Themselves)*, Channon Scott *(Jawbone)*, Robert Johnson *(Knifer)*, Sumner Spector *(Daddy)*.

Biker wars between black and white gangs. The Serpents, a gang of white bikers, discover that they have been infiltrated by a member of the Choppers (a real black motorcycle gang hired for the film) who is passing for white. An all-out war errupts between the two gangs. Terribly violent. The casting of actual bikers made considerable difference in making the fight scenes "realistic." Many of the same cast worked with Merrick on GUESS WHAT HAPPENED TO COUNT DRACULA later that year.

p, Leo Rivers; d,w&ph, Lawrence Merrick (Movielab Color); ed, Clancy Syrko; md, Lou Peralta.

Drama (PR:O MPAA:R)

BLACK ARROW*** (1948) 76m COL bw (GB:BLACK ARROW STRIKES)

Louis Hayward (*Richard Shelton*), Janet Blair (*Joanna Sedley*), George Macready (*Sir Daniel Brackley*), Edgar Buchanan (*Lawless*), Lowell Gilmore (*Duke of Gloucester*), Russell Hicks (*Sir Harry Shelton*), Paul Cavanagh (*Sir John Sedley*).

Murderous romance complete with villains and knights battling it out for the art of good entertainment. Based on a Robert Louis Stevenson tale, this film exaggerates in all the right places, making it an attention getter. Production, direction, and performances combined round off this high-jumping delight.

p, Edward Small; d, Gordon Douglas; w, Richard Schayer, David P. Sheppard, Thomas Seller (based on the novel by Robert Louis Stevenson); ph, Charles Lawton; ed, Jerome Thoms; art d, Stephen Goosson, A. Leslie Thomas.

Adventure (PR:A MPAA:NR)

BLACK BANDIT** (1938) 60m UNIV bw

Bob Baker (*Don/Bob*), Marjorie Reynolds (*Jane*), Hal Taliaferro (*Weepy*), Jack Rockwell (*Allen*), Forrest Taylor (*Sheriff*), Glenn Strange (*Johnson*), Arthur Van Slyke (*Ramsay*), Dick Dickinson (*Evans*), Schuyler Standish (*Young Bob*), Rex Downing (*Young Don*).

Twins separated during childhood meet unknowingly on opposite sides of the law and end up defending each other to the hilt like only kin can do. A banal effort.

p, Trem Carr; d, George Waggner; w, Joseph West; ph, Gus Peterson; md, Frank Sanucci.

Western (PR:A MPAA:NR)

BLACK BART**½ (1948) 80m UNIV c (GB: BLACK BART HIGHWAYMAN)

Yvonne DeCarlo (*Lola Montez*), Dan Duryea (*Charles E. Boles*), Jeffrey Lynn (*Lance Hardeen*), Percy Kilbride (*Jersey Brady*), Lloyd Gough (*Sheriff Gordon*), Frank Lovejoy (*Lorimer*), John McIntire (*Clark*), Don Beddoe (*J. T. Hall*), Ray Walker (*MacFarland*), Soledad Jimenez (*Teresa*), Eddy C. Waller (*Mason*), Anne O'Neal (*Mrs. Harmon*), Chief Many Treaties (*Indian*), Douglas Fowley (*Sheriff Mix*).

A precursor to George Roy Hill's BUTCH CASSIDY AND THE SUNDANCE KID (1969), BLACK BART stars Duryea and Lynn as two likable, but nonetheless violent, outlaws who make no apologies for their life of crime. Kilbride rescues the pair from a hanging party and all go their separate ways. Later the trio meet up again in California where Duryea has established himself as a wealthy, respected rancher who robs Wells Fargo trains, disguised as Black Bart, just for kicks. The three friends decide to go form a gang together, but Kilbride is jailed and Duryea and Lynn go down in a blaze of gunfire supplied by the sheriff's posse. BLACK BART is a ground-breaking western from a characterization standpoint. The villainous characters are made the central figures, and therefore, the most sympathetic to an audience. These men go to their deaths as outlaws who never make apologies for their crimes, nor do they ever give any hint of wanting to reform. This aspect of characterization is also used in the George Roy Hill film, and most frequently by Sam Peckinpah, especially in THE WILD BUNCH (1969). Loosely based on the life of Charles E. Bolton, the real Black Bart.

p, Leonard Goldstein; d, George Sherman; w, Luci Ward, Jack Natteford, William Bowers (based on a story by Ward, Natteford); ph, Irving Glassberg (Technicolor); m, Leith Stevens; ed, Russell Schoengarth; cos, Yvonne Wood; ch, Val Raset.

Western (PR:C MPAA:NR)

BLACK BEAUTY** (1933) 63m CHAD/MON bw

Esther Ralston (*Leila Lambert*), Alexander Kirkland (*Henry Cameron*), Hale Hamilton (*Bledsoe*), Gavin Gordon (*Captain Jordan*), Don Alvarado (*Renaldo*), George Walsh (*Junk Man*).

Stunning horse sired for racing gets tossed aside to be mistreated by an unappreciative and cruel owner. The horse is found by the original owners who did not authorize the sale and is returned to comfort and family love. Steady pacing from Rosen puts this tearjerker ahead of the B-film pack.

d, Phil Rosen; w, Anna Sewell (based on her novel); ph, Charles Stumar; ed, Carl Pearson.

Drama (PR:AAA MPAA:NR)

BLACK BEAUTY**½ (1946) 74m FOX bw

Mona Freeman (*Anne Wendon*), Richard Denning (*Bill Dixon*), Evelyn Ankers (*Evelyn Carrington*), Charles Evans (*Squire Wendon*), J. M. Kerrigan (*John*), Moyna Macgill (*Mrs.Blake*), Terry Kilburn (*Joe*), Thomas P. Dillon (*Skinner*), Arthur Space (*Terry*), John Burton (*Dr. White*), Olaf Hytten (*Mr. Cordon*), Leyland Hodgson (*Auctioneer*), Clifford Brooke (*Veterinary*), Highland Dale (*"Black Beauty"*).

Freeman stars as the nineteenth-century British girl who is given a colt by her father to teach her responsibility in this third adaptation of Anna Sewell's classic novel. The girl raises the pony into a prize horse, but tragedy strikes when the animal falls into the hands of an unscrupulous party who uses it as a workhorse. After a frantic search, Freeman finally locates "Black Beauty" in a burning stable but she is unable

to save the horse. Not a bad version of the story, but better performers and color photography might have helped.

p, Edward L. Alperson; d, Max Nosseck; w, Lillie Hayward, Agnes Christine Johnston (based on the book by Anna Sewell); ph, Roy Hunt; m, Dmitri Tiomkin; ed, Martin Cole; md, David Chudnow; art d, Arthur Lonergan; set d, Glenn P. Thompson.

Drama **Cas.** (PR:AA MPAA:NR)

BLACK BEAUTY** (1971, Brit./Ger./Span.) 90m PAR c

Mark Lester (*Joe*), Walter Slezak (*Hackenschmidt*), Peter Lee Laurence (*Gervaise*), Ursula Glas (*Maria*), Patrick Mower (*Sam*), John Nettleton (*Sir William*), Maria Rohm (*Anne*), Eddie Golden (*Evans*), Clive Geraghty (*Roger*), Johnny Hoey (*Muldoon*), Margaret Lacey (*Anna*).

Unremarkable adaptation of Sewell's novel, this time produced by German and Spanish studios, and shot in English. The international cast confuses the narrative, so the film has to rely on the skills of the beautiful horse (which are incredible) to pull it through.

p, Peter L. Andrews, Malcolm B. Heyworth; d, James Hill; w, Wolf Mankowitz (based on novel by Anna Sewell); ph, Chris Menges; m, Lionel Bart, John Cameron.

Drama (PR:AA MPAA:G)

BLACK BELLY OF THE TARANTULA, THE* (1972, Ital.) 88m MGM c

Giancarlo Giannini (*Inspector Tellini*), Stefania Sandrelli (*Anna Tellini*), Claudine Auger (*Laura*), Barbara Bouchet (*Maria Zani*), Rossella Falk (*Woman With Mole*), Silvano Tranquilli (*Paolo*), Annabella Incontrera (*Mirta*), Ezio Marano (*Masseur*), Barbara Bach (*Jenny*), Giancarlo Prete (*Mario*), Anna Saia (*Amica*), Eugene Walter (*Waiter*), Nino Vingelli (*Commissario*), Daniele Dublino (*Entomologist*), Giuseppe Fortis (*Psychiatrist*), Guerrino Crivello (*Informer*), Fulvio Mingozzi (*Director of Clinic*), Giorgio Dolphin (*Policeman*), Carla Mancini (*Beauty Parlor Client*).

Gory Italian murder mystery starring Giannini as a detective who searches for an unmotivated, psychopathic killer who murders his victims by stabbing them with a knife dipped in tarantula venom (hence the obnoxious title). Along the way he encounters Prete, a blackmailer who uses incriminating photos to collect his ransom, Auger, who runs a mysterious health spa, and two usually unclothed femmes who have appeared in James Bond movies, Bach and Bouchet. Musical score is by the brilliant Italian composer Ennio Morricone, and is the best thing about this Mediterranean potboiler.

p, Marcello Danon; d, Paolo Carvara; w, Lucille Saks (story by Danon); ph, Marcello Gatti (Eastmancolor); m, Ennio Morricone; ed, Mario Morra; art d, Piero Poletto; set d, Luigi Urbani.

Crime (PR:O MPAA:R)

BLACK BELT JONES** (1974) 85m WB c

Jim Kelly (*Black Belt Jones*), Gloria Hendry (*Sidney*), Scatman Crothers (*Pop*), Alan Weeks (*Toppy*), Eric Laneuville (*Quincy*), Andre Phillipe (*Don*), Vincent Barbi (*Big Tuna*), Nate Esformes (*Roberts*), Malik Carter (*Pinky*), Mel Novak (*Blue Eyes*), Eddie Smith (*Oscar*), Alex Brown (*Plumber*), Clarence Barnes (*Tango*), Earl Brown (*Jelly*), Esther Sutherland (*Lucy*), Sid Kaiser (*Ellis*), Doug Sides (*Militant*)..

Average chop-suey picture brought to you by the team (producers, Weintraub and Heller; director, Clouse) who made the masterpiece of the genre, ENTER THE DRAGON (1973) which co-starred Jim Kelly. This time out, Kelly stars as a martial arts expert who helps Crothers and his daughter, Hendry, save their karate studio from being torn down by slimy gangsters Phillipe, Barbi, and Carter, who want to use the real estate for illegal purposes. The usual lengthy scenes of swinging and kicking are done well enough, with Kelly plowing his way through dozens of stupid white gangsters who don't think to just shoot him. Though Kelly can't act, he's a likable guy and the supporting cast do their best with the cardboard roles they were assigned.

p, Fred Weintraub, Paul Heller; d, Robert Clouse; w, Oscar Williams (based on a story by Alex Rose, Weintraub); ph, Kent Wakeford (CFI Color); m, Luchi De Jesus, Dennis Coffy; ed, Michael Kahn; set d, Charles Pierce.

Crime **Cas.** (PR:O MPAA:R)

BLACK BIRD, THE*** (1975) 98m COL c

George Segal (*Sam Spade, Jr.*), Stephane Audran (*Anna Kemidon*), Lionel Stander (*Immelman*), Lee Patrick (*Effie*), Elisha Cook, Jr. (*Wilmer*), Felix Silla (*Litvak*), Signe Hasso (*Dr. Crippen*), John Abbott (*DuQuai*), Connie Kreski (*Decoy Girl*), Titus Napoleon (*Hawaiian Thug*), Harry Kenoi (*Hawaiian Thug*), Howard Jeffrey (*Kerkorian*), Ken Swofford (*McGregor*).

A funny satire of THE MALTESE FALCON written and directed by young David Giler, whose father, Berne Giler, was one of Hollywood's best screen writers in his day. Segal was never better then as Sam Spade Junior who inherits the detective agency, now in a desolate black area. Lee Patrick (she played Effie the first time around) is still the secretary, mainly because she hasn't been paid since Mary Astor went to jail. The plot concerns that elusive Falcon again and although this is a comedy, attention is paid to the antecedents and we never get the feeling that fun is being poked, only that fun is being had. Elisha Cook, Jr., reprises his Wilmer (the gunsel) role from the earlier film and we can be sure that if Sydney and Peter were still around, they would have been here as well. Playboy beauty Connie Kreski is delicious as a decoy girl and Signe Hasso quite believable as an aging historian. Hasso, who sprang to fame as the *male* villain in THE HOUSE ON 92ND STREET, is not seen often enough these days. She has always done good work. There are far too many jibes and jokes and more turns than Lombard Street in the screenplay detail. The one failing of the picture is the endinga cop-out if there ever was one.

Also, nowhere was the Dashiell Hammett original ever acknowledged in the credits. Not nice, fellas.

p, Michael Levee, Lou Lombardo; d&w, David Giler (based on a story by Gordon Cotler, Don Mankiewicz); ph, Phil Lathrop (Metrocolor); m, Jerry Fielding; ed, Margaret Booth, Walter Thompson, Lombardo.

Comedy   Cas.   (PR:A-C MPAA:PG)

BLACK BOOK, THE**1/2
                    (1949) 89m Walter Wanger bw (GB: REIGN OF TERROR)
Robert Cummings (Charles D'Aubigny), Arlene Dahl (Madelon), Richard Hart (Francois Barras), Arnold Moss (Fouche), Richard Basehart (Robespierre), Jess Barker (Saint Just), Norman Lloyd (Tallien), Wade Crosby (Danton), William Challee (Bourdon), Georgette Windsor (Cecile), Charles McGraw (Sergeant), Ellen Lowe (Farmer's Wife), John Doucette (Farmer), Frank Conlan (Gatekeeper).

War memorial about romance during the French Revolution laced with conspiracy, with both sides vying and scheming to obtain the tome with its vital information. Good action yarn with solid cast.

p, William Cameron Menzies; d, Anthony Mann; w, Phillip Yordan, Aeneas MacKenzie (based on their story); ph, John Alton; m, Sol Kaplan; ed, Fred Allen; md, Charles Previn; art d, Edward Ilou; set d, Armor Marlowe; makeup, Ern Westmore, Jack Pierce.

Adventure   (PR:A MPAA:NR)

BLACK CAESAR**1/2   (1973) 94m AIP c
Fred Williamson (Tommy Gibbs), Phillip Roye (Joe Washington), Gloria Hendry (Helen), Julius W. Harris (Mr. Gibbs), Val Avery (Cardoza), Minnie Gentry (Mama Gibbs), Art Lund (John McKinney), D'Urville Martin (Rev. Rufus), William Wellman Jr. (Alfred Coleman), James Dixon (Bryant), Myrna Hansen (Virgina Coleman), Don Pedro Colley (Crawdaddy), Patrick McAllister (Grossfield), Cecil Alonzo (Motor), Allen Bailey (Sport), Omer Jeffrey (Tommy as a Boy), Michael Jeffrey (Joe as a Boy).

Pretty good blacksploitation picture directed by the man who would later bring horror fans the low-budget cult classic IT'S ALIVE (1974), Larry Cohen. Story begins as we see a racist, corrupt cop, Lund, partially cripple a young black boy who later grows up to be Williamson. The adult rises to power and becomes the kingpin of crime in Harlem. Williamson now owns Lund because of a long list of incriminating evidence linking the recently promoted police captain to organized crime. Lund temporarily gets his hands on the list from Williamson's disgruntled girl friend Hendry. The cop declares war on the black gangster and sends some of his men out to assassinate the king of Harlem. After being seriously wounded by the cops, Williamson finds Lund and there is a bloody climax. Music provided by the "Godfather of Soul" James Brown. (Sequel: HELL UP IN HARLEM.)

p,d&w, Larry Cohen; ph, Fenton Hamilton, James Signorelli (DeLuxe Color); m, James Brown; ed, George Folsey Jr.; art d, Larry Lurin.

Crime   (PR:O MPAA:R)

BLACK CAMEL, THE**1/2   (1931) 67m FOX bw
Warner Oland (Charlie Chan), Sally Eilers (Julie O'Neil), Bela Lugosi (Tarneverro), Dorothy Revier (Shelah Fane), Victor Varconi (Robert Fyfe), Robert Young (Jimmy Bradshaw), Marjorie White (Rita Ballou), Richard Tucker (Wilkie Ballou), J. M. Kerrigan (Thomas MacMaster), Mary Gordon (Mrs. MacMaster), C. Henry Gordon (Van Horn), Violet Dunn (Anna), William Post Jr. (Alan Jaynes), Dwight Frye (Jessop), Murray Kinnell (Smith), Otto Yamaoka (Kashimo), Rita Roselle (Luana), Robert Homans (Chief of Police), Louise Mackintosh (Housekeeper).

The second Charlie Chan mystery featuring Oland as the Chinese detective. This one, shot on location in Hawaii, has Oland investigating the murder of a movie starlet who herself has murdered her director. The suspects are the dead girl's fortune teller, Lugosi, her maid, her ex-husband, and her butler. During the course of the investigation another murder is committed, and, believe it or not, the butler and the maid did it. The highlight of this Chan outing is a scene showing the detective eating breakfast with his wife and ten children. (See: CHARLIE CHAN series, Index)

d, Hamilton McFadden; w, Barry Conners, Philip Klein (based on characters created by Earl Derr Biggers); ed, Al De Gaetano.

Mystery   (PR:A MPAA:NR)

BLACK CASTLE, THE**   (1952) 82m UNIV bw
Richard Greene (Beckett), Boris Karloff (Dr. Meissen), Stephen McNally (Count Von Bruno), Paula Corday (Elga), Lon Chaney, Jr. (Gargon), John Hoyt (Herr Stieken), Michael Pate (Von Melcher), Nancy Valentine (Therese Von Wilk), Tudor Owen (Romley), Henry Corden (Fender), Otto Waldis (Krantz).

Two years after this horror film, producer William Alland was to make THE CREATURE FROM THE BLACK LAGOON, the title of which still stands as a "reference" for comedy writers. ("references" are like . . . my wife is so ugly she frightened "The Creature From The Black Lagoon" or . . . I dreamt I went dancing in my Maidenform bra—another reference—with The Creature From The Black Lagoon." But we digress . . .) In this melodrama, McNally is a suspicious count with a huge estate that seems to swallow up people. When two of handsome Greene's pals fail to return after a sojourn at McNally's property, Greene decides to investigate and quickly learns that McNally killed his friends and is now about to do the same to him. This understood, Greene grabs Corday, the count's unwilling spouse, and they try to flee the castle. Chaney helps McNally imprison them but Karloff, a doctor in residence at the castle, balks at this behavior and sacrifices himself so Greene and Corday can escape, after first having knocked off McNally. This is an odd gesture

because the only person anyone cares about in the film is Karloff. It's an okay picture if you're not too picky.

p, William Alland; d, Nathan Juran; w, Jerry Sackheim; ph, Irving Glassberg; md, Joe Gershenson; ed, Russell Schoengarth.

Mystery Horror   (PR:C MPAA:NR)

BLACK CAT, THE***1/2   (1934) 70m UNIV bw (DB: HOUSE OF DOOM)
Boris Karloff (Hjalmar Poelzig), Bela Lugosi (Dr. Vitus Verdegast), David Manners (Peter Allison), Jacqueline Wells [Julie Bishop] (Joan Allison), Lucille Lund (Karen), Egon Brecher (Majordomo), Henry Armetta (Sergeant), Albert Conti (Lieutenant), Anna Duncan (Maid), Herman Bing (Car Steward), Andre Cheron (Train Conductor), Luis Alberni (Train Steward), Harry Cording (Thalmar), George Davis (Bus Driver), Alphonse Martell (Porter), Tony Marlow (Patrolman), Paul Weigel (Stationmaster), Albert Polet (Waiter), Rodney Hildebrand (Brakeman).

The first and best team-up of Universal horror stars Karloff and Lugosi in this bizarre, haunting, fascinating little film by cult-director Edgar G. Ulmer. Story concerns a young couple, Manners and Wells, who venture to Budapest on their honeymoon. On the train in Austria they meet Lugosi, a mysterious scientist, who seems to be quietly possessed with a deep hatred. Lugosi is going to visit his old friend Karloff, who is an architect living at the top of a mountain. The trio share a bus ride from the train station, but the bus crashes, and the couple is forced to accompany Lugosi to Karloff's modernistic art-deco mansion. Karloff greets these visitors, who are taken aback by the strange appearance of their host. His hair is cut in a bizarre fashion, he is dressed in black robes, and even his lips are black. Soon it is revealed that Lugosi has come on a mission of revenge. During the war, Karloff and Lugosi had served in the military together. Karloff was in command and caused the capture of Lugosi, and the deaths of thousands of their countrymen in a bloody battle. Karloff has built his house on the battlefield, which he calls "The greatest cemetery in the world." While Lugosi rotted in prison, the architect stole his wife, who later died (he keeps her corpse in a glass case in the same manner Argentine dictator Juan Peron was to preserve the mummified body of his beloved Eva decades later). Karloff has also married Lugosi's daughter. Karloff informs the scientist that both women are dead, and keeps Lugosi's daughter hidden from him. Lugosi is about to strike Karloff when a black cat wanders by striking the angry scientist with paralyzing fear. Karloff explains that Lugosi has always had "all-consuming horror of cats." Meanwhile Karloff has designs on Wells and kidnaps her to use as a human sacrifice in a Black Mass that he and his army of followers perform in a hidden part of the castle. Lugosi saves the woman, but her husband (who has learned not to trust either of the eccentric and deadly men) misunderstands the scientist's intentions and shoots him. Wounded Lugosi helps the couple escape and captures Karloff, whom he skins alive in a particularly hair-raising sequence. As a finale, Lugosi finds a hidden switch, and blows the art-deco castle, himself, and the satanic remains of Karloff to Kingdom Come. Though at times the plotting and motivations of the characters get somewhat confused, the film has an overwhelming sense of uneasiness, eroticism, and horror to it which infuses every shot. The absolutely magnificent set design, superbly fluid camera work, and stunning performances by Karloff (whose character was inspired by Hedonist Aleister Crowley) and Lugosi (in one of his finest roles) give the film an almost timeless quality. The use of music is extremely effective. Most of the score was derived from the classical works of Tschaikovsky, Liszt, and Schumann and helps to create suspense and mystery. Ulmer had worked with the classic German expressionist filmmakers of the 1920s and their influence is packed into every frame, making this a fascinating picture to view. Karloff and Lugosi would never work as well together again. Ulmer would go on to direct some low-budget classics, but this is his masterpiece. Well worth seeing.

p, Carl Laemmle, Jr.; d, Edgar G. Ulmer; w, Ulmer, Peter Ruric (based on the story by Edgar Allan Poe); ph, John Mescall; ed, Ray Curtis; art d, Charles D. Hall; md, Heinz Roemheld; makeup, Jack P. Pierce.

Horror   Cas.   (PR:C MPAA:NR)

BLACK CAT, THE**   (1941) 70m UNIV bw
Basil Rathbone (Hartley), Hugh Herbert (Mr. Penny), Broderick Crawford (Hubert Smith), Bela Lugosi (Eduardo), Gale Sondergaard (Abigail Doone), Anne Gwynne (Elaine Winslow), Gladys Cooper (Myrna Hartley), Cecilia Loftus (Henrietta Winslow), Claire Dodd (Margaret Gordon), John Eldredge (Stanley Borden), Alan Ladd (Richard Hartley).

Inferior horror/comedy outing stars Rathbone, Ladd, Sondergaard, and Cooper as vicious relatives who gather to wait for their wealthy aunt to die so they can collect the inheritance. The action takes place in a large, dark mansion and Lugosi, as the caretaker, spends the movie looking around corners and peering through windows. One of the relatives can't wait and murders the dying woman, whereupon they all learn that the money won't be released until the deceased's dozens of cats have died. The rest of the film sees the relatives trying to eliminate one another, and the cats.

p, Burt Kelly; d, Albert S. Rogell; w, Robert Lees, Fred Rinaldo, Eric Taylor, Robert Neville (based on a story by Edgar Allan Poe); ph, Stanley Cortez; ed, Ted Kent.

Horror   (PR:A MPAA:NR)

BLACK CAT, THE*1/2   (1966) 91m Falcon/Hemisphere bw
Robert Frost (Lew), Robyn Baker (Diana), Sadie French (Lillith), Scotty McKay, George Russell, Tommie Russell.

Frost thinks his father has been reincarnated into a black cat. He gouges out its eye and kills the kitty. The film is all blood and gore from then on. He kills his wife, there's some decapitation, axes in the skull, etc. Considering its exploitation film aesthetics, this is suprisingly a faithful adaption of the Poe story.

p, Patrick Sims; d&w, Harold Hoffman; ph, Walter Schenk; ed, Charles Schelling; art d, Robert Dracub.

Horror (PR:O MPAA:NR)

BLACK CHRISTMAS* (1974, Can.) 93m Ambassador c

Olivia Hussey (Jess), Keir Dullea (Peter), Margot Kidder (Barb), Andrea Martin (Phyl), John Saxon (Lt. Fuller), Marian Waldman (Mrs. Mac), Art Hindle (Chris), Lynne Griffin (Clare Harrison), James Edmond (Mr. Harrison).

Rotten murder mystery by the man who would later go on to direct the rancid teenage sex film PORKY'S, Bob Clark. Action takes place at a university sorority where the girls are being bloodily murdered by a savage psychopath for no apparent reason. The film is slow and dull, the blood excessive, and none of the performances particularly inspired. Clark would also direct a minor holiday classic entitled A CHRISTMAS STORY (1983), which is a hilarious adaptation of Jean Shepherd's childhood tales and is as far removed from this trash as you can get.

p&d, Bob Clark; w, Roy Moore; ph, Reg Morris; m, Carl Zittrer; ed, Stan Cole; art d, Karen Bromley.

Horror (PR:O MPAA:R)

BLACK COFFEE*1/2 (1931, Brit.) 75m Twickenham bw

Austin Trevor (Hercule Poirot), Adrianne Allen (Lucia Amory), Richard Cooper (Capt. Hastings), Elizabeth Allan (Barbara Amory), C. V. France (Sir Claude Amory).

Another British thriller based on an Agatha Christie mystery. This one surrounds a house party where a scientist is murdered after his important papers have been stolen. Everyone is suspect and Poirot, played by Trevor, narrows it down to the one person nobody suspected. Surprise!

p, Julius Hagen; d, Leslie Hiscott; w, Brock Williams, H. Fowler Mear (based on the play by Agatha Christie).

Mystery (PR:A MPAA:NR)

BLACK DAKOTAS, THE** (1954) 65m COL c

Gary Merrill (Brock Marsh), Wanda Hendrix (Ruth Lawrence), John Bromfield (Mike Daugherty), Noah Beery, Jr. ("Gimpy" Joe Woods), Fay Roope (John Lawrence), Howard Wendell (Judge Baker), Robert Simon (Marshal Collins), James Griffith (Warren), Richard Webb (Frank Gibbs), Peter Whitney (Grimes), John War Eagle (War Cloud), Jay Silverheels (Black Buffalo), George Keymas (Spotted Deer), Robert Griffin (Boggs), Clayton Moore (Stone), Chris Alcalde (Burke), Frank Wilcox (Zachary Paige).

President Abe Lincoln would like to smoke the peace pipe with the Sioux Indians so he can get his troops out of that territory and down to the South, where they are needed for the Civil War effort. The Johnny Rebs hear of this and send a spy, Merrill, to pose as a Yankee, and swipe a mess of gold that the Indians had promised to the Northerners. Merrill's job is to snatch the yellow stuff for the Confederates. Then we learn that Merrill is not a Reb at all, nor is he a double agent for Lincoln's minions. Instead, he is operating on his own and has no loyalties to either side. An offbeat story handled in an on-beat way. Nazarro did a host of these second features and knows his stuff. Hendrix is the daughter of a southern spy and good-natured Bromfield is her fiance and does his customary solid work.

p, Wallace MacDonald; d, Ray Nazarro; w, Ray Buffum, DeVallon Scott (story by Buffum); ph, Ellis W. Carter (Technicolor); m, Mischa Bakaleinikoff; ed, Aaron Stell.

Western (PR:A-C MPAA:NR)

BLACK DEVILS OF KALI, THE
(SEE: MYSTERY OF THE BLACK JUNGLE, 1955)

BLACK DIAMONDS* (1932, Brit.) Hammer 53m bw

John Martin (The MP), John Morgan (The Miner), Mrs. Morgan (The Wife), Jenny Morgan (The Child), The Harmonious Miners, Barnborough Colliery Orchestra.

Tough old Yorkshire miner talks a film producer into making a movie depicting the hazards of pit life for all the world to see.

p,d&w, Charles Hammer.

Drama (PR:A MPAA:NR)

BLACK DIAMONDS** (1940) 60m UNIV bw

Richard Arlen (Walter Norton), Andy Devine (Barney Tolliver), Kathryn Adams (Linda Conner), Mary Treen (Nina Norton), Paul Fix (Matthews), Pat Flaherty (Johnson), Maude Allen (Mrs. Norton), Cliff Clark (Archie Connor).

Decent tale about a tough newspaper reporter, Arlen, who goes back to his home town to find that the local coal mine is extremely unsafe. He begins a crusade to improve conditions and is aided by Devine who plays a miner who is in love with the reporter's sister, Treen. Loose remake of the 1932 film.

p, Ben Pivar; d, Christy Cabanne; w, Clarence Upson Young, Sam Robins (based on a story by Robins); ph, William Sickner.

Drama (PR:A MPAA:NR)

BLACK DOLL, THE*1/2 (1938) 66m UNIV bw

Nan Grey (Marion Rood), Donald Woods (Nick Halstead), Edgar Kennedy (Sheriff Renick), William Lundigan (Rex), Doris Lloyd (Mrs. Laura Leland), Addison Richards (Mallison), Holmes Herbert (Dr. Giddings).

Tedious murder mystery somewhat redeemed by Kennedy's comic performance as the small-town sheriff who assists the young sleuth, Woods, in solving three murders. Kennedy plays the part for all the laughs it's worth, which helps the film glide to its inevitable conclusion.

p, Irving Starr; d, Otis Garrett; w, Harold Buckley (based on the novel by William Edward Hayes); ph, Ira Morgan; ed, Maurice Wright.

Comedy/Mystery (PR:A MPAA:NR)

BLACK DRAGONS** (1942) 61m MON bw

Bela Lugosi (Dr. Melcher Colomb), Joan Barclay (Alice), Clayton Moore (Don Martin), George Pembroke (Saunders), Robert Frazer (Hanlin), I. Stanford Jolley (The Dragon), Max Hoffman, Jr. (Kerney), Irving Mitchell (Van Dyke), Edward Peil (Wallace), Bob Fiske (Ryder), Kenneth Harlan (Colton), Joe Eggenton (Stevens).

Bizarre wartime horror/espionage film starring Lugosi as a Nazi plastic surgeon who is sent to Japan to turn Japanese spies into American-looking men so they can move about freely while committing their heinous acts of sabotage in the U.S. The surgery is a success, but the untrustworthy Japs throw Lugosi in the hoosegow to make sure the whole thing stays secret. The angry doctor eventually escapes and travels to America to seek his revenge on the sly Japanese. The whole thing is pretty silly (not to mention racist, as most of the films of this period were) and even includes a scene of a man being turned into a monster after being injected with a mysterious serum. Worth a look for the historically curious.

p, Sam Katzman, Jack Dietz; d, William Nigh; w, Harvey Gates; ph, Art Reed; ed, Carl Pierson.

Horror Cas. (PR:A MPAA:NR)

BLACK EAGLE** (1948) 76m COL bw

William Bishop (Jason Bond), Virginia Patton (Ginny Long), Gordon Jones (Benjy Laughton), James Bell (Frank Hayden), Trevor Bardette (Mike Long), Will Wright (Clancy), Edmund MacDonald (Si), Paul E. Burns (Hank Daniels), Harry Cheshire (The General), Al Ehen (Chicken), Ted Mapes (Sam), Richard Talmadge (Mort).

Bishop plays a vagabond hero in this adaptation of an O. Henry story. Bishop becomes a drifter because he wants to avoid contact with people who always cause him trouble. He boards a train, and unintentionally becomes embroiled in a western ranch war. First he's on the side of the good rancher, Jones, and then he ends up on the side of greedy rancher Bell. Eventually all is worked out and Bishop returns to his box car in search of some privacy.

p, Robin Cohn; d, Robert Gordon; w, Edward Huebsch, Hal Smith (based on the story "The Passing Of Black Eagle" by O. Henry); ph, Henry Freulich; ed, James Sweeney.

Drama/Western (PR:A MPAA:NR)

BLACK EYE*1/2 (1974) 98m WB c

Fred Williamson (Stone), Rosemary Forsyth (Miss Francis), Teresa Graves (Cynthia), Floy Dean (Diane Davis), Richard Anderson (Dole), Cyril Delevanti (Talbot), Richard X. Slattery (Bowen), Larry Mann (Avery), Bret Morrison (Majors), Susan Arnold (Amy).

Williamson almost saves this somewhat fuzzy detective movie about the murder of a silent film star who was involved in a dope smuggling ring. Williamson, an L.A. cop who was suspended for killing a dope pusher responsible for his sister's death, is reinstated to help find the killer of the former movie star. The trail leads him into a mess of episodic scenes, one of which has him tracking down a missing girl who is involved in the Jesus freak scene, drugs, lesbianism, and porno movies. This fails because it tries to appeal to too many of the sick fantasies of its limited audience.

p, Pat Rooney; d, Jack Arnold; w, Mark Haggard, Jim Martin (based on the novel Murder On The Wild Side by Jeff Jacks); ph, Ralph Woolsey (Technicolor); m, Mort Garson; ed, Gene Ruggiero; art d, Chuck Pierce, John Rozman.

Mystery/Action (PR:O MPAA:PG)

BLACK EYES** (1939, Brit.) 72m Associated British Films bw

Mary Maguire (Tania), Otto Kruger (Petroff), Walter Rilla (Roudine), John Wood (Karlo), Marie Wright (Miss Brown).

Melodrama set in Moscow concerns the efforts of a lowly waiter, Kruger, to improve his life for the benefit of his daughter, Maguire. Kruger works in a fancy restaurant that has private rooms for liaisons between rich men and their lady friends. The waiter keeps his eyes and ears open and has managed to make a number of good investments from overhearing stock-market tips from financiers who frequent the establishment. As far as his daughter knows, he is a successful businessman, and not a waiter. In an effort to make his dream come true, Kruger seeks out a rich banker to invest in his idea to purchase the restaurant. The banker and Maguire become attracted to each other, and unknowingly, the man takes the girl to the restaurant where her father works. Kruger enters the private dining room and is shocked to find his daughter and she to find him as a waiter. All works out in the end with the banker helping the waiter purchase the restaurant.

p, Walter C. Mycroft; d, Herbert Brenon; w, Dudley Leslie; ph, Gunther Krampf.

Drama (PR:A MPAA:NR)

BLACK FRIDAY** (1940) 70m UNIV bw

Boris Karloff (Dr. Ernest Sovac), Bela Lugosi (Eric Marnay), Stanley Ridges (Prof. George Kingsley/Red Cannon), Anne Nagel (Sunny Rogers), Anne Gwynne (Jean Sovac), Virginia Brissac (Margaret Kingsley), Edmund MacDonald (Frank Miller), Paul Fix (Kane), Murray Alper (Bellhop), Jack Mulhall (Bartender), Joe King (Police Chief), John Kelly (Taxidriver).

Bogus Karloff/Lugosi film in which the two horror stars have no scenes together, and the main character is actually a third actor, Ridges. Karloff plays a doctor who tries to save the life of his good friend Ridges, a college professor, who has sustained a potentially fatal injury to the skull in a car crash caused by gangsters. One of the gangsters was also killed in the crash and Karloff attempts to put a piece of the dead hood's brain into the head of Ridges and save his life. Unfortunately, the professor's evil section of gray matter takes over and he becomes a crook who seeks revenge on rival gang leader Lugosi. The script is by Curt Siodmak who later took the brain switching idea a step further and turned it into "Donovan's Brain," which was made into a terrifying radio broadcast starring Orson Welles, and two different movies, THE LADY AND THE MONSTER (1944) and DONOVAN'S BRAIN (1953).

p, Burt Kelly; d, Arthur Lubin; w, Curt Siodmak, Eric Taylor; ph, Elwood Bredell; ed, Phillip Cahn; md, Hans J. Salter; art d, Jack Otterson; set d, Russell Gausman; cos, Vera West.

Horror/Crime **(PR:A MPAA:NR)**

BLACK FURY* 1/2** (1935) 95m FN/WB bw

Paul Muni *(Joe Radek)*, Karen Morley *(Anna Novak)*, William Gargan *(Slim)*, Barton MacLane *(McGee)*, John Qualen *(Mike Shemanski)*, J. Carroll Naish *(Steve Croner)*, Vince Barnett *(Kubanda)*, Henry O'Neill *(J.W. Hendricks)*, Tully Marshall *(Tommy Poole)*, Mae Marsh *(Mary Novak)*, Sarah Haden *(Sophie Shemanski)*, Joe Crehan *(John Farrell)*, George Pat Collins *(Lefty)*, Willard Robertson *(Welsh)*, Effie Ellsler *(The Bubitschka)*, Wade Boteler *(Mulligan)*, Egon Brecher *(Alec Novak)*, Ward Bond *(Mac)*, Akim Tamiroff *(Sokolsky)*, Purnell Pratt *(Jenkins)*, Eddie Shubert *(Butch)*.

Like OUR DAILY BREAD, this film packs a walloping social message but also provides high drama, particularly in the form of one of the greatest actors to ever grace stage and screen, Paul Muni. He is a crude, unthinking miner hardly able to write his own name and when his sweetheart Morley runs away with Gargan, Muni gets drunk and then staggers out to a miner's meeting. Naish, an agitator trying to get the miners to reorganize their union, is addressing workers and Muni dumbly begins to echo his hortatory talk, then begins shouting louder than Naish until the miners respond to his wild encouragement, half of them breaking away from the old union and forming a new one under Muni's leadership. This group finds itself locked out of the mine the next day with strike-breaking thugs barring the path, the company goons headed by brutal MacLane (who, one wag pointed out, never talked when shouting would do). Thugs attack Qualen's daughter; when Muni and his friend Qualen go to the rescue Qualen is killed by MacLane and Muni is beaten up so badly he must be hospitalized. He learns that the strikebreakers have smashed the resolve of the union and the men are about to go back to work. He staggers from his bed, finds some dynamite and sneaks into the mine, aided by Morley, who now believes him. Muni barricades himself inside the mine after exploding the power plant and conducts his own strike. Newsmen make his stand famous overnight and Morley visits Muni inside the shaft, explaining that the world is now with him, that it is safe to come out. He does, to the cheers of his followers. MacLane, who has been held captive in the shaft by Muni, is turned over to the police and charged with Qualen's murder. Morley and Muni are in each other's arms at the finish. The film was a slice of real life, taken from a story about three company cops who had killed a rebellious miner in Imperial, Pennsylvania, in 1929, and also a hard-hitting play on the same subject by Henry R. Irving. Muni, as was his habit, researched his role with frenzy, going to Pennsylvania and working among miners for weeks, picking up the proper accent and mannerisms which resulted in another distinguished and powerful performance. But where Muni could be meticulous in building his own character, he was picky about those supporting him. He had been annoyed at the clowning of Vince Barnett as a fumbling little sidekick in SCARFACE and when he learned that Barnett was to again appear with him, Muni went to director Curtiz to have him removed from the cast. Curtiz, ever the iron-willed boss, refused and Barnett stayed in the film to provide vital comic relief in an otherwise heavy drama. Muni could not shuck himself of the little bald-headed comedian who would appear again with him in THE WOMAN I LOVE in 1937. Curtiz directs this film with his usual gusto, moving his scenes along with a ferocity that earned him the deserved reputation of Hollywood's top action director in the late 1930s and early 1940s. He was *the* Warner Brothers' workhorse. Curtiz loved work and making others meet his own exhausting efforts. But when excited, the Hungarian-born director would blurt malapropisms equal to those of the gentle Sam Goldwyn. On one occasion Curtiz sent an assistant for a prop and exploded on the set when the man failed to return within five minutes, raging: "The next time I send a dumb son-of-a-bitch to do something, I'll go myself!" BLACK FURY received a top budget and big production values, being shot at the Warner Brothers ranch where intricate mine shafts and heavy equipment were created and installed. Yet it failed at the box office. Too dreary, too brutal, too realistic, said the customers and critics alike. Moreover, the State of Pennsylvania officially banned the film because of its uncompromising profile of a mining city that could be none other than Pittsburgh. The Gargan-Morley-Muni lovemaking scenes were too torrid for many other states where local censorship boards refused to allow the film into theaters. (It is hard to believe today that these backwoods bureaucrats of the 1930s could so easily slip from their uncreative crannies to sit in judgment and exercise such horrible power.) The film remains, nevertheless, a great historic profile of the struggle early unions had in providing safety and decent wages for their people. Few studios other than Warner Brothers bothered with important social issues then and it is a credit to Jack Warner that he was willing to deal with any problem afflicting America's "little people," which was just about everyone.

p, Robert Lord; d, Michael Curtiz; w, Abem Finkel, Carl Erickson (based on the play "Bohunk" by Henry R. Irving, and the story "Jan Volkanik" by Judge M. A. Musmanno); ph, Byron Haskin; makeup, Perc Westmore.

Drama **Cas.** **(PR:C MPAA:NR)**

BLACK GESTAPO, THE* (1975) 88m Bryanston Pictures c

Rod Perry *(General Ahmed)*, Charles P. Robinson *(Colonel Kojah)*, Phil Hoover *(Vito)*, Ed Cross *(Delmay)*, Angela Brent *(Marsha)*, Wes Bishop *(Ernest)*, Lee Frost *(Vincent)*, Dona Desmond *(White Whore)*, Charles Howerton *(Joe)*, Rai Tasco *(Dr. Lisk)*, David Bryant *(Pusher)*.

This black exploitation picture profiles "The People's Army" in Watts, scene of the 1965 summer riots. Robinson is the second in command to Perry and wants to take over as top dog. The army was started to get the slumlords and bad dudes out of the ghetto but the Army becomes as corrupt as the people they have sought to get rid of. This picture is one disgusting, violent scene after another. The actors are only as good as the script . . . which is awful. This movie died a deservedly horrible death at the box office and it is doubtful that you will ever see it on TV, unless about an hour is cut . . . which would make it a 28-minute short subject.

p, Wes Bishop; d, Lee Frost; w, Frost, Bishop; ph, Derek Scott; ed, Jounnu Terbush.

Drama **(PR:O MPAA:R)**

BLACK GIRL** (1972) 97m Cinerama c

Brock Peters *(Earl)*, Leslie Uggams *(Netta)*, Claudia McNeil *(Mu' Dear)*, Louise Stubbs *(Mama Rosie)*, Gloria Edwards *(Norma)*, Loretta Greene *(Ruth Ann)*, Kent Martin *(Herbert)*, Peggy Pettit *(Billie Jean)*, Ruby Dee *(Netta's Mother)*.

Black family melodrama starring Stubbs as a mother who feels she's failed raising her own children and has turned to helping other girls. Uggams plays the foster daughter, Edwards and Greene play the jealous "real" daughters, and Peters plays the father. Stubbs gives a passionate performance as a woman trying to overcome her faults and weaknesses and make amends for her past mistakes. Adapted from a successful off-Broadway play. Betty Everett and Walter Hawkins provide the songs.

p, Lee Savin; d, Ossie Davis; w, J. E. Franklin (based on her play); ph, Glenwood J. Swanson; m, Ed Bogas, Ray Shanklin, Jesse Osborne, Merl Saunders; ed, Graham Lee Mahin; ch, Peggy Pettit.

Drama **(PR:A MPAA:PG)**

BLACK GLOVE* (1954, Brit.) 84m Hammer bw (GB: FACE THE MUSIC)

Alex Nicol *(James Bradley)*, Eleanor Summerfield *(Barbara Quigley)*, John Salew *(Max Marguiles)*, Paul Carpenter *(John Sutherland)*, Geoffrey Keen *(Maurice Green)*, Ann Hanslip *(Maxine)*, Fred Johnson *(Insp. Mackenzie)*, Martin Boddey *(Sgt. Mulrooney)*, Arthur Lane *(Jeff Colt)*, Gordon Crier *(Vic Parsons)*, Kenny Baker's Dozen.

American trumpet player accused of murdering a girl singer struggles to prove his innocence in a slow-moving melodrama that appeals little on production or acting levels, both being shallow.

p, Michael Carreras; d, Terence Fisher; w, Ernest Bornemann (based on the novel by Bornemann); ph, Jimmy Harvey.

Crime **(PR:A MPA:NR)**

BLACK GOLD** (1947) 90m MON c

Anthony Quinn *(Charley Eagle)*, Katherine DeMille *(Sarah Eagle)*, Elyse Knox *(Ruth Frazer)*, Kane Richmond *(Stanley Lowell)*, Ducky Louie *(Davey)*, Raymond Hatton *(Bucky)*, Thurston Hall *(Col. Caldwell)*, Alan Bridge *(Jonas)*, Moroni Olsen *(Dan Toland)*, H. T. Tsiang *(Davey's Father)*, Charles Trowbridge *(Judge Wilson)*, Jack Norman *(Monty)*, Darryl Hickman *(Schoolboy)*, Clem McCarthy, Joe Hernandez *(Themselves)*.

First starring role for Quinn after 46 appearances in the movies. He plays a kindly Indian man who one day finds an orphaned Chinese boy, Louie, and his horse. Quinn and his wife adopt the boy and mate his horse with their mare. Quinn falls in with an unscrupulous horse manager, Olsen, who talks him into entering the mare in a race. The horse wins, but Olsen shafts Quinn by grabbing the mare for $500 on a technicality. Quinn and his friend, Hatton, steal the horse back leaving the $500 in the stable. Soon after oil is struck on Quinn's property and the mare gives birth to a beautiful colt that the Indian names "Black Gold." Quinn and Louie raise the colt into a championship horse and enter it in the Kentucky Derby. Now an old man, Quinn goes off to die making Louie promise he will win the derby for him. The boy indeed does win in honor of the kind Indian who gave him a new life. Pretty melodramatic stuff, given poor technical production by the studio, but saved by Quinn's bravura performance.

p, Jeffrey Bernard; d, Phil Karlson; w, Agnes Christine Johnson (based on a story by Caryl Coleman); ph, Harry Neumann (Cinecolor); ed, Roy Livingston; md, Edward J. Kay; art d, E.R. Hickson.

Drama **(PR:A MPAA:NR)**

BLACK GOLD* 1/2 (1963) 98m WB bw

Philip Carey *(Frank McCandless)*, Diane McBain *(Ann Evans)*, James Best *(Jericho Larkin)*, Fay Spain *(Julie)*, Claude Akins *(Chick Carrington)*, William Phipps *(Albert Mailer)*, Dub Taylor *(Doc)*, Ken Mayer *(Felker)*, Iron Eyes Cody *(Charlie Two-Bits)*, Vincent Barbi *(Klein)*, Rusty Wescoatt *(Wilkins)*.

Carey (Granny Goose in later years) is the oil wildcatter, Akins is the heavy. Lots of wasted time in between the few moments of action. This was an introductory film in that it featured several performers heretofore unseen or only granted small roles. Under the direction of Martinson (among others) they don't get much of an opportunity to strut their stuff. The script is a softie to begin with and has every idea about oil that one can think of. The only problem is that the ideas were thought of long before this picture was made.

p, Jim Barnett; d, Leslie Martinson; w, Bob and Wanda Duncan (based on a story by Henry Whittington); ph, Harold Stine; m, Howard Jackson; ed, Leo H. Shreve.

Adventure/Drama **(PR:A-C MPAA:NR)**

BLACK GUNN* (1972) 94m COL c

Jim Brown *(Gunn)*, Martin Landau *(Capelli)*, Brenda Sykes *(Judith)*, Luciana Paluzzi *(Toni)*, Vida Blue *(Sam Green)*, Stephen McNally *(Laurento)*, Keefe Brasselle *(Winman)*, Timothy Brown *(Larry)*, William Campbell *(Rico)*, Bernie

Casey (Seth), Gary Conway (Adams), Chuck Daniel (Mel), Tommy Davis (Webb), Rick Ferrell (Jimpy), Bruce Glover (Ray Kriley), Toni Holt (Betty), Herbert Jefferson Jr. (Scott Gunn), Jay Montgomery (Junkie), Mark Tapscott (Cassidy), Gene Washington (Elmo), Jim Watkins (Lt. Jopper), Jonas Wolfe (Val), Tony Young (Dell), Sandra Giles (Prostitute), Kate Woodville (Louella), Gyl Roland (Celeste), Lavelle Roby (Jane), Jeanne Bell (Lisa), Tony Giorgio (Ben), Frank Bello (Robbo), Arell Blanton (Television Director), Manuel DePina (Bowling Alley Manager), Deacon Jones (Himself).

Poor blacksploitation film featuring Brown as a nightclub owner whose brother is involved in black militant activities. When his brother robs a white mobster's bookie joint to raise money for his militant army, the gangster leader, Landau, has him killed. Brown grabs his gun and seeks revenge on the hood and his gang. Explosions, bloody gun battles, and car chases are the only excuses for making this miserable film.

p, John Heyman, Norman Priggen; d, Robert Hartford-Davis; w, Franklin Coen (based on a screenplay by Robert Shearer from an idea by Davis); ph, Richard H. Kline; m, Tony Osborne; ed, David De Wilde, Pat Somerset; art d, Jack DeShields.

Crime   **(PR:O MPAA:R)**

BLACK HAND, THE***   (1950) 92m MGM bw

Gene Kelly (Johnny Columbo), J. Carrol Naish (Louis Lorelli), Teresa Celli (Isabella Gomboli), Marc Lawrence (Caesar Xavier Serpi), Frank Puglia (Carlo Sabballera), Barry Kelley (Capt. Thompson), Mario Siletti (Benny Danetta), Carl Milletaire (George Allani), Peter Brocco (Roberto Columbo), Eleonora Mendelssohn (Maria Columbo), Grazia Narciso (Mrs. Danetta), Maurice Samuels (Moriani), Burk Symon (Judge), Bert Freed (Prosecutor), Mimi Aguglia (Mrs. Sabballera), Baldo Minuti (Bettini), Carlo Tricoli (Pietro Riago).

An unusual film for Kelly, whose fortunes had dipped at MGM before he came back as a superstar with blockbusters like SINGIN' IN THE RAIN. To keep him busy, the studio produced THE BLACK HAND, one of the first films to take on the Mafia long before THE GODFATHER made it popular, although the script cautiously sets the time at the turn of the century and confines the criminal activities to NYC's "Little Italy," where organized secret groups terrorized their own by demanding money, threatening to blow up a pushcart or shop, always signing the extortion notes with an ink-coated handprint, ergo the notorious "Black Hand." Kelly's father, a conscientious Italian lawyer, is murdered by Black Handers and his mother takes him back to Italy where he grows to manhood, then returns to NYC to seek vengeance on his father's killers. Kelly intends to become a lawyer like his father, going to night school while working, but he fails to gather enough evidence on the gang until Naish, a NYC police inspector (the role based on real-life Lt. Joseph Petrosino) works with him. Several Black Handers are put away but to imprison the bosses, Naish must go to Naples to gather more information, which he does. He realizes that he is marked for death so he mails the vital letter to Kelly in NYC before being killed. (This is exactly what happened to Petrosino, but he went to Palermo, Sicily, to investigate the Mafia, not the Black Hand, and was murdered on the night of March 12, 1909, as he waited for an informant to meet him at the base of the Garibaldi Statue in Piazza Marina in the heart of Palermo, felled by more than 100 bullets fired at him from the darkness.) The letter mailed by Naish is sought after by both Kelly and the Black Handers, which leads Kelly into a wild fight with boss Lawrence, whom he beats up, then drags to the authorities, after an explosion almost kills both of them. Thorpe directs in a taut style that maintains the tension and Kelly is excellent as the Italian youth, while Naish gives one of his best character essays. Though of Irish ancestry, Naish was especially adept at Italian dialects and roles, with a long run in the radio series, "Life with Luigi.") Kelly's beautiful girl friend, Teresa Celli, was one of the many Italian talents recruited for this production. She is excellent, but, oddly, after making three more films that same year, disappeared from the screen. Vogel's lensing and Colombo's score present just the right film noir atmosphere and sound.

p, William H. Wright; d, Richard Thorpe; w, Luther Davis (based on a story by Leo Townsend); ph, Paul C. Vogel; m, Albert Colombo; ed, Irving Warburton; art d, Cedric Gibbons, Gabriel Scognamillo.

Crime Drama   **(PR:C MPAA:NR)**

THE BLACK HAND GANG*   (1930, Brit.) 63m BIP bw

Wee Georgie Wood (Georgie Robinson), Dolly Harmer (Mrs. Robinson), Violet Young (Winnie), Lionel Hoare (The Other Man), Junior Banks (Archibald), Viola Compton (Mater), Alfred Woods (Pater).

Burglar's attempt to rob a rich boy's home is thwarted by a bunch of enterprising children. A spoof that goes poof under the weak direction and lame script.

d, Monty Banks; w, R. P. Weston, Bert Lee (based on the play by Weston and Lee.)

Comedy   **(PR:A MPAA:NR)**

BLACK HILLS*   (1948) 60m EL bw

Eddie Dean (Eddie), Roscoe Ates (Soapy), Shirley Patterson (Janet), Terry Frost (Kirby), Steve Drake (Larry), Nina Bara (Chiquita), Bill Fawcett (Tuttle), Lane Bradford (Cooper), Lee Morgan (Sheriff), George Chesebro (Allen).

Dull western starring Dean and his sidekick Ates who avenge the murder of a struggling ranch owner who had found a gold mine on his property and was killed by saloon keeper Frost. The usual chases, shootouts, comedy, and songs occur with boring predictability.

p, Jerry Thomas; d, Ray Taylor; w, Joseph Poland; ph, Ernie Miller; ed, Hugh Winn; m/l, Dean Hal Blair, Pete Gates.

Western   **(PR:A MPAA:NR)**

BLACK HILLS AMBUSH*1/2   (1952) 53m REP bw

Allan "Rocky" Lane (Himself), Black Jack (His Stallion), Eddy Waller (Nugget Clark), Leslye Banning (Sally), Roy Barcroft (Bart), Michael Hall (Larry Stewart), John Vosper (Gaines), Edward Cassidy (Sheriff), John Cason (Jake), Wesley Hudman (Buck), Michael Barton (Clay Stewart).

Rocky Lane (born Harry Albershart) was a terrific athlete in his youth and that training stands him in good stead in this short, punchy film about a marshal (Lane) being called in by an old pal (Waller) to help him destroy a gang of brigands who are ruining his shipping business. Not much female activity in the picture except for a brief look at Banning. Fast-paced once it gets going.

p, Herbert J. Yates; d, Harry Keller; w, Ronald Davidson, M. Coates Webster; ph, Bud Thackery; m, Stanley Wilson; ed, Tony Martinelli.

Western   **(PR:A-C MPAA:NR)**

BLACK HILLS EXPRESS**   (1943) 55m REP bw

Don "Red" Barry (Lon Walker), Wally Vernon (Deadeye), Ariel Heath (Gale Southern), George Lewis (Vic Fowler), William Halligan (Harvey Dorman), Hooper Atchley (Jason Phelps), Charles Miller (Raymond Harper), Pierce Lyden (Carl), Jack Rockwell (The Sheriff), Bob Kortman (Dutch), Al Taylor (Denver).

Better than usual Barry outing sees him teamed up for the first time with new sidekick Vernon. Plot concerns Barry's efforts to clear himself from a string of stagecoach robberies by exposing the real culprits, the sheriff and a local banker. Fast-paced and inoffensive.

p, Eddy White; d, John English; w, Norman Hall, Fred Myton (based on an idea by Myton); ph, Ernest Miller; ed, Harry Keller.

Western   **(PR:A MPAA:NR)**

BLACK HOLE, THE***   (1979) 97m BV c

Maximilian Schell (Dr. Hans Reinhardt), Anthony Perkins (Dr. Alex Durant), Robert Forster (Capt. Dan Holland), Joseph Bottoms (Lt. Charles Pizer), Yvette Mimieux (Dr. Kate McGraw), Ernest Borgnine (Harry Booth), Tommy McLoughlin (Capt. S.T.A.R.)

Although technically superior to STAR WARS, STAR TREK, and CLOSE EN-COUNTERS OF THE THIRD KIND, THE BLACK HOLE failed to gather anything near the gross receipts of the aforementioned. Disney pictures have always had a patina of professionalism about them and this is no exception. Sometime in the future, five people in a spaceship encounter a Black Hole. Before attempting to flee, they see a spaceship near the Black Hole's entrance. Upon boarding it they discover the ship is manned by robots with one human, Schell, running things. Schell is a genius but somewhat bonkers and he plans to go into the Black Hole because he feels that is where all matter and energy begin. The five attempt to escape but are sucked in by the hole and to tell anything further would be to ruin an excellent picture. Peter Ellenshaw did the production design, and paintings by this Olympian artist now cost thousands. It is his vision that makes THE BLACK HOLE so incredibly wonderful to watch. The original story, by Barbash and Landau, was far superior to the rewrite by Rosebrook and Day, and Gary Nelson's direction of the actors is uninventive. The problem with THE BLACK HOLE is that the protagonist, Schell, is nuts and we find it difficult to root for him. Perkins, Forster, and the others are never fully realized as people and the picture becomes a triumph of style over substance. All technical credits are excellent and Barry's score is first-rate. If Walt were still alive, you may be sure that THE BLACK HOLE would have had a beating heart.

p, Ron Miller; d, Gary Nelson; w, Jeb Rosebrook, Gerry Day (based on a story by Bob Barbash, Richard Landau, Rosebrook); ph, Frank Phillips (Technovision, Technicolor); m, John Barry; ed, Gregg McLaughlin; prod d, Peter Ellenshaw; art d, John B. Mansbridge, Al Roelofs; cos, Bill Thomas.

Science Fiction   **Cas.**   **(PR:A-C MPAA:PG)**

BLACK HORSE CANYON**   (1954) 81m UNIV c

Joel McCrea (Del Rockwell), Mari Blanchard (Aldia Spain), Race Gentry (Ti), Murvyn Vye (Jennings), Irving Bacon (Doc), John Pickard (Duke), Ewing Mitchell (Sheriff), Pilar Del Rey (Juanita), William J. Williams (Graves).

This whoopie-ti-yi-yarn is about as diverting as one can be. McCrea and Gentry chase after a wild stallion that is stealing all the mares. They know this horse can be very valuable standing at stud. Vye also wants the horse that was once the property of Blanchard and Bacon, her uncle. McCrea and Gentry catch the horse, break it, and Blanchard joins McCrea at the fadeout. This is not a cowboys-and-Indians nor a shoot-em-up. Actually, it's closer to an adult version of BLACK BEAUTY or THE BLACK STALLION. (Why are these horses always black?) Better than most due to an intelligent script with believable dialogue by Geoffrey Homes.

p, John W. Rogers; d, Jesse Hibbs; w, Geoffrey Homes (based on the novel by Les Savage, adaptation by David Lang); ph, George Robinson (Technicolor); ed, Frank Gross.

Western   **(PR:A MPAA:NR)**

BLACK ICE, THE*   (1957, Brit.) 51m Parkside/Archway bw

Paul Carpenter (Greenslade), Gordon Jackson (Bert Harris), Ewen Solon (Capt. John Dodds), David Oxley (Tom).

While trying to save his ship from fog and ice, a trawler captain is trapped and must battle the elements. Good action yarn.

p, Jacque de Lane Lea; d, Godfrey Grayson; w, John Sherman, Roger Proudlock; ph, Jimmy Harvey.

Adventure   **(PR:A MPAA:NR)**

BLACK JACK (SEE: CAPTAIN BLACK JACK, 1952, Fr./U.S.)

BLACK JACK* (1973) 87m AIP c (AKA: WILD IN THE SKY)

Georg Stanford Brown (Lynch), Brandon De Wilde (Josh), Keenan Wynn (Gen. Harry Gobohare), Tim O'Connor (Sen. Bob Recker), Dick Gautier (Diver), Robert Lansing (Maj. Reason), Larry Hovis (Capt. Breen), Bernie Kopell (Penrat), Joseph Turkel (Corazza), Dub Taylor (Roddenberry), Phil Vandervort (Woody).

Awful black comedy about three radicals, Brown, De Wilde, and Vandervort, who hijack an Air Force bomber loaded with nuclear missiles. The trio decide to bomb Fort Knox to atomic oblivion as a symbol of protest against the establishment. Bad jokes, a fuzzy point of view, and mediocre performances make this a wasted effort. The film was actor Brandon (SHANE) De Wilde's last appearance before his tragic death.

p, William T. Naud, Dick Gautier; d, Naud; w, Gautier, Naud (story by Naud, Gautier, Peter Marshall); ph, Thomas E. Spaulding (Movielab Color); m, Jerry Styner; ed, Naud, Michael Kahn.

Comedy **(PR:C MPAA:PG)**

BLACK JACK ****1/2** (1979, Brit.) 106m Kestrel/National Film Finance c

Jean Franval (Black Jack), Stephen Hirst (Tolly), Andrew Bennet (Hatch), Louise Cooper (Belle), Packie Byrne (Dr. Carmody), John Young (Dr. Hunter), Russell Waters (Dr. Jones), Pat Wallis (Mrs. Gorgandy), William Moore (Mr. Carter).

A very fine family film that looks as though it should have cost ten times what it did. BLACK JACK is a Frenchman of few words in this eighteenth-century fable. He hires a young lad (Tolly) to speak for him after a miraculous escape from a hanging. It's endearing and quite believable, mainly because you probably have never seen any of the actors before, and so it seems to be really happening. A series of episodic adventures that almost strain credulity but stop just short of a hoax. The major problem is that the United States and England are two countries divided by the same language and in this case, the Yorkshire accent is almost unintelligible to the untrained ear. With a good ad campaign, this should have been rated as a young person's classic but it fell down in the publicity department and is now gathering dust on some TV station's shelf. Alas!

p, Tony Garnett; d, Kenneth Loach; w, Loach (based on the novel by Leon Garfield); ph, Chris Menges; m, Bob Pegg; ed, Bill Shapter; prod d, Martin Johnson; cos, Sally Nieper.

Adventure **(PR:AA MPAA:NR)**

BLACK JOY ****** (1977, Brit.) 110m Kastner/Milchan (Winkast) c

Norman Beaton (Dave), Trevor Thomas (Ben), Floella Benjamin (Miriam), Dawn Hope (Saffar), Oscar James (Jomo), Paul Medford (Devon).

Somewhat predictable but also pleasant programmer about a young black man from an unnamed Caribbean island who comes to Great Britain and gets bounced around in the left lane. In the broad sense of the word it's a Black Film but it doesn't have any large axe to grind, nor does it rub any white faces in the refuse of racism. It could just as easily have been about a Geordie coming to Manchester. A few laughs, a few tears, some good performances (especially by Thomas as Ben, the country cousin, and Beaton as Dave, a black version of Bilko) and an altogether too leisurely pace.

p, Elliott Kastner, Arnon Milchan; d, Anthony Simmons; w, Jamal Ali, Simmons (based on the play by Ali); ph, Philip Meheux (Eastmancolor); m, Reggae songs; ed, Terry Thom Noble; md, Lou Reizner.

Comedy **(PR:A-C MPAA:NR)**

BLACK KING ***1/2** (1932) 72m Southland bw

A. B. Comethiere (Charcoal Johnson), Vivianne Baber (Mary Lou), Knolly Mitchell (Sug), Dan Michaels (Longtree), Mike Jackson (Lawton), Mary Jane Watkins (Mrs. Bottoms), Len Tucker (Stephen Carmichael), Harry Gray (Deacon Jones), Trixie Smith (Delia).

Obscure all-black serio-comedy concerning the organization of a bogus back-to-Africa movement led by a con man who takes advantage of his fellow blacks who think him their savior. After the young army of followers go no further than New York, they realize they have been had after a disgruntled boy friend, whose girl had left him for the con man, blows the whistle on the whole operation. The plot closely resembles the life of historical black leader of the 1920s Marcus Garvey who preached black superiority and organized a back-to-Africa movement which went nowhere but enriched him personally.

d, Bud Pollard; w, Donald Heywood.

Comedy/Drama **(PR:A MPAA:NR)**

BLACK KLANSMAN, THE* (1966) 88m US Films c (AKA: I CROSSED THE LINE)

Richard Gilden (Jerry), Rima Kutner (Andrea), Harry Lovejoy (Rook), Max Julien (Raymond), Jackie Deslonde (Farley), Jimmy Mack (Lonnie), Maureen Gaffney (Carole Ann), Wm. McLennan (Wallace), Gino De Agustino (Sawyer), Tex Armstrong (Jenkins), Byrd Holland (Buckley), Whitman Mayo (Alex), Francis Williams (Ellis Madison), Ray Dennus (Sloane).

This tale of racial strife is brought to you by the man who would later go on to direct the equally vile THE ASTRO-ZOMBIES (1968), Ted V. Mikels. Story concerns Gilden, a light skinned black entertainer who goes into a rage when he learns that his young daughter has been killed in a Klan bombing of a black church in the South. Seeking revenge, Gilden is able to join the Klan (his skin is light enough to pass for white) and soon seduces the daughter of the Klan leader. Later, he brings his white mistress and black gangster acquaintances from Harlem to convince the white folks that they need to learn to live in harmony. Just awful.

p,d&ed, Ted V. Mikels; w, John T. Wilson, Arthur A. Names; ph, Robert Caraminco.

Drama **(PR:O MPAA:NR)**

BLACK KNIGHT, THE ****1/2** (1954) 85m COL c

Alan Ladd (John), Patricia Medina (Linet), Andre Morell (Sir Ontzlake), Harry Andrews (Earl of Yeonil), Peter Cushing (Sir Palamides), Anthony Bushell (King Arthur), Laurence Naismith (Major Domo), Patrick Troughton (King Mark), Bill Brandor (Bernard), Ronald Adam (The Abbot), Basil Appleby (Sir Hal), Thomas Moore (The Apprentice), Jean Lodge (Queen Guinevere), Pauline Jameson (Lady Yeonil), John Kelly (The Woodchopper), Elton Hayes (Minstrel), John Laurie (James), Olwen Brookes (Lady Ontzlake), David Paltenghi (High Priest).

They must have meant this to be a serious look at British history with all of the well-known names of the era; Arthur, Guinevere, Prince Hal, et al. Somewhere along the way, the movie got out of hand and it is almost as funny as START THE REVOLUTION WITHOUT ME although surely not intended to be. Ladd is a swordsmith (combination blacksmith and swordmaker) who is in love with Medina, daughter of Andrews, a belted earl. That romance will never do as the caste system is far too rigid to allow such a commoner to unify with a lady. Ladd sets out to prove himself worthy and with the help of Morell, strives to become a knight. He becomes The Black Knight of the title, a mysterious man who romps around the countryside jousting and foiling and thwarting the goals of Cushing and Troughton. It's all a lot of hooey and Ladd, who could be terrific in the right part (e.g., THIS GUN FOR HIRE, SHANE, SALTY O'ROURKE), is dreadful as practically the only American accent in a filmful of Britishers. Huge battle scenes, non-stop action and the knowledge that nobody took one minute of it seriously make this apparent mistake still worthy.

p, Irving Allen, Albert R. Broccoli, Phil C. Samuel; d, Tay Garnett; w, Alec Coppel; ph, John Wilcox (Technicolor); m, John Addison; ed, Gordon Pilkington; ch, David Paltenghi.

Historical Drama **(PR:A-C MPAA:NR)**

BLACK LASH, THE ***1/2** (1952) 57m Realart bw

Lash LaRue (U.S. LaRue), Fuzzy St. John (Fuzzy Q. Jones), Peggy Stewart (Joan), Kermit Maynard (Woodruff), Ray Bennett (Rago), Byron Keith (Leonard), Jimmy Martin (Pete), John Carson (Cord), Clarke Stevens (Johnson), Bud Osborne (Operator), Roy Butler (Mayor), Larry Barton (Judge).

Lash LaRue rides again in this lame oater concerning a U.S. Marshal's efforts to crush a band of stagecoach robbers. LaRue poses as an outlaw and convinces the dim gangleader that he has given up being a lawman for some quick, easy cash. He and sidekick St. John help pull enough robberies to snare the gang and bring them to justice. The sound effects department went a little crazy for this western and made the punches in the fist fights sound like howitzers going off.

p&d, Ron Ormond; w, Kathy McKeel; ph, Ernest Miller; m, Walter Greene.

Western **Cas.** **(PR:A MPAA:NR)**

BLACK LEGION, THE* (1937) 80m WB bw

Humphrey Bogart (Frank Taylor), Dick Foran (Ed Jackson), Erin O'Brien-Moore (Ruth Taylor), Ann Sheridan (Betty Grogan), Robert Barrat (Brown), Helen Flint (Pearl Davis), Joseph Sawyer (Cliff Moore), Addison Richards (Prosecuting Attorney), Eddie Acuff (Metcalf), Clifford Soubier (Mike Grogan), Paul Harvey (Billings), Samuel S. Hinds (Judge), John Litel (Tommy Smith), Alonzo Price (Alexander Hargrave), Dickie Jones (Buddy Taylor), Dorothy Vaughan (Mrs. Grogan), Henry Brandon (Joe Dombrowski), Charles Halton (Osgood), Pat C. Flick (Nick Strumpas), Francis Sayles (Charlie), Paul Stanton (Dr. Barham), Harry Hayden (Jones), Egon Brecher (Old Man Dombrowski).

Bogart is a happy-go-lucky auto worker who receives a jolt when Brandon, a hardworking Polish immigrant, gets the promotion he's been expecting. Sullen and bitter, Bogart is easily recruited into a secret organization known as The Black Legion which advocates hatred of foreigners and different races. Its leaders are sharpers who glean a fortune selling disgruntled workers outlandish Klan-like costumes (black robes instead of white), membership dues, badges, trinkets, even arms. Learning what happened at the plant, the leaders order Bogart and others to drive Brandon and his family out of town which they do, burning down the immigrant's house. Bogart gets Brandon's job and lavishes gifts on his family, a new washing machine for his wife, O'Brien-Moore, a car for himself. But his home life goes to pot as he spends more and more nights doing the Legion's dirty business. His wife confronts him and he slaps her, then takes to drink out of guilt. O'Brien-Moore packs up the kids and leaves to stay with her father. Bogart drinks more, taking up with trollop Flint. Foran, Bogart's best friend, tries to get him to reform and Bogie blurts out the atrocities he has committed with the Legion, outlining the secret group's activities. When sober Bogart panics, thinking Foran will inform on him, he tells Legion bosses and Foran is abducted. Taken to a remote spot where he is to be whipped, Foran breaks away and beats up several of the members before fleeing. Legion bosses order him shot and Bogart instinctively draws a pistol and kills his best friend. He runs wildly into the woods but later surrenders himself after being consumed by guilt. Legion lawyers visit him in prison and threaten to kill his wife and children if he talks. Bogart's trial is fixed. Flint goes on the stand to say that Bogart killed Foran after he was attacked; it was self-defense and she witnessed it, she says. It appears that Bogart will get off and the Legion go unscathed but, unexpectedly, Bogart insists upon taking the stand and blurts out his guilt, naming names and detailing the "whole rotten bunch's" activities. Sawyer, and other Legion members who have packed the courtroom, jump to their feet to flee but are immediately arrested and charged. All are later given long prison terms, Bogart receives life. A grim, often brutal film, this is one of Bogart's first starring roles and he made the most of his unsympathetic part. Foran is really the hero, sort of an all-American boy much like the role he essayed in THE PETRIFIED FOREST. Sheridan, as his wife, has a thankless part, almost a bit for the time she is on the screen. THE BLACK LEGION caused quite a bit of stir since it was taken right out of the headlines only months after authorities broke up a real-life Black Legion organized in Detroit. This was the essential Warner Brothers formula movie in the 1930s. Read the headline, then see the film.

p, Robert Lord; d, Archie Mayo; w, Abem Finkel, William Wister Haines (based on a story by Lord); ph, George Barnes; m, Bernhard Kaun; ed, Owen Marks; art d, Robert Haas; cos, Milo Anderson; spec eff, Fred Jackson, Jr., H.F. Koenekamp.

Crime Drama (PR:C MPAA:NR)

BLACK LIKE ME** (1964) 107m Continental bw

James Whitmore *(John Finley Horton)*, Dan Priest *(Bus Driver)*, Walter Mason *(Mason)*, John Marriott *(Hodges)*, Clifton James *(Eli Carr)*, Lenka Petersen *(Lucy Horton)*, Roscoe Lee Browne *(Christopher)*, Sorrel Booke *(Dr. Jackson)*, Richard Ward *(Burt Wilson)*, Llewellyn B. Skinner *(Stretch)*.

A very good idea that was technically lacking and the overdoing of several scenes put it into the exploitation category. BLACK LIKE ME is the true story of John Howard Griffin, a white man, who masqueraded as a black in order to see what it was like. A Texan by birth, Griffin (Whitmore) had a point to make with his book and it stood as a trend-setter in the early 1960s. All of that is lost in the pallid screenplay. Whitmore wears nice clothes, carries luggage Vuitton might envy, has plenty of money in his pocket and has a make-up job that looks as though it was done by an old minstrel show artist. Anyone who wasn't blind could spot that this was not a black man. It's too long, the sound is hard to hear, the hand-held camera only serves to annoy rather than heighten any attempt at realism. Jump cuts prevail and it's not easy to know when we're in the present or the past as there is no delineation of flashbacks. In later years, Whitmore was to achieve some of his greatest success doing stage biographies of Harry Truman and Will Rogers.

p, Jules Tannebaum; d, Carl Lerner; w, Gera and Carl Lerner (based on the book by John Howard Griffin); ph, Victor Lukens, Henry Mueller II; m, Meter Kupferman; ed, Lora Hayes.

Drama Cas. (PR:C MPAA:NR)

BLACK LIMELIGHT*¹/₂ (1938, Brit.) 60m Associated British Productions bw

Raymond Massey *(Peter Charrington)*, Joan Marion *(Mary Charrington)*, Walter Hudd *(Lawrence Crawford)*, Henry Oscar *(Inspector Tanner)*, Elliot Mason *(Jemima)*, Dan Tobin *(Reporter)*, Coral Browne *(Lily James)*, Leslie Brady *(Detective)*, Diana Beaumont *(Gwen)*.

Another loyal-wife-clears-her-husband-of-the-murder-of-his-mistress story starring Marion as the wife and Massey as the fugitive from justice. Real killer turns out to be psychopath Hudd, on whom Marion blows the whistle. Bad lead performance by Marion who seems to want to shout her lines.

p, Walter C. Mycroft; d, Paul Stein; w, Dudley Leslie, Walter Summers (based on the play by Gordon Sherry); ph, Claude Friese-Greene.

Mystery (PR:A MPAA:NR)

BLACK MAGIC** (1949) 105m UA bw

Orson Welles *(Cagliostro)*, Nancy Guild *(Marie Antoinette and Lorenza)*, Akim Tamiroff *(Gitano)*, Frank Latimore *(Gilbert)*, Valentina Cortesa *(Zoraida)*, Margot Grahame *(Mme. DuBarry)*, Stephen Bekassy *(DeMontagne)*, Berry Kroeger *(Alexandre Dumas, Sr.)* Gregory Gay *(Chambord)*, Raymond Burr *(Alexandre Dumas, Jr.)*, Charles Goldner *(Dr. Mesmer)*, Lee Kresel *(King Louis XVI)*, Robert Atkins *(King Louis XV)*, Nicholas Bruce *(De Remy)*, Franco Corsaro *(Chico)*, Aniello Mele *(Josef Balsamo, as a child)*, Ronald Adam *(Court President)*, Bruce Belfrage *(Crown Prosecutor)*, Alexander Danaroff *(Dr. Duval)*, Lee Lenoir *(Gaston)*, Tamara Shayne *(Maria Balsamo)*, Giovanni Van Hulzen *(Minister of Justice)*, Peter Trent *(Dr. Mesmer's Friend)*, Guiseppe Varni *(Bochmer)*, Tatiana Pavlowa *(The Mother)*.

Based on a real villain and ne'er-do-well of the eighteenth century, Cagliostro, profiled as Joseph Balsamo by Alexandre Dumas, this somber film offers Welles at his most extravagant, heavy-breathing, heavy-moving, heavy-handed. As a youth Cagliostro watches his parents executed for witchcraft and vows vengeance on the world. As a boy he knows he is gifted with hypnotic powers but does not know how to use them. Then, as a grown man, Welles, he meets Antoine Mesmer (Goldner) who is largely credited with the development of hypnotism (mesmerism) in the healing of the mentally ill. Goldner teaches Welles his art and then Cagliostro is off to make his name, curing supposedly incurable people, persuading one and all, including King Louis of France and Marie Antoinette to do his bidding, until he controls the destiny of Europe, as it were. Put on trial for stealing some of the crown jewels, Welles easily convinces the judges otherwise as he practices mass hypnosis, but he is undone at the last moment when Goldner appears and hypnotizes *him*, compelling him to admit his crime in court, which brings instant condemnation. He manages to break the spell, making a dash for freedom, the king's captain (Latimore) after him; the two duel to the death on a high rooftop and Welles is rapiered, tumbling downward and off the roof into the collected crowd below, an end identical to his demise in THE STRANGER. Producer Small and director Ratoff were obviously in awe of Welles and allowed him a free reign. The result is this oppressive overacting. Welles hits the viewer with everything, including a very heavy kitchen sink, and his supporting players infectiously duplicate the overbearing style. Apparently Welles was attempting to duplicate the exaggerated thesping of the period in which he was playing, a technique that makes the film unbelievable. The film is also edited in such a jerky fashion as to lose its already thin cohesion. Ratoff's direction is clumsy and Sawtell's score is overbearing. Cameramen Arata and Brizzi lens this one with imitation CITIZEN KANE lighting but the mood is all black. At one point, Welles intones: "Remember, I can afflict as well as heal," and in this film it's the viewer who is afflicted.

p, Edward Small; Gregory Ratoff; d, Ratoff; w, Charles Bennett (based on the novel *Joseph Balsamo* by Alexandre Dumas): ph, Ubaldo Arata, Anchise Brizzi; m, Paul Sawtell; ed, James McKay, Fred Feitshans.

Historical Drama Cas. (PR:C MPAA:NR)

BLACK MAMA, WHITE MAMA zero (1973) 87m AIP c

Pam Grier *(Lee Daniels)*, Margaret Markow *(Karen Brent)*, Sid Haig *(Ruben)*, Lynn Borden *(Densmore)*, Zaldy Zshornack *(Ernesto)*, Laurie Burton *(Logan)*, Eddie Garcia *(Capt. Cruz)*, Alona Alegre *(Juana)*, Dindo Fernando *(Rocco)*, Vic Diaz *(Vic)*, Wendy Green *(Ronda)*, Lotis M. Key *(Jeanette)*, Alfonso Carvajal *(Galindo)*, Bruno Punzalah *(Truck Driver)*, Ricardo Herrero *(Luis)*, Jess Ramos *(Alfredo)*.

Vile exploitation picture shot for cheap in the Philippines. Grier stars as a hooker and Markow as a radical revolutionary who are chained together at a women's rehabilitation center a la THE DEFIANT ONES (1958). While in prison they have to contend with the amorous advances of lesbian guards Borden and Burton. Soon the pair escape, murdering their tormenters in the process. The girls then meet up with island revolutionaries led by Zshornack, and dope dealers Diaz and Haig who all team up for a bloody gun battle with cop Garcia and his men.

p, John Ashley, Eddie Romero; d, Romero; w, H. R. Christian (based on a story by Joseph Viola, Jonathan Demme); ph, Justo Paulino (Movielab Color); m, Harry Betts; ed, Asagni V. Pastor; art d, Roberta Formoso.

Adventure (PR:O MPAA:R)

BLACK MARBLE, THE**¹/₂ (1980) 113m AE c

Robert Foxworth *(Sgt. Valnikov)*, Paula Prentiss *(Sgt. Natalie Zimmerman)*, James Woods *(Fiddler)*, Harry Dean Stanton *(Philo Sinner)*, Barbara Babcock *(Madeline Whitfield)*, John Hancock *(Clarence Cromwell)*, Raleigh Bond *(Capt. Hooker)*, Judy Landers *(Pattie Mae)*, Pat Corley *(Itchy Mitch)*, Paul Henry Itken *(Dr. Bambarella)*, Richard Dix *(Alex Valnikov)*, Lidia Kristen *(Russian Woman)*, Marilyn Chris *(Marvis Skinner)*, Doris Belack *(Married Woman)*, Dallas Alinder *(Chester Biggs)*, Elizabeth Farley *(Receptionist)*, Michael Dudikoff *(Millie's Houseboy)*, Lou Cuttell *(Limpwood)*, Anne Ramsey *(Bessie Callahan)*, Ion Teodorescu *(Iosif)*, Michael Gainsborough *(Capt. Packerton)*.

For some reason, the excellence of former cop Wambaugh's work doesn't ever seem to translate to the screen with the same impact that we see in the mind's eye of the novel's pages. In THE BLACK MARBLE, Wambaugh comes closest to the truth in a fictional work. His THE ONION FIELD was a true story so we don't count that. Foxworth and Prentiss make an unlikely loving couple and pull off the romance aspect perfectly. Where the picture fails is that it's segmented and is more an amalgam of little touches than a driving, forceful story. Foxworth is the drunken burnt-out case and Prentiss is the distaff dick (dickette?) he must team with. There's a fine performance by Babcock as a frustrated woman who places all of her sexuality in the care and feeding of her show dog. It's almost a comedy, but not quite. It's almost a hard-hitting true-to-life police film, but not quite. It's almost a hit . . . but not quite. Still, we liked it and it proves that Harold Becker's work in THE ONION FIELD was not a one-time occurrence. (Annoying is Prentiss' delivery, as if she were choking on a pork rind, or swallowing her words, a habit that undoes most of her roles, making her voice sound like that of a little girl bubbling out of the mouth of a large, mature woman, incongruous, distracting, weird.)

p, Frank Capra, Jr.; d, Harold Becker; w, Joseph Wambaugh (based on his novel); ph, Owen Roizman (DeLuxe Color); m, Maurice Jarre; ed, Maury Weintrobe; prod d, Alfred Sweeney; cos, Susan Becker.

Crime Drama Cas. (PR:C-O MPAA:PG)

BLACK MARKET BABIES*¹/₂ (1946) 71m MON bw

Ralph Morgan *(Dr. Jordan)*, Kane Richmond *(Eddie Condon)*, Teala Loring *(Evelyn Barret)*, Marjorie Hoshelle *(Donna Corbett)*, George Meeker *(Anthony Marco)*, Jayne Hazard *(Doris Condon)*, Dewey Robinson *(Barney)*, Alan Foster *(Jake)*, Selmer Jackson *(Mr. Andrews)*, Nana Bryant *(Mrs. Andrews)*, Maris Wrixon *(Helen Roberts)*, Addison Richards *(Hamilton)*, Parker Gee *(Paul Carroll)*, Terry Frost *(Sam)*.

Average crime tale concerning a gangster, a dishonest lawyer, and a shady doctor who run an illegal adoption agency. The crooks entrap women having illegitimate children, talk them into signing away the rights to their babies and later sell them to wealthy childless couples for large donations. The cops catch on to the scheme and the gangster sets up the doctor to take the fall, but the old doc kills the hood and is later acquitted.

p, Jeffrey Bernard; d, William Beaudine; w, George W. Sayre (based on a story by George Morris); ph, Harry Neumann; md, Edward J. Kay; ed, William Austin.

Crime (PR:A MPAA:NR)

BLACK MARKET RUSTLERS* (1943) 54m MON bw

Ray Corrigan *(Crash)*, Dennis Moore *(Dennis)*, Max Terhune *(Alibi)*, Evelyn Finley *(Linda)*, Steve Clark *(Prescott)*, John Merton *(Parry)*, Glenn Strange *(Corbin)*, Carl Sepulveda *(Sheriff)*, George Chesebro *(Slade)*, Hank Worden *(Slim)*, Frank Ellis *(Kyper)*, Frosty Royce *(Ed)*, Hal Price *(Bartender)*, Jean Austin, Ingrid Austin, Jim Austin, Art Fowler *(Specialty Acts)*, Stanley Price, Wally West, Carl Mathews, Tex Cooper, Claire McDowell, Foxy Callahan.

Ho-hum oater starring Corrigan, Moore, and Terhune who are employed by the Cattlemen's Association to end the activities of rustlers who are selling their cattle on the black market. Includes the song "You Wink At Me And I'll Wink At You." (See RANGE BUSTERS series, Index.)

p, George W. Weeks; d, S. Roy Luby; w, Patricia Harper; ph, Edward Kull; m, Frank Sanucci; ed, Roy Claire; md, Sanucci.

Western Cas. (PR:A MPAA:NR)

BLACK MASK*
(1935, Brit.) 67m WB bw

Wylie Watson (*Jimmie Glass*), Aileen Marson (*Jean McTavish*), Ellis Irving (*Verrell*), Wyndham Goldie (*Davidson*), Joyce Kennedy (*Lady McTavish*), Herbert Lomas (*Sir John McTavish*), John Turnbull (*Insp. Murray*), Kate Cutler (*Lady Mincott*).

Dapper gentleman burglar who only steals for charity is framed for the murder of a newspaper crusader. Tepid suspense film with mediocre production.

p, Irving Asher; d, Ralph Ince; w, Paul Gangelin, Frank Launder, Michael Barringer (based on the novel *Blackshirt* by Bruce Graeme); ph, Basil Emmott.

Crime **(PR:A MPAA:NR)**

BLACK MEMORY*
(1947, Brit.) 73m Ambassador bw

Michael Atkinson (*Danny Cruff*), Myra O'Connell (*Joan Davidson*), Jane Arden (*Sally* Davidson), Michael Medwin (*Johnnie Fletcher*), Frank Hawkins (*Alf Davidson*), Winifred Melville (*Mrs. Davidson*), Sidney James (*Eddie Clinton*).

Son of a man accused of murder poses as a juvenile delinquent in order to clear Dad's name. Weak story, poor dialog, everyone's just kiddin' around.

p, Gilbert Church; d, Oswald Mitchell; w, John Gilling; ph, S. D. Onions.

Crime **(PR:A MPAA:NR)**

BLACK MIDNIGHT* ½
(1949) 64m MON bw

Roddy McDowall (*Scott Jordan*), Damian O'Flynn (*Bill Jordan*), Lynn Thomas (*Cindy Baxter*), Kirby Grant (*Sheriff Gilbert*), Gordon Jones (*Roy*), Fay Baker (*Martha Baxter*), Rand Brooks (*Daniel Jordan*).

McDowall fans will like this story of a young man and his love for horses; specifically one horse named, you guessed it, Black Midnight. It's standard horsey fare; Roddy and his horse-rustling ne'er-do-well relative, Brooks, are the two major protagonists. There's a teeny weeny romance between Roddy and Thomas, lest you think there's something amiss. Boetticher's direction is as straightforward as the plot. Screenwriter Lazarus went on to become the doyen of daytime soap opera.

p, Lindsley Parsons; d, Oscar (Bud) Boetticher; w, Erna Lazarus, Scott Darling (based on a story by Clint Johnson); ph, William Sickner; ed, Ace Herman; md, Edward J. Kay; art d, Dave Milton.

Adventure **(PR:AA MPAA:NR)**

BLACK MOON* ½
(1934) 68m COL bw

Jack Holt (*Lane*), Fay Wray (*Gail*), Dorothy Burgess (*Juanita*), Cora Sue Collins (*Nancy*), Arnold Korff (*Dr. Perez*), Clarence Muse (*Lunch*), Lumsden Hare (*Macklin*).

Very bizarre tale concerning confused husband Holt whose wife, Burgess, becomes obsessed with weird voodoo rites of the West Indies natives. He follows her to the islands and watches helplessly as she dances in the heathen rituals and participates in human sacrificial rites. Finally Holt must shoot his wife in order to stop her from sacrificing their infant child. Very odd.

d, Roy W. Neill; w, Wells Root (based on a story by Clement Ripley); ph, Joseph August.

Drama **(PR:C MPAA:NR)**

BLACK MOON** ½
(1975, Fr.) 100m Nef/FOX c

Cathryn Harrison (*Lily*), Therese Giehse (*The Old Lady*), Alexandra Stewart (*Sister*), Joe Dallesandro (*Brother*).

A haunting, disturbing picture that is half-fantasy, half-reality but we are never certain which is which. Lily (played by Rex Harrison's granddaughter) drives down a lonely road and happens into an Alice-Through-the-Looking-Glass world with characters like an old woman (Giehse) who talks to a rat (no screen credit for this talented rodent), lots of nude children, a weird brother-sister act (Stewart and Dallesandro), a unicorn (left over from the Mankowitz classic A KID FOR TWO FARTHINGS) and more and more. Malle, who is sometimes boring and sometimes dull, but always provocative, has co-written and directed a small, tight film that will have cineastes and buffs of all ages arguing for many years. What it's about is a matter of conjecture. What it's *not* about is commercialism.

p&d, Louis Malle; w, Malle, Ghislain Uhry, Joyce Bunuel; ph, Sven Nykvist (Eastmancolor); ed, Suzanne Baron.

Drama/Fantasy **(PR:C MPAA:R)**

BLACK NARCISSUS****
(1947, Brit.) 100m Archer Prods/General Film c

Deborah Kerr (*Sister Clodagh*), Sabu (*Dilip Rai*), David Farrar (*Mr. Dean*), Flora Robson (*Sister Philippa*), Jean Simmons (*Kanchi*), Esmond Knight (*General Toda Rai*), Kathleen Byron (*Sister Ruth*), Jenny Laird (*Sister Honey*), Judith Furse (*Sister Briony*), May Hallatt (*Angu Ayah*), Shaun Noble (*Con*), Eddie Whaley, Jr. (*Joseph Anthony*), Nancy Roberts (*Mother Dorothea*), Ley On (*Phuba*).

Powell and Pressburger are two of the more interesting filmmakers to come out of England (STAIRWAY TO HEAVEN, THE RED SHOES, TALES OF HOFFMAN) and their choice of material has always been eclectic. BLACK NARCISSUS is a radical departure from an ever-changing norm. It concerns a coterie of Anglican nuns in the Himalayas as they seek to maintain a school and hospital. Kerr and Byron are the lead nuns and Farrar is their local bugaboo, a cynical British agent assigned to the area; his masculine presence disturbs the nuns. Sabu is a rich general who uses the dangerous Black Narcissus perfume to woo young Simmons, a native girl at her most nubile. In a melodramatic twist, Byron turns in her habit for a dress and makes a pass at Farrar who couldn't care less. Suspecting that he has eyes for Kerr, Byron attempts to kill Deborah, by pushing her from the bell tower but she only succeeds in killing herself. The Sisters realize that they can make no headway in this land and return to Calcutta. Wonderfully photographed, BLACK NARCIS-SUS took an Oscar for best color cinematography (Cardiff) and best color Set

Decoration (Junge). Kathleen Byron did a smashing job in this movie. Her career waffled afterwards and she never achieved the success one would have thought she merited after her superb performance.

p,d&w, Michael Powell, Emeric Pressburger (based on the novel by Rumer Godden); ph, Jack Cardiff (Technicolor); m, Brian Easdale; ed, Reginald Mills.

Drama **Cas.** **(PR:A-C MPAA:NR)**

BLACK OAK CONSPIRACY* ½
(1977) 92m New World c

Jesse Vint (*Jingo*), Karen Carlson (*Lucy*), Albert Salmi (*Sherriff*), Seymour Cassel (*Homer*), Douglas Fowley (*Bryan*), Robert Lyons (*Harrison*), Mary Wilcox (*Beulah*), James Gammon (*Deputy*), Janus Blyth (*Melba*), Will Hare (*Doc Rondes*), Jeremy Foster (*Billy Bob*), Peggy Stewart (*Virginia*), JoAnne Strauss (*Saide*), Vic Perrin (*Finch*), Darby Hinton (*Miner in Cafe*), Dana Derfus (*Miner*), Bill Cross (*Stunt Gaffer*), Rock Walker, Buff Brady (*Policeman*).

BLACK OAK CONSPIRACY, not to be confused with the pop group Black Oak Arkansas, is one of the pictures that has all of the standard corn-pone ingredients— dumb sheriff, a good-looking hero, lots of car chases, stolen kisses, feeble attempts at humor, etc. You've seen it all before in various Burt Reynolds pictures. Not that the Reynolds films were any better, they just had him in them. In this one, however, the talents of Cassel, Salmi (whose real name, by the way, is Imlas), and Perrin deserve better at the hands of the Vint-Hugh Smith script and the lame direction by Bob Kelljan. Lots of subplots that would have been better submarined.

p, Jesse Vint, Tom Clark; d, Bob Kelljan; w, Hugh Smith, Vint; ph, Chris Ludwig; m, Don Peake; ed, Sam Shaw; cos, Jerri Puhara.

Drama **(PR:C MPAA:NR)**

BLACK ORCHID***
(1959) 96m PAR bw

Sophia Loren (*Rose Bianco*), Anthony Quinn (*Frank Valente*), Ina Balin (*Mary Valente*), Jimmy Baird (*Ralphie Bianco*), Mark Richman (*Noble*), Naomi Stevens (*Giulia Gallo*), Virginia Stevens (*Alma Gallo*), Joe Di Reda (*Joe*), Frank Puglia (*Henry Gallo*).

A totally misleading title may have made this a flop at the box office because it had a lot to recommend it as a movie. Loren is a widow in a poor New York neighborhood who, quite rightly, blames herself for her gangster husband's death. She wanted material things and the late padrone sought to achieve that for her and was killed. Her son, Baird, is already into that life and confined on a state farm. She meets Quinn, a widower with Balin as his daughter, and they fall in love. Ina is livid when she hears her father is going to marry "the gangster's widow" and locks herself in her room, hoping to convince her father to give up the idea. Sophia is worried that Anthony will depart and that she and her son will not get the second chance at happiness she seeks so desperately. Baird escapes from the farm but he is found by Quinn who convinces him to return. Meanwhile, Sophia successfully convinces Balin that she is a good woman and will make Quinn a good wife. Loren won the Best Actress Award at the 1958 Venice Film Festival for this role but it failed to ignite any large commercial receipts despite superb performances by both stars, tight direction by Ritt, and what appeared to be a semi-autobiographical script from Joe Stefano, who went on to have enormous success with his screenplay for PSYCHO and his TV series "Outer Limits."

p, Carlo Ponti, Marcello Girosi; d, Martin Ritt; w, Joseph Stefano; ph, Robert Burks; m, Alessandro Cicognini; ed. Howard Smith; art d, Hal Pereira, Roland Anderson.

Drama **(PR:C MPAA:NR)**

BLACK ORPHEUS***
(1959 Fr./Ital./Braz.) 100m Lopert c (ORFEU NEGRO)

Breno Mello (*Orpheus*), Marpessa Dawn (*Eurydice*), Lourdes de Oliveira (*Mira*), Lea Garcia (*Serafina*), Adhemar da Silva (*Death*), Alexandro Constantino (*Hermes*), Waldetar de Souza (*Chico*), Jorge dos Santos (*Benedito*), Aurino Cassanio (*Zeca*).

The classic legend of Orpheus and Eurydice set during a carnival in Rio. Dawn is fleeing from her jilted lover and attempts to disappear into the chaos of the carnival. There she meets street-car conductor Mello and the couple fall in love. Her former lover, disguised as Death, seeks Dawn out and kills her. Mello enters the morgue (symbolic of Hades) and tries to revive his love using ancient Macumba rites. The samba music, colorful locations, and competent performances (mainly from an amateur cast) are very entertaining, but the film is overlong and drags somewhat. BLACK ORPHEUS won the Grand Prize at the Cannes Film Festival, and an Oscar as Best Foreign Film in 1959.

p, Sacha Gordine; d, Marcel Camus; w, Jacques Viot, Camus (based on the play "Orfeu da Conceicao" by Vinicius de Moraes); ph, Jean Bourgoin (CinemaScope, Eastmancolor); m, Antonio Carlos Jobim, Luis Bonfa; ed, Andree Feix.

Drama **Cas.** **(PR:C MPAA:NR)**

BLACK PANTHER, THE* ½
(1977, Brit.) 102m Impics Prod. c

Donald Sumpter (*Donald Neilson*), Debbie Farrington (*Lesley Whittle*), Marjorie Yates (*Neilson's Wife*), Sylvia O'Donnell (*Neilson's Daughter*), Andrew Brut (*Lesley's Brother*), Alison Key (*Lesley's Sister-in-law*), Ruth Dunning (*Lesley's Mother*), David Swift (*Detective Chief Superintendent*).

THE BLACK PANTHER is the true story of Donald Nielson, the British kidnapper and killer. His nefarious career lasted three brief years from 1972, when he began robbing post offices, until his arrest for the murder of a teenage heiress in 1975. As the title character, Sumpter does good work in allowing us a peek into the inner recesses of a madman's mind. The film was made in 1977, when the memory of the Panther was still fresh in the memory of the British public, thus lots of what is seen may seem unintelligible to someone looking at it years later. The libel laws in Great Britain are such that producers take great care when dealing with cases still pending. In the film, so much is glossed over or shunted aside that those viewers not familiar with the newspaper and television accounts of The Black Panther (so named because he wore a black hood with eye slits) will have a problem understanding much of the story. An earnest try at a docudrama but a misfire.

p&d, Ian Merrick; w, Michael Armstrong; ph, Joe Mangine; m, Richard Arnell; ed, Teddy Darvas; art d, Carlotta Barrow.

Crime-Docu-Drama   (PR:O   MPAA:NR)

BLACK PARACHUTE, THE**   (1944) 68m COL bw

John Carradine (Gen. von Bodenbach), Osa Massen (Marya Orloff), Larry Parks (Michael Lindley), Jeanne Bates (Olga), Jonathan Hale (King Stephen), Ivan Triesault (Col. Pavlec), Trevor Bardette (Nicholas), Art Smith (Joseph), Robert Lowell (Pilot), Charles Wagenheim (Kur Vandan), Charles Waldron (Erik Dundeen), Ernie Adams (Cobbler).

WW II espionage film set in an unnamed Eastern European country that has been taken over by ruthless Nazis. Carradine plays the evil German commander who sees the overthrow of the country's King, Hale. A nationalist guerrilla movement springs up to fight the invaders, and American agent Parks is parachuted in to rescue the king and spirit him out of the country so that he may broadcast the truth about the Huns to his people and they will continue to fight. Good performances by a competent cast of character actors make this worth a look.

p, Jack Fier; d, Lew Landers; w, Clarence Upson Young (based on a story by Paul Gangelin); ph, George Meehan; ed, Otto Meyer; art d, Lionel Banks, Carl Anderson; set d, William Kiernan.

Spy/War   (PR:A   MPAA:NR)

BLACK PATCH*   (1957) 82m WB bw

George Montgomery (Clay Morgan), Diane Brewster (Helen Danner), Tom Pittman (Flytrap), Leo Gordon (Hank Danner), House Peters, Jr. (Holman), Lynn Cartwright (Kitty), George Trevino (Pedoline), Peter Brocco (Harper), Ted Jacques (Maxton), Strother Martin (Petey), Gil Rankin (Judge Parnell), Sebastian Cabot (Frenchy De Vere), Stanley Adams (Drummer), John O'Malley (Colonel).

Gordon wrote and co-starred in this attempt at a psychological western. It was not one of Gordon's best efforts as a writer, although his acting ability is always on the money. Montgomery wears the black patch to cover an eye he lost in the Civil War. Gordon and wife, Brewster, come to the town where Montgomery, an old pal, is the marshal. Gordon is now a bank robber, so George tosses him in the clink. Cabot and Peters, two ne'er-do-wells of the village, agree to get Leo out of jail for half his loot. They attempt the breakout and Leo gets killed. Pittman gets Gordon's guns and they have sort of a magical effect on him as he becomes the fastest shooter in those parts. Next thing you know, he also gets Gordon's wife (an absurd bit of plotting) and the bad'uns convince the young punk to face down the marshal. Picture goes straight downhill from there as Brewster realizes her new love is being marionetted by Cabot and Peters and she saves the day by going to Montgomery. Some good cameos by Martin, Adams, and Gordon's real-life wife, Cartwright.

p&d, Allen H. Miner; w, Leo Gordon; ph, Edward Colman; m, Jerry Goldsmith; ed, Jerry Young; art d, Nicolai Remisoff; cos, Byron Munson.

Western   (PR:C   MPAA:NR)

BLACK PIRATES, THE*   (1954, Mex.) 72m Lippert c

Anthony Dexter, Martha Roth, Lon Chaney, Robert Clarke, Victor Mendoza, Alfonso Bedoya, Toni Gerry, Eddy Dutko.

Shabby yarn about buccaneers flitting about the West Indies in search of gold when the producers of this film should have been in search of a decent story.

p, Robert L. Lippert, Jr.; d, Allen Miner; w, Fred Freiberger, Al C. Ward; ph, (Anscocolor).

Adventure   (PR:C   MPAA:NR)

BLACK PIT OF DOCTOR M*
(1958, Mex.) United Releasing bw (MISTERIOS DEL ULTRATUMBA)

Raphael Bertrand, Mary Cortez, Gaston Santos.

A doctor in a madhouse contacts an old partner through a medium. Along comes a girl to claim an inheritance, but she ends up falling for the doctor and staying on as his nurse. Meanwhile, an attendant scarred by acid and passed on, returns from the dead with the spirit of the doctor's old partner. The attendant falls for the nurse and wants her to be as ugly as he is. Pretty gruesome stuff with a standard horror film premise, though there are some fun moments (the dead attendant plays the violin).

p, Alfred Ripstein, Jr.; d, Fernando Mendez; w, Raymond Obon

Horror   (PR:O   MPAA:NR)

BLACK RAVEN, THE*1/2   (1943) 62m PRC bw

George Zucco (Bradford), Wanda McKay (Lee Vinfield), Noel Madison (Mike Bardoni), Bob Randall (Allen Bentley), Byron Foulger (Horace Weatherby), Charles Middleton (Sheriff), Robert Middlemass (Tim Winfield), Glenn Strange (Sandy), I. Stanford Jolley (Whitey Cole).

Typical low-budget suspense film surrounds the actions at a lonely country inn named the Black Raven on a rainy night. The cast of mysterious customers that pass through its doors include: an ex-con with a score to settle, a dishonest bank cashier who has embezzled $50,000, a man who is after the cashier, and the money, a young couple who are trying to cross the border into Canada to get married, the girl's father who's trying to stop them, and a local cop who is trying to solve two recent murders. (Enough?) Lackluster cast and direction fail to inspire interest.

p, Sigmund Neufeld; d, Sam Newfield; w, Fred Myton; ph, Robert Cline; ed, Holbrook N. Todd.

Suspense   (PR:A   MPAA:NR)

BLACK RIDER, THE*   (1954, Brit.) 66m Balblair Butcher bw

Jimmy Hanley (Jerry Marsh), Rona Anderson (Mary), Leslie Dwyer (Robert), Lionel Jeffries (Brennan), Beatrice Varley (Mrs. Marsh), Michael Golden (Rakou), Valerie Hanson (Karen), Vincent Ball (Ted Lintott), Edwin Richfield (Geoff Morgan), Kenneth Connor (George Amble).

Smugglers "haunting" a ruined castle have their show closed by a bright young reporter and a motorcycle gang. The only thing spooky is the poor direction and inept acting.

p&w, A.R. Rawlinson; d, Wolf Rilla; ph, Geoffrey Faithfull.

Crime   (PR:A   MPAA:NR)

BLACK RODEO**   (1972) 87m Utopia/Cinerama c

Archie Wycoff (Bud), Clarence Gonzalez (Cleo), Pete Knight (Skeets), Marval Rogers (Rocky), Bailey Prairie Kid (Nelson), Reuben Heura (James), Moses Fields (Billy the Kid), Cornell Fields (Outlaw Kid), Chris Prophet (Alfred), Nat Purefoy, Gordon Hayes, Sandy Goodman, Joanne Eason, Lisa Bramwell, Betsy Bramwell, Dorothy Wright, Sandra Young, Muhammad Ali (Guest Stars), Woody Strode (Narrator).

Unusual rodeo film set in Harlem with a mostly black cast; the proving ground is the arena instead of the streets where skill replaces knife fights and muggings. Interesting premise but too far-fetched for the reality of the grim story beyond the rodeo. Shot in a semi-documentary style that proves more distracting than enhancing for a film that could have been a lot better.

p,d&ed, Jeff Kanew; ph, Luis San Andres, Amin Cahudri, John Stevens, John Wing, High Bell.

Western/Drama   (PR:C   MPAA:G)

BLACK ROOM, THE***   (1935) 73m COL bw

Boris Karloff (Baron Gregor de Berghmann/Anton de Berghmann), Marian Marsh (Thea Hassel), Robert Allen (Lt. Albert Lussan), Thurston Hall (Col. Hassel), Katherine De Mille (Mashka), John Buckler (Beran), Henry Kolker (Baron Frederick de Berghmann), Colin Tapley (Lt. Hassel), Torben Meyer (Peter), Egon Brecher (Karl), John Bleifer (Franz), Frederick Vogeding (Josef), Edward Van Sloan (Doctor).

Karloff is superb in a dual role as twin brothers (one evil, one good) in this rare horror film produced by Columbia. Action takes place in the early 1800s in Czechoslovakia where the twins are born to the ruling family of de Berghman. The good child is born with a paralyzed arm and is taken away when very young to be educated abroad. The evil brother grows to inherit the castle and develops an infamous reputation for mean and sadistic behavior. Many of the young women in the village have entered his domain, never to return, and the populace is beginning to turn nasty. The villagers rejoice when the good brother returns, and the evil brother steps down and allows his sibling to assume control of the castle to avoid being lynched by the peasants. But the evil Karloff has a plan. He takes his brother to a hidden part of the house known as the Black Room. In the room is a pit of long stakes where the evil twin has thrown his previous victims. Realizing what is about to happen, the good Karloff draws a knife to defend himself, but he is overpowered and hurled to his death. The evil brother then assumes the identity of his dead sibling and even fakes his paralyzed arm. Soon after Karloff proposes to his brother's beloved, who comes from a wealthy family. No one suspects the evil brother until the girl's father sees the twin use his supposedly paralyzed limb. Karloff kills the man and frames a young soldier for the killing. At the wedding ceremony the truth is revealed when the dead brother's faithful great Dane attacks the evil Karloff who is forced to defend himself using both his hands. The villagers chase Karloff back to his castle where he falls into the black pit and dies next to his good brother's corpse. Directed with a great sense of style by Neill, this gothic horror is first-rate.

p, Robert North; d, Roy William Neill; w, Arthur Strawn, Henry Myers (based on a story by Strawn); ph, Al Seigler; ed, Richard Cahoon; md, Louis Silvers; art d, Stephen Gooson; cos, Murray Mayer.

Horror   **Cas.**   (PR:C   MPAA:NR)

BLACK ROSE, THE****   (1950) 120m FOX c

Tyrone Power (Walter of Gurnie), Orson Welles (Bayan), Cecile Aubry (Maryam), Jack Hawkins (Tristram), Mary Rennie (King Edward), Finlay Currie (Alfgar), Herbert Lom (Anthemus), Mary Clare (Countess of Lessford), Bobby Blake (Mahmoud), Alfonso Bedoya (Lu Chung), Gibb McLaughlin (Wilderkin), James Robertson Justice (Simon Beautrie), Henry Oscar (Friar Roger Bacon), Laurence Harvey (Edmond).

Excellent adventure epic from the Thomas Costain novel has nobleman Power ostracized in thirteenth-century England for leading a revolt with Hawkins against King Edward (Rennie), a Norman whom Power, a Saxon, refuses to serve. Hawkins, a famous bowman (whose personal lore is similar to that of Robin Hood), and Power leave England as wanted men, traveling the long trade routes to the Far East, picked up in Antioch by Welles, a powerful warlord, and traveling with him to the court of Kublai Khan to pay homage. Welles allows them to accompany his caravan on the proviso that Hawkins teach his archers how to use the famous English longbow. One of the gifts Welles is taking to the Khan is Eurasian beauty Aubry, who falls in love with Power before reaching their destination. Once in the Chinese court, Power realizes that he and Hawkins are being held prisoner—they cannot leave the palace—but are still treated graciously. One day, attempting to take Aubry with them, flee through ancient underground tunnels from the palace with scores of guards in hot pursuit. Hawkins stays behind, killing dozens with his trusty longbow, to give Power and Aubry a chance to escape. He himself is killed but the pair get away, only to be separated. Power returns to England to instruct his people in the ways of paper-making, the use of the compass and explosives, knowledge he has learned in the Far East. His uncle, Currie, has disinherited him but accepts his return in the end. Completing Power's happiness is Aubry, who arrives at the last moment, sent by Welles as a gift to his young English friend. Loaded with action, beautifully photographed in England and North Africa, the film leans heavily on many adventure films, chiefly THE ADVENTURES OF ROBIN HOOD and THE ADVENTURES OF MARCO POLO, but it has its own fascinating subplots and is a lavishly mounted production. French actress Aubry, who had scored in the French-produced MANON, is a petite and lovely actress with considerable acting talent. She never again appeared on the screen after THE BLACK ROSE, marrying a Moroccan prince who visited the on-location shooting site in North Africa. The appearance of the Mexican character actor, Alfonso Bedoya (memorable for his bandit role in THE TREASURE OF THE SIERRA MADRE) is startling; he plays the part of a shifty, sneaky Oriental with an accent screaming for tamales. Fox made this film to employ almost $5 million of its frozen assets in England; executives had originally planned to make this sweeping historical romance as early as 1946, starring Cornel Wilde, but they could not use funds from Fox's British arm until four years later and then decided to make it an all-the-way epic with its top star, Power, one of the great filmic swashbucklers, which he proved to the swordhilt in this splendid production.

p, Louis D. Lighton; d, Henry Hathaway; w, Talbot Jennings (based on the novel by Thomas B. Costain); ph, Jack Cardiff (Technicolor); m, Richard Addinsell; md, Muir Mathieson; ed, Manuel Del Campo; art d, Paul Sheriff, W. Andrews; cos, Michael Whittaker; spec eff, W. Percy Day.

Historical Adventure/Romance   **(PR:A MPAA:NR)**

BLACK ROSES*¹/₂   (1936, Ger.) 93m UFA bw (AKA: DID I BETRAY?)

Lilian Harvey (Tania Fedorovna), Esmond Knight (Pavo Collin), Robert Rendel (Prince Avarov), Dennis Hoey (Niklander), Amy Veness (Annushka), Henry Wolston (Police Chief), Beatrice Munro (Maid).

Period piece set in Finland in the 1900s has a Russian ballerina sleeping with the Tsarist governor to save the life of the rebel sculptor she really loves. Good production, story and tight direction.

d, Paul Martin; w, Martin, Curt Braun, Walter Supper, John Heygate, Peter MacFarlane.

Drama   **(PR:A MPAA:NR)**

BLACK SABBATH***

         (1963, Ital.) 99m AIP bw (I TRE VOLTI DELLA PAURA)

THE DROP OF WATER: Jacqueline Pierreux (Helen Corey), Milli Monti (Maid); THE TELEPHONE: Michele Mercier (Rosy), Lidia Alfonsi (Mary); THE WURDALAK: Boris Karloff (Gorca), Susy Anderson (Sdenka), Mark Damon (Vladimir d'Urfe), Glauco Onorato (Giorgio), Rika Dialina (Wife), Massimo Righi (Pietro).

Good horror outing directed by Italian Mario Bava in three separate episodes introduced by Karloff who also stars in the last (and best) segment. The first story concerns a nurse, Pierreux, who is summoned to the home of a dying clairvoyant. Upon her arrival, she discovers that the medium has already died. The nurse greedily steals a diamond ring from the body and wears it home. That night the nurse is haunted by the ghost of the deceased woman and is found dead the next day with her finger badly mangled as if the ring had been torn off it. The second episode features Mercier as a call girl who is harassed with phone calls made by a man whom she had helped send to prison. The escaped killer murders the hooker's friend by mistake, giving Mercier a chance to kill him. Moments later, the phone rings and the voice of the dead man informs her that she will never be rid of him. The final episode stars Karloff as the head of an Eastern European family who has gone off to kill a local bandit. Before his departure he had informed his family that if he should be gone longer than five days, he may return as a Wurdalak, or vampire who thirsts for the blood of his loved ones, and that no matter how much he demands, they are not to let him into the house. Karloff returns on the fifth day with the severed head of the bandit. The children are also horrified to discover that their father has, indeed, returned as a Wurdalak. Karloff proceeds to kill the whole family, including his young grandson, turning them into vampires. One daughter flees with her lover, a young nobleman, but the old man finds her and she becomes one of the undead. Unknowingly, her lover embraces her and he too is killed. While all the episodes have terrifying moments, the finale is the standout, with the most disturbing scenes being those where Karloff has turned his grandson into a vampire, and uses the child's cries to lure the other members of the family out of the house and into his deadly trap.

p, Salvatore Billitteri; d, Mario Bava; w, Marcello Fondato, Alberto Bevilacqua, Mario Bava (based on "The Drop of Water" by Anton Chekov, "The Telephone" by F. G. Snyder, "The Wurdalak" by Leo Tolstoy); ph, Ubaldo Terzano; m, Roberto Nicolosi (Ital.), Les Baxter (US); ed, Mario Serandrei; art d, Giorgio Giovannini; set d, Riccardo Dominici; cos, Trini Grani; makeup, Otello Fava.

Horror   **(PR:O MPAA:NR)**

BLACK SAMSON**   (1974) 87m WB c

Rockne Tarkington (Samson), William Smith (Johnny Nappa), Connie Strickland (Tina), Carol Speed (Leslie), Carol Payne (Arthur), Joe Tornatore (Harry), Titos Vandis (Joseph Nappa), Napoleon Whiting (Old Henry), John Alderman (Michael Briggs).

Average exploitation vehicle starring Tarkington as a powerful black neighborhood leader who takes pride in the fact that his area of the city is free of dope dealers and gangsters. Smith plays the ambitious white mobster who sees the area as fresh territory to exploit and begins a war between the citizens of the neighborhood and his hoods. Smith and Tarkington are good as the rival leaders.

p, Daniel B. Cady; d, Charles Bail; w, Warren Hamilton Jr. (based on a story by Cady); ph, Henning Schellerup (Technicolor); m, Allen Toussaint; ed, Duane Hartzell; art d, Ed Cosby.

Drama   **(PR:O MPAA:R)**

BLACK SCORPION, THE*¹/₂   (1957) 85m WB bw

Richard Denning (Henry Scott), Mara Corday (Teresa), Carlos Rivas (Arturo Ramos), Mario Navarro (Juanito), Carlos Muzquiz (Dr. Velasco), Pascual Pena (Jose de la Cruz), Fanny Schiller (Florentina), Pedro Galvan (Father Delgado), Arturo Martinez (Major Cosio).

Richard Denning and Carlos Rivas are geologists investigating the eruption of a formerly dormant Mexican volcano. They find a huge scorpion nest (actually, a nest of huge scorpions). They explode a series of TNT charges to close the entrance to the nest, thinking they are shutting down the one and only entrance. Think again, Rich and Carlos. These scorpions are lots smarter than that and realize that if they were to allow themselves to be trapped this early in the film, there would be a host of viewers screaming "cheat." That decided, the chief Scorpion bites all of its lair-mates and exits for the nightlife of Mexico City where it intends to do the same damage Godzilla wreaks on Tokyo every few years. Denning and Rivas trap the Scorpion in the huge Mexico City stadium and do away with him. It's a variation of the KING KONG theme or THEM or any of several Bert I. Gordon films. The idea is by Paul Yawitz who ended his days writing weekly short stories for the Beverly Hills Courier newspaper, most of which were better than the story he wrote for THE BLACK SCORPION.

p, Frank Melford, Jack Dietz; d, Edward Ludwig; w, David Duncan, Robert Blees (based on a story by Paul Yawitz); ph, Lionel Lindon; m, Paul Sawtelle; ed, Richard Van Enger.

Monster/Horror/Science Fiction   **(PR:C MPAA:NR)**

BLACK SHAMPOO zero   (1976) 83m Dimension Pictures c

John Daniels (Jonathan Knight), Tanya Boyd (Brenda), Joe Ortiz (Mr. Wilson), Skip Lowe (Artie).

BLACK SHAMPOO is an obvious rip-off of the original SHAMPOO except that this one is set in a black-owned beauty salon. The similarity ends there as this film becomes one of the sleaziest films made in 1976 or any other year. John Daniels as "Mr. Jonathan" is supposed to be a black super-sexpot who woos and beds his wealthy white customers (and their offspring). His girl friend's ex-boy friend wants the babe back so he arranges to have Daniels' two gay assistants beaten up. Now if that makes any sense to you, good luck. There's sex, violence, chain saws, pool cues, anti-gay abuse, and just about anything else a red-blooded bigot (or the producers of this movie) might like to see. Lots of action but absolutely no content.

p, Alvin Fast; d, Graydon Clark; w, Fast, Clark; m, Gerald Lee; ed, Earl Watson, Jr.

Drama   **(PR:O MPAA:R)**

BLACK SHEEP**   (1935) 70m FOX bw

Edmund Lowe (John Dugan), Claire Trevor (Janette Foster), Tom Brown (Fred Curtis), Eugene Pallette (Col. Upton C. Belcher), Adrienne Ames (Mrs. Millicent Bath), Ford Sterling (Mather), Herbert Mundin (Oscar), Jed Prouty (Orville Schmelling), David Torrence (Capt. Savage).

Maudlin shipboard melodrama featuring Lowe as a professional gambler who discovers his long-lost son on board and in trouble. The boy is being framed by an evil woman for a jewel theft he didn't commit. Lowe helps the boy by using all his clever charms to get into the woman's cabin to obtain evidence to clear his son. Average tale is helped by the slick direction of veteran Allan Dwan.

p, Sol M. Wurtzel; d, Allan Dwan; w, Allen Rivkin (based on a story by Dwan); ph, Arthur Miller; m, Oscar Levant; md, Samuel Kaylin; m/l, Sidney Clare.

Drama   **(PR:A MPAA:NR)**

BLACK SHEEP OF WHITEHALL, THE*¹/₂   (1941 Brit.) 89m EAL/UA bw

Will Hay (Prof. Davis), John Mills (Bobby), Basil Sydney (Costello), Henry Hewitt (Professor Davys), Felix Aylmer (Crabtree), Frank Cellier (Innsbach), Joss Ambler (Sir John), Frank Allenby (Onslow), Owen Reynolds (Harman), Thora Hird (Secretary), George Woodbridge, Katie Johnson.

Uninspired comedy starring Hay as a correspondence course teacher who becomes embroiled in a Nazi plot to destroy an economic trade agreement between Britain and South America. Hay discovers that the Germans have substituted a phony economics expert (who will give bad advice to the countries, ruining the pact) and have held the real professor captive. He dons a variety of disguises while trying to find the real expert, who has been stashed by the Nazis in a nursing home. The only genuinely funny segment has Hay hiring a band to play every national anthem of the pact-signing countries under the window of the meeting hall to delay the signing of the bogus document. The humor is staged in a second-rate, silent slapstick style that tries to emulate the best of Chaplin, but Hay is not nearly as talented a performer as the little tramp.

p, Michael Balcon; d, Will Hay, Basil Dearden; w, Angus Macphail, John Dighton; ph, Gunther Krampf, Eric Cross; ed, Ray Pitt; art d, Tom Morahan.

Comedy   **(PR:A MPAA:NR)**

BLACK SHIELD OF FALWORTH, THE**¹/₂   (1954) 98m UNIV c

Tony Curtis (Myles Falworth), Janet Leigh (Lady Anne), David Farrar (Earl of Alban), Barbara Rush (Meg Falworth), Herbert Marshall (Earl of Mackworth), Rhys Williams (Diccon Bowman), Daniel O'Herlihy (Prince Hal), Torin Thatcher (Sir James), Ian Keith (King Henry IV), Patrick O'Neal (Walter Blunt), Craig Hill (Francis Gascoyne) with Leo Britt, Gary Montgomery, Robin Camp, Claud Allister.

Loosely based on Howard Pyle's novel, this swashbuckler was a disappointment to anyone who listens to dialog. Curtis still hadn't rid himself of his New York accent and was ludicrous as Myles, son of a disgraced knight and suitor for the hand of the fair Lady Anne (Leigh, who was his wife and mother of their daughter, Jamie Lee Curtis, queen of the 1980s horror movies). Farrar leads the conspiracy against King Henry IV (Keith). Myles enlists the aid of Marshall (Earl of Mackworth and Janet's Daddy) and O'Herlihy, the king's son (also known as Prince Hal and immortalized by Shakespeare some time earlier). The villains are thwarted and Curtis is restored to knighthood. Nice supporting bits turned in by Rush as Tony's sister and Hill as his best friend. Screenwriter Brodney (THE GLENN MILLER STORY, THE BRASS BOTTLE, FRANCIS) was out of his element here and the picture would have been better served if Brodney had been allowed to show some of his well-known penchant for badinage. Still, it might have been massacred by Curtis who, to his credit, eventually turned into a pretty fair light comedian. Lots of swordplay, wall-climbing, and romance.

p, Robert Arthur, Melville Tucker; d, Rudolph Mate; w, Oscar Brodney (based on the novel *Men Of Iron* by Howard Pyle); ph, Irving Glassberg (CinemaScope, Technicolor); m, Joseph Gershenson; ed, Ted J. Kent.

Swashbuckler   (PR:A-C MPAA:NR)

BLACK SIX, THE*   (1974) 90m Cinemation c

Gene Washington (*Bubba*), Carl Eller (*Junior Bro*), Lem Barney (*Frenchy*), Mercury Morris (*Bookie*), Willie Lanier (*Tommy*), Joe Greene (*Kevin*), Rosalind Miles (*Ceal*), John Isenbarger (*Moose*), Ben Davidson (*Thor*), Maury Wills (*Coach*).

A cast of real-life pro football players, and one baseball player (Wills), star as black bikers, all Vietnam vets, roaring through the West on R&R. This was one of the first all-black biker films so the group is extra nice to one and all, overly polite to whites, but tough on the white baddies they encounter. The dialog is no more than a series of "yeah, mans," and the story meanders like the on-racing motorcycle gang. A super bore.

p&d, Matt Cimber; w, George Theakos; ph, William Swenning; m, David Moscoe; ed, Swenning.

Adventure   **Cas.**   (PR:C MPAA:NR)

BLACK SLEEP, THE*½   (1956) 82m Bell-Air/UA bw

Basil Rathbone (*Sir Joel Cadman*), Akim Tamiroff (*Odo*), Lon Chaney, Jr. (*Mungo*), John Carradine (*Borg*), Bela Lugosi (*Casimir*), Herbert Rudley (*Dr. Gordon Ramsay*), Patricia Blake (*Laurie*), Phyllis Stanley (*Daphne*), Tor Johnson (*Curry*), Sally Yarnell (*Nancy*), George Sawaya (*K-6*), Claire Carleton (*Miss Daly*), Peter Gordon (*Investigative Sgt. Steel*), Louanna Gardner (*Angelina*), Clive Morgan (*1st Bobby*), John Sheffield (*Scotland Yard Detective*).

Basil Rathbone is a fine actor but it isn't easy thinking of him in any other role but his greatest, Sherlock Holmes. In THE BLACK SLEEP he is flanked by a veritable Who's Who in horror films. Carradine, Tamiroff, Lugosi, and Chaney lurk in and out of this gloomy and horrific tale of a mad medical man who invents a drug that produces a death-like trance without killing victims. Using this concoction, he performs brain surgery on several people (whether they need it or not). His wife is in a coma and he is about to operate on her but he needs an assistant so he frames Rudley for murder, then rescues him from the gallows with the drug. Rudley (who later went on to become a successful TV actor in "The Mothers-in-Law") then discovers the half-alive results of some of Rathbone's early experiments and wants to flee. The creatures get loose and intone "Kill, kill, kill" as they chase Herb and Blake who plays Chaney's daughter. It's a whole lot of hokum and an amateurish attempt to unite all of these marvelous horror actors in one film. A far miss.

p, Howard Koch; d, Reginald Le Borg; w, John C. Higgins; ph, Gordon Avil; m, Les Baxter; ed, John F. Schreyer; cos, Wesley V. Jeffries, Angela Alexander.

Horror   (PR:C MPAA:NR)

BLACK SPIDER, THE*½
                           (1983, Swit.) 98m PicaFilm/Europa c (DIE SCHWARZE SPINNE)

Beatrice Kessler, Walo Lueoend, Peter Ehrlich, Walter Hess, Michael Gempart, Sigfrit Steiner, Henrik Rhyn, Peter Scheider, Rosali Nydegger, Walter Krumm, Corinne Hirt, Sigmund Oberli, Christine Wipf, Hanny Scheuring, Rene Bill, Hans Wittwer, Greti-Jakob-Gugger, Curt Truninger, Sergio Catellani, Benjamin Kradolfer, Peter Luechinger, Hansjoerg Bahl, Peter Holliger.

This is the third time that Gotthelf's "The Black Spider" has been done but the first two efforts were operas by Willy Burkhard and Heinrich Sutermeister. It's a classic horror story about a woman who makes a deal with the devil for the soul of her unborn child. The tiny village is terrorized by a merciless knight and the devil agrees to thwart him in return for the baby. She foils Satan by baptizing the infant immediately. He gets even by sending a black spider to wreak havoc on the burghers of the town. Rissi (director) took that basic premise and contemporized it with the customary drug dealers, a chemical warehouse, and the accompanying ecological problems that accrue. While tripping out on drugs, one of the female addicts dreams the earlier story. An attempt at telling tales in two frames. A good try, but it falls short on several levels. The original work is interesting enough without the addition of the punks, but someone in Switzerland must have said: "Ja, but ve heff to get zer young pipple in der movie haus, zo let's make it modern." Whoever you are, mister, you were wrong.

p, Eduard Steiner; d, Mark M. Rissi; w, Walther Kauer (based on a story by Jeremias Gotthelf); ph, Edwin Horak; ed, Evelyn von Rabenau; cos, Edith Roth, Vernique Muller; spec eff, Giacomo Peier, Cornelius Defries, Bruno Reithaar.

Mystery-Horror   (PR:O MPAA:NR)

BLACK SPURS**   (1965) 80m PAR c

Rory Calhoun (*Santee*), Linda Darnell (*Sadie*), Scott Brady (*Tanner*), Lon Chaney, Jr. (*Kile*), Bruce Cabot (*Henderson*), Richard Arlen (*Pete*), Terry Moore (*Anna*), Patricia Owens (*Clare Grubbs*), James Best (*Sheriff Elkins*), Jerome Courtland (*Sam Grubbs*), De Forest Kelley (*First Sheriff*), James Brown (*Sheriff Nemo*), Joe Hoover (*Swifty*), Manuel Padilla (*Manuel*), Sandra Giles, Sally Nichols, Rusty Allen (*Sadie's Girls*), Jeanne Baird (*Mrs. Nemo*), Chuck Roberson (*Norton*), Guy Wilkerson, Read Morgan.

Good western filled with a cast of old veterans features Calhoun as a cynical bounty hunter who signs on to do heavy Chaney's dirty work. Chaney wants to ruin a small town's reputation so that the railroad will divert its path to run through his property. Calhoun invades the town bringing tough-guy Cabot, gambler Hoover, and Darnell (in her last screen performance) and her floozies to set up shop in the local saloon. The good townsfolk, led by sheriff Best, try to resist the demoralization of their settlement, but Cabot's men tar and feather the lawman. Calhoun is shocked by this turn of events (he has grown to respect Best) and switches sides to defend the town, which leads to a showdown. An enjoyable effort, and one of the last westerns to be made in the tradi tional style with a cast of oldtimers.

p, A. C. Lyles; d, R.G. "Bud" Springsteen; w, Steve Fisher; ph, Ralph Woolsey (Techniscope, Technicolor); m, Jimmie Haskell; ed, Archie Marshak; art d, Hal Pereira, Al Roelofs.

Western   (PR:A MPAA:NR)

BLACK STALLION, THE****   (1979) 118m UA c

Kelly Reno (*Alec Ramsey*), Mickey Rooney (*Henry Dailey*), Teri Garr (*Alec's mother*), Clarence Muse (*Snoe*), Hoyt Axton (*Alex's Father*), Michael Higgins (*Neville*), Ed McNamara (*Jake*), Doghmi Larbi (*The Arab*), John Burton, John Buchanan (*Jockeys*), Kristen Vigard (*Becky*), Fausto Tozzi (*Rescue Captain*).

THE BLACK STALLION is a "G" picture as in GREAT, as in GIFTED, as in "Gee whiz, I didn't think they made films like this anymore." It's a modern miracle when a diverse group of creators, actors, and craft people assemble, make a movie, and it works. The script must be perfect, the actors must be carefully cast, the editing must be crisp, the music complementary. Well, it all happens for the best in THE BLACK STALLION. Based on the Walter Farley book, the screenplay (one of the writers co-wrote E.T. and another did the 1984 COUNTRY) successfully combines suspense, wit, fantasy, and happiness with none of the mawkish sentimentality we've come to expect in films about horses and kids. There's one long stretch of about thirty minutes where not a word is spoken and all we hear are the natural sounds of a boy and a horse, counterpointed by Carmine Coppola's excellent score. (Carmine's son, Francis, is the exec producer, but here's a case where nepotism worked for the benefit of the film.) If you haven't read the novel, the plot is simply that Alec (Reno) and his father (Axton) are on board a ship that also carries the stallion, which is owned by a frightening Arab (Larbi). The boat catches fire and boy and horse surface on a deserted island. A rescue is effected and they are brought back to the USA. Horse escapes, is later found by Ramsey at the farm owned by Mickey Rooney (and if Rooney is not the best living American actor, then we'll eat our mother-in-law's cooking). Alec becomes a jockey, there's a big race and if you can't guess the end, stop going to moviesthey've made no impression on you. Yes, it's corny, but corn, when it's perfectly cooked with salt and pepper and butter, is one of the most delicious things you can eat. And this corn is one of the most delicious pictures you can see. It tugs the heart, delights the eye, and will take you through a series of emotional moments. Just a few flaws; It could have been a trifle shorter and director Ballard and Cinematographer Deschanel fell in love with their lenses, to the detriment of the story. Other than those nit-picks, this is something you will want to see at least ten times.

p, Tom Sternberg, Fred Roos; d, Carroll Ballard; w, Melissa Mathison, Jeanne Rosenberg, William Witliff (based on the novel by Walter Farley); ph, Caleb Deschanel; m, Carmine Coppola; ed, Robert Dalva.

Adventure   **Cas.**   (PR:AAA MPAA:G)

BLACK STALLION RETURNS, THE*½   (1983) 93m Zoetrope-MGM/UA c

Kelly Reno (*Alec*), Vincent Spano (*Raj*), Allen Goorwitz (*Kurr*), Woody Strode (*Meslar*), Ferdinand Mayne (*Abu Ben Ishak*), Teri Garr (*Alec's Mother*), Jodi Thelen (*Tabari*), Doghmi Larbi (*The Little Man*).

In this sequel to THE BLACK STALLION, good sense has been swept under the hay. Reno, who starred in the original, is now a teenager taking care of his beloved steed on a farm. Soon enough, some villainous Moroccans horsenap the stallion and bring him back to his true home in Africa. Meanwhile, some other Moroccans also want the horse. Teri Garr appears just long enough to rant and rave as Reno's mother and to make us wonder if she did this because she owed executive producer Francis Ford Coppola a favor after her performance in his ONE FROM THE HEART, the picture that apparently lost Zoetrope studios for him. The reason for all this chicanery is a once-every-five-years race that both tribes of Moroccans are pledged to win. Naturally, a race acts as the conclusion but after countless superfluous plot turns and a host of silly twists, nobody much cares. Gone is the joy and wide-eyed fun of the original. In its place is a hokey, ho-hum story that might have come out of a computer. Spano (Sheik in BABY, IT'S YOU) does a nice job as an Arab. Allen Goorwitz (who was born Goorwitz, changed his name to Garfield, then back to Goorwitz and now he's Garfield again) fails to impress as a Middle-Eastern type. (He's been terrific in just about everything else he's ever done, so he's entitled to one mediocre part.) The film falls between reality and fantasy and achieves neither.

p, Tom Sternberg, Fred Roos, Doug Claybourne; d, Robert Dalva; w, Richard Kletter, Jerome Kass (based on the book by Walter Farley); ph, Carlo DiPalma,

Caleb Deschanel; m, Georges Delerue; ed, Paul Hirsch; art d, Aurelio Crugnola.
Adventure **Cas.** **(PR:A-C MPAA:PG)**

BLACK SUN, THE*½ (1979, Czech.) 135m Barrandov (CERNE SLUNCE)

Radoslav Hrzobohary, Jiri Thomas, Rudolph Hrusinsky, Magda Vasaryova, Gunther Naumann, Vladimir Smeral.

Krakatit, a new energy source the size of a golf ball, is stolen from its creator by a young ambitious scientist. An American industry is also chasing after the krakatit for its own purposes. Eventually the younger scientist sets off a neutron bomb-type explosion that kills the population but leaves architecture intact. The older scientist starts his life over in a small village where the people still live traditional lives. This is an inferior remake of KRAKATIT, a 1948 film with the same story line by the same director. Rather than dreamy, lyrical passages as in the first film, THE BLACK SUN is overlong and fre quently resorts to spy movie aesthtics.

d, Otakar Varvra; w, Varvra, Jiri Sotala; ph, Miroslav Ondricek.
Drama **(PR:A MPAA:NR)**

BLACK SUNDAY*½ (1961, Ital.) 83m AIP bw

Barbara Steele *(Witch Princess Katia)*, John Richardson *(Dr. Gorobee)*, Ivo Garrani *(Prince)*, Andrea Cecchi *(Dr. Choma)*, Arturo Dominici *(Javutich)*, Enrico Olivieri *(Constantin)*, Antonio Pierfederici *(The Pope)*, Clara Bindi *(Innkeeper)*, Germana Dominici *(His Daughter)*, Mario Passante *(Nikita)*, Tino Bianchi *(Ivan)*.

If speedy, swooping camera moves don't make you dizzy and if you truly enjoy watching horror films, then BLACK SUNDAY is your meat. Not to be confused with the 1977 terrorist movie of the same name, this BLACK SUNDAY is about a vampirette (Steele) and her ghoulish sidekick who decide that they've slept enough and now want to go out and suck some more necks. They terrorize an old Russian castle and its inhabitants until the priest arrives and they burn the lady at the stake. Looking at this picture years after it was made, one wonders about the director, Bava, and if there might have been two men with the same name. He went on to make some terrible pictures, most notably BARON BLOOD, produced by the best-known shlockmeister of the genre, Alfredo Leone. This movie was Steele's first major role and she later became a cult figure. Married briefly to award-winning screenwriter James Poe (LILIES OF THE FIELD, THEY SHOOT HORSES, DON'T THEY?), she was to appear in the latter but lost the role to Susannah York. Shows you how much influence sleeping with a screenwriter has! Music by Les Baxter in the American version is better than the music by Roberto Nicolosi in the Italian version. The picture was banned for eight years in Britain, probably due to maggot scenes and some shots of a decomposed head. Definitely not a film to be seen after a hearty dinner.

p, Massimo de Rita; d, Mario Bava; w, Ennio De Coneine, Mario Serandrei (based on a story by Nikolai Gogol); ph, Bava, Ubaldo Terzano; m, Les Baxter; ed, Serandrei; art d, Giorgio Giovanni.
Horror **(PR:O MPAA:NR)**

BLACK SUNDAY*½** (1977) 143m PAR c

Robert Shaw *(Kabakov)*, Bruce Dern *(Lander)*, Marthe Keller *(Dahlia)*, Fritz Weaver *(Corley)*, Steven Keats *(Moshevsky)*, Bekim Fehmiu *(Fasil)*, Michael V. Gazzo *(Muzi)*, William Daniels *(Pugh)*, Walter Gotell *(Col. Riaf)*, Victor Campos *(Nageeb)*, Walter Brooke *(Fowler)*, James Jeter *(Watchman)*, Clyde Kusatsu *(Freighter Captain)*, Tom McFadden *(Farley)*, Robert Patten *(Vickers)*, Than Wyenn *(Israeli Ambassador)*, Joseph Robbie, Robert Wussler, Pat Summerall, Tom Brookshier *(Themselves)*.

This is one of the best genre films ever done. By "genre" we speak of the what-if disaster movie, but the plot of this borders so closely on reality that we sometimes shudder at the thought that we might be there when and if this happens. Keller and Fehmiu are Black September agents, not unlike those murderers at the 1972 Olympics. Their plan is to hijack the Goodyear Blimp, send it into the teeming Super Bowl crowd and fire thousands of steel darts from the blimp, thus inflicting carnage not seen since the last power struggle at Paramount pictures. Keller influences Dern, a deranged Vietnam veteran, and he becomes pilot of the blimp. Shaw scores, as always, in the role of an Israeli major, and Weaver is the first FBI agent anyone has admired in films for years. The plot is thwarted, just barely, but the scene where the blimp comes over the top of the Orange Bowl is one of the most memorable ever. There was a similar picture done in a stadium, TWO MINUTE WARNING, directed by Larry Peerce. Absolutely no comparison. That was exploitive, this was exceptional, a good story, many thrills, fully developed characterizations and the intelligence to cast it with actors, rather than stars. Most chilling is that gnawing feeling that someone, somewhere, is actually plotting to do exactly what they saw in BLACK SUNDAY. Just as Rod Serling wrote a story about the first skyjack and then it began to happen, the worry is always that life will imitate art. This would have merited four stars if they'd cut 20 minutes or so from it.

p, Robert Evans; d, John Frankenheimer; w, Ernest Lehman, Ivan Moffat, Kenneth Ross; ph, John A. Alonzo (Movielab Color); m, John Williams; ed, Tom Rolf; makeup, Bob Dawn, Brad Wilder.
Crime **Cas.** **(PR:C MPAA:R)**

BLACK SWAN, THE**** (1942) 85m FOX c

Tyrone Power *(James Waring)*, Maureen O'Hara *(Margaret Denby)*, Laird Cregar *(Capt. Henry Morgan)*, Thomas Mitchell *(Tommy Blue)*, George Sanders *(Capt. Billy Leech)*, Anthony Quinn *(Wogan)*, George Zucco *(Lord Denby)*, Edward Ashley *(Roger Ingram)*, Fortunio Bonanova *(Don Miguel)*, Stuart Robertson *(Capt. Graham)*, Charles McNaughton *(Fenner)*, Frederick Worlock *(Speaker)*, Willie Fung *(Chinese Cook)*, Charles Francis *(Higgs)*, Arthur Shields *(Bishop)*, Keith Hitchcock *(Majordomo)*, John Burton *(Capt. Blaine)*, Cyril McLaglen *(Capt. Jones)*, Clarence Muse *(Daniel)*, Olaf Hytten *(Clerk)*, Charles Irwin, David Thursby, Frank Leigh *(Sea Captains)*.

A sweeping pirate epic with Power as a swashbuckling aide to the notorious buccaneer Henry Morgan (Cregar). Cregar is pardoned from the gallows and sent to Jamaica as the new governor; his task is to prevent his former piratical associates from continuing their villainous activities. Power falls in love with O'Hara, the daughter of the former governor, but she is having none of this rough-hewn adventurer, spurning his advances. Renegade pirates Sanders and Quinn refuse to follow Cregar's authority. Power is sent to capture the renegades, taking O'Hara forcibly along on his warship, but when Sanders and company appear, outnumbering Power's ship, he tells them that O'Hara is his wife. Sanders is suspicious and, in a hilarious scene, enters their bedroom to make sure they are sleeping together. Quinn is more than suspicious; he believes Power is loyal to the reformed Cregar and says so. Sanders is finally convinced that Power is working against them and he ties him up in his cabin, throwing Power's crew, headed by aide Mitchell, into the hold. Then Sanders and Quinn attack Maracaibo Harbor, Cregar's headquarters; a savage battle between shore batteries and ships ensues. Just when all looks lost for Cregar's forces, Power frees himself and his crew, regains control of his ship after killing Sanders in a wild duel, and sinks Quinn's vessel. Thought to be a traitor by Cregar until the tide of battle turns, Power is honored at film's end, winning the hand of the lovely O'Hara. The story and dialog smack of CAPTAIN BLOOD and is a bit stilted in its attempt to capture the idiom of the period but the action is overwhelming once it starts and Power is full of marvelous dash and derring-do. Cregar is wonderful to behold, his enormous body bedecked in wigs and finery (this superb character actor, in an attempt to slim down for leading roles, literally starved himself to death in 1944, employing a diet so severe that it weakened his heart). Sanders, sporting a thick red beard, is his usual conniving self, made more fierce by his menacing makeup. Quinn is still playing the heavy role, using a snarl and a sneer to create his role. O'Hara is ravishing, her red hair blazing in this lush color film. Expensively produced, THE BLACK SWAN received several Academy Award nominations, including Newman for his score and one for the incredible special effects but it did take home one Oscar for Shamroy's bravura photography.

p, Robert Bassler; d, Henry King; w, Ben Hecht, Seton I. Miller (based on the novel by Rafael Sabatini); ph, Leon Shamroy (Technicolor); m, Alfred Newman; ed, Barbara McLean; art d, Richard Day, James Basevi; set d, Thomas Little; cos, Earl Luick.
Adventure **(PR:A MPAA:NR)**

BLACK TENT, THE** (1956, Brit.) 93m RANK c

Anthony Steel *(David Holland)*, Donald Sinden *(Charles Holland)*, Anna Maria Sandri *(Mabrouka)*, Andre Morell *(Sheik Salem)*, Ralph Truman *(Croft)*, Donald Pleasence *(Ali)*, Anthony Bushell *(Baring)*, Michael Craig *(Faris)*, Anton Diffring *(1st German Officer)*, Frederick Jaeger *(2nd German Officer)*, Paul Homer *(Khalil)*, Derek Sydney *(Interpreter)*, Terence Sharkey *(Daoud)*.

Unspectacular British desert epic starring Sinden who travels to North Africa to tidy up the affairs of his brother who was killed in a WW II campaign. Through flashbacks we see that the brother, Steel, was wounded in a tank battle and taken in by Bedouin tribesmen. The Sheik's daughter, Sandri, and the British soldier fall in love and they are allowed to marry. He soon discovers that he has been left behind by his division, so he decides to make his life among the nomads. Still carrying a passionate hate for the Nazis, Steel convinces the Sheik to help him conduct a guerrilla-style war against the Germans from behind their lines. The campaign is successful, but Steel is killed saving the life of his father-in-law during an ambush on a German convoy. Good production values and eye-catching locations help but the script suffers from the overly melodra- matic episodes.

p, William MacQuitty; d, Brian Desmond Hurst; w, Robin Maugham, Bryan Forbes; ph, Desmond Dickinson (Technicolor); m, William Alwyn; ed, Alfred Roome.
War **(PR:A MPAA:NR)**

BLACK 13** (1954, Brit.) 75m FOX bw

Peter Reynolds *(Stephen)*, Rona Anderson *(Claire)*, Patrick Barr *(Robert)*, Lana Morris *(Marion)*, Genie Graham *(Stella)*, Michael Balfour *(Joe)*, John Forest *(Wally)*, Viola Lyel *(Mrs. Barclay)*, Martin Walker *(Prof. Barclay)*, John Le Mesurier *(Inspector)*, Martin Benson *(Bruno)*.

Reynolds is a totally unsympathetic criminal whose sister falls in love with the detective assigned to catch him. Though he was raised in wealthy surroundings, Reynolds is attracted to a life of crime and proceeds to rob cafes and casinos. When caught red-handed, the slimy sibling grabs his sister and uses her as a shield to escape. Justice triumphs when the creep kills himself in a car crash while making his getaway. Potentially interesting material made maudlin by lackluster script, direction, and acting.

p, Roger Proudlock; d, Ken Hughes; w, Pietro Germi; ph, Gerald Gibbs; m, Carlo Rustichelli; ed, Sam Simmons.
Crime **(PR:A MPAA:NR)**

BLACK TIGHTS**** (1962, Fr.) 140m Magna Pictures c

Maurice Chevalier *(Narrator)*; THE DIAMOND CRUNCHER: Zizi Jeanmaire, Dirk Sanders; CYRANO DeBERGERAC: Moira Shearer, Roland Petit, George Reich; A MERRY MOURNING: Cyd Charisse, Roland Petit, Hans Van Manen; CARMEN: Zizi Jeanmaire, Roland Petit, Henning Kronstam.

Chevalier narrated this compilation that signaled the end of the ballet cycle of films. "The Diamond Cruncher" is a fairy tale about a young female mobster (Jeanmaire) who learns that it's more fun to eat cabbages with the man you love (Sanders) than it is to crunch diamonds. Choreographed by Zizi's husband, Roland Petit, with the English version's lyrics having been written by Herbert Kretzmer, today a TV critic in London and one-time translator-lyricist for Charles Aznavour. "Cyrano" was also choreographed by Petit with costumes by St. Laurent and music by Marius

Constant. Petit dances Cyrano, Reich is Christian and the radiant Shearer is Roxanne. "A Merry Mourning" is a story and ballet by Petit and concerns Van Manen twitting his wife for admiring an expensive frilly gown in a Paris window. He is challenged to a duel by Petit and promptly killed. Charisse, now a widow, buys the gown and immediately attracts the eye of Petit, killer of her husband. In "Carmen" the famous Bizet story is retold with dance instead of song. BLACK TIGHTS sounds more like a 1980s De Palma film and the title may have hurt it. You must be a balletomane to be able to sit through this much dance without wanting to get up and do a pirouette yourself, if only to work the kinks out of your legs. Technically brilliant and beautifully danced, BLACK TIGHTS will remain as one of the best of its genre.

p, Joseph Kaufman, Simon Schiffrin; d, Terence Young; cos, Yves St. Laurent; ch, Roland Petit.

Ballet **Cas.** **(PR:A MPAA:NR)**

BLACK TORMENT, THE** (1965, Brit.) 85m Compton-Tekli c

John Turner *(Sir Richard Fordyce)*, Heather Sears *(Lady Elizabeth)*, Ann Lynn *(Diane)*, Peter Arne *(Seymour)*, Raymond Huntley *(Col. Wentworth)*, Annette Whiteley *(Mary)*, Norman Bird *(Harris)*, Roger Croucher *(Apprentice)*, Joseph Tomelty *(Sir Giles)*, Patrick Troughton *(Ostler)*, Francis de Wolff *(Black John)*, Charles Houston *(Jenkins)*, Edina Ronay *(Lucy Judd)*, Cathy McDonald *(Kate)*.

Somewhat tedious gothic horror starring Turner as a nobleman who returns from his honeymoon with his second wife (the first had committed suicide) only to find that the villagers want his head on a platter. In his absence many of the citizens claim that he had raped a woman, committed crimes, and had been seen running from a woman on horseback dressed in white (who resembled his wife), who was screaming that he had murdered her. Turner claims he is innocent, but soon after his father is found hanged, and his new bride tries to shoot him to keep him away. In the end it turns out that his evil sister-in-law from his first marriage has been using Turner's crazed twin brother (the family skeleton-in-the-closet) to drive him insane so that she may get her revenge for the death of her sister. Average script and direction fail to spark the material. Good for gothic-horror nuts.

p, Tony Tenser, Michael Klinger, Robert Hartford-Davis; d, Hartford-Davis; w, Donald Ford, Derek Ford; ph, Peter Newbrook (Eastmancolor); m, Robert Richards; ed, Alastair McIntyre.

Crime/Horror **(PR:A MPAA:NR)**

BLACK TUESDAY** (1955) 80m UA bw

Edward G. Robinson *(Vincent Canelli)*, Peter Graves *(Peter Manning)*, Jean Parker *(Hatti Combest)*, Milburn Stone *(Father Slocum)*, Warren Stevens *(Joey Stewart)*, Jack Kelly *(Frank Carson)*, Sylvia Findley *(Ellen Norris)*, James Bell *(John Norris)*, Victor Perrin *(Dr. Hart)*, Hal Baylor *(Lou Mehrtens)*, Harry Bartell *(Boland)*, Simon Scott *(Parker)*, Russell Johnson *(Howard Sloane)*, Phil Pine *(Fiaschetti)*, Paul Maxey *(Donaldson)*, William Schallert *(Collins)*, Don Blackman *(Selwyn)*, Dick Rich *(Benny)*.

A very tough and dark film that foreshadowed things to come. Robinson and Graves are both on Death Row for assorted crimes. Graves has two hundred grand put away from a bank robbery so Robinson takes him and several hostages along when a jail break is made. They're trapped on the top floor of a warehouse and bloodthirsty Edward G. wants to kill a hostage every hour or so until the surrounding police leave. The cops won't depart and there's a stand-off until Graves kills Robinson when the latter is about to murder a priest (Stone). Graves then goes out with guns blazing and the picture is over. This is one of the later gangster films, almost twenty years after the Warner Brothers heyday of the genre. It's better than many, not as good as many others. By this time, Robinson was already doing an imitation of himself as the crime kingpin.

p, Leonard and Robert Goldstein; d, Hugo Fregonese; w, Sydney Boehm; ph, Stanley Cortez; m, Paul Dunlap; ed, Robert Golden; m/l, Black Tuesday," Robert Parrish.

Crime Drama **(PR:C MPAA:NR)**

BLACK TULIP, THE* 1/2 (1937, Brit.) 57m FOX bw

Patrick Waddington *(Cornelius)*, Ann Soreen *(Rosa)*, Campbell Gullan *(Boxtel)*, Jay Laurier *(Gryphus)*, Wilson Coleman *(Cornelius de Witte)*, Bernard Lee *(William of Orange)*, Florence Hunt *(Julia Boxtel)*, Ronald Shiner *(Hendrik)*, Aubrey Mallalieu *(Col. Marnix)*.

Period film set in Holland finds a merchant obsessed with black tulips. He frames the flower's cultivator in order to learn how to raise them, a zealously guarded secret, but the movie has little tension.

d, Alex Bryce; w, Alexandre Dumas (based on his novel *La Tulipe Noire*).

Adventure/Drama **(PR:A MPAA:NR)**

BLACK VEIL FOR LISA, A* 1/2 (1969 Ital./Ger.) 87m Commonwealth United c

John Mills *(Bulov)*, Luciana Paluzzi *(Lisa)*, Robert Hoffman *(Max)*, Renata Kasche *(Marianne)*, Tullio Altamura *(Ostermeyer)*, Carlo Hintermann *(Mansfeld)*, Enzo Fiermonte *(Siegert)*, Loris Bazzocchi *(Kruger)*, Giuseppe Terranova *("Rabbit")*, Rodolfo Licari *(Olaf)*, Bernadino Solitari *(Muller)*, Vanna Polverosi *(Ursula)*, Robert Van Daalen *(Dr. Gross)*, Carlo Spandoni *(Erick)*.

Contrived tale of a cop, Mills, who is distracted from his duties by the immoral activities of his cheating wife. The narcotics inspector is so obsessed with his bride's infidelity that he follows her movements during his working hours and even hires a hit-man to kill her. Things get complicated when the assassin falls in love with his intended victim.

p, Giorgio Venturini; d, Massimo Dallamano; w, Guiseppe Belli, Vittoriano Patrick, Dallamano, Audrey Nohra (based on a story by Belli); ph, Angelo Lotti (Eastmancolor); m, Dick Markowitz; ed, Harry Eisen, Daniele Alabiso, Mike Pozen, Stan Frazen; art d, Hans Hutter.

Crime **(PR:C MPAA:NR)**

BLACK WATCH, THE*** (1929) 91m FOX bw

Victor McLaglen *(Capt. Donald Gordon King)*, Myrna Loy *(Yassmini)*, David Rollins *(Lt. Malcolm King)*, Lumsden Hare *(Colonel of the Black Watch)*, Roy D'Arcy *(Rewa Chunga)*, Mitchell Lewis *(Mohammed Khan)*, Cyril Chadwick *(Maj. Twynes)*, David Torrence *(Field Marshal)*, Claude King *(General in India)*, Francis Ford *(Maj. McGregor)*, Walter Long *(Harrim Bey)*, Frederick Sullivan *(General's Aide)*, Richard Travers *(Adjutant)*, Pat Somerset, David Percy *(Black Watch Officers)*, Joseph Diskay *(Muezzin)*, Joyzelle.

This early John Ford talkie is loaded with the director's special action, his attention to military detail and protocol as precise as every setup shot he takes. McLaglen is a brawny captain of a Scottish regiment who is stopped from boarding the boat sailing for France at the last minute and given new orders. Instead of going to the front (it is WW I), he is to sail immediately to India to help put down an impending uprising in the Northern mountains. Upon arriving in India, however, McLaglen gets involved in a drunken brawl, ostensibly killing a fellow officer. He is arrested but escapes his British guards, racing down a crowded street. All of this is a ruse, however, to make it appear that he is a renegade so that he will be welcome in the sumptuous court of Loy, an Indian princess who is a descendant of Alexander the Great and is worshipped by her followers. It is McLaglen's job to find out her plans since it has been reported that she intends to lead a revolt, sending her native troops through the Khyber Pass to attack the British. Loy and McLaglen play a cat-and-mouse game, and Loy falls in love with the burly soldier, much to the chagrin of her advisers, D'Arcy and Long. There is, nevertheless, a pitched battle when Loy's orders are wrongly interpreted and she is captured by McLaglen after soldiers dressed as natives infiltrate her court. The action is plentiful and well-coordinated as the Black Watch, with kilts flowing and bagpipes bleating, is shown fighting in France and later in India, scenes certainly not lost on George Stevens when he was preparing GUNGA DIN. August's camera work is superb under Ford's watchful eye, but there was trouble with the primitive sound systems of the day, particularly in the action scenes. The reason Ford failed to blow up the ammunition dump coveted by both British and native troops in the final battle is that technicians didn't think the microphones could stand the strain. Other problems presented themselves. McLaglen had to tone down his silent film histrionics and had difficulty adjusting to sound. The timbre of his voice was fine, but his articulation left much to be desired. In one tender moment with Loy he pronounces her name "Yes, Minnie," when her name is "Yassmini." At the movie's premiere this caused the audience to erupt into laughter and Ford immediately cut the scene from the movie. (Loy's friends, however, joked so much about this *faux pas* that her nickname among close associates ever after was "Minnie.") Loy plays the mystical Indian princess to the exotic hilt, her slanted eyes further accented by heavy makeup, her wardrobe stunning, but too ancient for the period of the film's setting. She is a femme fatale through and through here, her private perversion being the capturing of British officers. She tortures them personally, whipping them and destroying their "man-hood," until McLaglen steals her heart. It is at this juncture that D'Arcy and company, accurately believing she is about to betray their cause, kill Loy, which brings about their own deaths at the hands of the raging bull McLaglen and his fierce Scottish troops. Rousing adventure from the man who brought the genre to perfection on the screen. (Remade as KING OF THE KHYBER RIFLES with Tyrone Power in 1953).

d, John Ford; w, John Stone, James Kevin McGuinness (based on the novel *King of the Khyber Rifles* by Talbot Mundy); ph, Joseph August; ed, Alexander Troffey; m/l, "Flames of Delight," William Kernell.

Adventure **(PR:C MPAA:NR)**

BLACK WATERS** (1929) 79m Sono Art-World Wide

James Kirkwood *(Tiger Larabee/Kelly)*, Mary Brian *(Eunice)*, John Loder *(Charles)*, Hallam Cooley *(Elmer)*, Frank Reicher *(Randall)*, Lloyd Hamilton *(Temple)*, Robert Ames *(Darcy)*, Ben Hendricks *(Olaf)*, Noble Johnson *(Jeelo)*.

Mad captain poses as a cleric and stalks his fogbound ship, murdering passengers. Though the dialog is stilted and poorly recorded in this early talkie, there are many chilling scenes to maintain the suspense.

p, Herbert Wilcox; d, Marshall Neilan; w, John Willard (based on his play Fog").

Crime **(PR:A MPAA:NR)**

BLACK WHIP, THE** (1956) 81m FOX bw

Hugh Marlowe *(Lorn)*, Coleen Gray *(Jeannie)*, Richard Gilden *(Dewey)*, Angie Dickinson *(Sally)*, Strother Martin *(Thorny)*, Paul Richards *(Murdock)*, Charles Gray *(Hainline)*, William R. Hamel *(Constable)*, Patrick O'Moore *(Governor)*, Dorothy Schuyler *(Delilah)*, Sheb Wooley *(Lasater)*, John Pickard *(Sheriff Persons)*, Adele Mara *(Ruthie)*, Harry Landers *(Fiddler)*, Howard Culver *(Dr. Gillette)*, Duane Thorsen *(Deputy Floyd)*, Rush Williams *(Jailer Garner)*, Sid Curtis *(Bartender)*, Rick Arnold, Robert Garvey, Bill Ward *(Red Legs)*.

Average oater following four women: Dickinson, Gray, Schuyler, and Mara, who are kicked out of town for helping a hated outlaw escape capture. The ladies are put on the next stagecoach, but the coach breaks down and the passengers must hole up in an out-of-the-way inn run by meek Marlowe. Soon after, an outlaw gang arrives led by whip-wielding crook Richards. The gang is awaiting the arrival of the next stage which bears the governor of Kentucky, whom the crooks plan to kidnap for a large ransom and run to Mexico. After taking much grief from the gang, Marlowe eventually outsmarts the hoods and helps the sheriff's posse dispose of the menace. (Loose remake of SHOW THEM NO MERCY, 1935, and RAWHIDE, 1951.)

p, Robert Stabler; d, Charles Marquis Warren; w, Orville Hampton; ph, Joseph Biroc (Regalscope); m, Raoul Kraushaar; ed, Fred W. Berger.

Western   **(PR:A MPAA:NR)**

BLACK WIDOW*½   (1951, Brit.) 62m Hammer bw

Christine Norden (*Christine Sherwin*), Robert Ayres (*Mark Sherwin*), Anthony Forwood (*Paul*), Jennifer Jayne (*Sheila Kemp*), John Longden (*Kemp*), John Harvey (*Dr. Wallace*).

Amnesiac recovers his memory long enough to realize his wife and her boy friend are trying to do him in. Some exciting moments.

p, Anthony Hinds; d, Vernon Sewell; w, Allan Mackinnon (based on the radio serial "Return From Darkness" by Lester Powell); ph, Walter Harvey; ed, James Needs.

Crime   **(PR:A MPAA:NR)**

BLACK WIDOW***   (1954) 95m FOX c

Ginger Rogers (*Lottie*), Van Heflin (*Peter*), Gene Tierney (*Iris*), George Raft (*Det. Bruce*), Peggy Ann Garner (*Nanny Ordway*), Reginald Gardiner (*Brian*), Virginia Leith (*Claire Amberly*), Otto Kruger (*Ling*), Cathleen Nesbitt (*Lucia*), Skip Homeier (*John*), Hilda Simms (*Anne*), Harry Carter (*Welch*), Geraldine Wall (*Miss Mills*), Richard Cutting (*Sgt. Owens*), Mabel Albertson (*Sylvia*), Aaron Spelling (*Mr. Oliver*), Wilson Wood (*Costume Designer*), Tony DeMario (*Bartender*), Virginia Maples (*Model*), Frances Driver (*Maid*), Michael Vallon (*Coal Dealer*), James F. Stone (*Stage Doorman*).

Garner is not unlike Eve Harrington in ALL ABOUT EVE in her insidious ways. She arrives from the South to visit with uncle Kruger. An aspiring writer, she quickly gets into the life of Great White Way impresario Heflin, who is married to Tierney, an actress who is out of town at the moment. When Garner says she needs a place to write, Heflin makes a tactical error and offers his apartment, a gorgeous flat overlooking Central Park. Tierney comes home and discovers Garner dead in the bedroom, hanging by her neck. The first suspicion is suicide, but detective Raft of the NYPD doesn't believe it for a second, especially after he learns that Garner was pregnant. Lots of suspects abound including Rogers, in an excellent portrayal of a phony, heartless stage personality, her husband Gardiner, a weakling playwright, Homeier, and a few others who've touched the young girl's life. Raft is not believable as the police officer, but all the other actors do wonderful work under Johnson's tight direction. The mystery is not quite what one might have hoped for but Johnson's dialog is bright and at 95 minutes, one doesn't squirm. Unfortunately, the title gives away the fact that the killer is a woman, otherwise there might have been somewhat more suspense.

p&d, Nunnally Johnson; w, Johnson (based on a story by Patrick Quentin); ph, Charles G. Clarke; m, Leigh Harline; ed, Dorothy Spencer.

Mystery   **(PR:C MPAA:NR)**

BLACK WINDMILL, THE**½   (1974, Brit.) 106m UNIV c

Michael Caine (*Maj. John Tarrant*), Joseph O'Conor (*Sir Edward Julyan*), Donald Pleasence (*Cedric Harper*), John Vernon (*McKee*), Janet Suzman (*Alex Tarrant*), Delphine Seyrig (*Ceil Burrows*), Joss Ackland (*Chief Superintendent Wray*), Clive Revill (*Alf Chestermann*), Edward Hardwicke (*Mike McCarthy*), David Daker (*Thickset M.I. 5 Man*), Denis Quilley (*Bateson*), Paul Moss (*David Tarrant*), Mark Praid (*James Stroud*), George Cooper (*Pincus*), Derek Newark (*Monitoring Policeman*), John Rhys-Davies (*Special Policeman*), Brenda Cowling (*Pleasant Secretary*), Preston Lockwood (*Ilkeston*), Nancy Gabrielle (*Manageress*), Murray Brown (*Doctor*), Hilary Sesta (*Ilkeston's Secretary*), Frank Henson (*S.P. Driver*), Catherine Schell (*Lady Julyan*), Derek Lord (*Sollars*), Michael Segal (*Postman*), Maureen Pryor (*Jane Harper*), Paul Humpoletz (*Tomkins*), Hermione Baddeley (*Hetty*), Patrick Barr (*Gen. St. John*), John Harvey (*Heppenstal*), Russell Napier (*Adm. Ballentyne*).

Spotty espionage film directed by Don Siegel and starring Caine as a secret agent whose son has been kidnaped by his own agency. Vernon and Seyrig play the kidnapers whose ransom is a fortune in diamonds in Caine's possession which are to be used as bait in the capture of an international smuggling ring. Pleasence is his usual malevolent self as the head of the "company" who can't stand Caine. Suzman is Caine's wife, who had left him because of his devotion to his job, but who returns to help him get their son back. The good opening half of the film bogs down during some lengthy voice-over exposition in the latter half and eventually plods on to a dissatisfying ending. Disappointing effort from Siegel, who is capable of turning out some very tight, engrossing films.

p&d, Don Siegel; w, Leigh Vance (based on the novel *Seven Days To A Killing* by Clive Egleton); ph, Outsama Rawi (Panavision, Technicolor); m, Roy Budd; ed, Anthony Gibbs; art d, Peter Murton; cos, Anthony Mendleson.

Spy Drama   **(PR:C MPAA:PG)**

BLACK ZOO*½   (1963) 88m AA c

Michael Gough (*Michael Conrad*), Jeanne Cooper (*Edna Conrad*), Rod Lauren (*Carl*), Virginia Grey (*Jenny*), Jerome Cowan (*Jeffrey Stengle*), Elisha Cook, Jr. (*Joe*), Warrene Ott (*Mary Hogan*), Marianna Hill (*Audrey*), Oren Curtis (*Radu*), Eilene Janssen (*Bride*), Eric Stone (*Groom*), Dani Lynn (*Art Student*), Susan Slavin (*Art Student*), Edward Platt (*Det. Rivers*), Douglas Henderson (*Lt. Duggan*), Jerry Douglas (*Lab Technician*), Claudia Brack (*Carl's Mother*), Daniel Kurlick (*Carl as Child*), Byron Morrow (*Officer Donovan*).

Sensational melodrama about a madman who belongs to a sect that worships animals and feels that the animals take on human souls. Gough runs a private zoo and uses his beasts to wreak havoc on anyone he feels deserves it. His son, Lauren,

eventually destroys him as his wife, Cooper, watches. Some unique touches include one scene where Gough takes several of his cats (lion, tiger, panther, cougar) and plays the organ for them to prove, we suspect, that music has charms to soothe a savage beast as well as a savage breast. Rod Lauren had a brief career as a rock singer/actor, then disappeared. Gough has always been a favorite of the Screaming Mimi Crowd and doesn't disappoint in this gory portrayal.

p, Herman Cohen; d, Robert Gordon; w, Cohen; ph, Floyd Crosby (Eastmancolor);; m, Paul Dunlap; ed, Michael Luciano.

Horror   **(PR:C MPAA:NR)**

BLACKBEARD THE PIRATE**½   (1952) 98m RKO c

Robert Newton (*Blackbeard*), Linda Darnell (*Edwina*), William Bendix (*Worley*), Keith Andes (*Maynard*), Torin Thatcher (*Sir Henry Morgan*), Irene Ryan (*Alvina*), Alan Mowbray (*Noll*), Richard Egan (*Briggs*), Skelton Knaggs (*Gilly*), Dick Wessel (*Dutchman*), Anthony Caruso (*Pierre La Garde*), Jack Lambert (*Tom Whetstone*), Noel Drayton (*Jeremy*), Pat Flaherty (*Job Maggot*).

There weren't many better villains than Robert Newton. From Bill Sikes in the original OLIVER to Long John Silver in TREASURE ISLAND to Pistol in HENRY V, Newton rolled his eyes and his R's and was always a pleasure to watch. BLACKBEARD is pestering the sea lanes again. The King of England dispatches Thatcher (As Sir Henry Morgan, a reformed pirate himself) to free the briny from the likes of Blackbeard. Andes, handsome and jut-jawed as always, allows himself to be Shanghaied and goes aboard a vessel in the harbor. Once on, he takes up with luscious Darnell, who is due to marry the captain of the ship. Andes and Linda team up and learn that the Captain has been killed and that the ship is really being run by Blackbeard and that Thatcher is in cahoots with him! Well, thank goodness Linda is only his "adopted" daughter and not a blood relation. Andes and Darnell wind up in a clinch after a series of piratical adventures, most of which you've seen before in at least ten other films. It's a lot of fun but Egan, Ryan, and especially Bendix are misused. Walsh didn't have a good grip on Newton, who went straight over the top in his portrayal and seemed to be doing a caricature of himself. Supposedly the role was to be played by Karloff with Val Lewton directing. But when Lewton died in 1951, Walsh took over and the result was what might be called "broad, bubbling, and hammy."

p, Edmund Grainger; d, Raoul Walsh; w, Alan LeMay (based on a story by DeVallon Scott); ph, William E. Snyder (Technicolor); m, Victor Young; ed, Ralph Dawson.

Adventure   **(PR:A-C MPAA:NR)**

BLACKBEARD'S GHOST***   (1968) 106m BV c

Peter Ustinov (*Captain Blackbeard*), Dean Jones (*Steve Walker*), Suzanne Pleshette (*Jo Anne Baker*), Elsa Lanchester (*Emily Stowcraft*), Joby Baker (*Silky Seymour*), Elliott Reid (*TV commentator*), Norman Grabowski (*Virgil*), Michael Conrad (*Pinetop Purvis*), Lou Nova (*Leon*).

Charming fantasy-comedy about a ghost (Ustinov) who comes back to Earth to help a group of little old ladies led by Lanchester. Some criminals (Baker is the prime heavy) want to take over a small resort island and turn it into a casino. Dean Jones is a track coach who finds a witch's book that lets him know the secret combination to evoking the ghost of the legendary pirate. Special effects abound (as in so many Disney films) but never take the place of old-fashioned story-telling. The story is standard; deserving people harassed by villains are saved by the intercession of a fantastic character. Artist Ellenshaw (his work on THE BLACK HOLE has become a legend) does marvelous art and special effects men Lycett and Mattey distinguish themselves. Michael Conrad is seen in a small role.

p, Bill Walsh; d, Robert Stevenson; w, Walsh, Don DaGradi (based on the novel by Ben Stahl); ph, Edward Colman (Technicolor); m, Robert F. Brunner; art d, Peter Ellenshaw; cos, Bill Thomas; spec eff, Eustace Lycett, Robert Mattey.

Comedy   **Cas.**   **(PR:AA MPAA:NR)**

BLACKBOARD JUNGLE, THE****   (1955) 100m MGM bw

Glenn Ford (*Richard Dadier*), Anne Francis (*Anne Dadier*), Louis Calhern (*Jim Murdock*), Margaret Hayes (*Lois Judby Hammond*), John Hoyt (*Mr. Warneke*), Richard Kiley (*Joshua Y. Edwards*), Emile Meyer (*Mr. Halloran*), Warner Anderson (*Dr. Bradley*), Basil Ruysdael (*Prof. A. R. Kraal*), Sidney Poitier (*Gregory W. Miller*), Vic Morrow (*Artie West*), Dan Terranova (*Belazi*), Rafael Campos (*Pete V. Morales*), Paul Mazursky (*Emmanuel Stoker*), Horace McMahon (*Detective*), Jameel Farah (*Santini*), Danny Dennis (*DeLiea*), Richard Deacon, Dorothy Neumann, Virginia Pherrin, Chris Randall, Henry Backus, David Alpert, Peter Miller, Yoski Tomita.

A powerful school drama that made stars out of several of the actors and served to point up the dangers in some big-city schools. Brooks received an Oscar nomination (as writer) and Harlan (as photographer) for this searing condemnation of juvenile delinquents facing earnest but underpaid teachers. Ford is a newly returned veteran who takes his first teaching job in a trade high school. He soons runs afoul of some of his tougher students, who are only staying inside until they are old enough to get out and get jobs. Morrow is brilliant as the leader of the pack of thugs. Poitier was already 31 years old when he played the high-schooler, but he still looks the same today, so he must be doing something right. There are several stories going at the same time in THE BLACKBOARD JUNGLE. Kiley thinks he can reason with the kids and soon learns how wrong he is; Anne Francis would love it if her husband (Ford) got out of there, but he is determined to make a go of it; Louis Calhern is excellent as the aging teacher who just wants to live out his days until he can retire and who will never rock any boat; Margaret Hayes impresses as a frightened but sensuous young teacher. The list never ends. Look for Mazursky (yes, the same one who became such a well-known director) as Stoker and a young Farr (while he still used his real name of Jameel Farah) and solid work by everyone. THE BLACKBOARD JUNGLE also introduced Bill Haley and His Comets to the movie audience. They sang "Rock Around The Clock" and rock 'n' roll music hasn't stopped since. It's a must-see film for anyone interested in the era. In a devastating scene for anyone who is a collector, Morrow smashes the prized jazz recording of Bix Biederbecke and His Gang that is owned by Kiley. That in itself is enough to make one want to kill the kid!

p, Pandro S. Berman; d&w, Richard Brooks (based on the novel by Evan Hunter); ph, Russell Harlan; m, Charles Wolcott; ed, Ferris Webster.

Drama (PR:C MPAA:NR)

BLACKENSTEIN*

(1973) 93m Exclusive International c (AKA: BLACK FRANKENSTEIN)

John Hart, Ivory Stone, Andrea King, Liz Renay, Roosevelt Jackson, James Cougar, Cardella Di Milo, Joe De Sue, Nick Bolin, Andy C.

Crazed scientist comes up with a beefy, black monster with an afro who has a penchant for tearing the blouses off his well-endowed female victims before killing them. Old horror film buffs will be disappointed to see old special effects expert Ken Strickfaden, who created the electronic gadgets in the original Universal FRANKEN-STEIN movies doing the same for this woefully inferior film.

p, Frank R. Saletri; d, William A. Levy; w, Saletri; ph, (DeLuxe Color).

Horror **Cas.** (PR:O MPAA:R)

BLACKJACK KETCHUM, DESPERADO** (1956) 76m COL bw

Howard Duff (Blackjack), Victor Jory (Jared Tetlow), Maggie Mahoney (Nita Riordan), Angela Stevens (Laurie Webster), David Orrick (Bob Early), William Tannen (Dee Havalik), Ken Christy (Sheriff Mach), Martin Garralaga (Jaime Brigo), Robert Roark (Ben Tetlow), Don C. Harvey (Mac Gill), Pat O'Malley (Doc Blaine), Jack Littlefield (Burl Tetlow), Sydney Mason (Matt Riordan), Ralph Sanford (Happy Harrow), George Edward Mather (Andy Tetlow), Charles Wagenheim (Jerry Carson), Wes Hudman (Grat Barbey).

When a big cattle baron tries to take over a peaceful valley, gunfighter Duff, trying to live down his reputation, is forced to strap on his sidearms once again to fight for the right. Before Duff can finally settle down with his girl he must face down the baddies. Realistically depicted romance scenes for this Louis L'Amour western, but there is no relationship with the facts about the real Ketchum and this mythical version of his life.

p, Sam Katzman; d, Earl Bellamy; w, Luci Ward, Jack Natteford (based on the story by Louis L'Amour); ph, Fred Jackman, Jr.; ed, Saul A. Goodkind.

Western (PR:A MPAA:NR)

BLACKMAIL* (1929, Brit.) 75m Elstree-BIP-Wardour/Sono Art bw

Anny Ondra (Alice White), John Longden (Frank Webber), Donald Calthrop (Tracy), Cyril Ritchard (The Artist), Sara Allgood (Mrs. White), Charles Paton (Mr. White), Harvey Braban (Inspector), Phyllis Monkman (Gossip), Hannah Jones (Landlady), Percy Parsons (Crook), Johnny Butt (Sergeant).

Early Hitchcock talkie where the master of suspense establishes a film formula that became distinctly his own, one where the leading player is the eternal victim, trapped by circumstances with apparently no way out of a menacing situation. In this case it's Ondra, who is dining with her fiance, Longden, a Scotland Yard detective. She flirts with a handsome artist, Ritchard, and, after Longden leaves in anger, goes to Ritchard's studio to see his etchings (a ploy that later became a cliche for seduction). She looks over his work, including some nudes, then naively agrees to pose for the artist. He begins to draw her scantily clad form, then moves in for the clinch. She resists, grabbing a bread knife and plunging it into the rake while Hitchcock swiveled his camera to show the painting of a grim court jester grinning strangely down upon the killing. Ondra flees in panic, leaving behind her gloves. One of these is found later by Longden, who is assigned to investigate the case. He recognizes the glove as that of his fiancee but does not turn her in, believing her innocent. The other glove is found by Calthrop who uses it to blackmail the detective. Meanwhile, Ondra is beset with guilt and every time she hears the word "knife" she cringes and winces, causing a similar reaction in the viewer, a grating but memorable technique typically Hitchcockian. Calthrop's game of blackmail backfires when Longden tells him on the phone that he knows who he is and he will soon be arrested. In a grand chase through historic London sites, a Hitchcock trademark to come, Longden and other detectives race after Calthrop, finally traversing the British Museum, past ancient artifacts, which culminates with the culprit scrambling over the building's huge Reading Room dome (here Hitchcock employed his favorite rear projection device) from which he finally falls to his death. Hitchcock shows his fall through a mirror technique; the director enjoyed the falling death routine, using it time and again, notably in SABOTEUR when Norman Lloyd takes his incredible drop from the top of the Statue of Liberty. Ondra, overcome with guilt, finally races to Scotland Yard to confess, but she is constantly interrupted and finally gives up. Longden arrives, hands her back her glove without comment, and the two go off together. A taut and suspenseful film, even though the early sound techniques are scratchy. The director disliked Ondra's reedy voice and so dubbed that of Joan Barry for that of the star. This procedure was crude in those early sound days; Barry had to crouch off camera next to Ondra and speak the lines as the leading lady mouthed them, causing Hitchcock to have many takes before they were in sync. His official "stamp" on the film was his bit part; Hitchcock appears in a subway car carrying Longden and Ondra, trying to read a book while being jostled, annoyed by a pesky boy who keeps jabbering at him.

p, John Maxwell; d, Alfred Hitchcock; w, Hitchcock, Benn W. Levy, Charles Bennett (based on the play by Bennett); ph, Jack Cox; m, Hubert Bath, Henry Stafford; m, John Reynders; ed, Emile de Ruelle; set d, Wilfred C. Arnold, Norman Arnold.

Mystery/Suspense **Cas.** (PR:A MPAA:NR)

BLACKMAIL ** 1/2 (1939) 81m MGM bw

Edward G. Robinson (John Ingram), Ruth Hussey (Helen Ingram), Gene Lockhart (William Ramey), Bobs Watson (Hank Ingram), Guinn Williams (Moose McCarthy), John Wray (Diggs), Arthur Hohl (Rawlins), Esther Dale (Sarah), Joe Whitehead (Anderson), Joseph Crehan (Blaine), Victor Kilian (Warden Miller), Gil Perkins (Kearney), Mitchell Lewis (1st Workman), Ted Oliver (2nd Workman), Lew Harvey 3rd Workman), Willie Best (Sunny), Art Miles (Driver), Robert Middlemass (Desk Sergeant), Ian Miller (Weber), Hal K. Dawson (Desk Clerk), Philip Morris (Local Trooper), Charles Middleton (1st Deputy), Trevor Bardette (3rd Deputy), Everett Brown (Prisoner), Ed Montoya (Juan), Joe Dominquez (Pedro).

Robinson plays a man framed for a crime he didn't commit. He is sentenced to serve his time on a southern chain-gang. He escapes and starts a new life, becoming a family man and opening an oil well fire-fighting business in Oklahoma. Soon after, Lockhart comes to town claiming that he committed the crime that Robinson is a fugitive from, and that he is willing to sign a confession. Lockhart double-crosses Robinson and turns him over to the authorities, who drag him back to the chain-gang. His treatment on the road-gang is worse than ever, and Robinson's hatred burns deep when he learns that the unscrupulous crook has taken over his business and left his wife and son poverty stricken. He escapes again and starts an oil-well fire to bring Lockhart out in the open. In front of the employees of the firm, Robinson extracts a confession from Lockhart, forcing the blackmailer toward the raging fire, and then puts out the fire himself. Good all-around effort, one of the first non-gangster roles for Robinson.

p, John Considine, Jr.; d, H.C. Potter; w, David Hertz, William Ludwig (based on a story by Endre Bohem, Dorothy Yost); ph, Clyde De Vinna; ed, Howard O'Neill.

Crime Drama (PR:A MPAA:NR)

BLACKMAIL* 1/2 (1947) 67m REP bw

William Marshall (Dan Turner), Adele Mara (Sylvia Duane), Ricardo Cortez (Ziggy Cranston), Grant Withers (Inspector Donaldson), Stephanie Bachelor (Carla), Richard Fraser (Antoine), Roy Barcroft (Spice Kellaway), George J. Lewis (Blue Chip Winslow), Gregory Gay (Jervis), Tristram Coffin (Pinky), Eva Novak (Mamie), Bud Wolfe (Gomez).

Sluggish private-eye drama starring Marshall as a detective hired by dashing playboy Cortez to protect him from a band of blackmailers. The immediate effect of the investigation sees the hoods up their demands from $50,000 to $150,000. Several fist fights, shootings, and tough-talk scenes later the extortionists are caught. Below average script and monotonous performances fail to hold much interest.

p, William J. O'Sullivan; d, Lesley Selander; w, Royal K. Cole, Albert DeMond (based on a story by Robert Leslie Bellen); ph, Reggie Lanning; ed, Tony Martinelli; md, Mort Glickman; art d, Frank Arrigo; set d, John McCarthy, Jr.; James Redd.

Crime (PR:A MPAA:NR)

BLACKMAILED* 1/2 (1951, Brit.) 85m GFD bw

Mai Zetterling (Carol Edwards), Dirk Bogarde (Stephen Mundy), Fay Compton (Mrs. Christopher), Robert Flemyng (Dr. Giles Freeman), Michael Gough (Maurice Edwards), James Robertson Justice (Mr. Sine), Joan Rice (Alma), Harold Huth (Hugh Saintsbury), Wilfrid Hyde-White (Lord Dearsley), Bruce Seton (Supt. Crowe), Cyril Chamberlain (PC).

Bad story structure saps this blackmail tale of any suspense that may have been exploited in a British drama concerning the victims of a dead blackmailer, Justice, who attempt to conceal the crime. The blackmailer is killed in the first fifteen minutes and the rest of the film deals with the extortion victims' tales of woe, every one of which demonstrates sufficent motive to bump off the deceased. Among the suspects: Flemy ing, a doctor who has committed some unethical behavior in his professional career, Bogarde, who is AWOL from the army, Bogarde's girl friend, Rice, who is an escapee from a women's reformatory, and Compton, a patroness of the hospital. None of this is particularly engrossing.

p, Harold Huth; d, Marc Allegret, w, Hugh Mills, Roger Vadim (based on the novel Mrs. Christopher by Elizabeth Myers); ph, George Stretton; m, John Wooldridge; ed, John Shirley.

Crime (PR:A MPAA:NR)

BLACKMAILER* 1/2 (1936) 66m COL bw

William Gargan (Peter Cornish), Florence Rice (Joan Rankin), H. B. Warner (Michael Rankin), Nana Bryant (Mrs. Lindsay), George McKay (Carney), Wyrley Birch (Nelson), Drue Leyton (Lydia Rankin), Paul Hurst (Inspector Killian), Kenneth Thompson (Mr. Porter), Boyd Irwin Sr. (D. Lindsay), Alexander Cross (Jack Donovan).

An uneasy mix of mystery and comedy fails to click in this tale of a blackmailed family whose daughter, Rice, falls for bumbling amateur detective Gargan. Gargan is forced to work with inept police inspector Hurst and the two play their roles strictly for comedy, which is successful, but it is when the film strays into serious drama that the flaws become apparent.

d, Gordon Wiles; w, Joseph Krumgold, Lee Loeb, Harold Buchman; ph, Allen E. Seigler.

Comedy/Mystery (PR:A MPAA:NR)

BLACKOUT ** 1/2 (1940, Brit.) 92m BN/UA bw (GB: CONTRABAND)

Conrad Veidt (Capt. Andersen), Valerie Hobson (Mrs. Sorenson), Esmond Knight (Mr. Pidgeon), Hay Petrie (Mate Skold/Chef Skold), Raymond Lovell (Van Dyne), Harold Warrender (Lt/Cdr Ellis), Charles Victor (Hendrick), Manning Whiley (Manager), Peter Bull (Grimm), Stuart Latham (Grimm), Leo Genn (Grimm), Dennis Arundell (Leinmann), Julian Vedey (Waiter), Paddy Browne (Singer).

Veidt is a Danish merchant captain who gets involved with a beautful agent. With the help of a group of waiters, they nab a gang of spies. Good suspense yarn with Veidt at the top of his form. Powell went on to direct THE RED SHOES. This was Deborah Kerr's first feature film; unfortunately, she was left on the cutting room floor as her scenes were deleted from the final print. No matter, she went on to score a huge success in MAJOR BARBARA (1941).

p, John Corfield; d, Michael Powell; w, Powell, Brock Williams (based on a story by Emeric Pressburger); ph, Frederick Young.

Drama **(PR:A MPAA:NR)**

BLACKOUT* 1/2 (1950, Brit.) 73m Tempean/Eros bw

Maxwell Reed *(Chris Pelley)*, Dinah Sheridan *(Patricia Dale)*, Patric Doonan *(Chalky)*, Eric Pohlmann *(Otto)*, Annette Simmonds *(Lila Drew)*, Kynaston Reeves *(Dale)*, Michael Brennan *(Mickey)*.

Once-blind man, having recovered his sight, stumbles upon girl's "once-dead" brother alive and well and running a smuggling gang. Contrived melodrama has little to offer in suspense.

p, Robert Blake, Monty Berman; d, Robert S. Baker; w, Baker, John Gilling; ph, Berman.

Crime **(PR:A MPAA:NR)**

BLACKOUT* 1/2
(1954, Brit.) 87m Hammer/Lippert bw (GB: MURDER BY PROXY)

Dane Clark *(Casey Morrow)*, Belinda Lee *(Phyllis Brunner)*, Betty Ann Davies *(Alicia Brunner)*, Eleanor Summerfield *(Maggie Doone)*, Andrew Osborn *(Lance Gorden)*, Harold Lang *(Travis)*, Jill Melford *(Miss Nardis)*, Alvis Maben *(Lita Huntley)*, Michael Golden *(Inspector Johnson)*, Alfie Bass *(Ernie)*.

Clark is a man who wakes up with blood on his clothes and booze on his breath and has no idea what happened. He then loses his bride-to-be (Lee), learns that his father-in-law is dead, and one complication piles onto another until the whole thing is a mish-mash and you no longer care. Landau, a good writer who, years later, supplied the idea for THE BLACK HOLE (with Bob Barbash), fails to adapt the Nielsen novel with the required simplicity. It's extremely convoluted and no one knows what's going on, least of all the viewer. They should have given the script assignment to the assistant director, Sangster, who distinguished himself with a host of film and TV credits as a writer, producer, and director (THE NANNY, THE MUMMY, FEAR IN THE NIGHT) in the mystery and horror fields in later years. Also wasted was comedian Bass (LAVENDER HILL MOB, A KID FOR TWO FARTHINGS, many more) in a role that gave him no chance to show his abilities.

p, Michael Carreras; d, Terence Fisher; w, Richard Landau (based on the novel by Helen Neilsen); ph, Jimmy Harvey; m, Ivor Slaney; ed, Maurice Roots; art d, Jim Elder Wills.

Mystery **(PR:A-C MPAA:NR)**

BLACKOUT** (1978, Fr./Can.) 89m New World/Cinepix c

Jim Mitchum *(Dan)*, Robert Carradine *(Christie)*, Belinda Montgomery *(Annie)*, June Allyson *(Mrs. Grant)*, Jean-Pierre Aumont *(Henry Lee)*, Ray Milland *(Mr. Stafford)*.

This is the scary version of WHERE WERE YOU WHEN THE LIGHTS WENT OUT. Mix in a bit of THE ANDERSON TAPES and you have BLACKOUT. Four nuts take over a posh Manhattan apartment building on the night when the NYC electricity fizzled. They pillage and sack the place, apartment by apartment, until stopped by police. Low-budget meller that has some very good photography, a lean script, and cameos by well-known actors. You won't remember much of the picture because you've seen it all in one form or another. June Allyson, Aumont and Milland are all excellent; Jim Mitchum is particularly strong in his role.

p, Nicole Boisvert, Eddy Matalon, John Dunning; d, Matalon; w, John Saxon; ph, J. J. Tarbes; m, Didier Vasseur; ed, Debbie Karen.

Crime Drama **(PR:A-C MPAA:NR)**

BLACKWELL'S ISLAND 1/2** (1939) 71m WB bw

John Garfield *(Tim Haydon)*, Rosemary Lane *(Sunny Walsh)*, Dick Purcell *(Terry Walsh)*, Victor Jory *(Thomas McNair)*, Stanley Fields *(Bull Bransom)*, Morgan Conway *(Steve Cardigan)*, Granville Bates *(Warden Stuart Granger)*, Anthony Averill *(Brower)*, Peggy Shannon *(Pearl Murray)*, Charley Foy *(Benny)*, Norman Willis *(Mike Garth)*, Joe Cunningham *(Rawden)*.

Garfield is the tough investigative reporter who makes a crusade of exposing and sending to prison big-time mobster Fields. Once Fields is there, however, Garfield hears that the powerful hood has set himself up as king of the cell block by using his influence with politicians and the warden. Outraged, the reporter gets himself thrown into prison to gather first-hand information and expose the corrupt dealings. Fields discovers his presence and trys to kill Garfield, but the reporter escapes and blows the whistle on the whole crooked operation. There is a very funny bit where Garfield is purposely given prison clothes too large for him, an identical scene occurring years earlier with Spencer Tracy in 20,000 YEARS IN SING SING. Warners was never a studio to throw away a good bit if one more guffaw could be squeezed out of it. A definite quickie for Garfield, who is good in the film, but by this point in his career he had proved himself to be capable of starring in better pictures. The script idea was based on actual prison conditions at New York's Welfare Island in 1934.

d, William McGann; w, Crane Wilbur (based on a story by Wilbur and Lee Katz); ph, Sid Hickox; ed, Doug Gould; md, Leo F. Forbstein; ph, Sid Hickox.

Crime **(PR:A MPAA:NR)**

BLACULA*** (1972) 92m AIP c

William Marshall *(Blacula)*, Vonette McGee *(Tina)*, Denise Nicholas *(Michelle)*, Thalmus Rasulala *(Gordon Thomas)*, Gordon Pinsent *(Lt. Peters)*, Charles McCauley *(Dracula)*, Emily Yancy *(Nancy)*, Lance Taylor Sr. *(Swenson)*, Ted Harris *(Bobby)*, Rick Metzler *(Billy)*, Jitu Cumbuka *(Skillet)*, Logan Field *(Barnes)*, Ketty Lester *(Juanita)*, Elisha Cook, Jr. *(Sam)*, Eric Brotherson *(Real Estate Agent)*.

One of the best blacksploitation films ever made. Marshall is outstanding in this subtle tongue-in-cheek version of the vampire legend. Action begins in the eighteenth century where an African prince, Marshall, is visiting Transylvania. There he is attacked by Count Dracula and made into one of the undead. Two hundred years later we pick up the story in Los Angeles where a couple of interior designers have bought the contents of Castle Dracula, including Marshall's coffin. Soon Blacula is romping around L.A. biting necks and chasing after McGee whom he thinks to be his reincarnated wife. Enter black doctor Rasulala who thinks he has a vampire on his hands and has a hard time convincing police lieutenant Pinsent that this is the case. Creative script and direction and a superb performance by Marshall make this an enjoyable outing. (Sequel: SCREAM, BLACULA, SCREAM)

p, Joseph T. Narr; d, William Crain; w, Joan Torres, Raymond Koenig; ph, John Stevens (Movielab Color); m, Gene Page; ed, Allan Jacobs; art d, Walter Herndon; m/l, Wally Holmes.

Horror **Cas.** **(PR:O MPAA:PG)**

BLADE** (1973) 90m Joseph Green/Pintoff c

John Marley *(Blade)*, Jon Cypher *(Peterson)*, Kathryn Walker *(Maggie)*, William Prince *(Powers)*, Michael McGuire *(Quincy)*, Joe Santos *(Spinelli)*, John Schuck *(Reardon)*, Peter White *(Freund)*, Keene Curtis *(Steiner)*, Karen Machon *(Connors)*, Raina Barrett *(Novak)*, Ted Lange *(Watson)*, Marshall Efron *(Fat Man)*, Arthur French *(Sanchez)*, Steve Landesberg *(DeBaum)*, James Cook *(Kaminsky)*, Jeanne Lange *(Melinda)*, Michael Pendrey *(Bentley)*, Vince Cannon *(Morgan)*, Fredrick Rolf *(Examiner)*, Hugh Hurd *(Attorney)*, Eddie Lawrence *(Producer)*.

Marley stars as a middle-aged detective who is trying to solve the murder of the daughter of an old nemesis, Prince, who is now a powerful, conservative politician. On the twisted, confusing, and bloody investigation trail, Marley encounters the man's uptight wife, his young son who hangs out with a bad crowd, and an angry black militant whose importance to the story is never fully explained. The field narrows to the suspect's brother who has become intent on eliminating all the obstacles from his sibling's political path, including his liberal, drug-taking daughter. The script is frustratingly oblique and meanders from situation to situation punctuated by some moments of graphic bloodletting. The cast of New York stage performers does the best it can to keep things from totally falling apart.

p, George Manasse; d, Ernest Pintoff; w, Pintoff, Jeff Lieberman; ph, David Hoffman (Eastmancolor); m, John Cacavas; ed, David Ray.

Mystery **Cas.** **(PR:O MPAA:R)**

BLADE RUNNER***** (1982) 114m WB c

Harrison Ford *(Deckard)*, Rutger Hauer *(Roy Batty)*, Sean Young *(Rachael)*, Edward James Olmos *(Gaff)*, M. Emmet Walsh *(Bryant)*, Daryl Hannah *(Pris)*, William Sanderson *(Sebastian)*, Brion James *(Leon)*, Joe Turkel *(Tyrell)*, Joanna Cassidy *(Zhora)*, James Hong *(Chew)*, Morgan Paull *(Holden)*, Kevin Thompson *(Bear)*, John Edward Allen *(Kaiser)*, Hy Pyke *(Taffey Lewis)*, Kimiro Hiroshige *(Cambodian Woman)*, Robert Okazaki *(Sushi Master)*, Caroly DeMirjian *(Sales Woman)*, Kelly Hine *(Showgirl)*, Thomas Hutchinson, Charles Knapp *(Bartenders)*, Rose Mascari, Sharon Hesky *(Bar Patrons)*, Steve Pope, Hiro Okazaki, Robert Reiter *(Policemen)*.

A futuristic, often terrifying film which has already become a *film noir* classic. Its $27 million price tag shows in astonishing sets of 21st-century Los Angeles where rain, mist, and fog swirl about titanic structures built upon the ruins of the city, mammoth space machines lumber about promoting the good life on other planets. Earth is in decay physically and psychologically; the best of the human race has departed for greener space pastures and only the dregs are left. Ford, a disobedient cop, is assigned to track down a group of killer androids known as "replicants" who have mutinied on a space colony and returned to Earth seeking to prolong their short life span by altering their programmed mechanisms through their sadistic scientific creator, Turkel. Rutger Hauer, as the superhuman replicant leader, is magnificent, but the film suffers at times from too much gore. (Definitely not for young viewers.)

p, Michael Deeley; d, Ridley Scott; w, Hampton Fancher, David Peoples (based on the novel *Do Androids Dream of Electric Sheep?* by Philip K. Dick); ph, Jordan Cronenweth (Panavision, Technicolor); m, Vangelis; ed, Terry Rawlings; art d, David Snyder; set d, Lawrence G. Paul; cos, Charles Knode, Michael Kaplan; spec eff, Douglas Trumbull.

Science Fiction/Crime **Cas.** **(PR:O MPAA:R)**

BLADES OF THE MUSKETEERS* 1/2 (1953) 54m Howco bw

Robert Clarke *(D'Artagnan)*, John Hubbard *(Athos)*, Mel Archer *(Porthos)*, Keith Richards *(Aramis)*, Paul Cavanagh *(Richelieu)*, Don Beddoe *(King Louis)*, Marjorie Lord *(Queen Anne)*, Lyn Thomas *(Constance)*, Kristine Miller *(Lady De Winter)*, Charles Lang *(Buckingham)*, Pete Mamakos *(Rochefort)*, James Craven *(De Treville)*, Byron Foulger *(Du Verges)*, Hank Patterson *(Fisherman)*.

Originally produced by Hal Roach, Jr., to be shown as an hour-long television show, BLADES OF MUSKETEERS presents strictly standard swashbuckler cliches. Based very loosely on Dumas' *Three Musketeers* characters, the usual horseplay, duels, romance, and court intrigues take place with monotonous regularity. Surprisingly, the film was directed by the famed low-budget western master Boetticher.

p, Hal Roach Jr.; d, Budd Boetticher; w, Roy Hamilton (based on *Three Musketeers* by Alexander Dumas); ph, Benjamin Kline; ed, Herb Smith.

Adventure **(PR:A MPAA:NR)**

BLAME THE WOMAN*1/2

(1932, Brit.) 66m Principal/Hakim bw (GB: DIAMOND CUT DIAMOND)

Adolphe Menjou (Dan Macqueen), Claude Allister (Jos Fragson), Benita Hume (Marda Blackett), Kenneth Kove (Reggie Dean), Desmond Jeans (Blackett), G. D. Manetta (Head Waiter), Roland Gillette (Cloak Room Attendant), Toni Bruce (Miss Loftus), Shayle Gardner (Spellman).

Totally vapid Menjou outing where Menjou and Allister play two crooks who have had to flee San Francisco due to the latter's problems with the ladies. The tables are turned when both the crooks end up on the rock pile after Menjou has let himself be conned into doing the dirty work on a jewel robbery by a clever con woman. Mediocre script and lackluster direction keep this effort from being as entertaining as it should be.

p, Eric Hakim; d, Fred Niblo; w, Viscount Castlerosse.

Crime   **(PR:A   MPAA:NR)**

BLANCHE**

(1971, Fr.) 90m Telepresse/France Abel & Charton c

Ligia Brancie (Blanche), Michel Simon (Chatelain), Jacques Perrin (Page), Georges Wilson (King), Lawrence Trimble (Nicola).

Medieval melodrama which is the second live-action feature film directed by famed Polish animator Walerian Borowczyk. Story concerns the young and innocent Brancie who is married to old nobleman Simon. Simon's son, Trimble, is in love with his young stepmother but keeps it to himself until a king, Wilson, and his wily page, Perrin, arrive. The page and the king have carnal designs on Brancie, but the stepson jealously guards her bedroom door at night, armed with a dagger. The king sneaks to the lady's room disguised in his page's robes, only to be attacked and wounded in the hand by Trimble. The loyal page cuts himself in the hand to clear the king of any suspicion. Soon after, the king sends Perrin out of the castle to deliver a message. While on his journey he is confronted by Trimble who forces a duel that ends in a stalemate. Perrin reads the note that he is to deliver and learns that the castle is about to be attacked. Together the two return to find the elderly Simon in a rage over the sexual intrigue going on under his roof and the page hides in fear in Brancie's room. Simon discovers him, accuses his innocent wife of infidelity, and drags the page out and begins to have him holed up in a wall alive. The king frees his page, who gets into another duel with Trimble. This time Trimble loses the contest and is killed. Brancie commits suicide, the page is dragged to his death by a horse, and the whole messy, complicated affair comes to an end. The production values are first rate, the material is given the proper treatment, but unless you enjoy this kind of brutal movie, you'll find it extremely overblown.

d&w, Walerian Borowczyk; ph, Andre Dubreuil (Eastmancolor); ed, Charles Bretoneiche; art d, Jacques D'Ovidio.

Historical Drama   **(PR:C   MPAA:NR)**

BLANCHE FURY**1/2

(1948, Brit.) 95m UNIV c

Stewart Granger (Philip Thorn), Valerie Hobson (Blanche Fury), Walter Fitzgerald (Simon Fury), Michael Gough (Lawrence Fury), Maurice Denham (Maj. Frazer), Sybilla Binder (Louisa), Edward Lexy (Col. Jenkins), Allan Jeayes (Wetherby), Suzanne Gibbs (Lavinia Fury), Ernest Jay (Calamy), George Woodbridge (Aimes), Arthur Wontner (Lord Rudford), Amy Veness (Mrs. Winterbourne), M. E. Clifton-James (Prison Governor).

A murder mystery based on the Rush Murder Case in the 1800s. This is a film noir, but in color, as director Allegret uses his camera as a palette in this expensive but shallow exercise. Hobson is a governess who marries a wealthy man, then arranges to have the husband knocked off with the help of the young man who takes care of the horses, Granger. There is no one to root for in this picture and the only sympathetic person is the victim. (Hobson was married to Havelock-Allan at the time but divorced him and then married politician John Profumo, who was the central figure in the Christine Keeler case—orgies, hookers, the lot—which brought down the British cabinet in 1963; Valerie never wavered in her loyalty to her husband during the travails.)

p, Anthony Havelock-Allan; d, Marc Allegret; w, Audrey Erskine Lindop, Hugh Mills, Cecil McGivern (based on the novel by Joseph Shearing); ph, Guy Green, Geoffrey Unsworth (Technicolor); m, Clifton Parker; ed, Jack Harris.

Crime Drama   **(PR:A-C   MPAA:NR)**

BLARNEY KISS*1/2

(1933, Brit.) 80m British & Dominion bw (GB: BLARNEY STONE, THE)

Tom Walls (Tim Fitzgerald), Anne Grey (Lady Anne Cranton), Robert Douglas (Lord Breethorpe), W. G. Fay, J. A. O'Rourke, George Barrett, Robert Horton, Haidee Wright, Dorothy Tetley, Zoe Palmer.

Trite poor-Irish-boy-makes-good-in-London tale directed by and starring Walls as a young Irishman who finds himself down and out in the big city. There he stumbles across a young lord having a drunken argument with a cab driver concerning his fare. Walls intervenes and settles the disagreement, much to the delight of the lord who takes the plucky Irishman on as a partner in his new firm. The business prospers and soon Walls falls in love with the lord's sister. Suddenly his happiness is shattered when he is accused of falsifying the company's accounts. In reality, the young lord had gambled away the money and Walls, out of love for his crooked partner's sister, takes the rap for the rascal. While Walls is in prison, the lord writes a note exonerating the Irishman and commits suicide, leaving the couple to marry.

p, Herbert Wilcox; d, Tom Walls; w, A. R. Rawlinson, Lennox Robinson (based on a story by Rawlinson).

Drama   **(PR:A   MPAA:NR)**

BLAST OF SILENCE**1/2

(1961) 77m Crown-Enright/UNIV bw

Allen Baron (Frank Bono), Molly McArthur (Lorrie), Larry Tucker (Big Ralph), Peter Clume (Troiano), Danny Meehan (Petey), Milda Memonas (Troiano's Girl), Dean Sheldon (Nightclub Singer), Charles Creasap (Contact Man), Bill DePrato (Sailor), Erich Kollmar (Bellhop), Ruth Kaner (Building Superintendet), Gil Rogers, Joe Bubbico, Jerry Douglas, Ernest Jackson, Bob Taylor (Gangsters), Don Saroyan (Lorrie's Boy Friend), Jeri Sopaner (Waiter), Mel Sponder (Drummer), Betty Kovac (Troiano's Wife).

Reviews for this film ranged from "pretentious" to "better luck next time" but we've al ways felt it was one of the better New York low-budget films. Baron, who also wrote and directed, is an assassin who has a contract to kill a racketeer. He has to work himself up to the deed and the film follows him as he meets his former sweetheart who tosses him aside, strangles the man who supplies him with the murder weapon, kills the racketeer and eventually gets double-crossed by the hoodlums who hired him. There's lots to recommend this shoestring picture, not the least of which is Baron's acting ability. The man was a triple threat and eventually gave up the typewriter and the makeup in favor of being behind the scenes. He still works often as a TV director. Tucker, who also became what he wasn't in this film, created BOB AND CAROL AND TED AND ALICE and a number of other films with his erstwhile partner, Paul Mazursky, is memorable as the fat man known as Big Ralph. (Tucker has had trouble with his weight all his life and topped the scales at nearly 500 pounds at one time.)

p, Merrill Brody; d&w, Allen Baron; ph, Erich Kollmar; m, Meyer Kupferman; ed, Peggy Lawson.

Crime Drama   **(PR:C   MPAA:NR)**

BLAST-OFF

(SEE: THOSE FANTASTIC FLYING FOOLS, 1967)

BLAZE O' GLORY**1/2

(1930) 78m Sono-Art bw

Eddie Dowling (Eddie Williams), Betty Compson (Helen Williams), Ferdinand Schumann-Heink (Carl Hummel), Frankie Darro (Gene Williams), Henry B. Walthall (Burke), William Davidson (District Attorney), Eddie Conrad (Abie), Frank Sabani (Tony), The Rounders (Themselves).

Strange film attempts to draw light parallels between war and crime in a failed attempt to put soldiers on trial for murder. Whithall recreates his role as counsel for the defense. Musical numbers are laced with ethnicity through flashback sequences where singing and dancing are inserted between battle scenes for relief. Music is snappy. You see, they were all entertainers before the war commenced. Constant return to court-room scenes has Whithall delineating the sacrifice these men have made for their country and why they should not be tried for crimes. Performances standard with singing above par, making this an entertaining venture. Songs include: "Welcome Home," "The Doughboy's Lullaby," "Put a Little Salt on the Bluebird's Tail," and "Wrapped in a Red, Red Rose."

d, Renaud Hoffman, George J. Crone; w, Hoffman, Henry McCarty (based on the story by Thomas Boyd); ph, Harry Jackson; m, James F. Hanley; ed, Arthur Huffsmith; m/l, Eddie Dowling, James Brockman, Ballard MacDonald, Joseph McCarty.

Musical   **(PR:A   MPAA:NR)**

BLAZE OF GLORY*

(1963, Brit.) 57m Argo bw

Gary Cockrell (Johnny de Bois), Geoffrey Toone (Roche), Ljubica Jovil (Yvette), Marian Spencer (Grandmother).

Last words of a dying company commander to the soldier who is trapped with him are that the soldier has shot his own brother. When you're dying, why should anybody else be happy? Trite story, bumbling performances.

p, Jack O. Lamont, David Henley; d, Robert Lynn; w, Paddy Manning O'Brine, Joy Garrison (based on O'Brine's story).

War   **(PR:A   MPAA:NR)**

BLAZE OF NOON**

(1947) 90m PAR bw

Anne Baxter (Lucille Stewart), William Holden (Colin McDonald), William Bendix (Porkie), Sonny Tufts (Roland McDonald), Sterling Hayden (Tad McDonald), Howard Da Silva (Gafferty), Johnny Sands (Keith McDonald), Jean Wallace (Poppy), Edith King (Mrs. Murphy), Lloyd Corrigan (Reverend Polly), Dick Hogan (Sydney), Will Wright (Mr. Thomas).

Four brothers (Holden, Tufts, Hayden, and Sands) begin as stunt men for a traveling air show and wind up carrying mail with veteran Da Silva. It's a tough life and Da Silva tries to explain it's not a job for a guy who wants a family. Holden doesn't heed that and marries Anne Baxter, who can't take the brothers who come along with the marriage, and the suspense of not knowing if her husband will return safely. She goes back to him after a while and Sands is killed while flying. Tufts quits flying, then changes his mind. Hayden has an accident and becomes a flight controller. Holden eventually dies and the film ends as they baptize his son. This might have been a terrific depiction of the early days of flying but it gets bogged down in too much soap opera and not enough aerial sequences. BLAZE OF NOON marked Holden's return to films after serving in the Army. Not auspicious but his fans flocked to see him anyhow. Co-author Sheekman was a most versatile writer whose other credits were as varied as WONDER MAN, MONKEY BUSINESS, ROMAN SCANDALS, SAIGON and many others.

p, Robert Fellows; d, John Farrow; w, Frank Wead, Arthur Sheekman (based on the novel by Ernest K. Gann); ph, William C. Mellor; m, Adolph Deutsch; ed, Sally Forrest; aer ph, Thomas Tutweiler; spec eff, Gordon and Devereux Jennings; chief pilot & aerial unit supervision, Paul Mantz.

Adventure   **(PR:A-C   MPAA:NR)**

BLAZING BARRIERS*   (1937) 65m MON bw

Frank Coghlan, Jr. (Tommy McGrath), Florine McKinney (Joan Martin), Edward Arnold, Jr. (Fats Moody), Irene Franklin (Fleurette), Guy Bates Post (Reginald), Herbert Corthell (Sheriff Martin), Milburn Stone (Joe Waters), Addison Randall (Arthur Forsythe).

Cheerleading propaganda film promoting Roosevelt's Civilian Conservation Corp. (C.C.C.). Coghlan and Arnold play two wayward city boys whose flirtations with a life of crime force a cop to chase them out of town. The pair land in a C.C.C. camp where they learn the values of hard work and good morals. Lengthy segments involving the singing of the C.C.C. marching song and the general Depression era flag-waving make the viewer feel as if a feature-length public service message is being shown.

d, Aubrey Scotto; w, Edwin C. Parsons; ph, Paul Ivano.

Drama   (PR:A MPAA:NR)

BLAZING FOREST, THE**   (1952) 90m PAR c

John Payne (Kelly Hanson), William Demarest (Syd Jessup), Agnes Moorehead (Jessie Crain), Richard Arlen (Joe Morgan), Susan Morrow (Sharon Wilks), Roscoe Ates (Beans), Lynne Roberts (Grace), Ewing Mitchell (Ranger), Walter Reed (Max), Jim Davies, Joey Ray, Joe Garcia, Brett Houston, Max Wagner (Lumberjacks).

John Payne is the tough guy whom Moorehead brings in to supervise the cutting down of the timber. She needs the money so she can give her niece, Morrow, enough money to make it in the big city and get off this boring land. Payne wants to get the job over with soon so he can get his money and go away. Morrow becomes interested in Payne but is turned off when she sees Payne with Roberts, whom she mistakes as a lover. But Roberts is, in fact, John's sister-in-law and married to his brother, Arlen, who has been a bad boy. Payne is working hard so he can pay off Arlen's debts before the police come after the man. There's some derring-do and you just *know* there's going to be a firewhy else call it THE BLAZING FOREST? If you like felling trees, then this is your movie.

p, William H. Pine, William C. Thomas; d, Edward Ludwig; w, Lewis R. Foster, Winston Miller; ph, Lionel Lindon (Technicolor); m, Lucien Cailliet; ed, Howard Smith.

Adventure   (PR:A-C MPAA:NR)

BLAZING FRONTIER*1/2   (1944) 59m PRC bw

Buster Crabbe (Billy The Kid), Al "Fuzzy" St. John (Fuzzy Jones), Marjorie Manners (Helen), Milt Kibbee (Barslow), I. Stanford Jolley (Sharp), Kermit Maynard (Pete), Frank Hagney (Tragg), George Chesebro (Slade), Frank Ellis (Biff).

Another ridiculous saga of Billy the Kid, this time played by FLASH GORDON fave Crabbe. Crabbe and sidekick St. John team up with a bunch of crooked railroad detectives who plan to rob settlers of their land. Do Crabbe and St. John actually share in the ill-gotten proceeds? No, they are really joining the gang to gather evidence against the criminals to smash their ring of conspiracy and deception. Needless to say, history does not show Billy the Kid to have ever been a part-time railroad detective dedicated to preserving the rights of western settlers. (See BILLY THE KID series, Index.)

p, Sigmund Neufeld; d, Sam Newfield; w, Patricia Harper; ph, Robert Cline; ed, Holbrook N. Todd.

Western   Cas.   (PR:A MPAAA:NR)

BLAZING GUNS*1/2   (1943) 53m MON bw

Ken Maynard (Ken), Hoot Gibson (Hoot), Kay Forrester (Betty), LeRoy Mason (Duke Wade), Roy Grant (Jim Wade), Lloyd Ingraham (Governor).

Technically inept Maynard-Gibson vehicle that looks cheaper than usual. Story line has the governor sending his two favorite marshals into a corrupt town to clean it up. Along the way the pair recruit an army of ex-cons to help them on their mission.

p&d, Robert Tansey; w, Frances Kavanaugh; ph, Marcel Le Picard; ed, Fred Bain.

Western   (PR:A MPAA:NR)

BLAZING SADDLES***   (1974) 93m WB c

Cleavon Little (Bart), Gene Wilder (Jim), Slim Pickens (Taggart), David Huddleston (Olson Johnson), Liam Dunn (Reverend Johnson), Alex Karras (Mongo), John Hillerman (Howard Johnson), George Furth (Van Johnson), Mel Brooks (Governor Lepetomane/Indian Chief), Harvey Korman (Hedley Lamarr), Madeline Kahn (Lili Von Shtupp), Dom DeLuise (Buddy Bizarre), Richard Collier (Dr. Sam Johnson), Count Basie (Himself).

The ultimate western spoof filled with inside jokes, toilet humor, several puns (see cast roles) and enough laughs to cover the fact that it is, essentially, a stupid movie. Little is a black sheriff who has been hired so the citizens of the town will panic and sell their land out cheap to speculators who plan a railroad through town. The village turns on Little and he must call on the jail's one con, Gene Wilder, at one time the fastest gun in the west. Madeline Kahn parodies Dietrich (DESTRY) and Dom De Luise parodies himself in every role he's ever played. The last fifteen minutes of the movie may be the biggest cop-out ever shot as they could not come up with a decent ending in the western genre so they opted to jump one hundred years in the future and . . . forget it. What's good is terrific: Karras, Korman, Kahn. Plenty of funny stuff but just as many misfires. The public loved it and it stands as the highest grossing western in film history—$45 million plus! Oscar nominations for Kahn and title song.

p, Michael Hertzberg; d, Mel Brooks; w, Brooks, Norman Steinberg, Andrew Bergman, Richard Pryor, Alan Uger (based on a story by Bergman); ph, Joseph

Biroc (Technicolor); m, John Morris; ed, John C. Howard, Danford Greene; prod d, Peter Wooley; ch, Alan Johnson; cos, N. Novarese; m/l, title song, John Morris, Brooks (sung by Frankie Laine).

Comedy Western   Cas.   (PR:C-O MPAA:R)

BLAZING SIX SHOOTERS**   (1940) 61m COL bw (GB: STOLEN WEALTH)

Charles Starrett (Jeff Douglas), Iris Meredith (Janet Kenyon), Dick Curtis (Lash Bender), Al Bridge (Bert Kargin), George Cleveland (Mark Rawlins), Henry Hall (Dan Kenyon), Bob Nolan (Bob), Stanley Brown (Cassidy), John Tyrell (Savage), Eddie Laughton (Bunyon), Francis Walker (Shorty), Edmund Cobb (Sheriff), Bruce Bennett (Winthrop), The Sons of the Pioneers.

Starrett rides again in this better-than-average horse opera that co-stars Meredith as the cowpoke's perennial sweetheart. Plot concerns the efforts of ambitious hood Curtis, who discovers a silver mine on the dividing line between two ranches, to gain control of the land on both sides of his discovery and hoard the silver for himself. Starrett, of course, is there to stop him. Crisp dialog and competent direction by Lewis keep the pace moving.

d, Joseph H. Lewis; w, Paul Franklin; ph, George Meehan; ed, Richard Fantl; m/l, Bob Noland, Tim Spencer.

Western   (PR:A MPAA:NR)

BLAZING SIXES*   (1937) 58m WB bw

Dick Foran (Red), Helen Valkis (Barbara), Mira McKinney (Aunt Sarah), John Merton (Jim Hess), Glenn Strange (Pewee), Kenneth Harlan (Major), Milton Kibbee (Mort), Gordon Hart (Flank), Harry Otho (Hank), Wilfred Lucas (Oneye).

Another lackluster singing oater starring dull cowboy star Foran as a government agent assigned to stop a rash of gold robberies. To fulfill his mission, the clever cowboy pretends to be an outlaw and joins the gang of crooks to catch them at their own game. Standard western cliches punctuated with the usual forgettable tunes.

d, Noel Smith; w, John T. Neville (story by Anthony Coldeway); ph, Ted McCord; ed, Frederick B. Richards; m/l M. K. Jerome, Jack Scholl.

Western   (PR:A MPAA:NR)

BLAZING SUN, THE**   (1950) 69m COL bw

Gene Autry (Himself), Pat Buttram (Mike), Lynne Roberts (Helen Ellis), Anne Gwynne (Kitty), Edward Norris (Doc Taylor), Kenne Duncan (Al Bartlett), Alan Hale, Jr. (Ben Luber), Gregg Barton (Trot Lucas), Steve Darrell (Sheriff Phillips), Tom London (Tom Ellis), Sandy Sanders (Carl Luber), Frankie Marvin (Deputy Sheriff).

Somewhat strange Autry oater that seems to be set in a time-warp. The standard western story line is normal, but modern devices such as automobiles and shortwave radio transmitters become very important to the plot which would seem to suggest that the action takes place circa 1950 instead of 1880. Plot concerns Autry's efforts to capture two bank robbers who have been working the territory. The film's climax takes place on a runaway train, pitting Autry against villain Duncan, who gets his just desserts. Well-paced and fairly interesting. Autry sings "Along The Navajo Trail" and "Brush Those Tears From Your Eyes." (See GENE AUTRY series, Index.)

p, Armand Schaefer; d, John English; w, Jack Townley; ph, William Bradford; ed, James Sweeney.

Western   (PR:A MPAA:NR)

BLAZING TRAIL, THE*1/2   (1949) 59m COL bw

Charles Starrett (Durango Kid/Steve Allan), Smiley Burnette (Himself), Marjorie Stapp (Janet Masters), Fred Sears (Luke Masters), Steve Darrell (Sam Brady), Jock O'Mahoney (Full House Patterson), Trevor Bardette (Jess Williams), Steve Pendleton (Kirk Brady), Robert Malcolm (Old Mike Brady), John Cason (Colton), Hank Penny, Slim Duncan.

Start humming "Red River Valley'" and you'll be in just the right mood to see THE BLAZING TRAIL. Charles Starrett is the Durango Kid. He is also the Marshal, Steve Allan. When Malcolm, a wealthy old land mogul is killed, the finger points at Darrell and Pendleton, Malcolm's siblings. By the time the film is over, we learn that it's not them at all but the true killer is . . .argh! (That's the usual scene in all these movies; just as you're about to reveal the name of the murderer, a shot rings out.) THE BLAZING TRAIL packs lots of action in an hour, plus has some time for a few funnies by Burnette, as well as a couple of tunes by Hank Penny and Slim Duncan. What more could a person want? (See DURANGO KID series, Index.)

p, Colbert Clark; d, Ray Nazzaro; w, Barry Shipman; ph, Ira H. Morgan; ed, Paul Borofsky.

Western   (PR:A MPAA:NR)

BLEAK MOMENTS**   (1972, Brit.) 110m Contemporary Films c

Anne Raitt (Sylvia), Sarah Stephenson (Hilda), Eric Allan (Peter), Joolia Cappleman (Pat), Mike Bradwell (Norman), Liz Smith (Pat's Mother).

Depressing, but somewhat engrossing, British melodrama starring Raitt as a lonely, overweight, but nonetheless attractive office worker dreaming of a possible marriage to a quiet schoolteacher she has been dating. Raitt lives with her retarded sister, whom she cares for. Her dreams are shattered during an uncomfortable dinner date at a Chinese restaurant, followed by a cold kiss and the revelation that her suitor is impotent. The only bright spot left in her life is a young hippie to whom she's rented out her garage. He runs an underground newspaper and entertains the retarded girl by strumming his guitar and singing the songs that he has written. He too moves on, leaving the women to their bleak existence. Good direction and fine performances keep the pace of this lengthy film moving and help the material from becoming too maudlin and sentimental.

p, Leslie Blair; d&w, Mike Leigh; ph, Bahram Manoochehri (Eastmancolor); ed, Blair; art d, Richard Rambaut; m/l, Mike Bardwell.

Drama (PR:C MPAA:NR)

BLESS 'EM ALL* (1949, Brit.) 79m Advance (Adelphi) bw

Hal Monty (*Skimpy Carter*), Max Bygraves (*Tommy Anderson*), Les Ritchie (*Sgt. Willis*), Stanley White (*Cpl.*), Jack Milroy (*Jock*), Patricia Linova (*Val Willis*), Sibyl Amiel (*Lisette*).

A private and sergeant in France during WW II vie for the attentions of the same girl. Good 1940 atmosphere at Dunkirk but the attempt to imitate WHAT PRICE GLORY falls through.

p&d, Robert Jordan Hill; w, C. Boganny, Hal Monty (based on a story by Aileen Burke, Leone Stuart, Arthur Dent); ph, S. D. Onions.

Comedy (PR:A MPAA:NR)

BLESS THE BEASTS AND CHILDREN* (1971) 109m COL c

Bill Mumy (*Teft*), Barry Robins (*Cotton*), Miles Chapin (*Shecker*), Darel Glaser (*Goodenow*), Bob Kramer (*Lally 1*), Marc Vahanian (*Lally 2*), Jesse White (*Sid Shecker*), Ken Swofford (*Wheaties*), Dave Ketchum (*Camp Director*), Elaine Devry (*Cotton's Mother*), Wayne Sutherlin (*Hustler*), Vanessa Brown (*Goodenow's Mother*), William Bramley (*Goodenow's Stepfather*).

Stanley Kramer can hardly make a movie without some sort of message, although it's somewhat buried in this story of six young men who set out to free a herd of buffalo scheduled to be shot the next day. They see some of the animals slain and are determined to save the remainder. In doing so, they learn something about themselves. All of the boys are "losers" at the private school they attend and thus identify with the fate of the doomed animals. An ensemble piece from start to finish, it's difficult to single out one particular actor for comment, either kind or otherwise. Since none of the boys (except for Mumy) is recognizable, it adds to the believability of the story. Kramer killed no animals for the film but purchased stock footage and shot his sequences around the purchased scenes. Ostensibly in Arizona, much of the movie was made in the lonelier reaches of Santa Catalina Island, in areas never before seen on film. After a series of critical failures, Kramer took his eyepiece and his family and moved to Seattle, Washington. A superb score that was better than the title song (sung by The Carpenters) which garnered an Oscar nomination but lost to the theme from SHAFT.

p&d, Stanley Kramer; w, Mac Benoff (based on the novel by Glendon Swarthout); ph, Michel Hugo (Technicolor); m, Barry De Vorzon, Perry Botkin, Jr.

Children's Drama Cas. (PR:A-C MPAA:PG)

BLESSED EVENT* 1/2** (1932) 82m WB bw

Lee Tracy (*Alvin*), Mary Brian (*Gladys*), Allen Jenkins (*Frankie Wells*), Ruth Donnelly (*Miss Stevens*), George Meeker (*Church*), William Halligan (*Flint*), Walter Miller (*Boldt*), Tom Dugan (*Cooper*), Isabel Jewell (*Dorothy*), Ned Sparks (*Moxley*), Dick Powell (*Harmon*), George Chandler (*Hanson*).

Excellent adaptation of the stage hit, with Tracy as a gossip columnist for a NYC paper who loves the power of the press. Obviously patterned after Walter Winchell, Tracy has the role of his life with some of the sharpest dialog he's ever had to speak. Action switches from light to heavy with nary a moment to breathe. Fast-paced byplay with young Powell as a crooner is followed by a scene where Tracy double-crosses a young chorine. Ned Sparks almost steals the picture with his underplaying of a woman-hating newspaperman. Sparks made more than 60 pictures and his former jobs as a Gold Rush miner, carnival barker, and medicine show man always stood him in good stead. This was Dick Powell's first picture after a brief career as a band singer. Not much was expected of him.

d, Roy Del Ruth; w, Howard J. Green (based on a play by Manuel Seff, Forrest Wilson); ph, Sol Polito; ed, Jim Gibbons.

Comedy (PR:A-C MPAA:NR)

BLIND ADVENTURE* (1933) 65m Radio bw

Robert Armstrong (*Richard Bruce*), Helen Mack (*Rose Thorne*), Roland Young (*Burglar*), Ralph Bellamy (*Jim Steel*), John Miljan (*Regan*), Laura Hope Crews (*Lady Rockingham*), Henry Stephenson (*Major Thorne*), Phyllis Barry (*Gwen*), John Warburton (*Reggie*), Marjorie Gateson (*Mrs. Thorne*), Beryl Mercer (*Chambermaid*), Tyrell Davis (*Gerald Fairfax*), Desmond Roberts (*Harvey*), Charles Irwin (*Bill*), Fred Sullivan (*General*), George K. Arthur (*Inebriated Guest*), Ivan Simpson (*Butler*).

Armstrong is his usual fast-talking self as an American in London who becomes embroiled in the scheme of a gang of kidnapers and extortionists who have acquired some very important papers that may be of international significance. Strong cast of veterans and a quick pace help gloss over some of the more unbelievable aspects of the story line.

d, Ernest B. Schoedsack; w, Ruth Rose; ph, Henry Gerard; m, Max Steiner.

Crime (PR:A MPAA:NR)

BLIND ALIBI* (1938) 62m RKO bw

Richard Dix (*Paul Dover*), Whitney Bourne (*Julia Fraser*), Eduardo Ciannelli (*Mitch*), Frances Mercer (*Ellen Dover*), Paul Guilfoyle (*Taggart*), Richard Lane (*Bowers*), Jack Arnold (*Dick*), Walter Miller (*Maitland*), Frank M. Thomas (*Larcon*), Solly Ward (*Al*), Tommy Bupp (*Freddie*), Ace the Wonder Dog.

Slightly bizarre extortion movie starring Dix as a sculptor living in Paris whose sister is being blackmailed with some steamy love letters she wrote in her youth. Dix retrieves the letters, but they are lost when accidentally shipped to a Los Angeles art museum with a cargo of antiques. The loyal brother travels to L.A. and hatches a clever plan that will give him unlimited access to the musuem. Dix acquires Ace, the

Wonder Dog, and feigns blindness to gain the sympathy of the young assistant curator, Bourne. She allows him to roam around feeling the sculptures so he may copy them in his own art. In reality, this scam gives him enough time to search for the missing letters. Dix and Bourne grow close over the days, but the extortionist in Paris hires a group of thugs to go to the museum and get the letters back. Dix and the dog beat the crooks and everything turns out fine in the end. This was Dix's first film for RKO in two years; his fortunes were declining and he hoped this programmer would put him back on top, which it didn't.

p, Cliff Reid; d, Lew Landers; w, Lionel Houser, Harry Segall, Ron Ferguson (based on a story by William Joyce); ph, Nicholas Musuraca.

Crime/Drama (PR:A MPAA:NR)

BLIND ALLEY* 1/2** (1939) 68m COL bw

Chester Morris (*Hal Wilson*), Ralph Bellamy (*Dr. Shelby*), Ann Dvorak (*Mary*), Joan Perry (*Linda Curtis*), Melville Cooper (*George Curtis*), Rose Stradner (*Doris Shelby*), John Eldredge (*Dick Holbrook*), Ann Doran (*Agnes*), Marc Lawrence (*Buck*), Stanley Brown (*Fred Landis*), Scotty Beckett (*Davy*), Milburn Stone (*Nick*), Marie Blake (*Harriet*).

Chilling psychological drama begins with Morris and other inmates breaking out of prison, then forcing Bellamy, a psychologist, and his family, to put them up while police are hunting for them (shades of THE DESPERATE HOURS). While Morris holds Bellamy's family prisoner, the doctor persuades the convict to undergo analysis, hypnotizing him. While under, Morris recounts his terrible experiences, seen in flashback, a subsconscious recitation which pinpoints Morris' mania for murder. A taut story, great moody lensing by Ballard, and sharp direction from Vidor, along with superlative acting by Morris and Bellamy, earn this *film noir* entry a top spot in the genre. (Remade as THE DARK PAST.)

p, Fred Kohlmar; d, Charles Vidor; w, Phillip MacDonald, Michael Blankfort, Albert Duffy (based on the play by James Warwick); ph, Lucien Ballard; m, Morris Stoloff; ed, Otto Meyer.

Crime Drama (PR:C MPAA:NR)

BLIND CORNER (SEE: MAN IN THE DARK, 1963, Brit.)

BLIND DATE* (1934) 71m COL bw (GB: HER SACRIFICE)

Ann Sothern (*Kitty Taylor*), Neil Hamilton (*Bob Hartwell*), Paul Kelly (*Bill*), Mickey Rooney (*Freddy*), Spencer Charters (*Pa Taylor*), Jane Darwell (*Ma Taylor*), Joan Gale (*Flora*).

Incredibly overblown and maudlin melodrama chronicling the love life of Sothern, the daughter of a ridiculous family. Dad is unemployed and likes to gamble, the smarty-pants younger brother and sister and the overly protective mother are all so predictable it's distracting. Sothern is engaged to Kelly, who runs the local garage. She dumps him and dates the wealthy Hamilton, who gets dumped when he fails to ask for her hand. She returns to Kelly and could kick herself when Hamilton returns to her on bended knee. The unbelievably noble Kelly forces a fight with Sothern to give her an excuse to break off their relationship again so that she can marry the man she really wants. The situation is stretched, cliche-ridden and dull; the Sothern character is petty and unappealing, and the whole movie is just plain lame.

d, Roy William Neill; w, Art Black (based on a story by Vida Hurst, Ethel Hill); ph, Al Seigler.

Drama (PR:A MPAA:NR)

BLIND DATE, 1959 (SEE: CHANCE MEETING, 1959, Brit.)

BLIND DEAD, THE** (1972, Span.) 81m Hallmark c (LA NOCHE DELL TERROR CIEGO, AKA: TOMBS OF THE BLIND DEAD)

Lone Fleming, Cesar Burner.

Blinded by crows for killing women during their weird rituals, a thirteenth-century religious sect returns to wreak havoc on twentieth-century Spain. The local population is terrorized by this group, reincarnated as mummified skeletons galloping through the streets on their horses. Eerie atmospherics, THE BLIND DEAD was a big hit in Europe and spawned three sequels.

p, Salvadore Romero; d&w, Armando De Ossorio.

Horror (PR:O MPAA:R)

BLIND DESIRE* 1/2** (1948, Fr.) 86m Discina International bw (LA PART DE L'OMBRE)

Jean-Louis Barrault (*Michel Kremer*), Edwige Feuillere (*Agnes Noblet*), Jean Wall (*Robert Ancelot*), Raphael Patorni (*Pierre Morin*), Line Noro (*Madame Berthe*), Helene Vervors (*Fanny*), Yves Denlaud (*Auguste*), Jean Yonnel (*Jerome Noblet*).

Barrault plays a violinist-composer who is a musical genius, but cannot find true happiness due to a series of romantic mistakes regarding his true love Feuillere. After a courtship in their youth, the musician breaks off the relationship and the couple do not see each other for ten years. Later when they are reunited, the musician finally decides to commit himself to his love, but his current mistress prevents the union. The two meet again, years later, but their love is thwarted by another jealous lover. Repetitious and boring, the film's musical sequences are well done, but the romance segments are lackluster. (In French; English subtitles.)

p, Michel Safra, Andre Paulve; d, Jean Dellannoy; w, Charles Spaak, Dellannoy; ph, Roger Hubert; m, Georges Auric.

Romance (PR:A MPAA:NR)

BLIND FOLLY*   (1939, Brit.) 78m George Smith/RKO bw

Clifford Mollison (George Bunyard), Lilli Palmer (Valerie), Leslie Perrins (Deverell), William Kendall (Raine), Gus McNaughton (Professor Zozo), Elliott Mason (Aunt Mona), David Horne (Mr. Steel), Gertrude Musgrove (Agnes), Roland Culver (Ford), Anthony Holles (Louis).

Thieves have to rob their own loot when a man inherits a roadhouse where the bandits have hidden their booty. The thieves prove themselves inept and comedy soon takes over.

p, George Smith; d, Reginald Denham; w, H. F. Maltby (based on John Hunter's story); ph, Geoffrey Faithfull.

Comedy   (PR:A MPAA:NR)

BLIND GODDESS, THE**   (1948, Brit.) 88m GFD bw

Eric Portman (Sir John Dearing), Anne Crawford (Lady Brasted), Hugh Williams (Lord Brasted), Michael Dennison (Derek Waterhouse), Nora Swinburne (Lady Dearing), Raymond Lovell (Mr. Mainwaring), Claire Bloom (Mary Dearing), Frank Cellier (Judge), Elspeth Gray (Daphne Dearing), Maurice Denham (Lord Brasted's Butler), Martin Benson (Count Mikla), Martin Miller (Mario), Marcel Poncin (Bertoni), Carl Jaffe (Meyer), Cecil Bevan (Morton).

Adaptation of a stage play written by noted British barrister Sir Patrick Hastings which concerns the efforts of a lord's secretary to have him convicted for diverting public funds for his own use. The lord denies the charges and sues the secretary for libel. Many forged notes, dishonest testimony and stolen documents later, the lord is cleared of the charges. Soon after, the truth comes out and the lord commits suicide rather than face another scandal. Good performances help keep this rather stagy and stiff adaptation moving.

d, Harold French; w, Muriel and Sydney Box (based on the play by Patrick Hastings); ph, Ray Elton, Dudley Lovell; m, Bernard Grun; ed, Gordon Hales.

Drama   (PR:A MPAA:NR)

BLIND JUSTICE**   (1934, Brit.) 73m Real Art bw

Eva Moore (Fluffy), Frank Vosper (Dick Cheriton), John Stuart (John Summers), Geraldine Fitzgerald (Peggy Summers), John Mills (Ralph Summers), Lucy Beaumont (Mrs. Summers), Hay Petrie (Harry), Roger Livesey (Gilbert Jackson), Charles Carson (Dr. Naylor).

Because her brother was shot as a coward, a young girl finds herself the victim of a blackmailer. Lively suspense film with good acting.

p, Julius Hagen; d, Bernard Vorhaus; w, Vera Allinson (based on Arnold Ridley's play "Recipe For Murder"); ph, Sydney Blythe.

Crime Drama   (PR:A MPAA:NR)

BLIND MAN'S BLUFF** (1936, Brit.) 72m Present Day British Fox/Apex bw

Basil Sydney (Dr. Peter Fairfax), Enid Stamp-Taylor (Sylvia Fairfax), Barbara Greene (Vicki Sheridan), James Mason (Stephen Neville), Iris Ashley (Claire), Ian Colin (Philip Stanhope), Wilson Coleman (Dr. Franz Morgenhardt), Warburton Gamble (Tracy), Tuff de Lyle (The Dog).

Blind scientist Sydney's sight is restored during an experiment in his efforts to create an invisibility ray. He returns home but does not tell his philandering wife Stamp-Taylor that his sight has been restored, hoping to use it in his attempt to "catch her in the act" with rival scientist Colin. Sydney confesses his newly regained vision to trustworthy assistant Mason and the two of them foil Colin's plot to steal the invisibility formula and force a quick elopement on Colin and Stamp-Taylor. Mundane mixture of a mad scientist idea tossed into a jealous husband-tramp wife story that gets its spark from its principal players, including a very young and charming James Mason.

d, Albert Parker; w, Cecil Maiden (based on the play "Smoked Glasses" by William Foster and B. Scott-Elder); ph, Stanley Grant; art d, W. Ralph Brinton; ed, Cecil Williamson.

Drama   (PR:AA MPAA:NR)

BLIND MAN'S BLUFF*   (1952, Brit.) 67m Present Day/Apex bw

Zena Marshall (Christine Stevens), Sydney Tafler (Rikki Martin), Anthony Pendrell (Roger Morley), Russell Napier (Stevens), Norman Shelley (Insp. Morley), John le Mesurier (Lefty Jones), Anthony Doonan (Charley), Barbara Shaw (Clare Raven).

Novelist son of an inspector proves he's a chip off the old block by breaking up a crime ring in a boarding house. Amateur sleuthing comparable to the acting.

p, Charles Reynolds; d, Charles Saunders; w, John Gilling; ph, Ted Lloyd.

Crime Drama   (PR:A MPAA:NR)

BLIND MAN'S BLUFF, 1967   (SEE: CAULDRON OF BLOOD, 1967)

BLIND SPOT*   (1932, Brit.) 75m WB-FN bw

Percy Marmont (Holland Janney), Muriel Angelus (Marilyn Janney), Warwick Ward (Hugh Conway), Laura Cowie (Anna Wiltone), Ivor Barnard (Mull), Mary Jerrold (Mrs. Herriott), George Merritt (Insp. Cadbury).

Amnesiac daughter of a gentleman thief falls in love and marries the state's attorney who tried to send Dad up the Thames. Contrived melodrama and weak production produce a yawner.

p, Irving Asher; d, John Daumery; w, Roland Pertwee, John Hastings Turner.

Crime Drama   (PR:A MPAA:NR)

BLIND SPOT*½   (1958, Brit.) 71m BUT bw

Robert Mackenzie (Dan Adams), Delphi Lawrence (Yvonne), Gordon Jackson

(Chalky), Anne Sharp (June), John le Mesurier (Brent), George Pastell (Schrieder), Ernest Clark (Fielding), Ronan O'Casey (Rushford).

U.S. Army officer who was framed by gem smugglers when he was blind regains his sight and tracks the blokes down. A few good turns, including final chase, can't pep up a tired script.

p, Robert Baker, Monty Berman, d, Peter Maxwell; w, Kenneth R. Hayles (based on a story by Robert Baker and John Gilling); ph, Arthur Graham.

Crime Drama   (PR:A MPAA:NR)

BLIND TERROR   (SEE: SEE NO EVIL, 1971, Brit.)

BLINDFOLD*½   (1966) 102m UNIV c

Rock Hudson (Dr. Bartholomew Snow), Claudia Cardinale (Vicky Vincenti), Jack Warden (General Pratt), Guy Stockwell (Fitzpatrick), Brad Dexter (Detective Harrigan), Anne Seymour (Smitty), Alejandro Rey (Arthur Vincenti), Hari Rhodes (Captain Davis), Vito Scotti (Michelangelo Vincenti), Angela Clarke (Lavinia Vincenti), John Megna (Mario Vincenti), Paul Comi (Barker), Ned Glass (Lippy), Mort Mills (Homburg), Jack De Mave (Homburg), Robert Simon (Police Lieutenant).

Brilliant but mentally disturbed scientist Rey is hidden away in a Southern swampland by Army general Warden, fearing that the current mental state of Rey could jeopardize national security. Warden enlists the aid of prominent New York psychologist Hudson who is flown to an airport, blindfolded, and taken to Rey every night in an effort to ease the strain on the scientist's mind. When an international group of spies tries to kidnap Rey, hoping to sell his secrets to the highest bidder, Hudson must blindfold himself and "feel his way" to the swampy hide-out in a last-ditch effort to save the crazed genius. Tongue-in-cheek espionage film that contains more than its fair share of preposterous scenes of derring-do. Nobody seems to take their roles very seriously, especially Hudson, and Cardinale isn't exactly around to capture the intellectual audience.

p, Marvin Schwartz; d, Philip Dunne; w, Dunne, W. H. Menger (based on the novel by Lucille Fletcher); ph, Joseph MacDonald (Panavision, Technicolor); m, Lalo Schifrin; ed, Ted J. Kent.

Spy Drama   (PR:A MPAA:NR)

BLINDMAN*   (1972, Ital.) 105m Abkco/FOX c

Tony Anthony (Blindman), Ringo Starr (Candy), Agneta Eckemyr (Pilar), Lloyd Batista (Domingo), Magda Konopka (Sweet Mama), Raf Baldassarie (Mexican General).

Anthony, a blind sharpshooter with a "seeing-eye" horse (it's supposed to be funny, see?) is hired to deliver 50 mail-order brides to some lonely Texans. On the way he encounters the hyper-active Starr and other Mexican banditos, who steal the women. With the help of his super-intelligent horse, Anthony tracks them down and kills the Mexicans, but the ladies decide to remain south of the border as free and independent spirits. Unbelievably stupid "comic" spaghetti western that screams, gouges, yells, and shoots its jokes out. Anthony, one of the more unappealing lesser Italian stars, spends most of his time making a fool out of himself and then looking at the camera and letting the audience know that he's been very foolish. A complete waste of time, except for those who want to see Starr participate in one of the dumbest career moves in history. Let's hope that his role in this film wasn't a contributing factor in the breakup of the Beatles.

p, Tony Anthony, Saul Swimmer; d, Ferdinando Baldi; w, Vincenzo Cerami, Piero Anchisi, Tony Anthony (based on a story by Anthony); ph, Riccardo Pallotini (Techniscope, Technicolor); m, Stelvio Cipriani; ed, Roberto Perpignani; art d, Gastoni Carsetti.

Western/Comedy   (PR:O MPAA:R)

BLISS OF MRS. BLOSSOM, THE***½   (1968, Brit.) 93m PAR c

Shirley MacLaine (Harriet Blossom), Richard Attenborough (Robert Blossom), James Booth (Ambrose Tuttle), Freddie Jones (Detective Sergeant Dylan), William Rushton (Dylan's Assistant), Bob Monkhouse (Dr. Taylor), Patricia Routledge (Miss Reece), John Bluthal (Judge).

Attenborough is a bra manufacturer who thinks that his search for the perfect brassiere will result in everlasting world peace. He spends his off-hours listening to classical music and conducting said recorded orchestras, as though his flailing arms could make a difference. MacLaine is his wife and she contents herself with sitting at the sewing machine until that machine breaks down. Attenborough sends one of his men home to repair it (Booth) and he and Shirley get on so well that she installs him as her lover in the attic! Scotland Yard starts looking for the man as he happily sits in his attic studying various self-help books and making the small area into a decorator's showplace. Meanwhile, Attenborough is plagued by thumps and bumps from above, none of which MacLaine claims to hear. Attenborough is eventually hospitalized for nervous exhaustion and Booth, who has read so much about the stock market that he is now an expert, passes on tips to MacLaine, who gives them to her husband and he promptly amasses a fortune. A few more twists until Attenborough finally learns the truth about his wife, announces his intention to divorce and to return to his music. He gives his bra factory to Booth as a wedding present. The end offers a startling machination we will not reveal. Freddie Jones as a gay cop and Bob Monkhouse, longtime British TV star, as a psychiatrist, add to the fun.

p, Josef Shaftel; d, Joseph McGrath; w, Alec Coppel, Denis Norden; ph, Geoffrey Unsworth; m, Riz Ortolani; ed, Ralph Sheldon; art d, George Lack, Bill Alexander; cos, Jocelyn Richards; makeup, Trevor Crole-Rees.

Comedy   (PR:C MPAA:NR)

BLITHE SPIRIT*****   (1945, Brit.) 96m Cineguild/Two Cities c

Rex Harrison (Charles Condomine), Constance Cummings (Ruth Condomine), Kay Hammond (Elvira), Margaret Rutherford (Madame Arcati), Hugh Wakefield (Dr. Bradman), Joyce Carey (Mrs. Bradman), Jacqueline Clark (Edith).

A delightful, sparkling fantasy from that wry satirist Coward, BLITHE SPIRIT radiates sophisticated wit and non-stop humor. Harrison is a novelist researching spiritualism for a new book, consulting a dinner guest and medium, Rutherford, for information. She conducts a seance and, acting as a "control," Rutherford conjures up the spirit of Harrison's first wife, Kay Hammond, who has been dead for some time. Hammond, once summoned from the beyond, refuses to return, insisting upon staying with her earth-bound husband, mostly to vex him for past transgressions. Only Harrison can see and hear Hammond and when he conducts wild conversations with her, his present wife, Cummings, begins to believe that he is going crazy or has become a secret alcoholic. Hammond is a playful ghost, pulling pranks on second wife Cummings out of other-world jealousy, annoying distractions Cummings attributes to her unbalanced husband. Harrison, beside himself, implores medium Rutherford to send Hammond back to the ghost world but try as she may, using every spell and incantation known to spiritualists, the eccentric Rutherford cannot shed Harrison of his visions. Hammond's jealousy of Cummings leads her to fix the brakes on Harrison's car so that he will be killed and join her in the spirit world where she can have him all to herself. The plan backfires. It is Cummings who takes the car and is killed. Now Harrison's problems double when the ghosts of both wives begin haunting him night and day. Rutherford is helpless to deal with the nagging ghosts but makes one last superhuman effort to rid Harrison of his nagging apparitions. It appears to work. Harrison sees no ghosts, hears no voices. He anxiously asks Rutherford if her spell will hold. The grand old medium tosses her serape about her shoulders, gathers up her old-fashioned skirts, juts her jaw in his direction and replies: "Quien sabe?" ("Who knows?") She departs with an apprehensive look around Harrison's large country house. Moments later doors open by themselves, wind blows through the rooms. The ectoplasmic wives are back. There is no escape. Harrison smiles; he'll outfox them. He'll travel around the world, write his books in foreign lands. He'll even marry again, he tells the hovering spirits, to a real live woman. He packs his bags, gets into his car, forgetting that it has been tampered with, and promptly crashes. Cummings and Hammond sit atop a garden wall, watching delightedly as Harrison's ghost leaves his body and joins them, decidedly unhappy at the prospect of going through eternity with two wives bickering at his transparent side. The acting by all the principals is a pleasure to behold, Cummings as the bewildered live wife, Hammond (who is all in white, her face and hands also a pasty white, only her lips and fingernails blood red) as the returning ghost, and Harrison, who established his widespread U.S. popularity with this film, is simply superb as the spiritually henpecked husband. Stealing almost every scene she's in, however, is the marvelous Rutherford, flamboyant, outlandish, and unforgettable in a role that will be forever hers; few actresses have ever been handed such a marvelous role and she made the most of it, even though Ruth Gordon, Beatrice Lillie and Mildred Natwick gave it their best in other versions. It is Rutherford who makes the film stay alive while fending off the very much dead. David Lean's direction is meticulously faithful to the play and lenser Neame presents spectacular color and just the right lighting for Coward's playful spirits. Coward himself owed some debt to the ghosts created earlier by American humorist Thorne Smith in his "Topper" novels, but, of course, Coward's plot is unique as is his witty dialog and sharply developed characterizations.

p&w, Noel Coward; d, David Lean; w, Lean, Anthony Havelock-Allan (based on Coward's play); ph, Ronald Neame (Technicolor); m, Richard Addinsell; ed, Jack Harris; md, Muir Mathieson; art d, C. P. Norman.

Fantasy   (PR:A MPAA:NR)

BLOB, THE*1/2   (1958) 85m PAR c

Steve McQueen (Steve), Anita Corseaut (Judy), Earl Rowe (Police Lieutenant), Olin Howlin (Old Man), with Stephen Chase, John Benson, Vince Barbi, Tom Ogen, Julie Cousins, Ralph Roseman, Diane Tabban.

Jack H. Harris, the cheapie producer who went on to make the forgettable MOTHER GOOSE A GO GO, struck it rich with this silly picture that gave McQueen his first starring role after a few supporting jobs in SOMEBODY UP THERE LIKES ME and NEVER LOVE A STRANGER. It's a teenage horror tale as McQueen and Corseaut tell their tiny Pennsylvania town that they've seen this purple goop that's eating people up. Naturally, no one believes them. (If they did, the movie would have been over in ten minutes—not a bad idea, when you come to think of it.) A sequel was made called BEWARE THE BLOB, also known as SON OF BLOB. The title was what brought the people in to see this otherwise undistinguished movie. McQueen plays his role with believability, as he did almost everything in his brief career. Oddest thing about the movie is the title song by Hal David and a 29-year-old composer named Burt Bacharach. It wasn't a bad ditty and got a number of novelty records. (Sequel: BEWARE THE BLOB)

p, Jack H. Harris; d, Irvin S. Yeaworth, Jr.; w, Theodore Simonson, Ruth Phillips (based on an idea by Irvine H. Millgate); ed, Alfred Hillman; ph, Thomas Spalding (DeLuxe Color); m, Jean Yeaworth; m/l, Hal David, Burt Bacharach.

Science Fiction   Cas.   (PR:A-C MPAA:NR)

BLOCK BUSTERS zero   (1944) 60m MON

Leo Gorcey (Muggs), Huntz Hall (Glimpy), Gabriel Dell (Skinny), Billy Benedict (Butch), Jimmy Strand (Danny), Bill Chaney (Tobey), Minerva Urecal (Amelia), Roberta Smith (Jinx), Noah Beery, Sr. (Judge), Harry Langdon (Higgins), Fred Pressel (Jean), Jack Gilman (Batter), Kay Marvis (Irma), Charles Murray, Jr. (Umpire).

Annoying East Side Kids entry has Gorcey, Hall, and the gang teaching a spoiled rich lad the values of democracy by bringing him into their group, pestering him with their inane antics, and driving him batty until he realizes his natural allegiance to other boys. Another bomb from one of the most irritating bunch of teenage males ever created. (See BOWERY BOYS series, Index)

p, Sam Katzman, Jack Dietz; d, Wallace Fox; w, Houston Branch; ph, Marcel Le Picard; ed, Carl Pierson.

Comedy   (PR:A MPAA:NR)

BLOCKADE**   (1928, Brit.) 78m New Era bw (GB: Q-SHIPS)

J. P. Kennedy (Adm. Sims), Roy Travers (Capt. von Haag), Johnny Butt, Philip Hewland, Douglas Herald, Charles Emerald, George Turner, Lionel d'Aragon, Alec Hurley, Terence O'Brien, Hugh Douglas, Val Gielgud, Earl Jellicoe.

Warships disguised to look like merchant vessels surprise and destroy U-boats in the English Channel off Flanders in 1917. Good action in a film that was originally made as a silent with sound and dialog added in 1932.

p, Gordon Craig; d, Geoffrey Barkas, Michael Barringer; w, Michael Barringer; ph, Sydney Blythe.

War   (PR:A MPAA:NR)

BLOCKADE zero   (1929) 70m RKO bw

Anna Q. Nilsson (Bess Maitland/Mona Van Slyke/Caravan), Wallace MacDonald (Vincent), James Bradbury, Sr. (Gwynn), Walter McGrail (Hayden).

Rum-runners in Florida are nabbed by tough female Revenue Agent Nilsson. Nilsson, who also plays one of the smugglers and a society girl, should get some kind of award for over-achievement in a bad movie. Only two scenes have dialog, a fairly standard procedure in the late silent, early sound transition period.

d, George B. Seitz; w, Harvey Thew (based on a story by Louis Sarecky and Harvey Thew); ph, Robert Martin; ed, Archie Marshek.

Crime Drama   (PR:A MPAA:NR)

BLOCKADE***   (1938) 73m UA bw

Madeleine Carroll (Norma), Henry Fonda (Marco), Leo Carrillo (Luis), John Halliday (Andre Gallinet), Vladimir Sokoloff (Basil, Norma's Father), Robert Warwick (General Vallejo), Reginald Denny (Edward Grant), Peter Godfrey (Magician), Katherine de Mille (Cabaret Girl), William B. Davidson (Commandant), Fred Kohler (Pietro), Carlos de Valdez (Major del Rio), Nick Thompson (Beppo), George Houston (Singer), Lupita Tovar (Palm Reader), Rosina Galli (Waitress).

The Spanish Civil War (1936-1939) was so hotly debated in neutral U.S. at the time that Hollywood shunned productions concerning this vital struggle, afraid to alienate either side. Then producer Walter Wanger decided to profile this distant war where an ill-equipped republic stood up to fascism for the first time. Yet Wanger produced a film that was so ambiguous that it is hard to tell where its sympathies really are. Fonda plays a peasant farmer being driven off his land by invading soldiers (adorned in uniforms that were purposely designed to represent no known country). He and his fellow farmers trudge along until Fonda turns to make an impassioned speech: "Stop! Turn back! This valley is ours, it's part of us! We were born here . . . our fathers were, and their fathers before them! Turn back and fight!" With that he becomes a leader of native troops and quickly earns a promotion, being sent to headquarters in what is probably Barcelona which is under blockade. Here he meets Carroll (the British leading lady was no doubt the most beautiful actress of her day and that's saying a lot and risking the wrath of many a fan). She is a reluctant spy for the other side, gathering information so that her loved ones in occupied territory will not be harmed. Both seek shelter in a building that is bombed and are trapped for hours while diggers work their way to them. Fonda, during this lull, describes in hortatory terms what her side is doing to the citizens of Spain, how they are being bombed and starved and slaughtered. He convinces her that his side (whatever that might be) represents that of a free people. Once free she works with him to help bring a much-needed supply ship into the harbor. This is achieved when Carroll sends a misleading message to blockading submarines. At film's end, Fonda addresses the viewer imploringly: "It's murder . . . murder of innocent people. There's no sense to it. The world can stop it. Where's the conscience of the world?" But the world was not moved by Fonda's speech in BLOCKADE (it was one of the actor's least favorite movies). The movie did badly at the box office and was banned in many fascist countries and in others supporting the Axis nations. The film obviously leans to the Loyalist side and condemns Franco's takeover (which he achieved mostly with Italian and German troops and weapons). Fonda and his men wear the traditional Basque berets, and civilian clothes, the basic uniform of Loyalists. The Loyalists were made up of Democrats, Socialists, Communists, and assorted volunteers from all over the world which made up the International Brigades (the American volunteers served in the Abraham Lincoln Brigade). To many right-wing or conservative Americans the Loyalists were Russian-sponsored, nothing more than Bolsheviks, and these groups lobbied against the film. So did the Catholic Church in America, condemning the film from the pulpit. (France had allied itself with the Catholic Church of Spain; here the church was one of the country's largest landowners and had traditionally supported regimes that protected its interests; the Catholic Church in Spain often operated much against the wishes of the Vatican.) Wanger was warned that he faced stiff opposition on BLOCKADE and risked the film being banned abroad. The short-tempered Wanger retorted: "I'm going to release this Spanish picture as is, and if it's banned in Europe, I'll have to take my loss." He did. When scripter Lawson later went before HUAC (he was blacklisted during the witch-hunting McCarthy era), this film was thrown in his face as representative of his leftist tendencies, an ironic charge in that BLOCKADE is so politically obtuse, one wonders what credo Lawson advocated.

p, Walter Wanger; d, William Dieterle; w, John Howard Lawson; ph, Rudy Mate; m, Werner Janssen; ed, Dorothy Spencer; md, Boris Morros; art d, Alexander Toluboff;

spec eff, Russell Lawson, James Basevi; m/l, Ann Ronell, Kurt Weill.

War Drama (PR:A MPAA:NR)

BLOCKHEADS***1/2 (1938) 58m MGM bw

Stan Laurel (Himself), Oliver Hardy (Himself), Patricia Ellis (Mrs. Gilbert), Minna Gombell (Mrs. Hardy), Billy Gilbert (Himself), James Finlayson (Mr. Finn).

Late in their brilliant careers, Stan and Ollie made this delightful comedy that begins with the absurd situation of Laurel guarding his WW I trench for 20 years, simply because nobody ever came back to give him the order to halt. Hardy discovers his old comrade on a return visit to the battlefield and brings Laurel back home to his wife with predictable but awfully funny results. Two of the greatest comic performers who ever lived, Laurel and Hardy easily made the transition from their silent classics to sound films, but their material in most of the sound pictures never equalled their great silents. BLOCKHEADS is an exception, with a few sequences that are among the duo's best. (See LAUREL & HARDY series, Index.)

p, Hal Roach; d, John G. Blystone; w, Charles Rogers, Felix Adler, James Parrott, Harry Langdon, Arnold Belgard; ph, Art Lloyd; ed, Bert Jordan.

Comedy **Cas.** (PR:AAA MPAA:NR)

BLOCKHOUSE, THE** (1974, Brit.) 93m Galactacus/Hemdale c

Peter Sellers (Roquet), Charles Aznavour (Visconti), Per Oscarsson (Lund), Peter Vaughan (Aufret), Jeremy Kemp (Grabinski), Leon Lissek (Kozhek), Nicholas Jones (Kramer), Alfred Lynch (Larshen).

Seven men of different nationalities and backgrounds find themselves trapped in an underground German blockhouse during WW II after bombs seal it. Although the place is well-stocked with food and wine, five of the men die over the six years that they remain enclosed. Based on a frighteningly true story, the film tries to be a character study of men in a terrible, claustrophobic setting, but it never reveals the true nature of the characters or a possible metaphysical reason for their predicament. A worthy idea that sadly goes nowhere.

p, Anthony Rufus Isaacs, Edgar M. Bronfman, Jr.; d, Clive Rees; w, Rees, John Gould (based on the novel by Jean Paul Ciebert); ph, Keith Goddard (Panavision, Eastmancolor); m, Stanley Myers; ed, Peter Gold.

Drama (PR:A MPAA:NR)

BLOND CHEAT* (1938) 87m RKO bw

Cecil Kellaway, Joan Fontaine, Lillian Bond, Derrick de Marney, Cecil Cunningham, Robert Coote, Olaf Hytten, John Sutton, Gerald Hamer, Charles Coleman.

That's enough, break it up and I'll back your show, is the cry of millionaire Kellaway, his bribe for Fontaine to separate aristocratic daughter Bond's romance with prominent wolf de Marney. Director Santley maintains a snail's pace in this comedy.

p, William Sistrom; d, Joseph Santley; w, Charles Kaufman, Paul Yawitz, Viola Brothers Shore, Harry Segall (based on the story by Aladar Lazlo); m/l, "It Must Be Love," David Dwyer, Herman Ruby.

Comedy (PR:A MPAA:NR)

BLONDE ALIBI* (1946) 62m UNIV bw

Martha O'Driscoll (Marian Gale), Tom Neal (Rick Lavery), Donald MacBride (Inspector Carmichael), Robert Armstrong (Williams), Samuel S. Hinds (Professor Slater), Elisha Cook, Jr. (Sam), Peter Whitney (Lt. Melody Haynes), Oliver Blake (Pat Tenny), John Barkes (Louie Carney).

Flyboy Neal is wrongly accused of murder thanks to the circumstantial evidence provided by dim-witted Hinds. Girl friend O'Driscoll then sets out to prove her lover innocent. Mindless whodunit.

p, Ben Pivar; d, Will Jason; w, George Bricker (based on a story by Gordon Kahn); ph, Maury Gertsman; ed, Edward Curtiss.

Mystery/Comedy (PR:A MPAA:NR)

BLONDE BAIT* (1956, U.S./Brit.) 70m Associated Film Distributing Corp. bw

Beverly Michaels (Angela Booth), Jim Davis (Nick Randall), Joan Rice (Cleo), Richard Travis (Kent Foster), Paul Cavanagh (Inspector Hedges), Thora Hird (Granny), Avril Angers (Bessie), Gordon Jackson (Percy), Valeria White (Prison Governor), April Olrich (Marguerite), Ralph Michael (Julian Lord).

In an attempt to find a murderer, Scotland Yard (working with the U.S. State Dept.) allows his girl friend to break out of prison, hoping that the girl will lead them to her killer-lover. U.S.-British co-production contains a few suspenseful moments, but fails to build up the excitement or allow its characters any room for creativity.

p, Anthony Hinds; d, Elmo Williams; w, Richard Landau, Val Guest; ph, Walter Harvey, William Whitley; m, Leonard Salzedo; ed, James Needs.

Crime Drama (PR:A MPAA:NR)

BLONDE BANDIT, THE*1/2 (1950) 60m REP bw

Dorothy Patrick (Gloria Dell), Gerald Mohr (Joe Sapelli), Robert Rockwell (James Deveron), Larry J. Blake (Capt. E. V. Roberts), Charles Cane (Lt. Metzger), Richard Irving (Benny), Argentina Brunetti (Mama Sapelli), Alex Frazer (Winters), Nana Bryant (Mrs. Henley), David Clarke (Lt. O'Connor), Jody Gilbert (Bertha Fannon), Monte Blue (Chief Ramsay), Eve Whitney (Marabelle), Norman Rudd (Gus), Bobby Scott (Mechanic), Bob Wilke (Walker), Philip Van Zandt (Arthur Jerome), Ted Jacques (Bartender), Walter Clinton (Waiter), Eva Novak (Jail Matron), Keith Richards (Detective), Lester Dorr (Ticket Taker), Roy Gordon (Thorndyke).

A pleasant programmer that features Patrick as a sweet young thing who has come West to marry a man. She then learns that the fiance has been married several more times than is usual and is already serving time as a bigamist. She meets Mohr, a bookie, falls in love, and gets involved in a hold-up. She then buckles under legal pressure and turns state's evidence on Mohr but promises she'll wait for him until he finishes his time inside the slammer. Fairly good acting in a story that doesn't go anywhere. Brunetti, who made a lifetime of playing these roles, is effective as Mama Sapelli.

p, Sidney Picker; d, Harry Keller; w, John K. Butler; ph, Ellis W. Carter; ed, Arthur Hilton.

Drama (PR:A-C MPAA:NR)

BLONDE BLACKMAILER* (1955, Brit.) 69m AA bw (GB: STOLEN TIME)

Richard Arlen (Tony Pelassier), Susan Shaw (Carole Carlton), Constance Leigh (Marie), Vincent Ball (Johnson), Andrea Malandrinos (Papa Pelassier), Alathea Siddons (Mama Pelassier), Clive St. George, Patricia Salonika, Reginald Hearne, Howard Lang, John Dunbar, Sidney Bromley, Claudia Carr, Arnold Adrian.

Arlen is released from prison after having served a term for the murder of a female blackmailer, a killing he did not commit. In an uninspired search and discovery, Arlen finally tracks down the man who framed him for the murder. Weak story undoes Arlen's considerable talent.

p,d&w, Charles Deane; ph, Geoffrey Faithfull.

Crime Drama (PR:A MPAA:NR)

BLONDE BOMBSHELL (SEE: BOMBSHELL, 1933)

BLONDE COMET* (1941) 65m PRC bw

Virginia Vale (Beverly Blake), Robert Kent (Jim Flynn), Barney Oldfield (Himself), Vince Barnett (Curly), William Halligan (Cannonball Blake), Joey Ray (Red), Red Knight (Tex), Diana Hughes (Jennie).

Mechanic/inventor Oldfield hires Kent to drive a car that contains his new carburetor hoping that some successful racing will make the gadget famous. Vale, the title driver, wheels her way around the track in order to save her father's failing tire business. The two racing rivals fall in love with each other and both Oldfield and Vale's old man wind up in the black. Very thinly plotted sports drama that makes the unbelievable mistake of casting racing great Oldfield as a simple mechanic.

p, George R. Batchellor; d, William Beaudine; w, Martin Mooney (based on a story by Philip Juergens and Robin Daniels); ph, Mervyn Freeman; ed, Holbrook N. Todd.

Sports Drama (PR:A MPAA:NR)

BLONDE CRAZY*** (1931) 78m Vitaphone/WB bw (GB: LARCENY LANE)

James Cagney (Bert Harris), Joan Blondell (Ann Roberts), Louis Calhern (Dapper Dan Barker), Noel Francis (Helen Wilson), Guy Kibbee (A. Rupert Johnson, Jr.), Ray Milland (Joe Reynolds), Polly Walters (Peggy), Charles Lane (Four-Eyes, the Desk Clerk), William Burress (Colonel Bellock), Peter Erkelenz (Dutch), Maude Eburne (Mrs. Snyder), Walter Percival (Lee), Nat Pendleton (Hank), Russell Hopton (Jerry), Dick Cramer (Cabbie), Wade Boteler (Detective), Ray Cooke, Edward Morgan (Bellhops), Phil Sleeman (Con Artist).

Cagney plays a non-violent con man who lives by his wits instead of the muscle he flexed earlier in THE PUBLIC ENEMY. He is a bellhop who connives to get his girl friend Blondell a job in the hotel's linen room. They next compromise a sucker in the old badger game; Blondell is caught necking with the sucker in a car where Cagney has planted a bottle of booze (then against the law, it being Prohibition). The investigating cop is a plant whom Cagney persuades to leave as he comes upon the scene, later demanding and getting a payoff from the sucker for the favor. Cagney and Blondell next move to the big time, NYC, where the tables are reversed; Calhern fleeces Cagney out of $5,000 belonging to Blondell. In anger, she takes up with another man, straight-laced Milland, marrying him. To vindicate himself, Cagney commits a robbery and is caught and sent to jail. Blondell's marriage fails; when she learns that Cagney has gone to prison trying to recoup her money, she visits him, promising to wait for him. It's a simple story but told with such gusto by director Del Ruth and acted with such verve by Cagney and Blondell that the charm and funny banter delighted audiences who flocked to see this new wisecracking love team. Cagney's delivery was still at an incredible speed and newcomer Milland matched the machinegun-like articulation with his own rapid-fire delivery. It was too much for Del Ruth. In the middle of production, he separated Cagney and Milland and bellowed (according to Milland in his biography, Wide-Eyed In Babylon): "You two remind me of a couple of goddamn woodpeckers. Now, tonight, get together somewhere and go over it so that tomorrow we can understand it. Right now I'm catching one word in four. Good night!" They had it right the next day. The film was a success, paying off well at the box office. Cagney, always a good businessman, advised by his brother Bill, went to Jack Warner after the release of BLONDE CRAZY, and told him the studio realized millions from his recent pictures and that he wanted a raise from his $450-a-week salary. Warner told him no, forget it. Cagney shrugged and walked, the first major star to buck the system, which created a furor in Hollywood. Cagney was still relatively new to the industry but his movies, THE PUBLIC ENEMY, SMART MONEY, and BLONDE CRAZY had made him box office dynamite. Warner knew it and, after public fulminations, capitulated, giving the feisty actor a new contract at $1,000-a-week. Cagney had achieved a major breakthrough for his fellow actors and his walk-out would be duplicated by others, including Bette Davis, as the talent continued to struggle against the traditional greed of the Hollywood producer. Songs: "When Your Lover Has Gone" (E. A. Swan); "Ain't That the Way It Goes" (Roy Turk, Fred Ahlert); "I Can't Write the Words" (Gerald Marks, Buddy Fields), "I'm Just a Fool in Love With You" (Sidney Mitchell, Archie Gottler, George W. Meyer).

d, Roy Del Ruth; w, Kubec Glasmon, John Bright; ph, Sid Hickox; ed, Ralph Dawson; md, Leo Forbstein.

Crime Drama/Romance (PR:A MPAA:NR)

BLONDE DYNAMITE*½   (1950) 66m MON bw

Leo Gorcey (Slip Mahoney), Huntz Hall (Sach), Adele Jergens (Joan Marshall), Gabriel Dell (Gabe Moreno), Harry Lewis (Champ), Murray Alper (Dynamite), Bernard Gorcey (Louie), Jody Gilbert (Sarah), William Benedict (Whitey), David Gorcey (Chuck), John Harmon (Professor), Michael Ross (Samson), Lynn Davies (Verna), Beverlee Crane (Bunny), Karen Randle (Tracy), Stanley Andrews (Mr. Jennings) Constance Purdy (1st Dowager), Florence Auer (2nd Dowager).

Typical Bowery Boys film. Although they were originally known as The Dead End Kids (from the movie DEAD END), legal restrictions and plagiarism charges forced the name change. In BLONDE DYNAMITE, Bernard Gorcey's candy store is transformed into an escort service (they were always changing Louie's place into something!). Dell makes the mistake of letting Jurgens con him out of several thousand dollars that belongs to the bank and now Adele's thug friends move into the escort service so they can tunnel through the building into the bank next door. They stupidly tunnel into the police station instead. (Producer Jan Grippo was well-known around Hollywood as being about the best nonprofessional magician in town and his brother, Jimmy Grippo, had a long magic career in Las Vegas.) (See BOWERY BOYS series, Index.)

p, Jan Grippo; d, William Beaudine; w, Charles Marion; ph, Marcel LePicard; m, Edward Kay; ed, William Austin.

Comedy   (PR:A MPAA:NR)

BLONDE FEVER**   (1944) 60m MGM bw

Philip Dorn (Peter Donay), Mary Astor (Delilah Donay), Felix Bressart (Johnny), Gloria Grahame (Sally Murfin), Marshall Thompson (Freddie Bilson), Curt Bois (Brillon), Elisabeth Risdon (Mrs. Talford), Arthur Walsh (Willie).

Restaurant owner Dorn gets a yearning for pretty waitress Grahame and contemplates leaving his wife, Astor. When Astor exposes the girl as a money-hungry tramp, Dorn wises up and Grahame is forced to leave town with boy friend Thompson. Familiar, uninspired middle-age lust story featuring an early, unrefined performance from Grahame and a very smart, textured one from Astor.

p, William M. Wright; d, Richard Whorf; w, Patricia Coleman (based on a play by Ferenc Molnar); ph, Lester White; ed, George Hively.

Drama   (PR:A MPAA:NR)

BLONDE FOR A DAY*   (1946) 67m PRC bw

Hugh Beaumont (Michael Shayne), Kathryn Adams (Phyllis Hamilton), Cy Kendall (Pete Rafferty), Marjorie Hoshelle (Helen Porter), Richard Fraser (Dilly Smith), Paul Bryar (Tim Rourke), Mauritz Hugo (Brenner), Charles Wilson (Henty), Sonia Sorel (Muriel Bronson), Frank Ferguson (Bronson), Claire Rochelle (Minerva).

Detective Beaumont saves a reporter from certain death at the hands of a bunch of hoods the writer has been exposing in a series of articles. Poor entry in the forgettable Mike Shayne detective series which featured Beaumont and his wife Adams as Shayne's pretty secretary.

p, Sigmund Neufeld; d, Sam Newfield; w, Fred Myton (based on the story "Mike Shayne, Detective" by Brett Halliday); ph, Jack Greenhalgh; ed, Holbrook N. Todd; md, Leo Erdody.

Crime Drama   (PR:A MPAA:NR)

BLONDE FROM BROOKLYN**   (1945) 65m COL bw

Robert Stanton (Dixon Harper), Lynn Merrick (Susan Parker), Thurston Hall ("Colonel" Hubert Farnsworth), Mary Treen (Diane Peabody), Walter Soderling (W. Wilson Wilbur), Arthur Loft (Daniel Frazier), Regina Wallace (Mrs. Frazier), Byron Foulger (Harey), Myrtle Ferguson (Miss Quackenfish), John Kelly (Bartender), Matt Willis (Curtis Rossmore), Eddie Bartell (Rickie Lester).

Ex-GI Stanton, a would-be crooner, meets up with singing New Yorker Merrick in a Southern bar and the two decide to pose as a hick couple in order to get a job with Hall promoting his Dixie brand of coffee. When the girl's assumed name coincides with that of a long-lost plantation heiress, Stanton and Merrick disappear to the bar where they first met, fearing confusion and legal action in the near future. After a few drinks, the two decide to make a second stab at show-biz as a legitimate vocal duo. Rather delightful Dixie comedy with Merrick and Stanton doing a fine job as a romantic but problem-laden couple.

p, Ted Richmond; d, Del Lord; w, Erna Lazarus; ph, Burnett Guffey; ed, Jerome Thoms.

Comedy   (PR:A MPAA:NR)

BLONDE FROM PEKING, THE*½

(1968, Fr.) Films Copernic-Atlas-Clesi Compania/Comacico/PAR c (LE BLONDE DE PEKIN; AKA: PEKING BLONDE)

Mireille Darc (Christine), Claudio Brook (Gandler), Edward G. Robinson (Douglas), Pascale Roberts (Secretary), Francoise Brion (Erika), Joe Warfield (Doctor), Georgia Moll (Ginny), Karl Studer (Hardy), Jean-Jacques Delbo (Olsen), Yves Elliot (Jackson), Valery Inkijinoff, Joseph Warfield (Tiny Young), Aime de March.

Could amnesia victim Darc be the missing ex-mistress of a noted Chinese nuclear scientist? Could she hold secrets that Russia and the U.S. would want to get and the Chinese would want to make sure aren't discovered? Could C.I.A. man Robinson hire out-of-work actor Brook to pose as Darc's husband to probe for information in her unstable mind? Could they fall in love while Brook discovers that Darc has a giant pearl the Chinese government is after, too? Could the mysterious ex-mistress be Darc's sister living in Hong Kong? Could the couple fly there only to see the sister killed in a Russian-Chinese shooting match that sees the pearl fall back into the ocean? Could this be one of the most confusing, idiotic, and unsuspenseful spy films ever made? You bet.

p, Raymond Danon; d, Nicolas Gessner; w, Gessner, Marc Behm, Jacques Vilfrid (based on a novel by James Hadley Chase, You Have Yourself A Deal); ph, Claude Lecomte (Eastmancolor); m, Francois de Roubaix; ed, Jean-Michel Gauthier; art d, Georges Petitot.

Spy Drama   (PR:A MPAA:NR)

BLONDE FROM SINGAPORE, THE*½

(1941) 67m COL bw (GB: HOT PEARLS)

Florence Rice (Mary Brooks), Leif Erickson (Terry Prescott), Gordon Jones (Waffles Billings), Don Beddoe (Sgt. Burns), Alexander D'Arcy (Prince Sali), Adele Rowland (Sultana), Lumsden Hare (Reginald Bevin), Richard Terry (Tada), Emory Parnell (Capt. Nelson).

Erickson and Jones, a couple of flyboys trying to get together enough money to buy their own plane and join the Far East branch of the RAF, decide to smuggle poached pearls. Erickson hides the jewels in the belongings of adventuress Rice and spends the rest of the film trying to get them back, falling in love, of course, while doing so. Likable but empty-headed adventure film from veteran director Dmytryk.

p, Jack Fier; d, Edward Dmytryk; w, George Bricker (based on a story by Houston Branch); ph, L. W. O'Connell; ed, Richard Fantl.

Adventure   (PR:A MPAA:NR)

BLONDE ICE*   (1949) 78m Film Classics bw

Leslie Brooks (Claire), Robert Paige (Les Burns), Walter Sande (Hack Doyle), John Holland (Carl Hanneman), James Griffith (Al Herrick), Russ Vincent (Blackie), Michael Whalen (Mason), Mildred Coles (June), Emory Parnell (Murdock), Rory Mallinson (Benson), Julie Gibson (Mimi), David Leonard (Dr. Klippinger).

Weird tale has disturbed socialite Brooks murdering her husbands and boy friends over the years because she enjoys the scandal and talk in the newspapers. Criminal psychologist Leonard finally worms a confession out of the crazed woman and she accidentally kills herself fleeing from police. Unusually strange, distasteful subject matter for the period is handled with an unsteady hand by director Bernhard.

d, Jack Bernhard; w, Kenneth Gamet (based on a story by Whitman Chambers).

Crime Drama   (PR:C MPAA:NR)

BLONDE IN A WHITE CAR   (SEE: NUDE IN A WHITE CAR, 1960, Fr.)

BLONDE INSPIRATION*½   (1941) 71m MGM bw

John Shelton (Jonathan Briggs), Virginia Grey (Margie Blake), Albert Dekker (Phil Hendricks), Charles Butterworth (Bittsy Conway), Donald Meek (Dusty King), Reginald Owen (Reginald), Alma Kruger (Victoria), Rita Quigley (Regina), Marion Martin (Wanda), George Lessey (C.V. Hutchins).

Western pulp writer Shelton gets into trouble when he tries to churn out more books than his publisher cares to pay for. Simplistic comedy that never finds its niche.

p, B. P. Fineman; d, Busby Berkeley; w, Marion Parsonnet (based on the play "Four Cents a Word" by John Cecil Holm); ph, Sidney Wagner, Oliver T. Marsh; m, Bronislau Kaper; ed, Gene Ruggiero.

Comedy   (PR:A MPAA:NR)

BLONDE NIGHTINGALE*½   (1931, Ger.) 67m UFA bw

Ernst Behmer (Gustav Schubert), Else Elster (Grete, His Daughter), Arthur Heil (Walter Heller), Walter Steiner (Bumke), Erich Kestin (Karl, Waiter), Leopold von Ledebur (Scheffelberg), Berthe Ostyn (Leonie, His Daughter), Siegfried Berisch (Goldstein), Wilhelm Bendow (Paime), Paul Kemp (Hirschfeld).

Hopeful nightclub singer Elster leaves her overbearing agents and gets a position in New York from the Europe-touring American impresario Kemp by just being herself. Light-hearted but forgettable German musical typical of the "backstage" series made at Ufa in the 1930s.

d, Johannes Meyer; w, Walter Wasserman, Walter Schlee; ph, Werner Brandes; md, Willi Schmidt-Gentner, Hans Salter; m/l, Willi Kollo.

Musical   (PR:A MPAA:NR)

BLONDE PICKUP*½   (1955) 81m Globe Roadshows bw

Timothy Farrell, Clare Mortensen, Rita Martinez, Peaches Page.

The mob and the U.S. Senate Crime Commission are both after Farrell, a gym owner who fixes horse races and lady wrestling matches. To complicate his problems, Farrell's got a suitcase full of money when he leaves town. There are some good, if sordid, wrestling scenes. A small, cheap film released by Globe, which was known for its art-house films.

p, George Weiss; d, Robert C. Dertano.

Crime   (PR:A MPAA:NR)

BLONDE RANSOM**   (1945) 66m UNIV bw

Donald Cook (Duke), Virginia Grey (Vicki), Pinky Lee (Pinky), Collette Lyons (Sheba), George Barbier (Uncle William), Jerome Cowan (Larson), George Meeker (Forbes), Ian Wolfe (Oliver), Joe Kirk (Bender), Charles Delaney (McDaily), Frank Reicher (Judge), Bill Davidson (Police Captain), Chester Clute (Clerk).

Nightclub owner Cook, about to lose his place to thugs who cheated him at cards, is bailed out at the last moment by girl friend Grey's understanding and wealthy relatives. Grey and Cook are married and the gangsters are sent walking. Pleasant romantic comedy highlighted by a truly delightful performance from Pinky Lee.

p, Gene Lewis; d, William Beaudine; w, M. Coates Webster (based on a story by Robert T. Shannon); ph, Maury Gertsman; m, Frank Skinner; m/l, Jack Brooks, Norman Berens, Al Sherman.

Comedy   (PR:A MPAA:NR)

BLONDE SAVAGE*   (1947) 62m Ensign/EL bw

Leif Erickson (Steve Blake), Gale Sherwood (Meelah), Veda Ann Borg (Connie Harper), Douglas Dumbrille (Mark Harper), Frank Jenks (Hoppy Owens), Matt Willis (Berger), Ernest Whitman (Tonga), Fay Forrester (Mary Comstock), John Dehner (Joe Comstock), Arthur Foster (Stone), Alex Fraser (George Bennett), Eve Whitney (Clarissa), James Logan (Inspector).

Adventurer Erickson, hired by Dumbrille to scout uncharted African territory, discovers Sherwood, a white jungle princess, living among the natives. Soon enough, Erickson uncovers the secret that Sherwood is the long-lost daughter of Dumbrille's murdered partner. Reworking of the Tarzan stories with a switching of the sexes tossed in for good measure. Poorly made jungle picture that never rises above a dime-novel mentality.

p, Lionel J. Toll; d, S. K. Seeley; w, Gordon Bache; ph, William Sickner; ed, Paul Landres.

Adventure   (PR:A   MPAA:NR)

BLONDE SINNER*   (1956, Brit.) 99m AA bw (GB: YIELD TO THE NIGHT)

Diana Dors (Mary Hilton), Yvonne Mitchell (Macfarlane), Michael Craig (Jim Lancaster), Geoffrey Keen (Chaplain), Olga Lindo (Hill), Mary Mackenzie (Maxwell), Joan Miller (Barker), Marie Ney (Governor), Liam Redmond (Doctor), Marjorie Rhodes (Brandon), Athene Seyler (Miss Bligh), Molly Urquhart (Mason), Harry Locke (Fred Hilton), Michael Ripper (Roy).

Dors on death row whiles away her time recalling the events that led to the murder of the rich mistress of her pianist lover. Maudlin story with an awful performance from British sexpot Dors.

p, Kenneth Harper, d, J. Lee Thompson; w, Joan Henry, John Cresswell (based on the novel Yield To The Night by Joan Henry); ph, Gilbert Taylor; m, Ray Martin.

Crime Drama   (PR:C   MPAA:NR)

BLONDE TROUBLE**   (1937) 67m PAR bw

Eleanore Whitney (Edna Baker), Johnny Downs (Fred Stevens), Lynne Overman (Joe Hart), Terry Walker (Eileen Fletcher), Benny Baker (Maxie Schwartz), William Demarest (Paul Sears), John Patterson (Danny Fox), El Brendel (Window Washer), Barlowe Borland (Goebel), Kittie McHugh (Goldie Foster), Helen Flint (Lucille Sears), Harvey Clark (Waiter), Spec O'Donnell (Fred's Friend), Eddie Davis (Crooner).

Optimistic small-town songwriter Downs moves to the Big Apple, breaks through the prevailing cynicism, falls in love with Whitney, and writes a hit song that catapults him to fame and fortune in Hollywood. Forgettable musical comedy that nonetheless features the high spirits and distinct talents of its young stars to a pleasant degree.

d, George Archainbaud; w, Lillie Hayward (based on the play "June Moon" by Ring Lardner, George S. Kaufman); ph, Henry Sharp; ed, Arthur Schmidt; md, Boris Morros; m/l, Burton Lane, Ralph Freed.

Musical/Comedy   (PR:A   MPAA:NR)

BLONDE VENUS****   (1932) 92m PAR bw

Marlene Dietrich (Helen Faraday), Herbert Marshall (Edward Faraday), Cary Grant (Nick Townsend), Dickie Moore (Johnny Faraday), Francis Sayles (Charlie Blaine), Robert Emmett O'Connor (Dan O'Connor), Gene Morgan (Ben Smith), Rita La Roy (Taxi Belle Hooper), Sidney Toler (Det. Wilson), Morgan Wallace (Dr. Pierce), Evelyn Preer (Lola), Mildred Washington (Black Girl), Gertrude Short (Receptionist), Harold Berquist (Big Fellow), Dewey Robinson (Greek Proprietor), Davison Clark (Night Court Judge/Bartender), Brady Kline (New Orleans Officer), Clifford Dempsey (Judge at Nightclub), Bessie Lyle (Grace), Sterling Holloway (Hitchhiker), Al Bridge (Bouncer), Mary Gordon (Landlady), Cecil Cunningham (Cabaret Owner), Hattie McDaniel (Cora, the Maid), Marcelle Corday (French Maid), Pat Somerset (Companion), Kent Taylor.

Made two years before American censors got out their heavy scissors, BLONDE VENUS, as a Dietrich opus, broadly suggests immorality and perversion in telling the story of a cabaret singer who meets Marshall, talented American chemist. He has fallen in love with her at first sight after seeing her bathe in a pond. He marries Dietrich and they sail for America where they have a son. Marshall slaves away in his laboratory, becoming contaminated by radium poisoning. Dietrich learns that her husband's only chance for a cure is to go to an expensive European clinic. They haven't enough money to pay for this treatment, so Dietrich goes back to work, singing in a posh nightclub. Here she meets Grant, a playboy politician who falls desperately in love with her. At first she is not interested, but then Dietrich invites his advances. When he learns that she is working to support her son (Moore) and pay for her husband's medical treatments, Grant magnanimously sets her up in a swanky penthouse apartment, giving her a great deal of money which she sends to Europe. Cured, Marshall returns from Europe to discover his wife's liaison with Grant. He angrily files for divorce and custody of his son, but Dietrich flees with Moore on an odyssey upon which Von Sternberg dwells too long, more than 30 minutes of film showing Dietrich on the move with her child through Baltimore, Washington, Nashville, Chattanooga, Savannah, and finally New Orleans. There she sinks to the gutter, becoming a common streetwalker to earn enough to support herself and her son. The most dogged detective on her trail, Toler, finds her living in the slums of New Orleans. Not as dedicated as he would later appear as Charlie Chan, Toler offers to forget Dietrich's address if she'll tryst with him. But even she, in her desperate situation, retains some honor and refuses the lecherous gumshoe. Moore is returned to his father and Dietrich is next shown in Paris, where, without any explanation, she has become the rage of the nightclub world. In one of the most outlandish performances of her career, or any other, Dietrich opens the show by appearing before a chorus line in a gorilla suit which she sheds to reveal herself in

a jungle outfit carrying a shield and spear, and wearing a ridiculous blonde wig (you have to see it to believe it), one similar to the hair-on-end topper worn by Elsa Lanchester in BRIDE OF FRANKENSTEIN. She proceeds to moan out a tune called "Hot Voodoo" (Sam Coslow, Ralph Rainer). In the crowd adoring her every movement is Grant, who again strikes up a relationship with her, going with her to America when the show moves to NYC. Dietrich's success means little to her; all she can think about is her son who is denied to her. Grant, feeling guilty for causing Dietrich's marital disaster, sets up a meeting between Marshall and Dietrich, making sure that the cuckolded husband knows why his wife was unfaithful. When learning that it was all a sacrifice for his cure, Marshall begs Dietrich to come back. At first she is disinclined but then returns to her husband and child before the fadeout. The film was the fourth Dietrich did with Von Sternberg; he coddled the aloof star with special lighting, moody shadows and soft focus which accentuated her remarkable, cold beauty. The story itself was made from nothing by the director, Furthman, and Lauren, and would have amounted to only a lowly programmer had it not been for the fascinating talents of its star. Grant and Marshall (this was Marshall's first film for Paramount) have little to do in this Dietrich vehicle except hover about her aura, waiting for her to bestow her favors upon them. Moore is splendid as her pensive child. Von Sternberg also has his star sing "You Little So-and-So" (Coslow, Rainger), and "I Couldn't Be Annoyed," (Leo Robin, Dick Whiting). In the former, Dietrich's stage costume consists of white top hat, tie and tails, a mannish outfit that soon become Dietrich's hallmark. (It was Dietrich and, a little later Katharine Hepburn, who made female slacks popular in the U.S.) At the time Dietrich was being promoted as Garbo's rival and this film is very close to Garbo's SUSAN LENOX, HER FALL AND RISE. It was good-looking hokum, slickly photographed by Glennon, an imaginative technical product where style replaced story.

d, Josef Von Sternberg; w, Jules Furthman, S. K. Lauren (based on a story by Von Sternberg); ph, Bert Glennon; m, Oscar Poteker; art d, Wiard Ihnen; cos, Travis Banton.

Drama   (PR:C-O MPAA:NR)

BLONDES AT WORK*   (1938) 63m WB bw

Glenda Farrell (Torchy Blane), Barton MacLane (Lt. Steve McBride), Tom Kennedy (Gahagan), Rosella Towne (Louise Revelle), Donald Briggs (Maitland Greer), John Ridgely (Regan), Betty Compson (Blanche Revelle), Thomas E. Jackson (Parker), Frank Shannon (Capt. McTavish), Jean Benedict (Salesgirl), Carole Landis (Carol), Suzanne Kaaren (Olive), Theodor Von Eltz (District Attorney), Charles Richman (Judge Wilson), Robert Middlemass (Boylan), Kenneth Harlan (Marvin Spencer), George Guhl (Desk Sergeant), Joe Cunningham (Maxie), Ralph Sanford (Healy), Milton Owen (Fashion Director).

Dim-witted reporter Farrell uses the diary of her cop boy friend's driver as a source of her miraculous scoops, much to the chagrin of the hard-boiled male writers on the staff of her paper. Dumb newspaper drama done with a light touch. (See TORCHY BLANE series, Index.)

d, Frank McDonald; w, Albert DeMond; ph, Warren Lynch; ed, Everett Dodd.

Drama   (PR:A   MPAA:NR)

BLONDES FOR DANGER**   (1938, Brit.) 68m BL bw

Gordon Harker (Alf Huggins), Enid Stamp-Taylor (Valerie), Janet Johnson (Ann Penny), Ivan Brandt (Capt. Berkeley), Percy Parsons (Quentin Hearns), Everley Gregg (Hetty Hopper), Henry Wolston (Doctor), Charles Eaton (Prince Boris).

Easy-going taxi driver Harker gets mixed up in the assassination attempt on a Middle East prince who could destroy a British tycoon's monopolization of the English oil industry. Nicely done suspense tale of international intrigue sparked with generous doses of comedy from the witty Harker.

p, Herbert Wilcox; d, Jack Raymond; w, Gerald Elliott (based on a novel by Evadne Price); ph, Frederick A. Young.

Spy Drama   (PR:A   MPAA:NR)

BLONDIE**1/2   (1938) 68m COL bw

Penny Singleton (Blondie), Arthur Lake (Dagwood), Larry Simms (Baby Dumpling), Gene Lockhart (C. P. Hazlip), Ann Doran (Elsie Hazlip), Jonathan Hale (J. C. Dithers), Gordon Oliver (Chester Franey), Stanley Andrews (Mr. Hicks), Danny Mummert (Alvin), Kathleen Lockhart (Mrs. Miller), Dorothy Moore (Dorothy), Fay Helm (Mrs. Fuddle), Richard Fiske (Nelson), Himself (Daisy), Irving Bacon (Mailman), Ian Wolfe (Judge).

First of the very successful "Blondie" series has harried Lake losing his job on the eve of his and Singleton's fifth anniversary. Not as exaggerated as the comic strip, the series was very simple in its approach to humor and managed to poke some fun at established suburban married-life values. Singleton and Lake, perfectly cast as the infamous husband and wife cartoon characters, bring charm and spontaneity to this film and each entry in the series. (See BLONDIE series, Index.)

p, Frank Sparks; d, Frank R. Strayer; w, Richard Flournoy (based on the comic strip created by Chic Young); ph, Henry Freulich; ed, Gene Havlick.

Comedy   (PR:AA MPAA:NR)

BLONDIE BRINGS UP BABY*1/2   (1939) 67m COL bw

Penny Singleton (Blondie), Arthur Lake (Dagwood), Larry Simms (Baby Dumpling), Himself (Daisy), Danny Mummert (Alvin Fuddle), Jonathan Hale (J. C. Dithers), Robert Middlemass (Abner Cartwright), Olin Howland (Book Agent), Fay Helm (Mrs. Fuddle), Peggy Ann Garner (Melinda Mason), Roy Gordon (Mason), Grace Stafford (Miss White), Helen Jerome Eddy (School Principal), Irving Bacon (Mailman), Robert Sterling (Salesman), Bruce Bennett (Chauffeur), Ian Wolfe (Police Judge).

An early entry in the BLONDIE series with all the standard plot elements: Mr. Dithers harasses Dagwood, Baby Dumpling harasses Blondie, and the dogcatcher harasses Daisy. A salesman convinces Singleton that her son is a juvenile genius, so he's enrolled in a school from which he promptly disappears. Daisy is recovered, Baby is recovered, and the Bumsteads fade out into happy chaos until the next installment. Only average, though Henry Freulich's camera work is particularly nice. (See BLONDIE series, Index)

p, Robert Sparks; d, Frank R. Strayer; w, Gladys Lehman, Richard Flournoy (based on a story by Robert Chapin, Karen de Wolf, Flournoy, and the comic strip created by Chic Young); ph, Henry Freulich; md, Morris Stoloff; ed, Otto Meyer; art d, Lionel Banks.

Comedy   **(PR:AA   MPAA:NR)**

BLONDIE FOR VICTORY* 1/2
(1942) 72m COL bw (GB: TROUBLES THROUGH BILLETS)

Penny Singleton (Blondie), Arthur Lake (Dagwood), Larry Simms (Baby Dumpling), Himself (Daisy), Majelle White (Cookie), Stuart Erwin (Herschel Smith), Jonathan Hale (J. C. Dithers), Danny Mummert (Alvin Fuddle), Danny Gargan (Sergeant). Renie Riano (Miss Clabber), Irving Bacon (Mr. Crumb), Harrison Greene (Mr. Green), Charles Wagenheim (Hoarder), Sylvia Field (Mrs. Williams), Georgia Backus (Mrs. Jones).

Singleton organizes housewives on the home front to guard the local dam, among their duties. Lake and the rest of the husbands don't much care for this patriotic fervor which keeps them at home at night with the kids and the cooking, so Dagwood pretends to join the Army. Singleton realizes where her real duty lies and disbands her Housewives of America in favor of home and family. Good work by entire cast slightly redeems this programmer. (See BLONDIE series, Index)

p, Robert Sparks; d, Frank R. Strayer; w, Karen De Wolf, Connie Lee (based on a story by Fay Kanin, and the comic strip created by Chic Young); ph, Henry Freulich; ed, Al Clark.

Comedy   **(PR:A   MPAA:NR)**

BLONDIE GOES LATIN**   (1941) 70m COL bw (GB: CONGA SWING)

Penny Singleton (Blondie), Arthur Lake (Dagwood), Larry Simms (Baby Dumpling), Himself (Daisy), Ruth Terry (Lovey Nelson), Tito Guizar (Don Rodriguez), Jonathan Hale (J. C. Dithers), Danny Mummert (Alvin Fuddle), Irving Bacon (Mailman), Janet Burston (Little Girl), Kirby Grant (Hal Trent), Joseph King (Captain), Eddie Acuff (Cab Driver), Harry Barris (Musician).

A cruise to South America provides the framework for this one, with Lake sneaking aboard by disguising himself as the drummer for the ship's conga band. Singleton gets a good chance to show off her Broadway origins by singing and dancing her way through several numbers that provide good reason to see another BLONDIE picture. (See BLONDIE series, Index)

p, Robert Sparks; d, Frank R. Strayer; w, Richard Flournoy, Karen De Wolf (based on a story by Quinn Martin, and the comic strip created by Chic Young); ph, Henry Freulich; md, Morris Stoloff; ed, Gene Havlick; m/l, Chet Forrest, Bob Wright.

Comedy   **(PR:AA   MPAA:NR)**

BLONDIE GOES TO COLLEGE* 1/2
(1942) 74m COL bw (GB: BOSS SAID NO)

Penny Singleton (Blondie), Arthur Lake (Dagwood), Larry Simms (Baby Dumpling), Himself (Daisy), Janet Blair (Laura Wadsworth), Jonathan Hale (J. C. Dithers), Danny Mummert (Alvin Fuddle), Larry Parks (Rusty Bryant), Adele Mara (Babs Connelly), Lloyd Bridges (Ben Dixon), Sidney Melton (Mouse Gifford), Andrew Tombes (J. J. Wadsworth), Esther Dale (Mrs. Dill), Bill Goodwin (Announcer).

When a football lands on Lake's lap at a college game, he gets the notion to further his own education. Singleton has her doubts but goes along with him, the pair enrolling as singles and keeping their marriage a secret. Simms is packed off to military school where he soon rises to top sergeant. Lake makes the rowing team and Singleton is hounded by the Big Man on Campus. Of slight significance to fans of the series is the disclosure of an impending second Bumstead child. Series was beginning to lose steam by the time, though it would struggle on for another nine years. (See BLONDIE series, Index)

p, Robert Sparks; d, Frank R. Strayer; w, Lou Breslow (based on a story by Warren Wilson and Clyde Bruckman and the comic strip created by Chic Young); ph, Henry Freulich; md, M. W. Stoloff; ed, Otto Meyer.

Comedy   **(PR:AA   MPAA:NR)**

BLONDIE HAS SERVANT TROUBLE* 1/2   (1940) 69m COL bw

Penny Singleton (Blondie), Arthur Lake (Dagwood), Larry Simms (Baby Dumpling), Himself (Daisy), Danny Mummert (Alvin Fuddle), Jonathan Hale (J. C. Dithers), Arthur Hohl (Eric Vaughn), Esther Dale (Anna Vaughn), Irving Bacon (Mailman), Ray Turner (Horatio Jones), Walter Soderling (Morgan), Fay Helm (Mrs. Fuddle), Murray Alper (Taxi Driver), Eddie Laughton (Photographer).

In order to dispel rumors that a certain unsalable property is haunted, Mr. Dithers (Hale) offers the house to the Bumsteads to live in, complete with creepy servants. Needless to say, strange things happen in the old mansion, with secret panels sliding away to reveal secret passages and the like. The trouble turns out to be the work of the servants, a magician-turned-butler and his wife, who figure that the house is rightfully theirs. Silly fluff. (See BLONDIE series, Index)

p, Robert Sparks; d, Frank R. Strayer; w, Richard Flournoy (based on a story by Albert Duffy and the comic strip created by Chic Young); ph, Henry Freulich; m, Leigh Harline; ed, Gene Havlick.

Comedy   **(PR:AA   MPAA:NR)**

BLONDIE HITS THE JACKPOT* 1/2
(1949) 66m COL bw (GB: HITTING THE JACKPOT)

Penny Singleton (Blondie), Arthur Lake (Dagwood), Larry Simms (Alexander), Marjorie Kent (Cookie), Jerome Cowan (Radcliffe), Lloyd Corrigan (J. B. Hutchins), Danny Mummert (Alvin), James Flavin (Brophy), Dick Wessel (Mailman), Ray Teal (Gus), Himself (Daisy).

BLONDIE HITS THE JACKPOT is the 27th film in the twenty-eight film series and by the time they got to this one, it had been more than 13 years since they began and everyone may have been getting tired. Lake's in a fix again; he's been fired for the umpteenth time and he has to get his job back at all costs. He makes a mistake in a construction deal and winds up on a hard-working labor gang. Not a very good example of the series. Lloyd Corrigan (Hutchins) was better served by the scripts for GHOST BREAKERS, YOUNG TOM EDISON and CYRANO DE BERGERAC. He was also a director and helmed THE BROKEN WING, NIGHT KEY, THE DANCING PIRATE, and many more. Penny Singleton went on to become very involved in the union movement and was eventually president of AGVA (The American Guild Of Variety Artists). (See BLONDIE series, Index)

p, Ted Richmond; d, Edward Bernds; w, Jack Henley (based on the comic strip by Chic Young); ph, Vincent Farrar; m, Mischa Bakaleinikoff; ed, Henry Batista.

Comedy   **(PR:AA   MPAA:NR)**

BLONDIE IN SOCIETY* 1/2   (1941) 77m COL bw (GB: HENPECKED)

Penny Singleton (Blondie), Arthur Lake (Dagwood), Larry Simms (Baby Dumpling), Himself (Daisy), Jonathan Hale (J. C. Dithers), Danny Mummert (Alvin Fuddle), William Frawley (Waldo Pincus), Edgar Kennedy (Doctor), Chick Chandler (Cliff Peters), Irving Bacon (Mailman), Bill Goodwin (Announcer), Garry Owen (Carpenter), Tommy Dixon (Saunders), and Robert Mitchell's Boys Choir.

Dagwood (Lake) gets into trouble when he brings home a pedigreed Great Dane, but soon an important client wants the dog and Singleton enters it in the big dog show. The canine burping display is a high point of this entry in the Bumstead chronicles. (See BLONDIE series, Index)

p, Robert Sparks; d, Frank R. Strayer; w, Karen De Wolf (based on a story by Eleanore Griffin and the comic strip created by Chic Young); ph, Henry Freulich; ed, Charles Nelson; md, M. W. Stoloff; art d, Lionel Banks.

Comedy   **(PR:AA   MPAA:NR)**

BLONDIE IN THE DOUGH*   (1947) 69m COL bw

Penny Singleton (Blondie), Arthur Lake (Dagwood), Larry Simms (Alexander), Marjorie Kent (Cookie), Jerome Cowan (George Radcliffe), Hugh Herbert (Llewellyn Simmons), Clarence Kolb (J. T. Thorpe), Danny Mummert (Alvin), Eddie Acuff (Mailman), Norman Phillips (Ollie), Kernan Cripps (Baxter), Fred Sears (Quinn), Himself (Daisy), Boyd Davis (lst Board Member), Mary Emery (Mrs. Thorpe).

Nine years into the series Lake and Singleton are beginning to show their age. So is the series in this programmer dealing with a sudden windfall for Singleton which creates family trouble. (See BLONDIE series, Index)

d, Abby Berlin; w, Arthur Marx, Jack Henley (based on a story by Jack Marx and the comic strip created by Chic Young); ph, Vincent Farrar; md, Mischa Bakaleinikoff; ed, Henry Batista.

Comedy   **(PR:AA   MPAA:NR)**

BLONDIE JOHNSON* 1/2   (1933) 67m EN bw

Joan Blondell (Blondie Johnson), Chester Morris (Curley Jones), Allen Jenkins (Louie), Claire Dodd (Gladys La Mann), Earle Foxe (Scannell), Mae Busch (Mae), Joseph Cawthorn (Jewelry Store Manager), Sterling Holloway (Red Charley), Olin Howland (Eddie), Arthur Vinton (Max Wagner), Donald Kirke (Joe), Tom Kennedy (Hype), Sam Godfrey (Freddie), Toshia Mori (Lulu).

Laughable gangster film with Blondell as a good girl forced into streetwalking after her mother dies, soon becoming the moll of mobster Morris. After being the impetus for a series of gun battles, she is packed off to the pen, leaving the audience with the stock message that crime doesn't pay. Silly at best.

d, Ray Enright; w, Earl Baldwin (based on a story by Baldwin); ph, Tony Gaudio; ed, George Weeks.

Crime Drama   **(PR:A   MPAA:NR)**

BLONDIE KNOWS BEST* 1/2   (1946) 69m COL bw

Penny Singleton (Blondie), Arthur Lake (Dagwood), Larry Simms (Baby Dumpling), Marjorie Kent (Cookie), Steven Geray (Dr. Schnidt), Jonathan Hale (J. C. Dithers), Shemp Howard (Jim Gray), Jerome Cowan (Charles Peabody), Danny Mummert (Alvin Fuddle), Ludwig Donath (Dr. Titus), Arthur Loft (Conroy), Edwin Cooper (David Armstrong), Jack Rice (Ollie), Alyn Lockwood (Mary), Carol Hughes (Gloria Evans), Kay Mallory (Ruth Evans).

This time Lake impersonates his boss to close a business deal while avoiding a half-blind process server (Shemp Howard). He falls into the hands of a pair of shrinks until the whole family—half a dozen dogs included—come to the rescue. (See BLONDIE series, Index)

p, Burt Kelly; d, Abby Berlin; w, Edward Bernds, Al Martin (based on a story by Bernds and the comic strip created by Chic Young); ph, Phillip Tannura; md, Mischa Bakaleinikoff; ed, Aaron Stell.

Comedy   **(PR:AA   MPAA:NR)**

BLONDIE MEETS THE BOSS* 1/2   (1939) 75m COL bw

Penny Singleton (Blondie), Arthur Lake (Dagwood), Larry Simms (Baby Dumpling), Dorothy Moore (Dot), Jonathan Hale (J. C. Dithers), Don Beddoe (Marvin),

Linda Winters (*Francine*), Danny Mummert (*Alvin*), Stanley Brown (*Ollie*), Joel Dean (*Freddie*), Richard Fiske (*Nelson*), Inez Courtney (*Betty Lou*), Irving Bacon (*Mailman*), James Craig, Robert Sterling.

Second film in the series has Singleton taking over her husband's job while he gets into trouble on a fishing trip. Things resolve themselves as usual. The series was predictable even this early. (See BLONDIE series, Index.)

p, Robert Sparks; d, Frank R. Strayer; w, Richard Flournoy (based on a story by Kay Van Riper and Flournoy and the comic strip created by Chic Young); ph, Henry Freulich; ed, Gene Havlick.

Comedy (PR:AA MPAA:NR)

BLONDIE OF THE FOLLIES**½ (1932) 97m MGM bw

Marion Davies (*Blondie McClune*), Robert Montgomery (*Larry Belmont*), Billie Dove (*Lottie Callahan*), Jimmy Durante (*Jimmy*), James Gleason (*Pa McClune*), ZaSu Pitts (*Gertie*), Sidney Toler (*Pete*), Douglass Dumbrille (*Murchenson*), Sarah Padden (*Ma McClune*), Louise Carter (*Ma Callahan*).

Davies and Dove both came out of the Follies so they were able to play these roles with more than the usual quota of believability. Picture leaves much to be desired, though, as it details the lives of two Follies girls, their loves, their on-again, off-again friendship. Davies produced this movie (but we all know who was behind it, don't we?) and cast herself in the more sympathetic role of the two, no fool she. Both girls chase Montgomery through the film and there's little doubt who will capture him. The highlight of the movie is an all-too-brief appearance by 39-year-old Jimmy Durante who teams with Davies in a devastating satire of Garbo and Barrymore in Ed Goulding's GRAND HOTEL. The rest of the movie pales by comparison. (Montgomery, born Henry Montgomery, Jr., was only 28 and already an established star.)

p, Marion Davies; d, Edmund Goulding; w, Frances Marion, Anita Loos; ph, George Barnes; m, Dr. William Axt; ed, George Hively; art d, Cedric Gibbons; cos, Adrian; m/l, Harry Tobias, Gus Arnheim, Jules Lemaire, Harry Link, Nick Kenny, Ray Egan, Ted Fiorito, Walter Samuels, Leonard Whitcup, Arthur Freed, Harry Barris, Dave Snell, Goulding.

Comedy (PR:A-C MPAA:NR)

BLONDIE ON A BUDGET*½ (1940) 72m COL bw

Penny Singleton (*Blondie*), Arthur Lake (*Dagwood*), Larry Simms (*Baby Dumpling*), Himself (*Daisy*), Rita Hayworth (*Joan Forrester*), Danny Mummert (*Alvin Fuddle*), Don Beddoe (*Marvin Williams*), John Qualen (*Mr. Fuddle*), Fay Helm (*Mrs. Fuddle*), Irving Bacon (*Mailman*), Thurston Hall (*Brice*), William Brisbane (*Theater Manager*), Emory Parnell (*Dempsey*), Willie Best (*Black Boy*), Hal K. Dawson (*Bank Teller*), Chester Clute (*Ticket Agent*), Dick Curtis (*Mechanic*), George Guhl (*Platt*), Janet Shaw, Claire James (*Usherettes*), Mary Currier, Rita Owin (*Saleladies*), Gene Morgan (*Man*), Jack Egan (*Elevator Man*), Ralph Peters (*Bartender*).

Blondie wants a fur coat and Dagwood wants to join the trout club. Blondie becomes jealous when an old flame of Dagwood's (Hayworth) rolls into town, but all is forgotten when a drawing at the local movie theater provides the money for the fur coat. Notable for the presence of Hayworth. (See BLONDIE series, Index)

p, Robert Sparks; d, Frank R. Strayer; w, Richard Flournoy (based on a story by Charles Molyneaux Brown and the comic strip created by Chic Young); ph, Henry Freulich; ed, Gene Havlick; md, Morris Stoloff; art d, Lionel Banks; cos, Ray Howell.

Comedy (PR:AA MPAA:NR)

BLONDIE PLAYS CUPID** (1940) 67m COL bw

Penny Singleton (*Blondie*), Arthur Lake (*Dagwood*), Larry Simms (*Baby Dumpling*), Himself (*Daisy*), Jonathan Hale (*J. C. Dithers*), Danny Mummert (*Alvin Fuddle*), Irving Bacon (*Mailman*), Glenn Ford (*Charlie*), Luana Walters (*Millie*), Will Wright (*Tucker*), Spencer Charters (*Uncle Abner*), Leona Roberts (*Aunt Hannah*), Tommy Dixon (*Saunders*), Rex Moore (*Newsboy*).

While the Bumsteads struggle through typical misadventures on the way to visit relatives in the country, Blondie encounters an eloping couple in need of help, which she provides. A very young Glenn Ford appears as half of the runaway duo. Delightful young lover pic. (See BLONDIE series, Index.)

p, Robert Sparks; d, Frank R. Strayer; w, Richard Flournoy, Karen De Wolf (based on a story by Charles M. Brown and De Wolf and the comic strip by Chic Young); ph, Henry Freulich; ed, Gene Milford.

Comedy/Romance (PR:AA MPAA:NR)

BLONDIE TAKES A VACATION** (1939) 68m COL bw

Penny Singleton (*Blondie*), Arthur Lake (*Dagwood*), Larry Simms (*Baby Dumpling*), Himself (*Daisy*), Danny Mummert (*Alvin Fuddle*), Donald Meek (*Jonathan Gillis*), Donald MacBride (*Harvey Morton*), Thomas W. Ross (*Matthew Dickerson*), Elizabeth Dunne (*Mrs. Dickerson*), Robert Wilcox (*John Larkin*), Harlan Briggs (*Holden*), Irving Bacon (*Mailman*), Milt Kibbee (*Creditor*).

The third installment in the BLONDIE saga finds the Bumsteads running a mountain hotel to keep the aging owners from losing their life savings. Air conditioning and arson also figure into this humorous piece of fluff. (See BLONDIE series, Index)

p, Robert Sparks; d, Frank R. Strayer; w, Richard Flournoy (based on a story by Karen De Wolf, Robert Chapin, Flournoy, and the comic strip created by Chic Young); ph, Henry Freulich; ed, Viola Lawrence.

Comedy (PR:AA MPAA:NR)

BLONDIE'S ANNIVERSARY** (1947) 67m COL bw

Penny Singleton (*Blondie*), Arthur Lake (*Dagwood*), Larry Simms (*Alexander*), Marjorie Kent (*Cookie*), Adele Jergens (*Gloria Stafford*), Jerome Cowan (*George Radcliffe*), Grant Mitchell (*Samuel Breckenbridge*), William Frawley (*Sharkey*),

Edmund MacDonald (*Burley*), Fred Sears (*Dalton*), Jack Rice (*Ollie*), Alyn Lockwood (*Mary*), Frank Wilcox (*Carter*), Eddie Acuff (*Mailman*), Larry Steers (*Parker*), Al Zeidman.

Blondie finds a watch which she mistakenly believes is her anniversary present, sending Dagwood into a flurry of activity to come up with something special to make amends. (See BLONDIE series, Index)

d, Abby Berlin; w, Jack Henley (based on the comic strip created by Chic Young); ph, Vincent Farrar; md. Mischa Bakaleinikoff; ed, Al Clark; art d, George Brooks.

Comedy (PR:AA MPAA:NR)

BLONDIE'S BIG DEAL** (1949) 66m COL bw

Penny Singleton (*Blondie*), Arthur Lake (*Dagwood*), Larry Simms (*Alexander*), Marjorie Kent (*Cookie*), Jerome Cowan (*Radcliffe*), Collette Lyons (*Norma*), Wilton Graff (*Dillon*), Ray Walker (*Stack*), Stanley Andrews (*Forsythe*), Alan Dinehart III (*Rollo*), Eddie Acuff (*Mailman*), Jack Rice (*Ollie*), Chester Clute (*Mayor*), George Lloyd (*Fire Chief*), Alyn Lockwood (*Mary*), Danny Mummert (*Alvin*).

"Competent" is the best way to describe many BLONDIE films. From the actors to the key grips, you'll seldom find anything fancy; just good, solid work from all involved. BLONDIE'S BIG DEAL is a shade better than most BLONDIE movies on all burners. Singleton and Lake do their customary good work in their time-tested roles. Dagwood is mixing chemicals in the kitchen when he discovers that he's created non-flammable paint. Two rival contractors (Graff and Walker) steal the stuff before the honest Bumstead can give it to his boss, Cowan. At a demonstration, Dagwood paints Cowan's cabin with the wrong paint (it was switched by the villains) and promptly burns down Cowan's place. Dagwood is disgraced until Blondie and newcomer Alan Dinehart III do some detective work and save the day. (See BLONDIE series, Index)

p, Ted Richmond; d, Edward Bernds; w, Lucile Watson Henley (based on the comic strip by Chic Young); ph, Vincent Farrar; ed, Henry Batista.

Comedy (PR:AA MPAA:NR)

BLONDIE'S BIG MOMENT** (1947) 69m COL bw (GB: BUNDLE OF TROUBLE)

Penny Singleton (*Blondie*), Arthur Lake (*Dagwood*), Larry Simms (*Alexander*), Marjorie Kent (*Cookie*), Anita Louise (*Miss Gray*), Jerome Cowan (*George M. Radcliffe*), Danny Mummert (*Alvin Fuddle*), Jack Rice (*Ollie*), Jack Davis (*Mr. Greenleaf*), Johnny Granath (*Slugger*), Hal K. Dawson (*Mr. Little*), Eddie Acuff (*Mailman*), Alyn Lockwood (*Mary*), Robert De Haven (*Pete*), Robert Stevens (*Joe*), Douglas Wood (*Theodore Payson*), Himself (*Daisy*), Dick Wessel (*Bus Driver*).

Blondie has the opportunity to become a star and turns the Bumstead household upside down; Dagwood is in a dither as usual, worrying over the attentions or lack of them from his beloved spouse. (See BLONDIE series, Index)

p, Burt Kelley; d, Abby Berlin; w, Connie Lee (based on the comic strip created by Chic Young); ph, Allen Siegler; ed, Jerome Thoms; md, Mischa Bakaleinikoff; art d, George Brooks.

Comedy (PR:AA MPAA:NR)

BLONDIE'S BLESSED EVENT** (1942) 69m COL bw

Penny Singleton (*Blondie*), Arthur Lake (*Dagwood*), Larry Simms (*Baby Dumpling*), Norma Jean Wayne (*Cookie*), Himself (*Daisy*), Jonathan Hale (*J. C. Dithers*), Danny Mummert (*Alvin Fuddle*), Hans Conried (*George Wickley*), Stanley Brown (*Ollie*), Irving Bacon (*Mr. Crumb*), Mary Wickes (*Sarah Miller*), Paul Harvey (*William Lawrence*), Dorothy Ann Seese (*Little Girl*), Arthur O'Connell (*Intern*), Don Barclay (*Waiter*).

Cookie is born, producing unmitigated joy in the Bumstead household. Adding to the chaos a new baby always creates is the appearance of Hans Conried as a cynical author who becomes caught up in the Bumstead lifestyle. (See BLONDIE series, Index)

p, Robert Sparks; d, Frank R. Strayer; w, Connie Leo, Karen De Wolf, Richard Flournoy (based on the comic strip created by Chic Young); ph, Henry Freulich; ed, Charles Nelson.

Comedy (PR:AA MPAA:NR)

BLONDIE'S HERO** (1950) 67m COL bw

Penny Singleton (*Blondie*), Arthur Lake (*Dagwood*), Larry Simms (*Alexander*), Marjorie Kent (*Cookie*), William Frawley (*Marty Greer*), Danny Mummert (*Alvin*), Joe Sawyer (*Sergeant Gateson*), Teddy Infuhr (*Danny Gateson*), Alyn Lockwood (*Mary Reynolds*), Iris Adrian (*Mae*), Frank Jenks (*Tim Saunders*), Dick Wessel (*Mailman*), Jimmy Lloyd (*Cpl. Biff Touhey*), Robert Emmett Keane (*J. Collins*), Edward Earle (*Richard Rogers*), Mary Newton (*Mrs. Rogers*), Pat Flaherty (*Recruiting Sergeant*), Ted Mapes (*Fruit Salesman*), Frank Wilcox (*Capt. Masters*), Frank Sully (*Mike McClusky*), Himself (*Daisy*).

Lake accidentally signs up for the Army reserve and gets caught up in basic training. Singleton, of course, goes to camp (much of the action was filmed at O.R.C. Training Center, Fort MacArthur, California) to watch hubby save the country and finds us almost thrown into civil war. (See BLONDIE series, Index)

p, Ted Richmond; d, Edward Bernds; w, Jack Henley (based on a story by Jack Henley and the comic strip created by Chic Young); ph, Vincent Farrar; ed, Henry Batista; md, Mischa Bakaleinikoff; art d, Perry Smith.

Comedy (PR:AA MPAA:NR)

BLONDIE'S HOLIDAY*½ (1947) 61m COL bw

Penny Singleton (*Blondie*), Arthur Lake (*Dagwood*), Larry Simms (*Alexander*), Marjorie Kent (*Cookie*), Jerome Cowan (*George Radcliffe*), Grant Mitchell (*Samuel Breckinridge*), Sid Tomack (*Pete Brody*), Mary Young (*Mrs. Breckinridge*), Jeff York

(*Paul Madison*), Bobby Larson (*Alvin Fuddle*), Jody Gilbert (*Cynthia Thompson*), Jack Rice (*Ollie*), Alyn Lockwood (*Mary*), Eddie Acuff (*Postman*), Tim Ryan (*Mike*), Anne Nagel (*Bea Mason*), Rodney Bell (*Tom Henley*).

Lake's bumbling attempts at achieving financial security get him in trouble with bookies, then land him in jail. The local bank manager comes to the rescue as a reward for Lake's getting his gambling-addicted wife out of the betting parlor just as the cops raid the joint. (See BLONDIE series, Index)

p, Burt Kelly; d, Abby Berlin; w, Constance Lee (based on the comic strip created by Chic Young); ph, Vincent Farrar; ed, Jerome Thoms; md, Carter DeHaven, Jr.

Comedy   **(PR:AA   MPAA:NR)**

BLONDIE'S LUCKY DAY* 1/2   (1946) 69m COL bw

Penny Singleton (*Blondie*), Arthur Lake (*Dagwood*), Larry Simms (*Alexander*), Marjorie Kent (*Cookie*), Robert Stanton (*Johnny*), Angelyn Orr (*Mary Jane*), Jonathan Hale (*J. C. Dithers*), Paul Harvey (*Mr. Butler*), Bobby Larson (*Tommy*), Jack Rice (*Ollie*), Charles Arnt (*Mayor*), Margie Liszt (*Mary*), Frank Orth (*Salesman*), Frank Jenks (*Postman*), Himself (*Daisy*).

In this late entry in the series, Lake takes over the office in the boss' absence and hires a former WAC (Orr) which leave Lake and the WAC unemployed. The Bumsteads start their own business and soon Lake is back at his old job. (See BLONDIE series, Index)

p, Burt Kelly; d, Abby Berlin; w, Connie Lee (based on the comic strip created by Chic Young); ph, L. W. O'Connell; ed, Aaron Stell; md, Mischa Bakaleinikoff.

Comedy   **(PR:AA   MPAA:NR)**

BLONDIE'S REWARD* 1/2   (1948) 65m COL bw

Penny Singleton (*Blondie*), Arthur Lake (*Dagwood*), Larry Simms (*Alexander*), Marjorie Kent (*Cookie*), Jerome Cowan (*George Radcliffe*), Gay Nelson (*Alice Dickson*), Ross Ford (*Ted Scott*), Danny Mummert (*Alvin*), Paul Harvey (*John Dixon*), Frank Jenks (*Ed Vance*), Chick Chandler (*Bill Cooper*), Jack Rice (*Ollie*), Eddie Acuff (*Postman*), Alyn Lockwood (*Mary*), Frank Sully (*Officer Carney*), Myron Healy (*Cluett Day*), Chester Clute (*Leroy Blodgett*).

Undistinguished program filler with Lake first buying the wrong property for his boss, then getting in deeper trouble when he is accused of punching out the son of an important client. Predictable comedy with ten-year-old gags. Mercifully brief. (See BLONDIE series, Index)

d, Abby Berlin; w, Edward Bernds (based on the comic strip created by Chic Young); ph, Vincent Farrar; ed, Al Clark; md, Mischa Bakaleinikoff.

Comedy   **(PR:AA   MPAA:NR)**

BLONDIE'S SECRET*   (1948) 68m COL bw

Penny Singleton (*Blondie*), Arthur Lake (*Dagwood*), Larry Simms (*Alexander*), Marjorie Kent (*Cookie*), Jerome Cowan (*Radcliffe*), Thurston Hall (*George Whiteside*), Jack Rice (*Ollie*), Danny Mummert (*Alvin*), Frank Orth (*Dog Pound Attendant*), Alyn Lockwood (*Mary*), Eddie Acuff (*Mailman*), Murray Alper (*Larry*), William ''Bill'' Phillips (*Chips*), Greta Granstedt (*Mona*), Grandon Rhodes (*Ken Marcy*), Himself (*Daisy*), Paula Raymond (*Nurse*), Allen Mathews (*Big Man*), Joseph Crehan (*Sergeant*).

One feeble device after another keeps the Bumsteads from their vacation, including the boss having their luggage stolen. Not one of the better entries of the series. (See BLONDIE series, Index)

d, Edward Bernds; w, Jack Henley (based on the comic strip created by Chic Young); ph, Vincent Farrar; ed, Al Clark; md, Mischa Bakaleinikoff; art d, George Brooks.

Comedy   **(PR:AA   MPAA:NR)**

BLOOD*   (1974, Brit.) 74m Bryanston c

Allan Berendt, Hope Stransbury, Eve Crosby, Patti Gaul, Pamela Adams.

In 1899 the upwardly mobile offspring of Dracula and Wolfman fall in love, marry and move to Staten Island where they happily plan to propagate the countryside by growing carnivorous plants. For dingbats only.

p, Walter Kent; d&w, Andy Miligan.

Horror   **(PR:C   MPAA:R)**

BLOOD ALLEY* 1/2   (1955) 115m Batjac/WB c

John Wayne (*Wilder*), Lauren Bacall (*Cathy*), Paul Fix (*Mr. Tso*), Joy Kim (*Susu*), Barry Kroeger (*Old Feng*), Mike Mazurki (*Big Han*), Anita Ekberg (*Wei Long*), Henry Nakamura (*Tack*), W. T. Chang (*Mr. Han*), George Chan (*Mr. Sing*).

Another Oriental adventure, typical of many made around this time. Wayne is a tough seafarer who is approached by the villagers of a Red Chinese hamlet. Bacall is the daughter of an American physician who was killed by the Red Chinese. She asks Wayne to take the villagers aboard a stolen ship and through BLOOD ALLEY, the straits of Formosa, to the relative freedom of the British colony of Hong Kong. Once on water they are chased by a Chinese gunboat and an enemy plane buzzes them. Wayne orders the decks covered with food so the seagulls flock all over the ship, thus making it difficult to spot from the sky. More trouble comes as a destroyer attacks them and the boat is almost sunk. It all winds up well as the villagers get to safety and Wayne and Bacall declare their love for each other. If you can believe the Amazonian sexpot Anita Ekberg as an Asian then you might enjoy this flag-waving film. If not, you'll find yourself laughing at the incredulity of the whole thing. In the middle of everything, Joy Kim takes time out to sing two songs. How silly can you get? Wellman's direction and Wayne's steadfast belief in what he is doing are what merit some attention.

d, William Wellman; w, A. S. Fleischmann (from his novel); ph, William H. Clothier (Warnercolor); m, Roy Webb; ed, Fred McDowell; cos, Gwen Wakeling, Carl Walker.

Adventure   **(PR:A-C   MPAA:NR)**

BLOOD AND BLACK LACE**   (1965, Ital.) 88m Lou Moss/AA c

Cameron Mitchell (*Max Marlan*), Eva Bartok (*Christina*), Thomas Reiner (*Inspector Silvester*), Arianna Gorini (*Nicole*), Dante De Paolo (*Frank Sacalo*), Mary Arden (*Peggy*), Franco Ressel (*Marquis Richard Morell*), Claude Dantes (*Taoli*), Lea Krugher (*Isabella*), Massimo Righi (*Marco*), Guiliano Raffaelli (*Zenchin*), Harriette White Medin (*Clarica*).

A stocking-masked killer dispatches a large number of glamorous models in the eternal city. Bava did these about as well as anybody and this is a typical work, well shot and stylish, despite plot inconsistencies.

p, Lou Moss; d, Mario Bava; w, Marcel Fondat, Joe Barilla, Bava; ph, Herman Tarzana (Technicolor); m, Carlo Rustichelli; ed, Mark Suran; art d, Harry Brest.

Horror   **Cas.**   **(PR:O   MPAA:NR)**

BLOOD AND GUTS** 1/2   (1978, Can.) Ambassador Films c

William Smith (*Dan O'Neil*), Micheline Lanctot (*Lucky Brown*), Henry Beckman (*Red Henkel*), Brian Patrick Clark (*Jim Davenport*), John McFadyen (*Jake McCann*), Ken James (*Harry Brown*).

There have been a number of attempts to recreate the ambiance of the wrestling arena on screen and BLOOD AND GUTS may be the closest to succeeding. Lynch directed the fast-moving film about a down-and-out wrestling troupe as it traverses the tank-town circuit. Smith, so good when he battled Clint Eastwood, plays an aging wrestler with lots of simpatico. The plot is nothing much to write home about; a love triangle between Smith and a young wrestler (Clark) and the radiant Lanctot. Henry Beckman, who can frequently be seen overacting on TV, gobbles up the Canadian scenery as the wrestling troupe's boss. It just misses being the definitive wrestling picture due to some bumps in the script and Beckman's histrionics. Otherwise, a worthwhile look at the mat game.

p, Peter O'Brian; d, Paul Lynch; w, Joseph McBride, William Gray, John Hunter; ph, Mark Irwin; m, Milton Barnes; ed, Gray; art d, Reuben Freed; cos, Delphine White.

Drama   **(PR:O   MPAA:R)**

BLOOD AND LACE**   (1971) 67m AIP/Contemporary Filmmakers-Carlin c

Gloria Grahame (*Mrs. Deere*), Melody Patterson (*Ellie*), Milton Selzer (*Mullins*), Len Lesser (*Tom Kredge*), Vic Tayback (*Calvin Carruthers*), Terri Messina (*Bunch*), Ronald Taft (*Walter*), Dennis Christopher (*Pete*), Peter Armstrong (*Ernest*), Maggie Corrie (*Jennifer*), Mary Strawberry (*Nurse*), Louise Sherrill (*Edna Masters*).

Gloria Grahame rules over her orphan asylum with an iron hand, not to mention a claw hammer and a cleaver. If her brutality kills a student or two, no problem, she simply freezes them to display to the social workers and so keep collecting her $150 a month for their maintenance. Manages to keep some tension despite murky photogra- phy and muddy sound.

p, Ed Carlin, Gil Lasky; d, Philip Gilbert; w, Lasky; ph, Paul Hipp (Movielab Color); m, John Rons; art d, Lee Fischer.

Horror   **(PR:O   MPAA:GP)**

BLOOD AND ROSES**
(1961, Fr./Ital.) 87m E.G.E.-Documento/PAR c (ET MOURIR DE PLAISIR)

Mel Ferrer (*Leopoldo De Karnstein*), Elsa Martinelli (*Georgia Monteverdi*), Annette Vadim (*Carmilla Von Karnstein*), Jacques-Rene Chauffard (*Dr. Verari*), Marc Allegret (*Judge Monteverdi*), Alberto Bonucci (*Carlo Ruggieri*), Serge Marquand (*Giuseppe*), Gabriella Farinon (*Lisa*), Renato Speziali (*Guido Naldi*), Edythe Peters (*The Cook*), Gianni De Benedetto (*Police Marshal*), Carmilla Stroyberg (*Martha*), Nathalie LeForet (*Marie*).

This version of Sheridan Le Fanu's CARMILLA (which had been the basis for the 1932 version of VAMPYR) abounds in atmosphere and recounts the story of Carmilla, a typical woman in modern-day Rome, obsessed with her vampire ancestor Mircalla. While celebrating her aristocratic cousin's engagement at a masked ball, Carmilla cannot resist reverting to type by killing a servant girl and biting her cousin's fiancee. The version dubbed for American audiences omits all references to lesbianism, pretty much destroying the story. (Remade as THE VAMPIRE LOVERS.)

p, Raymond Eger; d&w, Roger Vadim (based on the novel *Carmilla* by Sheridan LeFanu, adapted by Claude Brule, Claude Martin, Roger Vailland, Vadim); ph, Claude Renoir; m, Jean Prodomides; ed, Victoria Mercanton; prod d, Jean Andre; cos, Marcel Escoffier.

Horror   **(PR:C-O   MPAA:NR)**

BLOOD AND SAND****   (1941) 123m FOX c

Tyrone Power (*Juan Gallardo*), Linda Darnell (*Carmen Espinosa*), Rita Hayworth (*Dona Sol des Muire*), Anthony Quinn (*Manolo de Palma*), Alla Nazimova (*Senora Augustias*), J. Carrol Naish (*Garabato*), John Carradine (*Nacional*), Laird Cregar (*Natalio Curro*), Lynn Bari (*Encarnacion*), Vicente Gomez (*Guitarist*), Monty Banks (*Antonio Lopez*), George Reeves (*Capt. Pierre Lauren*), Pedro De Cordoba (*Don Jose Alvarez*), Fortunio Bonanova (*Pedro Espinosa*), Victor Kilian (*Priest*), Michael Morris (*La Pulga*), Charles Stevens (*Pabelo Gomez*), Ann E. Todd (*Carmen as a Child*), Rex Downing (*Juan as a Child*), Cora Sue Collins (*Encarnacion as a Child*), Russell Hicks (*Marquis*), Maurice Cass (*El Milquetoast*), John Wallace (*Francisco*), Jacqueline Dalya (*Gachi*), Cullen Johnson (*Manolo as a Child*), Schuyler Standish (*Nacional as a Child*), William Montague (*Sebastian*), Paco Moreno (*Conductor*),

Harry Burns (Engineer), Francis MacDonald (Friend), Kay Linaker (Woman), Alberto Morin (Attendant), Paul Ellis (Ortega), Fred Malatesta (Waiter), Rosita Granada (Singer), Mariquita Flores (Specialty Dancer), Armillita (El Matador), Cecilia Calleto, Esther Estrella (Street Gachis).

Magnificent color spectacle of the bull ring, BLOOD AND SAND had been a silent classic starring Rudolph Valentino, Nita Naldi, and Lila Lee in 1922. Fox wizard Zanuck had successfully revived THE MARK OF ZORRO, a Fairbanks silent, for Fox's top star, Tyrone Power, and thought to repeat the box-office formula. The romantic leading man plays the son of a famous matador who has been killed in the arena. The opening dwells long on Power and his friends, Carradine, Quinn, and Naish as the apprentice matador makes a name for himself while following in his father's footsteps. He returns home in triumph to marry Darnell, his childhood sweetheart, and buy a magnificent villa for his mother, Nazimova, and sister, Bari. Acknowledging Power's fame and furthering it with bombastic praise is Cregar, a bullfight critic who had once smeared his father. With fame and wealth, Power's fortunes begin to shatter, particularly after Cregar introduces him to sultry vamp Hayworth, who enchants him to the point where he begins a torrid affair with her. He pays less and less attention to his work in the arena, which causes him to make mistakes, and these errors inadvertently cause the deaths of his friends Carradine and Stevens, who are gored to death protecting him. His popularity wanes as Quinn's rises, the fickle crowds siding with their new hero. When Hayworth sees Power's fame evaporate she leaves him for Quinn. Darnell has already left him over his affair with Hayworth and the dissolute matador is now alone with his mother. His money is almost gone, servants dismissed, and Nazimova has taken to scrubbing the floor of the villa on hands and knees. Power resolves to make a comeback, promising his mother he will undo his disgrace in the arena. On the afternoon of his last battle with the bulls, Power kneels in a small chapel, as has always been his habit, to pray for protection. Darnell is there to tell him that she still loves him, that she will be waiting. Power goes into the arena and is devastating, putting on a show that brings the crowd instantly back to him; even Cregar is on his feet, mouthing his own cliche: "You are the greatest matador in the world!" After a dazzling display of brilliant passes, Power turns his back contemptuously on the bull to take his kudos. But the bull charges and gores him. He is carried from the arena to the chapel where he dies in the arms of Darnell, listening to the cheers of the crowd roaring from the arena, thinking this tribute is for him when it is being lavished upon the new hero, Quinn. Enraged, Power's faithful dresser, Naish, shouts out in anguish: "Listen! The crowd—that is the real beast!" (A paraphrase of BLOOD AND SAND's author Ibanez who had written: "The real beast in the arena is the crowd!") The old Technicolor process is opulent in this film, one where the brilliant colors match the extravagant costumes and beautiful scenery. Director Mamoulian, who did some shooting for the film in Mexico City, saw the production as a lavish, tragic mural. "Instead of just photographing the story," he was quoted as saying, "I tried to 'paint' it." This is evident in the sets, decorations, and costumes which reflect the brilliant work of Goya, Murillo, Velasquez, and El Greco. Darnell was cast opposite Power as a continuing film actor, having played with him in THE MARK OF ZORRO. The part of the wealthy seductress, however, was another matter. Many actresses were tested for the part, including Maria Montez, the exotic Mexican beauty. According to Mamoulian, she walked into his office and immediately lifted her skirts high to display a lot of leg, then gave him a sexy wink. Her screen test later proved unsatisfactory. Mamoulian and Zanuck all along wanted rising star Carole Landis to play the infamous femme fatale but when she learned that she would have to dye her hair red, Landis absolutely refused. She had been building herself up as a blonde bombshell and she had no intention of having a dye job that would ruin the image. Hayworth, who had been playing supporting parts up to this time, tested and won the part, especially for her dancing ability; there were a number of short seductive flamenco dances she had to perform in the movie. Ironically, BLOOD AND SAND catapulted Hayworth to superstar status and she was next given the lead in MY GAL SAL, a role which Landis thought she had been guaranteed. Landis wound up playing a supporting part in this movie and her career never did take off much beyond starlet status. The tragic actress would commit suicide, taking an overdose of sleeping pills in 1948, after reportedly breaking up with Rex Harrison, who was then married to Lilli Palmer. BLOOD AND SAND was a tour de force for the handsome Power, who looked for all the world to be the expert matador he was playing; bullfighting techniques were developed for the star by Budd Boetticher, an expert on the subject who later went on to direct MAGNIFICENT MATADOR and THE BULLFIGHTER AND THE LADY. His capework was impressive but Power, who wanted to actually do his own bullfighting, was never allowed near a bull, doubles standing in for him for the close work; the studio bosses were terrified that their top star would be injured. Power's star rose even higher with the triumph of this colorful, exciting production and he was never to forget his role. In later years he would enter a favorite San Francisco saloon where the head of a bull adorned a wall over the bar. Power would always stop before the stuffed menace, salute the horns, and shout jocularly: "Hola, bull! We meet again!"

p, Darryl F. Zanuck; d, Rouben Mamoulian; w, Jo Swerling (based on the novel Sangre y Arena by Vincente Blasco Ibanez); ph, Ernest Palmer, Ray Rennahan (Technicolor); m, Alfred Newman; ed, Robert Bischoff; art d, Richard Day, Joseph C. Wright; set d, Thomas Little; cos, Travis Banton; tech d, Natalie Kalmus, Morgan Padelford; torero cos, Jose Dolores Perez; paintings, Carlos Ruano Lopis; guitar m, Vicente Gomez; vocalist, Gracilla Pirraga; fiesta ch, Hermes Pan; "El Toro" number, Budd Boetticher.

Adventure   Cas.   (PR:C MPAA:NR)

BLOOD AND STEEL**   (1959) 62m FOX bw

John Lupton (Dave), James Edwards (George), Brett Halsey (Jim), John Brinkley (Cip), Ziva Rodann (Native Girl), Allen Jung (Head Jap), James Hong (Jap Draftsman), Bill Saito (Sugi).

Four Seabees sneak onto a Japanese-held island to scout out a location for an airstrip. They are helped by a native girl who leads them to an enemy transmitting station which they blow up. They flee to their boats, hounded by relentless pursuers, losing one dead, one badly shot up, and accidentally shooting the native girl. Routine heroics.

p, Gene Corman; d, Bernard L. Kowalski; w, Joseph C. Gillette; ph, Floyd D. Crosby; m, Calvin Jackson; ed, Anthony Carras.

War   (PR:A MPAA:NR)

BLOOD ARROW*½   (1958) 73m FOX c

Scott Brady (Dan Kree), Paul Richards (Brill), Phyllis Coates (Bess), Don Haggerty (Gabe), Rocky Shahan (Taslatch), Des Slattery (Ceppi), Bill McGraw (Norm), Patrick O'Moore (McKenzie), Jeanne Bates (Almee), Richard Gilden (Little Otter), John Dierkes (Ez), Diana Darrin (Lennie).

There's a smallpox outbreak in Blackfoot country and Bess, a Mormon girl played by Coates, must transport the serum across hostile Injun territory to save the lives of the other families in the valley where she lives. Brady (a scout), Haggerty (a trapper), and Richards (a gambler who thinks there may be gold in the valley) decide to help her. Lots of Indian attacks but it's generally a bore. Richards is totally wasted in this film as is Haggerty. Blame the usually-reliable Charles Marquis Warren who served as executive producer on such memorable western TV shows as "Gunsmoke," "Rawhide," and "The Virginian."

p, Robert Stabler; d, Charles Marquis Warren; w, Fred Frieberger; ph, Fleet Southcott (Regalscope); m, Raoul Kraushaar; ed, Michael Luciano.

Western   (PR:A-C MPAA:NR)

BLOOD BATH*   (1966) AIP/Jack Hill bw (AKA: TRACK OF THE VAMPIRE)

William Campbell (Alberto Sordi), Marissa Mathes (Daisy Allen), Lori Saunders (Dorian/Melissa), Sandra Knight (Donna Allen).

Feminist genre filmmaker Rothman made her directorial debut when executive producer Roger Corman pulled Jack Hill off this project. She was given Hill's footage and parts of a Yugoslavian vampire film Corman had picked up somewhere, and told to shoot just enough to make a feature out of it. Not surprisingly, the end result is a mess.

p, Jack Hill; d&w, Hill, Stephanie Rothman; ph, Alfred Taylor; m, Mark Lowry; ed, Mort Tubor.

Horror   (PR:C MPAA:NR)

BLOOD BATH*   (1976) 86m Cannon c

P.J. Soles, Harve Presnell.

An episodic film, similar in format to "The Twilight Zone." The set of strange tales was filmed in New York with Presnell as a horror film director. For the most part it's ineffectual and rather dull. It's probably best remembered for the debut of modern B movie queen Soles.

p, Anthony Fingleton; d&w, Joel Reed.

Horror   (PR:O MPAA:NR)

BLOOD BEACH*½   (1981) 89m Jerry Gross Org c

David Huffman (Harry Caulder), Mariana Hill (Catherine), John Saxon (Pearson), Otis Young (Piantadosi), Stefan Gierasch (Dimitros), Burt Young (Royko), Darrell Fetty (Hoagy), Lynne Marta (Jo), Eleanor Zee (Mrs. Elden), Lena Pousette (Marie), Pamela McMyler (Mrs. Hench), Harriet Medin (Ruth), Mickey Fox (Moose).

People keep disappearing on Santa Monica Beach. Saxon is the local police chief who wants to find out why. Seven hardy souls are sucked beneath the sand, which perplexes Saxon and Young, another cop. This should have been a satire of THE CREATURE FROM THE BLACK LAGOON but director/writer Bloom took himself grimly and attempted to scare the swimsuit off the viewer. It doesn't work. Not much suspense, a dumb-looking beach monster, silly premise, and a cast of veterans running around looking embarrassed. Run Run Shaw, together with brother Run Me Shaw, are two of the most successful producers in the Far East and have attempted to gain a foothold in the U.S. with several decent films. This is not one of them.

p, Steven Nalevansky; d, Jeffrey Bloom; w, Bloom (based on a story by Bloom, Nalevansky); ph, Steve Poster (Movielab Color); m, Gil Melle; ed, Gary Griffen; art d, William Sandell.

Horror   Cas.   (PR:C MPAA:R)

BLOOD BEAST FROM OUTER SPACE**½

(1965, Brit.) 84m World Entertainment/New Art bw (AKA: THE NIGHT CALLER)

John Saxon (Jack Costain), Maurice Denham (Professor Morley), Patricia Haines (Ann Barlow), Alfred Burke (Supt. Hartley), Jack Carson (Major), Jack Watson (Sgt. Hawkins), Stanley Meadows (Grant), Warren Mitchell (Lilburn), Ballard Barkeley (Cdr. Savage), Anthony Wager (Pvt. Higgins), Robert Crewdson (Medra).

Atomic mutant monster from Ganymede steals beautiful young women to take back to his world so that his dying, infertile race can reproduce. Intelligent script and high production values make this one worth checking out.

p, John Phillips, Ronald Liles; d, John Gilling; w, Jim O'Connaly (based on the novel The Night Callers, by Frank Crisp); ph, Stephen Dade; m, John Gregory; ed, Philip Barnikey.

Science Fiction   (PR:C MPAA:NR)

BLOOD BEAST TERROR, THE*

(1967, Brit.) 88m Tigon/Eastman c (AKA: VAMPIRE-BEAST CRAVES BLOOD, THE)

Peter Cushing (Insp. Quennell), Robert Flemyng (Prof. Mallinger), Wanda Ventham

(Clare Mallinger), Vanessa Howard (Meg Quennell), Roy Hudd (Morgue Attendant), David Griffin (William), Kevin Stoney (Grainger), Glynn Edwards (Sgt. Allan), John Paul (Warrander), Russell Napier (Landlord).

Flemyng is a mad professor whose daughter has the uncanny ability to change herself into a monster death's head moth. In a rather odd attempt to thwart his little girl from assaulting the entire village, Dad creates a giant moth for her to play with only to discover he now has two moths flapping around in search of more blood. Cushing plays a Victorian dectective trying to solve the gruesome murders with little help from a weak script, slack direction, and dire special effects.

p, Tony Tenser, Arnold Miller; d, Vernon Sewell; w, Peter Bryan.

Horror (PR:C MPAA:NR)

BLOOD CREATURE (SEE: TERROR IS A MAN, 1959).

BLOOD DEMON**
(1969, Ger.) 73m Hemisphere c (DIE SCHLANGENGRUBE UND DAS PENDEL; AKA: THE TORTURE CHAMBER OF DR. SADISM)

Christopher Lee (Count Regula), Karin Dor (Lilian Von Brandt), Lex Barker (Roger Montelis), Carl Lange (Anatole), Vladimir Medar (Fabian), Christiane Rucker (Babette), Dieter Eppler (Kutscher).

Outrageous fun with Lee as the gleefully sadistic Count who is put together by a loyal servant 40 years after being decapitated and dismembered for murdering 12 virgins. He's quickly back to his old habits, slinging Dor over a pit chock-full of spiders and strapping former Tarzan Barker beneath a razor-sharp pendulum. Very loosely based on Poe's "The Pit and the Pendulum," BLOOD DEMON has some interesting visual components including an eerie forest of the dead. A great makeup job on Lee.

p, Wolfgang Kuhnlenz; d, Harold Reinl; w, Manfred R. Kohler (based on Edgar Allen Poe's "The Pit and the Pendulum"); ph, Ernst W. Kalinke; m, Peter Thomas; ed, Hermann Haller; art d, Gabriel Pellon, Werner Achmann; cos, Irms Pauli.

Horror (PR:O MPAA:M)

BLOOD DRINKERS, THE* ½
(1966, U.S./Phil.) 79m Hemisphere bw/c (AKA: THE VAMPIRE PEOPLE)

Ronald Remy (Marco), Amalia Fuentes (Charita/Christine), Eddie Fernandez (Victor), Eva Montez, Jess Roma, Renato Robles.

Remy is a vampire with a dwarf, a girl, and a "carrier-pigeon" bat for assistants. His true love is dying so he decides to get her twin sister's heart for a transplant. Filmed in color and tinted black-and-white stock. Fuentes had a turn as a vampire a few years later in CREATURES OF EVIL.

p, Cirio H. Santiago; d, Gerardo de Leon; w, Cesar Amigo (based on a story by Rico Omagap); ph, Felipe Sacdalan; ed, Salvador; md, Tito Arevaldo; art d, Ben Ortico.

Horror (PR:O MPAA:NR)

BLOOD FEAST zero (1963) 58m Box Office Spectaculars c

Thomas Fair (Pete Thornton), Mal Arnold (Ramses), Connie Mason (Suzette), Scott H. Hall (Police Captain), Lyn Bolton (Mrs. Fremont), Toni Calvert (Trudy), Gene Courtier (Tony), Ashlyn Martin (Girl on Beach), Sandra Sinclair (Girl in Apartment), Jerome Eden (High Priest), Al Golden (Dr. Flanders), Craig Maudsley, Jr. (Truck Driver).

BLOOD FEAST has the dubious distinction of being the first film to openly wallow in gratuitous bloody gore. The insipid plot details the activities of an insane caterer, Arnold, who worships an Egyptian devil-cult. Seeking to resurrect the spirit of an ancient Egyptian princess, Arnold prowls about hacking the limbs, tongues, and brains of his female victims in bloody close-ups. After collecting his disgusting grue, he serves the whole mess to an unsuspecting former Playboy Playmate (June 1963) Mason at an "Egyptian feast" he has catered. Just as Arnold is about to vivisect Mason, policeman Wood arrives and chases the gore-crazed caterer into the blades of a garbage truck compactor. Totally reprehensible in all departments, BLOOD FEAST is a truly wretched work deserving none of the attention heaped upon it by misguided students of the horror film genre. Lewis' films are all worthless exercises in exploitation that bring nothing but degradation to the screen and the audience. To be sure, violence is quite effective on the screen, and at times even artistic, but films like BLOOD FEAST and the mindless imitations that followed are thoroughly repugnant, showing nothing but contempt for the cinema and humanity.

p, David F. Friedman, Stanford S. Kohlberg, Herschell Gordon Lewis; d, Lewis; w, Allison Louise Down; ph&m, Lewis; ed, Robert Sinise, Frank Romolo; spec eff, Lewis.

Horror (PR:O MPAA:NR)

BLOOD FEAST zero (1976, Ital.) 77m Cannon c (AKA: FEAST OF FLESH)
Barbara Bouchet

A thoroughly boring sleuthing film. Bouchet busies herself investigating a mysterious murder. Acting, writing and directing are worthless.

d, Emil P. Miragala; w, Frank Pitto.

Mystery (PR:O MPAA:NR)

BLOOD FEUD* (1979, Ital.) 112m AFD c (AKA: REVENGE)

Sophia Loren (Titina Paterno), Marcello Mastroianni (Spallone), Giancarlo Giannini (Nick), Turi Ferro (Baron).

Absurdly posturing film has Mastroianni, a lawyer, and petty thief Giannini vying for the sexual favors of Loren. She services both of them while trying to maintain the respectable image of a prudish widow. Although the 1920s background during Mussolini's rise in Italy is interesting, it adds not a tad to the story. The script is terrible and Loren looks nowhere near the alluring woman she is supposed to be

playing; she is heavy, hawkish, and horribly made-up like some frumpy harlot down on her luck. Director Wertmuller and the stars obviously rest on their long-past laurels. Not worth more than a glance.

d&w, Lina Wertmuller; ph, Tomino Delli Colli (Eastmancolor); m, Dangio Nando DeLuca; ed, Franco Fraticelli.

Drama Cas. (PR:O MPAA:R)

BLOOD FROM THE MUMMY'S TOMB** (1972, Brit.) 94m AIP/Hammer c

Andrew Keir (Professor Fuchs), Valerie Leon (Margaret/Tera), James Villiers (Corbeck), Hugh Burden (Dandridge), George Coulouris (Berigan), Mark Edwards (Tod Browning), Rosalie Crutchley (Helen Dickerson), Aubrey Morris (Dr. Putnam), David Markham (Doctor), Joan Young (Mrs. Caporal), James Cossins (Older Male Nurse), David Jackson (Younger Male Nurse), Jonathan Burn (Saturnine Young Man), Graham James (Youth in Museum), Tamara Ustinov (Veronica).

When a group of archaeologists excavate the tomb of Princess Tera and bring the treasures back to London, the princess reincarnates herself in the body of the expedition leader's daughter. Bloody vengeance follows on the transgressors. Polished but confusing, possibly due to director Holt's death in the final days of shooting. (Remade as THE AWAKENING.) (See MUMMY series, Index.)

p, Howard Brandy; d, Seth Holt; w, Christopher Wickling (based on the novel Jewel of Seven Stars, by Bram Stoker); ph, Arthur Grant (Technicolor); m, Tristam Cary; ed, Peter Weatherley.

Horror (PR:O MPAA:PG)

BLOOD IN THE STREETS**
(1975, Ital./Fr.) 111m Independent-International c (AKA: THE REVOLVER)

Oliver Reed (Vito Cipriani), Agostina Belli (Maria), Fabio Testi (Milo Ruiz), Daniel Baretta, Peter Berlin, Paol Pitagora, Frederic De Pasquale, Marc Mazza, Rene Kodehoff, Gunnar Warner.

BLOOD IN THE STREETS is one of those titles that someone felt sure would have hemophiliacs and vampires lining up at the box office. The original name of the film was THE REVOLVER and must have been altered because of the Link/Levinson film THE GUN. This tawdry meller is about Belli, Reed's wife, being kidnaped. He then releases Testi from jail in order to secure his wife's freedom. But the kidnapers don't want Testi alive, they want him dead. Reed, a prison official, and Testi team up to foil the villains. The fun is in the secondary characters who pop up and down while the primary people are in the midst of a chase. Some very well-done sidebar cameos. Would they had paid the same attention to the major roles. Near the end of the film, Reed makes a political speech that NRA enthusiasts will cheer, not realizing that it's anti-weapon, about the fact that, when all is done, justice is eventually boiled down to one finger, one trigger, one victim

p, Ugo Santalucia; d, Sergio Sollima; w, Arduino Maiuri, Massimo De Rita, Sollima; ph, Aldo Scavarda (DeLuxe Color); m, Ennio Morricone; ed, Sergio Montanara; art d,set d, Carlo Simi.

Crime Cas. (PR:C MPAA:R)

BLOOD LEGACY (SEE: LEGACY OF BLOOD, 1971)

BLOOD MANIA zero (1971) 88m Crown International

Peter Carpenter, Maria De Aragon, Reagan Wilson, Vicki Peters, Alex Rocco.

Sleazy story about a woman who plots to kill her abortion doctor father. Little does she know that the inheritance she wants is really to go to her sister. Vile with an advertised "shocking climax that will jolt you out of your seat." It doesn't. Rocco is a much better actor than what he has to work with here, which he proved in THE GODFATHER as the Bugsy Siegel-type gambling czar.

p, Peter Carpenter, Chris Marconi; d, Robert O'Neil; w, Toby Sacher, Tony Crechales.

Horror Cas. (PR:O MPAA:R)

BLOOD MONEY*** ½ (1933) 66m FOX/UA bw

George Bancroft (Bill Bailey), Judith Anderson (Ruby Darling), Frances Dee (Elaine Talbert), Chick Chandler (Drury Darling), J. Carroll Naish (Charley), Blossom Seely (Singer), Etienne Girardot (Bailey's Coworker), Joe Sawyer (Red), Sandra Shaw, Paul Fix.

Little-seen classic gangster film. Bancroft is a bailbondsman who jilts his nightclub owner girl friend (Anderson) for kinky, thrill-seeking rich girl Dee. Dee deserts Bancroft for an impetuous bank robber (Chandler), setting him up with stolen bonds which the police recover in a raid. A mobster chieftain decides to kill Bancroft during his daily pool game with an exploding eight ball. Just as he is about to sink the ball, Anderson warns him. Dee sees the two reconciled and turns away, setting off to meet a man she hopes will molest her. A fine underworld film lost for nearly 40 years.

d, Rowland Brown; w, Brown, Hal Long; ph, James Van Trees; m, Alfred Newman; ed, Lloyd Nosler.

Crime (PR:C MPAA:NR)

BLOOD MONEY zero
(1974, U.S./Hong Kong/Ital./Span.) 100m Shaw Bros.-Compagnia Cinematografica Champion-Midega Film-Harbor Prod. c

Lee Van Cleef, Lo Pieh, Karen Yeh, Yeh Ling Chih, Julian Ugarte, Goyo Peralta, Al Tung.

Stupid mishmash of spaghetti western and kung fu violence. Van Cleef wanders about collecting the information tattooed on the backs of four women which will lead him to a hidden treasure. Along the way he shoots a lot of people. Just plain bad.

p, Run Run Shaw, Gustave Berne; d, Anthony M. Dawson, Antonio Margheriti; w, Barth Jules Sussman; ph, Alejandro Ulloa.

Western   (PR:O   MPSA:NR)

BLOOD OF A POET, THE***
(1930, Fr.) 58m Vicomte de Noailles (LE SANG D'UN POETE)

Lee Miller, Pauline Carton, Odette Talazac, Enrico Rivero, Jean Desbordes, Fernand Dichamps, Lucien Jager, Feral Benga, Barbette.

An abstract film with wonderful imagery, the story line, such as it is, occuring as a chimney collapses. Many of the offbeat and unnerving scenes owe their creation to the Dadaistic rituals in France in the early 1920s, out of which came such surrealistic efforts. For those who like Cocteau's penetrating and curious mind this will edify; others will merely be confused.

d&w, Jean Cocteau; ph, Georges Perinal; m, Georges Auric; art d, Jean Gabriel d' Aubonne.

Drama   **Cas.**   (PR:C   MPAA:NR)

BLOOD OF DRACULA*¹/₂
(1957) 68m AIP bw (GB: BLOOD IS MY HERITAGE)

Sandra Harrison (Nancy Perkins), Louise Lewis (Miss Branding), Gail Ganley (Myra), Jerry Blaine (Tab), Heather Ames (Nora), Malcolm Atterbury (Lt. Dunlap), Mary Adams (Mrs. Thorndyke), Thomas B. Henry (Mr. Perkins), Don Devlin (Eddie), Jeanne Dean (Mrs. Perkins), Richard Devon (Sgt. Stewart), Paul Maxwell (Mike), Carlyle Mitchell (Stanley Mather), Shirley De Lancey (Terry), Michael Hall (Glenn).

Lewis is a teacher at a girls' school experimenting with a magical amulet from Transylvania. She places Harrison under her spell and makes her commit a series of murders. Harrison realizes what is happening to her and begs to be released. Lewis refuses so Harrison strangles her, then gets impaled on a stake. Could be worse, though not much.

p, Herman Cohen; d, Herbert L. Strock; w, Ralph Thornton; ph, Monroe Askins; m, Paul Dunlap; ed, Robert Moore.

Horror   (PR:O   MPAA:NR)

BLOOD OF DRACULA'S CASTLE zero
(1967) 84m Paragon Pictures c (AKA: DRACULA'S CASTLE)

John Carradine (George), Alex D'Arcy (Dracula), Paula Raymond (Countess), Ray Young (Mango), Vicki Volante, Robert Dix, John Cardos, Kent Osborne.

D'Arcy and Raymond play the infamous vampire and his wife, now relocated in modern America. Their cohorts include Carradine as a butler and Young as a hunchback assistant. Their job is to keep the Draculas in cocktails made from blood of young girls, conviently chained up in the basement. Occasionally one of the girls is sacrificed to the god Luna. Pretty cheap affair that is funny in its own peculiar way. Another of the cheap B films famed cinematographer Kovacs cut his teeth on.

p, Al Adamson, Rex Carlton; d, Adamson, Jean Hewitt; w, Carlton; ph, Laszlo Kovacs.

Horror   **Cas.**   (PR:O   MPAA:NR)

BLOOD OF FRANKENSTEIN**
(1970) 91m Independent-International bw (AKA: DRACULA VS. FRANKENSTEIN; THEY'RE COMING TO GET YOU)

J. Carroll Naish, Lon Chaney, Jr., Regina Carrol, John Bloom, Anthony Eisley, Zandor Vorkov, J. Forrest Ackerman.

Naish is Frankenstein, a wheelchair-bound curator of a horror museum. Chaney is a mad zombie who decapitates a girl. Eisley, along with Carrol, the girl's sister, stop the evil plans of Naish and Vorkov. A quickie exploitation film that has a good sense of crude fun about it. Adamson was well known for making these gleeful melanges. Don't miss the cameo by Ackerman, a noted science fiction historian.

p, Al Adamson, John Vandom; d, Adamson; w, William Pugsley, Samuel M. Sherman; ph, Gary Graver, Paul Glickman.

Horror   (PR:O   MPAA:NR)

BLOOD OF FU MANCHU, THE*
(1968, Brit.) 91m Udastex Films (AKA: KISS AND KILL)

Christopher Lee (Fu Manchu), George Gotz (Carl Janson), Richard Greene (Nayland Smith), Howard Marion Crawford (Dr. Petrie), Tsai Chin (Lin Tang), Maria Rohm (Ursula), Shirley Eaton (Black Widow), Frances Kahn (Carmen).

Lee stars as the evil villain he played in this irregular 1960s series. This time he has inoculated ten beautiful women with a special poison that will kill the ten world leaders he has assigned his flunkies to kiss. Greene is the first victim and he recovers from the poison and is able to stop the evil Lee. Poorly scripted and directed, this film lacks any sort of energy needed to make it the least bit fun. Also released in a badly butchered 61-minute version that was of no help at all in understanding the plot. (Sequel: CASTLE OF FU MANCHU.) (See FU MANCHU series, Index.)

p, Harry Alan Towers; d, Jess [Jesus] Franco; w, Peter Welbeck [Towers]; ph, Manuel Merino.

Crime   (PR:O   MPAA:NR)

BLOOD OF GHASTLY HORROR   (SEE: PSYCHO-A-GO-GO, 1965)

BLOOD OF THE VAMPIRE*¹/₂   (1958, Brit.) 84m UNIV c

Donald Wolfit (Callistratus), Vincent Ball (Dr. John Pierre), Barbara Shelley (Made leine), Victor Maddern (Carl), William Devlin (Kurt Urah), Andrew Faulds (Wetzler), Bryan Colman (Herr Auron), Hal Osmond (Sneakthief), Bernard Bresslaw (Sneak thief), Colin Tapley (The Judge), John LeMesurier (Chief Justice), Henry Vidon

(Meinster), John Stuart (Madeleine's Uncle), Cameron Hall (Drunken Doctor), Yvonne Buckingham (Serving Wench).

This is a wonderful cast of very funny veteran British comedians; the trouble is that the picture is a straight horror movie and they are all wasted. Maddern is a one-eyed hunchback mistakenly sentenced to death. He'd been attempting to save a person with a blood transfusion and the authorities saw it as murder. Just before that happened, Maddern revivified Wolfit, a doctor who'd been executed in 1880 for conduct unbecoming a vampire. Maddern is tossed into a jail for the criminally insane. There's lots of pain and torture and grisly scenes with some angry canines. The film was written by Jimmy Sangster, an excellent writer in this genre, but he must have run afoul of director Cass and the two producers because this one misses. Any film with Wolfit, Bresslaw, and LeMesurier should have been hysterical. This one wasn't.

p, Robert S. Baker, Monte Berman; d, Henry Cass; w, Jimmy Sangster; ph, Geoffrey Seahorn (Eastmancolor); m, Stanley Black; ed, Douglas Myers.

Horror   (PR:O   MPAA:NR)

BLOOD ON MY HANDS   (SEE: KISS THE BLOOD OFF MY HANDS, 1948)

BLOOD ON SATAN'S CLAW, THE**
(1970, Brit.) 100m Tigon/Cannon c (GB: SATAN'S SKIN; AKA: SATAN'S CLAW)

Patrick Wymark (Judge), Linda Hayden (Angel), Barry Andrews (Ralph), Michele Dotrice (Margaret), Wendy Padbury (Cathy), Anthony Ainley (Rev. Fallowfield), Charlotte Mitchell (Ellen), Tamara Ustinov (Rosalind), Simon Williams (Peter), Howard Goorney (Doctor), Avice Landon (Isobel), Robin Davis (Mark), James Hayter (Squire Middleton).

A coven of possessed children presided over by a seductive blonde serving the Devil wreaks havoc in 17th-century England. This is an effective witchcraft thriller with the devil being depicted as a hairy creature with claws, a somewhat interesting departure from his usual persona.

p, Peter Andrews, Malcolm Heyworth; d, Piers Haggard w, Robert Wynne Simmons; ph, Dick Bush; m, Marc Wilkinson.

Horror   **Cas.**   (PR:O   MPAA:R)

BLOOD ON THE ARROW**   (1964) 91m AA c

Dale Robertson (Wade Cooper), Martha Hyer (Nancy Mailer), Wendell Corey (Clint Mailer), Dandy Curran (Tim), Paul Mantee (Segura), Robert Carricart (Kai-La), Ted DeCorsia (Jud), Elisha Cook, Jr. (Tex), John Matthews (Mike), Tom Reese (Charlie), Blyce Wright (Capt. Stanhope), Michael Hammond, Leland Wainscott.

An Apache raid leaves all dead except an outlaw who later rescues the small boy taken by the Indians. A weak effort with little story and a ruthless portrait of Indians. The direction is miserable.

p, Leon Fromkess, Sam Firks; d, Sidney Salkow; w, Robert E. Kent (based on his story); ph, Kenneth Peach (DeLuxe Color); m, Richard La Salle; ed, William Austin.

Western   (PR:C   MPAA:NR)

BLOOD ON THE MOON***   (1948) 88m RKO bw

Robert Mitchum (Jim Garry), Barbara Bel Geddes (Amy Lufton), Robert Preston (Tate Biling), Walter Brennan (Kris Barden), Phyllis Thaxter (Carol Lufton), Frank Faylen (Jake Pindalest), Tom Tully (John Lufton), Charles McGraw (Milo Sweet), Clifton Young (Joe Shotten), Tom Tyler (Frank Reardan), George Cooper (Fred Borden), Richard Powers (Ted Eiser), Bud Osborne (Cap Willis), Zon Murray (Nels Titterton), Robert Bray (Bart Daniels).

Gunfighter Mitchum helps bad guy Preston get rich off a feud between ranchers and farmers, then has an outbreak of conscience and helps defeat him, winning Bel Geddes in the process. A tight, well-crafted adult western as moody and murky as Mitchum's intriguing personality.

p, Theron Warth; d, Robert Wise; w, Willie Hayward (based on an adaptation by Harold Shumate of a novel by Luke Short); ph, Nicholas Musuraca; ed, Samuel E. Beetley.

Western   **Cas.**   (PR:A   MPAA:NR)

BLOOD ON THE SUN***¹/₂   (1945) 98m UA bw

James Cagney (Nick Condon), Sylvia Sidney (Iris Hilliard), Wallace Ford (Ollie Miller), Rosemary De Camp (Edith Miller), Robert Armstrong (Col. Tojo), John Emery (Premier Tanaka), Leonard Strong (Hijikata), Frank Puglia (Prince Tatsugi), Jack Halloran (Capt. Oshima), Hugh Ho (Kajioka), Philip Ahn (Yamamoto), Joseph Kim (Hayashi), Marvin Miller (Yamada), Rhys Williams (Joseph Cassell), Porter Hall (Arthur Bickett), James Bell (Charley Sprague), Grace Lem (Amah), Oy Chan (Chinese Servant), George Paris (Hotel Manager), Hugh Beaumont (Johnny Clarke), Arthur Loft, Gregory Gay, Emmett Vogan, Charlie Wayne (American Newsmen in Tokyo).

A tough flag-waver set in the late 1920s where Cagney is a world-wise editor of the American-owned Tokyo Chronicle who prints a story sent to him by fellow news scribes Ford and De Camp. Japanese authorities demand that he print a retraction but he refuses, then learns that the couple who supplied the information were murdered trying to get out of the country with a secret document, the "Tanaka Plan," which proves Japan's aim of world conquest, outlining its tactics to invade Manchuria and other countries. When Cagney tries to investigate his friends' murders, he is arrested and kept in jail, authorities stating that he murdered the couple in a drunken brawl. Coming to his assistance is Sidney, an Anglo-Chinese double spy who is trying tosettle an old score with the Japanese. Cagney is freed but is constantly followed. He evades his trackers and obtains the much-wanted document, getting it out of the country to alert the world to the Japanese conspiracy.

There's a lot of action here as Cagney battles native thugs, besting them in jiu-jitsu, and a slam-bang fight with Halloran, a brutish Japanese secret service captain. The sets, moody lighting, and quick-paced direction by Lloyd are commendable, enhancing Cagney's electrifying performance. Sidney is beautiful, if not a bit too decorative, as the Eurasian spy. Emery, Armstrong, Puglia and Strong, all Caucasians, are unexpectedly convincing as members of the Japanese military cabal that set its country on the path to war. Most fascinating are the details surrounding the "Tanaka Plan," which was a real document stolen in 1927 and exposed in the international press. It contained maps and details for Japan's secretly planned war against China, Korea, and the U.S. but at the time of its revelation no one took the report seriously, even the suggestion that Japanese planes would some day bomb America's Pearl of the Pacific," the great naval base at Pearl Harbor.

p, William Cagney; d, Frank Lloyd; w, Lester Cole (based on a story by Garrett Fort); ph, Theodor Sparkuhl; m, Miklos Rosza; ed, Truman Wood, Walter Hanneman; art d, Wiard Ihnen; set d, A. Roland Fields; cos, Robert Martien; tech ad, Alice Barlow.

War Drama   **Cas.**   **(PR:C   MPAA:NR)**

BLOOD ORANGE*   (1953, Brit.) 76m Hammer bw

Tom Conway (*Himself*), Mila Parely (*Helen Pascall*), Naomi Chance (*Gina*), Eric Pohlmann (*Mercedes*), Andrew Osborn (*Capt. Simpson*), Richard Wattis (*Macleod*), Margaret Halstan (*Lady Marchant*), Eileen Way (*Fernande*), Delphi Lawrence (*Chelsea*).

Ex-FBI man keeps his hand in by solving the murder of a beautiful model, and a jewel robbery as well. Weak programmer saved by the suave Conway.

p, Michael Carreras; d, Terence Fisher; w, Jan Read; ph, Jimmy Harvey; m, Ivor Slaney; ed, Maurice Rootes; art d, J. Elder Wills.

Crime Drama   **(PR:A   MPAA:NR)**

BLOOD ORGY OF THE SHE-DEVILS*   (1973) 78m Gemini bw

Lila Zaborin (*Mara*).

Zaborin's a witch queen who brews her spells in California. During a seance she contacts an old Indian spirit and creates a wolf pack of voluptuous virgins." As worthless and forgettable as it sounds. From the director of THE ASTRO-ZOMBIES.

p, d&w, Ted V. Mikels.

Horror   **(PR:O   MPAA:NR)**

BLOOD RELATIVES*   (1978, Fr./Can.) 100m Filmcorp/SNS c (LES LIENS DE SANG)

Donald Sutherland (*Carella*), Aude Landry (*Patricia*), Lisa Langlois (*Muriel*), Laurent Malet (*Andrew*), Micheline Lanctot (*Mrs. Carella*), Stephane Audran (*Mother*), Donald Pleasence (*Doniac*), David Hemmings (*Armstrong*).

The story happens in Canada, where Sutherland plays an inspector investigating the death of a 17-year-old girl whom he suspects died at the hand of a maniac. Since Pleasence is in the film, we are preconditioned to think of this as another HALLOWEEN, or one of those other Pleasence monstrosities. Chabrol fools us, though, as he casts Pleasence in the role of a deviate who likes nymphets. The plot is meandering but never dull. Chabrol is not as scary as usual.

d, Claude Chabrol; w, Chabrol, R. Sydney (based on a novel by Ed McBain [Evan Hunter]); ph, Jean Rabier (Eastmancolor); m, Paul Jensen; ed, Yves Langlois.

Crime   **(PR:O   MPAA:NR)**

BLOOD ROSE, THE**(1970, Fr.) 87m AA c (AKA: LA ROSE ESCORCHEE)

Philippe Lemaire (*Frederic*), Annie Duperey (*Anne*), Howard Vernon (*Prof. Rohmer*), Elisabeth Tessier (*Barbara*).

This movie was billed as "the first horror-sex film," although lesbian scenes were deleted from American release. A wealthy painter living in a secluded chateau with his wife whose face was horribly burned, blackmails a plastic surgeon wanted by the police into performing grafting operations. Naturally, beautiful women are needed to contribute to the grafting process. An interesting addition to this eerie, atmosphoric production are two dwarf servants, dressed in animal skins, who are sexually active and underfoot throughout.

p, Edgar Oppenheimer; d, Claude Mulot; w, Mulot, Oppenheimer, Jean Carriaga; ph, (Eastmancolor).

Horror   **(PR:O   MPAA:NR)**

BLOOD SPATTERED BRIDE, THE*   (1974, Span.) 83m Europix Int. c

Simon Andrew, Maribel Martin, Alexandra Bastedo, Dean Selmier.

Another version of Sheridan le Fanu's CARMILLA, this film was made after the success of THE VAMPIRE LOVERS. A female vampire couple sleeping in a coffin built for two and a scene of a woman in a diving mask buried in the sand with only her breasts showing contribute to a rather bizarre rendition of what is basically a lesbian vampire love story.

p, Antonio Perez Olea; d&w, Vincent Aranda (Eastmancolor).

Horror   **Cas.**   **(PR:O   MPAA:NR)**

BLOOD SUCKERS (SEE: DR. TERROR'S GALLERY OF HORRORS, 1967)

BLOOD, SWEAT AND FEAR*   (1975, Ital.) 90m Cinema Shares c

Lee J. Cobb, Franco Gasparri, Giorgia Albertazzi, Sora Serati.

Cobb is the big boss of an international narcotics ring and Gasparri a dedicated drug agent; both play cat-and-mouse in a story that is mostly intrigue but offers little action. The plot is predictable and Cobb's end predestined. Another flat tire.

d, Stevio Massi.

Crime Drama   **(PR:C-O   MPAA:NR)**

BLOOD TIDE*   (1982) 82m 21st Century c (AKA: RED TIDE, THE)

James Earl Jones (*Frye*), Jose Ferrer (*Nereus*), Lila Kedrova (*Sister Anna*), Mary Louise Weller (*Sherry*), Martin Kove (*Neil*), Deborah Shelton (*Madeline*), Lydia Cornell (*Barbara*).

Originally lensed under the title THE RED TIDE, this beautiful-looking horror film made the mistake of allowing the actors to walk in front of the gorgeous Greek scenery. Standard underwater monster saga. It gets loose when a treasure hunter blows up the grotto where it's been living, presumably, since Plato. Lots of deaths, plenty of nubile, bikini-clad bodies. Jones chews up the scenery. Ferrer and Kedrova, both the ablest of players, seem to be there as window dressing. A generally embarrassing picture for all.

p, Nico Mastorakis, Donald Langdon; d, Richard Jeffries; w, Jeffies, Langdon, Mastorakis; ph, Ari Stavrou (Technicolor); m, Jerry Moseley; ed, Robert Leighton.

Horror   **Cas.**   **(PR:O   MPAA:R)**

BLOOD WATERS OF DOCTOR Z*   (1982) 99m Barton Film Capital c (AKA: ZAAT)

Marshall Grauer, Wade Popwell, Gerald Cruse, Sanna Ringhaver, Drew Dickerson, Gloria Brady.

Just as some movies are Two Years In The Making!", this one was ten years in the releasing! This film deserves to be a cult movie in the genre of PLAN NINE FROM OUTER SPACE or ATTACK OF THE KILLER TOMATOES. Done in Florida on a teeny budget, BLOOD WATERS OF DR. Z relates the saga of a man who drinks some heavy water, then becomes a human-sized walking catfish who attacks his fellow scientists for making fun of him and who attempts to get some women to try the water so he can have a female catfish to cavort with. It's unintentionally funny, thus funnier than many intentionally funny films. It owes its birth to CREATURE FROM THE BLACK LAGOON, which was produced by (now here's a bit of trivia for you) the same man who plays the reporter asking all the questions of the various actors in CITIZEN KANE. His name is William Alland and he had absolutely nothing to do with BLOOD WATERS OF DR. Z.

p&d, Don Barton; ph, Jack McGowan (Eastmancolor); m, Jami DeFrates, Barry Hodgin; ed, George Yarbrough.

Horror   **(PR:O   MPAA:PG)**

BLOOD WEDDING***   (1981, Sp.) 72m Libra c

Antonio Gades (*Leonardo*), Christina Hoyos (*Bride*), Juan Antonio Jimenez (*Groom*), Pilar Cardenas (*Mother*), Carmen Villena (*Wife*), El Guito, Elvira Andres, Marisa Nella, Lario Diaz, Azucena Flores, Antonio Quitana, Candy Roman, Enrique Esteve, Cristina Gombau, Quico Franco (*Wedding Guests*).

This flamenco ballet transformed from Garcia Lorca's passion and revenge play is brilliantly choreographed by Antonio Gades and filmed by Carlos Saura at an actual dress rehearsal, complete with backstage preparations, interview footage, and final briefing. The stark sets place the emphasis on the remarkable dancing by Gades and his company, making this an extraordinarily evocative and exciting film. Considered to be the dance film of the decade.

p, Emiliano Piedra; d, Carlos Saura; w, Antonio Areero (based on the play by Federico Garcia Lorca, adapted by Alfredo Manas); ph, Teo Escamilla (Eastmancolor); ed, Pablo del Amo.

Ballet   **(PR:A   MPAA:NR)**

BLOODBROTHERS**1/2   (1978) 116m Kings Road/WB c

Paul Sorvino (*Chubby DeCoco*), Tony Lo Biano (*Tommy DeCoco*), Richard Gere (*Stony DeCoco*), Lelia Goldoni (*Marie*), Yvonne Wilder (*Phyllis*), Kenneth McMillan (*Banion*), Floyd Levine (*Dr. Harris*), Marilu Henner (*Annette*), Michael Hershewe (*Albert*), Christine DeBell (*Cheri*), Pamela Myers (*Mrs. Pitt*), Gloria LeRoy (*Sylvia*), Bruce French (*Paulie*), Peter Iacangelo (*Malfie*), Kim Milford (*Butler*), Robert Englund (*Mott*), Raymond Singer (*Jackie*), Lila Teigh (*Jackie's Mother*), Eddie Jones (*Blackie*), Danny Aiello (*Artie*).

Rated R mostly for foul language, BLOODBROTHERS is an ambitious and sometimes incisive look at the inner workings of an Italian-American family. Odd that there doesn't seem to be one single person of Italian ancestry involved with the creation and production of this film, other than the actors. Gere is the son of LoBianco and Goldoni, and in the process of determining whether or not to stay in the macho world of construction, like his father and uncle, Sorvino, or to give it up and do something he wants to do, work with young children. It's a hard-edged film and the people are as real as the guys in the next truck. Gere is better than usual in a more demanding role than he customarily plays. He continues to be more mannered than natural, but it is held to a minimum. LoBianco and Sorvino, as the two brothers, are instantly recognizable as the boors one usually sees at the next table in a beer bar, making so much noise that conversation is an impossibility. It's not for the weak-eared. The trouble is, it may be just a bit too real to be entertainment.

p, Stephen Friedman; d, Robert Mulligan; w, Walter Newman (based on the novel by Richard Price); ph, Robert Surtees (Technicolor); m, Elmer Bernstein; ed, Shelly Kahn; prod d, Gene Callahan.

Drama   **Cas.**   **(PR:O   MPAA:R)**

BLOODEATERS*   (1980) 84m CM Prod/Parker National c (AKA: FOREST OF FEAR)

Charles Austin (*Cole*), Beverly Shapiro (*Polly*), Dennis Heffend (*Hermit*), Paul Haskin (*Briggs*), John Amplas (*Phillips*).

The government dumps chemicals on a marijuana plantation. The experimental herbicide causes anyone nearby to turn into a zombie-like creature and go after anyone who happens into this bucolic area. Not a bad idea, fairly current for the time, but so ineptly executed that people in the theater were waiting in line to get out! BLOODEATERS stars no one you ever heard of and, although some of the actors were believable in their roles, they would be wise to omit this one from their resumes.

p,d&w, Chuck McCrann; ph, David Sperling (Movielab Color); ed, McCrann, Sperling; makeup, Craig Harris.

Horror (PA:C MPAA:R)

BLOODHOUNDS OF BROADWAY***
(1952) 89m FOX c

Mitzi Gaynor (*Emily Ann Stackerlee*), Scott Brady (*Numbers Foster*), Mitzi Green (*Tessie Sammis*), Marguerite Chapman (*Yvonne*), Michael O'Shea (*Inspector McNamara*), Wally Vernon (*Poorly Sammis*), Henry Slate (*Dave the Dude*), George E. Stone (*Ropes McGonigle*), Edwin Max (*Lookout Louie*), Richard Allan (*Curtaintime Charlie*), Sharon Baird (*Little Elida*), Paul Wexler, Ralph Volkie, Charles Buchinski, Timothy Carey, Bill Walker, Alfred Mizner, Emile Meyer.

Fast-moving Damon Runyon story about a bookie (Brady) who leaves New York to avoid an investigating committee. He tries to lose himself deep in the marshes of Georgia and there he meets Gaynor, an adorable yokelette who is determined to make it big on the Great White Way. The little lady has some talent and after saving his life, she convinces Brady (brother of Lawrence Tierney) to take her back north where she can find fame and fortune. With some scene-stealing bloodhounds in tow, she suc- ceeds in the Apple and reforms the former bet-taker. He blabs before the committee and is sent away for a year. Vernon (Poorly Sammis) later became the resident comic at Disneyland's Pepsi-Cola show and lasted there for many years. Look for Buchinski as Pittsburgh Philo (a take-off on Pittsburgh Phil, who was really a killer in the 1930s and part of Murder Inc.). Buchinski is, of course, Charles Bronson. Mostly standard songs, good choreography by Bob Sydney who created some hip-slinging numbers for this film and who stayed with Gaynor well into the 1970s as her TV specials dance director.

p, George Jessel; d, Harmon Jones; w, Sy Gomberg (based on a story by Damon Runyon); ph, Edward Cronjager (Technicolor); m, Lionel Newman; ed, George A. Gittens; cos, Travilla; m/l, Eliot Daniel, Ben Oakland, Paul Webster.

Musical (PR:A MPAA:NR)

BLOODLINE**
(1979) 116m Geria/PAR c (AKA:SIDNEY SHELDON'S BLOODLINE)

Audrey Hepburn (*Elizabeth Roffe*), Ben Gazzara (*Rhys Williams*), James Mason (*Sir Alec Nichols*), Claudia Mori (*Donatella*), Irene Papas (*Simonetta Palazza*), Michelle Phillips (*Vivian Nichols*), Maurice Ronet (*Charles Martin*), Romy Schneider (*Helene Martin*), Omar Sharif (*Ivo Palazzi*), Beatrice Straight (*Kate Erling*), Gert Frobe (*Inspector Max Hornung*), Wolfgang Preiss (*Julius Prager*), Marcel Bozzuffi (*Man in Black*), Pinkas Braun (*Dr. Wal*), Wulf Kessler (*Young Sam Roffe*).

An all-star cast and a big-hit book combine to make a blah-blah film. Sheldon writes blockbuster books that seem to have trouble translating to the screen. Perhaps Sheldon, who began life as a screenwriter and won the Oscar in 1947 for THE BACHELOR AND THE BOBBY SOXER, should adapt his own work instead of leaving it to other hands. The novel BLOODLINE was a first-rate/third-rate book, filled with all sorts of high intrigue, fascinating characters (most notably Hornung, played by Frobe here) and a far-fetched plot that could be swallowed, provided one read the book at three sittings or more. However, when we are asked to see it all happen in 116 minutes, the inconsistencies assault the mind like wild Zulus. Hepburn as the young heiress to a pharmaceuticals fortune is the target of death threats and no one can figure out who the miscreant is. Lots of soap opera among the secondary characters; Morricone's music sounds better when the dialog is dialed out.

p, David V. Picker, Sidney Beckerman; d, Terence Young; w, Laird Koenig (based on the novel by Sidney Sheldon); ph, Freddie Young (Movielab Color); m, Ennio Morricone; ed, Bud Molin; prod d, Ted Haworth; cos, Enrico Sabbatini.

Drama/Mystery Cas. (PR:O MPAA:R)

BLOODLUST*
(1959) 89m Crown International bw

Wilton Graff (*Dr. Balleau*), June Kenney, Robert Reed, Lilyan Chauvin.

A ripoff of THE MOST DANGEROUS GAME with Graff as an evil doctor who stores his teenaged victims' cadavers in glass tanks. Does the Brady Bunch know father (Reed) started this way? A cheap little quickie with no real value.

p,d&w, Ralph Brooke.

Horror (PR:O MPAA:NR)

BLOODSUCKERS
(SEE: INCENSE FOR THE DAMNED, 1971)

BLOODSUCKING FREAKS zero
(1982) 88m Troma c (AKA: INCREDIBLE TORTURE SHOW, THE)

Seamus O'Brien (*Sardu*), Louie DeJesus (*Ralphus*), Niles McMaster (*Tom*), Viju Krim (*Natasha*), Alan Dellay (*Crazy Silo*), Dan Fauci (*Det. Sgt. Tucci*).

In 1976, this picture escaped (it couldn't have been released) under the name THE INCREDIBLE TORTURE SHOW. It has not gotten any better because of the name change. Inept, horrible, gory, it is an attempt to cash in on the basest of human natures; seeing people in pain. A so-called Theater of the Absurd is really a front for a NYC white slave trade. It's your basic sado-masochist film for all the flashers and whippers in the audience. Anyone with any taste, avoid this.

p, Alan Margolin; d&w, Joel M. Reed; ph, Gerry Toll; m, Michael Sahl; ed, Victor Kanefsky; ch, Gyles Fontaine; spec makeup eff, Bob O'Bradovich.

Horror Cas. (PR:O MPAA:R)

BLOODTHIRSTY BUTCHERS*1/2
(1970) 85m Constitution Films c

John Miranda, Annabella Wood, Berwick Kaler, Jane Helay, Michael Cox, Linda Driver, Jonathan Holt, Ann Arrow.

Gory re-telling of the Sweeney Todd legend. In Victorian London a barber and baker conspire for a series of brutal murders. Their assistant kidnaps and kills customers who end up in "meat pies." An unsuspecting salesgirl goes to the police when her boy friend disappears and the plot is revealed. Film ends with the barber and his assistant hacking each other to death. Vulgar and violent, the material was made into a much better macabre musical by Stephen Sondheim called "Sweeney Todd: The Demon Barber of Fleet Street."

p, William Mishkin; d, Andy Milligan; w, Milligan, John Borske; ph, Milligan; art d, James Fox.

Horror/Drama Cas. (PR:O MPAA:R)

BLOODY BROOD, THE zero
(1959, Can.) 80m AA/Key Films

Jack Betts (*Cliff*), Barbara Lord (*Ellie*), Peter Falk (*Nico*), Robert Christie (*Det. McLeod*), Ronald Hartmann (*Francis*), Anne Collins (*A Model*), William Brydon (*Studs*), George Sperdakos (*Ricky*), Ronald Taylor (*Dave*), Michael Zenon (*Weasel*), Billy Kowalchuk (*Roy*), Sammy Sales (*Louis*), Kenneth Wickes (*Paul, the Poet*), Carol Starkman (*Blonde Neighbor*), Rolf Colstan (*Stephanex*).

Sleazy tale of a man's search for the crazed beatniks who fed his brother a ground-glass-filled hamburger. Falk plays the hipster chief, killed by his own followers just before police arrive. A waste of good celluloid.

p&d, Julian Hoffman; w, Elwood Ullman, Ben Kerner (based on a story by Anne Edward Bailey); ph, Eugen Shuftan; m, Harry Freedman; ed, Robert Johnson.

Crime Cas. (PR:O MPAA:NR)

BLOODY KIDS**1/2
(1983, Brit.) 91m Black Lion/Palace-BFI c

Derrick O'Connor, Gary Holton, Richard Thomas, Peter Clark, Gwynneth Strong, Caroline Embling, Jack Douglas, Billy Colvill, Mel Smith, P. H. Moriarity, Richard Hope. Niall Padden, John Mulcahy, Terry Paris, Neil Cunningham, George Costigan, Stewart Harwood, Tammy Jacobs, Daniel Peacock, Paul Mari, Jimmy Hibbert, Kim Taylforth, Nula Conwell, Madeline Church, Gary Olson.

A wild, hyperkinetic story about two Southend kids who go off for a Saturday night spree. A surreal, high-energy street film with some intelligent social criticism, BLOODY KIDS was thrown onto British TV after its backers got scared with the content. Great visual style really helps the anarchic storytelling.

p, Barry Hanson; d, Stephen Frears; w, Stephen Poliakoff; ph, Chris Menges; m, George Fenton; ed, Peter Coulson; art d, Martin Johnson.

Drama (PR:O MPAA:NR)

BLOODY MAMA zero
(1970) 90m AIP c

Shelley Winters (*Kat "Ma" Barker*), Pat Hingle (*Sam Pendlebury*), Don Stroud (*Herman Barker*), Diane Varsi (*Mona Gibson*), Bruce Dern (*Kevin Kirkman*), Clint Kimbrough (*Arthur Barker*), Robert Walden (*Fred Barker*), Robert DeNiro (*Lloyd Barker*), Alex Nicol (*George Barker*), Michael Fox (*Dr. Roth*), Scatman Crothers (*Moses*), Stacy Harris (*Agent McClellan*), Pamela Dunlap (*Rembrandt*).

Sleazy, smutty story allegedly about Ma Barker and her kill-crazy sons, the notorious Barker gang of the early 1930s. Winters (big, fat, as repulsive as the lead in the disgusting PINK FLAMINGOS) is Ma, sleeping with one and all as she directs her lethal sons to rob banks, kidnap, and murder at will. Stroud, as Herman Barker, is about as obnoxious as Winters, with Walden a close third in the repugnant category. Varsi, a fairly good actress, disgraces herself in this slimy film (a true product of garbage-monger Corman) by playing the role of a sex plaything. In one scene she fornicates in a moving car with one brother, then hops into the back seat to have intercourse with another Barker offspring. All of the leads act like lunatics about to self-destruct at any second. Nothing in this film relates to the true story of the Barker clan (a film that should still be made) and nothing in the inane story or cretinous direction is redeemable. A dump heap filmed in color.

p&d, Roger Corman; w, Robert Thom (based on a story by Thom and Don Peters); ph, John A. Alonzo (Movielab Color); m, Don Randi; ed, Eve Newman; cos, Thomas Costich.

Crime Cas. (PR:O MPAA:R)

BLOODY PIT OF HORROR, THE zero
(1965, Ital.) 87m Pacemaker bw (AKA: CRIMSON EXECUTIONER; THE RED HANGMAN)

Mickey Hargitay (*Anderson*), Louise Barrett (*Edith*), Walter Brandt, Moa Thai, Ralph Zucker, Albert Gordon.

Sadistic film Hargitay made while in Italy with wife Jayne Mansfield (who was then working on PRIMITIVE LOVE). He's the proprietor of a castle that is visited by a publisher and horror novelist. They bring along a secretary, a photographer, and a quintette of sexy models for some book jacket photos. When they enter the private torture chamber for some gratuitous nude scenes, Hargitay takes on the persona of the castle's original owner, donning tights and face mask and indulging in various sadistic practices with his vistors. It's all ridiculous garbage. Supposedly, this is based on the writings of the Marquis de Sade, but even the cruel Marquis wouldn't subject anyone to this film.

p, Francesco Merli; d, Massimo Pupillo; w, Roberto Natale, Romano Migliorini; ph, Luciano Trasatti; m, Gino Peguri; ed, Robert Ardis; art d, Frank Arnold.

Horror (PR:O MPAA:NR)

BLOOMFIELD*1/2

(1971, Brit./Israel) 95m World Film Sales c (AKA: THE HERO)

Richard Harris (Eitan), Kim Burfield (Nimrod), Romy Schneider (Nira), Maurice Kaufman (Yasha), Robert Alexander.

Pretentious, incompetent story of an aging soccer star, the boy who idolizes him, and the artist he loves (Schneider). The big game at the end is embarrassingly bad. Harris' first attempt at directing; it appears he should stick with acting.

p, Wolf Mankowitz, John Heyman; d, Richard Harris; w, Mankowitz, Harris; ph, Otto Heller (Technicolor); m, Johnny Harris.

Drama　　　　　　　　　　　　　　　　　　　　　　**(PR:C　MPAA:NR)**

BLOSSOM TIME　　　　　　　　　(SEE: APRIL BLOSSOMS, 1937)

BLOSSOMS IN THE DUST**1/2　　　　　(1941) 100m MGM c

Greer Garson (Edna Gladney), Walter Pidgeon (Sam Gladney), Felix Bressart (Dr. Max Breslar), Marsha Hunt (Charlotte), Fay Holden (Mrs. Kahly), Samuel S. Hinds (Mr. Kahly), Kathleen Howard (Mrs. Keats), George Lessey (Mr. Keats), William Henry (Allan Keats), Henry O'Neill (Judge), John Eldredge (Damon McPherson), Clinton Rosemund (Zeke), Theresa Harris (Cleo), Charles Arnt (G. Harrison Hedger), Cecil Cunningham (Mrs. Gilworth), Ann Morriss (Mrs. Loring), Marc Lawrence (Bert La Verne), Frank Darien (Accountant), Will Wright (Senator), Edwin Maxwell (Board Member), Almira Sessions.

BLOSSOMS IN THE DUST is the true story of Edna Gladney, the woman who began the Texas Children's Home and Aid Society of Fort Worth. It was a noble deed and a noble effort to make a biography about a woman who was virtually unknown outside Texas but the picture was long, overly teary, and didn't excite too many people at the box office, although it did make money. Garson and Hunt are adopted daughters of a Wisconsin couple. Garson is about to get married, then meets Pidgeon, falls in love, and plans to go with him to Texas where he has a flour mill. Marsha is also about to get married but when it is learned that she's illegitimate, her fiance's parents say no. She promptly commits suicide. Garson and Pidgeon move to Texas, she has a child, then learns she can't have any more. Their little boy dies and Garson now needs a reason to live so she devotes herself to establishing the home cited above. Pidgeon dies after a series of business failures and Greer continues working for the Home. She succeeds in having the word "illegitimate" stricken from birth certificates and establishes herself as a Texas legend. The "blossoms" in the title refer to the children. Garson has one sensational scene with all the stops pulled out—sort of like something Capra would do. She makes an impassioned plea to the Texas Senate and when it's over, you'll want to cheer.

p, Irving Asher; d, Mervyn LeRoy; w, Anita Loos (based on a story by Ralph Wheelwright); ph, Karl W. Freund, W. Howard Green (Technicolor); m, Herbert Stothart; ed, George Boemler; art d, Cedric Gibbons, Urie McCleary; set d, Edwin B. Willis; cos, Adrian, Giles Steele.

Biography　　　　　　　　　　　　　　　　　　　　**(PR:A　MPAA:NR)**

BLOSSOMS ON BROADWAY**　　　　　(1937) 83m PAR bw

Edward Arnold (Ira Collins), Shirley Ross (Sally Shea), John Trent (Nell Graham), Rufe Davis (Sheriff Holloway), Weber and Fields (Themselves), William Frawley (Francis X. Rush), Frank Craven (P. J. Quinterfield, Sr.), John Arthur (P. J. Quinterfield, Jr.), Frederick Clarke (Chester), Edward Brophy (Mr. Prussic), Charles Halton (Dr. Gilgallon), Kitty Kelly ("Death Valley Cora" Keene), The Radio Rogues ("Eddie" and "Jimmy").

Ross is a sweet young thing whom Arnold promotes as a fabulous female gold miner fresh from the fields. The real gold-mining woman has been kidnaped by Arnold and is being held incognito (a nice job by Kelly) while Arnold plans to use the unsuspecting Ross as a foil to con millionaire Craven. Shirley falls in love with the man who is supposed to be her chauffeur and who turns out to be a G-Man. Kelly's boy friend, a Nevada sheriff, arrives and sees that Shirley is not Kitty, so he blows the whistle on the ruse. Lightweight script made somewhat heavier by Arnold's effective thesping. Songs by Manning Sherwin and Frank Loesser not memorable but just right for the picture. Weber and Fields, who are reputed to be the models for Neil Simon's "Sunshine Boys," do a funny turn. There was a time when Edward Arnold actually considered running for the U.S. Senate from California, thus predating George Murphy. Born Gunther Edward Arnold Schneider, he once served as President of the Screen Actors Guild, the same office once held by former actor Ronald Reagan.

p, B. P. Schulberg; d, Richard Wallace; w, Theodore Reeves; ph, Leon Shamroy; m/l, Manning Sherwin, Frank Loesser, Leo Robin, Ralph Rainger, Phil Boutelje, Ralph Freed.

Musical　　　　　　　　　　　　　　　　　　　　　**(PR:A　MPAA:NR)**

BLOW OUT zero　　　　　　　　　(1981) 108m Filmways c

John Travolta (Jack), Nancy Allen (Sally), John Lithgow (Burke), Dennis Franz (Karp), Peter Boyden (Sam), Curt May (Frank), Ernest McClure (Jim), Davie Roberts (Anchor Man), Maurice Copeland (Jack), Claire Carter (Anchor Woman), John Aquino (Detective), John Hoffmeister (McRyan), Patrick McNamara (Nelson), Terrence Currier (Lawrence Henry), Tom McCarthy (Policeman), Dean Bennett (Campus Guard).

BLOWOUT was supposed to be the movie that took beleaguered Filmways out of trouble. Knowledgeable people know that Filmways barely exists any longer. De Palma, the greatest-rip-off-of-Hitchcock director, has given us one of his most inept, disgusting pictures yet. DRESSED TO KILL and BODY DOUBLE have since surpassed BLOW OUT for stupidity and violence, but BLOW OUT—this time not a Hitchcock rip-off, but rather an Antonioni clone (BLOW-UP, 1966)—had to rank as the cock-a-doodle-doo of 1981. Travolta is a sound man who discovers that a blow out on a bridge was really a gunshot, followed by the car going over the side.

In the car is a male politician and with him is prostitute Allen (with a squeaky, fingernails-across-the-blackboard-voice) whom Travolta heroically saves from a watery death. This is sort of a reverse of the Kennedy incident at Chappaquiddick. The thing is that the story precis reads better than it plays. De Palma is a good photographer (or maybe that's Zsigmond) because all of his pictures look better than they are. When are De Palma and Colin Higgins going to leave poor Hitchcock alone? Hitch became a star director by his originality. De Palma and Higgins claim homages to the great Alfred but what they are doing is blatant copying, followed by excess. If someone offers you a free videotape of BLOW OUT, erase it immediately and use it to record BAMBI or CITIZEN KANE or DUEL IN THE SUN or anything else that hasn't been touched by De Palma.

p, George Litto; d&w, Brian De Palma; ph, Vilmos Zsigmond (Technicolor); m, Pino Donaggio; ed, Paul Hirsch; prod d, Paul Sylbert; set d, Jeannine Oppenwall; cos, Vicki Sanchez.

Mystery　　　　　　　**Cas.**　　　　　　　**(PR:O　MPAA:R)**

BLOW TO THE HEART**

(1983, Ital.) 105m RAI-Antea Cinematografica/Other Cinema c

Jean-Louis Trintignant, Laura Morante, Fausto Rossi, Sonia Gessner, Vanni Corbellini, Laura Nucci, Matteo Cerami, Vera Rossi.

Some nice things are going on in this film, though it's really a re-telling of old themes. A father and son have an emotional conflict over the political terrorism going on in modern Italy. There's an interesting casting reverse: the father is shaming his son with his terrorist activities. Still it's been done before under better hands.

p, Enzo Porcelli; d, Gianni Amelio; w, Amelio, Vincenzo Cerami; ph, Tonino Nardi; m, Franco Piersanti; ed, Ana Napoli; art d, Marco Dentici.

Drama　　　　　　　　　　　　　　　　　　　　　　**(PR:O　MPAA:NR)**

BLOW YOUR OWN TRUMPET*　　　　(1958, Brit.) 56m Cecil Musk CFF bw

Michael Crawford (Jim Fenn), Peter Butterworth (Mr. Duff), Gillian Harrison (Helen Fenn), Martyn Shields (Tony Holroyd), Arley Welfare Band.

A down-on-his-luck band conductor, fired from his job, does not let it make him bitter and goes on to help a young boy win a cornet contest. A few good musical moments.

d, Cecil Musk; w, Mary Cathcart Borer (based on a story by Geoffrey Bond); ph, Jo Jago.

Children　　　　　　　　　　　　　　　　　　　　　**(PR:A　MPAA:NR)**

BLOWING WILD**　　　　　　　　(1953) 89m WB bw

Gary Cooper (Jeff), Barbara Stanwyck (Marina), Ruth Roman (Sal), Anthony Quinn (Paco), Ward Bond (Dutch), Ian MacDonald (Jackson), Richard Karlan (Henderson), Juan Garcia (El Gavilan).

The producers got Cooper and Tiomkin (who teamed well in HIGH NOON), but it didn't help this ordinary movie get out of the doldrums. Cooper is a wildcatter in Mexico in the early 1930s. Times are bad because he's besieged by bandits. He turns to Quinn, a rich oilman, for a job but Quinn is wreaking revenge for the affair that Coop had with Stanwyck, Quinn's fiery wife. Barbara would like to bed Gary again, but he's being true to Roman, an American woman who's stranded south of the border. Garcia, the bandit leader, demands $50,000 or he'll blow up the oil field. Quinn tells him to take a walk. Stanwyck later pushes Quinn into a functioning oil well and the pump mashes him. Later, Cooper is shocked by Stanwyck when she admits what she did and says it was all for his love. Cooper can't believe his ears and is ready to turn her in when their argument is interrupted by Garcia who is on his way to fulfill his threat. Cooper kills Garcia and a dynamite explosion does the job to Stanwyck. Picture could have used some tighter editing and further exposition of Stanwyck's nymphomaniacal character. Movies like this and several of Joan Crawford's later pictures give women a bad name.

p, Milton Sperling; d, Hugo Fregonese; w, Phillip Yordan; ph, Sid Hickox; m, Dmitri Tiomkin; ed, Alan Crosland; m/l, Tiomkin, Paul Francis Webster, sung by Frankie Laine.

Adventure/Western　　　　　　　　　　　　　　　　**(PR:C　MPAA:NR)**

BLOW-UP*　　　　　　　　　　(1966, Brit.) 110m Premier Productions c

David Hemmings (Thomas), Vanessa Redgrave (Jane), Sarah Miles (Patricia), Jane Birkin, Gillian Hills (Teenagers), Peter Bowles (Ron), Harry Hutchinson (Antiques Dealer), John Castle (Painter), Susan Broderick (Antique Shop Owner), Mary Khal (Fashion Editor), Ronan O'Casey (Jane's Lover), Tsai Chin (Receptionist), Jill Kennington, Peggy Moffitt, Rosaleen Murray, Ann Norman, Melanie Hampshire (Models), The Yardbirds.

Overblown and overrated Antonioni film which offers an anemic-looking Hemmings as a chic London photographer who, while haphazardly snapping off human interest shots in the park, captures what he thinks is a murder in progress. He blows up several shots to unearth the foul play with less than conclusive results for the viewer. Most of the time Hemmings is frolicking in bed with assorted nude models. Redgrave is topless in a performance that could have been rendered by any nameless actress. The absence of a musical score through great portions of the film was thought to be artistic at the time but now it merely reaffirms the pedestrian techniques employed to make a dull story even duller. What was it all about? A notion in the director's head, one even he was unsure about. MGM was positive; after its executives took a look at this ambiguous product they said no, and let producer Ponti release the film on his own. The general public rejected the film and so Ponti played it to the so-called cognoscenti in the art houses. Naturally, it was a success there because it answered no questions, told a next-to-nothing story, and left everything up to the kind of viewer who likes to make up his own film. All of this does not preclude the film from being outright boring, terribly presumptuous, and a study in artistic fakery.

p, Pierre Rouve, Carlo Ponti; d, Michelangelo Antonioni; w, Antonioni, Tonino Guerra, Edward Bond (based on a story by Julio Cortazar); ph, Carlo di Palma (Metro Color); m, Herbie Hancock, The Yardbirds; ed, Frank Clarke; set d, Assheton Gorton; cos, Jocelyn Rickards; makeup, Paul Rabiger.

Crime **Cas.** **(PR:O MPAA:NR)**

BLUE* 1/2 (1968) 113m PAR c

Terence Stamp *(Blue/Azul)*, Joanna Pettet *(Joanne Morton)*, Karl Malden *(Doc Morton)*, Ricardo Montalban *(Ortega)*, Anthony Costello *(Jess Parker)*, Joe De Santis *(Carlos)*, James Westerfield *(Abe)*, Stathis Giallelis *(Manuel)*, Carlos East *(Xavier)*, Sara Vardi *(Inez)*, Robert Lipton *(Antonio)*.

BLUE is a waste of time from the outset. Stamp is the adopted son of Mexican bandido Montalban. He rescues Pettet and her father, Malden, from the bandits, then lives with the two for a year until he's discovered. Montalban wants him back. A fight. Lots of deaths. Boo. Pretentious direction by Narizzano with Leone-like close-ups and Peckinpah-like slow-motion. Stamp is miscast and his English accent shows through on those rare lines when he speaks at all. The only decent action comes out of Canutt's second unit. This movie cost about five million, more than two million over budget. A waste for everyone concerned. The acting is as good as can be expected with a rotten script and deadly direction. Nice photography by Cortez. Giallelis (Manuel) made such a splash in Kazan's AMERICA, AMERICA that great things were expected from him. He never should have taken this role. Winkler disliked the film so much that he took his name off the credits.

p, Judd Bernard, Irwin Winkler; d, Silvio Narizzano; w, Meade Roberts, Ronald M. Cohen (based on a story by Cohen); ph, Stanley Cortez (Technicolor), m, Manos Hadjidakis; ed, Stewart Linder.

Western **(PR:C MPAA:NR)**

BLUE ANGEL, THE***

(1930, Ger.) 99m UFA/PAR bw (DER BLAUE ENGEL)

Emil Jannings *(Professor Immanuel Rath)*, Marlene Dietrich *(Lola Frohlich)*, Kurt Gerron *(Kiepert, a Magician)*, Rosa Valette *(Guste, his Wife)*, Hans Albers *(Mazeppa)*, Eduard von Winterstein *(Principal of the School)*, Reinhold Bernt *(The Clown)*, Hans Roth *(Beadle)*, Rolf Muller *(Angst, a Student)*, Robert Klein-Lork *(Goldstaub, a Student)*, Karl Huszar-Puffy *(Publican)*, Wilhelm Diegelmann *(Captain)*, Gerhard Bienert *(Policeman)*, Ilse Furstenberg *(Rath's Housekeeper)*.

Jannings is a stern but respected professor who discovers some of his students passing postcards which show sexy photos of a cabaret singer appearing at a local den, The Blue Angel. That night, thinking to catch some of his students in the place, Jannings goes to the club and is caught up in the wild atmosphere, then entranced as he witnesses Dietrich as the sultry Lola-Lola vamp about the stage in stockings, garter belt, high heels and corset, her blonde bobbed hair covered with a top hat at a jaunty angle. Following her performance, Jannings finds himself in Dietrich's dressing room where she instantly captivates him. She later sings to him as he sips champagne in the guest-of-honor box. He wakes the next morning, embarrassed, in Dietrich's bed. Quickly the professor dresses in his old-fashioned clothes and scurries to his school. His students know how he has spent the night and they have drawn cruel, obscene cartoons of him and Dietrich on the blackboard. Jannings is shocked at this sight; the students jeer at him, and the principal, von Winterstein, is drawn to the commotion. He sees the drawings and quickly learns of the professor's indiscretion. He dismisses him from his post. Dumfounded, Jannings goes back to the club to see Dietrich, seeking sympathy. His savings and his courtly, ancient manners intrigue her. She comforts him and then quickly convinces him to marry her. The nuptials hold no bliss for Jannings; he is soon reduced to being Dietrich's servant, traveling with the troupe and making money by selling sexy photos of his wife to customers. Gerron, the opportunistic manager of the troupe, purposely schedules a visit to the town where Jannings once taught school, thinking to cash in on the professor's one-time standing in the community. Jannings is put on stage in front of his former students and ordered to play the buffoon. He is made up in a grotesque clown outfit and indignities are heaped upon him by other players; a raw egg is cracked upon his skull cap and the audience howls with laughter as the egg runs over his face. He then crows like a rooster, something Jannings had done earlier at his wedding. Now he is mortified and disgraced. Jannings is half mad with humiliation and runs offstage only to see his wife making love to another actor, Albers. He grabs the gold-digger who has ruined his life and begins to strangle her, but stagehands pull him away and toss him into the alley. Now he is utterly alone, a used-up human being. Jannings staggers to his old school and goes to the classroom where he once taught. He sits behind his desk peering hopelessly at the empty seats before him. Nothing but jeering ghosts greet his empty gaze. His spirits crushed, Jannings lowers his head and dies. The filming of this grim, ritualistic decline and fall of a respectable man at the hands of a scheming vamp is one of the most horrific studies of human degradation on filmic record, one so memorable that it made an overnight star of Dietrich and revived Janning's fading career; he had scored many a silent film triumph, THE LAST COMMAND, THE LAST LAUGH, but his thick, guttural German accent had prevented him from making an easy transition to the talkies. When casting about for a vehicle to return him to star status, Jannings first selected a script dealing with Rasputin and then asked director Josef von Sternberg, the man who had guided him through THE LAST COMMAND, and to an Oscar, Hollywood's first (and also for THE WAY OF ALL FLESH), von Sternberg said no to the Rasputin story, opting for a novel written by Heinrich Mann in 1904, originally selecting Brigit Helm to play the part of the manipulative singer. The author asked for Trude Hesterberg, a popular Berlin entertainer, but she was thought to be too obscure, having no audience recognition value. It was therefore paradoxical that Dietrich, a German leading lady of essentially B films, was selected or "discovered" by von Sternberg. The drector ordered his scriptwriters to keep only the bones of Mann's story and accent the role of the vamp, making her a sultry and irresistible love goddess. They went at their task with a vengeance, doubling the heroine's name to "Lola-Lola" because it was twice as sexy, according to one report. The movie was made both in German and English and released world-wide, although the English version did poorly the first time around because of the heavy German accents. Oddly, the German version with English subtitles, was much more popular and it remains so today. Jannings, considered at one time to be "the greatest actor in the world," more for his stage theatrics than the subtle style employed in films, stayed in Germany to become a willing propaganda tool for the Nazis, making race-slurring films for Josef Goebbels' Ministry of Propaganda. He would survive WW II, but die as much alone and in disgrace in 1950 as he did in THE BLUE ANGEL 20 years earlier. Two of his fellow actors in the von Sternberg masterpiece, Gerron and Huszar-Puffy, later died in Nazi concentration camps. Von Sternberg, having made his only German film, returned to the U.S. with his new star, Dietrich. Once back in Hollywood, von Sternberg quickly made MOROCCO with Dietrich and Gary Cooper, holding up THE BLUE ANGEL for American release until Dietrich had caught the public fancy in an American film, making THE BLUE ANGEL easier to promote when it was released a year after MOROCCO. From the moment she straddled a chair and low-moaned "Falling in Love Again," Dietrich became the epitome of a mystical woman capable of enslaving the passions of any man, an aloof beauty, cold as space, who could measure and master any male. This was seen by everyone except Jannings during the filming of THE BLUE ANGEL. Jannings considered the film *his* vehicle and told Heinrich Mann so as both watched the temptress go into her act. Mann pointed to the limp-eyed blonde with the stunning figure and whispered: "The success of this film will be found in the naked thighs of Miss Dietrich." (Remade in 1959.)

p, Erich Pommer; d, Josef von Sternberg; w, Robert Liebmann, Karl Vollmoller, Carl Zuckmayer (based on the novel *Professor Unrat* by Heinrich Mann); ph, Gunther Rittau, Hans Schneeberger; m, Friedrich Hollander; ed, Sam Winston; set d, Otto Hunte, Emil Hasler; m/l, "Nimm Dich in Acht vor Blonden Frauen," "Ich Bin Von Kopf Bis Fuss Auf Liebe Einestellt" ("Falling in Love Again"), "Kinder, Heut Abend Such Ich Mir Was Aus," "Ich Bin Die Fesche Lola" ("I'm Naughty Little Lola") by Friedrich Hollander, Robert Liebmann, English lyrics, Sam Lerner.

Drama **Cas.** **(PR:O MPAA:NR)**

BLUE ANGEL, THE 1/2** (1959) 107m FOX c

Curt Jurgens *(Prof. Immanuel Rath)*, May Britt *(Lola-Lola)*, Theodore Bikel *(Klepert)*, John Banner *(Principal Harter)*, Fabrizio Mioni *(Rolf)*, Ludwig Stossel *(Prof. Braun)*, Wolfe Barzell *(Clown)*, Ina Anders *(Gussie)*, Richard Tyler *(Keiselsack)*, Voytck Dolinski *(Mueller)*, Ken Walken *(Ertzum)*, Del Erickson *(Lohmann)*, Edit Angold *(Emilie)*.

Another remake that falls far short of the original. Jurgens is a middle-aged professor who falls madly in love with Britt, a gorgeous cafe singer. He is so crazy for her that he quits his respected position and joins her small performing company. She has little interest in him and when his savings run out, she couldn't care less. But Bikel, manager of the troupe, sees some value in having the old fellow playing the clown. Thus Jurgens is Pagliacci and he cries real tears when his now-wife begins having affairs with men closer to her own age. Eventually, he becomes enraged and tries to strangle Britt. This is stopped just in time when some of his intellectual schoolfriends convince him to let her be and return to the life he once knew. In 1959, the producers opted for a happy ending and Jurgens is saved. The 1930 original had Jannings die in his classroom. Excellent as the principal of Jurgens' school is Banner, who played Sgt. Shultz on the TV series "Hogan's Heroes." Oddly enough, Banner (who played Nazis so often that he used to cry when he heard "Lili Marlene") posed for a series of U.S. Army recruiting posters. Jurgens comes off well in the part but Britt (born Maybritt Wilkens in Sweden) did not have the necessary talent to make anyone forget Marlene Dietrich. The producers tried very hard to duplicate the original, even using the same songs, but they forgot the primary rule of remakes; never make a picture over unless you can make it better. In the case of the 1930 version, it would have been impossible to improve on it.

p, Jack Cummings; d, Edward Dmytryk; w, Nigel Balchin (based on the screenplay by Carl Zuckmayer, Karl Vollmoeller, Robert Liebmann, from the novel by Heinrich Mann); ph, Leon Shamroy (CinemaScope, DeLuxe Color); m, Hugo Friedhofer; ed, Jack W. Holmes; cos, Adele Balkan; ch, Hermes Pan.

Drama **Cas.** **(PR:O MPAA:NR)**

BLUE BIRD, THE** (1940) 83m Fox c

Shirley Temple *(Mytyl)*, Spring Byington *(Mummy Tyl)*, Nigel Bruce *(Mr. Luxury)*, Gale Sondergaard *(Tylette)*, Eddie Collins *(Tylo)*, Edwin Maxwell *(Oak)*, Thurston Hall *(Father Time)*, Sterling Holloway *(Wild Plum)*, Claire Du Brey *(Nurse)*, Dorothy Dearing *(Cypress)*.

This version of THE BLUE BIRD generally marked the end of Shirley Temple's careerjust the way it almost did the same for Liz Taylor in the later version. It was beautiful to look at in glorious Technicolor but was not enough of a fantasy to get the kiddie crowd and just too silly for the adults. The plot of Hansel and Gretel looking for the Blue Bird of Happiness and finding it's right there at home was too simplistic for even the smallest tots. It all takes place in a dream and that's what happened in the theaters as most of the patrons were falling asleep. One of the highlights is the performance of everyone's favorite villainess, Sondergaard. Gale was a Danish-American woman who specialized in playing the dark, swarthy types of mean ladies. Her career was irreparably damaged during the witch hunts of the fifties when she and her husband Herbert Biberman were blacklisted. Biberman had been a screen-writer of some note when he joined several other men in refusing to testify one way or the other about their political affiliations.

p, Darryl F. Zanuck; d, Walter Lang; w, Ernest Pascal, Walter Bullock (based on theplay by Maurice Maeterlinck); ph, Arthur Miller, Ray Rennahan (Technicolor); m, Alfred Newman; ed, Robert Bischoff; ch, Geneva Sawyer.

Fantasy (PR:AA MPAA:NR)

BLUE BIRD, THE*½ (1976) 100m Fox c

Elizabeth Taylor *(Mother, Witch)*, Jane Fonda *(Night)*, Ava Gardner *(Luxury)*, Cicely Tyson *(Cat)*, Robert Morley *(Father Time)*, Harry Andrews *(Oak)*, Todd Lookinland *(Tyltyl)*, Patsy Kensit *(Mytyl)*, Will Geer *(Grandfather)*, Mona Washbourne *(Grandmother)*, George Cole *(Dog)*, Richard Pearson *(Bread)*, Nadejda Pavlova *(The Blue Bird)*, George Vitzin *(Sugar)*, Margareta Terechova *(Milk)*, Oleg Popov *(Fat Laughter)*, Leonid Nevedomsky *(Father)*, Valentina Ganilaee Ganibalova *(Water)*, Yevgeny Scherbakov *(Fire)*, Pheona McLellan *(Sick Girl)*.

The third time was *not* the charm with the making of THE BLUE BIRD in 1975. It had been a successful play, then a book, but the 1918 silent version (by Maurice Tourneur) and the 1940 version (starring Shirley Temple) were flops. So, when it was decided to sink millions into something that had been sunk before, all the smart people at Fox agreed it was a good idea. A whole bunch of money came from the Soviet Union and this was to be the first Detente movie ever made with USA/USSR cooperation. If the resultant film is any example of American-Soviet relations and how well we work together, start looking for an island in the south seas to hide out. The story is simple; two peasant children are taken from their home to a fantasy world in search of the bulebird-of-happiness. After 100 minutes, they find that true happiness can be found in . . . oh, but why give away the surprise? Liz Taylor plays four parts, in between getting sick in Russia with dysentery, dehydration, and an incredible craving for Chasen's chili. Jane Fonda, as "Night," spent a lot of time talking politics on the set. Cicely Tyson couldn't be lit properly as there were no black women in Leningrad who could play stand-in for her while she changed costumes. James Coco got sick making the film and his replacement, George Cole, had to be flown in. Ava Gardner came out of Spanish retirement to collect a lot of money as "Luxury." It's an old saying that if the picture has a lot of trouble in the making, if there are arguments, shouting, recriminations, the film will surely be a hit. THE BLUE BIRD had more trouble than most pictures in recent history and managed to take in just a tiny percentage of the vast sums it cost to make. So much for old sayings.

p, Paul Maslansky; d, George Cukor; w, Hugh Whitemore, Alfred Hayes, Alexi Kapler (based on the novel by Maurice Maeterlinck); m, Irwin Kostal, Lionel Newman; ph, Freddie Young (DeLuxe Color); ed, Ernest Walter, Tatyana Shapiro, Stanford C. Allen; set d, Yevgeny Starikovitch.

Fantasy (PR:AA MPAA:G)

BLUE BLOOD*½ (1951) 72m MON c

Bill Williams *(Bill Manning)*, Jane Nigh *(Eileen)*, Arthur Shields *(Tim)*, Audrey Long *(Sue)*, Harry Shannon *(Buchanan)*, Lyle Talbot *(Teasdale)*, William J. Tannen *(Sparks)*, Harry Cheshire *(McArthur)*, Milton Kibbee *(Ryan)*.

After the success of BLUE GRASS OF KENTUCKY, they tried to do it again with BLUE BLOOD but fell short by several furlongs. Darling, who also wrote the screenplay for the aforementioned, adapted a story by Peter Kyne about the rescue of a horse from a dog food factory by Arthur Shields, playing an old horse trainer. If Shields looks and sounds like Barry Fitzgerald it's for good reason. They were brothers. So instead of becoming a can of Alpo, the horse becomes a winner. Bill and Jane don't know each other at the start of the picture but it might have been more interesting if their relationship had been carried over from the prior film.

p, Ben Schwalb; d, Lew Landers; w, W. Scott Darling (based on a story by Peter B. Kyne); ph, Gilbert Warrenton (Cinecolor); m, Ozzie Caswell; ed, Ray Livingston.

Sports Drama/Children (PR:AA MPAA:NR)

BLUE BLOOD* (1973, Brit.) 86m Mallard-Impact Quadrant c

Oliver Reed, Derek Jacobi, Fiona Lewis, Anna Gael, Meg Wynn Owen.

Reed is an evil-minded butler who intends to usurp his weak-willed employer's position and belongings at every turn until a German governess arrives to complicate matters. Not much of a story even for the scenery-chewing Reed, whose lines are so tepid that he can't manage to raise a wicked eyebrow.

d&w, Andrew Sinclair (based on the novel *The Carry-Cot* by Alexander Thynne); ph, Harry Waxman; m, Brian Gascoigne.

Drama (PR:C MPAA:NR)

BLUE CANADIAN ROCKIES* (1952) 58m COL bw

Gene Autry, Pat Buttram, Gail Davis, Carolina Cotton, Ross Ford, Tom London, Mauritz Hugo, Don Beddoe, Gene Roth, John Merton, David Garcia, Bob Woodward, W. C. Wilkerson, Cass County Boys, Campion, the horse.

The musical westerns were beginning to sink into the sunset by the time this lackluster Gene Autry feature was made, a limp oater about landgrabbers. Scripts were sparse and George Archainbaud, while competent, was a routine director. The cast, seeming to realize this, was not inspired to give its all and Autry himself, busy with radio, TV and movie series and business interests, was pretty much headed back to the corral. (See GENE AUTRY series, Index.)

p, Armand Schaefer; d, George Archainbaud; w, Gerald Geraghty; ph, William Bradford (Sepiatone); ed, James Sweeney.

Western Cas. (PR:A MPAA:NR)

BLUE COLLAR*** (1978) 110m T.A.T. Comm. Co./UNIV c

Richard Pryor *(Zeke)*, Harvey Keitel *(Jerry)*, Yaphet Kotto *(Smokey)*, Ed Begley, Jr. *(Bobby Joe)*, Harry Bellaver *(Eddie Johnson)*, George Memmoli *(Jenkins)*, Lucy Saroyan *(Arlene Bartowski)*, Lane Smith *(Clarence Hill)*, Cliff De Young *(John Burrows)*, Borah Silver *(Miller)*, Chip Fields *(Caroline Brown)*, Harry Northup *(Hank)*, Leonard Gaines *(IRS Man)*, Milton Selzer *(Sumabitch)*, Sammy Warren *(Barney)*, Jimmy Martinez *(Charlie T. Martinez)*, Jerry Dahlmann *(Superintendent)*, Denny Arnold *(Unshaven Thug)*, Rock Riddle *(Blonde Thug)*, Stacey Baldwin *(Debby Bartowski)*, Steve Butts *(Bob Bartowski)*, Stephen P. Dunn *(Flannigan)*, Speedy Brown *(Slim)*, Davone Florence *(Frazier Brown)*, Eddie Singleton *(Ali Brown)*, Rya Singleton *(Aretha Brown)*, Vermetta Royster *(Neighbor)*, Jaime Carreire *(Little Joe)*, Victoria McFarland *(Doris)*.

Schrader has done his best work in BLUE COLLAR. With a tight control over his stars and a well-drawn screenplay, he explores the boredom and apathy and rage of the factory workers who are known to TV announcers as "the rank and file." What Schrader and his brother show us is that these nameless faces are also human beings and the dehumanization of factory life exacts a terrible toll on anyone with any feelings. It's an urban film that will have trouble appealing to anyone from a farming community, because they might not be able to identify with the woes of unionism and life in the big city. Keitel, growing by giant strides in every film, and Pryor and Kotto are the trio Schrader focuses in on and we see the essential hopelessness of their lives, stopped dead in their tracks with jobs they can't stand and an existence they would love to quit. The language is crude but honest, not just tossed in to create a stir. It's the six-decades-later successor to Lang's METROPOLIS which was, in its day, the picture that portrayed what the future was to be. BLUE COLLAR is different in many ways, but the underpinning is the same.

p, Don Guest; d, Paul Schrader; w, Schrader, Leonard Schrader (based on materials by Sidney A. Glass); ph, Bobby Byrne (Technicolor); m, Jack Nitzche, Ry Cooder; ed, Tom Rolf; cos, Ron Dawson, Alice Rush.

Drama Cas. (PR:O MPAA:R)

BLUE COUNTRY, THE** (1977, Fr.) 102m GAU c (LE PAYS BLEU)

Brigitte Fossey *(Louise)*, Jacques Serres *(Mathias)*, Ginette Garcin *(Zoe)*, Armand Meffre *(Moise)*, Ginette Mathieu *(Manon)*, Roger Crouzet *(Fernand)*, Albert Delpy *(Armand)*.

The general theme of this picture is that the grass is *not* greener. It could have been shot in New York just as easily in that the story concerns city people seeking to free themselves of urban blight and sniff the clean air of the country. The second part of the tale is the country people who have had it up to here with the boredom of a small village and yearn to get to the city. Fossey (former juvenile actress) is the flirtatious city girl and Serres is the charming bumpkin. Good idea (what the heck, it's been good for two thousand years) that doesn't go anywhere. Director Tacchella (COUSINE, COUSINE) should have gotten himself a different writer.

p,d&w, Jean-Charles Tacchella; ph, Edmond Sechan (Eastmancolor); m, Gerard Anfosso; ed, Agnes Guillemot.

Drama/Romance Cas. (PR:C-O MPAA:PG)

BLUE DAHLIA, THE***** (1946) 96m PAR bw

Alan Ladd *(Johnny Morrison)*, Veronica Lake *(Joyce Harwood)*, William Bendix *(Buzz Wanchek)*, Howard da Silva *(Eddie Harwood)*, Doris Dowling *(Helen Morrison)*, Tom Powers *(Capt. Hendrickson)*, Hugh Beaumont *(George Copeland)*, Howard Freeman *(Corelli)*, Don Costello *(Leo)*, Will Wright *("Dad" Newell)*, Frank Faylen *(The Man)*, Walter Sande *(Heath)*, Vera Marshe *(Blonde)*, Mae Busch *(Jenny the Maid)*, Gloria Williams *(Assistant Maid)*, Harry Hayden *(Mr. Hughes, the Assistant Hotel Manager)*, George Barton *(Cab Driver)*, Harry Barris *(Bellhop)*, Paul Gustine *(Doorman)*, Roberta Jonay *(Girl Hotel Clerk)*, Milton Kibbee *(Night Hotel Clerk)*, Dick Winslow *(Piano Player at Party)*, Anthony Caruso *(Marine Corporal)*, Matt McHugh *(Bartender)*, Arthur Loft *(The Wolf)*, Stan Johnson *(Naval Officer)*, Ernie Adams *(Joe—Man in Coveralls)*, Henry Croom *(Master Sergeant)*, Harry Tyler *(Clerk in Bus Station)*, Jack Clifford *(Plainclothesman)*, George Sorel *(Paul, the Captain of Waiters)*, James Millican, Albert Ruiz *(Photographers)*, Charles A. Hughes *(Lt. Lloyd)*, Leon Lombardo *(Mexican Bellhop)*, Nina Borget *(Mexican Waitress)*, Douglas Carter *(Bus Driver)*, Ed Randolph *(Cop)*, Bea Allen *(News Clerk)*, Perc Launders *(Hotel Clerk)*, Jimmy Dundee *(Driver of Gangster Car)*, Tom Dillon *(Prowl Car Cop)*, Dick Elliott *(Motor Court Owner)*, Clark Eggleston *(Elevator Operator)*, George Carleton *(Clerk at DeAnza Hotel)*, Jack Gargan *(Cab Driver)*, Lawrence Young *(Clerk)*, Franklin Parker *(Police Stenographer)*, Noel Neill, Mavis Murray *(Hat Check Girls)*, Brooke Evans, Carmen Clifford, Audrey Westphal, Lucy Knoch, Audrey Korn, Beverly Thompson, Jerry James, Charles Mayon, William Meader *(Party Guests)*.

Hard-hitting *film noir* with Ladd at his toughest, THE BLUE DAHLIA has it all in the mystery/chiller category, emerging as one of slickest and most absorbing crime dramas in the 1940s. Ladd and his buddies Bendix and Beaumont have just been mustered out of the Navy and return to Los Angeles, Ladd to find his wife, Dowling, and his friends to look for jobs. The three enter a bar where Bendix gets a headache from listening to some loud music being played on a juke box by a Marine (Caruso); Bendix yanks the juke box's plug from the wall and almost gets into a fight until he explains that he has a plate in his head and that noise causes him to have incredible pain. Caruso, realizing Bendix is a wounded veteran, apologizes. Ladd goes off to see his wife, finding her living in an exclusive bungalow (not unlike those on the grounds of the Beverly Hills Hotel). He walks into a raucous party; Dowling is in the bedroom kissing Da Silva, owner of the Blue Dahlia nightclub and her sugar daddy. Dowling, realizing her husband has returned, tries to cover up her relationship with Da Silva but Ladd later notices his wife kissing him goodbye and slugs the nightclub owner, who suavely takes the punch without retaliating. Dowling creates a scene and the guests leave. Later Ladd tries to make up, but she is having none of it; they quarrel and Dowling tells him that their son was killed in a car accident while Ladd was in service; this he knows, but when she spitefully informs him that the cause of his death was due to her drunken driving, Ladd slaps her. House detective Wright appears to caution the couple to hold down the noise and later Ladd grabs his bags and leaves. Dowling begins drinking heavily and later goes to the complex's bar where she meets Bendix, who has been looking for Ladd. She attempts to seduce Bendix and they go back to the bungalow. Loud music is playing next door and Bendix seems to go a little crazy. Coupled to the racket, a violent rainstorm rages outside. That night, Ladd walks along a roadway in the rain and is picked up at Cahuenga Pass by blonde Lake (wearing her "Peek-a-Boo" haircut, a petite actess who was repeatedly teamed with Ladd for her size since he only stood 5'4"). They drive to Malibu where they take separate rooms and have breakfast the next day. Lake is a troubled lady searching for a good man and thinking Ladd is the guy, but he's on a bitter rebound and wants nothing to do with women. He leaves but learns that police are looking for him. Dowling has been found murdered in the bungalow, shot to death with Ladd's service automatic which he has left behind. As police look for him, Ladd begins his own investigation, learning that Lake is Da Silva's estranged wife, their meeting being devastatingly coincidental. House detective Wright goes to Da Silva and blackmails him so that he will keep quiet about his relationship with Dowling. When Ladd goes to see the cunning nightclub owner, he is warned by Lake that police are on his trail but he manages to contact Da Silva, who now believes Ladd knows too much about his background (he is wanted in the East for murder). Da Silva has two of his goons, Costello and Sande, kidnap Ladd; they take him to a lonely cabin for safekeeping until Da Silva arrives. Ladd breaks loose and, after a wild fight, knocks out Sande and shoots Costello. Da Silva arrives and is accidentally shot to death by one of the reviving goons before he or Ladd can learn anything from each other. Meanwhile, the police have picked up Bendix and Beaumont and are trying to pin Dowling's murder on the confused Bendix. He cannot remember what he did on the night of the killing, only the blaring sounds in his head that brought on his recurrent amnesia. Just as Bendix is about to confess to the murder out of loyalty to his friend Ladd, the hero bursts through the door. All of the suspects are present and Ladd proves that Bendix could not have committed the murder, that he would have shot his wife at long range because he had been an excellent marksman in the service (to demonstrate, Ladd dramatically holds up a kitchen match and Bendix lights it by shooting off the tip from across the room). Dowling, Ladd points out, was shot several times at close range by an inexpert killer. Police captain Powers has already figured out just who that is, Wright, the cynical blackmailing house detective. As he is about to leave, Powers stops him and accuses him of the murder, calling Wright a cheap blackmailer. Wright sneers and pulls a gun, spouting: "Cheap, huh? Sure—a cigar, a drink and a couple of dirty bucks, that's all it costs to buy me, that's what she thought. Found out a little different, didn't she? Maybe I could get tired of being pushed around by cops and hotel managers and ritzy dames in bungalows. Maybe I could cost a little something just for once. And if I do end up on a slab—." As Wright tries to escape, police officers gun him down. The film ends with Lake and Ladd going off together, the police content with solving the crime, and Bendix and Beaumont off to find a bar. Raymond Chandler began to write THE BLUE DAHLIA as a novel but got bogged down and turned it into an original screenplay, tailor-made for the dynamic near-emotionless Ladd, beautifully supported by the truculent Bendix. Chandler initially thought to have Bendix the killer, but the U.S. Navy objected to one of its wounded veterans being portrayed as a mad amnesiac turned killer because of battle wounds, so the stylish crime writer pinned it all on the house detective, in a rewrite of the ending. (Today Hollywood is impervious to governmental reaction, as drastically demonstrated in BLACK SUNDAY, 1977, where war hero Dern, a mental case due to battle trauma, plans to mass murder thousands of innocent people, a far cry from disposing of a cheating wife.) Chandler's dialog is simply great, full of biting retorts, wit, and black humor. The atmosphere and settings for the film—basically the bungalow complex and bar, the cheap rooming house where Bendix and Beaumont live, a dumpy northwoods cabin, and the Blue Dahlia nightclub—are lit with intruding shadows everywhere, giving the proper *film noir* feel. Marshall's direction is swift and economical as he rushes the story forward and all the cast members do outstanding jobs, even coy Lake whose role is basically incidental but obligatory as the love interest. No matter how sleazy these characters truly are, they maintain a higher level of humor, polish, and sophistication than is usually found at the end of any dark street leading to the underworld, to intrigue, mystery, and murder. This film was justifiably popular, so much so that Paramount reaped a $2.75 million profit, a vast sum at the time.

p, John Houseman; d, George Marshall; w, Raymond Chandler (based on his story); ph, Lionel Lindon; m, Victor Young; ed, Arthur Schmidt; art d, Hans Dreier, Walter Tyler; set d, Sam Comer, Jimmy Walters; cos, Edith Head.

Crime Drama **(PR:C MPAA:NR)**

BLUE DANUBE* (1932, Brit.) 68m British & Dominions/Mundus bw

Brigitte Helm *(Countess Gabrielle)*, Joseph Schildkraut *(Sandor)*, Dorothy Bouchier *(Yutka)*, Desmond Jeans *(Johann)*, Patrick Ludlow *(Companion)*, Alfred Rode and his Tzigane Band, Masine and Nikitina.

Plodding Gypsy romance musical concerns Schildkraut's efforts to reunite with his sweetheart despite their respective involvements with aristocrats. Violent overacting characterizes all performances.

p&d, Herbert Wilcox; w, Miles Malleson (based on a story by Doris Zinkeisen); ph, F. A. Young.

Musical **(PR:A MPAA:NR)**

BLUE DEMON VERSUS THE INFERNAL BRAINS*
(1967, Mex.) 85m Estudios America/Cinematografica Ra bw (BLUE DEMON CONTRA CEREBROS INFERNALES; CEREBRO INFERNAL; AKA: BLUE DEMON VERSUS EL CRIMEN)

Alejandro Cruz, David Reynoso, Ana Martin, Victor Junco, Noe Murayama, Dagoberto Rodriguez, Barbara Angely.

Cruz, in this quick sequel to ARANAS INFERNALES (1966), reprises his role as the grotesquely masked wrestler The Blue Demon. This time he's fighting an evil doctor who kills scientists and wrestlers for their superior intelligence that he saps from their brains. The doctor is assisted by his band of female zombies. This film was followed in turn by two other sequels, SANTO Y BLUE DEMON CONTRA LOS MONSTRUOS and SANTO CONTRA BLUE DEMON EN LA ATLANTIDA, both released in 1968. Director Urueta was famous for his nudie and wrestling pictures, but also dabbled in fantasy and horror films.

p, Rafael Perez Grovas; d, Chano Urueta; w, Antonio Orllana, Fernando Oses; ph, Alfredo Uribe.

Horror **(PR:O MPAA:NR)**

BLUE DENIM*** (1959) 89m FOX bw (GB:BLUE JEANS)

Carol Lynley *(Janet Willard)*, Brandon de Wilde *(Arthur Bartley)*, MacDonald Carey *(Maj. Malcolm Bartley, Ret.)*, Marsha Hunt *(Jessie Bartley)*, Nina Shipman *(Lillian Bartley)*, Warren Berlinger *(Ernie)*, Buck Class *(Axel)*, Vaughn Taylor *(Prof. Willard)*, Roberta Shore *(Cherie)*, Mary Young *(Aunt Bidda)*, William Schallert *(Vice President)*, Michael Gainey *(Hobie)*, Jennie Maxwell, Junie Ellis.

BLUE DENIM was the first of many troubled-teenager films and certainly one of the best. Lynley gets pregnant by de Wilde (only six years after he was such an innocent tyke in SHANE) and can't bring herself to tell her father (Taylor). De Wilde has very little in common with his selfish parents, Hunt and Carey, so he's not able to let them know how he feels about being a teenage father. With the aid of Berlinger, Lynley and de Wilde get enough money have an illegal operation performed on Carol. De Wilde tells his folks about it and they are incensed, stopping the operation, and telling him that he must do the honorable thing and marry her. The exciting chase sequence at the end of the film is to stop the abortionist from doing the deed. The movie's ending differs from the play in that the stage presentation has an abortion as the culmination. The film shows the kids going off to another city to have the child and to presumably live happily ever after. BLUE DENIM is essentially about alienation and the inability of parents to understand their children. It gets a bit simplistic in places, with all the sympathy on the side of the kids and no kind words for the long-suffering parents. Berlinger got his Broadway baptism in "Take A Giant Step" with Louis Gossett, Jr. in the lead (age 17). The film starred Johnny Nash as the producers felt Gossett had no appeal. Nash has dropped from sight and Gossett won an Oscar. So much for producers. In this picture, Berlinger (a cousin of Milton Berle) does well as de Wilde's fast-talking pal.

p, Charles Brackett; d, Philip Dunne; w, Edith Sommer, Dunne (based on the play by James Leo Herlihy and William Noble); ph, Leo Tovar; m, Bernard Herrmann; ed, William Reynolds.

Drama **(PR:C-O MPAA:NR)**

BLUE FIN** ½** (1978, Aus.) 90m South Australian Film Corp/Roadshow c

Hardy Kruger *(Bill Pascoe)*, Greg Rowe *(Steve "Snoek" Pascoe)*, Elspeth Ballantyne *(Mrs. Pascow)*, Liddy Clark *(Ruth Pascoe)*, John Jarratt *(Sam Snell)*, Hugh Keays-Byrne *(Stan)*, Ralph Cotterill *(Herbie)*, George Spartels *(Con)*, Alfred Bell *(Geordie)*, Wayne Rodda *(Andy Nelson)*, John Thompson *(Snitch)*, John Godden *(Ockie)*, Kelly Aitken *(Pamela)*, Terry Camilieri *(Truckie)*, Graham Rouse *(Bellamy)*, Peter Crossley *(Minister)*, Rob George *(Sid Hanna)*, John Frawley *(Governor)*, Anne Mullinar *(Lady Oswald)*, Brian Moore *(Oil Company Man)*, Max Cullen *(Pensioner)*.

Kruger is a captain of a tuna boat. Rowe is the son who doesn't get along with this thin-lipped, unforgiving father. (Come to think of it, except for one brief moment in SUNDAYS AND CYBELE, has anyone ever seen Hardy Kruger smile?) Rowe wants to prove himself to his father and when he gets the chance, he does. And that's about it except for a tiny subplot wherein Liddy Clark loses her boyfriend (Jarratt) in a sea-caused accident. It was a big hit in Australia but failed to make any noise in the U.S., despite the fact that the issues and the family-oriented problems laid bare are as universal as can be imagined. Beautifully photographed, well-acted and sharply edited.

p, Hal McElroy; d, Carl Schultz; w, Sonia Borg (based on the novel by Colin Thiele); ph, Geoff Burton; m, Michael Carlos; ed, Rod Adamson; spec eff, Chris Murray.

Action/Adventure **Cas.** **(PR:A MPAA:NR)**

BLUE GARDENIA, THE*** (1953) 90m WB bw

Anne Baxter *(Norah Larkin)*, Richard Conte *(Casey Mayo)*, Ann Sothern *(Crystal Carpenter)*, Raymond Burr *(Harry Prebble)*, Jeff Donnell *(Sally Ellis)*, Richard Erdman *(Al)*, George Reeves *(Haynes)*, Ruth Storey *(Rose)*, Ray Walker *(Homer)*, Nat "King" Cole *(Himself)*.

Baxter accepts a blind date with Burr after receiving a "Dear Jane" letter from her fiance in Korea. After drinking too much, Baxter returns with Burr to his apartment. When he attempts to seduce her, Baxter reaches for a poker in panic and clubs Burr unconscious, then flees. The next morning she reads through a hangover that Burr has been beaten to death and believes herself to be the killer. When newsman Conte begins writing open letters to the murderess in his paper, Baxter calls him, posing as a friend of the killer. They meet several times at Hollywood's Blue Gardenia restaurant and Baxter and Conte fall in love. Conte finally convinces Baxter to confess, first believing her guilty. Then he follows up a lead, discovering another woman, Storey, whom police find barely alive after a botched suicide attempt. She admits that she arrived at Burr's apartment after Baxter had left, telling him that she was pregnant with his child. When he refused to marry her she clubbed him to death with the poker. Conte and Baxter end up together as the real killer is charged with Burr's death. This is one of Fritz Lang's weaker efforts in the *film noir* field, although his great visual style is evident in every scene; it's the thin script, cliched lines, and the predictable twists it takes that limit this master filmmaker. To make up for story, Lang tried to tell it in craft, focusing upon Baxter, encircling her with his camera, closing in, like the long arm of the law reaching out for her. It's a commendable job, aided by Baxter's standout performance, but this film nowhere approaches Lang's memorable *film noir* works of that era, THE BIG HEAT, CLASH BY NIGHT, and HUMAN DESIRE. Musuraca's lensing is high-key and sometimes flat. Lingering long after the fading plot line is the unforgettable song "Blue Gardenia" sung by the great Nat "King" Cole with an arrangement by Nelson Riddle.

p, Alex Gottlieb; d, Fritz Lang; w, Charles Hoffman (based on the short story "Gardenia" by Vera Caspary); ph, Nicholas Musuraca; m, Raoul Kraushaar; ed, Edward Mann; art d, Daniel Hall; m/l, title song, Bob Russell, Lester Lee.

Crime Drama **(PR:C MPAA:NR)**

BLUE GRASS OF KENTUCKY 1/2** (1950) 69m MON c

Bill Williams *(Lin McIvor)*, Jane Nigh *(Pat Armistead)*, Ralph Morgan *(Maj. Randolph McIvor)*, Robert "Buzz" Henry *(Sandy McIvor)*, Russell Hicks *(Armistead)*, Ted Hecht *(Layton)*, Dick Foote *(Jim Brown)*, Jack Howard *(Armistead Jockey)*, Stephen S. Harrison *(Attendant)*, Pierre Watkin *(Head Steward)*.

Fast-moving racing story with romance, action, and lots of heart. Williams owns a horse with his father, Morgan. Their horse was sired by a horse belonging to Nigh's father. Jane is a millionairess who is in love with Bill and keeps proposing, but Williams is one of those honorable, old-fashioned men who won't marry a woman richer than he is. Lots of track action, with many scenes being shot at Churchill Downs in Kentucky. Very intelligent screenplay by Darling separates this from many others of the same ilk. Williams is totally believable in his part and Beaudine's direction is darn near perfect. Beaudine's career began in 1923 and continued well into the sixties. He was a first-rate second-feature director.

p, Jeffrey Bernerd; d, William Beaudine; w, W. Scott Darling; ph, Gilbert Warrenton (Cinecolor); ed, Otho Lovering, Roy Livingston.

Sports Drama **(PR:AA MPAA:NR)**

BLUE HAWAII** (1961) 103m PAR c

Elvis Presley *(Chad Gates)*, Joan Blackman *(Maile Duval)*, Nancy Walters *(Abigail Prentice)*, Roland Winters *(Fred Gates)*, Angela Lansbury *(Sarah Lee Gates)*, John Archer *(Jack Kelman)*, Howard McNear *(Mr. Chapman)*, Flora Hayes *(Mrs. Manaka)*, Gregory Gay *(Mr. Duval)*, Steve Brodie *(Mr. Garvey)*, Iris Adrian *(Mrs. Garvey)*, Darlene Tompkins *(Patsy)*, Pamela Akert *(Sandy)*, Christian Kay *(Beverly)*, Jenny Maxwell *(Ellie)*, Frank Atienza *(Ito O'Hara)*, Lani Kai *(Carl)*, Jose DeVarga *(Ernie)*, Ralph Hanalie *(Wes)*.

Elvis fans, rejoice! Here is Presley at his peak. This time they've moved Graceland mansion to Hawaii and Elvis plays the son of a pineapple mogul (Winters). Elvis wants to make his own way in life and forego those prickly fruits, so he takes a job in a tourist agency after returning home from the service. Lots of tunes, romance, and a good job of acting by Lansbury as Elvis' mother. Angela has always played characters much older than she is, and was, at the time, only ten years older than Elvis! Basically slim premise but plenty of clever lines from Hal Kanter, dean of Hollywood's after-dinner wits.

p, Hal B. Wallis; d, Norman Taurog; w, Hal Kanter (based on a story by Allan Weiss); ph, Charles Lang, Jr. (Technicolor); m, Joseph Lilley; ed, Warren Lew.

Musical **Cas.** **(PR:A MPAA:NR)**

BLUE IDOL, THE* (1931, Hung.) 74m Palatinus bw

Oscar Beregi, Paul Javor, Fyula Gozon, Nelly Redel, Sandor Pethes, Maklary, Venrey, Sarossy, Rosie Kiraly, Paul Fekete, Mimi Princz, Laszlo Dezsoffy, Sandor Peti.

First Hungarian talkie is, paradoxically, set in America. A down-on-his-luck baron works as a waiter. He wins a share in a farm and tries to marry the girl of his dreams, but is rebuffed as a fortune hunter. The financial straits back in Hungary suddenly clear up and the baron is rich again, and so can marry the girl. No hint can be seen here of the heights Hungarian cinema would later reach.

d, Lajos Lazar; w, Miklos Lorincz, Dezso Farago (based on a story by Andorjan Bonyi); ph, Istvan Elben; m/l, Laszlo Angyal, Imre Harmath.

Comedy **(PR:A MPAA:NR)**

BLUE LAGOON, THE 1/2** (1949, Brit.) 103m UNIV c

Jean Simmons *(Emmeline Foster)*, Susan Stranks *(Emmeline as Child)*, Donald Houston *(Michael Reynolds)*, Peter Jones *(Michael as Child)*, Noel Purcell *(Paddy Button)*, James Hayter *(Dr. Murdoch)*, Cyril Cusack *(James Carter)*, Nora Nicholson *(Mrs. Stannard)*, Maurice Denham *(Ship Captain)*, Philip Stainton *(Mr. Ansty)*, Patrick Barr *(Second Mate)*, Lyn Evans *(Trotter)*, Russell Waters *(Craggs)*, John Boxer *(Nick Corbett)*, Bill Raymond *(Marsden)*.

While not as ornate or visually attractive as its successor, this original version of THE BLUE LAGOON is surely more intelligent and less patently sexual. Simmons and Houston are supposed teenagers who were shipwrecked as children on a lush, tropical island. They grow from children (ably played by Stranks and Jones) to adults and, for the first few years, are accompanied by Purcell in the role later played by Leo McKern. Neither one of the films is particularly exciting, despite the gorgeous locations and the sure-handed direction. Perhaps there are some stories better left unfilmed.

p, Sidney Gilliat, Frank Launder; d, Launder; w, Launder, John Baines, Michael Hogan (based on a novel by Henry Devere Stacpoole) ph, Geoffrey Unsworth, Arthur Ibbetson (Technicolor); m, Clifton Parker; ed, Thelma Myers.

Drama/Romance **(PR:A-C MPAA:NR)**

BLUE LAGOON, THE* (1980) 102m Col c

Brooke Shields *(Emmeline)*, Christopher Atkins *(Richard)*, Leo McKern *(Paddy Button)*, William Daniels *(Arthur LeStrange)*, Elva Josephson *(Young Emmeline)*, Glenn Kohan *(Young Richard)*, Alan Hopgood *(Captain)*, Gus Mercurio *(Officer)*, Jeffrey Means *(Lookout)*, Bradley Pryce *(Little Paddy)*, Chad Timmermans *(Infant Paddy)*, Gert Jacoby, Alex Hamilton, Richard Evanson *(Sailors)*.

Director Kleiser (whose former credit was THE BOY IN THE GLASS BUBBLE, a TV movie with John Travolta) and Stewart, who went on to write the screenplay for AN OFFICER AND A GENTLEMAN, collaborated on this beautiful-to-watch but excruciating-to-listen-to remake of the picture of the same name done in 1949. Although this one was rated R, it was hardly more exciting than the original. Although there is as much nudity as one can get away with while using such a young actress, it is still a bore and there are story holes that one can drive an Amtrak train through. Often, Kleiser and Stewart drum up some false moments of danger but nothing really ever happens. The story is that of two young people who are shipwrecked on an island, grow to be adults, have a child, and so forth. It took a little over 100 minutes to tell and there were many times it felt as though huge hunks were edited out for pace. They edited the wrong hunks. McKern, as always, is good as the hard-drinking Paddy. Shields was just then learning how to act, at the expense of the viewer, of course. Chris Atkins would have been more at home on a surfboard.

p&d, Randal Kleiser; w, Douglas Day Stewart (based on the novel by Henry Devere Stacpoole); ph, Nestor Almendros (Metrocolor); m, Basil Poledouris; ed, Robert Gordon; cos, Jean-Pierre Dorleac.

Drama/Romance **Cas.** **(PR:O MPAA:R)**

BLUE LAMP, THE* 1/2** (1950, Brit.) 82m GFD bw

Jack Warner *(George Dixon)*, Jimmy Hanley *(Andy Mitchell)*, Dirk Bogarde *(Tom Riley)*, Robert Flemyng *(Sgt. Roberts)*, Bernard Lee *(Inspector Cherry)*, Peggy Evans *(Diana Lewis)*, Patrick Doonan *(Spud)*, Bruce Seton *(Constable Campbell)*, Frederick Piper *(Alf Lewis)*, Betty Ann Davies *(Mrs. Lewis)*.

THE BLUE LAMP is a perfect example of how an ordinary title can harm an excellent film. If you heard THE BLUE LAMP, what would you think it was about? An Arabian Nights Tale? The discovery of electricity? Well, it's an exciting story about the chasing down and apprehension of a cop-killer. Warner is an avuncular bobby whom everyone loves as he's never too busy to help a newcomer. He's murdered in the course of duty by Bogarde and Doonan. Hanley is a freshman cop and we can feel his fear and anguish as he learns his trade. Dearden loved to do these tight police dramas and will be best remembered for this film as well as SAPPHIRE, VICTIM, THE LEAGUE OF GENTLEMEN, and the wonderfully amusing THE SMALLEST SHOW ON EARTH. This is more of a suspense film than an action movie, but Dearden and screenwriter Clarke take a page from Hitchcock and build the suspense until it gets excruciating. A fantastic car chase is the highlight and today, despite all the Burt Reynolds-type chases that have glutted the screen, the chase in THE BLUE LAMP still stands out. Bogarde (born Derek Ven Den Bogaerd) is frightening as the criminal, and continued to play these roles until someone saw he could do comedy and starred him in DOCTOR IN THE HOUSE.

p, Michael Balcon; d, Basil Dearden; w, T. E. B. Clarke; ph, Gordon Dines; m, Ernest Irving; ed, Peter Tanner.

Crime Drama **(PR:C MPAA:NR)**

BLUE LIGHT, THE* 1/2
(1932, Ger.) 77m Leni Riefenstahl Studio/Aafa bw (AKA: DAS BLAUE LICHT)

Leni Riefenstahl, Beni Fuehrer, Max Holzboer, Mattias Weimann, Franz Maldacea, Martha Mair, the Sam Valley peasants.

Leni Riefenstahl (later to become Hitler's personal filmmaker) is thought to be a witch because only she can reach the top of a dangerous peak. When a love-struck artist follows her to the peak, he finds a crystal cave. The villagers below strip the cavern and when Riefenstahl sees what has happened she throws herself into a chasm. Beautiful photography doesn't overcome silly story.

p, Leni Riefenstahl, Bela Balacz, Hans Schneeberger; d, Riefenstahl; ph, Glaus Libucaberger; m, Guiseppe Becce; set d, Leopold Blonder.

Drama **(PR:A MPAA:NR)**

BLUE MAX, THE*** (1966) 155m FOX c

George Peppard *(Bruno Stachel)*, James Mason *(Count von Klugermann)*, Ursula Andress *(Countess Kasti)*, Jeremy Kemp *(Willi Von Klugermann)*, Carl Schell *(Richthofen)*, Karl Michael Vogler *(Heidemann)*, Loni Von Friedl *(Elfi Heidemann)*, Anton Diffring *(Holbach)*, Peter Woodthorpe *(Rupp)*, Harry Towb *(Kettering)*, Derek Newark *(Ziegel)*, Derren Nesbitt *(Fabian)*, Friedrich Ledebur *(Field Marshal Von Lenndorf)*, Roger Ostime *(Crown Prince)*, Hugo Schuster *(Hans)*, Tim Parkes, Ian Kingsley, Ray Browne *(Pilots)*.

Peppard is an infantry soldier desperate to escape the trenches of WW I, getting himself transferred to the German air force and becoming a fighter pilot. He is utterly ruthless and soon becomes an ace, but is never accepted by the other pilots who mostly represent the old Prussian aristocracy. He takes chances to mount a tally of downed planes so he can overtake aces Kemp and Vogler. Moreover, he meets his commander's wife, Andress, and carries on a blatant affair with her, apparently with her husband's (Mason) tacit approval. Obsessed with winning Germany's highest medal, The Blue Max, Peppard claims the "kill" of another pilot, Kemp, who has been killed while playing daredevil with Peppard. Mason awards the medal to Peppard, even though he has been informed by Vogler that the new ace has not earned it. Mason, who now resents Andress' notorious affair with the pilot, has other plans. At a large ceremony, he sends Peppard up to test a newly designed but dangerous plane. It crashes, killing Peppard, as Mason knew it would. A strange film which impressively records aerial battles and the terrible trench warfare of WW I, with a haunting score by Goldsmith, the story leaves a bad taste since there are no admirable characters in the lot. All the pilots are vainglorious killers and Mason, who appears to be reprising his role as Rommel, does only a serviceable job of acting. Andress displays as much of her sleek body as was then allowable which, of course, is the extent of her acting ability. Vogler, as the Prussian pilot attempting to maintain some sort of honor in a military system bent on worldwide destruction, gives the best performance in the film. Peppard is his usual arrogant, puffed-up self, sort of a German HUD but without the charm and style of Paul Newman. The excellent technical effort saves this expensive production from being an utter shell.

p, Christian Ferry; d, John Guillermin; w, David Pursall, Jack Seddon, Gerald Hanley (based on the novel by Jack D. Hunter); ph, Douglas Slocombe (CinemaScope, DeLuxe Color); m, Jerry Goldsmith; ed, Max Benedict; art d, Fred Carter; spec eff, Karl Baumgartner, Maurice Ayres, Ron Ballinger; aerial ph, Skeets Kelly.

War Drama   **Cas.**   **(PR:C MPAA:NR)**

BLUE MONTANA SKIES*½   (1939) 56m REP bw

Gene Autry (Gene), Smiley Burnette (Frog), June Storey (Dorothy), Harry Woods (Hendricks), Tully Marshall (Steve), Al Bridge (Marshall), Glenn Strange (Causer), Dorothy Granger (Mrs. Potter), Edmund Cobb (Brennan), Robert Winkler (Wilbur Potter), Jack Ingram (Frazier), Augie Gomez (Blackfeather), John Beach (N. W. M. Corporal), Walt Shrum and the Colorado Hillbillies (Themselves).

A clue written on a rock by a dying man leads Autry to capture a band of fur smugglers near the Canadian border, finding time also to sing three songs. These are: "I Just Want You," "Neath the Blue Montana Sky," and "Rockin' in the Saddle All Day." (See GENE AUTRY series, Index.)

p, Harry Grey; d, B. Reeves Eason; w, Gerald Geraghty; ph, Jack Marta; ed, Lester Orlebeck.

Western   **(PR:AA MPAA:NR)**

BLUE MURDER AT ST. TRINIAN'S**½   (1958, Brit.) 86m BL bw

Joyce Grenfell (Sgt. Gates), Terry-Thomas (Romney), George Cole (Flash Harry), Alastair Sim (Miss Fritton), Sabrina (Virginia), Lionel Jeffries (Joe Mangan), Lloyd Lamble (Superintendent), Raymond Rollett (Chief Constable), Thorley Walters (Major), Judith Furse (Dame Maude Hackshaw), Lisa Gastoni (Myrna), Josie Read (Cynthia), Rosalind Knight (Annabelle), Patricia Lawrence (Mavis), Dilys Laye (Bridget), Vikki Hammond (Jane), Marianne Brauns (Fluffy), Marigold Russell (Marjorie), Tony Scott, Ferdy Mayne, Cyril Chamberlain, Ronald Ibbs, Richard Wattis, Amanda Cosell, Alma Taylor, Peter Jones.

The further adventures of those madcap schoolgirls Searle loved to draw. Sim, in drag as Miss Fritton, the schoolmistress, is in jail, and the army and police have been called out to keep order at St. Trinian's school. The girls hate being stuck there so they enter a contest and, through cheating, win a trip to Europe. Next, a series of misadventures: diamonds are stolen by the father of one of the girls; the criminal dresses up as a woman and poses as the new headmistress in order to flee Europe; the jewels somehow get into a water polo ball and a mad match is played; and on and on and on, one slapstick joke after another in the 86 minutes with nary a chance to catch one's breath. Grenfell is delicious but Terry-Thomas is most memorable as the crooked owner of the bus company that takes the girls on their trip. All of the St. Trinian's films are recalled with fond memory, but they have not withstood the test of time the way some of the Sellers and Carmichael pictures have.

p, Frank Launder, Sidney Gilliat; d, Frank Launder; w, Gilliat, Launder, Val Valentine (inspired by drawings by Ronald Searle); ph, Gerald Gibbs; m, Malcolm Arnold; ed, Geoffrey Foot.

Comedy   **(PR:AA MPAA:NR)**

BLUE PARROT, THE*   (1953, Brit.) 69m ACT/Monarch bw

Dermot Walsh (Bob Herrick), Jacqueline Hill (Maureen), Ballard Berkeley (Supt. Chester), June Ashley (Gloria), Richard Pearson (Quincey), Ferdy Mayne (Stevens), Victor Lucas (Rocks Owen), Edwin Richfield (Taps Campbell), John Le Mesurier (Carson).

An American technician in England meets and falls in love with an English girl posing as a nightclub hostess. Their romance is briefly interrupted while they solve a murder in the nightclub where she works. Poor sleuthing matches a lame production.

p, Stanley Haynes; d, John Harlow; w, Allan Mackinnon (based on the story "Gunman" by Percy Hoskins); ph, Bob Navarro.

Crime Drama   **(PR:A MPAA:NR)**

BLUE PETER, THE   (SEE: NAVY HEROES, 1955, Brit.)

BLUE SCAR*   (1949, Brit.) 90m Outlook/BL bw

Emrys Jones (Tom Thomas), Gwyneth Vaughan (Olwen Williams), Rachel Thomas (Gweneth Williams), Anthony Pendrell (Alfred Collins), Prysor Williams (Ted Williams), Madoline Thomas (Granny), Jack James (Dai Morgan), Kenneth Griffith (Thomas Williams).

A Welsh mine manager eager for the excitement of the big city gives it a try and learns the hard way that life in his little village is better.

p, William MacQuitty; d&w, Jill Craigie; ph, Jo Jago.

Drama   **(PR:A MPAA:NR)**

BLUE SIERRA**   (1946) 93m MGM c

Elizabeth Taylor (Kathie Merrick), Frank Morgan (Harry McBain), Tom Drake (Sgt. Smitty), Selena Royle (Mrs. Merrick), Harry Davenport (Judge Payson), George Cleveland (Old Man), Catherine Frances McLeod (Alice Merrick), Morris Ankrum (Farmer Crews), Mitchell Lewis (Gil Elson), Jane Green (Mrs. Elson), David Holt

(Pete Merrick), William Wallace (Sgt. Mac), Minor Watson (Sheriff Ed Grayson), Donald Curtis (Charlie), Clancy Cooper (Casey), Carl "Alfalfa" Switzer (First Youth), Conrad Binyon (Second Youth), Lassie (Bill).

Collie raised in the mountains by Taylor is hit by a truck, taken by the driver to a vet in the big city, and winds up in the army. Sent to the Aleutians, the dog saves his group from a Japanese bombardment, but suffers shell shock. Repatriated, the heroic pooch makes his way back to Taylor, but is accused of chicken stealing. Kindly old shepherd Morgan defends the battle fatigue-stricken dog. Silly, but lovable.

p, Robert Sisk; d, Fred M. Wilcox; w, Lionel Houser; ph, Leonard Smith (Technicolor); ed, Conrad A. Nervig; animal sequence d, Basil Wrangel.

Children   **(PR:AA MPAA:NR)**

BLUE SKIES**   (1946) 104m PAR c

Bing Crosby (Johnny Adams), Fred Astaire (Jed Potter), Joan Caulfield (Mary O'Hara), Billy DeWolfe (Tony), Olga San Juan (Nita Nova), Mikhail Rasmuny (Francois), Frank Faylen (Mack), Victoria Horne (Martha Nurse), Karolyn Grimes (Mary Elizabeth).

Forty-two song cues and 30 full numbers highlight this musical romance about Crosby, Caulfield, and Astaire in a triangle where Crosby eventually takes Joan's hand. It's amazing they managed to get that much story sandwiched around all of the musical numbers. Astaire is a radio personality who had been one of the great dancers a few years back. He flashbacks the story to the time when he and Bing were after the hand of Joan. Bing and Joan finally married, but life was tough. He was an unstable businessman who couldn't make his life work. Eventually, Joan and Bing divorce after the birth of their daughter (Grimes), and she takes up with Astaire. Bing interrupts their plans and Joan leaves Fred to return to Bing, Fred makes friends with alcohol and begins to drown his sorrows in hooch. Astaire has a tragic accident and can dance no more. Story flashes forward to the radio station where Fred is recounting all this and Bing is there to sing. Now Joan arrives and the three pals exit arm in arm, a wholesome 1940s *menage a trois*. It's impossible to list all of the Irving Berlin songs in BLUE SKIES but a few include: "Puttin' On The Ritz," "White Christmas," "You Keep Coming Back Like A Song," and "A Couple Of Song And Dance Men." Billy DeWolfe does his famous "Mrs. Murgatroyd" number with good results and Olga San Juan scores with "You'd Be Surprised" as well as a few others. Solid musical fun all the way.

p, Sol C. Siegel; d, Stuart Heisler; w, Arthur Sheekman (based on an idea by Irving Berlin, adapted by Allan Scott); ph, Charles Lang, Jr., William Snyder (Technicolor); m, Robert Emmett Dolan; ed, LeRoy Stone; spec eff, Gordon Jennings, Paul K. Lepae, Farciot Edouart; ch, Hermes Pan.

Musical   **(PR:AA MPAA:NR)**

BLUE SKIES AGAIN**   (1983) 96m SB c

Harry Hamlin (Sandy), Mimi Rogers (Liz), Kenneth McMillan (Dirk), Robyn Barto (Paula), Dana Elcar (Lou), Joey Gian (Calvin), Doug Moeller (Carroll), Tommy Lane (The Boy), Andy Garcia (Ken), Marcos Gonzales (Brushback), Cilk Cozart (Wallstreet).

For those of us who grew up on IT HAPPENS EVERY SPRING (Ray Milland as a professor who invents a wood repellent that he lathers a baseball with and becomes a great pitcher) or ANGELS IN THE OUTFIELD (Paul Douglas as the foul-mouthed manager of the Pittsburgh Pirates who makes a deal with angels so he can win the pennant) or DAMN YANKEES, THE LOU GEHRIG STORY, and on and on, BLUE SKIES AGAIN is tame stuff indeed. Baseball films are not easy to do because the stories seldom compare with what's actually happening out there on the diamond, and the true fan scoffs and sneers when he sees someone as epicene as Tony Perkins playing Jimmy Piersall or a middle-aged Robert Redford attempting to convince us he's Malamud's THE NATURAL. BLUE SKIES AGAIN is a lighthearted attempt at a baseball comedy that features the world's first female player in the big time. Harry Hamlin is the single owner of the team, and his attraction to the player's manager is what causes him to think twice about his male chauvinism. The truth is that there are some marvelous female athletes and a number of distaff softball pitchers who could make Steve Garvey look silly at the plate. But this film will never prove to any real fan that a woman could take her place facing 97-mile-an-hour fast balls from veteran relievers or turn a double play when a 240-pound player is bearing down on her as she takes the throw from the shortstop. Still, it's a pleasant film, short on sweat and long on perfume, and it should bring smiles to the faces of any little girls who envy their brothers on the Little League field. THE BAD NEWS BEARS it ain't.

p, Arlene Sellers, Alex Winitsky; d, Richard Michaels; w, Kevin Sellers; ph, Don McAline (WarnerColor); ed, Dunford Greene; m, John Kander; art d, Don Ivey.

Comedy   **Cas.**   **(PR:A MPAA:PG)**

BLUE SMOKE*   (1935, Brit.) 74m FOX bw

Tamara Desni (Belle Chinko), Ralph Ince (Al Dempson), Bruce Seton (Don Chinko), Ian Colin (Chris Steele), Eric Hales (Tawno Herne), Hal Walters (Stiffy Williams), Beryl de Querton (Anna Steele), Wilson Coleman (Jasper Chinko), Jock McKay (Mac).

A Gypsy prizefighter and his rival take their battles beyond the ring in competition for the same girl. This one goes down for the count in the first round.

p, John Barrow; d, Ralph Ince; w, Fenn Sherie, Ingram d'Abbes (based on a story by Charles Bennett); ph, Alex Bryce.

Sports Drama   **(PR:A MPAA:NR)**

BLUE SQUADRON, THE*   (1934, Brit.) 74m WB/FN Steffano Pittaluga

Esmond Knight (Capt. Carlo Banti), John Stuart (Col. Mario Spada), Greta Hansen

(Elene), Cecil Parker *(Bianci)*, Ralph Reader, Barrie Livesey, Hay Plumb, Hamilton Keene.

After losing the woman he loves to a rival, a colonel proves his mettle as an officer and a gentleman by saving the rival's life in the Italian Alps. An utterly snowbound production.

p, Irving Asher; d, George King; w, Brock Williams.

Romance   **(PR:A MPAA:NR)**

BLUE STEEL*1/2   (1934) 54m MON/Lone Star bw

John Wayne *(John Carruthers)*, Eleanor Hunt *(Betty Mason)*, George "Gabby" Hayes *(Sheriff Jake)*, Ed Peil, Sr. *(Melgrove)*, Yakima Canutt *(Danti, The Polka Dot Bandit)*, George Cleveland *(Hank)*, George Nash *(Bridegroom)*, Lafe McKee *(Dad Mason)*, Hank Bell *(Stage Driver)*, Earl Dwire *(Henchman)*.

U.S. marshal Wayne infiltrates a gang of outlaws who are threatening everybody in town to get to the gold vein underneath. Canutt plays "The Polka Dot Bandit" and performs some amazing stunts.

p, Paul Malvern; d, Robert N. Bradbury; w, Bradbury; ph, Archie Stout; ed, Carl Pierson.

Western   **Cas.**   **(PR:A MPAA:NR)**

BLUE SUNSHINE**1/2   (1978) 97m Ellanby/Cinema Shares c

Zalman King, Deborah Winters, Mark Goddard, Robert Walden, Charles Siebert, Ann Cooper, Ray Young, Alice Ghostley, Stefan Gierasch, Bill Cameron, Richard Crystal.

As a result of LSD ingested ten years earlier while they were students at Stanford, a group of middle class citizens is transformed into hairless crazies wreaking havoc on their sleek neighbors by brutally murdering them, stopping at nothing until they die themselves. King is the unwilling hero who is being sought, after the murder of Crystal (whom he has killed in self-defense), and discovers the link between a rash of murders and the premature hair loss. This is Lieberman's second film (the first was SQUIRM, 1966, one of the best examples of the revenge-of-nature cycle of films of the 1970s). His style is reminiscent of Cronenberg (THE PARASITE MURDERS, 1974 and RABID, 1976) in that he reveals a concern with sexuality as opposed to the mere display of sex. His sense of humor and freneticism are evident in a hilarious scene depicting a conversation betewen Rodin the artist and Rodan the monster wherein their roles are momentarily confused. BLUE SUNSHINE has been wrongly touted as one of the best Science Fiction thrillers of the 1970s.

p, George Manasse; d&w, Jeff Lieberman; m, Charles Gross (Movielab Color).

Horror   **Cas.**   **(PR:A MPAA:R)**

BLUE THUNDER***   (1983) 108m COL c

Roy Scheider *(Murphy)*, Malcolm McDowell *(Cochrane)*, Candy Clark *(Kate)*, Warren Oates *(Braddock)*, Daniel Stern *(Lymangood)*, Paul Roebling *(Icelan)*, David Sheiner *(Fletcher)*, Ed Berhard *(Short)*, Jason Bernard *(Mayor)*, Joe Santos *(Montoya)*, Mario Machado *(Himself)*.

A rock-'em-sock-'em-shoot-'em-smash-'em commercial picture that starts out fast and winds up faster. Sure, it's on a par with Wile E. Coyote for its cartoonish quality, but there's absolutely no time to analyze BLUE THUNDER, so you just have to sit back and let the bullets whiz by. It's crammed with fade-in to fade-out action that doesn't even stop to refuel the amazing helicopter the film is named after. Roy Scheider is, of course, a Vietnam vet who learned how to pilot choppers Over There. McDowell is an old enemy. Don't ask why; just accept the fact. Blue Thunder has been brought to Los Angeles to combat any possible terrorist activities during the 1984 Olympics, and McDowell is out to sabotage the incredible machine that features goodies like microphones that can pick up sounds behind walls, a "whisper mode" that allows the copter to fly unheard, heat detectors, zoom lenses, and just about everything you'll be wanting on your next Cadillac. Blue Thunder is out on a run when it picks up the voice of McDowell and his cohorts as they discuss a cabal formed by a military group attempting to overthrow the U.S. Okay, it sounds like old stuff. We've seen it all before, yes. But here's a case where the execution overtook the explanation and, after awhile, you really don't care what the secret plot is as Blue Thunder goes through its paces and manages to provide more visual enjoyment than we've seen in many a film. Scheider is dandy as the hair-shirted pilot, McDowell is his customary vile self, Clark is adorable as Roy's girl friend (perhaps a bit young, though) and the late Warren Oates, to whom the film is dedicated, bows out with one of the best roles he's ever played. Director Badham again proves his incredible versatility, after making DRACULA and SATURDAY NIGHT FEVER.

p, Gordon Carroll; d, John Badham; w, Dan O'Bannon, Don Jakoby; ph, John Alonzo (Panavision, DeLuxe Color); m, Arthur B. Rubenstein; ed, Frank Morris, Edward Abroms; cos, Marianna Elliot; spec eff, Chuck Gaspar, Jeff Jarvis, Peter Albiez.

Crime Drama   **Cas.**   **(PR:C MPAA:R)**

BLUE VEIL, THE**

(1947, Fr.) 90m Compagnie Generale Cinematographique bw (LE VOILE BLEU)

Gaby Morlay *(Louise)*, Elvire Popesco *(Mona)*, Marcelle Genlat *(Mme. Breuilly)*, Alerme *(Ernest)*, Charpin *(Perrette)*, Larquey *(Antoine)*, Alme Clarlond *(Judge)*, Rene Devillers *(Doctor)*.

Static tale of widow Morlay who dedicates her life to caring for little children. Film ends with a reunion of all her former charges, after covering a 30-year span. Touching and sensitive. (In French; English subtitles.)

p, Raymond Artus; d, Jean Stelli; w, Francois Campaux; ph, Rene Caveau; m, A. Theurer.

Drama   **(PR:A MPAA:NR)**

BLUE VEIL, THE**1/2   (1951) 113m RKO bw

Jane Wyman *(Louise Mason)*, Charles Laughton *(Fred K. Begley)*, Joan Blondell *(Annie Rawlins)*, Richard Carlson *(Gerald Kean)*, Agnes Moorehead *(Mrs. Palfrey)*, Don Taylor *(Dr. Robert Palfrey)*, Audrey Totter *(Helen Williams)*, Cyril Cusack *(Frank Hutchins)*, Everett Sloane *(District Attorney)*, Natalie Wood *(Stephanie Rawlins)*, Vivian Vance *(Alicia)*, Carleton Young *(Mr. Palfrey)*, Alan Napier *(Prof. Carter)*, Warner Anderson *(Bill)*, Les Tremayne *(Joplin)*, Dan Seymour *(Pelt)*, Dan O'Herlihy *(Hugh Williams)*, Henry Morgan *(Charles Hall)*, Gary Jackson *(Robert Palfrey as Boy)*, Gregory Marshall *(Harrison Palfrey)*, Dee Pollack *(Tony)*.

An all-star cast of cameos is dominant in this remake of the French film LE VOILE BLEU about a governess, Wyman, who loses her husband and child during WW I and uses the rest of her life to take care of other people's offspring. Despite the surprisingly mawkish script by the normally unstinting Corwin, Wyman manages to play what might have been laughable into a believable and dignified character. It's very episodic, not unlike TALES OF MANHATTAN where a piece of clothing is followed. In this case, the clothing is Wyman as she goes from home to home, shedding a little sunshine everywhere she goes. Laughton is a rich manufacturer who hires her to care for his motherless son. He soon falls in love with Jane and when she says no thank you, he marries Vance, his secretary. Next, she goes to work for Moorehead and falls in love with Carlson, a tutor. His work sends him abroad, but she won't give up her duties and so he departs alone. Then she takes over the care of Natalie Wood, daughter of Joan Blondell, a Merman-like actress fallen upon hard times. Two more segments and then she's suddenly old and forgotten until one of her former "children," Taylor (now a very successful film and TV director in real life), arranges a party at which all of her "children" are in attendance. A similar film was done for TV, starring Mickey Rooney as a clown who had taken in a number of foster children. Both pictures have the same tearful ending and a feeling of having been manipulated by the writer and director.

p, Jerry Wald, Norman Krasna; d, Curtis Bernhardt; w, Norman Corwin (based on a story by Francois Campaux); ph, Franz Planer; m, Franz Waxman; ed, George J. Amy.

Romance/Drama   **(PR:A MPAA:NR)**

BLUE, WHITE, AND PERFECT**1/2   (1941) 74m FOX bw

Lloyd Nolan *(Michael Shayne)*, Mary Beth Reynolds *(Merle Garland)*, George Reeves *(Juan Arturo O'Hara)*, Steve Geray *(Vanderhoefen)*, Henry Victor *(Hagerman)*, Curt Bois *(Nappy)*, Marie Blake *(Ethel)*, Emmett Vogan *(Charlie)*, Mae Marsh *(Mrs. Toby)*, Frank Orth *(Mr. Toby)*, Ivan Lebedeff *(Alexis Fournier)*, Wade Boteler *(Judge)*, Charles Trowbridge *(Capt. Brown)*, Edward Earle *(Richards)*, Cliff Clark *(Inspector)*, Arthur Loft *(Capt. McCordy)*, Charles Williams *(Printer)*, Ann Doran *(Miss Hoffman)*.

Detective Nolan is put on the trail of a gang of spies who are smuggling industrial diamonds to the enemy disguised as buttons. Trail leads aboard a luxury liner bound for Honolulu. Released less than two weeks after Pearl Harbor, this was the first American movie to show a U.S. clearly involved in the war. Tough fast-paced sleuth yarn with hard-as-nails Nolan doing a great job. (See MICHAEL SHAYNE series, Index.)

p, Sol M. Wurtzel; d, Herbert I. Leeds; w, Samuel G. Engel (based on a story by Borden Chase and a character created by Brett Halliday); ph, Glen MacWilliams; ed, Alfred Day.

Crime Drama   **(PR:A MPAA:NR)**

BLUEBEARD**1/2   (1944) 71m PRC bw

John Carradine *(Gaston)*, Jean Parker *(Lucille)*, Nils Asther *(Insp. Lefevre)*, Ludwig Stossel *(Lamarte)*, George Pembroke *(Insp. Renard)*, Teala Loring *(Francine)*, Sonia Sorel *(Renee)*, Iris Adrian *(Mimi)*, Henry Kolker *(Deschamps)*, Emmett Lynn *(Le Soldat)*, Patti McCarty *(Bebette)*, Carrie Deven *(Constance)*, Anne Sterling *(Jeanette)*.

Carradine is an artist in 19th-century Paris fond of strangling his models after he paints their portraits. Jean Parker suspects something is wrong in this effective thriller, and undoes the charming monster. Many a harrowing scene.

p, Leon Fromkess; d, Edgar G. Ulmer; w, Pierre Gendron (based on a script by Arnold Phillips and Werner H. Furst); ph, Jockey A. Feindel; ed, Carl Pierson.

Horror   **Cas.**   **(PR:A MPAA:NR)**

BLUEBEARD, 1963   (SEE: LANDRU, 1963, Fr.)

BLUEBEARD*1/2   (1972) 123m Cinerama/Vulcano c

Richard Burton *(Bluebeard/Baron Von Sepper)*, Raquel Welch *(Magdalena)*, Joey Heatherton *(Anne)*, Virna Lisi *(Elga)*, Nathalie Delon *(Erika)*, Marilu Tolo *(Brigitte)*, Karin Schubert *(Greta)*, Agostina Belli *(Caroline)*, Sybil Danning *(The Prostitute)*, Edward Meeks *(Sergio)*, Jean Lefebvre *(Greta's Father)*, Mathieu Carriere *(The Violinist)*.

High camp retelling of the story of the man who marries and murders again and again. Heatherton finds a meat locker full of frozen beauties in husband Burton's estate, and he regales her with flashbacks that show the wide variety of fates befalling his wives, including drowning, guillotining, and shooting. Not very good.

p, Alexander Salkind; d, Edward Dmytryk; w, Ennio Di Concini, Dmytryk, Maria Pia Fusco; ph, Gabor Pogany (Technicolor); m, Ennio Morricone; ed, Jean Ravel; art d, Tomas Vayer; cos, Vicky Tiel, Jacques Fonteray.

Crime Drama   **Cas.**   **(PR:O MPAA:R)**

BLUEBEARD'S EIGHTH WIFE*1/2   (1938) 80m PAR bw

Claudette Colbert *(Nicole de Loiselle)*, Gary Cooper *(Michael Brandon)*, Edward Everett Horton *(de Loiselle)*, David Niven *(Albert De Regnier)*, Elizabeth Patterson

(Aunt Hedwige), Herman Bing (Monsieur Pepinard), Charles Halton (Monsieur de la Coste), Barlowe Borland (Uncle Fernandel).

A ridiculous farce starring Cooper as a spoiled millionaire who is so fond of married life that he's had seven wives, all of whom he coaxed into wedlock by his bank account. (This was patently a take-off on the infamous Tommy Manville, heir to the Johns-Manville fortune, who married his way into the headlines.) Visiting a Riviera shop, he meets Claudette and she rebuffs him. Daughter of impoverished but noble French parents, she is properly spunky, and her lack of interest only makes him more aggressive. Under a harangue by her father (Horton), she accepts Coop's proposal and makes it clear that it's only for the money, nothing else. She attempts to change him on their honeymoon and wins, but loses. He gives her a divorce but she's come to love him. She begins to chase him all over France and he hides in a sanitarium. She buys the place and has him put in a straitjacket so he *must* listen to her. Cooper never seemed at home in the role. Wilder's and Brackett's screenplay has some laughs and Lubitsch knows how to get the most out of the least, but this was a mistake to make in the first place. Some good bit parts with Pangborn in his usual role as a hotel executive, Drew as a secretary, and Ames as the former chauffeur. In a tiny bit is Joyce Matthews, who married several times in real life. She was wed to Milton Berle twice and Billy Rose twice.

p&d, Ernst Lubitsch; w, Charles Brackett, Billy Wilder (based on the play by Alfred Savoir, American version by Charlton Andrews); ph, Leo Tover; ed, William Shea.

Comedy (PR:A-C MPAA:NR)

BLUEBEARD'S TEN HONEYMOONS*½ (1960, Brit.) 90m AA bw

George Sanders (Landru), Corinne Calvet (Odette), Jean Kent (Mme. Guillin), Patricia Roc (Mme. Dueaux), Greta Gynt (Jeanette), Maxine Audley (Cynthia), Ingrid Hafner (Giselle), Selma Caz Dias (Mme. Boyer), Peter Illing (Lefevre), George Coulouris (Lacoste), Sheldon Lawrence (Pepi), Paul Whitsun-Jones (Station Master), Keith Pyott (Estate Agent), Jack Melford (Concierge), Robert Rietty (Bank Clerk), Mark Singleton (Advertising Clerk), Milo Sperber (Librarian), C. Denier Warren (Neighbor), Harold Berens (Jeweler), Ian Fleming (Attorney), Dino Galvani (Hardware Store Owner).

George Sanders was everybody's favorite swine until he took his own life in 1972 after leaving a note that said he was doing it because he'd done everything else and was bored. It was a mistake, George, you were good in everything you ever did, including this turkey retelling of the Bluebeard story which has been done on several other occasions and will, no doubt, continue to be retold as long as people are fascinated by mass murder. (BLUEBEARD starring John Carradine, 1944, BLUEBEARD with Richard Burton, 1972, and, of course, Charlie Chaplin's version, MONSIEUR VERDOUX.) Not even Sanders' suavity and Calvet's curves can make this version anything more than a potboiler. There's an actor named Ian Fleming who plays an attorney and many people confuse him with the author of the James Bond films who was also an actor in his early years. This is a different Ian, however. By the time this movie was made, Fleming the author was rolling in money and too above it all to work as an actor again.

p, Roy Parkinson; d, W. Lee Wilder; w, Myles Wilder; ph, Stephan Dade; m, Albert Elms; ed, Tom Simpson.

Mystery (PR:A-C MPAA:NR)

BLUEPRINT FOR MURDER, A***½ (1953) 76m FOX bw

Joseph Cotten (Whitney Cameron), Jean Peters (Lynne Cameron), Gary Merrill (Fred Sargent), Catherine McLeod (Maggie Sargent), Jack Kruschen (Hal Cole), Barney Phillips (Capt. Pringle), Fred Ridgeway (Doug, Jr.), Joyce McCluskey (Miss Brownell), Mae Marsh (Anna), Harry Carter (Wheeler), Jonathan Hale (Dr. Stevenson), Walter Sande (Henderson), Tyler McVey, Teddy Mangean, Aline Towne, Ray Hyke, Charles Collins, Eugene Borden, Carleton Young, Grandon Rhodes, Herb Butterfield, George Melford.

In this murder mystery Joseph Cotten is somewhat smitten with his beautiful widowed sister-in-law, sultry Peters, until he begins to suspect she may be responsible for the death of her stepdaughter. After an autopsy reveals strychnine poisoning and there is an inheritance involved as well as an existing stepson, Cotten is sure his hunch is correct and follows Peters on an ocean voyage, planning to entrap her before she does away with her nephew. Careful police work is well documented in the script. The basic premise that most poisoners get away with their crimes because poison is hard to trace makes this a provocative and compelling movie.

p, Michael Abel; d&w, Andrew Stone; ph, Leo Tover; md, Lionel Newman.

Crime Drama (PR:C MPAA:NR)

BLUEPRINT FOR ROBBERY*½ (1961) 88m PAR bw

J. Pat O'Malley (Pop Kane), Robert Wilke (Capt. Swanson), Robert Gist (Chips McGann), Romo Vincent (Fatso Bonneli), Jay Barney (Red Mack), Henry Corden (Preacher-Doc), Tom Duggan (James Livingston), Sherwood Price (Gus Romay), Robert Carricart (Gyp Grogan), Johnny Indrisano (Nick Tony), Joe Conley (Jock McGee), Marion Ross (Young Woman), Barbara Mansell (Bar Girl).

This compact little crime drama roughly parallels the Brink's caper. Lack of frills, nuances, and philosophical clutter create a businesslike tone to the production which should delight enthusiasts of this kind of picture. The script, while straightforward, is repetitious. The best moments are those without dialog, particularly a 15-minute scene where the thugs indulge in a bit of inside reconnaissance avoiding a night watchman and a maze of alarms and electric eyes to obtain the necessary impressions for the job of key-making. The preparatory stages of the heist, the $4,700,000 stick-up, and the deterioration of the plot through greed, impatience and inability to resist temptation for petty pilfering by gang members are the best scenes in the film.

p, Bryan Foy; d, Jerry Hopper; w, Irwin Winehouse, A. Sanford Wolf; ph, Loyal Griggs; m, Van Cleave; ed, Terry Morse; art d, Hal Pereira.

Crime Drama (PR:A MPAA:NR)

BLUES BROTHERS, THE*½ (1980) 133m UNIV c

John Belushi (Joliet Jake), Dan Aykroyd (Elwood), James Brown (Rev. Cleophus James), Cab Calloway (Curtis), Ray Charles (Ray), Carrie Fisher (Mystery Woman), Aretha Franklin (Soul Food Cafe Owner), Henry Gibson (Nazi Leader), John Candy (Burton Mercer), Murphy Dunne (Murph), Steve Cropper (Steve "The Colonel" Cropper), Donald "Duck" Dunn (Himself), Willie Hall (Willie "Too Big" Hall), Tom Malone ("Bones" Malone), Lou Marini ("Blue" Lou Marini), Matt Murphy (Matt "Guitar" Murphy), Frank Oz (Corrections Officer), Kathleen Freeman (Sister Mary Stigmata), Armand Cerani (Trooper Daniel), Steve Williams (Trooper Mount), Charles Napier (Tucker McElroy), Steve Lawrence (Maury Slime), Twiggy (Chic Lady), Steven Spielberg (Cook County Clerk).

THE BLUES BROTHERS is a monumental waste of money, time and energy. The premise for this $30 million dollar ho-hum is that Elwood and Jake (Belushi and Aykroyd) need to raise $5,000 for their old church. They keep talking about being on "A mission from God." And that's it. With no other motivation, they systematically destroy the city of Chicago in much the same way the hoodlums did it to Detroit after the Tigers copped the World Series in 1984. The only difference was that the Detroiters had better taste. One of the most self-indulgent films in recent years, THE BLUES BROTHERS shows us what can be done when untold sums of money are given to arrogant young directors who think they know it all. The highlights are few but telling; all of the black performers score in their brief sojourns. Henry Gibson is funny as a George Rockwell-type Nazi, and Frank Oz of Muppet fame makes a rare on-screen appearance in his true persona as the Corrections Officer. This film has one pace: breakneck. It doesn't allow the audience to breathe, rest, or care about anyone or anything; $30 million is more money than Chaplin, Keaton, Laurel and Hardy, Charlie Chase, Harry Langdon, and Ben Turpin used to make all of the films they ever made. Whoever said "nothing succeeds like excess" was wrong in the case of THE BLUES BROTHERS.

p, Robert K. Weiss; d, John Landis; w, Landis, Dan Aykroyd; ph, Stephen M. Katz (Technicolor); m, Ira Newborn; ed, George Folsey, Jr.; cos, Deborah Nadoolman.

Comedy **Cas.** (PR:C-O MPAA:R)

BLUES BUSTERS** (1950) 67m MON bw

Leo Gorcey (Slip Mahoney), Huntz Hall (Sach Debussy Jones), Adele Jergens (Lola Stanton), Gabriel Dell (Gabe Moreno), Craig Stevens (Rick Martin), Phyllis Coates (Sally Dolan), Bernard Gorcey (Louie Dumbrowsky), William Benedict (Whitey), Buddy Gorman (Butch), David Gorcey (Chuck), Paul Bryar (Bimbo), Matty King (Joe Ricco) William Vincent (Teddy Davis).

The Bowery Boys are up to some new tricks this time. Huntz Hall (whose name always sounded like a German catering establishment) has his tonsils taken out and wakes up to learn that he has a golden throat (looped off-stage by John Lorenz). Naturally, Leo Gorcey sees this as a way to make a million bucks so they redo the local candy store, owned by Bernard Gorcey, into a nightclub. It's an overnight success as the word gets out about Huntz's (born Henry Hall) fabulous pipes. Stevens owns a nightclub in the neighborhood that is suffering because of Hall's popularity. He sics comely Adele Jergens after Huntz and the young lad's head is turned. He joins her at Stevens' place. Coates is Hall's one-time flame and she tricks Adele into spilling the beans about Stevens. Everything works out for the best when Huntz loses his tones and his voice returns to its normally annoying timbre. Good fun all around. (Gorcey was half-Jewish and half-Catholic and was given a choice of religions by his liberal parents. The synagog of his father was six blocks away through hostile territory, but the church of his mother was on the next street. Leo became an altar boy and his brother Dave chose to go with father Bernard. So the family celebrated Christmas and Chanukah with the same enthusiasm.) (See BOWERY BOYS series, Index.)

p, Jan Grippo; d, William Beaudine; w, Charles R. Marion, Bert Lawrence; ph, Marcel LePicard; m, Edward J. Kay; ed, William Austin.

Comedy/Musical (PR:AA MPAA:NR)

BLUES FOR LOVERS** (1966, Brit.) 89m FOX c (AKA: BALLAD IN BLUE)

Ray Charles (Himself), Tom Bell (Steve Collins), Mary Peach (Peggy Harrison), Dawn Addams (Gina Graham), Piers Bishop (David), Betty McDowell (Mrs. Babbidge), Lucy Appleby (Margaret), Joe Adams (Fred), Robert Lee Ross (Duke Wade), Anne Padwick (Bus Conductress), Monika Henreid (Antonia), Brendan Agnew, Vernon Hayden, Leo McCabe, The Ray Charles Orchestra, The Raelets.

Ray Charles plays himself, helping a recently blinded English boy adjust in this sentimental tale. Worthwhile for extensive footage of Charles in performance. And, yes, the director/co-writer is Paul Henreid, the actor (Victor Lazlo in CASABLANCA, 1942, among many other fine films). Henreid directed a number of films and TV shows in his later years.

p, Herman Blaser; d, Paul Henreid; w, Burton Wohl (based on a story by Wohl and Henreid); ph, Bob Hike; m, Stanley Black; ed, Ray Poulton.

Drama/Musical (PR:A MPAA:NR)

BLUES IN THE NIGHT*** (1941) 89m WB bw

Priscilla Lane (Ginger), Betty Field (Kay Grant), Richard Whorf (Jigger Pine), Lloyd Nolan (Del Davis), Jack Carson (Leo Powell), Wally Ford (Brad Ames), Howard da Silva (Sam Paryas), Elia Kazan (Nickie Haroyan).

Musical melodrama about a jazz quintet featuring sharp dialog from the pens of Gilbert (who wrote the original play) and Rossen (screenplay), who went on to become an important director/writer. Lane toplines as the wife of Carson, leader of the group, and sings several of the tunes. Mercer and Arlen got an Oscar nomination for the title tune, but lost out to "The Last Time I Saw Paris." Field is the bad girl and Nolan is the heavy (an escaped convict lost in New Jersey. What a fate!) and whatever plot there is takes second position to the characterizations. Two well-known directors appeared in the cast: Elia Kazan (ON THE WATERFRONT, A FACE IN THE CROWD, VIVA ZAPATA) and Richard Whorf, who alternated between acting (Sam Harris in YANKEE DOODLE DANDY) and directing (CHAMPAGNE FOR CAESAR, TILL THE CLOUDS ROLL BY). Whorf's son was his assistant director in television. Whorf died while producing and directing the ill-fated "Tammy Grimes Show" for Fox.

p, Henry Blanke; d, Anatole Litvak; w, Robert Rossen (based on the play by Edwin Gilbert); ph, Ernie Haller; ed, Owen Marks; m/l, Harold Arlen, Johnny Mercer.

Musical   **(PR:A   MPAA:NR)**

BLUME IN LOVE*½   (1973) 115m SB c

George Segal (*Blume*), Susan Anspach (*Nina Blume*), Kris Kristofferson (*Elmo*), Marsha Mason (*Arlene*), Shelley Winters (*Mrs. Cramer*), Donald F. Muhich (*Analyst*), Paul Mazursky (*Blume's Partner*).

A very funny movie about a man who falls in love with his ex-wife. This is the masculine version of Mazursky's AN UNMARRIED WOMAN a few years later. Segal is splendid as the lovesick lawyer who lusts after his ex, Anspach, who has taken up with Kristofferson. Mason is formidable as a woman waiting for divorced men. Mazursky, working without Tucker for the first time, lets the picture get away from him a few times and does not edit with as tight an eye as his previous films. His jaundiced look at love in California allows him to have some fun satirizing early 1970s types like Gottlieb (the bass player in The Limelighters group) as a guru and Denison as a Yoga leader. Winters is hysterical in a small role as a wife trying to decide whether or not to divorce her lecherous husband. The last part of the movie takes place in Venice, scene of their first loving moments, and the city never looked more beautiful. It's so beautiful that it begins to resemble DEATH IN VENICE in many of the shots, perhaps deliberately. Mazursky likes to act and gives himself a role as Segal's partner. His acting background has stood him in good stead and he should do more of it. He also appeared in DEATHWATCH and THE BLACK-BOARD JUNGLE.

p,d&w, Paul Mazursky; ph, Bruce Surtees (Technicolor); ed, Donn Cambern; prod d, Pato Guzman; set d, Audrey A. Blaisdel.

Comedy   **Cas.**   **(PR:O   MPAA:R)**

BLUSHING BRIDES*½   (1930) 88m MGM bw

Joan Crawford (*Jerry*), Anita Page (*Connie*), Dorothy Sebastian (*Franky*), Robert Montgomery (*Tony*), Raymond Hackett (*David*), John Miljan (*Marty*), Hedda Hopper (*Mrs. Weaver*), Albert Conti (*M. Pantoise*), Edward Brophy (*Joe Munsey*), Robert E. O'Connor (*Detective*).

Three working girls (Crawford, Page, and Sebastian) set out to find husbands. Only Crawford keeps her honor and so naturally gets a rich hubby and lives happily ever after. 1930 audiences laughed at the silly moralizing and Montgomery's luxury treehouse.

d, Harry Beaumont; w, Bess Meredyth, John H. Lawson, Justin Mayer.

Drama   **(PR:A   MPAA:NR)**

BMX BANDITS*½   (1983) 90m Nilsen Premiere Pty. c

David Argue (*Duane*), John Ley (*Povic*), James Lugton (*Goose*), Brian Marshall (*The Boss*), Nicole Kidman (*Judy*), Angelo d'Angelo (*PJ*).

A trip into the Down Underworld as three young BMX bikers find a trove of two-way radios that belong to a mob of bank robbers. They take the radios and sell them to their friends. The radios are tuned to the police frequency and this causes general madness among the traffic cops. The chief robber sends two of his bumbling cohorts out to get the radios and erase the kids. The rest of the picture is a chase. If the above sounds simplistic, we haven't done it justice. This is a fun film that will light up the faces of people from eight to whatever. Lots of laughs here plus many thrills. BMX bikes are as popular as kangaroos in Australia but the craze hasn't yet hit the states. Perhaps this film will help. It's the kind of movie Disney used to make when Walt was still around and taking charge of the company himself. The kids are particularly good and have none of the cloying cuteness seen so often in American-made films. Somehow, the Aussies have a way with a chase film that we may have forgotten. The moves are all motivated and logical, with no gratuitous cars flipping over and burning. Have the kids see this one with you but don't be surprised when you find yourself laughing out loud.

p, Tom Broadbridge, Paul Davies; d, Brian Trenchard-Smith (based on the screenplay by Russell Hagg); ph, John Seale (Panavision); m, Colin Stead, Frank Strangio; ed, Alan Lake; prod d, Ross Major.

Comedy   **(PR:AA   MPAA:NR)**

BOARDWALK*½   (1979) 98m Atlantic Releasing Corp. c

Ruth Gordon (*Becky Rosen*), Lee Strasberg (*David Rosen*), Janet Leigh (*Florence*), Joe Silver (*Leo*), Eli Mintz (*Mr. Friedman*), Eddie Barth (*Eli*), Merwin Goldsmith (*Charlie*), Kim Delgado (*Strut*), Michael Ayr (*Peter*), Forbesy Russell (*Marilyn*).

Director, co-writer Stephen Verona has crafted an affecting, effective look at senior citizens in the Coney Island area of New York, seen most recently in THE WARRIORS. Lee Strasberg and Ruth Gordon are the Darby and Joan who refuse to leave the dangerous area or pay tribute to the swaggering gang leader (Delgado) who runs the neighborhood. Little by little, Strasberg's life is eaten away as his wife dies, his

cafeteria is firebombed, his neighbors are beaten, and his house of worship is desecrated. Verona manipulates the story so that we are straining in our seats to see the bad guys get theirs. And in the final scene, he delivers the goods. Yes, it's a revenge story not unlike so many others, but what is missing is gratuitous violence, 45-caliber madness, cars smashing bodies. What *is* seen is a most believable finale. Williams' photography is excellent and Coney Island has never looked more interesting; despite the rust and the dirt, it's a fascinating place and now the new home of many Russian emigres. Verona obviously loves his subject matter. It's evident in every frame.

p George Willoughby; d, Stephen Verona; w, Verona, Leigh Chapman; ph, Billy Williams.

Drama   **Cas.**   **(PR:C-O   MPAA:NR)**

BOAT, THE   (SEE: DAS BOOT, 1981)

BOAT FROM SHANGHAI* (1931, Brit.) 52m REA/MGM bw (GB: CHIN CHIN CHINAMAN)

Leon M. Lion (*The Mandarin*), Elizabeth Allan (*The Countess*), George Curzon (*Colley*), Dino Galvani (*Dolange*), Picot Schooling (*Marie*), Douglas Blandford (*Captain*).

Detectives Allan and Lion team up and go undercover as members of Chinese royalty to expose thieves of stolen jewels. They recover the gems and return to their normal lives where all's well that ends well, except for the viewer.

p, Julius Hagen; d, Guy Newall; w, Brock Williams, Newall (based on a play by Percy Walsh); ph, Basil Emmott.

Crime   **(PR:A   MPAA:NR)**

BOATNIKS, THE*½   (1970) 100m Disney/BV c

Robert Morse (*Ensign Garland*), Stephanie Powers (*Kate*), Phil Silvers (*Harry Simmons*), Norman Fell (*Max*), Mickey Shaughnessy (*Charlie*), Wally Cox (*Jason*), Don Ameche (*Cmdr. Taylor*), Joey Forman (*Lt. Jordan*), Vito Scotti (*Pepe Galindo*), Tom Lowell (*Wagner*), Bob Hastings (*Chief Walsh*), Sammy Jackson (*Garlotti*), Joe E. Ross (*Nutty Sailor*), Judy Jordan (*Tina*), Al Lewis (*Bert*), Midori (*Chiyoko Kuni*), Kelly Thordsen (*Motorcycle Cop*), Gil Lamb (*Mr. Mitchell*).

Jewel thieves Silvers, Fell, and Shaughnessy accidentally drop their take in a harbor and bungle all attempts to recover it. Coast Guard Officer Morse tries to figure out what's going on. Great sight gags and good casting make this a good Disney outing.

p, Ron Miller; d, Norman Tokar; w, Arthur Julian (based on a story by Marty Roth); ph, William Snyder (Technicolor); m, Robert F. Brunner; ed, Cotton Warburton; art d, Hilyard Brown; set d, Emile Kuri, Frank R. McKelvy.

Comedy   **Cas.**   **(PR:AAA   MPAA:G)**

BOB AND CAROL AND TED AND ALICE*½   (1969) 104m COL c

Natalie Wood (*Carol*), Robert Culp (*Bob*), Elliott Gould (*Ted*), Dyan Cannon (*Alice*), Horst Ebersberg (*Horst*), Lee Bergere (*Emelio*), Donald F. Muhich (*Psychiatrist*), Noble Lee Holderread, Jr. (*Sean*), K. T. Stevens (*Phyllis*), Celeste Yarnall (*Susan*), Carol O'Leary (*Sue*), Andre Phillipe (*Oscar*), Greg Mullavey (*Group Leader*).

A very funny movie about an intended mate-swapping incident that stays funny. Mazursky and Tucker (far afield from their TV work which included the creation/development of "The Monkees") have written an original screenplay reflecting the late 1960s and, while hitting the mark at the time, it becomes dated quickly by the light of later years. Bob and Carol and Ted and Alice are best friends. Bob and Carol (Culp and Wood) visit a psycho-babble retreat in California (not unlike the then-popular Esalen Institute) and come home spouting all sorts of "Love Generation" dogma. The larger the words they use, the funnier it becomes. Wood has an affair with a tennis pro and Culp, living by his new standards, congratulates her. Cannon seems the most conservative of the foursome but when Gould admits an affair *he* had, she seems to go wild and suggests they orgy together while they are on a short respite to Las Vegas. And so the four are nude in bed at the end and none of them knows how to get this thing started. The funniest scene in the picture is one between Gould and Cannon when Gould is amorous and Dyan is anything but. The dialog is wonderful and this movie should be seen for that alone. In later years, Mazursky settled down his directorial style and concentrated on the human element but in B&C&T&A he was still fascinated by the camera and somewhat indulgent with his lenses. Andre Phillipe (nee Everett Cooper) is Oscar and, if you look hard in most of Mazursky's films, you'll see Andre in some small role.

p, Larry Tucker; d, Paul Mazursky; w, Mazursky, Larry Tucker; ph, Charles E. Land (Technicolor); m, Quincy Jones; cos, Moss Mabry; ch, Miriam Nelson.

Comedy   **Cas.**   **(PR:O   MPAA:R)**

BOB MATHIAS STORY, THE*½   (1954) 79m AA bw

Bob Mathias (*Bob Mathias*), Ward Bond (*Coach Jackson*), Melba Mathias (*Melba Mathias*), Howard Petrie (*Dr. Mathias*), Ann Doran (*Mrs. Mathias*), Diane Jergens (*Pat Mathias*), Paul Bryar (*Andrews*).

Mathias does a good job portraying himself in the story of the first man to win the Olympic decathlon twice. Interesting use of documentary footage from the 1948 and 1952 Olympic Games makes this low-budget effort worth watching.

p, William E. Selwyn; d, Francis D. Lyon; w, Richard Collins; ph, Ellsworth Fredricks; ed, Walter Hanneman.

Sports Drama   **(PR:AA   MPAA:NR)**

BOB, SON OF BATTLE   (SEE: THUNDER IN THE VALLEY, 1947)

BOBBIE JO AND THE OUTLAW zero   (1976) 88m AIP c

Marjoe Gortner (*Lyle Wheeler*), Lynda Carter (*Bobbie Jo James*), Jesse Vint (*Slick*

Callahan), Merrie Lynn Ross *(Pearl James)*, Belinda Balaski *(Essie Beaumont)*, Gene Drew *(Sheriff Hicks)*, Peggy Stewart *(Hattie James)*, Gerrit Graham *(Magic Ray)*, John Durren *(Deputy Gance)*, Virgil Frye *(Joe Grant)*, Joe Toledo *(Indian)*.

Lester, whose career includes ROLLER BOOGIE and the ruination of the TV movie GOLD OF THE AMAZON WOMEN (meant to be a satire, directed into the jungle earth by Lester), teams up with screenwriter Zimmerman (FADE TO BLACK) for this putrid exploitation pic. Gortner toplines as a scum-of-the-earth killer who sucks in a group of admirers through a host of totally senseless and unmotivated murders. Second-billed is Lynda Carter, before scoring in TV's "Wonder Woman." Merrie Lynn Ross is probably the best actress in the film. Picture is rare in that there is not one socially redeeming moment in it at all.

p&d, Mark L. Lester; w, Vernon Zimmerman; ph, Stanley Wright (Movielab Color); m, Barry DeVorzon; ed, Michael Luciano; stunts, Speed Sterns.

Crime   **Cas.**   **(PR:C-O MPAA:R)**

BOBBIKINS**   (1959, Brit.) 90m FOX bw

Max Bygraves *(Benjamin Barnaby)*, Shirley Jones *(Betty Barnaby)*, Steven Stacker*(Bobbikins)*, Billie Whitelaw *(Lydia)*, Barbara Shelley *(Valerie)*, Colin Gordon *(Dr. Phillips)*, Charles Tingwell *(Luke)*, Lionel Jeffries *(Gregory Mason)*, Charles Carson *(Sir Jason Crandall)*, Rupert Davies *(Jock Fleming)*, Noel Hood *(Nurse)*, David Lodge *(Hargreave)*, Murray Kash *(Johnson)*, Arnold Diamond *(LeFarge)*, Charles Lloyd-Pack *(Stebbins)*, Bill Nagy *(Rogers)*, Trevor Reid *(Cavendish)*, John Welsh *(Admiral)*, Michael Ripper *(Naval Petty Officer)*, Ronald Fraser *(Sailor Joe)*, John Downing *(Sailor Jones)*.

Cutesy fantasy about a talking baby who passes stock market tips from the Chancellor of the Exchequer to his father, a struggling entertainer (Bygraves). When Baby sees the havoc the new-struck riches have wreaked on his once-happy family, he gives his father a bad tip and once again the family is reduced to its former happy poverty. A one-joke film that grows insufferable very quickly.

p, Oscar Brodney; d, Robert Day; w, Brodney; ph, Geoffrey Faithfull (CinemaScope); m, Philip Green; ed, Ralph Kamplen, Stanley Hawkes.

Comedy   **(PR:A MPAA:NR)**

BOBBY DEERFIELD**½   (1977) 124 m COL c

Al Pacino *(Bobby Deerfield)*, Marthe Keller *(Lillian)*, Anny Duperey *(Lydia)*, Walter McGinn *(Leonard Deerfield)*, Romolo Valli *(Uncle Luigi)*, Stephan Meldegg *(Karl Holtzmann)*, Jaime Sanchez *(Delvecchio)*, Norman Neilsen *(The Magician)*, Mickey Knox, Dorothy James *(Tourists)*, Guido Alberti *(Priest in Garden)*, Aurora Maris *(Woman in Gas Station)*, Gerard Hernandez *(Carlos Del Montanara)*.

Al Pacino may have been chosen to play this role because he is one of the few actors small enough to fit into the high-speed racing cars that form the backdrop for BOBBY DEERFIELD. Don't be put off by the milieu; it's a better picture than it starts out to be. Yes, tears are jerked. (Keller is an Italian jet-setter with an infuriating German accent and, sigh, a mysterious disease.) Putting all the cliches aside, there are sparks that fly in the relationship and that love story is what you will be caught up in. Pacino is a top-flight race driver who learns that it's lonely at the top. Keller is the complex lady of leisure. Ann Duperey is the groupie who follows Pacino from Gran Prix to Gran Prix. A gorgeous picture to look at, it's a trifle long at just over two hours and much of the racing footage could have been trimmed. Keller and Pacino find each other, then themselves. If some of the soapsuds could have been rinsed away, this would have been better.

p&d, Sidney Pollack; w, Alvin Sargent (based on the novel by Erich Maria Remarque); ph, Henri Decae, Tony Maylam (Metrocolor); m, Dave Grusin; ed, Frederic Steinkamp; cos, Bernie Pollack, Annalisa Masalli-Rocca; stunts, Remy Julienne.

Romance/Adventure   **Cas.**   **(PR:C MPAA:PG)**

BOBBY WARE IS MISSING*   (1955) 67m AA bw

Neville Brand, Arthur Franz, Jean Willes, Walter Reed, Paul Picerni, Kim Charney, Thorpe Whitman, Peter Leeds.

Sluggish kidnaping yarn where police lamely go about tracking down the abductors of a small boy. Uninspired performances and dumb cop mentality stereotypes a plot that will do nothing but unnerve the viewer.

p, Vincent M. Fenn; d, Thomas Carr; w, Daniel B. Ullman; m, Carl Brandt; cos, Bert Henrikson.

Crime Drama   **(PR:A MPAA:NR)**

BOBO, THE**   (1967, Brit.) 103m WB c

Peter Sellers *(Juan Bautista)*, Britt Ekland *(Olimpia Segura)*, Rossano Brazzi *(Carlos Matabosch)*, Adolfo Celi *(Carbonell)*, Ferdy Mayne *(Flores)*, Hattie Jacques *(Trinity)*, Alfredo Lettieri *(Eugenio)*, Kenneth Griffith *(Gamazo)*, Marne Maitland *(Castillo)*, Don Lurio *(Ramon)*, Giustino Durano *(Druggist)*, John Wells *(Major Domo)*, Alfredo Chetta *(Ilya)*.

THE BOBO was a bungle from start to finish. Sellers plays a half-baked torero who would like to be a singer. He is mad for Ekland (his wife in real life at the time), who is a woman who gives gold diggers a bad name. She is the most mercenary female that ever slinked across the earth. Sellers has three days to seduce Ekland and he will be rewarded with a contract to sing for a week at a place owned by Celi (who delivers one of the best performances of his life). She turns out to be underage and vicious as she dumps Sellers into some uncleanable dye after she learns he was only after her to get the singing job. A hodge-podge that's only made bearable by Sellers cavorting. In a small role is the usually tough Al Lettieri who went on to become a successful second banangster (a combination of banana and gangster) in

THE GODFATHER and THE GETAWAY. Music by Francis Lai was properly jaunty.

p, Elliott Kastner, Jerry Gershwin; d, Robert Parrish; w, David R. Schwartz; ph, Gerry Turpin (Technicolor); m, Francis Lai; ed, John Jympson; cos, Adriana Berselli.

Comedy   **Cas.**   **(PR:AC MPAA:NR)**

BOB'S YOUR UNCLE*   (1941, Brit.) 76m BUT bw

Albert Modley *(Albert Smith)*, Jean Colin *(Dolly Diehard)*, George Bolton *(Jeff Smith)*, Wally Patch *(Sgt. Brownfoot)*, H. F. Maltby *(Maj. Diehard)*, Bert Linden *(Cpl. Nelson)*, Clifford Cobbe *(Butler)*, Johnnie Schofield *(Stationmaster)*, Alfred Wright & Co., Pims's Comedy Navy.

WW II on the home front has Guardsman Modley vying for his commander's daughter, Colin. To show he is worthy, Modley arranges a community drive to fund the purchase of a tank for the village. He wins the girl's heart, but not the viewer's in this routine laugher.

p, F. W. Baker; d, Oswald Mitchell; w, Mitchell, Vera Allinson (based on a play by Allinson); ph, Stephen Dade.

Comedy   **(PR:A MPAA:NR)**

BOCCACCIO**   (1936, Ger.) 75m Ufa bw

Albrecht Schoenhals *(Cesare d'Este)*, Gina Falckenberg *(Francesca)*, Willy Fritsch *(Etruccicio)*, Heli Finkenzeller *(Fiametta)*, Paul Kemp *(Calandrino)*, Fita Benkhoff *(Bianca)*, Albert Florath *(Bartolomeo)*, Tina Ellers *(Pia)*, Ernst Waldow *(Ricco)*, H.H. Schaufuss *(First Judge)*, Helmuth Weiss *(Geronimo)*.

Renaissance Italy as seen (inaccurately) through the eyes of the officially sanctioned Nazi film industry, all in operetta form. When *The Decameron's* lusty stories mysteriously appear in Ferrara, they inspire all manner of amorous dalliances among the populace until nobody knows who is doing what to whom. Typical German pre-war craftsmanship is much in evidence. (In German; English subtitles.)

p, Max Pfeiffer; d, Herbert Maisch; w, E. Burri; m, Franz Doelle.

Musical   **(PR:A MPAA:NR)**

BOCCACCIO '70*   (1962/Ital./Fr.) 150m TCF/Francinex/Gray Films c

"The Raffle": Sophia Loren *(Zoe)*, Luigi Gillianni *(Gaetano)*, Alfio Vita *(Cuspet)* "The Job": Romy Schneider *(Pupe)*, Thomas Milian *(The Count)*, Romolo Valli, Paolo Stoppa; "The Temptation of Dr. Antonio": Anita Ekberg *(Anita)*, Peppino De Filippo *(Dr. Antonio)*, Dante Maggio, Giacomo Furia, Alberto Sorrentino.

Three unconnected episodes dealing with modern stories the producers would have you think Boccaccio might have written if alive; from the lack of content and characterization, Boccaccio would not have used a pseudonym for these turgid tales. The film is only an excuse to parade the Amazonian attributes of Ekberg and Loren, with Schneider thrown in for dramatic license. Ekberg is a billboard image that comes to life in a dream conjured by a middle-aged lecher, a gigantic voluptuary with mammaries exploding accross the screen. This gauche exposition of flesh is almost equalled by hefty Loren who operates a shooting gallery and is the sex prize of a Saturday night raffle. To accommodate a country bumpkin who begs to win the raffle, she fixes the drawing but does not deliver the goods; to show she is a noble slattern, however, Loren spreads the word that she has dallied with the clod so he will become a hero to his crowd. Loren exposes her considerable backside to the cameras in peepshow posture, strips to a blood red half-bra and sneers her way through a story unworthy of telling at a routine stag party. Schneider's segment is almost lost between these two beef trust stories, she being a secretary in love with the boss and sacrificing her personal life for the ungrateful wretch. The whole thing is abysmal, contrived, and about as interesting, when comparing the non-talents of Loren and Ekberg, as watching two battleships collide.

p, Carlo Ponti, Antonio Cervi; "The Temptation of Dr. Antonio," d, Federico Fellini; w, Fellini, Ennio Flaiano, Tullio Pinelli; ph, Otello Marelli; m, Nino Rota; "The Job," d, Luchino Visconti; w, Suso Cecchi D'Amico, Visconti; ph, Guiseppe Rotunno; m, Nino Rota; "The Raffle," d, Vittorio De Sica; w, Cesare Zavattini; ph, Marelli; m, Armando Trovajoli.

Fantasy/Drama/Comdey   **Cas.**   **(PR:O MPAA:NR)**

BODY AND SOUL***   (1931) 82m FOX bw

Charles Farrell *(Maj. Andrews)*, Elissa Landi *(Carla)*, Humphrey Bogart *(Jim Watson)*, Myrna Loy *(Alice Lester)*, Donald Dillaway *(Top Johnson)*, Crawford Kent *(Maj. Burke)*, Pat Somerset *(Maj. Knowles)*, Ian MacLaren *(Gen. Trofford Jones)*, Dennis d'Auburn *(Lt. Meggs)*, Douglas Dray *(Zane)*, Harold Kinney *(Young)*, Bruce Warren *(Sam Douglas)*.

Good though melodramatic story of American flyers in the RAF during WW I. Commanding officer MacLaren demands that the German observation balloons near the front be blown up, a dangerous mission since the balloonists are equipped with machineguns. Bogart makes a daredevil attempt to destroy a balloon and is killed in the process, but Farrell does the job and credits his slain pal with the deed. On leave in England, Farrell tries to find Bogart's widow through a seies of letters Bogart had received by somone signing the name "Pom-Pom." Landi answers Farrell's missives, saying she is Bogart's wife. She and Farrell fall in love but she is later suspected of being a German spy when secret information is leaked that causes the deaths of more American flyers. It turns out that Loy, another of Farrell's friends, is really "Pom-Pom" the spy, who is promptly imprisoned as Landi and Farrell are united. This was the American film debut of Elissa Landi, a ravishing brunette who had made a few European films. Hollywood made little use of this talented actress, reducing her to supporting roles within a few years of her arrival (she would die at age 44 in 1948). Bogart's role was brief but he made the most of it as a daring pilot. The action is brisk and the aerial battles well photographed.

d, Alfred Santell; w, Jules Furthman (based on the play "Squadrons" by A. E. Thomas and the story "Big Eyes and Little Mouth" by Elliott White Springs); ph, Glen MacWilliams: m, Peter Brunelli; ed, Paul Weatherwax; art d, Anton Grot; spec eff, Ralph Hammeras.

War/Spy Drama **(PR:A MPAA:NR)**

BODY AND SOUL******

(1947)104m Enterprise/UA bw (AKA: AN AFFAIR OF THE HEART)

John Garfield *(Charlie Davis)*, Lilli Palmer *(Peg Born)*, Hazel Brooks *(Alice)*, Anne Revere *(Anna Davis)*, William Conrad *(Quinn)*, Joseph Pevney *(Shorty Polaski)*, Canada Lee *(Ben)*, Lloyd Goff *(Roberts)*, Art Smith *(David Davis)*, James Burke *(Arnold)*, Virginia Gregg *(Irma)*, Peter Virgo *(Drummer)*, Joe Devlin *(Prince)*, Mary Currier *(Miss Tedder)*, Milton Kibbee *(Dan)*, Artie Dorrell *(Jack Marlowe)*, Cy Ring *(Victor)*, Tim Ryan *(Shelton)*.

Powerful and moving boxing drama with Garfield at his dynamic best. The film opens with Garfield fitfully remembering in flashback when he was a fledgling fighter promoted into an important match by his best friend Pevney (who went on to become director of such action films as DESERT LEGION, YANKEE PASHA, and AWAY ALL BOATS). Against his mother's wishes, Garfield becomes a professional fighter, managed by Conrad, a ring-wise veteran of the game. His motive is simple. After his father's candy store is bombed (as a result of gangsters destroying the speakeasy next door), his kindly father (Smith) is killed; Garfield is strapped for money. His mother (Revere, in a great role) applies for aid and when a social worker comes to review their financial situation, Garfield explodes at what he considers degrading questions. He drives the woman out of the apartment, yelling at her: "Tell them we don't want their money. Tell 'em we're dead!" He vows to get money and plenty of it, despite the pleadings of his mother and artist girl friend, Palmer. Conrad takes him on the road and Garfield displays an awesome ability to destroy all comers in the ring. Soon he returns to NYC as a leading contender, eager to take on the champion. He finally gets the bout with Canada Lee, an ailing champion (in a stirring performance), beating him badly, learning later that doctors have cautioned Lee that the blood clot on his brain might cause his death if he fights again. Becoming champion of the world has cost Garfield a great deal; he has had to give a big percentage of himself to gangster Lloyd Goff who introduces him to an enchantress who takes him away from Palmer. Garfield leads the lavish life, spending a fortune on women and booze, fighting only those boxers who are has-beens, winning easily. When Pevney tries to point out the error of his ways, Garfield mutely stands by while Goff's bodyguard beats his friend senseless, stepping in only at the last moment to save him. Pevney, half conscious, staggers into the street and is killed by a speeding car. Out of shape, anxious over a forthcoming fight with a tough opponent, Garfield tries to pick up the pieces, returning to Palmer who forgives him, and his mother. He hires Lee to become his trainer but is told by Goff that no amount of preparation will save the crown for him; the fight is to go to Dorrell, the challenger, so that the gamblers will cash in big. Lee begs Garfield to stay clean and fight to win and when Goff's thugs move in on him, the old boxer begins wildly shadow-boxing in the training ring, then dies as his clot explodes. Garfield panics and bets all his savings on his opponent. He goes to his mother's to get the money and is told by Palmer that she has put the money in the bank for their impending marriage. He demands it back, finally telling her and Revere, "the fight's fixed." Revere doesn't understand so he spells it out for her. She is in shock, pointing out that all "the little people" have made wagers on him and how could he do such a thing? Palmer is disgusted. When he shouts that she must return his money, she slaps him repeatedly in the face, saying: "I'll give you what everyone gives you!" It is the night of the big fight. Garfield takes a terrible beating from Dorrell, a cocky newcomer, and it looks like he will drop unconscious to the canvas at any moment. He is finished as a boxer and, more importantly, as a human being, corrupted through and through. Yet, there is a spark of self-respect left. At the last minute he decides he will fight to win and he literally, in the closing rounds, stalks his terrified opponent, before unleashing a furious attack that knocks Dorrell unconscious. Palmer arrives in the arena to see this, cheering him on. As he emerges from the arena, still champion, with Palmer at his side, after this, his last fight, Goff and his thugs stop him. Garfield juts his magnificent jaw at the gangster and spits out the memorable lines: "So—what are you going to do? Kill me? Everybody dies!" He and Palmer walk away, triumphant in and out of the ring, to the strains of the haunting tune, "Body and Soul." Garfield had left Warner Brothers at the time of this film, which he personally financed. It was a wise business decision since the movie was immensely popular and returned considerable profit. The story itself was nothing new, having all the boxing cliches—gangsters, corrupt ring practices, crooked managers and all the ordinary perversion, sort of a GOLDEN BOY with blood and scars. Rivaling this film is Kirk Douglas in CHAMPION and Robert Ryan in THE SET-UP. Garfield's riveting performance, however, lifted BODY AND SOUL to the masterpiece level, as did Rossen's superb direction and the marvelous photography of Howe, particularly the fight sequences, which brought a kind of realism to the genre that had never before existed (Howe wore skates and rolled around the ring shooting the fight scenes with a hand-held camera). A knockout on all levels.

p, Bob Roberts; d, Robert Rossen; w, Abraham Polonsky; ph, James Wong Howe; m, Hugo Friedhofer; ed, Robert Parrish; art d, Nathan Juran; set d, Edward J. Boyle; cos, Marion Herwood Keyes; spec montages, Guenther Fritsch; m/l, Johnny Green, Edward Hewman, Robert Sour, Frank Eyton; makeup, Gustaf M. Norin.

Sports Drama **Cas.** **(PR:C MPAA:NR)**

BODY AND SOUL zero (1981) 109m Cannon c

Leon Isaac Kennedy *(Leon Johnson)*, Jayne Kennedy *(Julie Winters)*, Perry Lang *(Charles Golphin)*, Nikki Swassy *(Kelly Johnson)*, Mike Grazzo *(Frankie)*, Kim Hamilton *(Mrs. Johnson)*, Muhammad Ali *(Himself)*, Peter Lawford *(Big Man)*.

Do not confuse this with the 1947 BODY AND SOUL; this bow-wow takes five minutes longer than the original and has as much drama in it as a worn-out piece of linoleum. Some films lend themselves to remakes but writer/actors like Kennedy should realize that you don't redo a film unless you can make it *better*. It's not enough to cast it black and think that will be sufficient. Best thing in the movie is Ali, making a few cameo appearances and showing why he is The Greatest. Ali, with no training, is a far better player than Kennedy, who took the reviews he received in PENITENTIARY too seriously and believed his own clippings. Jayne Kennedy is gorgeous and also a better actor than her then-husband. Matter of fact, just about everyone in this film, with the possible exception of Peter Lawford as the mobster, is a better actor than Kennedy.

p, Menaham Golan, Yoram Globus; d, George Bowers; w, Leon Isaac Kennedy; ph, James Forrest; m, Webster Lewis; ed, Samm Pollard, Skip Schoolnick; cos, Celia; fight ch, Bob Minor; ch, Hope Clarke.

Boxing **Cas.** **(PR:C MPAA:R)**

BODY DISAPPEARS, THE ½** (1941) 72m WB bw

Jeffrey Lynn *(Peter DeHaven)*, Jane Wyman *(Joan Shotesbury)*, Edward Everett Horton *(Prof. Shotesbury)*, David Bruce *(Jimmy Barbour)*, Herbert Anderson *(George "Doc" Appleby)*, Marguerite Chapman *(Christine Lunceford)*, Craig Stevens *(Robert Struck)*, Willie Best *(Willie)*, Ivan Simpson *(Dean Claxton)*, Charles Halton *(Prof. Moggs)*, Wade Boteler *(Insp. Deming)*, Sidney Bracy *(Barrett, the Butler)*, Natalie Schafer *(Mrs. Lunceford)*, Michael Ames *(Bill)*, DeWolfe Hopper *(Terrence Abbott)*, John Hamilton *(Judge)*, Frank Ferguson *(Prof. McAuley)*, Romaine Callender *(Prof.* Barkley), Vera Lewis *(Mrs. Moggs)*, Paul Stanton *(Prosecutor)*, Stuart Holmes *(Waiter)*, Charles Drake *(Arthur)*.

Fine special effects highlight this variation of the "invisible man" theme. Lynn is the butt of a bachelor party practical joke in which he is placed—unconscious and limp with drink—in the medical school morgue. There his comatose body is stolen by Best, assistant to a crackpot professor, Horton, to be injected with a substance that will restore the dead to life. Instead, it renders the benumbed Lynn invisible. He recovers and is naturally mortified at his condition. Horton promises to devise an antidote and Lynn has to remain at the professor's home. There he encounters Wyman, who has long loved Lynn from afar. Invisibility has its advantages and Lynn comes to discover that his fiancee, Chapman, is only going to marry him for mercenary reasons, and he dumps her for Wyman. A fine, funny B movie with Horton and wide-eyed Best giving fine comic performances.

p, Bryan Foy, Ben Stoloff; d, D. Ross Lederman; w, Scott Darling, Erna Lazarus (based on the story "Black Widow" by Darling and Lazarus); ph, Allen G. Siegler; ed, Frederick Richards; spec eff, Edwin A. DuPar.

Comedy **(PR:A MPAA:NR)**

BODY HEAT**** (1981) 113m Ladd Company/WB c

William Hurt *(Ned Racine)*, Kathleen Turner *(Matty Walker)*, Richard Crenna *(Edmund Walker)*, Ted Danson *(Peter Lowenstein)*, J.A. Preston *(Oscar Grace)*, Mickey Rourke *(Teddy Lewis)*, Kim Zimmer *(Mary Ann)*, Jane Hallaren *(Stella)*, Lanna Saunders *(Roz Kraft)*, Michael Ryan *(Miles Hardin)*, Carola McGuinness *(Heather Kraft)*, Larry Marko *(Judge Costanze)*, Deborah Lucchessi *(Beverly)*, Lynn Hallowell *(Angela)*, Thom J. Sharp *(Michael Glenn)*, Ruth Thom *(Mrs. Singer)*, Diane Lewis *(Glenda)*, Robert Traynor *(Prison Trustee)*, Meg Kasdan *(Nurse)*, Ruth P. Strahan *(Betty, the Housekeeper)*, Filomena Triscari *(Hostess at Tulios)*, Bruce A. Lee *(Man on the Beach)*.

Excellent, if slightly calculated, crime drama in the style of Chandler, Cain, and Hammett. Kasdan borrows liberally from the aforementioned in his style and substance and the plot is quite close to DOUBLE INDEMNITY in that it's the woman who plans knocking off her husband and enlists an unwitting and somewhat simple man as her accomplice. Major difference between this film and the *film noir* of the 1940s is that Kasdan is able to write double-entendres that the Hays Office would have frowned upon then. Kasdan uses an unidentifiable Florida town where you can almost feel the humidity and see the palmetto bugs running across the pavement. Hurt is a dimwitted attorney who is tricked by Turner into helping her murder Crenna. From then on, it's twist and turn and watch how the cabal falls apart. Hurt is superior in the role, and we can actually see the wood burning in his mental fireplace. How this yutz ever got out of law school is beyond us. Turner can be the next femme fatale if she spends some more time learning her craft and less time looking in the mirror. Still, for a first-time effort, she does mighty well and will be heard from often. Danson is excellent as Lowenstein, another attorney and a good pal of Hurt. Rourke, in one of his early screen appearances, shows the promise of things to come. Matter of fact, all of the secondary roles are well-cast and well-performed. The technical credits are first rate. Kasdan knows that stinting on the tech side can ruin even the most amibitious project. Every detail has been attended to and this is one of the best mysteries to come out of Hollywood (even though it was done in Florida) since CHINATOWN. But one can't help having the feeling about Kasdan that he is, at best, an emulator, rather than a creator. Still, even emulating well (unlike Higgins and De Palma) is an art and, in that, Kasdan is to be applauded. He will be a giant as soon as he starts thinking for himself, which he begins to prove in THE BIG CHILL.

p, Fred T. Gallo; d&w, Lawrence Kasdan; ph, Richard H. Kline (Technicolor); m, John Barry; ed, Carol Littleton; cos, Renie Conley.

Crime Drama **Cas.** **(PR:C MPAA:R)**

BODY SAID NO!, THE* (1950, Brit.) 75m New World Angel bw

Michael Rennie *(Himself)*, Yolande Donlan *(Mikki Brent)*, Hy Hazell *(Sue)*, Jon Pertwee *(Watchman)*, Valentine Dyall *(John Sutherland)*, Reginald Beckwith *(Benton)*, Arthur Hill *(Robin King)*, Cyril Smith *(Sergeant)*, Jack Billings *(Eddie)*,

Peter Butterworth (Driver), Margaret McGrath (Mrs. Rennie), Winifred Shotter (TV Announcer).

Suspicious comedy singer wrongly interprets cameras accidentally televising a rehearsal as a secret plot to murder one of the actors. An early inside glimpse of the television world, but a paranoid no-brainer.

p, Daniel M. Angel; d&w, Val Guest; ph, Bert Mason.

Comedy   (PR:AA MPAA:NR)

BODY SNATCHER, THE*   (1945) 79m RKO bw

Boris Karloff (John Gray), Bela Lugosi (Joseph), Henry Daniell (Dr. MacFarlane), Edith Atwater (Meg Camden), Russell Wade (Donald Fettes), Rita Corday (Mrs. Marsh), Sharyn Moffet (Georgina Marsh), Donna Lee (Street Singer).

Chilling, atmospheric tale of grave robbing in 1832 Edinburgh. Daniell is a doctor regularly buying cadavers delivered to his back door by menacing cabbie Karloff. When Karloff turns to murder in his quest for bodies—delivering the still-warm body of a young street singer Daniell has seen alive and well only that morning—the frightened doctor realizes he must do something. Daniell murders Karloff but is not rid of him, the grave robber's face appearing on the body of an old woman whose body Daniell is stealing, causing the doctor to panic and drive his carriage over a cliff. Lugosi and Karloff have only one scene together, but it's a great one, the last gasp of respectability in Lugosi's sad career.

p, Val Lewton; d, Robert Wise; w, Philip MacDonald, Carlos Keith (based on a short story by Robert Louis Stevenson); ph, Robert DeGrasse; m, Roy Webb; ed, J. R. Whittredge; md, Constantin Bakaleinikoff; art d, Albert S. D'Agostino, Walter Keller; set d, Darrell Silvera, John Sturtevant; cos, Renee.

Horror   **Cas.**   (PR:A MPAA:NR)

BODY STEALERS, THE*1/2   (1969, Brit.) 91m Tigon/AA c

George Sanders (Gen. Armstrong), Maurice Evans (Dr. Matthews), Patrick Allen (Bob Megan), Neil Connery (Jim Radford), Hilary Dwyer (Julie Slade), Robert Flemyng (W.C. Baldwin), Lorna Wilde (Lorna), Allan Cuthberton (Hindsmith), Michael Culver (Lt. Bailes), Sally Faulkner (Joanna), Shelagh Fraser (Mrs. Thatcher).

What could be causing our parachutists to disappear? Former Air Force investigator Sanders thinks it might be aliens. A waste of time as Sanders sloppily unearths outer-space visitors.

p, Tony Tenser; d, Gerry Levy; w, Michael St. Clair, Peter Marcus; ph, Peter Henry (Eastmancolor).

Science Fiction   (PR:A MPAA:NR)

BODYGUARD*1/2   (1948) 62m RKO bw

Lawrence Tierney (Mike Carter), Priscilla Lane (Doris Brewster), Philip Reed (Freddie Dysen), June Clayworth (Connie), Elizabeth Risdon (Gene Dysen), Steve Brodie (Fenton), Frank Fenton (Lt. Borden), Charles Case (Capt. Wayne).

Decent crime thriller with Tierney clearing himself of a murder charge. He is an ex-plainsclothes L.A. cop who has taken the job of protecting widow Risdon from blackmailers but soon discovers that his friends on the force want him for a killing. Tight script and quick pace keep this one on target.

p, Sid Rogell; d, Richard O. Fleischer; w, Fred Niblo Jr., Harry Essex (based on a story by George W. George, Robert B. Altman); ph, Robert De Grasse; ed, Elmo Williams.

Crime   (PR:A MPAA:NR)

BODYHOLD*1/2   (1950) 63m COL bw

Willard Parker (Tommy Jones), Lola Albright (Mary Simmons), Hillary Brooke (Flo Woodbury), Allen Jenkins (Slats Henry), Roy Roberts (Charlie Webster), Gordon Jones (Pat Simmons), Sammy Menacker (Red Roman), Frank Sully (Killer Cassidy), John Dehner (Sir Raphael Brokenridge), Billy Varga (Marvelous Milton), Henry Kulky (Mike Kalumbo), Wee Willie Davis (Azusa Assassin), Matt McHugh (Gus Stotz), George H. Lloyd (Chuck Hadley), Ruth Warren (Kitty Cassidy), Ray Walker (Professor Weaver), John R. Hamilton (Commissioner Harley), Ken Ackles (Terre Haute Terror), Ed "Strangler" Lewis (Referee).

The corrupt world of professional wrestling provides the backdrop for this exploitation film inspired by the boom in the sport after the advent of television coverage. Parker is a plumber who happens to be doing some repairs in the office of promoter Roberts just as the latter is looking for a new wrestler to replace the former champion (Jones), who was crippled by Roberts' men after he demanded a bigger share. Parker rises up through the ranks, but when he gets some ideas of his own, he is subjected to the same treatment as the former champ. This time, however, it backfires and Roberts is banned from the sport. Mercifully brief.

p, Rudolph C. Flothow; d, Seymour Friedman; w, George Bricker; m, Mischa Bakaleinikoff; ed, James Sweeney.

Sports Drama   (PR:A MPAA:NR)

BOEFJE*   (1939, Ger.) 69m NV City Film bw

Annie van Ees (Boefje), Guus Brox (Pietje Puck), Albert von Dalsum (Priest).

Homeless teenagers Ees and Brox hustle sailors in Rotterdam and Ees is caught by a priest and sent to a reformatory. Ees escapes and with Brox steals money and a map from the priest and they try to get to America. Ees is arrested instead and sent back to the juvenile home. Repentance follows and a new life begins after a reconciliation with the priest. Too much with too little.

d, Detlef Sierck [Douglas Sirk]; w, Sierck, Carl Zuckmayer (based on the novel Boefje by M.J. Brusse); ph, Akos Farkas; ed, Rita Roland.

Crime   (PR:AA MPAA:NR)

BOEING BOEING*   (1965) 102m PAR c

Tony Curtis (Bernard Lawrence), Jerry Lewis (Robert Reed), Dany Saval (Jacqueline Grieux), Christiane Schmidtmer (Lise Bruner), Suzanna Leigh (Vicky Hawkins), Thelma Ritter (Bertha), Lomax Study (Pierre).

Adaptation of hit play comes off all right on screen, helped by the most restrained performance yet seen from Mr. Lewis. Curtis is a swinging American newspaperman based in Paris who keeps three stewardesses on a rotating schedule in his apartment, unknown to the girls. This wonderful arrangement is threatened by Lewis, as Curtis' competitor, and by the Boeing Corporation's new, faster line of jets, which threatens to overlap the schedules of his harem. A first-class production.

p, Hal B. Wallis; d, John Rich; w, Edward Anhalt (based on a play by Marc Camoletti); ph, Lucien Ballard (Technicolor); m, Neal Hefti; ed, Warren Low, Archie Marshek; art d, Hal Pereira, Walter Tyler; cos, Edith Head.

Comedy   (PR:C MPAA:NR)

BOFORS GUN, THE*1/2   (1968, Brit.) 105m UNIV c

Nicol Williamson (O'Rourke), Ian Holm (Flynn), David Warner (Evans), Richard O'Callaghan (Rowe), Barry Jackson (Shone), Donald Gee (Crawley), John Thaw (Featherstone), Gareth Forwood (Lt. Packering), Geoffrey Hughes (Cook Private Samuel), John Herrington (German Painter), Barbara Jefford (NAAFI Girl).

A realistic adaptation of McGrath's play as directed by veteran TVer Jack Gold. Warner is a young, indecisive corporal about to take an officer's course. Williamson is a half-mad Irishman who drinks the way Dylan Thomas did before he died of it. Warner's job is to guard the rebel who wants to humiliate the young man and make certain he will never achieve promotion. Williamson commits suicide before the morning inspection, in hopes that Warner will be blamed. The film took lots of shots at the British military and it is not surprising that they received absolutely no help in shooting it. Salty dialog that smacks of absolute truth, flawless acting. A trifle lengthy at 105 minutes and not as emotionally engaging as one might wish.

p, Robert A. Goldston, Otto Plaschkes; d, Jack Gold; w, John McGrath (based on his play "Events While Guarding the Bofors Gun"); ph, Alan Hume (Technicolor); m, Carl Davis; cos, Duncan McPhee.

Drama   (PR:A-C MPAA:NR)

BOHEMIAN GIRL, THE*1/2   (1936) 75m MGM bw

Stan Laurel (Himself), Oliver Hardy (Himself), Antonio Moreno (Devilshoof), Jacqueline Wells (Arline as Adult), Darla Hood (Arline as Child), Mae Busch (Mrs. Hardy), James Finlayson (Capt. Finn), William P. Carleton (Count Arnheim), Thelma Todd (Gypsy Queen's Daughter), Zeffie Tilbury (Gypsy Queen), Harry Bowen (The Drunk), James C. Morton (Constable), Mitchell Lewis (Salinas), Eddie Borden (Foppish Nobleman).

This is the second version of the Balfe operetta, the first being a silent in the early 1920s starring Ivor Novello, Ellen Terry and C. Aubrey Smith. How they managed to do an operetta silently is beyond us but it had to have been funnier than this clunker from Laurel and Hardy. It's the old chestnut about the child of a nobleman being snatched by Gypsies and raised as one of the Romany tribe. This alleged comedy has kidnaping, torture, cheating on a spouse, burglary and a bad script. The photography is awful. Art Lloyd and Francis Corby were able to achieve the impossible; they made Thelma Todd look lousy. This was her last film and much of her work had to be cut because it wouldn't match the stand-in. Todd died of carbon monoxide poisoning at Santa Monica beach in circumstances that suggest murder. She made 40 pictures in her brief career. (See LAUREL & HARDY series, Index.)

p, Hal Roach; d, James W. Horne, Charles Rogers; w, Alfred Bunn (based on the opera by Michael Balfe); ph, Art Lloyd, Francis Corby; m, Nathaniel Shilkret; ed, Bert Jordan, Louis McManus.

Comedy   **Cas.**   (PR:A MPAA:NR)

BOHEMIAN RAPTURE*   (1948, Czech) 88m Artkino/National Film Studios

Jaromir Spol (Josef Slavik), Vaclav Voska (Frederick Chopin), Karel Dostal (Nicolo Paganini), Vlasia Fabianova (Anna Zasmucka), Libuse Zemkova (Henrietta Astfeldova), Jirinka Krelsova (Magdalenka), Marie Vasova (The Unknown Woman), Jiri Stelmar (Baron Astfeld), Karel Jellnek (Coco Cavelleno), Eduard Kohout (Pavel Adam Lazansky).

Poor account of the life of 19th-century Czech composer and violinist Josef Slavik. Spol is accused by Chopin (Voska) of stealing his mistress, Countess Fabianova. In addition, he frets about two other women, a simple country girl and a rich temptress. Could have been better. (In Czech; English subtitles.)

d&w, Vaclav Krska; ph, Ferd Pecenka; m, Frantisek Skvor.

Drama   (PR:A MPAA:NR)

BOILING POINT, THE*1/2   (1932) 62m Allied bw

Hoot Gibson, Helen Foster, Wheeler Oakman, Bill Robbins, Lafe McKee, Billy Bletcher, Tom London, George "Gabby" Hayes, Charles Bailey, Bill Nye.

Routine oater with hot-headed Hoot packed off to a friend's ranch by his father with the warning that if he gets into a fight he won't inherit the family spread. Naturally he finds it hard to restrain himself in the face of harassing bad guys, especially since romantic interest Foster thinks him a coward. Finally, Hoot foils the desperados when they try to rob the bank, and wins the girl. No surprises.

p, M. H. Hoffman; d, George Melford; w, Donald W. Lee; ph, Harry Neumann, Tom Gallaghan; ed, Mildred Johnson.

Western   **Cas.**   (PR:A MPAA:NR)

BOLD AND THE BRAVE, THE** (1956) 87m RKO bw

Wendell Corey (Fairchild), Mickey Rooney (Dooley), Don Taylor (Preacher), Nicole

Maurey (*Fiamma*), John Smith (*Smith*), Race Gentry (*Hendricks*), Ralph Votrian (*Wilbur*), Wright King (*Technician*), Stanley Adams (*Master Sergeant*), Bobs Watson (*Bob*), Tara Summers (*Tina*).

Routine war pic about three GIs on the Italian front. Nothing special except a good performance by Rooney, highlighted by a comic crap game in which Rooney wins $30,000 and is then killed on patrol while trying to protect it.

p, Hal E. Chester; d, Lewis R. Foster; w, Robert Lewin; ph, Samuel Leavitt (Superscope); m, Herschel Burke Gilbert; ed, Aaron Stell; cos, Dick Chaney; m/l, Ross Bagdasarian, Mickey Rooney.

War   **(PR:A   MPAA:NR)**

BOLD CABALLERO**1/2   (1936) 60m REP c (GB: THE BOLD CAVALIER)

Robert Livingston (*Zorro*), Heather Angel (*Isabella*), Sig Rumann (*Commandante*), Ian Wolfe (*Priest*), Robert Warwick (*Governor*), Emily Fitzroy (*Duenna*), Charles Stevens (*Vargas*), Walter Long (*Chate*), Ferdinand Munier (*Landlord*).

Sig Rumann is oppressing the Spanish colonists in southern California and at the first sound, Zorro (Livingstone) rides to the rescue. Zorro is charged with the murder of the arriving governor (Warwick), but the villainous Rumann gets his in the end. One of Republic's first efforts in color filmmaking.

p, Nat Levine; d, Wells Root; w, Root (based on an an idea by Johnston McCulley); ph, Alvin Wyckoff, Jack Marta (MagnaColor); m, Harry Grey; ed, Lester Orlebeck.

Western   **Cas.**   **(PR:A   MPAA:NR)**

BOLD FRONTIERSMAN, THE**   (1948) 59m REP bw

Allan "Rocky" Lane (*Himself*), Black Jack (*His Stallion*), Eddy Waller (*Nugget Clark*), Roy Barcroft (*Smiling Jack*), John Alvin (*Don Post*), Francis McDonald (*Adam Post*), Fred Graham (*Smokey*), Edward Cassidy (*Morton Harris*), Edmund Cobb (*Pete*), Harold Goodwin (*Cowboy*), Jack Kirk (*Rancher*), Ken Terrel (*Judd*), Marshall Reed (*Sam*), Al Murphy (*Professor*).

Lane and Black Jack, his stallion, protect the gold that drought-parched ranchers have raised to build a dam. Barcroft is the heavy come to steal it away. Tight direction, lots of action, and clear camera work put this a cut above the vast majority of B-westerns.

p, Gordon Kay; d, Philip Ford; w, Bob Williams; ph, Ernest Miller; ed, Arthur Roberts.

Western   **(PR:A   MPAA:NR)**

BOLDEST JOB IN THE WEST, THE*
(1971, Ital.) 101m Promofilm/Action/Les Films Number one c (EL MAS FABULOSI GOLPE DEL FAR WEST)

Mark Edwards, Carmen Sevilla, Fernando Sancho, Charly Bravo, Piero Lulli, Yvan Verella.

Edwards and Sancho lead a bank robbery that ends in a bloody shootout, then the loot is stolen by a gang member. Another bloody shootout recovers the money for Sancho and he is mistakenly given a hero's reception in the town where they think he has returned their money to them. Dull, humorless, and styleless, in fact, lacking all the features that make spaghetti westerns worth watching.

p, Jose Maria Carcasona; d&w, Jose Antonio de la Loma; ph, Hans Burmann, Antonio Millan.

Western   **(PR:A-C   MPAA:NR)**

BOLERO**1/2   (1934) 80m PAR bw

George Raft (*Raoul DeBaere*), Carole Lombard (*Helen Hathaway*), Sally Rand (*Arnette*), Frances Drake (*Leona*), William Frawley (*Mike DeBaere*), Ray Milland (*Lord Coray*), Gloria Shea (*Lucy*), Gertrude Michael (*Lady D'Argon*), Del Henderson (*Theatre Manager*), Frank G. Dunn (*Hotel Manager*), Martha Bamattre (*Belgian Landlady*), Paul Panzer (*Bailiff*), Adolph Miller (*German Beer Garden Manager*), Anne Shaw (*Young Matron*), Phillips Smalley (*Leona's Angel*), John Irwin (*Porter*), Gregory Golubeff (*Orchestra Leader*).

George Raft turned down HIGH SIERRA, THE MALTESE FALCON, and DEAD END. All three parts went to Bogart. Raft didn't want to die in a film, something he does very well in BOLERO. He dies of a heart attack after dancing the Bolero on an enormous drum with Lombard, and his dying words are "I'm too good for this joint." That's the way Raft felt about movie studios, and his battles and refusals are legendary. It's the story of a megalomaniacal dancer who ascends from low-brow cafes to become the owner of a posh Parisian boite. Raft knows that it's best to lay off one's dance partners, so he keeps them at arm's length, until he meets up with Lombard and falls head-over-patent-leather-heels for her. But she loves Milland and the feeling is mutual. One night, Raft reveals that he is going to enlist in the service (the start of the war had been announced that afternoon) but he later confesses that his announcement was just a ploy to get more business for the club. Enraged, Lombard, leaves to marry Milland. Several lap dissolves and the war ends with Raft returning with a weak heart. That sequence telescopes the war into under seven minutes. Would that could happen in real life! Raft is determined that he will dance again and reopens the club, hiring Sally Rand to be his new partner. She manages to do her famous fan dance, but when it's time to dance the Bolero, she's wacked on hooch. Seated in the audience are Milland and Lombard, and she volunteers to fill in for the drunken Rand. The dance is a huge success but before they can do the encore, Raft dies. Both Lombard and Raft enjoyed making this movie and a sequel followed soon after, RUMBA (1935). Although both were excellent dancers, Paramount used doubles in some long shots. Worth watching.

p, Benjamin Glaser; d, Wesley Ruggles; w, Carey Wilson, Kubec Glasmon (based on an idea by Ruth Ridenour, adapted by Horace Jackson); ph, Leo Tover; m, Ralph Rainger, Maurice Ravel; ed, Hugh Bennett.

Romance   **(PR:A-C   MPAA:NR)**

BOLERO*   (1982, Fr.) 173m Double 13 c

James Caan (*Glenn Sr. & Jr.*), Robert Hossein (*Simon Meyer/Robert Prat*), Nicole Garcia (*Anne*), Geraldine Chaplin (*Suzan/Sara Glenn*), Daniel Olbrychski (*Karl*), Jacques Villeret (*Jacques*), Jorge Donn (*Boris/Sergio*), Rita Poelvoorde (*Tatyana/ Tanya*), Evelyn Bouix (*Evelyne/Edith*), Macha Meril (*Magda*), Francis Huster (*Francis*), Raymond Pellegrin (*Raymond*), Jean-Claude Brialy (*Director of Lidao*), Fanny Dant (*Veronique*), Jean-Claude Bouttier (*Phillippe*), Richard Bohringer (*Richard*), Nicole Croisille (*Nicole*).

This production has nothing to do with the 1934 BOLERO or much of anything else for that matter, except that the characters, playing multiple roles in serveral generations during a 50-year time span, are music aficionados. The viewer will have a hard time determining who's who, let alone trying to follow an almost completely plotless film. The gifted director Lelouch (AND NOW MY LOVE), who also wrote the script, does not seem to have a handle on his subject, although he presents some attractive scenery, and some of the numbers are interesting.

p,d&w, Claude Lelouch; ph, John Boffety; m, Francis Lai, Michel Legrand; ed, Hughes Darmois, Sophie Bhaud; ch, Maurice Bejart.

Musical   **Cas.**   **(PR:A   MPAA:NR)**

BOMB IN THE HIGH STREET*1/2
(1961, Brit.) 60m Foxwarren-Elthea/Hemisphere bw

Ronald Howard (*Capt. Manning*), Terry Palmer (*Mike*), Suzanne Leigh (*Jackie*), Jack Allen (*Supt. Haley*), Peter Gilmore (*Shorty*), Russell Waters (*Trent*), Maurice Good (*Feeney*), Geoffrey Bayldon (*Clay*), Jack Lambert (*Sergeant*), Humphrey Lestocq (*Reporter*).

Teenagers Palmer and Leigh postpone their elopement to foil a bank raid. To do this, they expose the gang's cover as a phony bomb disposal squad. Weak effort, no explosion.

p, Ethel Linder Reiner, T. B. R. Zichy, Henry Passmore; d, Terence Bishop, Peter Bezencenet; w, Benjamin Simcoe; ph, Gordon Dines.

Crime   **(PR:A   MPAA:NR)**

BOMBA AND THE ELEPHANT STAMPEDE
(SEE: ELEPHANT STAMPEDE, 1951)

BOMBA AND THE HIDDEN CITY*   (1950) 71m MON bw

Johnny Sheffield (*Bomba*), Sue England (*Leah*), Paul Guilfoyle (*Hassan*), Smoki Whitfield (*Hadji*), Damian O'Flynn (*Dennis Johnson*), Leon Belasco (*Raschid*), Charles La Torre(*Abdullah*).

Bomba comes to the rescue of princess Sue England, rightful heir to the tribal throne unscrupulously seized by nasty Guilfoyle. Another mindless rumble in the jungle. (See BOMBA series, Index.)

p, Walter Mirisch; d, Ford Beebe; w, Carrol Young (based on characters created by Roy Rockwood); ph, William Sickner; md, Ozzie Caswell; ed, Roy Livingston.

Adventure   **(PR:A   MPAA:NR)**

BOMBA AND THE JUNGLE GIRL*1/2   (1952) 70m MON bw

Johnny Sheffield (*Bomba*), Karen Sharpe (*Linda*), Walter Sande (*Ward*), Suzette Harbin (*Boru*), Martin Wilkins (*Gamboso*), Morris Buchanan (*Kokoli*), Leonard Mudie (*Barnes*), Don Blackman (*Boru's Lieutenant*), Bruce Carruther (*Constable*), Jack Clisby (*Messenger*), Amanda Randolph (*Linasi*), Roy Glenn (*Kaje*), Bill Walker (*Bearer*).

Kimba the chimp gets equal billing with principal players in this unlikely tale where wildlife protector Sheffield accidentally finds human skeletons which turn out to be his parents. Western technology rivals Third World primitive weapons in jungle battle between poisonous darts and bullets. (See BOMBA series, Index.)

p, Walter Mirisch; d&w, Ford Beebe (based on characters created by Roy Rockwood); art d, Dave Milton; ph, Harry Neumann.

Adventure   **(PR:A   MPAA:NR)**

BOMBA ON PANTHER ISLAND*   (1949) 70m MON bw

Johnny Sheffield (*Bomba*), Allene Roberts (*Judy Maitland*), Lita Baron (*Losani*), Charles Irwin (*Andy Barnes*), Henry Lewis (*Robert Maitland*), Smoki Whitfield (*Eli*).

Sheffield tracks a maneating black panther and helps Roberts and Lewis, a brother and sister who are building an experimental farm in the jungle. (See BOMBA series, Index.)

p, Walter Mirisch; d&w, Ford Beebe (based on characters created by Roy Rockwood); ph, William Sickner; md, Edward Kay; ed, Richard Heermance.

Adventure   **(PR:A   MPAA:NR)**

BOMBA THE JUNGLE BOY*1/2   (1949) 70m MON bw

Johnny Sheffield (*Bomba*), Peggy Ann Garner (*Pat Harland*), Onslow Stevens (*George Harland*), Charles Irwin (*Andy Barnes*), Smoki Whitfield (*Eli*), Martin Wilkins (*Mufti*).

Johnny Sheffield, fresh from playing "Boy" in the Tarzan series, was immediately dropped into another jungle serial. The plot revolves around a father and daughter team of photographers (Garner and Stevens) who encounter a wild boy in the jungle. When the daughter becomes lost, it's Sheffield who finds her and brings her back to her party, despite locust plagues, jungle fires, and stock footage of dangerous animals. Without doubt the best of the Bomba films, but that isn't saying much. (See BOMBA series, Index.)

p, Walter Mirisch; d, Ford Beebe; W, Jack DeWitt (based on characters created by Roy Rockwood); ph, William Sickner; ed, Otho Lovering, Roy Livingston.

Adventure   **(PR:A   MPAA:NR)**

BOMBARDIER* (1943) 97m RKO bw

Pat O'Brien (*Maj. Chick Davis*), Randolph Scott (*Capt. Buck Oliver*), Anne Shirley (*Burt Hughes*), Eddie Albert (*Tom Hughes*), Walter Reed (*Jim Carter*), Robert Ryan (*Joe Connors*), Barton MacLane (*Sgt. Dixon*), Leonard Strong (*Jap Officer*), Richard Martin (*Chito Rafferty*), Russell Wade (*Paul Harris*), James Newill (*Capt. Rand*), John Miljan (*Chaplain Craig*), Charles Russell (*Instructor*), Joseph King, Charles D. Brown, Lloyd Ingraham, Lee Shumway, Edward Peil, Herbert Heyes, Robert Middlemass, Neil Hamilton, Abner Biberman.

O'Brien and Scott are officers at a bombardier training school, each arguing his own methods of killing the enemy. O'Brien is the team man sticking to precision bombing, Scott is a wildcatting pursuit pilot who goes his own way. Further complicating matters is Shirley, whom both men covet. Oddly, the action is kept mostly on the ground (with some fascinating training procedures covered), until the last reel when Pearl Harbor is bombed and a raid on Tokyo proves O'Brien's theories right, a raid patterned after Doolittle's 1942 sortie. Here fighter pilot Scott goes ahead in a single bomber, his mission to drop incendiary bombs about a huge ammunition dump. His plane is shot down instead and he and his crew members are captured and tortured by sadistic Leonard Strong (who made a short career of playing sadistic Japanese officers during WW II). Scott breaks free and is fatally wounded, but he manages to get behind the wheel of a burning gas truck, racing beneath the netting camouflaging the dump, setting it all on fire so that when O'Brien's planes arrive overhead they have a perfect target. O'Brien knows Scott has lit the dump (just *how* he knows we don't know) and drops his bombs on his best friend to destroy the enemy. Scott dies smiling in the truck, knowing he has done his duty and made up for past transgressions. This blatant propaganda movie was extremely popular when finally released. It was begun before Pearl Harbor and revised serveral times after war broke out so that when it finally appeared three years after beginning production, O'Brien's men had a real enemy to bomb. Robert Ryan made his screen debut in the film.

p, Robert Fellows; d, Richard Wallace; w, John Twist (based on a story by Twist and Martin Rackin); ph, Nicholas Musuraca; m, Roy Webb; ed, Robert Wise; md, C. Bakaleinikoff.

War Drama   Cas.   (PR:A MPAA:NR)

BOMBARDMENT OF MONTE CARLO, THE**

(1931, Ger.) 111m UFA bw (BOMBEN AUF MONTE CARLO; AKA: MONTE CARLO MADNESS)

Hans Albers (*Craddock*), Anna Sten (*Yola*), Heinz Ruhmann (*Peter*), Ida Wust (*Isabel*), Karl Etlinger (*Consul*), Rachel Devirys (*Diane*), Kurt Gerron (*Casino Manager*), Peter Lorre (*Pawlitschenk*), Otto Wallburg (*Minister*), Charles Kullman (*Street Singer*), Bruno Ziener (*Jeweler*).

Naval captain Albers rebels against orders to take Queen Sten on a pleasure cruise because he and his men haven't been paid in months. Sailing to Monte Carlo, he wins the money to pay his crew by gambling but then loses it again. He threatens to turn his ship's guns on the city unless the casino owners give him his money back, but is foiled when Queen Sten, who has been trying to seduce Albers, reveals herself and has him arrested. He sees a chance to escape and, diving overboard, is picked up by a ship bound for Honolulu. A ponderous political parable notable only for Sten's performance and Lorre's very brief appearance. Same story was filmed simultaneously on the same sets with an English-speaking cast and released as MONTE CARLO MADNESS.

p, Max Pfeiffer; d, Hanns Schwarz; w, Hans Muller, Franz Schulz (based on an idea by Jeno Heltai and the novel by Fritz Reck-Mallecewen); ph, Gunther Rittau, Konstantin Tschet; m, Werner R. Heymann; ed, Willy Zeyn, Jr.; art d, Erich Kettelhut; m/l, Heymann, Robert Gilbert.

Drama   (PR:A MPAA:NR)

BOMBAY CLIPPER** (1942) 60m UNIV bw

William Gargan (*Jim Wilson*), Irene Hervey (*Frankie Gilroy Wilson*), Lloyd Corrigan (*George Lewis*), Mary Gordon (*Abigail MacPherson*), Truman Bradley (*Dr. Gregory Landers*), Maria Montez (*Sonya Dietrich Landers*), Philip Trent (*Tom Hare*), Turhan Bey (*Capt. Chundra*), Charles Lang (*Tex Harper*), John Bagni (*Paul, the Purser*), Riley Hill (*Steward*), Peter Lynn (*Bland*), Warren Ashe (*R.C. Bradford*), Wade Boteler (*Ruggles*), Billy Wayne (*Jeremiah Lamb*), Keith Kenneth (*Hotel Clerk*), Connie Leon (*Chambermaid*), Mel Ruick (*Submarine Commander*), Harold Daniels (*Sam*), John Picorri (*Waiter*), Pat OMalley (*Chief Inspector*), C. Montague Shaw (*Capt. Caldwell*), Paul Dubov (*News Photographer*), Harry Strang (*Submarine Officer*), Jack Lee (*Sub-Inspector*), Shuran Singh (*Singapore Policeman*).

Journalist Gargan flies aboard the title aircraft over his bride's objections, and becomes entangled with spies stealing $4,000,000 worth of industrial diamonds bound from India to wartime England. When Bradley and his co-conspirators take over the plane, Gargan overwhelms the villains and is forgiven by his perturbed bride.

p, Marshall Grant; d, John Rawlins; w, Roy Chanslor, Stanley Rubin; ph, Stanley Cortez; ed, Otto Ludwig; md, Hans J. Salter.

Spy Drama   (PR:A MPAA:NR)

BOMBAY MAIL** (1934) 66m UNIV bw

Edmund Lowe (*Inspector Dyke*), Shirley Grey (*Beatrice Jones*), Onslow Stevens (*John Hawley*), Ralph Forbes (*William Luke-Patson*), John Davidson (*Xavier*), Hedda Hopper (*Lady Daniels*), Tom Moore (*Civil Surgeon*), John Wray (*Martini*), Ferdinand Gottschalk (*Sir Anthony Daniels*), Garry Owen (*Cuthbert Neal*), Huntley Gordon (*Burgess*), Herbert Corthell (*Edward Breeze*), Walter Armitage (*Maharajah of Zungore*).

Fine whodunit aboard title train. The governor of Bengal (Gottschalk) is poisoned, and CID man Lowe has it narrowed down to six suspects. Then the Maharajah of Zungore is shot in the back and the search takes on a new urgency.

d, Edwin L. Marin; w, Tom Reed, L. G. Blochman (based on a story by Blochman) ph, Charles Stumar.

Mystery   (PR:A MPAA:NR)

BOMBAY TALKIE* (1970, India) 105m Merchant/Ivory c

Shashi Kapoor (*Vikram*), Jennifer Kendal (*Lucia*), Zia Mohyeddin (*Hari*), Aparna Sen (*Mala*), Utpal Duff (*Bose*), Nadira (*Anjana*), Pincho Kapoor (*Swamiji*).

Two filmmakers in Bombay encounter a worldly American woman who has romantic interludes with both. A slow-paced programmer which offers interest chiefly in the movie-making techniques shown; otherwise it's pretty boring.

p, Ismail Merchant; d, James Ivory; w, Ruth Prawer Jhabvala, Ivory; ph, Subrata Mitra (Eastmancolor); m, Shankar-Jaikishan.

Romance   (PR:C MPAA:NR)

BOMBERS B-52** (1957) 106m WB c (GB: NO SLEEP TILL DAWN)

Natalie Wood (*Lois Brennan*), Karl Malden (*Sgt. Chuck Brennan*), Efrem Zimbalist, Jr. (*Col. Jim Herlihy*), Marsha Hunt (*Edith Brennan*), Don Kelly (*Sgt. Darren McKind*), Nelson Leigh (*Gen. Wayne Acton*), Robert Nichols (*Stuart*), Ray Montgomery (*Barnes*), Bob Hover (*Simpson*).

Paean to American strategic might in the 1950s. Wood wants her ground-crew-chief father Malden to leave the service after 20 years. Zimbalist is Malden's C.O., in love with Wood. Their respective entanglements are merely a back- ground for the story of the test flight of a B-52 Superfortress from the U.S. to Africa and back. Good aerial sequences can't overcome cliches back at the base.

p, Richard Whorf; d, Gordon Douglas; w, Irving Wallace (based on a story by Sam Rolfe); ph, William Clothier (CinemaScope, Warner Color); m, Leonard Rosenman; ed, Thomas Reilly; cos, Howard Shoup.

Drama   (PR:A MPAA:NR)

BOMBER'S MOON** (1943) 70m FOX bw

George Montgomery (*Capt. Jeff Dakin*), Annabella (*Lt. Alexandra Zoreich*), Kent Taylor (*Capt. Paul Husnik*), Walter Kingsford (*Friederich Mueller*), Martin Kosleck (*Maj. von Streicher*), Dennis Hoey (*Maj. von Grunow*), Robert Barrat (*Ernst*), Kenneth Brown (*Karl*), Victor Killian (*Henrik Vanseeler*), Robert Lewis (*Priest*), Mike Mazurki (*Kurt*), Christian Rub (*Johann*), Otto Reichow (*Hans*), Frank Reicher (*Dr. Hartman*), Gretl Dupont (*Elsa*).

American pilot Montgomery is shot down over Germany and put in a POW camp. He escapes along with a Czech (Taylor), and a Russian woman medic (Annabella). As they make their treacherous way to freedom Taylor is exposed as a Nazi spy and killed. Annabella flees to England in a fishing boat arranged by the underground, but Montgomery learns of a nearby airfield and, disguising himself as a German pilot, steals a bomber and flies it home, along the way shooting down the German who had killed his brother when he parachuted out of his plane earlier. A decent wartime programmer.

p, Sol M. Wurtzel; d, Charles Fuhr [Edward Ludwig], Harold Schuster; w, Kenneth Gamet, Aubrey Wisberg (based on a story by Leonard Lee); ph, Lucien Ballard; m, David Buttolph; ed, Robert Fritch; md, Emil Newman.

War Drama   (PR:A MPAA:NR)

BOMBS OVER BURMA* (1942) 67m PRC bw

Anna May Wong (*Lin Ying*), Noel Madison (*Me-hoi*), Leslie Denison (*Sir Roger Howe*), Nedrick Young (*Slim Jenkins*), Dan Seymour (*Pete Braganza*), Frank Lackteen (*Hallam*), Judith Gibson (*Lucy Dell*).

Grade-Z filler about gallant Chinese intelligence agents exposing a Nazi spy along the Burma Road. Anna May Wong is the most worthwhile thing here as a schoolteacher who heeds the call of patriotism.

p, Alfred Stern, Arthur Alexander; d, Joseph H. Lewis; w, Milton Raison, Joseph H. Lewis (based on a story by Raison); ph, Robert Cline; ed, Charles Hendle, Jr.; md, Lee Zahler.

War   (PR:A MPAA:NR)

BOMBS OVER LONDON1/2**

(1937, Brit.) 79m Grosvenor bw (GB: MIDNIGHT MENACE)

Charles Farrell (*Briant Gaunt*), Fritz Kortner (*Peters*), Margaret Vyner (*Mary Stevens*), Danny Green (*Socks*), Wallace Evennett (*Smith*), Monte de Lyle (*Pierre*), Dino Galvani (*Tony*), Dennis Val Norton (*Vronsky*), Arthur Finn (*Mac*), Lawrence Hanray (*Sir George*), Raymond Lovell (*Harris*).

This film prophetically promoted the concept of a remote-controlled bomb later used by Hitler in his efforts to conquer the world. Cartoonist Farrell discovers and exposes a Balkan minister's scheme to bomb London by using pilotless airplanes. Scary.

p, Harcourt Templeman; d, Sinclair Hill; w, G. H. Moresby-White, D. B. Wyndham Lewis (based on the book by Roger Macdougall, Alexander Mackendrick); ph, Cyril Bristow.

War   (PR:A MPAA:NR)

BOMBSHELL*1/2** (1933) 90m MGM bw (AKA: BLONDE BOMBSHELL)

Jean Harlow (*Lola*), Lee Tracy (*Space*), Frank Morgan (*Pops*), Franchot Tone (*Gifford Middleton*), Pat O'Brien (*Brogan*), Una Merkel (*Mae*), Ted Healy (*Junior*), Ivan Lebedeff (*Marquis*), Mary Forbes (*Mrs. Middleton*), C. Aubrey Smith (*Mr.

Middleton), Louise Beavers (*Loretta*), Isabel Jewell (*Junior's Girl*), Leonard Carey (*Winters*), June Brewster (*Alice Cole*).

Witty, hip, and fast-moving, BOMBSHELL gave Jean Harlow the opportunity to show that beautiful women can be funny, too. BOMBSHELL is so inside that many people outside the movie business didn't understand the nuances. Jean is a sexpot who becomes engaged to Lebedeff, an alleged marquis (who was, in real life, from Russia and a one-time diplomat). Tracy, a studio press agent, has the marquis arrested as an illegal alien. O'Brien, a studio film director, wants to marry Harlow but she'll have none of it. Jean is a confused young woman and decides to adopt a baby but her father, Morgan, and brother, Healy, give the adoption officials a hard time and that plan goes out the window. Harlow goes to Palm Springs to think, then meets and tumbles for Tone, a blueblood with a snobbish family. When Tone's family meets her father and looks down its collective nose at him, Harlow leaves. Back at the studio, Harlow sees Tone and the rest of his "family" and now realizes that they were all actors hired by Tracy. Tracy pleads with Jean and tells her that he only wanted her to realize that she belongs in movies, not married to some bluenosed boor. Jean looks at Tracy in another fashion and we get the feeling they'll be together long after the fadeout. The movie takes 90 minutes and packs more laughs and satire and punch than most of the so-called comedies made these days. (Harlow was only 26 when she died and she made two other films in 1933, one of which was DINNER AT EIGHT. She made 34 pictures, including shorts, in just nine years. Married three times and engaged to William Powell, who outlived her by 47 years.)

d, Victor Fleming; w, Jules Furthman, John Lee Mahin (based on a play by Caroline Francke, Mack Crane); ph, Chester Lyon, Harold Rosson; ed, Margaret Booth.

Comedy **(PR:A-C MPAA:NR)**

BOMBSIGHT STOLEN**1/2

(1941, Brit.) 90m Gainsborough/GFD bw (GB: COTTAGE TO LET)

Leslie Banks (*John Barrington*), Alastair Sim (*Charles Dimble*), John Mills (*Lt. George Perrey*), Jeanne de Casalis (*Mrs. Barrington*), Carla Lehmann (*Helen Barrington*), George Cole (*Ronald Mittsby*), Michael Wilding (*Alan Trentley*), Frank Cellier (*John Forrest*), Wally Patch (*Evans*), Muriel Aked (*Miss Fernery*), Muriel George (*Mrs. Trimm*), Hay Petrie (*Dr. Truscott*), Catherine Lacey (*Mrs. Stokes*).

A citizen evacuating Scotland during WW II discovers and sets out to thwart a spy plot to kidnap an inventor of a bombsight. Good triumphs over evil in this feeble attempt to bring wartime realism to the screen.

p, Edward Black; d, Anthony Asquith; w, Anatole de Grunwald, J. O. C. Orton (based on a play by Geoffrey Kerr); ph, Jack Cox.

War **(PR:A MPAA:NR)**

BON VOYAGE*1/2

(1962) 130m BV c

Fred MacMurray (*Harry Willard*), Jane Wyman (*Kate Willard*), Michael Callan (*Nick O'Mara*), Deborah Walley (*Amy Willard*), Tommy Kirk (*Elliot Willard*), Kevin Corcoran (*Skipper Willard*), Jessie Royce Landis (*La Comtesse*), Georgette Anys (*Madame Clebert*), Ivan Desny (*Rudolph*), Francoise Prevost (*The Girl*), Carol White (*Penelope*), Marie Sirago (*Florelle*), Alex Gerry (*Horace*), Howard I. Smith (*Judge Henderson*), Casey Adams (*The Tight Suit*), James Milhollin (*Librarian*), Marcel Hillaire (*Sewer Guide*), Richard Wattis (*Englishman*), Ana Maria Majalca (*Shamra*), Hassan Khayyam (*Shamra's Father*), Doris Packer (*Mrs. Henderson*).

Sluggish Disney offering with MacMurray as a Terre Haute, Indiana, plumbing contractor who takes his family to France. Typical misadventures occur, with predictable resolutions. Older siblings fall for exotic foreigners, youngsters keep wandering off, and the most notorious playboy in Europe chases MacMurray's wife. Pleasant family fare.

p, Walt Disney; d, James Neilson; w, Bill Walsh (based on a novel by Marrijane and Joseph Hayes); ph, William Snyder (Technicolor); m, Paul Smith; ed, Cotton Warburton; art d, Carrol Clark, Marvin Aubrey Davis; set d, Emile Kuri, Hal Gausman; cos, Chuck Keehne, Gertrude Casey; m/l, Richard M. and Robert B. Sherman.

Comedy **Cas.** **(PR:AA MPAA:NR)**

BON VOYAGE, CHARLIE BROWN (AND DON'T COME BACK)***

(1980) 75m PAR c

Character voices: Daniel Anderson, Scott Beach, Casey Carlson, Debbie Fuller, Patricia Patts, Laura Planting, Arrin Skelley, Bill Melendez, Annalisa Bortolin, Roseline Rubens, Pascale De Bardlet.

The fourth animated theatrical displaying the wonderful antics of the "Peanuts" gang is still great kids' stuff, although no longer the rage it once was. This time Charlie Brown fans get a bagful of surprises that include jet flights, spooky chateaus, and a dose of danger rarely seen in Peanuts films, as the gang is transported to France for two weeks in a student exchange program. It is there that Charlie Brown and Linus are invited to stay at a chateau where grim things happen. Not to worry, though. The dependable happy ending of cartoon shows rolls up and everybody goes home in great spirits, supported by some particularly endearing scenes between Woodstock and Snoopy. Peanuts fans will especially love Snoopy's first-class flight to London, and his stopover there where he plays tennis at fabled Wimbledon. As usual, Schultz and producers have worked another outstanding collaboration and Bogas again provides splendid background music in a film that was in production for three years.

p, Lee Mendelson, Bill Melendez; d, Melendez; w, Charles M. Schultz (based on his "Peanuts" characters); ph, Nick Vasu (Movielab Color); m, Ed Bogas, Judy Munsen; anim, Sam Jaimes, Hank Smith, Al Pabian, Joe Roman, Ed Newmann, Bill Littlejohn, Bob Carlson, Dale Baer, Spencer Peel, Larry Leichliter, Sergio Bertolli.

Comedy **Cas.** **(PR:AAA MPAA:NR)**

BONANZA TOWN*

(1951) 56m COL bw (GB: TWO FISTED AGENT)

Charles Starrett (*Steve Ramsey/The Durango Kid*), Smiley Burnette (*Smiley Burnette*), Fred F. Sears (*Henry Hardison*), Luther Crockett (*Judge Anthony Dillon*), Myron Healey (*Krag Boseman*), Charles Horvath (*Smoker*), Ted Jordan (*Bob Dillon*), Al Wyatt (*Bill Trotter*), Paul McGuire (*Marshal Reed*), Vernon Dent (*Whiskers*), and Slim Duncan.

Cheapie vehicle for Starret, pursuing the bad guys despite a crooked judge. This is more like two different movies, with a lengthy flashback from previous Starret westerns to pad out running time. (See DURANGO KID series, Index.)

p, Colbert Clark; d, Fred Sears; w, Barry Shipman, Bert Horswell; ph, Henry Freulich; ed, Paul Borofsky.

Western **(PR:A MPAA:NR)**

BOND OF FEAR*

(1956, Brit.) 66m Mid-Century/Eros bw

Dermot Walsh (*John Sewell*), Jane Barrett (*Mary Sewell*), John Colicos (*Dewar*), Jameson Clark (*Scotty*), John Horsley (*PC*), Anthony Pavey (*Michael Sewell*), Marilyn Baker (*Ann Sewell*), Avril Angers (*Hiker*).

A family of travelers in a trailer find themselves harboring an escaped killer when the badman forces them to hide him from the authorities. Confusing plot and characterless roles add up to a tedious time.

p, Robert Baker, Monty Berman; d, Henry Cass; w, John Gilling, Norman Hudis (based on a novel by Digby Wolfe); ph, Berman.

Crime **(PR:A MPAA:NR)**

BOND STREET**1/2

(1948, Brit.) 109m ABF/Pathe bw

Jean Kent (*Ricki Merritt*), Roland Young (*George Chester-Barrett*), Kathleen Harrison (*Mrs. Brawn*), Derek Farr (*Joe Marsh*), Hazel Court (*Julia Chester-Barrett*), Ronald Howard (*Steve Winter*), Paula Valenska (*Elsa*), Patricia Plunkett (*Mary*), Robert Flemyng (*Frank Moody*), Adrianne Allen (*Mrs. Taverner*), Kenneth Griffith (*Len Phillips*), Joan Dowling (*Norma*), Charles Goldner (*Waiter*), James McKechnie (*Yarrow*), Leslie Dwyer (*Barman*), Mary Jerrold (*Miss Slennett*), Marian Spencer (*Aunt Lottie*).

Twenty-four hours in the life of a London street as shown in four separate episodes, all revolving around Hazel Court and her wedding dress, her pearls, flowers, and veil. The last story is far and away the best, with the girl who helps an escaped British flier during the war arriving in London to search for him on the very day he is to be married.

p, Anatole de Grunwald; d, Gordon Parry; w, Grunwald, Terence Rattigan, Rodney Ackland (based on an idea by J. G. Brown); ph, Otto Heller, Brian Langley; ed, Gerald Turney-Smith.

Drama **(PR:A MPAA:NR)**

BONDAGE*1/2

(1933) 61m FOX bw

Dorothy Jordan (*Judy Paters*), Alexander Kirkland (*Dr. Nelson*), Merle Tottenham (*Ruth*), Nydia Westman (*Irma*), Jane Darwell (*Mrs. Wharton*), Edward Woods (*Earl Crawford*), Isabel Jewell (*Beulah*), Dorothy Libaire (*Maizie*), Rafaela Ottiano (*Miss Trigge*).

Department store clerk Jordan is seduced by a radio singer and committed to a home for unwed mothers ruled by tyrannical Ottiano. Heavily influenced by MAEDCHEN IN UNIFORM, but without any coherent point.

d, Alfred Santell; w, Arthur Kober, Doris Malloy (based on a novel by Grace S. Leake); ph, Lucien Andriot.

Drama **(PR:C MPAA:NR)**

BONJOUR TRISTESSE***

(1958) 93m COL bw/c

Deborah Kerr (*Anne Larsen*), David Niven (*Raymond*), Jean Seberg (*Cecile*), Mylene Demongeot (*Elsa Mackenbourg*), Geoffrey Horne (*Philippe*), Juliette Greco (*Nightclub Singer*), Walter Chiari (*Pablo*), Martita Hunt (*Philippe's Mother*), Roland Culver (*Mr. Lombard*), Jean Kent (*Mrs. Lombard*), David Oxley (*Jacques*), Elga Anderson (*Denise*), Jeremy Burnham (*Hubert Duclos*), Eveline Eyfel (*Maid*), Tutte Lemkow (*Pierre Schube*).

Hollow lives, promiscuity, and, eventually, tragedy on the French Riviera as seen through the eyes of a 17-year-old girl. Say bonjour to a lot of repressed attitudes in this often charming story. In flashback, Seberg, the daughter of a hedonistic father, Niven, is growing up to be his carbon copy. She recalls her last summer on the Riviera with her father and his newest mistress, Demongeot. Into this racy melange comes Kerr, a lovely but morally repressed woman who would soon be teetering between two worlds—the conventional society she comes from with its harsh codes and demands, and the Bohemian lives she has come upon. Niven promptly tries to bed her but finds that he must promise marriage to this one. Later Kerr discovers him in yet another illicit situation and in her distraught state jumps into a car, drives over a cliff, and dies, an apparent suicide. Seberg and Niven return to Paris but they cannot escape the fact that Kerr has illuminated the shallowness of their lives. In her first role since her disastrous film debut in Preminger's SAINT JOAN, Seberg regrettably comes off as the corn-fed middle-western beauty she was. As the movie progresses, however, she does exhibit some professionalism, but never enough to convey the character of a young girl influenced by a roue father who lives for today despite the dangers that lurk ahead. Niven's playboy role is one-dimensional and at times it is hard to believe he is a French rake waging a series of sexual conquests, and not the English gentleman he normally portrays. Kerr, of course, is a standout talent in spite of script deficiencies and Demongeot plays the role of a silly blonde well. The Riviera scenes are rich in eye appeal and Kerr's chic costuming by Givenchy adds another plus.

p, Otto Preminger; d, Preminger, John Palmer; w, Arthur Laurents (based on the novel by Francoise Sagan); ph, Georges Perinal (Videoscope, Technicolor); m, Georges Auric; ed, Helga Cranston; art d, Raymond Simm; set d, Georges Peitot; cos, Givenchy; ch, Tutte Lemkow.

Drama **(PR:C-O MPAA:NR)**

BONNE CHANCE** ½** (1935, Fr.) 75m Lehman/Rivers bw

Sacha Guitry *(Claude)*, Jacqueline Delubac *(Marie)*, Numes, Jr. *(Prosper)*, Robert Darthez *(Gastion Lepeltier)*, Pauline Carton *(Mother)*, Antoine *(Himself)*.

French actor Guitry finally ceased his long-standing opposition to the cinema by writing, directing, and starring (along with his wife, Delubac) in this story of a man who wins the French national lottery and goes on a vacation with the woman who gave him half her ticket, despite the fact that she is to be married to another. Direction shows stage origins of Guitry, but his personal charm carries the day.

p, Maurice Lehmann, Fernand Rivers; d&w, Sacha Guitry.

Drama **(PR:A MPAA:NR)**

BONNIE AND CLYDE****** (1967) 111m WB c

Warren Beatty *(Clyde Barrow)*, Faye Dunaway *(Bonnie Parker)*, Michael J. Pollard *(C. W. Moss)*, Gene Hackman *(Buck Barrow)*, Estelle Parsons *(Blanche)*, Denver Pyle *(Frank Hamer)*, Dub Taylor *(Ivan Moss)*, Evans Evans *(Velma Davis)*, Gene Wilder *(Eugene Grizzard)*, James Stiver *(Grocery Store Owner)*, Clyde Howdy *(Deputy)*, Garry Goodgion *(Billy)*, Ken Mayer *(Sheriff Smoot)*.

Although few scenes in this powerful film are representative of the true facts, BONNIE AND CLYDE was a landmark film that permanently established the stellar status of its stars, Beatty and Dunaway, along with its inventive director, Penn. (To the wrong- headed it made violence into an art form.) It is the story of the two most notorious outlaws of the early 1930s, who meet in a small town when Beatty tries to steal a car belonging to Dunaway's mother. (They actually met in a restaurant where Bonnie was slinging hash and turning tricks on the side.) The two walk along the streets talking like sophomoric kids, Beatty bragging that he once hacked off two toes to get off work detail in state prison. He next shows her a large automatic like some kid with a grownup toy, telling her he intends to rob the local store, which he promptly does. As he runs wildly to a car and hotwires it, jumping inside, Dunaway jumps into the car, and they race off laughing hysterically. He drives wildly into the country, but before he can bring the car to a halt Dunaway is all over him, ecstatic with excitement, smothering him with kisses, as if she has reached a sexual climax brought about by the robbery. Beatty pulls away from her, telling her that he is not "one of them glamour boys." She, feeling rejected, lashes back, saying he is not what he appears to be, that he has nothing to offer her sexually. (This, in fact, was not exactly true; Barrow was a practicing hetereosexual with homosexual tendencies which were sometimes pronounced with other younger male members of the gang.) She nevertheless goes off with Beatty, hiding in farmhouses, pulling a small-time job here and there, joined by a naive gas station attendant (Pollard) and then, here and there, Buck Barrow (Hackman) and his wife Blanche (Parsons). The gang robs a small-town bank and at this time Beatty is shown to be chivalrous in his country bumpkin way. A farmer withdrawing cash from a teller is asked by Beatty: "Is that your money or the bank's?" When the farmer tells him that it's his, Beatty tells him he can keep it. (This act of bravado was performed by John Dillinger at the Greencastle, Indiana bank he robbed in 1933, not by Clyde Barrow. The Barrows would have taken the farmer's money, his bib overalls, and the straw clenched between his teeth, then shot him to death for kicks as was their lunatic way.) The gang settles down in a cheap little apartment over a garage in Joplin, Missouri, but police discover their hideout and close in. The gang, in a wild shoot-out where several cops are killed (Penn does not spare the blood blisters), all escape, Parsons, in a particularly frenetic outburst, running after the gang's car, to be scooped up by Hackman leaning from an open door, much the same way western outlaws are shown to pick up a fallen outlaw to ride piggy-back on a horse. (This scene is perhaps the most accurate in the film, based on the actual facts of the Joplin shoot-out.) As the police nets draw closer around them, gang members begin to bicker. Parsons demands a share of their miserable loot which causes Dunaway to become jealous. Further, she can no longer stand being with Beatty and going without sex. She runs away, but Beatty quickly catches up with her, making love to Dunaway in an open field and then being congratulated by her for performing well. In a moment of caprice, the gang captures a Texas Ranger (Pyle), posing with him for pictures. (Gang members were indeed obsessed with taking each other's photos, but the famous photo of Bonnie with pistol and a cigar in her mouth was a gag.) Dunaway kisses Pyle and he spits in her face, which causes Beatty to almost drown him by throwing him into a lake, but he is stopped by Hackman. The sheriff, bound in his own handcuffs, is set adrift in a boat as they jeer at him. (This, of course, could only happen in the imaginations of writers Benton and Newman; Bonnie and Clyde murdered every cop who got near them, except those who finally executed them. On one occasion, in Oklahoma City, Bonnie Parker blew the head off a traffic cop for "fun" and to impress Barrow; on another occasion the two opened fire on a motorcycle cop routinely passing their car, killing him, then running their car back and forth over his corpse.) The gang steals another car which belongs to Wilder who, with Evans Evans (is this name for real?) chases after them, and is, in turn, chased by the gang, and is then made their prisoner, along with the girl friend, going on a joyride with the outlaws to swap jokes and eat hamburgers. When Dunaway learns that Wilder is a mortician, she abruptly orders him and his girl friend from the car. It is a telegraph to the viewer that she is aware of their eventual doom, a foreboding later emphasized by her mother at a family reunion when Dunaway fancifully babbles that Clyde will settle down and they'll live next door to her. "You live within a mile of me, honey, and you'll be dead," her ancient mother drones, clearly implying that she is watched constantly by the police, who will shoot the Barrows on sight. Down to their last two stolen cars, the gang is cornered at a cheap cabin court where police open fire. The outlaws fight their way free, but Hackman is mortally wounded and Parsons is blinded in one eye. They escape, stopping in a picnic field. The next morning an army of possemen open fire on them. Hackman is killed (actually Buck Barrow died some hours after this battle in Dexter, Iowa) and Parsons captured; later she inadvertently reveals to the dogged Pyle Pollard's name and through this Pyle locates Pollard's father. Fleeing from the dragnet, both Beatty and Dunaway are wounded, dragged to a stolen car by the ever-faithful Pollard (his name in the movie is C. W. Moss; the real name of this youthful accomplice was W. D. Jones). He drives them circuitously to his home town, stopping at "Okie" camps where the outlaws are given food and water, many of the displaced farmers gaping at the wounded outlaws in the back seat in awe and respect. (Another fable in the mythological script; Bonnie and Clyde were loathed by their relatives, friends, and neighbors whom they stole from, lied to, and shot; the writers, no doubt, were drawing upon the background of Charles Arthur "Pretty Boy" Floyd, who was sort of a Robin Hood to his native Oklahoma neighbors; when robbing a bank, Floyd made a habit of burning all unrecorded mortgages, a farm boy striking back against a system that was driving his people from their land.) Upon reaching Pollard's home, his father (Taylor) takes care of the wounded outlaws, but he later meets with Pyle and helps to set up the pair as they drive down a road alone. Penn has Beatty stop his car, get out, and go to Taylor, asking him if he can help him fix a flat tire on his truck. An army of police wait behind thick shrubbery across the road. When Taylor dives beneath the truck, a flock of birds suddenly erupt skyward from the bushes. Penn zooms his cameras in on the knowing faces of Beatty and Dunaway, who look lovingly at each other for the last time, their bloody death throes recorded down to the last twitch. (Bonnie and Clyde were ambushed outside of Gibland, Louisiana, on May 23, 1934. They did not get out of their car, which was raked by 187 shells. Clyde had been driving in his socks and Bonnie had a sandwich in her mouth. Both had been set up by a one-time confederate, Henry Methvin, and both died instantly without any long, furtive silent farewells.) The film, which does capture the era wonderfully in costume and props, in hardware, and cars, and in the music of the day, along with splendid photography, tells a fiction. Many of the rabid supporters of this film, who first identified with it as displaced persons of their own in the impersonal world of the late 1960s (it hasn't changed a tad) and the outsiders portrayed in the film feel that BONNIE AND CLYDE represented more than what it truly did, symbolizing the alienation and dehumanization of Americans (something like that). Through shrewd distribution, this film grossed $23 million and became Warner's second best box-office attraction up to that time, after MY FAIR LADY. All of its leading players—Beatty, Dunaway, Hackman, and Parsons—went on to greater fame, bigger films, and fatter paychecks, as did Wilder. Its director is still primarily known for this single filmic achievement. The approach was simple: Show the story everyone wants to see, forget the facts, and immerse the fiction in a heavy, colorful documentary atmosphere to make it appear factual, real, and, most important, significant.

p, Warren Beatty; d, Arthur Penn; w, David Newman, Robert Benton; ph, Burnett Guffey (Technicolor); m, Charles Strouse; ed, Dede Allen; art d, Dean Tavoularis; set d, Raymond Paul; cos, Theodora Van Runkle; spec eff, Danny Lee.

Crime Drama **Cas.** **(PR:O MPAA:NR)**

BONNIE PARKER STORY, THE** ½** (1958) 79m AIP bw

Dorothy Provine *(Bonnie Parker)*, Jack Hogan *(Guy Darrow)*, Richard Bakalyan *(Duke Jefferson)*, Joseph Turkel *(Chuck Darrow)*, William Stevens *(Paul)*, Ken Lynch *(Manager of Restaurant)*, Douglas Kennedy *(Tom Steel)*, Patt Huston *(Chuck's Girl)*, Joel Colin *(Bobby)*, Jeff Morris *(Marv)*, Jim Beck *(Alvin)*, Stanley Livingston *(Little Boy)*, Carolyn Hughes *(Girl)*, John Halloran *(Ranger Chief)*, Madeline Foy *(Ranger's Secretary)*, Sid Lassick *(Scoutmaster)*, Howard Wright *(Old Man)*, Karl Davis *(Texan)*.

Stanley Livingston of "My Three Sons" fame shows up as a little boy in this story about Provine's ("The Roaring Twenties") life of crime. When husband Bakalyan gets a 175-year prison term, the cigar chomping, voluptuous blonde waitress becomes rougher and more brutal than her male counterparts. She learns to handle a machine gun and kill with ease, adding murder to her long list of crimes. Good performances by cast and frenetic music emphasize the nerve-wracking lives of brainless fugitives. Camera work enhances the moods established by Ron Ament's intentionally sleazy period sets. No more based on the real facts than BONNIE AND CLYDE, this portrait, however, comes closer to the truth through the ruthless personalities shown.

p&w, Stanley Shpetner; d, William Witney; ph, Jack Marta; m, Ronald Stein; ed, Frank Keller.

Crime **(PR:O MPAA:NR)**

BONNIE PRINCE CHARLIE**** (1948, Brit.) 135m BL c

David Niven *(Bonnie Prince Charlie)*, Margaret Leighton *(Flora MacDonald)*, Judy Campbell *(Clementine Walkinshaw)*, Jack Hawkins *(Lord George Murray)*, Morland Graham *(Donald)*, Finlay Currie *(Marquis of Tullibardine)*, Elwyn Brook-Jones *(Duke of Cumberland)*, John Laurie *(Blind Jamie)*, Hector Ross *(Glenalandale)*, Hugh Kelly *(Lt. Ingleby)*, Charles Goldner *(Captain Ferguson)*, Henry Oscar *(James II)*, Martin Miller *(George II)*, Franklyn Dyall *(Macdonald)*, Herbert Lomas *(Kinloch Moidart)*, Ronald Adam *(Macleod)*, John Longden *(Capt. O'Sullivan)*, James Hayter *(Kingsburgh)*, Julien Mitchell *(General Cope)*, Guy Lefeuve *(Cameron of Lochiel)*, Stuart Lindsdell *(MacDonald of Apridale)*, Simon Lack *(Young Alan of Moidart)*, Tommy Duggan *(Clanranald)*, G. H. Mulcaster *(Duke of Newcastle)*, Kenneth Warrington *(Staff Officer)*, Nell Ballantyne *(Mrs. Kingsburgh)*, Patricia Fox *(Annie Kingsburgh)*, Molly Rankin *(Lady Margaret MacDonald)*, John Rae *(Duncan)*, Lola Duncan *(Effie)*, John Forrest *(Neil)*, Jane Gill Davies *(Lady Graham)*, Louise Gainsborough *(Madame d'Epoiles)*, Edward Lexy *(Lachlan)*, Bruce Seton *(Allan Macrae)*, Anthony Holles *(Colonel Warren)*, Mark Daly *(Ian*

MacQueen), Jean Stuart (Elspeth Patterson), Blanche Fothergill (Mary MacQueen), Margaret Gibson (Mysie), Alan Judd (Stewart of Ardshiel), Fred Hearn (Aeneas MacDonald), Bill Allison (Sir Francis Strickland), Charles Cullum (Sir John MacDonald), Norman Maitland (John Murray), Harry Schofield (Rev. George Kelly).

A rousing adventure film where Niven, in one of his best roles, plays Charles Stuart, who claimed through birthright the British crown, the Stuarts having been kings of Scotland and England for several hundred years until the House of Hanover took over the throne. The film opens with the young prince sailing from France and landing in Scotland in 1745. He has difficulty in persuading many clan members that he is, indeed, the real Prince Charles, but Leighton, a Scottish patriot to the marrow, Currie and others manage to convince the clan leaders that he is who he says he is. The clans rally to his side; in one stirring scene Niven addresses the collected thousands, urging them to follow him in overthrowing the cruel monarchy of George II (Miller). Wearing the colorful garb of the clansmen, kilts and cloaks of bright tartans, marching to the high whine of the bagpipes and flashing great swords, the clans march off with Niven toward England. The first battles with the British prove to be victories, but a powerful British army meets the Scots on the historic Culloden Moor near Inverness and destroys the clans (1746). Niven and his aides flee and the rest of the film becomes a long and often harrowing chase as British troops attempt to hunt down the Pretender. Leighton, who is in love with Niven, manages to assist him to the coast where he sails for France and historical oblivion. The film is a straightforward historical account of the last Stuart's attempt to reclaim the throne, although it drags in spots and Niven looks strange wearing a thick blonde wig. Alexander Korda reportedly spent more than $4 million mounting this epic, which does not really show in the sets. Korda took a sympathetic approach to the plight of the Pretender (Niven plays him as a kind-hearted, gentle soul to offset the brutish image of Miller's King George) and even directed some of the early scenes in the movie before hiring director Kimmins. The film, however, suffers from too much dialog in what is essentially an action movie. The British have a soft spot for Prince Charlie in their historic hearts, much the same way Americans look upon Robert E. Lee; both were noble and great men who led causes. Niven's superb performance sustains an otherwise empty epic.

p, Edward Black; d, Anthony Kimmins; w, Clemence Dane; ph, Robert Krasker (Technicolor); m, Ian Whyte; ed, Grace Garland; prod d, Vincent Korda, Wilfred Shingleton, Joseph Bato.

Adventure/Historical Drama   **(PR:A MPAA:NR)**

BONNIE SCOTLAND**   (1935) 70m MGM bw

Stan Laurel (Stanley McLaurel), Oliver Hardy (Himself), Anne Grey (Lady Violet Ormsby), David Torrence (Mr. Miggs), June Lang (Lorna McLaurel), William Janney (Alan Douglas), James Mack (Butler), James Finlayson (Sergeant Major), Mary Gordon (Mrs. Bickerdike), Maurice Black (Mir Jutra), Daphne Pollard (Millie), James May (Postman), Kathryn Sheldon (Schoolteacher), Minerva Urecal (Storekeeper).

Down on their luck, Laurel and Hardy travel to Scotland on a cattle boat to cash in on a dead uncle's will. After discovering that some bagpipes and a snuff box are all that the old geezer left his nephew Stanley, they wind up in the British army, on their way to India to join the fabled Lancers. Unimaginative Laurel and Hardy comedy highlighted by Stan's frustrating bouts with militaristic regimentation. (See LAUREL & HARDY series, Index.)

p, Hal Roach; d, James W. Horne; w, Frank Butler, Jefferson Moffit; ph, Art Lloyd, Walter Lundin; ed, Bert Jordan.

Comedy   **(PR:AAA MPAA:NR)**

BONZO GOES TO COLLEGE**   (1952) 78m UNIV bw

Maureen O'Sullivan (Marion Drew), Charles Drake (Malcolm Drew), Edmund Gwenn (Pop Drew), Gigi Perreau (Betsy Drew), Gene Lockhart (Clarence B. Gateson), Irene Ryan (Nancy), Guy Williams (Ronald Calkins), John Miljan (Wilbur Crane), David Janssen (Jack), Jerry Paris (Lefty Edwards), Frank Nelson (Dick), Richard Garrick (Judge Simpkins), Bonzo (Bonzo).

Sequel to smash BEDTIME FOR BONZO has the same simian antics but Ronald Reagan refused to do this one. Bonzo becomes the pet of Gigi Perreau, daughter of college professor Drake. He passes the entrance exams and then makes the football team. On the eve of the big game a pair of bad guys kidnap Bonzo. He escapes and wins the game in the nick of time. Reagan was smart to have avoided this one.

p, Ted Richmond; d, Frederick de Cordova; w, Leo Lieberman, Jack Henley (based on a story by Lieberman and a character created by Ralph David Blau and Ted Berkman); ph, Carl Guthrie; m, Frank Skinner; ed, Ted Kent.

Comedy   **(PR:AAA MPAA:NR)**

BOOBY TRAP*   (1957, Brit.) 71m Jaywell bw

Sydney Tafler (Hunter), Patti Morgan (Jackie), Harry Fowler (Sammy), Tony Quinn (Prof. Hasdane), Richard Shaw (Richards), Jacques Cey (Bentley), John Watson (Maj. Cunliffe), Michael Moore (Curate).

Unsuspecting drug dealer Tafler gets hold of a secret weapon. Unknown to him, it is an explosive pen activated by radio signals cueing broadcaster time changes, a booby trap which finally ends his program of crime.

p, Bill Luckwell, Derek Winn; d, Henry Cass; w, Peter Bryan, Luckwell (based on a novel by Bryan); ph, James Wilson.

Crime   **(PR:A MPAA:NR)**

BOOGENS, THE*   (1982) 95m Taft International/Sunn Classic c

Rebecca Balding (Trish), Fred McCarren (Mark), Anne-Marie Martin (Jessica), Jeff

Harlan (Roger), John Crawford (Brian), Med Flory (Dan), Jon Lormer (Blanchard), Peg Stewart (Victoria), Scott Wilkinson (Deputy), Marcia Reider (Martha).

Utah residents reopen a silver mine years after a cave-in caused by mysterious creatures. Locals probing the shaft end up dead, killed by the tentacled monsters protecting their home. The horrible creatures are not shown until the very end.

p, Charles E. Sellier, Jr.; d, James L. Conway; w, David O'Malley, Bob Hunt; ph, Paul Hipp; m, Bob Summers; ed, Michael Spence; art d, Linda Kiffe.

Horror   **(PR:A MPAA:NR)**

BOOGEY MAN, THE zero   (1980) 79m Jerry Ross c.

Suzanna Love (Lacy), Ron James (Jake), John Carradine (Doctor).

Lommel keeps making these dreadful pictures and starring his wife, Suzanna Love, in them. It's grounds for divorce on her part. This begins as a psychological look at a young murderer who grew up to be a mute. Now, a haunted mirror enters the scene and several gory murders occur. Then hayforks, knives, and broken windows begin to fly and the whole picture falls apart. At 79 minutes, it's still too long. John Carradine (born Richmond Reed Carradine) has a small part as a sane doctor (wonder of wonders) but seeing him in this bad a film is distressing. Carradine's film career began in 1930 and included memorable ones in STAGECOACH, THE GRAPES OF WRATH, and THE MAN WHO SHOT LIBERTY VALANCE. Soon enough, he began making pictures like THE FIEND WITH THE ELECTRONIC BRAIN, BILLY THE KID VERSUS DRACULA, and THE ASTRO-ZOMBIES. Now, he'll probably be best remembered for fathering David (BOUND FOR GLORY) and Keith (NASHVILLE, etc.) How the mighty have fallen.

p,d&w, Ulli Lommel; ph, David Sperling (Metrocolor); m, Tim Krog; ed, Terrell Tannen.

Horror   **Cas.**   **(PR:O MPAA:R)**

BOOGEYMAN II*1/2   (1983) 79m New West Films c

Suzanna Love (Lacey), Ulli Lommel (Mickey), Bob Rosenfarb (Bernie), Shannah Hall (Bonnie), Shoto von Douglas (Joseph), Ahley DuBay, Rhonda Aldrich, Sarah Jean Watkins, David D'Arnel, Leslie Smith, Mina Kolb, Rafael Nazario. Ann Wilkinson, Rock McKenzie. Flashback sequences include: Llewellyn Thomas, Nicholas Love, John Carradine, Ron James, Felicite Morgan.

Lommel is like "the little girl with a little curl" in that when he is good (BRAINWAVES) he is very good and when he is bad (BOOGEY MAN II) he is horrid. At 79 minutes, much of this mish-mash is devoted to flashbacks from THE BOOGEY MAN (1980) and when he's not doing that, he is waxing wroth (we hope Wroth doesn't mind) against the Hollywood establishment as he (Lommel) portrays a filmmaker who prattles on about the crass commerciality of films today. Lots of gore and attempts at black humor. It doesn't work. Lommel's wife (Love) and brother-in-law (Nicholas Love) are in the picture with him. They should have stayed home. There is no screenplay credit . . . . for good reason.

p, Ulli Lommel; d, Lommel, Bruce Starr; ph, Phillipe Carr-Foster, David Sperling (Pacific Color); m, Tim Krog, Wayne Love, Craig Hundley; ed, Terrell Tanen, spec eff, CMI Ltd.

Horror   **Cas**   **(PR:O MPAA:NR)**

BOOGIE MAN WILL GET YOU, THE***   (1942) 66m COL bw

Boris Karloff (Prof. Nathaniel Billings), Peter Lorre (Dr. Lorentz), Maxie Rosenbloom (Maxie), Larry Parks (Bill Leyden), Jeff Donnell (Winnie Leyden), Maude Eburne (Amelia Jones), Don Beddoe (J. Gilbert Brampton), George McKay (Ebenezer), Frank Puglia (Silvio Baciagalupi), Eddie Laughton (Johnson), Frank Sully (Officer Starrett), James Morton (Officer Quincy).

Parks and Donnell buy a decaying New England hotel from scientist Karloff in hopes of turning it into a tourist attraction, unaware of Karloff's experimenting in the building's basement lab. When Parks discovers a few corpses in the cellar, "miscalculations" in Karloff's attempts to create a race of super-men, he calls upon Lorre, the village's law enforcement official and financial powerhouse, to see that the fiend is taken into custody. Lorre, however, sees Karloff's experiments as a possible means of monetary gain and personal physical strength and refuses to arrest the crazed doctor. When two of the hotel's long-time inhabitants are discovered to be happy-go-lucky killers of guests over the years, Parks and Donnell just about explode with frustration amidst the madness. Suddenly, Puglia bursts onto the scene, a crazed radical Italian fascist who has strapped dynamite to himself. The police arrive, "the human bomb" turns out to be a dud, and the assorted loons are carted off to the local asylum. Unbeknownst to the police, Lorre is the joint's administrator, a little fact that makes Karloff quite happy. Columbia, trying to cash in on Karloff's success in the Broadway production of "Arsenic and Old Lace" before Capra's actual adaptation of the play to the screen, created this rather silly black comedy, pale in comparison to Capra's work, but still delightful.

p, Colbert Clark; d, Lew Landers; w, Edwin Blum (based on a story by Hal Fimberg and Robert E. Hunt, adapted by Paul Gangelin); ph, Henry Freulich; ed, Richard Fantl; art d, Lionel Banks; set d, George Montgomery; md, Morris W. Stoloff.

Comedy   **(PR:C MPAA:NR)**

BOOK OF NUMBERS**1/2   (1973) 81m AE c

Raymond St. Jacques (Blueboy Harris), Freda Payne (Kelly Simms), Philip Thomas (Dave Greene), Hope Clark (Pigmeat Goins), Willie Washington, Jr. (Makepeace Johnson), Doug Finell (Eggy), Sterling St. Jacques (Kid Flick), C.L. Williams (Blip Blip), D'Urville Martin (Billy Bowlegs), Jerry Leon (Joe Gaines), Gilbert Greene (Luis Antoine), Frank DeSal (Carlos), Temie Mae Williams (Sister Clara Goode), Pauline Herndon (Sister No. 2), Ethel Marie Crawford (Sister No. 3), Mimi Lee Dodd (Bus Station Prostitute), Charles F. Elyston (Mr. Booker), Queen Esther Gent

(Mrs. Booker), Irma Hall *(Georgia Brown)*, Chiquita Jackson *(Didi)*, Katie Peters *(Honey)*, Pat Peter son *(Becky)*, Ray McDonald, Charles Lewis *(Goons)*, Reginald Dorsey *(June Bug)*.

Decent black exploitation film about criminal operations in a small Southern town during the depression. St. Jacques and Thomas leave their jobs waiting tables in the city and try to establish a numbers racket in a small backwater town, running afoul of local white crime czar Greene. Shows the constraints of its low budget, but manages to get its points across. Worth watching.

p&d, Raymond St. Jacques; w, Larry Spiegel (based on a novel by Robert Deane Phaar); ph, Gayne Rescher (Eastmancolor); m, Al Schuckman; ed, Irv Rosenblum; art d, Bob Shepherd.

Crime **Cas.** **(PR:O MPAA:R)**

BOOLOO*½ (1938) 61m PAR bw

Colin Tapley *(Capt. Robert Rogers)*, Jayne Regan *(Kate Jaye)*, Michio Ito *(Sakal Chief)*, Herbert DeSouza *(Rod DeSouza)*, Fred Pullen *(Nah Laku)*, Mamo Clark *(Native Girl)*, Claude King *(Major Frenton)*, William Stack *(Col. Stanley Jaye)*, Ivan Simpson, Lionel Pape, Napier Raikes, Phil Smalley *(Governors)*, John Sutton *(Ferguson)*, Clive Morgan, Colin Kenny *(Radio Operators)*, Ah Lea *(Himself)*.

Tapley ventures to the jungles of Malaya to bring back a legendary white tiger sighted by his late father. Natives help him bag a large number of animals, but when they learn that his real quarry is their sacred feline they tie him up and prepare to kill him with poison darts. Will the colonial authorities arrive in time? Of course they will. Lots of documentary animal footage is by far the most interesting thing here.

p&d, Clyde E. Elliot; w, Robert E. Welsh (based on a story by Elliot); ph, Harry Sharp, Carl Berger, Ben Wetzler.

Adventure **(PR:A MPAA:NR)**

BOOM!* (1968) 112m UNIV c

Elizabeth Taylor *(Flora Goforth)*, Richard Burton *(Chris Flanders)*, Noel Coward *(Witch of Capri)*, Joanna Shimkus *(Blackie)*, Michael Dunn *(Rudy)*, Romolo Valli *(Doctor)*, Fernando Piazza *(Etti)*, Veronica Wells *(Simonetta)*, Claudye Ettori *(Manicurist)*, Howard Taylor *(Journalist)*.

Millionaire Taylor, slowly dying in her isolated palace on an island near Sardinia, spends most of her days swilling booze, popping pills, and swearing at her odd array of servants, which include a frigid secretary, a black giant, a sadistic dwarf, and sitar-playing Indian musicians. When wandering poet Burton stumbles onto the island one day, Taylor insists upon his removal until she learns that he is known as a somewhat mystical figure, nick-named the "Angel of Death" by the elite literary set. She then uses the poet as a plaything, a sort-of confidante with whom she can discuss personal philosophy before she passes on into the great beyond. As he watches Taylor's life wither away, Burton finds solace in the jewelry and fine brandy of the woman to whom he acted as friend, lover, and "saviour." Regarded as one of the biggest bombs in Hollywood history, BOOM! was intended to be a shot-in-the-arm for the sagging careers of Mr. and Mrs. Burton, but turned out to be yet another example of their self-indulgent, egocentric, pretentious "star" vehicles. Based on a rather poor Tennessee Williams play, "The Milk Train Doesn't Stop Here Anymore," that was a failure on the New York stage, BOOM! is probably the perfect film in which to analyze the ability of two actors capable of brilliance who instead chose to make utter fools out of themselves. With ridiculous treatments of "big" thematic ideas like Death, Christ's teachings, decadence, and the meaning of life, the film borders on unintentional comedy. Director Losey, whose imaginative visual style and continued treatment of odd subject matter has earned him a distinct cult following, appears to have been completely lost on this project. Known to have been intimidated by his stars, Losey's personality can only be seen in an occasional flourish of composition or camera movement. The one true delight in BOOM! is Noel Coward's brief role as Taylor's homosexual gossip pal, the Witch of Capri, a role originally written for a woman. However, even the great Coward connot save this unbelievable disaster.

p, John Heyman, Norman Priggen; d, Joseph Losey; w, Tennessee Williams (based on his play, "The Milk Train Doesn't Stop Here Anymore" and the short story, "Man, Bring This Up Road"); ph, Douglas Slocombe (Technicolor); m, John Barry; ed, Reginald Beck; prod d, Richard MacDonald; Indian music, Nazirali Jairazbnoy; Viram Jasani; m/l, John Dankworth, Don Black; cos, Tiziani.

Drama **(PR:O MPAA:NR)**

BOOM TOWN**** (1940) 117m MGM bw

Clark Gable *(Big John McMasters)*, Spencer Tracy *(Square John Sand)*, Claudette Colbert *(Betsy Bartlett)*, Hedy Lamarr *(Karen Vanmeer)*, Frank Morgan *(Luther Aldrich)*, Lionel Atwill *(Harry Compton)*, Chill Wills *(Harmony Jones)*, Marion Martin *(Whitey)*, Minna Gombell *(Spanish Eva)*, Joe Yule *(Ed Murphy)*, Horace Murphy *(Tom Murphy)*, Roy Gordon *(McCreery)*, Richard Lane *(Assistant District Attorney)*, Casey Johnson *(Little Jack)*, Baby Quintanilla *(Baby Jack)*, George Lessey *(Judge)*, Sara Haden *(Miss Barnes)*, Frank Orth *(Barber)*, Frank McGlynn, Sr. *(Deacon)*, Curt Bois *(Ferdie)*, Dick Curtis *(Hiring Boss)*.

A roaring, exciting film all the way, BOOM TOWN was a top-flight MGM production to which the studio gave its greatest stars, Gable and Tracy, with equally stellar ladies Colbert and Lamarr for added star power. It's the story of two oil wildcatters, Gable and Tracy, who arrive in the Texas oilfields, meeting on a muddy street and becoming friends. Though they are penniless, they manage to con some portable oil digging equipment out of skinflint supplier Morgan and, after debating where to dig, begin drilling. Morgan arrives later with the sheriff to reclaim his equipment but just then the well comes in, a huge gusher blowing away the top timbers of the derrick. Gable and Tracy are rich. Now Tracy can marry the girl back East. But Gable meets the schoolteacher Tracy has been writing to, not knowing who she is, and the two fall in love. Ever the gallant, Tracy bows out, blessing their marriage. But riches go to Gable's head and he begins carousing, leaving Colbert at home. Tracy, still in love with Colbert, finds Gable in a bar dancing with Marion Martin, a town floozie. Gable claims it's all innocent fun but Tracy takes a dimmer view and the two exchange blows but are interrupted when news comes that their oil field is on fire. The two, now bitter toward each other, rush to the scene where one oil derrick is in flames. Both men work their way into the roaring flames behind iron shields and manage to put out the fire. Following this, the partners toss a coin for the oil field. Gable loses and leaves with Colbert, who cannot bear to leave her husband now that he has lost everything. The couple move to an out-of-the-border oil field where Gable works as a regular hand. They live in a shack with their child but Gable soon prospers once more, going back to Texas where he finds an even larger oil field. Millions pour in. Then Tracy's fortunes turn sour, but he recoups his losses in South America with another oil strike. He meets Gable again and the two cement their friendship with a bottle. By then Gable has moved his offices to New York where he has gone into the distribution of oil, competing against the giants, allying himself with Eastern stock magnate Atwill and his sleek, worldly friend Lamarr, who soon becomes Gable's confidante and mistress. When Tracy learns of this liaison, he first threatens Lamarr, telling her to leave. When that fails, he tells Gable that he will throw his own fortune against him, ruin him, if it's the only way he can force him to be faithful to Colbert. He fails, going broke. Gable, because he will not work hand-in-glove with slippery Atwill, adopting his crooked procedures, is charged with anti-trust violations. (Atwill, of course, is behind the charges.) Brought into court, Gable tries to defend himself but it looks as if he will be convicted until Tracy testifies on his behalf, a magnificent speech which causes the charges to be dropped. Gable and Tracy are now back where they started, both broke, but happy. They set out, Gable, Colbert, their child, Tracy, and their faithful financial backer Morgan, for California to open the rich Kettleman Hills fields. This was the last film Gable and Tracy would do together, one that was as smashing a success as SAN FRANCISCO and TEST PILOT. Gable was by then the top talent at MGM, becoming "the king" of Hollywood. He admired Tracy's talent, always considering him superior in ability, and Tracy liked Gable, but he resented second billing. On other Gable-Tracy films there was a happy-go-lucky atmosphere on the set. Not this time. Tracy had had enough, wanted to be his own star. He was petulant and withdrawn throughout the making of BOOM TOWN, but this never showed on screen. Moreover, his attitude toward the aloof Lamarr was similar to the on-screen animosity he was supposed to show. When confronting her in one scene where he is trying to drive her off to protect Gable and Colbert's marriage, Tracy poked Lamarr very hard repeatedly. The actress, who liked working with Gable, later complained that Tracy was difficult and she couldn't wait until their scenes together were over. In one scene where Tracy's double (Gable didn't use one) was throwing round-house rights in their first fist fight, he accidentally landed a haymaker to Gable's jaw, cutting the star's lip and creating a large bruise. Worse, the blow broke Gable's dentures and he was away from the production for a week while they were being repaired. (Dentures figure in another Gable-Tracy story; in happier days together, the two were walking down an MGM studio street discussing their dictatorial boss, Mayer. They were standing beneath LBM's office windows when Gable, becoming upset at the mere thought of the benevolent mogul, and urged on by Tracy, withdrew his expensive false teeth and hurled them through Mayer's office window, smashing the glass. The story allegedly has Gable appearing moments later, sunken-cheeked and acting as if nothing unusual had happened, before the startled Mayer. Going to his desk where the teeth had landed and retrieving them nonchalantly, saying: "Excuse me, chief—I dropped something." He then left without waiting for the speechless Mayer to utter a word.) BOOM TOWN is a fast-moving film with director Conway keeping pace with the dynamic energy of its rollicking stars who turned routine scenes into sparkling gems. In one scene Tracy, at Gable's insistence, is being fitted for tailor-made clothes so he can look the part of a millionaire oil man. The effete tailor holds out a swatch of expen sive cloth from which the suit will be made. Tracy sniffs it suspiciously and says: "Smells a little gamy to me." The electricity flashes in the scenes where Gable and Tracy are together; they are both tough, alive, stubborn and loyal to each other unto death. Colbert is touching and sensitive as the faithful wife and Lamarr was never more convincing than as the calculating beauty bettering herself at the expense of other women's husbands. Great supporting players, Morgan at his gesticulating best, Wills, the country sage, Atwill the kid-gloved schemer, and a host of other MGM stalwarts, enliven every scene. Gable probably felt more at home with this vehicle than any other; he had begun working in the oil fields as a rigger when in his teens, long before he ever dreamed of acting. Moreover, his father William Gable was a wildcatter in the days of the Texas and Oklahoma oil booms and it was his rough-and-tumble father whom Gable used as a role model for a part that remains unforgettable as the film, full of blasting volcanic energy.

p, Sam Zimbalist; d, Jack Conway; w, John Lee Mahin (based on a story by James Edward Grant); ph, Harold Rosson; m, Franz Waxman; ed, Blanche Sewell; art d, Cedric Gibbons, Eddie Imazu; set d, Edwin B. Willis; cos, Adrian, Giles Steele.

Adventure **(PR:A MPAA:NR)**

BOOMERANG* (1934, Brit.) 82m Maude Productions/COL bw

Nora Swinburne *(Elizabeth Stafford)*, Lester Matthews *(David Kennedy)*, Millicent Wolf, Harvey Braban, Wallace Geoffrey, Charles Mortimer.

Blind author Matthews takes a break from writing when he discovers his wife is being blackmailed. His solution plots the end to the nefarious scheme, and he goes back to the grind.

d, Arthur Maude; w, John Paddy Carstairs (based on a play by David Evans).

Drama **(PR:A MPAA:NR)**

BOOMERANG**** (1947) 88m FOX bw

Dana Andrews *(Henry L. Harvey)*, Jane Wyatt *(Mrs. Harvey)*, Lee J. Cobb *(Chief*

Robinson), Cara Williams *(Irene Nelson)*, Arthur Kennedy *(John Waldron)*, Sam Levene *(Woods)*, Taylor Holmes *(Wade)*, Robert Keith *(McCreery)*, Ed Begley *(Harris)*, Phlip Coolidge *(Crossman)*, Lester Lonergan *(Cary)*, Barry Kelley *(Sgt. Dugan)*, Richard Garrick *(Mr. Rogers)*, Karl Malden *(Lt. White)*, Ben Lackland *(James)*, Helen Carew *(Annie)*, Wyrley Birch *(Father Lambert)*, Johnny Stearns *(Rev. Gardiner)*, Guy Thomajan *(Cartucci)*, Lucia Seger *(Mrs. Lukash)*, Dudley Sadler *(Dr. Rainsford)*, Walter Greaza *(Mayor Swayze)*, Helen Hatch *(Miss Manion)*, Joe Kazan *(Mr. Lukash)*, Ida McGuire *(Miss Roberts)*, George Petrie *(O'Shea)*, John Carmody *(Callahan)*, Clay Clement *(Judge Tate)*, E. J. Ballantine *(McDonald)*, William Challee *(Stone)*, Jimmy Dobson *(Bill)*, Lawrence Paquin *(Sheriff)*, Anthony Ross *(Warren)*, Bert Freed *(Herron)*, Royal Beal *(Johnson)*.

A chilling *film noir* gem which deals with the murder of a priest in Bridgeport, Connecticut, in front of many witnesses, BOOMERANG is the epitome of the realistic style developed by one of the leaders in semi-documentary (docudrama) filmmaking, producer de Rochemont who had created THE MARCH OF TIME series in 1934 and who went on to make theatrical films with the quality of you-are-there newsreels (THE HOUSE ON 92ND STREET, 13 RUE MADELEINE), based on real events and shot on the actual location whenever possible. The film opens with an elderly priest (Birch) walking down a dark street, greeting his parishioners. He pauses beneath a lamppost to light his pipe. A gun is suddenly put to the back of his head and he is shot dead in front of horrified passersby. A short time later police arrest a vagrant, Kennedy, and charge him with the murder. Andrews, the local state's attorney, is called upon to prosecute Kennedy, and is told by political bosses that convicting the man will appease the public outcry and greatly enhance his own political career. He begins to gather evidence and also interviews Kennedy, who is confused about the events on the murder night. He has been unemployed and hates life and society. He admits confessing the murder to police but claims that the admission was the result of not having eaten or slept in days. Many witnesses have positively identified Kennedy as the killer. The case appears overwhelming against the accused, and easy conviction for Andrews. But doubts and gaps in the evidential material nag Andrews so that he begins investigating on his own, unearthing facts contrary to his own case. In a surprise move, he takes the accused's side in court, knowing he is risking his political career, attempting to prove innocent the very man he is supposed to prosecute. He destroys the credibility of the witnesses, invalidates the confession, and, in a frightening scene, risks his own life before a stunned courtroom testing the so-called murder weapon (a gun owned by Kennedy) proving that the weapon could not have been used to kill the clergyman. Kennedy is freed and Andrews, in a captivating and understated performance, is vindicated. The film faithfully follows the actual murder (still unsolved) of Father Hubert Dahme in Bridgeport on the night of February 4, 1924, and the arrest and trial of a jobless drifter, Harold Israel, along with profiling the man who saved him from execution, a young state's attorney named Homer Cummings who later became U.S. Attorney General in the Roosevelt Administration. Director Kazan shot most of the film in Stamford, Connecticut, where he received great cooperation. His sharp, contrasting scenes, extremely mobile camera, and the actual offices, prison cells, and courtrooms he employed fill the screen with authenticity, accenting a sense of very real danger that an innocent man is about to forfeit his life for a crime he has not committed. The success of BOOMERANG spawned a new wave of realism in American films and established Kazan as a great directorial force.

p, Louis de Rochemont; d, Elia Kazan; w, Richard Murphy (based on the *Reader's Digest* article "The Perfect Case" by Anthony Abbott); ph, Norbert Brodine; m, David Buttolph; ed, Harmon Jones.

Crime Drama   **(PR:C MPAA:NR)**

BOOMERANG**
                                      (1960, Ger.) 92m UFA bw (BUMERANG; AKA: CRY DOUBLECROSS)
Hardy Kruger *(Robert Wegner)*, Mario Adorf *(Georg Kugler)*, Horst Frank *(Willy Schneider)*, Martin Held *(Police Inspector)*, Ingrid van Bergen *(Else)*, Peer Schmidt *(Police Sergeant)*, Cordula Trantow *(Helga)*.

Kruger, Frank, and Adorf plan to crack a safe, but one of them tips the police out of jealousy. Script flaws and bad acting by the principals bury this film's technical expertise and tight direction.

p, Luggi Waldleitner; d, Alfred Weidenmann; w, Herbert Reinecker (from a novel by Igor Sentjuro); ph, Kurt Hasse; m, Hans Martin-Majewski; ed, Lillian Seng.

Crime   **(PR:A-C MPAA:NR)**

BOOT HILL*
                                      (1969, Ital.) 87m Film Ventures c
Terence Hill, Bud Spencer, Woody Strode, Victor Buono, Lionel Stander, Eduardo Ciannelli.

Escapades of Hill and Spencer traditionally teamed up as the blue-eyed hard-jawed roustabout and his oversized bulky sidekick. Go-get-em comedy with spaghetti western action.

d, Gouseppe Colizzi.

Western   **(PR:A MPAA:NR)**

BOOTHILL BRIGADE**1/2
                                      (1937) 58m REP bw
Johnny Mack Brown *(Lon Cardigan)*, Claire Rochelle *(Bobbie Reynolds)*, Dick Curtis *(Bull Berke)*, Horace Murphy *(Calico Haynes)*, Frank La Rue *(Jeff Reynolds)*, Ed Cassidy *(John Porter)*, Bobbie Nelson *(Tug Murdock)*, Frank Ball *(Murdock)*, Steve Clark *(Holbrook)*, Frank Ellis *(Brown)*.

One of Brown's better vehicles due to careful plotting, polished direction, and careful cinematography. Homesteaders are having their land stolen by the scurrilous Cassidy, but Brown rides to the rescue using his fists rather than his guns in a number of good fight scenes.

p, A.W. Hackel; d, Sam Newfield; w, George H. Plympton (story by Harry W. Olmsted); ph, Bert Longenecker.

Western   **(PR:A MPAA:NR)**

BOOTLEGGERS*1/2
                                      (1974) 110m Howco Int'l c (AKA: BOOTLEGGER'S ANGEL)
Paul Koslo *(Othar Pruitt)*, Dennis Fimple *(Dewey Crenshaw)*, Slim Pickens *(Grandpa Pruitt)*, Betty Bluett *(Grandma Pruitt)*, Steve Ward *(Silas Pruitt)*, Seamon Glass *(Rufus Woodall)*, J.N. Houch, Jr. *(Bobby Joe Woodall)*, Jim Clem *(Big-un Woodall)*, Jaclyn Smith *(Sally Fannie Tatum)*, Darlyn Ann Lynley *(Leola Gauldin)*, Earl E. Smith *(The Sheriff)*.

Hick comedy about Koslo and Fimple running moonshine, raising hell, and looking for the rival 'shiners who shot Grandpa Pickens dead. Slow and stupid, with Fujimoto's glamorous and painstaking camera work totally out of place. Later reissued as BOOTLEGGER'S ANGEL to capitalize on the minor presence of Jaclyn Smith.

p&d, Charles B. Pierce; w, Earl E. Smith; ph, Tak Fujimoto (Eastmancolor); m, Jaime Mendoza-Nava; ed, Tom Boutross; art d, Tommy Hasson; m/l, Dorsey Burnette.

Crime   **(PR:A-C MPAA:PG)**

BOOTS AND SADDLES*
                                      (1937) 60m REP bw
Gene Autry *(Gene)*, Smiley Burnette *(Frog)*, Judith Allen *(Bernice Allen)*, Ra Hould *(Spud)*, Guy Usher *(Colonel Allen)*, Gordon Elliott *(Neale)*, John Ward *(Wyndham)*, Frankie Marvin *(Shorty)*, Chris Marvin *(Juan)*, Stanley Blystone *(Sergeant)*, Bud Osborne *(Joe Larkins)*.

Another indistinguishable Gene Autry vehicle. Allen is the romantic interest, and Burnette is the comic relief. Gene saves the homestead and sings the title song and "You're the Only Rose That's Left in My Heart." (See GENE AUTRY series, Index.)

p, Sol C. Siegel; d, Joseph Kane; w, Jack Natteford, Oliver Drake (based on a story by Natteford); ph, William Nobles.

Western   **Cas.**   **(PR:A MPAA:NR)**

BOOTS! BOOTS!*
                                      (1934, Brit.) 80m Blakeley's Productions/BUT bw
George Formby *(John Willie)*, Beryl Formby *(Beryl)*, Arthur Kingsley *(Manager)*, Tonie Forde *(Chambermaid)*, Lilian Keyes *(Lady Royston)*, Donald Reid *(Sir Alfred Royston)*, Betty Driver *(Betty)*, Harry Hudson and his Band.

A hotel shoeshine man and a scullery maid trade in their hard chores for the limelight when they star in a cabaret floor show. George Formby co-wrote and starred in this mediocre film.

p, John E. Blakely; d, Bert Tracy; w, George Formby, Arthur Mertz.

Musical   **(PR:A MPAA:NR)**

BOOTS MALONE***1/2
                                      (1952) 102m COL bw
William Holden *(Boots Malone)*, Johnny Stewart *(The Kid)*, Stanley Clements *(Stash Clements)*, Basil Ruysdael *(Preacher Cole)*, Carl Benton Reid *(John Williams)*, Ralph Dumke *(Beckett)*, Ed Begley *(Howard Whitehead)*, Hugh Sanders *(Matson)*, Henry [Harry] Morgan *(Quarter Horse Henry)*, Ann Lee *(Mrs. Gibson)*, Anthony Caruso *(Joe)*, Billy Pearson *(Eddie Koch)*, John W. Frye *(Foxy Farrell)*, Harry Hines *(Goofy Gordon)*, Toni Gerry *(Jenny West)*, Hurley Breen *(Rod)*, Whit Bissell *(Lou Dyer)*, Earl Unkraut *(Cabbage Head)*, Harry Shannon *(Colonel Summers)*, John Call *(Touting Clocker)*, Pat Williams *(Receptionist)*, Ken Christy *(Beanery Owner)*, Hank Worden *(Mechanic)*, Harlan Warde *(Private Investigator)*, Emory Parnell *(Evans)*, Ralph Volkie *(Soft Drink Man)*, Earle Hodgins *(Owner)*, Dewey Dick *(Bit)*, Franklyn Farnum *(Man)*, Snub Pollard *(Extra)*, Carleton Young *(Steward)*, Hal J. Moore *(Announcer)*, Milton Kibbee *(Conductor)*, Irving Smith *(Black Groom)*, Frank Ferguson *(Detective Agency Head)*.

Almost as much authentic race track lore is crowded into BOOTS MALONE as Dick Francis spins off in one of his novels about the racing business. Holden is down on his luck as a jockey's agent, and, like any of the world's luckless, is opportunistic as well. Into his life comes Stewart, a rich kid with a passion for racing and a thirst to learn how to ride. Holden decides to take him under his wing as long as the dough holds out but soon the two are attached to each other and their scenes together become very effective, a credit to Stewart, too, who is making his acting debut. Complications arise with the appearance of Stewart's mother, who is determined to rein in her son's blooming career. Another complication, this one more deadly, livens the pace when Holden must tell the kid to lose the big race or both will end up dead in a car trunk, victims of a racing syndicate which is betting on another horse in the race. The melodrama is unraveled successfully and plausibly when the crooks are thwarted and the boy's faith in his mentor is restored. Much of the photography was done at actual race tracks, and the prancing horses are fun to watch while a parade of seamy track characters—the touts, the phonies, the also-rans—give the whole an authentic feel. BOOTS MALONE was no giant step from Joe Bonaparte's GOLDEN BOY. At that point in Holden's life the film did nothing to advance his career. It did nothing to hinder it, either, and would lead, in the next year, to the turning point for him, as the maverick hero of STALAG 17.

p&w, Milton Holmes; d, William Dieterle; ph, Charles Lawton Jr.; m, Elmer Bernstein; ed, Al Clark.

Sports Drama   **(PR:A MPAA:NR)**

BOOTS OF DESTINY*
                                      (1937) 59m Grand National bw
Ken Maynard *(Ken)*, Claudia Dell *(Alice)*, Vince Barnett *(Acey Deucy)*, Ed Cassidy *(Harmon)*, Martin Garralaga *(Jose)*, George Morrell *(Pedro)*.

Cheapie western has Maynard and sidekick Barnett on the lam, coming to the rescue of ranch owner Dell, whose foreman is slowly wresting control from her. Nothing redeems this pic, unless it's the tricks of Maynard's horse Tarzan.

p, M. H. Hoffman; d, Arthur Rosson; w, Rosson (story by E. Morton Hough); ph, Tom Galligan; ed, Dan Malone.

Western   Cas.   (PR:A MPAA:NR)

BOP GIRL GOES CALYPSO★★   (1957) 80m UA bw (AKA: BOP GIRL)

Judy Tyler (Jo Thomas), Bobby Troup (Robert Hilton), Margo Woode (Marion Hendricks), Lucien Littlefield (Professor Winthrop), George O'Hanlon (Barney), Jerry Barclay (Jerry), Judy Harriet (Young Girl Singer), Gene O'Donnell (Drunk), Edward Kafafian (Taxi Driver), George Sawaya, Jerry Frank, Dick Standish (Record Company Reps), Mary Kaye Trio, The Goofers, Lord Flea Calypsonians, Nino Tempo, The Titans, The Cubanos (Musical Acts).

Musician Bobby Troup plays a psychologist whose essay "Mass Hysteria and the Popular Singer" proves that rock 'n' roll is fading away and calypso is the new youth beat. He convinces singer Tyler to forsake her rock roots for the Caribbean sound. Mercifully Mr. Troup and Miss Tyler were wrong. Judy Tyler's vaguely promising career came to an abrupt halt when she was killed in a car crash just days prior to the release of this curio.

p, Aubrey Schenck; d, Howard W. Koch; w, Arnold Belgard (based on a story by Hendrik Vollaerts); ph, Carl E. Guthrie; m, Les Baxter; ed, Sam Waxman.

Musical   (PR:A MPAA:NR)

BORDER, THE★★1/2   (1982) 107m UNIV c

Jack Nicholson (Charlie), Harvey Keitel (Cat), Valerie Perrine (Marcy), Warren Oates (Red), Elpidia Carrillo (Maria), Shannon Wilcox (Savannah), Manuel Viescas (Juan), Jeff Morris (J.J.), Mike Gomez (Manuel), Dirk Blocker (Beef), Lonny Chapman (Andy), Stacey Pickren (Hooker), Floyd Levine (Lou), James Jeter (Frank), Alan Fudge (Hawker), William Russ (Jimbo), Gary Grubbs (Honk), Gary Sexton (Slim), Billy Silva (George), William McLaughlin (Donny), David Beecroft (Kevin).

Despite some fine performances from Nicholson, Keitel, Perrine, and Oates, THE BORDER fails to involve the viewer beyond a perfunctory level of emotion. Nicholson top-lines as a decent sort who is married to one of the all-time grasping shrews, Perrine. She aspires to the middle-class and convinces him to take a job as a border guard in El Paso. There, he meets Keitel who shares the task of keeping Mexicans out of the United States. This is but one of several films in the last few years to deal with the plight of the guards and the Mexicans who want to find a better life north of the border. Difficulty with THE BORDER from the free-form story is that it jumps from place to place without settling in to tell us one tale. Nicholson hates the attitudes of his cohorts but, as in so many government jobs, he has to go along to get along and it gnaws at his innards. Keitel, a graduate of a small school in New York City that has produced more actors, writers, and performers than any other high school in the U.S. (Abraham Lincoln on Ocean Parkway in Brooklyn) is excellent, considering that Nicholson was allowed to nibble on the sets. Richardson (TOM JONES, TASTE OF HONEY, HAMLET) directed this as though he were double-parked.

p, Edgar Bronfman; d, Tony Richardson; w, Deric Washburn, Walon Green, David Freeman; ph, Ric Waite, Vilmos Zsigmond (Technicolor); m, Ry Cooder; ed, Robert K. Lambert; cos, Vicki Sanchez.

Drama   Cas.   (PR:O MPAA:R)

BORDER BADMEN★   (1945) 58m PRC bw

Buster Crabbe (Billy Carson), Al "Fuzzy" St. John (Fuzzy Jones), Lorraine Miller (Helen), Charles King (Merritt), Ralph Bennett (Deputy Spencer), Archie Hall (Gilian), Budd Buster (Evans), Marilyn Gladstone (Rosie), Marin Sais (Mrs. Bentley).

Buster and Fuzzy travel to the town where a distant cousin of Fuzzy's, a silver baron, has died. They arrive for the reading of his will. There they find desperadoes are killing off the heirs. Miller is the old man's closest relative, held prisoner by the heavies, until Buster and Fuzzy set her free. A series of fist fights round up the whole gang. Weak. (See BILLY CARSON series, Index.)

p, Sigmund Neufeld; d, Sam Newfield; w, George Milton; ph, Jack Greenhalgh; m, Frank Sanucci; ed, Holbrook N. Todd.

Western   (PR:A MPAA:NR)

BORDER BANDITS★   (1946) 57m MON bw

Johnny Mack Brown (Nevada), Raymond Hatton (Sandy), Riley Hill (Steve Halliday), Rosa Del Rosario (Celia), John Merton (Spike), Tom Quinn (Papper), Frank La Rue (John Halliday), Steve Clark (Doc Bowles), Charles Stevens (Jose), Lucio Villegas (Nogales), Bud Osborne (Dutch), Pat R. McGee (Cupid).

Slow, routine Brown oater with Johnny Mack hunting down the bad guys. He's a marshal sworn to do his duty but he proves it a boring job.

p, Scott R. Dunlop; d, Lambert Hillyer; w, Frank H. Young; ph, William A. Sickner; ed, Carroll Lewis.

Western   Cas.   (PR:A MPAA:NR)

BORDER BRIGANDS★1/2   (1935) 56m UNIV bw

Buck Jones (Lt. Tim Barry), Lona Andre (Diane), Fred Kohler (Conyda), Frank Rice (Roxy O'Leary), Edward Keane (Comm. Jim Barry), J. P. McGowan (Comm. Winston).

Buck Jones joins a gang of outlaws led by Kohler, but he's really an undercover Mountie hunting his brother's killer. Routine B.

p, Irving Starr; d, Nick Grinde; w, Stuart Anthony; ph, William Sickner.

Western   (PR:A MPAA:NR)

BORDER BUCKAROOS★   (1943) 60m PRC bw

Dave "Tex" O'Brien (Tex Wyatt), Jim Newill (Jim Steele), Guy Wilkerson (Panhandle Perkins), Christine MacIntyre (Betty Clark), Eleanor Counts (Marge Leonard), Jack Ingraham (Cole Melford), Ethan Laidlaw (Hank Dugan), Charles King (Rance Daggett), Michael Vallon (Seth Higgins), Kenne Duncan (Tom Bancroft).

Texas Rangers O'Brien, Newill, and Wilkerson sing some smooth tunes while keeping a mineral-rich ranch from falling into the wrong hands. (See TEXAS RANGERS series, Index.)

p, Alfred Stern, Arthur Alexander; d, Oliver Drake; w, Drake; ph, Ira Morgan; ed, Charles Henken, Jr.; md, Lee Zahler.

Western   (PR:A MPAA:NR)

BORDER CABALLERO★1/2   (1936) 57m Puritan bw

Tim McCoy (Tim Ross), Lois January (Goldie Ralph), Ralph Byrd (Tex Weaver), Ted Adams (Buff Brayden), J. Frank Glendon (Wiley), Earl Hodgins (Doc Shaw).

Lackluster Tim McCoy vehicle, interesting for meaty role given Lois January, who not only doesn't fall for McCoy, but gets shot and wounded in the climactic shootout.

p, Sig Neufeld, Leslie Simmonds; d, Sam Newfield; w, Joseph O'Donnell (based on a story by Norman S. Hall); ph, Jack Greenhalgh.

Western   (PR:A MPAA:NR)

BORDER CAFE★1/2   (1937) 67m RKO bw

Harry Carey (Tex), John Beal (Keith Whitney), Armida (Deminaga), George Irving (Senator Whitney), Leona Roberts (Mrs. Whitney), J. Carrol Naish (Rocky), Marjorie Lord (Janet), Lee Patrick (Ellie), Paul Fix (Dolson), Max Wagner (Shaky), Walter Miller (Evans).

Big-city mobsters try to muscle in on the ranching business, a Yankee falls for a senorita, and a rich dude from the East is forced to take an interest in his ranch, all in the title cantina. Ambitious but muddled effort.

p, Robert Sisk; d, Lew Landers; w, Lionel Houser (based on a story by Thomas Gill); ph, Nicholas Musuraca; ed, Jack Hively.

Western   (PR:A MPAA:NR)

BORDER DEVILS★★   (1932) 65m Supreme/Artclass bw

Harry Carey, Kathleen Collins, Al Smith, George Hayes, Niles Welch, Ray Gallager.

Interesting programmer with Carey breaking out of jail to prove himself innocent of the charges leveled against him by heavy Smith. In turn, Smith's strings are being pulled by a mysterious Chinaman who is seen only as a shadow on the wall until the last reel.

p, Louis Weiss; d, William Nigh; w, Harry C. Christ [Harry Fraser] (based on a novel by Murray Lenister); ph, William Dietz.

Western   (PR:A MPAA:NR)

BORDER FEUD★   (1947) 55m PRC bw

"Lash" La Rue (Cheyenne), Al "Fuzzy" St. John (Fuzzy), Bob Duncan (Barton), Brad Slavin (Jim Condon), Kenneth Farrell (Bob Hart), Gloria Marlen (Carol Condon), Casey MacGregor (Jed Young), Ian Keith (Doc Peters), Mikel Conrad (Elmore), Ed Cassidy (Sheriff Steele).

B-western in which Lash and Fuzzy are okay as lawmen breaking up a feud between the co-owners of a gold mine, a feud engineered by the fiendish Duncan.

p, Jerry Thomas; d, Ray Taylor; w, Joe O'Donnall, Patricia Harper; ph, Milford Anderson; ed, Joe Gluck.

Western   (PR:A MPAA:NR)

BORDER FLIGHT★★   (1936) 68m PAR bw

Frances Farmer (Ann Blane), John Howard (Lt. Dan Conlon), Robert Cummings (Lt. Bob Dixon), Grant Withers (Lt. Pat Tornell), Roscoe Karns (Calico Smith), Samuel S. Hinds (Commander Mosely), Donald Kirk (Heming), Matty Fain (Jerry), Frank Faylen (Jimmie), Ted Oliver (Turk), Paul Barrett (Radio Operator).

Coast Guard fliers Howard and Withers battle airborne smugglers and vie for the affections of Miss Farmer. Withers joins the smugglers when he is drummed out of the service but redeems himself by flying the smugglers' plane into their boat. Interesting for old airplanes and Frances Farmer at her freshest.

p, A. M. Botsford; d, Otho Lovering; w, Stuart Anthony, Arthur J. Beckhard (based on a story by Ewing Scott); ph, Harry Fishbeck; ed, Chandler House.

Adventure   (PR:A MPAA:NR)

BORDER G-MAN★1/2   (1938) 58m RKO bw

George O'Brien (Jim Galloway), Laraine Johnson (Betty Holden), Ray Whitley (Luke), John Miljan (Louis Rankin), Rita La Roy (Rita Browning), Edgar Dearing (Smoky Joslin), William Stelling (Leslie Bolden), Edward Keane (Col. Christie), Ethan Laidlaw (Curly), Hugh Sothern (Matt Rathburn), Bobby Burns (Sheriff).

Miljan and moll La Roy are organizing and arming a private army of hoodlums and ex-cons to plunder South America, but when La Roy tries to compromise Stelling, the son of a government official, G-man O'Brien is sent down to see what's going on. There is a bizarre final gun battle at sea amidst dozens of swimming horses.

p, Bert Gilroy; d, David Howard; w, Oliver Drake (based on a story by Bernard McConville); ph, Joseph H. August; ed, Frederic Knudston.

Western   (PR:A MPAA:NR)

BORDER INCIDENT*** (1949) 92m MGM bw

Ricardo Montalban (*Pablo Rodriguez*), George Murphy (*Jack Bearnes*), Howard da Silva (*Owen Parkson*), James Mitchell (*Juan Garcia*), Arnold Moss (*Zopilote*), Alfonso Bedoya (*Cuchillo*), Teresa Celli (*Maria*), Charles McGraw (*Jeff Amboy*), Jose Torvay (*Pocoloco*), John Ridgely (*Mr. Neley*), Arthur Hunnicutt (*Clayton Nordell*), Sig Ruman (*Hugo Wolfgang Ulrich*), Otto Waldis (*Fritz*).

American agent Murphy and Mexican agent Montalban join forces and go undercover to a ring smuggling Mexicans into California to work the fields of crooked rancher Da Silva. Murphy pretends to be a small-time hood joining Da Silva's gang while Montalban gets himself smuggled in as one of the workers. Murphy is found out and in a horrifying, effective scene is run over by a tractor while Montalban watches helplessly. But Montalban gets even in the climactic shootout in a quicksand-filled swamp. Mann's use of the Southwestern landscape foreshadows the westerns he began to make the following year.

p, Nicholas Nayfack; d, Anthony Mann; w, John C. Higgins (based on a story by Higgins, George Zuckerman); ph, John Alton; m, Andre Previn; ed, Conrad A. Nervig.

Crime   **(PR:C   MPAA:NR)**

BORDER LAW**1/2 (1931) 62m COL bw

Buck Jones, Lupita Tovar, James Mason, Frank Rice, Don Chapman, Glenn Strange, Louis Hickus, F. R. Smith, John Barnes.

Jones is a Texas Ranger infiltrating the robbers' gang to find the man who killed his brother. A long fist fight subdues the killer—gang leader Mason (no, not the English actor). One of the best films by the stoic Jones, and far better than the mass of B westerns.

p, Irving Briskin; d, Louis King; w, Stuart Anthony; ph, L. W. O'Connell.

Western   **(PR:A   MPAA:NR)**

BORDER LEGION, THE*1/2 (1930) 78m PAR bw

Richard Arlen (*Jim Cleve*), Jack Holt (*Jack Kells*), Fay Wray (*Joan Randall*), Eugene Pallette (*Bunco Davis*), Stanley Fields (*Hack Gulden*), E. H. Calvert (*Judge Savin*), Ethan Allen (*George Randall*), Sid Saylor (*Shrimp*).

Zane Grey's novel of an outlaw sacrificing himself for a pair of lovers doesn't come off very well in this antiquated production. Holt is the outlaw, Fay Wray and Arlen are the trouble-plagued lovers.

d, Otto Brower, Edwin A. Knopf; w, Percy Heath, Edward E. Paramore (based on the novel by Zane Grey); ph, Mack Stengler; ed, Doris Drought.

Western   **(PR:A   MPAA:NR)**

BORDER LEGION, THE*1/2 (1940) 58m REP bw

Roy Rogers (*Steve Kells*), George "Gabby" Hayes (*Honest John Whittaker*), Carol Hughes (*Alice*), Joseph Sawyer (*Gulden*), Maude Eburne (*Hurricane Hattie*), Jay Novello (*Santos*), Hal Taliaferro (*The Sheriff*), Dick Wessel (*Red*), Paul Porcasi (*Tony*), Robert Emmett Keane (*Officer Willets*).

Sappy, sanitized retelling of Zane Grey's novel. This time Rogers is the outlaw with a heart of gold who helps the young lovers stay together while simultaneously getting the best of his fellow bad guys. (See ROY ROGERS series, Index.)

p&d, Joseph Kane; w, Olive Cooper, Louis Stevens (based on a novel by Zane Grey, additional treatment by George Carleton Brown); ph, Jack Marta; ed, Edward Mann; md, Cy Feuer.

Western   **(PR:A   MPAA:NR)**

BORDER OUTLAWS*1/2 (1950) 57m EL bw (GB: THE PHANTOM HORSEMAN)

Spade Cooley (*Spade Cooley*), Maria Hart (*Jill*), Bill Edwards (*Mike Hoskins*), Bill Kennedy (*Carson*), George Slocum (*Turner*), John Laurenz (*Kevin*), Douglas Wood (*Kimball*), Bud Osborne (*Sheriff*), John Carpenter (*Keller*), The Six Metzetti Brothers.

Masked smugglers and rustlers are taught a lesson by Special Investigator Edwards. Cooley remains at the ranch and performs the Western Swing music where he made his real mark. Low budget and cliche-ridden, but the music is good. Producer/director Talmadge, a one-time stunt man, bounces around as one of the six tumbling "Brothers."

p, Richard Talmadge, Jack Schwarz; d, Talmadge; w, Arthur Hoerl.

Western   **Cas.**   **(PR:A   MPAA:NR)**

BORDER PATROL*1/2 (1943) 63m UA bw

William Boyd (*Hopalong Cassidy*), Andy Clyde (*California Carlson*), Jay Kirby (*Johnny Travers*), Russell Simpson (*Orestes Krebs*), Claudia Drake (*Inez*), Cliff Parkinson (*Don Enrique*), George Reeves, Duncan Renaldo (*Mexican Officers*).

Texas Rangers Boyd, Clyde, and Kirby attempt to break up an operation smuggling Mexicans into the U.S. to work as slaves in Simpson's silver mine. A kangaroo court sentences the trio to hang but they escape to free the laborers and round up the gang. Robert Mitchum's film debut, uncredited, as one of Simpson's minions. Also notable for bit roles played by Reeves, later to star as TV's "Superman," and Renaldo, who would make his mark as television's "The Cisco Kid" after playing the role in films. Writer Wilson, who scripted four of the Hopalong pictures, was one of the talented screenwriters blacklisted during the witch-hunts of the 1950s. (See HOPALONG CASSIDY series, Index.)

p, Harry Sherman; d, Lesley Selander; w, Michael Wilson (based on a story by Clarence E. Mulford); ph, Russell Harlan; ed, Sherman A. Rose; md, Irvin Talbot.

Western   **(PR:A   MPAA:NR)**

BORDER PATROLMAN, THE** (1936) 58m FOX bw

George O'Brien (*Bob Wallace*), Polly Ann Young (*Patricia Huntley*), Roy Mason (*Courtney Maybrook*), Mary Doran (*Myra*), Smiley Burnette (*Chuck Owens*), William P. Carleton (*Jeremiah Huntley*), Al Hill (*Frank Adams*), Tom London (*Johnson*), George MacQuarrie (*Riker*), Cyril Ring (*Hendricks*), John St. Polis (*Manning*).

Border Patrolman O'Brien arrests spoiled rich girl Young for smoking in a restricted area and her exasperated parents hire him to keep an eye on her. She gets entangled with a gang of jewel thieves but O'Brien comes to the rescue, winning her heart in the process.

p, Sol Lesser; d, David Howard; w, Dan Jarrett, Ben Cohen (based on their story); ph, Frank B. Good; ed, Robert Crandall.

Western   **(PR:A   MPAA:NR)**

BORDER PHANTOM**1/2 (1937) 60m REP bw

Bob Steele (*Larry O'Day*), Harley Wood (*Barbara*), Don Barclay (*Lucky*), Karl Hackett (*Obed Young*), Horace Murphy (*Sheriff*), Miki Morita (*Chang Lu*), Perry Murdock (*Slim Barton*), Hans Joby (*Dr. Von Kurtz*), Frank Ball (*Hartwell*).

Morita is a dapper oriental villain engaged in smuggling Chinese picture brides in from Mexico. Comic relief from Barclay is particularly good. One of Steele's better B westerns.

p, A. W. Hackel; d, S. Roy Luby; w, Fred Myton; ph, Jack Greenhalgh; ed, Roy Claire.

Western   **Cas.**   **(PR:A   MPAA:NR)**

BORDER RANGERS*1/2 (1950) 57m Lippert bw

Don Barry (*Bob Standish*), Robert Lowery (*Mugo*), Wally Vernon (*Hungry*), Pamela Blake (*Ellen Reed*), Lyle Talbot (*Capt. McLane*), Claude Stroud (*Randolph*), Ezelle Poule (*Aunt Priscilla*), Bill Kennedy (*Carlson*), Paul Jordan (*Tommy*), Alyn Lockwood (*Mrs. Standish*), John Merton (*Gans*), Tom Monroe (*Hackett*), George Keymas (*Raker*), Tom Kennedy (*Station Agent*), Eric Norden (*George Standish*), Bud Osborne (*Driver*).

Texas Ranger Barry, seeking to avenge the murders of his brother and sister-in-law, joins a band of outlaws in order to lure them back across the border to rob a bank where the Rangers lie in wait. Nothing new.

p&d, William Berke; w, Victor West, Berke; ph, Ernest W. Miller; ed, Carl Pierson.

Western   **(PR:A   MPAA:NR)**

BORDER RIVER**1/2 (1954) 80m UNIV c

Joel McCrea (*Clete Mattson*), Yvonne De Carlo (*Carmelita Caris*), Pedro Armendariz (*General Calleja*), Howard Petrie (*Newlund*), Erika Nordin (*Annina*), Alfonso Bedoya (*Captain Vargas*), Ivan Triesault (*Baron Von Hollden*), George Lewis (*Sanchez*), George Wallace (*Fletcher*), Lane Chandler (*Anderson*), Charles Horvath (*Crowe*), Nacho Galindo (*Lopez*).

McCrea plays a Confederate officer who leads a raid that gives him two million dollars in gold bullion. Taking the loot to Mexico, McCrea tries to buy arms and ammunition for the beleaguered Southern armies. But word of his fortune gets around and McCrea spends most of his time protecting it from a variety of unsavory types, including a slimy Mexican general and his even slimier German advisor. Not too bad.

p, Albert J. Cohen; d, George Sherman; w, William Sackheim, Louis Stevens (based on a story by Stevens); ph, Irving Glassberg (Technicolor); ed, Frank Gross.

Western   **(PR:A   MPAA:NR)**

BORDER ROMANCE* (1930) 61m Tiffany bw

Armida (*Conchita Cortez*), Don Terry (*Bob Hamlin*), J. Frank Glendon (*Buck*), Marjorie Kane (*Nina*), Victor Potel (*Slim*), Wesley Barry (*Victor Hamlin*), Nita Martan (*Gloria*), Harry von Meter (*Captain of Rurales*), William Costello (*Lieutenant of Rurales*).

Uninspired early B-western in which Terry is on the lam. He slips into Senorita Armida's house, the two fall for each other and sing a couple of songs about it. Vicious rustlers and the long arm of the law threaten the duo, but when Terry helps defeat the rustlers it wins him a pardon.

p, Lester F. Scott; d, Richard Thorpe; w, John Francis Natteford; ph, Harry Zech; ed, Richard Cahoon; md, Al Short; set d, Ralph de Lacy.

Western   **Cas.**   **(PR:A   MPAA:NR)**

BORDER SADDLEMATES zero (1952) 67m REP

Rex Allen (*Rex Allen*), Koko (*Koko*), Mary Allen Kay (*Jane Richards*), Slim Pickens (*Slim Pickens*), Roy Barcroft (*Steve Baxter*), Forrest Taylor (*Mel Richards*), Jimmie Moss (*Danny Richards*), Zon Murray (*Matt Lacey*), Keith McConnell (*Gene Dalton*), Mark Hanna (*Manero*), The Republic Rhythm Riders.

Rex is a crusading veterinarian breaking up a gang smuggling counterfeit U.S. currency from Canada. The phony money is hidden in cages shipped from villain Barcroft to Montana silver fox rancher Taylor. A sick fox leads Rex to slap a quarantine on the ranch and after a number of gunfights and fist fights the whole operation collapses. By this time B western writers were straining themselves in order to come up with some fresh variations, but this one fails utterly.

p, Herbert J. Yates; d, William Witney; w, Albert DeMond; ph, John MacBurnie; m, Stanley Wilson; ed, Harold Minter; m/l, "Roll On, Border Moon," Jack Elliott.

Western   **Cas.**   **(PR:A   MPAA:NR)**

BORDER STREET***

(1950, Pol.) 73m Globe/Film Polski bw (ULICA GRANICZNA; AKA: THAT OTHERS MAY LIVE)

M. Cwinklinska (Clara), J. Leszcynski (Dr. Bialek), W. Godik (Liberman), W. Walter (Cieplikowski), J. Pichelski (Kazimierz Wojtan), T. Fijewski (Bronek Cieplikowski), J. Muclinger (Kusmirak), R. Vrchota (Hans), S. Srodka (Nathan), E. Kruk (Freddie Kusmirak), J. Zlotnicki (David), D. Iczenko (Wladek Wojtan), M. Broniewska (Jadzia).

Good Polish offering about the Warsaw ghetto and the struggle against the Nazi oppressors. Presents a broad panorama of characters on both sides, concentrating primarily on the children, both Hitler Youth and Jewish. Aleksander Ford was one of the first Polish filmmakers to achieve international attention and this is one of his earliest films, shot in Czechoslovakia because the bombed-out Polish studios had not yet been rebuilt. (In Polish; English subtitles.)

d, Aleksander Ford; w, Ford, Jean Force, Ludwig Stolarski; ph, Jaroslav Tuzar; m, Roman Palester; art d, A. Radzinowicz, A. Sachicki.

War Drama (PR:A MPAA:NR)

BORDER TREASURE*

(1950) 60m RKO bw

Tim Holt (Ed Porter), Jane Nigh (Stella), John Doucette (Bat), House Peters, Jr. (Rod), Inez Cooper (Anita), Julian Rivero (Felipe), Ken MacDonald (Sheriff), Vince Barnett (Pokey), Robert Payton (Del), David Leonard (Padre), Tom Monroe (Dimmick), Richard Martin (Chito Rafferty).

Bandits are planning to rob a shipment of jewels and silver intended for disaster relief for victims of a Mexican earthquake. Their first attempt is foiled by Holt and sidekick Martin, but the second try succeeds, leaving Holt and Martin to recover the loot and round up the guilty parties, something they do with little difficulty.

p, Herman Schlom; d, George Archainbaud; w, Norman Houston; ph, J. Roy Hunt; m, Paul Sawtell; ed, Desmond Marquette.

Western (PR:A MPAA:NR)

BORDER VIGILANTES**

(1941) 61m PAR bw

William Boyd (Hopalong Cassidy), Russell Hayden (Lucky Jenkins), Andy Clyde (California Carlson), Victor Jory (Henry Logan), Morris Ankrum (Dan Forbes), Frances Gifford (Helen Forbes), Ethel Wales (Aunt Jennifer Forbes), Tom Tyler (Jim Yager), Hal Taliaferro (Ed Stone), Jack Rockwell (Henry Weaver), Britt Wood (Lafe Willis), Hank Worden (Wagon Driver), Edward Earle (Banker Stevens), Hank Bell (Liveryman).

An outlaw-plagued mining town sends for Boyd and his pals Hayden and Clyde to curb attacks which their own vigilante committee has been unable to do anything about. Boyd and company soon get to the bottom of things, discovering that the desperadoes are led by the town honcho, who incidentally also heads the vigilantes. More gunfire than usual, but otherwise nothing notable. (See HOPALONG CASSIDY series, Index).

p, Harry Sherman; d, Derwin Abrahams; w, J. Benton Cheney (based on characters created by Clarence E. Mulford); ph, Russell Harlan; ed, Carrol Lewis.

Western (PR:A MPAA:NR)

BORDER WOLVES*

(1938) 56m UNIV bw

Bob Baker (Rusty Reynolds), Constance Moore (Mary Jo Benton), Fuzzy Knight (Clem Barrett), Dickie Jones (Jimmie Benton), Willie Fung (Ling Wong), Glenn Strange (Deputy), Frank Campeau (Tom Dawson), Oscar O'Shea (Judge Coleman), Ed Cassidy (Jailer), Jack Montgomery (MacKay), Dick Dorrell (Jack Carson), Arthur Van Slyke (John Benton), Frank Ellis (McCone).

Muddled singing cowboy stuff, with Baker unjustly accused of attacking a wagon train, clearing his name, and bringing the real culprits to justice. Story changes direction a number of times, evidence of rewrites during the shooting, and there are so many songs that the whole thing just seems silly. This marked the screen debut of blonde singing star Constance Moore, whom reviewers of the time considered to have "future possibilities."

p, Paul Malvern; d, Joseph H. Lewis; w, Norton S. Parker (based on a story by Unie Hughes); ph, Harry Neumann.

Western (PR:A MPAA:NR)

BORDERLAND*1/2

(1937) 82m PAR bw

William Boyd (Hopalong Cassidy), James Ellison (Johnny Nelson), George Hayes (Windy), Stephen Morris [Morris Ankrum] (Loco), Charlene Wyatt (Molly Rand), Nora Lane (Grace Rand), Trevor Bardette (Col. Gonzales), Al Bridge (Dandy Morgan), George Chesebro (Tom Parker).

Hoppy goes undercover as an outlaw to bring to justice a gang prowling the border country. Morris is the lead baddie, diverting suspicion by pretending to be a halfwit. Hoppy seems to relish his villainous charade, which allows him to drink and be mean to children. At the time of its release, this fifth of the Hopalong movies ranked as the lengthiest western ever made. (See HOPALONG CASSIDY series, Index.)

p, Harry Sherman; d, Nate Wyatt; w, Harrison Jacobs (based on a story by Clarence E. Mulford); ph, Archie Stout; ed, Robert Warwick.

Western (PR:A MPAA:NR)

BORDERLINE**1/2

(1950) 88m UNIV bw

Fred MacMurray (Johnny Macklin), Claire Trevor (Madeleine Haley), Raymond Burr (Pete Richie), Roy Roberts (Harvey Gumbin), Jose Torvay (Miguel), Morris Ankrum (Whittaker), Charles Lane (Peterson), Don Diamond (Deusik), Nacho Galindo (Porfirio), Pepe Hern (Pablo), Richard Irving (Al).

Trevor is an L.A. cop going undercover to expose a Mexican dope ring. Disguised as a chorus girl she meets the gang chief, but a rival gang breaks in and carts off the drugs, along with Trevor. MacMurray is one of the rival gangsters, but, unknown to Trevor, he is really another undercover agent. The two fall for each other and make a run for the border, each reluctant to turn in the other. An exciting climax reveals their identities, and a shootout and fist fight subdue the gangsters, suave Raymond Burr among them. The script is occasionally confusing and director Seiter seems unsure whether to treat the material as comedy or drama.

p, Milton H. Bren, William A. Seiter; d, Seiter; w, Devery Freeman; ph, Lucien Andriot; m, Hans J. Salter; ed, Harry Keller.

Crime Cas. (PR:A MPAA:NR)

BORDERLINE***1/2

(1980) 97m ITC c

Charles Bronson (Jeb Maynard), Bruno Kirby (Jimmy Fante), Bert Remsen (Carl Richards), Michael Lerner (Henry Lydell), Kenneth McMillan (Malcolm Wallace), Ed Harris (Hotchkiss), Karmin Murcelo (Elena Morales), Enrique Castillo (Arturo), A. Wilford Brimley (Scooter Jackson), Enrique Castillo (Arturo), Norman Alden (Willie Lambert), James Victor (Mirandez), Panchito Gomez (Benito Morales), John Ashton (Charlie Monroe), Lawrence Casey (Andy Davis), Charles Cyphers (Ski), Katherine Pass (Mrs. Stine).

BORDERLINE predates the Nicholson/Keitel film on the same subject (THE BORDER) by two years but both films barely deliver enough. Bronson is a border patrolman battling a flesh smuggler (Harris) who runs Latinos across the dividing line for a large profit. The original film in this genre, BORDER INCIDENT, starring Ricardo Montalban and George Murphy, was better than both in execution and sincerity. Lots of night-shooting will make this a tough film to watch on TV in a semi-lit room, but it plays well in a theater. Bronson is his customary self, taciturn, crinkly-eyed, and heroic. Murcelo is the only female featured and thus stands out as a wetback who takes Bronson to the villain. Good programmer but not much.

p, James Nelson; d, Jerrold Freedman; w, Freedman, Steve Kline; ph, Tak Fujimoto (Eastmancolor); m, Gil Melle; ed, John Link.

Crime Drama Cas. (PR:C MPAA:PG)

BORDERTOWN***

(1935) 80m WB bw

Paul Muni (Johnny Ramierez), Bette Davis (Marie Roark), Margaret Lindsay (Dale El well), Eugene Pallette (Charlie Roark), Soledad Jiminez (Mrs. Ramirez), Robert Barrat (Padre), Gavin Gordon (Brook Mandillo), Henry O'Neill (Chase), Arthur Stone (Manuel Diego), Hobart Cavanaugh (Drunk), William B. Davidson (Dr. Carter), Oscar Apfel (Judge at Law School), Samuel S. Hinds (Judge at Trial), Edward McWade (Dean), Wallis Clark (Friend), John Eberts (Alberto), Chris-Pin Martin (Jose), Eddie Shubert (Marketman), Carlos Villar (Headwaiter), Marjorie North (Janet), Addie McPhail (Carter's Girl), Frank Puglia (Commissioner), Alphonse Ethier (Banker), Eddie Lee (Sam), Vivian Tobin (Woman), Arthur Treacher (Butler), Ralph Navarro (Defense Attorney).

That master of characterizations, Muni, is this time a swarthy Mexican lawyer whose lack of courtroom decorum and procedure, coupled with a volatile nature, gets him disbarred during his first case. He becomes a bouncer in a bordertown nightclub owned by Pallette. Davis is the portly owner's wife, who immediately begins to make a play for Muni, but he rebuffs her, pursuing Lindsay, a cultured woman from high society who loves slumming in the bordertown dives. (Lindsay calls the darkly-made-up Manuel "Savage.") In desperation, Davis thinks to free herself of Pallette so the discriminating Muni (he won't dally with a married woman) will feel proper in wooing her. Davis gets Pallette drunk, then leaves him sleeping it off in his car while locking the garage door so that carbon monoxide gas kills him. She then goes to Muni and tells him that she has done murder to be with him. Now he really doesn't want anything to do with her. Half crazy, Davis goes to the police to say that she and Muni killed Pallette. They are ar rested and are tried. But Davis becomes hysterical on the witness stand, her overwhelm ing guilt causing her to babble incoherently (it's one of Davis' most histrionic scenes). The court concludes that she's unbalanced but alone is guilty of the killing. Muni is released, inheriting the casino. When Lindsay drops by, he forces himself on her but she rejects him, running into the street, hopping into her roadster, and driving away at breakneck speed, crashing her car and killing herself. Thoroughly disillusioned, Muni sells the casino and gives the money to a school for underprivileged slum children as he had once been of their number. Other than the forced ending and Lindsay's absurd death, BORDERTOWN packs a stinging punch, chiefly because of Muni's frantic por trayal and Davis' extraordinary theatrics. (Muni lived with his Mexican chauffeur for weeks to perfect his speech patterns and gestures; Davis, of course, studied Davis.) The film was remade (at least in using the murder technique and motive) as THEY DRIVE BY NIGHT and BLOWING WILD. Gaudio's excellent photography greatly aided this improbable film.

p, Robert Lord; d, Archie Mayo; w, Laird Doyle, Wallace Smith (based on a novel by Carroll Graham, adapted by Lord); ph, Tony Gaudio; m, Bernard Haun; ed, Thomas Richards; art d, Jack Okey.

Crime Drama (PR:C MPAA:NR)

BORDERTOWN GUNFIGHTERS*1/2

(1943) 55m REP bw

Wild Bill Elliott (Himself), George "Gabby" Hayes (Gabby Whitaker), Anne Jeffreys (Anita Shelby), Ian Keith (Cameo Shelby), Harry Woods (Dave Strickland), Edward Earle (Daniel Forrester), Karl Hackett (Frank Holden), Roy Barcroft (Jack Gattling), Bud Geary (Buck Newcombe), Carl Sepulveda (Red Dailey).

Gang headed by devious gambler bilks Mexicans with a crooked lottery scheme, not to mention profiting from cattle swindles, stage holdups, and murder. Secret Service agent Wild Bill Elliot and sidekick Hayes bring them in. Run-of-the-mill B-western.

p, Eddy White; d, Howard Bretherton; w, Norman S. Hall; ph, Jack Marta; ed, Richard Van Enger.

Western Cas. (PR:A MPAA:NR)

BORIS GODUNOV***** (1959, USSR) 105m Mosfilm/Artkino c

A. Pirogov *(Boris Godunov)*, G. Nellep *(False Dmitri)*, A. Krivchenva *(Varlaam)*, I. Kozlovsky *(Fool)*, L. Avdeyeva *(Marina)*.

Emotional highs and lows come charging out of the screen in Stroyeva's disciplined adaptation of the slow-paced Moussorgsky opera. The story, such as it is, involves a conscience-stricken czar and a revolt against him by a false pretender, with the movement of the static plot accelerated brilliantly by the rich music and tangential scenes of pageantry, pomp, and spectacle that reach high art. Striking scenes include views of the Polish and Russian courts, crowds before the palace, and the coronation and mad scenes. The movie is a faithful recreation of the Moussorgsky-Pushkin stage work, with massive sets, rich costumes, and spectacular color shots, and the handling of crowds (both by the cameraman and the director) is eye-catching. Pirogov is a persuasive Boris, with a deep, stirring bass that conveys all the pathos and drama of his role, especially in a monolog about his guilt. Krivchenva is an imposing Varlaam, and also provides one of the high points in the film with her earthy drinking song in the inn. Nellep carries off both singing and acting roles as the false Dmitri convincingly, and Avdeyeva is an attractive Marina opposite him, with their duet in the garden of the Polish court another outstanding segment of the film. In a national history of triumphant shocks and shocking mistakes this film is a masterpiece.

d, V. Stroyeva; w, N. Golovanov, Stroyeva (based on Moussorgsky-Pushkin opera); ph, V. Nikolayev (Magicolor).

Opera **(PR:A MPAA:NR)**

BORN AGAIN 1/2** (1978) 110m AE c

Dean Jones *(Charles Colson)*, Anne Francis *(Patty Colson)*, Jay Robinson *(David Shapiro)*, Dana Andrews *(Tom Phillips)*, Raymond St. Jacques *(Jimmy Newsom)*, George Brent *(Judge Gerhard Gesell)*, Harold Hughes *(Senator Harold Hughes)*, Harry Spillman *(President Richard M. Nixon)*, Scott Walker *(Scanlon)*, Robert Gray *(Kramer)*, Arthur Roberts *(Al Quie)*, Ned Wilson *(Douglas Coe)*, Dean Brooks *(Dick Howard)*, Peter Jurasik *(Henry Kissinger)*, Christopher Conrad *(Chris Colson)*, Stuart Lee *(Wendell Colson)*. Alicia Fleer *(Emily Colson)*, Richard Caine *(H. R. Haldeman)*, Brigid O'Brien *(Holly Holm)*, Robert Broyles *(John Erlichman)*, Byron Morrow *(Archibald Cox)*, William Zuckert *(E. Howard Hunt)*, William Benedict *(Leon Jaworski)*.

They tried so hard to make this interesting. It's one more go-around on the Watergate participants. More money has been made by those involved with that heinous affair than anyone can imagine. ALL THE PRESIDENT'S MEN set the tone, then Liddy has his WILL done on TV, then Erlichman's thinly veiled story and on and on. In BORN AGAIN, Charles Colson (played by Dean Jones) realizes the error of his ways and is born again and his faith takes him through his prison term. In this sympathetic script, Colson emerges as an innocent who is woven into the devious fabric of Washington without actually doing anything terribly untoward. If Colson were as innocent as this movie purports him to be, he never would have been convicted, never would have gone to jail, never would have written the book, never would have a movie made of the book, and you wouldn't be sitting here reading this review because we never would have written it! So we all have to be thankful that Colson was a bad boy. Pretty good imitation of Nixon by Spillman, but when too many look-alikes get into a scene, it begins to resemble a late-night TV sketch.

p, Frank Capra, Jr.; d, Irving Rapper; w, Walter Block; ph, Harry Stradling, Jr. (Technicolor); m, Les Baxter; ed, Axel Hubert.

Drama **Cas.** **(PR:A MPAA:PG)**

BORN FOR GLORY 1/2**
(1935, Brit.) 70m GAU bw (GB: FOREVER ENGLAND; AKA: BROWN ON RESOLUTION)

Betty Balfour *(Elizabeth Brown)*, John Mills *(Albert Brown)*, Barry McKay *(Lt. Somerville)*, Jimmy Hanley *(Ginger)*, Howard Marion Crawford *(Max)*, H. G. Stoker *(Capt. Holt)*, Percy Walsh *(Kapitan von Lutz)*, George Merritt *(William Brown)*, Cyril Smith *(William Brown, Jr.)*.

Young English sailor Mills, bastard son of a Royal Navy officer, is captured by a German cruiser during WW I. Escaping from the ship, he steals a rifle and, hiding on the shore, begins sniping at the Germans. His sharpshooting delays the ship while they hunt him down and kill him, but the arrival of a British ship dooms the cruiser. Mills becomes a posthumous hero. The commander of the British ship discovers that the dead sailor was his unacknowledged son, and the British build a cross to him atop the bleak island. Reported to be a landmark in British seafaring films, the first of its kind to have the full cooperation of the Royal Navy, including ships and technical advisors.

p, Michael Balcon; d, Walter Forde; w, Michael Hogan, Gerard Fairlie, J. O. C. Orton (based on a novel by C. S. Forester); ph, Bernard Knowles; ed, Otto Ludwig.

War Drama **(PR:A MPAA:NR)**

BORN FREE*** (1966) 95m COL c

Virginia McKenna *(Joy Adamson)*, Bill Travers *(George Adamson)*, Geoffrey Keen *(Kendall)*, Peter Lukoye *(Nuru)*, Omar Chambati *(Makkede)*, Bill Godden *(Sam)*, Bryan Epson *(Baker)*, Robert Cheetham *(Ken)*, Robert Young *(James)*, Geoffrey Best *(Watson)*, Surya Patel *(Indian Doctor)*.

Heartwarming animal story in African locale. Shot in pseudo-documentary style, it tells the story of a Kenyan game warden and his wife (played by real-life married couple McKenna and Travers) who adopt the cubs of a slain lioness. One of the cubs, Elsa, is raised to adulthood and becomes a primary fixture in the couple's life. But soon they are faced with their inability to keep an enormous and dangerous (albeit domesticated) lion as a house pet. Rather than follow orders that Elsa be sent to a zoo, they set about teaching her the techniques of hunting and surviving in the wilderness. After a time the lion does return to life in the veldt, but in the final scene returns to her old home to show off her new-born cubs. A great success when released, the film won Academy Awards for score and the title song. The nature photography is excellent and, despite a few slips into maudlin sentimentality, the film maintains a fairly clear-eyed point of view. McKenna and Travers are very good, their real-life affection for each other transferring to the screen. The real Joy Adamson was later reported, ironically, to have been slain by a lion; investigation proved her death to be murder at the hands of a disgruntled ex-employee.

p, Sam Jaffe, Paul Radin; d, James Hill; w, Gerald L. C. Copley (based on books by Joy Adamson); ph, Kenneth Talbot (Technicolor); m, John Barry; ed, Don Deacon; animal supervisor, Peter Whitehead; technical adv, George Adamson; m/l, title song, Barry, Don Black.

Outdoors Drama **Cas.** **(PR:AAA MPAA:NR)**

BORN IN FLAMES 1/2** (1983) 80m First Run Features c

Honey *(Herself)*, Adele Bertei *(Isabel)*, Jeanne Satterfield *(Adelaide)*, Flo Kennedy *(Zella)*, Hillary Hurst, Sheila McLaughlin, Marty Pottenger *(Army Women)*, Pat Murphy, Kathryn Bigelow, Becky Johnston *(Editors)*, Ron Vawter, John Coplans *(FBI Agents)*, John Rudolph, Valerie Smaldone, Warner Schreiner *(Newscasters)* .

Set in a futuristic New York City after a revolution in the United States, another revolution begins among disenchanted party officials, the new women's army, and guerrillas. As in THE TERMINATOR, the new party underground developed following the death of its leader, Satterfield, who died in a detention cell after laying the groundwork for eliminating the new establishment. An explosion at the World Trade Center is outstanding for close-up images. This feminist film wins laurels for close attention to detail in a radical filmmaking effort.

p&d, Lizzie Borden; w, Hisa Tayo (based on a story by Borden); ph, Ed Bowes, Al Santana; m/l, The Bloods, Ibis, The Red Crayola.

Drama **(PR:O MPAA:NR)**

BORN LOSERS** (1967) 114m AIP bw

Tom Laughlin *(Billy Jack)*, Elizabeth James *(Vicky Barrington)*, Jane Russell *(Mrs. Shorn)*, Jeremy Slate *(Danny Carmody)*, William Wellman, Jr. *(Child)*, Robert Tessier *(Cue Ball)*, Jeff Cooper *(Gangrene)*, Edwin Cook *(Crabs)*, Tex *(Tex)*, Paul Prokop *(Speechless)*, Julie Cahn *(LuAnn Crawford)*, Susan Foster *(Linda Prang)*, Janice Miller *(Jodell Shorn)*, Stuart Lancaster *(Sheriff)*, Jack Starett *(Deputy)*, Paul Bruce *(District Attorney)*, Robert Cleaves *(Mr. Crawford)*, Ann Bellamy *(Mrs. Prang)*, Gordon Hobel *(Jerry Carmody)*.

Laughlin's "Billy Jack" character was introduced to movie audiences in this violent, shocking biker film, considered by some the best of the genre. When a gang of bikers invades a community, nobody will stand up to them. Law enforcement efforts are stymied because potential witnesses are frightened into silence. Only Laughlin, a half-breed, defies them, killing their leader before accidentally being slain by a deputy. Laughlin directed under his T. C. Frank pseudonym, and four years later his character was resurrected in the inane cult classic BILLY JACK, followed by two sequels.

p, Donald Henderson [Tom Laughlin], Delores Taylor; d, T. C. Frank [Tom Laughlin]; w, E. James Lloyd; ph, Gregory Sandor (Pathe Color); ed, John Wineld.

Crime **Cas.** **(PR:O MPAA:NR)**

BORN LUCKY* (1932, Brit.) 78m WEST/MGM bw

Talbot O'Farrell *(Turnips)*, Rene Ray *(Mops)*, John Longden *(Frank Dale)*, Ben Welden *(Harriman)*, Helen Ferrers *(Lady Chard)*, Barbara Gott *(Cook)*, Paddy Browne *(Patty)*, Roland Gillett *(John Chard)*, Glen Pointing.

Ray trades in her servant togs for a microphone when she shows off her voice. This changes her life and leads to stardom as a singer. Trite songfest in a draggy production.

p, Jerome Jackson; d, Michael Powell; w, Ralph Smart (based on the novel *Mops* by Oliver Sandys); ph, Geoffrey Faithfull.

Musical **(PR:A MPAA:NR)**

BORN RECKLESS 1/2** (1930) 73m FOX bw

Edmund Lowe *(Louis Beretti)*, Catherine Dale Owen *(Joan Sheldon)*, Lee Tracy *(Bill O'Brien)*, Marguerite Churchill *(Rosa Beretti)*, Warren Hymer *(Big Shot)*, William Harrigan *(Good News Brophy)*, Frank Albertson *(Frank Sheldon)*, Eddie Gribbon *(Bugs)*, Paul Page *(Ritzy Reilly)*, Ben Bard *(Joe Bergman)*, Mike Donlin *(Fingy Moscovitz)*, Paul Porcasi *(Pa Beretti)*, Joe Brown *(Needle Beer Grogan)*, Roy Stewart *(District Attorney Cardigan)*, Ferike Boros *(Ma Beretti)*, Pat Somerset *(The Duke)*, Jack Pennick, Ward Bond *(Soldiers)*, Yola D'Avril *(French Girl)*.

Suave gangster Lowe is apprehended for a robbery but he is offered a choice of either going to prison or to war to fight for his country; he opts for the military, goes off to war and becomes a hero. Upon returning, Lowe resumes his criminal career which bogs down when he falls in love with Owen, a high society lady. Hymer, in an act of reprisal against Lowe in their bootleg wars, kidnaps Owen's little girl, but Lowe goes to the rescue, retrieving the girl intact, killing Hymer. Although Lowe is not too convincing as an Italian gangster from NYC's "Little Italy," Ford's superb depiction of underworld settings and his fluid camera add greatly to this early gangster vehicle, a profile, based on the popular novel *Louis Beretti*, which shows underworld types in the fashion of the 1920s, a bit more civilized and conscious of the law than their brutal successors of the 1930s. (Remade loosely in 1937 with Brian Donlevy.)

d, John Ford; w, Dudley Nichols (based on the novel *Louis Beretti* by Donald Henderson Clarke); ph, George Schneiderman; ed, Frank E. Hull; art d, Jack Schulze.

Crime Drama **(PR:C MPAA:NR)**

BORN RECKLESS**   (1937) 60m FOX bw

Rochelle Hudson (Sybil Roberts), Brian Donlevy (Bob "Hurry" Kane), Barton MacLane (Jim Barnes), Robert Kent (Les Martin), Harry Carey (Dad Martin), Pauline Moore (Dorothy Collins), Chick Chandler (Windy Bowman), William Pawley (Mac), Francis McDonald (Louie), George Wolcott (Danny Horton), Joseph Crehan (District Attorney).

Donlevy is an auto racer who gets a job as a cabbie. The cab company is being pressured by racketeer MacLane, who is trying to take over all the taxi operations in the city. He frames anyone who stands in his way by planting stolen material in their cabs. His moll, Hudson, teams up with Donlevy to get the evidence to put him away. (Remake of John Ford's 1930 BORN RECKLESS.)

p, Sol M. Wurtzel; d, Mal St. Clair; w, John Patrick, Robert Ellis, Helen Logan (based on a story by Jack Andrews), ph, Daniel B. Clark; ed, Alex Troffey; md, Samuel Kaylin.

Crime Drama   (PR:A   MPAA:NR)

BORN RECKLESS*   (1959) 79m WB bw

Mamie Van Doren (Jackie), Jeff Richards (Kelly), Arthur Hunnicutt (Cool Man), Carol Ohmart (Liz), Tom Duggan (Wilson), Tex Williams (Himself), Donald Barry (Oakie), Nacho Galindo (Papa Gomez), Orlando Rodriguez (Manuel), Johnny Olenn and His Group.

A third-rate Marilyn Monroe clone, Van Doren, plays a rodeo star in love with aging rider Richards, who couldn't care less. The musical numbers aren't bad, but throughout her career Van Doren displayed a stunning lack of talent. Songs include "Song of the Rodeo" (Buddy Bregman, Stanley Styne); "Born Reckless," "A Little Longer," "Home Type Girl," "Separate The Men From The Boys," (Bregman); "Something to Dream About" (Charles Singleton, Larry Coleman); "You, Lovable You" (Johnny Olenn).

p, Aubrey Schenck; d, Howard W. Koch; w, Richard Landau (based on a story by Landau, Schenck); ph, Joseph F. Biroc; m, Buddy Bregman; ed, John F. Schreyer; art d, Jack T. Collis; cos, Marjorie O. Best.

Drama   (PR:A   MPAA:NR)

BORN THAT WAY*   (1937, Brit.) 64m Randall Faye bw

Elliott Mason (Aunt Emily), Kathleen Gibson (Pamela Gearing), Terence de Marney (Richard Gearing), Eliot Makeham (Prof. Gearing), Ian Colin (Hugh), Conway Palmer (Kenneth Danvers), John Laurie (McTavish).

Careless de Marney lets his Scottish wife's spinster sister take care of their children. Absent-mindedness runs rampant in comic bursts.

p&d, Randall Faye; w, V. C. Clinton-Baddeley, Diana Bourbon; ph, Geoffrey Faithfull.

Comedy   (PR:A   MPAA:NR)

BORN TO BE BAD*   (1934) 70m FOX/UA bw

Loretta Young (Letty Strong), Jackie Kelk (Mickey Strong), Cary Grant (Malcolm Trevor), Henry Travers (Fuzzy), Russell Hopton (Steve Karns), Andrew Tombes (Max Lieber), Howard Lang (Dr. Dropsy), Harry Green (Adolph), Marion Burns (Alice Trevor), Paul Harvey (Lawyer), Charles Coleman (Butler), Matt Briggs (Truant Officer), Geneva Mitchell (Miss Crawford), Eddie Kane (Headwaiter), George Irving, Mary Forbes, Edward Keane (Admirers at Club), Etienne Girardot (J. K. Brown), Guy Usher (Judge McAffee), Wade Boteler (Detective), John Marston (Doctor).

Unwed mother Young, constantly telling son Kelk to toughen up and take what you can in life, is horrified to learn one day that he has been hit by a truck. The horror, however, quickly dissipates when she learns that Kelk is alive and that the truck was being driven by millionaire Grant, who was simply trying to keep in touch with the transportation side of his dairy business. Greedy Young and her dishonest lawyer quickly plan a huge lawsuit, complete with faked doctors' reports, but when their plot is exposed, Young loses custody of the boy to the magnanimous Grant. Deciding that she can get her son back and a bit of Grant's fortune in one swift move, Young tries to seduce the adoptive father away from his devoted wife, Burns. Young succeeds in stirring Grant's passion and is about to expose his attraction, when Grant unsuspensefully informs his wife of the entire affair. When Burns saves Kelk from drowning in a swimming pool, Young becomes aware of the good nature of people and leaves her son with Grant, knowing that the boy will grow up to be a better person. Poorly scripted, manipulative attempt at social drama that fails to create any interest in the story or its people. Young tries to breathe some life into her unappealing character; Grant turns in one of his most uninspired performances.

d, Lowell Sherman; w, Ralph Graves; ph, Barney McGill; ed, Maurice Wright; md, Alfred Newman; art d, Richard Day, Joseph Wright.

Drama   (PR:A   MPAA:NR)

BORN TO BE BAD***1/2   (1950) 93m RKO bw

Joan Fontaine (Christabel), Robert Ryan (Nick), Zachary Scott (Curtis), Joan Leslie (Donna), Mel Ferrer (Gobby), Harold Vermilyea (John Caine), Virginia Farmer (Aunt Clara), Kathleen Howard (Mrs. Bolton), Dick Ryan (Arthur), Bess Flowers (Mrs. Worthington), Joy Hallward (Mrs. Porter), Hazel Boyne (Committee Woman), Irving Bacon (Jewelry Salesman), Gordon Oliver (Lawyer).

Heart-stealer Fontaine coaxes the wealthy Scott away from Leslie and plans to live off the businessman's riches while continuing her affair with moody novelist Ryan. When the proud Ryan refuses to play the witch's game and Scott discovers his "sweet" bride's true nature, Fontaine is left alone. She coldly brushes the dust of both men off her shoulders and moves on to other unsuspecting males. Commonplace story of a femme fatale is given an unorthodox treatment by gifted director Ray (REBEL WITHOUT A CAUSE, THE LUSTY MEN). Avoiding a cliche

punishment of retribution scene, Ray extinguished any hope for a typical Hollywood ending that would see such an evil woman wallowing in self-pity or dying as the credits roll. This characteristic is to be expected when dealing with the rebellious Ray and his work. Using artist Ferrer as an observer character during the film, Ray plays a bit too much with point-of-view and its relationship to conventional storytelling, creating a disassociated narrative that is hard to follow. However, Ray's interest in the psychological state of his protagonist and its relationship to visual style makes the film mesmerizing.

p, Robert Sparks; d, Nicholas Ray; w, Edith Sommer, Robert Soderberg, George Oppenheimer (based on the novel All Kneeling by Anne Parrish, adapted by Charles Schnee); ph, Nicholas Musuraca; ed, Frederic Knudson.

Drama   (PR:A   MPAA:NR)

BORN TO BE LOVED**   (1959) 82m UNIV bw

Carol Morris (Dorothy), Vera Vague (Mrs. Hoffman), Hugo Haas (Prof. Brauner), Dick Kallman (Eddie), Jacqueline Fontaine (Dame), Billie Bird (Drunk's Wife), Pat Goldin (Saxophone), Robert C. Foulk (Drunk), Mary Esther Denver (Woman), Margot Baker (Mother), Tony Jochim (Fred).

Miss Universe-1957 Morris plays a nearsighted seamstress and director Haas a music teacher in this low-budget romantic comedy. Haas encourages romance between Morris and one of his pupils, Kallman, while she encourages love to blossom between Haas and rich widow Vera Vague. A double wedding is the happy ending. Not very good in any objective sense, the picture is winning through sheer good-heartedness.

p,d&w, Hugo Haas; ph, Maury Gerstman; m, Franz Steininger; ed, Stefan Arnsten; cos, Rose Rockney; m/l, Steininger, Walter Bullock, Eddie Pola, Haas.

Comedy/Romance   (PR:A   MPAA:NR)

BORN TO BE WILD**   (1938) 66m REP bw

Ralph Byrd (Steve Hackett), Doris Weston (Mary Stevens), Ward Bond (Bill Purvis), Robert Emmett Keane (Davis), Bentley Hewlett (Wilson), Charles Williams (Spotter), Davison Clark (Stranger), Byron Foulger (Husband), George Anderson (Mayor), Edwin Stanley (Randolph), Ben Hendricks, Jr. (Deputy), Stelita (Manuela), Lew Kelly (Reilly), Harrison Greene (J. Carroll Malloy), George Magrill (Hank), Herbert Heywood (Stevens), Ann Demetrio (Cristobella), Stooge (Butch).

Byrd and Bond are truckers charged with delivering a shipment of dynamite to a distant town where it will be used to blow up a dam, an action that will foil a scheme by unscrupulous real estate brokers to steal the land below. A number of obstacles block the way and Byrd falls for Weston, but justice triumphs; the dam is destroyed, the ranchers are saved, and Byrd and Weston ride into the fadeout. Scripted by famed writer Nathanael West ("Miss Lonelyhearts," "The Day of the Locust"). West and his wife Eileen McKenney (whose early life was the basis for MY SISTER EILEEN, 1942, 1955) were killed in an automobile accident in 1940.

p, Harold Shumate; d, Joe Kane; w, Nathanael West; ph, Jack Marta; ed, William Morgan; md, Alberto Columbo; m/l, Jack Lawrence, Peter Tinturin, Eduardo Durant, Harold Peterson, Carlos Ruffino.

Adventure   (PR:A   MPAA:NR)

BORN TO DANCE***   (1936) 105m MGM bw

Eleanor Powell (Nora Paige), James Stewart (Ted Barker), Virginia Bruce (Lucy James), Una Merkel (Jenny Saks), Sid Silvers (Gunny Saks), Frances Langford (Peppy Turner), Raymond Walburn (Captain Dingby), Alan Dinehart (McKay), Buddy Ebsen (Mush Tracy), Juanita Quigley (Sally Saks), Georges and Jaina (Themselves), Reginald Gardiner (Policeman), Barrett Parker (Floorwalker).

Bare-bones script depicting the romance between high-spirited hoofer Powell and shy boy Stewart is merely used as a foundation for some outstanding song and dance work. Powell, in her first lead role, firmly established herself as one of the premier talents of the 1930s MGM musical. Although she is not remembered as well as Ginger Rogers, Powell's unpretentious charm combined with her dazzling tap work make her one of the most delightful musical personalities in film history. Ebsen is, as always, a simple pleasure, and Stewart does a fine job, although his crooning leaves a lot to be desired. He soon realized that the musical was not his forte. The Porter score is amazing.

p, Jack Cummings; d, Roy Del Ruth; w, Jack McGowan, Sid Silvers (based on a story by McGowan, Silvers, B. G. DeSylva); ph, Ray June; ed, Blanche Sewell; md, Alfred Newman; ch, Dave Gould; m/l, Cole Porter.

Musical/Comedy   (PR:A   MPAA:NR)

BORN TO FIGHT* 1/2   (1938) 64m Conn bw

Frankie Darro (Baby Face), Kane Richmond (Bomber), Jack LaRue (Smoothy), Frances Grant (Nan), Stella Manors (Ada), Monty Collins (Gloomy Gus), Eddie Phillips (Duffy), Snowflake (Snowflake), Philo McCullough (Goodall), Hal Price (Heckler), Donald Kerr (Broadcaster), Gino Corrado (Maitre de Hotel), Charles McMurphy (Cop), Bob Perry (Referee), Olin Francis (Hobo), Harry Harvey (Reporter).

Routine boxing film, with Richmond a trainer hiding from the crooked gambler he acci dentally hurt. He meets Darro, an up-and-coming contender, and manages him to a title.

d, Charles Hutchinson; w, Sascha Baranley (from a story by Peter B. Kyne); ph, Arthur Reed; ed, Richard G. Ray.

Drama   (PR:A   MPAA:NR)

BORN TO GAMBLE zero   (1935) 66m Liberty bw

Onslow Stevens (Ace Cartwright/Henry Mathews), H. B. Warner (Carter Mathews), Maxine Doyle (Cora Strickland), Eric Linden (Earl Mathews), Lois Wilson (Paula

Mathews), William Janney (*Fred Mathews*), Ben Alexander (*Paul Mathews*), Lucien Prival (*Al Shultz*).

Four brothers fight an inherited weakness for gambling. Three meet tragic fates, but Stevens, the youngest (who also plays an old-time gambler) beats the odds, avenging his brother's murder along the way. Weak, depressing melodrama.

p, M. H. Hoffman; d, Phil Rosen; w, E. Morton Hough (suggested by *The Greek Poropulos* by Edgar Wallace); ph, Gilbert Warrenton.

Drama **(PR:A MPAA:NR)**

BORN TO KILL**** (1947) 92m RKO bw (GB: LADY OF DECEIT)

Lawrence Tierney (*Sam*), Claire Trevor (*Helen*), Walter Slezak (*Arnett*), Phillip Terry (*Fred*), Audrey Long (*Georgia*), Elisha Cook, Jr. (*Marty*), Isabell Jewell (*Laury Palmer*), Esther Howard (*Mrs. Kraft*), Kathryn Card (*Grace*), Tony Barrett (*Danny*), Grandon Rhodes (*Inspector Wilson*).

Depressing, confusing *film noir* shows hot-headed Tierney committing a double murder in a fit of jealousy. The bodies are discovered by Trevor, who doesn't report them because she is leaving town. The two meet on a train bound for San Francisco and fall in love. Visiting her mansion, he learns she is engaged to be married, so he turns his attentions to her more available sister, Long. They get married, and then a detective turns up investigating the two murders. He is bought off by Cook, Tierney's friend, who Tierney then kills because he suspects him of having an affair with Trevor, whom he is still seeing on the side. Trevor convinces Tierney to shoot her sister, but he is stopped by the arrival of police. When he learns that Trevor sent for the police, he shoots her, and is gunned down by police.

p, Herman Schlom; d, Robert Wise; w, Eve Green, Richard Macaulay (based on novel *Deadlier Than The Male* by James Gunn); ph, Robert De Grasse; m, Paul Sawtell; ed, Les Millbrook; md, C. Bakaleinikoff.

Crime Drama **Cas.** **(PR:A MPAA:NR)**

BORN TO KILL**** (1975) 83m New World Pix c (AKA: COCKFIGHTER)

Warren Oates (*Frank Mansfield*), Richard B. Shull (*Omar Baradinsky*), Harry Dean Stanton (*Jack Burke*), Troy Donahue (*Randall Mansfield*), Millie Perkins (*Frances Mansfield*), Laurie Bird (*Dody White*).

BORN TO KILL, not to be confused with Robert Wise's BORN TO KILL (starring Lawrence Tierney), is a tight, fast-moving slice of death. The subject is cockfighting, not the average fare seen on ABC's "Wide World of Sports." Oates is a fanatic trainer of fighting cocks who has taken a vow of silence until one of his birds wins the championship. Thus, Oates' dialog is limited to voice-overs to indicate what he's thinking. A dull idea done in a dull fashion. BORN TO KILL had three titles prior to this one, WILD DRIFTERS, GAMBLIN' MAN, and COCKFIGHTER, and still no one seems to want to see the picture. Cockfighting may be big in the deep South, but making a film about it is like doing a picture about the game of Ring-a-lee-vio in the Northeast. Perkins (ANNE FRANK) makes a welcome return as the wife of Donahue. Both are good in their roles. Good photography by Almendros (Oscar for DAYS OF HEAVEN) and editing by Teague distinguish the picture beyond it's content. Hellman has done a handful of low-budget items, but he is better than the material he chooses.

p, Roger Corman, Sam Gellman; d, Monte Hellman; w, Charles Willeford (based on his novel *Cockfighter*); ph, Nestor Almendros (Metrocolor); m, Michael Franks; ed, Lewis Teague.

Drama **(PR:O MPAA:R)**

BORN TO LOVE**½ (1931) 79m RKO-Pathe bw

Constance Bennett (*Doris Kendall*), Joel McCrea (*Barry Craig*), Paul Cavanagh (*Sir Wilfred Drake*), Frederick Kerr (*Lord Ponsonby*), Anthony Bushell (*Leslie Darrow*), Louise Closser Hale (*Lady Agatha Ponsonby*), Mary Forbes (*Duchess*), Elizabeth Forrester (*Evelyn Kent*), Edmund Breon (*Tom Kent*), Reginald Sharland (*Foppish Gentleman*), Daisy Belmore (*Tibbetts*), Martha Mattox (*Head Nurse*), Fred Esmelton (*Butler*), Eddy Chandler (*Capt. Peters*), Robert Greig (*Hansom Cabby*), Billy Bevan (*Departing British Soldier*), Bill Elliott (*Extra at Hotel Desk*).

In WW I London, American nurse Bennett and fighter pilot McCrea meet and fall in love. Soon the pair take up housekeeping and conceive a child. Then one day McCrea doesn't return from a mission and shortly thereafter Bennett gives birth. After a time she accepts a proposal of marriage from disabled British officer Cavanagh, but then McCrea reappears and Bennett rushes to her true love. Cavanagh sues for divorce and wins custody of the child, who promptly dies. Bennett finds solace in McCrea's arms. Maudlin tearjerker designed for female audience.

d, Paul L. Stein; w, Ernest Pascal; ph, John Mescall; ed, Claude Berkeley.

Drama **(PR:A MPAA:NR)**

BORN TO SING* (1942) 82m MGM bw

Virginia Weidler (*Patsy Eastman*), Ray McDonald (*Steve*), Leo Gorcey ("*Snap*" *Collins*), "Rags" Ragland (*Grunt*), Douglas McPhail (*Murray Saunders*), Sheldon Leonard (*Pete Detroit*), Henry O'Neill (*Frank Eastman*), Larry Nunn (*Mike Conroy*), Margaret Dumont (*Mrs. E. V. Lawson*), Beverly Hudson (*Maggie Cooper*), Richard Hall (*Mozart Cooper*), Darla Hood (*Quiz Kid*), Joe Yule (*Ed Collera*).

Thin musical about a composer, despondent over the theft of his latest musical comedy effort, who is saved from suicide by three youngsters. Along with the composer's daughter, they manage to stage the production, and with the help of a forceful cabbie, steal the audience from a rival composer. Weak, stupid story is just an excuse to stage the number "Ballad for Americans," (Earl Robinson, John Latouche) the rights to which MGM bought with the intent of constructing a picture around it. Directed by Berkeley, the number looks completely overblown and out of place here. Other songs include "I Hate The Conga" (Earl Brent), "Alone," "You

Are My Lucky Star" (Arthur Freed, Nacio Herb Brown); "I Love Ya" (Brent, Lenny Hayton).

p, Frederick Stephani; d, Edward Ludwig; w, Harry Clork, Franz G. Spencer (based on a story by Spencer); ph, Sidney Wagner; ed, Robert J. Kern; md, David Snell, Lennie Hayton; ch, Sammy Lee.

Musical **(PR:A MPAA:NR)**

BORN TO SPEED*½ (1947) 61m PRC bw

Johnny Sands (*Johnny Randall*), Terry Austin (*Toni Bradley*), Don Castle (*Mike Conroy*), Frank Orth (*Breezy Bradley*), Geraldine Wall (*Mrs. Randall*), Joe Haworth (*Duke Hudkins*).

Midget auto racing is the backdrop to this familiar tale. Sands is the son of a driver who died in a fiery crash. With the help of old-time mechanic Orth he rebuilds his father's car and defeats his rival both in the big race and for the affections of Orth's daughter, Austin. Trite story, though race sequences are well done.

p, Marvin D. Stahl; d, Edward L. Cahn; w, Crane Wilbur, Scott Darling, Robert B. Churchill (based on the story "Hell On Wheels" by Churchill); ph, Jackson Rose; m, Albert Levin; ed, W. Donn Hayes; md, Irving Friedman.

Drama **(PR:A MPAA:NR)**

BORN TO THE SADDLE*½ (1953) 73m Astor c

Chuck Courtney, Donald Woods, Leif Erickson, Karen Morley, Rand Brooks, Glenn Strange, Dolores Priest, Bob Anderson, Lucille Thompson, Fred Kohler, Jr., Dan White, Milton Kibbee, Boyd Davis.

Young horse trainer goes to work training race horses for the man who may have been responsible for the death of his father. A muddled mudder.

p, Hall Shelton; d, William Beaudine; w, Adele Buffington (based on the story "Quarter Horse" by Gordon Young).

Western **(PR:A MPAA:NR)**

BORN TO THE WEST**½ (1937) 52m PAR bw (AKA: HELL TOWN)

John Wayne (*Rudd*), Marsha Hunt (*Nellie*), Johnny Mack Brown (*Fillmore*), John Patterson (*Hardy*), Monte Blue (*Hammond*), Sid Saylor (*Hooley*), Lucien Littlefield (*Buyer*), Nick Lukats (*Fallon*), James Craig (*Brady*), Johnny Boyle (*Sam*), Jack Kennedy (*Sheriff*), Lee Prather (*Stranger*), Alan Ladd (*Inspector*), Jack Daley (*Gambler*), Vester Pegg (*Bartender*).

Brown is a respected rancher courting Hunt. When his black-sheep cousin Wayne drifts in, Brown gives him a job as trail boss, and Wayne thanks him by stealing Hunt. On the drive, rustlers try to steal the herd but Wayne outwits them. Then in town, the rustlers try to cheat Wayne out of money with a rigged deck, but Brown exposes them and the pair, now reconciled, shoot it out with the villains. This film was a remake of a 1926 silent. Alan Ladd had a small role, well before his starring exposure in THIS GUN FOR HIRE (1942). The film was later reissued, with added outdoor footage, to take advantage of the growing popularity of both Wayne and Ladd.

d, Charles Barton; w, Stuart Anthony, Robert Yost (based on a story by Zane Grey); ph, J. D. Jennings; ed, John Link.

Western **(PR:A MPAA:NR)**

BORN TO WIN**½ (1971) 90m UA c

George Segal (*Jay Jay*), Karen Black (*Parm*), Jay Fletcher (*Billy Dynamite*), Hector Elizondo (*The Geek*), Marcia Jean Kurtz (*Marlene*), Irving Selbst (*Stanley*), Robert De Niro (*Danny*), Paula Prentiss (*Veronica*), Sylvia Syms (*Cashier*).

George Segal is very good in this black comedy about heroin addiction. An ex-hairdresser, he turns to crime to support a $100-a-day habit, gets arrested, and is released to work as an informant. Script is full of inconsistencies and the humor is strictly of the New York Nebbish school, but well worth checking out. The first American film by Czech director Passer.

p, Philip Langner; d, Ivan Passer; w, David Scott Milton; ph, Jack Priestly, Richard Kratina; m, William S. Fisher; ed, Ralph Rosenbaum; art d, Murray Stern; cos, Albert Wolsky.

Comedy **(PR:C MPAA:R)**

BORN WILD* (1968) 100m AIP c

Tom Nardini (*Tony*), Patty McCormack (*Janet*), David Macklin (*Bruce*), Zooey Hall (*Paco*), Joanna Frank (*Raquel*), Russ Bender (*Simms*), Arthur Petersen (*The Principal*), Keith Taylor (*Din-Din*), Sammy Vaughn, The American Revolution.

Any garbled idea that lends itself to loud music and violence is good enough for the youth trade, this film seems to say. Take a Mexican-American student strike for equality, stuff it with mayhem and steamy talk, and you have BORN WILD another shallow commentary on the time. Nardini is the strike leader seeking a peaceful solution while his vicious opposite number, Macklin, provokes bloody beatings, a rape, gang fights, and finally a visually interesting but pointless battle in an airplane junkyard. This so-called social study gets a "D" for dumb.

p&d, Maury Dexter; w, James Gordon White.

Drama **(PR:C MPAA:NR)**

BORN YESTERDAY******** (1951) 103m COL bw

Judy Holliday (*Billie Dawn*), Broderick Crawford (*Harry Brock*), William Holden (*Paul Verrall*), Howard St. John (*Jim Devery*), Frank Otto (*Eddie*), Larry Oliver (*Norval Hedges*), Barbara Brown (*Mrs. Hedges*), Grandon Rhodes (*Sanborn*), Claire Carleton (*Helen*), Smoki Whitfield (*Bootblack*), Helyn Eby Rock (*Manicurist*),

William Mays (Bellboy), David Pardoll (Barber), Mike Mahoney (Elevator Operator), John Morley (Native), Charles Cane (Policeman).

The whole show in this sprightly Broadway comedy (Kanin's play ran 1,642 nights on the Great White Way) is the most wonderful "dumb blonde" to ever grace the screen, Holliday, in a role she originally created on stage and almost didn't get to play on screen. She is the malaprop-tossing mistress of junk tycoon Crawford, who uses her ignorance for his own ends, having her sign countless papers that put her in charge of his empire and also allow him to shirk the responsibilities for his own shady wheelings and dealings. In Washington, to lobby for his special interests and buy available Congressmen, Crawford is ashamed to travel through the city's high society circles with his illiterate paramour (not that he's a paragon of culture, just managing to side-step his own gutter talk). He hires Holden, a professorial type who agrees to tutor the good-natured mistress, but secretly plans to write a series of articles exposing Crawford's slippery operations. The process of changing the tasteless Holliday into a woman of some enlightenment and intellectual bearing—she does have a street savvy mind to begin with—is loaded with laughs and sexual innuendoes that are not offensive. During this academic metamorphosis, not unlike the transformation of Liza Doolittle in PYGMALION, both Holliday and Holden fall in love and, by the time the blustering brute Crawford catches on and tries to prevent the union, he is the dumfounded loser, put adroitly in his place by the ex-chorus girl turned scholar. Crawford is perfect as the bullying tycoon (as was Paul Douglas in the stage version), rendering a performance that would frighten Attila the Hun, while Holden is subtly effective in playing his low-key role. But it is Holliday who is the film, a role she so welded to herself that she was, unfortunately, typecast as a dumb blonde in almost every subsequent film. But then she did create the part on Broadway, something Hollywood producers chose to ignore as they looked everywhere to replace her in the film version. After four years they gave up and accepted her. (Who else could duplicate that shrill squeak and noisy whine, while smiling broadly and blinking those enormous eyes in mock innocence?) Holliday's priceless characterization earned her an Oscar, a real feat in that she won against two giants, Gloria Swanson in SUNSET BOULEVARD and Bette Davis in ALL ABOUT EVE. A sheer delight, even if one only remembers the classic gin rummy scene where Holliday drives Crawford to the brink of madness, beating him royally while appearing to have nothing on her mind but millions of totally unused brain cells.

p, S. Sylvan Simon; d, George Cukor; w, Albert Mannheimer (based on the play by Garson Kanin); ph, Joseph Walker; m, Frederick Hollander; ed, Charles Nelson; md, Morris Stoloff; cos, Jean Louis.

Comedy   Cas.   (PR:A   MPAA:NR)

BORROW A MILLION*   (1934, Brit.) 50m FOX bw

Reginald Gardiner (Alastair Cartwright), Vera Bogetti (Adele Cartwright), Charles Cullum (Michael Trent), Wally Patch (Bodgers), Meriel Forbes (Eileen Dacres), Robert Rendel (Struthers), Roland Culver (Charles Nutford), Wilson Coleman (Blake), Gordon McLeod (Bowers), Dania Barrigo.

A poor man's dream comes to the screen. Here, the owner of a tea shop is befriended by a millionaire who backs him in a business venture. The befriended proprietor eventually winds up as owner of the restaurant chain.

d, Reginald Denham; w, Margaret McDonnell.

Comedy   (PR:A   MPAA:NR)

BORROWED CLOTHES*   (1934, Brit.) 70m Maude/COL bw

Anne Grey (Lady Mary Torrent), Lester Matthews (Sir Harry Torrent), Sunday Wilshin (Lottie Forrest), Joe Hayman (Herman Jacob), Renee Macready (Diana Arbuthnot), P. G. Clark (Donald MacDonald), Philip Strange (Clarence Ponsonby), Antony Holles (Gilbert Pinkley), Elizabeth Inglis (Barbara), Constance Shotter (Babette).

Grey plays an extravagant English lady who accidentally buys a failing fashion shop. With such a stable in hand, high couturier taste abounds in an agreeable farce.

d, Arthur Maude; w, Aimee and Philip Stuart (based on their play "Her Shop").

Comedy   (PR:A   MPAA:NR)

BORROWED HERO*1/2   (1941) 65m MON bw

Alan Baxter (Roger Andrews), Florence Rice (Ann Thompson), John Hamilton (William Brooks), Stanley Andrews (Mr. Taylor), Constance Worth (Mona Brooks), Wilma Francis (Carol Turner), Mary Gordon (Mrs. Riley), Richard Terry (Dixie Nelson), Jerry Marlowe (Johnny Gray), Paul Everton (Judge), John Maxwell (Editor), Guy Usher (District Attorney).

Uninspired programmer in which prosecutor Baxter cracks a mob hiding behind a reform group front. Hamilton is the villain and Rice the hard boiled newspaper reporter/love interest.

p, A. W. Hackel; d, Lewis Collins; w, Earle Snell (based on a story by Ben Roberts and Sidney Sheldon); ph, Marcel Le Picard; ed, Martin G. Cohn.

Crime   (PR:A   MPAA:NR)

BORROWED TROUBLE*1/2   (1948) 61m UA bw

William Boyd (Hopalong Cassidy), Andy Clyde (California Carlson), Rand Brooks (Lucky Jenkins), Elaine Riley (Mrs. Garvin), John Kellogg (Lee Garvin), Helen Chapman (Teacher).

Teacher Chapman opposes the saloon being built next to her schoolhouse, but until she is kidnaped by the saloon owner Hoppy can do little. Once stirred into action, though, he rescues the schoolmarm and forces the saloonkeepers to move elsewhere. Slow-paced Boyd vehicle. (See HOPALONG CASSIDY series, Index)

p, Lewis J. Rachmil; d, George Archainbaud; w, Charles Belden; ph, Mack Stengler; ed, Fred W. Berger; md, Darril Calker.

Western   (PR:A   MPAA:NR)

BORROWED WIVES*   (1930) 62m Tiffany bw

Rex Lease (Peter Foley), Vera Reynolds (Alice Blake), Nita Martan (Julia), Paul Hurst (Bull Morgan), Robert Randall (Joe Blair), Charles Sellon (Uncle Henry), Dorothea Wolbert (Aunt Mary), Sam Hardy (Parker), Harry Todd (Winstead), Tom London (Cop), Eddie Chandler (Sergeant).

Muddled failure about a young man who has to find a wife in order to collect an inheritance from his rich uncle. Early talkie suffers from sound problems but Hurst, as a screwball motorcycle cop, is memorable.

d, Frank Strayer; w, Scott Darling; ph, Andre Barlatier; ed, Bryon Robinson; set d, Ralph De Lacy.

Comedy   (PR:A   MPAA:NR)

BORROWING TROUBLE*   (1937) 59m FOX bw

Jed Prouty (John Jones), Shirley Deane (Bonnie Jones), Spring Byington (Mrs. John) Jones), Russell Gleason (Herbert Thompson), Kenneth Howell (Jack Jones), George Ernest (Roger Jones), June Carlson (Lucy Jones), Florence Roberts (Granny Jones), Billy Mahan (Bobby Jones), Marvin Stephens (Tommy McGuire), Andrew Tombes (Uncle George), Howard Hickman (Judge Walters), Cy Kendall (Chief Kelly), Joseph Downing (Charlie), George Walcott (Lester McGuire), Dick Wessel (Joe), Wade Boteler (Sgt. Callahan).

Seventh entry in the Jones Family series. This time they take in a juvenile delinquent (Stephens) in hopes a loving, family environment will rehabilitate him. Then their drugstore is robbed and the evidence points to Stephens. But his brother confesses to the crime and domestic bliss returns. (See JONES FAMILY series, Index.)

p, Max Golden; d, Frank R. Strayer; w, Robert Chapin, Karen DeWolf (based on characters created by Katherine Kavanaugh); ph, Edward Snyder; ed, Hanson Fritch; md, Samuel Kaylin.

Comedy   (PR:A   MPAA:NR)

BORSALINO**   (1970, Fr.) 123m PAR c

Jean-Paul Belmondo (Capella), Alain Delon (Siffredi), Michel Bouquet (Rinaldi), Catherine Rouvel (Lola), Francoise Christophe (Madame Escarguel), Corinne Marchand (Madame Rinaldi), Julien Guimoar (Boccace), Arnoldo Foa (Marello), Nicole Calfan (Ginette), Laura Adani (Siffredi's Mother), Christian de Tiliere (Dancer), Mario David (Mario), Daniel Ivernel (Police Superintendent), Dennis Berry (Nono), Andre Bollet (Poli), Helene Remy (Lidia), Odette Piquet (Singer), Lionel Vitrant (Fernand), Jean Aron (Accountant), Pierre Koulak (Spada).

Charming seriocomic movie about gang warfare in 1930s Marseilles. Delon is the ruthless brains and Belmondo the easygoing partner. Together they kill their way to the top. Belmondo is murdered when he tries to get out, leaving Delon to star in sequel BORSALINO AND CO. Catchy score by Claude Bolling.

p, Alain Delon; d, Jacques Deray; w, Jean Cau, Claude Sautet, Deray, Jean-Claude Carriere (based on The Bandits of Marseilles by Eugene Saccomano); ph, Jean Jacques Tarbes (Eastmancolor); m, Claude Bolling; ed, Paul Cayatte; art d, Francois De Lamothe; cos, Jacques Fonterey.

Crime   (PR:O   MPAA:NR)

BORSALINO AND CO.*1/2   (1974, Fr.) 110m CIC c

Alain Delon (Roch), Catherine Rouvel (Lola), Ricardo Cusiolla (Volpone), Reinhardt Kolidehoff (Sam), Daniel Ivernel (Inspector).

Sequel to BORSALINO opens with gangster Delon attending the funeral of his partner. He goes after the killers but winds up locked in an asylum. Escaping, he returns to wipe out his enemies in a number of bloody ways, the rival boss meeting his end by being shoved into a locomotive boiler. Not as good as the original, but still pretty interesting.

p, Alain Delon; d, Jacques Deray; w, Pascal Jardin, Deray; ph, Jean-Jacques Tarbes (Eastmancolor); m, Claude Bolling; ed, Henri Lanoe.

Crime   (PR:O   MPAA:NR)

BOSS, THE**   (1956) 88m UA bw

John Payne (Matt Brady), William Bishop (Bob Herrick), Gloria McGhee (Lorry Reed), Doe Avedon (Elsie Reynolds), Roy Roberts (Tim Brady), Rhys Williams (Stanley Millard), Robin Morse (Johnny Mazia), Gil Lamb (Henry), Joe Flynn (Ernie Jackson), Bill Phipps (Stitch), Bob Morgan (Hamhead), Alex Frazer (Roy Millard), John Mansfield (Lazetti), George Lynn (Tom Masterson), Harry Cheshire (Governor Beck).

The rise and fall of a powerful political boss and the corroding influence of the mob on government are brutally portrayed in this honest, hard-hitting drama which sees perennial B-rated actor Payne in one of his finest portrayals. Soldier Payne, made hard and ambitious by battle, returns from WW I to the "middle-class" city where his brother is boss. He gets drunk and stands up his girl friend, who then gives him the thumb. To get even, he grabs a stranger in a bar and convinces her to marry him. When the boss finds out about the misalliance they fight and the brother dies of a heart attack. Payne then takes over as boss. The machine he builds is more powerful than the brother's, and soon with the help of wartime buddy lawyer Bishop, he virtually controls the state. His arrogance and brutal methods bring on calls for reform which lead nowhere until his ties with the mob in the rackets bring on his downfall and he is jailed for income tax evasion. In this role Payne, who had adjusted to the hardening of his boyish facial features by switching to western and action pictures in the 1950s, registers most impressively in the later parts when he begins to age. As boss, he gets admirable assistance from Bishop, who finally is responsible for his conviction. McGhee wins raves as the wife he marries while drunk, and Avedon is good in her brief appearance as the angry fiancee.

p, Frank N. Seltzer; d, Byron Haskin; w, Ben L. Perry; ph, Hal Mohr; m, Albert Glasser; ed, Ralph Dawson.

Drama (PR:A MPAA:NR)

BOSS NIGGER*1/2 (1974) 87m Boss/Dimension c

Fred Williamson (*Boss Nigger*), D'Urville Martin (*Amos*), R. G. Armstrong (*Mayor*), William Smith (*Jed*), Carmen Hayworth (*Clara Mae*), Barbara Leigh (*Miss Pruitt*).

Black exploitation western with Williamson and partner Martin as a pair of bounty hunters terrorizing the town where their quarry is hiding. Violent but with touches of humor.

p, Fred Williamson, Jack Arnold; d, Arnold; w, Williamson; ph, Bob Caramico (Todd-AO 35).

Western (PR:C MPAA:PG)

BOSS OF BIG TOWN** (1943) 65m PRC bw

John Litel (*Michael Lynn*), Florence Rice (*Linda Gregory*), H. B. Warner (*Jeffrey Moore*), Jean Brooks (*Iris Moore*), John Miljan (*Craig*), David Bacon (*Dr. Gil Page*), Mary Gordon (*Mrs. Lane*), Frank Ferguson (*Bram Hart*), John Maxwell (*Foster*), Paul Duboy (*Graham*), Lloyd Ingraham (*Inspector Torrence*), Patricia Prest (*Francis Hart*).

Mobsters headed by Warner are trying to muscle into the milk business, but Litel, as a city market official, breaks up the ring. Average crime programmer.

p, Jack Schwarz; d, Arthur Dreifuss; w, Edward Dein (based on a story by Arthur Hoerl); ph, Marcel le Picard; m, Leo Erdody; ed, Charles Henkel, Jr.

Crime (PR:A MPAA:NR)

BOSS OF BULLION CITY*1/2 (1941) 61m UNIV bw

Johnny Mack Brown (*Tom Bryant*), Fuzzy Knight (*Burt*), Nell O'Day (*Martha*), Maria Montez (*Linda Calhoun*), Earle Hodgins (*Mike Calhoun*), Harry Woods (*Sheriff*), Melvin Lang (*Steve*), Dick Alexander (*Tug*), Karl Hackett (*Tug*), George Humbert (*Mario*), Frank Ellis (*Deputy*), Kermit Maynard, Tex Terry, Bill Nestell (*Cowboys*), Bob Kortman, Michael Vallon, The Guadalajara Trio.

It's a race to see who can get whom first when a tricky sheriff is exposed by Brown and his nit-witted stooge. Western shows Brown at his straight-shooting best.

p, Harry Sherman; d, Ray Taylor; w, Arthur St. Claire, Victor McLeod (based on a story by St. Claire).

Crime (PR:A MPAA:NR)

BOSS OF HANGTOWN MESA*1/2 (1942) 58m UNIV bw

Johnny Mack Brown (*Steve Collins*), Fuzzy Knight (*Dr. J. Wellington Dingle*), William Farnum (*Judge Ezra Binns*), Rex Lease (*Bert Lawler*), Helen Deverell (*Betty Wilkins*), Hugh Prosser (*Utah Kid*), Robert Barron (*Flash Hollister*), Michael Vallon (*Clint Rayner*), Henry Hall (*John Wilkins*), Fred Kohler, Jr. (*Clem*), The Pals of the Golden West with Nora Lou Martin.

Fewer fist fights than usual for Brown in this story of the struggle to complete a telegraph line. Deverell tries to get the line through after her uncle is murdered by heavies Farnum and Prosser. Knight sings "Pappy Was a Gun Man" and "Ain't Got Nothin'" and The Pals and Martin warble "Trail Dreamin'" and "Song of the Prairie."

p, Oliver Drake; d, Joseph H. Lewis; w, Drake; ph, Charles Van Enger; ed, Maurice Wright; m/l, Drake, Jimmy Wakely, Milton Rosen.

Western (PR:A MPAA:NR)

BOSS OF LONELY VALLEY* (1937) 60m UNIV bw

Buck Jones (*Steve Hanson*), Muriel Evans (*Retta Lowrey*), Harvey Clark (*Jim Lynch*), Walter Miller (*Jake Wagner*), Lee Phelps (*Peter Starr*), Ted Adams (*Slim*), Silver (*Silver*).

Bad Buck Jones offering. Miller and Phelps are the villains, forging papers to pick up the estates of dead folks. When they try this ploy to steal the ranch of Jones' girl friend, Buck takes a hand. Badly directed and incoherently scripted.

p, Buck Jones; d, Ray Taylor; w, Frances Guihan (based on a novel by Forrest Brown); ph, Allen Thompson, John Hickson.

Western (PR:A MPAA:NR)

BOSS OF THE RAWHIDE*1/2 (1944) 57m PRC bw

Dave "Tex" O'Brien (*Tex Wyatt*), Jim Newill (*Jim Steele*), Guy Wilkerson (*Panhandle Perkins*), Nell O'Day (*Mary Colby*), Edward Cassidy (*Henry Colby*), Jack Ingram (*Sam Barrett*), Billy Bletcher (*Jed Jones*), Charles King, Jr. (*Frank Hade*), George Chesebro (*Joe Gordon*), Robert Hill (*Capt. Wyatt*), Dan White (*Minstrel*), Lucille Vance (*Mrs. Periwinkle*).

Singing Texas Rangers O'Brien, Newill, and Wilkerson track down a gang that's killing off ranchers then buying their land from the grieving widows. Average. Songs include "High in the Saddle," "Ride On Vaquero," "I Ain't Got a Gal to Come Home To." (See TEXAS RANGERS series, Index.)

p, Alfred Stern; d&w, Elmer Clifton; ph, Robert Cline; ed, Charles Henkel, Jr.; md, Lee Zahler; m/l, Jim Newill, Dave O'Brien, Oliver Drake, Herbert Myers.

Western (PR:A MPAA:NR)

BOSS RIDER OF GUN CREEK* (1936) 60m UNIV bw

Buck Jones (*Lary Day/ Gary Elliott*), Harvey Clark (*Pop Greer*), Muriel Evans (*Starr Landerson*), Tom Chatterton (*Sheriff Blaine*), Josef Swickard (*Lafe Turner*), Lee Phelps (*Sheriff Marsden*), Ernest Hilliard (*Ed Randall*), Mahlon Hamilton (*Red Vale*), Alphonse Ethier (*Dr. Northrup*).

Jones is convicted of murder, but it's actually his double, whom Jones impersonates in order to clear his name. Confusing, below average B-western.

p, Buck Jones; d, Lesley Selander; w, Frances Guihan (based on a story by E.B. Mann); ph, Allen Thompson, Herbert Kirkpatrick.

Western (PR:A MPAA:NR)

BOSS'S SON, THE**1/2 (1978) 101m New American Cinema c

Asher Brauner (*Bobby*), Rudy Solari (*Joseph*), Rita Moreno (*Esther*), Henry G. Sanders (*Charles*), James Darren (*Buddy*), Richie Havens (*Albert*), Michelle Davison (*Cleo*), Gammy Burdett (*Bea*).

Keep an eye on writer/director Bobby Roth. He is a comer who will be one of the more important filmmakers soon enough. In THE BOSS'S SON, he gives evidence of his talent with a highly personal film that is probably very close to his own story. Brauner is a young man whose father owns a carpet company. Moreno is a Jewish mother nipping at the Johnny Walker and at her husband, Solari, would like the lad to go into Dad's business. Brauner would rather he lived a different life. He takes up with Sanders, a black truck driver for the firm, and they become best of friends until Brauner discovers that Sanders is part of a robbery scheme. The story is secondary to the emotions in this picture and it is clearly marked by a singular lack of selfindulgence, a trait often rampant in young directors.

p, Jeffrey White; d&w, Bobby Roth; ph, Alfonso Beato (Metrocolor); m, Richard Markowitz; ed, John Carnochan.

Comedy Cas. (PR:A MPAA:NR)

BOSTON BLACKIE AND THE LAW**1/2 (1946) 69m COL bw (GB: BLACKIE AND THE LAW)

Chester Morris (*Boston Blackie*), Trudy Marshall (*Irene*), Constance Dowling (*Dinah Moran*), Richard Lane (*Inspector Farraday*), George E. Stone (*The Runt*), Frank Sully (*Sgt. Matthews*), Warren Ashe (*Lampau Jani*), Selmer Jackson (*Warden Lund*), Fred Graff (*Clerk*), Ted Hecht (*Harry Burton*), Edward Dunn (*Peterson*), Ed Fetherston (*Reporter*), Frank O'Connor (*Cab Driver*), Brian O'Hara (*Cop*).

Series entry with Morris the crook-turned-sleuth. This time a woman convict takes advantage of Morris' magic show to escape and seek vengeance on her former partner, who let her take the fall for a crime they committed. She and the ex-partner are both murdered and Morris figures out whodunit. Fairly entertaining. (See BOSTON BLACKIE series, Index.)

p, Ted Richmond; d, D. Ross Lederman; w, Harry J. Essex; ph, George B. Meehan, Jr.; ed, James Sweeny; md, Mischa Bakaleinikoff; art d, Charles Clague.

Crime (PR:A MPAA:NR)

BOSTON BLACKIE BOOKED ON SUSPICION** (1945) 66m COL bw (GB: BLACKIE BOOKED ON SUSPICION)

Chester Morris (*Boston Blackie*), Lynn Merrick (*Gloria Mannard*), Richard Lane (*Inspector Farraday*), Frank Sully (*Sgt. Matthews*), Steve Cochran (*Jack Higgins*), George E. Stone (*The Runt*), Lloyd Corrigan (*Arthur Manleder*), George Carleton (*Wilfred Kittredge*), George Meader (*Porter Hadley*), Douglas Wood (*Alexander Harmon*), George Lloyd (*Diz*), Robert Williams (*Officer Lee*), Joseph Palma (*Policeman*), Dan Stowell (*Paisley*), Jessie Arnold (*Housekeeper*).

Posing as an auctioneer to help a friend, Morris accidentally sells a fake Charles Dickens first edition. Murder ensues and our hero is the prime suspect. Unfriendly Merrick doesn't help matters but adds interest to the caper. (See BOSTON BLACKIE series, Index.)

p, Michel Kraike; d, Arthur Dreifuss; w, Paul Yawitz (based on the novel by Malcom Stuart Boylan); ph, George B. Meehan, Jr; ed, Richard Fantl; art d, Perry Smith.

Crime (PR:A MPAA:NR)

BOSTON BLACKIE GOES HOLLYWOOD** (1942) 68m COL bw (GB: BALCKIE GOES TO HOLLYWOOD)

Chester Morris (*Boston Blackie*), George E. Stone (*Runt*), Richard Lane (*Inspector Farraday*), Forrest Tucker (*Whipper*), William Wright (*Slick Barton*), Lloyd Corrigan (*Arthur Manleder*), John Tyrrell (*Steve*), Walter Sande (*Sgt. Mathews*), Constance Worth (*Gloria Lane*), Shirley Patterson (*Stewardess*), Ralph Dunn (*Sergeant*), Charles Sullivan (*Cab Driver No. 3*), Al Herman (*Cab Driver No. 4*), Jessie Arnold (*Tenant*), Cy Ring (*Hotel Manager*).

Morris is mistaken for a safecracker by police who think he is stealing from a friend. Actually, the friend has asked him to take $60,000 from a safe and bring it to California immediately. When police catch wind of the plan, they go with him in hopes of discovering the location of the lost Monterey Diamond. Good whodunit. (See BOSTON BLACKIE series, Index.)

p, Wallace MacDonald; d, Michael Gordon; w, Paul Yawitz; ph, Henry Freulich; md, Morris Stoloff; ed, Arthur Seid.

Crime (PR:A MPAA:NR)

BOSTON BLACKIE'S CHINESE VENTURE** (1949) 59m COL bw

Chester Morris (*Boston Blackie*), Maylia (*Mei Ling*), Richard Lane (*Inspector Farraday*), Don McGuire (*Bus Guide*), Joan Woodbury (*Red*), Sid Tomack (*Runt*), Frank Sully (*Sgt. Matthews*), Charles Arnt (*Pop Gerard*), Luis Van Rooten (*Bill Craddock*), Philip Ahn (*Wong*), Peter Brocco (*Rolfe*), Benson Fong (*Ah Hing*), Edgar Dearing (*Reiber*), Fred Sears (*Chemist*), Pat O'Malley (*Jim*), George Lloyd (*Bartender*).

Chinatown caper has Morris and Tomack looking like homicidal maniacs when they are seen leaving a Chinese laundry where the proprietor is later found dead. Our breezy heroes solve the mystery when they catch the real murderer in a surprise ending. Plenty of action. (See BOSTON BLACKIE series, Index.)

p, Rudolph C. Flothow; d, Seymour Friedman; w, Maurice Tombragel (based on characters created by Jack Boyle); ph, Vincent Farrar; ed, Richard Fantl; art d, Paul Palmentola; md, Mischa Bakaleinikoff.

Crime (PR:A MPAA:NR)

BOSTON BLACKIE'S RENDEZVOUS**1/2

(1945) 64m COL bw (GB: BLACKIE'S RENDEZVOUS)

Chester Morris (Boston Blackie), Nina Foch (Sally Brown), Steve Cochran (James Cook), Richard Lane (Inspector Farraday), George E. Stone (The Runt), Frank Sully (Mathews), Iris Adrian (Martha), Harry Hayden (Arthur Manleder), Adelle Roberts (Patricia Powers), Joe Devlin (Steve Caveroni), Dan Stowell (Hotel Clerk), Phil Van Zandt (Dr. Fagle), Marilyn Johnson (Chambermaid), Robert Williams (First Cop), John Tyrrell (Second Cop), Joseph Palma (Third Cop), Dick Alexander (Second Bruiser).

A crazed killer (Cochran) escapes the asylum and goes on a strangling spree impersonating Morris, who deals with the threat in his usual suave manner. Pretty good, especially Cochran, who specialized in heels, lunatics, gangsters, and no-goodnik roles. (See BOSTON BLACKIE series, Index.)

p, Alexis Thurn-Taxis; d, Arthur Dreifuss; w, Edward Dein (based on a story by Fred Schiller), ph, George B. Meehan Jr.; ed, Aaron Stell; md, Mischa Bakaleinikoff; art d, Perry Smith.

Crime (PR:A MPAA:NR)

THE BOSTON STRANGLER, THE***

(1968) 116m FOX c

Tony Curtis (Albert DeSalvo), Henry Fonda (John S. Bottomly), George Kennedy (Phil DiNatale), Mike Kellin (Julian Soshnick), Hurd Hatfield (Terence Huntley), Murray Hamilton (Frank McAfee), Jeff Corey (John Asgeirsson), Sally Kellerman (Dianne Cluny), William Marshall (Edward W. Brooke), George Voskovec (Peter Hurkos), Leora Dana (Mary Bottomly), Carolyn Conwell (Irmgard DeSalvo), Jeanne Cooper (Cloe), Austin Willis (Dr. Nagy), Lara Lindsay (Bobbie Eden), George Furth (Lyonel Brumley), Richard X. Slattery (Ed Willis), William Hickey (Eugene T. Rourke), Eve Collyer (Ellen Ridgeway), Gwyda Donhowe (Alice Oakville), Alex Dreier (News Commentator), John Cameron Swayze (TV Commentator), Shelley Burton (David Parker), Elizabeth Baur (Harriet Fordin), Dana Elcar (Louis Schubert), James Brolin (Sgt. Lisi), George Ryne (Dr. Kramer).

The filmic approach to the maniac who murdered 13 women in the Boston area between 1962 and 1964 was anything but lurid. The producers and director Fleischer took the clinical way of looking at these mass killings, which was probably best; it was the only way rational viewers could accept such real-life horror. The film opens with several killings of elderly women, all seemingly related. Fonda, criminologist from the academy, is asked to head the investigative task force searching for the killer and he reluctantly accepts, later stating that the murders fascinate him, "they sucked me in." His work and that of his aides is painfully precise and even tedious as they follow up every minute clue and interview a host of psychopaths and sexual deviates (all of the women have been sexually attacked before, during, and after the killings). When the investigation bogs down, Fonda, in desperation, calls in pyschic Peter Hurkos (Voskovec) who puts on a dynamic and colorful show of "seeing" the killer, but he fails to pinpoint the right man. Then the film cuts away to focus upon the apparently quiet life of blue-collar worker Albert DeSalvo (Tony Curtis in an alarmingly well played, often terrifying performance). He is shown to quietly enjoy his meager life, his wife (Conwell) and small children. But he is next shown lying to lonely women, pretending to be a plumber sent to check the sinks, convincing them to let him inside their apartments, where he attacks and murders them. The last victim is Kellerman, whom he ties to a bed and rapes. She frees herself and bites him so hard she draws blood before he knocks her unconscious and flees. She survives to describe the assailant. Even while half the Boston police force is looking for him, the compulsion seizes Curtis and he tries again, this time breaking into an apartment where the husband is home. He flees, the husband in hot pursuit, and in a wild race down the streets Curtis slips and is hit by a car. Taken into custody, Curtis' mind snaps and authorities refuse to try him, committing him to an insane asylum. Fonda questions him, but is uncertain whether he is the strangler, even though Kellerman identifies him and the bite marks match those on his hand. Then Curtis attacks his wife when she comes to visit him and this convinces Fonda and his aides (but not everyone; experts still argue today that DeSalvo, stabbed to death on November 26, 1973 in Walpole State Prison, was not the killer and the real strangler was never apprehended). An unnerving film that chips away at the sensibilities, effectively shot in a semi-documentary style, but a movie that refuses to pander to the perverse.

p, Robert Fryer; d, Richard Fleischer; w, Edward Anhalt (based on the book by Gerold Frank), ph, Richard H. Kline (Panavision, DeLuxe Color); m, Lionel Newman; ed, Marion Rothman; art d, Jack Martin Smith, Richard Day; set d, Walter M. Scott, Stuart A. Reiss, Raphael Bretton; cos, Travilla; split screen image, Fred Harpman; spec eff, L. B. Abbott, Art Cruickshank, John C. Caldwell.

Crime Drama **Cas.** (PR:O MPAA:NR)

BOTANY BAY**1/2

(1953) 93m PAR c

Alan Ladd (Hugh Tallant), James Mason (Capt. Gilbert), Patricia Medina (Sally Munroe), Sir Cedric Hardwicke (Gov. Phillips), Murray Matheson (Rev. Thynne), Dorothy Patten (Mrs. Nellie Garth), John Hardy (Nat Garth), Hugh Pryse (Ned Inching), Malcolm Lee Beggs (Nick Sabb), Anita Bolster (Moll Cudlip), Jonathan Harris (Oakley), Alec Harford (Jenkins), Noel Drayton (3rd Mate Spencer), Brendan Toomey (Guard), Ben Wright (lst Mate Green).

Ladd, an American medical student studying in England during the 1780s, is swindled out of his tuition money by an unscrupulous accountant. When he tries to get the money back, he's accused of robbery and sentenced to join a group of prisoners sailing to a work colony in New South Wales, part of the recently acquired

land of Australia. Mason, the evil captain of the prison ship, takes an immediate dislike to the proud, hot-headed Ladd, and the hatred builds when Mason discovers that lovely Medina has fallen for Ladd and not him. The angry captain is informed of a pardon that had been granted to Ladd, but refuses to turn the ship around for just one man. Ladd tries to escape, but is captured and sadistically punished by Mason. Upon arrival in Australia, Ladd is greeted with open arms by the colony's governor, Hardwicke, who is in desperate need of a doctor for the colony's sick. Mason, however, insists that Ladd be taken back to mother England and tried for mutiny. Ladd again plots an escape and Mason's attempt to capture the fugitive doctor is interrupted by a group of frightened Aborigines who kill Mason in a misunderstanding. Ladd is granted a full pardon and chooses to remain in the colony with Medina at his side, finally overcoming his hesitancy about her morals. Ladd's final film for Paramount is a rather typical period adventure film in which the star can't seem to wait for the cameras to stop rolling. Medina is appealing in her minor role, but Mason steals the film with his powerful portrayal of the ruthless captain. A forceful presence that can still maintain a certain vulnerability, Mason, and his approach to acting, makes others appear pale in comparison.

p, Joseph Sistrom; d, John Farrow; w, Jonathan Latimer (based on the novel by Charles Nordhoff and James Norman Hall); ph, John F. Seitz (Technicolor); m, Franz Waxman; ed, Alma Macrorie.

Adventure (PR:C MPAA:NR)

BOTH ENDS OF THE CANDLE

1965 (SEE: HELEN MORGAN STORY, THE, 1957)

BOTH SIDES OF THE LAW*

(1953, Brit.) 94m LIP/RANK bw (GB: STREET CORNER)

Anne Crawford (Susan), Peggy Cummins (Bridget Foster), Rosamund John (Sgt. Pauline Ramsey), Terence Morgan (Ray), Barbara Murray (WPC Lucy), Ronald Howard (David Evans), Eleanor Summerfield (Edna), Michael Medwin (Chick Farrar), Sarah Lawson (Joyce), Charles Victor (Muller), Dora Bryan (Daughter of Joy), Eunice Grayson (Janet), Yvonne Marsh (Elsa), Michael Hordern (Inspector Heron), Lloyd Lamble (Sgt. Weston), John Warwick (Inspector Gray), Joyce Carey (Miss Hopkins), Maurice Denham (Mr. Dawson), Thora Hird (Mrs. Perkins), Marjorie Rhodes (Mrs. Foster), Anthony Oliver (Stanley Foster), David Horne (Judge), John Stuart (Magistrate).

Semi-documentary drama takes a long look at the roles and attitudes of police-women on the London force. The film is unexpectedly packed with adventure and provides glimpses of London life tourists seldom see. Crawford, John, and Murray are excellent as the lady cops, and the crooks equal their performances, Summerfield as a deserter-bigamist (an AWOL WAC), Cummins as the compulsive shoplifter, and Morgan as her sneak-thief boy friend.

p, Sydney Box, William MacQuitty; d, Muriel Box; w, Muriel and Sydney Box (based on a story by Jan Read).

Drama (PR:A MPAA:NR)

BOTTOM OF THE BOTTLE, THE ***

(1956) 88m FOX c (GB: BEYOND THE RIVER)

Van Johnson (Donald Martin), Joseph Cotten (P.M.), Ruth Roman (Nora Martin), Jack Carson (Hal Breckinridge), Margaret Hayes (Lil Breckinridge), Bruce Bennett (Brand), Brad Dexter (Stanley Miller), Peggy Knudsen (Ellen Miller), Jim Davis (George Cady), Margaret Lindsay (Hannah Cady), Nancy Gates (Mildred), Gonzales-Gonzales (Luis Romero), John Lee (Jenkins), Shawn Smith (Woman), Ted Griffin (Rancher), Ernestine Barrier (Lucy Grant), Walter Woolf King (Grant), Sandy Descher (Girl), Kim Charney (Boy).

Johnson, an escaped convict with a weakness for alcohol, turns to his well-known lawyer brother Cotten for assistance in his attempt to cross the border into Mexico. Fearing a lack of respect from his well-to-do neighbors, Cotten passes Johnson off as an old acquaintance, not a brother. Disheartened by his brother's reluctance to accept him, Johnson turns to drink and tries to make it on his own. After some prodding from his bored and frustrated wife, Roman, Cotten pushes his position aside and helps his brother. Entertaining story of pride and family honor from veteran director Hathaway. The pedestrian thematics are overshadowed by a pair of fine performances from Cotten and Johnson, who make the brothers' conflicts and love quite real.

p, Buddy Adler; d, Henry Hathaway; w, Sidney Boehm (based on a novel by Georges Simeon); ph, Lee Garmes (CinemaScope, DeLuxe Color); m, Leigh Harline; ed, David Bretherton.

Drama (PR:A MPAA:NR)

BOTTOMS UP***

(1934) 85m FOX bw

Spencer Tracy (Smoothie King), John Boles (Hal Reede), Pat Paterson (Wanda Gale), Herbert Mundin (Limey Brock), Sid Silvers (Spud Mosco), Harry Green (Louis Wolf), Thelma Todd (Judith Marlowe), Robert Emmett O'Connor (Detective Rooney), Del Henderson (Lane Worthing), Suzanne Kaaren (Secretary), Douglas Baldwin (Baldwin).

Tough, somewhat dishonest, but kind-hearted actors' agent Tracy convinces a film studio that Mundin and Paterson are a famous English lord and his daughter, anxious to get into American pictures. In reality, the two Britons are simple entertainers, but Tracy's plan works and the two become relatively successful. When Paterson strikes up a romance with box-office heart-throb Boles, Mundin, Tracy, and their crony Silvers all get fairly lucrative offers from the studio and decide that Paterson's qualities of innocence and honesty are the most beneficial qualities of all. Well-meaning musical comedy that is filled with charming, humorous moments. Intended as a vehicle in which to introduce English star Paterson to American audiences, the film mainly succeeds in strengthening Tracy's image as a calm, confident, engaging screen actor. Songs include "Waitin' at the Gate for Katie" (Richard A. Whiting, Gus Kahn); "Turn On the Moon," "Little Did I Dream," "I'm Throwin' My Love Away" (Burton Lane, Harold Adamson).

p, B. G. DeSylva; d, David Butler; w, DeSylva, Butler, Sid Silvers; ph, Arthur Miller; ed, Irene Marra; md, C. Bakaleinikoff; art d, Gordon Wiles; ch, H. Hecht; cos, Russell Patterson.

Musical Comedy   **(PR:A MPAA:NR)**

BOTTOMS UP*   (1960, Brit.) 89m Associated-British bw

Jimmy Edwards (*Prof. Jim Edwards*), Arthur Howard (*Oliver Pettigrew*), Martita Hunt (*Lady Gore-Willoughby*), Sydney Tafler (*Sid Biggs*), Raymond Huntley (*Garrick Jones*), Reginald Beckwith (*Bishop Wendover*), Vanda Hudson (*Matron*), Melvyn Hayes (*Cecil Biggs*), John Mitchell (*Wendover*), Donald Hewlett (*Hamley*), Richard Briers (*Colbourne*), Paul Castaldini (*Prince Hamid*), George Pastell (*Swarthy Man*), George Selway (*lst Man*), Richard Shaw (*2nd Man*), John Stuart (*Police Officer*).

Inane slapstick comedy set in an English boarding school. Headmaster Edwards fights to contain a student revolt, while his bookie's son pretends to be an enrolling Middle Eastern prince. Forced humor from a slapdash script and direction.

p&d, Mario Zampi; w, Michael Pertwee, Frank Muir, Denis Norden; ph, Gilbert Taylor; m, Stanley Black; ed, Richard Best.

Comedy   **(PR:A MPAA:NR)**

BOUDOIR DIPLOMAT*   (1930) 65m UNIV bw

Betty Compson (*Helene*), Ian Keith (*Baron Valmi*), Mary Duncan (*Mona*), Jeanette Loff (*Greta*), Lawrence Grant (*Ambassador*), Lionel Belmore (*War Minister*), Andre Beranger (*Potz*).

Precode sex comedy set in a mythical middle-European kingdom has little to recommend it except some flashes of silk underwear. Baron Keith seduces his way to a powerful post.

d, Malcolm St. Clair; w, Benjamin Glazer, Tom Reed (based on the play "Command to Love" by Rudolph Lothar and Fritz Gottwald); ph, Karl Freund; ed, Maurice Pivar.

Drama   **(PR:C MPAA:NR)**

BOUDU SAVED FROM DROWNING*1/2
(1967, Fr.) 84m Pathe Contemporary bw (AKA: BOUDU DAUVE DES EAUX)

Michel Simon (*Boudu*), Charles Grandval (*Monsieur Lastingois*), Marcella Hainia (*Madama Lastingois*), Severine Lerczynska (*Anne-Marie*), Jean Daste (*Student*), Max Dalban (*Godin*), Jean Gehret (*Vigour*), Jacques Becker (*Poet on Bench*), Jane Pierson (*Rose, Neighbor's Maid*), George Darnoux (*Marriage Guest*).

Wonderful early comedy from Renoir (made in 1932 but lost, then finally released in 1967 in the U.S.). It's a satire on middle-class morality and a major influence on the French new wave and Truffaut in particular. Simon is a protohippy tramp about to commit suicide in grief over the loss of his dog. He is saved by Gradval, who takes him home to try to start him on the road to a productive life. There he turns the place into a shambles, seduces the wife (Hainia), and when he strikes it rich in the lottery, marries the golddigging maid (Lerczynska). At the last minute, he reasserts his independence and chucks the whole thing in favor of his carefree life as a tramp. Not to be missed. Remade in 1986 as DOWN AND OUT IN BEVERLY HILLS. (In French; English subtitles).

p, Michel Simon, Jean Gehret; d, Jean Renoir; w, Renoir (based on a play by Rene Fauchois); ph, Jean-Paul Alphen; m, Leo Daniderff, Johann Strauss; ed, Marguerite Renoir; set d, Jean Castanier, Laurent.

Comedy   **(PR:C MPAA:NR)**

BOUGHT*1/2   (1931) 83m WB bw

Constance Bennett (*Stephany Dale*), Ben Lyon (*Nicky Amory*), Richard Bennett (*Dave Meyer*), Dorothy Peterson (*Mrs. Dale*), Ray Milland (*Charles Carter*), Doris Lloyd (*Mrs. Barry*), Maude Eburne (*Mrs. Chauncy*), Mae Madison (*Natalie Ransome*), Clara Blandick (*Miss Sprigg*), Arthur Stuart Hull (*Carter, Sr.*), Edward J. Nugent (*Jimmy Graham*), Paul Porcasi (*Rapello*).

Constance Bennett is a young girl trying to break into high society. She abandons her struggling writer boy friend, loses her virginity to the drunkard scion of a wealthy family (Milland), and returns to Lyon, her lesson learned. Bennett made a lot of these "women's pictures," none of them very interesting today.

d, Archie Mayo; w, Charles Kenyon, Raymond Griffith (based on the novel *Jackdaw's Strut* by Harriet Henry); ph, Ray June; ed, George Marks.

Drama   **(PR:A-C MPAA:NR)**

BOULDER DAM**   (1936) 70m WB bw

Ross Alexander (*Rusty Noonan*), Patricia Ellis (*Ann Vangarick*), Lyle Talbot (*Lacy*), Eddie Acuff (*Ed Harper*), Henry O'Neill (*Agnew*), Egon Brecher (*Pa Vangarick*), Eleanor Wessel Hoeft (*Ma Vangarick*), Joseph Crehan (*Ross*), Olin Howland (*Sheriff*), William Pawley (*Wilson*), Ronnie Cosby (*Peter Vangarick*), George Breakston (*Stan Vangarick*).

Alexander is on the run after accidentally killing his boss in Detroit. He drifts west and winds up as a laborer working on the title project. Through hard work and heroic deeds he rises to foreman, then with the support of his employers returns to Detroit to clear his name. Exciting in spots, but mostly as stimulating as watching poured concrete dry.

d, Frank McDonald; w, Sy Bartlett (story by Dan M. Templin); ph, Arthur Todd; ed, Tommy Richards.

Drama   **(PR:A MPAA:NR)**

BOULEVARD NIGHTS**1/2   (1979) 102m WB c

Richard Yniguez (*Raymond Avila*), Chuco Avila (*Danny De La Paz*), Marta Du Bois (*Shady Landeros*), James Victor (*Gil Moreno*), Betty Carvalho (*Mrs. Avila*), Carmen Zapata (*Mrs. Landeros*), Gary Cervantes (*Big Happy*), Victor Millan (*Mr. Landeros*), Roberto Covarrubias (*Toby*), Garret Pearson (*Ernie*), Jerado Carmona (*Wolf*), Jesse Aragon (*Casper*).

BOULEVARD NIGHTS is as close as anyone has gotten to the truth about East Los Angeles gang life, but still miles away from the reality, as voiced by several gang members who saw this film. Actually shot in the barrio, BOULEVARD NIGHTS uses a largely Latino cast and the absence of star faces makes this feel all the more believable. The story is what you might expect; sensitive young man, problems with gang violence, low rider cars, lots of idiotic Cheech and Chong "mans," earnest emotions, etc. It doesn't happen because all the good intentions in the world do not a good picture make.

p, Bill Benenson; d, Michael Pressman; ph, John Bailey; m, Lalo Schifrin; ed, Richard Halsey; prod d, Jackson DeGovia.

Drama   **(PR:O MPAA:NR)**

BOUND FOR GLORY**1/2   (1976) 147m UA c

David Carradine (*Woody Guthrie*), Ronny Cox (*Ozark Bule*), Melinda Dillon (*Mary Guthrie*), Gail Strickland (*Pauline*), John Lehne (*Locke*), Ji-Tu Cumbuka (*Slim Snedeger*), Randy Quaid (*Luther Johnson*), Elizabeth Macey (*Liz Johnson*), Allan Miller (*Agent*).

A moving, brilliantly photographed picture that portrays the legendary Woody Guthrie's eccentric ways in a Depression trip across an America that once was, and will never be again. Carradine is perfection as the penniless Guthrie who comes to California on a train and is then stopped at the border because too many Okies have already arrived and the state is having difficulty taking care of all the mouths to feed. Carradine sneaks across the border, meets Quaid, and they team up to look for work. Cox is an Ozark folk-singer who visits the labor camps from time to time to bring some enjoyment into these poor men's lives. At one of the meetings, Carradine joins in and sings. Cox is so impressed he gets Carradine a job on the radio. Success is almost immediate but Guthrie's social conscience gets the better of him and he begins using the radio as his personal pulpit for the travails of the farm workers he knows so intimately. He is told to cut out the politicking or get fired. He gets fired. Then he's offered the chance to play the big time at Hollywood's Coconut Grove . . . if he'll commercialize his work. Not Carradine. He takes off on the road, hoping to bring the message of his music to the many along the way. This is much more than a biography. Guthrie is shown, warts and all, and the fact that easily half the audience is too young to know who he was should not matter. It's the story of a man with principles, something in short supply these days. At 147minutes, this could lose a quarter of an hour or more with no loss to the drama. Haskell Wexler proves again that he is a master as he uses the camera to its best advantage in every frame.

p, Robert F. Blumofe, Harold Leventhal; d, Hal Ashby; w, Robert Getchell (based on autobiography of Woody Guthrie); ph, Haskell Wexler (DeLuxe Color); md, Leonard Rosenman; ed, Robert Jones, Pembroke J. Herring.

Biography   **(PR:A-C MPAA:PG)**

BOUNTIFUL SUMMER**   (1951, USSR) 80m Artkino/Kiev Film Studio c

N. Kryuchkov (*Nazar Protesenko*), N. Arkhipova (*Vera Groshko*), M. Kuznetsov (*Peter Sereda*), M. Bebutova (*Oksana Podpruzhenko*), V. Dobrovolsky (*Ruban*), K. Sorokin (*Tesluyk*), M. Krepkogorskaya (*Darka*), E. Maximov (*Kolodochka*).

Joyfully collectivized Russian peasants strive to see who can raise the most livestock and grain while singing folk songs. Lots of shots of waving wheatfields and grazing cattle. A strange propaganda film pretending to be a folk musical.

d, Boris Barnet; w, E. Pomeshnikov, N. Dalesky; ph, A. Mishurin (Magicolor); m, E. Zhukovsky.

Musical   **(PR:A MPAA:NR)**

BOUNTY HUNTER, THE**1/2   (1954) 79m WB c

Randolph Scott (*Jim Kipp*), Dolores Dorn (*Julie Spencer*), Marie Windsor (*Alice*), Howard Petrie (*Sheriff Brand*), Harry Antrim (*Dr. Spencer*), Robert Keys (*George Williams*), Ernest Borgnine (*Rachin*), Dub Taylor (*Danvers*), Tyler MacDuff (*Vance*), Archie Twitchell (*Harrison*), Paul Picerni (*Jud*), Phil Chambers (*Ed*), Mary Lou Holloway (*Mrs. Ed.*).

Scott is hired to track down train robbers Petrie, Windsor, and Taylor, who have taken up respectable positions in a small town. Pretty good action and a plausible story make this one above average.

p, Sam Bischoff; d, Andre De Toth; w, Winston Miller (based on a story by Miller and Finlay McDermid); ph, Edwin DuPar (Warner Color); m, David Buttolph; ed, Clarence Kolster.

Western   **(PR:A MPAA:NR)**

BOUNTY HUNTERS, THE**   (1970, Ital.) 106m P.E.A. Cinematografica c

Yul Brynner, Dean Reed, Pedro Sanchez, Gerard Herter, Sal Borgese, Franco Fantasia.

OK spaghetti western in which Brynner sets out to steal the gold bullion of an Austrian general in Mexico. He is double-crossed by Herter, who pays the price.

p, Alberto Grimaldi; d, Frank Kramer [Gianfranco Parolini]; w, Renato Izzo, Parolini; ph, Sandro Maniori (CinemaScope).

Western   **(PR:A-C MPAA:NR)**

BOUNTY KILLER, THE*** (1965) 93m Embassy/Premiere c

Dan Duryea *(Willie Duggan)*, Rod Cameron *(Johnny Liam)*, Audrey Dalton *(Carole)*, Richard Arlen *(Ridgeway)*, Buster Crabbe *(Mike Clayman)*, Fuzzy Knight *(Luther)*, Johnny Mack Brown *(Sheriff Green)*, Peter Duryea *(Youth)*, Bob Steele *(Red)*, Eddie Quillan *(Pianist)*, Norman Willis *(Hank Willis)*, Edmund Cobb *(Townsman)*, Duane Amont *(Ben Liam)*, Grady Sutton *(Minister)*, Emory Parnell *(Sam)*, Daniel J. White *(Marshal Davis)*, I. Stanford Jolley *(Sheriff Jones)*, John Reach *(Jeb)*, Red Morgan *(Seddon)*, Dolores Domasin *(Waitress)*, Dudley Ross *(Indian)*, Ronn Delanor *(Joe)*, Tom Kennedy *(Waiter)*.

Interesting, offbeat western brings a number of old time series stars out of retirement. When mild-mannered Duryea accidentally wipes out an outlaw gang he becomes a bounty hunter, but when his sidekick Knight is killed he turns into a drunken murderer. Finally he is killed by a youngster out to make a name for himself. Depressing but well worth watching.

p, Alex Gordon; d, Spencer G. Bennet; w, W. R. Alexander, Leo Gordon; ph, Frederick E. West (Techniscope, Technicolor); m, Ronald Stein; ed, Ronald Sinclair.

Western **(PR:A-C MPAA:NR)**

BOWERY, THE**** (1933) 92m FOX bw

Wallace Beery *(Chuck Connors)*, George Raft *(Steve Brodie)*, Jackie Cooper *(Swipes McGurk)*, Fay Wray *(Lucy Calhoun)*, Pert Kelton *(Trixie Odbray)*, George Walsh *(John L. Sullivan)*, Oscar Apfel *(Mr. Herman)*, Harold Huber *(Slick)*, Fletcher Norton *(Googy Cochran)*, John Kelly *(Lumpy Hogan)*, Lillian Harmer *(Carry Nation)*, Ferdinand Munier *(Honest Mike)*, Herman Bing *(Mr. Rummel)*, Tammany Young *(Himself)*, Esther Muir *(The Tart)*, John Bleifer *(Mumbo the Mute)*, Pueblo Jim Flynn, Al McCoy, Joe Glick, Phil Bloom, Joe Jerrick, Jack Herrick, Sailor Vincent, Kid Broad *(Pugs)*, Bobby Dunn *(Cockeyed Violinist)*, Heinie Conklin *(Drunk/Fight Spectator)*, Irving Bacon *(Hick with Tailors)*, Andrew Tombes *(Shill)*, Kit Guard *(Arsonist/ Henchman)*, Pat Harmon, Harry Tenbrook, Frank Mills *(Firemen)*, John Ince *(Crony)*, Hal Price *(Editor)*, Frank Moran *(Bettor)*, Lester Dorr *(Cynic)*, Harry Semels *(Artist)*, Charles McAvoy *(Waiter)*, James Burke *(Recruiting Sergeant)*, James Conlin *(Enlistee)*, Phil Tead *(Tout)*, Harvey Parry *(Raft's Double)*, Charles Middleton *(Detective)*, Fred Kelsey *(Detective Kelsey)*, Charles Lane *(Doctor)*.

Here's a rousing, frantic film with brass knuckles on it. THE BOWERY is the actionjammed story of two friendly enemies, Raft and Beery. Big man Beery owns a glittering saloon in the Bowery and takes care of kid Cooper on the side (Beery and Cooper almost do a reprise of their magnificent THE CHAMP) while Raft is the dapper and legendary Steve Brodie, the daredevil who reportedly jumped off the Brooklyn Bridge to make a name for himself. The two men are in constant competition, as are their gangs, armies of hooligans who are allied to political groups and social clubs, all of them taking great pride in their roles of volunteer firemen; in one fabulous scene where a building is being consumed by a raging fire, the two competing fire brigades arrive, led by Beery and Raft, but they fall to arguing about which company has the right to put out the fire. Then, a wild donnybrook ensues as the firemen beat each other senseless, completely ignoring the building which burns to a cinder. The competition even extends to the company Beery and Raft keep. When the blustering, pompous saloon owner befriends homeless, poverty-stricken Wray, the love interest, Cooper gets jealous and packs his things, going to live with Raft. The slick-haired hoofer soon wins Wray's heart after visiting the saloon, which causes Beery to seethe with anger. He goes to work on Raft's ego, daring him to do something spectacular that will impress Wray. He is finally urged into jumping off the Brooklyn Bridge to prove his manhood. Raft takes up the challenge but secretly tells Cooper he isn't insane; he plans to use a dummy. At the last minute, Beery appears on the famed bridge with a crowd of witnesses, making sure that Raft can't employ the dummy and must take the plunge personally. He does miraculously surviving, winning Beery's saloon in the bargain, a wager Raft judiciously made before his hazardous dive. With his saloon gone, Beery hits the skids. To impress Cooper, who is worried about his fortunes, Beery joins the Army, but before he sails for the war in Cuba, he storms ..to his old saloon and beats the potatoes out of Raft. Police later find the dandy in a shambles, but Raft, true to the code of the streets, refuses to identify assailant Beery. Cooper next plays peace-maker by convincing the two archrivals to shake hands. Raft then joins the Army himself and sails off to Cuba with Beery after Wray promises to wait for him. Cooper goes along with his pals, hiding in a gun wagon so he won't miss any of the further adventures of these colorful characters (in roles razor-close to those of Flagg and Quirt in WHAT PRICE GLORY?). This hell-for-leather film was directed by action packer Walsh, noted for his accelerated pace and quick takes. The script bent the facts considerably, having the time frame in the late 1890s; Brodie jumped off the Brooklyn Bridge on July 23, 1886, dropping 135 feet to the water, where a friend in a boat was waiting to pick him up, according to reporters for the *New York Times* who witnessed the leap, dismissing the charge that Brodie used a dummy. (Brodie died in 1901, age 37, of diabetes caused by acute alcoholism, and he never fought in the Spanish-American War. Yet he did use the $200 he won in the wager over his famous leap to buy a saloon, a raucous joint where celebrities gathered, so the film is on target when showing the great John L. Sullivan visiting the bar, though he did not fight for a $25 purse inside the saloon, nor did Temperance leader Carry Nation, as the film shows, march into the saloon wielding her ax and destroying, with other booze-hating females, every stick of furniture.) The rowdy antics on screen were representative of the offscreen animosities stirred by Beery and Raft. Raft, who had once been a truck driver delivering bootleg hooch from Canada for 1920s gangster Owney Madden before he decided that becoming a dancer was safer, met with many of his underworld friends at the on-location site in Manhattan when the film was being made, and convinced Walsh to hire many of these roughnecks for extra work. When two more gangsters showed up and asked to get in the picture for fun, Raft agreed. They said they'd be back to the location after lunch but they never returned; a half-hour later they were both machinegunned to death by a rival gang in a small restaurant. Raft had almost decided to join them, but stayed behind to prepare his wardrobe. The Raft goons were coached by their pal to really rough up the Beery minions in the scenes where the hoodlums do battle as the rival fire companies. The fight was for real, with bricks and clubs swinging against heads and bodies, and long after director Walsh yelled, "Cut!" the gangs were battling; in fact, they tore the set to pieces until nothing but splinters remained. Beery fumed over Raft's bully boys being in the film. He took his conniving revenge on the dandy the following day. He and Raft were supposed to stage a fight and Beery gave Raft a disarming smile, saying: "George, let me throw the first punch to get things rolling," and Raft shrugged agreement. To quote Raft (from his biography by Lewis Yablonsky): "The s.o.b. Beery threw the first punch and hit me with all his might, knocking me cold! When I came to, I got up and called him everything I could think of. I told him, 'I'm not afraid of you, you big tub of lard!' Then we squared off for real and I threw a few hard, fast punches into his fat belly. The crew jumped in and stopped the fight. But from then on, of course, we were at odds." Beery was not the only one toying with the touchy Raft. Director Walsh was an infamous practical joker. When it came time for Raft to jump off the Brooklyn Bridge—Walsh called over the feisty Raft and told him that the stunt man who was to perform the task was ill and, rather than hold up production which would cost a fortune, he, George Raft, would have to actually jump off the Brooklyn Bridge. "What?" gasped the incredulous Raft who was then fairly new to movies and did not know what demands could be made upon him. "You want *me* to take a dive off this thing?" Walsh nodded and motioned toward the rail. "Do I have to do that?" Raft questioned as he found himself walking to the rail. "Is that in my contract?" Raft said, climbing over the rail and holding on, looking down, talking rapidly. "Who'd put a thing like that in a contract?" Walsh held on to the actor's shoulder and replied: "There's nothing to it, George. See that little boat down there? It's waiting to pick you up. Just hold your middle and keep your legs stiff, and it'll all be over in seconds. Nothing to it." He could feel Raft tense up as he stared bug-eyed toward the water. "My agent must be crazy to let a thing like that get into my contract." But he was prepared to make the leap and, at the last second, Walsh grabbed his arm and told him to climb back over the rail for a few pointers. When Raft was safely back on the bridge, Walsh told him it was all a joke, they had planned on using a dummy all along. "A joke? That's a joke!" Raft had all he could do to contain his anger and keep from punching one of Hollywood's most powerful directors. Walsh knew it. He didn't laugh. But when THE BOWERY was released, it did produce laughter among the millions who relished its gaudy, colorful anything-goes story. Thanks to Walsh every scene bustles with jocular belligerence, reflecting the personality of its producer, Zanuck, as well as the era it represented. This was Zanuck's first film for Fox as its production chief, one that got great box office results and cemented Zanuck's position.

p, Darryl F. Zanuck, William Goetz, Raymond Griffith; d, Raoul Walsh; w, Howard Estabrook, James Gleason (based on the novel *Chuck Connors* by Michael L. Simmons and Bessie Roth Solomon); ph, Barney McGill; m, Alfred Newman; ed, Allen McNeil; art d, Richard Day.

Historical Drama **(PR:A MPAA:NR)**

BOWERY AT MIDNIGHT* ½ (1942) 60m MON

Bela Lugosi *(Prof. Brenner)*, John Archer *(Dennison)*, Wanda McKay *(Judy)*, Tom Neal *(Frankie Mills)*, Vincent Barnett *(Charlie)*, John Berkes *(Fingers Dolan)*, Ray Miller *(Big Man)*, J. Farrell MacDonald *(Capt. Mitchell)*; Lew Kelly *(Doc Brooks)*, Lucille Vance *(Mrs. Malvern)*, Anna Hope *(Mrs. Brenner)*.

Low-budget thriller with Lugosi using a mission as a front for criminal activities. When he feels threatened by his minions he bumps them off and buries them in the basement, where they are revived by a drug-addicted doctor and hidden in a cave, waiting for their chance at Lugosi. Lugosi's career was beginning the long slide downward by this time.

p, Sam Katzman, Jack Dietz; d, Wallace Fox; w, Gerald Schnitzer; ph, Mack Stengler; ed, Carl Pierson.

Thriller **Cas.** **(PR:A MPAA:NR)**

BOWERY BATTALION* (1951) 69m MON

Leo Gorcey *(Slip)*, Huntz Hall *(Sach)*, Donald MacBride *(Frisbie)*, Virginia Hewitt *(Marsha)*, Russell Hicks *(Hatfield)*, William Benedict *(Whitey)*, Bernard Gorcey *(Louie* Dumbrowsky), Buddy Gorman *(Butch)*, David Gorcey *(Chuck)*, John Bleifer *(Decker)*, Al Eben *(Conroy)*, Frank Jenks *(Recruiting Officer)*, Selmer Jackson *(Masters)*.

Better than average Bowery Boys entry is still unbearable. This time the gang has joined the army, engaging in their usual antics while breaking up a spy ring. (See BOWERY BOYS series, Index)

p, Jan Grippo; d, William Beaudine; w, Charles R. Marion; ph, Marcel Le Picard; ed, William Austin; md, Edward Kay.

Comedy **(PR:A MPAA:NR)**

BOWERY BLITZKRIEG*

(1941) 62m MON bw (GB: STAND AND DELIVER)

Leo Gorcey *(Muggs McGinnis)*, Bobby Jordan *(Danny Breslin)*, Huntz Hall *(Limpy)*, Warren Hull *(Tom Brady)*, Charlotte Henry *(Mary Breslin)*, Keye Luke *(Clancy)*, Bobby Stone *(Monk Martin)*, Donald Haines *(Skinny)*, Marsha Wentworth *(Mrs. Brady)*, David Gorcey *(Peewee)*, Ernest Morrison *(Scruno)*, Jack Mulhall *(Officer)*.

Gorcey is saved from a life of crime by becoming a Golden Gloves champ. This is no mean feat for Gorcey in that he gives his blood to a stricken pal in an emergency transfusion just before he steps into the ring! Awful series comedy. (See BOWERY BOYS series, Index) p, Sam Katzman; d, Wallace Fox; w, Sam Robins; ph, Marcel Le Picard; ed, Robert Golden.

Comedy   **(PR:A MPAA:NR)**

BOWERY BOMBSHELL zero   (1946) 65m MON

Leo Gorcey (Slip), Huntz Hall (Sach), Bobby Jordan (Bobby), Billy Benedict (Whitey), David Gorcey (Chuck), Teala Loring (Cathy Smith), James Burke (O'Malley), Sheldon Leonard (Ace Deuce), Vince Barnett (Street Cleaner), William Newell (Dugan), Milton Parsons (Prof. Schnackenberger), Bernard Gorcey (Louie), William "Wee Willie" Davis (Moose), Lester Dorr (Featherfingers), William Ruhl (Biff), Eddie Dunn (O'Hara), Emmett Vogan (Mr. Johnson), Dawn Kennedy (Maizie).

Another insipid series entry. This time the boys are after bank robbers led by Leonard to clear Hall. Huntz has been trying to sell his beat-up car in front of the bank when the bank is robbed and he is wrongly arrested as the getaway driver. The film is as improbable as it is insipid. (See BOWERY BOYS series, Index)

p, Lindsley Parsons, Jan Grippo; d, Phil Karlson; w, Edmond Seward, Tim Ryan (based on a story by Victor Hammond); ph, William Sickner; ed, William Austin.

Comedy   **(PR:A MPAA:NR)**

BOWERY BOY*   (1940) 71m REP

Dennis O'Keefe (Tom O'Hara), Louise Campbell (Anne Cleary), Jimmy Lydon (Sock Dolan), Helen Vinson (Peggy Winters), Roger Pryor (J. L. Mason), Paul Hurst (Blubber Mullins), Edward Gargan (Mr. Hansen), Selmer Jackson (Dr. Crane), John Kelly (Battler), Howard Hickman (Dr. Axel Winters), Frederick Burton (Dr. George Winters), Jack Carr (Flops).

Crusading doctor O'Keefe helps clear up tainted food epidemic while juvenile delinquent Lydon gets in trouble with mobsters. Artificial and trite, O'Keefe is wasted and clean-cut Lydon is unbelievable as a vicious street punk.

p, Armand Schaefer; d, William Morgan; w, Robert Chapin, Harry Kronman, Eugene Solow (based on a story by Sam Fuller, Sidney Sutherland); ph, Ernest Miller; m, Cy Feuer; ed, Edward Mann.

Drama   **(PR:A MPAA:NR)**

BOWERY BOYS MEET THE MONSTERS, THE*   (1954) 62m AA

Leo Gorcey (Slip), Huntz Hall (Sach), Bernard Gorcey (Louie), David Gorcey (Chuck), Bennie Bartlett (Butch), John Dehner (Derek), Lloyd Corrigan (Anton), Paul Wexler (Grissom), Ellen Corby (Amelia), Laura Mason (Francine), Norman Bishop (Gorgo), Steve Calvert (Cosmos), Rudy Lee (Herbie), Paul Bryar (Officer Martin), Pat Flaherty (O'Meara), Jack Diamond (Skippy Biano).

Another intolerable series entry, with the boys this time getting caught in a house full of mad scientists who want to put them to all sorts of ghoulish uses. Replete with gorilla suits, tin-can robots, and miserable malapropisms. (See BOWERY BOYS series, Index)

p, Ben Schwalb; d, Edward Bernds; w, Elwood Ullman, Bernds; ph, Harry Neumann; ed, Lester A. Sonsom, William Austin; art d, David Milton.

Comedy   **(PR:A MPAA:NR)**

BOWERY BUCKAROOS*1/2   (1947) 66m MON

Leo Gorcey (Slip), Huntz Hall (Sach), Bobby Jordan (Bobby), Gabriel Dell (Gabe), Billy Benedict (Whitey), David Gorcey (Chuck), Julie Briggs (Carolyn Briggs), Bernard Gorcey (Louie), Jack Norman (Blackjack), Minerva Urecal (Kate Barlow), Russell Simpson (Luke Barlow), Chief Yowlachie (Chief Hi-Octane), Iron Eyes Cody (Indian Joe), Rosa Turich (Ramona), Sherman Sanders (Rufe), Billy Wilkerson (Moose), Jack O'Shea (Jose), Bud Osborne (Spike).

The Bowery Boys go west to "prosecute for gold," clear Gorcey of a murder charge, and help Briggs recover the mine that heavy Norman has cheated her out of. One of the series' best. (See BOWERY BOYS series, Index)

p, Jan Grippo; d, William Beaudine; w, Tim Ryan, Edmond Seward; ph, Marcel Le Picard; md, Edward Kay; art d, Dave Milton.

Comedy   **(PR:A MPAA:NR)**

BOWERY CHAMPS*1/2   (1944) 61m MON

Leo Gorcey (Muggs), Huntz Hall (Glimpy), Billy Benedict (Skinny), Jimmy Strand (Danny), Bobby Jordan (Kid), Bud Gorman (Shorty), Anne Sterling (Jane), Gabriel Dell (Jim), Frank Jaquet (Cartwright), Francis Ford (Scoop), Evelyn Brent (Gypsy), Eddie Cherkose (Brother), Wheeler Oakman (Wilson), Ian Keith (Duncan), Thelma White (Diane), Bill Ruhl (Lieutenant).

Yet another dumb Bowery Boys film. Gorcey is a newspaper copy boy solving the murder of a nightclub owner, hiding his ex-wife, Brent, suspected of the killing, until he and his stooge-like pals pin the crime on Keith and White. (See BOWERY BOYS series, Index.)

p, Sam Katzman, Jack Dietz; d, William Beaudine; w, Earle Snell; ph, Ira Morgan; ed, John Link.

Comedy   **(PR:A MPAA:NR)**

BOWERY TO BAGDAD**   (1955) 64m AA bw

Leo Gorcey (Slip), Huntz Hall (Sach), David Gorcey (Chuck), Bennie Bartlett (Butch), Bernard Gorcey (Louie), Joan Shawlee (Velma), Robert Bice (Dolan), Rayford Barnes (Gus), Michael Ross (Tiny), Eric Blore (Genie), Rick Vallin (Selim), Paul Marion (Abdul), Jean Willes (Claire), Charlie Lung (Caliph), Leon Burbank (Man).

In an uncharacteristic spurt of good housekeeping, the Bowery Boys polish up an old magic lamp, and produce a genie who probably fervently hopes one of their wishes would put him right back in his lamp. This could explain why this was one of Eric Blore's (the genie) last roles. (See BOWERY BOYS series, Index.)

p, Ben Schwalb; d, Edward Bernds; w, Elwood Ullman, Edward Bernds; ph, Harry Neumann, ed, John C. Fuller; art d, David Milton, md, Marlin Skiles.

Comedy   **(PR:A MPAA:NR)**

BOWERY TO BROADWAY***   (1944) 94m UNIV

Maria Montez (Marina), Jack Oakie (Michael O'Rourke), Susanna Foster (Peggy Fleming), Turhan Bey (Ted Barrie), Ann Blyth (Bessie Jo Kirby), Donald Cook (Dennis Dugan), Louise Albritton (Lillian Russell), Frank McHugh (Joe Kirby), Rosemary De Camp (Bessie Kirby), Leo Carrillo (P.J. Fenton), Andy Devine (Fr. Kelley), Evelyn Ankers (Bonnie Latour), Thomas Gomez (Tom Harvey), Richard Lane (Walter Rogers), George Dolenz (George Henshaw), Mantan Moreland (Alabam), Ben Carter (No-More), Maude Eburne (Mme. Alda), Robert Warwick (Cliff Brown), Donald O'Connor, Peggy Ryan (Specialty Number).

Loosely connected story of Oakie and Cook, two rival Bowery showmen who eventually take their vaudeville-bred talents to 42nd Street. Although theft of ideas has separated them in the past, the two eventually collaborate on a show that turns out to be a tremendous success. When Cook breaks up the newly formed partnership to produce serious dramatic works for the lusty Montez, Oakie again turns sour on their relationship. After years of silence, the two reconcile during a revival of one of their classic productions. Essentially a vehicle to showcase the talents of Universal's singers and dancers of the 1940s, the film is undeniably up-beat and entertaining, but lacks the clarity, focus, and spontaneity of a classic musical. Songs: "Just Because You Made Dem Goo Goo Eyes At Me" (Hughie Cannon, John Queen); "The Love Waltz," "There'll Always Be A Moon" (Everett Carter, Edward Ward); "Montevideo," "Coney Island Waltz" (Kim Gannon, Walter Kent); "My Song of Romance" (Don George, Dave Franklin); "Under The Bamboo Tree" (Bob Cole, J. Rosamond-Johnson); "Daisy Bell" (Harry Dacre); "Yippie-I-Addy-I-Ay" (Will Cobb, John H. Flynn); "Wait Till The Sun Shines Nellie" (Andrew B. Sterling, Harry von Tilzer); "He Took Her For A Sleigh Ride" (traditional).

p, John Grant; d, Charles Lamont; w, Edmund Joseph, Bart Lytton, Arthur T. Horman (based on a story by Joseph, Lytton); ph, Charles Van Enger; ed, Arthur Hilton; m&md, Edward Ward; ch, Carlos Romero, Luis De Pron, John Boyle.

Musical Comedy   **(PR:A MPAA:NR)**

BOXCAR BERTHA**1/2   (1972) 88m AIP c

Barbara Hershey (Bertha), David Carradine (Bill Shelley), Barry Primus (Rake Brown), Bernie Casey (Von Morton), John Carradine (H. Buckram Sartoris), Victor Argo, David R. Osterhout (The McIvers), Chicken Holleman (Michael Powell), Graham Pratt (Emeric Pressburger), Harry Northup (Harvey Hall), Ann Morell (Tillie), Marianne Dole (Mrs. Mailer), Joe Reynolds (Joe Dreft), Gayne Rescher, Martin Scorsese (Brothel Clients).

Depression era crime story with Hershey taking to the road after her father dies in an airplane crash. She meets railroad union organizer Carradine and the two take up train robbing. Carradine ends up crucified on the side of a boxcar. Lots of violence, typical of the Roger Corman exploitation mill, still shows the budding talent of Scorsese in its use of moving camera and period detail.

p, Roger Corman; d, Martin Scorsese; w, Joyce H. Corrington, John William Corrington (based on Sister of the Road by Boxcar Bertha Thomson as told to Ben L. Reitman); ph, John Stephens (DeLuxe Color); m, Gib Guilbeau, Thad Maxwell; ed, Buzz Feitshans; prod d, David Nichols; cos, Bob Modes.

Crime   Cas.   **(PR:O MPAA:R)**

BOXER**   (1971, Pol.) 96m Polski Film bw

Daniel Olbrychski (Antoni), Tadeusz Kalinowski (Manager), Leszek Drogosz (Walczak), Malgorzata Wlodarska (Girl).

Well-done Polish film about a young boxer (Olbrychski). In flashbacks before the big fight he trains, gets drunk, gets thrown in jail, goes to the Olympics, and in the final bout, defeats a Russian fighter.

d, Julian Dziedzina; w, Bohdan Tomaszewski, Jerzy Suszko; ph, Miklaj Sprudin; ed, L. Romanis.

                                        (PR:A MPAA:NR)

Drama

BOXER, THE   (SEE: RIPPED OFF, 1971, Ital.)

BOXOFFICE*1/2   (1982) 93m Josef Bogdanovich Prod. c

Robin Clarke (Peter Malloy), Monica Lewis (Francesca), Eddie Constantine (Hugh Barren), Aldo Ray (Lew), Edie Adams (Carolyn), Carol Cortne (Eve Chandler), Peter Hurkos (Himself), Chuck Mitchell (Mr. Joy).

An inside-show-business story that manages to miss on just about every level. Cortne as an about-to-happen star strikes a wrong note at the beginning as she postures, struts and frets under the hand of Josef (no relation to Peter) Bogdanovich. The attempt at showing the sleaze of Hollywood is earnest, to be sure, but the execution is a failure. Coleman's score is too piercing, man, too piercing, even though the visual side of BOXOFFICE is good. Eric Saarinen (we can only surmise that he is related to the great Eliel Saarinen) had some interesting effects and unique lighting. Although made in 1982, it became dated early with the use of a special material song entitled "Ode To David Begelman," the deposed czar of Columbia pictures whose demise was chronicled so well in Indecent Exposure. One of the lines in the song asks "Where are you, David Begelman?" Only problem is that Begelman has already surfaced and has had several new jobs since then and will probably wind up being the man who runs all the studios in Hollywood simultaneously, if his luck keeps running this way.

p, Josef Bogdanovich, Bruce Chastain; d, Bogdanovich; ph, Eric Saarinen (DeLuxe Color); m, Ornette Coleman; ed, Bonnie Kozek, Edward Salier.

Musical Drama (PR:C-O MPAA:NR)

BOY . . . A GIRL, A zero (1969) 71m Jack Hanson c

Dino Martin, Jr. (*The Boy*), Airion Fromer (*The Girl*), Karen Steele (*Elizabeth*), Kerwin Mathews (*Mr. Christian*).

Wretched, amateurish film about 15-year-olds Martin and Fromer discovering love and sex. Fromer has an affair with neighbor Mathews, more than twice her age, then returns to Martin. Full of dreary, insipid meditations on life and love, with the characters staring off into space for long periods. Shot on 16mm stock, blown up, and sound looped, this was actor-turned-Renaissance-man Derek's second directorial effort. He later made a number of forgettable films starring his fourth wife, Bo.

p, Jack Hanson; d,w&ph, John Derek; m, Joe Greene; ed, John H. Post; m/l, Greene, Derek.

Drama (PR:O MPAA:NR)

BOY, A GIRL AND A BIKE, A* (1949, Brit.), 91m Gainsborough/GFD

John McCallum (*David Howarth*), Honor Blackman (*Susie Bates*), Patrick Holt (*Sam Walters*), Diana Dors (*Ada Foster*), Maurice Denham (*Bill Martin*), Leslie Dwyer (*Steve Hall*), Anthony Newley (*Charlie Ritchie*), Megs Jenkins (*Nan Ritchie*), John Blythe (*Frankie Martin*), Alison Leggatt (*Mrs. Howarth*), Julien Mitchell (*Mr. Howarth*), Hal Ozmond (*Mr. Bates*), Thora Hird (*Mrs. Bates*), Amy Veness (*Grandma Bates*).

A Yorkshire bicycle club and its adventures are the subject of this weak effort. A wealthy young man joins the club and causes jealousy between a young couple.

p, Ralph Keene; d, Ralph Smart; w, Ted Willis (story by Keene, John Sommerfield); ph, Ray Elton, Frank Bassill; m, Kenneth Pakeman; ed, James Needs.

Drama (PR:A MPAA:NR)

BOY, A GIRL, AND A DOG, A* (1946) 51m Film Classics

Jerry Hunter (*Kip*), Sharyn Moffett (*Button*), Harry Davenport (*Gramps*), Lionel Stander (*Jim*), Charles Williams (*Mr. Stone*), Charlotte Treadway (*Mrs. Foster*), Howard Johnson (*Lt. Stephens*), John Vosper (*Mr. Hamilton*), Nancy Evans (*Mrs. Hamilton*).

Low-budget programmer about a couple of children who volunteer their dog for combat duty. The canine goes on to beat the Japanese almost alone. Bad photography, bad acting, and bad writing add up to a bad movie.

p, W. R. Frank; d, Herbert Kline; w, Maurice Clark, Irving Fireman (based on a story by Leopold Atlas, adapted by Kline); ph, Edward Hull; ed, Marguerite Francisco.

Drama (PR:A MPAA:NR)

BOY AND HIS DOG, A zero (1975) 87m LQJaf c

Don Johnson (*Vic*), Susanne Benton (*Quilla June*), Tiger (*Blood*), Tim McIntire (*Voice of Blood*), Charles McGraw (*Preacher*), Jason Robards (*Mr. Craddock*), Alvy Moore, Helen Winston (*Committee Members*), Tiger (*Blood*).

At five feet four or so, Harlan Ellison is one of the best short short-story writers in the business today. So it came as a slice across the throat to see such a shambles made of his novella, *A Boy and His Dog*. This has no resemblance to LAD, A DOG or any other canine movie. This picture is a violent, vulgar attempt at black comedy that takes place in the future where civilization has gone the way of the doom-sayer. Johnson, who would go on to achieve great fame in TV's "Miami Vice," is a one-man sperm bank for all the sterile people. His telepathic dog (voiced by Tim McIntyre) is the only one with any sense in the picture. He is played by Tiger of "The Brady Bunch" and if it's possible for an animal to look embarrassed at his role, Tiger does. The best part of the picture is the dialog (taken directly from Ellison's work) between the Boy (Johnson) and his Dog (Tiger). The worst part of the picture is just about everything else. A sequel to this sometime cult film had been planned, but the dog died.

p, Alvy Moore; d&w, L. Q. Jones (based on the novella by Harlan Ellison); ph, John Arthur Morrill (Technicolor); m, Tim McIntyre; ed, Scott Conrad.

Science Fiction Cas. (PR:O MPAA:R)

BOY AND THE BRIDGE, THE (1959, Brit.) 91m Xanadu/COL

Ian Maclaine (*Tommy Doyle*), Liam Redmond (*Pat Doyle*), James Hayter (*Tugboat Skipper*), Norman MacOwan (*Tugboat Engineer*), Geoffrey Keen (*Bridge Master*), Jack MacGowran (*Market Porter*), Royal Dano (*Evangelist*), Bill Shine, Arthur Lowe, Jocelyn Britton (*Bridge Mechanics*), Andreas Malandrinos (*Organ Grinder*), Stuart Saunders (*Publican*), Chili Bouchier (*Publican's Wife*), Rita Webb (*Landlady*), Mead- ows White (*Yeoman Warder*), Winifred Kingston (*Tourist*), Jimmy Herbert (*Punch And Judy*), Jack Stewart (*Bridge Engineer*).

When London boy MacLaine sees his father arrested during a drunken brawl, he thinks it's for murder. He runs away from home and takes up residence inside Tower Bridge. Good-natured and technically adroit but dull.

p, Kevin McClory, David Eady; d, McClory; w, McClory, Desmond O'Donovan, Geoffrey Orme (from a story by Leon Ware); ph, Ted Scaife; m, Malcolm Arnold; ed, Jack Slade.

Drama (PR:A MPAA:NR)

BOY AND THE PIRATES, THE **1/2** (1960) 84m UA c

Charles Herbert (*Jimmy Warren*), Susan Gordon (*Katrina Van Keif*), Murvyn Vye (*Blackbeard*), Paul Guilfoyle (*Snipe*) Joseph Turkel (*Abu the Genie*), Archie Duncan (*Scoggins*), Than Wyenn (*Hunter*), Al Cavens (*Dutch Captain*), Mickey Finn (*Peake*), Morgan Jones (*Mr. Warren*), Timothy Carey (*Morgan*).

Children's film about a boy, Herbert, who finds genie Turkel. The genie zaps him aboard the pirate ship of Blackbeard (Vye). After numerous typical pirate adventures he and his newfound companion (Gordon), escape to safety. Not bad, but strictly kid stuff.

p&d, Bert I. Gordon; w, Lillie Hayward, Jerry Sackheim; ph, Ernest Haller (Eastman color); m, Albert Glasser; ed, Jerome Thomas; art d, Edward L. Ilou.

Adventure (PR:AA MPAA:NR)

BOY CRIED MURDER, THE* (1966, Ger./Brit./Yugo.) 86m Carlos-Avala-Luber/UNIV c

Veronica Hurst (*Clare Durrant*), Phil Brown (*Tom Durrant*), Fraser MacIntosh (*Jonathan Durrant*), Tim Barrett (*Mike*), Beba Loncar (*Susie*), Edward Steel (*Col. Wetherall*), Anita Sharpe-Bolster (*Mrs. Wetherall*), Sonja Hlebs (*Marianne*), Alex MacIntosh (*Sergeant*), Vuka Dundzerovic (*Mrs. Bosnic*).

It's the boy-who-cried-wolf story again, this time telling the tale of how an imaginative boy can convince no one but the criminal that he has witnessed a brutal murder. A tasteless, useless remake of the excellent THE WINDOW (1949), which was later remade as EYE WITNESS/SUDDEN TERROR (1970). The script is turgid and the direction appears as if the director's chair was empty throughout the shooting.

p, Philip N. Krasne; d, George Breakston; w, Robin Estridge (based on "The Boy Who Cried Murder" by Cornell Woolrich); ph, Milorad Markovic (Eastmancolor); m, Martin Slavin; ed, Milanka Nanovic.

Crime Drama (PR:C-O MPAA:NR)

BOY, DID I GET A WRONG NUMBER! **1/2** (1966) 98m UA c

Bob Hope (*Tom Meade*), Elke Sommer (*Didi*), Phyllis Diller (*Lily*), Cesare Danova (*Pepe*), Marjorie Lord (*Martha Meade*), Kelly Thordsen (*Schwartz*), Benny Baker (*Regan*), Terry Burnham (*Doris Meade*), Joyce Jameson (*Telephone Operator*), Harry Von Zell (*Newscaster*), Kevin Burchett (*Larry Meade*), Keith Taylor (*Plympton*), John Todd Roberts (*Newsboy*).

Usual Hope romp has himself as a glib, fast-talking real estate operator getting involved with Hollywood sex kitten Sommer, who has taken refuge in his Oregon town to escape her boy friend, director Danova, who keeps wanting to put her in movie bubble baths. Chaos abounds as Hope plays cat-and-mouse with his wife (Lord) in an effort to keep her from discovering Sommer. Add to this wing-ding Diller as Lily the family maid, wise-cracking her way throughout while she helps Hope in his attempts to hide Elke from the missus. Funny film with Hope playing it straight for the most part, Diller, zany as always, and Sommer, no slouch in comedy situations.

p, Edward Small; d, George Marshall; w, Burt Styler, Albert E. Lewin, George Kennett, (based on a story by George Beck), ph, Lionel Lindon (DeLuxe Color); m, Richard La Salle, "By" Dunham; ed, Grant Whylock; art d, Frank Sylos.

Comedy Cas. (PR:AA MPAA:NR)

BOY FRIEND* **1/2** (1939) 72m FOX

Jane Withers (*Sally Murphy*), Arleen Whelan (*Sue Duffy*), Richard Bond (*Jimmy Murphy*), Douglas Fowley (*Ed Boyd*), Warren Hymer (*Greenberg*), George Ernest (*Billy Bradley*), Robert Kellard (*Tommy Bradley*), Minor Watson (*Capt. Duffy*), Robert Shaw (*Cracker*), Ted Pearson (*Callahan*), William H. Counselman, Jr. (*Arizona*), Myra Marsh (*Mrs. Murphy*), Harold Goodwin (*Matchie Riggs*).

Jane Withers vehicle has Jane's brother, Bond, a rookie cop, pretending to go bad in order to infiltrate a gang. Jane is upset over what she sees as his desertion and she and her cadet boyfriend bust into the gang's H.Q. and stumble on the evidence to put them away. Mediocre mayhem.

p, John Stone; d, James Tinling; w, Joseph Hoffman, Barry Trivers (based on a story by Lester Ziffren, Louis Moore); ph, Lucien Andriot; ed, Norman Colbert; md, Samuel Kaylin; m/l, Sidney Clare, Harry Akst.

Comedy (PR:A MPAA:NR)

BOY FRIEND, THE* **1/2** (1971, Brit.) 108m MGM c

Twiggy (*Polly Browne*), Christopher Gable (*Tony Brockhurst*), Moyra Fraser (*Madame Dubonnet*), Max Adrian (*Max*), Bryan Pringle (*Percy*), Catherine Wilmer (*Lady Brockhurst*), Murray Melvin (*Alphonse*), Georgina Hale (*Fay*), Sally Bryant (*Nancy*), Vladek Sheybal (*De Thrill*), Tommy Tune (*Tommy*), Glenda Jackson (*Rita*), Antonia Ellis (*Masie*), Caryl Little (*Dulcie*), Graham Armitage (*Michael*), Brian Murphy (*Peter*), Ann Jameson (*Mrs. Peter*), Robert LaBassiere (*Chauffeur*), Barbara Windsor (*Hortense*).

Ken Russell's dizzy, affectionate homage to 1930s musicals and Busby Berkeley. Twiggy [Leslie Hornsby] is the assistant stage manager/gofer who gets her big chance when star Glenda Jackson hurts her ankle. "Come back a star" the director tells her, and that's just what she does. (The same utterings were made by Warner Baxter to Ruby Keeler in 42ND STREET.) Russell's bombastic direction has never looked so right. Musical numbers uniformly well done, include "I Could Be Happy," "The Boy Friend," "Won't You Charleston With Me?" "Fancy Forgetting," "Sur La Plage," "A Room In Bloomsbury," "Safety In Numbers," "It's Never Too Late To Fall In Love," "Poor Little Pierette," "Rivera," "The You Don't Want To Play With Me Blues" (Sandy Wilson), "All I Do Is Dream Of You," "You Are My Lucky Star" (Nacio Herb Brown, Arthur Freed); "Any Old Iron" (Charles Collins, E. A. Shepherd, Fred Terry).

p, Ken Russell; d, Russell; w, Russell (based on a play by Sandy Wilson); ph, David Watkin (Metrocolor); ed, Michael Bradsell; md, Peter Maxwell Davies; art d, Simon Holland; set d, Tony Walton; cos, Shirley Russell; ch, Christopher Gable, Terry Gilbert, Gillian Gregory.

Musical (PR:A MPAA:G)

BOY FROM INDIANA*½ (1950) 66m Ventura/EL bw (GB: BLAZE OF GLORY)

Lon McCallister *(Lon Decker)*, Lois Butler *(Betty Richards)*, Billie Burke *(Zelda Bagley)*, George Cleveland *(Mac Dougall)*, Rol Laughner *(Wilkinson)*, Victor Cox *(Thorne)*, Jerry Ambler *(Burke)*, Allen Church *(Corbett)*, Jeanne Patterson *(Pretty Girl)*, Texas Dandy *(Dandy)*.

Midwestern lad McCallister lands a job jockeying Cleveland's race horse unaware that the owner has been using drugs to push the pony along. After "Texas Dandy" is gored by a bull, his participation in the climactic race is jeopardized, but thanks to McCallister's tender loving care, the horse not only runs the race, but wins it. Familiar race-track drama complete with silly dialog, poor acting, and enough cliches for two or three movies.

p, Frank Melford; d, John Rawlins; w, Otto Englander; ph, Jack Mackenzie; ed, Merrill White.

Sports Drama **(PR:A MPAA:NR)**

BOY FROM OKLAHOMA, THE½** (1954) 87m WB c

Will Rogers, Jr. *(Tom Brewster)*, Nancy Olson *(Katie Brannigan)*, Lon Chaney, Jr. *(Crazy Charlie)*, Anthony Caruso *(Barney Turlock)*, Wallace Ford *(Wally Higgins)*, Clem Bevans *(Pop Pruty)*, Merv Griffin *(Steve)*, Louis Jean Heydt *(Paul Evans)*, Sheb Wooley *(Pete Martin)*, Slim Pickens *(Shorty)*, Tyler MacDuff *(Billy the Kid)*, Skippy Torgerson *(Johnny Neil)*, James Griffith *(Joe Downey)*, Charles Watts *(Harry)*.

Rogers, Jr., a mild-mannered fellow studying law in the Old West, drifts into a small town where tyrannical outlaw boss Caruso rules with an iron hand. Irritated by Caruso's corruption, Rogers, Jr. agrees to act as sheriff and rounds up the desperado gang using only his lariat and his faith in the Lord. Easy going, impossible-to-dislike western that shows the triumph of goodness over selfishness and violence. Rogers, Jr. cannot compare to his father, the old man's wit being a standard that few could come close to, but he manages to display the same simple virtues and calm manner that made Will, Sr. a national icon.

p, David Weisbart; d, Michael Curtiz; w, Frank Davis, Winston Miller (based on a *Saturday Evening Post* story by Michael Fessier); ph, Robert Burks (Warner Color); m, Max Steiner; ed, James Moore.

Western **(PR:A MPAA:NR)**

BOY MEETS GIRL*½** (1938) 86m WB bw

James Cagney *(Robert Law)*, Pat O'Brien *(J. Carlyle Benson)*, Marie Wilson *(Susie)*, Ralph Bellamy *(E. Elliott Friday)*, Dick Foran *(Larry Toms)*, Frank McHugh *(Rosetti)*, Bruce Lester *(Rodney Bevan)*, Ronald Reagan *(Announcer)*, Penny Singleton *(Peggy)*, Dennie Moore *(Miss Cruz)*, James Stephenson *(Major Thompson)*, Bert Hanlon *(Green)*, Harry Seymour *(Slade)*, George Hickman *(Office Boy)*, Cliff Saum *(Smitty)*, Carole Landis *(Commissary Cashier)*, Curt Bois *(Dance Director)*, Otto Fries *(Olaf)*, John Harron *(Extra)*, Hal K. Dawson *(Wardrobe Attendant)*, James Nolan *(Young Man)*, Jan Holm, Vera Lewis, Rosella Towne *(Nurses)*, Paul Clark *(Happy)*, Eddy Conrad *(Jascha)*, Peggy Moran *(N.Y. Operator)*, Nannette Lafayette *(Paris Operator)*, Janet Shaw *(Los Angeles Operator)*, Bert Howard *(Director)*, Bill Telaak *(Bruiser)*.

Zany comedy of screwball screenwriters Cagney and O'Brien who write every movie with a variation of "boy meets girl" theme and who are fast running out of ideas. To cover their "mental blanks," they create the most outlandish plots and characters based on their tried-and-true theme. The chief object of their incessant pranks and witness to their lunatic behavior is studio supervisor Bellamy, who is tearing his hair out in desperation to get them to write a logical script for the studio's pompous cowboy star Foran. The western star's career is fading fast and he is desperate for a punchy vehicle that will put him back on top fast. He implores Cagney and O'Brien to come up with an idea, but all they do is confuse him with the most elaborate and obtuse tales. "Yes," Foran begs, "but what's *the story* about?" Meanwhile dumb blonde Wilson, a studio commissary waitress, is worried about her infant child's future. Cagney and O'Brien, her self-appointed protectors, tell her not to worry, assuring that they'll take care of the child's destiny. To that end, they stop bamboozling Foran and Bellamy, sit down and bat out a completely preposterous script with Wilson's baby, whom they name Happy in the film, as the central character in a Foran western epic. The film is made and is a huge success, making Happy a superstar. BOY MEETS GIRL was a triumph, largely because the public flocked to see any film starring James Cagney. The film also satisfied a public desire to see what actually went on in the studio lots and offices where stars were made overnight. It got its fill as the film exposes the Warner sound stages, back lots, and front offices, showing the methods, technicians, and stars at work. Also delighting audiences was the thumb-nosing approach Cagney and O'Brien took toward their powerful bosses in a scathing satire of Hollywood producers and moguls, accurately shown to be a rather dim-witted, uncreative lot. (The fact that such a film was allowed to be made at the time is a minor miracle.) The role models for the Cagney-O'Brien team, of course, were the talented, irreverent Ben Hecht and Charles MacArthur, the greatest film-writing duo in the business. The story behind this laugh riot film is almost as fascinating as the quirkish film itself. A Broadway hit written by Sam and Bella Spewack in 1935, BOY MEETS GIRL was originally intended to be directed by George Abbott and to star Marion Davies, the colorful mistress of newspaper potentate William Randolph Hearst (Davies had a pronounced stammer but, oddly enough, she never stuttered a word when before the cameras). The madcap comedians Olson and Johnson were supposed to star as the writers but they were busy elsewhere and the studio brought in Cagney (then earning $150,000 per film with 10% of the gross) and O'Brien. Lloyd Bacon replaced Abbott, fortunately for the film, which he directed with a hectic pace that matches the whirlwind acting. Davies, who was to be the central character, began complaining about her role, saying it wasn't big enough and who were these two madman writers in the film anyway? She was replaced by Marie Wilson whose role was made even smaller. It was the last straw for temperamental Marion; she immediately retired from films altogether. Future film stars can be seen throughout the film. A cute, curvaceous manicurist with a few lines is Penny Singleton, who later made the BLONDIE series; the cashier in the studio commissary is Carole Landis. Even future President of the United States Ronald Reagan made the cast as an announcer heralding the arrival of stars at a premiere in BOY MEETS GIRL (at the Carthay Circle Theater in Los Angeles which was used in many movies to show premieres). Behind Reagan the theater marquee announces the premiere film as being THE WHITE RAJAH with Errol Flynn. This was another inside joke; Flynn had written a script years earlier called THE WHITE RAJAH but Warner Bros. found it too weak to film. When looking for something to represent the fictional premiere in BOY MEETS GIRL, director Bacon came across the old manu- script and slapped its title on the theater marquee. Flynn didn't think it funny.

p, Hal B. Wallis, Sam Bischoff; d, Lloyd Bacon; w, Bella and Sam Spewack (based on their play); ph, Sol Polito; ed, William Holmes; art d, Esdras Hartley; md, Leo Forbstein; cos, Milo Anderson; makeup, Perc Westmore; m/l, "With A Pain In My Heart," M. K. Jerome, Jack Scholl.

Satire **(PR:A MPAA:NR)**

BOY NAMED CHARLIE BROWN, A½** (1969) 86m NG c

Voices of: Peter Robbins *(Charlie Brown)*, Pamelyn Ferdin *(Lucy Van Pelt)*, Glenn Gilger *(Linus Van Pelt)*, Andy Pforsich *(Schroeder)*, Sally Dryer *(Patty)*, Anne Altieri *(Violet)*, Erin Sullivan *(Sally)*, Linda Mendelson *(Frieda)*, Christopher DeFaria *(Pig Pen)*, David Carey, Guy Pforsich *(Boys)*, Bill Melendez *(Snoopy)*.

Animated adventures of the Peanuts gang comes off surprisingly well in a feature-length treatment, largely because it leaves the comic strip's idea intact on the screen. Charlie Brown goes to the national spelling bee and, of course, loses. Not bad, though Rod McKuen's songs are hard to take. Musical numbers include "Piano Sonata Opus 13 (Pathetique)," Ludwig von Beethoven, played by Ingolf Dahl; title song, "Failure Face," "Champion Charlie Brown," "Cloud Dreams," "Charlie Brown And His All Stars," "We Lost Again," "Blue Charlie Brown," "Time To Go To School," "I Only Dread One Day At A Day," "By Golly I'll Show 'Em," "Class Champion," "School Spelling Bee," "Start Boning Up On Your Spelling, Charlie Brown," "You'll Either Be A Hero . . . Or A Goat," "Bus Station," "Do Piano Players Make A Lot of Money?" "I've Got To Get My Blanket Back," "Big City," "Found Blanket," "National Spelling Bee," "B-E-A-G-L-E," "Homecoming," "I'm Never Going To School Again," "Welcome Home, Charlie Brown" (Rod McKuen, Vince Guaraldi); "I Before E" (John Scott Trotter, Alan Shean).

p, Lee Mendelson, Bill Melendez; d, Melendez; w, Charles M. Schulz; ph, Nick Vasu (Technicolor); m, Vince Guaraldi; ch, Skippy Baxter; anim, Ed Levitt, Bernard Gruver, Ruth Kissane, Dean Spille, Eleanor Warren, Frank Smith, Faith Kovaleski, Rudy Zamora, Bill Littlejohn, Philip Roman, Richard Thompson, Frank Braxton, Everett Brown, Bob Matz, Ken O'Brien, Alan Shear; ed, Robert T. Gillis, Charles McCann, Steve Melendez.

Animated **Cas.** **(PR:AAA MPAA:NR)**

BOY OF THE STREETS** (1937) 75m MON bw

Jackie Cooper *(Chuck)*, Maureen O'Connor *(Nora)*, Kathleen Burke *(Julie)*, Robert Emmett O'Connor *(Rourke)*, Marjorie Main *(Mary Brennan)*, Guy Usher *(Fog Horn Brennan)*, Matty Fain *(Blackie)*, George Cleveland *(Tim Farley)*, Gordon Elliott *(Doctor)*, Don Latorre *(Tony)*.

Street punk Cooper, leader of a rebellious gang, plots to ease himself into the graft and corruption of a local branch of the city government. When a gangster's bullet hits him, Cooper wises up to the dangers of crime and decides to lead a good life with sweetheart O'Connor at his side. Intended to be a study of street life and its effects on a tough city boy, the film manages to capture the seedy atmosphere and harsh realities of urban life, but fails to breathe life into its characters. Cooper tries to bring some depth to his rough teen, but the faults of the script and direction fail to help one of the best child actors who ever appeared on screen.

p, George Kahn; d, William Nigh; w, Gilson Brown, Scott Darling; (based on a story by Rowland Brown); ph, Gilbert Warrenton; ed, Russell Schoengarth.

Drama **(PR:A MPAA:NR)**

BOY ON A DOLPHIN*** (1957) 103m FOX c

Alan Ladd *(Dr. James Calder)*, Sophia Loren *(Phaedra)*, Clifton Webb *(Victor Parmalee)*, Jorge Mistral *(Rhif)*, Laurence Naismith *(Dr. Hawkins)*, Alexis Minotis *(Government Man)*, Piero Giagnoni *(Niko)*, Charles Fawcett *(Bill B. Baldwin)*, Gertrude Flynn *(Miss Dill)*, Charlotte Terrabust *(Mrs. Baldwin)*, Margaret Stahl *(Miss Baldwin)*, Orestes Rallis *(Chief of Police)*, The Penegrysis Greek Folk Dance and Songs Society.

A lavish and lush adventure film, BOY ON A DOLPHIN could easily be dismissed as a variation of THE MALTESE FALCON shot under water, but for the considerable talents of its principal players, chiefly the resolute Ladd, the snide and sophisticated Webb, and the earthy and generously endowed Loren whose animalistic sex appeal wowed male viewers around the world in this, her first American film. While swimming off the coast of the Greek island Hydra, sponge diver Loren discovers a sunken ship in the deep, one lost for centuries, an ancient Greek galley boasting treasure and an exquisite statue of a boy on a dolphin. So awe-inspiring is this underwater marvel that Loren almost fails to surface. When she does she blurts her find to her boy friend, Mistral, a sleazy sort who immediately begins scheming to sell the find. They naively approach Ladd, an American archeologist working for the Greek museums, and he becomes excited. He will not pay for it, however, demanding that Loren and Mistral turn it over to their country as patriots who should want to see its heritage preserved. Mistral goes to greedy millionaire Webb, a collector of great treasures he begs, buys, or steals so he can have them all to himself. The two begin planning how to raise the ship's treasures secretly—only Loren and Mistral know the location—and smuggle it out of the country, a job for which Webb promises to pay handsomely. He is also taken with Loren and offers to make her his mistress, but she rejects him, leaving his yacht in a huff. Moreover, Loren has fallen in love with Ladd and is having patriotic pangs of guilt. She is encouraged to side with Ladd by her kid brother Giagoni whose innocent performance of an American-idolizing boy is captivating and funny. She finally leads Ladd to the spot and both dive for the treasure only to find it gone. Mistral has taken Webb to the location first and they have made off with the goods. Ladd believes Loren has betrayed him and will have nothing more to do with her. In a risky confrontation with her former boy friend and the avaricious Webb, Loren manages to recover the treasure with the help of Greek authorities; it is majestically delivered into the harbor, the bronze statue of the boy on a dolphin jutting from the government gunboat. Webb sails away empty handed, telling his yacht captain to steer a course for Monte Carlo. Ladd, realizing that Loren has been faithful to him, takes her into his arms as the Greek villagers cheer wildly at the restoration of their national treasure. Many in the cast and crew of BOY ON A DOLPHIN had produced the 1954 smash hit THREE COINS IN THE FOUNTAIN, shot on location in Rome. Director Negulesco, cinematographer Krasner and Webb had been involved with COINS and were enlisted for BOY ON A DOLPHIN three years later when Fox decided to recreate the same kind of exotic background that had proved so successful in COINS, but instead of Rome, it would be Greece. The film indeed is full of wonderful on-location shots of the Parthenon, the winding streets of Athens, the crumbling Epidaurus amphitheater and the stunning coastal towns along the azure Aegean Sea. Robert Mitchum was originally selected to play the role of the archeologist, but he was committed elsewhere and Fox desperately searched about for a big-name star, finding Ladd who was just completing THE BIG LAND. He agreed to do the film but his price was high, more than $275,000, according to one report, then a whopping sum. He was not too happy with Webb's presence, having run afoul of that actor's acerbic wit years earlier. (Webb would be cordial throughout the film but, when returning to Hollywood, complained of Ladd's temperament.) Yet Ladd's best scenes are with Webb as they play cat-and-mouse games about the treasure. Here he is animated and properly adversarial, but in almost all his scenes with Loren he is withdrawn, almost indifferent. Of course, he had reason to be. Loren was using the film to boost an international reputation as Italy's new sex symbol, her expansive physique advertised to be bigger and broader and more sumptuous than the considerable attributes of Gina Lollobrigida. Ladd, who stood only about 5′4″ was amazed when he first met Loren; no one had told him he would be acting with a giantess (albeit she stands about 5′8″ or so in bare feet). She was almost a head taller and their love scenes together had to be framed as special two-shots. At one point, the two walk along a beach. So that Ladd would appear taller, a trench was dug for Loren to walk in, a scene that embarrassed Ladd and made him even more distant from cast and crew, especially from Loren. Director Negulesco played all the scenes to the Italian sexpot, particularly her diving sequences where she grabs the hem of her skirt, tucks it between her legs and pins it, then dives into the water and emerges dripping wet, her voluptuous heavy-breasted body clearly outlined, a shot that would be used in the film's promotion and make Loren the rage. Ladd refused to be anything but polite to Loren who later claimed he was her only leading man who refused to become her friend. When they posed for publicity shots he was cold and indifferent, although she later said that Ladd was one of the sexiest men she had ever seen on the screen (Loren had studied his films before making BOY ON A DOLPHIN). To Ladd, "the full-lipped, almond-eyed" Loren was a talentless opportunist who was using him as a prop to establish a career in American movies. Moreover, Ladd hated being away from his children and the trip to Greece had proved unnerving; a burglar had slipped into his compartment on the Orient Express traveling from Paris to Athens and had stolen his dinner clothes and his wife's best jewelry. By picture's end, Ladd felt that the film had been a mistake, at least for him, and he blamed the director for handing Loren the film. "Negulesco fell 'in love' with her," he told a columnist, "so she got all the good closeups. All you ever saw of me in most scenes was the back of my head. I got fed up with it." Ladd also felt that Loren wanted publicity shots with him so that she could promote a new image that gave her status equal to a top-ranking star. No matter, the film remains as Loren's first smash American vehicle, with stunning photography and a haunting score by Friedhofer; it's a great travelog with a dramatic story thrown in for good measure.

p, Samuel G. Engel; d, Jean Negulesco; w, Ivan Moffat, Dwight Taylor (based on the novel by David Divine); ph, Milton Krasner (CinemaScope, DeLuxe Color); m, Hugo Friedhofer; ed, William Mace; ch, Dora Stratou; spec eff, Ray Kellogg; m/l, title song, based on "Tinafto" by Takes Morakis, J. Fermanglou, English lyrics by Paul F. Webster.

Adventure **(PR:C MPAA:NR)**

BOY SLAVES* 1/2 (1938) 70m RKO bw

Anne Shirley *(Annie)*, Roger Daniel *(Jesse)*, James McCallion *(Tim)*, Alan Baxter *(Graff)*, Johnny Fitzgerald *(Knuckles)*, Walter Ward *(Miser)*, Charles Powers *(Lollie)*, Walter Tetley *(Pee Wee)*, Frank Malo *(Tommy)*, Paul White *(Atlas)*, Arthur Hohl *(Sheriff)*, Charles Lane *(Albee)*, Norman Willis *(Drift Boss)*, Roy Gordon *(Judge)*.

Melodramatic expose of juvenile delinquents in forced labor camps. Daniel runs away from home, joins a gang headed by McCallion. They are arrested and sent to a privately run turpentine camp, where they are forced to work under inhuman conditions. They escape and when recaptured a kindly judge refuses to send them back. Tries to be the I AM A FUGITIVE FROM A CHAIN GANG of juvenile delinquency, but comes off preachy and dull.

p, P. J. Wolfson; d, Wolfson; w, Albert Bein, Ben Orkow (based on a story by Bein); ph, J. Roy Hunt; ed, Desmond Marquette.

Drama **(PR:A MPAA:NR)**

BOY TEN FEET TALL, A***
(1965, Brit.) 88m PAR c (AKA: SAMMY GOING SOUTH)

Edward G. Robinson *(Cocky Wainwright)*, Fergus McClelland *(Sammy Hartland)*, Constance Cummings *(Gloria Van Imhoff)*, Harry H. Corbett *(Lem)*, Paul Stassino *(Spyros Dracondopolous)*, Zia Mohyeddin *(The Syrian)*, Orlando Martins *(Abu Lubaba)*, John Turner *(Heneker)*, Zena Walker *(Aunt Jane)*, Jack Gwillim *(District Commissioner)*, Patricia Donahue *(Cathie)*, Jared Allen*(Bob)*, Guy Deghy *(Doctor)*, Marne Maitland *(Hassan)*, Steven Scott *(Egyptian Policeman)*, Frederick Schiller *(Head Porter)*.

When 10-year-old McClelland's parents are killed in an air raid in Egypt, the boy sets out to reach his aunt in Durban, South Africa, 5000 miles away. He meets a peddler in the desert who agrees to help him, but when the peddler goes blind he shackles himself to the boy, then dies. McClelland frees himself and moves on. He meets Robinson, a grizzled old diamond smuggler, who regales the boy with tales of his checkered past. Robinson is captured by police, also looking for McClelland, who escapes into the jungle. His Aunt arrives from South Africa, but Robinson tells her to go home and wait for the boy to finish his trek. Finally he reaches her door. Fine adventure film with Robinson very good.

p, Hal Mason; d, Alexander Mackendrick; w, Denis Cannan (based on the novel *Sammy Going South* by W. H. Canaway); ph, Erwin Hillier (Eastmancolor); m, Tristram Cary; ed, Jack Harris; art d, Edward Tester; set d, Scott Slimon.

Adventure **(PR:AAA MPAA:NR)**

BOY TROUBLE* 1/2 (1939) 75m PAR bw

Charlie Ruggles *(Homer C. Fitch)*, Mary Boland *(Sybil Fitch)*, Donald O'Connor *(Butch)*, Joyce Matthews *(Patricia Fitch)*, John Hartley *(Wyndham Wilson)*, Billy Lee *(Joe)*, Andrew Tombes *(Mr. Snively)*, Dick Elliott *(Dr. Benshlager)*, Zeffie Tilbury *(Mrs. Jepson)*, Sarah Edwards *(Mrs. Moots)*, Harlan Briggs *(Mr. Pike)*, Josephine Whittell *(Mother)*, Sonny Bupp *(Boy)*, Georgia Caine *(Mrs. Ungerlelder)*, Russell Hicks *(Magistrate)*, Grace Hayle *(Fat Mother)*, Charles Trowbridge *(Mr. Tatum)*, Spencer Charters *(Grocer Bradley)*.

Insipid heart-tugging melodrama starring Ruggles and Boland as a childless couple who have become sedate and set in their ways. Ruggles is a quiet man who enjoys his daily routine and becomes upset when minor changes occur. Boland, thinking her husband is unhappy due to their childless state, adopts two young boys. Upon his return from the department store where he works, Ruggles is shocked to find his home invaded by the urchins. He tells his wife to get the children out and will show no affection to them. The orphanage takes one of the boys back and the other runs off when it becomes clear to him that he is not wanted. The situation becomes even more melodramatic when Ruggles loses his job, separates from his wife, and then the younger boy comes down with a serious illness that finally cracks the old man's veneer, bringing the family back together.

d, George Archainbaud; w, Laura and S. J. Perelman (based on a story by Lloyd Corrigan, Monte Brice); ph, Henry Sharp; ed, Alma MacRorie.

Drama **(PR:A MPAA:NR)**

BOY! WHAT A GIRL* 1/2 (1947) 70m Herald bw

Tim Moore *(Bumpsie, The Girl)*, Elwood Smith *(Jim)*, Duke Williams *(Harry)*, Al Jackson *(Mr. Cummings)*, Shelia Guyse, Belli Mays *(Cummings Sisters)*, Sybil Lewis *(Mme. Deborah)*, Warren Patterson *(Mr. Donaldson)*, The Sam Stewart Trio, Deek Watson and his Brown Dots, Sid Catlett and Band, Ann Cornell and the International Jittebugs.

Weak black musical concerning the efforts of two shoestring producers, Smith and Williams, to get funding for a new production. Soon they meet a prospective investor, Jackson, with loads of money and two beautiful daughters. After some lame comedy provided by female-impersonator Moore, and a few decent musical numbers, the pair get the money and the girls. The film is hampered by a lack of genuine talent and a low budget.

p, Jack Goldberg; d, Arthur Leonard; w, Vincent Valentini; ph, George Webber; ed, Jack Kemp; m/l, Walter Bishop, Walter Fuller, Mary Lou Williams, Deek Watson.

Musical **(PR:A MPAA:NR)**

BOY WHO CAUGHT A CROOK* 1/2 (1961) 72m UA bw

Wanda Hendrix *(Laura)*, Roger Mobley *(Kid)*, Don Beddoe *(Colonel)*, Johnny Seven *(Rocky Kent)*, Robert Stevenson *(Sergeant)*, William Walker *(Keeper)*, Henry Hunter *(Flannigan)*.

Wearisome kid movie featuring Mobley as an irritatingly cute little tyke who finds a briefcase that belongs to a crook who had lost his loot when fleeing from the police. The kid, his helpful puppy, and a friendly hobo track down the thief, but luckily the cops arrive before anybody gets hurt.

p, Robert E. Kent; d, Edward L. Cahn; w, Nathan Juran; ph, Gilbert Warrenton; m, Richard La Salle; ed, Robert Carlisle.

Adventure/Children **(PR:AA MPAA:NR)**

BOY WHO CRIED WEREWOLF, THE** (1973) 93m UNIV c

Kerwin Matthews *(Robert Bridgeston)*, Elaine Devry *(Sandy Bridgeston)*, Scott Sealey *(Richie Bridgeston)*, Robert J. Wilke *(Sheriff)*, Susan Foster *(Jenny)*, Jack Lucas *(Harry)*, Bob Homel *(Brother Christopher)*, George Gaines *(Dr. Marserosian)*, Loretta Temple *(Monica)*, Dave Cass *(Deputy)*, Harold Goodwin *(Mr. Duncan)*, Tim Haldeman *(First Guard)*, John Logan *(Second Guard)*, Eric Gordon *(Hippy Jesus Freak)*, Paul Baxley *(1st Werewolf)*.

A new twist on the divorce melodrama starring Matthews and his women's lib wife Devry who separate, upsetting their son Sealey. The boy wants his parents back together, but while on a camping trip with his father, they are attacked by a werewolf and Matthews is bitten. Thoughts of a reconciliation between his folks disappear when it becomes apparent that dad has become a wolfman. The boy has the usual difficulties convincing the authorities that his pop is a werewolf, but eventually they see his point and dad is dealt the fatal blow. Not very horrifying, in fact, it's quite laughable and perhaps the producers should have taken a more satiric approach.

p, Aaron Rosenberg; d, Nathan H. Juran; w, Bob Homel; ph, Michael P. Joyce (Technicolor); m, Ted Stovall; ed, Barton Hayes.

Horror **(PR:A-C MPAA:PG)**

BOY WHO STOLE A MILLION, THE*** (1960, Brit.) 81m BL bw

Virgilio Texera *(Miguel)*, Maurice Reyna *(Paco)*, Marianne Benet *(Maria)*, Harold Kasket *(Luis)*, George Coulouris *(Bank Manager)*, Bill Nagy *(Police Chief)*, Warren Mitchell *(Pedro)*, Tutte Lemkow *(Mateo)*, Xan Das Bolas *(Knife Grinder)*, Francisco Bernal *(Blind Man)*, Edwin Richfield *(Commissionare)*, Barta Barri *(Gang Leader)*, Herbert Curiel *(Organ Grinder)*, Gaylord Cavallaro *(Reporter)*, Paul Whitsun Jones *(Desk Sergeant)*, Robert Rietty *(Detective)*, Mike Brendel *(Carlos I)*, Juan Olaguivel *(Carlos II)*, Victor Mojica *(Chico)*, Curt Christian *(Currito)*, Cyril Shaps *(Bank Clerk)*, Antonio Fuentes *(Assistant Organ Grinder)*, Andrea Malandrinos *(Shoemaker)*, Goyo Lebrero *(Street Vendor)*.

Charming tale, shot in Valencia, Spain, starring Reyna as a 12-year-old boy who "borrows" a million pesetas from the local bank to help his widowed father get his taxicab out of hock. The large amount robbed from the bank perks the interest of the underground and the police, who chase the boy to retrieve the money. Reyna takes it on the lam with his loyal dog and tries to elude capture. The chase leads him to a fiesta where he runs into all sorts of intimidating and bizarre characters, all of whom may want his money. The chase scenes have a Keystone Kops style to them that tends to get out of hand, but overall it is a lively and entertaining film from director Charles Crichton who is responsible for the Alec Guinness caper classic THE LAVENDER HILL MOB (1950).

p, George H. Brown; d, Charles Crichton; w, Crichton, John Eldridge (based on a story by Neils West Larsen and Antonio de Leon); ph, Douglas Slocombe; m, Tristram Cary; ed, Peter Bezencenet; art d, Maurice Carter.

Comedy **(PR:AA MPAA:NR)**

BOY WHO TURNED YELLOW, THE*

(1972, Brit.) 55m Roger Cherrill Ltd/Children's Film c

Mark Dightam, Robert Eddison, Helen Weir, Brian Worth, Esmond Knight, Laurence Carter.

Adventures of cowardly Dightam as he searches for his lost pet mouse in the Tower of London. There he encounters Eddison's alien, adding spice to his journey. Color effects well placed in this mish-mash of science fiction and fantasy. Film brings together once again the 1950s team of Powell, Pressburger, and Challis.

d, Michael Powell; w, Emeric Pressburger; ph, Christopher Challis.

Science Fiction/Fantasy **(PR:AA MPAA:NR)**

BOY WITH THE GREEN HAIR, THE*** (1949) 82m RKO c

Pat O'Brien *(Gramp)*, Robert Ryan *(Dr. Evans)*, Barbara Hale *(Miss Brand)*, Dean Stockwell *(Peter)*, Richard Lyon *(Michael)*, Walter Catlett *(The King)*, Samuel S. Hinds *(Dr. Knudson)*, Regis Toomey *(Mr. Davis)*, Charles Meredith *(Mr. Piper)*, David Clarke *(Barber)*, Billy Sheffield *(Red)*, John Calkins *(Danny)*, Teddy Infuhr *(Timmy)*, Dwayne Hickman *(Joey)*, Eilene Janssen *(Peggy)*, Charles Arnt *(Mr. Hammond)*, Russ Tamblyn, Curtis Jackson *(Students)*.

Quiet war orphan Stockwell wakes up one day to discover that his hair has turned green. Initially finding his new tresses delightfully intriguing, Stockwell soon discovers that the new coloring allows him to be singled out for ridicule and unacceptance in his small town. Although the sympathetic O'Brien tries to inject sympathy and understand- ing into the community, the townspeople call for a shaving of the boy's head. Feeling unloved and unwanted, Stockwell runs away. Pausing to sleep during his escape, Stockwell dreams of meeting other war orphans who urge him to return to the town to preach the stupidity of war and to make them aware of the horrible realities of how simple misunderstandings and the inability to accept what is different can lead to armed conflict. Well-intentioned but pretentious drama that, despite some distinct humanism from O'Brien, fails to create any sympathy because of its overblown profundity. An early work in the career of cult director Losey, the film points out its creator's penchant for laying it on thick. Notable is the song "Nature Boy" which appears for the first time in this film; it was written by eden ahbez who refused to employ capital letters, insisting that they be exclusively used for the word "God."

p, Dore Schary, Stephen Ames; d, Joseph Losey; w, Ben Barzman, Alfred Lewis Levitt (based on a story by Betsy Beaton); ph, George Barnes (Technicolor); m, Leigh Harline; ed, Frank Doyle; md, Constantin Bakaleinikoff; cos, Adele Balken

Drama **Cas.** **(PR:AA MPAA:NR)**

BOYD'S SHOP** (1960, Brit.) 55m Emmett Dalton/RFD bw

Eileen Crowe *(Miss McClure)*, Geoffrey Golden *(Andrew Boyd)*, Aideen O'Kelly *(Agnes Boyd)*, Vincent Dowling *(John Haslett)*, Aiden Crenwell *(Rev. Dunwoody)*, Rita O'Dea *(Miss Logan)*, May Craig *(Mrs. Clotworthy)*.

Crowe is the subject of conflict when a new grocer in town falls for his competitor's daughter. Beautiful Irish setting furthers romance of plot.

p, Robert S. Baker, Monty Berman; d, Henry Cass; w, Philip Howard (based on a play by St. John G. Ervine).

Comedy **(PR:A MPAA:NR)**

BOYS, THE** (1962, Brit.) 124m Gala bw

Richard Todd *(Victor Webster)*, Robert Morley *(Montgomery)*, Felix Aylmer *(Judge)*, Dudley Sutton *(Stan Coulter)*, Jess Conrad *(Barney Lee)*, Ronald Lacey *(Billy Herne)*, 05/8Tony Garnett *(Ginger Thompson)*, Wilfred Bramble *(Robert Brewer)*, Allan Cuthbertson *(Randolph St. John)*, Wensley Pithey *(Mr. Coulter)*, Colin Gordon *(Gordon Lonsdale)*, Kenneth J. Warren *(George Tanner)*, Betty Marsden *(Mrs. Herne)*, Patrick Magee *(Mr. Lee)*, Roy Kinnear *(Charles Salmon)*.

Somewhat slow, but nonetheless engrossing courtroom drama concerning the trial of four youths accused of murdering a garage night watchman. Todd is the prosecuting attorney who paints a picture of four juvenile delinquents who killed the man just for kicks. Morley is the defense attorney who tries to convince the jury that the boys are innocent. An interesting facet of British law is debated during the course of the trial, questioning the validity of allowing the death penalty for a murder involving money, but denying capital punishment for murders of passion or pleasure. Good performances all around, but the effect is muddled by a complicated flashback structure.

p, Kenneth Rive, Sidney J. Furie; d, Furie; w, Stuart Douglass; ph, Gerald Gibbs; m, The Shadows; ed, Jack Slade.

Crime **(PR:C MPAA:NR)**

BOYS FROM BRAZIL, THE*1/2** (1978) 123m FOX c

Gregory Peck *(Josef Mengele)*, Laurence Olivier *(Ezra Lieberman)*, James Mason *(Eduard Seibert)*, Lilli Palmer *(Esther Lieberman)*, Uta Hagen *(Frieda Maloney)*, Rosemary Harris *(Mrs. Doring)*, John Dehner *(Henry Wheelock)*, John Rubinstein *(David Bennett)*, Anne Meara *(Mrs. Curry)*, Steven Gutenberg *(Barry Kohler)*, Denholm Elliott *(Sidney Beynon)*, Jeremy Black *(Jack Curry, Simon Harrington, Erich Doring, Bobby Wheelock)*, David Hurst *(Strasser)*, Bruno Ganz *(Prof. Bruckner)*, Walter Gotell *(Mundt)*, Carl Duering *(Traustiner)*, Linda Hayden *(Nancy)*, Richard Marner *(Doring)*, Georg Marishka *(Gunther)*, Michael Gough *(Harrington)*, Wolfgang Preiss *(Lofquist)*, Joachim Hansen *(Fassler)*, Guy Dumont *(Hessen)*, Gunter Meisner *(Franbach)*, Prunella Scales *(Mrs. Harrington)*, Raul Faustino Saldanha *(Ismael)*, Jurgen Anderson *(Kleist)*, David Brandon *(Schmidt)*, Gerti Gordon *(Berthe)*, Mervin Nelson *(Stroop)*, Wolf Kahler *(Schwimmer)*, Monica Gearson *(Gertrud)*.

A sumptuous, fast-moving epic about Mengele/Peck (who may or may not still be alive) matching and losing his wits to Olivier (based, no doubt, on Nazi-hunter Elie Weisel) against a somewhat far-fetched plot having to do with the cloning of Hitler. Mengele's plan is to harvest all these young men who have been placed in environments like Hitler's (boring, civil-servant parents) in an attempt to recreate der Fuhrer's background as well as his genes. The picture jets all over the world and Peck, as Mengele, takes charge. His makeup seems a trifle Kabuki and his acting is a bit Noh, but he obviously relishes the chance to play a villain. Olivier, as Lieberman, uses his standard German/Jewish accent (he used the same one in MARATHON MAN) which seems to be a cross between the kosher butcher in Golders Green and Albert Basserman (THE RED SHOES, RHAPSODY IN BLUE, etc). The picture barrels along like a Mercedes for about 115 minutes, then spins and peters out near the end. Gutenberg, in one of his first roles, instantly achieves film recognizability in a small but telling role of a young member of a militant Jewish organization who spots a few ex-Nazis in Paraguay and is murdered for his efforts. Mengele and Seibert (Mason) are attempting to start a Fourth Reich (won't those people *ever* learn?) with the Hitler clones, all played with youthful menace by Black. All of the small parts are well cast and well done. Goldsmith's music is a rousing addition and the film might have merited more kudos were it not for the penultimate scene between Peck and Olivier, whereby the heinous Hun keeps firing bullets into the frail old fella, but that doesn't seem to daunt the aged Nazi-hunter who must get out all his dialog before he is rescued. Levin wrote a can't-put-down novel and Shaffner and Gould have fashioned a can't-turn-off picture.

p, Martin Richards, Stanley O'Toole; d, Franklin J. Schaffner; w, Heywood Gould (based on Ira Levin's novel); ph, Henri Becae (Panavision, DeLuxe Color); m, Jerry Goldsmith; ed, Robert E. Swink; cos, Anthony Mendleson.

Suspense Intrigue **Cas.** **(PR:C-O MPAA:R)**

BOYS FROM BROOKLYN, THE

(SEE: BELA LUGOSI MEETS A BROOKLYN GORILLA, 1952)

BOYS FROM SYRACUSE*** (1940) 72m Mayfair/UNIV bw

Allan Jones *(Antipholus of Ephesus/Antipholus of Syracuse)*, Martha Raye *(Luce)*, Joe Penner *(Dromio of Ephesus/Dromio of Syracuse)*, Rosemary Lane *(Phyllis)*, Charles Butterworth *(Duke of Ephesus)*, Irene Hervey *(Adriana)*, Alan Mowbray *(An gelo)*, Eric Blore *(Pinch)*, Samuel S. Hinds *(Aegon)*.

In ancient Greece, twin brothers and their twin slaves are separated at birth. One brother becomes emperor of Ephesus and conquers Syracuse. Proclaiming that all native Syracusans must die, the new ruler unknowingly sentences his own father, in town to seek out his long-lost sons, to death. When the twin brother arrives in Ephesus, the expected mix-up of identities pushes the comedy along until all is resolved between the relations. The Broadway updating of Shakespeare's "The Comedy of Errors" is given a light-hearted, free-spirited Hollywood treatment that manages to get some de lightful performances from its limited cast. Although the "modern" gags introduced during the film (stone newspapers, meters on taxi-chariots, etc.) may appear ridiculous, the sense of humor of the filmmakers is well-intentioned. Classic numbers include: "He And She," "This Can't Be Love," "Sing For Your Supper," "Falling in Love With Love," which were bowdlerized to inexplicably make room for new tunes "The Greeks Have A Word For It" and "Who Are You."

p, Jules Levey; d, Edward Sutherland; w, Leonard Spigelgass, Charles Grayson (based on the stage play by George Abbott, Richard Rodgers and Lorenz Hart, adapted from Shakespeare's *The Comedy of Errors*); ph, Joe Valentine; ed, Milton Carruth; md, Charles Previn; ch, Dave Gould;

Musical/Comedy **(PR:A MPAA:NR)**

BOYS IN BROWN*½

(1949, Brit.) 85m Gainsborough/GFD bw

Jack Warner (Governor), Richard Attenborough (Jackie Knowles), Dirk Bogarde (Alfie Rawlins), Jimmy Hanley (Bill Foster), Barbara Murray (Kitty Hurst), Patrick Holt (Tigson), Andrew Crawford (Casey), Thora Hird (Mrs. Knowles), Graham Payn (Plato Cartwright), Michael Medwin (Sparrow), John Blythe (Bossy), Alfie Bass (Basher), Cyril Chamberlain (Johnson).

Provincial Irish prison governor acts as a social worker when he attempts to reform teenage delinquents. All he succeeds in doing is allowing their mischief to disorganize his life.

p, Anthony Darnborough; d&w, Montgomery Tully (based on a play by Reginald Beckwith); ph, Gordon Lang, Cyril Bristow.

Crime **(PR:AA MPAA:NR)**

BOYS IN COMPANY C, THE***

(1978, U.S./Hong Kong) 125m COL c

Stan Shaw (Tyrone Washington), Andrew Stevens (Billy Ray Pike), James Canning (Alvin Foster), Michael Lembeck (Vinnie Fazio), Craig Wasson (Dave Bisbee), Scott Hylands (Capt. Collins), James Whitmore, Jr. (Lt. Archer), Noble Willingham (Sgt. Curry), Lee Ermey (Sgt. Loyce), Santos Morales (Sgt. Aquilla), Drew Michaels (Capt. Metcalfe), Karen Hilger (Betsy), Peggy O'Neal (Nancy Bisbee), Claude Wilson (Roy Foster), Chuck Doherty (George Pike), Cisco Oliver (Spoon), Stan Johns (Receiving Sergeant), Don Bell (Jr. D.I.), Bob Mallett (Hank), Parris Hicks (Oates), Frederick Matthews, Logan Clarke, Ray Wagner, Duane Mercier, Noel Kramer, Fred Smithson, Eazy Black, Rick Natkin, Helen McNeely, Charles Waters, Ken Metcalfe, Vic Diaz, Jose Mari Avellana, Victor Pinzon, Michael Cohen.

This was one of the first post-Vietnam pictures, none of which made any real money or any real dent in the psyche. It's the story of five young men and how their lives were altered by serving in the Far East. Shaw is a pusher who evolves from a profit-hungry dealer into a macho leader of men. Lembeck plays the kind of role his father, Harvey Lembeck, used to play—the smart-mouth street guy who is always on top of things. Canning is the Thomas Wolfe character, making notes for the novel he'll never publish. Wasson is the unreconstituted 1960s peacenick and Stevens is the athlete who turns to drugs. It's a little sluggish at just under two hours, and Furie thankfully does not get into all the tricks he used in various other films (THE IPCRESS FILE, THE LEATHER BOYS) that caused viewers to forget they were watching a story. Good performances and a solid screenplay (Furie and Rich Natkin) that does not aim to inspire or alter or illuminate the war and the reasons for it. With no pretensions to anything but what it is, an action picture with intelligence.

p, Andrew Morgan; d, Sidney Furie; w, Richard Natkin, Furie; ph, Godfrey A. Godar (Panavision, Technicolor); m, Jaime Mendoza-Nava; ed, Michael Berman, Frank J. Urioste, Allan Pattillo, James Benson.

War Drama **Cas.** **(PR:O MPAA:R)**

BOYS IN THE BAND, THE**

(1970) 117m Leo/Cinema Center/National General c

Kenneth Nelson (Michael), Frederick Combs (Donald), Leonard Frey (Harold), Cliff Gorman (Emory), Reuben Greene (Bernard), Robert La Tourneaux (Cowboy), Laurence Luckinbill (Hank), Keith Prentice (Larry), Peter White (Alan).

On the night of a birthday celebration for an old friend, homosexual Nelson receives a phone call from his old college roommate, White, who wants to drop by for a visit. Knowing that the "straight" White wouldn't appreciate a night with his gay cronies, Nelson tells his old pal that this particular night would be impossible. The guests, Gorman, Luckinbill, Combs, Prentice, and Greene, arrive and the men begin to discuss the tardiness of birthday boy Frey as well as Gorman's gift for Frey, La Tourneaux, a male prostitute who has been engaged to indulge in some birthday fantasies. The festivities are interrupted by the surprise appearance of White. At first the homosexual group is shy and uncomfortable with the heterosexual, but soon their problems and personalities emerge. White is at first surprised at, then fascinated by the gathering. After he confesses his own latent homosexual urges to Nelson, the group stabilizes just in time for Frey's arrival. Although the original theatrical version of the story was considered to be a daring off-Broadway work, one of the first plays to deal openly with homosexuality, that production, as well as the film version, suffers from pre-programmed, group-encounter-based dialog and simplistic moralizing. The usual types, the outrageous swish (Gorman), the family man turned gay (Luckinbill), the comer-out-of-the-closet (White), are all displayed with a disregard for true human emotion. The issue is dealt with in a sensitive manner, but a much less "meaningful" approach would have made the characters much more accessible. The direction by Friedkin is not cinematic at all, looking simply like a rendering of the stage play on celluloid. The action-oriented director, who can study a character while entertaining, had much greater success with THE FRENCH CONNECTION and THE EXORCIST. A more understanding, sensitive portrait of contemporary homosexuality can be found in SUNDAY, BLOODY SUNDAY.

p, Mart Crowley; d, William Friedkin; w, Crowley (based on his play); ph, Arthur J. Ornitz (DeLuxe Color); ed, Jerry Greenberg; prod d, John Robert Lloyd; set d, William C. Gerrity.

Drama **Cas.** **(PR:O MPAA:R)**

BOYS' NIGHT OUT***

(1962) 113m MGM c

Kim Novak (Cathy), James Garner (Fred Williams), Tony Randall (George Drayton), Howard Duff (Doug Jackson), Janet Blair (Marge Drayton), Patti Page (Joanne McIlleny), Jessie Royce Landis (Ethel Williams), Oscar Homolka (Dr. Prokosch), Howard Morris (Howard McIlleny), Anne Jeffreys (Toni Jackson), Zsa Zsa Gabor (Moss' Girl Friend), Fred Clark (Mr. Bohannon), William Bendix (Slattery), Jim Backus (Peter Bowers), Larry Keating (Mr. Bingham), Ruth McDevitt (Beulah Partridge).

Sociology student Novak, writing her thesis on the American male, poses as a lady of the night to obtain some inside information. She soon becomes the prospective plaything of Randall, Duff, Morris, and Garner, four businessmen who are desperate to fit into the "swinging suburbanite" mold. They set Novak up in an apartment and then proceed to do nothing but eat, complain, and chat with Novak, who, naturally, becomes surprised at the inability of the typical man to live up to his playboy status. The charming Garner finally sweeps the analytical Novak off her feet and the two quickly marry, reinforcing the old-fashioned monogamous relationship. Unpretentious social satire that manages to poke a few deserved jabs at modern man's ego. The laughs are a bit sparse, but the witty cast helps carry it along.

p, Martin Ransohoff; d, Michael Gordon; w, Ira Wallach (based on a story by Marvin Worth, Arne Sultan, adpated by Marion Hargrove); ph, Arthur E. Arling (Metrocolor); m, Frank DeVol; ed, Tom McAdoo.

Comedy **(PR:C MPAA:NR)**

BOYS OF PAUL STREET, THE**

(1969, Hung./US) 105m FOX c

Anthony Kemp (Nemecsek), William Burleigh (Boka), John Moulder-Brown (Gereb), Robert Efford (Csonakos), Mark Colleano (Csele), Gary O'Brien (Weisz), Martin Beaumont (Kolnay), Paul Bartlett (Barabas), Earl Younger (Leszik), Gyorgy Vizi (Richter), Julien Holdaway (Feriats), Peter Delmar (Older Pasztor), Miklos Jancso (Younger Pasztor), Attila Nemethy (Wendaver), Imre Ebergenyi (Szebenits), Sandor Kentner (Torok), Andras Avar (Szabo), Janos Pach (Younger Szabo), Istvan Seri (Bespectacled Boy), Orsolya Zeitler (Girl with Diabolo), Mari Torocsik (Nemecsek's Mother), Sandor Pecsi (Prof. Racz), Laszlo Zokak (Jano), Laszlo Paal (Nemecsek's Father), Arpad Teri (Doctor).

Anti-war allegory from Hungary dealing with rival street gangs in Budapest. One gang seizes territorial control over a vacant lot and another gang challenges their right to take it. Eventually, the city takes over the lot and bulldozes it to make way for new buildings.

p, Endre Bohem; d, Zoltan Fabri; w, Fabri, Bohem (based on the novel by Ferenc Molnar); ph, Gyorgy Illes (Agfascope, Eastmancolor); m, Emil Petrovics; cos, Judit Schaffer.

Drama **(PR:A MPAA:NR)**

BOYS OF THE CITY*½

(1940) 68m MON bw (AKA: THE GHOST CREEPS)

Bobby Jordan (Danny), Leo Gorcey (Muggs), Dave O'Brien (Knuckles), George Humbert (Tony), Holly Chester (Boy), Sunshine Sammy (Scruno), Frankie Burke (Skinny), Donald Haines (Pee Wee), Jack Edwards (Algy), Vince Barnett (Simp), Minerva Urecal (Agnes), Inna Gest (Louise).

Two Dead End Kids and a few East Side Kids are teamed up on a trip to the mountains. Meanwhile a judge has also taken a group up to the mountains to his retreat. The judge's life has been threatened by hoods to keep him from testifying to something that is never quite explained in the film, but the two groups of travelers are thrown together in the judge's mansion. That night the hoods knock off the judge and the city boys have to solve the murder. (See BOWERY BOYS series, Index)

p, Sam Katzman; d, Joe Lewis; w, William Lively; ph, Robert Cline; ed, Carl Pierson.

Comedy/Thriller **Cas.** **(PR:A MPAA:NR)**

BOYS' RANCH*½

(1946) 97m MGM bw

Jackie "Butch" Jenkins (Butch"), James Craig (Dan Walker), Skippy Homeier (Skippy), Dorothy Patrick (Susan Walker), Ray Collins (Davis Banton), Darryl Hickman (Hank), Sharon McManus (Mary Walker), Minor Watson (Mr. Harper), Geraldine Wall (Mrs. Harper), Arthur Space (Mr. O'Neil), Robert Emmett O'Connor (Druggist), Moroni Olsen (Judge Henderson).

Craig stars as a baseball player who gets a group of Texas ranchers interested in creating a retreat for wayward youth to help reform juvenile delinquents. The ball player works out a program of fresh air, farm work and exercise to teach the boys the proper values. Average treatment of the usual material, including the one boy, Homeier, who refuses to be reformed. (Loose sequel to BOYS TOWN)

p, Robert Sisk; d, Roy Rowland; w, William Ludwig; ph, Charles Salerno, Jr.; m, Nathaniel Shilkret; ed, Ralph E. Winters.

Drama **(PR:A MPAA:NR)**

BOYS' REFORMATORY*

(1939) 62m MON bw

Frankie Darro (Tommy), Grant Withers (Dr. Owens), David Durand (Knickles), Warren McCollum (Spike), Albert Hill, Jr. (Pete), Bob McClung (Blubber), George Offerman, Jr. (Joie), Frank Coghlan, Jr. (Eddie), Ben Welden (Mike Hearn), Lillian Elliot (Mrs. O'Mara).

Plodding crime drama concerning an orphaned boy who takes the rap for his weakling foster-brother so that his foster-mother won't lose faith in her son. The noble youngster is sent to a reformatory where the typical brutal and uncaring treatment is doled out. Soon the boy breaks out of the joint and searches for the crooks who framed him and his brother.

p, Lindsley Parsons; d, Howard Bretherton; w, Ray Trampe, Wellyn Totman (based on a story by Trampe and Norman S. Hall); ph, Harry Newman.

Crime **(PR:A MPAA:NR)**

BOYS TOWN*****

(1938) 96m MGM bw

Spencer Tracy (Father Edward Flanagan), Mickey Rooney (Whitey Marsh), Henry Hull (Dave Morris), Leslie Fenton (Dan Farrow), Addison Richards (The Judge), Edward Norris (Joe Marsh), Gene Reynolds (Tony Ponessa), Minor Watson (The Bishop), Jonathan Hale (John Hargraves), Bob Watson (Pee Wee), Martin Spellman *(Skinny)*, Mickey Rentschler *(Tommy Anderson)*, Frankie Thomas *(Freddie Fuller)*, Jimmy Butler *(Paul Ferguson)*, Sidney Miller *(Mo Kahn)*, Robert Keane *(Burton)*, Victor Killian *(The Sheriff)*.

When Father Edward J. Flanagan said there are no "bad boys," he meant it and then went about saving the homeless, underprivileged, and victimized youths of America by building a sanctuary called Boys Town in Omaha, Nebraska. Tracy begins picking up stray boys and housing them in a vacated building, borrowing and begging to get them food and clothes, his most loyal supporter being pawn shop owner Hull. In one early and precious scene Tracy asks for a dollar to help change one of his delinquent charges into a good American. Hull looks into his near-empty purse and asks Tracy: "Can't you make a good American for fifty cents?" Tracy hears the story of a murderer from his own lips and concludes that if he had been helped he would never have committed the crime. He helps the convict's brother, Rooney, a wisecracking poolhall shark, who is taken to the newly constructed Boys Town outside of Omaha. Here Rooney causes Tracy no end of headaches as he disrupts the boys' self-styled government. He runs away but returns when he is hungry. Next, Rooney gets the notion that if he "can't beat 'em, join 'em," and launches a campaign to become mayor of the community government, replete with brass bands, banners and slogans. He loses narrowly but graciously to a gentler boy, then runs away but returns when one of the small boys who idolizes him, Watson, is run over by a car (he survives). The third time Rooney leaves he joins his brother who has escaped from prison, finding him just as he is committing a robbery. He is wounded but Tracy saves him from prosecution, and helps capture the gang, which brings new rewards for Boys Town; Rooney returns to the home to embrace its wonderful ideals instead of sneer at them. BOYS TOWN was one of MGM's greatest hits to that time, millions going to see it, which surprised studio executives, especially mogul Louis B. Mayer who allowed only a modest budget for the film, which was shot on a short schedule. Mayer, despite his deep reservations about Catholicism, soon came to love the film and told one and all years after that it was his favorite, which may or may not have had something to do with the fortune it made for his studio. It also helped to make Tracy box office gold and, next to Gable, America's favorite actor, according to polls of the time. But the public also came to see that dynamic kid actor, Rooney, whose popularity was enormous. (Though he plays a child of about 14, Rooney was 17 at the time.) Much of the success for BOYS TOWN should be credited to director Taurog who specialized in directing children in movies and here put the child actors through their paces with the speed of light. When Tracy won his second consecutive Oscar for BOYS TOWN, having won in 1937 for CAPTAINS COURAGEOUS, he was as surprised as Mayer. No one argued about his right to have the award. He had studied long and hard to play the role of the saintly priest who made a crusade of saving boys. Tracy went to Boys Town before the production and spent long hours talking with the real Father Flanagan, finding him a strong but gentle man, without sanctimonious airs. Tracy emulated the man's attitudes to a blink before the cameras and when he won the Oscar he announced that it really belonged to the priest and he sent it to him, with an inscription which read: "To Father Edward J. Flanagan, whose great human qualities, kindly simplicity, and inspiring courage were strong enough to shine through my humble effort. Spencer Tracy." (Sequel: MEN OF BOYS TOWN.)

p, John W. Considine, Jr.; d, Norman Taurog; w, John Meehan, Dore Schary (based on a story by Schary and Eleanore Griffin); ph, Sidney Wagner; m, Edward Ward; ed, Elmo Vernon; spec eff, Slavko Vorkapich.

Drama **(PR:AAA MPAA:NR)**

BOYS WILL BE BOYS* (1936, Brit.) 75m Gainsborough/GAU bw

Will Hay *(Dr. Alec Smart)*, Gordon Harker *(Faker Brown)*, Claude Dampier *(Theo P. Finch)*, Jimmy Hanley *(Cyril Brown)*, Davy Burnaby *(Col. Crableigh)*, Norma Varden *(Lady Korking)*, Charles Farrell *(Louis Brown)*, Percy Walsh *(Governor)*.

School headmaster Hay discovers that the father of one of his students is a thief. He devises a plan to thwart the jewel-robbing hoodlum, and returns to his blackboard in peace. Not much of a caper nor too many laughs.

p, Michael Balcon; d, William Beaudine; w, Will Hay, Robert Edmunds (based on characters created by J. B. Morton); ph, Charles Van Enger.

Comedy **(PR:A MPAA:NR)**

BOYS WILL BE GIRLS* (1937, Brit.) 66m Leslie Fuller bw

Leslie Fuller *(Bill Jenkins)*, Nellie Wallace *(Bertha Luff)*, Greta Woxholt *(Roberta)*, Georgie Harris *(Roscoe)*, Judy Kelly *(Thelma)*, D. J. Williams *(George Luff)*, Tonie Edgar Bruce *(Mrs. Jenkins)*, Constance Godridge *(Ernestine)*, Syd Crossley *(Bookum)*, Olivette *(Dancer)*.

Heir to a fortune must kick his smoking habit and love of drinking to gain his inheritance. A tough way to make money, but it can be done, as Fuller demonstrates in this poor comedic effort.

p, Joe Rock; d, Gilbert Pratt; w, Clifford Grey, H. F. Maltby (based on a story by Evelyn Barrie); ph, Cyril Bristow.

Comedy **(PR:AA MPAA:NR)**

BRACELETS* (1931, Brit.) 50m GAU bw

Bert Coote *(Edwin Hobbett)*, Joyce Kennedy *(Annie Moran)*, D. A. Clarke-Smith *(Joe le Sage)*, Margaret Emden *(Mrs. Hobbett)*, Frederick Leister *(Slim Symes)*, Stella Arbenina *(Countess Soumbatoff)*, Harold Huth *(Maurice Dupont)*, George Merritt *(Director)*.

Jeweler who has been around the block a few times discovers crooks are posing as Russian royalty to pull off a robbery. The old-timer foils the swindlers for a happy ending. Dull sleuthing.

p, L'Estrange Fawcett; d&w, Sewell Collins (based on his play).

Crime **(PR:A MPAA:NR)**

BRAIN, THE* (1965, Ger./Brit.) 85m Governor bw

Anne Heywood *(Anna)*, Peter Van Eyck *(Dr. Corrie)*, Cecil Parker *(Stevenson)*, Bernard Lee *(Shears)*, Ellen Schwiers *(Ella)*, Maxine Audley *(Marion)*, Jeremy Spenser *(Martin)*, Siegfried Lowitz *(Walters)*, Hans Nielsen *(Immerman)*, Miles Malleson *(Dr. Miller)*, Jack MacGowran *(Furber)*, George A. Cooper *(Gabler)*, Irene Richmond *(Mrs. Gabler)*, Ann Sears *(Secretary)*, Victor Brooks *(Farmer)*, Alistair Williams *(Inspector Pike)*, Kenneth Kendall, John Junkin, Frank Forsythe, Bandana Das Gupta, Allan Cuthberton, Richard McNeff, John Watson, Patsy Rowlands, Brian Pringle, Dieter Borsche.

Mad doctor Van Eyck preserves the living brain of a cruel and ruthless tycoon after a plane crash takes the businessman's life. The bottled brain takes over the obsessed doctor's mind and uses him to discover who arranged the plane accident. Daughter of the dead man, Heywood, gets involved, adding to this third film version of Siodmak's DONOVAN'S BRAIN. Just an experiment, it seems.

p, Raymond Stross; d, Freddie Francis; w, Robert Stewart, Phil Mackie (based on the novel *Donovan's Brain* by Curt Siodmak); ph, Bob Huke; m, Ken Jones; ed, Oswald Hafenrichter; art d, Arthur Lawson; set d, Ted Barnes; cos, Jackie Cummins.

Science Fiction **Cas.** **(PR:A MPAA:NR)**

BRAIN, THE ½** (1969, Fr./U.S.) 115m PAR c (LE CERVEAU)

David Niven *(The Brain)*, Jean-Paul Belmondo *(Arthur)*, Bourvil *(Anatole)*, Eli Wallach *(Scannapieco)*, Silvia Monti *(Sofia)*, Fernand Valois *(Bruno)*, Raymond Gerome *(Le Commanissaire)*, Jacques Balutin *(Pochet)*, Jacques Ciron *(Duboeuf)*, Fernand Guiot *(Mazurel)*, Jean Le Poulain *(Man from Fifth Floor)*, Robert Dalban *(Belgian with a Cold)*.

Complex comedy/caper movie starring Niven as the title character who masterminded Britain's Great Train Robbery and who now sets his sights on France and a trainload of NATO money being shipped to Brussels. Meanwhile, two small-time French hoods, Belmondo and Bourvil, have decided that they too could rob the train. Enter Sicilian gangster Wallach who spends most of his time keeping his eyes on his beautiful sister Monti, who has set a date with Niven. Niven has gained control over the money shipment by using his old reserve status in the British army and the two Frenchmen follow him to steal the plans for the trip. Belmondo breaks into Niven's apartment and grabs the plans for the robbery, but he is attacked by a pet leopard and practically destroys the place trying to escape. When it comes time to actually rob the train the groups of crooks all converge and the loot keeps changing hands from one faction to another, slapstick style. Niven finally gets hold of the dough and hides it in the base of a 50-foot replica of the Statue of Liberty that is being shipped to America. Unfortunately the money falls out of the statue and into the ocean, but all the crooks escape capture. Niven and his new French partners discuss robbing the U.S. Treasury as the credits roll. Fun film with good comic moments and a fine cast, though at times it suffers from being a bit excessive.

p, Alain Poire; d, Gerard Oury; w, Oury, Marcel Julian, Daniele Thompson; ph, Armand Thirard (Eastmancolor); m, Georges Delerue; ed, Albert Jurgenson; art d, Jean Andre; cos, Tanine Autre.

Comedy **(PR:A MPAA:NR)**

BRAIN EATERS, THE* ½ (1958) 60m AIP bw

Edwin Nelson *(Dr. Kettering)*, Alan Frost *(Glenn)*, Jack Hill *(Senator Powers)*, Joanna Lee *(Alice)*, Jody Fair *(Elaine)*, David Hughes *(Dr. Wyler)*, Robert Ball *(Dan Walker)*, Greigh Phillips *(Sheriff)*, Orville Sherman *(Cameron)*, Leonard Nimoy *(Protector)*, Doug Banks *(Doctor)*, Henry Randolph *(Telegrapher)*.

Silly sci-fi film concerning a strange drill-shaped ship that burrows its way out of the earth and into a small town. Out of the ship swarm hairy parasites who attach themselves to the necks of the townsfolk and control them. Heroic scientist Nelson (who also served as the producer of the movie) spends most of his screen time arguing with the military on how to stop the invasion. After dozens of attempts to dispose of the creatures and their ship, Nelson comes up with the bright idea of throwing a live electric cable across the digger which explodes, killing all the little nasties. Nelson probably got the idea from watching THE SPIDER which AIP released at the same time (where the hero dealt with its monster by throwing a live electric cable on its web and frying it). Pretty typical stuff as "brain" movies go. Look hard and fast for "Star Trek's" Nimoy as the "Protector" of the alien craft.

p, Edwin Nelson; d, Bruno Ve Soto; w, Gordon Urquhart; ph, Larry Ralmond; m, Tom Jonson; ed, Carlo Lodato.

Science Fiction **(PR:C MPAA:NR)**

BRAIN FROM THE PLANET AROUS, THE* ½ (1958) 70m Howco bw

John Agar *(Steve)*, Joyce Meadows *(Sally Fallon)*, Robert Fuller *(Dan)*, Thomas B. Henry *(John Fallon)*, Henry Travis *(Col. Grogley)*, Kenneth Terrell *(Colonel)*, Tim Graham *(Sheriff Paine)*, E. Leslie Thomas *(Gen. Brown)*, Bill Giorgio *(Russian)*.

Agar stars as a nuclear physicist whose brain has been taken over by a giant, floating alien intelligence called Gor. Gor enters Agar's head and uses him to continue his plan to conquer the universe. Agar's friends notice a change in him (including his new black eyeballs that can explode airplanes) but they can't quite put their collective finger on it. Agar's gal-pal Meadows learns the truth from another floating brain, the good guy, who goes by the name of Vol. Vol enters the noggin of Agar's faithful pooch, and Gor and Vol battle it out through Agar and Fido until Meadows takes some initiative and whacks the scientist on the skull with an ax, knocking the evil brains out of him. Agar, doggy, and Meadows all return to normal and the universe is saved again. Really bad, but good fun for the cult of John Agar fanatics.

p, Jacques Marquette; d, Nathan Hertz; w, Ray Buffum; ph, Marquette; m, Walter Greene; ed, Irving M. Schoenberg.

Science Fiction **Cas.** **(PR:C MPAA:NR)**

BRAIN MACHINE, THE**   (1955, Brit.) 83m Merton Park/AA bw

Patrick Barr (*Dr. Geoffrey Allen*), Elizabeth Allan (*Dr. Philippa Roberts*), Maxwell Reed (*Frank Smith*), Russell Napier (*Insp. Durham*), Gibb McLaughlin (*Spencer Simon*), Edwin Richfield (*Ryan*), Neil Hallett (*Sgt. John Harris*), Vanda Godsell (*Mae*), Bill Nagy (*Charlie*), Mark Bellamy, Anthony Valentine, John Horsley, Donald Bissett, Gwen Bacon, Clifford Buckton.

Psychiatrist Allan discovers, by using an electroencephalograph, that amnesia victim Reed has the mind of a psychopathic murderer. When she reports her findings to the police, they show no interest until her patient kidnaps her and escapes from the hospital. In their search for Allan, police find a trail of bloody gang violence, the result of a drug-smuggling operation. Hughes' screenplay and direction bring out above-average performances.

p, Alec Snowden; d&w, Ken Hughes; ph, Josef Ambor.

Crime   (PR:A MPAA:NR)

BRAIN OF BLOOD*¹/₂   (1971, Phil.) 83m Hemisphere c (AKA: THE CREATURE'S REVENGE)

Kent Taylor, John Bloom, Regina Carroll, Angelo Rossitto, Grant Williams, Reed Hadley, Vicki Volante, Zandor Vorkov.

Mad scientist Taylor performs brain transplant experiments and unexpectedly creates Bloom, an ugly monster who threatens mayhem all around. Rossitto plays a dwarf assistant to Taylor whose sadistic tendencies lead him to insane laughter and poking chained women. Partly filmed in the Philippines.

p, Al Adamson, Sam Sherman; d, Adamson; w, Joe Van Rogers, Kane W. Lynn.

Horror   (PR:C MPAA:NR)

BRAIN THAT WOULDN'T DIE, THE**   (1959) 81m STER bw (AKA: THE HEAD THAT WOULDN'T DIE)

Herb [Jason] Evers (*Dr. Bill Cortner*), Virginia Leith (*Jan Compton*), Adele Lamont (*Doris*), Paula Maurice (*B-Girl*), Bruce Brighton (*Doctor*), Doris Brent (*Nurse*), Leslie Daniel (*Kurt*), Bonnie Shari (*Stripper*), Lola Mason (*Donna Williams*), Audrey Devereau (*Jeannie*), Eddie Carmel (*Monster*), Bruce Kerr (*Announcer*).

Another brain transplant flick that misses the mark. Brilliant surgeon Evers has created a monster so horrible to look at he keeps it locked in a dungeon. His fiancee, Leith, is decapitated in an auto accident and the doctor keeps her head alive to further his experiments. He finds model Lamont and renders her unconscious for a surgery he hopes will restore the life of his lover. The monster breaks out of the dungeon irritated by his seclusion, and makes off with Lamont cradled in his arms after killing Evers and setting the doctor's lab on fire. Not for the weak-stomached.

p, Rex Carlton; d&w, Joseph Green (based on a story by Carlton and Green); ph, Stephen Hajnal; m, Abe Baker, Tony Restaino; ed, Leonard Anderson, Marc Anderson; art d, Paul Fanning; spec eff, Byron Baer.

Horror   Cas.   (PR:O MPAA:NR)

BRAINSTORM***   (1965) 105m WB bw

Jeff Hunter (*Jim Grayam*), Anne Francis (*Lorrie Benson*), Dana Andrews (*Cort Benson*), Viveca Lindfors (*Dr. E. Larstadt*), Stacy Harris (*Josh Reynolds*), Kathie Brown (*Angie DeWitt*), Phillip Pine (*Dr. Ames*), Michael Pate (*Dr. Mills*), Robert McQueeney (*Sgt. Dawes*), Strother Martin (*Mr. Clyde*), Joan Swift (*Clara*), George Pelling (*Butler*), Victoria Meyerink (*Julie*), Stephen Roberts (*Judge*), Pat Cardi (*Bobby*).

Spooky suspense film stars Hunter as a young scientist who saves distraught Francis from committing suicide. The pair fall in love, but Francis' rotten husband Andrews (who drove her to the brink of suicide in the first place) digs up Hunter's old nervous breakdown file and gets his revenge by framing the doc on a number of strange incidents (obscene phone calls, etc.) to suggest he's cracking up again. Hunter has had enough and decides to murder Andrews and plead insanity since everyone is convinced he's loco anyway. Hunter figures that soon after his conviction he will be placed in a mental institution, suddenly "recover" after a decent interval, and walk off scot-free into the waiting arms of Francis. The plan goes haywire when Hunter realizes he can't take being locked up in the nut-house and he really starts to crack up. He desperately pleads with Francis to confess the scheme to the authorities so they will take him out of the asylum and back to a normal prison, but she won't stick her neck out to save him. Hunter finally escapes, only to have a true relapse of his breakdown and he gets dragged back to the institution. Great cast directed by actor Conrad—TV's "Cannon," of the great voice and great girth—in a clever and taut visual style. Good, sparse musical score by George Duning.

p&d, William Conrad; w, Mann Rubin (based on a story by Larry Marcus); ph, Sam Leavitt (Panavision); m, George Duning; ed, William Ziegler.

Suspense   (PR:C MPAA:NR)

BRAINSTORM***   (1983) 106m MGM/UA c

Christopher Walken (*Michael Brace*), Natalie Wood (*Karen Brace*), Louise Fletcher (*Lillian Reynolds*), Cliff Robertson (*Alex Terson*), Georgianne Walken (*Wendy*), Bill Morey (*James Zimbach*), Joe Dorsey (*Hal*), Alan Fudge (*Robert Jenkins*), Jason Lively (*Chris Brace*).

The last performance of Natalie Wood before her death at Catalina Island on November 29, 1981. She was a luminous performer but this final film had her cast more as a re-actress than an actress. It's Fletcher's picture as the chain-smoking scientist who manages to put her death on tape, from *inside* her head! The gimmick is this: Fletcher and Walken have been experimenting with a device that can get into the brain to record the emotions and all other sensations that can be played back and experienced by a second party. So imagine what it is to don the device and feel what it is to die! BRAINSTORM is chockablock with special effects that sometimes obscure, rather than enhance, the story. This *could* have been a wonderful film but

the makers fell in love with the hardware and forgot the humanity. The idea was big enough to sustain a closer look at the people and forego the high-tech. It cost $18 million and $6 million of that came from the insurance company that carried the policy on Ms. Wood's life. But for all that money, not enough of it shows up on screen. There's a lot of humor in the film to leaven the gritty moments, specifically when Walken watches (experiences?) a sexual orgasm through the machine. Robertson, in what seems like a reprise of his role as the duplicitous CIA man in THREE DAYS OF THE CONDOR, is about what you'd expect; earnest and a trifle wooden. Fletcher is a revelation to anyone who thought she'd left it all in the lap of Nurse Ratchet in ONE FLEW OVER THE CUCKOO'S NEST. Walken walks through his part as though he's just been awakened and Wood is, well, she was Natalie. And we'll never forget her.

p&d, Douglas Trumbull; w, Robert Statzel, Phillip Frank Messina (based on a story by Bruce Joel Rubin); ph, Richard Yurich (Super Panavision, Metrocolor); m, James Horner; ed, Edward Warschilka, Freeman Davies; prod d, John Vallone; art d, David L. Snyder; set d, Marjorie Stone; cos, Donfeld; sci-fi consultants, Durk Pearson, Sandy Shaw.

Science Fiction   Cas.   (PR:C-O MPAA:PG)

BRAINWASHED**¹/₂   (1961, Ger.) 102m AA bw (AKA: THE ROYAL GAME)

Curt Jurgens (*Werner von Basil*), Claire Bloom (*Irene Andreny*), Jorg Felmy (*Hans Berger*), Mario Adorf (*Mirko Centrowic*), Albert Lieven (*Hartmann*), Alan Gifford (*Mac Iver*), Dietmar Schonherr (*Rabbi*), Karel Stepanek (*Baranow*), Wolfgang Wahl (*Moonface*), Rudolf Forster (*Hotel Manager*), Albert Bessler (*Scientist*), Jan Hendriks (*First Officer*), Haralad Maresch (*Ballet Master*), Dorothea Wieck (*Countess*), Ryk De Gooyer (*Berger's Secretary*), Susanne Kolber (*Young Lady*), Hans Sohnker (*Bishop Ambrosse*).

Overlong, but fascinating, psychological drama starring Jurgens as an Austrian aristo- crat who is thrown into solitary confinement by the Nazis upon their takeover. While they mentally torture him to obtain vital secrets, he attempts to retain his sanity by stashing a book on chess in his cell and concentrating on the complexities of the chessboard to keep his mind clear. Eventually he cracks and becomes useless to the Nazis. Most of the film is told in flashback after we see Jurgens holding his own in a chess match with a worried champion. Complex and well-done visuals, coupled with a strong performance by Jurgens, keep this rather slow and deliberate film interesting.

p, Luggi Waldleitner; d, Gerd Oswald; w, Harold Medford (based on Stefan Zweig's novel *The Royal Game*, adapted by Herbert Reinecker); ph, Gunther Senfleben; m, Hans-Martin Majewski; art d, Wolfe Englert.

Drama   Cas.   (PR:A-C MPAA:NR)

BRAINWAVES**¹/₂   (1983) 81m Motion Picture Marketing c

Keir Dullea (*Julian*), Suzanna Love (*Kaylie*), Percy Rodrigues (*Dr. Robinson*), Vera Miles (*Marian*), Tony Curtis (*Dr. Clavius*), Paul Wilson (*Dr. Shroder*), Ryan Seitz (*Danny*), Nicholas Love (*Willy*), Corinne Alphen (*Lelia*), Eve Brent Ashe (*Miss Simpson*).

Ulli Lommel's BRAINWAVES is not unlike Douglas Trumbull's BRAINSTORM in that both detail devices which are able to electronically transfer thoughts between different people. The similarity ends there, though, as BRAINWAVES takes a left turn and eschews hardware and shock effects for a closer look at how the device affects human beings. Love has an auto accident that puts her into a coma. Dullea (husband) and Miles (mother) allow Clavius (Curtis) to attempt a new procedure on the tranced woman. The donor brain is from a murdered woman and Love is besieged with memories of the murder as well as the identity of the malfeasant. It's a solid suspense movie that falls short only because the cast was middle-ground rather than top-of-the-line. This is not to denigrate the actors, all of whom do a credible job. With Robert Reed and Diana Canova and Angie Dickinson in the three major roles, it would have been a TV film. With Al Pacino and Debra Winger and Liz Taylor, it would have been a feature. Same script, different casts. Love is the wife of the director and Nicholas Love is the brother of the wife of the director. The nepotism did not get in the way of a good picture. San Francisco locations a plus. Robert O. Ragland's music was exceptional to capture pace and mood.

p&d, Ulli Lommel; w, Lommel, Suzanna Love; ph, Jon Kranhouse (Getty Color); m, Robert O. Ragland; ed, Richard Brummer; spec eff, N. H. P. Inc.

Science Fiction   Cas.   (PR:O MPAA:PG)

BRAMBLE BUSH, THE**   (1960) 93m WB c

Richard Burton (*Guy*), Barbara Rush (*Mar*), Jack Carson (*Bert*), Angie Dickinson (*Fran*), James Dunn (*Stew Schaeffer*), Henry Jones (*Parker Welk*), Tom Drake (*Larry*), Frank Conroy (*Dr. Kelsey*), Carl Benton Reid (*Sam McFie*), Patricia Crest (*Betsy*), William Hansen (*Father Bannon*), Philip Coolidge (*Colin Eustis*), Russ Conway (*Sheriff Witt*), Joan Potter (*Ida Primmer*), Bern Hoffman (*Pico Salazar*), Grandon Rhodes (*Judge Manning*).

Overloaded New England soap-opera supposedly about a "mercy" killing, but the film becomes too embroiled in the sex lives of its characters to do the serious euthanasia subject justice. Burton plays the doctor who returns to his home town to care for friend Drake who is dying of Hodgkin's Disease. While treating his friend, Burton finds time to have an affair with the ill man's wife, Rush, who becomes pregnant. Not being able to watch his pal's suffering, Burton pulls the plug on his patient, killing him. The town is in an uproar over the incident and accuses the doctor of murder. It is obvious to the authorities that he bumped off Drake so that he could have Rush to himself. Burton is arrested and brought to trial. Meanwhile, nurse Dickinson, whose affections have been spurned by Burton, falls into an affair with Carson, a local politician. She is then forced to pose for nude photos taken by the town's newspaper editor, Jones, when he threatens to blow the whistle on the affair, which would ruin Carson politically. Burton is eventually cleared of the murder charge (the audience having lost interest in the case after watching all this sex) and is reunited with Rush. Okay acting, though Burton seems uncomfortable playing a New England doctor. Good cinematography by Ballard, and decent direction that somehow keeps the whole thing from becoming totally ridiculous. (The subject of euthanasia is better treated in AN ACT OF MURDER, 1948, with Fredric March.)

p, Milton Sperling; d, Daniel Petrie; w, Sperling, Philip Yordan (based on the novel by Charles Mergendahl); ph, Lucien Ballard (Technicolor); m, Leonard Rosenman; ed, Folmar Blangsted; cos, Howard Shoup.

Drama   **(PR:O MPAA:NR)**

BRAND OF FEAR*   (1949) 56m MON bw

Jimmy Wakely, Dub "Cannonball" Taylor, Gail Davis, Tom London, Marshall Reed, William H. Ruhl, William Bailey, Boyd Stockman, Joe Galbreath, Dee Cooper, Frank McCarroll, Holly Bane, Myron Healey, Bill Potter, Bob Woodward, Bob Curtis.

Routine oater has singing Wakely putting down his guitar long enough to chase rustlers off Davis' land. "Cannonball" is veteran actor Dub Taylor, best remembered for his conniving role as Michael J. Pollard's father in BONNIE AND CLYDE.

p, Louis Gray; d, Oliver Drake; w, Basil Dickey.

Western   **(PR:A MPAA:NR)**

BRAND OF THE DEVIL*1/2   (1944) 62m PRC c

Dave O'Brien, James Newill, Guy Wilkerson, Ellen Hall, Charles King, I. Stanford Jolley, Reed Howes, Budd Buster, Karl Hackett, Kermit Maynard, Ed Cassidy.

A gang of outlaws known as "the Brand of the Devil" terrorize a quiet community. The Texas Rangers discover that the gang's leader is secretly working as a foreman on a nearby ranch. Before the bad guys make their escape, the Rangers bring them down. (See TEXAS RANGERS series, Index.)

p, Arthur Alexander; d, Henry Fraser; w, Elmer Clifton; ph, Edward Kull; ed, Charles Henkel, Jr.; md, Lee Zahler.

Western   **(PR:A MPAA:NR)**

BRANDED*   (1931) 59m COL bw

Buck Jones, Ethel Kenyon, Wallace MacDonald, Philo McCullough, Al Smith, John Oscar, Bob Kortman, Fred Burns.

Jones' usual ramblings are interrupted when he inherits a ranch. The wandering cowboy intends to sell the spread and keep riding until he meets his neighbor-lady Kenyon. He falls for the gal, but the two have an argument over a strip of land and Jones erects a fence. She offers to buy him out, but he refuses because he wants to be near her. Kenyon's foreman, Smith, is also in love with his lady-boss and frames Jones on a rustling charge to get rid of him. Jones says adios and rides off when he sees the sheriff coming.

d, D. Ross Lederman; w, Randall Faye; ph, Benjamin Kline, Elmer Dyer.

Western   **(PR:A MPAA:NR)**

BRANDED***   (1951) 103m PAR c

Alan Ladd (Choya), Mona Freeman (Ruth Lavery), Charles Bickford (Mr. Lavery), Robert Keith (Leffingwell), Joseph Calleia (Rubriz), Peter Hansen (Tonio), Selena Royle (Mrs. Lavery), Tom Tully (Ransome), John Berkes (Tattoo), Milburn Stone (Dawson), Martin Garralaga (Hernandez), Edward Clark (Dad Travis), John Butler (Spig).

Ladd is super in this story of an outlaw who aids slimy crook Keith in a scheme to impersonate rich rancher Bickford's long-lost son, who was kidnaped by a bandit twenty-five years before, in order to bilk the old man out of his fortune. Ladd allows himself to have a birthmark tattooed on his shoulder to convince the rancher and his wife that he is indeed their offspring. Bickford and mother Royle welcome their "son" with open arms. Daughter Freeman finds herself extremely attracted to this stranger until she learns that he's her brother. Made to feel part of the family (feelings he hasn't had in years), Ladd begins to resent his role in the plot and reveals his true identity. As a good will gesture, he goes off in search of the couple's real son. He finds the young man, who was raised by the bandit as his son, and works out a compromise wherein the true son will split his visits between his biological parents and the aging bandit who raised him. Ladd, meanwhile, admits his feelings of love for Freeman, and the two ride off together. Ladd's performance is one of his best as a man who, over years of drifting, has become very cold and heartless, but when exposed to a loving atmosphere his facade melts and he becomes a caring person again. Good script and wonderful Technicolor photography by Charles B. Lang, Jr., enhance the effect.

p, Mel Epstein; d, Rudolph Mate; w, Sydney Boehm, Cyril Hume (based on the novel by Evan Evans); ph, Charles B. Lang, Jr. (Technicolor); m, Roy Webb; ed, Alma Macrorie.

Western   **(PR:A MPAA:NR)**

BRANDED A COWARD**   (1935) 58m Times/Superior bw

Johnny Mack Brown (Johnny Hume), Billie Seward (Ethel Carson), Lloyd Ingraham (Her Father), Syd Saylor (Oscar).

A potentially interesting psychological Johnny Mack Brown oater that is ruined by lousy camera work and poor direction. Film opens with a flashback (highly unusual for a B western) revealing why Brown falls apart under fire. His parents were gunned down by bandits in front of him when he was a child. Now he must conquer his fear to become a successful U.S. marshal. At this point, the narrative boils down to the typical shootings, chases, and general nonsense indistinguishable from any other horse opera. The twist ending nearly redeems this when, in another psychological

examination, the elusive villain that Brown has been pursuing turns out to be his own brother. A very odd little western.

p, A. W. Hackel; d, Sam Newfield; w, Earle Snell (story by Richard Martinsen); ph, William Nobles.

Western   **Cas.**   **(PR:A MPAA:NR)**

BRANDED MEN**   (1931) 60m TIF bw

Ken Maynard (Rod Whitaker), June Clyde (Dale Winters), Irving Bacon (Ramrod), Billy Bletcher (Half-A-Rod), Charles King (Mace), Donald Keith (The Brother).

Bletcher's small body coming out with his BIG voice and a young boy paired up with a runt, assisting big guy Maynard, bring plenty of laughs in this above-average western. Also, special recording techniques take masculine voices and make them soprano in emotional scenes. Unusual and excellent editing by Turner distinguishes this early talkie with big sound problems.

d, Phil Rosen; w, (based on a story by Earle Snell); ed, E. Turner.

Comedy   **Cas.**   **(PR:A MPAA:NR)**

BRANDY FOR THE PARSON**   (1952, Brit.) 79m Group 3/ABF bw

James Donald (Bill Harper), Kenneth More (Tony Rackham), Jean Lodge (Petronella Brand), Frederick Piper (Customs Inspector), Charles Hawtrey (George Crumb), Michael Trubshawe (Redworth), Alfie Bass (Dallyn), Wilfred Caithness (Mr. Minch), Lionel Harris (Mr. Frost), Richard Molinas (Massaud), Reginald Beckwith (Scout Master), Stanley Lemin (Customs Officer), Arthur Wontner (Major Glockleigh), Frank Tickle (Vicar).

Amusing little comedy about a young couple on a yachting vacation who suddenly become involved with a brandy smuggler. Soon events require the couple to run across the country because they are being chased by customs men. One of the many little vignettes concerning alcohol smuggling that Britain churned out in this period. This one's not the best, but it's far from the worst. Famed documentarist Grierson had a hand in this government-subsidized production.

p, John Grierson, Alfred O'Shaughnessy; d, John Eldridge; w, John Dighton, Walter Meade (based on the novel by Geoffrey Household); ph, Martin Curtis; m, John Addison; ed, John Trumper.

Comedy   **(PR:A MPAA:NR)**

BRANNIGAN***1/2   (1975, Brit.) 111m UA c

John Wayne (Jim Brannigan), Richard Attenborough (Commander Swann), Judy Geeson (Jennifer Thatcher), Mel Ferrer (Mel Fields), Del Henney (Drexel), Lesley-Anne Down (Luana), Barry Dennen (Julian), John Vernon (Larkin), Daniel Pilon (Gorman), John Stride (Traven), James Booth (Charlie), Brian Glover (Jimmy the Bet), Anthony Booth (Freddy), Ralph Meeker (Capt. Moretti), Jack Watson (Carter), Don Henderson (Geef), Kathryn Leigh Scott (Miss Allen), Arthur Batanides (Angell), Stewart Bevan (Alex).

Wayne in the title role is an Irish-American cop in Jolly Olde England hot on the trail of Ferrer's client, Vernon. Wayne comes up against Attenborough (now Sir Dickie) who is the 1975 equivalent of Inspector LeStrade as far as his way of doing things is concerned. These two unlikely allies solve the crime, nail the miscreants, and all is well. It's actually much the same plot as many films Wayne appeared in while wearing boots. Geeson is cute (why she didn't become a huge star still befuddles us), and all the secondary roles are well-drawn. Basically a formula film with all the usual car chases, knock-downs, booby traps, etc. If you like John Wayne, you'll love BRANNIGAN. If you hate John Wayne, you probably will never get to see BRANNIGAN. If you just think John Wayne is . . . well, only all right, you'll be better off reading a book. This is not one of the Duke's best.

p, Jules Levy, Arthur Gardner; d, Douglas Hickox; w, Christopher Trumbo, Michael Butler, William P. McGivern, William Norton (based on a story by Butler, Trumbo); ph, Gerry Fisher (Eastmancolor); m, Dominic Frontiere; ed, Malcolm Cooke; cos, Emma Porteous.

Crime Drama   **Cas.**   **(PR:A-C MPAA:PG)**

BRASHER DOUBLOON, THE***   (1947) 72m FOX bw (GB: THE HIGH WINDOW)

George Montgomery (Philip Marlowe), Nancy Guild (Merle Davis), Conrad Janis (Leslie Murdock), Roy Roberts (Lt. Breeze), Fritz Kortner (Vannier), Florence Bates (Mrs. Murdock), Marvin Miller (Blair), Houseley Stevenson (Morningstar), Bob Adler (Sgt. Spangler), Jack Conrad (George Anson), Alfred Linder (Eddie Prue), Jack Overman (Manager), Jack Stoney (Mike), Ray Spiker (Figaro), Paul Maxey (Coroner), Reed Hadley (Dr. Moss), Edward Gargan (Truck Driver), Ben Erway (Shaw).

Don't let the obscurity of the title scare you away. A stolen gold coin brings Raymond Chandler's hard-boiled private dick Philip Marlowe (Montgomery) into the employ of an eccentric and wealthy widow. While on the trail of the coin, he stumbles into blackmail and murder and suffers a savage beating at the hands of Kortner, one of the weird creatures populating Chandler's off-center world. Finally, while trying to straighten out a blackmail scheme involving Bates' mad secretary, Guild, who is bonded to her employer out of fear of being implicated in the murder of Bates' husband, Montgomery puts the pieces of an illogical and complicated puzzle together to discover that Bates herself is the murderer and the thief of the doubloon. In carrying over Chandler's complex story to the screen (the fourth and last of his novels to be put into film), the producers have presented a watered-down version of the author's tough prose and cast an actor in the central role who is wooden, uneasy in his lines, and cute and boyish instead of portraying a steel-eyed gumshoe loaded with dry wit and self-confidence. Guild comes off effectively as the bewildered secretary in an overwritten part, and the rest of the cast performs adequately in stock roles. Most distinguished is Kortner, a veteran German actor and playwright who was widely known in Europe before WW II for his unconventional interpretations of the classics—another great artist madman Hitler lost to America. In spite of its faults, THE BRASHER DOUBLOON achieves film noir status by its many low-keyed images and its dense and threatening backgrounds, and tricks of dialog and grotesque characterizations that distinguish a noir film from an ordinary thriller.

p, Robert Bassler; d, John Brahm; w, Dorothy Hannah (based on a novel by Raymond Chandler); ph, Lloyd Ahern; m, David Buttolph; ed, Harry Reynolds; md, Alfred Newman; art d, James Basevi, Richard Irvine; set d, Thomas Little, Frank E. Hughes; cos, Eleanor Behm; spec eff, Fred Sersen; makeup, Ben Nye.

Mystery   **(PR:A MPAA:NR)**

BRASIL ANNO 2,000*   (1968, Braz.) 95m Mapa bw

Annecy Rocha, Enio Goncalves, Iracema de Alencar, Ziembinsky, Manfredo Colasanti, Helio Fernandez.

Reporter Goncalves exposes developing hypocrisy of a new state rising out of the ruins of WW III amidst the desolation of the Brazilian countryside. From the remains come Rocha and mother de Alencar in search of food. To get it, they pose as peasant Indians who, in the new society, are now the privileged minority.

p,d&w, Walter Lima, Jr.; ph, Guido Cosulich.

Drama   **(PR:A MPAA:NR)**

BRASS BOTTLE, THE**   (1964) 89m UNIV c

Tony Randall (Harold Ventimore), Burl Ives (Fakrash), Barbara Eden (Sylvia), Kamala Devi (Tezra), Edward Andrews (Prof. Kenton), Richard Erdman (Seymour Jenks), Kathie Browne (Hazel Jenks), Ann Doran (Martha Kenton), Philip Ober (William Beevor), Parley Baer (Samuel Wackerbath), Howard Smith (Senator Grindle), Lulu Porter (Belly Dancer), Alex Gerry (Dr. Travisley), Herb Vigran (Eddie), Alan Dexter (Joe), Robert Lieb (Jennings), Jan Arvan (Seneschal), Nora Marlowe (Mrs. McGruder), Aline Towne (Miss Gidden).

Silly comedy featuring Randall as a young architect who buys an antique bottle that happens to contain genie Ives. Randall is surprised at this development, but he is an honest man and has no real use for a genie. Ives becomes frustrated with his master when he is not allowed to destroy any enemies and Randall works overtime keeping the mischievous genie in check. Unfortunately, he is not quick enough to prevent Ives from turning his girl friend Eden's father into a mule. Eden would later go on to star as a genie herself in television's "I Dream of Genie."

p, Robert Arthur; d, Harry Keller; w, Oscar Brodney (based on the novel by F. Anstey); ph, Clifford Stine; m, Bernard Green; ed, Ted J. Kent.

Comedy   **(PR:A MPAA:NR)**

BRASS LEGEND, THE**   (1956) 80m UA bw

Hugh O'Brian (Sheriff Wade Adams), Nancy Gates (Linda), Raymond Burr (Tris Hatten), Reba Tassell (Millie), Donald McDonald (Clay), Bob Burton (Gipson), Eddie Firestone (Shorty), Willard Sage (Tatum), Robert Griffin (Dock Ward), Stacy Harris (George Barlow), Norman Leavitt (Cooper), Dennis Cross (Carl Barlow), Russell Simpson (Jackson), Michael Garrett (Charlie), Jack Farmer (Earl Barlow).

Arizona Sheriff O'Brian acts on a tip from his fiancee's younger brother and captures infamous outlaw Burr as a result. The ruthless outlaw discovers the boy and has him killed, which leads to a gunfight between the sheriff and three of Burr's cronies, eventually allowing the captive to escape. Oswald's direction is lame and the script unimaginative.

p, Herman Cohen; d, Gerd Oswald; w, Don Martin (based on a story by George Zuckerman and Jess Arnold); ph, Charles Van Enger; m, Paul Dunlap; ed, Marj Fowler.

Western   **(PR:A MPAA:NR)**

BRASS MONKEY   1965 (SEE: LUCKY MASCOT, THE, 1948, Brit.)

BRASS TARGET**   (1978) 111m UA c

Sophia Loren (Mara), John Cassavetes (Maj. Joe DeLuca), George Kennedy (Gen. George S. Patton, Jr.), Robert Vaughn (Col. Donald Rogers), Patrick McGoohan (Col. Mike McCauley), Bruce Davison (Col. Robert Dawson), Edward Herrmann (Col. Walter Gilchrist), Max Von Sydow (Shelley/Webber), Ed Bishop (Col. Elton F. Stewart), Lee Montague (Lucky Luciano).

Another of those "What if this might have happened?" stories. In Len Deighton's SS-GB, the speculation was that Germany had won the war. In Higgins's THE EAGLE HAS LANDED, the target was Churchill. In Forsyth's DAY OF THE JACKAL, it was DeGaulle. In BRASS TARGET, we are asked to believe that George Patton (George Kennedy) did not die in a car accident, but at the hands of assassins. This film has a huge cast filled with big-name actors, a fine producer (Lewis), a good screenwriter (Boretz) and a boring director (Hough) which just goes to prove that all the great actors in the world are not going to triumph over lousy material. Boretz comes up lame in his adaptation of Frederick Nolan's "The Algonquin Project" by offering endless talking heads. There's a gold robbery, a love triangle between Cassavetes, Loren, and Von Sydow (who is beginning to specialize in playing assassins), there's McGoohan playing the chief of the OSS as though he'd been reading the script through blurred glasses. When seeing a film such as this, one often gets the feeling that it was made for tax reasons only.

p, Arthur Lewis; d, John Hough; w, Alvin Boretz (based on the novel The Algonquin Project by Frederick Nolan); ph, Tony Imi; m, Laurence Rosenthal; ed, David Lane; cos, Monika Bauert.

War/Mystery   **Cas.**   **(PR:A-C MPAA:PG)**

BRAT, THE*   (1930, Brit.) 84m Betty Balfour Pictures/UA bw (GB: THE NIPPER)

Betty Balfour (The Nipper), John Stuart (Max Nicholson), Anne Grey (Clarissa Wentworth), Alf Goddard (Alf Green), Gibb McLaughlin (Bill Henshaw), Percy Parsons (Joubert), Helen Haye (Lady Sevenoaks), Louis Goodrich (Woolf).

A homeless cockney child is made a star after trying to rob a wealthy producer of musicals. Early spinoff of the great "Pygmalion" story by Shaw.

p, Betty Balfour; d, Louis Mercanton; w, Reginald Berkeley, Donovan Parsons (based on the play "La Mome," by Michel Carre and A. Acremont).

Musical   **(PR:A MPAA:NR)**

BRAT, THE**   (1931) 60m FOX bw

Sally O'Neil (The Brat), Alan Dinehart (MacMillan Forester), Frank Albertson (Stephen Forester), Virginia Cherrill (Angela), June Collyer (Jane), J. Farrell MacDonald (Timson), Mary Forbes (Mrs. Forester), Albert Gran (The Bishop), William Collier, Sr. (The Judge), Louise Mackintosh (Lena), Margaret Mann (Housekeeper).

O'Neil plays a waif taken in by a wealthy land owner only to create conflict in his family with her candid comments. Her fight with a society girl secretly planning to undermine our heroine's chances for happiness is a down-on-the-ground brawl between the classes. Unfortunately, August's camera angles distract and interfere with the action. Not worthy of Ford's great directorial talent.

d, John Ford; w, Maude Fulton, Sonya Levien, S. N. Behrman; ph, Joseph August.

Drama   **(PR:A MPAA:NR)**

BRAVADOS, THE***   (1958) 99m FOX c

Gregory Peck (Jim Douglas), Joan Collins (Josefa Velarde), Stephen Boyd (Bill Zachary), Albert Salmi (Ed Taylor), Henry Silva (Lujan), Kathleen Gallant (Emma), Barry Coe (Tom), George Voskovec (Gus Steinmetz), Herbert Rudley (Sheriff Elroy Sanchez), Lee Van Cleef (Alfonso Parral), Ada Carrasco (Mrs. Parral), Andrew Duggan (Padre), Ken Scott (Primo), Gene Evans (Butler), Jack Mather (Quinn), Joe De Rita (Simms), Robert Adler (Tony Mirabel), Jason Wingreen, Robert Griffin, Juan Garcia, Jacqueline Evans, Alicia del Lago, The Ninos Cantores De Morelia Choral Group.

A harsh account of a vigilante in the old West who takes the law into his own hands, savagely extracts revenge, and lives to regret it. Peck arrives in town the night before the hanging of four outlaws whose trail he has been on for what he believes is the rape-murder of his wife. The four men escape the noose and the chase begins, with Peck catching them one by one and killing them as they scream out their innocence. Finally, the lone surviving fugitive convinces him that a trusted neighbor actually raped and killed his wife, and Peck realizes that his private lynch law has not only been legally wrong but has been ruthless murder. His moment of truth is a powerful one and he gives it all the value it deserves, though much of his acting up to then had been lackluster. He returns to the town and the acclaim of its citizens, and takes up with a former lady love, Collins, who tries to be convincing in a thankless role that apparently was written only to supply romantic interest. Outstanding in the film are color shots of gorges and precipitous mountains in remote areas of the Mexican states of Yucatan and Jalisco, where the film was made, and the church interior of a small Mexican town.

p, Herbert B. Swope, Jr.; d, Henry King; w, Philip Yordan (based on the novel by Frank O'Rourke); ph, Leon Shamroy (CinemaScope, DeLuxe Color); m, Lionel Newman; ed, William Ware; md, Bernard Kaun.

Western   **PR:C MPAA:NR**

BRAVE BULLS, THE****   (1951) 106m COL bw

Mel Ferrer (Luis Bello), Miroslava (Linda de Calderon), Anthony Quinn (Raul Fuentes), Eugene Iglesias (Pepe Bello), Jose Torvay (Eladio Gomez), Charlita (Raquelita), Jose Luis Vasquez (Yank Delgado), Alfonso Alvirez (Loco Ruiz), Alfredo Aguilar (Pancho Perez), Francisco Balderas (Monkey Garcia), Felipe Mota (Jackdaw), Pepe Lopez (Enrique), Jose Meza (Little White), Vicente Cardenas (Coyo Salinas), Manuel Orozco (Abundio de la O), Estevan Dominguez (Tacho), Silviano Sanchez (Policarpe Cana), Francisco Reiguera (Lara), E. Arozamena (Don Alberto Iriarte), Luis Corona (Pufino Vega), Esther Laquin (Senora Bello), M. du P. Castillo (Chona), Juan Assaei (Alfredo Bello), Delfino Morales (Indio), Rita Conde (Lola), Ramon D. Mesa (Don Tiburcio Balbuenna), Fanny Schiller (Mamacita), Fernando Del Valle (Don Felix Aldemas).

Popular matador Ferrer begins to doubt his prowess in the ring after a near-fatal attack by a bull. Quinn, Ferrer's cunning manager, convinces the champion to continue fighting using the pretty Miroslava to help bolster Ferrer's manhood. Unaware that Miroslava is Quinn's girl friend, Ferrer begins to fall for her and tries to impress her by returning to the arena. During his next bout, Ferrer wins clumsily and is met with harsh comments from the unappreciative crowd. When Quinn and Miroslava are killed in a car crash, Ferrer's world collapses and he loses all faith in himself. Labeled a coward by the press and the public, Ferrer nonetheless makes an appearance at younger brother Iglesias' first fight with a bull. In the first match, Ferrer acts like a frightened child and is chastised by the crowd. After his brother is gored during the second contest, Ferrer overcomes his fear, strikes out against the killer bull, and performs masterfully. An excellent film that takes on the difficult subjects of masculine pride, fear, jealousy, and death, and handles them in an intelligent, human manner. Quinn is outstanding as the tough, greedy, but vulnerable manager who places his faith in Ferrer's spirit. Ferrer gives his bullfighter a complexity, integrity, and sadness that makes his shift from coward to hero all the more remarkable. The ambiance of Mexico is captured with a clear passion by director Rossen and talented cinematographer James Wong Howe. The photographing of the bullfighting sequences effectively displays the hot, grimy, violent intensity of the situation. Two sad notes are associated with this film, the first being intriguing Czechoslovakian actress Miroslava's suicide soon after the film's release, and the second being director Rossen's falling victim to the McCarthy anti-communist hearings in Hollywood. After it became labeled as the product of a "Red," the film never found its deserved audience.

p&d, Robert Rossen; w, John Bright (based on a novel by Tom Lea); ph, Floyd Crosby, James Wong Howe; ed, Henry Batista.

Drama   **(PR:A MPAA:NR)**

BRAVE DON'T CRY, THE**   (1952, Brit.) 89m Group Three/ABF bw

John Gregson (John Cameron), Meg Buchanan (Margaret Wishart), John Rae (Donald Sloan), Fulton Mackay (Dan Wishart), Andrew Keir (Charlie Ross), Wendy Noel (Jean Knox), Russell Walters (Hughie Aitken), Jameson Clark (Dr. Andrew Keir), Eric Woodburn (Rab Elliottt), Archie Duncan (Walter Hardie), Jack Stewart (Willie Duncan), Anne Butchart (Biddy Ross), Mac Picton (Jim Knox), Jean Anderson (Mrs. Sloan), John Singer (Tam Stewart), Chris Page (George), Kelty Macleod (Mrs. Duncan), Hal Osmond (Sandy Mackenzie), Guthrie Mason (Jamie Knox).

Disaster film has trapped coal miners rescued by new technique after a cave-in. Keir teaches humor as self-preservation when he places a bet on a horse from the underground phone. Could have been more suspenseful but the direction drags.

p, John Grierson, John Baxter; d, Philip Leacock; w, Montagu Slater; ph, Arthur Grant, Ken Hodges.

Docudrama   **(PR:A MPAA:NR)**

BRAVE ONE, THE**   (1956) 100m RKO bw

Michel Ray (Leonardo), Rodolfo Hoyos (Rafael Rosillo), Elsa Cardenas (Maria), Carlos Navarro (Don Alejandro), Joi Lansing (Marion Randall), Fermin Rivera (Himself), George Trevino (Salvador), Carlos Fernandez (Manuel).

Blue-eyed Ray plays a Mexican boy who saves his pet bull from demise in the bull ring by obtaining a pardon from the president. Real-life drama purposefully directed by Rapper and filmed by Cardiff. Warms the heart with sensitivity and sweetness. Trumbo wrote this film under a pseudonym since he was currently under a blacklist because of his HUAC experiences.

p, Maurice and Frank King; d, Irving Rapper; w, Robert Rich [Dalton Trumbo], Harry Franklin, Merrill G. White; ph, Jack Cardiff; m, Victor Young; ed, White.

Children   **(PR:AAA MPAA:NR)**

BRAVE WARRIOR**   (1952) 73m COL c

Jon Hall (Steve Ruddell), Christine Larson (Laura Macgregor), Jay Silverheels (Chief Tecumseh), Michael Ansara (The Prophet), Harry Cording (Shayne Macgregor), James Seay (Gov. Harrison), George Eldredge (Barney Demming), Leslie Denison (Gen. Proctor), Rory Mallinson (Barker), Rusty Wescoatt (Standish), Bert Davidson (Gilbert), William P. Wilkerson (Chief Little Cloud), Gilbert V. Perkins (English Lieutenant).

Government agent Hall is on an action-filled quest to discover who is instigating resistance by the Indians. Production suffers from weak direction and poor attention to detail. Best of all is Silverheels who later became Tonto, the Lone Ranger's sidekick.

p, Sam Katzman; d, Spencer G. Bennet; w, Robert E. Kent; ph, William V. Skall; ed, Aaron Stell.

Western   **(PR:A MPAA:NR)**

BRAZIL**   (1944) 91m REP bw

Tito Guizar (Miguel Soares), Virginia Bruce (Nicky Henderson), Edward Everett Horton (Everett St. John Everett), Robert Livingston (Rod Walker), Veloz and Yolanda (Themselves), Fortunio Bonanova (Senor Renato Da Silva), Richard Lane (Edward Graham), Frank Puglia (Senor Machado), Aurora Miranda (Specialty Dancer), Alfredo De Sa (Master of Ceremonies), Henry Da Silva (Business Man), Rico de Montez (Airport Official), Leon Lenoir (Reporter), Roy Rogers (Guest Star).

Suave Guizar, a South American songwriter, having had initial success with the tune "Brazil," is in a desperate struggle to come up with a follow-up hit. His melody-making is interrupted when he takes it upon himself to convince the pretty Bruce of his abilities as a Latin Lover, the girl having just written a popular book that shatters the myth of the hot-blooded macho hombre. Although the jealous Horton tries to tell Bruce that Guizar is just toying with her, the two stubborn lovers finally realize that they do indeed love each other. When Guizar's second song wins the national Brazilian song contest, everything works out for the happy couple. Dim-witted but enjoyable musical comedy that could have benefited from more charismatic leads.

p, Robert North; d, Joseph Santley; w, Frank Gill, Jr., Laura Kerr (based on story by Richard English); ph, Jack Marta; ed, Fred Allen; m/l, Ary Barroso, Ned Washington, S. K. Russell, Hoagy Carmichael, Harolo Lobo, Milton de Olivera, Alvaro De S. Carvalho, Aloysio Oliveira.

Musical/Comedy   **(PR:A MPAA:NR)**

BREACH OF PROMISE*   (1942, Brit.) 64m Verschieser bw

Chester Morris (Pomeroy), Mae Clark (Hattie Pugmire), May Doran (Millie), Theodore Von Eltz (District Attorney), Charles Middleton (Joe Pugmire).

A politician's life is ruined when a teenage girl falsely charges him with sexual assault. The girl later relents and clears the man's name.

d, Paul Stein; w, Ben Verschieser, John Goodrich, Anthony Veiller (based on a story by Rupert Hughes); ph, Art Miller; ed Charles Kraft; art d, Edward Schulter.

Drama   **Cas.**   **(PR:A MPAA:NR)**

BREAD AND CHOCOLATE****1/2   (1978, Ital.) 112m Veronal/CIC c

Nino Manfredi (Nino), Anna Karina (Elena), Johnny Dorell (Italian Industrialist), Paolo Turco (Commis), Ugo D'Alessio (Old Man), Frederico Scrobogna (Grigory), Gianfranco Barra (The Turk), Giorgo Cerion (Police Inspector), Max Delys (Renzo), Francesco D'Adda (Rudiger), Geoffrey Copplestone (Boegli), Umberto Raho (Maitre), Nelide Giammarco (The Blonde).

Manfredi finds himself pushed down into the lower classes of Swiss society when he leaves Sicily hoping to find a better standard of living in a new country. Despite hardships, which force his family to live in the ghettos of Switzerland, there is lively merriment and colorful language which add refreshing spice to this bittersweet comedy.

p, Maurizio Lodi-Fe; d, Franco Brusati; w, Brusati, Iaia Fiastri, Nino Manfredi (based on a story by Brusati); ph, Luciano Tovali; m, Daniel Patrucci; ed, Mario Morra.

Comedy   **(PR:A MPAA:NR)**

BREAD, LOVE AND DREAMS****1/2   (1953, Ital.) Titanis/IFE bw

Vittorio De Sica (The Marshal), Gina Lollobrigida (The Girl "Frisky"), Marisa Merlini (The Midwife "Annarella"), Roberto Risso (The Carabiniere "Stelluti"), Virgilio Riento (Priest "Dom Emidio"), Maria Pia Casilio (Priest's Niece "Paoletta"), Memmo Carotenuto (Another Carabiniere), Tina Pica (Housekeeper "Caramel"), Vittoria Crispo (The Mother).

A peppery comedy of morals that breezes through to a pleasant conclusion finds De Sica as the new sergeant of police in a small rural village facing up to spicy Lollobrigida in his quest for a wife. Low-brow sex farce that helped to establish Gina as a box office favorite among American males, despite a next-to-nothing script.

d&w, Luigi Comencini (based on a story by Ettore Margadonna); ph, Arturo Gallea; m, Alessandro Cicognini.

Comedy   **(PR:O MPAA:NR)**

BREAD OF LOVE, THE***   (1954, Swed.) 90m Nordisk-Tonefilm/JANCO

Folke Sundquist (Prisoner), Sissi Kaiser (Lunnaja), George Rydeberg (Ledin), Nils Diarberg (Tom), Lennart Lindberg (Narrator), Erik Hell (Buteur), Dagny Lind (Mother).

Angry heartpounder has Sundquist captured by Finnish soldiers during the Finno-Russian war while he is talking intimately with the moon in a frozen wasteland attempting to reach his wife through psychic channels. The real and the unreal are fused when she is heard singing in the wilderness to her husband and is soon after killed by enemy soldiers. The ending reveals through excellent photography and subtly defined and directed performances the thrashing conflicts and ironies of war.

d, Arne Mattaon; w, W. Semitjov (based on a novel by Peder Sjogren); ph, Sven Ther maenius; m, Sven Skold; ed, Lennart Landheim.

Drama   **(PR:A MPAA:NR)**

BREAK, THE****1/2   (1962, Brit.) 76m Blakeley's Films/PLANET bw

Tony Britton (Greg Parker), William Lucas (Jacko Thomas), Eddie Byrne (Judd Tredegar), Robert Urquhart (Pearson), Sonia Dresdel (Sarah), Edwin Richfield (Moses), Gene Anderson (Jean Tredegar), Christian Gregg (Sue Thomas).

Story has all the components of an Agatha Christie mystery. Set in Devon, England, a detective, novelist, fugitive robber, and his sister make their way through crime as guests at a smuggler's farm. Tame whodunit.

p, Tom Blakeley; d, Lance Comfort; w, Pip and Jane Baker.

Mystery   **(PR:A MPAA:NR)**

BREAK IN THE CIRCLE, THE****1/2   (1957, Brit.) 72m Hammer/FOX bw

Forrest Tucker (Skip Morgan), Eva Bartok (Lisa), Marius Goring (Baron Keller), Guy Middleton (Hobart), Eric Pohlmann (Emile), Arnold Marle (Kudnic), Fred Johnson (Farquarson), David King-Wood (Patchway), Reginald Beckwith (Dusty), Guido Lorraine (Franz), Derek Prentice, Arthur Lovegrove, Marne Maitland, Standley Zevic, Andre Mikhelson.

Tucker plays an American in search of excitement which he finds after sailing his boat to Hamburg to smuggle a hunted Polish scientist to safety. Poor directing and acting undo an otherwise interesting escape yarn.

p, Mickey Delamar; d, Val Guest; w, Guest (based on a novel by Philip Lorraine); ph, Walter Harvey (Eastmancolor); m, Doreen Varwithen; ed, Bill Lenny.

Drama   **(PR:A MPAA:NR)**

BREAK OF DAY***   (1977, Aus.) 106m GUO/Clare Beach Films c

Sara Kestelman (Alice), Andrew McFarlane (Tom), Ingrid Mason (Beth), Tony Barry (Joe), Eileen Chapman (Susan), Ben Gabriel (Mr. Evans), Maurie Fields (Lou), Malcolm Phillips (Robbie), John Bell (Arthur), Dennis Olsen (Roger), Sean Myers (David), Kate Ferguson (Jean), Geraldine Turner (Sandy).

Slow, lazy beginning focuses on Australia's romantic countryside, Boyd's camera detailing the history-filled buildings of a once prosperous gold mining town. There, newspaper editor McFarlane settles with his pregnant wife Mason. Crippled in the abortive attempt to raid Turkey by Australian troops in the Gallipoli landings in 1915, he finds it difficult to adjust, thereby causing conflict in his home and an inability to communicate with his wife. His restlessness leads him to a river where he retreats each morning before work and reminisces about rabbiting as a child. He meets painter Kestelman and they become lovers. Her city friends intimidate him and at a picnic cricket match he becomes drunk, hobbling out into the night without his cane. He stumbles into a deserted mine shaft and reliving his Gallipoli experience, reveals that his wound was self-inflicted. He realizes that Kestelman can do without him, which gets him back into his daily routine at the town paper. Still, he suffers when Kestelman leaves the country town. Story parallels D. H. Lawrence writings with lots of room for interpretation below the surface. High level of acting with talented support from technical crew.

p, Pat Lovell; d, Ken Hannam; w, Cliff Green; ph, Russell Boyd (Eastmancolor); prod d, Wendy Dickson.

Drama   (PR:A MPAA:NR)

BREAK OF HEARTS**½   (1935) 78m RKO bw

Katharine Hepburn (Constance), Charles Boyer (Roberti), John Beal (Johnny), Jean Hersholt (Talma), Sam Hardy (Marx), Inez Courtney (Miss Wilson), Helene Millard (Sylvia), Ferdinand Gottschalk (Pazzini), Susan Fleming (Elise), Lee Kohlmar (Schubert), Jean Howard (Didi), Anne Grey (Phyllis).

Young, aspiring composer Hepburn meets and falls madly in love with prestigious orchestra conductor Boyer and the two marry, spending a romantic honeymoon in Europe. Hepburn soon discovers that Boyer's passion for music is equal to his passion for other women and she leaves him. Forsaking his career and his mistress, Boyer sinks into alocholic despair and near oblivion. Hepburn finds him in a seedy dive and lifts him out of his hole by playing "their" song on the honky tonk's cheap piano. The couple get back together and Boyer sets out to conquer the symphonic world once again. Hopelessly exaggerated drama that could have been unintentionally humorous if it had not been for the power and personality of its star. Boyer, playing his usual gigolo-wises-up role, does a credible job in bringing the counductor's intense feelings to the forefront, but it is Hepburn who steals the film with a charmingly innocent portrayal of a loving but strong-willed wife. Regrettably, the script and direction do nothing to equal Hepburn's insight into her character.

d, Phillip Moeller; w, Sarah Y. Mason, Victor Heerman, Anthony Veiller (based on a story by Lester Cohen); ph, Robert De Grasse. m, Max Steiner; ed, William Hamilton; art d, Van Nest Polglase; cos, Bernard Newman.

Drama   **Cas.**   (PR:A MPAA:NR)

BREAK THE NEWS****   (1941, Brit.) 72m Trio GFD/MON bw

Maurice Chevalier (Francois Verrier), Jack Buchanan (Teddy Enton), June Knight (Grace Gatwick), Marta Labarr (Sonia), Gertrude Musgrove (Helena), Garry Marsh (The Producer), Wallace Douglas (The Stage Manager), Joss Ambler (The Press Agent), Mark Daly (The Property Man), Gibb McLaughlin (The Superintendent), Robb Wilton (The Cab Driver), Felix Aylmer (Sir George Bickory), C. Denier Warren (Sir Edward Phring), George Hayes (President), Guy Middleton (Englishman), Athole Stewart (Governor), Charles Lefeaux (Interpreter), D.J. Williams (Judge), Elliot Mason (Dresser), J. Abercomie (Neighbor), W. Fazan (Passport Official), H.R. Hignett (Solicitor), Wally Patch, Hall Gordon (Prison Guards).

Egocentric Knight, the star of a musical revue, has song and dance pair Buchanan and Chevalier fired from the line-up fearing that the talented duo may become more popular than she. Hoping to get back in the public eye, Buchanan and Chevalier decide to stage a spectacular publicity stunt. Buchanan mysteriously disappears and Chevalier confesses to his murder. Knowing that his partner is hiding in a Balkan village and will miraculously reappear in time to save him, Chevalier patiently waits in his prison cell, glowing from the attention of the newspapers. Buchanan, however, gets mixed up with a group of revolutionaries who believe he is an enemy general and fails to make it to Chevalier's court appearance. Buchanan escapes and arrives in London on the day Chevalier is to be executed. Needing to enlist the aid of old foe Knight, Buchanan and the revue star save Chevalier. Knight is proclaimed a heroine by the public and the two frustrated hoofers return to obscurity. The always enchanting Buchanan and Chevalier are a pleasure to watch in this funny, energetic musical that features some hilariously suspenseful sequences. Although it may not rank with director Clair's French classics, this perfect piece of British entertainment holds its own special place. Songs include; "It All Belongs to You" (Cole Porter, sung by Chevalier), "We're Old Buddies" (Van Phillips, Jack Buchanan, sung by Chevalier and Buchanan).

p&d, Rene Clair; w, Geoffrey Kerr (based on an adaptation by Carlo Rima of the novel La Mort En Fuite by Lois le Guriadec); ph, Phil Tannura; m, Van Phillips.

Musical/Comedy   (PR:A MPAA:NR)

BREAK TO FREEDOM   (SEE: ALBERT, R.N, 1955)

BREAKAWAY*   (1956, Brit.) 72m Cipa/RKO bw

Tom Conway (Tom "Duke" Martin), Honor Blackman (Paula Grant), Michael Balfour (Barney), Bruce Seton (Webb), Brian Worth (Johnny Matlock), Freddie Mills (Pat), Alexander Gauge (McAllister), John Horsley (Michael Matlock).

Where, oh where is the secret formula and why has a gang of thieves kidnaped Blackman? To find the answer, obtain the secret potion which is supposed to eliminate metal fatigue. Absurd whodunit.

p, Robert S. Baker, Monty Berman; d, Henry Cass; w, Norman Hudis (based on a story by Manning O'Brine); ph, Berman.

Crime   (PR:A MPAA:NR)

BREAKDOWN*   (1953) 76m Realart bw

Ann Richards (June Hannum), William Bishop (Terry Williams), Anne Gwynne (Candy Allen), Sheldon Leonard (Nick Samson), Wally Cassell (Pete Samson), Richard Benedict (Punchy), John Vosper (Judge Hannum), Roy Engel (Al Bell), Joe McTurk (Longshot), Norman Rainey (Doc), Hal Bartlett (The Champ), Elena Strangelo (Mrs. Prescott), Michelle King (Girl in Honky Tonk), Gene Covelli (Newsboy), Al Cantor (DeVito).

Heavyweight boxer Bishop, is framed for murder. After serving part of his sentence, he proves the wealthy father of his girl friend Gwynne, and a ward boss set him up. Technical effort is down for the count in this weary programmer.

p&d, Edmond Angelo; w, Robert Abel (based on his play "The Samson Slasher"); ph, Paul Ivanho; m, Paul Dunlay; ed, Robert M. Leeds.

Drama   (PR:A MPAA:NR)

BREAKER! BREAKER!*½   (1977) 86m AIP c

George Murdock (Judge Trimmings), Terry O'Connor (Arlene Trimmings), Don Gentry (Sgt. Strode), Michael Augenstein (Billy Dawes), Dan Vandergrift (Wilfred), Ron Cedillos (Deputy Boles), John Difusco (Arney), Douglas Stevenson (Drake).

When everyone and his brother cashed in on the CB craze, several movies were made in an attempt to get the truckers off the highways and into the theatre. One notable flop was CONVOY (Kris Kristofferson) and BREAKER! BREAKER! was equally a flop, but somewhat less notable. This picture attempts to combine red-neck locales with Zen master philosophy. That combination is sort of like sushi and grits; both are pretty good but together they're awful. A martial arts trucker comes to a small town to rescue his kid brother who's been kidnaped by villains. In the course of inhuman events, he takes a bullet in his guts, destroys a few buildings, a few people, woos the waitress with a heart of gold and a cast iron stomach, and saves the day. The producer/director/composer was Don Hulette. It's hard enough to do one thing well in the movie business. Hulette proves that point in spades.

p&d, Don Hulette; w, Terry Chambers; ph, Mario Di Leo; m, Hulette; ed, Steven Zaillian.

Adventure/Crime   **Cas.**   (PR:C MPAA:PG)

BREAKER MORANT****

(1980, Aus.) 107m South Australian Film/New World c

Edward Woodward (Lt. Harry Morant), Jack Thompson (Maj. J. F. Thomas), John Waters (Capt. Alfred Taylor), Bryan Brown (Lt. Peter Handcock), Rod Mullinar (Maj. Charles Bolton), Lewis Fitzgerald (Lt. George Witton), Charles Tingwell (Lt. Col. Denny), Vincent Ball (Lt. Ian Hamilton), Frank Wilson (Dr. Johnson), Terence Donovan (Capt. Simon Hunt), Russell Kiefel (Christian Botha), Alan Cassell (Lord Kitchener), Judy Dick (Mrs. Shiels), Barbara West (Mrs. Bristow).

BREAKER MORANT is the true story of Harry Morant, an Englishman who went to Australia in the late 1800s and got a reputation as being the best breaker of horses around. When the Boers and the Australians put on the gloves in South Africa, Morant and several other Aussies volunteered to fight. The nature of war was changing. Gone was the formal type of battle. Guerrillas were the enemy and had to be dealt with differently than regular prisoners of war. Morant and his associates were accused of killing some innocent people. To prove a point, Morant and two others are taken from the crowd and put up for trial, much the same way that Turkel, Carey, and Meeker were put up for an example in PATHS OF GLORY. The first third of the film has to do with the action and the remainder comprises the trial and result. Performances are all first-rate, although some ears may have difficulty picking up the nuances of the Australian dialect. Woodward (YOUNG WINSTON, THE WICKER MAN) is superb in the title role and Jack Thompson, as the defense attorney, is a slimmer version of George Kennedy. It might have been called "A Man's Picture" years ago because it has virtually no women and the subject matter might have been an anathema back then. But today, morality and choice are everyone's business and BREAKER MORANT forces the viewer to take a stand, no matter the sex or political persuasion. A haunting film that will have you thinking and arguing for days after.

p, Matt Carroll; d, Bruce Beresford; w, Beresford, Jonathan Hardy, David Stevens (based on a play by Kenneth Ross); ph, Don McAlpine (Panavision, Eastmancolor); m, Phil Cunneen; ed, William Anderson; cos, Anna Senior; stunts, Heath Harris, Tony Smart.

War/Drama   **Cas.**   (PR:A-C MPAA:NRC

BREAKERS AHEAD*   (1935, Brit.) 58m Anglo-Cosmopolitan/Reunion bw

Barrie Livesey (George Kenyon), April Vivian (Stella Trevarthen), Billy Holland (Bob Pentreath), Roddy Hughes (Will), Cicely Oates (Aunt Martha), Richard Worth (Skipper), Francis Gregory (Champion).

High seas drive a jealous fisherman insane and he tries to drown his rival. In a split second, his twisted mind is restored, causing judgment day to close in as he dies saving his foe in the storm. Tempest in a British teapot.

p, Fraser Foulsham; d&w, Anthony Gilkison.

Adventure   (PR:A MPAA:NR)

BREAKERS AHEAD*

(1938, Brit.) 58m G.B. Instructional/GFD bw (AKA: AS WE FORGIVE)

Belle Chrystal (Mary), J. Fisher White (Harry), Arthur Seaton (Silas), Grant Sutherland (Joe), Michael Hogarth (Davy).

What a wreck! Set in Cornwall, England, a fisherman's wife alienates him from his brother until he saves the brother from a shipwreck. Nothing improved in this variation of the 1935 version.

d, Vernon Sewell; w, Leo Walmesley.

Drama   (PR:A MPAA:NR)

BREAKFAST AT TIFFANY'S****   (1961) 115m PAR c

Audrey Hepburn (Holly Golightly), George Peppard (Paul Varjak), Patricia Neal (2-E), Buddy Ebsen (Doc Golightly), Martin Balsam (O. J. Berman), Mickey Rooney (Mr. Yunioshi), Vilallonga (Jose da Silva Perriera), John McGiver (Tiffany's Clerk), Dorothy Whitney (Mag Wildwood), Stanley Adams (Rusty Trawler), Elvia Allman (Librarian), Alan Reed, Sr. (Sally Tomato), Beverly Hills (Stripper), Claude Stroud (Sid Arbuck), Putney (Cat).

Truman Capote's novella comes to glorious life on the screen as Audrey Hepburn gambols through the film portraying the ever-charming, fey Holly Golightly, insisting on living her own lifestyle with an indomitable spirit, yet showing a vulnerability which captures the heart of the viewer. In the opening sequence Hepburn leaves a sleek limousine on a deserted early morning in Manhattan to walk up to Tiffany's window, munching on a sweetroll while quietly contemplating the array of jewels on display. Peppard is her upstairs neighbor who is both intrigued and puzzled by Hepburn's errant behaviour; throwing all-night bashes for her dozens of friends on the one hand, then turning without warning into an isolated, lonely, neurotic hermit. Their relationship grows but still a mystery as Hepburn's visits to ganglord Reed in Sing Sing and her frequent trips to nightclub powder rooms, emerging with $50 in cash each time. Part of the mystery is solved when Ebsen as Doc Golightly, the deserted husband from rural Texas, shows up in the hope of retrieving his wayward wife whose real name is Lulumae Barnes. Hepburn's gentle treatment of this aging farmer, whom she married when she was 13, belies the sharp edge of sophistication she tries so hard to maintain when in the company of her cafe-society friends. Only the conclusion marks a departure from Capote's book, providing audiences with the obligatory happy Hollywood ending. Peppard is credible and low key as the young author who befriends Hepburn (a thinly disguised version of the author himself). Neal as the author's "sponsor" is aptly cast. Balsam as Holly's agent offers a significant insight into his client's personality half-way through the film when he describes her: "She's a phony, all right," he insists, "but a *real* phony." Rooney's participation as a much-harassed Japanese photographer adds an unnecessarily incongruous note to the proceedings. The film's song, "Moon River," won an Oscar and went on to become an enchanting and popular favorite. With this movie a new kind of woman made her first significant appearance on the screen; Hepburn stands as a precursor to the liberated woman who would appear in the films of the late 1960s, one who, in spite of her independence, realizes that she is not as tough as she would have us believe.

p, Martin Jurow, Richard Shepherd; d, Blake Edwards; w, George Axelrod (based on the novella by Truman Capote); ph, Franz E. Planer (Technicolor); m, Henry Mancini; ed, Howard Smith; cos, Edith Head; m/l, "Moon River," Mancini, Johnny Mercer.

Drama   **Cas.**   **(PR:A MPAA:NR)**

BREAKFAST FOR TWO★★1/2   (1937) 67m RKO bw

Barbara Stanwyck (*Valentine Ransome*), Herbert Marshall (*Jonathan Blair*), Glenda Farrell (*Carol Wallace*), Eric Blore (*Butch*), Etienne Girardot (*Meggs*), Donald Meek (*Justice of Peace*), Frank M. Thomas (*Sam Ransome*), Pierre Watkin (*Gordon Faraday*), Sidney Bracey (*Butler*), Harold Goodwin (*Chauffeur*), George Irving, Larry Steers, Bobby Barber, Monte Vandergrift, Edward Le Saint, William Gould, Lander Stevens, Tom Ricketts.

Funny screwball comedy has Stanwyck as a wealthy heiress who meets playboy Marshall. They become involved in a lot of slapstick situations as they toy with each other, but then Stanwyck meets his fiancee, brassie blonde Farrell who is blatantly after Marshall's big bucks. Marshall's indifference to the steamship line left to him causes Stanwyck to rebel against his squandering ways and, to teach him a lesson, she buys up controlling interest in the line, then directs him to reform. Bristling at Stanwyck's mannish attitude, Marshall sails off on one of his own ships with Farrell, attempting to have the captain wed them to the crass gold-digger. But Blore, in one of his best supporting roles as a snide aide to Marshall, blocks the marriage with an elaborate scheme. Stanwyck ends up with Marshall in a comedy that soars high then descends quickly in the final scenes. An amusing variarion of IT HAPPENED ONE NIGHT with forceful Stanwyck overshadowing the genteel Marshall.

p, Edward Kaufman; d, Alfred Santell; w, Charles Kaufman, Paul Yawitz, Viola Brothers Shore (uncredited Jack Mintz, Lawrence Pohle); ph, J. Roy Hunt; ed, George Hively; art d, Van Nest Polglase; set d, Darrell Silvera; cos, Edward Stevenson.

Comedy   **(PR:A MPAA:NR)**

BREAKFAST IN BED★★   (1978) 56m William Haugse Prod. c

Jenny Sullivan (*Sara*), John Ritter (*Paul*), V. Phipps Wilson (*Mimi*), Mitchell Breit (*Hairdresser*), Timothy Near (*Marcja*), Buckline Beery (*Man in Car*).

Ritter and Sullivan are a young Lotusland duo whose marriage is going the way of clear air in Los Angeles. They spend a fast-moving hour in a deep examination of what went wrong. It's honest, painful, sometimes funny, and often heart-tugging. Anyone who has ever gone through the pangs of separation will recognize themselves in this. One wishes that the ideas could have been developed to a larger extent instead of being satisfied with shorthand strokes in the characterizations. Still, it's better in many ways than such creakers as BEST FRIENDS in it's examination of a marriage. Ritter is the son of the well-known country singer Tex Ritter and is another of the graduates of the Harvey Lembeck Comedy workshop which includes Penny Marshall, Robin Williams, William Christopher, et al.

p, Catherine Coulson; d&w, William Haugse; ph, Frederick Elmes (Metrocolor); m, Tom Grant; ed, William Haugse.

Drama   **(PR:C MPAA:NR)**

BREAKFAST IN HOLLYWOOD★★
                          (1946) 90m Golden Pictures/UA bw (GB: THE MAD HATTER)

Tom Brenneman (*Himself*), Bonita Granville (*Dorothy Larson*), Beulah Bondi (*Annie*), Eddie Ryan (*Ken Smith*), Raymond William (*Mr. Cartwright*), Billie Burke (*Mrs. Cartwright*), ZaSu Pitts (*Elvira Spriggens*), Hedda Hopper, Andy Russell.

Mushy meddler Brenneman stages his daily radio show, this time getting a sailor and a girl to bounce together like puppy dogs in love. Three episodes of good deeds with corny gangs and hokey antics pull this film apart. Good technical contributions on camera and music. Songs include "If I Had A Wishing Ring," and "It's Better To Be Yourself," the latter sung beautifully by Nat "King" Cole.

d, Harold Schuster; w, Earl W. Baldwin; ph, Russell Metty; m, Nathanial W. Finston; ed, Bernard W. Burton; m/l, Lou Alter, Maria Shelton, Nat "King" Cole, Bob Levinson Howard Leeds, Spike Jones, Jack Elliott.

Comedy   **Cas.**   **(PR:A MPAA:NR)**

BREAKHEART PASS★★★   (1976) 95m UA c

Charles Bronson (*John Deakin*), Ben Johnson (*Nathan Pearce*), Richard Crenna (*Richard Fairchild*), Jill Ireland (*Marcia Scoville*), Charles Durning (*Frank O'Brien*), Ed Lauter (*Maj. Claremont*), David Huddleston (*Dr. Molyneux*), Roy Jenson (*Banlon*), Casey Tibbs (*Jackson*), Archie Moore (*Carlos*), Joe Rapp (*Henry*), Read Morgan (*Capt. Oakland*), Robert Rothwell (*Lt. Newell*), Rayford Barnes (*Bellew*), Scott Newman (*Rafferty*), Eldon Burke (*Ferguson*), William McKinney (*Rev. Peabody*), Eddie Little Sky (*White Hand*), Robert Tessier (*Sepp Calhoun*), Doug Atkins (*Jebbo*), Irv Faling (*Col. Scoville*), Bill Kiem (*Seaman Devlin*), John Mitchum (*Red Beard*), Keith McConnell (*Gabriel*).

BREAKHEART PASS is a Western mystery that never flags from the opening sequence to the closing credits. But if you don't like Bronson, forget this movie because he's in virtually every frame of it. Ireland (Bronson's wife) is the romantic interest, such as it is, because he eventually goes off without her at the conclusion. Bronson is an undercover agent after a murderous gang. Most of the action occurs on a magnificent old train. Bodies are tossed off the train, cars come loose, there's an epidemic that really isn't, there's a cabal between cowboys and Indians in which they are attempting to defeat the Army; matter of fact, there are more turns than a politician's speech. Alistair MacLean wrote the novel and the screenplay and Gries directed it with his customary professionalism. Durning and McKinney do well in a pair of small roles. Tibbs (the rodeo champ), Moore (boxing champ) and Kapp (football quarterback) seem to be in the film for no apparent reason other than adding some cameo marquee value. Second unit direction is by the dean, Yakima Canutt, and the train-top fight is a pip. (Canutt, whose real first name is Enos, spent half his life as a stunt man and the rest of it shooting other stunt men.)

p, Jerry Gershwin; d, Tom Gries; w, Alistair MacLean (based on his novel); ph, Lucien Ballard (DeLuxe Color); m, Jerry Goldsmith; ed, Buzz Brandt.

Western   **Cas.**   **(PR:C MPAA:PG)**

BREAKING AWAY★★1/2   (1979) 100m FOX c

Dennis Christopher (*Dave Stohler*), Dennis Quaid (*Mike*), Daniel Stern (*Cyril*), Jackie Earle Haley (*Moocher*), Barbara Barrie (*Mrs. Stohler*), Paul Dooley (*Mr. Stohler*), Robyn Douglass (*Katherine*), Hart Bochner (*Rod*), Amy Wright (*Nancy*), Peter Maloney (*Doctor*), John Ashton (*Mike's Brother*), Pamela Jane [P.J.] Soles (*Suzy*), Lisa Shure (*French Girl*), Jennifer K. Mickel (*Girl*), David K. Blace (*Race Announcer*), William S. Armstrong (*Race Official*), Howard S. Wilcox (*Race Official*), J. F. Briere (*Mr. York*), Eddy Van Guyse (*Italian Rider*), Carlos Saintes (*Italian Rider*), Jimmy Grant (*Black Student Leader*), Gail L. Horton (*Fight Spectator*), Woody Hueston (*Owner of Car Wash*), Jennifer F. Nolan (*Anthem Singer*), Nora Ringgenberry (*Race Starter*), Dr. John W. Ryan (*University President*), Morris Salzman (*Blond Guy*), Tom Schwoegler (*Team Captain*), Mike Silveus (*Homecoming Car Kid*), Alvin E. Bailey, Harold Elgar, Robert Woolery, Russell E. Freeman, Floyd E. Todd (*Stonecutters*).

BREAKING AWAY has to do with two things. Naturally, it means the jettisoning of one's parents, old ways, etc. It also means that moment in a bicycle race when one rider takes off from the pack. It's a pleasant film about the adjustment to life after high school. The story is set in Bloomington, Indiana where four recent high school graduates hang around and try to decide what to do with the rest of their lives. The quartet has a few run-ins with students from nearby Indiana University, while Christopher spends much of his time pursuing his main passion, bicycle racing. The climax comes when the foursome are allowed to enter the university's annual "Little 500" bicycle race. Some good perfromances and Tesich, who won an Oscar for his screenplay, provides some amusing dialog. Christopher is such a fan of Italian bike riders that he affects an Italian accent and attitude, something that drives his father, Dooley, wacko. Barrie does her usual excellent job. Pat Williams' music was good as were all technical credits but the sum of all the parts did not really measure up.

p&d, Peter Yates; w, Steve Tesich; ph, Matthew F. Leonetti (DeLuxe Color); m, Patrick Williams; ed, Cynthia Sheider; cos, Betsy Cox.

Comedy   **Cas.**   **(PR:C-O MPAA:PG)**

BREAKING GLASS★★1/2   (1980, Brit.) 104m GTO/PAR c

Phil Daniels (*Danny*), Hazel O'Connor (*Kate*), John Finch (*Woods*), Jonathan Pryce (*Ken*), Peter-Hugo Daly (*Mick*), Mark Wingett (*Tony*), Gary Tibbs (*Dave*), Charles Wegner (*Campbell*), Mark Wing-Davey (*Fordyce*), Hugh Thomas (*Davis*), Nigel Humphreys (*Brian*), Ken Campbell (*Publican*), Peter Tilbury (*Policeman*), Gary Holton (*Guitarist*), Derek Thompsn (*Andy*), Janine Duvitski (*Jackie*), Lowri Ann Richards (*Jane*), Gary Olsen (*Drunk*).

On paper, this movie should have been a smash. It predates FLASHDANCE and many other pop films by a few years and features an okay story with talented young people and lots of contemporary music. BREAKING GLASS is about the rigors and pains and highs of the record business; with excellent photography and very few false notes. Daniels (QUADROPHENIA), as the show-biz manager and Finch, as the producer, capture the tackiness of the time and place very well. O'Connor is the young performer who finally succumbs to the tortures of success. Good technical credits, some laughs, 1980s music that will date the picture soon enough but this film could serve as a good introduction to several new actors who might break out. It gets a bit silly at times and the story is as predictable.

p, Davina Belling, Clive Parsons; d&w, Brian Gibson; ph, Steven Goldblatt (Technicolor); m, Tony Viscont; ed, Michael Brandsell; ch, Eric G. Roberts.

Drama/Musical   **Cas.**   **(PR:C-O MPAA:PG)**

BREAKING POINT, THE***   (1950) 97m WB bw

John Garfield (*Harry Morgan*), Patricia Neal (*Leona Charles*), Phyllis Thaxter (*Lucy Morgan*), Juano Hernandez (*Wesley Park*), Wallace Ford (*Duncan*), Edmond Ryan (*Rogers*), Ralph Dumke (*Hannagan*), Guy Thomajan (*Danny*), William Campbell (*Concho*), Sherry Jackson (*Amelia*), Donna Jo Boyce (*Connie*), Victor Sen Yung (*Mr. Sing*), Peter Brocco (*Macho*), John Doucette (*Gotch*), James Griffith (*Charlie*).

Hollywood's second version of Hemingway's minor novel *To Have and Have Not* turns out to be a spanking good adventure story, ranging from California to Mexico and exploiting its coastal locations to the limit. Garfield is the ill-starred owner of a charter boat and is trying to support his wife, Thaxter, and two daughters, but business is abysmally bad. Dumke, a flashy sports fisherman, and his live-in lady friend, Neal, hire Garfield to take them to Mexico, where Dumke skips out without paying for the ride, leaving Garfield stranded with Neal and a docking fee he cannot pay. A seedy lawyer, Ford, induces him to smuggle Chinese into the United States for $200 a head, but Garfield is doublecrossed by the leader of the Chinese who is killed, leaving Garfield no choice but to dump the remaining Chinese into shallow Mexican waters. The Coast Guard gets wind of the smuggling attempt and impounds Garfield's boat, so he returns home despondent and has a brief sexual fling with the willing Neal. Ford meanwhile gets a court order freeing the boat and blackmails Garfield into taking a bunch of hoodlums to an island in international waters to deliver stolen race track receipts. Enroute, Garfield's alcoholic first mate and best friend, Hernandez, is killed by the crooks and Garfield in turn kills the hoods one by one in a brilliant action sequence on a moving fishing boat, with a complex arrangement of angles, set-ups, and cuttings. A Coast Guard cutter finds the wounded Garfield and brings him to home port, where he is reunited with his wife and kids. The final scene is the most eloquent in the film: the crowd on the dock drifts away as an ambulance takes Garfield to the hospital. The scene is empty except for a little black boy, Hernandez's son. The boy stands motionless, looking for his father along the dock, and the camera pulls away. In his last film for Warner Brothers, under Curtiz, a director who always brought out the best in his acting style, Garfield turns in a first-class performance as the strong man down by his failure. MacDougall's screenplay is admirably true to Hemingway's novel (its California setting in no way violates the book's intentions), and he keeps it a very realistic story with no pretensions, the kind Garfield worked best at, allowing the actor to drop some of his bad habits for a performance that is totally under control. Neal, as the whore, and Thaxter, whose secret is the fact that she knows all of her husband's faults and loves him only the more for it, are both excellent in their roles. (Remake of TO HAVE AND HAVE NOT; remade as THE GUN RUNNERS.)

p, Jerry Wald; d, Michael Curtiz; w, Ranald MacDougall (based on the novel *To Have and Have Not* by Ernest Hemingway); ph, Ted McCord; m, Ray Heindorf; ed, Alan Crosland, Jr.; art d, Edward Carrere; set d, George James Hopkind; cos, Leah Rhodes; makeup, Bill Phillips.

Drama   (PR:A   MPAA:NR)

BREAKING POINT, THE*   (1961, Brit.) 59m BUT bw

Peter Reynolds (*Eric Winlatter*), Dermot Walsh (*Robert Wade*), Joanna Dunham (*Cherry Winlatter*), Lisa Gastoni (*Eva*), Jack Allen (*Ernest Winlatter*), Brian Cobby (*Peter de Savory*), Arnold Diamond (*Telling*).

Printer's son Reynolds becomes a traitor when he helps Communists stop a shipment of foreign currency. Money talks, but not when it means putting your life on the line.

p&w, Peter Lambert (based on a novel by Lawrence Meynell); d, Lance Comfort.

Spy Drama   (PR:A   MPAA:NR)

BREAKING POINT**   (1976) 92m FOX c

Bo Svenson (*Michael*), Robert Culp (*Frank*), John Colicos (*Vincent*), Belinda Montgomery (*Diana McBain*), Stephen Young (*Peter Stratis*), Jeffrey Lynas (*Andy Stratis*), Richard Davidson (*Hirsch*), Jonathan White (*Redpath*), David Mann (*Policeman*), Bill Kemp (*Commissioner McGuire*), Ken James (*Hagerty*), Doug Lennox (*Gilligan*), Bud Cardos (*Fleming*), Joanna Noyes (*Sarah*), Ken Camroux (*Assistant D. A.*).

Similar plot to HIDE IN PLAIN SIGHT with a little bit of both versions of DEATH WISH tossed in. Svenson testifies as a witness in a murder case and that marks him as a victim right away. Culp sets up a new identity for Svenson in his capacity as a police officer. The Cosa Nostra somehow finds Svenson and the guy has to eliminate the mobsters by himself. Svenson is a teacher: Tall, muscular, but with the personality of an instructor, hardly the type who will take on heavy-jowled hoodlums with very thin gold watches. Still, he has to do it because the cops are shown to be helpless and ineffectual, thus leading viewers to believe that, in order to survive, the law must be taken into one's own hands. Don't believe it. This kind of stuff only happens in movies. And bad movies at that. Svenson is far better than the role as written. Culp probably wishes he could have rewritten his role, something he used to do while laboring in TV, but in films they don't let actors have that kind of latitude unless they are huge stars, which Culp is not. Bob Clark went on to later direct PORKY'S. It's a toss-up to decide which picture was funnier.

p, Bob Clark, Claude Heroux; d, Clark; w, Roger Swaybill, Stanley Mann (based on a story by Swaybill); ph, Marc Champion (DeLuxe Color); m, David McLey; ed, Stan Cole.

Crime Drama   (PR:C-O   MPAA:R)

BREAKING THE ICE**   (1938) 80m RKO bw

Bobby Breen (*Tommy Martin*), Charles Ruggles (*Samuel Terwilliger*), Dolores Costello (*Martha Martin*), Robert Barrat (*William Decker*), Dorothy Peterson (*Annie Decker*), John King (*Henry Johnson*), Billy Gilbert (*Mr. Small*), Charlie Murray

(*Janitor*), Margaret Hamilton (*Mrs. Small*), Jonathan Hale (*Kane*), Spencer Charters (*Farmer Smith*), Maurice Cass (*Mr. Jones*).

Breen plays a young boy who escapes from a domineering tobacco farmer who has taken in his wife's widowed sister and son. The kid runs away to Philadelphia and gains fame and fortune as a singer with the hopes of making his mother independent again. Admirable production and performing efforts make this a film where the viewer will cheer for the boy soprano, despite the weak script and dialog.

p, Sol Lesser; d, Edward F. Cline; w, Fritz Falkenstein, N. Brewster Morse, Mary McCall, Jr., Manuel Seff, Bernard Schubert; ph, Jack MacKenzie; md, Victor Young; ed, Arthur Hilton; ch, Dave Gould; m/l, Frank Churchill, Victor Young, Paul Webster.

Drama/Musical   Cas.   (PR:A   MPAA:NR)

BREAKING THE SOUND BARRIER***
         (1952) 115m BLPA bw (GB: THE SOUND BARRIER)

Ralph Richardson (*John Ridgfield*), Ann Todd (*Susan Garthwaite*), Nigel Patrick (*Tony Garthwaite*), John Justin (*Phillip Peel*), Dinah Sheridan (*Jess Peel*), Joseph Tomelty (*Will Sparks*), Denholm Elliott (*Christopher Ridgefield*), Jack Allen (*Windy Williams*), Ralph Michael (*Fletcher*), Vincent Holman (*A. T. A. Officer*), Douglas Muir, Leslie Phillips (*Controllers*), Robert Brooks Turner (*Test Bed Operator*), Anthony Snell (*Peter Makepeace*), Jolyon Jackley (*Baby John*).

Richardson, in his subtle understated way, is powerful, if not sometimes frightening, as an airplane factory magnet obsessed with breaking the sound barrier. To that end he sends aloft his son-in-law who is killed, but then continues to send pilot after pilot to achieve what American test pilot Chuck Yeager had already done secretly. But the production is marvelous for its technical achievements with masterful director Lean dwelling upon the aircraft and the incredible strain placed on pilots. Exciting and well-crafted.

p&d, David Lean; w, Terence Rattigan; ph, Jack Hildyard; m, Malcolm Arnold; ed, Geoffrey Foot; art d, Joseph Bato, John Hawkesworth; set d, Vincent Korda.

Drama   (PR:A   MPAA:NR)

BREAKOUT***   (1960, Brit.) 89m BL/Continental bw (GB: DANGER WITHIN)

Richard Todd (*Lt. Col. David Baird*), Bernard Lee (*Lt. Col Huxley*), Michael Wilding (*Maj. Charles Marquand*), Richard Attenborough (*Capt. Bunter Phillips*), Dennis Price (*Capt. Rupert Callender*), Donald Houston (*Capt. Roger Byford*), William Franklyn (*Capt. Tony Long*), Vincent Ball, Peter Arne.

A terrific cast make up the all-male British prisoners-of-war in an Italian internment camp, planning and executing a harrowing escape just before the arrival of Allied troops toward the end of WW II. In addition to shielding their secret activities from enemy guards, the plotters must deal with an insidious traitor in their midst. Attenborough would later reprise his role in THE GREAT ESCAPE and surely this film owes as much to STALAG 17 as VON RYAN'S EXPRESS owes much to it. Chaffey's direction is taut and swift and some droll British humor helps to break up the tension. A top notch effort.

p, Colin Lesslie; d, Don Chaffey; w, Bryan Forbes, Frank Harvey (based on the novel by Michael Gilbert); ph, Arthur Grant.

War Drama   (PR:A   MPAA:NR)

BREAKOUT*½   (1975) 96m COL c

Charles Bronson (*Nick Colton*), Robert Duvall (*Jay Wagner*), Jill Ireland (*Ann Wagner*), John Huston (*Harris Wagner*), Randy Quaid (*Hawk Hawkins*), Sheree North (*Myrna*), Alejandro Rey (*Sanchez*), Paul Mantee (*Cable*), Roy Jenson (*Spencer*), Alan Vint (*Helicopter Pilot*), Jorge Moreno (*Soza*), Sidney Clute (*Henderson*), Emilio Fernandez (*The Warden*).

BREAKOUT is a mistake that made it to the theaters. Something like this really did happen but it had to have been done a lot better than they did this movie. Bronson is the devil-may-care pilot who rescues Duvall from the south-of-the-border prison where he has been framed by John Huston. (Ireland is Duvall's wife in the film, Bronson's in real life.) It's one of those vigilante, simplistic stories that has audiences not screaming at the screen for the bad guys at all. Unmotivated, often plodding, and singularly without humor, this could have been terrific. Nice thesping from North, Quaid, and Rey, but Gries (WILL PENNY, HELTER SKELTER) didn't do his best work in this film.

p, Robert Chartoff, Irwin Winkler; d, Tom Gries; w, Howard B. Kreitsek, Marc Norman, Elliot Baker (based on the novel by Warren Hinckle, William Turner, Elliott Asinof); ph, Lucien Ballard (Eastmancolor); m, Jerry Goldsmith; ed, Bud Isaacs; spec eff, Augie Lohman.

Adventure   Cas.   (PR:C   MPAA:PG)

BREAKTHROUGH**½   (1950) 91m WB bw

David Brian (*Capt. Hale*), John Agar (*Lt. Joe Mallory*), Frank Lovejoy (*Sgt. Bell*), Bill Campbell (*Dominick*), Paul Picerni (*Pvt. Ed Rojeck*), Greg McClure (*Pvt. Frank Finley*), Richard Monahan (*"Four-Eff" Nelson*), Eddie Norris (*Sgt. Roy Henderson*), Matt Willis (*Pvt. Jumbo Hollis*), Dick Wesson (*Hansen*), Suzanne Dalbert (*Collette*), William Self (*Pvt. George Glasheen*), Danny Arnold (*Pvt. Rothman*), Dani Sue Nolan (*Lt. Janis King*), Howard Negley (*Lt. Col. Lewis*).

One particular infantry platoon of the thousands that went through the Normandy invasion during World War II provides the focus in this battle film, but it is the authentic as well as the manufactured war footage that sustains the action. A small group of veteran infantrymen march across Normandy, commanded by a tough captain, Brian, and led in the field by a green lieutenant, Agar. The scenes necessarily are episodic in nature as they show the fighting of individuals and the effect war has on the men, but they are enlivened by the staged and real clashes. Among the interesting portrayals are those by Campbell, a politically ambitious solder, and Agar, as the story deals mainly with his gaining battle experience. Lovejoy delivers a seasoned performance as the wise sergeant, and Brian the same as the tough company commander. The story was based on some true adventures of Breen, but the film scripters in attempting to show a balanced picture of the war weakened its impact and left a few holes and unclarified switches, such as Brian's suddenly becoming a psycho case at the end.

p, Bryan Foy; d, Lewis Seiler; w, Bernard Girard, Ted Sherdeman (based on a story by Joseph I. Breen, Jr.); ph, Edwin DuPar; m, William Lava; ed, Folmar Blangsted.

War Drama (PR:A MPAA:NR)

BREAKTHROUGH** ½**

(1978, Ger.) 115m Maverick Pictures Intl c (AKA: SERGEANT STEINER)

Richard Burton *(Sgt. Steiner)*, Rod Steiger *(Gen. Webster)*, Robert Mitchum *(Col. Rogers)*, Curt Jurgens *(Gen. Hoffmann)*, Helmut Griem *(Maj. Stransky)*, Michael Parks *(Sgt. Anderson)*, Klaus Loewitsch *(Corp. Krueger)*, Veronique Vendell *(Yvette)*, Joachim Hansen*(Capt. Kirstner)*.

BREAKTHROUGH is the sequel to CROSS OF IRON and a far better movie than the original, which was brilliantly photographed and emotionally unsatisfying. Richard Burton plays Sergeant Steiner (the alternate name of the film in some countries), a German but not a Nazi, who is embroiled in the plot to kill Hitler. Mitchum is a U.S. colonel whose life is saved by Steiner and Jurgens is particularly good as the German general who commits suicide after the plot to erase Der Fuehrer falls apart. Lots of suspense (although we all know how the war ended by this time) and good performances under the knowledgeable hand of McLaglen, who has done more than his share of these big-budget jobs. All that was missing for him was John Wayne, a man who starred in many McLaglen films. This film was not a hit and probably lost a pile of money.

p, Achim Sellus, Alex Winitzky; d, Andrew V. McLaglen; w, Tony Williamson; ph, Tony Imi (Eastmancolor); m, Peter Thomas; ed, Raymond Poulton.

War Drama Cas. (PR:C MPAA:PG)

BREATH OF LIFE* (1962, Brit.) 67m Norcon/BL bw

George Moon *(Freddie)*, Larry Martyn *(Tony)*, April Wilding *(Monica)*, Barry Halliday *(Spud)*, Vivienne Lacy *(Marilyn)*, Hugh Halliday *(Harry)*, Gabrielle Blunt *(Winnie)*.

Mechanic saves the life of a baby and brings it up with his own. The child returns the favor when it grows up and entices dad's real kiddies into a bank robbery. Callous production with no surpises.

p, Norman Cohen, Bill Luckwell; d&w, J. Henry Piperno.

Crime (PR:A MPAA:NR)

BREATH OF SCANDAL, A* ½ (1960) 97m PAR c

Sophia Loren *(Princess Olympia)*, Maurice Chevalier *(Prince Philip)*, John Gavin *(Charlie Foster)*, Isabel Jeans *(Princess Eugenie)*, Angela Lansbury *(Countess Lina)*, Robert Risso *(Aide)*, Frederick von Ledebur *(Count Sandor)*, Carlo Hintermann *(Prince Ruprecht)*, Tullio Carminati *(Albert)*, Adrienne Gessner *(Amelia)*, Milly Vitale *(Can-Can Girl)*.

Leading a wanton and reckless life, Princess Loren desires to consummate her passion but is rendered innocent by the Pittsburgh mining engineer and gentleman she hopes to seduce (Gavin). She meets this Yankee while living in exile in the country. She then is summoned to Vienna and told that a marriage has been arranged for her with Hintermann, Prince of Prussia. Jealous rival Lansbury attempts to prove Loren unworthy of Hintermann by exposing her lust for Gavin. As luck and the plot has it, Lansbury elopes with Gavin and Loren marries the prince. For Loren's performance, the light is on, but nobody is home. Also true for Chevalier, who doesn't identify with his character as her father. Director Curtiz and art directors Periera and Allen boost film with tasteful aesthetics. Elegant costuming by Bei and Knize capture romanticism of the Viennese, and the mood is enhanced by Cicognini's poetic music.

p, Carlo Ponti, Marcello Girosi; d, Michael Curtiz; w, Sidney Howard, Walter Bernstein (based on the play "Olympia" by Ferenc Molnar); ph, Mario Montouri (VistaVision, Technicolor); m, Alessandro Cicognini; ed, Howard Smith; art d, Hal Pereira, Eugene Allen; cos, Ella Bei, Knize.

Drama (PR:A MPAA:NR)

BREATHLESS****

(1959, Fr.) 89m Imperia Films bw (A BOUT DE SOUFFLE)

Jean-Paul Belmondo *(Michel Poiccard/Laszlo Kovacs)*, Jean Seberg *(Patricia Franchini)*, Daniel Boulanger *(Police Inspector)*, Jean-Pierre Melville *(Parvulesco)*, Liliane Robin *(Minouche)*, Henri-Jacques Huet *(Antonio Berrutti)*, Van Doude *(Journalist)*, Claude Mansard *(Claudius Mansard)*, Michel Fabre *(Plainclothesman)*, 10Jean-Luc Godard *(Informer)*, Jean Domarchi *(Drunk)*, Richard Balducci *(Tolmatchoff)*, Roger Hanin *(Carl Zombach)*, Jean-Louis Richard *(Journalist)*, Francois Moreuil *(Cameraman)*, Philippe de Broca.

"Anything goes" was the spirit behind BREATHLESS, and the portrayal of two characters lost in the labyrinths of existentialism burst like a thunderbolt on the turbulent era of the 1960s and early 1970s, making its director a god among youth and the movie the greatest filmic achievement of the New Wave. Godard's most popular film to date had its origins in an item Truffaut saw one day in a Paris newspaper: a motorcyclist killed a policeman and hid out with his girl friend, who betrayed him to the police. Unable to use the item for a film he had in mind, he gave the idea to Godard. With a $90,000 budget and a shooting goal of one month (which he kept), Godard cast a former boxer with a face so battered it was beautiful, Belmondo, as the rogue-hero, and Iowa-born actress Seberg (trying to recover from the disaster of her screen debut in Otto Preminger's SAINT JOAN four years earlier) as the girl friend who betrays him with a phone call made indifferently to the cops—a whore-virgin who is missing a soul. Disregarding formal conventions of filmmaking, Godard presents a fragmented narrative of petty thief Belmondo en route from Marseilles to Paris in a stolen car. Along the way he kills a cop who tries to arrest him for speeding, and in Paris persuades a reluctant Seberg—an American student who hawks newspapers—to hide him until he receives some money due him. Then they will go to Italy. Belmondo's crime has made the newspapers; he hides out in Seberg's apartment and there is an unforgettable scene in which they discuss books, they flirt, he talks about dying, she tells him she is pregnant by him (he answers: "You should have been more careful"). They make love. A genuine punk, Belmondo wears the tough-guy garb of sunglasses, suit, tie and hat, of the early 1940s American gangster movies (which Godard loved), and is completely without conscience. He robs parking meters, deflates tires, steals from a model's purse, steals cars, mugs a guy in a men's washroom. But events are about to catch up with him. Spotted on the street by an informer (Jean-Luc Godard), the cops are told and the final tragic chase begins. Inspector Boulanger visits Seberg at the *Herald Tribune* and shows her a news story about her criminal boy friend, warning her that if she does not cooperate with the law he will create passport trouble for her. A dragnet is spread for the cop-killer. Belmondo and Seberg go to a movie. Seberg helps him find the man who owes him money, and they spend the night in a friend's apartment. Next morning, she calls the inspector and tells him where Belmondo is. On the street, Belmondo is about to get his money when he is spotted by the inspector, who shoots him. As he collapses, Seberg standing on the sidewalk cooly watching him die, he utters his last laconic words: "It's truly disgusting." In keeping his story simple, Godard was able to do what he most wanted, liberate film from its inherited conventions and employ a collage of innovative film techniques—jump cuts, unusual camera angles, elliptical editing, then use of the hand-held camera in unusual ways (in one scene photographer Godard sat in a wheelchair and, camera on his lap, rolled along the street following the actors) to force the viewer to regard what is familiar in a new and unfamiliar manner and produce an immediacy that gave the film, as Godard said, "It's sense of living in the moment." BREATHLESS' style had a profound effect on the history of moviemaking, opening the way, as one critic observed, "to a freer, more personal kind of cinema." The film also demonstrated to filmmakers what novelists have always known, that the manner in which a story is told can be more important than the story itself. The status of BREATHLESS is now that of a cult film.

p, Georges de Beauregard; d&w, Jean-Luc Godard (based on an idea by Francois Truffaut); ph, Raoul Coutard; m, Martial Solal; ed, Cecile Decugis, Lila Herman; art d, Claude Chabrol.

Drama Cas. (PR:O MPAA:NR)

BREATHLESS** (1983) 100m Orion c

Richard Gere *(Jesse)*, Valerie Kaprisky *(Monica)*, Art Metrano *(Birnbaum)*, William Tepper *(Paul)*, John P. Ryan *(Lt. Parmental)*, Lisa Persky *(Salesgirl)*, Gary Goodrow *(Berrutti)*, Robert Dunn *(Sgt. Enright)*, James Hong *(Grocer)*, Eugene Lourie *(Dr. Boudreaux)*, Jack Leustig *(Policeman)*, Waldemar Kalinowski *(Tolmatchoff)*.

Remaking a movie is always a dicey proposition. Remaking a classic is even dicier. BREATHLESS burst upon the scene in 1959 and blew us all away. Godard took big chances with technique, content and the casting of an obscure actor named Belmondo and an actress from Iowa, the late, lovely Jean Seberg. The new BREATHLESS features Gere in the Belmondo role and Kaprisky in Seberg's part. But they've switched nationalities to accommodate the Los Angeles location. This version follows Godard's and Truffaut's (he wrote the original story) plotline but adds 1980s bizarre colors and more than a dozen pop tunes. It's a series of "I didn't mean-to's" whereby Gere keeps getting deeper and deeper into trouble, stealing cars, shooting people and it has more violence than a Tom & Jerry cartoon (which is sometime resembles). Gere shows us his (yawn) body again; it seems a Gere picture isn't complete these days unless he gives us some hairless nudity. It's unreal, manic, and thus an excellent depiction of Los Angeles in the 1980s. Very good music, some good performances but Kaprisky leaves much to be desired. The ending is one of the great cop-outs in modern moviedom.

p, Martin Erlichman; d, Jim McBride; w, McBride, L. M. Kit Carson (based on a screenplay by Jean Luc Godard and a story by Francois Truffaut); ph, Richard H. Kline (DeLuxe Color); m, Jack Nitzche; ed, Robert Estrin; prod d, Richard Sylbert; cos, J. Allen Highfill.

Crime Drama Cas. (PR:O MPAA:R)

BREED OF THE BORDER*

(1933) 53m MON bw (GB: SPEED BRENT WINS)

Bob Steele, Marion Byron, Ernie Adams, Wilfred Lucas, George "Gabby" Hayes, Henry Roquemore, Fred Cavens, Robert Cord, Perry Murdock.

Race car driver Steele is hired by an outlaw who needs protection getting across the border but finds he can't trust the crook and ends up working for the law instead. Good assortment of fist fights, car chases, and hard riding.

p, Paul Malvern; d, R. N. Bradbury; w, Harry O. Dean, ph, Faxon Dean.

Western (PR:A MPAA:NR)

BREEZING HOME** (1937) 63m UNIV bw

William Gargan *(Steve Rowan)*, Binnie Barnes *(Henrietta Fairfax)*, Wendy Barrie *(Gloria Lee)*, Raymond Walburn *(Clint Evans)*, Alma Kruger *(Mrs. Evans)*, Alan Baxter *(Joe Montgomery)*, William Best *(Speed)*, Michael Loring *(Eddie)*, Elisha Cook, Jr. *(Pete)*.

Socialite stable owner Barnes becomes a part of a romantic triangle involving devoted horse trainer Gargan and night club singer Barrie who receives a horse named Galaxy along with its trainer as a gift from her latest flame. Crooked gambling endangers the horse's life providing a comedic hole for Gargan to fill. Slow-paced racetrack programmer.

p, Edmund Grainger; d, Milton Carruth; w, Charles Grayson (based on the story "I Hate Horses" by Finley Peter Dunne, Jr. and Philip Dunne); ph, Gilbert Warrenton; m, Jimmy McHugh; m/l, "I'm Hitting the High Spots," "You're In My Heart Again," McHugh, Harold Adamson.

Drama **(PR:A MPAA:NR)**

BREEZY*** (1973) 106m UNIV c

William Holden *(Frank Harmon)*, Kay Lenz *(Breezy)*, Roger C. Carmel *(Bob* Henderson), Marj Dusay *(Betty)*, Joan Hotchkis *(Paula)*, Jamie Smith Jackson *(Marcy)*, Norman Bartold *(Man in Car)*, Lynn Borden *(Overnight Date)*, Shelley Morrison *(Nancy)*, Dennis Olivieri *(Bruno)*, Eugene Peterson *(Charlie)*, Lew Brown *(Police Officer)*, Richard Bull *(Doctor)*, Johnnie Collins III *(Norman)*, Don Diamond *(Maitre'd)*, Scott Holden *(Veterinarian)*, Sandy Kenyon *(Real Estate Agent)*, Jack Kosslyn *(Driver)*, Mary Munday *(Waitress)*, Frances Stevenson *(Saleswoman)*, Buck Young *(Paula's Escort)*, Priscilla Morrill *(Dress Customer)*, Earle *(Sir Love-A-Lot)*.

Divorced businessman Holden, frustrated with women and bitter over a separation from his wife, stays hidden away in his luxurious California home, unwilling to associate with anyone. When he discovers the pretty, outgoing free spirit Lenz sleeping on his doorstep one morning, he doesn't report her to the police, he simply chases her off his property. When the girl returns the next day to pick up a forgotten guitar, she convinces Holden to let her take a bath and spend the night in a comfortable bed. When the girl returns for a third time, this time accompanied by the police, Holden goes along with Lenz's story that he is her uncle and takes custody of her. The two begin to talk openly with one another and a true friendship develops. Sexual activity soon follows and an affair begins. Although he is certainly happy with the lively, spontaneous girl, Holden succumbs to pressure from his social peers and abandons his relationship with the much younger woman. When a female friend loses her husband in an auto accident, Holden realizes that life should be cherished and searches for Lenz. Finding her in a park, Holden apologizes to Lenz and asks her to come back to him. She accepts and the unusual couple settles down to an unpredictable life. Although the flawed script with its predictable situations and often cute dialog is a drawback, the direction by Eastwood and the performances he gets from Holden and newcomer Lenz are outstanding. His third film as director after PLAY MISTY FOR ME and HIGH PLAINS DRIFTER, BREEZY is a distinct change of pace for the action-oriented Eastwood. Concerning himself with compassion and understanding, Eastwood easily conveys the complexities of his actors. Eastwood's best films as director (THE OUTLAW JOSEY WALES, HONKYTONK MAN) deal with American values and the star's already established image. BREEZY is a small, personal film that allowed Eastwood to work with talented actors and experiment with directorial style. If Eastwood would have chosen a more intelligent script, he could have produced a minor classic.

p, Robert Daley; d, Clint Eastwood; w, Jo Heims; ph, Frank Stanley (Technicolor); m, Michel Legrand; ed, Ferris Webster; art d, Alexander Golitzen; set d, James Payne; m/l, Marilyn and Alan Bergman.

Drama **(PR:O MPAA:R)**

BREWSTER McCLOUD 1/2** (1970) 104m Lion's Gate/MGM c

Bud Cort *(Brewster McCloud)*, Sally Kellerman *(Louise)*, Michael Murphy *(Frank Shaft)*, William Windom *(Sheriff Weeks)*, Shelley Duvall *(Suzanne)*, Rene Auberjonois *(Lecturer)*, Stacy Keach *(Abraham Wright)*, John Schuck *(Policeman Johnson)*, Margaret Hamilton *(Daphne Heap)*, Jennifer Salt *(Hope)*, Corey Fischer *(Policeman Hines)*, G. Wood *(Police Capt. Crandall)*, Bert Remsen *(Policeman Breen)*, Angeline Johnson *(Breen's Wife)*, William Baldwin *(Week's Aide)*.

Cort, believing himself to be a bird in human form, spends his time hidden below the Houston Astrodome constructing a pair of wings that will enable him to fly around the famous sports arena. Although he usually turns to his bird-lady guardian angel Kellerman for advice, he falls victim to stadium usherette Duvall's seductions. She eventually turns him in to the police after learning that he is a suspect in a series of strangler murders that are being investigated by clothes-conscious cop Murphy. Intentionally confusing, surrealistic American satire that owes more to the anarchic structure of cartoons and the cinema of the French New Wave than to any type of normal American narrative. Director Altman's work can either fascinate or infuriate an audience, his lack of focus and spontaneous shooting style often becoming annoying. A mixed bag: unusually told and well-acted, it is, nevertheless, forgettable.

p, Lou Adler; d, Robert Altman; w, Doran William Cannon; ph, Lamar Boren, Jordan Croneweth (Metrocolor); m, Gene Page; ed, Louis Lombardo; songs, John Phillips, Rosamond and James Weldon Johnson; art d, George W. Davis, Preston Ames.

Comedy **Cas.** **(PR:C MPAA:R)**

BREWSTER'S MILLIONS* 1/2**
(1935, Brit.) 80m British and Dominion/UA bw

Jack Buchanan *(Jack Brewster)*, Lili Damita *(Rosalie)*, Nancy O'Neil *(Cynthia)*, Sydney Fairbrother *(Miss Plimsole)*, Ian McLean *(McLeod)*, Fred Emney *(Freddy)*, Allan Aynesworth *(Rawles, the butler)*, Lawrence Hanray *(Grant, a solicitor)*, Dennis Hoey *(Mario)*, Henry Wenman *(Pedro)*, Amy Veness *(Mrs. Barry)*, Sebastian Shaw *(Frank)*, Antony Holles *(Ferago, the Mayor)*.

High-spirited Buchanan is faced with the oh-so terrible task of having to spend 500,0000 pounds in order to collect his six million-pound inheritance from his recently dead uncle's estate. Thinking it will be easy and enjoyable, Buchanan faces a problem when every one of his throwaway investments makes money. The witty, energetic Buchanan has a field day with this craftily scripted comedy. The over-produced musical numbers and the elaborate Italian fiesta scenes are exaggerated delights, as is every scene of this classic example of British wit.

p, Herbert Wilcox; d, Thornton Freeland; w, Arthur Wimperis, Paul Gangelin, Douglas Furber, Clifford Grey, Donovan Pedelty, Wolfgang Wilhelm (based on the play by Winchell Smith and Byron Ongley and the novel by George Barr McCutcheon); ph, Bernard MacGill; m, Ray Noble.

Comedy **(PR:A MPAA:NR)**

BREWSTER'S MILLIONS**** (1945) 79m UA bw

Dennis O'Keefe *(Monty Brewster)*, Helen Walker *(Peggy Gray)*, Eddie "Rochester" Anderson *(Jackson)*, June Havoc *(Trixie Summers)*, Gail Patrick *(Barbara Drew)*, Mischa Auer *(Michael Michaelovich)*, Joe Sawyer *(Hacky Smith)*, Nana Bryant *(Mrs. Gray)*, John Litel *(Swearengen Jones)*, Herbert Rudley *(Nopper Harrison)*, Thurston Hall *(Colonel Drew)*, Neil Hamilton *(Mr. Grant)*, Byron Foulger *(Attorney)*, Barbara Pepper *(Cab Driver)*, Joseph Crehan *(Notary)*.

O'Keefe in one of his finest performances portrays Monty Brewster, the young, handsome, happy-go-lucky soldier returning to a grand life and a swell girl (played by Walker). Wouldn't you know, though, he finds he has inherited $8,000,000. Darn the luck. As if this didn't cause enough grief, he learns he has to spend $1,000,000 in two months under the provisions of the will or forfeit the entire estate. This is a real dilemma and Brewster embarks on a whirlwind of spending, racing around town in an effort to divest himself of this filthy lucre by investing in a flop musical show, a bankrupt banker, the stock market, the racetrack and a jewel-loving society gal. BREWSTER'S MILLIONS is a broad farce and comes across as such, providing laughs throughout. While the opening is somewhat slow and deliberate, once motivation has been established, this modestly budgeted production rockets along with one climax topping another. Sturdy performances are turned in by Eddie "Rochester" Anderson and Walker.

p, Edward Small; d, Allan Dwan; w, Siegfried Hersig, Charles Rogers, Wilkie Mahoney (based on the novel by George Barr McCutcheon and the play by Winchell Smith and Byron Ongley); ph, Charles Lawton; ed, Richard Heermance.

Comedy **Cas.** **(PR:A MPAA:NR)**

BRIBE, THE*** (1949) 98m MGM bw

Robert Taylor *(Rigby)*, Ava Gardner *(Elizabeth Hintten)*, Charles Laughton *(J. J. Bealler)*, Vincent Price *(Carwood)*, John Hodiak *(Tug Hintten)*, Samuel S. Hinds *(Dr. Warren)*, John Hoyt *(Gibbs)*, Tito Renaldo *(Emilio Gomez)*, Martin Garralaga *(Pablo Gomez)*.

Robert Taylor stars as Federal Agent Rigby sent to a banana republic to break up a ring dealing in contraband war surplus materials, headed by a naive American playboy-sportsman, Price, and the slovenly Laughton, a broken-down beachcomber type with aching feet, sly and sleazy, with a slightly humorous shading (perfect meat for Laughton). The story concerns the classic love/duty dilemma with Gardner, the femme fatale in her first star billing at MGM after a seven-year build-up. Agent Rigby tells his story in flashback, tipping off the plot too early, but the tropical locale is intriguing and the angle of war surplus racketeering was timely enough to save the picture. Hodiak is Gardner's sickly husband who owns the ship used to smuggle goods out of the country; he is killed by Price, leaving Taylor and Gardner free to pursue their hot love affair. This juicy chunk of melodrama was particularly notable for its climax, a fight between Taylor and villain Price, staged by Robert Z. Leonard amid a stupendous fireworks display. Gardner even sings a Nacio Herb Brown-William Katz tune, "Situation Wanted." Some of the frantic chase scenes during the fiesta and Price's hammy overacting which sometimes infects Laughton (who steals every scene) verges on the absurd, but much of the laughable camp is controlled through Ruggiero's skilled editing. The excellent cast, the exotic setting, and Leonard's pell-mell direction aided by Ruttenberg's moody graphics, firmly entrenches this production in the *film noir* field. (Steve Martin's sophomoric spoof DEAD MEN DON'T WEAR PLAID drew extensively from scenes in this film.)

p, Pandro S. Berman; d, Robert Z. Leonard; w, Marguerite Roberts (based on the short story by Frederick Nebel); ph, Joseph Ruttenberg; m, Miklos Rozsa; ed, Gene Ruggiero; art d, Cedric Gibbons, Malcolm Brown; set d, Edwin B. Willis, Hugh Hunt; cos, Irene; spec eff, Warren Newcombe, A. Arnold Gillespie.

Crime Drama **(PR:C MPAA:NR)**

BRIDAL PATH, THE 1/2** (1959, Brit.) 95m Kingsley-Union/BL bw

Bill Travers *(Ewan McEwan)*, Alex Mackenzie *(Finlay)*, Eric Woodburn *(Archie)*, Jack Lambert *(Hector)*, John Rae *(Angus)*, Roddy McMillan *(Murdo)*, Jefferson Clifford *(Wallace)*, Nell Ballantyne *(Jessie)*, George Cole *(Sgt. Bruce)*, Fiona Clyne *(Katie)*, Bernadette O'Farrell *(Siona)*, Patricia Bredin *(Margaret)*, Dilys Laye *(Isobel)*, Joan Fitzpatrick *(Sarah)*, Pekoe Ainley *(Craigie)*, Joan Benham, *(Barmaid)*, Annette Crosbie *(Good Looking Waitress)*, Nancy Mitchell *(Hotel Waitress)*, Lynda King *(Bank Clerk)*, Gordon Jackson *(Constable Alec)*, Robert James *(Inspector)*, Terry Scott *(Constable Donald)*, Duncan Macrae *(Sergeant)*, Jameson Clark *(Constable)*, Vincent Winter *(Neal)*, Elizabeth Campbell *(Kirsty)*.

Travers, a resident on a remote island, is ordered to go to the mainland to seek a wife so that no more first cousins marry in the cloistered community. In a series of comic adventures with pretty young ladies, Travers' life becomes more and more complicated, then turns serious when he is mistaken for a salmon poacher and must flee from police (in a sort of shallow parody of Hitchcock's THE 39 STEPS). Light-hearted fun paced with deft direction makes for an enjoyable production. Songs are provided by the Campbeltown Gaelic Choir.

p, Frank Launder, Sidney Gilliat; d, Launder; w, Nigel Tranter, Launder, Geoffrey Willans; ph, Arthur Ibbetson (Technicolor); m, Cedric Thorpe Davie; ed, Geoffrey Foot.

Comedy **(PR:A MPAA:NR)**

BRIDAL SUITE**   (1939) 69m MGM bw

Annabella (*Luise Anzengruber*), Robert Young (*Neil McGill*), Walter Connolly (*Dr. Grauer*), Reginald Owen (*Sir Horace Bragdon*), Gene Lockhart (*Cornelius McGill*), Arthur Treacher (*Lord Helfer*), Billie Burke (*Mrs. McGill*), Virginia Field (*Abbie Bragdon*), Felix Bressart (*Max*).

Uninspired wealthy playboy Young falls for independent business woman Annabella at her Swiss Alps Inn. She says yes to his proposal and they are married on the boat to America after Young jilts his gold-digging fiancee, Field. This production is poorly directed and unimaginatively filmed.

p, Edgar Selwyn; d, William Theile; w, Samuel Hoffenstein (based on a story by Gottfried Reinhardt and Virginia Faulkner); ph, Clyde De Vinna; m, William Budde and Gus Kahn; ed, Frank E. Hull.

Comedy   **(PR:A MPAA:NR)**

BRIDE, THE**

(1973, Can.) 85m Golden Gate/Unisphere c (AKA: THE HOUSE THAT CRIED MURDER)

Robin Strasser (*Barbara*), John Beal (*Father*), Arthur Roberts (*David*), Iva Jean Saraceni (*Ellen*).

Weird boss' daughter Strasser snares Roberts as a husband then catches him making love to old girl friend (Saraceni) on their wedding day. The house Strasser has built serves as a temple of punishment for the doomed two-timer and his lady friend when they take up residence there. Penny-pinching budget undoes this potentially good technical effort.

p, John Grissmer; d, Jean-Marie Pelissie; w, Grissmer, Pelissie; ph, Geoffrey Stephenson; m, Peter Bernstein; ed, Sam Moore.

Horror   **(PR:C-O MPAA:PG)**

BRIDE AND THE BEAST, THE*

(1958) 78m AA bw (AKA: QUEEN OF THE GORILLAS)

Charlotte Austin (*Laura*), Lance Fuller (*Dan*), Johnny Roth (*Taro*), Steve Calvert (*The Beast*), William Justine (*Dr. Reiner*), Jeanne Gerson (*Marka*), Gil Frye (*Capt. Cameron*), Slick Slavin (*Soldier*), Bhogwan Singh (*Native*), Jean Ann Lewis (*Stewardess*).

Austin marries Fuller, then finds him keeping a pet gorilla in a cage; she discovers herself attracted to the ape. Fuller kills the ape; then Austin, under hypnotic regression, discovers she was a gorilla in a former life, answering doubts about her peculiar infatuation. When she and hubby are on safari in Africa (exclusively stock footage), a gorilla makes off with her and that's the name of that tune. This one should never have fallen out of the tree.

p&d, Adrian Weiss; w, Edward D. Wood, Jr., Adrian Weiss; ph, Roland Price; m, Les Baxter; ed, George Merrick.

Horror   **(PR:C MPAA:NR)**

BRIDE BY MISTAKE*   (1944) 81m RKO bw

Alan Marshal (*Tony*), Laraine Day (*Norah*), Marsha Hunt (*Sylvia*), Allyn Joslyn (*Phil Vernon*), Edgar Buchanan (*Connors*), Michael St. Angel (*Corey*), Marc Cramer (*Ross*), William Post, Jr. (*Donald*), Bruce Edwards (*Chaplain*), Nancy Gates (*Jane*), Slim Summerville (*Samuel*), John Miljan (*Maj. Harvey*), Robert Anderson (*Lt. Wilson*).

When wealthy Day's hangers-on chase away her lover, she becomes infatuated with a convalescent pilot who thinks he has married the wrong woman until he sees her in a sexy negligee on their wedding night. Slow-moving film with tedious camerawork and direction. (Remake of THE RICHEST GIRL IN THE WORLD)

p, Bert Granet; d, Richard Wallace; w, Phoebe and Henry Ephron (based on a story by Norman Krasna); ph, Nicholas Musuraca; ed, Les Millbrook.

Drama   **(PR:A MPAA:NR)**

BRIDE CAME C.O.D., THE***   (1941) 90m WB bw

James Cagney (*Steve Collins*), Bette Davis (*Joan Winfield*), Stuart Erwin (*Tommy Keenan*), Jack Carson (*Allen Brice*), George Tobias (*Peewee*), Eugene Pallette (*Lucius K. Winfield*), Harry Davenport (*Pop Tolliver*), William Frawley (*Sheriff McGee*), Edward Brophy (*Hinkle*), Harry Holman (*Judge Sobler*), Chick Chandler (*1st Reporter*), Keith Douglas (*2nd Reporter*), Herbert Anderson (*3rd Reporter*), Creighton Hale, Frank Mayo, Jack Mower (*Reporters*), William Newell (*McGee's Pilot*), William Hopper (*Keenan's Pilot*), Eddy Chandler, Tony Hughes, Lee Phelps (*Policemen*), Reid Kilpatrick (*Announcer*), Cliff Saum (*Airport Mechanic*), Richard Travis (*Airline Dispatcher*), The Rogers Dancers (*Specialty*), Alphonse Martell (*Headwaiter*), Sol Gross (*Reporters' Pilot*).

Bette Davis, in her autobiography *The Lonely Life,* said of this picture: "Jimmy Cagney, with whom I'd always wanted to work in something fine, spent most of his time in the picture removing cactus quills from my behind. This was supposedly hilarious. We romped about the desert and I kept falling into cactus." Most critics did not agree, however, and lauded her performance in this departure from her usual dramatic fare. Cagney, of course, is tremendous as the pugnacious, rough-housing down-on-his-luck airline pilot who accepts the job of returning the daughter of a Texas oil tycoon to her father's ranch, unmarried, for the freight charge of $10 a pound. Through a ruse, Cagney keeps fiance Carson, a Hollywood bandleader Davis has known for only four days, and publicity hungry broadcaster Erwin from boarding his plane and flies off into the friendly skies with Davis who believes she is being kidnaped. She offers him a reward to take her back to Los Angeles but Cagney refuses, telling her he's getting a better price from her father. His plane develops engine trouble, however, and is forced to land in the desert, where they find a ghost town with one inhabitant, Davenport, a desert hermit who believes Davis' story of the kidnaping and locks Cagney in jail while putting Davis up in the

town's rundown hotel. Not to be outfoxed, Carson arrives the next morning with a Nevada justice of the peace and Davis marries him to spite Cagney, even though she now realizes she loves him. (Those oil heiresses are such a caution.) Pallette shows up and refuses to pay Cagney his freight charges until he discovers Davis' marriage is illegal because the ceremony was performed in California, not Nevada. All ends well when Cagney admits he loves Davis too, but jocularly insists the only reason he will consider marrying her is because her father is a millionaire. The teaming of Davis and Cagney in this broad farce provides a hefty package of laughs and shows Davis is capable of handling comedy roles with her usual elan.

p, Hal B. Wallis, William Cagney; d, William Keighley; w, Julius J. and Philip G. Epstein (based on a story by Kenneth Earl and M. M. Musselman); ph, Ernest Haller; m, Max Steiner; ed, Thomas Richards; md, Leo F. Forbstein; art d, Ted Smith; cos, Orry-Kelly.

Comedy   **(PR:A MPAA:NR)**

BRIDE COMES HOME***½   (1936) 83m PAR bw

Claudette Colbert (*Jeanette Desmereau*), Fred MacMurray (*Cyrus Anderson*), Robert Young (*Jack Bristow*), William Collier, Sr. (*Alfred Desmereau*), Donald Meek (*The Judge*), Richard Carle (*Frank*), Johnny Arthur (*Otto*), Bob McKenzie (*Painter*), Eddie Dunn (*Operator*), Jerry Mandy (*Waiter*), A. S. "Pop" Byron (*Cop*), Edgar Kennedy (*Henry*), Kate McKenna (*Emma*), James Conlon (*Len Noble*), Edward Gargan (*Cab Driver*).

After her wealthy father's business collapses, Colbert applies for a writing job on MacMurray's Chicago-based magazine. Contributing writer Young, attracted to the socialite, informs editor MacMurray of the girl's recent financial problems and he reluctantly hires her. The hard-edged MacMurray and the strong-willed Colbert soon develop a love/hate relationship that, despite constant arguing, ends up in a plan for marriage. When Colbert takes it upon herself to tidy up MacMurray's "lived-in" bachelor apartment, he explodes and sends his fiancee packing. Colbert falls into the arms of the still-adoring Young and the two run off to romantic Crown Point, Indiana to be married. MacMurray realizes the error of his actions, speeds off to Indiana on his motorcycle, interrupts the ceremony, and substitutes himself in the groom position. Pleasant comedy that has Colbert doing yet another variation on her role in IT HAPPENED ONE NIGHT. The battle of the sexes theme is familiar, but the chemistry between the spontaneous couple gives the routine plot a sparkle all its own.

p&d, Wesley Ruggles; w, Claude Binyon, (based on a story by Elizabeth Sanxay Holding); ph, Leo Tover; art d, Hans Dreier, Robert Usher.

Comedy   **(PR:A MPAA:NR)**

BRIDE COMES TO YELLOW SKY, THE   (SEE: FACE TO FACE, 1952)

BRIDE FOR HENRY, A*   (1937) 58m MON bw

Anne Nagel (*Sheila Curtis*), Warren Hull (*Henry*), Henry Mollison (*Eric*), Claudia Dell (*Helen*), Betty Ross Clark (*Mrs. Curtis*), Harrison Green (*Constable*).

Debutant Nagel teases and makes promises to men she is not willing to fulfill until she meets her match in Hull. Pitiful dialog with limp acting and boring direction.

p, Dorothy Reid; d, William Nigh; w, Dean Spencer (based on a play by Josephine Bentham); ph, Gilbert Warrenton.

Drama   **(PR:A MPAA:NR)**

BRIDE FOR SALE****   (1949) 87m Crest/RKO bw

Claudette Colbert (*Nora Shelly*), Robert Young (*Steve Adams*), George Brent (*Paul Martin*), Max Baer (*Litka*), Gus Schilling (*Timothy*), Charles Arnt (*Dobbs*), Mary Bear (*Miss Stone*), Ann Tyrrell (*Miss Swanson*), Paul Maxey (*Gentry*), Burk Symon (*Sitley*), Stephen Chase (*Drake*), Anne O'Neal (*Miss Jennings*), Eula Guy (*Miss Clarendon*), John Michaels (*Terry*), William Vedder (*Brooks*), Thurston Hall (*Mr. Trisby*), Michael Brandon (*Archie Twitchell*), Patsy Moran (*Sarah*), Harry Cheshire (*Haskins*), Robert Cautiero (*Manager of Jewelry Store*), Harry Wilson (*Bruiser*), Hans Conreid (*Jewelry Salesman*), Frank Orth (*Police Sergeant*) Stan Johnson (*Johnson*).

Colbert, an expert accountant working for Brent's firm, uses the company files as a resource center for finding the perfect, financially successful husband. Brent discovers her plan, and, anxious to keep her on his staff, gets museum curator friend Young to Sweep Colbert off of her feet, then drop her, teaching her the importance of remaining a single working girl. Naturally, Young can't help but fall in love with his unsuspecting victim. The affinity for the material and each other that is displayed by stars Colbert and Young make this screwball comedy a treasure. Although he was not Cary Grant, Young's easy-going style and wit made his presence here, and in many films of the 1940s, a welcome addition.

p, Jack H. Skirball; d, William D. Russell; w, Bruce Manning, Islin Auster (based on a story by Joseph Fields); ph, Joseph Valentine; ed, William Knudston; md, C. Bakaleinikoff; art d, Albert S. D'Agostino, Carroll Clark.

Comedy   **(PR:A MPAA:NR)**

BRIDE GOES WILD, THE***½   (1948) 97m MGM bw

Van Johnson (*Greg Rawlings*), June Allyson (*Martha Terryton*), Butch Jenkins (*Danny*), Hume Cronyn (*John McGrath*), Una Merkel (*Miss Doherty*), Arlene Dahl (*Tillie Smith*), Richard Derr (*Bruce Kope Johnson*), Lloyd Corrigan (*Pop*), Elisabeth Risdon (*Mrs. Carruthers*), Clara Blandick (*Aunt Pewtie*), Kathleen Howard (*Aunt Susan*).

New England school teacher Allyson, an aspiring commercial artist, wins a job illustrating the new book by a popular children's author known as "Uncle Bump." Upon arrival in New York she learns that "Uncle Bump" is Johnson, a hard-drinking, child-hating young writer. Feeling that Johnson has betrayed children everywhere, Allyson threatens to expose the hypocrite to the public. Seeing thousands of dollars flying out the window, Johnson's publisher friend Cronyn convinces Allyson that Johnson's attitude and habits are the result of his wife's death and current problems with their hostile son. Allyson swallows the fictitious story, but insists upon helping the troubled widower and meeting the little boy. Bribing tough orphan Jenkins to pose as Johnson's son, Cronyn is surprised to see the boy act as a catalyst in fueling the fires of romance between Johnson and Allyson. When Allyson discovers the true nature of the boy's relationship with the writer, she runs back home and prepares to marry long-time suitor Derr. Jenkins, having grown attached to the couple, convinces Johnson to track Allyson down and propose marriage. The two arrive in New England on the day of Allyson's wedding and Jenkins delays the ceremony by unleashing an army of ants on the outdoor festivities. Johnson's plea to Allyson is successful and the couple returns to New York, planning to adopt Jenkins as soon as they are married. Daffy comedy that manages to display some insight into the lonely world of children and lost adults amidst the broad, physical comedy. Allyson and Johnson do a remarkable job in blending character touches with slapstick action, although some may find the film's lack of sophistication a drawback.

p, William H. Wright; d, Norman Taurog; w, Albert Beich; ph, Ray June; m, Rudolph G. Kopp; ed, George Boemler; art d, Cedric Gibbons, Harry McAfee; set d, Edwin B. Willis, Arthur Krams.

Comedy **(PR:A MPAA:NR)**

BRIDE IS MUCH TOO BEAUTIFUL, THE** (1958, Fr.) 90m Ellis-Lax

Brigitte Bardot *(Chouchou)*, Micheline Presle *(Judith)*, Louis Jourdan *(Michel)*, Mar cel Amont *(Toni)*, Jean-Francois Calve *(Patrice)*, Roger Dumas *(Marc)*, Madeleine Lambert *(Tante Agnes)*, Marcelle Arnold *(Mme. Victoire)* Colette Regis *(Tante Yvonne)*, Roger Treville *(Designy)*, Nicole Gueden *(Juliette)*.

Weak story has France's one-time sex kitten as a top Paris model trying to snare her magazine editor boss but no matter what she does Jourdan, a romantic dunce, fails to respond. He has to be hit over the head so Bardot, at film's conclusion, runs wildly through the woods wearing only a thin negligee. Jourdan takes off after her and slavishly proposes. The only excuse for this sex farce is to have Bardot bounce around in the almost all-together.

p, Gaspard Huit; d, Fred Surin; w, Juliette Saint-Ginez, Odette Joyeux (based on a story by Joyeux).

Romance **(PR:O MPAA:NR)**

BRIDE OF FRANKENSTEIN, THE***** (1935) 80m UNIV bw

Boris Karloff *(The Monster)*, Colin Clive *(Henry Frankenstein)*, Valerie Hobson *(Elizabeth Frankenstein)*, Elsa Lanchester *(Mary Shelley/The Bride)*, O. P. Heggie *(The Hermit)*, Una O'Connor *(Minnie)*, Ernest Thesiger *(Dr. Septimus Pretorious)*, Gavin Gordon *(Lord Byron)*, Douglas Walton *(Percy Shelley)*, E. E. Clive *(Burgo master)*, Lucien Prival *(Otto)*, Dwight Frye *(Karl)*, Reginald Barlow *(Hans)*, Mary Gordon *(Hans' Wife)*, Anne Darling *(Shepherdess)*, Gunnis Davis *(Uncle Glutz)*, Tempe Piggott *(Auntie Glutz)*, Ted Billings *(Ludwig)*, Neil Fitzgerald *(Rudy)*, Walter Brennan *(Neighbor)*, Lucio Villegas *(Priest)*, Edwin Mordant *(Coroner)*, Grace Cunard *(Woman)*, Helen Gibson *(Woman)*, John Carradine *(Huntsman)*, Monty Montague *(King)*, Joan Woodbury *(Queen)*, Norman Ainsley *(Archbishop)*, Peter Shaw *(Devil)*, Billy Barty *(Baby)*, Kansas De Forest *(Ballerina)*, Josephine McKim *(Mermaid)*, Helen Parrish *(Girl)*.

Genuinely frightening, but also high and humorous camp is FRANKENSTEIN, a cultist's delight and one of the strangest films ever produced, far more eerie than the original FRANKENSTEIN with the emphasis on exaggeration. Everything in the film is blown out of proportion—the sets, the camera angles, the padded cell plot, actors wildly outbidding each other in hysterical histrionics. A huge palace is shown beneath a crackling thunderstorm and then a spacious chamber room where great poets Lord Byron (Gordon), and Percy Shelley (Walton) are urging Shelley's wife Mary to elaborate further on her fictional character, the Frankenstein monster. She is reluctant, telling Byron and her husband that the monster was killed when the old mill burned, as was shown in the finale of FRANKENSTEIN. Mary finally relents and begins to weave another tale of horror to amuse her companions. The monster did not die in the fire, but crashed through the old mill's fire-gutted ruins to an underground pond and survived the holocaust; his creator, Colin Clive, is not killed when his warped creation throws him from the top of the burning mill but his fall is cushioned by one of the moving mill blades. While Clive recuperates from the nightmare, believing the monster (Karloff) thankfully dead, the big guy crawls from the muddy waters and is discovered by two villagers who have stayed behind after the mill has crumbled to embers. They are the parents of the young girl the monster has murdered in FRANKENSTEIN. Before they can call the torch-carrying villagers back both are strangled by Karloff and hurled like rag dolls into the pond. Karloff then staggers off in his typically confused state. He comes upon Darling, a pretty shepherdess who is so frightened that she falls into a lake but Karloff, always a paradox as the monster, saves her from drowning. And, as always, his magnanimity is repaid with brutality which turns him once more into a bloodletter. The villagers arrive to capture Karloff and imprison him in the local dungeon-like jail, chaining him hand and foot and at the neck to a stone chair. His creator Clive is summoned to identify him and, with palsied hands and fearful look, he does, condemning the creature. Karloff later escapes and goes on a murder rampage, destroying one and all in his path. Off through the countryside he goes until finding the hut of a blind hermit (Heggie) who treats him with great kindness, offering him food, drink, and cigars, teaching him a few basic words. It appears that the monster has found, at last, a safe refuge with someone who understands him, but no. Two hunters come upon the scene, yelling at the hermit that he is entertaining the monster. Karloff cracks their skulls and off he goes to wreak havoc and terror. Clive is at home with what amounts to delerium tremens over the mere thought of his unleashed creature when his grim reveries are interrupted by an individual almost as alarming as Karloff, Clive's former teacher, Thesiger, a bizarre scientist quite off his nut. Thesiger's performance must be seen to be believed, that of a fruity, sinister, eccentric old man whose every ounce of manic energy is consumed by attempting to better his pupil's achievement in creating life. Conspiratorily, he takes Clive to his oddball workshop, a place of cavernous underground passages beneath a massive cemetery where human skeletons abound. Here he displays miniature people under belljars, alive but woefully inadequate in size. Thesiger insists that Clive work with him to produce another full-sized human from the scraps of the dead, stolen by his weird, rasping assistant Frye. When Clive refuses to duplicate his scientific monstrosity, Thesiger kidnaps Clive's wife Hobson, holding her incognito until Clive agrees to work with him. The two begin their frantic experiments in Clive's towering laboratory, which crackles and pops with electric charges snaking from strange machines. Thesiger scurries about, his tall thin frame flitting from machine to machine as he and Clive create a mate for the monster; Karloff has returned and is waiting in the lower dungeon for female companionship. The final product is Lanchester (who also plays Mary Shelley), as hideous a creature as Karloff, covered with scar tissue, slits for eyes, and a great shock of hair standing on end in the ancient style of Egyptian Queen Nefertiti. Karloff sits beside her, stroking her claw-like hand while she jerks her head about in grotesque muscular contractions. When he gives her a thin lustful smile, she pulls away, completely repelled by the monster's fearful countenance, hissing her hatred of him like a snake. Then, guided by Thesiger, she moves away from him, half gliding, half staggering, like a windup toy whose mechanism has gone haywire. With this rejection Karloff goes berserk and proceeds to destroy her, Thesiger, the labora- tory, and himself, although his new-found compassion allows him to let Clive live to rejoin Hobson before he brings down the roof. THE BRIDE OF FRANKENSTEIN was four years in the making after the worldwide success of FRANKENSTEIN in 1931. James Whale, who had directed the original FRANKEN-STEIN, was chosen to helm THE BRIDE; he initially wanted silent screen beauty Louise Brooks to play the mutilated mate, then later asked for German actress Brigitte Helm. He got neither, but he did transfer Helm's spasmodic movements from Fritz Lang's silent classic METROPOLIS in which Helm plays a robot to Lanchester. Viewers seeing this second man-made monster were even more petrified than they were by Karloff's appearance in 1931. BRIDE was originally intended to be called FRANKENSTEIN LIVES AGAIN! or THE RETURN OF FRANKENSTEIN but these titles were scrapped. Whale displays a devilish sense of humor in this macabre masterpiece. One of Thesiger's miniatures is a doppleganger of Henry VIII, whom Lanchester's husband Charles Laughton played to perfection. Whale's impish humor was further demonstrated when the wife of the peasant who finds the monster under the windmill reaches into the water to pull her husband ashore but her hand is clasped by the monster coming from the deep to yank her to a watery death. Whale allowed Thesiger to get away with any flamboyant gesture such as using a skull for an ashtray and toasting the comatose Karloff with lines like Gin is my only weakness," before cavalierly offering the monster a shot. Claude Rains was first selected by Whale to play the creepy Dr. Pretorious but he was busy elsewhere when the production started and Thesiger, who had acted with incredible hamminess in Whale's THE OLD DARK HOUSE in 1932, was a logical replace-ment. Karloff never liked this film or his role, later stating that he felt it wrong to humanize the monster by allowing him to speak, get tipsy from wine, and dizzy from cigar smoke. (Oddly, Bela Lugosi was offered the monster role in FRANKENSTEIN but rejected it for the very opposite reason, because it offered no dialog, only miserable grunting.) One of the writers of BRIDE, Balderston, later denounced his own work, declaring that he wrote it as a satire but producer Carl Laemmle, Jr., rearranged the script to emphasize horror. Brilliantly photograped by Mescall, there are a few minor flaws. Certain scenes were deleted and this hampers dialog before and after the missing frames. In the finale, Karloff, disgusted by the whole horror show, decides to send everyone, including himself, to perdition. He reaches for the main switch controlling the giant machines in the laboratory. Thesiger screams, "Don't touch that lever—you'll blow us all to atoms!" (Why such a lethal lever should exist in the first place is beyond wonder.) Before yanking the lever, Karloff looks to Clive and Hobson, grumbling, "You go!" allowing them to escape. The monster then turns to Thesiger and growls, "You stay! We belong dead." He looks to his bride Lanchester for one last time and is greeted with another vicious hiss. As a tear rolls down his face, Karloff pulls the lever, destroying them all. Yet a minute or two later Clive is shown still inside the collapsing laboratory being crushed by huge beams. No one seemed to notice; viewers were too much in awe of this incredible film to nit-pick. (Originally the monster killed his creator, along with himself, Lanchester, and Thesiger. Whale changed his mind at the last minute and allowed Clive to escape, but it was too late and too expensive to reshoot the destruction of the laboratory—thus a rather glaring error remains.) Universal, as was the studio's budget-minded way, later used stock footage from BRIDE in GHOST OF FRANKENSTEIN and HOUSE OF DRACULA and also used Wax man's spine-tingling score in its cheapie serials BUCK ROGERS and FLASH GORDON. This is, undoubtedly, James Whale's finest effort, yet it worked a great hardship on the poor monster. Karloff is beaten, whipped, shot, burned, and almost crucified on a cross by those pesky, torch-carrying villagers (and who in his right mind would go on living in a village where the population is drastically decreased daily by an undying monster?). In the scene where Karloff crashes through the burning windmill into the water below he bruised his left ribs and required infrared treatments for weeks after the production was completed. Moreover, he had to arrive first at the studio before any of the actors to undergo hours of makeup preparation and then thud around in specially made boots with ten pounds of lead in the soles of each so that he could affect that weird, uncertain lurch. After FRANKENSTEIN, THE BRIDE OF FRANKENSTEIN and its sequel, SON OF FRANKENSTEIN, Karloff had had enough of the indestructible creature with the square head and electrodes at the neck. He refused to play the role again. I could see the writing on the wall," he is quoted in *Dear Boris* by biographer Cynthia Lindsay, as to what was going to happen to the character of the monster. There is just so much you can develop in a part of that nature, and it was a case of diminishing returns. The monster was going to wind up as he did, a rather comic prop in the last act . . . '' (See FRANKEN-STEIN, Index)

p, Carl Laemmle, Jr,; d, James Whale; w, William Hurlbut, John L. Balderston (based on the novel by Mary Wollstonecraft Shelley); ph, John Mescall; m, Franz Waxman; ed, Ted Kent; art d, Charles D. Hall; spec eff, John Fulton; makeup, Jack Pierce.

Horror   **Cas.**   **(PR:C MPAA:NR)**

BRIDE OF THE DESERT*¹/₂   (1929) 50m Rayart bw

Alice Calhoun, LeRoy Mason, Ethan Laidlaw, Lum Chan, Walter Ackerman, Horace Carpenter.

Calhoun plays the lonely wife of gold prospector Laidlaw who harbors and then finds comfort in the arms of framed killer Mason. She then discovers her husband is the real murderer sought by the sheriff and posse. Technical effort is mediocre in this early talkie.

p, Trem Carr; d, Duke Worne; w, Arthur Hoerl; ph, Ernest Depew.

Western   **(PR:A MPAA:NR)**

BRIDE OF THE GORILLA*   (1951) 65m REA bw

Barbara Payton (Dina), Lon Chaney, Jr. (Taro), Raymond Burr (Barney Chavez), Tom Conway (Dr. Viet), Paul Cavanagh (Klass Von Gelder), Carol Varga (Larina), Paul Maxey (Van Heussen), Woody Strode (Policeman), Martin Garralaga (Native Man), Moyna MacGill (Mrs. Van Heussen), Felippa Rock (Van Heusen's Daughter).

Restless jungle wife Payton goes for hubby Cavanagh's plantation foreman Burr to escape loneliness. Hubby gets bitten by a poisonous snake and Burr turns gorilla by night after he weds the minx. Fair production with a few good moments but nothing outside the obvious.

p, Jack Broder; d&w, Curt Siodmak; ph, Charles Van Enger; m, Raoul Kraushaar; ed, Francis D. Lyon.

Adventure/Horror   **Cas.**   **(PR:A MPAA:NR)**

BRIDE OF THE LAKE**¹/₂

(1934, Brit.) 60m Ameranglo bw (GB: LILY OF KILLARNEY)

Gina Malo (Eileen O'Connor), John Garrick (Sir Patrick Cregeen), Stanley Holloway (Father O'Flynn), D. J. Williams (Danny Mann), Sara Allgood (Mrs. O'Connor), Dennis Hoey (Myles-Na-Coppaleen), Dorothy Boyd (Norah Cregeen), Hughes Macklin (Shan), Pamela May (Ann Chute), John Mortimer (Tim O'Brien), Pat Noonan (Commandant), McGinty (Pat Williams), Bromley Davenport (Lord Kenmore).

Garrick has to win a steeplechase in order to keep his castle and his girl. Fine musical with refreshing performances and songs.

p, Julius Hagen; d, Maurice Elvey; w, H. Fowler Mear (based on the play ''Colleen Bawn'' by Dion Boucicault); ph, Sidney Blyth, W. Luff; md, W. L. Trytell.

Musical   **(PR:A MPAA:NR)**

BRIDE OF THE MONSTER*

(1955) 68m Banner bw (AKA: BRIDE OF THE ATOM)

Bela Lugosi (Dr. Eric Vornoff), Tor Johnson (Lobo), Tony McCoy (Lt. Dick Craig), Loretta King (Janet Lawton), Harvey Dunn (Capt. Robbins), George Becwar (Prof. Strowski), Paul Marco (Kelton), Don Nagel (Martin), Bud Osborne (Mac), John Warren (Jake), Ann Wilner (Tillie), Delores Fuller (Margie), William Benedict (Newsboy), Ben Frommer (Drunk).

Mad scientist Lugosi captures twelve men he intends to make into supermen by using atomic energy. King gets lost in bad lines and over-direction as the snooping reporter destined to become the title of this flick. One of Lugosi's most dismal efforts.

p,d&w, Edward D. Wood, Jr.; ph, William C. Thompson, Ted Allan; m, Frank Worth; ed, Warren Adams.

Horror   **Cas.**   **(PR:A MPAA:NR)**

BRIDE OF THE REGIMENT**¹/₂   (1930) 79m FN bw

Vivienne Segal (Countess Anna-Marie), Allan Prior (Count Adrian Beltrami), Walter Pidgeon (Col. Vultow), Louise Fazenda (Teresa), Myrna Loy (Sophie), Lupino Lane (Sprotti), Ford Sterling (Tangy), Harry Cording (Sgt. Dostal), Claude Fleming (Capt. Stogan), Herbert Clark (The Prince).

Unremarkable musical comedy featuring Segal as the wife of a proud Italian count fighting off invading Austrians. When the Austrians, led by the imposing Pidgeon, take over the count's castle as a headquarters, he flees, leaving Segal to outwit the invaders. Pidgeon approaches the attractive countess with the proposition of trading her virtue for her husband's life; the sticky situation is resolved when Pidgeon, in a drunken stupor, thinks he has conquered the unwilling woman and leaves. An enthusiastic cast helps this easy-going, but forgettable musical. Pidgeon is enjoyable as the boisterous Hussar, but the routine direction and lackluster script does nothing to reinforce his energy.

d, John Francis Dillon; w, Humphrey Pearson (based on the operetta, ''The Lady in Ermine'' by Rudolph Schanzer and Ernest Welisch, adapted by Ray Harris); ph, Dev Jennings, Charles E. Schoenbaum; ed, Leroy Stone; m, Al Bryan, Eddie Ward, Al Dubin; ch, Jack Haskell.

Musical/Comedy   **(PR:A MPAA:NR)**

BRIDE OF VENGEANCE**¹/₂   (1949) 92m PAR bw

Paulette Goddard (Lucretia Borgia), John Lund (Alfonso D'Este), Macdonald Carey (Cesare Borgia), Albert Dekker (Vanetti), John Sutton (Bisceglie), Raymond Burr (Michelotto), Charles Dayton (Bastino), Donald Randolph (Tiziano), Rose Hobart

(Eleanora), Nicholas Joy (Chamberlain), Fritz Leiber (Filippo), Kate Drain Lawson (Gemma), William Farnum (Peruzzi), Anthony Caruso (Captain of the Guard), Douglas Spencer (The False Physician), Billy Gilbert (Beppo), Dean White (The Sentry), Ed Millard (Herald), Frank Puglia (Bolfi), Nestor Paiva (The Mayor).

Misguided costume drama has pretty Goddard plotting the deaths of an aristocratic clan after she learns that the family's head, Lund, may have been responsible for her beloved husband's death. When her evil brother Carey plots to control all of Italy, including the land owned by Lund, their diabolical plans become intertwined. A notorious box-office failure in its day, the film is a flawed but interesting tale of family intrigue and revenge. Leisen captures the eerie mood of the rich and twisted Borgias, but the treatment of his overwrought characters is unintentionally humorous in more than a few scenes.

p, Richard Maibaum; d, Mitchell Leisen; w, Cyril Hume, Michael Hogan, Clemence Dane (based on a story by Hogan); ph, Daniel L. Fapp; m, Hugo Friedhofer; ed, Alma Macrorie; art d, Hans Dreier, Roland Anderson; m/l, Troy Sanders, Livingston and Evans, Victor Young.

Drama   **(PR:A MPAA:NR)**

BRIDE WALKS OUT, THE**¹/₂   (1936) 75m RKO bw

Barbara Stanwyck (Carolyn Martin), Gene Raymond (Michael Martin), Robert Young (Hugh McKenzie), Ned Sparks (Paul Dodson), Helen Broderick (Mattie Dodson), Anita Colby, Vivian Oakland (Salesladies), Willie Best (Smokie), Robert Warwick (Mr. McKenzie), Billy Gilbert (Donovan), Eddie Dunn (Milkman), Ward Bond (Taxi Driver), Edgar Dearing (Cop), Wade Boteler (Field Manager), James Farley (Store Detective), Margaret Morris (Secretary), Hattie McDaniel (Maime).

Thinly plotted story of a young, working-class couple, Stanwyck and Raymond, who separate after Stanwyck begins to spend much more than Raymond earns. She latches onto the rich Young who can provide her with the stylish clothes she desires and jilted husband Raymond plans to forget his dilemma by running off to South America. Stanwyck realizes that her true love is Raymond and not fashion and she returns to her husband before he departs. The two settle down with Stanwyck keeping a careful eye on her spending. Run-of-the-mill comedy accentuated by some naturalistic, witty dialog between the delightful Stanwyck and the sadly humdrum Raymond.

p, Edward Small; d, Leigh Jason; w, P. J. Wolfson, Philip G. Epstein (based on a story by Howard Emmett Rogers); ph, J. Roy Hunt; ed, Arthur Roberts; md, Roy Webb; art d, Van Nest Polglase, Al Herman; cos, Bernard Newman.

Comedy   **Cas.**   **(PR:A MPAA:NR)**

BRIDE WITH A DOWRY**   (1954, USSR) 105m Artkino c

Vera Vashilieva (Olga), Vladimir Ushakov (Maxim), V. Dorofeyev (Avdei Spiridonovich), L. Kumicheva (Vasilisa Pavlovna), G. Kozhakina (Lyba), K. Kanayeva (Galya), D. Dubov (Muravlev), G. Ivanov (Semyon Ivanovich), A. Pribylovsky (Silanti Romanovich); T. Peitzer (Lukeria), Nikolai Kurochkin, V. Doronin, of the Maly Theatre.

Betrothed partners Vashilieva and Ushakov clash in farming methods which endangers their feelings for each other, then kiss and make up for a happy ending. Performances capture the idiosyncracies of the characters but technical support falls short in this Russian version of ''Oklahoma.''

d, T. Lukashevich, B. Ravenskikh; ph, N. Vlassov, S. Shenin; m, N. Budashkin.

Musical   **(PR:A MPAA:NR)**

BRIDE WORE BLACK, THE**

(1968, Fr./Ital.) 107m Films du Carrosse-DD/Artistes Associes c (LA MARIEE ETAIT EN NOIR)

Jeanne Moreau (Julie), Jean-Claude Brialy (Corey), Michel Bouquet (Coral), Charles Denner (Fergus), Claude Rich (Bliss), Daniel Boulanger (Holmes), Michel Lonsdale (Morane), Serge Rousseau (David), Jacques Robiolles (Charlie), Luce Fabiole (Julie's Mother), Sylvine Delannoy (Mrs. Morane), Jacqueline Rouillard (Maid), Van Doude (Inspector Fabri), Paul Pavel (Mechanic), Maurice Garell (Plaintiff), Frederique and Renaud Fontanarosa (Musicians).

An unconvincing Hitchcockian mystery where Moreau's fiance is brutally murdered and she spends all her waking moments tracking down and killing the five men who did it. Moreau's worldly and patient performance manages to sustain the mood if not the suspense.

p, Marcel Roberts; d, Francois Truffaut; w, Truffaut, Jean-Louis Richard (based on the novel by William Irish); ph, Raoul Coutard (DeLuxe Color); m, Bernard Herrmann; ed, Claudine Bouche; art d, Pierre Guffroy.

Mystery   **(PR:C MPAA:NR)**

BRIDE WORE BOOTS, THE***   (1946) 85m PAR bw

Barbara Stanwyck (Sally Warren), Robert Cummings (Jeff Warren), Diana Lynn (Mary Lou Medford), Patric Knowles (Lance Gale), Peggy Wood (Grace Apley), Robert Benchley (Tod Warren), Willie Best (Joe), Natalie Wood (Carol Warren), Gregory Muradian (Johnny Warren), Mary Young (Janet Doughton), Frank Orth (Judge), Charles D. Brown (Wells), Richard Gaines (Jeff's Attorney), Myrtle D. Anderson (Florence), James Millican (Kerwin Hayes), Minerva Urecal (Lady), Milton Kibbee (Hotel Manager).

Stanwyck, a top horse breeder, and her writer husband Cummings separate after a series of misunderstandings. Although Cummings hates horses, a cetain pony falls madly in love with him. When Cummings wins a prestigious steeplechase race by riding the lovesick horse, he and Stanwyck are brought back together. Screwy comedy that's a bit empty-headed, but undeniably funny. Cummings is hilarious as the timid wordsmith who finds himself in the middle of the equestrian world and Stanwyck is equally enjoyable as the strong-spirited horsewoman.

p, Seton I. Miller; d, Irving Pichel; w, Dwight Michael Wiley (based on a story by Wiley and a play by Harry Segall); ph, Stuart Thompson; m, Frederick Hollander; ed, Ellsworth Hoagland; art d, Hans Dreier, John Meehan; set d, Sam Comer, Jerry Welch; cos, Edith Head.

Comedy (PR:A MPAA:NR)

BRIDE WORE CRUTCHES, THE*

(1940) 54m FOX bw

Lynne Roberts (*Midge Lambert*), Ted North (*Johnny Dixon*), Edgar Kennedy (*Capt. McGuire*), Robert Armstrong (*Pete*), Lionel Stander (*Flannel Mouth*), Richard Lane (*Bill Daly*), Grant Mitchell (*E.J. Randall*), Harry Tyler (*Whispers*), Edmund MacDonald (*Dick Williams*), Horace MacMahon (*Brains*), Anthony Caruso (*Max*), Billy Mitchell (*Harvey*).

North makes a name for himself as a reporter when he witnesses a bank robbery, then tracks down the thieves. Eventually, through undercover efforts, North leads the police to the crooks' hideout. Technical efforts are not only lazy, but thrown together like a tossed salad.

p, Lucien Hubbard; d, Shepard Traube; w, Ed Verdier, Alan Drady; ph, Charles Clarke; md, Emil Newman.

Crime (PR:A MPAA:NR)

BRIDE WORE RED, THE***

(1937) 100m MGM bw

Joan Crawford (*Anni*), Franchot Tone (*Giulio*), Robert Young (*Rudi Pal*), Billie Burke (*Contessa di Milano*), Reginald Owen (*Admiral Monti*), Lynne Carver (*Magdalena Monti*), George Zucco (*Count Armalia*), Mary Phillips (*Maria*), Paul Porcasi (*Nobili*), Dickie Moore (*Pietro*), Frank Puglia (*Alberto*), Anna Demetrio (*Signora Milano*), Charles Judels (*Cordellera Bar Owner*), Ann Rutherford (*Peasant Girl*), Harry Wilson (*Sailor*), Rafael Storm, Bob Coutiere, Adrianna Cassellotti, Jean Lewis.

Crawford, a less-than-virtuous cabaret singer, is invited by wealthy aristocrat Zucco to spend a Cinderella-like two weeks at an exclusive resort in the Tyrol. Hoping to convince his snobby friends that anyone can appear to be a member of the upper crust if provided with the correct trappings, Zucco introduces Crawford as a mysterious socialite, secretly knowing that he will expose her true identity as a common tramp to them at the end of the two weeks. At the resort, Crawford plays her role to the hilt, making gentleman Young fall in love with her. She also meets the Bohemian Tone, village postman, who introduces Crawford to the simple wonders of nature. On the night that Zucco is to expose Crawford, she walks out in a sinful red dress, causing Young to abandon his plans of running off with her. Cast out by the tricked elite, Crawford is saved from emotional despair by the ever-adoring Tone, who has apparently been aware of her shady past all along. Above-average Crawford film that has a pleasing "love should know no bounds" message at its heart. Tone's disinterest in materialism and his appreciation of nature works as a nice complement to Zucco and company's stylish yet bored and frustrated world. Crawford is very calm and assured as the young, cynical woman who finally realizes the love that exists in the world around her.

p, Joseph L. Mankiewicz; d, Dorothy Arzner; w, Tess Slesinger, Bradbury Foote (based on the play, "The Girl From Trieste," by Ferenc Molnar); ph, George Folsey; m, Franz Waxman; ed, Adrienne Fazan; art d, Cedric Gibbons; cos, Adrian; ch, Val Raset; m/l, Waxman, Gus Kahn.

Drama (PR:A MPAA:NR)

BRIDEGROOM FOR TWO*

(1932, Brit.) 70m BIP bw (GB: LET'S LOVE AND LAUGH)

Gene Gerrard (*The Bridegroom*), Muriel Angelus (*The Bride Who Was*), Margaret Yarde (*Her Mother*), Frank Stanmore (*Her Father*), Dennis Wyndham (*Her Fiance*), Henry Wenman (*The Butler*), Rita Page (*The Bride Who Wasn't*), Ronald Frankau (*Her Father*), George Gee (*The Detective*).

Gerrard goes on a fling the night before his wedding and ends up married to Angelus instead of Page. Nothing to sing or laugh about in this contrived mess.

p&d, Richard Eichberg; w, Walter Mycroft, Frederick Jackson (based on the play "A Welcome Wife" by Fred Thompson and Ernest Paulton); ph, H. Gartner, B. Mondi.

Musical/Comedy (PR:A MPAA:NR)

BRIDES ARE LIKE THAT**1/2

(1936) 66m WB bw

Ross Alexander (*Bill McAllister*), Anita Louise (*Hazel Robinson*), Joe Cawthorn (*Fred Schultz*), Gene Lockhart (*John Robinson*), Kathleen Lockhart (*Mrs. Ella Robinson*), Mary Lou Treen (*Jennie*), Alma Lloyd (*Mary Coleridge*), Craig Reynolds (*Carter*), Richard Purcell (*Dr. Randolph Jenkins*).

Loafing nephew of a rich apple orchard owner strikes it rich with a girl who is also poor, but loves him anyway. Good performances in an amusing, well-produced film.

p, Bryan Foy; d, William McGann; w, Harry Conners, Ben Markson; ph, Sid Hickox.

Comedy (PR:A MPAA:NR)

BRIDES OF BLOOD zero

(1968, US/Phil.) 92m Hemisphere bw (AKA: GRAVE DESIRES; ISLAND OF LIVING HORROR)

John Ashley (*Jim Farrell*), Kent Taylor (*Dr. Paul Henderson*), Beverly Hills (*Carla Henderson*), Eva Darren (*Alma*), Mario Montenegro (*Stephen Powers*), Oscar Deesee.

Cartoonish blobs of monsters arise after exposure to nuclear radiation. The main monster eats naked girls. Idea here is that the victims enjoy sex with monsters. Sick, sick, sick.

p, Eddie Romero; d, Romero and Gerardo de Leon.

Horror (PR:O MPAA:NR)

BRIDES OF DRACULA, THE**1/2

(1960, Brit.) 85m Hammer-Hotspur/UNIV c

Peter Cushing (*Dr. Van Helsing*), Martita Hunt (*Baroness Meinster*), Yvonne Monlaur (*Marianne*), Freda Jackson (*Greta*), David Peel (*Baron Meinster*), Miles Malleson (*Dr. Tobler*), Henry Oscar (*Herr Lang*), Mona Washbourne (*Frau Lang*), Andree Melly (*Gina*), Victor Brooks (*Hans*), Fred Johnson (*Cure*), Michael Ripper (*Coachman*), Marie Devereux (*Village Girl*), Harold Scott (*Severin*), Vera Cook (*Landlord's Wife*), Norman Pierce (*Landlord*).

Peel is a teenager who has somehow inherited the trademark of the vampire Dracula. Mother Hunt takes note and locks him in the family castle to hide their secret and then goes about snaring victims for his ravenous appetite. She eventually becomes her son's victim. Peel is later aided in his escape by school teacher Monlaur who is in love with him. Cushing saves Monlaur from marriage to the vampire and the rest of the village too when he drives a wooden stake into Peel's heart. Chilling special effects highlight a rather gory production.

p, Anthony Hinds; d, Terence Fisher; w, Jimmy Sangster, Peter Bryan, Edward Percy (based on characters created by Bram Stoker); ph, Jack Asher (Technicolor); m, Malcolm Williamson; ed, Alfred Cox; spec eff, Sydney Pearson.

Horror (PR:O MPAA:NR)

BRIDES OF FU MANCHU, THE**

(1966, Brit.) 93m Anglo Amalgamated/Seven Arts c

Christopher Lee (*Fu Manchu*), Douglas Wilmer (*Nayland Smith*), Marie Versini (*Marie Lentz*), Heinz Drache (*Franz Baumer*), Howard Marion Crawford (*Dr. Petrie*), Tsai Chin (*Lin Tang*), Kenneth Fortescue (*Sgt. Spier*), Joseph Furst (*Otto Lentz*), Carole Gray (*Michele*), Harald Leipnitz (*Nikki Sheldon*), Rupert Davies (*Merlin*).

The evil Dr. Fu Manchu (this time Christopher Lee, in his second outing as this character) kidnaps the nubile daughters of government leaders in an effort to amass enough capital in ransom money to build a huge ray gun and take over the world. Ambitious plan is, of course, foiled, in the last minute, but not before the mean-spirited doctor lets us know, "You will hear from me again!" Oh, we will, we will. Best performance is offered by Tsai Chin, repeating her part as Manchu's evil daughter. Pedestrian screenplay, out of tune with the times but Lee's performance, while not as good as the late Warner Oland or Boris Karloff, is delightfully evil. (See FU MANCHU series, Index.)

p, Harry Alan Towers, Oliver A. Unger; d, Don Sharp; w, Peter Welbeck [Harry Alan Towers] (based on characters created by Sax Rohmer); ph, Ernest Stewart; m, Bruce Montgomery.

Crime Drama (PR:A MPAA:NR)

BRIDES TO BE*

(1934, Brit.) 68m PAR bw

Betty Stockfield (*Audrey Bland*), Constance Shotter (*Maisie Beringer*), Ronald Ward (*George Hutton*), Olive Sloane (*Phyllis Hopper*), Henry Oscar (*Laurie Randall*), Ivor Barnard (*John Boyle*), Gordon McLeod (*Snell*).

Shopgirl fears the end of her world when crooks frame her for stealing. You see, she's in love with a millionaire and this could spoil everything for the crooks. The world returns to normal when scheme is foiled. Nitwit script and awful acting make this a poor programmer.

p&d, Reginald Denham; w, Basil Mason (based on the story "Sign Please" by Mason).

Crime (PR:A MPAA:NR)

BRIDGE, THE***

(1961, Ger.) 106m AA bw

Volker Bohnet (*Hans Scholten*), Fritz Vepper (*Albert Mutz*), Michael Hinz (*Walter Forst*), Frank Glaubrecht (*Jurgen Borchert*), Karl Michael Balzer (*Karl Horber*), Volker Lechtenbrink (*Klaus Hager*), Guenther Hoffman (*Sigi Bernhard*), Cordula Trantow (*Franziska*), Wolfgang Stumpf (*Stern*), Gunther Pfitzmann (*Cpl. Heilmann*), Siegfried Schurenberg (*Lt. Colonel*), Ruth Hausmeister (*Mrs. Mutz*), Eva Vaitl (*Mrs. Borchert*), Edith Schulze-Westrum (*Mrs. Bernhard*), Hans Elvenspoeck (*Mr. Forst*), Trudy Breitschopf (*Mrs. Forst*), Kalus Hellmold (*Mr. Horber*), Inge Benz (*Sigrun*), Edeltraut Elsner (*Barbara*).

Boy soldiers stationed at an unimportant bridge end up defending it to the death, with the exception of one who escapes. Flawless first directing job from Wicki along with surprisingly good performances from no-name actors.

p, Dr. Herman Schwerin; d, Bernhard Wicki; w, Michael Mansfeld, Karl-Wilhelm Vivier (based on the novel by Manfred Gregor); ph, Gerd von Bonin; m, Hans Martin Majewski; ed, C. O. Bartning.

Drama (PR:A MPAA:NR)

BRIDGE AT REMAGEN, THE****

(1969) 116m UA c

George Segal (*Lt. Phil Hartman*), Robert Vaughn (*Maj. Paul Kreuger*), Ben Gazzara (*Sgt. Angelo*), Bradford Dillman (*Maj. Barnes*), E. G. Marshall (*Brig. Gen Shinner*), Peter Van Eyck (*Gen. Von Brock*), Matt Clark (*Col. Jellicoe*), Fritz Ford (*Col. Dent*), Tom Heaton (*Lt. Pattison*), Bo Hopkins (*Cpl. Grebs*), Robert Logan (*Pvt. Bissell*), Paul Prokop (*Capt. Colt*), Steve Sandor (*Pvt. Slavek*), Frank Webb (*Pvt. Glover*), Hans Christian Blech (*Capt. Carl Schmidt*), Joachim Hansen (*Capt. Otto Baumann*), Gunter Meisner (*S.S. Gen. Gerlach*), Richard Munch (*Field Marshal Von Sturmer*), Heinz Reinke (*Emil Holzgang*), Sonja Ziemann (*Greta Holzgang*), Vit Olmer (*Lt. Zimring*), Rudolf Jelinek (*Pvt. Manfred*), Anna Gael (*The Girl*).

As American forces move into Germany, the Nazi high command orders the Remagen bridge destroyed. Knowing that this will shut his troops off from safety in their home land, German officer Vaughn delays action on the bridge's demolition. American officer Segal, concerned with the welfare of his men, is ordered to capture Vaughn's troops or, if need be, destroy the bridge himself. The confusion and intensity of a single moment in war is captured amazingly well in this underrated WW II film. Containing exciting, tense battle scenes, THE BRIDGE AT REMAGEN balances the visceral excitement of violence with an emotional understanding of the sadness and harsh realities of war. Segal is excellent at portraying a simple man who has difficulties dealing with sending men into a no-win situation. In a smaller role, Gazzara is a treasure as a sleazy G.I. with the characteristics of a vulture. Vaughn, also, is quite good as the German officer who realizes the stupidity of the always-hopeful Third Reich. Veteran cinematographer Stanley Cortez does a breathtaking job of capturing the power of the battle scenes as well as creating the dark, haunting mood of the German countryside.

p, David L. Wolper; d, John Guillerman; w, Richard Yates, William Roberts (based on a story by Roger Hirson); ph, Stanley Cortez (DeLuxe Color); m, Elmer Bernstein; ed, William Cartwright; art d, Alfred Sweeney.

War Drama **(PR:C MPAA:M)**

BRIDGE OF SAN LUIS REY, THE**** (1929) 86m MGM bw

Lily Damita *(Camila)*, Ernest Torrence *(Uncle Pio)* Raquel Torres *(Pepita)*, Don Alvarado *(Manuel)*, Duncan Renaldo *(Esteban)*, Henry B. Walthall *(Father Juniper)*, Michael Vavitch *(Viceroy)*, Emily Fitzroy *(Marquesa)*, Jane Winton *(Dona Clara)*, Gordon Thorpe *(Jaime)*, Mitchell Lewis *(Capt. Alvarado)*, Paul Ellis *(Don Vicente)*, Eugenie Besserer *(Nun)*, Tully Marshall *(Townsman)*.

A quality production, with little dialog, set in Lima, Peru, in 1714, when a wornout bridge gives way, plunging five people to their deaths. The townspeople rush to church in terror thinking that St. Louis, patron saint of the ancient bridge, has deserted them. They see the collapsing of the bridge as punishment for their sins. In the forefront of wickedness is Damita, a Spanish country dancer, courtesan and social climber with a love 'em and leave 'em attitude. Excellent production supports excellent acting. Dialog is used only at the beginning and the end of this early talkie.

d, Charles Brabin; w, Alice D. G. Miller, Ruth Cummings, Marian Ainslee (based on Thornton Wilder's novel); ph, M. B. Gerstad; m, Carli Elinor; ed, Margaret Booth; art d, Cedric Gibbons.

Drama **(PR:A MPAA:NR)**

BRIDGE OF SAN LUIS REY, THE*½** (1944) 107m UA bw

Lynn Bari *(Michaela)*, Akim Tamiroff *(Uncle Pio)*, Francis Lederer *(Manuel & Esteban)*, Alla Nazimova *(The Marquesa)*, Louis Calhern *(The Viceroy)*, Blanche Yurka *(The Abbess)*, Donald Woods *(Brother Juniper)*, Emma Dunn *(Dona Mercedes)*, Barton Hepburn *(Don Rubio)*, Joan Lorring *(Pepita)*, Abner Biberman *(Malta)*, Minerva Urecal *(Servant to Uncle Pio)*.

Paralleling Thornton Wilder's novel closely, director Lee and screenwriter Estabrook turn in a classy example of dramatic entertainment. Superstition engulfs the lives of its citizens who think that when an ancient bridge collapses and kills five townsfolk they are doomed to continuing misfortune. Consolation is offered from the priest who learns that hypocrisy, violence, love, and hate swept the country with sin when Spaniards ruled the land. Symbolizing this tradition is Bari, a Spanish country dancer who has risen to fame and power as a Viceroy consort. Well-performed with close atten tion to idiosyncracies of character, a montage of sets, and startling costumes. High caliber all-around effort.

p, Benedict Bogeaus; d, Rowland V. Lee; w, Herman Weissman, Howard Estabrook (based on the novel by Thorton Wilder); ph, John Boyle; md, Dmitri Tiomkin; ed, Harvey Manager.

Drama **Cas.** **(PR:A MPAA:NR)**

BRIDGE OF SIGHS*½ (1936) 65m IN bw

Onslow Stevens *(Jeffery Powell)*, Dorothy Tree *(Marion Courtney)*, Jack LaRue *(Arny Norman)*.

Prosecuting attorney Stevens encounters complications when the innocent Tree confesses to murder in an attempt to clear her brother of the charge. Stevens carries a shallow production lacking in suspense.

p, Maury M. Cohen; d, Phil Rosen; w, Arthur T. Horman; ph, M. A. Anderson; ed, Ernest J. Nims.

Crime Drama **(PR:A MPAA:NR)**

BRIDGE ON THE RIVER KWAI, THE***** (1957) 161m COL c

William Holden *(Shears)*, Alec Guinness *(Col. Nicholson)*, Jack Hawkins *(Maj. Warden)*, Sessue Hayakawa *(Col. Saito)*, James Donald *(Maj. Clipton)*, Geoffrey Horne *(Lt. Joyce)*, Andre Morell *(Col. Green)*, Peter Williams *(Capt. Reeves)*, John Boxer *(Maj. Hughes)*, Percy Herbert *(Grogan)*, Harold Goodwin *(Baker)*, Ann Sears *(Nurse)*, Henry Okawa *(Capt. Kanematsu)*, K. Katsumoto *(Lt. Miura)*, M. R. B. Chakrabandhu *(Yai)*, Vilaiwan Seeboonreaung, Ngamta Suphaphongs, Javanart Punynchoti, Kannikar Wowklee *(Siamese Girls)*.

An absolutely gripping performance is registered by Guinness, a British colonel who has surrendered with his regiment to the Japanese in Burma in 1943. A martinet, Guinness insists that his men conduct themselves as soldiers in by-the-book conduct, even in prison, and he flatly refuses to cooperate with the equally bound-by-duty Japanese commander Hayakawa, who also renders a splendid characterization. Holden is an American already in the prison camp when Guinness and his tough jungle troops come marching in. He sits in wonder at the brassy Guinness who will not budge an inch when Hayakawa insists that his men construct an elaborate bridge over the canyon of the River Kwai. Hayakawa tries everything—persuasion, threats, and finally torture, sweating Guinness in a hot box for days on end. Then Guinness cracks, strutting his pride of military authority and the belief that his men can accomplish anything—his officers are professional engineers—the result being that he strides into Hayakawa's office and sneers at the architectual plans for the railroad bridge the Japanese have prepared. He points out the model's structural defects and boasts that his own men can build a much better bridge. He then orders his regiment to go to work and he drives them relentlessly to their task. Holden, meanwhile makes a successful escape but undergoes body-wracking rigors until reaching Australia where he impersonates an American officer to obtain the privileges of rank. Hawkins, the British officer in charge of guerrilla operations, comes to him, telling him that he knows Holden is not who he says he is. He makes no threat to expose him, only requests that Holden return to the jungle prison, guiding a small group of British soldiers, including Hawkins, so that they can destroy the bridge Guinness and his men are so frantically attempting to complete. At first Holden refuses, then he agrees when Hawkins makes veiled threats to turn his dossier over to American authorities. If Holden will lead his men to the bridge site, Hawkins promises that he will personally exonerate Holden upon their return. Holden accepts and the sabotage unit parachutes into the Burmese jungle, then, with local bearers, is led to the bridge by Holden, overcoming an impossible trek through jungles and over mountains. They arrive just in time. The bridge is completed and the Japanese plan to move troop trains over it the next day. That night Holden, Hawkins, and others plant their dynamite charges, waiting until the train arrives so that they can destroy the bridge and the train as well. At dawn, Guinness arrives at the bridge to inspect his masterpiece. He is by now, completely crazy, oblivious to the war and the enemy, his overwhelming ego insisting that the bridge be perfect. As he inspects the structure he spots a wire leading from the bridge, one exposed by the receding river below. He follows this wire to find the detonator and a British soldier. Seeing his beautiful bridge is about to be destroyed, he struggles with the soldier and is wounded and the soldier is killed by a guard. All hell breaks loose as the enemy troop train thunders toward the bridge. Hawkins, Holden, and others exchange fire with the Japanese guards, then Holden swims the river, attempting to set off the charges. He shouts at Guinness who has regained his feet as well as his senses. "My God, what have I done?" Guinness asks himself, realizing that he has aided the enemy, then at Holden, whose presence brings the reality of the war back to him. As Japanese mortar shells fall about them, Guinness is hit but staggers forward to the detonator, falling upon the plunger just as the train is crossing the bridge, blowing the structure, train, and enemy troops to pieces. Holden himself is killed, as is Hawkins. British soldier Donald witnesses the carnage and moans: "It's all madness." The camera pulls away to reveal the awful site of death to further emphasize the insanity of war. Lean's direction of this war epic is masterful as he juxtaposes action sequences with the psychological examination of war through his characters. Boule, who adapted his own novel for the screen, retains his terse, tough dialog laced with black humor, particularly through Holden's cowardly wise guy character. The film was shot in Ceylon and captures the lush colors of the dense jungles and craggy mountains. Like the book, the film was based on real events—the Japanese construction of what was called "the death railway," one being constructed from Bangkok to Rangoon in 1942 with Allied prisoners used as forced laborers, driven without food, drink, and shelter until they died on the roadbeds. This powerful, incisive film was a smash hit, yielding $30 million in grosses within three years (it cost $3 million to produce), which benefitted Holden enormously since he wisely chose to receive a percentage of profits in lieu of a higher salary. The film swept seven Oscars, including one for Guinness, another for Lean, Best Picture, writing, editing, cinematography, and music, all deserved.

p, Sam Spiegel; d, David Lean; w, Pierre Boule (based on his novel; Michael Wilson and Carl Foreman uncredited scenarists); ph, Jack Hildyard (CinemaScope, Technicolor); m, Malcolm Arnold; ed, Peter Taylor.

War Drama **Cas.** **(PR:C MPAA:NR)**

BRIDGE TO THE SUN½** (1961) 112m MGM bw

Carroll Baker *(Gwen Terasaki)*, James Shigeta *(Hidenari Terasaki)*, James Yagi *(Hara)*, Tetzuro Tamba *(Jiro)*, Hiroshi Tomono *(Ashi)*, Nori Elisabeth Hermann, Emi Florence Hirsch *(Mako Terasaki)*, Sean Garrison *(Fred Tyson)*, Ruth Masters *(Aunt Peggy)*.

American girl Baker, married to Japanese diplomat Shigeta, disregards the harsh comments of her family and friends and returns to Japan with her husband at the outbreak of WW II. Enduring numerous physical and social hardships during the war, an unexpected tragedy befalls the couple when the battles have ended. Compassionate but unexciting performances from Baker and Shigeta fail to elevate the film above its status as a well-intentioned but mediocre drama. The cultural, emotional, and social problems are evident, but a lack of focus in characterization and the inability, or unwillingness to take chances with the provocative subject matter, mark the film as a noble failure.

p, Jacques Bar; d, Etienne Perier; w, Charles Kaufman (based on an autobiography by Gwen Terasaki); ph, Marcel Weiss, Selichi Kizuka, Bill Kelly; m, Georges Auric; ed, Robert and Monique Isnardon; art d, Hiroshi Mizutani.

Drama **(PR:A MPAA:NR)**

BRIDGE TOO FAR, A*** (1977, Brit.) 176m UA c

Dirk Bogarde *(Lt. Gen. Browning)*, James Caan *(Sgt. Dohun)*, Michael Caine *(Lt. Col. Vandeleur)*, Sean Connery *(Maj. Gen. Urquhart)*, Edward Fox *(Lt. Gen. Horrocks)*, Elliott Gould *(Col. Stout)*, Gene Hackman *(Maj. Gen. Sosabowski)*, Anthony Hopkins *(Lt. Col. John Frost)*, Hardy Kruger *(Gen. Ludwig)*, Laurence Olivier *(Dr. Spaander)*, Ryan O'Neal *(Brig. Gen. Gavin)*, Robert Redford *(Maj. Cook)*, Maximillian Schell *(Lt. Gen. Bittrich)*, Liv Ullmann *(Kate ter Horst)*, Arthur Hill *(Tough Colonel)*, Wolfgang Preiss *(Field Marshall Von Rundstedt)*, Siem Vroom *(Underground Leader)*, Eric Vant Wout *(Child with Spectacles)*, Mary Smithuysen *(Old Dutch Woman)*, Marlies van Alcmaer *(Wife)*, Nicholas Campbell *(Cap. Glass)*,

Christopher Good *(Maj. Carlyle)*, Keith Drinkel *(Lt. Cornish)*, Peter Faber *(Cap. Harry)*.

At nearly three hours, A BRIDGE TOO FAR is a film too long. It's the true story of a military blunder that cost many lives and, in the end, meant little to the war effort. Montgomery and Eisenhower planned to drop 35,000 Allied troops into Holland to secure the six bridges leading to Germany. Next, a British force was to speed through Belgium to the last bridge at Arnhem. From there, the two groups were to smash into the Ruhr area and crush the already damaged factories of the Nazi war effort. Everything went wrong. The weather, bad judgement, panic, bad luck, all had their toll and the operation, code-named "Market Garden," was a total disaster. Why make a movie about such a terrible loss? Disaster movies are a different matter because EARTHQUAKE and THE POSEIDON ADVENTURE are conjecture; this is real. If you can swallow the premise that O'Neal is a brigadier general, you might be able to enjoy this picture on it's commercialized level. On a higher plane, this is one of the most ambitious war movies ever made, ranking with THE LONGEST DAY and THE BATTLE OF THE BULGE in sheer numbers of actors and crew people. There are so many cameo roles, all obviously attracted by enormous sums of Joseph Levine's money, that the film looks like dinner at the Beverly Hills Hotel. Attenborough used his abilities to greater success in GHANDI some years later but this was a definite forerunner of his capacity to make armies move. It's overproduced, over-starred and overly long but it should not be missed by any serious fan of the movies, just for the sheer scope and achievement of it. And yet, between all the huge exercises and troop advances, Goldman has added many little touches that make A BRIDGE TOO FAR quite human, despite the inhumanity of the theme.

p, Joseph E. Levine, Richard Levine, Michael Stanley-Evans; d, Richard Attenborough; w, William Goldman (based on the book by Cornelius Ryan); ph, Geoffrey Unsworth (Technicolor); m, John Addison; ed, Anthony Gibbs; cos, Anthony Mendelson.

War Drama **Cas.** **(PR:C MPAA:PG)**

BRIDGES AT TOKO-RI, THE**** (1954) 102m PAR c

William Holden *(Lt. Harry Brubaker, USNR)*, Fredric March *(Rear Adm. George Tarrant)*, Grace Kelly *(Nancy Brubaker)*, Mickey Rooney *(Mike Forney)*, Robert Strauss *(Beer Barrel)*, Charles McGraw *(Cdr. Wayne Lee)*, Keiko Awaji *(Kimiko)*, Earl Holliman *(Nestor Gamidge)*, Richard Shannon *(Lt. Olds)*, Willis B. Bouchey *(Capt. Evans)*, Nadene Ashdown *(Kathy Brubaker)*, Cheryl Lynn Calloway *(Susie)*, James Jankins *(Assistant C.I.C. Officer)*, Marshal V. Beebe *(Pilot)*, Charles Tannen *(M. P. Major)*, Teru Shimada *(Japanese Father)*.

Although hailed with much chauvinistic flag waving when it first came out as the most important studio film to deal with the Korean conflict, and already *deja vu* a year later when Americans were growing tired of the cloudy, complex situation it describes, THE BRIDGES AT TOKO-RI remains a major accomplishment because it was a feat of production skills and aerial photographic magic. A psychological study of a man called back to active duty who believes he has already done enough for his country in WW II, Holden resents the new war's intrusion on his life with his wife and kids but doggedly goes about his duty as a bomber pilot. The narrative drives toward the climactic bombing of the five bridges of Toko-Ri which span a strategic pass in Korea's interior. Along the way Holden gets in some intimate scenes with Kelly, the wife who waits for him in Tokyo. March, the dignified and solid admiral, makes an epic speech about the dangers of carrier flying, about men who fly off rolling decks, perform dangerous missions over strange territory, and return to find, from the air, a tiny speck in an endless sea that they must land upon. "Where do we find such men?" he asks, and promptly assigns Holden and his pals the job of demolishing the five bridges to forestall enemy movements. The men do their work in explosively exciting naval and aerial action (brilliantly photographed in color), but at the cost of their lives, including Holden's, whose plane is downed on the mission and who, despite the efforts of his entire squadron and helicopter relief units, is finally killed by enemy soldiers, along with loyal mechanic Rooney, who gives a sterling performance. Throughout the film, exceptionally realistic photography of naval operations (with the full cooperation of the U.S. Navy), described minutely by author Michener in his best seller, is recorded with a detached objectivity by the camera, making it a perfect backdrop for Holden. Technical credits are stolen by Charles G. Clarke's aerial photography crew, but there are second-unit photography exploits that advance cinema art in the war genre. Robson's direction is taut and as competent as the subject allows, and the production shows energy in all departments. Lavish settings are enhanced by the film's location sites—Tokyo and with a U. S. Navy task force in the China Sea.

p, William Perlberg; d, Mark Robson; w, Valentine Davies (based on a novel by James A. Michener); ph, Loyal Griggs; aerial ph, Charles G. Clarke; second unit ph, Wallace Kelley, Thomas Tutweiler (Technicolor); m, Lyn Murray; ed, Alma Macrorie; art d, Hal Pereira, Henry Bumstead; cos, Edith Head; makeup, Wally Westmore.

War Drama **(PR:A MPAA:NR)**

BRIEF ECSTASY* (1937, Brit.) 71m Phoenix bw

Paul Lukas *(Prof. Paul Bernardy)*, Hugh Williams *(Jim Wyndham)*, Linden Travers *(Helen Norwood)*, Marie Ney *(Martha Russell)*, Renee Gadd *(Girl Friend)*, Fred Withers *(Gardener)*, Howard Douglas *(Coleman)*, Fewlass Llewelyn *(Director)*, Peter Gawthorne *(Director)*.

Romantic tale of a young woman who marries an older man, then falls in love with his pilot son. Her husband is only the boy's legal guardian, which leads to further complications.

p, Hugh Perceval; d, Edmond T. Greville; w, Basil Mason; ph, Henry Harris, Ronald Neame.

Romance **(PR:A MPAA:NR)**

BRIEF ENCOUNTER***** (1945, Brit.) 86m Cineguild/EL bw

Celia Johnson *(Laura Jesson)*, Trevor Howard *(Alec Harvey)*, Cyril Raymond *(Fred Jesson)*, Stanley Holloway *(Albert Godby)*, Joyce Carey *(Myrtle Bagot)*, Everley Gregg *(Dolly Messiter)*, Margaret Barton *(Beryl Waters)*, Dennis Harkin *(Stanley)*, Valentine Dyall *(Stephen Lynn)*, Marjorie Mars *(Mary Norton)*, Nuna Davey *(Mrs. Rolandson)*, Irene Handl *(Organist)*, Edward Hodge *(Bill)*, Sydney Bromley *(Johnnie)*, Wilfrid Babbage *(Policeman)*, Avis Scott *(Waitress)*, Henrietta Vincent *(Margaret)*, Richard Thomas *(Bobbie)*, George V. Sheldon *(Clergyman)*, Wally Bosco *(Doctor)*, Jack May *(Boatman)*.

A touching and realistic film, one that deals with ordinary people in love, BRIEF ENCOUNTER is one of those poetically beautiful films that tells a simple story that could be that of any viewer. Howard is a doctor and Johnson a housewife, both happily married, who meet by chance in a railroad way station when he removes a cinder from her eye. They talk for a few minutes, having much in common, but then quickly separate to catch different trains. Each Thursday, Howard and Johnson find themselves looking for each other at the little tea shop in the station; this is her day to see a film and go shopping and his to perform one-day duties the next morning in a hospital other than the one to which he is regularly assigned. At each meeting they grow closer together, sharing moments of tenderness, tales of their families, the little problems that plague them, the pleasant memories that bring them joy. When Johnson fails to see Howard weeks later she becomes worried, then almost desperate. His train is late and when it arrives he races into the tea room, as frantic to see her as she is him. It is at this juncture that both realize they have fallen in love, a situation that troubles their family loyalties. Now they meet secretly, their actions guarded, their glances at fellow passen gers furtive, then compulsively, helplessly, they go to an apartment rented by one of Howard's friends, a less than edifying rendezvous, to consummate their clandestine affair. When both recognize that their relationship can go nowhere Howard and Johnson bid farewell, their love affair disappearing with trains going in opposite directions. Director Lean brilliantly cuts from sensitive scenes to the domestic tranquility of the lovers' homes, chiefly Johnson's, to show the contrast of their normal lives and the excitement of the affair, as well as the subsequent feelings of guilt and fear of discovery. Both Howard and Johnson give faultless performances in this always fascinating Noel Coward love story.

p, Noel Coward; d, David Lean; w, Coward, Lean, Anthony Havelock-Allan (based on Coward's play "Still Life"); ph, Robert Krasker; m, Rachmaninoff's Second Piano Concerto (played by Eileen Joyce); ed, Jack Harris.

Romance **Cas.** **(PR:A MPAA:NR)**

BRIEF MOMENT 1/2** (1933) 69m COL bw

Carole Lombard *(Abby Fane)*, Gene Raymond *(Rodney Deane)*, Monroe Owsley *(Sigrift)*, Donald Cook *(Franklin Deane)*, Arthur Hohl *(Steve)*, Reginald Mason *(Mr. Deane)*, Jameson Thomas *(Prince Otto)*, Theresa Maxwell Conover *(Mrs. Deane)*, Florence Britton *(Kay)*, Irene Ware *(Joan)*, Herbert Evans *(Alfred)*.

Nightclub singer Lombard marries wealthy Raymond, unaware that her new husband is a good-for-nothing living off of his father's riches. Continually preaching the importance of working for a living, Lombard finally forces Raymond to work when she convinces the father to cut off his son's allowance. When Raymond starts to spend more time at the race track than at his desk, Lombard leaves him in frustration. Finally coming to terms with his life, Raymond changes his prestigious name and takes on a demanding new job. Lombard's nightclub owner pal forces a meeting betwen the estranged couple and Lombard accepts her "new" man. A second-rate drama that could have been given some spirit if Lombard had felt up to turning in a clever, passionate performance instead of a merely entertaining one. The lackluster Raymond doesn't help much, either.

d, David Burton; w, Brian Marlow, Edith Fitzgerald (based on the play by S. N. Behrman); ph, Ted Tetzlaff; ed, Gene Havlick.

Drama **(PR:A MPAA:NR)**

BRIEF RAPTURE* 1/2 (1952, Ital.) 80m Jewel bw

Lois Maxwell *(Erika)*, Ermanno Randi *(Stefano)*, Amadeo Nazzari *(Commissioner)*, Umberto Spadaro *(Inspector)*, Juan De Landa *(The Boss)*, Massimo Sallusto *(Carlo)*.

Wicked pushers are lectured by police commissioner Nazzari on the evils of narcotics addiction after a fellow dealer cracks under captive questioning. Tired script and indifferent direction make a provocative subject boring. The music is performed by Teatro Dell'Opera Di Roma Orchestra.

d, Enzo Trapani; w, Andriano Bolzoni, Trapani; ph, Adalberto Albertini; md, Con stantino Ferri.

Crime Drama **(PR:C MPAA:NR)**

BRIEF VACATION, A* 1/2**

(1975, Ital.) 106m AA c (UNA BREVA VACANZA)

Florinda Bolkan *(Clara)*, Renato Salvatori *(Husband)*, Daneil Quenaud *(Luigi)*, Jose Maria Prada *(Ciranni)*, Teresa Gimpera *(Gina)*.

For his last film released in America, De Sica once more dealt with a person living what Thoreau called a life of "quiet desperation." Bolkan is a factory worker, barely able to support her disabled spouse, three children, brother-in-law, and senile mother. She grows disgusted with her life and a bureaucratic system that consistently fails to serve the common laborer. When she is diagnosed as tubercular, she is sent to a mountain-side spa to recuperate. There she thrives, physically as well as spiritually. Surrounded by people with similar ailments, Bolkan finds acceptance and engages in a love affair with another patient. Her "brief vacation" ends when she is released from the sanatorium and must return to her family and empty life, which she now finds more painful than ever before. Bolkan gives a touching portrayal, and her situation is handled with care and genuine sincerity by De Sica. Though not as thought-provoking as some of De Sica's other efforts, A BRIEF VACATION is nevertheless a warm and honest film from a director who consistently demonstrated his concern and his humanity throughout a distinguished career. (In Italian; English subtitles.)

d, Vittorio De Sica; w, Cesare Zavattini; ph, Ennio Guarnieri; m, Manuel De Sica.

Drama   **(PR:C   MPAA:PG)**

BRIGADOON***   (1954) 108m MGM c

Gene Kelly (*Tommy Albright*), Van Johnson (*Jeff Douglas*), Cyd Charisse (*Fiona Campbell*), Elaine Stewart (*Jane Ashton*), Barry Jones (*Mr. Lundie*), Hugh Laing (*Harry Beaton*), Albert Sharpe (*Andrew Campbell*), Virginia Bosier (*Jean Campbell*), Jimmy Thompson (*Charlie Crisholm Dalrymple*), Tudor Owen (*Archie Beaton*), Owen McGivney (*Angus*), Dee Turnell (*Ann*), Dody Heath (*Meg Brockie*), Eddie Quillan (*Sandy*).

MGM's decision to economize because of a waning public interest in musicals in 1954 was a bad one for BRIGADOON. By confining the screen version to a sound stage rather than filming on location, this whimsical fantasy lost a great deal of its allure and never recovered from it. The result was a production which contributed to the feeling of a filmed stage show rather than a motion picture musical. Other than a spirited dance to "I'll Go Home With Bonnie Jean," BRIGADOON offers very few pleasures. Johnson's dancing looks ponderous; Charisse moves exquisitely but her acting is colorless and even Kelly, usually adept in whimsical roles, gives a rather slug-like performance. The story tells of two bored New Yorkers who become lost while grouse hunting in Scotland and happen on Brigadoon on the one day that it is visible every 100 years. Given nights that are a 100 years long, the villagers are in a festive mood and preparing for a wedding. Our New Yorkers happily join in the dancing and festivities of the day, particularly Kelly who falls kilt over tam-o-shanter for Charisse and is faced with the tough decision of going back to the hustle of New York, or joining his lassie in the land of long ago. No such problem has Johnson, in his rather thankless role of a hard-drinking quipster. Kelly and Johnson return to New York to take up their humdrum lives and in the most brilliantly directed sequence in the picture, Minnelli cunningly runs the banal barroom chit chat a few frames out of sync, adding to Kelly's irritation and discontent with his empty New York existence. With this, he resolves to return to Brigadoon and such is the sincerity of his love for the fair Charisse that the village reappears and both disappear into the legend, singing and dancing "From This Day On." Adding to the problems of bringing this great stage hit to the screen was the decision to photograph not in Technicolor, but in Ansco Color and in CinemaScope. It is apparent that Minnelli was uncomfortable in his first encounter with the long rectangular frame. It would have been difficult to fill the frame with dancers and singers on location, but became an almost impossible feat in the confines of a studio.

p, Arthur Freed; d, Vincente Minnelli; w, Alan Jay Lerner (based on the musical play by Lerner and Frederick Loewe); ph, Joseph Ruttenberg (CinemaScope, Ansco Color); ed, Albert Akst; art d, Cedric Gibbons, Preston Ames; md, John Green; ch, Gene Kelly.

Musical   **Cas.**   **(PR:A   MPAA:NR)**

BRIGAND, THE***   (1952) 93m COL c

Anthony Dexter (*Carlos Delargo/King Lorenzo*), Jody Lawrence (*Princess Teresa*), Gale Robbins (*Countess Flora*), Anthony Quinn (*Prince Ramon*), Carl Benton Reid (*Triano*), Ron Randell (*Capt. Ruiz*), Fay Roope (*Mons. De Laforce*), Carleton Young (*Carnot*), Ian MacDonald (*Maj. Schrock*), Lester Matthews (*Dr. Lopez*), Barbara Brown (*Baroness Isabella*), Walter Kingsford (*Sultan*), Donald Randolph (*Don Felipe Castro*), Mari Blanchard (*Dona Dolores Castro*), Holmes Herbert (*Archbishop*).

Dexter stars in a dual role as a wounded king and a wanted adventurer who poses as the king until the ruler can recover. When zealous cousin to the king Quinn uses his mistress to uncover the whereabouts of the actual king, he kills both the girl and monarch. Before Quinn can expose Dexter as an impostor, Dexter kills Quinn in a climactic sword fight. Satisfied with the surrogate king's attitude and behavior, the court chamberlain and the lovely princess Lawrence, the only two to know of the switch, allow Dexter to carry on in charge of the kingdom. Fun, empty-headed swashbuckler that owes a great deal of thanks to Quinn's bravura in his non-starring role. (Loose remake of THE PRISONER OF ZENDA and THE MASK OF THE AVENGER.)

d, Phil Karlson; w, Jesse Lasky, Jr.; (based on a story by George Bruce adapted from *Brigand, A Romance of the Reign of Don Carlos* by Alexander Dumas); ph, W. Howard Greene (Technicolor); m, Mario Castelnuovo- Tedesco; ed, Jerome Thoms.

Adventure/Drama   **(PR:A   MPAA:NR)**

BRIGAND OF KANDAHAR, THE**   (1965, Brit.) 81m WB-Pathe/ABF c

Ronald Lewis (*Lt. Case*), Oliver Reed (*Ali Khan*), Duncan Lamont (*Col. Drewe*), Yvonne Romain (*Ratina*), Catherine Woodville (*Elsa*), Glyn Houston (*Marriott*), Inigo Jackson (*Capt. Boyd*), Sean Lynch (*Rattu*), Walter Brown (*Hitala*), Jeremy Burnham (*Connelly*), Carol Gardner (*Serving Maid*).

Arch-enemies Lewis and Lamont sharpen their differences when soldier Lewis joins a gang of roving bandits after being sacked by British Army Colonel Lamont in a frame up. Lewis fights the British with Reed, dueling against him in the end. Battle climax is fast, well staged, and entertaining. High action complete with hit men and skirmishes. Lamont wins out by killing all crossing his path.

p, Anthony Nelson Keys; d&w John Gilling; ph, Reg Wyer (Technicolor); m, Don Banks; ed, Tom Simpson.

Adventure   **(PR:A   MPAA:NR)**

BRIGGS FAMILY, THE*¹/₂   (1940, Brit.) 69m WB-FN bw

Edward Chapman (*Charley Briggs*), Jane Baxter (*Sylvia Briggs*), Oliver Wakefield (*Ronnie Perch*), Mary Clare (*Mrs. Briggs*), Peter Croft (*Bob Briggs*), Lesley Brook (*Alice*), Felix Aylmer (*Mr. Sand*), Jack Melford (*Jerry Tulse*), Austin Trevor (*John Smith*), George Carney (*George Downing*), Glynis Johns (*Shiela Briggs*), Muriel George (*Mrs. Brokenshaw*), Aubrey Mallalieu (*Milward*).

A lawyer's clerk defends his crippled son who has been charged with robbery. As good clerks do, he learns the boss's job and succeeds, exposing the real culprit along the way.

p, A.M. Salomon; d, Herbert Mason; w, John Dighton (based on a story by Brock Williams); ph, Basil Emmott.

Crime   **(PR:A   MPAA:NR)**

BRIGHAM YOUNG—FRONTIERSMAN***
                                        (1940) 112m FOX c (GB: BRIGHAM YOUNG)

Tyrone Power (*Jonathan Kent*), Linda Darnell (*Zina Webb*), Dean Jagger (*Brigham Young*), Brian Donlevy (*Angus Duncan*), Jane Darwell (*Eliza Kent*), John Carradine (*Porter Rockwell*), Mary Astor (*Mary Ann Young*), Vincent Price (*Joseph Smith*), Jean Rogers (*Clara Young*), Ann E. Todd (*Mary Kent*), Willard Robertson (*Heber Kimball*), Moroni Olsen (*Doc Richards*), Stanley Andrews (*Hyrum Smith*), Marc Lawrence (*Prosecutor*), Frank Thomas (*Hubert Crum*), Fuzzy Knight (*Pete*), Dickie Jones (*Henry Kent*), Russell Simpson (*Major*), Arthur Aylesworth (*Jim Bridges*), Tully Marshall (*Judge*), Chief Big Tree (*Big Elk*), Claire Du Brey (*Emma Smith*), Ralph Dunn (*Jury Foreman*), George Melford (*John Taylor*), Frederick Burton (*Mr. Webb*), Selmar Jackson (*Caleb Kent*), Charles Halton (*Prosecutor*), Frank LaRue (*Sheriff*), Dick Rich (*Mob Leader*), Philip Morris, Charles Middleton, Lee Shumway (*Henchmen*), Blackie Whiteford (*Court Spectator*), Cecil Weston (*Woman*), Edwin Marshall (*Leader*), Edmund McDonald (*Elger*).

An epic film of early American history, BRIGHAM YOUNG—FRONTIERSMAN is an admirable attempt to interest a wide audience in the story of the pioneering Mormons and their founding of Salt Lake City. Forced because of persecution to leave their settlement in Nauvoo, Illinois, Mormons set out under the capable leadership of Brigham Young (Jagger) across the plains to their eventual home on the Salt Lake. Adversity strikes at every turn, recalcitrants behave in a most un-Mormon-like way, hardships and starvation are endured, and, during an illness from which he almost dies, Young, rousing from a coma, has a revelation wherein he describes the promised land. "This is the place," he announces as the Great Salt Lake valley stretches out below them. The ensuing winter is one of incredible hardships but with the onset of spring a good harvest is expected and hopes rise, only to be dashed again when a plague of crickets descends on the fields. Broken and weary, Young despairs and summons his followers to prayer. Suddenly, in a vividly depicted sequence, millions of sea gulls appear in the sky, devouring the crickets and saving the crops. The matter of polygamy is delicately handled. It is not evaded, but so subtly dealt with that few would even be aware of its existence in the picture's unfolding. Jagger's portrayal of Young brings to the character of the Mormon leader a personable humaness and sympathy that will be long remembered, and would light a fire under Jagger's career as well, which had been flagging until this role. Power and Linda Darnell are the obligatory love interest turning in rather colorless performances, but they do not detract from the story. Walter Huston was scheduled originally to star as Brigham Young but his unavailability left Zanuck to cast the relatively unknown Jagger with veteran Astor in a brilliant coupling. The accent in the movie was on the historical rather than the religious in an effort not to scare off moviegoers and for that reason it was ordained the word "Frontiersman" be added to the title, but the picture still failed, even in Utah.

p, Darryl F. Zanuck; d, Henry Hathaway; w, Lamar Trotti (based on the story by Louis Bromfield); ph, Arthur Miller (Sepiatone); m, Alfred Newman; ed, Robert Bischoff; art d, William Darling, Maurice Ransford; set d, Thomas Little; cos, Gwen Wakeling.

Historical Drama/Biography   **(PR:A   MPAA:NR)**

BRIGHT EYES***   (1934) 84m FOX bw

Shirley Temple (*Shirley Blake*), James Dunn (*Loop Merritt*), Jane Darwell (*Mrs. Higgins*), Judith Allen (*Adele Martin*), Lois Wilson (*Mary Blake*), Charles Sellon (*Uncle Ned Smith*), Walter Johnson (*Thomas*), Jane Withers (*Joy Smythe*), Theodor von Eltz (*J. Wellington Smythe*), Dorothy Christy (*Anita Smythe*), Brandon Hurst (*Higgins*), George Irving (*Judge Thompson*), David O'Brien (*Tex*).

When Temple's mother dies, three people vie to become her new parent, rich old Sellon, his niece Allen, and adventurous flyboy Dunn, a friend of Temple's dead father. The always-cute Temple skips through a series of adventures with each of them until the parental question is resolved when Allen marries Dunn, Sellon moves in with them, and the entire group adopts Temple. Typically darling Shirley Temple picture that features her classic (for better or worse) rendition of "On the Good Ship Lollipop."

p, Sol Wurtzel; d, David Butler; w, William Conselman, Edwin Burke, Butler; ph, Arthur Miller.

Comedy   **(PR:AAA   MPAA:NR)**

BRIGHT LEAF***   (1950) 109m WB bw

Gary Cooper (*Brant Royle*), Lauren Bacall (*Sonia Kovac*), Patricia Neal (*Margaret Jane Singleton*), Jack Carson (*Chris Malley*), Donald Crisp (*Maj. James Singleton*), Gladys George (*Rose*), Elizabeth Patterson (*Tabitha Jackson*), Jeff Corey (*John Barton*), Taylor Holmes (*Lawyer Calhoun*), Thurston Hall (*Phillips*), Jimmy Griffith (*Ellery*), Marietta Canty (*Queenie*), William Walker (*Simon*).

Cooper returns to his southern home town after being kicked out years earlier by local tobacco tycoon Crisp who didn't want the somewhat unscrupulous Cooper dating his demure daughter, Neal. Anxious to do well in the business world, Cooper woos wealthy madame Bacall into investing in Corey's cigarette-making machine. Cooper and his cohorts make a fortune, driving the local tobacco monopolizers into near bankruptcy. Hoping to keep her father's business afloat, old flame Neal agrees to marry Cooper. Upon learning of their betrothal, anguished Crisp kills himself. Seeking revenge for her father's death, Neal informs the government of Cooper's monopolistic techniques and the never-happy couple separates. Cooper, about to leave town to escape federal investigation, bids farewell to Bacall, telling her that he's always loved her and will return someday. Although this type of period melodrama was Curtiz's forte, the passionate director missed the mark with this uninteresting tale of the Deep South. The underlying passions, betrayals, and greed could have been exploited to a highly emotional frenzy, but the film plays as a dull, lifeless affair. Cooper and Bacall do well with their roles, but Neal is a screaming failure as the frigid bitch Cooper is obsessed with. The lush look and feel of the film is the work of one of the great cinematographers, Karl Freund.

p, Henry Blanke; d, Michael Curtiz; w, Ranald MacDougall (based on the novel by Foster Fitz-Simmons); ph, Karl Freund; m, Victor Young; ed, Owen Marks; art d, Stanley Fleisher; set d, Ben Bone; makeup, Perc Westmore.

Drama (PR:A MPAA:NR)

BRIGHT LIGHTS* (1931) 73m WB/FN c

Dorothy Mackaill (*Louanne*), Noah Beery, Sr. (*Miguel Parada*), Frank Fay (*Wally Dean*), Inez Courtney (*Peggy North*), Eddie Nugent (*Windy Johnson*), Edmund Breese (*Franklin Harris*), Daphne Pollard (*Mame Avery*), Frank McHugh (*Fish*), Philip Strange (*Emerson Fairchild*), James Murray (*Connie Lamont*), Tom Dugan (*Tom Avery*), Jean Bary (*Violet Van Dam*), Edwin Lynch (*Dave Porter*), Virginia Sale (*Reporter*).

If it's happiness you're after, writer Pearson doesn't recommend marriage. Actress Mackaill gives up her stage career for the respectability of joint accounts, shared automobiles, dirty dishes, laundry, and raising children. But married bliss is practically nonexistent. Script misses the mark, saddling performers with trite lines and phrases. Early color feature. Songs include "Nobody Cares If I'm Blue," "I'm Crazy for Cannibal Love," "Chinatown," "Song of the Congo," "You're an Eyeful of Heaven."

p, Robert North; d, Michael Curtiz; w, Humphrey Pearson, Henry McCarthy (based on a story by Pearson); ph, Lee Garmes (Technicolor); ch, Larry Ceballos.

Musical/Drama (PR:A MPAA:NR)

BRIGHT LIGHTS**1/2 (1935) 82m WB bw

Joe E. Brown (*Joe Wilson*), Ann Dvorak (*Fay Wilson*), Patricia Ellis (*Peggy*), William Gargan (*Daniel Wheeler*), Joseph Cawthorn (*Otto Schlemmer*), Arthur Treacher (*Wilbur*), Gordon Westcott (*Wellington*), Joseph Crehan (*Airport Attendant*), William Demarest (*Detective*).

Vaudville comedy troupe leaders Brown and wife Dvorak make it to the big time only to fall back when Brown gets entrapped by a society woman who joins the show for fun. Brisk pace with a close eye for detail from Berkeley; basically a one-man show. Songs include "Toddling Along With You," "You're An Eyeful of Heaven," "Nobody Cares If I'm Blue," and "She Was An Acrobat's Daughter."

d, Busby Berkeley; w, Bert Kalmar, Harry Ruby, Ben Markson, Benny Rubin (based on a story by Lois Leeson); ph, Sid Hickox; m/l, Kalmar, Ruby, Mort Dixon, Allie Wrubel.

Comedy (PR:A MPAA:NR)

BRIGHT ROAD*** (1953) 68m MGM bw

Dorothy Dandridge (*Jane Richards*), Philip Hepburn (*C.T. Young*), Harry Belafonte (*School Principal*), Barbara Ann Sanders (*Tanya*), Robert Horton (*Dr. Mitchell*), Maidie Norman (*Tanya's Mother*), Renee Beard (*Booker T. Jones*), Howard McNeely (*Boyd*), Robert McNeely (*Lloyd*), Patti Marie Ellis (*Rachel Smith*), Joy Jackson (*Sarahlene Babcock*), Fred Moultrie (*Roger*), James Moultrie (*George*), Carolyn Ann Jackson (*Mary Louise*).

Hepburn plays a defiant, unruly boy whom teacher Dandridge seeks to win over. Dependable cast turns in fine performances along with excellent technical efforts to complement Mayer's snappy direction. The all-black cast radiates good humor.

p, Sol Baer Fielding; d, Gerald Mayer; w, Emmett Lavery (based on the *Ladies' Home Journal* story "See How They Run" by Elizabeth Vroman); ph, Alfred Gilks; m, David Rose; ed, Joseph Dervin.

Drama (PR:A MPAA:NR)

BRIGHT VICTORY**** (1951) 96m UNIV bw (GB: LIGHTS OUT)

Arthur Kennedy (*Larry Nevins*), Peggy Dow (*Judy Greene*), Julia Adams (*Chris Paterson*), James Edwards (*Joe Morgan*), Will Geer (*Mr. Nevins*), Minor Watson (*Mr. Paterson*), Jim Backus (*Bill Grayson*), Joan Banks (*Janet Grayson*), Nana Bryant (*Mrs. Nevins*), Marjorie Crossland (*Mrs. Paterson*), Richard Egan (*Sgt. John Masterson*), Russell Dennis (*Pvt. Fred Tyler*), Rock Hudson (*Cpl. John Flagg*), Murray Hamilton (*Pete Hamilton*), Donald Miele (*Moose Garvey*), Larry Keating (*Jess Coe*), Hugh Reilly (*Capt. Phelan*), Mary Cooper (*Nurse Bailey*), Ken Harvey (*Scanlon*), Phil Faversham (*Lt. Atkins*), Robert F. Simon (*Psychiatrist*), Jerry Paris (*Reynolds*), Ruth Esherick (*Nurse*), Bernard Hamilton (*Black Soldier*), Robert Anderson (*M.P.*), June Whitley (*Nurse at Oran*), Sydney Mason (*Dr. Bannerman*), Richard Karlan, Billy Newell (*Bartenders*), Virginia Mullen (*Mrs. Coe*), Glen Charles Gordon (*Lt. Conklin*), Alice Richey, Sara Taft (*Women*), Thaddeus Jones (*Pullman Porter*), John M. Robinson (*Medical Orderly*).

Kennedy is absolutely riveting in one of the most brilliant performances of his distinguished career as a blinded WW II veteran who returns home and begins the arduous process of not only adapting to civilian life but adjusting to his affliction.

Like John Garfield who was blinded in PRIDE OF THE MARINES, Kennedy is reluctant to leave the military hospital where he is recuperating to rejoin his family. And like Marlon Brando in THE MEN, he fights the involved and tedious training to equip himself for normal civilian life. Dow, a beautiful and patient nurse, helps Kennedy over-come his fear and bitterness until he returns home. But one disaster after another follows with his next-door girl friend Adams being embarrassed by Kennedy's disability and his parents, Geer and Bryant, feeling helpless and inadequate around their son. There is one devastating scene where a welcome-home party goes bust when Kennedy puts out a cigarette in a dish of food, the dish having been replaced for the ashtray. Kennedy, after undergoing a great deal of agony and self-examination, winds up with Dow whom he truly loves, and facing the future with no illusions. It's a bravura performance by Kennedy that should not be missed. (Look for Rock Hudson in a small role as an enlisted man.)

p, Robert Buckner; d, Mark Robson; w, Buckner (based on the novel *Lights Out* by Bayard Kendrick); ph, William Daniels; m, Frank Skinner; ed, Russell Schoengarth; art d, Bernard Herzbrun, Nathan Juran.

Drama (PR:A MPAA:NR)

BRIGHTON ROCK*** (1947, Brit.) 92m Boulting Bros/Associated British Picture Corp. bw (AKA: YOUNG SCARFACE)

Richard Attenborough (*Pinkie Brown*), Hermione Baddeley (*Ida Arnold*), William Hartnell (*Dallow*), Carol Marsh (*Rose Brown*), Nigel Stock (*Cubitt*), Wylie Watson (*Spicer*), Harcourt Williams (*Prewitt*), Alan Wheatley (*Fred Hale*), George Carney (*Phil Corkery*), Charles Goldner (*Colleoni*), Reginald Purdell (*Frank*).

A brutal look at the British underworld as seen through Attenborough's brilliant performance. Based upon the widely popular Graham Greene novel (which he called an "entertainment"), Attenborough heads a race track gang and commits a murder. He next uses Marsh, a pretty waitress, as an alibi. Worried that she still might betray him, Attenborough then marries the girl and plans her murder by driving her insane and to suicide, a scheme that eventually backfires. A moody film with meaty roles and a provocative theme that suffers from Boulton's somewhat plodding direction.

p, Roy Boulting; d, John Boulting; w, Graham Greene, Terence Rattigan (based on the novel by Greene); ph, Harry Waxman, Gilbert Taylor; m, Hans May; ed, Frank McNally.

Crime Drama (PR:C MPAA:NR)

BRIGHTON STRANGLER, THE**1/2 (1945) 67m RKO bw

John Loder (*Reginald*), June Duprez (*April*), Michael St. Angel (*Bob*), Miles Mander (*Allison*), Rose Hobart (*Dorothy*), Gilbert Emery (*Dr. Manby*), Rex Evans (*Shelton*), Matthew Boulton (*Inspector Graham*), Olaf Hytten (*Banke*), Lydia Bilbrook (*Mrs. Manby*), Ian Wolfe (*Mayor*).

Similar to Ronald Colman's A DOUBLE LIFE, Loder, an actor in a horror play, assumes the identity of his stage character after suffering a concussion in a London air raid. He meanders into Victoria Station where he hears a casual comment by a stranger which happens to be an exact line from the play. This leads him to carry out homicidal traits of the scripted individual and he strangles victims who match characters in the play. Good shock effect is well sustained.

p, Herman Schlom; d, Max Nosseck; w, Arnold Phillips, Nosseck; ph, J. Roy Hunt; m, Leigh Harline; ed, Les Milbrook; spec eff, Vernon L. Walker.

Crime Drama Cas. (PR:AA MPAA:NR)

BRIGHTY OF THE GRAND CANYON** (1967) 89m Feature Film Corp. c

Joseph Cotten (*Jim Owen*), Pat Conway (*Jake Irons*), Dick Foran (*Old Timer*), Karl Swenson (*Theodore Roosevelt*), Dandy Curran (*Homer Hobbs*), Jiggs (*Brighty, a Burro*).

Interesting programmer shot on location which beautifully details the glories of the Grand Canyon, Foran is a gold-seeking prospector who is repeatedly saved from disaster by a very smart mule named Brighty. Some humorous and touching moments.

p, Stephen F. Booth; d&w, Norman Foster (based on the book by Marguerite Henry); ph, Ted Saizis, Vincent Saizis; m, Richard Lavsky, Phyllis Lavsky; ed, Joseph Dervin.

Drama Cas. (PR:A MPAA:NR)

BRILLIANT MARRIAGE* (1936) 65m IN bw

Joan Marsh (*Madge Allison*), Ray Walker (*Garry Dane*), Inez Courtney (*Sally Patrick*), John Marlowe (*Richard Taylor*), Doris Lloyd (*Mrs. Allison*), Ann Codee (*Yvette Duval*), Olive Tell (*Mrs. Taylor*), Holmes Herbert (*Mr. Allison*), Robert Adair (*Thorne*), Barbara Bedford (*Brenda*), Dick Elliott (*Editor*), Herbert Ashley (*Captain*), Kathryn Sheldon (*Ellen*), Victor Wong (*Wong*), George Cleveland (*Bartender*), Lynton Brent (*Blaine*).

High society child Marsh gets involved with irresponsible, two-timing reporter Walker when he uncovers a scandal in the family's past. Thus, Marsh thinks her equally rich boy friend will alienate her, which is why she takes up with Marsh, but that is not the case in the end. Below-standard effort on all levels.

p, Maury M. Cohen; d, Phil Rosen; w, Paul Perez (based on the novel by Ursula Parrott); ph, M.A. Anderson.

Drama (PR:A MPAA:NR)

BRIMSTONE*** (1949) 90m REP c

Rod Cameron (*Johnny Tremaine*), Adrian Booth (*Molly Bannister*), Walter Brennan (*Pop Courteen*), Forrest Tucker (*Sheriff Henry McIntyre*), Jack Holt (*Marshal Walter Greenside*), Jim Davis (*Mick Courteen*), James Brown (*Bud Courteen*), Guinn "Big

Boy" Williams *(Art Benson)*, Jack Lambert *(Luke Courteen)*, Will Wright *(Martin Treadwell)*, David Williams *(Todd Bannister)*, Harry V. Cheshire *(Calvin Willis)*, Hal Taliaferro *(Dave Watts)*, Herbert Rawlinson *(Storekeeper)*, Stanley Andrews *(Mr. Winslow)*, Charlita *(Chiquita)*.

U.S. marshal Cameron is out to get once-wealthy stock man and now number one stagecoach robbing outlaw Brennan. Brennan's salty performance is a standout against Cameron's wooden characterization. Seasoned performers cover lame direction from Kane, through the story is well written.

p&d, Joseph Kane; w, Thames Williams (based on a story by Norman S. Hall); ph, Jack Marta; m, Nathan Scott; ed, Arthur Roberts.

Western **(PR:A MPAA:NR)**

BRIMSTONE AND TREACLE*** (1982, Brit.) 87m UA Classics c

Sting *(Martin Taylor)*, Denholm Elliott *(Thomas Bates)*, Joan Plowright *(Norma Bates)*, Suzanna Hamilton *(Patricia Bates)*, Mary McLeod *(Valerie Holdsworth)*, Benja- min Whitrow *(Businessman)*, Dudley Sutton *(Stroller)*, Tim Preece *(Clergyman)*.

Dennis Potter is surely one of the most interesting writers around today. He did the original PENNIES FROM HEAVEN for British TV as well as a host of other highly inventive works. As screenwriter for BRIMSTONE AND TREACLE he has crafted a psychological corker that will have goosebumps alternating with nervous laughter. Sting (QUADROPHENIA, RADIO ON) steps out of the rock group The Police to portray a con man who is so charming he can convince almost anyone that he's met them before. He attempts this ploy on Elliott, who sees through him and tries to get away. In doing so, Elliott drops his wallet and it's dutifully returned by Sting, knowing full well he can make a larger score if he plays out the line on this big fish. Plowright is Elliott's wife and she takes Sting into their home where the young man will help tend their handicapped daughter, Hamilton. The parents don't know it but Sting is doing vile things to the young woman who can't communicate with anyone. The picture is almost devoid of violence, but the suspense is excrutiating. Compared to most of the horror films, this could very well rank up there with Hitchcock.

p, Kenneth Trodd; d, Richard Loncraine; w, Dennis Potter; ph, Peter Hannan (Technicolor); m, Sting; ed, Paul Green.

Mystery/Suspense **Cas.** **(PR:C MPAA:R)**

BRING ME THE HEAD OF ALFREDO GARCIA**** (1974) 112m UA c

Warren Oates *(Bennie)*, Isela Vega *(Elita)*, Gig Young *(Quill)*, Robert Webber *(Sappensly)*, Helmut Dantine *(Max)*, Emilio Fernandez *(El Jefe)*, Kris Kristofferson *(Paco)*, Chano Urueta *(One-armed Bartender)*, Jorge Russek *(Cueto)*.

When the head of a prominent Mexican family (Fernandez) learns the identity of the uncaring stud who impregnated his daughter, he offers a million dollars to the man who can bring him the head of the culprit, Alfredo Garcia. Homosexual hitmen Young and Webber, working for Fernandez, enlist the aid of sleazy but good-natured bar owner Oates who convinces the pair that he can find Garcia. Learning from his hooker girl friend Vega that her former client Garcia is already dead from a car accident, Oates and the girl travel to the small town cemetery where Garcia is buried. Along the way, an odd jealousy of the dead man builds up in Oates and it prompts him to propose marriage to Vega. After killing two motorcycle rapists, Oates and the girl find Garcia's grave. Before they can cut off the head from the corpse they have dug up, Oates is knocked unconscious and Vega murdered by a mysterious Mexican clan. Oates recovers and vows to carry out the mission in honor of Vega. In a bloody confrontation, Oates aids Webber and Young in massacring the rival Mexican group, then turns on the gay killers and wipes them out also. Travelling through the hot Mexican desert with the head of Garcia in the passenger seat, Oates finally reaches the hacienda of Fernandez. With a great deal of thanks and money from the jefe in his possession, Oates explodes the "happy ending" by unleashing a gun-blazing fury on Fernandez and his men, sparing the daughter who gave Oates a nod of approval when he contemplated his actions, Appearing as though he will be able to walk out of the ranch unscathed, Oates is finally gunned down at the gate of the estate by the remaining henchmen of Fernandez. One of the most perversely fascinating cinema experiences of all time, the film is either appreciated as a bizarre classic or denounced as a piece of trash by anyone who sees it. It is a weird minor masterpiece. Having called it the only film experience during which he had complete control, notorious director Peckinpah creates a haunting, personal vision of a loser's quest for love and meaning in a harsh, brutal world. Using explicit screen violence as a means in which to explore the violence the director claims to be inherent in all men, Peckinpah's "philosophy" is often disregarded by those who are turned off by his stylized bloodletting. BRING ME THE HEAD is a dark, nihilistic, violent depiction of an existential quest. The "hero" of this quest is Oates, who holds the film together with an intense, likable, spellbinding performance as the broken-down American living out a meager, uneventful life in his seedy Mexican bar. Oates keenly portrays the obsession that drives his character on a suicidal pursuit of self-respect and importance. The macabre scenes in which Oates converses with the head as flies continually buzz around it are funny and telling. The head, which Oates affectionately calls Al, becomes the symbolic element that destroys Oates' world but forces him into an incredibly vital one. One of the finest American actors who ever lived, Oates was rarely given the chance at lead roles. His performances in many classic American films are sadly forgotten. Oates and Peckinpah's world is a difficult one for many to appreciate. It is a violent, sad, troubling nightmare atmosphere that forces men to act in ways that they never would have dreamed, alienating those who are unwilling to accept the darker side of the human character. BRING ME THE HEAD does have some sloppy photography, a few unintentionally humorous scenes, and an excess of Peckinpah's signature slow-motion violence, but it was this over-indulgence that fueled the fire in the director to create one of his most daring films. Perhaps the only true outlaw in American film history, Peckinpah's talent hits like a bullet, but the wound it creates exposes a highly volatile, emotional heart.

p, Martin Baum; d, Sam Peckinpah; w, Gordon Dawson, Peckinpah, (based on a story by Frank Kowalski); ph Alex Phillips (DeLuxe Color); m, Jerry Fielding; ed, Garth Craven, Robbe Roberts, Sergio Ortega, Dennis E. Dolan; set d, Enrique Estevez; m/l, Vega, Peckinpah, Javier Vega, Arturo Castro.

Crime Drama **(PR:O MPAA:R)**

BRING ON THE GIRLS*** (1945) 92m PAR c

Veronica Lake *(Teddy Collins)*, Sonny Tufts *(Phil North)*, Eddie Bracken *(J. Newport Bates)*, Marjorie Reynolds *(Sue Thomas)*, Grant Mitchell *(Uncle Ralph)*, Johnnie Coy *(Benny Lowe)*, Peter Whitney *(Swede)*, Alan Mowbray *(August)*, Porter Hall *(Dr. Efrington)*, Thurston Hall *(Rutledge)*, Lloyd Corrigan *(Beaster)*, Sig Arno *(Joseph)*, Joan Woodbury *(Gloria)*, Andrew Tombes *(Dr. Spender)*, Frank Faylen *(Sailor)*, Huntz Hall *(Sailor)*, William Moss *(Sailor)*, Norma Varden *(Aunt Martha)*, Spike Jones Orchestra.

Millionaire Bracken joins the Navy in order to escape the always-active clutches of vixens out for his money. As a sailor, he becomes attached to cigarette girl Lake, but dumps her when he discovers that she's aware of his true identity and fishing for his fortune. Just as he's about to write off women altogether, he falls in love with the sweet (and honest) Reynolds. Light-hearted musical that owes its quick pace and tempo to its never-ending barrage of entertaining song-and-dance numbers. Lake, as always, is a pleasure to watch in a delightfully nasty role and Bracken is a great deal of fun as the woman-weary hero.

d, Sidney Lanfield; w, Karl Tunberg, Darrell Ware; (based on a story by Pierre Wolff); ph, Karl Struss (Technicolor); ed, William Shea; md, Robert Emmett Dolan; art d, Hans Dreier, John Meehan; ch, Danny Dare; m/l, Jimmy McHugh, Harold Adamson.

Musical/Comedy **(PR:A MPAA:NR)**

BRING YOUR SMILE ALONG*** (1955) 83m COL c

Frankie Laine *(Jerry Dennis)*, Keefe Brasselle *(Martin Adams)*, Constance Towers *(Nancy Willows)*, Lucy Marlow *(Marge Stevenson)*, William Leslie *(David Parker)*, Mario Siletti *(Ricardo)*, Ruth Warren *(Landlady)*, Jack Albertson *(Jenson)*, Bobby Clark *(Waldo)*, Murray Leonard *(Dave)*, Ida Smeraldo *(Mama)*.

Timid schoolteacher Towers breaks away from her humble New England home and travels to New York in hopes of becoming a song lyricist. She latches onto tunesmith Brasselle and the two become partners. When their songs, as recorded by Laine, become popular hits, the working couple decide to become a romantic one, much to the dismay of Towers' hometown beau, Leslie. Although director Edwards had not yet perfected his wickedly funny style that made him one of the most popular comedy directors of the 1970s this early effort is still entertaining. Towers and Brasselle are likable, but unexciting; Laine is fantastic as the enthusiastic singer. Songs: "Bring Your Smile Along" (Benny Davis, Carl Fischer); "If Spring Never Comes" (Bill Corey, Fischer); "Gandy Dancers Ball" (Paul Mason Howard, Paul Weston); "Don't Blame Me" (Dorothy Fields, Jimmy McHugh); "Side By Side" (Harry Woods); "When A Girl Is Beautiful," "Every Baby Needs A Da Da Daddy" (Allan Roberts, Lester Lee); "Italian Mother Song" (Ned Washington, Lee).

p, Jonie Taps; d&w, Blake Edwards (based on a story by Edwards, Richard Quine); ph, Charles Lawton, Jr. (Technicolor); ed, Al Clark; md, Morris Stoloff.

Musical/Comedy **(PR:A MPAA:NR)**

BRINGING UP BABY***** (1938) 102m RKO bw

Katharine Hepburn *(Susan Vance)*, Cary Grant *(David Huxley)*, Charles Ruggles *(Maj. Horace Applegate)*, May Robson *(Aunt Elizabeth, Mrs. Carlton Random)*, Barry Fitzgerald *(Mr. Gogarty)*, Walter Catlett *(Constable Slocum)*, Fritz Feld *(Dr. Fritz Lehman)*, Leona Roberts *(Hannah Gogarty)*, George Irving *(Alexander Peabody)*, Virginia Walker *(Alice Swallow)*, Tala Birell *(Mrs. Lehman)*, John Kelly *(Elmer)*, Edward Gargan, Buck Mack *(Zoo Officials)*, William "Billy" Benedict, Buster Slaven *(Caddies)*, Geraldine Hall *(Maid)*, Stanley Blystone *(Doorman)*, Frank Marlowe *(Joe)*, Pat West *(Mac)*, Jack Carson *(Roustabout)*, Richard Lane *(Circus Manager)*, Frank M. Thomas *(Circus Barker)*, Ruth Alder *(Dancer)*, Ward Bond *(Motorcycle Cop)*, Pat O'Malley *(Deputy)*, Adalyn Asbury *(Mrs. Peabody)*, Judith Ford, Jeanne Martel *(Cigarette Girls)*, George Humbert *(Louis, Headwaiter)*, Billy Bevan *(Bartender)*, D'Arcy Corrigan *(Professor La Touche)*, Asta *(George, the Dog)*, Nissa *(Baby, the Leopard)*.

Hepburn and Grant are superb in this delightful screwball comedy with a plot that could have been hatched in a mental institution. Director Hawks refused to have one sane character in the film and directed with abandon, allowing his decided flair for the absurd to race to the ridiculous. The result is a laugh riot. Hepburn is an eccentric heiress with a wandering dog (Asta, the same as in the THIN MAN films) who steals a dinosaur bone from paleontologist Grant, a vital bone in that it is the last one he needs to complete his reconstruction of a prehistoric beast. Without the bone, Grant will not be able to finish his exhibit and get the $1 million from donors needed to open his museum. He follows Hepburn to her Connecticut farm in search of the relic and runs smack into the eccentric heiress' pet Brazillian leopard, Baby, who involves the couple in harrowing, harebrained moments. Then a real wild leopard escapes from the local zoo and the authorities comb the area, thinking Hepburn's pet is the dangerous beast. When Hepburn and Grant are caught harboring the big cat—after a while even they can't tell the difference between Baby and the wild leopard—they, relatives, and friends are all locked up in the local jail. Here Hepburn pretends to be a notorious gun moll, shocking jailer Catlett by saying she is going to inform on Grant, whom she claims is a much-wanted criminal, affecting a tough Brooklyn accent with: "Hey, flatfoot! I'm gonna unbutton my puss and shoot the woiks. An' I wouldn' be squealin' if he hadn' a give me the runaround for another twist." Even the supporting players are addlebrained if not out-and-out certifiable. Psychiatrist Fritz Feld explains irrational behavior to Hepburn as she nonchalantly pops one olive after another into her mouth. "All people," Feld says solemnly as his eyes spin crazily, "who behave strangely are not insane." In the end Grant, bewildered by events and then becoming an equal party to the zany goings-on, winds up with daffy heiress Hepburn, his museum gets its grant but, at the last moment, Hepburn finds the missing dinosaur bone and adds it to the huge reconstruction only to bring the entire skeleton crashing down, along with herself and her much-vexed betrothed. The dialog sizzles and Hawks' direction is fast and furious with inspired performances by all. Most of all, it's fun from beginning to end.

p&d, Howard Hawks; w, Dudley Nichols, Hagar Wilde (based on a story by Wilde; uncredited scenarists, Robert McGowan, Gertrude Purcell); ph, Russell Metty; m, Roy Webb; ed, George Hively; art d, Van Nest Polglase, Perry Ferguson; set d, Darrell Silvera; cos, Howard Greer; spec eff, Vernon L. Walker.

Comedy **(PR:A MPAA:NR)**

BRINGING UP FATHER*½ (1946) 65m MON bw

Joe Yule *(Jiggs)*, Renie Riano *(Maggie)*, George McManus *(Himself)*, Tim Ryan *(Dinty Moore)*, June Harrison *(Nora)*, Wallace Chadwell *(Danny)*, Tom Kennedy *(Murphy)*, Laura Treadwell *(Mrs. Kermishaw)*, William Frambes *(Junior Kermishaw)*, Pat Goldin *(Dugan)*, Jack Norton *(Norton)*, Ferris Taylor *(F. Newson Kermishaw)*, Tom Dugan *(Hod Carrier)*, Joe Devlin *(Casey)*, Fred Kelsey *(Tom)*, Charles Wilson *(Frank)*, Herbert Evans *(Jenkins)*, Dick Ryan *(Grogharty)*, Mike Pat Donovan *(Jerry)*, Bob Carleton *(Pianist)*, George Hickman *(Fogarty)*.

Yule's attempts to close Ryan's restaurant are foiled when socialite Riano gets in the picture with the restaurant owner's architect son. Good casting of main characters strengthens so-so technical effort. Not much of a stew.

p, Barney Gerard; d, Eddie Cline; w, Jerry Warner (based on a screenplay by Gerard and the comic strip by George McManus); ph, L.W. O'Donnell; m, Gerard, Eddie Cline, Edward Kay; ed, Ralph Dixon.

Comedy **(PR:A MPAA:NR)**

BRINK OF LIFE** (1960, Swed.) 83m Nordisk ToneFilm bw

Eva Dahlbeck *(Stina)*, Ingrid Thulin *(Cecila)*, Bibi Andersson *(Hjordis)*, Barbro Hiort Af Ornas *(Brita)*, Erland Josephson *(Anders)*, Max Von Sydow *(Harry)*, Gunnar Sjoberg *(Doctor)*, Ann-Marie Gyllenspetz, Inga Landgre, Margareta Krook, Lard Lind, Sissi Kaiser, Monika Ekberg, Gun Jansson, Inga Gill.

Trials and tribulations of three mothers in a maternity ward voicing their opinions about keeping and not keeping the child each is carrying. Not much actiontypical of Bergman filmsthough expertly acted and directed.

p, Gosta Hammerback; d&w, Ingmar Bergman (based on a story by Ulla Isaksson); ph, Max Wilen; ed, Carl Olov Skeppstedt; set d, Bibi Lindstrom.

Drama **Cas.** **(PR:C-O MPAA:NR)**

BRINK'S JOB, THE½** (1978) 118m UNIV c

Peter Falk *(Tony Pino)*, Peter Boyle *(Joe McGinnis)*, Allen Goorwitz *(Vinnie Costa)*, Warren Oates *(Specs O'Keefe)*, Gena Rowlands *(Mary Pino)*, Paul Sorvino *(Jazz Maffie)*, Sheldon Leonard *(J. Edgar Hoover)*, Gerard Murphy *(Sandy Richardson)*, Kevin O'Connor *(Stanley "Guss" Gusciora)*, Claudia Peluso *(Gladys)*, Patrick Hines *(H.H. Rightmire)*, Malachy McCourt *(Mutt Murphy)*, Walter Klavun *(Daniels)*, Randy Jurgensen, John Brandon, Earl Hindman, John Farrel *(FBI Agents)*.

This is The Gang Who Couldn't Rob Straight, not a genius among 'em; they were a bunch of klutzes who discovered that Brink's was not nearly as careful as it should have been, so they robbed the company. Falk is the nominal leader but he is so identified with "Colombo" by this time that it's hard to put him in the position of criminal rather than cop. Unless he decides to do some very weird part, like an Indian chief or a British diplomat, he will always suffer from the Colombo comparison. Boyle, Goorwitz (now Garfield again), Oates, Sorvino, Murphy and O'Connor make up this unlikely group of robbers. There's virtually no suspense or excitement. A bunch of guys get together, pull a job and that's about it. The film is loose at 118 minutes and might have had greater impact if less time were spent gathering the crooks and more energy was used in their characterizations. All technical credits are first rate but Friedkin doesn't make use of his copious cinematic talent. Since THE FRENCH CONNECTION, he seems to be going downhill. Either that, or he's decided that being a director is not good enough; he must now be an auteur. He still has some good work in him but you couldn't tell it by the yawning THE BRINK'S JOB produces.

p, Ralph Serpe; d, William Friedkin; w, Walon Green (based on the book *Big Stick Up At Brinks* by Noel Behn); ph, Norman Leigh (Technicolor); m, Richard Rodney Bennett; ed, Bud Smith, Robert K. Lambert; cos, Ruth Morley.

Crime/Comedy **(PR:A-C MPAA:PG)**

BRITTANIA HOSPITAL*** (1982, Brit.) 115m EMI/UNIV c

Leonard Rossiter *(Potter)*, Graham Crowden *(Millar)*, Malcolm McDowell *(Mike)*, Joan Plowright *(Phyllis)*, Marsha Hunt *(Amanda)*, Frank Grimes *(Fred)*, Jill Bennett *(MacMillan)*, Robin Askwith, John Bett, Peter Jeffrey, Fulton Mackay, John Moffatt, Dandy Nichols, Alan Bates, Brian Pettifer, Vivian Pickles, Marcus Powell, Barbara Hicks, Catherine Willmer, Mary MacLeod, Dave Atkins, Mark Hamill, Peter Machin, Gladys Crosbie, Rufus Collins, Ram John Holder, Jim Findlay, Pauline Melville, Kevin Lloyd.

BRITTANIA HOSPITAL is Anderson's version of Chayevsky's HOSPITAL. It's pointed, punchy, takes some sharp shots at the British establishment and went right over the heads of the public and directly into the john! Anderson, who had made O LUCKY MAN and IF, decided to apply his satirical eye to the medical establishment, doctors and unions included. Whereas the National Health Service is supposed to provide equally for all patients, the hospital is tipped over by the arrival of a member of royalty and the fawning and the toadying begins. Several incidents point up the huge waste and the foolish attitudes in the U.K. medical establishment; a cardiac death occurs when workers insist on their tea break, a crazed physician uses pilfered funds to experiment with Frankenstein-like results, a wimp arrives from the protocol office to teach the workers how to behave for the royal visitor. Hardly any part of hospital life escapes Anderson's direction and Sherwin's screenplay. It's a disturbing picture, especially if you've just come out of a hospital or are contemplating entering one. The story is enough to make a person sick, which means that BRITTANIA HOSPITAL did it's job in awakening viewers to the problems inherent in the British medical system. Only trouble is that no one wanted to learn the truth and the picture died as quickly as several patients in BRITTANIA HOSPITAL.

p, Davina Belling, Clive Parsons; d, Lindsay Anderson; w, David Sherwin; ph, Mike Fash (Technicolor); m, Alan Price; ed, Michael Ellis.

Comedy/Drama **Cas.** **(PR:C MPAA:NR)**

BRITANNIA MEWS

(SEE: AFFAIRS OF ADELAIDE, AKA: FORBIDDEN STREET)

BRITANNIA OF BILLINGSGATE*½ (1933, Brit.) 80m GAU/IDEAL bw

Violet Loraine *(Bessie Bolton)*, Gordon Harker *(Bolton)*, Kay Hammond *(Pearl Bolton)*, John Mills *(Fred)*, Walter Sondes *(Hogarth)*, Glennis Lorimer *(Maud)*, Gibb McLaughlin *(Westerbrook)*, Drusilla Wills *(Mrs. Wigglesworth)*, Anthony Holles *(Garibaldi)*, Joyce Kirby *(Joan)*, Grethe Hansen *(Gwen)*, Wally Patch *(Harry)*, Ernest Sefton *(Publicity Man)*, Jane Cornell *(Fay)*, George Turner *(Pal)*, Cecil Ramage *(Producer)*, Roy Fox and His Band, Ron Johnson, Gus Kuhn, Colin Watson, Tom Farndon.

A middle-class cockney fisherman's wife sets her sights on the bright lights and becomes a film star. An ironic and unlikely sea catch, but music helps the viewer rise to the bait.

p, Michael Balcon; d, Sinclair Hill; w, Ralph Stock (based on the play by Christine Jope-Slade and Sewell Stokes); ph, Mutz Greenbaum [Max Greene].

Drama/Musical **(PR:A MPAA:NR)**

BRITISH AGENT*½** (1934) 75m FN bw

Leslie Howard *(Stephen Locke)*, Kay Francis *(Elena)*, William Gargan *(Medill)*, Phillip Reed *(Gaston LaFarge)*, Irving Pichel *(Pavlov)*, Walter Byron *(Stanley)*, Cesar Romero *(Tito Del Val)*, J. Carrol Naish *(Commissioner for War)*, Ivan Simpson *(Evans)*, Gregory Gaye *(Kolinoff)*, Halliwell Hobbes *(Sir Walter Carrister)*, Arthur Aylesworth *(Farmer)*, Mary Forbes *(Lady Treherne)*, Doris Lloyd *(Lady Carrister)*, Alphonse Ethier *(Devigny)*, Paul Porcasi *(Romano)*, Addison Richards *(Zvododu)*, Marina Schubert *(Maria)*, George Pearce *(Lloyd George)*, Tenen Holtz *(Lenin)*, Thomas Braidon, Basil Lynn, Fred Walton, Winter Hall *(Cabinet Members)*, Olaf Hytten *(Undersecretary)*, Frank Lackteen, Robert Wilber, Lew Harvey *(Suspects)*, Frank Reicher *(Mr. X)*.

Technically and artistically perfect yarn about espionage during the early days of the Russian revolution shows Howard and Francis handling the curious star roles tellingly. Howard is spotted in Russia as the British consul-general just prior to the Bolshevik takeover of the Czarist government. Russia wants to break away from the Allies in WW I and sign a separate peace with Germany, which will then help it fight the revolutionaries, but Howard is so determined in his belief that Russia must remain an ally that he wages a one-man war on Bolshevism against his government's orders. Enter Francis, secre- tary to Lenin (Tenen Holtz). Howard accidentally saves her life and they fall in love. The romance continues through the revolution, although Francis is pitted against Howard politically, but at the finish she gives him information that is supposed to lead to his death. A phony finish shows Francis joining Howard in a building which is to be blown up, and both of them with it; they are saved when soldiers drop everything to celebrate the news that Lenin, who has been shot by a fanatic, will live. This contrived twist is the only element to mar the story. Howard is superb and good work is performed by the supporting cast. with William Gargan standing out in comedy.

d, Michael Curtiz; w, Laird Doyle (based on a novel by R. H. Bruce Lockhart); ph, Ernest Haller; m, Leo F. Forbstein; ed, Tom Richards; art d, Anton Grot.

Historical Drama **(PR:A MPAA:NR)**

BRITISH INTELLIGENCE** (1940) 62m WB bw

Boris Karloff *(Valdar)*, Margaret Lindsay *(Helene Von Lobeer)*, Maris Wrixon *(Dorothy)*, Bruce Lester *(Frank Bennett)*, Leonard Mudie *(James Yeats)*, Holmes Herbert *(Arthur* Bennett), Winifred Harris *(Mrs. Bennett)*, Lester Matthews *(Thompson)*, John Graham Spacey *(Crichton)*, Austin Fairman *(George Bennett)*, Clarence Derwent *(Milkman)*, Louise Brien *(Miss Risdon)*, Frederick Vogeding *(Kuglar)*, Carlos De Valdez *(Von Ritter)*, Willy Kaufman *(Corporal)*, Frank Mayo *(Brixton)*, Stuart Holmes *(Luchow)*, Sidney Bracy *(Crowder)*, Jack Mower *(Morton)*.

British agent Lindsay falls in love with British aviator Lester while working as a nurse in a French hospital, only to be separated from him, then find him again. Karloff turns in a chilling performance as a German master spy posing as a butler in the British War Office, planning to set off a bomb that will destroy the entire cabinet until Lindsay and Lester stop him by sacrificing their own lives. Excellent photography by Hickox. (Remake of THREE FACES EAST, 1930)

d, Terry Morse; w, Lee Katz, John Kangan (based on a story by Anthony Paul Kelly); ph, Sid Hickox; m, Heinz Roemheld; ed, Thomas Pratt.

Adventure **(PR:A MPAA:NR)**

BROADMINDED** (1931) 65m FN-WB bw

Joe E. Brown *(Ossie Simpson)*, Ona Munson *(Constance)*, William Collier, Jr. *(Jack Hackett)*, Marjorie White *(Penelope)*, Holmes Herbert *(John Hackett, Sr.)*, Margaret Livingston *(Mabel Robinson)*, Bela Lugosi *(Pancho)*, Thelma Todd *(Gertie Gardner)*, Grayce Hampton *(Aunt Polly)*.

Brown's antics are numerous and hit the mark on occasion as he is hired by Herbert to chaperon his younger cousin Collier, a spendthrift playboy. Lugosi has a small supporting part as a sophisticated South American who sports Todd about on his arm, a rare non-Dracula appearance for Lugosi, who is quite charming. The script is tepid and LeRoy's direction uncustomarily weak.

d, Mervyn LeRoy; w, Bert Kalmar, Harry Ruby; ph, Sid Hickox; ed, Al Hall.

Comedy **(PR:A MPAA:NR)**

BROADWAY*** (1929) 105m UNIV bw

Glenn Tryon *(Roy Lane)*, Evelyn Brent *(Pearl)*, Merna Kennedy *(Billie Moore)*, Thomas E. Jackson *(Dan McCorn)*, Robert Ellis *(Steve Crandall)*, Otis Harlan *(Porky Thompson)*, Paul Porcasi *(Nick Verdis)*, Marion Lord *(Lil Rice)*, Fritz Feld *(Mose Leavett)*, Leslie Fenton *(Scar Edwards)*, Arthur Housman *(Dolph)*, George Davis *(Joe)*, Betty Francisco *(Mazie)*, Edythe Flynn *(Ruby)*, Florence Dudley *(Ann)*, Ruby McCoy *(Grace)*.

Expensive production for its era was noted primarily for camera work in which director Fejos devised a camera crane capable of traveling at every possible angle and at a speed of nearly 600 feet per minute. This allowed for a spectacular polish which gave the film thrilling tenseness sustained without fraudulent material to expand its length. Bootlegger Ellis murders rival Porcasi, owner of the lively Paradise Night Club. Kennedy, who witnesses the killing but is covering for the gangster, breaks her silence when Ellis tries to frame Tyron, her dancing partner. She is kidnaped by Ellis but saved by the murdered man's mistress who shoots the villain dead. Kennedy then marries her dancing partner. Magnificent set complete with an excellent carnival night scene held fast by performers adds superfinesse to the nicely staged workmanship of this film. Songs include "Broadway," "The Chicken or the Egg," "Hot Footin' It," "Hittin' the Ceiling," "Sing a Little Love Song."

p, Carl Laemmle, Jr.; d, Paul Fejos; w, Edward T. Lowe Jr., Charles Furthman (based on the play by Jed Harris, Philip Dunning, George Abbott); ph, Hal Mohr; m, Howard Jackson; ed, Robert Carlisle, Edward Cahn, Maurice Pivar; art d, Charles D. Hall; cos, Johanna Mathieson; spec eff, Grant H. Booth; ch, Maurice L. Kusell; m/l, Con Conrad, Archie Goettler, Sidney Mitchell, Robert Carlisle, Edward Cahn.

Musical/Drama **(PR:A MPAA:NR)**

BROADWAY*** (1942) 89m UNIV bw

George Raft *(George)*, Pat O'Brien *(Dan McCorn)*, Janet Blair *(Billie)*, Broderick Crawford *(Steve Crandall)*, Marjorie Rambeau *(Lil)*, Anne Gwynne *(Pearl)*, S.Z. Sakall *(Nick)*, Edward S. Brophy *(Porky)*, Marie Wilson *(Grace)*, Gus Schilling *(Joe)*, Ralf Harolde *(Dolph)*, Arthur Shields *(Pete Dailey)*, Iris Adrian *(Maisie)*, Elaine Morey *(Ruby)*, Dorothy Moore *(Ann)*, Nestor Paiva *(Rinati)*, Abner Biberman *(Trado)*, Damian O'Flynn *(Scar Edwards)*, Mack Gray *(Himself)* Jennifer Holt *(TWA Hostess)*, Benny Rubin, Anthony Warde, Charles Jordan, Sammy Stein, Larry McGrath, Charles Sullivan, Tony Paton, Jimmy O'Gatty, Lee Moore *(Gangsters)*, Tom Kennedy *(Kerry the Cop)*, Joe Cunningham, Arthur Loft, Lee Phelps *(Detectives)*, Harry Seymour *(Piano Tuner)*, Jimmy Conlin *(Newsman)*, Bill Nelson *(Tommy)*, Harry Tyler *(Wingy)*, James Flavin *(Doorman)*, Byron Shores *(Manager)*, Henry Roquemore *(Will)*, John Sheehan *(Oscar)*, John Maxwell *(Ed)*, Jay Novello *(Eddie)*, Eve March *(Mary)*, John Harmon *(Harry)*, Walter Tetley *(Western Union Boy)*, A. Kenneth Stevens *(Himself)*, Fern Emmett *(Will's Wife)*, Pat Gleason, Frank Ferguson *(Reporters)*, Linda Brent *(Hat Check Girl)*, John Day *(Andy)*, Kernan Cripps *(Morgue Attendant)*, Grace Lenard *(Woman)*.

A trip down memory lane, in this case the Great White Way of the 1920s. Raft returns to NYC to visit his old stomping grounds, the Paradise Club of the Jazz Age. The film opens with Raft and his real-life sidekick and bodyguard Mack "Killer" Gray arriving in Manhattan by plane; after being swarmed over by members of the press who accompany him to his hotel suite, Raft strolls down Broadway, meeting old cronies, then discovering the nightclub where he worked as a dancer is being turned into a bowling alley. Raft begins to think back to his palmy days and, in flashback, the old club comes alive as Raft narrates his story to the building's night watchman. We see Raft as a young hoofer teamed with Blair in a club run by Sakall. Gangster Crawford, who covets Blair, arrives with his bootleg buddies to hide a load of hijacked booze in the club's basement. O'Flynn, another gangster, shows up, demanding Crawford return his booze; Crawford agrees, then shoots O'Flynn and hides the body. O'Brien, a Broadway detective, tries to pin the murder on Raft who had earlier argued with the dead mobster, but Blair provides an alibi for her dancing partner which angers Crawford. Before the bootlegger can wreak havoc upon Raft for stealing his girl friend, another dancer, Gwynne, who has hated the racket king for past transgressions, shoots him dead in his patent leather shoes. O'Brien considers the act good riddance and, instead of arresting Gwynne, announces that Crawford committed suicide. Blair and Raft are now free to continue their romance and their tango. The best part of this chestnut, remade from the bones of the 1929 film, are the 14 1920s tunes, and the brassy performance of Rambeau, who does a good impersonation of Texas Guinan for whom Raft actually worked as a dancer in the 1920s in her notorious El Fey Club (the story could have been Raft's biography to some degree). Songs include "Dinah," (Joe Young, Sam Lewis, Harry Akst), "Alabamy Bound" (Buddy De Sylva, Bud Green, Ray Henderson), "Sweet Georgia Brown" (Ben Bernie, Kenneth Casey, Maceo Pinkard), "The Darktown Strutters Ball," "Some of These Days" (Sheldon Brooks), "Yes Sir, That's My Baby" (Gus Kahn). Blair sings "I'm Just Wild About Harry" (Eubie Blake, Noble Sissle), and Raft does an incredibly wild Charleston which is almost a blur before the cameras as he legs it with the speed of mercury. Before going into this frantic dance, Raft announces to backstage cronies what his act will do to the audience: "I'm gonna cut 'em deep and let 'em bleed!" He sure does.

p, Bruce Manning [Frank Shaw]; d, William A. Seiter; w, Felix Jackson, John Bright (based on the play by Philip Dunning, George Abbott, adapted by Manning); ph, George Barnes; m, Charles Previn; ed, Ted Kent; ch, John Mattison.

Musical/Drama **(PR:A MPAA:NR)**

BROADWAY BABIES** (1929) 89m FN bw

Alice White *(Delight Foster)*, Charles Delaney *(Billy Buvanny)*, Fred Kohler *(Perc Gessant)*, Sally Eilers *(Navarre King)*, Marion Byron *(Florine Chandler)*, Tom Dugan *(Scotty)*, Bodil Rosing *(Sarah Durgen)*, Louis Natheaux *(August Brand)*, Maurice Black *(Nick the Greek)*, Jocelyn Lee *(Blossom Royale)*.

Chorus girl White gets involved with rumrunner Kohler, then decides to marry Delaney but not tell Kohler about it. The mobster goes after Delaney but a digruntled henchman gets Kohler first. Songs include "Wishing and Waiting for Love," "Jig, Jig, Jigaloo" (Grant Clarke, Harry Akst); "Broadway Baby Doll" (Al Bryan, George W. Meyer).

d, Mervyn Leroy; w, Monte Katterjohn, Humphrey Pearson (based on a story by Jay Gelzer); ph, Sol Polito; ed, Frank Ware; md, Leo F. Forbstein; art d, Jack Okey; cos, Max Ree.

Musical/Drama **(PR:A MPAA:NR)**

BROADWAY BAD** ½** (1933) 61m FOX bw (GB: HER REPUTATION)

Joan Blondell *(Tony Landers)*, Ricardo Cortez *(Craig Cutting)*, Ginger Rogers *(Flip Daly)*, Adrienne Ames *(Aileen)*, Allen Vincent *(Bob North)*, Phil Tead *(Joe Flynn)*, Francis McDonald *(Charley Davis)*, Spencer Charters *(Lew Gordon)*, Ronald Cosbey *(Big Fella)*, Frederick Burton *(Robert North, Sr.)*, Margaret Seddon *(Bixby)*, Donald Crisp *(Darrall)*.

Chorus girl Blondell is divorced by her jerk of a husband after he wrongly suspects her of infidelity. When he tries to gain possession of their son, whom Blondell adores, she tells him that the boy's father is really another man. Destroying her reputation but saving her child, Blondell lives happily on. Sappy attempt to portray a mother's hardship that manages to tug at a few heartstrings thanks to Blondell's understanding portrayal of a less-than-virtuous woman.

d, Sidney Lanfield; w, Arthur Kober, Maude Fulton (based on a story by William R. Lipman, A. W. Pezet); ph, George Barnes; ed, Paul Weatherwax; art d, Gordon Wiles.

Drama **(PR:A MPAA:NR)**

BROADWAY BIG SHOT** (1942) 63m PRC bw

Ralph Byrd *(Jimmy O'Brien)*, Virginia Vale *(Betty Collins)*, William Halligan *(Warden Collins)*, Dick Rush *(Tom Barnes)*, Herbert Rawlinson *(District Attorney)*, Cecil Weston *(Mrs. Briggs)*, Tom Herbert *(Carnation Charlie)*, Stubby Kruger *(Dynamite)*, Frank Hagney *(Butch)*, Jack Buckley *(Windy)*, Harry Depp *(Ben Marlo)*, Jack Roper *(Nipper)*, Al Goldsmith *(Coffee Cake George)*, Joe Oakie *(Sneaky)*, Alfred Hall *(Dr. Williams)*, Jimmy Aubrey *(Orderly)*, Dick Cramer *(Reilly)*, Jack Cheatham *(Tim)*, Jack Perrin *(Ed)*.

Wild story with improbable plot has Byrd, a crime reporter, as well as a star quarterback for a local college team, getting himself imprisoned so he can get a big story on an inmate. He gets the story, is elected president of the inmate's union and wins the heart of the warden's daughter, Vale. He is released to publish his scoop, marry Vale and look forward to a rewarding career. Well, anything was possible at poverty row's PRC where B-leading players were conceptually equal to William Randolph Hearst.

p, Jed Buell, d, William Beaudine; w, Martin Mooney; ph, Jack Greenhalgh; ed, Robert Crandall, Guy Thayer.

Drama **(PR:A MPAA:NR)**

BROADWAY BILL* ½**
(1934) 90m COL bw (GB: STRICTLY CONFIDENTIAL)

Warner Baxter *(Dan Brooks)*, Myrna Loy *(Alice)*, Walter Connolly *(J. L. Higgins)*, Helen Vinson *(Margaret)*, Douglas Dumbrille *(Eddie Morgan)*, Raymond Walburn *(Colonel Pettigrew)*, Lynne Overman *(Happy McGuire)*, Clarence Muse *(Whitey)*, Margaret Hamilton *(Edna)*, Frankie Darrow *(Ted Williams)*, Inez Courtney *(Mae)*.

Baxter, pressured by his witch of a wife Vinson into working in her family's business, abandons both his job and his marriage to start life anew as the owner of a racehorse, Broadway Bill. Baxter runs into trouble with fees, jockeys, gamblers, the law, and an often ill horse, but he receives emotional support from Vinson's understanding, charming sister Loy. Broadway Bill wins the climactic race, but dies in the Winner's Circle. Having lost his championship horse, Baxter finds solace in the loving arms of Loy. Enjoyable track picture is given an extra dash of excitement and humor by director Capra. Baxter is a likable hunk in the lead role, but Loy steals the show with her elegant wit.

p, Harry Cohn; d, Frank Capra; w, Robert Riskin (based on a story by Mark Hellinger); ph, Joseph Walker; ed, Gene Havlick.

Comedy **(PR:A MPAA:NR)**

BROADWAY GONDOLIER** ½** (1935) 100m WB bw

Dick Powell *(Richard Purcell)*, Joan Blondell *(Alice Hughes)*, Adolphe Menjou *(Professor De Vinci)*, Louise Fazenda *(Mrs. Twitchell)*, William Gargan *(Cliff)*, George Barbier *(Hayward)*, Grant Mitchell *(Richards)*, Hobart Cavanaugh *(Gilmore)*, James Burke *(Uncle Andy)*, Bob Murphy *(Irish Cop)*, Ted Fio Rito and Band *(Specialty)*, Mills Brothers *(Specialty)*, The Canova Family *(Specialty)*, June Travis *(Check Girl)*, Joe Sawyer *(Red)*, Mary Treen *(Woman)*, Jack Norton, Bill Elliot *(Reporters)*, Selmer Jackson *(Director)*, Sam Ash *(Singer)*, Ernie Wood *(Clerk)*, George Chandler *(Photographer)*.

Powell stars as a singing cab driver hired by a radio station to pose as an authentic Venetian gondolier for a cheese company's exotic radio ads. Eventually becoming fed up, Powell exposes the ruse on the air one day and is promptly fired. Although pretty radio exec Blondell is sympathetic, Powell runs off to Italy where he, oddly enough, becomes a crooning gondolier in Venice. When the eccentric head of the cheese company, Fazenda, and Blondell travel to the romantic city in search of a *real* gondolier, Fazenda gives the job to Powell unaware of his past indiscretion. Blondell and Powell rekindle their affair and return to the States with the pleased Fazenda. Silly, but entertaining minor musical that allowed Powell to stretch his vocal chords during some engaging numbers. Blondell works well as the love interest, and Fazenda is a weird treasure.

d, Lloyd Bacon; w, Warren Duff, Sig Herzig, Jerry Wald, Julius J. Epstein (based on a story by Herzig, E. Y. Harburg, Hans Kraly); ph, George Barnes; ed, George Amy; m/l, Al Dubin, Harry Warren.

Musical/Comedy **(PR:A MPAA:NR)**

BROADWAY HOOFER, THE** (1929) 63m COL bw

Marie Saxon *(Adele)*, Jack Egan *(Bobby)*, Louise Fazenda *(June)*, Howard Hickman *(Larry)*, Ernest Hilliard *(Morton)*, Gertrude Short *(Annabelle)*, Eileen Percy *(Dolly)*, Charlotte Merriam *(Mazie)*, Fred MacKaye *(Billy)*, Billy Franey *(Baggage Man)*.

Fantasy romance in a delightful tale leading to the ever-popular happy ending. Ziegfield Follies-type Broadway dancing star Saxon shows off her great legs while on a secluded vacation. In a small town they are having auditions for a burlesque show and guess who wanders in to capture the job? Right. Marie falls in love with Egan, the show's author-turned-manager, in part because of his innocence—that is, he doesn't recognize her. Once in the lineup, he notices her talent (she's just going along for the fun), and immediately promotes her to a duo dance number with him. When Saxon does not show up for her Broadway rehearsal, the stage manager finds her and exposes her. Egan feels ridiculed and fires her in front of the cast. Later, he makes his debut in New York and Saxon, still in love with him, sits in the audience. He freezes—Saxon saves him by assisting in the number they did in the burlesque show. Saxon's Broadway manager spots Egan's talent and hires him to join the troupe. Fine support from technical crew.

p, Harry Cohn; d, George Archainbaud; w, Gladys Lehman; ph, Joe Walker; ed, Maurice Wright.

Musical/Drama **(PR:A MPAA:NR)**

BROADWAY HOSTESS** (1935) 69m WB bw

Wini Shaw (Winnie Wharton), Genevieve Tobin (Iris Marvin), Lyle Talbot (Lucky Lorimer), Allen Jenkins (Fishcake Carter), Phil Regan (Tommy Blake), Marie Wilson (Dorothy Dubois), Spring Byington (Mrs. Duncan-Griswold-Wembly-Smythe), Joseph King (Big Joe Jarvis), Donald Rose (Ronnie Marvin), Frank Dawson (Morse), Harry Seymour (T. T. T.).

Shaw makes it to the top as a singer from a small town but can't find romance. Manager Talbot also has troublehe ends up with a brother-in-law who kills him for his money. Only the staging is well done by dance director Connolly in this lackluster production. Songs include "He Was Her Man, "Let It Be Me," "Weary," "Who But

You," "Playboy of Paree" (Mort Dixon, Allie Wrubel); "Only the Girl" (Herman Ruby, M.K. Jerome).

d, Frank McDonald; w, George Bricker; ph, Arthur Todd; ed, Jack Killifer; m/l, Allie Wrubel and Mort Dixon; ch, Bobby Connolly.

Musical **(PR:A MPAA:NR)**

BROADWAY LIMITED** (1941) 75m UA bw (GB: THE BABY VANISHES)

Victor McLaglen *(Mike)*, Marjorie Woodworth *(April)*, Dennis O'Keefe *(Dr. Harvey North)*, Patsy Kelly *(Patsy)*, ZaSu Pitts *(Myra)*, Leonid Kinskey *(Ivan)*, George E. Stone *(Lefty)*, Gay Ellen Dakin *(Baby)*, Charles Wilson *(Detective)*, John Sheehan *(Conductor)*, Edgar Edwards and Eric Alden *(State Troopers)*, Sam McDaniel *(Bartender)*.

Forced programmer has three Hollywood hopefuls traveling on the superliner from Chicago to New York to make it on Broadway, using as a prop a real baby whom they intend to promote to stardom. When police believe the infant has been kidnaped the problems mount for Woodworth, the would-be leading lady, Kelly, her wacky secretary, and Kinskey, an aspiring producer role modeling himself after actor Misha Auer. The implausible plot offers nothing for McLaglen's talents. Woodworth, who was being built up by United Artists as the next Jean Harlow, runs about scantily clad to reveal a torrid torso but her acting abilities make it evident that she was destined to remain in such B programmers as this.

p, Hal Roach; d, Gordon Douglas; w, Rian James; ph, Henry Sharp; md, Marvin Hatley; ed, Bert Jordan.

Comedy **(PR:A MPAA:NR)**

BROADWAY MELODY, THE*** (1929) 102m MGM bw

Anita Page *(Queenie)*, Bessie Love *(Hank)*, Charles King *(Eddie)*, Jed Prouty *(Uncle Jed)*, Kenneth Thompson *(Jock)*, Edward Dillon *(Stage Manager)*, Mary Doran *(Blonde)*, J. E. Beck *(Bebe Hatrick)*, Marshall Ruth *(Stew)*, Drew Demarest *(Turpe)*.

Midwesterners Page and Love, a sister song and dance team, travel to the Big Apple to meet up with Love's hoofer boy friend King and to take a stab at Broadway success themselves. King falls for younger sister Page, unaware that the girl has been using her feminine charms to further her and Love's careers. Love learns of King's passion for her sister, but before she can confront them with her knowledge, Page leaves in shame when King becomes aware of her association with a lecherous producer. Hoping to save at least one relationship, Love falsely tells King that her "love" for him was merely a way to get into the Broadway scene. With Love convincing him that he should forgive her sister, King sets out to find Page. This film, the first feature-length musical, is rather simplistic in its storytelling and visual techniques, but its historical significance is important. Not only did it pave the way for one of the most entertaining genres of all time, the American movie musical, it was, for a vast majority of its initial audience, the first sound film ever seen. THE JAZZ SINGER, 1927, and LIGHTS OF NEW YORK, 1928, and numerous sound shorts had preceded it, but BROADWAY MELODY was the first sound picture to be distributed to a wide range of theaters, many of which had just installed their sound systems. Immensely popular at the time of its release, the film's style, characters, and situations are less than memorable, making its significance a purely statistical one. Songs: "You Were Meant For Me," "The Wedding of the Painted Doll," "Broadway Melody," "Harmony Babies," "Love Boat," "Boy Friend" (Nacio Herb Brown, Arthur Freed); "Truthful Parson Brown" (Willard Robinson); "Give My Regards to Broadway" (George M. Cohan). (Remade as TWO GIRLS ON BROADWAY.)

d, Harry Beaumont; w, James Gleason, Norman Houston (based on a story by Edmund Goulding); ph, John Arnold; ed, Sam Z. Zimbalist; art d, Cedric Gibbons; cos, David Cox.

Musical **(PR:A MPAA:NR)**

BROADWAY MELODY OF 1936*** 1/2 (1935) 102m MGM bw

Jack Benny *(Bert Keeler)*, Eleanor Powell *(Irene Foster)*, Robert Taylor *(Bob Gordon)*, Una Merkel *(Kitty Corbett)*, Sid Silvers *(Snoop)*, Buddy Ebsen *(Ted)*, June Knight *(Lillian Brent)*, Vilma Ebsen *(Sally)*, Nick Long, Jr. *(Basil)*, Robert Wildhack *(Snorer)*, Paul Harvey *(Managing Editor)*, Frances Langford, Harry Stockwell *(Themselves)*.

Newshound for the New York theater scene Benny learns that the talentless Knight is financially backing producer Taylor's new show and prints his "suspicions" about Knight's worming her way into a lead role. Angered by his long-time enemy's comments, Taylor races to Benny's office and punches him in the nose, prompting a full-fledged feud between the two. Powell, Taylor's forgotten hometown girl friend, comes to New York hoping that her old flame will give her a chance to try out for a part in his production. Taylor dismisses the silly girl and Powell schemingly assumes the identity of mysterious (and fictitious) Parisian theater star, Mlle. Arlette, and wows Taylor with her tremendous singing and dancing capabilities. Benny, aware of Powell's ruse, threatens to expose the charade, but Powell herself unmasks "Mlle. Arlette," finally winning the approval of Taylor as well as his heart. The second of the BROADWAY MELODY series is the best, thanks to the engaging Powell in her first major role in a big-budget film. Her masterful dancing almost overshadows her energetic charm and wit in the nonmusical scenes. Benny is nastily wonderful as the scheming columnist and blossoming star Taylor handles the leading man responsibilities with a charming zeal. Containing some fine songs, including the memorable "You Are My Lucky Star" and "Broadway Rhythm," "I've Got a Feeling You're Fooling, "On a Sunday Afternoon," "Sing Before Breakfast" (Nacio Herb Brown, Arthur Freed).

p, John W. Considine, Jr.; d, Roy Del Ruth; w, Jack McGowan, Sid Silvers, Harry Cohn (based on a story by Moss Hart); ph, Charles Rosher; md, Alfred Newman; ch, Dave Gould, Albertina Rasch.

Musical/Comedy **Cas.** **(PR:A MPAA:NR)**

BROADWAY MELODY OF '38*** (1937) 115m MGM bw

Robert Taylor *(Steve Raleigh)*, Eleanor Powell *(Sally Lee)*, George Murphy *(Sonny Ledford)*, Binnie Barnes *(Caroline Whipple)*, Buddy Ebsen *(Peter Trot)*, Sophie Tucker *(Alice Clayton)*, Judy Garland *(Betty Clayton)*, Charles Igor Gorin *(Nicki Papaloopas)*, Raymond Walburn *(Herman Whipple)*, Robert Benchley *(Duffy)*, Willie Howard *(The Waiter)*, Charley Grapewin *(James K. Blakeley)*, Robert Wildhack *(The Sneezer)*, Billy Gilbert *(George Papaloopas)*, Barnett Parker *(Jerry Jason)*, Helen Troy *(Emma Snipe)*.

Broadway producer Taylor, in desperate need of financial backing for his new musical, is rescued when the racehorse of the show's star, Powell, wins a major race at Saratoga. Slim plot is there for the sole purpose of giving the producers a structure in which to incorporate an overabundance of song-and-dance numbers. Taylor, appearing very bored with the idea of being in another musical, and Powell, attempting to toss some enthusiasm into well-worn dance routines, are overshadowed by the mesmerizing young Garland, who hauntingly sings her classic "Dear Mr. Gable." Although some critics praised vaudeville star Tucker at the time, her overbearing, loud presence nicely points out the power in the gentle, emotional Garland, who was, of course, about to move on to become one of MGM's greatest stars. Other songs: "I'm Feeling Like A Million," "Yours And Mine," "Everybody Sing," "Follow In My Footsteps," "Your Broadway And My Broadway," "Broadway Rhythm," "Sun Showers" (Nacio Herb Brown, Arthur Freed); "Some Of These Days" (Shelton Brooks).

p, Jack Cummings; d, Roy Del Ruth; w, Jack McGowan (based on a story by McGowan, Sid Silvers); ph, William Daniels; ed, Blanche Sewell; md, Georgie Stoll; ch, Dave Gould.

Musical/Comedy **(PR:A MPAA:NR)**

BROADWAY MELODY OF 1940*** (1940) 102m MGM bw

Fred Astaire *(Johnny Brett)*, Eleanor Powell *(Clara Bennett)*, George Murphy *(King Shaw)*, Frank Morgan *(Bob Casey)*, Ian Hunter *(Bert C. Matthews)*, Florence Rice *(Amy Blake)*, Lynne Carver *(Emmy Lou Lee)*, Ann Morriss *(Pearl)*, Trixie Firschke *(Juggler)*, Douglas McPhail *(Masked Singer)*.

Aspiring dance team of Astaire and Murphy is separated professionally when, through a case of mistaken names, Murphy is offered the starring role in a big Broadway show. Astaire begins to coach the less-talented Murphy on the side and watches his former partner make an irritating fool out of himself as he becomes a hard-drinking egomaniac. When, on opening night, Murphy becomes too drunk to perform, a masked Astaire takes his place, impressing the audience and the show's leading lady, Powell. Murphy revels in his false success and Astaire remains in the shadows. At one point during the show's run, Murphy realizes the dishonesty in his "triumph" and feigns drunkenness, forcing Astaire to once again take his place, this time unmasked. As Astaire dances his way into the audience's and Powell's heart, Murphy joins the pair on stage, signaling his new honesty and appreciation of Astaire's humility and talent. This once-in-a- lifetime pairing of Astaire and Powell should have been a musical classic, but sadly, it is not. Their talents are given a great deal of exposure, but the film lacks the spontaneous sense of fun and grace that marked Powell's solo work and Astarie's partnership with Ginger Rogers. Some may consider Powell a superior dancer to Rogers, but when Rogers left the musical film to pursue a dramatic career, she left Astaire needing not only a dance partner, but someone who could recapture the sparkling communion the two had had in the nonmusical portions of their films. A different vehicle, or a different director, may have caused Astaire and Powell to generate some energy and affinity, but BROADWAY MELODY OF 1940 was the only chance to try, and, unfortunately, its creators were unsuccessful. Songs: "Begin the Beguine," "I've Got My Eyes On You," "I Am The Captain," "Please Don't Monkey With Broadway," "Between You And Me," "I Concentrate On You" (Cole Porter); "Il Bacio" (Luigi Arditi, sung by Charlotte Arren).

p, Jack Cummings; d, Norman Taurog; w, Leon Gordon, George Oppenheimer (based on a story by Jack McGowan, Dore Schary); ph, Oliver T. Marsh, Joseph Ruttenberg; ed, Blanche Sewell; md, Alfred Newman; ch, Bobby Connolly.

Musical **(PR:A MPAA:NR)**

BROADWAY MUSKETEERS** 1/2 (1938) 63m WB bw

Margaret Linday *(Isabel Dowling)*, Ann Sheridan *(Fay Reynolds)*, Marie Wilson *(Connie Todd)*, John Litel *(Stanley Dowling)*, Janet Chapman *(Judy Dowling)*, Dick Purcell *(Vincent Morrell)*, Anthony Averill *(Nick)*, Horace MacMahon *(Gurk)*, Dewey Robinson *(Milt)*, Dorothy Adams *(Anna)*, James Conlon *(Skinner)*, Jan Holm *(Schoolteacher)*.

Lindsay, Sheridan, and Wilson are three girls brought up together in an ophanage who go out together to conquer the world only to meet with suicide, gambling, kidnaping, and murder. Director Farrow misuses his outstanding talent to make only a routine melodrama.

p, Brian Foy; d, John Farrow, w, Don Ryan, Kenneth Gamet; ph, L. William O'Connell; ed, Thomas Pratt; m/l, M. K. Jerome, Jack Scholl.

Drama **(PR:A MPAA:NR)**

BROADWAY RHYTHM** (1944) 115m MGM c

George Murphy *(Johnnie Demming)*, Ginny Simms *(Helen Hoyt)*, Charles Winninger *(Sam Demming)*, Gloria DeHaven *(Patsy Demming)*, Nancy Walker *(Trixie Simpson)*, Ben Blue *(Felix Gross)*, Lena Horne *(Fernway De La Fer)*, Eddie "Rochester" Anderson *(Eddie)*, Hazel Scott *(Herself)*, Kenny Bowers *(Ray Kent)*, Russ Sisters *(Maggie, Aggie and Elmira)*, Dean Murphy *(Hired Man)*, Louis Mason *(Farmer)*, Bunny Waters *(Bunnie)*, Walter R. Long *(Doug Kelly)*, Tommy Dorsey and His Orchestra.

When film star Simms turns down offer by producer Murphy to join his musical comedy show, Winninger gets his chance at the big time. An elaborate production makes full use of massive sets but the film remains a stage expose of filmmaking. Songs: "All The Things You Are," "That Lucky Fellow," "In Other Words," "Seventeen," "All In Fun" (Jerome Kern); "Brazilian Boogie," "What Do You Think I Am?" (Hugh Martin, Ralph Blane); "Somebody Loves Me" (Buddy De Sylva, Ballard MacDonald, George Gershwin); "Milkman Keep Those Bottles Quiet," "Solid Potato Salad" (Don Raye, Gene De Paul); "Manhattan Serenade" (Louis Alter); "Pretty Baby" (Gus Kahn, Tony Jackson, Egbert Van Alstyne); "Oh You Beautiful Doll" (A. Seymour Brown, Nat D. Ayer); "Amor" (Sunny Skylar, Garbiel Ruiz, Ricardo Lopez Mendez); "National Emblem March" (E.E. Bagley); "Waltz In D Flat, Opus 64, No. 1" (Chopin); "Ida, Sweet As Apple Cider" (Edie Leonard, Eddie Munson); "A Frangesa" (P.M. Costa).

p, Jack Cummings; d, Roy del Ruth; w, Dorothy Kingsley, Harry Clork (based on a story by Jack McGowan and the musical "Very Warm For May" by Jerome Kern and Oscar Hammerstein II); ph, Leonard Smith (Technicolor); ed, Albert Akst.

Musical **(PR:A MPAA:NR)**

BROADWAY SCANDALS** (1929) 73m COL bw

Sally O'Neill *(Mary)*, Jack Egan *(Ted Howard)*, Carmel Myers *(Valeska)*, J. Barney Sherry *(Le Claire)*, John Hyams *(Pringle)*, Charles Wilson *(Jack Lane)*, Doris Dawson *(Bobby)*, Gordon Elliott *(George Halloway)*.

Two boys fall for the same girl and compete for her affections. Over-produced songs and garish staging make this film high camp. The chorus numbers provide armies of chorines thundering out tap numbers that are ear-shattering. Songs: "What Is Life Without Love?" (Fred Thompson, David Franklin, Jack Stone); "Does An Elephant Love Peanuts?" (James Hanley); "Can You Read In My Eyes?" (Sam Coslow); "Love's The Cause Of All My Blues" (Jo Trent, Charles Daniels); "Would I Love To Love You" (Dave Dreyer, Sidney Clare); "Rhythm Of The Tambourine," "Kickin' The Blues Away" (David Franklin).

p, Harry Cohn; d, George Archainbaud; w, Norman Houston (based on a story by Howard Green); ph, Harry Jackson; ed, Leon Barsha, Ben Pivar; art d, Harrison Wiley; ch, Rufus LeMaire.

Musical **(PR:A MPAA:NR)**

BROADWAY SERENADE 1/2** (1939) 111m MGM bw

Jeanette MacDonald *(Mary Hale)*, Lew Ayres *(James Geoffrey Seymour)*, IanHunter *(Larry Bryant)*, Frank Morgan *(Cornelius Collier, Jr.)*, Wally Vernon *(Joey, the Jinx)*, Rita Johnson *(Judy Tyrrell)*, Virginia Grey *(Pearl)*, William Gargan *(Bill)*, Katherine Alexander *(Harriet Ingalls)*, Al Shean *(Herman)*, Esther Dale *(Mrs. Olsen)*, Franklin Pangborn *(Gene)*, E. Allyn Warren *(Everett)*, Paul Hurst *(Reynolds)*, Frank Orth *(Mr. Fellowes)*, Esther Howard *(Mrs. Fellowes)*, Leon Belasco *(Squeaker)*, Kitty McHugh *(Kitty, the Maid)*, Kenneth Stevens *(Singer)*.

Poor but happy couple MacDonald and Ayres lose their jobs entertaining in a small cafe after Ayres blows up at the manager. When Ayres wins a scholarship to study music in Europe, he tries to sell a song to revue producer Morgan in hopes of making enough money to bring wife MacDonald along with him. The dashing financial backer of the show, Hunter, is impressed by MacDonald's vocal abilities; he offers her a spot in the production. Knowing that both opportunities should not be passed up, the couple separates. While abroad, Ayres hears rumors about a romance between MacDonald and Hunter and sends messages containing jealous accusations back to his wife. Upset with Ayres, and saddened by the distance between them, MacDonald seeks a divorce. Horribly saddened, Ayres tries to destroy his music, but with the help of friend Shean, sinks himself deeper into his work instead, creating an operetta that his colleagues agree will be a hit. He returns to America and producer Morgan agrees to do the show, as long as MacDonald can star. Although he and MacDonald had considered marriage, Hunter backs away from the girl when he realizes that the singer and composer are still very much in love. The operetta becomes a great success and MacDonald and Ayres happily reunite. Hopelessly melodramatic vehicle for MacDonald's thin lungs, one that fails to create any interest in its characters or its over-produced musical numbers. A mish-mash of visual stylizations during the different numbers creates an incoherent feeling to the film, rendering the emotional values of the story quite cold. Songs: "Broadway Serenade For Every Lonely Heart" (Herbert Stothart, Edward Ward, Gus Kahn, from Tschaikovsky's "None But The Lonely Heart"); "High Flyin'," "One Look At You" (Stothart, Ward, Bob Wright, Chet Forrest); "Time Changes Everything" (Kahn, Walter Donaldson); "Un Bel Di" (from Puccini's "Madame Butterfly"); "No Time To Argue" (Sigmund Romberg, Kahn), "Italian Street Song" (Victor Herbert, Rida Johnson Young); "Les Filles de Cadiz" (Delibes, De Musset); "Quando M'En Vo" ("Musetta's Waltz" from Puccini's "La Boheme"); "Musical Contract" (Stothart, Ward).

p&d, Robert Z. Leonard; w, Charles Lederer (based on a story by Lew Lipton, John Taintor Foote, Hans Kraly); ph, Oliver T. Marsh; ed, Harold F. Kress; ch, Seymour Felix, Busby Berkeley.

Musical **(PR:A MPAA:NR)**

BROADWAY THROUGH A KEYHOLE 1/2** (1933) UA/FOX 90m bw

Constance Cummings *(Joan Whelan)*, Russ Columbo *(Clark Brian)*, Paul Kelly *(Frank Rocci)*, Blossom Seeley *(Sybil Smith)*, Gregory Ratoff *(Max Mefooski)*, Texas Guinan *(Tex Kaley)*, Hugh O'Connell *(Chuck Haskins)*, Hobart Cavanaugh *(Peanuts Dinwiddie)*, C. Henry Gordon *(Tim Crowley)*, William Burress *(Thomas Barnum)*, Helen Jerome Eddy *(Esther)*.

As its title indicates, this is a small picture but nonetheless entertaining. Poultry racketeer Kelly falls for chorus girl Cummings and buys her a night club. In that club band leader Columbo's smooth and soft voice rings out. The lawbreaker loves Cummings but is willing to give her up at the cost of his life to the crooner whose love for her is even stronger. Kelly takes a bullet while trying to save Cummings from kidnapers on her wedding day. Lying in the hospital, he hears Walter Winchell hail him as a hero on the radio and learns that the rival who tried to kidnap his sweetheart is wiped out. Nothing to sing about.

d, Lowell Sherman; w, Gene Towne, Graham Baker (based on a story by Walter Winchell); ph, Barney McGill; m, Mack Gordon, Harry Revel; md, Alfred Newman.

Musical/Drama **(PR:A MPAA:NR)**

BROADWAY TO CHEYENNE**
(1932) 62m MON bw (GB: FROM BROADWAY TO CHEYENNE)

Rex Bell, Marceline Day, Mathew Betz, George Hayes, Robert Ellis, Huntley Gordon, Earl Dwire, John Elliott, Al Bridge, Harry Semels, Gwen Lee, Roy D'Arcy, Rae Daggett.

A gang of Broadway derelicts head west to conquer new territory but find a man they tried to kill out in New York is recovering on his father's ranch. This man, Bell, creates their eventual downfall as he runs them out of town. Action-filled, with hard riding, gun battles and fist fights galore.

p, Trem Carr; d, Harry Fraser; w, Wellyn Totman and Harry Fraser.

Western **(PR:A MPAA:NR)**

BROADWAY TO HOLLYWOOD 1/2**
(1933) 88m MGM bw (GB: RING UP THE CURTAIN)

Alice Brady *(Lulu Hackett)*, Frank Morgan *(Ted Hackett)*, Madge Evans *(Anne Ainslee)*, Russell Hardie *(Ted Hackett, Jr.)*, Jackie Cooper *(Ted Hackett, Jr., as a Child)*, Eddie Quillan *(Ted the Third)*, Mickey Rooney *(Ted the Third, as a Child)*, Tad Alexander *(David)*, Edward Brophy *(Joe Mannion)*, Ruth Channing *(Wanda)*, Jean Howard *(Grace)*, Jimmy Durante, Fay Templeton, May Robson, Claire DuBrey, Muriel Evans, Claude Kaye, Nelson Eddy, Una Merkel, Albertina Rasch Dancers.

Popular vaudeville couple Morgan and Brady take time off from show business when Brady learns that she is pregnant. Losing their headliner status because of their absence from the stage, Morgan and Brady get back in the limelight when their new-grown son Hardie catches the public's eye. Breaking up the family trip to join a very successful company and to marry pretty hoofer Evans, Hardie turns his back on his mother and father. Becoming a womanizer and a drunk, Hardie is not to be found when Evans has their child and commits suicide soon after the boy's birth. Hardie joins the army at the outbreak of WW I in an effort to cleanse his soul and is killed while fighting. Morgan and Brady raise the child and again become popular stage stars with the boy adding to their act. As a man, their grandson (Quillan) is invited to star in a Hollywood musical and flies to California. Tempted by the hedonistic lifestyle he sees there, and without his grandparent's guidance, he comes close to becoming a drunken loser like his father, before concentrating on his film work. On a visit to grandson Quillan's set during a shoot, Morgan dies in Brady's arms. Owing what little charm it has to Morgan's intelligent and sensitive performance, the film as a whole fails to create any interest in the trials and tribulations of its show business family. Although it was initially intended as a vehicle in which to include footage from MGM's ill-conceived Technicolor musical, THE MARCH OF TIME, BROADWAY TO HOLLYWOOD contains very little from that never-released epic. Songs: "We Are The Hacketts" (Al Goodhart); "When Old New York Was Young" (Howard Johnson, Gus Edwards); "Ma Blushin' Rosie" (Edgar Smith, John Stromberg); "Come Down Ma Evenin' Star" (Robert B. Smith, Stromberg); "The Honeysuckle And The Bee" (Albert H. Fitz, William H. Penn).

d, Willard Mack; w, Mack, Edgar Allan Woolf; ph, William Daniels, Norbert Brodine; ed, William S. Gray, Ben Lewis; md, Dr. William Axt; art d, Stanwood Rogers.

Musical **(PR:A MPAA:NR)**

BROKEN ARROW* 1/2** (1950) 93m FOX c

James Stewart *(Tom Jeffords)*, Jeff Chandler *(Cochise)*, Debra Paget *(Sonseeahray)*, Basil Ruysdael *(Gen. Howard)*, Will Geer *(Ben Slade)*, Joyce MacKenzie *(Terry)*, Arthur Hunnicutt *(Duffield)*, Raymond Bramley *(Col. Bernall)*, Jay Silverheels *(Goklia)*, Argentina Brunetti *(Nalikadeya)*, Jack Lee *(Boucher)*, Robert Adler *(Lonergan)*, Harry Carter *(Miner)*, Robert Griffin *(Lowrie)*, Bill Wilkerson *(Juan)*, Micky Kuhn *(Chip Slade)*, Chris Willow Bird *(Nochalo)*, J.W. Cody *(Pionsenay)*, John War Eagle *(Nahilzay)*, Charles Soldani *(Skinyea)*, Iron Eyes Cody *(Teese)*, Robert Foster Dover *(Machogee)*, John Marston *(Maury)*, Edwin Rand *(Sergeant)*, John Doucette *(Mule Driver)*.

Arizona is the background for this beautifully photographed story dealing with the conflict between whites and Apaches in the 1870s. This superb western is one of the earliest treating the problems of Indians seriously and sympathetically. Later films would lay the blame for the scandalous treatment of Indians at the door of the Indian Bureau and Washington business interests, but in this film it was renegades and crooked traders who were at fault. In a departure from the usual Indian fare, and based on some actual events, the script examines their ways, showing how Indians differ from the white culture and uses the artifacts of white and Indian existence, along with the Arizona landscape, to portray the story. Stewart, as the young frontiersman, tired of the mutual massacre of whites and Indians visits the feared Apache leader, Cochise (Chandler) to propose a truce. Not only does the meeting succeed but Stewart falls in love with an Indian maiden (Paget). Both truce and troth are impeded by treachery and peace only comes after the Indian girl, now married to Stewart, is killed by whites from ambush, incurring Stewart's wrath which is held in check by the wise Cochise. In scripting, direction, and performance this film is superior and Chandler invests a great deal of dignity in his role as Cochise. To give this film realism, cast and crew were transported to the site where the events actually occurred eighty years earlier. One of the problems in this isolated area was processing the film, since there were, of course, no film laboratories in the Arizona mountains. An Indian runner was used to rush the undeveloped stock on foot some thirty miles to a waiting car, which then raced it to a distant lab. It was returned as quickly as the runner could carry it. Researchers provided extensive information regarding the life style of the Apaches partly due to the fact that over 400 Apaches were working in the film, but one, Jim Red Finger, for his role in the film, had to wear a buckskin shirt due to the fact that his torso contained a large tattoo which read: "Remember Pearl Harbor." In another incident, when instructed to make fire grates and a bough bed in the traditional Apache manner, the stunned director Daves found his Indians consulting The Boy Scouts' "Handicraft Book." And as though there weren't already enough misconceptions, an archery expert had to teach many Apaches how to use a bow and arrow.

p, Julian Blaustein; d, Delmer Daves; w, Michael Blankfort (based on the novel *Blood Brother* by Elliott Arnold), ph, Ernest Palmer (Technicolor); m, Alfred Newman; ed, J. Watson Webb, Jr.; art d, Lyle Wheeler, Arthur Hogsett.

Western **(PR:A MPAA:NR)**

BROKEN BLOSSOMS* 1/2 (1936, Brit.) 78m Twickenham bw

Dolly Haas *(Lucy Burrows)*, Emlyn Williams *(Chen)*, Arthur Margetson *(Battling Burrows)*, Gibb McLaughlin *(Evil Eye)*, Donald Calthrop *(Old Chinaman)*, Ernest Sefton *(Manager)*, Jerry Verno *(Bert)*, Bertha Belmore *(Daisy)*, Ernest Jay *(Alf)*, C. V. France *(High Priest)*, Kathleen Harrison *(Mrs. Lossy)*, Basil Radford *(Mr. Reed)*.

D. W. Griffith made this story of a mystic romance between a young Chinese and a cockney maid as a silent when he was at the height of his success. He also conferred with the English organization before the remake was undertaken but after some preliminary work, bowed out, which may have contributed to the film's maudlin bathos and resultant failure. Based on Thomas Burke's Limehouse story, "The Chink and the Child," the film concerns the young couple who meet in the slums of London. The girl is fleeing her drunken and browbeating father and is befriended by a young Chinese youth who hides her, treats her with kindness, and dresses her up in Oriental costumes. Her father learns of her whereabouts and kills her. This production should never have been made in light of Griffith's silent masterpiece.

p, Julius Hagen; d, Hans Brahm; w, Emlyn Williams (based on the story "The Chink and the Child" by Thomas Burke and screenplay by D. W. Griffith); ph, Curt Courant.

Drama **(PR:A MPAA:NR)**

BROKEN DREAMS** (1933) 68m MON bw

Randolph Scott *(Dr. Robert Morley)*, Martha Sleeper *(Martha Morley)*, Joseph Cawthorn *(Pop)*, Beryl Mercer *(Mom)*, Buster Phelps *(Billy Morley)*, Adele St. Maur *(Madamoiselle)*.

Maudlin story has Scott rejecting his son Phelps, blaming him for his wife's death (she perishes in childbirth). Phelps is sent to live with relatives but after six years Scott wants his son back. The relatives give him a battle but he wins out only to deal with subsequent problems between his son and his second wife, Sleeper. An uninspiring tearjerker.

d, Robert Vignola; w, Olga Printzlau, Maude Fulton; ph, Robert Planck.

Drama **(PR:A MPAA:NR)**

BROKEN ENGLISH* 1/2 (1981) 93m Lorimar c

Beverly Ross *(Sarah)*, Jacques Martial *(Maas)*, Greta Rannigen *(Leslie)*, Mansour Sy

(Cheekh), Oona Chaplin *(Sarah's Mother)*, Frankie Stein *(Cecile)*, Sandy Whitelaw *(Arms Dealer)*, Assane Fall *(Amidau)*, Valery Kling *(Agency Woman)*, Michel Nicolini *(Merchant)*, Serge Rynecki *(Jacques)*, Reginald Huegenin *(Pat)*, Makhete Diallo *(Makhete)*.

Miscegenation saga about a white woman from the US and a black African from Nambia. Lots of locations from Paris to Senegal to Tunis to Marseilles, so it looks like a bigger picture than it actually is. It has to do with politics and the hell that the Africans go through, have gone through, and will continue to go through until a united Africa is formed. There are partial English subtitles and very little violence, gratuitous or otherwise. The big question is: what is Charlie Chapin's widow doing in this film? The luminous Oona O'Neil was approaching 60, didn't need the money, so why would she take a role in such an inconsequential film?

p, Keith Rothman, Bert Schneider; d, Michi Gleason; w, Gleason; ph, Elliot Davis; m, George Delerue; ed, Suzanne Senn.

Drama **(PR:O MPAA:NR)**

BROKEN HORSESHOE, THE* (1953, Brit.) 79m Nettlefold/BUT bw

Robert Beatty *(Dr. Mark Fenton)*, Elizabeth Sellars *(Della Freman)*, Peter Coke *(Insp. Bellamy)*, Vida Hope *(Jackie Leroy)*, Ferdy Mayne *(Charles Constance)*, James Raglan *(Supt. Grayson)*, Hugh Pryse *(Mr. Rattray)*, Hugh Kelly *(Dr. Craig)*, Janet Butler *(Sister Rogers)*, George Benson *(Prescott)*, Ronald Leigh Hunt *(Sgt. Lewis)*.

Doctor Beatty gets caught up with narcotic smugglers, which leads police to suspect he is involved. Femme fatale Sellars clears him of suspicion in the end.

p, Ernest G. Roy; d, Martyn C. Webster; w, A. R. Rawlinson (based on the TV serial by Francis Durbridge); ph, Gerald Gibbs, Noel Rowland.

Crime **(PR:A MPAA:NR)**

BROKEN JOURNEY*** (1948, Brit.) 89m Gainsborough/GFD bw

Phyllis Calvert *(Mary Johnstone)*, Margot Grahame *(Joanna Dane)*, James Donald *(Bill Haverton)*, Francis L. Sullivan *(Anton Perami)*, Raymond Huntley *(Edward Marshall)*, Derek Bond *(Richard Faber)*, Guy Rolfe *(Capt. Fox)*, Sonia Holm *(Anne Stevens)*, David Tomlinson *(Jimmy Marshall)*, Andrew Crawford *(Kid Cormack)*, Charles Victor *(Harry Gunn)*, Grey Blake *(John Barber)*, Gerald Heinz *(Joseph Romer)*, Sybilla Binder *(Lilli Romer)*, Amy Frank *(Frau Romer)*, Michael Allan *(Lt. Albert)*, R. Stuart Lindsell *(Mr. Barber)*, Mary Hinton *(Mrs. Barber)*.

Plane travelers from all walks of life, many in front of the public eye, find meaning in their lives when a crash in the Alps challenges their strength of character. A well-done disaster movie with top performances by Calvert, Grahame, Bond, Sullivan, and others; based upon an actual plane crash in the Alps and the dramatic rescue of survivors.

p, Sidney Box; d, Ken Annakin; w, Robert Westerby; ph, David Harcourt.

Drama/Adventure **(PR:A MPAA:NR)**

BROKEN LANCE*1/2** (1954) 96m FOX c

Spencer Tracy *(Matt Devereaux)*, Robert Wagner *(Joe Devereaux)*, Jean Peters *(Barbara)*, Richard Widmark *(Ben)*, Katy Jurado *(Senora Devereaux)*, Hugh O'Brian *(Mike Devereaux)*, Eduard Franz *(Two Moons)*, Earl Holliman *(Denny Devereaux)*, E. G. Marshall *(The Governor)*, Carl Benton Reid *(Clem Lawton)*, Philip Ober *(Van Cleve)*, Robert Burton *(Mac Andrews)*, Robert Adler *(O'Reilly)*, Robert Grandin *(Capitol Clerk)*, Harry Carter *(Prison Guard)*, Nacho Galindo *(Cook)*, Julian Rivero *(Manuel)*, Edmund Cobb *(Court Clerk)*, Russell Simpson *(Judge)*, King Donovan *(Clerk)*, Jack Mather *(Gateman)*, George E. Stone *(Paymaster)*, John Eppers *(Ranger)*, Paul Kruger *(Bailiff)*, James F. Stone *(Stable Owner)*.

On the day of his release from prison, Wagner recalls the events that led up to his imprisonment. Years earlier, his proud and stubborn cattle baron father, Tracy, led a destructive raid on a copper mine that was polluting the water on his land, threatening the welfare of his stock. Although Tracy had treated Wagner and his three brothers, Widmark, O'Brian, and Holliman, as nothing more than ranch hands, never showing them sympathy or understanding, Wagner claimed responsibility for the raid to save Tracy, whom he really loved. Now, after his jail stretch, Wagner returns to the ranch with the intent of violently getting back at his brothers who rebelled against Tracy and pushed him towards a fatal stroke. Tracy's Mexican wife Jurado persuades her son Wagner not to go through with his plans for revenge, but the twisted Widmark forces Wagner into a fight. In the struggle, Widmark is killed and Wagner regains control of the ranch. A western reworking of Joseph L. Mankiewicz's HOUSE OF STRANGERS, BROKEN LANCE succeeds in capturing the brutal intensity of a disrupted family. Tracy is marvelous as the hardened father who, while saddened by civilization's intrusion on the West, is determined to instill the hard-working, fighting spirit of the pioneers into his sons. His inability to express emotion to them creates dissension in the sadistic Widmark, but generates respect from the understanding Wagner. As the opposing sons, Widmark and Wagner do very well, with the former turning in one of his finest variations on his patented "ruthless male image." Director Dmytryk uses his CinemaScope compositions to convey the vast beauty and imposing qualities of the land around the family, nicely balancing the turmoil within the comparatively insignificant group.

p, Sol C. Siegel; d, Edward Dmytryk; w, Richard Murphy (based on a story by Philip Yordan); ph, Joe MacDonald (CinemaScope, DeLuxe Color); m, Leigh Harline; ed, Dorothy Spencer; md, Lionel Newman; art d, Lyle Wheeler, Maurice Ransford; set dr, Walter Scott, Stuart Reiss; cos, Travilla.

Western Drama **(PR:A MPAA:NR)**

BROKEN LAND, THE** (1962) 60m FOX c

Kent Taylor *(Marshall)*, Diana Darrin *(Waitress)*, Jody McCrea *(Deputy)*, Jack Nicholson, Gary Snead, Robert Sampson.

Harmless son of a famous gunfighter Nicholson escapes the clutches of overzealous sheriff Taylor with the aid of buddies Snead and Sampson. Nothing extraordinary and only mildly entertaining.

p, Leonard A. Schwartz; d, John Bushelman; w, Russ Bender, Edith Pearl, Edward Lasko; m, Richard LaSalle (CinemaScope, DeLuxe Color).

Western **(PR:A MPAA:NR)**

BROKEN LOVE** (1946, Ital.) 89m Suprafilm bw

Beniamino Gigli *(Luciano Riccardi)*, Emma Gramatica *(Letlzia)*, Camilla Horn *(Claudia Riccardi)*, Ruth Hellberg *(Corinna Delly)*, Herbert Wilk *(Alberto Vieri)*.

Daughter Horn of famous tenor Gigli has a weak heart but falls in love with bank clerk Wilk only to have the wimp snapped away by former mistress Hellberg. Production slick but the acting is only average. (In Italian, English subtitles.)

d, Guido Brignone; m, Giacomo Puccini.

Drama **(PR:A MPAA:NR)**

BROKEN LULLABY*** (1932) 77m PAR bw (GB: THE MAN I KILLED)

Lionel Barrymore *(Dr. Holderlin)*, Nancy Carroll *(Elsa)*, Phillips Holmes *(Paul)*, Tom Douglas *(Walter Holderlin)*, ZaSu Pitts *(Anna)*, Lucien Littlefield *(Schultz)*, Louise Carter *(Frau Holderlin)*, Frank Sheridan *(Priest)*, George Bickel *(Bresslauer)*, Emma Dunn *(Frau Muller)*, Tully Marshall *(Gravedigger)*, Lillian Elliott *(Frau Bresslauer)*, Marvin Stephens *(Fritz)*, Reginald Pasch *(Fritz's Father)*, Joan Standing *(Flower Shop Girl)*, Rodney McKennon *(War Veteran)*, Torben Meyer *(Waiter at Inn)*.

Urbane and charming Lubitsch gives up his sophisticated comedy style that became known as "the Lubitsch touch" for a deeply felt look at his native Germany after WW I, and the result is "the best talking picture that has yet been seen and heard," according to playwright Robert Sherwood. A somber, offbeat drama and a fierce antiwar document, BROKEN LULLABY tells the story of a young Frenchman who goes to Germany to seek out the family of a soldier he killed during the war and beg forgiveness. When he does find the man's kinfolk, they accept him as a friend. The film was Lubitsch's only dramatic sound film and surprised his international following of the time which was used to the wit of his escapist comedies, but it won a wide audience.

d, Ernst Lubitsch; w, Ernest Vajda, Samson Raphaelson (based on the play "L'Homme Que J'ai Tue," by Maurice Rostand, adpated by Reginald Berkeley); ph, Victor Milner; set d, Hans Dreier.

Drama **(PR:A MPAA:NR)**

BROKEN MELODY, THE*1/2

(1934, Brit.) 84m Twickenham/AP&D bw (AKA: VAGABOND VIOLINIST)

John Garrick *(Paul Verlaine)*, Margot Grahame *(Simone St. Clair)*, Merle Oberon *(Germaine)*, Austin Trevor *(Pierre)*, Charles Carson *(Dubonnet)*, Harry Terry *(Henri)*, Andrea Malandrinos *(Brissard)*, Tonie Edgar Bruce *(Vera)*.

A composer of classical music murders his wife's lover. From that action he finds the inspiration to write an opera after escaping from Devil's Island. Far-fetched yarn in a shallow production.

p, Julius Hagen; d, Bernard Vorhaus; w, Vera Allinson, Michael Hankinson, H. Fowler Mear (based on a story by Vorhaus); ph, Sydney Blythe.

Musical **(PR:A MPAA:NR)**

BROKEN MELODY*1/2 (1938, Aus.) 98m Cinesound/British Empire Films bw

Lloyd Hughes, Diana Du Cane, Rosalind Kennerdale, Frank Harvey, Alec Kellaway.

Outcast boat race winner with untapped musical ability Hughes finds happiness with the girl he lost when he writes a successful opera and is taken back into good graces. Confused script does not allow the cast members to shine.

p&d, Ken G. Hall; w, F. W. Thwaites, Frank Harvey; ph, George Heath; m, Alfred Hill; md, Hamilton Webber.

Drama **(PR:A MPAA:NR)**

BROKEN ROSARY, THE* (1934, Brit.) 85m BUT bw

Derek Oldham *(Giovanni)*, Jean Adrienne *(Maria)*, Vesta Victoria *(Vesta)*, Ronald Ward *(Jack)*, Marjorie Corbett *(Celia)*, Margaret Yarde *(Nanny)*, Evelyn Roberts *(Uncle Jack)*, Dino Galvani *(Carlo)*, Fred Rains *(Professor)*, Ian Wilson *(Hodge)*.

In a love triangle, an Italian singer loses his sweetheart to his best friend. Would play better with a libretto including the poem from which the story came. Archaic and uninspiring.

p, Wilfred Noy; d, Harry Hughes; w, Adelaide Proctor (based on her poem "Legend of Provence").

Musical **(PR:A MPAA:NR)**

BROKEN STAR, THE** (1956) 82m UA bw

Howard Duff *(Frank Smead)*, Lita Baron *(Conchita)*, Bill Williams *(Bill Gentry)*, Henry Calvin *(Thornton Wills)*, Douglas Fowley *(Hiram Charleton)*, Addison Richards *(Wayne Forrester)*, Joel Ashley *(Messendyke)*, John Pickard *(Van Horn)*, William Phillips *(Doc Mott)*, Dorothy Adams *(Mrs. Trail)*, Joe Dominguez *(Nachez)*.

Deputy marshal Duff crosses over to the crooked side of the law when he steals gold paid to a rancher by settlers for water rights. Direction sags in the middle but is covered by adequate acting by Duff and Baron. Fair fight at the finish.

p, Howard W. Koch; d, Lesley Selander; w, John C. Higgins; ph, William Margulies; m, Paul Dunlap; ed, John F. Schreyer.

Western **(PR:A MPAA:NR)**

BROKEN WING, THE* (1932) PAR 71m bw

Lupe Velez *(Lolita)*, Leo Carrillo *(Capt. Innocencio)*, Melvyn Douglas *(Phil Marvin)*, George Barbier *(Luther Farley)*, Willard Robertson *(Sylvester Cross)*, Claire Dodd *(Cecelia Cross)*, Arthur Stone *(Justin Bailey)*, Soledad Jiminez *(Maria)*, Julian Rivero *(Bassilio)*, Pietro Sosso *(Pancho)*, Chris-Pin Martin *(Mexican Husband)*, Charles Stevens *(Chicken Thief)*, Joe Dominquez *(Captain)*.

Outlaw Carillo is on the make for Velez but finds she's crazy for crashed aviator Douglas who accepts her affections. Velez is, as usual, fiery and animated but the tame script causes her to appear a bit slaphappy. The sophisticated Douglas is completely out of place in this oddball oater.

d, Lloyd Corrigan; w, Grover Jones, William Slavens McNutt (based on a play by Paul Dickey and Charles W. Goddard); ph, Henry Sharp.

Western **(PR:A MPAA:NR)**

BRONCO BILLY*** (1980) 119m WB c

Clint Eastwood *(Bronco Billy)*, Sondra Locke *(Antoinette)*, Geoffrey Lewis *(John Arlington)*, Sam Bottoms *(Leonard)*, Scatman Crothers *(Doc Lynch)*, Bill McKinney *(Lefty LeBow)*, Dan Vadis *(Chief Big Eagle)*, Sierra Pecheur *(Lorraine Running Water)*, Tanya Russell *(Doris Duke)*, William Prince *(Edgar)*, Tessa Richarde *(Mitzi Fritz)*, Walter Barnes *(Sheriff Dix)*, Beverlee McKinsey *(Irene)*, Woodrow Parfrey *(Dr. Canterbury)*, Douglas McGrath *(Lt. Wiecker)*, Hank Worden *(Mechanic)*, Pam Abbass *(Mother Superior)*, Edye Byrde *(Eloise)*, Michael Reinbold *(King)*, Douglas Copsey, Robert Dale Simmons *(Reporters at Bank)*, John Wesley Elliott, Jr.

(Sanatorium Attendant), George Orrison, Chuck Hicks, Bobby Hoy *(Cowboys at Bar)*, Jefferson Jewell *(Boy at Bank)*, Don Mummert *(Chauffeur)*, Lloyd Nelson *(Sanatorium Policeman)*, Sharon Sherlock *(License Clerk)*, James Simmerhan *(Bank Manager)*, Roger Dale Simmons, Jenny Sternling *(Reporters at Sanatorium)*, *Chuck Waters, Jerry Willis (Bank Robbers)*, Michael Reinbold *(King)*, Tessa Richarde *(Mitzi Fritts)*, Tanya Russell *(Doris Duke)*, Valerie Shanks *(Sister Maria)*.

BRONCO BILLY was Clint Eastwood's seventh directorial assignment and he believed that, after the success of his comedy EVERY WHICH WAY BUT LOOSE, this one would knock 'em dead. He was wrong. People stayed away and executives at the studio are still trying to figure out why. It's a human comedy about a Wild West show peopled by losers Billy has picked up in his travels. Eastwood is perfection as the New Jersey shoe clerk, like Miniver Cheevey, dreamed of an earlier day and took action to realize his dream. He could have gone over the top in satirizing the very character that he played so well in all the spaghetti westerns, but he preferred to exhibit superb taste and hewed so closely to truth that this should clam up detractors who thought Eastwood could only be a No Name drifter or Dirty Harry. Every single role is played with love and affection and reality in this paean of praise to days that once were. So why wasn't it a hit? Well, y'see, buckaroo, it's like this: The Public wants to see Clint shoot 'em up for *real*. Just as they won't buy Burt Reynolds as a sensitive human being (THE END, BEST FRIENDS) but flock to see him in mindless chase films (HOOPER, SMOKEY AND THE BANDIT), the same applies here. Actors like Eastwood are unfortunately typecast as stars, whereas actors like Alan Arkin are never typecast because they play so many roles and they never *become* stars. You can't have it all. The worst of it is that Eastwood, ever since he directed the Bill Holden/Kay Lenz BREEZY, has been getting better and better, but it will still be a while until the "establishment" takes him as a serious director. Eastwood made a wonderful movie with BRONCO BILLY and if he had dispensed with the services of the talentless Locke and hired a Goldie Hawn or equivalent, this film would have been better. Songs: "Misery and Gin" (J. Durrill, Snuff Garrett); "Cowboys and Clowns" (S. Dorff, G. Harju, L. Herbstritt, Garrett); title song (M. Brown, Dorff, Garrett); "Barroom Buddies" (Brown, C. Crofford, Dorff, Garrett); "Bayou Lullaby" (Crofford, Garrett).

p, Dennis Hackin, Neal Bobrofsky; d, Clint Eastwood; w, Hackin; ph, David Worth (DeLuxe Color); m, Snuff Garrett; ed, Ferris Webster, Joel Cox.

Comedy/Western Cas. (PR:C MPAA:PG)

BRONCO BULLFROG* (1972, Brit.) 86m Maya/BL bw

Del Walker *(Del)*, Anne Gooding *(Irene)*, Sam Shepherd *(Jo Bronco Bullfrog)*, Roy Haywood *(Roy)*, Freda Shepherd *(Mrs. Richardson)*, Dick Philpott *(Del's Father)*, Chris Shepherd *(Chris)*, Stuart Stones *(Sgt.)*, Geoff Wincott *(Geoff)*.

In their quest for excitement and adventure, East End teenagers in London get involved with a fugitive from Borstal prison in Ireland. Just plain silly.

p, Andrew St. John; d&w, Barney Platts-Mills.

Drama (PR:A MPAA:NR)

BRONCO BUSTER 1/2** (1952) 80m UNIV c

John Lund *(Tom Moody)*, Scott Brady *(Bart Eaton)*, Joyce Holden *(Judy Bream)*, Chill Wills *(Dan Bream)*, Don Haggerty *(Dobie)*, Dan Poore *(Elliott)*, Casey Tibbs, Pete Crump, Bill Williams, Jerry Ambler.

Champion rodeo rider Lund takes Brady under his wing, teaches him what he knows, and gets slapped and stomped on when Brady steals his long-time sweetheart Holden, then gets humbled after grandstanding when he permanently injures Wills, the father and rodeo clown. Excellent scripting and directing. Real rodeo footage adds authentic excitement.

p, Ted Richmond; d, Budd Boetticher; w, Horace McCoy, Lillie Hayward (based on a story by Peter B. Kyne); ph, Clifford Stine; ed, Edward Curtiss.

Western (PR:A MPAA:NR)

BRONTE SISTERS, THE** (1979, Fr.) 115m GAU c (LE SOEURS BRONTE)

Isabelle Adjani *(Emily)*, Isabelle Huppert *(Anne)*, Marie-France Pisier *(Charlotte)*, Pascal Greggory *(Branwell)*, Patrick Magee *(Father)*, Helen Surgere *(Mrs. Robinson)*, Roland Bertin *(Nicholls)*.

The tragic story of three sisters who might have been invented by Chekhov had they not actually lived. This picture, like most films about writers, is boring. How is a director supposed to show a brilliant writer creating? Chew the pencil, tear paper up and toss it in the trash? What does a writer do that would be interesting to see? Hemingway lived a wild life, so did Fitzgerald. In that, they are characters. But the three Bronte sisters sat around, argued with their Father, doted on their brother, wrote a few good books and died too early. Charlotte, author of *Jane Eyre*—lived to be all of 39 and she was the last one to go. Emily barely made 30 and Anne didn't survive tuberculosis at 29. As with so many writers, their work was more intriguing than their lives. THE BRONTE SISTERS accurately recreates the period, looks lovely and sheds no new light on the subject. Read the many biographies if you're that interested. Better yet, read their writings. Instead of rebelling against their existences, they wrote about it and the parallel of their lives, both real and fantasy, with their literary output, is the most fascinating part of the tale.

d, Andre Techine; w, Techine, Pascal Bonitzer, Jean Gruault; ph, Bruno Nuytten (Eastmancolor); m, Phillippe Sarde; ed, Claudine Merlin.

Biography (PR:A MPAA:NR)

BRONX WARRIORS (SEE: 1990: THE BRONX WARRIORS)

BRONZE BUCKAROO, THE** (1939) 57m Hollywood Productions bw

Herbert Jeffries, Artie Young, Rellie Hardin, Spencer Williams, Clarence Brooks, F.E. Miller

Jeffries and Brooks fight it out on the plains in a gun battle intended to avenge the murder of Young's father. Technical efforts nothing special, although the all black cast and crew, complete with singing hero, renders commendable performances.

p,d&w, Richard Kahn; ph, Roland Price.

Western (PR:A MPAA:NR)

BROOD, THE* 1/2 (1979, Can.) 91m New World c

Oliver Reed *(Dr. Raglan)*, Samantha Eggar *(Nola)*, Art Hindle *(Frank)*, Cindy Hinds *(Candice)*, Nuala Fitzgerald *(Julianna)*, Henry Beckerman *(Barton Kelly)*, Susan Hogan *(Ruth)*, Michael McGhee *(Inspector Mrazek)*, Gary McKeehan *(Mike Trellan)*, Bob Silverman *(Jan)*, Nicholas Campbell *(Chris)*.

Cronenberg is a young director who is establishing a cult of fans who pant expectantly for everything he does. After a slick start with RABID and THEY CAME FROM WITHIN, he seems to be getting worse instead of improving. THE BROOD is yet another of those movies where children are shown to be monsters. It's filled with creatures, malformations, and strange growths. (Cronenberg had his special effects yecchhh people working overtime on this one.) Reed is a mad doctor (well, angry, anyhow) who learns how to harness rage in people. This rage is manifested in creatures known as The Brood. Eggar is the woman who erupts. In the end, The Brood kills Reed, Eggar's husband strangles her, and there are enough disgusting doings to make any horrorphile happy. For such a rotten picture, it is fairly esoteric.

p, Claude Heroux; d&w, David Cronenberg; ph, Mark Irwin; ed, Allan Collins.

Horror Cas. (PR:C MPAA:R)

BROOKLYN ORCHID* (1942) 81m UA bw

William Bendix *(Tim McGuerin)*, Joe Sawyer *(Eddie Corbett)*, Marjorie Woodworth *(Lucy Gibbs)*, Grace Bradley *(Sadie McGuerin)*, Skeets Gallagher *(Tommy Goodweek)*, Florine McKinney *(Mable Cooney)*, Leonid Kinskey *(Ignatz Rochkowsky)*, Rex Evans *(Sterling)*, Jack Norton *(Jonathan McFeeder)*.

Romp at a mountain resort has fleet of taxi operators Bendix and Sawyer fishing Woodworth out of the river, saving her from a suicide attempt. Bradley, Bendix's wife, attempts to separate the threesome when the rescued maiden attaches herself to the buddies. Unfunny programmer.

p, Hal Roach; d, Earle Snell, Clarence Marks; ph, Robert Pittack; ed, Ray Snyder; spec eff, Roy Seawright.

Comedy (PR:A MPAA:NR)

BROTH OF A BOY* 1/2 (1959, Brit.) Emmett Dalton/BL 77m bw

Barry Fitzgerald *(Patrick Farrell)*, Harry Brogan *(Willie)*, Tony Wright *(Randall)*, June Thorburn *(Silin Lehane)*, Eddie Golden *(Martin Lehane)*, Maire Kean *(Molly Lehane)*, Godfrey Quigley *(Desmond Phillips)*, Bart Bastable *(Clooney)*, Dermot Kelly *(Tim)*, Cecil Barror *(O'Shaughnessy)*, Josephine Fitzgerald *(Mrs. O'Shaughnessy)*, Philip O'Flynn *(Father Carey)*, Dennis Brennan *(Bolger)*, Bill Foley *(Connolly)*.

Dumb film about a mean old poacher who refuses to accept an invitation to appear on television on his 110th birthday. Bad script, acting, and direction.

p, Alec Snowden; d, George Pollack; w, Patrick Kirwan, Blanaid Irvine (based onthe play "The Big Birthday" by Hugh Leonard); m, Stanley Black; ph, Walter J. Harvey.

Comedy (PR:A MPAA:NR)

BROTHER ALFRED* (1932, Brit.) 77m Wardour/BIP bw

Gene Gerrard *(George Lattaker)*, Molly Lamont *(Stella)*, Elsie Randolph *(Mamie)*, Bobbie Comber *(Billy Marshall)*, Clifford Heatherley *(Prince Sachsberg)*, Hal Gordon *(Harold Voles)*, Henry Wenman *(Uncle George)*, Blanche Adele *(Pilbeam)*, James Carew *(Mr. Marshall)*, Hugh E. Wright *(Sydney)*, Harvey Braban *(Denis Sturgis)*, Maurice Colbourne *(Equerry)*, Tonie Edgar Bruce *(Mrs. Vandaline)*.

In an effort to win back his fiancee, a man poses as his twin brother in Monte Carlo. Fun and games fall flat in this woeful production.

d, Henry Edwards; w, Edwards, Claude Guerney (based on the play by P.G. Wodehouse, Herbert Westbrook); ph, Walter Harvey, Horace Wheddon.

Comedy (PR:A MPAA:NR)

BROTHER JOHN** (1971) 94m COL c

Sidney Poitier *(John Kane)*, Will Geer *(Doc Thomas)*, Bradford Dillman *(Lloyd Thomas)*, Beverly Todd *(Louisa MacGill)*, Ramon Bieri *(Orly Ball)*, Warren J. Kemmerling *(George)*, Lincoln Kilpatrick *(Charley Gray)*, P. Jay Sidney *(Rev. MacGill)*, Richard Ward *(Frank)*, Paul Winfield *(Henry Birkhardt)*, Zara Cully *(Miss Nettie)*, Michael Bell *(Cleve)*, Howard Rice *(Jimmy)*, Darlene Rice *(Marsha)*, Harry Davis *(Turnkey)*, Lynn Hamilton *(Sarah)*, Gene Tyburn *(Calvin)*, E. A. Nicholson *(Perry)*, Bill Crane *(Bill Jones)*, Richard Bay *(Lab Deputy)*, John Hancock *(Henry's Friend)*, Lynne Arden *(Nurse)*, William Houze *(Motel Owner)*, Maye Henderson, Lois Smith *(Neighbors)*.

Poitier shoots for the perfect character once again as an angel who returns to his Alabama hometown finding the need to resolve all prejudice, hatred, and confusion (in Alabam?). Poitier's excellent performance leaves the audience with much to ponder. Clyde King sins "Children of Summer."

p, Joel Glickman; d, James Goldstone; w, Ernest Kinoy; ph, Gerald Perry Finnerman; m, Quincy Jones; art d, Al Brenner.

Drama (PR:A MPAA:NR)

BROTHER ORCHID* 1/2** (1940) 91m FN/WB bw

Edward G. Robinson *(Little John Sarto)*, Ann Sothern *(Flo Addams)*, Humphrey Bogart *(Jack Buck)*, Donald Crisp *(Brother Superior)*, Ralph Bellamy *(Clarence Fletcher)*, Allen Jenkins *(Willie the Knife)*, Charles D. Brown *(Brother Wren)*, Cecil Kellaway *(Brother Goodwin)*, Morgan Conway *(Philadelphia Powell)*, Richard Lane *(Mugsy O'Day)*, Paul Guilfoyle *(Red Martin)*, John Ridgely *(Texas Pearson)*, Joseph Crehan *(Brother MacEwen)*, Wilfred Lucas *(Brother MacDonald)*, Tom Tyler *(Curley Matthews)*, Dick Wessel *(Buffalo Burns)*, Granville Bates *(Pattonsville Supt.)*, Paul Phillips *(French Frank)*, Don Rowan *(Al Muller)*, Nanette Vallon *(Fifi)*, Tim Ryan *(Turkey Malone)*, Joe Caites *(Handsome Harry)*, Pat Gleason *(Dopey Perkins)*, Tommy Baker *(Joseph)*.

A gangster film with a unique twist, BROTHER ORCHID is a Robinson vehicle crammed with action and not a little bit of pathos. Big-shot gangster Robinson turns over his underworld empire to right-hand man Bogart and sails for Europe and culture. When he returns five years later he expects to take up his old position at the head of the board room table but he finds to his chagrin that Bogie is nailed to the biggest chair. He is told to get out of the rackets but Robinson vows to regain his fiefdom. Robinson finds Jenkins, his most loyal lieutenant, hiding out in a lunatic asylum and he quickly recruits him to begin a new gang. Aiding him is his old girl friend Sothern and a gangling Texas rancher, Bellamy (using the worst western accent ever recorded in films), who is taken with Sothern. But Robinson's inamorata Sothern unwittingly undoes the racketeer. She arranges a meeting between Bogie and Robinson where Bogart's minions snatch Robinson and take him for a ride. He flees into the woods when they stop the car to execute him but he is wounded in his escape. Robinson staggers through the woods and comes upon a retreat where he rings the bell and collapses. He has reached a remote monastery and the monks take him inside, tend to his wound, and allow him to recover. Like Jenkins, he realizes that he has the perfect hideout. He tells Crisp, the Brother Superior, that he wishes to stay on as an apprentice monk. Given chores in the garden, Robinson pays off a local boy to perform his work for him. When he is exposed and shamed before the monks, Robinson apologizes and asks for a chance to redeem himself. This time he goes to work for real, developing the monastery's flower garden, particularly adept at nurturing orchids, so much so that he takes the name of Brother Orchid. When he learns that the monks can no longer sell their flowers in the city, that Bogie's racketeers have taken over all flower distribution, Robinson discards his monk's robe, enlists the aid of Bellamy and fellow Texas ranchers, and invades Bogart's headquarters where a round-house fight ensues. Robinson and Bogart meet head-to-head and Bogie is killed in a gun duel. Robinson then gives up Sothern to Bellamy and returns to the monastery where he has found genuine peace. He enters the monastery dining hall and beams broadly, stating: "This . . . this is the real class." Offbeat, funny, and improbable, BROTHER ORCHID is almost an outright spoof of the gangster films of the 1930s and Robinson broadly caricatures himself in a rollicking farce of tough guys, molls, fast cars, and racket wars.

p, Hal Wallis, Mark Hellinger; d, Lloyd Bacon; w, Earl Baldwin (based on a *Collier's Magazine* article by Richard Connell); ph, Tony Gaudio; m, Heinz Roemheld; ed, William Holmes; art d, Max Parker; cos, Howard Shoup; spec eff, Byron Haskin.

Crime Drama **(PR:A MPAA:NR)**

BROTHER RAT* 1/2** (1938) 90m WB bw

Priscilla Lane *(Joyce Winfree)*, Wayne Morris *(Billy Randolph)*, Johnnie Davis *(A. Furman Townsend, Jr.)*, Jane Bryan *(Kate Rice)*, Eddie Albert *(Bing Edwards)*, Ronald Reagan *(Dan Crawford)*, Jane Wyman *(Claire Adams)*, Henry O'Neill *(Col. Ramm)*, Gordon Oliver *(Capt. "Lacedrawers" Rogers)*, Larry Williams *(Harley Harrington)*, William Tracy *(Mistol Bottom)*, Jessie Busley *(Mrs. Brooks)*, Olin Howland *(Slim)*, Louise Beavers *(Jenny)*, Isabel Withers *(Nurse)*, Robert Scott *(Tripod Andrews)*, Fred Hamilton *(Newsreel Scott)*, Oscar G. Hendrian *(Coach)*.

Two wild-spirited cadets at the Virginia Military Institute, Morris and Reagan, try to hold back their rule-breaking tendencies in the weeks before graduation but things get a bit harried and difficult when their buddy Albert, who is secretly married, learns that his wife is pregnant. When Reagan starts romancing the commandant's daughter Wyman and Morris woos Lane, the pair realize that they haven't shaped up at all and get mixed up in even worse circumstances when they try to hide Albert's wife in the barracks during the pre-graduation football game and prom. All three young men get their diplomas without any of the camp's officers *really* knowing what went on. Very enjoyable adaptation of the Broadway play that made the mistake of altering the original work's inclusion of Albert as the main character and not a secondary one. Although the humdrum Morris is given the leading role, Albert still manages to steal the show as the loving but frenzied cadet. Having won the hearts of New York audiences in the original production, Albert started his wonderful career in film and television with a delightful first appearance in this film. Reagan does well as the playful nice guy, as does Wyman as the restrained daughter of the strict camp commandant. Their meeting during this film prompted their famous romance and marriage.

p, Robert Lord; d, William Keighley; w, Richard Macaulay, Jerry Wald (based on the play by John Monk, Jr., Fred F. Finklehoffe); ph, Ernest Haller; m, Leo F. Forbstein; ed, William Holmes; art d, Max Parker.

Comedy **(PR:A MPAA:NR)**

BROTHER RAT AND A BABY 1/2**
(1940) 87m WB bw (GB: BABY BE GOOD)

Eddie Albert *(Bing Edwards)*, Wayne Morris *(Billy Randolph)*, Priscilla Lane *(Joyce Winfree)*, Jane Wyman *(Claire Ramm)*, Larry Williams *(Harley Harrington)*, Henry O'Neill *(Col. Ramm)*, Jessie Busley *(Mrs. Brooks)*, Peter B. Good *("Commencement")*, Paul Harvey *(Sterling Randolph)*, Berton Churchill *(Mr. Harper)*, Nana Bryant *(Mrs. Harper)*, Arthur Treacher *(McGregor)*, Edward Gargan *(Cab Driver)*, Mayo Methot *(Girl in Bus)*, Billy Wayne *(Expressman)*, Moroni Olsen *(Major)*, Irving Bacon *(Hospital Official)*, Richard Clayton, Alan Ladd, David Willock *(Cadets)*, Sally Sage *(Secretary)*, Tommy Bupp *(Small Boy)*, Granville Bates *(Doctor)*.

Having graduated from the Virginia Military Institute, three comrades settle into the "real" world. Reagan becomes an illustrator, Albert a football coach at a small school, and Morris sponges off of his wealthy publisher father. When Morris becomes deter mined to fulfill Albert's dream of becoming coach at their alma mater, he enlists the aid of Reagan and, after a variety of screw-ups, and finally resorts to placing Albert's precocious baby boy on a plane bound for Peru on a good will mission. The boy is returned and the resulting publicity makes the heads of the Institute offer Albert the position. Albert and Bryan are reunited with their child and Reagan and Morris finally win the hands of their long-time sweethearts, Wyman and Lane. Disappointing sequel to the successful BROTHER RAT. It failed to capture the charm of its predecessor, even though it included the same leading players and was scripted by the original writers. The nature of the humor was distinctly more "screwball" and sadly neglected the humanistic appeal of the first film.

p, Robert Lord; d, Ray Enright; w, Jerry Wald, Richard Macaulay (based on the play, "Brother Rat" by John Monks, Jr., Fred Finklehoffe); ph, Charles Rosher; m, Heinz Roemheld; ed, Clarence Kolster.

Comedy **(PR:A MPAA:NR)**

BROTHER SUN, SISTER MOON***
(1973, Brit./Ital.) 121m Euro International Films/Vic Film/PAR c

Graham Faulkner *(Francesco)*, Judi Bowker *(Clare)*, Alec Guinness *(Pope Innocent III)*, Leigh Lawson *(Bernardo)*, Kenneth Cranham *(Paolo)*, Michael Feast *(Silvestro)*, Nicholas Willatt *(Giocondo)*, Valentina Cortese *(Mother)*, Lee Montague *(Father)*, John Sharp *(Bishop)*, Adolfo Celi *(Consul)*, Francesco Guerrieri *(Deodato)*.

Faulkner, the son of a wealthy factory owner, returns home after fighting in the Crusades. Plagued with a terrible fever, Faulkner begins to have nightmarish visions about war and its inhumanity and his parents become worried. When the fever breaks, Faulkner becomes a changed man, pushing away material goods and opulence and concentrating his efforts on understanding nature and helping the poor. After selling some of his parents' valuables in an effort to raise money for the needy, Faulkner is severely beaten by his father and is ordered to confess the stupidity of his ways to the town. Faulkner refuses, dons very simple garments, and starts an order of monks with friends of his from the war. They travel from town to town, assisting the downtrodden and preaching the appreciation of the simplicity of life and the need to denounce materialism. Hoping to make their order legitimate, Faulkner and his followers travel to Rome and are granted an audience with the Pope, Guinness. Jeered at by the majority of the extravagantly dressed Catholic kingpins, Faulkner is praised by the understanding Guinness, who has become disillusioned by the indulgences of the Church. Kissing Faulkner's feet, Guinness symbolically gives importance and meaning to Faulkner and his ideas. Director Zeffirelli's attempt to relate the story of Francis of Assisi and his followers to the philosophy of the hippies and flower children of the 1960s is rather silly, but his emotional understanding of his characters, their feelings, and the world that they live in far outweigh his methaphorical urges. Beautifully visualized, the film vividly creates the atmosphere needed to contrast Faulkner's natural world and the harsh realities of the one he lives in. Faulkner is good at conveying the mysticism of Assisi's thoughts and desires, but does little to generate empathy for the *man.* Far superior is Judi Bowker as a beautiful, innocent girl who finally leaves her rich family to follow Faulkner. She effectively portrays the longing of a young girl and the appeal of forsaking everything she has been told to appreciate. Pretentious and slow-moving, the film is still entertaining thanks to the director's natural ability to care about his characters and his actors. Another version of this saint's life, FRANCIS OF ASSISI, with Bradford Dillman in the title role, uses the epic approach.

p, Luciano Perugia; d, Franco Zeffirelli; w, Suso Cecchi d'Amico, Kenneth Ross, Lina Wertmuller, Zeffirelli; ph, Ennio Guarniere (Technicolor); m, Donovan; ed, Reginald Hills, John Rushton; md, Ken Thorne; prod d, Lorenzo Mongiardino; art d, Gianni Quaranta; set d, Carmelo Patrono.

Historical Drama **Cas.** **(PR:A MPAA:PG)**

BROTHERHOOD, THE* 1/2** (1968) 96m PAR c

Kirk Douglas *(Frank Ginetta)*, Alex Cord *(Vince Ginetta)*, Irene Papas *(Ida Ginetta)*, Luther Adler *(Dominick Bertolo)*, Susan Strasberg *(Emma Ginetta)*, Murray Hamilton *(Jim Egan)*, Eduardo Ciannelli *(Don Peppino)*, Joe De Santis *(Pietro Rizzi)*, Connie Scott *(Carmelo Ginetta)*, Val Avery *(Jake Rotherman)*, Val Bisoglio *(Cheech)*, Alan Hewitt *(Sol Levin)*, Barry Primus *(Vido)*, Michele Cimarosa *(Toto)*, Louis Badolati *(Don Turridu)*.

Casting and fine performances make this a truly distinguished film, even if the subject matter, which deals with the home life and internal workings of the Mafia, sometimes revolts in its straining after the sympathy of the viewer. In a story that attempts to delineate the generational gaps within hoodlumdom, Douglas plays a middle-aged career crook dedicated to the old ways of the Mafia, pitted against his ambitious younger brother, Cord. When Cord broaches plans for Douglas to become a "modern" criminal, using sophisticated techniques of big business—stock control of companies, legitimate investments run by front men, and particularly a takeover of the burgeoning electronics and space industry—Douglas vetoes the plan, leading Cord's father-in-law, Adler, to start a move to replace him. An elderly, deposed head of the Mafia family, Ciannelli, reveals to Douglas that it was Adler who betrayed and caused the massacre of the previous syndicate leaders, including Douglas' father. Douglas then brutally murders Adler and flees with his wife and daughter to Sicily. Cord, playing the new generation hood to perfection, urbanely and coldly, gets the assignment to kill his brother. Douglas knows he is coming, and is braced to accept death. A kiss he bestows on Cord, the centuries old "kiss of death," seals his doom. The scene is played matter of fact, chillingly so, with Douglas' chauffeur driving Cord to the airport and sending him home. As the film's producer as well as its star, Douglas deserves praise on a number of counts, including the excellence of the casting. The old men who play the Mafia veterans look like old-style gangsters, especially Ciannelli, a character actor for almost 40 years appearing in the film at 87, the last year of his life. The Technicolor printing emphasizes darker tones, which gives the production a documentary flavor.

p, Kirk Douglas; d, Martin Ritt; w, Lewis John Carlino; ph, Boris Kaufman (Technicolor); m, Lalo Schifrin; ed, Frank Bracht; art d, Tambi Larsen.

Crime Drama **(PR:C-O MPAA:NR)**

BROTHERHOOD OF SATAN, THE* (1971) 92m COL c

Strother Martin *(Don Duncan)*, L. Q. Jones *(Sheriff)*, Charles Bateman *(Ben)*, Anna Capri *(Nicky)*, Charles Robinson *(Priest)*, Alvy Moore *(Tobey)*, Geri Reischl *(Kiti)*.

Slaughter of twenty-six people within seventy-two hours terrifies a small town cut off from all means of communication. Then someone gets the idea that witchcraft and demonic rituals are at work, further panicking the residents. Inept production turns a good horror idea into a boring vehicle. Jones is a miserable filmmaker.

p, L. Q. Jones, Alvy Moore; d, Bernard McEveety; w, William Welch (based on an idea by Sean McGregor); ph, John Arthur Morril; m, Jamie Mendoza-Nava; ed, Marvin Walowitz.

Horror **Cas.** **(PR:C-O MPAA:GP)**

BROTHERHOOD OF THE YAKUZA (SEE: YAKUZA, THE, 1975)

BROTHERLY LOVE 1/2**
(1970, Brit.) 112m MGM c (GB: COUNTRY DANCE)

Peter O'Toole *(Sir Charles Ferguson)*, Susannah York *(Hilary Dow)*, Michael Craig *(Douglas Dow)*, Harry Andrews *(Brigadier Crieff)*, Cyril Cusack *(Dr. Maitland)*, Judy Cornwell *(Rosie)*, Brian Blessed *(Jock Baird)*, Robert Urquhart *(Auctioneer)*, Mark Malicz *(Benny-the-Pole)*, Jean Anderson *(Marton)*, Lennox Milne *(Miss Mailer)*, Helena Gloag *(Auntie Belle)*, Marjorie Dalziel *(Bank Lissie)*, Madeleine Christie *(Bun Mackenzie)*, Rona Newton-John *(Miss Scott)*, Roy Boutcher *(James McLachlan Forbes)*, Ewan Roberts *(Committee Member)*, Peter Reeves *(Alex Smart)*, Paul Farrell *(Alec-the-Gillie)*, Helen Norman *(Cook)*, Bernadette Gallagher *(Ina)*, Maura Keeley *(Ina's Mother)*, John Kelly *(Ina's Father)*, Clare Mullen *(Second Barmaid)*, Alex McAvoy *(Andrew)*, John Molloy *(Slim Farmer)*, Geoff Golden *(Bearded Farmer)*, John Shedden *(Ginger-haired Farmer)*, Harry Jones *(Wee Farmer)*, Mary Larkin *(Hilary's Friend)*, Eamonn Keane *(Fred-who-is-Bob)*, Frances De La Tour *(District* Nurse), Patrick Gardiner *(Ambulance Driver)*, Desmond Perry *(Mental Health Officer)*.

After an argument, York leaves her husband Craig and goes to her family estate to stay with her brother O'Toole. Although the house and surrounding lands have been uncared for, York settles in, but must soon deal with her brother's amorous advances. Craig comes after his wife and an unusual triangle develops. It is learned that O'Toole has handled the family estate with disastrous financial results and his possession of the land is in jeopardy. Along with his incestuous yearning for York, O'Toole's longing for the old, stable ways on the estate cause him to become unbalanced. Sadly, the reunited Craig and York have him committed to an institution. Depressing film with some oddly placed humorous moments that fails to investigate the emotionally charged situation or the reasonings behind its protagonist's illness. The wordy script shoots off into a variety of directions, none of which add to or give another view of the essential conflict. O'Toole and York are good, but not exceptional, unable to overcome the limitations of the screenplay. The film's saving grace is its cinematography which nicely captures the somber mood of the hauntingly beautiful Scottish countryside.

p, Robert Emmett Ginna; d, J. Lee Thompson; w, James Kennaway (based on his play "Country Dance" and his novel *Household Ghosts*); ph, Ted Moore; m, John Addison; ed, Willy Kemplen; art d, Maurice Fowler; cos, Yvonne Blake.

Drama **(PR:O MPAA:R)**

BROTHERS** (1930) 63m COL bw (GB: BLOOD BROTHERS)

Bert Lytell *(Bob Naughton/Eddie Connolly)*, Dorothy Sebastian *(Norma)*, William Morris *(Dr. Moore)*, Richard Tucker *(Prosecutor)*, Maurice Black *(Lorenzo)*, Frank McCormack *(Oily Joe)*, Claire McDowell *(Mrs. Naughton)*, Howard Hickman *(Mr. Naughton)*, Francis MacDonald *(Tony)*, Rita Carlyle *(Mag)*, Jessie Arnold *(Maud)*.

Twin brothers, both played by Lytell, are separated as children, one brought up rich, the other poor. The rich brother commits a murder, for which the poor brother is blamed but rich brother's conscience won't let him take the rap, so he confesses, then conveniently dies. Poor brother gets rich kid's girl and money. Not the CORSICAN BROTHERS, but okay.

p, Harry Cohn; d, Walter Lang; w, Sidney Lazarus, John Thomas Neville, Charles R. Condon (based on the play by Herbert Ashton, Jr.); ph, Ira Morgan; ed, Gene Havlick; art d, Edward Jewell.

Drama **(PR:A MPAA:NR)**

BROTHERS** (1977) 104m WB c

Bernie Casey *(David)*, Vonetta McGee *(Paula)*, Ron O'Neal *(Walter)*, Rennie Roker *(Lewis)*, Stu Gillam *(Robinson)*, John Lehne *(Chief Guard McGee)*, Owen Pace *(Joshua)*, Joseph Havener *(Warden Leon)*, Martin St. Judge *(Williams)*.

The Brothers Warner began the prison movie way back when and they continue their tradition with BROTHERS except that this is as blatant a black exploitation film as has ever been made. What confounds the viewer is that there are several honest, real moments in between the preachiness and the violence that stand out like well thumbs in a sore hand. It's a thinly veiled account of the notorious Jackson brothers who were both eventually killed. Most of the inmates are black and all of the angry, mean, and vicious guards are white so we know how things stand straightaway. Lots of stereotypes and woe to the white patron who happens into a black theater where this film is showing. Rouse the "rabble" seem to be the bywords. Casey, McGee, and most everyone else is excellent with what little they are given. If the Lewises are black, then they are bigoted. If they are white, the knee-jerks of these liberals must have hit them in the forehead and knocked them on to Queer Street.

p, Edward and Mildred Lewis; d, Arthur Barron; w, Edward and Mildred Lewis; ph, John Morrill (Metrocolor); m, Taj Mahal; ed, William Dornisch.

Prison Drama **(PR:C MPAA:R)**

BROTHERS, THE** (1948, Brit.) 98m GFD bw

Patricia Roc *(Mary)*, Will Fyffe *(Aeneas McGrath)*, Maxwell Reed *(Fergus Macrae)*, Finlay Currie *(Hector Macrae)*, John Laurie *(Dugald)*, Andrew Crawford *(Willie McFarish)*, Duncan Macrae *(John Macrae)*, Morland Graham *(Angus McFarish)*, Megs Jenkins *(Angusina McFarish)*, James Woodburn *(Priest)*, David McAllister *(George McFarish)*, Patrick Boxil *(The Informer)*.

British version of the Hatfields and the McCoys has convent-bred servant girl Roc fought over and never conquered by the sons in both families. Fair effort with technical talent outweighing the performers.

p, Sidney Box; d, David MacDonald; w, Muriel and Sydney Box, David MacDonald, Paul Vincent Carroll (based on a novel by L. A. G. Strong); ph, Stephen Dade; m, Cedric Thorpe Davie.

Drama **(PR:A MPAA:NR)**

BROTHERS AND SISTERS** (1980, Brit.) 96m British Film Institute c

Carolyn Pickles *(Collins)*, Sam Dale *(David Barratt)*, Robert East *(James Barratt)*, Elizabeth Bennett *(Sarah Barratt)*, Jennifer Armitage *(Tricia Snow)*, Barry McCarthy *(Pete Gibson)*, Barrie Shore *(Helen Dawson)*, Norman Claridge *(Father)*, Mavis Pugh *(Mother)*, Fred Gaunt *(Detective)*, Nick Jensen *(Constable)*, Jack Platts *(Client)*, May Wray *(2nd Prostitute)*, David Theakston *(2nd Policeman)*, Nelson Fletcher *(Winston)*.

East is commendable in his effort to turn his wealthy character inside out as he changes from the kind of guy you just love to hate to the kind of guy you hate to love. Whodunit with Pickles in the dual role of a prostitute and her sister. The prostitute gets murdered, leaving the sister to secretly get involved with Dale. Although the killer's identity is not really certain, the crossover characters keep the story interesting. Artistic quality displayed by photographer MacFarlane, most notably of night exteriors. Fundamentally more honest than superficial characterizations.

p, Keith Griffiths; d, Richard Woolley; w, Woolley, Tammy Walker; ph, Pascoe MacFarlane; ed, Mickey Audsley; m, Trevor Jones; art d, Miranda Melville.

Crime **(PR:A MPAA:NR)**

BROTHERS IN LAW** ½ (1957, Brit.) 94m BC bw

Richard Attenborough *(Henry Marshall)*, Ian Carmichael *(Roger Thursby)*, Terry Thomas *(Alfred Green)*, Jill Adams *(Sally Smith)*, Miles Malleson *(Kendall Grimes)*, Raymond Huntley *(Tatlock)*, Eric Barker *(Alec Blair)*, Nicholas Parsons *(Charles Poole)*, Kynaston Reeves *(Judge Lawson)*, John Le Mesurier *(Judge Ryman)*, Irene Handl *(Mrs. Potter)*, Olive Sloane *(Mrs. Newent)*, Edith Sharpe *(Mrs. Thursby)*, Leslie Phillips *(Shopman)*, Brian Oulton *(Solicitor)*, George Rose *(Frost)*, Kenneth Griffith *(Undertaker)*, Basil Dignam *(Judge Emery)*, Henry Longhurst *(Roger's Father)*.

Rookie legal counsel Carmichael is thrown into the water to sink or swim by Judge Malleson and learns how to beat the law in the Queen's name. Good comedic effort with a wry, laugh-producing script.

p, John Boulting; d, Roy Boulting; w, Roy Boulting, Frank Harvey, Jeffrey Dell (based on a novel by Henry Cecil); ph, Max Greene; m, Benjamin Frankel; ed, Anthony Harvey.

Comedy **(PR:A MPAA:NR)**

BROTHERS IN THE SADDLE** (1949) 60m RKO bw

Tim Holt *(Tim Taylor)*, Richard Martin *(Chito Rafferty)*, Steve Brodie *(Steve Taylor)*, Virginia Cox *(Nancy Austin)*, Carol Foreman *(Flora Trigby)*, Richard Powers, aka Tom Keene *(Nash Prescott)*, Stanley Andrews, Robert Bray, Francis McDonald, Emmett Vogan and Monte Montague.

Two brothers are out to save each other from each other when Brodie gets framed with a murder rap and gets deeper into trouble. Then he goes haywire, actually killing an old enemy and holding up a stagecoach. This puts the brothers on opposite sides of the fence to duel it out with guns and fists. Flimsy script is saved by the action sequences.

p, Herman Schlom; d, Lesley Selander; w, Norman Houston; ph, J. Roy Hunt; ed, Sam Beetley.

Western **(PR:A MPAA:NR)**

BROTHERS KARAMAZOV, THE*** ½ (1958) 149m MGM c

Yul Brynner *(Dmitri Karamazov)*, Maria Schell *(Grushenka)*, Claire Bloom *(Katya)*, Lee J. Cobb *(Fyodor Karamazov)*, Richard Basehart *(Ivan Karamozov)*, Albert Salmi *(Smerdyakov)*, William Shatner *(Alexey Karamazov)*, Judith Evelyn *(Mme. Anna Hohlakov)*, Edgar Stehli *(Grigory)*, Harry Townes *(Ippoli Kirillov)*, Miko Oscard *(Illusha Snegiryov)*, David Opatoshu *(Capt. Snegiryov)*, Simon Oakland *(Mavrayek)*, Jay Adler *(Pawnbroker)*, Frank deKova *(Capt. Vrublevski)*, Gage Clarke *(Defense Counsel)*, Ann Morrison *(Marya)*, Mel Welles *(Trifon Borissovitch)*.

A roundhouse drama so meaty that this excellent cast gorges itself on the hearts of Dostoyevsky's characters. Brynner is superb as the callous older brother Dmitri, a ruthless army officer who lusts after the captivating slattern Grushenka, played wildly by Schell, who is his father's mistress. Matching Brynner scene for scene is Basehart in one of his finest performances as the disillusioned intellectual brother Ivan. Shatner is the holier-than-thou Alexey, the younger brother who has retreated into monkhood rather than face the raging dissolution of his father, Cobb. And Cobb plays old man Karamazov with a roar that signals his ever-present sexual craving, his lust for Schell and all other females, as well as an unquenchable thirst and an appetite for all things sensual, one never satisfied. He is the rich patriarch who hates and loves his sons, constantly baiting them, Brynner for his obvious attraction for Schell, Basehart for his ineffectual intellectualism, and even the good son Shatner, whom Cobb considers a coward hiding behind the sanctimony of the church. It is a chilling, churlish story of family conflict fat with Russian flamboyance, drinking, and orgies that rival the excesses of Rasputin while Schell goads all three sons, flaunting her ravishing beauty, taunting them, until finally Cobb is brutally murdered. Brynner is charged with the killing, but it is learned that the cretinous half-brother Salmi did the deed. Before this is revealed, a tense, taut trial ensues where Brynner comes close to conviction. The film is overlong and taxing for any viewer as on-screen emotions are drained as freely as the cutting of a steer's throat. It is worth seeing if only for Cobb's gargantuan performance. Of course, the strange and great Russian author Dostoyevsky was really all the brothers in one, each representing a facet of his personality, the noble, the courageous, the religious and the murderer. This story is all the more interesting to literary scholars who still wonder about the death of Dostoyevsky's own father who died under mysterious circumstances. It was a widely known fact that when this film was being cast Marilyn Monroe let it be known far and wide that she would do anything to play the role of the beautiful slut Grushenka. This desire was laughed at by producers then but MM might have given the role as much depth and understanding as Schell, perhaps more. Had Monroe enacted such meaningful roles in her brief career, she may not have ended so tragically; she may have found in herself the deep achievement and high art she mistakenly sought in others. Director Brooks does a journeyman job in handling the difficult material. He visually lingers upon Cobb and his strange sons at their most conflicting moments, yet appropriately cuts swiftly to action that realizes all the veiled threats and sexual innuendoes.

p, Pandro S. Berman; d&w, Richard Brooks (based on a adaptation by Julius J. and Phillip G. Epstein of the novel by Fyodor Dostoyevsky); ph, John Alton (Metrocolor); m, Bronislau Kaper; ed, John Dunning; cos, Walter Plunkett.

Drama **(PR:C-O MPAA:NR)**

BROTHERS OF THE WEST* (1938) 56m Victory bw

Tom Tyler *(Tom)*, Lois Wilde *(Celia)*, Dorothy Short *(Annie)*, Lafe McKee *(Sheriff Bob)*, Bob Terry *(Ed)*, Dave O'Brien *(Davy)*, Roger Williams *(Tracy)*.

Tyler's brother Terry gets involved with the Roger Williams gang whose forte is robbery. Tyler tries vainly to save his brother in this uninteresting oater.

p&d, Sam Katzman; w, Basil Dickey; ph, Bill Hyer; ed, Holbrook Todd.

Western **Cas.** **(PR:A MPAA:NR)**

BROTHERS O'TOOLE, THE* (1973) 90m CVD c

John Astin, Steve Carlson, Pat Carroll, Hans Conreid, Lee Meriwether, Allyn Joslyn, Richard Jury, Jesse White, Richard Erdman.

A sloppy slapstick western with a script as senseless as the dialog, replete with endless chases, gold-hunters and females threatened by sterotyped bad guys. Director Erdman gave himself a role in the movie; he should have stayed in front of the cameras.

p, Charles E. Sellier; d, Richard Erdman; ph, (Eastmancolor).

Western **Cas.** **(PR:A MPAA:G)**

BROTHERS RICO, THE** ½ (1957) 92m COL bw

Richard Conte *(Eddie Rico)*, Dianne Foster *(Alice Rico)*, Kathryn Grant *(Norah)*, Larry Gates *(Sid Kubik)*, James Darren *(Johnny Rico)*, Argentina Brunetti *(Mrs. Rico)*, Lamont Johnson *(Peter Malaks)*, Harry Bellaver *(Mike Lamotta)*, Paul Picerni *(Gino Rico)*, Paul Dubov *(Phil)*, Rudy Bond *(Gonzales)*, Richard Bakalyan *(Vic Tucci)*, William Phipps *(Joe Wesson)*, Mimi Aguglia *(Julia Rico)*, Maggie O'Byrne *(Mrs. Felici)*, George Cisar *(Dude Cowboy)*, Peggy Maley *(Jean)*, Jane Easton *(Nellie)*.

Conte is a businessman whose brothers are in the rackets. When he hears that rival gangsters have marked them for extinction, he begins searching for them. He then finds brother Picerni, learning that it is not rival gangsters but the syndicate boss himself, Gates, who has ordered their deaths. It was Gates who tipped Conte about the danger awaiting his brothers. Now Conte realizes that he has been used, that Gates' goons have followed him in hopes of tracking down Picerni, whom they later kill, and the younger brother Darren. Conte, in the kind of resignation that typified the 1950s belief that the syndicate was all-powerful, concludes that his brothers cannot be saved from a fate they somewhat deserve (they have murdered one of their own and absconded with the funds); he returns to his family to keep his mouth and eyes shut. A brutal film that offers no hope of ever dismantling an omnipotent crime cartel. Conte's performance is tension-packed and carries an otherwise depressing film, though it is expertly constructed and paced by veteran film noir director Karlson.

p, Lewis J. Rachmil; d, Phil Karlson; w, Lewis Meltzer, Ben Perry (based on the novelette *Les Freres Rico* by Georges Simenon); ph, Burnett Guffey; m, George Duning; ed, Charles Nelson; art d, Robert Boyle; set d, William Kiernan, Darrell Silvera; cos, Jean Louis.

Crime Drama **(PR:C MPAA:NR)**

BROWN ON RESOLUTION (SEE: BORN FOR GLORY, 1935)

BROWN SUGAR* (1931, Brit.) 70m Twickenham/WB bw

Constance Carpenter *(Lady Stella Sloane)*, Francis Lister *(Lord Sloane)*, Allan Aynesworth *(Lord Knightsbridge)*, Helen Haye *(Lady Knightsbridge)*, Cecily Byrne *(Lady Honoria Nesbitt)*, Eva Moore *(Mrs. Cunningham)*, Chili Bouchier *(Ninon de Veaux)*, Gerald Rawlinson *(Archie Wentworth)*, Alfred Drayton *(Edmondson)*, Wallace Geoffrey *(Crawbie Carruthers)*.

Snobby wealthy English landowners turn their noses up at their Lord's choice for a wife. She's an actress, and you see that just isn't the kind of profession acceptable for the bloodline. The loyal newlywed gains favor in their eyes when she takes the blame for a blueblood gambler. Bad no-brainer romance.

p, Julius Hagen; d, Leslie Hiscott; w, Cyril Twyford (based on the play by Lady Arthur Lever); ph, Ernest Palmer.

Romance **(PR:A MPAA:NR)**

BROWN WALLET, THE** (1936, Brit.) 68m FN/WB bw

Patric Knowles *(John Gilliespie)*, Nancy O'Neil *(Eleanor)*, Henry Caine *(Simmonds)*, Henrietta Watson *(Aunt Mary)*, Charlotte Leigh *(Miss Barton)*, Shayle Gardner *(Wotherspoone)*, Edward Dalby *(Minting)*, Eliot Makeham *(Hobday)*, Edward Dalby, Bruce Winston, June Millican, Louis Goodrich, Dick Francis, George Mills.

After finding 200 pounds, a bankrupt publisher is accused of killing a rich, old aunt. Justice prevails and his name is cleared by the film's end. One of many such small films that director Powell worked on before achieving some success with bigger projects.

p, Irving Asher; d, Michael Powell; w, Ian Dalrymple (based on a story by Stacy Aumonier); ph, Basil Emmott.

Drama **(PR:A MPAA:NR)**

BROWNING VERSION, THE**** (1951, Brit.) 90m Javelin GFD bw

Michael Redgrave *(Andrew Crocker-Harris)*, Jean Kent *(Millie Crocker-Harris)*, Nigel Patrick *(Frank Hunter)*, Wilfrid Hyde-White *(Frobisher)*, Brian Smith *(Taplow)*, Bill Travers *(Fletcher)*, Ronald Howard *(Gilbert)*, Paul Medland *(Wilson)*, Ivan Samson *(Lord Baxter)*, Josephine Middleton *(Mrs. Frobisher)*, Peter Jones *(Carstairs)*, Sarah Lawson *(Betty Carstairs)*, Scott Harold *(Rev. Williamson)*, Judith Furse *(Mrs. Williamson)*.

Not enough can be said of Michael Redgrave's brilliant portrayal of Andrew Crocker- Harris, the tragic, self-restricted martinet of England's public school system, forced by ill health to prematurely give up his long-time position as instructor of classic languages. The pitfalls in this role are many but Redgrave in his intelligent, cerebral way brings out even the subtlest of Crocker-Harris's emotions. Undermined for years as a man, a husband, and an instructor by his harridan of a wife, Millie (played by Jean Kent with a cloying mixture of callousness and coyness wonderfully suited for the role), the austere disciplinarian is finally beaten down and forced to retire without pension from his thankless job. Scorned by his students, pitied by his peers, Crocker-Harris is moved to uncharacteristic tears by a gift of Robert Browning's translation of the *Agamemnon* of Aeschuylus from his one sensitive student Taplow (Smith). But even this small pleasure is stripped from him by Millie who humiliates him by calling it a bribe for good grades in front of her none-too-secret lover (Patrick). Even Patrick is appalled by Millie's callous behaviour and breaks off the affair she has been flaunting for years. Millie departs in disgust, leaving her husband alone to deliver his farewell speech at the school's graduation ceremonies. Her departure has an invigorating effect on the old school master, however, and in a spurt of renewed strength of character he abandons his prepared text to speak from the heart, delivering a straightforward apology for his failure as a teacher. Stunned into silence by the final words ". . . I shall *not* find it so easy to forgive *myself* . . . Goodbye," the students collect themselves and burst into a belated applause, which builds into a tumultuous ovation, drowning out the headmaster's efforts to proceed with the program. The impact of this film is shattering, from Redgrave's heartbreaking Croker-Harris and Kent's hoydenish Millie to Patrick's sympathetic Hunter and Wilfrid Hyde-White's slyly manipulative Headmaster. Rattigan's skillful script defines and rounds out his characters. Redgrave won the Best Actor award and Terence Rattigan the writing prize at the 1951 Cannes Film Festival for this masterpiece.

p, Teddy Baird; d, Anthony Asquith, w, Terence Rattigan (based on his play), ph, Desmond Dickinson; ed, John D. Guthridge.

Drama **(PR:A MPAA:NR)**

BRUBAKER*½** (1980) 132m FOX c

Robert Redford *(Brubaker)*, Yaphet Kotto *(Dickie Coombes)*, Jane Alexander *(Lillian)*, Murray Hamilton *(Deach)*, David Keith *(Larry Lee Bullen)*, Morgan Freeman *(Walter)*, Matt Clark *(Purcell)*, Tim McIntire *(Huey Rauch)*, Richard Ward *(Abraham)*, Jon Van Ness *(Zaranska)*, Albert Salmi *(Rory Poke)*, Linda Haynes *(Carol)*, Everett McGill *(Caldwell)*, Val Avery *(Wendel)* Ronald C. Frazier *(Willets)*, David D. Harris *(Duane Spivey)*, Joe Spinell *(Birdwell)*, James Keane *(Pinky)*, Konrad Sheehan *(Glenn Elwood)*, Roy Poole *(Dr. Gregory)*, Nathan George *(Leon Edwards)*, Lee Richardson *(Warden Renfrew)*, John McMartin *(Senator Hite)*, Harry Groener *(Dr. Campbell)*, John R. Glover *(Ackroyd)*, Alex A. Brown, John Chappell, Brent Jennings, William Newman, Noble Willingham, Wilford Brimley, Jane Cecil, Ebbe Roe Smith, Young Hwa Han, Vic Polizos, Jack O'Leary, James Dukas, J. C. Quinn, Jerry Mayer.

Robert Redford is a man who likes to take chances. Sometimes they pay off, sometimes not. In BRUBAKER, Redford has to be very pleased at the result and annoyed at the audience's lack of response. BRUBAKER is about a man who is arrested and taken to a terrible jail (not unlike those places we hear about down South and close enough to the one in Sturges's SULLIVAN'S TRAVELS) where he sees man's inhumanity to man around every corner. After about an hour of this pain, we learn that Brubaker is not a convict at all; he's the new warden and has had himself incarcerated so he can see the prison from the convict's point of view. Good idea. Only problem is that no one much cares, these days, about prison reform—except the prisoners and their relatives. Many American citizens have the feeling that if a person's in jail, they deserve to be there. The prison depicted is hardly like Lewisburg in Pennsylvania or what Lompoc used to be in California: penal resorts where white collar crooks spent most of their time on the putting green. This is a very tough movie and not for the squeamish. Rosenberg has had a spotty career as a director with credits that range from MOVE to THE AMITYVILLE HORROR. This film moved him into a higher strata, but no matter who directs Redford, one cannot escape the feeling that Redford is the man behind the man behind the camera.

p, Ron Silverman; d, Stuart Rosenberg; w, W.D. Richter (based on a story by Richter, Arthur Ross); ph, Bruno Nuytten (DeLuxe Color); m, Lalo Schifrin; ed, Robert Brown.

Prison Drama **Cas.** **(PR:C-O MPAA:R)**

BRUCE LEE AND I zero (1976, Chi.) 106m SHAW BROS c

Betty Ting Pei *(Herself)*, Li Hsiu Hsien *(Bruce Lee)*.

Betty Ting Pei was the woman with Bruce Lee when he gave up the ghost. She has evidently made this movie for two reasons: to make a few yen and to get herself off the hook for such a popular star's death. How much truth and how much conjecture is in this film is not known. The acting on her part is nonsense. Hsien as Lee is one of the four or five lookalikes who have been making a fine living at it since Lee died. A B-movie, B for boring.

p, Run Run Shaw, Run Me Shaw; d, Lo Mar; ph, (Eastmancolor).

Biography **(PR:C-O MPAA:NR)**

BRUCE LEE—TRUE STORY*½ (1976, Chi.) 100m Eternal Film c

Ho Chung Tao, Unicorn Chan, Lia Siao Sung, Donnie William, David Chow, Roberta Ciappi, Mario Viadiano, Sham Chien Po, Tisui, Chung Shun.

Ever since Presley died, a huge cottage industry of Elvis imitators has flourished. The same could be said for Bruce Lee. BRUCE LEE—TRUE STORY is one of many that purports to be the truth, the whole truth, and nothing but the truth. They begin at the end and unspool Lee's life in many exotic locales including Rome, Thailand, Hong Kong, Seattle, Washington, and New York. Ho Chung Tao looks enough like the late master to fool most people and does a fair job in limning Lee. Bruce, in case you didn't know it, was a tiny man, all muscle, skin stretched over steel. (In Chinese; English subtitles.)

p, Pal Ming Production; d, Ng See Yuen; w, Ne see Yuen; ph, Chang Chee; m, Chow Foo Liang; ed, Sung Ming.

Biography **(PR:C-O MPAA:NR)**

BRUSHFIRE* (1962) 80m PAR bw

John Ireland *(Jeff Saygure)*, Everett Sloane *(Chevern McCase)*, Jo Morrow *(Easter Banford)*, Al Avalon *(Tony Banford)*, Carl Esmond *(Martin)*, Howard Caine *(Vlad)*.

American freedom fighters take up residence in the Southeast Orient with a plot to save POWS. A military mishmash.

p&d, Jack Warner, Jr.; w, Warner, Irwin Blacker; ph, Ed Fitzgerald; m, Irving Gertz; ed, Roy Livingston.

Adventure **(PR:A MPAA:NR)**

BRUTE, THE** (1952, Mex.) 80m Marceau bw (EL BRUTO)

Pedro Armendariz *(Pedro)*, Katy Jurado *(Manuela)*, Andres Soler *(Andres)*, Rosita Arena *(Michette)*, Roberto Meyer.

Murder and disappointment surround this yarn which has greedy female Jurado and wealthy landowner husband Armendariz instigating unrest among the tenants. Photography is outstanding, along with Armendariz's riveting performance.

p, Oscar Dancigers; d, Luis Bunuel; w, Luis Alcoriza, Bunuel; ph, Augustin Jimenez; m, Raul Lavista; ed, Jorge Bustos; set d, Gunter Gerzso.

Drama **(PR:C MPAA:NR)**

BRUTE AND THE BEAST, THE* (1968, Ital.) 85m AIP c

Franco Nero *(Tom)*, George Hilton *(Jeff)*, Nino Castelnuevo *(Jason)*, John M. Douglas *(Mr. Scott)*, Rina Franchetti *(Mercedes)*.

Six bloody bullets are required to kill each heavy in this horrid stab at portraying drunks and sadistic badmen. An abysmal script and direction, plus indifferent acting make for a sorry production.

d, Lucio Fulci, Terry Vantell; w, Fernando Di Leo; ph, Riccardo Pallottini (Anamorphic, Perfect Color); m, Lallo Gori; ed, Ornella Micheli; art d, Sergio Canevari.

Adventure **(PR:C MPAA:NR)**

BRUTE FORCE**** (1947) 94m UNIV bw

Burt Lancaster *(Joe Collins)*, Hume Cronyn *(Capt. Munsey)*, Charles Bickford *(Gallagher)*, Yvonne De Carlo *(Gina)*, Ann Blyth *(Ruth)*, Ella Raines *(Cora)*, Anita Colby *(Flossie)*, Sam Levene *(Louis)*, Howard Duff *(Soldier)*, Art Smith *(Dr. Walters)*, Roman Bohnen *(Warden Barnes)*, John Hoyt *(Spencer)*, Richard Gaines *(McCollum)*, Frank Puglia *(Ferrara)*, Jeff Corey *(Freshman)*, Vince Barnett *(Mugsy)*, James Bell *(Crenshaw)*, Jack Overman *(Kid Coy)*, Whit Bissell *(Tom Lister)*, Sir Lancelot *(Calypso)*, Ray Teal *(Jackson)*, Jay C. Flippen *(Hodges)*, James O'Rear *(Wilson)*, Howland Chamberlin *(Gaines)*, Kenneth Patterson *(Bronski)*, Crane Whitley *(Armed Guard in Drain Pipe)*, Charles McGraw *(Andy)*, John Harmon *(Roberts)*, Gene Stutenroth *(Hoffman)*, Wally Rose *(Peary)*, Carl Rhodes *(Strella)*, Guy Beach *(Convict Foreman)*, Edmund Cobb *(Bradley)*, Tom Steele *(Machine Gunner)*, Alex Frazer *(Chaplain)*, Will Lee *(Kincaid)*, Ruth Sanderson *(Miss Lawrence)*, Francis McDonald *(Regan)*, Jack S. Lee *(Sergeant)*, Virginia Farmer *(Sadie)*, Billy Wayne, Rex Dale, Frank Marlowe, William Cozzo *(Prisoners)*, Paul Bryar *(Harry)*, Glenn Strange *(Tompkins)*, Al Hill *(Plonski)*, Peter Virgo, Eddy Chandler, Kenneth R. MacDonald, Al Ferguson, Jerry Salvail *(Guards)*, Rex Lease *(Hearse Driver)*, Herbert Heywood *(Chef)*, Blanch Obronska *(Young Girl)*, Hal Malone *(Young Inmate)*, Don McGill *(Max)*, Harry Wilson *(Tyrone, Inmate in Yard)*, Sam Rizhallah *(Convict's Son)*, Kippee Valez *(Visitor)*.

A classic prison film, BRUTE FORCE is both an excellent character study as well as a scathing indictment of a penal system that allows for the dehumanization of inmates and the corruption of authority so that sadism and persecution flourish, encouraging bloody riot and lethal escape attempts. The prisoners housed in Cell R17 watch from their window to see Lancaster, one of the toughest convicts in the prison, crossing a rain-swept yard in company with guard captain Cronyn and his right-hand guard Teal. He has just been released from solitary confinement and once back in his cell he is congratulated for having survived the hole. "Everything's going to be all right," one of his cellmates says. "Nothin's all right," snaps Lancaster. "It'll never be all right until we're out!" With that he begins to plan a prison break, going to Bickford, the big boss of the inmates, publisher of the prison newspaper. Bickford sneers at Lancaster's escape notions. He takes him to an old inmate setting type, asking the inmate when *his* prison break is planned. "Next Tuesday," replies the inmate excitedly. Bickford walks away with Lancaster, saying sarcastically to Lancaster: "It's been all set for next Tuesday for the last ten years and it'll still be all set for next Tuesday in the next ten years." Undaunted, Lancaster begins to formulate his plan. First, he vists Smith, the prison doctor, careful to ask about the time. At that minute, in the prison workshop, Lancaster's cellmates take retribution from O'Rear, the informer who had sent Lancaster to solitary by planting a knife on him so that brutal Cronyn could discover it. Duff, Hoyt, Corey, Bissell, and Overman, the inmates of Cell R17, drive the informer back into a giant press by flaring blowtorches in his face. He is crushed to death just as Lancaster leaves Smith's office. That night Lancaster and cellmates talk about the women in their lives and we see in flashback Ella Raines, a harried housewife for whom Bissell, an accountant, has juggled the company books to buy her a mink coat, a crime which sends him to prison. Con man Hoyt's story depicts a con woman who outfoxes him. Duff, who is called Soldier, relates a faraway tale occurring in WW II Italy. Duff is a soldier in love with DeCarlo, an Italian beauty to whom he is smuggling food. Her father, a rock-ribbed fascist (Puglia), hates Duff but takes the black market items anyway. Then an American MP patrol arrives in front of the cottage and Puglia runs for the door, saying he will tell the police that he has had nothing to do with Duff's smuggled items. "You and your police can destroy each other!" he spits. Before he reaches the door DeCarlo shoots him with Duff's service forty-five. Duff takes the gun from her and assumes the guilt for the killing as the MPs close in, their flashlights bobbing toward the camera from the darkness. Then Lancaster recalls the pretty but wheelchair bound girl he loves. He is shown stopping in front of a country house to visit Blyth, encouraging her to hope that an impending operation will bring a cure. He then leaves to pull a job with his gang in order to get the money for the operation. Back in the cell, Lancaster worries about the girl; he later meets with his lawyer (Chamberlain) in the visitor's room, asking about his girl's health, then tells the lawyer to get some money and keep it in his office. Meanwhile, the warden (Bohnen) is tongue-lashed by political bigshot Gaines for not cracking down on the prisoners, for being too lenient. When Smith objects he is told that as an alcoholic doctor he is not fit for any job other than that of prison physician. Cronyn acts like a lickspittle toward Gaines and is the politician's obvious choice to replace Bohnen. When Gaines and Bohnen leave, Smith watches Cronyn sit in the warden's chair and accuses him of plotting to take over the job. Cronyn at first dismisses Smith's jibes but then the doctor works on him closely, telling him: "Your're obvious, Munsey, in everything you do, you're obvious.'" He accuses Cronyn of brutalizing the prisoners as slaves and for pleasure. (This is already evident in that Cronyn has caused Bissell to hang himself in his cell after lying to him about his wife's plan to divorce him.) Smith also tells Cronyn that he has a Napoleonic complex and is a closet psychopath. Cronyn erupts in a rage, knocking Smith down. From the floor, Smith smiles triumphantly: "That's it, Munsey, not logic, just force, brute force!" Bickford meanwhile finds that his parole has been denied: he opts for the break and alerts his men to prepare for an escape from inside the yard. Lancaster and his men will take the guard tower after emerging from the drainpipe where they are working just outside the prison wall. Once the guard tower is taken, the doors will be opened by Lancaster, the drawbridge lowered to a bridge spanning the bay and the entire population will escape. At least, that's the plan. But Cronyn suddenly knows about the break, though he doesn't know where it will happen or who is involved. He has Levene, one of Bickford's men, brought to his office where he plays blaring classical music while hitting Levene who is strapped to a chair. Levene tells him nothing before he is taken to Smith's infirmary. Smith next appears in the drainpipe, asking for Lancaster, saying he must check his heart since some recent examinations indicate problems. Under this pretext Smith whispers to Lancaster that Cronyn knows about the break, that there is an informer in their midst, one of his cellmates. When Smith leaves, Lancaster vows to go through with the escape attempt. He asks his cellmates what positions in the breakout they want. All reply that they will do as he says, all except Corey who asks to be last. At the chosen time, Bickford has a truck driven into the yard and he and others begin to hurl Molotov cocktails against the prison wall and the main tower. Lancaster and his men leave the drainpipe tunnel after overpowering their guards, climbing into an iron dump car which races down the tracks. Strapped to the front of the car is Corey, screaming that Cronyn made him turn informer. Two guards are waiting for them, sitting behind a fifty-calibre machinegun Cronyn has placed at the end of the tracks. The guards open fire, killing Corey, Hoyt, and wounding the powerful ex-prizefighter Overman. Duff and Lancaster leap from the car but Overman jumps on top of the machinegunners just as the car reaches their position. Duff picks up the machine gun and is about to follow Lancaster into the tower when another guard, Teal, shoots Duff dead. Lancaster then shoots Teal who fires a shot into him. Cronyn is now in the tower alone, manning a machinegun and shooting wildly into the inmates scurrying below. Bickford, in a futile attempt, crashes the truck into the huge gates but fails to dent them. Lancaster slowly struggles up the spiral staircase of the tower. Cronyn sees him too late, unable to turn the machinegun on him. He beats the wounded prisoner with a gun belt but Lancaster, in one last burst of energy, grabs the hated guard captain who has taken over the prison and lifts him high above his head, throwing him into the prison yard. He attempts to throw the levers that will open the gates but, ironically, the burning truck in which Bickford is dying blocks the doors. Lancaster, his goal almost accomplished, dies and the break dies with him. More guards rush into the yard throwing gas bombs and driving the surviving inmates back to their cells. In a final scene Smith is doctoring a wounded inmate, lamenting the disastrous escape attempt. "Why do they do it?" Smith asks. "I dunno, Doc," replies the inmate. "All I know is that when you lock people up they're gonna want to get out." Smith walks to the barred window, peering out into darkness sliced by the glaring spotlight sweeping from the tower. "Don't they know," he intones, "nobody escapes . . . nobody ever really escapes." BRUTE FORCE was a tour de force for Lancaster and it was Duff's debut; all of the male supporting players are excellent but Cronyn's study in evil, his role of the sadistic egomaniac Munsey, remains a chilling portrait that will not be forgotten. Dassin's direction is splendid, fast-moving and clearly organized, his expertly set scenes heavily underscored by Rozsa's rumbling offbeat score. Producer Hellinger had recently introduced Lancaster to viewers in his powerful THE KILLERS and he greatly furthered this fine actor's career by putting a first-class production behind BRUTE FORCE.

p, Mark Hellinger; d, Jules Dassin; w, Richard Brooks (based on a story by Robert Patterson); ph, William Daniels; m, Miklos Rozsa; ed, Edward Curtiss; art d, Bernard Herzbrun, John F. DeCuir; set d, Russell A. Gausman, Charles Wyrick; cos, Rosemary Odell; spec eff, David S. Horsley; makeup, Bud Westmore; tech adv, Jacques Gordon.

Prison Drama **(PR:C MPAA:NR)**

BRUTE MAN, THE ** (1946) 58m PRC

Rondo Hatton *(Hal Moffat)*, Jane Adams *(Helen)*, Tom Neal *(Clifford Scott)*, Jan Wiley *(Virginia)*, Peter Whitney, Donald MacBride.

Hatton is the renowned Creeper who was disfigured in the face by acid, now seeking revenge by murdering those he feels responsible. Like Mary Shelly's Frankenstein monster, he is kind to those who return his kindness. One such maiden is blind piano teacher Adams to whom he promises an eye operation intended to restore her sight. Unfortunately, before the operation can take place, the killer is captured. Not much stands out technically, nor do performances, only the presence of Hollywood curiosity Hatton.

p, Ben Pivar; d, Jean Yarbrough; w, George Bricker, M. Coates Webster (based on a story by Dwight V. Babcock); ph, Maury Gertsman; ed, Philip Cahn.

Horror **Cas.** **(PR:A MPAA:NR)**

BUBBLE, THE **

(1967) 112m Arch Oboler 3-D c (AKA: THE FANTASTIC INVASION OF PLANET EARTH)

Michael Cole *(Mark)*, Deborah Walley *(Catherine)*, Johnny Desmond *(Tony)*, Kassid McMahon, Barbara Eiler, Virginia Gregg, Victor Perrin, Olan Soule and Chester Jones.

When Walley goes into labor prematurely with hubby Cole by her side in a mountain cabin, the two decide it is best to get to a town. They employ the services of pilot Desmond who takes them to a strange village where the residents behave like zombies. The baby is delivered by a doctor and the new family discovers they cannot leave because they are in a bubble-covered town. Like trying to escape from a prison, they begin tunneling under the device, when they accidently cut the food supply and begin to starve. Astounding 3-D camera production is exciting for its technique, but the story is ridiculous.

p,d&w, Arch Oboler; ph, Charles Wheeler (Tri-Optiscope); m, Paul Sawtell and Bert Shafter; ed, Igo Kantor; art d, Marvin Chomsky.

Science Fiction **(PR:A MPAA:NR)**

BUCCANEER, THE*** (1938) 124m PAR bw

Fredric March *(Jean Lafitte)*, Franciska Gaal *(Gretchen)*, Akim Tamiroff *(Dominique You)*, Margot Grahame *(Annette)*, Walter Brennan *(Ezra Peavey)*, Ian Keith *(Crawford)*, Spring Byington *(Dolly Madison)*, Douglas Dumbrille *(Governor Claiborne)*, Robert Barrat *(Capt. Brown)*, Hugh Sothern *(Andrew Jackson)*, Beulah Bondi *(Aunt Charlotte)*, Anthony Quinn *(Beluche)*, Louise Campbell *(Marie De Remy)*, Montagu Love *(Adm. Cockburn)*, Eric Stanley *(Gen. Ross)*, Fred Kohler *(Gramby)*, Gilbert Emery *(Capt. Lockyer)*, Holmes Herbert *(Capt. McWilliams)*, Evelyn Keyes *(Madeleine)*, Francis McDonald *(Camden Blount)*, Frank Melton *(Lt. Shreve)*, Stanley Andrews *(Collector of Port)*, Jack Hubbard *(Charles)*, Richard Denning *(Capt. Reid)*.

Notorious pirate March refuses to attack and rob American ships in honor of his adopted home's regard for freedom. Hiding out in the Louisiana swamp country, March pines for New Orleans and the wealthy Grahame, whom he loves. After rescuing the pretty Gaal from a German ship that he has pillaged, March learns that the British are about to attack his beloved New Orleans. Coming to the aid of Southern and his American forces in what would be called the War of 1812, March helps defeat the attackers and is hailed as a hero. About to be decorated and accepted into the U.S., March's ceremony is interrupted by Grahame who announces that March's pirate pals have sacked and burned another ship, killing her sister who happened to be on board. With his past honor now destroyed, March returns to bayou country and the life of an adventuring rogue, with the adoring Gaal at his side. Fun, exciting typical DeMille film with plenty of over-indulgent, yet entertaining action. The lead women, Gaal and Grahame, turn in forgettable performances but it appears that DeMille was interested in them for decorative purposes, anyway, as he was with the majority of his actors. March manages to put some spirit into his role of the wild-living pirate with a passion for women and America, one that often comes across with fiery passion. Although not as epic and enchanting as a few of DeMille's historical dramas, THE BUCCANEER has a very patriotic, pleasant attitude that makes it a delight to watch.

p&d, Cecil B. DeMille; w, Edwin Justus Mayer, Harold Lamb, C. Gardner Sullivan (based on an adaptation by Jeanie Macpherson of *Lafitte the Pirate* by Lyle Saxon); ph, Victor Milner; m, George Antheil; ed, Anne Bauchens.

Historical Drama **(PR:A MPAA:NR)**

BUCCANEER, THE** (1958) 121m PAR c

Yul Brynner *(Jean Lafitte)*, Charlton Heston *(Andrew Jackson)*, Claire Bloom *(Bonnie Brown)*, Charles Boyer *(Dominique You)*, Inger Stevens *(Annette Claiborne)*, Henry Hull *(Ezra Peavey)*, E.G. Marshall *(Gov. Claiborne)*, Lorne Greene *(Mercier)*, Ted de Corsia *(Capt. Rumbo)*, Douglas Dumbrille *(Collector of Port)*, Robert F. Simon *(Capt. Brown)*, Sir Lancelot *(Scipio)*, Fran Jeffries *(Cariba)*, John Dierkes *(Deacon)*, Ken Miller *(Sentry)*, George Matthews *(Pyke)*, Leslie E. Bradley *(Capt. McWilliams)*, Bruce Gordon *(Gramby)*, Barry Kelley *(Commodore Patterson)*, Robert Warwick *(Capt. Lockyer)*, Steven Marlo *(Beluche)*, James Todd *(Whipple)*, Jerry Hartleben *(Miggs)*, Onslow Stevens *(Customs Inspector)*, Theodora Davitt *(Marie Claiborne)*, Wally Richard *(Lt. Shreve)*, Iris Adrian *(Wench)*, James Seay *(Creole Officer)*, Reginald Sheffield *(Tripes)*, Stephen Chase *(Col. Butler)*.

Lackluster remake of the 1938 film of the same name, this time starring Brynner as the pirate who comes to the aid of general Heston when the British attack New Orleans during the War of 1812. Brynner is very dashing and powerful as the pirate Lafitte and Heston very strong as the simple, yet forceful Andrew Jackson. The job of director was given to Quinn by his then father-in-law DeMille when the old epic-maker fell sick. The spectre of the old fellow is very much in the background amidst the incredibly gaudy costumes, sets, and trappings. A climactic battle scene is excitingly well-handled, but for the most part, Quinn's direction is sluggish and the narrative a bit sloppy.

p, Henry Wilcoxon; d, Anthony Quinn; w, Jesse L. Lasky, Jr., Bernice Mosk (based on a screenplay by Harold Lamb, Edwin Justus Mayer, C. Gardner Sullivan and Jeanie Macpherson's adaptation of *Lafitte the Pirate* by Lyle Saxon); ph, Loyal Griggs (VistaVision, Technicolor); m, Elmer Bernstein; ed, Archie Marshek.

Historical Drama **(PR:A MPAA:NR)**

BUCCANEER'S GIRL** (1950) 77m UNIV c

Yvonne De Carlo *(Deborah McCoy)*, Phillip Friend *(Frederic Baptiste)*, Robert Douglas *(Narbonne)*, Elsa Lanchester *(Mme. Brizer)*, Andrea King *(Arlene Villon)*, Nor- man Lloyd *(Patout)*, Jay C. Flippen *(Jared Hawkins)*, Henry Daniell *(Capt. Duvall)*, Douglas Dumbrille *(Capt. Matos)*, Verna Felton *(Dowager)*, John Qualen *(Vegetable Man)*, Connie Gilchrist *(Vegetable Woman)*, Ben Welden *(Tom)*, Dewey Robinson *(Kryl)*, Peggy Castle *(Cleo)*.

DeCarlo stows away on board a ship that turns out to be a freebooter under the command of pirate Friend. He tolerates her but, after they arrive in New Orleans, she falls in love with him. She learns, while attending Lanchester's school for refined young ladies, that Friend is the only one who stands up to mean tryant Douglas. She winds up with this Robin Hood and the loot, too. Good action movie with plenty of syrupy romance.

p, Robert Arthur; d, Frederick de Cordova; w, Harold Schumate, Joseph Hoffman (based on a story by Joe May and Samuel R. Golding); ph, Russell Metty (Technicolor); ed, Otto Ludwig; art d, Bernard Herzbrun, Robert F. Boyle; spec eff, David S. Horsley; ch, Harold Belfer; m/l, Walter Scharf, Jack Brooks.

Adventure/Romance (PR:A MPAA:NR)

BUCHANAN RIDES ALONE** (1958) 89m COL c

Randolph Scott *(Buchanan)*, Craig Stevens *(Abe Carbo)*, Barry Kelley *(Lou Agry)*, Tol Avery *(Simon Agry)*, Peter Whitney *(Amos Agry)*, Manuel Rojas *(Juan)*, L.Q. Jones *(Pecos Bill)*, Robert Anderson *(Waldo Peek)*, Joe de Santis *(Esteban Gomez)*, William Leslie *(Roy Agry)*, Jennifer Holden *(K.T.)*, Nacho Galindo *(Nacho)*, Roy Jensen *(Hemp)*, Don C. Harvey *(Lafe)*.

After staking a claim in Mexico, Scott makes his way back to a border town and befriends Rojas who ends up killing a pompous bully. Scott gets thrown in jail but, in his defense, ends up pitting the town's influential citizens against each other which results in his freedom. Scott co-produced this tough, witty western.

p, Harry Joe Brown, Randolph Scott; d, Budd Boetticher; w, Charles Land (based on the novel *The Name's Buchanan* by Jonas Ward); ph, Lucien Ballard (Technicolor); ed, Al Clark.

Western (PR:A MPAA:NR)

BUCK AND THE PREACHER* (1972) 102m COL c

Sidney Poitier *(Buck)*, Harry Belafonte *(Preacher)*, Ruby Dee *(Ruth)*, Cameron Mitchell *(Deshay)*, Denny Miller *(Floyd)*, Nita Talbot *(Mme. Esther)*, John Kelly *(Sheriff)*, Tony Brubaker *(Headman)*, Bobby Johnson *(Man Who Is Shot)*, James McEachin *(Kingston)*, Clarence Muse *(Cudjo)*, Lynn Hamilton *(Sarah)*, Doug Johnson *(Sam)*, Errol John *(Joshua)*, Ken Maynard *(Little Henry)*, Pamela Jones *(Delilah)*, Drake Walker *(Elder)*, Dennis Hines *(Little Toby)*, Fred Waugh *(Mizoo)*, Bill Shannon *(Tom)*, Phil Adams *(Frank)*, Walter Scott *(Earl)*, John Howard *(George)*, Enrique Lucero *(Indian Chief)*, Julie Robinson *(Sinsie)*, Jose Carlo Ruiz *(Brave)*, Jerry Gatlin *(Deputy)*, Ivan Scott *(Express Agent)*, John Kennedy *(Bank Teller)*.

Belafonte is a con man preacher who pushes his luck and the law, even though his lover Dee reminds him that some irate citizens will eventually stretch his neck. He reforms when teaming up with wagonmaster Poitier to provide some outlandish action in defeating the bad white guys. Stereotypes abound in this foolish, witless western, a production misusing the fine black talent in its cast.

p, Joel Glickman; d, Sidney Poitier; w, Ernest Kinoy (based on a story by Kinoy and Drake Walker); ph, Alex Phillips, Jr.; m, Benny Carter; ed, Pembroke J. Herring; spec eff, Leon Ortega; cos, Guy Berhille; m/l, Sonny Terry, Brownie McGee.

Western Cas. (PR:C MPAA:PG)

BUCK BENNY RIDES AGAIN** (1940) 82ms PAR bw

Jack Benny *(Jack Benny)*, Ellen Drew *(Joan Cameron)*, Eddie Anderson *(Rochester)*, Andy Devine *(Andy)*, Phil Harris *(Phil)*, Dennis Day *(Dennis)*, Virginia Dale *(Virginia)*, Lillian Cornell *(Peggy)*, Theresa Harris *(Josephine)*, Kay Linaker *(Brenda Tracy)*, Ward Bond *(1st Outlaw)*, Morris Ankrum *(2nd Outlaw)*, Charles Lane *(Charlie Graham)*, James Burke *(Taxi Driver)*, Merriel Abbott Dancers, Emil Pallenberg's "Carmichael."

After boasting about his skills as a cowboy on his program, radio star Benny is invited out west by ranch-owning pal Harris. At first declining the invitation, Benny later accepts when the pretty Drew turns his romantic offer down. Upon arriving in Nevada, Benny makes a fool out of himself trying to ride wild horses and challenging cowpokes to punching contests. He eventually becomes a true western hero when he unwittingly captures three outlaws with the assistance of Carmichael the polar bear. Witty 1940s comedy that unfortunately relies too heavily on the structure and wordplay of Benny's radio shows. Although funny, it is not cinematic in the least, lacking the physical charm of the work of Keaton, Chaplin, or the Marx Brothers. Benny's personality is a delight and his amusing cohorts from the radio programs are all present.

p, Mark Sandrich; d, Sandrich; w, William Morrow, Edmund Beloin (based on an adaptation by Zion Myers of a story by Arthur Stringer); ph, Charles Lang; ed, LeRoy Stone; ch, LeRoy Prinz; m/l, Frank Loesser, Jimmy McHugh.

Comedy (PR:A MPAA:NR)

BUCK PRIVATES** ½ (1941) 82m UNIV bw (GB: ROOKIES)

Lee Bowman *(Randolph Parker III)*, Alan Curtis *(Bob Martin)*, Bud Abbott *(Slicker Smith)*, Lou Costello *(Herbie Brown)*, The Andrews Sisters *(Themselves)*, Jane Frazee *(Judy Gray)*, Nat Pendleton *(Sgt. Michael Collins)*, Samuel S. Hinds *(Maj. Gen. Emerson)*, Harry Strang *(Sgt. Callahan)*, Nella Walker *(Mrs. Parker II)*, Leonard Elliott *(Henry)*, Shemp Howard *(Chef)*, Mike Frankovitch *(Announcer)*, Dora Clement *(Miss Durling)*, Jeanne Kelly, Elaine Morey, Kay Leslie, Nina Orla, Dorothy Darrell *(Camp Hostesses)*, Don Raye *(Dick Burnette)*, J. Anthony Hughes *(Capt. Williams)*, Hughie Prince *(Henry)*, Frank Cook *(Harmonica Player)*, James Flavin, Herold Goodwin *(Sergeants)*, Douglas Wood *(Mr. Parker)*, Charles Coleman *(Edmunds)*, Selmer Jackson *(Captain)*, Tom Tyler *(Instructor)*, Bud Harris *(Porter)*, Al Billings *(Tough Fighter)*.

While recent draftees Bowman and Curtis vie for the affections of pretty camp hostess Frazee, Abbott and Costello, also new recruits, wreak havoc on their boot camp and create a variety of headaches for their superiors. Although they had made their actual film debut in 1940s CARIBBEAN HOLIDAY, this was the film that launched the screen comedy careers of Abbott and Costello. Including some bits straight out of their vaudeville and radio shows, BUCK PRIVATES also contained the beginnings of the broad physical comedy and the clumsy, troublesome nature of their characters that would be "perfected" in films to come. The Andrews Sisters, of course, are on hand to sing, a presence which many considered to be the film's true delight. Songs: "Boogie Woogie Bugle Boy From Company B," "Bounce Me Brother With A Solid Four," "When Private Brown Meets A Sergeant," "Wish You Were Here" (Don Raye, Hughie Prince); "You're A Lucky Fellow Mr. Smith" (Raye, Prince, Sonny Burke); "I'll Be With You In Apple Blossom Time" (Neville Fleeson, Albert von Tilzer). (See ABBOTT & COSTELLO series, Index.)

p, Alex Gottlieb; d, Arthur Lubin; w, Arthur T. Horman, John Grant; ph, Milton Krasner; ed, Philip Cahn; ch, Nick Castle.

COMEDY Cas. (PR:AAA MPAA:NR)

BUCK PRIVATES COME HOME** ½

(1947) 77m UNIV bw (GB: ROOKIES COME HOME)

Bud Abbott *(Cpl. Slicker Smith)*, Lou Costello *(Herbie Brown)*, Tom Brown *(Bill Gregory)*, Joan Fulton *(Sylvia Hunter)*, Nat Pendleton *(Sgt. Collins)*, Beverly Simmons *(Yvonne LeBru)*, Don Beddoe *(Mr. Roberts)*, Don Porter *(Captain)*, Donald MacBride *(Police Captain)*, Lane Watson *(1st Lieutenant)*, William Ching *(2nd Lieutanant)*, Peter Thompson *(Steve)*, George Beban, Jr. *(Cal)*, Jimmie Dodd *(Whitey)*, Lennie Bremen *(Hank)*, Al Murphy *(Murphy)*, Bob Wilke *(Stan)*, William Haade *(Husband)*, Janna de Loos *(Wife)*, Buddy Roosevelt, Chuck Hamilton *(New York Cops)*.

Six years and 18 films later, Abbott and Costello return to their BUCK PRIVATES roles and help a little French girl sneak into America on their return trip home. Avoiding the cops and immigration officials, Bud and Lou find themselves in the middle of some wildly crazy situations including a classic sequence that has Lou dangling on a clothesline between two high-rises. Nothing spectacular, but a fine effort from the dim-witted clowns. (See ABBOTT & COSTELLO series, Index.)

p, Robert Arthur; d, Charles Barton; w, John Grant, Frederic I. Rinaldo, Robert Lees (based on a story by Richard Macauley and Bradford Ropes); ph, Charles Van Enger; m, Walter Schumann; ed, Edward Curtiss; art d, Bernard Herzbrun, Frank A. Richards.

Comedy (PR:AAA MPAA:NR)

BUCK ROGERS (SEE: DESTINATION SATURN, 1939)

BUCK ROGERS IN THE 25TH CENTURY* (1979) 89m UNIV c

Gil Gerard *(Buck Rogers)*, Pamela Hensley *(Princess Ardala)*, Erin Gray *(Wilma)*, Henry Silva *(Kane)*, Tim O'Connor *(Dr. Huer)*, Joseph Wiseman *(Draco)*, Duke Butler *(Tigerman)*, Felix Silla *(Twiki)*, Mel Blanc *(Twiki's Voice)*, Caroline Smith *(Young Woman)*, John Dewey-Carter *(Supervisor)*, Kevin Coates *(Pilot)*, David Cadiente *(Comtel Officer)*, Gil Serna *(Technician)*, Larry Duran, Kenny Endosoa *(Guards)*, Eric Lawrence *(Officer)*, H. B. Haggerty *(Tigerman Two)*, Colleen Kelly *(Wrather)*, Steve Jones, David Buchanan *(Pilots)*, Burt Marshall *(Wing Man)*.

Buck Rogers was fifty years old when this film was made. You'd think he would know better by that age. This began as a telefilm but someone in the Black Tower at Universal must have thought it had enough merit to be able to make it in the theaters. Lots of money was lavished on the production and it packs 89 minutes filled with fade in to fade out movement. But don't confuse movement with action. On the little screen, the eye is not discerning enough to see the obvious miniatures and shoddy special effects. It's all magnified by the big screen as are the comic strip lines put into the mouths of the wooden actors. There's nothing wrong with comic strips but they are newspaper items, not celluloid. This has pretensions to mediocrity, a goal far too high for it to reach.

p, Richard Caffey; d, Daniel Haller; w, Glen Larson, Leslie Stevens; ph, Frank Beascoechea (Technicolor); m, Stu Phillips; ed, John Dumas; cos, Jean-Pierre Dorleac; ch, Miriam Nelson.

Science Fiction Cas. (PR:A-C MPAA:PG)

BUCKAROO FROM POWDER RIVER** (1948) 55m COL bw

Charles Starrett *(Steve Lacy/The Durango Kid)*, Smiley Burnette *(Himself)*, Eve Miller *(Molly Parnell)*, Forrest Taylor *(Pop Ryland)*, Paul Campbell *(Clint Ryland)*, Doug Coppin *(Tommy Ryland)*, Phillip Morris *(Sheriff Barnell)*, Casey MacGregor *(Dave Ryland)*, Ted Adams *(Les Driscoll)*, Ethan Laidlaw *(Ben Trask)*, Frank McCarroll *(McCall)*, The Cass Country Boys.

Starrett aims to break up Taylor's gang of bank robbers but ends up saving outlaw's son Coppin who has been marked for death. Passable entertainment. (See DURANGO KID series, Index.)

p, Colbert Clark; d, Ray Nazzaro; w, Norman Hall; ph, George F. Kelley; ed, Paul Borofsky.

Western (PR:A MPAA:NR)

BUCKAROO SHERIFF OF TEXAS* (1951) 60m REP bw

Michael Chapin *(Red White)*, Eileen Janssen *(Judy Dawson)*, James Bell *(Tom Grampa White)*, Hugh O'Brian *(Ted Gately)*, Steve Pendleton *(Sam White)*, Tristram Coffin *(Jim Tulane)*, William Haade *(Mark Branigan)*, Alice Kelley *(Betty Dawson)*, Selmer Jackson *(Governor)*, Edward Cassidy *(Clint)*.

Coffin aims to take over as much property as possible while the owners are away fighting a war. Brainless horse opera with no style or story.

p, Rudy Ralston; d, Phillip Ford; w, Arthur Orloff; ph, John MacBurnie; ed, Arthur Roberts.

Western (PR:A MPAA:NR)

BUCKET OF BLOOD**

(1934, Brit.) 50m Clifton-Hurst/FOX bw (GB: THE TELL-TALE HEART)

Norman Dryden *(The Boy)*, John Kelt *(The Old Man)*, Yolande Terrell *(The Girl)*, Thomas Shenton *(1st Investigator)*, James Fleck *(2nd Investigator)*, Colonel Cameron *(Doctor)*.

A re-telling of the classic Poe story. Convinced he hears the heartbeat of his victim, a psychotic confesses to comitting murder. Weak production.

p, Harry Clifton; d, Brian Desmond Hurst; w, David Plunkett Greene (based on the story by Edgar Allan Poe).

Horror (PR:O MPAA:NR)

BUCKET OF BLOOD, A** (1959) 66m AIP bw

Dick Miller *(Walter)*, Barboura Morris *(Carla)*, Anthony Carbone *(Leonard)*, Julian Burton *(Brock)*, Ed Nelson *(Art Lacroix)*, John Brinkley *(Will)*, John Shaner *(Oscar)*,

Judy Bamber *(Alice)*, Myrtle Domerel *(Mrs. Surchart)*, Bert Convy *(Lou Raby)*, Jean Burton *(Haolia)*.

This beatnik horror comedy was done before the better known, though similar LITTLE SHOP OF HORRORS, by Roger Corman, guru of the 1950s horror buffs. Walter (Dick Miller), an inept busboy works in an expresso house where neighborhood beatniks hang out showing and talking about their sophomoric works of art. He longs to be one of the "crowd" and after accidentally killing a cat he's trying to rescue, covers up the deed by moulding clay around the cat's carcass. Intoxicated with success when his efforts are hailed by the beatniks as original works of art, the formerly scorned lackey is soon embarked upon his predictable career. Excellent performance by Miller who manages to sustain a sense of poignancy while committing his atrocities. Funny film with a good comical jazz score by Fred Katz.

p&d, Roger Corman; w, Charles B. Griffith; ph, Jack Marquette; ed, Anthony Carras; m, Fred Katz; art d, Dan Haller.

Horror **(PR:A MPAA:NR)**

BUCKSKIN** (1968) 98m PAR c

Barry Sullivan *(Chaddock)*, Joan Caulfield *(Nora Johnson)*, Wendell Corey *(Rep. Marlow)*, Lon Chaney, Jr. *(Sheriff Tangely)*, John Russell *(Patch)*, Barbara Hale *(Sarah Cody)*, Barton MacLane *(Do Raymond)*, Bill Williams *(Frank Cody)*, Richard Arlen *(Townsman)*, Leo Gordon *(Travis)*, Gerald Michenaud *(Akii)*, George Chandler *(Storekeeper)*, Aki Aleong *(Sung Li)*, Michael Larrain *(Jimmy Cody)*.

Frontier marshal Sullivan gathers the townspeople into rebellion against wealthy cattle owner Corey who has cut off the town's water supply and is holding it ransom. Slowmoving action and poor direction undoes a good cast.

p, A.C. Lyles; d, Michael Moore; w, Michael Fisher; ph, W. Wallace Kelley (Pathe Color); m, Jimmy Haskell; ed, Jack Wheeler.

Western **(PR:A MPAA:NR)**

BUCKSKIN FRONTIER** (1943) UA 78m bw

Richard Dix *(Stephen Bent)*, Jane Wyatt *(Vinnie Mar)*, Albert Dekker *(Gideon Skene)*, Lee J. Cobb *(Jeptha Marr)*, Victor Jory *(Champ Clanton)* Lola Lane *(Rita Molyneux)*, Max Baer *(Tiny)*, Joe Sawyer *(Brannigan)*, Harry Allen *(McWhinny)*, Francis McDonald *(Duvall)*, George Reeves *(Jeff Collins)*, Bill Nestell *(Whiskers)*.

Missouri Central Railroad wants to take the Santa Fe cutoff but is faced with a smalltime freight train owner blocking its effort. Fair action piece with excellent supporting players following Dix's strong lead.

p, Harry Sherman; d, Lesley Selander; w, Norman Houston, Bernard Schubert (based on a story by Harry Sinclair Drago).

Western **Cas.** **(PR:A MPAA:NR)**

BUCKSKIN LADY, THE *1/2 (1957) 66m UA bw

Patricia Medina *(Angela Medley)*, Richard Denning *(Dr. Bruce Merritt)*, Gerald Mohr *(Slinger)*, Henry Hull *(Doc)*, Hank Worden *(Lon)*, Robin Short *(Nevada)*, Richard Reeves *(Porter)*, Dorothy Adams *(Mrs. Adams)*, Frank Sully *(Jed)*, George Cisar *(Cranston)*, Louis Lettiere *(Ralphy)*, Byron Foulger *(Latham)*, John Dierkes *(Swanson)*.

Medina is a gambling lady who supports her drunken father Hull with her earnings, dallying with gunman Mohr. All this changes when Denning, a new and sober physician, arrives and Medina falls in love with him, leading to a confrontation between Mohr and Denning. Good action in a somewhat predictable oater.

p&d, Carl Hittleman; w, David Lang, Carl Hittleman (based on a story by Francis S. Chase, Jr.) ph, Ellsworth Fredericks; m, Albert Glasser; ed, Harry Coswick; m/l, Glasser, Maurice Keller.

Western **(PR:A MPAA:NR)**

BUCKTOWN zero (1975) 94m AIP c

Fred Williamson *(Duke)*, Pam Grier *(Aretha)*, Thalmus Rasulala *(Roy)*, Tony King *(T. J.)*, Bernie Hamilton *(Harley)*, Art Lund *(Chief Patterson)*, Tierre Turner *(Steve)*, Morgan Upton *(Sam)*, Carl Weathers *(Hambone)*, Jim Bohan *(Clete)*, Robert Burton *(Merle)*, Gene Simms *(Josh)*, Bruce Watson *(Bag Man)*.

Fred Williamson has done it again; starred in a film that did nothing to exploit his abilities. This is not just another footballer turned actor. He has a brain between those ears and proved it with some strong directing in later years. In BUCKTOWN, he plays a man who comes to a small southern town (sort of like PHENIX CITY) to wreak revenge for his brother's murder. The dead sibling was killed when he wouldn't pay off protection to the local white fuzz. Fred takes over the brother's tavern and the rest is the usual hokum. Fred then takes up with his brother's widow (Grier) and almost gets killed by the white cops. Now comes the one interesting moment,. Fred calls in some heavy black dudes to help him. These guys roll in, like what they see and decide this would be a nice town to push around. They murder the cops and take over the place. Using an armored tank, Fred becomes Clint Eastwood in tanface and decimates his former pals. An obvious black exploitation film, this could have been worth more if someone had exhibited any taste at all.

p, Bernard Schwartz; d, Arthur Marks; w, Bob Ellison; ph, Robert Virchall (Movielab Color); m, Johnny Pate; ed, George Fosley.

Crime **(PR:C MPAA:R)**

BUDDHA** (1965, Jap.) 139m Daiei/UA c

Kojiro Hongo *(Siddhartha)*, Charito Solis *(Yashodhara)*, Shintaro Katsu *(Devadatta)*, Machiko Kyo *(Yashas Nandabala)*, Raizo Ichikawa *(Kunala)*, Fujiko Yamamoto *(Usha)*, Keizo Kawaski *(Upali)*, Hiroshi Kawaguchi *(Ajatashatru)*, Katsuhiko Kobayashi *(Ananda)*, Tamao Nakamura *(Auttami)*, Junko Kano *(Matangi)*, Gen. Mitamura *(Shariputra)*, Mieko Kondo *(Amana)*, Tokiko Mita *(Sari)*, Hiromi Ichida *(Naecha)*, Matasburo *(Sonna)*, Kiezo Kawasaki *(Upali)*, Reiko Fujiwara *(Child's Mother)*, Ryuzo Shimada *(Bhutika)*, Joji Tsurumi *(Arama)*, Shiro Otsuji *(Kaloday)*, Yoshiro Kitahara *(Kaundinva)*, Jun Negami *(Mahakashyapa)*, Ganjiro Nakamura *(Ashoka)*, Toshio Chiba *(Graha)*, Ryuichi Ishii *(Bandhu)*, Yoichi Funak *(Maudgaliputra)*, Sanemon Arashi *(Rayana)*, Osamu Maryuama *(Jivaka)*, Michiko Ai *(Kilika)*.

Story revolves around the coming of a new Buddha. Hongo goes away for six years and is reborn, taking him on a journey touching the lives of his people. Obtuse and confusing to Western viewers. (In Japanese, English sub-titles.)

p, Masaichi Nagata; d, Kenji Misumi; w, Fuji Yahiro; ph, Hiroshi Imai (Technirama, Technicolor); m, Akira Ifukube; ed, Kanji Suganuma; spec eff, Tatsuyuki Yokota, Sohi-Ichi Aisaka; cos, Yoshio Ueno; ch, Kiitsu Sakakibara.

Drama **(PR:C MPAA:NR)**

BUDDIES1/2** (1983, Aus.) 99m PTY Ltd. c

Colin Friels *(Mike)*, Kris McQuade *(Stella)*, Harold Hopkins *(Johnny)*, Dennis Miller *(Andy)*, Simon Chilvers *(Alfred)*, Norman Kaye *(George)*, Lisa Peers *(Jennifer)*, Bruce Spence *(Ted)*, Andrew Sharp *(Peter)*, Dinah Shearing *(Merle)*.

BUDDIES is like one of those old-fashioned westerns where the male bonding triumphs over any woes that might befall the heroes. Set in remote Queensland, BUDDIES tells of two close friends scratching out a living mining diamonds with another male miner and one female. A villain arrives (we used to call them claimjumpers in Gabby Hayes' day) and the conflict begins. Superb characters in this film. Just when you think they are the cliche we've come to expect, they take a 180-degree turn and become totally different. Lots of comedy, action, fine location photography, superior stunts, and a happy ending. It's not THE TREASURE OF THE SIERRA MADRE, but it's a lot better than a many Burt Reynolds films that have been spewing forth of late.

p, John Dingwall; d, Arch Nicholson; w, Dingwall; ph, David Eggby (Panavision) m, Chris Neal; ed, Martyn Down.

Comedy/Adventure **(PR:A MPAA:NR)**

BUDDY BUDDY** (1981) 96m MGM/UA c

Jack Lemmon *(Victor Clooney)*, Walter Matthau *(Trabucco)*, Paula Prentiss *(Celia Clooney)*, Klaus Kinski *(Dr. Zuckerbrot)*, Dana Elcar *(Capt. Hubris)*, Miles Chapin *(Eddie the Bellhop)*, Michael Ensign *(Assistant Manager)*, Joan Shawlee *(Receptionist)*, Fil Formicola *(Rudy Disco Gambola)*, C. J. Hunt *(Kowalski)*, Bette Raya *(Mexican Maid)*, Ronnie Sperling *(Hippy Husband)*, Suzie Galler *(Pregnant Wife)*, Bill Manard *(Cop)*, John Schubeck, Ed Begley, Jr., Frank Farmer, Tom Kindle, Charlotte Stewart, Neile McQueen, Myrna Dell, Gene Price, Ben Lessy, Patti Jerome, Gary Allen, Frances Bay, Dean Bruce, Rod Gist, Steve Hirshon.

While Matthau sets himself up for a hit in one hotel room, Lemmon makes futile attempts on his own life following his wife's departure with a sex therapist in another. The usual slapstick chaos ensues with Lemmon and Matthau creating their by now stereotyped roles. A few good lines of dialog cannot save the fact that everybody is trying a little too hard to make this film work. As a black comedy the premise should work were it not for the fact that everyone capitalizes on the viewer's expectations of the "odd couple's" patent formula.

p, Jay Weston; d&w, Billy Wilder (based on the play and story by Francis Veber); ph, Harry Stradling, Jr.; m, Lalo Schifrin; (Panavision, Technicolor); ed, Argyle Nelson.

Comedy **Cas.** **PR:C MPAA:R)**

BUDDY HOLLY STORY, THE * 1/2** (1978) 113m COL c

Gary Busey *(Buddy Holly)*, Don Stroud *(Jesse)*, Charles Martin Smith *(Ray Bob)*, Bill Jordan *(Riley Randolph)*, Maria Richwine *(Maria Elena Holly)*, Conrad Janis *(Ross Turner)*, Albert Popwell *(Eddie Foster)*, Amy Johnston *(Jenny Lou)*, Jim Beach *(Mr. Wilson)*, John F. Goff *(T.J.)*, Fred Travalena *(Madman Mancuso)*, Dick O'Neil *(Sol Zuckerman)*, Stymie Beard *(Luther)*, M.G. Kelly *(M.C.)*, Paul Mooney *(Sam Cooke)*, Bill Phillips Murray *(Desk Clerk)*, Freeman King *(Tyrone)*, Steve Camp *(Cook)*, Jody Berry *(Engineer Sam)*, Bob Christopher *(Cadillac Salesman)*, Arch Johnson *(Mr. Holly)*, Neva Patterson *(Mrs. Holly)*.

Buddy Holly didn't live very long. His life ended in a snowstorm with The Big Bopper and Richie Valens in 1959. Their plane went down and it was later eulogized in Don McLean's song "The Day The Music Died." How much of a movie could be made about a young man who never survived his early twenties? The answer is . . . a hell of a lot of movie! Busey is perfect as Holly and all the small roles are well chosen. The story only spans a few years, from Holly's youth in Lubbock to his death. Lubbock is one of those quiet and conservative towns and Holly was chastized for his descent into rock and roll. The music was too black for their white sensibilities. Holly paid them no mind, started writing and recording, and was a star before he had to shave more than three times a week. If you are old enough to remember Buddy and The Crickets and their string of hits, you'll love this film. Busey did all his own singing and playing, as did Martin and Stroud as The Crickets, providing a welcome sense of realism. Busey's performance is terrific, and won him an Oscar nomination for Best Actor, though he lost to Jon Voight for COMING HOME. The film did win an Academy Award for best scoring. Songs include "That'll Be The Day," "Peggy Sue," "Every Day," "Oh Boy," all written by Holly and sung by Busey.

p, Fred Bauer; d, Steve Rash; w, Robert Gittler (based on the book by John Coldrosen); ph, Steven Larner; ed, David Blewitt; prod d, Joel Schiller; md, Joe Renzetti; set d, Tom Roysden; cos, Michael Butler; spec eff, Robbie Knott; ch, Maggie Rush; makeup, Marvin Westmore, Doris Alexaner.

Biography **(PR:A-C MPAA:PG)**

BUFFALO BILL* 1/2** (1944) 90m FOX c

Joel McCrea *(Buffalo Bill)*, Maureen O'Hara *(Louisa Cody)*, Linda Darnell *(Dawn* Starlight), Thomas Mitchell *(Ned Buntline)*, Edgar Buchanan *(Sgt. Chips)*, Anthony Quinn *(Yellow Hand)*, Moroni Olsen *(Sen. Frederici)*, Frank Fenton *(Murdo Carvell)*, Matt Briggs *(Gen. Blazier)*, George Lessey *(Mr. Vandevere)*, Frank Orth *(Sherman)*, George Chandler *(Trooper Clancy)*, Chief Many Treaties *(Tall Bull)*, Nick Thompson *(Medicine Man)*, Chief Thundercloud *(Crazy Horse)*, Sidney Blackmer *(President Theodore Roosevelt)*, William Haade *(Barber)*, Evelyn Beresford *(Queen Victoria)*, Edwin Stanley *(Doctor)*, John Dilson *(President Hayes)*, Cecil Weston *(Maid)*, Merrill Rodin *(Bellboy)*, Vincent Graeff *(Crippled Boy)*, Fred Graham *(Editor)*.

A slam-bang, hell-for-leather western epic, BUFFALO BILL opens with a racing stagecoach under Indian attack. Just when the Indians are about to close in and finish the driver, they are shot from their ponies by an unseen gunman, Buffalo Bill (McCrea), the noted frontier scout, Indian-fighter, and buffalo hunter. McCrea escorts the coach's passengers, Olsen, a U.S. Senator, and his daughter O'Hara to a nearby fort. Here McCrea meets railroad tycoon Lessey and Mitchell, playing the famous western journalist and dime novelist Ned Buntline. Lessey explains to commanding general Briggs that the army is needed to clear the Cheyennes from their lands so that his railroad can be completed. McCrea interrupts to warn the financier that if such action is taken the Indians will resist, but he is ignored. The army commander agrees to first set up a meeting with the Indians and senator Olson to negotiate a deal. Olsen is captured and McCrea risks his life to save the senator. McCrea is tortured but freed by the great chief Yellow Hand (Quinn) for past favors; he promises Quinn that he will bring about an equitable peace before returning Olsen to the fort and his daughter. When Olsen leaves for Washington O'Hara remains at the fort, marrying the scout. McCrea then heads a company selling buffalo robes, leading the slaughter of the great buffalo herds, while O'Hara gives birth to their child, Kit Carson Cody. When the Indians protest this mass killing of animals and are ignored by Washington, the western tribes rise to the warpath, destroying the Seventh Cavalry under Custer. Cody is called by Briggs to scout for his troops which are ordered to prevent the Cheyennes from joining the Sioux. O'Hara, fearful for his life, threatens to take their child and go East if McCrea rides off to battle the Indians. McCrea answers the call to duty and goes off with the troops. He purposely misleads them to War Bonnet Gorge against orders and here fights a hand-to-hand duel with Quinn, a stalling tactic until the main body of troops arrive. He kills Quinn and the troops rout and destroy the Cheyennes. Found among the dead by McCrea is Indian princess Darnell who had been in love with him. McCrea is called to Washington where he is to receive The Congressional Medal of Honor for his deeds at War Bonnet Gorge. As he travels East by train thousands of citizens mob him; he has been made famous by the many dime novels written by Mitchell heralding the feats of the great Buffalo Bill. Once in Washington, McCrea learns that his son is dying of diphtheria; he arrives at his bedside too late. This embitters McCrea after he learns from a doctor that diphtheria is "a disease of crowds, of civilization." O'Hara, he remembers, had taken the boy East to be educated and get the benefits of "civilization." Later, at a testimonial dinner, Cody attacks the Eastern Establishment for its ruthless treatment of Indians and is suddenly persona non grata with his sponsors. He stays in the East, separated from his wife, and his enemies soon mount a smear campaign that attempts to discredit McCrea's deeds and reputation. He is reduced to a pauper and makes his living in a shooting gallery as a marksman. O'Hara learns of his plight and goes to the gallery, holding up a dime which McCrea shoots out of her fingers. The crowd goes wild. O'Hara and McCrea are once again united. Mitchell arrives and proposes that McCrea "bring the West to the East." Buffalo Bill establishes his great Wild West Show, pleasing thousands of audiences, including President Theodore Roosevelt (Blackmer who is hardly recognizable behind his makeup), and the crowned heads of Europe. McCrea is swiftly shown to age so that his long hair is now white when he rides into the arena for the last time to bid his generations of fans farewell. "God bless you," he says while mounted on his magnificent horse. In poignant response a small boy on crutches struggles to his feet and yells: "And God bless you, too, Buffalo Bill!" The great scout bends his head, sweeps goodbye with his white Stetson, and rides out of the spotlight. Director Wellman, who did a marvelous job of filming this biography, as part of a deal with Fox so he could direct his classic THE OX-BOW INCIDENT, later denounced BUFFALO BILL as historic hokum, that the western scout was nothing more than a con man. "And when that little boy in the gallery struggled to his feet to say goodbye—God!" He claimed he fought against that ending and wanted to portray Cody in a more critical light but studio boss Zanuck vetoed the idea; he wanted the myth of the great hero preserved. It is true that Cody was a great self-promoter but Wellman was no doubt responding to then popular iconoclastic attitudes toward heroes of any kind when he besmirched Cody's character. Had he really investigated the career of Buffalo Bill, Wellman would have realized that much of the myth was true. Cody did fight, before many witnesses, a hand-to-hand duel with Chief Yellow Hand and did win The Congressional Medal of Honor. His incredible feats on the frontier were half fact and half legend and, as with all legends, Cody later embellished and exaggerated his career but none of his bragging was malicious; it was all part of the show by the greatest showman of his era. BUFFALO BILL, despite its slushy melodrama, remains a vivid, spacious, and exciting film, perfectly suited to Wellman's broad direction and McCrea's stoic personality, contrasting animation coming from the fiery O'Hara and the ebullient Mitchell. It also provided Quinn with a substantial role, albeit he had been playing Indians since his debut in THE PLAINSMAN (which also dealt with Buffalo Bill), and had played Chief Crazy Horse opposite Errol Flynn in THEY DIED WITH THEIR BOOTS ON.

p, Harry A. Sherman; d, William A. Wellman; w, Aeneas MacKenzie, Clements Ripley, Cecile Kramer (based on a story by Frank Winch); ph, Leon Shamroy (Technicolor); m, David Buttolph; ed, James B. Clark; md, Emil Newman; art d, James Basevi, Lewis Creger; spec eff, Frank Sersen.

Western/Adventure/Biography   Cas.   (PR:AAA MPAA:NR)

BUFFALO BILL AND THE INDIANS, OR SITTING BULL'S HISTORY LESSON zero
(1976) 120m UA c

Paul Newman (Buffalo Bill), Joel Grey (Nate Salsbury), Harvey Keitel (Ed), Kevin McCarthy (Maj. Burke), Mike Kaplan (Jules Keen), Bert Remsen (Crutch), Burt Lancaster (Ned Buntline), Geraldine Chaplin (Annie Oakley), John Considine (Frank Butler), Frank Kaquitts (Sitting Bull), Will Sampson (William Halsey), Robert Doqui (Wrangler), Denver Pyle (McLaughlin), Pat McCormick (Grover Cleveland), Shelley Duvall (Mrs. Cleveland), Evelyn Lear (Nina), Bonnie Leaders (Margaret), Noelle Rogers (Lucille), Fred Larsen (Cowboy King), Joy and Jerri Duce (Trick Riders), Humphrey Gratz (Old Soldier), Residents of The Stoney Indian Reserve.

The big question is: How does Robert Altman keep finding financiers gullible enough to allow him to engage in such cinema garbage as this film? Perhaps he should only make films with the letters A-S-H in the title. After all, M*A*S*H and NASHVILLE were both good. But since then, he has become so self-indulgent that it boggles the mind to see such tripe as THREE WOMEN, HEALTH, A WEDDING, QUINTET, A PERFECT COUPLE, and so on. Cynical, dumb, and in bad taste, Altman and screenwriter Rudolph take us through much the same territory that Irving Berlin did in his musical ANNIE GET YOU GUN. Newman has never been so charmless and Keitel, who seldom does anything bad on screen, does nothing good in this film. Look at that array of stars. Look at the producers. Look at the excellent technical people. And all of them must have believed that Altman knew what he was doing. Which just goes to prove . . . you can fool all of the cast and crew all of the time but you can't fool the public.

p&d, Robert Altman; w, Alan Rudolph (from the play "Indians" by Arthur Kopit); ph, Paul Lohmann (DeLuxe Color); m, Richard Baskin; ed, Peter Appleton, Dennis Hill.

Western   Cas.   (PR:C MPAA:PG)

BUFFALO BILL, HERO OF THE FAR WEST**
(1962, Ital.) 93m Gloria Film

Gordon Scott, Jan Hendriks, Mario Brega, Catherine Ribeiro, Mirko Ellis, Rolando Lupi.

Scott is sent by Gen. Grant to make peace with the Indians. Just plain good fun although nothing in particular is notable, except that this routine oater was the first Italian western to achieve international fame.

p, Solly Bianco; d, John W. Fordson [Mario Costa]; w, Nino Straesa, Luciano Martino: ph, Jack Dalmas [Massimo Dallamano].

Western   (PR:A MPAA:NR)

BUFFALO BILL IN TOMAHAWK TERRITORY**
(1952) 66m UA bw

Clayton Moore (Buffalo Bill), Slim Andrews (Cactus), Rod Redwing (Chief White Cloud), Sharon Dexter (Janet), Eddie Phillips (Lt. Bryan), Tom Hubbard (Stokey).

Moore is sent to Redwing with an offering to the Indians of a herd of cattle as part payment from the U.S. Government in a peace pact with the Sioux. Stock feature on all counts.

p, Edward Finney, Bernard B. Ray; d, Ray; w, Sam Neumann, Nat Tanchuck; ph, Elmer Dyer.

Western   (PR:A MPAA:NR)

BUFFALO BILL RIDES AGAIN*
(1947) 70m Screen Guild bw

Richard Arlen (Buffalo Bill), Jennifer Holt (Lale Harrington), Lee Schumway (Steve), Gil Patrick (Simpson), Edward Cassidy (Sheriff), Edmund Cobb (Morgan), Ted Adams (Sam), Shooting Star (Young Bird), Charles Stevens (White Mountain), Many Treaties (Chief Brave Eagle), John Dexter (Tom Russell), Hollis Baine (Rankin), Frank McCarroll (Hank), Carl Mathews (Pete), Clark Stevens (Jeff), George Sherwood (Mr. Smith), Fred Graham (Mr. Dawson), Paul Hill (Dawson's Daughter), Phillip Arnold (Scratchy), Tom Leffingwell (Senator), Frank O'Connor (Mr. Jordan), Fred Fox (Mr. Howard), Dorothy Curtis (Mrs. Dawson).

Arlen is sent by the U.S. Government to find out why the Indians are causing trouble, and is almost scalped for asking too many questions, a fate that should have befallen this poor film's producers.

p, Jack Schwartz; d, Bernard B. Ray; w, Barney Sarecky, Fran Gilbert; ph, Robert Cline.

Western   (PR:A MPAA:NR)

BUFFALO GUN*
(1961) 72m Globe bw

Marty Robbins, Webb Pierce, Carl Smith (Themselves), Wayne Morris (Rocca), Mary Ellen Kay (Clementine), Donald "Red" Barry (Murdock), Douglas Fowley (Sheriff), Harry Lauter (Telegrapher), The Jordanaires.

When Indians complain their government shipments are being raided, agents are sent to investigate. Background hillbilly music adds ironic twist to this western though its overpowering melodies are distracting rather than complementary.

p, A.R. Milton; d, Albert C. Gannaway; w, Milton; ph, Gerald Finnerman; m, Ramez Idriss; ed, Carl Pingitore; art d, George Troast.

Western   (PR:A MPAA:NR)

BUG*
(1975) 99m PAR c

Bradford Dillman (James Parmiter), Joanna Miles (Carrie Parmiter), Richard Gilliland (Metbaum), Jamie Smith Jackson (Norma Tacker), Alan Fudge (Mark Ross), Jesse Vint (Tom Tacker), Patty McCormack (Sylvia Ross), Brenden Dillon (Charlie), Fred Downs (Henry Tacker), James Greene (Rev. Kern), Jim Poyner (Kenny Tacker), Sam Jarvis (Taxi Driver), Bard Stevens (The Guard).

The best part of BUG is Charlie Fox's electronic music. If one could shut off the dialog and just listen to the music, it would be a neat album. Unfortunately, the actors keep talking. What they talk about is mutation of cockroaches due to a quake at the center of the earth. Bugs come out and eat carbon and are hot to the touch. They travel around in cars and hide out in the tail pipes. Dillman is a scientist who loses his wife to the bugs. Midway through the film, Dillman becomes a recluse and so the film goes to sleep along with him. A few scary moments but that's about it. Technical credits are good, actors are fair, direction is mediocre and BUG got squashed by the public's foot.

p, William Castle; d, Jeannot Szwarc; w, Castle, Thomas Page (based on the novel The Hephaestus Plague by Page); ph, Michel Hugo (Movielab Color); m, Charles Fox; ed, Alan Jacobs; cos, Guy Verhille.

Science Fiction   Cas.   (PR:A-C MPAA:PG)

BUGLE SOUNDS, THE**
(1941) 101m MGM bw

Wallace Berry (Hap Doan), Marjorie Main (Susie), Lewis Stone (Col. Lawton), George Bancroft (Russell), Henry O'Neill (Lt. Col. Seton), Donna Reed (Sally Hanson), William Lundigan (Joe Hanson), Guinn "Big Boy" Williams (Krims), Ernest Whitman (Cartaret), Roman Bohnen (Leech), Jerome Cowan (Nichols), Arthur Space (Hank), Jonathan Hale (Brigadier-General).

Beery is an old cavalryman caught up in the mechanization of the army with tanks. A good cast is wasted on a weak script and lame direction. Oddly, this film was released two weeks after Pearl Harbor, and made the fatal error of criticizing the U.S. Army's unpreparedness, something no one wanted to hear.

p, J. Walter Ruben; d, S. Sylvan Simon; w, Cyril Hume (based on a story by Lawrence Kimble and Hume); ph, Clyde De Vinna; ed, Ben Lewis; spec eff, Arnold Gillespie.

Military Drama   (PR:A MPAA:NR)

BUGLES IN THE AFTERNOON**
(1952) 85m WB c

Ray Milland (Kern Shafter), Helena Carter (Josephine Russell), Hugh Marlowe (Garnett), Forrest Tucker (Donavan), Barton MacLane (Capt. Myles Moylan), George Reeves (Lt. Smith), James Millican (Sgt. Hines), Gertrude Michael (May), Stuart Randall (Bannack Bill), William "Bill" Phillips (Tinney), Dick Rich (Biers), John Pickard (McDermott), John War Eagle (Red Owl), Sheb Wooley (Gen. Custer), Charles Evans (Gen. Terry), Nelson Leigh (Maj. Reno), Ray Montgomery (Osborne), Virginia Brissac (Mrs. Carson), John Doucette (Bill), Bud Osborne (Teamster), Hugh Beaumont (Lt. Cooke), Harry Lauter (Cpl. Jackson), Bob Steele (Horseman), Mary Adams, Lucille Shamburger (Women).

After striking fellow officer Marlowe, Milland quits the cavalry, planning to leave the East and re-enlist in the Wild West. When he arrives at Fort Lincoln, Milland is shocked to learn that his old enemy Marlowe is in command. Milland endures hardship after hardship as Marlowe gives him the most dangerous assignments, hoping that Milland will die on one of the dangerous assignments. When they both fall for Carter, the tension between the two builds to a frenzy. During the Battle of the Little Big Horn, the two rivals engage in a hand-to-hand fight while hundreds of soldiers and Indians battle around them. Marlowe is killed and Milland returns to Carter after Custer's devastating loss. Routine western containing a gutsy performance from Milland in his first action picture. Mediocre director Rowland manages to create a few thrilling fight sequences and gives the entire picture a fast rhythm and edgy quality.

p, William Cagney; d, Roy Rowland; w, Geoffrey Homes, Harry Brown (based on a novel by Ernest Haycox); ph, Wilfrid M. Cline (Technicolor); m, Dmitri Tiomkin; ed, Thomas Reilly.

Western **(PR:A MPAA:NR)**

BUGS BUNNY/ROAD-RUNNER MOVIE, THE
(SEE: GREAT AMERICAN BUGS BUNNY-ROAD RUNNER CHASE, 1979)

BUGS BUNNY, SUPERSTAR*** (1975) 90m WB c

Voices of Bob Clampett, Tex Avery, Friz Freleng, Mel Blanc; narration by Orson Welles.

Fans of the immortal, wisecracking rabbit will be entranced by the artistry of the "old-fashioned" realistic animation technique as well as the humor in this collection of ten cartoons.

d, Larry Jackson.

Animated Feature **(PR:AAA MPAA:NR)**

BUGS BUNNY'S THIRD MOVIE—1001 RABBIT TALES** (1982) 90m WB c

Voices, Mel Blanc.

Bugs, like ROCKY and SUPERMAN, seems to be on a sequel kick. This is the brilliant bunny's third compilation movie and, while it is not quite as good as the first two, it's still so much more fun than just about anything one sees on Saturday morning TV, unless, of course, you happen to be watching an old Bugs Bunny cartoon or some of the early Disney or Lantz. Some good yocks in this film as Bugs and Daffy are book salesmen for "Rambling House" (Bennett Cerf would be whirling at that) and the word play comes thick and fast. Bugs dreams of Jeanie, "She's a light brown hare" and the new segues take the Bunny and the Duck into the old adventures with hardly a seam showing. Mel Blanc is truly an amazing voice person and when he had a terrible auto accident many years ago and was laid up for several months, the line around Hollywood was that "400 animals are on unemployment." He'd been doing the voice of Barney on "The Flintstones" TV show and was temporarily replaced until he recovered. The odd part was that no one noticed. Blanc has been the voice of Bugs, Sylvester, Tweetie Pie and hundreds more. His greatest radio triumph was with Jack Benny. (Sequel: DAFFY DUCK'S MOVIE, FANTASTIC ISLAND)

p, Friz Freleng, d, David Detiege, Art Davis, Bill Perez; w, John Dunn, Detiege, Freleng; ph, Nick Vasu (Technicolor) m, Rob Walsh, Milt Franklyn, Bill Lava, Carl Stalling; animation, Warren Batchelder, Bob Bransford, Marcia Fertig, Terrence Lennon, Bob Matz, Norm McCabe, Tom Ray, Virgil Ross.

Animated Feature **Cas.** **(PR:AAA MPAA:G)**

BUGSY MALONE*1/2** (1976, Brit.) 93m PAR c

Scott Baio *(Bugsy Malone)*, Jodie Foster *(Tallulah)*, Florrie Dugger *(Blousey)*, JohnCassisi *(Fat Sam)*, Paul Murphy *(Leroy)*, Albin Jenkins *(Fizzy)*, Martin Lev *(Dandy* Dan), Davidson Knight *(Knuckles)*, Paul Chirelstein *(Smolsky)*, Paul Besterman *(Yonkers)*, Ron Melelu *(Doodle)*, Jorge Valdez *(Bronx Charlie)*, Michael Kirby *(Angelo)*, Donald Waugh *(Snake Eyes)*, Peter Holder *(Ritzy)*, John Lee *(Benny)*, Jon Zebrowski *(Shoulders)*, Michael Jackson *(Razamataz)*, Andrew Paul *(O'Dreary)*, Helen Corran *(Bangles)*, Dexter Fletcher *(Baby Face)*, Vivienne McKonne *(Velma)*, Jeffrey Stevens *(Louis)*, Kevin Reul, Brian Hardy, Bonita Langford, Mark Curry, Katherine Apanowicz, Lynn Aulbaugh, Nick Amend, John Williams, Herbert Norville, Louise English, Kathy Spaulding.

Charming, delightful, all the things a "G" rated picture should be, BUGSY MALONE is a gangster spoof of the 1920s replete with all of the cliche characters except that this is a musical and everyone in the film is a teenager or less. Hardly any of the boys' voices have changed so the songs are all in keys for altos or sorpranos. Paul Williams has written a lovely score and Alan Parker a lovely script. You've seen every single one of these characters played by Robinson or Cagney or Bogart or Steiger or Neville Brand but they come to life again when those tried and true lines like, "I thought I tol' ya ta stay outta da Sout' side, Blackie," are put into the mouths of babes. It was not the hit it might have been and Williams later took it to London as a live musical where it was, again, not the hit it might have been. Many of the juveniles are British but the few Americans have since gone on to some success. Scott Baio in several TV shows and Jodie Foster in films. When it comes around on TV or even in a revival house theater, make sure you see this one. And if you don't have any children of your own, rent a few and take them, then watch their faces as they enjoy BUGSY MALONE.

p, Alan Marshall; d,w Alan Parker; ph, Michael Seresin, Peter Biziou (Eastmancolor); ed, Gerry Hambling; cos. Monica Howe; ch, Gillian Gregory; m/l, Paul Williams.

Children's **Cas.** **(PR:AAA MPAA:PG)**

BUILD MY GALLOWS HIGH 1965 (SEE: OUT OF THE PAST, 1947)

BULLDOG BREED, THE*1/2 (1960, Brit.) 98m RANK bw

Norman Wisdom *(Norman Puckle)*, Ian Hunter *(Adm. Blyth)*, David Lodge *(C.P.O. Knowles)*, Robert Urquhart *(Cmdr. Clayton)*, Edward Chapman *(Philpotts)*, Eddie Byrne *(PO Fikins)*, Peter Jones *(Instructor)*, Liz Fraser *(Naafi Girl)*, John Le Mesurier *(Prosecution)*, Terence Alexander *(Defense)*, Sydney Taylor *(Owner)*, Penny Morrell *(Marlene)*, Brian Oulton *(Mr. Ainsworth)*, Joe Robinson *(Greenfield)*, Claire Gordon *(Girl on Yacht)*, Leonard Sachs *(Yachtsman)*, Julie Shearing *(Polynesian Girl)*, Glyn Houston *(Gym Instructor)*, Cyril Chamberlin *(Landlord)*, Sheila Hancock *(Doris)*, Rosemund Lesley *(Peggy)*.

After an attempt at suicide over the rejection of a celluloid blonde, Wisdom joins the Navy and is somehow idiotically chosen to man a space flight. Of course, he bungles the opportunity, as does the technical support in this one.

d, Robert Asher; w, Jack Davies, Henry Bligh, Norman Wisdom; ph, Jack Asher; m, Phillip Green; ed, Gerry Hambling.

Comedy **(PR:A MPAA:NR)**

BULLDOG DRUMMOND*** (1929) Goldwyn/UA bw

Ronald Colman *(Bulldog Drummond)*, Joan Bennett *(Phyllis Benton)*, Lilyan Tashman *(Erma Peterson)*, Montagu Love *(Carl Peterson)*, Lawrence Grant *(Doctor Lakington)*, Wilson Benge *(Danny)*, Claud Allister *(Algy Longworth)*, Adolph Milar *(Marcovitch)*, Charles Sellon *(John Travers)*, Tetsu Komai *(Chong)*, Donald Novis *(Singer)*, Tom Ricketts *(Colonel)*, Gertrude Short *(Barmaid)*.

By 1929, the dawn of the sound era, the detective stories of Bulldog Drummond by "Sapper" (H. C. McNeile) had become world famous. The silent era had contributed two earlier Drummond films, BULLDOG DRUMMOND with Carlyle Blackwell as the idling detective in 1922 and Jack Buchanan in the title role in BULLDOG DRUMMOND'S THIRD ROUND in 1925. In the Goldwyn production, matinee idol Colman would appear in his first talkie and the producer took great pains to make sure that his mellifluous voice came across, hiding microphones under every table and chair (the boom mike had yet to be invented and sound systems were crudely installed on sets so that staging required actors to be close to the mikes at all times). Drummond, a wealthy adventurer and WW I veteran, is approached by Bennett who asks that he rescue her father who is being held by a gang of thugs in a fake asylum, trying to beat him into telling them where his riches are hidden. Colman goes to the rescue but has the tables turned on him by villains Tashman and the phony asylum doctor. Grant. The urbane and witty detective just misses death on several occasions but manages to free himself from his captors, rescue Love and daughter Bennett, while rounding up the culprits for the police. The lack of action is offset by Colman's excellent performance. His pleasing, euphonic voice overwhelmed audiences who expected the handsome leading man to sound the way he actually did. Goldwyn was smart in having director Jones play down the love scenes, realizing that with talkies, unlike the wild histrionics of silent movies, such romantic scenes required restraint to be convincing. Colman did not really play Drummond as the author envisioned him. In print the detective is a wealthy, jaded war hero who seethes with hatred for Bolsheviks and sadistically goes about with his "Black Gang" capturing these bomb-throwers and torturing them. This brutal aspect of Drummond's character was abandoned by Colman who presents him as an elegant gentleman adventurer whose wits and fine manners are at the core of his character. This is the image the world would have of Drummond ever after and the one adopted by other actors playing the role. (See BULLDOG DRUMMOND series, Index.)

p, Samuel Goldwyn, F. Richard Jones; d, Jones; w, Wallace Smith, Sidney Howard (based on the play by H. C. McNeile and Gerald Du Maurier); ph, Gregg Toland, George Barnes; ed, Viola, Frank Lawrence; art d, William Cameron Menzies; m/l, "I Says to Myself, Says I," Jack Yellen, Harry Akst.

Crime Drama **(PR:A MPAA:NR)**

BULLDOG DRUMMOND AT BAY* (1937, Brit.) 63m Wardour/REP bw

John Lodge *(Hugh Drummond)*, Dorothy Mackaill *(Doris)*, Victor Jory *(Gregoroff)*, Claud Allister *(Algy Longworth)*, Hugh Miller *(Kalinsky)*, Leslie Perrins *(Greyson)*, Richard Bird *(Caldwell)*, Brian Buchel *(Meredith)*, Jim Gerald *(Veight)*, Maire O'Neill *(Norah)*, William Dewhurst *(Reginald Portside)*, Frank Cochrane *(Dr. Belfrus)*.

Drummond is played more for laughs than mystery by Lodge who busies himself by searching for international gun runners who are themselves searching for the secret plans of a remote-controlled British warplane. A feeble production. (See BULLDOG DRUMMOND series, Index.)

d. Norman Lee; w, James Parrish, Patrick Kirwan (from a novel by "Sapper"); ph, Walter Harvey.

Mystery **(PR:A MPAA:NR)**

BULLDOG DRUMMOND COMES BACK*1/2 (1937) 60m PAR bw

John Barrymore *(Col. Nelson)*, John Howard *(Bulldog Drummond)*, Louise Campbell *(Phyllis Clavering)*, Reginald Denny *(Algy Longworth)*, E. E. Clive *(Tenny)*, J. Carroll Naish *(Mikhail Valdin)*, Helen Freeman *(Irena Soldanis)*, Zeffie Tilbury *(Effie)*, John Sutton *(Sanger)*, Rita Page *(Barmaid)*, Iva Henderson *(Morris)*, John Rogers *(Blanton)*, John Ward *(Griswold)*, Forrester Harvey *(Barman-Landlord)*, Phyllis Barry *(Hortense)*, C. L. Sherwood *(Bartender)*, Otto Fries *(Sanghil Wun)*, Colin Kenny *(Policeman)*, Frank Baker *(Bobby)*.

Howard is a smooth but unimpressive Bulldog who is busy tracking down terrorists; he cannot compete with Barrymore's eccentric performance which assumes many disguises and is worth the whole film. (See BULLDOG DRUMMOND series, Index.)

d, Louis King; w, Edward T. Lowe (based on a story by "Sapper"); ph, Henry Mills.

Comedy **Cas.** **(PR:A MPAA:NR)**

BULLDOG DRUMMOND ESCAPES** (1937) 67m PAR bw

Ray Milland *(Capt. Drummond)*, Sir Guy Standing *(Inspector Nielson)*, Heather Angel *(Phyllis Clavering)*, Porter Hall *(Merridew)*, Reginald Denny *(Algy Longworth)*, E. E. Clive *(Dobbs)*, Fay Holden *(Natalie)*, Walter Kingsford *(Stanton)*, Patrick Kelly *(Stiles)*, Charles McNaughton *(Constable Higgins)*, Clyde Cook *(Alf)*, Frank Elliot *(Bailey)*, Doris Lloyd *(Nurse)*, David Clyde *(Gower)*, Colin Tapley *(Dixon)*, Zeffie Tilbury *(Drunk)*.

Policeman Standing is hustling after crooks who are attempting to bilk a woman's inheritance. They get bagged by the Bulldog and sent back to the rock pile for rehabilitation. Milland is a solid, sophisicated Drummong. (See BULLDOG DRUMMOND series Index)

d, James Hogan; w, H. C. McNeile, Gerard Fairlie, Edward T. Lowe; ph, Victor Milner.

Mystery **Cas.** **(PR:A MPAA:NR)**

BULLDOG DRUMMOND IN AFRICA** (1938) 58m PAR bw

John Howard *(Captain Hugh Drummond)*, Heather Angel *(Phyllis Clavering)*, H. B. Warner *(Col. Nielson)*, J. Carrol Naish *(Richard Lane)*, Reginald Denny *(Algie Longworth)*, E. E. Clive *(Tenny)*, Anthony Quinn *(Deane Fordline)*, Matthew Boulton *(Major Grey)*, Neil Fitzgerald *(McTurk)*, Michael Brooke *(Baron Nevsky)*, Jean De Briac *(Walter)*, Paul Porcasi *(Hotel Manager)*, William von Brincken *(Dr. Stern)*, Rollo Dix *(Acris)*, Evan Thomas *(Sergeant)*, Forrester Harvey *(Constable Jenkins)*, Gerald Rogers *(Tailor)*, Leonard Carey *(Phillips)*.

Howard tracks down kidnapers who have abducted Scotland Yard inspector Warner, torturing him in the wilds of Africa, to learn the whereabouts of a radio-wave disintegrator. Good atmosphere and direction puts this a notch above the usual Bulldog fare. (See BULLDOG DRUMMOND series, Index)

p, Harold Hurley; d, Louis King; w, Garnett Weston (based on the story "Challenge" by "Sapper"); m, Boris Morros; ph, William C. Mellor; ed, Anne Bauchens; art d, Hans Dreier, Earl Hedrick.

Mystery **(PR:A MPAA:NR)**

BULLDOG DRUMMOND STRIKES BACK**** (1934) 83m UA bw

Ronald Colman *(Capt. Hugh Drummond)*, Loretta Young *(Lola Field)*, C. Aubrey

Smith *(Insp. Nielsen)*, Charles Butterworth *(Algy Longworth)*, Una Merkel *(Gwen)*, Warner Oland *(Prince Achmed)*, George Regas *(Singh)*, Mischa Auer *(Hassan)*, Kathleen Burke *(Jane Sothern)*, Arthur Hohl *(Dr. Sothern)*, Ethel Griffies *(Mrs. Field)*, H. N. Clugston *(Mr. Field)*, Douglas Gerrard *(Parker)*, William O'Brien *(Servant at Banquet)*, Vernon Steele, Creighton Hale, Pat Somerset *(Men at Wedding)*, Gunnis Davis *(Man with Harsh Voice)*, Charles Irwin *(Cockney Drunk on Street)*, Halliwell Hobbes, E.E. Clive, Yorke Sherwood *(Bobbies)*, Wilson Benge *(Neilsen's Valet)*, Lucille Ball *(Girl)*, Bob Kortman *(Henchman)*, Doreen Monroe *(Woman in Hotel Room)*.

Colman repeats his successful 1929 Bulldog Drummond impersonation in this, his first film away from Goldwyn, whom he had refused to work for ever again. There were several Hollywood intimates, in fact, who found the title of the film more than a little apt. Fast-moving and smartly produced, this laugh-studded melodrama is as incredible as it is engrossing. Two main comedy veins flow through the narrative. First concerns the interrupted wedding night of Butterworth (whose interpretation of Drummond's sidekick Algy was a major factor in the film's success). Drummond's frequent calls for assistance keep the clapper on the wedding bells; at the same time his constant clash, futile to the end, is to convince Scotland Yard that something is afoot in London. Unfortunately, every time Drummond brings in a witness to prove his point, the witness mysteriously vanishes. The Commissioner naturally thinks Bulldog is drunk, crazy, or both, and, in the meantime, a cargo of cholera-contaminated furs, the cause of it all, goes up in flames at the wharf. Young's main function as Drummond's love interest is to look wide-eyed and beautiful while she is being kidnaped and returned over and over again. This is not a picture to be analyzed. It's strictly for enjoyment. The script is so polished and the characters so finely-honed that the action dovetails perfectly. This 1934 version is a much more polished product than the 1929 picture. Colman himself said in an interview that he had been delighted to repeat his Drummond role because the improvement in sound and the quality of films in general made it possible to get across the character with more polish and bite than the primitive 1929 version had permitted. "We spent so much time worrying about the mike and our voices that I am afraid we didn't give the original performances all we should have," he said with this characteristic modesty, even though he had received an Academy Award nomination for the earlier Drummond. Not for a moment does this movie lag and has, in fact, all the plausibility of a well-written mystery novel read in the middle of the night. (See BULLDOG DRUMMOND series, Index.)

p, Joseph M. Schenk; d, Roy Del Ruth; w, Nunnally Johnson; (based on the novel by "Sapper," adapted by Henry Lehrman); ph, Peverell Marley; ed, Allen McNeil.

Mystery **(PR:A MPAA:NR)**

BULLDOG DRUMMOND'S BRIDE*½ (1939) 55m PAR bw

John Howard *(Capt. Hugh Drummond)*, Heather Angel *(Phyllis Clavering)*, H. B. Warner *(Col. Nielson)*, Reginald Denny *(Algy Longworth)*, E.E. Clive *(Tenny)*, Elizabeth Patterson *(Aunt Blanche)*, Eduardo Ciannelli *(Henri Armides)*, Gerald Hamer *(Garvey)*, John Sutton *(Inspector Tredennis)*, Neil Fitzgerald *(Evan Barrows)*, Louis Mercier *(Maj. Dupres)*, Ada Kuznetzoff *(Gaston)*, Adrienne D'Ambricourt *(Therese)*.

Weak Bulldog entry has the famous sleuth's honeymoon interrupted in France when thieves rob a bank and Howard must recover the stolen loot. There is an exciting chase over the rooftops of a French village as Howard nabs the culprits. (See BULLDOG DRUMMOND series, Index)

p, Stuart Walker; d, James Hogan; w, Stuart Palmer, Garnett Weston (based on *Bulldog Drummond and the Oriental Mind* by "Sapper"); ph, Harry Fishbeck.

Mystery **Cas.** **(PR:A MPAA:NR)**

BULLDOG DRUMMOND'S PERIL*** (1938) 66m PAR bw

John Barrymore *(Col. Nielson)*, John Howard *(Bulldog Drummond)*, Louise Campbell *(Phyllis Clavering)*, Reginald Denny *(Algy Longworth)*, E. E. Clive *(Tenny)*, Porter Hall *(Dr. Botulian)*, Elizabeth Patterson *(Aunt Blanche)*, Nydia Westman *(Gwen Longworth)*, Michael Brooke *(Anthony Greer)*, Halliwell Hobbes *(Prof. Bernard Goodman)*, Matthew Boulton *(Sir Raymond Blantyre)*, Zeffie Tilbury *(Mrs. Weevens)*, David Clyde *(Constable McThane)*, Clyde Cook *(Constable Sacker)*, Austin Fairman *(Roberts)*, Gregory Gaye *(Raoul)*, Pat X. Kerry *(Expressman)*, Dave Thursby *(Expressman)*, Torben Meyer *(Hoffman)*.

John Barrymore, who brilliantly played Sherlock Holmes in the silent version (and first American production), is a bit reduced in rank here as a Scotland Yard operative Col. Nielson in this whodunit made only a few years before Barrymore's death. He gives the part some punch, with his usual offhand skill, but leaves the impression his mind is somewhere else. Dapper Drummond (John Howard), defender of womanhood, righter of wrongs, bothersome fruit-fly to Scotland Yard, has taken unto himself a bride in this yard, but before you can say "I do," the death of a detective sets up the usual seven-reel cops and robbers chase. Point of the plot is a secret formula for synthetic gems and the diamond merchant who tries to make off with the fake stones and destroy the formula. Culprits are caught, and one expects the real diamonds will find their way to the dainty fingers of the future Mrs. Bulldog. (See BULLDOG DRUMMOND series, Index)

d, James Hogan, w, Stuart Palmer (based on a story by "Sapper"); ph, Harry Fishbeck; ed, Edward Dmytryk.

Mystery **Cas.** **(PR:A MPAA:NR)**

BULLDOG DRUMMOND'S REVENGE*½ (1937) 55m PAR bw

John Barrymore *(Col. Nielson)*, Louise Campbell *(Phyllis Clavering)*, John Howard *(Capt. Drummond)*, E. E. Olive *(Tenny)*, Reginald Denny *(Algy Longworth)*, Frank Puglia *(Draven Nogals)*, Nydia Westman *(Gwen Longworth)*, Robert Gleckler *(Hardcastle)*, Lucien Littlefield *(Mr. Smith)*.

Amateur sleuth Howard uncovers the thief who stole the secret formula of a new explosive. Dialog is uninventive but succeeds in creating a few laughs with the aid of passable timing and direction. Fair Drummond effort. (See BULLDOG DRUMMOND series, Index)

d, Louis King; w, Edward T. Lowe (based on a story by "Sapper"); ph, Harry Fishbeck; ed, Arthur Schmidt.

Mystery **Cas.** **(PR:A MPAA:NR)**

BULLDOG DRUMMOND'S SECRET POLICE*½ (1939) 55m PAR bw

John Howard *(Capt. Hugh Drummond)*, Heather Angel *(Phyllis Clavering)*, H. B. Warner *(Col. Nielson)*, Elizabeth Patterson *(Aunt Blanche)*; Reginald Denny *(Algy Longworth)*, E.E. Clive *(Tenny)*, Leo Carroll *(Barjel Islanyant/Henry Seaton/Albert Boulton)*, Forrester Harvey *(Prof. Downie)*.

Mild action movie has Howard involved with a crackpot professor, following his wild escapades into danger. Poor Drummond showing. (See BULLDOG DRUMMOND series, Index)

p, Edward T. Lowe; d, James Hogan; w, Garnett Weston (based on a novel *Temple Tower* by "Sapper"); ph, Merritt Gersted; ed, Arthur Schmidt.

Mystery **Cas.** **(PR:A MPAA:NR)**

BULLDOG EDITION** (1936) 57m REP bw

Ray Walker *(Ken Dwyer)*, Evalyn Knapp *(Randy)*, Regis Toomey *(Hardy)*, Cy Kendall *(Enright)*, Billy Newell *(Charlie Hunter)*, Oscar Apfel *(Taggart)*, Betty Compson *(Billy)*, Robert Warwick *(Evans)*, Ivan Miller *(Johnson)*, Matty Fain *(Maxie)*, George Lloyd *(Manilla)*, Frank Puglia *(Tony)*, Ruth Gillette *(Gertle)*, Ed Le Saint *(Judge)*.

The Hatfields and the McCoys battle it out this time as newspapers searching for the ultimate in circulation figures. Rough and ready competition results in champagne when the winner gets the sweatheart.

p, Nat Levine; d, Charles Lamont; w, Richard English (based on the story "Back in Circulation" by Danny Ahearn); ph, Jack Marta.

Drama **(PR:A MPAA:NR)**

BULLDOG JACK (SEE: ALIAS BULLDOG DRUMMOND, 1935, Brit.)

BULLDOG SEES IT THROUGH* (1940, Brit.) 77m ABPC bw

Jack Buchanan *(Bill Watson)*, Greta Gynt *(Jane Sinclair)*, Sebastian Shaw *(Derek Sinclair)*, David Hutcheson *(Freddie Caryll)*, Googie Withers *(Toots)*, Robert Newton *(Watkins)*, Arthur Hambling *(Insp. Horn)*, Wylie Watson *(Dancing Professor)*, Polly Ward *(Miss Fortescue)*, Nadine March *(Gladys)*, Ronald Shiner *(Pug)*, Aubrey Mallalieu *(Magistrate)*.

Test pilot still smarting over his lost love nurses his wounds by enlisting the help of his butler (who also, wouldn't you know, just happens to be a secret agent) to expose his ex-fiancee's husband as an armaments saboteur.

p, Walter C. Mycroft; d, Harold Huth; w, Doreen Montgomery (based on the novel *Scissors Cut Paper* by Gerald Fairlie); ph, Claude Friese-Greene.

Mystery **(PR:A MPAA:NR)**

BULLET CODE½** (1940) 56m RKO bw

George O'Brien *(Steve Condon)*, Virginia Vale *(Molly Mathews)*, Slim Whitaker *(Pop Norton)*, Howard Hickman *(John Matthews)*, Harry Woods *(Cass Clantine)*, William Haade *(Scar Atwood)*, Walter Miller *(Gorman)*, Robert Stanton *(Bud Mathews)*.

O'Brien shoots a rustler, mistakenly thinking it's the son of his neighbor. When he arrives to apologize he becomes involved in chasing off rustlers from his neightbor's land and winds up with the rancher's daughter. Mighty neighborly.

p, Bert Gilroy; d, David Howard; w, Doris Schroeder; ph, Harry Wild; ed, Frederic Knudtson.

Western **(PR:A MPAA:NR)**

BULLET FOR A BADMAN½** (1964) 80m UNIV c

Audie Murphy *(Logan Keliher)*, Darren McGavin *(Sam Ward)*, Ruta Lee *(Lottie)*, Beverley Owen *(Susan)*, Skip Homeier *(Pink)*, George Tobias *(Diggs)*, Alan Hale, Jr. *(Leach)*, Berkeley Harris *(Jeff)*, Edward C. Platt *(Tucker)*, Kevin Tate *(Sammy)*, Cece Whitney *(Goldie)*.

Better-than-average Murphy western concerning our hero's efforts to track down and bring to justice an old friend, McGavin, who's now a crook. Murphy finds the villain and escorts him back to town with the stolen loot, while keeping one eye on his dishonest possemen who want to get their hands on the dough. Murphy is married to McGavin's ex-wife much to the bane of the crook who seeks revenge. Murphy is his usual stoic self, but McGavin is the real standout, playing his villainous role with zest.

p, Gordon Kay; d, R. G. Springsteen; w, Mary and Willard Willingham (based on the novel by Marvin H. Albert); ph, Joe Biroc (Eastmancolor); m, Frank Skinner; ed, Russell Schoengarth.

Western **(PR:A MPAA:NR)**

BULLET FOR JOEY, A½** (1955) 86m UA bw

Edward G. Robinson *(Inspector Raoul Leduc)*, George Raft *(Joe Victor)*, Audrey Totter *(Joyce Geary)*, George Dolenz *(Carl Macklin)*, Peter Hanson *(Fred)*, Peter Van Eyck *(Eric Hartman)*, Karen Verne *(Mrs. Hartman)*, Ralph Smiley *(Paola)*, Henri Letondal *(Dubois)*, John Cliff *(Morrie)*, Joseph Vitale *(Nick)*, Bill Bryant *(Jack Allen)*, Stan Malotte *(Paul)*, Toni Gerry *(Yvonne Temblay)*, Sally Blane *(Marie)*, Steven Geray *(Garcia)*, John Alvin *(Percy)*, Bill Henry *(Artist)*.

Canadian police Inspector Robinson links three murders to scientist Dolenz and thinks that the noted physicist could be the next victim. Unbeknownst to Robinson, Van Eyck, a sinister proponent of communism has hired infamous gangster Raft to "convince" Dolenz that he should join Van Eyck's group. Robinson tracks down Van Eyck who plans to get rid of the troubleseom inspector before he can destroy his fiendish plot. When Raft learns that Van Eyck is a Communist and that his "group" plans to take over the world, Raft himself saves Robinson and Dolenz, but dies in the process. Robinson finally rounds up the spy ring and saves the world. Unexciting espionage drama that is hampered by "Red Scare" thematics. Robinson and Raft enjoy themselves with a pair of nifty characters and Van Eyck is suitably creepy, giving credence to the otherwise ridiculous plotting.

p, Samuel Bischoff, David Diamond; d, Lewis Allen; w, Geoffrey Homes, A.I. Bezzerides (based on a story by James Benson Nablo); ph, Harry Neumann; m, Harry Sukman; ed, Leon Barsha.

Spy Drama **(PR:A MPAA:NR)**

BULLET FOR PRETTY BOY, A* (1970) 88m AIP c

Fabian Forte *(Floyd)*, Jocelyn Lane *(Betty)*, Astrid Warner *(Ruby)*, Michael Haynes *(Ned)*, Adam Roarke *(Preacher)*, Robert Glenn *(Hossler)*, Anne MacAdams *(Beryl)*, Camilla Carr *(Helen)*, Jeff Alexander *(Wallace)*, Desmond Dhooge *(Harvey)*, Bill Thurman *(Huddy)*, Hugh Feagin *(Jack)*, Jessie Lee Fulton *(Mrs. Floyd)*, James Harrell *(Mr. Floyd)*, Gene Ross *(William)*, Ed Lo Russo *(Bo)*, Charlie Dell *(Charlie)*,

Frank DeBenedett *(Lester)*, Eddie Thomas *(Ben)*, Ethan Allen *(Seth)*, Troy K. Hoskins *(Sheriff)*.

Pretty Boy Floyd's fall into crime is told in a ho-hum manner. Floyd, serving a six-year road-gang sentence on a manslaughter charge (having eliminated a jealous suitor for the hand of his wife) escapes after serving four years. Contacts from the joint lead Floyd to Kansas City madam Anne MacAdams who introduces him to a gang of bad guys and a sluggish parade of bank robberies until a weary G-man tracks him down and kills him. Production has an overall good look due primarily to Texas exteriors and a lot of period autos, indicating the BONNIE AND CLYDE influence had not played out as yet. But the story drags in this Depression-era melodrama.

p&d, Larry Buchanan; w, Henry Rosenbaum (based on a story by Enrique Touceda) ph, James R. Davidson (Movielab Color); m, Harley Hatcher; ed, Miguel Levin.

Crime **(PR:C MPAA:NR)**

BULLET FOR SANDOVAL, A** (1970, Ital./Span.) 91m UNIV c

Ernest Borgnine *(Don Pedro Sandoval)*, George Hilton *(Warner)*, Alberto De Mendozo *(Lucky Boy)*, Leo Anchoriz *(The Padre)*, Antonio Pico *(Sam)*, Jose Manuel Martin *(Guerico)*, Manuel De Blas *(Jose)*, Manuel Miranda *(Francisco)*, Gustavo Rojo *(Guadalupano)*.

Spaghetti western starring Hilton as a Confederate deserter who travels to Mexico to be with his girl, the daughter of feared bandit Borgnine, who is about to give birth to their child. Along the way, Hilton picks up two more deserters, De Mendozo and Pico, and they arrive at Bornine's village right in the middle of a cholera epidemic. The girl has already died, and Borgnine, who has always hated the gringo, hands him the baby and tells him to vamoose. Hilton takes his son and is forced to move quickly with the Confederate army and the epidemic hot on his heels. The child begins to fall ill and none of the villagers or ranchers in the area will help. One rancher breaks a botle of milk right in front of Hilton seeks revenge. He takes his gang, which now inludes a monk, Anchoriz, and goes on the rampage. They return to the nasty rancher and drown him in a bucket of milk, forcing his family to watch. He then seeks out and murders all others who refused him aid. Along the way the gang finds time to get in some robbing, drinking, and whoring. Hilton finally catches up with Borgnine and the showdown is a knife-fight in a bull's corral. Borgnine falls under the bull's horns and the Mexican army invades the stadium, fills the stands, and surrounds the gang. Typical bloody European oater, staged fairly well with some good but unusual action scenes. Poor english dubbing almost ruins the movie.

p, Elio Scardamaglia, Ugo Guerro; d, Julio Buchs; w, Guerro, Jose Luis Martinez Mollə, Frederic De Urratia; ph, Francisco Sempere (Movielab Color); ed, Daniele Alabisco; art d, Giancarlo Bartolini Salimbeni.

Western **(PR:C MPAA:GP)**

BULLET FOR STEFANO* 1/2 (1950, Ital.) 96m Lux bw (IL PASSATORE)

Valentina Cortese *(Barbara)*, Rossano Brazzi *(Stefano)*, Carlo Ninchi *(Priest)*, Carlo Campanini *(Gendarme)*, Lillian Laine *(Isola)*, Bella Starace Sainati *(Mother of Stefano)*, Camillo Pilotto *(Gigiazzo)*.

Nineteenth century Robin Hood tale starring Brazzi as a swordsman who kills his rival on his wedding day to steal the lovely Cortese away. Because of the murder, Brazzi is forced to become a bandit who steals from the rich and gives to the poor. Brazzi becomes preoccupied with his banditry (and a new mistress) causing the snubbed Cortese to get her revenge by turning the villagers against the robber. (In Italian; English subtitles.)

p, Giovanni Laterza; d, Duilio Coletti; w, T. Pinelli, F. Fellini; ph, Carlo Montuori; m, Enzo Masetti.

Romance/Adventure **(PR:A MPAA:NR)**

BULLET FOR THE GENERAL, A 1/2** (1967, Ital.) 135m MGM c (QUIEN SABE?)

Gian Maria Volonte *(Chuncho)*, Klaus Kinski *(Santo)*, Martine Beswick *(Adelita)*, Lou Castel *(Bill Tate)*, Jaime Fernandez *(Gen. Elias)*, Andrea Checchi *(Don Felipe)*, Spartaco Conversi *(Cirillo)*, Joaquin Parra *(Picaro)*, Jose Manuel Martin *(Raimundo)*, Santiago Santos *(Guapo)*, Valentino Macchi *(Pedrito)*.

Political spaghetti western starring Castel as an American mercenary hired by bandit Volonte and his brother Kinski to fight the revolution. Castel is really on a mission to assassinate the local revolutionary hero who has become too much of a symbol to the people. The assassin slowly distracts Castel from the cause by offering him blood money, but the Mexican bandit regains his senses and kills the American. (Original running time is a lengthy 135m, there is also a 77 minute cut in release.)

p, Bianco Manini; d, Damiano Damiani; w, Salvatore Laurani, Franco Solinas; ph, Toni Secchi (Techniscope, Technicolor); m, Luis Bacalov; cos, Marilu Carteny.

Western **(PR:C MPAA:NR)**

BULLET IS WAITING, A* 1/2 (1954) 83m COL c

Jean Simmons *(Cally Canham)*, Rory Calhoun *(Ed Stone)*, Stephen McNally *(Sheriff Munson)*, Brian Aherne *(David Canham)*.

Claustrophobic little film starring Calhoun as a criminal being brought to justice for a manslaughter charge by Sheriff McNally. On the way back to civilization, their plane crashes and the pair are forced to hole up in a small cabin owned by Simmons and her father, Aherne. Aherne has been out of town and a vicious storm has trapped the three in the cabin. McNally senses Simmon's attraction to Calhoun and warns her not to help him escape. Aherne finally returns and the sheriff borrows his jeep to bring Calhoun to trial. Overlong and very talky, there's not much action to show whether or not Calhoun really isn't the kind of man who would murder. Due to the locale the characters are forced to sit and say what they *think* about each other instead of showing it.

p, Howard Welsch; d, John Farrow; w, Thames Williamson, Casey Robinson (based on a story by Williamson); ph, Franz F. Planer (Technicolor); m, Dmitri Tiomkin; ed, Otto Ludwig.

Drama **(PR:A MPAA:NR)**

BULLET SCARS* (1942) 50m WB

Regis Toomey *(Dr. Steven Bishop)*, Adele Longmire *(Nora Madison)*, Howard Da Silva *(Frank Dillon)*, Ben Welden *(Pills Davis)*, John Ridgely *(Hank O'Connor)*, Frank Wilcox *(Mike)*, Michael Ames *(Joe Madison)*, Hobart Bosworth *(Dr. Carter)*, Roland Drew *(Jake)*, Walter Brooke *(Leary)*, Creighton Hale *(Jess)*, Hank Mann *(Gilly)*, Sol Gorss *(Dude)*, Don Turner *(Mitch)*.

Uninspired and cliche-ridden gangster tale concerning Toomey who has been kidnaped by a wounded mobster and forced to operate. The hood's sister, a nurse, is blackmailed by her brother and commanded to assist in the surgery. The pair manage to get a note off to the cops and the gang is blown to bits in a pitched gun-battle.

d, D. Ross Lederman; w, Robert E. Kent (based on a story by Charles Beldon, Sy Bartlett); ph, Ted McCord; m, Howard Jackson; ed, James Gibbon.

Crime **(PR:A MPAA:NR)**

BULLETS FOR O'HARA* (1941) 50m WB bw

Joan Perry *(Patricia Van Dyne)*, Roger Pryor *(Mike O'Hara)*, Anthony Quinn *(Tony Van Dyne)*, Maris Wrixon *(Elaine Standish)*, Dick Purcell *(Wicks)*, Hobart Bosworth *(Judge)*, Richard Ainley *(McKay Standish)*, DeWolf Hopper *(R. Palmer)*, Joan Winfield *(Marjorie Palmer)*, Roland Drew *(Bradford)*, Joseph King *(Maxwell)*, Victor Zimmerman *(Steve)*, Hank Mann *(Swartzman)*, Kenneth Harlan *(Jim)*, Frank Mayo *(Weldon)*, Jack Mower *(G-Man)*, Sidney Bracey *(Lamson)*, Leah Baird *(Police Matron)*.

Absolutely ridiculous crime melodrama that stars Perry as the naive wife who thinks that her husband Quinn is a walthy society type. She soon learns that her hubby is actually a big-time crook and is shocked and humiliated when he dares to rob their friends while on vacation with them. Quinn forces his bride to come back to Chicago with him and to keep her mouth shut. Clever detective, Pryor, is hot on the trail. Quinn dumps Perry and takes off. She divorces the creep and is arrested and charged with participating in the robbery. Her friends clear her and detective Pryor pressures her to fake a romance and wdding to him to bring the hubby out of hiding. Quinn kidnaps his ex-wifeand is killed in a shootout with the detective who then marries Perry for real. It staggers one's sensibilities that all this absurdity whizzes by in a running time of just 50 minutes.

d, William K. Howard; w, Raymond Schrock (based on a story by David O. Selznick, P. J. Wolfson); ph, Ted McCord; ed, James Gibbons.

Crime **(PR:A MPAA:NR)**

BULLETS FOR RUSTLERS* (1940) 57m COL bw (GB: SPECIAL DUTY)

Charles Starrett *(Steve Beaumont)*, Lorna Gray *(Ann Houston)*, Bob Nolan *(Bob)*, Dick Curtis *(Strang)*, Kenneth MacDonald *(Ed Brock)*, Jack Rockwell *(Sheriff Webb)*, Edward LeSaint *(Judge Baxter)*, Francis Walker *(Ellis)*, Eddie Laughton *(Shorty)*, Lee Prather *(Tom Andrews)*, Hal Taliaferro *(Eb Smith)*.

Starrett stars as another Cattleman's Association detective whc must crack a ring of rustlers. The only thing that distinguishes this oater from the others is that our hero doesn't hesitate or moralize over punching someone out or having a beer in the local saloon. These scenes probably shocked the sensibilities of the audience at the time but they don't make the film worth watching today.

d, Sam Nelson; w, John Rathmell; ph, George Meehan; ed, Charles Nelson; m/l, Bob Nolan, Tim Spencer.

Western **(PR:A MPAA:NR)**

BULLETS OR BALLOTS* 1/2** (1936) 68m WB bw

Edward G. Robinson *(Johnny Blake)*, Joan Blondell *(Lee Morgan)*, Barton MacLane *(Al Kruger)*, Humphrey Bogart *(Nick "Bugs" Fenner)*, Frank McHugh *(Herman)*, Joseph King *(Capt. Dan McLaren)*, Richard Purcell *(Ed Driscoll)*, George E. Stone *(Wires)*, Louise Beavers *(Nellie LaFleur)*, Joseph Crehan *(Grand Jury Spokesman)*, Henry O'Neill *(Bryant)*, Gilbert Emery *(Thorndyke)*, Henry Kolker *(Hollister)*, Herbert Rawlinson *(Caldwell)*, Rosalind Marquis *(Specialty)*, Norman Willis *(Vinci)*, Frank Faylen *(Gatley)*, Alice Lyndon *(Old Lady)*, Victoria Vinton *(Ticket Seller)*, Addison Richards *(Announcer's Voice)*, Harry Watson, Jerry Madden *(Kids)*, Al Hill, Dutch Schlickenmeyer, Jack Gardner, Herman Marks, Saul Gorss, George Lloyd, Benny the Gouge *(Men)*, Ray Brown *(Proprietor)*, Eddie Shubert *(Truck Driver)*, Max Wagner *(Actor Impersonating Kruger)*, Ed Stanley *(Judge)*, Milton Kibbee *(Jury Foreman)*, William Pawley *(Crail)*, Jack Goodrich *(Cigar Clerk)*, Alma Lloyd *(1st Beauty Attendant)*, Ralph M. Remley *(Kelly)*, Anne Nagel, Gordon [Bill] Elliott *(Bank Secretaries)*, Carlyle Moore, Jr. *(Kruger's Secretary)*, Virginia Dabney *(Mary)*.

Robinson is a tough Broadway cop in charge of a strong-arm squad feared by NYC racketeers. But he is a headstrong maverick and, in a confrontation with police commissioner King, Robinson slugs his superior and is kicked off the force, a widely publicized event which interests MacLane, the city crime boss. He hires the ex-cop as an advisor to show him how to beat the law. Bogart, MacLane's ruthless right-hand gunman, hates Robinson and doesn't believe for one moment that Robinson has really gone crooked but he fears killing the interloper because MacLane has threatened to shoot him if his "advisor" is harmed. MacLane is also the only man who knows the supreme heads of the crime syndicate controlling all underworld operations and Bogart fears reprisal from them if he kills MacLane in a takeover of the mobs. Robinson now acts with impunity, slugging a cop who sneers at his betryal of the force. He is jailed but is visited by King and it is at this moment the viewer realizes Robinson's wild conduct has all been an act so he could worm his way into the mobs and learn the identities of the syndicate chieftans. He is released but before MacLane takes him to his leaders, Bogart goes berserk and kills a man. MacLane throws him out and, in a rage, Bogart kills MacLane. By then Robinson has assumed leadership of the gangs, taking over the lucrative numbers (policy) racket from his girl friend Blondell which incurs her wrath. This he has done to prove to the unknown higherups that he can produce millions for their coffers. They send for him but he is fatally shot by Bogart who is killed by Robinson. Blondell finds Robinson walking down the street toward the secret sanctum of the syndicate leaders and, without knowing he is dying, drives him to his destination. Robinson enters the bastion of the wealthy crime cartel directors, followed by a horde of police he has arranged to follow him. As the big shots are arrested, Robinson collapses, dying in King's arms, a policeman having done his duty to the last. This tough though melodramatic crime vehicle allowed Robinson to display his flamboyant acting style while touching upon a conspiracy the public only suspected at the time, the existence of a national crime cartel. The prophetic film is enhanced by Keighley's swift direction, and a "March of Time"-like opening showing the far-reaching power of the 1930s mobsters.

p, Louis F. Edelman; d, William Keighley; w, Seton I. Miller (based on a story by Martin Mooney); ph, Hal Mohr; m, Heinz Roemheld; ed, Jack Killifer; art d, Carl Jules Weyl; spec eff, Fred Jackman, Jr., Warren E. Lynch.

Crime Drama **(PR:A MPAA:NR)**

BULLFIGHTER AND THE LADY*** (1951) 87m REP bw

Robert Stack *(Chuck Regan)*, Joy Page *(Anita de la Vega)*, Gilbert Roland *(Manolo Estrada)*, Virginia Grey *(Lisbeth Flood)*, John Hubbard *(Barney Flood)*, Katy Jurado *(Chelo Estrada)*, Antonio Gomez *(Antonio Gomez)*, Ismael Perez *(Panchito)*, Rodolfo Acosta *(Juan)*, Ruben Padilla *(Dr. Sierra)*, Dario Ramirez *(Pepe Mora)*.

John Wayne produced and Budd Boetticher directed this Mexican tale that illustrates the artistry and appeal in bullfighting. Stack finds himself in Mexico with Grey and Hubbard. He falls in love with local gal Page and to impress her he convinces matador Roland to show him the ropes. Stack begins to get the hang of it, gets cocky in a show-off moment, and causes Roland's death. To quell the hatred of Page and the Mexicans, Stack enters the ring again to slay a bull in honor of Roland. Good performances, lush visuals and a genuine love and feel for the country in which it was filmed.

p, John Wayne; d, Budd Boetticher; w, James Edward Grant (from a story by Budd Boetticher and Ray Nazarro); ph, Jack Draper; m, Victor Young; ed, Richard L. Van Enger; m/l, Young, Jack Elliot.

Drama Cas. (PR:A MPAA:NR)

BULLFIGHTERS, THE** (1945) 61m FOX bw

Laurel and Hardy *(Themselves)*, Margo Woods *(Tangerine)*, Richard Lane *(Hot Shot Coleman)*, Carol Andrews *(Hattie Blake)*, Diosa Costello *(Conchita)*, Frank McCown *(El Brilliante)*, Ralph Sanford *(Muldoon)*, Irving Gump *(Mr. Gump)*, Ed Gargan *(Vasso)*, Lorraine De Wood *(Spanish Girl)*, Emmett Vogan *(Prosecutor)*, Roger Neury *(Master of Ceremonies)*, Gus Glassmire *(Judge)*, Rafael Storm *(Hotel Clerk)*, Jay Novello *(Lusi)*, Guy Zanetto, Robert Ellmer *(Bullfighters)*, Max Wagner *(Attendant)*, Jose Portugal *(Waiter)*, Hank Worden *(Texan)*, Joe Domingues, Steven Darrell *(Mexican Policeman)*.

Depressingly mediocre Laurel and Hardy vehicle that has the pair as private detectives who travel down to Mexico in search of a mysterious woman. Stan, who happens to resemble a famous matador, finds himself battling el toro amid footage from BLOOD AND SAND. A few funny moments fail to relieve the tedium.

p, William Girard; d, Malcolm St. Clair; w, W. Scott Darling; ph, Norbert Brodine; m, David Buttolph; ed, Stanley Rabjohn.

Comedy Cas. (PR:A MPAA:NR)

BULLITT**** (1968) 113m WB c

Steve McQueen *(Bullitt)*, Robert Vaughn *(Chalmers)*, Jacqueline Bisset *(Cathy)*, Don Gordon *(Delgetti)*, Robert Duvall *(Weissberg)*, Simon Oakland *(Capt. Bennett)*, Norman Fell *(Baker)*, Georg Stanford Brown *(Dr. Willard)*, Justin Tarr *(Eddy)*, Carl Reindel *(Stanton)*, Felice Orlandi *(Rennick)*, Victor Tayback *(Pete Ross)*, Robert Lipton *(1st Aide)*, Ed Peck *(Wescott)*, Pat Renella *(John Ross)*, Paul Genge *(Mike)*, John Aprea *(Killer)*, Al Checco *(Desk Clerk)*, Bill Hickman *(Phil)*.

This is the film that sent McQueen to the top of the box office heap, a tough, cleverly plotted, and violent film of crime in San Francisco. He plays the title character, a colorful and unorthodox police lieutenant who is assigned to protect a government witness scheduled to inform on the national cirme syndicate. The informer is hidden in a fleabag hotel and guarded by McQueen's special aides, but killers break inside, wounding the cop on duty and mortally wounding the witness. McQueen rushes to the hotel and has the witness taken to a hospital where he later dies. To give himself time to investigate and also draw the killers back to complete unfinished business, McQueen orders the body kept in the morgue under a "John Doe" tag, later telling his superiors that he is holding the still-alive informer incognito (he trusts no one). Politician Vaughn, in a great characterization of a sleazy opportunist, explodes, demanding McQueen release his witness. He refuses, backed up for the time being by his superior, Oakland, who also gives a powerful performance of a good cop resisting political influence. Meanwhile, McQueen backtracks on the identity and actions of the murdered man, finally drawing the attention of the two killers who had invaded the hotel; they are following *him* in hopes that he will lead them to the man they have been assigned to kill, not knowing that the informer is dead. McQueen spots the hoodlums and follows in one of the most spectacular car chases ever filmed, up and down the hills of San Francisco while hand-held cameras record the perilous pursuit as each car narrowly misses intersecting autos, barriers, and buildings as they squeal, slide, and lurch along the narrow streets. Finally on the open highway, the killers try to blast McQueen off the road, firing shotgun loads into his car. He manages to slam his car into their speeding auto on one turn, sending the killers' car careening into a gas station where it strikes a pump and explodes the car, killers, station, and all. Still, McQueen has no real answers until a woman is found in a nearby motel with her throat cut. He and his partner Gordon investigate, finding luggage which tells them that the informer who has been killed is not the real witness, but a plant who had been paid to impersonate the syndicate informer, and that the real informer is now fleeing the country with millions stolen from syndicate offices in Chicago. McQueen and Gordon rush to the airport, frantically searching for the informer in the crowds. Vaughn arrives and warns McQueen that he wants his man alive, but the tough cop ignores him. McQueen finally corners the informer on a plane, but he jumps off through a rear exit, McQueen following across the runways as giant jets roar past and over them. Once back inside the terminal, McQueen locates the informer who pulls a gun and shoots a cop. McQueen returns fire, killing the man in front of horrified passengers. The case is closed. A disgruntled Vaughn climbs into his limousine and rides off. McQueen goes back to his apartment and his girl friend, Bisset, who has a relatively small role as the love interest. BULLITT was a return to the old, tough crime movies so expertly played by Bogart and Robinson, but made modern here by great technical advances and McQueen's taciturn, almost stoic presence. Yates' superb direction presents a fluid, always moving camera. All the performers are top-notch, from sour-faced Norman Fell to a curious bit part played by Robert Duvall as a cab driver who is seen almost entirely through a rear-view mirror. Aside from THE SAND PEBBLES, this fine *film noir* production stands as McQueen's top achievement in a lamentably short career.

p, Philip D'Antoni; d, Peter Yates; w, Alan R. Trustman, Harry Kleiner (based on the novel *Mute Witness* by Robert L. Pike); ph, William A. Fraker (Technicolor); m. Lalo Schifrin; ed, Frank P. Keller; art d, Albert Brenner; cos, Theodora Van Runkle.

Crime Drama Cas. (PR:C MPAA:NR)

BULLSHOT** 1/2** (1983) 85m Handmade Films c

Alan Shearman *(Bullshot Crummond)*, Diz White *(Rosemary Fenton)*, Ron House *(Count Otto von Bruno)*, Francis Tomelty *(Fraulein Lenya von Bruno)*, Ron Pember *(Dobbs)*, Mel Smith *(Crouch)*, Michael Aldridge *(Rupert Fenton)*, Christopher Good *(Lord Brancaster)*, Billy Connolly *(Hawkeye McGillicuddy)*.

BULLSHOT was a very funny play that somehow seems to have lost part of its spon taneity and good-natured romping when it was transferred to the screen. It's almost, but not quite, a send-up of the Bulldog Drummond flicks of the 1930s and the plot takes second position to the characters and the characterizations and the caricatures. Crummond is one of those jut-jawed, stiff upper-lipped types who yearns for the opportunity to meet his archrival from WW I once more on the field of battle. The heinous German is seeking a hush-hush secret discovered by the requisite damsel-in- distress' late father. The action takes place around one of those Agatha Christie DOMs (Dark Old Mansion) and culminates in a breakneck series of conclusions that range from battling a giant octopus to leaping onto a plane in mid-air. It's probably funnier to people who never saw any of the great Guinness or Sellers comedies, but in this day and age, when movie humor is either smarmy or Woody Allen, this sits somewhere in the middle and will make you smile, if not roar out loud. It's fast-moving, never flags, and will charm all but the most discerning.

p, Ian La Frenais; d, Dick Clement; w, Ron House, Alan Shearman, Diz White; ph, Alex Thomson (Technicolor); m, John Du Prez; ed, Allan Jones.

Comedy Cas. (PR:A-C MPAA:PG)

BULLWHIP** (1958) 80m AA c

Guy Madison *(Steve)*, Rhonda Fleming *(Cheyenne)*, James Griffith *(Karp)*, Don Beddoe *(Judge)*, Peter Adams *(Parnell)*, Dan Sheridan *(Podo)*, Burt Nelson *(Pine Hawk)*, Al Terr *(Lem)*, Tim Graham *(Pete)*, Hank Worden *(Tex)*, Rick Vallin *(Marshal)*, Wayne Mallory *(Larry)*, Barbara Woodell *(Mrs. Mason)*, Rush Williams *(Judd)*, Don Shelton *(Hotel Keeper)*, Jack Reynolds *(Sheriff)*, Frank Griffin *(Keeler)*, J. W. Cody *(Indian Chief)*, Jack Carr *(Trimble)*, Saul Gorss *(Deputy Luke)*.

Too-cute western version of "The Taming of the Shrew" stars Madison as a man about to hang for a crime he didn't commit. At the last moment he is saved if he will marry a woman, Fleming, and then disappear. The grateful man agrees, but his curiosity is peaked and he follows Fleming back to her home where he learns that she wanted a marriage so that she could own her own property. She is an ambitious woman who wants to become the richest fur trader in the territory, and has no place or desire for a man in her life. She enforces this lifestyle with a massive bullwhip she wields with skill. Madison doesn't give up that easily and slowly melts the icy woman's veneer. Beautiful color photography shows off stunning autumn locations that are unusual for westerns. (Remade as GOIN' SOUTH, 1978.)

p, Helen Ainsworth; d, Harmon Jones; w, Adele Buffington; ph, John J. Martin (CinemaScope, Technicolor): m, Leith Stevens; ed, Thor Brooks; cos, Marjorie D. Corso.

Western Cas. (PR:A MPAA:NR)

BUNCO SQUAD* 1/2** (1950) 67m RKO bw

Robert Sterling *(Steve)*, Joan Dixon *(Grace)*, Ricardo Cortez *(Anthony Wells)*, Douglas Fowley *(McManus)*, Elisabeth Risdon *(Jessica Royce)*, Marguerite Churchill *(Barbara)*, John Kellogg *(Reed)*, Bernadene Hayes *(Liane)*, Robert Bice *(Drake)*, Vivien Oakland *(Annie Cobb)*, Dante *(Dante)*.

The adventures of bunco squad detective Sterling are chronicled as he smashes all manner of con operations. Story concentrates on a seance parlor run by Cortez who trys to bilk old lady Risdon ont of her fortune. The film features the tricks of the seance trade for those interested.

p, Lewis J. Rachmil; d, Herbert I. Leeds; w, George Callahan (based on a story by Reginald Taviner); ph, Henry Freulich; ed, Desmond Marquette.

Crime (PR:A MPAA:NR)

BUNDLE OF JOY** (1956) 100m RKO c

Eddie Fisher *(Dan Merlin)*, Debbie Reynolds *(Polly Parrish)*, Adolphe Menjou *(J.B. Merlin)*, Tommy Noonan *(Freddie Miller)*, Nita Talbot *(Mary)*, Una Merkel *(Mrs. Dugan)*, Melville Cooper *(Adams)*, Bill Goodwin *(Mr. Creely)*, Howard McNear *(Mr. Appleby)*, Robert H. Harris *(Mr. Hargraves)*, Mary Treen *(Matron)*, Edward S. Brophy *(Dance Contest Judge)*, Gil Stratton *(Mike Clancy)*, Scott Douglas *(Bill Rand)*.

Fisher/Reynolds musical has Reynolds as a hyper salesgirl in a department store owned by Menjou and his son Fisher. One day Reynolds finds an infant left on the steps of a foundling home. She tries to give the child to the people in charge at the home but they refuse to believe the child is not hers. She decides to keep the baby and soon begins a romance with Fisher. Menjou notices the sudden romance and thinks that the baby is fathered by his son. All of this is played for laughs and the songs aren't half bad. Songs: "I Never Felt This Way Before," "Bundle Of Joy," "Lullaby In Blue," "Worry About Tomorrow," "All About Love," "Someday Soon," "What's So Good About Morning," "You're Perfect In Every Department" (Josef Myrow, Mack Gordon). (Remake of BACHELOR MOTHER.)

p, Edmund Grainger; d, Norman Taurog; w, Norman Krasna, Robert Carson, Arthur Sheekman (based on a story by Felix Jackson); ph, William Snyder (Technicolor); m, Josef Myrow; ed, Harry Marker; cos, Howard Shoup; ch, Nick Castle.

Musical/Comedy Cas. (PR:A MPAA:NR)

BUNGALOW 13* (1948) 70m FOX bw

Tom Conway *(Christopher Adams)*, Margaret Hamilton *(Mrs. Appleby)*, Richard Cromwell *(Patrick Macy)*, James Flavin *(Lt. Wilson)*, Marjorie Hoshelle *(Alice Ashley)*, Frank Cady *(Gus Barton)*, Eddie Acuff *(Jose Fernando)*, Jody Gilbert *(Mrs. Barton)*, Juan Varro *(Pedro Gomez)*, Lyle Latell *(Willie)*, Mildred Coles *(Hibiscus)*, John Davidson *(Mr. Eden)*.

Rambling and unconvincing private-eye drama featuring Conway as a detective searching for a rare piece of jade. When the cops kill his last suspect in a shoot-out, the frustrated detective goes to a motel to relax and puzzle over the evidence. Suddenly the owner of the motel, Cady, is involved in the mystery and arrested for two murders. Conway suspects there is more to this than meets the eye and sets a trap for the true criminal mastermind behind the plot.

p, Sam Baerwitz; d, Edward L. Cahn; w, Richard G. Hubler; ph, Jackson C. Rose; md, Edward J. Kay; ed, Lou Sackin.

Mystery (PR:A MPAA:NR)

BUNKER BEAN** (1936) 65m RKO bw (GB: HIS MAJESTY BUNKER BEAN)

Owen Davis, Jr. *(Bunker Bean)*, Louise Latimer *(Mary Kent)*, Robert McWade *(J. C.*

Kent), Jessie Ralph *(Grandmother)*, Edward Nugent *(Mr. Glab)*, Lucille Ball *(Miss Kelly)*, Berton Churchill *(Prof. Balthazer)*, Hedda Hopper *(Mrs. Kent)*, Pierre Watkin *(Mr. Barnes)*, Charles Arnt *(Mr. Metzger)*, Russell Hicks *(A. C. Jones)*, Ferdinand Gottschalk *(Mr. Meyerhauser)*, Sibyl Harris *(Countess)*, Joan Davis *(Telephone Operator)*, Edgar Dearing *(Cop)*, Edward LeSaint *(Bit)*.

When a shy, withdrawn office clerk is told by a fortune teller he is a reincarnation of both Napoleon and an Egyptian Pharoh, his personality goes through some radical and certainly comic changes. The once-mouse becomes a lion, taking on his boss and winning the heart of the boss's daughter. A nice little comedy with an excellent cast. Don't miss Ball in one of her first films. Two silent versions of the story were also made: the first by Paramount in 1918; the second by Warner Brothers in 1925.

p, William Sistrom; d, William Hamilton, Edward Kelly; w, Edmund North, James Gow, Dorothy Yost (based on the novel by Harry Leon Wilson and the play by Lee Wilson Dodd); ph, David Abel; ed, Jack Hively.

Comedy **(PR:A MPAA:NR)**

BUNNY LAKE IS MISSING* 1/2** (1965) 107m COL bw

Carol Lynley *(Ann)*, Keir Dullea *(Steven)*, Laurence Olivier *(Newhouse)*, NoelCoward *(Wilson)*, Martita Hunt *(Ada Ford)*, Anna Massey *(Elvira)*, Clive Revill *(Andrews)*, Finlay Currie *(Doll Maker)*, Richard Wattis *(Clerk in Shipping Office)*, Lucie Mannheim *(Cook)*, Megs Jenkins *(Sister)*, Victor Maddern *(Taxi Driver)*, Delphi Lawrence *(1st Mother)*, Suzanne Neve *(2nd Mother)*, Adrienne Corri *(Dorothy)*, Kika Markham *(Nurse)*, Jill Melford *(Teacher)*, Damaris Hayman *(Daphne)*, Patrick Jordan *(Policeman)*, Jane Evers *(Policewoman)*, John Sharp *(FInger Print Man)*, Geoffrey Frederick *(Police Photographer)*, Percy Herbert *(Policeman at Station)*, Michael Wynne *(Rogers)*, Bill Maxam *(Borman)*, Tim Brinton *(Newscaster)*, Fred Emney *(Man in Soho)*, David Oxley *(Doctor)*, John Forbes-Robertson *(Attendant)*, The Zombies *(Themselves)*.

Lynley, a neurotic American woman living in London, is shocked to learn that her little daughter has disappeared. When she contacts the local constable with the information, he and Lynley find out that the girl never showed up at school that day. In fact, Massey, the headmistress of the school, can find no record that says that the girl had *ever* attended the school. Olivier, a wise Scotland Yard inspector inexplicably trained in psychology, is assigned to the case and wonders if Lynley's "daughter" could be the product of an overactive, unstable mind. Dullea, Lynley's journalist brother, can offer no proof that his sister's child exists, but insists that she must. Suspicious of Dullea's mental state as well, Olivier is about to dismiss the case until Lynley finds a claim ticket for a doll of her daughter's that she has sent for repair. When he is alone with Lynley, Dullea exposes himself as the little girl's kidnaper and informs Lynley that he has become jealous of her devotion to her daughter. Before Dullea can harm Lynley and the girl, Olivier arrives on the scene and stops him. A truly compelling and interesting psychological suspense story from one of the strangest talents in film, Otto Preminger. Preminger has the ability to create truly haunting, elegant works or inane, sloppy junk, a paradox that seems rooted in his feisty egocentricity. BUNNY LAKE is one of his better efforts, a chilling depiction of the frailties of the human mind. Its questioning of what is real and what is an illusion has a nice parallel in the filmmaking process, a parallel that would be again explored in Michelangelo Antonioni's 1966 film, BLOW UP, also made in England. Although Lynley and Dullea show the worst side of the American-bred hyperactive acting style, Olivier is a sublime treasure as the analytical inspector, his easy-going grace a delightful contrast to the two stars.

p&d, Otto Preminger; w, John and Penelope Mortimer (based on a novel by Evelyn Piper); ph, Denys Coop (Panavision); m, Paul Glass; ed, Peter Thornton; prod d, Don Ashton; cos, Evelyn Gibbs.

Mystery **(PR:C MPAA:NR)**

BUNNY O'HARE** (1971) 91m AIP c

Bette Davis *(Bunny O'Hare)*, Ernest Borgnine *(Bill Green)*, Jack Cassidy *(Detective Greeley)*, Joan Delaney *(R. J. Hart)*, Jay Robinson *(Banker)*, Reva Rose *(Lulu)*, John Astin *(Ad)*, Robert Foulk *(Commissioner Dingle)*, Brayden Linden *(Frank)*, Karen Mae Johnson *(Lola)*, Francis R. Cody *(Rhett)*, Darra Lyn Tobin *(Elvira)*, Hank Wickham *(Speed)*, David Cargo *(State Trooper)*.

When senior citizen Davis is evicted by her unsympathetic banker Robinson, she teams up with plumber Borgnine, a former thief, and the pair decide to start a bank-robbing career. Dressed as hippies, the odd team successfully rips off quite a few financial institutions, including Robinson's. Wily detective Cassidy is assigned to the case and his old-fashioned ways are spruced up by modern criminologist Delaney. The two are found out, but through an ironic twist of fate, are freed. The former crooks then decide to settle down and get married, never forgetting their wild exploits. Clever script is ineptly directed by Oswald, who has no idea of how to embellish the comedy with pace, movement, or wit. Davis and Borgnine are excellent, though, showing that years of training and professionalism can overcome just about anything.

p&d, Gerd Oswald; w, Stanley Z. Cherry, Coslough Johnson (based on a story by Cherry); ph, Loyal Griggs, John Stephens (Movielab Color); m, Billy Strange; ed, Fred Feitshans, Jr.; cos, Phyllis Garr.

Comedy **(PR:C MPAA:PG)**

BUONA SERA, MRS. CAMPBELL** (1968, Ital.) 111m UA c

Gina Lollobrigida *(Mrs. Carla Campbell)*, Shelley Winters *(Shirley Newman)*, Phil Silvers *(Phil Newman)*, Peter Lawford *(Justin Young)*, Telly Savalas *(Walter Braddock)*, Lee Grant *(Fritzie Braddock)*, Janet Margolin *(Gia)*, Marian Moses *(Lauren Young)*, Naomi Stevens *(Rosa)*, Philippe LeRoy *(Vittorio)*, Giovanna Galletti *(Countess)*, Renzo Palmer *(Mayor)*, Dale Cummings *(Pete)*, James Mishler *(Stubby)*.

Lollobrigida plays an Italian woman who has conned three American WW II veterans (Savalas, Lawford, and Silvers), who were her lovers during the war, into supporting her and her illegitimate daughter, Margolin, for the past twenty years. The three former GIs are not aware of each other until their paths cross in Italy at a reunion of their old outfit. Once they figure out that between the three of them they have contributed over $200,000 to Lollobrigida, it's a contest to see who can keep the info from their wives the longest. Most of the humor is based on the men dashing in and out of rooms to keep from being spotted with Lollobrigida, but some genuine character study is accomplished by examining the old soldiers' personalities through their wives and families.

p&d Melvin Frank; w, Frank, Sheldon Keller, Denis Norden; ph, Gabor Pogany (Technicolor); m, Riz Ortolani; ed, William Butler; art d, Arrigo Equini; m/l, Ortolani, Frank, Andrew Frank.

Comedy **(PR:C MPAA:M)**

BUREAU OF MISSING PERSONS*** (1933) 75m FN/WB bw

Bette Davis *(Norma Phillips)*, Lewis Stone *(Captain Webb)*, Pat O'Brien *(Butch Saunders)*, Glenda Farrell *(Belle)*, Allen Jenkins *(Joe Musik)*, Ruth Donnelly *(Pete)*, Hugh Herbert *(Slade)*, Alan Dinehart *(Therme Roberts)*, Marjorie Gateson *(Mrs. Paul)*, Tad Alexander *(Caesar Paul)*, Noel Francis *(Alice)*, Wallis Clark *(Mr. Paul)*, Adrian Morris *(Irish Conlin)*, Clay Clement *(Kingman)*, Henry Kolker *(Mr. Arno)*.

Tough cop O'Brien is transferred to the department's missing persons bureau, of which Stone is in charge. Considering the bureau's duties as kid's work, not worthy of a *real* cop, O'Brien is looked down upon by the hardened Stone. When Davis walks into the office one day, she tells O'Brien that she would like the bureau to try to locate her husband who has been missing for a few weeks. Finding Davis attractive, O'Brien tells her that he will look into the matter personally and tries to make a date with her. When Stone notices Davis' name on O'Brien's initial report, he informs the dim O'Brien that Davis is wanted in Chicago for the murder of the man she claimed was her husband. Given 48 hours to find Davis, the confused O'Brien "borrows" a body from the morgue and informs the papers of Davis' unfortunate demise. Hoping that Davis will be curious enough to show up for her own funeral, O'Brien waits for her at the mortuary. Davis does arrive, but so does Dinehart, who resembles the man Davis is accused of killing. When O'Brien confronts them, he learns that Dinehart is the twin brother of the dead man *and* his killer. Capturing the real murderer and proving Davis innocent, O'Brien displays a remarkable adeptness at missing persons work and admits to Stone that it's not so easy after all. Amusing mystery film that is genuinely complex and intriguing. Davis and O'Brien bring some spontaneity and creativity to their not-too-serious roles, but are believable when the script demands them to be a bit more solemn.

p, Henry Blanke; d, Roy Del Ruth; w, Robert Presnell (based on the book *Missing Men* by John H. Ayres and Carol Bird); ph, Barney McGill; ed, James Gibbon; art d, Robert Haas.

Comedy **(PR:A MPAA:NR)**

BURG THEATRE* 1/2 (1936, Ger.) 120m Tobis-Europa bw

Werner Krauss *(Friedrich Mitterer)*, Willy Eichberger *(Josef Rainer)*, Hortense Raky *(Leni Schindler)*, Olga Tschechowa *(Baroness Seebach)*, Hans Moser *(Sedlmayer, Prompter)*, Carl Guenther *(Baron Seebach)*, Karl Skraup *(Schindler)*, Josephine Dora *(Mrs. Schindler)*, Franz Herterich *(Director of Burg Theatre)*, Camilla Gerzhofer *(Mrs. Von S.)*, Karl Paryla, Fred Steinbacher *(Young Actors)*.

Krauss plays a once-brilliant, now aging stage actor who falls in love with an up-and-coming young actress, Schindler. He professes his love and announces his retirement from the boards. Schindler pretends to return his affections for the sake of her real lover, Rainer, who is a struggling actor looking for a break. When the truth comes out, Krauss's ego is bruised, but he overcomes his shock and sees that the romance was never meant to be. Rainer, however, attempts suicide upon losing his job at the Burg Theatre, but the old actor saves him. Very lengthy and too melodramatic to maintain interest.

d, Willy Forst; w, Jochen Huth; m, Peter Krueder.

Drama **(PR:A MPAA:NR)**

BURGLAR, THE** (1956) 90m COL bw

Dan Duryea *(Nat Harbin)*, Jayne Mansfield *(Gladden)*, Martha Vickers *(Della)*, Peter Capell *(Baylock)*, Mickey Shaughnessy *(Dohmer)*, Wendell Phillips *(Police Captain)*, Phoebe Mackay *(Sister Sara)*, Stewart Bradley *(Charlie)*, John Facenda *(News Commentator)*, Frank Hall *(News Reporter)*, Bob Wilson *(Newsreel Narrator)*, Steve Allison *(State Trooper)*, Richard Emery *(Harbin as a Child)*, Andrea McLaughlin *(Gladden as a Child)*.

Self-conscious, badly paced film noir made during the last gasp of that genre. Duryea plays a thief that plans to steal a jewel necklace from the mansion of spiritualist Mackay. With the aid of cohorts Capell and Shaughnessy, he pulls off the robbery and obtains the trinket. Duryea's half-sister Mansfield is also along for the ride and falls into trouble when dishonest cop Bradley spots the gang and decides to kidnap her and make the jewels the ransom. Bradley manages to kill most of the gang and Duryea hands over the jewels to save her, but the cop kills him anyway. Soon after, Bradley is captured and led off to jail. The best part of the film is the opening robbery which is shot in tight close-ups with rapid cross-cuts, but soon after the pace drags and the character motivations become unsatisfying and generally choppy.

p, Louis W. Kellman; d, Paul Wendkos; w, David Goodis (based on his novel); ph, Don Malkames; m, Sol Kaplan; ed, Herta Horn.

Crime **(PR:A MPAA:NR)**

BURGLARS, THE** (1972, Fr./Ital.) 120m COL c (LA CASSE)

Jean-Paul Belmondo *(Azad)*, Omar Sharif *(Abel Zacharia)*, Dyan Cannon *(Lena)*, Robert Hossein *(Ralph)*, Nicole Calfan *(Helene)*, Renato Salvatori *(Renzi)*, Jean-Luis de Vilallonga *(Tasco)*, Myriam Colombi *(Mme. Tasco)*, Raoul Delfosse *(Caretaker)*, Steve Eckardt *(Malloch)*, Robert Duranton *(Johnny)*, Daniel Verite *(Playboy)*, Marc Arian *(Restaurant Owner)*.

Loose remake of the 1956 *film noir* THE BURGLAR, this time set in Europe and starring Belmondo as the leader of a gang that steals a valuable collection of emeralds. The gang is given chase by corrupt cop Sharif who does not want to arrest them, but to nab the loot for himself. Cannon plays an American nightclub owner who is forced to play stool pidgeon for the slimy copper. After a harrowing chase scene between Belmondo and Sharif, the thief manages to trap the crooked cop in a grain elevator and drown him. Action scenes well done, and the production values are generally high, but the film is too long for it's own good. Nice musical score by Ennio Morricone.

p&d, Henri Verneuil; w, Verneuil, Vahe Katcha (based on the novel by David Goodis); ph, Claude Renoir (Panavision, Eastmancolor); m, Ennio Morricone; ed, Pierre Gilette.

Crime **(PR:C MPAA:PG)**

BURIED ALIVE* (1939) 74m Producers Pictures bw

Beverly Roberts *(Joan Wright)*, Robert Wilcox *(Johnny Martin)*, George Pembroke *(Ernie Mathews)*, Ted Osborne *(Ira Hanes)*, Paul McVey *(Jim Henderson)*, Alden

Chase *(Dr. Robert Lee)*, Don Rowan *(Big Billy)*, Peter Lynn *(Gus Barth)*, Norman Budd *(The Kid)*, Robert Fiske, Bob McKenzie, Joe Coits, Edward Earle, James H. McNamara.

Wilcox stars as yet another innocent man sent to prison due to political reasons. After serving a term, he is denied parole because of the trumped up charges voiced by the man who wants to keep him locked up. Roberts plays the prison nurse who knows in her heart that Wilcox isn't really a bad guy. Trite and uninteresting.

d, Victor Halperin; w, George Bricker (story by William A. Ullman, Jr.) ph, Jack Greenhalgh; ed, Holbrook N. Todd; md, Dave Chudnow.

Drama (PR:A MPAA:NR)

BURIED ALIVE* (1951, Ital.) 83m Casolaro/Flora bw (LA SEPOLTA VIVA)

Milly Vitale *(Eva)*, Paul Muller *(Federico)*, Evi Maltagliati *(Elisa)*, Tina Lattanzi *(Elena)*, Piero Palermini *(Giorgio)*, Carlo Tamberlani *(Conte Capecci)*, Enzo Fiermonte *(Bruno)*, Luigi Garrone *(Silvestro)*, Cesare Palacco *(Ferdinando)*.

Plodding melodrama from Italy concerning a murderous man who kills his stepmother, tosses his stepsister into a dungeon, assists in the murder of a loyal servant, and then is finally killed by a heroic soldier. All of the action takes place as Garibaldi and his troops fight their way through Italy and Sicily on their way to unifying the country. (In Italian; English subtitles.)

d, Guido Brignone; w, L. Cevenini, V. Martino (based on the novel by Francesco Mastriani); ph, Mario Albertelli; English titles, Salvatore F. Billitteri.

Drama (PR:C MPAA:NR)

BURKE AND HARE* (1972, Brit.) 91m Armitage c

Harry Andrews, Derren Nesbitt, Glynn Edwards, Dee Sjendery, Alan Tucker, Yootha Joyce.

Amateur attempt at horror in telling the story of the two body snatchers who labored for anatomist Dr. Knox. Not much production value to what could have been a chilling film.

p, Kenneth Shipman; d, Vernon Sewell, w, Ernie Bradford; ph, Desmond Dickinson (DeLuxe Color); m, Roger Webb.

Horror (PR:O MPAA:NR)

BURMA CONVOY** (1941) 59m UNIV bw

Charles Bickford *(Cliff Weldon)*, Evelyn Ankers *(Ann McBrogal)*, Frank Albertson *(Mike Weldon)*, Cecil Kellaway *(Lloyd McBrogal)*, Willy Fung *(Smitty)*, Keye Luke *(Lin Tai Yen)*, Turhan Bey *(Mr. Yuchau)*, Truman Bradley *(Victor Harrison)*, Ken Christy *(Hank)*, C. Montague Shaw *(Maj. Hart)*, Harry Stubbs *(Hubert)*, Chester Gan *(Keela)*, Viola Vonn *(Maisie)*.

Enjoyable actioner starring Bickford as a convoy driver who works the vital supply area between Rangoon and Chungking. Feeling he has done his time in hazardous duty, Bickford decides to return to the states and set up shop as an auto mechanic. His departure is held up by the arrival of his younger brother Albertson who is entangled in some mysterious espionage. When Albertson is killed, big brother Bickford decides to stay and get to the bottom of the conspiracy. By the end of the film Bickford exposes a hijacking ring of Eurasians intent on short-circuiting the convoy shipments.

p, Marshall Grant; d, Noel M. Smith; w, Stanley Rubin, Roy Chanslor; ph, John W. Boyle; ed, Ted Kent.

Spy Drama (PR:A MPAA:NR)

BURN***

(1970) 112m Produzioni Europee Associates/Les Productions Artistes Associes/UA c (AKA: QUEMIMADA!)

Marlon Brando *(Sir William Walker)*, Evaristo Marquez *(Jose Dolores)*, Renato Salvatori *(Teddy Sanchez)*, Norman Hill *(Shelton)*, Tom Lyons *(Gen. Prada)*, Wanani *(Guarina)*, Joseph Persuad *(Juanito)*, Gianpiero Albertini *(Henry)*, Carlo Pammucci *(Jack)*, Cecily Browne *(Lady Bella)*, Dana Ghia *(Francesca)*, Maurice Rodriguez *(Ramon)*, Alejandro Obregon *(English Major)*.

Aristocratic English agent Brando is sent on a secret mission to the Caribbean island of Queimada where the Portugese have built a highly profitable sugar cane plantation worked by thousands of black natives. Once on Queimada, the intelligent and witty Brando befriends Marquez, a strong black dock worker. Instilling the revolutionary spirit in Marquez, Brando pushes Marquez into robbing a bank, an action which, thanks to Brando's publicity, turns Marquez into an outlaw hero. After enlisting the aid of Salvatori, a hotel clerk with political aspirations, Brando makes sure that Marquez and his guerrilla followers are ready to overthrow the Portugese. On the night of the annual Negro festival, Marquez and his men attack the city and its garrison, disguising themselves in parade costumes. Brando leads a hooded group to the governor's palace and steadies Salvatori's hand long enough for him to assassinate the governor, thus becoming the revolution's figurehead. Respecting Salvatori's intelligence and knowing that he could never lead a country, Marquez turns his troops over to Salvatori, giving him complete control of the island. Brando sees that Salvatori is given all the provisions needed to govern, and heads home for England, knowing that Queimada will now be the political puppet that his British merchant bosses wanted. Ten years later, a drunken and disillusioned Brando is hired to return to the island to halt a revolution led by his old friend Marquez which has erupted as a response to corruption in Salvatori's government. Brando and his crack British troops quickly and violently take control of Queimada, burning villages and killing hundreds. Sadly, Salvatori finally realizes that he has been a pawn of the British, but before he can say anything to his people, Brando has him executed for treason. A devastating little war springs up between Brando's forces and the ever-confident men under Marquez, a war that destroys nearly all of the precious sugar cane. Marquez is captured and Brando offers his old friend the chance to escape. Marquez refuses, telling Brando, "If a man gives you freedom, it is not freedom. Freedom is something you take for yourself." After Marquez's martyr-like assassination, Brando walks to the docks where he will board the boat that will take him back to England. A black dock hand offers to carry his bag, then stabs Brando, a murder that symbolizes the continuing revolutionary spirit still alive on the island. Wanting to work on a strong political film, Brando contacted Italian director Gillo Pontecorvo, whose brilliant BATTLE OF ALGIERS is considered to be one of the most powerful political films ever made. The two men, eager to work with each other, chose as their subject matter the Spanish intervention on the island of Quemada in the 1520s when a native uprising threatened sugar production. When the Spanish government protested the idea, the director simply changed the country in question to Portugal. Both Brando and Pontecorvo wanted to make a film that showed the purity of revolution, the cruelty of colonialism, and the inhumanity of slavery. They succeeded with BURN, but some of the quirks of the film make it less than classic cinema. Pontecorvo's insistence on using untrained actors in some of the key roles irritated Brando and their "natural" style is dull and uninteresting. Brando manages to turn in a finely crafted performance of a man whose spirit is pure and optimistic, but whose mind has been jaded by the realities of life. Brando became infuriated with the director's tedious, uncertain ways of shooting the film and left the project's Colombian location near the end of filming, threatening to kill Pontecorvo if he ever saw him again. Great art is often born out of such antagonism, and much of BURN is brilliant, but much of it is misguided and boring, too. Aside from its admirable political stance, much of the brilliance comes from the stunning color photography and a fantastic musical score by one of the greatest of all film composers, Ennio Morricone.

p, Alberto Grimaldi; d, Gillo Pontecorvo; w, Franco Solinas, Giorgio Arlorio (based on a story by Pontecorvo, Solinas, Arlorio; ph, Marcello Gatti (DeLuxe Color); m, Ennio Morricone; ed, Mario Morra; art d, Sergio Canevari.

Historical Drama Cas. (PR:O MPAA:NR)

BURN 'EM UP O'CONNER** (1939) 70m MGM bw

Dennis O'Keefe *(Jerry O'Conner)*, Cecilia Parker *(Jane Delano)*, Nat Pendleton *(Buddy Buttle)*, Harry Carey *(P. G. Delano)*, Addison Richards *(Ed Eberhart)*, Charley Grapewin *(Doc Heath)*, Alan Curtis *(Jose "Rocks" Rivera)*, Tom Neal *(Hank Hogan)*, Tom Collins *(Lefty Simmons)*, Frank Orth *(Tim McElvy)*, Frank M. Thomas *(Jim Nixon)*, Si Jenks *(Mr. Jenkins)*.

Weird race car movie that features Carey as a slightly manic car builder who is out to break speed records even if most of his drivers get killed. Enter bumpkin O'Keefe who loves to drive fast and enters a midget car race which Carey witnesses with his daughter Parker. The kid wins the race, Carey spots his man and signs him up, and Parker falls for her dad's new sucker. O'Keefe is determined to succeed where the other drivers have failed and stumbles across the real reason why so many others were killed driving Carey's cars. It seems that loyal friend of Carey, Dr. Grapewin, has been drugging the driver's drinks before they head out to the track, making them pass out at the wheel. Motivational factor is that Grapewin has been distraught and seeking revenge on his old pal ever since the car builder encouraged the doc's son to drive to his death on the race course. O'Keefe enters the race and wins, vindicating Carey's design skills, and getting the girl.

p, Harry Rapf; d, Edward Sedgwick; w, Milton Berlin, Byron Morgan (based on the book by Sir Malcolm Campbell); ph, Lester White; ed, Ben Lewis.

Drama (PR:A MPAA:NR)

BURN WITCH BURN**

(1962, Brit.) 87m AIP bw (GB: NIGHT OF THE EAGLE)

Peter Wyngarde *(Norman Taylor)*, Janet Blair *(Tansy Taylor)*, Margaret Johnston *(Flora Carr)*, Anthony Nicholls *(Harvey Sawtelle)*, Colin Gordon *(Prof. Lindsay Carr)*, Kathleen Byron *(Evelyn Sawtelle)*, Reginald Beckwith *(Harold Gunnison)*, Jessica Dunning *(Hilda Gunnison)*, Norman Bird *(Doctor)*, Judith Stott *(Margaret Abbott)*, Bill Mitchell *(Fred Jennings)*.

University professor delighted with the upward surge of his career discovers it is through none of his own doing and is being conjured up by his wife with the use of a little voodoo and witchcraft. Since he is a rational man and a good citizen he naturally destroys all her spiders, skulls, and dolls. Life, of course, falls apart. A student accuses him of rape, he almost dies in a car crash, and finds his wife nearly dead in a graveyard. An effective climax shows a stone eagle coming to life, proving once again that behind every great man, etc. For protection, American threater-goers were given a special pack of salt and words to an ancient incantation during the showing of this oddball, scary tale. This director was previously responsible for CHAMBER OF HORRORS and a 1944 Lon Chaney film, WEIRD WOMAN, was based on the same story.

p, Albert Fennell; d, Sidney Hayers; w, Charles Beaumont, Richard Matheson, George Baxt (based on the novel *Conjure Wife* by Fritz Leiber, Jr.).

Horror (PR:O MPAA:NR)

BURNING, THE zero (1981) 90m FILMWAYS c

Brian Matthews *(Todd)*, Leah Ayres *(Michelle)*, Brian Backer *(Alfred)*, Larry Joshua *(Glazer)*, Jason Alexander *(Dave)*, Ned Eisenberg *(Eddie)*, Carrick Glenn *(Sally)*, Carolyn Houlihan *(Karen)*, Fisher Stevens *(Woodstock)*, Lou David *(Cropsey)*.

THE BURNING should be given the cliche award as the film which has managed to use every single idea in every other movie of its kind and still managed to screw it up. Here's the story: Counselor returns to camp after having been burned by rotten kids five years ago. Skin grafts have been painful but didn't take so his face looks like the inside of a torn pocket. He's going to get even. Naturally, the villain will do his dirty work after the campers have been sexually active so we can get a glimpse of nipple. It's a waste of money and time and the one saving grace is that it takes only ninety minutes.

p, Harvey Weinstein; d, Tony Maylam; w, Peter Lawrence, Bob Weinstein (based on a story by Weinstein, Maylam, Brad Grey); ph, Harvey Harrison; m, Rick Wakeman; ed, John Sholder.

Horror Cas. (PR:O MPAA:R)

BURNING AN ILLUSION½** (1982, Brit.) 101m British Film Inst. c

Cassie MacFarlane, Victor Romero, Beverley Martin, Angela Wynter, Malcolm Fredericks, Trevor Laird.

Low-budget socio-drama about the plight of a young black woman (Cassie MacFarlane) in London's burgeoning Caribbean community. An excellent depiction of the way things are, done with no editorial comment or political posturing. There is humor, some violence, stirring performances by MacFarlane and Romero as her boy friend who goes astray after losing his job. If the same subject matter were covered by a large Pinewood or Ealing production, it couldn't have had half the impact that BURNING AN ILLUSION manages. Due to lack of money the producers were forced to use shortcuts such as voice-overs where dialog would have been superior but these are quibbles. Music by Nefta is particularly good and captures the mood.

p, Vivien Pottersman; d, Menelik Shabbazz; w, Shabbazz; ph, Roy Cornwall; m, Seyoum Nefta; ed, Judy Seymour.

Drama (PR:C MPAA:NR)

BURNING CROSS, THE*½
(1947) 77m Screen Guild bw

Hank Daniels (Johnny), Virginia Patton (Doris), Raymond Bond (Chester), Betty Roadman (Agatha), Dick Rich (Bud), Joel Fluellen (Charlie), Walden Boyle (Strickland), Alexander Pope (Gibbons), John Fostini (Tony), John Doncetto (Tobey), Jack Shulla (Hill), Maidie Norman (Kitty), Glen Allen (Bobby), Matt Willis (Dawson), Tom Kennedy (Police Sergeant), Dick Bailey (Pelham), Ted Stanhope (Elkins).

One of the first screen examinations of the evils of the Ku Klux Klan, starring Daniels as a bitter and disillusioned WW II vet who falls into the "America for Americans" mentality preached by the men of the white robes and burning crosses. The ex-GI is slowly sucked into the cult and we witness the initiation rites and ceremonial cross-burnings that strike terror into the hearts of non-whites. While all of this must have had the taste of expose in 1947, today it is stiff and dated and the film never really achieves any sort of insight into the kinds of characters that infest the KKK.

p&d, Walter Colmes; w, Aubrey Wisberg; ph, Walter Strenge; ed, Jason Bernie.

Drama (PR:C MPAA:NR)

BURNING GOLD*
(1936) 58m REP bw

Bill Boyd (Jim Thurston), Judith Allen (Caroline Long), Lloyd Ingraham (Calico), Fern Emmett (Lena), Frank Mayo (Brent Taylor).

Insipid drama starring Boyd as a poor oil driller who suddenly strikes it rich. Confident in his new-found wealth, he marries the local gal, spends a lot of dough at the local nightclub, overdraws his bank account, dumps his girl, then the oil well catches fire and he winds up broke. Down on his luck, his faithful wife returns and the couple reunite.

d, Sam Newfield; w, Earl Snell (based on a story by Stuart Anthony).

Drama (PR:A MPAA:NR)

BURNING HILLS, THE**
(1956) 93m WB c

Tab Hunter (Trace Jordan), Natalie Wood (Maria Colton), Skip Homeier (Jack Sutton), Eduard Franz (Jacob Lantz), Earl Holliman (Mort Bayliss), Claude Akins (Ben Hindeman), Ray Teal (Joe Sutton), Frank Puglia (Tio Perico), Hal Baylor (Braun), Tyler MacDuff (Wes Parker), Rayford Barnes (Veach), Tony Terry (Vincente Colton).

Western Romeo and Juliet tale detailing Hunter's efforts to get revenge on rotten cattle-baron Teal who had the boy's brother murdered to keep him off his land. The tables turn and the avenger is forced to run for the hills with half-breed Mexican Wood when the killers come after him. The vicious henchmen are led by the son of the cattle-baron, Homeier, who is just as nasty as his old man. Hunter manages to knock off most of their pursuers while climbing through the rough terrain of the hillside, until it's a final showdown on the jagged rocks above the wild river below.

p, Richard Whorf; d, Stuart Heisler; w, Irving Wallace (based on the novel by Louis L'Amour); ph, Ted McCord (Warner Color); m, David Buttolph; ed, Clarence Kolster; cos, Marjorie Best.

Western (PR:A MPAA:NR)

BURNING QUESTION, THE
(SEE: REEFER MADNESS, 1936)

BURNING UP*
(1930) 60m PAR bw

Richard Arlen (Lou Larrigan), Mary Brian (Ruth Morgan), Francis McDonald (Bullet McGhan), Sam Hardy (Windy Wallace), Charles Sellon (James P. Morgan), Tully Marshall (Dave Gentry).

Short and sweet early talkie concerning the trials and tribulations of maintaining a romance at the auto race track between Arlen and Brian. Arlen's racing rival McDonald is after the girl and the trophy. Luckily Hardy, Sellon, and Marshall are on the premises to lighten things up with their usual brand of hokey comedy.

d, Edward Sutherland; w, William Slavens McNutt, Grover Jones; ph, Allen Siegler; ed, Richard H. Digges, Jr.

Drama (PR:A MPAA:NR)

BURNING YEARS, THE**
(1979, Ital.) 90m Filmalpha/Megavision c

Fabio Traversi (Saverio), Laura Lenzi (Andreina), Gabriele Ferzetti (Father).

A shy boy, Traversi, bullied into becoming a small-town teacher by his overbearing father, travels to Rome to participate in some important qualifying exams. While in Rome, he meets and falls in love with Lenzi, missing his exams because he wants to stay in bed with her. He returns home in shame and is verbally abused by his frustrated father. Rebelling against the idea that he should follow in dad's footsteps, Traversi leaves the town and returns to Rome. Familiar story of youthful insurgence does not contain any scenes or characters that would distinguish it from a variety of predecessors.

d, Vittorio Sindoni; w, Nicol Badalucco, Sindoni, Mario Gallo; ph, Safai Teherani; ed, Angelo Curi.

Drama (PR:O MPAA:NR)

BURNT EVIDENCE**
(1954, Brit.) 61m Monarch/ACT Films

Jane Hylton (Diana Taylor), Duncan Lamont (Jack Taylor), Donald Gray (Jimmy Thompson), Meredith Edwards (Bob Edwards), Cyril Smith (Alf Quinney), Irene Handl (Mrs. Raymond), Hugo Shuster (Hartl), Kynaston Reeves (Pathologist).

Routine thriller about a husband who takes it on the lam after accidentally shooting the man with whom his wife has been fooling around.

p, Ronald Kinnoch; d, Dan Birt; w, Ted Willis (based on a story by Percy Hoskins); ph, Jo Jago.

Drama (PR:O MPAA:NR)

BURNT OFFERINGS*
(1976) 116m UA c

Karen Black (Marian), Oliver Reed (Ben), Burgess Meredith (Brother), Eileen Heckart (Roz), Lee Montgomery (David), Dub Taylor (Walker), Bette Davis (Aunt Elizabeth), Anthony James (Chauffeur), Orin Cannon (Minister), James T. Myers (Dr. Ross), Todd Turquand (Young Ben), Joseph Riley (Ben's Father).

Big stars, big effects, big bore. Dan Curtis, who made his name doing "Dark Shadows" on TV, then large mini-series such "Winds Of War," comes a cropper with this turgid, talky, and tiresome attempt at a classic Gothic. Nothing is burnt during the picture so we wonder if that was a scene that hit the cutting room floor. Reed, Black, Davis, and Montgomery move into the old house owned by Meredith and Heckart and things begin to happen. It's sort of The Amityville Ho-Hum from there on in. Money must be the reason these usually excellent actors took this job.

They couldn't have seen anything in the script. It's like a 2000-word scary short story that was somehow fed pituitary drugs and wound up grotesque and overblown.

p, Dan Curtis; d, Curtis; w, William Nolan (based on the novel by Robert Marasco) ph, Jacques Marquette, Steven Larner (DeLuxe Color); m, Robert Cobert; ed, Dennis Verkler.

Horror **Cas.** (PR:C-O MPAA:PG)

BURY ME AN ANGEL zero
(1972) 89m New World c

Dixie Peabody (Dag), Terry Mace (Jonsie), Clyde Ventura (Bernie), Stephen Wittaker (Killer), Maureen Math, Joanne Moore Jordan, Marie Denn, Dennis Peabody, Dianne Turley, Alan DeWitt, Janelle Pransky, Wayne Everett Chestnut, Dan Haggerty, Corky Williams, Beach Dickerson, David Atkins, Gary Littlejohn.

This movie has the unique distinction of being the first "biker" film directed by a woman. "A howling hellcat humping a hot hog on a roaring rampage of revenge" promised the ads, and sure enough six-foot Dixie Peabody, blonde hair flying and aided by two honchos and a sawed-off shotgun, is off on her bike in search of her brother's killer. Junk.

p, Paul Norbert; d&w, Barbara Peters; ph, Sven Walnum (Eastmancolor); m, Richard Hieronymus; ed, Tony De Aarraga.

Horror **Cas.** (PR:O MPAA:R)

BURY ME DEAD***
(1947) 68m EL bw

Cathy O'Donnell (Rusty), June Lockhart (Barbara Carlin), Hugh Beaumont (Michael Dunn), Mark Daniels (Rod Carlin), Greg McClure (George Mandley), Milton Parsons (Waters), Virginia Farmer (Mrs. Haskins), Sonia Darrin (Helen Lawrence), Cliff Clark (Archer).

Exceptionally well-done low-budget mystery that begins with Lockhart showing up at her own funeral. Determined to find out who killed the mysterious girl buried under her name, Lockhart begins to suspect her husband Daniels and her nymphomaniac sister O'Donnell. Enlisting the aid of her kindly lawyer, Beaumont, Lockhart uncovers the identity of the murderer and the dead girl. Containing some frankly sexual (for 1947) dialog and a nervous, edgy narrative structure, the film overcomes the limitations of its script and its budget, becoming an intriguing, craftily conceived piece of work.

p, Charles F. Reisner; d, Bernard Vorhaus; w, Karen de Wolf, Dwight V. Babcock (based on a story by Irene Winston); ph, John Alton; ed, W. Donn Hayes.

Mystery (PR:C MPAA:NR)

BURY ME NOT ON THE LONE PRAIRIE**
(1941) 57m UNIV bw

Johnny Mack Brown, Fuzzy Knight, Nell O'Day, Kathryn Adams, Lee Shumway, Frank O'Connor, Ernie Adams, Don House, Pat O'Brien, Bud Osborne, Ed Cassidy, Slim Whitaker, Kermit Maynard, William Desmond, Jack Rockwell, Bob Kortman, Jim Corey, Charles King, Ethan Laidlaw, Harry Cording, Frank Ellis, Jimmy Wakely's Rough Riders.

Brown is a mining engineer whose brother has been murdered. He goes after the group of claim jumpers responsible and avenges his brother's death. A routine western.

d, Ray Taylor; w, Sherman Lowe, Victor McLeod (based on a story by Lowe).

Western (PR:A MPAA:NR)

BUS IS COMING, THE**
(1971) 108m Thompson International c

Mike Simms (Billy Mitchell), Stephanie Faulkner (Tanya), Burl Bullock (Michael), Tony Sweeting (Dobie), Jack Stillman (John), Sandra Reed (Miss Nickerson), Bob Brubaker (Chief Jackson), Morgan Jones (Tim Naylor), Dick Ryal (Corie Smith), Eddie Kendrix, Juan Russell.

A young black man is killed in the Los Angeles suburb of Watts and a group of black militants demand that action be taken against the two sadistic cops who committed the murder. Sympathetic to the blacks, but forced into backing up the story of his two officers, police chief Brubaker must deal with a highly volatile situation. When Simms, the brother of the victim, returns from Vietnam, he is asked by the militants to join them in protest, but Simms refuses, wishing to remain neutral on the matter. When the two cops begin to harass him, Simms contemplates becoming a member of the militant organization. Independently made by blacks, the film manages to address the racial issues while telling an interesting, albeit melodramatic story. The unknown cast is quite good at portraying the anger and frustration of the situation without becoming overly preachy or forced.

p, Horace Jackson; d, Wendall James Franklin; w, Horace Jackson, Robert H. Raff, Mike Rhodes; ph, Rhodes; m, Tom McIntosh; ed, Donald R. Rode; art d, Haaga/Jacobsen.

Drama **Cas.** (PR:C-O MPAA:GP)

BUS RILEY'S BACK IN TOWN** ½
(1965) 93m UNIV c

Ann-Margret (Laurel), Michael Parks (Bus Riley), Janet Margolin (Judy), Brad Dexter (Slocum), Jocelyn Brando (Mrs. Riley), Larry Storch (Howie), Crahan Denton (Spencer), Kim Darby (Gussie), Brett Somers (Carlotta), Mimsy Farmer (Paula), Nan Martin (Mrs. Nichols), Lisabeth Hush (Joy), Ethel Griffies (Mrs. Spencer), Alice Pearce (Woman Customer), Chet Stratton (Benji), David Carradine (Stretch), Marc Cavell (Egg Foo), Parley Baer (Mr. Griswald).

Parks, doing a James Dean cum Marlon Brando impression, returns to his home town, searching for a purpose in life. Although he gets moral support from the understanding Margolin, Parks finds himself attracted to town tramp Margret who feeds his self-pity. A beautifully produced film (Metty's cinematography is breathtaking) that fails to create any interest in its protagonist's dilemma or the people that inhabit the town. The fault lies primarily with the casting of stoic Parks, whom the studio hoped would become a teen idol. His absence of a personality severely handicaps this hope. Margret is hopelessly misdirected as the town whore, giving a cartoon impersonation of a screaming bitch. The only shining light among the cast is Margolin who is nicely restrained as the quiet girl who wants to help the forlorn Parks.

p, Elliott Kastner; d, Harvey Hart; w, Walter Gage (based on a story by William Inge); ph, Russell Metty (Eastmancolor); m, Richard Markowitz; ed, Folmar Blangsted; cos, Jean Louis.

Drama (PR:A MPAA:NR)

BUS STOP*½   (1956) 94m FOX c (AKA: THE WRONG KIND OF GIRL)

Marilyn Monroe (*Cherie*), Don Murray (*Bo*), Arthur O'Connell (*Virgil*), Betty Field (*Grace*), Eileen Heckart (*Vera*), Robert Bray (*Carl*), Hope Lange (*Elma*), Hans Conreid (*Life Photographer*), Casey Adams (*Life Reporter*), Henry Slate (*Manager of Night Club*), Terry Kelman (*Gerald*), Linda Brace (*Evelyn*), Greta Thyssen (*Cover Girl*), Helen Mayon (*Landlady*), Lucille Knox (*Blonde*).

Among the countless fans of Marilyn Monroe are there any who can listen to "That Old Black Magic" without recounting Monroe's tinny, off-key, magically poignant rendition of that song in BUS STOP? In her energetic and warm portrayal of Cherie, the well worn chantoosie whose dream of Hollywood and Vine is interrupted by the reality of a layover in Phoenix, Monroe exposes her vulnerability without sacrificing any of her radiance. This movie proved to audiences that Monroe could act. In her year-long absence from the screen she pursued her craft under the firm hand of Lee Strasberg, prime exponent of the Method school of acting. It worked. Inge's rowdy play about a cowboy and a lady is lassoed into a screenplay by George Axelrod with delightful results. The Blue Dragon Cafe in Phoenix is where we meet Bo (Don Murray in his first screen role), a rambunctious cowboy who is in town to take part in a rodeo. He bullies the noisy patrons into a respectful silence during Cherie's big song and is rewarded with an innocent kiss of appreciation. From that moment on he is determined to make her his wife, in spite of her protestations and the dismay of his loyal sidekick O'Connell. Cherie boards a bus out of town to escape the noontime cowboy but Murray is not to be denied until the bus is stranded in a snow storm and the passengers forced to spend the night in a diner. A fight involving the bus driver, protecting his passenger, and the cowboy, claiming his woman, leaves Murray defeated and humiliated. By the time the road is cleared the next day a chastened Murray has calmed down to the point where he realizes he will get nowhere acting like a brute. A goodbye kiss brings spring back to the hearts of all and the happy couple board the bus to Montana and Murray's ranch. Inge's play, which had taken place on a single diner set, was moved to a ranch, a dance hall, a rodeo, and the countryside by Axelrod in this screen adaptation, without loss of humor or pathos. The film is further enhanced by some action-packed rodeo contesting. A warm, charming movie.

p, Buddy Adler; d, Joshua Logan, w, George Axelrod (based on the play by William Inge); ph, Milton Krasner (CinemaScope, DeLuxe Color); m, Alfred Newman, Cyril J. Mockridge.

Comedy   **Cas.**   **(PR:A MPAA:NR)**

BUSH CHRISTMAS**½   (1947, Brit.) GAU-GEN/UNIV bw

Chips Rafferty (*Long Bill*), John Fernside (*Jim*), Stan Tolhurst (*Blue*), Pat Penny(*Father*), Thelma Grigg (*Mother*), Clyde Combo (*Old Jack*), John McCallum (*Narrator*), Helen Grieve (*Helen*), Nicky Yardley (*Snow*), Morris Unicombe (*John*), Michael Yardley (*Michael*), Neza Saunders (*Neza*).

When their father's prize horses are stolen by thieves, a group of children set out to capture them. Utilizing techniques taught to them by their Aborigine servants, the kids finally subdue the rustlers in a ghost town after trekking across the barren Australian bush. Handsomely photographed kiddie adventure film that interestingly contrasts the harshness of the environment with the childrens' determination.

p, J. Arthur Rank; d, Ralph Smart; w, Smart; ph, George Heath.

Adventure   **(PR:AA MPAA:NR)**

BUSH CHRISTMAS**   (1983, Aus.) 91m Hoyts Release c

John Ewart (*Bill*), John Howard (*Sly*), Nicole Kidman (*Helen*), Mark Spain (*Michael*), Vineta O'Malley (*Mother*), James Wingrove (*Johnny*), Peter Sumner (*Father*), Manalpuy (*Manalpuy*).

Christmas in Australia is sort of like August in New Orleans; hot, steamy, and sweltering. Santa Claus must arrive in Bermuda shorts after several stops at the water hole for the exhausted, panting reindeer. That aside, BUSH CHRISTMAS is a joy. Freely adapted from the 1947 version (starring Australia's then only major star, Chips Rafferty), it tells the uplifting story of three dauntless kids who join with an Aboriginal (Manalpuy) to hunt the thieves who stole their horse. (THE BLACK STALLION sequel, which disintegrated into chaos, is oats compared to this feast for the eyes and emotions.) Nicole Kidman is a pleasure to watch, exhibiting many "star" qualities. Plenty of humor amidst the adventure and the picture has a high gloss to it that makes it appear much more expensive than it must have been. This is one of the rare remakes that's somewhat better than the original.

p, Gilda Baracchi, Paul Barron; d, Henri Safran; w, Ted Roberts (based on the prior version by Ralph Smart); ph, Malcolm Richards, Ross Berryman; m, Mike Perjanik; ed, Ron Williams.

Adventure/Comedy   **(PR:AA MPAA:NR)**

BUSHBABY, THE**½   (1970) 100m MGM c

Margaret Brooks (*Jackie Leeds*), Louis Gossett, Jr. (*Tembo*), Donald Houston (*John Leeds*), Laurence Naismith (*Prof. "Cranky" Crankshaw*), Marne Maitland (*The Hadj*), Geoffrey Bayldon (*Tilison*), Jack Gwillim (*Ardsley*), Noel Howlett (*Rev. Barlow*), Tommy Ansah (*Policeman*), Jumoke Debayo (*Bus Woman*), Harold Goodwin (*Steward*), Charles Hyatt (*Gideon*), Willy Jonah (*Police Sergeant*), Simon Lack (*First Officer*), Victor Maddern (*Barman*), Illario Pedro (*Policeman*), Martin Wyldeck (*Captain*).

Brooks, vacationing with her father in Africa, is given a bushbaby as a gift. She falls in love with the tiny, screaming beast and plans to take it back with her to England. As her ship leavs port, Brooks hops off the boat, hoping to leave the bushbaby in its natural home. Having missed the ship, Brooks and the little animal are helped by their former servant, Gossett, who agrees to accompany them on a trip across Africa, a journey that will link Brooks up with one of her father's friends. When local authorities assume that Brooks has been kidnaped by Gossett, he becomes a wanted man. Racist whites and white slavers pursue the girl, Gossett, and the animal, but they are saved when Brooks' father returns to clear matters up. Kiddie matinee fare that, naturally, avoids the race issue to a great extent. Gossett, a fine actor, is wasted here in a simple-minded role. Brooks, however, is not only simple-minded, but incredibly annoying as well.

p, Robert Maxwell, John Trent; d, Trent; w, Robert Maxwell, William H. Stevenson (from a novel by Stevenson); ph, Davis Boulton; m, Les Reed; ed, Raymond Poulton; art d, Jack Shampan.

Adventure/Drama   **(PR:AA MPAA:G)**

BUSHIDO BLADE, THE**   (1982 Brit./U.S.) 92m Aquarius Films/Trident c (AKA: THE BLOODY BUSHIDO BLADE)

Richard Boone (*Matthew Perry*), Sonny Chiba (*Prince Edo*), Frank Converse (*Capt. Hawk*), Laura Gemser (*Edo's Cousin*), James Earl Jones (*Harpooner*), Mako (*Friend*), Toshiro Mifune (*Shogun's Commander*), Timothy Murphy (*Robert Burr*), Michael Starr (*Cave Johnson*), Tetsuro Tamba (*Lord Yamato*), Mayumi Atano (*Yuki*).

Toshiro Mifune is going to continue doing these kind of films until he finds one that measures up to his talent. THE BUSHIDO BLADE is not that one. The story of Commodore Perry has been done any number of times on stage and screen and this film attempts it a new way; cartoon characters, yelling, derring-do, and a lot of derring-don'ts. Boone, who died shortly after completing the picture, is Perry and he hams it up. James Earl Jones is wasted as a harpooner. Frank Converse has a lot to do but never gets a chance to act much, just react to all the action around him. A bit of nudity, some violence, a few laughs, and a preposterous ending make THE BUSHIDO BLADE very dull.

p, Arthur Rankin, Jr.; d, Tom Kotani; w, William Overgard; ph, Shoji Ueda; m, Maury Laws; ed, Yoshitami Huroiwa.

Historical Drama   **Cas.**   **(PR:O MPAA:R)**

BUSHWHACKERS, THE**   (1952) 70m REA bw (GB: THE REBEL)

John Ireland (*Jeff Waring*), Wayne Morris (*John Harding*), Lawrence Tierney (*Sam Tobin*), Dorothy Malone (*Cathy Sharpe*), Lon Chaney, Jr. (*Mr. Taylor*), Myrna Dell (*Norah Taylor*), Frank Marlowe (*Peter Sharpe*), Bill Holmes (*Ding Bell*), Jack Elam (*Cree*), Bob Wood (*Gully*), Charles Trowbridge (*Justin Stone*), Stuart Randall (*Slocum*), George Lynn (*Guthrie*), Gordon Wynne (*Quigley*), Gabriel Conrad (*Kramer*), Norman Leavitt (*Yale*), Eddie Parks (*Funeral Franklin*), Evelyn Bispham (*Mrs. Lloyd*), Jack Harden (*Mr. Lloyd*), Venise Grove (*Woman*), Ted Jordan (*Soldier*), Kit Guard (*Oldster*).

As the Civil War ends, Ireland vows never to use a gun against a man again. Travelling west, he stops for awhile in a town in which Chaney is the local powerhouse. When Malone's newspaper publisher father is killed after printing some anti-Chaney articles, Ireland straps on his dusty gun and wipes out Chaney and his men. Winning the support of the townspeople and the love of Malone, Ireland settles down permanently. Good, simply constructed western that gets its character from Malone and Ireland, who perform admirably.

p, Larry Finley; d, Rod Amateau; w, Amateau, Thomas Gries; ph, Joseph Biroc; m, Albert Glasser; ed, Francis D. Lyon.

Western   **(PR:A MPAA:NR)**

BUSINESS AND PLEASURE**   (1932) 76m FOX bw

Will Rogers (*Earl Tinker*), Jetta Goudal (*Mme. Momora*), Joel McCrea (*Lawrence Ogle*), Dorothy Peterson (*Mrs. Tinker*), Peggy Ross (*Olivia Tinker*), Cyril Ring (*Arthur Jones*), Jed Prouty (*Ben Wackstle*), Oscar Apfel (*P. D. Weatheright*), Vernon Dent (*Charlie Turner*), Boris Karloff (*Sheikh*).

Rogers, a razor blade manufacturer hoping to corner the market, travels to the Middle East to meet the manufacturer of the steel he uses in production. When his rival uses a seductive female to lure Rogers into a trap, his wife and daughter, along with playwright McCrea, travel east to rescue Rogers. Rogers, however, using his own cornball ideas, escapes and meets up with the rescue party. Silly Will Rogers comedy that uses every possible chance to showcase its star's aw-shucks ingenuity. McCrea is very entertaining in an early role.

p, Al Rockett; d, David Butler; w, Gene Towne, William Conselman (based on the novel *The Plutocrat* by Booth Tarkington and the play of the same name by Arthur Goodrich); ph, Ernest Palmer.

Comedy   **(PR:A MPAA:NR)**

BUSMAN'S HOLIDAY*   (1936, Brit.) 64m GS/Bow Bell bw

Wally Patch (*Jeff Pinkerton*), Gus McNaughton (*Alf Green*), Muriel George (*Mrs. Green*), H. F. Maltby (*Mr. Bulger*), Isobel Scaife (*Daisy*), Robert Hobbs (*Harry Blake*), Norman Pierce (*Crook*), Michael Ripper (*Crook*).

Busmen on holiday run into trouble when they are mistaken for burglars, but their vacation turns out to be profitable anyway when they apprehend the real culprits.

p, A. George Smith; d, Maclean Rogers; w, Kathleen Butler, H. F. Maltby (based on a story by Wally Patch); ph, Geoffrey Faithfull.

Comedy   **(PR:A MPAA:NR)**

BUSMAN'S HONEYMOON**½   (1940, Brit.) 99m MGM bw (GB: HAUNTED HONEYMOON)

Robert Montgomery (*Lord Peter Wimsey*), Constance Cummings (*Harriet Vane*), Leslie Banks (*Inspector Kirk*), Seymour Hicks (*Bunter*), Robert Newton (*Frank Crutchley*), Googie Withers (*Polly*), Frank Pettingell (*Puffett*), Jean Kemp-Welch (*Angie Twitterton*), Louise Hampton (*Mrs. Ruddle*).

Montgomery injects some wit and charm into Dorothy Sayers' aristocratic detective in this otherwise tedious tale of Montgomery and newlywed bride Cummings investigating a murder on their honeymoon.

d, Arthur B. Woods; w, Monckton Hoffe, Angus MacPhail, Harold Goldman (based on the novel and play by Dorothy L. Sayers); ph, F. A. Young.

Mystery/Comedy   **(PR:A MPAA:NR)**

BUSSES ROAR**½   (1942) 59m WB bw

Richard Travis (*Sergeant Ryan*), Julie Bishop (*Reba Richards*), Charles Drake (*Eddie Sloan*), Eleanor Parker (*Norma*), Elisabeth Fraser (*Betty*), Richard Fraser (*Dick Remick*), Peter Whitney (*Hoff*), Frank Wilcox (*Detective Quinn*), Willie Best (*Sunshine*), Rex Williams (*Jerry Silva*), Harry Lewis (*Danny*), Bill Kennedy (*The Moocher*), George Meeker (*Nick Stoddard*), Vera Lewis (*Mrs. Dipper*), Harry C. Bradley (*Henry Dipper*), Lottie Williams (*1st Old Maid*), Leah Baird (*2nd Old Maid*), Chester Gan (*Yamanito*).

In WW II-era California, a German secret agent and his Japanese cohort plant a bomb on a passenger bus. Hoping that when the bomb explodes, it will be a clear beacon for a Japanese sub to target its bombs at, the spies wait patiently in the terminal. As travelers board the ill-fated bus, each of their personalities and dilemmas becomes evident. The plot is discovered as the bus is en route and the heroic Travis saves the day. Boring melodrama that plays its wartime spy paranoia to the hilt. An extremely low-budget production, most of the film takes place within the terminal, giving the entire production a weird, claustrophobic feel.

d, D. Ross Lederman; w, George R. Bilson, Anthony Coldewey (based on a story by Coldewey); ph, James Van Trees; ed, James Gibbon; spec eff, Edwin A. DuPar.

Spy Drama (PR:A MPAA:NR)

BUSTER KEATON STORY, THE* 1/2 (1957) 91m PAR bw

Donald O'Connor *(Buster Keaton)*, Ann Blyth *(Gloria)*, Rhonda Fleming *(Peggy Courtney)*, Peter Lorre *(Kurt Bergner)*, Larry Keating *(Larry Winters)*, Jackie Coogan *(Elmer Case)*, Richard Anderson *(Tom McAffee)*, Dave Willock *(Joe Keaton)*, Claire Carlton *(Myrna Keaton)*, Larry White *(Buster, age 7)*, *Dan Seymour (Indian Chief)*, Mike Ross *(Assistant Chief)*, Nan Martin *(Edna)*, Robert Christopher *(Nick)*, Richard Aherne *(Franklin)*, Tim Ryan *(Policeman)*, Joe Forte *(Theater Manager)*, Ralph Dumke *(Mr. Jennings)*, Larry Rio *(Holt)*, Constance Cavendish *(Wife)*, Ivan Triesault *(Duke)*, Pamela Jayson *(Leading Woman)*, Keith Richards *(Leading Man)*, Dick Ryan *(Susan's Father)*, Guy Wilkerson *(Boarder)*, Lizz Slifer *(Mrs. Anderson)*, Cecil B. DeMille.

Disappointing tribute to the great comedian, focuses mainly on romantic involvement with innocent and demure true love Blyth and seductively beautiful Fleming as his siren. Saddest part is that Hollywood made up its own facts to suit itself, offering an inaccurate impression of the film's brilliant subject. Disgraceful, with little comedy.

p, Robert Smith, Sidney Sheldon; d, Sheldon; w, Smith, Sheldon; ph, Loyal Griggs; m, Victor Young; ed, Archie Marshek.

Comedy Cas. (PR:A MPAA:NR)

BUSTIN' LOOSE** (1981) 94m UA c

Richard Pryor *(Joe Braxton)*, Cicely Tyson *(Vivian Perry)*, Alphonso Alexander *(Martin)*, Kia Cooper *(Samantha)*, Edwin DeLeon *(Ernesto)*, Jimmy Hughes *(Harold)*, Edwin Kinter *(Anthony)*, Tami Luchow *(Linda)*, Angel Ramirez *(Julio)*, Janet Wong *(Annie)*, Robert Christian *(Donald)*, George Coe *(Dr. Wilson T. Renfrew)*, Bill Quinn *(Judge)*, Roy Jensen *(Clan Leader)*, Fred Carney *(Alfred Schuyler)*, Peggy McCay *(Gladys Schuyler)*, Luke Andreas *(Loader)*, Earl Billings *(Man at Parole Office)*, Michael A. Esler *(Cop)*, Paul Gardner *(Anchorman)*, Ben Gerard *(Man)*, Gary Goetzman *(Store Manager)*, Joe Jacobs *(Watchman)*, Paul Mooney *(Marvin)*, Lee Noblitt *(Farmer)*, Inez Pedroza *(Herself)*, Morgan Roberts *(Uncle Humphrey)*, Vern Taylor, Rick Saways *(Patrolmen)*, Gloria Jewel Waggener *(Aunt Beedee)*, Shila Turna *(Girl in Card Game)*, Jonelle White *(Sales Clerk)*, Jewell Williams *(Thiss Thomas)* Sunny Woods *(Linette)*.

An old-fashioned, somewhat innocent account of a jailbird mechanic (Pryor) who reluctantly goes to the aid of Tyson, fixes her old bus, and drives her and eight children to Seattle where they will settle on a farm. The wayward bus winds up in several unusual places, breaks down regularly, etc. Delete the four-letter words and this might have been a Disney film, but Pryor likes to keep his mouth somewhere near the gutter and as long as people keep paying money to see him do that he will keep doing it. One would think that the movie-going public would tire of foul language for its own sake by this time. The center of the film is its funniest part, due to Pryor's ability to energize the screen with his presence. A sequence with the KKK is especially funny, but in the end this remains a minor effort from a major talent.

p, Richard Pryor, Michael S. Glick; d, Oz Scott; w, Roger L. Simon (based on an adaptation by Lonne Elder III of a story by Pryor); ph, Dennis Dalzell (Technicolor) m, Mark Davis, Roberta Flack; ed, David Holden; cos, Bill Whitten.

Comedy Cas. (PR:O MPAA:R)

BUSTING*** (1974) 91m UA c

Elliott Gould *(Keneely)*, Robert Blake *(Farrell)*, Allen Garfield *(Rizzo)*, John Lawrence *(Sgt. Kenflick)*, Cornelia Sharpe *(Jackie)*, Erin O'Reilly *(Doris)*, Richard X. Slattery *(Desk Sgt.)*, William Sylvester *(Lawyer)*, Logan Ramsey *(Dentist)*, Michael Lerner *(Bookstore Manager)*.

Blake and Gould, two cops frustrated with the criminal-conscious modern justice system, decide to pursue mob chief Garfield on their own, in complete disregard for the legal restrictions placed upon them by their supervisors. Exciting, well-paced police story whose vigilante thematics can be seen in director Hyams' later work, THE STAR CHAMBER. Blake and Gould are good, but have done better, the limitations of the script not allowing them to explore the eccentricities of their characters. The real star of the film is director Hyams' camera that manages to capture a frenzied sense of despair and sudden violence.

p, Irwin Winkler, Robert Chartoff; d, w, Peter Hyams; ph, Earl Rath (DeLuxe Color); m, Billy Goldenberg; ed, James Mitchell; set d, Ray Molyneaux.

Crime Drama (PR:C MPAA:R)

BUSYBODY, THE 1/2** (1967) 102m PAR c

Sid Caesar *(George Norton)*, Robert Ryan *(Charley Baker)*, Anne Baxter *(Margo Foster)*, Kay Medford *(Ma Norton)*, Jan Murray *(Murray Foster)*, Richard Pryor *(Whittaker)*, Arlene Golonka *(Bobbi Brody)*, Charles McGraw *(Fred Harwell)*, Ben Blue *(Felix Rose)*, Dom DeLuise *(Kurt Brock)*, Bill Dana *(Archie Brody)*, Godfrey Cambridge *(Mike)*, Marty Ingels *(Willie)*, George Jessel *(Mr. Fessel)*, Mickey Deems *(Cop)*, Paul Wesler *(Mr. Merriwether)*, Marina Koshetz *(Marcia Woshikowski)*, Norman Bartold, Mike Wagner, Larry Gelman, Don Brodie *(Board Members)*, Choo Choo Collins *(Woman)*.

Small-time crook Caesar, suspected of possessing Mafia money pilfered by bagman Dana, is hunted by gangland boss Ryan. A mix-up of dead bodies and a few cases of mistaken identity put Caesar into a few funny situations. After directing a few wonder fully ludicrous horror films, William Castle managed to inject a few laughs into this humorous look at the mob by using a talented cast of Vegas old-timers and gifted newcomers.

p&d, William Castle; w, Ben Starr (based on a novel by Donald E. Westlake); ph, Hal Stine (Techniscope, Technicolor); m, Vic Mizzy; ed, Edwin H. Bryant; m/l, Edward Heyman.

Comedy (PR:A MPAA:NR)

BUT NOT FOR ME 1/2** (1959) 105m PAR bw

Clark Gable *(Russell Ward)*, Carroll Baker *(Eleanor Brown)*, Lilli Palmer *(Kathryn Ward)*, Lee J. Cobb *(Jeremiah MacDonald)*, Barry Coe *(Gordon Reynolds)*, Thomas Gomez *(Demetrios Bacos)*, Charles Lane *(Atwood)*, Wendell Holmes *(Montgomery)*, Tom Duggan *(Roy Morton)*.

One of the most refreshing things about Clark Gable was that he was willing to act his age. What's more, he was willing to make jokes about it and let his script writers do the same. But that is about the only thing holding together this romantic-comedy based on Samson Raphaelson's play "Accent on Youth." A reluctantly aging Broadway producer is having script trouble with his latest play, "A May-December Romance." He is about to throw in the towel when his 22-year-old secretary (Baker) berates him for quitting while at the same time declaring her love for him. In a flash he sees the solution to his problem: reverse the situation and have the older man being pursued by the young girl instead of vice versa. He talks the author (Cobb), a disillusioned drunk, into sobering up long enough for a rewrite, and, of course, gives the girl friend the feminine lead. The play is a hit, but when, in his state of bliss he decides to marry Baker, she tells him she really loves a young actor, that the marriage would be a mistake, but blesses him for having "the wisdom that comes with age." Jolted back to reality, Gable decides to admit his age and start life anew by remarrying wonderfully mature and always desirable Lilli Palmer. The movie has some bright spots but generally does not click as a whole. Good performance by Gomez as a Hollywood film tycoon of Greek origin and the title song is beautifully sung by Ella Fitzgerald behind the main titles. (Remake of ACCENT ON YOUTH.)

p, William Perlberg, George Seaton; d, Walter Lang; w, John Michael Hayes (based on the play "Accent on Youth" by Samson Raphaelson); ph, Robert Burks; m, Leigh Stevens; ed, Alma Macrorie.

Romance/Comedy (PR:A MPAA:NR)

BUT NOT IN VAIN* (1948, Brit.) 73m Anglo-Dutch/BUT bw

Raymond Lovell *(Jan Alting)*, Carol Van Derman *(Elly Alting)*, Martin Benson *(Mark Meyer)*, Agnes Bernelle *(Mary Meyer)*, Julian Dallas *(Willem Bakker)*, Bruce Lister *(Fred Van Nespen)*, Ben Van Esselstyn [Eeslyn], Jordan Lawrence, Harry Croizet, Geoffrey Goodheart, Victor Colane, Henry Almar, Gerhard Alexander.

A Holland farmer provides a hiding place for patriots during WW II but is thwarted in his patriotic gesture when his greedy, selfish son threatens to betray them. Limp heroics.

p, Gus E. Ostwalt, Geoffrey Goodheart; d, Edmond T. Greville; w, Ben Van Eeslyn (based on his play); ph, William McLeod, Hone Glendinning, Ernest Palmer.

War (PR:A MPAA:NR)

BUT THE FLESH IS WEAK* (1932) 77m MGM bw

Robert Montgomery *(Max)*, Nora Gregor *(Rosine)*, Heather Thatcher *(Lady Joan)*, Edward Everett Horton *(Sir George)*, C. Aubrey Smith *(Florian)*, Nils Asther *(Prince Paul)*, Frederick Kerr *(Duke of Hampshire)*, Eva Moore *(Lady Ridgeway)*, Forrester Harvey *(Gooch)*, Desmond Roberts *(Findley)*.

Charismatic Montgomery and his devil-may-care father, intent on becoming members of Britain's upper crust, decide that the way to fortune and stature lies in Montgomery's ability to charm socialites. Unappealing adaptation of Ivor Novello's less-than-classic play "The Truth Game."

d, Jack Conway; w, Ivor Novello (based on his play); ph, Oliver T. Marsh; ed, Tom Held.

Drama (PR:A MPA:NR)

BUTCH AND SUNDANCE: THE EARLY DAYS* (1979) 110m FOX c

William Katt *(Sundance Kid)*, Tom Berenger *(Butch Cassidy)*, Jill Eikenberry *(Mary)*, Paul Plunkett *(Bobby)*, Wesley Burgess *(Sam)*, Jeff Corey *(Ray Bledsoe)*, Peter Weller *(Joe LeFors)*, Noble Willingham *(Capt. Prewitt)*, Arthur Hill *(Wyoming Governor)*, John Schuck *(Harvey Logan)* Brian Dennehy *(O.C. Hanks)*, Vincent Schiavell, Patrick Egan *(Guards)*, Sherril Lynn Katzman *(Annie)*, Elya Baskin *(Bookkeeper)*, Peter Brocco *(Old Robber)*, Liam Russell *(Banker)*, Carol Ann Williams *(Lilly)*, Charles Knapp *(The Telegrapher)*, Jane Austin *(Daisy Mullen)*, Paul Price *(Skinner)*, Michael C. Gwynne *(Mike Cassidy)*, Chris Lloyd *(Bill Carver)*, Hugh Gillan *(Cyrus Antoon)*, Will Hare *(Conductor)*.

Burns wrote this prequel to the William Goldman film and it suffers by comparison. Granted, it is no easy job to go back before the fact, but it has been done (Lillian Hellman: ANOTHER PART OF THE FOREST) and might have fared better had not Burns fallen back to his TV antecedents ("The Munsters") and plotted this film like a rank amateur. Surprisingly, Lester doesn't do his job very well either, but he had a sow's ear to begin with and there was little he could do to improve it. It's a series of predictable episodes with little glue holding them together. Katt and Berenger have the cinematic electricity and humor of Martin and Lewis together—Tony Martin and Huey Lewis. Small roles are well cast and several actors have advanced their careers since then, though not as a result of this film. Since it is impossible to do a sequel when your two stars have been riddled with South American bullets, someone said: "Hey, why don't we show what happened before, guys?" They should have left well enough alone.

p, Gabriel Katzka, Steven Bach; d, Richard Lester; w, Allan Burns; ph, Laszlo Kovacs (DeLuxe Color); m, Pat Williams; ed, Anthony Gibbs, George Trirogoff; prod d, Brian Eatwell; art d, Jack DeGovia; cos, William Theiss.

Comedy/Western Cas. (PR:C MPAA:PG)

BUTCH CASSIDY AND THE SUNDANCE KID**** (1969) 112m FOX c

Paul Newman *(Butch Cassidy)*, Robert Redford *(Sundance Kid)*, Katharine Ross *(Etta Place)*, Strother Martin *(Percy Garris)*, Henry Jones *(Bike Salesman)*, Jeff Corey *(Sheriff Bledsoe)*, George Furth *(Woodcock)*, Cloris Leachman *(Agnes)*, Ted Cassidy *(Harvey Logan)*, Kenneth Mars *(Marshal)*, Donnelly Rhodes *(Macon)*, Jody Gilbert *(Large Woman)*, Timothy Scott *(News Carver)*, Don Keefer *(Fireman)*, Charles Dierkop *(Flat Nose Curry)*, Francisco Cordova *(Bank Manager)*, Nelson Olmstead *(Photographer)*, Paul Bryar, Sam Elliott *(Card Players)*, Charles Akins *(Bank Teller)*, Eric Sinclair *(Tiffany's Salesman)*.

Forever etched in the public mind is the memorable portrait of these two offbeat outlaws whose lives spanned the eras of the Old West and the beginning of the modern era, unforgettably played by Newman and Redford. In a marvelous combination of slapstick and drama, the gun-toting, bank-robbing, train-blowing duo and their erstwhile companions present a West never quite seen before by the public, one of awkward and funny events, lethal personalities who are really dirt common folk like everyone else as well as gunslinging legends on the cheap side (except for the deadly accuracy of Sundance's guns). The film opens with Redford winning at poker so handily that his fellow players drop out, leaving only a professional gunman and gambler who accuses Redford of cheating, telling him to go for his guns. Newman, who hates gunplay and prides himself on using his brains to avoid problems, tries to convince Redford to leave his winnings and back away. Redford refuses, saying that the gambler must ask him to stay and then he will leave. The gambler laughs and stands up, preparing to kill Redford. Newman shrugs, saying: "Well, I can't help you, Sundance." The gambler stammers an apology at hearing the name of the legendary gunman and begs Redford to stay and take his winnings. Redford declines, and begins to leave the saloon. The curious gambler asks, "Just how fast are you?" With that Sundance whirls about, his guns spitting bullets; he shoots the gunbelt off the gambler and sends his gun flying to the other side of the room. He and Newman then ride to their hideout, the infamous Hole-in-the-Wall where Newman is challenged to a knife fight by one of his gang members. He beats up the challenger through a ruse then plans a train robbery, one that yields little after the gang blows the doors from the baggage car. Redford and Newman go to the farmhouse where schoolteacher Ross lives—she is Redford's woman—to relax. Here Newman sports a bicycle while Redford dallies with his lover. Next the boys are off to rob another train, and this time almost blow up the entire baggage car, sending money flying in all directions. Before they can scoop it up, another train comes into view and from this pours a super posse made up of the most feared lawmen in the West, all dedicated to tracking down Redford and Newman. A wild chase ensues, the relentless posse staying on the track of the outlaws no matter what ruses and tricks they employ. They can't lose their pursuers and finally Newman and Redford are cornered on a mountain top, their backs to a river below. Instead of fighting it out, they leap into the waters and are swept away to freedom. But they now know that they are marked men. A friendly lawmen, Corey, explains that their day in the West is all over, that progress will overcome the old outlaws. When they tell him they might join the army to serve in Cuba in the Spanish-American war, Corey laughs at them, telling them that they are too notorious to go on living. The pair realize they are doomed, that they will be hunted down no matter where they go, so Newman decides that the safest retreat would be South America. After enjoying the sights in New York, shown through some imaginative series of old tintype photos, Newman, Redford, and Ross arrive in Bolivia where the boys bungle their way through a series of small-time bank robberies because of their inability to speak the language. Later they become guards for a mining company, protecting gold shipments and, in one confrontation with peasant bandits, survive a wild shootout. Even in Bolivia their days are numbered now and Ross knows it, telling them that she will not stay to see them killed. She leaves by boat for the States. Redford and Newman ride into one more town to rob the little bank, but are met by fierce gunfire from the constabulary, which is joined by a whole regiment of troops looking for the "bandits Yanqui." Cornered in a building, each wounded a half dozen times, the pair plan their next exploits in another country. Of course, they know that in a matter of minutes they will be dead but they daydream through this reality, Newman joking Redford along and Redford, the stoic and loyal gunman friend, playing back Newman's fantasies to him. Finally, it is time to die. Both men load their weapons and, guns in hand, dash into the courtyard to be met with the roar of hundreds of rifles trained on them from all angles. Director Hill shows not their bloody end but freeze frames their last upright movement which fades to sepia tint and then out, the camera recording the legend, not the demise. The film stands today as a classic western with terrific performances from Redford and Newman, along with a superb rendering from Ross as their lady chum. Hill's sweeping direction captures the flavor of a fast-fading Old West while Goldman's wondrous script sparkles with wit, humor, and insight sans cliche. Oddly, Goldman had written the words, "Not that it matters, but the following story is true." These words appear before the viewer at film's opening. The writer's research of the real Butch Cassidy and Sundance Kid is astoundingly accurate and is faithfully enacted in a memorable screen experience. So, in reality, the fact that the film chronicles two memorable characters from real life matters very much, particularly to Newman, whose career was beginning to droop a bit, but was enhanced greatly by the smart-talking Cassidy role; Redford had practically no career at all until this film, one that properly made him an international star.

p, Paul Monash, John Foreman; d, George Roy Hill; w, William Goldman; ph, Conrad Hall (DeLuxe Color); m, Burt Bacharach; ed, John C. Howard, Richard C. Meyer; art d, Jack Martin Smith, Philip Jefferies; set d, Walter M. Scott, Chester L. Bayhi; cos, Edith Head; makeup, Dan Striepeke; spec eff, L. B. Abbott, Art Cruickshank; spec still photog, Lawrence Schiller; graphic montage, John Neuhart; m/l, "Raindrops Keep Falling on My Head" Bert Bacharach, Hal David.

Western **Cas.** **(PR:A MPAA:NR)**

BUTCH MINDS THE BABY 1/2**
(1942) 75m Damon Runyon Productions/UNIV bw

Virginia Bruce *(Susie O'Neill)*, Broderick Crawford *(Aloysius Grogan Butch)*, Dick Foran *(Dennis Devlin)*, Porter Hall *(Brandy Smith)*, Richard Lane *(Harry the Horse)*, Shemp Howard *(Squinty Sweeney)*, Rosina Galli *(Mrs. Talucci)*, Joe King *(Police Lieutenant)*, Fuzzy Knight *(Wyoming Bill)*, Grant Withers *(Cactus Pete)*, Russell Hicks *(J. Wadsworth Carrington)*, Baby Michael Barnitz *(Michael O'Neill)*.

Ex-safecracker on parole Crawford lands a job as a janitor at a New York brownstone and saves tenant Bruce from a suicide attempt. Learning that she has a baby and is finding it difficult to cope, Crawford offers to help Bruce in caring for the tot. Although cop Foran refuses to believe it, Crawford becomes as gentle as a lamb through his devotion to Bruce's baby. Engaging comedy that's stuffed with Runyon's street-wise sharp-tongued gamblers, hoods, and bootleggers, all, of course, with hearts as big as the Big Apple itself. Crawford is wonderful as the big, clumsy, dim-witted ex-con who learns the value of love.

p, Jules Levey; d, Albert S. Rogell; w, Leonard Spigelgass (based on a magazine story by Damon Runyon); ph, Woody Bredell; ed, Milton Carruth.

Comedy **(PR:A MPAA:NR)**

BUTCHER, THE (SEE: LE BOUCHER, 1971, Fr.)

BUTCHER BAKER (NIGHTMARE MAKER)*
(1982) 91m International Films c (AKA: NIGHT WARNING, AKA: NIGHTMARE MAKER)

Jimmy McNichol, Susan Tyrrell, Bo Svenson

McNichol (Kristy's little brother) is raised by a very fond aunt. She's so fond of him that she will stop at nothing to keep him around including violent and graphic murder. Pathetic little film directed by former "I Love Lucy" director Asher.

p, Stephen Breimer, Eugene Mazzola; d, William Asher; w, Breimer, Alan Jay Glueck man, Boon Collins.

Horror **(PR:O MPAA:R)**

BUTLER'S DILEMMA, THE** (1943, Brit.) 83m Shaftesbury bw

Francis L. Sullivan *(Leo Carrington)*, Judy Kelly *(Ann Carrington)*, Hermione Gingold *(Aunt Sophie)*, Henry Kendall *(Carmichael)*, Wally Patch *(Tom)*, Ronald Shiner *(Ernie)*, Andre Randall *(Vitello)*, Ralph Truman *(Bishop)*, Ian Fleming *(Sir Hubert Playfair)*, Marjorie Rhodes *(Mrs. Plumb)*, Frank Pettingell, Alf Goddard.

In order to collect their debts a group of gamblers force the double of a gem thief to masquerade as his fiancee's butler. Terribly tepid.

p, Elizabeth Hiscott, d, Leslie Hiscott; w, Michael Barringer; ph, Erwin Hillier.

Comedy **Cas.** **(PR:A MPAA:NR)**

BUTLEY* (1974, Brit.) 129m America Film Theatre c

Alan Bates *(Ben Butley)*, Jessica Tandy *(Edna Shaft)*, Richard O'Callaghan *(Joey Keyston)*, Susan Engel *(Anne Butley)*, Michael Byrne *(Reg Nuttall)*, Georgina Hale *(Miss Heasman)*, Simon Rouse *(Mr. Gardner)*, John Savident *(James)*, Oliver Maguire *(Train Passenger)*, Colin Haigh, Darien Angadi *(Male Students)*, Susan Woodridge, Lindsay Ingram, Patti Love, Belinda Low *(Female Students)*.

An overlong and overbearing study of the academy takes to task Tandy as an old-fashioned teacher who cannot comprehend her know-it-all students as well as Bates' homosexual affairs, which are nothing more than dull. This stagey and slowmoving piece seeks to justify itself in iconoclastic wordplays that are as soggy as the moors. This kind of philosophical gobbledygook has seen its day. Pinter directed this turgid tale, which was a mistake.

p, Ely A. Landau; d, Harold Pinter; w, Simon Gray (based on his play); ph, Gerry Fisher (Eastmancolor); ed, Malcolm Cooke; art d, Carmen Dillon.

Drama **(PR:O MPAA:R)**

BUTTERCUP CHAIN, THE* (1971, Brit.) 95m COL c

Hywel Bennett *(France)*, Leigh Taylor-Young *(Manny)*, Jane Asher *(Margaret)*, Sven-Bertil Taube *(Fred)*, Clive Revill *(George)*, Roy Dotrice *(Martin Carr-Gibbons)*, Michael Elphick *(Chauffeur)*, Jonathan Burn, Yutte Stensgaard, Susan Baker, Jennifer Baker.

Curious story of four inseparable friends; Bennett, an emotionally unstable young man, Asher, his depressed sister, Taube, a kind Swedish architect, and Taylor-Young, a free-spirited American student touring Europe. While Bennett and Asher continually battle their incestuous urges, Taube and Taylor-Young marry, an unhappy joining that sees its lowest moment in the death of their first child. Interesting, but emotionally void story of friendship, love, and dependency.

p, John Whitney, Philip Waddilove; d, Robert Ellis Miller; w, Peter Draper (based on a novel by Janice Elliott); ph, Douglas Slocombe (Technicolor); m, Richard Rodney Bennett; ed, Thelma Connell; prod d, Wilfrid Shingleton; art d, Fred Carter.

Drama **(PR:O MPAA:NR)**

BUTTERFIELD 8*** (1960) 109m MGM c

Elizabeth Taylor *(Gloria Wandrous)*, Laurence Harvey *(Weston Liggett)*, Eddie Fisher *(Steve Carpenter)*, Dina Merrill *(Emily Liggett)*; Mildred Dunnock *(Mrs. Wandrous)*, Betty Field *(Mrs. Fanny Thurber)*, Jeffrey Lynn *(Bingham Smith)*, Kay Medford *(Happy)*, Susan Oliver *(Norma)*, George Voskovec *(Dr. Tredman)*, Virginia Downing *(Clerk)*, Carmen Matthews *(Mrs. Jescott)*, Whitfield Connor *(Anderson)*, Dan Bergin *(Elevator Man)*, Beau Tilden *(Chauffeur)*, Don Burns *(Photographer)*, Richard X. Slattery *(State Trooper)*, Philip Faversham *(Man)*, Samuel Schwartz, John Armstrong *(Doormen)*, Robert Pastene *(Tipsy Man)*, Leon B. Stevens *(Policeman)*, Tom Ahearne *(Bartender)*, Rudy Bond *(Big Man)*, Marion Leeds *(Irate Woman)*, Helen Stevens *(Gossip)*, Joseph Boley *(Messenger)*.

Author John O'Hara was never noted for taking kindly to criticism. What he thought of the Charles Schnee and John Michael Hayes screenplay, loosely based on his novel *Butterfield 8* is probably better left unsaid. But he surely knew of Elizabeth Taylor's reluctance to take the part of Gloria Wandrous because she thought it cheap, commercial, and in bad taste; he must have been in a snit for years. The story, actually based on the real-life, never-solved murder case of a dissolute New York flapper named Starr Faithfull with whom O'Hara was obsessed, had long been on the "shelf" in MGM's library. Filmed entirely in New York, the story concerns the romantic life of a Manhattan beauty, day-time model, night-time call girl who, after many frenzied nights in the bedroom, finally falls upon Mr. Right, in this case Laurence Harvey, a married socialite. The affair, never an easy one for either of them, ends when Taylor, under the mistaken impression that Harvey will never leave his wife, takes off, driving recklessly, and crashes through a barricade to her death on a New England-bound parkway. The film is fraught with sexuality and tough language, but remains a weak story, saved only by direction and Taylor's performance which, in spite of her truculence throughout the whole project, is one of her best. (Even her insistence that Eddie Fisher, to whom she was married at the time, be given a role did nothing to soothe her belligerent nature.) One particularly strong scene gives us the first indication of the impending love affair. It is a battle of endurance in which Taylor slowly jams the sharp heel of her shoe into Harvey's foot as he squeezes her wrist, slowly increasing the pressure, both refusing to wince. Dunnock as Taylor's mother, unable to face the reality of what her daughter is, gives a fine performance, as does Field as the mother's not-quite-so-naive friend. Merrill, as Harvey's rich, chaste, totally understanding wife is blah, blah, blah, not even reacting when she sees Taylor prancing around in her own presumably "stolen" mink coat. That takes a lot of blah. Nevertheless, the film does has much has could be expected with the story.

P. Pandro S. Berman; d, Daniel Mann; w, Charles Schnee, John Michael Hayes (based on the novel by John O'Hara); ph, Joseph Ruttenberg; m, Bronislau Kaper; ed, Ralph E. Winters; art d, George W. Davis, Urie McCleary; set d, Gene Calahan, J. C. Delaney; cos, Helen Rose.

Drama **(PR:O MPAA:NR)**

BUTTERFLIES ARE FREE 1/2** (1972) 109m COL c

Goldie Hawn *(Jill)*, Edward Albert *(Don)*, Eileen Heckart *(Mrs. Baker)*, Michael Glasser *(Ralph)*, Mike Warren *(Roy)*.

Free-spirited Hawn helps timid, intelligent, young blind man Albert break away from the over-protection of his mother, Heckart. At first resenting the girl's intrusion into her son's life (which includes a few lessons in sex), Heckart finally realizes that her son needs to become self-reliant. Three good performances by the principal players help the film overcome the structural limitations placed on it as an adaptation from a play. Although the emotional conflicts are a bit too neatly settled at the story's conclusion, Albert, Hawn, and Heckart make it all seem believable. Heckart, a superb actress, won an Academy Award for her supporting role in the film.

p, M. J. Frankovich; d, Milton Katselas; w, Leonard Gershe (based on his play); ph, Charles B. Lang; m, Bob Alcivar; ed, David Blewitt; prod d, Robert Clatworthy; set d, Marvin Marsh; cos, Moss Mabry.

Drama **Cas.** **(PR:A MPAA:PG)**

BUTTERFLY** (1982) 107m Analysis c

Stacy Keach *(Jeff Tyler)*, Pia Zadora *(Kady)*, Orson Welles *(Judge Rauch)*, Lois Nettle ton *(Belle Morgan)*, Edward Albert *(Wash Gillespie)*, James Franciscus *(Moke Blue)*, Stuart Whitman *(Rev. Rivers)*, Ed McMahon *(Mr. Gillespie)*, June Lockhart *(Mrs. Gillespie)*, Paul Hampton *(Norton)*, Buck Flowers *(Ed Lamey)*, Peter Jason *(Allen)*, Kim Ptak *(Deputy)*, Leigh Christian *(Saleslady)*, Dr. Abraham Rudnick *(Court Steno grapher)*, John Goff *(The Truck Driver)*, Dylan Urquidi *(Danny)*.

Forget about all the Pia Zadora jokes. BUTTERFLY proves she can deliver if she has the right material and careful handling. Cimber, who is not known for much beyond being a soft porn filmmaker, does a good job co-authoring script and directing this story of a Lolita-like doll (Zadora) who has been tracking her Daddy (Keach) down and finally locates him in Nevada. Keach starts getting hot for his own daughter and incest rears its head until we learn (sigh) that someone else is her father and so Keach is allowed to let his sexuality go. Even so, there is a trial for incest over which a gorgon-like Orson Welles presides. James M. Cain wrote the original book and the producers might have done better had they deviated from the dated plot but it may have been that the estate of Cain would not allow it, especially after having seen the Rafelson version of THE POSTMAN ALWAYS RINGS TWICE. The picture was made for less than $2 million and Cimber, who is a master of wringing out production values with tiny budgets, does a lot with the slim figure and brings in a film that looks like three times the price.

p&d, Matt Cimber; w, John Goff, Cimber (based on the novel by James M. Cain); ph, Eddy van der Enden (Metrocolor); m, Ennio Morricone; ed, Brent Schoenfeld.

Drama **Cas.** **(PR:O MPAA:R)**

BUTTERFLY ON THE SHOULDER, A** (1978, Fr.) 95m GAU c

Lino Ventura *(Roland)*, Claudine Auger *(Woman)*, Paul Crauchet *(Raphael)*, Jean Bouise *(Doctor)*, Nicole Garcia *(Sonia)*, Laura Betti *(Carrabo)*, Xavier Depraz *(Miguel)*.

Deray attempted to use the middle-cut Hitchcock theory here . . . (with variations) . . . a man is accused of a crime he didn't commit and must get from point A to point B in order to prove his innocence. In doing so, he meets a woman who believes him to be guilty. He eventually convinces her that he is innocent and they get to point B only to learn that the man who could clear him of the charge is, in fact, the rotter behind the plot. If that all sounds familiar, it should. It's the story for about seven Hitchcock pictures and damned near the story for this one. Ventura jumps ship in Barcelona, gets involved in a series of incidents and more twists than Laurel Canyon in the Hollywood Hills. People come and go without much motivation and, in the end, old Lino is erased. With a bit more vigor, it could have had the driving force of TO THE ENDS OF THE EARTH (1948) and been a bit more memorable. As it is now, all you may recall is Ventura.

d, Jacques Deray; w, Jean-Claude Carriere, Tonino Guerra (based on the novel *The Velvet Well* by Jean Gearon); ph, Jean Boffety, Jean Charvein (Eastmancolor); ed, Henri Lanoe.

Suspense **(PR:C-O MPAA:NR)**

BUY ME THAT TOWN** ½ (1941) 68m PAR bw

Lloyd Nolan *(Rickey)*, Constance Moore *(Virginia)*, Albert Dekker *(Louie)*, Sheldon Leonard *(Chink Moran)*, Barbara Allen *(Henriette)*, Ed Brophy *(Ziggy)*, Warren Hymer *(Crusher)*, Horace MacMahon *(Fingers)*, Olin Howland *(Constable Sam Smedley)*, Richard Carle *(Judge Paradise)*, Rod Cameron *(Gerard)*, Jack Chapin *(Tom)*, Keith Richards *(Harry)*, Trevor Bardette *(George)*, John Harmon *(1st Heckler)*, Si Jenks *(2nd Heckler)*, Jane Keckley *(Woman)*, Pierre Watkin *(Charlton Williams)*, Guy Usher *(Norton)*, Broderick O'Farrell *(Moffett)*, J. W. Johnston *(Buckley)*, Lillian Yarbo *(Nancy)*, Russell Hicks *(Malcolm)*.

Small-time hood Nolan and a few of his crooked pals, frustrated by their inability to make it in the big-city rackets, decide to take over a small town, extorting protection money from everyone in the village. When the lovely Moore starts to charm boss Nolan, his conscience gets the better of him, and he devises a plan to put the collected protection money to use for the benefit of the citizenry. Good-natured souls at heart, Nolan's cronies start to feel a great sense of satisfaction from their charity. Delightful comedy, an early effort by legendary producer Sol Siegel, that honors the small-town warm-hearted spirit of America. Nolan and Moore are entertaining as the romantic couple but Albert Dekker is the real gem of the picture. His depiction of Nolan's dim-witted second-in-command is a minor tour-de-force.

p, Sol C. Siegel; d, Eugene Forde; w, Gordon Kahn (based on a story by Harry A. Gourfain, Murray Boltinoff, Martin Rackin); ph, Theodore Sparkuhl; ed, William Shea.

Comedy **(PR:A MPAA:NR)**

BWANA DEVIL** (1953) 79m Oboler/UA c

Robert Stack *(Bob Hayward)*, Barbara Britton *(Alice Hayward)*, Nigel Bruce *(Dr. Angus Ross)*, Ramsay Hill *(Maj. Parkhurst)*, Paul McVey *(Commissioner)*, Hope Miller *(Portuguese Girl)*, John Dodsworth *(Drayton)*, Pat O'Moore *(Ballinger)*, Pat Aherne *(Latham)*, Bhogwan Singh *(Indian Headman)*, Bhupesh Guha *(The Dancer)*, Bal Seirgakar *(Indian Hunter)*, Kalu K. Sonkur *(Karparim)*, Miles Clark, Jr. *(Mukosi)*.

During the construction of a railroad in Africa, workers are terrorized by a pair of hungry lions. After numerous people are eaten and attempts by local hunters to destroy the lions fail, American engineer Stack succeeds in killing the beasts. The first feature-length film to be shown in 3-D, Arch Oboler's "classic" brought thousands of Americans into theaters where they promptly donned annoying, ill-fitting glasses and proceeded to watch frightened natives, hurled spears, and angry lions leap off the screen and into their lap. Aside from the novelty of its presentation, the film is a tedious, less-than-thrilling action adventure.

p,d&w, Arch Oboler; ph, Joseph Biroc (Natural Vision 3-D, Anscocolor); m, Gordon Jenkins; ed, John Hoffman; 3-D super, M. L. Gunzburg.

Adventure **(PR:A MPAA:NR)**

BY APPOINTMENT ONLY* ½ (1933) 66m IN/CHES bw

Lew Cody, Aileen Pringle, Sally O'Neil, Marceline Day, Edward Morgan, Edward Martindel, Pauline Garon, Claire McDowell, Gladys Blake, Wilson Benge.

Physcian Cody becomes the guardian of O'Neil after the girl's mother has died, a death that could possibly have been prevented if Cody had gotten to the ailing woman in time. Although he is engaged to the mature Pringle, Cody finds himself attracted to the strong-spirited O'Neil. Cody realizes the stupidity of his yearnings and settles down with Pringle. Poorly acted, badly scripted melodrama that fails to convey any form of believable emotional tension.

d, Frank Strayer; w, Strayer, Robert Ellis; ph, M. A. Anderson.

Drama **(PR:A MPAA:NR)**

BY CANDLELIGHT** ½ (1934) 70m UNIV bw

Elissa Landi *(Marie)*, Paul Lukas *(Josef)*, Nils Asther *(Count von Bommer)*, Dorothy Revier *(Countess Von Rischenheim)*, Lawrence Grant *(Count Von Rischenheim)*, Esther Ralston *(Baroness Von Ballin)*, Warburton Gamble *(Baron Von Ballin)*, Lois January *(Ann)*.

Lukas, personal butler to Asther, a scoundrel nobleman, is mistaken to be of nobility himself by ladies' maid Landi. Lukas, in turn, thinks that Landi is a countess. As Lukas helps Asther out of a predicament brought on by his philandering ways, his and Landi's true, lower-class identities are exposed to each other. Still in love, they marry. Pleasant comedy given a sparkling look by talented, classy director Whale.

d, James Whale; w, Hans Kraly, F. Hugh Herbert, Karen de Wold, Ruth Cummings (based on a play by Siegfried Geyer); ph, John Mescall.

Comedy **(PR:A MPAA:NR)**

BY DESIGN** (1982, Can.) 90m Atlantic/BDF ALPHA c

Patty Duke Astin, Sara Botsford, Saul Rubinek, Sonia Zimmer, Mina Mina, Alan Durusissean, Clare Coulter, Robert Benson, Jeannie Elias, Anya Best, Patricia Best, Jan Filips, Joseph Flaherty, William Samples, Jim Hibbard, Ralph Benmurgie, Steve Witkin, Nabuko Hardychuck, Scott Swanson, Robin McCullough, Bill Reiter, Andrea Olch, Maria West.

Ambiguous look at the taboo topic of two lesbian lovers desiring to adopt a child. Their attempt fails, which forces them into sexual relations with a man in order to become pregnant. Treatment shows little understanding of the plight of female homosexuals but is to be commended for not dwelling on why the women are attracted to each other. Capable performances fall flat due to stereotyped scripting rather than acting talent.

p, Werner Aellen, Beryl Fox; d, Claude Jutra; w, Joe Weisenfeld, Jutra, David Eames; ph, Jean Boffety (Medallion Color); m, Chico Hamilton; ed, Tony Trow.

Drama **Cas.** **(PR:O MPAA:NR)**

BY HOOK OR BY CROOK 1965 (SEE: I DOOD IT, 1943)

BY LOVE POSSESSED** (1961) 115m Mirisch/Seven Arts/UA c

Lana Turner *(Marjorie Penrose)*, Efrem Zimbalist, Jr. *(Arthur Winner)*, Jason Robards, Jr. *(Julius Penrose)*, George Hamilton *(Warren Winner)*, Susan Kohner *(Helen Detweiler)*, Barbara Bel Geddes *(Clarissa Winner)*, Thomas Mitchell *(Noah Tuttle)*, Everett Sloane *(Reggie)*, Yvonne Craig *(Veronica Kovacs)*, Jean Willes *(Junie McCarthy)*, Frank Maxwell *(Jerry Brophy)*, Gilbert Green *(Mr. Woolf)*, Carroll O'Connor *(Bernie Breck)*.

Amid the calm pleasantry of his elite suburban east coast town, Zimbalist is plagued with a variety of emotional and social problems. After discovering that the head of his law firm, Mitchell, has been embezzling company money to pay back an old debt of honor, Zimbalist begins to feel stagnant in his marriage to Bel Geddes and his relationship with son Hamilton. He then finds himself in an adulterous affair with Turner, the wife of his crippled law partner, Robards. With Robards unable or unwilling to accept her love/pity, the alcoholic Turner finds understanding and love in the arms of Zimbalist. Although engaged to socialite Kohner, the sad Hamilton begins to associate with the town tramp who, starving for attention, accuses Hamilton of rape. Unable to cope with the hussy's accusations, Hamilton's fiancee kills herself. Coming to his son's aid, Zimbalist learns to appreciate the importance of family love and patches things up with the understanding Bel Geddes. Seeing how the inability to understand love can destroy life, Turner and Robards commit themselves to helping and loving each other. Based on a popular novel by James Gould Cozzens, which had the same "literary significance" that *Valley of the Dolls* did years later, the film is a hopelessly melodramatic soap-opera complete with psychologically inane television-bred dialog that manages to lump every "adult" situation into one big mess. Somewhat controversial at the time, both the book and the film fail to capture the essential human complexities that would be created in such extreme situations. Bel Geddes and Mitchell manage to overcome the ridiculous scripting and direction with a couple of finely crafted performances, and Turner is about as good as could be expected, but Zimbalist and Hamilton have the appeal of driftwood. Interestingly, the original screenwriter for the film was the Academy Award-winning Charles Schnee, who, after countless revisions by other writers, threatened to sue if he was not allowed to use a pseudonym in the film's credits.

p, Walter Mirisch; d, John Sturges; w, John Dennis Charles Schnee (based on the novel by James Gould Cozzens); ph, Russell Metty (DeLuxe Color); m, Elmer Bernstein; ed, Ferris Webster; art d, Malcolm Brown; set d, Edward G. Boyle; cos, Bill Thomas; makeup, Del Armstrong, Layne Britton.

Drama **(PR:O MPAA:NR)**

BYPASS TO HAPPINESS* (1934, Brit.) 74m Sound City/FOX bw

Tamara Desni *(Tamara)*, Maurice Evans *(Robin)*, Kay Hammond *(DInah)*, Mark Daly *(Wallop)*, Eliot Makeham *(Miller)*, Nellie Bowman *(Jane)*, John Teed *(Stephen)*, Billy Holland *(Jim)*.

Pilot gives up his career and purchases a garage which has fallen into partial ruin because of neglect. Romance ensues when a girl helps him make a success of the decayed shelter. Poorly constructed.

p, Ivar Campbell; d&w, Anthony Kimmins; ph, Hone Glendinning.

Romance **(PR:A MPAA:NR)**

BY THE LIGHT OF THE SILVERY MOON*** (1953) 101m WB c

Doris Day *(Marjorie)*, Gordon MacRae *(William Sherman)*, Leon Ames *(George Winfield)*, Rosemary DeCamp *(Mrs. Winfield)*, Billy Gray *(Wesley)*, Mary Wickes *(Stella)*, Russell Arms *(Chester Finley)*, Maria Palmer *(Miss LaRue)*, Walter Flannery *(Pee Wee)*, Geraldine Wall *(Mrs. Harris)*, John Maxwell *(Ike Hickey)*, Carol Forman *(Dangerous Dora)*.

In this sequel to ON MOONLIGHT BAY, the pretty Day anxiously awaits the arrival of her longtime sweetheart MacRae who has finished his stint in WW I. When he arrives, their marriage plans are delayed because MacRae insists on getting financially stable first. During this waiting period, a series of humorous misunderstandings builds up an unhealthy jealous state between the pair that, of course, is resolved at the film's conclusion. Entertaining musical comedy that uses Day's pert personality and exquisite voice to charming advantage. MacRae is in fine voice too, and his rugged manner is very appealing. Not pretending to be a classic, the simple film has a crisp, small-town attraction. Songs: "By The Light Of The Silvery Moon" (Gus Edwards, Edward Madden); "I'll Forget You" (Ernest R. Ball, Annelu Burns); "Your Eyes Have Told Me So" (Gus Kahn, Egbert Van Alstyne); "Be My Little Baby Bumble Bee" (Stanley Murphy, Henry I. Marshall); "If You Were The Only Girl In The World" (Clifford Grey, Nat D. Ayer); "Ain't We Got Fun" (Kahn, Richard Whiting); "King Chanticleer" (Ayer).

p, William Jacobs; d, David Butler; w, Robert O'Brien, Irving Elinson (based on Booth Tarkington's "Penrod" stories); ph, Wilfrid M. Cline (Technicolor); m, Max Steiner; ed, Irene Morra; md, Ray Heindorf; ch, Donald Saddler.

Musical/Comedy (PR:A MPAA:NR)

BY WHOSE HAND?* (1932) 63m COL bw

Ben Lyon (*Jimmy*), Barbara Weeks (*Alice*), William V. Mong (*Graham*), Ethel Kenyon (*Eileen*), Kenneth Thompson (*Chambers*), Tom Dugan (*Drunk*), William Halligan (*Detective*), Helene Millard (*Widow*), Dwight Frye (*Chick*), Lorin Baker (*Bridegroom*), Dolores Rey (*Bride*), Tom McGuire (*Conductor*), Nat Pendleton (*The Killer*).

A killer escapes from the police and tracks down the man who turned him in on a train going from Los Angeles to San Francisco. During the course of the trip the informer is murdered and an uninvolved man becomes intent on capturing the ruthless killer. Low-budget, forgotten crime drama is handled with a great amount of visual flair, giving an amazing intensity to the familiar plotting.

d, Ben Stoloff; w, Isadore Bernstein, Stephen Roe (based on a story by Harry Adler); ph, Teddy Tetzlaff, Joseph Walker; ed, Maurice Wright.

Crime Drama (PR:A MPAA:NR)

BY YOUR LEAVE* (1935) 81m RKO bw

Frank Morgan (*Henry Smith*), Genevieve Tobin (*Ellen Smith*), Neil Hamilton (*David Mackenzie*), Marian Nixon (*Andree*), Glen Anders (*Freddy Clark*), Gene Lockhart (*Skeets*), Margaret Hamilton (*Whiffen*), Betty Grable (*Frances Gretchell*), Lona Andre (*Miss Purcell*), Charles Ray (*Leonard*).

Morgan, somewhat disillusioned with his marriage and saddened by the onset of middle-age, convinces his wife, Tobin, that the two of them should take week-long separate vacations, and neither should feel obligated to talk about what went on after the week is over. Tobin is hesitant at first, then agrees, knowing that it will mean a great deal to him. Morgan's fantasies about being pestered by countless beautiful girls are completely unrealized during the vacation, but Tobin meets and falls in love with a charming young man. Tempted by his offers of marriage, Tobin refuses the man and returns to her true love, Morgan, who has had a rebirth of affection also. Very engaging comedy with some very serious overtones dealing with kindness, understanding, and marriage. Morgan and Tobin are wonderful as the couple, each bringing spirit and insight to their characters. The pace is fast and funny, but the emotional qualities of the script are never forgotten.

p, Pandro S. Berman; d, Lloyd Corrigan; w, Allan Scott (based on the play by Gladys Hurlbut and Emma B.C. Wells); ph, Nick Musuraca, Vernon Walker.

Comedy (PR:A MPA:NR)

BYE BYE BARBARA ** (1969, Fr.) 100m Parc Film-Marianne/PAR c

Ewa Swann (*Paula*), Philippe Avron (*Jerome*), Bruno Cremer (*Hugo*), Alexandra Stewart (*Eve*), Michel Duchaussoy (*Dimitri*).

A tattered but beautiful girl, Swann, approaches journalist Avron in a bar one night, telling him that she has been drugged and needs a place to sleep. Avron takes the girl to his apartment where, by the next day, she recovers. As they walk through Paris, Swann swears that she is being followed and disappears from Avron's sight. The day after, Avron reads in the paper that the girl's body had been discovered in a car wreck, but he refuses to believe it and sets out to track her down. He discovers that Swann's stepfather, Cremer, who is obsessed with Swann's beauty, staged the "death" with an imposter's body in order to collect on his stepdaughter's insurance policy. Avron saves the girl from the crazed man's clutches and the two declare their love for each other. Uneven mixture of laughs and oddly-based suspense keeps the film from finding its niche. The principals give passable performances and the direction is well-crafted, but the effort as a whole is unremarkable.

d, Michel Deville; w, Nina Companeez, Deville; ph, Claude Lecomte (Eastmancolor); ed, Companeez.

Suspense/Mystery (PR:A MPAA:NR)

BYE BYE BIRDIE* (1963) 120m COL c

Janet Leigh (*Rosie DeLeon*), Dick Van Dyke (*Albert Peterson*), Ann-Margret (*Kim McAfee*), Maureen Stapleton (*Mama*), Bobby Rydell (*Hugo Peabody*), Jesse Pearson (*Conrad Birdie*), Ed Sullivan (*Ed Sullivan*), Paul Lynde (*Mr. McAfee*), Mary LaRoche (*Mrs. McAfee*), Michael Evans (*Claude Paisley*), Robert Paige (*Bob Precht*), Gregory Morton (*Borov*), Bryan Russell (*Randolph*), Milton Frome (*Mr. Maude*), Ben Astar (*Ballet Manager*), Trudy Ames (*Ursula*), Cyril Delevanti (*Mr. Nebbitt*), Frank Albertson (*Mayor*), Beverly Yates (*Mayor's Wife*), Frank Sully (*Bartender*), Bo Peep Karlin (*Ursula's Mother*).

When a contest brings pop star Pearson to Sweet Apple, Iowa, for a final performance before going into the army, local songwriter Van Dyke becomes determined to get the idol to record one of his tunes. Van Dyke's perseverance in contacting Pearson is, however, outweighed by his pursuit of the lovely Leigh. On the night of the performance, with Ed Sullivan on hand to televise the event, local Pearson fanatic Ann-Margret wins the chance to meet Pearson and both of Van Dyke's wishes are granted. Fun, high-spirited look at rock 'n' roll's effect on small-town America that worked well on stage and is given a wonderful treatment on film. The hysteria of modern musician worship is given the perfect embodiment in the innocent, yet strongly sexual power of Ann-Margret. Her naive sensuality here is something lost in her later films where her obvious physical attributes were blatantly displayed. Van Dyke is very gentle and winning in one of his few lead feature film roles and Paul Lynde hilariously conveys the inability of the typical parent to understand teenagers and rock music. Not harshly critical of rock 'n' roll, the film instead captures the dizzy excitement and unpretentious power that the form is supposed to convey.

p, Fred Kohlmar; d, George Sidney; w, Irving Brecher (based on the musical comedy by Michael Stewart, m/l, Charles Strouse, Lee Adams); ph, Joseph Biroc (Panavision); m, Johnny Green; ch, Onna White; cos, Pat Barto.

Musical/Comedy Cas. (PR:A MPAA:NR)

BYE BYE BRAVERMAN* ½ (1968) 94m WB c

George Segal (*Morroe Rieff*), Jack Warden (*Barnet Weiner*), Jessica Walter (*Inez Braverman*), Phyllis Newman (*Myra Mandelbaum*), Godfrey Cambridge (*Taxi Cab Driver*), Joseph Wiseman (*Felix Ottensteen*), Sorrell Booke (*Holly Levine*), Zohra Lampert (*Etta Rieff*), Anthony Holland (*Max Ottensteen*), Susan Wyler (*Pilar*), Lieb Lensky (*Custodian*), Alan King (*Rabbi*).

Uninteresting story of four Jewish friends who get together to mourn for their never seen friend, Braverman. Although there is a hint of lust between widow Walter and Segal, the film is basically a character study of dull, sad people who care little about each other or themselves. Some of the Jewish humor could be seen as offensive, but the truly offending thing about the film is director Lumet's inability to create likable yet tragic characters instead of merely pitiful ones.

p&d, Sidney Lumet; w, Herbert Sargent (based on the novel *To An Early Grave* by Wallace Markfield); ph, Boris Kaufman (Technicolor); m, Peter Matz; ed, Gerald Greenberg; art d, Ben Kasazkow; cos, Anna Hill Johnson.

Drama (PR:A MPAA:NR)

BYE-BYE BRASIL* (1980, Braz.) 100m Carnaval Unifilm c

Jose Wilker (*Lord Gypsy*), Betty Faria (*Salome*), Fabio Junior (*Cico*), Zaira Zambelli (*Dasdo*), Principe Nabor (*Swallow*), Jofre Soares (*Ze da Luz*), Marcos Vinicius (*Gent*), Jose Maria Lima (*Assistant*), Emanoel Cavalcanti (*Mayor*), Jose Marcio Passos (*Mayor's Asst.*), Rinaldo Gines (*Indian Chief*), Carlos Kroeber (*Driver*), Oscar Reis (*Smuggler*), Rodolfo Arena (*Peasant*), Catalina Bonaki (*Widow*), Marieta Severo (*Social Worker*), Cleodon Gondin (*Customer*), Jose Carlos Lacerda (*Steward*).

BYE-BYE BRASIL should be subtitled HELLO BRAZIL because it talks about the end of Brasil (the Portuguese way of spelling it) and the beginning of Brazil (which is how the rest of the world spells it). This movie is sort of a staged documentary in that it takes viewers across this most diverse of all South American countries, visiting Rio, Brasilia, the Amazon interior and other spots. The point made is that television is what is ruining the individuality of this country. Four people form a caravan and explore the country, meeting various people and learning that TV takes over wherever there is electricity. The identity of the country is being submerged under the television aerial. Ain't it the truth? It's almost, but not quite, a tourist film. See it soon if you can, then see Brasil before it becomes USA, South.

p, Lucy Barreto; d&w, Carlos Diegues; ph, Lauro Escorel Filho; m, Roberto Menescal; ed, Anisio Medeiros.

Drama Cas. (PR:C-O MPAA:NR)

BYE BYE MONKEY ** (1978, Ital./Fr.) 114m GAU c

Gerard Depardieu (*Lafayette*), Marcello Mastroianni (*Nocello*), James Coco (*Flaxman*), Gail Lawrence (*Angelica*), Geraldine Fitzgerald (*Toland*), Avon Long (*Miko*).

One of the oddest pictures on record. Depardieu and Mastroianni are two foreigners living in New York. Coco is a man who either owns or runs a Roman museum. Depardieu works for him at the museum as well as part time at a feminist group. These women decide to raise their consciousness by raping Depardieu so the women can see how *he* feels about it. He evidently likes it because he and the girl who had her way with him become an item. A baby chimpanzee is found and Depardieu takes it in. Mastroianni, in a prankish mood, gets the chimp official status by arranging some false papers. Marcello, having nothing better to do, takes his own life and leaves his estate to the monkey. The monkey is then devoured by rats. And that's just part of it! Ferreri is the same man who made LA GRANDE BOUFFE in which a quartet of men ate themselves to death. In this film, allegory reigns supreme, if we could only discern what the allegory is and what the reality is. One of the more interesting parts was a scene with Geraldine Fitzgerald as an older woman who freely admits that she is still a sexual person and needs more than just kind affection from Depardieu. A most unique picture that takes a few viewings before you can understand it enough to dislike it.

d, Marco Ferreri; w, Ferreri, Gerard Brach, Rafael Azcona; ph, Lucianno Tavoli (Eastmancolor); m, Phillipe Sarde; ed, Ruggiero Mastroianni.

Comedy (PR:O MPAA:NR)